WORLD RADIO TV HANDBOOK

WRTH

THE DIRECTORY OF INTERNATIONAL BROADCASTING

2005

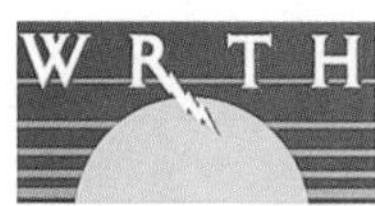

VOLUME 59 – 2005

Publisher:
Nicholas Hardyman

International Editor:
Sean Gilbert

Technical Editor:
John Nelson

Contributing Editors:
George Jacobs
Olle Alm
Bengt Ericson
Dave Kenny
Tore Larsson
Mauno Ritola
Bernd Trutenau
Torgeir Woxen

Cover Design:
Richard Boxall Design Associates

Advertising Sales Manager:
Beth Leinbach

Published in the UK by:
WRTH Publications Limited
PO Box 290
Oxford OX2 7FT
United Kingdom
Fax: +44 (0) 1865 514405
E-mail: wrth@wrth.com
Web: www.wrth.com
ISBN 0-9535864-7-2

Published in the USA by:
Watson-Guptill Publications
770 Broadway
7th Floor
New York, NY 10003-9595
USA
Web: www.watsonguptill.com
ISBN 0-8230-7794-2

Published in Germany by:
Gert Wohlfarth GmbH
Verlag Fachtechnik + Mercator-Verlag, Duisberg
Stresemannstrasse 20-22
47051 Duisberg
Tel: +49 (0) 203 30 52 70
Fax: +49 (0) 203 33 77 65
E-mail: info@wohlfarth.de
ISBN 3-87463-376-4

Printed and bound in Great Britain by Bath Press Limited

WORLD RADIO TV HANDBOOK

CONTENTS

Section Contents

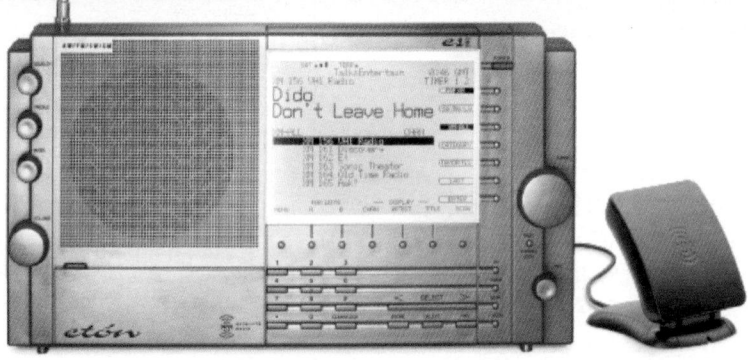

world's first & only
am/fm shortwave tuner with xm satellite radio
AM/FM/SW/XM
e1
Talk&Entertain
0:46 GMT
XM 156 VHI Radio
Dido
Don't Leave Home
XM 156 VHI Radio
XM 161 Discovery
XM 162 E!
XM 163 Sonic Theater
XM 164 Old Time Radio
XM 165 Ask!
SELECT
etón

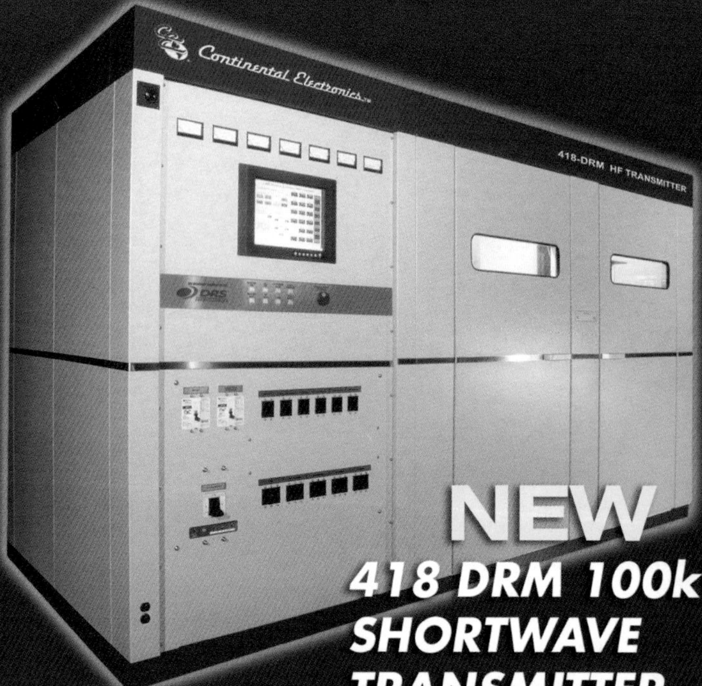

Editorial

THE FUTURE OF RADIO

This past year has, once again, been dominated by the advances of digital radio, and the steady decline of state-funded international shortwave broadcasts. In this edition we check up on the progress of digital radio and consider where these trends might lead: will commercial services take the place of state agencies, and how will digital services be delivered? The news that a European consortium is planning a satellite service, along the lines of the XM service in the USA, may well mark the future course for both these trends. As we outline in our 'Digital Update', there has been a significant advance in all the main digital services, although DRM and HD Radio seem to be having some difficulty getting up to speed. We see DRM's primary function as delivering high quality audio to those countries without ready access to the panoply of other digital systems. This being the case, it is our view that the DRM Consortium and the manufacturers must agree protocols that permit the development of inexpensive radios for mass distribution in these areas. There seems little point in only producing high-end DRM receivers. As for commercial shortwave; WMR has shown the way, and we wish them every success.

CONTRIBUTORS

We never tire of saluting the team of contributors who make it possible to produce this extraordinary reference book. This year we mourn the passing of one of our dedicated contributors, Bernt Erfjord, who's work on Norway was always immaculate. We also say farewell to Ruud Brand, but have the pleasure of welcoming Dave Kenny as a Contributing Editor and Tore B Vik, Svein Olaf Pedersen, and Max van Arnhem as country contributors.

REVIEWS & ARTICLES

In this edition we have reviewed the latest version of the estimable NRD-545, and the new offering from WinRadio, and we have considered five cheap portables for those who enjoy HF listening on a budget. Once again, however, no new heavyweight receivers have been released, although we are assured that we will see something during 2005.

Among a fine collection of articles we continue our series on the craft of radio receiving, with a look at the place of various pieces of 'Ancillary Equipment' in the modern receiving station.

CHANGES TO *WRTH*

While some of the changes we make to *WRTH*, such as the introduction of the COTB section, receive universal approval, others do not. Many readers wanted to know why we removed verification policy from most of the National Radio section. The reason is that most stations have stopped responding to reception reports and we decided we should only include details for stations that have recently responded. This year we have also removed the number of radio sets from the country heading. This is because in large parts of the world radios are being included not only in cars but also in pens and mousemats, and the figures were becoming meaningless.

WEB UPDATES

Putting the B03 updates and the 2004 summer schedules on our website was very popular and we intend to do the same for B04 and A05. So make sure you visit **www.wrth.com** to get updates and the A05 schedules.

PRIZE DRAW RESULTS

These winners were again drawn by members of the British DX Club.

RESULTS OF THE *WRTH* 2004 PRIZE DRAW

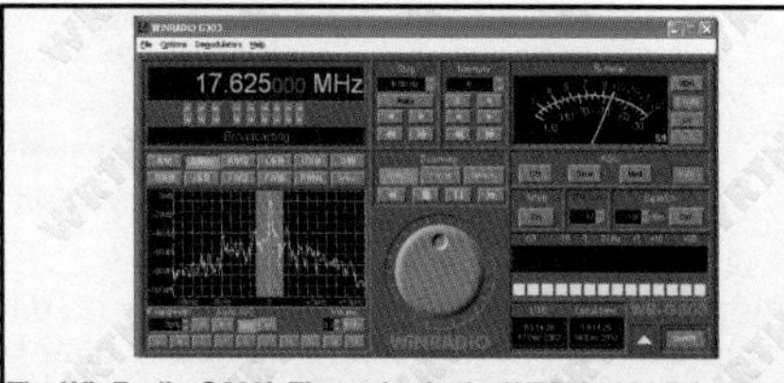

The WinRadio G303i. First prize in the WRTH 2004 Prize Draw

FIRST PRIZE
G Lorenz, Germany

RUNNERS-UP PRIZES (Copies of WRTH 2005)
A Sunde, New Zealand
O Galinsky, Russia
J Ervine, USA
T Patterson, The Philippines
S Hormann, USA

I hope you enjoy reading and using this new edition of *WRTH* as much as we have enjoyed compiling it.

Nicholas Hardyman
Publisher

WRTH Contributors 2005

The WRTH contributors come from all walks of life; yet share a common fascination with all aspects of global broadcasting. Each year we profile one of the people whose dedicated enthusiasm makes possible the enormous task of updating WRTH each year. This year it is the turn of Paul Ormandy, our contributor for New Zealand and the Pacific islands, to give an insight into what makes a WRTH contributor.

Paul Ormandy at his receiving station

The way I discovered DXing is probably no different to many fellow devotees. Around the age of 11 I started tinkering with crystal sets and, after hearing stations 100kms away, I became keen to hear even more distant stations. Thus I became a DXer by accident (although I did not there was a name for it!).

What's more, a chance glimpse of a MW loop led me to discover this hobby had a name and that there were other such hobbyists in my home town! The owner of the loop was a "DXer" and I was soon invited to join the New Zealand Radio DX League.

A job over the Christmas holidays gave me enough money to buy a decent receiver . . . the venerable Barlow-Wadley XCR-30. Now I had a receiver with real "grunt". This receiver served me well for a number of years until early 1981 when I bought a Kenwood R-1000. The R-1000 is an underrated receiver and would make a fine set for the average DXer. I swapped the R-1000 for a Drake SPR-4. The Drake was (and still is) rated as a top DX performer, and the SPR-4 served me very well, delivering many very good catches. I didn't really look to upgrading it until Bryan Clark brought his AOR 7030 to the shack! Not long after that, I bought an AOR and the Drake was 'retired from active service'.

I used to DX from home, until my parents were offered a bit of farm land to build a cabin on at Waianakarua. It was an ideal location for long aerials and up to 8 Beverages have graced the skyline. It's just 20km from home and has provided excellent catches time and again for visiting DXers and myself. From home, I have found a sloper antenna fed with coax via a matching transformer offers the best performance.

Although DXing can be regarded as a selfish hobby, I have always enjoyed the company of other DXers: sharing tips, hosting listeners at my Beverage site, and attending conventions. I have been a regular contributor to the *DX Times* since 1975 and have sub-edited various sections since 1985. I have also contributed technical articles, served as the League's Competitions Secretary, and now maintain the radiodx.com website. I started contributing to the *World Radio TV Handbook* in 1998.

Eight years ago, I was asked if I could provide a monthly programme of DX tips for ZLXA here in New Zealand. This led to the show being broadcast over AWR, Radio New Zealand International, HCJB and, more recently, Radio Korea International. I have just finished producing this programme.

I've always been a DXer, a chaser of exotic hard-to-hear stations and seeker of QSL cards, as opposed to a shortwave listener. On MW, I've verified 145 countries, and 250 stations from South America. On SW I have verified 242 countries, and many pirate stations of less than 50 watts.

I also spend a lot of time on the ham bands now, so keep an ear out for ZL4PW!

Paul Ormandy
Official *WRTH* contributor for New Zealand and the Pacific islands

A large project such as WRTH could not be produced without the help of many people from all over the world. The following organisations give invaluable help:

Asian Broadcasting Institute, British DX Club, Danish Shortwave Club International, Electronic DX Press, National Radio Club Inc (USA listings)

our Country Contributors provide us with updated entries for the countries for which they are responsible:

Olle Alm, Herman Boel, Swopan Chakroborty, Svetomir Cuckovic, Alok Dasgupta, Edward Dunne, Bengt Ericson, David Foster, Carlos Gonçalves, Victor Goonetilleke, Henrik Hargatai, Stig Hartvig Nielsen, Karel Honzik, Jose Jacob, Richard Jary, Dave Kenny, Tetsuya Kondo, Vashek Korinek, Tore Larsson, Kai Ludwig, Dario Monferini, Paul Ormandy, Svein Olaf Pedersen, Andy Reid, Mauno Ritola, Roberto Scaglione, Bernd Trutenau, Max van Arnhem, Thierry Vignaud, Tore B Vik

they and we are greatly aided by our other major contributors:

Teresa Beatriz Abreu, Rogildo Fontenele Aragão, Javaid Azim, Carlos Benoit, Erich Bergmann, Héctor García Bojorge, Jordi Brunet, Alfredo Cañote, Bryan Clark, Marcelo A. Cornachioni, Costa Constantinides, Alan Davies, Adalberto Marquea de Azevedo, Cesar Perez Dioses, Jack FitzSimons, Keith Gough, Noel Green, Rudolf Walter Grimm, Alokesh Gupta, Wolf Harranth, Hans Johnson, Anatoly Klepov, Hans-Joachim Koch, Erik Køie, Sergey Kolesov, Miroslav Krupieka, Andrej Kuznecov, Karl Leite, Zacharias Liangas, Carlos Maldonado, Björn Malm, Humberto Molina, Cláudio Rótolo de Moraes, Carlos Gamarra Moscoso, Adán Mur, Horacio Nigro, Tore Nilsen, Thomas Nilsson, L. Oberto, Alexey Osipov, Samuel Ouma, Rumen Pankov, Anker Petersen, James Robinson, Rafael Rodríguez, Célio Romais, Daniel Rosenzweig, Ibrahim Rustamov, Arnaldo Slaen, Paulo Roberto e Souza, George Touliatos, José Valdes, Numan Vasquez, Peter Wilson, Torgeir Woxen, Tarek Zeidan

We thank them, and also all our readers who have written or emailed us with useful ideas and information. Please keep sending your thoughts and updates to:

WRTH Publications Limited
PO Box 290
Oxford OX2 7FT
UK

or email to:

wrth@wrth.com

WRTH Receiver Reviews 2005

This year has been marked by the continuing spread of digital radio in a variety of forms, and for the first time a definite sense that analogue HF broadcast systems are in decline – at least in the context of domestic radio in the developed world. The affordable DAB receiver is now an everyday reality in the European market and satellite radio continues its inexorable growth in both North America and elsewhere. DRM developments continue apace, and there is evidence of massive growth in broadcast 'reception' via the internet now that affordable broadband is an everyday reality in many parts of the world. But as in previous years, the decline in the rate of introduction of new shortwave receivers has continued and almost no new models have come on to the market in the twelve months since the last edition of *WRTH* apart from very low-cost items which offer HF reception facilities as more of a marketing feature than anything else.

We said last year that "...it is clear that international television broadcasting is in some sense taking over from where HF radio broadcasts leave off". In the light of recent world events this trend is even clearer nowadays, although we also detect a considerable increase in the use of local FM and wider-spread satellite-based outlets by external broadcasters. However, there are (and for the foreseeable future will continue to be) several parts of the world where internet and satellite access to programme material are difficult, inordinately expensive or for political reasons unavailable. In these countries, reception of HF broadcasts will remain the only way of obtaining reliable sources of news and other information.

For much of the world, however, it appears that HF listening is increasingly the province of the hobbyist and the enthusiast driven by interest rather than necessity. And as will be evident from the data pages of *WRTH*, there continues to be a decline in the number of HF broadcast services; the recent complete closure of Swiss Radio International and the rumoured closure of several other large-scale European broadcasters are merely the most recent in a continuing trend. It is still argued in some circles that the introduction of digital HF broadcasts will increase the overall size of the audience for external programming, but it is far from clear that this is the case. Our estimate is that it may on the contrary take high-frequency broadcasting in a more commercial and less overtly nationalistic direction. The only growth area we envisage is religious broadcasting, which continues to make extensive use of the HF spectrum.

TYPES OF RECEIVER

This year we have looked at the latest development of the software-defined radio (SDR), the WinRadio G313i. In our view the advent of the SDR together with easy availability of low-cost digital signal processing and the spread of digital modes is a direct pointer to the way forward for broadcast reception. It is the way of the future, and not only in terms of conventional radio receivers. We have no doubt that as the internet continues its inexorable expansion and various forms of digital techniques come to dominate both broadcasting systems and those intended for local networks – even down to household and community level – the SDR in one form or another will in time shape the entire future of wireless modes. Adding new hardware always presents problems for manufacturers, whereas modifying software or (more correctly) firmware is trivially simple by comparison.

In sharp contrast to this advanced machinery, we have also assessed five low-cost portables of entirely traditional design. Two DAB receivers from Roberts Radio have been examined, as has the latest iteration of the NRD-545G and some of its many accessories. No new hand-held 'scanners' with HF coverage have come to market this year; in fact, with digital technology now the norm in modern non-broadcast radio systems, we rather suspect that the traditional scanning receiver has had its day. In terms of other radios, the usual crop of rumours of new models from major manufacturers have been as persistent (and regrettably as inaccurate) as usual. That said, several new radios of both conventional and software-defined architecture are known to be in the pipeline, as is a new high-grade receiver from Ten-Tec. We have also examined a commercially available preselector from MFJ and the latest iteration of the excellent Wellbrook loop antenna.

ABOUT THE AUTHOR

John Nelson is an author, editor and consultant specialising in audio, radio and communications technology. After graduation in 1974, John worked for the BBC and the Radio Society of Great Britain before becoming freelance in 1986 and has written, edited and contributed to a wide variety of publications. He now runs Crew Green Consulting Ltd, which specialises in electronic and communications systems design and assessment for a wide client base.

John's amateur radio callsign GW4FRX is often heard on the HF bands, where he currently has 316 DXCC countries confirmed, and on 144MHz. In his remaining spare time he enjoys aviation, music, literature and architecture. He lives in east Wales.

JRC NRD-545G

US$2200 £1295 €2800

OVERVIEW

Several years ago we reviewed the JRC NRD-545 HF receiver. This was one of the first DSP-based units to be available in the commercial market, and we were very enthusiastic about it. Since then other receivers have come and gone but the NRD-545 is still in production and now has a full line of accessories to accompany it. For this reason a re-visit seemed in order.

There are in fact three separate models of this receiver, and if you are considering purchase it is important to be aware of what you are buying. The NRD-545G, which is the subject of the present review, is the variant intended for Europe and has full CE approval. It is supplied with accompanying literature written in English and the mains voltage input is pre-set to 230V AC to suit most European countries. When used with the optional CHE-199 wideband converter (which extends coverage of the receiver from a 30MHz upper limit to 2GHz) there are no gaps in the range; this is because the receiver rather than the converter is programmed to prevent access to certain frequencies in some markets. The NRD-545U is for the American market and does not have CE approval, although it does have FCC approval for use in the USA. It is supplied with a manual in English and the mains-voltage selector is preset to 110V. When the CHE-199 converter is fitted, coverage of the American UHF cellular band is blocked. Finally, the NRD-545J is constructed for the Japanese home market. It is supplied with a Japanese manual and with its mains input selector preset to 100VAC. This version lacks CE approval, and when the CHE-199 converter is fitted there are several gaps in its coverage. Various internet sites suggest that in fact it is easy enough to modify the U and J models such that the VHF/UHF coverage becomes continuous, although we can neither vouch for nor condone such modifications. Given that most cellular telephone systems in the USA are now digital and cannot in any event be monitored by a conventional receiver, we confess to wondering why the FCC bothers to insist that the older UHF cellular analogue bands remain blocked.

Our understanding is that there are no other differences between the basic models of NRD-545. However, it should be pointed out that JRC does not offer any form of international warranty, so any rectification work under guarantee would have to be undertaken by the original supplier. In other words, if you live outside Europe but decide to purchase an NRD-545G because you require continuous coverage to 2GHz, you should be aware of the implications.

Messrs Waters & Stanton were kind enough to supply us with a G model for evaluation together with the CHE-199 converter, the NVA-319 external loudspeaker, an ST-3 headset and a CGD-197 high-stability TCXO. This latter is intended for users requiring better than the existing 2ppm/hr frequency stability and will provide 0·5ppm/hr or better. Our measurements actually suggested that this is a conservative specification and the measured stability appeared to be more like 0·1ppm/hr over the normal temperature range in our laboratory.

FEATURES

Whichever model is considered, the NRD-545 in its basic form offers continuous coverage of 100kHz to 30MHz. It embodies digital IF filtering and signal processing, a single-chip 1Hz-stepping DDS synthesizer, a powerful kit of tools for interference reduction including two noise blankers, a notch filter, continuously variable bandwidth control, passband shift and excellent facilities for ECSS reception. The front-end RF amplifier uses four parallel-connected JFETs and a quad-FET double-balanced mixer for good strong-signal handling. RTTY demodulation for 170, 425 and 850Hz shifts at baud rates between 37 and 75 is provided as standard, and the unit can be interfaced with an IBM-compatible PC. The NRD-545 measures 330 x 290 x 130mm and weighs just less than 8kg. It is very solidly built and beautifully finished in all respects. The front panel is initially rather daunting, and careful reading of the densely written and well illustrated manual is recommended before switching on for the first time. The panel is dominated by the display, which uses multiple colours for better legibility; the frequency display is yellow whereas the electronic S-meter shows levels up to S9 in a pale blue and levels above that (to +60dB) in red. Current settings of parameters such as filters, mode and AGC are shown along the upper edge of the display. A keypad for direct frequency entry is located to the right of the display, and the large rotary VFO knob lies underneath. All the other controls are more or less symmetrically disposed about the front panel, and we especially liked the way the timer facilities were interconnected with the power on/off switch. Probably the only criticism one could make of the unit's ergonomics is that the finger hole in the VFO knob is a little small and sharp-edged and does not contain an insert which can remain fixed in the plane of the finger whilst the knob rotates. Fast tuning is perhaps best carried out by the up/down keys either side of the knob. One other very trivial complaint is that the display brightness can be set to one of two levels but the difference between them is slight and we found the display rather dim even in a fairly dark room. It also 'washed out' almost entirely with even moderate backlighting. If we recall correctly, the original version had a much brighter display.

PERFORMANCE

The NRD-545G was available for about three weeks, during which time it was connected to a variety of antennas from a seven-element trapped array for the amateur HF bands to assorted dipoles, long wires and two Wellbrook loops. As with its predecessor, it was very unusual for any strong-signal problems to be encountered and measurements suggested that the third-order intermodulation intercept point referred to a 1V signal was +12dBm. This is an excellent figure, and other important parameters also measured very well.

In operational terms the NRD-545 was excellent throughout, and the combination of superb performance and overall ease of use was thoroughly beguiling. The audio output of the NRD-545 was very low in distortion, and lengthy periods of listening via the ST-3 headset were not at all fatiguing. The combination of well-judged sensitivity, excellent strong-signal handling and a 'quiet' synthesiser allowed signals to stand out from their background in a way which is very characteristic of the best receivers, and using the Wellbrook loops allowed full advantage to be taken of this. Even relatively weak stations were almost always highly intelligible, and the very well implemented noise blanking and passband tuning allowed severe interference to be effectively dealt with. The NVA-319 worked very well indeed and is one of the better external accessory speakers we have come across.

CONCLUSION

All in all, the JRC NRD-545G remains one of the finest HF receivers ever to come our way and we thoroughly enjoyed our time with it. And as with its illustrious precursor in 1999, perhaps the most eloquent tribute we can give to this excellent unit is that we were very sorry to have to return it to the distributors!

MEASUREMENTS

(all EMF at 1kHz, AM, 70% modulation for 10dB S/N + N)

Sensitivity

MHz	µV
5MHz	1·9µV
15MHz	1.2µV
25MHz	1.1µV

Selectivity: see text. Filter shape factor about 1.4 at most bandwidth settings

IF rejection in excess of 100dB

Image rejection in excess of 80dB

Rating table JRC NRD-545G

Mechanical design	★★★★½
Constructional quality	★★★★½
Ergonomics	★★★★½
Sensitivity	★★★★½
Dynamic range	★★★★★
RF intermodulation	★★★★½
IF filters	★★★★★
IF performance	★★★★★
Audio quality	★★★★½
Software	★★★★
Manual	★★★★
Versatility	★★★★
VFM – absolute	★★★★
VFM – comparative	★★★★
Overall rating	**★★★★★**

Key:

★ = Poor ★★ = Fair ★★★ = Average

★★★★ = Good ★★★★★ = Excellent

VFM = Value for money

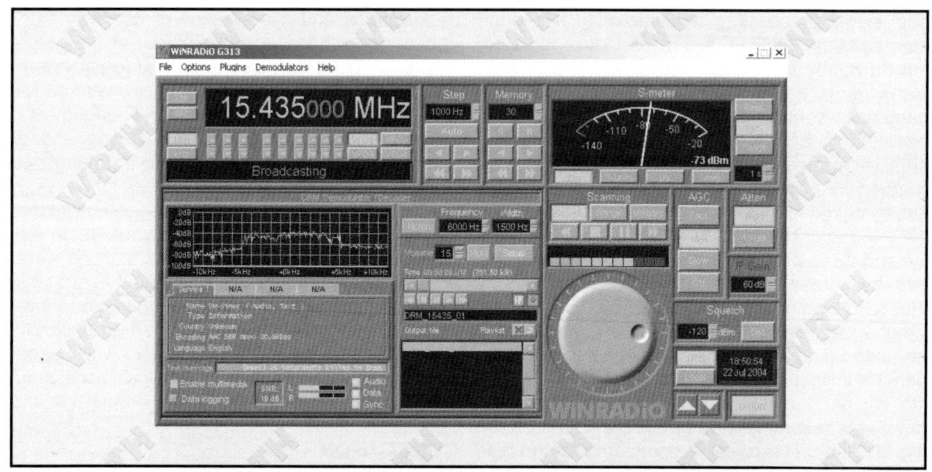

WinRadio G313i

US$950 £550 €800

OVERVIEW

In last years' WRTH we were very enthusiastic about the WinRadio G303i, which represented the first commercially available example of an essentially new type of receiver known as a software-defined radio (SDR). In essence this can be considered as an RF amplifier and frequency changer whose purpose is to derive a baseband IF for application to the computer's sound card. In the G303i the frequency conversion took place from the 9kHz–30MHz range to a first IF in the 45MHz region via switchable attenuators and front-end filters.

The G313i takes the evolution of the WinRadio SDR a stage further insofar as the unit embodies integral DSP and does not make use of the PC sound card for demodulation. As such, the G313i could be said to be entirely software-defined, which implies amongst other things that additional demodulation or decoding modes can be easily added by changes to the software. For example, WinRadio tell us that DRM software (which was written by themselves based on the work of the Fraunhofer Institute, but only available via VT Merlin for the foreseeable future because of the complexities of current DRM licensing arrangements) should be available by the time this is read. Indeed, our screenshot shows the receiver in 'DRM' mode and the ease with which the demodulator can be switched between modes with one mouse-click is one of the excellent features of an SDR. The G313i can also be factory-fitted with a 'hardware extension option' which allows continuous coverage of 9kHz-180MHz, together with other options for connection of an external reference oscillator and outputs at both the 45MHz and 107MHz intermediate frequencies. The G313i is otherwise very similar to the G303i and realised as a PCI card with extensive local screening. An external version, the G313e, will also be available shortly. The card is exceedingly well made, and what could be seen of the PCB suggests that it has been manufactured to the highest professional standards in all respects.

The minimum specification for the PC into which it should be installed is a 500MHz Pentium with 64MB of RAM, an SVGA display and at least 20MB of hard-drive space. The recommended specification is for a 1GHz Pentium 4 or Athlon processor with 256MB or more of RAM and at least 40MB of free hard-drive space. In the context of modern PCs these are all very modest requirements. The unit will run under Windows 98, ME, NT, 2000 or XP and all our tests were conducted with the latter.

As with the G303i, the local oscillator is a DDS and the first IF filter is a 4-pole component with a 15kHz bandwidth. The second mixer also uses a DDS as the local oscillator and down-converts to a 12kHz IF. Both DDSs use a common 20MHz reference oscillator. There are numerous demodulation modes, continuously variable IF bandwidth 1Hz to 15kHz (in 1Hz increments), a 20kHz wide real-time spectrum analyzer with 16Hz resolution, a noise blanker and a notch filter. AGC is performed in the first IF stage. There is also an integrated recorder, allowing instant recording and playback of the received signal. In addition the receiver can also record an entire 20kHz wide IF spectrum, making close analysis of the characteristics of the received signal possible. Even more delightful is the ability to 're-receive' the same signal with different IF filter bandwidths, notch filter, noise blanking or demodulator settings. In practice this proved to be an extremely useful feature which permitted good recovery of very weak or interference-degraded signals.

In addition to the real-time narrow-band spectrum analyser, there is also a wide-band analyser which contains additional professional instrumentation facilities. These include the ability to display minimum and maximum spectrum sweeps, search for peaks, average spectra, save and print spectra, marker mode, etc. Another useful feature, previously unavailable with receivers of this price class, is a test and measurement facility, performing measurements on the received signal including frequency accuracy, amplitude modulation depth, frequency deviation, THD (total harmonic distortion) and SINAD. An audio spectrum analyzer is also included, making it possible to observe the demodulated spectrum in real-time with a resolution of 5Hz.

FEATURES AND FUNCTIONALITY

The UK distributor was kind enough to provide the G313i for review already installed in a 'Shuttle' small-format PC with WinRadio branding, together with all necessary accessories including keyboard, mouse, amplified speakers, cables, software, manuals and so on. A Philips 15in LCD monitor was also provided. Everything was supplied in an impressive ruggedised transport case with copious packaging and a comprehensive packaging list.

We did not have a G303i and its software available for direct comparison, but the initial screen presentation appeared to be similar to what we saw last year insofar as it resembled a cross between the front panel of a conventional receiver and the display associated with an early software-controlled receiver such as the IC-PCR1000. A large and clear frequency display is at upper left, with small up/down keys lying below each numerical digit. Tuning step and memory controls are arranged to the right of the display and a very large and clear S-meter display is at upper right. Not only is its clarity exemplary but the ability to indicate in dBm, microvolts or 'S'-units is extremely useful. At centre left is a spectrum display centred on the frequency to which the receiver is tuned and extending either side. The centre portion of the display is greyed to represent the IF bandwidth currently in use, which can either be selected by one of several buttons lying below the display or by small up/down buttons and numerical readouts. Audio AGC controls are also located beneath the S-meter, as is the AF volume control and a mute button. A large 'rotary' tuning control (operated by the mouse buttons) is at centre-right with scanning and memory controls above it. There are several ways to tune the G313i, of which we found the easiest was a combination of the mouse wheel and the numeric keys beneath the frequency.

PERFORMANCE

As with the G303i, the G313i's lack of receiver spurious responses was quite astonishing given that the inside of a PC is hardly a hospitable electrical environment. The measured performance was generally similar to that of the G303i although the close-in reciprocal-mixing performance was somewhat improved; phase noise at 5 and 10kHz spacings was about 5dB better than in the G303i. The measured sensitivity was remarkably consistent over most of the frequency range at -119dBm for 10dB S+N: N. In our view this is still slightly higher than optimum, and better dynamic-range performance would in our view be obtained if the balance was shifted a little in favour of strong-signal performance. However, in practice there were very few problems and the switchable attenuator dealt very effectively with those that did arise.

CONCLUSION

As with the G303i, it is a pleasure to be able to say that the G313i and its software display an outstanding combination of performance, functionality, quality and value for money. It appears to us that the newer generation of WinRadio receivers are very much better in all respects than their predecessors, and the very favourable attention which they are receiving from a variety of quarters is richly deserved.

MEASUREMENTS

(all EMF at 1kHz, AM, 70% modulation for 10dB S/N + N)

Sensitivity

MHz	dBm
5MHz	-116
15MHz	-119
25MHz	-119

Selectivity: see text. Filter shape factor about 1.35 at most bandwidth settings

IF rejection	96dB
Image rejection	in excess of 80dB

Rating table WinRadio G313i

Mechanical design	★★★★★
Constructional quality	★★★★★
Sensitivity	★★★★
Dynamic range	★★★★
RF intermodulation	★★★★
Software	★★★★★
Manual	★★★★
VFM – absolute	★★★★★
VFM – comparative	★★★★★
Overall rating	**★★★★★**

Key:
★ = Poor ★★ = Fair ★★★ = Average
★★★★ = Good ★★★★★ = Excellent
VFM = Value for money

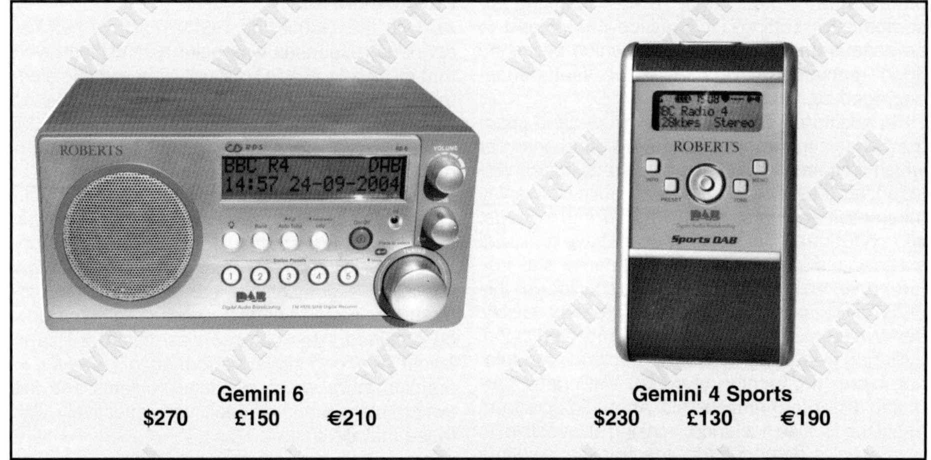

Gemini 6
$270 £150 €210

Gemini 4 Sports
$230 £130 €190

Roberts DAB Radios

INTRODUCTION

As noted elsewhere in this edition of *WRTH*, the market for DAB receivers is now growing apace. Many mains, transportable and portable models are available, although the number of DAB chipsets used in them could probably be counted on the fingers of one hand; conducting a group test of DAB receivers is liable to leave the reviewer with a severe case of *déja vu.*

One of the major players in the field is Roberts Radio, who are of course well known for their world-band receivers as well as a high-grade line of domestic portables and clock radios. Roberts nowadays has no manufacturing facilities of its own and all its contemporary products are made in the Far East. Some (such as its world-band portables) are rebadged Sangean items, and none the worse for that; others are purpose-built. Last year Roberts burst on to the DAB scene with no less than 11 different receivers, all with the 'Gemini' cognomen and almost all with an integral FM band as well.

The Roberts DAB range encompasses mains-only receivers, mains/battery and pure battery portables, a clock radio and a Fifties-style 'revival' portable closely resembling the popular R250 family. We chose to look at the 'Gemini 6' table-top mains-only unit and also the 'Gemini 4' personal portable, which were amongst the first of the new models available in the UK.

GEMINI 6

The Gemini 6 is a mains-powered table-top receiver with an integral PSU. It measures 240 x 160 x 120mm and is presented in a wrap-round cabinet finished in what is evidently a real wood veneer, apparently a species of cherry. The cabinet is very well finished and the entire unit is reassuringly heavy and solid; it turns the scales at almost 2kg and a sharp tap on the side of the unit suggests few or no mechanical resonances. It comes with a remote-control keypad.

There are five station presets allowing storage of five stations per band, making 10 in all. Whether this is enough, too many, or too few depends entirely on your personal preference and how you use the radio. We would prefer more, but anecdotal evidence suggests that a large proportion of DAB radio users listen only to two or three of their favourite stations and rarely re-tune. On the rear panel is a two-pin input for a non-latching mains connector and a TOSlink port for optical digital output. In a recess are the F-type socket for the telescopic antenna (which can, of course, be replaced by an external antenna connector if required), a socket for headphone output and a slide switch labelled 'DBB' which introduces Deep Bass Boost. This was left off for most of our testing.

The tuning range is channel 5A (174.928MHz) to 13F (239.2MHz), which makes the Roberts receiver usable for Band III DAB reception anywhere in the world. We spent some time tuning around the UK DAB allocation (11B-12D) with the receiver connected to either a three-element rotatable Yagi or a discone, both at about 60ft AGL, and were pleasantly surprised by the diversity of what could be heard. At the time of the review there was also considerable tropospheric enhancement of VHF and UHF signals, and for several evenings we were able to enjoy DAB transmissions from various parts of Europe.

These listening tests showed up one minor shortcoming of the Gemini 6, which is that its front-end is slightly less sensitive than might have been expected. Comparison tests with various other DAB receivers that were to hand at the time of the review, using the supplied telescopic antenna and also with the discone connected via a high-grade step attenuator, suggested that the 'boiling mud' quality associated with excessive DAB data rate errors set in rather early with the Roberts. Compared with a Pure Evoke-2 – with which it shares a good deal of design commonality – the Gemini 6 displayed between 4 and 6dB less sensitivity. In practical terms a slight lack of RF sensitivity is not a major issue but it does mean that care may have to be taken with the location of the radio to provide good results if it is used in conjunction with its telescopic antenna. We strongly recommend that the signal-strength function available via the 'Info' button is used each time the radio is moved to a different place.

On FM the Gemini 6 worked generally well. The RDS PS name was always slow to appear, even with signal strengths well in excess of the +54dBμV level that defines the primary service-area contour of an FM transmitter, and other RDS functions available via the 'Info' button consistently needed almost +60dBμV to display correctly. The receiver's RDS functions also struck us as inordinately sensitive to multipath. However, the audio quality was essentially as good as that from DAB. On both bands, incidentally, the tone control proved effective and useful but the DBB switch introduced an unwelcome 'honk' into the lower registers. There was ample audio available, even for noisy environments. The remote controller proved very useful, especially when it was necessary to site the radio near a window to acquire enough signal strength for good reception.

In conclusion, despite a few minor weaknesses, the Roberts Gemini 6 strikes us as a very good mains tabletop DAB receiver.

GEMINI 4 SPORTS DAB

At perhaps the other extreme from the large mains-powered Gemini 6, the Gemini 4 is the smallest DAB portable we have yet seen. It measures 120 x 66 x 22mm, which makes it a perfect fit in the breast pocket of the average shirt, and runs from three AA cells. Early DAB portables were criticized for their inordinate appetite for battery power, and it is fair to say that the Gemini 4 does not quite escape this charge. We went through no less than five sets of manganese-alkaline cells during testing and found that the useful battery life at normal listening level was about 14h, although the manufacturer claims 20h. In mitigation, there is a socket for an external 4V power supply and a suitable mains adaptor is supplied with the unit. This is not, incidentally, a charger but purely a power supply unit and the radio cannot be used with secondary cells without some external means to recharge them. We rather think that Roberts missed a trick here, and that it would have been more sensible to configure the PSU as a charger and supply suitable secondary cells with the unit.

The front panel and controls of the Gemini 4 are elementally simple. A large and clear dot-matrix display is backlit in orange for a few seconds on initial switch-on, and whenever a button is pressed. This shows the station name and an array of other symbology including battery state, signal strength, volume level, tone setting, time and so on. Unlike its bigger brother, the Gemini 4 always displays the correct time. Power is switched on via a button on top of the radio, with an adjacent slide switch to lock the unit by inhibiting all button functions. A four–way 'top-hat' rocker below the display selects the required station in its lateral plane and controls volume when operated vertically. By default, the scrolling function sequentially steps through all the stations available in a particular area. However, a 'Preset' button adjacent to it allows the user to select a sub-set of up to 10 preset stations which operating the rocker will step through. This is a delightfully elegant system which we liked very much. An 'Info' button adjacent to the preset button allows display of the station name, programme type, the name of the multiplex, the date, the channel and frequency, bit rate and the data error rate (expressed as a digit). A 'Tone' button to the right of the rocker allows six different settings to suit the earpiece and tastes of the current user. Finally, a 'Menu' button to the right of the tone button sets the station order, invokes an autoscan, reveals the software version, and allows manual tuning. This latter feature initially sounds quite interesting but the Gemini 4 is solely for the UK market and the tunable channels are only 11B to 12D. The headphone socket is on the right-hand side of the unit and the 4V input socket is on the left. Using the supplied earpiece, the volume available was more than enough for almost all situations. There is no external antenna, the earpiece lead doing double duty for the purpose.

We tested the unit extensively in the course of several rail and car journeys and in general the Gemini 4 performed extremely well. As always with digital systems, there is an 'all or nothing' quality about the results; the recovered audio was almost invariably either perfect or absent. Given the limitations of the simple earpiece supplied with the Gemini 4, the audio quality was actually rather good. Several concerts were much enjoyed with the help of the radio during evening railway journeys, and the audio was surprisingly natural and unfatiguing.

All in all, the Gemini 4 is an excellent digital travelling companion which we thoroughly recommend. It is slightly unfortunate that it appears to be designed with restricted frequency coverage, although presumably different markets are provided with models having the appropriate channelisation built in. The Roberts product is robust and well made, and we consider it very good value for money.

Low-cost Portables

INTRODUCTION

Of the questions *WRTH* is often asked about short-wave listening, a sub-set can be reduced to the form "what is the least amount of money which must be spent to allow me to hear station X?" It is inevitably disappointing to the enquirer to be advised that the question is unanswerable because there are so many variables. For example, if one lived almost literally next door to the transmitter of one's favourite AM station, the cost of receiving it would in principle reduce to the cost of a pair of headphones, a suitable length of wire and the procurement and assembly of a few simple electronic components. The result would be the modern-day equivalent of the 'crystal set' of yore, needing no batteries and giving excellent fidelity but little or no selectivity. At the other extreme is the professional monitoring organisation, using expensive receivers and extensive antenna systems so as to give itself the best possible chance of hearing anything it chooses whenever it wishes.

It might be more helpful to think about the question from another point of view. Many modern portable radios costing relatively little are available nowadays, and several embody HF reception facilities. Are they worth considering? If so, what is it reasonable to expect from them? Many (although not all) are made in China; does this automatically imply poor quality? Can a price-performance ratio be established?

Reduced to its lowest terms, the cost of a particular receiver – or indeed virtually any item of consumer electronics – is related to three main areas; mechanical, electrical and functional (ergonomic). In simple terms, mechanical robustness costs money because it implies better materials, or more of them. Reliability and performance are both chiefly electrical issues although both also require certain mechanical considerations to have been properly taken into account. Functionality and ergonomics are mainly matters of good design, although what economists call 'functional pricing' is all too often encountered in consumer goods; the addition of features which cost the manufacturer little or nothing is associated with a disproportionate price mark-up.

Although one might wish the situation to be different, the hard fact is that engineering and performance considerations come a long way behind the cost of production in the mind of the manufacturer of commercial electronic products. Much of what passes for a design process is imitative, derivative or based around reference circuitry provided by the makers of whatever integrated circuits are used in the unit. So there is little room for innovation and considerable commonality of circuit elements; the same chipsets will be found in a wide variety of units. To a large extent, therefore, one is buying on the basis of branding, visual appeal or price. But it should be remembered that the applied brand name may be misleading. One sees this most clearly in the world of car radios, where one China-based company (OPC) makes units for almost all the world's well-known brands, but it is not at all uncommon in other fields.

From the performance point of view, the low-cost receiver can be expected to be less good than its more expensive counterpart in two principal fields: *dynamic range* and *selectivity.* The first is a measure of the receiver's ability to separate weak signals from strong ones in the early stages of its circuitry, and amounts to the balance between sensitivity and strong-signal handling. A high-grade receiver displays a wide dynamic range, implying that it is both sensitive enough to receive weak signals and robust enough to do so when adjacent signals are very strong. In design terms it is easy to achieve sensitivity but much less easy to combine it with good strong-signal handling, with the result that inexpensive receivers are almost always compromised in this latter area.

The second issue is sometimes confused with the first, and as far as the listener is concerned can have the same effect. However, if the dynamic range of a receiver is such that a weak signal becomes corrupted by a stronger one in the RF amplifier or mixer, no amount of subsequent selectivity can do anything to ameliorate the situation. Selectivity is a measure of the performance of the intermediate-frequency circuitry of the receiver, and in particular the quality of whatever form of *filter* is fitted. In an ideal world, the bandwidth of the filter would be exactly equivalent to the bandwidth of the signal to which we wish to listen, and would reject everything else. Modern DSP filter systems can in fact approach this ideal, and indeed can be made variable so that they can cater for both relatively wideband transmissions (such as AM) and narrowband signals (such as SSB or CW) whilst maintaining excellent rejection of unwanted signals throughout. However, such systems are not yet to be found in low-cost receivers. These almost invariably rely on what are known as *ceramic* filters, which are produced in vast quantities at very low cost and can or can be made to perform quite well.

As far as the user is concerned, both shortcomings have rather similar effects. Strong stations can be easily received but weak stations are likely to suffer from what sounds like (and indeed is) interference or noise. One hallmark of a good receiver is the way in which even weak

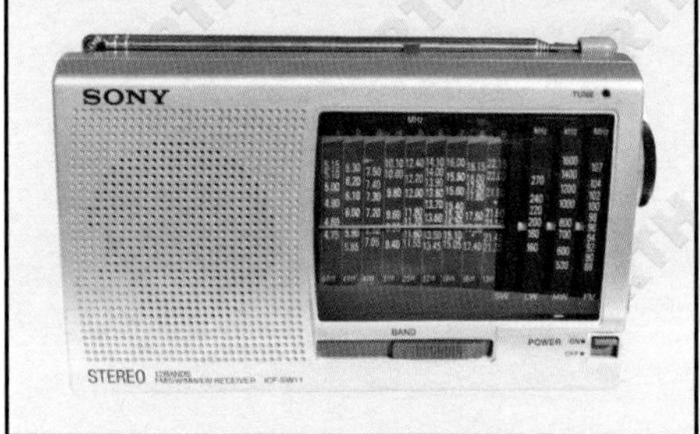

Sony ICF-SW11

US$40 £25 €35

Roberts R-9967

US$70 £40 €55

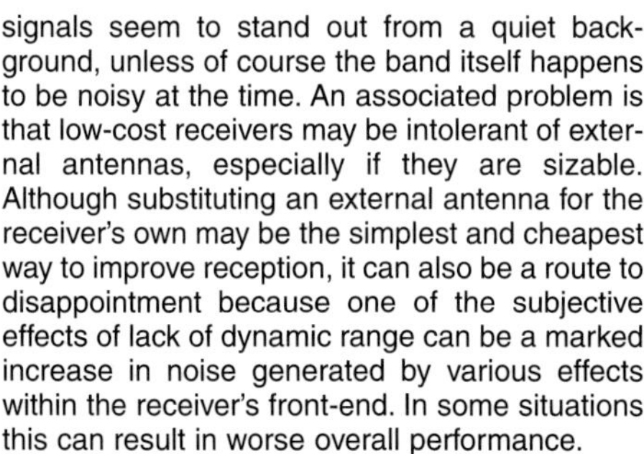

signals seem to stand out from a quiet background, unless of course the band itself happens to be noisy at the time. An associated problem is that low-cost receivers may be intolerant of external antennas, especially if they are sizable. Although substituting an external antenna for the receiver's own may be the simplest and cheapest way to improve reception, it can also be a route to disappointment because one of the subjective effects of lack of dynamic range can be a marked increase in noise generated by various effects within the receiver's front-end. In some situations this can result in worse overall performance.

For this edition of *WRTH* we decided to examine several currently available low-cost portables from Sony and Roberts to see how capable they actually are. We chose these manufacturers because of their good reputations and elected not to bother with the very low-end units originating in China and elsewhere, simply because their performance is such that a *WRTH* reader is unlikely to be interested in them. The list comprised the Sony ICF-SW11S (£24.95), Sony ICF-SW12S (£54.95), Sony ICF-SW35 (£69.95), Roberts R-9921 (£65) and Roberts R-9967 (£39.95). We carried out standard measurements of sensitivity and strong-signal handling to establish their usable dynamic range and also assessed other factors both by measurement and subjective judgment. Our findings were interesting and in certain ways surprising.

Incidentally, all quoted prices are manufacturer's recommended retail but there is some variation at this end of the market and on-line prices in particular may be higher or lower.

SONY ICF-SW11

Intuitively one might expect a receiver costing £25 or so to be considerably compromised, but within its limits the ICF-SW11 proved to be quite an impressive performer. It offers 12 bands; 88-108 MHz FM (with stereo reception via the earpiece), 141-290 kHz LW, 525-1620 kHz MW and nine SW bands (4750-5060, 5900-6200, 7100-7350, 9400-9990, 11600-12100, 13570-13870, 15100-15800, 17480-17900 and 21450-21750 MHz). Band selection is via a manual slide switch and tuning is performed with a side-mounted rotary control with very light action and some lost motion. There is a power on-off switch at lower right and a tuning-indicator LED at upper right. The 5·7cm diameter speaker takes up most of the left-hand half of the front panel. An internal ferrite-rod antenna is provided for MW and LW reception and a telescopic rod handles FM and HF signals. There is no provision for an external antenna. The unit operates from two internal AA cells, although there is an input for an external 3V DC supply.

An effective scale length of about 25mm coupled with mechanical tuning over a band covering several hundred kilohertz is not a recipe for accurate frequency resettability. It is not really feasible to tune the ICF-SW11 to a particular frequency, and effectively "what you hear is what you get". This is fine for strong stations but makes finding and holding the weaker ones very difficult. Sensitivity is adequate for use with the integral antennas, especially on the lower bands, but there are several spurious responses and internal 'birdies' which are not helpful. Strong-signal performance could perhaps be best described as indifferent. On the positive side, the LED tuning indicator works remarkably well and the audio quality – particularly on FM – is remarkably good, with exemplary clarity and adequate volume.

As a low-cost radio for tuning to your local domestic station and the occasional strong HF outlet, the ICF-SW11 can be recommended. However, it is not a receiver for the enthusiast.

ROBERTS R-9967

Occupying the middle ground between the two lower-cost Sony receivers, the R-9967 shares their manual tuning and no doubt many of their circuit elements but is rather better presented overall. It measures 150 x 80 x 35mm and feels pleasant in the hand, belying its low cost by the wrap-over leather case and elegant panel layout. Like the ICF-SW11, the R-9967 offers coverage of 12 bands; the only major difference is that the Roberts provides 75m (3900-4000 kHz) in place

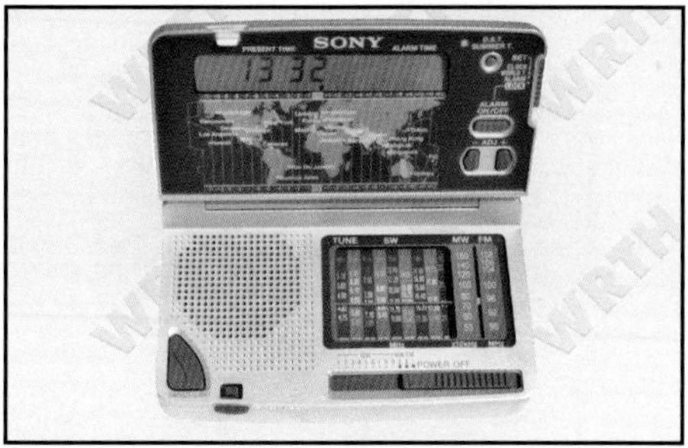

Sony ICF-SW12

US$80 £50 €70

Sony ICF-SW35

US$100 £65 €90

of 4750-5060 kHz. Tuning is by way of a rotary control on the upper right-hand edge, which has less lost motion and feels heavier that that in its Sony counterpart. The rotary volume control and toggle on-off switch are below the tuning knob. The horizontally oriented band and frequency display has an LED tuning indicator at upper left, and the left-hand half of the front panel is taken up with the speaker. The R-9967 operates from two internal AA cells. Sockets for headphones and an optional 3·6V external supply are on the left-hand edge together with a stereo/mono switch – a useful feature in noisy FM reception areas. There is an internal ferrite rod antenna for LW and MW and an external telescopic for HF and VHF/FM reception.

As with the manually tuned Sony receivers, it would be idle to pretend that an effective scale length of about 40mm at best can make for ease and repeatability of tuning. On some bands, indeed, the usable length is considerably less; on 75m it is only about 15mm. Quite why the designers did not pad all the tuned bands out to equivalent scale lengths is something of a mystery, since it is technically simple to achieve and need not have added to the cost of manufacture. In practice, the receiver cannot be 'tuned' to a particular frequency on any band; it is necessary to tune around, accept whatever is audible and decide whether or not it is wanted. Happily the receiver's balance of sensitivity and strong-signal handling is quite reasonable and signals that are relatively strong and 'in the clear' are nicely reproduced. FM sensitivity seemed a little lower that ideal, but stereo reproduction via the headphone socket was pleasant.

Overall, the Roberts R-9967 is likely to be adequate for those who are content with listening to a few stations regularly received at good strength. It is certainly good-looking and appears to be well made.

SONY ICF-SW12

Looking rather like the famous ICF-SW100, the ICF-SW12 is a 'flat-pack' radio with an upwards-opening lid. This reveals a 4·5cm speaker on the left-hand side and a band/frequency display resembling that in the ICF-SW11 but with an even smaller scale length. The unit covers the same bands as the latter but unaccountably omits any long-wave coverage, which seems unfortunate. Band selection is via a slide switch at lower right, and edge-mounted rotary volume and tuning controls are on the right-hand side. There is a digital clock display on the upper lid which is coupled with an alarm, and an LED tuning indicator in the upper left corner of the main display. The ICF-SW12 operates from two internal AA cells but there is no provision for operation from a mains PSU. There is also no provision for FM stereo via the earpiece. The unit is attractively small in size, measuring 110 x 85 x 30mm.

As might be expected, the ICF-SW12 performs very like the ICF-SW11 and displays the same strengths and weaknesses. Tuning to a particular frequency is not really possible, and using the receiver is a case of operating the tuning control and accepting or rejecting whatever you come across. The audio quality was quite reasonable, if a little thin, and there was adequate volume for most situations. FM reception via the earphone was noticeably more noisy than in the ICF-SW11. The clock and alarm facilities worked admirably.

Given that their performance is very similar and that the ICF-SW11 is less than half the price, it is a little difficult to see a good reason for opting for the ICF-SW12 unless you happen to need its particular combination of facilities and small size. Its price-performance ratio is the worst of the tested group, and it strikes us as more of an exercise in functional pricing than an attempt to provide value for money.

SONY ICF-SW35

For a little more money and an increase in the dimensions, we enter the world of the synthesised receiver with digital frequency readout, memory presets and vastly improved ergonomics. The ICF-SW35 is 165 x 100 x 30mm in size, and half of the front panel is taken up by the speaker. There is a large LCD display, five

Sangean ATS-305/Roberts R-9921

US$100 £65 €90

memory presets and manual/scan tuning buttons. These normally operate in the correct increments for the associated band (a switch in the battery compartment selects between 9 and 10 kHz steps for MW) but a fine-tuning switch allows tuning in 1 kHz steps if required. There is a digital clock with alarm facilities. The ICF-SW35 operates from three AA cells and there is provision for operation from an external 4·5V supply. Internal ferrite and external telescopic antennas are provided, and there is a switchable and variable attenuator. There is even a tone switch (news or music) next to the rotary volume control. A cloth travel case is supplied as standard.

The ICF-SW35 offers FM, MW, LW and continuous coverage between 2250 and 26100 kHz; the latter is also divided into 14 discrete bands selectable by a front-panel button. The ergonomics are a little unusual, but one rapidly becomes used to them.

In performance terms the ICF-SW35 worked very well. Sensitivity was well matched to the integral antennas and the strong-signal handling was quite reasonable; the unit could have taken advantage of a short external antenna, and it is unfortunate that there is no provision for connecting one. Audio quality was splendid, with excellent stereo reproduction available via the earpiece. Overall, our impression was of a well-designed receiver manufactured to a good standard. It offers excellent value for money and a very good balance of price and performance. Highly recommended.

SANGEAN ATS-305/ROBERTS R-9921

At the same price as the Sony ICF-SW35, of identical size and probably sharing much of its circuit architecture, the Roberts offers very similar functionality but adds some features of its own, notably RDS (or at least the RDS PS name and the CT clock-time function). This works reasonably well although it needs a fairly strong signal to operate reliably and the CT data can occasionally become corrupted.

Solidly made and provided with a high-quality vinyl travel case, the R-9921 operates from four AA cells or an optional AC adaptor. It covers FM, MW in selectable 9 or 10 kHz steps and continuous coverage between 5900 and 17900 kHz. This latter is sub-divided into seven bands, namely 5900-6200, 7100-7350, 9400-9900, 11600-12100, 13570-13870, 15100-15800 and 17480-17900 kHz. It is perhaps a little unfortunate that the HF coverage is restricted at both ends of the spectrum, and particularly that there is no 13m (21MHz) band; this can occasionally be useful to some listeners even at the present low point in the sunspot cycle. Stereo audio is available on FM via the headphone socket. The overall layout is simple and the ergonomics are excellent, as usual with most Roberts products. There are in effect 27 preset memories available, and the size and feel of all the controls is first-class. The only significant omission compared with the Sony ICF-SW35 is an attenuator, although the unit does not suffer unduly. The optionally backlit LCD is very crisp and clear and the three-position tone switch works well.

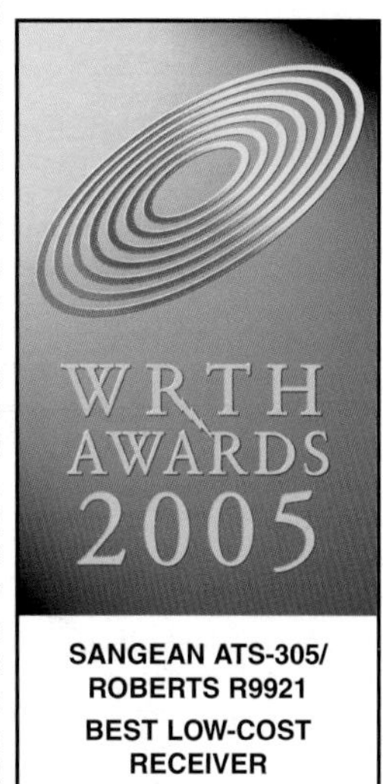

SANGEAN ATS-305/ ROBERTS R9921

BEST LOW-COST RECEIVER

Displaying very good sensitivity, slightly better IF selectivity than its Sony competitor and very good-quality audio, the R-9921 is a fine travelling companion; its comprehensive clock and alarm facilities are particularly useful. Its dynamic range was by a small margin the best of the tested radios, and front-end intermodulation and cross-modulation were seldom experienced except occasionally in the 49m band at night. Excellent value for money and strongly recommended.

CONCLUSION

Unless you are only interested in reception of one or two consistently strong stations, there seems little doubt that either of the two synthesised receivers in the tested group are very much easier to use and give better performance than their rotary-tuned counterparts. Certainly their ergonomics are far superior. Accepting that they are slightly more expensive, the Sony ICF-SW35 and Roberts R-9921 are much easier to handle than the others and are likely to provide considerably more long-term satisfaction. We slightly prefer the Roberts product to the Sony, chiefly because of marginally better ergonomics and performance and the addition of two useful RDS facilities, but both are well worth considering.

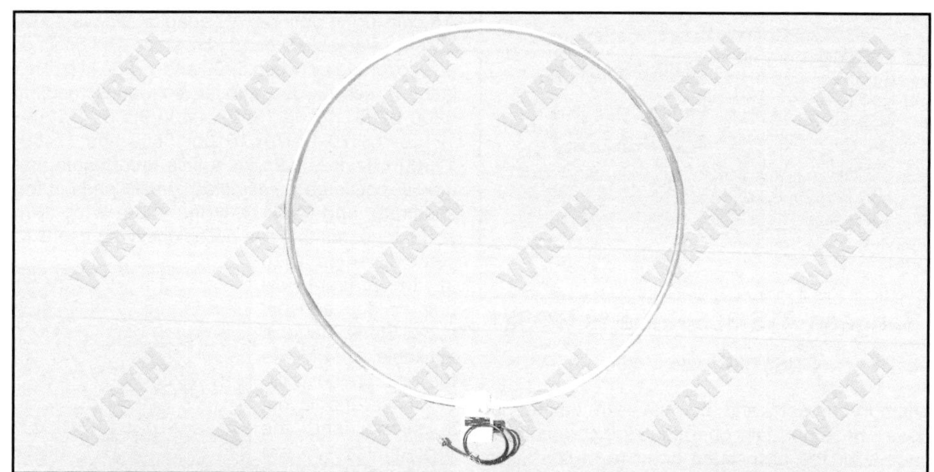

Wellbrook ALA-330S

US$190 £130 €190

OVERVIEW

Wellbrook Communications manufactures a range of active loop antennas which has achieved widespread popularity in the last few years, especially for those with restricted space and/or high levels of local noise and interference. We looked at the ALA-1530 last year and were extremely impressed with it. One year on, it has proved itself to be an extremely useful and versatile antenna. It has found extensive employment in our test and measurement laboratory, as well proving itself very useful indeed for a variety of general reception purposes.

In recent months Wellbrook has introduced an antenna of potentially great interest to the listener. This is the ALA-330S, which according to the manufacturer has about 10dB less gain on LW and the lower end of MW than the ALA1530 but more importantly the HF gain is 10-15dB higher. The claimed third-order intercept point at high frequencies is an astonishing +43dBm and the almost equally important second-order intercept is an even more striking +80dBm.

To understand the relevance of these figures, we need to define some terms. There exists a phenomenon called *intermodulation,* which in essence is the range of additional frequencies produced in a non-linear electronic system or circuit element when two signals are present. If we call these f1 and f2, spurious frequencies (f1 + f2) and (f1 – f2) will be generated, as will higher-order products. Intermodulation is the basis of operation of the circuit element in a receiver called the mixer, but it is also the basis of an important type of performance limitation in audio amplifiers and radio receivers, not to mention SSB transmitters. *Radio-frequency intermodulation* is a measure of mixer and (to a lesser extent) RF amplifier performance in the presence of strong signals. It is almost always assessed in terms of *odd-order* intermodulation performance, i.e. with input signals of the form (3f1 – 2f2), (5f1 – 3f2), (7f1 – 5f2) and so on. One measure of it is the third-order intermodulation intercept point, often written as IPI_3. This is a calculated intercept produced by extending a graph of the levels of intermodulation products produced by two test signals against their input levels to the point at which they cross. The ratio between each signal and its distortion products is the *intermodulation ratio.* The apparent level of a third-order distortion product increases by 3dB for every 1dB increase in input signal level. In very general terms, a typical HF portable might display a calculatedIPI_3 of somewhere between -20 and -10dBm, whereas a high-grade receiver could be expected to be between 10 and 40dB better.

The second-order intermodulation intercept point (IPI_2) is similar except that it is purely additive, i.e. of the form (f1 + f2). Generally speaking it is less of an issue in HF receivers butthe effect can manifest itself when listening on a band which is an octave higher than another band in which there are very strong signals. For example, amateurs using the upper part of their 14MHz band sometimes suffer from second-order intermodulation caused by strong 41m broadcast signals. In this instance, strong signals on 7105 and 7130 kHz might intermodulate to produce a spurious signal on 14235kHz.

If we are using a conventional antenna, any intermodulation-related effects of the type described above will be purely due to shortcomings in the receiver. However, the circuitry in an active antenna (i.e. one featuring some form of amplifying or matching circuitry using devices such as transistors, FETs or the like) can itself suffer from intermodulation problems. If this happens, nothing can be done in the receiver to deal with it and the overall station performance will be degraded. It is for this reason that Wellbrook's claimed intermodulation performance for the ALA-330S is highly important, especially if it to be used in conjunction with a high-grade receiver. To put it simply, even a very good receiver such as the NRD-545G will reach its IMD limit before the Wellbrook antenna amplifier does.

It might be worth recalling that the essence of a loop antenna is that it responds mainly to the magnetic-field component of an electromagnetic wave (the H-field) rather than the electric (E) field. Since local noise and interference are well within the near field of the antenna, they consist chiefly of E-field components and as such are rejected by it. Loop antennas also display quite sharp nulls off the sides, typically of the order of 20-26dB. This property can be exceedingly useful in rejecting either local noise or a distant interfering station. Active loops such as those in the Wellbrook family have the further advantage of a low and more or less constant impedance with frequency, which implies that they will match the associated receiver very well.

Physically the ALA-330S is almost identical to the ALA-1530 reviewed last year. It consists of an aluminium loop with a diameter of 94cm, a head unit containing a balun and wideband push-pull amplifier, mounting hardware and a 12V power supply. The interface box embodies an integral fuse and a 1m lead terminated in a PL259 connector which provides the input to the receiver. All necessary connectors and sundries are supplied. The head-end electronics are housed in a white PVC box which apparently is UV stabilised. The RF output from the loop amplifier emerges on a female BNC connector.

The mounting hardware is such as to allow easy mounting on a rotatable stub mast, which will permit advantage to be taken of the loop's ability to null-out interference at the lower frequencies. Alternatively, it can be easily secured to a suitable fixed support such as a fence post. Wellbrook recommends that the antenna is mounted at least 6m from a building to minimize local noise, although in practice we found the loop's siting to be entirely non-critical.

PERFORMANCE

We tested the ALA-330S against our reference ALA-1530 at the top of an existing rotatable Yagi array for the HF and 144MHz amateur bands and also on a garden fence post about 15m from the ground and 10m or so from the laboratory. The main receivers used for testing were the NRD-545G being reviewed for this year's *WRTH* and a Sangean ATS-909 portable, with occasional recourse to the Yaesu FT-1000D in the amateur station to check signal levels. For comparison purposes we used 11m and 24m long wires at heights of about 10m, a trapped 80/40m dipole at 15m and a rotatable seven-element Yagi for 14, 21 and 28MHz at 20m. An HP 8590 spectrum analyser was used for measurements of noise floor and absolute signal strength.

We first established some approximate comparative signal strengths at the test site, which is at approximately 52N43 003W and is electrically very quiet. In very general terms the ALA-330S was almost exactly -10dB with reference to the ALA-1530 at 198kHz and about -8dB at the upper end of the MW band. At about 4MHz the levels were approximately equal, and between about 8 and 20MHz the ALA-330S was generally about +12dB with respect to the ALA-1530. In all cases the antenna was between 8 and 10dB quieter than either long wire, and during the evening the difference was generally 10-14dB. These are very good results. In comparison with the trap dipole, the Wellbrook loop was very much quieter at all times and on both bands, the difference being anywhere between 9 to 22dB. The ability of the ALA-330S to null-out high-power broadcast stations near the band edges was exceedingly useful. It was noted in the course of testing that although the claimed response is only to 30MHz, the ALA-330S worked perfectly well in the 50MHz amateur band (where it displayed some very sharp nulls) and was still producing quite usable output at the lower end of Band II.

As to whether the ALA-330S was 'better' than the ALA-1530, the verdict depends somewhat on your interests and what kind of receiver you intend to use with it. The reduced gain at lower frequencies might be significant if you are particularly interested in MW and LW DX work, for which the ALA-1530 might be a better choice. However, if you have a high-grade HF receiver, the increase in gain at higher frequencies could well be useful in certain circumstances. A minor caveat is that the overall output level might prove rather too much for a small portable, for which the ALA-1530 might be more suitable.

CONCLUSION

Overall, we like the Wellbrook loop family very much; they are purposefully designed, well made and offer good value for money. They are ideal for anyone with a small garden or limited space for antennas, and all can give a good account of themselves in distinctly unpromising circumstances. Their ability to reject local interference, or to give a good 20dB of rejection to an adjacent MW transmitter, can be an extremely useful attribute. The ALA-330S is an excellent addition to the family and may be ideal for those whose interests lie mostly in the HF portion of the spectrum and whose receivers are such as to be able to take advantage of the extra gain offered over the ALA-1530 in this region.

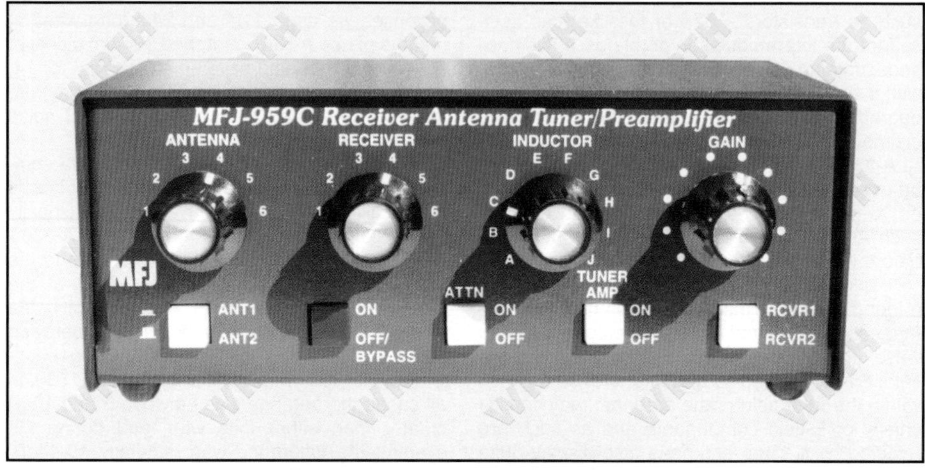

MFJ-959C

US$140 £100 €145

The issue of how preselectors work and why they are useful to the short-wave listener is discussed elsewhere in this issue of *WRTH* (see page 36). The MFJ-959C is an example of the type of preselector which is most likely to be useful to the listener, especially since it incorporates a switchable broadband preamplifier and attenuator together with provision for two separate antennas and receivers to be connected.

The unit consists of a black metal box measuring 165 x 100 x 65mm and with four rotary controls on the front panel. There are also five push-button switches. The circuit is conventional (a simple T-match) and employs two series variable capacitors and a tapped inductor. Controls for the variable capacitors are marked 'antenna' and 'receiver' and scaled from 1 to 6. The ten-position switch for the tapped inductor is marked A to J. A gain control for the broadband preamplifier, based on a single 2N3904 transistor, is provided. From left to right the push-button switches select between antennas 1 and 2; bypass the unit entirely; introduce a 20dB attenuator; select the preamplifier on or off; and select between receivers 1 and 2. The rear-panel connectors are four SO239s for receivers and antennas and a DC input socket for the preamplifier; a matching plug was not supplied, which seemed a curious omission although it is a standard 2·1mm type and should be easy to obtain. The use of SO239s implies that the unit is not suitable for use with antennas fed via balanced feeders and is best employed either in conjunction with long wires or a coaxial centre-fed dipole employing a balun. It was slightly surprising that no earth terminal was provided, since in certain circumstances this would be expected to give much improved results. However, external earths need to be used with caution when mains-driven receivers are in use, and MFJ may have felt it necessary to 'play safe'. Users who possess suitable experience in electrical wiring may find some benefit from experimentation in this area.

IN USE

The MFJ-959C was very easy to use and the instruction sheet describes setting-up and operation clearly. We tested the unit principally with the NRD-545G receiver reviewed in this edition (see page 16) and also with a Sangean ATS-909A portable and one or two other units. Formal measurements were made with standard laboratory instrumentation and our standard long-wire and dipole antennas were used for test purposes. In general terms the unit worked well and was particularly useful with the Sangean portable, where its ability to introduce considerable attenuation to strong out-of-band signals helped considerably in obtaining 'clean' reception of relatively weak transmissions. The preamplifier gave a measured 24dB of gain at frequencies between LF and well into the VHF region, but its strong-signal handling properties were not very good and it was necessary to use the facility with considerable caution. By contrast, the switchable attenuator worked well and was often employed to take the 'sting' out of strong 6/7MHz signals at night. Careful use of the preselector controls and attenuator results in good reception of some weak night-time signals which were entirely inaudible or swamped by noise when the unit was bypassed. The ability to switch between antennas for instant comparison was also well worth having.

All in all, the MFJ- 959C offers good value for money and is recommended.

Reviews Roundup 2005

TABLE-TOP

The **WinRadio G313i** builds on the success of the G303i reviewed last year and is a fine example of what can nowadays be achieved by combining good RF performance with the power of a modern PC and integrating everything via well-written software. The G313i is a truly excellent receiver by any standards, and one which points the way to the future. The **NRD-545G** is also excellent. As with its predecessor, it is still one of the world's high-grade HF receivers and displays a combination of fine performance and excellent build quality. It will be interesting to see whether its rumoured successor – which was supposedly to be marketed in early 2005 – will be as good or better. The other mains-powered receiver tested this year, the **Roberts Gemini 6** DAB/FM radio, worked well in most respects and is well worth considering. However, we still tend to admire the Pure DAB range, of which the Tempus-1 (not reviewed here but a clock-radio variant of the original Evoke-1) is our favourite. As befits their name, the current Pure designs seem to us to display a purity of design and an easy functionality that is wholly delightful.

PORTABLES

Of the five low-cost portables we tested, the **Roberts R9921** and **Sony ICF-SW35** justified their slightly higher price by being very much more versatile and easier to use. Both can be strongly recommended. The Roberts Gemini 4 DAB portable was also much liked; apart from the fact that its appetite for batteries is a little healthier than might be desirable, there is essentially nothing to criticize about this unit.

SATELLITE RECEIVERS

Most currently available receiver/control units for Sirius and XM respectively seem to be excellent examples of new-generation radios for satellite broadcasting. Our most recent direct experience was with the **Audiovox XR9**, which works very well and seem to us to offer excellent value for money. We said last year that we looked forward to the introduction of similar services in Europe, and it will be interesting to see whether they materialise. As far as WorldSpace is concerned, there were no new receivers apparently available this year and the future of what has largely become a subscription service remains unclear.

CONCLUSION

As usual, there is a wide spread of abilities and performance in the receivers tested this year, not to mention a considerable cost differential. So what follows is the usual highly subjective view of what I would like to have in my radio room.

I was very sorry to have to return the WinRadio G313i but delighted to see that WinRadio is now a company with a wholly admirable approach to product development. We were very rude about some of their earlier offerings, which seemed to us to offer poor performance and worse value for money; the G303 and 313 are in a completely different league and should be somewhere near the top of the shopping list of anyone looking for a high-performance receiver with essentially unlimited memory space. I have no doubt whatsoever that software-defined radio is the way of the future, and look forward with anticipation to whatever WinRadio serves up next.

I also liked the NRD-545G and its accessories and was deeply reluctant to return it; there was a profound temptation to send the suppliers a cheque instead. I have assessed several very high-grade receivers since the original NRD-545 was reviewed in 1999 but was pleasantly surprised by how well it compared. Indeed, the combination of the NRD-545G and the Wellbrook ALA-330S loop antenna provided some of the most impressive HF reception capability I have encountered in thirty years of working with radio. To be candid, I managed to underestimate the importance and value of active broadband HF loop antennas for rather longer than a professional radio engineer should have done. The simple fact is that whether or not you have the space to erect large conventional antennas, a well-designed active loop such as the Wellbrook is a very good antenna in its own right. It should emphatically not be considered merely as a potential solution for those with small gardens.

As far as the two Roberts DAB radios were concerned, the little Gemini 4 portable was an excellent travelling companion. The mains-driven Gemini 6 was also enjoyed. However, my ideal DAB radio would still be a fully featured mains/battery transportable with proper integration of DAB and FM and the inclusion of dynamic RDS and reversionary functions in the latter. Properly integrated alarm and clock functions (along the lines of those in the Tempus-1) would also be *de rigueur*. Sadly, no-one yet seems interested in making something along these lines.

Will next year bring a stand-alone DRM receiver? Will we see a combined DAB/DRM radio soon? As they used to say in American cinemas, watch this space.

WRTH HF Receiver Guide 2005

Budget, Hand-held & Travel Portables

Maker	Model	Size	SEL	DR	OV	US$	£	€
AOR	AR8200 MkII	H	****	***	***	650	450	650
Grundig	Yacht Boy 400	S	****	***	****	180	120	180
Icom	ICR-10	H	***	**	***	500	260	500
Roberts	R9914	S	****	***	****	180	100	145
Roberts	R861	S	****	****	****	315	175	250
Roberts	R9967	S	***	***	***	70	40	55
Sangean	ATS-305	S	***	***	****	100	65	90
Sangean	ATS-404	S	***	***	***	125	80	100
Sangean	ATS-606	S	***	***	***	160	130	160
Sangean	ATS-800A	S	***	***	***	75	50	75
Sangean	ATS-808	S	****	***	***	180	120	180
Sangean	ATS-818	S	****	****	****	200	160	250
Sony	ICF-SW07	S	****	****	****	330	220	330
Sony	ICF-SW11	S	***	***	***	40	25	35
Sony	ICF-SW12	S	***	**	*	80	50	70
Sony	ICF-SW30	S	****	***	****	125	80	125
Sony	ICF-SW35	S	***	***	****	100	65	90
Sony	ICF-SW40	S	****	***	****	120	90	120
Sony	ICF-SW100E/S	S	****	***	****	360	160	360
Sony	ICF-SW600	M	****	***	****	60	40	60
Sony	ICF-SW7600GR	S	****	****	****	225	149	225
Sony	ICF-SW1000T	S	****	****	****	540	380	540
Yaesu	VR-500	H	****	***	****	450	330	450
Yupiteru	MVT-7300	H	***	****	****	450	300	450
Yupiteru	MVT-9000EU Mk II	H	****	****	*****	550	369	550

PC Radios, Serious Short-wave & Semi-pro Receivers

Maker	Model	Size	SEL	DR	OV	US$	£	€
AOR	AR5000 + 3	M	***	***	***	2895	1550	2895
AOR	7030	M	*****	*****	****	1500	725	1500
AOR	7030 Plus	M	*****	*****	***	1700	950	1700
AOR	AR8600	L	**	***	***	1080	720	1080
Drake	SW-8	L	***	***	***	750	500	750
Drake	R8A	L	****	****	****	1200	995	1200
Drake	R8B	L	****	****	****	1200	995	1200
Fairhaven	RD500	M	***	***	***	1280	800	1280
Icom	IC-718	L	***	****	****	1050	700	1050
Icom	IC-746PRO/7400	L	***	****	****	2250	1550	2500
Icom	IC-R75	M	****	****	*****	1050	650	1050
Icom	ICR-8500	L	****	****	****	1500	1195	1600
Icom	IC-PCR100	C	***	***	****	325	200	325
Icom	IC-PCR1000	C	***	***	****	500	325	500
JRC	NRD 345	L	****	****	***	800	800	800
JRC	NRD 535	L	****	*****	****	1200	1750	1200
JRC	NRD 535D	L	*****	*****	****	1700	2000	1700
JRC	NRD 545G	L	*****	*****	*****	2200	1295	2895
K&D	KWZ 30	L	*****	*****	****	1800	1150	1800
Lowe	HF-150	M	***	****	****	500	425	500
Lowe	HF-225	M	***	***	****	850	500	850
Lowe	HF-250	M	***	***	***	1200	800	1200
Lowe	HF-250E	M	****	****	****	1100	525	1100
Palstar	R30	M	*****	*****	****	600	400	600
Roberts	R-861	M	****	****	***	210	140	210
Sangean	ATS-818C	L	***	***	****	150	150	150
Sangean	ATS-909	M	****	***	****	275	125	275
Ten-Tec	RX320	C	***	***	***	300	300	300
Ten-Tec	RX340	L	*****	*****	*****	4000	3800	5000
Ten-Tec	RX350	C	***	****	****	1200	1100	1600
Watkins	HF-1000	L	*****	*****	*****	3800	4500	3800
WinRadio	G303i	C	****	****	*****	500	350	500
WinRadio	G313i	C	*****	****	*****	950	550	800
Yaesu	FT-840	L	****	****	****	825	550	825
Yaesu	FRG-100B	L	****	****	***	600	450	600
Yaesu	VR-5000	L	****	***	****	1050	700	1050

KEY: SEL = Selectivity, DR = Dynamic Range, OV = Overall Value. H = Hand-held, C = PC radio, S = Small, easily portable. M = Medium, suitcase size. L = Large, table top use. * = Avoid ** = Poor *** = Fair **** = Good ***** = Outstanding.
NOTE: Prices are approximate due to exchange rate fluctuations. Some models may be unavailable in certain markets.

Ancillary Equipment

We continue our series of articles on the art of receiving, with an examination of the benefits and pitfalls afforded by ancillary equipment

Reduced to its lowest terms, reception of broadcast stations requires nothing more than a suitable receiver. In the case of a portable, such as those discussed on page 22 of this edition of *WRTH*, we have a single box which contains everything necessary; antenna, loudspeaker, power source and the approriate circuitry. However, if we want rather better results than are available from a simple portable, we need to consider some of its integral functions and pay attention to them as separate entities. The most obvious example is the *antenna*, which in a portable radio will inevitably be compromised by size and position. It will undoubtedly consist of an internal ferrite rod for LW and MW, perhaps in conjunction with some form of telescopic 'whip' for the higher frequencies. Both are compromises; they work well enough for reception of consistently strong signals but are of limited use for anything else. So the first separation we make is between receiver and antenna. We have discussed antennas a good deal in earlier editions of WRTH and make no apology whatsoever for asserting yet again that they are by far the most important part of any radio receiving installation. The finest and most expensive receiver ever made will not work well if it is fed from a few feet of wire, whereas an experienced user will wring miracles out of a modest receiver coupled to a good antenna.

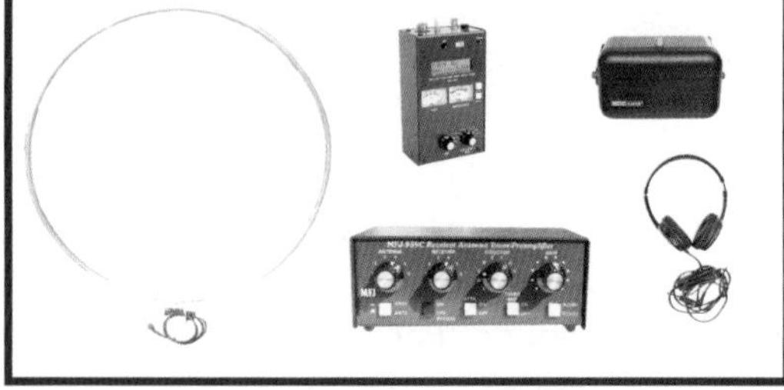

ANTENNA ANALYSERS

An item which is very useful for those who enjoy experimenting with antennas is the *antenna analyser*. To those brought up on noise bridges, impedance meters, Smith charts and similar impedimenta, the ability of the modern microprocessor-controlled portable analyser (such as the MFJ-259 or 269) to provide a formidable amount of information literally at the flick of a switch is quite astonishing. These units can make it almost child's play to set up even a complex multiband antenna and match it to its feeder in a matter of minutes. We freely confess that before we reviewed the MFJ-269 some years ago for *WRTH*, we were extremely sceptical of those devices and strongly suspected that they were not remotely worth the asking price. Nowadays we would not even consider attempting to set up a new antenna without one; it has become absolutely indispensable for a wide variety of jobs.

LOUDSPEAKERS

Another useful separation is in the *loudspeaker*. The position and size of the speaker in most radios is largely driven by cosmetic and visual considerations and in most cases the audio from them sounds somewhere between bearable and dreadful. Adding a decent-quality external speaker is one of the most cost-effective enhancements to a receiving system, and will have an immediate and dramatic effect in reducing listening fatigue. Unfortunately it may also immediately reveal some shortcomings in the audio amplifier stages of your receiver – hum, noise and rather too much distortion being the usual problems encountered. In some cases it may be possible to add an external amplifier driven from a line-level output, which again is likely to bring about a marked improvement. Many receiver manufacturers make external 'add-on' speakers for their products, and in our experience these range from being somewhere between very good and horrible. Our strong advice is to try before you buy, if at all possible.

In recent years there has been a tendency towards so-called *adaptive speakers* using onboard digital signal processing to tailor the frequency response to the optimum required for reception of a particular mode. These are usually sold as accessories by radio outlets, most of which seem to make inordinately extravagant claims for the level of performance produced by particular units. Our experience is that these items do not represent good value for money for the short-wave broadcast listener although they might well find a use in amateur stations. The reason is that adaptive speakers tend to be extremely adept at nulling-out heterodynes and assorted tuning-up noises, and such an ability can prove remarkably useful at times on the amateur bands. However, strong heterodynes are not commonly encountered during broadcast-band listening. The DSP-modified frequency response of all the examples we have auditioned also seems to detract from short-wave broadcast reception quality rather than adding to it. So all in all, it seems to us that adaptive speakers need not be very high on the shopping-list of the short-wave broadcast listener. In general terms we take the view that the best place for DSP circuitry is as far as possible towards the front-end of the receiver, not at the loudspeaker end.

HEADPHONES

Loudspeaker listening is fine if good-quality reception is available, but for reception of weak and noisy stations it may well be better to use *headphones*. All too often taken for granted, headphones are arguably one of the most vital components of the overall receiving system. The reason is that they act as the principal interface between the receiver's output and your ear-brain system, and also have an important role in excluding extraneous noise. So their electrical performance, comfort and acoustic insulation properties are all worth consideration.

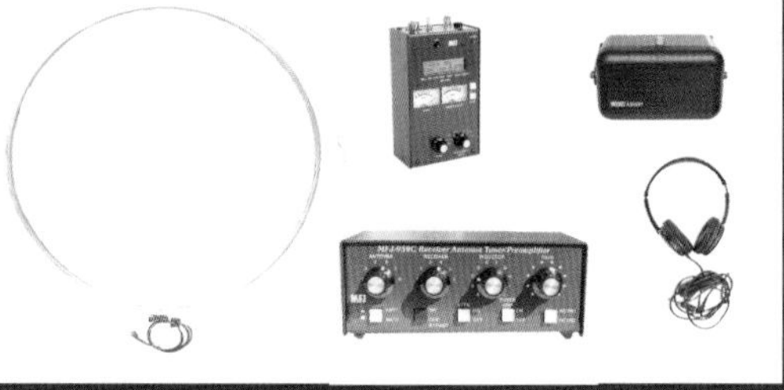

You might imagine that plugging an ordinary stereo headset into your receiver would produce perfectly good results, especially if you already own an expensive item which gives excellent hi-fi reproduction. Unfortunately this is far from being the case because your high-grade stereo headphones are likely to have an excellent frequency response extending to both ends of the AF spectrum. This will allow them to reproduce any shortcomings in your receiver's audio amplifier performance with the utmost fidelity. Many mains-powered receivers have some degree of low-level hum in the output. This originates in the power supply and is related to the mains frequency. The internal speaker may well not have enough low-frequency response to reproduce the hum, but a good-quality stereo headset will have no difficulty at all in doing so. Some receivers also display high levels of hiss, which is seldom audible on the internal speaker but is all too noticeable in a headset with an extended frequency response. Hum and hiss are very fatiguing to listen to for any length of time. To make matters worse, the distortion characteristics of the simple integrated-circuit power amplifiers commonly used in receivers are such that they also tend to be rather hard on the ears when experienced via wide-range headphones. The usual consequence of any or all of these issues is that headphone listening becomes something we do not much enjoy for long, although unless we have some insight into them we may well not know why.

Listening via headphones optimised for radio listening as opposed to sonic fidelity is likely to be a much more pleasant experience. These items tend to have responses that are curtailed at low and high frequencies and have a degree of 'tailoring' in the mid-band to enhance intelligibility. This implies a frequency response of perhaps 150-4000Hz to the -6dB points, and ideally a fairly steep roll-off thereafter. They should also display low inherent distortion.

The issue of comfort is all-important, and as with receivers as a whole there is no substitute for trying several different headphones before purchase. We all have differently dimensioned heads and strong personal preferences for how 'tight' the headphones should feel on the ears. Ideally the earpieces should be laterally and vertically adjustable for comfort. A related issue is the degree of isolation conferred by the headphones. Some people cannot tolerate feeling cut off from the outside world by earpieces with a high degree of acoustic isolation (usually by snugly fitting seals) whilst others positively welcome it.

As an aside, large quantities of ex-military headsets have appeared in recent times on the surplus market, and the eBay auction site, at extremely low prices. These tend to be very well made and give excellent performance. Our personal favourite is the 'Airlite 62' originally made for UK military and civil-aviation applications but now tending to be displaced in favour of noise-cancelling types. It is a simple task to remove the boom microphone and rewire the connecting cable to suit your particular receiver's connector, after which you are left with a rugged and reliable headset whose frequency response is beautifully tailored to communications-quality speech and which is very comfortable when worn for long periods.

PRESELECTORS

Another important add-on to a receiving station is the *preselector* or *antenna tuning unit (ATU)*. The main reason this is necessary – or at least very useful – is that a receiver is designed with an input impedance at its antenna input terminal which is quite low and constant over the bands it covers, whereas the impedance of the vast majority of antennas (apart from specifically broadband types, such as the log-periodic or discone) varies widely with frequency. This is especially the case with random-length long wires, which are apt to display highly reactive (i.e. very inductive or very capacitative) impedances that are nowhere near that of the receiver to which they are connected. For maximum power transfer from the antenna to the receiver to take place, the antenna impedance needs to be transformed to a value which is at least close to that of the receiver. This is usually done by means of a preselector, which acts as a species of continuously variable transformer. In effect, this can be considered as bringing the entire antenna system into resonance at the frequency of interest, and at the same time transforming its impedance to a value which a) approximately matches that of the receiver and b) is chiefly resistive. Using a preselector with a random-wire antenna can bring about a dramatic improvement in signal strength. Unfortunately many modern commercial preselectors do not have earth (ground) terminals, presumably for the good reason that injudicious earthing can in certain circumstances cause problems and *in extremis* result in a very real hazard of electric shock to the incautious user. The lack of a ground reference terminal may severely compromise the ability of a preselector to tune certain antennas on certain frequencies. In particular, some disappointment can ensue if operating a non-earthed preselector in conjunction with a long-wire antenna and a portable radio, and in this situation it might be worth obtaining specialist advice to achieve optimum results.

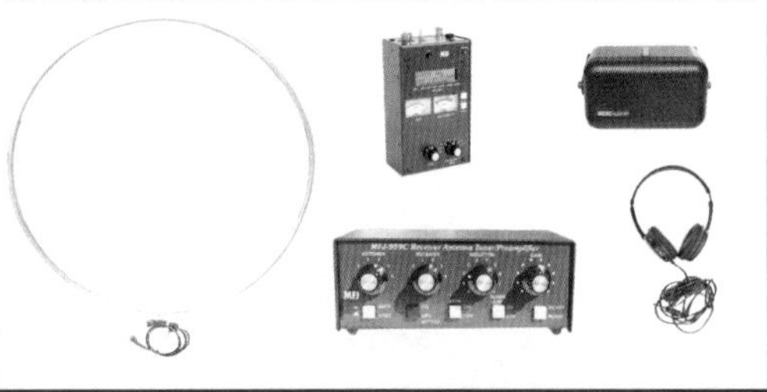

There are various forms of preselector but almost all incorporate one or more variable capacitors together with an inductor fitted with suitable switched taps. More expensive examples allow the use of either *balanced* or *unbalanced* feeder connections, which in certain circumstances can be extremely useful. An unbalanced antenna is one which is fed via coaxial line and has a *balun* (balance-to-unbalance transformer) at the feed point. A balanced antenna is fed via some form of flat line, usually open-wire feeder or ribbon. The advantages and disadvantages of each type are a little beyond the scope of this article, but the advanced listener with a large external antenna system may choose to use a balanced feed arrangement and requires a preselector which is capable of transforming this to the unbalanced input required by the receiver.

By virtue of the properties of circuits embodying capacitors and inductors, most preselectors will simultaneously act as either high-pass or low-pass *filters*. This makes them very useful for rejection of strong out-of-band signals, especially if the user happens to live near a high-power broadcast transmitter or has a radio-amateur neighbour. Equally, it is easy enough to incorporate a switchable *attenuator* into the preselector and this is often done in commercial items. Some units, such as the MFJ-959C reviewed on page 28, also embody broadband preamplifiers. These can be valuable if one happens to be using an older receiver which is perhaps a little short of sensitivity, especially at the higher frequencies. However, a preamplifier can be an outright liability if used with a receiver whose strong-signal handling is already marginal. Our strong recommendation is that if you purchase a preselector containing an RF preamplifier, make sure it can be switched out of circuit.

Incidentally, if you are considering the purchase of a preselector or ATU, there is no need to opt for the large and expensive items made for the amateur radio market. These are of course arranged to be capable of matching the amateur's *transmitter* to the antenna as well as the *receiver* – the principles of impedance matching outlined above apply to both – and as such they need to be able to handle high voltages and currents. Preselectors or ATUs for receive-only applications can be very much smaller and less elaborate. Having said that, the average amateur-type ATU will probably be capable of matching a rather wider range of impedances than a small unit intended for the listener, and would be well worth having if you have the budget and space for it. For those with a little experience and the willingness to look for suitable parts, a preselector can also represent an easy introduction to the world of home construction. There is nothing quite as satisfying as using equipment you have made yourself.

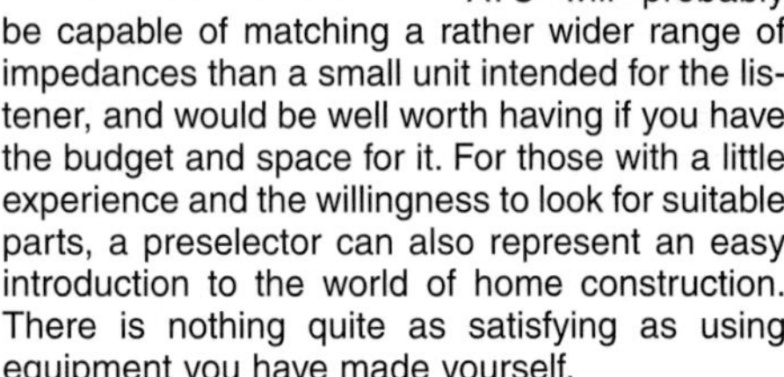

'HOME-BREWING'

If you are interested in what radio amateurs call 'home-brewing' you will need a *soldering iron* and the requisite skills to use it. Actually you will probably need one anyway, if only because you are likely to find yourself having to carry out tasks which positively require one, such as fitting coaxial connectors to cable. If you always use a good grade of multicore solder, keep the bit of the iron clean and set the operating temperature carefully, you will be surprised at how easy it is to do a good job every time. That said, the PL-259 or UHF connector taxes most of us since it seems to have been primarily designed as a wickedly difficult test for those who have to fit them. If you can reliably terminate coaxial cable with a PL-259 plug, you need no advice on soldering . . .

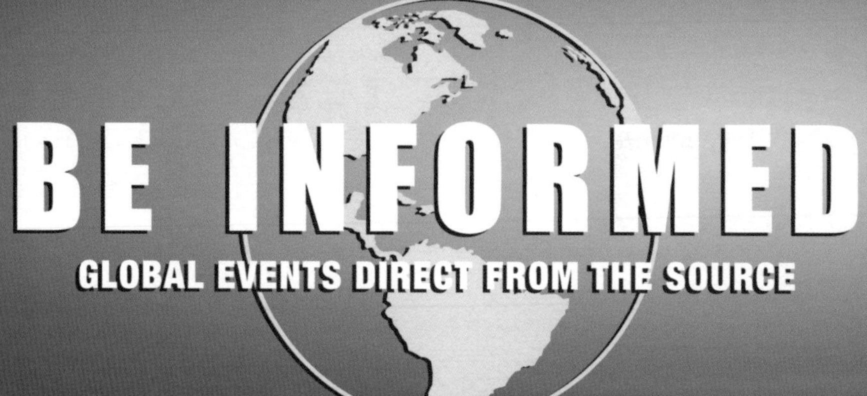
BE INFORMED
GLOBAL EVENTS DIRECT FROM THE SOURCE

S350

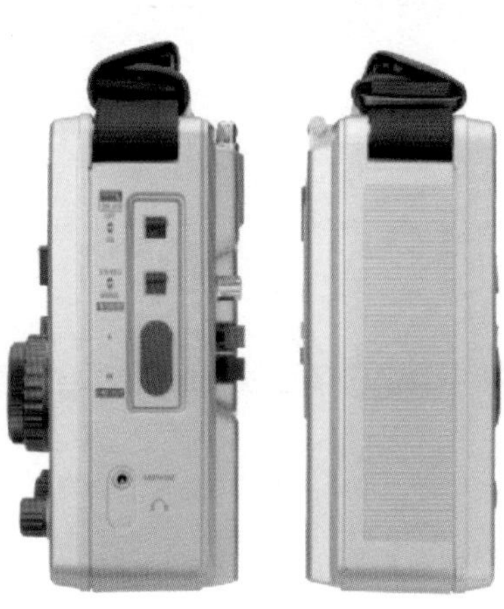

- Separate bass, treble, and RF gain controls
- Wide and narrow bandwidth filter controls
- Line-level audio outputs and external antenna input
- Alarm and sleep timer functions
- Illuminated multi-function LCD screen

Dimensions: 10.5"W x 6.5"H x 3.5"D **Weight:** 3lbs. 9oz.
Power Source: 4 D batteries (not included) or AC adaptor (included)

How to use *WRTH*

ORGANISATION OF THE BOOK

The book consists of three main areas: **Features**, consisting of equipment reviews, broadcasting predictions and informative radio-related articles; **Directory**, which is further divided into *National Radio, International Radio* and *TV* services; and finally **Reference** where miscellaneous information covering wider aspects of broadcasting can be found.

Each section is identified by a unique 'side-bar', which can be found both on the main contents page and on each individual page throughout the book. Each section starts with an alphabetical country listing and is followed by the appropriate 'by frequency' lists.

In the Directory, countries are listed alphabetically within each section so that they may be easily located by flicking forward to the relevant location. Alternatively, the index may be used to find the exact page number for a specific country of interest.

OPERATING TECHNIQUES

When operating their receivers, the majority of listeners tend to operate in one of two main modes, switching between them as and when they deem appropriate. One method is to 'target' a given station or country by monitoring known frequencies and the other is simply to 'cruise' a specific band and identify each station as they occur. We have designed WRTH in such a way that either of these methods can be accommodated.

TARGETING

When operating in the targeting mode there are two ways to find a particular country. The first option is to go to the main contents page and use the section 'side-bars' to direct you to the right area of the book. Once there, you then only have to flick forward a few pages to locate the country of interest. Alternatively you can use the country index at the back of the book, which will tell you the precise page number.

However, as you develop a 'feel' for the book and get used to the alphabetical layout, you will probably find that the side-bar method is simpler and quicker than using the country index.

BAND-SCANNING

Should you prefer to use band-scanning, there are listings of both medium wave and international short-wave broadcasts available at the end of the respective sections. These can also be useful for casual listening, but in either case can help to identify a station by frequency – whereupon further details can be obtained using the country entry to identify alternative frequencies for the station of interest.

BAND SELECTION

When choosing a band to monitor, it is well worthwhile refering to the *'Most Suitable Frequency'* table in this section, which recommends the most suitable frequency bands for a variety of locations. It is however important to bear in mind that such tables are only guides and cannot be considered to be 100% reliable – ionospheric events can not only enhance propagation conditions but also operate to their detriment – nevertheless, such tables remain an excellent starting point and their use is strongly recommended.

RECEPTION REPORTS

WRTH recommends use of the simple SINPO code using the following scale:

S	I N P	O
5=Excellent	5=None	5=Excellent
4=Good	4=Slight	4=Good
3=Fair	3=Moderate	3=Fair
2=Poor	2=Severe	2=Poor
1=Barely Audible	1=Extreme	1=Worthless

S=Signal Strength, I=Interference, N=Noise, P=Propagatioon-disturbance, O=Overall Merit

It is courteous to enclose return postage when writing to small domestic broadcasters. This can be in the form of an International Reply Coupon (IRC) available from post offices. Some DX clubs buy IRC's in bulk and sell them to members. In all cases, when writing to radio stations you must write clearly. Remember, if the station cannot read your address, then you cannot expect to receive a reply!

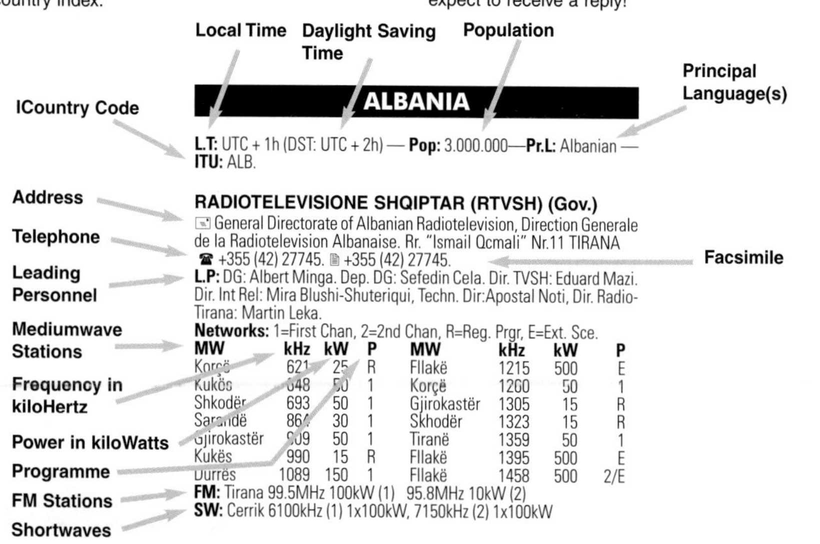

ALBANIA

L.T: UTC + 1h (DST: UTC + 2h) — **Pop:** 3.000.000—**Pr.L:** Albanian — **ITU:** ALB.

RADIOTELEVISIONE SHQIPTAR (RTVSH) (Gov.)

General Directorate of Albanian Radiotelevision, Direction Generale de la Radiotelevision Albanaise. Rr. "Ismail Qcmali" Nr.11 TIRANA
☎ +355 (42) 27745. +355 (42) 27745.
L.P: DG: Albert Minga. Dep. DG: Sefedin Cela. Dir. TVSH: Eduard Mazi. Dir. Int Rel: Mira Blushi-Shuteriqui, Techn. Dir:Apostal Noti, Dir. Radio-Tirana: Martin Leka.
Networks: 1=First Chan, 2=2nd Chan, R=Reg. Prgr, E=Ext. Sce.

MW	kHz	kW	P	MW	kHz	kW	P
Korçë	621	25	R	Fllakë	1215	500	E
Kukës	648	50	1	Korçë	1260	50	1
Shkodër	693	50	1	Gjirokastër	1305	15	R
Sarandë	864	30	1	Skhodër	1323	15	R
Gjirokastër	909	50	1	Tiranë	1359	50	1
Kukës	990	15	R	Fllakë	1395	500	E
Durrës	1089	150	1	Fllakë	1458	500	2/E

FM: Tirana 99.5MHz 100kW (1) 95.8MHz 10kW (2)
SW: Cerrik 6100kHz (1) 1x100kW, 7150kHz (2) 1x100kW

International Frequency Allocation Chart

LW MW 160m 120m 90m 80m (EU) 80m (NA) ←75m 60m 49m 40m (EU)→ 41m 40m (NA) 41m 31m

0 1 2 3 4 5 6 7 8 9 10
MHz

←30m 25m 22m 20m 19m 16m ←17m ←15m

10 11 12 13 14 15 16 17 18 19 20
MHz

15m 13m ←12m 11m 10m

20 21 22 23 24 25 26 27 28 29 30
MHz

= Broadcast Band
= Radio Amateur Band
= Utility - Other Services
= Standard Time & Frequency Transmission

Top face of each bar shows regional differences where appropriate

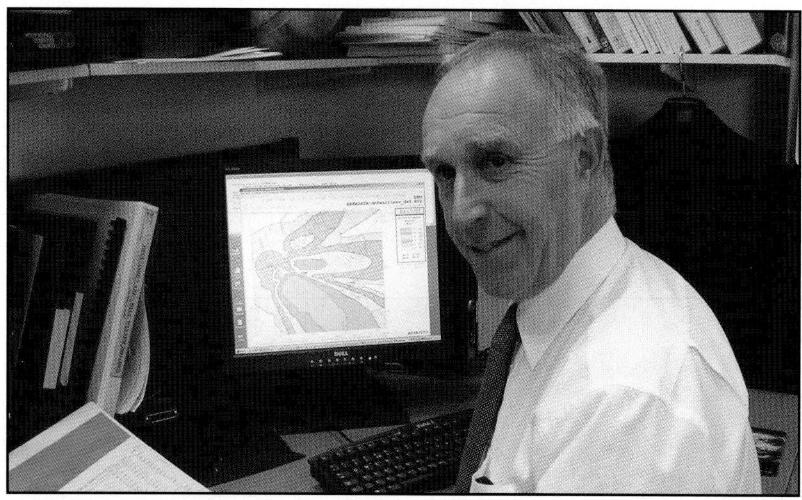

Managing the HF Spectrum

John Nelson talks to Mike Still of VT Communications

WRTH: Twenty-six years ago, when we were both with the BBC, I learnt the basic principles of frequency management with you and your colleagues. What has changed since then?

MS: Quite a lot. At that time there were four annual schedules, which made life very difficult at times. In the 1980s there were moves to introduce six-monthly schedules, and after that it was a case of trying to find a once-and-for-all plan. So by the 1992 WARC in Malaga, when the politics were changing very quickly and the former USSR had split up, it became possible to think in terms of much better co-ordination and flexibility. We all tend to talk to each other much more often and more freely than we did in the old days.

WRTH: How many transmitter sites does VT Communications have?

MS: We own four. There are the three ex-BBC HF sites at Skelton, Woofferton and Rampisham and the medium-wave site at Orfordness. Nowadays we tend to think of all three HF sites as being more or less completely interchangeable, although DRM is only on from Rampisham at present. I suspect that will change in time. The BBC owns the sites in Cyprus, Ascension, Seychelles, Kranji, Oman and Thailand. We have the operation and maintenance contracts for them, however, so we look after them for the BBC.

WRTH: The BBC site at Daventry closed in the early 1990s. I seem to remember that it was never a particularly good site.

MS: Daventry was really a general-purpose site. Rampisham was built to cover Eastern Europe and Russia. Skelton was organised for Western Europe and North Africa. Woofferton was mostly used by VOA, so it had lots of high-gain arrays looking at Eastern Europe. Daventry had a bit of everything; we could do most things from there.

WRTH: Is the trend of reducing frequency hours now being reversed?

MS: Good question; the answer is yes and no. The BBC is still reducing HF transmitter hours overall, but we keep the sites very busy with non-BBC services. The only real growth business in HF broadcasting *per se* is religious broadcasting. Having said that, the BBC broadcasts in a lot more languages overall than it did in our day. It's just that most of them aren't on shortwave. Many of the mainstream European language services have gone but there are lots of new ones and very much more rebroadcasting than there used to be. Since the break-up of Yugoslavia, for instance, there's Slovene, Macedonian, Serbian and Croatian. Albanian is new, as is Ukrainian. There are also the Central Asian languages – Azeri, Kazakh, Kirghiz, Uzbek and so on. All these are on rebroadcast FM, of course. Actually, some of them come and go. What tends to happen is that the service gets started and then something goes wrong; the transmitter breaks, or something. Then my phone rings and someone says "can you get us going on shortwave by tomorrow please?"

WRTH: How do you go about planning a service?

MS: Well, let's take a typical example. Let's assume you want to provide a service in Farsi for Iran. There are two questions to ask initially. Firstly, how much money do you want to spend? Secondly, how reliable do you want the service to be? If it's to be provided at low cost, we're talking about a single frequency out of the UK. You also need to think about the time of day. Will it be early morning or late evening, when it's dark in the UK? Or will it be in daylight? A transmission from the UK to Iran will be two hops, and we really want to avoid one of them coming down in an area of darkness and the other in daylight – that's a sure way to provide an unreliable service. Depending on what the customer wants, we might recommend moving the proposed time a couple of hours either way to make it an all-dark or all-light path. Generally speaking, if it's an all-dark path you're going to be looking at 6, 7 or 9MHz. If it's daylight, we're going to be thinking in terms of 13, 15 or 17MHz. But we can also look at what else is on to that area and how well it's working. On that basis we might go as low as 11MHz or as high as 21MHz in daylight. Having done that, we need to consider occupancy and congestion issues. If I go to a co-ordination conference and propose a new frequency that puts a hop down in Europe right in the middle of prime time, my colleagues will probably tell me not to be silly. And in Iranian prime time there will be an awful lot of transmitters which are much closer to the service area than mine in the UK and which will be putting in much louder signals. So I'm going to have a problem producing a signal from the UK that will be strong enough; the band I want to be on will almost certainly be congested in the target area. If the broadcaster has a little more money to spend, we can look at sites that are a bit closer. Lots of broadcasters and transmitter-site operators have opened up their facilities to other users. We can buy or barter time for our customers.

Let's take the case of an religious broadcaster who wants to put on a service to the Far East and who is a customer of ours. We can set up an exchange with a Far Eastern broadcaster who wants to provide a service into Europe. We could exchange transmitter time at Skelton for time somewhere in the Far East. So the Far Eastern broadcaster's programme would be sent from Skelton and our religious broadcast would go out of their site. We also have three-way models along the same lines. All in all, the world's transmitter networks are far more open and bartered than they used to be. Different routes and different areas of coverage require a few different things to be taken into account, but by and large that approach is valid for most situations. If more resources are available, one can add in other things, of course, like local FM rebroadcasting, satellite feeds and so on.

WRTH: So let's suppose you've got the service up and running. Do reception reports still matter?

MS: Oh yes. Very much so. I tell newcomers that the whole business of providing a service is a management process and it needs feedback. How am I doing? Was I successful? This is working well, don't change it; this isn't working, what do I need to do to make it work? We can't evaluate the results of what we do without good feedback. You probably remember that we used to rely on people turning on their radios and sending in reports. All very useful, but nowadays it's much more automated and mechanised, more reliable if you like. Thanks to the internet, we can have receivers in the target area and we don't have the gaps that we used to have. Some receivers are connected up to telephone lines; the organisations in the HFCC host them. But mostly we rely on a commercially available service. In essence this is a receiver and computer connected to the internet. We dial it up and tell the receiver what to listen to and when. The computer stores the audio, and from time to time it sends us an e-mail with the results. We still need people to listen to it and give what they hear an SIO score, so it isn't the computer that evaluates the results; it's a human. But all this means we don't have to have people listening in real time. And we can compare samples from various places, or listen to samples one after another.

WRTH: Will the HF broadcasting spectrum shrink or grow?

MS: Well, the pressure from broadcasters is still there. HF broadcasting is nowadays the main activity on short wave, and our bands are still generally over-used.

WRTH: Indeed, but when I tune round the non-broadcast shortwave bands these days, they sound very different: not much data, no Piccolo, very little teleprinting, not a lot of fax or point-to-point SSB and almost no ISB links.

MS: That's true. In general terms HF is a lot less busy than it used to be. But again, those users haven't actually gone away. They hang on to their old allocations as back-up. The other big present-day user is still aviation, with all the long-distance SSB traffic. I can't see that going anywhere for a long time yet, even with satellite systems taking up some of it. But the broadcasters will certainly keep the pressure on.

WRTH: So you can't see an end to short-wave broadcasting?

MS: No, because in some situations nothing can replace it. In tropical regions, for example, or in very large countries, there's no viable alternative.

WRTH: And what about DRM?

MS: It's early days yet. Lots of people are pushing for it, and from a technical and engineering point of view it works. It's easy enough to add it to a modern transmitter if the modulator is good enough; more or less anything built after the 1980s can handle it. Two of ours have it already. All the current DRM transmissions are experimental, as you know. In the short term, my guess is that one problem with DRM might be spectrum compatibility. However, there's no reason at all why DRM and analogue can't co-exist, given the will of the spectrum managers to co-ordinate frequencies. I am sure we will.

Mike Still is a frequency management consultant. He had a long and distinguished career with the BBC's Schedule Unit, where he was responsible for frequency planning and management in the External Services. He moved to VT Communications when the BBC's transmitter network was privatised in the 1990s.

Digital Radio Update

A round-up of what has been happening in the world of digital radio over the past year

DIGITAL AUDIO BROADCASTING

In the period since last year's edition of *WRTH*, digital radio in various forms has ceased to be tomorrow's technology and has without doubt become today's. In particular, DAB's time has arrived with a vengeance. It now appears quite likely that the end of domestic analogue radio broadcasting in the UK will take place in about eight years. In August 2004 the UK Secretary of State for Culture, Media and Sport said in answer to a recent Parliamentary question that later this year she would be reviewing the take-up of digital radio and ". . . considering how long it would be appropriate for sound digital broadcasting services to be provided in analogue form". It was also reported that OFCOM has reached a position on the issue, and that in its view analogue radio switch-off could take place soon after the changeover to digital television. In the UK this is intended to take place in 2012, and many European countries are understood to be working towards a similar time period. However, the industry's view – at least from a UK perspective – is that several criteria need to be met first. A major issue, both in the UK and elsewhere in Europe, is that of additional spectrum allocation for DAB.

In the past twelve months a number of relatively low-cost receivers have become available in quantity; in Europe they are now widely sold in supermarkets and other retail outlets. As this was written, almost 70 different models of DAB receiver were on sale worldwide and the audience for the service was about 320 million, with some 600 different DAB services available. A recent independent report by Eureca Research forecast that the installed base of DAB receivers in Europe would increase from around 512,000 at the end of 2003 to an astonishing 3955 million at the end of 2010, representing a Compound Annual Growth Rate (CAGR) of 861 per cent. The same report also predicted that the market value of DAB products would increase at a CAGR of 40 per cent in the period 2004-2010 and represent a €1·31 billion (US$1.57 billion/£875·7 million) market opportunity for receiver manufacturers in 2010. By any standards these are very impressive numbers.

As this was written, WorldDAB was due to host the first European demonstration of DMB (Digital Multimedia Broadcasting) on its stand at the IBC in Amsterdam, using hand-held receivers from Samsung, PersTel and onTimetek. DMB uses DAB technology to deliver television, video, audio and data to mobile devices. Earlier this year the Korean government approved the introduction of terrestrial DMB broadcasts of television programmes to mobiles, and commercial products are expected to be available by the end of 2004. The service will launch in Korea by the end of 2004 and will initially include 48 channels delivered to consumers free of charge.

We have discussed the technology of DAB in previous editions of *WRTH*, but in brief DAB stands for 'Digital Audio Broadcasting' and its origins date back to 1981 and the 'Eureka 147' project. In principle it offers near-CD quality sound, more stations, additional radio and data services, ease of tuning and interference-free reception for the listener. It also offers a vast improvement in spectrum efficiency over modulation methods such as FM and AM, which in an age of immense pressure on the radio spectrum is arguably its most important feature. DAB can be transmitted on frequencies in the existing FM band (also known as Band II and encompassing 88-108MHz) but the services that have been introduced in Europe, Canada and Australia, together with pilots in India and elsewhere, are using other frequencies. Some countries including the UK are using part of the upper portion of Band III (174-225MHz) formerly used for 405-line television. Others such as Germany and Canada are using L-band (1452-1492 MHz). Some DAB receivers currently on the market can receive both Band III and L-band transmissions although most of the current 'portables' are Band III only apart from a few some rather expensive units. The 1992 World Administrative Radio Conference allocated L-band spectrum to both terrestrial and satellite digital broadcasting. In practice, however, it seems likely that Band III will continue to be used in some countries for national networks and L-band (whose range is considerably shorter) for local stations. Ultimately this will be the position in the UK as well as other countries. Many European countries now have L-band allocations but relatively few are yet in use, and as yet there appears to be no likelihood of satellite-based DAB services. That said, it has been reported that a consortium including a UK-based commercial broadcaster has recently been considering the possibility of introducing an equivalent to the American Sirius and XM satellite radio services in Europe, using L-band DAB transmissions. The same consortium has apparently been considering the possibility of a parallel short-wave European service using DRM and subsidising the

cost of combined DRM and DAB integrated circuits, which would be interesting to say the least.

DIGITAL RADIO MONDIALE

All in all, DAB appears to have a bright future. In respect of the other major digital mode, DRM, it would seem fair to say that progress has been steady rather than spectacular. The essence of DRM is that it is an amalgam of existing digital technologies which aims to provide stereo audio, multimedia and text information in the same bandwidth as that currently used for AM broadcasting. Many of the world's major broadcasters have expressed an intention to adopt it, and test transmissions have been taking place for some time. The system actually uses four distinct modes, known as A, B, C and D. Mode A is intended for use on LW and MW during daylight hours and mode B – which is currently used for most of the test transmissions – is for MW at night and short wave. Modes C and D are for tropical bands, where most signals are vertical-incidence. The different modes all use quadrature amplitude modulation (QAM) in various combinations of amplitude and phase modulation and bit rate. Our experience to date is that DRM can work quite well but it is undoubtedly more vulnerable to various forms of interference and ionospheric effects than its proponents have insisted and some very strange effects have been heard. It is also exceedingly easy to jam. Taken together with what is undoubtedly a move away from HF broadcasting as a supplier of services and what appears to be its steady replacement by alternative forms of programme delivery, we still incline to the view that DRM's future is not necessarily guaranteed. As a senior BBC manager said to us recently, had DRM been available twenty years ago, its prospects would have looked very different.

Dedicated DRM receivers are still not commercially available but a software decoder is available from the DRM group or its licensees for a fee of €60 (US$70/£40). This can be used in conjunction with a modified receiver and a PC, or directly with a software-defined receiver such as the G313i (see page 18). A very useful web site listing modifications to receivers is at http://www.drmrx.org/ receiverods.htm and a good deal of background information is available from the DRM site www.drm.org. There is also a free software package known as 'Dream' which can be downloaded from www.sourceforge.net. This is more of a work-in-progress and requires considerable skill and software experience together with a degree of expertise in making hardware modifications.

XM & SIRIUS

For many years now it has been possible to receive radio stations from satellites. In Europe the 'Sky' constellation – which is principally intended for television – carries many domestic radio outlets and all are freely receivable as part of the subscription package. Other satellites carry radio as well. In the USA there are two satellite radio systems transmitting directly to the end user, both systems having been awarded SDARS (Satellite Digital Audio Radio Service) licences by the FCC in 1997. XM Satellite Radio launched its services in September 2001, with Sirius Radio beginning operations in February 2002. Both offer over 120 programme channels which are chiefly aimed at the mobile user, and many cars and car radios sold in the USA are now 'XM-ready' or 'Sirius-ready'. Both satellite operators have reached licensing agreements with a large number of vehicle and equipment manufacturers, and indeed at least one very large vehicle maker is a major shareholder in one of the systems. The channels are divided into 65 music streams, the majority of which are either commercial-free or include a small amount of advertising – far less than the average American radio station. There are also 50 streams of sport, news and entertainment including CNN, NBC, ESPN, NPR and BBC World Service.

The services operate on a subscription basis, with Sirius costing $12.95 per month, and XM $9.99 per month but with a one-off $14.95 activation fee. Sirius uses three satellites in non-geostationary orbits whereas XM uses two geostationary Model 702 'birds' referred to by the station as 'Rock' and 'Roll'. Built by Boeing, these are said by XM to be the most powerful civil satellites in service. They are located over the east and west coasts of the USA and are stated to produce S-band RF outputs of 18kW and generate overall ERPs in the region of 10MW. Both Sirius and XM use ground-based repeaters to fill-in reception in difficult urban situations. Neither XM nor Sirius transmissions are audible outside the continental US, and indeed their licences do not permit them to provide service elsewhere.

In the course of our visits to the USA we have extensively sampled Sirius and XM receiving systems and have been thoroughly impressed by both. All receivers have to be type-approved by the service provider and the resulting performance is to a very high standard indeed. Although intended mainly for in-car listening, both transmissions can be received in the home if an appropriate antenna is provided and 'home kits' are available for many of the currently available units. An example of a typical XM receiver, the XR9 from Audiovox, is illustrated.

HD RADIO

It seems certain that both Sirius and XM have a solidly viable commercial future. At the time of writing, XM had something over one million subscribers and Sirius had about 180,000; for services that have only been established for a few years these are quite remarkable figures. We mentioned last year that some competition was imminent from what is now referred to as 'HD Radio', the HD standing for 'High Definition'. This is the system which was hitherto was known as IBOC (in-band on-channel) and which allows existing AM and FM stations to transmit their output on existing frequencies in a digital format. After some initial political and technical hiccups, the FCC has now approved the standard and several stations are already transmitting.

Our experience with HD radio has been limited to several journeys within the coverage area of two FM stations, using a Kenwood KTC-HR100 in-car receiver. The quality seemed quite reasonable, but it could not be said to be any better than FM. Certain types of programme material displayed a rather hard and fatiguing quality, possibly due to the low bit-rate (a maximum of 96kbps, which compares rather unfavourably with the maximum of 256kbps available via DAB). There have reportedly been issues with HD transmissions causing adjacent-channel interference to other stations. Several colleagues have commented that the AM variant sounds considerably worse than good-quality analogue, and that it is heavily degraded by adjacent-channel interference. Apart from the Kenwood, the only other HD receivers available at the time of writing were from JVC and Panasonic, with others supposedly in the pipeline. However, it is still not clear whether HD radio has much of a future.

WORLDSPACE

The future for WorldSpace does not look particularly promising either. This satellite-based service provider started out with high ideals but much of its output is now encrypted and requires a monthly subscription of about US$10. Although it provides some of the output of the XM satellite system, now achieving enormous popularity in the USA, Noah Samara's original vision of low-cost radio for a Third World audience seems to have become lost. A few new receivers have been said by WorldSpace to have been introduced during the last twelve months, but they do not appear to be commercially available.

NORTH AMERICAN DIGITAL

We said last year that it would be a very brave person who predicted whether HD or one of the two satellite radio services will ultimately prevail in the USA. If we had to guess now, we suspect that XM has the brightest future and that HD radio probably has the dimmest. We also mentioned last year that DAB has no future whatsoever. Although the Eureka 147 system emerged very well indeed from laboratory and field tests carried out by CEMA (Consumer and Electronics Manufacturers Association), the National Association of Broadcasters opposes the adoption of DAB in the USA. The opposition is based on lack of new spectrum, dislike of sharing transmitters in the multiplex and concerns that DAB would introduce new competition. This makes for rather an unfortunate contrast with the situation in Canada, where DAB has been very well received. In recent visits we have again been enormously impressed by the variety of programming available and the excellent coverage. There is currently a total of 73 licensed stations, of which fifteen are in Ottawa (11 commercial and 4 public), 25 in Toronto (21 commercial and 4 public) 15 in Vancouver (11 commercial and 4 public), 12 in Montreal (8 commercial and 4 public) and 6 in Windsor (2 commercial and 4 public). These stations provide a service to about 11m potential listeners, which amounts to just over 35% of the population. Seven stations (4 commercial and 3 public) are field-testing in Halifax, Nova Scotia and a DAB-only station licensed for the Toronto area is scheduled to start operation soon.

CONCLUSION

Overall, it is safe to say the evidence suggests that radio broadcasting is inexorably moving towards a digital future – certainly for national and domestic services, and possibly for others.

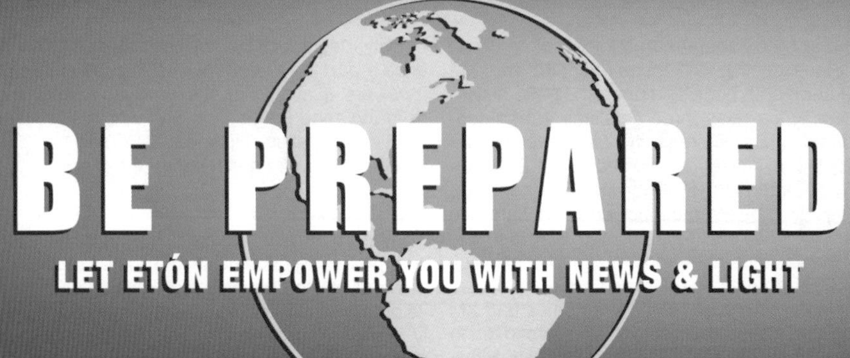
BE PREPARED
LET ETÓN EMPOWER YOU WITH NEWS & LIGHT

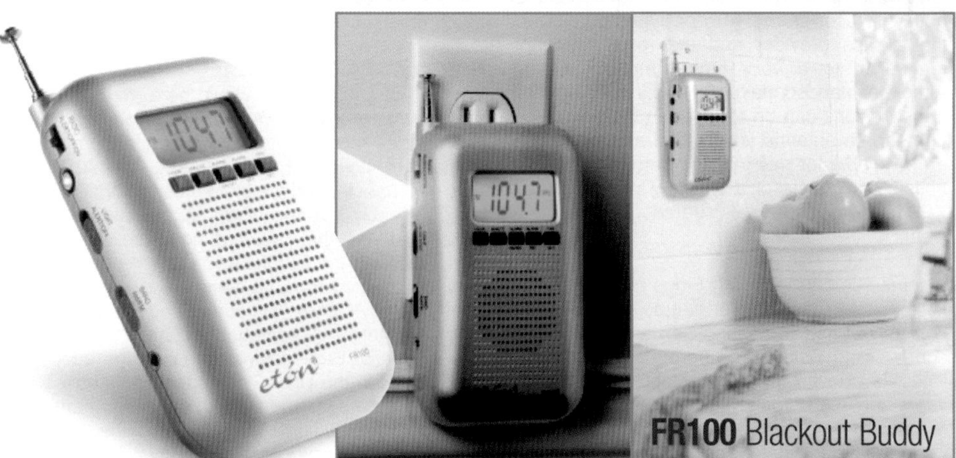
FR100 Blackout Buddy

Emergency

Plug-In AM/FM Radio with Blackout Alert

Plug the Blackout Buddy into AC sockets around your home. When the power fails, Blackout Buddy automatically shines to the rescue, with a brilliant beam of light that illuminates the room and its AM/FM radio to give you breaking news. Blackout Buddy also makes a perfect AM/FM clock radio & LED flashlight for everyday listening around the home.

- Automatically turns on radio/flashlight during power outages
- Super-bright LED flashlight
- Illuminated multi-function blue LCD screen and nightlight
- Patent-pending plug-in design recharges internal battery
- AM/FM radio with telescopic antenna
- Headphone jack and FM antenna input
- AC plug folds down for easy transportation

Dimensions:
3″W x 5″H x 1.4″D

Weight:
10oz.

Power Source:
AC power (direct plug-in)

HF BROADCAST RECEPTION CONDITIONS EXPECTED DURING 2005

George Jacobs, MSEE, Fellow IEEE, *Dean of* WRTH *Contibuting Editors, analyses likely listening conditions in the coming year*

Sunspot Cycle 23 Progress

The number of sunspots seen on the face of the sun follows an approximate 11-year cycle, from a minimum count to a maximum and back to a minimum again. There are corresponding variations in the ionosphere and its ability to reflect or propagate HF signals. When the sunspot count rises, the ionosphere is more intensively ionized. When the count falls there is a corresponding decrease in the intensity of ionization.

The present sunspot cycle is the 23rd to be observed by the Swiss Federal Observatory. It began during October 1996 with an official count of 8 and reached its peak intensity of 121 during April 2000. Cycle 23 has been slowly declining since then and is expected to continue to decrease during 2005. The predicted count for January is in the upper 20s, falling to the high teens by December. This marks the beginning of the Low Phase of Cycle 23. It will continue towards the end of the cycle, which solar experts now expect to occur during late 2006 or early 2007. *Figure 1* graphically plots the progress of Cycle 23 and its predicted future, against the background of a very active sun.

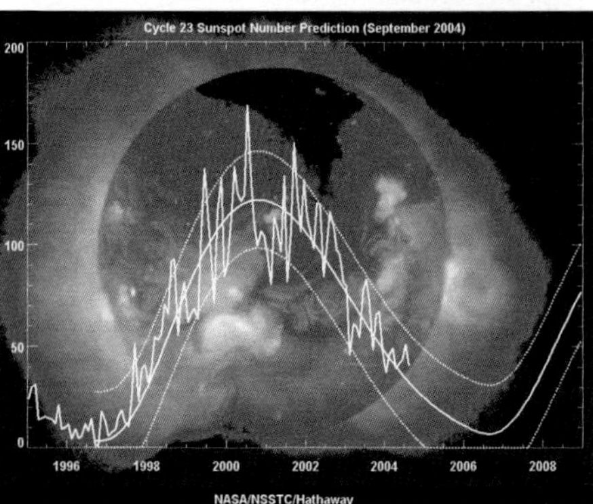

Picture: NASA

As the solar cycle diminishes, the 'window' of available HF spectrum also diminishes. This can be clearly seen from the trend shown in the percentage of the world's HF broadcasting in each broadcasting band. Usage in the bands above 11MHz declined steadily from 48% in 2000 to a planned 41% in 2005. Conversely, use of the bands below 10MHz increased from 52 to 59%.

2005 RECEPTION CONDITIONS

Table 1 is a general summary of the reception conditions expected in each high frequency broadcasting band during 2005.

TABLE 1

MHz	m.	%	Reception Characteristics
26	11	*	No usage in HFCC 2005 schedules
21	13	1.0	Day: long-distance, winter season
17	16	4.0	Day: mid- and long-distance, all seasons Night: occasional long-distance, summer
18	16	4.0	Day: mid- and long-distance, all seasons Night: occasional long-distance, summer
15	19	12.0	Day: mid and long-distance, all seasons Eve: mid and long-distance, not winter
13	22	5.0	Day: mid and long-distance, all seasons Eve: mid and long-distance, except winter
11	25	19.0	Day: short and mid-distance, all seasons Night: mid and long-distance,not winter
12	25	19.0	Day: short and mid-distance, all seasons Night: mid and long-distance,not winter
9	31	21.0	Day: short and mid-distance, all seasons Night: mid and long-distance, not winter
7	41	17.0	Day: short and mid-distance, all seasons Night: mid and long-distance, all seasons
6	49	18.0	Day: short and mid-distance, all seasons Night: mid and long-distance, all seasons
5	49	18.0	Day: short and mid-distance, all seasons Night: mid and long-distance, all seasons
4	120	3.0	Day: short distance, all seasons Night: mid-distance, all seasons
3	90	3.0	Day: short distance, all seasons Night: mid-distance, all seasons
2	60	3.0	Day: short distance, all seasons Night: mid-distance, all seasons

m. = Metre Bands % = % of overall reception
*** = negligible**
Short-distance: up to *c.* 1200 miles (2000 km)
Mid-distance: c. 1000-2400 miles (1600-4000 km
Long-distance, over 2400 miles (4000 km)

For specific times when reception of HF stations is expected to be optimum on various bands during 2005, refer to **Most Suitable Frequencies 2005** on the facing page.

ABOUT THE AUTHOR

This is the 42nd consecutive year that George Jacobs, has contributed editorials to *WRTH*. With 64 years of experience in the development of governmental and private international broadcasting systems, George is a legend in the field of International Broadcasting. He has received numerous awards and recognition from his peers, as well as a Presidential Commission for successfully combining innovative engineering talents and diplomacy with a fierce belief in the free flow of information.

Most Suitable Frequencies 2005

Prepared by George Jacobs, MSEE, Consulting Broadcast Engineer
P.O. Box 12298, Silver Spring, Maryland, USA 20908-0298
Email: broadcaster@gjainc.com Web: www.gjainc.com

TRANSMITTING STATION LOCATION

LISTENER'S AREA	LOCAL TIME	APPROX. UTC TIME	JAN/FEB & NOV/DEC								MAR/APR & SEPT/OCT								MAY-AUGUST							
			EUR/NAF	N.AM(E)	N.AM(W)	C/S.AM	C/S.AF	ME/S.AS	E.AS	AUS/NZ	EUR/NAF	N.AM(E)	N.AM(W)	C/S.AM	C/S.AF	ME/S.AS	E.AS	AUS/NZ	EUR/NAF	N.AM(E)	N.AM(W)	C/S.AM	C/S.AF	ME/S.AS	E.AS	AUS/NZ
EUROPE AND NORTH AFRICA	00:00-04:00	23:00-03:00	6	6	6	9	7	7	9	9	6	9	9	9	9	7	9	9	7	11	11	9	9	9	9	9
	04:00-08:00	03:00-07:00	4	6	6	6	9	7	9	9	6	6	6	9	9	9	9	9	7	9	9	11	11	9	11	9
	08:00-12:00	07:00-11:00	11	6	6	9	17	15	15	13	11	9	7	11	15	15	15	15	11	9	9	9	15	15	15	15
	12:00-16:00	11:00-15:00	11	15	9	15	15	15	15	15	11	9	9	15	17	15	15	13	11	15	11	15	17	15	15	15
	16:00-20:00	15:00-19:00	9	15	15	17	17	9	9	9	9	15	15	17	17	15	11	9	11	15	15	13	17	13	15	9
	20:00-00:00	19:00-23:00	6	9	9	11	11	7	9	9	6	13	13	15	11	9	9	9	9	13	13	15	11	9	11	9
NORTH AMERICA (EAST)	22:00-02:00	03:00-07:00	6	6	6	9	9	6	9	9	7	6	9	9	9	9	9	9	6	6	9	9	9	9	11	15
	02:00-06:00	07:00-11:00	6	6	6	9	9	9	9	9	9	6	9	6	9	9	9	11	9	6	9	9	11	11	11	11
	06:00-10:00	11:00-15:00	11	9	9	9	15	13	9	9	15	15	9	11	17	15	9	9	13	9	9	11	15	15	11	9
	10:00-14:00	15:00-19:00	15	15	15	17	17	15	11	11	15	15	13	17	17	15	11	15	15	15	15	17	17	15	15	11
	14:00-18:00	19:00-23:00	13	11	15	15	13	15	9	11	11	13	15	15	15	13	9	9	15	15	15	15	15	15	15	15
	18:00-22:00	23:00-03:00	7	6	9	9	9	7	13	15	9	6	13	9	9	9	13	15	11	9	13	9	11	7	15	15
NORTH AMERICA (WEST)	00:00-04:00	08:00-12:00	6	6	6	9	9	9	6	9	7	9	6	9	11	9	6	9	9	9	6	9	11	11	9	11
	04:00-08:00	12:00-16:00	7	9	9	9	11	9	9	9	9	9	6	11	15	11	6	9	9	9	6	11	11	11	9	9
	08:00-12:00	16:00-20:00	11	11	9	13	15	13	9	9	15	15	9	15	15	15	9	9	13	15	9	15	15	13	15	13
	12:00-16:00	20:00-00:00	11	13	15	15	15	9	13	17	11	15	11	13	13	9	13	15	15	15	15	15	15	15	15	15
	16:00-20:00	00:00-04:00	6	9	7	9	9	9	15	15	9	9	11	11	9	9	15	17	11	13	13	11	11	13	15	17
	20:00-00:00	04:00-08:00	6	6	6	9	9	7	9	13	6	6	9	9	9	9	11	11	9	9	9	9	9	11	15	13
CENTRAL AND SOUTH AMERICA	00:00-04:00	04:00-08:00	6	6	6	6	9	7	9	13	9	9	9	6	9	9	9	13	11	9	9	6	9	11	11	13
	04:00-08:00	08:00-12:00	9	6	6	9	15	11	9	11	11	9	9	9	11	11	9	11	11	9	9	9	11	11	11	13
	08:00-12:00	12:00-16:00	17	15	11	11	17	15	9	11	17	15	11	11	15	15	9	11	15	13	11	11	15	17	11	11
	12:00-16:00	16:00-20:00	15	15	13	13	15	15	9	11	15	17	15	15	15	15	13	11	17	17	15	15	15	15	13	9
	16:00-20:00	20:00-00:00	11	15	15	11	13	13	13	15	13	15	15	11	11	13	13	15	15	15	15	11	15	15	15	15
	20:00-00:00	00:00-04:00	6	9	7	9	11	9	15	15	9	9	15	6	11	11	15	15	11	13	13	6	11	13	15	15
CENTRAL AND SOUTH AFRICA	00:00-04:00	22:00-02:00	9	9	9	11	7	9	9	15	9	9	13	11	9	9	9	15	9	13	13	11	9	9	9	9
	04:00-08:00	02:00-06:00	9	9	9	9	9	11	11	15	9	9	11	9	9	11	11	15	9	9	9	9	7	11	9	15
	08:00-12:00	06:00-10:00	15	9	9	13	11	15	13	15	15	9	9	11	11	15	13	15	15	9	9	15	11	15	13	15
	12:00-16:00	10:00-14:00	17	15	15	15	11	15	15	11	17	15	15	17	15	15	15	15	17	15	15	17	11	15	15	15
	16:00-20:00	14:00-18:00	17	17	15	15	11	15	13	9	17	17	17	15	11	15	13	9	17	15	15	17	11	15	13	11
	20:00-00:00	18:00-22:00	9	13	9	15	11	11	7	15	11	15	15	15	11	11	9	13	13	15	15	15	11	15	9	9
MIDDLE EAST AND SOUTH ASIA	00:00-04:00	21:00-01:00	7	9	9	9	11	9	9	9	9	9	9	9	9	9	9	11	9	11	11	11	9	7	9	9
	04:00-08:00	01:00-05:00	7	6	9	9	11	9	15	15	9	9	9	9	9	9	13	15	9	11	11	11	9	9	13	15
	08:00-12:00	05:00-09:00	11	6	6	9	15	11	15	17	9	7	7	15	15	13	15	17	13	11	9	11	13	11	15	15
	12:00-16:00	09:00-13:00	15	6	6	11	17	13	15	11	17	9	9	11	17	13	13	11	15	15	9	11	15	15	13	11
	16:00-20:00	13:00-17:00	15	13	9	15	15	9	9	9	15	15	9	15	17	9	9	9	15	15	11	15	15	11	11	9
	20:00-00:00	17:00-21:00	9	11	11	15	13	9	9	9	13	13	11	15	13	9	9	9	13	15	11	15	9	7	9	9
EAST ASIA AND FAR EAST	00:00-04:00	16:00-20:00	9	9	9	11	11	9	6	11	9	11	13	11	9	9	9	9	13	13	15	15	9	9	9	11
	04:00-08:00	20:00-00:00	7	6	9	11	11	9	7	13	9	13	13	13	9	11	9	15	11	15	15	15	9	9	9	15
	08:00-12:00	00:00-04:00	7	6	7	11	9	9	13	15	7	15	15	15	9	13	13	15	9	15	15	13	9	13	13	15
	12:00-16:00	04:00-08:00	7	9	9	9	13	15	13	17	9	9	13	9	13	15	13	17	13	11	15	11	15	15	15	17
	16:00-20:00	08:00-12:00	13	9	7	9	15	13	11	15	13	9	9	9	17	15	11	15	15	9	11	11	15	17	11	15
	20:00-00:00	12:00-16:00	11	9	7	9	11	11	9	11	13	9	9	9	15	13	9	11	15	11	9	13	15	15	7	9
AUSTRALIA AND NEW ZEALAND	00:00-04:00	14:00-18:00	15	13	9	11	9	9	11	9	13	13	9	11	9	9	9	9	11	9	9	9	11	9	11	9
	04:00-08:00	18:00-22:00	9	13	11	11	11	9	9	9	9	11	11	13	9	9	11	9	9	13	11	11	11	7	11	9
	08:00-12:00	22:00-02:00	13	15	17	15	11	15	15	11	9	15	17	15	11	13	15	15	9	15	17	15	11	11	15	15
	12:00-16:00	02:00-06:00	9	9	11	15	15	15	15	15	9	13	15	15	15	15	17	15	9	13	15	15	15	15	17	15
	16:00-20:00	06:00-10:00	9	9	9	13	13	15	15	11	11	9	11	13	17	13	15	9	13	11	11	15	15	15	15	13
	20:00-00:00	10:00-14:00	17	9	9	11	11	11	15	9	15	9	9	11	15	11	11	9	17	9	11	13	13	11	11	9

Band Selections have been made taking into account both propagation conditions and station operating schedules.

Where the 6MHz band is shown as the most suitable, also check the 7MHz band and vice versa.

World Music Radio

Anker Petersen reports on the re-birth of a popular radio station and talks to the man behind the first commercial shortwave station in Denmark

Some readers of the *WRTH* will remember listening to World Music Radio (WMR) broadcasting good music each Sunday morning and afternoon on 6250 kHz back in the years 1967-73. It was one of the many 'Free Radio Stations' that flourished at the time, particularly on the 48-meter band. These stations were also known as 'Pirates', as a result of the fact that they operated without a broadcasting licence. They were very popular, particularly with the young people, because of their lively presentation and the fact that they played all the latest music which was sometimes ignored by the large, often state-controlled, broadcasters. In fact, they even succeeded in changing the format of State-run broadcasters, who were forced by this competition to introduce slick announcing with catchy jingles, and to play the kind of music that listeners actually wanted to hear.

Most of the Free Radio Stations no longer exist, but WMR is an exception. It has been on the air in with some breaks since 1967. In its first incarnation it was broadcast from a secret transmitter location in the Netherlands, and was run by young Theo Verstraeten. He started off with a 10W transmitter but steadily increased it to 250W. The postal address was in Lancashire, England, and it was from there I received my first WMR QSL and sticker.

WMR was a great success but it all ended on a Sunday in August 1973 when the Police and officials of the local regulation authority arrived and closed down the illegal transmitter. Theo Verstraeten had his equipment confiscated and was given a token fine of 100 Guilders.

After that, WMR leased airtime from stations in various countries. These stations included Radio Andorra, Radio Milano International, Radio Dublin International, and some local FM stations in Italy and France. This situation continued until the year 1989.

In 1997, the experienced Danish broadcast manager, DXer, and long-time *WRTH* contributor, Stig Hartvig Nielsen, took over WMR and the firm was officially registered in Denmark. During May to August 1997 the first WMR broadcasts under his ownership were aired on 3345 and 6290 kHz via the powerful Sentech transmitters at Meyerton in South Africa. Although Africa was the main target area, these broadcasts were heard worldwide.

Later on, Stig Hartvig Nielsen applied to the Danish regulatory authorities for permission to broadcast from WMR's own transmitters on 5815 and 15810 kHz and this was finally granted. While the shortwave transmitters were being prepared and shipped, new offices and a new on-air studio were completed in Kousted near Randers in Denmark. In April 2004 the two transmitters were installed at the village of Ilskov south of Karup in Central Jutland, and were tested successfully during May and June. Regular broadcasts began in August 2004 with programmes of good music 24 hours a day.

For the transmissions on 5815 kHz, a former 10 kW Collins mediumwave transmitter is used, which has been rebuilt for shortwave by a company in Canada. Until further notice 6 kW is

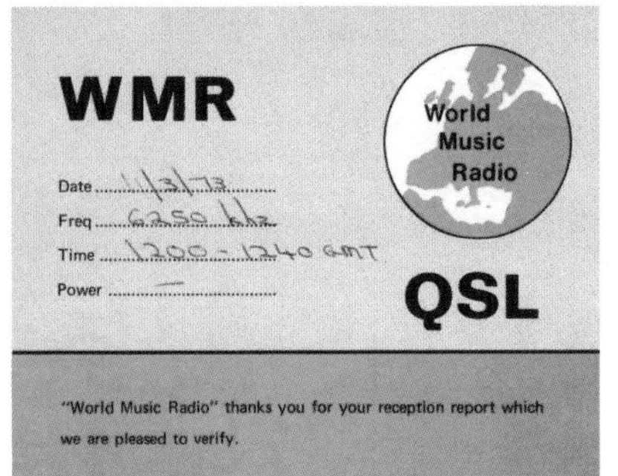

Anker Petersen's QSL card from WMR

radiated through an ordinary dipole antenna directed East-West at a height of about 24 metres. A former naval Siemens transceiver, with 500 watts of power, is used for the transmissions on 15810 kHz. This has been rebuilt for broadcasting and has an ordinary dipole antenna. The programmes are controlled by a computer in Kousted and sent as streaming audio via the internet to the transmitters at Ilskov. WMR programmes can also be heard via the internet on the website: www.wmr.dk

INTERVIEW

I asked Stig Hartvig Nielsen the following questions about the first private commercial shortwave station in Denmark:

AP: In August 2003 you announced the re-birth of WMR from Denmark at the Conference of the European DX Council in Germany, but it was May 2004 before it came on the air. What happened?

SHN: It took several months to have the frequency for the 6 MHz band cleared, and then it took several months to have the transmitter for 5815 delivered. When the transmitter finally arrived, a new filter had to be built because the transmitter didn't meet the technical requirements for spurious radiation.

AP: Who is your target audience?

SHN: WMR used to be a station aimed at DXers and other shortwave enthusiasts. While we still want to reach these groups, we also realise that they are rather small and that it is not commercially viable to base a radio station on them. Thus we are trying to reach 'ordinary' listeners – especially through our FM service and via the Internet. However, most listeners prefer their local or national stations, so we are aiming at those listeners with a broader outlook – those who have an international or global orientation.

AP: What kind of music are you playing? Some listeners might expect Danish music, or ethnic World Music.

SHN: When World Music Radio began broadcasting in the 1960s, there wasn't a music category called 'World Music' as there is today. And really we are not playing a lot of ethnic World Music from the interior of Africa or Northern Canada. However, we are playing popular, catchy, and contemporary music from the Caribbean, South America, Africa, India, Japan and Europe. Music from the UK and USA will still play an important role but is less dominant than on most other FM radio stations in the Western world. We are also featuring music from the past four decades – so 'oldies' music is an important part of our output. We are playing a lot of Soul, R'n'B and Reggae – but not very much rock music, and hardly any 'teenage music' with boy-bands, etc. In other words our music format is extremely wide and pretty unique.

AP: Are you going to broadcast DX programmes, as WMR did in the 70s?

SHN: No. For four reasons: Firstly, the number of DXers is very small. Second, a DX programme would mean that non-DXers would switch off their radios. Thirdly, DX news and loggings are easily available via the Internet. Finally, it would take a lot of time to produce such a programme.

AP: Do you verify reception reports with a QSL card?

SHN: We are surprised to see that DXers are still collecting QSL cards. I personally gave up collecting QSL-cards when the reply percentage got very close to nil. However, yes we are replying to reception reports with a non detailed QSL card. The address for sending in reports is: P. O. Box 112, 8900 Randers, Denmark, or by Email to this address: wmr@wmr.dk. Return postage is appreciated but not necessary.

AP: What is your present coverage with the shortwave transmitters?

SHN: Our 49-meter frequency of 5815 kHz provides very good reception up to around 1,000 km (625 miles) from Denmark day and night, obviously with some seasonal variations. At night the signals travel even further. Reception in South America, for instance, has been quite good after dark. The initial test transmissions with low power on 15810 kHz were disappointing, and we are considering either buying a stronger transmitter for this frequency or to give it up.

AP: What are your future plans with WMR?

SHN: Starting a radio station like WMR is obviously a crazy thing to do. It is a well-known fact that close to 100 percent of all advertising is carried out at a local or national level. International advertising is almost non-existant so it will be a tough job to make WMR survive, but that indeed is our top priority. Should we succeed in keeping the station on the air, I am hoping that in the future we can add a satellite service, more FM and MW frequencies, as well as shortwave services for listeners in Africa, the Americas, and possibly also for Asia. Should DRM ever begin to take off, we would love to broadcast in DRM as well.

BE PREPARED

LET ETÓN EMPOWER YOU WITH NEWS & LIGHT

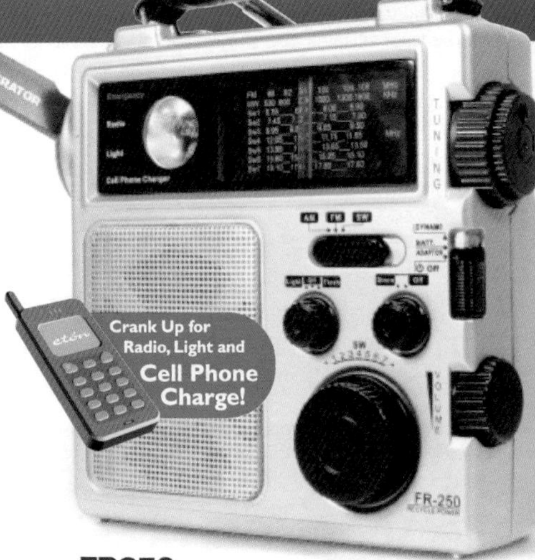

Emergency

AM/FM Shortwave Radio &

Cell Phone Charger

- AM/FM Shortwave with built-in antenna
- 7 international Shortwave bands
- Hand-Crank Power Generator
- Built-in Cell Phone Charger, flashlight, and emergency siren
- Rugged splash-proof ABS Body
- Inputs for AC adaptor and earphones

Dimensions: 6.7"W x 6.5"H x 2.5"D **Weight:** 1.3lbs. **Power Source:** Hand-Crank Power Generator with rechargeable battery pack, 3 AA batteries (not included) or AC adaptor (not included)

FR250

FR100
Blackout
Buddy

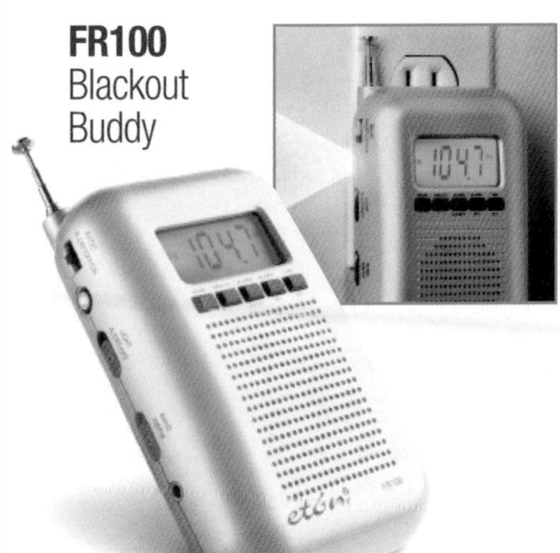

Emergency

Plug-In AM/FM Radio with

Blackout Alert

- Automatically turns on radio/flashlight during power outages
- Super-bright LED flashlight
- 16 hours of emergency flashlight use on single charge
- AM/FM radio with telescopic antenna
- Up to 8 hours of emergency radio use on single charge
- Illuminated multi-function blue LCD screen and nightlight
- Patent-pending plug-in design recharges internal battery
- Headphone jack and FM antenna input
- AC plug folds down for easy transportation

Dimensions: 3"W x 5"H x 1.4"D **Weight:** 10oz.
Power Source: AC power (direct plug in)

Bernt Erfjord

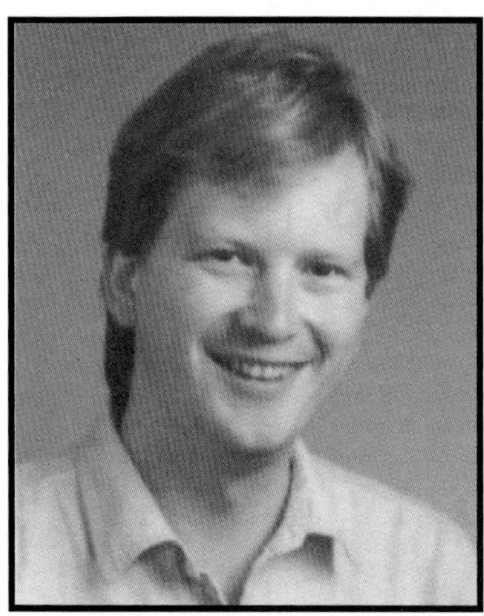

IN MEMORIAM

Well-known Norwegian DXer and long-time WRTH contributor, Bernt Erfjord, passed away after illness on 26 June 2004, aged 42. This volume is dedicated to his memory

Bernt joined the Norwegian DX-Listeners' Club in 1978 and quickly established himself as an active contributor and club member. For six years from 1982 he was DXLC chairman, before becoming editor of DX-News, the club magazine. He retained this post from 1988 until he died.

In this period Bernt was responsible for publishing more than 150 issues of DX-News. He compiled and edited contributions from club members, as well as producing more than one thousand pages of his own material.

The sheer volume of Bernt's contribution to the club was in itself outstanding, but even more impressive is the quality which was apparent in everything he did. Bernt was very knowledgeable and had contacts among radio stations and hobbyists all over the world. Under his stewardship, DX-News became a highly topical and professional magazine, and his dedicated work has been invaluable in securing a DXLC a loyal membership base.

Bernt also had friends in many countries outside Norway and his name is known to DXers all over the world. He was an active contributor to several other DX-clubs and bulletins – in the Nordic countries, the UK and elsewhere. He supplied relevant news and information from Norway, adding perspective from his professional career as a broadcast engineer. He also took a special interest in offshore radio, as well as the radio scene in the UK and Ireland.

Bernt was a country contributor to the WRTH for many years, as well as contributing to various other publications. He attended several EDXC conferences and other international DX-meetings, and twice served on the organizing committee for the Nordic DX Championships.

To fellow club members and hobbyists, Bernt was also a dear and loyal friend. His kindness, helpfulness and good spirits will be sorely missed by everyone who knew him. In this time of sorrow, our thoughts go to his wife, three daughters and the rest of his family.

Jan Alvestad *Svenn Martinsen* *Olav Nordli* *Svein Olav Pedersen*

NATIONAL
RADIO CLUB

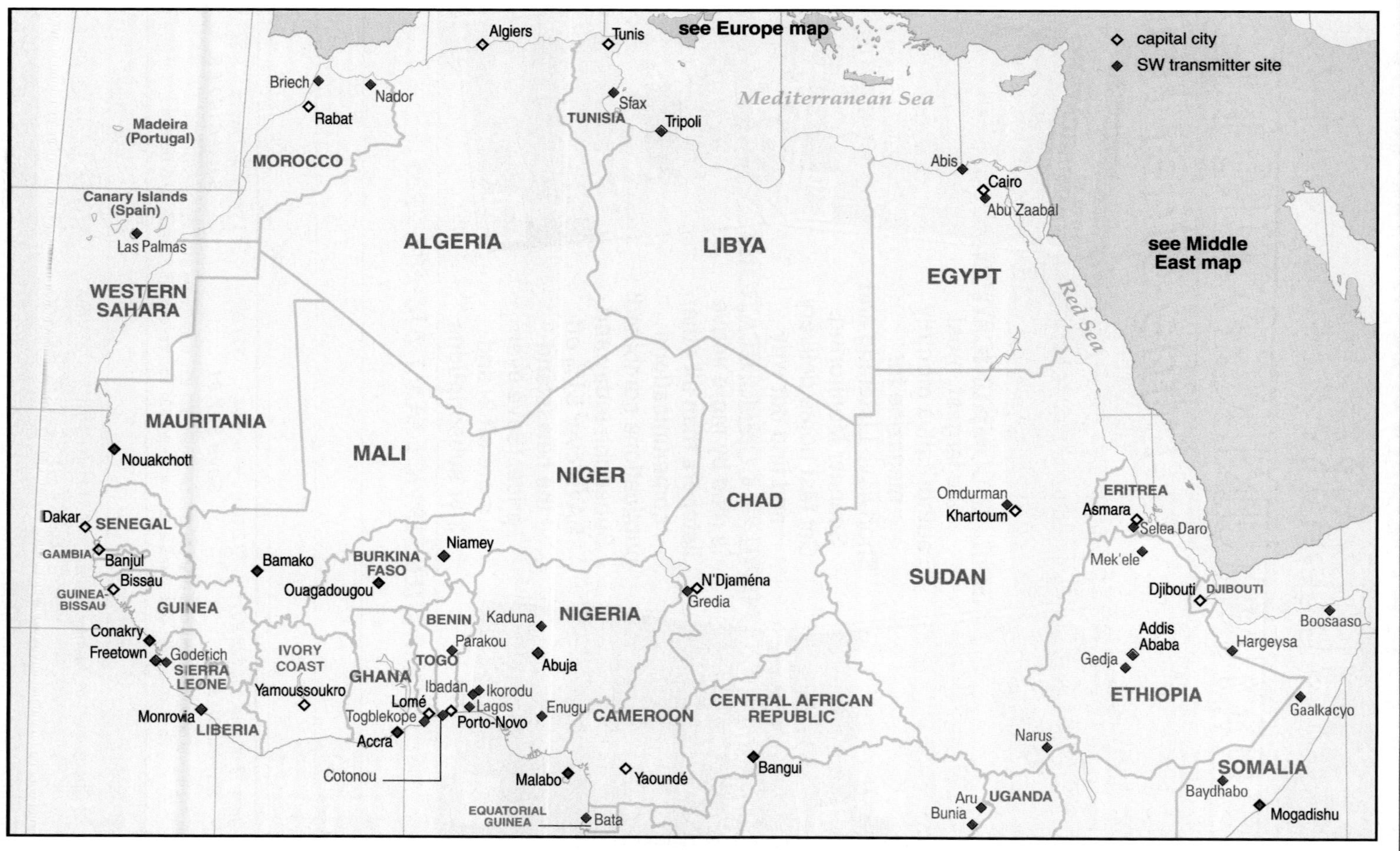
capital city
SW transmitter site
see Europe map
see Middle East map
Mediterranean Sea
Red Sea
Algiers
Tunis
Briech
Nador
Rabat
Sfax
TUNISIA
Tripoli
Madeira (Portugal)
MOROCCO
Canary Islands (Spain)
Las Palmas
ALGERIA
LIBYA
Abis
Cairo
Abu Zaabal
EGYPT
WESTERN SAHARA
MAURITANIA
Nouakchott
MALI
NIGER
CHAD
Omdurman
Khartoum
ERITREA
Asmara
Selea Daro
Mek'ele
Dakar
SENEGAL
GAMBIA
Banjul
Bamako
BURKINA FASO
Niamey
Ouagadougou
GUINEA-BISSAU
Bissau
GUINEA
N'Djaména
Gredia
SUDAN
Djibouti
DJIBOUTI
Boosaaso
BENIN
Kaduna
NIGERIA
Conakry
Freetown
Goderich
SIERRA LEONE
IVORY COAST
Yamoussoukro
GHANA
TOGO
Parakou
Abuja
Addis Ababa
Gedja
Hargeysa
Ibadan
Ikorodu
Lomé
Togblekope
Lagos
Porto-Novo
Enugu
Monrovia
LIBERIA
Accra
CAMEROON
CENTRAL AFRICAN REPUBLIC
ETHIOPIA
Gaalkacyo
Narus
Cotonou
Malabo
Yaoundé
Bangui
SOMALIA
Baydhabo
Aru
UGANDA
Bunia
Mogadishu
EQUATORIAL GUINEA
Bata

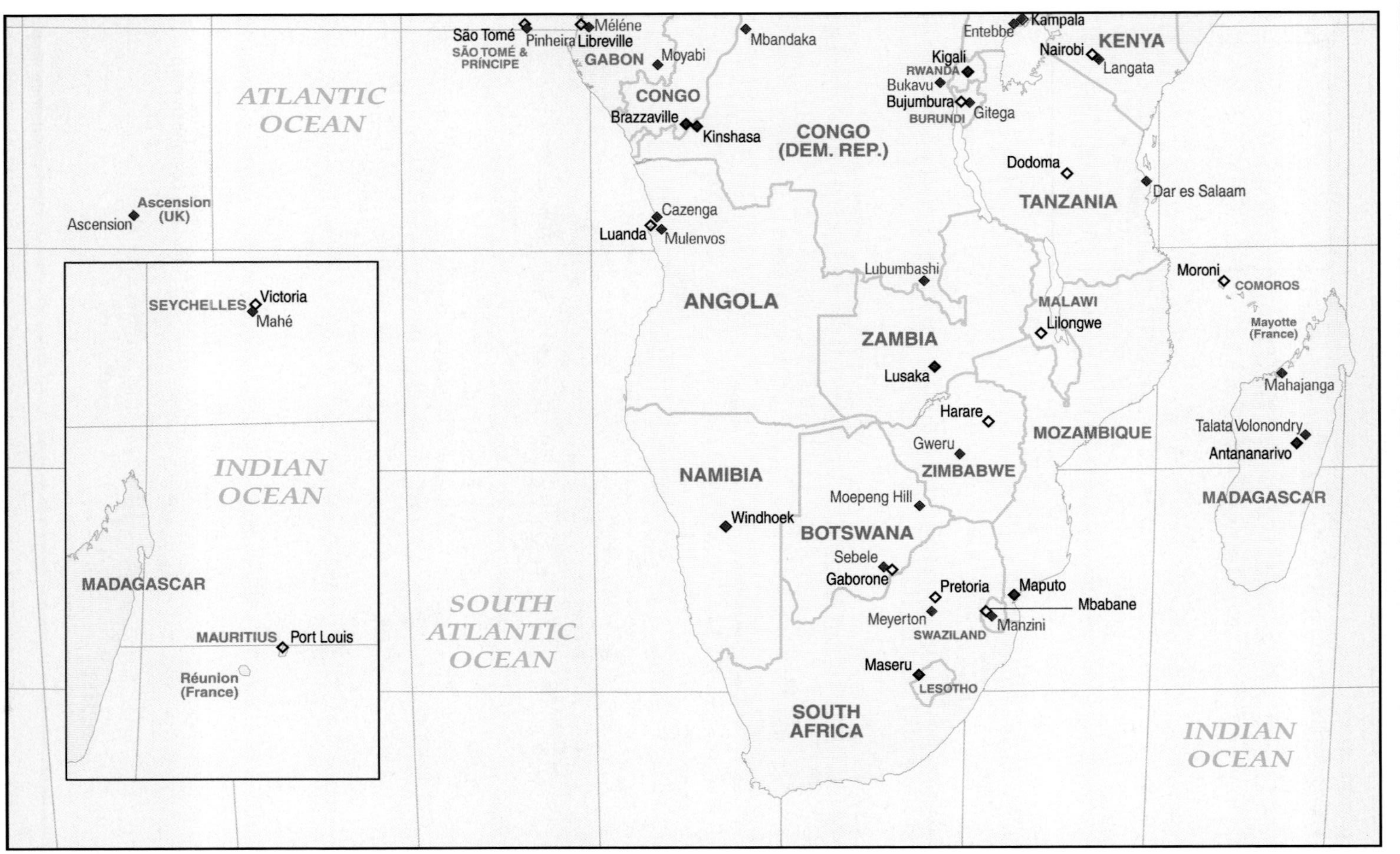
São Tomé
SÃO TOMÉ & PRÍNCIPE
Pinheira
Méléne
Libreville
GABON
Moyabi
Mbandaka
CONGO
Brazzaville
Kinshasa
CONGO (DEM. REP.)
Entebbe
Kampala
KENYA
Nairobi
Langata
Kigali
RWANDA
Bukavu
Bujumbura
BURUNDI
Gitega
Dodoma
TANZANIA
Dar es Salaam
ATLANTIC OCEAN
Ascension (UK)
Ascension
Cazenga
Luanda
Mulenvos
ANGOLA
Lubumbashi
ZAMBIA
Lusaka
MALAWI
Lilongwe
Moroni
COMOROS
Mayotte (France)
Mahajanga
Talata Volonondry
Antananarivo
MADAGASCAR
Harare
Gweru
ZIMBABWE
MOZAMBIQUE
NAMIBIA
Windhoek
Moepeng Hill
BOTSWANA
Sebele
Gaborone
Pretoria
Maputo
Mbabane
Meyerton
SWAZILAND
Manzini
Maseru
LESOTHO
SOUTH AFRICA
SOUTH ATLANTIC OCEAN
INDIAN OCEAN
SEYCHELLES
Victoria
Mahé
INDIAN OCEAN
MADAGASCAR
MAURITIUS
Port Louis
Réunion (France)

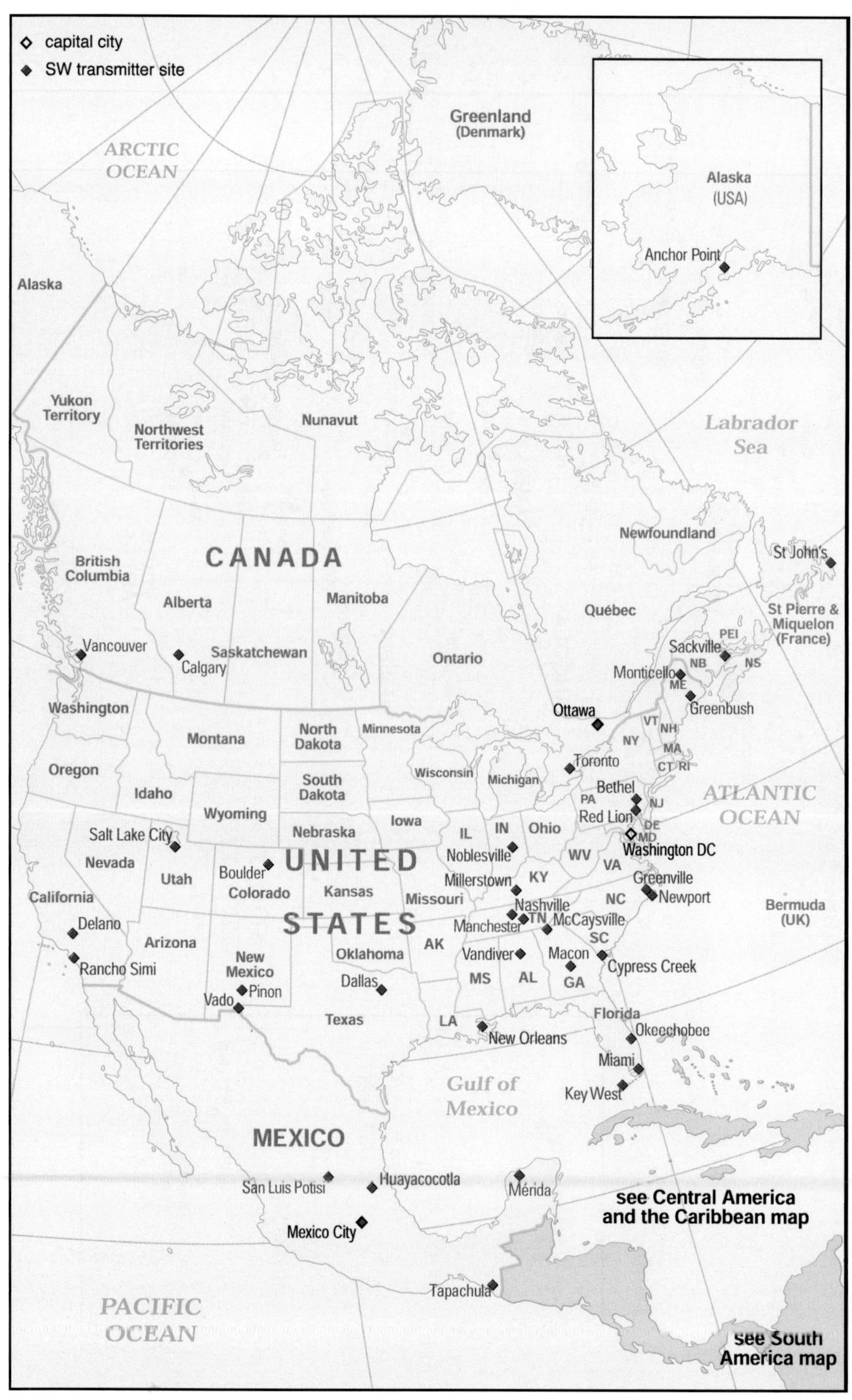

capital city
SW transmitter site
ARCTIC OCEAN
Greenland (Denmark)
Alaska (USA)
Anchor Point
Alaska
Yukon Territory
Northwest Territories
Nunavut
Labrador Sea
Newfoundland
St John's
CANADA
British Columbia
Alberta
Manitoba
Québec
St Pierre & Miquelon (France)
PEI
Sackville
NB
NS
Vancouver
Calgary
Saskatchewan
Ontario
Monticello
ME
Greenbush
Washington
Ottawa
Montana
North Dakota
Minnesota
VT
NH
NY
MA
Toronto
CT RI
Oregon
Idaho
South Dakota
Wisconsin
Michigan
Bethel
PA
NJ
ATLANTIC OCEAN
Wyoming
Iowa
Red Lion
DE
MD
Salt Lake City
Nebraska
IL
IN
Ohio
Washington DC
Nevada
UNITED STATES
Noblesville
WV
VA
Boulder
Utah
Colorado
Kansas
Millerstown
KY
Greenville
California
Missouri
Newport
Nashville
NC
Bermuda (UK)
Delano
Manchester
TN
McCaysville
SC
Arizona
AK
Rancho Simi
New Mexico
Oklahoma
Vandiver
Macon
Cypress Creek
Pinon
MS
AL
GA
Vado
Dallas
Texas
LA
Florida
New Orleans
Okeechobee
Miami
Gulf of Mexico
Key West
MEXICO
San Luis Potisi
Huayacocotla
Mérida
see Central America and the Caribbean map
Mexico City
Tapachula
PACIFIC OCEAN
see South America map

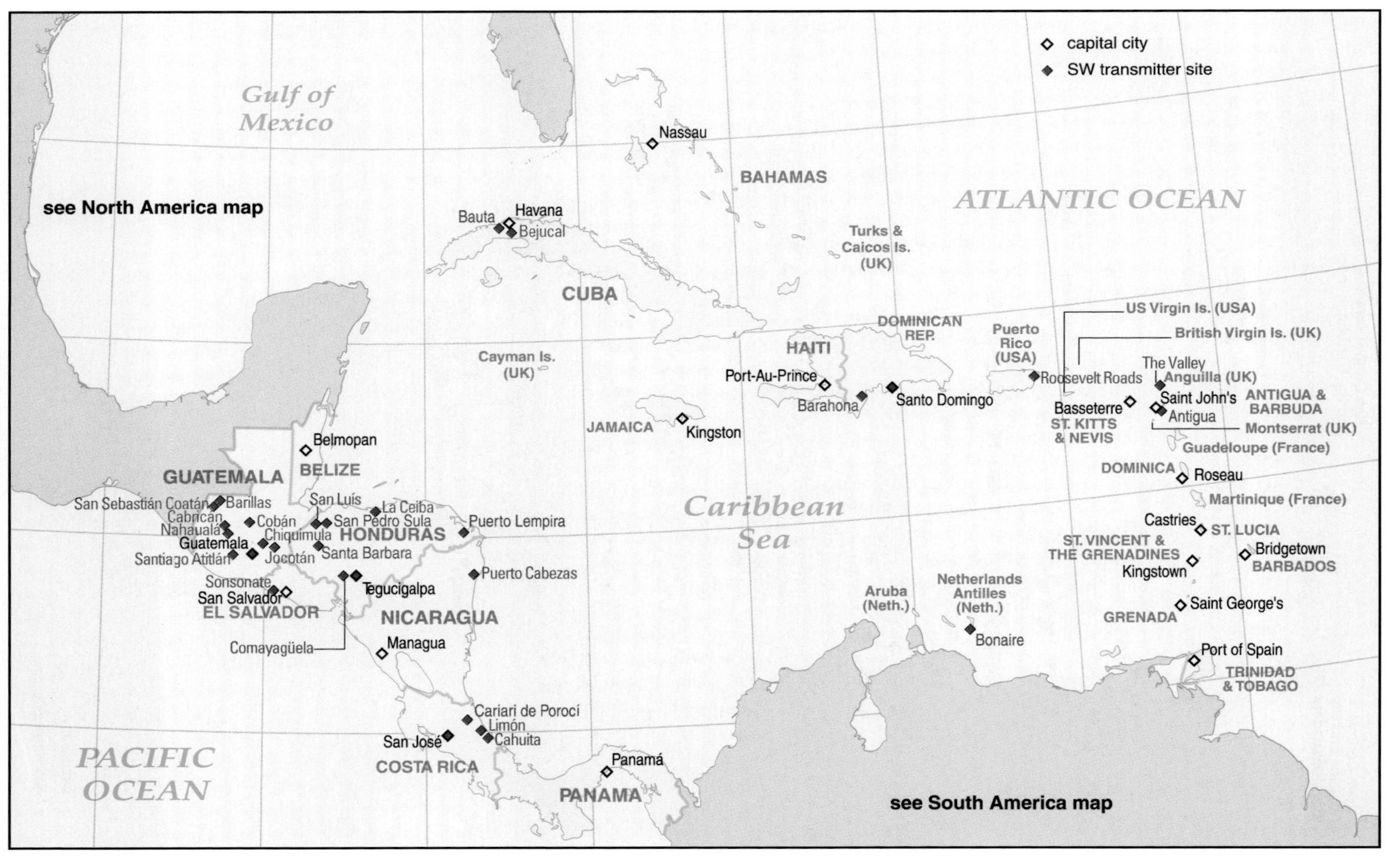
capital city
SW transmitter site
Gulf of Mexico
ATLANTIC OCEAN
Caribbean Sea
PACIFIC OCEAN
see North America map
see South America map
Nassau
BAHAMAS
Turks & Caicos Is. (UK)
Bauta
Havana
Bejucal
CUBA
Cayman Is. (UK)
JAMAICA
Kingston
HAITI
Port-Au-Prince
Barahona
DOMINICAN REP.
Santo Domingo
Puerto Rico (USA)
Roosevelt Roads
US Virgin Is. (USA)
British Virgin Is. (UK)
The Valley
Anguilla (UK)
Saint John's
Antigua
ANTIGUA & BARBUDA
Montserrat (UK)
Guadeloupe (France)
Basseterre
ST. KITTS & NEVIS
DOMINICA
Roseau
Martinique (France)
Castries
ST. LUCIA
ST. VINCENT & THE GRENADINES
Kingstown
Bridgetown
BARBADOS
Saint George's
GRENADA
Port of Spain
TRINIDAD & TOBAGO
Aruba (Neth.)
Netherlands Antilles (Neth.)
Bonaire
Belmopan
BELIZE
GUATEMALA
San Sebastián Coatán
Barillas
Cabricán
Nahualá
Cobán
Chiquimula
Guatemala
Santiago Atitlán
Jocotán
San Luís
La Ceiba
San Pedro Sula
HONDURAS
Santa Barbara
Puerto Lempira
Puerto Cabezas
Tegucigalpa
Sonsonate
San Salvador
EL SALVADOR
Comayagüela
NICARAGUA
Managua
Cariari de Porocí
Limón
Cahuita
San José
COSTA RICA
Panamá
PANAMA

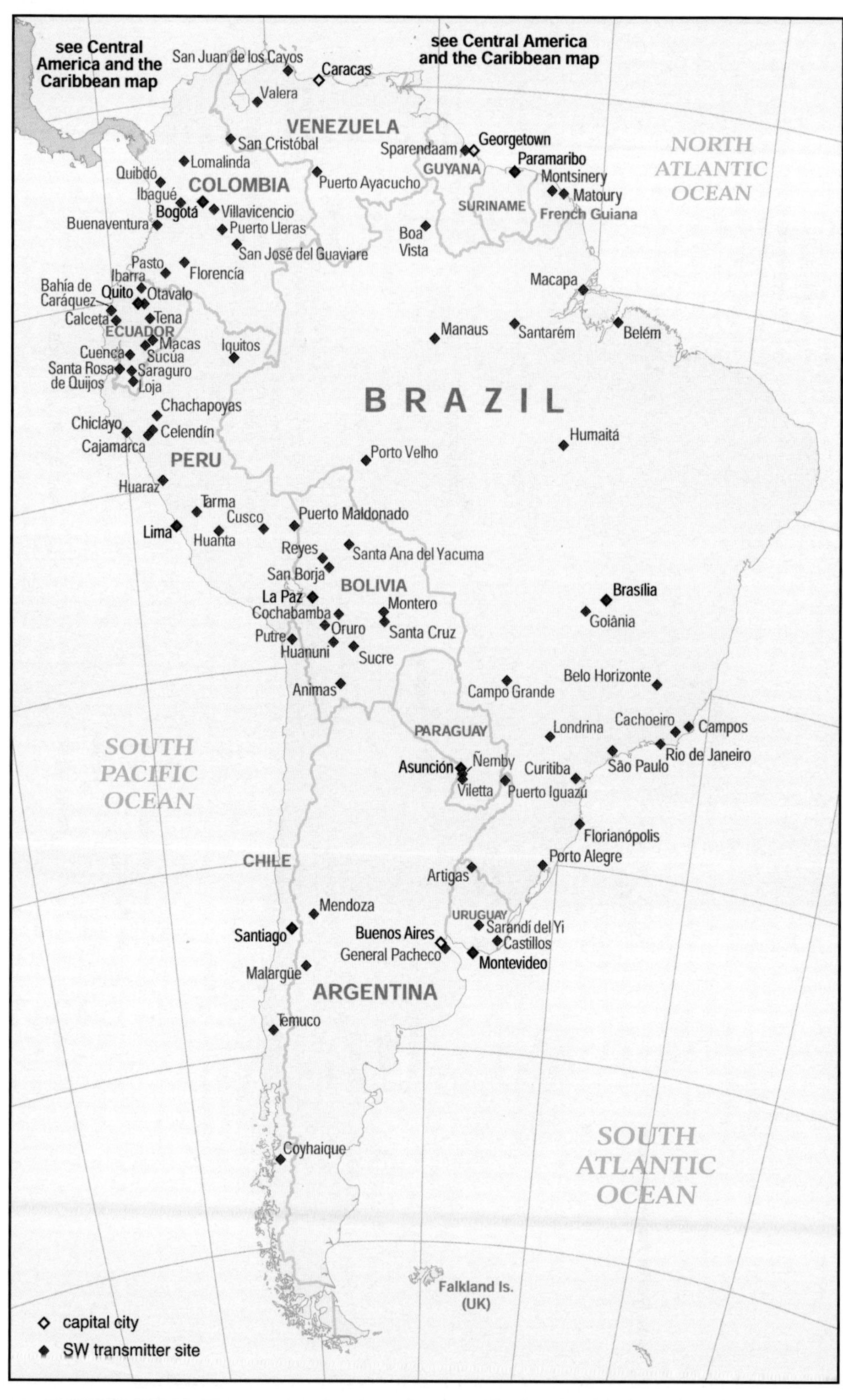

see Central America and the Caribbean map
see Central America and the Caribbean map
San Juan de los Cayos
Caracas
Valera
VENEZUELA
San Cristóbal
Lomalinda
Quibdó
Ibagué
COLOMBIA
Bogotá
Villavicencio
Puerto Lleras
Buenaventura
San José del Guaviare
Puerto Ayacucho
Sparendaam
Georgetown
GUYANA
Paramaribo
Montsinery
Matoury
SURINAME
French Guiana
NORTH ATLANTIC OCEAN
Boa Vista
Pasto
Florencía
Ibarra
Bahía de Caráquez
Quito
Otavalo
Calceta
Tena
ECUADOR
Macas
Sucúa
Cuenca
Santa Rosa de Quijos
Saraguro
Loja
Iquitos
Macapa
Manaus
Santarém
Belém
BRAZIL
Chachapoyas
Chiclayo
Celendín
Cajamarca
PERU
Humaitá
Porto Velho
Huaraz
Tarma
Cusco
Lima
Huanta
Puerto Maldonado
Reyes
Santa Ana del Yacuma
San Borja
BOLIVIA
La Paz
Cochabamba
Montero
Oruro
Santa Cruz
Putre
Huanuni
Sucre
Brasília
Goiânia
Belo Horizonte
Animas
Campo Grande
PARAGUAY
Londrina
Cachoeiro
Campos
Rio de Janeiro
Asunción
Ñemby
Curitiba
São Paulo
Viletta
Puerto Iguazú
SOUTH PACIFIC OCEAN
Florianópolis
Porto Alegre
CHILE
Artigas
Mendoza
URUGUAY
Sarandí del Yi
Castillos
Santiago
Buenos Aires
General Pacheco
Montevideo
Malargüe
ARGENTINA
Temuco
Coyhaique
SOUTH ATLANTIC OCEAN
Falkland Is. (UK)
capital city
SW transmitter site

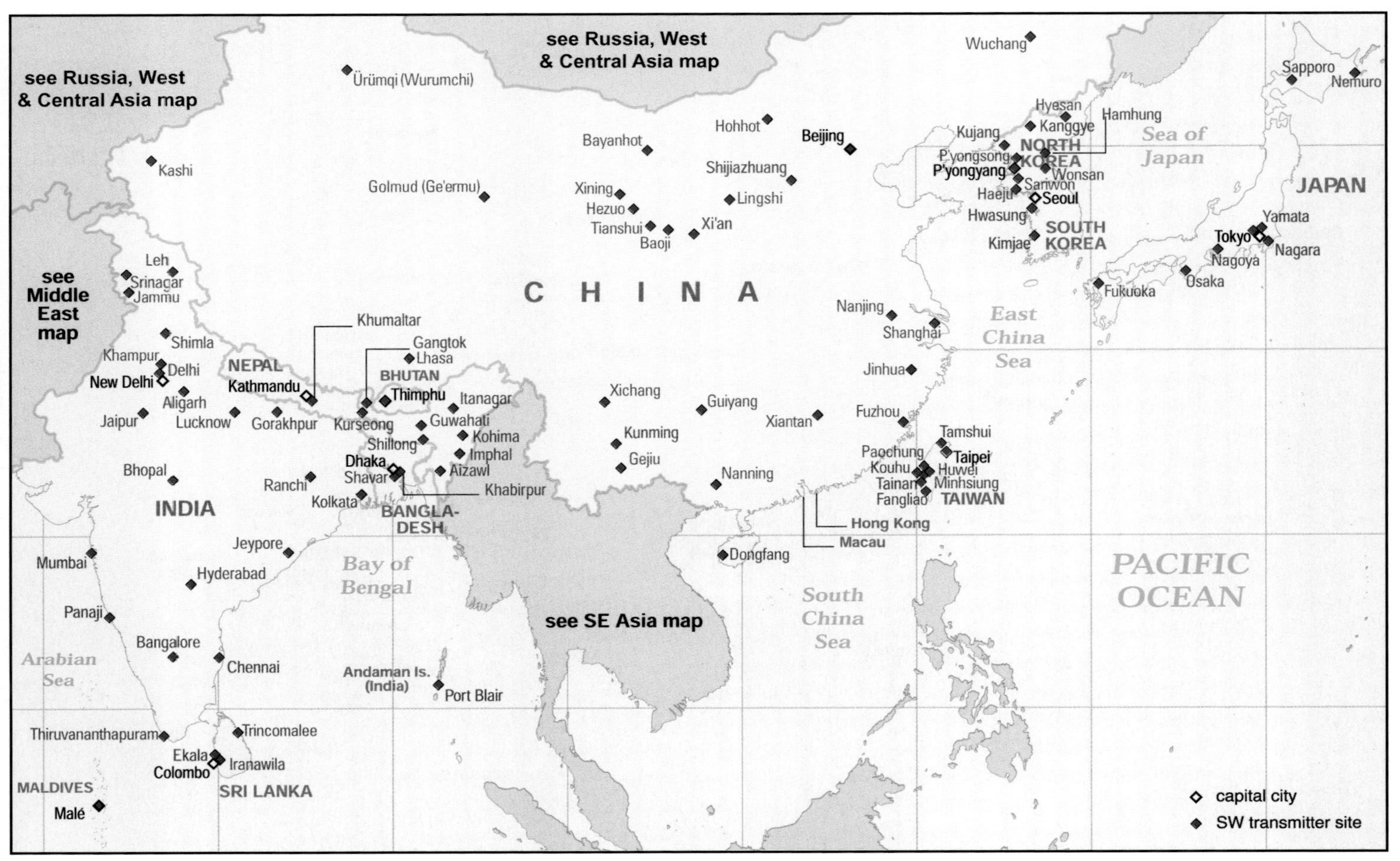
see Russia, West & Central Asia map
see Russia, West & Central Asia map
see Middle East map
see SE Asia map
CHINA
INDIA
NEPAL
BHUTAN
BANGLA-DESH
SRI LANKA
MALDIVES
JAPAN
NORTH KOREA
SOUTH KOREA
TAIWAN
Hong Kong
Macau
Sea of Japan
East China Sea
South China Sea
PACIFIC OCEAN
Bay of Bengal
Arabian Sea
Andaman Is. (India)
Port Blair
Ürümqi (Wurumchi)
Kashi
Golmud (Ge'ermu)
Bayanhot
Hohhot
Beijing
Shijiazhuang
Lingshi
Xining
Hezuo
Tianshui
Baoji
Xi'an
Xichang
Kunming
Gejiu
Guiyang
Nanning
Dongfang
Xiantan
Fuzhou
Jinhua
Nanjing
Shanghai
Wuchang
Tamshui
Taipei
Paochung
Kouhu
Huwei
Tainan
Minhsiung
Fangliao
Hyesan
Kanggye
Hamhung
Kujang
P'yongsong
P'yongyang
Wonsan
Sariwon
Haeju
Seoul
Hwasung
Kimjae
Fukuoka
Osaka
Nagoya
Tokyo
Yamata
Nagara
Sapporo
Nemuro
Leh
Srinagar
Jammu
Shimla
Khampur
Delhi
New Delhi
Aligarh
Jaipur
Lucknow
Gorakhpur
Kathmandu
Khumaltar
Gangtok
Lhasa
Thimphu
Itanagar
Kurseong
Guwahati
Shillong
Kohima
Imphal
Dhaka
Shavar
Aizawl
Khabirpur
Bhopal
Ranchi
Kolkata
Jeypore
Hyderabad
Mumbai
Panaji
Bangalore
Chennai
Thiruvananthapuram
Trincomalee
Ekala
Colombo
Iranawila
Malé
capital city
SW transmitter site

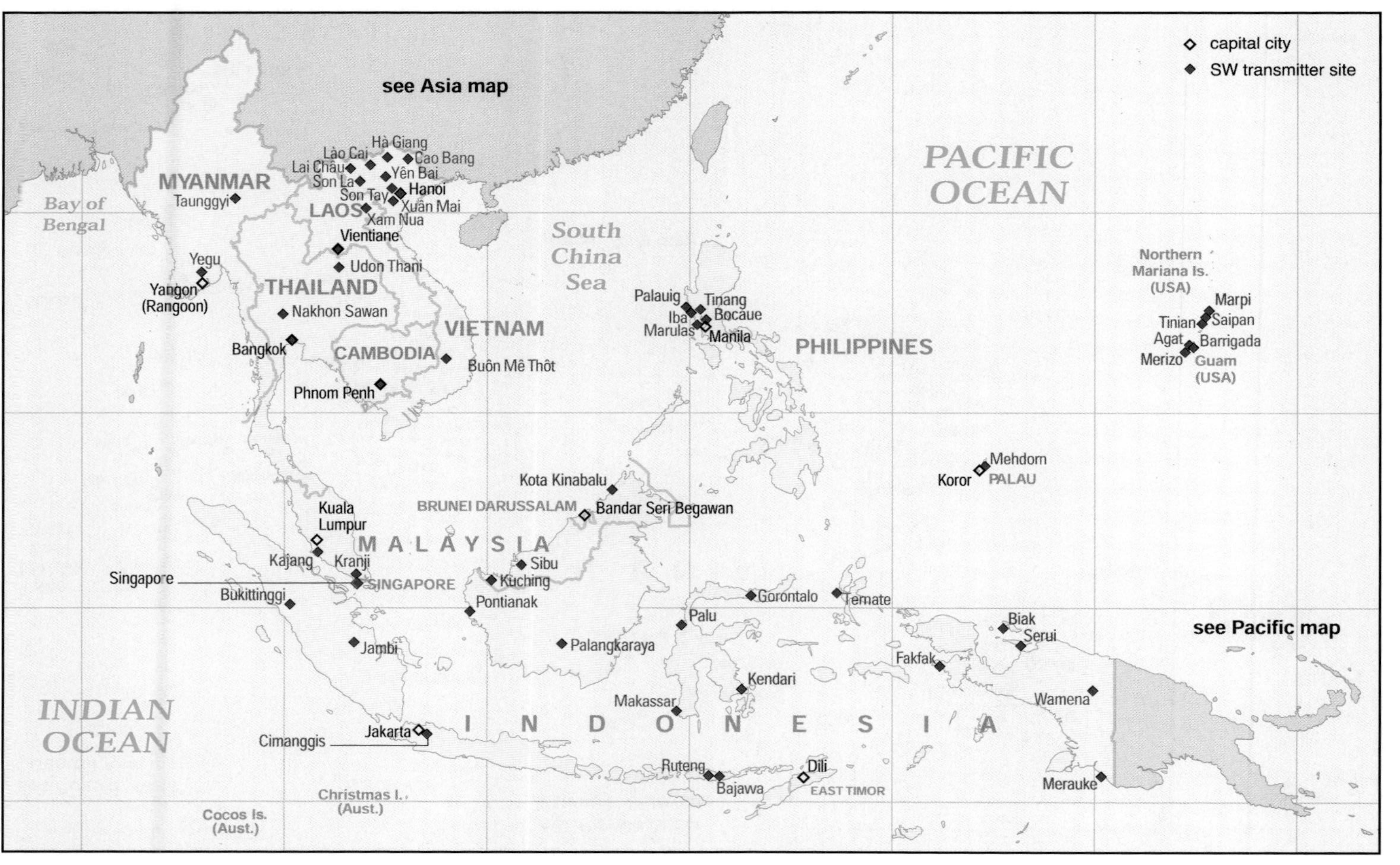

capital city
SW transmitter site
see Asia map
see Pacific map
PACIFIC OCEAN
South China Sea
Bay of Bengal
INDIAN OCEAN
MYANMAR
Taunggyi
Yegu
Yangon (Rangoon)
THAILAND
Nakhon Sawan
Bangkok
LAOS
Vientiane
Udon Thani
Lào Cai
Lai Châu
Sơn La
Hà Giang
Yên Bai
Cao Bang
Sơn Tây
Hanoi
Xuân Mai
Xam Nua
VIETNAM
CAMBODIA
Phnom Penh
Buôn Mê Thôt
Palauig
Iba
Marulas
Tinang
Bocaue
Manila
PHILIPPINES
Northern Mariana Is. (USA)
Marpi
Tinian
Saipan
Agat
Barrigada
Merizo
Guam (USA)
Mehdorn
Koror
PALAU
Kota Kinabalu
BRUNEI DARUSSALAM
Bandar Seri Begawan
Kuala Lumpur
MALAYSIA
Kajang
Kranji
Sibu
Kuching
Singapore
SINGAPORE
Bukittinggi
Pontianak
Gorontalo
Ternate
Palu
Biak
Serui
Jambi
Palangkaraya
Fakfak
Kendari
Makassar
Wamena
INDONESIA
Jakarta
Cimanggis
Ruteng
Bajawa
Dili
EAST TIMOR
Merauke
Christmas I. (Aust.)
Cocos Is. (Aust.)

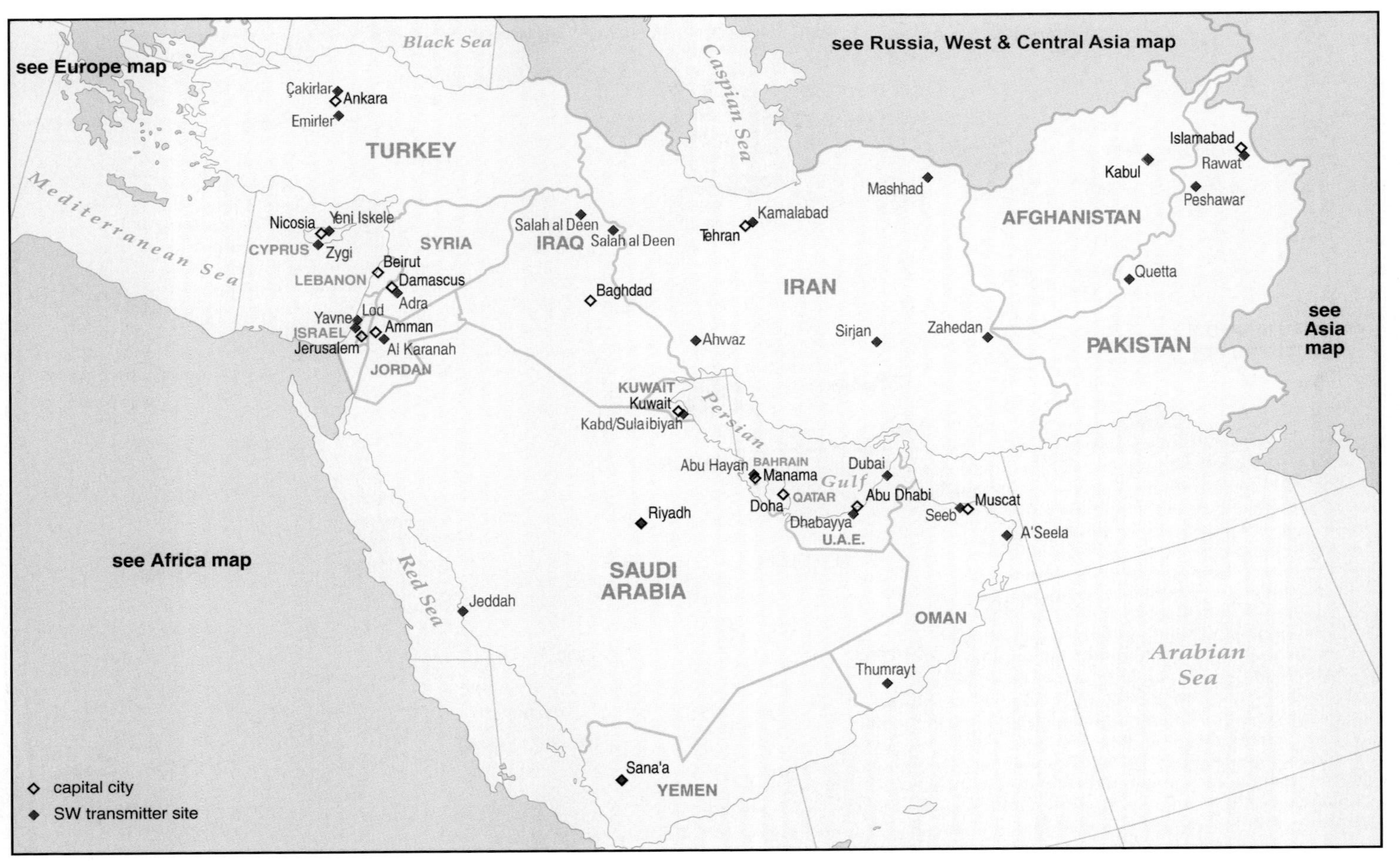

see Europe map
Black Sea
see Russia, West & Central Asia map
Caspian Sea
Çakirlar
Ankara
Emirler
TURKEY
Mediterranean Sea
Nicosia
Yeni Iskele
CYPRUS
Zygi
SYRIA
Beirut
LEBANON
Damascus
Adra
Lod
Yavne
ISRAEL
Amman
Jerusalem
Al Karanah
JORDAN
Salah al Deen
IRAQ
Salah al Deen
Baghdad
Tehran
Kamalabad
Mashhad
IRAN
Ahwaz
Sirjan
Zahedan
Islamabad
Kabul
Rawat
Peshawar
AFGHANISTAN
Quetta
PAKISTAN
see Asia map
KUWAIT
Kuwait
Kabd/Sulaibiyah
Persian Gulf
Abu Hayan
BAHRAIN
Manama
Dubai
QATAR
Doha
Abu Dhabi
Dhabayya
U.A.E.
Seeb
Muscat
A'Seela
Riyadh
see Africa map
Red Sea
Jeddah
SAUDI ARABIA
OMAN
Arabian Sea
Thumrayt
Sana'a
YEMEN
capital city
SW transmitter site

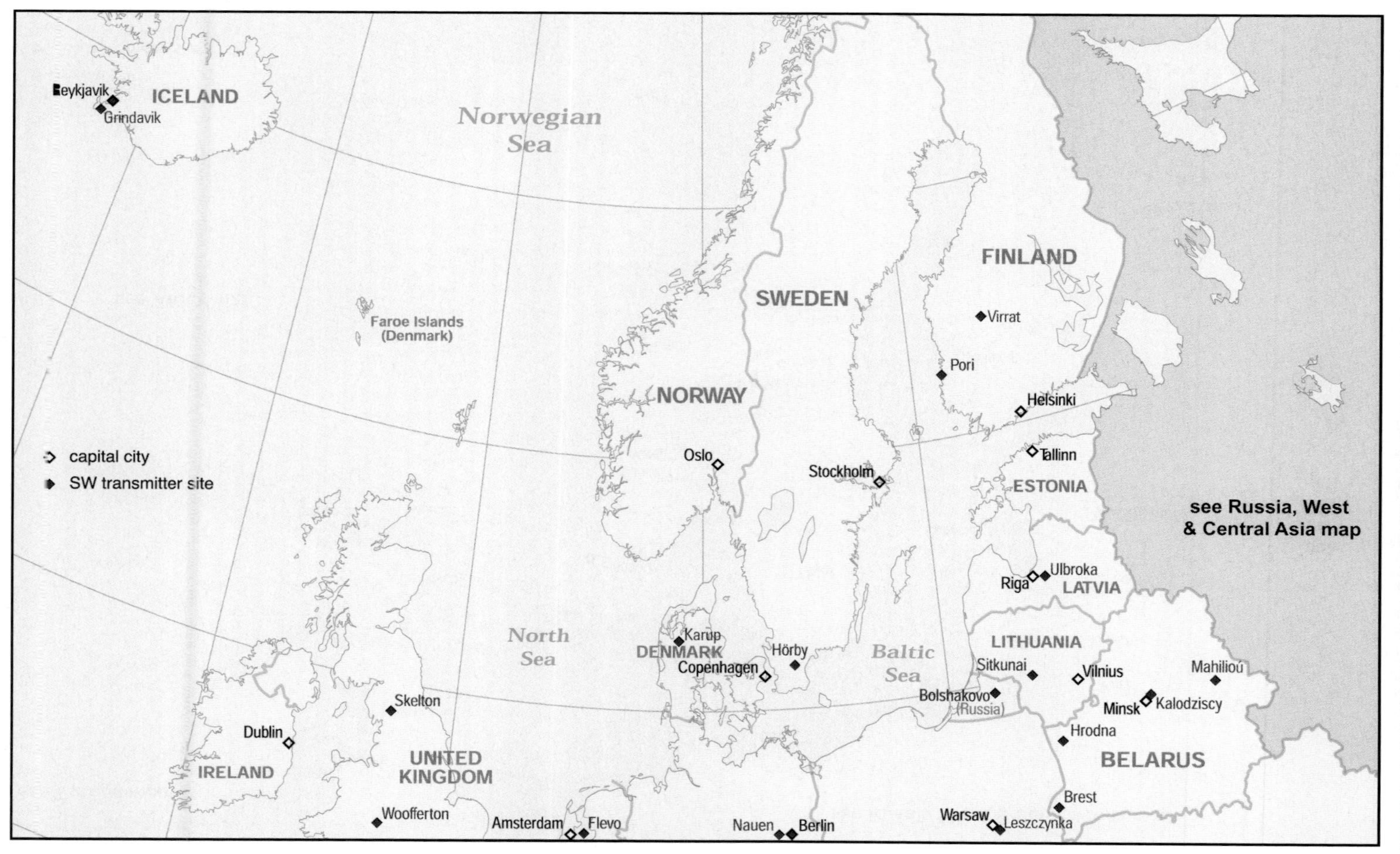
Reykjavik
Grindavik
ICELAND
Norwegian Sea
Faroe Islands
(Denmark)
SWEDEN
FINLAND
Virrat
Pori
NORWAY
Helsinki
capital city
SW transmitter site
Oslo
Stockholm
Tallinn
ESTONIA
see Russia, West
& Central Asia map
Riga
Ulbroka
LATVIA
North Sea
Karup
DENMARK
Copenhagen
Hörby
Baltic Sea
LITHUANIA
Sitkunai
Vilnius
Mahiliou
Bolshakovo
(Russia)
Minsk
Kalodziscy
Skelton
Dublin
Hrodna
IRELAND
UNITED KINGDOM
BELARUS
Brest
Woofferton
Amsterdam
Flevo
Nauen
Berlin
Warsaw
Leszczynka

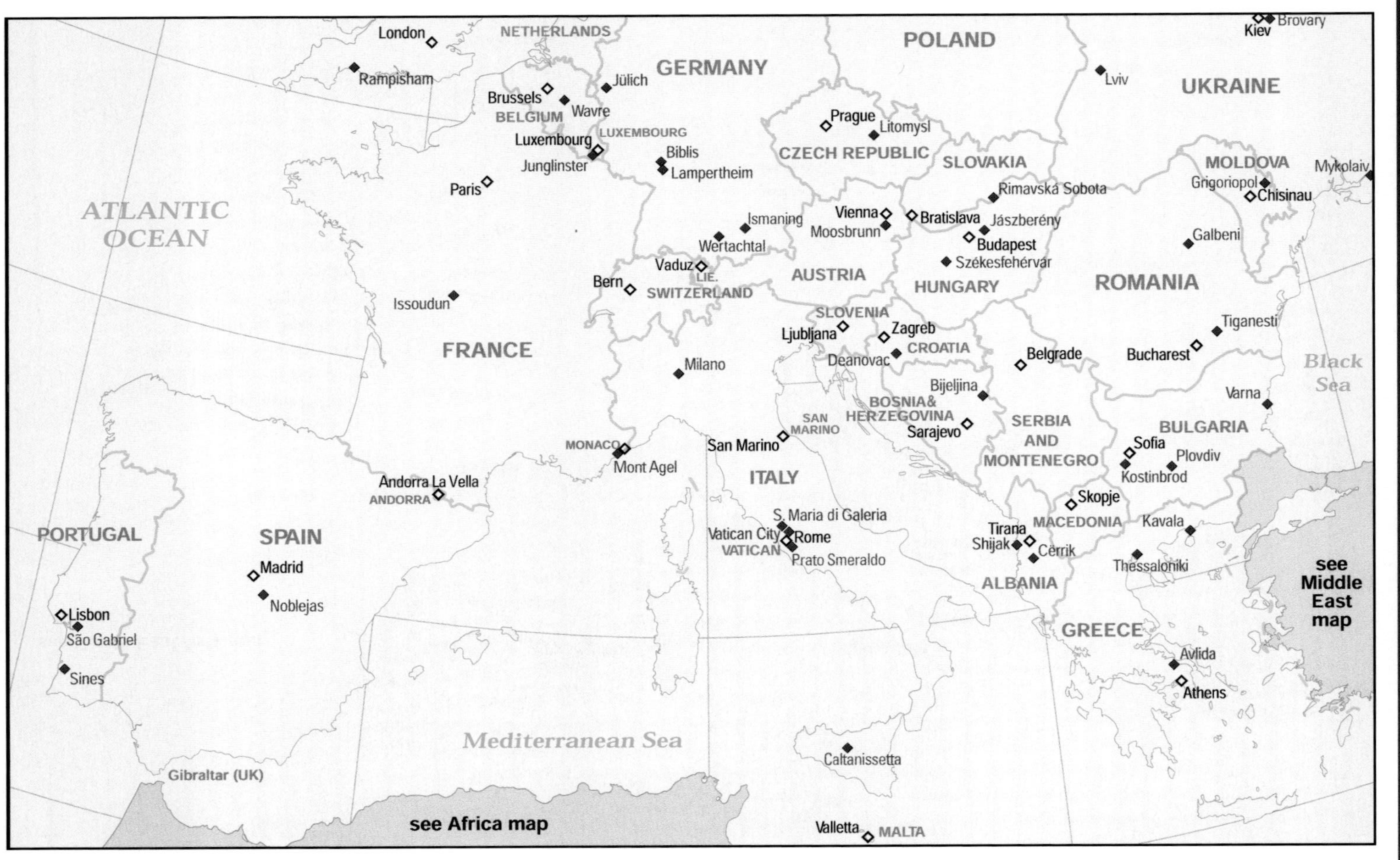

London
NETHERLANDS
GERMANY
POLAND
Kiev
Brovary
Rampisham
Brussels
BELGIUM
Wavre
Jülich
LUXEMBOURG
Luxembourg
Junglinster
Biblis
Lampertheim
Prague
Litomysl
CZECH REPUBLIC
SLOVAKIA
Lviv
UKRAINE
MOLDOVA
Grigoriopol
Chisinau
Mykolaiv
Paris
ATLANTIC OCEAN
Ismaning
Wertachtal
Vienna
Moosbrunn
Bratislava
Rimavská Sobota
Jászberény
Budapest
Székesfehérvár
Galbeni
Vaduz
LIE.
Bern
SWITZERLAND
AUSTRIA
HUNGARY
ROMANIA
Issoudun
SLOVENIA
Ljubljana
Zagreb
CROATIA
Deanovac
Tiganesti
Bucharest
Black Sea
FRANCE
Milano
Belgrade
Bijeljina
BOSNIA& HERZEGOVINA
Sarajevo
SAN MARINO
San Marino
Varna
SERBIA AND MONTENEGRO
BULGARIA
Sofia
Plovdiv
Kostinbrod
MONACO
Mont Agel
ITALY
Andorra La Vella
ANDORRA
Skopje
MACEDONIA
Kavala
S. Maria di Galeria
Vatican City
Rome
VATICAN
Prato Smeraldo
Tirana
Shijak
Cërrik
Thessaloniki
ALBANIA
PORTUGAL
SPAIN
Madrid
Noblejas
see Middle East map
GREECE
Lisbon
São Gabriel
Sines
Avlida
Athens
Mediterranean Sea
Caltanissetta
Gibraltar (UK)
see Africa map
Valletta
MALTA

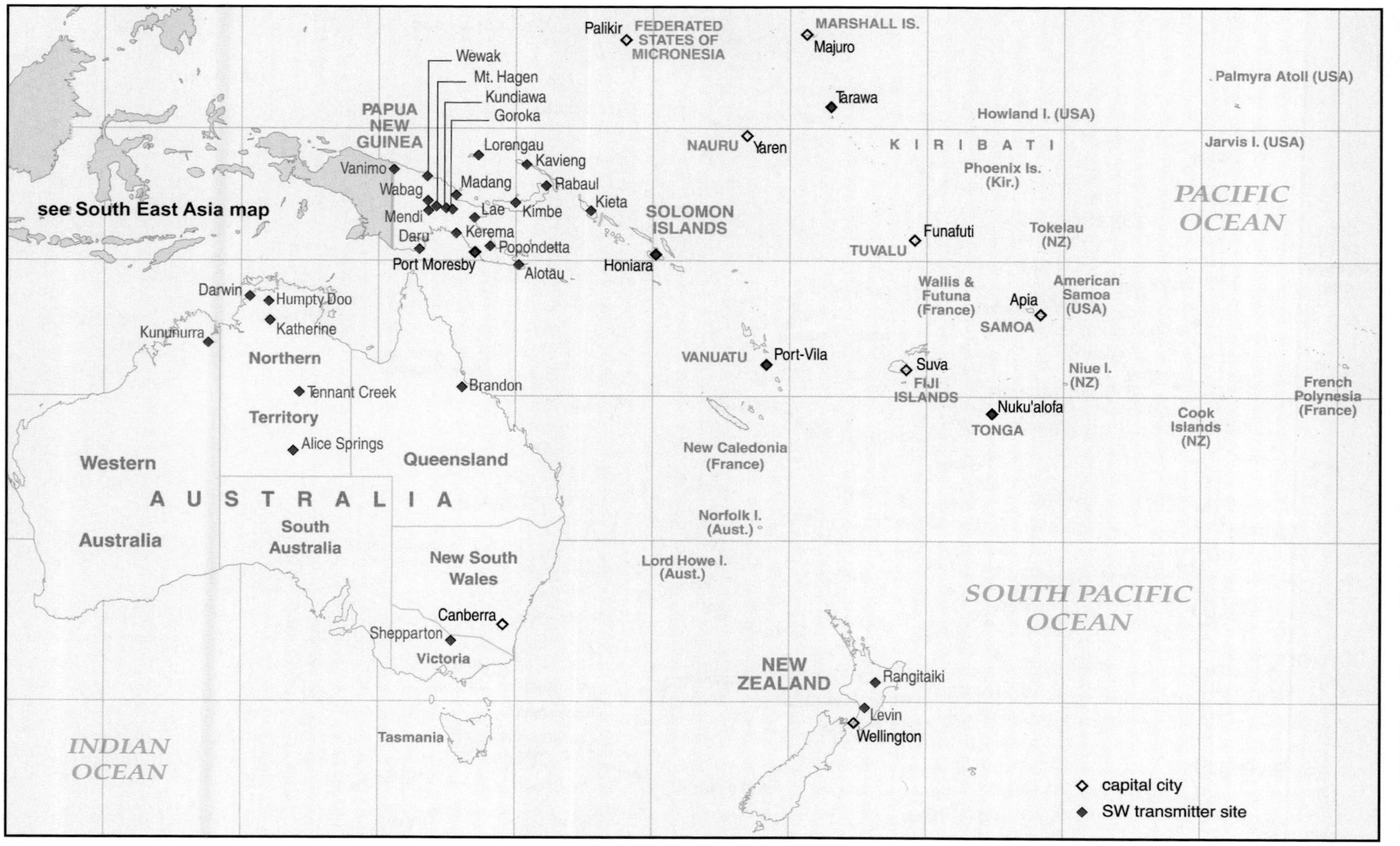

Palikir
FEDERATED STATES OF MICRONESIA
MARSHALL IS.
Majuro
Palmyra Atoll (USA)
Wewak
Mt. Hagen
Kundiawa
Goroka
PAPUA NEW GUINEA
Tarawa
Howland I. (USA)
Jarvis I. (USA)
NAURU
Yaren
K I R I B A T I
Lorengau
Kavieng
Vanimo
Phoenix Is. (Kir.)
Madang
Rabaul
Wabag
PACIFIC OCEAN
Kieta
see South East Asia map
Mendi
Lae
Kimbe
SOLOMON ISLANDS
Kerema
Tokelau (NZ)
Funafuti
Daru
Popondetta
TUVALU
Port Moresby
Honiara
Alotau
Wallis & Futuna (France)
American Samoa (USA)
Darwin
Humpty Doo
Apia
SAMOA
Katherine
Kununurra
Northern
VANUATU
Port-Vila
Suva
Niue I. (NZ)
French Polynesia (France)
Tennant Creek
Brandon
FIJI ISLANDS
Nuku'alofa
Cook Islands (NZ)
Territory
TONGA
Alice Springs
New Caledonia (France)
Western
Queensland
A U S T R A L I A
Norfolk I. (Aust.)
South Australia
Australia
New South Wales
Lord Howe I. (Aust.)
SOUTH PACIFIC OCEAN
Canberra
Shepparton
Victoria
NEW ZEALAND
Rangitaiki
Levin
Wellington
Tasmania
INDIAN OCEAN
capital city
SW transmitter site

ARCTIC OCEAN
East Siberian Sea
Barents Sea
Kara Sea
Laptev Sea
see Europe map
Monchegorsk
Baltic Sea
Arkhangelsk
Krasnyy Bor
Taldom
Lesnoy
Moscow
Kurovskaya
Perm
RUSSIA
Arman
Yakutsk
Yelizovo
Sea of Okhotsk
UKRAINE
Kharkiv
Zaporizhia
Samara
Yazykovo
Yekaterinburg
Tbilisskaya
Novosibirsk
Oyash
Krasnoyarsk
Komsomolsk-na-Amure
Vestochka
Khabarovsk
Soxum
GEORGIA
Dusheti
T'bilisi
Caspian Sea
Aral Sea
Astana
Kyzyl
Angarsk
Selenga
Atamanovka
ARMENIA
Yerevan
Gäncä
Gavar
Stepanakert
Baku
KAZAKHSTAN
Hailar
Mörön
Khonkhor
Ulaanbaatar
Shangzhi
Razdolnoye
AZERBAIJAN
UZBEKISTAN
TURKMENISTAN
Almaty
Bishkek
Qaraturyq
Altay
MONGOLIA
Sea of Japan
Ashgabat
Tashkent
KYRGYZSTAN
see Middle East map
Dushanbe
Yangiyul
Orzu
TAJIKISTAN
capital city
SW transmitter site
see Asia map

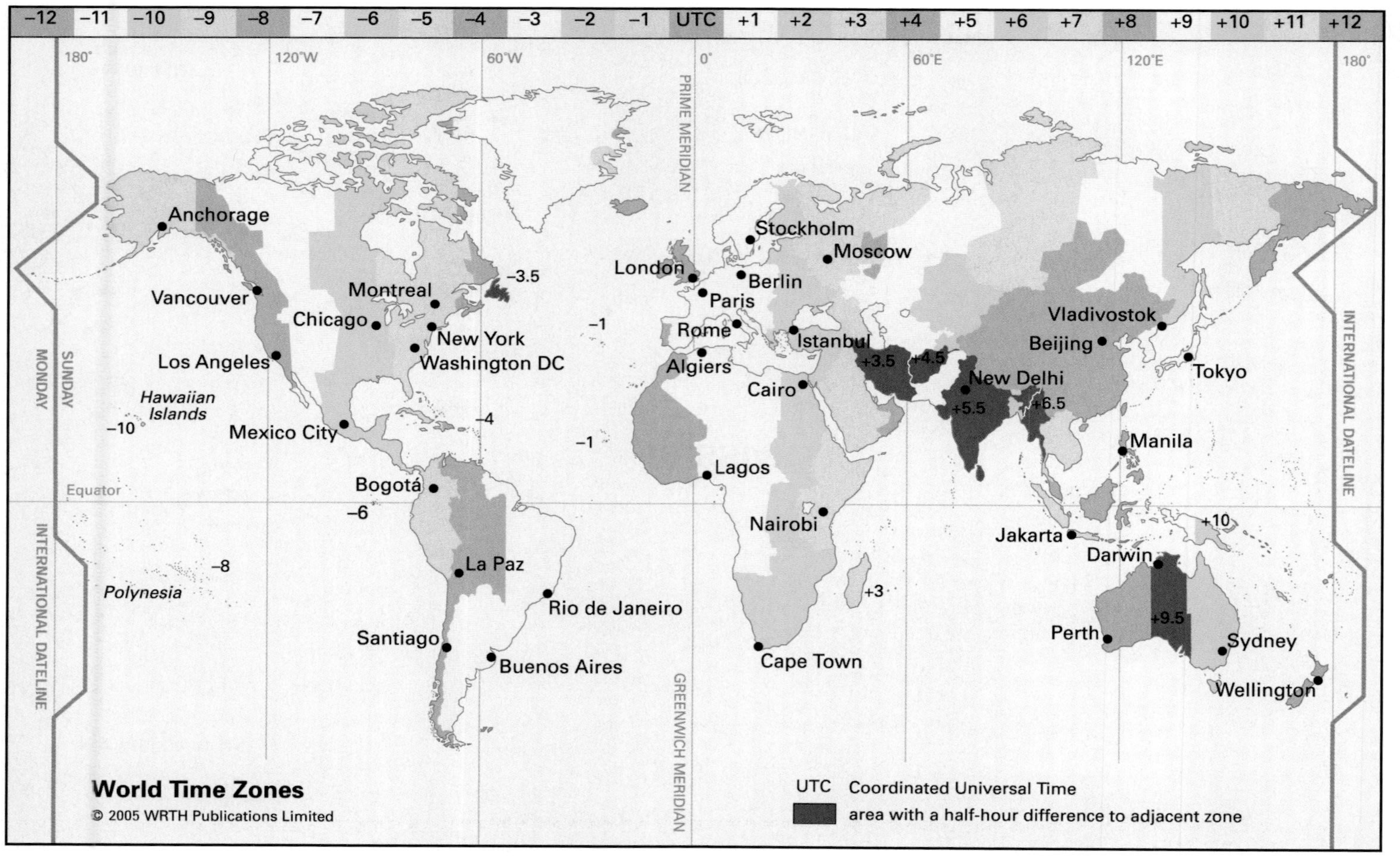

−12
−11
−10
−9
−8
−7
−6
−5
−4
−3
−2
−1
UTC
+1
+2
+3
+4
+5
+6
+7
+8
+9
+10
+11
+12
180°
120°W
60°W
0°
60°E
120°E
180°
PRIME MERIDIAN
GREENWICH MERIDIAN
INTERNATIONAL DATELINE
MONDAY
SUNDAY
INTERNATIONAL DATELINE
Equator
Anchorage
Vancouver
Los Angeles
Hawaiian Islands
−10
Montreal
Chicago
New York
Washington DC
−3.5
Mexico City
−4
−1
−1
Bogotá
−6
La Paz
Rio de Janeiro
Santiago
Buenos Aires
−8
Polynesia
Stockholm
Moscow
London
Berlin
Paris
Rome
Istanbul
Algiers
Cairo
+3.5
+4.5
New Delhi
+5.5
+6.5
Vladivostok
Beijing
Tokyo
Manila
Lagos
Nairobi
+3
Cape Town
Jakarta
+10
Darwin
+9.5
Perth
Sydney
Wellington
World Time Zones
© 2005 WRTH Publications Limited
UTC Coordinated Universal Time
area with a half-hour difference to adjacent zone

WORLD TIME TABLE

Differences marked + or - indicate the number of hours ahead of, or behind, UTC. Variations from Standard Time for part of the year (referred to as DST or Summer Time) are shown below; see the various country sections for the dates of operation.
N=Normal (Standard)Time; **D**=Daylight Saving Time (DST).

	N	D
Afghanistan	+4½	+4½
Alaska	–9	–8
Aleutian Is.	–10	–9
Albania	+1	+2
Algeria	+1	+1
American Samoa	–11	–11
Andorra	+1	+2
Angola	+1	+1
Anguilla	–4	–4
Antarctica		
(Argentinan)	–3	–3
(Chilenan)	–4	–3
(McMurdo)	+12	+13
Antigua	–4	–4
Argentina (Santiago)	–3	–3
(other regions see country section)		
Armenia	+4	+5
Aruba	–4	–4
Ascension I.	UTC	UTC
Australia		
W. Australia	+8	+8
N. Territory	+9½	+9½
S. Australia	+9½	+10½
Queensland	+10	+10
VIC, NSW, TAS	+10	+11
Austria	+1	+2
Azerbaijan	+4	+5
Azores	–1	UTC
Bahamas	–5	–4
Bahrain	+3	+3
Bangladesh	+6	+6
Barbados	–4	–4
Belarus	+2	+3
Belgium	+1	+2
Belize	–6	–6
Benin	+1	+1
Bermuda	–4	–3
Bhutan	+6	+6
Bolivia	–4	–4
Bosnia & Herzegovina	+1	+2
Botswana	+2	+2
Brazil (Brasília)	–3	–2
(other regions see country section)		
British Ind. Oc. Terr.	+5	+5
British Virgin Is.	–4	–4
Brunei	+8	+8
Bulgaria	+2	+3
Burkina Faso	UTC	UTC
Burundi	+2	+2
Cambodia	+7	+7
Cameroon	+1	+1
Canada		
NF (exc.S-E Labr.)	–3½	–2½
NF (S-E L.), NS, PE	–4	–3
NB, NU, ON, QC	–5	–4
MB	–6	–5
AB, NT, SK (parts)	–7	–6
SK (most parts)	–7	–7
BC, YT	–8	–7
Canary Is.	UTC	+1
Cape Verde	–1	–1
Cayman Is.	–5	–5
Ce. African Rep.	+1	+1
Chad	+1	+1
Chile	–4	–3
China (P.R.)	+8	+8
Christmas Is.	+7	+7
Cocos Is.	+6½	+6½
Colombia	–5	–5
Comoros	+3	+3
Congo (Kinshasa)	+1	+1
(other regions see country section)		
Congo (Rep.)	+1	+1
Cook Is.	–10	–10
Costa Rica	–6	–6
Côte d'Ivoire	UTC	UTC
Croatia	+1	+2
Cuba	–5	–4
Cyprus	+2	+3
Czech Rep.	+1	+2
Denmark	+1	+2
Djibouti	+3	+3
Dominica	–4	–4
Dom. Rep.	–4	–4
East Timor	+9	+9
Easter Is.	–6	–5
Ecuador	–5	–5
Egypt	+2	+3
El Salvador	–6	–6
Equatorial Guinea	+1	+1
Eritrea	+3	+3
Estonia	+2	+3
Ethiopia	+3	+3
Falkland Is.	–4	–3
Faroe Is.	UTC	+1
Fiji	+12	+12
Finland	+2	+3
France	+1	+2
French Guiana	–3	–3
French Polynesia	–10	–10
Gabon	+1	+1
Galapagos Is.	–6	–6
Gambia	UTC	UTC
Georgia	+3	+4
Germany	+1	+2
Ghana	UTC	UTC
Gibraltar	+1	+2
Greece	+2	+3
Greenland (Nuuk)	–3	–2
(other regions see country section)		
Grenada	–4	–4
Guadeloupe	–4	–4
Guam	+10	+10
Guatemala	–6	–6
Guinea	UTC	UTC
Guinea-Bissau	UTC	UTC
Guyana	–4	–4
Haiti	–5	–5
Hawaii	–10	–10
Honduras	–6	–6
Hong Kong	+8	+8
Hungary	+1	+2
Iceland	UTC	UTC
India	+5½	+5½
Indonesia (Jakarta)	+7	+7
(other regions see country section)		
Iran	+3½	+4½
Iraq	+3	+4
Ireland	UTC	+1
Israel**	+2	+3
Italy	+1	+2
Jamaica	–5	–5
Japan	+9	+9
Jordan	+2	+3
Kazakhstan (Astana)	+6	+7
(other regions see country section)		
Kenya	+3	+3
Kiribati	+12	+12
Korea (North, DPR)	+9	+9
Korea (South, Rep.)	+9	+9
Kuwait	+3	+3
Kyrgyzstan	+5	+6
Laos	+7	+7
Latvia	+2	+3
Lebanon	+2	+3
Lesotho	+2	+2
Liberia	UTC	UTC
Libya	+2	+2
Liechtenstein	+1	+2
Lithuania	+2	+3
Lord Howe I.	+10½	+11
Luxembourg	+1	+2
Macau	+8	+8
Macedonia	+1	+2
Madagascar	+3	+3
Madeira	UTC	+1
Malawi	+2	+2
Malaysia	+8	+8
Maldives	+5	+5
Mali	UTC	UTC
Malta	+1	+2
Marshall Is.	+12	+12
Martinique	–4	–4
Mauritania	UTC	UTC
Mauritius	+4	+4
Mayotte	+3	+3
Mexico (Mexico City)	–6	–5
(other regions see country section)		
Micronesia		
Chuuk, Yap	+10	+10
Kosrae, Pohnpei	+11	+11
Moldova	+2	+3
Monaco	+1	+2
Mongolia (U-baatar)	+8	+9
(other regions see country section)		
Montserrat	–4	–4
Morocco	UTC	UTC
Ceuta & Melilla	+1	+2
Mozambique	+2	+2
Myanmar	+6½	+6½
Namibia	+1	+2
Nauru	+12	+12
Nepal	+5¾	+5¾
Netherlands	+1	+2
Neth. Antilles	–4	–4
New Caledonia	+11	+11
New Zealand	+12	+13
Nicaragua	–6	–6
Niger	+1	+1
Nigeria	+1	+1
Niue	–11	–11
Norfolk I.	+11½	+11½
No. Mariana Is.	+10	+10
Norway	+1	+2
Oman	+4	+4
Pakistan	+5	+5
Palau	+9	+9
Panama	–5	–5
Papua N. Guinea	+10	+10
Paraguay	–4	–3
Peru	–5	–5
Philippines	+8	+8
Poland	+1	+2
Portugal	UTC	+1
Puerto Rico	–4	–4
Qatar	+3	+3
Réunion	+4	+4
Romania	+2	+3
Russia (Moscow)	+3	+4
(other regions see country section)		
Rwanda	+2	+2
Samoa	–11	–11
São Tomé & Princ.	UTC	UTC
San Marino	+1	+2
Saudi Arabia	+3	+3
Senegal	UTC	UTC
Serbia & Montenegro	+1	+2
Seychelles	+4	+4
Sierra Leone	UTC	UTC
Singapore	+8	+8
Slovakia	+1	+2
Slovenia	+1	+2
Solomon Is.	+11	+11
Somalia	+3	+3
So. Africa	+2	+2
Spain	+1	+2
Sri Lanka	+6	+6
St. Helena	UTC	UTC
St. Kitts & Nevis	–4	–4
St. Lucia	–4	–4
St. Pierre & Miq.	–3	–2
St. Vincent	–4	–4
Sudan	+2	+2
Suriname	–3	–3
Swaziland	+2	+2
Sweden	+1	+2
Switzerland	+1	+2
Syria	+2	+3
Taiwan	+8	+8
Tajikistan	+5	+5
Tanzania	+3	+3
Thailand	+7	+7
Togo	UTC	UTC
Tokelau	–10	–10
Tonga	+13	+13
Trinidad	–4	–4
Tristan da Cunha	UTC	UTC
Tunisia	+1	+1
Turkey	+2	+3
Turkmenistan	+5	+5
Turks & Caicos Is.	–5	–4
Tuvalu	+12	+12
Uganda	+3	+3
Ukraine	+2	+3
United Arab Em.	+4	+4
United Kingdom	UTC	+1
Uruguay**	–3	–2
USA		
Eastern* (CT, DE, FL, GA, KY, MA, MD, ME, MI, NC, NH, NJ, NY, OH, PA, RI, SC, VA, VT, WV)	–5	–4
*) exc. IN	–5	–5
Central (AL, AR, IA, IL, KS, LA, MN, MO, MS, ND, NE, OK, SD, TN, TX, WI)	–6	–5
Mountain* (N-E AZ, CO, ID, MT, NM, UT, WY)	–7	–6
*) exc. most of AZ	–7	–7
Pacific (CA, NV, OR, WA)	–8	–7
Uzbekistan	+5	+5
Vanuatu	+11	+11
Vatican City State	+1	+2
Venezuela	–4	–4
Vietnam	+7	+7
Virgin Is.	–4	–4
Wallis & Futuna	+12	+12
Yemen	+3	+3
Zambia	+2	+2
Zimbabwe	+2	+2

**) DST 2005/2006 to be confirmed

NATIONAL RADIO

Section Contents

Initial entries for each letter, see Main Index for full details

AFGHANISTAN

L.T: UTC +4½h — **Pop:** 24 million — **Pr.L:** Dari, Pashto, Turkmen, Uzbek — **E.C:** 50Hz, 220V — **ITU:** AFG

MINISTRY OF INFORMATION AND CULTURE
Web: www.afghanistangov.org **L.P:** Minister: Dr. Saeed Makhdom Raheen

RADIO-TELEVISION AFGHANISTAN
PO Box 544, Kabul. **L.P:** D.G: Mr. Ghulam Rasol Hazrati.

MW

Location	kHz	kW		kHz	kW
Kabul	909	10	Pol-e-Charkhi	1107	400
Kabul	1278	50			

FM: Kabul 93MHz 0.25kW.
D.Prgr: 0100-1830. Main **N**: Pashto 1430, Dari 1530.
ANN: Pashto: "Da Radyo Afghanistan". Dari: "Injá Radyoe Afghanistan Kabul ast" **F.Pl:** 100kW SW transmitter.

Regional stations:
R. Faryab, Maimana: 594/1188kHz 7kW, 99/104.3MHz 30W. **D.Prgr:** 1230-1430.
R. Paktia, Gardez: 621kHz 7kW, 104.6MHz 30W. **D.Prgr:** 0230-0430, 1330-1430.
R. Kandahar: 882kHz 7kW. **D.Prgr:** 0230-0430, 1130-1430.
R. Ghazni: 1017kHz 10kW. **D.Prgr:** 0230-0330, 1130-1530.
R. Farah: 1044kHz 7kW. **D.Prgr:** 0300-0430.
R. Khost: 1200kHz 0.5kW. **D.Prgr:** 0230-0630, 1130-1530.
R. Nangarhar, Jalalabad: 1530kHz 0.4kW, 93MHz 0.4kW. **D.Prgr:** 0130-0330, 1230-1500.
R. Bamiyan: 1500kHz 0.4kW, 88MHz 0.15kW. **D.Prgr:** 1330-1500.
R. Herat: 1512kHz 0.1kW, 95.5MHz 0.25kW. **D.Prgr:** 0300-0500, 1130-1330.
R. Nimroz, Zaranj: 1518kHz 2kW. **D.Prgr:** 0330-0530, 1230-1500 (Fri 1930)
R. Kunar, Asadabad: 1580kHz 0.1kW. **D.Prgr:** 0930-1230.
R. Balkh, Mazar-e-Sharif: 1584kHz 10kW, 101MHz 1kW. **D.Prgr** in Dari/Pashto/Tajik/Uzbek: 0230-0430 (Fri 0430-0730), 1230-1530.
R. Helmand, Lashkar Ga 1680kHz 0.1kW. **D.Prgr:** 1230-1500, Fri 0530-0630.
R. Taloqan: 91.2MHz 30W.
R. Badakhstan, Faizabad: 105.1MHz 30W.
R. Kabul: 105.2MHz 0.6kW. **Email:** radio.kabul.af@undp.org **D.Prgr:** 0330-0830 Sat-Thu.

RADIO FREE AFGHANISTAN/VOICE OF AMERICA
MW: Pol-e-Charkhi 1296kHz 400kW.
FM: Kabul 100.5MHz 0.8kW. **D.Prgr:** 24h in Dari/Pashto/English. For further details see International Radio section (USA).

PEACE RADIO (US Army PsyOp)
MW: Kandahar 864kHz 5kW. **SW:** Bagram 9365kHz 1kW.
FM: Kabul 88.5MHz.
D.Prgr: 0030-1830 in Pashto/Dari. **ANN**: Dari: "Inja Radyoe Soleh".

Other stations:
R. AMU, Faizabad: 91.5MHz 0.15kW – **R. Azad Afgan,** Kandahar: 88.5MHz 0.2kW. Also rel. BBC – **R. Arman FM,** Kabul: 98.1MHz 2kW. P.O. Box 1045, Central PO, Kabul. **Web:** www.arman.fm **Email:** info@arman.fm – **R. Istiqlal,** Baraki-Barak: 89.6MHz 0.2kW. **R. Killid,** Kabul: 88MHz 0.3kW. **Email:** zahinesh@yahoo.com – **R. Rabi'ah Balkhi,** Mazar-e-Sharif: 87.9MHz 50W – **R. Paygham-e-Melli,** Mohamad Agha: 94MHz 0.2kW – **R. Naw-e-Bahar,** Balkh: 88.5MHz 0.15kW – **R. Nedaye Solh,** Ghoreyan: 91.4MHz 0.15kW. **R. Sahar,** Herat: 88.7MHz 0.1kW – **R. Sedaye Adalat,** Chagcharan: 90.3MHz 50W – **R. Sedaye Javan (Voice of Youth),** Herat: freq. not known – **R. Sedaye Solh (Voice of Peace),** Jabul Saraj: 96.7MHz 0.5kW – **R. Sharq,** Jalalabad: 87.6MHz 1.2kW – **R. Shura'e,** Qarah Bagh: 91.3MHz 0.15kW – **R. Sulh-e-Paygham,** Khost: 93.1MHz 0.15kW – **R. Tiraj Mir,** Pol-e-Khumri: 91.3MHz. **R. Zohra,** Kunduz: 90.5MHz 50W – **University R.,** Kabul: 106.7MHz 1.2kW – **Voice of Women,** Kabul: 91.6MHz 1.2kW – **R. Yawali-Zhagh,** Sayedabad: 88MHz 0.15kW – **American Forces Network:** Bagram 103.1/105.7/107.3MHz 0.1kW, Kabul: 103.1/105.7/107 3MHz 0.2kW, Kandahar 103.1/105.1/ 107.3MHz 0.125kW.
BBC Afghan Sce in English/Pashto/Dari/Uzbek: Bamian, Herat, Jalalabad, Kabul, Kandahar, Khost, Kunduz, Maimana, Mazar-e-Sharif, Pol-e-Khomri on 89MHz, and Sheberghan 92.1MHz.
BFBS, Kabul: BFBS 1: 102.4MHz, BFBS 2: 104.9MHz.
German Forces Broadcasting Sce: 107.5MHz.
R. France Int: Kabul 89.5MHz 0.2kW.
Some Taliban mobile radio stations rep. operating along the Pakistani border. No further details available.

ALASKA (US State)

L.T: UTC -9h (3 Apr-30 Oct -8h) Aleutian Is. -10h (3 Apr-30 Oct -9h) — **Pop:** 627,000 — **Pr.L:** English — **E.C:** 60Hz, 120/240V — **ITU:** ALS

ALASKA BROADCASTERS ASSOCIATION
700 W. 41st Str, Anchorage, AK 99503. ☎ +1 907 258-2424. +1 907 258-2414.Web: www.akbroadcasters.org.

MW	Call	kHz	kW	h. of tr.
2)	KTZN	550	5	24h
3)	KVOK	560	1	24h
4)	KRSA	580	5++	24h
5)	KHAR	590	5	24h
6)	KGTL	620	5	W 1400-0906
7)	KJNO	630	5/1	1400-0900 (Fri/Sat 24h)
8)	KIAM	630	10/3.1	1600-0800
9)	KYUK*	640	10	1500 (Sun 1700)-0930 (Sat 1030)
2)	KENI	650	50	24h
11)	KFAR	660	10	24h
12)	KDLG*	670	10	1500-0900 (June-Aug: 24h)
13)	KBRW*	680	10	24h
14)	KBYR	700	10	24h
15)	KOTZ*	720	10	1400-0900 (su. 24h)
5)	KFQD	750	50	24h
17)	KCHU*	770	9.7	1300 (Sun 1400)-0900
18)	KNOM*	780	25/14	1455-1110
19)	KCAM	790	5	24h
20)	KINY	800	10/7.8	24h
11)	KCBF	820	10	24h
22)	KSDP*	830	1	as 12)
24)	KICY	850	50/10+	1445-0930
25)	KSKO*	870	10	24h
26)	KBBI*	890	10	1430 (Sat/Sun 1500)-0900
27)	KZPA*	900	5	24h
28)	KIYU*	910	5	24h
29)	KSRM	920	5	24h
30)	KTKN	930	5/1	1400-0900
31)	KNSA*	930	2.5	as 12)
32)	KSWD	950	1	**
33)	KIAK	970	5	24h
16)	KAXX	1020	10++	24h
2)	KUDO	1080	10	24h
35)	KAGV	1110	10	F.Pl.
29)	KSLD	1140	10	24h
37)	KJNP	1170	50/21	1400-1100
38)	KVAK	1230	1	24h
39)	KIFW	1230	1	1500-0900
40)	KLAM	1450	0.25	24h

*) non-comm – **) silent or irregular operation at editorial deadline. Stations below 250W not mentioned – +) 50kW directional 0800-1200 – ++) directional.

FM: Sts below 1kW not mentioned.

	Call	MHz	kW	City of licence
	KCUK	88.1	6	Chevak
	KAKL	88.5	11	Anchorage
	KTNA	88.5	1.9	Talkeetna
	KJHA	88.7	1	Houston
	KEUL	88.9	1.4	Girdwood
	KATB	89.3	4.90	Anchorage
	KUAC	89.9	38	Fairbanks
	KNBA	90.3	100	Anchorage
17)	KXGA	90.5	3.2	Glennallen
	KSKA	91.1	100	Anchorage
	KSUA	91.5	3	Fairbanks
	KWJG	91.5	1	Kasilof
	KDLL	91.9	4.9	Kenai
	KUHB-FM	91.9	15	St.Paul
	KQEZ	92.1	10	Houston
	KFAT	92.9	10	Anchorage
	KXBA	93.3	50	Nikiski
	KVAK-FM	93.3	1.2	Valdez
	KAFC	93.7	27	Anchorage
	KADX	94.7	51	Houston
11)	KXLR	95.9	25	Fairbanks
	KRPM	96.3	10	Houston

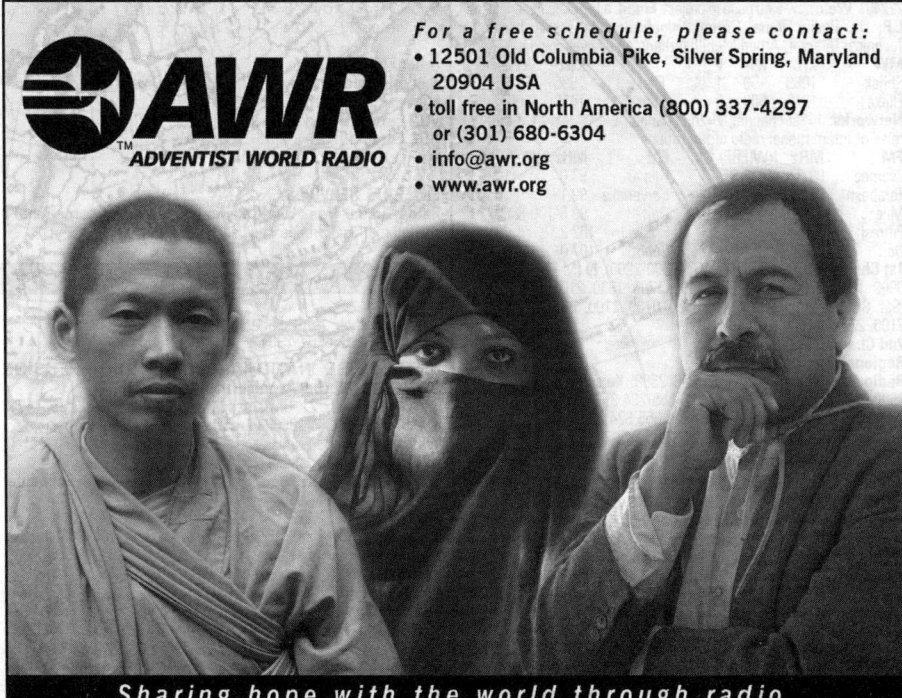

	Call	MHz	kW	City of licence
29)	KKIS-FM	96.5	10	Soldotna
5)	KEAG	97.3	100	Anchorage
	KLEF	98.1	25	Anchorage
11)	KWLF	98.1	28	Fairbanks
2)	KYMG	98.9	100	Anchorage
	KRUP	99.1	6	Dillingham
	KMBQ	99.7	51	Wasilla
8)	KYKD	100.1	7.7	Bethel
29)	KWHQ-FM	100.1	3	Kenai
	KMXT	100.1	3	Kodiak
37)	KJNP-FM	100.3	25	NorthPole
2)	KBFX	100.5	25	Anchorage
	KFMG	100.7	6	Juneau
	KCDV	100.9	1.2	Cordova
8)	KAKN	100.9	3	Naknek
	KFSK	100.9	2	Petersburg
33)	KAKQ-FM	101.1	50	Fairbanks
3)	KRXX	101.1	3.1	Kodiak
2)	KGOT	101.3	26	Anchorage
6)	KPEN-FM	101.7	25	Soldotna
	KSTK	101.7	3	Wrangell
	KDBZ	102.1	23	Anchorage
	KHNS	102.3	3	Haines
33)	KIAK-FM	102.5	100	Fairbanks
	KSRJ	102.7	6	Juneau
5)	KMXS	103.1	27	Anchorage
39)	KSBZ	103.1	3.1	Sitka
6)	KWVV-FM	103.5	100	Homer
11)	KUWL	103.9	2.95	College
5)	KBRJ	104.1	55	Anchorage
	KTOO	104.3	1.4	Juneau
	KKED	104.7	50	Fairbanks
	KCAW	104.7	4.9	Sitka
7)	KTKU	105.1	3.8	Juneau
14)	KNIK-FM	105.7	51	Anchorage
	KRBD	105.9	15	Ketchikan
	KPFN	105.9	3	Seward
20)	KSUP	106.3	10	Juneau
5)	KWHL	106.5	100	Anchorage
2)	KASH-FM	107.5	100	Anchorage

Addresses and other information for MW sts:
2) 800 E. Dimond Blvd, Ste. #3-370, Anchorage, AK 99515-2058 – **3)** P.O. Box 708, Kodiak, AK 99615-0708 – **4)** P.O. Box 650, Petersburg, AK 99833-0650 – **5)** 301 Arctic Slope Ave #200, Anchorage, AK 99518-3036 – **6)** P.O. Box 109, Homer, AK 99603-0109 – **7)** 3161 Channel Drive, #2, Juneau, AK 99801-7815 – **8)** P.O. Box 00474, Nenana, AK 99760-0474 – **9)** P.O. Box 468, Bethel, AK 99559-0468 – **11)** 1060 Aspen St, Fairbanks, AK 99709-5501 – **12)** P.O. Box 670, Dillingham, AK 99576-0670 – **13)** P.O. Box 109, Barrow, AK 99723-0109 – **14)** 1399 W. 34th Ave. #202, Anchorage 99503-3659 – **15)** P.O. Box 78, Kotzebue, AK 99752-0078 – **17)** P.O. Box 467, Valdez, AK 99686-0467 – **18)** Box 988, Nome, AK 99762-0988 – **19)** P.O. Box 249, Glennallen, AK 99588-0249 – **20)** 1107 W. 8th St, #2, Juneau, AK 99801-1896 – **22)** P.O. Box 328, Sand Point, AK 99661-0328 Mostly rel. 12) – **24)** P.O. Box 820, Nome, AK 99762-0820. Russian 0800-0930 – **25)** P.O. Box 70, McGrath, AK 99627-0070 – **26)** 3913 Kachemak Way, Homer, AK 99603.7618 – **27)** Box 50, Fort Yukon, AK 99740-0050. Mostly rel. KUAC-FM 89.9MHz – **28)** P.O. Box 165, Galena, AK 99741-0165. Mostly rel. 25) – **29)** 40960 Kalifornsky Beach Rd, Kenai, AK 99611-6445 – **30)** 526 Stedman St, Ketchikan, AK 99901-6629 – **31)** P.O. Box 178, Unalakleet, AK 99684-0178. Mostly rel. 12) – **32)** c/o 3098 Airport Way, Fairbanks 99709. (Lic. to Seward 99664) – **33)** 546 9th Ave, Fairbanks, AK 99701-4902 – **35)** Wasilla, AK (Lic. to Big Lake, AK) – **37)** P.O. Box 56359, North Pole, AK 99705-1359 – **38)** P.O. Box 367, Valdez, AK 99686-0367 – **39)** P.O. Box 299, Sitka, AK 99835-0299 – **40)** P.O. Box 60, Cordova, AK 99574-0060.

EXTERNAL SERVICES: Radio Station KNLS
see International Broadcasting section.

ALBANIA

L.T: UTC +1h (27 Mar-30 Oct UTC +2h) — **Pop:** 3.1 million — **Pr.L:** Albanian — **E.C:** 50Hz,220V — **ITU:** ALB

RADIO TELEVIZIONI SHQIPTAR (RTSH) (Public)
RADIO TIRANA

✉ General Directorate of Albanian Radiotelevision, Direction Generale de la Radiotelevision Albanaise.
Rruga Ismail Qemali Nr 11, TIRANA ☎ +355 4 222481. 🖷 +355 4

222481. **Web:** new web page in project. **Email**: aibro@albaniaonline.net **L.P:** Dir. Radio Tirana: Gezim Podgorica(gpodgorica@yahoo.com), Technical Director: Arben Mehilli (arbenmehilli@yahoo.co.uk)

MW	kHz	kW	P		kHz	kW	P
Shijak	1089	150	1	Fllakë	1395	500	E
Fllakë	1215	500	E	Fllakë	1458	500	E

Networks: 1=1st channel, 2=2nd channel, E=Ext. Sce (R. Tirana) or relay of international radio organizations.

FM	MHz	kW(ERP)	Ch.	FM	MHz	kW(ERP)	Ch.
Zvernec	88.3	2.5	1	Gllave	97.0	10	1
Tarabosh	91.0	5	1	Cervenake	99.1	10	1
Mile	93.0	5	1	Dajt	99.5	100 & 50	1
Petresh	95.4	3	1	Homesh	102.2	3	1
Dajt	95.8	10	2	Sopot	107.0	10	1

1st Channel: 0400-2300 (Mar-Oct 0300-2200). **N** (M-F): 0500, 0700, 0900, 1000, 1100, 1200, 1300, 1430, 1700, 1830, 2100, 2230. (Sat, Sun & national holidays): 0530, 0700, 1100, 1430, 1700, 1830, 2100, 2230.

2nd Channel FM: 24 h

Regional service FM(MHz):

Radio Gjirokastra ☎ + 355 846 2388. Kerculle 102.5 0.3 kW , 0600-1830.– **Radio Shkodra** ☎ +355 224 3593. Tarabosh 92.0 1.6 kW, 0600-2000 – **Radio Korca** ☎ + 355 824 2988/2417 Korce 89.5 0.9 kW, 24 h – **Radio Kukesi** ☎ +355 242 2493. Kukesi 100.4 0.9 kW, 0500-1800.

KKRT - KËSHILLI KOMBËTAR I RADIOS DHE TELEVIZIONIT NCRT - NATIONAL COUNCIL OF RADIO & TELEVISION

✉ Ish Hotel Drini, Tirana. ☎ +355 4 233326 🖷 +355 4 226287 **Web:** www.kkrt.gov.al. **Email:** tcobani@kkrt.gov.al

KKRT supervises private activities in the radio and television areas. **LP:** Chairman: vacant Technical Dir: Pirro Koci (pkoci@kkrt.gov.al)

National FM Private Stations

Radio+2

✉ Rruga Don Bosko, Vilat e reja, Tirana. ☎+355 4 251424 **Web:** www.plus2radio.com. **L.P:** Mgr: Leonard Gremi

FM	MHz	kW(ERP)	FM	MHz	kW(ERP)
Fushe	89.8	63	Zvernec	96.3	0.3
Cervenake	90.3	3.8	Gllave	97.6	3.2
Mide	94.3	6.3	Dajt	101.6	8.9

TOP ALBANIA RADIO

✉ Boulevard Dëshmorët e Kombit, Piramida-QNK-Qendra Nderkombetare e Kultures, Tirana. ☎+355 4247492. 🖷 +355 4247493 **Web:** www. topalbaniaradio.com. **Email:** topalbaniaradio@albaniaonline.net.

FM	MHz	kW(ERP)	FM	MHz	kW(ERP)
Kerculle	93.0	1.6	Mile	100.6	28.2
Tarabosh	94.1	3.2	Mide	101.3	22
Gllave	97.7	31.5	Zvernec	102.2	3.1
Cervenake	98.5	5	Ardenice	103.5	2.8
Dürres	99.0	1.6	Sopot	104.0	1.5
Tirana/Dajt	100.0	15	Preze	104.3	7.1

Local FM Private Stations (kW ERP):

	Station	MHz	kW		Station	MHz	kW
1)	R. Ngjallja	88.5	6.3	9)	R. ABC	98.0	1.8
1)	R. New Planet	89.0	3.2	1)	R. Koha	98.1	1.8
1)	R. Kontakt	89.3	1.6	1)	R. Aldo 03	98.8	1.6
1)	R. Love	90.7	1.6	1)	R. Super Star	99.0	-
2)	R. Alfa	90.9	0.7	10)	R. Saranda	100.0	0.5
3)	R. Argjiropoli	91.0	0.8	11)	R. E Pare	100.4	0.1
1)	R. Skorpion	91.4	0.3	1)	R. Club FM	100.4	12.6
4)	R. +3	91.6	0.8	12)	R. Prespa	100.8	0.3
1)	R. Italia	92.4	0.4	1)	R. Top Gold	100.8	56.1
5)	R. Planet	93.0	1.6	1)	R. Boom Boom	101.2	37.7
1)	R. Nacional AH	93.4	0.8	1)	R. Alfa & Omega	102.6	6.3
6)	R. Magic	93.8	0.3	1)	R. Alsat	103.1	3.2
2)	R. Klea	93.9	0.7	14)	R. Val e Kalter	103.3	1.9
7)	R. Alpo	94.1	0.1	2)	R. Club FM	104.3	0.7
1)	R. Eurostar	94.5	1.6	1)	R. Rock	104.6	25.2
6)	R. Fantasy	94.7	0.3	1)	R. Perla	105.0	0.8
8)	R. Ruzvelt	94.8	0.1	1)	R. Ime	105.4	0.5
9)	R. Emanuel	95.7	3.5	4)	R. Star	105.5	1.6
1)	R. Oxygen	96.1	3.2	15)	R. Perla	106.4	0.5
1)	R. Real	96.4	1.6	1)	R. NRG	106.6	1.6
2)	R. Eurostar	96.6	0.7	1)	R. Stinet	106.9	0.6
1)	R. Rash	97.0	3.2	9)	R. Magic Star	107.0	3.6
1)	R. Muzika Jone	97.3	1.6	4)	R. Fieri	107.2	0.8
1)	R. +7	97.7	6.3	1)	R. House of Arts	107.7	1.6

Locations: 1=Fushe Dajt, 2=Petresh, 3=Kerculle, 4=Fier, 5 =Tirana, 6=Kavaje, 7=Kerculle, 8=Memaliaj, 9= Korce 10 = Mile 11 =Burrel, 12 = Prespe, 13 = Shkoder, 14 = Zvernec, 15 = Dürres

Other FM stations)

Radio France International: 102.0 Fushe Dajt 1 kW; 102.0 Korca. RFI Musique, RFI in French & RFI in Albanian

VOA Europe: Tirana (Dajt) 107.4 0.8 kW.

BBC Europe: Tirana (Dajt) 103.9 2.2 kW

Deutsche Welle: Tirana (Dajt) 106.0 6.3 kW

EXTERNAL SERVICES

Radio Tirana, Trans World Radio, China Radio International see International Broadcasting section.

ALGERIA

L.T: UTC +1h — **Pop:** 34.5 million — **Pr.L:** Arabic, French, Berber dialects — **E.C:** 50Hz, 230V — **ITU:** ALG

ENTREPRISE NATIONALE DE RADIODIFFUSION SONORE (Radio Algérienne)

✉ Dir. Général, 21 Blvd. des Martyrs, Alger 16000. ☎ +213 21483790 🖷 +213 21230823 **Email:** technique@algerian-radio.dz **Web:** www.algerian-radio.dz.

L.P: DG:Zouaoui Benamadi

LW/MW	kHz	kW	Ch.	Schedule
Béchar	153	2x1000	1	24h
Ouargla	198	2x1000	1	24h
Tipaza	252	2x750*	3	0500-0100
Ain-Beida	531	2x300*	1	24h
S.Hamadouche	549	2x300*	1	24h
Béchar	576	400	1	0800-1600
R. Saoura, Tindouf	666	5	1	0800-1600
Reggane	693	5	2	0600-2400
Laghouat	783	20	3	0800-1600
Ghardaia	873	5	C	0800-1600
Alger	891	2x300*	1	24h
Timimoun	927	5	1	0800-1600
O. Fayet	981	2x300*	2	0600-2400
Touggourt	1017	5	1	0800-1600
Hassi-Messaoud	1026	5	3	0800-1600
Adrar	1089	5	1	0800-1600
Quargla	1098	5	1	0800-1600
El Golea	1287	5	C	0800-1600
O. Fayet	1422	40	C	0400-2000

*) half power used 1800-0600

FM (MHz)	1	2	3	B	kW
Adrar			91.9		2
Aflou	90.7				10
Ain N'sour	90.8				10
Akfadou		91.8			10
Baghlia		88.0			10
Bordj El Bahri	91.0		89.2	94.2	2/10/10
Chrea	94.7		88.4	91.5	10
El Ancor				88.0	10
Kef El Khal			87.6		10
M'cid-Souk Ahras	91.9	88.8	95.1		10
Mecheria	87.8				10
Meghriss	93.5				10
Nador		88.4	91.5		10
SbaaMokrane	88.0		91.1		10
Tebessa			91.0		2
Tessala	102.7			92.7	10
Tiaret	89.4				2

1=Chaine 1 24hr, Satellite Eutelsat 702 MHz. **2**= Chaine 2 0500-2400, Satellite Eutelsat 728 MHz. **3**=Chaine 3 0500-0100, Satellite Eutelsat 738 MHz. **B**=R. El Bahdja 24h, Satellite Eutelsat 756 MHz.

Local radio:

Station, location	MHz	kW	Ch.	Hr of tr
R. Essouhoub, Aflou	87.6	10	L+3	0800-1600
R. Chlef, Ain Sour	87.7	10	L+3	0800-1600
R Tebessa	87.9	10	L	0800-1600
R. Tassili, Illizi	88.0	0.1	L	0800-1600
R. Aurés, Metlili	88.1	10	L+2	0800-1600
R. Soummam, Akfadou	88.7	10	L+1	0800-1600
R. Adrar	88.8	2	L	0800-1600
R. Souf, El Oued	89.7	0.1	L	0800-1600
R. Soummam, Bejaia	90.0	10	L+2	0800-1600
R. El Hidhab, Meghriss	90.4	10	L+3	0800-1600

Station, location	MHz	kW	Ch.	Hr of tr
R. Naama, Mecheria	90.9	10	L+3	0800-1600
R. Zibane, Metlili	91.2	10	L+3	0800-1600
R Tiaret, Tiaret	92.5	10	L	0800-1600
R. Cirta, Kef El Khal	93.9	10	L+1	0800-1600
R. Tlemcen, Nador	94.7	10	L	0800-1600
R. Ahaggar, Tamanrasset	98.0	0.1	L	0800-1600
R. Ghardaia	98.0	0.1	L	0800-1600
R. B.Chougrane, Mascara	98.5	1	L+1	0800-1600
R. Sidi Bel Abbes, Tessala	99.2	10	L+1	0800-1600
R. Dahra, Mostaganem	100.1	1	L+1	0800-1600
R. Annaba, M'cid-Souk A.	100.3	1	L+3	0800-1600
R. Tlemcen, Nedroma	100.4	10	L+1	0800-1600
R. Dahra, Mostaganem	107.2	1	L+1	0800-1600

Most local sts transmit national prgrs at other times. Most of the regional FM sts transmit in stereo.

Ch.: 1=Arabic, 2=Tamazight, 3=French, 4=R. Algiers International, B=Radio El Bahia, Oran www.radioelbahia.com. C=R. Culture/ R.Koran/R.Mitidja, L=Local. **Ch. 1 in Arabic:** 24h. **N:** on the h. **Email:** chaine1@algerian-radio.dz. **Ch. 2 in Tamazight:** 0500-2400. **N:** on the h. **Email:** chaine2@algerian-radio.dz. **Ch. 3 in French:** 0500-0100. **N:** on the h. **Email:** chaine3@algerian-radio.dz. **C: R. Koran** 0400-0800. **R. Culture** 1600-2000; **R. Mitidja** 0800-1200 on 1422kHz and FM in Arabic. **R. El Bahdja**: 24h.

Addresses for local stations:
R. Locale de Tébéssa, Unité de Tébéssa, Parc des Loisirs, Tébéssa. – **R. Locale Cirta**, BP 28B El Koudia, Constanatine. **Email:** constantine@algerian-radio.dz. – **R. Locale Aurés**, BP 453, Batna.100.3 MHz 0.1 kW – **R. Locale Tassili**, BP 230, Illizi. 88.0 MHz 0.1 kW – **R. Locale El Hidab**, BP 54, Sétif. – **R. Locale Adrar**, BP 309, Adrar. – **R. Locale Soummam**, Boulevard Youcef Bouchebah, Béjaia. – **R. Locale Annaba**, 7, Boulevard Radji Mokhtar- Quartier Annasr, Annaba. – **R. Locale Tiaret**, Tiaret. – **R. Locale Souf**, El Oued. – **R. Tlemcen**, B.P. 44K, Tlemcen
Further information at **Web:** www.algerian-radio.dz/frequences.centre.htm
ANN: A: "Huna El Djazair, idha'atu-El Djoumhouriya El Djazairia". C: "al-Idha'atu al-Thaqafiyah". F: "Alger chaîne 3, Radiodiffusion Algerienne" **IS:** Oriental Lute (Ud)

Transmissions to Western Sahara (see Morocco):
RADIO NACIONAL DE LA R.A.S.D., Tindouf
✉ B.P. 10, El-Mouradia, DZ-16000 Alger. ☎ +213 49 923525. **Web**: http://web.jet.es/rasd. **Email:** rasradio@yahoo.es
MW(kHz): 1550 (v. freq.) 100 kW (Tindouf)
SW (kHz): 7460 (v. freq.) 20 kW (Rabuni)
D.Prgr: 0700-0800, 1700-2300 in Arabic and Spanish. (Su. 0600-0700, 1800-2400)

ANDORRA

L.T: UTC + 1h (27 Mar-30 Oct: UTC + 2h) — **Pop:** 73,000 — **Pr.L:** Catalan, French, Spanish — **E.C:** 50Hz, 230V — **ITU:** AND

ORGANITZACIÓ DE RADIOTELEVISIÓ D'ANDORRA (ORTA)
✉ Baixada del Moli, 24, Andorra la Vella. ☎ +376 873777. 🖷 +376863242. **Web:** www.andorra.ad/orta. **E.mail:** orta@andorra.ad

SERVEI DE TELECOMUNICACIONS D'ANDORRA
✉ Av. Meritxell 112, Andorra la Vella. ☎ +376 821021. 🖷 +376 864274. **Email:** sta.comer@andorra.ad
L.P: Admin Dir: Jaume Salvat. Tech. Dir: Joan Marc Lauga.
FM(MHz): France-Inter 101.8 1 kW, France-Musique 102.6 1 kW , France-Culture 104.0 1 kW, Catalunya R. 104.6 1 kW, RNE 4 Catalunya 106.0 1.2 kW, RNE-1 106.8 1.2 kW, RNE-3 107.9 1.2 kW.

RÀDIO NACIONAL D'ANDORRA (RNA)
✉ Baixada del Molí 22, Andorra la Vella. ☎ +376 873777. 🖷 +376 863242. **Web:** www.andorra.ad /rtvasa/rna/ra. **Email:** rtvasa@andorra.ad
L.P: DG: Enric Castellet Pifarré
FM: 91.4MHz 1kW, 94.2MHz 1 kW. **D.Prgr:** 24h in Catalan. Cultural & Social Information. 2300-0600 Musical program only.

ANDORRA MÚSICA
Web & **Email:** as RNA.**FM:** 97.0MHz 0.5kW. **D.Prgr:** 24h. Music.

RÀDIO VALIRA
✉ Carrer del Parnal 2, Escaldaes Engordany, Andorra la Vella. ☎ +376829600. 🖷 +376 828273. **Web:** www.radiovalira.ad **Email:** rvalira@radiovalira.ad **L.P:** SM: Gualberto Osorio.
FM (MHz): Pic de Corroi

Prgr. 1 on 93.3 0.3 kW/98.1MHz 0.5 kW: W 0700-2000, Sun 0900-1300 in Catalan exc. **French** 1300-1330, **English** 1330-1400. Other times rel. Onda Cero (Spain)

Other Stations:
RÀDIO TELETAXI ANDORRA, ✉ St. Coloma de Gramenet. **Web:** www.radioteletaxi.fm.com. **FM**: 90.1MHz. **D.Prgr**: 24 h
ONDA RAMBLA ANDORRA, ✉ See R. Valira. **FM**: 95.0MHz. **D.Prgr**.: 24 h
RÀDIO 7P, ✉ Avinguda Princep Benlloch 24, Baixos ☎+376 731414. **Web:** www.r7p.com. **FM**: 89.0, 89.5MHz. **D.Prgr**: 24 h
ANDORRA 1, ✉ Av. Meritxell 75, Andorra la Vella ☎+376 862288 🖷 +376 862287. **Web:** www.andorra1.ad. **Email:** andorra1@andornet.ad. **FM**: 96.0MHz 1 kW. **D.Prgr**: 24 h
RÀDIO PRINCIPAT, ✉16-18 de la Seu d'Urgell, E-25700 Lleida, Spain ☎ +34 973 354400 🖷+34 973 354211. **Web:** www.radioprincipat.com **Email:** radio@radopa.com. **FM** 107.5MHz 1.2 kW.

ANGOLA

L.T: UTC +1h — **Pop:** 10 million — **Pr.L:** Portuguese + ethnic — **E.C:** 50Hz, 220V — **ITU:** AGL

MINISTÉRIO DA COMUNICAÇÃO SOCIAL (MCS)
✉ Av. Comandante Valodia, CP. 2608, Luanda. **Web:** www.netangola.com/mcs **E:** mcs@netangola.com ☎ +244 2 443495 🖷 +244 2 392649.

RÁDIO NACIONAL DE ANGOLA (RNA)
✉ Rua Rainha Jinga, C.P. 1329, Luanda ☎ +244 2 323172/ 321258 🖷 +244 2 324647/391234 **Web:** www.rna.ao **Email:** rna@rna.ao
L.P: DG: Manuel Rabelais, PD: Júlio Mendonça. TD: Cândido R. Pinto.

MW:

Location	kHz	kW	Prgr.	H. of tr.
Mulenvos	702	10	A	24h
Mulenvos	945	25	N/A	24h
Luanda	1010	1	RL	24h
Mulenvos	1088	25	A	24h

SW:

Location	kHz	kW	Prgr.	H. of tr.
Mulenvos	4950	15	A	24h
Mulenvos	7215v	15	N/A	24h
Mulenvos	7245	50	A	0500-1800

FM (MHz): Luanda (4kW): 93.5 (A), 94.5 (5), 96.5MHz (FME), 99.9 (RL), 101.4MHz (N).
ANN: "Rádio Nacional de Angola".

Prgrs: A=Canal A in Portuguese (general coverage): 24h. **N:** on the h. **N=Rádio N'Gola Yetu** (ethnic): 0400-2000. **N:** rel. Canal A. **FME=Rádio FM Estéreo** (music): 1000-2400. **RL=Radio Luanda** (capital channel): 24h. **5=Rádio 5** (sports): 0500-2300. **P=Emissora Provincial:** 0400-2300, rel. A at night.

PROVINCIAL STATIONS
MW:

Location	kHz	kW	Pr	Location	kHz	kW	Pr
2) Benguela	774	50	A	7) Lubango	1313	1	P
3) Kuito	990	50	A	15) Namíbe	1314	10	P
1) Mulenvos	1134	10	P	12) Saurimo	1386	10	P
17) Mbanza Congo	1152	10	P	3) Kuito	1404	10	P
6) Huambo	1170	10	P	11) Dundo	1440	10	P
13) Malange	1188	10	P	14) Luena	v1458	10	P
7) Lubango	1233	10	P	8) Menongue	1467	10	P
9) N'dalatando	1260	10	P	10) Sumbe	v1485	10	P
4) Tenda	1278	25	A	2) Benguela	1503	10	P
16) Uige	1296	10	P	4) Tenda	1530	10	P
17) Soyo	1298	1	P				

FM:

Location	MHz	kW	Pr	Location	MHz	kW	Pr
4) Cabinda	88.3	0.1	N	8) Menongue	90.1	0.1	5
1) Caxito	88.5	0.25	A	11) Dundo	90.3	0.1	A
10) Sumbe	88.7	0.25	5	2) Benguela	90.4	1	5
9) Dondo	88.8	0.5	P	13) Malange	90.5	0.1	5
6) Huambo	89.0	0.25	5	3) Kuito	91.0	4	A
12) Saurimo	89.1	0.1	5	16) Uíge	91.0	4	P
5) Ondjiva	89.2	0.25	N	7) Lubango	91.1	4	P
15) Namíbe	89.5	0.1	A	4) Cabinda	91.3	4	P
14) Luena	89.6	0.25	A	1) Caxito	91.5	4	P
17) Mbanza Congo	89.7	0.25	5	10) Sumbe	91.7	4	P

Location	MHz	kW	Pr	Location	MHz	kW	Pr
9) N'dalatando	91.8	0.15	P	16) Uíge	94.5	0.25	5
6) Huambo	92.1	4	P	4) Cabinda	95.0	0.15	5
5) Ondjiva	92.2	4	A	10) Sumbe	95.1	0.25	A
3) Kuito	92.3	0.1	A	12) Saurimo	95.5	0.25	A
15) Namíbe	92.5	4	P	15) Tômbwa	95.9	0.25	P
12) Saurimo	92.5	0.25	P	14) Luena	96.0	2	P
16) Uíge	92.5	2	A	17) Mbanza Congo	96.1	2	A
14) Luena	92.6	0.15	5	8) Menongue	96.7	0.2	A
17) Soyo	92.7	0.1	P	13) Malange	96.9	0.25	A
2) Benguela	92.9	4	P	9) N'dalatando	97.2	0.1	A
8) Menongue	93.1	0.25	P	17) Mbanza Congo	97.7	0.5	P
11) Dundo	93.3	4	P	9) Ambaca	98.0	0.5	P
2) Lobito	93.5	0.25	P	5) Ondjiva	98.0	5	P
7) Lubango	93.5	0.1	A	6) Huambo	98.7	0.25	A
13) Malange	93.7	4	P	6) Huambo	99.8	0.1	N
16) Negage	94.4	0.25	P	9) Golungo Alto	100.4	0.2	P
11) Dundo	94.5	0.1	5	2) Lobito	101.4	1	5
7) Lubango	94.5	0.2	5	2) Benguela	101.7	2	A
15) Namíbe	94.5	0.15	5	7) Lubango	103.0	0.1	N
5) Ondjiva	94.5	0.25	5	2) Lobito	104.9	2	A

Addresses & other information:
1) EP de Bengo, Caxito – **2)** EP de Benguela, C.P. 19, Benguela – **3)** EP do Bié, C.P. 33, Kuito. Dir: Cordeiro Chimo – **4)** EP de Cabinda, Cabinda – **5)** EP de Cunene, Ondjiva – **6)** EP do Huambo, C.P. 125, Huambo – **7)** EP da Huíla, C.P. 111, Lubango – **8)** EP do Kuando-Kubango, C.P. 36, Menongue – **9)** EP do Kuanza Norte, C.P. 174, N'dalatando – **10)** EP do Kuanza Sul, C.P. 10, Sumbe – **11)** EP da Lunda Norte, Lucapa – **12)** EP da Lunda Sul, C.P. 116, Saurimo – **13)** EP de Malange, C.P. 83, Malange – **14)** EP do Mexico, C.P. 74, Luena – **15)** EP do Namíbe, C.P. 174, Namíbe – **16)** EP do Uíge, C.P. 140, Uíge – **17)** EP do Zaire, Mbanza Congo.

RÁDIO ECCLESIA (Rlg.)
✉ Rua Comandante Bula 118, São Paulo, CP-3579, Luanda ☎ +244 2 443041 📠 +244 2 443093 **Web:** www.recclesia.org **Email:** recclesia@recclesia.org
L.P: Exec. Dir: Father José Paulo. Admin. Dir: Sister Fátima Kavate.
FM: 97.5MHz 5kW: **D.Prgr** in Portuguese: 24h.
F.Pl: Direct shortwave broadcasts from Luanda pending restoration of license by Angolan gov.

Private stations: Antena Comercial, Luanda: 95.5MHz. **Web:** www.ebonet.net/lac **Email:** lac@ebonet.net **F.Pl: R. Vial,** Luanda. **R. Despertar**, nationwide on FM. No further details available.

ANGUILLA (British)

L.T: UTC -4h — **Pop:** 13,000 — **Pr.L:** English — **E.C:** 50Hz, 230V — **ITU:** AIA.

RADIO ANGUILLA (Gov. Comm.)
✉ P.O. Box 60, The Valley. ☎ +1 264 497 2218/0955. 📠 +1 264 497 5432. **Email:** radioaxa@anguillanet.com. **Web:** www.radioaxa.com.
L.P: Dir.: Kenneth Hodge. Chief Information Officer: Ivor Hodge. Engineer: Lester Richardson
FM: 95.5MHz
D.Prgr: Mon-Sat: 0925-0300, Sun: 1055-0200. **N:** MF only: Local: 1105, 1602, 2005, 2305. BBC: 1100, 1230, 1300, 1400, 1800, 2000, 2115, 2300. Sat: Local 1105. BBC 1100.

THE CARIBBEAN BEACON (Rlg.)
✉ P.O. Box 690, The Valley. ☎ +1 264 497 4340. 📠 +1 264 497 4311.
L.P: Owner: Dr. Gene Scott. GM & CE: Eddie Sutton.
MW: 690kHz (50kW), 1610kHz (50kW) – **SW:** 6090/11775kHz (100kW) – **FM:** 100.1MHz (35kW).
D.Prgr: 24h. Local prgrs 1000-1600 on 1610 kHz

PRIVATE FM STATIONS
Family Radio Network – **FM:** 90.5 MHz (relay Antigua)
GEM Radio – **FM:** 107.9 MHz (relay Trinidad).
HBR 107.5 - Heartbeat Radio, Sachasses, The Valley. ☎ +1 264 497 3354 📠 +1 264 497 5995. **FM:** 107.5 MHz.
Kool FM, P.O. Box 1300, The Valley. ☎ +1 264 497 0103. 📠 +1 264 497 0104. – **Web:** www.koolfm103.com. **FM:** 103.3 MHz.
New Beginning Radio - NBR, P.O. Box 1122, The Valley. ☎ +1 264 497 0977. 📠 +1 264 497 7977. **FM:** 99.3 MHz. **Format:** Rlg.
Voice of Creation - Radio J.E.S.U.S., The Valley. ☎ +1 264 497 0106. 📠 +1 264 497 0106. **FM:** 106.7 MHz. **Format:** Rlg.

ANTARCTICA

L.T: Antártida Argentina: UTC -3h; Antártida Chilena: UTC -4h (10 Oct-13 Mar: UTC -3h); McMurdo: UTC +12h (10 Oct-13 Mar: UTC +13h) — **Pop:** 4,120 (Su), 1,066 (Wi) — **ITU:** ATA

RADIO NACIONAL ARCANGEL SAN GABRIEL
✉ LRA36 Radio Nacional Arcangel San Gabriel, Base de Ejercito Esperanza, CP 9411-Antártida Argentina, Argentina. ☎ +54 967 444 5304. **Email:** esperanzaantar@infovia.com.ar, lra36@infovia.com.ar
L.P: Dir: Nestor Arguello, Op.: Mario Gallardo
SW: (G.C: 63S24 056W59): LRA36 15476kHz 10kW. **Spanish.:** Daily 1800-2100 – **V.** by QSL-card & letter only. Re. with 1 IRC to Dir.

SOBERANIA FM
✉ Villa Las Estrellas, Antartica Chilena, Chile. **FM:** 90.5MHz 0.1kW.

AMERICAN FORCES ANTARCTIC NETWORK (AFAN McMurdo)
✉ AFAN McMurdo, US Naval Support Force Antarctica, 651 Lyons Str, Port Hueneme, CA 93043-4345, USA.
FM: 93.9/104.5MHz 0.03/0.05kW.
D.Prgr: 24h on both freqs. Rel AFRTS exc. some local prgrs on 104.5MHz

ANTIGUA & BARBUDA

L.T: UTC -4h — **Pop:** 71,000 — **Pr.L:** English — **E.C:** 50/60Hz, 110/220V — **ITU:** ATG

ANTIGUA & BARBUDA BROADCASTING SERVICE (Gov. Comm.)
✉ P.O. Box 590, St. John's. ☎ +1 268 462 0010. 📠 +1 268 462 4442.
L.P: GM: Mark Bowers. SM: Alex Nicholas. PM: Lawrence Mason. CE: Denis Leandro.
MW: 620kHz (10kW) – **FM:** 90.3MHz (3kW)
D.Prgr: 24h. **BBC N:** 1100, 2300, 0400. **Local N:** 1600, 2310.
ANN: "You are listening to 620 - ABS"

CARIBBEAN RADIO LIGHTHOUSE (Rlg.)
✉ P.O. Box 1057, St.John's. ☎ +1 268 462 1454. 📠 +1 268 462 7420.
Email: cradiolight@candw.ag. **Web:** www.mannelli.com/lighthouse
L.P: Dir: Curtis L. Waite. Asst. Dir. & Tech. Dir: Jerry Baker.
MW: 1160kHz 10kW – **FM:** 92.5MHz 2kW.
D.Prgr: 0925-0145 on MW. 24h on FM. **BBC N:** 1100, 1200, 1300, 1600, 2000, 2300.
Format: Rlg. Owned by: Baptist International Missions Inc.

GRENVILLE RADIO LTD. (Comm.)
✉ P.O. Box 1100, St. John's. ☎ +1 268 462 1100. 📠 +1 268 462 1001. **Email:** news@zdkradio.com.
L.P: PD: Ivor Bird.
MW: 1100kHz 1kW (Inactive) - **FM:** 97.1 (1kW) / 100.1 (2.5kW) MHz.
ZDK Radio: 24h on 97.1MHz.
Sun FM: 24h on 100.1MHz.

OBSERVER RADIO (Comm.)
✉ P.O. Box 1318, Ryans Place, High Street, St. John's. ☎ +1 268 460 0911/481 9100. 📠 +1 268 481 9125.
FM: 'The Voice of the People - Radio 911FM – the Pulse of the Nation': 91.1MHz **Format:** 24h News/talk.

FAMILY RADIO NETWORK (Comm.)
✉ W1102, 1 Independence Drive, St. John's. ☎ +1 268 560 7578/9. 📠 +1 268 560 7577. **Web:** www.familyradionetwork.com. **Email:** family@caribmail.com. **L.P:** MD: John Silcott. CE: Shervin Bruno. GM: Ben Meade. OP's Mgr.: Kevin Alexander.
FM: 89.9/92.9MHz. Additional transmitters in Anguilla, St. Kitts & Nevis, Saba (Netherlands Antilles) and Montserrat.

CRUSADER RADIO (Comm.)
✉ Temple Street, P.O Box 2379, St. John's. **Web:** www.crusaderradio.com **Email:** crusaderradio@candw.ag **L.P:** SM: Conrad Pole
FM: 107.5MHz.

ABUNDANT LIFE RADIO (Rlg.)
✉ Codrington Village, Barbuda. ☎ +1 268 560 2676. 📠 +1 268 560 2676. **Email:** lifefm1031@hotmail.com. **L.P:** SM: Clifton Francois.

FM: 103.1MHz (1kW) Barbuda, 103.9MHz (1kW) Antigua.
D.PRGR: 24h

CARIBBEAN RELAY CO. LTD. (Deutsche Welle/BBC)
P.O. Box 1203, St. John's. ☎ +1 268 462 0436. Fax +1 268 462 0994. **Email:** cm-crc@candw.ag for Comp. Mgr. and acm-crc@candw.ag for Asst. Comp. Mgr.
L.P: Comp. Mgr: Dave Rayney. Asst. Comp. Mgr: Peter Ippendorf.
FM: 89.1MHz (rel. BBCWS & Caribbean Report).
SW (G.C: 17N06 061W48): 4 x 250kW tr's (only 2 used by BBC)
D.Prgr: see International Broadcasting section.

GEM RADIO NETWORK (Comm.)
FM: 93.9MHz (rel. Trinidad)

ARGENTINA

L.T: UTC -3h (Provinces C, Ct, LR, SJ, SL, SV DST: UTC -4h 1 May-17 Oct 2004) — **Pop:** 37 million— **Pr.L:** Spanish — **E.C.:** 50Hz, 220V — **ITU:** ARG

SECRETARIA DE COMUNICACIONES (SECOM)
Sarmiento 151, piso 4, (C1041AAC) CA Buenos Aires. ☎ +54 11 4347 9901. Fax +54 11 4312-1134. **Web:** www.secom.gov.ar
L.P: Lic. Mario Guillermo Moreno (Secretario de Comunicaciones).

COMISION NACIONAL DE COMUNICACIONES (C.N.C.)
Perú 103, (C1067AAC) CA Buenos Aires. ☎ +54 11 4347-9850. **Web:** www.cnc.gov.ar **L.P:** Interventor: Fulvio Mario Madaro.

COMITE FEDERAL DE RADIODIFUSION (COMFER)
Suipacha 765, 9° piso, (C1008AAO) CA Buenos Aires. ☎ +54 11 4320-4900. **Web:** www.comfer.gov.ar **L.P:** Interventor: Lic. Julio Donato Barbaro.
COMFER controls certain technical aspects of broadcasting, and also controls the prgrs. transmitted over all kinds of broadcasting stations.

SECRETARIA DE PRENSA Y DIFUSION
Subject directly to the Presidencia de la Nación. Controls and administers the media.

SISTEMA NACIONAL DE MEDIOS PUBLICOS S. E.
Av. Figueroa Alcorta 2977, (C1425CKI) CA Buenos Aires. ☎ +54 11 4808 2500, 4802 6001/2/3/4/5/6. Fax +54 11 4802 9878.
L.P: Interventor: Marcelo Simón.
All LRA st's belong to S.O.R. (incl. LRA36 in Antarctica). Common prgrs (originated from LRA1) in network called "Cadena Celeste y Blanca de Emisoras Argentinas".

MW: ° = also on SW, * = inactive, v = varying freq., CP = Construction Permit, rp = reported

	Call	kHz	kW	Name, location and h. of tr.
219)		530	3/1	R. República, San Justo
1)	LRA14	540	25/1	R. Nal., Santa Fé: 0700-0300
2)	LRA25	540	5	R. Nal.,Tartagal: 1000-0400
25)	LU17	540	10/5	R. Golfo Nuevo, Pto. Madryn: 24h
3)	LRA9	560	25/15	R. Nal., Esquel: 1000-0400
4)	LRA13	560	25/5	R. Nal., Bahia Blanca: 0900-0400
5)	LT15	560	10/5	R. del Litoral, Concordia: 0900-0500
6)	LV1	560	25/5	R. Colón, San Juan: 24h
7)	LRA16	560	25/1	R. Nal., La Quiaca: 0855-0400
239)		570	1	R. del Centro, Lomas de Mirador
8)	LU20	580	10	R. Chubut "La 20," Trelew:0800-0500
9)	LW1	580	25/5	R. Univ. Nal. de Córdoba, Córdoba: 0800-0500
10)	LS9	590	50/5	R. Continental, Buenos Aires: 24h
11)	LRA30	590	25	R. Nal., San Carlos de Bariloche: 0855-0400
12)	LV12	590	4	R. Independencia, San Miguel de Tucumán: 24h
69)	LU5	600	20/5	R.Neuquén, do 0900-0500
196)	LRK201	610	1	R. Solidaridad, Añatuya: Mon-Sat: 1000-2200, Sun 1000-2400
271)		610	5/1	R General San Martín, Villa Lynch
94)	LV4	620	10/5	R. San Rafael, do: 1000-0400
13)	LRA18	620	25/7	R. Nal., Río Turbio: 0845-0400
14)	LT17	620	25/5	R. Provincia de Misiones, Posadas:0900-0500
85)	LRA26	620	25/5	R. Nal., Resistencia: 0830-0300
15)	LRA28	620	25/5	R. Nal., La Rioja: 0900-0400 (nf. 1010)
16)	LS5	630	25/5	R. Rivadavia, Buenos Aires: 24h
52)	LW8	630	25/5	R. San Salvador de Jujuy: 0900-0400
65)	LU4	630	25/5	R. Dif. Patagonia Argentina, Comodoro Rivadavia: 0900-0500
17)	LRA24	640	25/5	R. Nal., Río Grande: 24h
18)	LU18	640	10/5	R. El Valle, "640 AM", General Roca: 0900-0300
19)	LV15	640	10/5	R. Villa Mercedes: 0900-0300
248)		650	3	La Nueva Radio, Florida
122)	LT41	660	1/0.25	R. LV del Sur Entrerriano, Gualeguaychú: 0900-0300
226)		660		R. Popular, Claypole
20)	LRA11	670	25/5	R. Nal., Comodoro Rivadavia: 24h
21)	LRA52	670	3	R. Nal., Chos Malal: 0900-0300
22)	LT4	670	25/5	R. Dif. Misiones, Posadas: 0800-0200
23)	LRI209	670	25/5	R. Mar del Plata, do: 24h
205)		680		R. Melody, Remedios de Escalada
110)	LT3	680	25	R. Cerealista "AM 680", Rosario: 24h
24)	LU12	680	25/5	R. Río Gallegos, do: 1000-0300
26)	LV6	680	25/5	R. Nihuil, Mendoza: 24h
27)	LRA4	690	25/5	R. Nal. Saltа: 0900-0400
28)	LU19	690	10/3	LV de Comahue, Cipoletti: 0900-0500
184)		690		R. Maranatha en las Nubes, Lomas del Mirador
99)	LV3	700	25/5	R. Córdoba: 24h
29)	LRA17	710	25/5	R. Nal., Zapala: 0900-0300
29x)	LRA19	710	25/5	R. Nal., Pto. Iguazú: 0900-0300
168)	LRL202	710	50	R. Diez, Buenos Aires: 24h
31)	LRA59	720	1	R. Nal., Gobernador Gregores: 1100-2300
32)	LV10	720	25/5	R. de Cuyo, Mendoza: 24h
33)	LRA3	730	20/5	R. Nal., Santa Rosa: 0900-0300
34)	LU23	730	10/1	Em. Lago Argentino, El Calafate:1000-0300
35)	LRA27	730	25/5	R. Nal., Catamarca: 0930-0300
206)		730		R. Excelsior, Monte Grande
36)	LRA55	740	1	R. Nal., Alto Río Senguer: 0900-0300
36x)	LRI200	740	1	R. Puerto Deseado: 24h
107)	LRH251	740	25/5	R. Chaco, Resistencia: 0800-0300
243)		740	5	R. Cooperativa, Buenos Aires
37)	LRA7	750	100/10	R. Nal., Córdoba: 0900-0500
249)		750	5/3	R. del Pueblo, Buenos Aires
81)	LU6	760	25/5	R. Atlántica, Mar del Plata: 24h
173)		770		R. Urbana, Lomas del Mirador
38)	LRA10	780	5/1	R. Nal., Ushuaía: 24h
39)	LRA12	780	5	R. Nal. Santo Tomé: 0900-0300
40)	LV8	780	25/5	R. Libertador, Mendoza: 0900-0500
224)	LRF210	780	5	R. Tres, Trelew: 24h
83)	LV19	790	5	R. Malargüe: 1100-0400
41)	LR6	790	25/5	R. Mitre "AM 80," Buenos Aires: 24h
42)	LRA22	790	25/5	R. Nal., San Salvador de Jujuy: 0945-0500
112)	LT46	790	5	R. Provincia, Bernardo de Irigoyen:0900-0300
44)	LU15	800	24/5	R. Viedma: 0900-0300
45)	LV23	800	1/0.25	R. Rio Atuel, General Alvear:1000-0400
50)	LT43	800	5/1	R. Mocoví, Charata: 0900-0300
46)	LRA8	820	25/5	R. Nal., Formosa: 0855-0400
48)	LU24	820	5/1	R. Tres Arroyos: 0900-0400
169)	LRI208	820	5	Estacion 820, Lomas de Zamora
117)	LRK221	820	1/0.25	R. Ciudad Perico, Perico: 1000-0400
49)	LT8	830	10/5	R. Rosario, do: 24h
114)	LV18	830	5/1	R. Municipal, San Rafael: 1030-0230
118)	LT21	830	1/0.5	R. Municipal, Alvear: 0900-0100
51)	LU14	830	25	R. Provincia de Santa Cruz, Río Gallegos: 0900-0500
319)		830		R. Filadelfia, Isidro Casanovas
54)	LT12	840	10/5	R. General Madariaga, Paso de los Libres: 0900-0300
56)	LU2	840	25/5	R. Bahía Blanca, do: 0900-0400
91)	LV9	840	25/5	R. Salta, do: 1000-0500
234)		840	1	R. General Belgrano, Buenos Aires
337)		850	10	LV de Amérca, San Miguel
57)	LRA56	860	1	R. Nal., Perito Moreno: 0955-0300
53)		860	5/1	R. Municipal, Chilecito: 1000-0400
58)	LRA1	°870	100	R. Nal., Buenos Aires: 24h
51)	LU14	880	10	R. Provincia de Santa Cruz, Las Heras (//LU14 830): 1000-0300
338)		880		R.Cualidad, Monte Grande
59)	LU33	890	25/5	R. Pampeana, Santa Rosa: 24h
60)	LV11	890	25/5	Emisora Santiago del Estero, do:0900-0530
281)		890		R. Soberania, Buenos Aires
61)	LT7	900	25/5	R. Provincia, Corrientes: 0900-0300
334)		900		R. Municipal, 25 de Mayo

Call	kHz	kW	Name, location and h. of tr.
62) LRA23	910	50/5	R. Nal.,San Juan: 0855-0400
63) LR5	910	25/5	R. La Red, Buenos Aires: 24h
80) LV7	930	25/5	R. Tucumán, San Miguel de Tucumán: 24h
126) LV28	930	5/1	R. Villa María, do: 0900-0300
258)	930		R. Alfa, Villa Ballester
113x) LRJ241	940	20/5	R. Dimensión, San Luís: 0900-0400
144) LRH200	940	3/5	R. Chajarí, do: 0900-0300
64) LR3	950	25/5	R. Belgrano, Buenos Aires: 24h
93) LT16	950	25/5	R. Esmeralda, Roque Saénz Peña:0900-0300
66) LRA6	°960	25/1	R. Nal., Mendoza: 1000-0500
68) LU13	960	10/3	R. Necochea, do: 0900-0400
70) LV2	970	25/15	R. General Paz, Córdoba: 24h
146) LT25	970	1/0.25	R. Guaraní, Curuzú Cuatiá:0900-0300
259)	970		NCN/Cadena de la Nueva Conciencia, Villa Insuperable
109) LU37	980	10/3	R. General Pico "R.37",: 0930-0300
136) LT39	980	5	R. Victoria: 0900-0300
263)	980	25/10	R. Luján AM, Valcheta
339)	980		Sintonia de Vida, El Talar
166) LR4	990	25/5	R. Splendid AM 990, Buenos Aires: 24h
70x) LRJ201	990	1	R. Calingasta, Barreal: 1000-0500
174) LRH203	990	25/5	AM 990, Formosa: 24h
71) LU16	1000	1/0.25	R. Río Negro, Villa Regina: 0900-0300
137) LT42	1000	1/0.25	R. del Iberá, Mercedes: 0900-0300
72) LV16	1010	20/10	R. Rio Cuarto, do: 1000-0500
130) LW2	1010	1/0.25	R. Emis. Tartagal: 1000-0300
238)	1010		R. Oasis, Victoria
212)	1010		R.Onda Latina, Buenos Aires
261)	*1010		Sintonia Ghost, Lanús
340) LRA28	1010	1	R. Nal., La Rioja // LRA28 - 620
73) LT10	1020	10/5	R. Univ. Nal. del Litoral, Santa Fé:0800-0500
74) LRA58	1020	1	R. Nal., Río Mayo: 1100-2300
76) LS10	1030	25/5	R. del Plata, Buenos Aires: 24h
165)	1050		R. Federal, Lanús
312)	1050		R. Conurbana, Gregorio de Laferrere
292)	1060		R. Restauración, Llavallol
77) LR1	1070	25/5	R. El Mundo, Buenos Aires: 24h
78) LU3	1080	25/5	R. del Sur, Bahía Blanca: 0900-0400
79)	1080	10/1	R. Departamento Minas, Andacollo: 1000 (SS 1200)-2300
145) LW4	1080	25/5	R. Orán/R.Maria: 1000-0600
250)	1090		R. Nuestras Raíces, Valentin Alsina
326)	1090		R.Sintonia, José C.Paz
222)	1100		R. Estilo, Glew: 24h
30) LS1	1110	25/5	R. de la Ciudad/La Once Diez, B. A: 24h
82) LV5	1120	25/5	R. Sarmiento, San Juan: 0900-0400
84) LRA21	1130	25/5	R. Nal., Santiago del Estero: 0900-0400
207)	*1130		R. Argentina, Buenos Aires
246)	1130	10	R. Tropicana, Buenos Aires (nom: 1620)
105) LU22	1140	5/1.5	R. Tandil, Tandil: 0900-0300
84x) LRA2	1150	10	R. Nal., Viedma: 0900-0400
86) LRA51	1150	1	R. Nal., Jáchal: 1030-0300
87) LT9	1150	10/5	R. Brigadier López, Santa Fé: 0700-0300
194) LRH202	1150	1	R. Tupá Mbaé, Posadas: 0800-0300
327)	1150		Concepto AM 11-50, Buenos Aires
88) LRA57	1160	1	R. Nal., El Bolsón: 0900-0300
89) LRH253	1160	5/10	R. Cataratas, Pto. Iguazú: 1000-1600
90) LU32	1160	10/2.5	R. Coronel Olavarría, Olavarría: 0900-0300
92) LRA29	1170	25/3	R. Nal., San Luis: 1000-0500
242)	1170	5	R. Mi País, Hurlingham
95) LRA15	1190	50	R. Nal., San Miguel de Tucumán: 24h
96) LR9	1190	25/5	R. América, Buenos Aires: 24h
66)	1200	1	R. Nal. Mendoza (r. LRA6 960), Valle de Uspallata: 1000-0500
97) LT6	1200	5/1.5	R. Goya: 0900-0300
159) LRI229	1210	5/1	R. Las Flores: 0900-0300
204)	1210		R. Mailín, Gregorio de Laferrere
215) LRL328	1220	5/1	LV del Aire – "Cadena Eco", BAires: 24h
320)	1220		R.del Norte, Pres. Roque Sanez Peña
100) LT2	1230	25/5	R. Gral. San Martín, "R. 2", Rosario: 24h
101) LW5	1230	5/1	R. Libertador, General San Martín
265)	1230		R. Litoral, Isidro Casanova
286)	1230		R. La Bendición, General Pico
186)	1240		R. Vida, Monte Grande
254)	1240	1	Onda Marina, Mar del Plata: 24h (r. LV del Aire 1220kHz)
164)	1250	1	AM 1250 R. Estirpe Nal. "La Radio" San Justo: 24h
102) LT14	1260	25/5	R. General Urquiza, Paraná: 0900-0500
187)	1260		R. Fortaleza Cristiana, Rafael Castillo

Call	kHz	kW	Name, location and h. of tr.
103) LRA20	1270	5	R. Nal., Las Lomitas: 0900-0300
104) LS11	1270	50/10	R. Provincia de Buenos Aires, La Plata: 24h
116) LU11	1280	10/5	R. Trenque Lauquén, Tr. Lauquén: 0900-0300
227)	1280		R. Eco Porteña, Buenos Aires
193) LRI371	1290	1	R. Amanacer, Reconquista
210)	1290		R. Cristal, Lanús: 24h
231)	1290		R. Provincia, Mariano Acosta
304) LRJ212	1290	5/1	R. Murialdo, Villa Nueva de Guaymallén
106) LRA5	1300	10/5	R. Nal., Rosario: 0853-0303
209)	1300		R. Metropolitana, Luís Guillón
314)	1300		R. Identidad, Buenos Aires
106x) LRA42	v1310	1	R. Nal., Gualeguaychú
106z)	1310	1	R. Dr. Gregorio Alvarez, "LV de la Comunidad", Piedra del Aguila: 24h
211)	*1310		R. Panamericana, Gregorio de Laferrere
331)	1310		R. Integracion, Buenos Aires
108) LU10	1320	5/3	R. Azul: 0900-0300
149) LV24	1320	0.25	R. Manantiales, Tunuyán: 1000-0600
236)	1320		R. Mística, Libertad
260)	1320		R. Sentir, Remedios de Escalada
253)	1330	3	R. Cadena Central, Bernal
252)	1340		R. Tradicional, Ituzaingó
111) LS6	1350	25/5	R. Buenos Aires, "RBA": 24h
269)	1350	5/1	R. Sucesos, Córdoba: 24h
176)	1350		R. Nuestra Señora de Itatí, Morón:0900-0300
113) LRA54	1370	1	R. Nal., Ingeniero Jacobacci: 0900-0300
241)	1370		AM-1370, Isidro Casanova: 24h
284)	1380		R. La Voz, Monte Chingolo
298)	1380		R. Los Toldos, Los Toldos
66) LRA6	1390	1	R. Nal., Mendoza (r. LRA6 960), Valle de Uspallata: 1000-0500
115) LR11	1390	10	R. Univ., La Plata: 0800-0300
285)	1390		R. Tradición, Isidro Casanova
315)	1390		R. Ribera Sud, Ingeniero Budge
270) LRG202	1400	10/1	R. Cumbre, Neuquén
228)	1400		R. Gama, Valentin Alsina
332)	1400		R.Fantastica, Lujan
182)	1410	5/0.25	R. Folklorismo, José Léon Suárez: 1100-0100
199) LRJ359	1420		R. Granaderos Puntanos, San Luis
218)	1420		R. Mágica, Lanús
305)	1420		R. Génesis 2000, General Conesa
119) LT24	1430	1/0.25	R. San Nicolás: 24h
120) LV26	1430	1/0.25	R. Río Tercero: 24h
121) LRI235	1430	0.25	R. Balcarce, do: 0900-0300
220)	1430		R. José de S. Martín, "la Pionera", El Jagüel
267)	1430		R. Imagén, Castelar
43) LRA53	1440	1	R. Nal., S. Martín de los Andes: 1000-0400
123) LU36	1440	0.25	R. Coronel Suárez: 1000-0300
124) LV20	1440	1/0.25	R. Laboulaye: 0900-0300
125) LV27	1440	1/0.25	R. Rural, San Francisco: 0900-0300
201)	1440		R. Impacto, Tapiales
272)	1440	1/0.5	R. General Obligado, Reconquista
183)	1450	0.5	R. Ciudad, Remedios de Escalada
275)	1450	5/1	R. Las Cuarenta, San Juan
293)	1450		R. Presencia, Martinez
127) LT29	1460	1/0.25	R. Venado Tuerto: 0930-0330
128) LU30	1460	0.25	R. Maipú: 0900-2400
129) LU34	1460	0.1	R. Pigüé: 1000-0300
181)	1460		R. Contacto, Ituzaingó: 24h
300)	1460		R. Nativa, Claypole
276) LRK146	1460	1	R. 21, Yerba Buena: 24h
296)	1460		R. Almirante Brown, San José
299)	v1460		R. luminemos el Mundo, Ezeiza
131) LT20	v1470	1/0.25	R. Junín: 0900-0300
132) LT26	1470	1/0.25	R. Nuevo Mundo, Colón: 0900-0300
133) LT28	1470	1/0.25	R. Rafaela: 0900-0300
134) LU26	1470	0.25	R. Coronel Dorrego: 1030-0300 (r. 1468)
135)	1470	1	R. Municipal, Luis Beltrán: 1200-0100
190)	1470		R. Mburucuya, José León Suarez
257)	1470		Cadena 14-70, Lanús
192) LU27	1480	0.25	R. Dolores: 1100-0300
217)	1480		La R. del Corazón, Tablada
138) LV22	1490	1	R. Huinca Renancó: 1000-0300
151) LU25	1490	0.1	R. Carhué, Carhué: 0900-0330
100)	1490		R. Canaán Celestial, Isidro Casanova
223)	1490		R. Vida AM, Mar del Plata
75) LRI214	1500	5/1	R. Bonaerense, Llavallol
138x)	1500	1/0.25	R. Municipal, Gral. Conesa: 1000-2400
140) LT34	v1500	0.25	R. Nuclear, Zárate: 0900-0000
141) LT45	1500	1/0.25	R. San Javier: 1100-0500; SS 1100-2100

	Call	kHz	kW	Name, location and h. of tr.
142)	LV25	1500	1/0.25	R. Unión, Bell Ville: 0900-0400
306)		1500		R. En Realidad, Capilla del Señor
307)	LU1	1500	0.04	R. Libertador General S. Martín, Lisandro Olmos
314)	LT22	1500	0.25	R. Nueva Era, Pehuajó
170)		1510		LV del Oeste,Libertad: 24h
143)	LV21	1510	1/0.25	R. Champaqui, Villa Dolores:1000-0100
237)		1510		R. Alabanza, Guernica
328)		1510		R.Sentimento Litoral, Banfield
240)		1550		R. Urkupiña, Buenos Aires
251)		1520		R. Modelo, Monte Grande
148)	LT38	1520	0.25	R. Gualeguay: 0900-0300
171)		1520		AM Reverendo Aquiles Acosta, S. Justo
180)		1520		R. Metropolitana, Ciudadela
279)		1520	5/1	R. Chascomús: 24h
150)	LRJ200	1530	1	R. Centro Morteros, Morteros: 0900-0300
308)		1530		LV del Futuro, Merlo
214)		1530		R. Contemporánea, Lomas de Zamora
152)	LT35	1540	0,25	R. Mon, Pergamino: 0930-0400
153)	LU28	1540	0.25	R. Tuyú, General Madariaga:1000-0300
329)		1540		AM 15 - 40, Buenos Aires
342)		1540		R. Fuego, Longchamps
154)	LT23	1550	5/0.25	R. Regional, San Jenaro Norte: 0900-0300
155)	LT32	1550	0.25	R. Chivilcoy: 1000-0400
156)	LT40	1550	0.25	R. LV de la Paz, La Paz: 0900-0100
294)		1550		R. Trompeta de Diós, Isidro Casanova
301)		1550		R. Tiempo, Mar del Plata
157)	LT11	1560	2.5/1.5	R. Gral. Francisco Ramírez, Villaguay
158)	LT33	1550	0.25	R. Nueve de Julio: 0900-0300
185)		1560		R. Castañares, Ituzaingó
283)		1560		R. Ebenezer, Ezeiza
323)		1560		R. Renecar, Quilmes Oeste
336)		1560		R. Almirante Brown, Rafael Calzada
202)		1570		R. Interactiva, Ciudad Madero
230)		1570	1	R. Rocha, La Plata
318)		1570		R. Nuevo Mundo, General Pinto
160)	LT27	1580	0.25	R. LV del Montiel, Villaguay: 0900-0300
161)	LT36	1580	0.25	R. Chacabuco: 1000-0400
302)		*1580		R. M.E.C., Caseros
189)		1580		R. Tradición, San Martín
244)		1580	1	R. Activa, Longchamps
324)		1580		R. Planeta, Rosario, SF
177)		1590		R. Jesucristo es el Rey, Lomas de Zamora
333)		1590		R. Guaviyú, Gregorio de Laferrere
175)		1600	1.2	R. Armonia, José Ingenieros: 24h
309)		1600		R. Fénix, General Viamonte
310)		1600		R. Belgrano, Junín
330)		1600		R. Copacabana, Gregorio de Laferrere
195)		1610	0.05	R. Luz del Mundo, Rafael Calzada
280)		1610		R. Exitos, Ituzaingó
322)		1610	0.5	R. Buenas Nuevas, Laboulaye
295)		°1610		R. Maranata AM, Puerto Iguazú: 24h
246)		1620	10	R. Tropicana, Buenos Aires (//1130)
325)		1620		R. Italia,Villa Martelli
245)		1630		AM Restauración, Hurlingham
288)		1630	1/5	R. Buen Ayre(Red 92), La Plata
247)		1640		R. Libre, Buenos Aires
311)		1640		R. Boanerges, Posadas
213)		1650		R. Fortaleza, Ezeiza
290)		1680		R. Getro, Lanús Oeste
303)		1690	1/0.25	R. Apocalipsis II, San Justo

SW: * = inactive

	Call	kHz	kW	Name, location and h. of tr.
58)	LRA31	6060	30	R. Nal. Buenos Aires: 2100-1500
83)	LV19	*6160	1	R. Malargüe, Malargüe
66)		*6180	7.5	R. Nal. Mendoza
295)		v6215		R. Baluarte, Puerto Iguazú: 24h

ASOCIACION DE RADIODIFUSORAS PRIVADAS ARGENTINAS (ARPA)

✉ Tte. Perón 1561, Piso 3, (C1050ACB) CA Buenos Aires. ☎ +54 11 4382 4412 +54 11 4382 4483. **Email:** arpaorg.@arpa.org.ar
L.P: Presidente: Edmundo Rébora.
ARPA is an association of privately owned commercial st's.

ASOCIACION DE RADIODIFUSORES CATOLICOS ARGENTINOS (ARCA)

✉ Tucumán 1993, (C1050AAM) CA Buenos Aires. **Email:** asinb@uol.com.ar ☎ +54 11 4375 0376/0664. **L.P.:** DG: Osvaldo Bufarini.

STATE ABBREVIATIONS *(Provincias):* BA = Provincia de Buenos Aires, C = Catamarca, Ca = Córdoba, Cs = Corrientes, Ch = Chaco, Ct = Chubut, ER = Entre Ríos, F = Formosa,J = Jujuy, LP = La Pampa, LR = La Rioja, Ms = Misiones, Ma = Mendoza, N = Neuquén, RN = Río Negro, S = Salta, SC = Santa Cruz, SE = Santiago del Estero, SF = Sante Fé, SJ = San Juan, SL = San Luis, T = Tucumán, (Territorio): TFAIA = Territorio Nacional de la Tierra del Fuego, Antártida e Islas del Atlántico Sur.
NB: These abbreviations should not be used for postal purposes.

1) Mendoza 2430, (S3000CHB) Santa Fé, SF. **Web:** www.nacionalsantafe.ceride.gov.ar ☎+54 342 453 3340. 📠+54 342 452 8640. - **Email:** santafe@radionacional.gov.ar - **FM:** 94.9. – **2)** Ruta Nal. 34,km. 1433, (A4560CJA) Tartagal, S. ☎+54 3875 421600. - **Email:** tartagal@radionacional.gov.ar - **FM:** 92.3. – **3)** Av. Alvear 1180, (U9200AXY) Esquel, Ct. ☎+54 2945 45 1900/3748. - **Email:** esquel@radionacional.gov.ar - **FM:** 88.7. – **4)** Moreno 30, (B8000FWB) Bahía Blanca, BA. ☎+54 291 453 2700, 452 9008. - **Email:** bahiablanca@ radionacional.gov.ar - **FM:** 99.3. – **5)** San Martín 371, (E3200FUG) Concordia, ER. ☎ 📠+54 345 421 5201/5507 +54 345 421 5506. **Email:** lt15am560@arnet.com.ar - **FM:** 89.3. – **6)** Mendoza 169 Sur, (J5402GUC) San Juan, SJ. - **Email**: colonsa@sinectis.com.ar ☎ +54 264 422 2344. - **FM:** 92.7, 98.5, 105.7, 106.3. – **7)** Av. España 700 Sur, (Y4650BAT) La Quiaca, J. ☎+54 3885 422356, 423488. **Email:** laquiaca@radionacional.gov.ar - **FM:** 92.5. – **8)** Av. Hipólito Yrigoyen 1735, (U9102BGM) Trelew, Ct. **Web:** www.lu20radiochubut.com.ar **Email:** info@lu20radiochubut.com.ar ☎+54 2965 483903. 📠+54 2965 425457. - **FM:** 95.7. – **9)** Fray Miguel de Mojica 1600, Barrio Marquez de Siobremonte, (X5008CCN) Córdoba, Ca. ☎📠+54 351 477 9000. **Web:** www.srtunc.com.ar/universidad580 **Email:** administracion@srtunc.com.ar - **FM:** 102.3. – **10)** Rivadavia 835, (C1002AAG) CA Buenos Aires. **Web:** www.continental.com.ar **Email:** oyentes@continental.com.ar ☎+54 11 4999 1500. 📠+54 11 4338 4469. – **11)** Av. 12 de Octubre 2421, (R8403AOH) San Carlos de Bariloche, RN. **Email:** bariloche@radionacional.gov.ar - **FM:** 95.5. – **12)** Rivadavia 120, 54 381 400 1212. **Web:** www.radiolv12.com.ar **Email:** radiolv12@yahoo.com.ar - **FM:** 98.9. – **13)** Comodoro Py 342, Planta Baja, (Z9407BFH) Río Turbio, SC. ☎📠+54 2902 421131. **Email:** rioturbio@radionacional.gov.ar - **FM:** 90.3. – **14)** Colón 1452, (372) (N3300LXF) Posadas, Ms. +54 3752 43 1430/31 - **FM:** 107.3. – **15)** Hipólito Yrigoyen 318/24, (F5300DIH) La Rioja, LR. **Email:** larioja@radionacional.gov.ar +54 3822 425396. - **FM:** 105.5. – **16)** Arenales 2467, (C1124AAM) Buenos Aires. **Web**:www.rivadavia.com.ar **Email:** contenidos@rivadavia.com.ar +54 11 5219 4760 +54 11 5219 4760 – **17)** Leonardo Rosales 490, (V9420CMJ) Río Grande, TF. **Web:** www.radionacionalrg.com.ar **Email:** riogrande@radionacional.gov.ar - **FM:** 88.1. – **18)** Tucumán 1074, (R8332HQV) General Roca, RN.☎ +54 2941 430640. **Web:** www.radioelvalle.com - **Email:** relvalle@infovia.com.ar or am640@radioelvalle.com - **FM:** 99.3. – **19)** Lavalle 291, Planta Alta, (D5732AEE) Villa Mercedes, SL. **Web**: www.lv15.com.ar **Email**: lv15@linfovia.com.ar ☎📠+54 2657 44400. - **FM:** 92.5 - 95.5. – **20)** 25 de Mayo 453, (U9000CXC) Comodoro Rivadavia, Ct. **Email:** comodororivadavia@radionacional.gov.ar +54 297 447 2125 +54 297 446 2564 - **FM:** 94.3. – **21)** Gral. Paz 536, (Q8353CGL) Chos Malal, N. - **Email:** chosmalal@radionacional.gov.ar +54 42 1198 - **FM:** 92.3. – **22)** Félix de Azara 2440, (N3300LQZ) Posadas,Ms. ☎+54 3752 430500. - **FM:** 104.5. – **23)** Hipolito Yrigoyen 2641, (B7600DPG) Mar del Plata, BA. **Web:** www.lacapitalnet.com.ar/lu9 **Email:** lu9-gtc@lacapitalnet.com.ar ☎+54 494 7700 +54 223 492 2020. - **FM:** 103.3. – **24)** Zapiola 25, (Z9400BCA) Río Gallegos, SC. **Web:** lu12radiogallegos.8m.net **Email:** eedloa@arnet.com.ar or eedloa@infovia.com.ar ☎ +54 2966 42 0023. 📠 +54 2966 42 2608 - **FM:** 92.9. – **25)** Estivariz 226, (U9120KEF) Pto. Madryn, Ct. ☎ +54 2965 45 1600. **Web:** www.radiogolfonuevo.com.ar **Email:** lu17@radiogolfonuevo.com.ar - **FM:** 88.3. – **26)** Echeverria 144, (M5500HED) Mendoza, Ma. **Web:** www.radionihuil.com.ar **Email:** radionihuil@radionihuil.com.ar ☎+54 261 430 1600. 📠+54 261 437 0148. - **FM:** 93.7. – **27)** Deán Funes 140, (A4400EDD) Salta, S. **Email:** salta@radionacional.gov.ar +54 387 427 2468/2730 - **FM:** 102.9. – **28)** Gral. Roca 365, 2° piso, (R8324BPG) Cipoletti, RN. **Email:** lu19@neuquenonline.com.ar +54 299 477 6333/6444 - **FM:** 102.9. – **29)** Av. San Martín 324, (Q8340EYQ) Zapala, N. ☎📠+54 2942 42 2960. **Email:** zapala@radionacional.gov.ar - **FM:** 93.9. – **29x)** Av. Victoria Aguirre Sur 809, (N3370AYI) Puerto Iguazú, Ms. ☎📠+54 3757 42 0999. **Email:** puertoiguazu@radionacional.gov.ar - **FM:** 99.1. – **30)** Sarmiento 1551, 8° piso, (C1042ABC) CA Buenos Aires. **Web**: www.oncediez.gov.ar. **Email:** oncediez@tournet.ar +54 11 5371 4646. – **31)** Av. San Martín 1114, (Z9311AVY) Governador Gregores, SC. **Email:** gobernadorgregores@radionacional.gov.ar +54 2962 491044 - **FM:** 99.9. – **32)** Rioja 1093, (M5500ALU) Mendoza, Ma. ☎+54 261 420 5100/3349. **Web:** www.elevdiez.com **Email:** eleve10@infovia.com.ar - **FM:** 100.9. – **33)** Rivadavia 402 – 4° piso, (L6300DWF) Santa Rosa, LP. ☎+54 2954 422456 +54 2954 42 5102. **Email:** santarosa@radionacional.com.ar - **FM:** 96.1. – **34)** Ruta Complementaria "0" s/n, (Z9405) El Calafate, SC. **Web:**

www.lu23.calafate.com **Email:** lu23@calafate.com +54 2902 49 1057 +54 2902 491 580 - **FM:** 88.1. – **35)** S.F. del Valle de Catamarca, C. **Email:** catamarca@radionacional.gov.ar ☎ +54 3833 42 4223 🖷 +54 3833 42 2251 - **FM:** 103.3. – **36)** Av. Comandante Fontana y Dr. Mariano Moreno, (U9033) Alto Río Chacabuco 762, (K4700BTP) Senguer, Ct. ☎🖷+54 2945 497050. **Email:** altoriosenguer@radionacional.gov.ar - **FM:** 93.5. – **36x)** Ramón Lista 36, (Z9050DLB) Puerto Deseado, SC. +54 297 487 2111. – **37)** Santa Rosa 241, (X5000ESF) Córdoba, Ca. ☎ +54 351 422 5663. +54 351 422 5665. **Email:** cordoba@radionacional.gov.ar - **FM:** 91.3. – **38)** Av. San Martín 331, (V9410BFD) Ushuaía, TFAIA. **Email:** ushuaia@radionacional.gov.ar - **FM:** 92.1. – **39)** Chacra 46, La Tablada, (W3340) Santo Tomé, Cs. **Email:** santotome@radional.gov.ar +54 3756 42 0090. - **FM:** 100.5. – **40)** Rioja 1484, (M5500AMD) Mendoza, Ma. **Email:** prensalv8@arlinkbbt.com.ar +54 261 429 2999. - **FM:** 92.7. – **41)** Mansilla 2668, (C1425BPD) CA Buenos Aires. +54 11 5777 1500 +54 11 5777 1504. **Web:** www.radiomitre.com.ar **Email:** tecnica@radiomitre.com.ar – **42)** Rio Bermejo y Olavarria, (Y4600) San Salvador de Jujuy, J. +54 388 422 3968 +54 388 422 6047. **Email:** jujuy@radionacional.gov.ar - **FM:** 94.3. – **43)** Rudecindo Roca 720, (Q8370EDN) San Martín de los Andes, N. **Email:** sanmartindelosandes@radionacional.gov.ar +54 2972 42 7566 - **FM:** 92.5. – **44)** Av. Alvaro Barros 1148, (R8500FFX) Viedma, RN. **Email:** lu15radioviedma@arnet.com.ar +54 2920 42 2081. – **Italian**: Sat 1500–1600. **FM:** 94.3. – **45)** Patricias Mendocinas 72/78, (M5620FYH) General Alvear, Ma. +54 2625 422123. - **FM:** 88.9. – **46)** Junín 665, (P3600IDM) Formosa, F. ☎+54 3717 42 6197. **Email:** formosa@radionacional.gov.ar - **FM:** 94.1. – **47)** Maestro Ferreyra 175, Barrio Parquq, (BC1663CHC) San Miguel Oeste, BA. ☎+54 11 4455 1408. - **FM:** 101.7.– **48)** Belgrano 457, (B7500EBE) Tres Arroyos, BA. **Web**: www.lu24.com.ar **Email:** lu24@3net.com.ar – ☎+54 2983 42 3504 +54 2983 42 7000. - **FM:** 95.3.. – **49)** Córdoba 1843, (S2000AXC) Rosario, SF. ☎+54 341 410 0600. 🖷+54 341410 0637. - **Web**: www.lt8.com.ar **Email:** lt8@lt8.com.ar - **FM:** 99.5//102.3. – **50)** Av. Güemes 1103, (H3730AML) Charata, Ch. **Web**: www.mocovi.com.ar **Email:** am800@mocovi.com.ar ☎ +54 3731 420150. 🖷 +54 3731 420735. - **FM:** 95.7. – **51)** Av. Pte. Julio A. Roca 823, 1°piso, (Z9400BAH) Río Gallegos, SC. **Web:** www.scruz.gov.ar/lu14/ **Email:** info@lu14radio.com.ar - +54 2966 42 2315 +54 2966 42 3510. - **FM:** 99.3. – **52)** Paraguay y Honduras, (Y4600) San Salvador de Jujuy, J. ☎+54 388 423 0035. **Email:** rvj@arnet.com.ar – **FM:** 97.7 – **53)** Arturo Marasso 170, (F5360CPF) Chilechito, LR. +54 3825 42 5025. – **54)** Juan Sitjanin 491, (W3230GEQ) Paso de los Libres, Cs. **Email:** lt12@sicnet.com.ar - +54 3772 42 1700. - **FM:** 92.7. – **56)** Sarmiento 55/64, (B8000HBQ) Bahía Blanca, BA. - **Web:** www.lu2.com.ar **Email:** radio@lu2.com.ar - ☎ +54 291 459 0002. 🖷 +54 291 455 5556. - **FM:** 105.7.– **57)** Saavedra 1318, (Z9040BQN) Perito Moreno, SC. +54 2963 43 2233 **Email:** peritomoreno@radionacional.gov.ar - **FM:** 93.5. – **58)** Maipú 555, (C1006ACE) Buenos Aires. ☎ +54 11 4327 3021. 🖷 +54 11 4325 9433. - **Web:** www.radionacional.gov.ar **Email:** buenosaires@radionacional.gov.ar – **International Sce:** see International Broadcasting section. – **59)** Lisandro de la Torre 474, (L6300BQJ) Santa Rosa, LP. - **Web**: www.lu33.com.ar **Email:** radiopampeana@ar.inter.net - ☎+54 2954 433505. - **FM:** 103.7. – **60)** 9 de Julio 390, (G4200DEH) Santiago del Estero, SE . ☎🖷 +54 385 421 3230 **Email:** lv11@nuevodiario_se.com.ar - **FM:** 89.5. – **61)** La Rioja 743, (W3400BZG) Corrientes, Cs. - **Web:** www.corrientesnoticias.com.ar/radio **Email**: radiocorrientes@impsat1.com.ar - ☎+54 3783 42 3560 🖷+54 3783 423149. - **FM:** 95.3. – **62)** Av. Ignacio de la Roza 293 Este, (J5402DBC) San Juan, SJ. ☎+54 264 421 4149. 🖷+54 264 421 4264. **Email:** sanjuan@radionacional.gov.ar - **FM:** 91.3. – **63)** Av.Paseo Colón 505, 1° piso, (C1063ACF) CA Buenos Aires. ☎+54 11 4338 0910 +54 11 4338 0900 - **Web:** www.lared.uol.com **Email:** lared@tyc.com.ar – **64)** Rivadavia 825, (C1002AAG) CA Buenos Aires. ☎+54 11 4345 0495 🖷 +54 11 4342 8249 - **Web:** www.am.belgrano.com **Email:** info@ambelgrano.com.ar – **65)** Cas. 229, (U9000AKP) Comodoro Rivadavia, Ct. **Email:** lu4radiopat@infovia.com.ar - **FM:** 101.7. – **66)** Emilio Civit 460, (M5502GVR) Mendoza, Ma. ☎+54 261 438 0596. **Email:** mendoza@radionacional.gov.ar - **FM**: 97.3. – **68)** Calle 64 No. 2946, (B7630CIR) Necochea, BA. ☎+54 2262 425630. **Web:** www.radionecochea.com.ar **Email:** radionecochea@hotmail.com - **FM:** 88.1. – **69)** Juan B. Alberdi 189, (Q8300HLC) Neuquén, N. **Web:** www.lu5am.com.ar **Email:** lu5@lu5am.com.ar +54 299 443 2772 - **FM:** 88.7, 94.7, 102.5, 103.3. – **70)** 25 de Mayo 424, (X5000ELJ) Córdoba, Ca. **Web:** www.am970.com.ar **Email**: info@am970.com.ar ☎🖷+54 351 411 0970. - **FM:** 99.7. – **70x)** Av. Belgrano y San Martin, (J5405AAA Barreal, SJ. ☎+54 2648 44 1260. – **71)** Remedios de Escalada 52, (R8336FED) Villa Regina, RN. ☎+54 2941 461102. 🖷+54 2941 462620. - **FM:** 92.7. – **72)** Constitución 399, (X5800BBB) Río Cuarto, Ca. ☎+54 358 463 8255. - **Web:** www.lv16.com **Email:** lv16@lv16.com - **FM:** 93.9, 106.9. – **73)** 9 de Julio 3560, (S3000EXB) Santa Fé, SF.- **Web:** www.unl.edu.ar **Email:** lt10@unl.edu.ar - +54 342 452 0187 - **FM:** 107.3. – **74)** Ruta 40 s/n, Barrio Gendarmería, (U9030) Río Mayo, Ch. **Email:** riomayo@radionacional.gov.ar +54 2903 42 0099 -**FM:** 88.1. – **75)** Doyhenard 316, (B1836EVH) Lavallol, BA. +54 11 4298 6580 +54 11 4231 3225. **Web:** www.am1500.com.ar. **Email:** radiobonaerense@am.1500.com ar or radiobonarense@yahoo.com – **76)** La Calle Olleros 3551, (C1427EEA) CA Buenos Aires. ☎+54 11 4556 9000. **Web:** www.amdelplata.com – **77)** Tacuarí 2035/7, (C1139AAQ) CA Buenos Aires. **Web**: www.radioelmundo.com.ar **Email:** mfioroni@radioelmundo.com.ar +54 11 4363 0070 🖷+54 11 4363 0071 – **78)** Av. Lamadrid 116, (B8000FKD) Bahía Blanca, BA. **Web:** www.radiodelsur.com.ar +54 291 452 0382 - **FM:** 94.1. – **79)** Ramón Elías Troitiño 624, Arroyo Atreuco, (Q8354) Andacollo, N. +54 2948 49 4025 – **80)** Mendoza 273, (T4000DAE) San Miguel de Tucumán, T. ☎+54 381 400 1930. **Web:** www.lv7radiotucuman.com.ar **Email:** lv7@lv7radiotucuman.com.ar - **FM:** 102.7 – **81)** Córdoba 1865, (B7600DVM) Mar del Plata, BA. ☎+54 223 491 7047. 🖷+54 223 491 2335. **Web:** www.lu6.com.ar **Email:** radioa@lu6.com.ar - **FM:** 93.3. – **82)** Mendoza 452 Sur, (J5402GUJ) San Juan, SJ. 🖷 +54 264 420 4024. **Email**: lv5 @radiolv5.com.ar - **FM:** 102.3, 103.7, 104.3, 104.7. – **83)** Esquivel Aldao 350, (M5613AEH) Malargüe, Ma. ☎+54 2627 471160/470658 - **Email:** lv19radio@infovia.com.ar - **FM:** 88.1. – **84)** Urquiza 332, (G4300DHH) Santiago del Estero, SE. **Email:** santiagodelestero@radionacional.gov.ar +54 385 421 2565 - **FM:** 93.5. – **84x)** Belgrano 710, (R8500FAP) Viedma, RN. - **Email:** viedma@radionacional.gov.ar - +54 2920 43 1697- **FM:** 93.5. – **85)** Av. Sarmiento 1255, (H3502COE) Resistencia, Ch. **Web:** www.radionacional.chaco.com.ar - **Email:** resistencia @radionacional.gov.ar +54 3722 43 2920. +54 3722 42 4937.– **Guaraní**: Sat. 1800. **FM:** 94.1. – **86)** Ruta Nal. 150, Km. 3, (J5460) San José del Valle de Jáchal, SJ. **Email:** jachal@radionacional.gov.ar +54 2647 42 0041 - **FM:** 102.1. – **87)** 4 de Enero 2153, (S3000FHY) Santa Fé, SF. - **Email**: lt9sfe@cerid.gov.ar **Web:** www.ceride.gov.ar/lt9 - +54 342 410 9940 - **FM:** 92.5. – **88)** San Martín y Salta, (R8430) El Bolsón, RN. **Email:** elbolson@radionacional.gov.ar +54 2944 49 2350 - **FM:** 92.5. – **89)** Av. Las Calandrias y Las Golondrinas, (N3370) Puerto Iguazú, Ms. - **Email:** radiocataratas@yahoo.com.ar - +54 3757 42 0060 - **FM:** 94.7. – **90)** Alsina 3377, (B7400COW) Olavarría, BA. ☎+54 2284 43 0911 - **Email**: info@lu32olavarria.com.ar **Web:** www.lu32radioolavarria.com.ar - **FM:** 98.7. – **91)** Deán Funes 28 (Cas. 113), (A4400EDB) Salta, S.+54 387 431 1140 +54 378 431 7030 - **Web:** www.radiosalta.com. **Email:** contacto@radiosalta.com - **FM:** 96.9. – **92)** Av. Lafinur 488, (D5700DCR) San Luís, SL. **Email:** sanluis@radionacional.gov.ar +54 2652 43 1318 - **FM:** 96.7. – **93)** Calle 19 No 151, (H3700) Presidencia Roque Sáenz Peña, Ch. ☎+54 3732 42 9651. **Email:** lt16@ciudad.com.ar - **FM:** 93.3. – **94)** Av. Hipólito Yrigoyen 627, (M5602HBC) San Rafael, Ma. **Web:** www.radiosanrafael.com **Email:** lv14@radiosanrafael.com ☎+54 2627 43 0055. 🖷+54 2627 43 0065. – **95)** San Martín 251, Piso 4, (T4000CVE) San Miguel de Tucumán, T. ☎+54 381 431 0131. 🖷+54 381 430 2409. **Email:** tucuman@radionacional.gov.ar - **FM:** 93.3. – **96)** Honduras 5691, (C1414BNE) CA Buenos Aires. +54 11 4779 7100 - **Web:** www.amradioamerica.com – **97)** Mariano I. Loza 231, (W3450BXE) Goya, Cs. ☎ +54 3777 42 3002. - **FM:** 98.3. – **99)** Alvear 139, (X5201EAC) Córdoba, Ca. ☎+54 351 526 2000. +54 351 526 0584 **Email**: audencia@cadena3.com.ar **Web:** www.lv3.com.ar – **FM:** 92.3, 100.5. – Satellite signal downlinked by 45 repeaters. – **100)** Av. Presidente Preón 8101, (S2010ACF) Rosario, SF. - **Web**: www.rosario3.com **Email:** radio2@rosario3.com - +54 341 457 5415 - **FM:** 92.3, 97.9– **101)** Jujuy 470, (Y4512ERJ) Tartagal, S. ☎+54 3886 42 3399. - **FM:** 104.5. – **102)** Rivadavia 126, (E3100GNO) Paraná, ER. **Web:** www.radiolt14.com.ar **Email:** lt14@radiolt14.com.ar +54 343 423 0101- **FM:** 93.3. – **103)** Intersección Ruta Nacional 81 y Provincial 32, (F3630) Las Lomitas, F. **Email:** laslomitas@radionacional.gov.ar +54 3715 43 2167 - **FM:** 93.5. – **104)** Calle 53 No. 810, (B1900BBQ) La Plata, BA. - **Web:** www.radioprovinciaba.com.ar **Email:** tecnica@radioprovinciaba.com.ar +54 221 424 9713 - **FM:** 97.1. – **105)** Gral. Rodriguez 762, PA, (B7000AOP) Tandil, BA. - **Web:** www.lu22radiotandil.com.ar **Email:** radiotandil@arnet.com.ar - +54 2293 42 7493 - **FM:** 97.1. – **106)** Peatonal Córdoba 1331 1° piso, (S2000AWS) Rosario, SF. ☎+54 341 440 2490. 🖷+54 341 411 8149. **Email:** rosario@radionacional.gov.ar - **FM** 104.5. – **106x)** Urquiza al Oeste, Parada 12, (E2820) Gualeguaychú, ER. **Email:** gualeguaychu@radionacional.gov.ar +54 3446 42 6159 - **FM** 98.7. – **106z)** Calle Las Rosas 81, Barrio Jardín, (Q8315AYA) Piedra del Aguila, N. ☎🖷+54 2942 493216 - **FM:** 99.5. – **107)** Córdoba 710, (H3500APP) Resistencia, Ch. **Web**: www.radiochaco.com.ar **Email:** radiochaco@arnet.com.ar ☎+54 3722 43 3900. 🖷+54 3722 43 3999. - **FM:** 101.5. – **108)** Av. Bartolomé Mitre 819/25, (B7300IKQ) Azul, BA. **Email:** lu10radioazul@latinmail.com - +54 2281 42 3224 - **FM:** 89.5. – **109)** Calle 40 esq. 29, (L6360) General Pico, LP. **Email:** radiolu37@infovia.com.ar +54 2302 43 0055- **FM:** 88.9. – **110)** Balcarce 840, (S2000DNR) Rosario, SF. ☎+54 341 411 8000/8516. – **Web:** www.lt3.com.ar **E.mail:** lt3@lt3.com.ar - **FM:** 102.7. – **111)** Av. Entre Ríos 1931, (C1133AAH) CA Buenos Aires. ☎+54 11 4307 2200. **Web:** www.radiobuenosaires.com.ar.– **112)** Av. Independencia s/n, (N3366) Bernardo de Irigoyen, Ms. - **FM:** 96.9. – **113)** Martín Coronado y José Hernández, (R8418) Ingeniero Jacobacci, RN. **Email:** ingenierojacobacci@radionacional.gov.ar +54 2940 43 2032. **FM:** 93.5. – **113x)** Av. Pte. Illia 128, (D5700IEO) San Luís, SL. ☎+54 2652 44 1088/1099. **Email:** dimensionsl@hotmail.com - **FM:** 102.5 "Maxima". – **114)** Cdte. Salas 287, (M5600DJE9 San Rafael, Ma. **Email:** lv18@sanrafael.gov.ar +54 2627 42 2449 - **FM:** 98.7 'FM Municipal'. – **115)** Plaza Rocha 133, 2° piso, (B1900DVA) La Plata, BA. - **Web:** www.lr11.com.ar ☎+54 221 42 20330 🖷+54 221 42 24165. - **FM:** 107.5. – **116)** Av. Pedro Garcia Salinas 1815, (B6400EIF) Trenque Lauquen, BA. - **Web:** www.lu11radio.com.ar **Email:** radiolu11@speedy.com.ar or radiolu11@ciudad.com.ar - +54 2392 42 5454 - **FM:** 88.5. – **117)** Villafañe y Calilegua, (Y4608) Perico, J. +54 388 491 1465/1509 **Email:** rvj@arnet.com.ar – **118)** Centenario 651, (W3344AOK) Alvear, Cs. +54 3772 47 0501. - **FM:** 98.7. – **119)** Av. Moreno 124, (B2900GPO) San Nicolás, BA. ☎+54 3461 42 5222 +54 3461 42 4479. **Web:** www.lt24online.com.ar **Email:** lt24@cablenet.com.ar - **FM:** 88.3. – **120)** Libertad 455 2° piso, (X5850KNI) Río Tercero, Ca. ☎+54 3571 42 1522. **Web:** www.lv26.com.ar **Email:** lv26@itc.com.ar - **FM:** 94.5. – **121)** Av. San Martín 2700, (B7620) Balcarce, BA. **Email:** radiobalcarce@telefax.com.ar - +54 2266 43 0780 +54 2266 43 0779 - **FM:** 89.7. – **122)** Carlos Pellegrini 106, (E2822EWD) Gualeguaychú, ER. ☎+54 3446 43 6651 **Web:** www.lt41.entrerios.net **Email:** lt41am660@entrerios.net - **FM** 90.3. – **123)** Avellaneda 1144, (B7540BBC) Coronel Suárez, BA. ☎+54 2926 43 2706. - **FM:** 100.1. – **124)** Tucumán 159, (X6120EOC) Laboulaye, Ca. ☎🖷+54 3385 42 6259. **Web:** www.lv20.com **Email:** lv20@arnet.com.ar - **FM:** 89.9. – **125)** Pasaje Peatonal 12 No 50,"Edifico Reggio II", (X2400) San Francisco, Ca. ☎+54 3564 422186. **Web:** www.sanfco.com.ar/lv27/ **Email:** radiolv27@cordoba.com.ar - **FM:** 88.7. – **126)** Santa Fe 1490, (X5900DTJ) Villa María, Ca. ☎+54 353 452 2699. - **Web:** www.radiovenadotuerto.com.ar **Email:** lt29t@radiovenadotuerto.com.ar - +54 3462 42 1524 - **FM:** 88.9. – **128)** Lavalle Sud 312, www.radiovillamaria.com **Email:** lv28@radiovillamaria.com - **FM:** 98.5. – **127)** Av. Casey 642, (S6400FJN) Venado Tuerto, SF. **Web:** (B7160BAH) Maipú, BA. **Email:** lu7ejm@latinmail.com +54 2268 42 1774 – **129)** Rivdavia 382, (B8170ACH) Pigüe, BA. - **Email:** lupigue@rcc.com.ar **Web:** www.ce.rcc.com.ar/pigueargentina/radiopigue.htm - +54 2923 47 2205 +54 2923 47 2709 - **FM:** 96.3 – **130)** Gorriti 524, (A4560BRL) Tartagal, S. - **Email:** lw2@fullnet.com.ar +54 3875 42 1150 - **FM:** 96.1. – **131)** Hipólito Yrigoyen 86, (B600DDB) Junín, BA - **Email:** redaccion@infovia.com.ar - +54 2362 44 4310 - **FM:** 89.1. – **132)** Av. Pte. Perón 117, (E3280CSB) Colón, ER. **Email:** radiomundo@ssdnet.com.ar +54 3447 42 1067 - **FM:** 93.7. – **133)** Bulevar Lehman 245, (S2300GSC) Rafaela, SF. ☎ +54 3492 42 8800 - **Web:** www.avizora.com/radiorafaela/ **Email:** radio@lt28.com.ar - **FM:** 96.5. – **134)** Uslenghí 592, (B8150EGD) Coronel Dorrego BA. +54 2921 45 3456 – **135)** Casa de Tucumán 481, (R8361BKO) Luis Beltrán, RN. +54 2946 48 0180 – **136)** Sarmiento 474, (E3153EZH) Victoria, ER. **Web:** www.lt39am980.arnet.com.ar **Email:** lt39am980@arnet.com.ar - +54 3436 421952 - **FM:** 96.3. – **137)** Av. Atanacio Aguirre Km 2 s/n, (W3470EHA) Mercedes, Cs. - **Email:** lt42@ibera.net - ☎+54 3773 42 0087. - **FM:** 93.5. – **138)** Santa Fé y La Pampa, (X6270) Huinca Renancó, Ca. ☎+54 2336 44 2007. **Email:** radiolv22@huincacoop.com.ar – **138x)** Julio A. Roca 570, (R8503BHL) General Conesa, RN. +54 2931 49 8653. – **140)** Independencia 501, (B2800JIG) Zárate, BA. **Web:** www.radionuclear.com.ar **Email:** radionuclear@delta.com.ar ☎+54 3487 42 3116. 🖷+54 3487 43 9500 – **FM:** 90.1. – **141)** Padre José Ordóñez 737, (N3357BMO) San Javier, Ms. **Email:** radiolt45@arnet.com.ar +54 3754 48 2420. – **142)** Intendente José Villalba s/n, (X2550) Bell Ville, Ca. +54 3534 42 4161. - **FM:** 105.5. – **143)** Belgrano 33, Galeria Central, (X5870ABA) Villa Dolores, Ca. ☎+54 3544 420226. - **FM:** 100.1. – **144)** Pablo Stampa 2430, (E3228FDD) Chajarí, ER. ☎+54 3456 42 0002. - **Web:** www.chajaridigital.com.ar **Email:** chajarialdia@bibyte.com.ar - **FM** 88.7. – **145)** 9 de Julio 163, (A4530XBF) San Ramón de la Nueva Orán, S +54 3878 42 1026. **Email:** radioran@oranaet.com.ar - **FM:** 90.9. – **146)** San Martín 1380, (W3461AKA) Curuzú Cuatiá, Cs. ☎ +54 3774 42 2540. **Email** radioguarani@ar.inter.net - **FM:** 107.1. – **148)** Chacabuco 38, (E2840BFB) Gualeguay, ER. **Email:** radiogualeguay@ciudad.com.ar **Web:** www.gualeguayer.com.ar/ radio - **FM:** 104.3. – **149)** Calles Alem y Juan B. Justo, (M5560) Tunuyán, Ma. - **Email:** neuro@yahoo.com.ar - +54 2622 42 2123. - **FM:** 88.5. – **150)** Bv. 25 de Mayo 133, (X2421ABB) Morteros, Ca. ☎+54 3562 42 2148 +54 3562 42 3176. **Email:** radiomorteros@yahoo.com.ar - **FM:** 90.3. – **151)** Av. Colón 985, (B6430BHF) Carhué, BA. **Email:** radiocarhue@yahoo.com.ar +54 2936 43 2560 – **152)** Dr. Alem 340, (B2700LHH) Pergamino, BA. ☎🖷+54 2477 424022. **Web:** www.lt35radiomon.com.ar **Emai:** lt35radiomon@ciudad.com.ar - **FM:** 90.3. – **153)** Av. San Martín 366, (B7163EGQ) General Madariaga, BA. **Email:** radiotuyu@infovia.com.a +54 2267 42 5795. - **FM:** 92.5. – **154)** Juan Chavarri 458, (S2147AUH) San Jenaro Norte, SF. ☎+54 3401 49 3069. **Email:** lt23@co19set.com.ar - **FM:** 92.1. – **155)** Av. Mitre 924, (B6620BMW) Chivilcoy, BA. +54 2346 43 0690. - **FM:** 101.1. – **156)** Roque Sáenz Peña 1082, (E3190FZJ) La Paz, ER. ☎🖷+54 3437 421568. **Email:** lt40@cabledos.com.ar - **FM:** 91.3. – **157)** Onésimo Leguizamón 269, (E3260FQE) Villaguay, ER. +54 3442 42 5661. - **FM:** 92.9. – **158)** Hipólito Irigoyen 969, (B6500DJQ) 9 de Julio, BA. +54 2317 43 0010. - **FM:** 89.9. – **159)** Av. Avellaneda 773, (B7200AOH) Las Flores, BA. **Web:** www.multimedialasflores.com.ar. **Email:** am1210@multimedialasflores.com.ar - +54 2244 45 2320 +54 2244 45 2838 - **FM:** 89.7. – **160)** Av. Vélez Sársfield 1111, (E3240AUL) Villaguay, ER. ☎+54 3455 42 1717. **Email:** lt27@clavis.com.ar - **FM:** 88.7. – **161)** Almirante Brown 135, (B6740DRB) Chacabuco, BA. ☎+54 2352 42 6346. **Email:** radiochacabuco@topmail.com.ar - **FM:** 91.7. – **164)** Juan Florio 3579, (B1754AJK) San Justo, BA. +54 11 4441 1400 +54 11 4482 1711. **Web:** www.estripenacional.com.ar **Email:** estirpe1250@yahoo.com.ar – **165)** Av. General Arias 1372, (B1824KPD) Lanús, BA. ☎+54 11 4247 8237. **Email:** radiofe@infovia.com.ar – **166)** San Martín 569, 2° piso "6", (C1004AAK) CA Buenos Aires. ☎+54 11 489 31701. **Web:** www.amsplendid.com.ar – **168)** Uriarte 1899, (C1414DAU) CA Buenos Aires. Web: www.radio10. com.ar **Email:** radio10@radio10.com.ar ☎+54 11 4833 8800. – **FM:** 98.3. – **169)** Sáenz 572, 2° piso, (B1832HUL) Lomas de Zamora, BA. ☎ +54 11 4243 7891. – **170)** Isla Soledad 2560, (B1716NXB) Libertad, BA. ☎+54 220 494 1300 - **FM:** 91.9. – **171)** Calle Balbastro 3881, (B1754GPM) San Justo, BA. ☎+54 11 4482 3230. – **173)** Roque Sáenz Peña 3241, (B1752CBQ) Lomas del Mirador, BA. ☎+54 11 4655 0400. **Web:** www.am770.com.ar **Email:** radiourbana@datafull.com – **174)** Av. 9 de Julio 165/9, (P3600BCB) Formosa, F. ☎+54 3717 42 8404. **Email:** cadena100formosa@arnet.com.ar - **FM:** 98.9. – **175)** Asuncion 3057, (B1703ATQ) José Ingenieros, BA. ☎+54 11 4653 5643. – **176)** Calle San Luís 991, (B1708JUE) Morón, BA. ☎+54 11 4627 7439 – **177)** Arroyo Santa Catalina 4067, Barrio Juan Manuel de Rosas, 1832 Lomas de Zamora, BA. ☎+54 11 4693 2789. – **180)** Julio A. Roca 3414, (B1702BCL) Ciudadela, BA. ☎+54 11 4488 3644. – **181)** Av. Rivadavia 22793, (B1714GJC) Ituzaingó, BA. ☎+54 11 4458 4974. – **182)** Calle Lacroze 7279, (B1655LVS) José León Suárez, BA. ☎+54 11 4720 2688. – **183)** Fray Mamerto Esquiú 2855, (B1826GBO) Remedios de 346, (B1752DPH) Lomas del Mirador, BA. ☎+54 11 4699 0584/3077. **Web:** www.radiomaranata.com **Email:** info@radiomaranata.com - Escalada, BA. ☎+54 11 4240 3544. - **Web:** www.radiociudad.mov.com.ar **Email:** radiociudad@movi.com.ar – **184)** Calle Coronel Dorrego **FM:** 89.3. – **185)** Calle Treinta y Tres 1033, Villa Ariza, (B1714NOS) Ituzaingó, BA. +54 11 4623 4549. – **186)** Carlos Pellegrini 1251, (B1842BCY) Monte Grande, BA. ☎+54 11 4281 4094 - **FM:** 104.9. – **187)** Juan Llerena 3036, 2° piso, (B1757GSF) Rafael Castillo, BA. ☎+54 11 4457 6583. – **188)** Juan Jofré 4243, (1765MOY) Isidro Casanova, BA. ☎+54 11 4694 8131. – **189)** Pueyrredón 3822, (B1650CVP) San Martin, BA +54 11 4754 8784. – **190)** Calle Santa Cruz 1312, (B1655THD) José León Suarez, BA. ☎+54 11 4720 0059. – **192)** Tte. Cnel. Manuel Rico 424, (B7100ABJ) Dolores, BA. +54 2245 44 3615 - **FM:** 94.9. – **193)** Lucas Funes 1258, (S3560ETZ) Reconquista, SF. - **Web:** www.radioamanecer.com.ar **Email:** radioamanecer@radioamanecer.com.ar - +54 42 8945 - **FM:** 92.7. – **194)** Domingo F.Sarmiento 1847, 7° piso, (N3300HUM) Posadas, Ms. ☎+54 3752 42 0203. - **Web.:**www.tupambaenoticias.com.ar **Email:** tupambae@tupambaenoticias.com.ar or tupambae@arnet.com.ar - **Guaraní:** Sun 0900–1500. - **FM:** 105.9. – **195)** Catamarca 2560, (B1847CXH) Rafael Calzada, BA. ☎ +54 11 4219 1150. – **196)** Av. 25 de Mayo sur 69, (G3760AEA) Añatuya, SE. **Web:** www.paulinas.org.ar/SaraRsolidaridad.htm ☎🖷+54 3844 42 1661. – **199)** Barrio Gastronomicos, Manzan 86, Casa 86, (D5700) San Luís, SL. ☎+54 2652 42 8138. 🖷+54 2652 43 8822. – **FM:** 98.5-97.3 -95.7 – **201)** Juncal 12, 1° piso, Of. 3, (B1770AOB) Tapiales, BA - **Email:** impactoam@hotmail.com - BA. ☎+54 11 4442 6333. – **202)** Mariquita Sánchez de Thompson 1850, (B1768BDP) Ciudad Madero, BA. ☎ +54 11 4622 1570. - **Email:** www.aminteractiva.com.ar – **204)** Fournier 4075, (B1757IDW) Gregorio de Laferrere, BA. ☎+54 11 4457 4513. – **205)** Las Piedras 2447, (B1826DJO) Remedios de Escalada, BA. ☎+54 11 4249 6047. **Email:** melody680@topmail.com.ar – **206)** Berasain 659, (B1842AMM) Monte Grande, BA. ☎+54 11 4296 5988. **Web:** www.am730.com.ar - **FM:** 91.7. – **207)** Rojas 2, 2° piso "2", (C1405AAB) CA Buenos Aires. ☎+54 11 4901 3363. **Email:** lanuevaargentina@latinmail.com – **209)** Robertson 1249, Of. 6, (B1838AIE) Luis Guillón, BA - **Web:** www,metropolitana1300.8k.com **Email:** metropolitana@datafull.com - ☎+54 11 4281 0804. – **210)** Fray Mamerto Esquiú 1161, (B1824BFQ) Lanús, BA. ☎+54 11 4225 2256. - **Web:** www.cristal1290.com.ar **Email:** cristal1290@argentina.com - – **211)** Zárate 5942, (B1757BML) Gregorio de Laferrere, BA. ☎+54 11 4626 1620. – **212)** Av. Callao 441, 17° piso "G", (C1022AAE) CA Buenos Aires. - **Web:** www.am1010-ondalatina.com.ar **Email:** am1010_ondalatina@fullzero.com.ar - ☎ +54 11 4372 5863. - **FM:** 88.3. – **213)** 12 de Octubre 537, PB, (B1804AAC) Ezeiza, BA. ☎+54 11 4232 9739. – **214)** Call Donizetti 140, (B1832CPF) Lomas de Zamora, BA. ☎ +54 11 4282 2627. – **215)** Av. Rivadavia 10561, 3° piso, (C1408AAF) CA Buenos Aires. - **Web:** www.cadenaeco.com.ar **Email:** cadenaeco@cadenaeco.com.ar - ☎+54 11 5631 1000. – **217)** José Morlote 895, (B1766FNG) La Tablada, BA. **Email:** laradiodelcorazon@hotmail.com - ☎+54 11 4652 5557. – **218)** Las Piedras 1544, (B1824QQJ) Lanús, BA. - **Email:** radiomagica1420@yahoo.com.ar - ☎+54 11 4247 3890. – **219)** Juan Florio 3579, (B1754AJK) San Justo, BA. **Web:** www.am530radiorepublica.com.ar **Email:** am530republica@argentina.com ☎+54 11 4482 3393/3588 +54 11 4482 0161. – **220)** Av. Enrique Santamarina 2642, (B1805AYF) El Jagüel, BA. ☎+54 11 4232 5635. – **222)** Florencio Sánchez 119, Barrio Los Alamos, (B1856FXE) Glew, BA. - **Email:** estilo1100@hotmail.com - ☎+54 11 4233

13 23/1. – **223)** Av. Jacinto Peralta Ramos 675, (B7608CFM) Mar del Plata, BA.+54 223 482 8617 – **224)** Calle 25 de Mayo 740, (U9100BRP) Trelew, Ct. **Web**: www.radio3patagonia.com.ar **Email**: radiotres@speedy.com.ar ☎+54 2965 42 2566. – **226)** Potrerillos 1246, (B1849DVX) Claypole, BA. **Web:** www.am660.com.ar **Email:** am660popular@hotmail.com ☎ +54 11 4219 4725. - **FM:** 89.1. – **227)** Av. Rivadavia 10561, 3° piso, (C1408AAF) CA Buenos Aires. - **Web:** www.cadenaeco.com.ar **Email:** cadenaeco@cadenaeco.com.ar - ☎+54 11 5631 1530. – **228)** Choele Choel 1233, (B1822DPY) Valentin Alsina, BA. - **Web:** www.cybergama.com.ar **Email:** radiogama@hotmail.com - ☎+54 11 4209 5487 – **229)** Juan Carlos Molina 830, (B1846BLE) José Marmol, BA. ☎+54 11 4241 2544. – **230)** Calle 39 No. 256, (B1902) La Plata, BA. - **Web:** www.radiorocha.com.ar **Email**: radiorocha@yahoo.com - ☎ +54 221 427 3360. – **231)** Calle Heredia 920, Augustin Ferrairi, (B1724EOT) Mariano Acosta, BA. ☎+54 220 498 1498. – **234)** Traful 3834, (C1437HML) CA Buenos Aires. - **Web:** www.am840generalbelgrano.com - ☎+54 11 4912 0497. – **236)** Congresales 570, 1° piso, (B1716) Libertad, BA. ☎+54 220 495 0245. – **237)** Santiago del Estero 73, (B1862SCA) Guernica, BA. ☎ +54 224 47 6963. – **238)** Av. Pte. Juan D. Perón 2514, (B1644CYP) Victoria, BA. ☎+54 11 4746 6856. **Web:** www.radiooasis.com.ar **Email:** radiooasis@mixmail.com – **FM:** 92.5 – **239)** Av. Mosconi 634, (B1752CXT) Lomas de Mirador, BA. ☎ +54 11 4699 1570. **Web:** www.am570radiodelcentro.com.ar **Email:** contacto@am570.com.ar - **FM:** 88.5 – **240)** Av. Saénz 459, (B1437DNE) CA Buenos Aires. ☎+54 11 4912 0819. **Web:** www.radiourkupina.com.ar **Email:** info@radiourkupina.com.ar – **241)** Av. Cristianía 3257, (B1765HOK) Isidro Casanova, BA. ☎+54 11 4694 5434 – **FM:** 92.1. – **242)** Jauretche 1052, 1° piso, (B1686FCD) Hurlingham, BA. - **Email:** mipais1170@ciudad.com.ar - ☎+54 11 4662 9534. – **243)** Cerrito 242, PB "B", (C1010AAF) Avellaneda, CA Buenos Aires, **Web:** www.am740.com.ar **Email:** direccion@am740.com.ar +54 11 4382 4650. – **244)** San Martín 513, (B1854FEM) Longchamps, BA. - **Web:** www.activa1580.com.ar **Email:** radio@activa1580.vom.ar - ☎+54 11 4233 4848. – **245)** Tgrl. Pedro E. Aramburu-ex Debussy-2948, (B1686FBB) Hurlingham, BA. - **Web:** www.radiorestauracion.com.ar **Email:** info@radiorestauracion.com.ar - ☎+54 11 4452 0167. – **246)** Av. San Juan 2461, (C1232AAG) CA Buenos Aires. ☎+54 11 4942 6913. – **247)** Av. Int. Francisco Rabanal 1465, PA, (C1437FPB) CA Buenos Aires. ☎+54 11 4919 2994. – **248)** Laprida 1680, (B1602EFD) Florida , BA. **Web**: www.am650.com.ar **Email:** info@am650.com.ar ☎+54 11 4796 3929. - **FM:** 105.7. – **249)** Calle Rodriguez Peña 408, 1° Piso "B", (C1020ADJ) CA Buenos Aires. ☎ +54 11 4371 1115. **Web:** www.750am.com.ar **Email:** tecnica_delpueblo@iplanmail.com.ar – **250)** Av. Pte. Domingo Perón 3939, (B1822AHM) Valentin Alsina, BA – **Email:** nuestrasraices@argentina.com.ar - ☎+54 11 4218 3099. – **251)** Av.Cervetti 301, (B1842HQG) Monte Grande, BA +54 11 4296 7214. – **FM:** 101.7. – **252)** Portugal 2154, (B1714ISR) Ituzaingó, BA. ☎+54 11 4621 5041. – **253)** Lebensohn 188, (B1876DCD) Mar del Plata, BA. ☎+54 223 479 0333. **Web:** www.cadenaeco.com.ar. **Email:** cadenaeco@cadenaeco.com.ar – **257)** 25 de Mayo 827, PB Bernal, BA. ☎+54 11 4251 0008 **Web:** www.am1330.com.ar **Email:** ofeliarosales@speedy.com.ar – **254)** Av. Libertad 4045, (B7600HJL) "1", (B1824NMI) Lanus, BA. ☎+54 11 4276 1436. - **Email:** cadena1470@yahoo.com.ar – **258)** San Martin – Calle 69 – No 50, (B1653LXB) Villa Ballester, BA +54 11 4768 2556 – **FM:** 97.7. – **259)** Av. General Paz 13869, (B1751BRG) Villa Insuperable, BA. - **Web:** www.radio970am.com.ar - ☎+54 11 4454 7799. - **FM:** 105.7. – **260)** Las Piedras 2306, (B1826DNJ) Remedios de Escalada, BA. **Web**: www.radiosentir.com.ar **Email**: info@radiosentir.com.ar ☎+54 11 4240 1323. – **261)** Av. General Arias 2160, (B1826DGJ) Remedios de Escalada, BA ☎+54 11 4247 5570. – **263)** Parroquia Nuestra Señora de Luján, Hipolito Yrigoyen s/n, (R8536) Valcheta, RN. ☎+54 2934 49 3283. - **FM:** 105.3. – **265)** Victorino de la Plaza 2829, (B1765LLW) Isidro Casanova, BA. +54 11 4485 7376. – **267)** Madrid 3987, Barrio San Juan, (B1712NMO) Castelar, BA. ☎+54 11 4692 4412. – **269)** Av. Concepción Arenale 1174, (X5000AAY) Córdoba, Ca. **Email**: sucesos@arnet.com.ar & radiosucesos@hotmail.com ☎+54 351 460 1010. 🖷+54 351 460 0056. - **FM:** 104.5. – **270)** Rivadavia 607, (Q8300HDM) Neuquén, N. ☎+54 299 443 0249. - **Email**: cumbre@cumbre1400.com.ar **Web:** www.cumbre1400.com.ar - **FM:** 97.9-104.7 – **271)** Av. General Paz 3755, (B1672AMA) Villa Lynch, BA. **Web:** www.radio610.com.ar ☎+54 11 4755 90 61/62. – **272)** Patricio Diez 374, (S3560FUH) Reconquista, SF. **Email:** am1440@trcnet.com +54 3482 42 2005 - **FM:** 96.1. – **275)** Bartolomé Mitre 11 este, (J5402CWA) San Juan, SJ. ☎+54 264 427 2740. - **FM**: 105.1. – **276)** Galaria Los Troncos, Av. Aconquija y Calle Belgrano, (T4107) Yerba Buena, T. - **Email:** radio21@am1460tucuman.com.ar **Web**: www.am1460tucuman.com.ar - ☎+54 381 400 0247. – **279)** Libres del Sur 128, (B7130ACD) Chascomús, BA. **Web**: - www.radiochascomus.com.ar **Email:** rch@radiochascomus.com.ar - ☎+54 2241 42 5367. - **FM**: 90.9 – **280)** Zufriâtegui 830, 11° piso, (B1714GDL) Ituzaingó, BA. ☎+54 11 4458 4603. **Email:** radioexitos1610@hotmail.com or radioexitos@yahoo.com.ar - **FM:** 94.7. – **281)** Av. Juan B. Alberdi 6693, 1° piso, (C1440) CA Buenos Aires. – **Web:** www.am890radiosobrina.com.ar - ☎+54 11 4686 5330. – **283)** Formosa 398, Villa Golf, (B1804DHH) Ezeiza, BA. ☎+54 11 4295 2246. – **284)** Magdalena 785, (B1825FVK) Monte Chingolo, BA. **Email:** am1380@hotmail.com - ☎+54 11 4230 8445. – **285)** Elias Bedoya 2024, (B1765LXH) Isidro Casanova, BA. ☎+54 11 4625 5357. – **286)** Calle 39 N° 1531, (L6360CNE) General Pico, LP. ☎+54 2302 43 4892. – **288)** Av. Circunvalación – Calle 32 No. 426, (B1902BKV) La Plata, BA. **Email**: am1630@red92.com **Web:** www.red92.com ☎+54 221 483 8998. – **FM:** 92.1 - 102.7. – **290)** Magallanes 3136, (B1824PYB) Lanús Oeste, BA. ☎+54 11 4267 2074. – **292)** Av. Alte. Francisco Seguí 1059, (B1836BYK) Llavallol, BA. ☎+54 11 4293 1144. – **293)** Av. Santa Fe 2470, (B1640IFY) Martinez, BA.- **Web:** www.presenciaderadio.com.ar - ☎+54 11 4798 7636. - **FM:** 99.3. – **294)** Juan Jofré 4243, (B1765MOY) Isidro Casanova, BA +54 11 4694 2538. – **295)** Hipólito Yrigoyen s/n esq. Andresito (Cas 45), (N3370) Puerto Iguazú, Ms. **Email**: icn.futuro@hotmail.com ☎+54 3757 42 2713. - **FM:** 101.7. – **296)** Bynnon 5074, (B1844EMP), BA. ☎+54 11 4211 5536. – **298)** Paso 1943, (B6015ASC) Los Toldos, BA. ☎+54 2358 44 3954. – **299)** Laprida 1237, (B1804AXY) Ezeiza, BA. ☎+54 11 4232 7673. – **300)** Amancio Alcorta 2552, (B1849HUD) Claypole, BA. ☎+54 11 4299 5344. – **301)** Salta 1155, (B7600DEW) Mar del Plata, BA. ☎+54 223 473 8266. - **FM:** 94.5. – **302)** Angel Cafferate 5199, (B1678BAI) Caseros, BA. ☎+54 11 4716 4734. **Web:** www.am1580.com.ar **Email:** radiomec@hotmail.com – **303)** Monseñor Bufano 3386, (B1754BZN) San Justo, BA. **Web:** www.apocalipsis2freeyellow.com **Email:** apocalipsis2@starmedia.com ☎+54 11 4484 4517. – **FM:** 90.7. – **304)** Arzobispado de Mendoza, Av. Bandera de los Andes 4404, (M5521AXL) Villa Nueva de Guaymallén, Ma. **Email:** murialdo@lanet.com.ar +54 261 421 3992 - **FM:** 90.5. – **305)** Dorrego y Artigues, (B7101) General Conesa, BA. ☎+54 2245 49 2140. – **306)** J.M. Estrada 329, 2812 Capilla del Señor, BA. ☎+54 2323 49 2110. – **307)** Unidad Penitenciara No 1,Calle 197 entre 52 y 53, (B1901) Lisandro Olmos, BA. +54 221 496 1504. – **308)** Calle Patricias Argentinas 456 (B1721BTD) Parque San Martin, Merlo, BA. +54 220 480 2134. – **309)** Manuela Molina 850, (B6015XAA) General Viamonte, BA. – **310)** Cabrera 877, (B6000FMA) Junín, BA. ☎+54 2362 42 1318. – **FM:** 95.3 – **311)** Avenida Santa Catalina 5330, (N3300PPO) Posadas, Ms. ☎+54 3752 45 4425. – **FM:** 94.5. – **312)** Av. Luro 6150, 3° piso "C", (B1757ARR) Gregorio de Laferrere, BA. **Email:** radioconurbana1050@yahoo.com.ar. ☎+54 11 4457 3674. – **314)** Bonpland 1114, (C1414CMJ) CA Buenos Aires. ☎+54 11 4856 8819. **Web:** www.am1300.com.ar **Email:** radioidentidad@argentina.co – **315)** Amazor 2858, (B1827AIX) Ingeniero Budge, BA. ☎+54 11 4273 1228. **Email:** riberasur@hotmail.com. – **318)** Rivadavia 99, (B6050AYA) General Pinto, BA. ☎+54 2356 42 0843. – **319)** Carlos Caseres 2886, (B1765MYN) Isidro Casanovas, BA +54 11 4466 LuisTozzini 40, (X6120DDB) Laboulaye, Ca. **Email:** buenasnuevas@arnet.com.ar +54 3385 42 6664 – **323)** Av. Hudson - Calle 893 No. 1115. – **FM:** 97.1 – **320)** (H3700) Presidente Roque Sanez Peña, Ch. - **Web:** www.radiodelnorte.com.ar - +54 3714 42 0994. – **322)** D. 1844, (B1897KWU) Quilmes Oeste, BA. +54 11 4212 8972. – **324)** Aaron Castellanos 2022, (S2003IRH) Rosario, SF – **Email:** marcel13@tutopia.com +54 341 421 7457. – **325)** Genral Guemez 5025, (B1603CUE) Villa Martelli, BA. +54 11 4709 1172. – **326)** Domingo F.Sarmiento 4154, (B1665KON) José C.Paz, BA. - **Web:** www.radiosintonia.com.ar **Email:** baguirecord@yahoo.com.ar +54 2320 42 3306. – **327)** Maipu 267 7° piso, (C1084ABE) CA Buenos Aires. - **Web:** www.conceptoam.com.ar **Email:** radio@concepto.com.ar - +54 11 4394 1450. – **328)** Mario Bravo 1284, Villa Fiorito, (B1821DWZ) Banfield, BA +54 11 4276 2396 – **FM:** 88.3. – **329)** Salguero 2745, 6° piso, (C1425DEL) CA Buenos Aires- **Web:** www.fmlaisla.com.ar **Email:** fmlaisla@fmlaisla.com.ar - +54 11 4803 4434 +54 11 4807 6006. – **330)** Calle Valentin Gomez 1762, (B1757JKD) Gregorio de Laferrere, BA. +54 11 4457 9882. – **331)** Av.Corrientes 1922 6° piso, Ofc. 63, (C1045AAO), CA Buenos Aires. +54 11 4951 2652 - **Web:** www.produccionescontar.com.ar **Email:** info@produccionescontar.com.ar – **332)** Las Heras 520, PA, (B6700ATL) Lujan. BA +54 11 2323 43 7801 – **FM:** 90.9 – **333)** Avenida Luro 6150, 3er Piso "C", (B1757ARR) Gregorio de Lafferrere, Buenos Aires - +54 11 4457 8712 – **334)** General Pico 690, (L8201BIK) 25 de Mayo, LP. +54 299 494 8086. – **336)** Bynnon 5047, 1847 Rafael Calzada, BA. +54 11 4211 5536. – **337)** Maestro Ferreyra 175, Barrio Trujui, (B1663CHC) San Miguel, BA. +54 11 4455 1408 – **FM:** 101.7 "Colieso". – **338)** Vicente López 234, PB A, (B1842AUE) Monte Grande, BA. – **Email:** am880claridad@argentina.com - +54 11 4284 3186. – **339)** Marcos Sastre y Sarmiento, (B1617) El Talar, BA. – **340)** Chilecito, LR. – **341)** Perito Moreno 696, (B6450GAN) Pehuajó, BA. - **Email:** lt22nuevare@yahoo.com.ar - **FM:** 88.1. – **342)** Florida 3168, (B1854HVH) Longchamps, BA. +54 11 4233 3990.

FM in Buenos Aires: 58) 87.9 R.Faro – **246)** 89.1 – **329)** 89.9 FM La Isla – **215)** 90.3 Eco Radio – 91.1 R.Abierta – **241)** 92.1 Mambo – 92.3 La Radio – **30)** 92.7 La Ciudad – 93.7 FM Federal – **77)** 94.3 Disney – 94.7 FM Palermo – **76)** 95.1 La Metro – **63)** 95.9 Rock & Pop – 96.3 R.Jai – **58)** 96.7 Clásica – **104)** 97.1 FM Europa – **79x)** 97.3 Contacto FM – 97.9 R.Cultura – 98.3 Mega – **58)** 98.7 FM Folklorica – 99.1 Cadena 3 Argentina – **41)** 99.9 Cadena 100 – 100.3 FM Cultural Musical – **64)** 100.7 Blue FM – 101.1 La Ciento Uno

– **63)** 101.5 Pop Radio – **96)** 102.3 Aspen Classic – **16)** 103.1 R. Uno – **168)** 103.7 Amadadeus FM – **10)** 105.5 FM Hit – **111)** 106.3 R.Alfa – 106.7 X4 – 107.3 Milenium – 107.9 Kabul Rock.

In the city area there are over 150 unlicensed LP FM st's, about 900 in the rest of the country.

FM in Córdoba: 88.1 FM Láser – 90.1FM Sur – **37)** 91.3 R.Nacional – 91.9 Hot FM – 92.9 FM Logos – 93.7 R.Vital – 94.3 R.Universidad – 95.1 Radiocentro Bar – 96.1 FM Shopping Classics – 96.3 FM Norte – 96.5 R.Suquia – 96.9 CNI – 98.5 FM Latinoamericana – 99.1 FM Amistad – 99.3 FM Impacto – **70)** 99.7 Estacion Tierra – **99)** 100.5 FM Córdoba – 101.5 R.Maria – **9)** 102.3 Power 102 – 102.7 FM Vision – 105.5 FM Cielo – 107.5 Box Music Station – 107.9 FM Potencia

FM in Mar del Plata: 87.7 R.Urbana – 87.9 R. 87.9 – 88.1 Graffiti FM – 88.3 LV del Puerto – 88.5 Onda Cero – 88.7 DeLaAzotea – 88.9 Mediterrano – 89.1 Red Impacto – 89.3 Láser – 89.7 d–Rock – 90.1 R. 90.1 – 90.5 Kids – 90.7 Rural – 90.9 Concierto FM – 91.3 La Red – 91.7 K.L.A. – 92.1 R. Maria – 92.3 Nova-92 – 92.7 Líder – 93.3 Atlantica Latina – 93.7 Lisán – 94.1 R. 94–1 – 94.5 Latina – 94.9 Mega – 95.3 R. Uno – 95.9 Compacto – 96.5 Residencias – 96.9 Red 92 – 97.1/ 97.5 R 97-1 – 97.5 Popular – 97.6 R. 97.6 – 97.7 Faro – 97.9 Estación 97 – 98.1 R.Disney – 98.5 Brisas – 98.9 Rock'n Pop – 99.1 R. 99.1 – 99.5 Más R. – 99.9 Coast – 101.1 Cadena Musica – 100.3 Cadena Latina – 100.7 Del Sol – 101.1 Red Master – 101.5 Arena Sports – 101.7 La Ola – 101.9 Concierto – 102.1 Bristol – 102.1 R.10 – 102.3 Municipal – 102.5 Nativa – 102.9 Ferimar – 102.9 Box – 102.9 La Nueva – 103.3 Universo – 103.7 Premium – 103.9 Canaan – 104.1 FM 104-1 – 104.5 Via – 104.7 Urbana – 104.9 LV Amiga – 104.9 Cosmos – 105.1 Señal – 105.5 Inolviable – 105.9 Coast–Melody – 106.3 Five – 106.5 Argentian – 106.7 Sur – 106.9 Veronica – 107.1 Cielo – 107.5 Radioactiva – 107.7 R.107.7 – 107.9 Trinidad.

FM in Rosario (Santa Fe): 89.5 R.Fisherton (CNN R.) – 90.9 Uruguay – 92.7 A-Z 927 – 92.9 Radioactiva – 93.7 Cordial – 94.5 Latina – 95.5 Corazon – 96.6 Rio – **100)** 97.9 Vida – 98.5 Tango – 98.9 FM Si – **49)** 99.5 Estacion del Siglo – 100.5 Radiofónica – 100.9 Meridiano – 101.3 Hollywood – 102.3 FM No – **106)** 104.5 R.Nacional – 105.5 Tiempo Libre – 107.1 R.Universidad – 107.9 Cristal FM

FM in Santa Fe: 89.9 Federal – 90.7 Eclipse – **87)** 92.5 Láser – 93.1 Estacion Rock – **1)** 94.9 R.Nacional – 98.1 Santa Fe Capital – 101.7 Cielo – 104.3 Plenitud – 104.5 Sensación – 105.1 Hot 105 – 105.5 News – 105.9 Ibiza FM – **73)** 107.3 La X – 107.9 R.Antena (CNN Radio)

ARMENIA

L.T: UTC +4h (27 Mar - 30 Oct 2005: UTC +5h) — **Pop:** 3,3 million — **Pr.L:** Armenian — **E.C:** 50Hz, 220V — **ITU:** ARM

HAYASTANI AZGAIN RADIO (Armenian Nat. Radio, Pub.)

A.Manukyan Str. 5, 375025 Yerevan. ☎ +374 1 551143. Fax +374 1 554600. **Email:** president@mediaconcern.am **Web:** www.armradio.am

L.P: Pres: Alexander Haroutunyan.

LW/MW	kHz	kW		kHz	kW
Gavar	234*	500	Yerevan	1395	150
Yerevan	4810*	100			
FM	**MHz**	**kW**		**MHz**	**kW**
Sisian	66.20	17	Vayk	103.9	1
Sevan	66.38	17	Charentsavan	104.4	1
Giumri	67.67	17	Ararat	104.6	1
Yerevan	71.00	17	Talin	105.2	1
Yerevan	102.0	0.1	Zovashen	106.8	1
Sevan	103.2	1	Vanadzor	107.2	1
Giumri	103.6	1	Jermuk	107.4	1

*) incl. foreign relays and/or F

D.PRGR: AR: 24h on FM; on LW/MW: 0200-2300 (s/off times may vary). On 4810: as filler between External Service (F) transmissions. Local channel in Yerevan: 24h on 107.6 MHz (1 kW).

EXTERNAL SERVICE: Voice of Armenia. See International Radio section.

OTHER STATIONS

FM	MHz	kW	Location	Station
1)	101.6	0.5	Yerevan	R. VEM
A)	102.4	1	Yerevan	RFI
2)	103.0	0.5	Yerevan	R. Van
3)	103.5	0.1	Yerevan	R. Ardzaganq
4)	103.8	0.1	Vanadzor	R. Interkap
5B)	104.1	1	Yerevan	Europa Plus
6)	104.1	1	Giumri	R. Shant
7)	104.9	1	Yerevan	Russkoye R.
8)	105.0	0.4	Giumri	R. TM 105
5A)	105.5	1	Yerevan	Hay FM
9)	106.0	0.5	Yerevan	Hit FM
10)	106.5	0.1	Yerevan	R. Impuls-Mayak
11)	107.0	1	Yerevan	Dinamit FM

Addresses & other information:

1) Koryun Str. 19, 375009 Yerevan. Email: info@vem.am – **2)** Hangyan Str. 13a, 375010 Yerevan. Email: radiovan@freenet.am – **3)** Tsitsernakaberd Park, Sports & Concert Complex , 375028 Yerevan. Email: ardzagank@media.am – **4)** Abegyan Str. 46a, 377200 Vanadzor. Email: radio@interkap.am – **5A,B)** Pavtos Buzandi Str. 3/1, 375010 Yerevan. Email: haifm@megacom.am. – **6)** Leningradyan Str., Radio-TV Center, 377524 Giumri. Email: shant@shirak.am – **7)** Nork, Nairi, 375047 Yerevan. Email: rryerevan@alfael.am – **8)** Paruyg Sevak Str. 10, 377524 Giumri. Email: tmr@media.am – **9)** Amaranotsain Str. 125, 375047 Yerevan. Email: hitfm@netsys.am – **10)** Tumanyan Str. 18-2, 375001 Yerevan. Email: mayak@freenet.am. Rel. R.Mayak from Russia. – **11)** Vagharsh Vagharshyan Str. 15, 375001 Yerevan. Email: dinamitfm@alfael.am – **A)** Nork, Ovsepyan Str. 95, 375047 Yerevan. Rel. RFI (see France).

ARUBA

L.T: UTC -4h — **Pop:** 70,000 — **Pr.L:** Dutch (official), Papiamento, English, Spanish — **E.C:** 50+60Hz, 127/220V — **ITU:** ABW

MW	kHz	kW	Station
2)	1270		Radio 1270
3)	1320	1	Radio Holland Aruba *

*** irregular**

FM	MHz	kW	Station, location
13)	88.1	1	Mega 88FM, Oranjestad
11)	88.9	-	Revolucion 88, Tanki Flip
3)	89.9	10	Canal 90FM, San Nicolas
1)	93.1	0.25	R. Victoria, Oranjestad (Rlg.)
12)	94.1	1	Hit 94 FM, Oranjestad
7)	95.1	2	Top 95.1 FM, Oranjestad
8)	96.5	-	Magic 96.5 FM, Oranjestad
6)	97.9	-	R. Carina FM, Oranjestad
10)	98.9	1	Radio 98.9 The New Cool FM, Oranjestad
9)	99.9	3.7	R. Galactica FM, Oranjestad
5)	102.7	0.3	R. Caruso Booy, Oranjestad
4)	106.7	6	R. Kelkboom, Oranjestad
2)	107.5		Radio 1270, San Nicolaas

Addresses and other information

1) Washington 23A, Noord. ☎/Fax +297 5873444.**Email:** radiovictoria@setarnet.aw **LP**: Pres. Nico J F Arts. 24h in English, Spanish, Papiamento and Dutch. **Web:** www.setarnet.aw/users/radiovictoria – **2)** Bernardstraat 138, P.O. Box 28, San Nicolas. ☎ +297 841075. Fax +297 845933 SM: J.A.C. Alders. Dir: F.A. Leauer. **Email:** radio1270@setarnet.aw – **3)** Van Leeuwenhoekstraat 26, Oranjestad ☎ +297 828952/824134, Fax +297 837340 **Email:** info@canal90fm.aw **Web:** www.canal90fm.com **MW:** 24h. Papiamento with nightly tourist programme "Radio Aruba" in E. – **4)** Bloemond 14, Paradera, (or P.O. Box 146), Oranjestad. ☎ +297 821899. Fax +297 834825 GM: C.A. Kelkboom. CE & PD: E.A.M. Kelkboom. Papiamento & E. 1000 (Sun 1200)-0400. **Dutch:** 1030-1100, 1230-1300. VOA relay M-F 2200-2300 **Web:** www.watapana-aruba.com – **5)** Generaal Majoor De Bruynewijk 49, Savaneta. ☎ +297 5847752 Fax +297 5843351 24h GM: Sira Booy **Email:** radiocarusobooy@hotmail.com **Web:** www.geocities.com/carusobooy – **6)** Datustraat 10A, Oranjestad. ☎ +297 821450 Fax +297 831955 **Web:** www.portalaruba.net/fm98_en.html – **7)** Santa Cruz 110, Oranjestad. ☎ +297 5859500 Fax +297 5850951 GM: Edmond Croes 24h **Email:** top@setarnet.aw **Web:** www.top95fm.aw – **8)** Caya G F Betico Croes 164, Oranjestad. ☎ +297 835353 Fax +297 835354. 24h **Web:** www.magic965.com – **9)** Italiestraat 40, 2nd floor, Suite 1, Oranjestad ☎ +297 5882534 Fax +297 5882536 GM: Maikel J. Oduber **Email:** radiogalactica@hotmail.com **Web:** www.galactica999fm.com – **10)** Caya Betico Croes 23, Oranjestad ☎ +297 5833100/5833111 Fax +297 5833101 GM: Alexander Ponson **Email:** coolaruba@hotmail.com **Web:** www.coolaruba.com – **11)** Tanki Flip 26B, ☎ +297 5873889 Fax +297 5875889 **Email**: revo88.9@setarnet.aw **Web:** www.revo88.9.aw – **12)** Caya Ernesto Petronia No. 68A , Oranjestad ☎ +297 5820694 Fax +297 5820494 GM: Johnny Habibe 24h **13)** Caya Ernesto Petronia No. 68A , Oranjestad ☎ +297 5820694 **Email:** mail@mega88fm.com **Web:** www.mega88fm.com

ASCENSION ISLAND (British)

L.T: UTC — **Pop:** 1.800 — **Radios:** 1.000 — **Pr.L:** English — **E.C:** 50Hz, 220V — **ITU:** ASC.

ASCENSION RADIO (USAF)

Ascension Radio Station, Ascension AAF, P.O. Box 4235, Patrick AFB, FL 32925-0235, USA.
MW: ZD8VR 1602kHz 0.1kW (1kW authorized) — **FM:** 95.1MHz 40W, 98.7MHz 0.4kW (stereo) — **Prgr. 1:** 24h on 1602kHz (95.1MHz inactive) — **Prgr. 2:** 24h on 98.7MHz (instrumental).

BBC ATLANTIC RELAY STATION

English Bay, Ascension Island, So. Atlantic.
Local Sce: MW: 1485kHz 0.5kW — **FM:** 93.2MHz 15W (24h relay of BBCWS in English plus occ. local prgrs).
SW (G.C: 07S54 014W23): 6 x 250kW tr's.
See International Broadcasting section for further details.

BFBS

BFBS 2 on 97.3 & 105.3MHz

VOICE OF AMERICA RELAY STATION

See International Broadcasting section.

AUSTRALIA

L.T: Victoria, New South Wales, Queensland, Tasmania: UTC +10h (VIC, NSW, TAS DST*: UTC +11h); South Australia: UTC +9½h (DST* UTC +10½h); Western Australia: UTC +8h; Northern Territory: UTC +9½h *DST: 31 Oct (TAS 3 Oct)-27 Mar — **Pop:** 20 million — **Pr.L:** English — **E.C:** 50Hz, 230V — **ITU:** AUS

ABORIGINAL RESOURCE & DEVELOPMENT SERVICES

Box 1671, Nhulunbuy NT 0881 ☎ +61 (08) 8987 3910. +61 (08) 8982 3499. **Web:** www.ards.com.au. **Email:** dale@ards.com.au.
L.P.: Radio Services Manager: Dale Chesson.
1530 kHz Humpty Doo 1kW 1530 kHz Nhulunbuy 400W 5050 kHz VKD963 Humpty Doo 400 W (G.C. 131.05E 12.34 S)
F.Pl: 1611 kHz VKD883 Milingimbi, 1611 kHz VKD884 Groote Eyland, 1620 kHz VKD885 Galiwin Ku (Elcho Island), 1629 kHz VKD886 Gapuwiyak

AUSTRALIAN BROADCASTING CORP. (ABC)

HQ: Ultimo Centre, 700 Harris Str, Ultimo, NSW 2007.(GPO Box 9994, Sydney NSW 2001) ☎ +61 (02) 9333 1500. +61 (02) 9333 5305. **Email:** howard.sue@ a2.abc.net.au. **L.P:** Sue Howard, Director of Radio
MW: N = R. National, R = Regional R, M = Metropolitan Sce, P = Parliamentary & News Netw. **Call letters:** 2 = NSW (exc. Canberra = A.C.T.), 3 = Victoria, 4 = Queensland, 5 = So. Australia, 6 = We. Australia, 7=Tasmania, 8=Northern Territory.

	Call	kHz	kW	Netw.	Location
36)	6DL	531	10	R	Dalwallinu
37)	4QL	540	10	R	Longreach
38)	2CR	549	50	R	Orange
39)	6WA	558	50	R	Wagin
40)	4JK	567	10d	R	Julia Creek
36)	6MN	567	0.1	R	Newman
36)	6PN	567	0.1	R	Pannawonica
36)	6PU	567	0.1	R	Paraburdoo
36)	6TP	567	0.1	R	Tom Price
2)	2RN	576	50	N	Sydney
6)	6PB	585	5	P	Perth
7)	7RN	585	10	N	Hobart
41)	3WV	594	50	R	Horsham
2)	2RN	603	10d	N	Nowra
37)	4CH	603	10d	R	Charleville
10)	6PH	603	2	R	Port Hedland
4)	4QR	612	50	M	Brisbane
6)	6RN	612	10	N	Dalwallinu
3)	3RN	621	50	N	Melbourne
2)	2PB	630	10	P	Sydney
40)	4QN	630	50	R	Townsville (Brandon)
13)	6AL	630	5	R	Albany
7)	7RN	630	0.4	N	Queenstown
14)	4MS	639	1	R	Mossman
15)	5CK	639	10	R	Port Pirie (Crystal Brook)
8)	8RN	639	2	N	Katherine
17)	2NU	648	10	R	Tamworth (Manilla)
18)	6GF	648	2	R	Kalgoorlie
38)	2BY	657	10d	R	Byrock
8)	8RN	657	2	N	Darwin
1)	2CN	666	5	M	Canberra ACT
20)	2CO	675	10	R	Albury (Corowa)
36)	6BE	675	5	R	Broome
21)	2KP	684	10	R	Kempsey (Smithtown)
22)	6BS	684	4	R	Busselton
8)	8RN	684	10	N	Tennant Creek
15)	5SY	693	2d	R	Streaky Bay
2)	2BL	702	50	M	Sydney
6)	6KP	702	10	R	Karratha
23)	4QW	711	10d	R	Roma/St.George
24)	7NT	711	10d	R	Launceston (Kelso)
25)	2ML	720	0.4	R	Murwillumbah
2)	2RN	720	0.05	N	Armidale
26)	3MT	720	2d	R	Omeo
14)	4AT	720	4	R	Atherton (Yungaburra)
6)	6WF	720	50	M	Perth
5)	5RN	729	50	N	Adelaide
25)	2NR	738	50	R	Grafton (Lawrence)
6)	6MJ	738	5d	R	Manjimup
23)	4QS	747	10	R	Toowoomba (Dalby)
7)	7PB	747	2	P	Hobart
8)	8JB	747	0.2	R	Jabiru
21)	2TR	756	5d	R	Taree
3)	3RN	756	10d	N	Wangaratta
3)	3LO	774	50	M	Melbourne
28)	8AL	783	2	R	Alice Springs
4)	4RN	792	25	N	Brisbane
14)	4QY	801	2	R	Cairns
29)	2BA	810	10	R	Bega
6)	6RN	810	10	N	Perth
17)	2GL	819	10	R	Glen Innes
36)	6KW	819	5	R	Kununurra
26)	3GI	828	10	R	Sale (Longford)
36)	6GN	828	10	R	Geraldton
30)	4RK	837	10	R	Rockhampton (Gracemore)
36)	6ED	837	1	R	Esperance
1)	2RN	846	10	N	Canberra
36)	6CA	846	2	R	Carnarvon
31)	4QB	855	10d	R	Pialba
31)	4QO	855	10	R	Eidsvold
6)	6DB	873	2	R	Derby
5)	5AN	891	50	M	Adelaide
4)	4PB	936	10	P	Brisbane
7)	7ZR	936	10d	M	Hobart
5)	5PB	972	2	P	Adelaide
3)	3RN	990	0.25	N	Albury-Wodonga
8)	8GO	990	0.5	R	Gove (Nhulunbuy)
32)	2NB	999	2d	R	Broken Hill
36)	6WH	1017	0.5	R	Wyndham
3)	3PB	1026	5	P	Melbourne
33)	2UH	1044	2d	R	Muswellbrook
14)	4WP	1044	0.5	R	Weipa
6)	6BR	1044	1	R	Bridgetown
14)	4TI	1062	2	R	Thursday Island
5)	5MU	1062	2	R	Renmark/Loxton
2)	2RN	1098	0.2	N	Goulburn
6)	6RN	1152	10d	N	Manjimup
34)	5PA	1161	10d	R	Naracoorte
24)	7FG	1161	1d	R	Fingal
6)	6XM	1188	2	R	Exmouth
6)	6NM	1215	0.5	R	Northam
6)	6RN	1224	5	N	Busselton
11)	2NC	1233	10	M	Newcastle
6)	6RN	1296	10	N	Wagin
5)	5RN	1305	2	N	Renmark/Loxton
38)	2LG	1395	0.2	R	Lithgow
2)	2RN	1431	2	N	Wollongong
1)	2PB	1440	2	P	Canberra
2)	2PB	1458	2	P	Newcastle
5)	5MG	1476	0.2	R	Mt. Gambier
2)	2RN	1485	0.1	N	Wilcannia
40)	4HU	1485	0.05	R	Hughenden
15)	5LN	1485	0.2	R	Port Lincoln
2)	2RN	1512	10	N	Newcastle
30)	4QD	1548	50	R	Emerald
12)	4GM	1566	0.2	R	Gympie
32)	2WA	1584	0.1	R	Wilcannia

	Call	kHz	kW	Netw.	Location
34)	5MG	1584	0.2	R	Mt.Gambier
15)	5WM	1584	0.05	R	Woomera
7)	7SH	1584	0.1	R	St. Helens
29)	2CP	1602	0.05	R	Cooma
16)	3WL	1602	0.25	R	Warrnambool
15)	5LC	1602	0.1	R	Leigh Creek South

FM stations (Transmitters of greater than 1kW)
Networks: N=Radio National, R/M=Regional or Metropolitan Network, FM=Fine Music Network, JJJ=Triple J Network (alternative).

	Area	State	N	R/M	FM	JJJ
5)	Adelaide	SA			103.9	105.5
5)	Adel. Foothills	SA	-		97.5	95.9
3)	Alexandra	Vic	104.5	102.9		
17)	Armidale	NSW		101.9	103.5	101.1
3)	Bairnsdale	Vic	106.3			
42)	Ballarat	Vic		107.9	105.5	107.1
29)	Batemans Bay	NSW	105.1	103.5	101.9	
2)	Bega/Cooma	NSW	100.9		99.3	100.1
12)	Bendigo	Vic		91.1	92.7	90.3
29)	Bombala	NSW		94.1		
2)	Bourke	NSW	101.1			
4)	Brisbane	Qld			106.1	107.7
5)	Broken Hill	NSW	102.9		103.7	102.1
6)	Broome	WA	107.7			
6)	Bunbury	WA			93.3	94.1
24)	Burnie	Tas		102.5		
14)	Cairns	Qld	105.1	106.7	105.9	107.5
14)	Cairns North	Qld	93.9	95.5	94.7	97.1
1)	Canberra	ACT		102.3	101.5	103.9
6)	Cen.Agricult	WA			98.9	98.1
5)	Central East	SA			105.1	101.9
2)	Cen.Table'nds	NSW	104.3		102.7	101.9
38)	Cen. Western	NSW	107.9	107.1	105.5	102.3
4)	Darling Downs	Qld	105.7		107.3	104.1
8)	Darwin	NT		105.7	107.3	103.3
2)	Deniliquin	NSW	99.3			
4)	Emerald	Qld	93.9		90.7	
6)	Esperance	WA	106.3		104.7	
6)	Geraldton	WA	99.7		94.9	98.9
2)	Glen Innes	NSW	105.1			
11)	Gold Coast	Qld	90.1	91.7	88.5	97.7
12)	Goulburn V.	Vic		97.7	96.1	94.5
25)	Grafton/Kemp.	NSW	99.5	92.3	97.9	91.5
31)	Gympie	Qld	96.9	95.3	93.7	
9)	Hay	NSW	88.9	88.1		
7)	Hobart	Tas			93.9	92.9
27)	Illawara	NSW	97.3	95.7	98.9	90.9
2)	Jerilderie	NSW	94.1			
6)	Kalgoorlie	WA	97.1		95.5	98.7
28)	Katherine	NT		106.1		
5)	Keith	SA	96.9			
24)	King Island	Tas		88.5		
3)	Latrobe Valley	Vic		100.7	101.5	96.7
7)	Launceston	Tas	94.1		93.3	90.9
24)	Lileah	Tas	89.7	91.3		
25)	Lismore	NSW	96.9	94.5	95.3	96.1
4)	Longreach	Qld	99.1			
19)	Mackay	Qld	102.7	101.1	97.9	99.5
21)	Manning River	NSW	97.1	95.5	98.7	96.3
4)	Meandarra	Qld	104.3			
3)	Melbourne	Vic			105.9	107.5
35)	Mildura	Vic	105.9	104.3	102.7	101.1
4)	Mission Beach	Qld	90.9	89.3		
4)	Monto	Qld	101.9			
30)	Moranbah	Qld	106.5	104.9		
4)	Mossman	Qld	90.1			
4)	Mount Isa	Qld	107.3	106.5	101.7	104.1
5)	Mt Gambier	SA	103.3		104.1	102.5
3)	Murray Valley	Vic		102.1	103.7	105.3
20)	Murrumbidgee	NSW	98.9	100.5	97.3	96.5
12)	Nambour	Qld		90.3	88.7	89.5
6)	Narrogin	WA			92.5	
2)	Newcastle	NSW			106.1	102.1
3)	Nhill	Vic	95.7			
6)	Perth	WA			97.7	99.3
6)	Port Hedland	WA	95.7			
2)	Port Stephens	NSW	98.3	95.7		
16)	Portland	Vic	98.5	96.9		
5)	Renmark	SA			105.1	101.9
4)	Rockhampton	Qld	103.1		106.3	104.7
6)	Roebourne	WA	107.5			
4)	Roma	Qld	107.3	105.7	97.7	
5)	Roxby Downs	SA	101.9	102.7	103.5	
6)	Salmon Gums	WA	100.7			
6)	S. Agricultural	WA	96.9		94.5	92.9
6)	South'n Cross	WA	107.9	106.3		
23)	South'n Downs	Qld	106.5	104.9	101.7	103.3
5)	Spencer Gulf N	SA	106.7		104.3	103.5
5)	Streaky Bay	SA	100.9			103.3
20)	SW Slopes	NSW	89.1	89.9	88.3	90.7
2)	Sydney	NSW			92.9	105.7
2)	Tamworth	NSW	93.9		103.1	94.7
4)	Townsville	Qld	104.7		101.5	105.5
5)	Tumby Bay	SA	101.9			
33)	Upper Hunter	NSW		105.7		
20)	Upper Murray	VIC		106.5	104.1	103.3
6)	Upper Namoi	NSW	100.7	99.1	96.7	99.9
3)	Warrnambool	Vic	101.7		92.1	89.7
8)	Western Vic.	Vic	92.5	94.1	93.3	94.9
31)	Wide Bay	Qld	100.9	100.1	98.5	99.3
4)	Winton	Qld	107.9			
5)	Wirrulla	SA	107.3			
5)	Wudinna	SA	107.7			105.3
3)	Yackandandah	Vic	99.9			

Note: Parliamentary News Network: 92.5 NE Tasmania (192d), 95/7 GoldCoast (26d)Darwin 102.5 MHz, Gold Coast on 95.7.
Reports for Radio National, Parliament, ABC-FM and Triple J should go to the capital city ABC office in that state (Addresses 1-8)

ABC regional addresses:
1) GPO Box 365, Canberra ACT 2601 – **2)** PO Box 487 Sydney NSW 2001 – **3)** GPO Box 1686, Melbourne VIC 3001 – **4)** GPO Box 293, Brisbane QLD 4001 – **5)** GPO Box 1419H, Adelaide SA 5001 – **6)** GPO Box 190D Perth WA 6001 – **7)** GPO Box 9994, Hobart TAS 7001 – **8)** PO Box 9994, Darwin NT 0800 – **9)** 100 Fitzmaurice St, Wagga Wagga NSW 2650 – **10)** PO Box 387 Port Hedland WA 6721 – **11)** PO Box 217, Mermaid Beach QLD 4217 – **12)** PO Box 1922, Shepparton VIC 3630 – **13)** PO Box 489 Albany WA 6330 – **14)** PO Box 932 Cairns QLD 4870 – **15)** PO Box 289 Port Pirie SA 5540 – **16)** Kepler St., Warrnambool VIC 3280 – **17)** PO Box 558 Tamworth NSW 2340 – **18)** PO Box 125 Kalgoorlie WA 6430 – **19)** PO Box 127, Mackay QLD 4740 – **20)** PO Box 321 Albury NSW 2640 – **21)** PO Box 76 West Kempsey NSW 2440 – **22)** PO Box 242 Bunbury WA 6230 – **23)** PO Box 358 Toowoomba QLD 4350 – **24)** PO Box 201 Launceston TAS 7250 – **25)** PO Box 435 Grafton NSW 2460 – **26)** PO Box 330 Sale VIC 3850 – **27)** cnr Kembla & Market Sts, Wollongong NSW 2520, – **28)** PO Box 1144 Alice Springs NT 0871 – **29)** PO Box 336 Bega NSW 2550 – **30)** PO Box 911 Rockhampton QLD 4700 – **31)** PO Box 376 Maryborough QLD 4650 – **32)** PO Box 315 Broken Hill NSW 2880 – **33)** 47 Newcomen St, Newcastle NSW 2300 – **34)** PO Box 448 Mount Gambier SA 5290 – **35)** PO Box 5051, Mildura VIC 3502 – **36)** PO Box 387 Geraldton WA 6530 – **37)** PO Box 318 Longreach QLD 4730 – **38)** PO Box 863 Orange NSW 2600 – **39)** PO Box 242 Bunbury WA 6230 – **40)** PO Box 694 Townsville QLD 4810 – **41)** PO Box 506 Horsham VIC 3400. – **42)** PO Box 637 Bendigo VIC 3550.

EXTERNAL SERVICE: Radio Australia
See International Broadcasting section.

DIGITAL RADIO – DAB

Digital Radio 2000 on 1483.7MHz. Regional stations on 202.928MHz

NORTHERN TERRITORY SHORTWAVE SERVICE

✉ Box 9994, Darwin, NT 0801.
VL8A Alice Springs: 2310 kHz (0830-2130), 4835 kHz (2130-0830), 3230 kHz (alt. freq) – **VL8T Tennant Creek:** 2325 kHz (0830-2130), 4910 kHz (2130-0830), 3315kHz (alt. freq) – **VL8K Katherine:** 2485kHz (0830-2130), 5025kHz (2130-0830), 3370kHz (alt. freq). Programming has been known to run over designated times.
D. PRGR. in English & Aboriginal languages:. Prgrs produced by Top End Aboriginal Bush Broadcasting Assoc. (TEABBA): VL8K: MF 2045-2330, 0730-0830. Rel. of ABC Alice Springs. All tr's 50kW

FEDERATION OF AUSTRALIAN RADIO BROADCASTERS

✉ PO Box 299, St. Leonards NSW 2065. ☎ +61 (2) 9906 5944. 🖷 +61 (2) 9906 5128. **L.P:** Federal Dir: Anthony M. King.
Abbreviations: N-1: News on the hour. N-2: News on the half hour. N-3: News on the hour and half hour. The numeral preceding the call letters indicates the state: 2=New South Wales,. 3=Victoria,

4=Queensland, 5=South Australia, 6=Western Australia; 7=Tasmania, 8=Northern Territory.
News: Additional newscasts are often carried during breakfast and drive times. t=translator (relays main station).

	Call	kHz	kW	Location
1)	2PM	531	5(d)	Port Macquarie
2)	3GG	531	5(d)	Warragul
3)	4KZ	531	5(d)	Innisfail
4)	7SD	540	5(d)	Scottsdale
5)	4AM	558	5(d)	Atherton
6)	4GY	558	5(d)	Gympie
7)	7BU	558	2	Burnie
8)	2BH	567	0.5	Broken Hill
164)	6EL	621	2	Bunbury
133)	2HC	639	5(d)	Coffs Harbour
33)	4CC(t)	666	2(d)	Biloela
103)	4LM	666	2	Mount Isa
160)	6LN	666	1	Carnarvon
105)	3EE	693	5(d)	Melbourne
9)	4KQ	693	5(d)	Brisbane
3)	4KZ(t)	693	0.5	Tully
103)	4LM(t)	693	0.5	Cloncurry
165)	6WR	693	5	Kununurra
31)	6FMS	747	1	Exmouth
131)	6SE	747	5	Esperance
166)	6TZ	756	2	Margaret River
10)	2EC	765	4(d)	Bega
73)	4GC(t)	765	0.5	Hughenden
134)	5CC	765	5(d)	Port Lincoln
88)	6SAT	765	0.1	Paraburdoo
88)	6SAT	765	0.1	Tom Price
147)	8HOT(t)	765	0.5	Katherine
11)	4TO	774	5(d)	Townsville
13)	6VA	783	2	Albany
14)	5RM	801	2	Berri
73)	4GC	828	1	Charters Towers
16)	7XS	837	0.5(d)	Queenstown
17)	4EL	846	5(d)	Cairns
18)	4GR	864	2	Toowoomba
19)	6AM	864	2	Northam
21)	2GB	873	5	Sydney
22)	3YB	882	2(d)	Warrnambool
24)	4BH	882	5(d)	Brisbane
23)	6PR	882	2	Perth
25)	2LM	900	5(d)	Lismore
107)	2LT	900	5(d)	Lithgow
58)	6BY	900	2	Bridgetown
27)	7AD	900	2	Devonport
28)	8HA	900	2	Alice Springs
29)	2XL	918	2	Cooma
153)	4VL	918	2	Charleville
164)	6NA	918	2	Narrogin
32)	3UZ	927	5	Melbourne
33)	4CC	927	5(d)	Gladstone
69)	4HI(t)	945	1(d)	Dysart
36)	2UE	954	5	Sydney
17)	4EL(t)	954	0.35	Gordonvale
38)	2RG	963	5(d)	Griffith
37)	4WK	963	5(d)	Warwick
93)	5SE	963	5(d)	Mt. Gambier
164)	6TZ	963	2	Bunbury
86)	2DU(t)	972	0.3	Cobar
39)	2MW	972	5	Murwillumbah
112)	2NM	981	5(d)	Muswellbrook
41)	3HA	981	2	Hamilton
42)	6KG	981	2	Kalgoorlie
43)	4RO	990	5(d)	Rockhampton
45)	2ST	999	5(d)	Nowra
46)	4TAB	1008	5(d)	Brisbane
48)	7TAB	1008	5(d)	Launceston
49)	2KY	1017	5	Sydney
139)	4MK	1026	5(d)	Mackay
52)	6NW	1026	2	Port Hedland
53)	5CS	1044	2	Port Pirie
54)	2CA	1053	5(d)	Canberra
55)	3EL	1071	5(d)	Maryborough
56)	4SB	1071	2	Kingaroy
151)	6WB	1071	2	Katanning
57)	2MO	1080	2	Gunnedah
167)	6IX	1080	2	Perth
59)	2EL	1089	5(d)	Orange
60)	3WM	1089	5(d)	Horsham
61)	4LG	1098	2	Longreach
62)	6MD	1098	2	Merredin
63)	7LA	1098	5(d)	Launceston
156)	3AK	1116	2	Melbourne
65)	4BC	1116	5(d)	Brisbane
135)	6MM	1116	2	Mandurah
43)	4RO(t)	1125	0.5	Gladstone
113)	5MU	1125	5(d)	Murray Bridge
66)	2AD	1134	2(d)	Armidale
67)	3CS	1134	5(d)	Colac
164)	6TZ(t)	1134	2	Collie
68)	2HD	1143	2	Newcastle
69)	4HI	1143	5(d)	Emerald
70)	2WG	1152	2	Wagga Wagga
30)	4FC	1161	2	Maryborough
72)	2CH	1170	5	Sydney
75)	2NZ	1188	2	Inverell
26)	4BI	1197	1	Brisbane
80)	2CC	1206	5(d)	Canberra
78)	2GF	1206	5(d)	Grafton
69)	4HI(t)	1215	0.25	Moranbah
82)	3TR	1242	5(d)	Sale
85)	4AK	1242	2	Toowoomba
84)	5AU	1242	2(d)	Port Augusta
86)	2DU	1251	2	Dubbo
164)	6NAN	1251	2	Narrogin
32)	3SR	1260	2	Shepparton
148)	4MW	1260	2	Thursday Island
88)	6KA	1260	1	Karratha
89)	2SM	1269	5	Sydney
90)	3AW	1278	5	Melbourne
91)	2TM	1287	2	Tamworth
32)	3BT	1314	5(d)	Ballarat
40)	5DN	1323	2	Adelaide
98)	3SH	1332	2	Swan Hill
99)	4BU	1332	5(d)	Bundaberg
102)	2LF	1350	5(d)	Young
37)	4WK(t)	1359	0.3	Toowoomba
104)	2GN	1368	2	Goulburn
105)	3MP	1377	5(d)	Melbourne
106)	5AA	1395	5(d)	Adelaide
108)	2PK	1404	2	Parkes
5)	4AM(t)	1422	1(d)	Port Douglas
111)	2MG	1449	5(d)	Mudgee
32)	3ML	1467	2	Mildura
115)	4ZR	1476	2	Roma
116)	2AY	1494	2	Albury
117)	2BS	1503	5(d)	Bathurst
142)	6BAY	1512	5	Morawa
119)	2QN	1521	2	Deniliquin
120)	2VM	1530	2	Moree
121)	2RE	1557	2	Taree
122)	3NE	1566	5(d)	Wangaratta
10)	2EC(t)	1584	0.2	Narooma
33)	4CC(t)	1584	0.5	Rockhampton
153)	4VL(t)	1584	0.2	Cunnamulla

FM Stations (1kW and higher)

	Call	MHz	kW	Location
3)	4KZ(t)	88.5	1(d)	Mission Beach
41)	3HFM_	88.9	20(d)	Hamilton
46)	4TAB	89.7	5(d)	Beaudesert
56)	4KRY	89.1	15	Kingaroy
71)	5CCC	89.9	6(d)	Port Lincoln
130)	5SSA (t)	90.3	2(d)	Adelaide Foothills
150)	4RBL	90.5	5(d)	Beaudesert
154)	4SEA	90.9	25(d)	Gold Coast
168)	4MCY	91.1	10(d)	Nambour
123)	2MAC	91.3	1	Campbelltown
120)	2NOW(t)	91.3	1	Lightning Ridge
17)	4HOT(t)	91.7	1	Mossman
52)	6HED	91.7	2	Port Hedland
55)	3BDG	91.9	120(d)	Bendigo
18)	4RDG	91.9	2	Warwick
15)	4SEE	91.9	10(d)	Nambour
169)	5ADL	91.9	20(d)	Adelaide
150)	4BRZ	92.1	5(d)	Beaudesert
16)	7AUS	92.1	20(d)	Queenstown/Zeehan
155)	4GLD	92.5	25(d)	Gold Coast

	Call	MHz	kW	Location
86)	2ZOO	92.7	10	Dubbo
15)	4SSS	92.7	10(d)	Nambour
29)	2SKI(t)	92.9	1	Thredbo
91)	2TTT	92.9	20(d)	Tamworth
120)	2VM(t)	92.9	1	Lightning Ridge
44)	6PPM	92.9	40(d)	Perth
70)	2WZD	93.1	80	Wagga Wagga
154)	4RGB	93.1	3(d)	Bundaberg
14)	5RIV	93.1	10(d)	Renmark/Loxton
163)	2DBO	93.5	10	Dubbo
104)	2SNO	93.5	40	Goulburn
35)	3BBO	93.5	120(d)	Bendigo
43)	4ROK	93.5	1(d)	Gladstone
41)	3HFM(t)	93.7	2	Portland
87)	3SUN(t)	93.7	1.2(d)	Mount Buller
87)	3SUN(t)	93.7	1(d)	Yea
150)	4SUN	93.7	4	Tenterfield (NSW)
47)	6PER	93.7	40(d)	Perth
102)	2LFF	93.9	40	Young
101)	3BAY	93.9	55(d)	Geelong
99)	4RUM	93.9	3.2(d)	Bundaberg
2)	3SEA	94.3	7	Warragul
79)	6MIX	94.5	40(d)	Perth
29)	2SKI(t)	94.7	2	Jindabyne
69)	4HIT(t)	94.7	5	Emerald
45)	2WSK	94.9	50(d)	Nowra
141)	4MIX	94.9	50(d)	Ipswich
88)	6KAN	94.9	5	Katanning
75)	2GEM	95.1	10	Inverell
43)	4RGK	95.1	1(d)	Gladstone
115)	4ROM	95.1	1	Roma
32)	3SRR	95.3	100(d)	Shepparton
162)	3YFM	95.3	20(d)	Warrnambool
13)	6AAY	95.3	50(d)	Albany
108)	2ROK	95.5	10	Parkes/Forbes
101)	3CAT	95.5	55(d)	Geelong
151)	6BUN	95.7	40(d)	Bunbury
73)	4CHT	95.9	1.5	Charters Towers
12)	2ONE	96.1	5	Katoomba
6)	4NNN	96.1	5(d)	Gympie
93)	5SEF	96.1	20	Mount Gambier
125)	6NOW	96.1	40(d)	Perth
29)	2XL(t)	96.3	2(d)	Jindabyne
95)	2UUL	96.5	40(d)	Wollongong
142)	6GGG	96.5	30(d)	Geraldton
19)	6NAM	96.5	10	Northam
40)	5ADD	96.7	2(d)	Adelaide Foothills
161)	2SYD	96.9	150(d)	Sydney
118)	3SUN	96.9	100(d)	Shepparton
159)	4BFM	97.1	12	Brisbane
135)	6CST	97.3	5(d)	Mandurah
57)	2GGG	97.5	20(d)	Gunnedah
29)	2SKI	97.7	50(d)	Cooma
170)	8SAT	97.7	3(d)	Coonalpyn
136)	3RMR	97.9	12(d)	Mildura
5)	4AMM	97.9	5(d)	Atherton
42)	6KAR	97.9	6	Kalgoorlie
112)	2VLY	98.1	20(d)	Muswellbrook
123)	2WIN	98.1	40(d)	Wollongong
142)	6BAY	98.1	30(d)	Geraldton
120)	2NOW	98.3	100(d)	Moree
11)	4TOO	98.3	2(d)	Townsville
3)	4ZKZ	98.3	20(d)	Innisfail
77)	5MMM(t)	98.3	2(d)	Adelaide Foothills
60)	3WWM(t)	98.5	1(d)	Ararat
98)	3SHI(t)	98.7	1	Kerang
158)	4RGM	98.7	100(d)	Mackay
113)	5EZY	98.7	20(d)	Murray Bridge
169)	5ADL	99.1	2(d)	Adelaide Foothills
117)	2BXS	99.3	10	Bathurst
114)	3MDA	99.5	20(d)	Mildura
82)	3TFM	99.5	20(d)	Sale
150)	4RBL	99.5	1	Meandarra
157)	4RGC	99.5	10(d)	Cairns
38)	2RGF	99.7	50	Griffith
113)	5EZY	99.7	1	Victor Harbour
132)	6CAR	99.7	10	Carnarvon
154)	7RGS	99.7	5(d)	Scottsdale
82)	3TFM(t)	99.9	5(d)	Bairnsdale
147)	8HOT	100.1	16	Darwin
66)	2NEB	100.3	10	Armidale
121)	2RE(t)	100.3	1.6	Forster
143)	3MEL	100.3	56(d)	Melbourne
51)	4MKY	100.3	100(d)	Mackay
113)	5EZY(t)	100.3	1	Mount Barker
88)	6BET	100.5	5	Bridgetown
164)	6NAN	100.5	5	Narrogin
1)	2PQQ	100.7	20(d)	Port Macquarie
18)	4RGD	100.7	10(d)	Toowoomba
11)	4RGR	100.7	100(d)	Townsville
25)	2ZZZ	100.9	32(d)	Lismore
144)	7TTT	100.9	36	Hobart
50)	3TTT	101.1	56(d)	Melbourne
140)	2CFM	101.3	16	Gosford
60)	3WWM	101.3	20(d)	Horsham
145)	6HED	101.3	2	Broome
43)	4RGK	101.5	10	Rockhampton
81)	2UUS	101.7	150(d)	Sydney
33)	4CCC	101.7	2	Charleville
20)	7HHO	101.7	36	Hobart
120)	2NOW(t)	101.9	1	Collarenebri
126)	3FOX	101.9	56(d)	Melbourne
149)	4CEE	101.9	10(d)	Maryborough
139)	4MMK	101.9	100(d)	Mackay
122)	3NNN	102.1	25(d)	Wangaratta
1)	2ROX	102.3	20	Port Macquarie
94)	3RBA	102.3	20(d)	Ballarat
11)	4TOO	102.3	100(d)	Townsville
40)	5ADD	102.3	20(d)	Adelaide
131)	6SEA	102.3	5	Esperance
10)	2EEE	102.5	5	Bega
119)	2MOR	102.5	50	Deniliquin
150)	4BRZ	102.5	1	Childers
96)	4CCA	102.7	10(d)	Cairns
109)	2KKO	102.9	20(d)	Newcastle
45)	2ST	102.9	2	Bowral
52)	6NW	102.9	2	Broome
94)	3BBA	103.1	20(d)	Ballarat
76)	4HTB	102.9	25(d)	Gold Coast
34)	4RAM	103.1	100(d)	Townsville
120)	2VM(t)	103.5	1	Collarenebri
96)	4HOT	103.5	10(d)	Cairns
149)	4MBB	103.5	10(d)	Maryborough
128)	2DAY	104.1	150(d)	Sydney
39)	2MW(t)	104.1	1(d)	Gold Coast
10)	2EEE	104.3	20(d)	Batemans Bay/Moruya
74)	3KKZ	104.3	56(d)	Melbourne
61)	4LRE	104.5	1(d)	Longreach
127)	4MMM	104.5	12	Brisbane
171)	2GOS	104.5	16	Gosford
78)	2CLR	104.7	20(d)	Grafton
138)	2ROC	104.7	20	Canberra
77)	5MMM	104.7	16(d)	Adelaide
116)	2AAY	104.9	100(d)	Albury
129)	2MMM	104.9	150(d)	Sydney
150)	4RBL	104.9	3	Bourke
146)	8MIX	104.9	15	Darwin
120)	2NOW(t)	105.1	1	Walgett
59)	2OAG	105.1	5	Orange
1)	2ROX	105.1	10(d)	Kempsey
124)	3MMM	105.1	56(d)	Melbourne
150)	4RBL	105.1	1	Monto
62)	6MER	105.1	10	Merredin
139)	2NEW	105.3	20(d)	Newcastle
92)	4BBB	105.3	12	Brisbane
133)	2CSF	105.5	15	Coffs Harbour
10)	2EC(t)	105.5	1	Eden
120)	2VM(t)	105.5	1	Mungindi
83)	2BDR	105.7	100(d)	Albury
10)	2EC(t)	105.9	20(d)	Batemans Bay/Moruya
84)	5AUU	105.9	20	Spencer Gulf North
137)	1CBR	106.3	20	Canberra
133)	2CFS	106.3	15	Coffs Harbour
67)	3CCS	106.3	10(d)	Colac
11)	4RGT	106.3	100(d)	Townsville
64)	2WFM	106.5	150(d)	Sydney
88)	6RED	106.5	1	Karratha
1)	2PQQ	106.7	10(d)	Kempsey
45)	2ST(t)	106.7	1.6	Ulladulla
120)	2VM(t)	106.7	1	Walgett

	Call	MHz	kW	Location
150)	4RBL	106.7	1	Childers
100)	2XXX	106.9	20(d)	Newcastle
146)	8MIX	106.9	1	Katherine
120)	2NOW(t)	107.1	1	Mungindi
130)	5SSA	107.1	16(d)	Adelaide
121)	2MVB	107.3	10(d)	Taree
152)	7XXX	107.3	36	Hobart
97)	2GGO	107.7	16	Gosford
98)	3SHI	107.7	10	Swan Hill
27)	7DDD	107.7	7(d)	Devonport
107)	2ICE	107.9	1	Lithgow
34)	4RAM(t)	107.9	2(d)	Bowen
43)	4ROK	107.9	10	Rockhampton

Addresses and other information (ARN:Australian Radio Network). **NB:** The term midnight-to-dawn refers to local time. Exact hours vary from st. to st.

1) PO Box 1161, Port Macquarie NSW 2444 (DMG). Supplementary st. on 102.3 and 105.1. – **2)** PO Box 253, Warragul Vic. 3820. (N-2) – **3)** PO Box 19, Innisfail, Qld. 4860 **Email:** zedamfm@4kz.com.au (N-1:) Translators: Tully 693kHz 0.5kW, Dunk Island 88.5MHz 0.5kW. – **4)** PO Box 189, Scottsdale, TAS. 7254 (N-1).Part of TASmanian Broadcasting Network – **5)** PO Box 177, Mareeba, QLD 4880 (N-1) Translators: Port Douglas 1422 kHz, Weipa 97.7 MHz. – **6)** PO Box 42, Gympie QLD 4370 (N-1). – **7)** PO Box 120, Burnie, TAS. 7320 (N-1) – **8)** 25 Garnet St, Broken Hill, NSW 2880 (N-3). Supplementary st. on 106.9 – **9)** PO Box 693, Newstead, QLD 4006 (N-1) – **10)** PO Box 471, Bega, NSW 2550 . Translators: 1584=Narooma, 105.9MHz = Batemans Bay. – **11)** PO Box 986, Townsville, QLD 4810. **Email:** fourto@ultra.net.au **Web:** www.ozemail.com.au/~asichter (N-1:). – **12)** PO Box 145, Penrith, NSW 2750 (N-1) – **13)** PO Box 293, Albany, WA 6330 . (N-1) – **14)** PO Box 321, Berri SA 5343 **Email:** fiverm@riverland.net. au. **Web:** www.riverland.net.au /~fiverm/ (N-1). – **15)** PO Box 828, Nambour, QLD 4560 (N-1) – **16)** PO Box 315, Queenstown, TAS 7467 (N-3). Translators at Strahan 105.1 MHz 25w & Rosebery 107.1 MHz 0.3kW – **17)** PO Box 6110, Cairns, QLD 4870. (N-1:Sky Radio) – **18)** PO Box 111, Toowoomba, QLD 4350 (N-1) – **19)** PO Box 256 Northam, WA 6401 – **20)** GPO Box 542F, Hobart, TAS 7001 (N-3) – **21)** GPO Box 4290, Sydney 2001 (N-3) – **22)** PO Box 485, Warrnambool, Vic. 3280 – **23)** GPO Box 6072, Perth, W.A. 6000 (N-1) – **24)** GPO Box 906, Brisbane, QLD 4001 (N-1) – **25)** PO Box 44, Lismore, NSW 2480 . (N-1) – **26)** Switch 1197, PO Box 1073, Fortitude Valley QLD 4006 – **27)** PO Box 635, Launceston TAS 7310 – **28)** PO Box 2106, Alice Springs 0871 (N-1).Translator at Yularaon 100.5MHz with 100w. Supplementary st. 8SUN on 96.9 MHz with 300w at Alice Springs – **29)** PO Box 651, Cooma, NSW 2630 (N-1) Relays 2UE 9:00am to 10:00am and AUSTEREO 4:00pm to 6:00pm. Translators: Thredbo 92.1 MHz 1kW, Jindabyne 96.3 MHz 2kW and Perisher 98.7 MHz 1kW – **30)** 625 Wyndham St, Shepparton, VIC 3630 – **31)** PO Box 665, Carnarvon WA 6701. – **32)** 3UZ Pty Ltd, PO Box 927, Carlton, VIC 3053 (N-1) ID's as "Sport 927" – **33)** PO Box 420, Gladstone, QLD 4680 . (N-1). Translator at Rockhampton on 1584 with 500w and at Biloela on 666kHz with 2.5 Kw – **34)** PO Box 986, Townsville, QLD 4810 (FM **Email:** hotfm@ultra.net.au) (N-1). 4RR: Racing format, programming 8:00am-midnight, also relays 4TAB 1008. 4RAM: Translator at Mt Stuart 107.9 MHz 1kW, ID's as "103.1 Hot FM" – **35)** PO Box 108, Golden Square, Vic. 3555 (N-1) – **36)** PO Box 950, North Sydney, NSW 2059 (N-3) – **37)** PO Box 195, Warwick, QLD 4370 (N-1) Rel 2TM 1287 7:00pm to 6:00am. Translator: Toowoomba 1359 kHz 0.3 kW – **38)** PO Box 493, Griffith, NSW 2680 (N-10) – **39)** PO Box 97, Coolangatta, QLD 4225 (N-1). Ids as "Radio 97" – **40)** 201 Tynte St, Nth Adelaide SA 5006. **Web:** www.5dn.com.au (N-1) – **41)** PO Box 981, Hamilton, VIC 3300 (N-1) – **42)** PO Box 440, Kalgoorlie, WA 6430 (N-1) – **43)** PO Box 159, Rockhampton, QLD 4700 (N-1) – **44)** PO Box 157, Subiaco, WA 6008 (N-1) – **45)** PO Box 540, Nowra 2540 (N-1). Translators: Uladulla 106.7MHz .Supplementary St. on 94.9 MHz. (N-1) – **46)** Radio 4TAB, PO Box 275, Albion, QLD 4010. Racing format – **47)** Level 1, 464 Hay St, Subiaco, WA 6008 – **48)** G.PO Box 572F, Hobart, TAS 7001 on 1008 kHz & 1080 kHz, 87.6 MHz 1W narrowcast throughout Queenstown, Strahan, Zeehan, Roseberry, Tullah, Stanley& Smithton (N-1:Sky Radio). Racing format. Rel 2UE M-F – **49)** PO Box 1303, Parramatta, NSW 2150 (N-3) Provides relays to over 100 NSW stations carrying racing: – **50)** Private Bag 1011, Richmond Vic. 3121 (N-1) – **51)** PO Box 183, Mackay, QLD 4740 (N-1). Airlie Beach on 94.7MHz. Bowen on 107.9MHz – **52)** PO Box 2216, South Hedland, WA 6722 . – **53)** PO Box 481, Pt. Pirie, SA 5540 (N-1) – **54)** G.PO Box 163, Canberra City, ACT 2601. **Web:** www.2ca.village.com.au (N-3). – **55)** PO Box 178, Bendigo VIC 3550. – **56)** PO Box 305, Kingaroy, QLD 4610 (N-1) ID's as "1071AM" and "Classic Gold" – **57)** PO Box 62, Gunnedah 2380 – **58)** 3 Gommes Lane, Yornup WA 6256.. – **59)** PO Box 88, Orange, NSW 2800 . (N-1:Sky Radio) – **60)** PO Box 606, Horsham, VIC 3400 . (N-1) – **61)** PO Box 20, Longreach, QLD 4730 – **62)** PO Box 264, Merredin, WA 6415. (N-1) – **63)** PO Box 835G, Launceston, TAS 7250 (N-3) – **64)** PO Box 1107, Neutral Bay NSW 2089 (N-1). ID's as "Mix 106.5 FM" – **65)** G.PO Box 95, Brisbane, QLD 4001 (N-1) – **66)** PO Box 270, Armidale, NSW 2350. **Email:** 2AD@mpx.com.au (N-1 – **67)** PO Box 63, Colac, Vic. 3250 (N-1). – **68)** PO Box 19, Mayfield, NSW 2304 (N-3) – **69)** PO Box 267, Emerald, QLD 4720 . (N-1). Translators: 945 kHz 1kW, 1215 kHz 0.1 kW, 88.1 MHz 30W, 92.5MHz 10W, 98.2 MHz 0.1 kW, 102.1 MHz 0.25 kW. Rel 4AM 558 kHz, 4ZR 1476 kHz, 4CC 927 kHz – **70)** PO Box 480, Wagga Wagga, NSW 2650. (N-1). Translator at Tumut on 107.9 MHz with 10w. Supplementary St. on 93.1 MHz. Both stns – **71)** PO Box 143, Maryborough, QLD 4650 . (N-1) – **72)** GPO Box 2516, Nth Sydney, NSW 2001 (N-1). – **73)** PO Box 381, Charters Towers, QLD 4820 Translator: Hughenden 765 kHz 0.5kW – **74)** Private Bag 1043, Richmond Vic. 3121 ID's as "Gold FM" – **75)** PO Box 770, Inverell, NSW 2360 . (N-3) – **76)** PO Box 10290, Southport BC, QLD 4215 – **77)** PO Box 1047, Unley, SA 5061 (N-1) Translator in Adelaide city on 98.3 MHz 0.5kW – **78)** PO Box 276, Grafton, NSW 2460 . (N-1). – **79)** PO Box 945, Subiaco, WA 6008 (N-1: BBC) – **80)** PO Box 1499, Canberra City, ACT 2601 (N-1) – **81)** PO Box 234, Seven Hills, NSW 2147 (N-1 – **82)** PO Box 160, Sale, Vic. 3850 (N-1) – **83)** 490 David Street, Albury NSW 2640 – **84)** PO Box 496, Port Augusta, SA 5700 (N-1) – **85)** PO Box 783, Toowoomba, QLD 4350 (N-1) – **86)** PO Box 1221, Dubbo, NSW 2830. **Email:** 2du@lisp.com.au . (N-1) FM station "ZOO FM" Dubbo 92.7 MHz, Cobar 103.7 MHz – **88)** PO Box 153, Karratha, WA 6714. (N-1) – **89)** 8 Jones Bay Road, Pyrmont NSW 2009 **Email:** contact@kick-am.com.au. **Web:** www.kick-am.com.au/ (N-1) ID's as "Kick AM" – **90)** GPO Box 369F, Melbourne 3001. **Web:** www.3aw.com.au/ – **91)** PO Box 497, Tamworth, NSW 2340 (N-1). Supplementary stn. on 92.9 MHz – **92)** PO Box 105, Albion, QLD 4010 (N-1) ID's as "B105" – **93)** PO Box 500, Mt. Gambier, SA 5290 (N-1) – **94)** PO Box 360, Ballarat, VIC 3350 . (N-1) – **95)** PO Box 1234, Wollongong, NSW 2500. **Email:** mike@w151.aone.net.au (N-1) – **96)** Abbott St Cairns QLD 4870 – **97)** PO Box 564, Gosford, NSW 2250 (N-1) – **98)** PO Box 504, Swan Hill, VIC 3585 (N-1) – **99)** PO Box 1059, Bundaberg, QLD 4670 (N-1) – **100)** PO Box 97, Charlestown, NSW 2290 (N-1) – **101)** PO Box 9550, Geelong, VIC 3220. **Email:** krock@slanreach.au (N-1). ID's as "K-Rock" – **102)** PO Box 31, Young, NSW 2594 (N-1). – **103)** PO Box 780, Mount Isa, QLD 4825 (N-1). Relays to 4GC 828. Translator: Cloncurry 693 kHz. Supplementary FM license at Mt. Isa . (N-1) – **104)** PO Box 115, Goulburn, NSW 2580 (N-1: Sky Radio) – **105)** PO Box 75, Frankston, Vic. 3199. **Email:** magic@magic.com.au (N-1). 3EE ID's as "Magic" – **106)** GPO Box 5AA, Adelaide SA 5001 (N-1) – **107)** Mailbag 90, Lithgow, NSW 2790. **Email:** 2lt@lisp.com.au . (N-1) (for QSL'ing purposes) c/o John Wright, 15 Olive Cres, Peakhurst NSW 2210. – **108)** PO Box 295, Parkes, NSW 2870 . (N-1) – **109)** PO Box 606, Charlestown, NSW 2290 . (N-1) – **111)** PO Box 17, Mudgee, NSW 2850 – **112)** PO Box 600, Muswelbrook, NSW 2333 (N-1) 2VLY 98.1 ID's as "Power FM" – **113)** PO Box 470, Murray Bridge, SA 5253 (N-1). Serves Murray Bridge, The Coorong and Meningie. – **114)** PO Box 539, Mildura, VIC 3500 (N-1). 3MA 99.5 ID's as "Today's Music 99.5FM" – **115)** PO Box 22, Roma, QLD 4455 . (N-1:Sky Radio) – **116)** PO Box 670, Albury, NSW 2640. **Web:** www.albury.net.au/ radio.albury.wodonga/2ay. html (N-1). Supplementary stn. on FM – **117)** PO Box 310, Bathurst, NSW 2795. **Email:** stereo@2bs.ix.net .au or 2bs@csu.edu.au. **Web:** www.2bs.ix.net.au (N-1) FM service on 99.3 MHz – **118)** PO Box 195, Shepparton, Vic. 3630 – **119)** PO Box 312, Deniliquin, NSW 2710 . (N-1) 2MOR 102.5 ID's as "Classic Rock 102.5" – **120)** PO Box 389, Moree, NSW 2400 . (N-1). Supplementary license on 98.3 MHz . Translator on 88.7 MHz with 250w r. (N-1) – **121)** PO Box 275, Taree, NSW 2430 (N-1). Translator: Gloucester 100.1MHz and Forster on 100.3 MHz – **122)** PO Box 449, Wangaratta, VIC 3677 (N-1). 3NE Translators: Mt. Hotham 89.3MHz 0.02kW, Mt. Buffalo 105.3MHz 0.2kW, Mt. Beauty 90.3MHz 10w. 3NNN ID's as "Edge FM" – **123)** Locked Bag 6198 Sth Coast Mail Centre NSW 2521 (N-1) ID's as "98FM" – **124)** GPO Box 105, Melbourne, VIC (N-1) – **125)** 111 Wellington Str, East Perth, WA 6004 . (N-1) – **126)** PO Box 1019, St. Kilda, Vic. 3182 (N-1) – **127)** GPO Box 1041, Brisbane, QLD 4001 . (N-1) – **128)** PO Box 920, Crows Nest, NSW 2065. **Web:** www.2dayfm.com.au (N-1) – **129)** GPO Box 442, Sydney, NSW 2001 (N-1). **Web:** www.mrock.com.au – **130)** PO Box 1071, Unley, SA 5061.24h (N-1) Translator South Tce, Adelaide on 91.1 MHz 1kW. ID's as "SAFM" – **131)** PO Box 527, Esperance, WA 6450 . N-1. Rel. 6PPM-FM 1000-2200 – **132)** PO Box 665, Carnarvon, WA 6701. 2200-1500 (N-1). Translator: Exmouth – **133)** PO Box 1950, Coffs Harbour, NSW 2450 (N-1). Rp – **134)** PO Box 483, Port Lincoln, SA 5606 . (N-1). – **135)** 141 Mandurah Tce, Mandurah, WA 6210 (N-1). – **136)** GPO Box 163, Canberra, ACT 2601 . Belongs to 54). **F.PI:** translator for Tuggeranong area – **137)** PO Box 106, Dickson, ACT 2602 . (N-1) ID's as "Mix 106.3" – **138)** GPO Box 163, Canberra, A.C.T. 2601 (N-1) – **139)** PO Box 185, Mackay QLD 4740 – **140)** PO Box 2101, Gosford, NSW 2250 . (N-1) – **141)** PO Box 7, Ipswich, QLD 4305 (N-1) ID's as "Mix 106.9 QFM" – **142)** PO Box 128 Geraldton, WA 6530. 24 h (N-1) – **143)** Nova 100, 678 Victoria Street, Richmond, VIC 3121 – **144)** G.PO Box 1800, Hobart, TAS. 7001 (N-1) – **145)** PO Box 810, Croydon VIC 3136 – **146)** GPO Box 2510, Darwin NT 0801 – **147)** 4 Peary St., Darwin, NT 0800 (N-1) Translators: Katherine 765 kHz 0.5 kW. – **148)** PO Box 385, Thursday Island QLD 4875 – **149)** 403 The Esplanade, Torquay QLD 4655 – **150)** PO Box 332, Beaudesert QLD 4285 – **151)** PO Box 148, Bunbury WA 6231 – **152)** GPO Box 1345, Hobart TAS 7001 – **153)** PO Box 84, Charleville, QLD 4470 (N-1) ID's as

"Outback Radio". Translator: Cunnamulla 1584 kHz 0.2 kW. – **154)** PO Box 5910 Gold Coast Mail Centre Bundall QLD 4217 r. (N-1) – **155)** Private Bag 925 Gold Coast Mail Centre QLD 4215 . (N-1). – **156)** Paul Taylor, 41 Allards Crt., Clifton Springs VIC 3222 – **157)** Sea FM, 320 Sheridan St Cairns QLD 4870 – **158)** Sea FM, Suncorp/Metway Building Suite 3, Level 3, 123 Victoria St Mackay QLD 4740 – **159)** 444 Logan Rd, Stones Corner QLD 4120 – **160)** PO Box 665 Carnarvon WA 6701 – **161)** 33 Saunders Road, Pyrmont NSW 2009 – **162)** Regional Communications Pty Ltd, PO Box 7515, St Kilda Road VIC 3004 – **163)** 47 Wingewarra St Dubbo NSW 2830 – **164)** DMG Regional Radio, Locked Bag 5000, Broadway NSW 2007 – **165)** Waringarri Media Aboriginal Corporation, PO Box 815 Kununurra WA 6743 – **166)** PO Box 112, Bunbury WA 6230 – **167)** PO Box 33, Tuart Hill WA 6060 **168)** cnr Plaza Pde & Carnaby St, Maroochydore QLD 4558 – **169)** Locked Bag 919, Adelaide SA 5001 – **170)** PO Box 579, Lilydale VIC 3140 - **171)** PO Box 3535, Erina NSW 2250.

COMMUNITY BROADCASTING ASSOCIATION OF AUSTRALIA

✉ Suite One, Level Three, 44-54 Botany Rd. Alexandria, NSW 2015. ☎ +61 (2) 9310 2999. 🖷 +61 (2) 9319 4545.

PRN: Public Radio Network, CBAA: Community Broadcasting Association of Australia. CBAA provides ComRadSat.

PUBLIC BROADCASTING STATIONS

MW	Call	kHz	kW	MW	Call	kHz	kW
1)	2WEB	585	5(d)	7)	1RPH	1125	2(d)
2)	6WR	693	5	9)	3RPH	1179	5
3)	3CR	855	2(d)	8)	4BI	1197	1
4)	7RPH	864	2	10)	5RPH	1197	2
210)	6FX	936	5	11)	2RPH	1224	5
6)	6RPH	990	2	12)	4RPH	1296	5(d)
				209)	3KND	1503	5

FM	Call	MHz	kW	Location
9)	3BPH	88.7	10	Bendigo
13)	2RBR	88.9	1(d)	Coraki
14)	2YOU	88.9	1(d)	Tamworth
15)	2SCR	89.1	1	Barham
148)	5BBB	89.1	1	Barossa Valley
16)	4CCC	89.3	2	Warwick
149)	5EFM	89.3	1	Victor Harbour
150)	5GFM	89.3	10	Arhurton
18)	3CCC	89.5	10	Bendigo
151)	3MFM	89.5	1(d)	Foster
19)	2TEN	89.7	4	Tenterfield
17)	4CRB	89.7	25(d)	Gold Coast
147)	5TCB(t)	89.7	1.6(d)	Naracoorte
152)	3TSC	89.9	56(d)	Melbourne
153)	5GSFM	90.1	1	Victor Harbour
20)	4DDD	89.9	2	Dalby
153)	3SYN	90.7	56(d)	Melbourne
21)	4CSB	90.7	5	Wondai
22)	5KIX	90.7	3(d)	Kangaroo Island
211)	8SAT	90.9	1(d)	Maitland SA
23)	1CMS	91.1	20	Canberra
24)	2CBD	91.1	5	Deepwater
25)	2MAX	91.3	10(d)	Narrabri
1)	2WEB	91.3	1(d)	Coonamble
26)	4GCR	91.5	1	Gympie
27)	1WAY	91.9	20	Canberra
28)	4RGL	91.9	1	Gladstone
29)	2ARM	92.1	2	Armidale
30)	2MFM	92.1	6	Sydney
31)	6RTR	92.1	10(d)	Perth
32)	7THE	92.1	4.8	Hobart
33)	2MCE	92.3	2	Bathurst
34)	3ZZZ	92.3	56(d)	Melbourne
35)	1ART	92.7	20	Canberra
155)	5FBI	92.7	20(d)	Adelaide
36)	2NCR	92.9	6	Lismore
37)	4GOD	92.9	4	Toowoomba
38)	2BBB	93.3	3.2	Dorrigo
156)	2MNO	93.3	2	Monaro
157)	2SNR	93.3	2	Gosford
9)	3RPH	93.5	1	Warragul
39)	2BAR	93.7	2	Bega
212)	2LND	93.7	1.5	Sydney
40)	5DDD	93.7	6.3	Adelaide
158)	2CCH	94.1	2	Gosford
41)	2LIV	94.1	4(d)	Wollongong/Nowra
42)	4RHI	94.1	2(d)	Gold Coast
43)	2DCB	94.3	10	Dubbo
213)	2FBI	94.5	150(d)	Sydney
9)	3RPH	94.5	5(d)	Warrnambool
44)	5CCR	94.5	1	Ceduna/Smoky Bay
45)	8KNB	94.5	15	Perth
33)	2MCE	94.7	1(d)	Orange
46)	3YYR	94.7	56(d)	Geelong
47)	4BCR	94.7	3(d)	Bundaberg
160)	2MIA	95.1	5	Griffith
161)	6EBA	95.3	16(d)	Perth
162)	7HRT	95.7	1(d)	Nthn Midlands TAS
214)	4___	95.9	1	Esk
48)	2CCC	96.3	2	Gosford
49)	3GGR	96.3	56(d)	Geelong
50)	2CHR	96.5	2(d)	Cessnock/Maitland
51)	3EON	96.5	1(d)	Bendigo (city)
52)	4FRB	96.5	12	Brisbane
215)	2QBN	96.7	5(d)	Queanbeyan
53)	2MAQ	97.3	1	Lake Macquarie
54)	3HCR	97.3	1	Omeo
165)	7TAS	97.7	1	Tasman Peninsula
55)	8GGG	97.7	15	Darwin
56)	2LVR	97.9	1(d)	Parkes/Forbes
57)	6DBY	97.9	2	Derby
58)	4EB	98.1	12	Brisbane
59)	1XXR	98.3	20	Canberra
60)	6MKA	98.3	1	Meekatharra
61)	2OOO	98.5	25(d)	Sydney
62)	3ONE	98.5	10(d)	Shepparton
167)	4YOU	98.5	1	Rockhampton
63)	6SON	98.5	16(d)	Perth
64)	2KRR	98.7	1	Kandos
65)	4CIM	98.7	10(d)	Cairns
66)	4AAA	98.9	9.5	Brisbane
67)	3RPC	99.3	2(d)	Portland
168)	7EDG	99.3	1	Hobart South
68)	2RFM	99.7	10(d)	Newcastle
69)	2UUU	99.7	1	Ulladulla
70)	3MCR	99.7	1	Mansfield
169)	4RED	99.7	2(d)	Redcliffe
71)	6GME	99.7	2	Broome
170)	2BAY	99.9	3	Byron Bay
72)	2PMQ	99.9	3	Port Macquarie
73)	3BBB	99.9	3	Ballarat
74)	4TCB	99.9	20	Townsville
171)	5MBS	99.9	2(d)	Adelaide Foothills
75)	2BCB	100.1	10	Bathurst
9)	3SPH	100.1	10(d)	Shepparton
172)	4RIM	100.1	1	Boonah
5)	6NR	100.1	6.5(d)	Perth
76)	2TLC	100.3	1	Maclean
216)	2YAS	100.3	2	Yass
77)	4BAY	100.3	4(d)	Wynnum/Redlands
1)	2WEB	100.7	1(d)	Nyngan
78)	3CH	100.7	1	Kyneton
79)	4US	100.7	1	Rockhampton
80)	6CRA	100.9	10	Albany
81)	4CBL	101.1	4(d)	Logan
82)	3WPR	101.3	2(d)	Wangaratta
83)	2GLA	101.5	10(d)	Forster
174)	4BSR	101.5	1	Beaudesert
84)	4OUR	101.5	1(d)	Caboolture
185)	5UV	101.5	20(d)	Adelaide
9)	2APH	101.7	2	Albury
85)	2GGZ	101.7	1	Muswellbrook
175)	4RRR	101.7	1	Roma
176)	6YMS	101.7	10(d)	Perth
177)	2PAR	101.9	1	Ballina
86)	4ZZZ	102.1	7.5(d)	Brisbane
87)	6WR	102.1	1	Wyndham
88)	2___	102.3	1	Nimbin
89)	2MBS	102.5	50(d)	Sydney
90)	3RRR	102.7	56(d)	Melbourne
178)	4DDB	102.7	4	Toowoomba
91)	2CVC	103.1	1	Grafton
92)	2WET	103.1	1	Kempsey
93)	5EBI	103.1	20(d)	Adelaide
94)	2CBA	103.2	8	Sydney
95)	2TLP	103.3	3(d)	Taree
97)	2CCB	103.5	5	Orange

	Call	kHz	kW	Location
98)	3MBR	103.5	4.8	Murrayville
99)	3MBS	103.5	56(d)	Melbourne
100)	2NUR	103.7	10(d)	Newcastle
101)	4MBS	103.7	12	Brisbane
179)	7LTN	103.7	3.2	Launceston
103)	2WAY	103.9	3	Port Macquarie
104)	3BGR	103.9	3	Ballarat
105)	4TTT	103.9	20	Townsville
106)	6ESP	103.9	5	Esperance
107)	2CHY	104.1	1.6	Coffs Harbour
108)	8TOP	104.1	16	Darwin
69)	2UUU	104.5	2	Nowra
147)	5TCB	104.5	1.6	Keith
109)	2BOB	104.7	5	Taree
110)	3GCR	104.7	7.9(d)	Latrobe Valley
111)	3GRR	104.7	5(d)	Echuca
112)	7DBS	104.7	2	Devonport
181)	4SDA	104.9	3	Nambour
182)	5RCB	104.9	20	Mt. Gambier
113)	4WBR	105.1	10(d)	Maryborough
114)	7WAY	105.3	3.2	Launceston
115)	4MET	105.7	1	Gold Coast
116)	2NVR	105.9	2(d)	Nambucca Heads
147)	5TCB	106.1	1.6	Bordertown
112)	7DBS	106.1	10(d)	Wynyard
117)	2CUZ	106.5	10	Bourke
183)	4CLG	106.5	1	Nambour
96)	7HFC	106.5	3	Hobart
118)	3PBS	106.7	16(d)	Melbourne
119)	2VOX	106.9	2(d)	Wollongong
120)	3UGE	106.9	1	Alexandra/Eildon
4)	7RPH	106.9	3.2	Launceston
121)	4KIG	107.1	16	Townsville
122)	2REM	107.3	2	Albury
123)	2SER	107.3	14	Sydney
124)	4CAB	107.3	10(d)	Gold Coast
125)	2EAR	107.5	1.6(d)	Moruya
9)	3MPH	107.5	1	Mildura
126)	4CRM	107.5	1	Mackay
127)	2AIR	107.9	5	Coffs Harbour
128)	2COW	107.9	1	Casino
129)	5RAM	107.9	7.9(d)	Adelaide
130)	6CCR	107.9	1(d)	Fremantle

HIGH POWER OPEN NARROWCAST STATIONS

These stations are licensed for a specific market such as horseracing or certain local audience that cannot be filled by commercial or other stations. Official callsigns are not issued for these stations but may be used.

	Call	kHz	kW	Location
188)	5RTI	531	0.5	Adelaide
141)	6—	657	2	Perth
187)	2RF	801	5(d)	Gosford
189)	4—	873	2	Innisfail
138)	4TAB	891	5(d)	Townsville
146)	3UZ	945	2	Bendigo
190)	2TAB	1008	0.3	Canberra
132)	6TAB	1008	2(d)	Geraldton
132)	6TAB	1017	1	Bunbury
141)	4—	1053	0.5	Brisbane
191)	7TAB	1080	5(d)	Hobart
132)	6TAB	1206	2	Perth
190)	2TAB	1215	0.35	Bowral
140)	8TAB	1242	2	Darwin
190)	2TAB	1314	5(d)	Wollongong
190)	2TAB	1341	5(d)	Newcastle'
192)	3—	1341	5(d)	Geelong
193)	3—	1359	0.2	Mildura
132)	6TAB	1404	4	Busselton
194)	3—	1413	0.5(d)	Shepparton
195)	3XY	1422	5	Melbourne
132)	6TAB	1422	2	Wagin
132)	6TAB	1431	2	Kalgoorlie
132)	6TAB	1449	2	Mandurah
186)	2—	1476	0.5	Penrith
187)	2RF	1539	1	Sydney
139)	5TAB	1539	10(d)	Adelaide
139)	5TAB	1557	0.5(d)	Renmark/Loxton
187)	2RF	1575	5(d)	Wollongong
154)	2—	1593	0.2	Murwillumbah
156)	3RG	1593	5(d)	Melbourne
196)	2NTC	1611	0.3	Armidale
196)	2NTC	1611	0.4	Tamworth
187)	2RG	1611	0.4	Griffith
201)	2—	1611	0.4	Sydney
197)	3XX	1611	0.4	Melbourne
199)	6AY	1611	0.4	Albany
200)	6GS	1611	0.4	Wagin
198)	6—	1611	0.4	Margaret River
187)	1RF	1620	0.4	Canberra
190)	2KM	1620	0.4	Sydney
202)	3GB	1620	0.4	Melbourne
203)	2HRN	1629	0.1	Newcastle
196)	2NTC	1629	0.4	Bathurst
204)	3—	1629	0.4	Melbourne
187)	3RF	1629	0.4	Shepparton
205)	4DB	1629	0.4	Dalby
187)	4RF	1629	0.4	Brisbane
187)	5RF	1629	0.4	Adelaide
196)	2ME	1638	0.4	Sydney
196)	3ME	1638	0.4	Melbourne
206)	2MM	1665	0.4	Sydney
207)	2—	1683	0.4	Sydney
196)	2NTC	1701	0.4	Sydney
208)	4—	1701	0.1	Brisbane

FM	MHz	kW	Location
131)	88.7	2(d)	Atherton QLD
132)	89.5	1.2	Esperance WA
142)	90.5	1(d)	Barossa Valley SA
133)	90.5	1(d)	Tamworth NSW
134)	90.9	1	Mossman QLD
133)	90.9	1	Mudgee NSW
135)	91.5	1	Toowoomba QLD
154)	91.9	8(d)	Latrobe Valley VIC
136)	92.3	10(d)	Maryborough QLD
132)	92.5	2	Port Hedland WA
133)	92.7	1	Inverell NSW
133)	92.7	3(d)	Port Macquarie NSW
133)	94.3	1	Goulburn NSW
137)	94.9	4	Broken Hill NSW
138)	95.5	3(d)	Bundaberg QLD
138)	95.5	4.5(d)	Emerald QLD
139)	95.5	5(d)	Renmark/Loxton SA
140)	95.9	1	Alice Springs NT
133)	95.9	20(d)	Gunnedah NSW
163)	96.5	1	Katherine NT
133)	96.9	1(d)	Cooma NSW
164)	97.5	2(d)	Bairnsdale VIC
138)	97.5	1	Blackwater QLD
165)	97.7	1(d)	Burnie TAS
141)	99.1	2(d)	Atherton QLD
133)	99.9	10	Parkes/Forbes NSW
138)	99.9	10	Rockhampton QLD
133)	100.5	4	Broken Hill NSW
132)	100.5	1	Wyndham WA
133)	100.9	10	Bathurst NSW
142)	101.1	10(d)	Nowra NSW
143)	101.3	2	Devonport TAS
133)	101.5	1	Grafton NSW
133)	101.5	1	Kempsey NSW
132)	101.7	1	Karratha WA
164)	102.1	1	Hamilton VIC
133)	102.7	2(d)	Jindabyne NSW
164)	102.9	2	Horsham VIC
133)	103.3	1	Muswellbrook NSW
138)	103.5	100(d)	Mackay QLD
140)	103.7	1	Katherine NT
133)	103.7	1	Moree NSW
133)	103.7	2(d)	Nowra NSW
133)	104.3	10	Armidale NSW
143)	104.3	10(d)	Cairns QLD
164)	105.3	1	Portland NSW
144)	105.3	2(d)	Wollongong NSW
133)	105.7	5	Taree NSW
145)	106.1	1	Deniliquin NSW
133)	106.7	5	Orange NSW
146)	106.9	10	Swan Hill VIC
133)	107.1	1	Eden NSW
184)	107.1	1	Alice Springs NT
133)	107.5	3	Glen Innes NSW

NB stations below 1kW are not mentioned.

Addresses and other information
1) Western Region Educational Broadc. Co. Ltd, PO Box 594, Bourke, NSW 2840 . – **2)** Radio Station 6WR. PO Box 162 Kununurra WA 6743. (N-1:CBAA) Aboriginal programs from National Indigenous Radio Service. – **3)** Community R. Federation Ltd, PO Box 277, Collingwood, VIC 3066 . Various foreign languages. – **4)** Radio 7RPH Broadcasting Services for Handicapped Inc. 136 Davey st Hobart TAS. 7000 . Information and reading service format. Relays BBCWS 11:00pm to 10:00am Mon-Sat, Sunday. – **5)** Curtin Univ of Technology, GPO Box U1987, Perth, WA 6001.. Rel. CBAA Network at times and BBCWS overnight. – **6)** Foundation for Information Radio, PO Box 101, Victoria Park WA 6100 . Information and print reading services. Rel selected programs from ComRadSat and relays BBCWS 11:00pm to 6:00am. **F.PI:** expansion to regional WA. – **7)** Print-Handicapped Radio of ACT Inc, Barton Highway, Gungahlin, ACT 2912 – relays BBCWS Mon-Fri 1:00pm to 6:00pm, Sa noon to Su 9:30am. – **8)** Switch FM, PO Box 173, Fortitude Valley, QLD, 4006 – **9)** Assoc. for the Blind, 454 Glenferrie Rd, Kooyong 3144 . Relays BBCWS overnight. – **10)** Radio 5RPH, 231 Morphett St. Adelaide SA 5000 . Relays BBCWS overnight. – **11)** R. for the Print-Handicapped (NSW) Co-op Ltd, 2/252 Illawarra Rd, Marrickville NSW 2204 . – **12)** Queensland Radio for the Print-Handicapped Ltd, 231 North Quay, Brisbane, QLD 4000 (N-3). Rel. BBCWS overnight. ID's as "Information Radio". – **13)** 50 Houghwood Rd, Bora Ridge NSW 2471 – **14)** PO Box 998, Tamworth NSW 2340 – **15)** PO Box 891, Barham NSW 2732 – **16)** Rainbow FM, PO Box 473, Warwick QLD 4370 – **17)** PO Box 86, Burleigh Heads QLD 4220 – **18)** 120 McCrae St, Bendigo VIC 3550 – **19)** PO Box 93, Tenterfield NSW 2372 – **20)** PO Box 483, Dalby QLD 4405 – **21)** Crow FM, PO Box 171, Emerald QLD 4606 – **22)** PO Box 90, Kingscote SA 5223 – **23)** PO Box 3882, Weston ACT 2611 (Ethnic) – **24)** Gough St, Deepwater NSW 2371 – **25)** PO Box 94, Narrabri NSW 2390 – **26)** The Positive Alternative, PO Box 774, Gympie QLD 4570 (Christian) – **27)** Canberra Christian Radio, PO Box 927, Fyshwick ACT 2609 (Christian) – **28)** 257 Goondoon St, Warwick QLD 4680 (Christian) – **29)** PO Box 707, Armidale NSW 2350 – **30)** Muslim Community Radio, PO Box 969, Bankstown NSW 1885 (Ethnic) – **31)** Arts Radio, PO Box 949, Nedlands WA 6009 – **32)** GPO Box 1324, Hobart TAS 7001 – **33)** Charles Sturt University, Locked Bag 30, Bathurst NSW 2795 – **34)** PO Box 1106, Collingwood VIC 3066 (Ethnic) – **35)** Artsound, PO Box 87, Curtin ACT 2605 – **36)** PO Box 5123, East Lismore NSW 2480 – **37)** The Light, PO Box 3367, Village Fair, Townsville QLD 4350 (Christian) – **38)** PO Box 304, Dorrigo NSW 2454 – **39)** Edge FM, PO Box 771, Bega NSW 2550 – **40)** 48 Nelson St, Stepney SA 5069 – **41)** Living Sound Broadcasters, PO Box 7, Coniston NSW 2500 (Christian) – **42)** Radio Hope Island, PO Box 16, Sanctuary Cove QLD 4212 – **43)** Radio Rhema, PO Box 1502, Dubbo NSW 2830 (Christian) – **44)** PO Box 271, Ceduna SA 5690 – **45)** Radio Larrakia, Shop 2, Alawa Shops, Alawa NT 0810 (Aboriginal) – **46)** PO Box 1276, Geelong VIC 3220 – **47)** PO Box 2678, Bundaberg QLD 4670 – **48)** PO Box 19, Gosford NSW 2250 – **49)** Rhema FM, PO Box 886, Belmont VIC 3216 (Christian) – **50)** PO Box 421, Cessnock NSW 2325 – **51)** Radio KLFM, PO Box 2997, Bendigo Delivery Centre VIC 3554 – **52)** Family Radio, PO Box 1700, Milton QLD 4064 – **53)** 30 Pillapai Rd, Brightwaters NSW 2264 – **54)** PO Box 86, Omeo VIC 3898 – **55)** Darwin Christian Broadcasters, PO Box 43146, Casaurina NT 0810 (Christian) – **56)** Parkes Road, Forbes NSW 2871 – **57)** PO Box 655, Derby WA 6728 – **58)** 140 Main St, Kangaroo Point QLD 4169 – **59)** 2XX, GPO Box 812, Canberra ACT 2601 – **60)** PO Box 259, Meekatharra WA 6642 – **61)** Radio 2000, 2/25 Belmore Rd, Burwood NSW 2134 (Ethnic) – **62)** PO Box 6824, Shepparton VIC 3630 – **63)** Sonshine FM, PO Box 6340, Morley WA 6062 (Christian) – **64)** PO Box 99, Kandos NSW 2848 – **65)** PO Box 1856, Cairns QLD 4870 (Aboriginal) – **66)** Box 6229, Fairfield Gardens QLD 4103 (Aboriginal) – **67)** PO Box 450, Portland VIC 3305 – **68)** Rhema FM, PO Box 2000, Dangar NSW 2309 (Christian) – **69)** PO Box 884, Nowra NSW 2541 – **70)** PO Box 667, Mansfield VIC 3724 – **71)** PMB Turkey Creek, via Kununurra WA 6743 (Aboriginal) – **72)** Radio Rhema, PO Box 1537, Port Macquarie NSW 2444 (Christian) – **73)** Voice FM, PO Box 149, Ballarat VIC 3350 – **74)** Live FM, PO Box 332, Aitkenvale QLD 4814 (Christian) – **75)** Radio Rhema, PO Box 615, Bathurst NSW 2795 (Christian) – **76)** PO Box 210, Yamba NSW 2464 – **77)** PO Box 1003, Cleveland QLD 4163 – **78)** PO Box 26, Kyneton VIC 3444 – **79)** PO Box 663, Rockhampton QLD 4700 (Aboriginal) – **80)** 211-217 North Road, Albany WA 6330 – **81)** PO Box 2101, Logan City DC, QLD 4114 – **82)** PO Box 605, Wangaratta VIC 3676 – **83)** PO Box 1015, Tuncurry NSW 2428 – **84)** PO Box 418, Caboolture QLD 4510 – **85)** PO Box 17, Willow Tree NSW 2339 – **86)** PO Box 509, Fortitude Valley QLD 4006 – **87)** PO Box 815, Kununurra WA 6743 (Aboriginal) – **88)** PO Box 522, Nimbin NSW 2480 – **89)** 76 Chandos St, St Leonards NSW 2065 – **90)** PO Box 304, Fitzroy VIC 3065 – **91)** PO Box 115, Grafton NSW 2460 (Christian) – **92)** PO Box 200, West Kempsey NSW 2440 – **93)** 10 Byron Pl, Adelaide SA 5000 (Ethnic) – **94)** PO Box 54, Five Dock NSW 2046 – **95)** Ngarralinyi, The Listening Place, PO Box 657, Taree NSW 2430 (Aboriginal) – **96)** PO Box 1033, New Town TAS 7008 – **97)** Radio Rhema, PO Box 974, Orange NSW 2800 – **98)** PO Box 139, Murrayville VIC 3512 – **99)** 146 Cotham Road, Kew VIC 3101 – **100)** University Dr, Callaghan NSW 2308 – **101)** 384 Old Cleveland Rd, Coorparoo QLD 4151 – **102)** PO Box 814, Dickson ACT 2602 (Racing) – **103)** PO Box 603, Port Macquarie 2446 – **104)** Good News Radio, PO Box 312, Ballarat VIC 3350 – **105)** PO Box 1033, Townsville QLD 4810 – **106)** PO Box 2154, Esperance WA 6450 – **107)** PO Box J233, Coffs Harbour NSW 2450 – **108)** PO Box 40146, Casaurina NT 0810 – **109)** PO Box 400, Taree NSW 2430 – **110)** PO Box 579, Morwell VIC 3840 – **111)** 1/15 Matong Rd, Echuca VIC 3564 – **112)** PO Box 333, Wynyard TAS 7325 – **113)** Rhema FM, PO Box 384, Hervey Bay QLD 4655 (Christian) – **114)** 93 Reatta Rd, Trevallyn TAS 7250 (Christian) – **115)** Radio Metro, PO Box 6530, GCMC QLD 9726 – **116)** PO Box 69, Bowraville NSW 2449 – **117)** PO Box 363, Bourke NSW 2840 (Aboriginal) – **118)** PO Box 2917, Fitzroy VIC 3065 – **119)** PO Box 1663, Wollongong NSW 2500 – **120)** PO Box 270, Alexandra VIC 3714 – **121)** PO Box 5483, Townsville QLD 4810 (Aboriginal) – **122)** Garland Ave, North Albury NSW 2640 – **123)** PO Box 123, Broadway NSW 2007 – **124)** Life FM, PO Box 948, Southport QLD 4125 (Christian) – **125)** PO Box 86, Moruya NSW 2537 – **126)** PO Box 1075, Mackay QLD 4740 – **127)** PO Box 2028, Coffs Harbour NSW 2450 – **128)** PO Box 1149, Casino NSW 2470 – **129)** Radio Alta Mira, PO Box 1079, North Adelaide SA 5006 (Christian) – **130)** Unit 4, 153 Rockingham Rd, Hamilton Hill WA 6163 – **131)** KIK FM, PO Bpx 1434, Edge Hill QLD 4870 – **132)** TAB WA, 14 Hasler Rd, Osborne Park WA 6017 – **133)** PO Box 1303, , NSW 2150 – **134)** 90.9 FM, Mossman & Port Douglas PO Box 383, Whakatane NEW ZEALAND – **135)** PO Box 111, Toowoomba QLD 4350 – **136)** PO Box 1059, Bundaberg QLD 4670 – **137)** Cross FM, Broken Hill Church of Christ, 232 Lane St, Broken Hill NSW 2880 – **138)** Radio 4TAB, PO Box 275, Albion, QLD 4010 – **139)** GPO Box 5AA, Adelaide SA 5001 – **140)** NT Racing Commission, PO Box 3170, Darwin NT 0800 – **141)** Rete Italia, PO Box 159, Clifton Hill VIC 3068 – **142)** Ambersky, PO Box 540, Nowra NSW 2541 – **143)** PO Box 5109, GCMC, Bundall QLD 9726 – **144)** 63 Minimbah Rd, Northbridge NSW 2063 – **145)** Rich Rivers Radio, PO Box 312, Deniliquin NSW 2710 – **146)** PO Box 927, Carlton, VIC 3053 – **147)** PO Box 526, Bordertown, SA 5268 – **148)** PO Box 654, Tanunda, SA 5352 – **149)** PO Box 591, Victor Harbour, SA 5211 – **150)** PO Box 390, Kadina, SA 5554 – **151)** PO Box 144, Inverloch, VIC 3996 – **151)** PO Box 899, Mont Albert, VIC 3127 – **152)** PO Box 999, Victor Harbour, SA 5211 – **153)** PO Box 12013, A'Beckett St, Melbourne, VIC 3000 – **154)** PO Box 5910 Gold Coast Mail Centre Bundall QLD 4217 – **155)** Level 2, 230-232 Angas St, Adelaide, SA 5000 – **156)** PO Box 28, Nimmitabel, NSW 2631 – **157)** PO Box 2050, Gosford, NSW 2250 – **158)** PO Box 2, The Entrance, NSW 2261 – **159)** PO Box 1962, Strawberry Hills, NSW 2012 – **160)** PO Box 2122, Griffith, NSW 2680 – **161)** PO Box 1005, Subiaco, WA 6904 – **162)** c/- PO, Gordon St, Poatina, TAS 7302 – **163)** PO Box 79, Earlwood, NSW 2206 – **164)** Vision FM, Locked Bag 3, Springwood, QLD 4127 – **165)** GPO Box 1345, Hobart, TAS 7001 – **166)** PO Box 1000, Nubeena, TAS 7184 – **167)** PO Box 5035, North Rockhampton MC, QLD 4701 – **168)** GPO Box 252-44, Hobart, TAS 7001 – **169)** PO Box 139, Redcliffe, QLD 4020 – **170)** PO Box 440, Byron Bay, NSW 2481 – **171)** PO Box 7016, Hutt St, Adelaide, SA 5000 – **172)** PO Box 243, Boonah, QLD 4310 – **173)** PO Box 51, Yass, NSW 2582 – **174)** PO Box 235, Beaudesert, QLD 4285 – **175)** PO Box 150, Roma, QLD 4455 – **176)** PO Box 312, South Perth, WA 6951 – **177)** PO Box 612, Ballina, NSW 2478 – **178)** PO Box 400, Toowoomba, QLD 4350 – **179)** 43 Tamar St, Launceston, TAS 7250 – **180)** CAAMA, PO Box 2608, Alice Springs, NT 0871 – **181)** 5 Desiree Cl, Buderim, QLD 4556 – **182)** Radio Rhema, PO Box 1465, Mt. Gambier, SA 5290 – **183)** Radio Rhema, PO Box 200, Woombye, QLD 4559 – **184)** 17 North St, Frewville, SA 5063 – **185)** 228-230 North Tce, Adelaide, SA 5000 – **186)** PO Box 259, Lane Cove, NSW 1595 – **187)** c/- John Wright, 29 Milford Rd, Peakhurst, NSW 2210 – **188)** GPO Box 1329, Adelaide, SA 5001 (Italian) – **189)** PO Box 19, Innisfail, QLD 4860 – **190)** PO Box 1303, Parramatta, NSW 2150 – **191)** GPO Box 572F, Hobart, TAS 7001 – **192)** PO Box 9550, Geelong, VIC 3220 – **193)** PO Box 1067, Mildura, VIC 3502 –**194)** Radio Rhema, PO Box 980, Shepparton, VIC 3630 – **195)** 1c Bell St, Preston, VIC 3072 – **196)** 5 Macquarie St, Parramatta, NSW 2150 – **197)** PO Box 173, Caulfield, VIC 3145 – **198)** 46 Ord St, West Perth, WA 6005 — **201)** 132 Ernest St, Crows Nest, NSW 2065 – **202)** PO Box 2160, Bayswater, VIC 3153 – **203)** Hospital Radio Network, 70 Dawson St, Cooks Hill, NSW 2300 – **204)** R. Salsa, PO Box 1141, Altona Meadows, VIC 3028 – **205)** PO Box 630, Dalby, QLD 4405 – **206)** Locked Bag 888, St. Peters, NSW 2044 – **207)** 1246 New Canterbury Rd, Roselands, NSW 2196 – **208)** 5 Cheviot Pl, Sinnamon ark, QLD 4073 – **209)** PO Box 507, Port Melbourne VIC 3207 – **210)** PO Box 52, Fitzroy Crossing WA 6765 – **211)** PO Box 579, Lilydale VIC 3140 – **212)** PO Box 966, Strawberry Hills NSW 2012 – **213)** PO Box 1962, Strawberry Hills NSW 2012 – **214)** PO Box 148, Toogoolwah QLD 4313 – **215)** PO Box 984, Queanbeyan NSW 2620 – **216)** PO Box 51, Yass NSW 2582.

SPECIAL BROADCASTING SERVICE (SBS)
✉ Locked Bag 028, Crows Nest, NSW 2065. ☎ +61 (02) 9430 2828. 🖷 +61 (02) 9430 3700 **L.P:** Head of Radio: Mr Quang Luu.

Call	kHz	kW	MHz	Location	Service
1) 2EA	1107	5		Sydney	Sydney 1.rs
1) 2EA	1413	5		Newcastle	National Prgr.rs

Call	kHz	kW	MHz	Location	Service
1) 2EA	1485	0.15		Wollongong	National Prgr.rs
1) 2SBS		50	105.5	Canberra	National Prgr.rs
1) 2SBS		150	97.7	Sydney	Sydney 2.rs
2) 3EA	1224	5		Melbourne	Melbourne 1.rs
2) 3SBS		100	93.1	Melbourne	Melbourne 2.rs
1) 4SBS		96	93.3	Brisbane	National Prgr.rs
1) 5SBS		32	106.3	Adelaide	National Prgr.rs
1) 5SBS		2(d)	95.1	Adel. Hills	National Prgr.rs
1) 6SBS		100	96.9	Perth	National Prgr.rs
1) 7SBS		56	105.7	Hobart	National Prgr.rs
1) 8SBS		32	100.9	Darwin	National Prgr.rs

Addresses and other information
1) Locked Bag 028, Crows Nest, NSW 2065.
2) 2 Kavanagh St, South Melbourne, VIC 3205.

AUSTRIA

L.T: UTC +1h (27Mar-30Oct: UTC +2h) — **Pop:** 7.8 million — **Pr.L:** German — **E.C:** 50Hz, 220V — **ITU:** AUT

ORF - ÖSTERREICHISCHER RUNDFUNK

✉ ORF-Funkhaus, Argentinierstr. 30A, 1040 Wien ☎ +43 1 50101 18699 🖷 +43 1 50101 82500 **Web:** www.orf.at
L.P: DG: Dr. Monika Lindner. MD: Dr. Wolfgang Buchner. PD: Kurt Rammerstorfer. Tech. Dir: Andreas Gall. Intl rel: Christiane Veigl

MW: Radio 1467 - Wien/Bissamberg 1476 kHz 60 kW.

FM (MHz)	Ö-1	Ö-Reg	Ö-3	FM4	kW
Bad Gleichen		94.9a			6
Bludenz	87.6	96.0h	98.8		4
Bregenz	93.3	98.2h	89.6	102.1	50
Bruck/Mur	87.6	93.2f	98.7	102.1	20
Graz	91.2	95.4f	89.2	101.7	67
Innsbruck	92.5	96.4g	88.5	101.4	45
				102.5	
Klagenfurt	92.8	97.8b	90.4	102.9	100
Kufstein	97.5	95.4g	103.9	99.9	5
Lienz	89.3	93.8b	99.3	101.0	2.6
		95.9g			2.6
Linz	97.5	95.2d	88.8	104.0	100
		90.1c		102.0	10
Mattersburg	89.0	96.2a	100.9		0.6/3/0.6
Rechnitz	90.6	93.5a	87.9	97.4	6
		100.1f			3
Salzburg	90.9	94.8e	99.0	104.6	100
		101.2d			7
St. Pölten	97.0	91.5c	89.4	98.8	100
Schärding	92.5	99.5d	88.2		3/4/3
Schladming	94.3	96.3f	101.3	103.3	3
Semmering	90.3	95.8c	88.2	92.4	9
Spittal/Drau	91.6	100.4b	87.9	103.6	3
Weitra	92.7	95.7c	98.1	101.4	2
Wolfsberg	96.7	94.5b	99.5	102.3	1.5
Wien	92.0	89.9i	99.9	103.8	100
		97.9c			100
		94.7a			2.4

+ more than 500 low power trs.

Österreich-1 (Ö1): 24h. **N:** on the h.
Österreich 2 (Ö2): Regional services
a) Burgenland – Buchgraben 51, 7001 Eisenstadt. **Web:** burgenland.orf.at **b)** Kärnten – Sponheimerstr. 13, 9010 Klagenfurt. **Web:** kaernten.orf.at **c)** Niederösterreich – Radioplatz 1, 3100 St. Pölten. **Web:** noe.orf.at **d)** Oberösterreich – Europaplatz 3, 4010 Linz. **Web:** linz.orf.at **e)** Salzburg – Nonntaler-Haupstr. 49d, 5020 Salzburg. **Web:** salzburg.orf.at **f)** Steiermark – Marburgerstr. 20, 8042 Graz. **Web:** steiermark.orf.at **g)** Tirol – Rennweg 14, 6010 Innsbruck. **Web:** tirol.orf.at **h)** Vorarlberg – Höchsterstrasse 38, 6851 Dornbirn. **Web:** vorarlberg.orf.at **i)** Wien – Argentinierstr. 30a, 1040 Wien. **Web:** wien.orf.at
Österreich 3 (Ö3): 24h. **N:** on the h.
FM4: Prgrs in English (0600-1300) and German (1300-0600). **Web:** http://fm4.orf.at
Radio 1476: special multilanguage prgrs Mon-Fri 1700-2308, Sat+Sun 1700-2305 on 1476 kHz. **Web:** fm4.orf.at. **Email:** 1476@orf.at
ANN: "Österreich 1", "Ö2…(Wien, Niederösterreich, Tirol…)", "Ö3"
IS: Österreich 1: composition by Werner Pirchner. Ö2: Composition by Bert Breit. Ö3: Electronic Music.

F.PI: Permission to use the following freq for commercial radio: 585, 630, 774, 891, 963, 1026, 1125, 1143, 1314, 1458, 1485, 1548 & 1602.

DIGITAL RADIO - DAB

National network provided by **ORF** on 227.360 & 229.072MHz.

PRIVATE STATIONS

KRONEHIT
Nationwide network with regional news windows
✉ Daumegasse 1, 1100 Wien **Web:** www.kronehit.at

Location	MHz	kW	Location	MHz	kW
Weitra	90.2	3	Mattersburg	103.4	1
Linz	92.6	4	Rechnitz	104.1	5
Gmunden	93.9	0.3	Schärding	104.9	4
Waidhofen	101.3	0.4	St. Pölten	105.3	100
Villach	101.6	0.5	Wien	105.8	100
Semmering	102.9	8	Innsbruck	106.5	0.6
B.Gleichenberg	103.2	1.5	Graz	107.5	1

+ 16 tr's below 1kW

Other Private Stations by Area:
BURGENLAND: HiT FM, 106.3 Mattersburg, 1 kW + 2rly
KÄRNTEN (Carinthia): Antenne Kärnten, 104.9 Klagenfurt, 125kW; 107.4 Spittal a.d.Drau, 4kW; 104.3 Wolfsberg, 2kW + 4rly – **Radio Agora / Radio Dva (ORF)** *(German/Slovenian programme)*, 105.5 Klagenfurt, 10kW; 106.8 Wolfsberg, 1kW + 8rly – **Radio Harmonie,** 95.2 Klagenfurt, 1kW + 3rly – **Radio CountryStar,** 102.5 Spittal a.d. Drau, 0.2kW – **Radio Real Radenthein-CMP,** 106.3 Radenthein, 0.02kW
NIEDERÖSTERREICH (Lower Austria): HiT FM, 104.9 Weitra/Nebelstein, 3kW; 103.3 Melk, 2kW; 100.8 St. Pölten, 0.3kW + 9rly – **Campus Radio 94.4,** 94.4 St. Pölten, 0,2kW – **106,7 Party FM,** 106.7 Hornstein, 1kW – **GymRadio 94,5,** 94.5 Hollabrunn, 0.1kW + 1rly – **Radio Maria,** 104.7 Waidhofen a.d.Y., 0.4kW – **Radio Arabella,** 99.4 Tulln-Judenau, 0.3kW
OBERÖSTERREICH (Upper Austria): Life Radio, 100.5 Linz, 100 kW; 102.6 Schärding, 3kW; 102.2 Bad Ischl, 0.6kW + 7rly – **Welle 1 Music Radio,** 102.6 Steyr, 1,6kW + 2rly – **Radio FRO,** 105.0 Linz, 0.3kW – **Life Radio Salzkammergut,** 100.2 Bad Ischl, 0.8kW; 107.3 Gmunden, 0.1kW + 2rly – **Antenne Wels,** 98.3 Wels, 0.1kW
SALZBURG: Antenne Salzburg, 101.8 Salzburg, 2 kW; 105.9 Zell an See, 1kW; 102.5 St. Michael i. Lungau, 0.5kW + 15rly – **Welle 1 Music Radio,** 106.2 Salzburg, 0.5kW; 107.5 St. Johann Pongau, 0.2kW – **Radiofabrik,** 107.5 Salzburg-Maria Plain, 0.5kW
STEIERMARK (Styria): Antenne Steiermark, 99.1 Graz/Schöckl, 67 kW; 105.7 Bruck a.d. Mur, 8kW; 92.0 Schladming, 3kW; 106.1 Rechnitz, 3kW + 17rly – **Das Soundportal,** 97.9 Graz, 0.4kW – **Radio Helsinki,** 92.6 Graz, 0.3kW – **89.6 Das Musikradio,** 89.6 Bruck a.d.Mur, 8kW – **A1 Radio,** 105.1 Knittelfeld, 0.3kW + 2rly – **Radio Grün-Weiss,** 102.6 Leoben, 0.1kW; 101.1 Altenmark a.d. Enns, 0.2kW + 1rly – **Radio West,** 107.3 Köflach, 0.1kW + 1rly – **Radio Freequenns,** 100.8 Liezen/Salberg, 0.2kW – **Radio Harmonie,** 106.3 Schladming, 2kW + 1rly – **Radio Nostalgie Raaba,** 94.2 Graz/Raaba, 0.5kW – **A1 Radio,** 105.1 Knittelfeld, 0.3kW + 2rly – **Radio Grün-Weiss,** 102.6 Leoben, 0.1kW + 4rly
TIROL (Tyrol): Antenne Tirol, 103.4 Inzing, 8kW; 100.8 Zirog, 1kW; 101.8 Innsbruck, 1kW; 104.4 Lienz, 1kW; 105.4 Haiming, 1kW; 106.0 Landeck, 1kW; 106.8 Kufstein, 1kW + 8rly – **Radio Arabella Innsbruck,** 105.1 Innsbruck, 0.2kW; 91.7 Wattens, 0.2kW + 4rly – **Oberländer Welle,** 103.9 Haiming(Telfs), 0.3kW; 104.3 Inzing, 0.2kW; 107.1 Landeck, 0.4kW + 5rly – **U1 Radio Unterland,** 89.2 Jenbach, 0.2kW + 10rly – **Radio Freirad,** 105.9 Innsbruck, 0.3kW – **Radio Osttirol,** 101.7 Matrei-Hopfgarten, 0.7kW; 107.8 Lienz, 0.4kW; + 5rly – **106fm,** Lienz 106.0, 0.3kW – **Ausserferner Welle,** 104.0 Reutte, 0.3kW + 2rly
VORARLBERG: Antenne Vorarlberg, 106.5 Bregenz, 50kW; 101.1 Bludenz, 1.5kW; 105.1 Feldkirch 0.2kW + 1rly – **Radio Arabella,** 95.9 Bregenz, 0.3kW – **Radio Pro-Ton,** 104.6 Bludenz, 0.5kW
WIEN (Vienna): 88,6 der Supermix, 88.6 MHz, 10kW – **Antenne Wien 102.5,** 102.5 MHz, 10kW – **R. Arabella 92.9,** 92.9 MHz, 3kW – **R. Energy 104,2,** 104.2 MHz, 1kW – **R. Stephansdom,** 107.3 MHz, 2kW – **R. Orange 94,0,** 94.0 MHz, 0.3kW

AZERBAIJAN

L.T: UTC +4h (27 Mar - 30 Oct 2005: UTC +5h) — **Pop:** 7,8 million — **Pr.L:** Azeri, Russian, Armenian — **E.C:** 50Hz, 220V — **ITU:** AZE

AZÄRBAYCAN DÖVLÄT TELERADIO VERILISLÄRI SIRKÄTI (State Radio-TV Broadcasting Company of Azerbaijan, Gov.)

✉ Mehdi Hüseyn küç. 1, AZ 1011 Baki. ☎ +994 12 928727. 🖷 +994 12 398505. **Email:** root@aztv.baku.az. **Web:** www.aztv.az
L.P: Chmn: Nizami Xudiyev.

MW	kHz	kW	Prgr.
Gäncä	549	50	AZR1
Pirsaat	801	150	AZR1
Quba	801	-	AZR1
Baki	891	30	AZR1
Pirsaat	1296	125	F, D
Gäncä	1359	-	AZR2
Pirsaat	1476	150	AZR2
Quba	1557	-	AZR2
FM (MHz)	**AZR1**	**AZR2**	**kW**
Baki	88.0	90.0	4

+ tx's in other parts of the country not mentioned.
D.PRGR: AZR1 (I-Respublika): 0200-2000 in Azeri, exc. Russian: 0710-0715 (Tue-Sat), 0755-0825 (Sun), 1110-1140 (Tue/Thu), 1110-1135 (Fri), 1145-1200 (Mon), 1400-1410, 1530-1700 (Sun). – **AZR2 (Araz):** 0200-2100 in Azeri & minority languages: Armenian (Mon 1440-1500, Wed 1330-1400, Fri 1530-1600, Sun 1535-1600), Georgian (Tue/Thu 1310-1330, Sat 1305-1325), Kurdish (Tue/Thu 1545-1600), Lezgian (Wed 1400-1415), Russian (Wed/Sat 1450-1500), Talysh (Tue/Thu 1445-1500).
EXTERNAL SERVICE: Voice of Azerbaijan. See International Radio section.

OTHER STATIONS

MW	MHz	kW	Location	Station
A)	801	15	Baki	BBC
D,5A)	1530	7	Baki	RFE-RL/Azad Azärb. R., F
FM	**MHz**	**kW**	**Location**	**Station**
5A)	69.53	17	Baki	Azad Azärbaycan R.
8)	95.0	1	Baki	CVI FM
1)	100.5	0.5	Baki	Burç FM
2)	101.0	1	Baki	Antenn 101
3)	102.0	1.5	Baki	R. ANS-ÇM
9)	102.7	-	Baki	Odlar Yurdu Radiosu
C)	103.0	4	Baki	R. Rossii
A)	103.3	4	Baki	BBC Baki
4)	104.0	1	Baki	R. Space
B)	105.0	0.5	Baki	RFI
5B)	106.0	0.5	Baki	R. 106 FM
6)	107.0	1	Baki	R. Lider
7)	107.7	1	Baki	Avropa plüs

Addresses & other information:
1) Atatürk pr. 28, AZ 1069 Baki. Email: webmaster@burc.fm – **2)** Tbilisi pr. 1, AZ 1072 Baki. Email: president@antenn.az – **3)** Mätbuat prosp. 28/11, AZ 1005 Baki. Email: radio.ans@ans-dx.com – **4)** Istiklaliyät küç. 31, AZ 1072 Baki. Email: space@azeri.com – **5A,B)** A.Abas-zade küç. 8, AZ 1001 Baki. 5B) Email: 106fm@106fm.azer-inet.az – **6)** Ä.Älekbärov küç. 83/23, AZ 1141 Baki. Email: lider@lider.fm – **7)** H.Zärdäbi küç. 88a, AZ 1012 Baki. Email: radio@europaplus.az – **8)** Baki. Email: cvi@mail.az – **9)** P.O. Box 81171, Burnaby, BC, V5H 3X5, Canada. Email: radioodlar@radioodlaryurdu.com – **A)** Azatliq prosp. 91, AZ 1001 Baki. Email: bbc@azdata.net – **B)** Rel. RFI (see France). – **C)** Rel. R.Rossii (see Russia). – **D)** Rel. RFE-RL (see USA): 0400-0500, 1600-1700, 1800-1830, 1900-2000 in Azeri ("R.Azadliq") on 1296/1530, 1830-1900 in Russian ("R.Svoboda") on 1530kHz.

MOUNTAINOUS KARABAKH (Artsakh/Dagliq Qarabag)

(autonomous territory, under seperatist administration)

ARTSAKHTELERADIO (Pub.)

✉ Tigran Mets Str. 23a, 374430 Stepanakert. ☎ +374 71 43848. **Email:** artv@ktsurf.net **L.P:** Dir: Garnik Grigoryan.
STATION: Stepanakert 102.1MHz. **D.PRGR:** in Armenian.

OTHER STATIONS

SW	kHz	kW	Location	Station
1)	9677v	5	Stepanakert	Ädälän Säsi Radiosu
FM	**MHz**	**kW**	**Location**	**Station**
3)	104.9	-	Stepanakert	R. Pace
2)	106.2	-	Stepanakert	Molodyozhnyy kanal
3)	106.7	-	n/a	R. Pace

Addresses & other information:
1) Tigran Mets Str. 23a, 374430 Stepanakert. In Azeri: Wed/Sat 0600-0630, Tue/Fri 1500-1530 (times vary). – **2)** Stepanakert. In Armenian, Russian. – **2)** Stepanakert. In Armenian, Russian.

AZORES (Portuguese)

LT: UTC -1h (27 Mar-30 Oct: UTC) — **Pop:** 315,000 — **Pr.L:** Portuguese — **E.C:** 50Hz, 220/380V — **ITU:** AZR

ANACOM-Autoridade Nacional de Comunicações, Delegação dos Açores
✉ Rua dos Valados, 9500-652 RELVA (São Miguel). ☎ +351-296 30 20 40, 🖷 +351-291 30 20 41

RDP-RADIODIFUSÃO PORTUGUESA - Centro Regional da RDP-Açores
✉ Rua de Castelo Branco, 9500-761 PONTA DELGADA ☎ +351-296 20 11 00 🖷 +351-296 20 11 20. **Email:** rdp@rdpacores.pt **Web** www.rdp.pt. **L.P:** Dir. Carlos Tavares

RDP Antena 1 Açores

MW	kHz	kW	Island
Santa Bárbara	693	10	Terceira
Monte das Cruzes	828	1	Flores
Pico da Barrosa	837	10	São Miguel

FM MHz	Ant. 1	Ant. 2	kW
Cabeço Gordo	88.9		9.1
Cabeço Verde	98.1		1
Cascalho Negro	92.2		1
Fajãzinha	100.4	103.7	1
Monte das Cruzes	99.8	97.4	1
Morro Alto	93.5	91.9	1
Pico Alto Stª Maria	96.7		1
Pico da Barrosa	97.9	101.7	33
Ponta Delgada	94.1	100.8	0.3/1.3
Santa Barbara	90.5	98.9	35

+ 13 trs below 1kW.
D.Progrs: both networks 24 h.
V: by QSL card via RDP in Lisboa.

RDP Antena 1 Açores carries its own progrs. Mon-Sat 0630-0100, Suns 0700-0100 LT; other times relays RDP-1 Lisboa; Antena 2 relays Lisboa 24 h.

DAB: RDP transmitters at Ponta Delgada, Espalamaca, Stª Bárbara, Pico da Barrosa, Monte das Cruzes, Pico Alto de Stª Maria, Serra do Cume, Cabeço Verde and Pico do Jardim, broadcasting Antena 1, 2, 3, RDP África and RDP Internacional on 225.648 MHz, ch. 12, block B.

Private MW stations:
RÁDIO CLUB DE ANGRA – "A VOZ DA TERCEIRA" (priv., comm.)
✉ Av. Tenente Coronel José Agostinho, 4, 9700 ANGRA DO HEROISMO. ☎ +351-295 21 31 01. 🖷 +351-295 21 31 02.
MW 909 kHz 10 kW (inactive), **FM** Santa Bárbara 101.1 MHz 0.4 kW

ESTAÇÃO EMISSORA DO CLUB ASAS DO ATLÂNTICO (priv., comm.)
✉ Aeroporto de Santa Maria, 9580 VILA DO PORTO. ☎ +351-296 88 64 68, 🖷 +351-296 88 64 59 **Email** asasdoatlantico@clix.pt
MW 1566 kHz 10 kW (inactive), **FM** Pico Alto, 103.2 MHz 2 kW.
D.Prgr.: 0700-2400 L time.

OTHER STATIONS
privately owned VHF-FM only local stations

	Island	MHz	kW	Name, tr. location
1)	São Miguel	91.0	0.5	R. Povoação, Pico Bartolomeu
7)	Faial	91.3	0.5	Antena Nove, Cabeço Gordo
3)	São Miguel	99.4	3	R. Comercial dos Açores/TSF, Pico da Barrosa
9)	Pico	100.2	0.5	R. Pico, Cabeço Gordo (Faial)
11)	São Jorge	100.5	0.5	R Canal, Calheta (Macelinha)
1)	São Miguel	102.4	0.5	Top Rádio, Pico da Barrosa
5)	Terceira	104.4	1	R. Horizonte-Açores 1, Santa Bárbara
8)	Pico	104.7	0.5	R. Nova Cidade, Lajes
1)	São Miguel	105.0	0.5	R. Vila Franca, Pico da Barrosa
2)	São Miguel	105.5	2	R.Nova Cidade,Pico da Barrosa
14)	Flores	105.5	0.5	R.Flores
1)	São Miguel	106.0	0.5	R. Nordeste, Pico Bartolomeu
10)	Pico	106.1	0.5	R. Cais, São Roque do Pico
4)	São Miguel	106.3	3	R.Atlântida, Pico da Barrosa
6)	Terceira	106.6	1	R. Ilha, Santa Bárbara
12)	São Jorge	107.1	0.5	R. Lumena, Pico Rebineu
1)	São Miguel	107.2	1	R. Horizonte-Açores 2, Pico da Barrosa

Island	MHz	kW	Name, tr. location
13) Graciosa	107.9	0.5	R.Graciosa, Serra Branca

+12 relays of 50 watt ERP used by certain stns.

Addresses & other information:
1) Rua Nova da Misericórdia, 271-r/c, 9500-336 PONTA DELGADA ☎ 296-65 39 11, 🖷 296-65 39 10 – **2)** Rua Adolfo Medeiros, 24, 9600 RIBEIRA GRANDE ☎296-47 28 02, 🖷 296-47 26 54 – **3)** (relays TSF Lisboa) Rua Dr. Bruno Tavares Carreiro, 34-2º, 9500-055 PONTA DELGADA ☎296 30 91 50, 🖷 296 62 90 18 **Email:** radioacores@acorianooriental.pt – **4)** Rua do Laureano, 444-4º, 9500 PONTA DELGADA ☎ 296-20 19 10, 🖷 296-62 48 56 **Email:** geral@radioatlantida.net, atlantida.radio@mail.telepac.pt **Web:** www.radioatlantida.net – **5)** São Carlos, 51, 9700 ANGRA DO HEROISMO ☎295-216011, 🖷 295 21 60 15 **Email:** noticias@horizonteacores.com, comercial@horizonteacores.com **Web:** www.horizonteacores.com – **6)** (see 5) – **7)** Rua de São João, 38-B, 9900 HORTA ☎292-29 33 90, 🖷 292-39 16 02 **Email:** antena9@clix.pt, nop43955@mail.telepac.pt – **8)** Rua Direita, 16, 9930-129 LAJES DO PICO ☎292-67 20 76 **Email:** rnc@acores.net – **9)** Av. Machado Serpa, 9950 MADALENA (Pico) ☎292-62 27 27 & 292-62 24 59, 🖷 292-622874 **Email:** radiopico@sapo.pt – **10)** Largo do Museu da Indústria da Baleia, Pico ☎292-642930, 🖷 292-64 29 34 – **11)** (relays TSF Lisboa) Largo do Cais (Casa da Junta), 9850 CALHETA (São Jorge) – **12)** Rua Cunha da Silveira, 25, 9800 VELAS ☎295-41 25 75, 🖷 295-41 28 10 **Email:** rlacores@net.spao.pt, radiolumena.iol.pt **Web:** www.radiolumena.com – **13)** Rua do Corpo Santo, 37, 9880-368 SANTA CRUZ DA GRACIOSA ☎295-71 25 18, 🖷 295 71 27 68 **Email:** radiograciosa@clix.pt **Web:** www.radiograciosa.com – **14)** Rua Almirante Gago Coutinho, 7, 9970 SANTA CRUZ DAS FLORES ☎296-20 19 10, 🖷 296-629856.

Other stations:

RÁDIO LAJES – A VOZ DA FAP-FORÇA AÉREA PORTUGUESA (The Voice of the Portuguese Air Force)
✉ Lajes, Terceira, 9760 PRAIA DA VITÓRIA, ☎. +351-295 54 27 70, 🖷 +351 295 542200.
Base Aérea das Lajes, **MW** (irr.) 648 kHz 1 kW & **FM** 93.5 MHz 150 watt. 24 h. Daytime : own progrs. Nighttime: relay of R. Renascença in Lisboa.

UNITED STATES AFRTS
✉ Lajes, Terceira, 9760 PRAIA DA VITÓRIA, ☎ +351-295 57 34 97. **Web:** www.lajes.af.mil
MW 1503 kHz 100 watt (1 kW nominal). **FM** 96.1 MHz 150 watt **D.Prgr.** Locally produced & relays of AFRTS.

BAHAMAS

L.T: UTC -5h (3 Apr-30 Oct: UTC -4h) — **Pop:** 326,000 — **Pr.L:** English — **E.C:** 60Hz, 120/220V — **ITU:** BAH.

BROADCASTING CORPORATION OF THE BAHAMAS (Comm., Gov.)
✉ P.O. Box N-1347, Nassau. ☎ +1 242 502 3800. 🖷 +1 242 322 3924. **Web:** www.znsbahamas.com.
L.P: GM: Anthony Foster. CEN: Donald Rolle.
MW: Nassau ZNS1 1540kHz 50kW (d), ZNS2 1240kHz 1kW – Freeport ZNS3 810kHz 1kW - **FM:** ZNS-FM 104.5MHz.
D.Prgr: 24h. **N.** (ZNS1): 0800, 1300, 1830, 0000, 0300.
ANN: ZNS1: "This is Radio Bahamas" or "National Voice of Bahamas". ZNS2: "Inspiration 1240". ZNS3: This is Northern Service, Radio Bahamas". ZNS-FM: "Power 104.5"

PRIVATE STATIONS:
Radio Abaco, P.O. Box AB-20418, Abaco. ☎ +1 242 367 4935. **Web:** www.radioabaco.com. **FM**: 93.5MHz.
Cool 96 FM: P.O. Box F-40773, Freeport. ☎ +1 242 352 7440. 🖷 +1 242 352 8709. **Web:** www.cool96fm.com. **L.P:** GM: Andrea Gottlieb. - **FM:** 96.1MHz.
Island FM, Nassau. ☎ +1 242 326 4378. - **FM:** Nassau 102.5MHz.
100 Jamz, P.O. Box N-3207, Nassau. ☎ +1 242 328 4771. 🖷 +1 242 356 5343. **Web:** www.100jamz.com. **L.P:** PD Eric Ward. - **FM:** Nassau 100.3, Freeport 100.3, Abaco: 100.1 and Coopers Town: 100.5MHz.
Joy FM. FM: Nassau 101.9MHz.
Love-97 FM, P.O. Box N-3909, Nassau. ☎ +1 242 356 4960. 🖷 +1 242 356 7256. **FM:** Nassau 97.5MHz.
More 94 FM: P.O. Box N-7030, Nassau. ☎ +1 242 361 2447. 🖷 +1 242 361 2448. **Web:** www.more94fm.com. - **FM:** Nassau 94.9MHz.
Splash FM, P.O. Box EL-27495, Spanish Wells, Eleuthera. ☎ +1 242 333 4638. **Web:** www.splashfmradio.com. - **FM:** Eleuthera; 89.9, Nassau 92.5MHz.

BAHRAIN

L.T: UTC +3h — **Pop:** 645,000 — **Pr.L:** Arabic — **E.C:** 50Hz, 230V(60/110 at Awala) — **ITU:** BHR

BAHRAIN RADIO & TELEVISION CORP.
✉ P.O.Box 702, Manama. **Web:** www.gna.gov.bh/brtc/radio.html. **Email:** info@bahrainradio.com. **L.P:** Dir of Broadcasting: Hamad Al-Manai
General Programme in Arabic: ☎ +973 781888, 629009. 🖷 +973 681544. **MW:** 801kHz 100 kW **SW:** (GC: 26N02 050E37): 9745 kHz (r. irr at 2-5kW). **FM:** 90.9 MHz 3 kW. Arabic service 24h. Main news bulletins: 0400, 0930, 1130, 1500 & 1800.
Second Programme in Arabic: MW: 612 kHz-100 kW. 0300-1700
Holy Quran Programme in Arabic: MW: 612 kHz 100 kW. Quran recitals & religous affairs 1700-2100.
Programme for the Indian community: FM: 104.2 (MHz): 24h of new and old Indian songs.
Foreign Language Sce (R. Bahrain in English): ☎ +973 629062/ 629085. 🖷 +973 780911. **MW:** 1584 kHz 1 kW. **FM:** 96.5 MHz 2.5 kW/101 MHz 0.5 kW.
ANN: A: "Idhaat al-Bahrain". E: "Radio Bahrain".
IS: Local composition on guitar and violin.

RADIO SAWA, Manama
FM(MHz): Manama 89.2
D. Prgr: 24 h in Arabic.

RADIO MONTE CARLO, Manama
FM(MHz): Manama 90.9
D. Prgr: 24 h in Arabic and French

BANGLADESH

L.T: UTC +6h — **Pop:** 141 million — **Pr.L:** Bengali — **E.C:** 50Hz, 220/440V — **ITU:** BGD

BANGLADESH BETAR (Gov.)
✉ National Broadcasting Authority, NBA House, 121 Kazi Nazrul Islam Ave, Dhaka-1000. ☎ +880 2 8625538, 8626175. 🖷 +880 2 8612021. **Email:** rrc@dhaka.net
L.P: DG: Aftab Hossain CE: Md. Aminur Rahman. DDG (Prgrs): Apel Mahmud. DG (News): Imman Hossai Khan Dir of Prgrs. Firoj Islam. Dir. of Monitoring: Nasimul Quader. Dir. Ext. Sces: M. A. Bashar Khan. Dir. Liaison: Amzad Hossain. Station Engineer (Research & Rec.): Ahmed Quaruzzaman.

MW	kHz	kW	Times
Khulna	558	100	0030-0400, 0600-1710
Dhaka-B	630	100	0030-0400, 0600-1710, 1800-2100
Dhaka-A	693	1000	0030-0610, 0830-1730
Bagura	846	10	0030-0400, 0530-1710
Chittagong	873	100	0030-0400, 0600-1710
Sylhet	963	20	0030-0400, 0800-1710
Thakurgaon	999	10	1000-1710
Rangpur	1053	20	0030-0400, 0800-1710
Rajshahi	1080	10	0030-0400, 0600-1710
Rangamati	1161	10	0800-0930, 1000-1130
Dhaka-C	1170	10	0900-1100
R. Metrowave	1170	10	0130-0430, 0600-0900, 1200-1500
Barishal	1287	10	0500-1010
Coxbazar	1314	10	0800-1010
Comilla	1413	10	1200-1710

SW: (G.C: Shavar: 23N27 090E12)

	kHz	kW	Times
Shavar	4880	100	0030-0505, 1200-1600
Shavar	15520	100	1200-1710

FM	MHz	Times
Rajshahi	102.0	0030-0400, 0530-1030, 0600-1710
R Metrowave	106.5	0130-0430, 0600-0900, 1200-1500
Sylhet	101.0	0030-0400, 0800-1710
Chittagong	102.5	0030-0400, 0600-1710
Rangpur	105.5	0030-0400, 0800-1710
Khulna	106.5	0030-0400, 0600-1710
BBC Dhaka	100.0	0000-0600, 1100-1700
VOA Dhaka	97.6	0000-0700, 1400-1700

FM	MHz	Times
VOA Khulna	105.0	0000-0700, 1400-1700
VOA Sylhet	105.0	0000-0700, 1400-1700
VOA Chittagong	105.4	0000-0700, 1400-1700

N. in English: 0200, 0700, 1100, 1530, 1805. **N. in Bengali:** 0100, 0300, 0400, 0500, 0600, 0800, 0900, 1000, 1200, 1430, 1700, 1800. F.Pl: New MW station at Bandarbon.

EXTERNAL SERVICE: see International Broadcasting section.

BARBADOS

L.T: UTC -4h — **Pop:** 265,000 — **Pr.L:** English — **E.C:** 50Hz, 110V — **ITU:** BRB.

CARIBBEAN BROADCASTING CORP. (Gov. Comm.)

The Pine, Wildey, St.Michael. ☎ +1 246 429 2041 . Fax +1 246 429 4795. **Web:** www.cbcbarbados.bb.
L.P: Chairman: John Williams. Dep. GM: Claude Graham. PD (Radio): Winfield Callender.
MW: 900kHz (10kW) - **FM:** 98.1/100.7MHz (5kW).
CBC Radio 900 AM on MW: 24h. **N:** 0915, 1015, 1215, 1615, 1715, 2015, 2115, 2215 – **Liberty FM 98.1**: 24h on 98.1 MHz. – **Quality 100.7** on 100.7 MHz.

BARBADOS BROADCASTING SERVICE (Comm.)

Astoria, St George. ☎ +1 246 437 9550. Fax +1 246 437 9203.
Web-stream: http://barbadosadvocate.com/bbs.ram
L.P: MD: Anthony T. Brian. GM: Shery Anne Padmore.
FM: 90.7/102.1MHz.
BBS-FM on 90.7MHz: 24h. **Local N:** 2045MF, 2200MF. **BBC N:** 1100 – **Faith FM** (Rlg.) on 102.1MHz: 24h.

STARCOM NETWORK INC. (Comm.)

River Road, Bridgetown. ☎ +1 246 430 7300. Fax +1 246 426 5377. **Web:** www.vob929.com.
L.P: CEO: Vic Fernandez. Mgr Ops: Lennox Edwards. PM (Radio): Patrick Gollop. **MW:** 790kHz (10kW). **FM:** 92.9/95.3/104.1MHz
Starcom Gospel 7-90 AM (Rlg.): 790kHz – **VOB Voice of Barbados**: 92.9MHz – **HOTT 95.3 FM**: 95.3MHz – **LOVE 104.1 FM**: 104.1MHz. All stations: 24h.

MIX 96.9 (Comm.)

Garden House, Upper Bay Street, St.Michael. ☎ +1 246 228 4183. Fax +1 246 228 3550. **Web:** www.mix969fm.com.
L.P: MD: Scott Weatherhead. **FM:** 96.9MHz

RADIO GED (Educ.)

Barbados Community College, Eyrie Howells Road, St. Michael. ☎ +1 246 426 2858. Fax +1 246 429 5935.
Web: www.bcc.bb/ged.html
FM: 106.1MHz. **D.Prgr:** 1500-1900MF during school terms only.

BELARUS

L.T: UTC +2h (27 Mar - 30 Oct 2005: UTC +3h) — **Pop:** 10,4 million — **Pr.L:** Belarusian, Russian — **E.C:** 50Hz, 220V — **ITU:** BLR

NACYJANALNAJA DZJARZAÚNAJA TELERADYJO-KAMPANIJA RESPUBLIKI BELARUS
(State TV & Radio Co. of Belarus, Gov.)

vul. Makaionka 9, 220807 Minsk. ☎ +375 17 2649286. Fax +375 17 2648182. **Email:** pr@tvr.by **Web:** www.tvr.by
L.P: Chmn: Uladzimir Macviaycuk.
Belaruskaje Radyjo: vul. Cyrvonaja 4, 220807 Minsk.
Radyus FM: vul. Zacharava 42, 220034 Minsk.

LW/MW	kHz	kW	Prgr.
Sasnovy	279	500	BR1
Babrujsk	1008	50	BR2
Hrodna	1008	7	BR2
Smiatanicy	1008	40	BR2
Ušacy	1008	50	BR2
Brest	1026	7	BR2
Heraniony	1026	5	BR2
Mahilioú	1026	50	BR2
Miadzel	1026	25	BR2
Pinsk	1026	7	BR2
Salihorsk	1026	5	BR2
Minsk	1125	150	BR2
Sasnovy	1170	700	BR1, F, Relays***
Baranavicy	1197	5	BR2
Braslaú	1197	5	BR2
Viciebsk	1197	40	BR2
Brest	1278	2.5	BR1
SW	**kHz**	**kW**	**Prgr.**
Brest	6010	5	BR1
Hrodna	6040	5	BR1, reg c
Brest	6070	5	BR1
Minsk	6080	150	BR1
Minsk	6115	75	BR1
Mahilioú	6190	5	BR1, reg d
Hrodna	7110	5	BR1, reg c
Mahilioú	*7145	5	BR1, reg d
Mahilioú	**7235	5	BR1, reg d
Hrodna	7265	2.5	BR2

*) 27 Mar - 30 Oct 2005, **) To 27 Mar/from 30 Oct 2005; ***) BR1 (non-dir.) 0500-0700, 1000-1100, 1600-1800 (incl. reg prgr's), other times (directional at 244 degr.) rel. Voice of Russia, R. Belarus.
NB. Further SW relays see International Radio section

FM (MHz)	*BR1	BR2	RSS	RFM	**REG	kW
Asipovicy	68.96	71.69	-	104.9	-	4
Babrujsk	71.45d	67.46	73.01	104.1	66.02d	4
Berazino	70.79	-	-	100.7	-	0.03/1
Brahin	67.37b	68.30	69.11	100.8	69.92b	4
Braslaú	69.08e	71.99	-	102.3	-	4
Brest	70.91a	71.69	72.47	-	69.68a	4
	100.0a	-	-	103.7	104.8a	4
Drahicyn	-	-	-	-	104.2a	-
Heraniony	72.32c	68.39	69.26	103.3	71.54c	4
Homiel	67.76b	69.26	66.20	-	66.98b	4
Homiel	105.1b	-	-	100.1	101.3b	4/4/1
Hrodna	66.98c	66.20	68.90	-	67.76c	4
	95.7c	-	-	100.5	101.2c	4
Kascjukovicy	66.47	68.03	-	102.2	-	4
Krycaú	70.34	-	-	-	-	-
Mahilioú	72.74d	71.96	71.18	-	70.10d	4
	105.9d	-	-	100.9	96.4d	4
Miadziel	68.69	70.31	66.86	103.9	67.64	4
Minsk	71.33	70.43	72.89	-	-	4
	106.2	102.9	-	103.7	-	4
Mscislaúl	-	-	-	102.9	100.4d	4
Pinsk	66.32a	67.10	67.88	102.0	69.08a	4
Salihorsk	70.22	72.23	-	102.8	-	4/4/2
Slonim	66.56a	67.34	-	104.0	69.44c	4
Slonim	68.12c	-	-	-	-	4
Smarhon	67.97	70.13	-	-	-	1
Smiatanicy	67.22b	68.00	70.28	103.8	66.44b	4
Ušacy	72.65e	66.74	70.94	102.7	68.30e	4
Viciebsk	70.67e	69.92	72.26	-	71.48e	4
	100.5e	-	-	105.5	91.2e	4
Vidzy	72.80	74.00	-	-	-	0.03
Vorša	67.85	69.14	-	100.2	-	4
Zlobin	69.68b	71.03	71.81	-	68.45b	4
Zlobin	101.6b	-	-	-	-	-

*) most freq's incl. reg.prgr's; **) only reg.prgr's (see below)
D.PRGR: BR1 (Peršy nacyjanalny kanal): 0400-2300 in Belarusian, Russian. Includes reg. prg's (see below). Freq's without reg prgr's relay RSS: W0440-0500 & 1600-1640 (Sat 1700), Sun 1600-1700. – **BR2 (Radyjokanal Kultura)**: 0500-2200 in Belarusian. – **RSS (Radyjostancyja Stalica):** 0400-2400 in Belarusian. – **RFM (Radyus FM):** 0300-0200 mainly in Russian.

EXTERNAL SERVICE: Radio Belarus
see International Radio section

REGIONAL STATIONS (Gov.)

D.PRGR: Via BR1 tx's (see tx table) W0440-0500, W1600-1640 (Sat 1700); and via own networks as shown below. All stn's broadcast in Belarusian and Russian.
a) TRK "Brest", vul. Kujbyšava 64, 224030 Brest: "R.Brest". Email: radio-brestgosti@tut.by. Via separate network: 0400-2200 on 69.08/69.68/104.2/104.8MHz. – **b) TRK "Homiel"**, vul. Puškina 8, 246050 Homiel: "R. Ekspres - Homielskaja chvalia". Via separate network: 0500-2000 on 66.44/66.98/68.45/69.92/101.3MHz. – **c) TRK "Hrodna"**, vul. Horkaha 85, 230015 Hrodna: "R.Hrodna". Email: radio@tvr.grodno.by.

Via separate network: 0300-1800 on 67.76/69.44/71.54/101.2MHz. – **d) TRK "Mahilioú"**, zav. Kamunistycny 1, 212030 Mahilioú: "R.Mahilioú". Email: radio-nrm@tut.by. Via seperate network: 0440-2000 on 66.02/70.10/96.4/100.4MHz. – **e) TRK "Viciebsk"**, vul. Kamunistycnaja 8, 210026 Viciebsk: "R.Viciebsk". Email: info@radio.vitebsk.by. Via seperate network: 0500-2000 on 68.30/71.48/91.2MHz.

OTHER STATIONS

FM	MHz	kW	Location	Station
7)	67.70	1	Minsk	Avtoradio
2B)	68.84	1	Minsk	Melodii veka
1A)	91.0	1	Homiel	R. BA
15)	92.4	2	Minsk	R. Minsk
2B)	96.2	1	Minsk	Melodii veka
19)	97.4	1	Minsk	Minskaja chvalia
16)	97.8	1	Viciebsk	Evropa pljus Viciebsk
17)	98.4	1	Minsk	Novaje R.
11)	98.6	1	Mahilioú	Nashe R.
3)	98.9	4	Minsk	Russkoye Radio
6)	99.5	4	Minsk	R. Unistar
13)	100.4	1	Minsk	Hit FM
2/3)	101.2	4	Brest	R. ROKS/Russkoye R.
5)	101.2	10	Minsk	Pilot FM
1A)	101.5	1	Slonim	R. BA
2)	102.1	1	Minsk	R. ROKS
14)	102.1	0.6	Polack	Evropa pljus Polack
2/3)	102.6	1	Homiel	R. ROKS/Russkoye R.
9)	102.7	0.1	Mazyr	R. Nelli-Info
2/3)	103.0	1	Viciebsk	R. ROKS/Russkoye R.
1A)	103.0	1	Hrodna	R. BA
2/3)	103.4	1	Mahilioú	R. ROKS/Russkoye R.
1A)	104.5	1	Mahilioú	R. BA
12)	104.6	4	Viciebsk	R. Ljuks 104.6FM
1A)	104.6	10	Minsk	R. BA
7)	105.1	1	Minsk	Avtoradio
1A)	105.3	1	Salihorsk	R. BA
10)	106.1	1	Pinsk	R. Variah
1A)	106.2	4	Brest	R. BA
2/3)	106.9	4	Hrodna	R. ROKS/Russkoye R.
8)	107.1	2	Minsk	R. Mir Belarus
18)	107.4	1	Homiel	Homielskaje Haradzkoje R.
4)	107.6	1	Viciebsk	Alfa-Radio
4)	107.9	2	Minsk	Alfa-Radio

Addresses & other information:
1A,B) vul. Ckalava 5, 220002 Minsk. Email: advert@radioba.nsys.by – **2)** vul. Kamunistycnaja 6a, 220029 Minsk. Email: radio@roks.com. In Russian. 24h on 101.2MHz; 0800-1700 via tx's timeshared with Russkoye R. – **3)** vul. Starazoúskaja 8a, 220002 Minsk. Email: stolzakov@tut.by. In Russian. 24h on 98.9MHz; 0500-0800, 1700-2200 via tx's timeshared with R.ROKS. – **4)** pr. Franciska Skaryny 181, 220125 Minsk. Email: alpharadio@alpharadio.com.by. In Russian. – **5)** vul. Kamunistycnaja 6a, 220029 Minsk. Email: radiostyle@belsonet.net. – **6)** pr. Franciska Skaryny 4, 220050 Minsk. Email: radio@unistar.by. In Russian. – **7)** P.O.Box 279, 220050 Minsk. Email: autoradio@belhard.com. In Russian. – **8)** vul. Kirava 17, 220030 Minsk. Email: mir@mir.belpak.minsk.by. In Russian. Own prgr's 0600-2230, rel. R. Retro from Russia 2230-0600. – **9)** vul. Vulianoúskaja 2-47, 247760 Mazyr. Email: nelly_info@mail.ru. In Russian. – **10)** vul. Karasiova 6, 225710 Pinsk. Email: wartv@bresttelecom.by. In Russian. – **11)** Mahilioú. Email: nashe_mogilev@tut.by. Rel. Nashe R. from Russia. – **12)** Viciebsk. – **13)** Minsk. Rel. Hit FM from Russia. – **14)** vul. Kastrycnickaja 77, 211400 Polack. Email: sammit@tut.by. Rel. Yevropa Plyus from Russia. – **15)** Minsk. – **16)** Maskaúski pr. 10, 210015 Viciebsk. – **17)** Minsk. – **18)** vul. Šašejnaja 41, 246004 Homiel. Email: gomelradio@tut.by.

BELGIUM

L.T: UTC +1h (27 Mar-30 Oct: UTC +2h) — **Pop:** 10 million — **Pr.L:** Dutch, French, German — **E.C:** 50Hz, 230V — **ITU:** BEL

FLANDERS Pop: 6.3 million — **Pr.L.:** Flemish

VLAAMSE RADIO EN TELEVISIEOMROEP (VRT) (Public Sector Public Limited Company) Flemish (Dutch) Language Network

Public Sce. grants by Flemish government.
✉ VRT, August Reyerslaan 52, B-1043 Brussels ☎ +32 2 741 3111 🖷 +32 2 734 9351 **Web:** www.vrt.be **Email:** info@vrt.be
L.P: MD: Tony Mary. Dir.Radio: Frans Ieven. PR: Paul De Meulder.
Regional Centres Radio 2:
Antwerpen: Jan Van Rijswijcklaan 157, 2018 Antwerpen ☎ 03-2479111 🖷 03-2378282 **Email:** redactieantwerpen@radio2.be
Vlaams-Brabant: Amerikaans theather, Dikke Lindelaan 2, 1020 Brussel ☎ 02-7411111 🖷 02-4782030 **Email:** redactievlaams brabant@radio2.be
Oost-Vlaanderen: Martelaarslaan 238, 9000 Gent ☎ 09-2247211 🖷 09-2253049 **Email:** redactieoostvlaanderen@radio2.be
West-Vlaanderen: Conservatoriumplein 1, 8500 Kortrijk, ☎ 056-247311, 🖷 056-221358 **Email:** redactiewestvlaanderen@radio2.be
Limburg: A. Rodenbachstraat 29, 3500 Hasselt ☎ 011-249611 🖷 011-242436 **Email:** redactielimburg@radio2.be

MW	kHz	Prgr	kW
Waver-Overijse	540	2	150
Wolvertem	927	1+Sporza	300
Kuurne	1188	2	5
Wolvertem	1512	RVI	25/300

FM: (all freqs. MHz, all prgrs stereo)

Stations	R1	R2	RK	SB	RD	kW
Antwerpen	-	-	92.0	-	-	1
Brussegem	-	90.7	-	-	-	2
Brussels	-	-	-	-	88.3	1
Diest	-	92.4	-	-	-	1
Egem O.+W.-Vl.	95.7	-	90.4	102.1	101.5	50/50/50/40
Egem O.-Vl	-	98.6	-	-	-	50
Egem W.-Vl.	-	-	-	100.1	-	50
Genk	99.9	97.9	89.9	101.4	102.0	20/20/20/40/40
	-	-	-	-	93.0	3
Gent	-	-	-	94.5	-	0.5
Leuven	98.5	-	-	88.0	-	0.5/0.5
N'kerken Waas	-	89.8	-	-	-	1
Schoten	94.2	97.5	96.4	100.9	89.0	20/20/3/40/20
St-Pieters-Leeuw	91.7	93.7	89.5	100.6	97.0	50/50/50/50/2
Veltem	-	88.7	-	-	94.8	1/1

+3 tr's under 1 kW
R1=Radio Een (information and music), **R2**=Radio Twee (light & popular music), **RK**=Radio Klara (classical music), **SB**=Studio Brussel (youth station), **RD**=Radio Donna (Hit music station)
Radio 2 Regional programmes: 0500-0700 (Mo-Fr), 1100-1200 (Mo-Fr), 1600-1700 (daily) on FM and MW frequencies (1188 kHz relays West-Vlaanderen reg. px)
Sporza: broadcasts on 927 Khz and replaces normal Radio 1 programming during sports events; www.sporza.be
D.Prgr: Night prgr on all frequencies. Until 0200 also on MW 540 kHz and on MW 1188 kHz all night.
DAB: 223.936MHz all services plus DAB Klassiek, Sporza, Donna Hitbits, and Nieuws+.
ANN: R1:"Radio Een", R2: "Radio Twee", RK: "Radio Klara", SB: "Studio Brussel", RD: "Radio Donna"

RADIO VLAANDEREN INTERNATIONAAL

See International Broadcasting section.

COMMERCIAL NETWORKS:

Note: For the latest information on all radio stations in Flanders, please visit **Web:** www.radioinvlaanderen.info

Q-MUSIC

✉ 1818 Vilvoorde **Web:** www.qmusic.be
Stations: Antwerpen 92.9 (0.5 kW) – Antwerpen 99.2 (10) – Berlaar 92.7 (0.316) – Brugge 103.3 (1) – Brussel 102.5 (1 kW) – Eeklo 104.8 (0.158) – Egem 103.0 (20) – Genk 102.5 (50) – Gent 88.6 (3.162) – Herentals 92.2 (2) - Heuvelland (Wijtschate) 93.2 (0.316) – Oostvleteren 88.3 (1) – Sint-Pieters-Leeuw 103.1 (50) – Turnhout 104.2 (0.2) – Veltem 95.8 (1) – Wuustwezel 100.0 (1)

4FM

✉ Gemeentestraat 44, 1083 Brussel **Web:** www.4fm.be
Stations: Aalst 104.2 (1 kW) – Antwerpen 103.4 (5) – Beringen 98.4 (0.5) – Bree 93.5 (1) – Brussegem 95.6 (1.26) – Brussel 103.4 (10) – Dendermonde 92.2 (3.162) – Diest 103.3 (1) – Egem 104.1 (50) – Geel 93.5 (2) – Gent 92.8 (1) – Herzele 90.9 (1) - Heusden-Zolder 88.8 (0.5) - Holsbeek (Nieuwrode) 90.3 (0.5) - Kasterlee (Tienen) 91.4 (0.316) – Leuven 99.7 (1) – Lommel 103.7 (3.162) – Mechelen 96.7 (2) – Ninove 99.7 (0.25) - Sint-Niklaas 93.5 (2) - Sint-Truiden 89.2 (0.5) - Sint-Pieters-Leeuw 95.5 (1) – Tongeren 89.1 (1) – Turnhout 90.6 (5) – Voeren 97.4 (0.25) – Wuustwezel 103.7 (1)

Provincial stations
Radio Contact Vlaams-Brabant
✉ Oorlogskruisenlaan 94, 1120 Brussel

Stations: Aarschot 104.4 (0.158 kW) – Brussel 98.1 (10) – Brussel 98.4 (0.2) – Diest 99.0 (0.5) – Leuven 103.8 (3.162)
Radio OVL
Visserij 201-203 te 9000 Gent
Stations: Aalst 104.8 (3.162 kW) – Gent 103.5 (20) – Oudenaarde 104.8 (0.316) – Ronse 103.3 (0.2)
Radio Mango
Westlaan 159 te 8800 Roeselare **Web:** www.mango.be
Stations: Brugge 88.1 (1 kW) – Egem 98.2 (3.162) – Kortrijk 88.0 (2) – Oostende 87.6 (3.162) – Oostvleteren 101.0 (20)
Antwerpen 1
Katwilgweg 2 te 2050 Antwerpen
Stations: Geel 104.6 (2 kW) – Mechelen 104.5 (1) – Schoten 102.9 (50) – Turnhout 104.5 (1)
FM Limburg
Kempische Steenweg 105, 3500 Hasselt **Web**: www.fmlimburg.be
Stations: Beringen 92.8 (1 kW) – Bree 103.0 (1) – Genk 94.7 (0.25) - Hamont-Achel 96.5 (0.5) – Hasselt 96.8 (0.5) – Lommel 95.9 (0.5) – Overpelt 104.2 (0.1 kW) - Sint-Truiden 96.9 (1) – Tongeren 94.8 (0.2)

Other networks:
RADIO CONTACT: Oorlogkruisenlaan 94, 1120 Brussel **Web:** www.radiocontact.be
TOPRADIO VLAANDEREN: 9000 Gent **Web:** www.topradio.be
BE ONE RADIO: Web: www.beoneradio.be
C-DANCE: Bredabaan 33, 2990 Wuustwezel **Web:** www.c-dance.be
RADIO NOSTALGIE: G. Legrellelaan 10, 2020 Antwerpen **Web:** www.radionostalgie.be
RGR: Postbus 77, 3000 Leuven **Web:** www.rgrfm.be

WALLONIA Pop: 4 million — **Pr.L.:** French, German

RADIO-TÉLÉVISION BELGE DE LA COMMUNAUTE FRANCAISE (R.T.B.F.)

French Language Network
Public sce. Grants by French Parliament.
Cité de la Radio-Television, B-1044 Brussels ☎ +32 (2) 737 21 11 📠 +32 (2) 737 4357 **Web:** www.rtbf.be
L.P: Admin. Gen: R. Stéphane. Dir. Radio: Ph. Dasnoy. Tech. Dept: Chief Eng: F. Fantuzzi. Head Int. Rel: C. Vial.
Regional & Local Centres: Brussels: Reyerslaan 52, 1044 Brussel; **Liège:** 203 rue de Verviers, 4821 Andrimont; **Hainaut:** Esplanade Anne-Charlotte de Lorraine, 7000 Mons; **Namur:** Av. Golenvaux 8, 5000 Namur; **Luxembourg:** Parc des Expositions, 6700 Arlon

MW	kHz	Prgr	kW
Wavre	621	1	300
Houdeng	1125	4	10
Liège	1233	4	0.2
Marche	1305	4	5

FM (MHz)	1	2	3	4	5	kW
Anderlues	93.4	92.3		99.1	96.6	0.6/40/40/40
Bruxelles		99.3	91.2	93.2		3/40/1
Léglise	96.4	91.5	94.1	87.6		10/10/10/10
Liège	96.4	90.5	99.5	95.6	92.5	5/40/40/13/?
Malmédy	89.2	91.6				1/0.1
Marche	93.3	95.2				0.5/4
Profondeville	102.7		92.8	90.8		25/10/10
Tournai	106.0	101.8	102.6	104.6	90.6	25/30/30/30/?
Verviers	91.3	103.0			87.9	1/3/?
Wavre	96.1	97.3			101.1	10/35/?

+ many tr's under 1kW

Network 1 (Première – information & musique)
Network 2 (Vivacité – light music)
Reg. Prgrs: W 0530-0800, 1200-1300, 1600-1800; Fri 1800-2100 – R. Hainaut (Mons) on 92.3/101.8MHz – R. Liège 90.5/103.0/94.6/89.1/89.4MHz – R. Namur on 97.3/92.8/89.3/91.5/89.4/90.2MHz – R. Bruxelles on 93.2MHz.
Local Prgrs: R. Verviers (Radiolène) on 103.0MHz.
Network 3 (Musiq 3 – classical music)
Network 4 (Classic 21 – oldies & rock classics)
Network 5 (Pure FM – youth station)
DAB: 225.648 MHz
ANN: "Vous écoutez R. Une, R. Deux, R. Trois, Radio 21, Bruxelles Capitale", "Pure FM"

BELGISCHES RUNDFUNK-UND FERNSEHZENTRUM DER DEUTSCHSPRACHIGEN GEMEINSCHAFT (BRF)

German Language Network (Public Sce.)
Grants by RDG-Rat (German speaking community council).
Kehrweg 11, B-4700 Eupen ☎ +32 (87) 59 1111 📠+32 (87) 591199 **Web:** www.brf.be **Email:** info@brf.be
Regional Blvd. Reyers 52, B-1044 Brussels – Malmedyer Str. 25, B-4780 St. Vith.
L.P: Pres. of Admin. Council: J-F Crucke; Dir. of BRF: H. Engels. Chief Editor: R Schroeder, PR:R. Ducomble.

Stations	MHz	kW	Stations	MHz	kW
Lüttich	88.5	50	Brussel*	95.2	2
Auel	92.2	0.16	Eupen	98.4	1
Recht	94.9	5	Recht	104.1	20

*: broadcasts joined programmes of Deutschlandfunk and BRF.
ANN: "Hier ist der Belgischer Rundfunk"

BRF Das HitRadio
Commercial station in co-operation with Radio Salu.
Kehrweg 11, B-4700 Eupen ☎ +32 (87) 591259 📠+32 (87) 591249 **Web:** www.hitradioworld.fm
Stations: Eupen 100.5 MHz

MAIN COMMERCIAL NETWORKS:
Note: The frequencies for national, provincial and local commercial stations are to change drastically sometime in 2004 or 2005. Little information is known about the allocated frequencies and starting date at time of publishing.
BEL-RTL: Rue Ariane 1, 1201 Bruxelles ☎ 02-7786911 **Web:** www.belrtl.be
RADIO CONTACT: Avenue des Croix de Guerre 94, 1120 Bruxelles ☎ 02-2442711 📠 02-2442710 **Web:** www.radiocontact.be
RADIO CONTACT 2: Avenue des Croix de Guerre 94, 1120 Bruxelles ☎ 02-2442711 📠 02-2442710 **Web:** www.contact2.be/fr/
RADIO NOSTALGIE: Quai Foin 55, 1010 Bruxelles ☎ 02-4259898 📠 02-4201969 (Also Avenue Ernest Mélot 12, 5000 Namur ☎ 081-248997 📠 081-241254). **Web:** www.nostalgie.be
BFM: Avenue des Croix de Guerre 94, 1120 Bruxelles ☎ 02-2442714 📠 02-2442703 **Web:** www.bfm.be
MUST FM: Web: www.mustfm.com
Radio NRJ: Chaussèe de Louvain 467, 1030 Bruxelles ☎ 02-5137575 📠 02-5114859 **Web:** www.nrj.be
FUN RADIO: Av. Telemaque 33, 1190 Bruxelles ☎ 02-3457575 **Web:** www.funradio.be
RADIO CIEL: Boulevard de la Sauvenière 56/21, 4000 Liége ☎ 041-210299 📠 041-210329 **Web:** www.cielfm.be
RCF: Rue des Trevires 3, 1070 Bruxelles ☎ 02-7333500 📠 02-7333390 **Web:** www.thgnet.com/Brussels/2137/Pub/Rcf1
SUDRADIO: 42, rue de la chaussée de Mons, 7000 Mons ☎ 065-401010 📠 065-401011 **Web:** www.sudradio.net

Other Networks:
AMERICAN FORCES NETWORK, SHAPE
Box 7, 7010 SHAPE. (APO AE 09700) ☎ +32 (65) 44 41 21.
L.P: Officer-in-charge: Cpt. G. Martel. Broadc. Superv: SFC C. Kubicek. Chief Eng: René Libre.
Stations: Kleine Broegel 106.2MHz 0.1kW, Brussels 101.7MHz 0.9kW, SHAPE 104.2/106.5MHz 4kW, Florennes 107.7MHz 0.1kW, Chievres 107.9.
D.Prgr: 24h on 101.7/104.2/107.7MHz. Own prgrs Mon-Fri 0500-0800, 1400-1700; Sat 0800-1200. Other times rel. AFN Europe.
AFN-2: 24h easy listening stereo prgr. on 106.5MHz.

BRITISH FORCES BROADCASTING SERVICE
Stations: SHAPE BFBS 1, 107.7MHz Casteau 0.05kW.
Wentworth B., Liststr., D-32049 Herford, Germany
D.Prgr: rel. BFBS Germany.

BELIZE

L.T: UTC -6h — **Pop:** 263,000 — **Pr.L:** English, Spanish — **E.C:** 60Hz, 110/220V — **ITU:** BLZ

BROADCASTING CORPORATION OF BELIZE (Gov. Semi-Comm.)

Albert Cattouse Bldg, Regent Str, Belize City. ☎ +501 (2) 72468. 📠 + 501 (2) 75040/75174. **Email:** rbgold@btl.net
FM: Ladyville 91.1MHz, Belize C. 92.MHz, Corozal 101.1MHz.
R. Belize Gold: 24h (0500-1200 rel. BBCWS). **N: English:** 1300,

1500, 1700, 1830, 2100, 2300, 0100, 0300. **Spanish:** 1845, 0115. **Friends FM** on 88.9/91.3/94.7MHz: 1600-1100.
V. by QSL-card. Rec.acc.

RADIO KREM Ltd. (Comm.)
✉ 3304 Partridge Str, c/o P.O. Box 15, Belize C. ☎ +501 (2) 75929. 🖷 +501 (2) 74079. **FM:** 96.5MHz 0.075kW, 89.9MHz (repeater). **D.Prgr:** 1100-0500.

MY REFUGE CHRISTIAN RADIO (Rlg.)
✉ P. O. Box 275, Belmopan. ☎ +501 (8) 21080. 🖷 +501 (8)22601. **Email:** myrefuge@btl.net **Web:** www.nauticom.net/www/jhorst/mrindex.htm **FM:** Belmopan 93.7MHz 0.5kW. Belize City 100.5 MHz 0.2 kW (repeater). **D.Prgr:** 24h.

GATEKEEPER FM (Rlg.), ✉ 1118 Vista del Mar, Ladyville. **FM:** 105.1MHz 0.5kW. **D.Prgr:** 24h.
RADIO EMANUEL, ✉ San Pedro, Ambergris Caye, Belize.**FM:** 101.7 MHz.
LOVE FM: Orange Walk 107.1MHz. **N:** 0100. **Web:** www.lovefm.com
ESTEREO MAR: Belize C. 97.9MHz (Spanish)
VOICE OF THE WEST: FM (no further details).

BRITISH FORCES BROADC. SCE. BELIZE
✉ BFBS Belize, Airport Camp, BFPO 12. ☎ +501 25 2333. 🖷 +501 25 2334. **Web:** www.ssvc.com/bfbs/radio/belize/index.htm
FM: 99.1MHz 3.5kW.

BENIN

L.T: UTC +1h — **Pop:** 7m — **Pr.L:** French + 18 ethnic — **E.C:** 50Hz, 220V — **ITU:** BEN

HAUTE AUTORITÉ DE L'AUDIOVISUEL ET DE LA COMMUNICATION (HAAC)
✉ 01 BP 3567, Cotonou ☎ +229 311745 🖷 +229 311742 **Web:** www.gouv.bj/institutions/haac

OFFICE DE RADIODIFFUSION ET TÉLÉVISION DU BENIN (ORTB)
✉ 01 BP 366, Cotonou ☎ +229 301096 🖷 +229 301437 **Web:** www.ortb.org **Email:** webmaster@ortb.org
L.P: Dir: Mr. Liahdy Mouafaliou. Chief Tech. Sces: Anastase Adjoko.
Regional ✉ B.P. 128, Parakou ☎ +229 610773/610881
MW: Cotonou 1476kHz 50/20kW, Parakou 963kHz 16/10kW (both rep. inactive).

SW	kHz	kW	Times
Cotonou	7210v	30	MF0500-0845, 1200-1400, 1600-2300 SS 0600-2300
Parakou	5025v	10	MF0500-0900, 1100-1400, 1700-2300 SS 0700-2300

(Alt freqs: Cotonou 4870 kHz, Parakou 7190 kHz).
FM: Cotonou 94.7/98.2MHz 10/0.05kW.
Radio Nationale: from Cotonou in French/ethnic.
N. in French: 0615MF, 0800SS, 1200SS, 1215MF, 1930, 2115.
R. Regionale Parakou: in French/ethnic.
(Cotonou & Parakou carry the same programme between 1900-2000).
Atlantic FM, Cotonou: 0700-2300 on 92.2MHz.
ANN: "Ici R. Bénin, Office de Radiodiffusion et Télévision du Bénin, émettant de Cotonou". "Ici Parakou, Office de Radiodiffusion et Télévision du Bénin, station regionale" **IS:** Bénin Tam-Tam.
Other stations:
R. Adja Ouèrè FM, 01 BP 1509, Cotonou: 92.6/100/100.6/107.6MHz – **R. Afrique Espoir**, 03 BP 203, Porto-Novo: 99.1MHz – **Benin Culture**: B.P. 21, Porto-Novo: 93.4MHz – **CAPP FM**, 06 BP 2076, Cotonou: 99.6MHz – **R. Carrefour**, 03 BP 432, Cotonou: 90.4MHz – **Cité Savalou Culture FM**: 01 BP 560, Cotonou: 87.8MHz – **Deeman R**, B.P. 163, Parakou: 90.2MHz – **FM Ahémé**, Possotome: 99.6MHz – **FM Alakétou**, Ketou: 95.8MHz – **FM Monts Kouffé**, Bassila: 103MHz – **FM Noon Sina**, B.P. 04, Bembereke: 90.8MHz – **FM Oré Ofé**, Tchetti: 102.1MHz – **Gerddes FM**, 01 BP 1258, Cotonou: 89.5MHz – **Golfe FM**, 06 BP 1624, Cotonou: 105.7MHz – **La Voix de la Lama**, B.P. 21, Porto-Novo: 103.8MHz – **La Voix de l'Islam**, 07 BP 134, Cotonou: 91.2MHz – **R. Immaculee Conception** (rlg.), 01 B.P. 491, Cotonou: 89.1/93.3/101MHz – **R. Liéma**, 01 BP 3609, Cotonou: 104MHz – **R. Planète**, 06 BP 537, Cotonou: 95.7MHz – **R. Maranatha**, 03 BP 4113, Cotonou: 103.1MHz – **R. Sedehon Allodalome**, 01 BP 1093, Cotonou: 97.4MHz – **R. Star**, 04 BP 0553, Cotonou: 94.3/96.3MHz – **R. Tokpa**, 01 BP 2445, C/n°233, Cotonou: 104.3MHz – **R. Tonassé**, Covè: 107.6MHz – **R. Wekê**, 03 BP 2753, Cotonou: 107MHz – **R. Rurale** (community st's set up by the development agency ACTT): st's are operating on FM(MHz) in Tanguiéta 90, Ouessè 97.7, Dogbo 100, Ouaké 101 & Banikoara 104.2MHz.
Africa No 1: Porto-Novo 102.6MHz (see main entry under Gabon).
BBC African Service: Cotonou 101.7MHz.
RFI Afrique: Cotonou 90MHz, Parakou 106.1MHz.

BERMUDA (British)

L.T: UTC -4h (3 Apr-30 Oct: UTC - 3h) — **Pop:** 64,000 — **Pr.L:** English — **E.C:** 60Hz, 115/230V — **ITU:** BER

BERMUDA BROADCASTING CO. LTD. (Comm., Gov.)
✉ 4 Fort Hill Road, Prospect, Devonshire DV 02, P.O. Box HM 452, Hamilton HM BX ☎ +1 441 295 2828. 🖷 +1 441 295 4282. **Email:** zbmzfb@bermudabroadcasting.com.
Web: www.bermudabroadcasting.com
L.P: CE: Ulric P Richardson. Ops. Mgr: E Delano Ingham. News Dir: Darlene Ming.
MW: ZFB AM 1230kHz (1kW), ZBM AM 1340kHz (1kW).
FM: ZBM-FM 89.1MHz (15kW), Power 95 Stereo FM 94.9MHz (1kW).
ZFB 1230 AM: 24h, easy listening & live prgr. – **ZBM 1340 AM:** 24h live & networked prgr. – **ZBM FM89:** 24h automated prgr. – **Power 95 FM:** 24h live & networked prgr.

DE FONTES BROADCASTING CO. LTD. (Comm.)
✉ P.O. Box HM 1450 (**studios:** 94 Reid Str.) Hamilton HM FX. ☎ +1 441 292 0050. 🖷 +1 441 295 1658. **Email:** vsbnews@ibl.bm. **Web:** www.vsb.bm.
L.P: CEO: Kenneth De Fontes. SM: Mike Bishop. N. Dir: Chris Lodge. TD: Ed. Tucker & Fred Blanchette.
MW: 1160/1280/1450kHz (1 kW) – **FM:** 106.1MHz (2.5kW).
1450 AM Gold on 1450kHz: 24h (oldies). **N:** 1045, 1115, 1145, 1215, 1245, 1300MF, 1500MF, 1615, 1645, 1715, 2045, 2115, 2145MF, 2215 – **Bible Broadcasting Network** on 1280kHz: 24h (rlg.) – **BBC World Service** on 1160kHz: 24h. Rel. BBCWS 24h except for special event prgrs. – **Mix 106.1 FM** on 106.1MHz: 24h (CHR).

BHUTAN (Kingdom of)

L.T: UTC +6h — **Pop:** 2 million— **Pr.L:** Dzongha, Sharchopkha, Nepali, English — **E.C:** 50Hz, 220V — **ITU:** BTN

BHUTAN BROADCASTING SERVICE (Corp.)
✉ P.O. Box 101, Thimpu. ☎ +975 2 2286/22533/23071. 🖷 +975 2 23073 **Web:** www.bbs.com.bt Email: request@bbs.com.bt **L.P:** Exec. Dir: Sonam Tshong.Tech. Dir: Dorji Wangchuk. Prgr. Dir: Tashi Dhendup. News Dir: Thinley Tobgye.
SW: 6035kHz 50kW (5030kHz in reserve)
FM(MHz): 88.1 Thimphu/92.0 Phuentsholing & Paro/93.0 Bumthang /96.0 Thimpu/98.0 Takti/ 100.0 Yonphula
D.Prgr: MF 0100-0600, 0800-1500; SS 0100-1300 on 6035kHz.
English: Daily 0500-0600 & 0800-0900. **N:** Daily: 0500(10'), 0530(05'), 0800(10'); **UN Radio Prgr:** Thurs 0820. **Dzongkha** Daily 0100-0300, 0600-0800(SS), Daily1100-1300 **Sharchhop** 0300-0400, 1000-1100, **Lhotsam** (Nepali**):** Daily 0400-0500 & 0900-1000 (N: 0400, 0900);
Relay of TV prog on SW 6035 kHz 1300-1500 Dzongkha, 1500-1600 English (this is irreg.)
V. by QSL-card. 15 min prgr details req. Rp. (2 IRCs).

BOLIVIA

L.T: UTC -4h — **Pop:** 8.8 million — **Pr.L:** Spanish, Quechua, Aymara — **E.C:** 50Hz, La Paz 110/220V, Santa Cruz 220/380V — **ITU:** BOL

SUPERINTENDENCIA DE TELECOMUNICACIONES - SITTEL
✉ Calle 13 entre Sauces y Costanera No. 8280 y 8260, Calacoto, La Paz. ☎ +591 2 772266. 🖷 +591 2 772299. **Web:** www.sittel.gov.bo
Email: informacion@sittel.gov.bo
LP: Superintendente: Ing. René Bustillo Portocarrero.

CAMARA NACIONAL DE MEDIOS DE COMUNICACION
✉ Casilla 2431, La Paz.
MW: ° = also on SW, * = inactive,.v = varying freq., CP = Construction Permit

	Call	kHz	kW	Name, location and h. of tr.
4)	CP-	*560	15	R. El Mundo, La Paz

	Call	kHz	kW	Name, location and h. of tr.
1)	CP91	°580	25	R. Panamericana, La Paz: 1100-0400 (Sun 1100-2400)
2)	CP190	600	10	R. ACLO, Sucre: 0900-0200
156)	CP-	600	1	Radioemisoras del Recobro, La Paz
3)	CP63	°620	20	R. San Gabriel, La Paz: 0900 (Sun 1000)-0200
5)	CP204	630		R.Tarija: 0900-0130 (n: 640)
5)	CP204	640		R.Tarija: 0900-0130 (r: 630)
17)	CP263	650	15	R. Dif. Integración, El Alto: 0900-0130
50)	CP-	°660	1	R. ABC, Santa Cruz: 0915-0500
114)	CP274	680	5	R. Andina, La Paz: 0900-0300
139)	CP50	710	10	R. Pío XII, Siglo Veinte: 0830-0230
8)	CP148	720	2.5	R. Yungas, Chulumani: 0900-1700,2000-0100
10)	CP27	°720	10	R. La Cruz del Sur, La Paz: 0930-0030
9)	CP165	*730	3	R. Mensaje, Montero
11)	CP29	°760	18	R. Fides, La Paz: 1000 (Sun 1100)-0300 (Sat 0500)
12)	CP116	770	5	R. Cosmos, Cochabamba: 1100-0300
213)	CP-	770		R.Popular, Santa Cruz (CP)
13)	CP265	°800	5	R. Libertad, La Paz: 1000-0200 (SS 2400)
14)	CP157	800	0.25	R. Santa Clara, Sorata: 0900-2400
214)	CP-	800	1	R. Churuquella, Sucre: 1000-0200
16)	CP35	820	10	Radiodifusoras Altiplano, La Paz: 1000-0200 (Sun 1100-0100)
19)	CP160	850	1	R. 21 de Diciembre, Mina Catavi: 1000-0100
20)	CP210	850	5	R. María Auxiliadora, Montero: 0900-0300 (Sun 1200-2400)
21)	CP8	860	10	R. Nueva América, La Paz: 1015-2400 (Sun 1100-0100)
22)	CP185	*°860		R. Paitití, Guayaramerín: 1030-0300
166)	CP-	°874	0.6	LV del Campesino, Sipe Sipe: 0700-2300 (n.f.: 870)
187)	CP-	875		R. Eucaliptos, Eucaliptos
216)	CP-	880		R. Inca, El Alto: 0900-0100
24)	CP79	900	0.25	R. Em. LV Nacional, Tarija: 1100-2300
165)	CP20	900		R. Popular, La Paz: 1000-0100
188)	CP-	902	1	R. Central Misionera, Cochabamba 1100-0100 (n. 900)
49)	CP83	°905	1.5	R. Norte, Montero: 0930-0200 (n. 990)
182)	CP-	920	1	R. Encuentro, Sucre: 1000-0200
248)	CP-	920	0.3	R. San Andres de Topohoco, Topohoco (CP)
217)	CP-	940	1	Chuquisaca XXI Comunicación, Sucre (CP)
25)	CP145	940		R. Metropolitana, La Paz: 0900-0500
26)	CP-	941	0.8	R. San Lorenzo, Colcapirhua: 0900 (Sun 1100)-0200 (n. 940)
7)	CP-	950	3	R. Yurac Molino, Chimboata
27)	CP93	960	1	R. Kollasuyo, Potosí: 0930-2400
218)	CP-	960		R. Huayna Potosí, Tiawanaku (CP)
28)	CP30	°970	10	R. Santa Cruz, Santa Cruz: 0900-0100
29)	CP118	980	2.5	R. Mar AM, La Paz: 1000-0200
30)	CP192	980	5	R. Esperanza, Aiquile: 0930-0200
219)	CP-	980		R. Concordia, Oruro (CP)
31)	CP119	°1000	3	R. Dif. Trópico, Trinidad:1300-0030
189)	CP	1000		R. Piraí, Santa Cruz
34)	CP220	1000	10	R. Bahá'í de Bolivia, Caracollo:0800-0200
23)	CP-	*1010		R. LV de Sipe Sipe, Sipe Sipe: 0900 (Sun 1000)-0200
220)	CP-	1000	1	R. Mística de Comunicaciones, La Paz (CP)
35)	CP4	°1020	10	R. Illimani, La Paz: 0930-0300
37)	CP113	1040	1	R. Villazón, Villazón:1100-0200(Sun 2200)
116)	CP208	1040	1	R. Sipe Sipe, Quillacollo: 1000-0300 (Sun 1100-0400)
221)	CP-	1040		R. Bolivianísima, La Paz (CP)
38)	CP233	°1050	5	R. El Mundo, Santa Cruz: 1000-0200
15)	CP-	1060	1.5	R. Noticias, Oruro: 1000-2200, 0200-0600
40)	CP181	1060	0.5	R. LV de la Frontera, Pto. Suárez: 0900-0300 (Sat 0230, Sun 2300)
191)	CP57	1060	10	R. Eco 2000, La Paz: 1100-0100
36)	CP173	1075	0.5	R. Agricultura, Portachuelo: 1000-0400 (n.f.: 1030)
43)	CP291	1080	1	R. Dif. Colosal, Sucre: 0900-0300 (n.f.: 1060)
222)	CP-	1080		R. Em.Comunitaria Pachacuti, Letanía (CP)
45)	CP45	1090	3	R. Cultura, Cochabamba: 0900-0400 (Sun 1200-2300)
48)	CP55	1100	1/ 0.75	R. Universidad de Oruro: 1100(Sun 1200)-2300 (n.f.: 620)
6)	CP137	1100	4	R. Mundial, La Paz: 0900-0330
121)	CP-	1100		R. Chaka, Pucarani: 0900-1300, 2030-0130
201)	CP-	1115	1	R. Difusoras Independencia, Atocha: 0930-0300
46)	CP184	1120	1	R. Estación El Dorado, Trinidad: 1000-0100
223)	CP-	1120	0.5	R. Em. Winay Khantati, Tiawanaku (CP)
224)	CP-	1120		R. Celestial El Milagro, El Alto: 1000-0100 (Sun 2400)
33)	CP-	1125	0.3	R. Em. Cooperativa Poopó, Poopó
44)	CP-	1125	0.5	R. Cruceña, Cotoca: 1130-2200 (n. 1530)
225)	CP-	1140	2	R. Pico Verde, Chulumani
184)	CP-	*°1143	1	R. Colonia, Yapacani
52)	CP19	1145	1	R. Chuquiago Musical, La Paz: 1000-0200
195)		1150		R. 24 de Noviembre, Eucaliptos
47)	CP194	1150	0.2	R. Chaco, Yacuíba: 1000-2400, Sun 1100-1600 (n. 1100)
53)	CP71	1150	0.5	R. El Cóndor, Oruro: 1100-2030
226)	CP-	1150	0.3	R. Guaqui, Guaqui
55)	CP317	°1160	5	R. Centenario, "La Nueva", Sta. Cruz: 0900-0100
56)	CP78	1160	3/1	R. RTC, Cochabamba: 1030-2400
57)	CP98	1160	1	R. Nuevo Mundo, Sucre: 1000-0300
141)	CP132	1160	10	R. Continental, La Paz: 0930-2400
39)	CP-	1180	5	R. Central, Oruro: 0900-2400
58)	CP235	1180	1	R. Emisora Ingavi, Viacha: 1000-0200 (Sun 1100-2400)
196)	CP-	1180	1	Radioemisora 20 de Septiembre, Arbieto: 1100-0200
66)	CP-	1180		R. Amanecer, Potosí: 0930-0200
59)	CP108	*1195	1	R. Independencia, Quillacollo: 1000-2300 (SS 1900) (n. 1200)
60)	CP32	1200	5	R. Oriental, Santa Cruz: 0930-0200
62)	CP171	1200	0.25	R. 24 de Noviembre, Arani: 1030-0400
247)	CP-	1200		R. Cuarzo de Comunicaciones, La Paz (CP)
63)	CP67	1220	1	R. Splendid, La Paz: 0900-0100
64)	CP162	°1220	1	R. Batallón Topáter, Oruro: 1000-0200 (Sat 1000-2300, Sun 1100-2300)
65)	CP-	r1220		R. El Cóndor, Arque
67)	CP180	1240	1	R. San Miguel, Arani: 1000-0300
70)	CP16	1240	2	R. Los Andes, Tarija: 1000-2200
227)	CP-	1240		R.Achocalla, Achocalla
69)	CP17	°1250	0.5	R. Sararenda, Camiri: 1000-0400
71)	CP26	1250	1	R. Amboró, Santa Cruz: 0845-0200 (Sun 1000-2400)
72)	CP69	*1250	0.5	R. Nacional, Cochabamba: 1200-2400
74)	CP65	1250	0.4	R. Oruro, Oruro: 1300-0400
76)	CP47	°1250	0.1	R. Frontera, Cobija: 1000-1800
68)	CP54	°1250	2.5	R. La Plata, "LV de la Capital", Sucre: 1000-0200
251)		1250		R.Uncia, Uncia
73)	CP14	1260	2	Radioemisoras Unidas, La Paz: 0900-0100
77)	CP-	1265	0.4	R. Uncía, Uncía: 1100-0300
78)	CP134	1270	1	R. Vanguardia, Colquiri: 1000-0300
79)	CP187	1275	0.5	R. Chané, Mineros:1000-0400(SS1100-2200)
81)	CP212	°1290	1	Radiodifusoras Minería, Oruro: 1000-2400
82)	CP51	°1300	2.5	R. Loyola, Sucre: 0900-2400 (Sun 1100-2200)
83)	CP127	*1300	0.15	R. Juan XXIII, Uyuni
84)	CP82	1300	1	R. Fides, Potosí: 1000-0100 (Sun 1100-0500)
85)	CP168	1300	0.3	R. Chichas, Siete Suyos: 1100-0400
86)	CP-	1300	1	R. Coronel Eduardo Avaroa, Sta. Cruz: 0930-0230
97)	CP-	1300	15/6	R. Sol, "Poder de Diós", La Paz: 1000-0100
228)	CP-	1300	5	R. Bandera Beniana, Trinidad
87)	CP68	1310	10	R. San Rafael, Cochabamba:1100-0200
229)	CP-	1320		R. Panorama, Achocalla
230)	CP-	1320		R. Tawantinsuyo, Taraco (CP)
54)	CP176	1330	3/3.5	R. América, Oruro: 0930-2400
80)	CP112	°1330	1	R. Frontera, Yacuíba: 0930-0330
90)	CP24	°1340v	1	R. Grigotá, Santa Cruz:1000(Sun 1100)-0100v
91)	CP146	1340	0.35	R. San Francisco, Apolo
198)	CP-	1340	0.5	R. Copacabana, Copacabana
199)	CP-	1340	0.5	R. Jach'a Suyu, Corocoro: 1000-1630, 2000-0100
231)	CP-	1340		R. Dif. La Misión, La Paz (CP)
32)	CP28	1350	25/0.1	R. Cochabamba, "CBA":1030-0200
92)	CP214	1350	2.5	R. Ichilo, Yapacaní: 0930-0135
93)	CP-	1350	1	América Radiodifusión, Sucre: 0800-0200
94)	CP154	1355v	0.25	R. Armonía, Cliza: 0900-0400v(n.f.: 1350)
95)	CP143	1360	1	R. Libertad, Villazón: 1100-0300v (Sun 2200)
41)	CP270	1360	5	Radiodifusoras Jiménez, El Alto: 0800- 0100
96)	CP158	1370	0.5	R. LV de Minero, Siglo XX:0900-1700, 2200-2300
75)	CP288	1370	5/3	Radiodifusoras Coral, Oruro: 1000-0400 (Sun 1100-2400)

	Call	kHz	kW	Name, location and h. of tr.
98)	CP133	1370	1	R. Agricultura, Achacachi: 1000-2400
99)	CP186	1370	0.15	R. Libertad, Cliza: 0930-0300
164)	CP342	1380	1.5	R. Bandera Tricolor, Cochabamba: 1100-0300
100)	CP221	*1380	0.25	R. 16 de Noviembre, Sacaba: 1000-2300
101)	CP227	1380	0.5	R. Luis de Fuentes, Tarija: 0930-0400
232)	CP-	1380		R. Em.Trunupa, Tiawanaku (CP)
233)	CP-	1380	1	R.Global AM, Sucre (CP)
250)	CP-	1380		R. Misericordia, El Alto: 0900-0330
103)	CP169	1390	0.25	R. LV Minera del Sud, Mina Telamayu: 1100-0300
144)	CP-	1395	0.1	R.Horizontes, Huanuni
102)	CP3	1400	5	R. Nacional de Bolivia, La Paz: 0900-0200
104)	CP174	*1400	1	R. Libertador, Santa Cruz
200)	CP-	1400		R. Comunidad, Patacamaya
105)	CP124	1410	0.25	R. Atlántida, Oruro: 1100-2400
106)	CP-	1410	0.25	R. Roboré, Roboré: 1000 (Sun 1100)-0400
89)	CP254	1420	1.5	R. Guadalquivir, Tarija: 0900-0100
108)	CP49	1420	1	R. Centro, Cochabamba: 1000-0300 (Sun 1100-0400)
234)	CP-	1420	1	R. Real Audiencia, Sucre: 0900-0200
235)	CP-	1420		R. Em. Omasuyo Andina, Achacachi (CP)
109)	CP141	1430	0.25	R. Nuestra Señora de Burgos, Mizque: 1000-0200
110)	CP193	*1430	0.25	R. 23 de Marzo, Tupiza
178)	CP-	1430	0.15	R. Centinela, Tupiza
111)	CP61	1440	1	R. Batallón Colorados, La Paz: 1100-0100 (Sun 2400)
112)	CP107	1440	2/1	R. Yaguarí, Vallegrande: 1000-0200
186)	CP-	1440	0.5	R. Oriente, Camiri
236)	CP-	1440		Sistema de Comunicaciones Horizontes, Sucre (CP)
237)	CP-	*1440	0.25	R. Bolivia, Cochabamba: 1000-1830, 2200-0200
238)	CP-	1440		R. LV de Juno, Tiraque (CP)
113)	CP-	1445	0.5	Super Broadcasting Alborada "SBA", Santa Cruz: 1000-0300 (n.1475)
88)	CP62	1450	1	R. Em. Bolivia, Oruro: 0900-0130
120)	CP262	1450	1	R. Verde y Blanco, Santa Cruz: 1000-0700
202)	CP-	1450		R. Amanacer, Huari
203)	CP-	1450		R. Amazonia, Cobija
204)	CP-	1455	0.5	R. Magnal, Capinota: M-Sat 1600-2400, Sun 1000-1800
193)	CP-	1461		R. LV del Pueblo de Dios, Cochabamba: 0900 (Sun 1100)-0100
239)	CP-	1480		R. Em. Ayni, Corapata (CP)
118)	CP215	1470	0.25	R. CORDECH, Alcalá: 1100-1600, 1900-0200
119)	CP-	r1475		R. Tiraque, Tiraque
115)	CP-	1480	0.1	Patrimonio Radiodifusión, Potosí: 0950-0100
185)	CP-	1480	1/0.8	R. Chiwalaki, Vacas: 0900-1400, 2100-0100
205)	CP-	1480		R. Domingo Savio, Villa Independencia(r:1495)
240)	CP-	1480		R. Amor de Diós, La Paz
241)	CP-	1480	1	R. Charcas AM, Sucre (CP)
122)	CP135	1485	1	R. LV del Valle, Punata: 1000-0300 (n.f.: 1580)
123)	CP172	1490	1	R. San José, San José, Oruro: 1100-2400 (Sun 2300)
124)	CP196	1490	0.25	R. Moxos, San Ignacio de Moxos
125)	CP198	1490	0.35	R. Pedro Domingo Murillo, Quime: 1000-1400
126)	CP-	1490	0.25	R. Mairana, Mairana: 1100-0300
117)	CP152	*1495	2.5	El Mundo Radiodifusión, Sacaba: 1000-0300
205)	CP-	1495		R. Domingo Savio, Villa Independencia (n: 1480)
127)	CP238	1500	1	R. Sagrado Corazón, Mineros: 0930-0100
130)	CP1	*1500	5/1	R. Chuquisaca, El Alto
129)	CP102	*1510	0.25	R. 27 de Diciembre, Villamontes: 1000-0200 (Sun 1100-0100)
131)	CP179	1520	1	R. Petrolera, Sta. Cruz: W 1200-0330, SS 1400-2300
132)	CP207	1520	0.25	R. LV del Cobre, Corocoro: 1000-0400
42)	CP-	1520		R. Melodía, Oruro
242)	CP-	1520		R. Nueva Esperanza, El Alto: 0900-2400
133)	CP111	1530	0.5	R. Em. Ballivián, San Borja: 1030-0100 (r:1535)
135)	CP200	1530	0.25	R. Litoral, Llica: 1400-0300
133)	CP111	1530	0.5	R. Em. Ballivián, San Borja: 1030-0100
148)	CP-	1540	0.8	R. Sariri, Escoma: 1000-1300, 2200-0200
243)	CP-	1540	0.25	R. Tutuka, Vilaque (CP)
136)	CP191	1545	0.35	R. Mejillones, Tarata: 1900-0400
158)	CP-	*1545		R. Emisoras Villamontes, Villamontes
137)	CP115	1550	10	R. Caranavi, Caranavi: 0930-1800, 2200-0200
138)	CP205	1550	1	R. Tamengo, Pto. Quijarro (n.f.: 1495)
169)	CP255	1560	1	R. Occidental, Oruro: 0930-2400
140)	CP-	1560	0.5	R. 1° de Octubre, Capinota:1030-0100
143)	CP-	1560	0.5	R. Urkupiña, Quillacollo: 1000-2400
142)	CP-	1570	0.5	R. 1° de Mayo, 1° de Mayo: 1000-0200 (Sun 1800)
134)	CP237	1578	1	R. Don Bosco, Kami: 0900-1330, 2100-0200 (n. 1530)
173)	CP-	1580	1	R. Andrés Ibáñez, Santa Cruz: 1000-0300
245)	CP-	1580		R. El Fuego del Espíritu Santo, El Alto: 1000-2400
244)	CP-	1590		R. Kollasuyo Marka, Tiawanaku
107)	CP155	1590	3	R. Bermejo, Bermejo: 0930-0100
128)	CP-	1590	0.5	R. Producciones Pusisuyu, Oruro: W 1000-1300, 0000-0400, Sun 1200-1300
206)	CP-	1590		R. Globo, La Guardia
145)	CP153	1600	0.5	R. Continental, Punata: 1000-0200
246)	CP-	1600	1	R. La Voz de Dios, El Alto: 0850-0200

SW: * = inactive, v = varying freq.

	Call	kHz	kW	Name, location and h. of tr.
146)	CP-	3310	10	R. Mosoj Chaski, Cochabamba: 0900-1300, 2100-0100
150)	CP-	*3344	0.5	R. Ayopaya, Independencia: 0900-1230, 2230-0130
129)	CP103	*3350	0.1	R. 27 de Diciembre, Villamontes: 2230-0200v
151)	CP167	*3380	1	R. Cumbre, Tazna
152)	CP175	3390	1	R. Emisoras Camargo "LV del Valle Cinteño, Camargo: 2200-0200
207)	CP-	*3420		R. Melodía, Bermejo
153)	CP-	*3493	0.5	R. Padilla, Padilla: 2200-0200
155)	CP-	4409	0.5	R. Eco, Reyes: 2230-0200
209)	CP-	4422		Radioemisora Reyes, Reyes
76)	CP59	*4450	0.25	R. Estación Frontera, Cobija
157)	CP142	4472v	1	R. Movima, Santa Ana del Yacuma: 1030-1600,2100-0200v (n.f. 4835) (v4471-4473)
160)	CP-	*4530	0.12	R.Hitachi, Guayaramerín: 1100-1600, 2200-2400v
158)	CP-	*4599	1	Radio Emisoras Villamontes: 0900-1730, 1900-2400 (Sun 0900-1700)
159)	CP-	4600	0.2	R. Perla del Acre, Cobija: W 0900-1100, 2130-0300
61)	CP89	4649	1	R. Santa Ana, Santa Ana del Yacuma: 1055-1700, 1930-0330 (n.f.:. 4805)
22)	CP185	v4682	1/0.2	R. Paitití, Guayaramerín: 1030-1900, 2100-0200 (n.f.: 4865)
154)	CP-	*4702		R. Eco, San Borja: W 1100-0300 (n. 4700)
162)	CP-	v4717	1	R. Yatun Ayllu Yura, Yura (n. 4715)
161)	CP136	*4720	0.5	R. Abaroa, Riberalta: 1000-0400 (Sun 0100) (n. 4760)
251)		4722		R.Uncia, Uncia
183)	CP-	*4732	0.7	R. La Palabra, Santa Ana del Yacuma: 1000-1300, 2200-0200
174)	CP-	v4762		R. Guanay, Guanay
253)		4763		R Chicha, Tocla
252)		4781		R.Tacana, Tumupasa
133)	CP152	4788	1	R. Em. Ballivián, S. Borja: 1030-0100 (n. 4785)
210)	CP-	v4796		R. Mallku, Uyuni: 0930-0005
180)	CP-	*4802	0.5	R. Mamoré, Guayaramerín: 1000-1700, 2100-0200 (n.f.: 4815)
90)	CP70	*4830	1	R. Grigotá, Santa Cruz
167)	CP-	*4864.	1	R. Em. 16 de Marzo, Mina Bolívar: 1000-0200 (SS 2300)
55)	CP318	4865	5	R. Centenario "La Nueva", Santa Cruz: 0900-0100 (Sat, Sun 1100-2300)
10)	CP75	4875	10	R. La Cruz del Sur, La Paz: Mon-Fri: 0930-1200, 2130-0030
69)	CP77	*4886	1	R. Sararenda, Camiri: W 1000-1200, 1800-2100 (n.f.: 4885)
168)	CP-	*4901	0.75	R. Em. San Ignacio, San Ignacio de Moxos: 1050-1200, 1600-2000 (n.f.:4900)
147)	CP114	v4904		R. San Miguel, Riberalta: 1000-0300 (Sun 0200)
49)	CP110*	4939	1.5	R. Norte, Montero: 0930-1300, 1600-1800, 2200-0100 (n.4935)
35)	CP7	*4945	10	R. Illimani, La Paz
64)	CP-	*4980	1	R. Batallón Topater, Oruro: 1000-0200
170)	CP163	*4991	1	R. Animas, Animas:1000-1800 (Sun1100-1300)
172)	CP218	*5153	0.2	R. Galaxia, Guayaramerín: 1100-0200 (SS 1800) (n.f.:5160)

	Call	kHz	kW	Name, location and h. of tr.
254)		v5500		R.Virgen de Remedios, Tupiza: 1300-1600 -2200v (test)
176)	CP-	5580	0.25	R. San José, San José de Chiquitos: 1100-1700, 2100-0200v
81)	CP213	v5927	1	Radiodifusoras Minería, Oruro: 1000-2400
254)		5945		R.Virgen de Remedios, Tupiza: v1300-v1600 -v2200 (test)
139)	CP60	v5952	5	R. Pío XII, Siglo Veinte: 0830-0230 (n. 5955)
179)	CP177	*5965	1	R. Nacional de Huanuni, Huanuni:
82)	CP41*	5996	1	R. Loyola, Sucre: 1000-0200 (n. 5955)
38)	CP234*	6015	10	R. El Mundo, Santa Cruz: 1000-0200
35)	CP5	6025	10	R. Illimani, La Paz: 0930-0300
50)	CP-	*6030	1	R. ABC, Santa Cruz
31)	CP120	v6037	1.5	R. Tropico, Trinidad: 1000-1300, 1600-1830, 2230-0100
13)	CP266	*6045	1	R. Libertad, La Paz
18)	CP90	v6054	3	R. Juan XXIII, San Ignacio de Velasco: 1030-2300 (n. 6055)
171)	CP-	*6065	1	R. Mauro Nuñez, Villa Serrano: 1000-0230 (n.f.: 6055)
3)	CP229	6085	5	R. San Gabriel, La Paz: 0900 (Sun 1000)-0200 (n. 6080)
1)	CP92	v6105	10	R. Panamericana, La Paz: 1100-0400 (Sun 2400)
28)	CP32	6135	10	R. Santa Cruz, Santa Cruz: 0900-0100
11)	CP12	6155	10	R. Fides, La Paz M-Th:1000-1800,2100-0200 Fr-Sat 1000-1800,2100-0500,Sun1100-1800
166)	CP-	v6537		R. LV del Campesino, Sipe Sipe
242)	CP-	6586		R. Nueva Esperanza, El Alto
11)	CP-	9625	15	R. Fides, La Paz: M-Th: 1000-1800, Fr- Sat: 1000-1800, 2100-0500, Sun 1100-1800
50)	CP-	*9660	1	R. ABC, Santa Cruz
68)	CP21*	9717	1	R. La Platal, Sucre:1400-1900 (Sun 2200)(n.f.: 9715)

Addresses and other information

ERBOL (Educación Radiofónica de Bolivia), Calle Ballivián 1323, 4° piso (✉ Cas. 5946), La Paz. ☎ +591 2 232 4606, 232 4768. 🖷 +591 2 239 1985. – Pte.: Jorge Trias S.J. Secr. Ejecutivo: Jorge Aliaga Murillo.
Affiliated st's: 2), 3), 5),18), 20), 28), 30), 92), 107), 121), 134), 139), 144), 147), 148), 185).

UNESBO (Unión de Emisoras Sindicales de Bolivia), Yanacocha 689, La Paz. ☎ +591 1 234 1881. Pte: Jorge Bustillo Burgos.
Affiliated st's: 4), 19), 23), 53), 60), 65), 74), 78), 85), 88), 103), 123), 132), 141), 151), 165), 166), 167), 170), 179).

1) Av. 16 de Julio, Edificio 16 de Julio, Of. 902, El Prado (✉ Cas. 503), La Paz. **Web:** www.panamericanabolivia.com **Email:** pana@panamericana.com ☎ +591 2 232 4606. 🖷 +591 2 232 5239 . **N:** "El Panamericano" relayed by many st's. – **2)** Loa 682 (or Cas. 538), Sucre. **Email:** aclo@mara.scr.entelnet.bo ☎ +591 4 646 0422. 🖷 +591 4 646 2618. Prgrs in **Quechua** except **Spanish** 1330-2030. – **3)** Gral. Lanza 2001, Cas. 4792, La Paz. ☎ +591 2 241 4371. 🖷 +591 2 241 1174. Prgrs in **Aymara** exc. Sp. & Quechua 1400-1430, Sat 2100-2130. – **4)** 16 de Julio 1295, La Paz. – **5)** Bolívar 1597 (or Cas. 1003), Tarija. **Email:** aclo.tja@olivo.tja.entelnet.bo ☎ +591 4 664 3425. - **FM:** 98.7. – **6)** Av. Sánchez Lima 2554, P. 2, La Paz. – **7)** Chimboata (Cochabamba). – **8)** Cas. 4535, La Paz. **Aymara:** 0930-1130, 2230-0030. - **FM:** 104.0. – **9)** Iglesia Metodista de Bolivia, Cas. 434, Santa Cruz. – **10)** Nicaragua 1759, Cas. 1408, La Paz. **Aymara:** 0900-1110, 2200-0030, otherwise in Sp. – **11)** Jenaro Sanjinés 799, Cas. 9143, La Paz. 🖷+591 2 240 6474, 240 6440. **Web:** www.radiofides.com - **N:** "La hora del país", relayed by many st's, at 1100, 1630, 2230, 0130. – **12)** Av. Heroinas O-467 (✉ Cas. 1092), Cochabamba. ☎ +591 4 425 0422, 425 0423. 🖷 +591 4 425 1173. **Quechua:** 0930-1030, 0000-0200. - FM: 95.1 "Fides". – **13)** Cas. 5324 or: Av. Sánchez Lima 2278, 3° piso (entre Fernando Guachalla y Rosendo Guttierez), La Paz. ☎ +591 2 236 1591. 🖷 +591 2 236 3069. **Aymara:** 0945-1015. – **14)** Cas. 2329, La Paz. – **15)** Calle Ayacucho 785 (Alto) (✉ Cas. 670), Oruro. ☎ +591 2 525 3534. 🖷 +591 2 525 2515. **Email:** cpi@coteor.net.bo **Aymara & Quechua:** 1130, 0230. – **16)** Galería Heriba, Evaristo Valle 140, or: Cas. 1081, La Paz. – **17)** Cas. 3-12472, La Paz. ☎ +591 2 810048. 🖷 +591 2 813424. **Aymara:** 0830-1200. – **18)** Vicariato Apostólico, Calle Santa Cruz, San Ignacio de Velasco (Santa Cruz). - **FM:** 100.3. – **19)** Plaza 6 de Agosto, Camamento Mina Catavi (Potosí). - **FM:** 105.7. **20)** Calle Potosí s/n (or Cas. 38), Montero (Santa Cruz). - FM: 105.7 "Concierto". – **21)** Calle Abdón Saavedra 1990 (or Cas. 2431), La Paz. ☎ +591 2 235 6622. – **22)** Cas. 172, Guayaramerín (Beni). - **FM:** 100.1. – **23)** Sipe Sipe (Cochabamba). – **24)** Cas. 404, Tarija. – **25)** Juan de la Riva 1527 (✉ Cas. 8704), La Paz. ☎ +591 2 236 3745. 🖷 +591 2 237 6785. **Aymara:** 0900-1000. – **26)** Cajón 21, Cochabamba. – **27)** Cobija 15, Potosí. – **28)** Calle Mario Flores esquina Güendá No. 20 (or Cas. 672-3213), Santa Cruz. **Email:** irfacruz@roble.scz.entelnet.bo ☎ +591 3 353 1817. 🖷 +591 3 353 2257. **Guaraní:** 1830-1900. - **FM:** 92.3. – **29)** Calle Jenaro Sanjinés 799, La Paz. – **30)** Loa Final s/n, Aiquile, or: Cas. 5716, Cochabamba. **Email:** aiquile@pino.cbb.entelnet.bo **Quechua:** 8 hours daily. - **FM:** 100.3. – **31)** Cas. 60, Trinidad (Beni). – **32)** Calle 25 de Mayo 230 entre Bolívar y Sucre (✉ Cas. 5500), Cochabamba. ☎ +591 4 425 1504. 🖷 +591 4 425 1561. - **FM:** 104.3 "Gaviota". – **33)** Cooperativa Minera Poopó, F. Fontanilla y Oblitas, Oruro. ☎ +591 2 511 2113. **Quechua & Aymara:** 0900-1100. – **34)** Cas. 1019, Oruro. ☎ +591 2 511 2259. **Email:** radbahia@nogal.oru.entelnet.bo **Aymara & Quechua:** 11 hours daily. – **35)** Av. Camacho 1485, Edificio La Urbana. P. 6, La Paz. ☎ +591 2 235 9275. **Email:** illimani@comunica.gob.bo – **36)** Calle Warnes s/n, Portachuelo, Provincia Sarah (Santa Cruz). – **37)** Cas. 58, Villazón (Potosí). – **38)** Parque Industrial Manzana No. 7 (or Cas. 1984), Santa Cruz. **Email:** diario@mail.elmundo.com.bo or radio@mail.elmundo.com.bo **Guarani:** 1115, 2315. – **39)** Montesinos 436 entre 6 de Octubre y Potosí, Oruro. **Quechua & Aymara:** 0900-1230. - **FM:** 98.7. – **40)** Cas. 18, Pto. Suárez (Sta. Cruz). – **41)** Av. Panamericana 93, Cd. Satélite, El Alto (La Paz) (or Cas. 6412, La Paz). – **42)** Oruro. – **43)** Cas. 335, Sucre. - **FM:** 90.7. – **44)** Victoriano Gutiérrez 200, Cotoca (Santa Cruz). – **45)** Santiváñez 172 casi Junín (✉ Cas. 719), Cochabamba. **Aymara & Quechua:** 1130-1300. – **46)** 18 de Noviembre 628 (✉ Cas. 720), Trinidad. – **47)** Inst. Politécnico Campesino, Cas. 42, Yacuíba (Tarija). – **48)** Calle Cochabamba esquiina 6 de Octubre (✉ Cas 49), Oruro. ☎ +591 2 525 0004. 🖷 +591 2 524 2215. – **49)** Warnes 195, Altos Cine Escorpio, Montero (Santa Cruz). ☎🖷 +591 3 992 0970. – **FM:** 99.9. – **50)** Warnes 334 (✉ Cas. 629), Santa Cruz. ☎ +591 3 336 3990. 🖷 +591 3 336 3992. - **FM:** 92.7. – **51)** Cochabamba. – **52)** Calle Nueva York 140, 1er Pasaje Chijini (or Cas. 8084), La Paz. – **53)** Junín 508, P.2, Oruro. – **54)** Calle Cochabamba 998 y Camacho (✉ Cas. 41), Oruro. ☎ +591 2 525 255, 525 4254. 🖷 +591 2 524 0035. – **55)** Cas. 818, Santa Cruz. ☎ +591 3 352 9265. 🖷 +591 3 352 4747. **Email:** mision.eplabol@scbbs-bo.com **Quechua & Guarani:** 0900-0945. - **FM:** 90.7 "R. Super Color". – **56)** Lanza esq. Ecuador N-0261 (✉ Cas. 846), Cochabamba. ☎ +591 4 425 7289. 🖷 +591 4 424 1414. – **57)** Cas. 25, Sucre. – **58)** Calle General Lanza 93, Viacha, Provincia Ingavi (La Paz). – **59)** Cochabamba esq. Heroes del Chaco, Quillacollo (Cochbamba) or: Cas. 108, Cochabamba. – **60)** Independencia 372 (✉ Cas. 186), Santa Cruz. ☎ +591 3 333 7194. 🖷 +591 3 333 5778. - **FM:** 96.3. – **61)** Calle Sucre 250, Santa Ana de Yacuma. – **62)** Arani (Cochabamba). – **63)** Cas. 1539, La Paz. Prgr in **Aymara**. – **64)** Calle Junín y 6 de Agosto, Oruro. ☎ +591 2 526 0200, 526 0462. **Aymara & Quechua:** 1000-1100. - **FM:** 98.3. – **65)** Arque (Cochabamba). – **66)** Plaza Alonso de Ibañez entre Pasaje Boulevard, Potosí. – **67)** Plaza Progreso 201 Arani (Cochabamba). – **68)** Abaroa 422, Cas. 276, Sucre. ☎ +591 4 645 3231. - **FM:** 92.1. – **69)** Cas. 7, Camiri (Santa Cruz). – **70)** Av. Las Américas 963, Edif. Radiofónico Los Andes (✉ Cas. 344), Tarija. - **FM:** 103.1. – **71)** Cas. 697, Santa Cruz. – **72)** Calle 16 de Julio S-0435 (✉ Cas. 4274), Cochabamba. – **73)** Calle Tumusla 765, La Paz. – **74)** Ayacucho 663 y La Plata, Oruro. – **75)** Av. 6 de Octubre 1042 y Montecinos (✉ Cas. 845), Oruro. **Email:** rdcoral@coteor.net.bo ☎ +591 2 525 4143. 🖷 +591 2 527 6645. – **Quechua** & **Aymara:** 1000-1130. - **FM:** 97.1. – **76)** Cas. 179, Cobija (Pando). – **77)** Cas. 15, Uncía (Potosí). – **78)** Cas. 154, Colquiri (La Paz). – **79)** Mineros (Santa Cruz). – **80)** Cas. 24, Yacuíba (Tarija). – **81)** San Felipe 493 entre Tarapacá y Tejerina (Cas. 247), Oruro. **Aymara:** 2200-2400. - **FM:** 107.7. – **82)** Calle Ayacucho 161, Sucre. ☎+591 4 645 3677, 645 4570. 🖷 +591 4 644 2555. - **FM:** 98.3 "Onda Joven". – **83)** Cas. 28, Uyuni (Potosí). – **84)** Cas 328, Potosí – **85)** Campamento Minero, Siete Suyos (Potosí). – **86)** Av. Charcas 1051 lado octava División del Ejército, Santa Cruz. ☎ +591 3 336 0447. 🖷 591 3 337 2242. - **FM:** 98.1. – **87)** Calle Calama E- 0315 (Cas. 546), Cochabamba. **Quechua/Aymara:** 0900-1100, 2300-0200. - **FM:** 92.3. – **88)** Av. Velasco Galvarro entre León y Rodriguez 1551, Oruro. – Prgrs. in **Sp., Aymara, Aymara & Poquina.** - **FM:** 105.1. – **89)** Daniel Campos 824, Tarija. ☎+591 4 663 4444. 🖷 +591 4 663 5555. - **FM:** 91.5. – **90)** Calle Colón 58, piso 5 Of. 501-2, Cas. 1399, Santa Cruz. ☎ +591 3 332 2142. - **FM:** 90.3. – **91)** Apolo, Pcia. Franz Tamayo (La Paz). – **92)** Calle Calama 118, Yapacani, Provincia Ichilo (Santa Cruz) or Cas.463, Santa Cruz. **Quechua:** 0930-1100. - **FM:** 101.1. – **93)** Calle Nataniel Aguirre 560, Sucre. ☎+591 4 645 2500, 645 5050. 🖷 +591 4 645 3500. **Email:** america@radioamerica.com.bo - **FM:** 97.5. – **94)** Calle 6 de Agosto 11, Cliza (Cochabamba). – **95)** Cas. 40, Villazón (Potosí). – **96)** Campamento Minero Siglo XX (Potosí). – **97)** Plaza del Estudiante 1905, La Paz. – **98)** Achacachi, Pcia. Omasuyos (La Paz). – **99)** Calle Santa Cruz 4, Cliza (Cochabamba). – **100)** Cas. 2522, Cochabamba. – **101)** Bolívar 376, Edificio Borda (Cas. 125), Tarija. - **FM:** 93.1. – **102)** Tumusla 612, 3° piso, or: Cas. 2532, La Paz. Prgr. mainly in **Aymara**. – **103)** Campamento Minero, Telamayu (Potosí). – **104)** Calle Cochabamba 255 (Cas. 1333), Santa Cruz. - **FM:** 107.5. – **105)** Linares 1160 entre Cochabamba y Caro, Oruro. – **106)** Roboré (Santa Cruz). – **107)** Av. Barrientos esq. Ameller, Bermejo (Tarija). ☎🖷 +591 4 696 1584. - **FM:** 99.1. – **108)** Cas. 839, Cochabamba. - **FM:** 96.3. – **109)** Cas. 893, Cochabamba. – **110)** Cochabamba s/n, Tupiza (Potosí). – **111)** Av. Saavedra esq. My. Zubieta Estado Mayor (Miraflores), La Paz. ☎ +591 2 237 2065. **Aymara:** 1100-

1200. – **112**) Florida esq. Montes Claros 143, Vallegrande (Santa Cruz). ☎ +591 3 942 2033, 942 2034. – **113**) Av. Perimetral 284 esq. Mutualista (or Cas. 2024), Santa Cruz. ☎ +591 3 347 0877. 🖷 +591 3 332 9180. – **114**) Av. 16 de Julio 1490, or: Cas. 5303, La Paz. – **115**) Victor Flores 410, Potosi. – **116**) Plaza de Granos 44, Quillacollo (Cochabamba). - **FM:** 99.1. – **117**) Plaza 6 de Agosto 44, Sacaba; Cas. 3230, Cochabamba. ☎ +591 4 428 6150. **English:** 1900-2230. – **118**) Cas. 156, Sucre. – **119**) Calle Junín s/n, Tiraque (Cochabamba). – **120**) Av. Paraguá 2465, Santa Cruz. – **121**) Casilla 204, Colegio Don Bosco, Pucarani (La Paz). Prgrs mainly in **Aymara**, but also in Spanish. – **122**) Cas. 1361, Cochabamba. – **123**) Caro 235 entre Pagador y Av. Velasco Galvarro, Oruro. – **124**) San Ignacio de Moxos (Beni). – **125**) Quime, Inquisivi (La Paz). – **126**) Correo Central, Mairana, Prov. de Florida (Santa Cruz). – **127**) Cas. 507, Santa Cruz. - **FM:** 89.5. Prgrs also in **Quechua**. – **128**) Cas. 812, Oruro. Prgr. In **Aymara & Quecua.** – **129**) Plaza del 15 de Abril, Villamonte (Tarija). – **130**) Cas. 3123, La Paz. – **131**) Barrio Petrolero 21 de Diciembre fte. Plaza Tarija, Santa Cruz. – **132**) Correo Central, Corocoro, Provincia Pacajes (La Paz). -**133**) Oruro 52, San Borja (Beni). ☎ +591 3 848 3020. – **134**) Congregación Salesiana, Kami (Cochabamba) or: Cas. 1151, Cochabamba. ☎🖷 +591 4 811 9295. Prgrs in Sp, **Aymara & Quechua**. – **135**) Llica, Pcia. Daniel Campos (Potosí). – **136**) Calle Esteban Arce 401, Tarata (Cochabamba). – **137**) Liga de Oración en Misión Mundial, Cas. 266, La Paz or: Correo Central, Caranavi. – **138**) Puerto Quijarro, Prov. Angel Sandoval (Santa Cruz). – **139**) Campamento Siglo XX, Llallagua (or Cas. 434), Oruro. **Email:** radiopio@nogal.oru.entelnet.bo – ☎ +591 2 582 0250. 🖷 +591 2 582 0554. **Aymara** & **Quechua** 6 hrs daily. - **FM:** 99.9. – **140**) Calle Bolívar 13, Capinota (Cochabamba). – **141**) Av. República 872, La Paz. – **142**) Calle 5 lado este, Villa 1° de Mayo (Santa Cruz). – **143**) Av. Suarez Miranda cuadra 10, Villa Moderna, Quillacollo (Cochabamba). – **144**) Plaza Fermín López, Huanuni (Potosí) or Cas. 147, Oruro. - **FM:** 93.5. – **145**) Ayacucho 138, Punata (Cochabamba). – **146**) Calle Abaroa S-0254 (Cas. 4493), Cochabamba. **Email:** chaski@bo.net ☎ +591 4 422 0651, 422 0644. 🖷 +591 4 425 1041. – **147**) Calle Fray Bernardino Ochoa 58 (✉ Cas. 102), Riberalta (Beni). - **FM:** 92.5 "Centenario". – **148**) Colegio Don Bosco, Plaza, Escoma (La Paz) or Cas. 204, La Paz. **Email:** escoma@caoba.entelnet.bo ☎ 🖷 +591 2 213 5336. - **FM:** 104.7. – **150**) Centro Cultural Ayopayamanta, Cas. 2433, Cochabamba. **Email:** culayo@supernet.com.bo ☎🖷 +591 4 424 4909. Prgrs mainly in **Quechua**. - **FM:** 96.5. – **151**) Campamento Minero Tazna, Pcia. Nor Chichas (Potosí). – **152**) Cas. 09, Camargo, Pcia. Nor Cinti (Chuquisaca). **Web:** www.radiocamargo.cjb.net - **FM:** 100.0. – **153**) Alcaldía Municipal, Padilla (Chuquisaca). – **154**) Av. Selim Majuli (✉ Correo Central), San Borja, Pcia. Ballivián (Beni). – **155**) Reyes, Pcia. Ballivián (Beni). – **156**) Calle Murillo 1379, La Paz. – **157**) Calle Baptista 24, Santa Ana del Yacuma (Beni). – **158**) Av. Méndez Arcos 157, Villamontes, Prov. Gran Chaco (Tarija). – **159**) Av. Prof. Alguira Gutierrez (✉ Cas. 209), Cobija (Pando). – **160**) Sucre 320, Guayaramerín. – **161**) Calle Nicanor Gonzalo Salvatierra 249, Riberalta (Beni). - **FM:** 91.1. – **162**) Cas. 326, Yura, Prov. Antonio Quijarro (Potosí). **Email:** cana118@cedro.pts.entelnet.bo. – **164**) Av. Oguendo N-0560 entre Pacieri y Pedro Blanco (Cas. 3655), Cochabamba. **Email:** latripple999@yahoo.com ☎ +591 4 425 3299, 452 0202. 🖷 +591 4 411 9729. **Quechua:** 1000-1200. - **FM: 99.9** "La Triple". – **165**) Calle Panama 11-53, Edufìcio Shopping Miraflores, 1 °piso, Oficina 1, La Paz. – **166**) Calle Rafael Urquidi 238, Comunidad Huañakahua, Prov. Sipe Sipe (Cochabamba). **FM:** 108.2. – **167**) Centro Minero Bolívar, Canadon Antequera, Provincia Poopo (Oruro). - **FM:** 106.3. – **168**) Ballivián s/n, San Ignacio de Moxos (Beni). – **169**) Av. Bakovic 1027 entre Caro y Montecinos, or Cas. 326, Oruro. **Aymara & Quechua:** 0930-1030. - **FM:** 93.1. – **170**) Dtto. Minero de Animas (Potosí). – **171**) CEDEC, Cas. 196, Sucre. ☎ +591 4 645 5008. 🖷 +591 (4) 646 2628. - **FM:** 103.1. – **172**) Cas. 395, Guayaramerín (Beni). – **173**) Calle España 572, 2°piso, Santa Cruz. - **FM:** 97.9. – **174**) Calle Boston de Guanay 123, Guanay (La Paz) or Casilla de Correo 15012, La Paz. – **176**) Cas. 15, San José de Chiquitos (Santa Cruz). – **178**) Cas. 180, Tupiza (Potosí). – **179**) Calle Sucre, Huanuni (✉ Cas. 681), Oruro. – **180**) Calle Beni s/n, Guayaramerín (Beni). – **182**) Calle La Paz 822, Sucre (Chuquisaca). – **183**) Plaza Fr. Martín Baltasar de Espinosa, Santa Ana del Yacuma (Beni). – **184**) Carretera Internacional Santa Cruz – Cochabamba (or Correo Central), Santa Fé de Yapacani, Prov. Ichilo (Santa Cruz). 🖷 +591 3 933 6000. – **Quechua:** 0900-1100. - **FM:** 99.7. – **185**) Misuk'ani, Vacas, Prov. de Arani (Cochabamba). **Email:** chiwalak@pino.cbb.entelnet.bo ☎🖷 +591 4 411 3111 or Calle Manko Kapaq 174 (or Cas. 80), Cochabamba. **Email:** incca@pino.cbb.entelnet.bo ☎🖷 +591 4 425 5390. Prgrs mainly in **Quechua**. – **186**) Cas. 30, Camiri (Santa Cruz). – **187**) Eucaliptos, Prov. Tomas Baron (Oruro). – **188**) Av. Heroinas Oeste 651, Cochabamba. – **189**) Cas. 1766, Santa Cruz. – **190**) Calle Aroma, Tiquipaya, Prov. Quillacollo (Cochabamba). – **191**) Plaza Alonso de Mendoza 500. 5° piso del Edificio Santa Anita, Ofic. 501 (or Cas. 4973), La Paz. ☎ +591 2 239 0542. – **192**) Calle Pablo Jaimes 188, Tiquipaya, Prov. Quillacollo (Cochabamba). - **FM:** 90.5. – **193**) Cochabamba. – **194**) Villa Tiquipaya, Prov. Quillacollo (Cochabamba). – **195**) Eucaliptos, Provincia Tomas Baron (Oruro). – **196**) Calle Sucre s/n, Arbieto, Provi. de Estaban Arce (Cochabamba). – **198**) Calle Professor Pedro F. Mejía 6, Esquina Plaza Central de la Basílica Nacional Nuestra Senora de Copacabana, Copacabana, Prov. Manco Capac (La Paz). – **199**) Plaza 15 de Agosto, Corocoro, Prov. Pacajes (La Paz). **Email:** tricolor-jachasuyu@hotmail.com ☎ +591 2 283 0192. Prgr. In **Aymara & Sp.** – **200**) Patacamaya (La Paz). – **201**) Mendez Arcos s/n, Atocha, Prov. Sud Chichas (Potosí). **Quechua:** M-F 1100-1200 - **FM:** 102.1. – **202**) Huari (Oruro). – **203**) Calle 9 de Octubre 2, Barrio Conavi, Cobija (Pando). – **204**) Augusto Larrain, Capinota (Cochabamba). – **205**) Villa Independencia, Prov. Ayopaya (Cochabamba). – **206**) El Toro s/n, La Guardia, Prov. Andrés Ibañez (Santa Cruz). – **207**) Av. Bolívar 608, Bermejo (Tarija). –**209**) Reyes, Prov. de Ballivián (Beni). – **210**) Calle Final Uruguay s/n (✉ Cas. 16), Uyuni, Prov. Antonio Quijarro (Potosí). ☎ +591 2 693 2145 – **213**) Calle Quijarro 74 esq. Av. Uruguay, Santa Cruz. - **FM:** 105.5. – **214**) Av. Hernando Siles 614, Sucre. – **215**) Cochabamba. – **216**) Av. Patriotica 3048, 1° piso, Zona Bolívar, El Alto. – **217**) Calle Kantuta 3, Barrio Ferroviario, Sucre. – **218**) Calle Jullio Tapia 962, Zona Gran Poder, La Paz. – **219**) Calle Adolfo Mier 1231, Oruro. – **220**) Calle Heroínas 1010 esq. 10 de Julio, El Alto, La Paz. – **221**) La Paz. – **222**) Comunidad Contorno Letania, Camino a Collana 30, Letania, Prov. Ingavi (La Paz). – **223**) Av. Manco Kapac 50, Tiawanaku, Prov. Ingavi (La Paz). – **224**) Calle Tarija 233, El Alto, La Paz. – **225**) Plaza Libertad s/n, Chulumani, Prov. Ingavi (La Paz). – **226**) Puerto de Guaqui, Prov. Ingavi (La Paz). – **227**) Achocalla (La Paz). – **228**) Calle Santa Cruz esq. Mamoré s/n, Trinidad (Beni). – **229**) Av. La Paz 90, Comunidad Pasajes, Localidad Achocalla (La Paz). – **230**) Plaza 16 de Julio s/n, Cantón Taraco, Taraco, Prov. Ingavi (La Paz). – **231**) Calle Noel Kempf 140, El Alto, La Paz. – **232**) Tiawanaku, Prov. Ingavi (La Paz). – **233**) Sucre. – **234**) Calle Avarioa 537, Sucre. – **235**) Calle Yanacocha 70, Achacachi (La Paz). – **236**) Sucre (Chuquisaca). – **237**) Calle Calama 0-0135, Cochabamba. – **238**) Calle Junín 309, Tiraque, Prov. Arani (Cochabamba). – **239**) Plaza 4 de Octubre, Rosario, Corapata, Prov. Los Andes (La Paz). – **240**) Edificio Hansa, piso 17, La Paz. – **241**) Sucre. – **242**) Raúl Salmón 92 entre Calle 4 y 5, Zona 12 de Octubre, El Alto, La Paz. ☎ +591 2 282 5269. – **243**) Plaza Principal, Cantón Villa Iquiaca, Vilaque, Prov. Los Andes (La Paz). – **244**) Av. Principal s/n, Tiawanaku, Prov. Ingavi (La Paz). – **245**) El Alto. – **246**) Av. Héctor Ormachea 5671 entre Calle 10 y 11, La Paz. – **247**) Calle Topater 830, La Paz. – **248**) Topohoco (La Paz). – **250**) Calle Jotan Save 3132 entre Bluniel, Zona 16 de Julio, La Paz. – **251)** Plaza 6 de Agosto y Calle Villazon, Uncia (Potosi) –**FM:** 105.3 – **252)** Tumupasa, Prov. Iturralde (La Paz) – **253)** Tocla, Prov. de Nor-Chicas (Potosi) – **254)** Casa Parroquial de Tupiza (Cas. 198),Tupiza (Potosi). **Email:** radiovirgenderemedios@hotmail.com +591 2 694 4662 – **FM:** 89.5

NB: Whenever listed, Casilla addresses should preferably be used for mailing purposes.

FM in La Paz: 87.7 87.7 FM – 25) 88.5 Doble 8 Latina – 88.9 Gente – 89.3 Sistema Cristiano de Comunicaciones – 89.7 Salesiana – 16) 90.1 Caliente FM – 90.5 Dimensión – 90.9 PCM – 91.3 Ciudad – 91.7 El Comercio – 92.1 Estudio 92 FM – 92.5 Estelar – 92.9 Galáctica – 93.3 Melodia – 93.7 Chacaltaya – 94.1 R La Voz de Bolivia – 94.5 Red Nuevo Tiempo – 94.9 Gigante – 10) 95.3 – 95.7 Digital Sur – 1) 96.1 – 96.5 La Paz – 96.9 Diferente – 97.3 Stereo 97 – 6) 97.7 – 11) 98.1 Láser – 98.5 Andina – 98.9 Restauración – 25) 99.3 Melodía – 99.7 Cristo Viene – 41) 100.1 FM Cien – 100.5 Constelación – 100.9 R. Color – 11) 101.3 – 101.7 Graffitti – 102.1 RRB – 102.5 Sintonia – 102.9 Cristal – 103.3 Cumbre FM – 103.7 San Francisco de Asis – 104.1 Cadena CNT – 104.5 RCN – 104.9 Fantástica – 105.3 Nuevo Amanacer – 105.7 Majestad – 106.1 Pachamama – 17) 106.5 – 106.9 Paris-La Paz – 107.3 Nueva Cosmos – 107.7 Central FM.

BOSNIA & HERZEGOVINA

L.T: UTC +1h (27 Mar - 30 Oct 2005: UTC +2h) — **Pop:** 3,9 million — **Pr.L:** Bosnian, Croatian, Serbian — **E.C:** 50Hz, 220V — **ITU:** BIH

REGULATORNA AGENCIJA ZA KOMUNIKACIJE

✉ Vilsonovo šetalište 10, 71000 Sarajevo. ☎ +387 33 250600. 🖷 +387 33 713080. **Email:** info@rak.ba **Web:** www.rak.ba
L.P: DG: Kemal Huseinovic.
NOTES: RAK is the regulatory authority for broadcasting.

JAVNI RTV SERVIS BOSNE I HERCEGOVINE (Public Broadcasting Service of Bosnia & Herzegovina, PBS-BiH)

✉ Bulevar Meše Selimovica 12, 71000 Sarajevo. ☎ +387 33 461101. 🖷 +387 33 464061. **Email:** kontakt@pbsbih.ba
Web: www.pbsbih.ba **L.P:** DG: Drago Maric.

BH Radio 1

MW	kHz	kW			
Sarajevo	612	600			
FM	**MHz**	**kW**	**FM**	**MHz**	**kW**
Ivornik	88.1	-	Drvar	94.7	0.4
Hadzica	89.7	-	Trebevic	94.5	0.25
Lipik	93.7	3	Vlašic	97.0	5

FM	MHz	kW	FM	MHz	kW
Forteca	97.3	0.5	Hum	101.7	-
V. Gomila	101.2	1	Kozara	103.1	0.5

D.PRGR: BH Radio 1 in Bosnian, Croatian, Serbian: 24h.
NOTE: PBS-BiH is the national public broadcasting service, producing the nationwide BH Radio 1. It is also the administrative roof for the regional public broadcasters R.FBiH and RTRS (see below).

Federacija Bosna i Hercegovina

RADIO FEDERACIJE BOSNE I HERCEGOVINE (RADIO FBiH) (Pub.)

✉ Bulevar Meše Selimovica 12, 71000 Sarajevo. ☎ +387 33 455102. 🖷 +387 33 455103. **Email:** rfbih@rtvbih.ba **Web:** www.rtvbih.ba
L.P: Prgr Dir: Cerovic Esad.

FM	MHz	kW	FM	MHz	kW
Tuzla	88.5	-	Lipik	95.6	1
Vlašic	89.3	10	Hum	95.7	1
Jablanica	90.0	-	V. Gomila	95.7	5
Gradacac	91.7	1	Hadzica	99.5	1
Forteca	91.8	0.5	Blagaj	99.5	0.01
Lisin	94.5	0.25			

D.PRGR: Radio FBiH in Bosnian, Croatian: 24h.

OTHER STATIONS

MW	kHz	kW	Location	Station
15)	774	2	Tuzla	R. Tuzla
23)	792	2	Banovici	R. Banovici
24)	1305	1	Bosanska Krupa	R. Buzim
25)	1503	1	Zavidovici	RTV Zavidovici
26)	1584	1	Bos. Petrovac	R. Bosanski Petrovac
27)	1602	1	Sanski Most	Nezavisni R. Boston
FM	**MHz**	**kW**	**Location**	**Station**
16)	88.2	2	Drvar	Radiopostaja Drvar
7)	90.3	5	Posušje	R. Livno
7)	90.8	5	Glamoc R.	R. Livno
13)	90.9	1	Sarajevo	R. Stari Grad
7)	91.5	5	Bos. Grahovo	R. Livno
5)	91.5	4	Sarajevo	R. Kalman
6)	91.8	2	Gradacac	R. Kameleon
20)	92,0	1.5	Sarajevo Centar	RTV Kometa
2)	93.1	5	Posušje	Hrvatski rp. Široki Brijeg
18)	94.7	1	Bihac	RTV Bihac
21)	96.2	4	Bihac	RTV USK
4)	96.2	1.5	Mostarsko Blato	R. Dobre vibracije
15)	96.5	3	Majevica Lipik	R. Tuzla
1)	96.9	3.5	Posušje	HRTV Mostar
13)	97.5	3.5	Zenica	R. Stari Grad
14)	97.6	2	Glamoc R.	R. Studio N
8)	98.7	1	Sarajevo	R. M
3)	99.3	2.5	Zenica	R. BM
7)	100.9	1	Livno	R. Livno
1)	100.9	7.5	Mostar	HRTV Mostar
19)	101.5	1	Gorazde	RTV Gorazde
7)	101.8	1	Bugojno	R. Livno
11)	101.9	3	Srebrenik K.	R. Sloboda
4)	102.5	1.5	Neum	R. Dobre vibracije
10)	103.7	2	Osjecenica	R. Sana
13)	104.3	16.5	Bjelašnica	R. Stari Grad
21)	105.1	31.5	Plješivica B.	RTV USK
9)	105.2	1	Fojnica	R. Q
12)	105.6	1	Sarajevo	R. Srpsko Sarajevo
22)	106.6	10	Zenica Lisac	RTV Zenica
17)	106.7	3	Bosanska Dubica	Radiop. Mir Medugorje

NB. Stn's below 1kW not mentioned.

Addresses & other information:
1) Dubrovacka 4, 88000 Mostar. Email: hrm.r@tel.net.ba – **2)** 88220 Široki Brijeg. – **3)** Talica brdo br.11 i 13, 72000 Zenica. Email: bmradio@bih.net.ba – **4)** Rudarska 212, 88000 Mostar. – **5)** Varazdinska 18, 71000 Sarajevo. Email: kalman_radio@hotmail.com – **6)** 75000 Tuzla. Email: kameleon@kameleon.ba – **7)** Kneza Mutimira 29, 80101 Livno. – **8)** fra Andjela Zvizdovica 1, 71000 Sarajevo. – **9)** Hazima Dedica 13, 71300 Visoko. Email: radioq@bih.net.ba – **10)** Banjalucka 2, 75260 Sanski Most. – **11)** Dr. Milana Jovanovica 6, 75000 Tuzla. Email: sloboda@kameleon.ba – **12)** Stefana Nemanje 8, 71123 Srpsko Sarajevo. Email: radioss@paleol.net – **13)** Zelenih Beretki 4, 71000 Sarajevo. Email: radiostarigrad@smartnet.ba – **14)** 80101 Livno. – **15)** ul. Mirze Delibašica 4, 75000 Tuzla. Email: radiotuzla@inet.ba – **16)** 80260 Drvar. – **17)** Gospin Trg 1, 88266 Medugorje. Email: radio-mir@medjugorje.hr – **18)** Krupska bb, 77000 Bihac. Email: rtvbihac@bih.net.ba – **19)** Zaima Imamovica 2, 73100 Gorazde. Email: czkrtvgo@bih.net.ba – **20)** Naselje starosjedilaca bb, Dobrinja IV, 71123 Srpsko Sarajevo. Email: kometa@paleol.net – **21)** Dom Kulture, 77000 Bihac. Email: rtvuskbi@bih.net.ba – **22)** 72000 Zenica. – **23)** Branislava Banovica 62, 75290 Banovici. – **24)** 505. viteske brigade bb., 77425 Buzim. – **25)** Prvomajska 12, 72220 Zavidovici. – **26)** Bosanska 134, 77250 Bosanski Petrovac.– **27)** Kljucka 7, 79260 Sanski Most.

Republika Srpska

RADIO TELEVIZIJA REPUBLIKE SRPSKE (RTRS) (Pub.)

✉ ul. Kralja Petra I Karadordevica 129, 78000 Banja Luka. ☎ +387 51 317661. 🖷 +387 51 301922. **Email:** marketing@rtrs.tv
Web: www.rtrs-bl.com

FM	MHz	kW	FM	MHz	kW
Kmur	87.8	-	Kozara	92.7	30
Trebevic	88.7	-	Leotar	92.8	30
Udrigovo	89.9	-	Banja Luka I	93.5	-
Veliki Zeb	90.3	30	Banja Luka II	95.9	1
Duge Njive	90.9	-			

D.PRGR: Radio RS in Serbian: 24h.

OTHER STATIONS

FM	MHz	kW	Location	Station
5)	88.4	6	Ugljevik	RTV Step
6)	89.9	2	Bosanska Dubica	RTV Vikom
10)	94.3	2.5	Gracanica	Obiteljski R. Valentino
3)	94.7	2	Bosanska Dubica	R. Feniks
11)	95.3	23	Kozara	R. Bobar
1)	95.6	1	Banja Luka	R. Balkan
2)	96.3	2	Doboj	R. Doboj
9)	99.3	2	Velika Kladuša	Nes R.
4)	99.9	9	Banja Luka	RTV BN
11)	100.9	9.5	Majevica	R. Bobar
9)	102.7	3	Banja Luka	Hard Rock R.
11)	102.8	8	Trebevic	R. Bobar
11)	104.7	30	Vlašic	R. Bobar
6)	105.3	3	Banja Luka	RTV Vikom
11)	105.4	4.5	Tušnica	R. Bobar
11)	105.5	22	Leotar	R. Bobar
11)	105.9	39	Velez	R. Bobar
9)	106.4	22.5	Kozara	Nes R.
7)	106.7	1	Drvar	TMK Radio
11)	107.3	12.5	Trovrh	R. Bobar
11)	107.8	77	Plješivica B.	R. Bobar

NB. Stn's below 1kW not mentioned.

Addresses & other information:
1) Macvanska 10, 78000 Banja Luka. Email: balkan@blic.net – **2)** Kneza Lazara 8, 74000 Doboj. – **3)** Svetosavska bb, 79240 Kozarska Dubica. Email: feniksfm@prijedor.com – **4)** Laze Kostica 146, 76320 Bijeljina. Email: rtvbn@rstel.net – **5)** Dvorovi-Hotel Sv. Stefan, 76320 Bijeljina. – **6)** Srpska 2/II, 51000 Banja Luka. Email: vikom@vikom-company.com – **7)** 78000 Banja Luka. – **8)** Majke knezopoljke 3, 78000 Banja Luka. – **9)** Petra I Karadordevica 83 A/II, 78000 Banja Luka. Email: nn_nesradio@teleklik.net – **10)** 76204 Bijela. – **11)** Filipa Višnjica 211, 76320 Bijeljina. Email: rbobar@rstel.net

FOREIGN MILITARY STATIONS
Foreign Armed Forces that are temporarily stationed in Bosnia & Herzegovina under UN mandate (SFOR) have established a number of relay stn's serving their military communities:

RADIO MIR (SFOR, multinational)
✉ SFOR, 71000 Sarajevo.
Sarajevo & Brcko 106.2MHz (separate prgr's).
D.PRGR: 24h for local listeners in Bosnian, Croatian, Serbian.

AFN BOSNIA (U.S.)
✉ CPIC Tuzla AB, Operation Allied Force, APO AE 09789, USA.

FM	AFN Balkans	Powernet
Butmir (Sarajevo)	88.0	91.1
Eagle Air Base (Tuzla)	88.1	99.1
Camp McGovern	100.1	-

D.PRGR: own prgr's (AFN Balkans) & rel. of AFN Germany.

BFBS BOSNIA (British)
✉ Chalfont Grove, Narcot Lane, Gerrards Cross, SL9 8TN, UK.

FM	BFBS1	BFBS2	FM	BFBS1	BFBS2
BLMF	102.7	105.3	MG Bus	101.2	105.6
Bos. Gradiska	101.2	105.2	MG Shoe	101.7	105.2
Glamoc	102.4	105.9	Prijedor	101.3	107.0
Knezovo	101.5	105.9	Prnjavor	101.5	106.7
Kotor Varos	101.8	105.9	Sarajevo	102.0	106.0
Manjaca	101.3	105.4	Sipovo	102.7	105.4

D.PRGR: relays of BFBS1 & 2 from studios in the United Kingdom.

RADIO ACCORD (French)
✉ SFOR, 88000 Mostar.
Mostar 106.2MHz.

RADIO ANDERNACH (German)
✉ General-Delius-Kaserne, Kürrenberger Steig 34, D-56727 Mayen, Germany.
Rajolvac 97.7, Sarajevo 104.8MHz.

BOTSWANA

L.T: UTC +2h — **Pop:** 1.5 million — **Pr.L:** English, Setswana — **E.C:** 50Hz, 220V — **ITU:** BOT.

DEPARTMENT OF INFORMATION AND BROADCASTING
✉ Private Bag 0060, Gaborone ☎ +267 3653086 🖷 +267 357792.
Web: www.gov.bw/government/ministry_of_state_president.html

RADIO BOTSWANA
✉ Private Bag 0060, Gaborone ☎ +267 3653000 🖷 +267 257138
Web: www.gov.bw/news/rb2.html **Email:** Rbeng@info.bw
L.P: Acting Dir. of Inf. & Broadc: Habuji Sosome. Chief Broadc. Officer: Mrs. Banyana Tshegoe, CE: Kingsley Reetsang.
G.C: Sebele: 25.58E/24.34S.

MW	kHz	kW	MW	kHz	kW
Maun	531	50	Sebele	972	50
Selebi Phikwe	621	100	Jwaneng	1071	25
Mopipi	648	50	Mahalapye	1215	50
Shakawe	693	25	Tshabong	1350	50
Gansti	873	50			
SW	**kHz**	**kW**	**SW**	**kHz**	**kW**
Sebele	4820	50	Sebele	7255	25

Note: 4820 rep. inactive, 7255: 0300-1800.

FM: all tr's 1kW

Location	RB1	RB2	Location	RB1	RB2
Francistown	103.6	90.5	Maun	94.2	104.6
Gaborone	89.9	103	Mahalapye	96.6	107
Lobatse	98.6	105.7	Orapa	89.9	98.6
Kasane	94.4	-	Serowe	99.4	92.9

National Sce. (RB1) in Setswana/English on MW/SW/FM: 24h.
N. in English: on the hour exc. **in Setswana:** 1100, 1600, 1900.
Commercial Sce. (RB2): 24h. **N**: rel. RB1.

ANN: E: "This is R. Botswana broadcasting from Gaborone", "RB", "RB1", "RB2". Setswana: "Se Ke Seromamowa Sa Botswana mo Gaborone".
IS: RB1: Cow Bells. Imitation of farm animals at s/on. National Anthem at opening and closing.

VOICE OF AMERICA RELAY STATION
MW Mopeng Hill 909kHz 600kW 0300-0630 1600-2200 & SW
For further details see International Radio section

BRAZIL

L.T: AL, AP, BA, CE, DF, ES, GO, MA, MG, PE, PI, PA-East, PB, PR, RJ, RN, RS, SC, SP: UTC -3h (DST*: UTC -2h). AM-East, MS, MT, PA-West, RO, RR: UTC -4h (DST*: UTC -3h). AC, AM-West: UTC -5h. *DST (only DF, ES, GO, MG, MS, PR, RJ, RS, SC, SP): 17 Oct-20 Feb) — **Pop:** 183 million — **Pr.L:** Portuguese — **E.C:** 60Hz, 220V — **ITU:** B.

AGÊNCIA NACIONAL DE COMUNICAÇÕES (ANATEL)
✉ SAS Quadra 06 Bloco H, Ed. Ministro Sérgio Motta, 2° andar, 70313-900 Brasília, DF. **Web:** www.anatel.gov.br **L.P:** Dir. Gen. Dr. Rubens Bussacos. Dir. of Radio: Roberto Blois Montes de Souza. Dir. Dept. of Authorizations: Domingo Poty Chabalgoity.

ASSOCIAÇÃO BRASILEIRA DE EMISSORAS DE RADIO E TELEVISÃO (ABERT)
✉ SAS Quadra 4 Bloco B No. 100, sala 501, Centro Empresarial Varig, 70170-500 Brasília, DF (C.P. 08780, 70312-970).
☎ +55 61 224 4600. 🖷 +55 61 321 7583. **Web:** www.abert.org.br
L.P: Presidente: Paulo Machado de Carvalho Neto. Exec. Dir: Antonio Abelin.
N.B: all st's carry "A Voz do Brasil" (official prgr.). Main tr. MF 2200-2300. Stations may transmit at other times during the day.

MW: Call ZY, ° = also on SW, * = inactive, ,
v = varying freq., ff = future frequency, CP = Construction Permit
The letters preceding the stn. number indicate the state or territory. Addresses are listed by state in alphabetical order.
H. of tr. usually 0800-0300. Larger st's may operate 24h.

	Call	kHz	kW	Name and location
BA01)	H481	540	1/0.25	R. Regional, Irecê
CE01)	H610	540	1/0.25	R. Jornal, Canindé
GO01)	H755	540	10/1	R. Riviera, Goiânia
MA01)	H894	540	1/0.25	R. Guajajara, Barra do Corda
MG151)	L331	540	1/0.5	R. Ipanema, Ipanema
MG188)	L...	540	0.5/0.25	R. Dif. Phoenix S/C Ltda.,Uberaba (CP)
MS37)		540	10	R. Nacional, Corumbá
PI31)	I914	540	1/0.25	R. Primeiro de Julho, Agua Branca
PR110)	J322	540	1/0.25	R. Nova Era, Borrazópolis
RJ01)	J450	540	10/2.5	R. Canção Nova, Niterói
RS01)	K226	540	1/0.5	R. Real, Canoas
RS02)	K322	540	10/1	R. Sepé Tiaraju, Santo Ângelo
SC01)	J778	540	10/1	R. Mirador, Rio do Sul
SE01)	J924	540	10/2.5	R. Jornal AM, Aracaju
SP01)	K697	540	1/0.25	R. Uirapuru, Biriguí
SP02)	K734	540	1/0.25	R. Nova Sumaré, Sumaré
CE59)	H644	550	1/0.25	R. Vale do Quinçoé, Acopiara
MG01)	L225	550	5/0.5	R. Cataguases, Cataguases
MG02)	L263	550	20/5	R. Soc. Norte de Minas,Montes Claros
MT29)	I429	550	1	R. Capital do Norte, Sinop
PE01)	I796	550	5/1	R. Meridional, Garanhuns
PI01)	I902	550	1/0.25	R. Serra da Capivara, São Raimundo Nonato
PI22)	I907	550	10/0.5	R. Igaraçu, Parnaíba
PR139)	J331	550	10/0.5	R. Banda B, Curitiba
RS03)	K287	550	2.5/0.25	R. Sta. Cruz do Sul, Sta. Cruz do Sul
SP03)	K578	550	5/0.5	R. Mantiqueira, Cruzeiro
SP04)	K696	550	5/0.5	R. Globo, Sertãozinho
AM09)		560	10	R.Educaão Rural,Coari (CP)
BA02)	H456	560	5/1	R. Jornal, Itabuna
CE41)	H604	560	1/0.25	R. Educ. Jaguaribana, Limoeiro do Nte.
GO25)	H769	560	5/0.25	R. Emissora Sul Goiana, Quirinópolis
MA02)	H887	560	25/5	R. Educadora do Maranhão, São Luís
MG05)	L277	560	5/0.25	R. Dif., Patrocínio
MT01)	I395	560	10/2.5	R. Em. Aruanã, Barra do Garças
MT24)	I419	560	10/1	R. Pioneira, Tangará da Serra
PB16)	I695	560	1/0.25	R. Potiguara, Mamanguape
PR01)	J214	560	1/0.5	R. Londrina, Londrina
PR02)	J281	560	2.5/0.25	R. Cultura AM, Guarapuava
RJ02)	J496	560	5/0.25	R. Costa do Sol, Araruama
RS04)	K231	560	5/1	R. São Francisco Sat, Caxias do Sul
SP213)	K761	560	25/10	R. Paulista AM, São Paulo
AL01)	H244	570	5/1	R. Novo Nordeste, Arapiraca
CE02)	H613	570	5/0.25	R. Vale do Cariri, Juazeiro do Norte
CE03)	H614	570	1/0.25	R. Uirapuru, Itapipoca
GO02)	H750	570	2.5/0.5	R. Cultura, Catalão
MA06)	H890	570	10/1	R. Imperatriz, Imperatriz
MG03)	L261	570	25/5	R. Capital, Belo Horizonte
MT30)	N407	570	1/0.25	R. Jornal, São José dos Quatro Marcos
PI48)		570	-	CBN Meio Norte, Teresina
PR146)	J349	570	1/0.5	R. Continental, Palotina
RS05)	K267	570	1/0.5	R. Planalto, Passo Fundo
SC02)	J735	570	5/0.5	R. Eldorado AM, Criciúma
SC99)	J794	570	1/0.25	R. Fronteira Oeste, Dionísio Cerqueira
SP05)	K595	570	1/0.25	R. Clube, Itapeva
SP06)	K672	°570	5/1	R. Dif., Taubaté
SP195)	K698	570	1/0.25	R. Jornal, Nhandeara
SP150)	K717	570	1/0.25	Bariri R. Clube, Bariri
AM01)	H290	580	10	R. Nacional, Tefé
BA03)	H477	580	1/0.25	R. Dif., Teixeira de Freitas
GO44)	H799	580	1/0.25	R. Serra Azul, Caiapônia
MG04)	L328	580	7/0.5	R. América, Uberlândia
MS01)	I387	°580	10/1	R. Educação Rural, Campo Grande
PE02)	I776	580	20/10	R. Boas Novas, Recife
PI12)	I905	580	5/1	R. Itamaraty, Piripiri
PR105)	J327	580	1/0.25	R. Auri Verde, Pitanga
PR03)	J330	580	1/0.25	R. Grande Lago, Santa Helena
RJ03)	J465	°580	50/5	R. Nova Relógio, Rio de Janeiro
RS06)	K299	580	2/0.5	R. São Gabriel, São Gabriel
RS07)	K318	580	10/5	R. Fátima, Vacarla
SP07)	K540	580	1/0.25	R. Noticia AM, Americana
SP08)	K724	580	1/0.25	R. Regional, Palmital
TO01)	H785	580	10/1	R. Tocantins AM, Porto Nacional
BA04)	H445	590	10/5	R. Cruzeiro da Bahia, Salvador
CE04)	H627	590	5/0.25	R. Vale do Rio Poty, Crateús

	Call	kHz	kW	Name and location
ES01)	I213	590	5/0.5	R. Tribuna, Vitória
GO03)	H798	590	10/1	R. Manchester, Anápolis
MG93)	L249	590	10/0.5	R. Cultura, João Monlevade
MT03)	I420	590	10/5	R. Gazeta, Cuiabá
PB25)	I692	590	5/0.25	R. Serrana, Araruna
PR04)	J234	590	10/5	R. Ouro Verde, Curitiba
RR01)	O700	°590	5	R. Dif. de Roraima, Boa Vista
RS08)	K210	590	5/0.5	R. Alegrete, Alegrete
SC03)	J809	590	2/1	R. Progresso, Descanso
SP09)	K534	590	10/1	R. Atlântica, Santos
SP10)	K612	590	1/0.25	R. Clube, Mirandópolis
SP11)	K643	°590	5/1	R. Ribeirão Preto, Ribeirão Preto
AM02)	H287	°600	10	R. Municipal, São Gabriel da Cachoeira
BA05)	H486	600	10/1	R. Vale do Rio Grande, Barreiras
BA64)	H...	600	1/0.25	R. Dif., Rio Real (CP)
CE38)	H627	600	1/0.25	R. Cultura, Aracati
MA38)	H...	600	10/1	R. Litoral Maranhense, São Luís
PE03)	I789	600	1/0.25	R. Cardeal Arcoverde, Arcoverde
RS09)	K278	°600	100	R. Gaúcha, Porto Alegre
AL10)	H249	610	10/2	R. Imperial AM, Marechal Deodoro
AM18)	H321	610	10	R. LBV Mundial, Iranduba
GO10)	H786	610	25/2	R. Mega AM, Luziânia
MG06)	L268	°610	100/25	R. Itatiaia, Belo Horizonte
MT04)	I425	610	10/5	R. Celeste, Sinop
PB01)	I678	610	1/0.25	R. Progresso, Sousa
PI02)	I899	610	10/1	R. Poty, Teresina
SC04)	J746	610	10/0.5	Super Condá, Chapecó
SP12)	K532	610	1/0.25	R. CBN, Mogi Mirim
SP13)	K577	610	1/0.25	R. Nova Voz AM, Catanduva
SP14)	K589	610	1/0.25	R. Piratininga, Guaratinguetá
SP15)	K726	610	1/0.25	R. Paranapanema, Piraju
CE05)	H590	620	10	R. Assunção Cearense, Fortaleza
GO04)	H777	620	1/0.25	R. Cristã Educativa, Pires do Rio
MG125)	L320	620	10/0.25	R. Educadora, Porteirinha
MG147)	L348	620	1/0.25	R. Ibiá, Ibiá
MG145)	L357	620	1/0.25	R. Catuaí, Manhuaçu
MT43)	I...	620	2.5	Pantal Som e Imagem, Cáceres (CP)
PR05)	J332	620	2.5/0.25	R. Cidade Jandaia, Jandaia do Sul
RS10)	K270	620	10/1	R. Pelotense, Pelotas
RS11)	K315	620	1/0.25	R. Municipal, Tenente Portela
SC05)	J779	620	5/0.25	R. Dif. Alto Vale, Rio do Sul
SP16)	K521	620	50/20	R. Jovem Pan, São Paulo
AC10)	H...	630	10	R. Fundação Cultural, Feijó (CP)
AP01)	H422	°630	25/10	R. Dif., Macapá
CE58)	H636	630	1/0.5	R. Cidade, Campos Sales
MA16)	H924	630	10/0.5	R. Macaru, Viana **(F.PI.** still on 650)
MG07)	L299	630	1/0.5	R. Dif., Uberaba
MS32)	N603	°630	10/1	R. Novo Tempo, Campo Grande
MT05)	I384	630	10/5	R. Dif. Bom Jesús, Cuiabá
PI03)	I904	630	1/0.5	R. Dif., Barras
PR06)	J284	630	10/0.5	R. Educativa AM, Curitiba
PR07)	J300	630	5/0.25	R. Educ. Marechal, Marechal Cândido Rondón
RJ04)	J466	630	25/10	R. Roquette Pinto, Rio de Janeiro
RS12)	K259	630	1/0.5	R. Cacique, Lagoa Vermelha
RS13)	K289	630	1/0.25	R. Santamariense, Santa Maria
SC06)	J800	630	1/0.25	R. Doze de Maio, São Lourenço d'Oeste
SE02)	J920	630	10/5	R. Aperipe, Aracaju
SP17)	K613	630	1/0.25	R. Mirassol, Mirassol
SP18)	K635	*630	5/0.25	R. Cidade Globo, Presidente Prudente
BA12)	H458	640	10/0.5	R. Dif. Sul da Bahia, Itabuna
ES02)	I204	640	10/0.5	R. Vitória, Vitória
GO05)	H757	640	50/5	R. Dif., Goiânia
MG08)	L308	640	3/0.25	R. Santa Cruz, Pará de Minas
MT06)	I406	640	10/5	R. Progresso, Alta Floresta
MT18)	I424	640	10/1	R. Tangará, Tangará da Serra
PI28)	I924	640	1/0.25	R. Cruzeiro, Pedro II
PR08)	J262	640	5/1	R. Auri Verde, Londrina
RJ05)	J489	640	5/1	R. Agulhas Negras, Resende
RN01)	J590	640	20/5	R. Globo Natal, Natal
RS14)	K277	640	50/10	R. Band AM, Porto Alegre
SP19)	K547	640	5/1	R. Morada do Sol, Araraquara
SP135)	K	640	2/0.5	R. CBN, Ribeirão Preto
BA06)	H462	650	5/0.5	R. Clube, Valença
GO06)	H790	650	1/0.25	R. Cultural do Araguaia, Jussara
MA16)	H924	650	1/0.25	R. Macaru, Viana (ff 630)
MG09)	L200	650	10/0.5	R. Princesa, Lagoa Formosa
MG85)	L309	650	5/0.5	R. Veredas, Unaí
MG142)	L372	650	10/1	R. Itatiaia AM Vale do Aço, Timóteo
MT19)	I414	650	5	R. Educadora, Colider
PA20)	I540	650	10/1	R. Tropical, Santarém
PB02)	I672	650	5/0.5	R. Alto Piranhas, Cajazeiras
PI26)	I925	650	1/0.25	R. Tapuio, Miguel Alves
PR09)	J202	650	1/0.5	R. Cultura, Cambará
PR91)	J250	650	5/1	R. Colméia, Cascavel
RS15)	K238	650	5/0.5	Radiodifusão Sul Riograndense, Erechim
SP20)	K508	650	1/0.25	R. Andradina, Andradina
SP22)	K518	650	5/1	R. News, Santos
SP21)	K524	650	5/0.25	R. Dif., Piracicaba
BA07)	H465	660	5/0.25	R. Jornal, Itapetinga
BA36)	H480	660	10/0.25	R. Bom Jesus AM, Bom Jesus da Lapa
BA66)	H510	660	1/0.25	R. Tribuna do Vale do São Francisco, Xique-Xique
BA65)	H...	660	1/0.25	R. Planalto, Euclides da Cunha (CP)
CE06)	H619	660	1/0.25	R. Rio das Garças, Itarema (Acaraú)
GO07)	H778	660	5/0.25	R. Primavera, Itapuranga
MG11)	L206	660	10/0.25	R. Clube, Curvelo
MT07)	I401	660	10/0.5	R. Amorim, Rondonópolis
PA21)	I552	660	1/0.25	R. Xinguara, Xinguara
PE04)	I787	660		R. Jornal, Limoeiro
PE05)	I795	660	1/0.25	R. da Grande Serra, Araripina
PI34)	I925	660	1/0.25	R. Tacarijus, São Miguel do Tapuio
RJ06)	J472	660	1	R. Friburgo, Nova Friburgo
RO01)	J673	660	10/5	R. Boas Novas AM, Porto Velho
RS16)	K286	660	1/0.25	R. Marajá, Rosário do Sul
RS17)	K319	660	10/0.25	R. Canão Nova, Vacaria
SP23)	K639	°660	10/0.5	R. Clube, Ribeirão Preto
SP112)	K656	°660	20/0.5	R. Mundial, São Paulo
AC11)	H...	670	0.25	Governo do Estado do Acre, Fundação Elias Mansour, Sena Madureira (CP)
AM04)	H288	670	1	R. Nacional, Tabatinga
AM03)	H297	°670	1/0.25	R. Vale do Rio Madeira, Humaitá
AP02)	H420	°670	10/1	R. Equatorial, Macapá
BA95)	H...	670	5/0.5	R. Cidade, Barreiras
CE07)	H606	670	1/0.25	R. Cultura, Várzea Alegre
GO08)	H747	670	10/1	R. São Francisco, Anápolis
MG12)	L310	670	10/2.5	R. Educadora, Montes Claros
MG126)	L347	670	1/0.25	R. Visão, Ponte Nova
MG123)	L361	670	5/0.25	R. Uberaba, Uberaba
MG135)	L3..	670	1/0.25	R. Cidade, Bambuí
MS23)	I408	670	1/0.25	R. Patriarca, Cassilândia
MS28)	N600	670	10	Super R. Fronteira, Ponta Porã
MT16)	I422	670	6/1	R. Transpantaneira, Poconé
MT44)	I...	670	1	R.Regional Centro Oeste Ltda., Lucas do Rio Verde (CP)
PA02)	I537	670	1/0.25	R. Rural, Altamira
PA22)	I539	670	5/0.25	R. Atalaia, Óbidos
PA27)	I546	670	1/0.25	R. Tropical AM, Paragominas
PI32)	I927	670	1/0.25	R. Livramento, José de Freitas
PR10)	J231	670	2.5/0.25	R. Canção Nova Esperança, Nova Esperança
PR11)	J248	670	10/2	R. Cidade, Curitiba
RS18)	K296	670	2.5/0.25	R. Cultura, Sta. Vitória do Palmar
RS19)	K370	670	10/0.5	R. Gazeta, Carazinho
SE03)	J921	670	10/5	R. Cultura de Sergipe, Aracaju
SP24)	K574	670	1/0.5	R. Oceânica, Caraguatatuba
SP25)	K585	670	1/0.25	R. Centro Oeste AM, Garça
SP26)	K598	670	1/0.5	R. Emissora Convenção, Itu
BA08)	H471	680	10/2	R. Clube, Sto. Antônio de Jesús
GO09)	H765	°680	10/0.5	R. Dif., Jataí
GO49	H787	680	5/1	R. Mantiqueira, Niquelândia (**F.PI.** still on 1570)
MA03)	H885	°680	10/5	R. Dif. do Maranhão, São Luís
MG173)	L270	680	2/0.25	R. Difusora, Ouro Fino
MG13)	L326	680	1/0.25	R. União, João Pinheiro
MS02)	I389	680	5/1	R. Cultura, Campo Grande
PB26)	I683	680	2.5/0.25	R. Integração do Brejo, Bananeiras
PE06)	I793	680	10/1	R. do Grande Rio, Petrolina
PR155)	J362	680	5/0.25	R. Poema, Pitanga
RJ07)	J452	°680	20/5	R. Copacabana, Rio de Janeiro
RS69)	K275	680	50	R. Farroupilha, Porto Alegre
SP27)	K576	680	1/0.25	R. Dif., Catanduva
SP28)	K628	680	2/0.25	R. Piratininga, Piraju
BA09)	H453	690	10/1	R. Cultura, Ilhéus
CE08)	H587	690	25/10	R. Dragão do Mar, Fortaleza
ES10)	I201	690	10/1	R. América, Vitória
GO48)	H780	690	10/0.25	R. Sociedade, Ceres
MG14)	L228	690	50/5	R. Mineira, Belo Horizonte
MS03)	I402	690	5/0.25	R. Cultura, Naviraí
MT31)	I451	690	5/1	R. Parecis, Diamantino
PA03)	I532	°690	12/5	R. Clube do Pará, Belém
PR13)	J229	°690	5/1	R. Dif., Londrina

	Call	kHz	kW	Name and location
PR14)	J252	690	1/0.25	R. Dif., Ponta Grossa
PR143)	J360	690	1/0.25	R. A Voz do Sudoeste, Coronel Vivida
RS21)	K252	690	5/0.5	R. Progresso, Ijuí
SC07)	J772	690	5/1	R. Clube, Lages
SP29)	K561	690	1/0.25	R. Bebedouro, Bebedouro
SP30)	K588	690	1/0.25	R. Clube, Guaratinguetá
SP31)	K625	690	1/0.25	R. Cidade, Pereira Barreto
SP220)	K646	690	1/0.25	R. Brasil, Santa Bárbara d'Oeste
TO12)	H...	690	25/1.5	R. Canção Nova do Coração de Jesus, Palmas
BA10)	H500	700	25/1	R. Cultura AM, Feira de Santana
MT21)	I428	700	25/1	R. Sorriso, Sorriso
GO47)	H801	700	25/0.5	R. Pouso Alto, Piracanjuba
PI04)	I890	700	10/5	R. Clube, Teresina
PR92)	J225	1450	1/0.25	R. Capital do Papei, Telêmaco Borba
RJ56)	J507	700	0.25	R. Aliança, Italva
RS123)	K247	700	1/0.5	R. Sideral, Getúlio Vargas (**F.PI.** still on 1400)
RS22)	K356	700	1/0.25	R. Batovi AM, São Gabriel
SP32)	K686	700	50	R. Eldorado Estadão, São Paulo
AL02)	H240	710	5/1	R. Novo Tempo, Maceió
BA46)	H490	710	10/0.25	R. Jacarandá, Eunápolis
CE09)	H628	710	1/0.25	R. Difusora Asa Branca, Boa Viagem
DF07)	H710	710	10/2.5	R. Nova Aliança, Brasília
MA12)	H891	710	1	R. Verdes Campos, Pinheiro
MA27)	H910	710	10/0.5	R. Verdes Vales, Grajaú
MG79)	L219	710	5/0.5	R. Cancella, Ituiutaba
MG15)	L258	710	20/0.5	R. Manhuaçu, Manhuaçu
MG80)	L319	710	1/0.25	R. Planeta, Carmo do Paranaíba
MG16)	L333	710	2/0.25	R. Difusora, Pouso Alegre
MT08)	I386	°710	5/0.5	R. Cultura, Cuiabá
MT23)	I436	710	5/1	R. Nova Xavantina, Nova Xavantina
PA04)	I534	°710	10/5	R. Rural, Santarém
PB03)	I685	710	5/0.25	R. Educadora, Conceição
PI19)	I901	710	1/0.25	R. Alvorada do Sertão, São João do Piauí
PI23)	I933	710	1/0.5	R. Clube, Barras
PR141)	J328	710	1/0.25	R. Alternativa, Cândido de Abreu
RJ09)	J451	710	10	R. Dif. Carioca, Rio de Janeiro
SC08)	J793	710	1/0.25	R. Fraiburgo, Fraiburgo
SP33)	K559	710	10/0.25	R. 710, Bauru
AC01)	H202	°720	10	R. Integração, Cruzeiro do Sul
AM05)	H281	720	1	R. Difusora, Itacoatiara
MG28)	L330	720	2.5/0.5	R. Divinópolis AM, Divinópolis
MS04)	I390	°720	5/1	R. Clube, Dourados
MT20)	I411	720	5/1	R. Difusora, Barra do Garças
PE07)	I770	720	100	R. Clube de Pernambuco, Recife
RS23)	K276	°720	100	R. Guaíba, Porto Alegre
SP34)	K575	720	1/0.25	R. Difusora, Casa Branca
SP35)	K701	720	1/0.25	R. Sentinela, Ourinhos
SP36)	K718	720	1/0.25	R. Cruzeiro, Cruzeiro
SP37)	K722	720	1/0.25	R. Menina, Olímpia
CE45)	H640	730	10/0.5	R. Sinal, Aracati
ES16)	I217	730	10/0.5	R. Novo Tempo, Vitória
GO31)	H759	730	25/5	R. K do Brasil, Goiânia
MA04)	H896	730	1/0.25	R. Eldorado, Codó
MG17)	L287	730	5/1	R. Soc. Triângulo Mineiro, Uberaba
MG18)	L297	730	10/1	R. Manchester AM, Juiz de Fora
MS38)	I452	730	1/0.5	R. Princesa do Vale, Camapuã
MT09)	I410	730	10/2.5	R. Jornal, Cáceres
PE08)	I780	°730	10/5	Em. Rural, A Voz do São Francisco, Petrolina
PR15)	J208	730	5/0.6	R. Marumby, Curitiba
PR16)	J323	730	1/0.25	R. Humaitá, Campo Mourão
PR147)	J353	730	5/0.25	R. Integração Oeste, Corbélia
RS24)	K268	730	5/1	R. Planalto, Passo Fundo
SC09)	J787	730	5/1	R. Super Tubá, Tubarão
SP38)	K523	730	10/0.25	R. Cidade, Jundiaí
SP39)	K610	730	10/1	R. Dirceu, Marília
AC02)	H206	°740	20/10	Super R. Alvorada, Rio Branco
BA11)	H446	740	100	R. Soc. da Bahia, Salvador
MT25)	N403	740	1/0.5	R. Cidade, Alto Araguaia
PR17)	J259	740	1/0.25	R. Goio-Erê, Goio-Erê
PR135)	J354	740	1/0.25	R. Placar, Ortigueira
RS25)	K265	740	2.5/0.25	R. Palmeira, Palmeira das Missões
RS26)	K283	740	10/0.25	R. Nativa, Rio Grande
SC10)	J753	740	10/1	CBN - Diário, Florianópolis
SP93)	K519	740	5/1	R. Assunção, Jales
SP40)	K553	740	1/0.25	R. Cultura, Bariri
SP41)	K650	740	25/0.5	R. Trianon, São Paulo
DF01)	H709	750	50/25	R. Jovem Pan, Brasília
MG19)	L213	750	50/5	R. América, Belo Horizonte
PA28)	I541	750	1/0.25	R. Ximango AM, Alenquer
PB04)	I682	750	1/0.25	R. Panati, Patos
PI05)	I897	750	1/0.25	R. Heróis do Jenipapo, Campo Maior
RS27)	K264	750	7.5/0.25	R. Osório, Osório
SC11)	J815	750	5/0.25	R. Aliança, Concórdia
SE04)	J927	750	10/0.25	R. Progresso, Lagarto
SP42)	K516	750	1/0.25	R. Clube, Osvaldo Cruz
SP43)	K642	750	12/0.5	R. CMN, Ribeirão Preto
SP44)	K661	750	2.5/0.25	Super R. Piratininga, São José dos Campos
SP169)	K708	750	5/0.5	R. News, Registro
TO03)	H792	750	1/0.25	R. Tocantins, Tocantinópolis
AL12)	H252	760	1/0.25	R. Pioneira, Delmiro Gouveia
AP03)	H424	760	5	Rede Amapaense de Radiodifusão, Macapá
BA44)	H461	760	5/0.5	R. Cidade, Vitória da Conquista
CE10)	H588	760	10	R. Uirapuru, Fortaleza
GO43)	H775	760	5/0.5	R. Rio Claro, Iporã
GO11)	H783	760	10/0.5	R. Pousada do Rio Quente, Caldas Novas
MG83)	L257	760	2.5/0.25	R. Difusora, Machado
MG137)	L360	760	10/0.5	R. Terra, Monte Claros
MT32)	N408	760	10/5	R. Central, Chapada dos Guimarães
PR12)	J343	760	10/0.25	R. Cacique, Guarapuava
RJ11)	J478	760	25/1	R. Manchete AM, Niterói
RS28)	K222	760	1/0.25	R. Princesa do Jacuí, Candelária
RS29)	K351	760	2.5/0.25	R. Ametista, Planalto
SC12)	J742	760	25/2	R. Nereu Ramos, Blumenau
SP149)	K541	760	1/0.25	R. Urubupungá, Andradina
SP45)	K560	760	10/0.5	R. Jovem Auriverde, Bauru
BA51)	H491	770	1/0.25	R. Rio Corrente, Santa Maria da Vitória
CE11)	H609	770	10/0.25	R. Vale do Salgado, Lavras da Mangabeira
ES03)	I211	770	5/0.25	R. Nova Difusora, Cachoeiro de Itapemirim
GO12)	H745	°770	1/0.25	R. A Voz do Coração Imaculado, Anápolis
MA28)	H922	770	1/0.25	R. Vitória, Coelho Neto
MA41)		770	10/0.25	Jundacao Prelazia, Balsas (CP)
MG20)	L209	770	2.5/0.25	R. Cultura d'Oeste, Lavras
MG21)	L302	770	10/0.5	R. Clube de Patos, Patos de Minas
MG108)	L315	770	5/0.5	R. Pontal do Triangulo, Iturama
MG22)	L337	770	1/0.25	R. Itabira AM, Itabira
MS11)	I412	770	10/0.5	R. Caiuás, Dourados
MT28)	N404	770	1	R. Cidade de Matupá, Matupá
MT45)	I...	770	5/1	LMR Telecomunicações, Jaciara (CP)
PA29)	I...	770	10/0.25	SNC-Sistema Norte de Comunicações ("R. Eldorado AM"), Marabá (CP)
PR131)	J344	770	1/0.25	R. Difusora, Cambé
SE05)	J922	770	10/5	R. Atalaia de Sergipe, Aracaju
SP46)	K506	770	5/0.5	R. Mix, Limeira
AM22)	H291	780	10	R. Nacional, Eirunepê
CE55)	H657	780	10/1	R. Difusora, Nova Russas
GO13)	H789	780	10/1	R. Soc. Vera Cruz, Goianésia
MA24)	H919	780	10/5	R. Alvorada, Zé Doca
MG23)	L246	780	1	R. Educadora, Uberlândia
MG103)	L259	780	10/1	R. Manhumirim, Manhumirim
PE09)	I771	780	20/10	R. Jornal do Comércio, Recife
PR18)	J247	780	1/0.25	R. Porta Voz, Cianorte
PR19)	J305	780	5/0.25	R. Chopinzinho, Chopinzinho
RS30)	K229	780	5/2	R. Diário da Manhã, Carazinho
RS31)	K279	780	25	R. Pampa, Porto Alegre
SC54)	J751	780	0.5	R. Brasil Novo, Jaraguá do Sul
SC13)	J788	780	1	R. Marconi, Urussanga
SP161)	K619	780	1/0.25	R. Difusora, Monte Aprazível
SP47)	K695	°780	50/10	R. CBN (Globo), São Paulo
BA13)	H484	790	10/1	R. Barreiras, Barreiras
BA14)	H505	790	1/0.25	R. Regional, Serrinha
CE12)	H629	790	1/0.25	R. Jornal Centro Sul, Iguatu
GO28)	H761	790	5/0.5	R. Xavantes, Ipameri
GO14)	H771	790	1/0.5	R. Eldorado, Mineiros
MA29)	H904	790	1/0.25	R. Pérola do Turi, ("R. Rio Turiaçu"), Santa Helena
MA20)	H915	790	1/0.25	R. Cultura, Açailândia
MA30)	H...	790	1/0.25	Sistema Clube de Comunicação, Tuntum (CP)
MG24)	L279	790	5/0.25	R. Soc. Ponte Nova, Ponte Nova
MG25)	L311	790	1/0.25	R. Treze de Junho, Mantena
MG26)	L314	790	5/1	R. Tropical, Lagoa da Prata
MT22)	I456	790	1	R. Difusora, Nortelândia
PB05)	I679	790	2.5/1	R. Cultura, Guarabira
PI36)	I931	790	1/0.25	R. Mafrense, Simplício Mendes
PR130)	J316	790	2.5/0.25	R. Clube, Faxinal

	Call	kHz	kW	Name and location
PR20)	J337	790	5/0.25	R. Nacional, Curitiba
RS32)	K285	790	1/0.25	R. Rio Pardo, Rio Pardo
SC14)	J789	790	1/0.25	R. Videira, Videira
SP48)	K538	790	1/0.25	R. Brasil, Adamantina (nf 1270)
SP49)	K546	°790	10/0.5	R. Cultura, Araraquara
SP162)	K674	790	5/0.25	R. Cultura, Taubaté
AC14)	H…	800	10	Líder Comunicações., Rio Branco (CP)
AL17)	H…	800	10	R. Sol Maior Ltda., Maceió (CP)
DF02)	H705	800	10/1	R. MEC, Brasília
MS53)	H…	800	10	CAMY Telecomunicacaões, Campo Grande (CP)
PI08)	I921	800	10	R. Antares, Teresina
RJ12)	J457	°800	100	R. MEC, Rio de Janeiro
RS33)	K292	800	10	R. Universidade, Santa Maria
BA54)	H528	810	10/0.25	R. Nossa Senhora de Guadalupe AM, Riacho de Santana
CE13)	H589	810	50/5	R. Verdes Mares, Fortaleza
GO15)	H767	810	5/0.5	R. Alvorada, Rialma
MG27)	L202	810	1	R. Aimorés, Aimorés
MG92)	L252	810	1/0.25	R. Educadora, Ubá
MG76)	L266	810	1/0.25	R. Clube, Nepomuceno
MG138)	L354	810	1/0.25	R. Capinópolis, Capinópolis
MG156)	L366	810	5/0.5	R. Rainha de Paz, Patrocínio
MG160)	L...	810	1/0.25	R. Princesa do Vale, Itaobim
MT33)	N402	810	1/0.25	Gaspar Radiodifusão, São José do Rio Claro
MT34)	N406	810	1/0.25	R. Floresta AM, Alta Floresta
PR111)	J336	810	5/0.5	R. Esperança, Prudentópolis
SP50)	K604	810	5/0.25	R. Dif. Jundiaiense, Jundiaí
SP89)	K655	810	1/0.5	R. Universal, Santos
SP51)	K732	810	5/0.5	R.Canão Nova, São José do Rio Preto
AC03)	H...	°820	1/0.25	R. Educadora 6 de Agosto, Xapuri
AC12)	H...	820	0.25	Governo do Estado de Acre, Fundação Elias Mansour, Tarauacá (CP)
AM06)	H294	820	1/0.25	R. Princesa do Solimões, Manacapuru
BA15)	H534	820	20/1	R. Cultura, Utinga
CE14)	H624	820	1/0.25	R. União, Camocim
CE60)	H655	820	1/0.25	R. Sul Cearense, Brejo Santo
ES04)	I212	820	10/2.5	R. Gazeta AM, Vitória
GO16)	H752	820	10/5	R. Jornal de Goiás, Goiânia
MG29)	L255	820	5/0.25	R. Globo, Barbacena
MG167)	L273	820	3/0.25	R. Bom Sucesso, Minas Movas
MG30)	L291	820	1/0.25	R. Dif. Paraisense, São Sebastião do Paraíso
MT10)	I400	°820	10/1	R. Difusora, Cáceres
PA05)	I543	820	5/1	R. Reg. do Araguaia, Conceição do Araguaia
PE10)	I775	820	5/1	R. Universitária, Recife
PI06)	I912	820	5/0.25	R. Cacique Bruenque, Regeneração
PR21)	J238	820	10/5	R. Cultura, Foz do Iguaçu
PR150)	J357	820	1/0.25	R. Princesa, Roncador (**F.PI** still on 1540)
RJ13)	J477	820	5/0.25	R. Jornal, Macaé
RS34)	K241	820	5/1	R. Alto Taquari, Estrela
SC15)	J738	820	10/5	CBN, Blumenau
SP52)	K542	°820	10/0.5	R. Aparecida, Aparecida
SP53)	K602	820	1/0.25	R. Jauense, Jaú
SP54)	K622	820	0.5/0.25	R. Clube, Ourinhos
SP55)	K624	820	1/0.25	R. Difusora, Penápolis
BA67)	H506	830	1/0.25	R. Extremo Sul da Bahia, Itamaraju
CE65)	H659	830	1/0.25	R. Pioneira, Forquilha
GO50)	H805	830	1/0.25	R. Cidade, Goiatuba
MA26)	H905	830	10/1	R. Mirante do Maranhão, Imperatriz
MA21)	H925	830	1/0.25	R. Boa Esperança, Esperantinópolis
MG31)	L244	830	50/5	R. Cultura, Belo Horizonte
MS07)	I396	830	15/0.5	R. Cidade Maracaju, Maracaju (**F.PI.** still on 1030)
MT11)	I430	830	5/0.25	R. Xavantes, Jaciara
MT26)	N401	830	1/0.25	R. Educadora, Juina
PA24)	I556	830	1/0.25	R. Guaraní de Marajó, Soure
PI07)	I906	830	1/0.25	R. Primeira Capital, Oeiras
PI37)	I934	830	1/0.25	R. União, União
PR22)	J224	830	5/0.5	R. Iguaçu, Araucária
PR24)	J266	830	10/0.5	R. Globo, Londrina
PR23)	J311	830	1/0.25	R. Progresso, Clevelândia
RJ39)	J488	830	10/0.5	R. Tropical, Nova Iguaçu
RN02)	J595	830	1/0.5	R. Rural do Caicó, Caicó
RS35)	K332	830	5/0.25	R. Independente, Cruz Alta
SC16)	J773	830	1/0.25	R. Cruz de Malta, Lauro Müller
SE06)	J926	830	20/1	R. Princesa da Serra, Itabaiana
SP56)	K681	830	10/1	R. Lider, Votuporanga
SP227)	K746	830	5/0.25	R. Novo Tempo, Nova Odessa
AL13)	H253	840	10/0.25	R. Quilombo, União dos Palmares
AM07)	H298	840	1/0.25	R. Rio Madeira, Manicoré
BA16)	H447	840	25/5	R. Excelsior da Bahia, Salvador
CE51)	H648	840	1/0.5	R. Campo Maior, Quixeramobim
PI38)	I930	840	1/0.25	R. Ribeirão, Demerval Lobão
PI39)	I...	840	1/0.25	R. Vitória, Batalha
PR75)	J320	840	10/1.2	R. Inconfidência, Umuarama
RO13)	J679	*840	50	R. Nacional, Porto Velho
RS36)	K248	840	10	R. Capital, Porto Alegre
SC17)	J750	840	10/1	R. Rural, Concórdia
SP57)	K687	°840	100/50	R. Bandeirantes, São Paulo
BA17)	H474	850	5/0.25	R. Caraiba, Senhor do Bonfim
CE15)	H599	850	1	R. Iracema de Juazerio, Juazeiro do Norte
GO17)	H776	850	10/5	R. Tropical, Porangatu
MA31)	H923	850	1/0.25	R. Cidade AM, Vitória do Mearim
MG32)	L233	850	1/0.25	R. Difusora Formiguense, Formiga
MG33)	L254	°850	10/0.5	R. Por Um Mundo Melhor, Governador Valadares
MG34)	L295	850	5/0.25	R. Tupaciguara, Tupaciguara
MS30)	I438	850	1/0.25	R. Difusora Nor'estado, São Gabriel
MT02)	I416	850	10/2	R. Cultura, Poxoréo
PA17)	I538	850	10/1	R. Itacaíunas, Marabá
PA06)	I555	850	1/0.25	R. Tocantins, Cametá (ff 910)
PA18)	I557	850	5/1	R. Itaituba, Itaituba
PB22)	I693	850	5/1	R. Rural, Guarabira
PI30)	I909	850	1/0.25	R. Grande Picos, Picos
PR50)	J254	850	5/0.25	R. Dif. Colméia, Campo Mourão
PR86)	J291	850	1/0.25	R. Alvorada do Sul, Rebouças
RJ31)	J470	850	10/0.5	R. Difusora, Campos dos Goytacazes
RO03)	J675	850	5/1	R. Ariquemes, Ariquemes
SC20)	J808	850	1/0.25	R. Cidade, Brusque
SC102)	J…	850	1/0.25	R. Atalaia, Campo Erê
SP59)	K563	850	1/0.5	R. Clube, Biriguí
SP58)	K644	850	1/0.25	R. Jornal, Rio Claro
CE16)	H592	860	25/10	R. Cidade, Maracanaú
RJ14)	J459	860	100	R. CBN, Rio de Janeiro
RS37)	K288	860	10/1	R. Guarathan, Santa Maria
AL03)	H245	870	5/1	R. Educ. Sampaio, Palmeira dos Indios
AM19)	H322	870	1/0.25	R. Cidade, Manacapuru
BA18)	H457	870	10/0.25	R. Nacional, Itabuna
BA84)	H499	870	5/1	R. da Cidade AM, Juazeiro
CE17)	H591	870	1/0.25	R. Iracema, Iguatu
CE66)	H658	870	1/0.25	R. Tabajara, São Benedito
ES20)	i…	870	1/0.25	Rádio e Televisão Ltda., Linhares (CP)
GO18)	H749	870	5/0.5	R. Lago Dourado, Uruaçu
GO32)	H754	870	20/0.5	R. Universitária, Goiânia
MA05)	H903	870	1/0.25	R. Mirante, Codó
MG78)	L304	870	10/0.5	R. Juriti, Paracatu
MG38)	L318	870	1/0.5	R. Cultura, Diamantina
MG66)	L324	870	5/0.25	R. Canção Nova 870 AM, Sacramento
MG128)	L349	870	5/0.25	R. Princesa da Mata, Muriaé
MG127)	L350	870	5/0.25	R. A Voz do São Francisco, Januária
MT35)	N409	870	1/0.5	R. Garça Branca, Guiratinga
PA11)	I547	870	1/0.25	R. Marajó, Breves
PR25)	J243	870	5/0.25	R. Nova Ingá, Maringá
SC96)	J784	870	10/0.25	R. São Francisco , São Francisco do Sul
SP60)	K620	870	1/0.25	R. Novo Horizonte, Novo Horizonte
SP61)	K705	870	5/1	R. Central, Campinas
TO04)	H762	°870	1/0.25	R. Anhanguera, Araguaína
MG35)	L275	°880	100	R. Inconfidência, Belo Horizonte
PB18)	I680	880	1/0.25	R. Maringá, Pombal
RS38)	K249	880	10/2.5	R. Itaí, Porto Alegre
RS87)	K317	880	2.5/0.25	R. Charrua, Uruguaiana
RS20)	K363	880	8/0.25	R. Seberi, Seberi
CE46)	H642	890	1/0.25	R. Itatiaia, Santa Quitéria
DF03)	H706	890	50/2.5	R. Planalto, Brasília
MA19)	H…	890	1/0.25	R. Portal de Caxias, João Lisboa (CP)
MG36)	L250	890	10/1	R. Santa Cruz, Jequitinhonha
MG154)	L370	890	5/0.25	R. Clube, Inhapim
MS33)	I453	890	10/0.5	R. Guaicurus, Fátima do Sul
PA13)	I536	890	5/1	R. Ponta Negra, Santarém
PE11)	I772	890	20/10	R. Tamandaré, Recife
PR117)	J287	890	5/0.25	R. Ubá, Ivaiporã
PR26)	J338	890	5/0.25	Super R. Itapuã, Pato Branco
RJ59)	J499	890	10	R.Musical, Cantagalo
RS39)	K215	890	5/0.25	R. Viva AM, Bento Gonçalves
RS40)	K295	890	1/0.5	R. Noroeste, Santa Rosa
SC52)	J745	890	1/0.25	R. Clube, Canoinhas
SC18)	J755	890	1/0.25	R. Santa Catarina, Florianópolis
SP62)	K690	°890	50/10	R. Canão Nova, São Paulo

	Call	kHz	kW	Name and location
SP127)	K703	890	2.5/0.25	R. Noticias, Matão
SP178)	K562	890	1/0.25	R. Clube, Bilac
BA19)	H488	900	1	R. Sisal, Conceição do Coité
GO41)	H768	900	10/1	R. Rio Verde AM, Rio Verde
MG86)	L207	900	5/0.25	R. Imbiara, Araxá
MG148)	L311	900	2.5/0.25	R. Carangola, Carangola
MG124)	L338	900	1/0.25	R. Vinícola, Andradas
MT36)	I455	900	10/2.5	R. Difusora Arco-Íris, Araputanga
MT41)	I431	900	5/1	R. Integração, Primavera do Leste
PA10)	I533	°900	25/5	R. Liberal, Belém (**F.Pl.** still on 1330)
PR27)	J272	900	5/0.25	R. Emiss. Sant'Ana, Ponta Grossa
PR28)	J295	900	5/0.25	R. União, Toledo
RJ15)	J454	900	50/10	R. Capital, Rio de Janeiro
RN03)	J591	900	10	R. Nordeste Evangélica, Natal
RO04)	J672	900	5/1	R. Alvorada de Rondônia, Ji-Paraná
RS41)	K211	900	2.5/0.5	R. Aratiba, Aratiba
RS179)	K...	900	5/0.5	R. ABC, Nôvo Hamburgo
RS164)	K303	900	1/0.25	R. Municipal, São Pedro do Sul
RS185)		900		R.Clube, Pedro Osório
SP63)	K511	900	5/0.25	R. Difusora, Presidente Prudente
SP64)	K664	900	10/0.8	R. CBN, São José do Rio Preto
SP65)	K742	900	1/0.25	R. Clube, Itapetininga
CE61)	H645	910	1/0.25	R. Assunção Cearense, Sobral
GO20)	H763	910	5/0.25	R. Paranaíba, Itumbiara
GO23)	H804	910	1/0.25	R. Cidade, Jaraguá
MG37)	L292	910	1/0.25	R. Teófilo Otoni, Teófilo Otoni
MG132)	L346	910	1/0.25	R. Difusora, Nova Serrana
MG149)	L...	910	5/1	R. Globo, Juiz de Fora
PA06)	I555	910	5/0.25	R. Tocantins, Cametá (**F.Pl.** still on 850)
PE12)	I785	910	5/1	R. Super Liberdade, Caruaru
PI41)	I935	910	10/1	R. Tropical, Teresina
PR29)	J207	910	1/0.25	R. Nova AM, Apucarana
RS43)	K320	910	5/0.5	R. Venâncio Aires, Venâncio Aires
SC19)	J811	910	4/0.5	R. Difusora, Içara
SC90)	J824	910	1/0.25	R. Rainha das Quedas, Abelardo Luz
SP66)	K536	910	5/0.25	R. Alvorada, Piracicaba
SP228)	K763	910	1/0.25	R. Princesa, Monte Azul Paulista
BA42)	H476	920	5/0.25	R. Educ. Santana de Caetité, Caetité
BA57)	H519	920	25/2	R. Novo Tempo, Salvador
ES05)	I207	920	10/5	R. Cultura, Linhares
GO33)	H788	920	5/1	R. Vale da Serra, São Luís de Montes Belos
MG39)	L271	920	5/0.5	R. Cultura, Visconde do Rio Branco
PB31)	I...	920	5/0.5	R. Cidade Verde, João Pessoa
PI11)	I893	920	10/0.5	R. Educadora, Parnaíba
PI09)	I895	920	1/0.25	R. Difusora, Picos
RJ41)	J494	920	1/0.5	R. CBN, Volta Redonda
RN04)	J600	920	1/0.25	R. Currais Novos, Currais Novos
RS44)	K348	920	20/2	R. Tramandaí, Tramandaí
SP67)	K584	920	5/0.25	R. Franca do Imperador, Franca
SP222)	K769	920	1/0.25	R. Bandeirantes, Penápolis
SP221)	K775	920	40/1	R. Nacional Gospel, Cotia
AM16)	H240	930	10	R. Boas Novas, Manaus – 24h
CE18)	H605	930	1/0.25	R. Salamanca, Barbalha
CE52)	H646	930	7/0.25	R. Metropolitana, Fortaleza
GO45)	H802	930	10/1	R. Caraiba AM, Aparecida de Goiânia
MG41)	L220	930	1/0.25	R. Clube, Campo Belo
MG42)	L229	930	5	R. Araguari, Araguari
MG87)	L237	930	20/1	R. Ibituruna, Governador Valadares
MS05)	I454	930	10/0.25	R. Capital, Campo Grande
MT12)	I423	°930	10/0.5	R. Clube, Rondonópolis
MT37)	N400	930	10/0.25	R. Jornal, Pontes e Lacerda
PA07)	I600	930	5/1	R. Liberal, Castanhal (ff 1330)
PR30)	J227	930	1/0.25	R. Cultura, Rolândia
PR31)	J232	930	10/1	R. Cultura, Curitiba
PR69)	J235	930	10/1	R. Princesa, Francisco Beltrão
RS45)	K230	930	20/2.5	R. Caxias, Caxias do Sul
RS46)	K298	930	10/0.5	R. Santo Ângelo, Santo Ângelo
SE07)	J923	930	20/5	R. Liberdade de Sergipe, Aracaju
SP71)	K500	930	1/0.25	R. Dinâmica de Sta. Fé, Sta. Fé do Sul
SP68)	K503	930	1/0.25	R. Cidade, Itapira
SP69)	K652	930	10/1	R. Cultura, Santos
SP70)	K713	930	5/1	R. Canão Nova, Agudos
SP214)	K747	930	1/0.25	R. Jóia, Adamantina
TO13)	H...	930	1/0.25	Kymo Filmes Produções Cinematograficas Ltda., Araguatins (CP)
AC04)	H204	°940	10/1	R. Verdes Florestas, Cruzeiro do Sul
PI25)	I911	940	10/0.25	R. Sete Cidades, Piracuruca
RJ16)	J453	940	100	R. LBV Mundial, Rio de Janeiro
BA50)	H489	950	1/0.25	R. Bahia Noroeste, Paulo Afonso
CE19)	H593	950	5/1	R. Educadora do Nordeste, Sobral
MA17)	H916	950	10/0.25	R. Capital, João Lisboa
MG43)	L212	950	25/10	R. Atalaia, Belo Horizonte
MG44)	L281	950	7/0.5	R. Independencia, Bueno Brandão
MT17)	I439	950	5/1	R. Tucunaré, Juara
PB17)	I681	950	1/0.25	R. Jornal, Sousa
PE13)	I782	950	25/5	R. Temurinha, Carpina
PI20)	I915	950	10/0.25	R. São José dos Altos, Altos
PI42)	I923	950	1/0.25	R. Boa Esperança, Padre Marcos
PR114)	J239	950	5/0.25	R. Difusora Cultural, Irati
RS47)	K260	950	5/0.25	R. Independente, Lajeado
SC21)	J736	950	1/0.25	R. Vale, Tijucas
SP72)	K510	950	5/0.25	R. 950, Marília
AL04)	H241	960	10	R. Difusora de Alagôas, Maceió
CE37)	H618	960	1/0.25	R. Cultura dos Inhamuns, Tauá
ES15)	I216	960	10/0.25	R. Diocesana, Cachoeiro de Itapemirim
GO21)	H764	960	5/0.25	R. Difusora, Itumbiara
MS44)	I...	960	5/1	R. AM Fronteira, Corumbá (CP)
PA26)	I551	960	5/1	R. Clube, Itaituba
PR109)	J217	960	2.5/0.25	R. Legendária, Lapa
PR32)	J257	960	1/0.25	R. Difusora, Maringá
RS48)	K291	960	10/1	R. Imembuí, Santa Maria
SC22)	J733	960	5/0.25	R. Guarujá, Orleães
SC23)	J813	960	8/0.25	R. Super Difusora, Xanxerê
SP73)	K689	960	50/10	R. São Paulo, São Paulo
TO09)	H793	960	25/5	R. Jovem Palmas, Palmas
BA20)	H451	970	10/5	R. Sociedade, Feira de Santana
CE20)	H612	970	5/0.25	R. Monólitos, Quixadá
MG45)	L243	970	5/0.25	R. Caratinga, Caratinga
MG46)	L285	970	2.5/0.25	R. São João del Rey, São João del Rey
MG47)	L321	970	1/0.5	R. Central, Monte Alegre de Minas
MS18)	I399	970	5/0.5	R. Vale do Taquari, Coxim
PB06)	I684	970	1/0.25	R. Princesa Isabel, Princesa Isabel
PI43)	I910	970	10/0.5	R. Vale do Parnaíba, Luzilândia
PR33)	J260	°970	5/1	R. Alvorada, Londrina
PR34)	J277	970	10/0.25	R. Difusora do Paraná, Marechal Cândido Rondón
RS49)	K201	970	50/10	R. Pampa, Porto Alegre
RS50)	K349	970	1/0.5	R. do Povo, Humaitá
SC24)	J730	970	1/0.25	R. Araguaia, Brusque
SP74)	K505	970	5/0.25	R. Difusora 2000, Itapetininga
SP75)	K529	970	1/0.25	R. Piratininga, São João da Boa Vista
SP76)	K684	970	1/0.25	R. Noticia, Franca
SP215)	K744	970	5/0.25	R. Alvorada, Estrela d'Oeste
DF04)	H707	°980	50/600	R. Nacional, Brasília
PR167)	J...	980	25	R. Foz Lago Comunicadora Ltda., Foz de Iguaçu (CP)
AM23)	H299	990	1/0.25	R. Independência, Maués
BA21)	H483	990	1/0.25	R. Alvorada de Teixeira de Freitas, Caravelas
PI44)	I922	990	1/0.25	R. Vale do Canindé, Oeiras
PR128)	J293	990	1/0.25	R. Najuá, Irati
PR121)	J321	990	5/0.25	R. Capital, Cianorte
RJ53)	J461	990	100/10	R. Record, Rio de Janeiro
RN05)	J596	990	10/1	R. Rural, Mossoró
RS51)	K314	990	1/0.25	R. Tupã, Tupanciretã
RS52)	K335	990	1/0.25	R. Sananduva, Sananduva
RS154)	K360	990	1/0.25	R. Clube, Pedro Osório
SC25)	J763	990	1/0.25	R. Ipiranga, Itapiranga
SC56)	J821	990	1/0.25	R. Cidade, Itaiópolis (**F.Pl** still on 1380)
SP239)	K579	990	10/0.25	R. Cultura Regional, Dois Córregos
PB30)	I...	1000	1/0.25	R. Oeste da Paraíba, Cajazeiras (**F.Pl.** still on 1460)
PE14)	I791	1000	1/0.25	R. Princesa Serrana, Timbaúba
SP77)	K522	°1000	200	R. Record, São Paulo
BA22)	H448	1010	25/5	R. Bahia, Salvador
CE21)	H625	1010	12.5/2.5	R. AM do Povo, Fortaleza
GO39)	H772	1010	10/0.5	R. Santelenense, Santa Helena de Goiás
MG50)	L230	1010	10/1	R. Educadora, Coronel Fabriciano
MG48)	L264	1010	5/0.5	R. Solar AM, Juiz de Fora
MG49)	L325	1010	5/0.25	R. Estância, Jacutinga
MT13)	I421	1010	5/1	R. Difusora, Mirassol d'Oeste
PR35)	J263	1010	25/5	R. Celinauta, Pato Branco
RS53)	K232	1010	7.5/0.75	R. Universidade, Caxias do Sul
RS54)	K344	1010	3/1	R. Missioneira Sete Povos, São Luíz Gonzaga
SC71)	J764	1010	10/0.25	R. Jaraguá, Jaraguá do Sul
SC26)	J807	1010	1/0.25	R. Verde Vale, Braço do Norte (ff 1050)
SC75)	J758	1010	1/0.25	R. Difusora, Imbituba
SP151)	K507	1010	5/0.5	R. Difusora, Lençóis Paulista
SP78)	K556	1010	1/0.5	R. Independente, Barretos
SP79)	K611	1010	1/0.25	R. Tuiuti, Martinópolis

	Call	kHz	kW	Name and location
AL05)	H247	1020	25/1	R. Maceió AM (Rede CBN), Maceió
AP04)	H. . .	1020	1/0.25	Beija Flor Radiodifusão, Santana
CE22)	H600	1020	5/1	R. Educadora Cariri, Crato
CE79)	H664	1020	1/0.25	R. Macambira, Ipueiras
ES06)	I205	1020	20/10	R. Difusora, Colatina
GO52)	H781	1020	1/0.25	R. Maranata, Firminópolis
MG55)	L224	°1020	10/1	R. Congonhas, Congonhas
MG51)	L260	1020	10/0.25	R. Cultura, Uberlândia
MS06)	I381	1020	10/0.25	R. Independente, Aquidauana
MT46)	I...	1020	10/0.5	R. Itaí de Rio Claro Ltda., Rondonópolis (CP)
PB19)	I686	1020	1/0.25	R. Cenecista, Picuí
PR36)	J244	1020	10/0.25	R. Colombo do Paraná, Curitiba
PR37)	J307	1020	1/0.25	R. Independência, Medianeira
PR142)	J359	1020	1/0.25	R. Campo Aberto, Laranjeiras do Sul
RJ42)	J484	1020	5/0.25	R. Santíssimo SalvadorCampos dos Goytacazes
RO02)	J680	1020	5/1	R. Educadora, Rolim de Moura
RR04)	O...	1020	10/5	Editora Boa Vista Ltda., Boa Vista (CP)
RS49)	K202	1020	25/5	R. Pampa, Porto Alegre
SC27)	J805	1020	2.5/0.25	R. Continental, Coronel Freitas
SP80)	K513	°1020	10/0.25	R. Canção Nova, Cachoeira Paulista
SP81)	K515	1020	5	R. Cultura, Assis
SP82)	K531	°1020	2.5/0.5	R. Educadora, Limeira
SP83)	K600	1020	5/0.25	R. Cultura, Jales
BA40)	H475	1030	10/1	R. Bahiana, Itaberaba
GO22)	H746	1030	10/1	R. Imprensa, Anápolis
MA07)	H892	1030	10/1	R. Jainara, Bacabal
MS07)	I396	1030	2.5/0.25	R. Cidade Maracaju, Maracaju (ff 830)
PE15)	I777	1030	20/5	R. Olinda, Olinda
PR38)	J240	1030	1/0.25	R. Difusora, Cruzeiro do Oeste
PR39)	J271	1030	5/0.25	R. Atalaia, Londrina
PR120)	J312	1030	2.5/0.25	R. Clube, Realeza
PR40)	J329	1030	1/0.25	R. Difusora do Xisto, São Mateus do Sul
RJ18)	J467	°1030	100/25	R. Capital, Rio de Janeiro
RN31)	J...	1030	1/0.25	R. Em. Vale do Apodi AM, Apodi
RO10)	J683	1030	5/1	R. Rondônia, Ariquemes
RS129)	K224	1030	1/0.25	R. Cultura, Canguçu
RS55)	K253	1030	10/0.5	R. Repórter, Ijuí
SC28)	J771	1030	2.5/0.5	R. Princesa, Lages
SP84)	K525	1030	5/0.25	R. Difusora de Franca, Franca
SP85)	K554	1030	1/0.25	R. Emissora da Barra, Barra Bonita
SP86)	K606	1030	1/0.25	Lins Rádio Clube, Lins
TO05)	H791	1030	1/0.25	R. Colinas, Colinas do Tocantins
SP87)	K537	1040	200/100	R. Capital, São Paulo
BA47)	H494	1050	10/0.5	R. Metropolitana da Bahia, Camaçari
CE54)	H647	1050	10/0.5	R. Primeira Capital, Aquiraz
ES07)	I203	°1050	100/10	R. Capixaba, Vitória
GO40)	H760	1050	1/0.25	R. Jornal, Inhumas (**F.PI** still on 1540)
MG52)	L236	1050	1/0.25	R. Rural, Tupaciguara
MS20)	I391	1050	10/0.5	R. Difusora Paranaibense, Paranaíba
PB07)	I676	1050	5/1	R. Caturité, Campina Grande
PI45)	I...	1050	1/0.25	Jet Radiodifusão, Teresina
PR66)	J226	1050	1/0.25	R. Dif. Platinense, Sto. Antônio da Platina
PR99)	J286	1050	5/0.25	R. Club de Palmas, Palmas
RJ19)	J497	1050	10/0.5	R. Angra, Angra dos Reis
SC26)	J807	1050	7/0.25	R. Verde Vale, Braço do Norte (**F.PI.** still on 1010)
SP160)	K601	1050	10/0.5	R. Show Jardinópolis
BA23)	H460	1060	5/1	R. Clube de Conquista, Vitória da Conquista
BA53)	H497	1060	2.5/0.25	R. Barra do Mendes, Barra do Mendes
BA68)	H520	1060	2.5/0.25	R. Clube, Itapicuru
GO59)	H...	1060	5/0.25	Soc. Serrados Vales de Comunicação, Minaçu (CP)
MG53)	L278	1060	50/5	R. Grande Belo Horizonte ("R. Grande Be Aga"), Belo Horizonte
MG54)	L306	1060	1/0.25	R. Itajubá, Itajubá
MS39)	N604	1060	5/1	R. Tupinambás, Dourados
PR42)	J246	1060	10/0.5	R. Paraná, Curitiba
PR43)	J298	1060	1/0.25	R. Colorado, Colorado
PR44)	J306	1060	10/0.5	R. Educadora, Francisco Beltrão
RJ20)	J495	1060	30/1.5	R. Tropical, Miguel Pereira
RN06)	J597	1060	5	R. Tapuyo, Mossoró
RS56)	K220	1060	5/0.25	R. Camaqüense, Camaquã
RS57)	K302	1060	2/0.25	R. São Luís, São Luís Gonzaga
RS81)	K307	1060	1/0.5	R. Cristal, Soledade
SC103)	J...	1060	1/0.25	R.Gazeta, Florianópolis
SP88)	K533	1060	5/0.25	R. Educadora, Piracicaba
SP229)	K765	1060	5/0.25	R. Universitária, Garça
BA48)	H492	1070	5/0.5	R. Rural ("R. Tropical"), Ipiaú
MG56)	L316	1070	1/0.25	R. Do Povo, Muzambinho
MG150)	L355	1070	5/0.25	Super R. Patos, Patos de Minas
MT14)	I427	1070	10/2.5	R. Industrial ("Antena 1"), Várzea Grande
PB08)	I673	1070	20/2.5	Difusora R. Cajazeiras, Cajazeiras
PR45)	J203	1070	5/0.25	R. Difusora União, União da Vitória
PR46)	J319	1070	1/0.25	R. Guaraniaçu, Guaraniaçu
RJ21)	J483	1070	10/0.25	R. Record, Campos dos Goitacazes
RS58)	K218	1070	2/0.25	R. Caçapava, Caçapava do Sul
RS59)	K343	1070	1/0.25	R. Metrópole, Crissiumal
RS60)	K357	1070	1/0.25	R. 1070, Bento Gonçalves
SC91)	J747	1070	1/0.25	R. Gralha Azul, Urubici
SP91)	K603	1070	1/0.25	R. Nova Piratininga, Jaú
SP145)	K615	1070	10/0.25	R. Metropolitana, Mogi das Cruzes
SP92)	K633	1070	5/1	R. Presidente Prudente , Presidente Prudente
SP212)	K758	1070	1/0.25	R. Jornal, Barretos
BA24)	H470	1080	10/0.5	R. Subaé AM, Feira de Santana
BA25)	H485	1080	1/0.25	R. Fascinação, Itapetinga
CE82)	H670	1080	2.5/0.25	R. Cultura, Quixadá
CE97)	H...	1080	1/0,25	R.FM Serrote, Ubajara (CP)
DF05)	H708	1080	25/5	R. Capital, Brasília
MG109)	L232	1080	2.5/0.5	R. Cultura, Dores do Indaiá
MG57)	L251	1080	10/0.5	R. Capital, Juiz de Fora
MT27)	I437	1080	1/0.25	R. Gaspar, Itiquira
PA32)	I540	1080	10/5	R. Novo Tempo, Belém
PE16)	I784	1080	5/1	R. Difusora, Caruaru
PE33)	I824	1080	1/0.25	R. Voluntários da Pátria, Ouricuri
PR47)	J201	1080	2.5/0.5	R. Clube Pontagrossense, Ponta Grossa
PR48)	J245	1080	1/0.25	R. Cultura do Norte, Paranavaí
PR49)	J261	1080	1/0.25	R. Educadora, Cornélio Procópio
RS61)	K254	1080	2.5/0.25	R. Marabá, Iraí
RS62)	K280	1080	10	R. da Univ. Federal do Rio Grande do Sul, Porto Alegre
SC29)	J759	1080	2/1	R. Clube, Indaial
SP94)	K557	1080	5/1	R. Difusora, Batatais
SP95)	K607	1080	1/0.25	R. Alvorada, Lins
SP96)	K669	1080	10/1	R. Boa Nova, Sorocaba
SP97)	K704	1080	1/0.25	R. Monumental, Aparecida
SP190)	K710	1080	1/0.25	R. Alvorada, Cardoso
AL15)	H...	1090	5/0.5	Radiodifusão Eldorado, Pão de Açucar
BA26)	H455	1090	1/0.25	R. Santa Cruz, Ilhéus
GO24)	H758	1090	10/1	R. Aliança, Goiânia
MA08)	H893	1090	10	R. Rio Balsas AM, Balsas
PR51)	J283	1090	1/0.25	R. Vicente Palotti, Coronel Vivida
RJ22)	J468	1090	25/5	R. Metropolitana, Rio de Janeiro
RN07)	J592	1090	10/5	R. Rural de Natal, Natal
RS63)	K216	1090	5/0.25	R. Cachoeira, Cachoeira do Sul
RS64)	K262	1090	1/0.25	R. Salette, Marcelino Ramos
RS65)	K341	1090	1/0.25	R. Giruá, Giruá
SC30)	J732	1090	1/0.25	R. Colón, Joinville
SC31)	J786	1090	5/0.5	R. Tabajara, Tubarão
SP98)	K609	1090	1/0.5	R. Clube, Marília
SP99)	K618	1090	1/0.25	R. Cultura, Monte Alto
SP233)	K768	1090	1/0.25	R. Canção Nova da Divina Providência, Paulínia
CE67)	H638	1100	1/0.25	R. Difusora dos Inhamuns, Tauá
CE73)	H668	1100	1/0.25	R. Difusora do Vale Acaraú, Acaraú
RN18)	J607	1100	1/0.25	R. A Voz do Seridó, Caicó
SP100)	K694	°1100	150	R. Globo, São Paulo
CE32)	H620	1110	5/0.25	R. Litoral, Cascavel
GO46)	H782	1110	25/2	R. Redentor AM, Sto. Antônio do Descoberto
MG58)	L205	1110	1/0.25	R. Planalto, Araguari
MG59)	L267	1110	1	R. Aurilândia, Nova Lima
MS08)	I392	1110		R. Ponta Porã, Ponta Porã
PB09)	I678	1110	20/10	R. Tabajara, João Pessoa
PR52)	J241	1110	10/1	R. Paiquerê, Londrina
PR151)	J356	1110	1/0.5	R. Clube, Ubiratã
RJ23)	J471	°1110	50/5	R. Cultura, Campos dos Goitacazes
RS66)	K257	1110	2.5/0.25	R. Cultura, Jaguarão
RS67)	K306	1110	1/0.25	R. Sobradinho, Sobradinho
RS68)	K325	1110	2.5/0.25	R. Cruzeiro do Sul, Itaqui
RS152)	K364	1110	1/0.25	R. Solaris, Antônio Prado
RS182)		1110	5	R.Universitária, Caxias do Sul
SC74)	J743	1110	1/0.25	R. Caçanjure, Caçador
SC32)	J752	1110	1/0.5	R. Cultura, Florianópolis
SC33)	J812	1110	2.5/0.25	R. São Carlos, São Carlos
SP101)	K544	1110	2.5/0.25	R. Tietê, Araçatuba
SP102)	K592	°1110	1/0.25	R. Ibitinga, Ibitinga
SP103)	K617	1110	1/0.25	R. Cultura, Mogi Mirim
BA72)	H658	1120	1/0.5	R. Belo Campo, Belo Campo

	Call	kHz	kW	Name and location
BA93)	H...	1120	1/0.25	R. Estrela de Ibiúna, Valente (CP)
CE23)	H598	1120	1	R. Tupinambá, Sobral
ES14)	I215	1120	10/1	R. Cricaré-AM, São Mateus
MG10)	L272	1120	10/0.5	R. Ouro Preto, Ouro Preto
MG60)	L301	1120	5/1	R. Sete Colinas, Uberaba
MG61)	L332	1120	1/0.25	R. Serra da Boa Esperança, Boa Esperança
MG177)	L...	1120	1/0.25	KMR Telecomunicações Ltda., Presidente Olegário (CP)
MS40)	N606	1120	25/1	R. Concordia AM, Campo Grande
PB10)	I687	1120	1/0.25	R. Independência, Catolé do Rocha
PE17)	I778	1120	5/1	R. Relógio Musical, Recife
PR53)	J253	1120	25/1	R. Eldorado, São José dos Pinhais
PR85)	J285	1120	5/0.5	R. Educadora, Laranjeiras do Sul
RS69)	K274	1120	50	R. Rural, Porto Alegre
RS156)	K367	1120	10/0.6	R. Querência, Santo Augusto (**F.PI**, still on 1540)
SP104)	K631	1120	1/0.25	R. Em. Portofelicense, Porto Feliz
SP105)	K660	1120	10/1	R. Bandeirantes, São José dos Campos
SP106)	K671	1120	5/1	R. Clube Imperial, Taquaritinga
CE72)	H667	1130	10/0.25	R. Paty, Senador Pompeu (**F.PI**, still 1390)
PA08)	I531	°1130	10	R. Marajoara, Belém
PE18)	I783	1130	5/1	R. Cultura do Nordeste, Caruaru
PR55)	J220	1130	1/0.25	R. Castro, Castro
PR54)	J333	1130	5/0.25	R. Ingamar, Marialva
RJ17)	J460	1130	100/50	R. Nacional, Rio de Janeiro
RO06)	J677	1130	5/0.25	R. Morimoto, Ji-Paraná
RS70)	K290	1130	5/1	R. Medianeira, Santa Maria
SC34)	J790	1130	10/1	R. Princesa d'Oeste, Xanxerê
SP107)	K676	1130	1/0.25	R. Tupã, Tupã
BA81)	H449	1140	10	R. Cultura da Bahia, Salvador
CE24)	H607	1140	10/1	R. Progresso, Russas
GO26)	H751	1140	1/0.25	R. Tapirapés, Formosa
MG62)	L204	1140	1/0.25	R. Minas, Divinópolis
MG63)	L248	1140	2.5/0.25	R. Dicesana, Campanha
MG64)	L253	1140	5/0.5	R. Muriaé, Muriaé
MG129)	L362	1140	10/0.5	R. Clube, Bocaiuva
MS22)	I398	1140	10/0.5	R. Globo Regional, Fátima do Sul
MS36)	I418	1140	5/0.25	R. Cidade, Aparecida do Taboado
MT47)	I...	1140	1/0.25	Radiodifusão Novo Mato Grosso Ltda., Juara (CP)
PR144)	J352	1140	2.5/0.25	R. San Thiago Dantas, Chopinzinho
RS71)	K228	1140	2/0.25	R. Cruz Alta, Cruz Alta
RS72)	K316	1140	5/0.25	R. 96 FM, Uruguaiana
RS73)	K330	1140	2/0.5	R. Sobral, Butiá
SC35)	J748	1140	10/0.5	R. Coroado AM, Curitibanos
SP108)	K550	1140	10/0.5	R. Difusora, Assis
SP109)	K555	1140	1/0.25	R. Barretos, Barretos
SP110)	K645	1140	1/0.25	R. Educação e Cultura, Rio Claro
SP111)	K709	1140	5/0.25	R. Costa Azul, Ubatuba
AL11)	H250	1150	20/1	R. Cultura, Arapiraca
CE47)	H643	1150	5/0.5	R. Cultura, Paracuru
MG65)	L283	1150	20/10	R. Globo Minas, Belo Horizonte
PI10)	I891	°1150	10/5	R. Pioneira, Teresina
RJ24)	J456	1150	10/0.5	R. Três Rios, Três Rios
RN25)	J617	1150	1/0.25	R. Cabugi do Seridó, Jardim do Seridó
SP232)	K777	1150	100/50	R. Tupi, São Paulo
AM24)	H323	1160	1/0.25	R. Sociedade TV Manauara, Boca do Acre
BA94)	H...	1160	5/0.25	R. São José Ltda., Itabuna (CP)
CE62)	H652	1160	1/0.25	R. Vale do Coreaú, Granja
CE80)	H660	1160	1/0.25	R. Montevidéu, Cedro
DF09)	H...	1160	1/0.25	R. Selvagem Ltda., Gama (CP)
ES08)	I202	1160	50/10	R. Espírito Santo, Vitória
GO42)	H784	1160	1/0.25	R. Itaberaí, Itaberaí
GO54	H...	1160	1/0.25	Vicente Propaganda e Publicidade, Caçu
MT15)	I385	1160	10/5	R. A. Voz d'Oeste, Cuiabá
PA30)	I558	1160	1/0.25	R. Guamá AM, São Miguel do Guamá
PB11)	I674	1160	1	R. Soc. Campina Grande, Camp. Grande
PR56)	J258	1160	10/1	R. Norte, Londrina
RS74)	K242	1160	5/0.5	R. Miriam, Farroupilha
RS75)	K245	1160	5/1	R. Luz e Alegria, Frederico Westphalen
RS76)	K256	1160	2.5/0.5	R. Jaguari, Jaguari
RS77)	K273	1160	1	R. Universidade Católica, Pelotas
SC36)	J741	1160	1	R. Globo, Blumenau
SC37)	J767	1160	1/0.25	R. Difusora, Laguna
SC38)	J776	1160	2.5/0.25	R. Difusora Colméia, Porto União (ff 1230)
SP113)	K502	1160	1/0.25	R. Presidente Venceslau, Presidente Venceslau
SP114)	K517	°1160	5/0.5	R. Cacique, Sorocaba
SP124)	K558	1160	2.5/1	R. Bandeirantes, Bauru
SP115)	K582	1160	5/0.25	R. Difusora, Fernandópolis
SP237)	K673	1160	4/0.25	R. Cacique, Taubaté
SP116)	K685	1160	1/0.25	R. Clube, Mococa
AC13)	H...	1170	1/0.25	R. Líder Comunicações, Brasiléia (CP)
AC15)	H...	1170	1/0.25	R. Líder Comunicações, Feijó (CP)
AM08)	H284	1170	5/2.5	R. Guaranópolis, Maués
AM25)	H...	1170	1/0.25	R. Difusora, Anori
AM21)	H...	1170	1/0.25	Juruá Comunicações, Carauari
BA27)	H473	1170	5/0.25	R. Jornal, Eunápolis
MG152)	L234	1170	1/0.25	R. Fronteira, Fronteira
MG104)	L269	1170	5/0.25	R. Sociedade, Oliveira
MG75)	L327	1170	10/0.25	R. Vanguarda do Vale do Aço, Ipatinga
MG67)	L336	1170	5/0.25	R. Cidade, Araxá
PR57)	J273	1170	20/10	R. Atalaia, Curitiba
PR154)	J363	1170	5/0.25	R. Colméia, Mandaguaçu
RN08)	J598	1170	10/1	R. Difusora, Mossoró
RS78)	K207	1170	1/0.25	R. Itapuí, Santo Antônio da Patrulha
RS79)	K213	1170	5/1	R. Difusora A Voz de Bagé, Bagé
RS80)	K359	1170	5/0.25	R. Uirapuru, Passo Fundo
RS155)	K380	1170	2/1	R. Pitangueira, Itaqui
SP117)	K569	1170	10/5	R. Bandeirantes, Campinas
TO14)		1170	1/0.25	R.Araguaia, Guarai (CP)
AL06)	H248	1180	1/0.25	R. Correio do Sertão, Santana do Ipanema
AM20)	H280	°1180	10/2.5	R. Difusora do Amazonas, Manaus: 24h
MA09)	H889	°1180	10/5	R. Capital, São Luís
MG118)	L203	1180	10/0.25	R. Cultura, Alfenas
MS34)	I602	1180	10	R. Guanandi AM, Campo Grande
MT38)	N405	1180	5/0.25	R. Enauan, Guarantã do Norte
PB20)	I690	1180	1/0.25	R. Bonsucesso, Pombal
PE19)	I797	1180	1/0.25	Radio Cult. de Vitória, Vitória de Sto. Antão
PR126)	J223	1180	2.5/0.5	R. Atalaia, Guarapuava
PR58)	J237	1180	15/0.5	R. Guaçu, Toledo
PR81)	J314	1180	1/0.25	R. Educadora, São João do Ivaí
RJ25)	J463	1180	50/10	R. Viva Rio, Rio de Janeiro
RS128)	K340	1180	10/0.5	R. Gazeta, Santa Cruz do Sul
SC39)	J737	1180	5/0.25	R. Integração d'Oeste, São José do Cedro
SC72)	J770	1180	1/0.5	R. Difusora, Lages
SP260)	K567	1180	1/0.25	R. Brotense, Brotas
SP179)	K647	1180	1/0.5	R. Difusora, Santa Cruz do Rio Pardo
SP217)	K749	1180	5/0.25	R. Nova, Bebedouro
BA28)	H459	1190	10/1	R. Juazeiro, Juazeiro
CE68)	H663	1190	5/0.25	R. Guaraciaba, Guaraciaba do Norte
GO35)	H800	1190	10/0.25	R. Rio Vermelho, Silvânia
MG68)	L221	°1190	10/1	R. Guarani, Belo Horizonte
MG40)	L276	1190	20/0.25	R. Mineira do Sul, Passa Quatro
PR59)	J309	1190	1/0.25	R. Pontal, Nova Londrina
PR136)	J355	1190	1/0.4	R. Cidade, Palmital (**F. PI.** still on 1550)
RN09)	J594	1190	10/1	CBN, Natal
RS82)	K234	1190	5/0.5	R. Cerro Azul, Cerro Largo
RS102)	K301	1190	1/0.25	R. São Lourenço, São Lourenço do Sul
RS83)	K354	1190	2.5/1	R. Rosário, Serafina Corrêa
SC40)	J783	1190	1/0.25	R. Clube, São João Batista
SC87)	J817	1190	1/0.25	R. Planalto, Major Vieira
SC41)	J820	1190	2.5/0.25	R. Clube, São Domingos
SP199)	K512	1190	2.5/0.25	R. Clube Marconi, Paraguaçu Paulista
SP118)	K700	1190	5/0.25	R. Cidade AM, Votuporanga
SP119)	K729	1190	10/0.25	R. 31 de Março, Sta. Cruz das Palmeiras
SP120)	K741	1190	1/0.5	R. Regional, Taquarituba
AL14)	H251	1200	10/1	R. Jornal, Maceió
BA29)	H482	1200	5/0.5	R. Clube Rio do Ouro, Jacobina
CE26)	H585	°1200	10	Ceará R. Clube, Fortaleza
RO07)	J...	1200	5/1	R. Tucumã, Ji-Paraná
RS84)	K239	1200	5/1	R. Erechim, Erechim
RS85)	K342	1200	1/0.5	R. Fundaão Cotrisel, São Sepé
RS181)		1200	1	R.Jornal Opinião Pública, Capão do Lrão
SP121)	K520	°1200	50/20	R. Cultura, São Paulo
BA30)	H452	1210	10/1	R. Carioca, Feira de Santana
BA58)	H498	1210	10/0.25	R. Canção Nova AM, Vitória da Conquista
CE50)	H637	1210	5/0.25	R. Principe Imperial, Crateús
CE48)	H641	1210	5/0.25	R. Boa Esperança, Barro
DF08)	H711	1210	50/2.5	R. Brasília, Brasília
ES09)	I200	1210	10/1	R. Cachoeiro, Cachoeiro de Itapemirim
MG69)	L238	°1210	10/0.5	R. Clube, Varginha
MG70)	L305	1210	10/1	R. Itatiaia do Triângulo, Uberlândia
PE20)	I786	1210	5/1	R. Jornal, Garanhuns
PR60)	J219	°1210	10/5	R. Tupi, Curitiba
PR140)	J325	1210	1/0.5	R. Brotense, Porecatu
RN29)	J620	1210	5/0.5	R. Vale do Potengi, São Paulo do Potengi
RS86)	K240	1210	10/5	R. Catedral, Porto Alegre
RS88)	K353	1210	1/0.5	R. Blau Nunes, Santa Bárbara do Sul

Call		kHz	kW	Name and location
RS186)		1210	1	R.Sananduva, Sananduva
SC42)	J785	1210	10/0.5	R. Super Santa, Tubarão
SP122)	K509	1210	1/0.25	R. Vida Nova, Jaboticabal
SP123)	K545	1210	5/0.25	R. Difusora, Araçatuba
SP125)	K668	1210	5/0.25	R. Vanguarda, Sorocaba
CE90)	H...	1220	1/0.25	Rede Sol de Comunicações, Jaguaruana (CP)
RJ25)	J458	°1220	150	R. Globo, Rio de Janeiro
BA59)	H...	1230	1/0.25	R. Jornal, Ubatã
CE85)	H...	1230	1/0.25	Rede Sol de Comunicações,Trairi (CP)
GO27)	H756	°1230	10/2.5	R. CBN Anhanguera, Goiânia
MA23)	H...	1230	1/0.25	R. Alecrim, Caxias
MG105)	L208	1230	5/0.25	R. Correio da Serra, Barbacena
MG102)	L216	1230	2.5/0.25	R. Passos AM, Passos
MG71)	L296	1230	5/0.5	R. Novo Tempo, Governador Valadares
MS45)	I...	1230	1/0.25	R. Pantanal de Coxim, Coxim (CP)
PB12)	I670	1230	10/1	CBN João Pessoa – Correio, João Pessoa
PR170)	J...	1230	1/0.25	R. Sesal Comunicação e Informatica, Ltda., Telêmaco Borba (CP)
RS146)	K297	1230	4/0.25	R. Santiago, Santiago
RS89)	K326	1230	1/0.25	R. Nonoai, Nonoai
RS90)	K333	1230	1/0.25	R. Prata, Nova Prata
RS91)	K352	1230	1/0.25	R. Encruzilhadense, Encruzilhada do Sul
SC38)	J776	1230	5/0.25	R. Difusora Colméia, Porto União (**F.Pl.** still on 1160)
SC88)	J816	1230	10/1	R. Guararema, São José
SP126)	K573	1230	1/0.25	R. Cidade, Capão Bonito
SP258)	K637	1230	10/0.25	R. Difusora, Rancharia
SP128)	K716	1230	5/0.5	R. Jequitibá AM, Campinas
SP223)	K766	1230	100/50	R. Atual AM, São Paulo
BA31)	H463	1240	10/0.5	R. Emiss. de Alagoinhas, Alagoinhas
CE49)	H654	1240	1/0.25	R. São Francisco, Canindé
MG97)	L294	1240	5/0.25	R. Três Pontas, Três Pontas
MG84)	L298	1240	1/0.25	Soc. R. Ubaense, Ubá
MG72)	L303	1240	1/0.25	R. Platina, Ituiutaba
MG116)	L317	1240	5/0.25	R. Pirapora, Pirapora
MS09)	I388	1240	5/1	CBN, Campo Grande - Pantanal
PE21)	I774	1240	5	R. Jovem Capi, Recife
PR112)	J215	1240	1/0.25	R. Arapongas, Arapongas
PR61)	J280	1240	2/0.25	R. Matelândia, Matelândia
PR94)	J301	1240	1/0.25	R. Difusora Ubiratanense, Ubiratã
RO08)	J...	1240	1	R. Verde, Jaru
RS92)	K200	1240	1/0.25	R. Aparados da Serra, Bom Jesus
RS93)	K251	1240	5/0.25	R. Ibirubá, Ibirubá
RS94)	K355	1240	1/0.25	R. São Jerônimo, São Jerônimo
SC43)	J774	1240	5/0.5	R. São José AM, Mafra
SC44)	J810	1240	1/0.25	R. Iracema, Cunha Porã
SP129)	K565	1240	10/0.25	R. Municipalista, Botucatu
SP130)	K621	1240	5/0.25	Orlândia R. Clube, Orlândia
SP131)	K653	1240	10/2.5	R. Clube, Santos
SP132)	K711	1240	5/0.25	R. Vale do Rio Tietê, José Bonifácio
AM09)	H289	°1250	1/0.25	R. Educação Rural, Coari
CE27)	H594	1250	1	R. Educadora, Crateús
CE69)	H669	1250	1/0.25	R. Liberdade, Itarema
ES18)	I218	1250	10/0.25	R. CBN, Vitória
GO29)	H748	1250	1/0.25	R. Difusora São Patricio, Ceres
MG73)	L282	°1250	5/1	R. Difusora, Poços de Caldas
MG153)	L367	1250	50/0.25	R. Metropolitana, Belo Horizonte
MS10)	I394	1250	1/0.25	R. Difusora, Três Lagoas
PB27)	I...	1250	1/0.25	R. Sociedade de Soledade, Soledade
PI47)	I932	1250	1/0.25	R. João de Paiva, Altos
PR62)	J211	1250	5/0.5	R. Difusora, Guarapuava
PR63)	J233	1250	1/0.25	R. Paranavaí, Paranavaí
PR64)	J313	1250	2.5/0.25	R. Danúbio Azul, Sta. Isabel do Oeste
RJ50)	J500	1250	15/0.5	R. Litoral, Casimiro de Abreu
RS95)	K233	1250	10/1	R. Difusora Caxiense, Caxias do Sul
RS96)	K272	1250	1	R. Tupanci, Pelotas
RS142)	K361	1250	5/0.25	R. Aguas Claras, Catuípe
SC45)	J766	1250	5/0.25	R. Cultura, Joinville
SE08)	J925	1250	10/1	R. Esperança, Estância
SP133)	K702	1250	5/0.5	R. Difusora do Grande Vale, Caçapava
AL07)	H242	1260	50/5	R. Gazeta de Alagoas, Maceió
CE28)	H596	1260	10/0.25	R. Vale do Jaguaribe, Limoeiro do Norte
MG77)	L273	1260	25/5	R. Record, Uberlândia (ff 1290)
RO09)	J670	°1260	5	R. Educadora, Guajará Mirim
RS97)	K204	1260	1/0.25	R. Cultura, São Borja
RS98)	K327	1260	5/0.25	R. Fandango, Cachoeira do Sul
RS99)	K345	1260	1/0.25	R. Gaurama, Gaurama
SC46)	J740	1260	10/0.5	R. Blumenau, Blumenau
SP257)	K629	1260	1/0.25	Pirajuí R. Clube, Pirajuí
SP134)	K688	1260	100/25	R. Morada do Sol, São Paulo

Call		kHz	kW	Name and location
AM10)	H282	°1270	2.5	R. Educação Rural, Tefé
GO30)	H753	°1270	50/10	R. Brasil Central, Goiânia
MG74)	L227	1270	5/1	R. Carijós, Conselheiro Lafaiete
MG107)	L300	1270	2.5/0.5	R. Estância, São Lourenço
MG155)	L240	1270	5/1	R. Libertas do Vale do Aço, Ipatinga
PA09)	I530	1270	10/2.5	R. TransPaz, Belém
PB28)	I696	1270	5/0.25	R. Cidade, Sumé
PR65)	J222	1270	5/0.5	R. Guairacá, Mandaguari
PR67)	J236	1270	10/0.7	R. Capital, Curitiba
PR68)	J289	1270	5/0.5	R. Cidade AM, Cascavel
RJ26)	J474	1270	10/0.5	R. Continental, Campos dos Goitacazes
RN10)	J593	°1270	5/0.5	R. Poty, Natal
RS131)	K206	1270	5/0.5	R. América, Montenegro
RS101)	K250	1270	5/0.5	R. Vera Cruz, Horizontina
SC47)	J765	1270	12/1	R. Catarinense, Joaçaba
SC48)	J768	1270	5/0.5	R. Garibaldi, Laguna
SP136)	K678	°1270	5/0.5	R. Brasil, Campinas
PB21)	I688	1280	10/1	R. Sinhauá, Bayeux
RJ27)	J455	1280	100	Super R. Tupi, Rio de Janeiro
AM11)	H286	°1290	10/2.5	R. Rio Mar, Manaus
BA32)	H450	1290	10/1	R. Clube, Salvador
MA10)	H888	°1290	50/5	R. Timbira do Maranhão, São Luís
MG77)	L273	1290	10/0.25	R. Record, Uberlândia (**F.Pl.** still on 1260)
MG164)	L345	1290	1/0.25	R. Cidade, Arcos
PR73)	J310	1290	25/0.5	R. Brasil Sul, Londrina
RN26)	J619	1290	1/0.25	R. Caicó AM, Caicó
RS103)	K331	1290	5/2	R. Planetário, Espumoso
SC81)	J734	1290	5/1	R. Araranguá, Araranguá
SC49)	J804	1290	5/1	R. Camboriú, Balneário Camboriú
SP240)	K662	1290	5/0.5	R. Difusora, São José do Rio Pardo
SP137)	K663	1290	5/1	R. Novo Tempo, São José do Rio Preto
SP216)	K745	1290	1/0.5	R. Vale, São José dos Campos
CE29)	H586	1300	10	R. Iracema, Fortaleza
ES11)	I210	1300	5/1	R. Novo Tempo, Afonso Cláudio
MG143)	L339	1300	5/1	R. Eldorado, Sete Lagoas
PE22)	I799	1300	1/0.25	R. Guarany AM Stereo, Camarajibe
PR71)	J278	1300	1/0.25	CBN, Ponta Grossa
PR127)	J288	1300	5/0.25	R. Educadora, Dois Vizinhos
RS104)	K203	°1300	50/13	R. RGS , Porto Alegre
RS105)	K337	1300	1/0.25	R. Regional, Santo Cristo
RS106)	K347	1300	5/0.5	R. Cidade, Santana do Livramento
SC89)	J819	1300	1/0.25	R. Alvorada, Santa Cecília
SP138)	K535	1300	50/1	R. Universo, São Bernardo do Campo
SP252)	K649	1300	5/0.25	R. Cultura Regional, Santo Anastácio
SP226)	K762	1300	2/0.25	R. Realidade AM, São Carlos
AP05)	H...	1310	1/0.25	R. Mazagão AM, Mazagão
BA33)	H454	1310	1/0.25	R. Bahiana, Ilhéus
BA63)	H501	1310	5/0.25	R. Canto da Sereia, Jacobina
CE30)	H602	1310	1	R. Progresso de Juazeiro, Juazeiro do Nte.
CE63)	H656	1310	1/0.25	R. Liberdade, Boa Viagem
MG168)	L351	1310	10/0.25	R. Difusora, Salinas
MG144)	L359	1310	1/0.25	R. Montanhesa, Vazante
MS31)	I426	1310	5/1	R. Pindorama, Sidrolândia
PB23)	I691	1310	10/0.5	R. Cidade Esperança, Esperança
PR70)	J274	1310	10/0.5	R. Atalaia, Maringá
RJ28)	J504	1310	1/0.25	R. Difusora Coroados, São Fidélis
RO17)	J684	1310	10/5	R. Tropical AM, Porto Velho
RS107)	K305	1310	5/1	R. Sarandi, Sarandi
RS124)	K329	1310	2.5/0.25	R. Integração, Restinga Seca
RS160)	K371	1310	5/0.5	R. Horizonte, Capão da Canoa
SC85)	J801	1310	10/0.5	R. Sintonia 1310 AM, Ituporanga
SP141)	K566	1310	5/0.25	R. Bragança, Bragança Paulista
SP139)	K596	1310	2/1	R. Difusora, Itápolis
AL08)	H243	1320	10/0.25	R. Milênio, Maceió
BA69)	H503	1320	5/1	R. Regional, Cícero Dantas
CE31)	H597	1320	5/1	R. Regional, Sobral
CE70)	H672	1320	1/0.5	R. Vento Leste AM, Aracati
CE86)	H...	1320	1/0.25	Sistema de Comunicação Terra do Sol Ltda., Assaré (CP)
MG136)	L322	°1320	5/0.25	R. Mucuri, Teófilo Otoni
PE31)	I823	1320	1/0.25	R. Cultura, São José do Egito
PR72)	J255	1320	8/0.5	R. Brasil Tropical, Curitiba
PR145)	J351	1320	5/0.5	R. Foz, Foz do Iguaçu
RJ29)	J475	1320	25/5	R. Difusora Boas Novas, Rio de Janeiro
RS108)	K223	1320	1/0.25	R. Clube, Canela
RS109)	K266	1320	3/0.25	R. Sulbrasileira, Panambi
RS110)	K271	1320	5/1	R. Cultura, Pelotas
SC104)	J...	1320	1/0.25	R. Vale do Contestado Ltda., Videira (CP)
SP140)	K630	1320	1/0.25	R. Difusora, Pirassununga
SP241)	K675	1320	1/0.25	R. Clube, Tupã

	Call	kHz	kW	Name and location
BA34)	H468	1330	5/1	R. Difusora, Serrinha
CE91)	H...	1330	1/0.25	R. São Bento de Amontada, Milhã (CP)
MG178)	L...	1330	5/0.25	R. e TV Libertas Ltda., Uberlândia (CP)
PA10)	I533	°1330	25/5	R. Liberal, Belém (ff 900)
PA07)	I600	1330	5/1	R. Liberal, Castanhal(**F.PI**, still on 930)
PB33)	I. . .	1330	5/0.25	Sistema de Comunicação do Cabo de Sto. Agostinho, Cabo de Sto. Agostinho
PR74)	J264	1330	10/0.5	R. Jaguariaíva, Jaguariaíva
RN27)	J621	1330	10/0.5	R. Eldorado, Natal
RS111)	K236	1330	1/0.25	R. Upacaraí, Dom Pedrito
RS112)	K323	1330	1/0.5	R. Diplomata, São Marcos
SC50)	J739	1330	12/0.5	R. Clube, Blumenau
SC51)	J749	1330	10/0.25	R. Chapecó, Chapecó
SP142)	K638	1330	5/0.25	R. Paulista, Regente Feijó
SP143)	K641	1330	20/1	R. Cultura, Ribeirão Preto
SP187)	K736	°1330	50/5	R. Tupi, Osasco
CE71)	H661	1340	2.5/0.25	R. Pitaguary, Maracanaú
MA11)	H886	1340	10/2	R. Clube de São Luís, São Luís
MG81)	L241	1340	10/0.25	R. Cultura, Itabirito
MG139)	L352	1340	5/1	R. Minas Liberdade, Passos
MG156)	L366	1340	1/0.5	R. Capital do Triângulo, Patrocínio (ff 810)
MS12)	I380	°1340	1	R. Difusora, Aquidauana
PB13)	I671	1340	5/1	R. Arapuan, João Pessoa
PR76)	J205	1340	2.5/0.25	R. Difusora, Rio Negro
PR77)	J249	1340	1/0.25	R. Cultura, Arapongas
PR41)	J368	1340	20/0.25	R. Capital AM, Cascavel
RJ40)	J490	1340	5/0.5	R. Transamérica, Rio Bonito
RS113)	K227	1340	10/1	R. CBN, Porto Alegre
SP144)	K543	1340	5/1	R. Cultura, Araçatuba
SP203)	K571	1340	5/0.25	R. Em. Campos do Jordão, Campos do Jordão
SP146)	K738	1340	1/0.25	R. Canoa Grande, Igaraçu do Tietê
AC05)	H201	1350	10/5	R. Capital, Rio Branco
BA70)	H520	1350	50/10	R. Cristal, Salvador
CE56)	H662	1350	1/0.25	R. Liberal, Morada Nova
GO56)	H...	1350	1/0.25	R. Britto Ltda., Anicuns (CP)
MG82)	L214	1350	10/5	R. Cultura, Poços de Caldas
PB14)	I675	°1350	5/0.5	Super R. Borborema, Campina Grande
RS114)	K205	1350	1/0.25	R. Aurora, Guaporé
RS115)	K313	1350	5/1	R. Difusora, Três Passos
RS116)	K336	1350	1/0.25	R. Agudo, Agudo
SC53)	J760	1350	1/0.25	R. Clube, Itajaí
SP265)	K...	1350	10/0.25	R. Excelsior, Ibiúna
BA35)	H469	1360	10/1	R. Cultura, Paulo Afonso
CE57)	H650	1360	5/0.25	R. Iracema, Ipu
CE92)	H...	1360	1/0.25	FM Serrote Ltda., Milagres (CP)
MS14)	I383	1360	2	R. Difusora Matogrossense, Corumbá
PR165)	J265	1360	10/0.25	R. Cidade, Pato Branco
PR78)	J268	1360	1/0.25	R. Pepita de Ouro, Assaí
PR79)	J302	1360	5/0.25	R. Cultura, Iporã
RJ30)	J464	1360	50/10	R. Bandeirantes, Rio de Janeiro
RN11)	J605	1360	1/0.5	R. Ouro Branco, Currais Novos
RS117)	K261	1360	5/0.5	R. Alvorada, Marau
RS151)	K281	1360	3/0.25	R. Navegantes, Porto Lucena (**F.PI** still on 1590)
RS183)		1360	5	R.Cerro Azul, Cerro Largo
SP147)	K581	1360	5/1	R. Aguas Quentes, Fernandópolis
SP148)	K739	1360	1/0.25	R. Regional, Dracena
SP235)	K759	1360	1/0.25	R. Luzes da Ribalta, Santa Bárbara d'Oeste
BA82)	H555	1370	0.25	R. Piquaraca, Monte Santo
CE81)	H...	1370	1/0.25	R. Vanguarda, Caridade
GO57)	H...	1370	1/0.25	Rede Brasileira de R. e TV 8, Edéia (CP)
PE34)	I800	1370	1/0.25	R. Vale do Capibaribe, Sta. Cruz do Capibaribe
PI13)	I892	1370	10/1	R. Difusora, Teresina
PR80)	J267	1370	50/7	R. Independência, Curitiba
RN28)	J618	1370	2.5/0.25	R. Difusora AM,São Miguel
RS118)	K243	1370	25/0.5	R. Mãe de Deus, Flores da Cunha
RS119)	K334	1370	1/0.25	R. Gazeta, Alegrete
RS173)	K377	1370	4/0.25	R. Jornal da Manhã, Ijuí
SC55)	J782	1370	5/0.25	R. Peperí AM, São Miguel do Oeste
SE09)	J929	1370	5/0.5	R. Capital do Agreste, Itabaiana
SP266)	K. . .	1370		R. Boa Vontade, São Paulo
AM12)	H283	°1380	5/1	R. Alvorada, Parintins
BA83)	H495	1380	5/0.25	R. União, Gandu
MA40)	H. . .	1380	1/0.25	MR Radiodifusão Ltda., Caxias (CP)
MG172)	L218	1380	1/0.25	R. Cidade, Brasópolis
MG120)	L284	1380	5/0.25	R. Paranaíba, Rio Paranaíba
MG130)	L323	1380	1/0.25	R. Gorutubana AM, Janaúba
MG176)	L. . .	1380	1/0.25	R. Estrela de Ibiúna, Campina Verde
MT49)	I. . .	1380	1/0.25	Sistema Plug de Comunicações, Nova Brasilândia (CP)
PA31)	I...	1380	1/0.25	R. Tocantins, Tucuruí
PE23)	I773	1380	10/5	R. Globo, Recife
PR122)	J276	1380	2/0.25	R. Bom Jesus, Siqueira Campos
PR152)	J367	1380	1/0.25	R. Integração, Toledo
RS120)	K293	1380	1/0.25	R. Cultura, Santana do Livramento
RS134)	K311	1380	1/0.5	R. Maristela, Torres
RS121)	K350	1380	1/0.25	R. Cultura, Tapera
RS165)	K372	1380	1/0.25	R. Chiru Comunicações, Palmitinho
SC56)	J821	1380	1/0.25	R. Cidade, Itaiópolis (ff 990)
SC93)	J827	1380	1/0.25	R. Barriga Verde, Capinzal
SC105)	J. . .	1380	1/0.25	Frequência Brasileira de Comunicações, Garopaba (CP)
SP152)	K616	1380	1/0.5	R. Difusora, Mogi Guaçu
SP247)	K623	1380	1/0.25	R. Cultura, Pedemeiras (**F.PI**, still on 1550)
SP224)	K751	1380	5/1	R. Globo, Presidente Prudente
SP234)	K772	1380	1/0.25	R. República, Morro Agudo
BA76)	H. . .	1390	1/0.25	Grupo Integração de Comunicações, Xique-Xique (CP)
CE72)	H667	1390	10/0.25	R. Paty, Senador Pompeu (ff 1130)
MG157)	L358	1390	2.5/0.25	R. Ouro Verde, São Sebastião do Paraíso
MT50)	I. . .	1390	1/0.25	Sistema Gois de Radiodifusão Ltda., Agua Boa (CP)
PA12)	I535	°1390	10/1	R. Educadora, Bragança
PE24)	I788	1390	1	R. Jornal O Povo, Pesqueira
PR82)	J242	1390	10/1	R. Cultura, Maringá
PR83)	J335	1390	1/0.25	R. Independência, Salto do Lontra
RJ32)	J473	1390	5/0.5	R. Sul Fluminense, Barra Mansa
RN32)	J. . .	1390	1/0.25	R. Farol, Touros
RO18)	J687	1390	5/1	R. Itapirema, Ji-Piraná
RR02)	O701	1390	10/5	R. Roraima, Caracaraí
RS122)	K209	1390	10	R. Esperança, Porto Alegre
RS166)	K368	1390	8/0.25	R. Atlântica, Constantina
SC57)	J769	1390	1/0.25	R. Diário da Manhã, Lages
SP153)	K570	1390	25/0.5	R. Globo, Campinas
SP90)	K594	1390	2.5/0.25	R. Alfa, Itanhaém
SP154)	K636	1390	1/0.25	R. Cultura, Promissão
AC06)	H200	°1400	10/1	R. Dif. Acreana, Rio Branco
BA71)	H529	1400	1/0.25	R. Vale do Vasa-Barris, Jeremoabo
CE93)	H...	1400	1/0.25	R. FM Serrote, Coreaú (CP)
PB15)	I677	1400	5/1	R. Espinharas, Patos
PI27)	I926	1400	1/0.25	R. Cantagalo, Jaicós
PR84)	J256	1400	1/0.25	R. CBN Londrina, Londrina
PR87)	J299	1400	1/0.25	R. Fronteira d'Oeste, Terra Roxa
PR119)	J339	1400	10/0.25	R. Difusora, Balsa Nova
PR148)	J346	1400	2/0.45	R. Jornal São Miguel, São Miguel do Iguaçu (**F.PI.** still on 1450)
RJ33)	J462	1400	50/5	R. Rio de Janeiro ("R. Rio AM"), Ri
RS123)	K247	1400	1/0.25	R. Sideral, Getúlio Vargas (ff 700)
RS170)	K376	1400	1/0.4	R. Educadora, São João da Urtiga (**F.PI.** still on 1510)
SC58)	J775	1400	1/0.25	R. Entre Rios, Palmitos
SP155)	K527	1400	1/0.25	R. Difusora, Lucélia
SP156)	K658	1400	5/0.25	R. Clube, São Carlos
SP157)	K682	1400	5/0.25	R. Metrópole AM, São José do Rio Preto
TO08)	N660	1400	1	Radiodifusão Guaraí, Guaraí
BA37)	H467	1410	10/0.5	R. São Gonçalo, São Gonçalo dos Campos
CE25)	H639	1410	10/1	R. Boa Nova, Pacajus
GO19)	H803	1410	10/1	R. Fraternidade Universal, Santo Antônio do Descoberto
MS15)	I382	1410	5/1	R. Clube, Corumbá
RJ34)	J486	1410	10/0.5	R. Itaperuna, Itaperuna
RN21)	J614	1410	5/0.5	R. Santa Cruz AM, Santa Cruz
RS137)	K246	1410	5/1	R. Garibaldi, Garibaldi
RS125)	K284	1410	1/0.25	R. Minuano, Rio Grande
RS126)	K294	1410	5	R. Santa Rosa, Santa Rosa
SC100)	J799	1410	0.5	R. Namba, Ponte Serrada
SP158)	K691	1410	50/10	R. América, São Paulo
SP264)	K. . .	1410	1/0.25	R. Excelsior, Rio Claro
AL18)	H...	1420	1/0.25	Alagoas Comunicação, Palmeira dos Indios (CP)
BA60)	H504	1420	1/0.25	R. Difusora, Irecê
CE87)	H. . .	1420	1/0.25	Sistema de Comunicações Terra do Sol Ltda., Bela Cruz (CP)
MG88)	L286	1420	1/0.25	Multisom R. São João Nepomuceno, São João Nepomuceno
MG89)	L288	1420	5/1	R. Cultura, Sete Lagoas
MG90)	L313	1420	1/0.25	R. Montanhês Botelhos, Botelhos
MS16)	I397	1420	1/0.25	R. Difusora Cacique, Nova Andradina

	Call	kHz	kW	Name and location
PA38)	I...	1420	10	Sistema Lagrado de Comunicação, Belém (CP)
PB35)	I…	1420	1/0.25	R. Cajazeiras, Campina Grande (CP)
PR88)	J269	1420	5/0.25	R. Cultura, Umuarama
PR89)	J282	1420	1/0.25	R. Educadora, Jacarezinho
PR90)	J334	1420	1/0.25	R. Entre Rios, Sto. Antônio do Sudoeste
RN12)	J609	1420	1/0.25	R. Tapuyo, Alexandria
RS149)	K258	1420	5/0.25	R. 14 de Julho, Júlio de Castilhos
RS171)	K308	1420	3/0.3	R. Tapense, Tapes (**F.PI**, still on 1500)
SC60)	J744	1420	6/0.5	R. Cultura, Campos Novos
SC59)	J754	°1420	5/2.5	R. Guarujá, Florianópolis
SP159)	K597	1420	2.5/0.5	C.R.N., Itatiba
SP163)	K733	1420	1/0.25	R. Nova São Manuel, São Manuel
SP267)	K…	1420	1/0.25	EBC Empresa Bauruense de Comunicação Ltda., Ribeirão Preto (CP)
CE94)	H...	1430	1/0.25	Sistema Maior de Radiodifusão Pucujá
ES21)	I…	1430	1/0.25	R. Itaí de Rio Claro Ltda., Iúna (CP)
MG91)	L239	1430	1/0.25	R. Clube, Guaxupé
MG158)	L371	1430	2.5/0.25	R. Planalto, Perdizes
PE32)	I826	1430	5/0.25	R. Goiana AM, Goiana
PR134)	J200	°1430	50/10	R. Clube Paranaense, Curitiba
RN13)	J604	1430	10/0.5	R. Libertadora Mossoroense, Mossoró
RO11)	J671	1430	10/1	R. Caiari, Porto Velho
RS167)	K366	1430	1/0.25	R. Guarita, Coronel Bicaco
SP164)	K666	1430	1/0.25	R. Serra Negra, Serra Negra
AM13)	H285	°1440	10	R. Bare, Manaus
BA38)	H466	1440	10/0.5	R. Independência, Santo Amaro
CE33)	H603	1440	10/1	R. Araripe, Crato
MG159)	L365	1440	1/0.25	Empreendimentos Guimarães e Franzão ("R. Som 200"), Santa Vitória
MS41)	I407	1440	1/0.25	R. Bela Vista, Bela Vista
MS47)	I…	1440	1/0.25	Sistema de Radiodifusão Ribas do Rio Pardo Ltda., Bandeirantes (CP)
RJ35)	J469	1440	20/5	R. Super 1440, Rio de Janeiro
RS168)	K221	1440	1/0.25	R. Ceres, Não-Me-Toque
RS130)	K328	1440	1/0.25	R. Excelsior, Gramado
RS153)	K362	1440	1/0.25	R. Caibaté, Caibaté
SC69)	J757	1440	7/0.3	R. Sentinela de Alto Vale, Ibirama (**F.PI.**, still on 1490)
SC61)	J792	1440	1/0.25	R. Difusora, Maravilha
SE11)	J930	1440	5/0.25	R. Educadora, Frei Paulo
SP253)	K568	1440	1/0.25	R. Cultura, Cajuru
SP165)	K634	1440	10/0.5	R. Comercial, Presidente Prudente
SP218)	K752	1440	1/0.25	R. Azul Celeste, Americana
SP268)	K…	1440	0.5/0.25	R. Clarim de Palmas, Itaí (CP)
BA73)	H531	1450	1/0.25	R. Ipirá, Ipirá
CE34)	H601	1450	1/0.25	R. Difusora Cristal, Quixeramobim
CE35)	H623	1450	1/0.25	R. Pinto Martins, Camocim
CE95)	H...	1450	1/0.25	Sistema Lages de Comunicações, Acopiara (CP)
ES12)	I208	1450	1/0.5	R. Gaeta, Guarapari
GO51)	H794	1450	1/0.25	R. Alvorada, Quirinópolis
MA32)	H900	1450	1/0.25	R. Boa Esperança, São João dos Patos
MA13)	H901	1450	1/0.25	R. Cultura, Pedreiras
MG93)	L249	1450	5/0.25	R. Cultura, João Monlevade
MG94)	L312	1450	10/0.25	R. Diamante, Coromandel
MS13)	I417	1450	1/0.25	R. Difusora, Rio Brilhante
MS48)	I…	1450	1/0.25	Sistema de Radiodifusão Ribas do Rio Pardo Ltda., Bataguassu (CP)
PA33)	I559	1450	1/0.25	R. Juruá, São Felix do Xingu
PA39)	I...	1450	1/0.25	Sistema Lagrado de Comunicação, Castanhal (CP)
PB29)	I699	1450	1/0.25	R. Itatiunga, Patos
PE25)	I794	1450	1/0.25	R. Cultura, Palmares
PE38)	I…	1450	1/0.25	R. Felicidade, Petrolândia (CP)
PI21)	I908	1450	1/0.25	R. Cultura do Gurguéia, Bom Jesus
PI35)	I917	1450	1/0.25	R. Confederação Valenciana ("R. Valenciana"), Valença do Piauí
PR93)	J279	1450	1/0.25	R. Cabiúna, Bandeirantes
PR95)	J317	1450	1/0.25	R. Rainha d'Oeste, Altônia
PR148)	J346	1450	1/0.25	R. Jornal São Miguel, São Miguel do Iguaçu (ff 1400)
PR171)	J…	1450	1/0.25	R. AM Banda 1, Sarandi (CP)
RJ36)	J480	1450	5/0.25	R. do Comércio, Barra Mansa
RJ37)	J503	1450	1/0.25	R. Feliz, Santo Antônio de Pádua
RO12)	J674	1450	1/0.25	R. Vilhena AM, Vilhena
RR03)	O...	1450	1/0.25	LHM Comunicação, Alto Alegre
RS132)	K346	1450	1/0.25	R. Cassino, Rio Grande
SC62)	J802	1450	1/0.25	R. São Bento, São Bento do Sul
SC63)	J822	1450	10/0.25	R. Soc. Hulha Negra, Criciúma
SC97)	J828	1450	2.5/0.25	R. Belos Montes, Seara
SE12)	J...	1450	1/0.25	R. Abais, Estância
SP238)	K526	1450	1/0.25	R. Cultura, Ituverava
SP166)	K587	1450	1/0.25	R. Difusora, Guararapes
SP167)	K591	1450	50/5	R. Boa Nova, Guarulhos
SP168)	K657	°1450	1/0.25	R. São Carlos, São Carlos
TO15)		1450	1/0.25	R.Tocantins, Pedro Alfonso (CP)
AM17)	H300	1460	5	R. Clube, Parintins
BA39)	H472	1460	1/0.25	R. Baiana, Jequié
BA85)	H523	1460	1/0.25	R. Ferro Doido, Morro do Chapéu
BA74)	H536	1460	1/0.25	R. Alvorada, Cruz das Almas
CE53)	H595	1460	1/0.25	R. Dragão do Norte, Massapé
CE36)	H616	1460	1/0.25	R. Uirapuru, Morada Nova
GO34)	H766	*1460	1/0.25	R. Morrinhos, Morrinhos
MA33)	H917	1460	1/0.25	R. Vanguarda, Santa Luzia (ff 1480)
MG95)	L201	1460	1/0.25	R. Cultura de Porto Novo, Além Paraíba
MG161)	L356	1460	1/0.25	R. Buritis, Buritis
MG131)	L363	1460	1/0.25	R. Entre Rios, Raul Soares
MG166)	L…	1460	0.25	R. Matinada, Paraguaçu (CP)
MS49)	I…	1460	1/0.25	Maia & Oliveira Ltda., Costa Rica (CP)
PB30)	I...	1460	1/0.25	R. Oeste da Paraíba, Cajazeiras (ff 1000)
PI14)	I903	1460	1/0.25	R. Cultura, Amarante
PR96)	J204	1460	1/0.25	R. Difusora, Paranaguá
PR97)	J228	1460	1/0.25	R. Central do Paraná, Ponta Grossa
PR98)	J251	1460	1/0.25	R. Cultura, Apucarana
PR100)	J297	1460	1/0.25	R. Guaíra, Guaíra
PR101)	J308	1460	1/0.25	R. Ampere, Ampere
PR102)	J318	1460	1/0.25	R. Educadora, Loanda
RN20)	J615	1460	10/1	R. Agreste, Santo Antônio
RS133)	K214	1460	1/0.25	R. Cultura, Bagé
RS135)	K312	1460	1/0.25	R. Colonial, Três de Maio
RS175)	K373	1460	1/0.25	R. Campinas , Campinas do Sul
RS176)	K...	1460	1/0.25	R. Mostardas, Mostardas
RS188)		1460	1/0.25	R.Calhandra, Uruguaiana (CP)
SC64)	J756	1460	2.5/0.25	R. Sentinela do Vale, Gaspar
SP242)	K548	1460	3/0.5	R. Clube Ararense, Araras
SP170)	K608	1460	1/0.25	R. Cultura, Lorena
SP171)	K707	1460	25/0.25	R. Universal, São Roque
TO02)	H774	1460	1/0.25	R. Independência do Tocantins, Paraíso do Tocantins
TO16)			1/0.25	R.Alvorada, Arraias (CP)
BA86)	H509	1470	0.25	R. Morro Verde, Mairi
CE64)	H665	1470	1/0.25	R. Guanancés de Itapajé, Itapajé
ES17)	I214	1470	1/0.25	R. São Francisco, Barra de São Francisco
GO36)	H773	1470	1/0.25	R. Dif. Serra dos Cristais, Cristalina
GO37)	H779	1470	1/0.25	R. Cidade, Goiás
MA34)	H908	1470	1/0.25	R. Paranoá, Presidente Dutra
MA25)	H…	1470	1/0.25	MR Radiodifusão Ltda., Turiaçu (CP)
MA39)	H…	1470	1/0.25	MR Radiodifusão,Urbano Santos
MG96)	L247	1470	1/0.25	R. Difusora, Ituiutaba
MS29)	I413	1470	1/0.25	R. Alvorada, Dourados
PA25)	I548	1470	1/0.25	R. Moreno Braga, Vigia
PE35)	I822	1470	1/0.25	R. Educadora de Belém, Belém de São Francisco
PE37)	I827	1470	1/0.25	R. Papacaça AM, Bom Conselho
PI15)	I900	1470	1/0.25	R. Difusora Vale do Uruçuí, Uruçuí
PI24)	I913	1470	1/0.25	R. Ingazeira, Paulistana
PI33)	I928	1470	1/0.25	R. AM Cidade, Castelo do Piauí
PR103)	J294	1470	1/0.25	R. Educadora, Ibaiti
PR104)	J304	1470	2/0.25	R. Jornal, Assis Chateaubriand
PR172)	J…	1470	1/0.25	Rede Panorama de Comunicações Ltda., Itapejara d'Oeste (CP)
PR173)	J…	1470	1/0.25	R. Tradição, Rio Branco do Sul (CP)
RJ08)	J476	1470	1/0.25	R. Jornal Fluminense, Campos dos Goitacazes
RJ38)	J481	1470	1/0.25	R. Vale do Paraíba, Barra do Piraí
RN23)	J616	1470	1/0.25	R. Rural AM de Parelhas, Parelhas
RO05)	J676	1470	1/0.25	R. Soc. Rondônia, Cacoal
RR05)	O…	1470	1/0.25	Editora Boa Vista Ltda., Bonfim (CP)
RS138)	K208	1470	2.5/0.25	Radiodiusão Assisense, São Francisco de Assis (**F.PI** still on 1490)
RS169)	K219	1470	1/0.25	R. Cult. Cacequiense, Cacequi (ff 1490)
RS136)	K324	1470	2.5/0.25	R. 1470, Campo Bom
RS42)	K263	1470	2.5	R. 1470, Novo Hamburgo
SC65)	J781	1470	10/1	R. Mais, São José
SC66)	J798	1470	1/0.25	R. Líder do Vale, Herval d'Oeste
SP172)	K586	1470	1/0.25	R. Cultura, Guaíra
SP173)	K599	1470	1/0.25	R. Mensagem, Jacareí
SP174)	K632	1470	1/0.25	R. Primavera, Porto Ferreira
SP175)	K712	1470	1/0.25	R. Jornal, Indaiatuba
SP243)	K771	1470	1/0.25	R. Bastos AM, Bastos
BA61)	H508	1480	5/1	R. Alvorada, Guanambi

	Call	kHz	kW	Name and location
BA75)	H...	1480	1/0.25	R. Santana, Santana
BA76)	H...	1480	1/0.25	R.Tribuna, Xique-Xique
CE74)	H671	1480	1/0.25	R. Universal, Morrinhos
MA14)	H897	1480	10/0.5	R. Itapecuru, Colinas
MA33)	H917	1480	10/0.5	R. Vanguarda, Sta. Luzia (**F.PI** still 1460)
MG98)	L235	1480	1/0.25	R. Nova Frutal AM, Frutal
MG99)	L265	1480	5/0.25	R. Difusora, Nanuque
MG100)	L307	1480	2.5/0.25	R. Emboabas, Tiradentes
MS17)	I393	1480	1/0.25	R. Caçula, Três Lagoas
MS50)	I...	1480	1/0.25	Bonito Comunicação, Bonito (CP)
MT51)	I...	1480	0.25	R. Som da Terra, Alto Taquari (CP)
MT52)	I...	1480	1/0.25	JEA Comunicações Ltda., Aripuanã (CP)
MT57)	I...	1480	1/0.25	R. Educ. Nova Geração, São Joaquím (CP)
MT58)	I...	1480	1/0.25	Continental Comunicações, Campo Verde
PE26)	I790	1480	1/0.25	R. A Voz do Sertão, Serra Talhada
PE36)	I825	1480	5/0.25	R. Canção Nova, Gravatá
PI29)	I929	1480	1/0.25	R. Vale do Coroatá, Elesbão Veloso
PR153)	J221	1480	1/0.25	R. Brotas, Piraí do Sul
PR106)	J230	1480	1/0.25	R. Astorga, Astorga
PR107)	J270	1480	5/0.25	R. Educadora, União da Vitória
PR174)	J...	1480	1/0.25	R. Cl. Entre Amigos, Pérola d'Oeste(CP)
RJ55)	J485	1480	0.25	R. Duque de Caxias, do
RN14)	J601	1480	1/0.25	R. Princesa do Vale, Açu
RO15)	J681	1480	1/0.25	R. Soc Rondônia, Pimenta Bueno
RS100)	K244	1480	2.5/0.25	R. São Roque, Faxinal do Soturno
RS127)	K321	1480	5/0.25	R. Veranense, Veranópolis
RS178)	K...	1480	2.5/0.25	R. Guaramano, Guarani das Missões
RS184)		1480	5	R.Dif.Garibaldi, Garibaldi
SC67)	J731	1480	1/0.25	R. Difusora, Joinville
SC68)	J762	1480	1/0.25	R. Difusora 26 de Abril, Imaruí
SC94)	J826	1480	2.5/0.25	R. Caibi, Caibi
SE10)	J928	1480	1/0.25	R. Atalaia, Simão Dias
SP176)	K539	1480	1/0.25	R. Clube, Altinópolis
SP177)	K551	1480	1/0.25	R. Atibaia, Atibaia
SP255)	K767	1480	0.25	R. Boituva AM, Boituva
TO06)	H795	1480	1/0.25	R. Anhanguera, Miracema do Tocantins
AL09)	H246	1490	5/1	Em. Rio São Francisco, Penedo
BA41)	H478	1490	1/0.25	R. Educadora, Ipiaú
BA77)	H507	1490	1/0.25	R. Rio São Francisco, Bom Jesus da Lapa
BA87)	H512	1490	0.25	R. Planalto d'Oeste, Correntina
BA88)	H...	1490	2.5/0.5	R. Antena Um, Ribeira do Pombal
BA97)	H...	1490	1/0.25	Brumado Radiodifusão Sertaneja, Brumado (CP)
MG162)	L231	1490	0.25	R. Cacique, Araguari
MG163)	L274	1490	1/0.25	R. Paraisópolis, Paraisópolis
MG165)	L353	1490	1/0.25	R. Pirapetinga, Pirapetinga
MG179)	L...	1490	1/0.25	Momento de Comunicação,Santa Luzia
MS19)	I404	1490	1/0.25	R. Nova Paiaguás, Glória de Dourados
MT53)	I...	1490	1/0.25	Sistema Plug de Comunicações Ltda., Vila Ruca (CP)
MT54)	I...	1490	1/0.25	Sistema Góis de Radiodifusão Ltda., Terra Nova do Norte (CP)
PE39)	I...	1490	1/0.25	R. Felicidade FM Ltda., Cabrobó (CP)
PI40)	I...	1490	1/0.25	R. Lagoa, Buriti dos Lopes
PR108)	J210	1490	1/0.25	R. Cornélio, Cornélio Procópio
PR149)	J347	1490	1/0.25	R. Difusora, São Jorge d'Oeste
RO20)	J...	1490	0.25	Rede Brasileira de R. e TV Ltda., Ouro Preto d'Oeste (CP)
RS138)	K208	1490	1/0.25	Rádiodifusão Assisense, São Francisco de Assis (ff 1470)
RS169	K219	1490	1/0.25	R. Cultura Cacequiense, Cacequi (**F.PI**, still on 1470)
RS139)	K225	1490	1/0.25	R. Liberdade, Canguçu
RS140)	K309	1490	3/0.25	R. Taquara, Taquara
SC69)	J757	1490	1/0.25	R. Sentinela de Alto Vale, Ibirama (ff 1440)
SC70)	J791	1490	1/0.25	R. Cultura, Xaxim
SP180)	K530	1490	1/0.25	R. Difusora, Olímpia
SP181)	K580	1490	1/0.25	R. Nova Dracena, Dracena
SP182)	K583	1490	1/0.25	R. Educadora Santa Rita, Fernandópolis
SP244)	K680	1490	1/0.25	R. Cultura, Vargem Grande do Sul
SP183)	K764	1490	10/0.25	R. Imaculada Conceição, Mauá
BA49)	H487	1500	0.25	R. Jacuípe, Riachão do Jacuípe
BA52)	H493	1500	5/0.5	R. Difusora do Descobrimento, Porto Seguro
CE39)	H615	1500	2.5/0.25	R. Macico, Baturité
MG101)	L215	1500	5/0.25	R. Montanhosa, Viçosa
MG140)	L340	1500	1/0.25	R. Aparecida do Sul, Ilicínea
PA19)	I542	1500	1/0.25	R. Floresta, Tucuruí
PE27)	I779	1500	1/0.25	R. Pajeu, Afogados da Ingazeira
PI46)	I919	1500	1/0.25	R. Voz do Longa, Esperantina
PR163)	J366	1500	1/0.25	R. Marqueirinha, Margueirinha

	Call	kHz	kW	Name and location
RS171)	K308	1500	0.5	R. Tapense, Tapes (ff 1420)
RS161)	K365	1500	3/0.25	R. Simpatia , Chapada
RS180)	K...	1500	2	R.Caapava, Caapava do Sul
SC106)	J...	1500	1/0.25	R. O Guri AM, Balneário Camboriú (CP)
SP184)	K549	1500	1/0.25	R. Fraternidade, Araras
SP185)	K626	1500	1/0.25	R. Difusora, Pindamonhangaba
SP186)	K706	1500	1/0.25	R. Vale do Rio Grande, Miguelópolis
SP211)	K773	1500	1/0.25	R. Nova Uni, Guarulhos
SP236)	K776	1500	1/0.25	R. Cidade, Apiaí
CE40)	H608	1510	1/0.25	R. Planalto da Ibiapaba, São Benedito
CE84)	H...	1510	0.25	Rede Fortal de Comunicações Ltda., Pedra Branca (CP)
GO38)	H770	1510	1/0.25	R. Goiatuba, Goiatuba
GO55)	H...	1510	1/0.25	RBN Rede Brasil Norte de Comunicação Ltda., Posse (CP)
MG180)	L...	1510	1/0.25	KMR Telecomunicações Ltda., Araçuaí
MG181)	L...	1510	1/0.25	Sistema Cariris de Radiodifusão Ltda., Pirapora (CP)
MS51)	I...	1510	1/0.25	Empresa de Radiodifusão Pantanense, Mundo Novo (CP)
PA01)	I544	1510	1/0.25	R. Oriente de Redenção, Redenção
PA35)	I...	1510	1/0.25	Brasil Amazonia Comunicação e Empreendimentos, Abaetetuba
PI16)	I894	1510	1/0.25	R. Difusora, Floriano
PI17)	I896	1510	1/0.25	R. Progresso, Corrente
PI49)	I...	1510	1/0.25	R. Nordeste Ltda., Picos (CP)
PR113)	J216	1510	1/0.25	R. Educadora, Venceslau Brás
PR115)	J326	1510	1/0.25	R. União, Céu Azul
RJ43)	J492	1510	1/0.25	R. Teresópolis, Teresópolis
RN15)	J602	1510	1/0.25	R. Centenário, Caraúbas
RO21)	J...	1510	0.25	Comunicações Cone Sul, Jaru (CP)
RS170)	K376	1510	5/1	R. Educadora, São João da Urtiga
SC73)	J795	1510	1/0.25	R. Centro Oeste, Pinhalzinho
SC82)	J797	1510	5/0.25	R. Educadora, Taió
SP188)	K654	1510	10/1	R. Cacique, Santos
SP189)	K665	1510	1/0.25	R. Clube, São Manuel
SP256)	K770	1510	0.5/0.25	R. Vale do Tietê, Salto
SP230)	K...	1510	1/0.25	R. Rural, Rinópolis
SP269)	K...	1510	1/0.25	Sistema Athenas Paulista de Radiodifusão Ltda., Jaboticabal (CP)
TO17)		1510	1/0.25	R.Alvorada, Natividade (CP)
BA78)	H530	1520	5/1	R. Bela Vista, Poções
CE75)	H635	1520	1/0.25	R. Araripe, Ipu
CE83)	H653	1520	1/0.25	R. Cachoeira, Solonópole
GO53)	H806	1520	1/0.25	R. Campos Belos, Campos Belos
MA15)	H899	1520	1/0.25	R. Ribamar, Pindaré Mirim
MA35)	H928	1520	1/0.25	R. Mirante AM, Chapadinha
MG174)	L223	1520	0.25	R. Cultura, Cássia
MG106)	L245	1520	1/0.25	R. Clube, Itaúna
MS21)	I405	1520	1/0.25	R. Jornal, Amambaí
MS42)	N605	1520	1/0.25	R. Campo Alegre, Rio Verde de Mato Grosso
PE28)	I801	1520	1/0.25	R. Surubim AM, Surubim
PR116)	J218	1520	2.5/0.25	R. Serra do Mar, Antonina
PR118)	J292	1520	1/0.25	R. Cultura Palotinense, Palotina
PR132)	J340	1520	1/0.25	R. Internacional, Quedas do Iguaçu
PR156)	J358	1520	1/0.25	R. Guairacá, Terra Rica
RJ44)	J491	1520	10/0.5	R. Continental, Rio de Janeiro
RJ10)	J499	1520	0.25	R. Musical; Cantagalo
RN22)	J610	1520	1/0.25	R. Salinas, Macau
RS141)	K217	1520	1/0.25	R. Difusora Cachoeirense, Cachoeira do Sul
RS177)	K338	1520	1/0.25	R. Cultura, Arvorezinha
RS187)		1520	0.25	R. Tapense, Tapes
SC76)	J806	1520	2.5/0.25	R. Cultura, Timbó
SE13)	J931	1520	1/0.25	R. Imperatriz dos Campos, Tobias Barreto
SP191)	K614	1520	10/1	R. News, Mogi das Cruzes
SP192)	K627	1520	1/0.25	Pinhal R. Clube, Espírito Sto. do Pinhal
SP225)	K760	1520	1/0.25	R. Manchester, Sorocaba
SP270)	K...	1520	1/0.25	R. Difusora Torre Forte Ltda., Buritana
SP271)	K...	1520	0.25	R.Veradouro AM Ltda., Viradouro (CP)
TO07)	H797	1520	1/0.25	R. Cristal, Cristalândia
BA43)	H479	1530	10/0.5	R. Cultura, Guanambi'
BA96)	H...	1530	0.25	Grupo Frajola de Comunicação Ltda., Copim Grosso
CE76)	H666	1530	1/0.25	R. Tres Fronteiras, Campos Sales
CE96)	H...	1530	1/0.25	Rede Sol de Comunicação Ltda., Granja
GO58)	H...	1530	1/0.25	R. Vale das Esmeraldas Ltda., Pontalina
MG175)	L262	1530	0.25	R. Progresso, Monte Santo de Minas
MG110)	L280	1530	1/0.25	R. Clube, Pouso Alegre
MG182)	L...	1530	1/0.25	Magui Comunicações e Marketing

	Call	kHz	kW	Name and location
				Ltda., Almenara (CP)
MS46)	I...	1530	1/0.25	R. AM Atalaia, Sete Quedas (CP)
MT42)	I...	1530	1/0.25	DMD Associados Assessoria e Propaganda, Peixoto de Azevedo
MT59)	I...	1530	1/0.25	Sistema de Comunicações Keller Ltda., Campo Novo do Parecís (CP)
PE29)	I781	1530	1/0.25	R. Bitury, Belo Jardim
PR157)	J348	1530	2.5/0.25	R. Vale do Iguaçu, Verê
RJ57)	J482	1530	1/0.25	R. Búzios, Cabo Frio
RJ45)	J502	1530	1/0.25	R. Princesinha do Norte, Miracema
RN16)	J603	1530	1/0.25	R. Curimataú, Nova Cruz
RO16)	J685	890	1	R. Planalto, Vilhena
RO22)	J...	1530	0.25	Rede Brasileira de R. e TV Ltda., Pimenta Bueno (CP)
RS143)	K235	1530	1/0.25	R. Sulina, Dom Pedrito
RS144)	K300	1530	5/0.25	R. São Leopoldo, São Leopoldo
RS145)	K304	1530	4/0.25	R. Tapejara, Tapejara
SC77)	J761	1530	1/0.25	R. Difusora, Itajaí
SC78)	J780	1530	1/0.25	R. Difusora, São Joaquim
SC79)	J796	1530	2.5/0.25	R. Porto Feliz, Mondaí
SP193)	K677	1530	1/0.25	R. Difusora Digital, Tupi Paulista
SP194)	K699	1530	1/0.25	R. Noticias, Tatuí
SP231)	K755	1530	1/0.25	R. Universal, Teodoro Sampaio
BA79)	H...	1540	0.25	R. Jornal, Souto Soares
BA89)	H...	1540	0.25	R. Sociedade, Itiruçu
CE42)	H611	1540	1/0.5	R. Sant'Ana, Tianguá
CE77)	H631	1540	1/0.25	R. Sertões, Mombaça
CE78)	H...	1540	1/0.25	R. Aratanha, Pacatuba
ES19)	I206	1540	0.25	R. Agricultura, Santa Teresa
GO40)	H760	1540	1/0.25	R. Jornal, Inhumas (ff 1050)
MA36)	H921	1540	1/0.25	R. Santa Maura, Lago da Pedra
MG111)	L217	1540	1/0.25	R. Bomdespachense, Bom Despacho
MG112)	L226	1540	1/0.25	R. Clube de Minas Gerais, Conselheiro Lafaiete
MG113)	L293	1540	2/0.25	R. Tropical, Três Corações
MS35)	N601	1540	1/0.25	R. Regional Piravevê, Ivinhema
MT55)	I...	1540	1/0.25	Soc. Barrabugrense de Comunicação Ltda., Barra do Bugre (CP)
PA14)	I545	1540	1/0.25	R. Boa Vista, São Sebastião da Boa Vista
PB24)	I694	1540	1/0.5	R. Santa Maria, Monteiro
PR168)	J306	1540	1/0.25	R. Litorânea, Guaratuba
PR150)	J357	1540	1/0.25	R. Princesa, Roncador (ff 820)
PR175)	J...	1540	0.25	R. e TV Rotiones Ltda., Icaraima (CP)
PR178)		1540	1/0.25	R.Tres de Maio, Imbutuva (CP)
RJ54)	J...	1540	1/0.25	R. Clube, Paraíba do Sul
RN30)	J611	1540	1	R. Baixa Verde, João Câmara
RS157)	K282	1540	1/0.25	R. Quaraí, Quaraí
RS156)	K367	1540	1/0.25	R. Querência, Santo Augusto (ff 1120)
SC80)	J803	1540	1/0.25	R. Capinzal, Capinzal
SP245)	K514	1540	1/0.25	R. Cultura, Leme
SP196)	K564	1540	2/1	R. Em. de Botucatu, Botucatu
SP197)	K723	1540	50/1	Nova Difusora AM, Osasco
SP246)	K737	1540	0.5/0.25	R. Central, Pompéia
BA80)	H518	1550	5/0.25	R. Independência do São Francisco, Juazeiro
MA37)	H926	1550	1/0.25	Sistema Janaina de Radiodifusão, Vargem Grande
MG114)	L211	1550	1/0.25	R. Cultura, Monte Carmelo
MG169)	L222	1550	1/0.25	R. Difusora, Carmo do Rio Claro
MG115)	L289	1550	1/0.25	R. Difusora Santarritense, Santa Rita do Sapucaí
MG183)	L...	1550	1/0.25	Agência Guanhaense de Comunicação Ltda., Guanhães (CP)
PA34)	I550	1550	1/0.25	R. Cabano, Maracanã
PB32)	I700	1550	10/0.25	R. Jardim do Brejo, Areia
PR133)	J213	1550	1/0.25	R. Ipiranga, Palmeira
PR123)	J303	1550	1/0.25	R. Pioneira de Formosa, Formosa do Oeste
PR124)	J315	1550	1/0.25	R. Cristal, Marmeleiro
PR136)	J355	1550	1/0.25	R. Cidade, Palmital (ff 1190)
PR169)	J...	1550	1/0.25	R. Itaí de Rio Claro Ltda., Tibagi (CP)
RJ46)	J479	1550	1/0.25	R. Imperial, Petrópolis
RN19)	J606	1550	1/0.25	R. Gazeta do Oeste, Areia Branca
RO23)	J...	1550	0.25	Suprema Comêrcio e Empreendimentos Ltda., Cacoal (CP)
RS162)	K377	1550	1/0.25	R. Jornal, Capão do Leão
RS159)	K...	1550	1/0.25	Em. Soledadense de Radiodifusão Ltda., Soledade (CP)
SC92)	J814	1550	5/0.25	R. Imigrantes, Turvo
SP198)	K501	1550	1/0.25	R. Clube, Itararé
SP259)	K528	1550	1/0.25	R. Tambaú, Tambaú
SP200)	K572	1550	1/0.25	R. Cacique, Capivari
SP201)	K590	°1550	5/1	R. Guarujá Paulista, Guarujá
SP247)	K623	1550	1	R. Cultura, Pederneiras (ff 1380)
SP202)	K659	1550	1/0.25	R. São Joaquim, São Joaquim da Barra
SP219)	K740	1550	1/0.25	R. Auriflama, Auriflama
AL16)	H...	1560	1/0.25	R. Princesa das Matas, Viçosa
BA90)	H526	1560	1/0.25	R. Educ. Sta. Tereza AM, Ribeira do Pombal
CE43)	H622	1560	1/0.25	R. Difusora Vale de Curu, Pentecoste
CE88)	H...	1560	1/0.25	Sistema de Comunicações Terra do Sol Ltda., Araripe (CP)
MA18)	H902	1560	1/0.25	R. Agua Branca, Vitorino Freire
MG117)	L256	1560	1/0.25	R. Jornal, Leopoldina
MG184)	L...	1560	1/0.25	Paraopeba Comunicações Ltda., Mateus Leme (CP)
MT56)	I...	1560	1/0.25	Sistema Plug de Comunicações Ltda., Paranaita (CP)
PA36)	I...	1560	0.25	RBN Rede Brasil Norte de Comunicação Ltda., Almeirim (CP)
PA37)	I...	1560	1/0.25	Rede Brasileira de R. e TV Ltda., Igarapé Miri (CP)
PR125)	J275	1560	1/0.25	R. Capanema, Capanema
PR161)	J361	1560	1/0.25	R. Cultura Serpin, Ribeirão do Pinhal
PR162)	J364	1560	1/0.25	R. Clube, Mallet
PR177)	J...	1560	0.5/0.25	R. Barigui, Almirante Tamandaré (CP)
RJ47)	J501	1560	5/0.25	R. Grande Rio, Itaguaí
RN17)	J608	1560	1/0.25	R. Cultura do Oeste,Pau dos Ferros
RS158)	K310	1560	2.5/0.25	R. Açoriana, Taquari
RS172)	K369	1560	5/0.25	R. Poata, São José do Ouro
SC95)	J825	1560	1/0.25	R. Cidade, São Miguel d'Oeste
SP261)	K593	1560	1/0.25	R. Show, Igarapava
SP248)	K679	1560	1/0.25	R. Valparaíso, Valparaíso
SP249)	K725	1560	0.25	R. Regional AM, Pedreira
SP250)	K...	1560	1/0.25	R. Vale do Rio Paraná, Presidente Epitácio
BA56)	H496	1570	1/0.25	R. Educadora Jaguaquara
BA91)	H533	1570	0.25	R. Lider, Central
CE44)	H621	1570	1/0.25	R. Sertão Central,Senador Pompeu
GO49)	H787	1570	1/0.25	R. Mantiqueira, Niquelândia (ff 680)
MA22)	H907	1390	10/0.5	R. Cultura do Rio Jordão, Coroatá
MG146)	L242	1570	1/0.25	R. Universitária, Itajubá
MG141)	L344	1570	1/0.25	R. Cidade, Corinto
MG170)	L364	1570	10/0.25	R. Difusora, Piranga
MG185)	L...	1570	1/0.25	KMR Telecomunicações Ltda., Pedra Azul
MG189)		1390	1/0.25	Rede Brasileira, Uberlandia (CP)
MS24)	I409	1570	1/0.25	R. Caarapó, Caarapó
PE30)	I798	1570	5/1	R. Asa Branca, Salgueiro
PR158)	J324	*1570	0.25	R. Brasileira, Bela Vista do Paraíso
PR137)	J341	1570	1/0.25	R. Club, Nova Aurora
PR159)	J365	1570	1/0.25	R. Arapoti, Arapoti
PR166)	J...	1570	0.25	Porto de Cima R. e TV Ltda., Paranaguá (CP)
RJ48)	J493	1570	1/0.25	R. Cultura, Valença
RJ49)	J498	1570	1/0.25	R. Bom Jesus, Bom Jesus de Itabapoana
RN33)	J...	1570	1/0.25	RIR Rede Integrada de Radiodifusão, Angicos
RO19)	J678	1570	1/0.25	R. Soc. Espigão, Espigão d'Oeste
RS147)	K358	1570	5/0.25	R. Metrópole, Cachoeirinha
SC83)	J777	1570	1/0.25	R. Rio Negrinho, Rio Negrinho
SC98)	J829	1570	1/0.25	R. Modelo, Modelo
SC107)	J...	1570	1/0.25	Frequência Brasileira de Comunicaões Ltda., Tangará (CP)
SP204)	K552	1570	1/0.25	R. Avaré, Avaré
SP205)	K605	1570	1/0.25	R. Junqueirópolis, Junqueirópolis
SP262)	K648	1570	1/0.25	R. Zequinha de Abreu, Santa Rita do Passa Quatro
SP206)	K651	1570	10/0.25	R. Emissora ABC, Santo André
SP207)	K667	1570	1/0.25	R. Socorro, Socorro
SP208)	K670	1570	1/0.25	R. Clube, Tanabi
TO10)	H...	1570	1/0.25	Sistema de Comunicação Rio Bonito, Gurupi
TO11)	H...	1570	1/0.25	RBN Rede Brasil Norte de Comunicação Ltda., Dianópolis (CP)
BA45)	H464	1580	1/0.25	R. Emissora Radiovox, Muritiba
BA62)	H502	1580	1/0.25	R. Atalaia, Canavieiras
BA92)	H...	1580	0.25	R. União, Teolândia
ES13)	I209	1580	5/0.25	R. Educadora, Afonso Cláudio
MG119)	L210	1580	1/0.25	R. Liberdade AM, Itapecirica
MG121)	L290	1580	1/0.25	R. Cultura, Santos Dumont
MG122)	L329	1580	1/0.25	R. Educadora, Espinosa
MG133)	L335	1580	1/0.25	R. Rural, Guaranésia
MS25)	I415	1580	1/0.25	R. Laguna, Jardim
MS43)	I...	1580	1/0.25	R. Difusora, Ivinhema

	Call	kHz	kW	Name and location
PI18)	I898	1580	1/0.25	R. Santa Clara, Floriano
PR164)	J342	1580	1/0.25	R. São João do Sudoeste, São João
PR176)	J...	1580	0.25	Sesal Comunicação e Informatica, Cambé
RJ51)	J487	1580	1/0.25	R. Popular Fluminense, Conceição de Macabu
RJ58)	J505	1580	0.25	R. Geração 2000, Teresópolis
RN24)	J613	1580	1/0.25	R. Novos Tempos, Ceará Mirim
RS148)	K237	1580	1/0.25	R. Encantado, Encantado
RS150)	K339	1580	1/0.25	R. Difusora Fronteira, Arroio Grande
SC84)	J818	1580	1/0.25	R. Pomerode, Pomerode
SP251)	K504	1580	1/0.25	R. Difusora, Amparo
SP209)	K743	1580	0.25	R. Trans Universal, Itaporanga
BA55)	H...	1590	0.25	R. Vale do Jiquiriçá, Jiquiriça
CE89)	H...	1590	1/0.25	R. Bom Jesus Ltda., Camocim (CP)
CE98)	H...	1590	1/0.25	R.FM Benza, Eusebio (CP)
ES22)	I...	1590	1/0.25	SM Comunicação Ltda., Cachoeiro de Itapemirim (CP)
MG171)	L368	1590	1/0.25	R. Cidade Carinho, Ubá
MG134)	L369	1590	10/1	R. Guaicuí, Várzea da Palma
MG186)	L...	1590	0.25	R. Sistema Maua de Comunicação Ltda., Itapagipe (CP)
MG187)	L...	1590	0.25	R. Alternativa, Lambari (CP)
MS26)	I403	1590	1/0.25	R. Independência, Eldorado
MS52)	I...	1590	1/0.25	R. Nova FM Anastácio, Anastácio (CP)
PB34)	I. . .	1590	1/0.25	R. Correio do Vale, Itaporanga
PE40)	I...	1590	1/0.25	Radiodifusão Rainha do Céu Ltda., Bezerros (CP)
PR129)	J290	1590	1/0.25	R. Cultura, Andirá
PR160)	J296	1590	1/0.25	R. Princesa, Capitão Leônidas Marques
RJ52)	J506	1590	1/0.25	R. Resende AM, Resende
RS174)	K212	1590	0.25	R. Clube, Bagé
RS151)	K281	1590	1/0.25	R. Navegantes, Porto Lucena (ff 1360)
SC101)	J823	1590	10/0.5	Floresta Negra AM, Joinville
SP254)	K774	1590	1/0.5	R. Japi, Cabreúva
SP263)	K779	°1600	100/20	R. Nove de Julho, São Paulo

SW: * = inactive, ff = future frequency.

	Call	kHz	kW	Name and Location, h. of tr.
SP82)	ZYG852	2380	0.25	R. Educadora, Limeira: 24h
SP168)	ZYG862	2420	0.5	R. São Carlos, São Carlos
AC02)	ZYF204	2460	1	Super R. Alvorada, Rio Branco: 1000-0400
SP114)	ZYG851	2470	0.25	R. Cacique, Sorocaba: 24h
SP210)	ZYG866	2491	0.25	R. Oito de Setembro, Descalvado: 0900-2300
AM03)	ZYF279	*3205	5	R. Vale do Rio Madeira, Humaitá
SP11)	ZYG861	3205	1	R. Ribeirão Preto: 0700-0400
SP201)		3235	1	R. Guarujá Paulista, Guarujá
MG69)	ZYG203	3245	1	R. Clube, Varginha: 0830-0210
AC03)	ZYF...	3255	1	R. Educ. 6 de Agosto, Xapuri: 1000-0400
AC07)	ZYF202	*3255	5	R. Transamazônica, Senador Guiomard
SP112)	ZYG867	3325	2.5	R. Mundia, São Paulo
SP49)	ZYG855	3365	1	R. Cultura, Araraquara: 0700-0300
AM02)	ZYF276v	*3375	5	R. Municipal, São Gabriel da Cachoeira
MS04)	ZYF907	3375	5	R. Clube, Dourados: 0800-0400
AP02)	ZYF361	*3375	5	R. Equatorial, Macapá
RO09)	ZYG792	3375	5	R. Educadora, Guajará Mirim: 0900-1300, 2000-2200
AC08)	ZYF....	v3560	1.5	R. Difusora, Brasiléia: W 1000-0400, Sun 1100-0300 (n. 3315)
AC09)	ZYF....	*4116	0.25	R. Difusora, Sena Madureira (occ.)
MA03)	ZYF810	4754	5	R. Dif. do Maranhão, São Luís: 24h
MS01)	ZYF904	4755	10	R. Educação Rural, Campo Grande: 0700-0300
AC01)	ZYF200	*4765	10	R. Integração, Cruzeiro do Sul: 0900-0300
PA04)	ZYG363	4765	5	R. Rural, Santarém: 0800-0500
MG55)	ZYG207	4775	1	R. Congonhas, Congonhas: 0800-0300
MT39)	ZYF902	4775	1	R. Portal da Amazônia, Cuiabá: 0700-0300
PA10)	ZYG430	*4775	5	R. Liberal, Belém
RO14)	ZYG794	4775	5	R. Amarela, Rolim de Moura (CP)
MA09)	ZYF812	*4785	5	R. Ribamar, São Luís
RO11)	ZYG790	4785	10	R. Caiari, Porto Velho: 0900-1400, 1900-0300
SP136)	ZYG857	4785	1	R. Brasil, Campinas: 0800-0200
MS12)	ZYF900	4795	1	R. Difusora, Aquidauana: 0755-0400
AM20)	ZYF273	4805	10/5	R. Dif. do Amazonas, Manaus: 0930-1330, 1530-0100
MG06)	ZYG209	4805	0.5	R. Itatiaia, Belo Horizonte: 0800-1900
PR13)	ZYG640	4815	10	R. Difusora, Londrina: 0755 (Sun 0900)-0355
SP80)	ZYG868	4825	10	R. Canção Nova, Cachoeira Paulista: 24h
PA12)	ZYG364	4825	5	R. Educadora, Bragança: 0930-0300
MS27)	ZYF908	*4835	5	R. Atalaia, Corumbá
SP102)	ZYG869	4845	1	R. Meteorologia Paulista, Ibitinga: 0700-2300 (relays R. Ternura FM)
AM14)	ZYF278	4845	10	R. Cultura, Manaus: 1000-0200
MG33)	ZYG202	4855	1	R. Por Um Mundo Melhor, Governador Valadares:
MT40)	ZYF905	4855	2.5	R. Tropical da Barra, Barra do Garças: 0900-0130
AC04)	ZYF203	4865	5	R. Verdes Florestas, Cruzeiro do Sul: 0930-1230, 2100-0100
PA23)	ZYG366	4865	5	R. Missões da Amazônia, Óbidos: 0900-0200
PR33)	ZYG641	4865	5	R. Alvorada, Londrina: 0700-0300
RR01)	ZYG810	4875	10	R. Roraima, Boa Vista: 0800-0400
GO12)	ZYF692	4885	1	R. A Voz do Coração Imaculado, Anápolis: 0800-1200, 2000-0300
AC06)	ZYF201	4885	5	R. Dif. Acreana, Rio Branco: 1000-0400
PA03)	ZYG362	4885	10	R. Clube do Pará, Belém: 0800-0500
AM13)	ZYF270	4895	5	R. Bare, Manaus: 2000-1200
MS32)	ZYR200	4895	5	R. Novo Tempo, Campo Grande: 24h
RJ03)	ZYG683	4905	5	R. Nova Relógio, Rio de Janeiro: 0730-0330
TO04)	ZYF693	4905	1	R. Araguaia, Araguaína: 0800-0100
AP01)	ZYF360	4915	25/10	R. Dif., Macapá: 2100-0700
GO27)	ZYF691	4915	10	R. CBN Anhanguera, Goiânia: 0900-0300
SP06)	ZYG684	4925	0.5	R. Difusora, Taubaté: 24h
AM10)	ZYF271	4925	5	R. Educação Rural, Tefé: 1000-1530, 2000-0200
ES07)	ZYF641	4935	1	R. Capixaba, Vitória: 24h
GO09)	ZYF694	4935	2.5	R. Difusora, Jataí: 0900-1300, 1900-2200
MG73)	ZYG201	4945	1	R. Difusora, Poços de Caldas: 0800-0400
PE08)	ZYG525	4945	1	Emiss. Rural A Voz do São Francisco, Petrolina: 0700-0300
RO13)	ZYG791	4945	7.5	R. Progresso, Porto Velho: 0900-0200
MT12)	ZYF906	4955	2.5	R.Clube, Rondonópolis: W 0800-0200, Sun 0900-0300
PA08)	ZYG361	*4955	10	R. Marajoara, Belém
RJ23)	ZYG682	4956	1	R. Cultura, Campos dos Goitacazes: 0700-0300
AM12)	ZYF275	4965	5	R. Alvorada, Parintins: 0900-0200
RN10)	ZYG761	*4965	1	R. Poty, Natal
MA10)	ZYF813	4975	5	R. Timbira do Maranhão, São Luís: 0800-0300
SP112)	ZYG865	4975	1	R. Mundial, São Paulo: 24h
SP187)	ZYG685	*4975	1	R. Iguatemi, Osasco
GO30)	ZYF690	4985	10	R. Brasil Central, Goiânia: 0700-0300
PI10)	ZYG595	5015	1	R. Pioneira, Teresina: 0800-0200
MT08	ZYF903	5015	1	R. Brasil Tropical, Cuiabá: 24h (at night rel. R. Cultura FM)
RJ07)	ZYG685	5015	1	R. Copacabana, Rio de Janeiro: 24h
PA15)	ZYG365	5025	5	R. Vale do Xingu, Altamira,
PB14)	ZYG481	*5025	1	Super R. Borborema, Campina Grande
RO06)	ZYG793	5025	5	R. Morimoto, Ji-Paraná
SP52)	ZYG853	5035	10	R. Aparecida, Aparecida:0700-0300
AM09)	ZYF272	5035	5	R. Educação Rural, Coari:0945-0100
SP201)	ZYG850	5045	1	R. Guarujá Paulista, Guarujá
PA16)	ZYG360	5045	10	R. Cultura do Pará, Belém:0800-0300
AM15)	ZYF274*	5055	5	R. Jornal A Crítica, Manaus
MT10)	ZYF901	5055	1	R. Difusora, Cáceres: 0800-0400
SP201)		5930	1	R. Guarujá Paulista, Guarujá
SP62)	ZYE965	5955	10	R. Gazeta, São Paulo: 0900-0300
RS163)	ZYE858	5965	7.5	R. Nova Visão, Santa Maria: 0700 - 0100 (rel. R. Transmundial)
MG06)	ZYE523	5970	10	R. Itatiaia, Belo Horizonte: 0800-1900
SC59)	ZYE891	5980	10	R. Guarujá, Florianópolis: 24h
DF10)	ZYE773	5990	250	R. Senado, Brasília: M-F 1000-2400
RS23)	ZYE852	6000	10	R. Guaíba, Porto Alegre: 0800-0400
MG35)	ZYE521	6010	5	R. Inconfidência, Belo Horizonte: 1200-1600, 1800-2000
RS09)	ZYE850	6020	10	R. Gaúcha, Porto Alegre: 0900-0400
RJ25)	ZYE770	6030	10	R. Globo, Rio de Janeiro: 0900-0330
PR134)	ZYE725	6040	7.5	R. Clube Paranaense, Curitiba: 0900-2200 (Sun 2300)
MG08)	ZYE520	6050	10	R. Guarani, Belo Horizonte
PR60)	ZYE726	6060	10	R. Tupi, Curitiba: 24h
RJ18)	ZYE765	6070	7.5	R. Capital, Rio de Janeiro: 0800-0300
GO27)	ZYE441	6080	5	R. CBN Anhanguera, Goiânia: 0900-0300
PR15)	ZYE726	6080	10	R. Novas de Paz, Curitiba: 1000-0300
SP57)	ZYE956	6090	10	R. Bandeirantes, São Paulo: 24h
PR138)	ZYE728	6105	5	R. Cult. Filadelfia, Foz do Iguaçu:

	Call	kHz	kW	Name and Location, h. of tr.
				0800-0300
SP80)	ZYE971	6105	5	R. Canção Nova, Cachoeira Paulista: 24h
SP100)	ZYE968	6120	10	R. Globo, São Paulo: 0900-0200
SP52)	ZYE954	6135	25	R. Aparecida, Aparecida: 0800-0300
SP77)	ZYE950	6150	7.5	R. Record, São Paulo: 0800-0215
AM11)	ZYE245	6160	10	R. Rio Mar, Manaus: 1000-1600, 2000-0000
RS104)	ZYE854	6160	1	R. RGS, Porto Alegre (Sistema LBV Mundial hires airtime 24h)
SP121)	ZYE959	6170	7.5	R. Cultura, São Paulo: 0800-0400
DF06)	ZYE365	6180	250	R. Nacional da Amazônia, Brasília (r. 6190)
DF10)		6190		R. Senado Federal, Brasília:1000-2400
SP77)	ZYE951	9505	7.5	R. Record, São Paulo: 0900-2400
PR15)	ZYE726	9515	10	R. Novas de Paz, Curitiba: 0800-2100
RS163)	ZYE858	9530	10	R. Nova Visão, Santa Maria: 0700 – 0100 (rel. R. Transmundial)
RS104)	ZYE855	9550	10	R. RGS, Porto Alegre (Sistema LBV hires airtime 24h)
PR60)	ZYE727	9565	20	R. Tupi, Curitiba: 24h
SP47)	ZYE969	9585	10	R. CBN (Globo), São Paulo: 0900-1500
RJ12)	ZYE772	9600	7.5	R. MEC, Rio de Janeiro
SP121)	ZYE960	9615	7.5	R. Cultura, São Paulo: 0800-0300
SP52)	ZYE954	9630	10	R. Aparecida, Aparecida:
SP57)	ZYE957	9645	7.5	R. Bandeirantes, São Paulo: 24h
SC86)	ZYE890	9665	10	R. Marumby, Florianópolis: 0900-0100
SP80)	ZYE971	9675	10	R. Canção Nova, Cachoeira Paulista: 1000-2100
SP62)	ZYE963	9685	7.5	R. Gazeta, São Paulo: 0900-0300
AM11)	ZYE245	9695	7.5	R. Rio Mar, Manaus: 1000-2000
RJ17)	ZYE768	*9705	7.5	R. Nacional, Rio de Janeiro
PR134)	ZYE725	9725	7.5	R. Clube Paranaense, Curitiba: 0900-2200 (Sun 2300)
SP263)	ZYE...	*9820	10	R. Nove de Julho, São Paulo (CP)
PR15)	ZYE726	11725	10	R. Novas de Paz, Curitiba: 0900-2100
RS163)	ZYE858	11735	50	R. Nova Visão, Santa Maria 0700 - 0100 (rel. R. Transmundial)
PR60)	ZYE726	11765	20	R. Tupi, Curitiba: 0900-0300
DF06)	ZYE365	11780	250	R. Nal. da Amazônia, Brasília: 0900-0200
RS23)	ZYE853	11785	7.5	R. Guaíba, Porto Alegre: 0800-0400
RJ25)	ZYE775	11805	10	R. Globo, Rio de Janeiro: 0900-0330
GO30)	ZYE440	11815	7.5	R. Brasil Central, Goiânia: 0700-0300
GO27)	ZYE441	11830	10	R. CBN Anhanguera, Goiânia: 0900-0300
SP52)	ZYE954	11855	1	R. Aparecida, Aparecida: 0800-0300
RS104)	ZYE856	11895	10	R. RGS, Porto Alegre (Sistema LBV Mundial hires airtime 24h)
RS09)	ZYE851	11915	10	R. Gaucha, Porto Alegre: 0900-0300
SP57)	ZYE958	11925	10	R. Bandeirantes, São Paulo: 24h (R. Juratel hires airtime)
PR134)	ZYE725	11935	7.5	R. Clube Paranaense, Curitiba: 0900-2200 (Sun 2300)
DF06)	ZYE773	11950	250	Radiobrás, Brasília
SP77)	ZYE952*	11965	7.5	R. Record, São Paulo
SP77)	ZYE953*	15135	7.5	R. Record, São Paulo
MG35)	ZYE522*	15190	5	R. Inconfidência, Belo Horizonte
DF06)	ZYE365*	15200	250	R. Nacional da Amazônia, Brasília
MA10)	ZYE480*	15215	2.5	R. Timbira, São Luís
DF06)	ZYE365*	15265	250	Radiobras, Brasília
SP100)	ZYE970*	15265	1	R. Globo, São Paulo
SP62)	ZYE964	15325	1	R. Gazeta, São Paulo: 0900-0300
SP23)	ZYE955*	15415	1	R. Clube, Ribeirão Preto
SP121)	ZYE961	17815	10	R. Cultura, São Paulo: 0800-0300

RADIO NETWORKS:
In Brazil there are several radio networks. Below are listed just some of them. The affiliated outlets are often subject to alterations.

JOVEM PAN
✉ Av. Paulista 807, 24° andar, 01311-915 São Paulo, SP.
Web: www.jovempan.uol.com.br
Stations: AL05, AL10, AP05, CE21, CE62, DF01, ES08, ES12, ES14, ES17, GO04, GO31, MA11, MG54, MG56, MG60, MG82, MG98, MT14, PB09, PI04, PI47, PR18, PR48, PR81, PR98, PR108, PR131, PR143, PR161, RJ34, RJ35, RJ48, RN31, SC45, SC57, SP05, SP33, SP37, SP43, SP56, SP64, SP75, SP83, SP88, SP92, SP97, SP98, SP101, SP102, SP107, SP109, SP111, SP126, SP129, SP130, SP132, SP136, SP140, SP147, SP148, SP152, SP159, SP166, SP169, SP191, SP199, SP203, SP207, SP217, SP219, SP226, SP231, SP234, SP235, SP239, SP241, SP244, SP247, SP256, SP261, SP264.

REDE GAÚCHA SAT
✉ Av. Erico Veríssimo 400, Edificio Maurício Sirotsky Sobrinho, 90169-900 Porto Alegre, RS. **Web:** www.rbs.clicrbs.com.br
Stations: AC06, AL14, MT18, MT41, PR03, PR37, PR90, PR125, PR146, RS02, RS07, RS09, RS12, RS15, RS18, RS19, RS20, RS22, RS28, RS29, RS40, RS41, RS47, RS51, RS57, RS58, RS59, RS61, RS65, RS71, RS72, RS80, RS81, RS82, RS85, RS88, RS92, RS97, RS98, RS99, RS101, RS102, RS103, RS107, RS109, RS114, RS117, RS123, RS124, RS130, RS133, RS135, RS142, RS143, RS145, RS146, RS152, RS155, RS156, RS161, RS166, RS168, RS170, RS175, RS177, SC03, SC14, SC17, SC34, SC39, SC47, SC51, SC58, SC74, SC97, SC99, SC100.

SISTEMA GUAÍBA SAT
✉ Rua Caldas Jr. 219, 2° andar, 90019-900 Porto Alegre, RS.
Web: www.guaiba.com.br
Stations: RS06, RS08, RS23, RS24, RS35, RS37, RS46, RS52, RS54, RS55, RS68, RS84, RS106, RS111, RS116.

REDE PAULUS SAT
✉ Rua Doutor Pinto Ferraz 183, Vila Mariana, 04117-900 São Paulo, SP. **Web:** www.radioamericasp.com.br/paulussat.htm
Stations: AL14, BA37, BA81, CE35, ES15, GO29, GO40, MG04, MG07, MG26, MG31, MG33, MG45, MG93, MG107, MG135, MG139, MG156, MS40, MT08, PA27, PB01, PB13, PB24, PE15, PE19, PR42, PR43, PR49, PR56, PR65, PR102, PR121, PR152, RJ09, RJ34, RJ56, RN11, RO11, RS44, RS117, RS147, SC59, SC95, SE06, SP15, SP36, SP59, SP114, SP142, SP153, SP157, SP158, SP171, SP174, SP193, SP201, SP248, SP254, SP255.

RCR – REDE CATÓLICA DE RÁDIO
✉ RCR – Rede Católica de Rádio – UNDA BRASIL, União de Radiodifusão Católica, Rua Vergueiro 3086, Conj. 91, Vila Mariana, 04102-001 São Paulo, SP. **Web:** www.rcrunda.com.br
Email: rcr@rcrunda.com.br
Stations: AL07, AM10, AM11, AM12, AP01, BA03, BA08, BA16, BA20, BA36, BA37, BA54, BA58, BA69, BA71, CE19, CE25, CE38, CE42, DF07, ES10, ES15, GO02, GO05, GO08, GO09, GO12, GO13, GO14, GO18, GO20, GO21, GO25, GO28, GO29, GO33, GO34, GO35, GO37, GO38, GO39, GO43, GO49, MA02, MG04, MG08, MG15, MG16, MG19, MG26, MG27, MG28, MG31, MG33, MG36, MG50, MG63, MG64, MG66, MG78, MG103, MG107, MG108, MG127, MG163, MS01, MT01, MT05, MT08, MT34, PA04, PA12, PB15, PB26, PE08, PE09, PE33, PE36, PI10, PI18, PR33, PR46, PR79, PR86, PR89, PR91, PR96, PR99, PR109, PR116, PR120, PR121, PR122, PR127, PR128, PR133, PR134, PR137, PR142, PR154, PR155, PR160, RN02, RN05, RN07, RO09, RO11, RS07, RS12, RS24, RS25, RS26, RS41, RS44, RS70, RS74, RS77, RS81, RS83, RS107, RS114, RS118, RS127, RS134, RS137, SC09, SC20, SC27, SC67, SC88, SE03. SE11, SP34, SP43, SP52, SP93, SP148, SP161, SP162, SP174, SP178, SP182, SP183, SP196, SP229, SP252, SP259, SP263, TO01.

SISTEMA LBV MUNDIAL
✉ Legião da Boa Vontade, Rua Doraci 90, Bairro Bom Retiro, 01134-020 São Paulo, SP. **Web:** www.lbv.org.br
Stations: AM18, BA70, DF08, GO19, MG02, RJ02, RJ16, RS104, SP04, SP48, SP101, SP232, SP266.

REDE CANÇÃO NOVA DE RÁDIO
✉ Rua João Paulo II s/, Alto da Bela Vista, 12630-000 Cachoeira Paulista, SP. ☎ +55 12 250 2000. 🖷 +55 12 561 2074.
Web: www.cancaonova.org.br **Email:** radio@cancaonova.com
Stations: BA58, MG66, MG156, MT05, PE36, PR10, RJ01, RN07, SC27, SP62, SP80, SP176, SP233, TO12.

REDE SOMZOOM SAT
✉ Av. Herois do Acre 590, Passaré, 60743-760 Fortaleza, CE☎ +55 85 295 1238. **Web:** www.somzoom.com.br
Email: somzoomsat@somzoom.com.br
Stations: AL06, AL11, AL13, CE36, CE41, CE44, CE46, CE59, CE69, MA05, MA21, MA28, MA31, MA35, PB01, PB28, PI25, PI43, RJ39, RN11, RN12, RN16, RN17, RN18, RN21, RN22, RN24, RN28, RN30, RS117, SE04, TO04.

Addresses and other information
AC00) ACRE
AC01) Rua Alagoas 270, 69980-000 Cruzeiro do Sul. **Email:** rtvi@omega-sul.com.br +55 68 322 4637 +55 68 322 6511 – **AC02**) Av. Ceará 2150, Jardim Nazle, 69900-460 Rio Branco. **Email:** severian_jose@brturbo.com ☎+55 68 226 2301. – **AC03**) Rua Pio Nazario 31, 69930-000 Xapuri. +55 68 542 3063. – **AC04**) Rua Mário Lobão 81, 69980-000 Cruzeiro do Sul. ☎🖷 +55 68 322 3309, 322 2634. **Email:** verdesflorestas@yahoo.com.br – **AC05**)

Rua Epaminondas Jacome 236, 69908-420 Rio Branco. – **AC06**) Rua Benjamin Constant 1232, 69900-161 Rio Branco. ☎ +55 68 223 9696. 🖷 +55 68 223 8610. **Email:** comercial.difusora@ac.gov.br – **AC07**) Av. Castelo Branco 329, 69925-000 Senador Guiomard. .– **AC08**) Rua Genni Assis s/n, 69932-000 Brasiléia.– **AC09**) Rua Avelino Chaves 707, 69940-000 Sena Madureira. – **AC10**) Governo do Estado do Acre, 69960-000 Feijó. – **AC11**) Governo do Estado do Acre, 69940-000 Sena Madureira. – **AC12**) Governo do Estado do Acre, 69970-000 Tarauacá. – **AC13**) 69930-000 Brasiléia. – **AC14**) 69900-000 Rio Branco. – **AC15**)69960-000 Feijó.

AL00) ALAGOAS

AL01) Av. Coronel Wilson Santa Cruz 6, 57314-000 Arapiraca. – **AL02**) Via Expressa 4360, Serraria, 57080-000 Maceió. ☎ +55 (82) 328 3066. 🖷 +55 (82) 328 3771. – **AL03**) Rua José Maria Passos 25, 57600-030 Palmeiras dos Indios. - **FM:** 92.5. – **AL04**) Rua Barão José Miguel 400, Farol, 57055-160 Maceió. – **AL05**) Rua Miguel Palmeira 1513, 7° andar, Farol, 57055-330 Maceió. – **AL06**) Praça Senador Eneas Araújo 61, 57500-000 Santana do Ipanema. – **AL07**) Rua Aristeu de Andrade 355, Farol, 57021-900 Maceió. **Web:** www.oam.com.br/gazetaam/ – **AL08**) Rua Barão de Penedo 258, 57020-340 Maceió. – **AL09**) C.P. 6, 57201-970 Penedo.- **AL10**) Quadra A lote 04, 57160-000 Marechal Deodoro. – **AL11**) Rua Porcos s/n, 57300-000 Arapiraca. – **AL12**) Parque Industrial Delmiro Gouveia ao lado da Rodovia BR-423, 57480-000 Delmiro Gouveia. – **AL13**) BR-104 Km. 36, Bairro Roberto Correia de Arajuó, 57800-000 União dos Palmares. – **AL14**) Rua Aldeir Lima Peixoto 123, 3° andar, Farol, 57051-110 Maceió – **AL15**) Av. Braulio Cavalcante s/n, 57400-000 Pão de Açucar. – **AL16**) 57700-000 Viçosa. – **AL17**) 57100-000 Maceió. – **AL18)** 57600-000 Palmeira dos Indios.

AM00) AMAZONAS

AM01) Rua Brasília s/n, 69470-000 Tefé. – **AM02**) Av. Alvaro Maia s/n, 69750-000 São Gabriel da Cachoeira. **Email:** rmunicipal@yahoo.com.br ☎🖷 +55 97 471 1768. – **AM03**) Rua Júlio de Oliveira 1323, São Pedro, 69800-000 Humaitá. ☎🖷 +55 97 373 2073. **Email:** radiovrm@dnknet.com.br – **AM04**) a/c Prefeitura Municipal de Tabatinga, 69640-000 Tabatinga. ☎🖷 +55 97 412 4078. – **AM05**) Rua Solimões 809, 69100-000 Itacoatiara. ☎🖷 +55 92 521 1273/1635/2500. **Email:** difusora@italig.com.br – **AM06**) Rua Joana D'Angelo 2255, 69400-000 Manacapuru. – **AM07**) Av. Major Santana 2502, 69280-000 Manicoré. – **AM08**) Estrada dos Morães 1455, 69190-000 Maués. – **AM09**) Praça São Sebastião 228, 69460-000 Coari. ☎ +55 97 561 2474 🖷 +55 97 561 2633. **Email:** radiocoari@portalcoari.com.br – **AM10**) Rua Benjamin Constant 343 (CP 21), 69470-000 Tefé. ☎ +55 97 343 3017. 🖷 +55 97 343 2663. **Email:** rert@osite.com.br – **AM11**) Rua José Clemente 500, 69010-070 Manaus. ☎+55 92 632 5005 +55 92 232 7763. **Email:** decom@click21.com.br – **AM12**) Rua Governador Leopoldo Neves 516, 69151-460 Parintins. ☎ +55 92 533 2002/3097 +55 92 533 2004. **Email:** alvorada@parintinsnet.com.br **Web:** www.jcam.com.br - **FM:** 100.1. – **AM13**) Tefe 3025, Japiim, 69078-000 Manaus, ☎ +55 92 231 1299/1379 🖷 +55 92 614 5556. **Web:** www.radiobare.com.br **Email:** proclip@argo.com.br - **AM14**) Rua Barcelos s/n, Praça 14, 69020-200 Manaus. **Web:** www.tvcultura-am.com.br **Email:** radiocultura.hotmail.com ☎ +55 92 621 0015. 🖷 +55 92 663 3332/2829. – **AM15**) Av. Andre Araujo 1924 A, 69060-001 Manaus. ☎ +55 92 2123 1000. - **FM:** 93.1. – **AM16**) Rua Santo Antonio 108, Santo Antônio , 69029-230 Manaus. ☎ +55 92 671 4030. 🖷 +55 92 671 4182. **Email:** radioboasnovas@hotmail.com – **AM17**) Av. Amazonas 1958, 69151-000 Parintins. +55 92 533 1564 +55 92 533 2456. – **AM18**) Rodovia Manoel Urbano, km. 02, 69405-000 Iranduba. – **AM19**) Boulevard Pedro Rate 176, São José, 69400-000 Manacapuru. ☎ +55 92 361 2192. 🖷 +55 92 361 2453. – **AM20**) Av. Eduardo Ribeiro 639, 20° andar, 69010-001 Manaus. ☎ +55 92 633 1001. 🖷 +55 92 234 3750. **Web:** www.difusoramanaus.com.br **Email:** difusora@internext.com.br – **AM21**) Estrada do Gavião, km. 05, 69500-000 Carauari. – **AM22**) 69880-000 Eirunepê. – **AM23**) Praça Coronel João Vercosa 47, Centro, 69190-000 Maués. ☎ +55 92 542 1036. 🖷 +55 92 542 1668. – **AM24**) Av. Leopoldo Neves 360, 69850-000 Bôca do Acre. – **AM25**) Rua Anori/Anama 327, 69440-000 Anori.

AP00) AMAPÁ

AP01) Rua Cândido Mendes 525, 68900-100 Macapá. **Email:** difusora_ap@hotmail.com +55 96 212 1120 +55 96 212 1116 – **AP02**) Rua Major Eliezer Levy 684, 68900-140 Macapá. – **AP03**) Av. Nações Unidas 256, 68906-100 Macapá. – **AP04**) 68925-000 Santana. – **AP05**) 68930-000 Mazagão.

BA00) BAHIA

BA01) Rua M. Dourado Sobrinho 78, 44900-000 Irecê. – **BA02**) Praça José Bastos 2, 45600-000 Itabuna. – **BA03**) Praça da Independência 244, 45995-000 Teixeira de Freitas. – **BA04**) Rua Gabriel Soares 23, Ladeira dos Aflitos, 40060-040 Salvador. – **BA05**) Rua Luis Augusto Fernandes Borges 306, 47800-000 Barreiras. – **BA06**) Av. Nilo Peçanha 572, 45400-000 Valença. – **BA07**) Praça Duque Caxias 3, 45700-000 Itapetinga. – **BA08**) Rua dos Sururu s/n, 44570-000 Santo Antônio de Jesus. – **BA09**) Rua Joana Angélica 125, 45660-000 Ilhéus. – **BA10**) Rua Germiniano Costa 47, 44025-070 Feira de Santana. – **BA11**) Rua Ferreira Santos 5, Federacão, 40230-040 Salvador. – **BA12**) C.P. 19, 45601-970 Itabuna. – **BA13**) Marechal Deodoro 639, 47800-000 Barreiras. ☎ +55 (73) 811 4188. **Web:** www.rb.am.br/ – **BA14**) Praça Luiz Nogueira 385, 48700-000 Serrinha. – **BA15**) Rodovia BA-052, km. 48, 46810-000 Utinga. – **BA16**) Rua Martin Afonso de Souza 270, Bairro Garcia, 40100-050 Salvador. – **Web:** www.arquissa.org.br/radio – **BA17**) Av. Visconde do Rio Branco 68, 48970-000 Senhor do Bonfim. ☎ +55 74 541 4078. 🖷 +55 74 541 4617. – **BA18**) Travessa da Catedral s/n, 45600-000 Itabuna. – **BA19**) Rua Wercelêncio da Mota 81, 48730-000 Conceição do Coité. **Web:** www.radiosisal.hpg.ig.com.br/ – **BA20**) Rua Frei Hermenegildo 300, Capuchinos, 44052-250 Feira de Santana. - **FM:** 96.9. – **BA21**) Gleba Fazenda Ouro Verde, 45900-000 Caravelas. – **BA22**) Rua Gabriel Soares 23, 40060-040 Salvador. – **BA23**) Praça Barão do Rio Branco 42, 45100-000 Vitória da Conquista. – **BA24**) Av. Maria Quitéria 223, 44062-630 Feira de Santana. - **FM:** 95.3 "Nordeste FM". – **BA25**) Rua Santos Dumont 22, 45700-000 Itapetinga. – **BA26**) Rua Marquês de Paranaguá 259, 45660-000 Ilhéus. 🖷 +55 73 231 3612. – **BA27**) C.P. 29, 45825-000 Eunápolis. – **BA28**) Rua Aprigo Duarte 4, 48900-000 Juazeiro. – **BA29**) Morro do Peru Pelado, 44700-000 Jacobina. – **BA30**) Rua Monte Castelo 45, Sobradinha, 44018-210 Feira de Santana. – **BA31**) Rua Dom Pedro II 98, 48100-000 Alagoinhas. – **BA32**) Rua Lima e Silva 216, Liberdade, 40375-010 Salvador. – **BA33**) Av. 2 de Julho 140, 45660-000 Ilhéus. **Email:** radiobahianadeilheus@bol.com.br – **BA34**) Praça Luiz Nogueira 385, 48700-000 Serrinha. – **BA35**) Rua São Francisco 159, 48600-000 Paulo Afonso. – **BA36**) Praça da Bandeira s/n, Centro, 47600-000 Bom Jesus da Lapa. ☎ +55 77 481 5179. – **BA37**) Av. Getúlio Vargas 394, 44330-000 São Gonçalo dos Campos. – **BA38**) Rua Marechal Deodoro 16, 44200-000 Santo Amaro. – **BA39**) Rua 2 de Julho 20, 45200-000 Jequié. – **BA40**) Rua Sítio Escurinha s/n, BR-242, km. 90, 46880-000 Itaberaba. – **BA41**) Rua Castro Alves 207, 45570-000 Ipiaú. – **BA42**) Av. Contorno s/n, 46400-000 Caetité. – **BA43**) Rua Otavio Mangabeira 1026, Fazenda Piranha, 46430-000 Guanambi. – **BA44**) Av. Santa Maria 422, Sumaré, 45100-000 Vitória da Conquista. – **BA45**) Rua Ramiro Costa 41, 44340-000 Muritiba. – **BA46**) Av. Porto Seguro 718, 1° andar, 45820-000 Eunápolis. **Email:** jacaranda@euinanet.com.br ☎ +55 73 281 5883. 🖷 +55 73 281 7103. –**BA47**) Rua da Bandeira 27, 42800-000 Camaçari. – **BA48**) Travessa do Contorno 26, 45570-000 Ipiaú. – **BA49**) Pe. A. Guimarães 32, 44640-000 Riachão do Jacuípe. – **BA50**) Av. Getúlio Vargas s/n, 48600-000 Paulo Afonso. – **BA51**) Rua Rio Corrente s/n, 47640-000 Santa Maria da Vitória. – **BA52**) Travessa Luis Viana Filho s/n 45820-000 Porto Seguro. – **BA53**) Rua Alvaro Campos 83, 44990-000 Barra do Mendes. – **BA54**) Av. Dom Avelar Brandão Vilella s/n, Sítio São Félix, 46470-970 Riacho de Santana. **Web:** www.micks.com. br/guadalupe **Email:** guadalupe@micks.com.br ☎🖷 +55 74 457 2104. – **BA55**) Rua Coronel Vicente s/n, 45470-000 Jiquiriça. – **BA56**) Praça Guilherme Silva 85, 1° andar, 45345-000 Jaguaquara. ☎ +55 73 534 1422. 🖷 +55 73 534 2220. – **BA57**) Rua Professor Severo Pessoa 170, Federação, 40210-170 Salvador. – **BA58**) Av. Regis Pacheco 534, Centro, 45100-000 Vitória da Conquista. – **BA59**) Rua Gonçalo Martins 19, 45550-000 Ubatã. – **BA60**) Rua Reggio Emilia 32, 44900-000 Irecê. – **BA61**) C.P. 45, 46430-000 Guanambi. – **BA62**) Rua General Pedemeiras 62, 45860-000 Canavieiras. – **BA63**) Rua Margem do Rio do Ouro 115, 44700-000 Jacobina. – **BA64**) Rua Farias Goes 164, 48330-000 Rio Real. – **BA65**) Rua Otavio Mangabeira 13, 48500-000 Euclides da Cunha. – **BA66**) Rua Rui Barbosa 119, 47400-000 Xique-Xique. – **BA67**) Praça Castelo Branco 294 – Centro, 45830-000 Itamaraju. ☎ +55 73 294 1106. – **BA68**) Av. José Candido dos Santos 20, 48475-000 Itapicuru. – **BA69**) Rua Frei Apolônio de Todi 10, 48410-000 Cícero Dantas. **Email:** regional@fallnet.com.br ☎ +55 75 278 2298. 🖷 +55 75 278 2252. – **BA70**) Terreiro de Jesus 13, Centro Histórico, 40025-010 Salvador. – **BA71**) Rua Vicente Paula Costa 16, 48540-000 Jeremoabo. – **BA72**) Rua 2 de Julho s/n, 45160-000 Belo Campo. ☎🖷 +55 77 4372233. – **BA73**) Praça São José 279 44600-000 Ipirá. ☎ +55 75 2541450. – **BA74**) Rua Anisio Teixeira 157, 44380-000 Cruz das Almas. ☎🖷 +55 75 721 2716. – **BA75**) Rua Teixeira de Freitas s/n, 47700-000 Santana. – **BA76**) 47400-000 Xique-Xique. – **BA77**) Rua Barão do Rio Branco s/n, 47600-000 Bom Jesus da Lapa. – **BA78**) Rua Dulce Pazzi 6, Alto da Bela Vista, 45260-000 Poções. ☎ +55 73 4311135. – **BA79**) Rua Idalina Pinto s/n, 46990-000 Souto Soares. – **BA80**) Rua José Inácio 31, 48700-000 Juazeiro. – **BA81**) Rua Machado de Assis 16, Brotas, 40285-280 Salvador. 🖷 +55 71 2550195. – **BA82**) Rua Desembargador Salvio Martins 321, 48800-000 Monte Santo. – **BA83**) Parque Emilia Costa s/n, 45450-000 Gandu. – **BA84**) Praça da Bandeira 47, 3° andar, Centro, 48900-000 Juazeiro. – **BA85**) Rua Coronel Dias Coelho 249, 44850-000 Morro do Chapéu. – **BA86**) Travessa Juracy Magalhaes 4, 2° andar, 44630-000 Mairi. **Email:** jjowe@uol.com.br. ☎🖷 +55 74 632 2086. – **BA87**) Rua Dr. Guerra 91, 47650-000 Correntina. – **BA88**) Rua Espírito Santo s/n, 48400-000 Ribeira do Pombal. – **BA89**) Rua João Brandão 233, Centro, 45350-000 Itiruçu. – **BA90**) Praça Getúlio Vargas 211, 48400-000 Ribeira do Pombal. ☎ +55 75 276 1164. – **BA91**) Rua do Comércio 31, 44940-000 Central. – **BA92**) 45465-000 Teolândia. – **BA93**) 48890-000 Valente. – **BA94**) 45600-000 Itabuna. – **BA95**)47800-000 Barreiras. – **BA96**) 44695-000 Capim Grosso. – **BA97)** 46100-000 Brumado.

CE00) CEARÁ
CE01) Rua Romeu Martins, Ed. 29 de Julho, 62700-000 Canindé. – **CE02**) Rua São Pedro 918, 63010-010 Juazeiro do Norte. – **CE03**) Av. Monsenhor Tabosa 2514, 62500-000 Itapipoca. ☎ +55 88 6312173. 🖷 +55 88 6310469. – **CE04**) Rua Carlos Rolim/Praça da Matriz, 63700-000 Crateús. – **CE05**) Rua Marcondes Pereira 684, 60130-060 Fortaleza. – **CE06**) Praça da Matriz s/n, 62590-000 Itarema. – **CE07**) Rua Major Joaquim Alves 221, 63540-000 Várzea Alegre. – **CE08**) C.P. 2651, 60121-970 Fortaleza. – **CE09**) Rua Agronomando Rangel 475, 63870-000 Boa Viagem. **Email:** asabranca@daterranet.com.br ☎ +55 88 427 1104. 🖷 +55 88 427 1456. – **CE10**) Rua Marcondes Pereira 426, 60130-060 Fortaleza. ☎ +55 88 272 3733. 🖷 +55 88 272 3749.- **CE11**) Rua Hilda Augusto 201, 63300-000 Lavras da Mangabeira. – **CE12**) Av. Agenor Araujo 1194, 63500-000 Iguatu. – **CE13**) C.P. 851, 60001-970 Fortaleza. – **CE14**) Praça Vicente Aguilar 16, 62400-000 Camocim. – **CE15**) Rua São Luís 68, 62040-450 Juazeiro do Norte. – **CE16**) Av. Senador Virgilio Tavoar 2279, 60170-251 Fortaleza.- **CE17**) Rua Floriano Peixoto 358, 63500-000 Iguatu. – **CE18**) Rua Totonho Figueiras 244, 63180-000 Barbalha. – **CE19**) Av. Dom José 947, 62030-630 Sobral.- **CE20**) C.P. 87, 63901-970 Quixadá. – **CE21**) Av. Aguanambi 282, 60055-402 Fortaleza. ☎ +55 88 2314233. – **CE22**) Rua Coronel Antônio Luiz 1068, Bairro do Pimenta, 63100-000 Crato. – **CE23**) Rua Conselheiro José Júlio 126, 62010-820 Sobral. – **CE24**) Rua Raul Vieira 562, 62900-000 Russas. – **CE25**) Rua Conego Eduardo Araripe 1692, 62870-000 Pacajus. ☎ +55 88 3480005. – **CE26**) Av. Senador Virgilio Távora 2279, 60170-251 Fortaleza. **Web:** www.radioclubeam.com.br – **CE27**) Rua Coronel Zezé 1158, 63700-000 Crateús. ☎ +55 88 691 2180. 🖷 +55 88 691 1693. – **CE28**) Rua Coronel Malveira 1122, 62930-000 Limoeiro do Norte. – **CE29**) Av. Santos Dumont 1687, Aldeota, 60150-160 Fortaleza. – **CE30**) Rua São Francisco 374, 63010-210 Juazeiro do Norte. – **CE31**) Praça Duque de Caxias 552, 62011-300 Sobral. – **CE32**) Av. Dr. Pedro de Queiroz Ferreira 2129, 62850-000 Cascavel. – **CE33**) Rua São Francisco 139, 63100-000 Crato. – **CE34**) Rua Monsenhor Salviano Pinto 71, 63800-000 Quixeramobim. – **CE35**) Praça Pinto Martins 260, 62400-000 Camocim. – **CE36**) Av. Manoel Castro 815, 62940-000 Morada Nova. – **CE37**) Rua Moacir Pereira Gondim 333, 63650-000 Tauá. – **CE38**) Rua Coronel Alexanzito 835, 62800-000 Aracati. – **CE39**) Rua Hildo Furtado s/n, 62760-000 Baturité. – **CE40**) Rua Italiano Júlio Filizola 512, 62370-000 São Benedito. – **CE41**) Rua Coronel Antônio Joaquim 2148, 62930-000 Limoeiro do Norte. – **CE42**) Rua Maestro Quincas Bezerril s/n, 62320-000 Tianguá. – **CE43**) Rua Poeta A. Martins, 62640-000 Pentecoste. – **CE44**) Av. Santos Dumont 414, 63600-000 Senador Pompeu. ☎ +55 88 829 0206. – **CE45**) Praça Adolfo Caminha 247, 62800-000 Aracati. – **CE46**) Maria de Lourdes 545, 62280-000 Santa Quitéria. – **CE47**) Rua Coronel Meireles 35, 62680-000 Paracuru. – **CE48**) Rua Firmino Tavares 246, 63380-000 Barro. – **CE49**) Travessa Mercedes Santos 762, 62700-000 Canindé. – **CE50**) Rua Coronel Lucio 489, 63700-000 Crateús. ☎ +55 88 811 0060. – **CE51**) Rua Monsenhor Salviano Pinto 507, 63800-000 Quixeramobim. **Email:** campo@disovermet.com.br ☎ +55 88 441 0263. 🖷 +55 88 441 1209. – **CE52**) Av. Barão de Studart 2820, Aldeota, 60120-002 Fortaleza. ☎ +55 88 2722922, 2727635. – **CE53**) Rodovia Massapê/Sobral (Mumbaba), 62140-000 Massapê. – **CE54**) Rua Tibúrcio Targino 155, 61700-000 Aquiraz. – **CE55**) Rua Dr. Almir Farias 446, 62200-000 Nova Russas. **Web:** www.rd780.com.br ☎ +55 88 672 1221. 🖷 +55 88 672 1050. – **CE56**) Rua Raimundo Nonato 81 – Centro, 62940-000 Morada Nova. – **CE57**) Rua Coronel Felix 1237 altos, 62250-000 Ipu. – **CE58**) Travessa 10 de Novembro 198, 63150-000 Campos Sales. – **CE59**) Rua Cazuzinha Marques 87, 63560-000 Acopiara. – **CE60**) Rua Manoel Inacio de Lucena 249, 63260-000 Brejo Santo. – **CE61**) BR-222 Km 220, 62100-000 Sobral. – **CE62**) Rua Conrado Pinto 180, 62430-000 Granja. – **CE63**) Rua Antônio Queiroz 343, 63870-000 Boa Viagem. – **CE64**) Rua Major Barreto 3000, 62600-000 Itapajé. – **CE65**) Loteamento Pioneiro, Estrada Sobral Santa Quitéria km. 03, 62115-000 Forquilha. – **CE66**) Rua Capitão Carapeba 67, Centro, 62370-000 São Benedito. **Email:** tabajara@bol.com.br ☎ +55 88 626 2266/2268. 🖷 +55 88 626 2166. – **English**: 2200 – 2400. – **CE67**) Rua Monsenhor Joviniano Barreto 22, 2° andar, 63660-000 Tauá. – **CE68**) Rua Monsenhor Eurico 300, 62380-000 Guaraciaba do Norte. – **CE69**) Av. Rios 92, 62590-000 Itarema. – **CE70**) Av. Coronel Alexanzito 369, 62800-000 Aracati. – **CE71**) Av. José de Borba Vasconcelos 3589, 61900-000 Maracanaú. – **CE72**) Rodovia BR-226 km. 20, Distrito de Bonfim, 63600-000 Senador Pompeu. – **CE73**) Rua Dom Pedro II 141, 62580-000 Acaraú. – **CE74**) Rua Padre Antônio Tomaz s/n, 62550-000 Morrinhos. – **CE75**) Rua Major Liberalino s/n, 62250-000 Ipu. – **CE76**) Rua Joaquim Távora 333, 63150-000 Campos Sales. ☎ +55 88 533 1530. – **CE77**) Rua Manoel Alencar 35, 63610-000 Mombaça. – **CE78**) Rua Caio Prado 406 – Centro, 61800-000 Pacatuba. – **CE79**) Rua Raul Catunda Fontenele 61, 62230 000 Ipueiras. – **CE80**) Margem Direita da Ferrovia Cedro – Fortaleza, 63400-000 Cedro. – **CE81**) Rua Placido Pinho 294, 62730-000 Caridade. – **CE82**) Rua Ovidio Maia 213, Centro, 63900-000 Quixadá. – **CE83**) Av. Cachoeira do Riacho do Sangue s/n, 63620- 000 Solonópole. – **CE84**) 63630-000 Pedra Branca. – **CE85**) 62690-000 Trairi. – **CE86**) 63140-000 Assaré. – **CE87**) 62570-000 Bela Cruz. – **CE88**) 63170-000 Araripe. – **CE89**) 62400-000 Camocim.- **CE90**) 62823-000 Jaguaruana. – **CE91**) 63635-000 Milhã. – **CE92**) 63250-000 Milagres. – **CE93**) 62160-000 Coreaú. – **CE94**) 62180-000 Pacujá. – **CE95**) 63560-000 Acopiara. – **CE96**) 62430-000 Granja. – **CE97**) 62350-000 Ubajara. – **CE98**) 61760-000 Eusebio.

DF00) DISTRITO FEDERAL
DF01) SRTS, Qd. 701, Ed. Assis Chateaubriand, Bl. 2, salas 701 a 716, 70340-906 Brasília. ☎ +55 61 316 9530. 🖷 +55 61 9223 0532. – **DF02**) Setor de Rádio e TV Sul, Palácio do Rádio, Bloco 1 6° andar, 70340-901 Brasília. – **DF03**) Av. W-3, Q-16, lotes 26/28-Gr. 314, 70340-000 Brasília. – **DF04**) SCRN 702/03, B1 "B", Edificio Radiobrás, 70710-750 Brasília. – **DF05**) SRTV/Sul, Q-701, bloco E, Térreo, 70340-000 Brasília. – **DF06**) **Radiobras.** C.P. 070.747, 70359-970 Brasília. ☎ +55 61 321 3949. ✆ 061-1682. **Web:** www.radiobras.gov.br/ – Pres: Marcelo Netto. Dir. Radio: Iolando Lourenço. Dir. News: Miriam Moura. Dir. Adm: Januário Procópio. Dir. Tec: Toshihiro Kanagae. Dir. SW: Renato Geraldo de Lima. – **DF07**) SRTV-Sul, Q. 701, Conj. "E", Bloco 2 e 4, sala 316, 70340-902 Brasília. ☎ +55 61 226 0265/322 2963. – **DF08**) SCS-Quadra 05, Bl. B, Lotes 47 a 57, Ns. 39/40, 70340-000 Brasília. – **DF09**) 72401-970 Gama. – **DF10**) Senado Federal, Praça dos Tres Poderes, Anexo II, Bloco B -Térreo, 70165-900 Brasília. **Web:** www.senado.gov.br/radio

ES00) ESPÍRITO SANTO
ES01) Av. Alberto Torres 345, 29040-700 Vitória. – **ES02**) C.P. 700, 29001-970 Vitória. – **ES03**) Rua Dr. Deolindo 65, Baiminas, 29305-440 Cacheiro de Itapemirim. – **ES04**) Rua Chafic Murad 902, Ilha de Monte Belo, 29050-901 Vitória. ☎ +55 27 3218333. 🖷 +55 27 2231525. - **FM:** 92.5 "Antena Um", 102.3 "Litoral FM". – **ES05**) C.P. 125, 29900-971 Linhares. ☎ +55 27 373 2000. 🖷 +55 27 373 1598. - **FM**: 98.7. – **ES06**) C.P. 178, 29700-971 Colatina. – **ES07**) Av. Santo Antônio 366, 29025-000 Vitória. **Email:** radiocap@terra.com.br – **ES08**) C.P. 809, 29001-970 Vitória. **Email:** radioespirito@gol.com.br – **ES09**) Rua 7 de Setembro 2/4, Centro, 29300-901 Cachoeiro de Itapemirim. – **ES10**) Rua Alberto de Oliveira Santos 42, 19° andar, salas 1916-1920, Centro, 29010-901 Vitória. **Email:** america@ebr.com.br ☎ +55 27 322 0082. - **FM:** 101.5 "Cidade". – **ES11**) Rua José Cupertino 120, 29600-000 Afonso Cláudio. – **ES12**) Rua da Matriz 85, 29200-000 Guarapari. – **ES13**) Av. Presidente Vargas 449, 29600-000 Afonso Cláudio. – **ES14**) C.P. 132, 29930-000 São Mateus. – **ES15**) Rua Costa Pereira 39, Centro, 29300-090 Cachoeiro de Itapemirim. **Web:** www.radiodiocesana. com.br ☎ +55 27 5227056. – **Italian:** Sun 1300-1600. – **ES16**) Rua Graciano Neves 250, 29156-050 Cariacica. – **ES17**)Av. Perfeito Manoel Vila 660, 29800-000 Barra de São Francisco. – **ES18**) Rua Chafic Murad 902, Ilha de Monte Belo, 29050-902 Vitória. **Email:** ana.nogureira@ redegazeta.com.br – **ES19**) 29650-000 Santa Teresa. – **ES20**) 29900-000 Linhares. – **ES21**) 29390-000 Iúna. – **ES22**) 29300-000 Cachoeiro de Itapemirim.

GO00) GOIÁS
GO01) Av. Goiás 636, 74010-010 Goiânia. **Web:** www.radio-riviera.com.br – **GO02**) Av. João XXIII 381, Centro, 75702-130 Catalão. ☎ +55 62 411 7500, 441 2700. 🖷 +55 62 441 3435. **Email:** radiiocultura@com.br – **GO03**) Rua Coronel Barbosa 420, 75025-060 Anápolis. – **GO04**) Av. Egídio Francisco Rodrigues 54, Centro, 75200-000 Pires do Rio. – **FM:** 102.3 "Rio FM". – **GO05**) Av. 24 de Outobro 1854, Campinas, 74505-011 Goiânia. ☎ +55 62 8334000. 🖷 +55 62 8334019. – **GO06**) Av. Marechal Rondón, Q. 18 Lote 9, 76270-000 Jussara. – **GO07**) Rua 48 esq. 47A no. 498, Praça Castelo Branco, 76680-000 Itapuranga. – **GO08**) C.P. 670, 75001-970 Anápolis. - **FM:** 96.3. – **GO09**) C.P. 33, 75800-000 Jataí. **Web:** www.difusora.am.br/ – **GO10**) Rua Evangelino Meireles 26, 72800-000 Luziânia. – **GO11**) Rua Coronel Gonzaga 400, 56900-000 Caldas Novas. – **GO12**) C.P. 354, 75001-970 Anápolis. – **GO13**) Av. Brasil 272, 76380-000 Goianésia. – **GO14**) Rua 03 No. 30, Praça Coronel Carrijo, Centro, 75830-000 Mineiros. ☎ +55 (62) 661 1353. ☎🖷 +55 62 661 1044. – **GO15**) Av. Bernardo Sayao 371, 76310-000 Rialma. – **GO16**) Av. Anhanguera 3511, 74610-010 Goiânia. – **GO17**) Av. Floriano Peixoto 17, 76550-000 Porangatu. – **GO18**) Av. Tocantins 2011, 76400-000 Uruaçu. – **GO19**) C.P. 17, 72900-000 Santo Antônio do Descoberto (or Av.São João Batista 23, 77223-000 Cidade Eclética). ☎ +55 61 626 1391. 🖷 +55 61 502 8777. – **GO20**) C.P. 149, 75503-970 Itumbiara. – **GO21**) Praça da Bandeira 94, 75500-000 Itumbiara. – **GO22**) C.P. 501, 75001-970 Anápolis. – **GO23**) Rua do Contorno 702, 76330-000 Jaraguá. – **GO24**) Rua 148 No. 326, 74170-110 Goiânia. – **GO25**) Av. Lazaro Xavier 18, 75860-000 Quirinópolis. 🖷 +55 62 6511538. – **GO26**) Rua Herculano Lobo 80, 73800-000 Formosa. – **GO27**) Rua Thomaz Edson Qd 07, Setor Serrinha, 74835-130 Goiânia. **Email:** anhanguera@radioexecutiva.com.br ☎ +55 62 250 1110. 🖷 +55 62 250 1247. - **FM:** 92.7 "Executiva FM" and 97.1 "Araguaia". – **GO28**) C.P. 34, 75781-970 Ipameri. – **GO29**) Rua 15 No. 83, 76300-000 Ceres. – **GO30**) Rua Dona Adelaide 430, Jardim Bela Vista,74001-070 Goiânia. - **FM:** 90.1. – **GO31**) Av. Goiás 174, Quadra 4, Lote 24, 16° andar, 74010-970 Goiânia. – **GO32**) Alameda das Rosas 2200, Setor Oeste, 74126-010 Goiânia. – **GO33**) Av. Amazonas 367, 76100-000 São Luís de Montes Belos. – **GO34**) Rua Barão do Rio Branco 989, 75650-000 Morrinhos. - **FM:** 94.5 "Integração FM". – **GO35**) Praca Rui Barbosa 471, 75180-000 Silvânia. – **GO36**) Rua Kisleu Maciel 113, 73850-000 Cristalina. **Email:**

figueiredo.radio@zaz.com.br ☎ +55 62 612 1078, 612-2929. 🖷 +55 62 612 1461. – **GO37**) C.P. 60, 76601-970 Goiás. – **GO38**) C.P. 70, 75601-970 Goiatuba. – **GO39**) Praça Dr. Pedro Ludovico Teixeira 137, 75920-000 Santa Helena de Goiás. **Email:** rs1010@betangt.com.br ☎ +55 62 641 1555. – **GO40**) C.P. 117, 75401-970 Inhumas. – **GO41**) C.P. 131, 75901-970 Rio Verde. - **FM:** 95.3. – **GO42**) Praça Alves Castro s/n, 76630-000 Itaberaí. – **GO43**) Rua Catalão 182, 76200-000 Iporã. – **GO44**) Av. Lindolfo Alves Dias 571, Centro, 75850-000 Caiapônia. – **GO45**) Rua São Domingos 376, 75300-000 Aparecida de Goiânia. – **GO46**) Quadra 33, Lotes 23/24, 72900-000 Santo Antônio do Descoberto (C.P. 06-799, 71701-970 Brasília, DF). ☎ +55 61 626 1266. 🖷 +55 61 626 1052. – **GO47**) Rua José Alves Ferreira 250, 75640-000 Piracanjuba. – **GO48**) C.P. 185, 76301-970 Ceres. – **GO49**) Praça Silva Junior 184, 76420-000 Niquelândia. – **GO50**) Rua Xingu 625, 75600-000 Goiatuba. – **GO51**) Av. Brasil 100, 75860-000 Quirinópolis. – **GO52**) Av. Joaquim David Ferreira 1390, 76105-000 Firminópolis. – **GO53**) Av. Santana, Qd. 55, lote 01, Sector Vila Baiana, 78340-000 Campas Belos. – **GO54**) 78505-000 Caçu. – **GO55**) 73900-000 Posse. – **GO56**) 76170-000 Anicuns. – **GO57**) 75940-000 Edéia. – **GO58**) 75620-000 Pontalina. – **GO59**) 76450-000 Minaçu.

MA00) MARANHÃO

MA01) Av. Eliézer Moreira s/n, Incra, 65950-000 Barra do Corda. – **MA02**) Praça Dom Pedro II s/n, 65030-000 São Luís. **Web:** www.educadora.elo.com.br – **MA03**) Av. Camboa 120, Bairro Camboa, 65020-260 São Luís. **Web:** www.sistemadifusora.com.br –**FM:** 94.3. – **MA04**) Rua Henrique de Figueiredo 485, 65400-000 Codó. – **MA05**) Av. São Benedito 1075, Bairro São Benedito, 65400-000 Codó. – **MA06**) Rua Simplicio Moreira 1686, 1° andar, Centro, 65901-490 Imperatriz. **Email:** radioimp@aeronet.com.br **Web:** www.radioimperatriz.com.br ☎ +55 98 523 2633. 🖷 +55 98 525 1779. – **MA07**) Rua Manoel Alves de Abreu 373, 65700-000 Bacabal. – **MA08**) Av. Coronel Fonseca 200, 65800-000 Balsas. – **MA09**) Parque do Bom Menino s/n, 65025-180 São Luís. – **MA10**) Av. Jerônimo de Albuquerque 73, Cohafuma, 65071-750 São Luís. **Email:** radiotimbira.raimundofilho@bol.com.br – **MA11**) Av. Presidente Médici 77, 65031-410 São Luís. 🖷 +55 98 221 4141. – **FM:** 102.5. – **MA12**) Rua Albino Paiva 655, 65200-000 Pinheiro. – **MA13**) Rua Manoel Trindade 410, 65725-000 Pedreiras. – **MA14**) Av. Keened, 65690-000 Colinas. – **MA15**) BR-316 km 115, 65370-000 Pindaré Mirim. – **MA16**) Fazenda São João, BR-14 Km 37, 65215-000 Viana. – **MA17**) Rua Guarani 3, Parque das Laranjeiras, 65922-000 João Lisboa. – **MA18**) Rua A. Bandeira 831, 65320-000 Vitorino Freire. – **MA19**) 65922-000 João Lisboa. – **MA20**) Rua Piauí 895, 65930-000 Açailândia. – **MA21**) C. Carneiro 177, 65750-000 Esperantinópolis. – **MA22**) Travessa Tiradentes 338, Centro, 65415-000 Coroatá. – **MA23**) Rua Aarão Reis s/n, 65604-060 Caxias. – **MA24**) Av. Coronel Stanley Fortes Batista 454, 65365-000 Zê Doca. – **MA25**) 65278-000 Turiaçu. – **MA26**) Rua Alagoas 497, 65900-490 Imperatriz. – **MA27**) Av. Amaral Raposo s/n, 65940-000 Grajaú. – **MA28**) Rua Rui Barbosa s/n, 65620-000 Coelho Neto. – **MA29**) Rua Dr. Paulo Ramos 495, 65208-000 Santa Helena. – **MA30**) Rua Frederico Coelho esquina com Av. Frei Aniceto, 65763-000 Tuntum. – **MA31**) Rua do Puraqueu s/n, 65350-000 Vitória do Mearim. – **MA32**) Parque da Bandeira 222, Edificio Ariana, Centro, 65665-000 São João dos Patos. – **MA33**) Praça do Guarim s/n, 65390-000 Santa Luzia. – **MA34**) Rua Terra esquina com Rua Jupiter s/n, 65760-0000 Presidente Dutra. – **MA35**) Praça Coronel Luis Vieira 25, 65500-000 Chapadinha. ☎ +55 98 471 1337. 🖷 +55 98 471 2156. – **MA36**) Rua Cel. Pedro Bogéa 227 – Centro, 65715-000 Lago da Pedra. – **MA37**) Rua Hemeterio Leitão 103, 65430-00 Vargem Grande. – **MA38**) Av. Ana Jansen 200, 65000-000 São Luís. – **MA39**) 65530-000 Urbano Santos. – **MA40**) 65600-000 Caxias. – **MA41**) 65800-000 Balsas.

MG00) MINAS GERAIS

MG01) C.P. 123, 36771-970 Cataguases. - **FM:** 89.5. – **MG02**) Rua General Carneiro 10, Edificio Milinardo, s 200 à 305, 39400-095 Montes Claros. – **MG03**) Av. Sinfronio Brochado 805, 30640-000 Belo Horizonte. – **MG04**) Praça Nossa Senhora Aparecida 134, Bairro Aparecida, 38406-063 Uberlândia. **Email:** radioamerica@triang.com.br **Web:** www.radio.triang.net/menu.html ☎ +55 34 3214 4342, 3214 3222. 🖷 +55 34 3214 4503. - **FM:** 98.7. – **MG05**) Av. Padre Matias 1089, Bairro Marciano Brandão, 38740-000 Patrocínio. ☎ +55 34 3831 1546. 🖷 +55 34 3831 1896. - **FM:** 98.9. – **MG06**) Rua Itatiaia 117, Bairro Bonfim, 31210-170 Belo Horizonte. ☎ +55 31 3421 3588. 🖷 +55 31 3422 8588. **Email:** itatiaia@itatiaia.com.br **Web:** www. itatiaia.com.br – **MG07**) Rua Alvares Cabral 73, 38065-240 Uberaba. – **MG08**) Av. Presidente Vargas 372, Centro, 35661-000 Pará de Minas. – **MG09**) Rua Euripides Ribeiro 739, 38720-000 Lagoa Formosa. – **MG10**) Rua Padre Antônio Gabriel Carvalho 17, 35400-000 Ouro Preto. – **MG11**) C.P. 30, 35791-970 Curvelo. – **MG12**) Rua Prof. Monteiro Fonseca 119, 39400-149 Montes Claros. – **MG13**) Praça Coronel Hermógenes 292, 38770-000 João Pinheiro. – **MG14**) Rus Entre Rios 33, Bairro Carlos Prates, 30710-080 Belo Horizonte. – **MG15**) Praça 15 de Novembro 388, 36900-000 Manhuaçu. – **MG16**) C.P. 37, 37551-970 Pouso Alegre. – **MG17**) Rua Guilherme Ferreira 650, salas 81/82, 38022-200 Uberaba. **Email:** sociedade@ldc.com.br – **MG18**) Rua Dr. João Penido Filho 269, 36021-600 Juiz de Fora. – **MG19**) Av. Itaú 515, Bairro Dom Cabral, 30730-280 Belo Horizonte. **Web:** www.arqui-bh.org.br/radiotv **Email:** radioamerica-diretoria@ pucminas.br ☎ +55 31 3464 8355. 🖷 +55 31 3411 1243. – **MG20**) Praça Leonardo Venerando Pereira 200, 37200-000 Lavras. – **MG21**) C.P. 69, 38701-970 Patos de Minas. – **MG22**) C.P. 10, 35901-970 Itabira. - **FM:** 93.3. – **MG23**) Av. Prof. José Ignácio de Souza 2710, 38405-550 Uberlândia. ☎ +55 34 3212 0010. 🖷 +55 34 3232 2044. – **MG24**) Praça Getúlio Vargas 10, 35430-002 Ponte Nova. – **MG25**) C.P. 153, 35291-970 Mantena. – **MG26**) Rua Luz 235, Bairro Américo Silva, 35590-000 Lagoa da Prata. ☎ +55 37 261 1999. 🖷 +55 37 261 2544. – **MG27**) Praça Aloys Benz 34, 35200-000 Almorés. - **FM:** 90.3 – **MG28**) Rua Minas Gerais 655, 35500-007 Divinópolis. – **MG29**) Praça Dom Pedro Teixeira 49, 36200-000 Barbacena. **Email:** rbq@prower.com.br – **MG30**) Travessa Padre Benatti 1200, 37950-000 São Sebastião do Paraíso. ☎ +55 35 3531 5154. 🖷 +55 35 3531 1351. – **MG31**) Rua Itatiaia 117, Bairro Bonfim, 31210-170 Belo Horizonte. **Web:** www.culturabh.com.br/ – **MG32**) Rua Barão de Piunhi 31, 37290-000 Formiga. – **MG33**) Av. Brasil 2770, 35020-070 Governador Valadares. +55 33 3271 17322 **Email:** radiomundomelhor@wkve.com.br - **FM:** 97.7. – **MG34**) Rua Coronel Joaquim Mendes 19. Ed. Cine T. Helena, 38430-000 Tupaciguara. ☎ +55 34 281 2034, 281 2146. - **FM:** 91.9. – **MG35**) Av. Raja Gabáglia 1666, Bairro Luxemburgo, 30350-540 Belo Horizonte. **Email:** inconfidencia@plugway.com.br ☎+55 31 3297 7344. 🖷 +55 31 3297 7379. – **MG36**) Rua Dr. Olinto Martins 207, 39960-000 Jequitinhonha. ☎ +55 33 3741 1521. 🖷 +55 33 3741 1332. – **MG37**) Rua Benedito Valadares 139, 39800-000 Teófilo Otoni. – **MG38**) Praça Dom João 122, Centro, 39100-000 Diamantina. ☎ 🖷 +55 38 3531 1408. – **MG39**) Praça 28 de Setembro 95, 36520-000 Visconde do Rio Branco. – **MG40**) Rua Tenente Viotti 131, 37460-000 Passa Quatro. ☎ +55 35 371 1260/1129. – **MG41**) Av. Afonso Pena 795, 2° andar, 37270-000 Campo Belo. **Web:** www.radioculturacampobelo.hpg.ig.com.br/ ☎🖷 +55 35 3832 2700. – **MG42**) Av. Teodolino Pereira de Araújo 731, 38440-000 Araguari. – **MG43**) Av. Ferroviaria s/n, 30520-480 Belo Horizonte. ☎ +55 31 3361 0205. – **MG44**) Av. Bom Jesus 464, 37578-000 Bueno Brandão. ☎🖷 +55 35 4631160. – **MG45**) Rua dos Viajantes 81, 35300-000 Caratinga. – **MG46**) Av. Tirandentes 209, A 217, 36300-000 São João del Rei. – **MG47**) Rua Rio Barbosa 259, 38420-000 Monte Alegre de Minas. ☎🖷 +55 34 3281 2100. – **MG48**) Rua Espírito Santo 95, 36020-000 Juiz de Fora. ☎ +55 32 3215 1620. 🖷 +55 32 3215 4360. - **FM:** 88.9. – **MG49**) Rua Afonso Pena 340, 37590-000 Jacutinga. ☎ +55 35 3443 2121, 3443 2828. 🖷 +55 35 3443 1625. – **MG50**) Rua Dr. Querubino 303, 35170-001 Coronel Fabriciano. ☎ +55 31 842 1112, 842 1492. 🖷 +55 31 842 1400. – **MG51**) C.P. 557, 38409-970 Uberlândia. – **MG52**) Rua Bueno Brandão 26, 38430-000 Tupaciguara. – **MG53**) Rua Tamoios 200, 21° andar, 30120-050 Belo Horizonte. **Email:** radiomundomelhor@wkve.com.br – **MG54**) Rua Olegário Maciel 200, Bairro Vila Podis, 37500-000 Itajubá. **Web:** www.radioitajuba.com.br – **MG55**) Praça da Basílica 130, 36404-000 Congonhas. ☎+55 31 3731 9000/9001. 🖷 +55 31 3731 1342. – **MG56**) Av. Dr. Américo Luz 153, 37890-000 Muzambinho. – **MG57**) C.P. 262, 36001-970 Juiz de Fora. – **MG58**) C.P. 85, 38441-970 Araguari. – **MG59**) Rua Areião do Matadouro s/n, Parque da California, 34000-000 Nova Lima. – **MG60**) C.P. 253, 38001-970 Uberaba. 🖷 +55 34 313-3400. Email: sete@ldc.com.br **Web:** www.ldc.com.br/sete/ - **FM:** 98.1. – **MG61**) Av. Juscelino Kubstchek 740, 37170-000 Boa Esperança. ☎ +55 35 831 1000. 🖷 +55 35 851 1475. – **MG62**) Av. Antonio Olímpio de Morais 545, 35500-900 Divinópolis. **Email:** industriaaudio@divinet.com.br ☎ +55 37 222 0001. 🖷 +55 37 222 0005. - **FM:** 95.3. – **MG63**) Rua João Bressane 1, 37400-000 Campanha. ☎ +55 35 261 1985 **Email:** radiodio@uaisol.com.br. – **MG64**) Av. Constantino Pinto 90, 36880-000 Muriaé. **Email:** radio96@imicro.com.br ☎ +55 32 722 1951. - **FM:** 96.3 "R. 96". – **MG65**) Av. Raja Gabáglia 3502, 4° andar, Estoril, 30350-540 Belo Horizonte. ☎ +55 31 3298 9303. 🖷 +55 31 3298 9305. – **MG66**) Rua do Rádio 60, Bairro Pepétuo Socorro, 38190-000 Sacramento. **Email:** radiosac@sacranet.com.br ☎ +55 34 3351 1735. 🖷 +55 34 3351 1432. – **MG67**) Rua Cassiano Lemos 87, 38180-000 Araxá. – **MG68**) Av. Assis Chateaubriand 499, Floresta, 30150-101 Belo Horizonte. **Web:** www.guarani.com.br/ ☎ +55 31 3237 6000. 🖷 +55 31 3237 6699. – **MG69**) Praça Cleber de Holanda 111, Jardim Sion, 37048-370 Varginha. **Email:** sistemaclube@varginha.com.br - **FM**: 99.3. – **MG70**) Av. Brasil 4460, 38405-378 Uberlândia. – **MG71**) Av. Brasil 3049, 35020-070 Governador Valadares. – **MG72**) C.P. 110, 38301-970 Ituiutaba.Retransmits Sistema LBV Mundial: 2100-2200. – **MG73**) Rua Rio Grande do Sul 631. 1° andar, 37701-001 Poços de Caldas. **Web:** www.difusorapocos.com.br/ ☎ 🖷 +55 35 37222 1530. - **FM:**104.1. – **MG74**) Rua Capitão Henrique Albuquerque 55, 36400-000 Conselheiro Lafaiete. **Web**: www.radiocarijjos.com.br br 🖷 +55 31 3763 1752. - **FM:** 89.9. – **MG75**) Rua Itajubá 80, 35160-035 Ipatinga. – **MG76**) Rua Francisco Ribeiro 59, 37250-000 Nepomuceno. – **MG77**) Rua Duque de Caxias 450, 16° andar, Edificio Chams, 38400-066 Uberlândia. ☎ +55 34 236 6320. 🖷 +55 34 236 2079. – **MG78**) Rua Alexandre Silva 295, 38600-000 Paracatu. – **MG79**) Av. 13 No. 658, 6° andar, Edifício Ituiutaba, 38300-140 Ituiutaba. **Email:** radiocancella@mgt.com.br br ☎ +55 34 3268 1813, 3261 2851. 🖷 +55 34 3251 7071. - **FM:** 93.7. – **MG80**) Av. Costa Junior 467, 38840-000 Carmo do Paranaíba. – **MG81**) Rua José Benedito 441, Santa Efigenia, 35450-000 Itabirito. – **MG82**) Av. João Pinheiro 596, 1° andar,

37701-386 Poços de Caldas. **Web:** www.radioculturapocos.com.br ☎ +55 35 722 1687. 🖷 +55 35 722 2687. – **MG83**) Rua Prof. Maria Justiana 26, 37750-000 Machado. – **MG84**) Praça Guido Marliere 30, 36500-000 Ubá. – **MG85**) Rua Calixto Martins de Melo 391, 38610-000 Unaí. – **MG86**) Rua Calimeiro Guimarães 308, 38180-000 Araxá. – **MG87**) Rua Antônio Dias Adorno 1290, 35045-040 Governador Valadares. - **FM:** 100.1 "Imparsom". – **MG88**) Rua Dr. Péricles de Mendonça 91, 36680-000 São João Nepomuceno. ☎ +55 32 261 1344, 261 2596. – **MG89**) Rua Niquel 457, 35701-107 Sete Lagoas. **Email:** musirama@mrnet.com.br - **FM:** 92.1 "Musirama". – **MG90**) Av. Major Antônio Alberto Fernandes 445, 37720-000 Botelhos. – **MG91**) Av. Conde Ribeirão do Vale 661, 37800-000 Guaxupé. – **MG92**) Rua XV de Novembro 62, 36500-000 Ubá. ☎ +55 32 532 2433. 🖷 +55 32 532 2521. - **FM:** 94.5. – **MG93**) Praça Minas Gerais 50, 35930-259 João Monlevade. **Email:** rcultura@robynet.com.br – **MG94**) Rua Gerson Coutinho da Silva 1001, 38550-000 Coromandel. – **MG95**) Rua Juliano Marques Duarte 110, 36660-000 Além Paraíba. ☎ +55 32 3462 7400. - **FM:** 95.5 "Juventude". – **MG96**) Av. 17 No. 1045, 38300-000 Ituiutaba. ☎ +55 34 261 1417, 261 7118. 🖷 +55 34 261 1829. – **MG97**) Rua Cônego Victor 73, 37190-000 Três Pontas. – **MG98**) Rua Coronel Domiciano Ferreira 314, 38200-000 Frutal. – **MG99**) Av. Belo Horizonte 108, 39860-000 Nanuque. – **MG100**) Av.Presidente Tancredo Neves 425-fundos, 36300-000 São João del Rei. – **MG101**) Rua Floriano Peixoto 31, 36570-000 Viçosa. ☎ +55 31 891 1242. 🖷 +55 31 891 3421. - **FM:** 97.9. – **MG102**) C.P. 28, 37901-970 Passos. **Web:** www.passos. com.br/radiopassos – **MG103**) C.P. 61, 36971-970 Manhumirim. – **MG104**) Rua Dr. Coelho de Moura 158, Centro, 35540-000 Oliveira. **Web:** www.radiosociedade.com.br ☎ +55 37 3331 1170. 🖷 +55 37 3331 1510. – **MG105**) Rua 13 de Maio 425, 36200-000 Barbacena. – **MG106**) Praça Dr. Augusto Gonçalves 146, salas 411/412, Centro, 35680-054 Itaúna. ☎ +55 37 3742 1910. 🖷 +55 37 3241 2890. – **MG107**) C.P. 189, 37471-970 São Lourenço. **Web:** www.radioestancia.com.br **Email:** estancia@radioestancia.com.br - **FM:** 94.3. – **MG108**) Rua Ribeirao São Domingos 689, 38280-000 Iturama. – **MG109**) Av. Magalhães Pinto 829, 35610-000 Dores do Indaiá. ☎ +55 (37) 551 1622. – **MG110**) Rua Adalberto Ferraz 50, 2° andar, 37550-000 Pouso Alegre. – **MG111**) Rua Dr. José Gonçalves 17, 35600-000 Bom Despacho. – **MG112**) Praça Getúlio Vargas 81,(C.P. 123) 36400-000 Conselheiro Lafaiete. – **MG113**) Rua Casemiro Avelar Filho 143, Centro, 37410-000 Três Corações. ☎ +55 35 231 1000/1540/1941. – **FM:** 95.5. – **MG114**) Praça Nossa Senhora do Carmo 224, 38500-000 Monte Carmelo. – **MG115**) Rua Sancho Viderla 19, Centro, 37540-000 Santa Rita do Sapucaí. –**FM:** 95.3. – **MG116**) Av. Brasil 508, Bairro Santo Antônio, 39270-000 Pirapora. **Web:** www.itatiaia.com.br/pirapora – **MG117**) Praça João XXIII 15, salas 303/307/308, 36700-000 Leopoldina. **Web:** www.leopoldina.com.br/ radiojornal/ – **MG118**) Rua Bias Fortes 366 A, 37130-000 Alfenas. **Web:** www.radioculturaalfenas.com.br/ – **MG119**) Rua JK 108, 35500-000 Itapecerica. – **MG120**) Rua Anastácio José Gonçalves 139, 38810-000 Rio Paranaíba. ☎ +55 34 3855 1240. 🖷 +55 34 3855 1433. – **MG121**) Rua Antonio Ladeira 175, Centro, 36240-000 Santos Dumont. – **MG122**) Av. Minas Gerais 584, 39510-000 Espinosa. ☎ +55 38 812 1299. 🖷 +55 38 812 1444. – **MG123**) Praça Nossa Senhora da Abadia 490, Abadia, 38025-430 Uberaba. ☎ +55 34 3322 6200. 🖷 +55 34 3322 6430. – **MG124**) Av. Hermenegildo Donatti 199, 37795-000 Andradas. **Email:** vinicola@andradas-net.com.br ☎ +55 35 731 2291. 🖷 +55 35 731 1303. - **FM:** 94.9. – **MG125**) Praça Coronel Odilon Coelho s/n, 39520-000 Porteirinha. – **MG126**) Rua Ordalino Rodrigues 351, 35430-148 Ponte Nova. – **MG127**) Travessa Dona Santinha 20, 39480-000 Januária. – **MG128**) Rua Benedito Valadares 423, 36880-000 Muriaé. – **MG129**) Rua Padre Pedro 53, 39391-000 Bocaiúva. – **MG130**) Rua Rui Barbosa 74, 39440-000 Janaúba. – **MG131**) Av. Getúlio Vargas 205, Centro Shopping Luziana, 35350-000 Raul Soares. – **MG132**) Praça José Batista de Frieitas 78, 3° andar, 35519-000 Nova Serrana. – **MG133**) Rua Quimino Bocaiuva 735, 37810-000 Guaranésia. – **MG134**) BR-496 Km 33, 39260-000 Várzea da Palma. – **MG135**) Rua dos Quarteis s/n, 38900-000 Bambuí. – **MG136**) Rua Alto da Catedral s/n, 39800-000 Teófilo Otoni. ☎ +55 33 521 2938. **Web:** www2/triang.com.br – **MG137**) Rua Major Honor Sarmento 393, Alto São João, 39400-103 Montes Claros. ☎ +55 38 3223 5666. 🖷 +55 (38) 3221 5590. – **MG138**) Rua 102 No. 498, 38360-000 Capinópolis. – **MG139**) Praça Monsenhor Messias Bragança 80, sala 203, 37900-000 Passos. ☎ +55 35 521 6767, 521 6196. – **MG140**) Rua Padre João Lourenço Leite 100, 37175-000 Ilicínea. – **MG141**) Rua Astor Goulart de Moura 51, 39200-000 Corinto. – **MG142**) BR-381 Km. 195, Bairro Cachoeira do Vale, 35180-000 Timóteo. **Email:** am650@gold.com.br. – **MG143**) Rua Coronel Américo Teixeira Guimarães, 35700-181 Sete Lagoas. – **MG144**) Rua Alves Rosa 255, 38780-000 Vazante. – **MG145**) Rua Leandro Gonçalves 88, 3° andar, 36900-000 Manhuaçu. – **MG146**) Rua Coronel Rennó 7, 37500-000 Itajubá. – **MG147**) Praça São Pedro 49, 38950-000 Ibiá. – **MG148**) Praça Getúlio Vargas 108, 36800-000 Carangola. - **FM:** 102.7 "Caparaó". – **MG149**) Rua Oscar Vidal 416, 36016-290 Juiz de Fora. – **MG150**) Rua Ceará esquina com Rua Alagoas, 38700-000 Patos de Minas. – **MG151**) Av. 7 de Setembro 55-A, 36950-000 Ipanema. – **MG152**) Rua Julio Cosi 5, 38230-000 Fronteira. – **MG153**) Av. José Maria de Alckmim 1700, Bairro Serra Verde, 30320-210 Belo Horizonte. ☎ +55 31 455 2066/1133. 🖷 +55 31 455 2070. – **MG154**) Praça Lindolfo Barbosa Vieira 40, 35330-000 Inhapim. – **MG155**) Rua João Valentim Pascoal 669, 5° andar, 35160-000 Ipatinga. – **MG156**) Av. Rui Barbosa 621, 5° andar, Conj. 501, 38740-000 Patrocínio. **Web:** www.radiorainhadapaz.com.br – **MG157**) Praça Comendador José Honorio 100, 37950-000 São Sebastião do Paraiso. – **MG158**) Rua Pref. Terêncio Pereira Vale 10, 38170-000 Perdizes. - **FM:** 96.1. – **MG159**) Av. Joaquim Ribeiro de Gouveia 1651, 38320-000 Santa Vitória. – **MG160**) Rua Belo Horizonte 461, 39625-000 Itaobim. – **MG161**) Rua das Acacias 672, 38660-000 Buritis. – **MG162**) Rua João Peixoto 100, 38440-000 Araguari. – **MG163**) Travessa Cônego Benedito Profício 95, 37660-000 Paraisópolis. – **MG164**) Av. Progresso 177, Olaria, 35588-000 Arcos. ☎ +55 37 351 2100. – **MG165**) Rua Antônio Ribeiro da Costa Junior 16, 36730-000 Pirapetinga. – **MG166**) 37120-000 Paraguaçu. – **MG167**) Praça Dr. Badaró 112, 39650-000 Minas Novas. ☎ +55 33 3764 1181, 🖷 +55 33 3764 1185. – **MG168**) Rua Marcos Vinícius Ferreira 226, São Miguel, 39560-000 Salinas. – **MG169**) Av. Rondón Pacheco 450, 37150-000 Carmo do Rio Claro. – **MG170**) Rua Vereador Maria Anselmo 33, 36480-000 Piranga. – **MG171**) Rua Coronel Carlos Brandão 98, sala 07/08, 36500-000 Ubá. – **MG172**) Av. Dr. Pedro Rosa s/n, 37530-000 Brasópolis. ☎ +55 35 3641 1317. – **MG173**) Rua Silviano Brandão 795, 37570-000 Ouro Fino. ☎ +55 35 441 1433. 🖷 +55 35 441 1800. – **MG174**) Praça Vital Brasil 56, 37980-000 Cássia. – **MG175**) Praça Coronel Silverio de Melo 172, 37958-000 Monte Santo de Minas. – **MG176**) 38270-000 Campina Verde. – **MG177**) 38750-000 Presidente Olegário. – **MG178**) 38400-000 Uberlândia. – **MG179**) 33100-000 Santa Luzia. – **MG180**) 39600-000 Araçuaí. – **MG181**) 39270-000 Pirapora. – **MG182**) 39900-000 Almenara. – **MG183**) 39740-000 Guanhães. – **MG184**) 35670-000 Mateus Leme. – **MG185**) 39970-000 Pedra Azul. – **MG186**) 38240-000 Itapagipe. – **MG187**) 37480-000 Lambari. – **MG188**) 38100-000 Uberaba. – **MG189**) 38400-000 Uberlandia.

MS00) MATO GROSSO DO SUL

MS01) Av. Mato Grosso 530, Centro, 79002-233 Campo Grande. **Web:** www.radioeducacaorural.com.br **Email:** radioeducacao@radioeducacaorural.com.br – **MS02**) Av. Senador Felinto Müller 59, 79080-190 Campo Grande. – **MS03**) C.P. 104, 79951-970 Naviraí. – **MS04**) Rua Ciro Melo 2045, 79805-000 Dourados. **Web:** www.radioclubeam720.com.br – **MS05**) Rua Anchieta 871, 79081-180 Campo Grande. – **MS06**) Rua 15 de Agosto 98, 79200-000 Aquidauana. – **MS07**) Rua Melanio Garcia Barbosa 749, 79150-000 Maracaju. – **MS08**) Rua Joaquim Pereira Teixeira 135, 79900-000 Ponta Porã. – **MS09**) Rua 15 de Novembro 2649, Jardim dos Estados, 79020-300 Campo Grande. **Email:** cbnms@terra.com.br. ☎ +55 67 384 1240. – **MS10**) C.P. 37, 79601-970 Três Lagoas. – **MS11**) Av. Marcelino Pires 1404, 79801-002 Dourados. – **MS12**) C.P. 18, 79201-970 Aquidauana. ☎ +55 (67) 241 3956. – **MS13**) Rua Antônio Lino Barbosa 1130, 79130-000 Rio Brilhante. – **MS14**) C.P. 138, 79301-970 Corumbá. – **MS15**) C.P. 217, 79301-970 Corumbá. – **MS16**) Rua Walther Hubachi 643, 79750-000 Nova Andradina. – **MS17**) Av. Aldair Rosa de Oliveira 1045, 79640-100 Três Lagoas. ☎ +55 67 521 2305. – **MS18**) Rua Ferreira 69 B, Piracema, 79400-000 Coxim. – **MS19**) Rua Angélica 455, 79730-000 Glória de Dourados. ☎🖷 +55 67 466 2040. – **MS20**) Rua Visconde de Taunay 895, 79500-000 Paranaíba. – **MS21**) C.P. 126, 79991-970 Amambaí. – **MS22**) Av. 9 de Julho 1557, 79700-000 Fátima do Sul. ☎ +55 67 467 2045. 🖷 +55 67 467 1222. – **MS23**) C.P. 200, 79541-970 Cassilândia. – **MS24**) Av. Presidente Vargas 669, 79940-000 Caarapó. ☎🖷 +55 67 453 1248. – **MS25**) Rua Dr. A. Coelho de Oliveira 549, 79240-000 Jardim. – **MS26**) Rua Rui Barbosa 753, 79970-000 Eldorado. – **MS27**) C.P. 129, 79301-970 Corumbá. – **MS28**) C.P. 199, 79901-970 Ponta Porã. – **MS29**) C.P. 68, 79804-970 Dourados. – **MS30**) Rua São Paulo 1359, 79490-000 São Gabriel d'Oeste. – **MS31**) Rua Marquês de Tamandaré 349, Bairro São Bento, 79170-000 Sidrolândia. **Web:** www.sidronet.com.br/pindorama/ ☎ +55 67 272 1514, 272 1543. 🖷 +55 67 272 1868. – **MS32**) Rua Amando do Oliveria, Bairro Amambai, 79005-280 Campo Grande (C.P.146 79002-970 Campo Grande). **Web:** www.asm.org.br **Email:** ellen.ramos@usb.org.br – **MS33**) Rua Severino de Araujo Ferreira 1375, 79700-000 Fátima do Sul. **Web:** www.fifasul.com.br/guaicurus ☎ +55 67 467 1566. 🖷 +55 67 467 1833. – **MS34**) Av. Calogeras 1932, 79012-003 Campo Grande. – **MS35**) Av. Costa Rica 654, 79740-000 Ivinhema. ☎ 🖷 +55 67 442 1450. – **MS36**) Av. João Pedro Pedrossian 4058, 79570-000 Aparecida do Taboado. ☎ +55 67 565 1075 – **English & Spanish:** 1100-1400. – **MS37**) 79300-000 Corumbá. – **MS38**) Rua Candido Severino 462, 79420-000 Camapuã. ☎ +55 67 286 1366. 🖷 +55 67 286 1239. – **MS39**) Rua 01 No. 1550, Altos do Indaiá, 79823-500 Dourados. **Email:** tepims@menthor.com.br 🖷 +55 67 421 0276. – **Spanish & Guaraní**: Sat 1400-1600. – **MS40**) Rua José Antônio Pereira 1488, sala 23, 79010-190 Campo Grande. – **MS41**) Rua Antônio Maria Coelho 289, 79260-000 Bela Vista. – **MS42**) Rua Porfirio Gonçalves 1240, 79480-000 Rio Verde de Mato Grosso. – **MS43**) Rua Atilio Reginato 355, 79740-000 Ivinhema. – **MS44**) 79300-000 Corumbá. – **MS45**) 79400-000 Coxim. – **MS46**) 79935-000 Sete Quedas. – **MS47**) 79430-000 Bandeirantes. – **MS48**) 79780-000 Bataguassu. – **MS49**) 79550-000 Costa Rica. – **MS50**) 79290-000 Bonito. – **MS51**) 79980-000 Mundo Novo. – **BA52**) 79210-000 Anastácio. – **MS53**)

79100-000 Campo Grande
MT00) MATO GROSSO
MT01) Rua Boróros 45, 78600-000 Barra do Garças. ☎ +55 65 861 1345. – **MT02)** Av. Brasil 27, 78600-000 Poxoréo. – **MT03)** Professora Tereza Lobo 30, 78048-700 Cuiabá. **Web:** www.gazetadigital.com.br/gazetaam/ ☎ +55 65 321 4144, 624 6699. – **MT04)** Av. Gov. Júlio Campos 300, 78550-000 Sinop. – **MT05)** Praça do Seminário 239, 78015-140 Cuiabá. **Email**: difusoracab@cancaonova.com ☎ +55 65 623 7000. – **MT06)** Av. Leste s/n, 78580-000 Alta Floresta. ☎ +55 65 521 2999. – **MT07)** C.P. 401, 78700-970 Rondonópolis. ☎ +55 65 423 2806. – **MT08)** Rua Joaquim Murtinho 1456, Palacio do Rádio, 78020-830 Cuiabá. **Web:** www.solunet.com.br/rcultura/ ☎ +55 65 321 6226, 321 6882. – **MT09)** Rua São Pedro 806, 78200-000 Cáceres. ☎ +55 65 223 1885. 🖷 +55 65 223 1663. – **MT10)** C.P. 297, 78201-970 Cáceres. - **FM:** 102.3. – **MT11)** C.P. 227, 78821-970 Jaciara. – **MT12)** Av. Cuiabá 829, Edifício Mikerinos, 12° andar, 78700-090 Rondonópolis. ☎ +55 65 421 3666/3451. – **MT13)** Rua 28 de Outobro 1445, 78280-000 Mirassol d'Oeste. ☎ +55 65 241 1288, 241 1770. – **MT14)** Rua Benedito Monteiro 68, 78110-390 Várzea Grande. – **MT15)** Rua Zulmira Canavarros 285, 78005-390 Cuiabá. ☎ +55 65 321 1210, 321 1223. – **MT16)** Rua 2 No. 32, 78175-000 Poconé. ☎ 🖷 +55 65 345 1577. – **MT17)** Rua Sorocaba 716 B, 78575-000 Juara. ☎ 🖷 +55 65 556 1478. – **MT18)** Av. Brasil 780, 78300-000 Tangará da Serra. ☎ +55 65 726 2080. – **MT19)** Av. T. Neves 1682, 78500-000 Colider. ☎ +55 65 541 1233. – **MT20)** Rua Waldir Rabelo 789, 78600-000 Barra do Garças. ☎ +55 65 861 2361. 🖷 +55 65 861 1760. – **MT21)** Rua Criciúma 165, 78890-000 Sorriso. **Web:** www.radiosorriso.com.br ☎ +55 65 544 2595. – **MT22)** Praça Brigadeiro Eduardo Gomes 28, 78430-000 Nortelândia. – **MT23)** Av. Mato Grosso 133, 78690-000 Nova Xavantina. ☎ +55 65 438 1218. – **MT24)** Rua 6 No. 498, 78300-000 Tangará da Serra. ☎ +55 65 726 1084. – **MT25)** Rua Benjamim Constant s/n, 78780-000 Alto Araguaia. – **MT26)** Av. 9 de Maio 65, 78320-000 Juina. – **MT27)** Av. Mario Correa 350, 78790-000 Itiquira. – **MT28)** Av. Agricolo Pães de Barros 924, 78525-000 Matupá. – **MT29)** Rua das Primaveras 3574, 78550-000 Sinop. – **MT30)** Av. Amazonas s/n, 78285-000 São José dos Quatro Marcos. ☎ +55 65 251 1317. – **MT31)** Rua 6 s/n, 78400-000 Diamantino. ☎ +55 65 736 1316. – **MT32)** Rua Perimetral s/n, Bairro Bom Clima, 78195-000 Chapada dos Guimarães. – **MT33)** Santa Catarina 1284, 78435-000 São José do Rio Claro. ☎ +55 65 786 1363. – **MT34)** Rua U-2 s/n – Canteiro Central, 78580-000 Alta Floresta. **Web:** www.radiofloresta.com.br/ – **MT35)** Rua Jovino Lopes 1292, 2° andar, Bairro Santa Maria Bertila, 78760-000 Guiratinga. ☎ +55 65 431 2002, 1944. 🖷 +55 65 431 1268. – **MT36)** Rua Joaquim Nabuco 450, 78260-000 Araputanga. **Email:** radioarcoiris@terra.com.br ☎ +55 65 261 1460. 🖷 +55 65 261 1813. – **MT37)** Rua São Paulo 1440, 78250-000 Pontes e Lacerda. ☎ +55 65 266 2598. – **MT38)** Margem Esquerda BR-163 km 723, Quadra 05, Lote 01, 78520-000 Guarantã do Norte. – **MT39)** Rua Dom Antônio Malan 674, 78015-600 Cuiabá. – **MT40)** Rua Carajás 69, 76800-000 Barra do Garças. – **MT41)** 78850-000 Primavera do Leste. – **MT42)** 78530-000 Peixoto de Azevedo. – **MT43)** 78200-000 Cáceres. – **MT44)** 78455-000 Lucas do Rio Verde. – **MT45)** 78820-000 Jaciara. – **MT46)** 78700-000 Rondonópolis. – **MT47)** 78575-000 Juara. – **MT49)** 78860-000 Nova Brasilândia. – **MT50)** 78635-000 Agua Boa. – **MT51)** 78785-000 Alto Taquari. – **MT52)** 78325-000 Aripuanã. – **MT53)** 78645-000 Vila Ruca. – **MT54)** 78505-000 Terra Nova do Norte. – **MT55)** 78390-000 Barra do Bugre. – **MT56)** 78590-000 Paranaita. – **MT57)** 78306-000 São Joaquím. – **MT58)** 78840-000 Campo Verde. – **MT59)** 78360-000 Campo Novo do Parecís.
PA00) PARÁ
PA01) Av. Araguaia 247, 68551-000 Redenção. **Email:** roriente@realonline.com.br ☎ 🖷 +55 91 424 1306. – **PA02)** C.P. 119, 68371-970 Altamira. – **PA03)** Av. Almirante Barroso 2190 1° andar, 66095-000 Belém. **Web:** www.radioclubedopara.com.br **Email:** rba13@expert.com.br ☎ +55 91 235 3579 +55 91 3084 0101. – **PA04)** Av. São Sebastião 622-Bloco A, 68005-090 Santarém. ☎ +55 93 523 1006. 🖷 +55 93 523 2685. **Email:** radioeducadora@uol.com.br – **PA05)** Av. Marechal Rondón 786, 68540-000 Conceição do Araguaia. – **PA06)** Praça dos Notáveis 1006, 68400-000 Cametá. – **PA07)** Rodovia BR-316 Km 58, 68741-740 Castanhal. – **PA08)** Travessa Campos Sales 370, 66019-050 Belém. ☎ +55 83 241 2103. - **FM:** 100.9. – **PA09)** Travessa Vileta 2193, 66093-380 Belém. – **PA10)** Av. Nazaré 319, Nazaré, 66035-170 Belém. **Web:** www.radioliberal.com.br **Email:** radio@radioliberal.com.br ☎ +55 91 213 1500. 🖷 +55 91 224 5240 **FM:** 97.5 – **PA11)** C.P. 038, 68801-970 Breves. – **PA12)** Praa das Bandeiras s/n, 68600-000 Bragança. **Email:** educadora@eletronet.com.br +54 91 425 1295 +54 91 425 1702 – **FM:** 102.9 – **PA13)** Av. Mendonça Furtado 1481, 68005-100 Santarém. **Email:** rtvpontanegra@trtvpontanegra.com.br ☎ +55 91 523 3348. 🖷 +55 91 523 2144. – **PA14)** Av. Coronel Monfredo 42, 68820-000 São Sebastião da Boa Vista. – **PA15)** Rua Primeiro de Janeiro 1359 Catedral 68371-020 Altamira (C.P. 226, 68371-970 Altamira). **Email:** radiotv@valedoxingu.com.br +55 93 515 1182/4899/4411– **FM:** 93.1 – **PA16)** Av. Almirante Barroso 735, 66090-000 Belém. - **FM:** 93.7. – **PA17)** Margem da Rodovia PA-130 Km 8/9, 68500-000 Marabá. – **PA18)** Rodovia Transamazonica Km. 01, 68180-010 Itaituba. – **PA19)** Rua Lauro Sodré 722, 68456-000 Tucuruí. – **PA20)** Av. Rui Barbosa 825, 68005-080 Santarém. – **PA21)** Av. Xingu s/n, 68555-010 Xinguara. – **PA22)** Travessa E. Simões 230, 68250-000 Óbidos. – **PA23)** Travessa Dr.Lauro Sodré 299, 68250 000 (C.P. 8 - 68251-970) Óbidos. **Web:** www.kaleb.hpg.ig.com.br **Email:** radiomissoes@eunet.com.br +54 93 547 1699 – **PA24)** Travessa 18 No. 1863, entre 4 e 5 ruas, 68870-000 Soure. – **PA25)** Av. Visconde de Sousa Franco 116, Centro, 68780-000 Vigia. – **PA26)** Rodovia BR-230 (Transamazônica) Km 01, 68180-010 Itaituba. – **PA27)** Av. Tropical s/n, 68625-000 Paragominas. – **PA28)** Rua 2 de Outobro s/n, 68200-000 Alenquer. – **PA29)** Rodovia Transamazônica Km 04, 68502-290 Marabá. – **PA30)** Rodovia BR-010 Km. 09, Bairro Industrial, 68660-000 São Miguel do Guamá. – **PA31)** 68460-000 Tucuruí. – **PA32)** Travessa Mauriti 1006, Bairro da Pedreira, 66080-650 Belém. – **PA33)** Av. Beira Rio s/n, 68380-000 São Felix do Xingu. – **PA34)** Av. Augusto Montenegro s/n, 68710-000 Maracanã. – **PA35)** 68440-000 Abaetetuba. – **PA36)** 68230-000 Almeirim. – **PA37)** 68430-000 Igarapé Miri. – **PA38)** 66000-000 Belém. – **PA39)** 68740-000 Castanhal.
PB00) PARAÍBA
PB01) Rua Pres. João Pessoa 25, 58800-010 Sousa. – **PB02)** C.P. 26, 58900-970 Cajazeiras. **Email:** gazeta@openline.com.br 🖷 +55 83 531 1334. – **PB03)** Rua Padre Manoel Otaviano 340, 58970-000 Conceição. – **PB04)** Rua Presidente Epitácio Pessoa 242, 58700-020 Patos. – **PB05)** C.P. 40, 58200-970 Guarabira. – **PB06)** Praça Pres. Epitácio Pessoa 167, 58755-000 Princesa Isabel. – **PB07)** C.P. 134, 58100-970 Campina Grande. – **PB08)** Rua Coronel Juvêncio Carneiro 160, 58900-000 Cajazeiras. ☎ +55 83 531 1497, 531 1237. – **PB09)** C.P. 1089, 58001-970 João Pessoa. – **PB10)** Rua Manoel Pedro s/n, 58884-000 Catolé do Rocha. – **PB11)** Rua Venâncio Neiva 287, 58100-060 Campina Grande. – **PB12)** Av. Pedro II 523, Centro, 58013-420 João Pessoa. ☎ +55 83 216 5000. – **PB13)** Rua das Trincheiras 198, Centro, 58011-000 João Pessoa. – **PB14)** C.P. 160, 58100-970 Campina Grande. – **PB15)** C.P. 57, 58700-970 Patos. **Email:** espinharas@openline.com.br ☎ +55 83 421 3791/3792. 🖷 +55 83 221 3795. – **PB16)** Rua Antônio Martins s/n, 58290-000 Mamanguape. – **PB17)** Rua Dr. Carlos Pires 17, 58804-200 Sousa. – **PB18)** Rua Monsenhor Valeriano s/n, 58840-000 Pombal. – **PB19)** Rua Antônio Firmino 344, 58187-000 Picuí. – **PB20)** Rua Cândido de Assis 421, 58840-000 Pombal. – **PB21)** Rua Osvaldo Cruz 161, 58309-490 Bayeux. – **PB22)** Rua Epitácio Pessoa 8, 58200-000 Guarabira. – **PB23)** Rua Monsenhor Palmeira s/n, 58135-000 Esperança. – **PB24)** Rua Getúlio Vargas 129, 58500-000 Monteiro. – **PB25)** Rua Coronel Pedro Targino s/n, 58233-000 Araruna. – **PB26)** Rua Castro Pinto 234, 58220-000 Bananeiras. – **PB27)** Rua Prefeito Inacio Claudino 121, 58155-000 Soledade. – **PB28)** Rua João Sabiá 56, 58540-000 Sumé. – **PB29)** Praça Frei Martinho s/n, 1° andar, Centro, 58700-100 Patos. ☎ +55 83 421 4531. 🖷 +55 (83) 421 3704. - **FM:** 102.9. – **PB30)** Rua Epifanio Sobreira 14, 58900-000 Cajazeiras. – **PB31)** Av. Almirante Barroso 918, 58040-220 João Pessoa. – **PB32)** Rua Epitácio Pessoa 35, 58397-000 Areia. **Web:** www.radiojardim.hpg.ig.com.br **Email:** radiojardim@areianet.com.br – **PB33)** 54500-000 Cabo de Santo Agostinho. – **PB34)** 58780-000 Itaporanga. – **PB35)** 58100-000 Campina Grande.
PE00) PERNAMBUCO
PE01) Av. Santo Antônio 324, 55290-000 Garanhuns. – **PE02)** Rua Floriano Peixoto 780, São José, 50020-060 Recife. ☎ +55 81 224 4118. 🖷 +55 81 224 2077. – **PE03)** Av. Joaquim Nabuco 322, 56500-000 Arcoverde. – **PE04)** Praça da Bandeira s/n, 55700-000 Limoeiro. – **PE05)** Rodovia Araraipina – Picos Km 3, 56280-000 Araripina. – **PE06)** Av. Sete de Setembro s/n, Bairro Km. 02, 56300-000 Petrolina. **Email:** granderioam@uol.com.br ☎ +55 81 861 2311. 🖷 +55 81 862 2366. – **PE07)** Rua do Veiga 590, Santo Amaro, 50040-908 Recife. – **PE08)** Praça Maria Auxiliadora 205, 56300-000 Petrolina. - **F.PI**: FM. – **PE09)** Rua Capitão Lima 250, Santo Amaro, 50040-080 Recife. ☎ +55 81 421 1588. 🖷 +55 81 421 3868. – **PE10)** Cidade Universtitária, 50670-901 Recife. – **PE11)** Av. Pres. Kennedy 3092, Bairro Peixinhos, 53260-640 Olinda. ☎ +55 81 444 8282. 🖷 +55 81 433 5400. – **PE12)** Rua da Conceição 16/22, 2° andar, Centro, 55000-000 Caruaru. **Web:** www.liberdade.com.br/ - **FM:** 94.7. – **PE13)** Av. Padre Rocha s/n, 55810-000 Carpina. – **PE14)** Av. Maria Emília Cavalcanti 570, 55870-000 Timbaúba. – **PE15)** Estrada do Passarinho 1415, 53170-110 Olinda. – **PE16)** C.P. 88, 55001-970 Caruaru. – **PE17)** Rua Floriano Peixoto 780, 1° andar, 50020-060 Recife. – **PE18)** Rua do Expedicionário 30, 55000-000 Caruaru. – **PE19)** Rua dos Ferreiros s/n, Granja Fazenda Nova, 55600-000 Vitória de Santo Antão. – **PE20)** C.P. 13, 55301-970 Garanhuns. – **PE21)** Rua Coronel Urbano Ribeiro de Sena 956, 52221-000 Recife. – **PE22)** Rua Lindaura Marinho Dias 95, 54750-000 Camarajibe. – **PE23)** Rua Pajussara 225, Bairro Tigipió, 50920-121 Recife. – **PE24)** Av. F. Pessoa de Queiróz s/n, 55200-000 Pesqueira. – **PE25)** BR-101 Km. 117, Eng. São Manoel, 55540-000 Palmares. **Web:** www.onlife.com.br/radiocultura/cultura.htm ☎ 🖷 +55 81 662 1020/1288/1082. – **PE26)** Rua Inocencio Gomes de Andrade 619, 56900-000 Serra Talhada. – **PE27)** Rua 03 de Maio 5, 56800-000 Afogados da Ingazeira – **PE28)** Rua Benjamim Constant 16, 55750-000 Surubim. – **PE29)** Rua José Lopes da Silva s/n, São Pedro, 55150-000 Belo Jardim. – **PE30)** Rua Antônio Figueira Soares s/n, 56000-000 Salgueiro. – **PE31)** Av. C. Colombo 16, 56700-000 São José do Egito. – **PE32)** Praça Duque de Caxias

818, 55900-000 Goiana. – **PE33**) Av. Fernando Bezerra 1123, 56200-000 Ouricuri. – **PE34**) Rua Manoel Balbino 184, 55190-000 Santa Cruz do Capibaribe. – **PE35**) Av. Coronel Trapia s/n, 56440-000 Belém de São Francisco. – **PE36**) Rua São Francisco de Assis s/n, Centro , 56440-000 Gravatá. **Email:** cancaope@vitorialink.com.br – **PE37**) Rua José do Amaral 12, 55330-000 Bom Conselho. – **PE38**) 56460-000 Petrolândia. – **PE39**)56180-000 Cabrobó. – **PE40**) 55660-000 Bezerros.

PI00) PIAUÍ

PI01) Praça Júlio Paixão s/n, 64770-000 São Raimundo Nonato. – **PI02**) Rua Alvaro Mendes 972, 64000-060 Teresina. - **FM:** 94.1. – **PI03**) Rua Taumaturgo de Azevedo 995, 64100-000 Barras. – **PI04**) Av. Valter Alencar 2120, Monte Castelo, 64017-500 Teresina. - **FM:** 99.1. – **PI05**) Av. Heróis do Jenipapo 37, 64280-000 Campo Maior. – **PI06**) Praça Pres. Kennedy 233, 64490-000 Regeneração. – **PI07**) Praça do Comércio 400, 1° andar, 64500-000 Oeiras. – **PI08**) Av. Prof. Valter Alencar 2021, 64017-500 Teresina. – **PI09**) Rua Joaquim Baldoíno 40, 64600-000 Picos. – **PI10**) Rua 24 de Janeiro 150 – Sul, 64001-230 Teresina. **Web:** www.radiopioneira.com.br ☎ +55 86 221 8121. ℻ +55 86 221 8122. – **PI11**) Av. Presidente Getúlio Vargas 266, 64200-000 Parnaíba. – **PI12**) Rua 18 de Setembro 678, 64260-000 Piripiri. – **PI13**) Av. Miguel Rosa 3775 Sul, 64001-490 Teresina. – **PI14**) Av. Prefeito J. de Carvalho, 64400-000 Amarante. – **PI15**) Av. Rio Branco 314, 64860-000 Uruçuí. – **PI16**) Rua Clementino Ribeiro 56, 2° andar, 64800-000 Floriano. – **PI17**) Praça Emilio Cavalcante 29, 64980-000 Corrente. – **PI18**) Rua Antônio Neto 1065, 64800-000 Floriano. – **PI19**) Rua Sabino Paulo 696, 64760-000 São João do Piauí. – **PI20**) Av. João de Paiva 94, 64290-000 Altos. – **PI21**) Rua Arsénio Santos 555, 64900-000 Bom Jesus. – **PI22**) Rua Riachuelo 770, 64200-280 Parnaíba. – **PI23**) Rua General Taumaturgo de Azevedo 800, 64100-000 Barras. – **PI24**) Praça Presidente Castelo Branco s/n, 64750-000 Paulistana. – **PI25**) Rua Fernando Bacelar 480, 64240-000 Piracuruca. – **PI26**) Av. José de Deus Lacerda 584, 64130-000 Miguel Alves. – **PI27**) Av. Governador Chagas Rodrigues s/n, 64575-000 Jaicós. – **PI28**) Rua Corrinto de Andrade s/n, 64255-000 Pedro II. – **PI29**) Praça da Independência 69, 64325-000 Elesbão Veloso. – **PI30**) Rua Joaqium Baldoíno 48, 64600-000 Picos. - **FM:** 94.5. – **PI31**) Av. João Ferreira 199, 64460-000 Agua Branca. – **PI32**) Rua Hugo Napoleão 940, 64110-000 José de Freitas. – **PI33**) Rua Pedro II 695, 64340-000 Castelo do Piauí. – **PI34**) Rua Pedro II s/n, 64330-000 São Miguel do Tapuio. – **PI35**) Rua Coronel Anibal Martins 481, 64300-000 Valença do Piauí. ☎ +55 86 4651244. – **PI36**) Rua Matias Gomes 510, 64700-000 Simplício Mendes. – **PI37**) Rua Coronel Narciso 728, 64120-000 União. – **PI38**) Rua Padre Joaquim Nonato s/n, 64390-000 Demerval Lobão. – **PI39**) Rua Coronel Messeas Melo s/n, 64190-000 Batalha. – **PI40**) Estrada Barra do Longa, Periferia de Cidade, 64230-000 Buriti dos Lopes. – **PI41**) Av. Antonino Freire 1356, 64001-040 Teresina. – **PI42**) Praça Waldemar Leal 42, 64680-000 Padre Marcos. – **PI43**) Rua Sete de Setembro 471, 64160-000 Luzilândia. – **PI44**) Praça da Bandeira 93, 64500-000 Oeiras. – **PI45**) Rua Professor Alceu Brandão 2397, Bairro Monte Castelo, 64016-150 Teresina. – **PI46**) Rua Coronel José Fortes 549, 64180-000 Esperantina. – **PI47**) Rodovia BR-343 s/n, 64290-000 Altos. – **PI48**) Av. Professor Alceu Brandão 2750, 64016-150 Teresina. **Web:** www.servo.com.br/gmn/iradios.htm – All news. – **FM:** 91,1. – **PI49**) 64600-000 Picos.

PR00) PARANÁ

PR01) Rua Quintino Bocaiuva 41, 86020-100 Londrina. **Email:** radiolondrina@onda.com.br ☎ +55 43 323 5666, 344 2038. – **PR02**) Rua XV do Novembro 3466, 85010-000 Guarapuava. **Email:** cultura@gol.psi.br **Web:** www.centralcultura.com.br ☎ +55 42 723 6423. ℻ +55 42 723 7269. - **FM:** 93.7. – **PR03**) C.P. 10, 85892-970 Santa Helena. **Web:** www.radiograndelago.com.br ☎ +55 45 268 1112, 268 1212, 268 1425. ℻ +55 45 2681135. – **PR04**) C.P. 202, 80001-970 Curitiba. – **PR05**) Av. Anunciato Sonni 1673, 86900-000 Jandaia do Sul. – **PR06**) Rua Cruz Machado 55, 80410-170 Curitiba. – **PR07**) Rua 7 de Setembro 520, 85960-000 Marechal Cândido Rondón. **Web:** www.radioeducadoraam.com.br ☎ +55 45 284 1212. – **PR08**) C.P. 337, 86001-970 Londrina. – **PR09**) Rua Octavio Rodrigues Ferreira Filho 1303, 86390-000 Cambará. **Email:** radiocultura@cainet.com.br ☎ ℻ +55 43 732 4050. – **PR10**) C.P. 218, 87600-970 Nova Esperança. – **PR11**) Rua Afonso Pedri 65, 80820-680 Curitiba. – **PR12**) Rua Marechal Floriano Peixoto 1670, Centro, 85010-250 Guarapuava. – **PR13**) Rua Sergipe 843, sala 05, 86010-360 Londrina. ☎ +55 43 322 1105. ℻ +55 43 324 7369. – **PR14**) Rua 15 de Novembro 433, Centro, 84010-905 Ponta Grossa. – **PR15**) Av. Paraná 1896, Bairro Boa Vista, 82510-000 Curitiba. **Web:** www.iensen.cjb.net **Email:** dafaie@ig.com.br – **PR16**) Av. Irmãos Pereira 1960, 87300-000 Campo Mourão. **Web:** www.radiohumaita.com.br **Email:** radiohumaita@onda.com.br – **PR17**) Av. 19 de Agosto 522, 1° andar, 87360 000 Goio-Erê. **Email:** rgam@visaonete.com.br – **PR18**) C.P. 209, 87201-970 Cianorte. – **PR19**) Rua Frei Everaldo 445, 85560-000 Chopinzinho. **Email:** radiochopinzinho@chnet.com.br ☎ +55 46 242 1148, 242 1789. – **PR20**) Rua Bruno Filgueira 1210, 80440-220 Curitiba. – **PR21**) Rua Marechal Floriano Peixoto 1123, 85851-020 Foz do Iguaçu. ☎ +55 45 523 1133. – **PR22**) Rodovia do Xisto Km. 20 No. 2018, 83705-740 Araucária. – **PR23**) Rua Coronel Manoel Ferreira Bello 64, 85530-000 Clevelândia. **Web:** www.rdprogresso.com.br **Email:** rdprogresso@pinet.com.br – **PR24**) Rua Anita Garibaldi 43, Centro, 86020-410 Londrina. – **PR25**) Av. Getúlio Vargas 266, 87013-130 Maringá. – **PR26**) Rua Iguaçu 808, Centro, 85501-270 Pato Branco. ☎ +55 46 225 1087. ℻ +55 46 224 1319. – **PR27**) Praça Marechal Floriano Peixoto 581, 84010-910 Ponta Grossa. **Web:** www.dioceseponta-grossa.com.br **Email:** radiosantana@uol.com.br – **PR28**) Av. Largo São Vicente de Paulo 1085, 85900-210 Toledo. **Email:** radiouniao@uol.com.br ☎ +55 45 252 7488. ℻ +55 45 252 1841. – **PR29**) Rua Gastão Vidigal 777, 86800-050 Apucarana. **Email:** novaam@uol.com.br ☎ +55 43 423 1100. – **PR30**) C.P. 178, 86600-970 Rolândia. **Email:** radiocultura@onda.com.br – **PR31**) Rua João Negrão 558, 80010-200 Curitiba. – **PR32**) Rua Joubert de Carvalho 623, 87013-200 Maringá. – **PR33**) Edificio Júlio Fuganti, Rua Senador Souza Naves 9, 9° andar, salas 903 á 911, 86010-170 Londrina. **Web:** www.radioalvorada.com.br **Email:** mater@sercomtel.com.br ☎ +55 43 336 0606. ℻ +55 43 321 4745. – **PR34**) Rua Santa Catarina 970, 85960-000 Marechal Cândido Rondón. **Web:** www.radiodifusora.com.br - **FM:** 95.1. – **PR35**) Rua Tocantins 1991, 85505-140 Pato Branco. – **German:** Sun 2200-2300. – **PR36**) Praça Generoso Marques 90, 1° andar, Galeria Andrade, 80020-230 Curitiba. **Web:** www.radiocolombo.com.br – **PR37**) Av. Pedro Soccol 542, São Cristovão, 85884-000 Medianeira. **Web:** www.medianeira.com.br/independencia/ **Email:** independencia@ar-net.com.br – **PR38**) Rua Paraná 650, Centro, 874-000 Cruzeiro do Oeste. **Email:** radiodifusoraam@cianet.com.br – **PR39**) Km. 6 da Estrada de Cambé, 86010-040 Londrina. – **PR40**) Rua Ulisses Faria 1077, 83900-000 São Mateus do Sul. ☎ +55 42 532 1644. ℻ +55 42 532 1777. – **PR41**) Rua Maranhão 2955, 85805-220 Cascavel. **Web:** www.capitalfm.com.br/ - **FM:** 102.7. – **PR42**) Rua Rockefeller 1311, Porto Velho, 80230-130 Curitiba. – **PR43**) Rua Bahia 667, 86690-000 Colorado. ☎ +55 44 323 1003. – **PR44**) Rua Porto Alegre 21, 1° andar, 85601-480 Francisco Beltrão. **Email:** educadora@win.com.br ☎ +55 46 524 2255. – **PR45**) Rua Dario Antônio Bordin 313, Centro, 84600-000 União da Vitória. – **PR46**) C.P. 09, 85400-970 Guaraniaçu. – **PR47**) Rua 15 de Novembro 344, Centro, 84010-020 Ponta Grossa. – **PR48**) Rua Getúlio Vargas 1050, 87772-000 Paranavaí. – **PR49**) C.P. 101, 86300-000 Cornélio Procópio. **Email:** educa1080@uol.com.br ☎ +55 43 524 1581. – **PR50**) Av. Capitão Indio Bandeira 1400, 5° andar, Centro Empresarial Antares, 87300-000 Campo Mourão. **Web:** www.radiocolmeia.com.br/ – **PR51**) Rua das Américas 255, 85550-000 Coronel Vivida. **Email:** pallotti@win.com.br – **PR52**) Av. Higienópolis 2100, 86015-905 Londrina. **Web:** www.paiquere.com.br **Email:** paiquere@paiquere.com.br ☎ +55 43 323 5500. ℻ +55 43 339 1175. - **FM:** 98.9. – **PR53**) Rua Visconde do Rio Branco 2905, 83005-420 São José dos Pinhais. **Email:** eldorado@softone.com.br - **FM:** 97.9. – **PR54**) Av. Cristóvão Colombo 1055, 86990-000 Marialva. – **PR55**) Praça Manoel Ribas 112, 84165-000 Castro. **Email:** radiocastro@convoy.com.br – **PR56**) C.P. 56, 86001-970, Londrina. **Email:** radionorte@onda.com.br ☎ +55 43 348 4141. – **PR57**) Rua João Negrão 595, Centro, 80010-200 Curitiba. – **PR58**) Rua Raimundo Leonardi 1301, 85900-110 Toledo. **Email:** radioguacu@uol.com.br ☎ +55 45 378 3161, 378 4930. – **PR59**) Av. Londrina 500, 87970-000 Nova Londrina. ☎ +55 44 432 1540. – **PR60**) Rua Basilio Itiberê 1001, Rebouças, 80215-140 Curitiba. – **PR61**) Av. Paraná 596, 85887-000 Matelândia. **Email:** radiomatelandia@matelnet.com.br – **PR62**) Rua Saldanha Marinho 1489, 85010-290 Guarapuava. **Email:** difusora@gol.psi.br – **PR63**) Rua Pernambuco 1560, 87705-000 Paranavaí. **Email:** rpvai@uol.com.br – **PR64**) Rua do Cedro s/n, 85650-000 Santa Isabel do Oeste. **Email:** danubioazul@qualinet.com.br – **PR65**) C.P. 239, 86975-970 Mandaguari. **Web:** www.radioguairaca.com.br **Email:** guairaca@bwnet.com.br ☎ +55 44 233 1180. – **PR66**) C.P. 91, 86430-970 Santo Antônio da Platina. **Email:** valedosol@uol.com.br – **PR67**) Rua Pedro Eloy de Souza 51, 82820-130 Curitiba. **Email:** radiocapitalpr@uol.com.br – **PR68**) Rua Rio Grande do Sul 1110, 85806-010 Cascavel. **Email:** radiocidade@certto.com.br – **PR69**) C.P. 71, 85601-600 Francisco Beltrão. **Email:** seleski@win.com.br or 105@wmail.com.br - **FM:** 105.1 "FM Super Jovem". – **PR70**) C.P. 1300, 87001-970 Maringá. **Email:** radioatalaia@wnet.com.br – **PR71**) Rua XV de Novembro 591,Sobreloja, Centro, 84010-020 Ponta Grossa. – **PR72**) Rua Desembargador Westphalen 295, 80010-110 Curitiba. **Email:** radiobrasiltropical@radiobrasiltropical.com.br – **PR73**) Rua Miguel Couto 67, Xangri Lá, 86070-640 Londrina. – **PR74**) C.P. 26, 84201-970 Jaguariaíva. – **PR75**) C.P. 13, 87502-970 Umuarama. **Email:** inconfidencia@fenixnet.com.br – **PR76**) Rua Bom Jesus 511, 83880-000 Rio Negro. – **PR77**) Rua Flamingos 357, 86701-390 Arapongas. **Web:** www.transnorte.com.br – **PR78**) Av. Paul Harris 50, 86220-000 Assaí. – **PR79**) Rua Pedro Alvares Cabral 1609, 87560-000 Iporã. – **PR80**) Rua André Zanetti 340, Mercês, 81810-280 Curitiba. **Web:** www.radioindependencia.com.br – **PR81**) Rua Paraíba 168, 86930-000 São João do Ivaí. **Email:** radioeducadora@ligbr.com.br – **PR82**) Av.Mauá, Vila Operária, 87050-020 Maringa (C.P. 76, 87001-970 Maringá). ☎ +55 44 222 3413. ℻ +55 44 222 4969. - **FM:** 102.5. – **PR83**) Rua Juventino Bonetti 288, 85670-000 Salto do Lontra. **Email:** ri@win.com.br – **PR84**) Rua Anita Garibaldi 43, Centro, 86020-410 Londrina. **Web:** www.cbnlondrina.com.br **Email:** cbnlondrina@sercomtel.com.br ☎ +55 43 323 9363. ℻ +55 43 321 3501. – **PR85**) Av. Dep. Ivan Ferreira do Amaral Filho 86, Centro, 85303-000 Laranjeiras do Sul.

Web: www.radioeducadora1120.com.br – **PR86**) Rua Simão Domingues 26, 84550-000 Rebouças. **Email:** radioalvorada@convoy.com.br – **PR87**) Rua Vereador Vicente Balan 12, 85990-000 Terra Roxa. – **PR88**) Av. Tiradentes 2113, 87505-090 Umuarama. ☎ +55 44 622 1014, 622 1286. 🖷 +55 44 622 1091. – **PR89**) Rua Antônio Lemos 807, 86400-000 Jacarezinho. **Email:** educadora@uol.com.br ☎ +55 43 525 0773. 🖷 +55 43 527 2029. – **PR90**) Av. Brasil 702, 85710-000 Santo Antônio do Sudoeste. **Email:** radioer@win.com.br ☎ +55 46 563 1541. – **PR91**) C.P. 66, 85801-970 Cascavel. **Web:** www.radiocolmeia.com.br **Email:** colmeia@unimidia.com.br – **PR92**) Av. Horácio Klabin 383, 2° andar, 84261-000 Telêmaco Borba. ☎ +55 422 72 1515/1381. - **FM:** 92.9. – **PR93**) Av. Bandeirantes 958, 86360-000 Bandeirantes. – **PR94**) Rua Herculino Otaviano 817, 1° andar, 85440-000 Ubiratã. **Email:** difusora@ubinet.com.br ☎ +55 44 543 1317, 543 1717. – **PR95**) C.P. 171, 87550-970 Altônia. **Email:** rainhaam@bol.com.br – **PR96**) Rua Prof. Cleto 281, Centro, 83221-320 Paranaguá. – **PR97**) Rua XV de Novembro 522, 84010-908 Ponta Grossa. **Email:** centralam@interponta.com.br ☎ +55 42 225 1267. – **PR98**) C.P. 777, 86800-970 Apucarana. **Email:** amcultura @uol.com.br – **PR99**) Rua Jesuino Alves da Rocha Loures 1764 (C.P. 66) 85555-000 Palmas. **Web:** www.radioclubeamfm.com.br **Email:** comercial@radioclubeamfm.com.br ☎🖷 +55 46 263 1818/1299. – **FM:** 96.5 "Horizonte". – **PR100**) C.P. 217, 85980-970 Guaíra. – **PR101**) Rua Londrina 410, 85640-000 Ampére. **Email:** radioampere@ampernet.com.br – **PR102**) C.P. 171, 87900-970 Loanda. – **PR103**) C.P. 16, 86590-970 Ibaiti. – **PR104**) Praça Nossa Senhora do Carmo 99, 85935-000 Assis Chateaubriand. **Email:** radiojornal@visaonet.com.br **Web:** www.radiojornalam.com.br ☎ 🖷 +55 44 528 4477. – **PR105**) Rua Ebano Pereira 157, 85200-000 Pitanga. – **PR106**) C.P. 45, 86730-970 Astorga. – **PR107**) Rua Ipiranga 91, 84600-000 União da Vitória. ☎ +55 42 522 1340. 🖷 +55 42 522 1098. - **Polish & German:** Sat, Sun 1500. – **PR108**) C.P. 230, 86300-000 Cornélio Procópio. **Email:** radiocor@onda.com.br – **PR109**) Rua 7 de Setembro 42, 83750-000 Lapa. **Email:** am960@matrix.com.br ☎ +55 41 622 1918. 🖷 +55 41 622 1428. – **PR110**) C.P. 195, 86925-970 Borrazópolis. **Email:** radionovaera@uol.com.br – **PR111**) C.P. 121, 84400-970 Prudentópolis. **Email:** radioes@visionet.com.br – **PR112**) Rua Rouxinol 752, 86701-150 Arapongas. ☎ +55 43 252 2133. 🖷 +55 43 252 3577. – **PR113**) C.P. 72, 86500-970 Venceslau Brás. – **PR114**) Rua Coronel Emilio Gomes 281, Terreo, 84500-000 Irati. – **PR115**) Rua Florianópolis 1636, 85840-000 Céu Azul. **Email:** uniao@netceu.com.br – **PR116**) Travessa Vale Porto 240, 83370-000 Antonina. – **PR117**) Av. Souza Naves 1265, 86870-000 Ivaiporã. ☎ +55 43 472 4366. 🖷 +55 43 472 4856. – **PR118**) Rua 5 de Julho 1065, 85950-000 Palotina. ☎ +55 44 649 5266. – **PR119**) Rua D. Pedro II 1889, 834601-610 Campo Largo - **Email:** radiorbn@uol.com.br. - +55 41 292 2670. +55 41 393 3734. – **PR120**) Rua Mauá 2518, 85770-000 Realeza. **Email:** radioclube@wim.com.br – **PR121**) C.P. 358, 87200-970 Cianorte. **Email:** radio.capital@uol.com.br – **PR122**) Praça Frei Alfredo J. Lazzaroto, 89490-000 Siqueira Campos. **Email:** fmcanaverde@uol.com.br ☎ +55 43 571 1125. – **PR123**) C.P. 11, 85830-970 Formosa do Oeste. – **PR124**) C.P. 10, 85615-970 Marmeleiro. **Email:** radiocristal@wim.com.br – **PR125**) Av. Brasil 502, 85760-000 Capanema. – **PR126**) Rua Senador Pinheiro Machado 1536, Centro, 85010-100 Guarapuava. – **PR127**) Rua do Comércio 654, 85660-000 Dois Vizinhos. **Web:** www.vizifm.com.br ☎ +55 46 536 3131. 🖷 +55 46 536 3003. – **FM:** 100.7 "Vizinhança". – **PR128**) C.P. 199, 84500-970 Irati. **Email:** radionajua@irati.com.br – **PR129**) Rua Bandeirantes 165, 86380-000 Andirá. – **PR130**) Rua São Paulo 489, 86840-000 Faxinal. **Email:** radioclub@folnet.com.br – **PR131**) Rua Noruega 98, 86182-000 Cambé. – **PR132**) Praça São Pedro 999, 85460-000 Quedas do Iguaçu. – **PR133**) Praça Marechal Floriano 108, 84130-000 Palmeira. **Email:** radioipiranga@convoy.com.br **Web:** www.radioipiranga.com.br ☎🖷 +55 42 252 3669/3939. – **PR134**) Rua Rockefeller 1311, Prado Velho, 80230-130 Curitiba. – **PR135**) Av. Brasil 740, 84350-000 Ortigueira. ☎ +55 42 277 1366. – **PR136**) Av. Maximiliano Vicentin 240, 85270-000 Palmital. **Email:** cidadeam@ig.com.br ☎ +55 42 657 1442. – **PR137**) Rua Melissa 520, 85410-000 Nova Aurora. **Email:** raclubna@sercopa.com.br ☎ +55 45 243 1233. 🖷 +55 45 243 1793. – **PR138**) Rua Dom Pedro II 196, 85852-520 Foz do Iguaçu. ☎ +55 45 574 3030. – **PR139**) Rua Oyapock 649, Cristo Rei, 80050-450 Curitiba. **Web:** www.radiobandab.com.br ☎ +55 41 264 9945. – **PR140**) Rua Urbano Lunardelli 875, 86160-000 Porecatu. **Email:** radiobrotense@com.br ☎ +55 43 623 1611. – **PR141**) Av. Paraná 220, 84470-000 Cândido de Abreu. **Email:** radioalternativa @matrix.com.br ☎🖷 +55 43 476 1244. – **PR142**) Av. Santos Dumont 2505, 85302-080 Laranjeiras do Sul. **Email:** rca@orangenet.com.br – **PR143**) Av. Genoroso Marques 599, 2° andar, 85550-000 Coronel Vivida. **Email:** radiovoz@win.com.br – **PR144**) Rua 7 de Setembro 540, 85560-000 Chopinzinho. **Email:** difusora_america @chnet.com.br – **PR145**) Av. Paraná 201, 85852-000 Foz do Iguaçu. **Email:** radio.foz@fnn.net ☎ +55 45 523 2211. – **PR146**) Av. Presidente Kennedy 170, Norte, 85950-000 Palotina. **Web:** www.graunafm.com.br **Email:** grauna@graunafm.com.br ☎ +55 44 649 5253. 🖷 +55 44 649 6084. - **FM:** 93.5. – **PR147**) Rua Amor Perfeito 1827, 85420-000 Corbélia. **Email:** integracao @realplus.com.br ☎ +55 45 242 1799, 242 1999. – **PR148**) Rua Farroupilha 80, 2° andar, 85877-000 São Miguel do Iguaçu. **Email:** radiojornal@innet.com.br – **PR149**) Av. Iguaçu 288, Centro, 85575-000 São Jorge d'Oeste. **Email:** difusora@whiteduck.com.br – **PR150**) Av. Santo Antônio 826, 87320-000 Roncador. – **PR151**) Av. Yolanda Loureiro de Carvalho 1021, 87350-000 Ubiratã. – **PR152**) Rua XV de Novembro 1670, 85900-000 Toledo. **Web:** www.radioeldoradotoledo.com.br – **PR153**) Rua Perfeito Pedro Rolim de Moura 104, 84240-000 Piraí do Sul. ☎ +55 42 237 2508. 🖷 +55 42 237 1174. – **PR154**) Rua Bernardino Bogo 68, 87160-000 Mandaguaçu. **Web:** www.sgcp.com.br/radiocolmeia **Email:** rcolmeia@iwnet.com.br ☎ +55 44 245 1776. – **PR155**) Rua Rosalvo Petrechem 551, 85200-000 Pitanga. **Email:** poema@convoy.com.br – **PR156**) Av. Euclides da Cunha s/n, 87890-000 Terra Rica. **Email:** guairaca@vsp.com.br ☎ +55 44 441 1991. – **PR157**) Av. Iguaçu 858, Ed. Fabiane, 85585-000 Verê. **Email:** rvaledoiguacu@gualinet.com.br ☎🖷 +55 46 535 1305. – **Italian:** Sat mornings. – **PR158**) Rua Independência s/n, Prox. Escola de Aplica, 86130-000 Bela Vista do Paraíso. – **PR159**) Rua Luiz Pinheiro 1446, 84990-000 Arapoti. – **PR160**) Av. Iguaçu 366, 85790-000 Capitão Leônidas Marques. **Email:** hawai@certto.com.br – **PR161**) Rua Antonio Rosa 1170, 86490-000 Ribeirão do Pinhal. **Email:** am@radioserpin.com.br – **PR162**) Rua Vicente Machado 385, 84570-000 Mallet. – **PR163**) Rua Marechal Deodoro 22, 85540-000 Mangueirinha. **Email:** radioaraucaria@qualinet.com.br – **PR164**) Rua São Miguel 922, 85570-000 São João. **Email:** saojoao@win.com.br ☎ +55 46 533 1474. – **PR165**) Rua Guarani 829, sala 01, 85501-000 Pato Branco. **Email:** radiocidade@qualinet.com.br – **PR166**) 83200-000 Paranaguá. – **PR167**) 85850-000 Foz de Iguaçu. – **PR168**) 83280-000 Guaratuba. – **PR169**) 84300-000 Tibagi. – **PR170**) 84260-000 Telêmaco Borba. – **PR171**) 86985-000 Sarandi. – **PR172**) 85580-000 Itapejara d'Oeste. – **PR173**) 83540-000 Rio Branco do Sul. – **PR174**) 85740-000 Pérola d'Oeste. – **PR175**) 87530-000 Icaraima. – **PR176**) 86180-000 Cambé. – **PR177**) 83500-000 Almirante Tamandaré. – **PR178**) 84430-000 Imbutuva.

RJ00) RIO DE JANEIRO

RJ01) Rua Visconde de Itaborai 184, 24030-091 Niterói. – **RJ02**) Rua Costa Rica 151, Parque Hotel, 28970-000 Araruama. – **RJ03**) Rua Paramopama 131, Ribeira, Ilha do Governador, 21930-110 Rio de Janeiro. **Web:** www.radiorelogio.com.br – **RJ04**) Praça Mauá 7, 21° andar, 20083-900 Rio de Janeiro. – **RJ05**) Rodovia Presidente Dutra Km 303, Paraíso, 27536-000 Resende. - **FM:** 93.9. – **RJ06**) Praça Demerval Barbosa Moreira 28, 28610-160 Nova Friburgo. – **RJ07**) Rua Visconde de Inhaúma 37, 20091-000 Rio de Janeiro. – **RJ08**) Av. 24 de Outubro 201, 28100-000 Campos dos Goitacazes. – **RJ09**) Rua México 111, Sobreloja, 20031-145 Rio de Janeiro. – **RJ10**) Av. Djalma Beda Coube 719, 28500-000 Cantagalo. ☎ +55 24 555 4455. – **RJ11**) Rua do Russel 804, 22210-010 Rio de Janeiro. – **RJ12**) Praça da República 141-A, 3° andar, sala 306, 20211-350 Rio de Janeiro. ☎ +55 21 221 7447, 252 8413, 242 6328. 🖷 +55 21 232 1931. – **RJ13**) Av. Rui Barbosa 749, 3° andar, 27910-260 Macaé. – **RJ14**) Rua do Russel 434, Glória, 22210-010 Rio de Janeiro. – **RJ15**) Av. Portugal 96, Urca, 22291-050 Rio de Janeiro. ☎ +55 21 295 8770, 295 0332. 🖷 +55 21 295 3920. – **RJ16**) Av. Meriti 2584, Vila da Penha, 21250-000 Rio de Janeiro. – **RJ17**) Praça Mauá 7, 21° andar, 20081-240 Rio de Janeiro. – **RJ18**) Rua do Bispo, 20261-060 Rio de Janeiro. – **RJ19**) Rua Julio Maria 10, Centro, 23900-900 Angra dos Reis. – **RJ20**) Rua Machado Bittencourt 300, 26900-000 Miguel Pereira. – **RJ21**) Av. Sete de Setembro 380, 28013-000 Campos dos Goitacazes. – **RJ22**) Estrada Velha da Pavuna 3517, 20765-170 Rio de Janeiro. – **RJ23**) Av. Dep. Alair Ferreira 201, Turf-Club, 28022-000 Campos dos Goitacazes. – **RJ24**) Rua Duque de Caxias 627, 25802-120 Três Rios. ☎🖷 +55 242 52 0720, 52 1797. – **FM:** 89.7. – **RJ25**) Rua do Russel 434, Glória, 22210-010 Rio de Janeiro. **Web:** www.radioglobo.com.br – **RJ26**) Rua Carlos Lacerda 75, 28013-030 Campos dos Goitacazes. – **RJ27**) Rua do Livramento 189, 8° andar, 20221-191 Rio de Janeiro. **Web:** www.tupi-am.com.br – **RJ28**) Rua Alberto Torres 410, 28400-000 São Fidelis. – **RJ29**) Av. 28 de Setembro 258, 20551-031 Rio de Janeiro. – **RJ30**) Av. Treze de Maio 23, 6° andar, 20031-000 Rio de Janeiro. – **RJ31**) Rua Carlos de Lacerda 52, 2° andar, 28013-030 Campos de Goytacazes. – **RJ32**) Rua 9 No. 12, Alto Cristo Redentor, Bairro Santa Teresa, 27400-000 Barra Mansa. – **RJ33**) Estrada do Dende 659, Ilha do Governador, 21920-000 Rio de Janeiro. ☎ +55 21 396 6969. – **Esperanto:** Wed 2330, Sun 1100. – **RJ34**) Av. Cardoso Moreira 422, Sobrado, Centro, 28300-000 Itaperuna. ☎ +55 24 3824 1410. – **RJ35**) Rua do Mercado 34/1101, 20010-120 Rio de Janeiro. – **RJ36**) Av. Joaquim Leite 279, 2° andar, Centro, 27330-042 Barra Mansa. – **RJ37**) Rua Dr. Temistocles de Almeida 97, 28470-000 Santo Antônio de Pádua. – **RJ38**) Praça Nilo Peçanha 42, 27123-020 Barra do Piraí. – **RJ39**) Praça Procópio Ferreira 22, 26000-000 Nova Iguaçu. – **RJ40**) Rodovia BR-101 km. 270, 28800-000 Rio Bonito. ☎ +55 21 734 0069/0929. – **RJ41**) Rua 100 No. 01, Bairro Laranjal, 27255-000 Volta Redonda. – **RJ42**) Rua Tenente Coronel Cardoso 359, Centro, 28013-460 Campos dos Goytacazes. – **RJ43**) Rua José Augusto da Costa 14, 25953-160 Teresópolis. – **RJ44**) Rua Comandante Vergueiro da Cruz 151, Olaria, 21021-020 Rio de Janeiro. – **RJ45**) Rua Paulino Padilha 80, 28460-000 Miracema. – **RJ46**) Rua Alencar Lima 26, 25620-050 Petrópolis. – **FM:** 88.5. – **RJ47**) Rua Vereador Darcy Teixeira Fontes 556, 23815-270 Itaguaí. ☎ +55 21 688 2267. 🖷 +55 21 688 1684. – **RJ48**) Rua Carneiro de Mendonça 29-A, 27600-000 Valença. – **RJ49**) Praça Governador Portela 18, 28360-000

Bom Jesus do Itabapoana. – **RJ50**) Av. Amaral Peixoto 366, 28860-000 Casimiro de Abreu. – **RJ51**) Rua Frei Valerio 58, 28740-00 Conceição de Macabu. – **RJ52**) Rua Nilo Peçanha 320, 27542-210 Resende. – **RJ53**) Rua Visconde de Inhaúma 37, 12° andar, 20091-000 Rio de Janeiro. – **RJ54**) Praça Carmelo Dutra 155, 28540-000 Paraíba do Sul. – **RJ55**) Av. Presidente Kennedy 1763, 25010-001 Duque de Caxias. – **RJ56**) Rua Figueiras de Barros 100, 28210-000 Italva. – **RJ57**) Praça Porto Rocha 56, Grupos 102/110, 28905-250 Cabo Frio. **Email:** radiocabofrio@mar.com.br – **RJ58**) Rua Coronel Santiago 250, 25950-000 Teresópolis. – **RJ59**) Rua México – Sala 811, 28500-000 Cantagalo.

RN00) RIO GRANDE DO NORTE

RN01) Av. Duque de Caxias 106, Ribeira, 59010-200 Natal. **Web:** www.cabugi.globo.com/radioglobonatal/ ☎ +55 84 221 3480/3485. 🖷 +55 84 211 1117/6978. – **RN02**) Praça Dom José de Madeiros Delgado s/n, 59300-000 Caicó. **Web:** www.radioruraldecaico.com.br ☎ +55 84 421 2270, 417 1887. 🖷 +55 84 421 1229. – **RN03**) Rua Dos Transmissores 10, Bairro Nordeste, 59042-070 Natal. ☎ +55 84 653 3780. **Web:** www2.eol.com.br/clientes/ieadem.central.htm – **RN04**) Rua João Pessoa 22, 1° andar, 59380-000 Currais Novos. **Web:** www.radiocurraisnovosam.com.br ☎ +55 84 431 1844. 🖷 +55 84 431 1907. – **RN05**) Praça Vigário Antonio Joaquim 39, 59600-160 Mossoró. **Email:** rrural@serv2000.com.br ☎ +55 84 321 1001. 🖷 +55 84 321 3820. – **RN06**) Rua Dr. Almeida Castro 49, 59600-160 Mossoró. ☎ +55 84 321 3849. 🖷 +55 84 321 3850. – **RN07**) Rua Açú 335, Tirol, 59020-110 Natal. ☎ +55 84 206 6256. – **RN08**) Rua Dr. Cunha Mora s/n, 59600-160 Mossoró. ☎ 🖷 +55 84 317 5247. – **RN09**) Rua Romualdo Galvão 973, Tirol, 59056-100 Natal. **Email:** tropical@digi.com.br **Web:** www.redetropical.com.br ☎ +55 84 211 6400. 🖷 +55 84 211 6918/6507. – **RN10**) Av. Deodoro 245, 59012-600 Natal. ☎ +55 84 214 2025. – **RN11**) Praça Des. Tomás Salustino 42, 59380-000 Currais Novos. ☎ +55 84 431 1596. 🖷 +55 84 431 1266. – **RN12**) Rua Francisca Delfina 30, Centro, 59860-620 Alexandria. ☎ +55 84 381 2320/2321. – **RN13**) Praça Bento Praxedes 104, 59600-620 Mossoró. ☎ 🖷 +55 84 321 3133/1430. – **RN14**) Rua Otávio Amorim 643, 59650-000 Açu. ☎ +55 84 331 1222. – **RN15**) Rua Reinaldo Pimenta 56, Centro, 59780-300 Caraúbas. ☎ 🖷 +55 84 337 2229. – **RN16**) Rua Frei Alberto Cabral 08, 59215-000 Nova Cruz. ☎ 🖷 +55 84 281 2123. – **RN17**) Rua Getúlio Vargas 1296, Centro, 59900-000 Pau dos Ferros. ☎ 🖷 +55 84 351 2388/2389. – **RN18**) Av. Augusto Monteiro 415, Centro, 59300-300 Caicó. ☎ +55 84 421 2500. 🖷 +55 84 421 1988. – **RN19**) Rua Barão do Rio Branco 173, 59615-000 Areia Branca. ☎ 🖷 +55 84 332 2200/2025. – **RN20**) Rua Ana de Pontes 419, 59255-000 Santo Antônio. ☎ +55 84 282 2347. 🖷 +55 84 282 2346. – **RN21**) Rua Odorico Ferreira de Souza 70, 59200-000 Santa Cruz. **Email:** radiosantacruz@inhare.com.br ☎ +55 84 291 2300. 🖷 +55 84 291 2201. – **RN22**) Rua Esperidião Coimbra 22, Centro Macau, 59500-000 Macau. – **RN23**) Rua Cícero Tomás de Acevedo 1050, Cruz do Monte, 59360-000 Parelhas. ☎ 🖷 +55 84 471 2401. – **RN24**) Rua Heráclito Vilar s/n, 59570-000 Ceará Mirim. ☎ +55 84 274 2794. 🖷 +55 84 274 2119. – **RN25**) Rua Sebastião Guilherme Caldas s/n, 59343-000 Jardim do Seridó. ☎ 🖷 +55 84 472 2450. – **RN26**) Rua Coronel Martiniano 1077, 59300-000 Caicó. ☎ +55 84 421 1848. 🖷 +55 84 417 1112. – **RN27**) Rua São Jorge 1290, Vale Dourado, 59104-200 Natal. ☎ +55 84 664 1330. – **RN28**) Rua Padre Cosme 45, Centro, 59930-000 São Miguel. ☎ +55 84 353 2166. 🖷 +55 84 353 2112. – **RN29**) Rua Coronel Freire 242, Centro, 59460-000 São Paulo do Potengi. ☎ +55 84 251 2263. 🖷 +55 84 251 2381. – **RN30**) Av. 21 de Abril 460, BR-460, 59550-000 João Câmara. ☎ 🖷 +55 84 262 2189. – **RN31**) Rua Joel do Amaral Gurgel s/n, Bairro Cohab, 59700-000 Apodi. ☎ +55 84 333 2528. – **RN32**) Rua do Chafariz 1390, Bairro Novo Horizonte, 59584-000 Touros. ☎ +55 84 263 2121. 🖷 +55 84 263 2526. – **RN33**) 59515-000 Angicos.

RO00) RONDÔNIA

RO01) Rua Joaquim Nabuco 1573, 79815-350 Porto Velho. – **RO02**) Av. Rondônio s/n, 78987-000 Rolim de Moura. – **RO03**) Av. Jamari 4218, 78932-000 Ariquemes. – **RO04**) Rua Capitão Silvio 145, 78961-730 Ji-Paraná. **Email:** rd-alvorada@ulbrajp.com.br ☎ +55 (69) 421 5233/5293. – **RO05**) Rua Rui Barbosa 3375, 78975-000 Cacoal. – **RO06**) Rua Costa e Silva 1297, Vila Jotão, 78964-140 Ji-Paraná. +55 69 421 0054 **Email:** radioji-parana@bol.com.br. – **RO07**) Rua Dom Augusto 681, Centro, 78958-000 Ji-Paraná. – **RO08**) Rua Ricardo Catanhede esquina com a Rua Goiás s/n, 78941-000 Jaru. – **RO09**) Praça Mario Correa 90, 78957-000 Guajará Mirim. ☎ +55 69 541 2274. **Email:** radioeducadora@uol.com.br - **FM:** 93.7. – **RO10**) Rua Dourados 4, Setor de Areas Especiais, 78932-000 Ariquemes. – **RO11**) Rua das Crianças 4646, Areal da Floresta, 78912-210 Porto Velho. **Web:** www.radiocaiari.com.br **Email:** caiari@radiocaiari.com.br +55 69 210 3621. – **RO12**) Rua Princesa Isabel 128, 78995-000 Vilhena. – **RO13**) C.P. 005, 78900-970 Porto Velho. – **RO14**) Loteamento Monte Alegre, Quadras 35, 36, 38, 39, 41 e 42, 78987-000 Rolim de Moura. – **RO15**) Rua Carlos Doneje esquina com Monteiro Lobato, 78984-000 Pimenta Bueno. – **RO16**) Setor Prefeitura de Characas – Ara de Faculdade, 78995-000 Vilhena. **Web:** www.radioplanalto.com.br – **RO17**) Rua Miguel Chakian 1300, Bairro Embratel, 78906-300 Porto Velho. ☎ +55 69 225 3053. 🖷 +55 69 225 3002. – **RO18**) Rua 06 de Maio 211, Bairro Casa Preta, 78960-000 Ji-Paraná. – **English:** 0000-0200. – **RO19**) Rua Sergipe 1766, Morada do Sol, 78983-000 Espigão d'Oeste. – **RO20**) 78949-000 Ouro Preto d'Oeste. – **RO21**) 78941-000 Jaru. – **RO22**) 78984-000 Pimenta Bueno. – **RO23**) 78975-000 Cacoal.

RR00) RORAIMA

RR01) Av. Capitão Ene Garcez 860, São Francisco, 69301-160 Boa Vista. ☎🖷 +55 95 623 2259. **Email**: radioadm@technet.com.br **Web:** www.radiororaima.com.br - **F.Pl**: new tr's. – **RR02**) Rua Sebastião Diniz 363, 69360-000 Caracaraí. – **RR03**) 69350-000 Alto Alegre. – **RR04**) 69300-000 Boa Vista. – **RR05**) 69380-000 Bonfim.

RS00) RIO GRANDE DO SUL

RS01) Av. Vitor Barreto 3056, Conj. 207, 92010-901 Canoas. ☎+55 51 472 4000 +55 51 476 5077 **Web:** www.radiororaima.com.br **Email:** radioreal@terra.com.br – **RS02**) Av. Antunes Ribas 1535, 98801-630 Santo Angelo. – **RS03**) Rua Marechal Deodoro 1157, 96800-000 Santa Cruz. **Email:** radiosantacruz@viavale.com.br +55 51 3715 5958 – **RS04**) Rua General Sampaio 161, Bairro Rio Branco, 95097-000 Caxias do Sul. **Email:** comercial@maisnova.fm.br ☎+55 54 226 2222 🖷+55 54 226 1003 - **FM:** 98.5 – **RS05**) Av.Scarpelini Guezzi 353, 99072 000 Passo Fundo **Email:** info@radioplanalto.com +55 54 313 2587 +55 54 311 3088 – **RS06**) Rua Mascarenhas de Morães 586,, 97300-000 São Gabriel. **Email:** comercial-redecomunidade@brturbo.com.br +55 55 232 6336 +55 55 232 6440 – **RS07**) Rua Moreira Paz 726, 95200-000 Vacaria. **Email:** rdfatima@radiofatima.am.br **Web:** www.radiofatima.am.br +55 54 232 2218 - **FM:** 101.5. "R. Mais Nova FM" – **RS08**) Praça Oswaldo Aranha 39, 97540-000 Alegrete. +55 55 242 1600 +55 55 422 1235. – **RS09**) Av. Ipiranga 1075, 2° andar, 90160-093 Porto Alegre. **Email:** gaucha@rdgaucha.com.br **Web:** www.clicrbs.com.br ☎ +55 51 3218 6600. 🖷+55 51 3218 6680. – Satellite signal downlinked via 165 st's in southern Brazil forming Rede Gaúcha Sat. – **RS10**) C.P. 284, 96001-970 Pelotas. – **RS11**) Rua Suécia 255, 98500-000 Tenente Portela. **Email:** municipal@redemeganet.com.br ☎+55 55 551 1395 +55 55 551 1211 – **RS12**) Rua 14 de Julho 588, 95300-000 Lagoa Vermelha. **Web:** www.radiocacique.am.br **Email:** rcacique@radiocacique.am.br +55 54 358 1788. – **RS13**) Rua Venâncio Aires 1851, 97010-003 Santa Maria. – **RS14**) Rua Delfino Riet 183, 90660-120 Porto Alegre. **Email:** ouvinte@bandrs.com.br .Web: www.bandrs.com.br ☎+55 51 3218 2100/2190 – **RS15**) Av. Mauricio Cardoso 88, 1° andar, 99700-000 Erechim. ☎🖷+55 54 321 2243. **Email:** radiodifusao@clicalpha.com.br - **FM:** 94.9 – **RS16**) Rua Voluntários da Patria 1432, 97590-000 Rosário do Sul. ☎+55 55 231 2533 🖷+55 55 231 4141 – **RS17**) Rua Farroupilha 110, 95200-000 Vacaria. **Email:** produrora@radioesmeralda.com.br +55 54 231 2961 +55 54 231 3803 – **RS18**) Rua Neita Ramos 217, 96230-000 Santa Vitória do Palmar. **Email:** rcultura@planetsul.com.br +55 53 263 1660 – **RS19**) Rua Domingos Secchi s/n, 99500-000 Carazinho. **Email:** gazeta670@ciinet.com.br +55 54 330 1396 +55 54 330 2800 – **RS20**) Travessa 4 de Junho 84, 98380-000 Seberi. **Email:** radiseb@fesau.psr.br – **RS21**) Rua XV de Novembro 275, 9° andar, 98700-000 Ijuí. **Email:** rpi.iju@terra.com.br **Web:** www.radioprogresso.com.br ☎+55 55 332 8888. 🖷+55 55 332 9999. – **RS22**) Rua Marechal Mascarenhas de Morães 298, 97300-000 São Gabriel. ☎+55 232 2244 +55 55 232 5920. **Email:** rbatovi.comerciais@terra.com.br – **RS23**) Rua Caldas Jr. 219, 2° andar, 90019-900 Porto Alegre. **Email:** portela@cpovo.net **Web:** www.guaiba.com.br ☎+55 51 3215 6222. 🖷+55 51 215 6223. – **RS24**) Av. Scarpelini Ghezzi 353, 99072-000 Passo Fundo. - **FM:** 105.9. – **RS25**) Av. Júlio de Castilhos 435, 98300-000 Palmeiradas Missões **Email:** rp101@mksnet.com.br +55 55 742 1082 +55 742 2626. – **RS26**) Av. Silva Paes 363 "A", 96200-340 Rio Grande. **Email:** nativa@vetorialnet.com.br ☎+55 53 231 5188. – **RS27**) Av. Marechal Floriano 920, Sala 301, 95520-000 Osório. **Web:** www.litoralgaucho.com.br/radioosorio **Email:** radioosorio@gln.com.br ☎+55 51 663 3435/663 3436. 🖷+55 51 663 3344. – **RS28**) Rua Botucaraí 911, 96930-000 Candelária. **Email:** radioprincesa@teksa.com.br +55 51 3743 1031 – **RS29**) Av. Duque de Caxias 736, 98470-000 Planalto +55 55 3794 1025. – **RS30**) Rua Santiago Matiotti 670, 99500-000 Carazinho. – **RS31**) Rua Orfanatrófio 711, 90840-440 Porto Alegre. **Web:** www.pampa.com.br **Email:** pampa@pampa.com.br ☎+55 51 3233 8311. – **RS32**) Rua São João 567, 96640-000 Rio Pardo **Email:** sucursalpoa@gazetadosul.com.arg +55 51 731 2199. – **RS33**) Campus de Universidade Federal de Santa Maria, 10° andar, Reitoria, 97105-900 Santa Maria. – **RS34**) Rua Fernando Abott 427, 2° andar, 95880-000 Estrela. **Email:** radioaltotaquari@bewnet.com.br. – **RS35**) Rua Voluntários da Pátria 805, 98025-770 Cruz Alta. – **RS36**) Rua Silveiro 1321, 90850-000 Porto Alegre. ☎+55 51 3227 6809. – **RS37**) Rua Dr. Bozano 1336,3° andar, Galeria do Comércio (C.P. 278), 97010-902 Santa Maria. **Email:** ze.f@terra.com.br ☎🖷+55 55 223 0187. – **RS38**) Rua Coronel Correa Lima 1831, 90850-250 Porto Alegre. ☎ +55 51 3231 0127, 3233 4009. – **RS39**) Rua Marechal Deodoro 101, Galeria Central, 7° andar, 95700-000 Bento Gonçalves. **Email:** progeral@dsk.com.br +55 54 451 3999 +55 54 451 3578 - **FM:** 94.5. – **RS40**) Praça da Bandeira 36, 2° andar, 98900-000 Santa Rosa. **Email:** noroeste@viabrazil.com.br ☎+55 55 3512 5757. – **RS41**) Rua 15 de Novembro 336, 99770-000 Aratiba. – **RS42**) Rua Nações Unidas 1876, 93310-500 Nôvo Hamburgo. ☎+55 51 593 3311/593 9845. – **RS43**) Rua 7 de Setembro 1441, 95800-000 Venâncio Aires. **Email:** gravacao@gruporva.com.br - **FM:** 105.1. – **RS44)** Rua Saihydi Abrahão 315, 95590-000 Tramandaí. – **RS45)** Rua Garibaldi 789,21° andar, 95084-900 Caxias do Sul. **Web:** www.radiocaxias.am.br/ – **RS46)** Av. Brasil 523, 98801-590 Santo Ângelo. **Email:** radiosan@radiosantoangelo.com.br **Web:** home.missoes.com.br/radio_ sto_angelo/+55 55 313 2440/5397. – **RS47)** Av. Alberto Müller 242, 95900-000 Lajeado **Email:** comercial@independente.com.br – **RS48)** Rua Venâncio Aires 1980, 97010-004 Santa Maria. **Email:** radioimembui@pro.viars.com.br +55 55 221 3475 +55 55 221 3476. – **RS49)** Rua Orfanatrófio 711, 90840-440, Porto Alegre. **Email:** pampa@pampa.com.br **Web:** www.pampa.com.br ☎+55 51 3233 8311. – **RS50)** Av. Getúlio Vargas 412, 98670-000 Humaitá. **Email:** radioaltouruguai@mousenet.com.br +55 55 525 1212 +55 55 525 1222 – **RS51)** Rua Otacílio Tupanciretã de Azevedo 2, 98170-000 Tupanciretã. ☎+55 55 272 1753 ☎℻+55 55 352 1865 - **FM:** 92.5. – **RS52)** Av. Fiorentino Bachi 791, 99840-000 Sananduva. ☎+55 54 343 1438. ℻+55 54 343 1682. **Email:** radiosananduva@terra.com.br - **FM:** 97.7. – **RS53)** Rua Garibaldi 789, 21° andar, 95084-900 Caxias do Sul. – **RS54)** Rua Julio de Castilhos 2236, 97800-000 São Luís Gonzaga. **Email:** missioneira@viacom.com.br ☎+55 55 3352 4141. ℻+55 55 3352 4562. – **RS55)** Av. David José Martins 1206, 98700-000 Ijuí. **Email:** radioreporter@ijuinet.com.br ☎℻+55 55 3332 8000. - **FM:** 101.5 "Iguatemi". – **RS56)** Rua General Zeca Netto 1396, 96180-000 Camaquã. **Email:** radiorc@terra.com.br ☎+55 51 671 2144. – **RS57)** Rua São João 1894, 97800-000 São Luís Gonzaga. **Email:** radioslg@terre.com.br. +55 55 3352 4440 +55 55 3352 4444 – **RS58)** Rua 15 de Novembro 236, 96570-000 Caçapava do Sul. **Web:** www.radiocacapava.com.br/ **Email:** radiocacapava@farrapo.com.br – **RS59)** Rua Tucunduva 758, 98640-000 Crissiumal. **Email:** metrópolo@virnet.com.br +55 55 524 1212 +55 55 524 1223 – **RS60)** Rua Marechal Deodoro 101,Galeria Central, 7° andar, 95700-000 Bento Gonçalves. **Email:** grabento@dsk.com.br +55 54 451 3999 +55 54 451 3578 - **FM:** 92.5 "Serrana". – **RS61)** Rua João Carlos Machado 645, 98460-000 Iraí. **Email:** maraba@speedrs.com.br +55 55 745 144. – **RS62)** Rua Sarmento Leite 426, 90046-900 Porto Alegre. **Web:** www.ufrgs.br/radio **Email:** radio@orion.ufgrs.br ☎+55 51 3221 5047, 3316 3417. - **Spanish:** Fri 2400. – **RS63)** Rua Ramiro Barcelos 2092, 96508-070 Cachoeira do Sul. **Email:** radiocachoeira@netcentro.com.br ☎+55 51 3722 4022 ℻+55 51 3722 4313 - **German & Italian:** 3 h weekly. – **RS64)** Praça Pe. Basso 95, 99800-000 Marcelino Ramos +55 54 372 1389. – **RS65)** Av. Bento Gonçalves 733, 98870-000 Giruá. ☎+55 55 361 2065 +55 55 3361 2020 **Email:** radio@srgirua.com.br – **RS66)** Rua Dr. João Azevedo 220, 96300-000 Jaguarão. – **RS67)** Rua Padre Oswaldo Stracke 56, 96900-000 Sobradinho. ☎+55 51 742 1089, 742 1090. **Email:** radiosobradinho@terra.com.br - **FM:** 97.3. – **RS68)** Rua Borges do Canto 1056, 97650-000 Itaqui **Email:** frontur@bnet.com.br +55 55 433 2233 +55 55 433 1933 – **RS69)** Rua Ten. Cel. Corrêa Lima 1960, 90850-250 Porto Alegre. **Web:** www.clicrbs.com.br ☎+55 51 3218 5759. ℻+55 51 3218 6680. – **RS70)** Av. Rio Branco 809, 97010-122 Santa Maria. **Web:** www.infoway.com.br/medianeira **Email:** radiomed@terra.com.br +55 55 222 9500 +55 55 222 0310. – **RS71)** Rua Pinheiro Machado 628, 98005-000 Cruz Alta. **Email:** gravadorarca@comnet.com.br ☎+55 55 3322 7222. - **FM:** 105.1. – **RS72)** Rua Santana 2499/501, 97500-004 Uruguaiana. **Email:** fm96@fm969.com.br – **RS73)** Rua André Kopaeff 02, 96750-000 Butiá. **Email:** radiosob@terra.com.br +55 51 652 1140 – **RS74)** Rua Ruy Barbosa 96, 95180-000 Farroupilha. **Email:** radiomiriam@radiomiriam.com.br ☎+55 54 261 1204/261 2121 – **RS75)** Rua Tenente Lira 950, 98400-000 Frederico Westphalen. **Web:** www.luzealegria.com.br **Email:** radio@luzealegria.com.br ☎ +55 55 744 6003. - **Italian & Polish:** Sun 0930 & 1600. - **FM:** 95.9. – **RS76)** Rua General Osório 1160, 97760-000 Jaguari. **Email:** rjaguar@santiagonet.com.br +55 55 255 1474. – **RS77)** Rua Félix da Cunha 328, 3° andar, 96010-000 Pelotas **Email:** opcalfa@ig.com.br +55 53 222 6584 +55 53 225 7742. – **RS78)** Av. Coronel Victor Villa Verde 491, 95500-000 Santo Antônio da Patrulha. **Email:** elinesouza@terra.com.br – **RS79)** Av. 7 de Setembro 1115, 96400-001 Bagé. **Email:** difusora@difusorabage.com.br. +55 53 242 5211 – **RS80)** Rua 7 de Setembro 366,(C.P. 326) 99010-121 Passo Fundo. **Web:** www.rduirapuru.com.br **Email:** comercial@rduirapuru.com.br ☎℻+55 54 313 6611. – **RS81)** Av. Maurício Cardoso 697, 99300-000 Soledade. ☎+55 54 381 1144 +55 54 381 4360 **Email:** cristal@gampnet.com.br - **FM:** 99.1. – **RS82)** Rua da Anunciação s/n, Morro do Convento, 97900-000 Cerro Largo. ☎+55 55 3359 2022. ℻+55 55 3359 1291. – **German:** Tuesday 1230-1330. - **FM:** 105.9 "Shamballa". – **RS83)** Rua João Batista Scalabrini 346, 99250-000 Serafina Corrêa. ☎+55 54 244 1212, 244 1089. – **Dialeto Veneto:** Sun 1030-1230. – **RS84)** Rua Torres Gonçalves 33, 99700-000 Erechim. **Email:** radio.erechim@pro.viars.com.br +55 54 522 1389 +55 54 522 1289 – **RS85)** Próximo ao Km 233 da BR-392, 97340-000 São Sepé. **Email:** radfunco@plugnet.psi.br +55 55 233 1163 – **RS86)** Travessa Francisco de Leonardo Trudo 40, 90010-050 Porto Alegre. ☎+55 51 3221 8711. – **RS87)** Rua Domingos de Almeida 2194, 97500-003 Uruguaiana. ☎+55 55 412 1731 +55 55 412 3046 **Email:** amfmradiocharrua@uol.com.br – **RS88)** Rua Coronel Vitor Dumoncel 1756, 98240-000 Santa Bárbara do Sul. **Email:** blume@express.com.br +55 55 372 1453 +55 55 372 1136 – **RS89)** Rua Rui Barbosa 373, 99600-000 Nonoai **Email:** radiononoai@pro.via-rs.com.br +55 54 362 1591 +55 54 362 1384 – **RS90)** Av. Luiz Fernando Luzatto 42, 95320-000 Nova Prata. **Email:** radioprata@netprata.com.br +55 54 242 1684 +55 54 242 1212. – **RS91)** Praça Dr. Ozy Teixeira 45/57, Cj. 2, 96610-000 Encruzilhada do Sul. **Email:** radien@viavale.com.br – **RS92)** Rua Júlio de Castilhos 430, 95290-000 Bom Jesus. **Email:** sectur@m2m.com.br ☎+55 54 237 1755. ℻ +55 54 237 1728. – **RS93)** Rua General Osório 1134, 98200-000 Ibirubá. **Email:** radioibiruba@coprel.com.br +55 54 324 1758 +55 54 324 1501 - **FM:** 96.6. – **RS94)** Rua Ponciano Ramos 74, 96700-000 São Jerônimo. **Email:** radiosaojeronimo@terra.com.br +55 51 651 4592. – **RS95)** Av. Júlio de Castilhos 1511, 8° andar, salas 81/84, 95010-003 Caxias do Sul. **Email:** radiodifusoracxs1250@terra.com.br +55 54 221 2658 +55 54 223 6788. – **RS96)** Rua 15 de Novembro 717, 96015-000 Pelotas **Email:** malhao@atlas.ucpel.tche.br +55 53 225 0930 +55 53 222 6167. – **RS97)** Rua Riachuelo 928, 97670-000 São Borja. – **RS98)** Rua Moron 1520, 95290 000 Cachoeira do Sul. **Web:** www.radiofandango.com.br/ **Email:** radiofandango@radiofandango.com.br - **FM:** 102.5. – **RS99)** Rua José Sponchiado 418, 99830-000 Gaurama. **Email:** radiogaurama@awo.com.br ☎℻+55 54 391 1134. - **Italian & Polish:** 1300-1400. – **RS100)** Rua Benjamim Santo Zago 601, 97220-000 Faxinal do Soturno. +55 55 263 1021 +55 55 263 1335 – **RS101)** Rua Balduino Schneider 254, 98920-000 Horizontina. **Email:** radioveracruz@mksnet.com.br +55 55 3537 1212 +55 55 3537 1414. – **RS102)** Rua Dr. Pio Ferreira 453, 96170-000 São Lourenço do Sul. +55 53 251 1303. **Email:** radio@cybersul.com.br - **German:** Sun 1100-. – **RS103)** Av. Angelo Macalós 246, 99400-000 Planetário. **Email:** liderfm@razaoinfo.combr ☎ +55 54 383 1082. - **German:** Sun 1600. - **FM:** 95.3. – **RS104)** Av. São Paulo 722, 3° andar, 90230-160 Porto Alegre. **Web:** www.lbv.org ☎+55 51 3337 6416 – **RS105)** Rua 25 de Julho 39, 98960-000 Santo Cristo. +55 55 541 1188/1205. – **RS106)** Rua João Goulart 131/102, 97574-001 Santana do Livramento. **Email:** radiocidade@bnet.com,.br +55 55 242 4544 – **RS107)** Av. Duque de Caxias 1320, 99560-000 Sarandi. ☎+55 54 361 1455 - **German & Italian:** Sat 1800, Sun 1100. – **RS108)** Av. Júlio de Castilhos 232, 95680-000 Canela. **Email:** radioclube@pdh.com.br +55 54 282 2000 +55 54 282 3632 – **RS109)** Rua General Osório 1276, 98280-000 Panambi **Email:** sulbrasileira@profnet.com.br +55 55 3375 33538 - **Italian:** 1300-1330 - **German:** Sun 1230-1255 – **RS110)** Rua Sete de Setembro 353, 96015-300 Pelotas.**Email:** radiopel.sul@terra.com.br +55 53 229 3174 +55 53 227 2382 – **RS111)** Av. Rio Branco 401, 96450-000 Dom Pedrito. **Email:** upacarai@provesul.com.br +55 53 243 3400/243-2658 +55 53 243 1257 – **RS112)** Rua Osvaldo Aranha 1052, 95190-000 São Marcos. **Email:** diplomata@nsol.com.br +55 54 291 1497 +55 54 291 2422 – **RS113)** Av. Ipiranga 1075, 2° andar, 90160-093 Porto Alegre. **Web:** www.clicrbs.com.br **Email:** cbn@rbsradios.com.br ☎+55 51 3218 6600. ℻+55 51 3218 6680 – **RS114)** Av. Scalabrini 777, 99200-000 Guaporé. **Email:** radioaurora@mastertek.com.br ☎+55 54 443 1212 +55 54 443 4624 - **Italian:** Sat 1700-1800 – **RS115)** Rua Daltro Filho 417, 98600-000 Três Passos. – **RS116)** Av. Concordia 1480, 96540-000 Agudo. **Email:** radioagudo@terra.com.br – **RS117)** Rua Tiradentes 402, 99150-000 Marau **Email:** producao@alvorada.am.br +55 342 3300 +55 54 342 3438 - **FM:** 94.7 "Kosmos" – **RS118)** Rua Frei Eugenio 657, 95270-000 Flores da Cunha. – **RS119)** Rua Gaspar Martins 55, 97542-000 Alegrete. ☎ +55 55 422 1829 – **RS120)** Rua Conde de Porto Alegre 521, 97573-581 Santana do Livramento. **Email:** cultura@v-expressa.com.br +55 55 242 3136 – **RS121)** Praa 15 de Novembro 1369 2° andar, 99490-000 Tapera. +55 54 385 1166 – **RS122)** Rua Chaves Barcelos 36/705, 90030-120 Porto Alegre. ☎+55 51 3228 9903 – **RS123)** Rua Pedro Toniollo 529, Centro, 99900-000 Getúlio Vargas. **Email:** sideral@itake.com.br ☎+55 54 341 1555 +55 54 341 1554 – **RS124)** Rua Augusto Rossi 316, 97200-000 Restinga Seca. **Email:** radioint@piq.com.br ☎+55 55 261 1270 +55 55 261 1030 – **RS125)** Rua Marechal Floriano Peixoto 178, 96205-190 Rio Grande. **Email:** minuanorg@terra.com.br +55 53 232 5597. – **RS126)** Rua São Francisco 246, 98900-000 Santa Rosa. **Email:** lidersom@vuabrazil.com.br +55 55 512 5265 – **RS127)** Rua Dr. Montaury 617, 95330-000 Veranópolis. **Email:** publicidade@radioveranense.com.br +55 54 4411877 – **RS128)** Rua Ramiro Barcelos 1206 - Centro, 96901-900 Santa Cruz do Sul. **Email:** gazeta1180@viavale.com,.br +55 51 711 2211/715 7814- **FM:** 101.7. – **RS129)** Rua General Osorio 1080, 96600-000 Canguçu. **Web:** www.supersul.com.br/radiocultura/ ☎℻+55 53 252 1144. – **RS130)** Av. das Hortencias 78, 95670-000 Gramado +55 54 286 1902 +55 54 286 4718 – **RS131)** Rua São João 1637, 95780-000 Montenegro **Email:** r.am.fm@terra.com.br – **RS132)** Rua Benjamin Constant 327, 96200-400 Rio Grande. ☎℻+55 53 231 3169 **Email:** cassinoam@vetorial.net – **RS133)** Av. Sete de Setembro 672, 96400-000 Bagé. ☎+55 53 242 1471 ℻+55 53 242 1211 – **RS134)** Rua Borges de Medeiros 401, 95560-000 Torres. **Email:** studion@terra.com.br – **RS135)** Travesa Dr. Bruno Dockhorn 18, 98910-000 Três de Maio. **Email:** radiocolonial@mksnet.com.br ☎+55 55 535 1022 ℻+55 55 535 2488 – **RS136)** Rua José Arnoldo Klaus 60, Sl. 03, 93700-000 Campo Bom. **Email:** radio1470@gruposinos.com.br – **RS137)** Rua Julio de Castilhos 325, 95720-000 Garibaldi. **Web:** www. radiogaribaldi.com.br ☎+55 54 462 1557 ℻+55 54 462 5522 - **Italian:** Sat 1800-1900, Sun 1030-1200. - **FM:** 88.1 – **RS138)** Rua Gabriel Machado 1590, 4° andar,

97610-000 São Francisco de Assis. **Email:** radiodifusão@terra.com.br +55 55 252 1166 +55 55 252 1455 – **RS139**) Rua General Osorio 943, 96600-000 Canguçu. **Email:** liberdade@supersul.com.br +55 53 252 1515 – **RS140**) Rua Rio Branco 1006, 95600-000 Taquara. **Web:** www.jornalpanorama.com.br/am **Email:** panorama@faccat.br ☎+55 51 542 2288 +55 51 542 2222 – **RS141**) Rua São Vicente 345, 96501-180 Cachoeira do Sul. **Email:** rdc@netcentro.com.br +55 51 3723 1465 – **RS142**) Av. Rio Branco 616, 98770-000 Catuípe. **Email:** aguasclaras@san.psi.br +55 55 336 1042 – **RS143**) C.P. 144, 96450-970 Dom Pedrito. – **RS144**) Rua Independência 197, 3° andar, 93010-001 São Leopoldo. ☎+55 51 592 1483 +55 51 592 1214 **Email:** rdsaoleo@zaz.com.br – **RS145**) Rua Cel. Amâncio Cardoso 596, 99950-000 Tapejara. ☎+55 54 344 1185/1600. **Email:** tapejaraam@netvisual.com.br - **Italian & German:** Sat 1230-1400, Sun 1300-1400 – **RS146**) Trav. Jaime Pinto 136, 97700-000 Santiago. **Email:** zyk297@radiosantiago.com.br +55 55 251 1487 – **RS147**) Av. Flores da Cunha 4402, Conjuntos 301 e 303, 94950-001 Cachoeirinha. **Email:** radiometropole@terra.com.br – **RS148**) Rua 7 de Setembro 792, 95960-000 Encantado. **Email:** becker@encantadoam.com.br – **RS149**) Rua Assis Brasil 263, 98130-000 Júlio de Castilhos. **Email:** radio14@datanews.com.br +55 55 271 1414 – **RS150**) Rua José Bonifácio 41, 96330-000 Arroio Grande. **Email:** miguel@dominet.com.br ☎ +55 53 262 1008. – **RS151**) Rua Paraguai 42, 98980-000 Porto Lucena **Email:** radnaveg@uol.com.br ☎+55 55 565 1200 🖷+55 55 565 1221 – **RS152**) Av. Valdomiro Bocchese 872, 95250-000 Antônio Prado. **Email:** radiosolaris@nol.com.br ☎+55 54 293 1110 +55 54 293 1099. – **RS153**) Av. Padre Reus 1344, 2° andar, 97930-000 Caibaté. **Email:** radiocaibate@viacom.com.br +55 55 355 1349 – **RS154**) Rua Rui Barbosa 46, 1° andar, 96360-000 Pedro Osório. – **RS155**) Av. Borges de Medeiros 1462, 97650-000 Itaqui **Email:** pirfm@itaqui.com.br +55 55 433 2292. – **RS156**) C.P. 241, 98590-970 Santo Augusto. **Email:** querencia@abol.com.br ☎ +55 55 781 1255, 781 1675, 781 1439. – **RS157**) Rua Baltazar Brum 343, 97560-000 Quaraí **Email:** quarai@terre.com.br +55 55 423 3001. – **RS158**) Rua José Porfirio 663 (C.P. 80), 95860-000 Taquari. **Email:** radioacoriana@taquari.com.br – **RS159**) 99300-000 Soledade. – **RS160**) Rua Pery 625, Conjunto. 201, 95555-000 Capão da Canoa. ☎+55 51 625 2300. **Email:** radiohor@terra.com.br – **RS161**) Rua da República 220, 99530-000 Chapada. **Email:** radiosimpatia@chapadanet.inf.br – **RS162**) Av. Narciso Silva 1791, 96160-000 Capão do Leão. – **RS163**) Ao lado do Açude Pozobom, Distrito de Camobi, 97110-150 Santa Maria. **NB:** re. to R. Transmundial, C.P. 18300, 04626-970 São Paulo, SP. – **RS164**) Rua Coronel Scherer 195, 97400-000 São Pedro do Sul. **Email:** rsj4507@pro.viars.com.br +55 55 276 1311 +55 55 276 1255 – **RS165**) Rua Duque de Caxias 255, 98430-000 Palmitinho **Email:** radiochiru@mksnet.com.br +55 55 791 1244 +55 55 791 1175 – **RS166**) Rua João Maffesoni 10, 99680-000 Constantina. +55 54 363 1300. +55 54 363 1122. **Email:** atlantica@infe.com.br – **RS167**) Rua Severino Dias 599, 98580-000 Coronel Bicaco.+55 55 3557 1195. +55 55 3557 1220. – **RS168**) Av. Alto Jacuí 435, Terreo, 99470-000 Não Me Toque **Email:** radioceres@annex.com.br +55 54 332 1488 +55 54 332 1498. – **RS169**) Praça Getúlio Vargas 35, 97450-000 Cacequi. +55 55 254 1398 +55 55 254 1366 – **RS170**) Rua Sanaduva 178, 99855-000 São João da Urtiga. +55 54 532 1247. – **RS171**) Av. Borges de Medeiros 407, 96760-000 Tapes. **Email:** radiotapense@terra.com.br – **RS172**) Av. Antônio Finco 700 (C.P. 19), 99870-000 São José do Ouro. +55 54 352 1008 +55 54 352 1108 **Email:** radiopoata@ouronetonline.com.br – **RS173**) 98700-000 Ijuí. – **RS174**) Rua General Sampaio 18, Edificio Consorcio, Bl. Central, Conj. 09, 96400-370 Bagé. – **RS175**) Rua Pedro Alvares Cabral 164, 99660-000 Campinas do Sul. **Email:** radiocampinas@toirs.com.br +55 51 366 1266 – **RS176**) 96270-000 Mostardas. – **RS177**) Av. Barão do Triunfo 584, 95995-000 Arvorezinha. - **FM:** 92.3. – **RS178**) Rua Comandaí 615, Centro, 97950-000 Guarani das Missões. **Email:** radiogua@aterca.com.br +55 55 3353 1721. +55 55 3353 1722. – **RS179**) Rua Jornal NH 99, 93334-350 Novo Hamburgo. **Email:** radioabc@gruposinos.com.br +55 51 587 4000, 594 0470. – **RS180**) Rua 15 de Novembro 236, 96570-000 Caapava do Sul. +55 55 281 1495 **Email:** radiocapava@farrapo.com.br – **RS181**) Rua Duque de Caxias 963, Pelotas +55 53 221 0248. – **RS182**) Rua Francisco Getulio Vargas 1130, Petropols. **Email:** ucsradio@ucs.tch.br +55 54 218 2567 +55 54 218 2194 – **RS183**) Rua Anunciacão s/no M.Concento, 97900-000 Cerro Largo **Email:** radioshamballafm@pro.via.rs.com.br +55 55 359 1291 - **FM** - 105.9 – **RS184**) Rua Júlio de Castilhos 325, 95720 000 Garibaldi. **Email:** comercial@radiogaribaldi.com.br +55 54 462 1557 – **RS185**) Rua Rui Barbosa 46 1° andar, 96369 000 Pedro Osório **Email:** rclube@kerneonline.com.br +55 53 255 1397 +55 53 255 1228 – **RS186**) Av. Fiorentino Bachi 791, 99840-000 Sananduva. **Email:** radiosananduva@terre.com.br +55 54 343 1438 +55 54 343 1662 – **RS187**) Rua Borges de Medelros 407, 96760-000 Tapes. **Email:** radiotense@terra.com.br +55 51 672 1031/1266 – **RS188**) 97500- 000 Uruguaiana.

SC00) SANTA CATARINA

SC01) Rua Aristiliano Ramos 36, 89160-000 Rio do Sul. **Web:** www.grupomirador.com.br ☎ +55 478 22 2111 - **FM:** 93.3. – **SC02**) C.P. D2, 88801-970 Criciúma. – **SC03**) Av. Martin Piaseski 25, 89910-000 Descanso. ☎🖷 +55 498 23 0307. – **SC04**) Rua Benjamin Constant 286-D, 3. e 4. andares, 89801-070 Chapecó. – **SC05**) Rua Carlos Gomes 12, Centro, 89160-000 Rio do Sul. **Web:** www.superdifusora.am.br/ **Email:** difusora@softhouse.com.br ☎ +55 47 521 1155. 🖷 +55 47 521 1245. - **FM**: 94.9 "Amanda FM". – **SC06**) Rua João Beux Sobredinho 350, 89990-000 São Lourenço d'Oeste. **Web:** www.rdm.cmnnet.com.br ☎ +55 49 344 1544. 🖷 +55 49 344 1748. – **SC07**) Rua Carlos Jofre do Amaral 67, 88501-010 Lages. ☎ +55 49 221 3000. 🖷 +55 49 221 3030. – **SC08**) Av. Sete de Setembro 155, 89580-000 Fraiburgo. ☎ +55 492 46 2775, 46 2754, 46 3294. 🖷 +55 492 46 2877. – **SC09**) Rua Gustavo Richard 90, 88701-220 Tubarão. **Email:** rtuba@tro.matrix.com.br – **SC10**) Av. Antão s/ni, 88025-150 Florianópolis. **Email:** cbndiario@rbsradios.com.br ☎ +55 48 216 2500. 🖷 +55 48 216 2535. – **SC11**) Rua Leonel Mosele 275, 89700-000 Concórdia. ☎🖷 +55 49 442 1366, 442 1217. - **Italian & German:** Sun 1130, 1600. – **SC12**) Rua Angelo Dias 251, 89010-020 Blumenau. **Email:** neruam@terra.com.br – **SC13**) Rua da Criança s/n, 88840-000 Urussanga. **Email**: marconi@ceusanet.com.br ☎ +55 48 465 1055. 🖷 +55 48 465 1116. – **SC14**) Rua Venereanos dos Passos 385, 89560-000 Videira. **Web:** www.radiovideira.com.br/ – **SC15**) Rua Angelo Dias 207, 89010-020 Blumenau. **Email:** rfc@flynet.com.br ☎ +55 47 326 9699. 🖷 +55 47 326 6155. – **SC16**) Rua Itagiba 215, 88880-000 Lauro Müller. **Email:** radiocm@matrix.com.br ☎🖷 +55 48 464 3004. - **Italian:** Sat 1600. – **SC17**) C.P. 71, 89700-970 Concórdia. ☎ +55 494 42 2611. - **FM:** 96.3. – **SC18**) Rua Jaú Guedes da Fonseca 17, Coqueiros, 88080-080 Florianópolis. **Web:** lucio.jornalismo@radiosantacatarina.com.br - **FM:** 101.7 "Transamérica". – **SC19**) Rodovia SC-444 km. 3, 88820-000 Içara. – **SC20**) Rua Rodrigues Alves 111, 88350-000 Brusque. **Web:** www.radiocidadeam.com.br ☎ +55 47 351 4511. – **SC21**) Loteamento Jardim Portobello, Rua A, 88200-000 Tijucas. – **SC22**) Rua Barão de Rio Branco 229, 88870-000 Orleãns. – **SC23**) Rua José de Miranda Ramos 100, sala 105, 89820-000 Xanxerê. – **SC24**) C.P. 96, 88350-970 Brusque. **Web:** www.blumenau.zaz.com.br/970/ ☎🖷 +55 47 351 1744. - **FM:** 107.7. – **SC25**) Rua São Bonifacio 280. 89896-000 Itapiranga. **Web:** www.peperi.com.br ☎ +55 49 677 0238. – **SC26**) Rua Vereador Severiano F. Sombrio 684, 88750-000 Braço do Norte. – **SC27**) Av. Santa Catarina 25, 89840-000 Coronel Freitas. – **SC28**) Rua Otacilio Vieira da Costa 40, 88501-050 Lages. ☎ +55 492 22 3040, 22 3011, 22 4784. - **FM:** 95.7 "Amizade". – **SC29**) Av. Getúlio Vargas 234, 89130-000 Indaial. – **SC30**) C.P. 25, 89201-970 Joinville. – **SC31**) Rua Princesa Isabel 300, 2° andar, 88702-200 Tubarão. **Web:** www.redetabajara.com.br ☎ +55 48 626 5266. - **FM:** 98.9 "Band FM". – **SC32**) C.P. 1477, 88010-970 Florianópolis. – **SC33**) Av. Santa Catarina 828, 2° andar, 89885-000 São Carlos. **Email:** am1110@sancasnet.com.br ☎ +55 49 325 4355. 🖷 +55 49 325 4483. – **SC34**) Rua João Winkler 15, 89820-000 Xanxerê. ☎ +55 494 33 1110, 33 1115. 🖷 +55 494 33 0682. - **FM:** 101.3. – **SC35**) Rua Florianópolios 271, 89520-000 Curitibanos. **Email:** coroado@baroni.com.br **Web:** www.baroni.com.br/coroado ☎ +55 49 241 1140. 🖷 +55 49 241 0928. - **FM:** 98.9. – **SC36**) Rua 15 de Novembro 600, sala 401, 89010-000 Blumenau. – **SC37**) Rua Conselheiro Jeronimo Coelho 48, 88790-000 Laguna. – **SC38**) Rua Siqueira Campos 33, 89400-000 Porto União. – **SC39**) Rua Padre Auréliop 260, 89930-000 São José do Cedro. – **SC40**) Rua Otavianpo Dadan, 355-Centro, 88240-000 São João Batista. – **SC41**) C.P. 59, 89835-970 São Domingos. – **SC42**) Av. Patricio Lima 3073, Bairro São Bernardo, 88708-201 Tubarão. ☎ +55 48 628 0658, 628 0020. 🖷 +55 48 628 0638. – **SC43**) Rua Tenente Ary Rauen 1361, 89300-000 Mafra. - **FM:** 104.5 "Nova Era". – **SC44**) Rua Rui Barbosa 136, 89890-000 Cunha Porã. – **SC45**) Rua 9 de Março 737, 8° andar, 89201-400 Joinville. – **SC46**) Empresa Blumenauense de Comunicaão Ltd. Rua Indaial 208, 89012-060 Bluemau +55 47 3401260 **Web:** radiobluemau.com.br **Email:** radioblu@bnu.nutecnet.com.br. – **SC47**) Av. XV de Novembro 608, 89600-000 Joaçaba. **Web:** www.radiiocatarinense.com.br ☎ +55 49 522 0433. – **Italian:** Sun 1215-1500. - **FM:** 92.3. – **SC48**) Rua Osvaldo Cruz 68, Centro, 88790-000 Laguna. – **SC49**) Rua 400 No. 585, 88330-000 Balneário Camboriú. ☎ +55 473 67 1044, 67 1045, 67 2733. 🖷 +55 473 67 4949. – **SC50**) Rua Buenos Aires 131, 89051-050 Blumenau. – **SC51**) Rua Marechal Floriano Peixoto 161-0, Centro, 89802-010 Chapecó. **Email:** soesca@redamp.com.br ☎ +55 49 722 0688, 722 0658. 🖷 +55 49 722 0429. - **FM:** 107.1. – **SC52**) Rua Princesa Isabel 311, 89460-000 Canoinhas. – **SC53**) Av. Gov. Adolfo Konder 1500, Bairro São Vicente, 88308-000 Itajaí. – **SC54**) Rua Olivio D. Brugnago s/n, Bairro Vila Nova, 89259-260 Jaraguá do Sul. – **SC55**) Rua Duque de Caxias 1302, 2° andar, 89900-000 São Miguel d'Oeste. **Web:** www.peperi.com.br ☎ 🖷 +55 49 622 1877. - **FM:** 104.9. – **SC56**) Rua José Gonçalves 333, 89340-000 Itaiópolis. ☎ 🖷 +55 47 652 2279. - **Polish:** Sat 1030-1100. – **SC57**) Rua Carlos Jofre do Amaral 67, 88501-010 Lages. ☎ +55 49 221 3000. 🖷 +55 49 221 3030. – **SC58**) Rua Visconde do Rio Branco 1028, 89887-000 Palmitos. – **SC59**) Rua Nunes Machado 14, 10° andar, 88010-460 Florianópolis. – **SC60**) Rua Marechal Deodoro 298, Ed. Pe. Quintílio Costini, 89620-000 Campos Novos. **Web:** www.cnx.com.br/cultura/ **Email:** cultura@cnx.com.br ☎ 🖷 +55 49 541 0391. – **SC61**) Rua 7 de Setembro 341, 89874-000 Maravilha. – **SC62**) C.P. 307, 89290-970 São Bento do Sul. –

SC63) Av. Centenario 6050, Bairro Prospera, 88815-000 Criciúma. – **SC64**) Rua São Pedro 245, 89110-000 Gaspar. **Web:** www.braznet.com.br/sentinela **Email:** radiosentinela@ terra.com.br ☎ +55 471 332 0783. ☎ 📠 +55 47 332 1200. – **SC65**) Rua Ademar da Silva 106, Ed. Sarita, Térreom, 88101-091 São José. **Email:** radio.gazeta.am@com.br – **SC66**) Rua Santos Dumont 193, Centro, 89610-000 Herval d'Oeste. ☎ +55 49 544 1579. 📠 +55 49 554 1817. - **Italian:** Sat 1530-1730. – **SC67**) Av. Procópio Gomes 1155, 89202-300 Joinville. – **SC68**) Rua Izau Luiz de Bittencourt s/n, 88770-000 Imaruí. – **SC69**) Rua Getúlio Vargas 183, 89140-000 Ibirama. – **SC70**) Av. Plínio Arlindo de Nes 476, 89825-000 Xaxim. ☎ +55 49 753 2425. – **SC71**) Rua Max Wilhelm 373, 89256-000 Jaraguá do Sul. **Web:** www.jaraguaam.com.br **Email:** jaraguaam@jaraguaam.com.br ☎ +55 47 371 1010. 📠 +55 49 275 0304. – **SC72**) C.P. 104, 88502-970 Lages. – **SC73**) Av. Belém 500, 89870-000 Pinhalzinho. **Web:** www.rco.com.br – **SC74**) Rua Altamiro Guimarães 230, 89500-000 Caçador. – **SC75**) Praça Henrique Lage 797, 88780-000 Imbituba. – **SC76**) Rua Equador 245, 89120-000 Timbó. – **SC77**) Praça Vidal Ramos 3, 15° andar, 88300-000 Itajaí. – **SC78**) Rua Egidio Martorano 300, 88600-000 São Joaquim. – **SC79**) Av. Porto Feliz 151, 89893-000 Mondaí. ☎ +55 498 74 0122. 📠 +55 498 74 0023. - **German & Spanish:** Sun 1300-1400. – **SC80**) C.P. 160, 89665-970 Capinzal. – **SC81**) Av. Getúlio Vargas 429, 88900-000 Araranguá. **Email:** transa.ara@contacto.com.br ☎ 📠 +55 48 524 0137. – **FM:** 92.5. – **SC82**) C.P. 3, 89190-970 Taió. – **SC83**) Rua Carlos Weber 228, 89295-000 Rio Negrinho. – **SC84**) Av. 21 de Janeiro 966, Centro, 89107-000 Pomerode. **Web:** www.radiopomerode.com.br – **SC85**) Rua João Steffens 260, 88400-000 Ituporanga. ☎ +55 47 833 1311. – **SC86**) Rua Angelo Laporta 155, 88020-600 Florianópolis. – **SC87**) Rua João Florentino de Souza s/n, 89480-000 Major Vieira. – **SC88**) C.P. 1477, 88103-970 São José. – **SC89**) Rua Sargento Juvenil Pereira de Souza 476, 89540-000 Santa Cecília. – **SC90**) Av. Getúlio Vargas 860, 89830-000 Abelardo Luz. – **SC91**) Av. Antônio Francisco Guizoni s/n, 88650-000 Urubici. – **SC92**) Rua Rui Barbosa 1321, 88930-000 Turvo. **Email:** imigrant@aru.matrix.com.br ☎📠 +55 48 525 0321. – **SC93**) Rua Professor João Sobotka 222, Bairro São Cristovão, 89665-000 Capinzal. ☎📠 +55 495 55 1799, 55 1369. - **Italian:** Sun 1500-1600. – **SC94**) Av. Progresso s/n, 89888-000 Caibi. – **SC95**) Rua Duque de Caxias 1302, 2° andar, 89900-000 São Miguel d'Oeste. **Web:** www.peperi.com.br ☎ +55 49 622 1877. – **SC96**) Rua Rafael Pardinho 249, 3° andar, 89240-000 São Francisco do Sul. **Web:** www.bueri.com.br **Email:** bueri@saofranciscodosul.com.br ☎ +55 47 444 2235. 📠 +55 47 444 2900. – **SC97**) Rua Vicente Rech 399, 89770-000 Seara. – **SC98**) Rua do Comércio 214, 89872-000 Modelo. – **SC99**) Rua 7 de Setembro 495, 89950-000 Dionísio Cerqueira. – **SC100**) Rua José Bertolucci 201, 89683-000 Ponte Serrada. – **SC101**) Av. Dr. Albano Schultz 925, 2° andar (C.P. 669), 89201-220 Joinville. **Web:** www.florestanegra.com.br **Email:** publicidade@florestanegra.com.br ☎📠 +55 47 433 3000. - **FM:** 103.1. – **SC102**) Av. Getúlio Vargas 97, 89980-000 Campo Erê. – **SC103**) Rua Santos Saraiva 1098, 88070-101 Florianópolis. – **SC104**) 89560-000 Videira. – **SC105**) 88495-000 Garopaba. – **SC106**) 88330-000 Balneário Camboriú. – **SC107**) 89642-000 Tangará.

SE00) SERGIPE

SE01) Rua Claudio Batista 334, Bairro Santo Antônio, 49060-100 Aracaju. – **SE02**) Rua Propria 124, 49010-020 Aracaju. **Web:** www.aperipe.se.gov.br/ - **FM:** 104.9. – **SE03**) Rua Simão Dias 643, 49010-430 Aracaju. **Email:** cultura@infonet.com.br ☎ +55 79 211 3239/6849. 📠 +55 79 211 8900. – **SE04**) Praça Dr. Filomeno Mora 4, 49400-000 Lagarto. – **SE05**) C.P. 409, 49001-970 Aracaju. – **SE06**) Rua João Pessoa 85, 49500-000 Itabaiana. – **SE07**) Rua Pacatuba 254, Ed. Paulo Figueiredo, sala 1116, 49010-900 Aracaju. ☎📠 +55 79 211 7129. – **SE08**) Praça Coronel Gonçalo Prado s/n, 49200-000 Estância. ☎ +55 79 522 1411. 📠 +55 79 522 2327. – **SE09**) Av. Dr. Luíz Magalhães 346, 49500-000 Itabaiana. – **SE10**) Rua Presidente Vargas 280, 49480-000 Simão Dias. – **SE11**) Av. José da Cunha 6, 49510-000 Frei Paulo. – **SE12**) Rua Barão do Rio Branco 262, 49200-000 Estância. – **SE13**) Travessa Santa Luzia 69, 49300-000 Tobias Barreto.

SP00) SÃO PAULO

SP01) Rua Padre Geraldo Goseling 798, 16200-000 Biriguí. – **SP02**) Rua Antônio do Vale Mello 807, Centro, 13170-011 Sumaré. – **SP03**) Av. Nesralla Rubez 353, 12700-000 Cruzeiro. **Web:** www.radiomantiqueira.com.br/ **Email:** mantamfm@fastnet.com.br ☎ +55 12 544 1364/1439. - **FM:** 100.7. – **SP04**) Rua José Bonini 1415, 14160-000 Sertãozinho. – **SP05**) Rua Cafélândia 161, Vila Nova, 18400-000 Itapeva. - **FM:** 93.5 "Cristal". – **SP06**) Rua Dr. Sousa Alves 960, 12020-030 Taubaté. – **SP07**) Rua Rui Barbosa 474, 13465-280 Americana. **Email:** noticiafm@noticiafm.com.br ☎ +55 19 461 7056/7106/7031. 📠 +55 19 461 7081 - **FM:** 88.9 "Notícia". – **SP08**) Av. Rotary 05, 19970-000 Palmital. – **SP09**) Rua Pedro Lessa 1640, sala 808, 11025-002 Santos. **Web:** www.rederic.com.br/santos.htm ☎ +55 13 238 6218. 📠 +55 13 238 6912. – **SP10**) Rua das Nações Unidas 127, 16800-000 Mirandópolis. **Email:** clubeam@expressnet.com.br ☎ +55 18 3701 4084. 📠 +55 18 3701 4143. – **SP11**) Av. Jerônimo Gonçalves 640, 14010-040 Ribeirão Preto. – **SP12**) Av. Luíz Gonzaga de Amoedo Campos 28, 13800-000 Mogi Mirim. – **SP13**) Rua Pará 155, Centro, 15800-000 Catanduva. ☎ +55 175 22 7311. - **FM:** 94.9. – **SP14**) Rua Conselheiro Rodrigues Alves 104, 3° andar, 12500-000 Guaratinguetá. – **SP15**) C.P. 150, 18800-970 Piraju. 📠 +55 143 51 1066. – **SP16**) Av. Paulista 807, 24° andar, 01311-915 São Paulo. **Email:** info@jovempan.com.br **Web:** www.jovempan.com.br – **SP17**) Rua Capitão Neve 18/40, 15130-000 Mirassol. – **SP18**) Av. Marcondes Filho 1130, 19013-160 Presidente Prudente. – **SP19**) Praça José Palamone Lepre 99, 14804-010 Araraquara. ☎ +55 16 236 3622. 📠 +55 16 236 0114. **Email:** radiomorada@ sunrise.com.br **Web:** radiomorada.com.br – **FM:** 98.1. – **SP20**) Rua Homero Rodrigues Silva 1090, 16900-000 Andradina. - **FM:** 97.9 "Cidade Andradina". – **SP21**) Praça José Bonifácio 815, 13400-340 Piracicaba. – **SP22**) Rua João Pessoa 129, 9° andar, 11013-900 Santos. ☎ +55 13 219 4543. - **FM:** 105.5. – **SP23**) Av. Nove de Julho 606, 14025-000 Ribeirão Preto. **Web:** www.clube.com.br - **FM:** 100.5. – **SP24**) Rua Teotonio Tibiriçá Pimenta 380, 11660-230 Caraguatatuba. ☎ +55 12 422 4633. 📠 +55 12 422 5000. – **SP25**) Rua Heitor Penteado 173, 17400-000 Garça. – **SP26**) Praça Regente Feijo 167, 13300-000 Itu. – **SP27**) Rua 13 de Maio 720, 15800-000 Catanduva. – **SP28**) Av. Dr. Alvaro Schmidt Gallo 317, 18800-000 Piraju. – **SP29**) Rua Francisco Inácio 257, 14700-000 Bebedouro. – **SP30**) Praça Conselheiro Rodrigues Alves 170, Centro, 12500-020 Guaratinguetá. **Email:** rclube@provale.com.br ☎ +55 12 522 2531. 📠 +55 12 522 2633. – **FM:** 97.1 – **SP31**) Rua Humberto Liedtke 1936, 15370-000 Pereira Barreto. **Email:** radiocidadeam@clubinter.com.br br ☎ +55 18 3704 2121. – **SP32**) Rua Pires da Mota 820/830, 01529-000 São Paulo. ☎ +55 11 3274 6800. 📠 +55 11 3274 6858. **Web:** www.radioeldorado.com.br/ – **SP33**) Rua 1 de Agosto 927, 17010-011 Bauru. – **SP34**) Rua dos Pelegrini s/n, Bairro do Desterro, 13700-000 Casa Branca. ☎ +55 19 671 2101, 671 1143. 📠 +55 19 671 1048. – **SP35**) C.P. 355, 19900-970 Ourinhos. – **SP36**) C.P. 25, 12700-970 Cruzeiro. – **SP37**) C.P. 361, 15400-970 Olímpia. – **SP38**) Rua Siqueira de Morães 578, 10° andar, Ed. Marijú, 13201-803 Jundiaí. **Email:** cidade@radiojundiai.com.br **Web:** www.radiojundial.com.br +55 11 4586 09969 – **SP39**) C.P. 324, 17500-970 Marília. – **SP40**) C.P. 88, 17250-970 Bariri. – **SP41**) Av. Paulista 900, 01310-100 São Paulo. ☎ +55 11 289 3765/3592. 📠 +55 11 289 3768. – **SP42**) Rua Itapura 06, Jardim América, 17700-000 Osvaldo Cruz. **Web:** www.radioosvaldocruz.com.br ☎📠 +55 18 561 2326. - **FM:** 97.3 "California FM". – **SP43**) Rua Visconde do Rio Branco 401, 14015-000 Ribeirão Preto. – **SP44**) Rua Euclides Miragaia 394, 12245-550 São José dos Campos. **Web:** www.superradio.com.br - **FM:** 99.7. – **SP45**) C.P. 621, 17001-970 Bauru. **Web:** www.auriverde.com.br/ – **SP46**) Rua Santa Cruz 655, 13480-041 Limeira. - **FM:** 100.7. – **SP47**) Rua das Palmeiras 315, Santa Cecília, 01269-901 São Paulo. ☎ +55 11 3824 3200. 📠 +55 11 3825 8844. **Web:** www.radioclick.globo.com.br/cbn/ **Email:** contato@globonoar.com.br – **SP48**) Av. Armando de Sales Oliveira 575, 17800-000 Adamantina. – **SP49**) Av. Feijó 583, Centro, 14801-140 Araraquara. ☎ +55 16 232 1177, 232 3790. 📠 +55 16 232 3475. **Email:** cultura@culturafmam.com.br **Web:** www.culturafmam.com.br - **FM:** 97.3. – **SP50**) C.P. 30, 13200-970 Jundiaí. – **SP51**) Rua Benjamim Constant 3327, 15015-600 São José do Rio Preto. – **SP52**) Av. Getúlio Vargas 185, 12570-000 Aparecida. **Web:** www.radioaparecida.com.br ☎ +55 12 565 1133. 📠 +55 12 565 1138. - **FM:** 90.9. – **SP53**) Rua Tenente Lopes 191, 17201-460 Jaú. —**FM:** 101.1. – **SP54**) Rua José Galvão 359, 19900-260 Ourinhos. – **SP55**) Rua Dr. Mário Sabino 131, 16300-000 Penápolis. – **SP56**) Rua Bahia 1468, 15500-011 Votuporanga. **Email:** club92fm@votuporanga.com.br ☎ +55 17 422 3232. - **FM:** 92.1. – **SP57**) Rua Radiantes 13,.Morumbi, 05699-900 São Paulo. **Web:** www.bandeirantes.com.br ☎ +55 11 845 7211. – **SP58**) Av. Visconde do Rio Claro 2128, 13500-580 Rio Claro. – **SP59**) C.P. 154, 16200-970 Birigui. – **SP60**) Rua Prudente de Morães 418, 14960-000 Novo Horizonte. – **SP61**) Rua Romualdo Andreazzi 516, Jd. Leonor, 13041-030 Campinas. **Web:** radiocentral.com.br **Email:** redecentral@terra.com.br +51 19 3272 1400- **FM:** 103.7 "Nova". – **SP62**) Av. Paulista 900, 01310-100 São Paulo. – **SP63**) C.P. 5, 19001-970 Presidente Prudente. – **SP64**) Rua Siqueira Campos 3223, 15010-210 São José do Rio Preto. ☎ +55 172 32 0101. 📠 +55 172 32 0089. - **FM:** 102.1 "R. Onda Nova FM". – **SP65**) Rua Dr. Virgilio de Rezende 400, Centro, 18200-180 Itapetininga. 📠 +55 15 272 4202, 271 8207. – **SP66**) Rua Alferes José Caetano 1039, 13400-120 Piracicaba. – **SP67**) Rua Major Claudiano 1393, 14400-690 Franca. – **SP68**) Rua XV de Novembro 18, 13970-000 Itapira. **Web:** www.radioclubeitapira.com.br **Email:** radioclube@dglnet.com.br ☎ +55 19 3863 3899. 📠 +55 19 3863 4233. – **FM:** 91.1 "Clube FM". – **SP69**) Av. Ana Costa 532, 11060-002 Santos. **Web:** www.radiocultura.com.br ☎ +55 13 3289 5757. 📠 +55 13 3289 4758. - **FM:** 106.7. – **SP70**) Avenioda Aviador Marques 11-13, Barrio Jd. Europa, 17015-310 Bauru. – **SP71**) Rua Sete 1057, 15775-000 Santa Fé do Sul. **Email:** radiodinamica@sfsmelfinet.co.br ☎ +55 17 631 1521. 📠 +55 17 631 2410. - **FM:** 104.7. – **SP72**) Av. Sampaio Vidal 185, 17501-040 Marília. – **SP73**) Alameda Ministro Rocha Azevedo 395, 01410-000 São Paulo. – **SP74**) C.P. 56, 18200-970 Itapetininga. – **SP75**) Rua Joaquim Goulardins 225, Santo André, 13870-000 São João da Boa Vista. **Email:** radio970@dglnet.com.br – **SP76**) C.P. 34, 14400-970 Franca. - **FM:** 96.5 "R. 10". – **SP77**) Rua São Carlos do Pinhal 696, 9° andar, 01333-000 São Paulo. **Web:** www.rederecord.com.br ☎ +55 11 253 1566. 📠 +55 11 284 7710. –

SP78) Praça Joel Waldo Dal Moro 1, 14781-574 Barretos. – **SP79**) Rua José Maria Sanches 539, 19500-000 Martinópolis. ☎ +55 182 52 1333. – **SP80**) Rua João Paulo II s/n,12630-000 Alto da Bela Vista (C.P. 57, 12630-070 Cachoeira Paulista). **Web:** www.cancaonova.org.br **Email:** radio@cancaonova.org.br ☎ +55 12 560 2022. 🖷 +55 12 561 2074. – **FM:** 96.3 – **SP81**) Rua Benjamin Constant 33, 10° andar, Centro, 19800-000 Assis. ☎ +55 18 3322 8811. 🖷 +55 18 3322 1319. - **FM:** 100.1. – **SP82**) Rua Profa. Aparecida M.Faveri 988, Jd.Fumagalli, 13485-316 Limerira (C.P. 105, 13480-970 Limeira). **Web:** educadoraam.com.br **Email:** radio@educadoraam.com.br +55 19 3441 3760 – **SP83**) C.P. 16, 15700-970 Jales. – **SP84**) Rua Tomáz Gonzaga 1869, 14400-00+0 Franca. **Email:** difusora@difusora.com.br **Web:** www.difusora.com.br – **SP85**) Rua Antônio Franco Pompeu 261, 17340-000 Barra Bonita. ☎ +55 14 641 0131. - **FM:** 97.7. – **SP86**) Av. Floriano Peixoto 1840, 16400-101 Lins. ☎ +55 14 522 1881. - **FM:** 103.1. – **SP87**) Av. 9 de Julho 3939, 01407-900 São Paulo. **Email:** administra@radiocapital.am.br ☎ +55 11 887 4436/9963/6760. – **SP88**) Rua Boa Morte 1122, 13400-140 Piracicaba. ☎🖷 +55 19 434 9444. - **FM:** 103.1. – **SP89**) Av. Ana Costa 90, 11060-000 Santos. – **SP90**) C.P. 31, 11740-970 Itanhaém. – **SP91**) Rua Marechal Bitencourt 346, 17201-430 Jaú. – **SP92**) Rua Tenente Nicolau Maffei 357, 19010-010 Presidente Prudente. ☎ +55 18 221 3030. - **FM:** 101.1. – **SP93**) Rua Vinte 3011, 15700-000 Jales. Web: www.regionalfm.com.br - **FM:** 103.5 "Regional FM". – **SP94**) Rua Santos Dumont 239, Centro, 14300-000 Batatais. **Web:** www.difusoraam.com.br ☎ +55 16 3761 3600. 🖷 +55 16 3761 3623. – **SP95**) Rua Olavo Bilac 693, 16400-000 Lins. – **SP96**) C.P. 565, 18001-970 Sorocaba. – **SP97**) Av. Monumental Papa João Paulo II 221, 12570-000 Aparecida. – **SP98**) C.P. 326, 17500-970 Marília. – **SP99**) Rua Jeremias de Paulo Eduardo 916, 15910-000 Monte Alto. – **SP100**) Rua das Palmeiras 315, 01221-010 São Paulo. **Email:** contato@globonoar.com.br – **SP101**) Rua Nossa Senhora do Rosario 233, Jardim Nova Iorque, 16065-420 Araçatuba. – **SP102**) C.P. 91, 14940-970 Ibitinga. **Web:** www.ibinet.com.br/radioibitinga/ - **FM:** 99.3 "Ternura FM". – **SP103**) Av. Luíz Gonzaga de Amoêdo Campos 28, 13800-000 Mogi Mirim. - **FM:** 93.9. – **SP104**) C.P. 95, 18540-970 Porto Feliz. ☎ +55 152 62 1219. – **SP105**) Av. Dr. Mário Galvão 463, Jardim Bela Vista, 12209-400 São José dos Campos. - **FM:** 97.5 "Band FM". – **SP106**) Rua Duque de Caxias 260, 15900-000 Taquaritinga. ☎ +55 16 352 2200, 352 2999. – **SP107**) C.P. 258, 17600-970 Tupã. – **SP108**) Rua Gonçalves Dias 208, 19800-000 Assis. – **SP109**) Praça Joel Waldo Dal Moro 1, Centro, 14781-574 Barretos. – **SP110**) C.P. 139, 13500-970 Rio Claro. – **SP111**) C.P. 153, 11680-970 Ubatuba. – **SP112**) Rua Nadir Dias de Figueiredo 1329, 02110-000 São Paulo. **Web:** www.tupi-am.com.br – **SP113**) Rua Almirante Barroso 456, Sobre Loja, 19400-000 Presidente Venceslau. - **FM:** 95.1 "R. Jovem Som". – **SP114**) C.P. 486, 18001-970 Sorocaba. **Web:** www.radiocacique.com.br/ – **SP115**) Rua São Paulo 731, 15600-000 Fernandópolis. – **SP116**) Rua Barão de Monte Santo 1211, 3° andar, 13730-000 Mococa. ☎ +55 196 55 0223. 🖷 +55 196 55 1598. – **SP117**) Rua Eng. Antonio Francisco de Paula Souz 2799, Jd.São Gabriel, 13044-370 Campinas. **Web:** redebandcampinas.com.br **Email:** jornalam@redebandcampinas.com.br +55 19 3779 7404. – **SP118**) C.P. 380, 15500-970 Votuporanga. – **SP119**) Av. XV de Novembro 715, (C.P. 75) 13650-000 Santa Cruz das Palmeiras. ☎ +55 19 672 1959. – **SP120**) Rodovia SP-255 Km 384, 18740-000 Taquarituba ☎ +55 14 3762 1560. 🖷 +55 14 3762 1009. – **SP121**) Rua Cenno Sbrighi 378, 05036-900 São Paulo. **Web:** www.tvcultura.com.br **Email:** dpt@tvcultura.com.br ☎ +55 11 3874 3332. 🖷 +55 11 3611 0965. – **SP122**) Rua Rui Barbosa 546, 4° andar, 14870-000 Jaboticabal. ☎ +55 163 22 0266. 🖷 +55 163 22 0866. – **SP123**) Rua Tupinambás 115, Bairro São João, 16025-180 Araçatuba. – **SP124**) C.P. 209, 17001-970 Bauru. – **SP125**) Praça Coronel Fernando Prestes 45, 11° andar, Centro, 18010-060 Sorocaba. - **FM:** 94.9. – **SP126**) Rua Floriano Peixoto 375, 18300-000 Capão Bonito. – **SP127**) Rua João Pessoa 1990, 15990-000 Matão. – **SP128**) Rua Dr. Miguel Penteado 585, Jardim Chapadão, 13073-180 Santos. – **SP129**) Praça Comendador Emilio Pedutti 28, 18600-410 Botucatu. – **SP130**) Rua 8 No. 472, 14620-000 Orlândia. ☎ +55 (16) 726 2230, 726 2060, 726 5000. – **SP131**) Rua José Caballero 60, 11055-300 Santos. – **SP132**) Av. Nove de Julho 265, 15200-000 José Bonifácio. – **SP133**) Av. da Saudade 200, 12280-000 Caçapava. – **SP134**) Av. Prof. Alceu Maynard Araújo 153, 7° andar, Santo Amaro, 04726-160 São Paulo. – **SP135**) Av. Maurílicio Biagi 2103, Ribeirânia, 14096-160 Ribeirão Preto. ☎🖷 +55 16 624 2929. – **SP136**) Av. Benjamin Constant 1214, 5° andar, Centro, 13010-141 Campinas. – **SP137**) Rua Bernardino de Campos 3180, 15015-300 São José do Rio Preto. – **SP138**) Rua Carina 05, 09732-060 São Bernardo do Campo. – **SP139**) C.P. 66, 14900-970 Itápolis. – **SP140**) Rua Duque de Caxias 154, 13630-000 Pirassununga. – **SP141**) Rua Coronel Osório 84, 12900-000 Bragança Paulista. **Web:** www.radiobraganca.com.br/ – **SP142**) Rua Brigadeiro Tobias 911, 19570-000 Regente Feijó. – **SP143**) Av. Costabile Romano 2201, Ribeirania, 14096-380 Ribeirão Preto. – **SP144**) C.P. 246, 16001-970 Araçatuba. **Web:** cult.am@terra.com.br ☎ +55 (18) 623 8466, 623 2052. 🖷 +55 18 622 6024. – **FM:** 95.5. – **SP145**) Rua Barão de Jaceguai 468, 08710-905 Mogi das Cruzes. – **SP146**) C.P. 20, 17350-970 Igaraçu do Tietê. – **SP147**) C.P. 173, 15600-970 Fernandópolis. ☎ +55 174 42 1811. - **FM:** 90.5. – **SP148**) Av. José Bonifácio 1229, 17900-000 Dracena. – **SP149**) Rua Cuiabá 2790, 16900-000 Andradina. – **SP150**) Av. Antônio J. de Carvalho 1671, 17250-000 Bariri. **Web:** www.baririradioclube.com.br – **SP151**) Rua Pedro Natalia Lorenzetti 172, 18680-030 Lençóis Paulista. **Web:** www.difusora.lpnet.com.br ☎ +55 14 263 0139. 🖷 +55 14 263 2434. – **SP152**) Rua Guanabara 144, 13840-000 Mogi Guaçu. – **SP153**) Rua Benjamin Constant 1214, 3° andar, 13010-141 Campinas. **Email:** cbncultura@supernet.com.br. **Web:** www.supernet. com.br/cbncultura/ ☎ +55 19 231 4277. 🖷 +55 19 231 8156. – **FM:** 99.1. – **SP154**) Rua Dr. Erico de Abreu Sodré 542, 16370-000 Promissão. – **SP155**) Av. Brasil 1119, 17780-000 Lucélia. – **SP156**) C.P. 96, 13560-970 São Carlos. - **FM:** 104.7. – **SP157**) C.P. 755, 15001-970 São José do Rio Preto. – **SP158**) Rua Doutor Pinto Ferraz 183, Vila Mariana, 04117-900 São Paulo. **Web:** www.radioamericasp.com.br ☎ +55 11 252 6272. – Satellite signal downlinked to 44 stations forming Paulus Sat Network. – **SP159**) Ladeira Prof. Irineu Lopes de Lima 418, Centro, 13250-241 Itatiba. **Email:** crn@betwave.com.br ☎ +55 11 4524 1594. 🖷 +55 11 4534 4417. – **SP160**) Rua Cerqueira Cesar 481, 14010-130 Ribeirão Preto. – **SP161**) Rua Oswaldo Aranha 1040, 15150-000 Monte Aprazível. – **SP162**) Rua Dr. Souza Alves 960, 12020-030 Taubaté. – **SP163**) Rua Coronel Joaquim Floriano 287, 18650-000 São Manuel. – **SP164**) Praça Lourenço Franco de Oliveira 81, 13930-000 Serra Negra. – **SP165**) Av. Manoel Goulart 291, 1° andar, Centro, 19010-270 Presidente Prudente. **Web:** www.rederic.com.br/presidenteprudente.htm ☎ +55 18 221 0081. 🖷 +55 18 221 8959. – **SP166**) Praça Nossa Senhora da Conceição 434, 16700-000 Guararapes. – **SP167**) Av. André Luís 723, Picanço, 07082-050 Guarulhos. **Email:** radioboanova@.com.br – **SP168**) C.P. 115, 13560-970 São Carlos. ☎ +55 162 71 1248. 🖷 +55 162 71 3498. – **SP169**) Av. Clara Gianetti de Souza 1124, 11900-000 Registro. – **SP170**) Rua Duque de Caxias 53, salas 24, 26 e 28, 12600-040 Lorena. – **SP171**) Rua Enrico dell'Aqua 332, 18130-000 São Roque. – **SP172**) Av. 15 No. 225, 14790-000 Guaíra. – **SP173**) Av. Malek Assad 535, Jardim Santa Maria, 12300-000 Jacareí. – **SP174**) C.P. 40, 13660-970 Porto Ferreira. – **SP175**) Rua 13 de Maio 2680, Jardim Avaí, 13330-000 Indaiatuba. ☎ +55 19 3875 9141. 🖷 +55 19 3875 6270. – **SP176**) Rua Renato Jardim 511, 14350-000 Altinópolis. – **SP177**) Rua Adolfo André 478, 2° andar, 12940-280 Atibaia. – **SP178**) Praça Oswaldo Martins 218, 16210-000 Bilac. ☎ +55 18 681 1339. – **SP179**) Rua Conselheiro Antônio Prado 518, 18900-000 Santa Cruz do Rio Pardo. – **SP180**) Av. Governador Dr. Ademar Pereira de Barros 134, 15400-000 Olímpia. **Web:** www.difusoraolimpia.com.br – **SP181**) Rua Monte Castelo 941, 17900-000 Dracena. – **SP182**) Rua Brasil 1712, Centro, 15600-000 Fernandópolis. ☎🖷 +55 17 462 1112. **Email:** educadorasr@acif.com.br – **SP183**) Rua Sorocaba 150, Matriz, 09370-150 Mauá. – **SP184**) Riodovia SP-191 Km. 51, 13600-000 Araras. - **FM:** 97.9. – **SP185**) Av. Coronel Fernando Prestes 28, 12400-000 Pindamonhangaba. – **SP186**) Av. Leopoldo Carlos de Oliveira 1038, 14530-000 Miguelópolis. – **SP187**) C.P. 66, 06001-970 Osasco. – **SP188**) Rua Euclides da Cunha 5, sala 702/705, 11065-100 Santos. – **SP189**) C.P. 13, 18650-970 São Manuel. – **SP190**) Av. Romeu Viana Romaneli 1510, 15570-000 Cardoso. ☎ +55 17 453 1376, 456 1330. – **SP191**) Rua Dr. Ricardo Vilela 568, 08710-150 Mogi das Cruzes. ☎ +55 11 4796 1478. 🖷 +55 11 461 6005. – **Japanese:** 0800-0900. – **SP192**) C.P. 66, 13990-970 Espírito Santo do Pinhal. - **FM:** 102.7. – **SP193**) C.P. 125, 17930-970 Tupi Paulista. – **SP194**) Rua Capitão Lisboa 1080, 18270-000 Tatuí. – **FM:** 93.9 "Ternura". – **SP195**) Rua Benedito Carlos dos Reis 700, 15190-000 Nhandeara. – **SP196**) Rua Marechal Deodoro 320, 18600-320 Botucatu. ☎ +55 14 822 1332, 822 1227. – **FM:** 93.1. – **SP197**) C.P. 300, 06001-970 Osasco. – **SP198**) Rua Dom José Carlos Aguirre 567, 18460-000 Itararé. – **SP199**) Rua Pedro de Toledo 205, 19700-000 Paraguaçu Paulista. **Web:** www.radiomarconi. com.br – **SP200**) Rua Regente Feijó 121, 13360-000 Capivari. – **SP201**) Rua José Vaz Porto 175, Vila Santa Rosa, 11431-190 Guarujá. **Email:** radioguarujaam@radioguarujaam.com.br – DX-programme Sat.: 2330-0000 – rpts.: to Orivaldo Rampazo, Presidente-Director – **SP202**) C.P. 135, 14600-970 São Joaquim da Barra. – **SP203**) Av. Dr. Januario Miraglia 2818, Vila Jaguaribe, 12460-000 Campos do Jordão. - **FM:** 94.9. – **SP204**) Rua A.G. Guerra 175 18700-000 Avaré. – **SP205**) C.P. 221, 17890-970 Junqueirópolis. – **SP206**) Rua Tatuí 321, Bairro Casa Branca, 09015-620 Santo André. – **SP207**) Rua Dr. Vicente D´Anna 473, 13960-000 Socorro. – **SP208**) C.P. 68, 15170-970 Tanabi. – **SP209**) Rua Dr. Felipe Vita 1616, 18480-000 Itaporanga. – .**SP210**) C.P. 8, 13690-970 Descalvado. – **SP211**) Rua Benedito Rodrigues de Freitas 95 – Centro, 07094-000 Guarulhos. – **SP212**) Av. 17 No. 560, 14780-000 Barretos. – **SP213**) Av. Paulista 2202, 8° andar, Conj. 81/82, 01310-300 São Paulo. – **SP214**) Av. Capitão José Antônio de Oliveira 544, 17800-000 Adamantina. ☎ +55 18 521 3547. - **FM:** 93.7 "Antena 1". – **SP215**) Av. São Paulo 788, 15650-000 Estrela d'Oeste. – **SP216**) Av. João Guilhermino 429, 12210-131 São José dos Campos. – **SP217**) Rua Brandão Veras 1274, 14700-000 Bebedouro. – **SP218**) Rua Antônio Lobo 237, 13465-000 Americana. – **SP219**) Estrada Serrinha Km 200, 15350-000 Auriflama. – **SP220**) Rua Duque de Caxais 520, 13450-000 Santa Bárbara d'Oeste. ☎ +55 194 63 5255, 63 5068. – **SP221**) Rua Almerim 435, Gramado, 06700-000 Cotia. (24h Gospel prgrs). – **SP222**) Rua Dr. Mário Sabino 131, 16300-000 Penápolis. – **SP223**) Rua Jacofer 2615, 02712-070 São Paulo. ☎ +55 11 265 0667, 265

6208, 252 6544. – **SP224**) Rua Kametaro Morishita 95, 2° andar, 19050-700 Presidente Prudente. ☎ 🖷 +55 18 229 0309. - **FM:** 106.7. – **SP225**) Rua Paula Ney 79, 18110-000 Votorantim. – **SP226**) Rua Bento Carlos 61, 13560-660 São Carlos. - **FM:** 96.9 "Jovem Pan FM". – **SP227**) Rua Duque de Caxais 33, Centro, 13460-000 Nova Odessa. **Email:** radiolib@dglnet.com.br ☎ +55 19 466 2198. – **SP228**) Rua Américo Vespúcio 20, 14730-000 Monte Azul Paulista. – **SP229**) Av. Dr. Labiano da Costa Machado 1735, 17400-000 Garça. – **SP230**) Rua Professor Sud Menucci 464, 17740-000 Rinópolis. – **SP231**) Alameda Juscelino Kubitschek 1914, 19280-000 Teodoro Sampaio. – **SP232**) Praça Vicente Rodrigues 90, Butantã, 05507-030 São Paulo. **Web:** www.radiomundial.com.br – **SP233**) Av. 9 de Julho 304, 13140-000 Paulínia. **Email:** pauliniacn@dglnet.com.br ☎ +55 19 3874 3742, 3844 8500. – **SP234**) Rua Carlos Gomes 534, 14640-000 Morro Agudo. – **SP235**) Rua General Câmara 733, 2° andar, 13450-221 Santa Bárbara d'Oeste. **Email:** radioluzes@netsbo.com.br ☎ 🖷 +55 19 463 3490. – **SP236**) Rua Joaquim Eliziário de Campos 126, 18320-000 Apiaí. ☎ +55 15 552 1968. 🖷 +55 15 552 1060. – **SP237**) Rua 5 No. 170, Bairro Cristo Redentor, 12100-000 Taubaté. – **SP238**) Rua Ademar de Barros 275, 14500-000 Ituverava. – **SP239**) Av. Frederico Ozanan 554, 17300-000 Dois Córregos. – **SP240**) Av. Olinda Ralston 411B, Vila Formosa, 13720-000 São José do Rio Pardo. **Email:** cidlivreadm@vd.com.br - **FM:** 88.7 "R. 88". – **SP241**) Rua Bororos 344, 17600-020 Tupã. – **SP242**) Av. Washington Luís 214, 13600-000 Araras. ☎ +55 19 541 1265/3714. 🖷 +55 19 541 0477. **Email:** radioclube@ radio-clube.com.br **Web:** www.radioclube.com.br/ – **SP243**) Av. 18 de Junho 367, 17690-000 Bastos. – **SP244**) Rua Santana 440, Centro, 13880-000 Vargem Grande do Sul. – **SP245**) Rua Rafael de Barros 126, 13610-300 Lemé. – **SP246**) Rua Francisco Geraldino 71, 17580-000 Pompéia. ☎ +55 144 52 1142. – **SP247**) Rua 7 de Setembro S-73, 17280-000 Pederneiras. - **FM:** 88.3. – **SP248**) Rua Tenente Adolfo Padilha 157, 16880-000 Valparaíso. – **SP249**) Rua 15 de Novembro 52, 13920-000 Pedreira. 🖷 +55 19 893 2520. – **SP250**) Rua Vitória 162, 19470-000 Presidente Epitácio. – **SP251**) Av. Dr. Carlos Burgos 1680, 13901-300 Amparo. – **SP252**) Rua Engenheiro Maylaski 308, Centro, 19360-000 Santo Anastácio. ☎ +55 18 261 1202. 🖷 +55 18 261 2132. **Web:** www.culturaregional.com.br – **SP253**) Rua 7 de Setembro 911, 14240-000 Cajuru. – **SP254**) Av. São Paulo 1220, 13310-000 Cabreúva. – **SP255**) Rua Manoel dos Santos Freire 629, 18550-000 Boituva. – **SP256**) Rua José Revel 477, Centro, 13320-020 Salto. ☎ +55 11 483 2015. – **SP257**) Rua 9 de Julho 666, 16600-000 Pirajui. ☎ +55 14 572 1352. 🖷 +55 14 572 1941. – **SP258**) Rua dos Operários 1441, Vila Guaçu, 19600-000 Rancharia. – **SP259**) Rua Coronel João de Carvalho 39, 1° andar, 13710-000 Tambaú. – **SP260**) Av. Rodolfo Guimarães 635, 1° andar, 17380-000 Brotas. – **SP261**) Rua Benjamim Constant 543, 14540-000 Igarapava. – **SP262**) Rua Inácio Ribeiro 592, 13670-000 Santa Rita do Passa Quatro. – **SP263**) Rua Manoel de Arzão 85, 02730-030 São Paulo. **Web:** www.arquid-iocese-sp.org.br/radio9ju/radio9jul/aprse.html – **SP264**) Rua 6 No. 1460, 4° andar-Ed. São Lucas, 13500-151 Rio Claro.- **SP265**) Av. São Sebastião 162, 3° piso, sala 1, 18150-000 Ibiúna. – **SP266**) 01000-000 São Paulo. – **SP267**) 14100-000 Ribeirão Preto. – **SP268**) 18730-000 Itaí. – **SP269**) 14870-000 Jaboticabal. – **SP270**) 15290-000 Buritana. – **SP271**) 14740-000 Viradouro.

TO00) TOCANTINS

TO01) Av. Joaquim Aires 2393, 77500-000 Porto Nacional. ☎ +55 63 863 1608. – **TO02**) Praça José Tôrres 03, Centro, 77600-000 Paraíso do Tocantins. 🖷 +55 63 861 1135. – **TO03**) Av. Nossa Senhora de Fátima 894, 77900-000 Tocantinópolis. – **TO04**) BR-157 Km. 1103, Zona Rural, 77804-970 Araguaína. -**FM:** 99.7 "Araguaia". – **TO05**) Rua Raul do Espírito Santo 1334, 77760-000 Colinas do Tocantins. **Email:** elgb@zipmail.com.br ☎ 🖷 +55 63 476 1180. – **TO06**) Av. Tocantins 422, 77650-000 Miracema do Tocantins. – **TO07**) Almeda João Pires Querido 07, 77490-000 Cristalândia. – **TO08**) Av. Bernardo Sayão 2201, 77700-000 Guaraí.- **TO09**) 77054-970 Palmas. – **TO10**) 77402-970 Gurupi. – **TO11**) 77300-000 Dianópolis. – **TO12**) Quadra 105N, NHM Lote 01 CR, 77054-970 Palmas. – **TO13**) 77950-000 Araguatins. – **TO14**) 77700-000 Guarai. – **TO15**) 77710-000 Pedro Alfonso. – **TO16**) 77330-00 Arraias. – **TO17**) 77370-000 Natividade.

FM Stations in principal cities

Belo Horizonte: 88.7 Scala FM – 90.7 Cidade – 91.7 Horizontes de Minas – 94.9 Alvorada – MG06) 95.7 – MG68) 96.5 – MG53) 97.3 Altaneira FM – 98.3 98 (Del Rey) – 99.9 Terra – MG35) 100.9 – 102.1 BH FM – MG06) 103.9 – 105.1 Antena Um – MG65) 106.1 – 107.5 FM

Brasília: 89.9 Brasília Super FM – 91.7 Brasília Comunicação – 93.7 Atlântida FM – DF01) 95.3 – DF04) 96.1 – 96.9 Dest Câmara Deputados 97.7 Manchete FM – 99.3 Antena 9 – 100.1 Transamérica – DF02) 100.9 Cultura FM – 101.7 R Jornal de Brasília – 105.5 FM 105 (Planalto) – 106.3 Sigma Radiodifusão – DF03) 107.1 Atividade.

Curitiba: PR15) 88.5 – PR139) 90.1 – 91.3 Transamerica Hit – 92.3 Scala FM – 93.9 Capital – 95.1 Transamérica Light – 96.3 Studio 96 – PR06) 97.1 – 97.9 Melodia – 98.7 FM 98 – PR42) 99.5 Paraná FM – 100.3 Transamérica – PR134) 101.5 – 102.3 Caioba – 103.9 Jovem Pan – 105.5 Ouro Verde – 106.5 R Novo Tempo.

Fortaleza: 88.9 FM Jangadeiro – 89.9 Capital – 92.9 Tropical – 93.9 FM 93 – 94.7 Jovem Pan – CE21) 95.5 FM do Povo – 99.1 Cidade FM – CE08) 99.9 Dragão FM – 100.9 Pajeu – 101.7 FM Casablanca – 103.9 FM O Tempo – 105.7 Atlântico Sul FM – 106.7 Hoje – 107.9 Universitária.

Porto Alegre: 89.3 Antena Um – 90.3 Transamérica FM – 91.3 Metropolitana – 92.1 Cidade – 92.9 Alegria FM – 94.1 Atlântida – 94.9 Ipanema – 95.9 Liberdade FM – 96.7 Eldorado – 97.5 Jovem Pan FM – 98.3 Continental – 99.3 Band FM – 99.9 Novo Tempo FM – 100.5 Capital – RS23) 101.3 – RS09) 102.3 – 104.1 FM 104 (Rede Pampa) – 106.3 Aliança – 107.7 Cultura.

Recife: 88.7 Antena Um – 90.3 J.C. FM – 91.9 Rede Aleluia – 92.7 Transamérica – 94.3 Manchete – 95.9 Cidade – 97.5 Recife FM Stereo – 99.1 Caetes – PE10) 99.9 – 100.7 Evangélica do Brasil – 103.9 Maranata FM – 107.9 JMB Empreendimentos.

Rio de Janeiro: 88.5 Tribuna – RJ11) 89.3 – 90.3 M.P.B. FM – 91.1 Diário – RJ25) 92.5 – 93.3 El Shaddai FM – RJ04) 94.1 – 94.9 Jovem Rio FM – 95.7 Alvorada FM – RJ27) 96.5 – 97.3 Melodia FM – RJ25) 98.1 FM 98 – RJ12) 98.9 – RJ16) 99.7 – RJ35) 100.5 FM O Dia – 101.3 Transamérica FM – 102.1 Jovem Pan – 102.9 Cidade – 103.7 Antena Um – 104.5 Tropical – RJ16) 105.1 105 FM – 106.3 Universidade – 106.7 Catedral – 107.1 107 – 107.9 Universidade.

Salvador: BA57) 90.1 Globo FM – 91.3 Itaparica – 92.3 Salvador FM – 94.3 Piata – 95.9 FM 96 (Aratu) – 97.5 Itapuã – 99.1 Bandeirantes – 100.1 Transamérica – 101.3 BA32) Metrópole – BA04) 102.3 – 103.9 104 FM (R FM a Tarde) – 104.7 Manchete – BA55) 107.5.

São Paulo: SP62) 88.1 – 89.1 FM 89 – SP77) Nova FM 89.7 – SP47) 90.5 CBN – 91.3 Manchete FM – 92.1 Lider FM – SP32) 92.9 – 93.7 R. USP – 94.1 Deus e Amor – 94.7 Antena Um FM – 95.3 Nativa FM – 95.7 Scala FM – SP57) 96.1 Band FM – 96.9 Cidade FM – 97.7 FM 97 – SP232) 98.1 – 98.5 Metropolitana FM – 99.3 99 FM – 100.1 Transamérica – SP16) 100.9 – 101.7 Alpha FM – 102.1 Kiss FM – 102.5 Imprensa – SP121) 103.3 – 104.1 Apolo FM – 104.7 Transcontinental – 105.1 105 FM – 105.7 Musical FM – SP41) 106.3 Mix FM – 106.9 Nova Omega FM – 107.3 Brasil 2000 – 107.5 Antena 1 – 107.9 Tropical FM.

BRITISH INDIAN OCEAN TERRITORY

L.T: UTC + 5h — **Pr.L:** English — **Pop:** variable (US & British military personnel). The original population of approx. 3000 was removed to Mauritius — **E.C:** 60Hz, 110/220V — **ITU:** BIO **Diego Garcia ITU**: DGA

ARMED FORCES RADIO AND TELEVISION SERVICE (U.S. Mil.)

✉ Naval Media Center Detachment-Diego Garcia, PSC 466 Box 14, FPO, AP 96595-0014. ☎ +246 370 3680/3685 🖷 +246 370 3681

Email: Dgar@mediacen.navy.mil

MW: Island Talk, 1485kHz 200W, news, sports & talk

FM: Power 99, 99.1MHz 200W, weekdays 0600-1400, rock & roll, live DJ. **Island Variety,** 101.9MHz 200W, mixture of rock, alternative, urban & country. – **D.Prgr:** 24h – **V.** by letter.

BRUNEI DARUSSALAM

L.T: UTC +8h — **Pop:** 344,000 — **Pr.L:** Malay, English, Chinese, Gurkha — **E.C:** 50Hz, 240V — **ITU:** BRU

RADIO TELEVISION BRUNEI (Gov.)

✉ Prime Minister's Office, Jalan Elizabeth II, Bandar Seri Begawan BS8610. ☎ +673 2243111. 🖷 +673 2241882. **Email** (International and Public Relations): rtbipro@brunet.bn. **Web**: www.rtb.gov.bn.

L.P: Dir: Pengiran Dato Ismail Mohamed. Superintendent Eng: Lim Sam Lee. Acting Assistant Director (Radio): Mr Haji Osman Mohammad. Head of Int. & Pub. Rel. & CBA/COMBROAD Liaison Officer: Haji Hussain Abdul Rahman.

MW	kHz	kW	Netw.	H. of tr.
Tutong 1)	594	200d	RN	2030-1600
Serasa 2)	675	200	RN	2030-1600
Sungei Hanching 2)	710v	20	RPi	2200-1600

FM (MHz)	RN	RPi	RPe	RH	NI	kW
Andulau 1)	93.8	96.9	91.0	97.7	94.9	5
Bukit Subok 2)	92.3	95.9	91.4	94.1*	93.3	5/0.5
Kuala Belait (?)	96.3					

1) Kuala Belait & Tutong areas. 2) Bandar Seri Begawan (BSB) area. *) a 2nd tr. in the BSB region rep. on 88.5MHz (irr.). **RN** = Rangkaian Nasional in Malay: 2030-1600. **RPi** = R. Pilihan. English: 2200-0100, 0300-0800, 1200-1600. Chinese: 0100-0300, 0800-1100. Gurkhali: 1100-1200. **RPe** = Rangkaian Pelangi (prgr's for young people): 2200-

1600. **RH** = Rangkaian Harmoni (music sce.): 2200-1600. **NI** = Rangkaian Nur-i-Islam (rlg. talk channel): 2200-1400.
ANN: (RN in Malay) "Rangkaian Nasional, Radio Brunei".
IS: Synthesized chimes.

DST NETWORK SDN. BHD. (KRISTAL RADIO) (Comm.)

✉ P. O. Box 55, Mail Processing Centre Berakas, Bandar Seri Begawan BB3577 **Web**: www.dst-group.com **Email**: kristalfm@dst-group.com

FM (MHz)	KFM	RQ	CFM	CG
Andulau 1)	98.7	99.7	94.4	100.9
Bukit Subok 2)	90.7	89.1	100.1	92.9

KFM=Kristal FM. RQ=Recital of Al-Quran. CFM=Capital FM. CG=Capital Gold. 1), 2) as above.
D.Prgr: Kristal FM: 2200-1600(Sat 2200) in English/Malay (50/50%). CFM, CG: 24h live relay via satellite of Capital Radio, London.

DAB: Radio Television Brunei on 225.648MHz

BRITISH FORCES BROADCASTING SERVICE

✉ BFBS Brunei, BFPO 11. ☎ +673 3223424.
Web: www.ssvc.com/bfbs/radio/gurkhabrunei
Prgr.: 24h in English on 92.0MHz 0.25kW, in Nepali on 89.05MHz 0.25kW. Location: Belait district.

BULGARIA

L.T: UTC +2h (27 Mar-30 Oct: UTC +3h) — **Pop:** 7.9 million — **L:** Bulgarian — **E.C:** 50Hz, 220V — **ITU:** BUL

BÂLGARSKO NATSIONALNO RADIO (BNR)

✉ P.O. Box 900, 1000 Sofia. Visiting address: Dragan Tsankov 4, 1504 Sofia. ☎ +359 2 652871 📠 +359 2 650560. **Web:** www.bnr.bg. **Email**:bnr@bnr.bg
L.P: DG:Polya Stancheva.

LW/MW	Prgr.	kHz	kW	H. of tr.
Sofia	H+K	261	75	24h
Vidin	C	576	500	0400-2200
Pleven	H	594	250	0400-2200
Plovdiv	C+L	648	30	24h
Pirin	C	702	10	24h
Petrich	H+F	747	500	0400-2300
Salmanovo	H+T	747	10	24h
Varna	V	774	75	24h
Shumen	C	828	500	0400-2200
Sofia	C	828	50	24 h
Blagoevgrad	B	864	150	0400-2200
Samuil	H+T	864	10	24h
Stara Zagora	C+Z	873	60	0300-0100
Shumen	H+S	963	75	0300-0100
Sofia	H	963	40	24h
Pirin	H	963	40	24h
M. Tarnovo	H	963	5	24h
Kardzhali	H+T	1017	50	0300-0100
Varna	H	1143	40	24h
Stara Zagora	H	1161	500	0400-2200
Targovishte	H+T	1161	10	24h
Dulovo	H+T	1161	10	24h
Vidin	H+F	1224	500	0400-2300
Kardzhali	C	1296	150	0400-2200
Pleven	C	1296	30	24h
Suvorovo	H	1485	5	24h
Haskovo	C	1485	3	24h
Dobrich	H	1584	10	24h

FM(MHz):	H	C	kW	FM(MHz):	H	C	kW
Belogradchik	102.3	88.2	10/1	Plovdiv	-	91.7	1
Burgas	102.5	95.3	10/1	Ruse	103	95.7	10/1
Dobrich	104.3	102.3	3/1	Shumen	102	100.4	10/1
G. Delchev	100.3	98.5	10/1	Sliven	87.8	98.7	1
Kârdzhali	105	99.2	10/1	Smolyan	101.8	96	5/1
Kyustendil	102.1	99.3	10/1	Sofia	103	92.9	10/1
Montana	101.4	-	10	St. Zagora	-	98.3	1
Mt. Botev	100.9	92.2	10/1	Svilengrad	99.7	94.9	3
Pleven	102.7	100.2	1	Varna	100.9	104.8	5/1

+ 10 (H), 5 (C) freq's below 1 kW

SW: Varna 7400 kHz 100kW. Relay of R. Varna: Sun 2200-Mon 0400.
National Prgrs. C = Hristo Botev, 24h culture & arts. **Email**: hrbotev@bnr.bg. F = Foreign Service, R. Bulgaria (see International Radio section) on 747kHz 1730-2300 & 1224kHz 0400-0700 (0900SS), 1300-2300. H = Horizont, 24h news & music. **Email**: horizont@bnr.bg. K = Parliament Channel, direct from parliament 0800-1700Tu-Th, 0900-1200 F exc. August. Also on Sofia 69.26 MHz 3 kW. T = Home Service in Turkish, 0600-0630 (SS 0700),1300-1330, 1800-1900 on 747, 864, 1017, 1161kHz & 69.80MHz 3 kW (Shumen).
Regional Prgrs. B = R. Blagoevgrad, ul. Ivan Mihaylov 56, BG-2700 Blagoevgrad. **Web**:www.radiobl.com , **Email**: radio@radiobl.com), 0400-2200 on 864 kHz & on 72.92 MHz (G. Delchev 6 kW), 90.9 MHz (Yakoruda 0.1 kW), 103.2 MHz (Blagoevgrad 0.25 kW), 105.2 MHz (Kresna 1 kW). L = R. Plovdiv, ul.Knyaz Dondukov korsakov 2, BG-4000 Plovdiv. **Web**: www.radioplovdiv.bg, **Email**: director@radioplovdiv.bg. 0400-2200 on 648kHz & 94.0 (Plovdiv 1 kW), 103.1MHz (Smolyan 1 kW). S = R. Shumen, ul.Dobro Volnikov 7, BG 9700 Shumen. **Web**: www.radioshumen.net, **Email**: sovi@radioshumen.net.) 0400-2200 on 963kHz & 87.6MHz (Shumen 10 kW) & 90.3MHz (Silistra 0.25 kW). V = R.Varna, Bul.Primorski 22, BG-9000 Varna (www.radiovarna.com. Email:bnr@radiovarna.com) 0200 -2400 on 774 kHz & 24h on 88.5 (Burgas 1 kW), 88.7 (Dobrich 1 kW), 88.9 (Provadiya 0.1 KW) , 103.4MHz (Varna 1 kW). Special prgr for ships on the Black Sea ("Zdravey, more!") on SW, see above. Z= R. Stara Zagora, ul. Knyaz Boris 175, BG-6000 Stara Zagora (Email: radio.sz@sz.bia-bg.com), 0400-2200 on 873 kHz & 88.3MHz(Stara Zagora 1 kW).
NB: Most reg. stn's relay National Prgr H or C outside own prgrs at night.

EXTERNAL SERVICE: Radio Bulgaria
see International Radio section.

FM relays of International Broadcasters:
British Broadcasting Corporation, ✉ BBC Centre, Box 81, Sofia 1606. ☎ +359 2 9877130. 📠 +359 2 9806232. - **FM:** Sofia 91.0MHz 1kW 24h. Relay of BBC World Service in English and Bulgarian.News in Bulgarian is relayed by several private stations.
Deutsche Welle, ✉ Bulgarian Service., PO Box 622, 1000 Sofia. **FM:** Sofia 95.7MHz 1kW 24h. Relay of Deutsche Welle in German and Bulgarian. German 1600-1800.
R. France Internationale, ✉ Ul. Vasil Levski 4, 1000 Sofia. **Web**: www.rfi.bg ☎ +359 2 9810272. 📠 +359 2 9802741, - **FM:** Sofia 103.6MHz 1.5 kW. 24h.Relay RFI in French & Bulgarian. RFI in Bulgarian is relayed by some commercial stn's.
Voice of America, VOA programs in English are relayed by some commercial stn's, e.g. R. Vitosha, Sofia 97.6 MHz.and Bulgarian are relayed. - **FM (MHz)**: 92.6 Varna, 97.0 Plovdiv, 97.6 Sofia, 98.9 Blagoevgrad, 103.9 Burgas & 106.5 Pleven.
Trans World Radio, ✉ P.O. Box 38, 1202 Sofia. Prgr: see International Radio Section under Monaco.
Adventist World Radio, ✉ Ul. Antim I 22, 4000 Plovdiv. Prgr: see International Radio Section under USA..

Private Commercial Networks (all 24h exc. Where indicated):
BG RADIO: ✉ ul. Sofiyski geroy 3A, 1612 Sofia. Web: www.bgradio.net FM(MHz): 89.0, 91.9, 93.6, 94.6, 94.9, 95.7. 97.4, 97.8, 104.2
CLASSIC FM: ✉ ul. Panayot Volov 3, 1504 Sofia. **Web:** www.clasicfmradio.com **FM:** (MHz): 87.9, 89.1, 95.9, 97.8, 100.1, 102.1, 103.7, 105.1, 105.7. Carries prgrs produced by R. Nova Evropa (see below) & BBC
DARIK RADIO: ✉ bul. Knyaz Alexander Dondukov 82, 1504 Sofia. **Web:** www.darik.net **FM**(MHz): 88.4, 91.0, 91.5, 91.6, 93.2, 96.4, 96.7, 97.3, 99.3, 100.6, 100.7, 101.2, 104.0, 104.5, 104.9, 105.0, 105.4, 106.2, 106.6, 106.8, 107.0, 107.3, 107.7, 107.9.
FM+ GROUP: ✉ bul. Yerusalim 51, 1784 Sofia. **Web**: www.fmplus.net **FM**(MHz): 89.9, 90.3, 94.1, 94.2, 94.4, 94.6, 94.9, 98.1, 99.4, 99.9, 100.3, 100.4, 102.1.
INFO RADIO: ✉ ul. A. Zhendov 1, 1113 Sofia. **Web:** www.inforadio.bg **FM:** (MHz): 89.7, 90.9, 93.7, 96.2, 97.7, 101.1, 102.7, 103.6, 103.9, 105.6, 105.7, 107.1.
JAZZ FM: ✉ ul. Panayot Volov 3, 1504 Sofia. **Web:** www.jazzfm.bg.com **FM:** (MHz): 90.6, 101.6, 101.8, 101.9, 102.0, 103.9, 104.0, 106.2.
RADIO CITY: ✉ ZhK "Bokar", Evrotsentâr, 1404 Sofia. Web: www.radiocity.bg **FM**(MHz): 91.1, 95.0, 95.2, 96.8, 99.7
RADIO EKSPRES: ✉ bul. N. Vabtsarov 26, 1407 Sofia. **Web**: www.express.vratza.net **FM**(MHz): 90.2, 90.9, 91.2, 91.8, 96.2, 97.2, 106.0, 107.5
RADIO FRESH: ✉ bul. Yerusalim 51, 1784 Sofia. **Web**: www.radiofresh.bg **FM**(MHz): 89.9, 90.5, 91.9, 92.5, 93.6, 98.9, 100.3, 100.5, 103.3, 104.5, 104.6, 104.8, 105.7, 107.0
RADIO NOVA EVROPA: ✉ bul. Vitosha 18, 1000 Sofia. **Email**: radio@novaevropa.net **FM**(MHz): see Classic FM. **D. Prgr**: 0530-0730, 0900-1000, 1100-1200, 1400-1600 via trs of Classic FM.

RADIO SPORT
stadion V. Levski, sector V, etazh 4, 1000 Sofia. **Web**: www.radio.sportbg.com **FM**(MHz): 89.5, 90.6, 90.8
RADIO VESELINA: bul. Cherni vrah 43, 1000 Sofia. **Web**: www.radioveselina.bg **FM**(MHz): 88.7, 91.2, 91.4, 94.8, 95.8, 97.7, 99.1
RADIO 1: bul. Tsar Boris III 23, 1612 Sofia. **Web**: www.radio1.bg **FM**(MHz): 88.8, 88.9, 89.5, 90.3, 90.5, 93.8, 94.7, 95.5, 102.3, 104.5, 105.6, 106.0
RETRO RADIO: bul. Knyaz A. Dondukov 82, 1504 Sofia. **Web**: www.retroradio.bg **FM**(MHz): 88.3, 98.0, 98.3, 99.3, 101.5, 103.4, 104.3, 105.2, 105.9

LOCAL RADIO STATIONS
More information can be found on the webpage of Association of Bulgarian Broadcasters ABBRO,. **web:**www.abbro.bulmedia.com. Details of Bulgarian FM-sts can be found at **web**: www.radio.dir.bg/en_index.htm and www.devabroadcast.com.

BURKINA FASO

L.T: UTC — **Pop:** 12m — **Pr.L:** French + 16 ethnic — **E.C:** 50Hz, 220V — **ITU:** BFA.

CONSEIL SUPÉRIEUR DE L'INFORMATION (CSI)
01 BP 6437, Ouagadougou ☎ +226 33 41 98/99 ☎ +226 33 50 39 **Web**: www.csi.bf **Email**: info@csi.bf

RADIODIFFUSION NATIONALE DU BURKINA (RNB)
03 BP 7029, Ouagadougou ☎ +226 324302/324303 ☎ +226 310441. **Email:** rnb@cenatrin.bf
L.P: MD: Marcel Toe. Head of Tr. Centre: Marcel Teho. Prgr.Dir: Taheré Ouedraogo.
STATIONS: Ouagadougou (G.C: 12N22 001W31):
MW:

kHz	kW	times
747	100	0530-0900, 0900-1200SS, 1200-2400
1341	1	standby tr.

SW: (GC: 12N22 001W31):

kHz	kW	times
4815	100	alt. to 5030
5030	100	0530-0800, 1700-2400
7230	100	0800-0900, 0900-1200SS, 1200-1700

FM: 88.5/92.0/99.9MHz 0.02kW.
D.Prgr in French/Vernaculars. N. in French: 0630MF, 1000SS + Thurs, 1245 (regional), 1300, 1900, 2200. **N. in English:** W1920 (approx). **ANN:** "Ici Radio Burkina". **IS:** Balafon.

REGIONAL STATIONS
Radio Bobo, BP 392, Bobo-Dioulasso. ☎ +226 991158
MW: 1008kHz 10kW - **FM:** 92.0MHz 0.02kW - **D.Prgr:** MF 0600-0800, 1200-1400, 1600-2400, SS 0800-2400.
Radio Gaoua, Gaoua. ☎ +(226)870348/870198 - **FM:** 90.1MHz.
R. Rurale: FM tr's in Diapaga, Djibasso, Gassan, Kongoussi, Orodara & Poura.
Canal Arc-en-Ciel, 03 BP 7045, Ouagadougou. **FM:** Ouagadougou 96.6MHz, Bobo-Dioulasso 89.8MHz.

Other stations:
R. de l'Alliance Chrétienne, Bobo-Dioulasso: 95.9MHz – **R. Balafon**, Bobo-Dioulasso: 102.7MHz – **Bankuy FM**, Dédougou: 107.7MHz – **R. FM Boulgou**, Garango: 101.1MHz – **R. Cascade**, Banfora: 98MHz – **R. Daande Sahel**, Dori: 104.6MHz – **R. Djongo**, Pô: 106.4MHz – **Echo des Cotonniers**, Solenzo: 95.1MHz – **R. Djibasso:** 94.6MHz – **R. Ènergie**, 01 BP 6437, Ouagadougou - **FM:** Kaya 92.2MHz, Yako 94.9MHz, Fada N'Gourma 98.8MHz – **R. de l'Espoir**, Réo: 102.8MHz – **R. Évangile Développement**, 04 BP 8050, Ouagadougou. **FM:** Ouagadougou 93.4MHz 0.1kW, Koudougou 95.4MHz, Leo 97.8MHz, Bobo-Dioulasso 103.6MHz, Ouahigouya 104.6MHz **Web:** www.autre.net/red – **R. Evangile du Sud-Ouest**, Gaoua: 99.7MHz – **R. Fréquence Espoir**, Dédougou: 96.8MHz – **R. Frontière**, Tenkodogo: 97.6MHz – **R. Gambidi**, Ouagadougou: 97.7MHz – **R. Gassan:** 105.5MHz – **R. du Grand Nord**, Dori: 97.5MHz – **Horizon FM**, 01 BP 2710, Ouagadougou. **FM:** Tenkodogo 97.6MHz, Banfora 98MHz, Koudougou 98.7MHz, Ouayigouya 100.4MHz, Dédougou 102.7MHz, Ouagadougou 104.4MHz, Dori 104.6MHz – **R. Kadoadb**, Ziniare: 107.7MHz – **R. Kongoussi:** 93.2MHz – **R. Kouritta**, Koupela: 93.7MHz – **Laafi FM**, Zorgho: freq. unknown – **R. Lotamou**, Solenzo: on FM 0.5kW, freq. unknown – **R. Lumière,** 01 BP 108, Ouagoudougou: 98.1MHz – **R. Manegda**, Kaya: 99.4MHz – **R. Maria**, 01 BP 90, Ouagadougou. **FM:** Ouagadougou 91.6MHz 1kW, Kaya 99.4MHz, Koupêla 96.9MHz 1kW. **Web:** www.radiomaria.org – **Media Star**, Bobo-Dioulasso: 96.7MHz – **R. Munuy FM**, Banfora: 94.7MHz – **R. Naboswende**, Pouytenga: 103.7MHz – **R. Natigmeb Zanga**, Yako: 98.2MHz – **R. Notre Dame du Sahel**, Ouahigouya: 102.6MHz – **R. Ouaga FM**, Avenue Loudun-Immeuble Obouf, Ouagadougou: 105.2MHz. **Web:** http://www.netaccess.bf/radioouagafm.htm – **R. Palabre**, B.P. 196, Kougougou: 92.2MHz – **R. Poura:** 98.2MHz – **R. Pulsar**, 01 BP 5976, Ouagadougou: 94.8MHz 0.4kW – **R. Salankoloto**, 01 BP 1716, Ouagadougou: 97.3MHz – **R. Sanmentenga**, Kaya: 96.1MHz – **R. Savane**, Ouagadougou: 103.4MHz – **La Voix du Sud-Ouest**, Diébougou: 101.5MHz – **R. Taanba**, Fada N'Gourma: 98.8MHz – **R. Tapao**, Diapaga: 95.8MHz – **R. Unitas**, Diébougou: 94.7MHz – **R. Vive le Paysan**, B.P. 74, Saponé: 107MHz – **R. la Voix du Passoré**, Yako: 105.3MHz – **R. la Voix du Paysan**, Ouahigouya: 97MHz – **R. la voix du Verger**, Orodara: 91.2MHz – **R. Zoodo**, Ouahigouya: 100.4MHz.
Africa No. 1: Ouagadougou 90.3MHz (see main entry under Gabon).
BBC African Sce: Ouagadougou 99.2MHz.
RFI Afrique: Ouagadougou 94MHz, Bobo-Dioulasso 99.4MHz.
Voice of America: Ouagadougou 102.4MHz

BURUNDI

L.T: UTC +2h — **Pop:** 6.2m — **Pr.L:** Kirundi, Swahili, French, English — **E.C:** 50Hz, 220V — **ITU:** BDI.

MINISTÈRE DE L'INFORMATION
Web: www.burundi-gov.org

RADIODIFFUSION NATIONALE DU BURUNDI (RTNB)
B.P. 1900, Bujumbura ☎ +257 22 3742 ☎ +257 22 6547
Email: rtnb@cbinf.com **LP:** D.G.: Innocent Muhozi
SW: Gitega (G.C: 03S29 29E56): 6140kHz 60kW (inactive).
FM: 89.8/92.9/98.9/102.9MHz.
D.Prgr: W 0300-0700 & 0900-2100, Sun 0300-2100. (RTNB1 in Kirundi, RTNB2 in French/Swahili/English). **N.** in French: 0530, 1200, 1500, 1900. **N.** in Swahili: 0630, 1245, 1800. **N.** in Kirundi: 0500, 0700, 1130, 1800, 2000. **N.** in English: 0445, 1230, 1600, 1845.
ANN: "Ici Bujumbura, Radiodiffusion Nationale de la République du Burundi". **IS:** Drums.

Other stations:
R. CCIB FM, Bujumbura: 99.4MHz, nationwide 102.4MHz – **R. Culture**, Bujumbura: 88.2/99.9MHz – **R. Sans Frontiers Bonesha FM**, B.P. 5314, Bujumbura: 0400-2100 96.8/107.5MHz – **R. Scolaire Nderagakura**: Bujumbura 87.9MHz – **R. Ivyizigiro**, B.P. 6445, Bujumbura: 90.9/104.8MHz.
RFI Afrique: Bujumbura 96.1MHz, nationwide 92.4MHz.
BBC African Sce, Bujumbura. 90.2MHz.

CAMBODIA

L.T: UTC +7h — **Pop:** 13 million — **Pr.L:** Khmer (Cambodian) — **E.C:** 50Hz, 230V — **ITU:** CBG

NATIONAL RADIO OF CAMBODIA
Street 106, Phnom Penh 12202. ☎ +855 23 722869. ☎ +855 23 427319.

MW	kHz	kW	MW	kHz	kW
Steung Treng *)	585	20	Sihanoukville *)	1255	20
Phnom Penh	740	150	Phnom Penh **)	1300	1
Phnom Penh a)	918	120	Phnom Penh **)	1360	1
Battambang	999	20			

a) Location: Steung Meanchey. *) presumed inactive.**) inactive.
SW: Steung Meanchey (Phnom Penh): 11940kHz (v.) 50kW.
National sce: 2230-1530 on 918kHz. 740kHz used as standby. N. in English: 0600-0615.

FM-96 (comm.): Phnom Penh 96.0MHz: 2200-1300/1400v.
Provincial sce's on AM: Battambang 999kHz: 1200-1405.
Provincial sce's on FM: (MHz) Battambang 96.1, Kampong Cham 92.5, Kampot 93.25, Pailin 90.5, Preah Vihea 99.0, Pursat 98.5.
Foreign language service on 11940kHz (irr.): 0000-0115, 1200-1315. 15 mins each in English, French, Thai, Laotian & Vietnamese.
ANN: HS (Khmer): "Thini Sathani Vithayu Cheat Kampuchea".
Other stations

FM	Location	MHz	kW	Station
1)	Phnom Penh	88.0		Sweet FM in Khmer/Chinese
2)	Phnom Penh	89.5		V. of New Life R. (Samlang Chivit Thmey)
3)	Phnom Penh	90.0	10	FM90 (Reach Sey, Big Bird)
19)	Phnom Penh	90.5		Ta Phrom Radio
4)	Battambang	91.0		R. FM Khemara
6)	Takhao	91.0		rel. Phnom Penh 95.0
7)	Phnom Penh	92.0		R. France Int. (French)
5)	Sihanoukville	92.0	1.6	FM92 (mostly rel. Phnom Penh 95.0, 97.0)
7)	Siem Reap	92.0		R. France Int. (unconfirmed)
6)	Siem Reap	93.0	3	R. Bayon FM 93
9)	Kampot	93.25		
19)	Phnom Penh	93.5		FM 93.5
7)	Sihanoukville	94.5		R. France Int. (French)
6)	Phnom Penh	95.0	10	R. Bayon FM (Eagle 95)
18)	Sisopohon	96.5	10	FM 96.5,
8)	Phnom Penh	97.0	10	R Apsara
9)	Phnom Penh	97.5	1	Love FM (English)
10)	Phnom Penh	98.0	10	FM98
11)	Phnom Penh	99.0	10	FM99 (Chroo FM?)
9)	Preah Vihear	99.0		
12)	Phnom Penh	99.5	0.5	FEBC
13)	Phnom Penh	100.0		BBC World Service (E.)
9)	Kompong Cham	100.5	1	FM 100.5
9)	Siem Reap	100.5		Sweet FM
9)	Sihanoukville	100.5		
20)	Phnom Penh	101.5		Radio Australia: 24h
15)	Phnom Penh	102.0	10	WMC R.
15)	Kompong Thom	102.2		WMC R.
9)	Phnom Penh	103.0	10	Municipality R. (Khmer)
9)	Battambang	103.25		Sweet FM
9)	Svey Rieng	103.75		Sweet FM
16)	Phnom Penh	105.0	5	Sombok Ka Mum (R. Beehive)
17)	Phnom Penh	107.0	1	Planet FM

Addresses and other information
1) Nº 29, Street 335, Phnom Penh – **2)** PO Box 1426 Phnom Penh. Operated by Final Frontiers Foundation – **3)** Chamkadong, Phnom Penh 12401 – **6)** Near Holiday Hotel, Phnom Penh – **7)** Centre Culturel Français, No 218, Keo Chea (Street 184), Phnom Penh – **8)** No 69, Street No 57 (Corner Street No 370), Phnom Penh – **9)** No 02, Confédération de la Russie, Sankat Monorom, Khann 7 Makara, Phnom Penh – **10)** No. 27B, Street 472 Phnom Penh 12312. Owned by the Royal Cambodian Armed Forces, operated by the Kantana Group (Bangkok, Thailand) – **11)** No 41, Street 360, Phnom Penh – **12)** F.PI: 10kW on 99.5MHz. Trs on 810 and 1413kHz – **15)** Women's Center of Cambodia, 488, Sangkat Phsar Demthkov, Khan Chamcar Morn, Phnom Penh 12307 – **16)** No 44G, Street 360, Sangkat Boeung Keng Kang III, Khan Chamkarmorn, Phnom Penh 12304 – **17)** No 18, Rd. 562, Phnom Penh 12151 – **18)** Phum Svay Hill, Kou Than Village, O Ampil Commune, Sispohon, Banteay Meanchey Province – **19)** No 27B Street 472, Phnom Penh 12312. Owned by Funcinpec Party.

CAMEROON

L.T: UTC +1h — **Pop:** 16m — **Pr.L:** French, English, ethnic — **E.C:** 50Hz, 220V — **ITU:** CME.

MINISTRY OF COMMUNICATION (MINCOM)
Yaoundé ☎ +237 2 223155 🖷 +237 2 233022
Web: www.mincom.gov.cm **Email:** mincomonline2002@yahoo.fr

CAMEROON RADIO TELEVISION (CRTV)
B.P. 1634, Yaoundé ☎ +237 214077/88 🖷 +237 204340
Web: www.crtv.cm **L.P:** GM: Prof. Gervais Mendo Ze. Dir. of Prgrs: Dr. Gervais Mbarga. Tech. Dir: Emmanuel Agbor.
FM: 1) Yaoundé 88.8MHz 10kW – **2)** Douala 89.2/91.3/94.5/98.0/104.9MHz 10/10/3/10kW – **3)** Buéa 94.5/98.6/107.9MHz – **4)** Garoua 102.3MHz 10kW – **5)** Bertoua 89.8/92.9MHz 10/10kW – **6)** Bafoussam 91.1/93.5MHz 10/10kW – **7)** Bamenda 107.1MHz 10kW – **8)** Ebolowa 96.0MHz 10kW – **9)** Adamaoua 102.5MHz 10kW – **10)** Maroua 94.8MHz – **11)** Suelada 105MHz.

Addresses & other information
1) Poste National. N. in French: 0500, 0600, 1200, 1600, 1900. **N. in English:** 0530, 0630, 1400, 1830, 2300. **ANN:** E: "This is Yaoundé, the national station of CRTV". F: "Ici Yaoundé, poste nationale de la CRTV" – **CRTV du Centre** on 101.9MHz – **Yaoundé FM 94 in French** on 94.0MHz (rel. National Sce. 0600-1700). – **2) CRTV Littoral**, B.P. 986, Douala. - **FM 105** on 104.9MHz – **ANN:** E: "This is Douala, the Littoral provincial st. of CRTV. "Ici Douala, CRTV, station provinciale de la Cameroon Radio Television du Sud-Ouest". – **3) CRTV Sud-Ouest**, P.M.B, Buéa. **Local N. in French/English:** 0610, 0830, 1615, 1850, 2130. **Mount Cameroon** - **FM** on 107.9MHz – **ANN:** F: "Ici Buea, station provinciale de la Cameroon Radio-Television, du Sud-Ouest". E: "This is Buea, the So.We. provincial st. of the Cameroon Radio-Television". – **4) CRTV Nord**, B.P. 103, Garoua. **Local N: English:** 1330. **French:** 0600 – **ANN:** E: "This is Garoua, provincial st. of CRTV". F: "Ici Garoua, station provinciale de la C.R.T.V. du nord". –**5) CRTV Est**, B.P. 230, Bertoua, Eastern Province. Provincial Sce: 0430-0910 & 1100-2300 on 92.9MHz. **Local N. in English:** 1715. Rel National Sce: 0430-2400 on 89.8MHz – **ANN:** E: "This is Bertoua, the Eastern provincial st. of CRTV, Cameroon Radio & Television Corporation". F: "Ici Bertoua, station provinciale de la CRTV" – **6) CRTV Ouest**, B.P. 970, Bafoussam, Western Province – **ANN:** E: "This is Bafoussam, the Western provincial st. of R. Cameroon". F: "Ici Bafoussam, station provinciale de R.Cameroon". – **7) CRTV Nord-Ouest**, B.P. 4049, Bamenda, North-Western Province. **Local N: English:** 0515. 1705, 2130. **French:** 0720, 1840 – **ANN:** E: "This is Bamenda, the North Western provincial st. of R. Cameroon". F: "Ici Bamenda, station provinciale de la Cameroun Radio Télévision, CRTV". – **8) CRTV Sud**, Ebolowa. – **9) CRTV Adamaoua**, Ngaoundéré. – **10) CRTV Extrême-Nord**, Maroua. – **11)** Suelada.

Other stations:
Fem-FM, Mbalmayo: 107.1MHz. 0500-2000. **Web:** www.gcnet.cm/afac/Fem-FM.htm – **R. Bonne Nouvelle**, Yaoundé: 97.7MHz. – **R. Lumière**, Yaoundé: 91.9MHz. – **R. Reine**, Yaoundé: 103.7MHz. – **R. Rurale de Tana**, Yagoua. – **RTV Siantou**, B.P. 4, Yaoundé: 90.5MHz. Tel/Fax: 306271. **Web:** www.gcnet.cm/siantou/rst.htm **Email:** rts@gcnet.cm – **R. Venus**, Yaoundé: 95.4MHz – **R. Veritas,** Douala: 96.9MHz – **Real Time Music**, Douala: 103.5MHz.

BBC African Sce: Douala 93.6MHz, Yaoundé 98.4MHz.
RFI Afrique: Yaoundé 105.5MHz, Douala 97.8MHz, Bafoussam 101.1MHz in French & English.
Africa No 1, Douala: 102MHz (see main entry under Gabon).

CANADA

L.T: See World Time Table (DST 3 Apr - 30 Oct where applicable) — **Pop:** 32 million — **Pr.L:** English, French — **E.C:** 60Hz, 120V. — **ITU:** CAN

CANADIAN RADIO-TELEVISION AND TELECOMMUNICATIONS COMMISSION (CRTC)
Ottawa, ON K1A 0N2. ☎ +1 819 997 0313. 🖷 +1 819 994 0218.
Web: www.crtc.gc.ca
L.P: Chair: Charles Dalfen. Vice-Chair, Broadcasting: Andrée Wylie. Commissioners: Jean-Marc Demers, J. Stuart Langford, Joan Pennefather. Executive Director, Broadcasting Directorate: Marc O'Sullivan.
The CRTC is an independent public authority vested with the authority to regulate and supervise all aspects of the Canadian broadcasting system.

CANADIAN BROADCASTING CORPORATION SOCIÉTÉ RADIO-CANADA (Publicly owned)
Head Office: 181 Queen St., P.O. Box 3220, Station C, Ottawa ON K1Y 1E4. ☎ +1 613 288 6000. 🖷 +1 613 288 6335.
Web: www.cbc.radio-canada.ca
L.P: President and CEO, Robert Rabinovitch. Chair, Board of Directors: Carole Taylor. Vice-President and Chief Technology Officer: Raymond Carnovale. Vice-President, Comm.: Bill Chambers. Sen. Dir. Corporate Comm.: Martine Ménard.
English Networks: P.O. Box 500, Station A, Toronto ON M5W 1E6. ☎ +1 416 205 3311. **Web:** www.cbc.ca
L.P: Vice-President, English Radio: Jane Chalmers. Editor in Chief CBC News (radio & TV) Current Affairs, Newsworld & cbc.ca, Tony Burman. Deputy Dir., English Comm.: Bridget Hoffer.
French Networks: P.O. Box 6000, Montreal PQ H3C 3A8. ☎ +1 514 597 6000. **Web:** www.radio-canada.ca
L.P: Vice-President, French Radio and New Media: Sylvain Lafrance. Senior Dir., Comm. (radio): Guylaine Bergeron. Gen. Dir. of French Information Radio: Alain Saulnier.

English Radio

CBC Radio One (mono): *=also on Shortwave.

MW:	Location	kHz	kW	Call
1)	Grand Falls NL	540	10	CBT
2)	Regina SK	540	50	CBK
3)	Whitehorse YT	570	5/1	CFWH
4)	St. John's NL	640	10	CBN
5)	Vancouver BC*	690	50	CBU
7)	Edmonton AB	740	50	CBX
36)	Fort Smith NT	860	0.099	CBDI
10)	Inuvik NT	860	1	CHAK
11)	Prince Rupert BC	860	10	CFPR
15)	Corner Brook NL	990	10	CBY
16)	Winnipeg MB	990	50/46	CBW
17)	Calgary AB	1010	50	CBR
18)	Moncton NB	1070	50	CBA
19)	Sydney NS	1140	10	CBI
21)	Iqaluit NU	1230	1	CFFB
23)	Yellowknife NT	1340	2.5	CFYK
24)	Gander NL	1400	4	CBG
25)	Windsor ON	1550	10	CBE

FM:	Location	MHz	kW	Call
8)	Thunder Bay ON	88.3	23.7	CBQT-FM
13)	Montreal QC	88.5	16.9	CBME-FM
30)	Kelowna BC	88.9	4.7	CBTK-FM
6)	Kitchener/Waterloo ON	89.1	5	CBLA-FM-2
22)	Goose Bay NL*	89.5	4.5	CFGB-FM
9)	Halifax NS	90.5	91	CBHA-FM
31)	Victoria BC	90.5	3	CBCV-FM
32)	St. John NB	91.3	80	CBD-FM
12)	Ottawa ON	91.5	84	CBO-FM
33)	Prince George BC	91.5	100	CBYG-FM
13)	Sherbrooke QC	91.7	25	CBMB-FM
6)	London ON	93.5	69.3	CBCL-FM
6)	Huntsville ON	94.3	70	CBLU-FM
34)	Charlottetown PE	96.1	100	CBCT-FM
38)	Sept Îles QC	96.9	15	CBSE-FM
18)	Allardville NB	97.9	50	CBAA-FM
16)	Brandon MB	97.9	90	CBWV-FM
6)	Peterborough ON	98.7	10.17	CBCP-FM
6)	Toronto ON	99.1	55.1	CBLA-FM
14)	Fredericton NB	99.5	3.2	CBZF-FM
35)	Sudbury ON	99.9	50	CBCS-FM
17)	Lethbridge AB	100.1	100	CBRL-FM
29)	Chicoutimi QC	102.7	30	CBJE-FM
13)	Quebec QC	104.7	24.9	CBVE-FM
20)	Rankin Inlet NU	105.1	0.087	CBQR-FM
37)	La Ronge SK	105.9	0.08	CBKA-FM
9)	Middleton NS	106.5	93.4	CBHM-FM
9)	Mulgrave NS	106.7	93.4	CBHB-FM
6)	Kingston ON	107.5	100	CBCK-FM

SW:

	Location	kHz	kW	Call	Times
5)	Vancouver BC	6160	0.5	CKZU	1400(Sun 1500)-0905 (relays CBU)
22)	St. John's NL	6160	1	CKZN	0930-0500 (relays CFGB-FM)

+ 374 relay tr's

CBC Radio Two (stereo):

FM:	Location	MHz	kW	Call
5)	Kelowna BC	89.7	6	CBU-FM-3
13)	Sherbrooke QC	89.7	25	CBM-FM-1
25)	Windsor ON	89.9	100	CBE-FM
35)	Sudbury ON	90.1	50	CBBS-FM
1)	Grand Falls NL	90.7	100	CBN-FM-1
6)	Kitchener/Waterloo ON	90.7	4	CBL-FM-2
7)	Edmonton AB	90.9	100	CBX-FM
15)	Corner Brook NL	91.1	3	CBN-FM-2
17)	Lethbridge AB	91.7	100	CBBC-FM
31)	Victoria BC	92.1	74	CBU-FM-1
16)	Brandon MB	92.7	90	CBWS-FM
6)	Kingston ON	92.9	1.6	CBBK-FM
9)	Middleton/Kentville NS	93.3	8	CBH-FM-1
13)	Montreal QC	93.5	24.6	CBM-FM
6)	Toronto ON	94.1	38	CBL-FM
23)	Yellowknife NT	95.3	0.114	VF2146
10)	Moncton NB	95.5	77	CBA-FM
13)	Quebec QC	96.1	0.31	CBM-FM-2
2)	Regina SK	96.9	100	CBK-FM
16)	Winnipeg MB	98.3	160	CBW-FM
6)	London ON	100.5	22.5	CBBL-FM
14)	Fredericton NB	101.5	100	CBZ-FM
8)	Thunder Bay ON	101.7	23.5	CBQ-FM
17)	Calgary AB	102.1	100	CBR-FM
9)	Halifax NS	102.7	81	CBH-FM
9)	Mulgrave/Antigonish NS	103.1	40.5	CBH-FM-2
12)	Ottawa ON	103.3	84	CBOQ-FM
6)	Peterborough ON	103.9	17.3	CBBP-FM
34)	Charlottetown PE	104.7	100	CBCH-FM
6)	Huntsville ON	104.7	70	CBL-FM-1
19)	Sydney NS	105.1	61.7	CBI-FM
5)	Kamloops BC	105.3	4.75	CBU-FM-4
2)	Saskatoon SK	105.5	98	CBKS-FM
5)	Vancouver BC	105.7	50	CBU-FM
4)	St. John's NL	106.9	100	CBN-FM

+ 14 relay tr's

French Radio – Radio Canada

Première Chaîne (mono):

MW:	Location	kHz	kW	Call
25)	Windsor ON	540	2.5/5	CBEF
7)	Edmonton AB	680	10	CHFA
2)	Saskatoon SK	860	10	CBKF-2
6)	Toronto ON	860	50	CJBC
16)	Winnipeg MB	1050	10	CKSB

FM:	Location	MHz	kW	Call
18)	Moncton NB	88.5	22	CBAF-FM
26)	Rimouski QC	89.1	19.4	CJBR-FM
12)	Ottawa ON	90.7	84	CBOF-FM
39)	Rouyn-Noranda QC	90.7	16	CHLM-FM
9)	Halifax NS	92.3	91	CBAF-FM-5
29)	Chicoutimi QC	93.7	50	CBJ-FM
13)	Montreal QC	95.1	16.86	CBF-FM
40)	Trois Rivières QC	96.5	66.7	CBF-FM-8
2)	Regina SK	97.7	13.7	CBKF-FM
5)	Vancouver BC	97.7	46	CBUF-FM
38)	Sept Îles QC	98.1	96.75	CBSI-FM
35)	Sudbury ON	98.1	50	CBON-FM
41)	Sherbrooke QC	101.1	35	CBF-FM-10
28)	Matane QC	102.1	42.93	CBGA-FM
18)	Fredericton/St.John NB	102.3	84	CBAF-FM-1
18)	Allardville NB	105.7	50	CBAF-FM-2
27)	Quebec QC	106.3	20	CBV-FM

+ 147 relay tr's

La chaîne musicale (stereo):

FM:	Location	MHz	kW	Call
18)	Fredericton/St.John NB	88.1	78.5	CBAL-FM-4
2)	Saskatoon SK	88.7	100	CKSB-FM-2
2)	Regina SK	88.9	96.4	CKSB-FM-1
39)	Rouyn-Noranda QC	89.9	17.2	CBFX-FM-4
16)	Winnipeg MB	89.9	61	CKSB-FM
7)	Edmonton AB	90.1	100	CBCX-FM-1
6)	Toronto ON	90.3	3.5	CJBC-FM
41)	Sherbrooke QC	90.7	25	CBFX-FM-2
35)	Sudbury ON	90.9	50	CBBX-FM
5)	Vancouver BC	90.9	1.28	CBUX-FM
9)	Halifax NS	91.5	77.5	CBAX-FM
27)	Quebec QC	95.3	24.9	CBVX-FM
38)	Sept Îles QC	96.1	84.8	CBRX-FM-2
18)	Moncton NB	98.3	77	CBAL-FM
13)	Montreal QC	100.7	100	CBFX-FM
29)	Chicoutimi QC	100.9	50	CBJX-FM
26)	Rimouski QC	101.5	50	CBRX-FM
18)	Allardville NB	101.9	13.3	CBAL-FM-1
12)	Ottawa ON	102.5	84	CBOX-FM
40)	Trois Rivières QC	104.3	43	CBFX-FM-1
28)	Matane QC	107.5	31.7	CBRX-FM-1

+ 13 relay tr's

Addresses:

1) 2 Harris Ave., Grand Falls-Windsor NL A2A 2J7. **Web:** stjohns.cbc.ca/morningshow/morning_central.jsp – **2)** 2440 Broad St., Regina SK S4P 4A1. **Web:** sask.cbc.ca **Web (F):** www.radio-canada.ca/regions/saskatchewan/ – **3)** 3103 3rd Avenue, Whitehorse YT Y1A 1E5. **Web:** north.cbc.ca – **4)** P.O. Box 12010, Station A, St. John's NL A1B 3T8. **Web:** stjohns.cbc.ca – **5)** P.O. Box 4600, Vancouver BC V6B 4A2. **Web:** vancouver.cbc.ca **Web (F):** www.radio-canada.ca/regions/colombie-britannique/ – **6)** P.O. Box 500, Station A, Toronto ON M5W 1E6. **Web:** toronto.cbc.ca **Web (F):** www.radio-canada.ca/regions/ontario/ – **7)** P.O. Box 555, Edmonton AB T5J 2P4. **Web:** edmonton.cbc.ca **Web (F):** www.radio-canada.ca/regions/alberta/ – **8)** 213 East Miles St., Thunder

Bay ON P7C 1J5. **Web:** nwo.cbc.ca – **9)** P.O. 3000, Halifax NS B3J 3E9. **Web:** novascotia.cbc.ca – **10)** 155 Mackenzie Rd., Bag Service 8, Inuvik NT X0E 0T0. **Web:** north.cbc.ca – **11)** 222 3rd Ave., W, Prince Rupert BC V8J 1L1. **Web:** vancouver.cbc.ca/daybreaknorth/– **12)** P.O. Box 3220, Station C, Ottawa ON K1Y 1E4. **Web:** ottawa.cbc.ca **Web (F):** www.radio-canada.ca/regions/ottawa/ – **13)** P.O. Box 6000, Montreal QC H3C 3A8. **Web:** montreal.cbc.ca **Web (F):** www.radio-canada.ca/regions/montreal/ – **14)** P.O. Box 2200, Fredericton NB E3B 5G4. **Web:** nb.cbc.ca/fredericton – **15)** P.O. Box 610, Corner Brook NL A2H 6G1 – **16)** 541 Portage Ave., Winnipeg MB R3B 2G1. **Web:** winnipeg.cbc.ca **Web (F):** www.radio-canada.ca/regions/manitoba/ – **17)** P.O. Box 2640, Calgary AB T2P 2M7. **Web:** calgary.cbc.ca – **18)** P.O. Box 950, Moncton NB E1C 8N8. **Web:** nb.cbc.ca/moncton **Web (F):** www.radio-canada.ca/regions/atlantique/ – **19)** 285 Alexandra St., Sydney NS B1S 2E8. **Web:** novascotia.cbc.ca/capebreton/ – **20)** Box 130, Rankin Inlet NU X0C 0G0. **Web:** north.cbc.ca – **21)** P.O. Box 490, Iqaluit NU X0A 0H0. **Web:** north.cbc.ca – **22)** P.O. Box 1029, Station C, Happy Valley – Goose Bay NL A0P 1C0. **Web:** stjohns.cbc.ca/morningshow/morning_goosebay.jsp – **23)** P.O. Box 160, Yellowknife NT X1A 2N2. **Web:** north.cbc.ca – **24)** P.O. Box 369, Gander NL A1V 1W7. **Web:** stjohns.cbc.ca/morningshow/ morning_central.jsp – **25)** 825 Riverside Dr. W., Windsor ON N9A 5K9. **Web:** windsor.cbc.ca – **26)** 273 St. Jean Baptiste Ouest, Rimouski QC G5L 4J8. **Web (F):** www.radio-canada.ca/regions/bas-st-laurent/ – **27)** 250 Grande-Allee Ouest, Room 005, Quebec QC G1R 2H4. **Web (F):** www.radio-canada.ca/regions/quebec/ – **28)** 155, rue Saint-Sacrement, Matane QC G4W 1Y9. **Web (F):** www.radio-canada.ca/regions/ gaspesie-lesiles/ – **29)** 2303, rue Sir Wilfrid-Laurier, Jonquière QC G7X 5Z2. **Web (F):** www.radio-canada.ca/regions/saguenay-lac/ – **30)** 243 Lawrence Ave., Kelowna BC V1Y 2Y4. **Web:** www.vancouver.cbc.ca/daybreaksouth/ – **31)** 1025 Pandora Avenue, Victoria BC V8V 3P6. **Web:** vancouver.cbc.ca/ontheisland – **32)** P.O. Box 2358, St. John NB E2L 3V6. **Web:** www.nb.cbc.ca/saintjohn – **33)** 1268 - 5th Ave., Prince George BC V2I 3L2. **Web:** vancouver.cbc.ca/daybreaknorth – **34)** P.O. Box 2230, Charlottetown PE C1A 8B9. **Web:** pei.cbc.ca – **35)** 15 MacKenzie St., Sudbury ON P3C 4Y1. **Web:** sudbury.cbc.ca – **36)** Box 1439, Fort Smith NT X0E 0P0. **Web:** north.cbc.ca – **37) Web:** sask.cbc.ca/radio/keewatincountry – **38)** 350 rue Smith Bureau 30, Sept Iles QC G4R 3X2. **Web (F):** www.radio-canada.ca/regions/cote-nord/ – **39)** 70, rue Principale, Rouyn-Noranda J9X 4P2. **Web (F):** www.radio-canada.ca/regions/abitibi/ – **40)** 25, rue des Forges Bureau 101, Trois-Rivières QC G9A 6A7. **Web (F):** www.radio-canada.ca/regions/mauricie/ **41)** 65, rue Belvedère Nord Bureau 190, Sherbrooke QC J1H 4A7. **Web (F):** www.radio-canada.ca/regions/estrie/

DIGITAL RADIO (DAB): All four domestic CBC radio networks are available in Montreal, Ottawa, Toronto and Vancouver on freq. from 1452.810-1482.464MHz

Provinces & Terrritories: AB=Alberta, BC=British Columbia, MB=Manitoba, NB=New Brunswick, NL=Newfoundland & Labrador, NS=Nova Scotia, NT=North West Territories, NU=Nunavut, ON=Ontario, PE=Prince Edward Island, QC=Quebec, SK=Saskatchewan, YT=Yukon

SW: CBC NORTH QUEBEC: 9625kHz, 1155-0610 in English/French/Inuktitut/Cree. Via R. Canada International transmitter at Sackville.

INTERNATIONAL SERVICES:
Radio Canada International

see International Broadcasting section

PRIVATELY OWNED STATIONS

Tr's below 100W not mentioned. *=also Shortwave, f=mainly French prgrs, e=mainly English prgrs, b=bilingual E/F, m=multilingual/ethnic. +=inactive or F.Pl. c=will change to FM.

SW:

MW:	Call	kHz	kW
464)	CIAO	530	1/0.25m
500)	CHLN	550	10/5f
2)	CHTK	560	1/0.25e
402)	CFOS	560	7.5/1e
901D)	CHVO	560	5e
4A)	CKWL	570	1e
212)	CKSW	570	10e
401)	CKGL	570	10e
900)	CFCB	570	1e
6)	CKXR	580	10/1e
100)	CKUA	580	10e
403)	CFRA	580	50/10e
404)	CKPR	580	5/1e
406)	CKWW	580	0.5e
7)	CFTK	590	1e
302)	CFAR	590	10/1e

MW:	Call	kHz	kW
407)	CJCL	590	50e
503)	CKRS	590	25/5f
608)	CJCW	590	1/0.25e
901)	VOCM	590	20e
8)	CKBD	600	10e
200)	CJWW	600	25/8e
408)	CKAT	600	10/5e
9)	CHNL	610	25/5e
90)	CKRW	610	1e
101)	CKYL	610	10e
303)	CHTM	610	1e
409)	CKTB	610	10/5e
505)	CHNC	610	10/5f
201)	CKRM	620	10e
502)	CFRP	620	1f
901B)	CKCM	620	10e

MW:	Call	kHz	kW
12)	CKOV	630	5/1e
102)	CHED	630	50e
411)	CFCO	630	10/6e
507)	CHLT	630	10/5f
700)	CFCY	630	10e
412)	CFMJ	640	50e
38)	CISL	650	10/9e
208)	CKOM	650	10e
901c)	CKGA	650	5e
108)	CFFR	660	50e
305)	CJOB	680	50e
407)	CFTR	680	50e
504)	CINF	690	50f
416)	CJRN	710	5/2.5e
509)	CKVM	710	10/1f
901E)	CKVO	710	10e
700)	CHTN	720	10/7.5e
13)	CHMJ	730	50e
306)	CKDM	730	10/5e
510)	CKAC	730	50f
449)	CHWO	740	50e
901A)	CHCM	740	10e
211)	CKJH	750	25e
414)	CKGB	750	10/5e
24A)	CFLD	760	1e
104)	CHQR	770	50e
802)	CFDR	780	50/15e
103)	CFCW	790	50e
419)	CIGM	790	50e
900R)	CFNW	790	1e
14)	CKOR	800	10/0.5e
202)	CHAB	800	10e
406)	CKLW	800	50e
423)	CJBQ	800	10e
425)	CKDR	800	1/0.7e
511)	CHRC	800	50f
512)	CJAD	800	50/10e
902)	VOWR	800	10/2.5e
307)	CKJS	810	10m
603)	CJVA	810	10f
440)	CHAM	820	50/10e
127A)	CKKY	830	10/3.5e
4B)	CKBX	840	1/0.5e
129B)	CKBA	850	1e
6R)	CKIR	870	1/0.25e
24)	CFBV	870	1/0.5e
900B)	CFSX	870	0.5e
10A)	CKKC	880	1/0.7e
102)	CHQT	880	50e
312)	CKLQ	880	10e
30)	CJDC	890	10e
16)	CKMO	900	10e
203)	CKBI	900	10e
424)	CHML	900	50e
516)	CKTS	900	10e
803)	CKDH	900	1e
106)	CKDQ	910	50e
4)	CKCQ	920	10/1e
308)	CFRY	920	25/15e
428)	CKNX	920	10/1e
802)	CJCH	920	25e
107)	CJCA	930	50e
605)	CFBC	930	50e
903)	CJYQ	930	50/25e
204)	CJGX	940	50/10e
504)	CINW	940	50e
309)	CFAM	950	10e
606)	CKNB	950	10/1b
805)	CHER	950	10e
108)	CFAC	960	50e
430)	CFFX	960	10/5e
806)	CHNS	960	10e
109)	CJYR	970	10e
19)	CKNW	980	50e
205)	CJME	980	10/5e
431)	CFPL	980	10/5e
432)	CKRU	980	10/7.5e
521)	C...	+980	10f
519)	CKGM	990	50e
433)	CFRB	*1010	50e
129C)	CKVH	1020	1/0.4e

MW:	Call	kHz	kW
15)	CKST	1040	50e
520)	CJMS	1040	5/1.1f
206)	CJNB	1050	10e
434)	CHUM	1050	50e
111)	CKMX	*1060	50e
20)	CFAX	1070	10e
436)	CHOK	1070	10e
438)	CKKW	1090	10e
21)	CKWX	1130	50e
122)	CHRB	1140	50/46e
22)	CKFR	1150	10e
440)	CKOC	1150	50e
505R)	CHGM	1150	5f
522)	CJRC	1150	50/5f
207)	CFSL	1190	10/5e
403)	CFGO	1200	50e
129A)	CKWA	1210	1e
210A)	CFYM	1210	1/0.5e
905)	VOAR	1210	10e
309A)	CJRB	1220	10e
442)	CHSC	1220	10e
443)	CJRL	c1220	5/1e
444)	CJUL	1220	1e
500A)	CKSM	1220	10/2.5f
535)	CFVM	1220	10/5f
9A)	CJNL	1230	1e
109A)	CIYR	c1230	1e
410R)	CHYK-2	1230	1/0.6f
900C)	CFGN	1230	0.25e
900D)	CFLN	1230	1e
23)	CKMK	1240	1e
14A)	CJOR	1240	1e
26)	CJAV	1240	1e
33B)	CFNI	1240	1e
206A)	CJNS	1240	1e
302A)	CJAR	1240	1e
447)	CJCS	1240	1e
526)	CFLM	1240	1f
527)	CJMD	1240	1f
901BR)	CKIM	1240	1e
309B)	CHSM	1250	10e
449)	CJYE	1250	10/5e
119)	CFRN	1260	50e
610)	CKHJ	1260	10e
120)	CHAT	1270	10e
530)	CFGT	1270	10/5f
805)	CJCB	1270	10e
33C)	CHQB	1280	1e
207A)	CJSL	1280	10e
534)	CFMB	1280	50m
311)	CFRW	1290	10e
451)	CJBK	1290	10e
127)	CHLW	1310	10e
453)	CIWW	1310	50e
29)	CHMB	1320	50m
449A)	CJMR	1320	20e
809)	CKEC	1320	25e
210)	CJYM	1330	10e
6A)	CKCR	1340	1e
9R)	CINL	1340	1e
11)	CIVH	1340	1e
10)	CFKC	1340	0.25e
106A)	CIBQ	1340	1e
127B)	CJCM	c1340	1e
527R)	CFED	1340	0.25f
900E)	CFLW	1340	0.25e
907)	CKHV	1340	1e
456)	CKDO	1350	10/5e
812A)	CKAD	1350	1e
609)	CKBC	1360	10e
129)	CFOK	1370	10e
458)	CKLC	1380	10e
459)	CKPC	1380	10e
6B)	CKGR	1400	1e
14D)	CIOR	1400	1e
9R)	CHNL-1	1400	1e
106B)	CKSQ	1400	1e
32)	CFUN	1410	50e
451)	CKSL	1410	10e
463)	CKPT	1420	10/5e
812B)	CKDY	1420	1e

MW:	Call	kHz	kW	MW:	Call	kHz	kW
470)	CHKT	1430	50m	117)	CJPR	c1490	1e
121)	CKJR	1440	10e	212A)	CJSN	1490	1e
14C)	CHOR	1450	1e	402R)	CFPS	1490	1e
109R)	CKYR	c1450	0.25e	472)	CKOT	1510	10/0e
467)	CHUC	1450	8/1e	473)	CHIN	1540	50/30m
812C)	CFAB	1450	1e	309C)	CKMW	1570	10e
468)	CJOY	1460	10e	537)	CFAV	1570	10f
34)	CJVB	1470	50m	467)	CHUC	+1580	10e
33A)	CFWB	1490	0.875e	536)	CJWI	1610	1f

	Call	kHz	kW	Relays
111)	CFVP	6030	0.1	CKMX, Calgary: 24h
433)	CFRX	6070	1	CFRB, Toronto: 24h

Addresses and other information for MW and SW stations: **Station Networks:** There are several regional networks. The st's of a network often transmit a common prgr. during part of the broadcast day. The main st has been given a pure number, under which details common to all st's or pertaining to the main st only are found, while the other st's have been given the same number with an individual capital letter added, under which details pertaining only to this st are found. R. means a pure relay st. – **Hours of transmission:** Most st's are on the air 24h. – **Programme Networks: French:** MW: Radiomédia. FM: Télémédia, Radiomutuel. **English:** Broadcast News, Standard Broadcast News, Telemedia Network, Western Information Network, Pelmorex Radio Network. These networks provide news and/or other prgrs. – **Station information on the Internet:** strategis.ic.gc.ca/epic/internet/insmt-gst.nsf/en/h_sf01842e.html (government site, technical database of Industry Canada). www.rcc.ryerson.ca/rta/ccf/CCF_Listings_and_Histories/Radio (university site, station histories).

British Columbia
2) 215 Cow Bay Road #212, Prince Rupert, BC V8J 1A2 – **4)** 160 Front Str, Quesnel, BC V2J 2K1 – **4A)** 83 S. First Ave, Williams Lake, BC V2G 1H4. Own prgrs 1400-1800 – **4B)** P.O. Box 939, 100 Mile House, BC V0K 2E0. Own prgrs: Mon-Fri 1500-2100. Sat 1500-1700, 2000-2100 – **6)** P.O. Box 69, Salmon Arm, BC V1E 4N2. Ann: "Columbia Shuswap R." – **6A)** P.O. Box 1420, Revelstoke, BC V0E 2S0. Own prgrs Mon-Fri 1400-2000, Sat 1400-1700 – **6B)** P.O. Box 1403, Golden, BC V0A 1H0. Own prgrs: As 6A) – **6R)** = Invermere – **7)** 4625 Lazelle Ave, Terrace, BC V8G 1S4 – **8)** 1401 West 8th Ave, Vancouver, BC V6H 1C9 – **9)** 611 Lansdowne St, Kamloops, BC V2C 1Y6. 1340=Ashcroft/Cache Creek, BC, 1400=Clearwater, BC – **9A)** P.O. Box 925 Stn Main, Merritt, BC V1K 1B8. Own prgrs Mon-Sat 1400-1800, 2000-2100 – **10)** P.O. Box 310, Creston, BC V0B 1G0. Own prgrs: 1200-0600. (Key st: CJAT Radio, 1560 2nd Ave, Trail, BC V1R 1M4. On FM 95.7.) Ann: "KBS" – **10A)** 1560-2nd Avenue Trail, Nelson, BC V1R 1M4 – **11)** P.O. Box 1370, Vanderhoof, BC V0J 3A0. Own prgrs Mon-Fri 1400-1700, 2300-0200, at other times rel. CJCI-FM 97.3 (1940-3rd Ave, Prince George, BC V2M 1G7) – **12)** 3805 Lakeshore Rd, Kelowna, BC V1W 3K6 – **13)** 700 West Georgia Street #2000, Vancouver, BC V7Y 1K9 – **14)** 33 Carmi Ave, Penticton, BC V2A 3G4. Ann: "OR Network" – **14A)** P.O. Box 539, Osoyoos, BC V0H 1V0. Own prgrs W 1400-0200 (Sat 2200) – **14C)** P.O. Box 170, Summerland, BC V0H 1Z0. Own prgrs 1400-0200 (Sat 2200) – **14D)** P.O. Box 1400, Princeton, BC V0X 1W0. Own prgrs Mon-Fri 1400-1800, 2300-0200, Sat. 1400-1800 – **15)** 300-380 West 2nd Avenue, Vancouver, BC V6B 2W5 – **16)** Village 900, 3100 Foul Bay Road, Victoria, BC V8P 5J2 – **19)** #2000-700 West Georgia St, Vancouver, BC V7Y 1K9 – **20)** 825 Broughton Str, Victoria, BC V8W 1E5 – **21)** 2440 Ash St, Vancouver, BC V5Z 4J6 – **22)** 300-435 Bernard Ave, Kelowna, BC V1Y 6N8 – **23)** 124 - 403 Mackenzie Blvd, Mackenzie, BC V0J 2C0 – **24)** P.O. Box 335, Smithers, BC V0J 2N0 – **24A)** P.O. Box 600, Burns Lake, BC V0J 1E0. Own prgrs 1700-2000 – **26)** 2970 3rd Ave, Port Alberni, BC V9Y 7N4 – **29)** #100-1200 West 73rd Ave, Vancouver, BC V6P 6G5. Prgr's mostly in Chinese – **30)** 901-102nd Ave, Dawson Creek, BC V1G 2B6 – **32)** 300-380 W. 2nd Ave, Vancouver, BC V5Y 1C8 – **33)** 1625-A McPhee Ave, Courtenay, BC V9N 3A6. 24h on FM + 1240/1280/1490kHz. (Stn 33) on FM only.) – **33A)** 909 Ironwood St, Campbell River, BC V9W 3E5 – **33B)** P.O. Box 1240, Port Hardy, BC V0N 2P0 – **33C)** 6816 Courtenay Str, Powell River, BC V8A 1X1 – **34)** A1-525 West Broadway, Vancouver, BC V5Z 4K5. Prgr's in E and 21 other languages. Chinese: W0400-1700, English 2000-0200. and within foreign language prgr's – **38)** 20-11151 Horseshoe Way, Richmond, BC V7A 4S5.

Yukon Territory
90) 203-4103 4th Ave, Whitehorse, YT Y1A 1H6.

Alberta
100) 400-10526 Jasper Ave, Edmonton, AB T5J 1Z7 – **101)** Bag 300, Peace River, AB T8S 1T5 – **102)** 5204-84th Str, Edmonton, AB T6E 5N8 – **103)** 4752-99th Str, Edmonton, AB T6E 5H5 – **104)** Shaw Court 105 630 - 3rd Ave. SW, Calgary, AB T2P 4L4 – **106)** P.O. Box 1480, Drumheller, AB T0J 0Y0 – **106A)** 8 - 403 2nd Ave. W, Brooks, AB T1R 0S3 – Own prgrs Mon-Fri 1300-2000, Sat 1400-1900 – **106B)** 4703-58 Str, Stettler, AB T0C 2L1 – Own prgrs: Mon-Fri 1300-0100, Sat 1400-1900) – **107)** #206, 4207-98th Street, Edmonton, AB T6E 5R7 – **108)** 240-2723 37th Avenue, N.E, Calgary, Alberta T1Y 5R8 – **109)** P.O. Box 7800, Edson, AB T7E 1V8 – **109A)** 506 Carmichael Lane, Hinton, AB, T7V 1S8. Own prgr's 1700-2200 – **111)** P.O. Box 2750, Stn. Main, Calgary, AB T2P 4P8 – **117)** P.O. Box 840, Blairmore, AB T0K 0E0. Own prgrs: W 1300-1600 (Sat 2000). Other times rel. CJOC FM – **119)** #100-18520 Stony Plain Rd, Edmonton, AB T5S 2E2 – **120)** 1111 Kingsway Avenue S.E, Medicine Hat, AB T1A 2Y1 – **121)** 5220-51st Ave, Wetaskiwin, AB T9A 3E2 – **122)** #11-5th Ave S.E, High River, AB T1V 1G2 – **127)** #201, 4341-50th Ave, St. Paul, AB T0A 3A3. Partly in netw. with st. 129) – **127A)** #2, 1037-2nd Ave, Wainwright, AB T9W 1K7 – **127B)** P.O. Box 433, Cold Lake, AB T9M 1R5 – **129)** 201-10030 106th St, Westlock, AB T7P 2K4 – **129A)** P.O. Box 2470, Slave Lake, AB T0G 2A0. Local prgrs: Mon-Fri 1400-2000 2200-0200, Sat 1400-1800 – **129B)** 1-4818 49th St, Athabasca, AB T9S 1C3. Own prgrs: 1400-0600 – **129C)** P.O. Box 2219, High Prairie, AB T0G 1E0. Local IDs inserted into netw. prgr's for all st's.

Saskatchewan
200) 345-4th Ave. S, Saskatoon, SK S7K 5S5 – **201)** 2060 Halifax St, Regina, SK S4P 1T7 – **202)** 1704 Main St. N, Moose Jaw, SK S6H 4P5 – **203)** P.O. Box 900, Prince Albert, SK S6V 7R4 – **204)** 120 Smith Str. E, Yorkton, SK S3N 3V3 – **205)** 210-2401 Saskatchewan Dr, Regina, S4P 4H8 – **206)** P.O. Box 1460, North Battleford, SK S9A 2Z5 – **206A)** P.O. Box 1660, Meadow Lake, SK S9X 1L5 – Own prgrs: W1500-1800, 1930-2400 – **207)** P.O. Box 340, Weyburn, SK S4H 2K2 – **207A)** 1134-5th St, Estevan, SK S4A 0Z4 – **208)** 715 Saskatchewan Crest West, Saskatoon, SK S7M 5V7 – **210)** P.O. Box 490, Rosetown, SK S0L 2V0. 1200-0700 (Sun 0600) – **210A)** Kindersley, SK (all correspondence to Rosetown) – **211)** P.O. Box 750, Melfort, SK S0E 1A0 – **212)** 134 Central Ave. N, Swift Current, SK S9H 0L1 – **212A)** P.O. Box 1176, Shaunavon, SK S0N 2M0. Own prgrs: Mon-Fri 1330-1800.

Manitoba
302) 316 Green St, Flin Flon, MB R8A 0H2 – **302A)** P.O. Box 2980, The Pas, MB R9A 1R7 – **303)** 201 Hayes Rd, Thompson, MB R8N 1M5 – **305)** 930 Portage Ave, Winnipeg, MB R3G 0P8 – **306)** 27-3rd Ave. N.E, Dauphin, MB R7N 0Y5 – **307)** 520 Corydon Ave, Winnipeg, MB R3L 0P1 – **308)** 1500 Saskatchewan Ave. W, Portage la Prairie, MB R1N 0N6 – **309)** R. Southern Manitoba, Box 950, Altona, MB R0G 0B0 – **309A)** P.O. Box 1220, Boissevain, MB R0K 0E0 – **309B)** P.O. Box 1250, Steinbach, MB R0A 2A0 – **309C)** P.O. Box 399, Winkler, MB R6W 4A6 – **311)** 1445 Pembina Hwy, Winnipeg, MB R3T 5C2 – **312)** 624-14th Str. E, Brandon, MB R7A 7E1.

Ontario
401) 305 King Str. W, Kitchener, ON N2G 4E4 – **402)** 270 9th St. E, Owen Sound, ON N4K 1N7. CFPS=Port Elgin repeater – **403)** 87 George St, Ottawa, ON K1N 9H7 – **404)** 87 N. Hill Str, Thunder Bay, ON P7A 5V6 – **406)** 1640 Ouellette Ave, Windsor, ON N8X 1L1 – **407)** 777 Jarvis Street, Toronto, ON M4Y 3B7 – **408)** P.O. Box 3000, North Bay, ON P1B 8K8 – **409)** 12 Yates Str, St. Catharines, ON L2R 6X7 – **410)** Kapuskasing, ON. c/o CHMT-FM, 202-32 Mountjoy Str. N, Timmins, ON P4N 4V6. (On FM 93.1MHz.) – **411)** P.O. Box 100, Chatham, ON N7M 3H3 – **412)** 1 Dundas Street West #1600, Toronto, ON M5G 1Z3. (Lic. to Richmond Hill, ON.) – **414)** 260 Second Ave, Timmins, ON P4N 2K3 – **416)** 316 4th St, Niagara Falls, ON L2E 3S8 – **419)** 880 Lasalle Blvd, Sudbury, ON P3A 1X5 – **423)** P.O. Box 488, Belleville, ON K8N 5B2 – **424)** 875 Main Str. West, Hamilton, ON L8S 4R1 – **425)** P.O. Box 580, Dryden, ON P8N 2Z3 – **428)** 215 Carling Terrace, Wingham, ON N0G 2W0 – **430)** 170 Queen, Kingston, ON K7K 1B2 – **431)** P.O. Box 2580, Station B, London, ON N6A 4H3 – **432)** 159 King St, Peterborough, ON K9J 2R8 – **433)** 2 St. Clair Ave. West #200, Toronto, ON M4V 1L6 – CE: David Simon. CFRX special ID twice an hour on 6070kHz – **V.** by QSL-card. Re. to ODXA, P.O. Box 161, Willowdale Station A, North York, ON M2N 5S8 – **434)** 1331 Yonge Str, Toronto, ON M4T 1Y1 – **436)** 1415 London Rd, Sarnia, ON N7S 1P6 – **438)** 255 King St. N. #207, Waterloo, ON N2J 4V2. (Lic. to Kitchener, ON.) – **440)** 883 Upper Wentworth St. #401, Hamilton, ON L9A 4Y6 – **442)** 36 Queenston St, St. Catharines, ON L2R 2Y9 – **443)** 128 Main St. S, Kenora, ON P9N 1S9 – **444)** Box 969, Cornwall, ON K6H 5V1 – **447)** 376 Romeo St. South, Stratford, ON N5A 4T9 – **449)** 284 Church St, Oakville, ON L6J 7N2. (QSL requests to ODXA, P.O. Box 161, Willowdale Stn A, North York, M2N 5S8.) – **449A)** P.O. Box 1320, Port Credit Postal Sta, Mississauga, ON L5G 4M3. (QSL requests: as above.) **451)** 743 Wellington Road S, London, ON N6C 4R5 – **453)** 2001 Thurston Drive, Ottawa, ON K1G 6C9 – **456)** 207-1200 Airport Blvd, Oshawa, ON L1J 8P5 – **458)** P.O. Box 1380, Kingston, ON K7L 4Y5 – **459)** 571 West St, Brantford, ON N3T 5P8 – **463)** P.O. Box 177, Peterborough, ON K9J 6Y8 – **464)** 5302 Dundas St. West, Etobicoke, ON M9B 1B2 – **467)** P.O. Box 520, Cobourg, ON K9A 4L3 – **468)** 75 Speedvale Ave, Guelph, ON N1E 6M3 – **470)** 8-135 East Beaver Creek Road, Richmond Hill, ON L4B 1E2 – Chinese: "Fairchild Radio" – **472)** P.O. Box 10, Tillsonburg, ON N4G 4H3. Daytime only (Jan. 1300-2215, July 1000-0100) – **473)** 622 College Str, Toronto, ON M6G 1B6.

Quebec
500) 1350 rue Royal, bureau 1200, Trois-Rivières, QC G9A 4J4 – **500A)** 6183 boul. Royal, bur. 130, Shawinigan, QC G9N 8O3 – **502)** c/o CHLC, 399 rue de Puyjalon, Baie Comeau, QC G5C 2Z7. Location: Forestville, QC – **503)** 121 Racine Est, Chicoutimi, QC G7H 5G4. Lic. to Jonquière, QC. – **504)** 215 St. Jacques St, suite 333, Montreal, QC H2Y 1M6. CINF=Info 690, CINW=940 News – **505)** C.P. 610, New Carlisle, QC G0C 1Z0. CHGM=Gaspé, QC – **507)** 4020 blvd. de Portland, Sherbrooke, QC J1L 2V6 – **509)** 62 rue Ste-Anne, Ville-Marie, QC J0Z 3W0 – **510)** 1411 rue Peel, bur. 400, Montréal, QC H3A 3L5 – **511)** 2136 Chemin Ste-Foy, Ste-Foy, QC G1V 1R8 – **512)** 300-1411 Fort St, Montreal, QC H3H 2R1 – **516)** 901 Galt Str. East, Sherbrooke, QC J1G 1Y6. Reportedly simulcasting CJAD-800kHz or silent – **519)** 300 - 1310 Greene Ave, Montréal, QC H3Z 2B5 – **520)** 200-B Saint-Pierre, Suite 104, Saint-Constant, QC J5A 2G9 – **521)** Saint-Nicolas, QC — **522)** 150 rue d'Edmonton, Gatineau, QC J8Y 3K6 – **526)** C.P. 850, La Tuque, QC G9X 3P6 – **527)** 455-3e rue, Chibougamau, QC G8P 1N6. CFED=Chapais – **530)** 200-460 Place Sacre-Coeur O, Alma, QC G8B 1L9 – **534)** R. Montréal, 35 York St, Westmount, QC H3Z 2Z5 Prgr's in Italian and several other languages – **536)** 10 St-Jacques St. #807, Montréal, QC H2Y 1LR – **537)** 10 rue St-Jacques #807, Montréal, QC H2Y 1L3 or 3733 rue Jarry E 2e et, Montréal, QC H1Z 2G1.

New Brunswick
603) 195 rue Main, Bathurst, NB E2A 1A7 – **605)** P.O.Box 930, Saint John, NB E2L 4E2 – **606)** P.O. Box 340, Campbellton, NB E3N 3G7 – **608)** P.O. Box 5900, Sussex, NB E4E 5M2 – **610)** 206 Rookwood Ave, Fredericton, NB E3B 2M2.

Prince Edward Island
700) 5 Lower Prince Str, Charlottetown, PE C1A 3P4.

Nova Scotia
802) P.O. Box 9316, Station A, Halifax, NS B3K 6B2 – **803)** P.O. Box 670, Amherst, NS B4H 4B8 – **805)** 318 Charlotte Street, Sydney, NS B1P 1C8 – **806)** P.O. Box 400, Halifax, NS B3J 2R2 – **809)** P.O. Box 519, New Glasgow, NS B2H 5E7 – **812)** CKEN-FM, P.O. Box 310, Kentville, NS B4N 1H5. On 97.7MHz. Netw. st's carry local prgrs Mon-Fri 1300-1600 – **812A)** P.O. Box 550, Middleton, NS B0P 1J0 – **812B)** P.O. Box 1420, Digby, NS B0V 1A0 – **812C)** 169-A Water St., Windsor, NS B0N 2T0.

Newfoundland & Labrador
900) P.O. Box 570, Corner Brook, NL A2H 6H5 (CFNW Port au Choix repeater) – **900B)** 60 West Street, Stephenville, NL A2N IC9. Own prgrs 0930 (Sat 1030, Sun 1630)-2130 – **900C)** P.O. Box 1230, Port aux Basques, NL A0M 1C0. Own prgrs: Mon-Fri 1230-2130 – **900D)** P.O. Box 4000, Stn "C", Goose Bay, Lab, NL A0P 1C0. Own prgrs: Mon-Sat 1100-2130 (studio in Corner Brook) – **900E)** P.O. Box 6000, Wabush, Lab, NL A0R 1B0. Own prgrs: 1100-2130 (studio in Corner Brook) – **901)** P.O. Box 8-590, Station A, St. John's, NL A1B 3P5 – **901A)** P.O. Box 560, Marystown, NL A0E 2M0. Own prgrs: 0930-2130, rel. 901D) 2130-0330 – **901B)** P.O. Box 620, Grand Falls, NL A2A 2K2. Own prgrs: 0930-2100. CKIM=Baie Verte – **901C)** P.O. Box 650 (TCH), Gander, NL A1V 1X2. Own prgrs: 0930-2130 – **901D)** #1 CHVO Drive, Carbonear, NL A1Y 1A2 – **901E)** Clarenville, NL. Own prgrs 0930-2130, rel. 901D) 2130-0330 – **902)** P.O. Box 7430, St. John's, NL A1E 3Y5 – **903)** P.O. Box 8010, Station A, St. John's NL A1B 3M7 – **905)** 1041 Topsail Rd, Mt. Pearl, NL A1N 5E9 – **907)** Goose Bay, NL. c/o CKOK, P.O. Box 160, Nain, NL A0P 1L0. CKOK=Nain, NL, 610kHz, 40W.

FM: Listed by province-city-freq. Tr's below 5kW not mentioned.

Call	City of licence	Prov.	MHz	kW
CHFB-FM	Bonnyville	AB	98.7	18.7
CKLM-FM-1	Bonnyville	AB	99.7	50
CKSA-FM-1	Bonnyville	AB	101.3	25
CJSI-FM	Calgary	AB	88.9	40
CJAY-FM	Calgary	AB	92.1	100
CKUA-FM-1	Calgary	AB	93.7	100
CHKF-FM	Calgary	AB	94.7	65
CHFM-FM	Calgary	AB	95.9	100
CKIS-FM	Calgary	AB	96.9	100
CIBK-FM	Calgary	AB	98.5	100
CIQX-FM	Calgary	AB	103.1	100
CKRY-FM	Calgary	AB	105.1	100
CFGQ-FM	Calgary	AB	107.3	100
CJXK-FM	Cold Lake	AB	95.3	100
CIBW-FM	Drayton Valley	AB	92.9	7.4
CKUA-FM-13	Drumheller	AB	91.3	100
CKNG-FM	Edmonton	AB	92.5	100
CKUA-FM	Edmonton	AB	94.9	100
CKRA-FM	Edmonton	AB	96.3	100
CIRK-FM	Edmonton	AB	97.3	100
CFBR-FM	Edmonton	AB	100.3	100
CKER-FM	Edmonton	AB	101.9	100
CHZN-FM	Edmonton	AB	102.9	100
CISN-FM	Edmonton	AB	103.9	100
CFMG-FM	Edmonton	AB	104.9	100
CJRY-FM	Edmonton	AB	105.9	100
CJOK-FM	Fort McMurray	AB	93.3	15.3
CJXX-FM	Grande Prairie	AB	93.1	100
CFGP-FM	Grande Prairie	AB	97.7	100
CKUA-FM-4	Grande Prairie	AB	100.9	100
CKHL-FM	High Level	AB	102.1	34
CFKX-FM	High Level	AB	106.1	34
CFXL-FM	High River/Okotoks	AB	100.9	100
CHLB-FM	Lethbridge	AB	95.5	100
CKUA-FM-2	Lethbridge	AB	99.3	100
CFRV-FM	Lethbridge	AB	107.7	100
CJRX-FM	Lethbridge/Taber	AB	106.7	100
CKSA-FM	Lloydminster	AB	95.9	100
CKLM-FM	Lloydminster	AB	106.1	100
CFMY-FM	Medicine Hat	AB	96.1	100
CKUA-FM-3	Medicine Hat	AB	97.3	100
CKLJ-FM	Olds	AB	97.7	13
CKUA-FM-5	Peace River	AB	96.9	100
CFWE-FM-2	Peigan/Blood River	AB	89.3	10.2
CKGY-FM	Red Deer	AB	95.5	100
CIZZ-FM	Red Deer	AB	98.9	100
CKUA-FM-6	Red Deer	AB	101.3	100
CHUB-FM	Red Deer	AB	105.5	100
CJBZ-FM	Taber	AB	93.3	100
CFYR-FM	Whitecourt	AB	96.7	9
CKSR-FM	Chilliwack	BC	98.3	5
CKLR-FM	Courtenay	BC	97.3	11.6
CFCP-FM	Courtenay	BC	98.9	5
CHRX-FM	Fort St. John	BC	98.5	50
CKNL-FM	Fort St. John	BC	101.5	40
CHSU-FM	Kelowna	BC	99.9	35
CILK-FM	Kelowna	BC	101.5	33.3
CKLZ-FM	Kelowna	BC	104.7	36
CFMI-FM	New Westminster	BC	101.1	75
CIGV-FM	Penticton	BC	100.7	10.6
CIRX-FM	Prince George	BC	94.3	11.5
CJCI-FM	Prince George	BC	97.3	12
CKDV-FM	Prince George	BC	99.3	9.3
CKKN-FM	Prince George	BC	101.3	9.1
CISQ-FM	Squamish	BC	107.1	30
CJAT-FM	Trail	BC	95.7	13.5
CJJR-FM	Vancouver	BC	93.7	75
CFBT-FM	Vancouver	BC	94.5	90
CKZZ-FM	Vancouver	BC	95.3	71.3
CHKG-FM	Vancouver	BC	96.1	100
CKLG-FM	Vancouver	BC	96.9	75
CFOX-FM	Vancouver	BC	99.3	75
CFRO-FM	Vancouver	BC	102.7	5.5
CHQM-FM	Vancouver	BC	103.5	100
CKCL-FM-2	Vancouver	BC	104.9	31
CICF-FM	Vernon	BC	105.7	100
CKIZ-FM	Vernon	BC	107.5	100
CIOC-FM	Victoria	BC	98.5	100
CKKQ-FM	Victoria	BC	100.3	100
CHTT-FM	Victoria	BC	103.1	20
CHBE-FM	Victoria	BC	107.3	20
CIWM-FM	Brandon	MB	91.5	100
CKLF-FM	Brandon	MB	94.7	100
CKX-FM	Brandon	MB	96.1	88.7
CKXA-FM	Brandon	MB	101.1	100
CFRY-1-FM	Portage La Prairie	MB	93.1	27
CKPG-FM	Portage La Prairie	MB	96.5	24
CFQX-FM	Selkirk	MB	104.1	100
CICY-FM	Selkirk	MB	105.5	100
CKXL-FM	St. Boniface	MB	91.1	61
CILT-FM	Steinbach	MB	96.7	100
CJEL-FM	Winkler/Morden	MB	93.5	100
CITI-FM	Winnipeg	MB	92.1	140
CHIQ-FM	Winnipeg	MB	94.3	100
CHVN-FM	Winnipeg	MB	95.1	100
CJKR-FM	Winnipeg	MB	97.5	310
CJZZ-FM	Winnipeg	MB	99.1	100
CFWM-FM	Winnipeg	MB	99.9	100
CKY-FM	Winnipeg	MB	102.3	100
CKMM-FM	Winnipeg	MB	103.1	100
CKLE-FM	Bathurst	NB	92.9	100
CKBC-FM	Bathurst	NB	104.9	33.5
CJEM-FM	Edmundston	NB	92.7	40.8
CFXY-FM	Fredericton	NB	105.3	78

Call	City of licence	Prov.	MHz	kW
CIBX-FM	Fredericton	NB	106.9	78
CIKX-FM	Grand Falls	NB	93.5	5.3
CKRO-FM	Inkerman/Pokemouche	NB	97.1	44.4
CFAN-FM	Miramichi City	NB	99.3	17.8
CKCW-FM	Moncton	NB	94.5	19
CJXL-FM	Moncton	NB	96.9	100
CHOY-FM	Moncton	NB	99.9	9.5
CJMO-FM	Moncton	NB	103.1	46.8
CFQM-FM	Moncton	NB	103.9	70
CHSJ-FM	Saint John	NB	94.1	100
CHWV-FM	Saint John	NB	97.3	100
CJYC-FM	Saint John	NB	98.9	12
CIOK-FM	Saint John	NB	100.5	100
CHTD-FM	St. Stephen	NB	98.1	40
CJCJ-FM	Woodstock	NB	104.1	10
CJOZ-FM	Bonavista	NL	92.1	6.7
CKOZ-FM	Corner Brook	NL	92.3	50
CKXX-FM	Corner Brook	NL	103.9	47
CKXD-FM	Gander	NL	98.7	6
CKXG-FM	Grand Falls	NL	102.3	20
CIOZ-FM	Marystown	NL	96.3	31.3
CKMY-FM	Rattling Brook	NL	95.9	50
CHOZ-FM	St. John's	NL	94.7	100
VOCM-FM	St. John's	NL	97.5	100
CKIX-FM	St. John's	NL	99.1	100
CKSJ-FM	St. John's	NF	101.1	20
CJFX-FM	Antigonish	NS	98.9	75.4
CJLS-FM-2	Barrington	NS	96.3	5.5
CKBW-FM	Bridgewater	NS	98.1	32
CFRQ-FM	Dartmouth	NS	104.3	100
CIEZ-FM	Halifax	NS	96.5	100
CIOO-FM	Halifax	NS	100.1	100
CHFX-FM	Halifax	NS	101.9	91
CKWM-FM	Kentville	NS	94.9	18
CKEN-FM	Kentville	NS	97.7	18
CKBW-1-FM	Liverpool	NS	94.5	8.7
CIGO-FM	Port Hawkesbury	NS	101.5	19
CKBW-2-FM	Shelburne	NS	93.1	8.6
CKPE-FM	Sydney	NS	94.9	61
CKTY-FM	Truro	NS	99.5	16.8
CKTO-FM	Truro	NS	100.9	50
CJLS-FM	Yarmouth	NS	95.5	18
CIFA-FM	Yarmouth	NS	104.1	39.3
CJKX-FM	Ajax	ON	95.9	50
CHMS-FM	Bancroft	ON	97.7	50
CHAY-FM	Barrie	ON	93.1	100
CFJB-FM	Barrie	ON	95.7	70
CKMB-FM	Barrie	ON	107.5	50
CJOJ-FM	Belleville	ON	95.5	100
CIGL-FM	Belleville	ON	97.1	50
CHCQ-FM	Belleville	ON	100.1	32
CKJJ-FM	Belleville	ON	102.3	45
CFBG-FM	Bracebridge	ON	99.5	12
CFNY-FM	Brampton	ON	102.1	35.4
CKPC-FM	Brantford	ON	92.1	50
CJPT-FM	Brockville	ON	103.7	100
CFJR-FM	Brockville	ON	104.9	7.7
CJXY-FM	Burlington	ON	107.9	26.1
CJDV-FM	Cambridge	ON	107.5	6
CKSY-FM	Chatham	ON	94.3	50
CKUE-FM	Chatham	ON	95.1	42
CKSG-FM	Cobourg	ON	93.3	6.3
CFMX-FM	Cobourg	ON	103.1	86.7
CHOD-FM	Cornwall	ON	92.1	45.6
CFLG-FM	Cornwall	ON	104.5	28.2
CKEY-FM	Fort Erie	ON	101.1	50
CFOB-FM	Fort Frances	ON	93.1	21
CIMJ-FM	Guelph	ON	106.1	50
CIWV-FM	Hamilton/Burlington	ON	94.7	10
CING-FM	Hamilton	ON	95.3	100
CKLH-FM	Hamilton	ON	102.9	40.3
CINN-FM	Hearst	ON	91.1	5.5
CFBK-FM	Huntsville	ON	105.5	5
CKAP-FM	Kapuskasing	ON	100.9	12
CFMK-FM	Kingston	ON	96.3	28
CFLY-FM	Kingston	ON	98.3	95.5
CIKR-FM	Kingston	ON	105.7	50
CJKL-FM	Kirkland Lake	ON	101.5	23
CHYM-FM	Kitchener	ON	96.7	100
CFCA-FM	Kitchener	ON	105.3	100
CKBT-FM	Kitchener/Waterloo	ON	91.5	10
CKWR-FM	Kitchener/Waterloo	ON	98.5	27
CHYR-FM	Leamington	ON	96.7	91
CKLY-FM	Lindsay	ON	91.9	27.5
CKNR-FM	Little Current	ON	94.1	90
CJBX-FM	London	ON	92.7	50
CHRW-FM	London	ON	94.9	5.3
CFPL-FM	London	ON	95.9	300
CIQM-FM	London	ON	97.5	50
CHST-FM	London	ON	102.3	12.1
CFNO-FM	Marathon	ON	93.1	50
CICZ-FM	Midland	ON	104.1	20
CJTT-FM	New Liskeard	ON	104.5	10
CKDX-FM	Newmarket	ON	88.5	30
CFLZ-FM	Niagara Falls	ON	105.1	30
CHUR-FM	North Bay	ON	100.5	100
CKFX-FM	North Bay	ON	101.9	68
CIDC-FM	Orangeville	ON	103.5	30.7
CICX-FM	Orillia	ON	105.9	50
CKGE-FM	Oshawa	ON	94.9	50
CHUO-FM	Ottawa	ON	89.1	18.1
CIHT-FM	Ottawa/Hull	ON	89.9	27
CKCU-FM	Ottawa	ON	93.1	12
CKKL-FM	Ottawa	ON	93.9	95
CJLL-FM	Ottawa	ON	97.9	6
CHRI-FM	Ottawa	ON	99.1	66
CJMJ-FM	Ottawa	ON	100.3	100
CISS-FM	Ottawa	ON	105.3	84
CHEZ-FM	Ottawa	ON	106.1	100
CKQB-FM	Ottawa	ON	106.9	84
CKYC-FM	Owen Sound	ON	93.7	31.6
CIXK-FM	Owen Sound	ON	106.5	100
CJIQ-FM	Paris	ON	88.3	10.6
CKLP-FM	Parry Sound	ON	103.3	46.6
CHVR-FM	Pembroke	ON	96.7	100
CKWF-FM	Peterborough	ON	101.5	48.5
CKQM-FM	Peterborough	ON	105.1	50
CFGX-FM	Sarnia	ON	99.9	26
CHKS-FM	Sarnia	ON	106.3	50
CHAS-FM	Sault Ste. Marie	ON	100.5	13.9
CJQM-FM	Sault Ste. Marie	ON	104.3	100
CHCD-FM	Simcoe	ON	98.9	50
CJET-FM	Smiths Falls	ON	92.3	17
CKBY-FM	Smiths Falls	ON	101.1	100
CHTZ-FM	St. Catharines	ON	97.7	50
CHRE-FM	St. Catharines	ON	105.7	50
CFHK-FM	St. Thomas	ON	103.1	50
CHGK-FM	Stratford	ON	107.7	6
CJRQ-FM	Sudbury	ON	92.7	100
CHNO-FM	Sudbury	ON	103.9	100
CJMX-FM	Sudbury	ON	105.3	100
CJKX-FM-1	Sunderland	ON	89.9	5
CJSD-FM	Thunder Bay	ON	94.3	93
CJLB-FM	Thunder Bay	ON	105.3	100
CKOT-FM	Tillsonburg	ON	101.3	50
CJQQ-FM	Timmins	ON	92.1	40
CKGB-FM	Timmins	ON	99.3	40
CIUT-FM	Toronto	ON	89.5	15
CJRT-FM	Toronto	ON	91.1	40
CJAQ-FM	Toronto	ON	92.5	13
CFXJ-FM	Toronto	ON	93.5	5
CFMX-FM-1	Toronto	ON	96.3	30
CJEZ-FM	Toronto	ON	97.3	28.9
CHFI-FM	Toronto	ON	98.1	44
CKFM-FM	Toronto	ON	99.9	40
CHIN-FM	Toronto	ON	100.7	8.5
CHUM-FM	Toronto	ON	104.5	40
CILQ-FM	Toronto	ON	107.1	40
CJTN-FM	Trenton	ON	107.1	15
CHOW-FM	Welland	ON	91.7	50
CIMX-FM	Windsor	ON	88.7	100
CIDR-FM	Windsor	ON	93.9	100
CKNX-FM	Wingham	ON	101.7	100
CKDK-FM	Woodstock	ON	103.9	52
CHLQ-FM	Charlottetown	PE	93.1	75
CJRW-FM	Summerside	PE	102.1	50
CKYK-FM	Alma	QC	95.7	100
CHLM-FM-1	Amos/Val d'Or	QC	91.5	50
CHOA-FM-1	Amos/Val d'Or	QC	103.5	100
CHGO-FM	Amos/Val d'Or	QC	104.3	100

Call	City of licence	Prov.	MHz	kW
CFVM-FM	Amqui	QC	99.9	23.8
CJAN-FM	Asbestos	QC	99.3	11.1
CFIM-FM	Cap-aux-Meules	QC	92.7	6.3
CIEU-FM	Carleton	QC	94.9	37.6
CJAB-FM	Chicoutimi	QC	94.5	100
CFIX-FM	Chicoutimi	QC	96.9	100
CION-FM-2	Chicoutimi	QC	106.7	46
CFVD-FM	Dégélis	QC	95.5	12.5
CHVD-FM	Dolbeau	QC	100.3	50
CHIP-FM	Fort-Coulonge	QC	101.7	11.9
CKTF-FM	Gatineau/Hull	QC	104.1	19
CIMF-FM	Hull	QC	94.9	84
CHOX-FM	La Pocatière	QC	97.5	25.2
CFIN-FM	Lac-Etchemin	QC	100.5	9.6
CFGL-FM	Laval	QC	105.7	41
CHMP-FM	Longueuil	QC	98.5	40.8
CHOE-FM	Matane	QC	95.3	30
CHRM-FM	Matane	QC	105.3	30
CINI-FM	Mistassini	QC	95.3	50
CFLO-FM	Mont-Laurier	QC	104.7	16.9
CFEL-FM	Montmagny	QC	102.1	8.7
CISM-FM	Montréal	QC	89.3	10
CKUT-FM	Montréal	QC	90.3	5
CIRA-FM	Montréal	QC	91.3	36.2
CFQR-FM	Montréal	QC	92.5	41.4
CKMF-FM	Montréal	QC	94.3	41.4
CJFM-FM	Montréal	QC	95.9	41.2
CHOM-FM	Montréal	QC	97.7	41.2
CJPX-FM	Montréal	QC	99.5	8.7
CITE-FM	Montréal	QC	107.3	42.9
CHLX-FM	Ottawa-Hull	QC	97.1	12.6
CIPC-FM	Port-Cartier	QC	99.1	13
CION-FM	Québec	QC	90.9	5.7
CJEC-FM	Québec	QC	91.9	31
CJMF-FM	Québec	QC	93.3	33
CHOI-FM	Québec	QC	98.1	40
CHIK-FM	Québec	QC	98.9	41
CITF-FM	Québec	QC	107.5	37
CKMN-FM	Rimouski	QC	96.5	6.4
CIKI-FM	Rimouski	QC	98.7	100
CJOI-FM	Rimouski	QC	102.9	33.6
CIEL-FM	Rivière-du-Loup	QC	103.7	60
CIBM-FM	Rivière-du-Loup	QC	107.1	100
CHRL-FM	Roberval	QC	99.5	50
CHLM-FM	Rouyn	QC	90.7	25
CHGO-FM-1	Rouyn	QC	95.7	44
CHOA-FM	Rouyn-Noranda	QC	96.5	61.1
CHYZ-FM	Sainte-Foy	QC	94.3	6
CKCN-FM	Sept-Îles	QC	94.1	11.3
CFGE-FM	Sherbrooke	QC	93.7	5
CITE-FM-1	Sherbrooke	QC	102.7	92
CFNJ-FM	St-Gabriel-Brandon	QC	99.1	9.75
CHJM-FM	St-Georges-de-Beauce	QC	99.7	100
CIME-FM	St-Jérôme	QC	103.9	39.3
CFJO-FM	Thetford Mines	QC	97.3	100
CKLD-FM	Thetford Mines	QC	105.5	6
CIRA-FM-2	Trois-Rivières	QC	89.9	6
CHEY-FM	Trois-Rivières	QC	94.7	100
CJEB-FM	Trois-Rivières	QC	100.1	81.1
CIGB-FM	Trois-Rivières	QC	102.3	11
CJMV-FM	Val-d'Or	QC	102.7	63.1
CKOI-FM	Verdun	QC	96.9	307
CKVM-FM	Ville-Marie	QC	93.1	34
CJRH-FM	Waskaganish	QC	92.5	7.1
CFNE-FM	Waswanipi	QC	93.9	6.2
CJVR-FM-1	Dafoe	SK	100.3	100
CHSN-FM	Estevan	SK	102.3	100
CJVR-FM	Melfort	SK	105.1	100
CILG-FM	Moose Jaw	SK	100.7	100
CJNE-FM	Nipawin	SK	94.7	14.8
CJCQ-FM	North Battleford	SK	97.9	100
CHXL-FM	Okanese Indian Reser.	SK	95.3	50
CFMM-FM	Prince Albert	SK	99.1	100
CHQX-FM	Prince Albert	SK	101.5	100
CHMX-FM	Regina	SK	92.1	100
CKCK-FM	Regina	SK	94.5	100
CIZL-FM	Regina	SK	98.9	100
CFWF-FM	Regina	SK	104.9	100
CFQC-FM	Saskatoon	SK	92.9	100
CFMC-FM	Saskatoon	SK	95.1	100
CJMK-FM	Saskatoon	SK	98.3	100
CJDJ-FM	Saskatoon	SK	102.1	100
CIMG-FM	Swift Current	SK	94.1	100
CFGW-FM-2	Wapella	SK	102.9	14
CJVR-FM-2	Waskesiu Lake	SK	106.3	11
CFGW-FM	Yorkton	SK	94.1	100

BRITISH FORCES BROADCASTING SERVICE

BFBS Suffield, Alberta. ✉ BFBS Canada, BATUS, BFPO 14, UK. ☎ 001 403 544 4104 – BFBS 1: 98.1, 104.1MHz. BFBS 2: Not broadcast. www.ssvc.cdm/bfbs/radio/canada

CANARY ISLANDS

L.T: UTC (27 Mar-30 Oct: UTC +1h) — **Pop:** 1.7 million — **Pr.L:** Spanish — **E.C:** 50Hz, 220V — **ITU:** CNR

Abbreviations: GC=Gran Canaria, GCF=Fuerteventura, GCL=Lanzarote, TF=Tenerife, TFP=Isla de la Palma, TFG=Isla de la Gomera, TFH=Hierro. (For network abbreviations please refer to Spain).

MW	kHz	kW	Net	Location	Island
1.1)	576	20	RNE-1	Las Palmas	GC
1)	621	300	RNE-1	Santa Cruz	TF
1)	720	10	RNE-5	Santa Cruz	TF
1.1)	747	25	RNE-5	Las Palmas	GC
4)	837	10	COPE	Las Palmas	GC
5)	882	20	COPE	La Laguna	TF
6)	1008	10	OCR	Las Palmas	GC
9)	1179	20	SER	Radio Club Tenerife	TF
8)	1269	20	ECCA	Las Palmas	GC

FM	MHz	kW	Net	Location	Island
1)	87.7	1	RNE-2	Temejereque	GCF
33)	87.8		DIAL	La Laguna	TF
1)	88.6	10	RNE-5	La Isleta	GC
7)	89.6	1	RNE-5	Santa Cruz	TFP
1)	88.8	10	RNE-5	La Montañeta	TF
28)	89.7	4	SER	Lanzarote,Arrecife	GCL
1)	90.0	5	RNE-3	Izaña	TFHH
8)	90.4	2	ECCA	Las Palmas	GC
12)	90.7	4	SER	Arrecife	GCL
13)	91.0	8	M80 Radio	Santa Cruz	TF
36)	91.2		OCR X	Fuenteventura	GC
6)	91.2	-	Dance FM	Las Palmas	GC
33)	91.6	2	Cadena Dial	Los Realejos	TF
4)	91.8	1	C100	Las Palmas	GC
8)	91.8	1	ECCA	Santa Cruz	TF
41)	92.0	-	R. Gaoré	La Frontera	TFH
1)	92.3	5	RNE-1	Izaña	TF
1)	92.5	1	RNE-1	Montaña Mina	GCL
1)	92.6	1	RNE-2	Los Cristianos	TF
-	92.7	-	OCR	Los Llanos de Aridane	GC
1)	92.8	10	RNE-1	La Isleta	GC
8)	93.0	1	ECCA	Pto del Rosario	GCF
9)	93.2	25	Cadena 40	La Laguna	TF
9)	93.3	2.5	SER	La Gomera	TCF
37)	94.0	8	OCR	Santa Cruz	TF
14)	94.4	8	Cadena 40	Las Palmas	GC
32)	94.4	2	OCR	Tacoronte	TF
1)	94.6	1	RNE-1	Temejereque	GCF
1)	94.8	10	RNE-1	La Montañeta	TF
1)	94.9	1	RNE-2	Montaña Mina	GCL
1)	95.1	10	RNE-2	La Isleta	GC
5)	95.1	2	COPE	Santa Cruz	TFP
15)	95.3	4	Top Radio	Maspalomas	GC
1)	95.4	1	RNE-3	Los Cristianos	TF
6)	95.8	8	Top Radio	Las Palmas	GC
1)	96.2	5	RNE-2	Izaña	TF
16)	96.8	5	Radio Insular	Arrecife	GCL
5)	97.1	2	Cadena 100	La Laguna	TF
7)	98.4	1	RNE-5	El Paso	TFP
1)	98.5	10	RNE-3	La Isleta	GC
-	98.9	-	OCR	Vecindario	GC
18)	99.1	2	Cadena 40	Pto. la Cruz	TF
6)	99.3	-	R. Marca	Las Palmas	GC
8)	99.5	2	ECCA	Santa Cruz	TFP
41)	99.7	-	COPE	Lanzarote	GCL
19)	99.8	2	Radio Club Norte	La Orotava	TF
13)	100.1	8	M 80 R.	Santa Cruz	TF

FM	MHz	kW	Net	Location	Island
1)	100.2	1	RNE-5	Montaña Mina	GCL
11)	100.3	2	SER	Las Palmas	GC
1)	100.6	1	RNE-3	Temejereque	GCF
5)	100.9	-	COPE	Tenerife	TF
9)	101.1	-	SER R.	Tenerife,Santa Cruz	TF
22)	101.4	2	Cadena Dial	Las Palmas	GC
40)	101.6	-	SER R	La Palma,Santa Cruz	TFP
1)	102.1	10	RNE-2	La Montañeta	TF
23)	102.2	-	R.Fuerteventura	Pto.del Rosario	GCF
10)	102.4	1	Maxima FM	Playa del Inglés	GC
1)	102.7	1	RNE-1	El Paso	TFP
1)	102.8	1	RNE-3	Montaña Mina	GCL
11)	103.0	3.7	SER	Las Palmas	GC
-	103.4	-	OCR	Arrecife	GCL
25)	104.0	4	R. Olé Tropical	Arrecife	GCL
1)	104.0	5	RNE-5	Los Cristianos	TF
26)	104.1	2	DIAL	Llanos de Aridane	TF
1)	104.5	1	RNE-2	El Paso	TFP
1)	104.8	1	RNE-5	Temejereque	GCF
29)	105.0	1	R. Archipiélago	Pto. del Rosario	GC
1)	105.6	1	RNE-1	Los Cristianos	TF
1)	105.7	10	RNE-3	Las Mesas	TF
1)	106.1	1	RNE-3	El Paso	TFP
-	106.4	-	OCR	Santa Cruz	TFP
30)	106.8	8	OCR	Las Palmas	GL
39)	107.4	-		R. Isora	

Addresses and other information

1) R. Nacional de España**,** San Martín 1, 38001 Sta. Cruz de Tenerife ☎ +34 (922) 288400 🖷 +34 922 283363 **R.1:** 24h on 621kHz. **N:** On the h. **R.2:** (classical music) 24h. **R.3:** 24h. **R.5:** 24h. – **1.1)** R. Nacional de España, 1 de Mayo 21, 35002 Las Palmas de G. Canaria ☎ +34 928 364 088 🖷 +34 928 362 754. – **4)** R. Popular de Las Palmas, Av. Escaleritas 60, Las Palmas 35011. ☎ +34 928 286970 **Email:** laspalmas@cadenacope.net. Dir: Antonio Miguel Díaz.. **D.Prgr:** 24h. **N.** summaries in English, German & Swedish between 1330 & 1830, produced by Canary Tourist R, Paseo de Chil 117, 35014 Las Palmas. Dir: Xavier Palin. - **FM:** 91.8 R. Insular. . – **4.1)** COPE Lanzarote, Fred Olsen 6 (Edif.E) Isolete 1 35500 Lanzarote Islas Canarias. . – **5)** R. Popular de Tenerife, Darías y Padrón, 1-2°-38003 Santa Cruz de Tenerife ☎ +34 922 236900/05/09 🖷 +34 922 236911 **Email:** c-tenerife@arrakis.es. Dir: José Carlos Marrero Gonzá. **D.Prgr:** 24h. – **6)** Punto Radio, Sao Paulo 40, 35008 Las Palmas de Gran Canaria. **Web**: www.puntoradio.com ☎ +34 928 462066. 🖷 +34 928 462057 Dir:María Enma Hernández Martín. **D.Prgr:** 24h. – **7)** R. Nacional de España, Plaza de la Constitución 4, Santa Cruz de la Palma 38700. ☎ +34 922 288400. Dir: Julio Marante Diaz. **D.Prgr:** 0800-2300. – **8)** R. ECCA, Av. Mesa y López 38 (or: Aptdo. 994), Las Palmas 35007. ☎ +34 928 275454. Dir: Luis Espina Cepeda. **D.Prgr:** 0655-2300 (Sun 2100). - **FM** 91.8: Lope de Vega 5, 38700 Sta, Cruzde Tenerife. - **FM 93.0:** Plaza de España, Pto. del Rosario, Fuerteventura. - **FM 99.5:** Av. Francisco de Abreu 6, Santa Cruz de la Palma 38700. **Email:** jefatura@radioecca.org **Web:** www.radioecca.org. – **9)** R. Club Tenerife, Av. de Anaga 35, Santa Cruz de Tenerife 38001. ☎ +34 922 270400 🖷 +34 922 281043. **Email:** radioclubtenerife@unionradio.es. Dir: Mª José Pérez. – **9.1)** Radio Garoé, a orredera 5, 38911 La Frontera, El Hierro. – **11)** SER Las Palmas, C/ General Balmes, s/n, Edificio Mapfre 4ª plta, Las Palmas de Gran Canaria 35008. ☎ +34 928 463007.**Email**:serlaspalmas@unionradio.es. – **12)** R. Lanzarote, Fred Olsen 14, 2°, Apdo. 234, 35500 Arrecife. ☎ +34 928 811517. Dir: Agustín Cruz. **D. Prgr.** in Spanish 0700-2400 exc: Mon-Fri 1530-1630 **German,** 1830-2000 **English**. – **13)** M 80 Radio Tenerife, R.J. Hamilton 14, Santa Cruz de Tenerife 38001. ☎ +34 922 240227. Dir: Gabriel Mesa Barrera. **D. Prgr:** 24h. – **14)** Cadena 40, José Franchy Roca 5, Las Palmas 35007. ☎ +34 928 279911. Dir: Gabriel Mesa Barrera. **D.Prgr:** 24h. **DX Prgrs** produced by José Luis Martín: Sat 1300-1330 "El Mundo de las Ondas", Mon 2030-2100 "Radioaficionados", Mon 1205-1220 "Historia de la Radio".– **15)** R. Maspalomas, Morro Besudo s/n, Maspalomas 35100. ☎ +34 922 765853. Dir: Juan José Roda. **D.Prgr.** in Spanish 24h. exc: W. 0830-0900, 1705-1800 **German,** 0905-0930 **English,** 0930-1000 **Swedish.** – **16)** R. Onda Insular, García Escámez 159, Arrecife 35580. ☎ +34 928 815750. Dir: Armando de León Expósito. **D.Prgr:** 0700-2400. – **18)** Cadena 40, Pl. de los Reyes Católicos 3, Pto. la Cruz 38400. ☎ +34 922 380012. Dir: Ignacio Baute España. – **19)** R. Club Sur, Av. Marítima s/n, Playa de Américas 38660. **D.Prgr:** 0800-0100 (Fri 0300, Sat 0200). – **20)** R. Tourist Lanzarote, Av. Fred Olsen 14 (or: Aptdo. 260), Arrecife 35580. Prgr. Dir: Barbara Graf. **D.Prgr:** 0655-2300. **N.** in English on the h., in German on the halfhour. **German** 0740-0930, 1530-1630, **Scandinavian** 1630-1730, **English** 0930-1100, 1800-2000. – **23)** R. Fuerteventua, Cervantes 122, 35600 Pto. del Rosario. – **25)** R. 106, Aptdo. 28, Arrecife 35580 (Lanzarote). – **26)** Dial Llanos de Aridane, Av. Anaga 35, 38001 Sta. Cruz de Tenerife. – **27)** Guiniguada R., Ap. 67, 35080 Las Palmas, Las Palmas de Gran Canaria. – **28)** SER Lanzarote, José Antonio 114, 35500 Arrecife (Lanzarote). **Email:** serlanzarote@unionradio.es. – **29)** R. Archipielago, La Juventud 31, 35600 Fuerteventura. – **30)** Onda Cero Color, León y Castillo 41, 35005 Las Palmas. – **31)** Onda Cero R., C.C. San Eugenio Adeje, 38660 Playa Las Américas. – **32)** Onda Cero, R. 21, Crtra/ Gral. Norte 29, 38350 Tacoronte. – **33)** Dial Norte, Av.Av. Anaga 35, 38001 Sta. Cruz de Tenerife. ☎ +34 922 270408. – **34)** R. ECCA Pto. del Rosario, Dr. Fleming s/n, 35600 Pto. del Rosario. – **35)** Dial Tenerife, Av. Anaga 35, 38001 Sta. Cruz de Tenerife. – **36)** Canal 28 Fuente-ventura, Calle Segura 29, 3°, 35600 Pto. del Rosario. ☎ +34 928 530255. – **37)** Salamanca 5, 38006 Sta. Cruz de Tenerife. – **38)** Canal 28 Las Palmas, Dr. Juan Dominguez Pérez 12, 1°. 35008 Las Palmas. – **39)** Radio Isora, Apto de correo 76, Guia de Isora, 0 38680. ☎ +34 228 50302. **Web:** toolbox.com/rc/owa/freeweb.page?id=1038768. – **40)** R. La Palma, Santa Cruz de la Palma. **41)** La Corredera 5, La Frontera, El Hierro.

CAPE VERDE

L.T: UTC -1h — **Pop:** 405,000 — **Pr.L:** Portuguese, Crioulo — **E.C:** 50Hz, 220V — **ITU:** CPV.

INSTITUTO DAS COMUNICAÇÕES E TECNOLOGIAS DE INFORMAÇÃO(ICTI)

✉ Ponta Belém, C.P. 07, Praia ☎ +238 615779 🖷 +238 614141.

RÁDIO TELEVISÃO CABOVERDIANA (RTC)

✉ Archada Santo Antão, Praia, Santiago ☎ +238 615755/6/7 🖷 +238 623206/623054, ✉C.P. 29, Av. Marginal, Mindelo, São Vicente ☎ +238 311513/311731 🖷 +238 311006, ✉C.P. 40, Espargos, Ilha do Sal ☎ +238 411333 🖷 +238 411444. **Email:** rtcfm@cvtelecom.cv
L.P: Dir: Manuela Fonseca. PD: Giordano Custodio. Dir. Inf: Mario Almeida. Dir. Tec: Francisco Lopes Monteiro.
FM: Monte Verde 87.6MHz 1kW, Morro Curral 89.7MHz 0.25kW, Monte Tchota 91.6MHz 1kW, Mindelo 95.6MHz 0.5kW, Praia 98.1MHz 0.1kW + 12 relays below 0.1kW. **D.Prgr:** 24h.

RÁDIO NOVA - EMISSORA CRISTÃ DE CABO VERDE

✉ C.P. 426, Mindelo, São Vicente. ☎ +238 317819 (office), 311480 (studios). 🖷 +238 311475 **Email:** radionova@cvtelecom.cv – **L.P:** Dir: António Fidalgo Barros.
FM: Monte Vermelho 94.1MHz, unk. location 94.9MHz, Monte Tropetona 99.1MHz, Santiago 101.6MHz 0.25kW, São Vicente 104.3MHz 0.5kW, Sal 106.4MHz – **D.Prgr:** 14h daily, also rel. Vatican R.

Other stations:
R. Comercial, CP 507, Praia or Prédo Gomirmãos, 3 E Archada, Santo Antão. - **FM**: Santiago 92.9 1 kW, Punta Rachada 96.1MHz, Praia 99.9MHz 0.5kW. **Web:** www.radiocomercial.net – **R. Morabeza**, Mindelo, São Vicente, 90.7MHz – **R. Mosteiros FM**, Mosteiros, Ilha do Fogo. 96.1/97.3MHz – **Praia FM,** 1,4-A Rua.Justino Lopes, Plateau: 94.1MHz – **RFI Afrique**, Praia 99.3MHz 1kW, Mindelo 100.7MHz 0.25kW in French and Portuguese – **RDP África**, Dr. Socotril, Av. Cidade Lisboa, Várzea, Praia. **Email:** rtpacv@cvtelecom.cv - **FM**: Monte Verde 93.9MHz 3kW, Sal-Rei 95.1MHz 0.03kW, Pinhão 95.7MHz 0.3kW, Morro Curral 97.0MHz 0.1kW, Pedra Rachada 105.2MHz 1kW, Monte Tchota 105.2MHz 3kW

CAYMAN ISLANDS (British)

L.T: UTC -5h — **Pop:** 49,000 — **Pr.L:** English — **E.C:** 60Hz, 110V — **ITU:** CYM.

RADIO CAYMAN (Gov. Comm.)

✉ 71B Elgin Av, Box 1110, George Town, Grand Cayman. ☎ +1 345 949 7799. 🖷 +1 345 949 6536. **Email:** radiocym@candw.ky
L.P: Dir. Broadc: Loxley Banks. Dep. Dir: Norma McField. Sales Mgr: Paulette Conolly-Taylor.
FM: Grand Cayman 105.3 MHz (5 kW), 89.9 MHz (3 kW) – Cayman Brac: 91.9/93.9 MHz (0.25kW).
R. Cayman One on 89.9/93.9MHz: music, current affairs, news. 1100-0500. **N:** 1100*, 1200W/Sat, 1300W, 1300Sun*, 1500W/Sat, 1700, 2000, 2215MF, 2300*, 0300*.
R. Cayman Two on 91.9/105.3MHz: music and news. **N:** 1130W, 1230W. R. Cayman 1 & 2 0500-1100*, 1100*, 1500W/Sat, 1700, 2000, 2300*, 0300. *= BBC

ZFZZ (Comm.)

✉ 375 Walkers Rd, Box 30110 SMB, George Town, Grand Cayman. ☎ +1 345 945 1166. 🖷 +1 345 945 1006. **Web:** www.z99.ky and www.rooster101.ky. **L.P:** Pres. & GM: Randy Merren. PD: Scott Hamilton
FM: George Town 99.9MHz (15kW) and 101.9MHz

Z99 on 99.9MHz. **D.Prgr:** 24h. **Format:** CHR
Roster 101.9 on 101.9MHz. **D.Prgr.:** 24h. **Format:** Country

PARAMOUNT MEDIA GROUP (Comm.)

✉ Fort Street, Box 10236 APO, George Town, Grand Cayman. ☎ +1 345 949 8423/947 0095. 📠 +1 345 946 9867. **Email:** info@vibefm.ky and sales@oceanfm.ky. **Web:** www.vibefm.ky and www.oceanfm.ky. **L.P:** MD: Kenneth Rankin. Sales Mgr.: Kirk Rampersad. Marketing Mgr.: Tina Trumbach. **FM:** George Town 95.5 and 98.9MHz.
Vibe 98.9 on 98.9MHz. **D.Prgr**: 24h. **Format**: Urban Caribbean
Ocean 95.5 MHz. **D.Prgr**: 24h. **Format:** Oldies

ICCI-FM (Educ.)

✉ International College of the Cayman Islands, Newlands, P.O. Box 136 SAV, Savannah Post Office, Grand Cayman. **College** ☎ +1 345 947 1100. 📠 +1 809 947 1230. **Station** ☎ +1 (345) 947 1212 (request line). **L.P:** College Pres. & GM: Elsa M. Cummings, Ph.D.
FM: 101.1MHz (0.5kW). **D.Prgr:** 24h. Locally produced prgrs in English & Spanish for Grand Cayman residents, or continuous music, acc. to availability of student volunteers. **ANN:** "This is ICCI-FM, Newlands", "FM 101.1 ICCI".

HEAVEN 97 (Rlg.)

✉ Box 31481 SMB, George Town, Grand Cayman. ☎ +1 345 945 2797. 📠 +1 345 945 2707. **Email:** heaven97@candw.ky.
L.P: SM: Steve Koranda. **FM:** George Town 97.7MHz (2kW)
D.Prgr: 24h. Continuous Christian music.

STYLE 96.5 (Comm.)

✉ Godfred Nixon Way, Box 192 GT, Grand Cayman.
L.P: Dir: Dave Martins. **FM:** George Town 96.5MHz

DMS BROADCASTING (Comm.)

✉ Box 31910 SMB, Grand Cayman. **Web:** www.dms.com.ky
L.P: MD: Don Seymour. **HOT 104.1** – **MIX 106.1** – **ISLAND 107.1**.

CENTRAL AFRICAN REPUBLIC

L.T: UTC +1h — **Pop:** 3.5m — **Pr.L:** French, Sango, Zande — **E.C:** 50Hz, 220V — **ITU:** CAF.

MINISTÈRE DES POSTES ET DES TÉLÉCOMMUNICATIONS

✉ B.P. 814, Bangui ☎ +236 61 29 66 📠 +236 61 23 13. **L.P:** Parfait Mbay, Minister.

RADIODIFFUSION-TÉLÉVISION CENTRAFRICAINE

✉ B.P. 940, Bangui ☎ +236 61 2588/1650
L.P: MD: Delphine Zouta. Dir. of Inf: Christian Ndotah.
MW: 1440kHz 20/50kW - **FM:** 106.9MHz.
SW: Bangui-Bimbo (G.C: 04N21 018E35) 7220kHz (alt. 5035/ 6100kHz) 100kW 0430-2100.
D.Prgr in French/Vernaculars: 0430-2300. **N. in French:** 0500, 0600, 0700, 0800, 1300, 1800. **ANN:** F: "Ici Bangui, Radio Centreafrique". **IS:** Repeated piano chord. Opens and closes with National Anthem.

RADIO NDEKE LUKA

(joint initiative between the UN Development Programme, CAF government and Hirondelle Foundation)
✉ c/o PNUD, Av. de l'Indépendance, B.P. 872, Bangui ☎ +236 61 06 52 **Web:** www.hirondelle.org **Email:** ndekeluka@hotmail.com
L.P: Michael Künzli, Jean Laverdière. **FM:** 100.8MHz 1kW. **D.Prgr:** 24h in Sango/French. **SW:** see International radio section.

Other stations:
R. Rurale (community st's set up by the development agency ACTT): st's are operating in Bouar, Nola, Berberati & Bambari.
R. Evangile Nehemie (rlg), Bangui: freq. not known.
R. Notre Dame (rlg.): Bangui 103.3MHz.
Africa No. 1: Bangui 94.5MHz (see main entry under Gabon).
BBC African Sce: Bangui 100.6MHz.
RFI Afrique: Bangui 99.8MHz.

CHAD

L.T: UTC +1h — **Pop:** 9m — **Pr.L:** French, Arabic, 8 ethnic — **E.C:** 50Hz, 220V — **ITU:** TCD.

HAUT CONSEIL DE LA COMMUNICATION(HCC)

✉ N'Djaména. **L.P:** Moussa Dago, president.

RADIODIFFUSION NATIONALE TCHADIENNE (RNT)

✉ B.P. 892, N'Djaména ☎ +235 514253
L.P: Dir: Nguérébaye Adoum Saleh. S/Dir. of Tech. Sces: Raphael Mbaye Sané. **Station:** N'Djaména-Gredia (G.C: 15.03E/12.08N)
MW: 840kHz 20kW
SW: (GC:12N08 015E03) 6165 kHz 100kW.
FM: 94.05MHz 0.1kW
D.Prgr: in French/Arabic/Vernaculars MF 0425-0730 & 1000-2230, Sat 0425-2230, Sun 0425-2230. **N. in French:** 0530, 1300, 1330, 1830, 1900, 2100. **ANN:** "Ici N'Djaména, Radiodiffusion Nationale Tchadienne" **IS:** Balafon.

REGIONAL STATIONS
R. Moundou, B.P. 122, Moundou. ☎ +235 691322 - **FM:** 94.05/98.3MHz 200/450W. **D.Prgr:** 0500-0800, 1400-1830.
R. Sarh, B.P. 270, Sarh. ☎ +235 681361/681422 - **FM:** 100.1MHz **MW:** 850kHz 1kW **D.Prgr:** 1500-1800.
R. Abéché, B.P. 105, Abéché. ☎ +235 698149 **L.P:** Dir: Sanoussi Saïd - **FM:** 101MHz **D.Prgr:** 0500-0600, 1630-1800.
R.Faya-Largeau: FM 99.1MHz.

Other stations:
Dja FM, B.P. 1312, N'Djaména: 96.9 MHz 0.5kW – **R. Duji Lohar**, B.P. 61, Mondou: 101.8MHz – **R. Lotiko,** B.P. 87, Sarh: 97.6MHz (also r. BBC). **Web:** www.lotiko.org/fr/save/lotiko.htm **Email:** lotiko@intnet.td – **La Voix du Paysan**, B.P. 22, Doba: 96.2MHz – **Africa No. 1:** N'Djaména 103MHz (see main entry under Gabon) – **BBC African Sce:** N'Djaména 90.6MHz – **RFI Afrique**: N'Djaména 100.2MHz.

CHILE

L.T: UTC -4h (10 Oct-13 Mar: UTC -3h) — **Pop:** 15 million— **Pr.L:** Spanish — **E.C:** 50Hz, 220V — **ITU:** CHL.

SUBSECRETARIA DE TELECOMUNICACIONES

Offices: Amunátegui 139, Santiago. ✉ Clasificador 120, Correo 21, Santiago. ☎ + 56 2 672 6503. 📠 +56 2 699 5138. **Web:** www.subtel.cl **L.P:** Subsecr of Telecommunocations: Roberto Pliscoff Vásquez.

ASOCIACION DE RADIODIFUSORES DE CHILE

✉ Cas. 10476, Santiago de Chile ☎ +56 2 6398755.
📠 +56 2 6394205. . **Web:** www.galeon.com/redarca
L.P: Pres: César Molfino Mendoza. Dir: Alfredo Matte L.

STATIONS: MW: Call letters CA, CB, CC and CD indicate: A=No. Zone, B=Central Zone, C=So. Zone and D=Antarctic Zone. The figures indicate the freq. in kHz minus one cipher, f. inst. CB82 = Central Zone 820kHz. **SW:** Call letters CE are used for all zones.

MW: ° = also on SW, * = inactive, v=varying freq.

	Call	kHz	kW	Name, location and h. of tr.
1)	CB54	540	1	R. Ignacio Serrano, Melipilla: 1100-0400
2)	CD54	540	1	R. Calle Calle Saval, Valdivia: 1000-0400
170)	CC55	*550		Radiodifusión Americana, Penco
2x)	CD55	550	1	R. LV. de la Tierra, Angol
3)	CB57	*570	50	R. Agricultura, Santiago: 1000-0400
4)	CA59	590	1	R. Santa Maria de Guadalupe, Antofagasta: 1000-0430
5)	CC59	590	1	R. Hebrón, Concepción: 24h
6)	CD59	590	10	R. Chilena "Solonoticias", Punta Arenas: 1000-0430
6x)	CB60	600	10	R. Monumental, Santiago: 24h
65)	CD60	600	10	R. Tricolor, Osorno: 1000-0500
24)	CD61	610	5	R. Puerto Aysen, Puerto Aysén
7)	CA62	620	1	R. Norte Verde, Ovalle: 1100-0400
8)	CC62	620	1	R. Bío-Bío, Concepción: 24h
9)	CB63	630	10	R. Stela Maris, Valparaíso: 1100-0500
10)	CD64	640	10	R. Temuco Cooperativa AM, Temuco: 1000-0430
11)	CB66	660	50	R. Chilena "Solonoticias", Santiago: 24h
12)	CA68	680	10	R. Chilena "Solonoticias", Calama: 1000-0400
13)	CC68	680	10	R. Cooperativa, Concepción
14)	CB69	690	10	R. Santiago, Santiago: 1000-0600
15)	CD69	690	10	R. Estrella del Mar, Ancud: 1100-0330
15x)	CA70	700	1	R. Nibsan, Copiapó: 1030-0300
28)	CD70	700	1	R. Valdivia, Valdivia: 1030-0500
63)	CD70	700	5	R. Magallanes, Punta Arenas
16)	CB73	730	10	R. Cooperativa AM, Valparaíso: 1000-0430
17)	CD73	730	1	R. Camila, Los Angeles
18)	CD73B	730	1	R. Aysén, Pto. Aysén: 1100-0400

	Call	kHz	kW	Name, location and h. of tr.
16)	CB76	760	50	R. Cooperativa, Santiago: 24h
75)	CD77	770	10	R. Agricultura, Temuco: 1000-0400
81)	CD77	770	1	R. Cooperativa, Castro
19)	CD78	780	10	R. Sago AM, Osorno: 1000-0400
20)	CB80	*800	5/1	R. Santa Maria de Guadalupe, Viña del Mar
21)	CA82	820	10/1	R. Gabriela Mistral, La Serena: 1000-0400
127)	CB82	820	10/5	Radioemisora Carabineros de Chile, Santiago: 24h
22)	CC82	820	1	R. Maria Inmaculada, Concepción
23)	CD82	820	1	R. Concordia, La Unión: 1100-2330
25)	CA82	820	0.25	R. Pampa, Pedro de Valdivia
26)	CB84	840	10	R. Portales, Valparaíso: 1000-0500
27)	CD84	°840	10	R. Santa María, Coyhaique: 1030-0230
95)	CC86	860	10	R. Nueva Inés de Suárez, Concepción: 24h
29)	CB88	880	10	R. Colo Colo, Santiago: 24h
30)	CA89	890	10	R. León XIII, Pozo Almonte: 1100-0200
31)	CC89	890	1	R. Interamericana, Concepción: 1030-0400
32)	CD89	890	20	R. Nal., Punta Arenas: 1000-0400
33)	CA90	900	5	R. Manantial, Copiapó: 1100-0400
69)	CB90	900	1	Cablenoticias, Valparaíso: 1100-0500
34)	CC90	900	1	R. Ñuble, Chillán: 1100-0400
35)	CD90	900	1	R. LV de la Costa, Osorno: 1030-0400
35x)	CD92	920	1	R. 920, Temuco
36)	CA93	*930	10	R. El Cobre, Antofagasta
37)	CB93	930	10	R. Nuevo Mundo, Santiago: 1000-0530
38)	CD93	930	10	R. Reloncaví, Puerto Montt: 1100-0400
48)	CB94	940	1	R. Valentín Letelier, Valparaíso
152)	CA94	*940	1	R. 9-40, Copiapó
39)	CB96	960	10	R. Carrera, Santiago: 1100-0400
40)	CD96	960	10	R. Polar, Punta Arenas: 24h
41)	CA97	970	1	R. Calama, Calama: 1000-0400
42)	CC97	970	1	R. Lautaro, Talca: 1000-0500
43)	CD97B	°970	1	R. Patagonia Chilena, Coyhaique: 1000-0400
44)	CD97A	970	1	R. Austral, Valdivia: 1030-0400
45)	CA98	*980	1	R. Univ. Católica del Norte, Arica
3)	CB98	980	5	R. Agricultura, Valparaíso
145)	CC99	990	1	R. El Roble, Parral (n. 1590)
46)	CB100	1000	10	R. RRB, Santiago: 1030-0500
47)	CD101	1010	10	R. Chilena "Solonoticias", Temuco: 1000-0430
91)	CC102	1020	5	R. Amiga, Talca: 1000-0500
49)	CC103	1030	10	R. Chilena "Solonoticias", Concepción: 1100-0430
139)	CB103	1030	1	R. Progreso, Talagante
50)	CD103A	1030	1	R. Chiloé, Castro: 1100-0330
51)	CD104	1040	1	R. Payne AM, Puerto Natales
52)	CD104	1040	1	R. Raíces, Curacautín: 1100-0100
107)	CD105	1050	1	R. Armonía, Osorno: 1030-0630
53)	CB106	1060	50	R. Santa Maria de Guadalupe.Santiago: 1000-0500
54)	CA108	1080	1	R. Río Elqui, Vicuña
55)	CD108	1080	1	R. Los Confines, Angol: 1100-0300
56)	CC109	1090	5/1	R. Chilena "Solonoticias", Talca: 1000-0400
58)	CA110	*1100	1	R. La Portada, Antofagasta
59)	CB110	1100	10	R. Integridad, Viña del Mar: 1100-0500
60)	CD111	1110	10	R. La Frontera, Temuco: 1000-0400
61)	CB114	1140	75	R. Nal., Santiago: 1000-0600
62)	CC116	1160	1	R. Ancoa, Linares: 1000-0600
99)	CD116	1160	1	R. Baha'i, Temuco: 1030-0230
98)	CD117	1170	3	R. Natales, Puerto Natales: 1200-0400
172)	CB118	1180	50	R. Portales, "la primera de Chile", Santiago: 1030-0430
64)	CA120	*1200	1	R. Almirante Blanco Encalada, Tocopilla
3)	CD120	1200	10	R. Agricultura, Los Angeles: 1000-0400
66)	CB121	1210	5	R. Valparaíso, Valparaíso: 0930-0600
67)	CC121	1210	1	R. Universidad de Talca, Talca: 1100-0400
161)	CD121	1210	10	R. Armonía, Puerto Montt
169)	CA122	*1220	1	Soc. Morales y Morales y Cia., La Serena
162)	CD122	1220	10	R. Santa Maria de Guadalupe, Temuco
68)	CB124	1240	10	R. Universidad de Santiago, Santiago: 1100-0400
163)	CA124	1240	0.25	R. Principal Chuquicamata, Calama: 0950-0500
70)	CA125	1250	1	R. Santa Maria de Guadalupe, La Serena
71)	CD125	1250	10	R. Armonía, Valdivia: 1100-0400
72)	CA126	*1260	10	R. Nal., Arica
73)	CC126	1260	1	R. Condell, Curicó: 1100-0500
57)	CD126	1260	10	R. Santa Maria de Guadalupe, Punta Arenas: 1100-0400
74)	CB127	v1270	10	R. Festival, Viña del Mar: 1000-0700
151)	CC128	1280	1	R. Arturo Prat Chacón AM, San Carlos: 1050-0405
164)	CD128	1280	10	R. del Sur "En Voz Alta", Osorno
150)	CA129	1290	0.25	R. Coya, María Elena
165)	CD129	1290	1	R. Mulchen, Mulchen
76)	CB130	1300	5	R. Tierra, Santiago: 1300-0100
77)	CD130	1300	10	R. Chilena "Solonoticias", Valdivia: 1000-0430
78)	CD130	1300	1	R. Cabo de Hornos, Pto. Williams:1100-0500
79)	CA132	1320	0.25	R. Estrella del Norte, Vallenar
80)	CD132	1320	1	R. Lincoyan, Mulchén: 1100-0300
46)	CB133	v1330	3	R. Metropolitana, Santiago
83)	CD133	1330	3/1.5	R. Vicente Pérez Rosales, Puerto Montt: 1055-0400
85)	CB134	1340	10	R. Caracola, Valparaíso: 0930-0300
86)	CC134	v1340	1	R. La Discusión, Chillán: 24h
87)	CD134	1340	1	R. Panguipulli, Panguipulli: 1200-0100
89)	CD135	1350	1	R. San Carlos, Ancud: 1130-0400
90)	CA135	1350	1	R. Riquelme, Coquimbo: 1030-0430
92)	CC136	1360	5	R. Universidad del Bío Bío, "UBB", Concepción: 1040-0300
153)	CD137	1370	1	R. Conun Huenu "La Popular", Temuco: 1100-0400 (Sat 0800)
93)	CB138	1380	50	R. Corporación, Santiago: 24h
154)	CD140	1400	5	R. La Amistad, Los Angeles: 1030-0400
94)	CA140	v1400	1	R. Tarapacá, Iquique: 1045-0600
166)	CD140	1400	5	R. Belén, Puerto Montt
96)	CB141	1410	3	R. Quinta Región, Valparaíso
97)	CD141	1410	1	R. Loncoche, Loncoche: 1100-0330
82)	CB142	v1420	1	R. Panamericana, Santiago: 1100-0400
100)	CC142	1420	1	R. Maule, Cauquenes: 1050-0430
101)	CC143	1430	1	R. Chilena "Solo Noticias", Rancagua: 1030-0500
102)	CA144	1440	1	R. Santa Maria de Guadalupe, Arica: 1000-0430
103)	CA144	1440	1	R. Agricultura, La Serena: 1000-0400
104)	CC144	1440	1	R. El Sembrador, Chillán: 1030-0430
105)	CB145	1450	1	R. Universidad Técnica "Federico Santa María", Valparaíso: 1100-0300
106)	CC145	1450	5	R. Libertad, Curicó: 1000-0400
108)	CD145	v1450	1	R. Santa Maria de Guadalupe, Puerto Varas: 24h
109)	CA146	1460	10	R. Antofagasta, Antofagasta: 1130-0300
110)	CB146	1460	1	R. Yungay, Santiago: 1100-0400
111)	CC146	1460	1	R Armonía, Concepción
112)	CB147	*1470	1	R. Sargento Aldea, San Antonio
113)	CA148	1480	1/0.25	R. Amanecer, Ovalle: 1100-0400
114)	CB148	1480	1	R. La Amistad AM, Tomé: 1100-0230
115)	CD148	1480	1	R. General Baquedano, Valdivia
116)	CA149	1490	5	R. Alicanto, Salvador: 1000-0400
117)	CB149	1490	1	R. El Canelo de Nos AM, San Bernardo: 1100-0400
88)	CD149	1490	5	R. Malleco, Victoria: 0300
118)	CA150	1500	1	R. Santa Maria de Guadalupe, Iquique: 1100-0500
119)	CC150	1500	1	R. Centenario, San Javier: 1100-0300
120)	CD150	1500	1	R. Tierra del Fuego, Puerto Porvenir: 1100-0400
136)	CB150	1500	1	R. Trasandina, Los Andes: 1100-0400
149)	CA151	1510	1/0.5	R. Luís Alvarez Sierra. Illapel: 1100-0400
121)	CC151	1510	1	R. Rancagua, Rancagua: 1100-0400
122)	CD151	1510	1	R. Teniente Merino, Lebu: 1130-0300
123)	CC152	1520	1	R. Nueva Soberanía, Linares: 1030-0430
124)	CD152	1520	0.1	R. Aníbal Pinto, Lautaro
155)	CB152	v1520	1	R. Integración, San Antonio: 0900-0500
125)	CA153	*1530	1	R. Juan Godoy, Copiapó
156)	CB153	1530	1	R. Nexo, Quillota: 1100-0600
126)	CC153	1530	1	R. Corporación, Lota
167)	CD153	1530	1	R. Calbuco, Calbuco
128)	CB154	1540	1	R. Sudamérica, Santiago: 1200-0030
157)	CC154	1540	1	R. Central, Chillán
129)	CD154	1540	1	R. San José de Alcudia, Río Bueno: 0955-0300
130)	CB155	1550	1	R. Provincia AM, Putaendo
131)	CC155	v1550	1	R. Manuel Rodríguez, San Fernando (r 1555): 1100-0400
132)	CD155	1550	0.25	R. Regional, Tralguén
133)	CA156	°1560	5/3	R. Parinacota, Putre: 24h
134)	CB156	1560	1	R. Manantial, Talagante: 1100-0400
135)	CD156	1560	1	R. Parque Nacional, Villarrica: 1100-0400
137)	CC157	v1570	1	R. Niebla, Rancagua: 24h

	Call	kHz	kW	Name, location and h. of tr.
159)	CC157	1570	7	R. Familia del Maule, "La Voz de la Región", Talca: 24h
138)	CD157	1570	0.25	R. Acuarela, Nueva Imperial: 1155-1810, 2200-0200
140)	CC158	v1580	1	R. Colchagua, Santa Cruz
141)	CD158A	1580	0.25	R. Millaray, Cañete
142)	CD158B	1580	0.5	R. Continental, Collipulli: 1100-0430
143)	CB159	v1590	1	R. Aconcagua, San Felipe: 1100-0430
144)	CC159	v1590	0.25	R. Rengo, Rengo: 1000-0400
168)	CD159	1590	5	Em. Tepual, Llanquihue
146)	CB160A	1600	0.25	R. Nuevo Tiempo, Santiago
147)	CB160B	1600	0.25	Radiocable, Viña del Mar
148)	CC160A	v1600	0.25	R. Llacolén, Concepción: 1000-0430
171)	CD160	*1600	0.25	Millalebu-La Regalona AM, Temuco

SW: * = inactive

	Call	kHz	kW	Name, location and h. of tr.
160)	CE582	5825	0.1	R. Triunfal Evangélica, Santiago
133)	CE601	6010	1	R. Parinacota, Putre: 24h
27)	CE603	6030	10	R. Santa María, Coyhaique: 1045 (Sun 1130)-0230 (n. 6030)
43)	CE608	6080	1	R.Patagonia Chilena,Coyhaique: 0930 (Sun 1000)-2400
158)	CE609	6090	10	R. Esperanza, Temuco: 24h
3)	CE963	*9630	10	R. Agricultura, Santiago

Addresses and other information

A complete list of Chilean radio stations is maintained by Chilnet as part of the Chilean yellow pages, with links to the Web pages of individual stations and a *free* Internet Fax service to each station at **Web:** www.chilnet.cl/rubros/radioeo1.

1) Cas. 110, Melipilla. - **FM:** 104.5 "Caricia FM". – **2)** Chacabuco 210, piso 3, Validivia. ☎ 📠 +56 63 225087. – **2x)** Av. Bernardo O'Higgins 294, piso 2 (✉ Cas. 268), Angol. **Email:** vozdelatierra@123click.cl ☎ 📠 +56 45 712331, 714706. – 3) CB57: Av. Manuel Rodriguez 15, Santiago. 📠 +56 2 6722749.; CD120: Colón 143, Los Angeles, ☎ +56 43 312538. 📠 +56 43 322663. - **FM:** 97.5, 100.5 "San Cristóbal"; CB98: Cas. 90, Valparaíso. - **FM:** 97.3. – **4)** Washington 2562, Depto. 204 (✉ Cas. 1060), Antofagasta. – **5)** Cas. 486, Concepción. – **6)** Cas. 97-D, Punta Arenas. – **6x)** Av. Condell 910, Santiago. ☎ +56 2 2224500. 📠 +56 2 2223093. – **7)** Cas. 355, Ovalle. – **8)** O'Higgins 680, Concepción. ☎ +56 41 225660. 📠 +56 41 620621. **Email:** rbiobio@reuna.cl **Web:** www.reuna.cl/rbiobio/ – **9)** Pedro Montt 1766 (Cas. 3304), Valparaíso. ☎ +56 32 745537. 📠 +56 32 596064. – **10)** Portales 775, Temuco. ☎ +56 43 311015. - **FM:** 93.5 "Temuco Rock & Pop FM". – **11)** Phillips 40, 2° piso, (✉ Cas. 10277), Santiago. **Web:** www.radiochilena.com **Email:** radio@radiochilena.cl ☎ +56 2 463 5000. 📠 +56 2 463 5100. – **12)** Calle Domeyko esquina Los Pimientos, Calama. - **FM:** 104.7 "Aurora". – **13)** Paicavi 119, 2° piso, (Paza Peru) (or Cas. 2337), Concepción. ☎ +56 41 223207, 242563. 📠 +56 41 234697. - **14)** Triana 868, Providencia (or Cas. 10195), Santiago. – **15)** Ramírez 207, or Cas. 260, Ancud. ☎ +56 65 622905. 📠 +56 65 622722. – **15x)** Vallejos 650, Departamento 11, Copiapó. - ☎ +56 52 214133. – **16)** CB76: Antonio Bellet 353, Providencia, Santiago. **Web:** www.cooperativa.cl **Email:** info@cooperativa.cl ☎ +56 2 364 8000. 📠 +56 2 364 8010; CB73: Lira 543, Valparaíso. ☎ +56 32 213342. 📠 +56 32 255027 - **FM:** 93.1 "Viña del Mar Rock & Pop FM". – **17)** Cas. 51, Los Angeles. ☎ +56 43 311015. – **18)** Carrera 545, 2° piso, Puerto Aysén. **Email:** radioaysen@yahoo.com ☎ +56 67 332626. – **19)** Juan Mackenna 904, entrepiso (or Cas. 35-0), Osorno. **Email:** sago@telsur.cl ☎ +56 64 232160. 📠 +56 64 233881. - **FM:** 94.5. – **20)** 5 Norte 168, Viña del Mar. ☎ +56 32 971201. – **21)** Los Carrera 525, 3° piso, Departamento C, La Serena. **Web:** www.radiogabrielamistral.8m.com ☎ 📠 +56 51 211987. - **FM:** 98.5 "Intima". – **22)** Angol 81, piso 2, Talcahuano. – **23)** Arturo Prat 466 (or Cas. 312), La Unión. ☎ +56 64 322275. ☎ 📠 +56 64 322322. – **24)** Puerto Aysén. – **25)** Of. SOQUIMICH, Pedro de Valdivia. – **26)** Cas. 89-V, Valparaíso. - **FM:** 98.9 "Carolina". – **27)** Francisco Bilbao 691, Coyhaique. ☎ +56 67 232398. 📠 +56 67 231306. – **28)** Caupolicán 597, of. 31, Valdivia. – **29)** Philips 56, 6° piso (or Cas. 56042), Santiago. **Web:** www.radiocolocolo.cl ☎ +56 2 6396825, 6394774. 📠 +56 2 6396826. – **30)** Ap. 6, Pozo Almonte, Iquique. - **31)** Calle Barros Arana 871, 5° piso, Of. 51, Concepción. ☎ +56 41 224704, 245705. – **32)** Errazuriz 889, piso 3, Punta Arenas. – **33)** Cas. 355, Copiapó. ☎ +56 52 226094, 222598. 📠 +56 52 211245. - **FM:** 96.5. – **34)** 5 de Abril 655 (✉ Cas. 267), Chillán. **Web:** www.chillan2000.cl/radionuble.htm **Email:** radionuble@entelchile.net ☎ +56 42 226226. 📠 +56 42 215530. - **FM:** 89.7. – **35)** Cochrane 746 (✉ Cas. 5-0), Osorno. ☎ 📠 +56 64 233366. – **35x)** Gral. Cruz 551 (or Cas. 1499), Temuco. ☎ +56 45 212707. – **36)** Cas. 1298, Antofagasta. – **37)** Estados Unidos 246, Santiago. **Web:** www.radionuevomundo.cl ☎ +56 2 460 8215. – **38)** Illapel 60 (✉ Cas. 67), Puerto Montt. **Email:** radio-rr@telsur.cl ☎ +56 65 252946. 📠 +56 65 256523. – **39)** Eleodoro Flores 2475, Nunoa, Santiago. ☎ +56 2 2692255, 2692256. 📠 +56 2 2692257. – **40)** Bories 871, Punta Arenas. **Web:** www.radiopolar.com **Email:** radiopolar@chilecontrol.cl ☎ +56 61 241417. 📠 +56 61 228344. - **FM:** 105.7 "Finísima". – **41)** Rafael Vargas 1875, Calama. - **FM:** 104.7 "Aurora FM". – **42)** Cas. 214, Talca. ☎ +56 71 220061. 📠 +56 71 231344. – **43)** Simón Bolívar 26, Coyhaique. ☎ 56 67 232240. 📠 +56 67 233287. - **FM:** 99.3 "Acro Iris". – **44)** Arauco 363 3° piso, Valdivia. – **45)** Cas. 6-D, Arica. ☎ +56 58 222380. 📠 +56 58 222278. - **FM:** 95.9. – **46)** Av. Bulnes 120, Oficina 89 (or Cas. de Correo 14351), Santiago. – **47)** Arturo Prat 215 (✉ Cas. 640), Temuco. ☎📠 +56 45 212039. - **FM:** 97.9 "Aurora". – **48)** Av. Errazuriz 2120, Valparaíso. - **FM:** 97.3. – **49)** Aníbal Pinto 215, of 801, Concepción. - **FM:** 90.1 "Galaxia", 106.5 "Aurora". – **50)** O' Higgins 486 (✉ Cas. 106), Castro. ☎ +56 65 632260. - **FM:** 90.1 "Martin Ruiz de Gamboa". – **51)** Puerto Eberhard 229, Puerto Natales. – **52)** Cas. 136, Curacautín, Malleco. – **53)** Calle Miguel Claro 161, Providencia, Santiago. **Web:** www.santamariadeguadalupe.com **Email:** radio@santamariadeguadalupe.com ☎ +56 2 236 6375. 📠 +56 2 236 6405. – **54)** San Marín 205, piso 2, Oficina 4, Vicuña. – **55)** Lautaro 124 (✉ Cas. 211), Angol ☎ +56 45 711511. 📠 +56 45 711297. - **FM:** 94.9. – **56)** Uno Poniente 1239 (✉ Cas. 516), Talca. - **FM:** 98.9 "Aurora". – **57)** Faguano 548 A, Punta Arenas. – **58)** Cas. 410, Antofagasta. – **59)** Plaza Vergara 172, Oficina 22, Viña del Mar. **Email:** vina@rrb.org ☎ +56 32 885524. – **60)** Claro Solar 536, Temuco. - **FM:** 95.9 "La Araucana". – **61)** Cas. 244-V, Santiago. – **62)** Independencia 631 (or Cas. 500), Linares. - **FM:** 90.7. – **63)** Errazuriz 675, 2° piso, Punta Arenas. ☎📠 +56 (61) 223210. – **64)** Cas. 2001, Tocopilla. – **65)** Cas. 923, Osorno. – **66)** Juana Ross 28, Valparaíso. ☎ +56 32 216950, 216400, 594098. 📠 +56 32 216400. – **67)** 2 Norte 685, Talca. - **FM:** 102.1. – **68)** Cas. 442, Correo 2, Santiago. **Web:** www.radio.usach.cl – **69)** Valparaíso 633, piso 3, Valparaíso. ☎ +56 32 695485. – **70)** Matta 591, La Serena. – **71)** Caupolicán 588, Valdivia. **Web:** www.armonia.cl ☎ +56 63 204415. - **FM:** 90.1. – **72)** Baquedano 575, (✉ Cas. 49-D), Arica. - **FM:** 90.9 "Pukara FM". – **73)** Cas. 492, Curicó. - **FM:** 89.9 "Futura". – **74)** Paseo Cousiño 8, Viña del Mar. **Web:** www.radiofestival.cl – **75)** Colón 143, piso 2, Los Angeles. ☎ +56 45 213854. - **FM:** 105.7 "San Cristóbal". – **76)** Purísima 251, Barrio Bellavista, Ricoleta, Santiago. ☎ +56 2 442 9635. 📠 +56 (2) 7773840. – **Italian:** Sat 1400-1500. – **77)** Cas. 597, Valdivia. – **78)** Calle Cabo de Hornos, Puerto Williams. ☎📠 +56 61 621122. - **FM:** 98.5. – **79)** Cas. 13, Vallenar. – **80)** Gana 360, Mulchén. – **81)** Thompson 255 (✉ Cas. 174), Castro. – **82)** Gran Av. José Miguel Carrera 5848, 4° piso, Santiago. 📠 +56 2 5216302. – **83)** Cas. 166, Puerto Montt. – **85)** Plaza de la Justicia 45, Of. 702, Valparaíso. – **86)** 18 de Septiembre 721 (or Cas. 479), Chillán. **Web:** www.diarioladiscusion.cl **Email:** radiotv@ladiscusion.cl ☎ +56 42 211667. 📠 +56 42 213578. - **FM:** 94.7. – **87)** Bernard O'Higgins 793, Panguipulli. – **88)** Cas. 267, Victoria. – **89)** Cas. 283, Ancud, Isla de Chiloé. – **90)** Aldunate 1619, Coquimbo. ☎ +56 51 321948, 321051. 📠 +56 51 327367. – **91)** Diagonal Isidoro del Solar 285, Talca. **Email:** chb@entelchile.net ☎ +56 71 224333. 📠 +56 71 225175. - **FM:** 100.7 "Futura FM", 107.1 "Logika FM". – **92)** Cas. 5-C, Concepción. **Web:** www.ubiobio.cl/radioubb – **93)** Portugal 810, Santiago. ☎ +56 2 665 1032. – **94)** Cas. 614, Iquique. ☎ +56 (57) 426606. – **95)** Castellón 477, 3° piso (or Cas. 862), Concepción. ☎ +56 41 212280. – **96)** Pasaje Ross 149 Dpto. 1201, Valparaíso. – **97)** Ignacio Serrano 264 (✉ Cas. 61), Loncoche. - **FM:** 105.9 "Vibración". – **98)** Eberhard 212, Puerto Natales. ☎ +56 61 414746. ☎ 📠 +56 61 410157. – **99)** Cas. 56-D, Temuco. **Email:** kalimat@telsur.cl ☎ +56 45 375142. 📠 +56 45 323657. - **Mapuche:** 1030-1400, 1600-2100, 0000-0230. – **100)** Claudina Urrutia 707, Interior (or Cas. 196), Cauquenes. ☎ +56 73 514303. - **FM:** 101.9 "Dinastia". – **101)** Cas. 102, Rancagua. ☎ +56 72 236602. 📠 +56 72 230796. – **102)** General Lagos 678 (✉ Cas. 225), Arica. – **103)** Cas. 536, La Serena. – **104)** Cas. 336, Chillán. - **FM:** 104.7 "Aurora FM". – **105)** Av. España 1680, Valparaíso. **Web:** www.radioutfsm.cl ☎ +56 32 654122. - **FM:** 99.7. – **106)** Yungay 737, Curicó. - **FM:** 101.1MHz (rel. AM), 92.7 "Opus". – **107)** Manuel Rodríguez 741, Osorno. – **108)** San Francisco 248, Of. 2, Puerto Varas. – **109)** Gloria Postrera, Colectivo Peru, Ofic. 1, Antofagasta. 📠 + 56 55 262572. – **110)** Irarrazaval 2821, Of. 427, Edif. Century, Santiago. – **111)** Aníbal Pinto 399, Talcahuano. **Web:** www.armonia.cl – **112)** Av. Barros Luco 1678 (✉ Cas. 68, Correo 2), San Antonio. ☎📠 +56 35 211321. - **FM:** 90.9 "Cristalina". – **113)** Libertad 786 (✉ Cas. 34), Ovalle. ☎ 📠 +56 53 620651. – **114)** Sotomayor 652, Tomé. ☎ +56 41 650657. – **115)** Av. Ramón Picarte 4215 (or Cas. 35), Valdivia. – **116)** Av. El Tofo 535, El Salvador. - **English:** 2100-2300. – **117)** Av. Portales 3020 (✉ Cas. 380), San Bernardo. ☎ +56 2 8571943. 📠 +56 2 8571160. – **118)** Esmeralda 594 (✉ Cas. 290), Iquique. ☎ +56 57 422693. – **119)** Cas. 18-D, San Javier. - **FM:** 105.5 "Musical FM". – **120)** Bulnes 449, Puerto Porvenir. – **121)** Pasaje Hoffman 61, Rancagua. **Web:** www.radiorancagua.cl – **122)** Cas. 76, Lebu. – **123)** Diputado Dario Dueñas 340 (or Cas. 67), Linares. – **124)** O'Higgins 828, 2° piso, Of. 5 (✉ Cas. 15), Lautaro. – **125)** Colipí 371, Copiapó. ☎ +56 52 212031. – **126)** Cas. 66, Lota. – **127)** Av. Presidente Bulnes 80, Of. 127, Santiago. **Web:** www.carabinerosdechile.cl **Email:** radio@carabineros.cl ☎ 📠 +56 2 698 8141. – **128)** Cas. 1346, Santiago. **Web:** www.radiosudamerica.cl3 ☎ +56 2 527 3999. – **129)** Pedro Lagos 295, Río Bueno. – **130)** Cas. 75, Putaendo. – **131)** Chacabuco Esq. España, San Fernando. ☎📠 +56 72 714267. – **132)** General

Lagos 662 (✉ Cas. 186), Traiguén. - **FM:** 101.3 "Granero". – **133)** Calle José Miguel Carrera 350 esquina Av. Circulación O'Higgins, Putre (✉ Cas 82, Arica). ☎ +56 58 222521. - **FM:** 94.5. – **134)** Cas. 223, Talagante. - **FM:** 102.9 "Embrujo FM". – **135)** Pedro Montt 478 (✉ Cas. 110), Villarrica. – **136)** Papudo 155 (or Cas. 307), Los Andes. ☎🖷 +56 34 514343. – **137)** Calvo 447, Rancagua. - **FM:** 101.3 "FM San Fernando". – **138)** Cas. 18, Nueva Imperial. – **139)** Enrique Alcalde 1081, Talagante. ☎ +56 2 8151666. - **FM:** 103.9 "Contacto". – **140)** Rafael Casanova 146, Santa Cruz. - **FM:** 105.5 "Ensueño". – **141)** Arturo Prat 399, Cañete. - **FM:** 98.5 "Cañete". – **142)** Alcázar 1158, 2º piso, Collipulli. ☎ +56 45 811623. – **143)** Cas. 100, San Felipe. - **FM:** 91.7 "Colunquén FM". – **144)** Urriola 485, Rengo. – **145)** Cas. 37, Parral. – **146)** María Luisa Santander 0292, Providencia, Santiago. ☎ +56 2 223 7048, 223 7031. 🖷 +56 2 204 0529. – **147)** Cas. 972, Viña del Mar. – **148)** Cas. 2311, Concepción. – **149)** Independencia 175, Illapel. ☎ +56 53 522831. 🖷 +56 53 522726. - **FM:** 100.9. – **150)** Of. SOQUIMICH, María Elena. – **151)** Cas. 265, San Carlos. – **152)** Maipú 370, Copiapó. – **153)** Rudecindo Ortega 691 (or Cas. 12), Temuco. ☎ +56 45 220408. – **154)** Cas. 541, Los Angeles. – **155)** Cas. 33, Llolleo, San Antonio. – **156)** Cas. 529, Quillota. - **FM:** 104.7 "Libra Stereo FM". – **157)** Bulnes 220 (✉ Cas. 35), Chillán. – **158)** Luis Durand 3057 (or Cas. 830), Temuco. ☎ +56 45 367070. 🖷 +56 45 213790. - **English:** 0800-0830. **German:** Sun 1230-1300. - **FM:** 106.9. – **159)** 1 Poniente 1239 (or Cas. 516), Talca. **Email:** radiofamilia'a'hotmail.com ☎ +56 71 227255. 🖷 +56 71224916. – **160)** Las Araucarias 2757, Villa M. Larrain, Santiago. – **161)** La Serena 97, Puerto Montt. – **162)** Antonio Varas 920, Temuco. – **163)** Cas. 127, Calama. ☎ +56 65 258097. - **FM:** 99.7 "Sensación El Abra FM". – **164)** Patricio Lynch 1814-B, Osorno. ☎ +56 64 330400. - **FM:** 101.5 "La Palabra". – **165)** Aníbal Pinto 720, Mulchen (Bío Bío). – **166)** Benavente 385, Puerto Montt. **Email:** puertomontt@episcopado.cl ☎ +56 65 258909. 🖷 +56 65 258048. - **FM:** 92.3 "Aurora". – **167)** Camino Pte. Ibáñez, Calbuco (Llanquihue). – **168)** E. Ramirez y Pte. Ibáñez, Llanquihue (Puerto Montt). – **169)** Parcela 510, La Serena. – **170)** Penco. – **171)** Ziem 2676, Temuco. ☎ +56 45 220271. – **172)** Fanor Velasco 11, Santiago. ☎ +56 2 673 2288. 🖷 +56 2 6957159.

FM in Santiago. **Power** 1-10 kW. **Slogans:** Name + "FM".
11) 88.1 Aurora – 88.5 Concierto – 61) 88.9 R. Futuro – 89.3 Maria – 11) 89.7 Duna – 90.5 Pudahuel – 91.3 El Conquistador – 91.7 Amistad – 3) 92.1 – 92.5 Radioactiva – 92.9 Romance – 93.3 La Cooperativa – 93.7 Universo – 16) 94.1 Rock & Pop – 68) 94.5 – 95.3 40 principales – 76) 95.9 Tiempo – 96.5 Beethoven – 97.1 Caracol – 97.7 Zero – 98.5 FM 2 – 29) 99.3 Carolina – 99.7 Bío Bío – 76) 100.1 Infinita – 11) 100.9 – 101.3 Corazón – 101.7 FM Hit – 102.1 Oasis – 102.5 Univ. de Chile – 103.3 Horizonte – 103.9 Maria – 104.1 Romantica – 104.9 Nina – 105.7 Para ti – 106.3 Armonía – 46) 106.9 Sintonía – 107.5 Fantasía

CHINA (People's Rep. of)

L.T: UTC +8h — **Pop:** 1,336 million —**Pr.L:** Mandarin, Amoy, Cantonese, Chaozhou, Hakka, Kazakh, Korean, Mongolian, Tibetan, Uighur, Zhuang, a.o. — **E.C:** 50Hz, 220V — **ITU:** CHN.

MINISTRY OF INFORMATION AND INDUSTRIES

✉ 13 Xi Chang'an Jie, Beijing 100804. **L.P:** Minister: Wang Xudong.

THE STATE ADMINISTRATION OF RADIO, FILM AND TELEVISION (SARFT) (Gov.)

✉ 2 Fuxingmenwai Dajie, Beijing 100866 or P.O.Box 4501, Beijing. ☎ +86 10 6851 3409. 🖷 +86 10 6851 2174.
Web: www.chinasarft.gov.cn **L.P:** Dir: Xu Guangchun.

Official P.R.C Abbreviations: The 31 regions of People's Republic of China, with their abbreviations and names in Pinyin (Chinese Phonetic Alphabet) version followed by the old spelling in brackets:
AH: Anhui (Anhwei) – BJ: Beijing M. (Peking) – CQ: Chongqing M. (Chungking) – FJ: Fujian (Fukien) – GD: Guangdong (Kwangtung) – GS: Gansu (Kansu) – GX: Guangxi Zhuang A.R. (Kwangsi) – GZ: Guizhou (Kweichow) – HAN: Hainan (Hainan) – HB: Hubei (Hupeh) – HEB: Hebei (Hopeh) – HEN: Henan (Honan) – HL: Heilongjiang (Heilungkiang) – HN: Hunan (Hunan) – JL: Jilin (Kirin) – JS: Jiangsu (Kiangsu) – JX: Jiangxi (Kiangsi) – LN: Liaoning (Liaoning) – NM: Nei Menggu A.R. (Inner Mongolia) – NX: Ningxia Hui A.R. (Ningsia) – QH: Qinghai (Tsinghai) – SC: Sichuan (Szechwan) – SD: Shandong (Shantung) – SH: Shanghai M. (Shanghai) – SN: Shaanxi (Shensi) – SX: Shanxi (Shansi) – TJ: Tianjin M. (Tientsin) – XJ: Xinjiang Uighur A.R. (Sinkiang) – XZ: Xizang A.R.(Tibet) – YN: Yunnan (Yunnan) – ZJ: Zhejiang (Chekiang).

Regional Services: Add "Renmin Guangbo Diantai" (People's Broadcasting Station) to the station name shown in the table below to obtain the full name in Standard Chinese.

Abbreviations: 1 = 1st prgr, 2 = 2nd prgr, 3 = 3rd prgr; E = Economic ch/st, ED = Educational ch/st, G = General ch/st, I = Information ch/st, L = Literary ch/st, LF = Life ch/st, M = Music ch/st, N = News ch/st, T = Traffic ch/st; EBS = Economic Broadcasting Station, IBS = Information Broadcasting Station, LBS = Literary Broadcasting Station, MBS = Music Broadcasting Station, TBS = Traffic Broadcasting Station.
Languages: Standard Chinese (Putonghua), based on the Beijing dialect, is used in broadcasts throughout China. Various dialects and minority languages are included in the relevant regional services and in broadcasts to Taiwan.
Abbreviations: Ch = Standard Chinese, Kg = Kirghiz, Ko = Korean, Kz = Kazakh, Mo = Mongolian, Tb = Tibetan, Ug = Uighur.

MW:

	kHz	kW	Station	Location
ZJ1)	531	10	Zhejiang N	ZJ, Jinhua
1)	540		CNR 1	
NM18)	540		Genhe	NM
QH4)	540		Haixi-Mo/Tb	QH, Da Qaidam
1)	549	1200	CNR 5	FJ, Putian
NM5)	549	10	Chifeng-Ch	NM
NM12)	549	10	Alxa-Ch	NM, Bayanhot
EN2)	549	10	Zhengzhou N	HEN
FJ1)	558	50	Fujian N	FJ
XJ1)	558	120	Xinjiang-Ug	XJ, Urumqi
NM3)	558	10	Baotou N	NM
NM17)	558	1	Zalantun	NM
1)	567		CNR 1	
TJ1)	567	20	Tianjin T	TJ
ZJ1)	576v		Zhejiang N	ZJ, Jiaojiang
YN1)	576	10	Yunnan Sat.	YN
FJ5)	576		Quanzhou N	FJ
EN4)	576	1	Luoyang N	HEN
JS1)	585	50	Jiangsu E	JS, Nanjing
14)	585	200	Southeast BC	FJ, Fuzhou
SX6)	585	10	Jincheng N	SX
EN14)	585	10	Nanyang	HEN
JX5)	585	1	Xinyu G	JX
GS3)	585		Jinchang	GS
SD1)	594	50	Shandong E	SD, Jinan
XZ1)	594	300	Xizang-Tb	XZ, Lhasa
13)	603		V.O.Pujiang	SH
BJ1)	603	10	Beijing Capital	BJ
EB1)	603		Hebei T	HEB, Shijiazhuang
SH2)	603		Dongfang E	SH
ZJ1)	603		Zhejiang Travel	ZJ, Hangzhou
AH1)	603		Anhui T	AH, Hefei
AH1)	603		Anhui LF	AH, Suzhou
EN1)	603		Henan I	HEN, Zhengzhou
GD1)	603		Guangdong ED	GD, Guangzhou
GZ1)	603	10	Guizhou E	GZ, Guiyang
SN1)	603		Shaanxi E	SN, Xi'an
NX1)	603	10	Ningxia EBS	NX, Yinchuan
SX4)	603	1	Yangquan	SX
NM8)	603	50	Hulun Buir-Ch	NM, Hailar
NM10)	603	10	Ordos BS-Mo	NM, Ulanhot
JL3)	603		Jilin-shi E	JL
JL10)	603		Yanbian-Ko	JL
JS9)	603	1	Nantong E	JS
ZJ4)	603	10	Ningbo T	ZJ
JX9)	603		Ji'an	JX
SD5)	603		Zaozhuang EBS	SD
SD10)	603		Jining L	SD
HB3)	603	10	Wuhan T	HB
SN7)	603		Yan'an	SN
XJ9)	603	1	Ili-Ug	XJ, Yining
XJ10)	603		Shihezi EBS	XJ
LN1)	612	10	Liaoning Sat.	LN, Dandong
FJ1)	612	100	Fujian N	FJ
SC1)	612	10	Sichuan 1	SC
HL1)	621	200	Heilongjiang N	HL, Harbin
HB9)	621	10	Yichang N	HB
SC9)	621		Guangyuan	SC
YN11)	621	1	Zhaotong	YN
QH4)	621	20	Haixi-Ch	QH, Da Qaidam
1)	630	200	CNR 2	JX, Nanchang
1)	639	200	CNR 1	BJ
SH1)	648		Shanghai T	SH
AH1)	648		Anhui LF	AH, Wuhu
GD1)	648	150	Guangdong Sat.	GD, Guangzhou
LN16)	648		Chaoyang EBS	LN
AH3)	648	1	Huainan	AH

	kHz	kW	Station	Location
XJ7)	648		Kashi-Ch	XJ
EN1)	657	300	Henan N	HEN, Zhengzhou
JL7)	657	1	Baishan	JL
ZJ6)	657		Jiaxing N	ZJ
11)	666		V.O.Strait N	FJ
QH1)	666	200	Qinghai-Ch	QH, Xining
LN8)	666	2	Jinzhou N	LN
JL4)	666		Siping	JL
HL10)	666	10	Jiamusi	HL
ZJ5)	666	7.5	Wenzhou G	ZJ
AH2)	666	10	Hefei	AH
SD10)	666	1	Jining N	SD
GZ5)	666	1	Anshun	GZ
YN10)	666	1	Dongchuan	YN
NM1)	675	200	Nei Menggu-Ch	NM, Hohhot
ZJ9)	675		Jinhua	ZJ
YN12)	675	1	Gejiu	YN
1)	684	1200	CNR 6	FJ, Putian
AH1)	684		Anhui LF	AH, Xuancheng
HB2)	684		Chutian Sat.	HB, Jingmen
GS1)	684		Gansu 1	GS
EB8)	684	10	Tangshan N	HEB
LN5)	684	10	Fushun N	LN
HL9)	684	50	Mudanjiang N	HL
ZJ11)	684	10	Zhoushan	ZJ
AH13)	684		Suzhou	AH
XJ6)	684		Hotan-Ch	XJ
SN1)	693	200	Shaanxi N	SN, Xianyang
LN16)	700		Chaoyang	LN, Lingyuan
2)	702		CRI DS	GD, Zhuhai
JS1)	702	150	Jiangsu N	JS, Nanjing
XJ1)	702		Xinjiang-Ch	XJ
NM6)	702	10	Ulanqab-Ch	NM, Jining
NM15)	702	1	Manzhouli	NM
JL3)	702		Jilin-shi LF	JL
SC11)	702	1	Neijiang	SC
YN5)	702	10	Honghe	YN, Gejiu
QH1)	711	10	Qinghai-Ch	QH, Golmud
ZJ10)	711		Quzhou N	ZJ
ZJ12)	711		Lishui N	ZJ
AH12)	711	3	Fuyang E	AH
AH16)	711		Lu'an	AH
EN2)	711	10	Zhengzhou E	HEN
SC5)	711	1	Panzhihua	SC
SC8)	711	1	Mianyang	SC
1)	720	200	CNR 2	BJ
JX1)	729	150	Jiangxi N	JX, Nanchang
EN15)	729		Shangqiu N	HEN
JL1)	738	150	Jilin Sat.	JL, Changchun
HN1)	738	150	Hunan N	HN, Changsha
XJ1)	738	120	Xinjiang-Ch	XJ, Urumqi
ZJ8)	738		Shaoxing G	ZJ
1)	747		CNR 9	BJ
2)	747		CRI DS 1	AH, Hefei
TJ1)	747		Tianjin L	TJ
EB1)	747		Hebei LF	HEB, Shijiazhuang
SC1)	747		Sichuan Women	SC, Chengdu
SN1)	747		Shaanxi L	SN, Xi'an
EB12)	747		Hengshui L	HEB
NM4)	747	1	Wuhai	NM
NM9)	747	10	Tongliao-Ch	NM
LN5)	747		Fushun M	LN
LN10)	747		Yingkou E	LN
JS6A)	747		Yancheng E	JS
JS11)	747		Changzhou T	JS
ZJ4)	747		Ningbo E	ZJ
ZJ11)	747		Zhoushan E	ZJ
FJ6)	747		Longyan	FJ
JX8)	747		Ganzhou N	JX
SD5A)	747		Zaozhuang TBS	SD
SD11)	747		Rizhao T	SD
SD15)	747	10	Binzhou G	SD
EN5)	747	10	Pingdingshan	HEN
HB10)	747	3	Jingmen Health	HB
SC14)	747		Nanchong	SC
SC15)	747		Jiudu MBS	SC, Yibin
YN6)	747	100	Xishuangbanna	YN, Jinghong
SN6)	747	1	Weinan N	SN
SX8)	750	1	Xinzhou	SX
LN16)	750		Chaoyang	LN, Jianping
1)	756		CNR 1	
1)	765	600	CNR 5	FJ, Fuzhou
NM1)	765	10	Nei Menggu-Ch	NM, Baotou
GZ1)	765	10	Guizhou Sat.	GZ, Zunyi
AH7)	765	1	Bengbu N	AH
GD8)	765	10	Shaoguan Can.	GD
GZ3)	765	1	Liupanshui	GZ
HB1)	774	100	Hubei Sat.	HB, Wuhan
SX2)	774		Taiyuan E	SX
LN8)	774		Jinzhou E	LN
15)	783	200	China Huayi BC	FJ, Fuzhou
EB1)	783	100	Hebei 1	HEB, Baoding
GD10)	783		Meizhou	GD
SH2)	792	50	Dongfang City	SH
GX1)	792	200	Guangxi Sat.	GX, Nanning
NM10)	792		Ordos BS-Ch	NM, Otog
LN2)	792	10	Shenyang N	LN
EN18)	792		Xinmi	HEN
SC3)	792		Chengdu N	SC
GS5)	792	1	Jiayuguan	GS
XJ2)	792		Urumqi N	XJ
2)	801		CRI DS 2	AH, Hefei
2)	801		CRI DS	SD, Zibo/Weifang
AH1)	801		Anhui M	AH
HB1)	801		Hubei Health	HB, Wuhan
GD2)	801	50	Zhujiang EBS	GD, Maoming
EB8)	801	10	Tangshan E	HEB
JS2)	801		Nanjing T	JS
JS3)	801		Xuzhou E	JS
JS5)	801		Huai'an	JS
JS7)	801		Yangzhou EBS	JS
ZJ5)	801		Wenzhou E	ZJ
AH12)	801	3	Fuyang E	AH
AH15)	801		Chizhou	AH
SD4)	801		Zibo E	SD
SD8)	801	10	Yantai E	SD
SD10)	801		Jining E	SD
SD13)	801		Linyi T	SD
SD14)	801		Liaocheng E	SD
EN8)	801		Xinxiang	HEN
EN13)	801	10	Sanmenxia N	HEN
NX2)	801	10	Yinchuan	NX
XJ7)	801		Kashi-Ug	XJ
ZJ1)	810	200	Zhejiang N	ZJ, Hangzhou
LN16)	810	1	Chaoyang	LN
JL5)	810	1	Liaoyuan	JL
EN17)	810		Zhumadian	HEN
SN2)	810	10	Xi'an N	SN
SX1)	819	200	Shanxi	SX, Taiyuan
XJ11)	819		Korla-Ch	XJ
XJ12)	819		Kuytun-Kz	XJ
BJ1)	828	50	Beijing N	BJ
EN1)	828	10	Henan Sat.	HEN
GD1)	828	50	Guangdong Sat.	GD, Heyuan
EN16)	828v		Zhoukou N	HEN
HB8)	828	10	Jingzhou L	HB
HB23)	828v	1	Xiantao	HB
1)	837		CNR 1	
XJ1)	837	10	Xinjiang E	XJ, Urumqi
LN14)	837	1	Liaoyang G	LN
HL2)	837	10	Harbin	HL
2)	846		CRI DS 3	BJ
12)	846		Jiangsu Health	JS, Nanjing
HB2)	846		Chutian Sat.	HB, Xianning
EB10)	846		Cangzhou N	HEB
EB11)	846	10	Langfang T	HEB
SX1)	846	20	Shanxi	SX, Changzhi
JL1)	846	10	Jilin LF	JL, Changchun
EN1)	846		Henan E	HEN
GX1)	846	10	Guangxi E	GX, Qinzhou
XZ1)	846		Xizang-Ch	XZ, Lhasa
LN8)	846		Jinzhou T	LN
LN13)	846	10	Fuxin Mo BS	LN
JS11)	846	10	Changzhou N	JS
JS13)	846	5	Suzhou T	JS
AH4)	846		Huaibei 1	AH
SD2)	846		Jinan E	SD
SD3)	846		Qingdao L	SD
SD7)	846		Weifang T	SD
SD9)	846		Weihai L	SD
EN4)	846		Luoyang L	HEN
EN5)	846		Pingdingshan LBS	HEN

	kHz	kW	Station	Location
EN6)	846		Jiaozuo	HEN
EN7)	846		Hebi EBS	HEN
XJ6)	846		Hotan-Ug	XJ
1)	855	50	CNR 2	YN, Anning
XJ1)	855		Xinjiang-Ug	XJ
ZJ1)	864		Zhejiang N	ZJ, Ninghai
AH1)	864	50	Anhui E	AH, Hefei
ZJ15)	864		Jiangshan	ZJ
EN19)	864		Qinyang	HEN
11)	873		V.O.Strait Amoy	FJ
HL1)	873	200	Heilongjiang Ko	HL, Harbin
GS1)	873	50	Gansu 1	GS, Lanzhou
EB13)	873v		Xinji	HEB
ZJ7)	873		Huzhou N	ZJ
SD13)	873	10	Linyi N	SD
EN3)	873v	1	Kaifeng N	HEN
HB3)	873	50	Wuhan	HB
XJ8)	873		Changji	XJ
FJ1)	882	100	Fujian N	FJ, Fuzhou
EB2)	882	10	Shijiazhuang N	HEB
NM2)	882	10	Hohhot	NM
LN2)	882	10	Shenyang E	LN
LN3)	882	50	Dalian N	LN
EN9)	882		Anyang	HEN
GZ6)	882	1	Duyun	GZ
QH3)	882	10	Yushu	QH
XJ4)	882		Karamay-Ch	XJ
XJ9)	882	1	Ili-Kz	XJ, Yining
NX1)	891	200	Ningxia N	NX, Yinchuan
NM13)	891	10	Hinggan-Ch	NM, Ulanhot
LN7)	891	1	Dandong T	LN
1)	900	10	CNR 2	QH, Golmud
2)	900		CRI DS 2	BJ
EB1)	900		Hebei L	HEB, Baoding
SX1)	900		Shanxi E	SX, Taiyuan
HL1)	900	50	Heilongjiang N	HL, Bei'an/Jiamusi
EN1)	900	10	Henan T	HEN, Zhengzhou
HB2)	900		Chutian Sat.	HB, Xiangfan
HN1)	900		Hunan E	HN, Changsha
SN1)	900	10	Shaanxi Farm	SN, Xi'an
EB6)	900		Zhangjiakou L	HEB
EB9)	900		Qinhuangdao N	HEB
SX3)	900	10	Datong G	SX
NM5)	900	10	Chifeng EBS	NM
LN6)	900	1	Benxi T	LN
LN19)	900	1	Haicheng	LN
JL2)	900	10	Changchun	JL
JL16)	900	1	Yanji	JL
JS2)	900		Nanjing E	JS
JS10)	900		Zhenjiang N	JS
JS12)	900		Wuxi M	JS
ZJ11)	900		Zhoushan L	ZJ
EN12A)	900		Luohe EBS	HEN
GD6)	900		Zhuhai T	GD
YN9)	900	100	Dehong	YN, Luxi
SN4)	900		Baoji EBS	SN
1)	909	100	CNR 6	FJ, Quanzhou
TJ1)	909	50	Tianjin N	TJ
SC1)	909	120	Sichuan 1	SC, Fuling
QH1)	909	10	Qinghai-Ch	QH
JL6)	909	10	Tonghua	JL
HL8)	909	7.5	Yichun	HL
SD1)	918	200	Shandong N	SD, Yantai
GX2)	918	1	Nanning N	GX
1)	927		CNR 6	FJ
SH1)	927		Shanghai L	SH
BJ1)	927	50	Beijing Sports	BJ
LN1)	927	12.5	Liaoning T	LN, Shenyang
JX1)	927	10	Jiangxi LF	JX, Nanchang
HB2)	927		Chutian Sat.	HB, Suizhou
GD1)	927		Guangdong Stock	GD, Guangzhou
GZ1)	927	200	Guizhou Sat.	GZ, Kaili
NM7)	927	10	Xilingol-Mo	NM, Xilinhot
JL3)	927	10	Jilin-shi G	JL
JL19)	927	1	Hunchun	JL
JS8)	927		Taizhou EBS	JS
JS11)	927		Changzhou E	JS
JS16)	927	1	Changshu E	JS
ZJ6)	927		Jiaxing E	ZJ
ZJ7)	927		Huzhou E	ZJ
EN11)	927		Xuchang E	HEN
EN14)	927	1	Nanyang E	HEN
EN15)	927		Shangqiu City	HEN
HB12)	927	1	Xiaogan N	HB
XJ3)	927		Urumqi EBS	XJ
ZJ1)	930		Zhejiang L	ZJ
AH1)	936	200	Anhui N	AH, Hefei
NM10)	936	10	Ordos BS-Ch	NM, Dongsheng
1)	945	400	CNR 1	JL, Jiaohe
HB2)	945		Chutian Sat.	HB, Jingzhou
SD10)	945		Jining T	SD
HA1)	954	30	Hainan	HAN, Haikou
SC1)	954	10	Sichuan LF	SC, Chengdu
EB12)	954	1	Hengshui	HEB
NM8)	954	50	Hulun Buir-Mo	NM, Hailar
LN4)	954	10	Anshan	LN
ZJ2)	954	25	Hangzhou N	ZJ
SC6)	954		Luzhou N	SC
GS2)	954	10	Lanzhou N	GS
LN1)	963	50	Liaoning N	LN, Dalian
ZJ1)	963	10	Zhejiang N	ZJ
EB3)	963	10	Handan 1	HEB
HB5)	963	10	Huangshi N	HB
EN1)	972	150	Henan E	HEN, Zhengzhou
HL2A)	972	10	Harbin EBS	HL
1)	981	200	CNR 1	JL, Changchun
SH1)	990	50	Shanghai N	SH
YN1)	990	20	Yunnan Sat.	YN, Kunming
EB9)	990		Qinhuangdao N	HEB
LN1)	999	200	Liaoning E	LN, Shenyang
GD1)	999	7.5	Guangdong Health	GD, Guangzhou
XZ1)	999		Xizang-Ch	XZ, Lhasa
SC1)	999		Sichuan Health	SC, Chengdu
XJ1)	999		Xinjiang-Ch	XJ
GZ2)	999	10	Guiyang	GZ
1)	1008	200	CNR 1	YN, Anning
2)	1008		CNR DS 3	BJ
TJ1)	1008		Tianjin M	TJ
SN1)	1008	10	Shaanxi N	SN, Hanzhong/Yan'an
EB3)	1008		Handan T	HEB
JS2)	1008		Nanjing N	JS
JS12)	1008		Wuxi T	JS
SD12)	1008		Dezhou E	SD
EN2)	1008		Zhengzhou LBS	HEN
EN5)	1008		Pingdingshan IBS	HEN
EN13)	1008		Sanmenxia LF	HEN
HN7)	1008v	1	Yueyang EBS	HN
HN9)	1008v		Yiyang E	HN
GD22)	1008		Chenghai	GD
1)	1017		CNR 1	
1)	1017	200	CNR 8	JL, Changchun
GD1)	1017		Guangdong Sat.	GD, Shaoguan/Shantou
EB5)	1017	10	Baoding LF	HEB
1)	1026		CNR 6	FJ
BJ1)	1026	50	Beijing E	BJ
GZ1)	1026	200	Guizhou Sat.	GZ, Jianhe
LN10)	1026	2	Yingkou N	LN
JS6)	1026		Yancheng N	JS
JS14)	1026		Yizheng	JS
1)	1035	50	CNR 1	
XJ1)	1044	10	Xinjiang-Ug	XJ
YN8)	1044	1	Dali N	YN
ZJ1)	1050		Zhejiang L	ZJ
JS1)	1053		Jiangsu L	JS, Nanjing
EB15)	1053	1	Shahe	HEB
EB17)	1053	1	Zhuozhou	HEB
JL10)	1053	20	Yanbian-Ch	JL, Yanji
AH2)	1053		Hefei T	AH
SD2)	1053	10	Jinan G	SD
EN3)	1053		Kaifeng E	HEN
EN4)	1053		Luoyang T	HEN
EN17)	1053		Zhumadian EBS	HEN
HN7)	1053		Yueyang	HN
YN4)	1053	1	Wenshan	YN
GD2)	1062	150	Zhujiang EBS	GD, Guangzhou
HL11)	1062		Qitaihe	HL
TJ1)	1071	50	Tianjin E	TJ
ZJ1)	1071	10	Zhejiang M	ZJ, Hangzhou
FJ1)	1071v		Fujian N	FJ
GX1)	1071	10	Guangxi Sat.	GX, Ninming
LN4)	1071	2	Anshan E	LN
AH13)	1071		Suzhou	AH

	kHz	kW	Station	Location
SN4)	1071	10	Baoji	SN
XJ3)	1071		Urumqi-Ug	XJ
ZJ1)	1080v		Zhejiang N	ZJ
HL7)	1080	1	Daqing	HL
JS13)	1080	10	Suzhou N	JS
GD7)	1080	5	Shantou N	GD
1)	1089	600	CNR 6	FJ, Fuzhou
LN1)	1089	200	Liaoning N	LN, Shenyang
HN3)	1089	1	Zhuzhou N	HN
TJ1)	1098		Tianjin Binhai	TJ
NM1)	1098	10	Nei Menggu-Mo	NM
EN1)	1098		Henan I	HEN, Zhengzhou
LN8)	1098		Jinzhou LF	LN
JS10)	1098		Zhenjiang T	JS
JS17)	1098	1	Zhangjiagang N	JS
ZJ11)	1098	10	Zhoushan E	ZJ
AH7)	1098v		Bengbu EBS	AH
AH17)	1098		Dangtu Xian	AH
SD12)	1098		Dezhou N	SD
EN5)	1098		Pingdingshan L	HEN
EN14)	1098	1	Nanyang T	HEN
EN16)	1098		Zhoukou E	HEN
HN5)	1098	10	Hengyang	HN
GD4)	1098		Guangzhou E	GD
GD19)	1098	5	Maoming	GD
SC7)	1098	1	Deyang	SC
XJ5)	1098		Hami-Ug	XJ
JL1)	1107		Jilin Sat.	JL
HA1)	1107	10	Hainan	HAN, Tongshi
XJ1)	1107	120	Xinjiang-Kz	XJ, Urumqi
ZJ6)	1107		Jiaxing N	ZJ
AH6)	1107	1	Tongling	AH
FJ3)	1107		Xiamen E	FJ
JX4)	1107	1	Pingxiang N	JX
EN7)	1107		Hebi	HEN
1)	1116	120	CNR 2	HL
1)	1116	600	CNR 5	FJ, Shaowu
SC1)	1116	50	Sichuan 1	SC
AH12)	1116	1	Fuyang N	AH
EB1)	1125		Hebei E	HEB, Shijiazhuang
HB4)	1125v	50	Changjiang EBS	HB, Wuhan
1)	1134	1200	CNR 1	QH, Golmud
ZJ1)	1134v		Zhejiang N	ZJ, Ningbo
GD18)	1134	10	Zhanjiang 1	GD
SN3)	1134	10	Tongchuan	SN
GS9)	1134	1	Yumen	GS
XJ9)	1134	1	Ili-Ch	XJ, Yining
1)	1143	10	CNR 8	BJ
ZJ1)	1143v		Zhejiang N	ZJ, Yuhuan
EN1)	1143		Henan L	HEN, Zhengzhou
HA1)	1143		Hainan T	HAN, Haikou
QH1)	1143		Qinghai E	QH, Xining
EB8)	1143		Tangshan T	HEB
EB10)	1143	10	Cangzhou E	HEB
EB18)	1143	1	Dingzhou	HEB
NM16)	1143	1	Yakeshi	NM
LN5)	1143		Fushun City	LN
LN10)	1143		Yingkou T	LN
LN14)	1143		Liaoyang E	LN
JL17)	1143	1	Tumen	JL
HL10)	1143		Jiamusi E	HL
JS2)	1143		Nanjing T	JS
JS3)	1143		Xuzhou L	JS
JS11)	1143		Changzhou E	JS
AH14)	1143v		Chaohu	AH
SD4)	1143	1	Zibo N	SD
SD13)	1143	10	Linyi E	SD
SD14)	1143	1	Liaocheng	SD
EN5)	1143		Pingdingshan EBS	HEN
SC9)	1143		Guangyuan	SC
SC11)	1143		Neijiang EBS	SC
SC16)	1143	1	Dazhou	SC
GZ5)	1143		Anshun	GZ
GS4)	1143	10	Tianshui	GS
EN6)	1147		Jiaozuo EBS	HEN
HN1)	1152		Hunan N	HN, Hengyang
NM11)	1152	10	Bayannur	NM, Linhe
NM13)	1152	10	Hinggan-Mo	NM, Ulanhot
LN3)	1152	2	Dalian City	LN
1)	1161		CNR 1	
GX1)	1161	7.5	Guangxi E	GX, Beihai
JS12)	1161		Wuxi N	JS
SD7)	1161	10	Weifang N	SD
HB10)	1161	10	Jingmen N	HB
SD5)	1170	1	Zaozhuang N	SD
SD15)	1170	10	Binzhou LF	SD
SD17)	1170	1	Qingzhou	SD
HB2)	1179		Chutian N	HB, Wuhan
HL5)	1179	1	Shuangyashan	HL
JS7)	1179		Yangzhou N	JS
XJ4)	1179		Karamay-Ug	XJ
EB4)	1188		Xingtai	HEB
EB19)	1188	1	Botou	HEB
SH1)	1197		Shanghai Play	SH
HL3)	1197	10	Qiqihar	HL
FJ5)	1197v		Quanzhou T	FJ
SD16)	1197	10	Heze-shi N	SD
12)	1206		V.O.Jinling	JS, Nanjing
NX1)	1206		Ningxia N	NX, Zhongning
EB3)	1206	10	Handan LF	HEB
JL10)	1206	150	Yanbian-Ko	JL, Yanji
SD9)	1206v	1	Weihai N	SD
EN20)	1206	1	Huixian	HEN
1)	1215		CNR 2	
1)	1215		CNR 7	GD, Zhuhai
XJ1)	1215	10	Xinjiang E	XJ, Urumqi
1)	1224		CNR 6	FJ
GX1)	1224	100	Guangxi E	GX, Nanning
EB11)	1224	10	Langfang N	HEB
JS10)	1224		Zhenjiang E	JS
HN1)	1233		Hunan N	HN, Yueyang
XJ1)	1233	120	Xinjiang-Mo	XJ, Urumqi
JS9)	1233	10	Nantong N	JS
YN1)	1242		Yunnan Minor.	YN, Kunming
LN9)	1242	1	Huludao N	LN
AH16)	1242v		Lu'an	AH
JX9)	1242		Ji'an Diqu	JX, Ji'an
HB20)	1242		Macheng	HB
HB24)	1242v	1	Qianjiang	HB
ZJ10)	1250		Quzhou T	ZJ
AH8)	1250		Ma'anshan	AH
2)	1251		CRI DS 1	BJ
ZJ1)	1251		Zhejiang Travel	ZJ, Jinhua
SD1)	1251		Shandong 6	SD, Jinan
HB1)	1251		Hubei E	HB, Xianning
QH1)	1251	100	Qinghai-Tb	QH, Xining
LN4)	1251		Anshan T	LN
JL3)	1251		Jilin-shi IBS	JL
JS4)	1251		Lianyungang E	JS
JS5A)	1251		Huai'an EBS	JS
JS12)	1251		Wuxi E	JS
ZJ7)	1251		Huzhou L	ZJ
ZJ8)	1251		Shaoxing E	ZJ
SD3)	1251		Qingdao E	SD
SD7)	1251		Weifang E	SD
SD18)	1251		Longkou EBS	SD
EN9)	1251v		Anyang EBS	HEN
EN10)	1251		Puyang N	HEN
EN12)	1251	10	Luohe N	HEN
EN21)	1251	1	Yima	HEN
HN2)	1251		Changsha M	HN
SN8)	1251		Hanzhong G	SN
ZJ13)	1254v		Xiaoshan	ZJ
LN1)	1260		Liaoning N	LN
HN8)	1260		Changde	HN
XZ2)	1260	1	Shannan	XZ, Nedong
11)	1269	200	V.O.Strait N	FJ
SX1)	1269	10	Shanxi	SX, Xinzhou
JL18)	1269	1	Dunhua	JL
JS3)	1269		Xuzhou N	JS
EB1)	1278	100	Hebei 1	HEB, Shijiazhuang
HL13)	1278	7.5	Daxing'anling	HL, Jagdaqi
FJ3)	1278	10	Xiamen N	FJ
JX2)	1278	10	Nanchang N	JX
1)	1287		CNR 1	
ZJ1)	1287		Zhejiang N	ZJ, Dongtou
NX1)	1287		Ningxia N	NX, Sanying
EB20)	1287v	1	Renqiu	HEB
LN12)	1287		Fuxin	LN
EN11)	1287		Xuchang N	HEN
GD5)	1287		Shenzhen T	GD
YN7)	1287	10	Chuxiong A.P.	YN, Chuxiong

	kHz	kW	Station	Location
SH2)	1296	20	Dongfang N	SH
EB16)	1296		Qinghe	HEB
LN6)	1296	10	Benxi	LN
LN20)	1296		Xingcheng	LN
SC10)	1296		Suining	SC
SN5)	1296	10	Xianyang	SN
1)	1305		CNR 2	
SD2)	1305		Jinan L	SD
JS1)	1314	10	Jiangsu N	JS, Suzhou
CQ1)	1314	15	Chongqing N	CQ
SD8)	1314	10	Yantai N	SD
HB6)	1314	10	Xiangfan G	HB
HB14)	1314		Xianning	HB
SN1)	1323	10	Shaanxi T	SN, Xi'an
LN17)	1323	1	Wafangdian	LN
JL9)	1323	10	Baicheng	JL
ZJ4)	1323	20	Ningbo N	ZJ
SD16A)	1323	1	Heze T	SD
HN2)	1323	10	V.O.Xingsha	HN, Changsha
EN1)	1332	10	Henan N	HEN
JL2)	1332	2	Changchun EBS	JL
FJ2)	1332	10	Fuzhou N	FJ
GS6)	1332	7.5	Gannan	GS, Hezuo
HL1)	1341	10	Heilongjiang N	HL, Shuangyashan
SD1)	1341	10	Shandong 6	SD, Liaocheng
LN2)	1341	10	Shenyang Sports	LN
JS8)	1341	5	Taizhou	JS
SD19)	1341	1	Qufu	SD
HB19)	1341	1	Yingcheng	HB
HB21)	1341	1	Chibi	HB
JX1)	1350v		Jiangxi N	JX
NM9)	1350	50	Tongliao-Mo	NM
LN19)	1350		Haicheng EBS	LN
YN2)	1350	50	Kunming Sun.	YN
1)	1359		CNR 1	
FJ1)	1368v		Fujian N	FJ
HL6)	1368	10	Jixi	HL
HB18)	1368	1	Guangshui	HB
1)	1377	600	CNR 1	HEN, Yingyang
15)	1377	200	China Huayi BC	FJ
XZ1)	1377		Xizang-Ch	XZ
QH1)	1377		Qinghai T	QH, Xining
EB5)	1377	10	Baoding N	HEB
LN21)	1377	1	Beipiao	LN
AH11)	1377		Chuzhou	AH
SD3)	1377	10	Qingdao N	SD
NX5)	1377	1	Qingtongxia	NX
TJ1)	1386	20	Tianjin LF	TJ
JS15)	1386	1	Jiangyin	JS
HB11)	1386	1	Ezhou	HB
HB17)	1386	1	Shishou	HB
GX3)	1386	5	Liuzhou N	GX
NM1)	1395		Nei Menggu-Mo	NM
AH1)	1395		Anhui N	AH
AH1)	1395	10	Anhui LF	AH, Hefei
NM7)	1395	10	Xilingol-Ch	NM, Xilinhot
ZJ1)	1404		Zhejiang N	ZJ, Wenling
HB1)	1404		Hubei Sat.	HB
LN7)	1404	10	Dandong	LN
JS1)	1413		Jiangsu N	JS, Wuxi
XJ1)	1413	100	Xinjiang-Ug	XJ
LN15)	1413		Tieling N	LN
HL4)	1413v	1	Hegang	HL
NX4)	1413		Wuzhong	NX
13)	1422	20	V.O.Pujiang	SH
SH2)	1422	20	Dongfang E	SH
SX2)	1422	10	Taiyuan N	SX
SC4)	1422	10	Zigong	SC
EB2A)	1431	10	Shijiazhuang E	HEB
NM14)	1431	1	Fengzhen	NM
JL8)	1431		Songyuan N	JL
AH4)	1431v	1	Huaibei 1	AH
AH10)	1431v	1	Huangshan	AH
HB16)	1431	1	Danjiangkou	HB
HN10)	1431	1	Jinshi	HN
GX1)	1440	50	Guangxi Sat.	GX, Bose
NM5)	1440	50	Chifeng-Mo	NM
NM12)	1440	10	Alxa-Mo	NM, Bayanhot
LN18)	1440		Zhuanghe	LN
JX1)	1449	20	Jiangxi N	JX
SD6)	1449	10	Dongying N	SD
SD11)	1449	10	Rizhao N	SD
NM1)	1458	200	Nei Menggu-Mo	NM, Hohhot
JS4)	1458	5	Lianyungang N	JS
FJ1)	1467v	50	Fujian E	FJ, Fuzhou
SD1)	1467	1	Shandong N	SD, Dezhou
JX3)	1467	1	Jingdezhen N	JX
1)	1476	200	CNR 2	HL, Shuangyashan
ZJ1)	1476		Zhejiang N	ZJ, Leqing
JL14)	1476	1	Qian Gorlos	JL
HL9)	1476		Mudanjiang E	HL
SD4)	1476		Zibo T	SD
HB15)	1476v	1	Laohekou	HB
SC12)	1476		Leshan	SC
QH2)	1476	10	Xining	QH
XJ10)	1476		Shihezi	XJ
SD1)	1485	1	Shandong N	SD, Weihai
GX1)	1485	1	Guangxi Sat.	GX, Lingshan
GS1)	1485		Gansu 1	GS
LN11)	1485	1	Panjin N	LN
JL11)	1485	1	Gongzhuling	JL
JX6)	1485	1	Jiujiang N	JX
HB7)	1485	1	Shiyan N	HB
GX4)	1485	1	Guilin N	GX
GX5)	1485		Wuzhou	GX
SC3)	1485	1	Chengdu T	SC
YN5)	1485	1	Honghe	YN, Jinping
YN13)	1485	1	Chuxiong	YN
XJ5)	1485		Hami-Ch	XJ
XJ12)	1485		Kuytun-Ch	XJ
NM1)	1494		Nei Menggu-Ch	NM
AH5)	1494v		Wuhu	AH
XJ11)	1494		Korla-Ch	XJ
ZJ1)	1503		Zhejiang N	ZJ, Huzhou
AH12)	1503v		Fuyang E	AH
HN4)	1503	1	Xiangtan N	HN
NM5)	1512	1	Chifeng-Ch	NM, Lindong
SD2)	1512		Jinan T	SD
GS7)	1512	10	Linxia	GS
EB1)	1521		Hebei T	HEB, Langfang
HL1)	1521	1	Heilongjiang N	HL, Jingbohu
EN1)	1521		Henan L	HEN
SC1)	1521		Sichuan ED	SC, Chengdu
SN1)	1521	1	Shaanxi N	SN, Shangzhou
SX5)	1521	1	Changzhi	SX, Qinxian
NM6)	1521	10	Ulanqab-Mo	NM, Jining
JL15)	1521	1	Taonan	JL
JS7)	1521		Yangzhou T	JS
JS11)	1521		Changzhou L	JS
JS12)	1521		Wuxi Health	JS
JS13)	1521		Suzhou M	JS
JS17)	1521		Zhangjiagang T	JS
ZJ7)	1521		Huzhou E	ZJ
FJ3)	1521		Xiamen M	FJ
SD2)	1521		Jinan T	SD
SD16)	1521	10	Heze-shi E	SD
GD20)	1521	1	Zhaoqing I	GD
GZ5)	1521		Anshun	GZ
YN5)	1521	1	Honghe	YN
YN3)	1521	1	Qujing	YN
JL1)	1530		Jilin Sat.	JL, Yanji
ZJ1)	1530	50	Zhejiang City	ZJ, Hangzhou
1)	1539	10	CNR 1	
SD1)	1548	200	Shandong N	SD, Jinan
HN6)	1548		Shaoyang	HN
EB10)	1557		Cangzhou T	HEB
EB14)	1557	1	Nangong	HEB
EB6)	1566	10	Zhangjiakou N	HEB
SX9)	1566	1	Yuncheng	SX
GS8)	1566		Pingliang	GS
LN3)	1575	2	Dalian M	LN
JL12)	1575		Lishu	JL
EB7)	1584	1	Chengde 1	HEB
SX5)	1584	10	Changzhi	SX
SX7)	1584	1	Jinzhong	SX
JL13)	1584	1	Meihekou	JL
ZJ14)	1584		Rui'an	ZJ
AH8)	1584v	1	Ma'anshan	AH
AH9)	1584v	1	Anqing N	AH
JX7)	1584		Yingtan	JX
HB22)	1584	1	Suizhou	HB
GZ4)	1584	1	Zunyi	GZ

	kHz	kW	Station	Location
1)	1593	600	CNR 1	
HL1)	1593	10	Heilongjiang N	HL
HL12)	1593	1	Suihua	HL
JS1)	1602	1	Jiangsu N	JS, Hongze

SW:

	kHz	kW	Station	Location	Times
FJ1)	2340		Fujian N	Fuzhou	2050-2215, 1030-1600
13)	3280		V.O.Pujiang	Shanghai	1155-1600
NM8)	3900	7.5	Hulun Buir-Ch	Hailar	as 603kHz
XJ1)	*3950	50	Xinjiang-Ch	Urumqi	Nov-Apr only
1)	3985	100	CNR 2	Golmud	1300-1605
GS6)	3990	15	Gannan	Hezuo	as 1332kHz
XJ1)	*3990	50	Xinjiang-Ug	Urumqi	Nov-Apr only
NM1)	4000	50	Nei Menggu-Ch	Hohhot	2150-0115, 0905-1605
1)	4190	50	CNR 8	Beijing	2100-2300
QH1)	4220	15	Qinghai-Tb	Xining	as 1251kHz
XJ1)	*4330	15	Xinjiang-Kz	Urumqi	Nov-Apr only
1)	4460	100	CNR 1	Beijing	2000-2330, 1300-1735
XJ1)	*4500	50	Xinjiang-Mo	Urumqi	Nov-Apr only
NM1)	4525	50	Nei Menggu-Mo	Hohhot	2150-0115, 0835-1605
NM1)	4620	50	Nei Menggu-Ch	Hohhot	2150-0115, 0905-1605
QH1)	4750	15	Qinghai-Ch	Xining	as 666kHz
NM1)	4785	50	Nei Menggu-Mo	Hohhot	2150-0115, 0805-1605
1)	4800	100	CNR 1	Golmud	2000-2400, 1100-1735
XZ1)	4820	50	Xizang-Ch	Lhasa	as 999kHz
15)	*4830	15	China Huayi BC	Fuzhou	Winter only
HL1)	4840	15	Heilongjiang N	Shangzhi	as 621kHz
11)	*4900	50	V.O.Strait Amoy	Fuzhou	Winter only
XZ1)	4905	50	Xizang-Tb	Lhasa	as 594kHz
XZ1)	4920	50	Xizang-Tb	Lhasa	as 594kHz
YN5)	v4930	15	Honghe	Gejiu	as 702kHz
11)	*4940	15	V.O.Strait N	Fuzhou	Winter only
13)	4950		V.O.Pujiang	Shanghai	1155-1600
FJ1)	4975	10	Fujian N	Fuzhou	2255-2330, -1040
XJ1)	*4980	50	Xinjiang-Ug	Urumqi	Nov-Apr only
HN1)	4990	10	Hunan N	Xiangtan	as 738kHz
1)	5030	100	CNR 1	Beijing	2000-2300, 1200-1735
FJ1)	5040	10	Fujian N	Fuzhou	-2325, -1030
11)	*5050	50	V.O.Strait L	Fuzhou	Winter only
21)	5050	15	Guangxi FBS	Nanning	2300-0100, 1000-1600
XJ1)	*5060	50	Xinjiang-Ch	Urumqi	Nov-Apr only
13)	*5075		V.O.Pujiang	Shanghai	Winter only
XZ1)	5240	50	Xizang-Tb	Lhasa	as 594kHz
1)	5420	50	CNR 8	Beijing	2100-2300, 1200-1300
12)	5860	50	V.O.Jinling	Nanjing	1200-1400
1)	5925	50	CNR 5	Beijing	0955-0005
XZ1)	v5935	50	Xizang-Ch	Lhasa	as 999kHz
1)	*5945	100	CNR 1	Beijing	Winter only
HL1)	5950	15	Heilongjiang Ko	Wuchang	as 873kHz
YN1)	5960	50	Yunnan ED	Kunming	0030-0400, 1045-1200
XJ1)	5960	50	Xinjiang-Ch	Urumqi	2300-0300, 1200-1800
GS6)	5970	15	Gannan	Hezuo	as 1332kHz
QH1)	5990	15	Qinghai-Tb	Xining	as 1251kHz
1)	6010	100	CNR 2/8	Tianshui	2100-2300, 1200-1605
XJ1)	6015	15	Xinjiang-Kz	Urumqi	2330-0300, 1200-1800
NM12)	v6025	15	Alxa-Ch	Bayanhot	as 549kHz
1)	6030	100	CNR 1	Beijing	2000-1735
22)	6035	50	Yunnan BS	Kunming	2230-0130, 1000-1300
NM1)	6045	50	Nei Menggu-Ch	Hohhot	2150-0115, 0905-1605
XZ1)	6050	50	Xizang-Ch	Xi'an	as 999kHz
SC1)	v6060	15	Sichuan LF	Xichang	as 954kHz
1)	6065	150	CNR 2	Beijing	2100-2330, 1200-1605
QH3)	6075	50	Yushu		as 882kHz
1)	6080	100	CNR 1	Golmud	1500-1735
NM8)	6080	7.5	Hulun Buir-Mo	Hailar	as 954kHz
1)	6090	100	CNR 2	Golmud	2100-2300, 1200-1605
XZ1)	6110	50	Xizang-Tb	Lhasa	as 594kHz
11)	6115	50	V.O.Strait Amoy	Fuzhou	2225-1700
XJ1)	6120	50	Xinjiang-Ug	Urumqi	2300-0300, 1200-1800
1)	6125	100	CNR 1	Shijiazhuang	2000-2400, 1200-1735
XZ1)	6130	50	Xizang-Tb	Lhasa	as 594kHz
1)	6140	50	CNR 6	Beijing	2055-2300
QH1)	6145	15	Qinghai-Ch	Xining	as 666kHz
1)	6155	150	CNR 2	Beijing	2100-2300, 1400-1605
1)	6165	100	CNR 1	Golmud	0800-1500
1)	6165	50	CNR 6	Beijing	1200-1805
1)	6175	100	CNR 1	Beijing	2000-2200, 1130-1735
SN1)	6176	15	Shaanxi N	Xi'an	as 693kHz
15)	6185	15	China Huayi BC	Fuzhou	2230-1700
1)	6190	100	CNR 2	Golmud	2100-2300
XJ1)	6190	15	Xinjiang-Mo	Urumqi	2330-0330, 1230-1800
NM1)	6195	50	Nei Menggu-Mo	Hohhot	2150-0115, 0805-1605
XZ1)	6200	50	Xizang-Tb	Xi'an	as 594kHz
QH1)	6260	15	Qinghai-Ch	Xining	as 666kHz
QH1)	6500	7.5	Qinghai-Tb	Xining	as 1251kHz
YN1)	v6937	20	Yunnan Minor.	Kunming	2225-0045, 0355-0545, 1100-1500
1)	6950	100	CNR 1	Shijiazhuang	2000-2400
NM1)	7105	50	Nei Menggu-Ch	Hohhot	0120-0900
1)	7110	100	CNR 1	Shijiazhuang	1200-1735
1)	7120	50	CNR 8	Lingshi	0200-0300, 1000-1100, 1400-1700
XJ1)	*7120	15	Xinjiang-Kg	Urumqi	Nov-Apr only
XZ1)	7125	50	Xizang-Tb	Xi'an	2100-0200
1)	7130	150	CNR 2	Xi'an	2000-2300, 1500-1605
1)	7140	150	CNR 2	Beijing	2000-2300, 1300-1605
1)	7140	100	CNR 2	Golmud	2300-0300, 0800-1300
1)	7150	100	CNR 2	Tianshui	2100-2400, 1230-1605
XJ1)	7155	50	Xinjiang-Ch	Urumqi	as 738kHz
NM1)	7165	50	Nei Menggu-Ch	Hohhot	0120-0900
XZ1)	7170	50	Xizang-Ch	Lhasa	2000-0300, 1200-1730
XJ1)	7195	50	Xinjiang-Ug	Urumqi	2300-0200, 1400-1800
NM1)	7210	50	Nei Menggu-Mo	Hohhot	0120-0800
XZ1)	7215		Xizang-Ch	Lhasa	as 999kHz
1)	7230	120	CNR 1	Beijing	2000-1735
XJ1)	7230	15	Xinjiang-Mo	Urumqi	as 1233kHz
XZ1)	7240	50	Xizang-Ch	Lhasa	2000-0200, 1100-1730
NM1)	7270	50	Nei Menggu-Mo	Hohhot	0120-0830
1)	7275	100	CNR 1	Beijing	2000-2230, 1100-1735
GZ1)	7275	7.5	Guizhou Sat.	Guiyang	0140-0600
XJ1)	7275	50	Xinjiang-Ug	Urumqi	as 558kHz
11)	7280	50	V.O.Strait L	Fuzhou	2225-1700
1)	7290	100	CNR 1	Beijing	2000-2400, 1200-1735
1)	7305	100	CNR 1	Shijiazhuang	2000-2330, 1130-1735
XJ1)	7310	50	Xinjiang-Ch	Urumqi	2300-0300, 1400-1800
1)	7315	120	CNR 2	Xi'an	2100-2300, 1100-1605
1)	7335	100	CNR 2	Tianshui	2100-0030, 1200-1605
XJ1)	7340	15	Xinjiang-Kz	Urumqi	as 1107kHz
1)	7345	100	CNR 1	Beijing	2000-2300, 1230-1735
1)	7350	100	CNR 2	Tianshui	1400-1605
HL1)	7350	15	Heilongjiang N	Wuchang	2205-0540, 0840-1130
1)	7360	100	CNR 2/8	Tianshui	2100-2400
1)	7375	150	CNR 2	Beijing	1400-1605
XZ1)	7385	50	Xizang-Tb	Lingshi	as 594kHz
1)	7620	50	CNR 6	Beijing	0955-0005
1)	7935	100	CNR 1	Lingshi	2000-2300, 1530-1735
1)	9170	50	CNR 6	Beijing	2055-0105, 1130-1805
1)	9380	50	CNR 5	Beijing	0955-0005
1)	9440		CNR 8	Lingshi	1400-1700
1)	9455	100	CNR 1	Lingshi	2000-2400, 1300-1735
1)	9460	100	CNR 1/8	Lingshi	1200-1700
XJ1)	9470	15	Xinjiang-Kz	Urumqi	0300-1200
1)	9480	100	CNR 2/8	Tianshui	2100-0100
XZ1)	9490	50	Xizang-Tb	Xi'an	0200-1800
1)	9500	100	CNR 1	Shijiazhuang	2000-1735
XJ1)	9510	15	Xinjiang-Mo	Urumqi	0530-1030
1)	9515	50	CNR 2	Beijing	2100-2400, 1100-1605
NM1)	9520	50	Nei Menggu-Ch	Hohhot	0120-0900
1)	9530	100	CNR 2/8	Tianshui	0000-1200
XJ1)	9560	50	Xinjiang-Ug	Urumqi	0300-1200
1)	9570	100	CNR 2	Golmud	2300-0300, 0800-1200
1)	9590	100	CNR 1	Golmud	0000-0300, 0800-1100
XJ1)	9600	50	Xinjiang-Ch	Urumqi	0300-1400
1)	9610	50	CNR 8	Beijing	0200-0400, 0700-0800, 1000-1100
1)	9620	150	CNR 2	Beijing	2100-1605
1)	9630	100	CNR 1	Golmud	2000-0300
1)	9645	100	CNR 1	Beijing	2330-1300
1)	9655	100	CNR 1	Lingshi	2000-2400
1)	9675	100	CNR 1	Beijing	2300-1200
1)	9690	100	CNR 8	Lingshi	1100-1200
13)	9705		V.O.Pujiang	Shanghai	1155-1600
XJ1)	9705	15	Xinjiang-Kg	Urumqi	0330-0530, 1030-1230
1)	9710	100	CNR 1	Shijiazhuang	2000-2330, 1300-1735
1)	9720	150	CNR 2	Baoji	0100-1000
1)	9730	100	CNR 2	Tianshui	1400-1605
NM1)	9750	50	Nei Menggu-Mo	Hohhot	0120-0800
1)	9755	100	CNR 2	Tianshui	2000-0200, 1300-1605
1)	9775	150	CNR 2	Beijing	2100-0100, 1130-1605
QH1)	9780		Qinghai-Ch	Xining	0400-0600
1)	9810	100	CNR 1	Nanning	2000-2200, 1300-1735

	kHz	kW	Station	Location	Times
1)	9810	100	CNR 2	Xi'an	0000-1230
1)	9820	150	CNR 2	Xi'an	2100-2400, 1000-1605
21)	9820		Guangxi FBS	Nanning	2300-0100, 1000-1600
1)	9830	100	CNR 1	Beijing	2000-2300, 1500-1735
XJ1)	9835	50	Xinjiang-Ch	Urumqi	0300-1200
1)	9845	100	CNR 1	Beijing	2000-0100, 1130-1735
1)	9860	100	CNR 1	Beijing	1400-1735
1)	9890	100	CNR 1	Lingshi	2000-0200, 1300-1735
1)	9900	100	CNR 1	Beijing	2000-2230
11)	11590	15	V.O.Strait N	Fuzhou	2225-1700
1)	11610	150	CNR 2	Beijing	2300-1300
1)	11620	50	CNR 5	Beijing	0055-0615
1)	11630	100	CNR 1/8	Lingshi	2000-1600
1)	11660	120	CNR 2	Xi'an	2300-1100
1)	11670	150	CNR 2	Beijing	2330-1200
1)	11685	100	CNR 2/8	Tianshui	0100-1400
1)	11710	100	CNR 1	Beijing	2000-2200, 1200-1735
1)	11720	100	CNR 1	Shijiazhuang	2330-1300
1)	11740	50	CNR 2	Beijing	2100-2400, 1300-1605
1)	11750	100	CNR 1	Shijiazhuang	2330-1130
1)	11760	100	CNR 1	Shijiazhuang	0000-1200
XJ1)	11770	50	Xinjiang-Ch	Urumqi	as 738kHz
1)	11780	50	CNR 8	Lingshi	0500-0700, 0900-1000
1)	11800	150	CNR 2	Beijing	2100-1400
1)	11810		CNR 8	Lingshi	0000-0200
1)	11815	50	CNR 8	Beijing	0300-0400, 0700-0800
1)	11835	150	CNR 2	Xi'an	2300-0900
1)	11845	150	CNR 2	Xi'an	0000-1000
1)	11860	100	CNR 1	Beijing	2000-2300
XZ1)	11860	50	Xizang-Ch	Lhasa	0300-1200
XJ1)	11885	50	Xinjiang-Ug	Urumqi	as 558kHz
1)	11905	50	CNR 6	Beijing	2300-0105, 0355-1200
1)	11915	100	CNR 2	Tianshui	0030-1200
1)	11925	100	CNR 1	Lingshi	2300-2400, 1000-1735
1)	11935	50	CNR 5	Beijing	0055-0615
XZ1)	11950	50	Xizang-Ch	Lhasa	0200-1100
1)	11960	100	CNR 1	Beijing	2200-1130
XJ1)	11975	15	Xinjiang-Kg	Urumqi	0330-0530, 1030-1230
1)	12055	100	CNR 1/8	Lingshi	0200-1300
1)	12080	100	CNR 2	Tianshui	0200-1300
1)	13610	100	CNR 1	Nanning	2200-1300
XJ1)	13670	50	Xinjiang-Ug	Urumqi	0200-1400
1)	13700	100	CNR 1	Lingshi	0200-1300
1)	15180	100	CNR 1	Lingshi	2300-1300
1)	15270	150	CNR 2	Beijing	0000-1200
1)	15300	100	CNR 1	Beijing	2230-1400
1)	15370	100	CNR 1	Shijiazhuang	0100-1100
1)	15380	100	CNR 1	Beijing	2230-1100
1)	15390	100	CNR 1/8	Lingshi	0000-0900
1)	15415		CNR 8	Lingshi	0000-0200, 0500-0600
1)	15480	100	CNR 1	Beijing	2300-1300
1)	15500	150	CNR 2	Beijing	2300-1400
1)	15540	50	CNR 2	Beijing	0000-1300
1)	15550	100	CNR 1	Beijing	0000-1230
1)	15570	100	CNR 2/8	Tianshui	0100-1300
1)	15670	50	CNR 8	Lingshi	0600-0700, 0900-1000
1)	15710	50	CNR 5	Beijing	0055-0615
1)	15880	50	CNR 6	Beijing	0355-1130
1)	17550	100	CNR 1	Beijing	0100-0600, 0700-1130
1)	17565	100	CNR 1	Beijing	2300-1100
1)	17580	100	CNR 1	Lingshi	0300-1200
1)	17605	100	CNR 1	Beijing	0300-1200
1)	17615	100	CNR 1	Shijiazhuang	0000-1200
1)	17625	50	CNR 2	Beijing	0000-1100
1)	17890	100	CNR 1	Beijing	0000-1200

*) inactive.

Addresses and other information:

1) CHINA NATIONAL RADIO (CNR)

✉ 2 Fuxingmenwai Dajie, Xicheng Qu, Beijing 100866. ☎ +86 10 8609 2610. **Web:** www.cnradio.com.

L.P: Gen. Dir: Yang Bo. CE: Sun Yingnian.

V.O. China (1st Prgr): 2000-1735 (exc. Tues 0600-0850) on MW/SW/FM. **V.O. the Economy (2nd Prgr):** 2100-1605 (exc. Wed 0600-0900) on MW/SW/FM. **V.O. the Music (3rd Prgr):** 2200-1600 (exc. Tues 0600-0855) on FM stereo only. **V.O. the City (4th Prgr):** 2155-1600 (exc. Tues 0500-0855) on 101.8MHz. **V.O. Zhonghua (5th Prgr)**: 0055-0615, 0955-0005 on MW/SW. **V.O. Shenzhou (6th Prgr)** in Chinese, Amoy and Hakka: 2055-0105, 0355-1805 on MW/SW. **V.O. Huaxia (7th Prgr)** for the Zhujiang Delta: Chinese Ch. on 87.8MHz 2100-1800 (exc. Tues 0600-0855), Bilingual Ch. on 1215kHz/104.9MHz 2100-1800 (exc. Tues 0600-0855) in Chinese and Cantonese. **V.O. the Literary (9th Prgr):** 2200-1800 on 747kHz. **V.O. Minorities (8th Prgr):** 2100-1700 on MW/SW – +) relayed by regional sts.

Kazakh

0100-0200	XJ	15415, 15390, 11810, 11630, 9455, 1143
0500-0600+	XJ	15415, 15390, 12055, 11780, 11630, 1143
0900-1000	XJ	15670, 12055, 11780, 11630, 1143
1400-1500+	XJ	11630, 9460, 9440, 7120, 1143

Korean

0200-0300	JL/HL	9610, 7120, 1143
1000-1100+	JL/HL	9610, 7120, 1143, 1017
2100-2200	JL/HL	5420, 4190, 1143

Mongolian

0300-0400+	NM	11815, 9610, 1143
0700-0800	NM	11815, 9610, 1143
1200-1300	NM	9610, 5420, 1143
1600-1700+	XJ	9460, 9440, 7120, 1143
2200-2300	NM	5420, 4190, 1143

Tibetan

0400-0500+	XZ/QH	15570, 11685, 9530, 1143
0800-0900	XZ/QH	15570, 11685, 9530, 1143
1300-1400+	XZ/QH	11685, 6010, 1143
2300-2400+	XZ/QH	9480, 7360, 1143

Uighur

0000-0100	XJ	15415, 15390, 11810, 11630, 9455, 1143
0600-0700+	XJ	15670, 15390, 12055, 11780, 11630, 1143
1100-1200	XJ	12055, 11780, 11630, 9690, 1143
1500-1600+	XJ	11630, 9460, 9440, 7120, 1143

2) CHINA RADIO INTERNATIONAL (CRI)

(Zhongguo Guoji Guangbo Diantai)

✉ Jia 16, Shijingshan Lu, Shijingshan Qu, Beijing 100040. ☎ +86 10 6889 1001. **Web:** www.cri.com.cn. **L.P:** Gen. Dir: Li Dan.

Domestic Sce:

Prgrs in English: News, current affairs, features, music, weather and 5 minutes' news in French/German/Spanish /Japanese/Korean/Russian/Arabic for visitors and resident foreigners.

Beijing 1 "Easy FM" (1251kHz/91.5MHz): 2200-1600. – **Beijing 2 "Hit FM"** (900kHz/88.7MHz): 2200-1600. N: in English 0000-0005, 0100-0105, 0400-0405, 0900-0905; in Spanish 0200-0205, 0300-0305; in French 0500-0505, 0600-0605; in German 0700-0705, 0800-0805; in Japanese 1000-1005, 1100-1105; in Korean 1200-1205, 1300-1305; in Russian 1400-1405; in Arabic 1500-1505. – **Beijing 3** (846/1008kHz): 24h. – **Shanghai** (87.9MHz): 2200-1600. – **Hefei 1** (747kHz/92.4MHz): 2230-1000, 1100-1500. – **Hefei 2** (801kHz): 2200-1600. – **Xiamen** (107.0MHz): 2200-1600. – **Jingdezhen** (102.0MHz): 0900-1200, 1300-1500, 2300-0500. – **Zibo** (801kHz): 0000-0100, 1300-1500. – **Weifang** (801kHz): 1100-1200, 1300-1500, 2300-0100. – **Guangzhou** (88.5MHz): 2200-1600. – **Lanzhou** (98.2MHz): 1300-1400, 2300-1200.

Special Prgr:

Zhuhai (702kHz/107.1MHz): English 2200-2300, 0100-0400, 0700-0800, 1300-1700; Chinese 2300-0100, 0800-1100; Cantonese 0400-0700, 1100-1300.

DAB: Radio, Film & TV Bureau of Guangdong on 209.936MHz (test transmission).

EXTERNAL SERVICES: China Radio International

See International Broadcasting section

BROADCASTS TO TAIWAN

11) Voice of the Strait (Haixia zhi Sheng), Xindian, Fuzhou or P.O.Box 187, Fuzhou, Fujian 350012. Operated by the People's Liberation Army of China. News and Politics Ch. on 666/1269/4940/11590kHz 2225-1700 (exc. Wed 0400-0955) in Ch. – Literary and Life Ch. on 5050/7280kHz/90.6MHz 2225-1700 (exc. Wed 0400-0955) in Ch. – Amoy Ch. on 873/4900/6115kHz 2225(Wed 0955)-1700 in Amoy. – Music and Information Ch. on 99.6MHz 2230-1330. – **12)** Voice of Jinling (Jinling zhi Sheng), P.O.Box 268, Nanjing, Jiangsu 210002. 1200-1400 on 5860kHz. – Travel Sce. on 1206kHz 24h. – **13)** Voice of Pujiang (Pujiang zhi Sheng), 1376 Hongqiao Lu, Shanghai or P.O.Box 518, Shanghai 200051. On 603/1422/3280/4950/9705kHz 1155-1600. – **14)** China Southeast Broadcasting Company, 2 Gutian Lu, Fuzhou, Fujian 350001. On 585kHz/97.6/106.2MHz and via Satellite 0955-1600 in Ch and Amoy. – **15)** China Huayi Broadcasting Corporation, P.O.Box 251, Fuzhou, Fujian 350001. On 783/1377/4830/ 6185kHz/107.1MHz for Taiwan, Hong Kong, Macao and Southeast Asia. 24h (exc. Wed 2125-1000).

BROADCASTS TO VIETNAM

21) Guangxi Foreign Broadc. St, 75 Minzu Dadao, Nanning, Guangxi 530022. On 5050/9820kHz 2300-0100, 1000-1200, 1400-1600 in Vietnamese, 1200-1400 in Cantonese. – **22)** Yunnan Broadc. St, 73 Renmin Xilu, Kunming,

Yunnan 650031. On 6035kHz 2230-2320, 0030-0120, 1030-1100, 1130-1200, 1230-1300 in Vietnamese; 2320-2330, 0120-0130, 1000-1030, 1100-1130, 1200-1230 in Ch. Rel. CRI Vietnamese prgr. 2330-0030.

ANHUI PROVINCE

AH1) 355 Tongcheng Nanlu, Hefei, Anhui 230065. News General Sce. on 936/1395kHz/FM and via Satellite 2100-1700. N in English: 1500-1510. – Economic Sce. on 864kHz/97.1MHz and via Satellite 2120-0600, 0900-1650. – Traffic Sce. on 603kHz/90.8MHz. 24h. – Life Sce. on 1395/603/648/684kHz/105.5MHz 2130-1650. – Music Sce. on 801kHz/FM. 24h. – **AH2)** 114 Rongshida Dadao, Hefei, Anhui 230001. On 666kHz/91.5MHz 2120-1600. – Traffic St. on 1053kHz/102.6MHz. 24h (exc. Tues 0605-0900). – Literary St. on 87.6/98.8MHz 2200-1600. – **AH3)** Dongshan Zhonglu, Huainan, Anhui 232001. On 648kHz/103.7MHz 2120-0010, 0255-0510, 0855-1300. – Traffic and Literary St. on 97.9MHz. – **AH4)** 336 Huaihai Donglu, Xiangshan Qu, Huaibei, Anhui 235000. 1st Prgr. on 1431/846kHz/94.5MHz 2115-0600, 0855-1500. – Traffic and Music St. on 100.4MHz. – Huaibei EBS: on 89.3MHz 2110-1600. – **AH5)** 61 Beijing Xilu, Wuhu, Anhui 241000. On 1494kHz/100.4MHz 2158-0020, 0155-0510, 0850-1430. – Wuhu EBS: on 96.3MHz. – **AH6)** Yi'an Beilu, Tongling, Anhui 244000. On 1107kHz/100.0MHz 2120-0005, 0155-0510, 0855-1305. – Literary St. on 88.7MHz 2255-1100. – **AH7)** 150 Zhongrong Jie, Bengbu, Anhui 233000. News St. on 765kHz/107.9MHz 2200-1400. – Bengbu EBS: on 1098kHz/104.2MHz 2150-1430. – **AH8)** Yushan Zhonglu, Ma'anshan, Anhui 243011. On 1584/1250kHz/105.1MHz 2150-1500. – Traffic Music St. on 92.8MHz 2155-1500. – FM Stereo Sce. on 88.7MHz 0355-0520, 0945-1100. – **AH9)** 23 Guanyue Miao, Anqing, Anhui 246004. News General Ch. on 1584kHz/90.3MHz 2200-0530, 0930-1400. – **AH10)** 27 Qianyuan Nanlu, Tunxi Qu, Huangshan, Anhui 245000. 2200-0600, 0920-1400. – **AH11)** 225 Langxie Lu, Chuzhou, Anhui 239000. 2125-?, 0925-1330. – **AH12)** 73 Yingzhou Beilu, Fuyang, Anhui 236014. News General St. on 1116kHz/91.6MHz 2150-0700, 0825-1500. – Economic St. on 711/801/1503kHz/94.1MHz 2145-0700, 0830-1505. – Traffic Sce. on 90.0/103.5MHz. – **AH13)** Huaihai Lu, Suzhou, Anhui 234000. On 1071kHz/105.0MHz 1015-?. – Traffic and Music St. on 96.1MHz. – **AH14)** 107 Dongfeng Lu, Juchao Qu, Chaohu, Anhui 238000. 2135-?, 0245-0500, 0815-1120. – **AH15)** 11 Qiupu Xilu, Guichi Qu, Chizhou, Anhui 247100. 2120-2325, 0315-0515, 0950-1310. – **AH16)** 45 Gaocheng Lu, Lu'an, Anhui 237006. 0955-1230. – **AH17)** Dangtu Xian, Anhui 243100. 0250-0450.

BEIJING MUNICIPALITY

BJ1) 14 Jianguomenwai Dajie, Chaoyang Qu, Beijing 100022. News Sce. on 828kHz/100.6MHz and via Satellite 2130-1700(Tues 1600) (exc. Thurs 0600-0800). – Economic Sce. on 1026kHz/107.3MHz 2150-1700(Mon 1600) (exc. Thurs 0600-0800). – Sports Sce. on 927kHz 2155-1600 (exc. Thurs 0600-0800). – Traffic Sce. on 103.9MHz. 24h (exc. Mon 1600-2130). – Capital Life Sce. on 603kHz 2130-1700(Tues 1600) (exc. Thurs 0600-0800). – Literary Sce. on 87.6MHz 2155-1730. – Music Sce. on 97.4MHz. 24h (exc. Mon 1800-2100).

CHONGQING MUNICIPALITY

CQ1) 159 Zhongshan 3 Lu, Yuzhong Qu, Chongqing 400015. News Ch. on 1314kHz/96.8MHz 2200-1800. – Economic Ch. on 101.5/107.7MHz 2100-1800. – Traffic Ch. on 95.5/88.9/92.7MHz 2200-1805. – City Ch. on 93.8MHz. – Music Ch. on 88.1MHz. 24h.

HEBEI PROVINCE

EB1) 203 Yuhua Donglu, Shijiazhuang, Hebei 050012. 1st Prgr. on 783/1278kHz/FM 2130-1700 (exc. Tues 0530-0825). – Economic Sce. on 1125kHz/FM 2130-1700 (exc. Tues 0530-0900). – Life Sce. on 747kHz/89.0MHz 2100-1900. – Traffic Sce. on 603/1521kHz/FM 2130-1700. – Literary Ch. on 900kHz/89.3/90.7/95.3MHz 2130-1700. – **EB2)** 302 Tiyu Nan Dajie, Shijiazhuang, Hebei 050021. News St. on 882kHz/96.5MHz 2155-0600, 0825-1500. – Economic St. on 1431kHz/100.9MHz 2125-1600 (exc. Tues 0600-0830). – Literary Ch. on 106.7MHz 2225-0530, 0825-1400. – Shijiazhuang Traffic Information BS: on 94.6MHz. – **EB3)** 246 Renmin Lu, Handan, Hebei 056002. 1st Prgr. on 963kHz/101.0MHz 2155-?, 0335-0600, ?-1305. – Life Ch. on 1206kHz/102.8MHz 2200-1230. – Traffic Ch. on 1008kHz/104.8MHz ?-1600. – Educational Ch. on 96.4MHz ?-1600. – Literary Ch. on 90.9MHz. – **EB4)** 12 Ankang Jie, Dahuoquan Lu, Xingtai, Hebei 054000. On 1188kHz/93.0/102.0/104.0MHz 2220-2400, 0255-0535, 1020-?. – **EB5)** 30 Wusi Donglu, Baoding, Hebei 071000. News General Ch. on 1377kHz/99.7MHz 2210-1500 (exc. Tues 0600-0925). – Fashion Life Ch. on 1017kHz/93.7MHz 2230-1500 (exc. Tues 0600-0930). – Music Ch. on 101.7MHz ?-0600. – **EB6)** 17 Jianguo Lu, Qiaodong Qu, Zhangjiakou, Hebei 075000. News General Sce. on 1566kHz/107.4MHz 2155-1505. – General Literary Sce. on 900kHz/100.0MHz 2155-0505, 0655-1500. – Traffic and Life Sce. on 98.6MHz 2155-1500 (exc. Tues 0500-0900). – **EB7)** 120 Guangdian Lu, Chengde, Hebei 067000. 1st Prgr. on 1584kHz/93.8MHz 2155-0540, 0950-1400. – 2nd Prgr. (Traffic Literary Ch) on 97.6MHz 2255-0540, 1055-1500. Rel. CRI English prgr: 2300-0500, 1300-1500. – **EB8)** 1 Guangda Jie, Wenhua Lu, Tangshan, Hebei 063000. News General Sce. on 684kHz/91.7MHz 2100-1535. – Economic Life Sce. on 801kHz/95.5MHz 2130-1530 (exc. Tues 0600-0830). – Traffic and Literary Sce. on 1143kHz/102.0MHz 2230-1430. – **EB9)** 23 Wenhua Beilu, Haigang Qu, Qinhuangdao, Hebei 066000. News General St. on 990/900kHz/99.5MHz 2100-1500 (exc. Tues 0630-0855). – Traffic and Literary Sce. on 91.0/100.4MHz. – Music and Health Sce. on 102.6MHz. – **EB10)** 12 Jiefang Xilu, Cangzhou, Hebei 061001. News General Ch. on 846kHz/104.0MHz 2057-1500. – Economic Life Ch. on 1143kHz/88.5MHz 2200-1600. – Traffic and Music Ch. on 1557kHz/97.0MHz 2225-1330. – **EB11)** 8 Yongfeng Dao, Langfang, Hebei 065000. News General Ch. on 1224kHz/95.1MHz 2055-1600. – Traffic and Storytelling Ch. on 846kHz/100.3MHz. – **EB12)** 49 Hongqi Dajie, Hengshui, Hebei 053000. On 954kHz 2225-0535, 0825-1400. – Literary and Information St. on 747kHz. – **EB13)** 167, Bei Duan, Xinghua Lu, Xinji, Hebei 052360. 2225-2355, 0255-0500, 1025-1250. – **EB14)** Xitou, Shengli Dajie, Nangong, Hebei 055750. 2225-0045, 1005-1400. – **EB15)** 36 Yingxin Dajie, Shahe, Hebei 054100. – **EB16)** Sanyang Dongjie, Qinghe Xian, Hebei 054800. 2210-?, 0910-1230. – **EB17)** Beiguan, Zhuozhou, Hebei 072750. – **EB18)** Zhongshan Xilu, Dingzhou, Hebei 073000. – **EB19)** 393 Xiguan Xijie, Botou, Hebei 062150. 2225-2355, 0345-0450, 1025-1235. – **EB20)** 12-1 Xihuan Lu, Renqiu, Hebei 062550. 2230-1500.

HENAN PROVINCE

EN1) 18 Zhenghua Lu, Zhengzhou, Henan 450008. News Sce. on 657/1332kHz/FM and via Satellite 2100-1700. – Economic Sce. on 972/846kHz/103.2MHz and via Satellite 2100-1600. – Traffic Sce. on 900kHz/104.1MHz 2200-1700 (exc. Tues 0600-1000). – Music Sce. on 88.1MHz. – Literary Sce. on 1143/1521kHz/90.0MHz 2100-1700. – Information Sce. on 603kHz/96.7MHz. 24h. – Infromation Sce. FM Prgr. on 1098kHz/96.2/103.4/105.6MHz. 24h. – **EN2)** 67 Huaihe Donglu, Zhengzhou, Henan 450057. News General Sce. on 549kHz/91.2MHz. 24h (exc. Tues 0600-1000, Thurs 1600-2200). – Economic Life Sce. on 711kHz/93.1MHz W2150-1600, Sun2220-1430. – V.O. the City: on 88.9MHz. – Music Sce. on 91.8MHz. – Zhengzhou LBS: on 1008kHz/94.4MHz 2200-1600. – **EN3)** 78 Songcheng Lu, Kaifeng, Henan 475004. News General Ch. on 873kHz/105.1MHz MF2155-1420 (exc. Tues 0600-1000), SS2155-0600. – Economic Life Ch. on 1053kHz/100.2MHz MF2225-1400 (exc. Tues 0600-1000), SS2225-0600. – **EN4)** Fu 67, Jiudu Lu, Luoyang, Henan 471009. News Sce. on 576kHz/88.1MHz 2155-0600, 0955-1600. – Economic St. on 97.0MHz 2225-0600, 1200-1500. – Traffic Sce. on 1053kHz/106.5MHz 2250-0500, 1120-1430. – Literary St. on 846kHz 2225-0500, 0955-1400. – **EN5)** Zhong Duan, Kuanggong Lu, Pingdingshan, Henan 467000. On 747kHz/104.3MHz 2155-0630, 0855-1505. – V.O. FM: on 96.4MHz 2200-1400 (exc. Thurs 0030-0400). – Pingdingshan EBS: on 1143kHz 2155-0630, 0855-1500. – Pingdingshan IBS: on 1008kHz 2155-1500 (exc. Tues 0700-0900). – Pingdingshan LBS: on 846kHz 2150-1500. – **EN6)** 43 Jiefang Zhonglu, Jiaozuo, Henan 454150. On 846kHz/89.4/103.0MHz ?-0030, 0345-?. – Travel and Traffic Sce. on 99.5MHz. – Jiaozuo EBS: on 1147kHz. – **EN7)** Zhong Duan, Chunlei Lu, Hebi, Henan 458000. On 1107kHz/99.4/100.3MHz 2200-2400, 0350-0535, 0925-1430. – Hebi EBS: on 846kHz 2155-?. – **EN8)** Renmin Lu, Xinxiang, Henan 453000. 2200-0600, 0755-1500. – **EN9)** Zhong Duan, Wenfeng Dadao, Anyang, Henan 455000. On 882kHz/94.2MHz 2155-1530. – Anyang EBS: on 1251kHz/104.3MHz 2225-1400. – **EN10)** Dong Duan, Renmin Lu, Puyang, Henan 457001. News General Sce. on 1251kHz/100.1MHz 2140-0610(SS0640), 0830-1445. – Economic Sce. on 91.0MHz. – **EN11)** 72 Balong Lu, Xiao Nanhai, Xuchang, Henan 461000. News Sce. on 1287kHz/93.8MHz 2120-1500. – Economic Sce. on 927kHz 2200-0530, 1000-1345. – Xuchang Literary and Information BS: on 92.6MHz. – **EN12)** Daxue Lu, Luohe, Henan 462000. News Sce. on 1251kHz/100.0MHz 2130-0730, 0915-1400. – **EN12A)** 1 Wenhua Lu, Luohe, Henan 462000. – **EN13)** Zhong Duan, Wenming Lu, Sanmenxia, Henan 472000. News General Ch. on 801kHz/90.8/98.9MHz 2155-1555 (exc. Tues 0530-0955). – Life General Ch. on 1008kHz/104.0MHz 2255-1500 (exc. Tues 0530-1000). – **EN14)** Zhong Duan, Funiu Lu, Nanyang, Henan 473000. On 585kHz/93.6MHz 2130-1600. – Economic St. on 927kHz 2130-1600. – Traffic and Music St. on 1098kHz/97.7MHz 2155-1500. – **EN15)** 35 Xinjian Nanlu, Shangqiu, Henan 476600. News General Ch. on 729kHz/92.4MHz 2205-0150, 0355-0555, 0840-1330. – City Ch. on 927kHz/100.7MHz 2155-1505. – Traffic Ch. on 94.5MHz 2200-1600. – **EN16)** 10, Dong Duan, Jianshe Lu, Zhoukou, Henan 466000. News General Ch. on 828kHz/90.6MHz 2130-1500. – Economic Life Ch. on 1098kHz/89.3MHz 2130-1500. – **EN17)** 209 Wenhua Lu, Zhumadian, Henan 463000. – Zhumadian EBS: on 1053kHz. – **EN18)** Qingping Lu, Xinmi, Henan 452370. – **EN19)** Lianmeng Xiaoqu, Chengguan Zhen, Qinyang, Henan 454550. – **EN20)** 25 Xi Dajie, Huixian, Henan 453600. – **EN21)** 10 Qianqiu Lu, Yima, Henan 472300.

FUJIAN PROVINCE

FJ1) 2 Gutian Lu, Fuzhou, Fujian 350001. News Sce. on 558/612/882kHz/SW/FM and via Satellite. 24h (exc. Tues 0600-0900) in Ch and Amoy. – City Life Ch. on 98.7/101.5MHz. 24h. – Traffic Sce. on 100.7MHz. 24h. – Music Sce. on 91.3MHz. 24h (exc. Tues 0600-0855) – Fujian EBS "Fortune Broadcast": on 1467kHz/FM. 24h (exc. Tues 0600-0850) in Ch and Amoy. – **FJ2)** Fuzhou Radio and TV, 16 Shengmiao Lu, Gulou Qu, Fuzhou, Fujian 350001. News Ch. on 1332kHz/94.4MHz. 24h (exc. Wed 0605-0925) in Ch and Fuzhou dialect. – Music Ch. on 89.3MHz. 24h (exc.

Thurs 0600-0900). – Business and Traffic Ch. on 87.6MHz. 24h. – **FJ3)** 121 Hubin Beilu, Xiamen, Fujian 361012. News St. on 1278kHz/99.6MHz 2130-1700 in Ch and Amoy. – Economic and Traffic Ch. on 1107kHz/105.2MHz 2130-1700 (exc. Tues 0600-0900). – Music St. on 90.9MHz. 24h in Ch and Amoy. – **FJ4)** 347 Puyang Lu, Chengxiang Qu, Putian, Fujian 351100. On 91.1MHz 2155-1600 (exc. Tues 0700-0930) in Ch and Puxian dialect. – Life St. on 93.7MHz. – Music St. on 103.0MHz. – **FJ5)** Citong Lu, Quanzhou, Fujian 362000. News Ch. on 576kHz/88.9MHz 2155-1905 in Ch and Quanzhou dialect. – Economic Life Ch. on 92.3MHz 2200-1900. – V.O. the Traffic: on 1197kHz/90.4MHz. 24h (exc. Tues 0500-0900) in Ch and Quanzhou dialect. – **FJ6)** 62 Heping Lu, Longyan, Fujian 364000. 2158-1620 (exc. Tues 0600-1000).

GUANGDONG PROVINCE

GD1) 686 Renmin Beilu, Guangzhou, Guangdong 510012. Satellite St. on 648/828/1017kHz/FM and via Satellite 2200-1900 (exc. Tues 0015-0355). – V.O. the City: on 103.6MHz 2200-1700. – V.O. the Health: on 999kHz/93.6MHz. 24h (exc. Mon 0400-1000). – V.O. the Education "Channel E": on 603kHz/107.6MHz. 24h in Ch, Cantonese and English. – Stock Sce. on 927kHz/95.3MHz. – V.O. the Music: on 99.3/93.9/96.8MHz. 24h (exc. Fri 1600-2130). – **GD2)** Zhujiang EBS, 686 Renmin Beilu, Guangzhou, Guangdong 510012. On 1062/801kHz/FM. 24h in Cantonese. – "Liuxing 1057": on 105.7MHz 2200-1800. – **GD3)** Yangcheng TBS, 686 Renmin Beilu, Guangzhou, Guangdong 510012. On 105.2MHz. 24h. – **GD4)** 231 Huanshi Zhonglu, Guangzhou, Guangdong 510010. FM Sce. "Fengyun 962": on 96.2MHz. 24h (exc. Sun 1700-2200) in Cantonese. English Prgr: Fri 1300-1400. – Golden Hit Sce. "Jinqu 1027": on 102.7MHz. 24h (exc. Sun 1600-2200) in Cantonese. – Economic and Environment Sce. "Jihuo 1061": on 1098kHz/106.1MHz 2200-1600 (exc. Mon 0600-0900). – **GD5)** Yijing Lu, Shenzhen, Guangdong 518021. News Ch. on 89.8MHz. 24h (exc. Tues 0530-0930) in Ch and Cantonese. – Music Ch. "Feiyang Music FM" on 97.1MHz. 24h in Ch and Cantonese. – Traffic Ch. on 1287kHz/106.2MHz 2230-1800. – **GD6)** 1129 Dong, Jiuzhou Dadao, Xiangzhou Qu, Zhuhai, Guangdong 519015. V.O. the City: on 95.1MHz 2225-1700 in Ch and Cantonese. – Traffic Music Sce. "Feiyue 875" on 900kHz/87.5MHz 2225-1700 in Ch and Cantonese. – **GD7)** Chaoshan Lu, Shantou, Guangdong 515021. News Ch. on 1080kHz/99.3MHz 2200-1600 in Ch and Chaozhou dialect. – Economic Ch. on 102.5MHz 2300-1600. – Music Ch. on 107.1MHz. 24h (exc. Wed 0600-0900). – **GD8)** 57 Huimin Beilu, Shaoguan, Guangdong 512026. Chinese Ch. on 105.7MHz 2225-1600. – Cantonese Ch. "V.O. Beijiang" on 765kHz/95.2MHz 2225-1600. – **GD9)** Heyuan PBS, Shanyuan Lu, Yuancheng Qu, Heyuan, Guangdong 517000. On 92.2/97.8MHz in Ch and Cantonese. – **GD10)** 42 Dong Jiaochang Bei, Meizhou, Guangdong 514011. 2155-1600 in Ch and Hakka. – **GD11)** Huizhou PBS, Ehu Lu, Huicheng Qu, Huizhou, Guangdong 516001. On 100.0MHz 2230-1630 (exc. Tues 0030-0830) in Ch and Cantonese. – **GD12)** Shanwei PBS, Zhong, Shanwei Dadao, Shanwei, Guangdong 516600. On 90.0MHz 0940-? in Ch and Hakka. – **GD13)** Dongguan PBS, 35 Xizheng Lu, Cheng Qu, Dongguan, Guangdong 523001. General Ch. on 100.8MHz 2225-1600 in Cantonese. – Music Ch. on 106.9MHz 0100-1600 in Cantonese. – **GD14)** Zhongshan BS, 4 Xingzhong Dao, Dong Qu, Zhongshan, Guangdong 528403. 1st St. on 96.7MHz 2225-0605, 0755-1800 in Cantonese. – Music St. (2nd St.) on 89.3MHz. – **GD15)** Jiangmen PBS, 19 Jianshe Lu, Jiangmen, Guangdong 529000. On 100.2MHz 2200-1600 in Cantonese. – **GD16)** Foshan PBS, Jihua Lu, Foshan, Guangdong 528000. Zhen'ai Ch. (Love FM) on 94.6MHz. 24h in Cantonese. – Qianse Ch. (Color FM) on 98.5MHz. 24h in Cantonese. – **GD17)** Yangjiang PBS, 114 Mojiang Lu, Yangjiang, Guangdong 529500. V.O. the City: on 95.6MHz in Ch and Cantonese. – **GD18)** 93 Yuejin Lu, Chikan Qu, Zhanjiang, Guangdong 524038. 1st St. on 1134kHz/95.1MHz 2220-1700 in Ch, Cantonese and Leizhou dialect. – 2nd St. on 98.1MHz 2220-1700. – Zhanjiang EBS: on 104.6MHz 2200-0600, 0800-1600. – **GD19)** 13 Gaoliang Zhonglu, Hedong Qu, Maoming, Guangdong 525000. News St. on 1098kHz/106.1MHz 2230-1500 in Ch and Cantonese. – Music St. on 97.6MHz. – **GD20)** 41 Ganyuan Beilu, Zhaoqing, Guangdong 526040. Information Sce. on 1521kHz/90.9MHz 2200-1600 in Ch and Cantonese. – Golden Hit Ch. on 92.9MHz 2200-1600 in Ch and Cantonese. – **GD21)** Qingyuan PBS, 30 Xianfeng Lu, Qingyuan, Guangdong 511500. On 88.7/96.7MHz 2225-1600 in Ch and Cantonese. – **GD22)** Wenci Donglu, Chenghai Qu, Shantou, Guangdong 515800. 2250-1600 in Ch and Chaoshan dialect.

GANSU PROVINCE

GS1) 226 Donggang Xilu, Lanzhou, Gansu 730000. 1st Prgr. on 684/873kHz/FM 2150-1600 (exc. Tues 0600-0855). – City FM: on 102.2/106.6MHz and via Satellite 2230-1830 (exc. Tues 0600-0855). – Gansu EBS "V.O. Yellow River": on 93.4MHz 2255-1600. – **GS1A)** Gansu Traffic BS, 55 Zhanjia Guaizi, Chengguan Qu, Lanzhou, Gansu 730000. On 103.5/104.8MHz 2150-1800 (exc. Tues 0600-0855). – **GS2)** 34 Qingyang Lu, Lanzhou, Gansu 730030. News St. on 954kHz W2220-0255, Sun0000-0530, W0355-0855, 1000(Sun 0920)-1300. – Music St. on 99.5MHz 2300-1600 (exc. Mon 0600-1000). – **GS3)** Yan'an Xilu, Jinchang, Gansu 737100. – **GS4)** 11-5 Huancheng Zhonglu, Qincheng Qu, Tianshui, Gansu 741000. – **GS5)** Wuyi Nanlu, Jiayuguan, Gansu 735100. – **GS6)** 49 Renmin Xilu, Hezuo, Gansu 747000. On 1332/3990/5970kHz/97.2MHz 2220-0030(Sun0040), 0350-0620, 0950-1400 in Ch and Tb. – **GS7)** 109 Tuanjie Lu, Linxia, Gansu 731100. 2255-0130(Sun 0230). – **GS8)** 29 Hongqi Jie, Pingliang, Gansu 744000. – **GS9)** Gongyuan Lu, Zhongping Qu, Yumen, Gansu 735200.

GUANGXI ZHUANG AUTONOMOUS REGION

GX1) 75 Minzu Dadao, Nanning, Guangxi 530022. Satellite Sce. on 792/1071/1440/1485kHz/FM and via Satellite 2200-1600 (exc. Tues 0425-1000). – Economic Sce. on 846/1161/1224kHz/FM 2200-1600 (exc. Tues 0500-0830) in Ch and Guangxi dialect. – Education and Life Sce. on 90.1/93.0MHz 2250-0500, 1000-1700. – Literary Sce. on 95.0/105.0MHz 2250-1700 (exc. Tues 0500-1000). – **GX2)** 25 Gecun Lu, Nanning, Guangxi 530012. News General Ch. on 918kHz/101.4MHz 2055-1700 in Ch and Guangxi dialect. – Traffic and Music Ch. on 107.4MHz 2240-1600. – **GX3)** 1 Guizhong Dadao, Liuzhou, Guangxi 545001. News General Ch. on 1386kHz/102.9MHz. 24h in Ch and Liuzhou dialect. – Traffic and Life Ch. on 99.1MHz. – Music Sce. on 94.5MHz. – **GX4)** Anxin Beilu, Xiangshan Qu, Guilin, Guangxi 541002. News General Sce. on 1485kHz/97.7MHz 2225-0525(Sun 0350), W0910-1400, Sun1025-1410. – Travel and Music Sce. on 88.3MHz. – **GX5)** 1-1 Dieshan Li, Dieshan 2 Lu, Wuzhou, Guangxi 543002. On 1485kHz/100.8MHz 2200-1600 in Ch and Guangxi dialect. – Wuzhou EBS: on 107.5MHz 2200-1300 (exc. Mon). – **GX6)** Beihai PBS, 36 Guizhou Nanlu, Beihai, Guangxi 536000. On 93.5/101.5MHz 2220-1700 in Ch and Guangxi dialect.

GUIZHOU PROVINCE

GZ1) 302 Qingyun Lu, Guiyang, Guizhou 550002. Satellite Sce. (General Ch.) on 765/927/1026/7275kHz/FM and via Satellite 2150-1705 (exc. Tues 0600-0900). – Economic Sce. on 603kHz/98.9MHz. 24h (exc. Tues 0700-1000). – V.O. the City: on 97.2MHz and via Satellite. 24h. – Traffic Sce. on 95.2MHz. 24h. – Health Sce. on 106.2MHz. 24h (exc. Tues 0700-1000). – Music Sce. on 91.7MHz 2300-1600 (exc. Tues 0600-0900). – **GZ2)** 21 Zunyi Lu, Guiyang, Guizhou 550002. News St. on 999kHz/88.9MHz 2150-1800. – V.O. the Commerce: on 104.0MHz 2150-1800. – Guiyang Traffic and Literary BS: on 102.7MHz 2250-1800. – **GZ3)** 31 Minghu Lu, Zhongshan Qu, Liupanshui, Guizhou 553000. 2225-0030, 0325-0530, 0955-1330. – **GZ4)** 11 Wenmiao Xiang, Fenghuang Lu, Zunyi, Guizhou 563000. – **GZ5)** 14 Waihuan Xinan Lu, Anshun, Guizhou 561000. – **GZ6)** 86 Pu'an Lu, Duyun, Guizhou 558000. 2225-2400, 0400-0500, 1000-1400.

HAINAN PROVINCE

HA1) Hainan Radio and TV St, Nansha Lu, Haikou, Hainan 570206. On 954/1107kHz/FM 2130-1530 (exc. Tues 0610-0920) in Ch and Hainan dialect. – Economic Sce. on 89.8/99.0/103.8/106.8MHz 2200-1600. – Traffic Sce. on 1143kHz/100.0MHz 2255-1805 (exc. Tues 0530-0900). – **HA2)** Haikou Radio and TV St, 42 Yusha Lu, Haikou, Hainan 570125. Radio Ch. on 101.8MHz. 24h in Ch and Hainan dialect. – **HA3)** Sanya PBS, 4 Jiaoyu Xiang, Hedong 1 Lu, Sanya, Hainan 572000. General Ch. on 104.6MHz. – Traffic Ch. on 100.3MHz.

HUBEI PROVINCE

HB1) 563 Jiefang Dadao, Hankou, Wuhan, Hubei 430022. MW Satellite Ch. on 774/1404kHz/FM 2000-1730 (exc. Tues 0615-0850). – Economic Ch. on 1251kHz/FM 1945-1800. – Health and Entertainment Ch. on 801kHz/96.6MHz 2100-1730. – Traffic Music Ch. on 107.8/90.4MHz 2150-1700. – Music Ch. on 103.8MHz 2100-1700 (exc. Tues 0730-0900). – **HB2)** Chutian BS, 563 Jiefang Dadao, Hankou, Wuhan, Hubei 430022. News St. on 1179kHz 2000-1700 (exc. Tues 0630-0855). – Satellite St. on 684/846/900/927/945kHz/91.6/103.8/104.8MHz and via Satellite 1955-1630 (exc. Tues 0630-0855). – Traffic and Sports St. on 92.7MHz 2125-1630 (exc. Tues 0630-0855). – Music St. on 105.8MHz. 24h (exc. Tues 0630-0855). – **HB3)** 620 Jianshe Dadao, Hankou, Wuhan, Hubei 430015. On 873kHz 2155-1700 (exc. Wed 0600-0925). – Traffic Netw. on 603kHz/89.6MHz 2200-1530 (exc. Tues 0500-0900). – Literary Netw. on 101.8MHz 2300-1600 (exc. Tues 0600-1000) . – **HB4)** Changjiang EBS, 620 Jianshe Dadao, Hankou, Wuhan, Hubei 430015. 2055-1600(Sun 1630) (exc. Thurs 0600-0900) . – **HB5)** 188 Wuhan Lu, Huangshi, Hubei 435000. News St. on 963kHz/101.2MHz 2145-0530, 0845-1600. – Traffic and Music St. on 103.3MHz 2230-1605 (exc. Tues 0500-0855) . – **HB6)** 78 Zhongshan Houjie, Fancheng Qu, Xiangfan, Hubei 441021. General Ch. on 1314kHz/90.9MHz 2150-1600. – Literary St. on 105.3MHz 2200-1630. – Traffic and Music St. on 89.0MHz 2155-1630. – **HB7)** 4 Renmin Beilu, Shiyan, Hubei 442000. News St. on 1485kHz/106.2/107.3MHz 2100-1600. – V.O. Checheng (Mobile City): on 99.1MHz 2200-1600. – Music and Traffic St. on 101.9MHz 2200-1700 (exc. Tues 0600-1000). – **HB8)** 32 Yuanlin Lu, Shashi Qu, Jingzhou, Hubei 434100. News St. on 90.1MHz 2100-1700. – Traffic and Music St. on 96.3MHz. – Literary and Life St. on 828kHz/97.2/98.4MHz 2225-1655. – **HB9)** 2 Guoyuan 1 Lu, Yichang, Hubei 443000. News St. on 621kHz/97.6MHz 2127-1600. – City Life St. on 100.6MHz 2122-1630. – Traffic St. on 105.9MHz 2227-1630. – **HB10)** 100 Xiangshan Dadao, Dongbao Qu, Jingmen, Hubei 448000. News and Economic St. on 1161kHz/89.7MHz 2120-1600. – Health and Music St. on 747kHz/93.2MHz 2120-0500, 0930-1500. – Traffic and Literary St. on 103.0MHz 2120-1600. –

HB11) 71 Mingtang Lu, Ezhou, Hubei 436000. 2100-1600. – **HB12)** 13 Changzheng Lu, Xiaogan, Hubei 432100. News General Ch. on 927kHz/91.2MHz 2155-1530 (exc. Tues 0500-1000). – Traffic and Music Ch. on 87.7MHz 2255-1505. – **HB13)** 169 Dongmen Lu, Huanggang, Hubei 438000. On 101.8MHz 2150-0005, 0425-0605, 0955-1340. – Traffic and Music St. on 107.6MHz. – Huanggang Education and Literary BS: on 91.4MHz. – **HB14)** 129 Ganhe Dadao, Xianning, Hubei 437000. ?-0800, 0930-?. – **HB15)** 32 Xuefu Lu, Laohekou, Hubei 441800. 2155-2400, ?-1255. – **HB16)** 4 Renmin Lu, Danjiangkou, Hubei 441900. 2200-2355, 0955-1155. – **HB17)** 2 Shannan Xiaoqu, Shishou, Hubei 434400. 2200-0005, 0955-1235. – **HB18)** 56 Guang'an Lu, Yingshan Zhen, Guangshui, Hubei 432700. 2155-0055, 0355-0515, 0955-1235. – **HB19)** 146 Puyang Dadao, Yingcheng, Hubei 432400. 2155-0120, 0955-1305. – **HB20)** 1 Xinjian Jie, Macheng, Hubei 436100. – **HB21)** 50 Chunchuan Daqiao Lu, Chibi, Hubei 437300. 0950-1340. – **HB22)** 8 Lieshan Dadao, Suizhou, Hubei 441300. 2130-2330, 0330-0500, 1030-1305. – **HB23)** 117 Mianyang Dadao, Xiantao, Hubei 433000. 2225-0715, 0945-1445. – **HB24)** 16 Jianghan Lu, Yuanlin Zhen, Qianjiang, Hubei 433100. 2150-0445, 0955-1600.

HEILONGJIANG PROVINCE

HL1) 181 Zhongshan Lu, Nangang Qu, Harbin, Heilongjiang 150001. News Sce. on 621/900/1341/4840/7350kHz/FM and via Satellite 2055-1500. – Life and Literary Sce. on 93.5/97.5/104.5MHz 2155-1600. – Traffic Sce. on 93.9/97.1/99.8/106.0/106.9MHz 2155-1600 (exc. Tues 0500-?). – Women and Children Sce. on 102.1MHz 2200-1600. – Music Netw. on 95.8/94.0MHz 2300-1600. – Heilongjiang Korean BS: on 873/5950kHz/96.1MHz W2100-2300, Sun0100-0400, W0400-0500, D0900-1100 and on 95.8MHz 2100-2400, 1000-1300 in Ko. – **HL2)** 1 Huashan Lu, Xiangfang Qu, Harbin, Heilongjiang 150036. On 837kHz 2100-0520, 0855-1445. – Literary Sce. on 98.4MHz 0100(SS 0000)-0500, 0900-1200. – **HL2A)** 2 Wenzheng Jie, Dongli Qu, Harbin, Heilongjiang 150040. On 972kHz 2130-1500 (exc. Tues 0500-0900). – Investment Sce. on 92.5MHz. 24h. – **HL3)** 99 Yong'an Dajie, Qiqihar, Heilongjiang 161005. On 1197kHz/103.1MHz 2125-0010, 0340-0610, 0855-1335. – Traffic Sce. on 94.1MHz. – **HL4)** Bama Lu, Xiangyang Qu, Hegang, Heilongjiang 154100. On 1413kHz/97.2MHz 2125-0030, 0325-?, 0840-1430. – Traffic Sce. on 106.1MHz. – Life and Literary Sce. on 93.3MHz. – **HL5)** 74 Xinxing Dajie, Shuangyashan, Heilongjiang 155100. 2120-0120, 0320-0530, 0905-1230. – **HL6)** 11 Diantai Lu, Jiguan Qu, Jixi, Heilongjiang 158100. On 1368kHz 2130-0600, 0850-1350. – Traffic St. on 95.9MHz. – **HL7)** Jia 1, Dongfeng Lu, Daqing, Heilongjiang 163311. On 1080kHz/96.7MHz 2125-0105, 0250-?, 0925-1430. – Traffic Sce. on 95.0MHz 2125-1430. – **HL8)** Tongshan Lu, Yichun Qu, Yichun, Heilongjiang 153000. 2050-0040, 0325-0520, 0855-1315. – **HL9)** 138 Taiping Lu, Mudanjiang, Heilongjiang 157000. News and Politics Ch. on 684kHz/87.9MHz 2105-1400 (exc. Tues 0800-0855). – Economic Life Ch. on 1476kHz/91.6MHz 2200-0520, 0855-1250. – Traffic and Literary Ch. on 98.2MHz 2300-1300. – **HL10)** 17 Shunhe Lu, Jiamusi, Heilongjiang 154002. On 666kHz/88.0MHz 2055-0530, 0855-1400. – Economic Sce. on 1143kHz/95.0MHz 2055-1600. – Traffic and Literary Sce. on 98.0MHz 2225-1600. – **HL11)** 2 Shanhu Dajie, Taoshan Qu, Qitaihe, Heilongjiang 154600. 0820-1100. – **HL12)** Bei Wusi Lu, Suihua, Heilongjiang 152054. – **HL13)** 47-2 Xing'an Dajie, Jagdaqi Zhen, Heilongjiang 165000. 2120-0155, 0255-0535, 0825-1430.

HUNAN PROVINCE

HN1) 167 Yuhua Lu, Changsha, Hunan 410007. Satellite Ch. (News Ch) on 738/1152/1233/4990kHz/FM and via Satellite 2130-1700 (exc. Tues 0500-0900). – Economic Ch. on 900kHz/90.1/91.0MHz 2200-1600 (exc. Tues 0500-0900). – Literary Ch. "Smile FM": on 97.5/90.8/96.9MHz 2230-1700 (exc. Tues 0500-0900). – Traffic Ch. on 91.8/100.3/102.0MHz 2255-1600. – **HN2)** 368 Laodong Xilu, Changsha, Hunan 410007. V.O. Xingsha: on 1323kHz/105.1MHz. 2200-1700 (exc. Tues 0600-0900). – Music Ch. on 1251kHz/106.1MHz. 24h (exc. Tues 0600-0900). – **HN3)** Caotangba Xiang, Jianshe Zhonglu, Zhuzhou, Hunan 412000. News Ch. on 1089kHz/101.2MHz 2150-1600. – Traffic Ch. on 98.4MHz. – **HN4)** Shaoshan Zhonglu, Xiangtan, Hunan 411100. News and Traffic Ch. on 1503kHz/104.2MHz 2155-0015, 0325-0555, 0925-1510. – V.O. the Music: on 98.6MHz. – **HN5)** 114 Xianfeng Lu, Hengyang, Hunan 421001. 2150-1705. – **HN6)** 373 Zhangshulong, Baoqing Xilu, Daxiang Qu, Shaoyang, Hunan 422000. On 1548kHz 2225-0530, 0955-1600. – Traffic Ch. on 95.4MHz. – **HN7)** Nanhu Dadao, Yueyang, Hunan 414000. On 1053kHz/95.5/104.1MHz 2200-0530, 0925-1340. – Yueyang EBS: on 1008kHz ?-1500. – **HN8)** 69 Wuling Dadao, Changde, Hunan 415000. On 1260kHz 2200-2355, 0400-0500, 0925-1100. – Traffic Ch. on 97.1MHz. – **HN9)** Chaoyang Lu, Yiyang, Hunan 413002. Economic Ch. on 1008kHz/99.7MHz 2220-1600 (exc. Wed 0800-1000) – **HN10)** 51 Renmin Lu, Jinshi, Hunan 415400.

JILIN PROVINCE

JL1) 2 Xi'an Dalu, Changchun, Jilin 130051. Satellite Sce. on 738/1107/1530kHz/FM 2050-1535 (exc. Tues 0500-0900). – Popular Life St. on 846kHz/95.3MHz 2200-1600. – Health and Entertainment St. on 101.9MHz 2135-1630. – Traffic and Literary St. on 103.8MHz. 24h. – Northeast Asia Music St. on 92.7MHz. 24h (exc. Tues 1500-1800). – **JL2)** 3 Baicao Lu, Changchun, Jilin 130061. On 900kHz/88.9MHz. 24h. – V.O. the Traffic BS: on 96.8MHz. 24h. – Changchun EBS: on 1332kHz/90.0MHz 2125-1600. – Changchun Wire Broadc. Literary St. on 99.6MHz. 24h. – **JL3)** 149 Jilin Dajie, Jilin-shi, Jilin 132011. General Ch. on 927kHz/88.3MHz 2055-1430. – Economic Ch. on 603kHz. – Popular Life Ch. on 702kHz ?-1530. – Traffic and Music St. on 105.3MHz. 24h. – Jilin-shi IBS: on 1251kHz/90.3MHz. – **JL4)** 56 Nan Xinhua Dajie, Siping, Jilin 136000. 2135-0030, 0300-0600, 0855-1300. – **JL5)** 15 Hebin Lu, Longshan Qu, Liaoyuan, Jilin 136200. – **JL6)** 24 Cuiquan Lu, Longquan Jie, Tonghua, Jilin 134001. On 909kHz 2150-0530, 0920-1310. – Traffic Sce. on 104.7MHz. – **JL7)** 36 Hunjiang Dajie, Badaojiang Qu, Baishan, Jilin 134302. On 657kHz/106.5MHz 2125-0540, 0930-1240. – Traffic and Literary St. on 107.7MHz. – **JL8)** 71 Linjiang Lu, Ningjiang Qu, Songyuan, Jilin 131200. News General Ch. on 1431kHz/89.9MHz 2150-?, ?-0900. – **JL9)** 99 Zhongxing Dong Dalu, Baicheng, Jilin 137000. News General Ch. on 1323kHz/103.0MHz 2100-1400 (exc. Tues 0630-0940). – Traffic and Literary Ch. on 96.5MHz. – **JL10)** 166 Juzi Jie, Yanji, Jilin 133000. Ch Prgr. on 1053kHz 2130-1630. – Ko Prgr. on 1206kHz/89.5MHz 2125-0210(SS0235), 0255-0515(SS0535), 0930-1450. – Music and Life St. on 98.3MHz. 24h. – Traffic and Literary St. on 105.9MHz 2130-1600. – **JL11)** 45 Dong Huancheng Lu, Gongzhuling, Jilin 136100. – **JL12)** 18 Nan Dalu, Lishu Xian, Jilin 136500. – **JL13)** 70 Henan Jie, Meihekou, Jilin 135000. – **JL14)** Yucai Jie, Qian Gorlos, Jilin 131100. 2125-2330, 0325-0500, 0955-1230 in Ch and Mo. – **JL15)** 29 Gushu Nanjie, Taonan, Jilin 137100. – **JL16)** 7 Yongle Jie, Yanji, Jilin 133000. Ch Prgr. on 900kHz. 24h. – Ko Prgr. on 88.0MHz 2200-1300. – V.O. the Traffic: on 93.5MHz. – **JL17)** 12 Xiangshang Jie, Tumen, Jilin 133100. 2155-2400, 0330-0500, 0855-1230 in Ch and Ko. – **JL18)** 1-8 Xinhua Xilu, Dunhua, Jilin 133700. 2130-1500 in Ch and Ko. – **JL19)** Jinghe Jie, Hunchun, Jilin 133300. 2150-2355, 0315-0540, 0955-1200 in Ch and Ko.

JIANGSU PROVINCE

JS1) Jiangsu Prov. Radio and TV Headquarters, 8 Xi Citang Xiang, Zhongshan Donglu, Nanjing, Jiangsu 210002. News General Ch. on 702/1314/1413/1602kHz/FM and via Satellite 2020-1600 (exc. Tues/Thurs 0600-0850). – Economic Ch. "Caifu 585" on 585kHz 2100-1700. – Economic Ch. "Shangye 937" on 93.7MHz 2100-1700. – Health Sce. on 846kHz. 24h (exc. Tues/Thurs 0600-0855). – Traffic Netw. on 101.1MHz. 24h. – Music Ch. "Joy FM": on 89.7/107.8MHz 2130-1700 (exc. Tues 0600-0900). – Literary Ch. on 1053kHz/97.5MHz and via Satellite 2200-1700. – **JS2)** 50 Yanling Xiang, Nanjing, Jiangsu 210002. News St. on 1008kHz 2000-1800. – Economic St. on 900kHz. 24h. – Traffic St. on 801/1143kHz/102.4MHz 2100-1800. – Music St. on 105.8MHz. 24h. – Sports and Entertainment Ch. on 104.3MHz. 24h. – **JS3)** 223 Zhongshan Nanlu, Xuzhou, Jiangsu 221003. News General Ch. on 1269kHz/93.0MHz 2100-1600. – Economic Life Service Ch. on 801kHz/91.6MHz 2115-1520. – Literary and Traffic Ch. on 1143kHz/103.3MHz 2200-0545, 0900-1230. – **JS4)** 6 Jiefang Xilu, Xinpu Qu, Lianyungang, Jiangsu 222003. News General Ch. on 1458kHz/93.6/98.3MHz 2100-1530 (exc. Tues 0600-0855). – Economic Life Ch. on 1251kHz/90.2/90.7MHz 2200-1410. – Traffic and Music Ch. on 900kHz/90.0/102.1MHz 2200-1600. – **JS5)** 6 Dazhi Lu, Huai'an, Jiangsu 223001. On 801kHz/96.5MHz. 2000-1600. – **JS5A)** 80 Beijing Beilu, Huai'an, Jiangsu 223001. On 1251kHz/105.0MHz 2120-1500 (exc. Tues 0600-0840). – **JS6)** 4 Shengyuan Lu, Yancheng, Jiangsu 224001. News General Ch. on 1026kHz/99.6MHz 2125-0530, 0900-1500. – **JS6A)** 88 Huanghai Zhonglu, Yancheng, Jiangsu 224002. Economic Ch. on 747kHz/105.3MHz 2200-0540, 0955-1400. – **JS7)** 8 Meiling Donglu, Yangzhou, Jiangsu 225002. News St. on 1179kHz/98.5/105.5MHz 2120-1530 (exc. Tues 0600-0930). – Traffic St. on 1521kHz/103.0MHz 2120-1600. – Yangzhou EBS: on 801kHz/94.9MHz 2200-1530. – **JS8)** 20 Qingnian Lu, Taizhou, Jiangsu 225300. On 1341kHz/106.2MHz 2050-1700 (exc. Tues 0530-0855). – Taizhou EBS: on 927kHz/97.3MHz 2100-1700. – **JS9)** 100 Renmin Zhonglu, Nantong, Jiangsu 226001. News General Ch. on 1233kHz 2130-1510. – Economic Life Ch. on 603kHz/103.0MHz 2130-0500, 0925-1400. – Music and Traffic Ch. on 92.9MHz. – **JS10)** 94 Zhongshan Xilu, Zhenjiang, Jiangsu 212004. News General Ch. on 900kHz/99.4MHz 2125-1500. – Economic Life Ch. on 1224kHz/104.5MHz 2100-1600. – Traffic Ch. on 1098kHz/96.3MHz 2200-1600. – **JS11)** 88 Guangshi Lu, Changzhou, Jiangsu 213016. News St. on 846kHz/103.4MHz 2059-1600 (exc. Tues 0600-0900). – Economic St. on 1143/927kHz/105.2MHz 2200-1600. – Traffic and Music St. on 90.0MHz 2100-1600. – Traffic and Music St. "Health Time": on 747kHz 2110-1600 (exc. Tues 0600-0900). – Literary St. "Popular Ch": on 1521kHz/100.1MHz 2150-1600. – **JS12)** 4 Hubin Lu, Wuxi, Jiangsu 214061. News St. on 1161kHz/89.4MHz 2110-1605. – Economic St. on 1251kHz/104.0MHz 2100-1700. – Traffic St. on 1008kHz/106.9MHz 2130-1800. – Music Ch. on 900kHz/91.4MHz 2200-1800. – Health St. on 1521kHz/98.7MHz 2130-1700. – V.O. Jiangnan: on 92.6MHz. – **JS13)** Suzhou Radio and TV Headquarters, 4 Gongyuan Lu, Suzhou, Jiangsu 215006. News General Ch. on 1080kHz/91.1MHz 2030-1630 (exc. Tues 0600-0730) in Ch and Suzhou dialect. – Traffic and Economic Ch. on 846kHz/104.8MHz 2115-1600. – Music Ch. "Enjoy Radio" on 1521kHz/94.8MHz 2155-1505 (exc. Tues 0600-1000). – **JS14)** 43 Gongnong

Lu, Yizheng, Jiangsu 211400. 2125-0100, 0255-0530, 0925-1240. – **JS15)** 79 Zhongshan Nanlu, Jiangyin, Jiangsu 214400. 2200-1600. – **JS16)** 43 Shuyuan Nong, Yushan Zhen, Changshu, Jiangsu 215500. News General Ch. on 1116kHz 2130-1400 (exc. Sat 0600-0700). – Economic Service Ch. on 927kHz 2150-1430 (exc. Sat 0600-0700). – Traffic and Music Ch. on 747kHz/100.8MHz 2130-1430 (exc. Sat 0600-0700). – **JS17)** Chenjiachang Nong, Yangshe Zhen, Zhangjiagang, Jiangsu 215600. News General Ch. on 1098kHz/100.4MHz 2150-1420 (exc. Wed 0600-0830). – Traffic and Music Ch. on 1521kHz/102.0MHz 2150-1405 (exc. Wed 0530-0955).

JIANGXI PROVINCE

JX1) 207 Hongdu Zhong Dadao, Nanchang, Jiangxi 330046. General News Ch. on 729/1350/1449kHz/FM and via Satellite 2000-1700 (exc. Tues 0600-0855). – Life and Economic Ch. on 927kHz/88.7/99.5/106.5MHz and via Satellite 2200-1600 (exc. Tues 0600-0900). – Traffic Sce. on 96.9/105.4MHz. 24h. – Literary and Music Ch. on 94.7/97.9/103.4/107.6MHz. 24h. – **JX2)** 241 Ruzi Lu, Nanchang, Jiangxi 330009. News General Ch. on 1278kHz/91.7MHz 2030-1800 (exc. Tues 0500-0900). – V.O. the Traffic and Music: on 95.1MHz. 24h (exc. Tues 0500-0900). – **JX3)** 525 Cidu Dadao, Jingdezhen, Jiangxi 333000. News General Sce. on 1467kHz/96.5/107.3MHz 2200-1600. – **JX4)** 2 Yingbin Lu, Pingxiang, Jiangxi 337005. News General Ch. on 1107kHz/96.8/106.8MHz 2155-1500. – Traffic and Literary Ch. on 88.8MHz. 24h. – **JX5)** 8 Xianlai Zhong Dadao, Xinyu, Jiangxi 338000. General Ch. on 585kHz/94.0MHz 2130-1800. – Traffic and Literary Ch. on 96.2MHz 2200-1800. – **JX6)** 84 Changhong Dadao, Jiujiang, Jiangxi 332000. News General Ch. on 1485kHz/90.0/91.6MHz 2200-0600, 0855-1500. – Traffic and Music Ch. on 88.4/88.9MHz 2255-1500 (exc. Tues 0530-0855). – **JX7)** 22 Shengli Xilu, Yingtan, Jiangxi 335200. On 1584kHz/104.8MHz 2200-1605. – Traffic and Music St. on 95.6MHz. – **JX8)** 58 Hongqi Dadao, Ganzhou, Jiangxi 341000. News St. on 747kHz/93.7MHz 2130-1700 (exc. Tues 0600-0830) in Ch and Hakka. – V.O. the City: on 95.9MHz 2200-1700. – **JX9)** 191 Beimen Jie, Ji'an, Jiangxi 343000.

LIAONING PROVINCE

LN1) 10 Guangrong Jie, Heping Qu, Shenyang, Liaoning 110003. News St. on 612/963/1089/1260kHz/FM and via Satellite. 24h (exc. Tues 0530-0905). – Economic St. on 999kHz/FM 2125-1700 (exc. Tues 0540-0855). – Life and Entertainment St. on 102.9MHz 2130-1800 (exc. Tues 0530-0830). CNR Ko Prgr: 1700-1800. – Traffic St. on 927kHz/97.5MHz. 24h (exc. Tues 0540-0850). – Literary St. "Music Radio": on 95.9MHz. 24h (exc. Tues 0540-0900). – **LN2)** 89 Nan Sanhao Jie, Heping Qu, Shenyang, Liaoning 110003. News St. on 792kHz/103.4MHz 2100-1700. – Ecomonic St. on 882kHz/90.4MHz 1955-1800 (exc. Tues 0500-0855). – Traffic St. on 98.6MHz. 24h (exc. Thurs 0500-0855). – Sports and Health St. on 1341kHz/105.9MHz. 24h. – Literary St. on 92.1MHz 2055-1700. – **LN3)** 162 Minquan Jie, Shahekou Qu, Dalian, Liaoning 116022. News Ch. on 882kHz/100.8MHz 2030-1700 (exc. Tues 0630-0830). – "Fortune 99.1": on 99.1MHz. 24h (exc. Tues 0630-0800). – V.O. the City: on 1152kHz/93.1MHz 2030-1700 (exc. Tues 0630-0800). – Traffic Ch. on 103.3MHz. 24h (exc. Tues 0630-0800). – Culture and Sports Ch. on 105.7MHz. 24h (exc. Tues 0630-0800). – Music Ch. on 1575kHz/89.1MHz 2100-1600 (exc. Tues 0630-0900). Rel. CRI Prgr: D0400-0900, Sat1000-1200, D1300-1500. – **LN4)** 3, 219 Lu, Tiedong Qu, Anshan, Liaoning 114002. On 954kHz/101.0MHz. 24h. – Economic St. on 1071kHz/89.7MHz. 24h. – Traffic St. on 1251kHz/105.1MHz 24h. – **LN5)** 2 Hunhe Beilu, Shuncheng Qu, Fushun, Liaoning 113006. News St. on 684kHz/93.0MHz 2100-1430. – V.O. the City: on 1143kHz/106.1MHz 2155-0130, 0355-0610, 0925-1230. – V.O. the Music: on 747kHz/100.6MHz 2230-0600, 0800-1300. – **LN6)** 15 Tiyu Lu, Mingshan Qu, Benxi, Liaoning 117000. On 1296kHz 2125-1500. – Traffic and Economic St. on 900kHz/107.4MHz 2155-1600. – Life and Entertainment St. on 96.4MHz ?-1500. – **LN7)** 1 Shanshang Jie, Zhenxing Qu, Dandong, Liaoning 118000. On 1404kHz 2120-0600, 0850-1300. – Traffic Ch. on 891kHz/101.7MHz 2155-1300. – **LN8)** 3, 4 Duan, Beijing Lu, Jinzhou, Liaoning 121000. News St. on 666kHz 2125-1500 (exc. Tues 0530-0855). – Economic St. on 774kHz 2125-1500 (exc. Tues 0530-0855). – Popular Life St. on 1098kHz/97.7MHz 2125-1500 (exc. Tues 0530-0855). – Traffic and Literary St. on 846kHz/100.3MHz 2125-1500 (exc. Tues 0530-0855). – **LN9)** 23 Haixing Lu, Longwan Dajie, Huludao, Liaoning 125000. News St. on 1242kHz/95.2MHz 2125-1430. – Traffic and Literary St. on 87.8MHz 2150-1330 (exc. Tues 0540-0955). – **LN10)** 10, Dong, Bohai Dajie, Yingkou, Liaoning 115000. News General Sce. on 1026kHz/106.2MHz 2050-1500. – Economic Life Sce. on 747kHz/91.1MHz 2200-1315. – Traffic and Literary Sce. on 1143kHz/95.1MHz 2130-1600. – **LN11)** 7 Shifu Dajie, Xinglongtai Qu, Panjin, Liaoning 124010. News Ch. on 1485kHz/88.2MHz 2115-0155, 0330-0540, 0925-1400. – Traffic and Literary Ch. on 90.1MHz 2100-1500. – Life and Entertainment Ch. on 104.2MHz 2100-1600. – **LN12)** 61 Zhonghua Lu, Haizhou Qu, Fuxin, Liaoning 123000. On 1287kHz 2115-0625, 0755-1245. – Economic Life Sce. on 89.3MHz 0855-?. – **LN13)** Fuxin Mongolian BS, 52-2 Yan'an Lu, Haizhou Qu, Fuxin, Liaoning 123000. 2155-0015, 0325-0530, 1040-1300 in Mo. – **LN14)** 93 Qingnian Jie, Liaoyang, Liaoning 111000. General Ch. on 837kHz 2125-1500 (exc. _Tues 0540-0800). – Economic St. on 1143kHz/102.0MHz 2125-1500 (exc. Tues 0600-0800). – Traffic and Literary St. on 107.8MHz. – **LN15)** 45 Gongren Jie, Yinzhou Qu, Tieling, Liaoning 112000. News General Ch. on 1413kHz/98.5MHz 2150-0610, 0850-1300. – Traffic and Literary St. on 95.2MHz 2200-1300. – Life and Entertainment Ch. on 90.8MHz 2200-?. – **LN16)** 19 Jianshe Lu, Shuangta Qu, Chaoyang, Liaoning 122000. On 810/700/750kHz/96.1MHz 2155-1305 (exc. Tues 0630-0920). – Traffic and Literary Sce. on 104.4MHz. – Chaoyang EBS: on 648kHz/107.7MHz 2150-0600, 1155-1600. – **LN17)** 67 Jinluan Lu, Wafangdian, Liaoning 116300. 2130-0500, 0810-1345. – **LN18)** 385, 1 Duan, Huanghai Dajie, Zhuanghe, Liaoning 116400. 2100-0100, 0855-1200. – **LN19)** 15 Zhengfu Lu, Haicheng, Liaoning 114200. On 900kHz/90.4MHz 2120-?, 0315-0505, 0850-1230. – Haicheng EBS: on 1350kHz/106.9MHz. – **LN20)** 18, 2 Duan, Xinghai Beilu, Xingcheng, Liaoning 121600. – **LN21)** 6 Qingnian Lu, Nanshan Jie, Beipiao, Liaoning 122100. ?-0500, 0920-?.

NEI MENGGU AUTONOMOUS REGION

NM1) 55 Xinhua Dajie, Hohhot, Nei Menggu 010058. Chinese News General Prgr. on 675/765/1494kHz/SW/FM and via Satellite 2150-1605. – Mongolian News General Prgr. on 1458/1098/1395kHz/SW/FM and via Satellite 2150-1605. – Economic Life Sce. on 101.4MHz 2255-1600. – V.O. the Traffic: on 105.6MHz 2220-1600. – V.O. the Music: on 93.6MHz 2255-1600. – **NM2)** 159 Gongyuan Xilu, Hohhot, Nei Menggu 010035. On 882kHz/107.4MHz 2200-0130, 0150-0530, 0830-1400 in Ch and Mo. – Traffic Sce. on 107.3MHz 2250-1600. – **NM3)** 12, Dong Duan, Gangtie Dajie, Qingshan Qu, Baotou, Nei Menggu 014030. News General Ch. on 558kHz/94.9MHz 2155-1600 (exc. 0630-0950). – Baotou Stereo Traffic and Literary St. on 89.2MHz. – **NM4)** 17 Ordos Dongjie, Haibowan Qu, Wuhai, Nei Menggu 016000. W2225-0025, Sun0025-0515, W0325-0520, D1025-1305(SS 1405). – **NM5)** 125 Gangtie Xijie, Hongshan Qu, Chifeng, Nei Menggu 024000. Ch Prgr. on 549/1512kHz/91.4/100.0MHz 2130-1430. – Mo Prgr. on 1440kHz/102.8MHz 2205-0010, 0230-0545, 1000-1300. – Traffic and Literary St. on 105.7MHz 2200-1530. – Chifeng EBS: on 900kHz/100.7MHz 2150-1330 (exc. Tues 0600-0925). – "Lark" FM Stereo Sce. on 89.4MHz 2220-1400. – **NM6)** 86 Qiaoxi Shahe Lu, Jining Qu, Ulanqab, Nei Menggu 012000. Ch Prgr. on 702kHz 2150-0100, 0340-0540, 1005-1500. – Mo Prgr. on 1521kHz 2125-0100, 0330-0600, 1010-1505. – **NM7)** 89 Xilin Dajie, Xilinhot, Nei Menggu 026000. Ch Prgr. on 1395kHz 2225-2400, 0255-0550, 0955-1305. – Mo Prgr. on 927kHz 2220-0035, 0240-0450, 1025-1335. – **NM8)** 11 Shengli Dajie, Hailar Qu, Hulun Buir, Nei Menggu 021008. Chinese News General Ch. on 603/3900kHz/99.9MHz 2130-0700(Tues 0210), 0900-1440. – Mongolian News General Ch. on 954/6080kHz 2150-2400, 0355-0600, 0920-1500. – Life and Literary Ch. on 104.6MHz. – **NM9)** 29 Heping Lu, Tongliao, Nei Menggu 028001. Ch Prgr. on 747kHz 2150-0520, 0930-1330. – Mo Prgr. on 1350kHz 2225-0500, 0925-1330. – **NM10)** Ordos BS, 2 Hongbo Hutong, Baoritaohai Dongjie, Dongsheng Qu, Ordos, Nei Menggu 017000. Ch Prgr. on 936/792kHz/98.9MHz 2220-0020, 0320-0600, 1000-1320. – Mo Prgr. on 603kHz. – **NM11)** 26 Xinhua Xijie, Linhe Qu, Bayannur, Nei Menggu 015000. – **NM12)** 1 Elute Donglu, Bayanhot Zhen, Alxa Zuoqi, Nei Menggu 750306. Ch Prgr. on 549/6025kHz 2220-0020, 0350-0600, 1000-1320. – Mo Prgr. on 1440kHz 2220-0020, 0340-0530, 1050-1345. – **NM13)** 73 Hinggan Bei Dalu, Ulanhot, Nei Menggu 137400. Ch Prgr. on 891kHz 2155-2400, 0955-1400. – Mo Prgr. on 1152kHz. – V.O. the Traffic: on 99.0MHz. – **NM14)** Xuegang Shan, Xinchengwan Xiang, Fengzhen, Nei Menggu 012100. 2225-0020, 0355-0505, 0955-1215. – **NM15)** 1 Dianshi Jie, Manzhouli, Nei Menggu 021400. – **NM16)** 1 Xing'an Dongjie, Yakeshi, Nei Menggu 022150. – **NM17)** 3 Shengli Lu, Shiqiao Jie, Zalantun, Nei Menggu 162650. ?-0635, 0925-?. – **NM18)** Zhongyang Dajie, Genhe, Nei Menggu 022350.

NINGXIA HUI AUTONOMOUS REGION

NX1) 16 Beijing Donglu, Xixia Qu, Yinchuan, Ningxia 750021. News Sce. on 891/1206/1287kHz/FM 2130-1655 (exc. Tues 0630-0955). – City Sce. on 103.7MHz 2225(SS2325)-1635 (exc. Tues 0630-0955). – Traffic and Music Ch. on 98.4MHz W2225-1605 (exc. Tues 0600-0955), Sun2355-1510. – Ningxia EBS: on 603kHz W2220-1600 (exc. Tues 0630-1000), Sun2330-0630, Sun1230-1600. – **NX2)** 5 Zhongshan Beijie, Xingqing Qu, Yinchuan, Ningxia 750004. On 801kHz W2225-0145, Sun0000-0500, W0355-0530, D1025-1310(Sun 1330). – Traffic Sce. on 100.6MHz 2225-1800. – **NX2A)** Yinchuan City Economic St, 11 Zhongshan Beijie, Xingqing Qu, Yinchuan, Ningxia 750001. On 95.0MHz 0000-1705. – **NX3)** Shizuishan PBS, 359 Youyi Xijie, Dawukou Qu, Shizuishan, Ningxia 753000. – **NX4)** 54 Yumin Jie, Wuzhong, Ningxia 751100. – **NX5)** Wenhua Jie, Xiaoba Zhen, Qingtongxia, Ningxia 751600.

QINGHAI PROVINCE

QH1) 96 Kunlun Lu, Xining, Qinghai 810001. 1st Prgr. (Satellite Sce.) on 666/711/909/4750/6145/6260/9780kHz and via Satellite 2220-0600, 0925-1505. – Tb Prgr. on 1251/4220/5990/6500kHz and via Satellite 2255-0055, 0355-0545, 1025-1520. – Economic Sce. on 1143kHz 2225-0030, 0410-0640, 1005-1350(Sun 1405). – Traffic and Music Sce. on 1377kHz/97.2MHz. – **QH2)** 43 Nanguan Jie, Xining, Qinghai 810000. 2225-0530(Tues 0015), 1025-1330(Sun/Mon 1400). – **QH3)** 31 Hongwei Lu, Jiegu Zhen, Yushu Xian, Qinghai 815000. On 882/6075kHz 2255-0100, 1025-1230 in Ch and Tb. Rel. CNR 1: 1135-1230. – **QH4)** 24 Renmin Lu, Delingha, Qinghai 817000. Ch Prgr. on 621kHz. Mo/Tb Prgr. on 540kHz.

SICHUAN PROVINCE
SC1) 119-1 Hongxing Zhonglu, Chengdu, Sichuan 610017. 1st Prgr. (Satellite Sce) on 612/909/1116kHz/FM 2155-1605. – Economic Ch. "Times Broadcast": on 94.0MHz 2300-1700. – Economic Ch. "Popular Broadcast" on 89.4MHz. 24h. – V.O. the Health: on 999kHz 2200-1700 (exc. Tues 0600-0800). – Life, Travel and City Sce. on 954/6060kHz/97.0MHz 2230-1300 in Ch, Tb and Yi. – Educational Prgr. on 1521kHz/98.1MHz 0900-1030, 1330-1500. – Sichuan Women & Children BS: on 747kHz 2200-1640 (exc. Tues 0600-1000). – **SC2)** Minjiang Music BS, 119-1 Hongxing Zhonglu, Chengdu, Sichuan 610017. On 95.5MHz 2230-1700 (exc. Tues 0700-1000). – City FM: on 102.6MHz. – **SC3)** 99 Shuanglin Lu, Chengdu, Sichuan 610021. News Ch. on 792kHz/99.8MHz 2130-1700. – Traffic and Literary Ch. on 1485kHz/91.4MHz 2200-1700 (exc. Tues 0500-0800). – Music Sce. "Love Radio": on 105.6MHz 2200-1700. – **SC4)** 1 Wenhua Lu, Huidong Xinqu, Zigong, Sichuan 643000. On 1422kHz/99.4MHz 2220-1505 (exc. Tues 0600-1000). – Yandu MBS: on 97.7MHz 2150-1530. – **SC5)** Linjiang Lu, Bingcaogang, Panzhihua, Sichuan 617000. 2225-0530, 0955-1505. – **SC6)** Chengbei Xinqu, Luzhou, Sichuan 646000. News General Sce. on 954kHz/89.8/97.0MHz 2155-1600. – Traffic and Music Sce. on 96.0/100.6MHz 2155-1600. – **SC7)** 63, 1 Duan, Taishan Nanlu, Deyang, Sichuan 618000. – **SC8)** 98 Hongxing Jie, Fucheng Qu, Mianyang, Sichuan 621000. 2200-1500. – **SC9)** 81 Jianshe Lu, Guangyuan, Sichuan 628017. 2200-1300. – **SC10)** 358 Suizhou Beilu, Suining, Sichuan 629000. 2200-1500. – **SC11)** 33, 1 Xiang, Xianglong Lu, Neijiang, Sichuan 641000. – Neijiang EBS: on 1143kHz/101.4MHz. – **SC12)** Wujia shan, Shizhong Qu, Leshan, Sichuan 614000. – **SC13)** Jiazhou EBS, 40 Dingdong Jie, Leshan, Sichuan 614000. On 95.7MHz 2200-1405 (exc. Wed 0500-1000) . – **SC14)** 12 Sichou Lu, Nanchong, Sichuan 637000. 2155-0015, 0355-0520, 1155-1415. – **SC15)** 24 Renmin Lu, Yibin, Sichuan 644000. News General Ch. on 92.8/97.0/101.4MHz 2210-1500 (exc. Tues 0630-1000). – Jiudu MBS: on 747kHz/105.9MHz. – **SC16)** Zhangjiawan, Tongchuan Qu, Dazhou, Sichuan 635000.

SHANDONG PROVINCE
SD1) 81 Jing 10 Lu, Lixia Qu, Jinan, Shandong 250062. News Ch. on 918/1467/1485/1548kHz/FM 2125-1700 (exc. Tues 0530-0900). English Prgr: 1630-1700. – Economic Ch. on 594kHz/FM. 24h. – Life Ch. on 104.7/105.0/107.8MHz 2155-1600. – V.O. the Traffic and Music "Love FM": on 101.1/106.0MHz. 24h. – Literary Ch. "My FM": on FM 2155-1600 (exc. Tues 0500-0900). – 6th Ch. (Storytelling Ch): on 1251/1341kHz/91.9MHz 2125-1700 (exc. Tues ?-0900). – **SD2)** 32 Jing 11 Lu, Lixia Qu, Jinan, Shandong 250014. News Ch. on 1053kHz/106.6MHz. 24h (exc. Tues 0410-0850). – Economic Ch. on 846kHz/90.9MHz 2055-1700. – Traffic Sce. on 1521kHz/103.1MHz. 24h (exc. Tues 0400-0850). – Literary Sce. on 1305kHz/93.6MHz. 24h (exc. Tues 0400-0900). – **SD3)** 200 Ningxia Lu, Qingdao, Shandong 266071. News Ch. on 1377kHz/107.6MHz 2100-1600. – Economic Ch. on 1251kHz/102.9MHz 2125-1630. – Traffic Ch. on 900kHz/89.7MHz. 24h. – Literary Ch. on 846kHz/96.4MHz 2200-1600 (exc. Tues 0600-0900). – **SD4)** 10 Xi 2 Xiang, Liuquan Lu, Zhangdian Qu, Zibo, Shandong 255008. News Ch. on 1143kHz/89.0MHz 2150-1530. – Economy Ch. on 801kHz/106.7MHz 2155-1530. – Traffic and Literary Sce. on 1476kHz/100.0MHz 2145-1700 (exc. Tues 0500-0900). – **SD5)** 6 Xinsheng Lu, Zaozhuang, Shandong 277101. News St. on 1170kHz/97.6MHz 2050-0100, 0310-0600, 0925-1400. – Zaozhuang EBS: on 603kHz/103.7MHz. – **SD5A)** Zaozhuang Traffic Information BS, Guangming Donglu, Zaozhuang, Shandong 277101. – **SD6)** 1229 Nan 1 Lu, Dongying, Shandong 257031. News Ch. on 1449kHz/102.2MHz 2155-1430. – Economic Ch. on 105.3MHz. – Traffic and Music Ch. on 94.9MHz 2200-1430. – Literary Ch. on 97.3MHz. – **SD7)** 248 Dongfeng Dajie, Kuiwen Qu, Weifang, Shandong 261041. News General Ch. on 1161kHz/100.2MHz 2155-1600. – Economic Ch. on 1287kHz/93.3MHz 2200-1600. – Traffic and Music Ch. on 846kHz/95.9MHz 2200-1600. – **SD8)** 32 Wenhua 2 Xiang, Yantai, Shandong 264000. News General Ch. on 1314kHz/95.3/101.0/101.4MHz 2125-1530 (exc. Tues 0540-0855). Rel. CRI Korean news: 1300-1315. – Economic Life Ch. on 801kHz/105.9/102.7MHz 2125-1530. – Traffic and Literary Ch. on 103.0/89.1MHz 2155-1600. Rel. CRI English prgr: 2230-2300, 0300-0330, 0700-0705, 1400-1500. – **SD9)** 99 Guzhai Donglu, Weihai, Shandong 264200. News Ch. on 1206kHz/97.5/105.1MHz 2100-1530 (exc. Tues 0600-0825). Ko Prgr: 0530-0600, 1430-1500. – Traffic and Literary Ch. on 846kHz/96.1/101.7MHz 2125-1500 (exc. Tues 0600-0855). – **SD10)** Changqing Lu, Jining, Shandong 272137. News St. on 666kHz/104.2MHz 2200-1600. – Economic St. on 801kHz/99.3MHz. – City Information St. on 93.1MHz. – Traffic and Literary St. on 945kHz/101.9MHz 2155-1600. – **SD11)** 115 Haiqu Donglu, Rizhao, Shandong 276800. News General Ch. on 1449kHz/95.0MHz 2150-1500. – Traffic and Life Ch. on 747kHz/88.1MHz 2200-1500. – **SD12)** 224 Tianqu Donglu, Dezhou, Shandong 253000. News Information Ch. on 1098kHz/92.9MHz. – Economic Life Ch. on 1008kHz. – **SD13)** 33 Jinqueshan Lu, Lanshan Qu, Linyi, Shandong 276003. News St. on 873kHz/97.6MHz 2155-1410 (exc. Tues 0530-1020). – Economic St. on 1143kHz/93.2MHz 2155-1405. – Life Ch. on 101.0MHz. – Traffic and Music St. on 801kHz/89.9MHz 2155-1305 (exc. Tues 0600-0950). – **SD14)** 6 Caigan Lu, Liaocheng, Shandong 252051. On 1143kHz/96.8MHz 2130-1500. – Economic St. on 801kHz/92.4MHz. – **SD15)** 502 Huanghe 8 Lu, Binzhou, Shandong 256602. General Ch. on 747kHz/99.4MHz 2130-1535. – Life Ch. on 1170kHz/93.1MHz 2130-1530. – **SD16)** Heze-shi PBS, 68 Dongfanghong Dajie, Heze, Shandong 274000. News St. on 1197kHz/100.4MHz 2150-1500. – Economic and Literary St. on 1521kHz/94.8MHz 2155-1530. – **SD16A)** Heze PBS, 1 Guangfu Beijie, Heze, Shandong 274015. Traffic and Music Ch. on 1323kHz/104.0MHz 2155-1555. – **SD17)** 21 Fangongting Xilu, Qingzhou, Shandong 262500. 2145-0535, 0755-1350. – **SD18)** Yantai Longkou Economic and Literary BS, Huangcheng Xihuan Lu, Longkou, Shandong 265701. 2228-0200, 0500-0700. – **SD19)** 4 Gulou Beijie, Qufu, Shandong 273100. 2215-0025, 0355-0530, 1045-1300.

SHANGHAI MUNICIPALITY
SH1) 1376 Hongqiao Lu, Shanghai 200051. News Ch. on 990kHz/93.4MHz 24h (exc. Thurs 1705-2100). – Traffic Ch. on 648kHz/105.7MHz. 24h (exc. Thurs 1700-2100). – Traditional Play Ch. on 1197kHz/92.4MHz 2125-1500 (exc. Wed 0530-0830) in Ch and Shanghai dialect. – Literary Ch. "Kaixin 968": on 927kHz/96.8MHz 2200-1600 (exc. Wed 0530-0830). – **SH2)** Shanghai Dongfang BS (Eastern Radio), 1376 Hongqiao Lu, Shanghai 200051. News St. on 1296kHz/104.5MHz. 24h (exc. Thurs 1600-2100). Rel. CRI English prgr: 1540-1600. – "City 792": on 792kHz/89.9MHz. 24h (exc. Thurs 0500-0700, 1600-2100). – First Financial and Ecomonic Ch. on 1422/603kHz/97.7MHz 2158-1600. – Popular Music Ch. "Donggan 101": on 101.7MHz 2200-1800 (exc. Fri 0600-0800). – "Liuxing Weili 103": on 103.7MHz. 24h (exc. Thurs 1600-2100). – Classical Music Ch. on 94.7MHz 2200-1700.

SHAANXI PROVINCE
SN1) 336 Chang'an Nanlu, Xi'an, Shaanxi 710061. News General Sce. on 693/1008/1521/6176kHz/FM and via Satellite 2100-1710 (exc. Tues 0600-0900). – Economic Sce. "Fortune Broadcast": on 603kHz/89.6MHz 2200-1710 (exc. Tues 0600-0900). – Life Sce. on 101.8MHz 2210-1700. – Traffic Sce. "Inspiring FM": on 1323kHz/91.6MHz. 24h (exc. Tues 0600-0855). – Farm Sce. on 900kHz 2210-1700 (exc. Tues 0600-0900). – Literary Sce. on 747kHz/99.4MHz 2200-1700. – Music Sce. on 98.8MHz. 24h. – **SN2)** Fu 7, Zhenxing Lu, Xi'an, Shaanxi 710068. News Sce. on 810kHz 2100-1600. – Traffic and Travel Sce. on 104.3MHz 2150-1800. – Music Ch. on 93.1MHz. 24h. – **SN3)** Miaopu Lu, Hongqi Jie, Tongchuan, Shaanxi 727000. 2210-0015, 0330-0515, 0915-1405. – **SN4)** 47 Hongqi Lu, Baoji, Shaanxi 721000. On 1071kHz 2145-2400, 0325-0610, 0930-1500. – Music St. on 105.3MHz 2255-1700. – Baoji EBS: on 900kHz/102.8MHz 2155-0600, 0955-1400. – **SN5)** Fuan Lu, Xianyang, Shaanxi 712000. 2220-1740. – **SN6)** 13 Zhong Duan, Dongfeng Dajie, Weinan, Shaanxi 714000. News General Ch. on 747kHz/102.6MHz. – Music Ch. on 90.9MHz. – **SN7)** Dabian Gou, Yan'an, Shaanxi 716000. 2210-1500 (exc. Wed 0630-0910). – **SN8)** 200 Nan Tuanjie Jie, Hanzhong, Shaanxi 723000. General Ch. on 1251kHz/95.6MHz. – Music St. on 97.1/99.5MHz. 24h (exc. Wed 0700-0930).

SHANXI PROVINCE
SX1) 318 Yingze Dajie, Taiyuan, Shanxi 030001. On 819/846/1269kHz/FM 2159-1700. – Changcheng Economic Sce. on 900kHz/95.8MHz. 2200-1700 (exc. Tues 0600-0900). – V.O. the Health: on 105.9MHz 2220-1700 (exc. Mon 0600-0900). – Traffic Sce. on 89.3/88.0MHz 2200-1600. – Literary Sce. on 101.5MHz 2200-1600. – **SX2)** 2 Yifen Jie, Taiyuan, Shanxi 030024. News Ch. on 1422kHz/91.2MHz 2200-1600. – Economic Life Ch. on 774kHz/104.4MHz 2200-1600. – V.O. the City: on 94.0MHz. – Traffic Ch. on 107.0MHz 2250-1600. – **SX3)** 178 Yingbin Xilu, Datong, Shanxi 037006. General St. on 900kHz/103.8MHz 2200-1605. – Health St. on 91.1MHz 2200-1605. – Traffic St. on 99.6MHz 2200-1605. – **SX4)** 79 Bei Dajie, Yangquan, Shanxi 045000. 2150-2400, 0300-0535, 0955-1355. – **SX5)** 124 Yingxiong Lu, Changzhi, Shanxi 046000. 2210-0600, 0915-1500. – **SX6)** Fengtai Xijie, Jincheng, Shanxi 048000. News General Ch. on 585kHz/89.8MHz 2155-0800, 0955-1600. – Traffic and Health Ch. on 93.5MHz. – **SX7)** 37 Taishan Miao Jie, Yuci Qu, Jinzhong, Shanxi 030600. 2220-0015, 0355-0605, 0955-1400. – **SX8)** 1 Xingsi Jie, Xinzhou, Shanxi 034000. – **SX9)** Hongqi Donglu, Yuncheng, Shanxi 044000.

TIANJIN MUNICIPALITY
TJ1) 143 Weijin Lu, Heping Qu, Tianjin 300070. News St. on 909kHz/97.2MHz. 24h (exc. Mon 1600-2055). – Economic St. on 1071kHz/101.4MHz 2055-1800(Mon 1600). – Traffic St. on 567kHz/106.8MHz. 24h (exc. Mon 1600-2100). – Life St. on 1386kHz/91.1MHz 2055-1800(Mon 1600). – Literary St. on 747kHz/104.6MHz. 24h (exc. Mon 1600-2155). – Music St. on 1008kHz/99.0MHz. 24h (exc. Mon 1600-2155). – Binhai St. on 1098kHz/92.0MHz 2155-1800(Mon 1600).

XINJIANG UIGHUR AUTONOMOUS REGION
XJ1) 84 Tuanjie Lu, Urumqi, Xinjiang 830044. Ch Prgr. on 702/738/999kHz/SW/96.1MHz 2300-1800 (exc. Tues 0800-1100). – Ug Prgr. on 558/855/1044kHz/SW/101.7MHz 2300-1800 (exc. Tues 0800-1100). – Kz Prgr. on 1107kHz/SW 2330-1800 (exc. Tues/Thurs 0800-1100). – Mo Prgr. on 1233kHz/SW 2330-0330, 0530-1030(Tues/Thurs 0800), 1230-1800. – Kirghiz Prgr. on 1233kHz/SW 0330-0530, 1030(Tues/Thurs 1100)-1230. – Satellite Economic Sce. on 837/1215kHz/92.9MHz and via Satellite 2330-1800. –

Satellite Music Sce. on 94.9/101.8MHz and via Satellite 2330-1800. – FM Stereo Sce. on 88.9/105.3MHz MF0600-0700, SS0730-1030, MF1330-1430 in Ug. – **XJ2)** 28 Xinmin Lu, Urumqi, Xinjiang 830002. News Ch. on 792kHz/106.5MHz 2345-1720. – Traffic and Music Ch. on 100.7MHz 2345-1730. – Uighur General Ch. on 1071kHz 2345-1630. – **XJ3)** Urumqi EBS, 11 Nanchang Lu, Urumqi, Xinjiang 830002. Health and Life Ch. on 927kHz 2345-1800. – Traffic and Music Ch. on 97.4MHz 2345-1800. – **XJ4)** 42 Tianshan Xilu, Karamay, Xinjiang 834000. Ch Prgr. on 882kHz 0025-0240, 0600-0800, 1155-1505. – Ug Prgr. on 1179kHz. – **XJ5)** 2 Hongxing Xilu, Hami, Xinjiang 839000. Ch Prgr. on 1485kHz 2200-1800. – Ug Prgr. on 1098kHz. – City FM: on 103.5MHz 2300-1800. – **XJ6)** Wenhua Lu, Hotan, Xinjiang 848000. Ch Prgr. on 684kHz. – Ug Prgr. on 846kHz/92.2MHz. – **XJ7)** Tiyu Lu, Kashi, Xinjiang 844000. Ch Prgr. on 648kHz 2355-0215, 0455-0710, ?-1335. – Ug Prgr. on 801kHz 2355-?. – **XJ8)** Beijing Beilu, Changji, Xinjiang 831100. W2335-0235, Sun0155-0540, W0500-0730, Sun1115-1350, W1135-1430. – **XJ9)** 5 Hongqi Lu, Yining, Xinjiang 835000. Ch Prgr. on 1134kHz/105.9MHz 2350-0200, 0550-0700, 1150-1600. – Ug Prgr. on 603kHz/96.3MHz 2350-0200, 0550-0700, 1150-1600. – Kz Prgr. on 882kHz 2350-0200, 0550-0700, 1220-1500. – **XJ10)** 33 Xiaoqu, Bei 2 Lu, Shihezi, Xinjiang 832000. – Shihezi EBS: on 603kHz. – **XJ11)** Renmin Donglu, Korla, Xinjiang 841000. – **XJ12)** Korla Donglu, Kuytun, Xinjiang 833200. Ch Prgr. on 1485kHz W2355-0230, Sun0025-0335, Sun0528-0720, W0558-0740, D1123-1425. – Kz Prgr. on 819kHz.

XIZANG AUTONOMOUS REGION

XZ1) 180 Beijing Zhonglu, Lhasa, Xizang 850000. Chinese News General Ch. on 999/1377kHz/SW/93.3MHz and via Satellite 2000-1730 (exc. Tues 0600-1000). Rel. CNR 1: MF2030-2100. – Tibetan News General Ch. on 594/846kHz/SW/101.6MHz and via Satellite 2100-1805 (exc. Tues 0600-1000). English Prgr. "Holy Tibet": 0700-0730, 1630-1700. – Kham (Tibetan dialect) Ch. on 594kHz and via Satellite 2200-1605 (exc. Tues 0600-1000). – City Life Ch. on 98.0MHz 2300-1700 (exc. Tues 0600-1000). – **XZ2)** 25 Nedong Lu, Zetang Zhen, Nedong, Xizang 856000. 2335-0135, 0405-0535, 1005-1340 in Ch and Tb.

YUNNAN PROVINCE

YN1) 182 Renmin Xilu, Kunming, Yunnan 650031. Satellite Sce. on 576/990kHz/94.4/105.8MHz and via Satellite 2200-1700. – Economic Life Sce. on 88.7MHz 2250-1700. Rel. CRI English prgr: 1300-1500. – Educational St. on 5960kHz W0030-0400, D1045-1200. – Minority Language St. on 1242/6937kHz 2225-0045, 0355-0545, 1100-1500 in Lahu, Jingpo, Lisu, Dehong Dai and Xishuangbanna Dai. – Traffic and Travel Sce. on 91.8MHz 2240-1600. – Music Sce. on 97.0/100.0MHz 2300-1600 (exc. Tues 0600-0900). – **YN2)** Danxia Lu, Kunming, Yunnan 650118. Sunlight Ch. on 1350kHz/100.8MHz 2225-1600 (exc. Tues 0400-0800). – City FM: on 102.8MHz. 24h. – **YN3)** 121 Qilin Xilu, Qujing, Yunnan 655000. – **YN4)** 172 Zhudianpo, Wenshan Xian, Yunnan 663000. 2225-0100, 0225-0500, 0955-1400 in Ch, Zhuang, Miao and Yao. – **YN5)** 31 Jianshe Donglu, Gejiu, Yunnan 661000. On 702/1521/4930kHz/101.4MHz 2200-1800 in Ch, Hani and Yi. – City FM: on 92.9MHz. – Music Sce. on 97.5MHz 2200-1900. – **YN6)** 10 Jinghong Donglu, Jinghong, Yunnan 666100. 2210-0100, 0250-0600, 1030-1540 in Ch, Xishuangbanna Dai and Hani. – **YN7)** 144 Lucheng Donglu, Chuxiong, Yunnan 675000. News General St. on 1287kHz/93.9MHz 2225-0050, 0310-0625, 0955-1355. – Economic and Music St. on 96.7MHz 2300-1600. – **YN8)** Renmin Jie, Xiaguan Zhen, Dali, Yunnan 671000. News General Ch. on 1044kHz. – Cang'er FM: on 99.9/105.5MHz 2200-1600. – **YN9)** 31 Yingjian Lu, Mangshi Zhen, Luxi, Yunnan 678400. 2230-0110, 0330-0700, 1030-1530 in Ch, Dehong Dai, Jingpo and Zaiwa. – **YN10)** Donghuan Lu, Dongchuan Qu, Kunming, Yunnan 654100. – **YN11)** 6 Longquan Lu, Zhaotong, Yunnan 657000. – **YN12)** Baohua Lu, Gejiu, Yunnan 661400. – **YN13)** 38 Xueqiao Jie, Chuxiong, Yunnan 675000. W2225-2400, Sun2325-0200, D0325-0600, D0955-1405.

ZHEJIANG PROVINCE

ZJ1) 111 Moganshan Lu, Hangzhou, Zhejiang 310005. News General Ch. on MW/FM and via Satellite. 24h (exc. Tues 0600-0858). – Economic Ch. on FM and via Satellite. 24h. – V.O. the City: on 1530kHz/107.0/99.1MHz. 24h. – V.O. the Traffic: on 93.0/93.6MHz. 24h. – Music FM: on 1071kHz/96.8/89.8MHz. 24h (exc. Tues 0600-0800). – Literary St. on 930/1050kHz/99.6MHz. 24h (exc. SS1600-2200). – V.O. the Travel: on 603/1251kHz/FM 2100-1800. – **ZJ2)** 86 Moganshan Lu, Hangzhou, Zhejiang 310005. News General Ch. on 954kHz/89.0MHz 2000-1600. – City FM: on 97.9MHz 2130-1600. Rel. CNR 2: 2130-0600, 1100-1600. – **ZJ2A)** V.O. the Economy St, 5 Qingchun Donglu, Hangzhou, Zhejiang 310016. On 91.8MHz. 24h. – **ZJ3)** V.O. Xihu, 86 Moganshan Lu, Hangzhou, Zhejiang 310005. On 105.4MHz. 24h. – **ZJ4)** 109 Heyi Lu, Ningbo, Zhejiang 315000. News General Ch. on 1323kHz/98.6MHz 2120-1600 (exc. Tues 0500-0900). English N: MF0100-0130, D1500-1515. – Economic and Entertainment Ch. on 747kHz/102.9MHz 2130-1830 (exc. Tues 0500-0900). – Traffic and Music Ch. on 603kHz/93.9MHz. 24h (exc. Tues 0500-0900). – **ZJ5)** 19 Xianxue Qian, Lucheng Qu, Wenzhou, Zhejiang 325000. News St. on 666/2415kHz/94.9MHz 2155-1610 (exc. Tues 0610-0900) in Ch and Wenzhou dialect. – Economic St. on 801kHz/88.8MHz 2155-1610 (exc. Tues 0600-0855). – V.O. the Music: on 100.3MHz. 24h (exc. Tues 0600-0855). – **ZJ6)** 6 Dongsheng Lu, Jiaxing, Zhejiang 314001. News St. on 1107/657kHz/104.1MHz 2110-1600. Rel. Shanghai Dongfang BS on 657kHz: 2300-1100. – Economic St. on 927kHz/92.2MHz 2130-1600 (exc. Tues 0500-0700). – Suburban St. on 88.2MHz 2155-1330. – **ZJ7)** 628 Xinhua Lu, Huzhou, Zhejiang 313000. News General Ch. on 873kHz/105.0MHz 2100-1700 (exc. Tues 0600-0730). – Economic Ch. on 927/1521kHz/89.6MHz 2222-1400. – Literary Ch. on 1251kHz/98.5MHz 2225-1600. – **ZJ8)** 508 Yan'an Donglu, Shaoxing, Zhejiang 312000. General St. on 738kHz/96.0MHz 2130-1500 (exc. Tues 0600-0900). – Economic St. on 1251kHz/94.1MHz 2200-1600 (exc. Tues 0600-0900). – Music and Health Ch. on 92.5/102.5MHz 2130-1400. – Traditional Play St. on 103.5MHz 2100-1330. – **ZJ9)** 238 Renmin Xilu, Jinhua, Zhejiang 321000. On 675kHz/94.2MHz 2145-1605 (exc. Tues 0600-0900). – Jinhua EBS: on 101.4MHz. – **ZJ10)** 35 Nanjie, Quzhou, Zhejiang 324000. News General Ch. on 711kHz/105.3MHz 2155-1505 (exc. Tues 0500-0855). – Traffic and Music Ch. on 1250kHz/97.5MHz 2200-1600. – **ZJ11)** 137 Changguo Lu, Dinghai Qu, Zhoushan, Zhejiang 316000. On 684kHz/99.8MHz 2135-1400 (exc. Tues 0530-0855). – Economic St. on 1098kHz/94.8/97.0MHz 2255-1330 (exc. Tues 0500-0855). – Literary St. on 900kHz/91.0MHz 2255-1500 (exc. Tues 0530-0855). – **ZJ12)** 149 Zhongdong Lu, Liandu Qu, Lishui, Zhejiang 323000. News General Ch. on 711kHz/94.0/96.4MHz 0855-1600. – Traffic and Music Ch. on 106.9MHz 2200-1600. – **ZJ13)** 99 Renmin Lu, Xiaoshan Qu, Hangzhou, Zhejiang 311200. 2200-1400. – **ZJ14)** Xishan, Chengguan, Rui'an, Zhejiang 325200. ?-1305. – **ZJ15)** 121 Zhongshan Lu, Jiangshan, Zhejiang 324100.

CHRISTMAS ISLAND (Australian)

L.T: UTC +7h — **Pop:** 3,000 — **Pr.L:** English, Malay, Cantonese, Mandarin — **E.C:** 50Hz, 240V — **ITU:** CHR.

CHRISTMAS ISLAND COMMUNITY RADIO SERVICE

MW: Phosphate Hill VLU2 1422kHz 0.5kW. (relays ABC R National)
FM: VLU2-FM 102.1MHz 0.015kW & 105.3MHz (relays ABC R National, local programs & PMFM from Perth, WA). Relays WAFM 98.9MHz, R Australia 100.5MHz
D.Prgr: continuous music & local prgrs. The tr. is on the air continuously for shipping, aircraft and weather information. Programs in English, Chinese & Malay. **ANN:** "The Power Station" – **V.** by letter.

COCOS (Keeling) ISLANDS (Australian)

L.T: UTC +6½h — **Pop:** 650 — **Radios:** 200 — **Pr.L:** English, Cocos Malay — **E.C:** 50Hz, 220V — **ITU:** ICO.

RADIO VKW (Gov.)

✉ P.O. Box 70, Cocos (Keeling) Islands, Indian Ocean 6799, Australia — **L.P:** SM: S. O'Neill. TD: K. Beard. PD: Ms. A.Parker.
MW: 1404kHz 0.1kW (relays ABC R National, Triple J & WAFM)— **D.Prgr:** 24h. Rel. BBCWS 1300-1730. Rel. R.Australia 1730-2400 — **V.** by QSL-card.

COLOMBIA

L.T: UTC -5h — **Pop:** 45 million— **Pr.L:** Spanish — **E.C:** 60Hz, 110V — **ITU:** CLM.

MINISTERIO DE COMUNICACIONES Dirección General de Telecomunicaciónes y Servicios Postales

✉ Edificio Murillo Toro, Cras 7 y 8, Calles 12A y 13, Santafé de Bogotá, DC. ☎+57 1 286 6911.

MW:
° = also on SW, * = inactive, (r) = repeater, v = varying fq,
SF de Bogotá=Santafé de Bogotá.
The letters preceding the st. number indicate the Departamento. Addresses are listed by Departamento in alphabetical order.

	Call	kHz	kW	Name and h. of tr.
DC01)	HJKA	540	20	R. Auténtica, SF de Bogotá: 24h
DC02)	HJHF	550	50	R. Dif. Nal., Marinilla (rel: 570)
DC02)	HJZQ	550	50	R. Dif. Nal., Neiva (rel: 570)
DC02)	HJGS	560	10	R. Dif. Nal., Tunja (rel: 570)
GU01)	HJPF	560	25/10	LV de la Pampa, Maicao: 0900-0300
DC02)	HJND	°570	100	R. Dif. Nacional de Colombia, SF de

	Call	kHz	kW	Name and h. of tr.
				Bogotá: 0900-0500
DC02)	HJHP	580	50/10	R. Dif. Nal., Cali (rel: 570)
AN01)	HJCR	590	50	W Radio, Medellín: 24h
AT01)	HJHJ	600	50	R. Libertad, Barranquilla: 24h
NA13)	HJZ95	600	2	R. UWA Unipa, Ricaurte el Diviso: 1300-2300
DC02)	HJD90	610	50	R. Dif.Nal., Uríbia
DC03)	HJKL	610	30	La Cariñosa 6-10, SF de Bogotá: 24h
BO01)	HJVP	620	10	Colmundo, Cartagena: 24h
VA01)	HJEL	620	50/20	Colmundo, Cali: 24h
CL01)	HJFD	630	10	R. Manizales, Manizales: 24h
GN01)	HJWC	630	10	LV del Guainía, Puerto Inírida
MA01)	HJBJ	640	10	RCN, Santa Marta: 1000-0300
DC03)	HJKH	650	100	RCN Antena 2, SF de Bogotá: 24h
NS01)	HJQS	660	25	Colmundo, Cúcuta: 24h
VA02)	HJJM	660	20	R. Auténtica, Cali: 24h
AN02)	HJPL	670	50	RCN Antena 2, Medellín: 1100-0500
SS28)	HJR33	670	10	R. U.I.S - Universidad Industrial
				de Santander, Bucaramanga
DC04)	HJCZ	690	50/12	R. Recuerdos, SF de Bogotá: 24h
VA03)	HJCX	700	120	W Radio, Cali: 24h
AN03)	HJNX	710	10	R. Super, Medellín: 24h
BY14)	HJYD	710	5	R. La Paz, Paipa: 1000-0400
AT01)	HJAN	720	30	Emisoras Unidas, Barranquilla
DC02)	HJZX	720	50	R. Dif. Nal., Rionegro (rel: 570)
QU01)	HJVO	720	25	Transmisora Quindío, Armenia
CO03)	HJTJ	730	15	R. Uno, Montería: 1000-0100 (cfr.1050)
DC05)	HJCU	730	100	Radio Lider, SF de Bogotá: 24h
CE01)	HJNS	740	50	R. Guatapurí, Valledupar: 0900-0300
NA01)	HJHB	740	10	Ecos de Pasto, Pasto: 1000-0200
AN01)	HJDK	750	50	Caracol Colombia, Medellín: 24h
CS01)	HJLH	750	5	LV de Yopal, Yopal: 1000-0500
AT02)	HJAJ	760	30/10	RCN, Barranquilla: 24h
DC03)	HJJX	770	100	RCN, SF de Bogotá: 24h
GU02)	HJZW	780	10/5	R. Almirante, Riohacha: 1000-0300
VA04)	HJZG	780	10	LV del Valle, Cali: 1100-0400
AN01)	HJDC	790	50	R. Caracol, Medellín: 24h
				(Múnera Eastman Radio)
DC02)	HJBU	790	50	R. Dif. Nal., Zambrano (rel: 570)
DC02)	HJZR	790	50	R. Dif. Nal., Villavicencio (rel: 570)
SS01)	HJBW	800	100	RCN, Bucaramanga
DC04)	HJCY	°810	200	Caracol Colombia, SF de Bogotá: 24h
BO02)	HJAD	v820	10	R. Vigía, Cartagena: 1000-0500
VA03)	HJED	820	50	Caracol Colombia, Cali: 24h
AN01)	HJDM	830	25	R. Reloj, Medellín: 24h
HU01)	HJKK	840	30	H J Doble K, Neiva: 24h
MA02)	HJBI	840	30	Ondas del Caribe, Santa Marta: 0945-0500
DC23)	HJKC	850	50	W Radio, SF de Bogotá: 24h
CE02)	HJNJ	860	50	LV del Cañaguate, Valledupar
VA05)	HJFP	860	10	Voces de Occidente, Buga: 1100-0500
AN09)	HJZH	870	5	Vida AM, Medellín: 24h
AT03)	HJSB	870	25	R. Mar Caribe Internacional, Barranquilla:
				0900-0400
BY17)	HJGD	870	5	Em. Reina de Colombia, Chiquinquirá:
				0930-0300
TO01)	HJLA	870	10	LV del Tolima, Ibagué: 0900-0400
CL04)	HJFH	880	10	R. Regional Independiente, Anserma:
				0900-0300
SS02)	HJGE	880	20	Caracol Colombia, Bucaramanga: 24h
AT13)	HKO93	890	0.25	R. Ecos de Soledad, Soledad
DC06)	HJCE	890	10	R. Continental, SF de Bogotá: 24h
MA03)	HJPM	v890	20	R. Galeón, Santa Marta: 24h
NS02)	HJDD	900	15/5	R. Super, Cúcuta: 1000-0400
VA04)	HJEY	v900	10	LV de Cali, Cali: 1000-0300 (SS -0400)
AN04)	HJDO	v910	10	LV del Rio Grande, Medellín: 24h
BY12)	HJTT	910	1	Ondas del Porvenir, Samacá: 0900-0300
DC24)	HJS52	910	15	Colombia Mía, Florencia, CA
IS01)	HJMY	910	30	RCN, San Andrés: 24h
BO03)	HJAA	v920	30	Emisoras Fuentes, Cartagena: 1000-0420
NA02)	HJJN	v920	10	Ondas del Mayo, Pasto: 1000-0100
TO02)	HJSJ	920	10	Colmundo, Ibagué: 24h
DC07)	HJCS	930	10	LV de Bogotá, SF de Bogotá: 24h
NS03)	HJTL	940	25	RCN, Cúcuta: 24h
VA04)	HJGB	v940	10	R. Calima, Cali: -0300
BY19)	HJUJ	950	1	Armonias Boyacenses, Motavita
RI01)	HJFN	950	15	Caracol Colombia, Pereira: 24h
BO08)	HJHN	960	50	Caracol Colombia, Magangué: 24h
SS23)	HJHX	960	1	Candela AM, Bucaramanga: 1000-0500
				(cfr.1510)
CA01)	HJVK	°970	30	Armonias del Caquetá, Florencia: 1000-0300
DC08)	HJCI	970	10	R. Super, SF de Bogotá: 24h
GU03)	HJME	970	10	RCN Guajira, Maicao: 24h
QU09)	HKX59	970	0.25	R. Quimbaya, Calarca
NS04)	HJJV	v980	15	La Vallenata, Cúcuta
VA06)	HJES	980	100	RCN, Cali: 24h
AN02)	HJDB	990	100	RCN, Medellín: 24h
BY07)	HJHI	990	5	LV de Garagoa, Garagoa: 1000-0330
BO04)	HJAQ	1000	15	RCN, Cartagena: 24h
DC02)	HJZP	1000	50	R. Dif. Nal., Yopal (rel: 570)
CC01)		1000	0.8	R. Panamericana, Cajibío: 1300-2300
DC02)	HJJG	v1000	10	R. Dif. Nal., Manizales (rel: 570)
AT04)	HJOP	1010	10	Caracol Barranquilla, Barranquilla: 24h
CO01)	HJZD	v1010	20	R. Panzenú, Montería: 1000-0400
DC04)	HJCN	1010	10	R. Reloj, SF de Bogotá
HU02)	HJJR	v1010	15	Caracol Colombia, Neiva: 24h
NA03)	HJBN	v1010	10/5	LV del Galeras, Pasto: 24h
SS03)	HJIX	1010	10	R. Yarima, Barrancabermeja
AN04)	HJDQ	1020	10	Emisora Claridad, Medellín: 24h
ME01)	HJKS	°1020	10	LV del Llano, Villavicencio: 24h
RI02)	HJFQ	1020	10	RCN, Pereira: 24h
SS04)	HJDZ	v1020	15	R. Primavera, Bucaramanga: 0900-0400
TO03)	HJFT	1020	10	R. Super, Ibagué: 24h
BY01)	HJDJ	1030	10	LV de los Libertadores, Duitama: 24h
CE03)	HJRF	1030	15	Ondas del Cesar, Aguachica
CO02)	HJGX	1030	1	R. Progreso de Córdoba, Lorica: 1000-0400
VA06)	HJER	1030	30	RCN Antena 2, Cali: 24h
VP01)		1030	5	Ondas del Vaupés, Mitú
AT05)	HJAI	1040	15	R. Tropical, Barranquilla: 24h
CC02)	HJSY	v1040	10	La Caucana 10-40, Popayán: 1000-0400
DC10)	HJCJ	°1040	15	Colmundo, SF de Bogotá: 24h
NA04)	HJUB	v1040	15	Colmundo, Pasto: 0900-0500
NS05)	HJBF	1040	15	LV del Norte, Cúcuta
QU02)	HJFM	1040	15	LV de Armenia, Armenia: 24h
AN04)	HJDR	1050	10	R. Unica, Medellín: 24h
AR01)	HJLZ	1050	10	LV del Cinaruco/Caracol, Arauca: 24h
CE04)	HJBB	1050	15	Caracol Colombia, Valledupár: 0900-0500
CO03)	HJTJ	1050	15	R. Uno, Montería: 1000-0100 (cfr.730)
ME02)	HJIO	1050	5	LV de la Conquista, Granada: 24h
SS05)	HJGU	1050	10	R. Bucarica, Bucaramanga
TO04)	HJFZ	1050	10	La Cariñosa del Centro, Espinal: 24h
VA07)	HJNG	1050	10	R. Palmira, Palmira: 1000-0500
AN05)	HJMG	1060	1	Caracol Colombia, Turbo
BY02)	HJMV	v1060	10	R. Furatena, Chiquinquirá: 0900-0600
CL02)	HJFJ	1060	15	RCN Caldas, Manizales: 24h
GU04)	HJLY	1060	5	R. Delfín, Riohacha: 0930-0400
HU03)	HJOV	1060	15	R. Surcolombiana, Neiva: 0955-0530
SU11)	HJYX	1060	1	Caracoli, Sincelejo: 1030-0200
AT06)	HJAH	v1070	20	Em. Atlántico, Barranquilla: 1000-0455
CC03)	HJVR	1070	15	R. Super, Popayán: 24h
DC11)	HJCG	1070	30	R. Santa Fé, SF de Bogotá: 24h
AN01)	HJAX	v1080	10	R. Recuerdos, Medellín: 24h
CL03)	HJJS	1080	15	R. Pontoná, La Dorada: 1000-0500
CO04)	HJAW	v1080	10	LV de Montería, Montería: 1000-0300
ME03)	HJKT	°1080	10	R. Autentica/R. Macarena, Villavicencio: 24h
SS06)	HJMH	1080	10	Melodía AM, Floridablanca
VA04)	HJJF	1080	10	R. Popular, Cali: 24h
BO05)	HJOM	1090	5	R. Bucanero, Cartagena
BY03)	HJIH	1090	10	Caracol Colombia, Sogamoso: 24h
CA02)	HJIG	1090	10	Caracol Colombia, Florencia
CL01)	HJIA	1090	10	Ondas del Nevado, Manizales: 24h
NS06)	HJBC	1090	15	Caracol Colombia, Cúcuta: 24h
TO05)	HJJB	1090	1	LV de los Pijaos, Guamo: 1000-0300
AT04)	HJAT	v1100	15	Caracol Colombia, Barranquilla: 24h
CO05)	HJMK	1100	5	Emisora Ideal, Planeta Rica
DC04)	HJCN	1100	10	Caracol, SF de Bogotá: 24h
				Prgr: Radiodifusión Biblica
HU04)	HJYZ	1100	15	R. Super, Neiva
SS07)	HJGI	1100	5/1	Em. José António Galán/LV de Colombia,
				Socorro: 0930-0300
VI01)	HJEF	*1100	2	LV del Vichada, Puerto Carreño
AN06)	HJGQ	1110	5	Transmisora Surandes, Andes: 1100-0500
AN07)	HJDI	1110	10	R. Bolivariana, Medellín: 24h
AR02)	HJGP	1110	5	LV del Río Arauca, Arauca
IS02)	HJPA	1110	1	LV de las Islas, San Andrés: 24h
ME04)	HJJP	1110	10	RCN, Villavicencio: 24h
SU02)	HJZE	1110	15	R. Piragua, Sincelejo
TO03)	HJNC	v1110	1	Ecos del Combeima, Ibagué: 1000-0400
VA03)	HJEW	1110	10	R. Reloj, Cali: 24h
BY04)	HJKQ	1120	10	Caracol Colombia, Tunja
DC24)	HJQ92	1120	5	Colombia Mía, Yopal, CS
NS01)	HJTI	1120	10	Colmundo R. 24, Cúcuta

	Call	kHz	kW	Name and h. of tr.
RI03)	HJJC	1120	5	R. Matecaña, Pereira: 24h
SS02)	HJGH	1120	15	R. Reloj, Bucaramanga
AT07)	HJAC	1130	10	Em. Riomar, Barranquilla: 0930-0500
BO06)	HJNN	1130	1	Ondas del Río, Magangué
DC12)	HJVA	1130	15	Vida AM, SF de Bogotá: 24h
NA05)	HJQQ	1130	15	R. Reloj, Pasto
AN02)	HJDL	1140	10	R. Paisa "La Cariñosa de Antioquia", Medellín: 24h
BO07)	HJKO	1140	10	LV de la Victoria, Cartagena
CC12)		1140		R. Piendamo, Piendamo
CU01)	HJCL	1140	10	R. Girardot, Girardot
ME05)	HJRW°	1140	10	Caracol Villavicencio, Villavicencio: 0900-0500
SS08)	HJRN	1140	10	RCN, Barbosa: 24h
BY05)	HJGJ	1150	1	La Vallenata, Duitama: 24h
CH01)	HJTE	1150	1	LV del Chocó, Quibdó: 24h
HU05)	HJFP	1150	5	RCN, Neiva: 24h
NS07)	HJBT	1150	10	R. Catatumbo, Ocaña
QU03)	HJFI	1150	15	Caracol Colombia, Armenia: 24h
VA24)	HJSQ	1150	5	R. Robledo/RCN Antena 2, Cartago: 1100-0500 (cfr.1580)
AT01)	HJBL	1160	10	R. Aeropuerto, Barranquilla
CA03)	HJAU°	1160	15	Ondas del Orteguaza, Florencia: 1030-0300
CO06)	HJAZ	1160	5	Meridiano Radio, Montería
DC13)	HJOC	v1160	15	Ecos de Colombia, SF de Bogotá: 24h (prgr: La Voz de Liberación)
NA06)	HJZV	1160	5	R. Las Lajas, Ipiales: 1100-0200
NS08)	HJEC	1160	10	R. San José de Cúcuta, Cúcuta:
RI04)		v1160		Ondas del Puerto, La Virginia
SS09)	HJS31	1160	10	Colombia Mía, Barrancabermeja
VA04)	HJEV	v1160	10	R. Unica, Cali: 24h
AN04)	HJKW	1170	10	R. Nutibara, Medellín: 24h
AR04)	HJE74	1170	10	Meridiano 70, Arauca
BO08)	HJNW	1170	10	Caracol Colombia, Cartagena: 24h
BY04)	HJGA	1170	10	R. Recuerdos, Tunja
CE06)	HJPB	1170	10	Ondas de Macondo, Valledupar
GV01)	HJWA°	1170	5	LV del Guaviare, San José del Guaviare: 0900-0400
ME01)	HJBX	1170	10	Ondas del Meta, Villavicencio
VA08)	HJJE	1170	1	RCN, Tuluá: 24h
AN08)		1180		Em. Coorpurabá, Apartadó
CL05)	HJFX	1180	15	Caracol Colombia, Manizales: 24h
SS10)	HJGK	1180	20	R. Santander 2, Bucaramanga: 24h
TO06)	HJJT	1180	10/5	RCN, Ibagué: 24h
AT05)	HJCT	1190	10	LV de la Costa, Barranquilla: 1030-0200
CO07)	HJKI	1190	1	R. Barají, Sahagún: 1000-0500
DC07)	HJCV	1190	10	R. Cordillera, SF de Bogotá: 24h
NA07)	HJKG	1190	10	R. Mira, Tumaco: 1100-0400
VA09)	HJEO	1190	15	Ondas del Valle, Cartago: 24h
GU05)		v1195		Ondas del Ranchería, Barrancas
AN49)	HJIJ	1200	15	R. 1200 "LV de la Raza", Medellín: 24h
BO09)	HJBV	1200	10	Caracol Colombia, Cartagena: 24h
BY06)	HJLR	1200	10	La Cariñosa, Sogamoso: 1100-0500
CU02)	HJCD	1200	10	Em. Nueva Epoca, Fusagasugá: 0900-0400
GU06)	HJBZ	1200	10	Ondas del Riohacha, Riohacha
VA10)	HJNF	v1200	10	R. Super, Cali: 24h
HU02)	HJFR	1210	10	R. Recuerdos, Neiva: 24h
NS03)	HJBE	1210	10	La Cariñosa, Cúcuta: 24h
RI02)	HJBQ	1210	10	RCN Antena 2, Pereira: 24h
AT05)	HJFF	1220	15	R. Reloj, Barranquilla: 1030-0200
CO08)	HJAV	1220	10	RCN, Montería: 24h
DC22)	HJKR	1220	10	R. María, "LV Católica de su Hogar", SF de Bogotá: 24h
NA08)	HJNM	v1220	10	R. Viva Cultural Bolívar, Ipiales: 1100-0200
SS11)	HJMT	1220	10	RCN, San Gil: 24h
AN10)	HJIL	1230	10	Minuto de Dios, Medellín: 24h
BO13)		1230	10	Minuto de Dios, Cartagena: 24h
BY04)	HJBR	1230	10	Caracol Tunja, Tunja: 1100-0500
CU03)	HJTP	1230	1	R. Colina, Girardot: 18h
GU03)	HJMJ	1230	1	RCN Antena 2, Maicao
SS12)	HJGV	1230	15	Colmundo, Bucaramanga
VA06)	HJKL	1230	10	R. Calidad "La Cariñosa", Cali: 24h
AR03)	HJGO	1240	1	R. Caribabare, Saravena
QU04)	HJFG	1240	10	RCN, Calarca: 24h
SS13)	HJGN	1240	5	R. Barrancabermeja: 1000-0300
VA11)	HJJA	1240	5	R. Buenaventura, Buenaventura: 1030-0500
AI07)	HJOK	1250	10	Em. ABC, Barranquilla: 24h
DC14)	HJCA	1250	10	R. Capital, SF de Bogotá: 24h
NA15)	HJFV	v1250	1.5	R. Viva Canal 12-50, Pasto: 1100-0500
NS06)	HJHS	1250	15	R. Reloj, Cúcuta: 24h
SU03)	HJEM	1250	1	LV de Corozal, Corozal: 1100-0500

	Call	kHz	kW	Name and h. of tr.
AM01)	HJOU	1260	2	Ondas del Amazonas, Leticia: 1000-0500
AN11)	HJDA	1260	5	R. Autentica, Medellín: 24h
BY05)	HJNO	1260	5	Bésame AM, Duitama: 24h
CE08)	HJOH	1260	5	RCN Cesar, Valledupar: 24h
IS03)	HJHU	1260	1	Caracol Colombia, San Andrés
ME06)	HJLX	1260	5	Minuto de Dios Eco Llanero, Villavicencio: 24h
NS10)	HJTM	1260	5	R. Sonar, Ocaña: 1030-0300
TO07)	HJDV	1260	5	Caracol Colombia, Ibagué: 24h
VA29)	HJET	1260	5	R. María, Cali: 24h
BO04)	HJAR	1270	2	RCN Antena 2, Cartagena: 24h
CE05)	HJKJ	1270	1.5	LV de Curumaní, Curumaní: 1000-0100
CU04)	HJXQ	1270	1	R. Melodía, Ubaté
DC24)	HJQ99	1270	5	Colombia Mía, San José del Guaviare, GV
HU05)	HJKD	1270	5	La Cariñosa, Neiva
PU01)	HJSV	1270	1	LV de Orito, Orito: 1100-2300
RI05)	HJIM	v1270	1	Colmundo, Pereira: 0930-0515
SS02)	HJTX	1270	5	Bésame AM, Bucaramanga: 24h
TO12)	HJBM	1270	5	R. Internacional, Honda: 1000-0300 (cfr.1440)
AN12)	HJMB	1280	5	R. Suroeste, Concordia
AT01)	HJSO	1280	5	R. Playa Mendoza, Barranquilla
DC07)	HJKN	1280	5	R. Unica, SF de Bogotá: 24h
GU07)	HJHO	1280	5	Impacto Popular, San Juan del Cesar
HU06)	HJCM	1280	5	R. Sur, Pitalito: 0900-0400
NA05)	HJLR	1280	5	Caracol Colombia, Pasto: 24h
NS11)	HJRP	1280	5	Ecos de Tibú, Tibú: 1000-2400
SS14)	HJNQ	1280	1	LV del Río Suárez, Barbosa: 0730-2330
VA12)	HJTK	1280	5	R. Super, Caicedonia
AN13)	HJTH	1290	5	LV de las Estrellas "R.Ritmos", Medellín: 24h
DC24)	HJSZ	1290	5	Colombia Mía, Saravena, AR
CU05)	HJKY	v1290	5	RCN, Girardot: 24h
MA04)	HJEB	1290	5	LV del Turismo, Santa Marta: 1000-0200
ME07)	HJNE	1290	5	LV del Ariari, Granada: 24h
SU04)	HJOI	1290	5	R. Chacurí, Sampués: 1100-0300
VA13)	HJMC	v1290	5	R. Viva 12-90, Cali: 1000-0500
BO10)	HJOG	1300	5	LV de las Antillas, Cartagena: 24h
BY08)	HJRB	1300	5	R. Super, Tunja
CC04)	HJIN	1300	5	R. Eucha, Belalcázar: 1000-2400
PU02)	HJUA	1300	5	R. Sindamanoy, Mocoa: 0900-0300
RI01)	HJLD	1300	5	R. Reloj, Pereira: 24h
SS02)	HJNB	1300	5	Onda 5, Bucaramanga: 24h
TO08)	HJEA	1300	5	R. Lumbí, Mariquita
AN14)	HJLM	1310	5	R. Santa Bárbara: 1000-0500
AN15)	HJIR	1310	5	RCN Urabá, Apartadó: 24h
AT08)	HJAK	1310	5	LV de la Patria, Barranquilla: 0900-0500
CO09)	HJDG	1310	5	Caracol Colombia, Monteria
DC09)	HJJZ	1310	5	Colorín ColorRadio, SF de Bogotá: 1100-0300
HU07)	HJWD	1310	5	Micrófono Civico, Palermo: 0900-0300
NS12)	HJTQ	1310	5	R. Tasajero, Cúcuta: 1000-0500
AN16)	HJTA	v1320	1	R. María, Medellín: 24h
BY09)	HJHT	1320	5	R. Guateque, Guateque: 1000-0300
CU06)	HJNO	1320	5	La Cariñosa, Girardot: 24h
IS04)	HJQI	1320	5	R. Leda Internacional, San Andrés: 1100-0500
MA05)	HJLV	1320	5	R. Onda Fantastica, Fundación
SS15)	HJMS	1320	5	R. El Sol, Barrancabermeja: 0900-0400
VA14)	HJNK	1320	1	R. Luna, Palmira: 1000-0400
AN17)	HJRD	1330	1	R. Coopeñol, El Peñol
BO02)	HJAP	1330	5	R. Autentica, Cartagena: 24h (cfr.1420)
CE09)	HJMP	1330	1	LV de Aguachica, Aguachica (cfr.1500)
CC05)	HJLS	1330	5	Caracol Colombia, Popayán: 24h
CL17)	HKR33	1330	0.25	Alcadía de Salamina, Salamina
RI02)	HJFE	1330	5	La Cariñosa Amiga, Pereira: 24h
SS16)	HJNR	v1330	5	La Caliente 13-30, San Gil: 0900-0300
AN18)	HJNP	1340	1	R. Comunal, Nariño: 1100-0100
AT03)	HJFA	1340	5	R. Olimpica AM, Barranquilla: 24h
DC03)	HJFB	1340	5	R. Uno, SF de Bogotá: 24h
NA10)	HJHA	1340	5	RCN Nariño, Pasto: 24h
NS04)	HJPY	1340	5	R. Lemas, Cúcuta
NS13)	HJVL	1340	0.5	Brisas del Catatumbo, Tibú: 1030-1700, 2100-0200
SS05)	HJNY	1340	1	R. Unica, Bucaramanga
SU05)	HJHY	1340	5	RCN Sucre, Sincelejo: 24h
VA15)	HJIS	1340	5	La Cariñosa, Buenaventura: 24h
AN19)	HJDS	1350	5	R. Ondas de la Montaña, Medellín: 24h
AN20)	HJLO	1350	5	RCN Antena 2/R. Uno, Caucasia: 24h
BY10)	HJHW	1350	5/1	Em. Ecos del Río, Puerto Boyacá: 0900-0400
CE10)	HJMN	1350	1	R. Perijá, Codazzi
CE12)		1350	1	R. Cultural 2001, Pailitas
MA01)	HJOC	1350	5	RCN Antena 2, Santa Marta: 1000-0300
TO09)	HJHL	v1350	5	R.Reloj, Ibagué
VA16)	HJEN	v1350	10	R. Fabulosa, Cali: 24h

	Call	kHz	kW	Name and h. of tr.
VA30)	HKZ98	1350	0.25	Alcaldía de Caicedonia, Caicedonia
AN21)	HJPK	1360	10/5	LV de Abejorral, Abejorral: 0900-0500
AN22)		1360	0.5	R. Segovia, Segovia: 1100-0300
BO08)	HJTU	1360	5	Caracol Cartagena, Cartagena
BY21)	HJRX	1360		LV de la Comarca, Miraflores
ME08)	HJSD	1360	1	R. Morichal, San Martín
RI06)	HJRA	1360	1	Eco 13-60 "La Superestación", Pereira: 24h
SS17)	HJKV	1360	1	R. Láser, Zapatoca
TO18)	HJMI	1360	5	R. Autentica, Melgar: 0900-0500
AN23)	HJNU	1370	2.5	RCN, Rionegro
AT09)	HJBO	1370	10	Minuto de Dios, Barranquilla: 24h
CC06)	HJEQ	1370	10	RCN Cauca, Popayán: 24h
DC01)	HJKX	1370	5	R. Mundial, SF de Bogotá: 24h
NS15)	HJBD	1370	1	La Nueva R. Guaimaral, Cúcuta: 1000-0500
VA17)	HJJQ	1370	1	RCN Antena 2, Zarzal: 24h
AN24)	HJJD	1380	2.5	Armony Records, Medellín: 24h
BY11)	HJEE	1380	5	RCN, Tunja: 24h
CE13)	HJMM	1380	5	R. Recuerdos, Valledupar: 24h
CL06)	HJLG	1380	3	LV de La Dorada, La Dorada: 0930-0500
HU08)	HJID	1380	5	R. Potencia Latina, La Plata: 1000-0100
VA18)	HJEJ	1380	1	Armonías del Palmar, Palmira: 1130-0300
AN25)		1390	0.1	R. Ciudad de Antioquia, Santa Fé de Antioquia: 1100-2300
CL07)	HJFO	v1390	5	LV de los Andes, Manizales: 24h
CU07)	HJYW	1390	5	R. Autentica, Pacho: 24h
SS18)	HJZY	v1390	1	LV de la Misericordia, Bucaramanga: 24h
TO10)	HJFY	1390	5	R. Avenida, Espinal: 1000-0400
AN26)	HJLL	1400	1	RCN Antena 2, Santa Bárbara: 24h
AT02)	HJAS	1400	5	RCN Antena 2, Barranquilla: 24h
CC07)	HJWY	1400	1	LV de los Samanes: Quilichao: 1100-2400
CC13)		1400	0.45	R. Cañaveral, Morales: 1130-1700, 1900-2200
CH02)	HJIT	°1400	1	Ecos del Atrato, Quibdó: 1000-0400
CO10)		1400	0.25	Brisas del Sinú, Tierralta
CO11)	HJDF	1400	5	LV de Niquel, Montelíbano
DC16)	HJKM	1400	5	Em. Mariana de Bogotá "R.Multi-Cultural" SF de Bogotá: 1100-0130
NA11)	HJJJ	1400	5	R. Ipiales, Ipiales: Sat -0730
NA12)		1400	1.5	LV de Samaniego, Samaniego
NS16)	HJBK	1400	1	Voz Grancolombia, Cúcuta: 24h
QU04)	HJHM	1400	5	RCN Antena 2, Calarca: 24h
SS19)	HJD31	1400	2.5	LV de Cimitarra, Cimitarra: 0900-0300
SS20	HJTY	v1400	1	Caracol Colombia, Vélez: 24h
SU12)	HKZ25	1400	0.25	Alcaldía de Ovejas, Ovejas
SU13)	HKZ22	1400	0.25	Alcaldía de Majagual, Majagual
AN27)	HJDU	1410	5	Em. Cultural Universidad de Antioquia, R. Universidad, Medellín: 1100-0500
BY18)	HKP79	1410	1	R. Universidad, Tunja
BY23)	HKP86	1410	0.25	Alcaldía de Chiquinquira, Chiquinquira
GU08)	HJP79	1410	2	R. Evangélica, Uribia
TO11)	HJFS	1410	5	RCN Antena 2, Honda: 24h
VA19)	HJEI	1410	5	R. Guadalajara, Buga
AN28)	HJD23	1420	1	Ecos de Frontino, Frontino
BO02)	HJAP	1420	5	R. Autentica, Cartagena: 24h (cfr.1330)
CL05)	HJHK	1420	5	R. Reloj, Manizales: 24h
MA06)	HJBH	1420	5	Caracol Colombia/R. Magdalena, Santa Marta: 24h
SS21)	HJSN	1420	1	R. Lenguerque, Zapatoca
TO06)	HJLE	1420	1	La Cariñosa, Ibagué
AN29)	HJCK	1430	1	R. Sensación, Yarumal
AN30)	HJMF	1430	2	R. Venus, Puerto Berrío
AN47)	HJG42	1430	0.5	R. Alejandría, Alejandría
AT10)	HJPW	1430	5	Colmundo, Barranquilla: 24h
CC08)	HJEG	1430	1	LV de Belalcázar, Popayán: 0930-0400
CL08)	HJIU	1430	1	Armonías del Ingrumá, Riosucio: 1100-0300
DC17)	HJKU	1430	5	Em. Kennedy, SF de Bogotá: 1055-0300 (prgr: LV de María)
NS17)	HJBP	1430	2	R. Cariongo, Pamplona: 0900-0300
PU03)	HKK38	1430	0.5	R. Manantial, Sibundoy: 1300-2300
QU08)	HJX61	1430	0.25	R. Dif. Cultural del Quindío, Armenia
RI08)	HKX73	1430	0.25	R. Ciudad de Pereira, Pereira
SU07)	HJQX	1430	5	R. Majagual, Corozal
AN46)	HJNZ	1440	5	Colmundo, Medellín: 1100-0600
BY06)	HJGM	1440	5	RCN, Sogamoso
CA04)	HJIB	1440	1	RCN Caquetá, Florencia: 24h
CU19)	HKT58	1440	0.25	Alcaldía de Ubala, Ubala
TO12)	HJBM	1440	5	R. Internacional, Honda: 1000-0300 (cfr.1270)
VA20)	HJEK	1440	5	R. Reloj, Tuluá: 1000-0500
CU08)		1445	0.5	Em. R. Unión, La Palma
AN31)	HJE20	1450	1	R. María, Urrao: 0900-0300
AN32)		1450	0.2	R. LV del Nordeste, Remedios: 1100-2400
BO11)	HJMX	1450	1	R. Mancomoján, Carmen de Bolívar: 1030-0400
CC09)		1450	0.5	LV del Cauca, El Bordo
CL02)	HJNL	1450	5	La Cariñosa, Manizales: 1000-0500
SS22)	HJHH	1450	5	R. Católica Metropolitana, Bucaramanga: 24h
TO13)	HJBY	1450	5	R. Ciudad de Flandes, Flandes
AN33)	HJTF	1460	5	Ondas del Darién, Turbo: 1000-0400
AN34)	HJMN	1460	1	LV de Amalfi, Amalfi: 1000-0300
AN45)	HJE26	1460	1	R. Capiro, La Ceja: 1100-0300 (Sun -0100)
AT02)	HJVH	1460	5	R. Uno, Barranquilla
DC18)	HJJW	1460	5	Em. Nuevo Continente, SF de Bogotá: 24h
HU09)	HJFL	1460	2.5	Agustiniana Minuto de Dios, San Agustín: 1100-0300
NA10)	HJZU	1460	5	RCN Antena 2, Pasto: 24h
NS18)	HJIW	1460	1	R. Monumental, Cúcuta: 1000-0400
QU06)	HJJH	1460	5	R. Ciudad Milagro, Armenia: 1000-0500
SU08)	HJAL	1460	1	R. Sincelejo, Sincelejo: 1000-0400
AN04)	HJIM	1470	5	R. Popular, Medellín: 24h
AT14	HKO96	1470	0.25	Alcaldía de Baranoa, Baranoa
BO12)	HJPX	1470	5	Colmundo, Cartagena: 24h
BY13)	HJB63	1470	1	R. Uno, Iza: 24h
CU09)	HJHQ	1470	5	R. Futurama, Pacho: 0930-0400
PU04)	HJIF	1470	1	R. Tres Fronteras, Puerto Asís: 1100-0200
TO14)	HJTB	1470	5	Ondas de Ibagué, Ibagué: 1000-0400
TO21)	HJS20	1470	0.25	Ecos de Palo Cabildo, Palo Cabildo
VA26)	HJNT	1470	5	R. Restauración, Cali: 1100-0500
AN35)	HJTC	1480	1	R. Sonsón, Sonsón (n.f.1490)
CL18)	HKR44	1480	0.25	Alcaldía de Victoria, Victoria
MA07)	HJOD	1480	2.5	R. Rodadero, Santa Marta: 1100-0300
NS14)		1480	0.25	LV del Samán, Bochalema: 1100-0500
RI03)	HJFC	1480	5	R. Unica, Pereira: 1000-0500
SS10)	HJTZ	1480	5	RCN Antena 2, Bucaramanga: 24h
TO15)	HJVB	*1480	1	R. Guayabal, Armero, Guayabal
AT11)	HJAY	1490	5	Onda Nueva, Barranquilla: 1100-0500
BO14)	HJJ76	1490	0.2	Alcaldía de El Peñon, El Peñon
DC19)	HJBS	1490	5	Em. Punto Cinco, SF de Bogotá: 1100-2300
HU10)	HJAG	v1490	8	R. Garzón, Garzón: 1000-0300
NA18)	HKW24	1490	0.2	Alcaldía de Guaitarilla, Guaitarilla
SU09)	HJJO	1490	1	LV de San Marcos, San Marcos
VA21)	HJZB	1490	5	LV de los Robles, Tuluá: 1100-0500
BY15)	HJSH	v1500	5	Ecos del Ricaurte, Moniquirá: 1030-0300
CE09)	HJMP	1500	1	LV de Aguachica, Aguachica (cfr.1330)
CL09)	HJUW	1500	5	R. María, Manizales: 1015-0500
CU10)	HJTW	1500	5	R. Sumapaz, Fusagasugá: 0900-0300
CU16)	HKT71	1500	1	Macheta
VA22)	HJLJ	v1500	5	La Básica 1500, Cali: 24h
AN37)	HJD24	1510	5	LV de La Unión, La Unión: 1000-0200
BY16)	HJA22	1510	1	LV de San Luis, San Luis de Gaceno: 0900-0300
DC24)	HKY41	1510	1	Colombia Mía, Barrancabermeja, SS
QU07)	HJZA	1510	1	R. Estrella, Armenia: -0300
SS23)	HJHX	1510	1	Candela AM, Bucaramanga: 1000-0500 (cfr.960)
TO16)		1510	0.5	LV de los Cedros, Libanó: 1000-0300
VA28)	HKZ98	1510	0.25	Alcaldía de Caicedonia, Caicedonia
VA31)	HKZ94	1510	0.25	Alcaldía de Buenaventura, Buenaventura
VA32)	HKZ93	1510	0.25	Alcaldía de Versalles, Versalles
AN38)		1520	0.3	Brisas del Palmar, Caucasia: 1130-0400
AN39)	HJMA	1520	1	LV de Suroeste, Jericó: 1000-0500
AT03)	HJLQ	v1520	5	R. Minuto, Barranquilla: 24h
CC11)	HKS24	1520	0.5	R. Cristalares Timbío, Timbío: 1200-2400
CL10)		1520		Sonoradio 1520 AM, Viterbo
CO13)	HKT20	1520	0.25	Alcaldía de Montería, Montería
CU14)	HJV37	1520	1	R.Pueblo Viejo, Zipacon
DC20)	HJLI	1520	5	Estación Latina, SF de Bogotá: 1100-0500
DC24)	HJT21	1520	0.25	Colombia Mía, Tierralta, CO
NA16)	HKW37	1520	1	R. Universidad, Pasto
NA19)	HKW43	1520	0.1	Alcaldía de Tangua, Tangua
NS19)	HJJ98	1520	1	Em. Una Voz de la Frontera, Puerto Santander: 1000-2200
RI07)	HJRL	1520	15	Antena de los Andes, Santa Rosa de Cabal: 1000-0300
SU10)	HJMZ	1520	1	Ecos de la Sierra Flor, Sincelejo: 1030-0430
TO17)	HJAM	1520	1	R. Altamizal, Dolores: 0945-0300
AN24)	HJDN	1530	5	LV de la Misericordia, Medellín: 24h
AN50)	HKN57	1530	0.25	Alcaldía de San Juan de Uraba, SJdU
AN53)	HKN85	1530	0.25	Alcaldía de Anza, Anza
CE11)	HKS56	1530		Fascinación AM, Becerril
CE15)	HKS58	1530	0.1	Alcaldía de El Copey, El Copey
CC14)		1530		R. Integración, Morales

	Call	kHz	kW	Name and h. of tr.
DC24)	HKN65	1530	0.25	Colombia Mía, Caucasia, AN
GU09)	HJOZ	1530	5	LV de la Prov. de Padilla, San Juan del Cesar: 1000-0400
ME10)	HJV82	°1530	0.25	Alcaraván Radio, Puerto Lleras
VA23)	HJJB	1530	1	Caracol Sevilla, Sevilla
VA25)	HKR73	1530	1	Ecos del Pacífico, Guapí: 1300-2300
AN40)		1540	0.25	LV Dorada, Segovia
AN41)	HJB89	1540	1	Em. Brisas del Río Chico, Belmira
BO15)	HKP50	1540	0.25	Alcaldía de Arjona, Arjona
CL11)	HJZF	1540	5	R. Cóndor "Em. Universitaria", Manizales: 1200-0355
CS02)	HKR80	1540	0.15	Alcaldía de Sacama, Sacama
DC24)	HKZ52	1540	1	Colombia Mía, Chaparral, TO
NA09)	HJRQ	1540	2	R. Austral, Túquerres: 0900-0400
SS24)		1540	0.25	R. El Sur, San Vicente de Chucurí
SS25)	HJHD	1540	1	LV del Petróleo, Barrancabermeja: 1000-0400
TO18)	HJD89	1540		LV del Nevado Cumbal, Melgar
AN36)		v1550	0.5	Ondas del Nechí, Campamento: 1100-2300
AT02)	HJCB	1550	5	R. El Sol, Barranquilla: 1000-0300
CL16)	HJUN	v1550	5	LV del Río Arma, Aguadas: 1000-0300
DC21)	HJZI	1550	5	MCI Radio 15-50, SF de Bogotá: 24h
DC24)	HKV38	1550	1	Colombia Mía, Pitalito, HU
DC24)	HKX29	1550	0.25	Colombia Mía, Tibú, NS
NA20)	HKW53	1550	0.1	Alcaldía de El Tablón, El Tablón
NA21)	HKW55	1550	0.1	Alcaldía de Guachucal, Guachucal
NA22)	HKW50	1550	0.25	Alcaldía de Mallama, Mallama
QU03)	HJQD	1550	5	Caracol Armenia, Armenia: 24h
VA33)	HJLT	1550	1	R. Renacer en Cristo, Cali: 1100-0400
AN42)		1555	0.5	R. Parroquial, El Santuario: 1230-1500, 2200-2400
AN52)	HJXZ	1560	1	Sta María de la Paz, Medellín
AN54)	HKO35	1560	0.25	Alcaldía de Cañasgordas, Cañasgordas
CE07)	HKS65	1560	0.5	R. Tamalameque, Tamalameque
CE14)	HJPZ	1560	1	R. Codazzi, Codazzi
CU11)	HJCP	1560	5	RCN Antena 2, Arbelaez: 24h
ME09)	HKV90	1560	0.2	Villavicencio
ME11)	HKV90	1560	0.25	Alcaldía de Villavicencio, Villavicencio
SS26)	HJHE	1560	5	Voces Rovirenses, Málaga: 1000-0200
VA08)	HJLP	v1560	5	La Cariñosa, Tuluá: 1000-0300
AN43)	HJC22	1570	1	R. Ciudad Dabeiba, Dabeiba: 0900-0300
BO16)	HKP58	1570	0.25	Alcaldía de Sta Rosa Sur, Sta Rosa Sur
BY24)	HKQ83	1570	0.25	Alcaldía de Maripi, Maripi
BY25)	HKQ82	1570	0.25	Alcaldía de Sta María, Sta María
CA05)	HKR66	1570	0.2	R.Universidad de la Amazonia, Florencia
CA06)	HJR66	1570	0.5	Timbiqui Estéreo, Timbiqui
CL12)	HJZT	v1570	1	R. Sensación, Manizales
CU18)	HKU42	1570	0.15	Alcaldía de Cajica, Cajica
DC22)	HJTG	1570	1	R. María, Machetá
DC24)	HJE96	1570	1	Colombia Mía, Palmira, VA
DC24)	HKX52	1570	2	Arc. Armada de Colombia, Pto Leguizamo
NS09)		1570		LV de Fomeque, Fomeque: 1000-1700, 2200-0100
RI09)	HKX80	1570	0.1	R. Marsella, Marsella
RI11)	HKX78	1570	0.25	Alcaldía de Balboa, Balboa
SS29)	HKY73	1460	0.25	Alcaldía de San Andrés, San Andrés
AT12)	HJQZ	1580	5	R. María, Barranquilla: 0930-0130
CC16)	HKS46	1580	0.15	R. Alcaldía de Padilla, Padilla
CO12)	HKT34	1580	0.25	Alcaldía de San Antero, San Antero
CU17)	HKU42	1580	0.25	Alcaldía de Cajica, Cajica
DC25)	HJQT	1580	5	R. Mar, SF de Bogotá: 24h
HU11)		1580		Alcaldía de Yaguará, Yaguará
MA08)	HJLC	1580	1	LV del Banco, El Banco: 1000-0400
NA23)	HKW74	1580	0.1	Alcaldía de Pupiales, Pupiales
NS20)	HJKB	1580	1	R. Zulima, Villa del Rosario
SU01)	HJRM	1580	5	Caracol Colombia, Sincelejo: 1000-0430
TO19)	HJDE	1580	1	R. Miraflores, Rovira
VA24)	HJSQ	v1580	5	R. Robledo/RCN Antena 2, Cartago: 1100-0500 (cfr 1150)
AN44)	HJIP	1590	5	Em. Nuevo Continente, Envigado: 24h
CE16)	HKS72	1590		Alcaldía de La Gloria, La Gloria
CL13)	HJQM	1590	1	Ecos de la Miel, Samaná: 1100-0100
CU14)		1590		Ondas del Rioseco, Rioseco
SS27)	HJWB	1590	5	Minuto de Dios Sra del Socorro, Socorro: 1000-0200
VA25)		1590		R. Espacial, Andalucía
AN51)	HKO63	1600	0.25	Alcaldía de Jardín, Jardín
BY20)		1600		R. Fortaleza, Sogamoso
BY22)		1600		R. Bello Horizonte, Pesca (r. 1620-1630)
CC15)		1600	0.25	R. Impacto Cristiano, Popayán: 1000-0500
CL14)		v1600	0.25	LV de Aranzazu: 1100-1300, 1700-1900, 2100-2300
CL15)	HKR52	1600	0.25	LV de Colina, Risaralda
CO14)	HKT39	1600	0.25	Alcaldía de Valencia, Valencia
CU13)	HJHV	v1600	5	Armonías Zipaquireñas, Zipaquirá
CU15)		1600	1	LV del Rosario, Junín
DC24)	HKO72	1600	5	Colombia Mía, Carepa, AN
RI10)	HKX84	1600		Em. Mundial, Dosquebradas
RI12)	HKX83	1600	0.25	Alcaldía de La Celia, Celia
TO20)	HKZ79	1600	0.15	Alcaldía de Cajamarca, Cajamarca
TO22)	HKZ77	1600	0.15	Alcaldía de Venadillo, Venadillo
VA27)	HJF33	1600	0.25	R. Restauración, Cali: 24h
AN48)		1610		Armonías de Occidente, Medellín
BY26)		v1613	1	R. Ideal, Umbita (nom 1600)

SW:

Stations with (*) are reported to be inactive, but may occasionally be reactivated for variable periods of time.

	Call	kHz	kW	Name and h. of tr.
TO03)	HJLW	*4785	5	R. Super, Ibagué
VA11)	HJAM	*4835	1	R. Buenaventura, Buenaventura
ME01)	HJIE	*4885	5	Ondas del Meta, Villavicencio
DC24)		*4895		Colombia Estéreo/Em de Creer, Melgar (Tolima)
CA01)	HJRI	v4915	3	Armonías del Caquetá, Florencia: irr
CA03)	HJQA	4975	1	Ondas del Orteguaza, Florencia: irr
CH02)	HJCP	v5020	1	Ecos del Atrato, Quibdó: irr, often // with 850 kHz (Caracol)
NA17)	HJV44	v5585	0.3	R. Juventud, Pasto: Sun 0100-0500, irr
DC26)	HJDH	5910		LV de tu Conciencia, Lomalinda (Meta)
ME05)	HJKW	v5955	5	LV de los Centauros, Villavicencio: M-F 1100-1200, Sat-Sun 1500-1700, irr
ME03)	HJHZ	v5975	5	R. Autentica, Villavicencio: irr
DC26)	HJDH	v6010	0.4	LV de tu Conciencia, Lomalinda (Meta): 24h
GV01)	HJOY	v6035	5	LV del Guaviare, San José del Guaviare: 1000-0300
ME01)	HJIQ	v6115	10	LV del Llano, Villavicencio: 0900-0400
DC05)	HJQE	v6140	5	Melodía Bogotá, SF de Bogotá: 24h, irr
ME03)	HJHZ	v6090		R. Macarena, Villavicencio

CARACOL (Primera Cadena Radial Colombiana)
✉ Cra. 39A N° 15-81, Santafé de Bogotá, DC. ☎+57 1 337 8866. 🖷+57 1 337 7126. **Web:** www.caracol.com.co **Email:** caracolcolombia @caracol.com.co

RADIONET (All-news 24h.)
✉ Diagonal 22A N° 43-77, Santafé de Bogotá, DC. ☎+57 1 268 6700, 269 4123. 🖷+57 1 269 4770. **Web:** www.radionet.com.co

RCN (Radio Cadena Nacional)
✉ Cra. 13A N° 37-32, Santafé de Bogotá, DC. ☎+57 1 314 7070. 🖷+57 1 314 7070. **Web:** www.rcn.com.co

SUPER RADIO
✉ Calle 39A N° 18-12 (or: Ap. 23316), Santafé de Bogotá, DC. ☎+57 1 338 2166. 🖷+57 1 287 8678. **Web:** www.super.com.co

TODELAR (Circuito Todelar de Colombia)
✉ Ap. 27344 (Av. 13, Autopista Norte, N° 84-42), Santafé de Bogotá, DC. ☎+57 1 621 6621 - 🖷+57 1 616 0056. **Web:** www.todelar.com.co **Email:** todelar@telesat.com.co

COLMUNDO
✉ Diagonal 58 N° 26A-29, Santafé de Bogotá, DC. ☎+57 1 217 8911. 🖷+57 1 217 9358 **Email:** colmundo@latino.net.co

CADENA RADIAL AUTENTICA DE COLOMBIA (Rlg.)
✉ Ap. 18350, (Calle 32 N° 16-12), Santafé de Bogotá, DC. ☎+57 1 285 3360. 🖷+57 1 285 2505 **Web:** www.cmb.org.co/cra/index.html **Email**: cmbvillavo@andinet.com

WV RADIO
✉ Calle 56 N° 37-34, Santafé de Bogotá, DC. ☎+57 1 222 0001. 🖷+57 1 222 4188. **Web**: www.wv-radio.com.co

RED SONORA (Sistema Nacional de Comunicaciónes)
✉ Av. Roosevelt N° 34-37, Cali, Valle del Cauca. ☎+57 92 558 9000. **Email**: redsonora@hotmail.com

State abbreviations: (Departamentos) AM = Amazonas, AN = Antioquia, AR = Arauca, AT = Atlántico, BO = Bolívar, BY = Boyacá, CA = Caquetá, CC = Cauca, CE = Cesar, CH = Chocó, CL = Caldas, CO = Córdoba, CS = Casanare, CU = Cundinamarca, DC = Distrito Capital, GN = Guainía, GU = Guajira, GV = Guaviare, HU = Huila, IS = Islas San

Andrés y Providencia, MA = Magdalena, ME = Meta, NA = Nariño, NS = Norte de Santander, PU = Putumayo, QU = Quindío, RI = Risaralda, SS = Santander del Sur, SU = Sucre, TO = Todelar, VA = Valle del Cauca, VI = Vichada, VP = Vaupés.
N.B: These abbreviations are not officially recognized by the Colombian Post Office. Letters should therefor carry full name.

Addresses and other information:
AM00) AMAZONAS
AM01) Cra. 6A N° 10-104 (or: Ap. 236), Leticia.
AN00) ANTIOQUIA
AN01) Cra. 79A N° 39-45, Medellín. **Web:** www.radiomunera.com **Email:** munera@munera.eastman.com – **AN02)** Ap. 1244, Medellín. – **AN03)** Calle 50 Colomb N° 67-141, Medellín. – **AN04)** Av.13 N° 84-42 (or: Ap. 1431), Medellín. – **AN05)** Cra. 19 N° 20-66, Turbo. – **AN06)** Ap. 1431, Andes. – **AN07)** Circular 1a N° 70-01, Bloque 6, P7 U.P.B. Laureles, Medellín **Web:** www.ubicar.com/radiobolivariana - **FM:** 92.4. – **AN08)** Apartadó. – **AN09)** Cra. 77B N° 48-144, Medellín ☎+57 421 0102. **Web:** www.vidaam.com **Email:** info@vidaam.com – **AN10)** Calle 56 N° 41-57, Medellín. **Web:** www.infonetway.com/minuto/ or www.1230amradio.com - **Email:** mdradiomedellin @epm.net.co – **AN11)** Calle 41 N° 80B-46, P2, Medellín. – **AN12)** Cra. 3 Calles 2 y 3, Concordia. – **AN13)** Ap. 4300, Medellín. – **AN14)** Cra. 51 N° 51-38 (or Ap. 3854) , Medellín. – **AN15)** Calle 94 N° 99-51, Apartadó. – **AN16)** Calle 50 N° 67-141 (or: Ap. 65103), Medellín. – **AN17)** Centro Cooperativo, Parque Principal, El Peñol. – **AN18)** Cra. 11 N° 10-34, Nariño. – **AN19)** Calle 44 N° 94-15, P3, Medellín. **Email:** ondasm@cis.net.co – **AN20)** Cra. 2 N° 21-54, Caucasia. – **AN21)** Cra. 51 N° 50-09, Abejorral. – **AN22)** Segovia. – **AN23)** Cra. 51 N° 49-09, Rionegro. – **AN24)** Calle 48B N° 79-38, Medellín. – **AN25)** Casa de la Cultura, Santa Fé de Antioquia. – **AN26)** Cra. Bolívar, Calle López, Santa Bárbara. – **AN27)** Ap. 1226 (or: Cra. 44 N° 48-72), Medellín.**Web:** www.udea.edu.co/emisora/ - **FM:** 101.9. – **AN28)** Cra. 32 N° 30-05, Frontino. – **AN29)** Cra. 20 N° 20-21, Yarumal. – **AN30)** Calle 6 N° 1-23, Puerto Berrio. – **AN31)** Urrao. – **AN32)** Remedios. – **AN33)** Ap. 1289, Medellín. – **AN34)** Calle 19 N° 19-78, Amalfi - **FM:** 103.9. – **AN35)** Calle 8 N° 6-60, Sonsón. – **AN36)** Casa Cural, Campamento. – **AN37)** Plaza Principal N° 9-37, La Unión (or: Ap. 4897, Medellín). – **AN38)** Batallón de Infantería N° 29 "Rifles", Barrio El Palmar, Caucasia. – **AN39)** Calle 7, Cras. 3 y 4, Jericó. – **AN40)** Batallón Bomboná, Segovia. – **AN41)** Cra. 20 N° 20-14, Belmira. – **AN42)** Parroquia de Nuestra Señora de Chiquinquirá, El Santuario. – **AN43)** Edif.Restrepo, P3, Plaza Principal, Dabeiba. – **AN44)** Ap. 81095 (or: Cra. 44A N° 31 Sur-16, Medellín), Envigado. – **AN45)** Calle 20 N° 27-20, La Ceja. **Email:** radiocapiro@yahoo.com –☎ +57 4 5531528. 🖷+57 4 5530785. – **AN46)** Cra. 80 N° 46-74, Medellín. – **AN47)** Junta de Acción, Comunal Central, Alejandría –**AN48)** Calle 100 N° 14-06, Turbo. **AN49)** Cra.73 N° 47-35, Medellín. – **AN50)** Palacio Municipal de San Juan de Uraba, San Juan de Uraba. – **AN51)** Palacio Municipal de Jardín, Jardín.– **AN52)** Calle 10 N° 42-22, Medellín. **Web:** www.santamariadelapaz.org/index.html **Email:** webmaster@santamariadelapaz.org – **AN53)** Palacio Municipal de Anza, Anza. – **AN54)** Palacio Municipal de Cañasgordas.
AR00) ARAUCA
AR01) Calle 19 N° 19-62 P2, Arauca. – **AR02)** Cra. 20 N° 19-09, P5, Arauca (or: Ap. 16555, SF de Bogotá). – **AR03)** Calle 20, Cra. 27 (or: Ap. 6558), Saravena –**AR04)** Ap. 18227, Arauca (or: Parque Bolívar, Edif. Banco Bogotá, SF de Bogotá). **Web:** meridiano70.com **Email:** info@meridiano70.com
AT00) ATLÁNTICO
AT01) Cra. 53 N° 15-166 (or: Ap. 3143), Barranquilla. **FM:** 96.9. – **AT02)** Ap. 1883, Barranquilla. – **AT03)** Calle 72 N° 41C-64, Ofc 301 y 302, Barranquilla. **Web:** www.oro.com.co/ – **AT04)** Ap. 1688, Barranquilla. – **AT05)** Cra. 53 N° 82-132, Barranquilla. – **AT06)** Ap. 51266, Barranquilla. – **AT07)** Cra. 48 N° 72-25, Ofc. 306, (or: Ap. 2010), Barranquilla. – **AT08)** Calle 38 N° 22-37 (or: Ap. 231), Barranquilla. – **AT09)** Calle 53 N° 50-11, P2, Barranquilla. **Web:** www.minutodedios.org or www.1370am.org/ **Email:** aj1370@latinmail.com – **AT10)** Cra. 44 N° 70-61, Barranquilla. – **AT11)** Cra 54 N° 55-127, P12, Ofc.1104 (or: Ap. 2647), Barranquilla. – **AT12)** Calle 74 N° 45-31, Barranquilla (or: Transversal 34 N° 149-23, Cedro Golf, SF de Bogotá). – **AT13)** Palacio Municipal de Soledad, Soledad. – **AT14)** Palacio Municipal de Baranoa, Baranoa.
BO00) BOLÍVAR
BO01) Av. Venezuela, Edif. Banco Internacional, La Matuna 8B-05, Cartagena. – **BO02)** Calle Real 20-217, Cartagena. – **BO03)** Calle Mayor N° 6-34 (or: Ap. 1771), Cartagena. – **BO04)** Ap. 246, Cartagena. – **BO05)** Banco Popular, Ofc 1103 Mutana, Cartagena. – **BO06)** Ap. 180, Magangué. – **BO07)** Calle 32 N° 5-09, Banco Comercio 702 (or: Ap. 2456), Cartagena. – **BO08)** Ap. 97, Cartagena. – **BO09)** Av. 3 N° 21-62, La Manga, Cartagena. – **BO10)** Cra. 21 N° 29B-10, Cartagena. – **BO11)** Calle 56 N° 26-01, Carmen de Bolívar. – **BO12)** Av. Venezuela, Edif. Suramericana, Of. 801, Cartagena. – **BO13)** Av. Miramar, Calle 24 N°20-203, Cartagena. – **BO14)** Palacio Municipal de El Peñon, El Peñon. – **BO15)** Palacio Municipal de Arjona, Arjona. – **BO16)** Palacio Municipal de Sta Rosa Sur, Sta Rosa Sur.
BY00) BOYACÁ
BY01) Calle 16 N° 15-21, P8, Edif.Camara de Comercio, Duitama. – **BY02)** Cra. 10 N° 16-36, Chiquinquirá. – **BY03)** Ap. 282, Sogamoso. - **FM:** 88.5+107.3. – **BY04)** Calle 20 N° 8-54, Tunja. – **BY05)** Cra. 15 N° 14-47, Duitama. – **BY06)** Ap. 019, Sogamoso. - **FM:** 106.1. – **BY07)** Cra. 9 N° 8-65, Garagoa (or: Ap. 13729, SF de Bogotá). – **BY08)** Calle 20 N° 10-64, Tunja. – **BY09)** Cra. 7 N° 9-57, Guatepeque (or: Ap. 17387, SF de Bogotá). – **BY10)** Cra. 3 N° 13-74, P2, Puerto Boyacá. – **BY11)** Cra. 10 N° 17-50, P5, Tunja. – **BY12)** Calle 5,N° 5-25, P2, Parque Santander, Samacá. – **BY13)** Iza (or: Cra. 7 N° 17-51, Of. 610, SF de Bogotá). – **BY14)** Cra. 6 N° 6-93, Paipa. – **BY15)** Calle 7 N° 3-61, Moniquirá. – **BY16)** Calle 6 N° 5-42, San Luis de Gaceno. – **BY17)** Calle 18 N° 12-81, P2, Chiquinquirá. - **FM:** 92.6. – **BY18)** Universidad Pedagogica y Técnico de Colombia, Tunja. – **BY19)** Calle 20 N° 10-64, Ofc.307, Motavita. – **BY20)** Cra. 10 N° 1495, Sogamoso. – **BY21)** Calle 4 N° 8-66, Miraflores. – **BY22)** Pesca. – **BY23)** Palacio Municipal de Chiquinquira, Chiquinquira. – **BY24)** Palacio Municipal de Maripi, Maripi. – **BY25)** Palacio Municipal de Sta María, Sta María. – **BY26)** Calle 16A N° 3-58, Umbita.
CA00) CAQUETÁ
CA01) Cra.14 N° 12-129, Casa Episcobal, P2 (Ap. 285), Florencia. – **CA02)** Ap. 465, Florencia. – **CA03)** Calle 17 N° 10-40, P2, (Ap. 209), Florencia. – **CA04)** Ap. 150, Florencia. – **CA05)** Ap. 192, Florencia **Web:** www.uniamazonia.edu.co - **FM:** 98.1. – **CA06)** Timbiqui.
CC00) CAUCA
CC01) Barrio El Porvenir, Cajibío (or: Ap. 945, Popayán). – **CC02)** Cra 8 N° 3-17 (or: Ap. 1321), Popayán. – **CC03)** Cra. 8 N° 5-41, Popayán. – **CC04)** Casa Cural, Parque Principal, Belalcázar (or: Ap. 987, SF de Bogotá). – **CC05)** Calle 5A N° 11-25, Popayán. – **CC06)** Ap. 535, Popayán. – **CC07)** Cra. 13 N° 9-20, Santander de Quilichao. – **CC08)** Calle 2a N° 1-06 (or: Ap. 759), Popayán. – **CC09)** Batallón José Hilario López, Bordo. – **CC11)** Calle 15 Cra. 17 Esq. Casa de la Cultura, Timbío (or: Calle 12B N° 13B-22, Popayán). – **CC12)** Cra. 4 N° 9-42, Piendamo. – **CC13)** Barrio Sagrada Familia, Cra. 3 esq., Morales. – **CC14)** Casa de la Cultura, Morales. – **CC15)** Ap. 789, Popayán. – **CC16)** Palacio Municipal de Padilla.
CE00) CESAR
CE01) Calle 17 N° 15-67, Valledupar. – **CE02)** Cra. 5 N° 13-52, Valledupar. – **CE03)** Calle 7 N° 16-39, Aguachica. – **CE04)** Ap. 22, Valledupar. – **CE05)** Calle 6 N° 19-66, Curumaní. - **FM:** 95. 7. – **CE06)** Calle 16B N° 13-74, Valledupar. – **CE07)** Casa de la Cultura, Tamalameque. – **CE08)** Ap. 250, Valledupar. – **CE09)** Cra. 10a N° 4-38, P2, Aguachica. – **CE10)** Cra. 16 N° 11-102, Codazzi. – **CE11)** Becerril. – **CE12)** Pailitas. – **CE13)** Cra. 9 N° 5-02, Valledupar. – **CE14)** Calle 12 N° 15-08, Codazzi. – **CE15)** Palacio Municipal de El Copey, El Copey. – **CE16)** Palacio Municipal de La Gloria.
CH00) CHOCÓ
CH01) Calle 28 N° 1-04, P2 (or: Ap. 482), Quibdó. – **CH02)** Cra. 4 N° 25-18, P2, (or: Ap. 196), Quibdó.
CL00) CALDAS
CL01) Ap. 67, Manizales. – **CL02)** Ap. 244, Manizales. – **CL03)** Cra. 2 N° 13-31, P3, La Dorada. – **CL04)** Cra. 4 N° 8-58, P3, Anserma. – **CL05)** Ap. 2000, Manizales. – **CL06)** Calle 11 N° 3-58 (or: Ap. 34), La Dorada. – **CL07)** Calle 22 N° 21-40, Plaza Bolívar, Manizales. – **CL08)** Cra. 5 N° 11-102, Av. Los Fundadores, Riosucio. – **CL09)** Cra. 23 N° 71-03 (or: Ap. 990), Manizales. – **CL10)** Viterbo. – **CL11)** Ap. 441, Manizales. **Web:** www.autonoma.edu.co/emisora.html – **CL12)** Cra. 23 N° 71-03, Av.Sant, Manizales. – **CL13)** C. A. M, Samaná. – **CL14)** La Parroquia de Nuestra Señora del Rosario, Aranzazu. – **CL15)** Av. Joaquín 1-09, Salida a San José, Risaralda. – **CL16)** Cra. 3 N° 7-31, Aguadas. – **CL17)** Palacio Municipal de Salamina, Salamina. – **CL18)** Palacio Municipal de Victoria, Victoria.
CO00) CÓRDOBA
CO01) Cra. 3A N° 30-12, P2, Montería. – **CO02)** Av. Olaya Herrera, Edif. Jatin, Lorica. – **CO03)** Calle 23 N° 1-53, Montería. – **CO04)** Cra 2 N° 28-53, P2, (or: Ap. 497), Montería. – **CO05)** Cra. 8 N° 17-56, Planeta Rica. – **CO06)** Ap. 148, Montería. – **CO07)** Calle de Comercio, Sahagún. – **CO08)** Calle 27 N° 8-25, Montería. – **CO09)** Ap. 364, Montería. – **CO10)** Brigada N° 11, Tierralta. – **CO11)** Cra. 5 N° 14-85, Montelibano. – **CO12)** Palacio Municipal de San Antero, San Antero. – **CO13)** Palacio Municipal de Montería, Montería. – **CO14)** Palacio Municipal de Valencia, Valencia.
CS00) CASANARE
CS01) Calle 9 N° 22-63, Edif. Cine Casanare, P2, Yopal. **Web:** www.lavozdeyopal.com.co **FM:** 97.7. – **CS02)** Palacio Municipal de Sacama, Sacama.
CU00) CUNDINAMARCA
CU01) Calle 14 N° 11-23, P2, Ofc.202, Girardot. – **CU02)** Av. Las Palmas N° 5-08, P5, Fusagasugá. – **CU03)** Calle 14 N° 9-100, Of. 302, Girardot. – **CU04)** Cra. 6 N° 6-38, Ubaté. – **CU05)** Ap. 416, Girardot. – **CU06)** Calle 16

N° 10-38, P3, Girardot. - **FM:** 93.6. – **CU07)** Calle 7 N° 14-83, Pacho. – **CU08)** La Palma. – **CU09)** Calle 3 N° 16-39, Pacho. – **CU10)** Calle 8 N° 5-59, Fasagasugá. – **CU11)** Cra. 3 N° 2-36, Arbeláez (or: Av. 37 N° 75-84, SF de Bogotá). – **CU13)** Calle 3 N° 7-56, Zipaquirá. – **CU14)** Zipacon. – **CU15)** Alcaldia Municipal, Junín. – **CU16)** Macheta. – **CU17)** Palacio Municipal de Cajica, Cajica. – **CU18)** Palacio Municipal de Cajica, Cajica. – **CU19)** Palacio Municipal de Ubala.

DC00) DISTRITO CAPITAL

DC01) Calle 32 N° 16-12 (or: Ap. 18350), SF de Bogotá. ☎+57 1 285 3360. 🖷 +57 1 285 2505. – **DC02)** Edif. Inravisión, CAN, Av. El Dorado, SF de Bogotá. **Web:** www.inravision.com.co – **DC03)** Cra. 13A N° 37-32, SF de Bogotá. – **DC04)** Cra. 39A N° 15-81, SF de Bogotá. Red de Radiodifusión Biblica address: Cra. 10 N° 19-65, Edif.Camacol, Ofc.902, SF de Bogotá – **DC05)** Calle 45 N° 13-70 (or: Ap. 19823), SF de Bogotá. ☎+57 1 323 1500. 🖷+57 1 288 4020. – **DC06)** Calle 48 N° 18-77, SF de Bogotá. – **DC07)** Av. 13 N° 84-42, SF de Bogotá. – **DC08)** Calle 39A N° 18-12, SF de Bogotá. ☎+57 1 338 2166. – **DC09)** Ap. 10556, SF de Bogotá. **Web:** www.caracol.com.co/colorin – **DC10)** Diagonal 58 N° 26A-29, SF de Bogotá. – **DC11)** Calle 57 N° 17-48, SF de Bogotá. ☎+57 1 345 6781. 🖷+ 57 1 345 7080. **Web:** www.radiosantafe.com – **DC12)** Cra. 16 N° 43-09, SF de Bogotá. ☎+57 1 288 3766. 🖷+57 1 288 7720. **Email:** radiok@multiphone.net.co – **DC13)** Cra. 13 N° 46-72, SF de Bogotá. – **DC14)** Cra. 30 N° 91-84 (or: Ap. 250649), SF de Bogotá. ☎+57 1 610 2079. 🖷+57 1 218 0312. – **DC15)** Ap. 9291, SF de Bogotá. – **DC16)** Calle 6 N° 7-22, (or: Ap. 3201), SF de Bogotá. (alt.address: Calle 38S N° 75-31, Cd. Kennedy, SF de Bogotá) **Web:** www.emisoramariana.com – **DC17)** Ap. Cd. Kennedy 72825, SF de Bogotá. – **DC18)** Cra. 27 N° 49-48, SF de Bogotá. – **DC19)** Av. 15 N° 123-61, Of. 408, SF de Bogotá. – **DC20)** Diagonal 88 bis N° 26-40 (or: Ap. 90883), SF de Bogotá. – **DC21)** Calle 22C N° 31-01, SF de Bogotá. ☎+57 1 368 7431. **Email:** mciradio@latino.net.co – **DC22)** Transversal 34 N° 149-23, Cedro Golf, SF de Bogotá. ☎+57 1 216 9839. 🖷 +57 1 614 3730. **Web:** www.radiomariacol.org **Email:** info.col@radiomaria.org – **DC23)** Diagonal 22A N° 43-77, SF de Bogotá. – **DC24)** Escuela de Cadetes José María Cordoba, Calle 80 N° 38-00, SF de Bogotá. 🖷+57 1 240 7374. – **DC25)** Catedral de la Fé, Av. Caracas N° 20-17 Sur, SF de Bogotá. – **DC26)** Colombia para Cristo, Calle 44 N° 13-69, Local 1, Barrio Palermo, (or: Ap.95300), SF de Bogotá. **Email:** Colombia-para-Cristo@neutel.com.co or rms05001@neutel.com.co ☎+57 1 338 4716.

GN00) GUAINÍA

GN01) Casa Cultura, Calle 6 con Cra. 3, Puerto Inírida. - **FM:** 88.9 Super Estación.

GU00) GUAJIRA

GU01) Cra. 9 N° 12-31, Maicao. – **GU02)** Cra. 8 N° 3-27, Riohacha. **Email:** mercorio@col3.telecom.com.co – **GU03)** Ap. 125 & 256, Maicao. – **GU04)** Calle 15, Salida a Maicao, Riohacha. – **GU05)** Barrancas. – **GU06)** Cra 8A N° 3-27 (or: Ap. 3), Riohacha. – **GU07)** Cra. 6 N° 6-60, San Juan del César. – **GU08)** Cra. 18 N° 13-54, Uribia. – **GU09)** Calle 1 N° 5-63, San Juan del Cesar.

GV00) GUAVIARE

GV01) Cra 22 con Calle 9, San José del Guaviare. **Email:** mercorio@col3.telecom.com.co

HU00) HUILA

HU01) Calle 7 N° 10-36 (or: Ap. 727), Neiva. – **HU02)** Ap. 150, Neiva. – **HU03)** Ap. 496 (or: Cra. 7, Calles 21 y 22), Neiva. – **HU04)** Cra. 13 N° 3A-24, Neiva. – **HU05)** Cra. 4 N° 2-21, Of. 501-502, Neiva. – **HU06)** Calle 6 N° 5-36, P4, Pitalito. – **HU07)** Cra 8 N° 8-60, P2, Palermo. – **HU08)** Calle 4a N° 5-59, La Plata. – **HU09)** Cra. 14 N° 2-47, San Agustín. **Email:** – **HU10)** Cra. 7 N° 7-05, Garzón. –**HU11)** Palacio Municipal de Yaguará, Yaguará.

IS00) ISLAS SAN ANDRÉS Y PROVIDENCIA

IS01) Ap. 354, San Andrés Isla. – **IS02)** Ap. 1034, San Andrés Isla. – **IS03)** Edif. Bermuda, P2, Av. de las Américas, San Andrés Isla. – **IS04)** Av. Providencia N° 1A-48, (or: Ap. 665), San Andrés Isla.

MA00) MAGDALENA

MA01) Av. Libertadores 27-101, Santa Marta. – **MA02)** Cra. 5 N° 18-32 (or: Ap. 757), Santa Marta. – **MA03)** Calle 17 N° 5-83 (or: Ap. 103), Santa Marta. – **MA04)** Calle 18 N° 5-58, Santa Marta. – **MA05)** Cra. 9 N° 14-13, Fundación. – **MA06)** Ap. 1240, Santa Marta. – **MA07)** Calle 11 C N° 18a-34, Santa Marta. –**MA08)** Ap. 45, El Banco.

ME00) META

ME01) Calle 41B N° 30-11, Barrio La Grama, Villavicencio. –
ME02) Cra. 13 N° 15-52, Granada. – **ME03)** Calle 38 N° 32-41, P7, Edif. Prollano, Ofc 702, Villavicencio. **Web:** www.cmb.org.co/cra/ index.html **Email:** cmbvillavo@andinet.com – **ME04)** Cra. 30 N° 36-14, P4, Villavicencio. – **ME05)** Cra. 31 N° 37-71, Of.1001, (Ap. 2472), Villavicencio. – **ME06)** Cra. 40 N° 34-34, Baltazar Alto, Villavicencio. – **ME07)** Calle 13 N° 28-05 (Ap. 001), Granada. – **ME08)** Vía Villavio km 3, San Martín. – **ME09)** Villavicencio. – **ME10)** (See DC26). **Web:** www.fuerzadepaz.com - **FM:** 88.8 Marfil Stereo. – **ME11)** Palacio Municipal de Villavicencio, Villavicencio.

NA00) NARIÑO

NA01) Cra. 29 N° 17-30 (or: Ap. 375), Pasto. – **NA02)** Ap. 635 (or: Cra.20A N° 16-73, P2), Pasto. – **NA03)** Ap. 454, Pasto. – **NA04)** Calle 20 N° 24-73, Of 603, P6, Pasto. – **NA05)** Cra. 27 N° 19-30, Pasto. – **NA06)** Ap. 1005, Ipiales. – **NA07)** Parque Colón (or: Ap. 165), Tumaco. – **NA08)** Cra. 8 N° 4-48, Ipiales. – **NA09)** Calle 20 N° 15-13, Túquerres. – **NA10)** Ap. 516, Pasto. – **NA11)** Cra. 6A N° 9-14, P2, Ipiales. – **NA12)** Cra. 5 N° 3-15, Samaniego. – **NA13)** Fundación Tomás Cipriano de Mosquera, Ricaurte el Diviso. – **NA14)** Nevado Cumbal. – **NA15)** Cra. 25 N° 19-12, Pasto. – **NA16)** Universidad de Nariño, Cra. 25 N° 19-12, Pasto. – **NA17)** Cra. 1 N° 21-36, Pasto. – **NA18)** Palacio Municipal de Guaitarilla, Guaitarilla. – **NA19)** Palacio Municipal de Tangua, Tangua. – **NA20)** Palacio Municipal de El Tablón, El Tablón. – **NA21)** Palacio Municipal de Guachucal, Guachucal. – **NA22)** Palacio Municipal de Mallama, Mallama. – **NA23)** Palacio Municipal de Pupiales, Pupiales.

NS00) NORTE DE SANTANDER

NS01) Calle 5 N° 3-26 (or: Ap. 1650), Cúcuta. – **NS02)** Centro Comercial Bolívar, Local E4 y E5, Cúcuta. – **NS03)** Ap. 400, Cúcuta. – **NS04)** Calle 5A N° 0-45, Cúcuta. – **NS05)** Av. 0. N° 10-54, P2 (or: Ap. 624), Cúcuta. – **NS06)** Ap. 519, Cúcuta. – **NS07)** Cra. 13 N° 9-10, P6, Ocaña. –**NS08)** Calle 7N N° 4-117 (or: Ap. 2284), Cúcuta. – **NS09)** Cra. 4 Calle 5 junto Almacén Fotorubio, Fomeque. – **NS10)** Calle 11 N° 15-24, Ocaña. – **NS11)** Calle 7 N° 4-50, Tibú. – **NS12)** Calle 16 N° 2-17 (or: Ap. 473), Cúcuta. – **NS13)** Base Militar "San Jorge", Tibú. – **NS14)** Av. 2 N° 4-11, Bochalema. – **NS15)** Calle 12 N° 4-19, Ofc. 214, (or: Ap. 2582), Cúcuta. – **NS16)** Av. 0A N° 12-75, Ofc. 101 (or: Ap. 1303), Cúcuta. – **NS17)** Cra. 6 N° 4-59, P3 (or: Ap. 1074), Pamplona. – **NS18)** Av. 4 N° 11-17, Ofc. 303, Cúcuta. – **NS19)** Cra. 2 N° 1-10, Puerto Santander. – **NS20)** Av. 5 N° 9-58, P2, Edif. Mut.Aux (or: Ap. 151), Villa del Rosario.

PU00) PUTUMAYO

PU01) Calle Principal, Orito. – **PU02)** Calle 10 N° 6-01 (or: Ap. 011), Mocoa. – **PU03)** 19A Barrio Oriental, Sibundoy. - **FM:** 107.3. – **PU04)** Calle 11 N° 17-18 (or: Ap. 9), Puerto Asís.

QU00) QUINDÍO

QU01) Cra 16 N° 19-23, P10, Armenia. – **QU02)** Calle 9 N° 13-50 (or Ap. 2361), Armenia. – **QU03)** Ap. 2481, Armenia. – **QU04)** Ap. 556, Calarca. – **QU06)** Cra. 14 N° 21-26, P2, (or: km 2 via al Aeropuerto), Armenia. - **FM:** 104.7 Robles FM Stereo. – **QU07)** Calle 21 N° 16-31, Ofc 702, (or: Ap. 617), Armenia. – **QU08)** Universidad del Quindío, Av.Bolívar Cra.15 Calle 12 Norte, Armenia. **Web:** www.uniquindio.edu.co **Email:** uq@uniquindio.edu.co - **FM:** 102.1. – **QU09)** Cra.24 N° 39-52, Calarca. – **QU10)** Palacio Municipal de Armenia, Armenia.

RI00) RISARALDA

RI01) Ap. 354, Pereira. – **RI02)** Ap. 045, Pereira. – **RI03)** Ap. 221, Pereira. – **RI04)** La Virginia. – **RI05)** Cra. 7a N° 18-21, Of. 1103, Pereira. – **RI06)** Cra. 7 N° 15-10, P3 (or: Ap. 1262), Pereira. – **RI07)** Cra. 15 N° 11-80, Santa Rosa de Cabal (or: Calle 19 N° 8-74, Pereira). – **RI08)** Palacio Municipal, Pereira. – **RI09)** Calle 17 N° 9-10, Marsella. – **RI10)** Centro Administrativo Municipal, Dosquebradas. – **RI11)** Palacio Municipal de Balboa, Balboa. – **RI12)** Palacio Municipal de La Ceila La Ceila.

SS00) SANTANDER DEL SUR

SS01) Ap. 915, Bucaramanga. – **SS02)** Ap. 223, Bucaramanga. – **SS03)** Calle 50 N° 17-71, P3, Barrancabermeja. – **SS04)** Cra. 27 N° 45-80, Bucaramanga. – **SS05)** Ap. 007, Bucaramanga. – **SS06)** Calle 36 N° 14-58, Ofc.707, Floridablanca. – **SS07)** Calle 16 N° 15-01, Socorro. – **SS08)** Transv. 6 N° 9-56, Barbosa. – **SS09)** Batallón de Artillería de Defensa Aerea N° 2 "Nueva Granada" (or: Ap. 036), Barrancabermeja. – **SS10)** Ap. 1100, Bucaramanga. – **SS11)** Calle 10 N° 9-71, San Gil. – **SS12)** Calle 48 N° 35A-25, Bucaramanga. – **SS13)** Edif.Súper Estrellas, Ofc.409 (or: Ap. 23), Barrancabermeja. – **SS14)** Calle 7 N° 17-44, Barbosa. – **SS15)** Ap. 578, Barrancabermeja. – **SS16)** Calle 12 N° 10-30, San Gil. – **SS17)** Calle 16 N° 4-47, Zapatoca. –**SS18)** Calle 35 N° 20-39 (or: Ap. 3104), Bucaramanga. – **SS19)** Cra. 4 N° 4-118, P2, Cimitarra. – **SS20)** Cra. 3 N° 3-42, Vélez. – **SS21)** Calle 20 N° 6-36, Zapatoca. –**SS22)** Cra. 20 N° 36-06, P9, Edif.De La Sagrada Familia, Bucaramanga. **Email:** radiocatolica1450@hotmail.com – **SS23)** Calle 41 N° 19-87, Bucaramanga. – **SS24)** Batallón Luciano D'Ahuyar, San Vicente de Chucurí. – **SS25)** Calle 12 N° 17-10, Ofc.302 (or: Ap. 250), Barrancabermeja. – **SS26)** Pasaje Carrillo Casas 13-15, P3, Málaga. – **SS27)** Cra. 13 N° 34, Esquina Socorro. – **SS28)** Cra.27, Calle 9, Televis, Bucaramanga. – **SS29)** Palacio Municipal de San Andrés, San Andrés.

SU00) SUCRE

SU01) Ap. 167, Sincelejo. – **SU02)** Cra. 18 N° 20-48 (or: Ap. 448), Sincelejo. – **SU03)** Cra. 24 N° 29-50 (or: Ap. 100), Corozal. –
SU04) Cra. 20 N° 16-40 (or: Ap. 191), Sincelejo. – **SU05)** Calle 20 N° 24-93, Av. las Penitas, Sincelejo. – **SU07)** Cra. 20 N° 25-82 (or: Ap. 542), Corozal. – **SU08)** Cra. 20 N° 21-46 (or: Ap. 303), Sincelejo. – **SU09)** Cra. 28 Calle 18, San Marcos. – **SU10)** Calle 25A N° 18, Sincelejo. – **SU11)** Cra. 20 N° 25-92, P2, Sincelejo. – **SU12)** Palacio Municipal de Ovejas,

Ovejas. – **SU13)** Palacio Munivipal de Majagual, Majagual.
TO00) TOLIMA
TO01) Calle 12 N° 1-17, P5, Ibagué. - **FM:** 96.3. – **TO02)** Calle 14 N° 2A-14, P2, Ibagué. – **TO03)** Parque Murillo Toro N° 3-29, P4, Ibagué. – **TO04)** Cra 7 con Calle 10, Espinal. – **TO05)** Calle 11 N° 10-22, Guamo. – **TO06)** Ap. 2419, Ibagué. – **TO07)** Ap. 1094, Ibagué. **FM:** 93.9. – **TO08)** Calle 5 N° 6-25, Mariquita. – **TO09)** Calle 9 N° 1-124, P3, Ibagué. – **TO10)** Calle 11 N° 4-26 (or: Ap. 64), Espinal. – **TO11)** Ap. 536, Honda. – **TO12)** Ap. 509, Honda. – **TO13)** Cra. 2 N° 11-27, Flandes. – **TO14)** Cra 3 N° 12-76, Ofc.801 (or: Ap. 589), Ibagué. – **TO15)** Armero, Guayabal. – **TO16)** Cra. 13 N° 5-61, Libanó. – **TO17)** Cra. 7a N° 5-36, Dolores. – **TO18)** Calle 7 N° 20-70, Melgar. – **TO19)** Cra. 2 N° 3-74, Rovira. –**TO20)** Palacio Municipal de Cajamarca, Cajamarca. – **TO21)** Palacio Municipal de Palo Cabildo, Palo Cabildo. – **TO22)** Palacio Municipal de Venadillo, Venadillo.
VA00) VALLE DEL CAUCA
VA01) Cra. 26 N° 5C-25, San Fernando, Cali. – **VA02)** Cra. 38D Diagonal 37A-52B/Santa Isabel, Cali. – **VA03)** Ap. 1941, Cali. **Email:** Gerencia: caracolra@emcali.net.co – Dir.Técnico: caracol@emcali. net.co – **VA04)** Ap. 4666, Cali. – **VA05)** Cra. 14 N° 2-25, P2 (or: Ap. 96), Buga. **Web:** www.pablus.net/vocesdeoccidente – **VA06)** Av. 5B Norte N° 21-02, Cali. 🖷 +57 92 667 5536. – **VA07)** Cra. 33 N° 28-51 (Ap. 280), Palmira. **Email:** radiopalmira@uni **Web**.net.co – **VA08)** Ap. 126, Tuluá. – **VA09)** Cra. 4A N° 10-75 (or: Ap. 145), Cartago. – **VA10)** Calle 21 Nte N° 3N-49, P5, Cali. **Email:** superam@telesat.com.co – **VA11)** Calle 12-39, Ofc 301, Edif.R.Buenaventura (Ap 383), Buenaventura. ☎ +57 92 242 4387. 🖷+57 092 242 2969. **Email:** fdradbue@col2.telecom.com.co – **VA12)** Cra. 16 N° 6-22, P2, Caicedonia. – **VA13)** Autopista Cali-Yumbo, km 4, Harinera de Occidente, Cali. – **VA14)** Cra. 30 N° 29-09, Palmira. – **VA15)** Cra 6 N° 54-08, Av. Simon Bolívar, Buenaventura. – **VA16)** Av. 3 Bis. N° 23CN-71, Cali – Mon and Fri "Manantial de Vida" rel. from Miami. – **VA17)** Cra. 11 N° 11-43, P2, Zarzal. – **VA18)** Cra. 29 N° 32-88/90 (or: Ap. 201), Palmira. – **VA19)** Cra. 14 N° 5-77, Buga. – **VA20)** Cra. 26 N° 28-72, Tuluá. – **VA21)** Calle 27 N° 33-35, Tuluá. – **VA22)** Av. Roosevelt N° 34-37, Cali. **Email:** redsonora@hotmail.com – **VA23)** Cra. 51 N° 49-21, Sevilla. – **VA24)** Calle 10 N° 6-87, P3, Cartago. – **VA25)** Calle 14 N° 4A-63, Andalucía. – **VA26)** Centro Fe y Esperanza, Cra 23A N° 13-60, Barrio Junín , Cali. – **VA27)** Cra. 13 N° 10-58, Cali. – **VA28)** Palacio Municipal de Caicedonia, Caicedonia. –**VA29)** Av.Roosevelt N° 28, Cali. (Or: Transversal 34 N° 149-23, Cedro Golf, SF de Bogotá) ☎+57 52 514 2641. 🖷+57 52 558 1113. – **VA30)** Palacio Municipal de Caicedonia, Caicedonia. – **VA31)** Palacio Municipal de Buenaventura, Buenaventura. – **VA32)** Palacio Municipal de Versalles, Versalles. – **VA33)** Cra. 13 N° 10-58, San Bosco, Cali.
VI00) VICHADA
VI01) Av. Orinoco, Puerto Carreño.
VP00) VAUPÉS
VP01) Mitú.

FM in Santafé de Bogotá: 88. 9 Super Estación (Super) – 89. 9 HJCK El Mundo en Bogotá – 90.4 Universidad Distrital (University) – 90. 9 La Mega (RCN) – 91. 9 Javeriana (Univrsity)– 92. 4 Policía Nacional – 92. 9 La Z (Todelar) – 93.4 Colombia Estéreo (Colombian Army) – 93. 9 Amor Estéreo (RCN) – 94. 9 La FM (RCN) – 95. 9 Nacional – 96. 9 Melodía – 97. 4 40 Principales (Caracol) – 97.9 Radioactiva (Caracol) – 98. 5 Universidad Nacional (University) – 99. 1 Canal Joven Nacional – 99. 9 W Radio (Caracol) – 100.4 Bésame (Caracol) – 100. 9 Caracol Colombia (rel. 810 kHz) – 101. 9 Candela (W Radio) – 102. 9 Tropicana (Caracol) – 103. 9 La X (Todelar) – 104.4 La Vallenata (Caracol) – 104. 9 Vibra Bogotá (W Radio) – 105.4 Rumba Stereo (RCN) – 105. 9 Olímpica – 106. 9 Universidad Jorge Tados Lozano (University) – 107. 9 Minuto de Dios (rel).

COMOROS

L.T: UTC +3h — **Pop:** 596,200 — **Radios:** 61,000 — **Pr.L:** French, Comorian, Arabic — **E.C:** 50Hz, 220V — **ITU:** COM.

RADIO COMORO (Gov.)

🖃 BP 452, Moroni, Grand Comoro. ☎ +269 (73) 2531. 🖷 +269 (73) 0303. **LP**: Tech. Dir: Abdulkader Radjab.
MW/SW: transmitters inactive
FM: Moroni, R.Studio 1 101.2MHz. Nkazi, R.Nkazi 107.0MHz. 6 x 1kW, 3 x 0.5kW tr's.
D.Prgr: 0300-1900. **N. in French:** 1030, 1700.
ANN: F: "Ici Radio Comoro" – **V.** by letter. Rp. Rec.acc.

Other stations:
R. Anjouan: 88.0/94.0/102MHz
R. Dziyalandze: Anjouan 90.0MHz (rel. RFI 1700-1030).
R. Ndzouani: freq. not known
R. France Intl: 103.0MHz.

CONGO (Dem. Rep.)

L.T: Kinshasa & western part: UTC +1h, eastern part: UTC +2h — **Pop:** 54m — **Pr.L:** French, Lingala, Swahili, Tshiluba, Kikongo — **E.C:** 50Hz, 220V — **ITU:** COD

HAUTE AUTORITÉ DES MÉDIAS (HAM)

🖃 Kinshasa. **L.P:** President: Modeste Mutinga.

RADIO-TÉLÉVISION NATIONALE CONGOLAISE (RTNC)

🖃 B.P. 3171,Kinshasa-Gombe ☎ +243 12 23171-5. **L.P:** D.G: E. K. Mukambilwa, Deputy D.G: M. Makuala.
Stations:
SW: 2) v7435kHz (irr.).
FM: 1) 91.8/100.4MHz – **3)** 88.9MHz 1.5kW – **4)** 93.3MHz 1.5kW/90MHz 0.05kW – **6)** 89.1MHz 50kW – **9)** 94.8MHz – **11)** 93.7MHz.
Addresses and other information
1) B.P. 3171, Kinshasa-Gombe. 24h in French/Swahili/Lingala/Tshiluba/Kikongo. **N. in French:** 0100, 0300, 0500, 0600, 0700, 0900, 1000, 1130, 1300, 1400, 1500, 1800, 2000, 2200, 2300 – also rel. by other sts. **ANN:** "RTNC, Radio-Télévision Nationale Congolaise, emettant de Kinshasa" – **2)** B.P. 7296, Lubumbashi. W 0300-0700, 1000-1245, 1500-2100v; Sun 0300-1830v. – **3)** RTNC Kivu, B.P. 475, Bukavu. W 0300-0700, 1000-1245, 1500-1830; Sun 0300-1830 in French/Swahili - **Regional N. in French:** 0430, 0630, 1030, 1630. – **4)** B.P. 1061, Mbandaka. W 0500-0800, 1000-1200, 1600-2100; Sat 0500-0800, 1000-2200; Sun 0500-2200. **N.** 0430 1030 1630. – **5)** B.P. 1232, Mbuji-Mayi – **6)** B.P. 708, Kananga, Kasai Occidental – **7)** B.P. 704, Matadi – **8)** B.P. 1745, Kisangani. 0400-2200 – **9)** Butembo, Nord-Kivu. In Swahili – **10)** Goma, Nord-Kivu. On FM in French/ Swahili – **11)** Ulvira, Sud-Kivu. In French.
F.PI: 10 kW SW transmitters in Goma and Bukavu and 100 kW FM transmitters in all main cities.

RADIO CANDIP

🖃 Centre d'Animation et de Diffusion Pedagogique, B.P. 373, Bunia.
SW: Bunia 5066v kHz 1kW.
FM: 91.4/95/98MHz 0.02kW.
D.Prgr: 0400-0700, 1300-1600.

RADIO KAHUZI (Rlg.)

Web: www.besi.org **Email:** besi@alltel.net
SW: Bukavu 6210v kHz 0.8kW. **FM:** 91.1MHz. **D.Prgr:** 0500-1630 in English, French, Kikongo, Mashi, Lingala and Swahili.

RADIO OKAPI

(joint initiative between the UN Mission in the DRC [MONUC] and Hirondelle Foundation)
🖃 QG Monuc, 12 Av. des Aviateurs, Kinshasa-Gombe ☎ +243 896 4258 **Web:** www.radiookapi.net **Email:** info@monuc.org
L.P: Dir: David Smith. Station Mgr: Philippe Dahinden. Head of Tech. Sces: Georges Schleger.
SW: Kinshasa 6030/9550/11690kHz 10kW (irr.).
FM (MHz, powers 1-5kW): Isiro 90.1, Beni 92, Butembo 92.9, Kananga/Gbadolite 93, Mbuji-Mayi 93.8, Kisangani 94.8, Bukavu 95.3, Lubumbashi 95.8, Kanya Bayonga/Mahagi 96, Kindu/Mbandaka 103, Kinshasa 103.5, Bunia 104.9, Kalemie 105, Goma 105.2, Uvira 105.5.
D.Prgr: 0430-2200 in in French/Lingala/Swahili/Tshiluba.

RADIO TANGAZENI KRISTO (RTK)

(joint operation of Communauté Evangélique au Centre de l'Afrique (CECA-20) and Die Gute Nachricht für Afrika (DIGUNA)).
🖃 c/o DIGUNA e.V., Am Lohgraben 5, D/35708 Haiger, Germany. **Email:** buero@diguna.de
SW: Aru 4845kHz 0.3kW. **FM:** Bunia 88.6MHz, Aru/Kwandruma 90MHz. **D.Prgr** Swahili/French/English/local languages: D 0330-0515, Mon-Fri 1400-1930, SS 1155-1930.

Other stations:
R. Artemis, Bunia: 90.2MHz.
R. Butembo: 100MHz.
Canal Congo pour Christ, Bukavu: 97.3MHz.
R. Canal Révélation, Bunia: freq. unk.
R. Congo FM, Kinshasa 96.4MHz.
R. Elikya (rlg.), Kinshasa: 97.5MHz.
R. Maria Malkia wa Amani: Bukavu 94 & 97MHz. **Web:** www.radiomaria-bukavu.best.cd
R. Moto: Kivu 103MHz 1.2kW, Butembo 106MHz (also rel. RFI).
R. Raga FM: Kinshasa 90.5MHz 1.1kW. (Also rel. BBC & VOA). **Web:**

www.raga.net/RagaFm.htm **Email:** webmaster@raga.net
R. Rehema, Bukavu: 99.7MHz.
R. Reveil FM, 503 Blvd. du 30 juin, Kinshasa-Gombe: 105.4MHz. 0430-2330. **Web:** reveilfm.itgo.com
R. RTKM, Kananga: 97.5MHz (also rel. RFI).
R. Télé Mosaïque, Likasi: 88.5MHz (also rel. RFI).
R. Tomisa, B.P. 7245, Kikwit: 97.5MHz 0.5kW (also rel. RFI).
Africa No. 1: Kinshasa 102MHz (see main entry under Gabon).
BBC African Sce: Kinshasa 92.7MHz.
RFI Afrique: Bunia 90.2MHz, Bukavu/Kisangani/Lubumbashi/ Matadi 98MHz, Kinshasa 105MHz.

CONGO (Rep.)

L.T: UTC +1h — **Pop:** 3m — **Pr.L:** French, Lingala, Kikongo — **E.C:** 50Hz, 230V — **ITU:** COG.

ADMINISTRATION CENTRALE DES POSTES ET TÉLÉCOMMUNICATIONS (DGACPT)

🖃 Avenue Paul Doumer B.P. 2490, Brazzaville ☎ +242 811693 🖷 +242 814554.

TELEDIFFUSION DU CONGO

🖃 Direction Générale, B.P. 2912, Brazzaville ☎ +242 810608.
L.P: Pres: Jean Gilbert Foutou. DG: Jean Médard Bokatola. English Sce: Roger Olingou. Admin.&Financial Dir: Felix Lossombo.
MW: Brazzaville 1476kHz 20kW (inactive).
SW: Brazzaville (G.C: 04S15 015E18) 50kW.

kHz	H. of tr.	kHz	H. of tr.
5985*	0430-0600, 1700-2130	6115	0600-0830, 1700-2030
9610	0600-1700		

*alt. 4765kHz
FM: 90.1/94.0/96.4MHz
National Network: 0430-2130. **Main N. in French:** 0500, 0700, 0800, 1200, 1400, 1800, 2100. **N. in English:** SS 1835, Mon-Thurs 1900, Fri 1930. **ANN:** "Radio Congo, Chaîne Nationale".
IS: Zansi solo. Opens and closes with National Anthem.

Other stations:
R. Rurale (community st's set up by the development agency ACTT): st's are operating in Sembé, Étoumbi, Nkayi & Mossendjo.
R. Brazzaville: 98.0MHz.
BBC African Sce: Brazzaville 103.8MHz.
RFI Afrique: Brazzaville/Pointe-Noire 93.2MHz.
Africa No. 1: Brazzaville 89.6MHz (see main entry under Gabon).

COOK ISLANDS

L.T: UTC -10h — **Pop:** 20,611 — **Pr.L:** English, Maori — **E.C:** 50Hz, 220V — **ITU:** CKH.

ELIJAH COMMUNICATIONS

🖃 P.O. Box 126, Avarua, Rarotonga. ☎ +682 29460. 🖷 +682 21907.
L.P: C.E.O: George Pitt. **Web:** http://radio.co.ck.
Email: jeanne@ oyster.net.ck
MW: Matavera 630kHz 2.5kW (2.5kW reserve).
D.PRGR: 1630-0930 weekdays, 1730-0930 Sun, 1630-1030 Fri, Sat.
National N: 1600W, 1645W, 2230, 0130, 0330, 0530, 0730. **N. in English** (rel. R. NZ): 1730, 1830, 1930. **ANN:** "This is Radio Cook Islands calling". **IS:** Symphony of Drums – **V.** by QSL-card. Rp.

KIA ORANA COUNTRY RADIO (Comm.)

🖃 P.O. Box 521, Avarua, Rarotonga. ☎ +682 23203.
L.P: Pres. & GM: David Schmidt.
FM: Penrhyn 95.3MHz 1kW, Rarotonga 103.3MHz 1kW.
D.PRGR: MF 1600-0900, Sat 1600-1000, Sun 1700-0800. **N:** on the h (rel. R. NZ or ABC) – **V.** by letter.

COSTA RICA

L.T: UTC -6h (Su: UTC -5h) — **Pop:** 4.3 million — **Pr.L:** Spanish — **E.C:** 60Hz, 120V — **ITU:** CTR.

CONTROL NACIONAL DE RADIO (CNR)

🖃 Ministerio de Gobernación y Policia, Ap.10006, 1000 San José. ☎ +506 221 0992, 221 9910.

CAMARA NACIONAL DE RADIO (CANARA)

🖃 Ap.1583, 1002 San José. ☎ +506 233 1845. 🖷 +506 255 4483.
Email: canara@sol.racsa.co.cr

MW: Call TI–,
° = also on SW, * = inactive, (r) = repeater, v = varying fq.

	Call	kHz	kW	Name and h. of tr.
1)	CAL	v530	18	R. Sinfonola, Cartago: (r: FM 90.3)
2)	SCL	550	20/2	R. Santa Clara, Cd. Quesada: 1100-0300
3)	CDL	570	6.5	R. Libertad, Desamparados: 24h
4)	RN	590	5	R. Nacional, San José: 24h
6)	RSU	610	4	R. María, San José
5)	AD	640	20	R. Rica, San José: 1130-0400
7)	RM	670	10	R. Monumental, San José: 24h
12)	JC	700	10	R. Sonora, San José: 1100-0400
8)	HB	*730	20	R. 730, San José: 24h
9)	LX	760	20	R. Columbia, San José: 24h
10)	RA	780	10	R. América, San José: 1000-0500 (Sun -0400)
59)	W	800	5	R. Unica, San José: 24h
11)	GC	820	2.5	R. Centro AM, San José: 1130-0600
58)	W	850	20	R. Tigre, San José
13)	UCR	°870	5	R. Universidad de Costa Rica, San José: 1300-0600
7)	HOT	890	10	R. Fabulosa, San José: 1100-0500
14	)QM	910	1	R. Metrópolis, San José: 24h
53)	RCR	930	5	R. Costa Rica, San José: 24h (Prgr: Telemundo Internacional 0400-1300)
54)	CS	960	5	Premium Radio, San José: 24h
7)	RI	980	20	R. Favorita, San José: 1100-0500
17)	MIL	1000	10/1	Mil FM, San José: 24h
29)	TIC	v1020	2	R. Mil Veinte, San José: 1100-0500
18)	AC	1040	10	R. Fides, San José: 1000-0500
60)	HG	1040	2	R. Nosara, Hojancha: 1100-1400, 2100-2300
9)	LX	1060	1	R. Columbia, San Isidro del General (r: 760)
9)	LX	1060	1	R. Columbia, Liberia (r: 760)
19)	FC	°1080	19	Faro del Caribe, San José: 24h
20)	SCR	1100	5	R. Chorotega, Santa Cruz: 0900-0600
16)		1120		Unción Radio, San José: 24h
15)	VAL	1140	1.5	R. Nueva, Guápiles
9)	LX	1160	3	R. Columbia, Puntarenas (r: 760)
22)	PJ	1180	20	R. Victoria, Heredia: 1100-0400
23)	AM	1200	5	R. Cucú, San José: 1000-0600
21)	Q	°1220	1	R. Casino, Limón: 1030-0600
9)	LX	1240	1	R. Columbia, Nicoya (r: 760)
24)	HM	1260	5	R. Emaús, San Vito de Coto Brus: 1100-0300
25)	HT	v1280	2	R. Alajuela, Alajuela: 1030-0300 (F.Pl: Estéreo Visión, San José)
26)	LC	1300	7.5	La Fuente Musical, Cartago: 0500-1300
27)	HR	1340	6	R. Sideral, San Ramón: 1000-0400
53)	CA	1360		R. Celestial, San José: 24h
28)	MS	1380	1	R. Guanacaste, Liberia: 1000-0500
28)	MS	1380	1	R. Guanacaste, San José (r: 1380)
61)	CJ	1400	12	R. Sinaí, San Isidro del General: 1000-0400
33)	RP	1420	5	R. Pampa, Nicoya: 1000-0300
30)	RSC	1430	12	R. San Carlos, Cd. Quesada: 1100-0400
9)	LX	1460	2	R. Columbia, Limón (r: 760)
49)	AW	1480	1	R. Caracol, Puntarenas: 1200-0400
55)	RC	1500	15	R. Cima, Cd. Quesada: 1100-0300
62)	ECC	1520	2	R. Cartago, Cartago: 1100-0400
52)		1540		Enlace Radio, Pavas
32)	RN	1560	6	R. Nicoya, Nicoya: 1000-0300
26)		1580	10	R. Mi País, Siquirres
34)	RCLS	1580	0.25	R. Cultural Los Santos, San Marcos
35)	RCC	1580	0.25	R. Cultural de Corredores, Cd. Neily
36)	RCLC	1580	0.25	R. Cultural, La Cruz
37)	RCM	1580	0.25	R. Cultural Maleku, Tonjibe
38)	RCL	1580	0.25	R. Cultural, Los Chiles
45)	LGJ	1590	2	R. 16, Grecia: 1100-0400
39)	RCN	1600	0.25	R. Cultural Nicoyano, Nicoya
40)	RCT	1600	0.25	R. Cultural, Turrialba
41)	RCBA	1600	0.25	R. Cultural, Buenos Aires
42)	RCP	v1600	0.25	R. Cultural, Pital
43)	RCU	1600	0.25	R. Cultural, Upala
44)		1600	0.25	LV de Talamanca
50)	JV	1600	3/2	R. 88 Stereo, San Isidro del General: 1100-0300
46)	MMCH	1600	2/1	R. Golfito, Pto Golfito: 24h
47)	MQ	1600	1.5	R. Pococí, Guápiles: 1100-0400
51)		1600	0.25	R. Quepos, Pto Quepos

SW:
Stations with a (*) are reported to be inactive, but may occasionally be reactivated for variable periods of time.

	Call	kHz	kW	Name and h. of tr.
49)		3040		R. Puntarenas (r: 91.9 FM)
19)	FC	*5055	5	Faro del Caribe, San José
21)	Q	*5954	1	R. Casino, Limón

Call	kHz	kW	Name and h. of tr.
13) UCR	6105	10	R. Universidad de Costa Rica "R. U", San José
19) FC	*6175	2.5	Faro del Caribe, San José
19) FC	*9645	5	Faro del Caribe, San José

EXTERNAL SERVICES: R. Exterior de España, University Network and **Radio For Peace International** see International Broadcasting section

Addresses and other information:
1) Ap. 140, 7050 Cartago. – **2)** Ap. 221, 4400 Cd. Quesada. **Email:** notirsc@racsa.co.cr ☎ +506 460 7360. 🖷 +506 460 2151. – **3)** Ap. 301, 2400 Desamparados. ☎ +506 259 7090. – **4)** Ap. 7-1980 (or: La Uruca 1 km Oeste Parque Diversionales), 1000 San José ☎+506 220 0072. 🖷+506 290 4373. **Email:** sinart@racsa.co.cr ☎ +506 231 3333. 🖷 +506 231 6604. **Web:** www.sinart.com/Radio/Radionacional.htm **Email:** sinart@sol.racsa.co.cr – **5)** Ap. 3835, 1000 San José. – **6)** 1000 San José. – **7)** Ap. 800 (or: Costado Oeste del Puente Juan Pasco II), 1000 San José. **Email:** radio@monumental.co.cr - **Web:** www.monumental.co.cr ☎ +506 296 6093. 🖷 +506 296 6042. – **8)** Ap. 341 (or: 700 metros al sur del Parque de La Paz, Carr. a Desamparados), 1000 San José. **Email:** info@radioreloj.co.cr **Web:** www.radioreloj.co.cr ☎ +506 286 2636. 🖷+506 226 5579. – **9)** Ap. 708, 1000 San José. **Web:** www.columbia.co.cr – **10)** Ap. 1951, 2100 Guadalupe. ☎+506 222 8036. **Web:** www.radioamerica780am.com – **11)** Ap. 6133, 1000 San José. ☎+506 240 7373 – **12)** Family Christian Network, Ap. 60-2020, Zapote. – **13)** Cd. Universitaria Rodrigo Facio, 2060 San Pedro de Montes de Oca. **Web:** http://cariari.ucr.ac.cr/~radioucr **Email:** radioucr@cariari.ucr.ac.cr ☎ +506 225 3936. 🖷 +506 207 5459. – **14)** Ap. 2006, 1100 San José. **Web:** www.rrb.org ☎+506 286 5272 – **15)** Casa Cultural de Guápiles, 7210 Guápiles. ☎ +506 710 3113. 🖷 +506 710 7321. – **16)** De la rotonda de la Y, 200 m al este y 25 m sur, San José. ☎+506 226 6832 – **Email:** uncionradio@yahoo.com – **17)** Ap. 10. 001, 1000 San José. ☎+506 225 1000 – **18)** Ap. 5079, 1000 San José. ☎ +506 258 1415. 🖷 +506 233 2387. **Web:** www.radiofides.co.cr – **19)** Ap. 2710, 1000 San José. ☎+506 227 1725. **Web:** www.farodelcaribe.org **Email:** tifc@farodelcaribe.org – **20)** Ap. 92, 5175 Santa Cruz. ☎/🖷 +506 680 0447. – **21)** Ap. 287, 7301 Puerto Limón. ☎ +506 758 0029. 🖷 +506 758 3029. - **FM:** 98.3. – **22)** Ap. 298, 3000 Heredia. – **23)** Ap. 1128, 1000 San José. ☎+506 257 1314 – **24)** Ap.266, 8257 San Vito de Coto Brus. **Email:** rademaus@racsa.co.cr or radioemaus@sol.racsa.co.cr ☎ +506 773 3101. 🖷+506 773 4035. - **FM:** 103.9. – **25)** Ap. 122, (or: Lotes Aguilar) 4050 Alajuela **Email:** radioala@sol.racsa.co.cr ☎ +506 440 2627.🖷 +506 441 9666. – **26)** Ap. 596, 7050 Cartago. – **27)** Ap. 73, 4250 San Ramón. – **28)** Ap. 27, 5600 Liberia, (or: Ap. 6462, 1000 San José). – **29)** Ap. 8130, 1002 San José. – **30)** Ap. 25, 4400 Cd. Quesada. – **32)** Ap. 50, 5200 Nicoya. – **33)** Ap. 66, 5200 Nicoya. – **34-44)** St`s are affiliated to Instituto Costarricense de Enseñanza Radiofónica, Ap.132, 2050 San Pedro de Montes de Oca (Ministerio de Educación Pública). – **45)** Ap. 16, 4100 Grecia. ☎+506 494 5356. 🖷+506 494 2031. **Web:** www.radio16.com **Email:** gerencia@radio16.com – **46)** Ap. 11, Pto Golfito, (or: Ap. 1954, 2100 Guadalupe) **Email:** crystal@sol.racsa.co.cr ☎ +506 224 1119.🖷 +506 225 3437. – **47)** Ap. 160, 7210 Guápiles. – **49)** Ap. 708, 1000 San José (or: Puntarenas Centro, Puntarenas). – **50)** Ap. 827, 8000 San Isidro del General. **Web:** www.88stereo.com ☎+506 771 6094 🖷 +506 771 6093. – **51)** 6350 Quepos. – **52)** Ap. 23, 1200 Pavas. **Web:** www.enlace.org **Email:** radio@enlace.org – **53)** Ap. 6462, 1000 San José. **Email:** radiocelestial@costarricense.cr – **54)** 100 metros Norte, 50 metros al Oeste, entrada de Emergencia del Hospital Calderón Guardia, 1000 San José. ☎ +506 257 3131. – **55)** Ap. 300, 4400 Cd. Quesada. – **58)** Ap. 695, 2100 Guadalupe. – **59)** 1000 San José. – **60)** Casa Cultural de Hojancha, Hojancha, Guanacaste. ☎ +506 659 9028. 🖷 +506 659 9038. – **61)** Ap. 262, 8000 San Isidro del General. ☎ +506 771 4367. 🖷 +506 771 0598. – **62)** Altos de Apolo, frente al Palacio Municipal, Cartago.

FM in San José and vicinities: 88.3 El Mundo – 88.5 88 Stereo – 88.7 Lira – 89.1 Momentos – 89.5 Sendas de Vida – 89.9 Bésame 8 99 – 90.3 Sinfonola – 90.7 Ritmo 907 – 91.1 911 – 91.5 Activa – 91.9 Puntarenas – 92.3 EXA-FM – 92.7 Columbia Stereo – 93.1 Fides – 93.5 Monumental – 93.9 Sonido Latino – 94.3 Reloj – 94.7 "94.7" – 95.1 Z-FM – 95.5 95 Cinco Jazz – 95.9 Eco – 96.3 Centro – 96.7 "U" – 97.1 Faro del Caribe – 97.5 Musical – 97.9 Conexión – 98.3 Visión – 98.7 Columbia – 99.1 Sabrosa – 99.5 R. Dos – 99.9 R. Azul – 100.3 La Paz del Dial – 100.7 Mil FM – 101.1 Sonido 101 – 101.5 Nacional – 101.9 "U" – 102.3 Super – 102.7 Uno – 103.1 "103" – 103.5 Punto Cinco – 103.9 Sinai – 104.3 Los 40 Principales – 104.7 R. Emperador – 105.1 Omega – 105.5 Omega – 105.9 Puntarenas – 106.3 Vox FM – 106.7 Rumba 106.7 – 107.1 Estéreo Actual – 107.5 Real Rock – 107.9 Bahía Puntarenas.

CROATIA

L.T: UTC +1h (27 Mar - 30 Oct 2005: UTC +2h) — **Pop:** 4.3 million — **Pr.L:** Croatian — **E.C:** 50Hz, 220V — **ITU:** HRV

HRVATSKA AGENCIJA ZA TELEKOMUNIKACIJE

✉ Jurišiceva 13, 10002 Zagreb. ☎ +385 1 4896000. 🖷 +385 1 4920227. **Email:** info@telekom.hr **Web:** www.telekom.hr
L.P: Chmn: Gašper Gacina.
NOTES: HZT is the regulatory authority for broadcasting.

HRVATSKI RADIO (Pub.)

✉ Prisavlje 3, 10000 Zagreb. ☎ +385 1 6342634. 🖷 +385 1 6343712. **Email:** ird@hrt.hr **Web:** www.hrt.hr
L.P: Dir: Ivanka Lucev

MW	kHz	kW	Prgr	MW	kHz	kW	Prgr
Osijek	594	20	HR GH	Hvar	774	50	HR GH
Buje	783	10	HR GH	Deanovec	1125	100	HR GH
Zadar	1134	600	HR GH	Osijek	1557	20	HR R. Osijek

FM (MHz)	HR1	HR2	HR3	kW
Beli Manastir	93.3	98.1	-	50
Biokovo	89.7	98.9	-	80
Borinci	88.3	96.1	-	3
Brac	99.8	-	88.8	3
Buje	91.3	103.7	93.2	1
Celavac	95.1	98.1	-	80
Drenovci	92.1	104.4	-	3
Gruda	101.7	106.1	-	2
Ivanšcica	102.4	106.4	96.1	15/15/30
Kalnik	90.8	105.8	107.8	15
Labinština	91.3	96.1	-	30
Licka Plješivica	87.7	90.5	-	50
Limski kanal	90.2	102.6	-	1
Mirkovica	91.3	93.3	-	30
Pag	98.5	103.4	-	3
Papuk	94.9	106.8	97.7	10
Psunj	97.3	99.7	-	80
Pula	91.4	102.1	94.2	5
Slavonski Brod	91.3	105.1	107.9	15/0.3/-
Sljeme	92.1	98.5	101.0	120
Srdj	88.9	98.5	-	30
Stipanov Gric	102.3	97.5	89.7	15
Ucka	99.3	105.3	-	80
Ugljan	91.6	87.6	-	5
Uljenje	95.1	103.0	105.6	3

NB. Tx's with outlets below 1kW not mentioned.
D.PRGR: HR1 (Prvi program): 24h. – **HR2 (Drugi program):** 24h. – **HR3 (Treci program):** 24h. – **HR GH (Glas Hrvatske):** 24h. Relays of HR1 & news in English, Hungarian, Italian, Spanish. Details see International Radio section: **Voice of Croatia (Glas Hrvatske).**

HR REGIONAL STATIONS (Pub.)
D.PRGR: all stn's 24h (incl. relays of HR1)
HR R. Dubrovnik: Dr. Ante Starcevica 21, 20000 Dubrovnik. ☎ +385 20 411411. 🖷 +385 20 411314. Email: redakcija@radiodubrovnik.com, Web: www.radiodubrovnik.com. On (MHz) 88.2 (Rota), 89.5 (Gruda), 97.2 (Blato), 101.1 (Vela Luka), 103.7 (Slano), 103.8 (Korcula), 105.0 (Srd), 106.2 (Lastovo), 106.5 (Lopud) – **HR R. Knin:** Kralja P. Krešimira IV 30, 23400 Knin. ☎ +385 22 660410. 🖷 +385 22 660523. Email: radio_knin@hrt.hr. On (MHz) 90.2 (Knin), 94.4 (Promina) – **HR R. Osijek:** Šamacka 13, 31000 Osijek. ☎ +385 31 225500. 🖷 +385 31 204660. Email: radioosijek@hrt.hr. On1557kHz + (MHz) 102.0 (Psunj), 102.4 (Drenovci & Osijek), 102.8 (Beli Manastir), 105.3 (Borinci), 105.6 (Zlatarevac), 105.8 (Ilok). Incl. Hungarian ("Eszéki Rádió"): 1730-1800 – **HR R. Pula:** Riva 10, 52100 Pula. ☎ +385 52 211936. 🖷 +385 52 210810. Email: radio_pula@hrt.hr. On (MHz) 93.8 (Novigrad), 93.9 (Limski kanal), 96.3 (Koromacno), 96.4 (Buje), 100.0 (Pula & Vrsar), 101.3 (Vcka), 103.8 (Raša) – **HR R. Rijeka:** Korzo 24, 51000 Rijeka. ☎ +385 51 657777. 🖷 +385 51 657745. Email: radiori@ri.tel.hr. On (MHz) 94.5 (Brgud), 95.1 (Pulac), 97.9 (Cres), 98.1 (Kupjacki Vrh), 100.3 (Licka Plješivica), 101.7 (Prezid), 102.7 (Mirkovica), 104.0 (Fuzine), 104.7 (Ucka), 107.4 (Mali Lošinj II), 107.5 (Mrkopalj). Incl. Italian: 0900-0903, 1100-1103, 1400-1403, 1500-1530. – **HR R. Sljeme:** Prisavlje 3, 10000 Zagreb. ☎ +385 1 6343258. 🖷 +385 1 6343202. Email: radio_sljeme@hrt.hr. On 88.1MHz (Sljeme) – **HR R. Split:** Mazuranicevo šetalište 24a, 21000 Split. ☎ +385 21 366666. 🖷 +385 21 366646. Email: radio_split@hrt.hr. On (MHz) 88.4 (Komiza), 100.2 (Hvar), 101.0 (Labinštica), 102.0 (Biokovo), 104.5 (Brac), 105.3 (Orlovaca), 105.8 (Vrlika) – **HR R. Zadar:** Poljana Šime Budinica 3, 23000 Zadar. ☎ +385 23 316111. 🖷 +385 23 313430. Email: radio_zadar@hrt.hr. On (MHz) 101.8 (Ugljan), 103.0 (Celevac), 105.9 (Pag).

OTHER STATIONS

FM	MHz	ERP	Location	Station
13)	87.8	1.85	Brac	R. Dalmacija
7)	88.0	3	Beli Monastir	R. Baranja
26)	88.6	3	Slavonski Brod	R. Slavonija
45)	89.0	1	Valpovo	Hrvatski R. Valpovština
49)	89.3	5.5	Zadar	Novi R.
25)	89.4	2	Sisak	R. Sisak
11)	89.6	1	Porec	R. Centar Porec
50)	89.7	4.68	Sljeme	Obitelski R.
34)	90.2	1	Vinkovci	Radio postaja Vincovci
28)	90.2	1	Slavonska Pozega	R. Vallis aurea
22)	90.3	1	Dugo Selo	R. Martin
44)	90.4	1	Vrlika	Hrvatski R. Sinj
48)	90.5	1	Komiza	Nautic R. Vis
35)	91.0	1	Dakovo	Slavonski R. Osijek
31)	91.6	5	Vinkovci	R. VFM
19)	91.7	5	Koprivnica	R. Koprivnica (RKC)
44)	92.2	1	Krizice	Hrvatski R. Sinj
37)	92.4	2	Alaginci	Zupanijski R. Pozega
2)	92.6	2	Zagreb	Otvoreni R.
32)	92.9	1.9	Virovitica	R. Virovitica
11)	93.6	7	Rusnjak	R. Centar Porec
18)	93.8	1	Jastrebarsko	R. Jaska
42)	94.4	6	Cetingrad	Hrvatski R. Karlovac
47)	94.7	1	Hvar	Megamix R. Hvar
24)	94.8	1	Rovinj	R. Rovinj
30)	94.9	5	Velika Gorica	R. Velika Gorica (RVG)
1)	95.3	3	Osijek	Narodni R.
45)	95.4	5	Drenovci	Hrvatski R. Vukovar
23)	95.4	1	Duga Resa	R. Mreznica
19)	95.5	5	Kalnik	R. Koprivnica (RKC)
3)	95.5	1	Ugljan	Hrvatski Katolicki R.
27)	95.6	2	Donja Stubica	R. Stubica
21)	96.4	1	Zagreb	R. Marija
52)	96.5	1	Rijeka	Primorski R.
4)	96.5	1	Varazdin Breg	R. 042
17)	96.9	5	Ucka	R. Istra
20)	97.6	4	Bogomolje	R. Makarska Rivijera (RMR)
3)	97.9	1	Split	Hrvatski Katolicki R.
51)	98.0	5	Zagreb	Plavi R.
17)	98.0	5	Pula	R. Istra
43)	98.1	1	Nova Gradiska	Hrvatski R. Nova Gradiska
36)	98.4	1	Rijeka	Svid R.
3)	98.6	1	Osijek	Hrvatski Katolicki R.
19)	98.8	5	Zabno	R. Koprivnica (RKC)
15)	99.1	2	Bijele Vode	R. Glina
40)	99.1	1	Osijek	Gradski R. Osijek
33)	99.5	1	Zapresic	R. Zapresic
41)	99.5	1	Sveta Marija	Hrvatski R. Cakovec
39)	100.1	5	Moslavacka Gora	Bjelovarsko-Bilogorski R.
14)	100.2	1	Djakovo	R. Djakovo
35)	100.6	1	Osijek	Slavonski R. Osijek
38)	100.7	3	Zirje	Zupanijski R. Sibenik
1)	101.2	3	Metkovic	Narodni R.
10)	101.3	1	Slavonski Brod	R. Brod
19)	101.5	5	Sedlarica	R. Koprivnica (RKC)
22)	101.8	1	Zagreb	R. Martin
37)	102.4	2	Pakrac	Zupanijski R. Pozega
9)	102.7	1	Brac	R. Brac
3)	103.5	3	Sljeme	Hrvatski Katolicki R.
3)	103.9	3	Psunj	Hrvatski Katolicki R.
6)	104.0	1	Sveti Martin	R. 105
3)	104.1	1	Licka Plješivica	Hrvatski Katolicki R.
45)	104.1	1	Zupanja	Hrvatski R. Vukovar
2)	104.4	5	Papuk	Otvoreni R.
12)	104.5	1.85	Zagreb	R. Cibona
38)	104.9	5	Sibenik	Zupanijski R. Sibenik
8)	105.5	1	Okucani	R. Bljesak
5)	105.6	1.5	Cakovec	R. 1
16)	105.7	1.5	Stipanov Gric	R. Gospic
35)	106.2	5	Beli Manastir	Slavonski R. Osijek
3)	106.7	3	Ucka	Hrvatski Katolicki R.
21)	106.8	1	Zagreb	R. Marija
27)	106.9	2	Ostri Hum	R. Stubica
13)	106.9	1.85	Labinstica	R. Dalmacija
29)	107.1	4	Varazdin Breg	R. Varazdin
46)	107.2	5	Vinkovci	Hrvatski R. Vukovar
3)	107.9	3	Biokovo	Hrvatski Katolicki R.

NB. Tx's below 1kW not mentioned.

Addresses & other information:
1) Avenija Dubrovnik 15, 10000 Zagreb. Email: marketing@narodni.hr – **2)** Cebini 28, Buzin, 10000 Zagreb. Email: otvoreni@otvoreni.hr – **3)** Vocarska cesta 106, 10000 Zagreb. Email: hkr@hkr.hr – **4)** Trstenjakova 3, 42000 Varazdin. Email: radio-042@vz.tel.hr – **5)** Nova ulica 7, 40000 Cakovec. Email: marketing@radio1.hr – **6)** B. Radica 23, 40314 Selnica. Email: info@radio105.hr – **7)** Trg slobode 32/III, 31300 Beli Manastir. Email: radio@radio-baranja.hr – **8)** Blazenog kardinala A. Stepinca 24, 35430 Okucani. Email: radio-bljesak@sb.hinet.hr – **9)** Mladena Vodanovica 3, 21400 Supetar. Email: radio-brac@st.htnet.hr – **10)** Dr. Mile Budaka 1, 35 000 Slavonski Brod. Email: radio-brod@sb.hinet.hr – **11)** Vitomira Širole - Paje 18, 52440 Porec. Email: radio-centar-studio-porec@pu.tel.hr – **12)** Palmoticeva 7/I, 10000 Zagreb. Email: marketing@radio-cibona.hr – **13)** Kralja Zvonimira 14/2, 21000 Split. Email: marketing@radiodalmacija.hr – **14)** Bana Jelacica 6/5, 31400 Djakovo. Email: radio-djakovo@os.htnet.hr – **15)** Antuna i Stjepana Radica 8, 44400 Glina. Email: radio-glina@sk.htnet.hr – **16)** Trg Stjepana Radica 4, 53000 Gospic. Email: radio-gospic1@gs.htnet.hr – **17)** Jurja Dobrile 6, 52000 Pazin. Email: radioistra@radioistra.hr – **18)** Strossmayerov trg 5, 10450 Jastrebarsko. Email: radio-jaska@zg.hinet.hr – **19)** Zagrebacka b.b., 48000 Koprivnica. Email: radio-koprivnica@kc.htnet.hr – **20)** Don Mihovila Pavlinovica 1, 21300 Makarska. Email: radio-makarska-rivijera@st.hinet.hr – **21)** Jordanovac 110, 10000 Zagreb. Email: info@radiomarija.hr – **22)** Josipa Zorica 17, 10370 Dugo Selo. Email: radio.martin@zg.htnet.hr – **23)** Jozefinska cesta 8, 47250 Duga Resa. Email: radio-mreznica@ka.htnet.hr – **24)** Carducci 13, 52210 Rovinj. Email: arting-radio-rovinj@pu.tel.hr – **25)** Antuna i Stjepana Radica 2, 44000 Sisak. Email: radio-sisak@sk.htnet.hr – **26)** Mile Budaka 1, 35 000 Slavonski Brod. Email: radioslavonija@radioslavonija.hr – **27)** Toplicka 5, 49240 Donja Stubica. Email: radio-stubica@ht.hinet.hr – **28)** Cehovska 8/I, 34000 Pozega. Email: radio-vallis-aurea@po.tel.hr – **29)** Uršulinska 5, 42000 Varazdin. Email: info@radio-varazdin.hr – **30)** Zagrebacka 3, 10410 Velika Gorica. Email: radio@globalnet.hr – **31)** Trg Franje Tudjmana 2, 32100 Vinkovci. Email: vfm@vfm.hr – **32)** F. Rusana 1/IX, 33000 Virovitica. Email: rtv@icv.hr – **33)** Trg zrtava fašizma 6, 10290 Zapresic. Email: info-centar-zapresic@zg.tel.hr – **34)** Jurja Dalmatinca 29, 32100 Vinkovci. Email: radio-vinkovci@vk.htnet.hr – **35)** Hrvatske Republike 20, 31000 Osijek. Email: slavonski-radio@glas-slavonije.tel.hr – **36)** Trpimirova 2, 51000 Rijeka. Email: svid-radio@hi.hinet.hr – **37)** Antuna Kanizlica 3/I, 34000 Pozega. Email: radio.pozega@inet.hr – **38)** Bozidara Petranovica 3, 22000 Šibenik. Email: info@radiosibenik.hr – **39)** Trg E. Kvaternika bb, 43000 Bjelovar. Email: bbr@bbr.hr – **40)** Trg Ante Starcevica 7/1, 31000 Osijek. Email: marketing@eter.hr – **41)** Trg republike 5, 40000 Cakovec. Email: info@radio-cakovec.hr – **42)** Ambroza Vraniczanya 2, 47000 Karlovac. Email: radio.karlovac@ka.tel.hr – **43)** Relkoviceva 4, 35400 Nova Gradiška. Email: hr-nova-gradiska@sb.hinet.hr – **44)** Glavicka 29, 21230 Sinj. Email: radio-sinj@st.tel.hr – **45)** Kralja Petra Krešimira IV br.1, 31550 Valpovo. Email: hrvatski-radio-valpovstina@os.htnet.hr – **46)** Trg Drazena Petrovica 1, 32010 Vukovar. Email: hrvatski-radio-vukovar@vk.hinet.hr – **47)** Šime Ljubica 30, 21000 Split. Email: megamix@st.htnet.hr – **48)** V. Nazora 19, 21480 Vis. Email: nautic-radio@st.tel.hr – **49)** Opatice Vekenege 2, 23000 Zadar. Email: noviradio@noviradio.hr – **50)** Avenija Dubrovnik 15, 10000 Zagreb. Email: kontakt@obiteljski-radio.hr – **51)** Slavonska avenija 2, 10000 Zagreb. Email: marketing@plaviradio.hr – **52)** Barciceva 4a, 51000 Rijeka. Email: marketing@primorski-radio.hr.

DAB: 227.360 on 12C from Sljeme. Operated by OIV (HRT)

BFBS: Zagreb BFBS 1 on 106.0MHz

CUBA

L.T: UTC -5h (Su: UTC -4h) — **Pop:** 11.9 million — **PR. L:** Spanish — **E.C:** 60Hz, 110/120V — **ITU:** CUB.

MINISTERIO DE COMUNICACIONES (MC)
Dirección General de Telecomunicaciones
Plaza de la Revolución, Ciudad de la Habana.

INSTITUTO CUBANO DE RADIO Y TELEVISION (ICRT)
Edif.Radiocentro, Av. 23 N° 258, Vedado, Habana 4. ☎ +53 32 1568 +53 31 1723.

MW: Call CM-, v = varying fq.

	Call	kHz	kW	Primary network and location
1)		530		R. Rebelde
1)	HV	540	1	R. Rebelde, Sancti Spiritus, SS
1)	DN	550	10	R. Rebelde, Guantánamo, GU
1)		550	30	R. Rebelde, Pinar del Río, PR
1)		550	1	R. Rebelde, Manzanillo, GR
1)		560	5	R. Rebelde, Moa, HO

	Call	kHz	kW	Primary network and location
2)	DC	570	30	R. Reloj, Santa Clara, VC
1)	DF	580	5	R. Rebelde, Baracoa, GU
1)	AM	580	10	R. Rebelde, Mantua, PR
1)	HI	590	30	R. Rebelde, Santa Clara, VC
1)	KV	600	150	R. Rebelde, Urbano Noris, HO
1)	AN	610	1	R. Rebelde, Bahía Honda, PR
2)	HI	610	1	R. Reloj, Trinidad, SS
1)	KF	620	1	R. Rebelde, Moa, HO
1)	GN	620	30	R. Rebelde, Colón, MA
4)		630	5	R. Progreso, Pinar del Río, PR
4)	BC	640	50	R. Progreso, Guanabacoa, HA
4)	DQ	640	10	R. Progreso, Las Tunas, LT
1)	DD	640	5	R. Rebelde, Las Mercedes, GR
1)	KU	650	1	R. Rebelde, Stgo de Cuba, SC
1)	DC	650	1	R. Rebelde, Media Luna, GR
4)	HG	660	30	R. Progreso, Santa Clara, VC
1)	BA	670	50	R. Rebelde, Arroyo Arenas, CH
1)	JV	680	10	R. Rebelde, Ciego de Ávila, CA
4)	HN	680	1	R. Progreso, Cienfuegos, CI
4)	DB	680	1	R. Progreso, Stgo de Cuba, SC
4)		690	20	R. Progreso, Jovellanos, MA
5)	DU	700	1	R. Enciclopedia, Guantánamo, GU
4)		700		R. Progreso, Baracoa
1)	GA	700	1	R. Rebelde, Sancti Spíritus, SS
1)	W	710	150	R. Rebelde, La Julia, HA
1)	KJ	710	10	R. Rebelde, Holguín, HO
1)	HQ	710	50	R. Rebelde, Santa Clara, VC
1)	JN	710	30	R. Rebelde, Camagüey, CM
1)	HC	720	1	R. Rebelde, Cienfuegos, CI
4)	BB	730	10	R. Progreso, Nueva Gerona, IJ
4)	JL	740	20	R. Progreso, Camagüey, CM
1)	HV	750	1	R. Progreso, Trinidad, SS
2)	CD	760	10	R. Reloj, Las Mercedes, GR
2)		760	1	R. Reloj, La Habana, HA (occasional)
1)		780		R. Rebelde
2)	AQ	v790	30	R. Reloj, Pinar del Río, PR
4)	DT	v800	1	R. Progreso, Manzanillo, GR
4)	DW	810	10	R. Progreso, Guantánamo, GU (rep on 814kHz)
4)	JT	820	10	R. Progreso, Ciego de Avila, CA
11)	CA	820	10	R. Ciudad de la Habana, Santa Catalina, CH
2)		830	5	R. Reloj, Holguín
4)	DQ	840	1	R. Progreso, Las Tunas, LT
5)	BQ	840	1	R. Enciclopedia, La Fé, IJ
12)	HW	840	10	Doblevé, Santa Clara, VC
13)	KC	840	1	R. Revolución, Stgo de Cuba, SC
4)	HL	850	1	R. Progreso, Trinidad, SS
2)		850	1	R. Reloj, Nueva Gerona, IJ
2)	DB	860	1	R. Reloj, Baracoa, GU
4)	BL	860	10	R. Progreso, Arroyo Arenas, CH
2)	DT	870	1	R. Reloj, Sancti Spíritus, SS
4)	AF	880	30	R. Progreso, Pinar del Río, PR
3)	HD	890	1	R. Progreso, Santa Clara, VC
4)	DZ	890	80	R. Progreso, Chambas, CA
4)	KP	900	50	R. Progreso, Cacocum, HO
2)	GL	910	5	R. Reloj, Bolondrón, MA
11)	CA	910		R. Ciudad de la Habana
14)	BL	910	10	R. Metropolitana, La Lisa, CH
15)	FA	910	10	R. Cadena Agramonte, Camagüey, CM
2)	GL	920	1	R. Reloj, Moa, HO
4)		920	1	R. Progreso, Pilón, GR
2)	GB	930	1	R. Reloj, La Jaiba, MA
2)	JS	930	10	R. Reloj, Ciego de Ávila, CA
2)	KN	930	1	R. Reloj, Stgo de Cuba, SC
2)	GU	940	10	R. Reloj, Central España, MA
2)		940	10	R. Reloj, Holguín, HO
4)		940	1	R. Progreso, Sancti Spíritus, SS
2)		950	10	R. Reloj, La Habana, HA
2)		950	1	R. Reloj, Mayarí Arriba, SC
5)	GF	960	1	R. Enciclopedia, Matanzas, MA
2)	DJ	960	10	R. Reloj, Guantánamo, GU
3)	JD	960	0.25	R. Musical, Ciego de Avila, CA
2)	DE	980	1	R. Reloj, Bayamo, GR
16)	CO	980	5	El Periodico del Aire, Sapo, CH
17)	KR	980	1	La Voz del Níquel, Moa, HO
18)	AP	990	1	R. Guamá, San Luís, PR
3)	HB	1000	1	R. Musical, Sancti Spíritus, SS
3)	JB	1000	1	R. Musical, Camagüey, CM
18)	AC	1000	10	R. Guamá, Los Palacios, PR
3)	KM	1010	1	R. Musical, Holguín, HO
2)		1010	5	R. Reloj, Jobabo, LT
18)	AP	1010	10	R. Guamá, Guane, PR

	Call	kHz	kW	Primary network and location
18)	AP	1020	1	R. Guamá, Bahía Honda, PR
2)		1020		R. Reloj
18)	AX	1030	1	R. Guamá, La Palma, PR
3)		1030		R. Musical
19)	KT	1040	1	R. Victoria, Puerto Padre, LT
19)	KT	1050	10	R. Victoria, Las Tunas, LT
19)	KT	1060	1	R. Victoria, Amancio Rodríguez, LT
20)	DX	1060	5	Cadena CMKS, Baracoa, GU
26)		1060		R. 26, Matanzas
18)	AS	1070	1	R. Guamá, Pinar del Río, PR
20)	KS	1070	10	Cadena CMKS, Guantánamo, GU
21)	CH	1080	10	R. Cadena Habana, Güines, HA
18)	AP	1090	1	R. Guamá, Santa Lucia, PR
21)	CH	1090	1.5	R. Cadena Habana, La Salud, CH
22)	KO	1090	1	R. Angulo, Moa, HO
22)	KO	1100	1	R. Angulo, Banes, HO
21)	CH	1100	1	R. Cadena Habana, La Habana, CH
21)		1110		R. Cadena Habana
22)	KO	1110	10	R. Angulo, Holguín, HO
1)		1120		R. Rebelde
21)	CH	1120	5	R. Cadena Habana, Artemisa, HA
22)	KO	1120	1	R. Angulo, Mayarí, HO
5)	HA	1130	1	R. Enciclopedia, Santa Clara, VC
22)	KO	1130	5	R. Angulo/Ecos del Sagua, Sagua de Tánamo, HO
5)	CG	1140	5	R. Enciclopedia, Loma de la Cruz, HA
23)	KX	1140	1	R. Bayamo, Media Luna, GR
21)	CH	1140	5	R. Cadena Habana, La Habana, CH
43)		1140		R. Ciudad Banderas
23)	KX	1150	10	R. Bayamo, Entronque Bueycito, GR
23)	KX	1160		R. Bayamo, Pilón, GR
20)	KS	1170	10	Cadena CMKS, Maisí, GU
1)	BA	1180	50	R. Rebelde, Villa María, CH
2)	DB	1180	1	R. Reloj, Mayarí Arriba, SC
24)	GL	1190	1	R. Sancti Spíritus, Trinidad, SS
26)		1190	1	R. 26, La Caridad, MA
25)	BS	1200	1	R. Ariguanabo, San Antonio de los Baños, HA
13)	KC	1200	10	R. Revolución, Palma Soriano, SC
24)	GL	1200	1	R. Sancti Spíritus/LV de Yaguajay, Yaguajay, SS
24)	GL	1210	10	R. Sancti Spíritus, Sancti Spíritus, SS
13)	KC	1210	1	R. Revolución, Chivirico, SC
13)	KC	1210	1	R. Revolución, Mayarí Arriba, SC
26)	GY	1220	10	R. 26, Central España, MA
26)	GJ	1230	3	R. 26, Unión de Reyes, MA
26)	GW	1240	10	R. 26, Bolondrón, MA
27)	HS	1250	1	R. Caibarién, Caibarién, VC
23)	KS	1250	0.25	R. Bayamo, Imías, GU
3)	BF	1260	5	R. Enciclopedia, Arroyo Arenas, CH
28)	GH	1260	1	R. Victoria de Girón, Torriente
2)		1270	10	R. Reloj, Camagüey, CM
5)	GF	1270	1	R. Enciclopedia, Varadero, MA
29)	BN	1270	10	R. Caribe, Nueva Gerona, IJ
30)	KW	1280	1	R. Mambí, Stgo de Cuba, SC
31)	JC	1280	1	R. Rectángulo/R.Guaimaro, Guaimaro, CM
4)	CS	1290	5	R. Progreso, La Pastora, HA
5)	BQ	1290	5	R. Enciclopedia, La Habana, HA
12)	HW	1290	1	Doblevé, Rancho Veloz, VC
6)		1290	1	R. Taino, La Habana, HA
36)		1300		R. Portada de la Libertad, Niquero, GR
5)	DA	1300	1	R. Enciclopedia, Las Tunas, LT
12)	HW	1310	1	Doblevé, Sagua La Grande, VC
42)	JW	1310	1	R. Santa Cruz, Santa Cruz del Sur, CM
32)	AD	1320	0.5	R. Artemisa, Artemisa, HA (cfr 1330)
5)	DA	1320	1	R. Enciclopedia, Stgo de Cuba, SC
5)	HA	1320	1	R. Enciclopedia, Sancti Spíritus, SS
32)	AD	1330	0.5	R. Jaruco, Artemisa, HA (cfr 1320)
36)		1330	1	R. Portada de la Libertad, Holguín, HO
33)	DO	1340	1	R. Banes, Banes, HO
34)	FL	1340	10	R. Ciudad del Mar, Palmira, CI
34)	FL	1350	1	R. Ciudad del Mar, Aguada de Pasajeros, CI
35)	KY	1350	10	R. Libertad, Puerto Padre, LT
15)	FA	1360	1	R. Cadena Agramonte, Rodolfo Ramírez Esquível, CM
15)	FA	1370	1	R. Cadena Agramonte, Nuevitas, CM
37)	DV	1370	1	R. Siboney, Stgo de Cuba, SC
53)	DF	1370	1	R. Granma, Manzanillo, GR
15)	FA	1380	10	R. Cadena Agramonte, Central Brasil, CM
32)	BT	1390	1	R. Jaruco, Jaruco, HA
3)	GX	1400	1	R. Musical, Matanzas, MA
15)	FA	1400	1	R. Cadena Agramonte/R. Guaimaro, Guaimaro, CM
5)	AL	1410	1	R. Enciclopedia, Pinar del Río, PR

	Call	kHz	kW	Primary network and location
42)	JW	1410	1	R. Cadena Agramonte, Sta Cruz
38)		1420	0.25	R. Llanuras, Colón, MA
54)	JH	1420		R. Grito de Baire, Contramaestre, SC
39)	JY	1430	10	R. Surco/R. Amanecer, Primero de Enero, CA
39)	JP	1440	10	R. Surco, Ciego de Avila, CA
40)	JF	1450	1	R. Maboa, Amancio Rodríguez, LT
41)	BU	1450	1	R. Güines, Güines, HA
15)	HZ	1460	1	R. Cadena Agramonte/R. Cubitas, Sola, CM
43)	GE	1470	1	R. Ciudad Banderas, Cárdenas, MA
44)	JI	1480	0.25	R. Florida, Florida, CM
45)	LW	1490	1	R. Camoa, San José de las Lajas, HA
46)	DH	1490	1	R. Mayarí, Mayarí, HO
5)	DA	1500	1	R. Enciclopedia, Holguín, HO
47)	KQ	1500	0.25	R. Majaguabo, San Luis, SC
5)	DA	1510	1	R. Enciclopedia, Moa, HO
48)	KZ	1520	1	R. Pitan, Mella, SC
49)	IX	1530	1	R. Morón, Morón, CA
50)	ES	v1540	1	R. Sagua, Sagua La Grande, VC
51)		1540	1	R. Juvenil, Holguín, HO
52)	JQ	1550	1	R. Nuevitas, Nuevitas, CM
5)	BQ	1560	1	R. Enciclopedia, Ciego de Avila, CA
5)	BQ	1570		R. Enciclopedia, Las Tunas, LT
15)	FA	1580	1	R. Cadena Agramonte,Santa Cruz del Sur, CM
4)	BQ	1590		R. Progreso, Manzanillo, GR

SW:	kHz	kW	Station
1)	v5025	10	R. Rebelde
1)	6120	10	R. Rebelde/Reloj
1)	6140	10	R. Rebelde/Reloj
1)	9655	10	R. Rebelde/Reloj
1)	11655	10	R. Rebelde/Reloj
1)	13680		R. Reloj
1)	15570		R. Rebelde

Provinces: CA=Ciego de Avila, CH=Ciudad Habana, CI=Cienfuegos, CM=Camagüey, GR=Granma, GU=Guantánamo, HA=Habana, HO=Holguín, IJ=Isla de laJuventud, LT=Las Tunas, MA=Matanzas, PR=Pinar del Río,SC=Santiago de Cuba, SS=Sancti Spíritus, VC=Villa Clara.

N.B.: Some stations relay different networks at different times of the day. This applies especially to the three major networks; Progreso, Rebelde and Reloj. Radio Rebelde carries sports events which are relayed by many stations.

EXTERNAL SERVICE: R. Habana Cuba
see International Broadcasting section.

FM in La Habana: 90.3 R. Progreso – 91.7 CMCK R. COCO – 93.3 R. Taíno – 94.1 R. Enciclopedia – 94.9 R.Ciudad de la Habana – 96.7 R. Rebelde – 98.3 Metropolitana – 99.1 R. Musical Nacional – 99.9 R. Cadena Habana – 100.9 Habana FM –101.5 R. Reloj – 104.7 R. Rebelde – 106.3 R. Progreso – 106.9 Habana R – 107.9 R. Rebelde.

National networks
1) R. Rebelde, Ap. 6277, La Habana 10600 (or: Edif.Radiocentro, Av. 23 N° 258, Vedado, La Habana 10400). **Web:** www.cuba.cu/RRebelde or: www.radiorebelde.com.cu/ – **2)** R. Reloj, P y 23, Vedado, La Habana 10400. **Web:** www.radioreloj.cu – **3)** R. Musical Nacional, Infanta 105, La Habana 10300. – **4)** R. Progreso, Infanta 105, La Habana 10300. **Web:** www.radioprogreso.cu – **5)** R. Enciclopedia, Calle N.N° 255 e/23 y 21, Vedado, La Habana 10400. **Web:** www.radioenciclopedia.cu – **6)** R. Taíno, Av. 23 N° 258, Vedado, La Habana 10400.

Other stations
11) Calle N.N° 266, Vedado, La Habana 4. **Web:** www.radiociudad.islagrande.cu – **12)** Ap. 376, (or: Parque Vidal el Martha Abreu y Pao Chao), Santa Clara 50100, VC. **Web:** www.cmhw.islagrande.cu/ – **13)** Ap. 232, Stgo de Cuba, SC. **Web:** www.cmkc.co.cu/ – **14)** Edif. Focsa, Calle 17 esq.N.Vedado, 10400 La Habana. **Web:** www.metropolitana.islagrande.cu – **15)** Calle Cisneros N° 310, entre Ignacio Agramonte y General Gomez, (or: Ap. 140), Camagüey 70100, CM. **Web:** www.cadenagramonte.cubaweb.cu – **16)** Edif. Focsa, Calle 17 esq.N.Vedado, 10400 La Habana. – **17)** Moa, HO. – **18)** Ap. 14 (or: Colón entre Adela Azuay y Juan Gualberto Gómez), Pinar del Río 20100, PR. **Web:** www.rguama.co.cu – **19)** Ap. 21, Las Tunas 72510, LT – **Web:** www.tiempo21.islagrande.cu – **20)** Donato Mármol 409, Guantánamo 95100, GU. – **21)** Av. 51 el 128 y 130, La Habana. **Web:** www.cadenahabana.islagrande.cu/ – **22)** Ap. 14, Holguín 80100, HO. **Web:** www.radioangulo.cu – **23)** Ap. 74, Bayamo 85100, GR. **Web:** www.radiobayamo.islagrande.cu – **24)** Circunvalación Olivos 1, Sancti Spíritus 60100, SS. **Web:** www.radiosanctispiritus.islagrande.cu/ – **25)** Av. 41 N° 5614, San Antonio de las Baños 32500, HA. – **26)** Ap. 51 (or: Contreras 69), Matanzas 40100, MA. **Web:** www.atenas.inf.cu/servicios/radio26.htm – **27)** Caibarién, VC. – **28)** Torriente. **Web:** www.tiempo21.islagrande.cu – **29)** Nueva Gerona, Isla de la Juventud, IJ. – **30)** Stgo de Cuba, SC. – **31)** Guáimaro, CM. – **32)** Av. 25 N° 1810, Jaruco 32800, HA. – **33)** Banes, HO. – **34)** Ap. 290, (or: Av. 58 N° 3311), Cienfuegos 55100, CI. **Web:** www.rcm.cu – **35)** Av. de la Libertad 95, Puerto Padre, LT. – **36)** Niquero, GR. – **37)** Stgo de Cuba, SC. – **38)** Ap. 97, Colón 42400, MA. – **39)** Ap. 183, Ciego de Avila, CA. **Web:** www.radiosurco.islagrande.cu/ – **40)** Amancio Rodríguez, LT. – **41)** Calle 76 N° 7707, Güines 33900, HA. – **42)** Calle F.N° 31, Santa Cruz del Sur 73200. – **43)** Calle 13 y 5a Av. Cárdenas, MA. – **44)** Florida, CM. – **45)** Av. 47 N° 10202, San José de las Lajas 32700, HA. – **46)** Mayarí, HO. – **47)** San Luis, SC. – **48)** Mella, SC. – **49)** Ap. 157, Morón 67210, CA. – **50)** Sagua La Grande, VC. – **51)** Holguín 80100, HO. – **52)** Ap. 46, Nuevitas 72510, CM. **Web:** www.cadenagramonte.cubaweb.cu/radionuevitas/ –**53)** Ap. 220, Manzanillo 87510, GR. – **54)** Contramaestre, SC.

AFRTS (US Navy)
✉ FPO New York, NY 09595, USA.
MW: Guantánamo Bay: 1340kHz 0.25kW
FM: 102.1 MHz 0.5kW (stereo), 103.1 MHz 0.5kW – D.Prgr: 24h on 1340kHz/102.1 MHz. Rel AFRTS satellite sce on 103.1 MHz.

CYPRUS

L.T: UTC +2h (27 Mar-30 Oct: UTC +3h) — **Pop:** 950,000 — **Pr.L:** Greek, Turkish, Armenian — **E.C:** 50Hz, 240V — **ITU:** CYP.

CYPRUS BROADCASTING CORPORATION
✉ Cyprus Broadcasting Corporation, CyBC Street, Athalassa, Nicosia 2110. ☎ +357 2 862000. 🖷 +357 2 314050.
Web: www.cybc.com.cy. **Email:** rik@cybc.com.cy.
L.P: Chmn: Andreas Aloneftis. Director: Marios Mavrikios.

MW	kHz	kW	Ch.	MW	kHz	kW	Ch.
Paphos	558	10	1	Paphos	918	10	3
Nicosia	603	100	3	Nicosia	963	100	1
Limassol	693	10	1	Limassol	1044	10	3

FM (MHz)	Ch. 1	Ch. 2	Ch. 3	kW
Larnaca	90.2	92.4	96.0	7
Mt. Olympos	97.2	91.1	94.8	30
Paphos	93.3	96.5	99.8	7
Paralimni	91.4	94.2	97.9	4

Ch. 1 in Greek: 24h. **Main N:** 0430, 0500, 0530, 0600, 0800, 1000, 1100, 1130, 1300, 1400, 1600, 1700, 1900, 2000, 2100, 2200 – **Ch. 2: Multilingual 2**4h. Programs in English 1030-1040, 1500-0300. **N. in English:** 1030, 1700 & 1900. **Turkish** 0300-1400. **Armenian:** 1400-1500. – **Ch. 3 in Greek:** 24h.
Ext. Sce. in Greek: see International Broadcasting section.
ANN: Greek: "Radiofonikon Idryma Kyprou". Turkish: "Burasi Kibris Radyo Yayin Korporasyonu" **IS:** "Avkoritssa" (guitar).

RADIO MONTE CARLO MIDDLE EAST (Comm.)
✉ B.P. 2026, Nicosia.
L.P: SM: A.Pavlides **MW:** Cape Greco 1233kHz 600kW.
D.Prgr. in French/Arabic: 0500-2040. **N. in Arabic:** on the h, also 0530 & 1730. **N. in French:** 1000, 1830. **V.** Re. to B.P. 128, Monte Carlo.

TRANS WORLD RADIO (Rlg.)
✉ TWR, BP 349, MC 98007 Monte Carlo, Monaco. **Web:** www.gospelcom.net.
MW: Cape Greco 1233kHz 600kW. D.Pr. in Arabic, Iraqi and Sudanese.
External Services- see International Broadcasting section (Monaco).

Other stations:
FM(MHz):Radio Love, Limassol 88.2 – Mega R, Larnaca 88.4 – R.Anastasis, Nicosia 88.6 – Athena Radio, Limassol 88.7 – R.Anastasi, Paphos 88.8 Cosmos, Lakatamia 89.0 – Kiss FM, Nicosia 89.0 – Auto Radio, Limassol 89.05 – First FM, Lefkosa 90.0 – R. Napa 90.9 – Coast FM, Limassol 91.4. Web: www.91-4coastfm.com. Email: information@91-4coastfm.com – Kokkinochoria, Paralimni 91.5 – Astra FM, Paphos 91.7 – Niata, Larnaca 92.0 – R. Paphos 92.5 – Astra FM 92.8 – Zenon, Larnaca 93.2 – R. Eraklis, Nicosia 93.6 – Super 93.9 – R. Klik, Nicosia 94.0 – Kiniras, Paphos 95.6 – Cosmos FM, Paphos 95.7 – R.Kronos, Nicosia 95.7 – Capital Radio, Limassol 96.1 – R. Zenith, Nicosia 96.4 – R. Sfera, Nicosia 96.8 – R.Lemesos, Limassol 98.2 – Cannel 7, Nicosia 98.4 – Channel 98.6, Limassol 98.6 – Intercollage Radio, Larnaca 99.0 – R.Proto 99.3 – R. Top, Nicosia 99.9 – Pyrkos,

Limassol 100.2 – R.Pirgos, Paphos 100.2 – Gastro, Larnaca 100.3 – Yialloussa, Paphos 100.5 – Athina FM, Nicosia 100.7 – R.Logos,.Nicosia 101.1 – R.Logos (repeater) 101.6 – Radio Power, Larnaca 101.8 – Epilogi,.Paphos 102.0 – R.Asteras, Limassol 102.2 – Magic, Larnaca 102.4 – Logos, Paphos 102.4 – Tymbou, Larnaca 102.7 – R.Freterick, Nicosia 103.0 – Ammochostos FM, Nicosia 103.6 – R. Camares, Larnaca 103.9 – Astromeritis, Nicosia 104.0 – Epistrofi, Nicosia 104.3 – Choice Radio, Limassol 104.3 – R.Arts, Paphos 105.0 – Astra, Larnaca 105.1 – Disastasi, Nicosia 105.4 – R. City, Limassol 105.7 – Proton, Larnaca 105.7 – R.Proto, Paphos 105.7 – Aphrodite, Larnaca 106.0 – R. Afrodite, Larnaca 106.0 – R.Ena, Nicosia 106.0 – R. Contact, Peristeron 106.3 – R. Freedom, Limassol 106.3 – R.Epafi, Nicosia 106.3 – Radio EMU, Lefkosa 106.5 – R. Sfera, Limassol 106.5 – R.Tamptadon, Nicosia 106.6 – R. Grammar, Nicosia 107.0 – Athena Radio, Nicosia 107.0 –_R. Amore, Limassol 107.2 – R. Lykos, Nicosia 107.3 – R. Elios, Vavatsinia 107.6 – Voice of Potamia, Dali(Nicosia) 107.9.
N.B.: A List of logged FM-stations in Cyprus can be found on www.skywaves.info/cyprus.html.

BFBS FORCES RADIO, CYPRUS
✉ BFBS Akrotiri, BFPO 57. ☎ +357 5 96 8518. 🖷 +357 5 96 8580. **Web:** www.bfbs.com. **Email:** patrick.eade@bfbs.com
L.P: GM: Patrick Eader. Eng.Mgr: J.Dunlop.

Location	**Ch.1** (MHz)	**Ch.2** (MHz)	**kW**
Akrotiri	92.1	89.9	25
Dhekelia	99.6	95.3	25
Nicosia	89.7	91.7	1.5

Ch.1 is Forces Radio BFBS and Ch.2 is BFBS Radio 2.
D.Prgr: 24h. **ANN:** "Forces FM". **V.** by QSL-folder.

BRITISH EAST MEDITERRANEAN RELAY STATION
see International Broadcasting section.

RADIO SAWA
Web: www.ibb.gov/radiosawa. **Email:** comment@radiosawa.com. **MW**: 990 kHz 600kW (Cape Greco). **D.Prgr**: 24h. (see USA entry for full details)

NORTHERN CYPRUS

BAYRAK RADIO TELEVISION CORPORATION
✉ BRT Sitesi, Dr. Fasýl Kücük Bulvary, Lefkosa, Turkish Republic of Northern Cyprus, via Mersin 10, Turkey. ☎ +90 392 225 5555. 🖷 +90 392 225 4991. **Web:** www.brtk.org. **Email:** brt@brtk.net.
L.P: DG:Hüseyin Cobanoglu. **MW:** Yeni Yskele 1098kHz 2x50 kW
SW: Yeni Yskele (G.C. 33.55E/35.13N) 6150 kHz 25 kW 0430-2300.

FM (stereo)	**1**	**FM**	**Int**	**Klasik**	**Klasik Turk**	**kW**
Kantara	90.6	98.1	87.8		93.4	10/10/10/1
Selvilitepe	102.0	92.1	105.0	88.4	94.6	5/5/0.5/1/0.5

Radyo 1 in Turkish: 0420-2300 on 1098kHz +FM 24h. **N:** 0400, 0500, 0600, 0700, 0800, 0900, 1030, 1200, 1300, 1400, 1530, 1800, 1930. **Bayrak FM** in Turkish 24h. **Bayrak International in Greek/English/ Arabic/German:** 24h on FM. **N. in English:** 1215, 1730. **N. in Greek:**1200, 1800. News in Arabic, German & Russian: 1600. News headlines in English/Greek: 1000, 1400. Klassik Turk: 0600-2200.
ANN: E: "This is Bayrak International, the Voice of the Turkish Republic of Northern Cyprus". **V.** by QSL-folder.

KIBRIS FM
✉Dr.Fazil Kucuk Boulevard, Yeni Sanayi Bolgesi, Lefkosa, Turkish Republic of Northern Cyprus, via Mersin 10, Turkey. ☎ +90 392 2252555. 🖷 +90 392 2253707
L.P: Head of Broadc. Exec. Council: Asil Nadir.
FM: Selvilittepe 103.4MHz 10kW, Kantara 100.2MHz 2.5kW, Lefkosa 102.0MHz 0.2 kW. **D.Prgr:** 24h

OTHER STATIONS FM (MHz):

	Station	**W**	**E**	**L**	**kW**
1)	Laü FM	97.4			
2)	YDÜ FM	88.0			1
3)	Akdeniz FM	88.6	105.0		1.2/0.25
4)	Kuzey FM	106.7			1.5
5)	Sim FM	98.6		89.5	1.5/1
6)	Asram FM	97.7	95.2		1/1
7)	Radyo Vatan	87.5	104.3	100.4	5/5/1
8)	Günes FM	101.4			0.3
9)	Dance FM	95.5	95.8		1/0.3
10)	Radyo Daü		106.5		0.5
11)	Gaü FM	105.7			0.3
12)	Cool FM		97.5		1
13)	Ukü FM			103.5	0.25
14)	Radyu Plus			106.0	0.25
15)	First FM	90.0	96.6		1/0.2
16)	Radyo T	96.6			1
17)	Kral FM			107.0	1

Transmitter sites:W (west) = Selvilitepe, E (east)= Kantara, L = local. All sts transmit 24h

Location and contact:
1) Lefke 🖷 +903927277528 – **2)** Lefkosa 🖷 +903922232867 – **3)** Lefkosa 🖷 +903922237768 – **4)** Lefkosa 🖷 +903922284623 – **5)** Lefkosa 🖷 +903922237710 – **6)** Lefkosa 🖷 +903922252870 – **7)** Lefkosa 🖷 +903922284112 – **8)** Lefkosa 🖷 +903922289776 – **9)** Gazi-Magusa 🖷 +903923668839 – **10)** Gazi Magusa 🖷 +903923660743 – **11)** Girne 🖷 +903928222153 – **12)** Magusa 🖷 +903923661378 – **13)** Lefkosa 🖷 +903923661376 – **14)** Lefkosa 🖷 +903922278327 – **15)** Lefkosa 🖷 +903922276363 – **16)** Lefkosa 🖷 +903922234257 – **17)** Lefkosa **Web:** www.kralfm.com.tr

CZECH REPUBLIC

L.T: UTC +1h (27 Mar-30 Oct UTC +2h) — **Pop:** 10.5 million — **Pr.L:** Czech — **E.C:** 50Hz, 230V — **ITU:** CZE

CESKÉ RADIOKOMUNIKACE, a.s.
✉ U nákladového nádrazí 4, 130 00 Praha 3 ☎ +420 267 005 111
L.P: Gen. Dir: Miroslav Curín.
Operates the TV and radio transmission facilities.

CESKY ROZHLAS (CZECH RADIO)
✉ Vinohradská 12, 120 99 Praha 2 ☎ +420 221 551 111 🖷 +420 224 222 223 **Email:** webmint@cro.cz **Web:** www.rozhlas.cz
L.P: DG: Václav Kasík. PD: Josef Havel. TD: Martin Zadrazil.

LW & MW:	**kHz**	**kW**	**Prgr.**
Uherské Hradiste	270	650	CRo 1
Praha (Liblice)	639	1500	CRo 2 + CRo 6
Ostrava-Svinov	639	30	CRo 2 + CRo 6
Hradec Kralové	774	2.5	DRM test
Brno (Dobrochov)	954	200	CRo 2 + CRo 6
Ceské Budejovice	954	30	CRo 2 + CRo 6
Karlovy Vary	954	20	CRo 2 + CRo 6
Moravské Budejovice	1332	50	CRo 2 + CRo 6

FM (MHz)

Reg	**Location**	**CRo 1**	**CRo 2**	**CRo 3**	**CRo 5**	**kW**
9)	As	107.9			96.7	0.1/0.2
1b)	Benesov				99.0	1
6)	Brno	95.1		102.0	106.5	72/91/72
6)	Brno (city)		92.6	90.4	93.1	6/6/0.4
2)	C. Budejovice	91.1	103.7	96.1	106.4	80/1/40/80
	Cheb			106.2		1
4)	Chomutov	98.9	94.2	96.3	103.1	10
3)	Domazlice	98.0			105.3	10
6)	Hodonín	106.2	107.8	100.4	93.6	9/3/9
5)	Hradec Králové				95.3	1
11)	Hradec Králové				104.7	10
9)	Jáchymov				103.4	1
8)	Jeseník	91.3	88.7	98.2	106.8	20/0.2/20/20
	Jicín		106.9			1
10)	Jihlava	90.7	107.1	95.4	87.9	20/10/20/10
	Kaplice			105.9		0.2
9)	Karlovy Vary	102.6		105.7	91.0	0.1/0.2/1
	Kasperské Hory			107.2		0.5
1b)	Kladno				100.5	0.2
3)	Klatovy	99.8	90.3	88.6	102.4	10
1b)	Kutná Hora		102.2		100.5	1/3
13)	Liberec	95.9	89.9	103.9	102.3	20/20/20/1
13)	Liberec				91.3	0.5
8)	Lipník n.Becvou				88.7	0.1
9)	Marián. Lázne	97.6			100.8	1
1b)	Mladá Boleslav				100.3	0.5
	Nové Hrady		102.2			1
8)	Olomouc		107.2		92.8	0.5/1
7)	Opava				102.6	0.5
7)	Ostrava	101.4		104.8	107.3	43/43/3
11)	Pardubice	89.7	100.1	102.7	101.0	90/90/90/1
	Písek	97.0	98.9	105.2		1
	Plzen (North)	89.1	101.7	95.6		80

Reg	Location	CRo 1	CRo 2	CRo 3	CRo 5	kW
3)	Plzen (East)	99.2		93.3	106.7	10
3)	Plzen (city)				91.0	1
1b)	Praha				100.7	50
1a)	Praha (city)	94.6	91.2	105.0	92.6	5/3/5/7
1b)	Príbram	102.2	107.0		100.0	0.4/1/1
1b)	Rakovník				100.4	1
5)	Rychnov n.K.				96.5	1
2)	Slavonice		103.3		88.2	1
	Susice	90.6				1
11)	Svitavy				102.4	1
7)	Trinec	92.1	101.9		105.3	1
5)	Trutnov	88.5		101.9	90.5	10/10/20
10)	Uher. Hradiste				99.1	0.2
6)	Uhersky Brod	93.0			107.3	1
4)	Ustí nad Labem	90.9		104.5	88.8	80
7)	Val. Mezirící	92.5	89.9	96.8	99.0	7/1/7/7
4)	Varnsdorf			88.4	98.5	0.2
	Votice	93.1	103.2			95
7)	Vrbno pod Prad.		103.6		95.5	1
7)	Vsetín	92.1		98.3	89.5	0.1
3)	Zelezná Ruda				95.8	0.2
6)	Zlín	99.5	107.7	94.8	97.5	6
6)	Znojmo	101.2		99.2	97.3	1/3/1

CRo 1 (Radiozurnal): 24h (LW: Mon-Sat 0400-2300, Sun 0500-2300). **N:** on the h – **CRo 2 (Praha):** 24h (MW: Mon-Fri 0300-1700, Sat+Sun 0400-1700) – **CRo 3 (Vltava):** 24h. – **CRo 6:** 1700-2300. **N:** on the h. – **CRo 5 REGIONAL STATIONS** – own prgrs as listed, otherwise relays of CRo 2.

Addresses:
1a) CRo Regina Praha, Hybesova 10, 186 72 Praha 8: 24h. Web: www.rozhlas.cz/regina – **1b)** CRo Region - Strední Cechy, Hybesova 10, 186 72 Praha 8: 24h. Web: www.rozhlas.cz/regina – **2)** CRo Ceské Budejovice, U Trí lvu 1, 370 29 Ceské Budejovice: 0400-2000 (Sun - 2100). Web: www.rozhlas.cz/cb – **3)** CRo Plzen, Nám. Míru 10, 320 70 Plzen: 24h. Web: www.rozhlas.cz/plzen – **4)** CRo Sever (=North), Na schodech 10, 400 91 Ustí nad Labem: 24h. Web: www.rozhlas.cz/usti – **5)** CRo Hradec Králové, Havlíckova 292, 501 01 Hradec Králové: 0400-2100. Web: www.rozhlas.cz/hradec – **6)** CRo Brno, Beethovenova 4, 657 42 Brno: Mon-Fri 0400-1900, Sat+Sun 0500-1700. Web: www.rozhlas.cz/brno – **7)** CRo Ostrava, Dr. Smerala 2, 729 91 Ostrava: 0400-1900. Web: www.rozhlas.cz/ostrava – **8)** CRo Olomouc, Horní námestí 21, 771 06 Olomouc: 0400-2100. Web: www.rozhlas.cz/ol – **9)** CRo Karlovy Vary, Karla Capka 4, 360 00 Karlovy Vary: Mon-Fri 0400-0500, 1300-1700, otherwise CRo Plzen. Web: www.rozhlas.cz/plzen – **10)** CRo Region - Vysocina, Masarykovo nám. 42, 586 01 Jihlava: 0400-1700. 1700-0400: relay of CRo Region (1b). Web: www.rozhlas.cz/vysocina – **11)** CRo Pardubice, Sv. Anezky Ceské 29, 530 02 Pardubice: 24h. Web: www.rozhlas.cz/pardubice – **13)** CRo Liberec (future plan)

FOREIGN SERVICE: See International Broadcasting section.

MAJOR PRIVATE STATIONS/NETWORKS:

RADIO IMPULS (Comm.)
✉ Kovárská 15, 190 00 Praha 9 ☎ +420 255 700 700 📠 +420 255 700 727 **Email:** info@radioimpuls.cz **Web:** www.radioimpuls.cz
L.P: DG: Jirí Hrabák. PD: Hana Andelová. Mus. Dir.: Jan Hanousek. CE: Roman Culek.
FM: see list below **D.Prgr:** 24h.

RADIO FREKVENCE 1 (Comm.)
✉ Wenzigova 4, 120 00 Praha 2 ☎ +420 257 001 111 📠 +420 257 314 183 **Email:** frekvence1@frekvence1.cz
Web: www. frekvence1.cz
L.P: Pres: Michel Fleischmann. MD: Katerina Fricová. PD: Ivo Mravinac. Mus. Dir.: René Hnilicka. CE: Jirí Dostalík.
FM: see list below **D.Prgr:** 24h

EVROPA 2 (Comm.)
✉ Wenzigova 4, 120 00 Praha 2 ☎ +420 257 001 111 📠 +420 257 001 807 **Email:** info@evropa2.cz **Web:** www.evropa2.cz
L.P: Pres: Michel Fleischmann. MD: Katerina Fricová. PD: Petr Zizka. Mus. Dir: René Hnilicka. CE: Jirí Dostalík.
FM: see list below **D.Prgr:** 24h

RADIO KISS FM (Comm.)
✉ Rícanská 3, 101 00 Praha 10-Vinohrady ☎ +420 267 009 800 📠 +420 267 009 811 **Email:** radio@kiss.cz
L.P: DG: Andrew Dower. PD: Miroslav Albrecht. Mus. Dir.: Karel Rychly. CE: Pavel Polák. **FM:** see list below **D.Prgr:** 24h

Regional branches: R. KISS 98 FM, ✉ Rícanská 3, 101 00 Praha 10-Vinohrady ☎ +420 267 009 800 📠 +420 267 009 811 **Web:** www.kiss98.cz – **R. KISS Hády,** ✉ Stefánikova 38, 612 00 Brno 12 ☎ +420 541 221 143 📠 +420 541 211 117 **Web:** www.kisshady.cz – **R. KISS Jizní Cechy** ✉ U Vystaviste 15A, 370 05 Ceské Budejovice ☎ +420 385 510 888 📠 +420 385 510 990. **Web:** www.kissjiznicechy.cz – **R. KISS Morava** ✉ Starobelská 13, 700 30 Ostrava-Zábreh ☎ +420 596 708 401 📠 +420 596 708 400 **Web:** www.kissmorava.cz – **R. KISS ProTon** ✉ Husova 58, 301 24 Plzen 1 ☎ +420 377 235 808 📠 +420 377 235 810 **Web:** www.kissproton.cz – **R. KISS Publikum** ✉ Bartosova 45, 760 01 Zlín ☎ +420 577 009 036. 📠 +420 577 009 033 **Web:** www.kisspublikum.cz – **R. KISS Delta** ✉ Jana Palacha 1025, 293 01 Mladá Boleslav 1 ☎ +420 326 720 000. 📠 +420 326 721 342 **Web:** www.kissdelta.cz

RADIO FM PLUS (Comm.)
✉ Box 40 (Zikmunda Wintra 21), 320 90 Plzen ☎ +420 377 676 111 📠 +420 377 422 221 **Email:** info@fmplus.cz **Web:** www.fmplus.cz
L.P: DG: Václav Jezek. MD: Zbynek Suchy. PD: Václav Voborník. CE: Václav Voborník. **FM:** see list below **D.Prgr:** 24h

RADIO PROGLAS (Relig.)
✉ Barvicova 85, 602 00 Brno ☎ +420 543 217 241-3. 📠 +420 543 217 245 **Email:** radio@proglas.cz **Web:** www.proglas.cz
L.P: Dir.: Martin Holík. Chief Editor: Marie Blazková. CE: Lubor Prikryl.
FM: see list below **D.Prgr:** 24h

COUNTRY RADIO (Comm.)
✉ Zenklova 34, 180 00 Praha 8. ☎ +420 251 024 111.
📠 +420 251 024 224 **Email:** info@countryradio.cz
Web: www.countryradio.cz
L.P: MD: Zdenek Petera. PD: Jan Srámek. CE: Miroslav Kasan.
MW: Praha 1062kHz 20/1kW **FM:** Praha 89.5 MHz. **D.PRrgr:** 24h

BBC WORLD SERVICE + BBC CZECH
✉ Opletalova 5, 110 00 Praha 1 ☎ +420 224 190 811 📠 +420 224 190 827 **Web:** www.bbc.uk.co/czech
D.Prgr: 24h (BBC World Service + own programmes in Czech produced in studios in Prague)

FM Stations:

MHz	kW	Station	Location
87.6	70	R. Impuls	Brno
87.8	1	R. Blaník	Praha
87.8	1	R. Cerná hora	Králíky
88.0		R. Evropa 2/Radioclub	Ustí nad Labem
88.1	1	R. Evropa 2	Liberec
88.1	10	R. Orion	Jeseník
88.2	5	R. Evropa 2	Praha
88.3	10	R. Kiss Hády 88 FM	Brno
88.4		Eldorádio	Ceské Budejovice
88.7	1	R. Proglas	Tábor
88.9	10	R. Jih	Breclav
89.0	1	R. Prácheň	Písek
89.0	45	R. Impuls	Ostrava
89.0		Info Radio (?)	Praha (F.Pl.)
89.3	5	R. Novy Preston	Benesov
89.5	1	R. Cas	Trinec
89.5	5	Country R.	Praha
89.6	1	R. Frekvence 1	Plzen
89.6	7	AZ Rádio	Zlín
89.8	1	BBC World Service	Ceské Budejovice
90.0	1	R. Dragon	Cheb
90.0	1	R. Rubi	Sumperk
90.0	10	R. Kiss ProTon	Plzen
90.2	1	R. Kiss Delta	Kutná Hora
90.3	5	R. Expres	Praha
90.3	3	R. Kiss Publikum	Zlín
90.6	4	R. Most	Chomutov
91.0	70	R. Frekvence 1	Ostrava
91.0	1	R. Evropa 2	Mariánské Lázne
91.4	66	R. Impuls	Plzen
91.6	1	R. Decín	Decín
91.6	5	R. Life	Opatovice
91.7	4	R. Zlín	Zlín
91.9	1	R. 1	Praha
92.1	10	R. Impuls	Trutnov
92.3	1	R. Relax	Kladno
92.3	5	R. Haná	Pohorany
92.5	5	R. Egrensis	Mariánské Lázne
92.8	5	R. Cas	Ostrava

MHz	kW	Station	Location
92.8	1	R. Metuje	Náchod
92.9	1	R. Kiss Delta	Mladá Boleslav
93.2	1	R. Egrensis	Cheb
93.3	20	R. Proglas	Jeseník
93.4	20	R. Frekvence 1	Jihlava
93.5	50	R. Frekvence 1	Ustí nad Labem
93.6	1	R. Faktor	Písek
93.7	5	R. City	Praha
93.7	45	R. Hellax	Ostrava
93.8	1	R. Evropa 2	Karlovy Vary
93.9	80	R. OK	Pardubice
94.0	10	R. Impuls	Klatovy
94.1	7.2	R. Frekvence 1	Valasské Mezirící
94.1	50	R. Frekvence 1	Ceské Budejovice
94.3	10	R. Vysocina	Jihlava
94.7	1	R. Hey	Ostrava
94.9	1	R. Hey	Opava
95.0	95	R. Blaník	Votice
95.2	1	R. North Music	Ustí nad Labem
95.2	1	R. Sumava	Klatovy
95.3	5	R. Beat	Praha
95.8	1	R. Vysocina	Trebíc
96.2	1	R. Twist (Slovakia)	Praha
96.2	1	R. Zlín	Uherský Brod
96.4	4	R. Orion	Ostrava
96.5	1	R. Kiss Morava	Sumperk
96.6	5	R. Impuls	Praha
96.7	4	BBC World Service	Jihlava
96.8	1	R. Hey	Brno
96.9	1	R. Profil	Pardubice
97.1	5	R. Rubi	Pohorany
97.2	5	R. Fajn	Praha
97.4	50	R. Frekvence 1	Pardubice
97.4		Radiohrad	Terlicko (F.Pl.)
97.7	50	R. Kiss Jizní Cechy	Votice
97.9	20	R. Proglas	Liberec
98.1	1	R. Agara	Chomutov
98.1	1	R. Kiss 98 FM	Praha
98.3	1	R. Cas	Trinec
98.4	20	R. Frekvence 1	Trutnov
98.4	5	R. Impuls	Kasperské Hory
98.6	1	BBC World Service	Plzen
98.7	1	R. Orion	Trinec
98.7	5	R. Classic FM	Praha
99.0	1	AZ Radio	Brno
99.1	1	BBC World Service	Hradec Králové
99.2	1	BBC World Service	Liberec
99.3	1	Kiss Jizní Cechy	Cesky Krumlov
99.3	10	R. Evropa 2 - Morava	Jeseník
99.5	1	R. Evropa 2 - V.Cechy	Pardubice
99.7	1	R. Dragon	Karlovy Vary
99.7	1	R. Gold	Ceské Budejovice
99.7	5	R. Bonton	Praha
99.8	1	R. Apollo	Valasské Mezirící
99.9	1	R. Crystal	Ceská Lípa
100.3	20	R. Impuls	Jihlava
100.5	7	R. Impuls	Valasské Mezirící
100.6	2	R. Blaník / R. Tep	Teplice
100.9	12.5	R. Impuls	Jeseník
101.1	1	R. Kiss Morava	Frydek-Místek
101.1	3	BBC World Service	Praha
101.3	10	R. Evropa 2	Plzen
101.4	20	R. Contact (RCL)	Liberec
101.8	1	R. Classic FM	Tábor
102.0	50	R. Impuls	Ustí nad Labem
102.5	5	R. Frekvence 1	Praha
102.8	5	R. Dragon	Mariánské Lázne
102.8	1	R. Labe	Ustí nad Labem
102.9	50	R. Impuls	Ceské Budejovice
103.0	10	R. Krokodyl	Brno
103.4	1	R. OK	Hradec Králové
103.4	5	R. Petrov	Brno
103.6	1	R. Profil	Chotebor
103.7	1	R. Olympic	Praha
103.8	10	R. Frekvence 1	Klatovy
103.9	7	R. Orion	Valasské Mezirící
104.1	50	R. Frekvence 1	Plzen
104.2	1	R. Blanik - Jiz. Morava	Znojmo
104.3	20	R. Frekvence 1	Jeseník
104.3	31.5	R. Faktor	Ceské Budejovice
104.5	50	R. Frekvence 1	Brno
104.7	10	R. Karolína	Plzen
104.9	1	R. Karolína	Klatovy
105.0	5	R. Frekvence 1	Zlín (F.Pl.)
105.3	3	R. Cerná hora	Trutnov
105.4	1	R. Rubi	Vrbno pod Pradedem
105.5	95	R. Evropa 2	Votice
105.7	1	R. Jizera	Mladá Boleslav
105.8	8	R. FM Plus	Klatovy
105.9	1	R. Cas	Frenstát p. Radh.
106.0	50	R. Impuls	Pardubice
106.1	1	R. FM Plus	Plzen
106.3	1	BBC World Service	Ostrava
106.4	1	R. Evropa 2	Vrchlabí
106.5	10	R. Blaník	Chomutov
106.6	1	R. Fajn	Kutná Hora
106.7	1	R. Evropa 2	Znojmo
107.2	1	R. Evropa 2	Ustí nad Labem
107.5	2.8	R. Proglas	Brno
107.5	2	R. Proglas	Nové Hrady

+75 tr's below 1kW

RADIO FRANCE INTERNATIONALE / FRANCE MUSIQUE
Praha 99.3 MHz 1kW 24 h (relay station only, no office). Relay of France Musique during evening and night hours.

DENMARK

L.T: UTC +1h (27 Mar-30 Oct UTC +2h) — **Pop:** 5.4 million — **Pr.L:** Danish. — **E.C:** 50Hz, 230/380V — **ITU:** DNK

BROADCAST SERVICE DENMARK A/S

✉ Banestrøget 21, DK-2630 Taastrup. ☎+45 70118011. 🖷 +45 43711143.
Broadcast Service Denmark, a joint DR and TV 2 company, is responsible for the operation of the tr's carrying the prgrs. of DR, TV 2 and Sky Radio.

DR RADIO (Gov.)

✉ Radio House, Rosenørns Alle 22, DK-1999 Frederiksberg C. ☎+45 35203040. 🖷 +45 35202644. Listeners' Sce: ☎ +45 35203520. **Web:** www.dr.dk **Email:** dr@dr.dk
L.P: DG: vacant. Dir. radio: Leif Lønsmann. Dir. production (radio & TV): Lars Vesterløkke. Dir. News (radio & TV): Lisbeth Knudsen. Head of News (radio): Jens Holme. Head of Programme Dept.: Jesper Grunwald. Head of P1: Anders Kirch-Jensen. Head of P2 & DR Klassisk: Hans Peter Larsen. Head of P3: Thomas Sande Pedersen. Head of P4: Ole Damgaard. Head of DAB: Katja Moeslund. Head of Technology and Distribution: Karen Marie Zeuthen. Head of Music: Alex Nyborg Madsen

LW/MW: Kalundborg 243kHz (300kW), 1062kHz (250kW).

FM (stereo)	P1	P2	P3	P4	kW
Bornholm	96.2	103.5	90.0	99.3	30
Copenhagen	90.8	102.3	93.9	96.5	60
Funen	89.0	100.5	92.6	96.8	60
Holstebro	90.2	100.3	92.9	98.5	60
Nakskov	89.4	98.8	94.1	92.2	5/15/8/30
Næstved	94.8	101.6	99.6	97.5	100
Skamlebæk	88.4	101.1	94.3	92.0	3/15/3/3
So. Jutland	95.1	102.1	97.2	99.9	60
Thisted	91.4	101.3	99.2	95.6	2/3/2/2
Tolne, N.Jutland	91.0	100.7	96.6	94.4	8/10/8/8
Ølgod	88.7	102.5	92.3	99.0	10
Vejle	95.5	100.9	90.7	94.0	10
Ølgod				97.7	10
Aalborg	93.3	102.7	89.7	98.1	60
Aarhus	88.1	103.0	91.7	95.9	60

+ 16 FM tr's below 1kW

DAB: DAB1: 35 transmitters on ch.12C (227.360MHz). 98% nat'l coverage. DAB2: approx. 35 transmitters: ch.11C (220.352MHz) on Sealand & Funen & ch.13B (232.496MHz) in Jutland. For DAB2 almost 98% national coverage is expected by the end of 2004

P1 on 243 kHz (0433-2330) + FM (24h) + DAB2 (24h). **N:** 0500, 0600, 0700, 0800, 1100, 1500MF, 1600, 1700, 1800, 2200MF & 2300. Chimes of the Copenhagen Town Hall: 1100.
P2 on FM: Classical & jazz music and cultural programmes. (24h). Rlg.: Mon-Sat 0707-0730, Sun 0855-1005

P3 on 1062 kHz (MF: 0349-1100 & 1700-2329, SS: 0349-1100 & 1700-2329) + FM (24h) + DAB2 (24h): Popular music, news and sport. **N:** on the h. + MF: 0529, 0629, 0729, 1529, 1629.
P4 on 1062 kHz (MF: 1100-1500, SS: 1100-1700) + FM: 0400-2300. National version on DAB2. News, entertainment and regional prgrs. **N:** national news on the hour and regional news on the half hour. Relays P3 at night.
DR Klassisk on satellite + DAB1: Classical music: 24h. Relays from P2 at 2300-0700 – **DR Boogie** on DAB1: Continuous current chart hits. 24h – **DR Plus** on DAB1: Cultural all-talk. 24h – **DR Nyheder** on DAB1: All news. 24h – **DR Sport** on DAB1: All sport. 24h – **DR Rock** on DAB1: Continuous rock music. 24h – **DR Soft** on DAB1: Continuous soft pop. 24h – **DR Jazz** on DAB1: Continuous Jazz. 24h – **DR Litteratur** on DAB1: Readings: 1100-2300 – **DR Demokrati** on DAB1: debates from Parliament when in session – **DR Erhverv** on DAB2: Business news – **DR Kanon Kamelen** on DAB 2: For children 3-6 years old. 0600-1800 – **DR Gyldne Genhør** on DAB: For elderly people

Regional stations:
MF: 0507-0600, 0610-0700, 0707-0800, 0807-0900, 0903-1000 (excl. Wed), 1030-1032, 1130-1200, 1403-1500, 1510-1550 & 1610-1700. Sat 0603-0700, 0707-0800, 0807-0900, 0903-1000, 1030-1032, 1130-1132, 1303-1400 & 1403-1500. Sun: 0603-0700, 0703-0800, 0807-0900, 0930-0932, 1030-1032, 1130-1132, 1530-1532 & 1630-1700. At other times national P4 programmes are carried.
Nordjyllands Radio, Frederik Bajers Vej 9, DK-9220 Aalborg: on 94.4 /96.7/98.1MHz – **Radio Midt- & Vest**, Vestergade 1, DK-7500 Holstebro: on 95.6/97.7/98.5/102.2MHz. – **Østjyllands Radio**, Olof Palmes Alle 10-12, DK-8200 Aarhus N: on 88.9/89.1/95.9/102.0MHz. – **Kanal 94**, Karl Bjarnhofs Vej 2, DK-7120 Vejle: on 94.0/96.4MHz. – **Radio Syd**, H.P. Hansensgade 11, DK-6220 Aabenraa: on 96.6/99.0/ 99.9/103.7MHz. – **Radio Fyn**, Lille Tornbjergvej 10, DK-5220 Odense S: on 96.8MHz. – **Regionalen**, Vadestedet 1, DK-4700 Næstved: on 92.0/ 92.2/97.5MHz. – **Københavns Radio**, Landskronagade 68, DK-2100 Copenhagen: on 96.5MHz. – **Bornholms Radio**, Aakirkebyvej 52, DK-3700 Rønne: on 93.7/99.3MHz

Special Prgrs. on 243/1062kHz: **Wrp:** 0445, 0745, 1045, 1645, 2145. **Navigational Warnings**: 1700. **Gymnastics**: 0730-0740.
Special Prgrs on 1062kHz: **N** in **English**: MF 0930, 1605 & 2100. **N** in **Arabic**: MF 0935, 1610 & 2105. **N** in **Urdu**: MF 0940, 1615 & 2110. **N** in **Turkish**: MF 0945, 1620 & 2115. **N** in **Somali**: MF 0950, 1625 & 2120. **N** in **Serbo-Croat**: MF 0955, 1630 & 2125. **N** in **Faroese**: Sat 1800-1830. **N in Danish from KNR, Greenland**: MF 1755-1800.
Radio Data System: RDS & TMC signals are broadcast on all tr's
ANN: DR P (or: Du lytter til P) et/to/tre/fire (1st, 2nd, 3rd & 4th prgr).

MAJOR NETWORKS:

SKY RADIO (Comm.)
Lille Strandstræde 20C, DK-1254 Copenhagen K. ☎ +45 133 950. Fax +45 132 950. **Email:** info@skyradio.dk. **Web:** www.skyradio.dk
L.P: MD: Kasper Krüger. PD: Lasse Roldkær. Comm Dir. Morten Bentzen. CEN: Pierre Soelberg.
FM: Ølgod 87.8MHz (10kW), So. Jutland 89.3MHz (3kW), Copenhagen 91.4MHz (10kW), Bornholm 92.2MHz (1kW), Funen 93.4MHz (1kW), Broager 98.9MHz (1kW), Tolne N. Jutland 102.4MHz (1kW), Holstebro 103.4MHz (60kW), Næstved 103.9MHz (100kW), Aalborg 106.0MHz (5kW) + 13 st's below 1 kW.
D.Prgr: 24h **F.Pl.:** DAB2

TALPA RADIO INTERNATIONAL (Comm.)
Rådhuspladsen 45, DK-1550 Copenhagen V. ☎ +45 33378900. Fax +45 33378967. **Email:** info@radio100fm.dk. **Web:** www.radio100fm.dk
L.P: Executive Chairman: Jesper Sehested Lund. MD: Jim Receveur. PD: Niklas Nordén. Comm. Dir.: Derrick Wilkie
FM: Randers 99.9MHz (0.5kW), Hove Copenhagen 100.0MHz (60kW), 106.5 Antenne Århus (0.16kW) **D.Prgr:** Radio 100FM: 24h. **F.Pl.:** DAB2

SBS Radio (Comm.)
Magstræde 10, DK-1204 Copenhagen K. ☎ +45 33376666. Fax +45 33930807. **Email:** info@thevoice.dk. **Web:** www.thevoice.dk
L.P: MD: Henrik Knaack. PD: Tobias Nielsen. Comm. Dir.: René Slatanach. CEN: Jan Andersen
The Voice on FM. 20 low power tr's in major cities. 24h. CHR
Radio 2 on FM. 15 low power tr's in major cities. 24h. AC
Pop FM on FM in metropolitan Copenhagen. 24 h. Hot AC
Nyhedsradioen 24-7 on FM in metropolitan Copenhagen. 24 h. All News.

MIX FM (Comm.)
Markedsgade 8,1. DK-4300 Holbæk. ☎ +45 70227069. Fax +45 59444074. **Email:** kontakt@mixfm.dk. **Web:** www.mixfm.dk
FM: 20 low power tr's primarily in major cities. 24h. Hot AC.

WMR - WORLD MUSIC RADIO (Comm.)
P.O. Box 112, DK-8900 Randers. ☎ +45 70222222. Fax +45 70222888. **Email:** wmr@wmr.dk. **Web:** www.wmr.dk
L.P: MD: Stig Hartvig Nielsen.
FM: Galten 104.2MHz (0.16kW)
SW: Karup 5815kHz 10kW & 15810kHz **D.Prgr:** 24h

Private stations (local radio):
Approx. 240 organizations are operating low-powered FM tr's. (0.16kW-0.5kW ERP at 40 m. height). Currently approx. 370 transmitters are on the air. A full listing of these st's can be obtained from Hartvig Media ApS, P.O. Box 112, DK-8900 Randers.
Major sts in the main cities are as follows:
Aabenraa: Radio Mojn, Box 44, 6200 Aabenraa: 102.6/104.0/104.5/ 105.1/106.2/107.6/107.8MHz
Aalborg: ANR Hit FM, Box 7089, 9200 Aalborg SV: 87.6/88.5/103.2/103.8/ 105.6/106.8/107.9 MHz a.o. – ANR Guld FM, Box 7089, 9200 Aalborg SV: 89.0/90.5/94.1/105.1/105.3/105.4/107.0/107.1/107.6MHz a.o. – Radio 2, Box 47, 9490 Pandrup: 102.2MHz. – MixFM, Box 72, 9490 Pandrup: 97.4/104.4/107.8MHz – The Voice, Toftevej 9, 9440 Aabybro: 98.9MHz. – Various community sts: 92.2/106.5/107.4MHz
Århus: The Voice, Søren Frichs Vej 42 B, 8230 Åbyhøj: 93.1/93.7/106.2MHz – Radio 2, Søren Frichs Vej 42 B, 8230 Åbyhøj: 90.9/92.2/94.6/98.3MHz – WMR, Box 112, 8900 Randers: 104.2MHz – Various community sts: 98.7MHz
Copenhagen: The Voice, Magstræde 10, 1204 Copenhagen K: 104.9/ 105.4MHz – Radio 2, Magstræde 10, 1204 Copenhagen K: 89.2/91.8/ 105.6MHz – NRJ, Bispevej 4,1., 2400 Copenhagen NV: 88.6/107.1MHz. – Nyhedsradioen 24-7, Børsbygningen, 1217 Copenhagen K: 90.4/96.1/ 106.6MHz. – Pop FM, Magstræde 10, 1204 Copenhagen K: 98.6/104.4MHz. – Sky Radio, Ll. Strandstræde 20, 1254 Copenhagen K: 95.0MHz – Mix FM, Box 131, 4300 Holbæk: 104.1MHz. – Various community sts: 87.6, 90.2, 90.4, 92.9, 94.5, 95.2, 95.5, 97.7, 98.9, 100.9, 102.9, 103.4, 105.9, 106.3, 107.4MHz.
Esbjerg: Radio Victor Esbjerg, Banegårdspladsen, 6700 Esbjerg: 90.0/101.7/105.4MHz – Skala FM Esbjerg, Banegårdspladsen, 6700 Esbjerg: 106.8MHz. Skala FM Holsted, Banegårdspladsen, 6700 Esbjerg: 94.6/98.2/101.5/ 104.0/104.6/104.8/105.0/105.1/107.5/107.7MHz.
Frederikshavn: ANR Frederikshavn, Tordenskjoldsgade 4, 9900 Frederikshavn: 105.7/107.5/107.6MHz a.o.
Herning: Midtjylland Hit FM, Østergade 25, 7400 Herning: 89.5/95.3/101.8/104.9/106.7/107.2/107.4MHz – Midtjylland Guld FM, Østergade 25, 7400 Herning: 88.4/99.7/105.8MHz.
Hillerød: Radio MEGA, Ndr. Banevej 6, 3400 Hillerød: 89.4/90.0/106.2/ 106.9MHz
Holbæk: MixFM, Box 131, 4300 Holbæk: 105.2/105.6/106.1/106.7MHz.
Holstebro: Bergske Radioer, Lægårdsvej 86, 7500 Holstebro: Guld FM: 96.6/104.1/104.6/105.1/106.1 - Hit FM: 106.2MHz
Horsens: Radio Horsens, Nørregade 42, 8700 Horsens: 91.1/97.9/104.4/ 104.8MHz
Kolding: Skala FM, Dalbygade 40, 6000 Kolding: 87.6/98.0/105.2MHz. – MixFM, Helligkorsvej 14,2., 6000 Kolding: 91.3/102.7/107.2MHz.
Nykøbing F: Radio Sydhavsøerne, Tværgade 18, 4800 Nykøbing Falster: 87.8/90.4/90.6/105.0/107.8MHz
Nykøbing M: Radio Limfjord, Gasværksvej 10, 7900 Nykøbing Mors: 94.7/ 104.7/106.9/107.8MHz
Næstved: Radio SLR, Dania 28, 4700 Næstved: 98.1/106.5/107.9MHz a.o.
Odense: The Voice, Vestergade 11, 3, 5100 Odense C: 90.4/98.0/105.1/ 107.6MHz – Radio 3, Box 312, 5100 Odense C: 91.1/99.1/101.0/105.7MHz – MixFM, Kochsgade 31,1., 5100 Odense C: 103.5MHz. – Radio 2, Vestergade 11, 3, 5100 Odense C: 101.2/104.2/106.7MHz – Various community sts: 107.1MHz
Randers: Radio ABC Box 174, 8900 Randers: 89.5/95.3/104.4/104.6/105.0/ 105.7/106.3/106.7/106.9/107.0MHz – Radio Alfa, Box 174, 8900 Randers: 95.2/97.1/97.9/99.5/102.4/103.6/104.5/ 104.7/107.4/107.7MHz – Radio ABC Solo FM, Box 174, 8900 Randers: 96.4/104.1/105.4/105.8/107.8MHz.
Roskilde: Sky Radio, Hestetorvet 8, 4000 Roskilde: 104.3/105.7/107.7MHz.
Silkeborg: Radio Silkeborg, Fredensgade 1, 8600 Silkeborg: 89.2/90.0/ 106.6/106.8/107.7MHz – Radio Silkeborg Guld, Fredensgade 1, 8600 Silkeborg: 94.5/101.2MHz.
Slagelse: Radio SLR, Korsgade 4, 4200 Slagelse: 91.6/ 101.0/104.4MHz.
Vejle: The Voice, Nyboesgade 36, 7100 Vejle: 89.9/90.0/104.1/104.5/ 104.7/105.0/105.9MHz. – VLR, Nyboesgade 36, 7100 Vejle: 88.5/101.7/105.4/107.3/107.9 a.o.
Viborg: Radio Viborg, Box 501, 8800 Viborg: 100.6/101.5/104.1/105.0/ 105.6/106.1/106.8MHz. – Viborg Guld FM, Box 501, 8800 Viborg: 93.8/94.2/ 101.7/104.7/106.4/106.5/107.3/107.5 MHz.

DJIBOUTI

L.T: UTC +3h — **Pop:** 700,000 — **Pr.L:** Arabic, French (official), Somali, Afar — **E.C:** 50Hz, 220V — **ITU:** DJI.

MINISTÈRE DE LA COMMUNICATION ET DE LA CULTURE CHARGÉ DES POSTES ET DE TÉLÉCOMMUNICATIONS (MCCPT)

1 Rue de Moscou, B.P. 32, Djibouti ☎+253 355 672 +253 353 957 **Web:** www.mccpt.dj **Email:** mccpt@intnet.dj **L.P:** Minister: Rifki Abdoulkader Bamakhrama

RADIODIFFUSION TÉLÉVISION DE DJIBOUTI (RTD)

1 Rue St. Laurent du Var, B.P. 97, Djibouti ☎+253 350484 +253 356502 **Web:** www.rtd.dj **Email:** rtd@intnet.dj
L.P: DG: M. Abdi Atteyeh Abdi. Dir. Tec: Mohamed Moussed Yaya. PD: Nabil Dorani. Dir. Inf: Ms. Hasna Maki.
MW: Djibouti (Doraleh) 1116kHz 40kW, 1539kHz 40kW.
SW: Djibouti (Doraleh) 4780kHz 50kW
FM: Djibouti 91.3/95.25MHz 1kW, Arta 93.5/89.5MHz 5kW.
Chaîne Nationale in Afar/Arabic/Somali: 0300-0700, 0900-2000 (Fri 0300-2200) on 1539 & 4780kHz + 91.3 & 93.5MHz. **Chaîne Internationale** in French: 1000-1200, 1530-1800 on 1116kHz and 95.25MHz. **ANN:** "RTD-Djibouti".

Other stations:
BBC African Sce: Djibouti 99.2MHz 1kW.
RFI Afrique: Arta 92MHz 2kW, Djibouti 104MHz 0.5kW.
RMC Moyen-Orient: Arta 97.2MHz 5kW.
R. Sawa (see USA): Arta 1431kHz 600kW & 100.8MHz 5kW.
Voice of America: Djibouti 102MHz 1kW

DOMINICA

L.T: UTC -4h — **Pop:** 70,000 — **Pr.L:** English, Patois — **E.C:** 50Hz, 240V — **ITU:** DMA.

DOMINICA BROADCASTING CORP. (Gov. Comm.)

Victoria Str, PO. Box 148, Roseau. ☎ +1 767 448 3282/3. +1 767 448 2918. **Email:** dbsradio@cwdom.dm **Web:** www.dbcradio.net
L.P: GM: Mariette Warrington. PD: Shermaine Green-Brown. CE: Kurt Matthew. Chaiman: Ian Munro.
MW: Hillsborough 590kHz (10kW).
FM: Roseau 88.1 (1kW), Grand Ford 88.5 (0.03kW), Marigot 89.5 (0.3kW), Grand Bay 103.1 (0.1kW) and Portsmouth 103.5MHz (0.1kW)
D.Prgr: Own prgs: 0900-0300. BBC relay: 0300-0900. **N:** 1000, 1030, 1100 (BBC), 1400, 1715, 2000, 2100, 2200. **Patois:** 1800-1930MF
ANN: "DBS Radio".

KAIRI FM (Comm.)

P.O. Box 931, Roseau. ☎ +1 767 448 7330/7331. +1 767 448 7332. **Web:** www.kairifm.com **L.P:** Mgr: Frankie Bellot.
FM: 88.7/93.1/107.9MHz (1kW).

Q95 (Comm.)

18 Hanover Str., Roseau. ☎ +1 (767) 449 1095. +1 (767) 449 3097. **Web**: http://q95fm.com **L.P:** CEO: Sheridon Gregoire.
FM: 89.7/95.1/105.7MHz.

RADIO CARIBBEAN INTERNATIONAL (Comm.)

FM: 98.1MHz 24h (see St. Lucia).

DOMINICAN REPUBLIC

L.T: UTC -4h — **Pop:** 8.5 million — **Pr.L:** Spanish — **E.C:** 60Hz, 110V — **ITU:** DOM

INDOTEL - INSTITUTO DOMINICANO DE LAS TELECOMUNICACIONES

Abrahan Lincoln N° 962, Edif. Osiris 1, Planta, Santo Domingo. Web: www.indotel.org ☎ +1 809 732 5555 +1 809 732 3904.

MW: Call HI–
° = also on SW, * = inactive, (r) = repeater, v = varying fq.

	Call	kHz	kW	Name and h. of tr.
1)	CM	540	5	R. ABC, Sto Domingo: 0900-0400
2)	AA	*560	5	R. Ritmos, Santiago
52)	MS	570	10/5	R. Cristal, Sto Domingo: 1000-0400
8)	AS	580	3	R. Montecristi, Montecristi: 24h
4)	DV	590	10/5	R. Santa María, La Vega: 0900-0300
7)	SD	600		R. Televisión Dominicana, El Seybo (r: 620)
53)		600		R. Studio 600 AM, Sto Domingo
60)	JR	610	5/1	R. Amanecer, Santiago (r: 1570)
7)	SD	610	1	R. Televisión Dominicana, Pedernales: (r: 620)
7)	SD	620	10	R. Televisión Dominicana, Sto Domingo: 0900-0400
7)	SD	630	1	R. Televisión Dominicana, San Juan (r: 620)
7)	SD*	640	10	R. Televisión Dominicana, Santiago
9)	AT	650	15/5	R. Universal, Sto Domingo: 24h
62)	AM	660	3	R. Visión Cristiana, Santiago: (r: 1330)
59)	BS	670	5	R. Dial, San Pedro de Macorís: 24h
7)	SD	670	1	R. Televisión Dominicana, Barahona (r: 620)
11)	JX	680	3	R. Zamba, San Ignacio de Sabaneta: 0900-0300
12)	AW	690	10	R. Guarachita, Sto Domingo: 0900-0400
13)	DC	700	1.5	R. Mao, Mao, Valverde: 1000-0400
104)	WP	710		Onda del Caribe, San Cristóbal
14)	AQ	720	5	R. Norte, Santiago: 24h
15)	Z	730	10	R. HIZ, Broadcasting Nacional, Sto Domingo: 1100-0500
87)	EF	740	1	R. Cayacoa, Higüey: 0900-0400
16)	DB	750	5	R. Cristo es el Señor, Santiago
17)	CO	760	5	R. Cordillera, Sto Domingo
18)	MD	770	10	R. Popular, Santiago: 1000-0400
19)	BO	780	0.5	R. Constanza, Constanza: 1100-0200
20)	L	790	5	LV del Trópico, Sto Domingo: 24h
70)	VM	800		R. Bonao, Bonao: 1000-0400
24)	AV	810	1	R. Baní, Baní: 1100-0300
106)	RN	810		R. Novel, Santiago
21)	AZ	820	5/1	Bachatera 8-20, Santiago: 24h
22)	JB	830	10	R. HIJB, Sto Domingo: 1100-0300
23)	AB	840	1	R. Isabel de Torres, Puerto Plata: 0930-0330
72)	GA	850	5	R. Guarocuya, Barahona: 1000-0400
5)	UA	850	5	R. Clarín, Santiago (r: 860)
5)	UA	860	10	R. Clarín, Sto Domingo: 1100-0300
25)	VG	870	10	R. La Vega, La Vega: 1000-0300
26)	OR	880	1	AM-88, Mao, Valverde: 1000-0400
27)	PJ	890	4/5	R. Continental, Sto Domingo: 1000-0500
28)	EN	900	5/1	R. Puerto Plata, Puerto Plata: 0900-0400
60)	AJ	900	5	R. Amanecer, San Pedro de Macorís (r: 1570)
107)	FK	900		R. Super Mega, Neiba
29)	LB	910	5	R. 91 "La Grande", Bonao: 0930-0300
9)	BA	920	10	R. 9-20 AM-Stereo "Power", Sto Domingo: 24h
31)	CK	930	10	Ondas del Yaque, Santiago: 0945-0400
32)	G	950	10	R. Popular, Sto Domingo: 24h
33)	FF	960	5/1	LV del Atlántico, Puerto Plata: 1000-0500
25)	VP	970	10	R. Olímpica, La Vega: 1000-0300
35)	FA	*980	5	LV Cultural de las Fuerzas Armadas, Sto Domingo
36)	SA	990	5	R. Cibao, Santiago: 1000-0400
37)	HG	*1000	5/1	R. Beller, Dajabón: 1000-0300
38)	JA	1010	10	R. Comercial, Sto Domingo: 1100-0600
30)	TS	1020	10	R. Enriquillo, Tamayo: 0900-0400
39)	DL	1030	10	R. Novedades, Santiago: 24h
40)	ON	1040	10	La Mezcla, Sto Domingo: 24h (Sometimes r: Cadena de Noticias TV Ch 37)
14)	CB	1050	10	R. Hispaniola, Santiago: 0930-0400
60)	AJ	1060		R. Amanecer, San Francisco de Macorís (r: 1570)
42)	XF	1060	1	R. Azua, Azua: 1000-0200
43)	RV	1060	1	R. Mar, San Pedro de Macorís: 0900-0300
44)	BI	1070	5/1	HIBI R. 1070, San Francisco de Macorís: 0900-0400
45)	MC	*1080	1	R. Ambar, Sto Domingo
46)	JM	1090	3/1	R. Amistad, Santiago: 24h
50A)	RB	1090	1	R. Jimaní, Jimaní: 0900-0400
47)	HD	1100	1	R. Oriente, San Pedro de Macorís: 0900-0400
48)	MP	1100	1	R. Ocoa, San José de Ocoa: 1200-0200
49)	PS	1100	1	R. Nagua, Nagua: 0900-0200
51)	TC	1110	2.5	R. Jarabacoa, Jarabacoa: 1000-0400
95)	OS	*1110	1/0.5	R. Marién, Dajabón
52)	CN	1120	10	R. Metro 1120 AM Stereo, Sto Domingo: 24h
52)	CN	1120		R. Metro, Samaná (r: 1120)
109)		1120		R. Antillas, Barahona
40)	RL	1130	10/1	La Mezcla, Santiago: 24h (r: 1040) (Sometimes r: Cadena de Noticias TV Ch 37)
54)	RA	1140	5	R. Anacaona, San Juan de la Maguana: 1100-0400
55)	AS	1150	5	Onda Musical, Sto Domingo: 1100-0500
56)	BE	1160	5/1	Radiolandia, Santiago: 0900-0400 (Occ r: 1180kHz)
110)	JS	1170		Cadena Espacial, Azua
57)	BE	1180	10	R. Mil, Sto Domingo: 1000-0500
58)	AG	*1190	10	Azul 11-90 Bachatisima, Santiago

	Call	kHz	kW	Name and h. of tr.
50B)	MR	1200	1	R. Caracol, Azua: 1000-0400
98)	AH	1210		R. VEN - Voz Evangelica Nacional, Sto Domingo: 1000-0400 (Sun 1100-2300)
61)	CJ	1210	5	R. Merengue, San Francisco de Macorís: 18h
100)		1220		R. Bemba, Sto Domingo
63)	PM	1230	1	R. Moca, Moca: 1000-0300
64)	AU	1240	1	R. Revelación, Puerto Plata: 0900-0300
50C)	CV	°1240	5/1	R. Barahona, Barahona: 0900-0400
66)	BC	1250	5	LV del Progreso, San Francisco de Macorís: 1000-0400
67)	RJ	1250	5	El Sonido del Este "Digital", La Romana: 0930-0430
38)	T	1260	1	R. Recuerdos, Sto Domingo: 0900-0400
52)	DA	1270	5	R. Hit 12-70, Santiago: 24h (Occ. r: 1120 kHz as "Metro Hit")
69)	TA	1270	1	R. Ambiente, Baní: 1000-0400
110)	JH	1280		Cadena Espacial, Sto Domingo
71)	HZ	1280	1	R. Clave, Monte Plata: 1000-0300
6)	BD	*1290		R. Jánico, Jánico
74)	KQ	1300	1	R. Dos, Sto Domingo: 24h
75)	MH	1310	1	R. Real, La Vega: 1100-0400
76)	BZ	1320	1/0.5	R. Centro, San Juan de la Maguana: 1000-0400
62)	VC	1330	3	R. Visión Cristiana, Sto Domingo: 24h
35)	FA	*1340	3	LV Cultural de las Fuerzas Armadas, Moca (r: 980)
77)	PM	1350	1	R. Rutas Musical, La Romana: 1000-0400
102)	JD	1350	1	Ondas del Yuna, Bonao
108)	XZ	1360		R. Listín, Sto Domingo
35)	FA	*1370	5	LV Cultural de las Fuerzas Armadas, Elías Piña (r: 980)
79)	RP	1370	5	R. Seybo, El Seybo: 24h
80)	SC	1380	5/1	R. Nacional, Santiago: 1000-0300
81)	AR	1390	1	R. San Cristóbal: 1100-0300
82)	AC	1400	1	Ondas del Valle, La Vega: 1100-0200
65)	AE	1410	1	R. Revelación en América, Sto Domingo: 1200-0200
84)	RM	1410	3	R. Sol, Higüey: 1000-0300
85)	JJ	1410	1/0.5	R. Grí-Grí, Río San Juan: 1000-0300
50D)	CH	1410	3/0.5	R. 14-10, Barahona: 0900-0400
86)	FD	1420	15	R. Oro, Cotuí: 18h
34)	JC	1430	3	R. Emanuel, Santiago: 24h
88)	FS	v1440	1	R. Bahía, Nagua: 1000-0500
89)	AD	1440	5	R. San Juan, San Juan de la Maguana: 1000-0300
90)	AK	1440	5	R. Cristocéntrico, Sto Domingo: 1000-0400
83)		1450		R. Alfa y Omega, Sto Domingo
91)	AC	1450	10	R. Util, Salcedo: 0900-0400
92)	AN	1460	0.5	R. Renacimiento, Hato Mayor del Rey
93)	DE	1470	1	LV de la Alabanza, San Francisco de Macorís: 1000-0400
105)	CH	1470		R. Sur, Barahona
50D)	CV	1470		R. Emisoras Unidas, Duvergé
68)	AH	°1480	5	R. Villa, Sto Domingo: 1000-0400 (Sun 1100-2300)
96)	AP	1490	1	LV del Cibao, Santiago: 24h
97)	PA	1500	0.5	R. Color, Higüey: 0900-0400
111)	RD	1500		R. Juan Pablo Duarte, Elías Piña
98)	BL	°1510	10/3	R. Pueblo, Sto Domingo: 1000-0300 (Occ. R.Cristal Int v5010kHz)
99)	WJ	1520	1	R. Samaná "R. 15-20", Samaná: 0930-0400
112)	JN	1530		R. 1530, Santiago: 24h (r: TV Ch 25 UHF)
38)	FP	1540	1	R. Criolla Comercial, Sto Domingo
41)	BU	v1540	1	LV de La Romana, La Romana: 0930-0400
50E)	PZ	1560	1/0.5	R. Pedernales, Pedernales: 0900-0400
101)	GL	1560	1	R. Unica, Santiago: 24h
60)	AJ	°1570	10	R. Amanecer, Sto Domingo: 1000-0400
50F)	PK	1580	1	R. Neiba, Neiba 0900-0400
101)	AC	1590	5	R. Libertad, Santiago: 24h
65)	FG	1600	5	R. Revelación en América, Sto Domingo: 1200-0200
103)	SR	1620		R. Taina/Planeta, San Pedro de Macorís
10)		1640	1/0.5	R. Juventus Don Bosco, Sto Domingo

SW:

Stations with a (*) are reported inactive, but may be reactivated for variable periods of time.

	Call	kHz	kW	Name and h.of tr.
50C)	CV	*4930	1	R. Barahona, Barahona
68)	VR	4960	5	R. Villa/Cima 100/Super Q FM, Santo Domingo: irr
3)	MI	v5010	1	R. Cristal Int., Sto Domingo: 0900-1200, 2100-0430 (occ. r: R.Pueblo 1510)
60)	IJ	v6025	1	R. Amanecer Internacional, Sto Domingo: 0900-0300.

Addresses and other information

1) Ap. 517, Sto Domingo. ☎+1 809 684 2888. Web: www.vida105.com – **2)** Ap. 581, Santiago. – **3)** Ap. 894 (or: Calle Pepillo Salcedo 18, Altos) Sto Domingo. **Email:** cristalinternacional@hotmail.com – **4)** Ap. 55, La Vega. - **FM:** 97.9. – **5)** Ap. 205-2, Sto Domingo. – **6)** Jánico. – **7)** Ap. 869 (or: Dr.Tejada Florentino N° 8), Sto Domingo. ☎+1 809 689 2121. 🖷+1 809 688 6208. – **8)** Ap. 52, Montecristi. – **9)** Ap. 2000, Sto Domingo. – **10)** Calle Juan Evangelista Jiménez 49, Urbanización María Auxiliadora, Sto Domingo. ☎+1 809 538 4647 – **11)** Ap. 2, San Ignacio de Sabaneta. ☎+1 809 580 2455. 🖷 +1 809 580 2808. - **FM:** 92.3. – **12)** Calle Palo Hincado 302, Sto Domingo. – **13)** Ap. 20, Valverde Mao (or: Ap. 789, Santiago). – **14)** Ap. 454, Santiago. - **FM:** 107.3. – **15)** Ap. 68, Sto Domingo. **Web:** www.hiz730.com – **16)** USA-address. Se Web: www.misionerosdejesus.org – **17)** Calle Emilio A. Morel esq. Luis Pérez, Ensanche La Fé, Sto Domingo. – **18)** Ap. 1636 (or: Calle El Sol 51, 3a Planta, Edif. Lamarche Alvarez), Santiago. – **19)** Calle Duarte 17, Constanza. – **20)** Ap. 335, Sto Domingo. – **21)** Ap. 282, Santiago. - **FM:** 99.1. – **22)** Edif. Teleantillas, Carr. Duarte km 7.5, Sto Domingo. – **23)** Ap. 146, Puerto Plata. – **24)** Calle Pres. Billini esq. Duarte, Baní. – **25)** Ap. 203, La Vega. ☎+1 809 573 2872. 🖷+1 809 573 2317. - **FM:** 100.7+104.9. – **26)** Ap. 80, Valverde Mao. - **FM:** 106.7. – **27)** Ap. 156, Sto Domingo. – **28)** Calle Beller 35, Puerto Plata. – **29)** Calle Mella 50, Boano. – **30)** Ap. 99, Tamayo. – **31)** Ap. 225, Santiago. – **32)** Ap. 928, Sto Domingo. – **33)** Duarte 65, altos, Puerto Plata. – **34)** Ap. 42, Santiago. - **FM:** 89.1. – **35)** Ap. 1350, Sto Domingo. – **36)** Ap. 141, Santiago. – **37)** Hno. Martin Juffermans, Dajabón. – **38)** Ap. 1322 (or: E. A. Morel 27), Sto Domingo. – **39)** Av.Juan Duarte, Santiago. ☎+1 809 583 1030 – **40)** Unicentro Plaza. Av. 27 de Febrero N° 350, Esq. A. Lincoln, Sto Domingo. **Web:** www.cdnradio.com.do – **41)** Ap. 213, La Romana. – **42)** Calle Emilio Prud'homme 17A, Azua. – **43)** Ap. 476, San Pedro de Macorís. – **44)** Ap. 201, San Francisco de Macorís. - **FM:** 102.3. – **45)** Edif. Jaar, Calle El Conde esq. Espaillat, Sto Domingo. – **46)** Ap. 561, Santiago. **Web:** www.radioamistadfm.com - **FM:** 101.9. – **47)** Ap. 64, San Pedro de Macorís. – **48)** Calle Canada, San José de Ocoa. – **49)** Calle Colón 66, Nagua. – **50A-F)** Empresas Radiofónicas SA, Ap. 20339, Sto Domingo. **Web:** www.suprafm.com/informativo.htm – **Email:** f.suprafm@codetel.net.do 50A) 27 de Febrero 1, Jimaní; 50B Félix del Rosario 1, Azua;50C-D) Ap. 20339, Barahona; 50E) Duarte 1, Pedernales; 50F) Cambronal 8, Neiba. – **51)** Ap. 10, Jarabacoa. - **FM:** 98.7. – **52)** Av. 27 de Febrero 514, Sto Domingo. – **53)** Santo Domingo – **54)** Ap. 37, San Juan de la Maguana. – **55)** Ap. 860 (or: Pablo Hincado 204 Altos), Sto Domingo. – **56)** Ap. 187, Santiago. - **FM:** 93.1. – **57)** Ap. 1372, Sto Domingo. – **58)** Ap. 79, Santiago. – **59)** Ap. 142, San Pedro de Macorís. - **FM:** 90.7 Sultana + 98.7 Estéreo 98. – **60)** Ap. 1500, Sto Domingo. (Owned and operated by the Seventh Day Adventist Church) – **Email:** amanecer@tricom.net **Web:** www.tricom.net/ amanecer/ – F.PI: 10 kW SW. – **61)** Ap. 57, San Francisco de Macorís. **Web:** www.circuitomerengue.com - **FM:** 94.7. – **62)** P O Box 2908, Paterson, NJ 07509-2908, USA. Email: radiovision@sprintmail.com – **63)** Corazón de Jesús 61, Moca. – **64)** Av. Circunvalación Norte, Puerto Plata. – **65)** Av. 25 de Febrero 144, Ensanche Las Américas, P3 Hotel Hostal Puerto Rico, Sto Domingo. **Web:**www.radiorevelacionenamerica.org.do – **66)** Ap. 264 (or: Calle San Francisco 50), San Francisco de Macorís. – **67)** Ap. 151, La Romana. - **FM:** 107.5. – **68)** Av.27 de Febrero N° 265, Ofc.201, Ensanche, Sto Domingo. **Web:** www.cima100fm.com. cima100.htm – **69)** Sánchez esq. Mella, Baní. – **70)** Calle Libertad 97, Bonao. - **FM:** 88.7 Latina 88. – **71)** Miguel A. Monclús, Monte Plata. – **72)** Padre Billini esq. Jaime Mota, Barahona. – **74)** Conde esq. 19 Marzo, Edif. El Palacio, Sto Domingo. – **75)** Juan Rodríguez 76-A, La Vega. – **76)** Ap. 65, San Juan de la Maguana. **Web:** www.Radiocentroam.8k.com - ☎/🖷 + 1 809 557 2777. - **FM:** 100.1 Santome FM. – **77)** Ap. 207, La Romana. - **FM:** 94 5. – **79)** Ap. 266 (or: Libertad 9), El Seybo. ☎+1 809 552 3614. 🖷+1 809 552 3274. - **FM:** 93.7. – **80)** Av. Las Carreras, Santiago. - **FM:** 106.1. – **81)** Calle Padre Borbón 16, San Cristóbal. – **82)** Restauración 64, La Vega. – **83)** Ap. 2674, Sto Domingo. – **84)** Carr. Mella Km 1.5, Higüey. – **85)** Ap. 003, Río San Juan. - **FM:** 98.9. – **86)** Mª Trinidad Sánchez 75, Cotuí. - **FM:** 97.3. – **87)** Calle General Santana 65, Higüey. – **88)** Calle Duarte 84, Nagua. - **FM:** 99.3 R. Trebol. – **89)** Ap. 88, San Juan de la Maguana. – **90)** Prol. Av. Bolívar 49, Sto Domingo. – **91)** Ap. 2, Salcedo. – **92)** Calle Felipe de Castro, Hato Mayor del Rey. – **93)** Carr.salida a Nagua al lado del Hospital del Seguro Social, San Francisco de Macorís. – **95)** Pres. Henriquez 53, Dajabón. - **FM:** 105.1. – **96)** Plaza Alejo, Av.Estrella Sadhala, Santiago. **FM:** Comando 88 – **97)** Calle 16 de Agosto, Higüey. – **98)** Ap. 30011 (or: Calle Pepillo Salcedo 18, La Fé), Sto Domingo. – **99)** Av. Malecón, Samaná. – **100)** Sto Domingo. – **101)** Ap. 1091, Santiago. **Web:** www.radiopoder.com/ index.html – **102)** Bonao. – **103)** Circuito Telesonido, Mella N° 177, San Pedro de Macorís. – **104)** San Cristóbal. – **105)** Empresa Sur, Barahona. – **106)** Santiago. – **107)** Neiba. – **108)** C/Paseo de Los Periodistas N° 52, Sto Domingo. – **109)** Barahona. – **110)** Sto Domingo. – **111)** C/La Lira N° 18, Ens.Vergel, Elias Piña. – **112)** Santiago.

FM in Sto Domingo: Antena 100, 100.1 – Caliente 104, 104.1 – Clasica R., 97.7 – Dominicana FM, 98.9 – Escape FM, 88.9 – Estrella 90, 90.5 – Fiesta FM, 105.7 – Fuego FM, 90.1 – Galaxia FM, 97.3 – Hits 92, 92.1 – Kiss 95, 94.9 – KQ-94, 94.5 – La 91, 91.1 – La Brava, 88.5 – La Nota Diferente, 95.7 – La Rocka, 91.7 – La Voz de la Luz, 88.7 – La Voz de la Verdad, 89.7 – La X 102, 102.1 – LV de las FF AA, 106.9 – Mania FM, 92.9 – Millenium FM, 103.3 – Power FM, 103.7 – Primera FM, 88.1 – Proyecciones, 107.3 – R. ABC, 105.3 – R. Alfa & Omega, 93.7 – R. Cima, 100.5 – R. Disco, 106.1 – R. Listin,

99.7 – R. Universal, 98.1 – R. WAO, 89.3 – Radeco, 95.3 – Ritmo 96, 96.5 – RTVD, 96.1 – Rumba FM, 98.5 – Sonido Suave, 99.3 – Super Potente, 104.5 – Super Q, 100.9 – Supra FM, 101.7 – Viva FM, 94.1 – Z-101, 101.3 – Zol 106, 106.5

EAST TIMOR

L.T: UTC +9h — **Pop:** 1 million — **Pr.L:** Tetum, Indonesian, Portuguese — **E.C:** 50 Hz, 220V — **ITU:** TMP

TECNOLOGIA DE INFORMAÇÃO, CORREIOS E TELECOMUNICAÇÕES DE TIMOR-LESTE

✉ Secção de Radiodifusão, TICT, Edifício das Telecomunicações, 1° andar, Av. Bispo de Medeiros, Díli. ☎ +670 3339343. 🖷 +670 3339393. **Email:** jdsousa73@hotmail.com
L.P: Freq Mgr: Jesuina I.R. de Sousa.

RÁDIO E TELEVISÃO TIMOR-LESTE (RTTL) (Pub.)

✉ Rua de Caicoli, Díli. ☎ +670 3321827. **Web:** www.rttl.org **Email:** admin@rttl.org **L.P:** Acting Mgr: Virgílio da Silva Guterres. RTTL administers Rádio Timor-Leste (RTL) and TV Timor-Leste (TVTL)

RADIO TIMOR-LESTE (RTL)

✉ Edifício da Rádio e Televisão, Rua de Caicoli, Díli. ☎ + 670 3321826. **Email:** radio@rttl.org or radiotimorleste@hotmail.com
L.P: Prgr Mgr: Rosário Martins.
MW (kHz): Díli (Mt. Kutulau) 684 1 kW
FM (MHz): Díli 91.5 4kW, Aileu 90.9 0.3kW, Baucau 105.1 1kW, Cutalau 99.1 0.3kW, Lospalos 97.1 0.5kW, Maliana 88.7 0.5kW, Manatuto 94.5 0.3kW, Oecussi 92.1 0.3kW, Same 96.3 1kW, Suai 93.1 0.3kW, Viqueque 98.5 0.3kW.
D.Prgr in Tetum, Indonesian and Portuguese: 2045-1300. Regional station hours may be limited due to restricted electricity supply.
N. in Tetum: 2200, 0800. **N. in Indonesian:** 0000,1000. **N. in Portuguese:** 2300, 0700. All N. Mon-Fri only.

COMMUNITY STATIONS
A Voz da Esperança (Rádio Falintil) (Community/ Comm.) ✉ Díli. ☎ +670 7237151. **L.P:** Coordinator: Nilton Gusmão; Mgr: Januário. - **FM:** 88.10 MHz 1kW. **D.Prgr** in Tetum, Indonesian: 2100-1400. Relays Voice of America in Indonesian, Portuguese and English 2¼ hours daily – **Rádio Klibur** ✉ Instituto para Comércio, Díli. ☎ +670 3317073. **L.P:** Pedro Ximenes. - **FM:** 102.7 MHz. **D.Prgr** 2200-1300 6 days weekly – **Rádio La Luna** ✉ Díli. ☎ +670 7245923 - **FM:** frequency unk. Currently inactive. **Rádio Lorico Lian** ✉ RENETIL, Rua Gov. Serpa Rosa, Palapaso, Díli. **Email:** arktlcra@yahoo.com **L.P:** Mgr: Akau Guterres. - **FM:** 105.5 MHz 0.01kW. **D.Prgr** in Tetum and Indonesian. Currently inactive. – **Rádio Rakambia** ✉ Kampung Alor, Díli. ☎ +670 7243674. **Web:** www.radio-rakambia.org **Email:** cacatua@eudoramail.com or info@radiorakambia.org. **L.P:** Coordinator: Eurico Pereira. Tech. Mgr: Lindo. - **FM:** 99.50 MHz 0.4kW. **D.Prgr** in Tetum, Indonesian: 2000-1400 6 days weekly. **F. Pl:** add MW transmitter – **Rádio Timor Kmanek** ✉ Rua Foho Na'in Feto-Maloa, Ailook Laran, (Caixa Postal 40), Díli. ☎ +670 7236763. **Email:** imonemnasi@yahoo.com **L.P:** Acting Mgr: Padre Venancio. - **MW:** 1404kHz 2.5/5kW. - **FM:** 98.5MHz 0.1kW. **D.Prgr** in Tetum, Indonesian: 2030-1500. Relays program Timor Lorosa'e in Portuguese and Tetum from RDP Internacional (Portugal) 1000-1100 (Mon-Fri) and 2100-1300 (Sat/Sun) – **Rádio Comunidade Atoni Lifau** ✉ Rua de Santa Rosa, Oecussi, Distrito de Ambeno. ☎ +670 7240163 **L.P:** Mgr: Domingos Sasi; Coordinator: Anis Leki. - **FM:** 93.3 MHz 0.1 kW. **D.Prgr:** in Tetum, Indonesian, Maikenu: 2100-2400, 1000-1300 – **Rádio Comunidade Café Ermera** ✉ Traseiras do Campo de Futebol, Gleno, Distrito de Ermera. **L.P:** Mgr: Pedro de A.G. - **FM:** 92.3 MHz 0.1 kW. **D.Prgr** in Tetum, Indonesian, Mambae: 0700-1100 – **Rádio Comunidade Cova Taroman** ✉ Suai, Distrito de Covalima. ☎ +670 7247843. **L.P:** Coordinator: Rosa. - **FM:** 94.1 MHz 0.1 kW. **D.Prgr:** in Tetum, Indonesian, Bunak. Currently inactive – **Rádio Comunidade Ili Uai** ✉ Posto Manatuto, Distrito de Manatuto. ☎ +670 7257174. **L.P:** Coordinator: Azanu. - **FM:** 96.1 MHz 0.1 kW. **D.Prgr:** in Tetum, Indonesian, Galolen: 0900-1400 – **Rádio Comunidade Lian Matebian** ✉ Campus Universitário, Kota Baru, Baucau, Distrito de Baucau. ☎ +670 7243424. **L.P:** Coordinator: Syamsul. - **FM:** 99.9 MHz 0.1 kW. **D.Prgr:** in Tetum, Indonesian, Makassae: 0800-1300 6 days weekly – **Rádio Comunidade Lian Tatamailau** ✉ Posto de Ainaro, Ainaro, Distrito de Ainaro. ☎ +670 7258263. **L.P:** Coordinator: Celcia. - **FM:** 98.1 MHz 0.1 kW. **D.Prgr:** in Tetum, Indonesian, Mambae. Currently inactive – **Rádio Comunidade Lian 1912 Dom Boaventura** ✉ Rua de Posto, Same, Distrito de Manufahi. ☎ +670 7258878. **L.P:** Coordinator: Xisto Pineiro. - **FM:** 95.1 MHz 0.1 kW. **D.Prgr:** in Tetum, Indonesian, Mambae: 0800-1300. – **Rádio Comunidade Lospalos** ✉ Rua SD 3, Lospalos, Distrito de Lautém. ☎ +670 7238720, 7239901. **Web:** www.smallvoices.org/rcl **Email:** daveyjulia@yahoo.com **L.P:** Stn Mgr: Alfredo de Araújo. - **FM:** 100.1 MHz 1.2kW. **D.Prgr** in Indonesian, Fataluku, Tetum: 2130-0100, 0830-1300. **N:** 2300, 1000. **ANN:** "The Voice of the People" – **Rádio Comunidade Maliana** ✉ Maliana, Distrito de Bobonaro. ☎ +670 7258183. **L.P:** Mgr: Aze Armindo; Asst.Mentor: Atoi. - **FM:** 91.7 MHz 0.5kW. **D.Prgr** in Tetum, Indonesian, Bunak, Kemak: 0800-1300 Tues, Thurs, Sat. **N:** 1130, 1230. Relay transmitter in Balibo. **ANN:** "Aqui Rádio Comunidade Maliana 100 MHz FM" – **Rádio Comunidade Rai Husar** ✉ Posto Aileu, Distrito de Aileu. ☎ +670 7257100. **L.P:** Coordinator: Ameilia. - **FM:** 97.1 MHz 0.1 kW. **D.Prgr:** in Tetum, Indonesian, Mambae: 0900-1200 – **Rádio Comunidade Tokodede** ✉ Liquiça, Distrito de Liquiça. ☎ +670 7249428, 7257206. **Email:** radio_tokodede@hotmail.com **L.P:** Asst.Mgr: Helio Lobauto. - **FM:** 92.3MHz 0.1kW. **D.PRGR:** in Tetum, Indonesian, Tokodede: 2230-0300, 0800-1300 – **Rádio Kolele Mai** ✉ Bukoli, Distrito de Baucau. ☎ +670 7235108, 7247581. **L.P:** Coordinator: Guilerme; Mgr. Sahe Popular Media: Coki Nasution. - **FM:** 102.5 MHz 0.01kW. **D.Prgr:** in Makassae, Tetum, Indonesian – **Rádio Povo Viqueque** ✉ Viqueque, Distrito de Viqueque. ☎ +670 7238769, 7255281, 7259359. **L.P:** Coordinator: Florindo; Liaison Officer: Elio. - **FM:** 97.9 MHz 12kW. **D.Prgr:** 2200-0115, 0700-1100 Tues, Thurs, Sat – **Voz FM** ✉ Christian Voice East Timor (Voz Cristã Timor-Leste), Rua Mundo Perdido II 28, Delta, Díli (Caixa Postal 153, Díli). ☎ +670 7231074. 🖷 +670 3307071. **Email:** cvetimor@aol.com **L.P:** Dir: Pr Davi Rodrigues Sampaio. - **FM:** 89.5 MHz 0.5kW. **D.Prgr:** Portuguese, Tetum, Indonesian and English: 24h. **ANN:** "Voz FM, uma vida melhor para Timor-Leste".

OTHER STATIONS:
RDP Internacional and local prgr: Díli (Marabia) 105.3 MHz and Baucau (Lamegoa) 94.1 MHz. **RDP Antena 1:** Díli (Marabia) 103.1 MHz. **Australian Broadcasting Corp (ABC): JJJ Triple J Network:** Díli 103.5MHz 0.025kW: 24 h **Metropolitan Sce:** Díli 106.5 MHz (0.025 kW): 24 h. Relays ABC Perth. Broadcasts are intended for Australian service personnel in East Timor.

EASTER ISLAND (Chile)

L.T: UTC -6h (10 Oct-13 Mar: UTC -5h) — **Pop:** 3,000 — **Pr.L:** Spanish, Rapa Nui — **E.C:** 50Hz, 220V (Hotel Hangaroa: 60Hz, 220V) — **ITU:** PAQ

MW Call	kHz	kW
1)	580	0.25

FM Call	MHz	kW	Call	MHz	kW
2) XQB207	88.3	1	1)	101.8	
3) XQB222	88.9	1	5) XQB297	104.3	1
4) XQB???	98.5				

Addresses:
1) R Manukena (operated by Chilean Air Force volunteers), ✉ Municipalidad Isla de Pascua, Correo Isla de Pascua, Chile. ☎ +5639 100 245 Fax: +5639 100 339 – **2) R Activa** (relayed from Chile) **Web:** www.radioactiva.cl – **3) R Manueka**, ✉ Calle Apina s/n, Correo Isla de Pascua, Chile – **4) R. Valkava** (Armada de Chile), ✉ Gobernación Marítima, Hanga Roa, Isla de Pascua, Chile – **5) R Amistad** (relayed from Chile) **Web:** www.radioamistad.cl

ECUADOR

L.T: UTC -5h — **Pop:** 13 million — **Pr.L:** Spanish, Quichua — **E.C:** 60Hz, 110/127 V — **ITU:** EQA.

SUPERINTENDENCIA DE TELECOMUNICACIONES DEL ECUADOR

✉ 9 de Octubre y Berlin, Quito. ☎+593 2 2221 500.

MW: Call HC–, ° = also SW, * = inactive, (r) = repeater, v = varying fq.
The letters preceding the st. number indicate the Province. Addresses are listed by Province in alphabetical order.

	Call	kHz	kW	Name and h. of tr.
PI01)	DC1	530	1	R. Iris "LV de la Comunidad", Quito: 1000-0500
GU01)	FA2	540	25	R. Tropicana "Canal 540", Guayaquil: 1100-0600
PI02)	GM1	550	50	R. Reloj "5-50", Quito: 1100-0400
GU01)	RN2	560	25	C. R. E. Satelital, Guayaquil: 0900-0400
PI03)	CE1	570	10	R. El Sol, Quito: 24h
GU02)	PC2	580	10	R. Uno, Guayaquil: 24h
PI04)	SP1	590	10	R. Carrousel, Quito: 1100-0200
GU03)	XY2	600	50	R. Nal. del Ecuador, Guayaquil: 1100-0400

	Call	kHz	kW	Name and h. of tr.
PI05)	MJ1	610	10	R. Caravana, Quito: 24h
LO01)	XY3	620	50	R. Nal. del Ecuador, Loja: 1100-0400
LR01)	HA2	630	10	Ondas Quevedeñas, Quevedo: 24h
GU04)		640		R. Morena, Guayaquil
PI06)	XY1	640	50	R. Nal. del Ecuador, Quito: 1100-0400
MA01)	FD4	650	5	R. Visión Manta, Manta: 0900-0500
GU05)	LG2	660	30	R. Carrousel, Guayaquil: 24h
PI07)	FF1	670	12/5	R. Jesús del Gran Poder, Quito: 0945-0500
GU06)	VP2	680	25/12	Sistema de Emis. Atalaya, Guayaquil: W 0900-0500, Sun 1000-0300
MA02)	FA4	690	5	Sucre Portoviejo, Portoviejo
PI08)	JB1	°690	50d	LV de los Andes, Quito: 1030-0500
GU07)	RS2	700	50	Sucre Guayaquil, Guayaquil: 24h
CR01)	ER5	710	8	Escuelas Radiofónicas Populares, Riobamba: 0900-0300
EO01)	UE3	720	10	R. Unica, Machala
LO02)	MO3	720	5	R. Matovelle "HCM-3", Loja: 1000-0200
MA03)	GB4	v720	10	LV de Portoviejo, Portoviejo: 1000-0400
PI09)	IC1	720	5	R. Municipal, Quito: 1100-0300
GU08)	MG2	730	10	R. Guayaquil, Guayaquil: 24h
MA04)	SE4	v740	10	R. Libertad, Chone: 1100-0600
PI15)	GC1	740	10	R. Melodía "Canal 7-40", Quito: 1100-0400
GU09)	RC2	750	30	Caravana, Guayaquil: 24h
PI10)	QR1	°760	25	R. Quito "LV de la Capital", Quito: 24h
GU10)	MF2	770	25/12	R. El Telégrafo, Guayaquil: 1000-0500
MA05)	RG4	*780	1.5	R. Mía, Manta: 1000-0200
PI20)	CM1	780	10/2	Nueva R. Colón, Quito: 24h
PI12)		790		R. Paraíso, Maldonado
IM01)		790		Su Radio 790 AM, Otavalo
GU05)	ML2	800	25	K 800, Guayaquil: 1200-0500
PI13)	FB1	800	5	R. Sensación 800, Quito: 1000-0300
GU11)	VT2	810	5	R. Atalaya, El Milagro: 2300-0300
TU01)		810		Sucre Ambato, Ambato
CA01)	VI5	820	5	R. LV de Ingapirca, Cañar: 0900-0330
MA06)	RF4	820	1	Canal Manabita, Portoviejo
PI54)	UP1	820	25	R. Unión, Quito: 1100-0100
CR02)	RP5	830	4.5	R. Promoción, Riobamba: 0900-1400, 2200-0200
GU12)	RM2	830	25	R. Huancavilca, Guayaquil: 24h
MA07)	EM4	840	1	R. Costa Azul, Portoviejo: 1100-0500
PI16)	PN1	840	50	R. Vigía "LV de la Policia Nacional", Quito: 1100-0300
GU13)	VS2	v850	20/12	R. San Francisco, Guayaquil: M-F 0945-0500, Sat -0300 Sun -0100
PA01)	GB7	*850	0.5	R. Nal. Espejo, El Puyo
PI17)	PC1	v860	10	R. Positiva, Quito: 1015-0400
GU14)	NY2	870	20	R. Cristal "RCQ", Guayaquil: 1000-0600
TU02)	GS6	870	1	R. Píllaro, Píllaro: 1100-0400
PI18)	RP1	880	50/40	R. Católica Nacional, Quito: 1000-0200
CR03)	TL5	890		Ondas del Chimborazo, Riobamba: 1100-0500
EO02)	RS3	v890	25/20	R. Superior, Machala: 0900-0500
AZ01)	RR5	900	1	R. Carrousel, Cuenca: 1100-0200
MA08)	OF4	v900	5	R. Chone, Chone: 1100-0400
PI19)	VA1	v900	10	Sucre Quito, Quito: 1100-0400
CR04)	GE5	910	5	R. Mundial, Riobamba: 1000-0400
GU15)	BO2	910	2	R. Espectáculo, Guayaquil: 24h
EO03)	RU3	920	10	CRO - Compañía Radiofonica Orense, Machala: 0930-0430
GU16)		*920		R. Peripa, El Empalme
PI40)	AB1	920	1	R. Democrácia "La Cariñosa", Quito: 1000-0400
GU12)	VI2	v930	5	Canal Tropical, Guayaquil: 24h
TU03)	BA6	930	5	R. Ambato, Ambato: 24h
AZ21)		940		R. Austral del Ecuador, Cuenca
PI21)	BZ1	940	5	R. Dif. de la Casa de la Cultura Ecuatoriana, Quito -0200
CR05)	UE5	950	3	R. Colta "LV de la Asociación", Colta: 0900-0200
GU17)	DE2	950	10	GRD - Grupo Radial Delgado, Guayaquil
IM02)		950		Chasquis del Norte, Ibarra
AZ02)	SA5	960	1	Sononda Internacional, Cuenca: W 0925-0430, Sun 1200-0400
PI22)	NC1	v960	10	R. Cosmopolita, Quito: 1100 0500
TU04)	JX6	960	1	LV del Santuario, Baños: 1000-0300
PI23)	OT1	965	10	R. Católica Nacional, Sto Domingo de los Colorados (r: 880)
GU18)	AW2	970	20	R. Católica Nal. del Ecuador, Guayaquil: 1000-0500
IM03)	MB1	970	1	R. Imperio, Ibarra: 1030-0300
CR06)	JI5	980	1	R. El Prado, Riobamba
AZ03)	OL5	*990	4	R. América, Cuenca: 1000-0300
PI24)	GH1	990	25	R. Tarquí, Quito: 1015-0400
GU19)	EW2	990	15	Frecuencia Mil, Guayaquil: 24h
LO03)	NT3	1000	1	Dinamita Mil, Catamayo: 1030-2330
PI25)	CR1	*1000	1	R. Alegría, Sto Domingo de los Colorados: 1000-0500
AZ04)	RV5	1010	2.5	R. Visión, Cuenca
GU20)	RZ2	1010	3	R. Amiga, Guayaquil: 1100-0500
MA09)	RC4	*1010	1	R. Cenit, Portoviejo: 1200-0500
TU05)	NR6	1010	15	TSB R. Lider, Ambato: 0945-0300
BO01)	CR6	1020	5/3	R. Surcos, Guaranda: 1030-0100
EO04)	GO3	1020	3	Canal Estelar, Santa Rosa
PI26)	HR1	1020	5	R. Quitumbe "LV del Orgullo", Quito: 24h
GU21)	RF2	1030	5	R. Punto 1030, Guayaquil: 1100-0500
AZ05)	EV5	v1040	10/5	R. Splendit, Cuenca: 24h
PI27)	CW1	1040	3	LV del Valle, Machachi: 1130-0100
TU06)	GB6	1040	3	R. Colosal, Ambato: 0930-0500
GU49)	RQ2	1050	5	R. Motivación, Guayaquil: 1030-0400
IM04)	IM1	1050	5/3	R. Municipal, Ibarra: 1000-0100
CP01)	MG6	v1060	5	R. Ecos del Pueblo, Saquisilí: 1045-0330
EO19)		1060		R. Fiesta, Machala
LR02)		1060		R. Richi, El Empalme
AZ06)	CJ5	1070	5	R. LV de Tomebamba, Cuenca: 1000-0500
PI28)	VP1	1070	1	R. Libertad, Quito: 24h
PI29)	RS1	1070	1	R. Lubakán, Santo Domingo de los Colorados: 0950-0200 (Sun -2300)
CP02)	BH6	1080	10	R. Latacunga, Latacunga: 0900-0230
GU22)	KD2	1080	10	R. Tigre, Guayaquil: 1100-0500
MA11)	AB4	v1080	1	R. Contacto, Manta: 0900-0300
PI30)	VI1	v1090	5	R. Irfeyal "Fe y Alegría", Quito
CP03)	GR6	1100	5/2	R. Novedades, Latacunga: 1000-0500
GU23)	FW2	v1100	10	R. Alegría, Guayaquil: 24h
NA02)	LE7	°1100	1.5	R. Oriental, Tena: 0900-0400
AZ07)	JC5	1110	5	R. Ondas Azuayas, Cuenca: 1100-0200
PI31)	JR1	1110	10	Hoy La Radio, Quito: 24h
TU07)	RP6	v1110	5	R. Pelileo, Pelileo: 1100-0400
CC01)	EB1	*1120	2	Canal 1120, San Gabriel
GU24)	FV2	1120	5	Estación Intercontinental, Guayaquil: 1100-0500 (rep. on 1220 kHz)
PA02)	AS7	1120	3	R. Variedades del Puyo, El Puyo
PI32)	LE1	1120	10	R. Dif. Marañon, Sto Domingo de los Colorados: 1300-0200
IM05)	RD1	1130	5/3	R. Punto, Ibarra: 1000-0400
LR03)		1130		R. Sibimbe, Ventanas
TU08)	PV6	*1130	5	R. Centro, Ambato: 24h
AZ08)	AZ5	1140	1	R. Alfa Musical, Cuenca: 1100-0600
GU25)	FB2	1140	1.5	R. Cóndor, Guayaquil: 1130-0500
MA12)	MF4	1140	4	R. Rumbos, Portoviejo
PI33)	IR1	v1140	5	Raíz 11-40, Quito: 1130-0400
CR07)	GB5	v1150	10	LV de Riobamba "Antena 1", Riobamba: 24h
LO06)	AV3	°1150	10	R. Luz y Vida, Loja: 1000-0330, (Sat -0400, Sun -0700)
SU01)	BC7	*1150	1	R. El Cisne, Nueva Loja: 1000-0200
CA02)		1160		LV del Pueblo, Azoguez
CP04)	UR6	1160	1	R. Runatacuyaj "LV de la Asociación". Latacunga: W 1000-0200
EO05)	VR3	1160	2	R. Vía, Machala
MA13)	WD4	v1160	1	R. Cenit, Portoviejo: 1200-0500
PI34)	CP1	v1160	2	R. Presidente, Quito: 24h
CR08)	JV5	1170	5	R. Central, Riobamba: 0900-0500
ES01)	JM4	1170	10	R. Antena Libre, Esmeraldas
GU26)	RV2	1170	5	R. Filadelfia, Guayaquil: 24h
AZ09)	DP5	1180	4	R. Cuenca, Cuenca: 1200-0300
CC02)	RV1	1180	1.2	R. Familiar, Julio Andrade: 1100-1800, 2200-0200
EO06)		1180	5	R. Trébol AM, Zaruma: 1130-0200
PI35)	LR1	1180	12.5	Nueva Em. Central, Quito: 1100-0400
CP05)	RF6	1190	5	R. El Sol, Pujilí: 1100-0200
GU22)	DE2	1190	2	Estudio 11-90, Guayaquil: 24h
AZ10)	RM5	1200	5	R. El Mercurio, Cuenca: 0900-0500
EO07)		1200		R. U Cadena Sur, Sta Rosa
LR04)	RE2	1200	5	LV del Trópico, Quevedo: 1000-0400
MA14)	MP4	*1200	1	R. La Grande, Bahía de Caráquez
PI11)		1200		R. Filadelfia, Quito
PI36)	CS1	v1200	5	R. Super K, Sangolquí: 1000-0100
GU27)	BJ2	1210	20	R. El Mundo, Guayaquil: 1200-0300, Sat -0100, Sun -0400)
LO07)	VC3	°1210	10	R. Centinela del Sur "CDS", Loja: 1100-0300
TU09)	JM6	1210	3	R. Sira, Ambato: 1000-0700
BO03)	EB6	1220	3/5	Ecos de Bolívar, Guaranda: 0930-0130

	Call	kHz	kW	Name and h. of tr.
PI32)	AP1	1220	10	Sistema de Radiodifusoras Marañon, Quito: 1000-0300
AZ11)	MV5	1230	3	R. Popular, Cuenca: 1045-0500
CP06)	RL6	°1230	1	LV de Saquisilí y Libertador, Saquisilí: 1045-0300
ES02)	FG4	*1230	5	Sucre Esmeraldas, Esmeraldas
GU48)	FV2	1230	15	R. Galáctica, Guayaquil: 1000-0400
IM06)	RI1	°1230	3	CRI-Centro Radiofónico de Imbabura, Ibarra: 1100-0300
CR09)	LA5	v1240		R. Sonorama, Riobamba
EO08)	RF3	1240	5	R. Fenix, Zaruma: 1000-0100
PI37)	PA1	1240	1	R. Metropolitana, Quito: 1200-0300
CC03)	EM1	1250	10	Ondas Carchenses, Tulcán: 1000-0400
GU28)	HB2	1250	10	R. Tricolor, Guayaquil: 24h
PI38)	MY1	1250	3	LV del Triunfo, Sto Domingo de los Colorados: 1000-0500
AZ12)	PB5	1260	2	R. Contacto XG, Cuenca: 1100-0300
EO09)	RB3	1260	1	R. Benemérita, Sta Rosa: 1030-0100
PI39)	MO1	1260	10	LV del Santuario del Quinche, Quito: 1100-0300
TU10)	RO6	1260	3	R. Calidad, Ambato: 0930-0600
GU22)	UM2	1270	15	R. Universal, Guayaquil: 0900-0500
MA15)	LD4	1270	3	R. Junín, Junín: 1100-0500
CR10)	NW5	1280	1	R. Canal Tropical, Riobamba: 1100-0100
EO10)	RP3	*1280	2	R. Continental, Arenillas
MA16)	IN4	1280	1	LV del Sur de Manabí, Jipijapa: 1000-0500
AZ13)	JA5	1290	3	LV del Río Tarqui, Cuenca: 0900-0200
CP08)	VM6	1290	0.5	R. Once de Noviembre, Latacunga: 1200-0400
GU29)	OF2	1290	1	Canal Milagreño, El Milagro
IM07)	NS1	1290	1	R. Popular, Atuntaqui: 1100-0300
BO04)		1300		R. La Paz, Guaranda
GU30)	DC2	1300	5	R. Cenit, Guayaquil: 1200-0400
PI41)	RV1	1300	5	R. Festival, Sto Domingo de los Colorados: 0930-0300
SU02)	RS7	1300	2/1	R. Sucumbios, Nueva Loja: 1100-2400
CA03)	CI5	1310	3	T. V. O. "El Poder Mágico de la Fé", Biblián
CR20)	AI5	1310	0.5	Eco de los Andes, Cumanda: 1000-0200
EO11)	CP3	v1310	1	LV de El Oro, Pasaje
PI58)	GB1	°1310	20	R. Nal. Espejo, Quito: 24h
LR05)	FR2	1320	3	R. Guayaquil, Babahoyo: 1030-0300
MA24)	VO4	°1320	1	R. Stéreo Carrizal, Calceta: 1130-0300
MS02)	OB7	*1320	0.5	R. Nacional Limón, Limón Indanza: 2100-0300
TU11)	JD6	1320	10	R. Continental, Ambato: 0930-0400
AZ14)	LW5	1330	2	R. Misión Cristiana Internacional, Cuenca
CC04)	OV1	1330	3	GRC AM-Grupo Radial Carisma, El Angel
EO12)	RV3	1330	5	R. El Oro, Machala: 1000-0600
GU31)		1330		Lomas Stereo 2000, Guayaquil
PI42)		v1330	3	R. Misión Cristiana Internacional, Quito
CR11)	VP5	*1340	2.5	LV del Volcan, Penipe
ES03)		1340		LV de su amiga "Esté Musical", Esmeraldas
LO08)		1340	1	R. Regional, Loja: 1100-0300
LR06)	SF2	*1340	1	R. Fluminense, Babahoyo: 1100-0500
TU12)	RT6	1340	5	R. Paz y Bien, Ambato: 0930-0130
AZ15)	SF5	1350	2/1	R. San Fernando, San Fernando: 1000-0300
CC05)	PZ1	*1350	5	R. Rumichaca, Tulcán: 1045-0415
GU47)	VP2	1350	3	Teleradio AM, Guayaquil: 24h
PI43)	PU1	v1350	1	LV de Sto Domingo, Sto Domingo de los Colorados
CR12)	RJ5	1360	1	R. América, Riobamba: 1100-0300
EO13)	HG3	1360	5	R. Jerusalem AM, Machala
MA18)	EG4	*1360	3	LV del Carmen, El Carmen
PI44)	MT	v1360	3	Oyambaro AM, Tumbaco: 1000-0300
CA04)		v1370		R. El Rocio, Biblián
GU32)	VO2	1370	5	LV del Milagro, El Milagro
IM08)	JS1	*1370	2	Ecos Andinos, Pimampiro
LO09)	ER3	1370	5	R. Progreso, Loja: 1000-0315
PA03)	RP7	1370	2	R. Pastaza, El Puyo: 1100-0100 (Sun 1200-2300)
CC06)	VL7	1380	7	R. Multicolor, Tulcán
EO14)	OA3	1380	1	Impacto AM, Piñas: 1000-0400
MS03)	WV7	*1380	3	R. Morona, Macas
PI45)	CV1	1380	5	R. Cristal "RCQ", Quito: 0830-0300
TU13)		v1380	5	R. Mera, Ambato: 24h
AZ16)	EA5	1390	5	R. Tropicana "Canal 13-90", Cuenca: 1200-0300
CR13)	DN5	1390	3	R. Atenas, Riobamba: 0900-0500
ES04)	HE4	*1390	1	LV de Esmeraldas, Esmeraldas
IM09)	IE1	1390	1.5	R. Uno, Urcuquí
CP09)		1400		Impacto 1400 AM, Latacunga
GU02)	FL2	v1400	10	R. Z Uno, Guayaquil: 24h

	Call	kHz	kW	Name and h. of tr.
ZC01)	VZ7	*1400	5	R. LV de Zamora, Zamora
AZ17)	GC5	1410	1	R. Centro Gualaceo, Gualaceo: 1200-0300 (Sun 1100-2300)
CR14)		1410	1	Ondas Cisnerias, Riobamba: 2000-2300
ES05)	FR4	1410	1	LV de Quinindé, Quinindé
GU33)	CQ2	1410	1	R. Presidente "LV del Pueblo", El Milagro
PI59)	EC1	v1410	1	R. El Tiempo "Em.del Amor", Quito
CP10)	MA6	v1420	1	R. Nuevos Exitos, Salcedo: 1000-0400
EO15)	NR3	*1420	1	LV de Huaquillas, Huaquillas
IM10)	RN1	°1420	3	R. Bahá'í, Otavalo: 0900-1500, 1930-2300
NA06)	VN7	1420		LV del Napo, Tena
BO05)	JC6	1430	5	R. Guaranda, Guaranda: 1100-0300
GU34)	MB2	1430	10	R. Federal, Virgen de Fátima: 24h
LO10)	CV3	1430	5	Ondas del Zamora, Loja: 1130-0330
PI46)	GF1	1430	3.5	R. Futura 14-30, Quito: 1300-0200
BO06)	RC6	*1440	2	R. Antología, Caluma: 0900-0400
CA05)	OV5	1440	2.8	Ondas del Volante, Azogues: 1000-0400
CP11)	AQ6	1440	3/5	R. Fenix, Latacunga: 24h
ES06)	DY4	1440	2.5	R. Iris, Esmeraldas: 1000-0400
IM11)	DF1	v1440	5	R. Panorama, Ibarra: 1030-0400
PA04)	MD7	*1440	5	R. Puyo, El Puyo
CR15)	SC5	1450	10	R. Calidad, Riobamba: 0800-0400
GU35)	DR	v1450	1	R. Minutera, Guayaquil
GU36)	SE2	1450	1	R. Santa Elena, Santa Elena: 2200-0200
PI47)	SC1	1450	1	AS La Radio, Tabacundo
CP12)	IC6	1460	5	R. Nuevos Horizontes, Latacunga: 1000-0200
LO11)	CL3	1460	5	R. Cariamanga, Cariamanga: 1000-0400
MS04)	AA7	1460	5	LV de Gualaquiza, Gualaquiza: 1000-0300
GU37)	LD2	1470	1.5	R. Ecos de Naranjito, Naranjito: 1200-0300
PI48)	JC1	1470	5	Ecos de Cayambe, Cayambe: 1000-0330
TU18)		1470	5	R. San Juan, Ambato
CR16)	WP5	v1480	3	R. Atlántida, Alausí: 1000-0400
CP13)	CY6	1480	5	R. Popular de La Maná, La Maná
EO16)	BS3	v1480	3	Sucre Machala, Machala
IM12)	MC1	1480	1	R. Municipal, Cotacachi
MA20)	JV4	1480	3	R. LV de Jipijapa, Jipijapa: 1100-0400
CA06)	SM5	1490	5	R. Santa María, Azogues: 0930-0330
ES07)	AE4	1490	2.5	R. Unión, Esmeraldas: 1000-0300
GU38)	VY2	1490	1	La R. Dinámica, Guayaquil
TU14)	AI6	1490	3	R. Moderna, Píllaro: 1300-0200
IM13)	RO1	1500	1	R. Otavalo, Otavalo: 1200-0300
LR09)	HG2	1500	5	LV del Río Vinces, Vinces: 1100-0500
MA21)	AD4	1500	5	R. Satélite, El Carmen: 1000-0500
ZC02)	OY7	*1505	1.5	Ondas del Río Yacuambí, Yacuambí: 1000-1400, 2000-2400
BO07)	RY6	1510	1	R. Runacunapac Yachana "R. El Saber del Hombre", Simiátug
CA07)	RC5	1510	0.5	LV de la Juventud, Cañar
GU39)	HD2	°1510	0.5	Inst. Oceanográfico de la Armada, Guayaquil: time signals 24h
LO13)	UC3	1510	10	R. Unión Calvense, Cariamanga
PI56)		1510	5	R. Monumental, Quito: 1300-0400
SU03)	JV7	1510	3	R. Ecos del Oriente, Lago Agrio: 1030-0100
TU19)		1510		R. Net, Ambato
CR18)	RI5	1520	2.5	LV de Guamote, Guamote
GU40)	RN2	1520	1	LV de Naranjal, El Naranjal
IM14)	TI1	1520	1	R. Ibarra, Ibarra: 1000-0400
MA22)	EB4	*1520	5	R. Manta, Manta: 1100-0500
CA08)	CC5	1530	5	Ondas Cañaris AM, Azogues: 1030-0400
CR19)	VP5	v1530	3	R. LV de Pallatanga, Pallatanga: 1100-0300
ES08)	JY4	*1530	5	R. Uno, La Concordia: 1000-2400
GU41)	MP2	v1530	5	LV de la Península, La Libertad: 1100-0300
TU15)	MZ6	1530	1	R. Dorado, Pelileo: 1130-0230
CC07)	PV1	1540	1	R. Mira. Mira
CP14)	MH	v1540	0.5	Cotopaxi Digital, Latacunga: 1000-0400
EO18)		1540		R. Flecha AM, Machala
LR10)	FM2	1540	3	R. Cristal, Babahoyo
MS05)	VB7	°1540	0.25	LV del Upano, Macas: 1030-0300
PI49)	DP1	1540	1	R. Caracol, Quito: 1000-0400
AZ18)	AD5	1550	5	LV de Chaguarurco, Santa Isabel: 1000-0300
GU42)	AD2	1550	2	LV del Triunfo, El Triunfo: 1100-0400
NA05)	RA7	*1550	1	R. Amazonas, Archidona
TU16)	EI6	1550	2	R. Montalvo, Ambato: 1130-0300
EO17)	TR3	1560	2	LV del Guabo, El Guabo: 1100-1300, 2300-0400
GU43)	CS2	1560	2	R. Sideral, Daule: 1300-0500
IM15)	ZD1	1560	1.5	Ecos Culturales de Urcuquí, Urcuquí
MA23)		1570	1	R. LV Espirítu Santo de Dios, Manta: 1100-0100
PI51)	PG1	1570	10	R. Nucanchic, Maldonado
TU20)		1570	0.5	Ondas Quereñas, Quero: 1100-0300

	Call	kHz	kW	Name and h. of tr.
AZ19)	TP5	v1580	3	Ecos del Portete, Girón: 1200-0330 (rep on 1610kHz)
ES09)	VA4	*1580	5	Estación de la Alegría, Esmeraldas
GU44)	CP2	*1580	0.5	Canal del Pueblo, Samborondón
LO14)	AB3	1580	0.25	Ondas de Paltas, Catacocha
PI52)	LF1	*1580	1	Ecos de Orellana, Machachi: 1030-0230
GU45)	AS2	v1590	0.25	R. Record, La Libertad
PI53)	RZ1	1590	1	R. Mensaje, Cayambe: 1000-1400, 2130-0130
TU17)	QT6	1590	1	R. Panamericana, Quero: 1000-0200(Sun-2400)
AZ20)	PB5	*1600	3	R. Intiñán, Girón: 1100-0300
BO09)		v1600		Ondas de Caluma "R.del Pueblo", Caluma
GU46)	JP2	v1600	1	R. Consular, Playas: 1200-0100
PI57)		1600		Ilusión AM, Quito
AZ19)	TP5	v1610	3	Ecos del Portete, Girón: 1200-0330 (nom 1580kHz)

SW:
Stations with a (*) are reported to be inactive, but may occasionally be reactivated for variable periods of time.

	Call	kHz	kW	Name and h. of tr.
PI08)	JB1	3220	8	LV de los Andes/TWR, Quito
MA24)	RN4	*3260	1	R. Stéreo Carrizal, Calceta
NA06)	VN7	v3280	2.5	LV del Napo, Tena: 0900-1115, 1300-1400, 2200-0300 Prgrs: R. María
TU08)	PV6	*3290	0.5	R. Centro, Ambato
MS05)	VB7	3360	2.5	LV del Upano, Macas: irr
IM06)		v3380	1	Centro Radiofónico de Imbabura, Ibarra: irr
LO07)	VC3	v4770	5	R. Centinela del Sur, Loja: irr.
NA02)	LE7	v4781	3	R. Oriental, Tena
MS06)	SK7	4785	10	R. Federación Shuar, Sucúa: irr
MA25)	AS4	*4795	3	LV de los Caras, Bahía de Caráquez
LO15)	AX3	4815	1	R. Buen Pastor, Saraguro 1000-1600, 2100-0355
LO06)	AV3	*4850	3	R. Luz y Vida, Loja
MS06)	SK7	4860	10	R. Federación Shuar, Sucúa: irr
MS05)	VB7	4870		LV del Upano, Macas: Prgrs: R.María: irr
CP06)	RL6	4900	1	LV de Saquisilí y Libertades, Saquisilí: irr.
PI10)	QR1	v4919	12	R. Quito "LV de la Capital", Quito: 24h
IM10)	RN1	*4950	1	R. Bahá'í, Otavalo
MS06)	SK7	v4960	5	R. Federación Shuar, Sucúa: irr
MS05)	VB7	v5040	10	LV del Upano, Macas: irr
MS05)	VB7	*5965		LV del Upano/Deal Tena, Tena
MS06)	SK7	*5980	10	R. Federación Shuar, Sucúa
MS05)	VB7	*6000		LV del Upano, Macas

LV de los Andes: see International Broadcasting section.

Province-abbreviations: AZ=Azuay, BO=Bolívar, CA=Cañar, CC=Carchi, CP=Cotopaxi, CR=Chimborazo, EO=El Oro, ES=Esmeraldas, GU=Guayas, IM=Imbabura, LO=Loja, LR=Los Ríos, MA=Manabí, MS=Morona Santiago, NA=Napo, PA=Pastaza, PI=Pichincha, SU=Sucumbios, TU=Tungurahua, ZC=Zamora Chinchipe.
N.B.: These abbreviations are not recognized by the Ecuadorian Post Office. Letters should therefore carry the full name.

Addresses and other information:
AZ00) AZUAY
AZ01) Bolívar 368, Cuenca. – **AZ02)** Av.Remigio Crespo y Calle La Libertad, Cuenca. – **AZ03)** Cas. 01-01-0820 (or: Av.de las Américas s/n y México), Cuenca. ☎/🖷+593 7 452022. – **AZ04)** Cas. 198, Cuenca. – **AZ05)** Cas. 01-01-1352, Cuenca. - **FM:** 90.5+92.5. – **AZ06)** Cas. 01-01-0493, Cuenca. **Web:** www.tomebamba.satnet.net - **Email:** tomebamba@cue.satnet.net - **FM:** 94.9 102.1. – **AZ07)** Cas. 01-01-4980 (or: Av. Héroes de Verdeloma 9-15), Cuenca. ☎+593 7 823911. 🖷+593 7 839067. **Email:** oazuayas@cue.satnet.net - **FM:** 93.7 Sunny. – **AZ08)** Simon Bolívar 226, Cuenca. – **AZ09)** Bomboiza 1-83, entre Loja-Pastaza, Cuenca. – **AZ10)** Av.de las Américas, Edif.Mercurio, Cuenca. – **AZ11)** La Gloria de Nanuncay, Av.Loja 2408, Cuenca. – **AZ12)** J. Dávila y C. Merchán, Cuenca. – **AZ13)** Manuel Vega 653 y Presidente Córdoba, Cuenca. – **AZ14)** Edif.Alfa, P4, Gran Colombia 739 y A Borrero, Cuenca. – **AZ15)** Av. José María Quito y Santiago de San Fernando, San Fernando. ☎+593 7 279187. – **AZ16)** Cas. 830 (or: Pumapungo 5-50), Cuenca. – **AZ17)** Gran Colombia y 9 de Octubre 3102, Frente al Parque Central, Gualaceo. – **AZ18)** Cas. 01-01-46 (or: Calle Bolívar 7-64), Aperado (or: Calle 24 de Mayo y Abdon Calderón, Cuenca). **Email:** chaguarurco60@hotmail.com – **AZ19)** Antonio Flor 6-57, Girón. – **AZ20)** Girón. – **AZ21)** J. Roldos 480, Edif. El Consorcio, Cuenca.
BO00) BOLÍVAR
BO01) Johnson City 204 y Sucre, Parraquia San Vicente, Guaranda - **FM:** 97.3. – **BO03)** 10 de Agosto 612, Guaranda - **FM:** 93.9. – **BO04)** G. Moreno y 7 de Mayo, Guaranda. – **BO05)** Federico Paez, Frente al Parque Cen, (or: Cas. 86), Guaranda. – **BO06)** 23 de Agosto y Heroes del Cenepa Cerquina, Caluma. ☎+593 3 974607 🖷+593 3 974267. – **BO07)** Simiátug. – **BO09)** Av. La Naranja 169, Atras-Coliseo, Caluma.
CA00) CAÑAR
CA01) Av. Ingapirca, Cdla. El Vergel, Cañar (or: Cas. 01-01-0447, Cuenca). Quichua: 0900-1300 - **FM:** 94.3. – **CA02)** General Vintimilla 1-10 y Oriente, Azogues. – **CA03)** Mariscal Sucre 722 y B. Ochoa, Biblián (or: Cas. 729, Azogues). – **CA04)** Calle Mariscal Sucre 202 y Tarquí, Biblián. – **CA05)** Bolivar y Azuay, Azogues. ☎+593 7 240274 🖷+593 7 240898. – **CA06)** Cas. 03-01-730, Azogues. ☎+593 7 240616 🖷+593 7 243247. **Web:** www.radiosantamaria.com **Email:** stamaria@satnet.net – **CA07)** Av. San Antonio y A. Cordoba, Cañar. – **CA08)** Calle Rivera 613, Azogues.
CC00) CARCHI
CC01) Atahualpa 166 y Aristizava, San Gabriel. – **CC02)** Calle 13 de Abril, Convento parroquial, Julio Andrade. – **CC03)** Olmedo 52-025 y Ayacucho (or: Cas. 30), Tulcán. – **CC04)** Olmedo s/n y Bolívar, El Angel. ☎+593 6 977075. – **CC05)** Cas. 42, Tulcán. – **CC06)** Antigua vía Tulcán Ipiales (or: Cas. 60), Tulcán. – **CC07)** González Suarez 824, Mira.
CP00) COTOPAXI
CP01) Imbabura 2333 y 9 de Octubre, Saquisilí. – **CP02)** Cas. 05-01-392 (or: Calle Quito 14-56, Pasaje La Catedral), Latacunga. ☎+593 3 810287. 🖷+593 3 802329. **Email:** latacunga@andinanet.net - **FM:** 97.1+102.1. – **CP03)** J.Echeverra 42-64 y Quito, Latacunga. – **CP04)** Bel.Quevedo Caserio Illuchi, Latacunga. – **CP05)** B. Quevedo 555, Pujilí. – **CP06)** Av.24 de Mayo 669, Saquisilí. – **CP08)** Cas. 286, Latacunga. **Web:**www.radio11denoviembre.com **Email:** programacion@ radio11.net or radio11@radio11denoviembre.com – **CP09)** General Maldonado 379 y 2 de Mayo, Latacunga. – **CP10)** García Moreno N° 543 y Sucre, Salcedo. ☎+593 3 726228 - **FM:** 95.3. – **CP11)** Juan Abel Echeverria 6-56 y Quito, Latacunga. ☎/🖷 +593 3 812258. **Email:** ehquintana@hotmail.com – **CP12)** Faustino Sarmiento 5046 y Vela, Latacunga. – **CP13)** Calavi y Gonzalo Albarracin, La Maná. – **CP14)** António Clavijo, P3, Latacunga.
CR00) CHIMBORAZO
CR01) Cas. 06-01-693 (or: Juan de Velasco N° 20-60 y Guayaquil), Riobamba. Quichua: 0900-1100, 2300-0300. ☎+593 3 961608 🖷+593 3 961625. **Web:** www.ferpe.org - **Email:** - **FM:** 91.7. – **CR02)** Cas. 06-01-0242, Riobamba. – **CR03)** Pichincha 1363 y Cardondelet, Riobamba. – **CR04)** Cas. 06-01-572 (or: Av.Daniel León Borja 30-44), Riobamba. ☎+593 3 960101. 🖷+593 3 940464. **Email:** radiomundial@soccer.com or camelosg@yahoo,com – **CR05)** Cas.87A, Majipamba, Colta. Prgrs. in Quichua only. – **CR06)** Francia 1857 y Villaroel, Riobamba. – **CR07)** Cardondelet 2952 y J.Montalvo, Riobamba. – **CR08)** 10 de Agosto 1742 y Benalcazar, Riobamba. – **CR09)** M. E. Flor 4009, Riobamba. – **CR10)** Ayacucho 3234 (or: Cas. 06-01-0471), Riobamba. – **CR11)** Padre Mancero y Av. Amazonas (Parque Central), Penipe. ☎+593 3 940494 - **FM:** 99.3. – **CR12)** Calle Pichincha 24-26 y Veloz (or: Cas. 82), Riobamba - **FM:** 100.1. – **CR13)** Av.C.Norte y Av. Circunvalación, Riobamba. – **CR14)** Cas. 334 (or: La Paz y México Esq.), Riobamba. ☎+593 3 961331 🖷+593 3 961330. – **CR15)** Cas. 06-01-0376, Riobamba. – **CR16)** Cas. 06-03-0805, Alausí. – **CR18)** Comunidad Sta Cruz, Guamote. – **CR19)** Panamericana y Eloy Alfaro, Pallatanga. – **CR20)** 1 Constituyente y G. Rendon, Cumanda.
EO00) EL ORO
EO01) Bolívar Madero 1313, via Pto Bolívar, Machala. ☎+593 7 929845 – **EO02)** Cas. 221, Machala. – **EO03)** Bolívar 601, Edif.Encasa, Machala. – **EO04)** Libertad y Vega Davila, Santa Rosa. – **EO05)** Cas. 07-01-0086, Machala (or: 9 de Octubre y Paéz), Machala. – **EO06)** Av. Honorato Márquez, Zaruma. ☎+593 7 972565. 🖷+593 7 972165. – **EO07)** 9 de Octubre y 1 Diagonal, Santa Rosa. – **EO08)** San Francisco 114 y Sucre, Zaruma. – **EO09)** El Oro y Cuenca, Sta Rosa. ☎/🖷 +593 7 943139. – **EO10)** Cap. Chiriboga y J. J. Olmedo s/n, Arenillas. – **EO11)** San Martín 720, Entre Municipalidad y Och, Pasaje. – **EO12)** 9 de Octubre y Sta Rosa, Machala. – **EO13)** Calle Pasaje s/n y Costa Oeste, Machala. – **EO14)** Av.Heroes de Panupali y Av.Loja, Piñas. ☎+593 7 976165 🖷+593 7 976983. – **EO15)** Cdla. Jaime Roldós, Calle Martha Bucaram, Huaquillas. – **EO16)** Machala. (see also GU07) – **EO17)** Av. del Ejército, El Guabo. – **EO18)** Av. del Periodista y Calle Jon, Machala. –**EO19)** Av. 9 de Octubre y 23 de Abril, Machala. ☎+593 7 962300.
ES00) ESMERALDAS
ES01) Sucre y Catedral (or: Cas. 08-01-65), Esmeraldas. **Email:** lepla@latinmail.com - **FM:** 105.9. – **ES02)** Malecón 805 y Cañizares, Esmeraldas. (se also GU07) – **ES03)** Manuela Cañizares y Olmedo, Esmeraldas - **FM:** 96.3. – **ES04)** Edif.Mutualisat. Vargas Torres,, Esmeraldas. – **ES05)** Simon Plata Torres y Maclovio Velazco, Quinindé. – **ES06)** Bolívar s/n, Esmeraldas. – **ES07)** Gustavo Becerra y Piedrahita, Esmeraldas. – **ES08)** Edif. Venegas, P5, Parque Principal, La Concordia. – **ES09)** Bolívar 513 y Piedrahita, Esmeraldas.
GU00) GUAYAS
GU01) Cas. 4144 (or: Boyaca 642 y Padre Solano), Guayaquil. **Web:** www.cre.com.ec/cre htm **Email:** cresat@gye.satnet.net ☎+593 4 2564290. 🖷+593 4 560386 - **FM:** 105.7. – **GU02)** Cas. 2119, Guayaquil (or:

Amazonas 743 y Veintemilla, P8, Quito). **Web:** www.radiocadenauno.com/ – **GU03)** Quisquis 316 y Garaicoa, Edif. Huancavelica, Guayaquil. – **GU04)** Quisquis 316 y Garaicoa, Guayaquil. – **GU05)** Cas 9974 (or: Av. de Las Américas junto Canal 10), Guayaquil. **Web:** http://superk800.com/ – **GU06)** Rumichacha 934 y Velez, Guayaquil. – **GU07)** Cas. 11714 (or: Av.Francisco de Orellana y Juan Tanca Marengo), Guayaquil. ☎+593 4 2680588. 🖷+593 4 2680592.**Web:** www.radiosucre.com.ec – **Email:** rsucre@radiosucre.com or: info@radiosucretv.com - **FM:** 95.3. – **GU08)** Cas. 2440 (or: Escobedo 1504 y Aguirre, P9), Guayaquil. – **GU09)** Cas. 716, (or: P. Icaza 437 y Córdoba), Guayaquil. ☎+593 4 2561220. 🖷+593 4 564570. **Email:** caravana@gye.satnet.net - **FM:** 88.1. – **GU10)** Cas. 09-01-4203 (or: Colón 548 y Boyacá, P7), Guayaquil. – **GU11)** Juan Montalvo 1042, El Milagro. – **GU12)** Cas. 856 (or: Edif. Gran Pasaje. Of. 906/908), Guayaquil. – **GU13)** Cas. 09-01-5762, Guayaquil. **Email:** sfrancisco@telconet.net ☎+593 4 2530058. – **GU14)** Cas. 5062 (or: Laque 1407 y Antepara), Guayaquil. **Email:** rcristal@ecua.net.ec – **GU15)** Malecón 206 entre Juan Montalvo y Loja, Guayaquil - **FM:** 92.9. – **GU16)** Pista Papín, El Empalme. – **GU17)** García Moreno y Hurtavbo, en los Altos, Ofc.Delgado Travel P3, Guayaquil. – **GU18)** 10 de Agosto 504 y Chimborazo, P3), Guayaquil. ☎+593 4 2322495. ☎+593 4 2329695. **Email:** servidor1000@hotmail.com – **GU19)** Urdesa, Av.Circunvalación Sur 111-B, frente al parque, Guayaquil. ☎+593 4 2885449. – **GU20)** José de Antepara 4415 y Nicolas González, Guayaquil. – **GU21)** Cas. 09-01-4719 (or: García Moreno 913), Guayaquil. – **GU22)** Bolivia 713 y Noguchi, Guayaquil. – **GU23)** Cas. 856, Guayaquil. – **GU24)** Aguirre 931 y L.de Garaycoa, Guayaquil. – **GU25)** Febres Cordero 315 y Chile, Guayaquil. – **GU26)** Veléz 905, Edif.Forum, P16 (or: Cas. 8729), Guayaquil. ☎+593 4 2530288 ☎+593 4 2530059. **Email:** ife@interactive.net.ec – **GU27)** Jiguas 500 y V.Emilio Estrada, Guayaquil. – **GU28)** Lorenzo de Garaycoa 2615, Guayaquil. ☎+593 4 2412533. 🖷+593 4 2412533. – **GU29)** Laurel y Guayacanes, El Milagro. – **GU30)** Luis Urdaneta 202 y Cordoba, Guayaquil. – **GU31)** Simon Bolívar, entre Gonzales y Telégrafo, Guayaquil. – **GU32)** Av. 17 de Septiembre, El Milagro. – **GU33)** García M 1135 y 9 de Octubre, El Milagro. – **GU34)** Km 26.5 vía Duran-Tambo, Virgen de Fátima. – **GU35)** Quito 1520 entre Sucre y Colón, Guayaquil. – **GU36)** Guayaquil y 9 de Octubre, Santa Elena. – **GU37)** Av. 5 de Octubre 150, Naranjito. ☎+593 4 2720212. – **GU38)** Av. 25 de Julio cdla 7 Lagos C, Guayaquil. – **GU39)** Cas. 5940, Guayaquil. ☎+593 4 2481300. 🖷+593 4 2485166. **Web:** www.inocar.mil.ec **Email:** inocar@inocar.mil.ec **GU40)** Pastaza y 15 de Octubre, El Naranjal. **Email:** jpinoargote@hotmail.com – **GU41)** 4a Av. 619 y Robles, La Libertad. ☎+593 4 2785129. 🖷+593 4 2786296. **Email:** lvp@porta.net – **GU42)** Jaime Roldos 700 y Av.8 de Abril, El Triunfo. – **GU43)** Cdla.Belén Piedrahita y 1era, Daule. – **GU44)** El Oro y Los Ríos, Samborondón. – **GU45)** 12 de Octubre 1032, La Libertad. **GU46)** Gral. Villamil, Playas (or: Cas. 10983, Guayaquil). – **GU47)** 9 de Octubre y Baquerizo Moreno, Edif.Plaza, P1, Guayaquil. ☎+593 4 2565615. – **GU48)** Edif. El Forum, P5, Ofic. 508, Guayaquil. 🖷 +593 4 2533885. **GU49)** Eloy Alfaro Duran en la Av. Samuel Cisneros, via al Secap, Guayaquil.

IM00) IMBABURA

IM01) . Morales 408 y Sucre, Otavalo. – **IM02)** Celiano Aguinaga y Panamericana Sur, Atuntaqui, Ibarra. – **IM03)** Cas. 413 (or: Olmedo 1178 y Av.Peréz Guerrero), Ibarra. – **IM04)** Cas. 10-01-0179 (or: Bolívar y García Moreno), Ibarra. – **IM05)** Calle Ramón Teanga y Calle s/n, Ibarra - **FM:** 98.5. – **IM06)** Río Chinchipe 397 y Río Daule, Ibarra. – **IM07)** Cas. 3, Atuntaqui. – **IM08)** G. Suarez s/n y Montufar, Pimapiro. – **IM09)** Matovelle s/n, Urcuquí. – **IM10)** Cas. 10-02-1464, Otavalo. Quicha: 0900-1200, 1930-2300, Sp: 1200-1500. – **IM11)** Juan José Flores 11-26 y Jaime Rivadeneira, Ibarra. ☎+593 6 956008. 🖷+593 6 950828. **Web:** www.imbanet.net/panorama/ panorama.html - **FM:** 93.7. – **IM12)** Av.Reales Tamarindos y Calle Tenis Club, Portoviejo. – **IM13)** Rocafuerte 1-10 y Guayaquil, Otavalo. – **IM14)** Pedro Moncayo 781 y Sanchez y Cifuentes, Ibarra. – **IM15)** Antonio Ante s/n, Urcuquí.

LO00) LOJA

LO01) Av.J.A Eguiguirren y Bolívar, Loja. – **LO02)** Cas. 474 (or: Bernardo Valdiviezo 1054, entre Miguel Riofrio y Azuay), Loja. **FM:** 100.3. – **LO03)** 24 de Mayo y Eloy Alfaro, Catamayo. ☎/🖷 +593 7 677067 - **FM:** 93.7. – **LO06)** Cas. 11-01-222, Loja. **FM:** 88.3. **Email:** Luzyvida@easynet.net.ec – **LO07)** Cas. 196 (or: Olmedo 11-56 y Mercadillo), Loja. ☎+593 7 561166. 🖷+593 7 562 270 - **FM:** 88.9. – **LO08)** Lourdes y Mercadillo s/n, Loja. – **LO09)** Av. Gran Colombia 2663 y Ibarra, Loja. – **LO10)** B. Valdiviezo 08-59, Loja. – **LO11)** 18 de Noviembre s/n, Cariamanga. ☎+593 7 687320. 🖷+593 7 687322. **Email:** rcmga@loja.telconet.net – **LO13)** Sucre y García Moreno, Cariamanga. – **LO14)** Coop. Ahorro y Crédito 3 de Diciembre, Isidro Ayora 235, Catacocha. – **LO15)** Asociación Cristiana de Indigenas Saraguros, Saraguro – Quichua 1200-1400, 2100-2300, Sp: 1400-1600, 2300-0100. ID in Quichua: "R. Alli Michic" - **FM:** 93.1.

LR00) LOS RÍOS

LR01) 12 Calle N° 207 y 7 de Octubre, Quevedo. – **LR02)** Av. Manabí y Juan León Mera, El Empalme, Quevedo. – **LR03)** Av. Velasco Ibarra 1012, Ventanas. – **LR04)** Av.7 de Octubre 727, Quevedo. – **LR05)** Cdla. El Mamey, Babahoyo. – **LR06)** Cas. 31, Babahoyo - **FM:** 100.9. – **LR09)** Olmedo 109, Vinces. – **LR10)** Malecón 407 y Av. Seminario, Babahoyo.

MA00) MANABÍ

MA01) Av.10ma y Calle 17, P2,, Manta. – **MA02)** 10 de Agosto 609 y Olmedo, Portoviejo. (see also GU07) – **MA03)** Ricaurte y P.Moreira, Portoviejo. – **MA04)** Av. Lascano, Chone. – **MA05)** Cas. 4810, Manta. – **MA06)** Pedro Gual, Edif.Servicentro,, Portoviejo. – **MA07)** Colón 180, Portoviejo. – **MA08)** 18 de Octubre 404, Chone. – **MA09)** Calle 13 y Avenida 12, Portoviejo. – **MA11)** 9 y Malecón, Edif. "Jacob Vera", P1 Ofc. 7, Manta. ☎+593 5 622714. 🖷+593 5 628718. – **MA12)** C. Central, Portoviejo. – **MA13)** Bolívar y Espejo, Portoviejo. – **MA14)** Bolívar 1219, Bahía de Caráquez. – **MA15)** 10 de Agosto 180 y Eloy Alfaro, Junín. – **MA16)** Cas. 13-04-0705 (or: 9 de Octubre en Mejía y Rocafuerte), Jipijapa. ☎+593 5 600679. 🖷+593 5 601477. – **MA18)** Chone y Carlos Aray, El Carmen. – **MA20)** Noboa y Colón, Jipijapa. – **MA21)** 4 de Diciembre y Alfaro, El Carmen. – **MA22)** Cas. 13-05-4869, Manta. – **MA23)** 306 Entre Las Avenidas 204 y 205, Manta. ☎+593 5 923666. 🖷+593 5 921635. **Email:** diosvenami@aol.com or esdvami@hotmail.com – **MA24)** Flavio Alfaro 718 Ciudadela San Bartolo, Calceta. ☎+593 5 685169 🖷+593 5 685126. – **MA25)** Cas. 13-02-0629 (or: Montufar N° 1014 y Aguilera), Bahía de Caráquez. ☎+593 5 690370. 🖷+593 5 690305 - **FM:** 95.3.

MS00) MORONA SANTIAGO

MS02) Quito s/n, Limón Indanza. – **MS03)** Tarquí 6-34 y 24 de Mayo, Macas (or: 10 de Agosto 4106 y Rumipampa, Quito). – **MS04)** Luia Casiragui s/n y Amazonas, Gualaquiza. ☎+593 7 780227 - **FM:** 91.7+96.5. – **MS05)** Misión Salesiana de Oriente, Calle 10 de Agosto s/n, Macas. Shuar: 1200-1230, 2230-2300 on SW. ☎ +593 7 700186. 🖷 +593 7 701838. **Email:** radioupano@cue.eolnet.net or radioupano@easynet.net.ec - **FM**: 90.5. For **Radio María del Ecuador** address, se NA06 – **MS06)** Federación de Centros Shuar, Domingo Comín 17-38, Sucúa (or: Cas. 17-01-4122, Quito). Educational prgr. in Shuar only. ID in Shuar: "Shuar Achuara Tuntuiri".

NA00) NAPO

NA02) Cas. 260 (or: Av.Jumandy 536, Barrio 2 Rios), Tena. – **NA05)** El Chaco, Parque Central, Archidona. – **NA06)** Misión Josefina, Juan Montalvo s/n y P. Central, Tena. **Email:** coljav20@yahoo.es **Radio Maria del Ecuador:** Calles Baquerizo Moreno 281 y Leonidas Plaza, Quito. ☎+593 2 564714 🖷+593 2 237630. **Web:** www.radiomaria ecuador.org. **Email:** radiomaria@andina.net or info.ecu@ radiomaria.org

PA00) PASTAZA

PA01) Cas. 744, El Puyo. – **PA02)** Vía Macas km 1. 5, El Puyo. – **PA03)** Cas. 728 (or: Ceslaos Marín 391), El Puyo. – **PA04)** Cas. 06-01-777 (or: Ceslaos Marín Junto al Hospital del Iess), El Puyo. ☎+593 3 885385. 🖷+593 3 883099 - **Email:** Radiopuyofm@yahoo.es **FM:** 89.1.

PI00) PICHINCHA

PI01) Ulloa 611 y Acuña, La Fincha, P1, Quito. ☎+593 2 2551 423 – **PI02)** Panamericana Sur km 14.5 (teléfono 2 691 573), Quito. ☎+593 2 2691 573 – **PI03)** Av.Maldonado 688 y Calvas, Quito. – **PI04)** Conde Ruíz de Castilla 997 y Muregeón, Quito. ☎+593 2 2442 650 – **PI05)** Pasaje A 689 y Vasco de Contrera, Quito. ☎+593 2 2442 951. ☎+593 2 2443 147. **Web:** www.geocities.com/~crespo/ – **PI06)** Cas. 60 (or: Mariano Echeverria y Brasil), Quito. – **PI07)** Cuenca 477 y Sucre (El convento de San Francisco), Quito. ☎+593 2 2953 077 – **PI08)** Cas. 17-17-691(or: Villalengua 884 y Av.10 de Agosto), Quito. ☎+593 2 2266808. International service: See Int. Broadcasting section. – **PI09)** García Moreno 751 entre Sucre y Bolívar, P3, Quito. **Web:** www.quito.gov.ec/homequito/ municipio/com – **PI10)** Cas. 17-21-1971 (or: La Coruña 2104 y Whimper, Edif.Aragones) Quito. ☎+593 2 508 301. **Email:** radioquito@elcomercio.com ☎+593 2 2508 301. – **PI11)** (See GU26). – **PI12)** Av. Principal s/n, Maldonado. – **PI13)** Amazonas 1638 y La Pinta, Quito. ☎+593 2 2559 383. – **PI15)** Panamericana Sur km 14.5 (teléfono 2 678 989), Quito. ☎+593 2 2678 989 – **PI16)** Ramírez Dávalos 612 y 10 de Agosto, Quito. – **PI17)** Av.Amazonas y Colón, Edif.España, P4, Ofc.42, Quito ☎+593 2 2905 471 – **PI18)** Cas. 17-03-540 (or: Av.América 1830 y Mercadillo),Quito. ☎+593 2 2245 770. **Web:** www.radiocatolica-ecuador.org **Email:** buenanoticia@radiocatolica.org.ec – **PI19)** Palacio 303 y Av. La Gasca, Quito. (see also GU07) – ☎+593 2 2484591 **PI20)** Avellanas E5-107 y Av.Eloy Alfaro, Quito ☎+592 2 2484 574. **Web:** www.colonfm.com - **Email:** escucha@colonfm.com – **PI21)** Cas. 17-01-67, Quito. – **PI22)** Morales 1224 y García Moreno, Quito. ☎+593 2 2283 096. – **PI23)** Calle Ibarra y Babahoyo esq, Sto Domingo de los Colorados. – **PI24)** García Moreno 1315 y Olmedo, Quito. – **PI25)** Cas. 045, Sto Domingo de los Colorados. – **PI26)** Edif. Sevilla, P9, J. L. Mera 565 y Carrión, Quito. – **PI27)** García Moreno 446, Machachi. ☎+593 2 2315 025. 🖷+593 2 2315 473. – **PI28)** Tarquí 785 y Estrada,Edif.de Cosi, P2, Quito. ☎+593 2 2903 306 – **PI29)** Guayaquil 124 y Tsachilas, Sto Domingo de los Colorados. – **PI30)** Cas. 17-03-31 (or: Carrión 1288 y Av 10 de Agosto), Quito. **Email:** Irfeval@ecuanex.net.ec or Radioirf@ecuanex.net.ec ☎+593 2 2903 756 – **PI31)** Av.América 4829 y Naciones Unidas, Quito. ☎+593 2 2563 560. 🖷+593 2 2543 625. **Web:** www.explored.com.ec/radio/ index.htm – **PI32)** Cas. 17-11-2263 (or:

Bolivar 359 entre García Moreno y Venezuela), Quito. ☎+593 2 2950 060. 🖷+593 2 2951 018. (In Sto Domingo de los Colorados, studios at Av. Quevedo 405) – **PI33)** Cas. 17-01-638 (or Av. Amazonas N35-89 y Corea, P4), Quito. ☎+593 2 2255 999. 🖷+593 2 2462 562. **Web:** www.radio-eres.com - **Email:** izurieta@ecuafast.com – **PI34)** Marquesa de Solanda 722, Quito. ☎+593 2 2583 942. – **PI35)** Central Roca 331 y Av. 6 de Diciembre, Quito. ☎+593 2 2524 158 – **PI36)** Cas. 17-23-47 (or: Av. General Enriquez N° 29-35 y Río Chinchipe), Sangolquí. ☎+593 2 2331 064. 🖷+593 2 2330736. – **PI37)** 12 de Octubre 227, Quito. – **PI38)** Cas. 17-24-0043 (or: Primera circunvalación y Esmer), Sto Domingo de los Colorados. – **PI39)** Cas. 17-01-3386 (or: García Moreno N 11-184 y Carchi), Quito. **Email:** hcmunomat@hotmail.com – **PI40)** Edif. Doral Mariscal, Of. 86, Páez y Mercadillo, Quito. **Web:** www.radiodemocracia.com – **PI41)** San Miguel s/n y 29 de Mayo, Sto Domingo de los Colorados. ☎+593 2 2750 284. 🖷+593 2 2750 187. **Email:** r.velastegui@andinanet.net - **FM:** 89.7. – **PI42)** Reina Victoria 447 y Roca, Quito – **PI43)** Edif. Vidal Gómez, P3, Sto Domingo de los Colorados. – **PI44)** Carvajal e Interoceania, Barrio Sta Rosa, Tumbaco - **FM:** 104.1. – **PI45)** Av. de la Prensa N°60-22 y Av.de la Prensa, Quito. ☎+593 2 2595 219. 🖷+593 2 2532262. **Email:** rcq_1380@yahoo.com – **PI46)** Av.Amazonas 3911 y Corea, Unicormio 2, P10, Ofc.1008, Quito. – **PI47)** Calle Bolívar y Alfredo Boada (sobre el Banco del Pichincha), Tabacundo ☎+593 2 2365 556. – **PI48)** Cas.17-25-5 (or: Terán 409 y Av 10 de Agosto, Cayambe. ☎+593 2 2360047 – **PI49)** Venezuela 701 y Espejo, Quito. ☎+593 2 2956 679 – **PI51)** Pedro Vicente, Maldonado (or: Concejo Provincial de Pichincha, Manuel Larrea y Antonio Ante, Cas. 298, Quito). – **PI52)** Luis Cordero 557 y J.Mejia, Machachi. – **PI53)** Av.Natalia Jarrín 2-77 y Vivar, Cayambe. ☎+593 2 2360516. **Email:** acayambe@uio.satnet.net – **PI54)** Iñaquito 133-E2 y Unión Nacional de Periodistas, Quito. ☎+593 2 2254782. – **PI56)** Manuel Cajias E 14-09 y Toribio Hidalgo, Quito. ☎+593 2 2234 234. – **PI57)** Yanez Pinzón 257 y Colón, Quito. – **PI58)** Panamericana Sur km 14.5 (teléfono 2 245 300), Quito ☎+593 2 2245 800. – **PI59)** Gonzalo Díaz de Pineda 290 y Pedro del Alfaro, Quito. ☎+593 2 2660 580.

SU00) SUCUMBIOS
SU01) Cas. 21-01-45, Nueva Loja - **FM:** 101.7. – **SU02)** Cas. 21-01-14 (or: Venezuela y Progreso), Nueva Loja. ☎+593 6 830423 🖷+593 6 830425. **Email:** radiosuc@andinanet.net **FM:** 105.3. – **SU03)** Cas. 40 (or: Mariscal Sucre y 12 de Febrero), Lagos Agrio – ☎+593 6 830201 - **FM:** 99.3.

TU00) TUNGURAHUA
TU01) Cevallos 345, Ambato. (see also GU07) – **TU02)** Bolívar 537 y Fund.del Canton, Píllaro (or: Cas. 18-01-244, Ambato). – **TU03)** Cas. 18-01-181 (or: Sucre 09-42 y Quito), Ambato. ☎+593 3 822450. 🖷+593 3 822450. **Web:** www.radioambato.com **Email:** radioambato@radioambato. com - **FM:** 96.7 R. Amor. – **TU04)** 12 de Noviembre y Ambato, Edif.El Pelegrino, Baños. **Email:** radiosantuario@yahoo.es ☎+593 3 740962. – **TU05)** Cas. 18-01-0674 (or: Av.Cevallos 15-57 y Mera, P10, Ofc. 1001), Ambato. ☎+593 3 823128 🖷+593 3 823097. **Email:** radiolider@uio.telconet.net – **TU06)** Bolívar y Martinez, Ambato. – **TU07)** Cas. 005, (or: Av. 22 de Julio y Padre Jorge Chacón 4-47), Pelileo. ☎/🖷 +593 3 871155. **Email:** radiopelileo@hotmail.com – **TU08)** Cas. 18-01-0574 (or: Castillo entre 12 de Noviembre y Olmedo, Edif.R.Centro), Ambato - **FM:** 93.7. – **TU09)** Cevallos 1624 y Maldonado, Ambato. – **TU10)** Cevallos 754 y Martinez (or: Cas. 18-01-0198), Ambato. – **TU11)** Cotacachi 176 e Iliniza, Ambato. – **TU12)** Cas. 18-01-115 (or: Fray Fausto Suárez, Francisco Flor 321), Ambato - **FM:** 92.9/104.5/106.9. – **TU13)** Cas. 618 (or: Calle Ayllón 1753 y Darquea), Ambato. – **TU14)** Barrio El Censo via San Miguelito, Píllaro. – **TU15)** Quisquis 343 y A.Clavijo, Pelileo. – **TU16)** Av.El Rey, Ciudadela Oriente, Ambato. – **TU17)** Montalvo 106, Quero. – **TU18)** Av. El Rey s/n, Frente al Parque Central, Mocha, Ambato. – **TU19)** Calle Montalvo y Av. Cevallos, Ambato. ☎+593 3 421789 – **TU20)** Sector Kiambe, Quero.

ZC00) ZAMORA-CHINCHIPE
ZC01) Sevilla de Oro 3-12 y Pasaje San Francisco, Zamora. **Web:** www.lvzradio.org.ec **Email:** lvzradio@yahoo.es - **FM:** 102.7. – **ZC02)** Parroquia 28 de Mayo, Cantón Yacuambí.

FM in Quito: 88.1 FM88 – 88.5 Metro – PI08) 89.3 – 89.7 Majestad – 90.1 Tropicalida – 90.5 Concierto – 90.9 Platinum – 91.3 Sabormix – PI17) 91.7 – 92.1 Azuca – 92.5 La Genial – PI33) 93.3 Eres 93.3 – 93.7 Galaxia – PI18) 94.1 – 94.5 Rumba – 94.9 Radio Q – 95.3 Teleonda Musical – 95.8 G.R.D.Int – 96.1 Onda Cero – 96.5 Pasión – 96.9 Paraíso – PI31) 97.3 – 97.7 Centro – 98.1 Proyección – 98.5 Alfa – 98.9 Colón – 99.3 La Luna – 99.7 La Rumbera – 100.1 María – PI23) 100.5 – 101.3 Onda Azul – 101.7 "101.7" – 102.1 R.La Red – PI07) 102.5 Francisco Estéreo – 102.9 Armonía – 103.7 Sonorama – 104.5 América – 104.9 Ecuashyris – 105.3 Kiss – 105.7 CRE – 106.1 Fuegottit 106 – 106.5 Bonita – 106.9 USFQ – 107.3 La Bruja (JC Radio).

EGYPT

L.T: UTC +2h (29 Apr-30 Sep UTC +3h) — **Pop:** 70 million — **Pr.L:** Arabic — **E.C:** 50Hz, 220V — **ITU:** EGY.

EGYPTIAN RADIO & TV UNION (Gov.)

✉ P.O. Box 1186, Cairo 11511 (Street: Radio & TV Building, Cornish El Nil, Cairo). ☎ +20 2 5789461, 5789145, 57577155.
Email: freqmag@menanet.net **Web:** www.ertu.gov.eg (Arabic)
L.P: Pres. ERTU: Hassan Hamed, Chmn Eng. Sector: Hamdy Emara, Chmn Broadc. Sector: Omar Batisha

MW	kHz	kW	P	Times
Cairo	558	100	8a	1200-2400
			8c	0400-1200
Barnis	603	100	1	0300-2400
Batra	621	1000	6a	24h
Asswan	702	10	2e	0400-2000
			4	0200-0400, 2000-2200
El Kharga	702	10	2h	0400-1000, 1130-2000 (Fri 0400-2000)
			4	2000-2200
			9	1000-1130 (not Fri)
Tanta	711	100	9	24h
Qena	756	10	2e	0400-2000
			4	0200-0400, 2000-2200
Abis	774	500	5	24h
Batra	819	1000	1	24h
Santah	864	500	4	24h
Halayeb	882	7	2i	0500-0900, 1700-2100
Matruh	882	10	1	1100-0700 (Fri 24h)
Bawti	918	10	1	24h
Hurghada	918	10	4	0200-0500, 2000-2200
			8a	1300-2000
			9	0500-1300
Salum	936	10	1	24h
Abu Simbel	981	1	1	24h
Assiut	981	10	2d	0400-2000
			4	0200-0400, 2000-2200
Baris	981	1	1	0300-2400
El Arish	1008	100	6a	2200-0600, 0800-1000
			6c	0600-0800, 1200-1500
			7	1500-2200
El Farafra	1008	1	1	24h
El Fayoum	1008	10	2d	0400-2000
Cairo	1071	100	2a	0350-0100
El Minya	1080	10	1	0300-2400
Luxor	1080	10	1	0300-2400
Batra	1107	600	6a	1800-0500
			6b	0500-0600, 1500-1800
			6c	0600-1500
Sohag	1143	10	1	0300-2400
Tanta	1161	100	2c	0400-2200
Quena	1179	10	1	0300-2400
Ras Gharib	1188	10	1	0300-2400
Alexandria	1197	25	2b	0400-2300
Asswan	1278	10	1	0300-2400
Assuit	1305	10	1	0300-2400
Abu Simbel	1314	1	2e	0400-2000
			4	0200-0400, 2000-2200
Hurghada	1314	10	1	0300-2400
Nag Hamadi	1314	1	1	0300-2400
Bawiti	1341	10	4	0200-0500, 2000-2200
			8a	1300-2000
			9	0500-1300
Cairo	1341	100	3c	1700-0100
			8b	0500-1700
Idfu	1341	10	1	0300-2400
Siwa	1341	10	1	24h
Quseir	1350	10	1	0300-2400
El Farafra	1368	1	4	0200-0500, 2000-2200
			8a	1300-2000
			9	0500-1300
El Kharga	1368	10	1	0300-2400
El Dakhla	1386	10	1	0300-2400
Luxor	1386	10	2e	0400-2000
			4	0200-0400, 2000-2200
Ras Gharib	1422	10	4	0200-0500, 2000-2200
			8a	1300-2000
			9	0500-1300
Salum	1422	10	2j	0400-2000

MW	kHz	kW	P	Times
			4	0200-0400, 2000-2200
El Minya	1476	10	2d	0400-2000
			4	0200-0400, 2000-2200
Sohag	1476	10	2e	0400-2000
			4	0200-0400, 2000-2200
El Tur	1485	1	4	0200-0500, 2000-2200
			8a	1300-2000
			9	0500-1300
El Arish	1503	25	2f	0400-2200
Quseir	1575	10	4	0200-0500, 2000-2200
			8a	1300-2000
			9	0500-1300
Baris	1584	1	2h	0400-1000, 1130-2000 (Fri 0400-2000)
			4	2000-2200
			9	1000-1130 (not Fri)
Idfu	1584	10	2e	0400-2000
			4	0200-0400, 2000-2200
Matruh	1593	10	2j	0400-2000
			4	0200-0400, 2000-2200
El Dakhla	1602	10	2h	0400-1000, 1130-2000 (Fri 0400-2000)
			4	2000-2200
			9	1000-1130 (not Fri)
Nag Hamadi	1602	10	2e	0400-2000
		1	4	0200-0400, 2000-2200
Siwa	1602	10	2j	0400-2000
			4	0200-0400, 2000-2200

Prgrs: 1=General Prgr, 2=Local Prgr (2a=Greater Cairo, 2b=Alexandria, 2c=Mid-Delta,2d=North Upper Egypt, 2e=South Upper Egypt, 2f=North Sinai, 2h=El Wady El Gadid, 2i=Halayeb, 2j=Matruh), 3c=Cultural Prgr, 4=Holy Koran Prgr, 5=Middle East Prgr, 6a=Voice of the Arabs, 6b=Wadi El Nile Prgr, 6c=Palestine Prgr, 7=Hebrew Prgr, 8a=Educational Prgr: 8b=Songs Prgr, 8c=Adult Prgr, 9=Youth and Sports Prgr.

FM (MHz)

Site	D	E	G	K	M	N	R	S	Y
AbuS				95.4					
Alx		94.3	104.7	90.1	88.0		101.1	97.6	
Al F				88.6					
Al H								102.2	
Asy	99.1			95.8	89.1			92.6	99.1
Asw	98.6	92.1		95.3	89.0				98.6
Baris				88.8					
Baw				87.6					
Cairo†		95.4	107.4	98.2	98.8	91.5	102.2	105.8	108.0
El A	87.8	94.1		87.8	90.9		97.4		87.8
El D				88.0					
El K				88.4					
El M	91.0	94.2		101.0	87.9				91.0
El Tur	89.4		95.7	89.4	92.5		99.0		89.4
Hal			96.7						
Hga	101.7	94.9		91.7	88.6			98.2	101.7
Ism		93.5			90.4		96.7		
Kat			90.0	87.8					
Lux	93.1	96.3		103.1	90.0				93.1
Mah				99.6	93.1			89.2	
Mat				99.1	95.8		102.6	92.6	
NaH				87.8					
Nuw	99.1		92.6	99.1	89.5		95.8		99.1
Pt S		98.0			101.5		91.5		
Qena	100.1	96.8		90.5	93.6				100.1
Qus				87.6					
Raf				102.0					
SeS	97.6		91.1	97.6	88.0		94.3		97.6
Siwa				90.6					
Shg	99.3			89.7	96.0			92.8	99.3
Suez		91.2			88.1		97.7		

†=Also Cultural Prgr & Middle East Prgr on 89.5MHz.

Stations & Power (kW ERP): AbuS=Abu Simbel (0.3), Alx=Alexandria (58.6), Al F=Al Farfra (0.3), Al H=Al Hammam (0.3), Asy=Assyout (11.2), Asw=Aswan (11.9), Baris (0.3), Baw=Bawiti (0.3), Cairo (100), El A=El Arish (54.5), El D=El Dakhla (0.3), El K=El Kharga (0.3), El M=El Minyah (18), El Tur (11.9), Hal=Halayb (0.3), Hga=Hurghada (7.96), Ism=Ismailia (61.5), Kat=Katherina (0.3), Lux=Luxor (11.7), Mah=Mahalla (155), Mat=Matruh (9.77), NaH=Naga Hammady (0.3), Nuw=Nuweiba (9.53), Pt S=Port Said (10), Qena (28.6), Qus=Quseir (0.3), Raf=Rafah (0.3), SeS=Sharm El Sheikh (7.41), Siwa (0.3), Shg=Sohag (38), Suez (8.71).

Prgrs: D=Educational Prgr, E-European Prgr, G=General Prgr, K=Koran, M=Musical Prgr, N=News & Music Prgr, R=Regional Prgr, S=Songs Prgr, Y=Youth and Sport

ANN: General Prgr: "Idha'atu jumhuriya misr al'arabbiya min al-qahira". Voice of the Arabs: "Saut al-'arab, min al-qahira". Holy Koran prgr: "Idha'atu-l-Quran min al-qahira" – **V.** by QSL-card. Re. to P.O. Box 1186, Cairo. Schedules available on request.

EXTERNAL SERVICES: Radio Cairo
see International Broadcasting Section.

Other FM Stations
Three new private stations have been reported:
Negoom FM, Cairo 100.6MKHz. Arabic music, 24h
Nile 1 FM, Cairo 104.2MHz. Mainly English music, 24h
Radio Orient, Alexandria 88.7MHz

AFRTS Low-power broadcasts of NPR and AFN to US contingent of UN MFO in Sinai rep. on wide range of freq. from 92.7 to 106.1. Also 107.0 at Gebel Musa.

EL SALVADOR

L.T: UTC -6h — **Pop:** 6.3 million— **Radios:** 2,080,000 — **Pr.L:** Spanish — **E.C:** 60Hz, 115V — **ITU:** SLV.

SUPERINTENDENCIA GENERAL DE ENERGÍA Y TELECOMUNICACIONES (SIGET)

✉ Sexta Décima Calle Poniente y 3°Av.Sur N° 2001, Colonía Flor Blanca, San Salvador. 🖷 +503 254438 (+503 25SIGET)
Web: www.siget.gob.sv

ASOCIACION SALVADORENA DE RADIODIFUSION (ASDER)

✉ Ap.210, San Salvador.

MW: Call YS–,° = also on SW, * = inactive, (r) = repeater, v = varying fq
H.of tr: 1100-0400 exc.where indicated.

	Call	kHz	kW	Name and h. of tr.
1)	HV	540	5	R.Restauración, San Salvador: (r: 98.1)
2)	FG	550	2	R.Variedades, Sonsonate
3)	KT	*570	10	R.Cadena Central, La Libertad (r:103.7)
4)	NK	600	3	Vox FM, San Salvador (r:94.5)
5)	SS	*610	10	R.El Salvador, Morazán (r:655)
64)	LN	630	10	R. Promesa, San Salvador: 1130-0400
5)	SS	*655	10	R.El Salvador, San Salvador
7)	UU	*700	5	Más Hits FM, San Salvador
9)	RA	720	1	R. Paz, San Salvador (r:88.9)
5)	SS	*750	10	R.El Salvador, Santa Ana (r:655)
10)	KL	770	10	R.Cadena YSKL,San Salvador: 1030-0530
10)	KL	780	5	R.Cadena YSKL, San Miguel (r:770)
10)	KL	780	1	R.Cadena YSKL, Sonsonate (r:770)
10)	KL	780	1	R.Cadena YSKL, Usulután (r:770)
10)	KL	780	1	R.Cadena YSKL, Sta Ana (r:770)
11)	AX	800	10	R.María El Salvador, San Salvador: 24h
12)	FA	810	2	R.Lorenzana, San Vicente
44)	DA	°810	1	R.Imperial, Sonsonate: 1100-0300
13)	PX	*830	5	R.Pax, San Miguel
14)	FB	840	10	R.Santa Bíblia, San Salvador: 1030-0300
15)	RC	860	1	R.Tecana, Sta Ana
16)	AR	870	10	R.Renacer, San Salvador: 24h
8)	CD	880	1	R.Ritmo, Stgo de María
17)	LA	890	3	R.Musical, Sta Ana: 1000-0500
18)	QJ	*900	2	R.El Tiempo, San Salvador
19)	TG	930	5	R.Cadena Sonora, San Salvador: 1100-0500
19)	TG	930	1	R.Cadena Sonora, Sonsonate (r:930)
19)	TG	930	1	R.Cadena Sonora, San Miguel (r:930)
19)	TG	930	1	R.Cadena Sonora, Sta Ana (r:930)
19)	TG	930	1	R.Cadena Sonora, Ahuachapán (r:930)
19)	TG	930	1	R.Cadena Sonora, Usulután (r:930)
62)	HG	950	1	R.Cristo Te Llama, San Miguel
21)	TW	960	0.5	R.Centro, Sonsonate
47)	MS	970	5	R.UTEC–R.Universidad Tecnológica, San Salvador: 1200-0400
63)	AT	990	1	R.UPA "La radio de los niños", San Salvador: 1200-0700 (r:90.9)
24)	HH	1000	1	Estación H, Sta Ana
25)	CA	v1020	5	R.Internacional, San Salvador: 1100-0300
27)	RM	1030	1	R.Frontera, Ahuachapán: 1200-0400
26)	AN	1070	1	LV de los Ausoles, Ahuachapán
61)	ME	1080	5	R.CRET, San Salvador

	Call	kHz	kW	Name and h. of tr.
61)		1080	1	R.CRET, Sta Ana
28)	MG	v1090	3	R.1090, Atiquizaya
29)	RF	*1100	3	R.Ranchera, San Salvador
30)	CL	*1110	2.5	R.Horizonte, San Miguel (r.1160)
58)	LR	1120	3	R.Voz que Clama en Desierto, San Salvador: 1130-0400
20)	LG	1130	1	R.Chaparrastique, San Miguel
31)	AJ	1130	1	R.Moderna, Sta Ana: 1200-0400
23)	TS	1140	10	R.El Mundo, San Salvador: 1130-0600 (r:93.7)
32)	CF	1150	1	Estéreo Mi Consentida, San Miguel: 1930-0200
48)	RG	1160	1	R.Corporación, Sta Ana
30)	CL	*1160	3	R.Horizonte, San Salvador
55)	CR	1170		R.Cristo Viene, San Miguel
2)	CB	1175	0.5	LV del Pacifico, Sonsonate (n.1170)
33)	VG	1180	5	R.VEA–Voz Evangélica de América, San Salvador: 1200-0300
29)	MM	*1200	10	R.Familiar, San Salvador
34)	KJ	*1200	1	R.Sirama, San Miguel
22)	CG	1210	1	R.La Paz, Zacatecoluca
49)	MT	1240	0.5	R.Metapán, Metapán
50)	QN	1240	1	R.Norteña, San Miguel
35)	AA	*1260	3	R.Abba, San Salvador
34)	QZ	1270	1	R.W "LV de la Verdad en Oriente", San Miguel
36)	QV	1280	1	R.Galaxia, Sta Ana
57)		1280		R.Emaús, San Vicente
37)	MA	1290	1	R.Chalatenango, Chalatenango
38)	LV	1300	5	W-LV de la Verdad, San Salvador
56)	KG	1300		R.Llanera "La Campechana", San Miguel
51)	RV	1310	5	R.Veritas, Stgo de María
52)	AH	1320	1	R.Emanuel, La Unión
39)	HQ	1330	5	R.Cristo Te Llama, San Salvador: 24h
40)	XW	1340	1	R.Novedades, Usulután
46)	FM	1360	5	Super Radio, San Salvador -0400
53)	KO	1370	1	R Lluvia de Bendición, San Miguel:1100-0300
59)		1390		R.Sinaí, San Salvador
41)	JI	1400	1	LV del Litoral, Usulután
42)	UCA	*1420	1	R.Universitaria, San Salvador
54)	KR	1450	1	R.Restauración, San Miguel: 1000-0400
43)	CS	1500	1	R.Fides, Usulután
60)		1550	5	R.Sanidad Divina, San Salvador: 1000-0500
45)	CZ	1580	5	R.Cadena Cuscatlán, San Salvador (r:98.5)

SW:

	Call	kHz	kW	Name and h. of tr.
44)	DA	v17835	1.5	R.Imperial, Sonsonate

Addresses and other information:
1) Ap.2854 (or: Calle al Matazano N° 1, Final Col.Sta Lucía, Ilopango), San Salvador. – **2)** Av.Sta Monica 9, Sonsonate. – **3)** Blvd.Orden de Malta N° 3, Urb.Sta Elena, Antiguo Cuscatlán, La Libertad. ☎+503 289 5686. 🖷+503 289 5523. **Web:** www.cadenacentral.com **4)** Edif.TV2, Alameda Dr.Manuel E.Araujo, San Salvador. – **5)** Edif. Ministerio del Interior, P6, Centro de Gobierno, San Salvador. **Web:** www.radionacional.com.sv/ ☎ +503 222 9670. 🖷 +503 222 7907. – **6)** 65 Av. S. y Av.Olipica, 192 Edif.Corporación YSKL, San Salvador. ☎+503 223 9267. **Web:** www.radiofmmonumental.com – **7)** Av.Olimpica y Alameda Dr.Manuel E.Araujo, Col.Escalón, San Salvador. **Web:** www.ysuradiocadena.com.sv – **8)** 2a Av.Norte 24, Stgo de María, Usulután. – **9)** Ap.720, San Salvador. – **10)** 65 Av. S. y Av.Olimpica, 192 Edif.Corporación YSKL, San Salvador. **Web:** – **11)** Urb.General Escalon, Pasaje Beethoven 8/E, San Salvador. ☎+503 262 0800. 🖷+503 262 0692. **Email:** president.sal@radiomaria.org or info.sal@radiomaria.org –**12)** Carr.Amapulapa km 1, San Vicente. – **13)** 10 Calle Oriente 102 Bis, San Miguel. – **14)** Iglesia San Pablo, Final 5a Calle Poniente, Colonia Escalón, San Salvador. ☎+503 263 0666.– **15)** Altos del Cine Tecana, Sta Ana. – **16)** 27 Calle Poniente 544, San Salvador. ☎+503 248 1683. **Web:** www.renacer.org – **17)** 4a Av.Sur, Entre 7a y 9a Calle Poniente, Edif.Plaza de Vidrio, Sta Ana. – **18)** Ap.2156, San Salvador. – **19)** Urb.La Esperanza. Diagonal Principal 1322, San Salvador. – **20)** 4a Av.Sur 303 bis, San Miguel. ☎+503 661 3640. 🖷+503 661 7644. – **21)** 5a Calle Oriente 44, Sonsonate. – **22)** 2a Calle Poniente 22, Zacatecoluca. – **23)** Ap.06-210, San Salvador. **Web:** www.radioelmundo.com.sv – **24)** 9a Calle Poniente 25, Sta Ana. – **25)** Av.España y 23 Calle Oriente, Ex Cine Fausto, San Salvador. – **26)** Av.Morazán km 101, Ahuachapán. – **27)** Av.2 de Abril y 8a Calle Poniente, Ahuachapán. – **28)** Esq.2a Av.Sur y 1a Calle Oriente 3-93, Atiquizaya. – **29)** Calle y Col.Roma, Edif.3-B, San Salvador. ☎+503 238 6489. – **30)** 4a Calle Poniente, Entre 43 y 45 Av.Sur, Col.Flor Blanca, San Salvador. – **31)** 8a Calle Poniente 11A, Sta Ana. – **32)** Ap.19, San Miguel. – **33)** Carr. Panamericana km 18.5, Cantón La Palma, San Martín, San Salvador – **34)** Carr.Litoral km 134, Cantón Jalacatal, San Miguel. – **35)** Col.San Benito, Pasaje Las Palmas 182, San Salvador. – **36)** 2a Calle Poniente 43-B, Col.Sta Lucía, Sta Ana. – **37)** 4a Calle Poniente 11, Chalatenango. – **38)** 17 Calle Oriente 143, Barrio San Miguelito, San Salvador. – **39)** Misión Evangelístyica Cristo Te Llama, Ap.855, San Salvador. **Email:** cristotellama@navegante.sv – **40)** 1a Oeste 18, Usulután. – **41)** 12 Av.Sur y final 5a Calle Oriente, Col.Sta Rosa, Usulután. **FM:** 90.1. – **42)** UCA, Universitaria, Autopista Sur, San Salvador. – **43)** 4a Calle Oriente N° 2, Usulután. – **44)** Ap.56, Sonsonate. 🖷+503 450 0189 – **45)** Ap.2147 (or: Carr.Sta Tecla km 5.5, Contiguo Al Circulo Militar), San Salvador. ☎/🖷 +503 298 0365. – **46)** 12 Av.Norte 1712, San Salvador. – **47)** Universidad Tecnológica, 17 Av.Norte 130, San Salvador. – **48)** Sta Ana. – **49)** Calle Principal, Costado Norte Centro Judical, Col. Lomas de Montecristo, Metapán, Sta Ana. – **50)** Col.Hirleman 14 C P Block 6 N° 9, San Miguel. – **51)** Bo. El Centro, C.Bolivar y 4 Av.S, Stgo de María, Usulután. – **52)** La Unión. – **53)** Carr.Panamericana, Crio El Alto, 300 mts al Norte, El Jalacatal, San Miguel. ☎+503 669 8303 – **54)** Ap.210, San Miguel. – **55)** San Miguel. – **56)** Col.Hirleman, 14 Calle Poniente, Bloque 6, N° 9, Col.Hirleman, San Miguel. ☎+503 669 5151. 🖷+503 669 5150. – **57)** 2 Av. N N° 10, San Vicente. – **58)** San Salvador. – **59)** Calle a Plan del Pino, Fca El Rosario ½ Cuadra de Ciudadela Don Bosco, Soyapango, San Salvador. – **60)** Col. La Chacra, Calle Principal 2518, San Salvado. ☎+503 293 3762. – **61)** Barrio La Cruz, 10 Av. Norte N° 203-Bis, San Miguel. – **62)** Misión Evangelística Cristo Te Llama, Barrio El Calvario, 4a Av.Sur 303 bis, San Miguel. ☎+503 661 3283. – **63)** Final 5a Av.Norte, Col.Universitaria Norte Mejicanos, San Salvador. ☎+503 225 9204. – **64)** 75 Av. Norte, Prolongación Juan Pablo II, Col. Jardines de Escalón, final Pasaje KL, San Salvador.

FM in San Salvador: 88.5 Paz – 88.9 Qué Buena – 89.3 Cool – 89.7 Bautista – 90.1 Láser (español) – 90.5 Progreso – 90.9 UPA – 91.3 Pulsar – 91.7 YSUCA – 92.1 La Klave – 92.5 Club – 92.9 Láser (inglés)– 93.3 Globo – 93.7 El Mundo – 94.1 Fama – 94.5 Vox – 94.9 Astral – 95.3 Feliz – 95.7 Verdad – 96.1 Scan – 96.5 Adventista – 96.9 Nacional – 97.3 Corazón – 97.7 Luz – 98.1 Restauración – 98.5 Cuscatlán – 98.9 La Mejor FM – 99.3 Mesías – 99.7 La Guapa – 100.1 ABC – 100.5 100.5 – 100.9 La Chévere – 101.3 Monumental – 101.7 Mil 80 – 102.1 "102.1" –102.5 Femenina – 102.9 102 Nueve – 103.3 Clásica – 103.7 Cadena Central – (6) 104.1 YSKL – 104.5 Sonora – 104.9 Fiesta – 105.3 DM Radio – 105.7 YXY – 106.1 El Camino – 106.5 Ranchera – 106.9 Maya Visión – 107.3 YSU – 107.7 Más Hits FM.

FM in San Miguel: 90.5 Siglo 21– 91.7 YSUCA – 94.1 Cadena Central – 97.3 Carnaval – 09.1 La Pantera – 102.9 102 Nueve.

FM in Santa Ana: 91.7 YSUCA – 92.5 Musical – 96.5 La Conga – 102.9 Doble H.

EQUATORIAL GUINEA

L.T: UTC +1h — **Pop:** 490,000 — **Pr.L:** Spanish, French, ethnic — **E.C:** 50Hz, 220V — **ITU:** GNE.

MINISTERIO DE INFORMACIÓN, TURISMO Y CULTURA

✉ Barrio Nzalang (antiguo África 2000), Malabo ☎ +240 98221 🖷 +240 92444 **Email:** nkat_fuen@hotmail.com
Web: ceiba-guinea-ecuatorial.org/guineees/indexbienv1.htm
L.P: Minister: Don Alfonso Nsue Mokuy

RADIO NACIONAL DE GUINEA ECUATORIAL

✉ Ap. 749, Bata ☎ +240 8 2592 🖷 +240 8 2093 ✉ Av. 3 de Agosto 90, Ap. 195, Malabo. ☎ +240 9 2260 🖷 +240 9 2097/3122
L.P: DG of Information: Frederico Abaga Ondo. Dir. Tech. Radio & TV: Hermengildo Moliko Chele. **Bata:** GM: Sebastian Aloh Aseko. Tech.Dir: Simeon Ndong Mozui. **Malabo:** Dir: Juan Eyene Ekua. PD: Román Manuel Mañe.

SW:

Location	kHz	kW	Times
Bata	5005	50	0500-2300 (irr.)
Malabo	6250v	10	0500-2300

FM: Bata 99.9MHz, Malabo 102MHz.
F.Pl: R. 2 in Bata on FM, Malabo 20kW on 6250kHz.
D.Prgr: in Spanish/French/ethnic. N: 0600, 1415, 2100.
Radio Rural in Ebebiyín, Mongomo and Evinayong, freq's not known
Ann (Malabo): "Radio Uno desde Malabo, capital de la Republica de Guinea Ecuatorial".

Other stations:
Africa No. 1: Malabo 102MHz (see main entry under Gabon).
RFI Afrique: Malabo 88/97.5MHz in French/Spanish.
R. Asonga: freq. not known.

ERITREA

L.T: UTC +3h — **Pop:** 4 million — **Pr.L:** Afar, Amharic, Kunama, Tigre, Tigrigna — **E.C:** 50Hz, 230V — **ITU:** ERI.

MINISTRY OF INFORMATION

✉ Asmara **Web:** shabait.com **Email:** nesredin@tse.com.er

VOICE OF THE BROAD MASSES OF ERITREA

✉ P.O. Box 242, Asmara ☎ +291 1 117111/118711 🖷 +291 1 124847
L.P: DG: Mahmud Chirum. Dir. (Tech.): Mehreteab Tesfagiorgis. Dir (Prog.): Abdu Heji. Dir. (Radio Eng.): Berhane Gerezgiher.
Station: Asmara (Sela'i Da'iro): (G.C: 15N32 038E55)
MW: 837kHz 100kW (Prgr.2), 945kHz 100kW (Prgr.1).
SW: 7100kHz 100kW (Prgr.1), 7180 kHz 100kW (Prgr.2).
Prgr. 1 in Tigrigna/Tigre/Kunama/Hdareb/Nara: 0330-0630, 0930-1030, 1400-1830.
Prgr. 2 in Arabic/Saho/Afar/Blien/Oromo/Amharic: 0330-0700, 0930-1100, 1400-1800.
Zara FM: 100MHz.
ANN: Amharic:"Yeh be Asmera ketema yemigegne yesifiw yeritrea hezeb demts yeamarigna agelgilot new". Arabic: "Huna Asmara, Idha'at Sawt al-Jamahir al-Iritriyyah". Tigrigna: "Ezi kab Asmara Zemehalalef Medeber Radio Demtsi Hafash Eritrea Eyu".

ESTONIA

L.T: UTC +2h (27 Mar - 30 Oct 2005: UTC +3h) — **Pop:** 1,5 million — **Pr.L:** Estonian, Russian — **E.C:** 50Hz, 220V — **ITU:** EST

KULTUURIMINISTEERIUM (Ministry of Culture)

✉ Suur-Karja 23, 15076 Tallinn. ☎ +372 6282208. 🖷 +372 6282200.
Email: peeter.sookruus@kul.ee **Web:** www.kul.ee
L.P: Media & Copyright Department Head: Peeter Sookruus.
NOTES: The Ministry of Culture is issuing broadcasting licenses.

EESTI RAADIO (Pub.)

✉ Gonsiori 21, 15020 Tallinn. ☎ +372 6114115. 🖷 +372 6114457.
Email: raadio@er.ee **Web:** www.er.ee **L.P:** Dir. Gen: Margus Allikmaa.

FM (MHz)	**ER1**	**ER2**	**ER3**	**ER4**	**kW**
Haapsalu	105.3	102.9	106.3	93.6	0.7
Koeru	105.1	102.6	107.6	93.4	30
Kohtla-Nõmme	105.4	102.9	90.4	95.3	11.2
Kuressaare	105.6	103.1	107.0	-	1
Narva	104.7	102.3	89.4	*100.9	0.5
Orissaare	105.9	103.4	107.8	-	20/10/10
Pärnu	104.8	102.3	107.3	94.8	10
Tallinn	104.1	101.6	106.6	94.5	30
Tartu	-	-	103.0	94.4	0.5
Valgjärve	106.1	103.6	-	-	40
Viljandi	105.8	103.3	107.0	95.5	1

*) incl. reg.prgr (see below)
D.PRGR: ER1 (Vikerraadio) in Estonian: 24h. - **ER2 (Raadio 2)** in Estonian: 24h. – **ER3 (Klassikaraadio)** in Estonian: 24h. – **ER4 (Raadio 4/Radio Chetyrye)** in Russian: 24h. Reg prgr ER Narva Stuudio (Pushkini 12, 20308 Narva): on Narva 100.9 in Russian 0605-0700. – **ER Raadio Tallinn** 103.5 MHz (0.3 kW): 24h. N. in English & Esperanto; relays of BBC World Sce, RFI, DW, R. Sweden.

OTHER STATIONS

MW	**kHz**	**kW**	**Location**	**Station**
6B)	1035	50	Tartu	Tartuskoe Semeinoe R.

FM	**MHz**	**ERP**	**Location**	**Station**
4)	88.1	1	Paide	Star FM
1C)	88.3	0.75	Tallinn	Capital R.
5)	88.6	3	Pärnu	Raadio 7
8)	88.7	0.75	Otepää	Kuressaare Pereraadio
6A)	88.7	0.3	Kärdla	Tartu Pereraadio
2D)	88.8	2	Tallinn	RadioMania
6A)	88.9	1.5	Pada	Tartu Pereraadio
6A)	89.0	3	Tartu	Tartu Pereraadio
8)	89.0	3	Vätta	Kuressaare Pereraadio
1B)	89.4	3	Rakvere	Raadio Uuno
8)	89.4	0.4	Palivere	Kuressaare Pereraadio
12)	89.6	1	Tallinn	Tallinna Pereraadio
1A)	89.9	2	Pärnu	Raadio Kuku
1D)	90.2	1	Tallinn	Dinamit FM
14)	90.5	1	Kuressaare	Raadio Kadi
2C)	90.6	3	Tallinn	Russkoe R.
1B)	91.0	3	Pärnu	Raadio Uuno
7A)	91.2	10	Valgjärve	Raadio Elmar
7A)	91.5	0.3	Tallinn	Raadio Elmar
7A)	91.5	1	Kuressaare	Raadio Elmar
7A)	91.7	10	Koeru	Raadio Elmar
5)	92.1	0.3	Puja	Raadio 7
7A)	92.2	3	Linnamäe	Raadio Elmar
4)	92.2	3	Pada	Star FM
17)	92.5	1	Rakvere	Raadio Viru
2B)	92.6	1.4	Anna	Sky Plus
13)	92.7	3	Pärnu	Raadio Pärnu
4)	92.9	3	Linnamäe	Star FM
1F)	93.2	3	Tallinn	Energy FM
4)	93.3	0.75	Kuressaare	Star FM
2B)	95.1	1	Rapla	Sky Plus
2B)	95.2	0.6	Tartu	Sky Plus
2B)	95.4	3	Tallinn	Sky Plus
6A)	95.7	3	Võru	Tartu Pereraadio
5)	96.1	3	Tamsalu	Raadio 7
2B)	96.3	1.5	Vätta	Sky Plus
21B)	96.3	1	Kohtla-Järve	R. 100FM Narva
2B)	96.5	0.15	Põltsamaa	Sky Plus
10)	96.6	0.3	Sangaste	Raadio Ruut
4)	96.6	1	Tallinn	Star FM
2B)	96.8	1.6	Pärnu	Sky Plus
2B)	96.9	3	Palade	Sky Plus
1B)	97.2	0.75	Tallinn	Raadio Uuno
1B)	97.3	0.7	Tartu	Raadio Uuno
1B)	97.4	10	Koeru	Raadio Uuno
1B)	97.5	3	Kuressaare	Raadio Uuno
2B)	97.6	1	Rohuküla	Sky Plus
3)	97.8	2	Tallinn	European Hit R.
3)	97.9	1.2	Viljandi	European Hit R.
3)	98.0	0.3	Varbola	European Hit R.
3)	98.1	1.3	Paide	European Hit R.
3)	98.3	3	Pärnu	European Hit R.
2A)	98.4	3	Tallinn	Sky Radio
3)	98.5	1.2	Vinni	European Hit R.
14)	98.6	0.5	Orissaare	Raadio Kadi
3)	98.6	1.2	Ilmatsalu	European Hit R.
7A)	99.0	3	Pärnu	Raadio Elmar
2B)	99.1	0.3	Otepää	Sky Plus
2C)	99.2	3	Assamalla	Russkoe R.
11)	99.3	0.3	Tallinn	Nõmme Raadio
4)	99.4	3	Ilmatsalu	Star FM
2B)	99.6	0.25	Orissaare	Sky Plus
2B)	99.7	3	Viljandi	Sky Plus
1B)	99.8	2.4	Linnamäe	Raadio Uuno
21A)	100.0	0.75	Tallinn	R. 100FM
21B)	100.0	0.4	Narva	R. 100FM Narva
7B)	100.2	3	Tartu	Tartu Kuku
4)	100.3	3	Seljametsa	Star FM
17)	100.4	1.4	Jõhvi	Raadio Viru
1B)	100.4	1	Kärdla	Raadio Uuno
9)	100.5	3	Paide	Järva Kuku
16)	100.7	3	Põlva	Raadio Marta
1A)	100.7	3	Tallinn	Raadio Kuku
1A)	100.8	1.5	Viljandi	Raadio Kuku
1A)	100.9	2.5	Linnamäe	Raadio Kuku
5)	100.9	0.1	Elva	Raadio 7
23)	101.0	3	Paide	Kuma Raadio
15)	101.2	1	Tartu	Tartumaa Raadio
2B)	101.3	3	Assamalla	Sky Plus
18)	101.7	1	Võru	Raadio Ring
2A)	102.1	0.7	Kohtla-Nõmme	Sky Radio
19)	102.1	1	Tallinn	Power Hit R
7B)	102.4	0.2	Otepää	Tartu Kuku
5)	103.1	0.5	Tallinn	Raadio 7
4)	103.2	3	Parksepa	Star FM
2C)	103.6	0.3	Narva	Russkoe R.
19)	103.9	0.1	Pärnu	Power Hit R
18)	104.7	1	Tartu	Raadio Ring
20)	104.9	1	Tallinn	Euro FM
1C)	105.6	0.7	Tartu	Capital R
1A)	105.8	1	Tallinn	Raadio Kuku
2A)	107.9	0.3	Narva	Sky Radio

Addresses & other information:
1A,B,C,D,E) Narva mnt. 63, 10152 Tallinn. Email: 1A) kuku@kuku.ee; 1B) uuno@uuno.ee; 1C) info@capitalfm.ee; 1D) in Russian. – **2A,B,C,D)** Pärnu mnt. 139c, 11317 Tallinn. Email: skymedia@sky.ee. In Russian, exc. 2B. 2C)

rel. Russkoye R. from Russia. 2D) Email: reklaam@mania.ee – **3)** Tartu mnt 80c, 10112 Tallinn. Email: radio@superfm.lv – **4)** Peterburi tee 81, 11415 Tallinn. Email: starfm@starfm.ee – **5)** PK 3396, 10115 Tallinn. Email: raadio7@raadio7.ee – **6A,B)** Annemõisa 8, 50708 Tartu. Email: tartu@pereraadio.ee; 6B) Religious prgr's in Russian: 24h. Email: am1035@bk.ru – **7A,B)** Õpetaja 9a, 51003 Tartu. Email: 7A) elmar@elmar.ee; 7B) raadio@tartukuku.ee – **8)** Tallinna mnt. 45, 93811 Kuressaare. Email: famrakur@tt.ee – **9)** Pärnu tn. 18, 72712 Paide. Email: kukupai@estpak.ee – **10)** Pikk 3A, 68206 Valga. Email: ruutfm@ruutfm.ee – **11)** Jaama 2, 11621 Tallinn. Email: nommeraadio@infonet.ee – **12)** Endla 29, 10129 Tallinn. Email: tallinn@pereraadio.ee – **13)** Esplanaadi 10-409, 80010 Pärnu. Email: raadio@pfm.ee – **14)** Pikk tn. 62, 93815 Kuressaare. Email: raadio@kadi.ee – **15)** Tartu. – **16)** Kesk tn. 39, 63308 Põlva. Email: kaguraadio@kaguraadio.ee – **17)** Lai 9, 44308 Rakvere. Email: raadio.viru@mail.ee – **18)** Lembitu tn. 2, 65608 Võru. Email: mail@raadioring.ee – **19)** Peterburi tee 81, 11415 Tallinn. Email: info@power.ee – **20)** Tallinn. – **21A,B)** Email: urho@100fm.ee. In Russian. 21A) Narva mnt. 63, 10152 Tallinn; 21B) Kangelaste 2a, 20605 Narva. – **22)** Prääma tee 11, 72720 Paide. Email: kuma@kuma.ee

DAB: Ch 10D **MHz** 215.072 **Location:** Tallinn **Operator:** Levira

ETHIOPIA

L.T: UTC +3h — **Pop:** 66m — **Pr.L:** Amharic, Somali, Tigre, Tigrinya, Oromo — **E.C:** 50Hz, 220V — **ITU:** ETH

RADIO ETHIOPIA

P.O. Box 1020, Addis Ababa ☎ +251 1 711111/714104 Fax +251 1 713222 **Web:** www.angelfire.com/biz/radioethiopia **L.P:** GM: Ato Fikadu Yimeru. SM: Kasa Miloko. CE: Kebede Gobena. Head of English Prgrs: Melesse Edea.

MW	kHz	kW		kHz	kW
Bahir Dar	594	100	Addis Ababa	873	100
Metu	684	100	Robe	972	100
Arba Minch	828	100	Unk. location	1322v	-
Harar	855	100	3 st's	1485	1

SW: Gedja (G.C: 08N47 038E38): 100kW on 5990/7110/9704v kHz.
FM: Addis Ababa 93.2/97.1MHz.
National Programme in Amharic/Vernaculars: MF 0300-0600, 0800-2000, SS 0400-2000. **In English:** MF 1030-1100.
ANN: Nat. Sce: Amharic: "Yeh Ye-Ethiopia Radio Naw". E: "This is R. Ethiopia broadcasting in English". **IS:** Electronic keyboard.
International Service: see International Radio section.

RADIO FANA

P.O.Box 30702, Addis Ababa ☎ +251 1 518655 Fax +251 1 515039 **Email**: rfana@telecom.net.et **L.P**: GM: Woldu Yemessel.
MW: Addis Ababa 1080kHz.
SW: Addis Ababa 6210 & 6940kHz 10 kW.
D.Prgr in Amharic/Oromifa/Somali/Afar: MF 0330-0530, 0900-1100, 1500-2000, SS 0330-0800, 0900-1100, 1200-1400, 1500-1800.

VOICE OF THE TIGRAY REVOLUTION

P.O.Box 450, Mekelle, Tigray. **L.P:** Fre Tesfamichael, Dir.
SW: Mekelle 5500 & 6350kHz 10kW.
D.Prgr in Tigrinya/Afar: MF 0400-0500, 0930-1030, 1500-1900, SS 0400-0900, 1100-1630.

FALKLAND ISLANDS (British)

L.T: UTC - 4h (5 Sept-17 Apr: UTC -3h) — **Pop:** 2,895 (excl. military personnel) — **Pr.L:** English — **E.C:** 50Hz, 220V — **ITU:** FLK

FALKLAND ISLANDS BROADC. STATION (Gov.)

John Str, Stanley. ☎ +500 27277. Fax +500 27279. **Email:** fibs.fig@horizon.co.uk — **L.P:** Broadc. Officer: Patrick Watts, MBE. Asst. Prod: Carina Goss. Secr: Linda Clarke.
MW: 530kHz, 15kW. **FM**(MHz): 88.3 Stanley, 96.5 & 102.0 Mt Maria

BRITISH FORCES BROADCASTING SERVICE

Rockhopper Road, RAF Mount Pleasant. BFPO 655. ☎ +500 32179. Fax +500 32193. **Email:** adriana@bfbs.com **L.P:** SM: Steve. Eng. Mgr: Adrian J. Almond.
MW: Bush Rincon 550kHz 10kW.
FM: Pt. Stanley 96.5MHz (BFBS 1), MPA 98.5MHz (BFBS2)
D.Prgr: 24h **N:** 24h every hour from Independent Radio News by satellite from London. **ANN:** "This is BFBS in the Falklands". **V.** by QSL-card. Rp.

FAROE ISLANDS (Danish)

L.T: UTC (27 Mar-30 Oct: UTC +1h) — **Pop:** 49,000 — **Pr.L:** Faroese — **E.C:** 50Hz, 220/380V — **ITU:** FRO

ÚTVARP FØROYA (Gov.)

P.O. Box 328, FR-110 Tórshavn. ☎ +298 342000. Fax +298 342002. **Email:** uf@uf.fo **Web:** www.uf.fo
L.P: SM: Jógvan Jespersen. PD: Jógvan Arge. TD: Hans Andor Johannesen. Head of News: Jóhann Mortensen. Head of Music: Ove Olsen.
MW: Akraberg 531kHz 200kW (usually operates at 100kW).
FM: Tórshavn 89.9MHz (5kW), Klaksvík 94.3MHz (3kW), Hesturin Suðurðy 97.5MHz (3kW), 100.0MHz Støðlafjall (0.5kW) + 11 st's low power.
D.Prgr: MF 0700-2310, Sat 0715-0100, Sun 1000-1900.

RÁS 2 (Comm.)

Hoyvíksvegur 61, FR-110 Tórshavn. ☎ +298 359999. Fax +298 359990. **Email:** ras2@ras2.fo. **Web:** www.ras2.fo
L.P: SM: Petur Jacobsen. Head of Engineering: Ronny Petursson.
FM: Tórshavn 102.0MHz, Vestmanna 102.5MHz, Suðurðy 102.6MHz, Streymoy 106.0MHz, Eysturoy 106.5MHz, Klaksvik: 107.0MHz, Miavagur 107.5MHz, Eusturhøvdi 107.5MHz.
D.Prgr: MF: 0945-2300, SS: 0945-2130

LINDIN KRISTILIGT KRINGVARP (Rlg.)

Bøkjaragøta 9, Box 2163, FR-110 Tórshavn. ☎ +298 321377. Fax +298 321379. **Email**: lindin@post.olivant.fo **Web:** www.lindin.fo.
L.P: Chairman: Preben Hansen
FM: Tórshavn 101.0MHz, Klaksvik: 103.0MHz, Fróbia nakkur 104.0MHz, Hestin Há Vági 105.5MHz
D.Prgr: MF: 1300-0700, SS: 0900-0700

FIJI

L.T: UTC +12h — **Pop:** 900,000 — **Radios:** 450,000 — **Pr.L:** English, Fijian, Hindustani — **E.C:** 50Hz, 240V — **ITU:** FJI.

FIJI BROADCASTING CORPORATION LTD. (Independent Statutory Body)

P.O. Box 334, Suva. ☎ +679 331 4333. Fax +679 330 1643. **Web:** www.radiofiji.org **Email:** fbcl@is.com.fj
P.O. Box 606, Lautoka. ☎ +679 666 2121. Fax +679 666 5855.
P.O. Box 1241, Labasa. ☎ +679 82888. Fax +679 63450.
L.P: Chmn: Daniel Whippy. CEO: Simeli Kimi. Mgr. Eng. & Tech. Resources: Ram Deo Raj.

MW	kHz	kW	N	MW	kHz	kW	N
Suva	558	12	RF1	Sigatoka	927	2.5	RF1
Lautoka	639	10	RF1	Rakiraki	1152	2.5	RF1
Labasa	684	2.5	RF1	Sigatoka	1206	2.5	RF2
Labasa	810	10	RF2	Rakiraki	1467	2.5	RF2

FM

Location	Bula 98	Bula100	Bula 102	RF 1	RF 2	BBC WS
Koro-O		93.0	94.6	91.4	92.2	89.8
Sabeto	98.4	100.0	102.4		105.4	106.8
Vunatavou	98.2	100.6	103.0			
Ba	98.2					
Nakobalevu	98.0	100.4	102.0	107.6	105.2	
Rakiraki	98.0	100.0	102.0			
Delaikoro	98.4	100.0	102.4			106.8
Devoux Peak		98.2	100.6	103.0		

RF1 = **R. Fiji 1** 24hrs in Fijian & English; **RF2** = **R. Fiji 2** 24hrs in Hindustani; **Bula 98** = Hindi 24hrs ; **Bula 100** = English 24hrs; **Bula 102** = Fijian 24hrs. **BBC N. in English** 0700. **IS:** Fijian Lali (Log-Drum) - **V.** by QSL-card. Rp. **BBC World Service Relay, FM:** Lambasa 106.8MHz; Lautoka/Nadi 106.8MHz.

COMMUNICATIONS FIJI LTD (CFL)

231 Waimanu Rd, Suva (Private Mail Bag, Suva). ☎ +679 331 4766. Fax +679 330 3748. **Web:** www.fijivillage.com/radio/fm96/index.html, www.fijivillage.com/radio/navtarang/index.html, www.fijivillage.com/radio/viti/index.html **Email:** commfiji@is.com.fj
75 Drasa Ave (P O Box 4190), Lautoka. ☎ +679 666 4966 Fax +679 666 4996. 10 Rowasa St, Labasa. ☎ +679 881 2791. Fax +679 881 2177.
L.P: M.D: William Parkinson. G.M: Ian Jackson. P.D (FM96): Charles Taylor. P.D (Navtarang): Anirudh Diwarkar P.D (VitiFM): Malakai Veisamsama

FM (MHz)	**FM96**	**Navtarang**	**Viti FM**
Ba	99.2	101.6	103.2
Lautoka	95.4	97.4	99.6
Sigatoka	96.6	102.2	107.8
Suva	96.0	98.8	102.8
Rakiraki	95.4	98.8	
Labasa	95.4	97.4	99.6

FM 96 in English, **Navtarang** in Hindi, **Viti FM** in Fijian: all 24h.

RADIO PASIFIK FM 88.8

✉ USP Students' Association, Univ. of the So. Pacific, P.O. Box 1168, Suva. ☎ +679 313900 🖷 +679 312591. **Email:** schuster_a@usp.ac.fj
L.P: GM: Alfred Schuster.
FM: 88.8MHz. **D.PRGR:** MF 1800-2000, 2200-0200, 0400-0800.

RADIO LIGHT FM 106 (Priv.)

✉ P.O. Box 319, Pacific Harbour, Fiji. ☎/🖷 +679 450 007. **L.P:** SM: Arnie Dykes. **Email:** radiolight@is.com.fj
FM: Deuba 106.0Mhz 0.2kW
D.Prgr: Gospel music.

BBC WORLD SERVICE
Lambasa **FM:** 106.8MHz – Lautoka/Nadi **FM:** 106.8MHz – Suva **FM:** 106.8MHz
RADIO FRANCE INTERNATIONAL
Suva – **FM:** 91.8MHz
VOICE OF HOPE
FM: Hope FM – Suva 97.6MHz; Lautoka 91.8MHz; Taveuni 92.2MHz; Sigatoka 107.0MHz **D.Prgr:** Contemporary Christian in Hindi & Fijian.

FINLAND

L.T: UTC +2h (27 Mar-30 Oct: UTC +3h) — **Pop:** 5.2 million — **Pr.L:** Finnish, Swedish — **E.C:** 50Hz, 230V — **ITU:** FIN

VIESTINTÄVIRASTO (FICORA, Finnish Communications Regulatory Authority)

✉ PL 313, 00181 Helsinki ☎ +358 9 69661 🖷 +358 9 6966410 **Web:** www.ficora.fi **Email:** info@ficora.fi **L.P:** DG: Rauni Hagman. Dir. of Radio Adm.: Kari Koho. Dir. of Communications Networks: Tapani Rantanen. Dir. of Television Fee Administration: Esko Kotilainen. Dir. of Communications Markets and Services: Jorma Koivunmaa.

DIGITA OY (programme distributor)

✉ Jämsänk. 2, 00520 Helsinki ☎ +358 20411711 🖷 +358 204117234 **Web:** www.digita.fi **Email:** Comm. Mgr: Riitta.Kontula@digita.fi **L.P:** DG: Pauli Heikkilä. Vice Pres, Mediacasting: Mrs. Sirpa Ojala. Vice Pres, Media Systems Mgmt: Mr. Pekka Mattila. Vice Pres, Netw. & Site Sces: Ilari Anttila.

YLEISRADIO OY (YLE, Finnish Broadcasting Company)

✉ 00024 YLEISRADIO ☎ +358 9 14801 🖷 +358 9 14803216 **Web:** www.yle.fi/fbc **Email:** fbc@yle.fi
L.P: DG: Arne Wessberg. Dep. DG: & Dir. of Radio: Heikki Peltonen. Dir. Corporate Affairs: Jussi Tunturi. Dir. Finance: Marja-Riitta Kaivonen. Dir. Radio 1: Olli Alho. Dir. Radio 2: Jukka Haarma. Dir. Radio 3: Reijo Perälä. Dir. Radio 4 (Swedish language R.): Annika Nyberg-Frankenhaeuser. Head of Int. Rel.: Ulla-Kristiina Haarma. Int. Rel. (Radio): Pirjo Rintakoski. Head of Communic.: Leena Jaakkola.

MW: Helsinki 558kHz 50kW (rel. YLE Puhe & FM1/FM3)
Pori 963kHz 600kW (r. FM1/FM3 &YLEQ/R. Peili). Both 24h.

FM (MHz)	**1**	**2**	**3**	**4**	**5**	**6**	**kW**
Aavasaksa	87.9	89.8	94.7				3
Ahvenanmaa			100.3		93.1		10
Anjalankoski	88.5	92.8	96.9	99.5b*			30
Espoo	87.9	91.9	94.0	98.9	101.1		60
Eurajoki	87.7	92.0	94.8	99.4	103.0		30/3
Fiskars	90.9	93.1	97.0	102.5	99.7		3
Haapavesi	89.0	96.1	98.4				30
Iisalmi	87.7	92.8	96.5				2
Inari	88.4	92.8	98.8			101.9	50
Joutseno	88.0	90.9	98.5				30
Jyväskylä	89.9	92.5	99.3	103.5			30
Karigasniemi	89.5	93.4	96.8			100.8	2
Kerimäki	90.5	95.8	99.1				30
Kiihtelysvaara	88.4	94.9	97.2				5
Koli	90.2	93.4	99.6	102.4b			30
Kruunupyy	91.4	94.0	97.6	99.7	102.7		60
Kuopio	91.6	93.9	98.1	100.2b			50
Kuttanen	94.1	97.2	99.6			102.2	3
Lahti	93.2	95.5	97.9	100.6b			50
Lammaskoski	88.5	91.4	98.7			101.2	5
Lapua	88.2	90.1	93.1	95.2	101.5		60
Mikkeli	88.9	92.1	94.6				30
Nuorgam	88.6	93.9	97.7			101.2	3
Oulu	90.4	93.2	97.3	100.3b			50
Pello	90.2	97.0	99.7				3
Pernaja	89.5	92.3	95.0	102.2	98.3		3
Pieksämäki	89.4	95.3	97.4				2
Pihtipudas	88.6	91.1	97.0	100.8b			50
Posio	87.6	91.5	98.6				30
Pyhätunturi	91.0	97.6	99.9				50
Pyhävuori	88.9	91.0	94.2	98.6	102.6		30
Rovaniemi	88.2	94.0	96.7			103.0	30
Ruka	90.7	92.8	95.1				3
Taivalkoski	89.2	91.9	99.2				60
Tammela	89.2	91.3	96.0				5
Tampere	90.7	93.7	99.9	102.1b			60
Tenola(NOR)	89.0	94.1	95.8			100.5	0.02
Tervola	88.6	92.6	95.6				30
Turku	89.8	92.6	94.3	98.2	101.4		50
Utsjoki	90.7	93.1	99.4			102.6	2
Vaasa	87.8	89.6	94.8	97.3	101.0		1
Vuokatti	92.3	94.3	98.9				60
Vuotso	87.8	90.1	94.3			101.3	3
Ylläs	92.2	95.3	98.1			103.8	60
Ähtäri	91.9	94.6	96.6				3

+14 st's under 1 kW not mentioned.
*b = "FSR Mix", mixture of FM4 & FM5

Additional transmitters

Location	**MHz**	**kW**	**Programme**
Espoo	97.5	3	Capital FM
Espoo	103.7	60	YLEQ (r. R Peili/Capital FM at night)
Haapavesi	101.9	3	Reg. (R. Keski-Pohjanmaa)
Joensuu	100.4	1	Reg. (Pohjois-Karjalan R.)
Jyväskylä	87.6	3	YLE Puhe (rel. R Peili/Capital FM at night)
Kerimäki	97.7	6	Reg. (Pohjois-Karjalan R.)
Kerimäki	103.2	6	Reg. (Etelä-Karjalan R.)
Kuopio	88.1	5	R Kantti (mostly r. R Peili/Capital FM)
Lahti	90.3	0.2	R Masto (mostly r. R Peili/Capital FM)
Pyhävuori	97.2	30	Reg. (Satakunnan R.)
Taivalkoski	103.6	60	Reg. (Kainuun R.)
Tampere	88.3	6	YLE Puhe (rel. R Peili/Capital FM at night)
Turku	96.7	6	R Aurora (mostly r. R Peili/Capital FM)

FM1 "YLE Radio 1" (classical music, culture, actualities): 24h. **N:** 0400, 0500, 0600, 0900, 1100, 1400, 1600, 1700, 2000, 2200.**N. in English:** 1525. **N. in Russian:** 2055. **N. in Latin:** Fri 0755, Sat 1055 – **FM2 "YleX"** (rock & pop culture for youth): 24h (r. FM1 W00-04).**N:** on the h – **FM3 "Radio Suomi"** (news, sports, popular music and regional prgrs): 24h. **N:** on the h – **FM4 "Radio eXtrem"** (Swedish language prgr for young people). 24h (simultaneous night prgr. with R Vega) – **FM5 "Radio Vega"** (Swedish language prgr for elderly people and regional prgrs). 24h – **"FSR Mix"** carries R eXtrem MF 0400-0650, 1415-1700, 2000-2200 Sat 1500-0000 Sun 1500-2200. At other times R Vega – **FM6 "Sámiradio"** (Sámi language network). 24 h. Carries YLE, SR & NRK Sámiradio: MF: 0515-0830, 1100-1130, 1300-1630 Sat 1700-1800 Sun 1700-1830, at other times FM3 – **"Capital FM"** (on fq´s mentioned above), 24h. Carries R Finland & relays of international broadcasters.BBC WS, RA, RFI, NBC, DW, CBC, RTE & RNE – **"Radio Peili"** (digital network carried on FM fq´s mentioned above). 24h – **"YLE Puhe"** (rel. R. Peili, Capital FM and R. Finland in Russian). 24h – **"YLEQ"** (digital network carried on FM fqs above). 24h.

Regional & local prgrs:
In Finnish on FM3: MF 0430-1530, Sat 0503-1400 excl. nationwide news on the h. – **Ylen aikainen,** Radiok. 5, 00240 Helsinki: 94.0MHz. – **R. Itä-Uusimaa,** Rihkamak. 2, 06100 Porvoo: 90.3/95.0MHz. (also r. 94.0MHz) – **Ylen läntinen,** PL 86, 08101 Lohja: 97.0/105.0MHz. (also r. 94.0MHz)-94.0MHz) – **Tampereen R,** PL 110, 33101 Tampere: 99.9MHz. – **Lahden R,** PL 120, 15111 Lahti: 97.9MHz. – **R. Häme,** Viipurint. 4 E, 13200 Hämeenlinna: 96.0/97.3/99.2MHz. – **Turun R,** PL 400, 20101 Turku: 94.3/100.3/107.1MHz. – **Satakunnan R,** PL 113, 28101 Pori: 94.8/97.2MHz. – **R. Keski-Suomi,** PL 3, 40101 Jyväskylä: 87.6/97.0/99.3MHz. – **Kymenlaakson R,** PL 192, 45101 Kouvola: 96.9MHz. – **Etelä-Karjalan R,** PL 100, 53101 Lappeenranta: 97.2/98.5/103.2MHz. – **Pohjois-Karjalan R,** PL 206, 80101 Joensuu:

97.2/97.7/99.6MHz. – **Etelä-Savon R,** PL 361, 50101 Mikkeli: 94.6/97.4/99.1MHz. – **R. Savo,** PL 99, 70101 Kuopio: 96.5/98.1MHz. – **Pohjanmaan R,** PL 1000, 65101 Vaasa: 93.1/94.2/94.8/96.6MHz. – **R. Keski-Pohjanmaa,** PL 1000, 67101 Kokkola: 97.6/101.9MHz. – **Oulu-R,** PL 277, 90101 Oulu: 95.1/97.3/98.4/99.2/102.5MHz. – **Kainuun R,** PL 111, 87101 Kajaani: 98.9/103.6MHz. – **R. Perämeri,** PL 202, 94101 Kemi: 94.7/ 95.6MHz. – **Lapin R,** PL 8113, 96101 Rovaniemi: on 16 FM freqs. **In Swedish on FM5:** MF 0510-0800, 1103-1500. **R. Vega Mellannyland,** PB 87, 00024 Yleisradio: 101.1MHz. – **R. Vega Östnyland,** Krämareg. 2, 06100 Borgå: 91.4/98.3MHz. – **R. Vega Västnyland,** Långg. 13, 10601 Ekenäs: 99.7MHz. – **R. Vega Åboland,** PB 400, 20101 Åbo: 93.1/101.4/103.0MHz. – **R. Vega Österbotten,** PB 1000, 65101 Vasa: 101.0/101.5/102.6/102.7MHz.

DAB: YLE DAB covers the southern part of the country. DAB carries R Peili (actualities), YLEQ (general coverage prgr. for young adults), Ylen klassinen (classical music), YLE Mondo (multilingual) and YLE World (English). The programmes can also be heard on the Internet at www.yle.fi/dab

COMMERCIAL RADIO

Main Networks

FM (MHz)	**1)**	**2)**	**3)**	**4)**	**5)**	**6)**	**7)**	**8)**
Anjalankoski	105.7	102.7		89.3		90.0		
Espoo	106.2							
Eurajoki	106.0					101.7		
Forssa		103.3	97.7					
Haapavesi	104.1							
Hamina			94.4					
Hanko		96.2		104.5				
Harjavalta			93.9					
Heinola			87.6					
Helsinki		104.6	96.2	98.1	96.8	94.9	89.0	92.9
Hämeenlinna		106.5	101.7		97.3	92.3	105.9	88.1
Iisalmi		103.1						
Ikaalinen			92.9					
Imatra			105.3		102.5			
Joensuu		87.9	103.7	102.9	96.4			
Joutseno	103.8	94.2						
Jyväskylä	105.8	101.6	107.1	104.9	97.3	97.7	94.1	96.2
Jämsä		94.4	100.3					88.8
Kajaani		102.8	96.3					
Kannus			92.7					
Karjalohja					88.8			
Kaustinen			103.7					
Kemi		105.2	98.8					
Kemijärvi	104.7							
Kerimäki	107.7							
Kokkola		99.1	96.7				104.3	
Koli	104.3						107.4	
Kotka			87.7		101.5			
Kouvola			100.1		93.8			
Kruunupyy	107.2							
Kuopio	106.7	93.0		105.3	101.6	100.9	106.1	94.8
Lahti	104.4	105.0	103.0	102.4	96.6	89.7	106.4	107.4
Lappeenranta			93.5		96.5			
Lapua	106.5						89.4	
Lohja			96.5					
Loimaa			106.8					
Mikkeli	106.3	100.5	89.7	96.2			87.8	107.5
Mäntsälä				103.4				
Mäntyharju				93.0				
Nokia			95.0					
Orivesi		101.2	103.8					
Oulu	104.8	101.4	89.4	96.4	99.1	95.8	106.9	99.6
Pieksämäki		101.3						
Pietarsaari			94.6					
Pihtipudas	105.1		107.5					
Pohja			95.1	89.4				
Pori		104.5	90.4			96.5	95.7	101.0
Porvoo								90.8
Pyhätunturi	105.8				104.7			
Pyhävuori	107.6							
Raahe		107.0	92.5		87.7			
Riihimäki		107.2						
Rovaniemi	105.5				89.3		93.4	
Ruka	100.8				104.3			
Ruovesi			94.9					
Salo			105.2					
Savonlinna		104.2	96.7		105.2			
Seinäjoki				103.3				
Siuntio			98.0					
Taivalkoski	106.5				105.0			
Tampere	104.7	89.6	100.9	91.6	90.0	104.2	97.2	92.2
Tervola	107.5				100.1			
Turku	103.9	98.7	105.5	106.8	104.6	97.6	107.3	103.4
Uusikaupunki			97.5					
Vaasa		104.4		102.0	93.9	91.6		96.7
Valkeakoski			96.7					
Vammala			89.5					
Varkaus				91.0				
Vihti			105.6					
Vilppula			95.4					
Virrat			99.0					
Vuokatti	105.7				101.2			
Ylivieska		88.3						
Ylläs	107.9				100.7			
Ähtäri		102.9						
Äänekoski			90.5					

1) R. Nova ✉ PL 123, 00241 Helsinki ☎ +358 9 88488700 📠 +358 9 88488710 **Web:** www.radionova.fi Powers 1–60kW – **2) Kiss FM** ✉ Tallbergink. 1C 7. krs, 00180 Helsinki ☎ +358 9 98096501 📠 +358 9 68096521 **Web:** www.kiss.fi Powers 0.1–30kW – **3) Iskelmäradio** ✉ Hallituskatu 11 A, 33200 Tampere ☎ +358 3 31420200 📠 +358 3 31420245 **Web:** www.iskelma.net Powers 0.1–1kW – **4) R. Suomipop** ✉ Lintulahdentie 10, 00500 Helsinki ☎ +358 9 6126911 📠 +358 9 61269130 **Web**: www.radiosuomipop.fi Powers 0.1–1kW – **5) R. NRJ (Energy)** ✉ Kiviaidankatu 2 I, 00210 Helsinki ☎ +358 9 681900 📠 +358 9 68190102 **Web:** www.nrj.fi Powers 0.1–1kW – **6) R. City** ✉ SBS Finland Oy, Tallberginkatu 1 C, 00180 Helsinki. ☎ +358 9 680 960 📠 +358 9 68096522 **Web:** www.radiocity.fi Powers 0.1–10kW – **7) R. Dei (Rlg.)** ✉ Ilmalankuja 2 i, 00240 Helsinki ☎ +358 9 75144511 📠 +358 9 75144555 **Web:** www.radiodei.fi Powers 0.2–5kW – **8) Clasic R.** ✉ PL 800, 00101 Helsinki ☎ +358 9 4767800 📠 +358 9 47678767 **Web:** www.classicradio.fi Powers 0.2–1kW

Note: about 50 more stations are in operation.

ÅLAND (autonomous province)

SVERIGES RADIO cf. Sweden

FM (MHz)	**P1**	**P2**	**P3**	**P4**	**kW**
Mariehamn	95.0	97.1	88.6	102.3	10/7

RIX FM cf. Sweden

FM: Mariehamn, 101.8MHz, 3kW

RADIO SCANDINAVIA 603

✉ Box 14006, S-200 24 Malmö, Sweden ☎ +46 40495000 📠 1-425-795-95 03 **Web:** www.amradio.se (www.603am.com) **Email:** scandinavia603@hotmail.com

MW: Mariehamn 603kHz 1kW. Rep. irr. with non-stop music.

FRANCE

L.T: UTC +1h (27 Mar-30 Oct: UTC +2h) — **Pop:** 60 million — **Pr.L:** French — **E.C:** 50Hz, 220V — **ITU:** F

CONSEIL SUPÉRIEUR DE L'AUDIOVISUEL (CSA)

✉ 39/43 quai André Citroën, 75739 Paris cedex 15. ☎ +33 1 40 58 38 00. 📠 +33 1 45 79 00 06 . **Web:** www.csa.fr

L.P: Pres.: Dominique Baudis

The CSA regulates TV and radio and issues broadcast licenses.

TÉLÉDIFFUSION DE FRANCE (TDF)

✉ 10 rue d'Oradour sur Glane, 75732 Paris cedex 15. ☎ +33 1 55 95 10 00. 📠 +33 1 55 95 20 00 **Web:** www.tdf.fr

L.P: Pres. & DG: Bruno Chetaille.

TDF operates radio transmitters used by Radio France, Radio France International, RFO, and tv transmitters used by FranceTelevisions, ARTE, TF1, M6 and around 1500 private FM tx's.

RÉSEAU FRANCE OUTRE-MER (RFO)

✉ 35/37 rue Danton, 92240 Malakoff. ☎ +33 1 55 22 71 00. 📠 +33 1 55 22 74 46 **Web:** www.rfo.fr **L.P:** DG: François Guilbeau.

RFO is a part of France Televisions and products public service programmes (radio & TV) in the French overseas territories.

RADIO FRANCE

✉ 116 Av. du Président Kennedy, 75220 Paris cedex 16. ☎ +33 1 56 40 22 22. **Web:** www.radiofrance.fr

L.P: Pres. & DG: Jean-Paul Cluzel.

HOME SERVICES

MW	N	kHz	kW	MW	N	kHz	kW
Allouis	A	162	2000(*)	Lille	I	1377	300
Paris	F	585	10	Ajaccio	B+L	1404	20
Lyon	I	603	300	Brest	I+L	1404	20
Rennes	I+L	711	300	Dijon	I	1404	5
Paris	E	738	5	Grenoble	I	1404	20
Limoges	I	792	300	Pau	I	1404	20
Nancy	I	837	200	Bastia	B+L	1494	20
Paris	B+L	864S	300	Bayonne	I	1494	4
Toulouse	I+L	945	300	Besançon	I	1494	5
Bordeaux	I	1206	300	Clermont-Ferrand	I	1494	20
Marseille	I	1242	150	Nice	I	1557	300
Strasbourg	B+L	1278	300				

N=Networks: A=France Inter, B=France Bleu, E=rel. Ext. Sce (RFI), F=FIP, I = France Info, L=rel. local st's at certain times. S=testing AM stereo C-QUAM. (*)1000 kW 1700-0500 (Wi. time) 1900-0400 (DST)

FM:

Station	C	D	E	F	kW
Abbeville	93.1	97.4	89.8	105.8	2.5
Ajaccio	92.4	97.6	88.0		11
Ajaccio (La Punta)	88.6	103.9		105.6	4
Albi				105.5	1
Alençon	93.0	88.0	91.0	105.5	10
Ales	87.6	96.1	98.6	105.1	1
Amiens (St Just)	95.4	102.5	99.4		20
Amiens (Dury)	92.6	97.0	89.3		2
Angers	93.2	91.4	97.4	105.5	10
Angoulême	92.4	87.6	95.1	105.5	2
Arcachon	87.7	97.0	91.0	105.5	1.2
Argenton	101.9	89.8	97.2		5
Arles				105.0	1
Arnay le Duc	94.6	90.3	100.3		3
Aurillac	94.5	98.0	91.9	105.5	7
Autun	88.1	97.3	94.1		10
Auxerre	99.5	89.5	92.8	105.5	5
Avignon	97.4	90.7	93.2	105.2	4
Bar le Duc	90.9	88.4	92.7	104.5	10
Bastia	95.9	89.2	93.9	105.5	10
Bayonne	89.0	96.1	92.7	105.5	20
Beaucaire				105.2	1
Beauvais				105.6	1
Bergerac	92.3	94.0	97.1	105.5	50
Besançon (Town)	98.7	89.3	95.0	104.4	10
Besançon (Lomont)	90.0	97.7	92.9		18
Beziers				105.1	1
Bordeaux	89.7	97.7	93.5	105.5	6
Boulogne sur Mer	103.3	99.9	89.4	106.5	1
Bourges	94.9	88.5	91.8	105.5	160
Brest	95.4	97.8	89.4	105.5	170
Briançon	91.5	97.8	89.5	105.4	1
Brignoles	106.7	104.0	105.5		1.5
Caen	99.6	91.5	95.6	105.5	100
Calais	104.7			105.6	1
Cannes				105.3	1
Carcassone	88.3	96.5	90.9	105.1	80
Castres				105.5	2
Chalon sur Saône				105.0	5
Chambéry	93.5	90.5	98.6	105.1	8
Champagnole	88.5	91.7	98.3		1
Chantilly				105.4	1
Charleville-Mézières	95.8	90.1	93.5	105.9	10
Chartres	94.6	98.1	89.7	105.7	50
Chateaubriant				105.5	1
Châteauroux				105.5	1
Chaumont	96.5	90.4	93.3	105.5	15
Cherbourg	94.1	89.2	92.3	105.6	1
Cholet				105.9	1
Clermont-Ferrand	90.4	98.4	95.5	105.5	35
Compiègne				105.3	1
Corse (East)	96.8	92.3	103.5		17
Corte	98.2	91.0	94.8		1.3
Creil				105.6	1
Dijon	95.9	93.7	99.2	105.1	20
Dunkerque				99.0	1
Epinal	98.6	92.4	89.4	106.5	10
Evreux	87.7	98.9	102.0	105.5	1
Gap	98.3	88.5	95.3	105.5	5
Gex	94.4	96.7	89.6	101.1	20
Grenoble (Chamrousse)	99.4	88.2	91.8		

Station	C	D	E	F	kW (ERP)
Grenoble (T. sans Venin)	89.9	92.8	95.5	105.1	1.3
Guéret	100.7	98.8	90.8	105.5	12
Hirson	94.4	99.7	97.2		5
Hyères	91.6	97.5	94.5	107.1	1.5
Laval	95.1	88.3	92.1	105.5	5
La Rochelle				105.5	1
Laon				105.3	1
Le Havre	88.9	93.3	98.5	105.5	1
Le Mans	92.6	89.0	97.0	105.5	270
Le Puy	99.3	89.3	92.8	105.5	10
Lesparre	92.4	90.3	95.1		1.3
Lille (Bouvigny)	103.7	98.0	88.7	105.2	400
Limoges	93.0	89.5	97.5	105.5	150
Longwy	98.1	88.3	91.0	104.3	5
Lourdes				105.3	3.5
Lyon (Mont Pilat)	99.8	88.8	92.4	103.4	150
Lyon (Town)	101.1	94.1	98.0	105.4	1
Mantes	95.0	92.4	97.1		5
Marseille	91.3	99.0	94.2	105.3	400
Marseille (town)	91.7	98.6	94.7		1
Maubeuge				106.2	2
Melun				106.2	1
Mende	90.1	96.9	93.7		13
Menton	97.0	89.6	91.7	105.5	5
Metz	99.8	94.5	89.7	106.8	145
Millau	94.9	99.2	88.9		6
Mont de Marsan				105.5	6
Montargis	102.9	98.8	94.1	105.5	1
Montauban				105.7	1
Montereau				106.2	1
Montlieu la Garde	87.8	104.8	98.8		3
Montluçon				105.5	1
Montpellier	89.4	97.8	92.9		18
Montpellier (Town)			102.7	105.1	1
Morosaglia	97.1	88.8	93.4		1
Mulhouse	95.7	88.6	91.6	105.5	100
Nancy	96.9	88.7	91.7	105.9	5
Nantes	90.6	94.2	98.9	105.5	200
Neufchateau	96.3	100.3	91.5		1
Neufchatel-en-Bray	92.7	96.0	90.2		5
Nevers				105.5	1
Nice	100.2	101.9	92.2	105.7	100
Nimes				105.1	5
Niort	99.4	96.4	91.1	105.5	276
Orléans	99.2	95.8	90.7	105.5	4
Paris	87.8	93.5	91.7	105.5	10
Parthenay	93.8	87.9	98.5	105.5	13
Pau				105.5	1
Perpignan	92.1	99.8	97.2	105.1	10
Poitiers				105.1	1
Porto Vecchio (Col de Mela)	96.8	90.8	98.9		1.5
Porto Vecchio (Punto di a Varra)	92.6	87.9	94.6		1
Privas	89.8	96.5	94.7	105.2	1
Reims	96.8	98.8	89.2	105.5	170
Rennes	93.5	98.3	89.9	105.5	100
Roanne				105.5	1
Rouen	96.5	94.0	92.0	105.7	100
Saint Brieuc				105.5	1
Saint Etienne	88.0	91.7	97.1	105.6	1
Saint-Nazaire	95.2	92.2	102.6	105.5	1.5
Saint-Quentin				105.6	1
Saint-Raphaël	96.3	88.7	99.6	105.4	50
Sarrebourg	93.1	99.4	90.3		10
Sens	96.3	98.5	93.8	94.3	10
Soissons				105.7	1
Strasbourg	97.3	87.7	95.0	104.4	48
Toulon	92.0	97.1	94.9	105.8	2
Toulouse (town)	103.5	90.5	93.1	105.5	1
Toulouse (Pic du Midi)	87.9	95.7	91.5		72
Tours	99.9	97.8	92.2	105.5	10
Troyes	95.3	97.9	91.4	105.5	50
Ussel	96.0	88.2	99.7		10
Valence				105.4	3
Vannes	88.6	96.0	91.8	105.5	20
Verdun	92.1	99.3	97.4	106.3	6
Villebon sur Yvette	95.4	94.1	97.6		1
Villers-Cotterets	91.1	89.6	92.9		10
Vittel	98.2	89.0	94.0		8

Station	C	D	E	F	kW (ERP)
Voiron	91.5	89.2	107.2	105.4	1

+1458 sts under 1kW

C=France Inter (stereo), D=France-Culture (stereo), E=France-Musiques (stereo), F=France Info (mono). RDS on all tr's.

France Inter Network A on **LW**, C on **FM**; Allouis 162 kHz: **D.Prgrs**:24h exc. Tues 0005-0358. FM tr's: 24h. **N:** Hourly, plus 0530, 0630

France Culture (Network D) (stereo) **D.Prgrs**:24h. **N:** 0600, 0700, 0800, 1130, 1700, 2100

France Musiques (Network E) (stereo): **D.Prgrs**:24h. **N:** 0600, 0700, 0800, 1130, 1700

France Info (Network F) News and informations **D.Prgrs**:24h.

Le Mouv'

78 allée Jean Jaurès, 31009 Toulouse Cedex 6. ☎ +33 5 34 41 70 00 +33 5 34 41 70 06

Station	MHz	kW	Station	MHz	kW
Ajaccio	92.0	4	Marseille (town)	96.4	1
Angers	103.0	1	Mende	107.2	0.2
Brest	94.0	3	Nantes	96.1	3
Cannes	101.1	1	Paris	92.1	8
Clermont-Fd	97.5	2	Reims	101.1	0.5
Dijon	88.9	1	Rennes	107.3	2
Lille	91.0	1	Toulouse	95.2	5
Lyon	87.8	4	Valence	100.7	0.5
Marseille	96.8	2.5			

D.Prgrs: 24h. RDS on all tr's. (stereo)

Local Stations "F.I.P."

F.I.P. Bordeaux, 95 rue Judaïque, 33000 Bordeaux. ☎ +33 5 56 24 13 13 : 96.7 MHz 2,5 kW

F.I.P. Nantes, 1 rue d'Alger, 44100 Nantes. ☎ +33 2 40 73 14 14 . Nantes 95.7 MHz 20 kW, St Nazaire 97.2 MHz 1.5 kW.

F.I.P. Paris, 116 avenue du Président Kennedy, 75220 Paris Cedex 16. ☎ +33 1 42 20 12 34 : 585 kHz 10 kW, 105.1 MHz 10 kW.

F.I.P. Strasbourg, 4 rue Joseph Massol, 67000 Strasbourg. ☎ +33 3 88 35 24 00 : 92.3 MHz 4 kW.

RDS on all tr's. **D.Prgrs:** 24h. Prgrs consist of music and News.

France Bleu

116 av. du Président Kennedy, 75220 Paris Cedex 16.

☎ +33 1 56 40 11 11. **D.Prgrs :** 24h, uninterrupted music 2200-0400

Stations : **MW** Network B + **FM**

France Bleu Local Stations (F.B. = France Bleu) - At certain times, local stations relay a national France Bleu programme.

F.B. Alsace, 4 rue Joseph Massol, 67000 Strasbourg. ☎ +33 3 88 76 20 00 : Strasbourg 101.4 MHz 48 kW, Mulhouse 102.6 MHz 100 kW.

F.B. Armorique, 14 av. Janvier, 35031 Rennes Cedex. ☎ +33 2 99 67 43 21 : Vannes 101.3 MHz 20 kW, Rennes 103.1 MHz 125 kW.

F.B. Auxerre, B.P. 101, 89002 Auxerre Cedex. ☎ +33 3 86 72 34 56 Sens 100.5 MHz 10 kW, Auxerre 101.3 MHz 5 kW, Nevers 104.0 MHz 1 kW.

F.B. Azur, 2 place Grimaldi, 06012 Nice Cedex 1. ☎ +33 4 97 03 36 36 : Nice 103.8 MHz 100 kW, Menton 94.8 MHz 5 kW, Saint Raphaël 100.7 10 kW.

F.B. Basse Normandie, 75 rue Basse, 14053 Caen Cedex. ☎ +33 2 31 47 14 14 : Le Havre 102.2 MHz 2.5 kW, Caen 102.6 MHz 50 kW.

F.B. Béarn, 2 rue O'Quin, 64000 Pau. ☎ +33 5 59 98 30 30 : Oloron Sainte Marie 93.2 MHz 1.5 kW, Pau 102.5 MHz 10 kW.

F.B. Belfort, Centre commercial des 4 as, BP 439, 90008 Belfort Cedex. ☎ +33 3 84 57 90 90 : Belfort 106.8 MHz 2 kW.

F.B. Berry Sud, 10/12 rue de la République, 36000 Châteauroux. ☎ +33 2 54 60 60 60 : Argenton 93.5 MHz 5 kW, Bourges 103.2 MHz 160 kW.

F.B. Besançon, 2 Place Granvelle, BP 591, 25027 Besançon Cedex. ☎ +33 3 81 21 25 25 : Besançon 101.4 MHz 18 kW + 102.8 MHz 10 kW.

F.B. Bourgogne, 29 rue Guillaume Tell, 21000 Dijon. ☎ +33 3 80 59 21 21 : Troyes 87.8 50 kW, Arnay le Duc 103.4 MHz 3 kW, Dijon 103.7 MHz 20 kW.

F.B. Breiz Izel, rue de Falkirk, BP1119, 29101 Quimper Cedex. ☎ +33 2 98 55 29 29 : Brest 93.0 MHz 170 kW.

F.B. Champagne, 28 bd du Maréchal Joffre, BP 1094, 51054 Reims Cedex. ☎ +33 3 26 84 51 51: Charleville-Mézières 100.9 MHz 10 kW, Châlons en Champagne 94.8 MHz 1 kW, Troyes 100.8 MHz 1 kW.

F.B. Cotentin, Place du Général de Gaulle, 50100 Cherbourg. ☎ +33 2 33 88 50 50 : 100.7 MHz 4 kW.

F.B. Creuse, 4 rue de Stalingrad, BP 249, 23005 Guéret Cedex. ☎ +33 5 55 61 23 23 : Guéret 94.3 MHz 12 kW.

F.B. Drôme Ardèche, 7 rue Poncet, BP 519, 26005 Valence Cedex. ☎ +33 4 75 81 33 33 : Valence 87.9 MHz 10 kW, Privas 98.4 MHz 1.5 kW.

F.B. Gard Lozère, 12 av. Carnot, 30020 Nîmes Cedex. ☎ +33 4 66 36 30 30 : Nîmes 90.2 MHz 5 kW, Alès 91.6 MHz 2 kW, Mende 104.9 MHz 10 kW.

F.B. Gascogne, 13 place Jean Jaurès, 40000 Mont de Marsan. ☎ +33 5 58 85 40 40 : Mont de Marsan 98.8 MHz 20 kW, Bayonne 100.5 MHz 38 kW, La Bouheyre 103.4 MHz 12 kW.

F.B. Gironde, 95 rue Judaïque, BP 585, 33006 Bordeaux Cedex. ☎ +33 5 57 81 20 20 : Bordeaux 100.1 MHz 6 kW, Lesparre 101.6 MHz 1,3 kW, Arcachon 101.8 MHz 1.2 kW.

F.B. Haute Normandie, 45 bd. des Belges, 76000 Rouen. ☎ +33 2 35 07 31 07 : Le Havre 95.1 MHz 1 kW, Rouen 100.1 MHz 115 kW, Neufchâtel en Bray 101.6 MHz 5 kW, Evreux 89.5 MHz 1 kW.

F.B. Hérault, 9 rue de la République, BP 1256, 34011 Montpellier Cedex 1. ☎ +33 4 67 06 65 65 : Montpellier 101.1 MHz 18 kW.

F.B. Isère, 10 rue Etienne Forest, BP 154, 38003 Grenoble Cedex. ☎ +33 4 76 86 38 38 : Chambéry 99.1 MHz 5 kW, Lyon 101.8 MHz 45 kW, Grenoble 102.8 MHz 1 kW.

F.B. La Rochelle, 5 av. Michel Crépeau, 17025 La Rochelle Cedex 01. ☎ +33 5 46 35 17 17 : Royan 101.1 MHz 1 kW, Saintes 103.9 MHz 60 kW, Angoulême 101.5 MHz 2 kW, La Rochelle 98,2 MHz 1 kW.

F.B. Limousin, 23 bd Gambetta, BP 422, 87012 Limoges Cedex. ☎ +33 5 55 11 38 11 : Chateauponsac 92.5 MHz 1 kW, Ussel 101.4 MHz 10 kW, Limoges 103.5 MHz 150 kW.

F.B. Loire Océan, 11 rue Flandres-Dunkerque, 44053 Nantes Cedex 04. ☎ +33 2 40 44 45 46 : Saint Nazaire 88.1 MHz 1.5 kW, Nantes 101.8 MHz 220 kW.

F.B. Lorraine Nord, 5, rue d'Austrasie – B.P. 50071, 57003 Metz cedex 03. ☎ +33 3 87 68 22 22 : Metz 98.5 MHz 1 kW.

F.B. Mayenne, 41 av. Robert Buron, 53000 Laval. ☎ +33 2 43 49 50 50 : Laval 96.6 MHz 5 kW.

F.B. Melun, 24 place Saint Jean, 77000 Melun. ☎ +33 1 64 87 77 77 : Corbeil Essonnes 92.3 MHz 16 kW.

F.B. Nord, 14 rue Léon Trulin, 59002 Lille Cedex. ☎ +33 3 20 13 59 62 : Lille (town) 87.8 MHz 1 kW, Lille (Bouvigny) 94.7 MHz 400 kW, Boulogne sur Mer 95.5 MHz 1 kW, Etaples 97.8 MHz 2 kW, Calais 106.2 MHz 1 kW.

F.B. Orléans, 8 rue d'Illiers, 45057 Orléans Cedex 1. ☎ +33 2 38 71 45 45 : Blois 93.9 MHz 1 kW, Orléans 100.9 MHz 4 kW, Montargis 106.8 MHz 1 kW.

F.B. La City Radio de Paris, 116, av. du Président Kennedy, 75220 Paris 16. ☎ +33 1 56 40 11 11: Paris 107.1 MHz 1 kW, Chartres 97.3 MHz 4 kW, 864 kHz 300 kW (C-QUAM stereo)

F.B. Pays Basque, 46 allées Marines, 64116 Bayonne Cedex. ☎ +33 5 59 46 64 64 : Bayonne 101.3 MHz 15 kW.

F.B. Pays d'Auvergne, 80 bd François Mitterand, BP 277, 63008 Clermont-Ferrand Cedex 01. ☎ +33 4 73 34 63 63 : Clermont-Ferrand 102.5 MHz 37 kW, Aurillac 100.2 MHz 1 kW

F.B. Pays de Savoie, 45 place de la Brigade de Savoie, 73000 Chambéry. ☎ +33 4 79 70 73 74 : Annecy 95.2 MHz 1 kW, Chambéry 103.9 MHz 8 kW, Gex 106.1 MHz 20 kW.

F.B. Périgord, 28 rue Ernest Guillier, BP 3033, 24003 Périgueux Cedex. ☎ +33 5 53 06 20 00 : Limoges 91.7 MHz 100 kW, Bergerac 99.0 MHz 50 kW.

F.B. Picardie, Rue du Maréchal de Lattre de Tassigny, 80000 Amiens. ☎ +33 3 22 71 15 15 : Amiens 100.2 MHz 2 kW, Abbeville 100.6 MHz 5 kW, Hirson 101.3 MHz 2 kW, Sailly Saillisel 102.8 MHz 20 kW.

F.B. Poitou, 27, bd de Solférino, 86000 Poitiers. ☎ +33 5 49 60 39 18 : Niort 101,0 MHz 1 kW.

F.B. Provence, 560 av. Mozart, 13617 Aix en Provence.Cedex 01 ☎ +33 4 42 99 13 13 : Brignoles 102.1 MHz 1.5 kW, Hyères 102.5 MHz 1.5 kW, Toulon 102.9 MHz 5 kW, Marseille 103.6 MHz 100 kW.

F.B. Radio Corse Frequenza Mora, 4 rue Favalelli, 20200 Bastia ☎ +33 4 95 32 95 32 : Corse (east) 88.2 MHz 17 kW, Ajaccio 97.0 MHz 4 kW, Corte 100.0 MHz 1.33 kW, Ajaccio 100.5 MHz 11 kW, Bastia 101.7 MHz 10 kW, Porto Vecchio 101.8 MHz 1.5 kW + 105.4 MHz 1 kW, Morosaglia 104.6 MHz 1 kW.

F.B. Roussillon, 34 av. du Général de Gaulle, 66000 Perpignan. ☎ +33 4 68 51 90 00 : Perpignan 101.6 MHz 10 kW.

F.B. Sud Lorraine, 21/23 bd du Recteur Senn, 54042 Nancy Cedex. ☎ +33 3 83 19 54 88 : Epinal 100.0 MHz 1 kW, Nancy 100.5 MHz 5 kW, Vittel 102.6 MHz 1 kW, Neufchateau 103.0 MHz 1 kW.

F.B. Touraine, Les Halles, BP 3231, 37032 Tours Cedex 1. ☎ +33 2 47 36 37 37 : Tours 105.0 MHz 8 kW.

F.B. Vaucluse, 25 rue de la République, BP 320, 84021 Avignon Cedex. ☎ +33 4 90 14 13 12 : Avignon 100.4 MHz 2 kW.

+ 337 tr's less than 1kW not mentioned. Stereo and RDS on all tr's.

Special Programmes (MW)

Lyon 603 kHz religious prgr Sun 1700-1800.

Strasbourg 1278 kHz (religious prgr) Sun 0700-0900. First Sun 1200-1300 prgr in cooperation with SWF4.
Rennes 711 kHz + Brest 1404 kHz Prgr in Breton language. Sat 1100-1300.
Toulouse 945 kHz.. Prgr in Occitan language. Sat 1100-1200.

RADIO FRANCE INTERNATIONALE

116 av. du Président Kennedy, 75016 Paris. ☎ +33 1 56 40 12 12.
Web: www.rfi.fr
LP: Pres. & DG: Antoine Schwarz
RFI1 (French service): Paris **FM** 89 MHz 10 kW (stereo) – RFI2 (foreign service): Paris **MW** 738 kHz 5 kW. **D.Prgrs:** 24h.

FOREIGN SERVICE: Radio France International
See International Broadcasting section.

PRIVATE FM STATIONS

Station	MHz	kW	Station	MHz	kW
17) Besançon	87.6	1	8) Caen	88.7	2
23) Castres	87.6	1	18) Châteauroux	88.7	1
4) Laval	87.6	1	19) Étampes	88.7	1
17) Besançon	87.6	1	9) Ghisonaccia	88.7	4
23) Castres	87.6	1	3) Gray	88.7	1
4) Laval	87.6	1	18) Saint Flour	88.7	1
22) Niort	87.6	1	22) Toulouse	88.7	5
7) Orléans	87.6	2	8) Condom	88.8	1
17) Romilly sur Seine	87.6	1	6) Mantes la Jolie	88.8	2
22) Vannes	87.6	1	8) Nantes	88.8	3
8) Yssingeaux	87.6	1	6) Reims	88.8	2
7) Bourges	87.7	1	17) Saint Dizier	88.8	1
13) Clermont Ferrand	87.7	1	17) Bordeaux	88.9	1
7) Corte	87.7	1	7) Boulogne sur Mer	88.9	1
5) Figeac	87.7	1	13) Montluçon	88.9	1
19) Nice	87.7	2	23) Rennes	88.9	1
21) Saint Omer	87.7	1	6) Valence d'Agen	88.9	1
9) Tours	87.7	2	6) Aurillac	89.0	1
19) La Flèche	87.8	1	6) Avignon	89.0	1
1) Le Blanc	87.8	1	17) Brest	89.0	3
7) Montluçon	87.8	1	17) Clamecy	89.0	1
6) Verdun	87.8	1	13) Moulins	89.0	1
6) Avranches	87.9	1	1) Bourges	89.1	1
6) Dijon	87.9	1	18) Perpignan	89.1	3
21) Menton	87.9	1	8) Saint Nazaire	89.1	1
17) Reims	87.9	2	22) Valenciennes	89.1	1
5) Saint Raphaël	87.9	1	9) Beauvais	89.2	1
2) Toulon	87.9	1	19) Brive la Gaillarde	89.2	1
7) Yvetot	87.9	1	23) Châteaubriant	89.2	1
17) Châteauroux	88.0	1	9) Châtellerault	89.2	1
23) Colmar	88.0	1	9) Decazeville	89.2	1
18) Provins	88.0	1	22) Lille	89.2	2
17) St Gilles Croix de Vie	88.0	1	18) Marseille	89.2	10
17) Vesoul	88.0	1	17) Nevers	89.2	1
3) Villefranche sur Saône	88.0	1	23) Ussel	89.2	1
9) Vitry le François	88.0	1	17) Vichy	89.2	1
17) Angers	88.1	1	17) Castres	89.3	1
3) Avignon	88.1	1	17) Cholet	89.3	1
6) Brive la Gaillarde	88.1	1	13) Longwy	89.3	1
18) Châtellerault	88.1	1	4) Niort	89.3	1
6) Nice	88.1	5	9) Nogaro	89.3	1
6) Soissons	88.1	1	23) Rouen	89.3	2
10) Nancy	88.2	1	18) Bayeux	89.4	1
6) Saint Quentin	88.2	1	18) Bayonne	89.4	2
9) Strasbourg	88.2	4	6) Chambéry	89.4	1
22) Tours	88.2	2	23) Marmande	89.4	1
17) Dijon	88.3	1	6) Roanne	89.4	1
9) L'Ile Rousse	88.3	1	23) Chaumont	89.5	1
17) Roanne	88.3	1	4) Mayenne	89.5	1
5) Laon	88.4	1	6) Strasbourg	89.5	4
9) Lure	88.4	1	18) Ajaccio	89.6	8
17) Lyon	88.4	4	14) Angers	89.6	2
6) Mont de Marsan	88.4	1	6) Clermont Ferrand	89.6	2
19) Nantes	88.4	2	23) Le Havre	89.6	1
21) Sarreguemines	88.4	1	4) Marseille	89.6	4
5) Tonnerre	88.4	1	21) Mende	89.6	1
3) Nogent le Rotrou	88.5	1	7) Vierzon	89.6	1
17) Annecy	88.6	1	13) Mauriac	89.7	1
17) Châlons en Champagne	88.6	1	13) Nevers	89.7	1
6) Châteaubriant	88.6	1	23) Perpignan	89.7	3
8) Chaumont	88.6	1	18) Saint Nazaire	89.7	1
19) Confolens	88.6	1	6) Troyes	89.7	1
16) Paris	88.6	4	6) Agen	89.8	1
18) Villeneuve sur Lot	88.6	1	6) Brioude	89.8	1
10) Alençon	88.7	1	23) Gray	89.8	1
7) Avallon	88.7	1	18) Quimper	89.8	1

Station	MHz	kW	Station	MHz	kW
21) Roanne	89.8	1	6) Laval	91.2	1
6) Sablé sur Sarthe	89.8	1	22) Mulhouse	91.2	1
18) Toulon	89.8	4	17) Orléans	91.2	2
17) Cognac	89.9	1	6) Saint Tropez	91.2	1
18) Douai	89.9	1	19) Cahors	91.3	1
19) Montpellier	89.9	3	9) Cambrai	91.3	1
3) Périgueux	89.9	1	3) Paris	91.3	10
6) Saint Dizier	89.9	1	6) Valence	91.3	1
20) Saint Girons	89.9	1	19) Amiens	91.4	1
18) Saint Raphaël	89.9	1	13) Bastia	91.4	4
17) Bayeux	90.0	1	17) Brive la Gaillarde	91.4	1
22) Brest	90.0	3	7) Beaune	91.5	1
13) Cosne Cours sur Loire	90.0	1	6) Beauvais	91.5	1
23) Marseille	90.0	10	6) Boulogne sur Mer	91.5	1
21) Quimperlé	90.0	1	22) Le Puy en Velay	91.5	1
18) Saint Quentin	90.0	1	10) Roanne	91.5	1
22) Sartene	90.0	1	5) Béthune	91.6	1
3) Vichy	90.0	1	17) Clermont Ferrand	91.6	1
6) Béthune	90.1	1	3) Compiègne	91.6	1
18) Étampes	90.1	3	9) Corte	91.6	1
22) Évreux	90.1	1	5) Dunkerque	91.6	1
18) Nantes	90.1	3	17) Epernay	91.6	1
19) Perpignan	90.1	3	17) La Châtre	91.6	1
5) Poligny	90.1	1	5) Perpignan	91.6	3
9) Toul	90.1	1	13) Royan	91.6	1
23) Bar le Duc	90.2	1	3) Tours	91.6	2
10) Châteauroux	90.2	1	23) Apt	91.7	1
9) La Ferté sous Jouarre	90.2	1	18) Bourgoin Jallieu	91.7	1
18) Mimizan	90.2	1	23) Cholet	91.7	1
10) Nevers	90.2	1	17) Mortagne au Perche	91.7	1
14) Pau	90.2	1	17) Villefranche sur Saône	91.7	1
9) Thionville	90.2	1	7) Amiens	91.8	1
17) Vannes	90.2	2	7) Bordeaux	91.8	4
5) Bastia	90.3	4	8) Brioude	91.8	1
18) Decazeville	90.3	1	3) Castres	91.8	1
17) Montargis	90.3	1	18) La Rochelle	91.8	1
4) Montmorillon	90.3	1	21) Montélimar	91.8	1
24) Pamiers	90.3	1	7) Montpellier	91.8	3
3) Saumur	90.3	1	7) Saint Malo	91.8	1
19) Valence	90.3	2	7) Saint Quentin	91.8	1
18) Auch	90.4	1	7) Bressuire	91.9	1
10) Caen	90.4	2	9) Chalon sur Saône	91.9	1
21) Longwy	90.4	1	19) Chaumont	91.9	1
13) Paris	90.4	10	4) Civray	91.9	1
13) Aurillac	90.5	1	7) Le Puy en Velay	91.9	1
9) Bourges	90.5	1	7) Lessay	91.9	1
23) Le Mans	90.5	2	9) Porto Vecchio	91.9	1
9) Mont de Marsan	90.5	1	8) Salon de Provence	91.9	1
6) Narbonne	90.5	1	7) Arcachon	92.0	1
4) Lourdes	90.6	3	23) Auxerre	92.0	1
7) Maubeuge	90.6	1	6) Lille	92.0	2
8) Millau	90.6	1	22) Pau	92.0	1
13) Creil	90.7	1	8) Saint Affrique	92.0	1
7) Dijon	90.7	1	10) Saintes	92.0	1
18) Figeac	90.7	1	19) Soissons	92.0	1
6) Soustons	90.7	1	21) Cambrai	92.1	1
13) Troyes	90.7	1	6) Menton	92.1	1
9) Château Thierry	90.8	1	18) Nontron	92.1	1
9) La Flèche	90.8	1	19) Troyes	92.1	1
9) Melun	90.8	1	22) Béthune	92.2	1
3) Vannes	90.8	1	10) Bordeaux	92.2	1
23) Vesoul	90.8	1	7) Colmar	92.2	1
17) Annonay	90.9	1	7) Dunkerque	92.2	1
19) Brest	90.9	3	4) Lannemezan	92.2	1
9) Brive la Gaillarde	90.9	1	9) Laon	92.2	1
13) Montreuil sur Mer	90.9	1	7) Limoges	92.2	2
17) Segré	90.9	1	22) Metz	92.2	1
7) Villefranche sur Saône	90.9	1	22) Mont de Marsan	92.2	1
5) Ajaccio	91.0	8	5) Montélimar	92.2	1
19) Besançon	91.0	1	7) Mimizan	92.3	1
17) Bourges	91.0	1	10) Rennes	92.3	1
10) Chambéry	91.0	1	13) Vitry le François	92.3	1
9) Colmar	91.0	1	23) Albi	92.4	1
13) Fleurance	91.0	1	14) Montpellier	92.4	3
24) Le Puy en Velay	91.0	1	22) Romilly sur Seine	92.4	1
4) Sarrebourg	91.0	1	6) Vannes	92.4	1
7) Sens	91.0	1	23) Avignon	92.5	1
10) Vichy	91.0	1	4) Cahors	92.5	1
23) Dunkerque	91.1	1	17) Fontenay le Comte	92.5	1
8) Nancy	91.1	1	17) Issoudun	92.5	1
19) Orange	91.1	1	9) Le Havre	92.5	1
23) Pau	91.1	1	5) Lille	92.5	2
4) Saint Gaudens	91.1	1	7) Lourdes	92.5	3
3) Villeneuve sur Lot	91.1	1	19) Rodez	92.5	1
6) Grenoble	91.2	1	7) Tonnerre	92.5	1

Station	MHz	kW
1) Aix en Provence	92.6	1
3) Charolles	92.6	1
10) Clermont Ferrand	92.6	1
17) Quimper	92.6	1
7) Saint Raphaël	92.6	1
3) Bastia	92.7	4
23) Boulogne sur Mer	92.7	1
13) Montélimar	92.7	1
22) Montluçon	92.7	1
22) Rennes	92.7	1
9) Béthune	92.8	1
22) Castres	92.8	1
8) Châteauroux	92.8	1
22) Nice	92.8	5
23) Vannes	92.8	1
3) Cambrai	92.9	1
4) Château Gontier	92.9	1
13) Lyon	92.9	10
7) Montauban	92.9	3
10) Orléans	92.9	2
13) Ajaccio	93.0	8
21) Beauvais	93.0	1
22) Bonifacio	93.0	1
5) Courtenay	93.0	1
18) Hirson	93.0	1
21) Lille	93.0	2
9) Lourdes	93.0	3
22) Saint Raphaël	93.0	1
9) Verdun	93.0	1
13) Annecy	93.1	1
13) Arcachon	93.1	1
10) Bastia	93.1	4
13) Bourg en Bresse	93.1	1
21) Châlons en Champagne	93.1	1
7) Coutances	93.1	1
8) Ernée	93.1	1
23) Fontenay le Comte	93.1	1
23) Royan	93.1	1
13) Saint Étienne	93.1	2
7) Toulon	93.1	4
6) Bergerac	93.2	1
9) Commercy	93.2	1
5) Évreux	93.2	1
23) Nevers	93.2	1
21) Romilly sur Seine	93.2	1
5) Ussel	93.2	1
13) Arras	93.3	1
13) Grenoble	93.3	1
7) Lyon	93.3	1
4) Montauban	93.3	3
8) Montluçon	93.3	1
18) Orléans	93.3	2
5) Pamiers	93.3	1
3) Poitiers	93.3	1
17) Argentan	93.4	1
21) Epernay	93.4	1
6) Le Chambon sur Lignon	93.4	1
13) Lille	93.4	1
8) Marseille	93.4	4
7) Moulins	93.4	1
10) Narbonne	93.4	1
7) Niort	93.4	1
23) Quimper	93.4	1
6) Vic Fezensac	93.4	1
22) Ajaccio	93.5	4
18) Dax	93.5	1
6) Amiens	93.6	1
8) Brest	93.6	1
7) Calvi	93.6	1
18) Évreux	93.6	1
23) La Roche sur Yon	93.6	1
19) Laon	93.6	1
17) Mazamet	93.6	1
9) Pau	93.6	1
21) Saint Gaudens	93.6	1
22) Grenoble	93.7	1
10) Le Havre	93.7	1
8) Lyon	93.7	1
6) Montreuil sur Mer	93.7	1
17) Nancy	93.7	1
13) Orléans	93.7	2
20) Saint Nazaire	93.7	1
6) Saintes	93.7	1
13) Toulon	93.7	4
6) Chaumont	93.8	1

Station	MHz	kW
2) Marseille	93.8	4
18) Montauban	93.8	3
7) Orange	93.8	1
22) Aurillac	93.9	1
21) Avallon	93.9	1
17) Bourg en Bresse	93.9	1
19) Bourges	93.9	1
7) Carcassonne	93.9	1
13) Château Gontier	93.9	1
20) Condom	93.9	1
9) Epernay	93.9	1
20) Jonzac	93.9	1
3) Lille	93.9	1
7) Nogent le Rotrou	93.9	1
13) Saint Brieuc	93.9	1
7) Verdun	93.9	1
6) Pau	94.0	1
9) Rochefort	94.0	1
22) Saint Flour	94.0	1
19) Decazeville	94.1	1
18) Grenoble	94.1	1
8) Mayenne	94.1	1
24) Mont de Marsan	94.1	1
13) Montmorillon	94.1	1
13) Soissons	94.1	1
23) Tours	94.1	2
3) Chaumont	94.2	1
5) Saint Omer	94.2	1
23) Tarbes	94.2	1
6) Bordeaux	94.3	4
18) La Côte Saint André	94.3	1
17) Le Havre	94.3	1
18) Le Mans	94.3	2
23) Lille	94.3	1
23) Lorient	94.3	1
15) Paris	94.3	1
1) Saint Étienne	94.3	2
8) Le Puy en Velay	94.4	1
22) Loches	94.4	1
19) Orléans	94.4	1
4) Parthenay	94.4	1
18) Pau	94.4	1
6) Saint Hilaire de Riez	94.4	1
9) Saintes	94.4	1
19) Toulouse	94.4	1
5) Gournay en Bray	94.5	1
7) La Rochelle	94.5	1
9) Mazamet	94.5	1
9) Montmorillon	94.5	1
9) Nevers	94.5	1
7) Rennes	94.5	2
17) Arcachon	94.6	1
13) Chambéry	94.6	1
5) Colmar	94.6	1
6) Lannemezan	94.6	1
22) Perpignan	94.6	3
13) Pouzauges	94.6	1
23) Romilly sur Seine	94.6	1
7) Saint Lô	94.6	1
18) Fougères	94.7	1
13) Le Havre	94.7	1
7) Mende	94.7	1
6) Nantes	94.7	3
4) Poitiers	94.7	1
8) Quimper	94.7	1
17) Saint Étienne	94.7	2
3) Vesoul	94.7	1
6) Angers	94.8	2
20) Chalon sur Saône	94.8	1
9) Chaumont	94.8	1
22) Forbach	94.8	1
6) Longwy	94.8	1
13) Montpellier	94.8	2
5) Mulhouse	94.8	1
22) Nancy	94.8	1
5) Avignon	94.9	1
17) Caen	94.9	1
13) Hirson	94.9	1
9) La Roche sur Yon	94.9	1
13) Le Puy en Velay	94.9	1
19) Lyon	94.9	1
7) Chambéry	95.0	1
6) Cholet	95.0	1
19) Clermont Ferrand	95.0	1
8) Dinan	95.0	1

Station	MHz	kW
19) Grenoble	95.0	1
10) Lorient	95.0	1
13) Mimizan	95.0	1
9) Montauban	95.0	3
7) Nice	95.0	5
13) Niort	95.0	1
13) Porto Vecchio	95.0	1
17) Macon	95.1	1
17) Pithiviers	95.1	1
10) Saint Étienne	95.1	2
9) Sens	95.1	1
3) Ussel	95.1	1
3) Béziers	95.2	1
21) Dunkerque	95.2	1
21) Fontenay le Comte	95.2	1
5) Jussey	95.2	1
9) Périgueux	95.2	1
24) Tarascon	95.2	1
3) Bordeaux	95.3	5
7) Dax	95.3	1
21) Évreux	95.3	1
13) Fontainebleau	95.3	1
10) Le Puy en Velay	95.3	1
2) Lyon	95.3	10
13) Nancy	95.3	1
3) Tarbes	95.3	1
3) Toulon	95.3	4
18) Cahors	95.4	1
18) Chambéry	95.4	1
19) Le Mans	95.4	2
3) Montpellier	95.4	3
23) Orléans	95.4	2
17) Pouzauges	95.4	1
8) Angers	95.5	1
3) Annonay	95.5	1
24) Bergerac	95.5	1
23) Besançon	95.5	1
13) Calvi	95.5	1
17) La Rochelle	95.5	1
6) Macon	95.5	1
19) Marseille	95.5	10
8) Mazamet	95.5	1
7) Ales	95.6	1
6) Niort	95.6	1
11) Paris	95.6	4
9) Saint Tropez	95.6	1
19) Vannes	95.6	1
23) Le Puy en Velay	95.7	1
22) Lyon	95.7	4
3) Nancy	95.7	1
17) St Amand Montrond	95.7	1
22) Chambéry	95.8	1
6) Montpellier	95.8	3
3) Nice	95.8	5
21) Saint Brieuc	95.8	1
6) Toulon	95.8	4
10) Bourges	95.9	1
17) Bourgoin Jallieu	95.9	1
13) Brioude	95.9	1
18) Cavaillon	95.9	1
18) Commercy	95.9	1
10) Limoges	95.9	2
22) Mazamet	95.9	1
3) Saint Étienne	95.9	2
3) Annecy	96.0	1
9) Brignoles	96.0	1
13) Châtillon sur Seine	96.0	1
3) Cognac	96.0	1
23) Grenoble	96.0	1
7) Lisieux	96.0	1
13) Marseille	96.0	4
23) Paris	96.0	10
23) Valence	96.0	2
22) Auxerre	96.1	1
22) Béziers	96.1	2
8) Decazeville	96.1	1
6) Le Puy en Velay	96.1	1
23) Lyon	96.1	4
23) Montauban	96.1	3
6) Nancy	96.1	1
13) Saint Dizier	96.1	1
6) Tours	96.1	2
17) Vire	96.1	1
19) Alençon	96.2	1
18) Brive la Gaillarde	96.2	1

Station	MHz	kW
22) Châteauroux	96.2	1
23) Clermont Ferrand	96.2	1
13) Compiègne	96.2	1
6) Dunkerque	96.2	1
8) Lesparre	96.2	1
6) Saint Brieuc	96.2	1
13) Sedan	96.2	1
23) Annonay	96.3	1
6) Bourg en Bresse	96.3	1
7) Caen	96.3	2
9) Montluçon	96.3	1
6) Morlaix	96.3	1
17) Rennes	96.3	1
7) Saint Étienne	96.3	2
22) Bastia	96.4	4
7) Epernay	96.4	1
13) Granville	96.4	1
2) Lille	96.4	2
6) Lorient	96.4	1
13) Mont de Marsan	96.4	1
2) Paris	96.4	1
9) Saint Quentin	96.4	1
22) Sarrebourg	96.4	1
20) Bourges	96.5	1
6) Brest	96.5	3
10) Lyon	96.5	4
20) Marmande	96.5	1
23) Saint Flour	96.5	1
23) Saint Nazaire	96.5	1
23) Saint Omer	96.5	1
5) Auxerre	96.6	1
6) Châteauroux	96.6	1
7) Clermont Ferrand	96.6	2
3) Nîmes	96.6	1
9) Toulon	96.6	4
6) Yssingeaux	96.6	1
23) Abbeville	96.7	1
23) Limoges	96.7	2
13) Montargis	96.7	1
22) Thionville	96.7	1
6) Caen	96.8	2
6) Cahors	96.8	1
17) Cannes	96.8	1
20) Châtellerault	96.8	1
14) Dreux	96.8	1
7) Lille	96.8	1
18) Mont de Marsan	96.8	1
13) Nantes	96.8	3
13) Roanne	96.8	1
13) Rochefort	96.8	1
13) Valence	96.8	1
7) Arras	96.9	1
7) Montbard	96.9	1
17) Moulins	96.9	1
18) Rennes	96.9	1
1) Toulouse	96.9	1
21) Chambéry	97.0	1
3) Mazamet	97.0	1
7) Albi	97.1	1
9) Bar le Duc	97.1	1
21) La Ferté sous Jouarre	97.1	1
6) Montluçon	97.1	1
6) Pouzauges	97.1	1
10) Bourg en Bresse	97.2	1
18) Chaumont	97.2	1
7) Pithiviers	97.2	1
18) Saint Omer	97.2	1
21) Auch	97.3	1
8) Beauvais	97.3	1
13) Bordeaux	97.3	5
22) Le Havre	97.3	1
7) Poitiers	97.3	1
8) Rodez	97.3	1
6) Vire	97.3	1
13) Brest	97.4	1
21) Grenoble	97.4	1
23) Mont de Marsan	97.4	1
4) Morhange	97.4	1
21) Nice	97.4	5
19) Paris	97.4	1
18) Saint Malo	97.4	1
3) Toulouse	97.4	1
18) Béziers	97.5	1
23) Carmaux	97.5	1
13) Corte	97.5	1

Station	MHz	kW
13) Dijon	97.5	1
7) Mayenne	97.5	1
3) Rouen	97.5	2
18) Avallon	97.6	1
23) Caen	97.6	2
5) Chambéry	97.6	1
22) Fontenay le Comte	97.6	1
7) L'Ile Rousse	97.6	1
3) Le Mans	97.6	2
18) Menton	97.6	1
6) Metz	97.6	1
13) Montauban	97.6	3
7) Pamiers	97.6	1
3) Perpignan	97.6	1
13) Rennes	97.6	3
6) Bayonne	97.7	1
9) Castres	97.7	1
7) Compiègne	97.7	1
4) Dreux	97.7	1
4) Figeac	97.7	1
5) Maubeuge	97.7	1
9) Montargis	97.7	1
22) Nantes	97.7	3
8) Ussel	97.7	1
24) Brive la Gaillarde	97.8	1
6) Chalon sur Saône	97.8	1
1) Grenoble	97.8	1
6) Saint Étienne	97.8	2
6) Villeneuve sur Lot	97.8	1
4) Bastia	97.9	1
13) Parthenay	97.9	1
4) Toulouse	97.9	5
9) Angers	98.0	2
6) Montélimar	98.0	1
23) Montluçon	98.0	1
9) Vannes	98.0	1
23) Ajaccio	98.1	8
18) Besançon	98.1	1
6) Dax	98.1	1
9) Saint Flour	98.1	2
20) Saintes	98.1	1
13) Samatan	98.1	1
13) Auxerre	98.2	1
9) Avignon	98.2	1
19) Bordeaux	98.2	1
22) Bourges	98.2	1
3) La Flèche	98.2	1
19) Limoges	98.2	2
6) Lourdes	98.2	3
13) Macon	98.2	1
17) Narbonne	98.2	1
23) Niort	98.2	1
12) Paris	98.2	4
8) Quimperlé	98.2	1
1) Toulon	98.2	1
13) Aix en Provence	98.3	1
18) Bar le Duc	98.3	1
9) Gien	98.3	1
17) Montpellier	98.3	3
22) Rouen	98.3	2
23) Amiens	98.4	1
13) Chaumont	98.4	1
18) Mazamet	98.4	1
8) Royan	98.4	1
18) Agen	98.5	1
23) Alençon	98.5	1
17) Béziers	98.5	1
21) Hirson	98.5	1
5) Albi	98.6	1
9) Cognac	98.6	1
20) Dax	98.6	1
18) Vannes	98.6	1
7) Auch	98.7	1
10) Chartres	98.7	1
13) La Rochelle	98.7	1
9) Le Puy en Velay	98.7	2
1) Rouen	98.7	2
13) Argentan	98.8	1
20) Cannes	98.8	1
21) Castres	98.8	1
7) Grenoble	98.8	1
20) Nice	98.8	1
19) Toulon	98.8	4
7) Valence	98.8	1
3) Arcachon	98.9	1

Station	MHz	kW
6) Auxerre	98.9	1
7) Brest	98.9	3
6) Le Creusot	98.9	1
3) Lyon	98.9	1
9) Mende	98.9	1
3) Montauban	98.9	3
3) Vierzon	98.9	1
9) Amiens	99.0	1
22) Bayonne	99.0	2
5) La Ferté Macé	99.0	1
18) Metz	99.0	1
22) Poitiers	99.0	1
7) Royan	99.0	1
17) Saint Raphaël	99.0	1
6) Ussel	99.0	1
3) Aurillac	99.1	1
9) Cervione	99.1	2
7) Châteauroux	99.1	1
5) Châtillon sur Seine	99.1	1
9) Limoges	99.1	2
18) Toulouse	99.1	5
3) Abbeville	99.2	1
23) Aubusson	99.2	1
22) Calais	99.2	1
4) Châtellerault	99.2	1
7) Condom	99.2	1
20) Narbonne	99.2	1
9) Nice	99.2	2
23) Vichy	99.2	1
22) Cambrai	99.3	1
13) L'aigle	99.3	1
19) Monthléry	99.3	2
18) Montpellier	99.3	3
6) Saint Nazaire	99.3	1
10) Avignon	99.4	1
7) Bastia	99.4	4
5) Charolles	99.4	1
5) Fontainebleau	99.4	2
3) Macon	99.4	1
7) Mazamet	99.4	1
10) Montluçon	99.4	1
13) Mulhouse	99.4	1
5) Saint Malo	99.4	1
3) Châteaudun	99.5	1
13) Eauze	99.5	1
13) Toulouse	99.5	1
6) Abbeville	99.6	1
18) Bordeaux	99.6	4
6) Bourges	99.6	1
3) Carcassonne	99.6	1
17) Carmaux	99.6	1
22) Cholet	99.6	1
18) Dijon	99.6	1
5) Ile de re	99.6	1
17) Limoges	99.6	2
17) Quimperlé	99.6	1
7) Salon de Provence	99.6	1
9) Vichy	99.6	1
6) Bagnères de Bigorre	99.7	1
3) Brest	99.7	3
22) Montauban	99.7	3
2) Orléans	99.7	1
3) Troyes	99.7	1
6) Ajaccio	99.8	8
21) Chartres	99.8	1
17) Lavaur	99.8	1
9) Menton	99.8	1
18) Montargis	99.8	1
6) Mulhouse	99.8	1
21) Parthenay	99.8	1
9) Auxerre	99.9	1
17) Chaumont	99.9	1
9) Mimizan	99.9	1
9) Quimper	99.9	1
7) Belfort	100.0	1
23) Béziers	100.0	1
13) Limoges	100.0	2
9) Montélimar	100.0	1
9) Poitiers	100.0	1
22) Porto Vecchio	100.0	1
3) Rodez	100.0	1
13) Romilly sur Seine	100.0	1
23) Toulouse	100.0	1
18) Angers	100.1	1
13) Châteauroux	100.1	1

Station	MHz	kW
3) Marseille	100.1	4
22) Reims	100.1	2
13) Ales	100.2	1
7) Chinon	100.2	1
13) Gien	100.2	1
9) La Rochelle	100.2	1
3) Orthez	100.2	1
18) Ploumoguer	100.2	1
9) Troyes	100.2	1
9) Valence	100.2	2
6) Angoulême	100.3	1
7) Le Mans	100.3	2
6) Lyon	100.3	4
13) Mende	100.3	1
9) Paris	100.3	10
19) St Gilles Croix de Vie	100.3	1
6) Besançon	100.4	1
21) Bourges	100.4	1
22) Chaumont	100.4	1
4) Corte	100.4	1
13) Lens	100.4	1
6) Limoges	100.4	2
9) Niort	100.4	1
22) Royan	100.4	1
21) Toulon	100.4	4
9) Toulouse	100.4	5
17) Tours	100.4	2
6) Annecy	100.5	1
3) Bourgoin Jallieu	100.5	1
21) Brive la Gaillarde	100.5	1
9) Château Gontier	100.5	1
6) Compiègne	100.5	1
9) Nogent le Rotrou	100.5	1
8) Pontivy	100.5	1
18) Rodez	100.5	1
9) Rouen	100.5	2
22) Saint Étienne	100.5	2
9) Saint Nazaire	100.5	1
20) Vichy	100.5	1
9) Albi	100.6	1
9) Avallon	100.6	1
7) Blois	100.6	1
3) Bourg en Bresse	100.6	1
3) Brioude	100.6	1
9) Carcassonne	100.6	1
9) Dijon	100.6	1
3) Douarnenez	100.6	1
5) Parthenay	100.6	1
9) Reims	100.6	2
17) Saint Brieuc	100.6	1
20) Villeneuve sur Lot	100.6	1
13) Béziers	100.7	1
6) Decazeville	100.7	1
13) Le Mans	100.7	2
3) Le Puy en Velay	100.7	1
4) Paris	100.7	10
9) Bastia	100.8	4
20) Castres	100.8	1
23) Chambéry	100.8	1
3) Clermont Ferrand	100.8	1
2) Grenoble	100.8	1
5) Lisieux	100.8	1
7) Saint Gaudens	100.8	1
8) Thouars	100.8	1
9) Bayonne	100.9	5
9) Besançon	100.9	1
10) Marseille	100.9	10
23) Nancy	100.9	1
3) Amiens	101.0	1
24) Aurillac	101.0	1
9) L'aigle	101.0	1
5) Lourdes	101.0	3
6) Quimper	101.0	1
9) Agen	101.1	1
9) Aubusson	101.1	1
7) Bar le Duc	101.1	1
9) Châteauroux	101.1	1
6) La Roche sur Yon	101.1	1
10) Laval	101.1	1
11) Le Havre	101.1	1
13) Metz	101.1	1
10) Paris	101.1	10
23) Poitiers	101.1	1
9) Saint Malo	101.1	1
9) Ajaccio	101.2	8

Station	MHz	kW
24) Albi	101.2	1
13) Blois	101.2	1
21) Chaumont	101.2	1
9) Clermont Ferrand	101.2	1
7) Epinal	101.2	1
7) Bourgoin Jallieu	101.3	1
3) Chambéry	101.3	1
21) Châtellerault	101.3	1
22) Dreux	101.3	1
9) Dunkerque	101.3	1
4) Forbach	101.3	1
6) Jonzac	101.3	1
22) La Rochelle	101.3	1
9) Lille	101.3	2
20) Orange	101.3	1
19) Saint Étienne	101.3	2
9) Sarlat la Canéda	101.3	1
10) Amiens	101.4	2
9) Caen	101.4	2
17) Longwy	101.4	1
21) Marseille	101.4	10
5) Nice	101.4	5
21) St Gilles Croix de Vie	101.4	1
24) Toulouse	101.4	
18) Ales	101.5	1
9) Cahors	101.5	1
5) Montbard	101.5	1
18) Nevers	101.5	1
14) Paris	101.5	10
13) Poitiers	101.5	1
21) Redon	101.5	1
21) Rodez	101.5	1
17) Valence	101.5	1
18) Cambrai	101.6	1
5) Chaumont	101.6	1
3) Dijon	101.6	1
18) Issoudun	101.6	1
10) Le Mans	101.6	2
5) Macon	101.6	1
20) Montargis	101.6	1
23) Périgueux	101.6	1
10) Quimper	101.6	1
21) Saint Malo	101.6	1
13) Valence d'Agen	101.6	1
21) Albi	101.7	1
5) Bayonne	101.7	5
18) Compiègne	101.7	1
6) Cosne Cours sur Loire	101.7	1
17) Le Puy en Velay	101.7	1
22) Limoges	101.7	2
7) Reims	101.7	2
9) Romilly sur Seine	101.7	1
22) Tarascon	101.7	1
6) Aubusson	101.8	1
9) Aurillac	101.8	1
9) Bergerac	101.8	1
23) Brest	101.8	3
6) Le Havre	101.8	1
9) Châtillon sur Seine	101.9	1
6) Cognac	101.9	1
9) Coutances	101.9	1
4) Martigues	101.9	1
9) Mayenne	101.9	1
18) Moulins	101.9	1
7) Paris	101.9	10
7) Abbeville	102.0	1
6) Bar le Duc	102.0	1
17) Beaune	102.0	1
6) Falaise	102.0	1
23) La Rochelle	102.0	1
4) Metz	102.0	1
22) Quimper	102.0	1
6) Rennes	102.0	3
21) Saint Quentin	102.0	1
24) Toulouse	102.0	70
7) Annecy	102.1	1
20) Avallon	102.1	1
9) Charolles	102.1	1
18) Limoges	102.1	2
22) Melun	102.1	1
9) Mulhouse	102.1	1
6) Nîmes	102.1	1
7) St Amand Montrond	102.1	1
18) Strasbourg	102.1	4
9) Arcachon	102.2	1

Station	MHz	kW
9) Blois	102.2	1
21) Dole	102.2	1
7) Montargis	102.2	1
9) Thouars	102.2	1
7) Troyes	102.2	1
9) Avranches	102.3	1
13) Cahors	102.3	1
17) Chambéry	102.3	1
6) Forbach	102.3	1
7) Laval	102.3	1
21) Le Puy en Velay	102.3	1
6) Marseille	102.3	10
9) Montbard	102.3	1
18) Nancy	102.3	1
21) Nevers	102.3	1
3) Quimperlé	102.3	1
9) Saint Brieuc	102.3	1
9) Saint Omer	102.3	1
10) Tours	102.3	2
7) Auxerre	102.4	1
9) Bordeaux	102.4	5
9) Brest	102.4	3
3) Chalon sur Saône	102.4	1
20) Chaumont	102.4	1
3) Decazeville	102.4	1
10) Grenoble	102.4	1
6) Haguenau	102.4	1
5) Montmorillon	102.4	1
9) Nantes	102.4	3
7) Perpignan	102.4	3
9) Romorantin Lanthenay	102.4	1
6) Toulouse	102.4	5
3) Vienne	102.4	1
22) Angers	102.5	1
18) Calais	102.5	1
24) Carmaux	102.5	1
5) Chartres	102.5	1
6) Commercy	102.5	1
7) Fontainebleau	102.5	1
18) Gourdon	102.5	1
8) Les Sables d'Olonne	102.5	1
8) Niort	102.5	1
6) Sarrebourg	102.5	1
18) Angoulême	102.6	1
13) Bergerac	102.6	1
21) Carcassonne	102.6	1
21) Montauban	102.6	3
9) Orléans	102.6	2
3) Quimper	102.6	1
9) Saint Gaudens	102.6	1
20) Troyes	102.6	1
9) Abbeville	102.7	1
22) Avallon	102.7	1
3) Limoges	102.7	2
5) Morlaix	102.7	1
3) Nérac	102.7	1
8) Paris	102.7	40
9) Saint Dizier	102.7	1
5) Saint Flour	102.7	1
9) Annecy	102.8	1
5) Annonay	102.8	1
13) Avignon	102.8	1
23) Bordeaux	102.8	5
9) Bourg en Bresse	102.8	1
22) Brive la Gaillarde	102.8	1
21) Dax	102.8	1
17) Lorient	102.8	1
20) Parthenay	102.8	1
9) Saint Étienne	102.8	2
7) Tours	102.8	2
13) Charolles	102.9	1
1) Le Mans	102.9	2
21) Lourdes	102.9	3
9) Lunéville	102.9	1
23) Nantes	102.9	3
24) Villeneuve sur Lot	102.9	1
17) Carcassonne	103.0	1
9) Chambéry	103.0	1
9) Châteaudun	103.0	1
13) Colmar	103.0	1
6) Condom	103.0	1
18) Le Puy en Velay	103.0	1
9) Lyon	103.0	4
3) Metz	103.0	1
21) Moulins	103.0	1

Station	MHz	kW
17) Neufchâtel en Bray	103.0	1
12) Poitiers	103.0	1
23) Angoulême	103.1	1
17) Charensat	103.1	1
7) Marseille	103.1	4
20) Mont de Marsan	103.1	1
20) Paris	103.1	10
24) Saint Affrique	103.1	1
3) Saint Dizier	103.1	1
13) Saint Flour	103.1	1
10) Toulouse	103.1	5
22) Amiens	103.2	1
21) Belfort	103.2	1
17) Dole	103.2	1
6) Douarnenez	103.2	1
9) Grenoble	103.2	1
9) Mirande	103.2	1
20) Montmorillon	103.2	1
19) Niort	103.2	1
24) Perpignan	103.2	10
20) Albi	103.3	1
18) Aurillac	103.3	1
21) Avesnes sur Helpe	103.3	1
6) Carpentras	103.3	1
6) Chartres	103.3	1
9) Compiègne	103.3	1
20) La Rochelle	103.3	1
7) Nancy	103.3	1
7) Nérac	103.3	1
19) Rouen	103.3	2
5) Strasbourg	103.3	4
10) Toulon	103.3	1
13) Carcassonne	103.4	1
7) Nantes	103.4	3
20) Rodez	103.4	1
13) Tours	103.4	2
7) Dinan	103.5	1
6) Epinal	103.5	1
19) Le Havre	103.5	1
6) Le Mans	103.5	2
9) Morlaix	103.5	1
6) Paris	103.5	10
9) Saint Affrique	103.5	1
23) Angers	103.6	2
21) Blois	103.6	1
7) Longwy	103.6	1
5) Montluçon	103.6	1
20) Saint Gaudens	103.6	1
7) Saint Nazaire	103.6	1
20) Châteauroux	103.7	1
17) Grenoble	103.7	1
23) Laval	103.7	1
18) Niort	103.7	1
21) Bergerac	103.8	1
17) Chinon	103.8	1
17) Cosne Cours sur Loire	103.8	1
24) Figeac	103.8	1
22) Lorient	103.8	1
20) Lourdes	103.8	3
4) Nantes	103.8	2
18) Troyes	103.8	1
9) Ussel	103.8	1
24) Bayonne	103.9	10
18) Epinal	103.9	1
18) Le Havre	103.9	1
20) Le Mans	103.9	2
5) Montpellier	103.9	3
18) Paris	103.9	10
9) Rennes	103.9	3
21) Saint Dizier	103.9	1
21) Toulouse	103.9	5
21) Vierzon	103.9	1
17) Avignon	104.0	1
21) Besançon	104.0	1
3) Ghisonaccia	104.0	2
3) Mauriac	104.0	1
18) Millau	104.0	1
18) St Gilles Croix de Vie	104.0	1
21) Tours	104.0	2
24) Villefr. de Rouergue	104.0	1
21) Abbeville	104.1	1
9) Bressuire	104.1	1
18) Chartres	104.1	1
21) Châteauroux	104.1	1
20) Compiègne	104.1	1

Station	MHz	kW
17) Confolens	104.1	1
9) Laval	104.1	1
24) Mazamet	104.1	1
8) Menton	104.1	1
20) Montauban	104.1	3
20) Montélimar	104.1	1
21) Montluçon	104.1	1
2) Nancy	104.1	1
22) Rethel	104.1	1
6) Rouen	104.1	2
20) Annecy	104.2	1
20) Bordeaux	104.2	4
21) Dijon	104.2	1
20) Grenoble	104.2	1
20) Lyon	104.2	4
20) Mende	104.2	1
10) Niort	104.2	1
21) Troyes	104.2	1
20) Ajaccio	104.3	8
21) Amiens	104.3	1
21) Angers	104.3	1
20) Arles	104.3	1
20) Bastia	104.3	4
20) Bayonne	104.3	10
20) Béziers	104.3	1
21) Brest	104.3	3
21) Cholet	104.3	1
21) Clermont Ferrand	104.3	2
13) Epinal	104.3	1
21) La Rochelle	104.3	1
21) Le Havre	104.3	1
21) Le Mans	104.3	2
21) Limoges	104.3	2
21) Lorient	104.3	1
20) Marseille	104.3	10
17) Montbard	104.3	1
20) Montpellier	104.3	3
21) Nantes	104.3	3
20) Nîmes	104.3	1
21) Orléans	104.3	2
21) Paris	104.3	10
20) Pau	104.3	1
21) Péronne	104.3	1
20) Perpignan	104.3	3
21) Poitiers	104.3	1
21) Quimper	104.3	1
21) Rennes	104.3	3
20) Saint Affrique	104.3	1
21) St Amand Montrond	104.3	1
21) Saint Nazaire	104.3	1
21) Soissons	104.3	1
20) Toulon	104.3	4
20) Toulouse	104.3	5
20) Valence	104.3	1
21) Vannes	104.3	1
21) Auxerre	104.4	1
7) Bourg en Bresse	104.4	1
20) Le Puy en Velay	104.4	1
19) Montargis	104.4	1
2) Nice	104.4	5
21) Reims	104.4	2
24) Rodez	104.4	1
18) Romorantin Lanthenay	104.4	1
20) Saint Étienne	104.4	2
20) Agen	104.5	1
21) Aurillac	104.5	1
20) Avignon	104.5	1
7) Baccarat	104.5	1
20) Chambéry	104.5	1
11) Chartres	104.5	1
21) Compiègne	104.5	1
5) Forbach	104.5	1
17) La Roche sur Yon	104.5	1
13) Laval	104.5	1
9) Le Creusot	104.5	1
20) Provins	104.5	1
17) Redon	104.5	1
21) Rouen	104.5	2
5) Tours	104.5	2
1) Ales	104.6	1
22) Alta rocca	104.6	1
5) Bordeaux	104.6	4
5) Grenoble	104.6	1
5) Lyon	104.6	4
5) Nevers	104.6	1

Station	MHz	kW
20) Saint Flour	104.6	1
21) Saint Raphaël	104.6	1
5) Amiens	104.7	1
5) Angers	104.7	1
5) Brest	104.7	3
24) Carcassonne	104.7	80
5) Cholet	104.7	1
5) Clermont Ferrand	104.7	2
5) Dijon	104.7	1
22) Ghisonaccia	104.7	4
5) La Rochelle	104.7	1
5) Le Mans	104.7	10
5) Limoges	104.7	2
5) Lorient	104.7	1
24) Montpellier	104.7	1
5) Nantes	104.7	3
5) Orléans	104.7	2
5) Paris	104.7	10
5) Poitiers	104.7	1
5) Quimper	104.7	1
5) Rennes	104.7	2
5) Saint Nazaire	104.7	1
5) Soissons	104.7	1
5) Toulon	104.7	4
5) Troyes	104.7	1
5) Vannes	104.7	1
3) Argentan	104.8	1
20) Aubusson	104.8	1
5) Cambrai	104.8	1
5) Châlons en Champagne	104.8	1
4) Gourdon	104.8	1
5) Marseille	104.8	10
21) Metz	104.8	1
18) Neufchâteau	104.8	1
13) St Amand Montrond	104.8	1
5) Saint Étienne	104.8	2
21) Valence	104.8	1
5) Abbeville	104.9	1
5) Agen	104.9	1
5) Besançon	104.9	1
7) Chartres	104.9	1
5) Compiègne	104.9	1
7) La Roche sur Yon	104.9	1
22) Laval	104.9	1
5) Mont de Marsan	104.9	1
7) Montereau	104.9	1
5) Moulins	104.9	1
7) Parthenay	104.9	1
24) Périgueux	104.9	1
5) Rouen	104.9	2
21) Royan	104.9	1
20) Auch	105.0	1
21) Bar le Duc	105.0	1
21) Caen	105.0	2
24) Cahors	105.0	1
13) Luxeuil les Bains	105.0	1
21) Lyon	105.0	4
7) Morlaix	105.0	1
23) Reims	105.0	2
21) Alençon	105.1	1
3) Angers	105.1	2
20) Aurillac	105.1	1
21) Bayonne	105.1	5
9) Bonifacio	105.1	1
21) Bordeaux	105.1	4
21) Charolles	105.1	1
20) Clermont Ferrand	105.1	2
9) Dinan	105.1	1
20) Limoges	105.1	2
21) Nancy	105.1	1
20) Niort	105.1	1
17) Toulon	105.1	4
7) Ajaccio	105.2	8
20) Brive la Gaillarde	105.2	1
9) Issoudun	105.2	1
3) Lons le saunier	105.2	1
5) Montauban	105.2	3
21) Saint Étienne	105.2	2
13) Saint Lô	105.2	1
3) Chartres	105.3	1
19) Cholet	105.3	1
5) Metz	105.3	1
13) Rouen	105.3	2
13) Sens	105.3	1
13) Strasbourg	105.3	4

Station	MHz	kW	Station	MHz	kW
13)Dole	105.4	1	5) Blois	106.5	1
5) Nancy	105.5	1	5) Châteauroux	106.5	1
9) Béziers	105.7	1	9) Fougères	106.5	1
7) Lannemezan	105.7	1	17)Lons le saunier	106.5	1
21)Le Creusot	105.7	1	13)Nogent le Rotrou	106.5	1
17)Loches	105.7	1	22)Périgueux	106.5	1
9) Redon	105.7	1	5) Reims	106.5	2
3) Saint Flour	105.7	2	23)Saint Étienne	106.5	2
21)Sens	105.7	1	22)Tarbes	106.5	1
21)Strasbourg	105.7	4	17)Yvetot	106.5	1
13)Vesoul	105.7	1	22)Albi	106.6	1
17)Argenton sur Creuse	105.8	1	10)Brest	106.6	3
5) Carcassonne	105.8	1	20)Cahors	106.6	1
10)Dijon	105.8	1	5) Châtellerault	106.6	1
3) Grenoble	105.8	1	17)Châtillon sur Seine	106.6	1
19)Henrichemont	105.8	1	9) Gournay en Bray	106.6	1
23)Segré	105.8	1	13)La Flèche	106.6	1
5) Caen	105.9	2	6) La Rochelle	106.6	1
22)Clermont Ferrand	105.9	1	5) Le Puy en Velay	106.6	1
9) Le Mans	105.9	2	20)Montluçon	106.6	1
18)Lesneven	105.9	3	4) Nîmes	106.6	1
18)Mende	105.9	1	23)Quimperlé	106.6	1
22)Paris	105.9	10	13)Saint Malo	106.6	1
7) Pau	105.9	1	8) Toulon	106.6	1
20)Périgueux	105.9	1	9) Vire	106.6	1
9) Perpignan	105.9	3	18)Alençon	106.7	1
13)Saint Nazaire	105.9	1	5) Angoulême	106.7	1
21)Saintes	105.9	1	18)Bourges	106.7	1
7) Toulouse	105.9	5	10)Carcassonne	106.7	1
23)Troyes	105.9	1	5) Chalon sur Saône	106.7	1
5) Valence	105.9	1	5) Condom	106.7	1
21)Ajaccio	106.0	8	8) Lisieux	106.7	1
22)Besançon	106.0	1	15)Lyon	106.7	1
24)Bordeaux	106.0	4	5) Mende	106.7	1
8) Bourges	106.0	1	10)Nantes	106.7	4
8) Limoges	106.0	2	1) Paris	106.7	4
7) Lorient	106.9	1	3) Roanne	106.7	1
9) Lorient	106.0	1	5) Saint Gaudens	106.7	1
3) Marseille	106.0	1	20)Ussel	106.7	1
20)Mauriac	106.0	1	6) Vitry le François	106.7	1
21)Montargis	106.0	1	8) Avallon	106.8	1
21)Niort	106.0	1	22)Bordeaux	106.8	4
20)Rennes	106.0	3	20)Brioude	106.8	1
8) Roanne	106.0	1	4) Chartres	106.8	1
13)St Gilles Croix de Vie	106.0	1	13)Château Renault	106.8	1
23)Agen	106.1	1	20)Grasse	106.8	1
3) Albi	106.1	1	17)La Côte Saint André	106.8	1
13)Angers	106.1	2	22)Marseille	106.8	4
8) Aubusson	106.1	1	21)Montpellier	106.8	3
22)Beaumont sur Oise	106.1	2	5) Niort	106.8	1
5) Brive la Gaillarde	106.1	1	5) Pau	106.8	1
22)Chartres	106.1	1	13)Perpignan	106.8	1
9) Montpellier	106.1	3	3) Rennes	106.8	3
10)Rouen	106.1	2	5) Rethel	106.8	1
5) Saint Dizier	106.1	1	18)Saint Affrique	106.8	1
5) Sarrebourg	106.1	1	8) Auch	106.9	1
13)Tarbes	106.1	1	23)Béthune	106.9	1
7) Argentan	106.2	1	21)Bourg en Bresse	106.9	1
19)Avignon	106.2	1	19)Châteauroux	106.9	1
5) Bergerac	106.2	1	22)Compiègne	106.9	1
13)Morlaix	106.2	1	8) Grenoble	106.9	1
3) Nantes	106.2	2	8) La Roche sur Yon	106.9	1
6) Neufchâteau	106.2	1	7) Le Havre	106.9	1
18)Tonnerre	106.2	1	8) Le Mans	106.9	2
22)Toulon	106.2	1	9) Mantes la Jolie	106.9	2
13)Vendôme	106.2	1	5) Mazamet	106.9	1
21)Arras	106.3	1	3) Mers les bains	106.9	1
13)Bourges	106.3	1	8) Périgueux	106.9	1
5) Castres	106.3	1	18)Poligny	106.9	1
20)Moulins	106.3	1	5) Romilly sur Seine	106.9	1.2
21)Pau	106.3	1	2) Strasbourg	106.9	1
13)Quimper	106.3	1	5) Bar le Duc	107.0	1
22)Saint Brieuc	106.3	1	10)Beauvais	107.0	1
5) Toulouse	106.3	5	8) Bressuire	107.0	1
8) Vannes	106.3	1	7) Château Thierry	107.0	1
15)Bordeaux	106.4	2.7	2) Clermont Ferrand	107.0	1
13)Caen	106.4	2	19)Le Puy en Velay	107.0	1
8) Chambéry	106.4	1	21)Mont de Marsan	107.0	1
18)Clermont Ferrand	106.4	2	8) Montauban	107.0	1
9) Marseille	106.4	10	17)Montluçon	107.0	1
5) Montargis	106.4	1	23)Nice	107.0	5
10)Troyes	106.4	1	10)Rodez	107.0	1
10)Valence	106.4	1	10)Arcachon	107.1	1
7) Agen	106.5	1	5) Bourges	107.1	1
5) Aurillac	106.5	1	2) Caen	107.1	2

Station	MHz	kW	Station	MHz	kW
23)Dijon	107.1	1	2) Bordeaux	107.3	1
8) Laval	107.1	1	2) Brest	107.3	3
21)Mulhouse	107.1	1	10)Brive la Gaillarde	107.3	1
9) Nancy	107.1	1	10)Chantilly	107.3	4
10)Poitiers	107.1	1	3) Châteauroux	107.3	1
7) Quimper	107.1	1	21)Colmar	107.3	1
18)Saint Étienne	107.1	2	7) Creil	107.3	4
21)Saint Flour	107.1	1	8) Dax	107.3	1
21)Avignon	107.2	1	23)Évreux	107.3	1
21)Figeac	107.2	1	3) Lens	107.3	1
14)Limoges	107.2	2	18)Lorient	107.3	1
19)Macon	107.2	1	9) Metz	107.3	1
2) Nantes	107.2	3	5) Millau	107.3	1
10)Pau	107.2	1	10)Montpellier	107.3	3
8) Rochefort	107.2	1	20)Orléans	107.3	1
7) Soissons	107.2	1	9) Parthenay	107.3	1
2) Toulouse	107.2	1	21)Perpignan	107.3	3
20)Tours	107.2	2	18)Roanne	107.3	1
24)Ussel	107.2	1	23)Saint Brieuc	107.3	1
7) Arnay le Duc	107.3	1	23)Saint Raphaël	107.3	1
10)Auxerre	107.3	1	21)Cherbourg	107.5	1

As of August 2004, a total of 3631 licenses (transmitters) were allocated to private commercial and non-commercial FM st's. Approx. 2450 st's are affiliated to one of the following private commercial national networks.

Stations under 1kW not mentionned.

1) Beur FM ✉ 89 rue Oberkampf, B.P. 249, 75524 Paris Cedex 11. ☎ +33 1 48 06 55 33. ℻+33 1 48 06 06 62. **Web:** www.beurfm.net. + 1 tr less than 1kW – **2)** BFM ✉ 12 rue d'Oradour sur Glane, 75015 Paris. ☎ +33 1 71 19 11 81. ℻ +33 1 56 97 27 61. **Web:** www.radiobfm.com. + 5 tr's less than 1kW. – **3)** Chérie FM ✉ 22 rue Boileau, 75116 Paris. ☎ +33 1 40 71 40 00. ℻ +33 1 40 71 41 24 **Web:** www.cheriefm.fr.+ 48 tr's less than 1kW. – **4)** COFRAC 11 rue Rosenwald, 75015 Paris. ☎+33 1 56 56 44 44 ℻ +33 1 56 56 44 55. **Web:** www.cofrac-media.com. + 10 tr's less than 1kW. – **5)** Europe 1 ✉ 26 bis rue François 1er, 75008 Paris. ☎ +33 1 44 31 90 00. ℻ +33 1 47 23 88 13. **Web:** www.europe1.fr. **LW:** 183 kHz 2000 kW see Germany. + 77 tr's less than 1kW. – **6)** Europe 2 ✉ 28 rue François 1er, 75008 Paris. ☎ +33 1 47 23 10 63. ℻ +33 1 47 23 24 55. **Web:** www.europe2.fr. + 84 tr's less than 1kW. – **7)** Fun Radio ✉ 20 rue Bayard, 75008 Paris. ☎ +33 1 40 70 48 48. ℻ +33 1 40 70 48 00. **Web:** www.funradio.fr. + 79 tr's less than 1kW. – **8)** MFM ✉ 104 avenue du Président Kennedy, 75016 Paris. ☎ +33 1 53 67 67 67. ℻ +33 1 53 67 67 74. **Web:** www.mfm.fr. + 30 tr's less than 1kW. – **9)** NRJ ✉ 22 rue Boileau, 75116 Paris. ☎ +33 1 40 71 40 00. ℻ +33 1 44 14 92 92. **Web:** www.nrj.fr. + 117 tr's less than 1kW. – **10)** Radio Classique ✉ 12 bis place Henri Bergson, 75008 Paris. ☎ +33 1 40 08 50 00. ℻ +33 1 40 08 50 80. **Web**: www.radioclassique.fr. + 17 tr's less than 1kW. – **11)** Radio Courtoisie ✉ 61 bd Murat 75016 Paris. ☎ +33 1 46 51 00 85. ℻ +33 1 46 51 21 82. **Web**: www.radiocourtoisie.com + 3 tr's less than 1kW. – **12)** Radio FG ✉ 51 rue de Rivoli, 75001 Paris. ☎ +33 1 40 13 75 31 ℻ +33 1 40 13 88 01. **Web**: www.radiofg.com. + 2 tr's less than 1kW. – **13)** Nostalgie ✉ 22 rue Boileau, 75116 Paris. ☎ +33 1 40 71 40 00. ℻ +33 1 40 71 40 40. **Web**: www.nostalgie.fr. + 77 tr's less than 1kW. – **14)** Radio Nova ✉ 33 rue du faubourg Saint Antoine, 75011 Paris. ☎ +33 1 53 33 33 15. ℻ +33 1 43 47 33 39. **Web**: www.novaplanet.com. + 1 tr' less than 1kW. – **15)** Radio Orient ✉ 98 bd Victor Hugo, 92110 Clichy. ☎ +33 1 41 06 16 00. ℻ +33 1 41 06 16 19. **Web**: www.radioorient.com. + 1 tr' less than 1kW. – **16)** Radio Soleil ✉ 57 rue Avron, 75020 Paris. ☎ +33 1 43 48 43 43. ℻ +33 1 43 48 55 58. **Web**: www.radio-soleil.com. + 2 tr's less than 1kW. – **17)** RCF ✉ 7 place Saint Irénée, 69321 Lyon Cedex 05. ☎ +33 4 72 38 20 22. ℻ +33 4 72 38 20 57. **Web:** www.radiorcf.com/. + 91 tr's less than 1kW. – **18)** RFM ✉ 28 rue François 1er, 75008 Paris. ☎ +33 1 42 32 20 00. ℻ +33 1 42 32 20 01. **Web**: www.rfm.fr. + 66 tr's less than 1kW. – **19)** Rire et Chansons ✉ 22 rue Boileau, 75116 Paris. ☎ +33 1 40 71 42 11. ℻ +33 1 40 71 41 24. **Web**: www.rireetchansons.fr. + 22 tr's less than 1kW. – **20)** RMC Info ✉ 12 rue d'Oradour sur Glane, 75015 Paris. ☎ +33 01 71 19 11 91. ℻ +33 01 71 19 11 90. **Web**: www.rmcinfo.fr. **LW:** Roumoules 216kHz 1400kW. See Monaco. + 69 tr's less than 1kW. – **21)** RTL ✉ 22 rue Bayard, 75008 Paris. ☎ +33 1 40 70 40 70. ℻ +33 1 40 70 44 50 **Web**: www.rtl.fr. **LW**: 234 kHz 2000 kW see Luxembourg. + 48 tr's less than 1kW. – **22)** RTL 2 ✉ 22 rue Bayard, 75008 Paris. ☎ +33 1 40 70 40 00. ℻ +33 1 40 70 43 67. **Web:** www.rtl2.fr. + 41 tr's less than 1kW. – **23)** Skyrock ✉ 37 bis rue Greneta, 75002 Paris. ☎ +33 1 44 88 82 00 ℻ +33 1 40 26 26 43 **Web:** www.skyrock.com. + 43 tr's less than 1kW. – **24)** Sud Radio ✉

4 place Alfonse Jourdain, 31071 Toulouse Cedex. ☎ +33 5 61 63 20 20. 🖷 +33 5 61 63 20 64. **Web:** www.sudradio.fr. + 25 tr's less than 1kW.

DAB: L band multiplexes are operating in Lyon, Marseille, Nantes, Paris, Toulouse and Tours on 1461.520 - 1466.656 MHz

PRIVATE MW STATIONS

	Location	kHz	kW		Location	kHz	kW
5)	Marseille	675	100	1)	Paris	1314	5
4)	Toulouse	819	1	2)	Nice	1350	10
5)	Paris	999	10	3)	Paris	1575	5
6)	Paris	981	3	2)	Nîmes	1602	1

Addresses

1) Loisirs AM, 50 avenue du Président Wilson, 93210 La Plaine Saint Denis Cedex. ☎ +33 1 49 17 84 00. 🖷 +33 1 49 17 84 01. **Web:** www.airprod.com/airprodcom – **2)** Radio Orient, see entry under FM – **3)** R. Nouveaux Talents, 31/32 quai de Dion Bouton, 92800 Puteaux. ☎ +33 1 49 17 84 00. 🖷 +33 1 49 17 84 01. **Web:** www.radiont.com – **4)** Sud Radio, see entry under FM – **5)** Superloustic, B.P. 32, 75462 Paris cedex 10. ☎ +33 1 47 20 77 40. 🖷 +33 1 47 20 65 18. **Web:** www.superloustic.net.**6)** Ciel AM, 25 rue St Sulpice, 75006 Paris ☎ +33 1 72 296969. 🖷 +33 1 53 103282. **Web:** www.cielradio.com.

FRENCH GUIANA

L.T: UTC -3h — **Pop:** 197,000 — **Pr.L:** French — **E.C:** 50Hz, 127/220V — **ITU:** GUF.

R.F.O. GUYANE (RADIODIFFUSION FRANÇAISE D'OUTRE-MER)

✉ B.P. 7013, F-97305 Cayenne ☎ +594 301500 🖷 +594 302649.
L.P: Dir: Anastasie Bourquin. Dir. Tec: Serge Sulpice-Timothe. PD: Jean-Pierre Karam

MW: Matoury 1070kHz 10kW, St. Laurent du Maroní 1060kHz 0.05kW.
SW: Matoury (G.C: 04N54 052W20): 5055kHz 10kW.
FM: Cayenne 91.5/95.2MHz 0.05kW, 94.0MHz 0.3kW + 5 relays.
D.PRGR: 24h on 1060/5055kHz + FM. **N:** 1030, 1630, 2230.
Rel. France-Inter: 24h on 1070kHz + 91.5MHz.
ANN: "Ici Cayenne, R. F.O. Guyane".
IS: "Nos richesses" on guitar. **V.** by QSL-folder. Rec. acc.

Local Radio: 6 private FM-st's are operating.

RADIO FRANCE INTERNATIONALE RELAY STATION

✉ TDF Montsinery, B.P. 97307, Cayenne Cedex.
FM: Cayenne 98.7MHz.

FRENCH POLYNESIA

L.T: UTC -10h — **Pop:** 254,000 — **Radio sets:** 105,000 — **Pr.L:** French, Tahitian — **E.C:** 60Hz, 220V — **ITU:** OCE

RADIO TAHITI

✉ B. P. 585, Papeete, Tahiti ☎ +689 430551 🖷 +689 45 1650
Web: www.rfo.fair/polynesie/homepoly; www.radiobleue.pf
L.P: Dir: Claude Ruben . Editor-in-Chief: Patrick Durand-Gaillard. Dir. of Prgrs: Jean-Raymond Bodin.
MW: Mahina 738kHz 20kW

FM: RFO Radio Polynesia (most 0.01/0.05/0.1kW) – Archipel des Australes: Rairua 89.6MHz, Moerai 89.6MHz, Amaru 99.4MHz, Matarua 99.4MHz, Ahurei 99.4MHz. Archipel de Marquises: Atuona 88.2MHz, Mont Muake 89.0MHz, Tapeata 89.5MHz, Taiohae 90.5MHz, Vaipaee 91.0MHz, Hakahua 91.5MHz. Moorea: Mahatea 89.0MHz, Papetoai 89.6MHz. Iles Sous le Vent: Uturoa 94.0MHz, Bora Bora 96.6MHz. Tahiti: Papeete 89.0MHz, Punaauia 89.6MHz, Tiarei 90.5MHz, Mont Marau 91.8MHz, Papara 95.2MHz, Mahaena 95.3MHz, Taravao 99.0MHz, Mahina 99.0MHz, Archipel des Tuamotu: Arutua 90.5MHz, Napuka 93.6MHz, Mataiva 93.6MHz, Kaukura 93.6MHz, Takaroa 93.6MHz, Nukutavake 94.0MHz, Rangiroa 94.0MHz, Faaite 94.0MHz, Makemo 94.0MHz, Manihi 94.4MHz, Fakareva 94.4MHz, Rikitea 94.4MHz, Fakahina 94.4MHz, Hao 94.4MHz, Reao 94.4MHz, Anaa 94.8MHz, Fangatau 94.8MHz, Takapoto 94.8MHz, Tureia 94.8MHz, Tikehau 94.8MHz, Tatakoto 94.8MHz, Pukarua 95.2MHz, Apataki 95.2MHz **D.Prgr: 24h**. **Local N. in French:** 1730. **Rel. France-Inter:** on the h. (N.) and during the evening/night hours. **ANN:** F: "Ici Radio Tahiti". Tahitian: "O Radio Tahiti". **IS:** Tahitian flute (vivo) and drums **V.** by QSL-card.
Other RFO stations: Radio Bleue – Moorea: Mahatea 101.0MHz. Iles Sous le Vent: Bora Bora 100.3MHz. Tahiti: Papeete 93.3MHz, Mahina 96.0MHz, Taiarapu 96.0MHz, Papeete 102.0MHz. **D.Prgr: 24h**. **Local N. in French:** 1730. **Rel. France-Inter:** on the h. (N.) and during the evening/night hours. **ANN:** F: "Ici Radio Tahiti". Tahitian: "O Radio Tahiti". **IS:** Tahitian flute (vivo) and drums **V.** by QSL-card.

OTHER STATIONS

1) Star FM ✉ Papeete, Tahiti 96.4MHz, Moorea 96.4MHz, Papeete 105.9MHz, Cote Ouest 97.8MHz ?: +689 434100 ? +689 422421 – **2)** Radio 1 ✉ B.P. 3601, Fare Ute, Papeete: ☎ +689 434100 🖷 +689 423406 **Web:** www.radio1.pf - **FM:** Fare Ute 100.0MHz, 98.7MHz, 103.8MHz, 90.9MHz, 100.9MHz – **3)** Radio Maohi ✉ Maison des Jeunes de Pirae ☎ +689 439595 🖷 +689 433101 - **FM:** 88.2MHz, 94.8MHz, 101.7MHz, 99.7MHz, 92.3MHz – **4)** Radio Te Reo O Tefana ✉ BP 6295, Faa'a, Tahiti ☎ +689 819797 🖷 +689 825493 - **FM:** Papeete 92.8MHz, Tahiti 97.4MHz, Presqu'ile 107MHz, Isle Sur le Vent 90MHz – **5)** Radio Tiare ✉ Fare Ute, Papeete ☎: +689 434100 🖷 +689 422421. **Email:** **Web:** www.tiarefm.pf - **FM:** Papeete 89.9MHz, Taravao 98.3MHz, Tahiti 104.2MHz, Moorea 105.9MHz **6)** Radio NRJ ✉ BP 50, Papeete ☎ +689 464346 🖷 +689 464346 **Web:** www.nrj.pf - **FM:** 88.6MHz & 103.0MHz **7)** Radio Te Vevo No Papara - **FM:** 102.2MHz **8)** Radio Te Vevo O Te Tiaturiraa ✉ BP 1817, Papeete, Tahiti - **FM:** Papeete 91.4MHz, Moorea 91.4MHz, Presqu'ile 93.5MHz, Iles Sur le Vent 97.2MHz **9)** Radio Fara ✉ Chemin Graffe Taunoa, Papeete **Email:** make.roti@mail.pf - **FM:** 100.5MHz.

GABON

L.T: UTC +1h — **Pop:** 1.2 million — **Pr.L:** French, Fang, Bopounou, Obamba, Djebi — **E.C:** 50Hz, 220V — **ITU:** GAB.

CONCEIL NATIONAL DE LA COMMUNICATION(CNC)

✉ B.P. 6437, Libreville ☎ +241 762796
L.P: Pierre-Marie Dong, President.

RADIODIFFUSION TÉLÉVISION GABONAISE (RTG)

✉ B.P. 10150, Libreville ☎+241 732459 🖷 +241 739775
L.P: DG RTG-1: Willy Kombény. DG RTG-2: Jules Legnongo. Asst. DG's: Radio: Gilles Terence Nzoghe. Tech: Claude Nganga. Provincial St's: Robert Aloli.

MW	kHz	kW	N	Times
Oyem	549	20	2	0430-0630, 1030-1430, 1600-2230

FM (MHz): Libreville 87.7/96.54(1) 92.5(2) Franceville 87.86(2), Makokou 100.5(2), Oyem 87.94(2), Pt. Gentil 88.03(2), Tchibanga 91.04(2).
1=RTG Chaîne 1 in French. **N:** 0500, 0530, 0600, 0700, 0800, 0900, 1000, 1200, 1400, 1500, 1700, 1800, 1830, 2100.
2=RTG Chaîne 2 (provincial network) in French & ethnic languages.
FM Prgr: 0500-2305 on FM only.
ANN: 1: "Ici Libreville, vouz écoutez Radio Gabon, châine 1".
IS: Indigenous instruments. Opens and closes with National Anthem.

AFRICA No. 1

✉ B.P. 1, Libreville ☎ +241 760001 🖷 +241 742133 ✉ **in France:** 193 Rue du Faubourg Poissonnière, F-75009 Paris ☎ +33 1 55075801 🖷 +33 1 55079748 **Web:** www.africa1.com
L.P: Pres: Louis Barthélémy Mapangou. Dir. Tec: Gaston Ombolo Ki-Obo. Dir. Prgrs. & Adv: Augustin Letamba. Dir. Inf: Jean Valère Mbina Mandza. Chief Editor: Eugène Ellang Mba.
FM: Libreville 94.5MHz + relays in Benin, Burkina Faso, Cameroon, Central African Rep, Chad, Congo (Rep.), Congo (Dem. Rep.), Equatorial Guinea, France, Ivory Coast, Mali, Niger, Senegal, Togo.
Main N: 0530, 0630, 0730, 1115W, 1215, 1700, 1830, 2200.
Africa Plus Gabon on 99.5MHz.
SW: see International Radio section.

Other stations:
R. Émergence, B.P. 06, Libreville: 91.6MHz 30W. 1200-1900.
Web: f-i-a.org/emergence
R. Génération Nouvelle, B.P. 727, Libreville: 97.4MHz.
R. Mandarine, B.P. 511, Libreville: 106.6MHz.
R. Nostalgie, B.P. 13050, Libreville: 93.0MHz.
R. Notre-Dame de Sainte-Marie, B.P 20348, Libreville: 99MHz.
R. Soleil FM, B.P. 5420, Libreville: 107.7MHz.
Top FM, B.P. 6554, Libreville: 105.5MHz (also rel. VOA).
R. Unité, B.P. 2676, Libreville: 100.5MHz.
RFI Afrique in Franceville, Libreville & Port-Gentil on 104MHz.

International relays via Africa No.1:
see International Radio section.

GALAPAGOS ISLANDS (Ecuador)

L.T: UTC -6h — **Pop:** 13,000 — **Pr.L:** Spanish — **E.C:** 60Hz 110/220V — **ITU:** EQA (**WRTH**: GAL)

LA VOZ DE GALAPAGOS (Rlg)

☎ +593 5 520144. 🖷 + 593 5 520372.
MW: La Voz de Galapagos 530kHz 5kW (inactive at the moment). **FM: Galapagos Stereo** 97.1MHz. **V.** by QSL card.

LA VOZ DE SAN CRISTÓBAL

🖃 Misión Franciscana, Pto. Baquerizo Moreno, Isla San Cristobal.
MW: 1320khz 5 kW 1300-0200

RADIO SANTA CRUZ (Rlg)

🖃 Av.Charles Darwin, frente al Parque de San Francisco, Isla Santa Cruz. ☎ + 593 5 526109. 🖷 + 593 5 526342
Web: www.puertoayora.com/radiosantaceuz.
Email: radiosantacruz@gpsinter.net
FM: HCSC8 92.1MHz.

RADIO CRISTO SALVADOR (Rlg)

🖃 Puerto Villamil ☎+593 5 529244 🖷+593 5 529108.
FM: 100.1

GAMBIA

L.T: UTC — **Pop:** 1.4 million — **Pr.L:** English, Mandinka, Fula, Wollof, Jola, Sarahullay — **E.C:** 50Hz, 230V — **ITU:** GMB

DEPARTMENT OF STATE FOR COMMUNICATION, INFORMATION & TECHNOLOGY (DOSCIT)

🖃 Private Mail Bag, State House, Banjul ☎ +220 223851 **Web:** www.newgambia.gm/infotech.htm
L.P: Amadou Scattred Janneh, Secretary of State.

GAMBIA RADIO AND TELEVISION SERVICE (GRTS)

🖃 Mile 7 Studios, P.O. Box 387, Banjul ☎ +220 4495101/4497419 🖷 +220 4495102 **Web:** www.grts.gm **Email**: info@grts.gm
L.P: DG: Mr. Bora Mboge. Deputy DG: Mrs. Neneh Macdouall-Graye. Radio Eng. Mgr: Famara Dampha.
MW: Bonto 648kHz 50kW, Basse 747kHz 10kW - **FM:** 91.4/98.6MHz.
D.Prgr: Mon-Thurs 0555-1400, 1655-2400. Fri-Sun 0555-2400.
N. in English: (SS)0700, 1300, 1800, 1900,2200.
ANN: "You are tuned to Gambia Radio & Television Services from Banjul".**IS:** Cora (harp).
Other stations:
City Limits R, Serrekunda: 93,6MHz 0.25kW.
R. One FM, 44 Kairaba Ave, Serrekunda: 102.1MHz 0.5kW.
Email: george.radio1@qanet.gm
Sud FM Sen R, P.O. Box 65, Banjul: 92.1MHz **Web:** www.sudonline.sn
West Coast R, P.O. Box 2687, Serrekunda: 95.3MHz.
Web: www.westcoast.gm **Email:** info@westcoast.gm
RFI Afrique: Banjul 89MHz in French/English.
F.PI: R. Syd on FM.

GEORGIA

L.T: UTC +3h (27 Mar - 30 Oct 2005: UTC +4h) — **Pop:** 5 million — **Pr.L:** Georgian, Russian, Abkhaz, Ossetic — **E.C:** 50Hz, 220V — **ITU:** GEO

GEORGIAN NATIONAL COMMUNICATIONS COMMISSION (GNCC)

🖃 Ave. Al. Kazbegi 42, T'bilisi 0177. ☎ +995 32 921667. 🖷 +995 32 921625. **Email:** post@gncc.ge **Web:** www.gncc.ge
L.P: Chmn: Dimitri Kitoshvili.
NOTES: GNCC is the regulatory authority for broadcasting.

SAQARTVELOS TELERADIO KORPORACIA (Georgian National Broadcasting Corp., Pub.)

🖃 M. Kostava Str. 68, T'bilisi 0171. ☎ +995 32 368362. 🖷 +995 32 368665. Email: office@geotvr.ge Web: www.geotvr.ge
L.P: Dir: Guram Kuciava.

LW/MW	kHz	kW	Prgr
Dusheti	189	250	1
Batumi	909	5	1*
Dusheti	1215	125	1

*) Also rel. R. Ajaria (see below).

FM (MHz)	Prgr 1	Prgr 2	kW
Batumi	102.4	-	-
Ch'iatura	102.4	-	-
Gori	100.6	-	-
T'bilisi	102.4	100.9	5/4
Zugdidi	101.3	-	-

D.PRGR: Prgr 1 (R. Erti): 24h in Georgian. On LW/MW: 0300-2300, schedule may vary. – **Prgr 2 (R. Ori):** 0400-2400.

EXTERNAL SERVICE: Radio Georgia
See International Radio section

OTHER STATIONS

MW	MHz	kW	Location	Station
27)	4875	100	Dusheti	R. Hara
FM	**MHz**	**kW**	**Location**	**Station**
10)	98.0	-	T'bilisi	Georgian Culture R.
22)	99.0	5	Batumi	R. Ajaria
7B)	99.6	-	T'bilisi	Europa Plus
22)	99.9	0.5	T'bilisi	R. Ajaria
23)	100.3	0.3	T'bilisi	R. 100.3
14)	100.5	-	Poti	R. Poti Plus
9)	100.9	5	Qutaisi	R. Imedi
2)	101.4	5	T'bilisi	R. 101
3)	101.9	0.1	T'bilisi	R. Evrika
15)	102.0	-	Zestaponi	R. Argo
26)	102.8	5	Lagodekhi	R. Hereti
16)	102.9	-	Zugdidi	R. Eurasia
4)	102.9	0.1	T'bilisi	R. Sanet
5B)	103.4	5	T'bilisi	R. Fortuna+
6)	103.9	0.1	T'bilisi	R. Univers
17)	104.0	-	Samtredia	R. Zari
7A)	104.3	5	T'bilisi	R. Ar Daidardo
21)	105.0	-	Tsnori	R. Atleti
25)	105.0	1	Qutaisi	R. Nostalgia
8)	105.0	5	T'bilisi	R. 105
1)	105.4	1	Qutaisi	R. Iveria
1)	105.4	0.5	Gori	R. Iveria
1)	105.4	0.5	Zugdidi	R. Iveria
1)	105.4	5	T'bilisi	R. Iveria
18)	105.5	-	Qutaisi	R. Viva Plus
9)	105.9	0.5	T'bilisi	R. Imedi
19)	105.9	-	Zugdidi	R. Atinati
11)	106.4	10	T'bilisi	Pirveli R. (R. 106)
5A)	106.9	5	T'bilisi	R. Fortuna
12)	107.4	10	T'bilisi	R. Mtsvane talga
24)	107.5	-	Zugdidi	R. Odishi
13)	107.9	5	T'bilisi	R. Saqartvelos xma
20)	107.9	-	Qutaisi	R. Dzelvi kalaki

Addresses & other information:
1) Mepe Erekle II Sq. 1, Tbilisi 0005. – **2)** Agladze Str. 39, T'bilisi 0019. Email: info@radio101.ge – **3)** Tsinamdzgvrishvili Str. 95, T'bilisi 0064. Email: evrika@geo.net.ge – **4)** T'bilisi. – **5A,B)** Marshal Gelovani Str. 2, T'bilisi 0059. Email: radiofortuna@access.sanet.ge – **6)** M.Kostava Str. 77, T'bilisi 0075. Email: universe@posta.ge – **7A,B)** Marshal Gelovani Str. 2, T'bilisi 0059. – **8)** Agladze Str. 31 Tbilisi 0019. Email: n1001@geo.net. ge – **9)** M.Kostava Str. 14, T'bilisi 0096. Email: imedi@access.sanet.ge – **10)** Tbilisi. – **11)** Zoia Ruxadze Str. 1, T'bilisi 0093. Email: radio1@com.ge – **12)** Vazha-Pshavela Ave 45, T'bilisi 0077. Email: gwave@access.sanet.ge – **13)** Shartava Str. 7, T'bilisi 0122. – **14)** Tsminda Giorgi Str. 16, Poti 4401. Email: potitv@gol.ge – **15)** Argonavtebi Str. 1, Zestaponi. – **16)** Agmashenebili Str. 29, Zugdidi 2100. Email: eurazia@zugdidi.ge – **17)** Javakhishvili Str. 8, Samtredia. – **18)** Pushkini Str. 16, Qutaisi 4600. Email: rioni@posta.ge – **19)** Rustaveli Str. 89, Zugdidi 2100. Email: atinati2001@gol.ge – **20)** pr. Rustaveli 37a, Qutaisi 4600. Email: radio107.9@sanetk.ge – **21)** Tsotne Dadiani Str. 12, Tsnori. – **22)** Stalini Ave. 57, Batumi 6000. Shares 909kHz with Georgian National Radio. – **23)** T'bilisi. – **24)** Aghmashenebeli Str. 17, Zugdidi 2100. Email: odishitv@yahoo.com – **25)** Tamar Mepe Ave. 56, Qutaisi 4600. Email: nostalgiarad@posta.ge – **26)** Merab Kostava Str. 1, Lagodekhi. Email: radiohereti@posta.ge – **27)** Rustaveli Ave. 52, Tbilisi 0008. Prgr's in Abkhaz: Tue/Fri 0600-0630, Mon/Thu 1800-1830.

ABKHAZIA (Apsny/Ap'khazet'i)
(autonomous territory, under separatist administration)

APSUA XÖYNTKARRATÄ TELERADIOKOMPANIA
(Abkhaz State Radio & TV Company)
✉ Aydghylara Str. 34, 384900 Soxum. ☎ +995 122 24867. 📠 +995 122 21144. **L.P:** Dir: Zurab Argun.

Station	kHz	kW	Station	kHz	kW
Soxum	1350	30	Soxum	9495v	5

D.PRGR: 0440-2100 in Abkhaz, Russian. Times may vary. Apart from own prgr's, rel. R. Rossii from Russia (incl. regional prgr from Krasnodar/Sochi, Krasnodarskiy kray).
NB. The native name in Abkhaz for "Soxum" is "Aqwa".

OTHER STATIONS

FM	MHz	kW	Location	Station
2)	105.6	-	Soxum	Avtoradio
1)	107.9	-	Soxum	R. Soma

Addresses & other information:
1) Zvanba Str. 9, 384900 Soxum. Email: info@radiosoma.com
2) Soxum. Rel. Avtoradio from Russia.

SOUTH OSSETIA (Xussar Iryston/Samkhret' Oset'i)
(self-proclaimed territory, under separatist administration)

STATE COMMITTEE FOR RADIO & TV
✉ Tsxinval. **L.P:** Chmn: Robert Kulumbekov.
Stations: n/a. **D.PRGR:** in Ossetic, Russian.

OTHER STATIONS

FM	MHz	kW	Location	Station
1)	104.7	-	Tsxinval	R. Nau Ulan

GERMANY

L.T: UTC +1h (27 Mar-30 Oct: UTC +2h) — **Pop:** 80 million— **Pr.L:** German — **E.C:** 50Hz, 230V — **ITU:** D

REGULIERUNGSBEHÖRDE FÜR POST UND TELEKOMMUNIKATION (RegTP)
Authority responsible for frequency allocation matters.
✉ Postfach 8001, 53105 Bonn (office location: Tulpenfeld 4) ☎ +49 (228) 14 0 📠 + 49 (228) 14 8872 **Web:** www.regtp.de

NOTE: Due to the complexity of the broadcasting system in Germany, AM-transmitters (public service, commercial and military) are listed in a combined frequency table below. FM stations and other info can be found under the respective public radio station (section I) or federal state (section II), resp. military station (section III).

LW/MW/SW

	Stn kHz	kW	Site	Prgr.
A)	153	500/250	Donebach	DLF (1)
A)	177	500	Zehlendorf (Oranienbg.)	DLRB (2)
	183	2000	Felsberg (Saarlouis)	Europe 1 (3)
A)	207	500/250	Aholming (Deggendorf)	DLF (1)
	531		Burg	(silent) (4)
A)	549	100	Nordkirchen	DLF
A)	549	100	Thurnau	DLF
G)	567	1.8	Berlin Stallupöner Allee	RBB Radio Multikulti
I)	576	95	Mühlacker	SWR cont.ra
C)	594	250	Rodgau-Weiskirchen	hr-info
C)	594	90	Hoher Meißner	hr-info
	603	20	Zehlendorf (Oranienbg.)	Voice of Russia
	612		Kiel-Kronshagen	(silent) (5)
I)	666	150	Rohrdorf	SWR cont.ra
E)	702	5	Flensburg	NDR Info Spezial
	702	5	Jülich	TruckRadio
I)	711		Heidelberg	(silent) (6)
I)	711	5	Heilbronn	SWR cont.ra
I)	711	5	Ulm	SWR cont.ra
J)	720	85	Langenberg	WDR 2/VERA
B)	729	1	Hof	Bayern 1
B)	729	1	Würzburg	Bayern 1
	729	10	Putbus (Rügen)	DRM test
J)	774	5	Bonn	WDR 2/VERA
A)	756	200	Königslutter	DLF (7)
A)	756	100	Ravensburg	DLF
D)	783	100	Wiederau (Leipzig)	MDR Info
E)	792	5	Lingen	NDR Info Spezial
B)	801	100	Ismaning (München)	Bayern 1
B)	801	10	Dillberg (Nürnberg)	Bayern 1
E)	828	20/5	Hannover-Hemmingen	NDR Info Spezial (8)
I)	828	10	Freiburg	SWR cont.ra
	855	25	Berlin-Britz	special (9)
	855	5	Nordkirchen	TruckRadio
	873	150	Weißkirchen (Oberursel)	AFN Power Network
D)	882	20	Wachenbrunn (Themar)	MDR Info (10)
F)	936	50/10	Bremen Oberneuland	Bremen Eins
E)	972	100	Hamburg Billwerder	NDR Info Spezial
A)	990	100	Berlin-Britz	DLRB
I)	1017	100	Wolfsheim (Mainz)	SWR cont.ra
D)	1044	20	Wilsdruff (Dresden)	MDR Info (11)
	1107	10	Kaiserslautern	AFN Power Network
	1107	10	Grafenwöhr	AFN The Big Gun
	1107	1	Vilseck	AFN The Big Gun
	1107	0.3	Amberg	AFN The Big Gun
	1143	1	Mönchengladbach	AFN SHAPE
	1143	1	Bitburg-Spangdahlem	AFN Power Network
	1143	0.3	Gießen	AFN Power Network
	1143	0.3	Bamberg	AFN Big Red Radio
	1143	0.3	Bad Kissingen	AFN Big Red Radio
	1143	0.3	Schweinfurt	AFN Big Red Radio
	1143	0.3	Würzburg	AFN Big Red Radio
	1143	10	Stuttgart-Hirschlanden	AFN Power Network
	1143	1	Heidelberg	AFN Power Network
D)	1188	3	Reichenbach (Görlitz)	MDR Info
	1197	150/300	Ismaning (München)	VOA/RFE
A)	1269	300	Arpsdorf (Neumünster)	DLF (2)
	1323	800/150	Wachenbrunn (Themar)	Voice of Russia (12)
A)	1422	600	Heusweiler	DLF
	1485	1	Baden-Baden	SWR cont.ra
	1485	1	Kaiserslautern	DRM test
	1485	0.3	Ansbach	AFN Big Red Radio
	1485	0.3	Hohenfels	AFN The Big Gun
	1485	0.3	Regensburg	AFN Bavaria A.M.
	1539	120/700	Mainflingen (13)	Evangeliums-Rundfunk
A)	6005	100	Berlin-Britz	DLRB (2)
I)	6030		Mühlacker	(silent) (6)
B)	6085	100	Ismaning (München)	B5 aktuell (14)
A)	6190	15	Berlin-Britz	DLF (2)
I)	7265		Rohrdorf	(silent) (6)

Stn: Public Radio Stations **A-J** see section I. – Commercial and other stations see section II: **Europe 1** see Saarland, **Evangeliums-Rundfunk** see Hessen, **TruckRadio** see Nordrhein-Westfalen. – **AFN** (American Forces Network Europe) see section III, except for Mönchengladbach 1143kHz: rel. AFN SHAPE, see under Belgium. Power Network tr's may carry short insertions from local affiliates. – **Voice of Russia and VOA/RFE** see International Broadcasting section (Russia and USA, respectively).

Notes: 1) Day 500kW non-directional, night 250kW directional. 153kHz occ. rel. special broadcasts. – **2)** carries sea weather forecasts and navigational warnings at 0005, 0540 and 1005. 177kHz also rel. some of the 855kHz special prgr. – **3)** Directional, beam 220 deg. Rel. 0300-0000 prgr. of Europe 1 from Paris (see under France). – **4)** DRM tests have been concluded. – **5)** Power 612 has been closed down in 2004. Freq. to be reallocated. – **6)** Tr. has been closed down in 2004. – **7)** Nights screened towards Romania. – **8)** 1800-0500 5kW, otherwise 20kW. – **9)** Tests in digital DRM mode and special broadcasts (often rel. TV soundtracks) in AM mode. – **10)** Also parliament coverage from Erfurt. – **11)** Also parliament coverage from Dresden. – **12)** s/on-1600 800kW beam 310 deg., 1600-1800 800kW beam 220 deg., 1800-s/off 150kW beam 220 deg. – **13)** 0600-1900 120kW, 0400-0600 and 1900-2300 700kW. **14)** 0500-2300, overnight open carrier.

PUBLIC STATIONS:

A) DEUTSCHLANDRADIO
National public broadcasting corporation. Operates two nationwide networks:
Deutschlandfunk (DLF): ✉ Raderberggürtel 40, 50968 Köln ☎ +49 (221) 345 0 📠 +49 (221) 345 4803 **Web:** www.dradio.de
DeutschlandRadio Berlin (DLRB): ✉ Hans-Rosenthal-Platz, 10825 Berlin ☎ +49 (30) 8503 0 📠 +49 (30) 8503 6168 **Web:** www.dradio.de

FM (MHz)	DLF	DLRB	kW
Baden-Württemberg			
Biberach	100.5	–	0.5
Blauen	105.1	–	10
Esslingen	96.7	–	0.1
Freiburg	–	90.6	0.2
Geislingen	–	87.7	0.2
Göppingen	99.8	–	0.1
Heidelberg	106.5	–	0.4
Heidenheim	–	100.8	0.1
Heilbronn	91.3	97.3	0.1
Hornisgrinde	106.3	–	100
Kirchheim	91.3	–	0.1
Schwäb. Hall	95.8	–	0.1
Schwarzwald	106.3	–	100
Stuttgart	96.0	87.9	0.5
Ulm	103.5	94.0	0.5/0.1
Witthoh	100.6	–	40
Wörth	–	96.6	0.2
Bayern			
Amberg	–	107.9	0.1

FM (MHz)	DLF	DLRB	kW
Ansbach	92.7	102.7	0.2
Aschaffenbg.	–	94.8	0.1
Augsburg	101.5	100.0	0.5/15
Berchtesgd.	91.6	103.4	0.1
Brotjacklrieg.	100.1	–	100
Burgbernhm.	106.3	94.3	0.2/0.3
Burglengenf.	–	107.3	0.1
Cham	–	101.4	0.1
Freilassing	100.3	–	15
Füssen	87.6	103.4	0.1
Hof Waldst.	–	89.3	20
Ingolstadt	107.0	88.6	0.5/0.6
Kempten	89.3	89.8	0.1
Landshut	95.9	100.5	0.2
München	101.7	96.8	0.3/0.1
Nürnberg	90.1	105.6	0.1
Oberstdorf	92.0	96.5	0.1
Ochsenkopf	100.3	–	100
Passau	–	97.7	0.5
Regensburg	95.5	101.3	0.2
Rhön	103.3	–	100
Rosenheim	97.2	96.2	0.1
Starnberg	87.9	94.7	0.1
Traunstein	–	88.3	0.1
Weiden	–	103.7	0.1
Würzburg	100.3	101.3	0.1
Berlin & Brandenburg			
Berlin A'platz	97.7	–	100
Berlin-Britz	–	89.6	100
Calau	–	90.8	10
Casekow	105.2	–	6
Cottbus	88.6	–	3
Eisenhütt.st.	100.2	–	1
Frankfurt (Bo.)	–	92.7	5
Herzberg/Els.	94.5	–	0.3
Rhinow	–	103.7	0.2
Bremen			
Bremen	107.1	100.3	100/1
Bremerhaven	103.4	106.2	0.5/5
Hamburg			
Hmb.-Moorfl.	88.7	–	3.2
Hessen			
Alsfeld	104.0	–	0.1
Bad Camberg	99.8	–	0.2
Bad Hersfeld	102.9	–	0.3
Darmstadt	102.0	91.1	0.2/0.1
Eschwege	100.6	–	0.5
Frankfurt/M.	97.6	91.2	0.3
Friedberg	89.9	–	0.3
Fritzlar	96.0	106.6	0.1
Fulda	88.5	90.7	0.3
Gelnhausen	93.9	–	0.2
Gießen	103.1	107.5	0.6/0.3
Hanau	92.4	107.7	0.3
Hofgeismar	106.9	–	0.3
Kassel	107.5	–	1
Korbach	92.8	–	0.1
Limburg	103.3	105.1	0.3
Mainz-Kastel	–	107.2	0.4
Marburg	103.5		0.5
Michelstadt	100.5	107.2	0.2
Reinhardsh.	92.9	–	0.2
Wetzlar	103.7	97.3	0.5/0.3
Wiesbaden	103.7	–	0.5
Mecklenburg-Vorpommern			
Anklam	107.4	–	1
Barth	100.3	–	0.1
Dargun	89.8	–	0.5
Greifswald	104.3	106.8	0.2
Güstrow	106.0	–	0.8
Helpterberg	96.5	97.1	10/30
Heringsdorf	98.4	107.1	0.5
Marlow	–	96.7	30
Neukloster	90.6	–	0.3
Neustrelitz	97.9	–	1
Ribn.-Damg.	102.1	–	0.2
Röbel	102.4	90.0	3
Rostock	106.5	–	1
Sassnitz	104.0	101.4	8
Schwerin	106.3	95.3	2/100
Waren/Mü.	91.3	–	0.2
Niedersachsen			
Aurich	101.8	106.9	100/1
Cuxhaven	101.6	107.7	2/20
Emden	–	93.4	1
Göttingen	101.0	–	0.1
Hannover	94.0	–	0.1
Hann. Münd.	98.5	–	0.5
Höhbeck	102.2	–	95
Lingen	102.0		25
		91.6	0.4
		102.9	0.3
Lübbecke	–	97.7	0.2
Meppen	–	100.7	0.1
Norden	–	105.3	0.3
Oldenburg	–	102.8	1
Osnabrück	101.8	–	0.5
Soltau	89.3	–	0.1
Stadthagen	106.1	–	1
Tecklenburg	–	101.1	0.5
Torfh./Harz	103.5	–	100
Uelzen	107.5	–	0.5
Visselhövede	–	88.8	1
Warendorf	107.2	–	1
Nordrhein-Westfalen			
Aachen	102.7	–	0.5
Beckum	91.5	–	0.2
Bielefeld	95.5	106.2	0.1
Bochum	–	89.3	0.3
Bonn	89.1	–	5
Dorsten	–	97.0	0.2
Düsseldorf	–	106.0	0.3
Eifel-Bärbelk.	–	106.1	20
Essen	–	88.3	0.1
Gronau	–	94.6	0.2
Hagen	–	89.4	0.3
Hückeswagen	–	106.0	0.2
Kleve	–	90.1	1
Köln	91.3	89.9	0.1
Lemgo	92.2	88.9	0.3
Münster		97.5	0.1
Nordhelle	102.7	–	20
Olsberg	–	106.1	10
Paderborn	94.5	–	0.2
Recklinghs.	–	101.9	0.2
Rheinberg	–	105.1	0.5
Schwerte	104.4	–	0.2
Stadthagen	106.1	–	1
Steinfurt	–	91.0	0.2
Warendorf	107.2	–	1
Wesel	102.8	–	100
Rheinland-Pfalz			
Bingen	–	106.3	0.2
Bitburg	–	95.3	0.1
Boppard	90.5	88.9	0.1
Idar-Oberst.	–	94.7	0.2
Kaiserslaut.	105.1	98.1	0.2
Koblenz	99.8	105.3	0.5
Ludwigshafen	–	97.3	0.1
Mayen	100.8	–	0.2
Saarburg	104.6	105.3	20/0.1
Traben-Trarb.	88.7	106.2	0.3
Trier	–	94.3	0.2
Wörth	–	96.6	0.2
Saarland			
Lebach	–	107.9	0.1
Neunkirchen	–	105.0	5
Oberperl	–	106.2	5
Saarbrücken	107.5	–	0.1
Saarlouis	–	96.3	0.1
Völklingen	–	88.6	0.1
Sachsen			
Bad Düben	–	99.4	0.2
Bärenstein	–	104.3	1
Belgern	–	101.1	1
Chemnitz	–	106.3	0.5
Collmberg	–	96.1	0.3
Döbeln	–	101.3	1
Dresden	97.3	93.2	100/1
Eilenburg	–	92.0	0.2
Freiberg	–	100.7	1
Geyer (Erzg.)	97.0	–	100
Grimma	–	91.6	0.1
Hoyerswerda	–	89.7	0.5
Leipzig-Holzh.	–	100.4	2
Löbau	99.5	103.0	5/2
Pulsnitz	–	106.7	0.5
Schöneck	94.5	–	3
Weißwasser	–	97.7	2
Wiederau	96.6	–	100
Zwickau	–	104.6	0.2
Sachsen-Anhalt			
Brocken/Harz	–	97.4	100
Dessau	107.1	–	0.3
Dequede	–	96.9	7
Schönebeck	102.0	–	20
Wittenberg	89.3	107.7	1
Zeitz	–	91.8	0.5
Schleswig-Holstein			
Bungsberg	101.9	103.1	95/0.2
Flensburg	103.3	92.1	20/1
Garding	102.3	101.7	0.2/0.5
Heide	104.4	92.2	0.4/0.1
Husum	–	101.0	0.1
Itzehoe	102.2	97.5	0.4/0.1
Kaltenkirchen	–	105.5	0.1
Kiel	–	104.7	0.2
Neumünster	–	107.8	0.5
Niebüll	–	104.2	0.6
Rendsburg	–	95.2	0.3
Schleswig	–	105.0	0.2
Sylt	90.3	103.9	0.2
Thüringen			
Bleßberg	–	94.2	100
Eisenach	106.5	–	0.5
Erfurt	103.1	–	2
Gera	–	93.6	0.3
Ilmenau	99.9	–	0.1
Inselsberg	–	97.2	100
Jena	104.5	98.2	0.3/0.2
Mühlhausen	107.0	–	1
Saalfeld	98.7	–	0.1
Suhl	98.8	–	0.1
Weimar	89.7	–	0.5

+ 13 sts below 0.1kW

ARBEITSGEMEINSCHAFT DER ÖFFENTLICH-RECHTLICHEN RUNDFUNKANSTALTEN DEUTSCHLANDS (ARD)

Ubrella organization of the public broadcasting institutions below. ✉ Arnulfstraße 42, 80335 München ☎ +49 (89) 5900 3344 **Web:** www.ard.de Significant radio activities:

Overnight programming: ARD-Nachtexpress (light music, from 0300 as ARD-Radiowecker); ARD-Popnacht (pop music, often in fact a relay of the delivering stn.); ARD-Nachtkonzert (classical music); produced on a rota system and rel. at night by certain stn's.

B) BAYERISCHER RUNDFUNK (BR)

Public broadcasting institution of the state of Bayern.
✉ Bayerischer Rundfunk, 80300 München (headquarter location: Rundfunk platz 1) ☎ +49 (89) 5900 01 🖹 +49 (89) 5900 2375 **Web:** www.br-online.de

FM (MHz)	B. 1	B.2R	B. 3	B. 4	B5	kW
Augsburg Haberk.	–	–	–	–	105.3	0.5
Bad Reichenhall	91.8	89.9	96.7	98.3	105.0	0.3
Bamberg Geisberg	94.8N	98.6	99.8	102.9	97.4	25/5
Berchtesgaden	90.4	99.6	96.9	94.2	106.4	0.3/0.1
Brotjacklriegel	92.1R	96.5	94.4	100.9	106.9	100/50
Büttelberg	91.4N	88.2	99.3	95.5	104.0	25/10
Coburg	93.5N	88.3	99.2	97.7	92.8	5/0.3
Dillberg	88.9N	92.3	97.9	87.6	102.0	25
	104.5R					5
Eichstätt Gelbelsee	101.6	90.5	97.6	89.0	106.1	25/10
Garmisch-Partenk.	89.2	93.5	97.7	95.9	104.9	0.1
Grünten (Allgäu)	90.7U	88.7	95.8	101.0	106.9	50/100
Herzogstand	88.1	97.0	91.0	–	106.7	0.1
Hochberg-Traunst.	98.0	91.5	95.9	97.0	107.1	5/0.5
Hohenpeißenberg	92.8	94.2	99.2	100.4	–	25
Hoher Bogen	96.8R	91.6	94.7	88.3	104.4	50/5
Hühnerberg	91.9U	96.1	99.5	93.1	107.6	25/11
Kreuzberg (Rhön)	98.3W	93.1	96.3	107.9	105.3	100/50
Landshut	90.2R	97.8	95.3	93.2	106.6	0.1
Lindau Hoyerberg	88.1U	92.0	94.0	87.6	100.4	0.5/0.1
München-Ismaning	91.3	88.4	97.3	103.2	90.0	25
Ochsenkopf	90.7N	96.0	99.4	102.3	107.1	100/50
	91.2R					20
Passau	87.7R	93.2	90.4	95.6	105.9	0.5/0.3
Pfaffenberg	95.6W	88.4	93.4	98.0	106.4	25/1
Regensburg	95.0R	93.0	99.6	97.0	105.0	25/5
Untersb. Geiereck*)	87.8	92.9	96.1	100.7	–	0.1
Wallberg	94.0	87.7	99.7	97.9	101.8	0.1
Wendelstein	93.7	89.5	98.5	102.3	105.7	100
Würzburg	90.9W	90.0	97.6	89.0	105.7	5/0.2

+ 8 tr's less than 0.1kW *) Tr. in Austria.

Bayern 1: On 729/801kHz, FM and satellite, light music format, at night rel. ARD-Nachtexpress. **Bayern2Radio**: On FM and satellite, various prgr., at night rel. ARD-Nachtkonzert. **Bayern 3**: On FM and satellite, pop, 24 hours. **Bayern 4 Klassik**: On FM, DAB and satellite, classical music, at night rel. ARD-Nachtkonzert. **B5 aktuell**: On 6085kHz, FM, DAB and satellite, all-news, monaural only, rel. 2300-0500 MDR Info. **Special DAB prgr.:** Bayern mobil; Das Modul; BR Traffic News; BR News+Wetter; BR Business; all via DAB ch. 12D (229MHz) only.

C) HESSISCHER RUNDFUNK (HR)

Public broadcasting institution of the state of Hessen.
60222 Frankfurt am Main (headquarter location: Bertramstraße 8)
☎ +49 (69) 155 1 🖹 +49 (69) 155 2900 **Web:** www.hr-online.de

FM (MHz)	hr1	hr2	hr3	hr4	kW
Bensheim Hemsb.	–	–	–	91.2R	0.06
Biedenkopf	91.0	99.6	87.6	104.3M	100
				102.3N	10
Bingen	–	–	91.1	–	0.3
Feldberg (Taunus)	94.4	96.7	89.3	102.5R	100
Fulda	–	–	–	103.9N	0.3
Habichtswald	–	–	101.2	103.2N	20
Hardberg (Odenw.)	90.6	95.3	92.7	101.6R	50
Heidelstein*)	104.8	–	106.2	107.3N	50
Hoher Meißner	99.0	95.5	89.5	101.7N	100
Kassel-Wilhelmsh.	94.3	–	–	–	0.5
Limburg Schafsberg	–	–	–	97.1M	0.2
Marburg	–	–	–	102.8M	1
Rimberg	91.3	95.0	97.7	91.9N	50/20
Weilburg	–	–	–	97.9M	0.05
Wetzlar	–	–	–	90.5M	0.3
Wiesbaden	98.3	–	–	–	0.1
Würzberg (Odenw.)	88.1	97.4	89.7	103.8R	5

FM (MHz)	hr-klassik	YOU FM	hr-info	kW
Alsfeld-Homberg	105.6	–	–	0.1
Bad Hersfeld	88.9	106.9	–	0.3
Bensheim Hemsb.	–	90.2	–	0.2
Bingen*)	–	92.3	–	0.3
Darmstadt	–	98.2	107.0	0.25/5
Eltville-Erbach	96.2	–	–	0.5
Eschwege	–	106.6	–	0.1
Frankfurt/Main	87.9	90.4	103.9	0.1/0.5/0.5
Fulda	106.6	93.6	89.7	0.3/0.3/0.2
Gelnhausen	–	99.4	–	0.3
Gießen	97.9	–	99.2	0.5/0.3
Kassel-Wilhelmsh.	93.7	100.1	–	0.5
Korbach	102.6	–	–	1
Limburg	100.8	90.7	99.2	0.3/0.2/0.3
Marburg	–	93.9	–	1
Michelstadt	–	91.0	–	0.2
Rotenburg	105.7	96.8	–	0.3
Schlüchtern	–	88.2	–	0.3
Seeheim-Jungenh.	–	–	88.2	0.05
Sontra	–	90.8	–	0.05
Wetzlar	–	105.5	–	0.3
Wiesbaden	93.1	99.7	97.2	0.1/0.2/0.1
Witzenhausen	–	91.1	–	0.3

*) Heidelstein tr. site in Bayern, Bingen tr. site in Rheinland-Pfalz.

hr1: On FM and satellite, information and pop, at night rel. ARD-Popnacht. **hr2**: On FM and satellite, culture, 2305-0500 rel. ARD-Nachtkonzert. **hr3**: On FM and satellite, pop, at night rel. ARD-Popnacht. **hr4**: Produced at Kassel (Wilhelmshöher Allee 347, 34131 Kassel). On FM and satellite, light music format. Regional prgr. Nordhessen (N; Kassel/Fulda), Mittelhessen (M; Gießen) and Rhein-Main (R; Frankfurt/Darmstadt) Mon-Fri only 0830-0835, 1105-1200 and 1505-1600; 2305-0500 rel. ARD-Nachtexpress. **hr-klassik**: On FM (lp.) and satellite, classical music, rel. hr2 at times. **YOU FM**: Former hr-XXL, relaunched in 2004. On FM (lp.) and satellite. **hr-info**: Former hr-skyline, relaunched in 2004. On 594kHz, FM (lp.) and satellite, all-news, 2100-0500 rel. MDR Info. 594kHz and separate satellite ch.: MW edition with live coverage of parliament sessions, sports and other events, 1800-2100 foreign language broadcasts in Italian, Turkish, Serbocroatian, Greek and Spanish.

D) MITTELDEUTSCHER RUNDFUNK (MDR)

Public broadcasting institution of the states of Sachsen, Sachsen-Anhalt and Thüringen.
Kantstraße 71-73, 04360 Leipzig (administration) **Web:** www.mdr.de
Gerberstraße 2, 06110 Halle/Saale ☎ +49 (345) 300 0 🖹 +49 (345) 300 5544. (radio, except MDR 1 prgr's, see below)

FM (MHz)	MDR1	Jump	Figaro	Info	Sputnik	kW
Altenburg	–	–	–	101.5	–	1
Annaberg-Buchholz	–	–	–	91.2	–	0.2
Apolda	–	–	–	91.2	–	1
Arnstadt	–	–	–	106.1	–	0.5
Aue	–	–	–	95.1	–	1
Auerbach	–	–	–	101.7	–	0.4
Bad Salzungen	–	–	–	94.0	–	0.1
Bautzen	–	98.8	–	87.9	–	0.2/0.1
Bleßberg	91.7T	96.9	–	–	–	100/20
Brocken	94.6A	91.5	107.8	–	–	60/100/10
Burg Kapaunberg	96.1A	–	107.4	–	–	10/30
Burg (town)	–	–	–	89.6	–	1
Chemnitz-Reichenh.	–	–	–	94.7	–	0.5
Collmberg	101.8S	103.7	98.9	105.9	–	2x3/0.5/5
Dequede	94.9A	98.9	89.4	–	–	10
Dessau-Mildensee	–	–	–	90.0	–	0.3
Döbeln-Mockritz	–	–	–	99.6	–	0.1
Dresden-Wachwitz	92.2S	90.1	95.4	106.1	–	3x100/0.5
Eilenburg	–	–	–	92.4	–	0.2
Eisenach	–	–	–	100.0	–	0.2
Erfurt	94.4T	–	–	97.8	–	2/1
Fleetmark	–	–	–	90.1	105.0	2/1
Freiberg	99.1S	–	–	93.7	–	1/0.2
Freital	–	–	–	95.6	–	0.2
Gera	–	–	–	91.1	–	1
Gernrode	–	–	–	91.0	–	0.1
Geyer (Erzgebirge)	92.8S	89.8	87.7	–	–	100
Grimma-Hohnstädt	–	–	–	100.6	–	0.2
Görlitz	–	–	–	106.9	–	1
Gotha	–	–	–	88.8	–	0.1
Greiz	–	–	–	93.3	–	0.2
Haidberg	–	–	–	–	100.7	5
Haldensleben	–	–	–	99.1	–	1
Halle Petersberg	100.8A	–	–	95.3	104.4	5/2/10
Halle city	–	89.6	107.3	–	–	0.1
Heiligenstadt	93.6T	–	–	90.5	–	0.1
Hergisdorf	92.9A	–	–	–	–	1
Hoyerswerda	93.0S	89.0	94.7	94.2	–	1/0.5/1/1
	100.4So					30
Ilmenau	–	–	–	93.0	–	0.1
Inselsberg	92.5T	90.2	87.9	–	–	100/100/60
Jena-Oßmaritz	88.2T	101.9	96.4	89.5	–	1/0.2
Jerichow	–	–	–	–	90.5	1
Jessen	–	–	–	87.6	–	1
Keula	98.5T	–	–	–	–	20
Klingenthal	93.7S	–	98.4	–	–	0.2
Klötze	–	–	–	–	100.7	5
Leipzig city	–	–	–	95.6	–	0.5
Löbau	98.2S	91.8	96.2	–	–	5
Lobenstein	107.9T	–	–	–	–	2
Magdala	92.9T	–	–	99.2	–	0.01/0.05
Markneukirchen	104.8S	–	106.4	–	–	0.5
Meißen-Korbitz	–	–	–	94.9	–	1
Meiningen	–	–	–	94.7	–	0.2
Mühlhausen	–	–	–	105.8	–	0.1
Naumburg	92.3A	–	–	–	93.1	1/0.5
Nordhausen	88.3T	–	–	93.7	–	0.1
Plauen	–	–	–	102.0	–	1
Pößneck	–	–	–	101.6	–	0.2
Raschau	–	–	–	91.6	–	0.2
Remda	103.6T	105.6	100.7	–	–	60
Ronneburg	97.8T	100.9	103.9	–	–	10/30/30
Saalfeld	–	–	–	104.6	–	0.1
Sangerhausen	101.1A	–	–	99.9	–	0.1/1
Schönebeck	–	–	–	91.1	105.2	2/1.5
Schleiz	–	–	–	105.1	–	0.2
Schmalkalden	–	–	-	100.0	–	0.1
Schmölln	–	–	–	107.9	–	0.2
Seifhennersdorf	94.5S	96.9	103.4	–	–	0.25/0.3
Schneidlingen	–	–	–	106.7	–	0.5
Schöneck	88.7S	101.2	98.7	–	–	3/30/3
Sondershausen	–	–	–	95.1	–	0.1
Sonneberg	–	–	–	105.8	–	0.1
Stendal-Borstel	–	–	–	87.8	104.8	1
Suhl Erleshügel	93.7T	91.1	89.8	97.5	–	1/0.1/0.2/5
Torgau	88.9S	–	93.0	–	–	0.5/0.2
Weimar Ettersberg	93.3T	–	–	–	–	5
Weimar Belvedere	–	–	–	102.6	–	2
Wernigerode	–	–	–	98.6	–	1
Weißenfels	–	–	–	88.8	–	1
Weißwasser	–	–	–	90.5	–	1
Wiederau (Leipzig)	93.9S	90.4	88.4	–	–	100
	106.5A					30*)
Wittenberg	88.1A	101.6	104.0	–	–	30/55/55
Zeitz-Hainichen	–	–	–	–	89.4	0.5
Zittau	87.7S	107.1	95.4	–	–	0.2/2x0.5
Zschopau	–	–	–	99.5	–	0.2
Zwickau	–	–	–	91.4	–	1

*) directional towards Halle/Saale.

MDR 1 – Radio Sachsen: Königsbrücker Straße 88, 01099 Dresden; on freq. marked S. **MDR 1 – Radio Sachsen-Anhalt**: Stadtparkstraße 8, 39114 Magdeburg; on freq. marked A. **MDR 1 – Radio Thüringen**: Humboldstraße 36a, 99425 Weimar; on freq. marked T. MDR 1 prgrs. light music format, incl. short insertions from local studios, 2300-0400 common prgr. called "MDR-Dreiländernacht". **Jump**: On FM and satellite, pop. **MDR Figaro**: Former MDR Kultur, relaunched in 2004. On FM and satellite, rel. 2300-0500 ARD-Nachtkonzert. **MDR Info**: On 783/882/1044/1188kHz, FM and satellite, all-news. At night rel. by BR, HR and SWR, see there. **Sputnik**: On FM (Sachsen-Anhalt only) and satellite, youth. Produces also three further prgrs. for webcasting only. **MDR Klassik**: Only on DAB (ch. 12, except in eastern Sachsen: ch. 5), classical music. **Sorbian language broadcasts**: MDR-Studio Bautzen, Am Postplatz 2, 02607 Bautzen. On Hoyerswerda 100.4MHz Mon-Fri 0405-0700, Sat 0505-0800, Sun 1000-1130 (also on Calau 93.4MHz). "Radio Satkula" for young listeners Mon 1900-2100. **N.B** Sorbian broadcasts from Cottbus see under RBB.

E) NORDDEUTSCHER RUNDFUNK (NDR)

Public broadcasting institution of the states of Hamburg, Mecklenburg-Vorpommern, Niedersachsen and Schleswig-Holstein. ✉ Rothenbaumchaussee 132, 20149 Hamburg ☎ +49 (40) 4156 0 🖹 +49 (40) 447 602 **Web:** www.ndr.de **N.B** Adresses for regional NDR 1 services see below.

FM (MHz)	NDR 1	NDR 2	NDR-K	Info	N-Joy	kW
Anklam	94.6M	–	–	–	103.0	6.3/1.25
Aurich-Popens	95.8	98.1	90.0	96.4	92.7	25/10/1
Bad Doberan	94.3M	–	–	–	103.7	0.2/5
Bad Rothenfelde	–	–	–	97.9	91.2	0.2/0.1
Barth	87.6M	–	–	–	95.0	0.4/0.3
Braunschweig	–	–	–	–	100.3	15
Bremen-Walle	–	–	–	95.0	–	1
Bremerhaven	–	–	–	98.9	92.8	0.5/0.05
Bungsberg	97.8K	91.9	89.9	96.6	99.0	50/1/0.5
Cloppenburg	–	–	–	103.7	93.5	1
Cuxhaven	105.4	97.9	94.6	93.1	91.6	20/10/1/10
	98.4H					1
Damme	–	–	–	106.5	105.0	0.5/1
Dannenberg	91.2	96.4	93.3	90.7	94.0	25/10/3/1
Dömitz	88.3M	–	–	–	–	1
Flensburg	89.6K	93.2	96.1	87.7	91.0	25/10/0.5
Garding-Katingsiel	–	–	–	–	88.8	0.5
Garz/Rügen	102.5M	99.8	91.5	88.6	95.5	50/10
Goslar	88.2	93.7	95.1	96.0	96.5	0.1
Göttingen	88.5	94.1	96.8	99.9	95.9	5/0.5/5/0.5
Greifswald	101.0M	–	–	–	–	0.16
Grevesmühlen	100.7M	–	–	–	103.4	0.5/5
Güstrow-Strentz	92.5M	–	–	–	104.4	1.25/0.63
Hamburg-Moorfleet	90.3H	87.6	99.2	92.3	94.2	80/5/1
	89.5K					10
Hannover-Hemm.	90.9	96.2	98.7	88.6	92.6	15/5/15/0.5/25
Heide-Welmbüttel	90.5K	96.3	99.4	87.9	94.9	15/0.5
Helpterberg	90.5M	99.1	96.0	101.8	103.2	100/1.25
	94.2M*)					6.3
Heringsdorf	97.6M	94.0	102.7	100.5	92.3	1
Hildesheim	–	–	–	–	95.7	0.5
Holzminden	92.7	96.0	98.4	88.6	99.7	0.5/0.1
Jever	–	–	–	–	97.3	0.3
Kiel-Kronshagen	91.3K	98.3	95.7	99.7	94.5	15/1/0.4/15
Königslutter-Elm	–	–	–	88.7	–	0.2
Lauenburg	94.7K	–	–	96.8	99.8	0.3
Lingen	92.8	97.8	90.2	88.9	96.6	15/0.2/0.5
Lübeck	93.1K	90.7	88.0	95.9	94.0	0.5/0.1/0.5
Malchin	–	–	–	103.5	94.4	1
Marlow	91.0M	93.5	88.2	102.8	–	100/30/100
Mölln	104.5K	–	–	–	90.9	20/0.5
Neubrandenburg	–	–	–	–	89.5	1
Neumünster	106.4K	–	–	90.8	98.7	20/1/0.5
Niebüll-Süderlügum	–	–	–	–	91.5	0.2
Osnabrück	92.4	89.2	98.8	87.6	96.4	8/2x0.2
Pasewalk	93.7M	–	–	–	94.8	2.5/1.25
Ribnitz-Damgarten	–	–	–	–	99.4	0.3
Rinteln	–	–	–	95.3	105.2	0.1/0.04
Röbel	88.5M	107.0	94.7	100.4	97.4	10/60/4
Rosengarten	103.2	–	–	–	91.4	20/0.3
Rostock	95.8M	–	–	–	88.9	0.16/2
Schwerin	92.8M	98.5	89.2	105.3	99.5	30/100/2
Seesen	–	–	–	90.4	96.6	0.2/0.05
Stadthagen	100.8	102.6	104.4	98.2	91.3	25/1
Steinkimmen	91.1	99.8	94.4	98.6	92.9	100/3/1
Stralsund	92.1M	–	–	–	–	0.4
Sylt	90.9K	98.7	94.3	92.7	95.6	5
Torfhaus	98.0	92.1	89.9	99.5	–	100/50
Ueckermünde	90.1M	–	–	–	104.1	4/1.5
Visselhövede	91.8	95.9	87.8	98.4	90.1	5/2/5/1
Wedel	–	–	–	–	95.6	0.2
Wismar	96.2M	–	–	–	–	0.2
Wolfsburg	–	–	–	88.2	–	0.1
Wolgast-Moeckow	89.0M	–	–	–	93.2	0.4/0.3

+ 8 tr's less than 0.1kW *) with different local insertions

NDR 1 Niedersachsen: Postfach 45 60, 30045 Hannover (studio location: Rudolf-von-Bennigsen-Ufer 22). On freq. not marked and on DAB (224MHz). Special "Messeradio" during Hannover Messe trade fairs on 90.9MHz. **NDR 90,3:** From Hamburg headquarter, on freq. marked H and DAB (Hamburg, 227MHz). **NDR 1 Welle Nord:** Postfach 34 80, 24033 Kiel (studio location: Eggerstraße 16). On freq. marked K and DAB (Kiel only, 229MHz). **NDR 1 Radio MV:** Schloßgartenallee 61, 19061 Schwerin. On freq. marked M and DAB (Schwerin only, 226MHz). At night all with common prgrg. called "NDR 1 Nacht". **NDR 2**: On FM, DAB and satellite, pop. **NDR Kultur:** On FM and satellite, classical music, rel. 2305-0500 ARD-Nachtlonzert. **NDR Info:** On FM, DAB and satellite, Mon-Fri 0500-1850 and Sat 0500-1700 all-news format, remaining time diverse prgr. **NDR Info Spezial:** On 702/792/828/972kHz and satellite. Rel. Mon-Fri 1500-1700 Funkhaus Europa (WDR/RB), 1700-1730 BBC-Worldservice, 1730-1800 RFI, 1800-1830 prgr. in Italian, 1830-1900 Greek, 1900-1930 Serbocroatian. Sun 0500-0700 Hamburger Hafenkonzert. Sea weather forecasts on 702/972kHz only: 2305 (also via NDR Info FM tr's in Mecklenburg-Vorpommern), 0730 and 2105. **N-Joy:** On FM and satellite, youth.

F) RADIO BREMEN (RB)

Public broadcasting institution of the state of Bremen.
✉ Bürgermeister-Spitta-Allee 45, 28329 Bremen ☎ +49 (421) 246 0 🖹 +49 (421) 246 1010 **Web:** www.radiobremen.de

FM (MHz)	Eins	NWRadio	Vier	Europa	kW
Bremen-Walle	93.8	88.3	101.2	96.7	100/50
Bremerhaven	89.3	95.4	100.8	92.1	25

Prgr (all networks also on satellite):
Bremen Eins: Oldie format, also on 936kHz. Rel. 2305-0400 (Sun til 0500) SWR1. **Nordwestradio:** Culture, co-produced with NDR. Rel. 2305-0500 ARD-Nachtkonzert. **Bremen Vier:** Pop, at night rel. ARD-Popnacht. **Funkhaus Europa:** Multicultural prgrg., together with WDR, see also there.

G) RUNDFUNK BERLIN-BRANDENBURG (RBB)

Public broadcasting institution of the city of Berlin and state of Brandenburg.
Potsdam branch: ✉ Marlene-Dietrich-Allee 20, 14482 Potsdam-Babelsberg ☎ +49 (331) 731 0 🖹 +49 (331) 731 3571
Berlin branch: ✉ 14046 Berlin (studio location: Masurenallee 8-14) ☎ +49 (30) 3031 0 🖹 +49 (30) 3015 062 **Web:** www.rbb-online.de

FM (MHz)	Ant.B.	Eins	Fritz	Kultur	kW
Belzig	106.2	99.3	91.9	100.2	100/10
Berlin Alexandplatz	99.7	95.8	102.6	–	100
Berlin Scholzplatz	–	–	–	92.4	80
Booßen (Frankf.)	87.6F	89.1	101.5	96.8	5/30
Calau	98.6C	95.1	103.2	104.4	100/10
Casekow-Luckow	91.1F	106.1	100.1	104.4	63/10
Guben	100.9C	–	–	–	6.3
Prenzlau	99.4F	–	–	–	0.5
Pritzwalk-Buchh.	106.6	99.9	103.1	91.7	100/10
Zehlendorf	90.8F	–	–	–	1.3
FM (MHz)	**88acht**	**Info**	**Multik**	**Serb**	**kW**
Berlin Scholzplatz	88.8	93.1	96.3	–	80/25/80
Booßen (Frankf.)	–	102.0	99.3	–	1.6/0.8
Calau	–	–	–	93.4	30
Cottbus Klein Oßnig	–	99.9	91.6	–	1/0.5
Lübben	–	92.9	–	–	0.4
Perleberg	–	92.3	–	–	1
Prenzlau	–	98.6	–	–	0.5
Pritzwalk-Buchholz	–	94.2	–	–	0.5
Wittstock	–	97.7	–	–	1.3

Prgrs from Berlin: 88acht, Berlin city prgr. on 88.8MHz, DAB Berlin (199MHz) and satellite, rel. ARD-Nachtexpress at night. **Inforadio** on FM, DAB Berlin and satellite, all-news. **Radio Multikulti** on 567kHz, FM, DAB Berlin and satellite, multicultural prgr., incl. foreign language broadcasts. **Kulturradio** on FM, DAB Berlin and satellite, at night rel. ARD-Nachtkonzert.
Prgr's from Potsdam: Antenne Brandenburg, Brandenburg state prgr. on FM, DAB Brandenburg (229MHz, except Frankfurt/Oder: 220MHz) and satellite, includes local prgr. from Frankfurt/Oder (freq. marked F) and Cottbus (freq. marked C), at night rel. ARD-Nachtexpress. **Radio Eins**, on FM, DAB Brandenburg and satellite, rock/pop orientated. **Fritz**, on FM, DAB Berlin and satellite, youth prgr. **Bramborske Serbske Radio**: On 93.4MHz, Sorbian language prgr. from Cottbus , Mon-Fri 1100-1200 and 1800-1900, Sundays and holidays 1130-1300, otherwhise rel. Sorbian language prgr. from MDR and Inforadio.

H) SAARLÄNDISCHER RUNDFUNK (SR)

Public broadcasting institution of the state of Saarland.
✉ Funkhaus Halberg, 66100 Saarbrücken ☎ +49 (681) 602 0 🖷 +49 (681) 602 3874 **Web:** www.sr-online.de

FM (MHz)	SR 1	SR 2	SR 3	UnserDing	kW
Bliestal-Webenheim	92.3	98.0	89.1	–	5
Göttelborner Höhe	88.0	91.3	95.5	–	100
Homburg	–	–	–	98.6	0.2
Merzig-Hilbringen	89.3	92.1	98.0	–	0.1
Mettlach	98.6	88.5	96.0	–	0.01
Neunkirchen	–	–	–	–	5
Oberperl	91.9	88.6	96.1	–	5
Saarbrücken Halberg	98.2	–	–	–	0.01
Saarbr. Schocksberg	–	–	–	103.7	100
Sankt Wendel	–	–	–	90.3	0.1

Prgr: SR 1 Europawelle Saar: Pop, at night rel. ARD-Popnacht. **SR 2 KulturRadio:** Culture, at night rel. ARD-Nachtkonzert. **SR 3 Saarlandwelle:** Light music, at night rel. ARD-Nachtexpress. News in French at 0805. **Unser Ding:** Prgr. for teenagers, at times rel. Das Ding (SWR). SR 1 und SR 2 also on satellite. All prgr. plus special SR Info also on DAB (198MHz).

I) SÜDWESTRUNDFUNK (SWR)

Public broadcasting institution of the states of Baden-Württemberg and Rheinland-Pfalz.
✉ 76522 Baden-Baden (Location: Hans-Bredow-Straße) ☎ +49 (7221) 929 0 🖷 +49 (7221) 929 2010
Broadcasting house Mainz: ✉ Postfach 3740, 55122 Mainz (Location: Am Fort Gonsenheim 39) ☎ +49 (6131) 929 0
Broadcasting house Stuttgart: ✉ Postfach 106040, 70049 Stuttgart (Location: Neckarstraße 230) ☎ +49 (711) 929 0

FM (MHz)	SWR1	SWR2	SWR3	SWR4	DasDing	kW
Aalen Braunenberg	95.1B	91.1	98.1	96.9Sc	–	50/5
Albstadt-Mahlesfeld	–	–	–	99.5Tü	–	0.1
Annweiler Trifels	–	–	–	91.0L	–	0.03
Bad Bellingen	–	–	–	96.6Br	–	0.1
Bad Kreuznach	95.8R	–	98.2	90.9M	–	0.05
Bad Mergentheim	87.8B	93.2	99.7	105.5F	100.5	10/0.04
Baden-Baden	90.9B	98.9	99.6	88.5B	–	0.8/0.4
Baiersbronn	–	–	–	87.9O	–	0.1
Basel St. Crischona*)	87.9B	92.0	98.3	89.5H	–	5
Blauen-Hochblauen	89.2B	92.6	97.0	–	–	8.4
Bleialf-Buchet	88.3R	99.7	98.9	94.6T	–	0.1
Buchen-Walldürn	91.9B	97.1	94.1	107.5Ku	100.6	0.1/25
Daun-Scharteberg	91.1R	–	98.5	93.6T	–	8
Diez-Geisenberg	88.4R	93.4	98.2	87.9K	–	0.01/0.1
Donnersberg	99.1R	92.0	101.1	105.6Ka	–	60
Elzach Hörnleberg	–	–	–	101.8Br	–	0.1
Feldberg	89.8B	97.9	93.8	104.0Br	–	5
Freiburg-Lehen	107.0B	91.1	99.2	100.7Br	–	0.1/1
Geislingen	93.0B	88.5	95.5	107.9S	–	0.5/0.1
Grünten	98.7B	–	103.0	–	–	30
Haardtkopf	97.7R	93.0	90.0	107.1T	–	50/25
Hausach Brandenkopf	95.4B	–	99.7	97.6O	–	0.5/0.1
Heidelberg Königstuhl	97.8B	88.8	99.9	104.1Ku	–	100
Hohe Wurzel	–	–	–	107.9M	–	6.2
Hornisgrinde	93.5B	96.2	98.4	94.0O	–	80/5
Karlsruhe-Ettlingen	–	–	–	97.0B	–	20
Kaiserslautern Bornberg	90.8R	93.9	97.5	99.6Ka	–	25/0.5
Klettgau Wannenberg	95.1B	92.8	98.5	87.7H	–	2.6
Koblenz-Waldesch	96.1R	94.0	91.6	107.4K	99.4	10/40/0.2
Kreuzweiler	–	–	–	97.3T	–	0.3
Lichtenstein	99.1B	–	–	89.0Tü	–	0.1
Linz-Ginsterhahn	92.4R	–	94.8	97.4K	–	50
Mainz-Kastel	87.7R	103.2	93.7	91.4M	–	1
Mainz-Wolfsheim	–	–	–	94.9M	–	0.5
Mannheim	–	–	–	–	91.5	2.5
Marienberger Höhe	89.8R	95.4	92.8	106.3K	91.3	25/0.1
Mühlacker	–	–	–	95.7B	–	2
Nierstein-Oppenheim	–	–	–	92.9M	–	0.1
Pirmasens Kettrichhof	100.8R	–	107.2	104.2Ka	–	5
Pforzheim	92.9B	88.1	99.3	87.6B	–	5/0.2/0.5
Raichberg	88.3B	91.8	94.3	107.3Tü	–	40/25
Saarburg-Geisberg	99.2R	93.8	90.6	101.2T	–	5
Schiltach-Simonsberg	90.8B	–	94.5	99.2O	–	0.1
Schussental	99.0B	–	87.9	–	107.2	0.1
Schwäbisch Gmünd	–	–	–	100.9Sc	–	0.1
Sigmaringen	–	–	–	101.2Bo	–	0.1
Stuttgart-Degerloch	94.7B	105.7	92.2	90.1S	90.8	100/2
Stuttgart (town)	–	93.1	–	–	–	0.2
		91.5+)				0.3
Trier Markusberg	94.9R	89.4	98.2	98.8T	91.7	0.1/0.3
Tübingen Herrenberg	–	–	97.2	87.6Tü	90.5	1
Ulm Kuhberg	92.6B	89.2	97.4	94.5Sc	89.9	10/1
Vaihingen	–	98.6	–	–	–	0.1
Villingen-Schwenningen	–	–	–	91.1Br	–	1
Waldenburg Hohenau	98.8B	93.8	96.5	106.6F	–	100/50
Waldburg Galgenberg	–	94.9	–	99.5F	–	60
				91.2Bo		25
Weinbiet	89.9R	102.2	–	95.9L	–	25
Weinheim Hirschkopf	97.1B	99.5	–	100.7Ku	–	0.04/0.1
Wertheim	96.9B	91.8	94.6	101.2F	–	0.1
Witthoh	92.4B	90.4	97.1	89.0Bo	–	40/5
Zell Hohe Möhr	87.6B	–	96.8	–	–	0.1
	100.2Br					0.1
Zwiefalten	93.7B	–	92.8	87.6Bo	–	0.1

+ 20 tr's less than 0.1kW *) Site in Switzerland. +) rel. SWR cont.ra

Prgr (all networks also on satellites):
SWR1 Baden-Württemberg (on freq. marked B and DAB Baden-Württemberg – 226MHz) from Stuttgart and **SWR1 Rheinland-Pfalz** (on freq. marked R and DAB Rheinland-Pfalz – 224MHz) from Mainz; oldies/pop and information, at night common prgr. produced at Baden-Baden. **SWR2:** Culture, at night rel. ARD-Nachtkonzert. **SWR3:** Pop. **SWR4 Baden-Württemberg:** Light music format, includes regional prgr.: Baden-Radio (B, produced at Karlsruhe), Bodensee-Radio (Bo, Friedrichshafen), Radio Breisgau (Br, Freiburg), Franken-Radio (F, Heilbronn), Hochrhein-Radio (H, Lörrach and Waldshut-Tiengen), Kurpfalz-Radio (Ku, Mannheim), Ortenau-Radio (O, Offenburg), Schwaben-Radio (Sc, Ulm), Radio Stuttgart (S), Radio Tübingen (Tü). **SWR4 Rheinland-Pfalz:** Light music format, includes regional prgr.: Kaiserslautern (Ka), Koblenz (K), Ludwigshafen (L), Trier (T), at night rel. ARD-Nachtexpress. **DasDing:** Also on DAB. Aiming at teenagers. Also produces three music prgr. for webcasting only. **SWR cont.ra:** On 576/666/711/828/1017/1485kHz, Stuttgart 91.5MHz and local DAB (1.5GHz; F.Pl.: move to ch.12 services). News and other spoken word. 2100-0500 rel. MDR Info.

N.B: The shortwave trs of SWR (6030/7265kHz) were closed 2004.

J) WESTDEUTSCHER RUNDFUNK (WDR)

Public broadcasting institution of the state of Nordrhein-Westfalen.
✉ 50600 Köln (Location: Appellhofplatz 1) ☎ +49 (221) 220 1 🖷 +49 (221) 220 4800 **Web:** www.wdr. de

FM (MHz)	ELive	WDR 2	WDR 3	WDR4	WDR5	kW
Aachen-Stolberg	106.4	100.8A	95.9	93.9	101.9	20
Arnsberg	96.0	99.4S	97.5	91.7	88.5	0.1
Bad Oeynhausen	107.7	99.1B	92.7	90.1	87.7	0.1
Bergheim	–	88.4K	–	–	–	0.5
Bonn Venusberg	102.4	100.4K	93.1	90.7	88.0	50
Dortmund	–	87.8D	–	–	–	2
Ederkopf	107.2	101.8S	–	100.7	95.8	15/20
Eifel-Bärbelkreuz	105.5	101.0	96.3	104.4	89.6	20/10/20/10
Gummersbach	–	91.8W	–	–	–	10
Hallenberg	105.7	–	–	96.1	88.3	0.1
Höxter Hasselberg	107.3	96.4B	95.2	87.8	93.9	0.5
Ibbenbüren	102.5	96.0M	97.3	99.5	88.5	0.5
Klever Berg	103.7	93.3Dü	97.3	101.7	99.7	2
Köln	–	98.6K	–	–	–	0.5
Langenberg	106.7	99.2Dü	95.1	101.3	88.8	100
					103.3*)	100
Lübbecke	93.6	96.0B	91.7	99.6	88.6	0.1
Münster-Baumberge	107.9	94.1M	89.7	100.0	92.0	25
Nordhelle	104.7	93.5S	98.1	103.8	90.3	35
Olsberg	107.0	102.1S	–	104.1	98.6	10
Remscheid	–	95.7W	–	–	–	1
Schmallenberg	100.1	93.8S	97.8	101.1	90.0	0.1
Siegen	107.5	97.1S	98.4	101.2	97.6	0.5/1/0.5/1
Teutoburger Wald	105.5	93.2B	97.0	100.5	90.6	100
Warburg	98.2	91.8B	94.3	104.5	88.4	0.5
Wittgenstein	–	92.3S	88.7	–	–	15
Wuppertal	–	99.8W	–	–	–	1

+ 1 tr less than 0.1kW *) Funkhaus Europa.

Prgr (all networks also on satellite):
Eins Live: Youth. **WDR 2:** Pop and information, incl. local prgr. from Aachen (A), Bielefeld (B), Köln (K), Dortmund (D), Düsseldorf (Dü), Münster (M), Siegen (S), Wuppertal (W). **WDR 3:** Culture (mostly classical music), at night rel. ARD-Nachtkonzert. Also on 720kHz. **WDR 4:** Light music, at night rel. ARD-Nachtexpress. **WDR 5:** Special prgrg. at night rel. Funkhaus Europa. **Funkhaus Europa:** Multicultural prgrg. together with Radio Bremen (see there), at night common prgr. with RBB Radio Multikulti.

DAB (229MHz): Eins Live, WDR 2, Funkhaus Europa and special prgr.: VERA (continuous traffic jam information, at times also on 720kHz), WDR 2 Klassik (spoken content of WDR 2 with classical music), WDR 2 Sport, Eins Live Diggi (music only).

COMMERCIAL AND OTHER STATIONS

NOTE: In Germany supervision and frequency allocation for commercial broadcasting services is the responsibility of the federal states. Each state (listed below)has its own media institution, with the exception of a common institution for Berlin and Brandenburg. As a result of this situation most commercial stations broadcast on the territory of one state only.

BADEN-WÜRTTEMBERG

Media institution: Landesanstalt für Kommunikation (LfK) ✉ Rotebühlstraße 121, 70178 Stuttgart ☎ +49 (711) 669910 🖷 +49 (711) 6699111 **Web:** www.lfk.de

Commercial stations:

FM MHz	kW	Site	Station
2) 87.8	1	Mannheim	big FM
6) 88.6	2	Langenburg	Radio Ton
18) 88.6	1	Stuttgart-Münster	F.Pl.
3) 89.1	0.5	Heilbronn	Hit-Radio Antenne 1
3) 89.3	0.03	Bad Urach	Hit-Radio Antenne 1
2) 89.5	10	Stuttgart-Frauenkopf	big FM
2) 89.7	1	Tübingen	big FM
11) 90.4	2	Karlsruhe	Klassik Radio
9) 90.5	2	Achern	Hitradio Ohr
2) 90.9	0.1	Heidelberg city	big FM
15) 91.4	3	Lützenhardt	R. TV Radio
7) 91.4	0.5	Pforzheim	Hit 1
19) 92.4	1	Hockenheimring	Rennradio
2) 92.7	1	Horb	big FM
9) 93.0	0.1	Haslach	Hitradio Ohr
17) 93.1	1	Rottweil-Zimmern	Radio Neckarburg
16) 94.7	0.5	Freiburg-Lehen	antenne südbaden
6) 95.6	1	Balingen	Radio Ton
6) 96.0	0.1	Künzelsau	Radio Ton
10) 96.4	1	Überlingen	Radio Seefunk
4) 96.9	0.1	Schussental	Radio 7
12) 97.2	1	Stuttgart-Münster	chart-radio
2) 97.2	0.5	Sinsheim	big FM
13) 97.5	0.5	Esslingen	Die Neue 107.7
8) 97.6	0.3	Rudersberg	Energy Baden-Württ.
2) 99.0	0.5	Rottweil	big FM
6) 99.0	0.1	Bad Urach	Radio Ton
15) 99.2	0.2	Herrenberg	R. TV Radio
9) 99.2	0.1	Oberkirch	Hitradio Ohr
10) 99.3	5	Friedrichshafen	Radio Seefunk
2) 99.7	1	Ulm	big FM
3) 100.1	50	Schwäbisch Hall	Hit-Radio Antenne 1
6) 100.1	0.1	Hechingen	Radio Ton
2) 100.3	5	Geislingen	big FM
1) 100.4	80	Hornisgrinde	Radio Regenbogen
8) 100.7	20	Güglingen	Energy Baden-Württ.
6) 100.9	1	Tübingen	Radio Ton
7) 100.9	0.8	Baden-Baden	Hit 1
1) 101.1	8.4	Blauen-Müllheim	Radio Regenbogen
4) 101.2	0.1	Villingen-Schwenningen	Radio 7
3) 101.3	75	Stuttgart Frauenkopf	Hit-Radio Antenne 1
9) 101.6	0.5	Brandenkopf	Hitradio Ohr
7) 101.8	25	Karlsruhe	Hit 1
4) 101.8	10	Ulm-Ermingen	Radio 7
10) 101.8	10	Konstanz	Radio Seefunk
8) 101.8	1	Backnang	Energy Baden-Württ.
10) 101.9	0.1	Schopfheim	Radio Seefunk
17) 102.0	3	Villingen-Schwenningen	Radio Neckarburg
5) 102.1	25	Mudau	sunshine live
10) 102.4	0.2	Laufenburg [Switzerl.]	Radio Seefunk
4) 102.5	40	Witthoh-Tuttlingen	Radio 7
6) 102.6	0.5	Schwäbisch Hall	Radio Ton
10) 102.6	0.3	Ravensburg	Radio Seefunk
15) 102.6	0.1	Bad Wildbad	R. TV Radio
15) 102.7	0.1	Nagold	R. TV Radio
1) 102.8	50	Heidelberg.Königstuhl	Radio Regenbogen
2) 102.8	0.5	Freiburg	big FM
11) 103.0	1	Göppingen	Klassik Radio
15) 103.0	0.3	Calw	R. TV Radio
15) 103.0	0.01	Wildberg	R. TV Radio
10) 103.1	5	Rheinfelden	Radio Seefunk
3) 103.1	0.1	Reutlingen	Hit-Radio Antenne 1
6) 103.2	25	Heilbronn	Radio Ton
3) 103.4	50	Raichberg	Hit-Radio Antenne 1
6) 103.5	20	Bad Mergentheim	Radio Ton
4) 103.7	50	Aalen	Radio 7
17) 103.7	0.1	Schramberg	Radio Neckarburg
2) 103.8	2	Baden-Baden	big FM
10) 103.9	10	Iberger Kugel	Radio Seefunk
11) 103.9	2	Stuttgart-Münster	Klassik Radio
6) 104.2	0.1	Heidenheim	Radio Ton
15) 104.3	1	Sindelfingen	R. TV Radio
10) 104.3	0.1	Lörrach	Radio Seefunk
8) 104.5	2	Waiblingen	Energy Baden-Württ.
8) 104.5	0.1	Winnenden	Energy Baden-Württ.
17) 104.6	1	Oberndorf	Radio Neckarburg
14) 104.6	0.3	Biberach	Donau 3 FM
1) 104.6	0.1	Buchen	Radio Regenbogen
2) 104.7	0.2	Heilbronn	big FM
6) 104.7	0.1	Wertheim	Radio Ton
13) 104.7	0.1	Geislingen	Die Neue 107.7
6) 104.8	1	Reutlingen	Radio Ton
9) 104.9	5	Offenburg-Ohlsbach	Hitradio Ohr
5) 104.9	1	Stuttgart-Münster	sunshine live
4) 105.0	50	Grünenbach	Radio 7
2) 105.1	0.2	Aalen	big FM
2) 105.2	20	Pforzheim	big FM
10) 105.3	0.5	Singen	Radio Seefunk
3) 105.4	1	Geislingen	Hit-Radio Antenne 1
3) 105.4	0.3	Balingen	Hit-Radio Antenne 1
10) 105.4	0.1	Waldshut-Tiengen	Radio Seefunk
9) 105.5	0.5	Bühl	Hitradio Ohr
14) 105.9	10	Ulm-Ermingen	Donau 3 FM
16) 106.0	8.4	Blauen-Müllheim	antenne südbaden
3) 106.0	0.1	Bad Mergentheim	Hit-Radio Antenne 1
5) 106.1	1	Heidelberg-Königstuhl	sunshine live
13) 106.1	1	Göppingen	Die Neue 107.7
14) 106.2	0.5	Riedlingen	Donau 3 FM
16) 106.6	0.1	Titisee-Neustadt	antenne südbaden
13) 106.8	1	Nürtingen	Die Neue 107.7
3) 106.9	0.1	Leonberg	Hit-Radio Antenne 1
10) 107.0	5	Wannenberg-Klettgau	Radio Seefunk
3) 107.0	1	Pforzheim	Hit-Radio Antenne 1
6) 107.1	20	Aalen	Radio Ton
5) 107.1	0.1	Wiesloch	sunshine live
7) 107.3	0.1	Bruchsal	Hit 1
9) 107.4	5	Lahr	Hitradio Ohr
13) 107.4	0.1	Gosbach	Die Neue 107.7
13) 107.7	4	Stuttgart Frauenkopf	Die Neue 107.7
16) 107.7	0.5	Freiburg-Littenweiler	antenne südbaden
5) 107.7	0.1	Weinheim	sunshine live
5) 107.9	0.1	Mosbach	sunshine live
7) 107.9	0.1	Bretten	Hit 1

Addresses and other information:

1) P.O.-Box 10 26 55, 68026 Mannheim (studio location: Dudenstr. 12-26); Web: www.regenbogenweb.de. Also on local DAB (1.5GHz). – **2)** Kronenstr. 24, 70173 Stuttgart; Web: www.bigfm.de. Also on DAB (226MHz). **N.B** See also Rheinland-Pfalz. – **3)** Plieningerstr. 150, 70567 Stuttgart; Web: www.antenne1.de. Also on DAB. – **4)** Gaisenbergstr. 29, 89073 Ulm; Web: www.radio7.de – **5)** 68721 Schwetzingen (studio location: Scheffelstr. 55); Web: www.sunshine-live.de. Also on local DAB. On satellite, DAB in Sachsen and cable nets throughout Germany with different prgr. than on FM. – **6)** Allee 2, 74072 Heilbronn; Web: www.radioton.de. Also on local DAB. – **7)** Albert-Nestler-Str. 26, 76131 Karlsruhe; Web: www.hit1radio.de – **8)** Anton-Schmidt-Str. 36, 71332 Waiblingen; Web: www.energy.de/stuttgart/home/ – **9)** P.O.-Box 20 80, 77610 Offenburg (studio location: Hauptstr. 83a); Web: www.hitradio-ohr.de – **10)** Konzilstr. 1, 78462 Konstanz; Web: www.radio-seefunk.de – **11)** See under Hamburg (stn. 1). Also on local DAB. – **12)** Augustaplatz 8, 76530 Baden-Baden; Web: www.chart-radio.de – **13)** Königstr. 2, 70173 Stuttgart; Web: www.dieneue1077.de. Also on local DAB. – **14)** Basteistr. 37, 89073 Ulm; Web: www.donau3fm.de – **15)** Otto-Lilienthal-Str. 24, 71034 Böblingen; Web: www.rtvradio.de – **16)** Sasbacher Str. 12, 79111 Freiburg; Web: www.antenne-suedbaden.com – **17)** August-Schuhmacher-Str. 10, 78664 Eschbronn-Mariazell; Web: www.radio-neckarburg.de – **18)** allocated to Radio Wilantis; Web: www.wilantis.de – **19)** special stn. during Hockenheimring races only

Noncommercial stations:

FM MHz	kW	Site	Station
1) 89.6	0.1	Mannheim	bermuda.funk
6) 96.6	1	Tübingen	Wüste Welle
2) 97.5	0.1	Schwäbisch Hall	Radio StHörfunk
4) 99.2	0.3	Stuttgart-Münster	Freies R. f. Stuttg.
7) 100.0	0.5	Freudenstadt	Freies R. Freudens.
8) 102.3	1	Freiburg Vogtsberg	Radio Dreyeckland
5) 102.6	1	Ulm-Ermingen	Radio FreeFM
7) 104.1	0.1	Baiersbronn	Freies R. Freudens.
9) 104.5	0.5	Hohe Möhr	Radio Kanal Ratte
3) 104.8	1	Karlsruhe	Querfunk
2) 104.8	0.1	Crailsheim	Radio StHörfunk
1) 105.4	0.05	Heidelberg-Königstuhl	bermuda.funk

Addresses and other information:

1) Brückenstr. 2-4, 68167 Mannheim; Web: www.bermudafunk.org. Also rel. Radio Aktiv (Universität Mannheim, Postfach 144, 68131 Mannheim); Web: www.radioaktiv-online.de; Mon-Wed 0600-1000 and 1700-1900, Thu 0600-1900, Fri and Sat 2300-0500, Sun 1900-

2100. – **2)** Haalstr. 9, 74523 Schwäbisch Hall; Web: www.sthoer-funk.de – **3)** Steinstr. 23, 76133 Karlsruhe; Web: www.querfunk.de. Also rel. LernRadio, Hochschule für Musik, Postfach 6040, 76040 Karlsruhe (studio location: Wolfartsweierer Str. 7a); Web: www.lern-radio.de. Mon-Thu 1600-2100. Radio aus Bruchsal (commercially orientated), Karlsruher Str. 20, 76646 Bruchsal; Web: www.radio-aus-bruchsal.de. Mon-Fri 0600-1100; Mon-Thu 0900-1000 also on Heidelberg 105.4MHz. – **4)** Freies Radio für Stuttgart, Rieckestr. 24, 70190 Stuttgart; Web: www.freies-radio.de. Also rel. Hochschulradio Stuttgart (Nobelstr. 10, 70569 Stuttgart; Web: www.horads.de) Mon/Tue/Wed 0600-1000, Thu 0000-1000, Fri/Sat 0500-1000 and R. Kormista (details n/a) Wed 1900-2100 N.B Frequency splitting was subject of legal action at time of editing. – **5)** Söflinger Str. 206, 89077 Ulm; Web: www.freefm.de – **6)** Hechinger Str. 203, 72072 Tübingen; Web: www.wueste-welle.de. Also rel. Uniwelle Tübingen (Gmelinstr. 6/1, 72076 Tübingen; Web: www.uni-tuebingen.de/uniradio/) Wed 1600-1900 and Sun 0900-1300; helle welle (religious; Seestr. 6-8, 72764 Reutlingen; Web: www.hellewelle.de) Tue-Thu 0700-0800. – **7)** Freies Radio Freudenstadt, Forststr. 23, 72250 Freudenstadt; Web: www.radio-fds.de – **8)** Adlerstr. 12, 79098 Freiburg; Web: www.rdl.de – **9)** Bahnhofstr. 3, 79650 Schopfheim; Web: www.kanalrattefm.de. 1400-0200, otherwise rel. Radio Dreyeckland

BAYERN

Media institution: Bayerische Landeszentrale für Neue Medien (BLM) Heinrich-Lübke-Straße 27, 81737 München ☎ +49 (89) 638 080 🖹 +49 (89) 63808140; **Web:** www.blm.de

FM networks:

Location	Ant.B.	Rock	Klass	Melodie	Galaxy	kW
Ansbach	–	–	–	–	105.8	0.1
Aschaffenburg	103.0	–	–	–	91.6	25/0.5
Augsburg	104.2	87.9	92.2	94.8	–	0.1/0.3
Bad Reichenhall	103.7	–	–	–	–	0.3
Balderschwang	97.3	–	–	–	–	0.05
Bamberg	101.1	–	–	–	104.7	25/0.5
Berchtesgaden	107.9	–	–	–	–	0.3
Breithart	101.5	–	–	–	–	25
Brotjacklriegel	103.5	–	–	–	–	100
Cham Hoher B.	101.9	–	–	–	–	50
Coburg	103.8	–	–	–	90.4	5/0.2
Dillberg	100.6	–	–	–	–	25
Eichstätt	100.2	–	–	–	–	25
Enterbach	101.1	–	–	–	–	0.5
Grünten	104.4	–	–	–	–	50
Heidelstein	101.9	–	–	–	–	100
Herzogstand	102.0	–	–	–	–	0.1
Hochrieshaus	107.7	–	–	–	–	50
Hof Labyrinthbg.	–	–	–	–	94.0	0.2
Hof-Münchberg	–	–	–	–	98.1	0.1
Högl-Freilassing	105.3	–	–	–	–	1
Hohenpeißenb.	103.8	–	–	–	–	25
Ingolstadt	–	–	–	–	107.9	0.1
Kempten	–	–	–	–	88.1	0.3
Konradsreuth	–	–	–	–	98.1	0.1
Landshut	99.3	–	–	–	99.8	0.1/0.2
Lindau Hoyerb.	99.0	–	–	–	–	0.5
München	101.3	(F.Pl.)	107.2	104.0	–	0.3/1/0.1
Naila Finkenflug	–	–	–	–	96.5	0.1
Nördlingen	103.3	–	–	–	–	25
Nürnberg	–	–	105.1	103.6	–	0.5/0.3
Oberaudorf	94.6	–	–	–	–	0.3
Ochsenkopf	103.2	–	–	–	–	100
Passau	102.1	–	–	–	91.7	1/0.2
Pfaffenhofen	92.6	–	–	–	–	0.5
Regensburg	103.0	–	91.1	107.5	–	25/0.3/0.3
Reit im Winkel	101.6	–	–	–	–	0.1
Rosenheim	–	–	–	–	106.6	0.1
Selb	–	–	–	–	93.4	0.1
Traunstein	103.7	–	–	–	–	5
Weiler Simm.	106.0	–	–	–	–	0.1
Wunsiedel	–	–	–	–	97.3	0.2
Würzburg	104.4	–	92.1	95.8	–	5/0.3
Zugspitze	102.7	–	–	–	–	2

Addresses and other information:

Antenne Bayern, Rockantenne: Münchener Straße 101c, 85737 Ismaning; Web: www.antenne.de; www.rockantenne.de. Both also via satellite, Rockantenne also via DAB (229MHz). – **Klassik Radio:** see stn. 1) under Hamburg.– **Radio Melodie:** Muthmannstraße 4, 80939 München, Web: www.radio-melodie.de. Also on satellite and cable nets throughout Germany. – **Radio Galaxy:** Lilionthalstraße 3c, 93049 Regensburg, Web: www.radiogalaxy.de. Also on DAB. Includes local insertions.

Local stations:

FM MHz	kW	Site	Station
39) 87.9	0.3	Straubing Bogenberg	R. AWN
44) 87.9	0.1	Erding	Hitwelle Erding
35) 88.0	5	Großer Waldstein	extra~rad. / Euroherz
19) 88.1	0.1	Krumbach-Kirchberg	R. Prima 1
18) 88.2	0.2	Kaufbeuren	R. Ostallgäu
51) 88.2	0.1	Bad Reichenhall	R. Untersberg
32) 88.5	0.5	Bamberg Rothof	R. Bamberg
36) 88.5	0.1	Tirschenreuth	R. Ramasuri
27) 88.6	0.1	Karlstadt	R. Charivari
5) 89.0	0.3	München Olympiaturm	2DAY/Neues Europa
42) 89.0	0.1	Dingolfing	R. Trausnitz
51) 89.0	0.1	Högl-Freilassing	R. Untersberg
26) 89.1	0.1	Wassertrüdingen	R. 8
31) 89.2	0.5	Coburg Eckardtsberg	R. EINS
17) 89.3	0.1	Oberstdorf-Steinach	RSA R.
40) 89.3	0.2	Regen Geiskopf	Unser R. Deggendorf
26) 89.4	0.5	Ansbach Ludwigshöhe	R. 8
24) 89.7	0.1	Dillingen	RT.1 Nordschwaben
38) 89.7	0.3	Regensburg Ziegetsberg	gong fm
41) 89.7	0.3	Bad Griesbach	Unser R. Passau
26) 89.8	0.1	Dinkelsbühl	R. 8
45) 89.8	0.1	Landsberg-Stoffen	R. 106.4
31) 90.0	0.1	Kronach-Neuses	R. EINS
19) 90.2	0.32	Bad Grönenbach	R. Prima 1
26) 90.2	0.1	Gunzenhausen	R. 8
47) 90.2	0.1	Miesbach-Bergham	R. Alpenwelle
21) 90.3	0.1	Günzburg	Hitradio X
26) 90.4	0.2	Neuastadt / Aisch	R. 8
27) 90.4	0.1	Gemünden / Lohr	R. Charivari
49) 90.4	0.1	Mühldorf	Inn-Salzach-Welle
30) 90.5	0.1	Bad Kissingen	R. PrimaTon
29) 90.8	0.2	Alzenau	R. Primavera
15) 91.0	0.2	Fürth	Vil R.
47) 91.7	0.1	Holzkirchen Jasberg	R. Alpenwelle
42) 91.8	0.2	Pfeffenhausen-Stollnried	R. Trausnitz
47) 92.0	0.1	Wolfratshausen	R. Alpenwelle
6) 92.4	0.3	München Olympiaturm	(shared freq.)
16) 92.7	0.1	Weiler Simmerberg	Welle Bodensee
37) 92.7	0.4	Hoher Bogen	Charivari Regensbg.
49) 92.7	0.3	Reichertsheim	Inn-Salzach-Welle
13) 92.9	0.3	Nürnberg	Hi R. N1
17) 93.0	0.1	Immenstadt	RSA R.
49) 93.1	0.1	Burgkirchen-Gendorf	Inn-Salzach-Welle
2) 93.3	0.3	München Olympiaturm	Energy 93.3
33) 93.3	0.1	Pegnitz	R. Mainwelle
23) 93.4	0.3	Augsburg	R. Fantasy
9) 93.6	0.3	Erlangen	Energy Nürnberg
36) 93.6	0.1	Waidhaus Fischerberg	R. Ramasuri
19) 93.9	0.3	Mindelheim-Altensteig	R. Prima 1
41) 93.9	0.3	Vilshofen-Otterkirchen	Unser R. Passau
30) 94.0	0.1	Bad Brückenau	R. PrimaTon
37) 94.0	1	Seubersdorf Göschberg	Charivari Regensbg.
7) 94.5	0.1	München Blutenburgstr.	M 94,5
11) 94.5	0.3	Nürnberg	R. F / Jazztime
43) 94.6	0.1	Schrobenhausen	R. IN / R. ND1
47) 95.0	0.2	Bad Tölz	R. Alpenwelle
35) 95.1	0.1	Marktredwitz	extra~r. / Euroherz
36) 95.3	1	Hirschberg Rothbühl	R. Ramasuri
31) 95.4	0.3	Lichtenfels	R. EINS
43) 95.4	0.1	Ingolstadt	R. IN
3) 95.5	0.3	München Olympiaturm	Charivari 95.5
24) 95.6	1	Harburg Hühnerberg	RT.1 Nordschwaben
30) 95.7	0.1	Haßfurt/Main	R. PrimaTon
39) 95.7	0.1	Mallersdorf-Hofkirchen	R. AWN
14) 95.8	0.3	Nürnberg	R. Z / aladin
4) 96.3	0.3	München Olympiaturm	R. Gong 96,3
38) 96.3	0.32	Burglengenfeld	gong fm
32) 96.6	0.1	Forchheim Pinzberg	R. Bamberg
45) 96.6	0.1	Starnberg	R. 106.4
17) 96.7	0.1	Kempten town	RSA R.
22) 96.7	0.3	Augsburg	Kit R. RT.1
48) 96.7	0.3	Flintsbach Dandlberg	Charivari Rosenheim
12) 97.1	0.3	Nürnberg	Gong 97.1
24) 97.1	0.1	Donauwörth	RT.1 Nordschwaben
41) 97.2	0.1	Grafenau Liebersberg	Unser R. Passau
26) 97.3	0.3	Feuchtwangen	R. 8
38) 97.3	0.1	Schwandorf Weinberg	gong fm
46) 97.5	0.1	Weilheim	R. Oberland
17) 97.6	1	Kempten Blender	RSA R.
18) 98.0	0.1	Füssen	R. Ostallgäu
51) 98.1	0.1	Berchtesgaden	R. Untersberg
37) 98.2	0.3	Regensburg Ziegetsberg	Charivari Regensb.
41) 98.3	0.2	Passau-Haidenhof	Unser R. Passau
10) 98.6	0.3	Nürnberg	Charivari 98.6
40) 98.7	0.1	Deggendorf-Hochobernd.	Unser R. Deggendorf
37) 98.8	0.5	Burglengenfeld	Charivari Regensbg.

FM MHz	kW	Site	Station
34) 98.9	0.1	Stadtsteinach	R. Plassenburg
25) 99.0	0.2	Lauf Moritzberg	star fm
27) 99.0	0.1	Marktheidenfeld	R. Charivari
43) 99.1	0.1	Eichstätt-Seuversholz	R. IN
50) 99.4	0.3	Haslach-Einham	R. Chiemgau
36) 99.9	0.2	Weiden Fischerberg	R. Ramasuri
47) 99.9	0.1	Herzogstand	R. Alpenwelle
29) 100.4	1	Aschaffenburg	R. Primavera
30) 100.5	0.5	Schweinfurth	R. PrimaTon
1) 100.8	0.1	München Blutenburgstr.	R. Arabella
26) 100.8	0.1	Burgbernheim	R. 8
43) 101.2	0.2	Neuburg/Donau	R. IN / R. ND1
46) 101.2	0.1	Oberammergau	R. Oberland
46) 101.4	0.3	Sindelsdorf	R. Oberland
30) 101.5	1	Bad Neustadt-Unsleben	R. PrimaTon
41) 101.5	0.1	Freyung Geyersberg	Unser R. Passau
50) 101.5	0.3	Trostberg	R. Chiemgau
34) 101.6	5	Kulmbach Rehberg	R. Plassenburg
27) 102.4	0.3	Würzburg	R. Charivari
37) 102.6	0.32	Waldmünchen Perlhütte	Charivari Regensbg.
16) 103.6	0.5	Lindau Hoyerberg	Welle Bodensee
36) 103.9	0.1	Amberg Eisberg	R. Ramasuri
37) 103.9	0.5	Kelheim Leitenberg	Charivari Regensbg.
42) 104.1	1	Landshut	R. Trausnitz
48) 104.2	0.3	Oberaudorf-Hölzelsau	Charivari Rosenheim
33) 104.3	10	Oschenberg	R. Mainwelle
47) 104.3	0.5	Enterbach-Ringberg	R. Alpenwelle
46) 104.6	0.1	Herzogstand	R. Oberland
43) 104.8	0.2	Pfaffenhofen Wolfsberg	R. IN
36) 105.1	0.5	Wiesau-Fuchsmühle	R. Ramasuri
1) 105.2	25	München-Isen	R. Arabella
18) 105.2	0.1	Obergünzburg	R. Ostallgäu
43) 105.4	0.1	Beilngries	R. IN
37) 105.5	0.3	Lam-Koppenhof	Charivari Regensbg.
42) 105.5	0.32	Landau	R. Trausnitz
20) 105.9	5	Ulm-Ermingen	R. Donau 1
37) 105.9	0.32	Nabburg Galgenberg	Charivari Regensbg.
32) 106.1	0.1	Burglesau Reisberg	R. Bamberg
8) 106.2	0.2	Erlangen	afk max
46) 106.2	0.3	Garmisch-Partenkirchen	R. Oberland
47) 106.2	0.1	Schliersbergalm	R. Alpenwelle
18) 106.3	0.5	Eisenberg Schloßberg	R. Ostallgäu
36) 106.4	0.1	Königstein Gr. Ossinger	R. Ramasuri
45) 106.4	2	Fürstenfeldbruck	R. 106.4
49) 106.4	0.3	Lohkirchen	Inn-Salzach-Welle
8) 106.5	0.1	Nürnberg	afk max
28) 106.9	5	Würzburg	R. Gong 106,9
9) 106.9	0.3	Nürnberg	Energy Nürnberg
42) 107.4	1	Pfarrkirchen-Postm.	R. Trausnitz
25) 107.8	0.2	Schwabach Heidenberg	star fm
40) 107.9	0.2	Brotjacklriegel	Unser R. Deggendorf

+ 28 tr's less than 0.1kW

Adresses and other information:

Dienstleistungsgesellschaft für Bayerische Lokal-Radioprogramme (BLR) Rosenheimer Straße 145c, 81671 München **Web:** www.blr.de and www.radiodienst.de. Program supplier for many of the above listed stn's. Nationwide content delivery under the brand RadioDienst.

1) Paul-Heyse-Str. 2-4, 80336 München, Web: www.radioarabella.de – **2)** Pestalozzistr. 15-19, 80469 München, Web: www. energy.de/muenchen/ – **3)** Postfach 20 16 09, 80016 München (studio location as stn. 1), Web: www.charivari.de – **4)** Franz-Joseph-Str. 14, 80801 München, Web: www.radiogong.de – **5)** Schneemanstr. 25, 81369 München, Web: www.radio2-day.de. Tr. rel. instead Sat 2300-Mon 0500 R. Neues Europa: Konviktstr. 1, 85049 Ingolstadt – **6) Radio Horeb**, Postfach 1165, 87501 Immenstadt; Web: www.radiohoreb.de. Religious. On 92.4MHz Mon-Fri 2300-1500, Sat/Sun 2300-0500, Sun 0900-1730. 24 hours on satellite and cable nets in Germany, Austria, Switzerland, Luxembourg and Liechtenstein- – **Lora München**, Gravelottestr. 6, 81667 München, Web: home.link-m.de/lora/. Non-commercial. Mon-Sat 1700-2300. – **Feierwerk München**, Hansastr. 39, 81373 München; Web: www.feierwerk.de. Non-commercial. Mon-Fri 1600-1700, Sun 0500-0600 and 0800-0900. – **Net.FM**, Bavariaring 8, 80336 München; Web: www.net-fm.de. Sun 1730-2000. – **7)** Öttingenstr. 67, 80538 München, Web: http://m945.afk.de. Journalist training stn., housed in the former RFE/RL promises. – **8)** Fürther Str. 212, 90429 Nürnberg, Web: www.afkmax.de. Journalist training stn. – **9)** Ostendstr. 100, 90482 Nürnberg, Web: www.energy.de/nuernberg/. Also on DAB (1.5GHz). – **10),11),12),13)** Funkhaus Nürnberg, Senefelder Str. 7, 90409 Nürnberg, Web: www.funkhaus.de. 92,0MHz also rel. Camillo 92.9 (Mon, Tue, Sun 2000-2200), R. AREF (Sun 0900-1100), Pray 92.9 (Sun 1100-1200), R. Meilensteine (Sun 0800-0900), 94.5MHz also rel. Jazztime Nürnberg (Mon 2100-2200, Thu 2000-2100). – **14)** 1300-0100 R. Z, Kopernikusplatz 12, 90459 Nürnberg, Web: www.radio-z.net. Non-commercial. 0100-1300 radio aladin, Postfach, 90614 Ammerndorf, Web: www.radioaladin.de – **15)** Platnersgasse 1, 90403 Nürnberg, Web: www.vilradio.de. Also on DAB (1.5GHz). – **16)** Web: www.welle-bodensee.de – **17)** Rottachstr. 17, 87439 Kempten, Web: www.allgaeu-seite.de/rsa_radio – **18)** Web: www.roal.de – **19)** Hirschgasse 1, 87700 Memmingen, Web: www.prima1.de – **20)** Leipzigstr. 26, 88400 Biberach, Web: www.radiodonau1.de – **21)** Augsburger Str. 1 ½, 89312 Günzburg, Web: www.hitradiox.de – **22)** Curt-Frenzel-Str. 4, 86167 Augsburg, Web: www.radio-rt1.de – **23)** Ludwigstr. 1, 86150 Augsburg, Web: www2.fantasy.de. Rel. Mon 2100-2400 Kanal C (university stn.): Eichleitnerstr. 30, 86159 Augsburg, Web: www.kanal-c.de – **24)** Artur-Proeller-Str. 1, 86609 Donauwörth, Web: www.rt1-nordschwaben.de – **25)** O´Brien Str. 2, 91126 Schwabach; Web: www.rocksender.de/rocksender_nuernberg/ – **26)** Postfach 8, 91510 Ansbach (studio location: Schalkhäuser Landstr. 5), Web: www.radio8.de – **27),28)** Semmelstr. 15, 97070 Würzburg, Web: http://charivari.fm and www.gong.fm Also rel. Radio Opera. Also on DAB (1.5GHz). – **29)** Am Funkhaus 1, 63743 Aschaffenburg, Web: www.radio-primavera.de – **30),31)** Seifartshofstr. 21, 96450 Coburg, Web: www.radioeins.com – **32)** Gutenbergstr. 5, 96050 Bamberg, Web: www.radio-bamberg.de – **33)** Postfach 10 11 61, 95411 Bayreuth (studio location: Richard-Wagner-Str. 33), Web: www.mainwelle.de – **34)** E.C.-Baumann-Str. 5, 95326 Kulmbach, Web: www.radio-plassenburg.de – **35)** 0900-1000, 1200-1300 and 1800-2000 extra-radio, Postfach 1745, 95016 Hof (studio location: Kreuzsteinstr. 2-6), Web: www.extra-radio.de; otherwhise: R. Euroherz, Pfarr 1, 95028 Hof, Web: www.euroherz.de – **36)** Unterer Markt 35, 92637 Weiden, Web: www.ramasuri.de – **37),38)** Lilienthalstr. 3c, 93049 Regensburg, Web: www.radiocharivari.de and www.gongfm.de – **39),40)** Bahnhofstr. 28, 94469 Deggendorf, Web: www.unserradio.de – **41)** Medienstr. 5, 94036 Passau, Web: as stn. 40). – **42)** Altstadt 361, 84028 Landshut, Web: www.radio-trausnitz.de – **43)** Donaustr. 11, 85049 Ingolstadt, Web: www.radio-in.de, rel. 0500-0900 on 94.6/101.2MHz R. ND1 – **44)** Postfach 1155, 84420 Isen, Web: www.hitwelle.de – **45)** Schöngeisingerstr. 11, 82256 Fürstenfeldbruck, Web: www.radio1064.de – **46)** Postfach 1752, 82467 Garmisch-Partenkirchen (studio location: Marienplatz 17), Web: www.radio-oberland.de – **47)** Web: www.radio-alpenwelle.de – **48)** Hafnerstr. 5-7, 83022 Rosenheim, Web: www.radio-charivari.de. – **49)** Mozartstr. 3a, 84508 Burgkirchen/Alz, Web: www.inn-salzach-welle.de – **50)** Rupertistr. 40-42, 83278 Traunstein, Web: www.radio-chiemgau.de – **51)** www.untersberg.de **N.B** Stn's 49), 50), 51) also rel. prgr. of independent producers.

DAB-only services in Munich: Nova Radio, Radio Deluxe, Digital Classix, Radio Gong Mobil on ch. LG (1463MHz).

BERLIN & BRANDENBURG

Media institution: Medienanstalt Berlin-Brandenburg (MABB) Kleine Präsidentenstraße 1, 10178 Berlin ☎ +49 (30) 264 9670 +49 (30) 264 96730 **Web:** www.mabb.de

Berlin-based transmitters:

FM MHz	kW	Site	Station
13) 87.9	1	Alexanderplatz	(shared freq.)
15) 90.2	20	Alexanderplatz	BBC-Worldservice
2) 91.4	100	Alexanderplatz	Berliner Rundfunk
9) 93.6	3	Alexanderplatz	JAM FM
3) 94.3	25	Alexanderplatz	94'3 r.s.2
14) 94.8	4	Schäferberg	94.8 metropol FM
12) 97.2	0.1	Kreuzberg	(shared freq.)
8) 98.2	8	Scholzplatz	R. Paradiso
10) 98.8	1	Alexanderplatz	98 8 KISS FM
4) 100.6	10	Alexanderplatz	Hundert,6
8) 101.3	5	Alexanderplatz	Klassik R.
11) 101.9	0.5	Alexanderplatz	Jazz R.
5) 103.4	10	Alexanderplatz	Energy 103.4
17) 104.1	0.2	Kreuzberg	Twen FM / JoyFM
6) 104.6	10	Alexanderplatz	104.6 RTL
7) 105.5	5	Alexanderplatz	Spreeradio
16) 106.0	1	Alexanderplatz	RFI
1) 107.5	13	Schäferberg	BB-Radio

Transmitters in Brandenburg:

FM MHz	kW	Site	Station
8) 87.6		Brandenburg	Klassik R.
6) 88.0	1	Crinitz	104.6 RTL
4) 89.2		Templin-Ludwigshof	(silent)
6) 89.5	0.5	Elsterwerda-Hohenl.	104.6 RTL
18) 90.3	0.5	Spremberg	94.5 Radio Cottbus
1) 90.9	0.8	Rhinow	BB-Radio
8) 91.0		Booßen (Frankf./O.)	Klassik R.
3) 91.3	1	Lauchhammer West	94'3 r.s.2
5) 91.6	1.3	Casekow	Energy 103.4
5) 91.7	0.1	Herzberg/Elster	Energy 103.4
4) 91.8	1.3	Zehlendorf	Hundert,6
18) 92.1	1	Guben-Reichenbach	94.5 Radio Cottbus

FM MHz	kW	Site	Station
4) 92.7		Prenzlau	(silent)
4) 93.3		Casekow	(silent)
18) 94.5	0.3	Cottbus-Madlow	94.5 Radio Cottbus
3) 94.7	3	Booßen (Frankf./O.)	94'3 r.s.2
3) 95.6	1.3	Cottbus-Klein Oßnig	94'3 r.s.2
1) 95.4	1.25	Zehlendorf	BB-Radio
3) 96.7	1	Crinitz	94'3 r.s.2
8) 96.9		Luckenwalde	Klassik R.
3) 100.1	3	Lübben	94'3 r.s.2
2) 100.9	5	Casekow	Berliner Rundfunk
1) 102.1	20	Casekow	BB-Radio
2) 102.2	3	Cottbus-Klein Oßnig	Berliner Rundfunk
18) 102.7	0.5	Forst	94.5 Radio Cottbus
1) 103.7	0.6	Eisenhüttenstadt	BB-Radio
3) 103.9	6.3	Forst	94'3 r.s.2
2) 104.2	20	Booßen (Frankf./O.)	Berliner Rundfunk
1) 104.3	100	Pritzwalk-Buchholz	BB-Radio
1) 105.0	3	Brandenburg-Krahne	BB-Radio
3) 106.3	4	Spremberg	94'3 r.s.2
4) 107.0		Angermünde	(silent)
1) 107.2	100	Calau	BB-Radio
3) 107.3	20	Casekow	94'3 r.s.2
1) 107.8	30	Booßen (Frankf./O.)	BB-Radio
1) 107.9	5	Zehlendorf	BB-Radio

Addresses and other information:
1) Großbeerenstraße 185, 14482 Potsdam; Web: www.bbradio.de. Also on DAB Brandenburg (229MHz). Bc's short local insertions (different ones on both Zehlendorf tr's). – **2)** Leipziger Straße 62, 10117 Berlin; Web: www.berliner-rundfunk.de – **3)** Voltastraße 5, 13355 Berlin; Web: www.rs2.de. – **4)** Katharina-Heinroth-Ufer 1, 10787 Berlin; Web: www.hundert6.de. Alternative prgr. on 91.8MHz. 89.2/92.7/93.3/107.0MHz also allocated but silent at time of editing. – **5)** Potsdamer Straße 88, 10785 Berlin: Web: www.energyonline.de/Berlin – **6)** Kurfürstendamm 207-208, 10719 Berlin: Web: http://104.6rtl.com. F.Pl.: Tr. via DVB-T. – **7)** Rosenstraße 2, 10178 Berlin; Web: www.spreeradio.de – **8)** see under Hamburg (stn. 10). 87.6/91.0/96.9MHz allocated but silent at time of editing. – **8)** Am Kleinen Wannsee 5, 14109 Berlin; Web: www.paradiso.de – **9)** Haynauer Straße 60, 12249 Berlin; Web: www.jamfm.de. Also on satellite. See also under Saarland. **10)** Voltastraße 5, 13355 Berlin; Web: www.kissfm.de – **11)** Sophienstraße 20-21, 10178 Berlin; Web: www.jazzradio.net – **12) Radio Russkij Berlin**, Rosenstraße 2, 10178 Berlin; Web: www.radio-russkij-berlin.de. Prgr. in Russian. Mon-Fri 0600-1500, Sat/Sun 0600-1200. – **Offener Kanal Berlin**, Voltastraße 5, 13355 Berlin; Web: www.okb.de. Citizen radio, operated by MABB. On 97.2MHz Mon-Thu 1500-2200, Fri 1500-1900, Sat/Sun 1200-1900; cable net tr. 24 hours. – **BluRadio**, Neue Schönhauser Straße 20, 10178 Berlin; Web: www.bluradio.de. Gay stn. Fri-Sun 1900-0100. – **WRN Deutsch**, rel. German ch. of World Radio Network (London) Mon-Thu 2200-0600, Fri-Sun 0100-0600. – **13) Star.FM**, Rosenstraße 2, 10178 Berlin; Web: www.rocksender.de. 2000-1800. – **UniRadio**, Thielallee 50, 14195 Berlin; Web: www.uniradio.de. 1800-2000. – **14)** Potsdamer Straße 131, 10783 Berlin, Web: www.metropolfm.de. Prgr. in Turkish. – **15)** Rel. BBC-Worldservice in English. – **16)** Rel. R. France Internationale in German and French. – **17) Twen FM**, Web: www.twenfm.de. Electronical music. On 104.1MHz 1900-0500, Sat/Sun also 1400-1600. 24 hours on DAB (ch. LE, 1460MHz). – **JoyFM**, Lietzenburger Straße 71, 10719 Berlin; Web: www.joyfm.de. Pop. On 104.1MHz when TwenFM is not on. 24 hours on DAB (ch. LE). **N.B** 104.1MHz available as additional outlet for DAB licence holders and special stations. Usage may change anytime. – **18)** Schloßkirchplatz 3, 03046 Cottbus; Web: www.radio-cottbus.de
On DAB in Berlin only: ch. 8C (199MHz) WDR 2 and Deutsche Welle (foreign language prgr.); ch. LA (1453MHz) BBC and Digital One multiplexes from the UK, alternating each week (promotional sce.); ch. LE (1460MHz) Mallorca 95.8, RadiJoJo (childrens prgr.; Web: www.radijojo.de), Kaufradio (home shopping; Web: www.kaufradio.de); ch. LI (1467MHz) Roadradio.

BREMEN

Media institution: Bremische Landesmedienanstalt ✉ Grünenweg 26, 28215 Bremen ☎ +49 (421) 334940 🖷 +49 (421) 323533 **Web:** www.bremische-landesmedienanstalt.de

FM MHz	kW	Site	Station
1) 89.8	1	Bremen-Walle	Energy Bremen
3) 90.7	0.2	Bremerhaven	Bremerhaven/radioWSM
2) 92.5	0.2	Bremen Neuenstr.	OK Bremen
1) 104.3	10	Bremerhaven	Energy Bremen

Addresses and other information:
1) Erste Schlachtpforte, 28195 Bremen; Web: www.energy.de/bremen/. Former R, Wir von hier, relaunched in 2003. – **2)** Findorffstraße 22-24, 28215 Bremen; Web: www.ok-bremen.de – **3)** Hafenstraße 156, 27576 Bremerhaven; **Web:** www.ok-bremerhaven.de; on Wednesdays radioWSM from Nordenham studio. **N.B** stn. 2) and 3) open access (citizen radio)

HAMBURG

Media institution: Hamburgische Anstalt für Neue Medien ✉ Kleine Johannisstraße 10, 20457 Hamburg ☎ +49 (40) 3690050 🖷 +49 (40) 36900555 **Web:** www.ham-online.de

FM MHz	kW	Site	Station
6) 88.1	0.1	Bergedorf	Oldie 95
5) 91.7	0.04	H.-Hertz-Turm	106!8 rock'n' pop
8) 93.0	0.04	H.-Hertz-Turm	Freies Sender Kombinat
3) 93.4	2	H.-Hertz-Turm	delta radio
6) 95.0	0.1	H.-Hertz-Turm	Oldie 95
9) 96.0	0.1	H.-Hertz-Turm	TIDE 96.0 / HLR
7) 97.1	0.1	H.-Hertz-Turm	Energy 97.1
1) 98.1	0.1	H.-Hertz-Turm	Klassik Radio
2) 100.0	2	H.-Hertz-Turm	R.SH
7) 100.9	0.1	Bergedorf	Energy 97.1
2) 102.0	0.1	Bergedorf	RSH
4) 103.6	80	Moorfleet	R. Hamburg
4) 104.0	0.16	H.-Hertz-Turm	R. Hamburg
5) 106.8	40	Rahlstedt	106!8 rock'n pop
3) 107.7	0.1	Bergedorf	delta radio

N.B Further R. Hamburg and 106!8 rock'n pop tr's see under Niedersachsen.
Addresses and other information:
1) Postfach 57 03 60 22772 Hamburg (studio location: Planckstr. 15); Web: www.klassikradio.de. Also on satellite and FM tr's in other states. **2), 3)** see under Schleswig-Holstein. – **4)** Postfach 10 01 23, 20001 Hamburg (studio location: Speersort 10); Web: www.radiohamburg.de – **5)** Former Alster R., relaunched in 2004. Rödingsmarkt 29, 20459 Hamburg; Web: www.106acht.de – **6)** Speersort 10, 20095 Hamburg; Web: www.oldie95.de – **7)** Winterhuder Marktplatz 6-7, 22299 Hamburg; Web: www.energyonline.de/hamburg/ – **8)** Schulterblatt 23c, 20357 Hamburg; Web: www.fsk-hh.org. Non-commercial. – **9) TIDE 96.0**, Uferstraße 2, 22081 Hamburg; Web: www.tidenet.de. Run by Hamburg Media School. Mon 0500-2300 and thorough Tue 0500 til Sun 0500. – **Hamburger Lokalradio**, Kulturzentrum LOLA, Lohbrügger Landstraße 8, 21031 Hamburg; Web: www.hhlr.de. Non-commercial. On 96.0MHz Sun 0500 til Mon 0500 and night Mon/Tue 2300-0500. Satellite tr. via WRN Deutsch Sun 1000-1100.

HESSEN

Media institution: Hessische Landesanstalt für Privaten Rundfunk (LPR) ✉ Wilhelmshöher Allee 262, 34131 Kassel ☎ +49 (561) 935860 🖷 +49 (561) 9358630; **Web:** www.lpr-hessen.de
FM networks:

Location	FFH	plan.	Kla.	Sky	Main	harm	kW
Alsfeld	88.1	–	–	101.5	–	94.1	4/0.1
Bad Hersfeld	100.3	88.4	93.8	99.8	–	–	50/0.2
Bad Nauheim	–	104.6	–	106.6	–	100.4	0.5/1
Bensheim	–	–	–	103.3	–	107.5	0.2
Bingen	106.9	–	(F.Pl.)	–	–	101.8	0.3
Butzbach	–	–	96.0	–	–	–	0.08
Darmstadt	–	–	–	92.4	–	–	0.2
Dieburg	–	90.1	–	99.5	–	–	1/0.2
Dillenburg	100.0	–	–	–	–	–	30
Dridorf	106.8	–	–	–	–	–	30
Eltville	90.3	–	–	–	–	–	0.2
Eschwege	–	104.6	–	103.0	–	–	0.5
Feldberg	105.9	–	–	–	–	–	100
Frankfurt	–	100.2	107.5	97.1	95.1	(F.Pl.)	1/0.1
Fulda	–	99.9	102.8	105.7	99.2	95.7	0.2/0.3
Gießen	–	93.7	–	92.6	105.2	–	0.2/0.1
Habichtsw.	103.7	–	–	–	–	–	20
Hanau	–	–	–	–	–	106.8	0.5
Heidelstein	100.9	–	–	–	–	–	50
Hofgeismar	–	–	–	88.8	–	–	0.1
H. Meißner	105.1	–	–	–	–	–	100
Kassel	–	104.6	–	96.6	(F.Pl.)	–	0.5/0.3
Krehberg	105.0	–	–	–	–	–	20
Korbach	107.7	94.0	–	96.5	–	107.4	20/0.2
Limburg	–	97.6	102.0	90.2	–	92.1	0.5/0.2
Marburg	–	101.0	–	103.9	–	–	0.1
Michelstadt	96.1		–	90.5	–	104.8	0.1/1
Rotenburg	–	–	–	93.5	–	104.5	0.05
Wetzlar	–	–	(F.Pl.)	88.2	105.0	101.3	0.3/0.5
Wiesbaden	102.0	90.1	–	–	–	–	0.1/0.5

Addresses and other information:
Hit-Radio FFH, planet radio, harmony.fm: FFH-Platz 1, 61111 Bad Vilbel; **Web:** www.ffh.de, www.planet-radio.de, www.harmonyfm.de

planet radio and harmony.fm also on satellite. – **Klassik Radio** see under Hamburg (stn. 1) – **Sky Radio**, Friedrich-Ebert-Str. 2, 34117 Kassel; Web: www.skyradio.de – **Main FM**, Rüsselsheimer Str. 22, 60326 Frankfurt am Main; Web: www.mainfm.de. Former Frankfurt Business Radio, relaunched in 2004.

Evangeliums-Rundfunk (German branch of Trans World Radio) ✉ Postfach 1444, 35573 Wetzlar (studio location: Berliner Ring 62) ☎ +49 (6441) 9570, 🖷 +49 (6441) 957120; **Web:** www.erf.de German prgr. 0400-2300 on 1539kHz, 24 hours on satellite and local 103.2MHz (1W). Broadcasts via RMC/TWR tr's see International Radio section. Also produces TWR programming in other languages.

Non-commercial stations:

FM	MHz	kW	Site	Station
5)	90.1	0.1	Marburg-Lahnberge	R. Unerhört
3)	90.9	0.32	Rüsselsheim	R. Rüsselsheim
2)	92.5	0.1	Wiesbaden	R. RheinWelle 92,5
7)	96.5	0.32	Witzenhausen	RundFunk Meißner
7)	99.4	0.05	Sontra	RundFunk Meißner
7)	99.7	0.5	Eschwege	RundFunk Meißner
1)	101.4	0.2	Frankfurt-Ginnheim	R. X
7)	102.6	0.32	Hessisch Lichtenau	RundFunk Meißner
4)	103.4	0.32	Darmstadt	R. Darmstadt
6)	105.8	0.5	Kassel Tannenwäldchen	Freies R. Kassel

Adresses and other information:
1), 2) Postfach 49 20, 65039 Wiesbaden, Web: www.rheinwelle.de – **3)** Ludwigstraße 13-15, 65428 Rüsselsheim, Web: www.radiok2r.de – **4)** Steubenplatz 12, 64293 Darmstadt, Web: www.radiodarmstadt.de – **5)** Rudolf-Bultmann-Straße 2b, 35039 Marburg, Web: www.radio-rum.de – **6),7)** Niederhoner Straße 1, 37269 Eschwegem, Web: www.eschwege.de/rfm

MECKLENBURG-VORPOMMERN

Media institution: Landesrundfunkzentrale Mecklenburg-Vorpommern, ✉ Bleicheufer 1, 19053 Schwerin ☎ +49 (385) 5588 10 🖷 +49 (385) 5588 130 **Web:** www.lrz-mv.de

FM networks:

Location	Ant.MV	Ostseewelle	kW
Garz (Rügen)	105.1	107.6	50
Grevesmühlen-Hamberge	105.8	94.7	0.1
Güstrow-Strentz	107.7	98.0	1.25/0.4
Helpterberg	103.8	105.8	100
Heringsdorf (Usedom)	105.4	103.3	10/2
Marlow	100.8	104.8	100
Röbel/Müritz	93.8	92.2	5/0.1
Rostock-Stadtweide	97.3	105.6	2/0.16
Schwerin-Zippendorf	101.3	107.3	100
Waren/Müritz	98.3	93.0	0.2/0.1
Wismar	88.7	93.7	0.2/0.1
Wolgast-Moeckow	–	100.0	0.5

Adresses and other information:
Antenne Mecklenburg-Vorpommern, 19086 Plate, **Web:** www.antennemv.de – **Ostseewelle**, Kröpeliner Straße 83, 18055 Rostock, **Web:** www.ostseewelle.de.

Noncommercial stations:

FM	MHz	kW	Site	Station
1)	88.0	0.8	Neubrandenburg	Radiotreff 88,0
2)	98.1	0.2	Greifswald	Radio 98eins
	103.3		Ahrenshoop	F.Pl.
3)	107.9	0.1	Rostock-Stadtweide	LOHRO

Adresses and other information (only stn. 1) on air at time of editing):
1) Treptower Straße 9, 17033 Neubrandenburg; Web: www.nb-radiotreff.de – **2)** Domstraße 12, 17489 Greifswald; Web: www.98eins.de. F.Pl.: From 2005 regular sce., to rel. NB-Radiotreff 88,0 when no own prgr. is on air. – **3)** Margaretenstraße 43, 18057 Rostock; Web: www.lohro.de. F.Pl.: From 2005 regular sce., probably on 90.2MHz instead.

NIEDERSACHSEN

Media institution: Niedersächsische Landesmedienanstalt für privaten Rundfunk, ✉ Seelhorststraße 18, 30175 Hannover ☎ +49 (511) 28477 0 🖷 +49 (511) 28477 36 **Web:** www.nlm.de

FM networks:

Location	ffn	HR. Ant.	R. 21	kW
Aurich-Popens	103.1	104.9	–	25
Bad Rehburg	–	–	89.4	0.5
Barsinghausen	101.9	103.8	–	25
Braunschw.-Broitzem	103.1	106.9	104.1	15/13/1
Cuxhaven-Otterndorf	102.6	104.6	–	20
Dannenberg-Zernien	102.7	106.1	–	25
Delmenhorst	–	–	107.6	0.1
Goslar	–	–	87.7	0.5
Göttingen	102.8	106.0	93.4	2x5/1
Hannoversch Münden	100.7	106.7	–	0.5
Hannover	–	–	104.9	0.5
Helmstedt	–	–	94.1	0.5
Hildesheim	–	–	105.8	1
Holzminden	102.2	105.7	–	0.5
Leer-Nüttermoor	–	–	104.5	0.3
Lingen-Damaschke	101.5	104.3	–	15
Oldenburg	–	–	104.1	0.24
Osnabrück-Bramsche	103.4	105.9	–	10
Rosengarten	100.6	105.1	–	20
Seesen	–	100.9	–	0.05
Steinkimmen	102.3	105.7	–	100
Torfhaus (Harz)	102.4	106.3	–	100
Visselhövede	101.7	104.2	–	10
Wolfsburg	–	–	95.1	0.1

Addresses and other information:
radio ffn, Stiftstraße 8, 30159 Hannover; Web: www.ffn.de – **Hit-Radio Antenne**, Goseriede 9, 30159 Hannover; Web: www.antenne.com – **Radio 21**, An der Feuerwache 3-5, 30823 Garbsen; Web: www.radio21.de. F.Pl: More FM tr's.
DAB only: Klassik digital (bouqet on ch. 12A, 224MHz)
Relay tr. for Hamburg-based stations (details see there):

MHz	kW	Site	Station
88.5	2	Cuxhaven-Otterndorf	R. Hamburg
93.6	2	Cuxhaven-Otterndorf	106!8 rock'n pop

Noncommercial stations:

	MHz	kW	Site	Station
4)	87.7	0.2	Emden	Radio Ostfriesland
3)	87.8	1	Wilhelmshaven	Radio Jade
1)	88.0	1	Uelzen	Radio ZuSa
1)	89.7	0.5	Dannenberg-Zernien	Radio ZuSa
4)	94.0	1	Aurich-Haxtum	Radio Ostfriesland
8)	94.8	0.05	Bad Pyrmont	Radio Aktiv
2)	95.2	0.2	Nordhorn	Ems-Vechte-Welle
1)	95.5	1	Lüneburg	Radio ZuSa
5)	95.6	1	Lingen-Schepsdorf	Ems-Vechte-Welle
5)	99.3	1	Molbergen-Cloppenburg	Ems-Vechte-Welle
8)	100.0	0.3	Hameln	Radio Aktiv
10)	104.6	0.5	Braunschweig-Broitzem	Radio Okerwelle
6)	104.8	1	Osnabrück	OS Radio 104,8
11)	105.3	1	Hildesheim	Radio Tonkuhle
2)	106.5	1	Oldenburg-Wahnbek	Oldenburg Eins
7)	106.5	0.3	Hannover	Radio Flora
9)	107.1	1	Göttingen	StadtRadio Gött.

Adresses and other information:
1) Ilmenauufer 47, 29525 Uelzen and Scharnhorststraße 1, 21335 Lüneburg; Web: www.zusa.de – **2)** Bahnhofstr. 11, 26122 Oldenburg; Web: www.uni-oldenburg.de/ok_ol/ – **3)** Kieler Str. 31, 26382 Wilhelmshaven; Web: www.radio-jade.de – **4)** VHS Emden, An der Berufsschule 3, 26721 Emden; Web: www.radio-ostfriesland.net – **5)** Halle IV, Kaiserstr. 10a, 49809 Lingen; Web: www.emsvechtewelle.de – **6)** Lohstr. 45a, 49074 Osnabrück; Web: www.os-radio.de – **7)** Zur Bettfedernfabrik 1, 30451 Hannover; Web: http://radioflora.apc.de – **8)** Hefehof 23, 31785 Hameln; Web: www.radio-aktiv.de – **9)** Groner Str. 2, 37073 Göttingen; Web: www.stadtradio-goettingen.de – **10)** Rebenring 18, 38106 Braunschweig; Web: www.okerwelle.de – **11)** Andreas-Passage 1, 31134 Hildesheim; Web: www.tonkuhle.de
Permanent special stn's: Radio SWS (Web: www.radio-sws.de), Norderney 104.0MHz; **Radio S.A.S.** (Web: www.radio-sas.de), Stadthagen 94.5MHz; **Lamberti-Kirchenfunk** (Web: www.soerenkoenig.com/Radlam/), Aurich 106.0MHz; **Kirchenfunk Esterwegen**, 106.6MHz; **Kirchenfunk Lorup**, 107.6MHz; **Kirchenfunk Herzlake**, 106.1MHz; **Pfarrfunk Breitenberg**, 98.4MHz.; **Kirchenfunk Meppen**, 95.0MHz. All tr's 6W.

NORDRHEIN-WESTFALEN

Media institution: Landesanstalt für Rundfunk Nordrhein-Westhalen (LfR) ✉ Postfach 10 34 43, 40025 Düsseldorf (office location: Zollhof 2) ☎ +49 (211) 77 007 0 🖷 +49 (211) 727 170 **Web:** www.lfr.de

FM	MHz	kW	Site	Station
5)	87.7	0.2	Krefeld-Oppum	Welle Niederrhein
43)	87.8	0.1	Geilenkirchen	Welle West
26)	88.1	4	Eggegebirge	R. Hochstift
19)	88.2	0.5	Lüdinghausen	R. Kiepenkerl
37)	88.2	0.5	Siegen	R. Siegen
35)	88.3	0.1	Meinerzhagen	R. MK
16)	88.4	1	Bocholt	Westmünsterlandw.
36)	89.1	0.2	Schmallenberg	R. Sauerland
7)	89.4	1	Düsseldorf Rheinturm	NE-WS 89.4
6)	90.1	0.25	Mönchengladbach-Holt	R. 90,1

FM	MHz	kW	Site	Station
31)	90.8	0.1	Herne	Herne 90acht
35)	90.8	0.03	Letmathe	R. MK
30)	91.2	0.2	Dortmund	R. 91.2
39)	91.2	0.2	Siegburg	R. Bonn/Rhein-Sieg
42)	91.4	0.1	Bergheim	R. Erft
35)	91.5	0.1	Altena	R. MK
33)	91.5	0.1	Hattingen-Schierken	R. en
3)	91.7	0.1	Moers-Meerbeck	R. K.W.
23)	91.7	0.1	Vlotho	R. Herford
4)	92.2	0.1	Duisburg	R. Duisburg
35)	92.5	0.32	Iserlohn	R. MK
20)	92.6	1	Sendenhorst	R. WAF
44)	92.7	0.5	Düren-Hürtgenwald	R. Rur
13)	92.9	0.5	Mülheim-Saarn	Antenne Ruhr
29)	92.9	0.1	Selm	antenne unna
16)	93.0	0.5	Ahaus	Westmünsterlandw.
26)	93.7	0.1	Paderborn	R. Hochstift
39)	94.2	0.1	Much-Wersch	R. Bonn/Rhein-Sieg
9)	94.3	0.2	Solingen	R. RSG
15)	94.6	0.1	Recklinghausen	R. FiV
35)	94.6	0.02	Balve	R. MK
20)	94.7	0.2	Warendorf	R. WAF
36)	94.8	0.1	Marsberg	R. Sauerland
23)	94.9	0.5	Herford	R. Herford
18)	95.4	0.16	Münster	Antenne Münster
15)	95.6	0.1	Berghaltern	R. FiV
24)	95.7	0.5	Minden Jakobsberg	R. Westfalica
20)	95.7	0.25	Beckum	R. WAF
14)	96.1	0.1	Gelsenkirchen	REL
36)	96.2	0.4	Olsberg-Antfeld	R. Sauerland
20)	96.3	0.25	Oelde	R. WAF
38)	96.9	0.5	Leverkusen-Opladen	R. Berg
1)	97.2	0.1	Simmerath	Antenne AC
35)	97.2	0.1	Werdohl	R. MK
37)	97.3	0.1	Bad Laasphe	R. Siegen
11)	97.6	4	Langenberg	R. Neandertal
16)	97.6	1	Borken	Westmünsterlandw.
22)	97.6	0.4	Friedrichsdorf	R. Bielefeld
2)	98.0	1	Kleve	Antenne Niederrhein
43)	98.3	0.5	Erkelenz	Welle West
22)	98.3	0.1	Bielefeld	R. Bielefeld
32)	98.5	0.5	Bochum	R. 98.5
14)	98.7	0.5	Bottrop	REL
39)	98.9	0.1	Bonn Venusberg	R. Bonn/Rhein-Sieg
37)	98.9	0.1	Neunkirchen	R. Siegen
35(	99.5	0.05	Plettenberg	R. MK
45)	99.7	0.1	Euskirchen	R. Euskirchen
38)	99.7	0.5	Gremberg	R. Berg
39)	99.9	0.5	Bonn-Königswinter	R. Bonn/Rhein-Sieg
46)	100.0	0.1	Köln-Neumarkt	Kölncampus
1a)	100.1	0.4	Aachen-Karlshöhe	Aachen 100,eins
35)	100.2	0.5	Lüdenscheid	R. MK
27)	100.9	1	Soest-Möhnesee	Hellweg R.
25)	101.0	0.5	Schieder-Schwalenbg.	R. Lippe
7)	102.1	0.25	Grevenbroich	NE-WS 89.4
12)	102.2	0.32	Essen-Werden	R. Essen
29)	102.3	1	Schwerte Sommerberg	Antenne Unna
5)	102.5	0.32	Viersen Süchtelner Höhe	Welle Niederrhein
16)	103.6	0.1	Gronau	Westmünsterlandw.
27)	103.6	0.1	Lippstadt	Hellweg R.
17)	104.0	1	Tecklenburg	R. RST
8)	104.2	1	Düsseldorf	Antenne Düsseldorf
33)	104.2	0.1	Witten-Stockum	R. en
26)	104.8	0.5	Neuhaus-Hasselberg	R. Hochstift
26)	104.8	0.1	Büren	R. Hochstift
36)	104.9	0.1	Meschede	R. Sauerland
12)	105.0	0.1	Essen-Holsterhausen	R. Essen
28)	105.0	0.2	Hamm	R. Lippewelle
1)	105.0	0.05	Monschau	Antenne AC
38)	105.2	4	Lindlar	R. Berg
17)	105.2	4	Schöppingen	R. RST
15)	105.2	0.1	Dorsten	R. FiV
37)	105.4	4	Aue Hohe Hessel	R. Siegen
38)	105.7	1	Waldbröl	R. Berg
2)	105.7	0.5	Geldern	Antenne Niederrhein
33)	105.7	0.1	Gevelsberg	R. en
42)	105.8	1	Köln Colonius	R. Erft
13)	106.2	0.1	Oberhausen	Antenne Ruhr
36)	106.5	0.5	Hallenberg	R. Sauerland
36)	106.5	0.25	Arnsberg	R. Sauerland
25)	106.6	1	Lemgo	R. Lippe
24)	106.6	0.1	Lübbecke	R. Westfalica
21)	106.8	0.4	Borgholzhausen	R. Gütersloh
45)	106.9	4	Schleiden (Eifel)	R. Euskirchen
41)	107.1	0.5	Köln Neumarkt	R. Köln
33)	107.2	0.1	Herdecke	R. en
27)	107.3	0.2	Wickede	Hellweg R.
19)	107.4	1	Coesfeld	R. Kiepenkerl
25)	107.4	1	Linderhofe-Dörenberg	R. Lippe
10)	107.4	0.5	Wuppertal	R. Wuppertal
45)	107.4	0.1	Bad Münstereifel	R. Euskirchen
21)	107.5	1	Oelde	R. Gütersloh
44)	107.5	0.1	Linnich	R. Rur
29)	107.5	0.01	Fröndenberg	Antenne Unna
36)	107.6	0.5	Sundern	R. Sauerland
3)	107.6	0.2	Wesel-Büderich	R. K.W.
40)	107.6	0.1	Leverkusen-Wiesdorf	R. Leverkusen
27)	107.7	0.2	Belecke-Sennhöfe	Hellweg R.
34)	107.7	0.2	Hagen	R. Hagen
1)	107.8	0.4	Aachen-Stolberg	Antenne AC
39)	107.9	0.1	Herchen-Rosbach	R. Bonn/Rhein-Sieg
9)	107.9	0.1	Remscheid	R. RSG

+ 5 repeaters 50W or less.

Addresses and other information:

Radio NRW, Essener Straße 55, 46047 Oberhausen, **Web:** www.radionrw.de.

Note: All stn's except 1) rel. at times Radio NRW with own identifications inserted automatically.

1) Merzbrück 214, 52146 Würselen; Web: www.diehitgarantie.de and www.antenne-ac.de – **1a)** Bahnhofstraße 18-20, 52064 Aachen; Web: www.diehitgarantie.de – **2)** Stechbahn 2-8, 47533 Kleve, Web: www.antenneniederrhein.de – **3)** Rheinstraße 24-26, 47495 Rheinberg, Web: www.radiokw.de – **4)** Ruhrorter Straße 187, 47119 Duisburg, Web: http://medien.freepage.de/guidojansen/ – **5)** Uerdinger Straße 543, 47800 Krefeld, Web: www.welleniederrhein.de – **6)** Lüpertzender Straße 159, 41061 Mönchengladbach, Web: www.radio901.de – **7)** Moselstraße 16, 41464 Neuss, Web: www.news894.de – **8)** Kaistraße 7, 40221 Düsseldorf, Web: www.antenneduesseldorf.de – **9)** Postfach, 42621 Solingen (studio location: Alleestraße 1), Web: www.radiorsg.de – **10)** Friedrich-Engels-Allee 426, 42283 Wuppertal, Web: www.radiowuppertal.de – **11)** Elberfelder Straße 81, 40804 Mettmann, Web: www.radioneandertal.de – **12)** Sachsenstraße 36, 45128 Essen, Web: www.radioessen.de – **13)** Viktoriastraße 26-28, 45468 Mülheim/Ruhr, Web: www.antenne-ruhr.de – **14)** Hochstraße 68, 45894 Gelsenkirchen, Web: www.radio-emscher-lippe.de – **15)** Schaumburgstraße 14, 45657 Recklinghausen, Web: www.radiofiv.de – **16)** Heinrich-Hertz-Straße 6, 46325 Borken, Web: www.radiowmw.de –**17)** Poststraße 3, 48431 Rheine, Web: www.radiorst.de – **18)** Nevinghoff 14/16, 48147 Münster, Web: www.antennemuenster.de – **19)** Tiberstraße 21, 48249 Dülmen, Web: www.radio-kiepenkerl.de – **20)** Am Schweinemarkt 3, 48231 Warendorf, Web: www.radiowaf.de – **21)** Feldstraße 14, 33330 Gütersloh, Web: www.radioguetersloh.de – **22)** Niedernstraße 21-27, 33602 Bielefeld, Web: www.radiobielefeld.de – **23)** Berliner Straße 30, 32052 Herford, Web: www.radioherford.de – **24)** Johanniskirchhof 2, 32423 Minden, Web: www.radiowestfalica.de – **25)** Lagesche Straße 17, 32756 Detmold, Web: www.radiolippe.de – **26)** Frankfurter Weg 22, 33106 Paderborn, Web: www.radiohochstift.de – **27)** Jakobistraße 46, 59494 Soest, Web: www.hellwegradio.de – **28)** Königstraße 39, 59065 Hamm, Web: www.lippewelle.de – **29)** Mozartstraße 1, 59423 Unna, Web: www.antenneunna.de – **30)** Karl-Zahn-Straße 11, 44141 Dortmund, Web: www.radio912.de – **31)** Bahnhofstraße 45, 44623 Herne, Web: www.radio-herne.de – **32)** Westring 26, 44787 Bochum, Web: www.ruhrwelle-bochum.de – **33)** Mühlenstraße 25, 58285 Gevelsberg, Web: www.radio-en.de – **34)** Rathausstraße 23, 58095 Hagen, Web: www.radio-hagen.de – **35)** Vinckestraße 9-13, 58636 Iserlohn, Web: www.radio-mk.de – **36)** Steinstraße 32, 59872 Meschede, Web: www.radio-sauerland.de – **37)** Postfach 10 02 42, 57002 Siegen (studio location: Obergraben 33), Web: www.radio-siegen.de – **38)** Friedrich-Ebert-Straße, 51429 Bergisch Gladbach, Web: www.radioberg.de – **39)** Kennedybrücke 4, 53225 Bonn, Web: www.radio-bonn.de – **40)** Bismarckstraße 71, 51373 Leverkusen, Web: www.radioleverkusen.de – **41)** Stolberger Straße 374, 50933 Köln, Web: www.radiokoeln.de – **42)** Hürth Park, 50354 Hürth, Web: www.radioerft.de – **43)** Hochstraße 167, 52525 Heinsberg, Web: www.wellewest.de – **44)** August-Klotz-Straße 21, 52349 Düren, Web: www.radiorur.de – **45)** Rheinstraße 55, 53881 Euskirchen, Web: www.radioeuskirchen.de

Via cable, satellite and DAB (229MHz): **Domradio**, Domkloster 3, 50667 Köln; Web: www.domradio.de. Run by Catholic Church.

Planned for 702/855kHz: TruckRadio, Karolinenstraße 32, 90762 Fürth, web: www.truckradio.de. At time of editing only via local DAB in Sachsen-Anhalt, date for launch of MW sce. not known.

University and other stn's: Kölncampus (Web: www.koelncampus.com) on 100.0MHz (0.1kW); **Hochschulradio Düsseldorf** (Web: www.hochschulradio.uni-duesseldorf.de) on 97.1MHz (40W);

Eldoradio (Dortmund; Web: www.eldoradio.de) on 93.0MHz (50W); **CT – Das Radio** (Bochum; Web: www.radioct.de) on 90.0MHz (0.2kW); **Radio Q** (Münster; Web: www.radioq.de) on 90.9MHz (5W); **Hertz 87,9** (Bielefeld; Web: www.radiohertz.de) on 87.9MHz (50W); **Antenne Bethel** (curch; Bielefeld; Web: www.antenne-bethel.de) on 94.3MHz (50W); **Radio St. Laurentius** (church; Clarholz; Web: www.laurentius-clarholz.de/radio/index.htm) on 106.4MHz (10W); **Teutoradio Plus** (shopping centre; Bad Oeynhausen; Web: www.teutoradioplus.de) on 88.5MHz (5W). **F.Pl.:** University stn. at Bonn on 96.8MHz (0.5kW).

RHEINLAND-PFALZ

Media institution: Landeszentrale für private Rundfunkveranstalter (RPR) ✉ Postfach 21 73 63, 67072 Ludwigshafen (office location: Turmstraße 8) ☎ +49 (621) 5252 0 🖷 +49 (621) 5252 152 **Web:** www.lpr-online.de

FM networks:

Location	RPR Eins	BigFM	Rockl.	RiT	kW
Bad Bergzabern	103.3	–	–	–	0.25
Bad Dürkheim	98.1	96.4	–	–	0.05/0.1
Bad Kreuznach	89.7	104.8	88.3	–	0.1/0.2/0.1
Bad Marienberg	102.9	–	–	–	25
Bernkastel-Kues	–	100.5	–	–	0.1
Betzdorf	–	107.7	–	–	0.5
Bitburg	–	–	107.9	–	0.1
Bornberg-Eßweiler	103.1	107.6	–	–	25
Daun (Eifel)	102.1	106.6	92.2	–	20/10/0.8
Diezer Hain	101.2	100.4	–	–	0.1
Eisenberg	–	–	94.8	–	0.1
Grünbach	103.3	106.5	–	–	0.05
Haardtkopf	100.1	–	–	–	50
Heckenbach	103.5	104.9	–	–	30
Hermeskeil	–	–	–	88.4	0.4
Hohe Wurzel	–	–	107.9	–	6
Idar-Oberstein	100.3	101.9	87.6	–	2/0.2
Kaiserslautern	103.1	107.6	96.9	–	25/0.5
Kalmit	103.6	106.7	–	–	25
Kirchheimbolanden	–	–	97.1	–	0.2
Kleinkarlbach	91.1	90.3	–	–	0.1
Koblenz Kühkopf	101.5	104.0	–	–	40
Koblenz-Bendorf	–	–	88.3	–	0.25
Landau	–	–	94.8	–	0.1
Linz	–	–	96.9	–	0.2
Mainz Ober-Olm	100.6	104.5	–	–	20
Mainz (city)	98.1	106.6	–	–	0.2/0.32
Mannheim	–	–	93.2	–	1
Naurath	–	–	–	88.2	0.05
Neustadt	–	–	94.2	–	1
Nürburgring	–	–	87.7*)	–	0.05
Oberemmel	–	–	–	100.5	0.2
Pirmas. Kettrichhof	104.7	–	–	–	5
Pirmasens (city)	–	96.7	88.4	–	0.4/0.2
Rivenich	–	95.8	–	88.6	0.2/0.04
Rockenhausen	–	–	87.6	–	0.5
Saarburg	–	96.5	–	95.1	0.25/0.04
Schoden-Geisberg	102.6	–	–	–	20
St. Vieth (Belgium)	–	–	–	101.7	1
Trier Petrisberg	102.9	106.4	105.8	88.4	3x0.1/0.5
Trierweiler	–	–	–	94.7	0.05
Welschbillig	–	–	–	87.8	0.01
Zweibrücken	103.3	106.6	–		2/0.2

*) Carries Nürburgring Radio during car races. N.B Hohe Wurzel tr. in Hessen.

Addresses and other information:

Hit-Radio RPR Eins, Turmstraße 8, 67059 Ludwigshafen; Web: www.radiorpr.de – **BigFM:** See under Baden-Württemberg. Rel. of adopted BigFM version in responsibility of Radio RPR. – **Rockland Radio**, Neuffer am Park, 66953 Pirmasens, Web: www.rockland.de – **Radio in Trier**, Metternichstr. 6, 54292 Trier; Web: www.radio22.de. Former Radio 22, renamed in 2004.

Antenne Koblenz, Friedrich-Ebert-Ring 54, 56068 Koblenz; Web: www.antenne-koblenz.de. On 98.0MHz (1kW).

Metropol FM, see stn 14) under Berlin & Brandenburg. Rel. on Ludwigshafen 88.3MHz (10W).

SAARLAND

Media institution: Landesmedienanstalt Saar (LMS) ✉ Postfach 11 01 64, 66070 Saarbrücken (office location: Nell-Breuning-Allee 6) ☎ +49 (681) 389880; 🖷 +49 (681) 3898820; **Web:** www.lmsaar.de

FM networks:

Location	Radio Salü	JAM FM	(F.Pl.)	kW
Merzig	103.0	92.6	105.1	0.1/0.5
Mettlach	104.2	–	106.1	0.1/0.01
Neunkirchen	–	94.6	–	0.6
Oberperl	100.3	–	–	5
Saarbrücken Schoksberg	101.7	–	–	100
Saarbrücken Halberg	–	94.2	–	1
Saarbrücken-Rotenbühl	–	99.6	–	0.1
St. Ingbert	–	–	100.6	0.1
Sulzbach	–	96.8	–	0.1
Webenheim	100.0	–	–	5

Addresses and other information:

Radio Salü, Postfach 10 08 44, 66008 Saarbrücken (studio location: Richard-Wagner-Str. 58-60), Web: www.salue.de – **JAM FM**: see stn. 12) under Berlin & Brandenburg. – **F.Pl:** Allocation procedures under way at time of editing. Applicants for these freq. were Radio Salü Gold, Hit Mix FM, TruckRadio and Radio in Trier.

Europe 1 (Europäische Rundfunk und Fernseh AG), Postfach 10 08 32, 66008 Saarbrücken. Rel. Europe 1 prgr. from Paris on 183kHz (tr. station: Postfach 1365, 66713 Saarlouis).

SACHSEN

Media institution: Sächsische Landesanstalt für privaten Rundfunk und neue Medien (SLM) ✉ Postfach 100 551, 01075 Dresden ☎ +49 (351) 814040 🖷 +49 (351) 5670523; **Web:** www.slm-online.de; office location: Carolinenstraße 1.

FM networks:

Location	PSR	R.SA	RTL	Energy	kW
Annaberg-Buchholz	–	104.8	–	–	0.5
Auerbach	–	107.9	–	–	0.1
Chemnitz-Reichenh.	–	91.0	–	97.5	3
Collmberg	98.0	–	104.7	–	5/10
Döbeln	–	107.9	–	98.3	1/0.2
Dresden-Wachwitz	102.4	89.2	105.2	100.2*	100/2/100/5
Flöha	–	98.4	–	–	0.1
Freiberg	–	90.6	–	96.4	0.2/0.5
Freital	–	88.3	–	–	0.2
Geyer (Erzgebirge)	100.0	–	105.4	–	100
Görlitz	–	105.1	–	–	1
Grimma	–	107.4	–	93.3	2/0.3
Hoyerswerda-Zeißig	–	96.9	–	87.6	0.2/0.32
Leipzig-Holzhausen	–	97.6*	–	99.8	4
Markneukirchen	–	89.6	–	–	1
Löbau	101.0	–	105.6	–	30
Mittelherwigsdorf	–	100.0	–	–	0.5
Niederschöna	–	94.4	–	–	0.5
Nossen	–	91.4	–	–	0.2
Oschatz	–	89.1	–	–	0.25
Plauen	–	93.5	–	–	1
Riesa	–	106.4	–	91.7	2/1
Schöneck	92.0	–	106.0	–	10/30
Stollberg	–	93.4	–	–	1
Torgau	–	91.1	–	–	0.2
Wiederau (Leipzig)	102.9	–	106.9	–	100
Wilkau-Haßlau	–	92.3	–	–	0.5
Wilthen	–	106.5	–	104.9	1/0.5
Wurzen	–	95.0	–	–	0.4
Zwickau-Ebersbrunn	–	–	–	98.2	0.3

*) Time-sharing with non-commercial stn's, see below

Addresses and other information:

Radio PSR and **R.SA**: Delitzscher Straße 97, 04129 Leipzig; Web: www.radiopsr.de; www.rsa-sachsen.de – **Hitradio RTL**: Breitscheidstraße 40, 01237 Dresden; Web: www.hitradio-rtl.de. Former Hit-Radio Antenne Sachsen, relaunched in 2004. F.Pl.: Merger with SLP with possible move of studios. – **ENERGY Sachsen**: Nonnenstraße 17-21, 04229 Leipzig; Web: www.nrj.de – **Apollo Radio:** plus Freita

Other stations:

FM	MHz	kW	Site	Station
9)	88.2	0.4	Auerbach	Vogtlandradio
10)	88.9	1	Chemnitz-Reichenhain	BBC/RFI
8)	89.2	1	Weißwasser	Radio WSW
4)	89.2	0.1	Meerane	Zwickau 96 Punkt 2
11)	89.2	0.1	Leipzig-Reudnitz	Radio Blau / Apollo
2)	90.9	0.3	Grimma-Hohnstädt	Leipzig 91 Punkt 3
4)	90.9	0.3	Werdau	Zwickau 96 Punkt 2
10)	91.1	1	Dresden-Gompitz	BBC/RFI
2)	91.3	4	Leipzig-Holzhausen	Leipzig 91 Punkt 3
3)	91.7	0.3	Zschopau	Chemnitz 102 Punkt 1
5)	94.3	0.32	Mittelherwigsdorf	Lausitz 107 Punkt 6
11)	94.4	0.25	Leipzig-Stahmeln	Radio Blau / Apollo
8)	94.9	0.2	Wilthen	Radio WSW
9)	95.4	2	Plauen	Vogtlandradio
3)	95.8	1	Neukirchen	Chemnitz 102 Punkt 1
4)	96.2	0.5	Zwickau-Ebersbrunn	Zwickau 96 Punkt 2

FM MHz	kW	Site	Station
10) 96.4	0.1	Pirna	BBC/RFI
10) 98.2	1	Leipzig-Paunsdorf	BBC/RFI
3) 99.0	0.1	Flöha	Chemnitz 102 Punkt 1
11) 99.2	0.5	Leipzig-Connewitz	Radio Blau / Apollo
13) 99.3	0.1	Freital	Apollo Radio
2) 99.5	0.1	Borna	Leipzig 91 Punkt 3
9) 100.5	1	Kuhberg (Reichenbach)	Vogtlandradio
3) 102.1	3	Chemnitz-Reichenhain	Chemnitz 102 Punkt 1
12) 102.7	1	Chemnitz-Reichenhain	Radio T / Apollo
7) 102.8	0.5	Hoyerswerda-Zeißig	Elsterwelle
4) 103.4	0.5	Wilkau-Haßlau	Zwickau 96 Punkt 2
1) 103.5	2	Dresden-Wachwitz	Dresden 103 Punkt 5
1) 104.2	0.2	Freiberg	Dresden 103 Punkt 5
1) 107.0	0.2	Freital	Dresden 103 Punkt 5
3) 107.3	0.1	Limbach-Oberfrohna	Chemnitz 102 Punkt 1
1) 107.5	0.2	Meißen	Dresden 103 Punkt 5
5) 107.6	30	Löbau	Lausitz 107 Punkt 6
6) 107.7	2	Fichtelberg (Erzgebirge)	R. Erzgebirge

Addresses and other information:
1), 2), 3), 4), 5) SLP, Ammonstraße, 01067 Dresden; Web: www.lokalrundfunk.net. Stn's run under ID's shown above. At times local prgr. from studios Friedrich-List-Platz 1, 04103 Leipzig (2); Carolastraße 4-6, 09111 Chemnitz (3); Leipziger Straße 176, 08058 Zwickau (4); Untermarkt 19, 02828 Görlitz 5). F.Pl.: Merger with Hitradio RTL. – **6)** Vierenstraße 11, 09484 Oberwiesenthal; Web: www.radioerzgebirge-online.de. At times rel. R.SA. – **7)** Walter-Rathenau-Straße 27, 02977 Hoyerswerda; Web: www.elsterwelle.de – **8)** Werner-Seelenbinder-Straße 54a, 02943 Weißwasser; Web: www.radiowsw.de – **9)** Haselbrunner Straße 114, 08525 Plauen; Web: www.vogtlandradio.de – **10)** BBC Radiocom Deutschland GmbH c/o The British Trade Office, Gohliserstraße 7, 04105 Leipzig. Own prgr. in German Sun only 0800-0830. Rel. RFI German prgr. 0730-0800, 1130-1200, 1730-1830, RFI Service Mondiale 1830-2400, otherwise BBC-Worldservice. – **11)** Paul-Gruner-Straße 62, 04107 Leipzig; Web: www.radioblau.de. Mon-Thu 1700-2100, Fri 1700-2300, Sat 1100-2300, Sun 1100-1800, otherwise rel. stn. 13). Non-commercial. – **12)** Karl-Liebknecht-Straße 19, 09111 Chemnitz; Web: www.radiot.de. Daily 1800-2300, otherwise rel. stn. 13). Non-commercial. – **13)** Carolastraße 4-6, 09111 Chemnitz; Web: www.apolloradio.de. Backed by Radio PSR, Hitradio RTL and SLP.
Non-commercial stn's on shared freq's: mephisto 97.6, on 97.6MHz Mon-Fri 0900-1100 and 1700-1900: c/o Universität Leipzig, internes Postfach 89 00 99, Augustusplatz 9, 04109 Leipzig; Web: www.uni-leipzig.de/~mephisto/ – **coloRadio**, on 100.2MHz Thu 1900-2300: Jordanstraße 5, 01099 Dresden; Web: www.coloradio.de
Radio Novum, Leisniger Straße 9, 09648 Mittweida; Web: www.radio-novum.de. College stn. via cable net and webstream. F.Pl.: FM tr. (planned: 99.3MHz).
Via DAB only (224MHz, exc. eastern Saxonia: 178MHz): 89.0 RTL (see under Sachsen-Anhalt), RadiJoJo (Web: www.radijojo.de), sunshine live (see under Baden-Württemberg).

SACHSEN-ANHALT

Media institution: Medienanstalt Sachsen-Anhalt ✉ Reichardtstraße 9, 06114 Halle/Saale ☎ +49 (345) 52550 🖹 +49 (345) 5255 121 **Web:** www.lra.de
FM networks:

Location	R Bro	RTL	SAW	Rock	kW
Blankenburg	99.9	–	95.7	–	0.5/0.1
Brocken	–	89.0	101.4	–	60/100
Dequede	101.0	–	95.6	–	60/1.5
Dessau-Mildensee	90.6	–	94.1	92.6	0.8/0.3/2
Fleetmark-Lüge	–	–	103.9	–	5
Halle Petersberg	93.5	–	–	103.3	5
Hergisdorf-Wolferode	93.7	–	–	–	1
Köthen	–	–	97.1	–	1
Magdeburg-Buckau	–	–	–	98.7	0.2
Naumburg	98.8	–	95.1	–	10/0.5
Schneidlingen	–	–	–	107.2	2.4
Schönebeck	105.7	–	100.1	–	15/4
Weißenfels	–	–	88.0	–	1
Wernigerode	105.4	–	90.8	–	0.5/1
Wiederau (Leipzig)	–	–	104.9	–	*100
Wittenberg-Gallun	102.3	–	98.4	–	4/10
Zeitz-Hainichen	99.1	–	–	–	0.5
Ziesar	–	–	102.8	–	1.5

*) directional towards Halle/Saale.
Addresses and other information:
Radio Brocken, 89.0 RTL: Brachwitzer Straße 16, 06118 Halle; Web: www.brocken.de, www.89.0rtl.de. 89.0 RTL also via state-wide DAB (227MHz), Radio Brocken via local DAB Halle (1463MHz) and Magdeburg (1455MHz). – **Radio SAW, Rockland Sachsen-Anhalt**: Hansapark 1, 39116 Magdeburg; Web: www.radiosaw.de, www.rockland-digital.de. Both stn's also via 227MHz DAB.
Local Halle/Magdeburg DAB only: Nova Radio (see under Bayern), TruckRadio (see under Nordrhein-Westfalen).

Non-commercial stations:

FM MHz	kW	Site	Station
3) 92.5	1	Aschersleben	radio hbw
1) 95.9	0.6	Halle Petersberg	R. Corax
2) 99.6	1	Naumburg	R. FRN

Adresses and other information:
1) Unterberg 11, 06108 Halle; Web: www.radiocorax.de – **2)** Salzstr. 35, 06618 Naumburg/Saale; Web: www.radio-frn.de – **3)** Herrenbreite 9, 06449 Aschersleben; Web: www.89.0rtl.de

SCHLESWIG-HOLSTEIN

Media institution: Unabhängige Landesanstalt für das Rundfunkwesen ✉ Schloßstraße 19, 24103 Kiel ☎ +49 (431) 974560 🖹 +49 (431) 9745660 **Web:** www.ulr.de
FM networks:

Location	R.SH	delta	Nora	K.R.	kW
Ahrensburg	–	96.5	–	–	2
Bredstedt	–	–	98.1	–	0.1
Bungsberg (Eutin)	100.2	104.1	106.2	97.2	2x50/0.13/0.2
Flensburg-Freienwill	101.4	105.6	–	–	20
Flensburg-Harrislee	–	–	88.5	106.5	0.5
Garding	–	–	94.1	91.7	0.5
Heide-Welmbüttel	103.8	100.4	–	–	15
Heide (town)	–	–	96.9		0.3
Helgoland (island)	100.0	103.5	101.6	89.8	0.1
Henstedt-Ulzburg	102.9	107.4	–	–	20
Husum	–	–	92.0	–	0.1
Itzehoe	–	–	104.9	92.7	1/0.5
Kaltenkirchen	102.9	107.4	101.1	–	20
Kiel	102.4	105.9	97.0	97.4	2x15/0.1/0.3
Lauenburg	102.5	105.6	97.4	–	1/1/0.25
Lübeck	–	–	91.5		0.32
Mölln-Berkenthin	101.5	107.9	91.5	93.6	2x20/0.32/1
Neumünster	–	–	88.9	–	0.5
Niebüll	–	–	107.2	94.7	0.16/0.2
Rendsburg	–	–	93.6	92.9	0.5
Schleswig (town)	–	–	92.4	100.8	1/0.5
Schleswig-Borgwedel	–	–	–	93.9	0.5
Westerland (Sylt)	102.8	104.8	89.1	89.8	5/5/1/0.5

N.B Further R.SH and delta radio tr's see under Hamburg.
Addresses and other information:
R.SH, Funkhaus Wittland, 24109 Kiel; Web: www.rsh.de. Also broadcasts short local insertions. – **delta radio**, Werftstr. 214, 24143 Kiel; Web: www.deltaradio.de. – **Radio Nora**, Im Saal 2, 24145 Kiel; Web: www.radionora.de – **Klassik Radio**: See stn. 1) under Hamburg – **Power 612**, Andreas-Gayk-Str. 13, 24103 Kiel; Web: www.power-radio.de (offline at time of editing). 0500-1800 on 612kHz.

Non-commercial stations:

FM MHz	kW	Site	Station
2) 97.6	0.5	Garding	OK Westküste
2) 98.8	0.03	Husum	OK Westküste
3) 98.8	0.5	Lübeck-Stockelsdorf	OK Lübeck
1) 101.2	0.1	Kiel	Kiel FM
2) 105.2	0.05	Heide-Dithmarschen	OK Westküste

Addresses and other information:
1) Hamburger Chaussee 36, 24113 Kiel; Web: www.kielfm.de – **2)** Landvogt-Johannsen-Str. 11, 25746 Heide; Web: www.okwestkueste.de – **3)** Kanalstr. 42-48, 23554 Lübeck; Web: www.ok-luebeck.de

THÜRINGEN

Media institution: Thüringer Landesmedienanstalt (TLM) ✉ Am Häckerstieg 12, 99310 Arnstadt ☎ +49 (3628) 6116 0 🖹 +49 (3628) 6116 26 **Web:** www.tlm.de.
FM networks:

Location	Ant.T.	LW.	Top 40	kW
Altenburg	–	–	98.4	0.5
Bleßberg	102.7	106.7	–	60
Dingelstädt	103.9	–	–	5
Eisenach	–	–	93.5	0.2
Erfurt Windischh.	100.2	99.7		3/0.5
Erfurt Hochheim	–	–	88.6	0.5
Gera	–	105.8	95.3	1/0.5
Gotha	–	–	90.8	0.06
Heiligenstadt	–	88.7	–	0.1
Ilmenau	–	–	94.8	0.1
Inselsberg	102.2	104.2	–	100

Location	Ant.T.	LW.	Top 40	kW
Jena-Oßmaritz	90.9	106.1	–	1
Jena Kernberge	–	–	94.8	0.2
Keula	–	104.5		10
Kulpenberg	104.7	96.8	–	3
Lobenstein	93.2	98.5	–	1/2
Meiningen	–	–	99.5	0.2
Mühlhausen	–	–	93.8	0.2
Nordhausen	106.8	105.8	103.0	0.1
Pößneck	–	–	98.9	0.2
Remda Kalmberg	107.6	95.7	–	60/10
Ronneburg	102.5	94.9	–	30/3
Saalfeld	–	–	88.8	0.08
Sömmerda	–	–	91.0	0.1
Sondershausen	–	–	90.7	0.2
Suhl	101.3	88.6	92.1	2x1/0.05
Weimar Ettersberg	107.2	89.2	–	0.25
Weimar Belvedere	–	–	97.9	0.1

Addresses and other information:
Antenne Thüringen, Top 40: Belvederer Allee 25, 99425 Weimar; Web: www.antennethueringen.de, www.radiotop40.de. Top 40 also on DAB (226MHz). – **LandesWelle Thüringen**: Mehringstr. 5, 99086 Erfurt; Web: www.landeswelle.de.

Non-commercial and other stations:

FM	MHz	kW	Site	Station
7)	92.4	0.2	Schleiz	Rennstadt-Radio
1)	96.2	0.6	Erfurt-Hochheim	Funkwerk, F.R.E.I.
4)	96.5	0.2	Eisenach	Wartburg-R.
3)	98.1	0.1	Ilmenau	hsf Studentenradio
6)	100.4	0.1	Nordhausen	Offener Kanal Nordh.
5)	103.4	0.32	Jena-Oßmaritz	Offener Kanal Jena
2)	106.6	2	Weimar Belvedere	Funkwerk, Lotte, b11

Addresses and other information:
1) Funkwerk, Juri-Gagarin-Ring 96, 99084 Erfurt; Web: www.radio-funkwerk.de. Mon-Fri 1200-2000, Fri 2300- Sat 2300. **F.R.E.I.**, Gotthardstr. 21, 99084 Erfurt; Web: www.radio-frei.de. Mon-Thu 0600-1200 and 2000-2400, Fri 0600-1200 and 2000-2300, Sat 2300- Sun 2400 – **2) Radio Lotte**, Herderplatz 14, 99423 Weimar; Web: www.radiolotte.de. Mon 0600-1200 and 2300-2400, Tue-Thu 0600-1200 and 2000-2400, Fri 0600-1200 and 2000-2300, Sat 2300- Sun 2400. **studio b11**, Bauhaus-Universität, Bauhausstr. 11, 99421 Weimar; Web: http://radiostudio.org. Mon 1900-2300 only. Also rel. Funkwerk from Erfurt – **3)** Postfach 100 565, 98684 Ilmenau; Web: www.hsf.tu-ilmenau.de – **4)** Georgenstr. 43, 99817 Eisenach; Web: www.wartburg-radio.de – **5)** Helmboldstr. 1, 07749 Jena; Web: www.jenaonline.de/okj – **6)** August-Bebel-Platz 6, 99734 Nordhausen; Web: www.ok-nordhausen.de – **7)** Alte Poststraße 2, 07907 Schleiz; Web: www.rennstadtradio.de. Periodically on air (latest licence: Nov 19-Dec 05 2004).
BBC-Worldservice rel.: On all stn's exc. 7) when no own prgr. is on air.

III. ARMED FORCES STATIONS

FM	MHz	kW	Site	Station
Baden-Württemberg				
4)	102.3	100	Stuttgart Frauenkopf	AFN HOT FM
4)	104.6	0.4	Heidelberg-Wieblingen	AFN HOT FM
Bayern				
1)	90.0	0.1	Amberg	AFN Power Network
2)	104.9	0.4	Illesheim	AFN Big Red Radio
1)	104.9	0.2	Würzburg	AFN Power Network
3)	107.4	0.3	Fürth	AFN The Big Gun
1)	107.6	0.2	Vilseck	AFN Power Network
Bremen				
1)	107.9	0.3	Bremerhaven	AFN Power Network
Hessen				
1a)	98.7	50	Feldberg (Taunus)	AFN Z-98
Niedersachsen				
8)	93.0	40	Braunschweig	BFBS Radio 1
8)	95.4	0.2	Celle	BFBS Radio 2
8)	97.6	30	Visselhövede	BFBS Radio 1
8)	99.3	0.1	Hameln	BFBS Radio 1
8)	104.7	0.2	Bergen-Belsen	BFBS Radio 2
8)	106.3	0.1	Osnabrück	BFBS Radio 2
Nordrhein-Westfalen				
8)	96.5	35	Langenberg	BFBS Radio 1
8)	97.8	0.5	Bonn Venusberg	BFBS Radio 1
8)	101.6	0.3	Bielefeld	BFBS Radio 2
8)	102.2	0.3	Münster	BFBS Radio 2
8)	103.0	70	Bielefeld	BFBS Radio 1
8)	104.3	0.3	Mönchengladbach	BFBS Radio 2
8)	105.0	0.3	Paderborn	BFBS Radio 2
6)	106.1		Kalkar	(silent)
1)	107.6	0.3	Bonn (US embassy)	AFN Power Network
6)	107.7		Kalkar	(silent)

N.B Brunssum tr's of AFN, BFBS and CFN, also serving Geilenkirchen, see under Netherlands.

FM	MHz	kW	Site	Station
Rheinland-Pfalz				
5)	100.2	1	Kaiserslautern	AFN Z100.2
5)	103.0	0.5	Pirmasens	AFN Z100.2
7)	105.1	1	Spangdahlem	AFN Eifel

+10 trs less than 0.1kW

Addresses and other information:
1) AFN Europe, Bertramstraße 6, 60320 Frankfurt am Main ☎ +49 (69) 15688 403, **Web:** www.afneurope.net. Affiliates: 2)...6), AFN SHAPE (see under Belgium) and AFN stn's in Italy (see there). Prgr.: AFN Power Network (talk format, includes rel. of NPR and commercial US stn's) and Z-FM (music). – **1a) AFN Hessen** (on-air slogan: Z-98, produced in AFN Europe headquarter), Web: www.afneurope.net/hessen/. On 98.7MHz. – **2) AFN Würzburg** (on-air slogan: Big Red Radio; studio location: Würzburg, Leighton Barracks), Web: www.afneurope.net/wuerzburg/. On 1143/1485kHz and Illesheim 104.9MHz, own prgr. Mon-Fri 0400-0800 and 1400-1700, otherwhise rel. Power Network and other AFRTS feeds. Alternate Service on Würzburg 104.9MHz: Mixture of Power Network and Z-FM – **3) AFN Bavaria** (on-air slogan: The Big Gun; studio location: Vilseck, Rose Barracks), Web: www.afneurope.net/bavaria/. On 1107/1485kHz and 90.3/107.4MHz, own prgr. Mon-Fri 0500-0800 and 1400-1700, otherwhise rel. Z-FM. – **4) AFN Heidelberg** (on-air slogan: HOT FM), Web: www.afneurope.net/heidelberg/. On 102.3/104.6/107.3MHz. Own prgr. Mon-Fri 0400-0800 and 0200-0500, otherwhise rel. Z-FM and other AFRTS feeds. – **5) AFN Kaiserslautern** (on-air slogan: Z100.2), Web: www.afneurope.army.mil/kaiserslautern/. On 100.2/103.0MHz. Local prgr. Mon-Fri 0500-0900 and 1300-1700, Sat 0700-1100. Otherwhise rel. Z-FM, 103.0MHz Sat 1100-Mon 0500 Power Network instead. – **6)** Kalkar tr's of AFN have been closed down in 2004. – **7) AFN Eifel** (studio location: Spangdahlem airbase near Bitburg), Web: myafn.dodmedia.osd.mil/affiliates/detail.asp?affil_id=40 Own prgr. Mon-Fri 0500-0800, 1000-1200 and 1500-1700, Sat 0800-1000. Otherwise rel. Z-FM. **8) BFBS Germany**, Wentworth Barracks, Vlothoer Straße, 32049 Herford; Web: www.ssvc.com/ bfbs/radio/germany/index.htm. Own prgr. from Herford on BFBS Radio 1 network: Mon-Fri 0500-1300 and 1500-1800, Thu 0000-0200, Fri 1800-2000, Sat/Sun 0600-0900 and 1100-1300, Sat 2200-2400, Sun 1800-2000. – **9) Canadian Forces Network**, Slot 6041 PO Box 5053 STN FORCES, Belleville, Ontario K8N 5W6, Canada; Web: www.cfsue.de/cfn/. – **10) Radio Andernach** (German forces broadcasting sce.): Bundeswehr, Zentrum Operative Information, Kürrenberger Steig 34, 56727 Mayen; Web: www.radio-andernach.de. On 107.0MHz sporadic tr. tests only. Regular FM tr's at present in Bosnia (Rajlovac 97.7MHz), Serbia (Suva Reka 89.9MHz, Prizren 106.9MHz) and Afghanistan (Kabul 107.5MHz), carrying satellite feeds from Mayen and local shows.

GHANA

L.T: UTC — **Pop:** 20 million — **Pr.L:** English, Akan, Dagbani, Ga, Ewe, Hausa, Nzema, others — **E.C:** 50Hz, 230V — **ITU:** GHA

NATIONAL COMMUNICATIONS AUTHORITY (NCA)
✉ P.O. Box C1568, Cantonments, Accra ☎ +233 21 776621 ☎ +233 21 763449 **Web:** www.communication.gov.gh

GHANA BROADCASTING CORPORATION (GBC)
✉ Broadcasting House, P.O. Box 1633, Accra ☎ +233 21 221161-9 ☎ +233 21 221153 **Web:** www.gbc.com.gh
L.P: Interim board of directors: Chairman: Prof Kwame Karikari. Other members: George Dawson-Amoah and Georgette Francois.

SW: Accra (G.C: 05N31 000W10):

kHz	kW	Times
4915	50	D 0525-0915, SS 0915-1200, D 1200-2400

D.Prgr in **English & Vernaculars. French:** MF 1330-1500.
Network N. in E (relayed by all GBC stations)**:** 0600, 0700, 0900, 1100SS, 1300, 1400, 1800, 2000, 2200, 2345.
ANN: "This is Radio Ghana in Accra". **IS:** Sign on with drum beat.

Principal GBC FM regional stations:

Location	MHz	Name	Region
Accra	95.7	Uniiq FM	Greater Accra
Accra	96.5	Obonu FM	Greater Accra
Bolgatanga	89.8	URA Radio	Upper East
Cape Coast	92.5	R.Central	Central
Ho	91.5	Volta Star	Volta
Kumasi	92.1	Garden City R.	Ashanti
Sekondi-Takoradi	94.7	Twin City R.	West

Location	MHz	Name	Region
Tamale	91.2	R.Savanna	North
Wa	93.9	Upper West R.	Upper West
Koforidua	106.7	Sunrise FM	East

FM stations in Accra:
Atlantis R, P.O. Box 14629, Accra: 87.9MHz 4.5kW. Email: atlantis@ghana.com – **Channel R**, Accra: 92.7MHz – **Choice FM**, P.O. Box 18167, Accra: 102.3MHz. **Email:** choice@ncs.com.gh – **R. Gold FM**, P.O. Box 17298, Accra: 90.5MHz – **Happy FM**, Accra: 98.9MHz – **R. Hits**, Accra: 103.7MHz – **Joy FM**, PO Box 17202, Accra: 99.7MHz. **Web:** www.joy997.com.gh – **Peace FM**, Accra: 104.3MHz 5kW. **Web:** www.peacefmonline.com – **Sunny FM**, Accra: 88.7MHz – **R. Universe**, P.O. Box 436, Legon: 105.7MHz – **Vibe FM**, PO Box 3613, Accra 91.9 MHz. **Web:** www.vibefm.com.gh

BBC African Service: Accra 100.3MHz.
RFI Afrique: Accra 89.5MHz, Kumasi 92.9Mhz in French/English.
VOA relayed at times via private stations on 93.5/96.7/97.9/98.7/100.5/102.9/103.9MHz.

GIBRALTAR (British)

L.T: UTC +1h (27 Mar-30 Oct: UTC +2h) — **Pop:** 28,000 — **Pr.L:** English, Spanish — **E.C:** 50Hz, 240V — **ITU:** GIB

THE GIBRALTAR BROADCASTING CORP.
Broadcasting House, 18 South Barrack Rd, Gibraltar. ☎ +350 79760. 🖷 +350 78673. **Web:** www.gbc.gi. **Email:** gbc@ gibraltar.gi
L.P: GM: George Valarino.
MW: 1458kHz 2 kW.
FM: 92.6MHz 1kW, 91.3 & 100.5MHz 0.2kW (stereo).
Local sce. in English: 0600-1300 & 1500-1800. **Spanish:** 1300-1500. **Rel. BBC World Sce:** 1800-0600. **ANN:** "Radio Gibraltar".

Rock FM: 106.9MHz 0.3kW.

BRITISH FORCES BROADC. SCE. GIBRALTAR
BFBS Gibraltar, BFPO 52. ☎ +350 53720. 🖷 +350 55528.
Web: www.bfbs.com **Email:** nicky.ness@bfbs.com
FM:
BFBS Radio 1: North Mole 93.5 MHz; O'Hara's Battery 97.8 MHz 1 kW
BFBS Radio 2: North Mole 89.4 MHz; O'Hara's Battery 99.5 MHZ 0.25 kW
Local Prgrs: 0700-0900, 1200-1400, 1600-1800, 2200-2300.
Rel BBC World Sce: 0000(SS 2300)-0500.
ANN: "BFBS Community Radio on the Rock, BFBS 1/2 FM".

GREECE

L.T: UTC +2h (27 Mar-30 Oct: UTC +3h) — **Pop:** 11 million — **Pr.L:** Greek — **E.C:** 50Hz, 220V — **ITU:** GRC

ELLINIKI RADIOPHONIA TELEORASSI S.A. (ERT)
Messogeion 432, Aghia Paraskevi-Attikis, GR-15342 Athens ☎ +30 1 6066365 🖷 +30 1 6066309 **L.P:** Pres. & MD: Eugenios Giannakopolous **Web:** www.ert.ntua.gr **Email:** info@ert.gr

GREEK RADIO – ERA
P.O. Box 60019, Aghia Paraskevi-Attikis, GR-15310 Athens. ☎ +30 1 606 6700. 🖷 +30 1 606 6309 — **L.P:** DG: Apostolos Kossonas. Dir. Local R: Alexandris Arglias. Head of ERA 1: Christoforos Kontaxis. Head of ERA 2: Takis Psaridis. Head of ERA 3: Giorgos Tsangaris. Head of ERA 4: Makis Papazissis. Head of ERA 5: Filotas Gianottas. Dir. of Int. Rel: Evi Demiri. Head of Engineering Dept.:Kostantinidis Tsiakalos **Web:** www.ert.gr/radio **Email:** ktsiakalos@ert.gr

	MW	kHz	kW	Prgr.
	Athens	666	15	F
	Athens 1	729	150	1
2)	Ioannina	765	10	R
	Kavala	792	600	5
3)	Zakynthos	927	50	R
4)	Larisa	945	5	R
5)	Heraklion	954	10	R
	Athens 4	981	200	4
6)	Corfu	1008	50	R
7)	Thessaloniki 1	1044	150	M1
8)	Nea Orestiada	1080	10	R
7)	Thessaloniki 2	1179	50	M2, 4
	Rhodes	1260	500	5
9)	Florina	1278	10	R
10)	Tripolis	1314	10	R
11)	Pyrgos	1350	3	R
	Athens	1386	50	2,F
12)	Komotini	1404	100	R
13)	Patras	1485	1	R
14)	Volos	1485	1	R
	Nea Orestiada	1485	1	1
15)	Rhodes	1494	100	R
16)	Chania	1512	100	R
18)	Serres	1584	1	R
19)	Kavala	1601v	1	R
20)	Kozani	1602	1	R
	Samos	1602	1	1

Prgrs: 1=ERA NET, 4=ERA SPOR, M1=Macedonia, M2=Macedonia 2, R=Regional prgrs & rly. ERA 1,2 & 4. F= Filia Radio (mainly foreign-language broadcasts).

FM(MHz)	ERA1	ERA2	ERA3	ERA4	kW(ERP)
Akarnanika Mts	88.9	100.3	102.5	99.3	35
Alexandroupolis	89.8	91.8			3
Athens	91.6	103.7	90.9	101.8	100
	105.8		95.6		100
Chania	92.9	94.9			3
Corfu	91.8	93.8	89.9	101.1	10
Corinth	97.9	99.9			3
Euboea Isl.	107.4	88.8			3
Heraklion	94.4	96.4	91.3		3
Ioannina	97.8	99.8			3
Kalamata	92.2	94.2	89.3	100.4	3
Kastoria	88.6	90.6			10
Kavalla	89.2	91.2			10
Kephallonia Isl.	96.9	98.9	104.3	105.4	10
Larnia	104.2				10
Mytilini	92.3	94.3			3
Rhodes Isl.	88.4	90.4			3
Santorini	96.9	98.9			10
Thessaloniki	88.0	90.0	92.0		10
Tripolis	88.3	90.3			10
Volos	92.8	94.8	96.8	107.1	10

ERA REGIONAL STATIONS ON FM(MHz):
1) Northern Aegean: Chios 95.2/97.2, Ikaria Isl. 89.1, Lesbos 99.4, Limnos 96.5, Mytilini 102.1/103.0/104.4, Samos Isl. 89.7/103.9. All 35kW – **15) Southern Aegean:** Rhodes: 92.7/93.1 10kW, Kos/Thasos/Thira Isl. 93.3/98.4 – **6) Corfu:** 99.3 10kW – **16) Chania:** 95.2/99.3/104 35kW – **5) Heraklion** 97.5/103.6 3kW – **9) Florina:** 96.6 3kW – **2) Ioannina:** 102.1 3kW – **17) Kalamata:** 105.4 3kW – **19) Kavala:** 96.3 3kW – **12) Komotini:** 98.1/98.4 10kW – **20) Kozani** 100.2 3kW, Kozani 100.6 10kW – **4) Larisa** 98.3 13kW – **8) Nea Orestiada:** 103.5 3kW – **13) Patras:** 92.5 3 kW – **11) Pyrgos:** 102.4 3kW – **18) Serres:** 96.4/101.5 3kW – **10) Tripolis:** 95.2 10kW – **14) Volos:** 100.7 1.5kW, Pilion 101.2 10kW – **3) Zakynthos:** 95.2 3kW

Other ERT Stations:
Athens: Cosmos Radio 93.6MHz 100kW
Athens & Corinth: Filia Radio 666kHz & 107MHz

D.PRGR: All 24h. **1st prgr (ERA NET):** News, talk, current affairs. **N:** every hr. 0400-2300 except 0700 & 1600. **ERA 2** Mainly music. **N:** every hr. Foreign language N: Arabic 1703, Russian 1705, Polish 1803, Albanian 1805, English 1808, French 1903, Bulgarian 1905. 1386kHz: 0400-1400 ERA2, 1400-2000 relay of Filia R. **ERA 3** Classical music, arts & drama. **ERA 4 (ERA Spor) N:** every half hour, Sport N: every hour. Common night programme all channels 2300-0400UTC. **Regional programmes:** typically MF 0500-0800, 1600-1800, at other times relays of various national networks.

Regional station addresses:
1) Mytilini **2)** N. Papadoupoulou 2, GR-45444 Ioannina **3)** Ampelokipoi, GR-29100 Zakynthos **4)** Iroon Politehniou 1, GR-41222 Larisa **5)** Platia Deskalogianni, GR-71201 Heraklion-Kritis **6)** Ethniki Lefkimis, GR-49100 Kerkyra **8)** Euripidou 15, GR-68200 Nea Orestiada **9)** Megarovou 18, GR-53100 Florina **10)** Erithrou Staurou 1, GR-22100 Tripolis **11)** Diakou 16, GR-27100 Pyrgos **12)** 3 Km Komotinis-Kosmioi, GR-69100 Komotini **13)** Riga Feraiou 104, GR-

26001 Patras **14)** Plateja Aghiou Konstantinou, GR-32222 Volos **15)** 50 km Rodou-Kallitheas, GR-85100 Rhodes **16)** Ellis 40, GR-73200 Souda **17)** Anataliko Kentro 10-11, T.F. 98, GR-24100 Kalamata **18)** Stratopedou Kolokotroni, GR-62100 Serres **19)** Karakosta-Aghia Paraskevi, GR-65100 Kavala **20)** Tranta 19, GR-65000 Kozani.

7) RADIOPHONIKOS STATHMOS MAKEDONIAS

🖃 2 Angelaki, 54636 Thessaloniki ☎ +30 2310 299400 🖹 +30 2310 299655 **L P:** Dir.: Klearhos Tsaousidis, Head of Int. Rel.: Lefty Kongalides, Tech. Dir.: Papagiannis Vouras. **Web:** www.ert3.gr **Email:** p.vouras@ert3.gr *or* pr@ert3.gr
Macedonia 1 on MW 1044kHz + FM 102.0MHz 10kW.
Macedonia 2 on MW 1179kHz + FM 95.8MHz 10kW.
Relays abroad on shortwave: see International Radio section.
ANN: "Elliniki Radiophonia, Radiophonikos Stathmos Makedonias"

Radiophonikos Stathmos Amaliadas

🖃 Riga Feraiou-Aghio Trifonos 5, GR-27200 Amalias
MW: Amalias 1584kHz 1kW.

THE VOICE OF GREECE (ERA 5th Prgr.)

MW: 792kHz: 1000-1800, 1830-1900, 2100-2230, 2300-2400.
1260kHz: 1000-1500.
For details and shortwave usage see International Radio section.

PRIVATE RADIO

Main Networks

FM (MHz)	**1)**	**2)**	**3)**	**4)**	**5)**	**6)**	**7)**	**8)**
Aitoloakarnania		97.2	105.1	105.8	98.7		107.1	91.5
Akhaia	92.2	104.2	89.4	97.1	92.2	94.4	92.6	89.7
Alexandroupolis								106.0
Argolidos	105.2	106.3		97.5	104.7	102.3	98.1	
Arkadia	94.6			97.1		102.8	99.8	
Arta	106.8	100.1	101.5	103.1	95.6	96.0		
Athens	89.5	96.0	100.3	97.2	92.9	98.9		97.5
Chania		96.1	100.2	97.1		98.8	92.1	88.0
Corfu		101.1		92.6	94.8		103.5	107.9
Corinth						104.0		
Cyclades Isl.	89.9		92.6					
Dodecanese						96.9		98.5
Drama		96.9				95.5		
Evros					106.0			
Florina		89.6						
Fthiotida	89.7	107.6	96.3	101.6		100.5	90.0	
Grevena				94.0			106.0	
Heraklion	99.4	91.0	92.1	95.8	96.1	106.2	91.6	
Ileia	98.0	107.2					104.6	
Imathia						99.7		
Ioannina	89.0		105.1	102.7	104.7		87.8	105.7
Kalimnos	96.3	100.8						
Kastoria				102.9	97.5	94.7		92.0
Karbitsa					99.5			
Kavala		95.7	88.6	90.5		88.3	107.2	
Kefalonia					100.1			
Khalkidiki	93.7							
Khios	93.1							
Kilkis			106.3					
Kos		99.7					107.4	
Kozani		90.1	99.0			89.2		88.9
Laconias	89.1	93.5	89.7	97.9		96.7	95.8	
Lamia		95.5						
Larisa			100.4	101.9	99.5		106.2	
Lasithi	90.1					106.0		
Leros			103.1					
Levkada					95.6			
Lesbos		99.8	97.2			98.7		
Limnos	93.3	95.7						
Magnisia			103.0	97.3		88.6		105.5
Messinia	89.6		93.0	99.6	89.0		91.5	90.5
Mytilini	105.4	96.3			101.3			88.3
Nausis	88.8							
Preveza		100.1						
Pyrgos					103.3			
Rethimno								99.0
Rodopi		103.1						
Rhodes	104.0	99.5	100.9		107.8		90.0	
Samos	95.0	103.4	102.4					106.9
Santorini		106.4				100.0		97.2
Serres	107.2	99.6				90.9		
Simi					100.7			
Siros		95.8						
Sporades				102.3				
Thessaloniki	106.8	99.4			96.5		105.2	
Tinos	106.2							
Trikala			104.9	97.3	99.5	99.0		
Veroias	90.6							
Voiotia	106.9			102.9		104.1		
Xanthi	93.8					107.4		
Zakynthos		88.5	90.2					97.2

1) Radiofonikos Stathmos tis Ekklisias tis Ellados (rlg.), Athens. **Web:** www.ecclesia.gr/greek/ecclesiaradio **Email:** contact@ecclesia.gr – **2) Flash 96** 🖃 Leoforos Kifisias 64, 15125 Maroussi ☎ +30 1 6896100 🖹 +30 1 6896116 **Web:** www.flash.gr **Email:** flash@flash.gr – **3) Skai 100.3 FM** 🖃 Falireos 2-Eth. Makariou, 18547 Piraeus ☎ +30 1 4800170 🖹 +30 1 4800120 **Web:** www.skairadio.gr **Email:** skai@skairadio.gr – **4) Antenna Radio** 🖃 Kifisias 10-12, 15125 Maroussi ☎ +30 1 6842220 🖹 +30 1 6834349 **Web:** radio.antenna.gr **Email:** webmaster@antenna.gr – **5) Kiss FM** 🖃 Vas. Sofias 85, 15126 Maroussi ☎ +30 1 8050000 🖹 +30 1 8105000 **Web:** www.kiss.gr **Email:** info@kisss.gr – **6) Alpha Radio** 🖃 Pavlou Mela 25, 182 33 Rentis ☎ +30 1 4897507 🖹 +30 1 4897790 **Web:** www.alpharadio989.gr **Email:** radio@alphanews.gr – **7) Hristianismos FM** (rlg.) 🖃 P.O. Box 10530, 54110 Thessaloniki ☎ +30 31 0566362 **Web**: www.christians.gr **Email:** christians@christianity.gr – **8) Love Radio** 🖃 Dimitros 31, 17778 Tavros ☎ +30 1 3412607 🖹 +30 1 3412608 **Web:** www.loveradio.gr **Email:** info@loveradio.gr

ARMED FORCES RADIO & TV SERVICE (United States Air Force)

🖃 Det 4, Air Force European Broadc. Squadron (AFEBS), APO AE 09846, USA — SM: MSgt. Scott W. Kirby.
FM: Gournes 106.1MHz: 24h — **ANN:** "This is EBS Iraklion".

BBG relays:

MW: Kavala 792kHz 600kW: 3 hours daily.
MW: Rhodes 1260kHz 500kW: R. Sawa 1600-0900.
For details and shortwave relays see International Radio section.

GREENLAND

L.T: UTC -3h (DST*: UTC -2h). Pituffik/Thule area: UTC -4h(DST*: UTC -3h, not Thule), Ittoqqortoormiit/Danmarkshavn: UTC -1h (DST*: UTC) *DST: 27 Mar-30 Oct — **Pop:** 57,000 — **Pr.L:** Greenlandic, Danish — **E.C:** 50Hz, 220V — **ITU:** GRL

KALAALIT NUNAATA RADIOA – KNR (Gov. Comm.)

🖃 P.O. Box 1007, DK-3900 Nuuk. ☎ +299 361600. 🖹 +299 326238. **Web:** www.knr.gl
L.P: MD: Lars Lennert-Sandgreen. Head of programming: Stina Skifte. Head of News: Maria Simonsen. Head of radio: Stephen Heilmann.

MW	**kHz**	**kW**	**MW**	**kHz**	**kW**
Nuuk	570	5	Upernavik	810	5
Qeqertarsuaq	650	5	Uummannaq	900	5
Simiutaq	720	10			
FM	**MHz**	**kW**	**FM**	**MHz**	**kW**
Nuuk*	90.5	0.05	Aasiaat	95.5	0.1
Sisimiut	95.0	0.1	Ilulissat	96.0	0.05
Kangerlussuaq	96.0	0.01	Tasillaq	96.0	0.05
Uummannaq	95.0	0.05			

+ 60 additional st's 0.05 kW or less. *) = stereo
SW: 3815kHz USB (0.2kW) Tasiilaq: 1500-1615, 2100-2215. N: Greenlandic: 1515, 2130. Danish: 1530, 2200
D.Prgr: MF 0930-0130, SS 1000-0130. Relays DR P1, Denmark, daily from 0500.
ANN: "Kallaallit-Nunaata Radioa", "Grønlands Radio" **IS:** "Sunnia Kalippoq" (The Whaleboat "Sonja" drags whale) played on celeste.
DR P1, Denmark. Sat. relay 24h: Nuuk 98.0MHz (0.1kW)

Private stations (local radio):
Aasiaat: Tusaat Aasiaat, Box 20, 3950 Aasiaat: 93.0MHz (0.1kW). – **Grønnedal**: R. Grønnedal, Grønlands Kommando, 3930 Kangilinnguit: 91.5MHz (0.015kW). – **Ilulissat:** Ilulissat Radio-at 99 MHz, Box 1004, 3952 Ilulissat: 99.0MHz (0.1kW). – **Kangerlussuaq:** KLR Kangerlussuaq Lokal Radio, Box 37, 3910 Kangerlussuaq: 98.5MHz (0.025kW). – **Maniitsoq:** Maniitsup Tusaataa Akisuasoq, Box 29, 3912 Maniitsoq: 90.5MHz (0.1kW), 93.0MHz (0.1kW), 99.0MHz (0.1kW. – **Nuuk:** Nuuk FM, Box 1462, 3900 Nuuk: 93.0MHz (0.1kW) – **Paamiut**: Paamiut Tusaataat, Box 229, 3940 Paamiut:

93.0MHz (0.02kW). – **Pituffik/Thule Air Base:** Radio OZ520, Den Danske Radio, SPE, Box 139, Thule Air Base, 3970 Pituffik: 97.1MHz (0.1kW) – **Qaanag:** Qaanaaq Radiunga, Box 57, 3971 Qaanag: 93.5MHz (0.02kW). – **Sisimiut:** Sisimiut Tusaataat, Box 312, 3911 Sisimiut: Sarfannguit 91.0MHz (0.02kW), Sisimiut 93.0MHz (0.05kW), Kangerlussuaq 93.0MHz (0.02kW), Sarfannguit 98.0MHz (0.02kW). – **Tasiilaq:** Tasiilap Tusaalaa, Ittimiini B.883, 3913 Tasiilaq: 93.0MHz (0.02kW). – **Uummannaq:** Tusaat Uummannaq, Box 195, 3961 Uummannaq: 98.2MHz (0.075kW)

GRENADA

L.T: UTC -4h — **Pop:** 94,000 — **Pr.L:** English — **E.C:** 50Hz, 230/400V — **ITU:** GRD

GRENADA BROADCASTING NETWORK – G.B.N. Radio (Gov, Comm.)

Observatory Road, P.O. Box 535, St. George's ☎ +1 473 440 3826. 🖷 +1 473 444 5054. **Web:** www.klassicgrenada.com. **Email:** gbn@caribsurf.com. **L.P:** MD: Richard Purcell. PD: Andre Jerome. CE: Kennedy Bowen. N Dir: Odette Campbell.
MW: 535kHz (2 x 10kW) **FM:** 98.5/105.5MHz.
Klassic 535: 535kHz and 105.5MHz: 24h. – **Sun FM:** 98.5MHz: 24h.

THE HARBOUR LIGHT OF THE WINDWARDS (Rlg.)

Carriacou ☎ +1 473 443 7628 🖷 +1 473 443 7628. **Web:** www.harbourlightradio.org & www.lastchanceministries.com/harbourlight.htm. **Email**: harbourlight@caribsurf.com.
L.P: SM: Randy Cornelius.
MW: 1400kHz (5kW) **FM:** 92.3 (Lp.) & 94.5MHz (1kW).
D.Prgr: MW: 0953-0235. FM: 24h. **N:** rel. BBC & VOA.
ANN: "This is the Harbour Light of the Windwards broadcasting from beautiful and friendly Carriacou"

PRIVATE STATIONS
City Sound, River Road, St. George's. ☎ +1 473 440 9616. **L.P.:** Mgr Alphonses Strachan. **FM:** 97.5MHz.
CR-FM Community Radio: Morne Jaloux, St. George's. ☎ +1 473 440 4848. 🖷 +1 473 440 4991. **L.P.:** Mgr Rawl Ghatt. **FM:** 89.5MHz.
GN FM - Good News FM, Marrast Hill, St. George's. ☎ +1 473 435 1301. 🖷 +1 473 435 1278. **FM:** 96.3MHz. **Format**: Rlg., regional.
GNG – Good News Grenada Radio, Box 224, St. George's. ☎ +1 473 435 0143. **L.P.**: Cyril Hopkin. **FM**: 99.5MHz (+ 1 planned). **Format**: Rlg.
Kayack 106 FM, Church Street, Hillsborough, Carriacou. ☎ +1 473 443 7733. 🖷 +1 473 443 6262. **FM:** 106.3MHz.
SAC FM, St. Andrews Connection, Grenville. ☎ +1 473 442 4745. 🖷 +1 473 438 0338. **L.P.:** Mgr. Bernard La Mothe. **FM:** 104.7MHz.
Spice Capital Radio, PO Box 90, St. George's. ☎ & 🖷 +1 473 440 3601. **L.P.:** Mgr Paul Roberts. **FM:** 90.1MHz.
VOG – Voice of Grenada, Lagoon Road, St. George's. ☎ +1 473 440 8171. 🖷 +1 473 440 8505. **L.P.:** Mgr Errol Maitland. **FM:** 88.9/95.7/103.3MHz.
WEE FM, Grenada Wireless Comm. Network, Lower Depradine St, PO Box 555, Gouyave, St. John's. ☎ +1 473 437 4933 / 444 3473. 🖷 +1 473 437 0521. **L.P.:** GM: Alvin Dabreo. **FM:** 93.3/93.9MHz

GUADELOUPE (French)

L.T: UTC -4h — **Pop:** 431,000 — **Pr.L:** French, Créole Patois — **E.C:** 50Hz, 220V — **ITU:** GDL

RADIO GUADELOUPE

Morne Bernard-Destrellan, B.P. 180, F-97122 Baie-Mahault. ☎ +590 939696. 🖷 +590 939682. **L.P:** Dir: R.Surjus. Editor-in-Chief: Philippe Goudé. PD: L.Francil. Head Communications Dept: Sonia Gémieux.
MW: Point-à-Pitre 640kHz 40kW.
FM: Point-à-Pitre 88.9 MHz, Marie Galante 89.1 MHz, Deshaies 96.8MHz, Basse-Terre 97.0MHz, Pointe-Noire 97.4 MHz.
D.Prgr: 24h. **N:** 1100, 1700, 2230, plus relays of France-Inter.
ANN: "Ici Point-à-Pitre, RFO Guadeloupe" or "RFO".
IS: "Biguin" (guitar) — **V.** by QSL-card. Rp.

RCI - RADIO CARAÏBES INTERNATIONAL GUADELOUPE (Comm.)

RCI Guadeloupe, B.P. 1309, F-97187 Point-à-Pitre Cédex. ☎ +590 839696. 🖷 +590 839697 — **FM:** 95.1/98.6/106.MHz.
D.Prgr: 24h. **N:** on the h. (rel. Europe 1).

RCI 2 (Comm.)

FM: 96.3/100.6/102.6MHz (rel. RCI 2 St. Martin) — **D.Prgr:** 24h.
Europe 2: Basse Terre 96.6MHz, Point-à-Pitre 103.4MHz.
R. France Internationale: via R. Basse Terre 98.2MHz and Ile FM 103.0MHz.
Other stations: over 30 FM st's are operating.

SAINT MARTIN & SAINT BARTH

RADIO GUADELOUPE

FM: St. Martin 88.9MHz, St. Barth 88.6MHz (see main entry above)

RCI - RADIO CARAÏBES INTERNATIONAL GUADELOUPE (Comm.)

FM: St. Martin 105.0MHz (see main entry above)

RCI2 (Comm.)

RCI2 Saint Martin, B.P. 173, Marigot, F-97150 Saint Martin. ☎ +590 875406. 🖷 +590 878887.
FM: 102.1MHz + relays in Guadeloupe & Martinique.

RADIO SAINT MARTIN (Comm.)

Port de Marigot, F-97150 Saint Martin — Mgr: H. Cocks.
FM: 95.3MHz — **D.Prgr:** 1000-0500(Sun 0400) in French & English exc. **Spanish:** 2000-2100W.

RADIO VOIX CHRETIENNES DE ST. MARTIN (Rlg.)

B.P. 103, Marigot, F-97150 Saint Martin. ☎ +590 873159.
L.P: Mgr: Father Cornelius Charles — **FM:** 106MHz 0.25kW.
D.Prgr: 0845-0530 in English & French.

R. France Internationale: via R. St. Barth 100.7MHz.

GUAM (U.S. Territory)

L.T: UTC +10h — **Pop:** 158,000 — **Pr.L:** English, Chamorro, Filipino — **E.C:** 60Hz, 110/220V — **ITU:** GUM

	MW	kHz	kW		MW	kHz	kW
2)	KGUM	567	10	6)	KTWG	801	10
1)	KUAM	612	10/1				
	FM	**MHz**	**kW**		**FM**	**MHz**	**kW**
9)	KHMG	88.1	8	2)	KZGZ	97.5	40
7)	KPRG	89.3	6.6	4)	KOKU	100.3	5
8)	KOLG	90.9	5.7	2)	KTKB	101.9	50
5)	KSDA	91.9	3.8	11)	KISH	102.9	25
1)	KUAM	93.9	5.2	2)	KGUM	105.1	12
3)	KSTO	95.5	25				

Addresses and other information
1) Box 368, Agana, Guam 96910. **Web:** www.kuam.com/isla61 – Pres. & GM: Joey Calvo. Asst. SM: James Castro. CE: Richard Garman. PD (AM): Lynda Evangelista. **Email:** lyndae@isla61.com. KUAM-AM: "Isla 61" Chamorro Music. KUAM-FM: "94 Jamz". (10kW 1400-0800, 1kW 0800-1400). – **2)** Sorensen Pacific Broadcasting Inc, P.O. Box GM, Agana, Guam 96932. ☎ +671 477-5700 🖷 +671 477-3982 **Web:** www.radiopacific.com **Email:** k.sorenson@spbguam.com – Pres: Rex Sorensen. GM Jon Anderson. VP: Kathleen Sorensen. CE: Marvin Palmer. KGUM-AM: 24h news/talk in English. KZGZ: 24h CHR. KGUM-FM: 24h rock **N.** on the h (rel. CBS). Ann: "Newstalk 57 AM", "Power 98 FM" "The Rock". – **3)** KSTereO FM 95.5, Inter-Island Communications, 4th Flr, Bank of Hawaii Bldg, Agana (or P.O. Box 20249, GMF 96921). **N:** rel. AP. **Email:** ksto@ite.net. – **4)** Hit Radio 100, 530 W. O'Brien Dr, Hagatna, Guam 96910 – GM & Sales Mgr: E.Galito. PD: C. Cruz. 24h CHR. **N.** at :55. **Web:** www.hitradio100.com **Email:** hr100@netpci.com – **5)** Joy 92, 290 Chalan Palasyo, Agana Heights, Guam 96919. ☎ +671 477 4678 🖷 +671 472 5732 **Web:** www.joy92.net **Email:** mail@ joy92.net – SM: John Geli. **N:** rel CNN Radio N. Ann: "Family Friendly Radio" – **6)** see Trans World Radio Pacific (below). – **7)** Guam Educational Radio Foundation, Univ. of Guam, Bldg. 13, Dean's Circle, UOG Station, Mangilao 96923 (NPR affiliate). **Web:** www.guam.net/kprg – **8)** Light 91, Catholic Educational R, Archdiocese Agana, P.O. Box DZ, Agana 96910 – GM: Fr. David Quitugua. – **9)** Harvest Family Radio, Box 23-189 Barrigada 96921. ☎ +671 477 6341 🖷 +671 477 7136 LP: Pres: Pastor Marty Herron. Stn Mgr: John Collier. **Web:** www.harvestministries.net **Email:** khmg@havestministries.net – Format: Christian music. News from American Family Radio Tues – Sat mornings – **10)** KM Communications Inc, 3654 W. Jarvis Ave., Skokie, IL. 60076. **Web:** www.kmcommunications.com/Radio/agana,_gu_.htm **Email:** kevinbae@kmcommunications.com – **11)** Inter Island Communi-cations Inc. (comm). P.O. Box 914, Saipan, CM 96950. ☎ +670 234 7239. 🖷 +670 234 0447. **L.P:** GM: Hans W. Mickelson. PD: Ken Warnick. CE: Angel Ocampo. N. Dir: Ken Phillips. **Web:** www.itecnmi.com/news.

ADVENTIST WORLD RADIO - ASIA (Rlg.)
See International Broadcasting section.

TRANS WORLD RADIO PACIFIC (Rlg.)
✉ P.O. Box CC, Agana,.Guam 96910-8980 ☎ +1 (671) 477 9701 🖷 +1 (671) 477 2838 **Email:** ktwg@twr.hafa.net.gu **Web:** www.ktwg.com
L.P: MD: Harry Bettig. PD: Jim Elliott. CE: Robert Chick. Head of PR: Glenn Scheyhing.
MW: KTWG 801kHz 10kW: 2000-1300 in English exc. International Hour Mon-Fri 1100-1200 (Mon, Tagalog, Tues, Mandarin, Wed, Korean, Thurs, Chamorro, Fri, Japanese).
SW: see International Broadcasting section.
IS: "We've a Story to Tell the Nations" played on an organ. **V.** by QSL-card. 3 IRC's for airmail reply, one for surface mail. Rec. acc.
PUB: Frequency schedule on request.

GUATEMALA

L.T: UTC -6h — **Pop:** 12 million — **Pr.L:** Spanish — **E.C:** 60Hz, 120V — **ITU:** GTM

SUPERTEL
✉ 14 Calle N° 3-51, Z-10, Edif. Murano, Nivel 16, Guatemala
☎ +502 366 5880.

MW: Call TG-,° = also on SW, * = inactive, (r) = repeater, v = varying fq.

Call	kHz	kW	Name and h. of tr.
AV01)	540	1	R. Cobán, Cobán
SO03)	540	0.025	R. Amistad, San Pedro de Laguna
GU01) RV	560	10	R. 5-60, Guatemala: 1200-0500
SM01)	560	1	R. Quetzal, Malacatán
ES01) PA	570	1	R. Palmeras, Escuintla
GU02) Y	580	5	R. Progreso, Guatemala: 1100-0600
QU01) RQ	590	5	R. Quiché, Sta Cruz del Quiché: 1100-0400
ES02) RC	600	1	Emisoras Unidas Campesina, Escuintla
GU03) GA	610	0.5	R. Alianza, Guatemala: 1130-0300
TO01) PQ	620	5	R. 6-20, San Cristóbal: 1200-0400
PE01) EL	630	1	R. El Porvenir, Sta Elena: 1000-0400
GU04) W	640	10	R. Nacional "LV de Guatemala", Guatemala: irr
QE01) Q	660	3	R. Nacional "LV de Quetzaltenango", Quetzaltenango: 1100-0400
GU05) RT	670	10	Emisoras Unidas Central, Guatemala
AV02) VP	680	10	R. Norte, Cobán: 1100-0400
JU01) VB	690	1	R. Tamazulapa, Jutiapa
GU06) HR	700	15	R. Mundial, Guatemala: 1000-0600
QE02) XL	710	1	R. Tecún Umán, Quetzaltenango: 1030-0400
IZ01) RO	720	1	R. Corona, Morales: 24h
GU07) N	°730	10	R. Cultural, Guatemala: 24h
SM02) HF	740	1	Emisoras UnidasTacaná, San Marcos
ES03) AJ	750	1	R. Tropicana "Circuito Dos", Escuintla
GU08) HB	760	5	Nueva R. Super, Guatemala: 1000-0500
QE03) BX	770	1	R. Fraternidad, Quetzaltenango: 1000-0600
ZA01) CK	780	1	R. Sultana del Oriente, Zacapa
GU09) O	790	3	R. Festival, Guatemala: 1100-0400
SR01) YZ	800	1	R. Rosa, Chiquimulilla: 24h
PE02)	810		R. Moapán, Sta Elena
GU10) TO	820	10	R. Internacional, Guatemala: 1000-0600
SU01) AV	830	5	R. Satélite, Mazatenango: 1100-0400
SM03) SM	840	0.35	LV de San Marcos, San Marcos: 1300-0400
GU11) X	850	10	R. Ciro, Guatemala: 1000-
PE03) FP	*860	1	R. Nal. Tikal, Flores
SU02) L	v870	0.5	R. Victoria, Mazatenango
GU12) J	880	10	R. Nuevo Mundo, Guatemala: 1030-0500
ES04) HU	890	1	R. Escuintla, Escuintla
IZ02) MA	900	1	R. Amatique, Puerto Barrios
GU30) KL	910	10	R. Emperador, Guatemala: 1130-0600
ES05) RS	920	0.2	R. Sur, Escuintla
AV03) JL	v930	5	Emisoras Unidas Imperial, San Pedro Carchá
GU13) TL	940	5	LV del Hogar "R.Paz", Guatemala: 1200-0500
GU13) TL	940	1	LV del Hogar "R.Paz", Sacatepeque (r: 940)
SU03) AF	950	1	R. Indiana, Mazatenango
QU02) RU	960	1	Emisoras Unidas Utatlán, Sta Cruz del Quiché
GU14) AX	970	5	R. Continental, Guatemala: 1200-0430
SM04) MQ	980	1	R. Retama, San Marcos: 1200-0500
CH01) AL	990	1	R. Perla de Oriente, Chiquimula: 24h
IZ06)	1010	1	R. Caribe, Izabal
QU03) XI	1010	1	R. Emmanuel, Nebaj: 1100-0200
SM05) CM	1020	5	R. Frontera, Pajapita: 1100-0400
GU15) UX	1030	10	R. Panamericana, Guatemala: 1145-0500
JA01) JP	1040	1	R. Oriental, Jalapa
HU01) SL	1050	5/1	LV de los Cuchumatanes, Huehuetenango: 1100-0600
GU16) T	1060	10	R. Favorita, Guatemala: 1100-0600
QE04) D	1070	3/2	LV de Occidente, Quetzaltenango: 1200-0400
ZA02) LU	1080	1	R. Viva, Zacapa
GU05) Z	1090	10	Emisoras Unidas Central, Guatemala
QE05) SR	1100	1	R. Superior, Coatepeque
AV04) MK	1110	1	R. Verapaz, Cobán
GU17) C	1120	0.5	R. Uno 120 AM, Guatemala
RE01) VR	1130		Emisoras Unidas LV de la Costa Sur, Retalhuleu
GU18) RR	1150	1	R. Fiesta, Guatemala: 24h
IZ03) RI	1160	1	R. Izabal, Morales: 1100-0130
QE06) RL	1170	5	R. Cadena Landívar, Quetzaltenango: 0900-0300
GU17) T	1180	10	R. Sonora, Guatemala: 1100-0600 (r: 1060)
JU02) RJ	1200	1	R. Jutiapa, Jutiapa
GU19) MX	1210	10/5	Coco Radio, Guatemala: 24h
SA01) MT	1220	1	R. Amiga, Antigua: 1100-0300
IZ04) AT	1230	1	R. Atlántida, Puerto Barrios: 1130-0500
SU04)	1230		R. América, Cuyotenango
GU20) K	1240	5	R. Luz, Guatemala: 1200-
CH02) PY	1250	1	R. Payakí, Esquipulas: 1100-0300
TO04)	1250		LV Cristiana, Totonicapán
GU21) CQ	1270	2.5	R. Exclusiva, Guatemala: 24h
BV01) VY	1280	2.5	R. Zamaneb, Salamá: 1100-0200
TO02) TU	1290	0.5	R. Nal. de Totonicapán, Totonicapán: 0000-0400
ZA03)	1290		R. Miramundo "LV del Ejercito", Zacapa
QE07) AN	1310	1	R. LV de los Altos, Quetzaltenango: 1100-0500
JU03) ME	1320	1	R. Quesada, Jutiapa
GU22) MU	°1330	5.5	Unión Radio "LV de la Esperanza", Guatemala: 1100-2330
QE08) CO	1340	10	Emisoras Unidas LV del Trópico, Coatepeque
AV05) MC	1350	1	R. Monja Blanca, Cobán
GU16) LK	1360	10	R. Tic Tac "LV del Tiempo", Guatemala: 1100-0500
QE09) AC	1370	1	LV de Colomba, Colomba: 1200-0300
TO03) EB	1380	1	R. Momostenango Educativa, Momostenango: 1100-1900
GU23) YC	1390	5	R. Istmania, Guatemala: 1130-0330
IZ05) RB	1400	1	R. Porteña, Puerto Barrios: 24h
QE10) GH	1410	5	R. Xelajú, Quetzaltenango: 1200-0600
GU24) RP	1420	1	R. Verdad, Guatemala: 1130-0600
HU02) AG	1430	1.2	LV de Huehuetenango: 1100-0400
SU05) MS	1440	0.5	R. Nal., Mazatenango: 0000-0400
GU06) LG	1450	1	R. Epoca, Guatemala
PE04) RN	1460	2.5	R. Petén, Flores: 1100-0500
GU25) HB	1480	5	R. Buenas Nuevas, Guatemala: 1030-
RE02) RE	1490	1	R. Modelo, Retalhuleu: 0900-0300
SO01) DS	1490	1	R. LV de Atitlán, Santiago Atitlán
GU26) DX	1510	5	R. Centroamericana "Nueva RCA", Guatemala: 1130-0500
PE05)	1520	1	R. Taysal, Sta Elena de la Cruz
QE11) RS	1520	1	R. Superior, Coatepeque
GU29)	1540	1	R. Cultura y Deportes, Guatemala
GU27) VE	1570	10	VEA - Voz Evengélica de América, Guatemala: 1030-0600
CM01) XC	1590	1	R. Triunfadora, Chimaltenango
GU28) ML	1600	5	R. María "LV de la Familia", Guatemala: 1130-0500

SW:
Stations with a (*) are reported to be inactive, but may occasionally be reactivated for variable periods of time.

Call	kHz	kW	Name and h. of tr.
GU07) NC	*3300	10	R. Cultural, Guatemala
HU03) BA	v3325	0.2	R. Maya, Barillas: 0900-1230, 2100-0330
SO02) VN	*3360	1	R. LV de Nahualá, Nahualá
CH03) CH	*3380	1	R. Chortís, Jocotán: 1055-1300, 2100-0330
CH04) AV	v4052	0.8	R. Verdad, Chiquimula: 1130-0500 (rep: 4052.5)
SO03)	*4699	0.5	R. Amistad, San Pedro La Laguna:
HU04) LT	4780	1	R. Cultural Coatán, San Sebastián Coatán: 1100-1500, 2200-0230
HU05) MI	v4800	1	R. Buenas Nuevas, San Sebastián, Huehuetenango: 1930-1545, 2130-0230
QE12) MN	*4825	0.5	R. Mam, Cabricán
AV07) VC	4845	1.25	R. K'ekchi, Fray Bartolomé de las Casas: irr
GU07) NA	*5955	0.5	R. Cultural, Guatemala

State abbreviations: (Departamentos) AV = Alta Verapaz, BV = Baja Verapaz, CH = Chiquimula, CM = Chimaltenango, ES = Escuintla, GU = Guatemala, HU = Huehuetenango, IZ = Izabal, JA = Jalapa, JU =

Jutiapa, PE = Petén, QE = Quetzaltenango, QU = Quiché, RE = Retalhuleu, SA = Sacatepéquez, SR = Santa Rosa, SM = San Marcos, SO = Solola, SU = Suchitepequez, TO = Totonicapán, ZA = Zacapa. **N.B:** These abbreviations are not recognized by the Post Office. Letters should therefore carry the full name.

Addresses and other information:
AV00) ALTA VERAPAZ
AV01) 5 Calle 1-06, Z-3, 16001Cobán. – **AV02)** 2 Calle 5-57, Z-3, 16001Cobán. – **AV03)** 5 Calle 7-53, Z-1, San Pedro Carchá. – **AV04)** 2 Calle 5-57, Z-3, 16001Cobán. – **AV05)** Edif. Municipalidad, 5a Calle 1-06, 16001Cobán. – **AV07)** 3 Calle 7-15, 2-1, 16015 Fray Bartolomé de las Casas (or: Ap. 25, 53140 Bulevares, Edo Mex., México). Prgrs in Spanish and Q'eqchí.
BV00) BAJA VERAPAZ
BV01) Inst. de Educación Básica, Barrio Abajo San Jerónimo, 15001Salamá. Prgrs. in Spanish, Achi and Q'eqchí.
CH00) CHIQUIMULA
CH01) 7 Calle Av. 4-00, Z-1, 20001Chiquimula (or: 6 Av. 0-60, Z-4, Torre Prof. II, Of. 904, 01004 Guatemala). – **CH02)** 5 Av. 6-37, Z-1, 20007 Esquipulas. - **FM:** 91.5. – **CH03)** Centro Social, 20004 Jocotán. **Email:** chortifmtierra@hotmail.com **FM:** 89.5 – **CH04)** Estación Educativa Evangélica, Ap. 5 (or: 4 Av. 2-24, Z-1), 20901 Chiquimula. **Email:** radioverdad@chiquimula.zzn.com ☎ +502 9 425689. 🖷+502 9 420362 - **FM:** 102.7.
CM00) CHIMALTENANGO
CM01) 2 Calle 3-33, Z-3, 04001Chimaltenango.
ES00) ESCUINTLA
ES01) 15 Calle 2-48, Z-3, 05001Escuintla. – **ES02)** Col. 15 de Junio, Z-3, Tiquisate, 05001Escuintla. - **FM:** 92.3. – **ES03)** 4 Av. 6-26, Z-1, 05001Escuintla. – **ES04)** 4 Av. 11-38, Z-1, 05001Escuintla. – **ES05)** Central American Benevolent Association, 05001Escuintla - **FM:** 96.3.
GU00) GUATEMALA
GU01) 8 Calle 1-11, Z-1, 01001Guatemala. – **GU02)** 9 Av. 0-32, Z-2, 01002 Guatemala. ☎ +502 2 542440. 🖷+502 2 542541. – **GU03)** 34 Av. "A" 7-60, Z-7, 01007 Guatemala. – **GU04)** 18 Calle 6-72, Z-1, 01001Guatemala. – **GU05)** 4 Calle 6-84, Z-13, 01013 Guatemala. **Web:** www.emisorasunidas.com – **GU06)** 6 Av. 2-80, Z-1, 01001Guatemala – **GU07)** Ap. 601 (or: 4 Av. 30-09, Z-3), 01901 Guatemala. **English:** 0300-0430.☎+502 4 710807. 🖷+502 4 400260. **Web:** www.radiocultural.com **Email:** tgna@guate.net – **GU08)** 30 Av. 3-86, Z-11, Utatlán II, 01011 Guatemala. – **GU09)** 11 Calle 2-43, Z-1, 01001Guatemala. – **GU10)** 11 Av. 18-55, Z-2, Ciudad Nueva, 01002 Guatemala. – **GU11)** Calzada San Juan 7-90, Edif.Acuario, Z-7, 01007 Guatemala. – **GU12)** 6 Av. 10-45, Z-1, 01001Guatemala. – **GU13)** Ap. 31, 01901 Guatemala. – **GU14)** 15 Calle 3-45, Z-1, 01001Guatemala. – **GU15)** 1 Av. 35-48, Z-7, Col. Toledo, 01007 Guatemala. ☎ +502 5 958504. 🖷+502 5 912293. – **GU16)** 10 Calle 5-20, Z-1, 01001Guatemala. **Web:** www.infovia.com.gt/sonora/ – **GU17)** Ruta 105, Guatemala. – **GU18)** Grupo Radial El Tajín, 2 Av. "A" 13-45, Z-1, 01001 Guatemala. – **GU19)** 4 Av. 1-14, Z-1, 01001Guatemala. – **GU20)** Ap. 281, 01901 Guatemala. – **GU21)** 4 Calle 35-76, Utatlán 2, Z-11, 01011Guatemala. – **GU22)** Ap. 51-C, 01015 Guatemala. Owned and operated by Adventist World Radio. – **GU23)** 24 Av.del Ferrocarrill 23-39, Z-12, Centro San Pablo, 01012 Guatemala. – **GU24)** 4 Av. 0-60, Z-4, 01004 Guatemala. – **GU25)** 17 Av.21, Cnt.Com Las Pergolas, Z-11, 01011Guatemala. – **GU26)** 3 Av. 6-32, Z-1, 01001Guatemala. – **GU27)** Ap. 1213 (or: 30 Av. "A" 7-33, Z-7, Col. Tikal, 01007 Guatemala) 01901 Guatemala. **Email:** radiovea@yahoo.com – **GU28)** Carr. Roosevelt km 15, Z-2, Mixco, Entrada por el Convento de la Visitación de Sta María, 01002 Guatemala. ☎+502 5 979618. 🖷+502 4 718815. Prgrs in Cakchiquel and Quiché. – **GU29)** Guatemala – **GU30)** Av. 14 Calle 11-63, Z-1, Guatemala.
HU00) HUEHUETENANGO
HU01) 2 Calle 4-42, Z-1, 13001 Huehuetenango. – **HU02)** Ap. 13, 13901Huehuetenango. – **HU03)** 4 Av. 0-14, Z-1, 13026 Barillas. ☎/🖷 +502 7 802132. – **HU04)** San Sebastián Coatán. –
HU05) 13020 San Sebastián H, Huehuetenango.
IZ00) IZABAL
IZ01) Calle Principal, Morales. – **IZ02)** Ruta Atlántico km 291, 18001 Puerto Barrios. – **IZ03)** Barrio El Carrizal, Morales. – **IZ04)** Ap. 425, 18901Puerto Barrios. – **IZ05)** 8 Av. 15 y 16 Calle, 18001 Puerto Barrios. – **IZ06)** Izabal.
JA00) JALAPA
JA01) Av. Chipilapa "A" 1-03, Z-2, 21001 Jalapa.
JU00) JUTIAPA
JU01) Calle 15 Septiombre, Sta Cruz, 22001 Jutiapa. – **JU02)** Carr. Interamericana km 117, 22001 Jutiapa. – **JU03)** Quezada.
PE00) PETÉN
PE01) Sta Elena de la Cruz. **FM:** 96.9. – **PE02)** Sta Elena de la Cruz. – **PE03)** 17001 Flores. – **PE04)** Isleta Sta Bárbara, 17001 Flores (or: 1 Av 1-22, Z-1, Guatemala). **Email:** radiopeten@hotmail.com ☎/🖷+502 2 515516. **FM:** 105.3. – **PE05)** Ministerio de la Defensa Nacional, Sta Elena de la Cruz.
QE00) QUETZALTENANGO
QE01) Ap. 113 (or: 13 Av. 8-19, Z-1), 09901Quetzaltenango. –
QE02) 6 Av. 6-41, Z-1, 09001 Quetzaltenango. – **QE03)** Ap. 90, 09901 Quetzaltenango. - **FM:** 99.1.– **QE04)** 7 Av. 0-26, Z-2, 09002 Quetzaltenango. ☎+502 7 610582. 🖷+502 7 612062. – **QE05)** 3 Calle 3-38, Z-1, Coatepeque. – **QE06)** 14 Av. "A" 0-78, Z-1, 09002 Quetzaltenango. – **QE07)** Ap. 107, 09901 Quetzaltenango. – **QE08)** 2 Av. 2-02, Z-3, Barrio San Francisco, Coatepeque. – **QE09)** Calle Principal, Z-2, Colomba. ☎+502 7 723050. 🖷+502 7 723075. -**FM:** 99.1. – **QE10)** 4 Calle 15A-62, Z-1, 09002 Quetzaltenango. – **QE11)** 3 Calle 3-38, Z-1, Coatepeque, Retalhuleu. – **QE12)** Acu'Mam, Cabricán - **FM**:105.1.
QU00) QUICHÉ
QU01) 7 Calle 3-67, Z-5, 14001 Sta Cruz del Quiché. **Email:** rquiche@intelnet.net.gt - **FM:** 91.5. – **QU02)** 5 Av. 4-22, Z-2, 14001 Sta Cruz del Quiché. – **QU03)** 5 Av. 1-32, Canton Batzbaca, 14013 Nebaj.
RE00) RETALHULEU
RE01) Ap. 84, 11901Retalhuleu. – **RE02)** 7 Av. 6-72, 11001 Retalhuleu (or: Ap. 183-A, Guatemala).
SA00) SACATEPÉQUEZ
SA01) Av. del Desengaño 20, 03001 Antigua Guatemala.
SR00) SANTA ROSA
SR01) Edif. Municipal, Chiquimulilla.
SM00) SAN MARCOS
SM01) 5 Calle 3-58, Z-1, Malacatán. – **SM02)** 8 Calle 8-01, Z-2, 12001 San Marcos. – **SM03)** Palacio Maya, 12001 San Marcos. – **SM04)** 5 Calle 8-21, Z-1, San Pedro. – **SM05)** Pajapita, 12001 San Marcos.
SO00) SOLOLA
SO01) Cantón Xechivoy, 07019 Santiago Atitlán. - **FM**: 103. 5. – **SO02)** Asociación Pro-Desarollo y Educación Popular, 4 Av.4-62, Z-4, Nahualá. ☎+502 7 630163. **FM:** 93.1. –**SO03)** Iglesia Bautista Getsemani, San Pedro La Laguna (or: International Mission Board, SBC, Ap. 25, Bulevares, MX 53140, México) - **FM:** 97.6.
SU00) SUCHITEPEQUEZ
SU01) 10001 Mazatenango. – **SU02)** La Libertad 9-91, Z-1, 10001 Mazatenango. – **SU03)** 6 Av. 10-54, Z-1, 10001 Mazatenango. – **SU04)** 13 Av. 23-60, Z-12, 10012 Coyotenango. – **SU05)** Calle 30 de Junio 1a y 2a, Z-5, 10001 Mazatenango.
TO00) TOTONICAPAN
TO01) Barrio La Cienaga, 08002 San Cristóbal Totonicapán. – **TO02)** Palacio Municipal, 08001 Totonicapán. – **TO03)** Momostenango, 08001 Totonicapán. – **TO04)** Totonicapán.
ZA00) ZACAPA
ZA01) 4 Calle 12-54, Z-1, 19001 Zacapa. – **ZA02)** 4 Calle 10-34, Z-1, 19001 Zacapa. – **ZA03)** Zona Militar N° 7, 19001 Zacapa.

FM in Guatemala City: 88.5 Galaxia – 89.3 Estrella – 89.7 Em.Unidas – 90.3 Sideral – 90.5 Punto – 91.3 KeBuena – 91.9 Fiesta – 92.3 Universidad – 92.7 Cristal – 93.5 Sonora – 93.9 Jazz 94 – 94.1 94 Su FM – 94.5 Coco – 94.9 "FM95" – 95.3 Viva – 95.9 Ranchera – 96.1 Nuevo Mundo – 96.9 Sonora – 97.3 Alfa Sigma – 98.1 Doble S – 98.9 Globo – 99.7 Conga – 100.5 Cultural – 101.0 Fresca – 101.7 Exa – 102.1 Stereo 102 – 102.3 Eco la Cariñosa – 102.9 Metroestéreo – 103.3 R. María – 103.7 R. Fiesta – 105.7 Union – 106.1 Máxima – 106.5 Clásica – 106.9 Internacional – 107.3 Nacional – 107.5 Fama

GUINEA

L.T: UTC — **Pop:** 8 million — **Pr.L:** French, Fulah, Maninké, Soussou — **E.C:** 50Hz, 220V — **ITU:** GUI

MINISTÈRE DE LA COMMUNICATION
🖃 Conakry.

RADIODIFFUSION TELEVISION GUINEENNE (RTG)
🖃 B. P. 391, Conakry ☎ & 🖷 +224 451408.
L.P: Dir: Mr. Issa Condé.
SW: Conakry (G.C: 09N32 013W40) 6155/7125kHz 50kW.
FM: Conakry 88.55/91.7MHz.
D.Prgr. on SW/FM in French/Vernaculars: W 0555-2400, Sun 0800-2400. **N: French:** 0645, 0915Sun, 1200Sun, 1245W, 1300Sun, 1615W, 1945W, 2000Sun, 2200, 2350. **English:** 1845 (irr.).
ANN: F. "Ici Conakry", "R. Guineé". **IS:** Guitar.

RADIO RURALE
🖃 B.P. 391, Conakry ☎ +224 412717/211409 🖷 +224 414797
R. Rurale de la Moyenne Guinée ("R. Fouta Internationale [RFI]"),

B.P.169, Labé. **MW**: 1386v kHz 50kW. **FM**: 87.6MHz. **D.Prgr**: 0555-2300 in French/Pular/Malinke/others.
R. Rurale de la Haute Guinée: Mandiana 88.2MHz, Kankan 92.1MHz, Dabadou 93MHz, Siguiri 97MHz, Douabou 99MHz.
R. Rurale de Kindia: 88.3MHz, Kakoulima 98.7MHz, Koliadi 99.9MHz.
R. Rurale de N'Zerekore: 89MHz.

GUINEA-BISSAU

L.T: UTC — **Pop:** 1.3 million — **Pr.L:** Portuguese, Crioulo — **E.C:** 50Hz, 220V — **ITU:** GNB

INSTITUTO DAS COMUNICAÇÕES DA GUINÉ-BISSAU (ICGB)

✉ Av. Domingos Ramos 53, C.P. 1372, Bissau ☎ +245 20 4873/74 🖷 +245 20 4876 **Web:** www.icgb.org **Email:** icgb@mail.bissau.net
L.P: Teófilo Lopez, Chief of Registrations and Licensing Dept.

RADIODIFUSÃO NACIONAL

✉ C.P. 191, Bissau ☎ +245 212426 **L.P:** DG: Calilo Jandi
Web: www.guine-bissau.net/rdn
FM: 88/91.5/93.7/98MHz.
D.PRGR: 0600-1330, 1530-2400. **N:** 1320 (Portuguese), 1500, 1900, 2200 (Crioulo).
ANN: "Escutam a Radiodifusão Nacional da República de Guiné-Bissau".

OTHER STATIONS:
R. Mavegro: 100MHz. Also rel. BBC Portuguese sce.
R. Pindjiguiti: Bairro Ajuda 95MHz.
RFI Afrique: Bissau 94.7MHz in French/Portuguese.
RDP África: Nhacra 88.4MHz 25kW.

GUYANA

L.T: UTC -4h — **Pop:** 870,000— **Pr.L:** Creole, English, Hindi, Urdu, Amerindian dialects — **E.C:** 50Hz, 240V — **ITU:** GUY

PUBLIC UTILITIES COMMISSION

✉ Parliament Buildings, Brickdam, Georgetown ☎ +592 2 227 3293 🖷+592 2 227 3534.

NATIONAL COMMUNICATIONS NETWORK INC. (ex. GUYANA BROADCASTING CORP)

✉ Broadcasting House, P.O. Box 10760, Georgetown ☎ +592 2 58734 🖷+592 2 58756
L.P: Ag. Chmn: Earl Bousquet. GM: Fazil Azeez. Prgr. Mgr: Margaret Lawrence. CE: Shiroxley Goodman.
MW: Georgetown 560/760kHz 10kW, Linden 700kHz 1kW
SW: Sparendaam (G.C: 06N49 058W10): 3290/*5950kHz 10kW
FM: Georgetown 100.1/102.5MHz, Linden 106.5MHz.
R. Roraima: 0800-0200 on 760kHz + 100.1MHz. **N:** 0900, 1000, 1100, 1330, 1500, 1900, 2100, 2230 (Sun), 2300 (W), 0100.
Voice of Guyana: 24h on 560/700kHz + 102.5/106.5MHz, 0900-2200 on 5950kHz, 2200-0900 on 3290kHz. **N:** as R. Roraima.
V. by letter.

HAITI

L.T: UTC -5h — **Pop:** 9 million — **Pr.L:** Créole, French — **E.C:** 50+60Hz, 110V — **ITU:** HTI

CONSEIL NATIONAL DES TELECOMUNICATIONS (CONATEL)

✉ B.P.2002 (or: Cité de l'Exposition 16), Port-au-Prince ☎ +509 22 0300 🖷+509 22 0579

Abbreviations: P-au-P = Port-au-Prince, Rdf = Radiodiffusion, V = Voix, * = inactive, v = varying fq.

MW	kHz	kW	Station and location
1)	570	10	Vision 2000,P-au-P
2)	590	1	R. Ti Moun,P-au-P
3)	610	0.2	R. L'Eternal est Grand, P-au-P
4)	630	1	Rdf Jeremienne, Jeremie
5)	630	1	V. des ODS, P-au-P
6)	660	5	R. Lumiere, P-au-P: 1000-0200
7)	690	10	V. des Travailleurs, P-au-P
6)	720	1	R. Lumiere, Petite Riv.
6)	740	1	R. Lumiere, Pignon
6)	760	2	R. Lumiere, Cayes
6)	780	0.5	R. Lumiere, Jeremie
8)	780	10	Eben-Ezer, Mirebalais
9)	810	0.05	R. Atlantique, Gonaives
10)	820	10	R. Tropicale, P-au-P
11)	840	10	R. 4VEH, Cap Haitien
12)	850	0.25	R. Petion-Ville, P-au-P
13)	860	3	R. Men Kontre, Cayes
14)	870	1	R. Express, Jacmel
15)	880	0.3	R. Independance, Gonaives
16)	890	0.5	R. Trans Artibonite, Gonaives
17)	890	1	V. du Nord'est, Forte Liberte
18)	910	0.5	R. Kyskeya, P-au-P
19)	910	0.5	R. Neg Combit, P-au-P
20)	930	5	R. Cap Haitien, Cap Haitien
21)	930	0.1	R. Echo 2000, Val. de Jacmel
22)	940	0.25	R. St Marc, St marc
23)	940	0.2	Rdf Jacmelienne, Jacmel
24)	960	0.3	R. Carillon, P-au-P
25)	990	0.2	R. Cacique, P-au-P
66)	v1030		R. Guinen, P-au-P (nom 1050 kHz)
27)	1080	20	R. Nationale, P-au-P
28)	1120	10	R. Magic, P-au-P
29)	1150	0.25	R. Caraibes, P-au-P
30)	1170	10	R. Soleil, P-au-P
31)	1190	0.3	R. Grand Anse, Jeremie
32)	1210	1	R. Plus, P-au-P
33)	1220	1	V. du Plateau Central, Hinche
34)	1230	1	V. de L'ave Maria, Cap Haitien
35)	1240	1	Haiti Internationales, P-au-P
36)	*1280	3	R. Metropole, P-au-P
67)	1300	1	R. Vision Nouvelle, P-au-P
37)	*1330	10	R. Haiti Inter, P-au-P
38)	1350	0.25	R. Dame Marie, Dame Marie
39)	1360	5	R. Liberte, P-au-P
40)	1370	0.5	R. Citadelle, Cap Haitien
41)	1370	1	Rdf Cayenne, Cayes
42)	1380	0.7	R. Port au Prince, P-au-P
43)	1410	1	V. de Nord-ouest, Port de Paix
44)	1420	0.5	R. Messie Continental, Dessalines
45)	1430	0.8	R. MBC, P-au-P
46)	1460	0.2	V. du Nord, Cap Haitien
47)	1470	0.5	R. Lakansyel, P-au-P
48)	1500	10	Haiti Flambeau Caraibes, P-au-P
49)	1560	10	V. de L'esperance, P-au-P: 24h

FM	MHz	kW	Station, location and h. of tr.
6)	88.1	1	R. Lumiere, P-au-P: //630 kHz
18)	88.5	1.5	R. Kyskeya, P-au-P: 24h
49)	89.5	1	V. de L'esperance, P-au-P: 24h //1560 kHz
51)	90.1	1	R. Phare, P-au-P
52)	90.5	1	R. Signal FM, P-au-P: 24h
2)	90.9	1	R. Ti Moun, P-au-P
53)	91.3	1	Tropic FM, P-au-P: 24h
5)	91.7	1	V. de ODS, P-au-P
54)	92.5	1	R. Boussole, P-au-P
66)	92.9	1	R.Guinen, P-au-P
35)	93.5	1	Haiti International, P-au-P: 1000-0300
39)	94.1	1	R. Liberte, P-au-P
11)	94.7	1	R. Horizon, Cap Haitien
45)	94.9	1	R. MBC, P-au-P: 24h
20)	96.1	1	R. Cap Haitien, Cap Haitien
55)	96.1	1	R. Verite, P-au-P
56)	96.7	1	R. Delta, P-au-P: 24h
35)	96.9	1	Haiti International, P-au-P: 1000-0300
57)	98.5	1.5	R. Ibo, P-au-P
1)	99.3	1	Vision 2000, P-au-P: 24h
36)	100.1	1	R. Metropole, P-au-P: 24h
58)	100.5	80	R. Rotation, P-au-P
28)	100.9	1	R. Magic Stereo, P-au-P: 24h
59)	101.3	10	R. Super Gemini, St. Marc: 24h
64)	101.7	1	Energie FM, P-au-P
1)	101.7	1	Vision 2000, Les Cayes
27)	102.1	2.5	R. Nationale, P-au-P: 0900-0200
60)	102.9	1	R. Super Star, P-au-P: 24h
20)	103.1	1.5	R. Cap Haitien, Cap Haitien
61)	103.3	1	Melodie FM, P-au-P: 24h
62)	104.5	1	R. Galaxie, P-au-P:24h
27)	105.1	1	R. Nationale, P-au-P: 0900-0200
1)	105.7	1	Vision 2000, Cap Haitien

FM	MHz	kW	Station, location and h. of tr.
35)	106.1		R. Haiti, P-au-P
63)	106.9	1	R. Kadans, P-au-P
65)	107.5		R. Solidarité, P-au-P: 24h

+ 66 st's less than 1kW.

Addresses and other information:
1) 184, Lalue (Etage Mapharmacie), P-au-P. **Web:** www.radiovision2000.com – **2)** 27, Rue Camille Leon, P-au-P. – **3)** 22, Angle rte de Delmas et Delmas, P-au-P. – **4)** 82, Rue Eugene Magron, Jeremie. – **5)** 42, Rue Faustin, P-au-P. – **6)** Cote Plage, P-au-P. – **7)** Rue Chareron, P-au-P. – **8)** 27, Rue Clair Heureuse, P-au-P. – **9)** Rllw Laporte, Gonaive. – **10)** Delmas 29, Dubois Shopping Centre, P-au-P. – **11)** Box 1, Cap-Haitien (or: Radio 4VEH, P.O.Box 24638, West Palm Beach, FL 33416, USA). **Web:** www.radio4veh.org – **12)** 71, Rue Rigau, P-au-P. – **13)** 137, Rue Simon, Cayes. – **14)** 31, Rue Stenio Vincent, Jacmel. – **15)** Rue Egalite, Gonaives. – **16)** Rue du Quai, Gonaives. – **17)** Rue Bourbons, Forte Liberte. – **18)** Rue Pavee, P-au-P. – **19)** Rue de St Nicolas, P-au-P. – **20)** 30 Rue 10A, Cap Haitien. – **21)** 32 Rue Titus, Vallee de Jacmel. – **22)** 20 Rue A Thoby, St marc. – **23)** 32, Rue D'Orleans, Jacmel. – **24)** 159, Rue Dr Aubrey, P-au-P. – **25)** 5, Rue Bellevue, Pacot, P-au-P. – **26)** Vaudreuil, Cap Haitien – **27)** Rue du Magasin de L'etat, P-au-P. – **28)** 346, Route de Delmas, P-au-P. – **29)** 19, Rue Chavannes, P-au-P. – **30)** B.P. 538, P-au-P. – **31)** 54, Rue Eugene Magron, Jeremie. – **32)** 85, Bicentenaire, P-au-P. – **33)** 657, Rue Toussant L'Ouverture, Hinche. – **34)** Rue 19H, Cap Haitien. **Email:** radiovoixavemaria@hotmail.com – **35)** 175, Rue du Centre, P-au-P. – **36)** 10, Delmas 52, P-au-P. – **37)** Route de Delmas, P-au-P. – **38)** 252, Rue Frere Portier, Dame Marie. – **39)** Rue des Miracles, P-au-P. **Email:** fmliberte@aol.com – **40)** Rue 10-11-E, Cap Haitien. – **41)** 77, Rue du Vivier-Hall, Cayes. – **42)** Rue Oswald Durand, P-au-P. – **43)** 84, Rue Christophe, Port de Paix. – **44)** 15, Rue Jacque 1er, Marchands Dessalines, Dessalines. – **45)** Rue du Quai, P-au-P. – **46)** Rue 10-11-E, Cap Haitien. – **47)** Route de Delmas, P-au-P. – **48)** 48, Bois Moquette ptv., P-au-P. – **49)** Seminarie Adventiste, Diquini, P-au-P. – **51)** 30, Rue Bigot, Delmas 4, P-au-P. – **52)** 85, Rue des Fronts Forts, P-au-P. – **53)** 6, Avenue John Brown, P-au-P. – **54)** 249, LaLue, P-au-P. – **55)** n/a. – **56)** 7, Avenue John Brown, P-au-P. – **57)** 51, Route Canapevert, P-au-P. – **58)** 37, Rue S Rouzier, P-au-P. – **59)** 128, Rue Pierre Pinchinat, St. Marc. – **60)** 38, Rue Safran, Delmas 68, P-au-P. – **61)** Rue Capois, P-au-P. – **62)** 17, Rue Pavee, P-au-P. – **63)** 3, Rue Marcelin, Delmas – **64)** P-au-P. – **65)** P-au-P. – **66)** 9 Bis, Delmas 31, P-au-P. – **67)** 406, Route Delmas a L'Etage, P-au-P.

RADIO FRANCE INTERNATIONALE
B.P. 1126, Port-au-Prince ☎ +509 22-4724 🖷 +509 22-9140
Email: ablanc@acn2.net. **FM:** Port-au-Prince 89.3.

HAWAII (U.S. State)

L.T: UTC -10h — **Pop:** 1.2 million — **Radios:** 1,000,000 (est) — **Pr.L:** English, Japanese, Filipino — **E.C:** 60Hz, 120V — **ITU:** HWA.

HAWAIIAN ASSOCIATION OF BROADCASTERS, INC.
P.O. Box 22112, Honolulu HI 96823-2112. **Pres:** Mark Haworth.

MW	Call	kHz	kW	Location
1)	KMVI	550	5	Wailuku
2)	KQNG	570	1	Lihu'e (FPl. 3kW)
3)	KSSK	590	7.5	Honolulu
4)	KIPA	620	5	Hilo (inactive)
4)	KIPA-1	620	10	Kalaoa-Kona (inactive)
4)	KIPA-2	620	5	Na'alehu (inactive)
5)	KHNR	650	5	Honolulu
6)	KPUA	670	10	Hilo
7)	KORL	690	10	Honolulu
8)	KUAI	720	5	'Ele'ele
5)	KGU	760	10	Honolulu
4)	KKON	790	5	Kealakekua
3)	KHVH	830	10	Honolulu
9)	KHLO	850	5	Hilo
5)	KAIM	870	5	Honolulu
1)	KNUI	900	5	Kahului
11)	KHCM	940	10	Honolulu
3)	KHBZ	990	5	Honolulu
12)	KLHT	1040	10	Honolulu
13)	KHBC	1060	5	Hilo
14)	KWAI	1080	5	Honolulu
15)	KAOI	1110	5	Kihei
41)	KRUD	1130		Honolulu (CP)
16)	KJPN	1170	5	Honolulu (r. KAIM 95.5)
17)	KZOO	1210	5	Honolulu
18)	KNDI	1270	5	Honolulu
45)	KITT	1370	5	Pearl City
20)	KKEA	1420	5	Honolulu
20)	KHRA	1460	5	Honolulu
22)	KUMU	1500	10	Honolulu
23)	KREA	1540	5	Honolulu
24)	KUAU	1570	0.5	Ha'iku (irreg.)

FM	Call	MHz	kW	Location
19)	KHPR	88.1	45	Honolulu
46)	KAKU	88.5	0.1	Kahului (CP)
25)	KHJC	88.9	100	Lihu'e
19)	KIPO	89.3	100	Honolulu
42)	KLVN	89.3	0.25	Hilo
26)	KCIF	90.3	14	Hilo
27)	KTUH	90.3	3	Honolulu
47)	KPHL	90.5	50	Pahala (CP)
19)	KKUA	90.7	7	Wailuku
28)	KKCR	90.9	0.9	Hanalei
19)	KANO	91.1	26	Hilo
27)	KTUH	91.3	0.01	North Shore
43)	KEAO	91.5	0.1	Wailuku
28)	KAQA	91.9	0.95	Kilauea
3)	KSSK	92.3	100	Waipahu
4)	KHWI	92.7	50	Hilo
7)	KQMQ	93.1	100	Honolulu
30)	KPOA	93.5	69	Lahaina
2)	KQNG	93.5	100	Lihue
31)	KLUA	93.5	3	Kailua
31)	KLUA	93.7	6.6	Kailua
3)	KIKI	93.9	100	Honolulu
31)	KLUA	93.9	32	Kailua-Kona
15)	KDLX	94.3	3	Makawao
6)	KWXX	94.7	100	Hilo
22)	KUMU	94.7	100	Honolulu
15)	KAOI	95.1	100	Wailuku
5)	KAIM	95.5	99	Honolulu
31)	KPVS	95.9	50	Hilo
2)	KSRF	95.9	100	Po'ipu-Koloa
15)	KDLX	95.9		Makawao
48)	KPVS	95.9	39	Hilo
20)	KRTR	96.3	74	Kailua
15)	KAOI	96.7		Wailuku
32)	KFMN	96.9	100	Lihu'e
6)	KNWB	97.1	40	Hilo
49)	KLUI	97.3	0.1	Kula
7)	KPOI	97.5	100	Honolulu
9)	KKBG	97.9	35	Hilo
33)	KAWV	98.1	100	Lihu'e
1)	KJMD	98.3	50	Pukalani
3)	KDNN	98.5	100	Honolulu
34)	KITH	98.9	100	Princeville
35)	KAGB	99.1	42	Kamuela
7)	KHUI	99.5	100	Honolulu
1)	KNUI	99.9	100	Kahului
36)	KTOH	99.9	100	Princeville
4)	KAPA	100.3	100	Hilo
4)	KAPA	100.3	7.1	Puueo
20)	KCCN	100.3	100	Honolulu
30)	KLHI	101.1	70	Lahaina
4)	KAOY	101.5	7.1	Kealakekua
3)	KUCD	101.9	100	Pearl City
7)	KDDB	102.7	100	Waipahu
50)	KCSK	102.3	0.1	Hanamalou
51)	KDDB	102.7	60	Waipahu
2)	KSHK	103.3	100	Kekaha
52)	KIHL	103.3	0.1	Hilo
1)	KNUQ	103.7	70	Pa'auilo
20)	KXME	104.3	75	Kane'ohe
37)	KONI	104.7	29	Lana'i City
44)	KINE	105.1	100	Honolulu
53)	KBGX	105.1	28	Keaau
21)	KRTR	105.5		Kona
38)	KPMW	105.5	6	Hali'imaile
39)	KAHA	105.9	100	Honolulu
9)	KLEO	106.1	7.3	Kahalu'u-Kona
40)	KWYI	106.9	5.5	Kawaihae
54)	KJHI	107.3	0.1	Honokaa
9)	KKOA	107.7	18	Volcano
20)	KGMZ	107.9	100	'Aiea

All sts comm. except 19, 26 and 28
+ 7 st's less than 1 kW

Addresses and other information:
Abbreviations: See under U.S.A. commercial sts.
Addresses: Add state abbreviation HI between location and zip code.
1) 311 Ano Street, Kahului, Maui 96732-1304. Format: KMVI - Sports, KNUI-AM - Hawaiian; KNUI-FM - contemporary hits; KNUQ – Jawaiian; KJMD – urban hits/Jawaiian. **Web:** KMVI - www.sportszone55.com/; KNUI - www.vibe99.com/; KNUI - www.knuiam900. com; KNUQ - www.q103.com – **2)** 4271 Hale Nani Street; Lihu'e, Kaua'i 96793-1312. Format: KQNG-AM - Newstalk; KQNG-FM – contemporary hits; KSRF - Hawaiian; KSHK - rock'n'roll. **Web:** www.hawaiian.net/~kong – **3)** 650 'Iwilei Road, Suite 400, Honolulu 96817-5317. Format: KSSK - Adult contemporary music/news; KDNN island music; KIKI – CHR/rap/dance; KUCD - modern rock; KHVH - news/talk; KHBZ – news/talk **Web:** www.ksskradio.com; http://star1019fm.com; www.khvh830am.com; www.khbz.com – **4)** 688 Kino'ole Street; Hilo, Big Island 96720-3868. Format: KIPA - popular standards, Tagalog Mon-Sat 1400-1445, Japanese Mon-Sat 1445-1530; KKON - //850 KHLO; KHWI – classic rock'n'roll; KAPA – Hawaiian. – **5)** 114-B Genty Pacific Center, 560 North Nimitz Highway, 96817. Format: KHNR - Talk, KGU - Relig; KAIM – Relig. **Web:** www.hawaii-radio.net/khnr; www.hawaiian-radio.net/kgu – **6)** 1145 Kilauea Avenue; 96720-4203. Format: KWXX - contemporary hits/island music; KNWB – classic hits; KPUA – news/talk/sports. **Web:** www.kwxx.com – **7)** 500 Pacific Business News Building, 1833 Kalakaua Avenue, Suite 500, 96815-1527. Format: KORL-AM - //940 KJPN days (Japanese) light jazz nights. KQMQ-FM - oldies, KPOI - modern rock; KDDB - urban contemporary hits. **Web:** www.kqmq.net; www.975kpoi.com; www.dabombhawaii.com – **8)** 'Ele'ele Shopping Center; 1-4469 Wai'alo Road; 'Ele'ele, Kaua'i 96705-0720. Format: adult contemporary/Hawaiian/country/news/ sports. Mon-Sat 1500-1000, Sun. 1500-0900. **Web:** www.hawaiian-net/~kuai – **9)** 913 Kanoelehua Avenue; Hilo, Big Island 96720-5116. Format: KHLO - oldies; KKBG - hot adult contemporary/Hawaiian; KLEO – adult contemporary/Hawaiian; KKOA – T40. **Web:** www.emeraldcityradio.com – **11)** 750 Pacific Park Plaza, 711 Kapi'olani Boulevard; 96813-5215. Format: Country music. **Web:** www.kjpn.net – **12)** 1190 Nu'uanu Avenue; 96817-5122. Format: Christian music & religious programming **Web:** http://calvarychapel.com/honolulu/ klht/page1.htm – **13)** P.O. Box 4727; Hilo, Big Island 96720-0727. Format: Hawaiian, some Japanese. Irreg hours of operation – **14)** 401 Chinatown Cultural Plaza Shopping Center, Building III; 100 North Beretania Street; 96817-4712. Format: CNN Newstalk. Filipino Mon-Fri 1500-1600; Samoan Mon 0700-0800; Tongan Fri 0700-0900. **Email:** kwai@aloha.net – **15)** Box 38, Kahului, Maui 96733-0038. Format: KAOI-AM - newstalk, sports, CNN; KAOI-FM – adult contemporary/Hawaiian; KDLX – country. **Web:** www. kaoi.com. – **16)** new, under construction. – **17)** 209 Ward Court Building, 250 Ward Avenue; 96814-4066. Format: Japanese Sun-Thu 1530-1000, Fri-Sat 1530-1030. **Web:** www.kzoohawaii.com. – **18)** 1734 South King Street; 96814-2042. Format: Ethnic/Filipino. – **19)** 738 Kaheka Street, Suite 101; Honolulu 96814-3726. Format: non-commercial National Public Radio/classical music & news **Web:** www.hawaiipublicradio.org – **20)** 900 Fort Street Mall, Suite 700; 96813-3797. Format: KCCN-AM – sports; KCCN-FM - island music; KRHA - //KRTR 96.3.; KRHA – Korean (relays KYPA Los Angeles); KRTR-FM - adult contemporary; KXME - CHR/urban hits; KGMZ – oldies. **Web:** www.oldiesradio.net; www.krater96.com, http://xtremeradio.net; http://kccn1420am.com; http://kccnfm100.com – **22)** 765 'Amana Street, Suite 206; 96814. Format: KUMU-AM – news talk; KUMU-FM - light rock. **Web:** www.kumu.com – **23)** 860 Interstate Building, 1314 South King Street; 96814-1943 Format: Korean, some relays of KYPA-1230 Los Angeles. Daily 1600-1000 (1000-1600 period leased to kWAI-1080). – **24)** 490 'Ulumalu Road, Ha'iku, Maui 96708-9230. –0800. Format: religious. – **25)** KOAM Broadcasting, 1585 Kapiolani Blvd, 12th floor, Honolulu HI. Korean. – **25)** 2970 Kele St, Suite 117, Lihu'e, Kaua'i 96766 – **26)** Hemenway Hall #203, University of Hawai'i, 2445 Campus Road; 96822-2224. Format: religious (non commercial) **Web:** www.ktuh.org – **27)** 310 Plaza Building, 180 Kino 'ole Street; Suite 310; 96720-2827. Format: various.– **28)** P O Box 825, Hanalei, 96714. Format: music/news, non-commercial. **Web:** www.kkcr.org. – **30)** 505 Front Street, Suite 215; Lahaina, Maui 96761-1116 Format: KPOA - Jawaiian; KLHI – alternative rock **Web:** www.kpoa.com; www.thepointfm101.com/ – **31)** B-7 Ka'ahumanu Plaza, 74-5605 Luhia Street; Kailua-Kona, Big Island 96740-1659. Format: KLUA - adult contemporary/contemporary Hawaiian – **32)** Leleiona and Shop Roads; P.O. Box 1566; Lihu'e, Kaua'i 96766-5566. Format: adult contemporary. – **33)** c/o Ohana Radio Partners, 530 Wilshire Blvd, Santa Monica CA 90401, Lihu'e, Kaua'i 96766 (F.Pl.). – **34)** Princeville, Kaua'i 96722. Format: traveller information radio – **35)** Kamuela, Big Island 96743. Format: Hawaiian //KAPA 100.3 – **36)** Princeville, Kaua'i 96722. Format: classic hits. – **37)** C-318 Kihei Commecial Center, 300 Ohukai Road; Kihei, Maui 96753-8967. Format: KONI – T40/soul **Web:** www.konifm.com – **38)** 230 Hana Highway, Suite 4; Kahului, Maui 96732-2304. Format: KPMW – hip-hop/dance/Filipino – **39)** 64-1040 Mamalahoa Highway, Suite 4; Kamuela, Big Island 96743-6540. Format: alternative rock **Web:** www. lavarock1059.com – **40)** 64-1040 Mamlahoa Hwy, Kamuela, Format: contemporary hits – **41) KRUD,** new. – **42)** c/o 1425 North Market Blvd, Sacramento, CA 95834, USA. Format: contemporary Christian. **Web:** www.klove.com – **44)** 900 Fort Str, Suite 700, Honolulu, 96813. Format: contemporary Hawaiian music **Web:** http://hawaiian105.com – **45)** P O Box 1450, St George UT 84771-1450 USA. Format: Japanese ("K-Japan") – **46)** Maui County Community TV, 333 Dairy Rd, Kahului 96732 – **47)** 188 South Bellevue, Suite 222, Memphis TN 38104 – **48)** 2447 Makiki Heights Dr, Honolulu 96822 – **49)** P O Box 842, Makawao 96768 – **50)** P O Box 192, Eleele 96705 – **51)** 1833 Kalakaua Ave, Suite 500, Honolulu 96815 – **52)** P O Box 4250, Hilo 96720 – **53)** 3180 N Mountain View Dr, San Diego CA 92116 – **54)** P O Box 2026, Honokaa 96727

HONDURAS

L.T: UTC -6h — **Pop:** 6.5 million — **Pr.L:** Spanish — **E.C:** 60Hz, 110V — **ITU:** HND

EMPRESA HONDURENA DE TELECOMUNICACIONES (HONDUTEL)

Ap. 1794, Tegucigalpa.

ASOCIACION NACIONAL DE RADIODIFUSORES DE HONDURAS (ANARH)

Ap. 4039, Tegucigalpa.

MW: Call HR–
° = also on SW, * = inactive, (r) = repeater, v = varying fq. H. of tr. 1100-0500 exc. where indicated.

	Call	kHz	kW	Name and h. of tr.
203)		540		R. Nuevo Mundo, Tegucigalpa
154)	OW	540	1	R. Atlántida, La Ceiba
155)	XT	550	1	R. X, Tegucigalpa: 0945-0445
2)	XD	550	0.5	R. Manantial, Sta Rosa de Copán: 1115-0300
76)	OY	560	1	R. Jupiter, Comayagua
3)	RZ	560	5	R. Juticalpa, Juticalpa: 1100-0400
4)	PX	560	1	R. Tropical "Cadena Radial Reloj", San Pedro Sula
156)	OS	560	1	R. Castilla, Tocoa
160)	OT	560	1	R. Montserrat, Danlí
157)	OX	570	1	R. El Triunfo, Choluteca
6)	ZQ	580	3	R. Tegucigalpa, Tegucigalpa
112)	EO	580		Super Estrella de Occidente, Sta Rosa de Copán
158)	OU	580	1	R. Unión, Gracias
159)	OV	590	1	LV de Lepaguare, Juticalpa
186)		590		R. Agricola, El Zamorano
5)	LD	610	10	R. América "LV Informativo del Pueblo", Tegucigalpa: 1000-0500
5)	LD	610	10	R. América, Sta Rosa de Copán (r:610)
5)	LD	620	1	R. América, Comayagua (r:610)
5)	LD	620	1	R. América, Juticalpa (r:610)
28)	LP17	620	1	R. Continental, San Pedro Sula
5)	LD	630	1	R. América, Choluteca (r:610)
5)	LD	630	1	R. América, La Ceiba (r:610)
7)		640		LV de Centroamérica, Sta Rosa de Copán (r:650)
8)	NN4	640	1	R. Televisión, Tegucigalpa: 24h.
185)		640		R. Estéreo Canaan, Sta Bárbara
7)	VW	650	25	LV de Centroamérica, San Pedro Sula
7)		650		LV de Centroamérica, Siguatepeque (r:650)
7)		650		LV de Centroamérica, La Ceiba (r:650)
5)	LD	650	15	R. América, Danlí (r:610)
182)		650		R. Turquesa, Siguatepeque
198)		650	1	R. Católica Olancho, Olanchito
8)	NN18	660	3	LV de Honduras, La Ceiba (r:670)
8)	N	670	10	LV de Honduras, Tegucigalpa: 1045-0500
8)	NN20	670	1	LV de Honduras, Sta Rosa de Copán (r:670)
8)	NN8	680	10	LV de Honduras, San Pedro Sula (r:670)
8)	NN11	680	10	LV de Honduras, Tocoa (r:670)
8)	NN2	680	10	LV de Honduras, Siguatepeque (r:670)
8)	NN7	680	1	LV de Honduras, Danlí (r:670)
8)	NN10	680	1	LV de Honduras, Juticalpa (r:670)
8)	NN3	690	1	LV de Honduras, Choluteca (r:670)
8)	NN9	690	1	LV de Honduras, Tela (r:670)
203)	GP	700	5	R. Reloj, Tegucigalpa
9)	RH	710	3	LV de Occidente, Sta Rosa de Copán
14)	UP	710	1	Estéreo Rey, San Pedro Sula: 1100-0600
10)	LK	710	2	R. Comayagua/LV Católica, Comayagua: 1200-0300
11)	KN	710	2.5	LV de Olancho, Catacamas: 24h
8)	NN13	710	1	LV de Honduras, Olanchito (r:670)

	Call	kHz	kW	Name and h. of tr.
79)	NN3	720	1	R. Caribe, La Ceiba
161)	NG	720	1	Super Stereo Costa Sur, Choluteca
8)	TG	730	1	R. Exitos, Tegucigalpa
162)	XG	730	0.25	R. Cadena Dial, Sta Bárbara
12)	QQ	740	1	R. Intibucañá, La Esperanza: 1100-0100
13)	IH	740	1	7-40 La Super, Juticalpa: 1200-0400
14)	NN23	740	1	R. Satélite, San Pedro Sula: 24h.
85)	TU	750	1	R. Trujillo, Trujillo
16)	XK	°750	1	LV de la Mosquitia, Puerto Lempira
18)	XW	760	2.5	R. Comayagüela/Stereo Azul, Comayagüela: 1200-0600
137)	CG	760	1	R. Copán Galel, La Entrada
14)	NN21	v770	10	R. Norte, San Pedro Sula
19)	MV	770	0.5	R. Aguán, Olanchito
30)		770		R. Sui Generis, Comayagua
135)	RO	770	1	R. Majestad "LV del Guayape", Juticalpa: 1100-0300
5)		780		R. Sonora, La Ceiba
163)	SE	780	1	Estéreo Sol 2000, Choluteca
195)		780		R. Amapala, Amapala
20)	IR	790	1	R. Feliz, Sta Bárbara
8)	TG2	790	3	R. Satélite, Tegucigalpa: 24h
21)	DL	v800	1	R. Corporación, Comayagua 1100-0400
22)	LP26	800	1	R. Sonora, Danlí
17)	MA	810	3	R. Mundial, San Pedro Sula
90)	VC	810	1	LV Evangélica, La Ceiba (r:1390)
25)	LP24	810	3	R. Valle, Choluteca: 1000-0400
5)	LD	820	5	R. Moderna, Tegucigalpa: 24h
84)	KW	820	7/3	R. Sultana, Sta Rosa de Copán: 1100-0400
24)	RU	830	1	R. Uno, San Pedro Sula
26)	JB	830	1	Cadena Radial Impacto, Comayagua
27)	VQ	830	1	R. Excelsior, Juticalpa: 1100-0400
18)	CR	840	1	Dif. Cristiana de Radio "DCR", Choluteca
8)	UP	850	10	R. Centro, Tegucigalpa: 1100-0400
165)	IF	850	0.5	R. Inspiración, La Entrada: 1100-0300
190)		850		R. Misionera, Sta Bárbara
28)	BS	860	10	R. San Pedro, San Pedro Sula
110)	LS	860	0.5	R. Dinorama, La Paz: 1200-0300
1)	H9	870	5	R. Honduras, La Ceiba (r:880)
1)	H10	870	5	R. Honduras, Puerto Lempira (r:880)
1)	H4	870	3	R. Honduras, Nacaome (r:880)
1)	H	880	10	R. Honduras, Tegucigalpa
1)	H5	880	10	R. Honduras, Sta Rosa de Copán (r:880)
23)	MD	880	5	R. Yoro, Yoro
1)	H3	890	10	R. Honduras, San Pedro Sula (r:880)
1)	H7	890	10	R. Honduras, Juticalpa (r:880)
1)	H9	890	10	R. Honduras, Siguatepeque (r:880)
1)	H2	890	1	R. Honduras, Comayagua (r:880)
1)	H6	890	1	R. Honduras, El Paraíso (r:880)
1)	H8	890	1	R. Honduras, Olanchito (r:880)
8)	UP5	890	1	R. Satélite, Danlí
8)	UP6	900	1	R. Satélite, La Ceiba
8)	UP7	900	1	R. Satélite, Choluteca
29)	VS	910	10	R. Católica "LV de Suyapa", Tegucigalpa: 24h
151)	NM	910	2.5	R. Comunidad, Ocotepeque: 1100-0300
166)	VH	910	0.5	R. Corona, La Entrada
21)	RM	920	1	R. Sistema, Comayagua: 1300-0300
31)	ZV	920	1	R. Variedades, San Pedro Sula: 1200-0500
32)	SK	920	5	R. Catacamas, Catacamas: 1200-0400
1)	H11	920	1	R. Honduras, Danlí (r:880)
18)	CR	940	1	R. Dif. Cristiana de Radio "DCR", Tegucigalpa: 1200-0400
15)	BO	940	1	R. Cadena Occidental, La Entrada
34)	QL	950	1	Centro Radial Hondureño, Siguatepeque: 1100-0300
35)	ZE	950	1.5	R. Cortés AM, Puerto Cortés: 24h
138)	PS	950	0.5	R. Sistema Popular, Danlí
36)	YF	960	1	R. Fergusón, Choluteca
37)	RD3	960	1	R. Sangrelaya, Sangrelaya
38)	TL	970	2	R. Milenium, Tegucigalpa: 24h.
139)	AS	970	0.25	LV de la Frontera, Ocotepeque
189)		970		R. Copán, Copán
41)	YG	980	1	R. Tocoa, Tocoa
39)	ZC	980	2	R. Monumental, San Pedro Sula: 1200-0600
42)	RD2	980	1	R. Emperador, Campamento
90)	VC	980		LV Evangélica, Siguatepeque (r:1390)
140)	VO	990	3.5	R. Paz, Choluteca: 1000-0400
44)	XZ	1000	1	Unión R., Tegucigalpa: 1000-0600
43)	MH	1000	0.5	LV del Junco, Sta Bárbara: 1200-0400
5)		1010		R. Sonora, San Pedro Sula

	Call	kHz	kW	Name and h. of tr.
89)	CD	1010	1	R. Constelación. Juticalpa: 1200-0400
46)	LP23	1010	1	R. Moderna, El Progreso
48)	UW	1020	1	R. Michel, La Ceiba
167)	MP	1020	1	R. Moropocai, Nacaome
152)	YF	1030	1	R. Ticante, Ocotepeque: 1200-0400
8)	UP3	1030	1	Estéreo Mil, Tegucigalpa
14)	NN22	1040	3	Exitos, San Pedro Sula
11)	FX	1040	1	R. Musical, Catacamas: 1200-0200
33)	MJ	1040	1	R. Renovación, Comayagua: 1100-2400
49)	ZX	1040	10/5	La Primerísima, Olanchito
90)	VC	1040		LV Evangélica, Juticalpa (r:1390)
178)		1050	1	Estéreo Ceiba, La Ceiba
7)	VW	1060	2	LV de Centroamérica, Tegucigalpa (r:650)
50)	FA	1060	0.5	R. Peña Blanca, Sta Barbara
179)		1060		R. Mineria, Sta Cruz de Yojoa
52)	GR	1070	3	Cadena Guaymuras, El Paraíso: 1100-0400
53)	LE	1070	1	R. Unica AM, San Pedro Sula
54)	LP26	1070	2.5	R. Siguatepeque, Siguatepeque 1055-
55)	XM	1070	1	R. Meridiano, Choluteca 1200-
180)		1070		R. Unión Evangélica, Catacamas
184)		1070		R. ZAZ Stereo, Danlí
56)	ID	1080	1	R. Miramar, Tela: 1200-0400
8)	NN27	*1090	1	Exitos, Sta Rosa de Copán (r:640)
90)	WC	*1090	1	Cadena Radial Samaritano, Tegucigalpa: 24h.
58)	ND	1100	1	R. Esperanza, La Esperanza: 1100-0300
59)	VA	1100	1	R. Tiempo/R. Fama, San Pedro Sula
60)	VL	1100	1	R. Lux, Olanchito: 1000-0400
29)	VS	1100	1	LV de Suyapa "R. Católica", Juticalpa: 1030-0400
5)		1110		R. Sonora, Choluteca
87)	ME	1110	0.5	R. El Patio, La Ceiba
38)	YL	1120	2	R. Fiesta, Tegucigalpa
62)	DG	1120	1	R. Oriental "RCO", Danlí: 1100-0600
196)		1120		R. Marchala, Ocotepeque
61)	PL	1130	5	R. Progreso, El Progreso: 1000-0300
63)	BT	1130	1	R. San Francisco, San Francisco de la Paz: 1100-0200
99)	HP	1130	1	R. Pinares, Siguatepeque 1155-
64)	AP	1140	1	R. Mercurio, Choluteca
65)	UN	1140	1	R. Palmeras, La Ceiba
90)	VC	1140		LV Evangélica, Choluteca (r: 1390)
5)		1150		R. Universal, Tegucigalpa
66)	AV	1150	5	Ondas del Ulúa, Sta Bárbara: 0900-0400
67)	QN	1160	5	R. LV del Atlántico, Puerto Cortés: 24h
68)	GF	v1160	0.5	R. El Paraíso, El Paraíso
34)	QL2	1160	1	R. Sentimentos, Siguatepeque
201)	HZ	1160	1	R. Bethel, Taujica
47)	AZ3	1170	1	R. Hits, La Ceiba: 24h.
45)	AF	1170	2	R. Atenea "La Internacional", Choluteca: 1000-0400
149)	CY	1180	1/0.8	R. Congolon, Gracias: 1100-0500
188)	AZ	1180	1	R. Taxi, Tegucigalpa
197)		1180		Sta Bárbara Estéreo, Sta Bárbara
70)	PO	1190	1	R. Sta María de la Luz, Gualaco
6)	ZQ	1190	1	R. Tegucigalpa, San Pedro Sula: 1030-0500 (r:580)
134)	GK	1190	1	R. Brassabola, Minas de Oro: 1000-0300
169)	FS	1190	0.5	R. Familiar, Morazan
71)	DS	1200	1	R. Nacaome, Nacaome
72)	SI	1210	1	R. Impacto, Tela: 1200-0400
73)	RO	1210	1	R. Capital, Comayagüela
114)	HO	1210	1	Estéreo Maya, La Entrada
74)	QO	°1220	1	R. Costeña Ebenezer, San Pedro Sula: 1100-0600
75)	YS	1220	1	R. Suari, Marcala
148)	JM	1220	0.5	R. Destellos de Luz, Sabá
170)	GW	1220	10/1	R. Patria, Catacamas: 1000-0400
56)	QW	1230	10	R. Tela, Tela: 1200-0200
171)	SM	1230	0.25	R. Samaritano, San Marcos de Colón
133)	ZC	1240	1	R. Monumental, Tegucigalpa
172)	VN	1240	1	R. Venus, Sta Bárbara
40)	AT	1250	1	Super R., San Pedro Sula
51)	CC	1250	1	R. Cadena Continental, Comayagua
115)	YN	v1250	1	R. Latina, Danlí (cfr 1310)
141)	QV	1250	0.5	R. Subirana, Yoro
200)		1250		R. Sonaguera, Sonaguera (rep on 1270)
77)	YF2	1260	1	R. San Marcos, San Marcos de Colón
116)	ZR	1260	1	R. 1260, La Ceiba
5)	NQ	1270	1	R. Sonora, Tegucigalpa
117)	OF	1270	1	Ecos del Celaque, Gracias
78)	AM	1280	1	R. Olanchito, Olanchito

	Call	kHz	kW	Name and h. of tr.
136)	BU	1280	1	R. Digital, San Pedro Sula
107)	BN	1280	1	R. San Miguel, Marcala: 1000-0400
191)		1280		R. Monserrat, El Paraíso
81)	NN26	1290	1	R. Choluteca, Choluteca: 1050-0400
118)	GS	1290		R. HRGS/Bay Island Christian Network, Utila
82)	LR	1300	5	R. Sta Rosa, Sta Rosa de Copán
83)	LH	1300		LV de la Amistad, Tegucigalpa
90)	VC	1310	2.5	LV Evangélica, San Pedro Sula (r:1390)
103)	RL	1310		R. Libertad, Marcala, La Paz: 1200-0500
115)	YN	1310	1	R. Latina, Danlí (cfr 1250)
142)	JH	1310	0.5	R. Colón, Tocoa
119)	MG	1320	1	R. Bahía "La Super Grande", La Ceiba
126)	GM	1320	1	R. Ilusión, Choluteca
150)		1320		R. Super K, Nacaome
86)	SW	1330	1	R. Evangélica, Tegucigalpa
173)	FL	1330	1	R. Florida, La Entrada
153)	HH	1340	10	R. El Mundo, San Pedro Sula
120)	JC	1340	1	R. Colonial, Comayagua
174)	ED	1340	1	R. Red, Olanchito
143)	JV	1350	1	LV de San Lorenzo, San Lorenzo
193)		1350		R. Estelar, La Ceiba
28)	BS	1360	1	R. San Pedro, Tegucigalpa (r:860)
197)	GH	1360	5	R. Sta Bárbara, Sta Bárbara: 1200-0400
199)		1360		R. Continente, Trinidad
175)	SZ	1370	1	R. Sta Bárbara, Siguatepeque
69)	TR	*1370	1.5	R. Danlí, Danlí
88)	ST	1370	1	R. Fraternidad, San Pedro Sula
127)	AH	1380	0.5	R. Redención, Jutiapa: 1200-0600
176)	EJ	1380	1	R. Voz Evangélica, Choluteca
90)	VC	°1390	10/5	LV Evangélica, Tegucigalpa: 24h
90)	VC	1390	1	LV Evangélica, Sta Rosa de Copán (r:1390)
91)	JJ	1400	1	R. Estéreo Punto, Comayagua
80)	YT	1400	1	R. Estrella de Oro, San Pedro Sula: 1100-0200
177)	AU	1400	1	R. Alegre, Sava Colón
187)	JU	1400		R. Punto, Comayagua
92)	DD	1410	1	LV de Atlántida, La Ceiba
93)	SY	1410	1	R. Voz Evangélica del Pacifico, San Lorenzo
94)	SL	*1420	1	R. Stereo Actualidad, Trinidad
168)		1420	1	LV de las Fuerzas Armadas, Comayagüela
95)	IC	1430	1	La R. del 70, Puerto Cortés
96)	SJ	1430	1	R. Futura, Tocoa: 1100-0400
97)	VM	1430	1	R. Maranatha, La Paz
164)	TP	1430		R. Recuerdos, Juticalpa
98)	RD	1440	5	Dimensión R, La Ceiba
121)	RY	1440	0.5	R. Mía, San Marcos de Colón
44)	XZ2	1450	1	R. Titania, Tegucigalpa: 1200-0600
144)	BR	1450	1	R. Cultural, La Entrada
202)	GC	1460	2.5	R. Conga, San Pedro Sula
100)	QX	1460	1	Radiolandia, Comayagua
122)	CX	1460	0.5	LV de Patuca, Catacamas: 1000-0400
113)	OC	1460	0.5	R. Ranchera, Yoro
123)	SA	1470	0.5	R. Luz y Verdad, La Ceiba
145)	WP	1480	1	R. Soberanía, San Marcos, Ocotepeque:
102)	MI	°1480	1	LV de Misiones "R. MI", Comayagüela: 1100-0300
35)	GO	1490	1.2	R. Porteña, Puerto Cortés: 1200-0300
104)	OM	1490	1	R. Omega "Sonido Internacional", La Esperanza: 1100-0400
129)	RA	1490	1/0.5	R. Juventud, Sonaguera: 1200-0300
105)	TX	1500	1	R. Victoria, Choluteca
109)		1500		R. Sion, La Ceiba
124)	YK	1510	1	R. Gualcho, Tegucigalpa
106)	EM	1510	1	R. Emanuel, Ocotepeque
130)	RG	1520	5	R. Providencia, Danlí
108)	CR	1520	1	Dif. Cristiana de Radio "DCR", San Pedro Sula: 1200-0400
131)	HJ	1520	1	R. Santiago, Yoro
183)		1520		R. Rios de Agua Viva, Siguatepeque
192)		1520		R. Manantial de Vida Eterna, Juticalpa
194)	YK	1540		R. Nuevo Mundo "Cadena Radial Reloj", Tegucigalpa
132)	JX	1550	1	R. Nueva Vida, San Pedro Sula: 1000-0200
146)	KR	1550	1	R. Kristel, Juticalpa
101)	JO	1550	1	R. Campeona, Comayagua
57)	RF	v1570	2.5	R. Cadena Nacional de Noticias "RCN", Tegucigalpa: 24h.
18)	CR	1580	1	Dif. Cristiana de Radio "DCR", La Esperanza
125)	IK	1590	1	R. San Antonio, San Pedro Sula
181)		1590	1	R. Perla, El Progreso
111)	PC	°1600	1	R. Luz y Vida, San Luís: 1100-0400

SW:

Stations with a (*) are reported to be inactive, but may occasionally be reactivated for variable periods of time.

	Call	kHz	kW	Name and h. of tr.
111)	PC	v3250	1	R. Luz y Vida, San Luís: 1100-1600, 2200-0400
102)	MI	3340		R. Misiones Int. "R.MI", Comayagüela
90)	VC	*4819	5	LV Evangélica, Tegucigalpa
147)	LW	v4832	0.5	R. Litoral, La Ceiba: 1100-1600, 2200-0500
16)	XK	*4910	0.5	LV de la Mosquitia, Puerto Lempira
74)	QO2	*4930		R. Costeña Ebenezer, San Pedro Sula:
128)	ET	*4960	1	R. Buenas Nuevas, Puerto Lempira
102)	MI	5010	1	R. Misiones Int., Comayagüela: 1200-0500

Addresses and other information:

1) Ap. 403, Tegucigalpa. – **2)** 1a Av. 439, Barrio San Martín, Sta Rosa de Copán. ☎ +504 662 0318. – **3)** Ap. 3, Juticalpa. - **FM:** 98.9. – **4)** Ap. 24, San Pedro Sula. – **5)** Edif. Audio Video, Ap. 259, Tegucigalpa. **Web:** www.radioamerica.hn ☎+504 232 1009. 🖷+504 232 2923. – **6)** Cadena Corp. de Radiodifusión, Edif. Landa Blanca, Calle la Fuente, Tegucigalpa. – **7)** Corpocentro, Ap. 120 (or: 10 A. 9 y 10 Calle, Barrio Guamilito), San Pedro Sula. - **FM:** 89.5. – **8)** Emisoras Unidas, Col. Florencia, Blv. Suyapa (or: Ap. 642), Tegucigalpa. **Web:** www.radiohrn.hn **Email:** noticias@radiohrn.hn – **9)** Ap. 206, Sta Rosa de Copán. - **FM:** 92.1. – **10)** Ap. 347, Comayagua. - **FM:** 90.3. – **11)** 3a Calle, S.E.N° 46, Catacamas, Olancho (or: Ap.T-30046 (Toncontín), Tegucigalpa, M.D.C.).**Email:** razahrkn@hondutel.hn - **FM:** 91.9 La Super Voz. – **12)** Barrio El Way, Calle Principal, La Esperanza, Intibucá. ☎ -504 783 0171. – **13)** Ap. 9, Juticalpa. – **14)** Emisoras Unidas, Ap. 163, San Pedro Sula. – **15)** Atras de Gasolinera Shell, La Entrada, Copán. ☎ +504 661 2425. – **16)** Barrio El Centro, Puerto Lempira (or: Global Outreach, Box 1, Tupelo, MS 38802, USA). – **17)** Av. New Orleans 20C, San Pedro Sula. – **18)** Ap. 3448 (or: Col.15 de Septiembre, 8 Calle, 3 Av.), Tegucigalpa. – **19)** Coyoles Central, Olanchito, Yoro. – **20)** Ap. 26, Sta Bárbara. - **FM:** 90.9. – **21)** Barrio San Francisco, Fte Parque, Comayagua. - **FM:** 99.9. – **22)** Danlí, El Paraíso. – **23)** Yoro, Yoro. – **24)** Edif.Maranata, Calle 8 y 9, San Pedro Sula. ☎ +504 350 4614. – **25)** Ap. 29, Choluteca. – **26)** Ap. 33, Comayagua. – **27)** Ap. 28, Juticalpa. ☎ +504 885 1277. – **28)** Ap. 364 (or Av.New Orleans), San Pedro Sula. – **29)** Ap. 480 (or: Edif. Radio Católica, Av. Paz Barahona), Tegucigalpa. **Email:** rcatolica@unete.com ☎+504 237 2848. 🖷+504 237 2017. – **30)** Comayagua. – **31)** Ap. 2918 (or: 5 Calle, 10 y 11 Av. S.O. 91), San Pedro Sula. **Email:** radiofabulosa@sigmanet.hn - **FM:** 102.1 Radio Fabulosa. ☎ +504 553 1228. – **32)** Ap. 50, Catacamas. - **FM:** 104.5. ☎ +504 899 4891. – **33)** Ap 10, 12101 Comayagua. ☎ +504 772 6581. 🖷+504 772 1926. - **FM:** 89.1 R.Vida. – **34)** Barrio Abajo, 2da Ave, 2 y 3 Calle, Siguatepeque. - **FM:** 95.7. ☎ +504 773 1632. – **35)** 3 Av. entre 7 y 8 Calles N° 772, Puerto Cortés. **Email:** radiocortes@lemaco.hn – ☎ +504 665 2810. - **FM:** 88.9+105.7. – **36)** Calle Vicente Williams, Edif. Fergusón, Choluteca. **Web:** http://hometown.aol.com/djrubbik/stereoF.html - **FM:** 103.3. – **37)** Municipio de Iriona, Sangrelaya, Colón. – **38)** Ap. 2821, Tegucigalpa. ☎ +504 237 7927. – **39)** Ap. 996 (or: 9 Calle, S.O. 44, Entre 8 y 9 Av), San Pedro Sula. - **FM:** 98.5 Estéreo Mass. – **40)** Barrio Las Acacias, 10 Calle 2 Av., San Pedro Sula. – **41)** Tocoa, Colón. – **42)** Campamento Olancho. – **43)** Ap. 6, Sta Bárbara. – **44)** Ap. 614 (or: Barrio Abajo, 6 Calle), Tegucigalpa. – **45)** Ap. 78, Choluteca. ☎+504 990 3796. - **FM:** 97.3. – **46)** Col. Brisas del Ulúa, El Progreso, Yoro. – **47)** Barrio La Isla, 4 Calle, La Ceiba. – **48)** 14 Calle, Barrio Solares Nuevos, Av. 14 de Julio, La Ceiba. - **FM:** 96.9 Stereo Michelle. – **49)** Av. Francisco J. Mejía, Barrio Sofoco, Olanchito, Yoro. – **50)** Peña Blanca, 10 km al norte de Las Vegas, Sta Bárbara. – **51)** Barrio Costado Norte Cine Valladolid, Comayagua. – **52)** Barrio Sta Clara, El Paraíso. – **53)** 9 Av. 4 Calle, Edif. Las Fuentes, San Pedro Sula. - **FM:** 88.3. – **54)** Barrio Fatima, Edif. Audiovideo, Siguatepeque. – **55)** Calle San Marcos, Choluteca. – **56)** Av. Panamá, Edif. Canales N° 861, Tela, Atlántida. - **FM:** 104.7. ☎ +504 448 2957. – **57)** Ap. 2250, Tegucigalpa. – **58)** Ap. 25, La Esperanza, Intibucá. ☎+504 783 0025. 🖷+504 783 0644. – **59)** Ap. 906, San Pedro Sula. -**FM:** 97.9. – **60)** Calle El Calvario Frente Al Parque, Edif. Plaza, Olanchito, Yoro. - **FM**: 88.7. – **61)** Ap. 20, El Progreso, Yoro. - **FM**: 103.3 Stereo Alegría. – **62)** Ap. 21, Danlí, El Paraíso. – **63)** San Francisco de la Paz, Olancho. – **64)** Contiguo Cine Rey, Choluteca. – **65)** Barrio La Isla, La Ceiba. – **66)** Ap. 004, Sta Bárbara. ☎+504 643 2406. 🖷+504 643 2940. - **FM:** 97.5. – **67)** 12 Calle 2,3 ave Bo, Copen, Puerto Cortés. **Web:** http://radioatlantico.8m.com - **FM:** 104.5. – **68)** Barrio San Isidro, El Paraíso - **FM:** 93.3. – **69)** Ap. 29, Danlí, El Paraíso. ☎+504 883 21 49. 🖷+504 883 3245 – **Web:** www.grupoastro.com - **FM:** 94.5+98.1. – **70)** Iglesia Católica, Gualaco, Olancho. – **71)** Barrio El Centro, Nacaome, Valle. – **72)** Calle José Trinidad Cabañas, Edif. Hotel Presidente, Tela. - **FM:** 89.9. – **73)** Col. El Prado 1C-107A, Comayagüela. ☎ +504 239 2228. – **74)** Iglesia de Cristo, Ministerio Ebenezer, 14 Calle A, Costado Sur de Wendy's Circunvalación (or: Ap. 34-76), San Pedro Sula. – **Web:** www.ebenezer.hn - **FM:** 91.9+93.7. – **75)** Calle Principal, Marcala, La Paz. – **76)** Barrio Abajo,

Comayagua. – **77)** San Marcos de Colón, Choluteca. – **78)** Olanchito, Yoro. – **79)** Emisoras Unidas, Solares Nuevos, Av. República, La Ceiba. – **80)** Ap. 303, San Pedro Sula. **Email:** efmhonduras@globalnet.hn - **FM:** 97.3. – **81)** Barrio Campo Luna, Choluteca. – **82)** Ap. 203, Sta Rosa de Copán. - **FM:** 94.5. – **83)** Ap. 955, Tegucigalpa. – **84)** Ap. 204, Sta Rosa de Copán. - **FM:** 90.3. Rosa de Copán. – **85)** Barrio El Centro, Trujillo. – **86)** Ap. 3405, Tegucigalpa. – **87)** Av. San Isidro, La Ceiba. – **88)** Colonía Fesitran, San Pedro Sula. – **89)** Juticalpa. – **90)** Ap. 3252, Tegucigalpa – (Owned and operated by Conservative Baptist Home Mission Society, Box 828, Wheaton, IL 60187, USA). **Web:** www.hrvc.org - **Email:** hrvc@infanet.hn – **91)** 1a Av. N° 189, Camayagua. – **92)** Ap. 17, La Ceiba. – **93)** Barrio El Centro, San Lorenzo, Valle. – **94)** Barrio El Centro, 22115 Trinidad, Sta Bárbara. ☎+504 664 1706. 🖷+504 664 1663. - **FM:** 105.3. – **95)** 12 Calle 2a Ave 206, Barrio La Curva, Puerto Cortés. – **96)** Barrio El Centro, Tocoa, Colón. – **97)** Santiago de la Paz, La Paz (or: Col.21 de Octubre, Sector 3, Bloque 2, Casa 5, Tegucigalpa). – **98)** Av. San Isidro, Entre Calles 9 y 10, La Ceiba. – **99)** Casa 269, Barrio Abajo, Siguatepeque. - **FM:** 91.5. – **100)** Calle Boulevar, Comayagua. – **101)** Barrio Abajo 229, Comayagua. – **102)** Ap. 20583, Comayagüela (or: IMF World Misiones, PO Box 6321, San Bernardino, CA 92412, USA). – **103)** Barrio San Miguel, Calle Principal, Marcala, La Paz. ☎ +504 764 5377. – **104)** Av. España, La Esperanza, Intibucá. ☎ +504 898 2063. – **105)** Barrio La Cruz, Calle Chorotega, Choluteca. - **FM:** 96.2. – **106)** Barrio San Andrés, Ocotepeque. – **107)** Barrio Concepción, Marcala, La Paz (or: Palacio Arzobispal, Av.Cervantes, Barrio El Centro, Tegucigalpa). – **108)** Ap. 2017, San Pedro Sula. – **109)** La Cruzada del Evangélico de Honduras, La Ceiba. – **110)** Parque Central, La Paz. – **111)** Barrio Luz y Vida, San Luis, Sta Bárbara (or: Ap. 303, San Pedro Sula). **English:** Sat 0300-0400, Sun 0230-0400 - **Email:** efmhonduras@globalnet.hn – **112)** Sta Rosa de Copán – **113)** Ap.23301, Olanchito, Yoro. – **114)** Barrio El Progreso, 2da y 3ra Calle, Av.La Entrada, La Entrada, Copán – ☎ +504 661 2049. – **115)** Barrio El Centro, Danlí, El Paraíso. – **116)** 4a Calle N° 1185, La Ceiba. – **117)** 2a Av. 9C N° 9, Gracias, Lempira. ☎ +504 686 1087. – **118)** Col. de Jerico, Utila – **Web:** www.ibnet.org/ – **119)** Barrio La Bara, Calle Pavimentada, Casa 1185, La Ceiba. ☎ +504 443 2481. – **120)** Calle del Comercio 12A, Comayagua. – **121)** San Marcos de Colón, Choluteca. – **122)** Barrio La Mora, Catacamas, Olancho. - **FM:** 99.1. – **123)** Barrio Loma Jackson N° 3, La Ceiba. – **124)** Col. 21 de Octubre, Sector 3, Bl. 1, Casa 4, Tegucigalpa. – **125)** San Pedro Sula. – **126)** Barrio Cafetal, San Marcos de Colón, Choluteca. - **FM:** 91.3. – **127)** 1 Av. Calle Principal, Jutiapa, Atlántida. - **FM:** 95.7. ☎ +504 898 4918. – **128)** Radio Ensenanzas Evangelicas, Puerto Lempira. – **129)** Barrio Abajo, Sonaguera, Colón. - **FM:** 93.5. – **130)** Barrio El Centro Contiguo a Banadesa, Danlí, El Paraíso. - **FM:** 104.7. – **131)** Yoro – Dir: Jamil N. Hawit Castro. – **132)** Ap. 2424, San Pedro Sula. – **133)** Ap. 914, Tegucigalpa. – **134)** Barrio La Manzana, Minas de Oro, Comayagua. – **135)** Ap. 15, 16101 Juticalpa. - **FM:** 106.3. Prgrs in Sp. and E. – **136)** Col. Río Piedras, 5 Calle 26 Av., San Pedro Sula. – **137)** La Entrada. – **138)** Fte. Supermercado Demar, Danlí, El Paraíso. **FM:** 98.1. – **139)** Barrio Concepción, Fte Coop, Ocotepeque. - **FM:** 99.9. ☎ +504 653 3306. – **140)** Ap. 40, Choluteca. - **FM:** 95. 5. – **141)** Barrio El Centro, Yoro. – **142)** Tocoa, Colón. – **143)** San Lorenzo. – **144)** La Entrada, Copán. – **145)** Barrio San Sebastián 2 Calle, San Marcos, Ocotepeque. – **146)** Barrio Jesús, Juticalpa. – **147)** Ap. 888, (or: Centro Comercial San José), La Ceiba. ☎+504 441 5973. **Web:** www.applegatefellowship.org/missions/honduras.asp - **Email:** radiolitoral@psinet.hn **English:** Weekends 0400-0500 – **148)** Barrio La Pava, Sabá, Colón. ☎ +504 424 82 49. – **149)** Frente al Parque "Lempira", Gracias, Lempira (or: Ap.1579, Tegucigalpa). - **FM:** 95.1 R. Galaxia 21 FM Stereo. ☎ +504 656 1068. – **150)** Barrio Las Brisas, Contiguo a Comercial Dorado, Nacaome, Valle. - **FM:** 99.1. – **151)** Ocotepeque, Ocotepeque **Web:** www.cauaguanca.com/radiocomunidad **Email:** radiocomunidad910@yahoo.es ☎+504 653 3994 – **152)** Media Cuadra Al Norte del ParWque, B:o El Centro, Ocotepeque. - **FM:** 92.1. – **153)** Ap. 210 (or: 5 Calle, 10 y 11 Av S.O., Barrio Beuque), San Pedro Sula. - **FM:** 90.7. – **154)** Av. 19 de Julio, La Ceiba. – **155)** Col. Miraflores, Tegucigalpa. ☎+504 661 2327. – **156)** Calle Principal, Tocoa, Colón. – **157)** Calle Vicente Williams 345, Choluteca. – **158)** Barrio El Centro, Gracias, Lempira. – **159)** Barrio El Centro, Juticalpa. – **160)** Calle del Comercio, Danlí, El Paraíso. – **161)** Barrio Sanpile, Carr. a Guasaule, Choluteca. – **162)** 2 Av. Calle 38, Trinidad, Sta Bárbara. ☎ +504 664 1681. – **163)** Barrio La Esperanza 4A N° 142, Choluteca. - **FM:** 98.5. – **164)** Barrio Jesus, Juticalpa. – **165)** Barrio El Banco, La Entrada. ☎+504 661 2327. - **FM:** 103.5. – **166)** Barrio El Progreso, La Entrada. – **167)** Barrio Sta Rosario, Nacaome, Valle. – **168)** Las Torres, Comayagüela. – **169)** Barrio San José, Morazán, Yoro. – **170)** Calle del Estadio, Barrio El Campo, Catacamas. – **171)** San Marcos de Colón, Choluteca. – **172)** Av. Independencia, Sta Bárbara. - **FM:** 89.7. – **173)** Barrio Miraflores, La Entrada. – **174)** Olanchito, Yoro. – **175)** Barrio El Centro, Siguatepeque. – **176)** Barrio Guadalupe, Choluteca. - **FM:** 100.9. – **177)** Barrio El Coyol, Sava Colón. – **178)** Atrás del Estadio, Barrio La Isla, ½ Cdra del Colegio Bethel, La Ceiba. – **179)** Calle Principal, Frente a Parque Central, Sta Cruz de Yojoa, Cortés. – **180)** Barrio La Cruz, Contiguo a la Iglesia el Encuentro, Catacamas, Olancho. ☎ +504 899 4329. – **181)** 4 y 5 Ave, 3 Calle 442, Barrio Las Delicias, El Progreso, Yoro. ☎ +504 898 4803. – **182)** Barrio El Campo, Frente a la Ferreteria San António, Sigiatepeque. – **183)** Barrio El Centro, Valle del Boulevard, Contiguo a la Iglesia Adventista, Siguatepeque. – **184)** Ap 79, Danlí, El Paraíso. – **185)** Barrio El Centro, Contiguo al Banco Atlántida, Las Vegas, Sta Bárbara. ☎ +504 659 3156. – **186)** Escuela Agricola Panamericana, Valle El Zamorano, Francisco Morazán. ☎ +504 235 8227. – **187)** Balneareo Pasada del Sol, Barrio Arriba, Comayagua. ☎ +504 772 0565. – **188)** Tegucigalpa. – **189)** Copán. – **190)** Sta Bárbara. - **FM:** 103.5. – **191)** El Paraíso. – **192)** Barrio de Jesús, Casa 7, Calle Principal, Juticalpa. – **193)** Col.Irias, Primera Calle, 5 Casas a Mano Izquierda, La Ceiba. ☎ +504 441 0238. – **194)** Radio Industrias de Honduras, Tegucigalpa. – **195)** Amapala, Valle. – **196)** Barrio San José, Ocotepeque. ☎ +504 443 0435. – **197)** Ap. 004, Sta Bárbara. ☎+504 643 2740. 🖷+504 643 2940. - **FM:** 102.9. – **198)** Olanchito, Yoro. – **199)** Trinidad, Sta Bárbara – **200)** Sonaguera, Colón. – **201)** Taujica. **202)** Ap 534, San Pedro Sula. **203)** Edif. Tovar López y Asociados, Col. Florencia Norte, 1 Av, 2 Calle, Tegucigalpa. **Email:** radioreloj@hondudata.hn

FM in Tegucigalpa: 88.1 Satélite – 88.3 Aeropuerto – 88.7 Reloj – 89.3 Power – 89.9 Saturno/Sonora – 90.5 La Fórmula – 91.0 Estéreo Mil – 91.7 R. Fiesta – 92.3 Mil – 92.9 HRN Cadena de Noticias – 93.3 Estéreo Fantasía – 93.5 Tic Tac – 94.1 FM 94 – 94.7 América – 95.3 Digital FM – 95.9 R. Panamericana – 96.5 Sonorama – 96.9 Estéreo Dimensión – 97.1 Tic Tac/Titania – 97.7 Azul – 98.3 Concierto FM – 98.9 La Exitosa – 99.5 Suprema – 100.1 Super 100 – 100.7 Unión — 101.3 LV Suyapa – 101.5 Monumental/Norte – 101.9 Satélite – 102.5 Suave – 103.1 DCR – 103.7 Luz/Fiesta – 104.1 FM104 – 104.3 Momentos FM – 104.9 Amor/Exitos – 105.5 Actión – 106.1 Romántica – 106.7 LV Evangelica – 107.3 W107 – 107.9 Tegucigalpa.

AFRTS (Air Force)
🖃 JTF-B, APO AA 34042, USA **Email:** PAO@jtfb-emh1.army.mil
FM: 106.5 Soto Cano Air Base, 0.25 kW, **D.Prgr:** 24h.

HONG KONG (China, SAR)

L.T: UTC +8h — **Pop:** 6.8 million — **Pr.L:** Cantonese, English — **E.C** 50Hz 200/220v — **ITU:** HKG

RADIO TELEVISION HONG KONG (Gov.)

🖃 Broadcasting House, 30 Broadcast Drive, Kowloon, Hong Kong ☎ +852 2339 6300 🖷 +852 2336 9314 **Email:** ccu@rthk.org.hk **Web:** www.rthk.org.hk
L.P: Dir. of Broadc: Mr. Chu Pui-hing. Asst. Dir. of Broadc. (Radio): Mr. Peter Shiu-Lo-sin.
MW:

kHz	Network	Location	kW
567	Radio 3	Golden Hill	20
621	P. Ch	Golden Hill	20
675	Radio 6	Peng Chau	10
783	Radio 5	Golden Hill	20
1584	Radio 3	Chung Hom Kok	0.2

P. Ch = Putonghua Channel
FM:

MHz	Network	kW	Tr. Location	Target Div.
92.6	Radio 1	1	Mt. Gough	Kowloon
92.9	Radio 1	0.1	Golden Hill	Tsuen Wan
93.2	Radio 1	0.5	Cloudy Hill	Fan Ling
93.4	Radio 1	0.5	Castle Peak	Tuen Mun
93.5	Radio 1	0.1	Beacon Hill	Sha Tin
93.6	Radio 1	0.3	Lamma Island	HK Island south
94.4	Radio 1	0.5	Kowloon Peak	HK Island north, Sai Kung
94.8	Radio 2	1	Mt. Gough	Kowloon
95.3	Radio 2	0.5	Cloudy Hill	Fan Ling
95.6	Radio 2	0.1	Golden Hill	Tsuen Wan
96.0	Radio 2	0.3	Lamma Island	HK Island south
96.3	Radio 2	0.1	Beacon Hill	Sha Tin
96.4	Radio 2	0.5	Castle Peak	Tuen Mun
96.9	Radio 2	0.5	Kowloon Peak	HK Island north, Sai Kung
97.6	Radio 4	1	Mt. Gough	Kowloon
97.8	Radio 4	0.5	Cloudy Hill	Fan Ling
97.9	Radio 3	0.01	Mt. Nicholson	Jardine's Lookout
98.1	Radio 4	0.1	Beacon Hill	Sha Tin
98.2	Radio 4	0.3	Lamma Island	HK Island south
98.4	Radio 4	0.1	Golden Hill	Tsuen Wan
98.7	Radio 4	0.5	Castle Peak	Tuen Mun

MHz	Network	kW	Tr. Location	Target Div
98.9	Radio 4	0.5	Kowloon Peak	HK Island north, Sai Kung
99.4	Radio 5	0.015	Jank Bay	Jank Bay
100.9	P. Ch	0.01	Jardine's Lookout	Happy Valley
103.3	P. Ch	0.015	Jank Bay	Jank Bay
106.8	Radio 5	0.01	Castle Peak	Tuen Mun
106.8	Radio 3	0.06	Chung Hom Kok	HK Island south
107.8	Radio 3	0.015	Jank Bay	Jank Bay

RTHK Radio 1 in Cantonese/Chinese: 24h. Merged with Radio 2: 1830-2230(2300 on Sat). Merged with Radio 5: 1000-1030(Sat & Sun 1015), 1400-1800(Mon-Fri), 2230-0200(0300 on Sat) exc Sun. Merged with Putonghua Channel: 1200-1400.and 1800-1830
RTHK Radio 2 in Cantonese: 24h. Merged with Radio 1 : 1830-2200. Merged with Radio 5: 1530-2230(Mon to Fri) , 1200-2300 on Sat. and 1400-2200 on Sun.
RTHK Radio 3 in English: 24h AM-stereo.
RTHK Radio 4 in English/Cantonese: 24h. Merged with Radio 3 1600-2200.
RTHK Radio 5 in Cantonese/Chinese: 24h AM-stereo. Merged with Radio 1: 1000-1030(Sat & Sun 1015), 1400-1800(Mon-Fri), 2230-0200. Merged with Radio 2: 1530-2230(Mon to Fri) 1200-2300 on Sat.1500-2200
RTHK Radio 6 Relay BBCWS English: 24h.
RTHK Putonghua Channel in Chinese: 24h. Merged with Radio 1 1200-1400 (Mon-Fri). and 1800-1830. Merged with Radio 2 1830-2300(Mon to Fri) ,1830-2200(Sat & Sun).

HONG KONG COMMERCIAL BROADC. CO. LTD

✉ 3 Broadcast Drive, Kowloon, Hong Kong ☎ +852 2336 5111 🖷+852 2338 0021 **Email:** cs@881903.com **Web:** www.881903.com

MW:

kHz	Location	Prgr.	kW
864	Peng Chau	Quote AM	10

FM:

MHz	Network	kW	Tr. Location	Target Div.
88.1	CR1	1	Mt.Gough	Kowloon
88.3	CR1	0.5	Cloudy Hill	Fan Ling
88.6	CR1	0.5	Castle Peak	Tuen Mun
88.9	CR1	0.1	Golden Hill	Tsuen Wan
89.1	CR1	0.3	Lamma Island	HK Island south
89.2	CR1	0.1	Beacon Hill	Sha Tin
89.5	CR1	0.5	Kowloon Peak	HK Island north, Sai Kung
90.3	CR2	1	Mt.Gough	Kowloon
90.7	CR2	0.5	Cloudy Hill	Fan Ling
90.9	CR2	0.1	Golden Hill	Tsuen Wan
91.1	CR2	0.1	Beacon Hill	Sha Tin
91.2	CR2	0.5	Castle Peak	Tuen Mun
91.6	CR2	0.3	Lamma Island	HK Island south
92.1	CR2	0.5	Kowloon Peak	HK Island north, Sai Kung

HKCR CR1 (Supercharged 881) in Cantonese. 24h **N:** half-hourly. Rel CR2 1800(Sat 1700)-2200.
HKCR CR2 (Ultimate 903) in Cantonese. 24h **N:** hourly.
HKCR AM864 in English. 24h **N**:On the hour from 2200-1500.

METRO BROADCAST CORPORATION LTD.

✉ Basement 2, Site 6, Whampoa Gardens Hunghom, Kowloon, Hong Kong ☎ +852 2123 9888 🖷+852 2123 9877 **Email:** tech@metroradio.com.hk, **Web:** www.metroradio.com.hk

MW:

kHz	Network	kW	Location
1044	Metro Plus	10	Peng Chau

FM:

MHz	Network	kW	Tr. Location	Target Div.
99.7	Metro Showbiz	1	Mt.Gough	Kowloon
100.0	Metro Showbiz	0.5	Cloudy Hill	Fan Ling
100.4	Metro Showbiz	0.5	Castle Peak	Tuen Mun
100.5	Metro Showbiz	0.1	Beacon Hill	Sha Tin
101.6	Metro Showbiz	0.1	Golden Hill	Tsuen Wan
101.8	Metro Showbiz	0.5	Kowloon Peak	HK Island north, Sai Kung
102.1	Metro Showbiz	0.3	Lamma Island	HK Island south
102.4	Metro Finance	0.1	Beacon Hill	Sha Tin
102.5	Metro Finance	0.5	Castle Peak	Tuen Mun
104.0	Metro Finance	1	Mt.Gough	Kowloon
104.5	Metro Finance	0.3	Lamma Island	HK Island south
104.7	Metro Finance	0.5	Cloudy Hill	Fan Ling
105.5	Metro Finance	0.1	Golden Hill	Tsuen Wan
106.3	Metro Finance	0.5	Kowloon Peak	HK Island north, Sai Kung

Metro Plus in English (Partly Filipino, Indonesian and Hindi). 24h. AM-Stereo music, news and information. **Metro Showbiz** in Cantonese. 24h. **Metro Finance** in Cantonese. 24h.

HUNGARY

L.T: UTC +1h (27 Mar-30 Oct: UTC +2h) — **Pop**: 10.1 million — **Pr.L**: Hungarian — **E.C**: 50Hz, 220V — **ITU**: HNG

MAGYAR RÁDIÓ

✉ Bródy Sándor u. 5-7, H-1800 Budapest. ☎ +36 1 3287000 or 3288388. 🖷 36 1 3288908. **Web**: www.radio.hu Prgr guide: www.musor.radio.hu Audio archive for past 6 months: www.radio.hu/index.php?rovat_id=1011

Kossuth Rádió
☎ +36 1 3287945 Petőfi Rádió: ☎ +36 1 3288555 Bartók Rádió: ☎ +36 1 3288772. **L.P**: Pres.: Katalin Kondor

Regional network (RNI) ☎ +36 1 328-8438, 🖷 +36 1 328-7018 **b)** Debrecen Civis Rádió ✉ 4024 Debrecen, Piac u. 28./c ☎ +36 52 412-311 🖷 36 52 413-348 **c)** Györi Regionális Stúdió + Régió R. ✉ 9027 Győr, Nagy Imre u. 28. ☎ +36 96 412-722 🖷 36 96 412-722 **d)** Miskolci Regionális Stúdió ✉ 3527 Miskolc, Bajcsy-Zsilinszky u. I5. ☎ +36 46 343-666 🖷 36 46 341-688 **e)** Nyíregyházi Regionális Stúdió ✉ 4400 Nyíregyháza, Szent István u. 42. ☎+36 42 410-611 🖷 +36 42 410-472 **f)** Pécsi Regionális Stúdió ✉ 7621 Pécs, Szent Mór u. 1. ☎ +36 72 210-666 🖷 36 72 210-424 **Web:** www.radio-pecs.hu **g)** Szeged Partiscum Rádió ✉ 6720 Szeged, Stefánia 7. ☎ +36 62 475-725 🖷 36 62 475-725 **h)** Szolnoki Regionális Stúdió ✉ 5000 Szolnok, Kolozsvári u. 2. ☎ +36 56 421-133 🖷 36 56 425-610 **i)** Zala Rádió Nagykanizsa ✉ 8800 Nagykanizsa, Petőfi S. u. 5. ☎ +36 93 326-410 🖷 36 93 326-412 **j)** Szombathely: ✉ 9700 Szombathely, Thököly út 14. ☎ +36 94 313-850 🖷 36 94 313-850

MW	kHz	kW	Prgr+Reg.
Solt	540	2000/1000	1
Lakihegy	873	22	1+ethn.
Pécs	873	20	f
Miskolc	1116	15	1d
Mosonmagyaróvár	1116	5	c
Szombathely	1251	25	1c,i
Nyíregyháza	1251	25	1e
Györ	1350	5	c

FM (MHz):	1*	1	2	3	Reg	kW
Budapest	67.40	107.8	94.8	105.3		10
Csávoly			89.4			3
Debrecen		99.7	89.0	106.6	91.4b	1
Györ	72.86c		93.1	106.8		3/1
Kabhegy	72.98c	102.3	93.9	105.0		10/3/10/10
Kékestetö	71.21d		102.7	90.7		3
Kiskörös			95.1	105.9		3/1
Komádi	66.14g	89.9p	96.7	105.1		3
Miskolc	66.80d	103.8	102.3	107.5		3
Nagykanizsa	71.03ij	106.7	94.3	104.7		10
Pécs	71.81f	104.6	103.7	107.6	101.7f	10
Sopron	72.86c	91.8p	99.5	107.9		10/10/1
Szeged		101.9p	104.6	105.7	93.1g	0.5/2/1
Szentes	66.29g	91.6	98.8	107.3		3/1/10/
Szolnok					101.2	-
Tokaj	71.33d	88.3	92.7	105.5		10/5/10/
Úzd			90.3	106.9		3
Vasvár		103.6	98.2	106.9		3

* "Kossuth URH", mono. Also carries ethnic pgrs and parliamentary broadcasts
Additional trs below 1kW for Kossuth R: Telkibánya (90.2), Sátoraljaújhely (91.9), Siófok (93.5), Szolnok (94.3),, Aggtelek (94.6), Mosonmagyaróvár (95.0), Kaposvár (96.7), Békéscsaba (97.3), Kazincbarcika (97.7), Szekszárd (99.0), Kékesteto (99.8), Salgótarján (99.8), Rábaszentandrás (105.2), Fehérgyarmat (105.9)

DAB: Budapest Prgrs 1+2+3: 230.016-231.552 MHz 90W. ☎ +36 (1) 203-6060/2821 🖷: 464-2550

Prgrs: 1=**Kossuth** R. (news, talk) 2=**Petöfi** R. (family enterntainm.) 3=**Bartók** R. (classical+literature) **NB**: All sts 24h. Kossuth Rel. BBC Hungarian 0704-0714.
Regional Prgrs: b) Debrecen, c) Györ, d) Miskolc, e) Nyíregyháza, f) Pécs, g) Szeged, h) Szolnok, i) Nagykanizsa j) Szombathely. Local pgrms on AM: 0430-2100, on FM: 0430-0800 Relays Kossuth R.: 0600-0615, 0700-0715, 1200-1240, 1800-1830.
Ethnic Prgrs: ☎ +36 (1) 328-8672, 🖷 +36 (1) 328-8682. Nationwide on Kossuth OIRT FM + Regional AM/FM trs: Slovak: 1730-1800; Romanian: 1800-1830; German: 1830-1900; Croatian 1900-1930;

Serbian 1930-2000; Roma 2000-2030 (exc. Pécs, Szeged: 2200-2230). 2030-2100 Slovenian, Tu: Rusin, W: Bulgarian, Th: Greek, F: Ukranian, Sa: Armenian, Su: Polish (☎+36-1-328-7018). Local: Slovene 0500-0530 Sun (j), Serbian 1200-1300, 2000-2030 (f) German 0930-1100 (f) **ANN**: "Kossuth Rádió, Budapest" or "Itt a Kossuth Rádió" (Tune signal: from Kossuth-song), "Petőfi Rádió, Budapest", Bartók Rádió, Budapest" (Tune signal from Bartók: 3rd Concerto).

EXTERNAL SERVICE: Radio Budapest
See International Broadcasting Section

National Radio and Television Commission (ORTT)
✉ 1088 Budapest, Reviczky u. 5. ☎ +36 1 429-8600, 267-2590. ℻ +36 (1) 267-2612. **Web**: www.ortt.hu

National Communications Authority, Hungary (NCAH)
✉ 1015 Budapest, Ostrom utca 23-25 ☎ +36 1 468-0673 **Web**: www.hif.hu.

Hungarian Federation of Free Radios (SZARÁMASZER)
✉ 1066 Budapest Ó utca 11. I/6. ☎/℻ +36 1 3111855. **L.P**: MD: Peterfi Ferenc. **Web**: www.szabadradio.hu

National Association of Hungarian Local Radios
✉ 8200 Veszprém, Zrínyi utca 3. ☎/℻ +36 88 422-944, 425-056 Pres: Mészáros Zoltán

DANUBIUS RÁDIÓ (Comm.)
✉ H-1138 Budapest, Vaci u. 141. ☎ +36 (1) 452 6100. ℻ +36 (1) 452 6180.

FM:	MHz	kW	FM:	MHz	kW
Szeged	94.9	0.5	Sopron	102.0	3
Miskolc	98.3	3	Budapest	103.3	10
Kabhegy	100.5	10	Tokaj	103.5	10
Debrecen	101.1	1	Kékes	104.7	3
Györ	101.4	3	Pecs	105.5	10
Komádi	101.6	3			

SLÁGER RÁDIÓ (Comm.)
✉ 2040 Budaörs, Szabadság út 117 ☎ +36 (23) 400-400. ℻ +36 (23) 507-444. Format: Oldies

FM:	MHz	kW	FM:	MHz	kW
Debrecen	87.6	1	Csávoly	96.7	3
Györ	87.6	3	Sopron	96.8	10
Kiskörös	88.4	1	Miskolc	97.1	3
Nagykanizsa	90.2	10	Tokaj	97.5	10
Szeged	90.3	0,5	Szentes	100.4	3
Vasvár	91.6	3	Budapest	100.8	10
Kékes	95.5	3	Úzd	101.5	3
Pécs	95.9	10	Komádi	103.0	3
Kabhegy	107.2	10			

Major Networks of Local Stations

RÁDIÓ 1
✉ 1062 Budapest, Andrássy út 86. ☎ +36 (1) 473-2600. ℻ +36 (1) 473-2620 **NB.** All sts have local prgrming

FM:	MHz	kW	FM:	MHz	kW
Budapest	103.9	5	Orosháza	90.2	0.8
Békéscsaba	100.9		Pécs	90.6	0.1
Debrecen	92.3	0.1	Székesfv.	101.8	
Eger	101.9		Veszprém	94.6	
Komló	99.4	0.02	Gyula	90.5	
Szarvas	95.2		Szeghalom	99.4	

KÉK DUNA RÁDIÓ
✉ 2501 Esztergom, Pf.4 00 ☎ +36 (33) 400 925 ℻ +36 (33) 400 111. **Email:** ttb@kekduna.hu **NB**: All sts have local prgming

FM:	MHz	kW	FM:	MHz	kW
Esztergom	92.5	0.1	Pápa	92.7	
Györ	91.5	1	Tatabánya	107.0	0.84
Komárom	90.5	0.8			

ALISCA RÁDIÓ
✉ 7100 Szekszárd, Szent László u. 19. ☎ +36 (74) 410-191 **Email:** aliscaradio@terrasoft.hu

FM:	MHz	kW	FM:	MHz	kW
Szekszárd	91.1	0.1	Paks	107.5	0.25
Bonyhád	92.8	0.25	Tamási	101.9	1
Baja	94.3	0.05	Dunaföldvár	106.5	1

JUVENTUS RÁDIÓ
✉ 1134 Budapest, Róbert Károly körút 82/84 ☎+36 (1) 237 5300 ℻ +36 (1) 320-1299

FM:	MHz	kW	FM:	MHz	kW
Budapest	89.5	10	Szeged	100.2	0.17
Siófok	92.6	-	Pécs	101.2	0.1
Szentes	95.7	0.25			

Note: 18 local stations, part of Juventus network, are not mentioned, incl. R. Ga-Ga and R. Jam.

MAGYAR KATOLIKUS RÁDIÓ (Eger)
✉ 3301 Eger, Pf. 86. ☎ +36 (36) 510-610. ℻ +36 (36) 510-614 . **Web**: www.mkr.hu **NB.** All sts rel. Eger

FM:	MHz	kW	FM:	MHz	kW
Eger	91.8	1	Hatvan	94.0	
Sátoraljaújhely	90.6	1	Miskolc	95.1	1

MAGYAR KATOLIKUS RÁDIÓ (National)
✉ 1062 Budapest, Délibáb u. 15-19. ☎ +36 (1) 255-3366. ℻ +36 (1) 255-3399 **Web**: www.katolikusradio.hu

MW	kHz	kW	kHz	kW
Lakihegy	810†	12	Siófok 1341†	-
Szolnok	1341	135		

D.Prgr: 03:30-23:30. † trs from Apr. 2005

Other Local Stations

MW	kHz	kW	Name & Location	Times
78)	1485	0.25	Party Rádió, Mohács	0600-1900

FM	MHz	kW	Name & Location
6)	88.1	0.1	Budapest R., Budapest (+97.3 Göd)
95)	88.8	0.1	Rádió C, Budapest (roma ethnic)
110)	90.3	1	Tilos Rádió, Budapest (community)
29)	92.9	0.15	Radio Deejay, Budapest (CHR)
112)	93.6	1	Másik Rádió, Gödöll (talk+music)
113)	94.2		R. Extrém, Budapest
42)	95.3	0.25	Klubrádió, Budapest (talk)
44)	95.8c	0,25	Info R., Budapest (news mono)
50)	96.4	2.5	Roxy R., Budapest (hot CHR)
93)	97.7	1	Partner Rádió, Kecskemét (CHR)
55)	98.0	1	Fiksz R., Budapest (Su-Tu) (community)
56)	98.0	1	Civil R., Budapest (We-Sa) (community)
58)	98.6	1.2	Radiocafé, Budapest (alt. rock)
72)	102.1	1	Sztár FM, Budapest (CHR)
81)	104.0a	1	Csaba R., Békéscsaba (CHR)
75)	106.6	0.13	Szlovén R., Szentgotthárd 1600-1700 (ethnic)
111)	105.9		Gazdasági R., Budapest (news)

+ c. 100 local st's below 0.5kW

Addresses and other information
6) ✉ 1146 Budapest, Hungária krt. 162. 10. em.☎+36 (1) 471-93-56 ℻ +36 (1) 471-93-54. – **29)** ✉ 1024 Budapest, Lövöház u. 2-6. ☎ +36 (1) 438-6058, 438-6055 ℻ +36 (1) 438-6065 – **42)** ✉ 1024 Budapest, Rómer Flóris utca 4/a ☎ +36 (1) 315 1204 ℻ +36 (1) 315 1205 – **44)** ✉ 1088 Budapest, Múzeum u. 9. ☎ +36 (1) 4832950 ℻ +36 (1) 4832625. **NB** Rel. BBC Hungarian 2005 – **50)** ✉ Budapest, Fény u. ☎ +36 (1) 466 03 44 ℻ +36 (1) 466 06 73 – **55)** ✉ 1111 Budapest, Müegyetem rakpart 3. ☎ +36 (1) 463 4313 – **56)** ✉ 1011 Budapest, Corvin tér 8. ☎ +36 (1) 201 1417 – **58)** ✉ 1064 Budapest, Vörösmarty u. 67 ☎ +36 (1) 301 2170 ℻ (36 1) 301 2190 **SMS** (36 20) 9 986 986 – **72)** ✉ 1149 Budapest, Róna u. 120-122. – **75)** ✉ 9970 Szentgotthárd, Gárdonyi Géza utca 1. ☎ +36 (94) 383 111. ℻ (36 94) 383-100 **Email:** radiomonoster@matavnet.hu **NB** In Slovenian language – **78)** ✉ 7700 Mohács, Bakács u.5. ☎ +36 (69) 311-447 ℻ +36 (69) 311-733 – **81)** ✉ 5600 Békéscsaba, Teleki utca 5. ☎ +36 (66) 441-111. ℻ +36 (66) 441-112. – **93)** ✉ 6000 Kecskemét, Kandó Kálmán u. 1. ☎ +36 (76) 503-970 ℻ +36 (76) 509-770 **Email:** partnerradio@axelero.hu – **95)** ✉ 1086 Budapest, Teleki tér 6 . ☎ +36 (1) 4590095. ℻ +36 (1) 4590094 **Email:** radioc@radioc.hu **SMS**:20/956-8888 – **110)** ✉ 1092 Budapest, Kinizsi u. 28. **NB:** Some English prms – **111)** ✉ 1133 Budapest, Váci út 78/B ☎ +36 (1) 8873500 ℻ +36 (1) 8873501 – **112)** ✉ 2101 Gödöllo, Pf 336 ☎ +36 (28) 511936 ℻ +36 (28) 511939 **Web**: www.tuloldal.hu – **113)** ✉ 1118 Budapest, Citadella sétány ☎℻ +36 (1) 2791145
NB. For up-to-date ✉☎info, see www.matav.hu, DX info: www.eter.hu **Web:** usually www.[stationname with or without "radio"].hu

Small-Community Radio
23 new, local, low-power stations (max. 1W) have been granted licences in both cities and country villages in 2004. For more info: http://www.kkapcsolat.hu/szabadradio/hkiskoz.htm

VOA, RADIO FREE EUROPE, RADIO LIBERTY
MW: Marcali 1188kHz 500kW

BBC/RFI
✉ 1054 Budapest, Szabadság tér 7. ☎+36 (1)3010471
FM: 92.1 MHz Budapest, Óbuda 24h 1kW
BBC broadcasts in English (0130-0630, 1800-2300) and Hungarian (1500-1700), RFI in French (0630-1500, 2300-0130) and German (0730, 1130, 1700-1800)

ICELAND

L.T: UTC — **Pop:** 275,277 — **Pr.L:** Icelandic — **E.C:** 50Hz, 230V — **ITU:** ISL

RÍKISÚTVARPIÐ (Icelandic National Broadcasting Service, Pub.)

Efstaleiti 1, 150 Reykjavík. ☎ +354 515 3000. 🖷 +354 515 3010. **Email:** isradio@ruv.is **Web:** www.ruv.is
L.P: Dir Gen: Markús Örn Antonsson.

LW	kHz	kW		kHz	kW
Gufuskálar	189	300	Eiðar	207	100

SW: Relays of RÚV newscasts: see International Radio section.

FM (MHz)	Rás 1	Rás 2*	kW
Almannaskarð	90.3	104.8a	1
Auðsholt	91.3	95.3d	2.5
Borgarland	88.0	96.3	3/3.5
Gagnheiði	98.8	87.7b	8.8/11.8
Girðisholt	92.9	-	3.5
Háfell	93.8	98.7d	14/34
Hegranes	90.6	98.8b	3.1/5
Hnjúkar	89.1	95.5b	6/6.2
Skálafell	92.4	99.9	24/24
Vaðlaheiði	91.6	96.5b	9.3
Vatnsendi	93.5	90.1	3.4
Vestmannaeyjar	97.1	88.1d	17/24
Viðarfjall	88.1	96.1b	3.3

NB. Tx's below 1kW not listed. *) Carries reg. prgrs (see below)
D.PRGR: Rás 1: 0600-0010. Rel. Rás 2: 0010-0600. – **Rás 2**: 24h.
LW schedule (189/207 kHz): MF: 0000-0700 Rás 1, 0700-0900 Rás 2, 0900-1400 Rás 1, 1400-1600 Rás 2, 1600-1615 Rás 1, 1615-1930 Rás 2, 1930-1945 Rás 1, 1945-2200 Rás 2, 2200-2400 Rás 1. Sat/Sun: 0000-1615 Rás 1, 1615-1930 Rás 2, 1930-1945 Rás 1, 1945-2200 Rás 2, 2200-2400 Rás 1.
Regional Prgrs (on Rás 2 tx's): **a)** Svæðisútvarp Austurlands, Miðvangi 2-4, 700 Egilsstaðir: Tue-Fri 1730-1800. – **b)** Svæðisútvarp Norðurlands, Kaupvangsstræti 1, 602 Akureyri: 1730-1800. – **c)** Svæðisútvarp Vestfjarðar, Aðalstræti 22, 400 Ísafjörður: Tue-Fri 1730-1800.– **d)** Svæðisútvarp Suðurlands, Austurvegi 4, 800 Selfoss: Tue-Fri 1730-1800.

OTHER STATIONS

MW	kHz	kW	Location	Station
9)	1530	0.25	Keflavík	Thunder 1530 (AFN)
FM	**MHz**	**kW**	**Location**	**Station**
2)	88.9	0.5	Vestmannaeyjar	Lindin
6)	89.5	2	Reykjavík	KissFM
1C)	90.4	2	Vestmannaeyjar	Radíó X
A)	90.9	2	Rjúpnahæð	BBC World Service
1A)	92.7	2	Vaðlaheiði	Bylgjan
1B)	93.1	2	Vestmannaeyjar	FM957
1E)	93.3	0.5	Vaðlaheiði	Útvarp Saga
1A)	93.9	0.5	Flatey	Bylgjan
1E)	94.3	2	Rjúpnahæð	Útvarp Saga
1A)	94.5	2	Háfell	Bylgjan
1B)	94.7	1	Egilsstaðir	FM957
1B)	95.1	1	Hegranes	FM957
1B)	95.7	10	Vatnsendi	FM957
1B)	95.7	0.5	Vaðlaheiði	FM957
4)	96.3	2	Vestmannaeyjar	Útvarp Suðurland
1A)	96.4	1	Skáneyjarbunga	Bylgjan
1D)	96.7	2	Rjúpnahæð	Létt 96.7
8)	96.7	0.5	Blönduós	Kántrý FM
1C)	97.7	2	Vatnsendi	Radíó X
1A)	97.9	1	Hegranes	Bylgjan
1A)	97.9	0.5	Arnabæli	Bylgjan
1A)	98.9	2	Vatnsendi	Bylgjan
1A)	98.9	1	Hnjúkar	Bylgjan
1A)	100.9	2	Vestmannaeyjar	Bylgjan
1B)	101.7	2	Vestmannaeyjar	FM957
8)	102.1	0.5	Hofsós	Kántrý FM
1F)	102.2	2	Vatnsendi	Barnaútvarpið
1B)	102.5	1	Skáneyjarbunga	FM957
2)	102.9	2	Vatnsendi	Lindin
1B)	103.2	1	Arnabæli	FM957
10)	103.7	2	Rjúpnahæð	3 ABN Radio
1C)	104.1	0.5	Vaðlaheiði	Radíó X
4)	104.5	2	Reykjavík	Radíó Reykjavík
5)	105.0	0.5	Reykjavík	Útvarp Boðun
3)	107.0	0.5	Vatnsendi	KFM107

NB. Tx's below 0.5kW not mentioned.
Addresses & other information:
1A-1E) Lynghálsi 5, 110 Reykjavík. Email: 1A) bylgjan@bylgjan.is, 1B) fm957@fm.is, 1C) radiox@radiox.is, 1D) lett@lett.is, 1E) saga@utvarp-saga.is – **2)** Krókhálsi 4a, 110 Reykjavík. – **3)** Hrafnhólum 8, 111 Reykjavík. Email: kfm@simnet.is – **4)** Eyravegi 2, 800 Selfoss. Email: utvarp@eyjar.is – **5)** Laugavegi 28, 101 Reykjavík. Email: 1045@radioreykjavik.is – **6)** Hverfisgötu 46, 101 Reykjavík. – **7)** Hlíðasmári 9, 200 Kópavogur. Email: bodunarkirkjan@bodunarkirkjan.is – **8)** Brimnes, 545 Skagaströnd. – **9)** US Naval Air Station, 235 Keflavíkurflugvöllur. Email: keflavik@mediacen.navy.mil. On 1530kHz: "Thunder 1530", rel. AFN (cf. USA) & own prgr's; on 104.1MHz: "Power 104" (mainly own prgr). – **10)** Reykjavík. – **A)** Lynghálsi 5, 110 Reykjavík. Rel. BBCWS (see UK).

INDIA

L.T: UTC +5½h — **Pop**: 1,030 million — **Pr.L**: Assamese, Bangla, Bodo, Dogri, English, Gujarati, Hindi, Kannada, Kashmiri, Maithili, Marathi, Malayalam, Nepali, Oriya, Punjabi, Santhali, Sindhi, Tamil, Telugu & Urdu — **E.C**: 50Hz 220/400V — **ITU**: IND

MINISTRY OF INFORMATION & BROADCASTING

Main Secretariat: A-Wing, Shastri Bhawan, New Delhi-110001.
L.P: Minister for Inf.& Broadc: S.Jaipal Reddy

PRASAR BHARATI (BROADCASTING CORPORATION OF INDIA) (Public Corporation)

2nd Floor, PTI Building, Parliament Street, New Delhi-110001
☎ +91-11-23382094/5/7/8/9, 🖷 +91-11-23386507.
☎91-11-23737603, 23352558 🖷91-11-23352549
Email: kssarma@prasarbharati.org.in
L.P: Chairman: M.V.Kamath, CEO: K.S. Sharma

AKASHVANI – ALL INDIA RADIO (Gov, semi-comm.)

Administration/Engineering: Directorate General of All India Radio, Akashvani Bhawan, 1 Sansad Marg, New Delhi-110001.
☎+91-11-23421006,23715413 🖷+91-11-23711956.
Email: airlive@air.org.in **Web:** www.allindiaradio.org.
Live Audio: www.allindiaradio.org/live.html.
L.P: DG: Brijeshwar Singh ☎+91-11-23710300/23421006 🖷 91-11-23421956 Email: dgair@air.org.in. Eng-in-Chief: K.M.Paul ☎+91-11-23421058, 23421459 🖷 +91-11-23421459, **Email:** einc@air.org.in Dir.(Spectrum Management & Synergy) Y.K.Sharma ☎+91-11-23421062, 23421145. Dy .Dir.: Devendra Singh **Email:** spectrum-manager@air.org.in
Programming: Broadcasting House, 1 Sansad Marg, New Delhi-110001.☎+91-11-23715411. Dir. Transcription & Prgr. Exchange Sces: V.A.Magazine ☎ +91-11-23421927.
News Services Division: Broadcasting House, 1 Sansad Marg, New Delhi-110001. Newsroom: ☎ +91-11-23421006, 23715413 🖷+91-11-23711956. **Email:** nsdair@giasdl01.vsnl.net.in.
Spl.DG (News): B.I.Saini ☎ +91-11- 23710084,23731510, News on phone: English ☎ +91-11-23324343, Hindi 23324242.
Commercial Sce: Vividh Bharati Sce, AIR, PO Box 11497, 101 M.K. Rd, Mumbai-400020. ☎ +91-22-22037193
Audience Research: Audience Research Unit, AIR, 2nd Floor, PTI Building, Sansad Marg, New Delhi-110001. ☎ +91-11-23710033, 23719215. Dir: Ramesh Chandra ☎ +91-11-23386506
National Channel: AIR, Gate 22, Jawaharlal Nehru Stadium, Lodhi Road, New Delhi-110003. ☎ +91-11-25843825
Dir: J.K.Das St.Eng: V.D. Sharma ☎ +91-11-25843207
Research & Development: Office of the Chief Eng R & D, All India Radio, 14-B Ring Road, Indra Prashta Estate, New Delhi-110002. ☎ +91-11-23378211, 23378212. Chief Eng: B.L.Mathur.
☎ +91-11-23379255, 23379329
Monitoring: International Monitoring Stn., All India Radio, Dr. K.S. Krishnan Rd, Todapur, New Delhi-110097. ☎ +91-11-25842939
Central Monitoring Station, All India Radio, Ayanagar, New Delhi-110047. Dir: P.S.Bhatnagar ☎ +91-11-26502955, 26501763
Regional Headquarters:
North Zone: AIR, Jamnagar House, Shahjahan Road, New Delhi-110011 ☎ +91-11-23382519
East Zone: AIR, 4th Floor, Akashvani Bhawan, Eden Gardens, Kolkata-700001 ☎ +91-33-22480158
North-East Zone: AIR, Dr P Kakati's Building, Nr. Ganeshguri

Flyover, G.S. Road, Guwahati-781006, Assam ☎ +91-361-2598276
West Zone: AIR, Old CGO Building, 101 M.K.Road, (P.O. Box 11452), Mumbai-400020, Maharashtra ☎ +91-22-22014287
South Zone: AIR, Swami Sivanada Salai, Chepauk, Chennai-600005. ☎ +91-44-25383253

Mediumwaves:
c) Vividh Bharati, e) Ext.Sce. n) National Channel, r) Relay Station

KHz	Station	kW	reg	KHz	Station	kW	reg
531	Jodhpur A	300	N	1143	Ratnagiri	20	W
540	Aizawl	20	NE	1143	Rohtak	20	N
549	Ranchi A	100	E	1161	Thiruvanathapuram	20	S
558	Mumbai B	100	W	1170	Hyderabad	1	S
567	Dibrugarh	300	NE	1179	Rewa	20	W
576r	Alappuzha	200	S	1188c	Mumbai C	50	W
585	Nagpur A	300	W	1197	Shillong	1	NE
594er	Chinsurah	1000	E	1197	Tirunelveli	20	S
603r	Ajmer	200	N	1206	Bhawanipatna	200	E
612	Bangalore A	200	S	1215n	New Delhi	20	N
621	Patna A	100	E	1215	Pudducherri	20	S
630	Thrisoor	100	S	1224	Kolkata	20	E
639	Kohima	100	NE	1233	Tura	20	NE
648	Indore A	200	W	1242	Varanasi	100	N
657	Kolkata A	200	E	1251	Sangli	20	W
666	New Delhi B	100	N	1260	Ambikapur	20	W
675	Chhattarpur	20	W	1269	Agartala	20	NE
675	Itanagar	100	NE	1269c	Jaipur B	1	N
684	Kozhikode A	100	S	1269	Madurai	20	S
684	Port Blair	100	S	1278c	Lucknow C	10	N
684	Srinigar C	10	N	1287	Panaji A	100	W
702e	Jalandhar A	200	N	1296	Darbhanga	10	E
711	Siliguri	200	E	1305	Parbhani	20	W
720	Chennai A	200	S	1314	Bhuj	20	W
729	Guwahati A	100	NE	1314c	Cuttack B	1	E
738	Hyderabad A	200	S	1323c	Kolkata C	20	E
747	Lucknow A	300	N	1332	Tezu	10	NE
756	Jagdalpur	100	W	1341	Kohima	1	NE
765	Dharwad A	200	S	1350c	Dharwad B	1	S
774	Shimla	100	N	1359	Bhadravathi	20	S
783c	Chennai C	20	S	1368c	New Delhi C	20	N
792	Pune A	100	W	1377	Hyderabad B	20	S
801	Jabalpur	200	W	1386	Gwalior	20	W
810	Rajkot A	300	W	1395	Bikaner	20	N
819	New Delhi A	200	N	1404	Gangtok	20	E
828	Silchar	20	NE	1440	Kurseong	1	E
837	Vijayawada A	100	S	1440	Port Blair (St'by)	1	S
846	Ahmedabad A	200	W	1449c	Kanpur	1	N
864	Shillong	100	NE	1458	Barmer	20	N
873	Jalandhar B	300	N	1458	Bhagalpur	20	E
882	Imphal	300	NE	1467	Jeypore	100	E
891	Rampur	20	N	1476	Jaipur A	1	W
900	Kadapa	100	S	1485	Adilabad	1	S
909	Gorakhpur	100	N	1485	Ahwa	1	W
918	Suratgarh	300	N	1485	Baripada	1	E
927	Visakhapatnam	100	S	1485	Diphu	1	NE
936	Tiruchirapalli A	100	S	1485	Gopeshwar	1	N
945	Sambalpur	100	E	1485	Joranda	1	E
954	Najibabad	100	N	1485	Nongstoin	1	E
963	Jalgaon	20	W	1503c	Vijayawada B	1	S
972	Cuttack A	300	E	1512	Kokrajhar	20	NE
981	Raipur	100	W	1521	Aurangabad	1	W
990	Jammu A	300	N	1521	Tawang	10	NE
999	Almora	1	N	1530	Agra	20	N
999	Coimbatore	20	S	1539c	Panaji B	20	W
1008	Kolkata B	100	E	1566nr	Nagpur	1000	W
1017	Chennai B	20	S	1584	Jamshedpur	1	E
1017	New Delhi	10	N	1584r	Kalpa	1	N
1026	Allahabad A	20	N	1584	Kargil	1	N
1035	Guwahati B	10	NE	1584	Kavaratti	1	S
1044	Mumbai A	100	W	1584	Keonjhar	1	E
1053	Leh	20	N	1584	Kota	1	N
1053e	Tuticorin	200	S	1584	Mathura	1	N
1062	Pasighat	10	NE	1584	Mon	1	NE
1071e	Rajkot	1000	W	1593	Bhopal A	10	W
1089r	Udipi	20	S	1602	Oottacamund	1	S
1107	Gulbarga	20	S	1602	Pauri	1	N
1116	Srinagar A	200	N	1602r	Pithoragarh	1	N
1125	Tezpur	20	NE	1602	Saiha	1	NE
1125	Udaipur	20	W	1602	Solapur	1	W
1134ne	Chinsurah	1000	E	1602	Tuensang	1	NE
1602r	Uttarkashi	1	N	1602	William Nagar	1	NE
1602c	Varanasi B	1	N	1602	Zero	1	NE

D.Prgr: Varies from station to station. Most stations have 3 transmissions daily ie Morning/Noon/Evening. Some smaller stations have only 1 or 2 transmissions. Extended coverage during sports or special events.
National Channel: 1325-0043 on 1215, 1566, 9425, 9470 kHz & 107.2 MHz Kasauli, (1134 from 1730)
Vividh Bharati (Entertainment Channel): 0025-1200, 1245-1730
F.Pl: New stations: 1kW at Car Nicobar, Champawat, Dharchulla, Drass, Dungarpur, Garison, Khaltsi, Lahul Spiti, Manendragargh, New Tehri, Padam, Pauri Srinagar, Rairangpur, Rudraprayag & Soro; 10kW at Hyderabad; 20kW at Chhatarpur, Darbhanga, Kota & Kupwara; 100kW at Kadapa & Delhi; 200 kW at Guwahati, Kargil, Najibabad & Tura; 300kW at Itanagar; 1000kW at Rajkot.

Regional Domestic SW stations:

kHz	KW	Station	Times
3223	50	Shimla	0025-0200,1300-1730 (Sat,Sun 1741)
3315	50	Bhopal	0025-0215,1130-1742
3365	50	Delhi	1220-1841
3390	10	Gangtok	0100-0400,1030-1600
3945†	50	Gorakhpur	0230-0300
4760	10	Leh	s0100/w0215-0430, 1130-1630/1700
4760	10	Port Blair	2355-0300,1030-1630/1700/1730
4775	50	Imphal	0030-0215,1030-1700/1730
4800	50	Hyderabad	0020-0215,1130(Sun 1140)-1744
4820	50	Kolkata	0025-0215,1220-1744
4830	50	Jammu	0025-0445, 1030-1100, 1130-1741
4840	50	Mumbai	2355-0400,1230-1730
4850	50	Kohima	0000-0450,1000-1600/1630/1700
4860†	50	Delhi	0025-0440,1220-1330
4880	50	Lucknow	0025-0400,1215-1741
4895	50	Kurseong	0055-0400,1130(Sun1030)-1700/1741
4910	50	Jaipur	0025-0415,1130-1741
4920	50	Chennai	0015-0245,1200-1736
4940	50	Guwahati	0015-0415,1150-1700/1741
4950	50	Srinagar	2330-0010(Ramzan Dec-Jan), s0025/w0120-0200,1130-1736
4960	50	Ranchi	0025-0435,1125(Sun 1130)-1741
4970	50	Shillong	0025-0400,1056-1630
4990	50	Itanagar	0020-0400,1000-1630
5010	50	Thiruvananthap.	0020-0215 1115(Sun 1130)-1735
5040	50	Jeypore	0025-0435(Sun 0445, Sat 0545v), 1130(Sun 1030)-1741
5050	50	Aizawl	0025-0400,1130(Sun 1125)-1630/1700
5965	50	Jammu	0630-0930
5985	50	Ranchi	0700-0945 (Sun 0630-1130)
6000	10	Leh	0655-0900 (Sun 1130)
6020	50	Shimla	0215-0400, (Sun 0415-1230), 0700-0936,1130-1230
6030	50	Delhi	0200-0310 1215-1430
6040	50	Jeypore	0700-0935
6065	50	Kohima	0430-0510, 0700-0900
6085	10	Gangtok	0700-0930
6085	50	Delhi	1220-1310, 1330-1340,1345-1420, 1430-1440, 1445-1615/1630/1700/1730v, 1730-1740
6110	50	Srinagar	0215-0453(Sun 1115),0600-1115
6150	50	Itanagar	0700-0900
6190	50	Delhi	0730-1030
7105	50	Lucknow	0630(Sun 0415)-0930, 0935-0936, (Sun 1030-1130)
7115	10	Port Blair	0315-0346(Sat 0415,Sun 0505), 0700-0930(Sun 1015)
7120	50	Jaipur	(Sun v0420-0600), 0700(Sun 0630)- 0941, (Sun 1030-1120)
7130	50	Shillong	0655-0930
7140	50	Hyderabad	0225-0445(Sat, Sun 0500), 0610-0930/ 0935, Sun 0530-1130
7140	100	Delhi	1550-1615/1630/1700/1730v,1730-1740
7150	50	Delhi	0030-0040
7150	50	Imphal	0230-0430/0530, 0630-1010
7160	50	Chennai	0300-0400(Hol 0445/Sun 0530), 0710(Hol 0610,Sat/Sun 0630)-0930 (Sun 1130)
7180	50	Bhopal	0225-0447(Sun 1115), 0700-0931
7190	50	Guwahati	0630-1730 (Tests)
7195	100	Mumbai	0025-0430, 0700-1330, 1430-1730 (Tests)
7210	50	Kolkata	0230-0401(Sat/Sun 0430), 0700-1000
7230	50	Kurseong	0619-1030 (Sun 1115)

kHz	KW	Station	Times
7235	50	Delhi	0215-0320, 0330-0355
7240	50	Mumbai	0530(Sun 0415)-1035
7250†	50	Gorakhpur	1130-1140
7255†	250	Aligarh	1530-1545
7270	100	Chenai	0025-0430, 0700-1330, 1430-1730 (Tests)
7280	50	Guwahati	0600-0930, 0945-1145, (Sun 0530-1145)
7290	50	Thiruvananthap.	0230-0415 (Sun 1030), 0630-0930
7295	50	Aizawl	0700-0930
7360	100	Delhi	0025-0430, 0700-1330, 1430-1730 (Tests)
7420	50	Guwhati	0025-0430, 0700-1330, 1430-1730 (Tests)
9425	500	Bangalore	1320-0043
9470	250	Aligarh	0130-0530 0930-1230 1320-0043
9575†	50	Delhi	1330-1420, 1430-1440, 1445-1615/ 1630/1700/1730v, 1730-1740
9595†	250	Aligarth	0800-0830, 1130-1140
9820†	250	Panaji	1530-1545
9835†	50	Delhi	1330-1420, 1430-1440, 1445-1615/ 1630/1700/1730v, 1730-1740
9910†	250	Aligarh	1530-1545
10330	500	Bangalore	0025-0435, 0900-1200, 1245-1740
11620†	250	Delhi	1130-1140
11710	50	Delhi	1115-1140
11740†	250	Panaji	1530-1545
11830	50	Delhi	0125-0355
15135	500	Delhi	0125-0205, 0215-0355
15185†	50	Delhi	0700-0930, 1115-1140
15260†	50	Delhi	0700-0930
17860†	100	Delhi	1220-1245

† = Used by External Service at other times, s = summer, w = winter, v = timing varies.

N in English originating in Delhi and relayed by most stations: 0035-0040, 0245-0300, 0335-0340, 0435-0440, 0630-0635, 0730-0735, 0830-0900, 0935-0940, 1030-1035, 1135-1140, 1230-1235, 1430-1435, 1435-1440(Sports), 1530-1545, 1730-1735. Extended broadcasts for special events, sports and on January 26 (Republic Day) and August 15 (Independence Day)

V. by QSL-card. Reception Reports to: Director (Spectrum Management & Synergy), All India Radio, Room No.204, Akashvani Bhavan, New Delhi-110001. 91-11-23421062, 23421145. **Email:** spectrum-manager@air.org.in. In charge of processing reception reports: Director: Y.K. Sharma Local stations also verify directly in many cases by letter or email. No return postage is necessary.

F.PI: News channel on SW.

FM Stations:

c) Vividh Bharati (Entertainment Channel) at 0025-1200, 1245-1730, n) National Channel r) Relay Station

MHz	location	kW	reg	MHz	location	kW	reg
93.9c	Vadodara	10	W	101.0	Bhaderwah	6	N
95.8c	Rajkot	10	W	101.0	Nagercoil	10	S
96.7c	Ahmedabad	10	W	101.0c	Pune	6	W
100.1	Ahmednagar	6	W	101.1	Bathinda	6	N
100.1	Kothagudem	6	S	101.1	Jowai	6	NE
100.2	Haflong	6	NE	101.1	Nanded	6	W
100.2	Patiala	6	N	101.1	Surat	6	W
100.2	Shivpuri	6	W	101.2	Khandwa	6	W
100.2	Kolkata II	5	E	101.3r	Aligarh	6	N
100.3c	Allahabad	10	N	101.3	Balaghat	6	W
100.3r	Asansol	6	E	101.3c	Bangalore I	10	S
100.3c	Jaipur	6	N	101.3	Banswara	6	N
100.3	Jammu A	3	N	101.3	Cuttack	6	E
100.3	Karaikal	6	S	101.3	Osmanabad	3	W
100.3	Mangalore	10	S	101.4	Devikulam	6	S
100.4	Bangalore		S	101.4	Kurukshetra	6	N
100.4	Bareilly	6	N	101.4c	Siliguri	10	E
100.5	Dhule	6	W	101.4	Nasik	6	W
100.5	Hospet	10	S	101.5	Kannur	6	S
100.5	Kodaikanal	10	S	101.5	Markapur	6	S
100.6	Berhampur	6	E	101.5	Sawai Madhopur	6	N
100.6c	Nagpur	6	W	101.6c	Indore	6	W
100.6	Mysore	10	S	101.6	Raipur	10	W
100.7	Churu	6	N	101.7	Anantapur	6	S
100.7	Lucknow	10	N	101.7	Chaibassa	6	E
100.7	Mumbai II	10	W	101.8	Bijapur	6	S
100.7	Poonch	6	N	101.8	Hamirpur	6	N
100.7	Raigarh	6	W	101.8	Jaisalmer	10	N
100.8c	Guwahati	10	NE	101.9	Bolangir	3	E
100.8c	Jamshedpur	6	E	101.9	Faizabad	6	N
100.9	Mukokchung	6	NE	101.9	Lungleh	6	NE

MHz	location	kW	reg	MHz	location	kW	reg
101.9	Rajouri	6	N	103.0	Chandrapur	6	W
101.9c	Thiruvanantha.	10	S	103.0c	Coimbatore	10	S
102.0	Shahdol	6	W	103.0	Daltonganj	6	E
102.0c	Visakhapatnam	10	S	103.0c	Dharwad	10	S
102.1	Hazaribagh	3	E	103.0	Jhansi	6	N
102.1c	Jodhpur	6	N	103.1	Alwar	6	N
102.1r	Musoorie	10	N	103.1	Betul	6	W
102.1	Raichur	6	S	103.1c	Chandigarh	3	N
102.1c	Tiruchirapalli	10	S	103.1	Madikeri	6	S
102.2	Chindwara	6	W	103.1	Satara	6	W
102.2	Godhra	6	W	103.1	Shanthi Nikethan	3	E
102.2	Hassan	6	S	103.2	Bilaspur	6	W
102.2	Kathua	10	N	103.2	Jhalawar	6	N
102.2	Murshidabad	6	E	103.2	Kailashahar	3	NE
102.3	Daman	3	W	103.2	Nizamabad	6	S
102.3	Guna	6	W	103.2	Tirupati	10	S
102.3	Hissar	6	N	103.3r	Dhubri	6	NE
102.3	Karwar	3	S	103.3c	Ranchi	6	E
102.3	Kochi A	6	S	103.4	Dharamsala	10	N
102.3	Purnea	6	E	103.4	Jorhat	10	NE
102.4	Akola	6	W	103.4	Puri	3	E
102.4	Kurnool	6	S	103.4	Sasaram	6	E
102.5r	Kullu	6	N	103.5c	Bhopal	6	W
102.5c	Patna	6	E	103.5	Mount Abu	6	N
102.6	Chitradurga	6	S	103.5	Warangal	10	S
102.6	Delhi I	10	N	103.6c	Kozhikode	10	S
102.6	Rourkela	6	E	103.7	Belonia	6	NE
102.6	Sagar	5	W	103.7	Nagaur	6	N
102.6c	Srinagar	10	N	104.1	New Delhi	0.1	N
102.7	Jalandhar	10	N	104.5c	Jammu B	10	N
102.7	Kolhapur	6	W	105.0	Chennai II	5	S
102.7c	Manjery	10	S	105.4	Panaji	6	W
102.7	Nagaon	6	NE	106.4	Delhi II	5	N
102.7	Obra	6	N	107.0	Kolkata I	10	E
102.7	Yeotmal	6	W	107.1	Chennai I	10	S
102.8c	Hyderabad	6	S	107.1	Mumbai I	10	W
102.9	Bangalore II	10	S	107.2nr	Kasauli	10	N
102.9	Beed	6	W	107.5c	Kochi B	10	S
102.9	Chittorgarh	6	N	107.5	Tirupati II	3	S
102.9c	Jabalpur	10	W				

F.PI: New stations at: Along, Chamba, Dharmanagar, Dharmapuri, Himmatnagar, Kathihar, Manubazar, Rajouri etc. and 3 in Lakshadeep. **1kW:** Anini, Bomdila, Champai, Daporijo, Dawki, Goalpara, Khonsa, Lumding, Nutan Bazar, Phek, Tamenglong, Tuipang, Udaipur (Tripura), Ukhrul, Wokha & Zunhebeto. **3 kW:** Macherla. **5 kW:** Bageshwar, Bankunthpur, Bhatwari, Danteware, Deogarh, Dumka, Gumla, Jashpurnagar, Kanchipuram, Karimgani, Karimnagar, Konny, Oros, Parlakimidi, Purulia, Rajnandgaon, Rayagada, Shirdi, Silchar, Srikakulam, Tamluk & Ujjain. **Change of 1kW MW to 5kW FM:** Mon & Tuensang. **6kW:** Aizawl, Churachandpur, Faridabad, Hamirpur (U.P.), Junagarh, Longtherai, Mandi & Shimoga. **Replacement of 10kW:** Jorhat. **Change of 1kW MW stations to 10kW FM:** Adilabad, Aurangabad, Kanpur, Mon, Sholapur,Tuensang, Varanasi & Vijayawada. **Upgrade to 10kW:** Alwar, Banswara, Chittorgarh, Hyderabad, Jorhat, Kochi, Kurukshetra, Nagpur, Pune & Surat. **10kW:** Agartala, Agra, Ahmedabad, Ambala, Amravati, Balurghat, Banda, Banka, Bardhaman, Behar, Bellary, Bhubaneswar, Bikaner, Chandigarh, Cooch Darjeeling Dehradun, Dhanbad, Fazilka, Gangtok, Gaya, Ghazipur, Gorakhpur, Gulbarga, Gwalior, Haldwani/Kaldhungi, Imphal, Itanagar, Jalandhar, Jamnagar, Junagadh, Kakinada, Kasargode, Kavaratti, Kheri, Kohima, Kota, Lakhimpur, Lucknow, Madhubani, Madurai, Mahaboobnagar, Malda, Motihari, Mussorie, Nellore, Patna, Pondicherry, Port Blair, Raipur, Ranchi, Sangli, Shillong, Shimla, Srigeri, Tirunelveli & Udaipur (Rajasthan). **20kW:** Amritsar, Delhi FM 1 & II, Chennai FM 1 & II & Kolkata FM II.

Addresses of regional stations

Adilabad-504002, Andhra Pradesh – Palace Compound, North Gate – **Agarthala**-799001, Tripura – Vivbhav Nagar, **Agra**-282001, Uttar Pradesh – Ashram Rd, Navarangpura, **Ahmedabad**-380009, Gujarat – **Ahmednagar**-414001, Maharashtra – **Ahwa**-394710, Dangs Dist., Gujarat – Radio Tila, Tuikhuahtlang, **Aizawl**-796001, Mizoram Email: airzawl@sancharnet.in – 21/10 Vaishali Nagar, **Ajmer**-305001, Rajasthan – **Akola**-444001, Maharashtra – **Alappuzha**-688001, Kerala – Anoopshahar Road, **Aligarh**-202001, Uttar Pradesh Email: airaligarh@lycos.com – Z-9 Dayanand Marg, **Allahabad**-211001, Uttar Pradesh – **Almora**-263601, Kumaon Dist., Uttaranchal – Scheme No 6, Mangal Vihar, **Alwar**-301001, Rajasthan – Kumar Palace, **Ambikapur**-497001, Surguja Dist., Chhatisgarh – Near, Collectorate, **Anantapur**-

515001, Andhra Pradesh – **Asansol**-713301, Burdwan Dist., West Bengal – Jalna Rd, **Aurangabad**-431005, Maharashtra – **Balaghat**-481001, Madhya Pradesh – Raj Bhavan Rd, **Bangalore**-560001, Karnataka (SW: Super Power Transmitters, Yelahanka New Town, Bangalore-560064, Karnataka. Email: spairyn@vsnl.net – **Banswara**-327001, Rajasthan – No 15, Lal Phatak, Badaun Road, **Bareilly**-243004, Uttar Pradesh – **Baripada**-757001, Mayurbhanj Dist., Orissa – Laxmi Nagar, **Barmer**-344001, Rajasthan – Khandeshwari Road, **Beed**-431122, Maharashtra – **Bellary**-583101, Karnataka – **Belonia**-799155, Tripura – **Berhampur**-760001, Ganjam Dist., Orissa – **Betul**-460001, Madhya Pradesh – J.P.S.Colony, Paper Tower, **Bhadravati**-577302, Karnataka – Port Campus, **Bhagalpur**-812001, Bihar – **Bathinda**-151005, Punjab – **Bhaderwah**-182222, Doda Dist., Jammu & Kashmir –_ **Bhawanipatna**-766001, Nektiguda, Kalahandi Dist., Orissa – Shyamla Hills, **Bhopal**-462002, Madhya Pradesh Email: airbpl@sancharnet.in – **Bhuj**-370001, Kutch Dist., Gujarat – **Bijapur**-586101, Karnataka – **Bikaner**-334001, Rajasthan – Nutan Colony, **Bilaspur**-495001, Chhattisgarh – **Bolangir**-767001, Palach Linew Line, Orissa – Tungri Maidan, **Chaibasa**-833201, Singhbhum Dist., Jharkhand – **Chandrapur**-442401, Maharashtra – Sector-19B, **Chandigarh**-160019 – Avadi, **Chennai**-600062, Tamilnadu Email: airavadi@.vsnl.com – **Chhatarpur**-471001, Madhya Pradesh – **Chindwara**-480001, Madhya Pradesh – **Chinsurah**-712102, West Bengal – **Chitradurga**-577501, Karnataka – Sector 4, Gandhi Nagar, **Chittorgarh**-312001, Rajasthan – **Churu**-331001, Rajasthan – Trichy Rd, Ramanathapuram, **Coimbatore**-641045, Tamilnadu – Cooperative Colony, **Cuddapah**-516001, Andhra Pradesh – Madhupur House, Bakshi Bazar, Cantonment Rd, **Cuttack**-753001, Orissa – **Daltonganj**-822101, Jharkhand – Opp. Varkunt, Mota Fliya, **Daman**-396210, Daman & Diu – **Darbhanga**-846004, Bihar – **Devikulam**-685613, Idukki Dist., Kerala – **Dharmasala**-176215, Kangra Dist., Himachal Pradesh – Saptapur, **Dharwar**-580008, Karnataka – **Dhubri**-783301, Assam – **Dhule**-424001, Maharashtra – Malakhubasa, **Dibrugarh**-786001, Assam – **Diphu**-782460, Kabri Anglong Dist., Assam – Begumganj Garahiya, **Faizabad**-224001, Uttar Pradesh – Old MLA Hostel, **Gangtok**-737101, Sikkim Email: argtk@dte.vsnl.net.in – **Godhra**-389001, Gujarat –**Gopeshwar**-246401, Uttaranchal – Town Hall, **Gorakhpur**-273001, Uttar Pradesh – Aiwan-e-Shahi, Municipal Garden, **Gulbarga**-585103, Karnataka – **Guna**-473001, Madhya Pradesh – Chandmari, **Guwahati**-781003, Assam Email: airgau@sancharnet.in – Gandhi Rd, **Gwalior**-474002, Madhya Pradesh – **Haflong**-788819, Assam – **Hamirpur**-177001, Himachal Pradesh – Salagame Road, **Hassan**-573201, Karnataka – Jail Road, **Hazaribagh**-825301, Jharkhand – **Hissar**-125001, Haryana – **Hospet**-583201, Karnataka – Rocklands, Saifabad, **Hyderabad**-500004, Andhra Pradesh Email: airhyd@hd2.vsnl.net.in – Palace Compound Rd, **Imphal**-795001, Manipur Email: airimfal@sancharnet.in – Malwa House, Residency Area, **Indore**-452001, Madhya Pradesh – 'C' Sec., **Itanagar**-791111, Arunachal Pradesh Email: airitan@sancharnet.in – 373 Napier Town, **Jabalpur**-482001, Madhya Pradesh – Collectorate Rd, **Jagdalpur**-494 001, Bastar Dist., Chhattisgarh – 5 Park House, Mirza Ismail Rd, **Jaipur**-302001, Rajasthan Email: airjpr@datainfosys.net – Akashvani Bhawan, Vyas Colony, **Jaisalmer**-345001, Rajasthan – **Jalandhar**-144001, Punjab – Jilhapet, **Jalgaon**-425001, Maharashtra – Radio Kashmir, Begum Haveli, Old Palace Rd, **Jammu**-180001, Jammu & Kashmir Email: airjammu2002@yahoo.co.uk – Adityapur, Gamharia Rd, **Jamshedpur**-831013, Jharkhand – **Jeypore**-764005, Orissa airjeyp@sancharnet.in – Jungle Road, **Jhalawar**-326001, Rajasthan – Kanpur Road, **Jhansi**-284128, Uttar Pradesh – Paoata 'C' Road, **Jodhpur**-342006, Rajasthan – **Joranda**, Dhenkanal Dist., Orissa – **Jorhat**-785001, Assam – **Jowai**-793150, Jaintia Hills, Meghalaya – Cooperative Colony, **Kadapa**-516001, Andhra Pradesh – **Kailashsahar**-799277, Tripura – **Kalpa**-172108, Kinnaur Dist., Himachal Pradesh – **Kannur**-670001, Kerala – **Kanpur**-208001, Uttar Pradesh – **Kargil**-194103, Jammu & Kashmir – Radio Avenue, Nehru Ngr., **Karaikal**-609606, Puducherri – **Karwar**-581301, Karnataka – **Kasauli**-173204, Solan Dist., Himachal Pradesh – **Kathua**-184104, Jammu & Kashmir – **Kavaratti**-682555, Lakshadeep – **Keonjhar**-758001, Orissa – **Khandwa**-450001, Nimar Dist., Madhya Pradesh – BMC PO, **Kochi**-682021, Ernakulam Dist., Kerala – Anandagiri, **Kodaikanal**-624101, Tamilnadu – **Kohima**-797001, Nagaland Email: airkohima@rediffmail.com – **Kokrajhar**-783370, Assam – Sardar Cly, Taravai Park, **Kolhapur**-416003, Maharashtra – Eden Gardens, **Kolkata**-700001, West Bengal Email: aircal@cal.vsnl.net.in – Jawahar Rd, **Kota**-324001, Rajasthan – Ramavaram, **Kothagudam**-507118, Khammam Dist., Andhra Pradesh – Beach Rd, **Kozhikode** 673001, Kerala – **Kulu**-175101, Himachal Pradesh – Bellary Road, **Kurnool**-518003, Andhra Pradesh – Mehta Club Bldg, **Kurseong**-734203, Darjeeling Dist., West Bengal Email: airkurseong@justmailz.com – **Kurushetra**-132118, Haryana – Radio Kashmir, **Leh**-194101, Ladakh Dist., Jammu & Kashmir Email: seairladakh2002@yahoo.co.in – 18 Vidhan Sabha Marg, **Lucknow**-226001, Uttar Pradesh Email: airlko@sancharnet.in – **Lungleh**-796701, Mizoram – **Madikeri**-571201, Kodagu Dist., Karnataka – Lady Doak College Rd, Chokkikulam, **Madurai**-625002, Tamilnadu – Kadri Hills, **Mangalore**-575004, Dakshin Kanara Dist., Karnataka – **Manjeri**-676121, Kerala –_**Markapur**-523316, Prakasam Dist., Andhra Pradesh – Vrindavan Rd, Gaytri Tapobhumi, **Mathura**-281003, Uttar Pradesh – **Mokokchung**-798601, Nagaland – **Mount Abu**, Rajasthan – 'B' Casting House, Backbay Reclamation, **Mumbai**-400020, Maharashtra Email: mindiran@yahoo.co.uk, sdairmumbai@vsnl.net – **Murshidabad**-742101, West Bengal – **Mussoorie**-248179, Dehradun Dist., Uttaranchal – Yadavagiri, **Mysore**-570020, Karnataka – **Nagaon**-782002, Assam – Basni Rd, **Nagaur**-341001, Rajasthan – Konam, **Nagercoil**-629004, Kanya Kumari Dist., Tamilnadu – Civil Lines, Palam Rd, **Nagpur**-440001, Maharashtra (National Channel: Seminary Hills, **Nagpur** 440006, Maharashtra) – Kotwali Rd, **Najibabad**-246763, Bijnor Dist., Uttar Pradesh – Vasrania, **Nanded**-431601, Maharashtra – 1, Sansad Marg, **New Delhi**-110001 Email: faair@nda.vsnl.net.in – **Nizamabad**-503012, Andhra Pradesh – **Nongstoin**-793119, West Khasi Hills, Meghalaya – **Obra**-314401, Rajasthan – Finger Post, Udhagamandalam, **Ooty**-643006, Tamilnadu – Tambri Vibhag, **Osmanabad**-413501, Maharashtra – Altinho, **Panaji**-403001, Goa. Email: airtrgoa@sancharnet.in – Jamakar Colony, Nawa Mondha, **Parbhani**-431401, Maharashtra – **Pasighat**-791102, East Siang Dist., Arunachal Pradesh – Phase-I, Urban Estate, Rajpura Rd, **Patiala**-147002, Punjab –Frazer Road, Chhaju Bagh, **Patna**-800001, Bihar – **Pauri**-246001, Uttaranchal – **Pithorgarh**-262501, Uttaranchal – **Poonch**-185101, Jammu & Kashmir – Haddo Post, Dilanipur, **Port Blair**-744102, Andaman & Nicobar Islands Email: pblairpb@sancharnet.in – 24 Coubert Avenue, Gorimedu, **Puducherri**-605001 – University Rd, Shivaji Nagar, **Pune**-411005, Maharashtra – **Puri**-751001, Orissa – **Purnea**-854302, Bihar – **Raichur**-584101, Karnataka – Chote Atarmude, **Raigarh**-496001, Chhattisgarh – Kamla Nehru Marg, Civil Lines, **Raipur**-492001, Chhattisgarh – Opposite Race Course, Sitaram Pandit Marg, **Rajkot**-360001, Gujarat – **Rampur**-244901, Uttar Pradesh – 6 Ratu Rd, **Ranchi**-834001, Jharkhand Email: seairran@yahoo.co.in – Thiba Palace Rd, **Ratnagiri**-415612, Maharashtra – 6 Civil Lines, **Rewa**-486001, Madhya Pradesh – Subhash Rd, **Rohtak**-124001, Haryana – **Rourkela**-769001, Orissa – **Sagar**-470001, Madhya Pradesh – **Saiha**-796901, Chhimtuipui Dist., Mizoram – 3, Kuchery Rd, **Sambalpur**-768001, Orissa – Market Yard, Kolhapur Rd, **Sangli**-416416, Maharashtra – **Sasaram**-821115, Rohtas Dist., Bihar – **Satara**-415001, Maharashtra – Pali Road, **Shahdol**-484001, Madhya Pradesh – **Shanthi Nikethan**, West Bengal – Pomdngiem, Opposite GPO, **Shillong**-793001, Meghalaya Email: airmegh@sancharnet.in, airnews@sancharnet.in – Choura Maidan, **Shimla**-171004, Himachal Pradesh – Physical College, **Shivpuri**-473551, Madhya Pradesh – **Silchar**-788001, Cachar Dist., Assam – 2 Mile Sevoke Rd, **Siliguri**-734401, Darjeeling Dist., West Bengal – **Solapur**-413006, Maharashtra – Radio Kashmir, Sherwani Rd, **Srinagar**-190001, Jammu & Kashmir – **Surat**-395001, Gujarat – **Suratgarh**-335804, Sriganganagar Dist., Rajasthan – **Swai Madhopur**-322001, Rajasthan – **Tawang**-790104, Arunachal Pradesh – **Tezpur**-784001, Sonitpur Dist., Assam – **Tezu**-792001, Lohit Dist., Arunachal Pradesh – Bhakti Vilas, Vazuthacaud, **Thiruvanathapuram**-695014, Kerala Email: airtvpm@sancharnet.in – Ramavarmapuram, **Thrissur**-680631, Kerala – 28-3 Promenade Rd, **Tiruchirapalli**-620001, Tamilnadu – Sarojini Park, Palayamkottai, **Tirunelveli**-627006, Tamilnadu – **Tirupati**-517501, Andhra Pradesh – **Tuensang**-798612, Nagaland – Lower Chandmari, **Tura**-794001, Meghalaya – Millerpuram, Playamkottai Road, **Tuticorin**-628008, Tamilnadu – Chetak Circle, **Udaipur**-313001, Rajasthan – Brahmavar, **Udipi**-576213, Dakshina Kanara Dist., Karnataka – **Uttar Kashi**-249193, Uttaranchal – Makarpura Rd, **Vadadora**-390009, Gujarat – Mahmoorganj, **Varanasi**-221010, Uttar Pradesh – Bandar Rd, Punnammathota, **Vijayawada**-520010, Andhra Pradesh – **Visakhapatnam**-530003, Andhra Pradesh – **Waranagal**-506002, Andhra Pradesh – **William Nagar**, Meghalaya – **Yeotmal**-445001, Maharashtra – **Zero**-791120, Lower Subansiri Dist., Arunachal Pradesh.

EXTERNAL SERVICES: All India Radio
see International Broadcasting section.

Private FM Stations:

MHz	Station & location	MHz	Station & location
90.4	Anna FM, Chennai	104.2	Gyan Vani, Chennai
91.0	Radio City, Bangalore	104.8	Radio City, Lucknow
91.0	Radio City, Mumbai	105.0	Gyan Vani, Bhopal
91.0	Radio City, New Delhi	105.1	Suriyan FM, Chennai
91.9	Gyan Vani, Coimbatore	105.4	Gyan Vani, Kolkata
91.9	Radio Mirchi, Ahmedabad	105.6	Gyan Vani, Lucknow
92.5	Go 92.5, Mumbai	105.6	Gyan Vani, Mumbai
93.5	Red FM, Kolkata	105.6	Gyan Vani, New Delhi
93.5	Red FM, Mumba	105.6	Visakha FM, Visakhapatnam
93.5	Red FM, New Delhi	105.8	Suriyan FM, Coimbatore
93.9	Radio Mirchi, Pune	106.2	Amar 106.2, Kolkata

MHz	Station & location	MHz	Station & location
94.6	Win 94.6, Mumbai	106.4	Gyan Vani, Visakhapatnam
98.3	Radio Mirchi, Chennai	106.8	Suriyan FM, Tirunelveli
98.3	Radio Mirchi, Kolkata	107.4	Gyan Vani, Allahabad
98.3	Radio Mirchi, Mumbai	107.6	Gyan Vani, Bangalore
98.3	Radio Mirchi, New Delhi	107.8	Power 108, Kolkata
98.4	Radio Mirchi, Indore		

F.PI: 30 more Gyan Vani (Educational Channel) FM stations by Indira Gandhi National Open University, New Delhi. More details from **Web:** www.gyandarshan.ernet.in

INDONESIA

L.T: We. Indonesia (Java, Sumatra, We. & Ce. Kalimantan): UTC +7h; Ce. Indonesia (So. & Ea. Kalimantan, Sulawesi, Bali, Nusa Tenggara): UTC +8h; Ea. Indonesia (Maluku, Papua): UTC +9h — **Pr.L:** Bahasa Indonesia (Indonesian) — **Pop:** 235 million — **E.C:** 50 Hz, 230V — **ITU:** INS

DIRECTORATE GENERAL OF POSTS & TELECOMMUNICATIONS (Direktorat Jenderal Pos dan Telekomunikasi (Departemen Perhubungan)
Gedung Sapta Pesona, Medan Merdeka Barat 17, Jakarta 10110 ☎ +62 21 3835912 🖷 +62 21 3860754 **Web:** www.postel.go.id **Email:** admin@postel.go.id

FEDERATION OF INDONESIAN NATIONAL COMMERCIAL BROADCASTERS (Persatuan Radio Siaran Swasta Nasional Indonesia)
Pengurus Pusat, Persatuan Radio Siaran Swasta Nasional Indonesia, Jl. Raya Pondok Gede 96, Jakarta 13810 ☎ +62 21 8414311 🖷 +62 21 8414314. **Web:** www.radioprssni.com **Email:** radioprssni@radioprssni.com or ppjkt @indosat.net.id.
LP: Chmn: Drs. H. Gandjar Suwargani. PRSSNI has 821 members (338 on AM, 483 on FM).

MW	kHz	kW	Station
JB01)	540	2/10	RRI Bandung
KS02)	540	0.25	R. Dirgahayu, Barabai
LA02)	540		R. Dei Marganusa, Trimurjo
BA13)	558		RSPDT2 Gianyar (R. Gelora Pemerintah Kabupaten Gianyar)
BN01)	558		R. Swara Angkasa Megah, Pandeglang
JA02)	558	0.25	R. Manggis B.S., Jambi
JH04)	558	0.25	R. Suara Jalesveva Juana Sakti, Pati
JH05)	558		R. Diantara Vita Kharisma (D.V.K.), Kebumen
SL02)	558		R. Rosa, Makassar *
JH06)	567	0.25	RSPDKDT2 Semarang
KS03)	576		R. Swara Tapin Raya, Rantau
JT01)	585	50	RRI Surabaya
LA05)	594		R. Suara Pramudya Lestari (Puri), Sukadana
JB04)	603	0.5	RDKDT2 Sumedang
JK02)	603		R. Namlapanha, Jakarta
KH02)	603		R. Riwut Melawen, Buntok
BN02)	612	0.25	R. Gema Bahari Selatan, Rangkasbitung
JB05)	612		R. Geswara Pamanukan (G.S.P.), Pamanukan
JH08)	612	0.25	R. Suara Banyumas Asli (Subali), Purwokerto
JH09)	612		R. Bahurekso Sakti (B.O.S.), Weleri
KB02)	612		R. Kijang Berantai (Kiber) Perkasa, Sambas
KS04)	612		R. Swara Barabai, Barabai
SS02)	612		R. Swara Betung Indah, Betung-Musi Banyuasin
JH71)	621		RSPDT2 Salatiga (Suara Salatiga)
JT06)	621		R. Citra Airlangga, Pare-Kediri
LA06)	630		R. Gema Swarna Dwipa (Slendro), Terbanggi Besar
SL01)	630	50	RRI Makassar
YG02)	630		R. Swara Adiloka, Gunung Kidul
JB06)	639	0.25	R. Gita Kanari Ria, Purwakarta
BN03)	648		R. Suara Minangkabau, Tangerang
JA03)	648		R. Batanghari Permai (B.H.P.), Muarabulian
JB07)	648		R. Bestari, Sukabumi
JH10)	648		R. Santo Bernadus D.S., Pekalongan
JH11)	648		R. Suara Palagan Semesta Sehati (S.P.S.),Ambarawa
JH12)	648		R. Roro Djonggrang B.S., Prambanan
JH13)	648		R. Wijaya Adikusuma, Cilacap
JT08)	648	0.5	RKPDT2 Lamongan
KS05)	648		R. Citraswara Pelangi Indah, Banjarmasin
NB05)	648		R. Suara Hamzanwadi, Selong
JH14)	657	0.25	RSPD Kotamadya Magelang
BN04)	666	2	RDKDT2 Pandeglang
JB08)	666	0.22	R. Linggarjati Utama (Rasilima), Kuningan
JH15)	666	0.25	R. Ramakusala, Surakarta
JH16)	666	0.25	R. Borobudur Siebra Patria, Semarang
JH17)	666		R. Tunggul Suara Dirgantara, Purbalingga
JK10)	666		R. Sekuntum Bunga Yang Indah (SBY), Jakarta
JT09)	666		R. Gita Nada Tebu Ireng, Jombang
KB03)	666		R. Bengkayang Sentra Nusa, Bengkayang
LA07)	666		R. Den Bang, Bandar Jaya
GO02)	684		R. Swara Gorontalo Permai, Gorontalo
JB10)	684		R. Swara Pakusarakan Pratika, Sawangan
JB23)	684		R. Angkasa Media, Kadipaten
JH36)	684	0.25	RSPDT2 Pati (Suara Pati)
JT10)	684		R. Wisata Panataran (Wita), Blitar*
KS06)	684		R. Purnama Nada, Kandangan
LA08)	684		R. Patrol Radika, Bandar Lampung
NB02)	684		R. Putri Mandalika, Praya
BB01)	693	1	RRI Sungai Liat
JH20)	693	0.25	RSPDKDT2 Purworejo (R. Suara Irama)
JH21)	693		RSPKDT2 Jepara (R. Kartini)
JT12)	693		RSPDK Kediri (R. Canda Bhirawa)
BA03)	702		R. Besakih Rasisonia, Amlapura
JB12)	702		R. Swara Prima Sonata, Cirebon
JH22)	702		R. Swara Zenith Angkasa, Salatiga
JH76)	702		R. Aji Satria, Ajibarang
KH03)	702		R. Mitrabarito Nadaswara, Tamiang Layang
PA08)	702		RRI Manokwari
SL03)	702		R. Al Kawakib, Makassar *
YG03)	702		R. Suara Konco Tani, Sidokarto-Sleman
PA10)	703		R. Suara Kasih Agung, Jayapura
JT15)	711		Suara Besuki Indah, Situbondo
JH26)	720		R. Purnamasidi, Wonosobo
JH27)	720	0.25	R. Lusiana Namberwan, Semarang
JH28)	720		R. Gagah Sehat Berbobot (Gasebo), Majenang
JH29)	720		R. Gita Swara Alfina, Pemalang
JT16)	720		RKPDT1 Jawa Timur, Surabaya *
KS07)	720	0.1	R. Telerama, Banjarmasin
LA09)	720		R. Bhara Kharisma Suryajaya, Talangpadang
MA01)	720	10	RRI Ambon
SL04)	720		Suara Simpati Angkasa (Susia), Pinrang
SS03)	720		R. Suara Mitra Bayu Buana, Belitang
YG04)	720	0.35	RSPDT2 Kulonprogo (R. Rosala), Wates*
NB10)	729		R.Dewi Anjani, Selong
BN06)	738		R. Bharata Bhakti Nusa, Tangerang
JB14)	738	0.25	R. Galuh Surya Kencana,Tasikmalaya
JH30)	738		R. Konservatori, Surakarta
JT03)	738	1	RRI Jember*
JT17)	738		R. Suara Pamekasan Indah, Pamekasan
KB04)	738		R. Swara Melati Gramedia, Mempawah
KB05)	738		R. Swara Pinohperkasa, Sintang
KS08)	738	0.25	R. Kharisma Nada Rasisonia (La Fuzsy), Banjarmasin
LA10)	738		R. Duta Paramita, Metro
NT10)	738		RSPDT2 Timor Tengah Selatan, Soe
SL05)	738		R. Rina Bestari, Rantepao
SS04)	738		R. Aditya Nada Jaya, Indralaya
JA04)	740		RSPDT2 Batanghari, Muarabulian
NT02)	743	0.3	RPDT2 Sumba Barat, Waikabubak
BE01)	747	5	RRI Bengkulu
JH31)	747	0.25	RSPDT2 Kudus (Suara Kudus)
JT18)	747		R. Swara Nabawi, Pasuruan
JT19)	747		R. Canka Bhalaria, Ngawi
BA10)	756		R. Bali Mandala Perkasa, Gianyar
JB64)	756		R. Ratna Palupi (R. Virgin), Karawang
JH03)	756	2/10	RRI Purwokerto
JT20)	756	0.5	RKPDKDT2 Magetan (R. Magetan Indah)
JT21)	756	0.5	RKPKDT2 Mojokerto*
KS09)	756		R. Gema Meratus, Batulicin
SS18)	756		R. Raja Paksi Lolita, Pasar Lama
JB11)	765		R. Buana Sari, Kuningan
JH32)	765	0.25	RSPDT2 Boyolali
KS01)	765	0.2	RRI Banjarmasin *
LA12)	765		R. Dian Rajabasa, Kota Dalam
MA02)	765	1	RRI Tual
BA04)	774		R. Citrah Anugerah, Negara
BN07)	774	0.5	RDK Tangerang
JH33)	774		R. P.T.D.I. Walisongo, Pekalongan
JH35)	774	0.2	R. Leonardus Buana Suara, Salatiga
JT23)	774		R. Pesona 2000, Sumenep
KS10)	774		R. Ruhui Rahayu,Rantau
PA07)	774		RRI Fak-Fak
SB03)	774	0.35	RSPD Kotamadya Payakumbuh

MW	kHz	kW	Station
SL06)	774		R. Suara Adyafiri, Watansoppeng
SS05)	774		R. Suara Kristal Baru, Pagar Alam
JH37)	783		RSPDT2 Tegal (Suara Slawi Ayu), Slawi
KS11)	783		R. Dakwah Masjid Raya Sabilal Muhtadin Banjarmasin
BN14)	792		R. Swara Lebak Ria, Rangkasbitung
JB17)	792		R. Cempaka Angkasa, Ciamis
JB18)	792		R. Swara Citra Cianjur Mandiri, Cianjur
JH38)	792		R. Swara Graha Jelita, Surakarta
JH39)	792		R. Bayu Sakti, Purwokerto
JK14)	792		R. Assyafi'yah, Jakarta
JT25)	792	0.5	RKPDK Jombang
LA14)	792		R. Suara Dwi Amanda, Gadingrejo
NB03)	792		R. Mitra Idola Kita, Pancor
SL07)	792		R. Padaidi Padaelo Sipatuo Sipatokkong (PIPOSS), Makassar *
SS06)	792		R. Suara Ria Jaya Sentosa (S.R.J.S.), Baturaja
JH01)	801	10	RRI Semarang
SU01)	801	1	RRI Medan
AC04)	810		R. Amanda Rasisonia, Takengon
JB19)	810		R. Indraswara Cakrawala Nada, Majalengka
JB20)	810		RSPDK Bandung
JH40)	810		R. Suara Maung Sakti, Banjarnegara
JK11)	810		R. Universitas Mercu Buana, Jakarta
KS12)	810		R. Gema Kuripan, Amuntai
LA15)	810		R. Saburai Alam Permai, Liwa
PA02)	810	7.5	RRI Merauke
SL08)	810		R. Megapesona, Enrekang
SS07)	810	0.25	R. Warastra Bewara Swara, Palembang
SU04)	810		R. Suara Tanjung Berjaya, Tanjungbalai
JH41)	819		R. Pancabayu Madugondo (Suara R.P.M.)Sukoharjo
BA05)	828	0.25	R. Suara Yudha, Denpasar
BN13)	828		RSPDK Lebak, Rangkasbitung
JB21)	828	0.25	R. Leidya Swara Utama, Bandung
JB22)	828	0.25	R. Prabu Kiansantang, Tasikmalaya
JB24)	828		R. Adhika Pariwara, Pelabuhanratu
JB59)	828		R. Gema Remaja, Kuningan
JH42)	828		R. Bahurekso Sakti, Semarang *
JH44)	828		R. S.B.S., Purbalingga
JT26)	828		R. Tritara Yaksa (T.T.-77), Malang
KB06)	828		R. Mahkota Ngabang Gemaswara, Ngabang
KH04)	828		R. Babayaga, Sampit
SB05)	828		R. TASSA, Lubuk Alang
SL09)	828		R. Swara Christy Ria, Makassar
JH46)	837	0.25	R. Immanuel, Surakarta
JB25)	846		R. Suara Galunggung Giri Sakti, Tasikmalaya
JB26)	846		R. Menara Buana Suara Indah, Sukabumi
JH45)	846		R. Cipta Bentala Swara (CBS), Magelang
JH47)	846		R. Swara Caraka Ria, Semarang
JH48)	846		R. Suara Karangbolong, Gombong
JH49)	846		R. Swara Anggada Senatama, Purbalingga
JH50)	846		R. Suara Tegal Agung Raya (Star), Tegal
JT07)	846		R. Gending G.K.P., Kediri
JT28)	846	0.5	RKPDT2 Ponorogo (R. Suara Ponorogo)
JT34)	846		R. Miniwati Pesona Indah, Surabaya
KH05)	846		R. Pantaikubu Bahagia, Pangkalan Bun
KS13)	846		RSPDT2 Kotabaru
JB02)	850	1	RRI Bogor*
JB27)	855	0.75	RSPDT2 Bekasi (R. Patriot)
JH51)	855	0.25	RSPDKDT2 Cilacap
LA16)	855		R. Surya Gita Paramarta (S.G.P.), Labuhan Maringgai
NB01)	855	2/10	RRI Mataram
SU01)	855	50	RRI Medan, Padang Cermin
JB03)	864	2/10	RRI Cirebon
JB16)	864		R. Bogor Swaratama (R. B.O.S.), Bogor
JH52)	864	0.25	RSPD Kotamadya Salatiga
JT29)	864		R. Menara III, Surabaya
KB07)	864		R. Prominda Dirgantara, Pontianak
SL10)	864		Suara AsAdiyah, Sengkang
JB29)	873		R. Sipatahunan (Suara Bogor), Bogor
JH53)	873	0.5	RSPDKDT2 Sragen (R. Suara Buana Asri), Sragen
LA17)	873		R. Sari Bunga Sadari (S.B.S.), Sidomulyo
JT31)	879	0.5	RSPD Sidoarjo
JB28)	882		R. Suara Anggada Senatama (S.A.S.), Banjarsari
JB30)	882	0.3	R. Nusantara Bharata Citra (N.B.C.), Garut
JH55)	882		R. Swara Kranggan Persada, Temanggung
JK03)	882		R. Pelangi Nusantara, Jakarta
JT32)	882		R. Citra Wisnu Wardhani Mojopahit (CWM), Mojokerto*
JT33)	882		R. Gema Panca Arga, Pacitan
KS14)	882	0.25	R. Chandra Rasisonia, Banjarmasin
LA18)	882		R. Ragam Tunas Lampung (Ratula), Kotabumi
SG01)	882		RRI Kendari
SL11)	882	0.5	R. Bambapuang, Pangkajene
PA03)	886	0.5	RRI Serui
JT02)	891	10	RRI Malang
AC03)	900		R. Siaran Cempaka Nadacitra, Desa Tonjong
AC07)	900		R. Siaran Nada Karya Semesta, Lhok Sukon
BA06)	900	0.25	R. Gema Megantara Pratama, Tabanan
JA05)	900	0.25	R. Gema Nugraha, Sungai Penuh
JB31)	900		RPKDT2 Cianjur
JH56)	900		R. Permata Swaratama, Boyolali
JH89)	900		R. Rona Puspita, Sukorejo
JT13)	900		R. Jayabaya, Kediri
KB08)	900		R. Aries Sanggau Perkasa, Sanggau
KS15)	900		R. Gematara Batakan, Peleihari
LA19)	900		R. Swara Alfina Shakti, Kalianda
SB04)	900		R. Elkartika Angkasa Niaga, Padang
NB04)	905	0.25	RPDKDT2 Sumbawa, Sumbawa Besar
JT35)	909	0.25	RKPDKDT2 Pamekasan (Suara Dian Lestari)
PA04)	909	10	RRI Sorong
BA07)	918		R. Dhirgantara, Negara
JB32)	918		R. Gema Nury (El Nury), Bogor
JH57)	918	0.25	R. Chandra Kusuma, Pekalongan
JH58)	918		R. Suara Selomanik (R.S.S.), Banjarnegara
JK04)	918		R. P.T.D.I., Jakarta
JT36)	918	0.5	RKPKDT2 Gresik
JT37)	918		R. Suara Semeru Permai, Lumajang
KS16)	918		R. Gema Amandit, Kandangan
NT03)	918		R. Balistik, Kupang
SU05)	918		R. Gelora Pertiwi, Medan
JB34)	925		RDK Subang (R. Benteng Pancasila – Benpas)
LA20)	927		R. Primanada, Gisting
RI01)	927	25	RRI Pekanbaru
BA14)	936		R. Pesona Bali, Singaraja
JB36)	936	0.25	R. Budaya Sari, Bandung
JH59)	936		R. Pasopati Andalan, Semarang
JH61)	936		R. Widya Bhakti, Magelang
JH62)	936		RSPDKDT2 Karanganyar (Swara Intanpari Baru)
JH65)	936		R. Kelana Sumbangsihku (Kasihku), Bumiayu
JK05)	936	0.25	R. Puspa Dwi Swara Cipta (P2SC), Jakarta
JT40)	936		R. Suara Fiskarama, Bondowoso
KB09)	936		R. Swara Dermagaria Persada Cakrawala, Sekadau
JH25)	945	0.5	RSPDT2 Blora
JH63)	945		R. Swara Buana Asri, Wonosobo
JH79)	945		RSPDT2 Pemalang (Suara Widuri)
SB06)	945		R. Galundi Pradana, Gando Sulit Air
SU06)	945		R. Tuah Swara Murni, Lubukpakam
BA08)	954		R. Batur (Raba), Bangli
JB37)	954	0.25	R. Sena Bahana Cakrawala, Sukabumi
JB38)	954		R. Ewangga, Kuningan
JB39)	954		R. Suara Terunajaya, Pemeungpeuk
JH64)	954		R. Gita Nusantara Perkasa (Studio 99), Purbalingga
JT41)	954	0.25	R. El Bayu, Gresik
KS18)	954		R. Gema Persada, Banjarmasin *
SG01)	954	10	RRI Kendari
SL12)	954		R. Gandaria (Anging Mamiri), Makassar *
SS09)	954	0.15	R. Garuda Kenten Jaya, Palembang
JT03)	963	2/10	RRI Jember
SU07)	966		RPDK Deli Serdang, Medan
JH02)	972	50	RRI Surakarta
JH66)	972	0.25	R. Suara Alas Roban (A.R.O.), Batang
JT42)	972		R. Megantara Bhinneka, Nganjuk
JT43)	972		R. Suara Harmoni, Situbondo
SS08)	972		R. Nada Santika, Pagar Alam
JB41)	981		R. Antares, Garut
JH67)	985	0.25	RSPDKDT2 Magelang
AC05)	990		R. Cakra Donya Multi Swara, Lhokseumawe
BA09)	990		R. Suara Calvary, Klungkung
JH68)	990		R. Gita Lestari, Brebes
JH115)	990		R. Pesona Bahari, Weleri
JT44)	990		Suara Probolinggo, Probolinggo*
JT45)	990		R. Citra Wanodya Angkasa, Jombang
JT77)	990		Suara Kartika, Jember
KS19)	990		R. Bahana Nirmala, Martapura
KT06)	990		RSPD Balikpapan
NT04)	990		R. Gema Suara Gloria (G.B.S.), Kupang
SL14)	990		R. Suara Sowerigading, Wonomulyo
SU09)	990		R. Nias Mitra Dharma, Gunungsitoli

MW	kHz	kW	Station
JK01)	999	1/150	RRI Jakarta
KT02)	1005		RPDT2 Kutai, Tenggarong
AC06)	1008		R. Siaran Dwieka Swara, Beureunuen
JT04)	1008	10	RRI Madiun
JT46)	1008		R. Swara Rebana, Malang *
KB11)	1008		R. Suara Pemangkat, Pemangkat
NB06)	1008		R. Kharisma Lombok Perkasa, Aikmel
SU10)	1008		R. Citra Tebingtinggi Idola Nada, Tebingtinggi
JH70)	1017		R. Suara Gajah Mungkur, Ngadirejo
SU11)	1017		R. Kardopa, Medan
NT05)	1024	0.25	RPDT2 Belu, Atambua
AC08)	1026		R. Gema Cakrawala Utama, Kuala Simpang
AC09)	1026		R. Dutakencana Suara Banda Aceh, Banda Aceh
JB42)	1026		R. Fortuna, Sukabumi
JB43)	1026		R. Ummat, Bandung
JK12)	1026		Suara Multazam, Jakarta Utara
JT47)	1026	0.25	R. Taurus Adiswara, Kediri
KS20)	1026		R. Siaga Indah Marista (Santanimo), Banjarmasin
PA03)	1026	5	RRI Serui
SS11)	1026		R. Suara Enim Jaya Perkasa, Muara Enim
JB44)	1029	0.5	RPKDT2 Ciamis
NT06)	1034		RPDT2 Ngada, Bajawa
JH73)	1035		R. Suara Sendang Mas, Banyumas
JH74)	1035		RSPDT2 Temanggung
JT48)	1035	0.5	RKPDT2 Malang
LA01)	1035	1/5	RRI Bandar Lampung
SH01)	1035		RRI Palu
BA11)	1044	0.25	R. Cakra Swara Perkasa, Singaraja
JB45)	1044		R. Duta Angkasa, Pangandaran
JB46)	1044	0.25	R. Purnayudha, Sukabumi
JB47)	1044		R. Lima Swara Mandiri (Purnayudha), Bekasi
JH75)	1044	0.25	R. Raka, Tegal
JT49)	1044		R. Arena Duta Swara, Trenggalek
KB13)	1044		R. Ramagentara, Sungai Pinyuh
PA05)	1044	10	RRI Biak
RI02)	1044		R. Soreram Indah, Pekanbaru
RI03)	1044		R. Bagan Batu Citra Nuansa, Bagan Batu
SU02)	1044		RRI Sibolga
AC10)	1050		RPDT2 Aceh Timur, Langsa
PA01)	1053	10	RRI Jayapura
JH02)	1055	1	RRI Surakarta
JB48)	1062		R. Swakarya Niaga (SKN), Cianjur
JB49)	1062	0.5	RPKDT2 Tasikmalaya
JH77)	1062		R. P.T.D.I. Kalimasadha Sakti, Semarang
JK06)	1062	0.25	R. Cendrawasih Pusat, Jakarta
JT51)	1062		R. Sangkakala, Surabaya
JT74)	1062	0.5	RKPDK Tulungagung
KH06)	1062		RPDK Kapuas (R. Ekasapta Kapuas), Kuala Kapuas
NB07)	1062	0.25	R. Suta Remaja, Mataram
SB07)	1062	0.25	Suara Subuh, Padang
SS12)	1062	0.25	R. Gema Mutiara, Palembang
SU12)	1062		R. Tembang Perbaungan Indah, Perbaungan
YG05)	1062		R. R.B., Yogyakarta
JH78)	1071	0.25	RSPDKDT2 Pekalongan (R. Kota Santri)
KH07)	1071		R. Gita Pesona Swara Pandaran, Sampit
AC11)	1080		R. Katalina, Sigli
BA02)	1080	2/10	RRI Singaraja
GO01)	1080	1	RRI Gorontalo
JB50)	1080		R. K.C.B.S., Losali
JK13)	1080		R. Safari, Jakarta
JT53)	1080	0.25	R. Carolina Arjuno, Surabaya
KH08)	1080		R. Bahana Nusantara, Ampah
KH15)	1080		R. Citra Barito, Muarateweh
LA21)	1080		R. Idola Nada, Tulang Bawang
SG05)	1080		R. Gema Gersamata, Kolaka
SS13)	1080		R. Minat Tradisi Jaya, Pembantu Lempuing
SU13)	1080		R. Ropades, Kisaran
JA01)	1098	2/10	RRI Jambi
JH82)	1098		R. Gelora Indah Swara (I.S.), Wonogiri
JK07)	1098		R. Media Mahasiswa Tarumanegara, Jakarta
JT05)	1098	0.5/10	RRI Sumenep
NT01)	1107	1/5	RRI Kupang
SU14)	1107	0.25	R. Bintang Niaga, Kisaran
YG01)	1107	1/10	RRI Yogyakarta
JB09)	1116		R. Barami, Cileunyi-Lembang, Bandung
JB33)	1116		R. Adhika Swara (R. Alawiyah), Bekasi
JH83)	1116	0.3	RSPKDT2 Kendal
JH84)	1116	0.25	R. Bhakti Dirgantara Suara Batang, Batang
JH85)	1116		R. Indah Sragen Asri, Sragen
RI01)	1116	0.3	RRI Pekanbaru

MW	kHz	kW	Station
SL15)	1116		R. Mitra Bayu Suara Utari, Bantaeng
SS14)	1116		R. Dian Bahagia Sentosa, Prabumulih Barat
SU15)	1116	0.25	RPDT2 Kotamadya Binjai
KB01)	1125		RRI Pontianak
SL16)	1125	0.25	RPDT2 Luwu, Palopo
SU16)	1127	0.2	RPDT2 Kotamadya Medan
JB51)	1134		R. Kauman, Bogor
JH86)	1134		R. Swara Delanggu, Delanggu
JT54)	1134		R. Duta Nusantara Suara Ponorogo, Ponorogo
KS01)	1134	1/25	RRI Banjarmasin
JB52)	1135		R. Ria Cindelaras, Indramayu
AC12)	1140		R. Siaran Niaga dan Budaya Milanda, Meulaboh
JT55)	1143	0.25	R. Pariwisata Senaputra, Malang
AC13)	1145		R. Daerah Perdajaya Bebas Sabang, Sabang
AC14)	1152		R. Citraganda Kencanaswara, Bireun
JB15)	1152		R. Rama Sutra, Sukamandi-Subang
JB53)	1152		R. Pasundan Citra Angkasa (PAS), Cianjur
JH116)	1152		R. Pertiwi, Semarang
JT57)	1152		R. Yasmara, Surabaya
SS15)	1152	0.25	R. Enes Duabelas Ulu, Palembang
JH87)	1161	0.1	RSPD Kotamadya Tegal
AC15)	1170		R. Kazuma Bawana Swara, Lhokseumawe
AC21)	1170		R. Swara Fatali Nusajaya, Blangpidie
BN11)	1170	0.25	R. Swara Rama Lokantara, Serang
JB35)	1170		R. Swara Irama Kusuma Sena (R. Elpas), Bogor
JH01)	1170	50	RRI Semarang *
JT58)	1170		R. Rajawali, Surabaya
PA11)	1170		R. Suara Nusa Bahagia, Jayapura
SH02)	1170v		R. Gema Angkasa Swara Al Khairaat, Palu
SL17)	1170		R. Lariang Indah, Mamuju
JT05)	1175		RRI Sumenep
JB55)	1179		R. Kotamadya Cirebon (R. El Thema), Cirebon
SB01)	1179	2/10	RRI Padang
JH23)	1180v	0.5	RSPDKDT2 Wonogiri
NT07)	1185		RSPDT2 Ende (Suara Kelimutu)
AC22)	1188		R. Rapeja, Lamno
BA12)	1188	0.25	R. La Barong, Singaraja
BE04)	1188	0.25	R. Namora Swara Pratama, Curup
BN12)	1188		R. Kawula Muda, Tangerang*
JB56)	1188		R. Swara Selabintana Permai (S.S.P.), Sukabumi
JB65)	1188		R. Duta Swara Parahyangan (D.S.P.), Bekasi
JH88)	1188		R. Suara Ayukarya Banjaran Adiwerna (RSA-Abadi),Tegal
JT59)	1188		R. Swara Perak Jaya P.T.D.I., Surabaya
JT60)	1188		R. Kutilang, Malang
RI01)	1188	0.3	RRI Pekanbaru
ST01)	1188	1	RRI Manado
YG06)	1188	0.25	R. Arma Sebelas, Yogyakarta
NB01)	1194	0.5	RRI Mataram
KH01)	1197	1/5	RRI Palangkaraya
MA04)	1197		R. Sangkakala, Sonya Atas
SU18)	1197	0.5	RSPDT2 Labuhan Batu, Rantau Prapat
RI04)	1200		RSPDT2 Indragiri Hulu, Rengat
SU19)	1205	0.2	RPDT2 Simalungun, Pematang Siantar
AC16)	1206		R. Geunta Suara, Geudong
AC17)	1206		R. Mariba Raya (Maya), Kuala Simpang
BA01)	1206	0.5/10	RRI Denpasar
JB57)	1206		R. Histori Gita Jaya, Karawang
JH90)	1206	0.25	RSPKDT2 Purbalingga
JT01)	1206	1	RRI Surabaya *
SB08)	1206		R. Suara Dikara Bawana (Dirgan Bravo), Padang
SU20)	1206		R. Suara Langkat Tanjung Persada, Tanjungpura
JT61)	1211	0.5	RKPDT2 Bondowoso
KT01)	1215	0.5/10	RRI Samarinda
JB13)	1221		R. Suara Risalah, Cirebon
JB40)	1224		R. Sonata 47, Bandung
JB58)	1224	0.25	R. Buana Jaya, Tasikmalaya
JH91)	1224		R. Angkasa Bahana Citra (A.B.C.), Surakarta
JH92)	1224		RSPDT2 Banyumas, Purwokerto
JH93)	1224		R. Prima Ukir Utama, Jepara
JT62)	1224	0.5	RKPDT2 Bojonegoro
JT63)	1224		Suara Tawang Alun, Banyuwangi
RI05)	1224		R. Pariwara Citra Swara Riau, Duri-Mandau
SU03)	1224		R. Barisan Nauli, Sidikalang
SU21)	1224		R. Alnoria Dirgantara, Tebingtinggi
SU22)	1224		R. Cipta Anindya Guna, Binjai
AC18)	1233v	0.3	RPD Kotamadya Sabang
JB01)	1233		RRI Bandung *
JT65)	1233		RKPDT2 Sumenep (R. Dinamika Suara Pariwisata)
KB01)	1233	02/1/5	RRI Pontianak

MW	kHz	kW	Station
BE01)	1242	1	RRI Bengkulu
JB02)	1242	0.5/5	RRI Bogor
JB60)	1242		R. Swara Rugeri, Garut
JH94)	1242		R. Duta Suara Garuda Sakti, Blora
JT66)	1242		R. La Victor, Surabaya
SL18)	1242		R. Suara Bulusaraung, Pangkep
SU23)	1242		R. Suara Sibolga Indah Sempurna, Sibolga
SU24)	1242		R. Langkat Jaya, Binjai
JB02)	1250	1	RRI Bogor *
AC01)	1251	10	RRI Banda Aceh
BA02)	1251	1	RRI Singaraja*
NB01)	1251	1	RRI Mataram*
JH95)	1260		R. P.T.D.I. Suara Kaliwungu Dirgantara, Kaliwungu
JH96)	1260		R. Citra Angkasa Ikhsaniya (R.C.A.), Tegal
JT68)	1260		R. Gabriel, Madiun
KH09)	1260		R. Cinderanada Awigra, Palangkaraya
KT03)	1260		R. Rajawali Sakti, Balikpapan
SL13)	1260		R. Molina Indah Pesona, Sinjai
SU25)	1260	0.25	R. Khamasutra, Medan
SU26)	1260		R. Swara Jupti Indah, Sibolga
SH03)	1268		R. Aribawana Semesta Prabaswara, Donggala
JB61)	1278		RPDK Bogor (R. Tegar Beriman)
JH97)	1278	0.25	R. Mandalika Rasiswana, Jepara
JH98)	1278	0.25	RSPDK Grobogan, Purwodadi
JT70)	1278		R. Antariksa Radang IV, Surabaya
NB08)	1278		RPDT2 Lombok Timur, Selong
SG02)	1278		R. Ringan Mutiara, Kendari
SU27)	1278		R. Suaratama Citra Mitra, Bandar Pulau
SU28)	1278		R. Cempaka Selaras Silindung, Tarutung
KH10)	1287		R. Gema Kahayan, Pangkalan Bun
SS01)	1287	20/25	RRI Palembang
SU29)	1290	0.2	RPDT2 Kotamadya Pematang Siantar
JH99)	1296		R. R.B.B., Rembang
JT01)	1296		RRI Surabaya *
KH11)	1296		R. Merak Jaya, Muarateweh
NB09)	1296	0.5	R. Duta Gita Bhyomantara Sinta Rama, Cakranegara
SB09)	1296		R. Gapilar Rasisonia, Solok
SL19)	1296		R. Suara Kelandka, Palopo
SU30)	1296		R. Begita, Kabanjahe
JT71)	1304	0.5	RKPDKDT2 Nganjuk
JA07)	1305		R. Kerinci Giri Swara (K.G.S.), Sungaipenuh
JB62)	1305	0.25	RDKDT2 Sukabumi (Programa Dua)
BE05)	1314		R. Shinta Wahana, Bengkulu
JB63)	1314		R. Mutiara, Bandung
JH100)	1314		Suara Sion Perdana, Karanganyar
JH101)	1314		R. Bintoro Karya, Demak
JH102)	1314		R. Gema Sritanjung Mediatama (G.S.M.), Jatibarang
JT72)	1314		R. Suara Ronggohadi, Lamongan
JT73)	1314	0.5	RKPDKDT2 Lumajang
SG03)	1314		R. Buana Sutra, Kendari
SU32)	1314		R. Suara Tanjung Berjaya (Suara Al Falah), Tanjung Balai
LA23)	1324		RDK Lampung Selatan, Kalianda
JK01)	1332	10	RRI Jakarta
JT52)	1332		RKPDT2 Ngawi (Suara Ngawi)
JT75)	1332		RKPD Kotamadya Surabaya (R. Gelora Surabaya)
KH12)	1332		R. Granada Tara Indah, Kuala Kapuas
SB10)	1332		R. Swara Carano Batirai Indah, Batusangkar
SG04)	1332		R. Suara Bhakti Nusantara, Bau-Bau
SH04)	1332		R. Atma Cipta, Palu
SU33)	1332		R. Suara Asahan, Kisaran
KR01)	1341	1/5	RRI Tanjung Pinang
SH05)	1341		R. Bittara Indah, Toli-Toli
JT78)	1350		R. Puspa Jaya, Bojonegoro
JT79)	1350	0.5	RKPDT2 Situbondo
SS17)	1350		R. Baturaja Mutiara Wahana (B.M.W.), Baturaja
SU34)	1350	0.75	RPDT2 Tapanuli Utara, Balige
SU35)	1351		R. Delijaya, Tebingtinggi
SL01)	1359	1	RRI Makassar *
SU36)	1359		R. Surya Da'wah Muhammadiyah (S.D.M.), Medan
JT81)	1365	0.5	RKPDKDT2 Pacitan
JT82)	1365	0.5	RKPDT2 Trenggalek
AC19)	1368		R. Sonya Manis, Bireuen
JB67)	1368	0.5	RPKDT2 Cirebon
JT85)	1368	0.25	RKPDK Tuban (R. Gelora Ronggolawe)
KH13)	1368		R. Hay Citra Ria, Palangkaraya
SL20)	1368		R. Suara Daya Indah, Watampone
SU37)	1368		R. Swaratama Jatayu, Limapuluh-Asahan
SU38)	1368		R. Gundaling, Brastagi
JH103)	1377	0.25	RSPDK Sukoharjo (R. Sukoharjo Makmur)
SU39)	1377		R. Kharisma Swararia, Balige
JB68)	1385	0.25	RPKDT2 Majalengka
JB69)	1386		R. Citra Lestari, Sukabumi
JT80)	1386		RKPDT2 Bangkalan (Suara Bangkalan Ceria)
KB16)	1386		R. Mudhita Buana B.S., Pontianak
SB11)	1386		R. Dhara Perbawa Swara Pada, Pariaman
SH06)	1386		R. Swara Maya Prastha, Poso
PA06)	1395		RRI Wamena
SU08)	1395		R. Deli Indah Swara Diah, Tebingtinggi
JT83)	1400	0.5	RKPDKDT2 Banyuwangi (R. Swara Blambangan)
JH104)	1404	0.25	RPDT2 Brebes
SH07)	1404		Suara Ramayana Jelita, Palu
SS19)	1404		R. Puspa Irama, Belitang Oku
KH14)	1405		R. Swara Nava Ria Gemilang, Palangkaraya
BB01)	1413		RRI Sungai Liat
SH08)	1415		R. Swara Magaga, Toli-Toli
JH105)	1422		R. Suara Purwodadi Bersemi (Pursemi), Purwodadi
JT84)	1422		R. Perkasa Muda Agung (P.M.A.), Kraksaan
KR03)	1422		R. Karastina, Tanjung Pinang
SB12)	1422		R. El Em Bahama, Padangpanjang
SG01)	1422		RRI Kendari
SU40)	1422	0.25	R. Citra Kisarannada, Kisaran
SU41)	1431		R. Buana Serdang, Dolok Masihul
JH106)	1440	0.25	R. Muria, Kudus
JH107)	1440		R. Dian Sindoro Suara Semesta (D.S.S.), Temanggung
JT86)	1440	0.25	R. Nada Kemala Jaya, Sumenep
JT87)	1440	0.25	R. Gema Surya, Ponorogo
RI06)	1440		RPDT2 Bengkalis
RI07)	1440	0.25	R. Indra Kencana, Tembilahan
SH09)	1440		R. Setia Nada, Luwuk
ST02)	1440		Suara Totabuan Ria, Kotamobagu
SU42)	1440		R. Bahana Kusuma, Kabanjahe
JK08)	1445		R. A.W.N., Jakarta
RI08)	1450	0.2	RPDT2 Kampar, Bangkinang
JB70)	1458	0.5	RSPDT2 Indramayu
JB71)	1458		R. Swara Cakrawala Sangkuriang, Bandung
JT89)	1458		R. Sritanjung Setia, Rogojampi
SS23)	1458	0.5	R. Lematang Indah, Bandar Agung
SU43)	1465		R. Kencana Perkasa, Pematang Siantar
JT88)	1467v		R. Khusus Informasi Pertanian, Surabaya
JB72)	1475	1	RKDT2 Karawang
JH108)	1476	0.25	R. Siaran Niaga Hiukencana (R.H.K.), Semarang
JA08)	1485	0.25	R. Dian Irama, Jambi
JH109)	1494		R. Blora Sakti (R.B.S.), Cepu
JK09)	1494		R. Angkatan Bersenjata (Suara Jakarta), Jakarta
SH10)	1494	0.25	R. Toddo Puli (Topsi), Palu
SU44)	1494		R. Al Rona Bahana, Padangsidempuan
JT50)	1503		R. Pendidikan Jawa Timur, Surabaya
JT90)	1503	0.5	RKPDT2 Kotamadya Kediri (R. Gema Kediri)*
KT04)	1512	0.25	R. Swara Mitra Dirgantara (Ramona Jelita), Balikpapan
SB02)	1512		RRI Bukittinggi
AC20)	1521		R. Dirgantara, Langsa
JH110)	1521	0.1	RSPDK Klaten
JH111)	1521	0.3	RSPDKDT2 Wonosobo
JT91)	1521		R. Antares, Sidoarjo *
SS24)	1521		R. Suara Musijaya Pratama, Sekayu
SU46)	1521		R. Cendrawasih Karya Murni, Pematang Siantar
NT08)	1530		R. Swara Rhamagong, Kupang
RI09)	1539	0.25	R. Esti Elita, Pekanbaru
JH113)	1548		R. Swara Manggala Sakti, Kudus
RI10)	1550	0.06	R. Programa Hiburan dan Informasi DT2 Indragiri Hilir, Tembilahan
ST01)	1551	0.1	RRI Manado *
JB73)	1557	0.25	R. Miraka Yunior, Bogor
JB74)	1557	0.25	R. Fantasy 70, Jatiwangi
JH114)	1557	0.25	RSPDT2 Demak (Suara Kota Wali)
JB75)	1563	0.3	RPDT2 Garut
JB76)	1565		R. Swara Primadona Mahardika, Cikampek
JB77)	1584		R. Gema Bhakti Yudha Seroja, Bekasi
KS21)	1584		Swara Al Karomah Pratama, Martapura
KT05)	1584		R. Pangkalan Remaja Derap Bhakti (PRDB), Samarinda
SD14)	1584		R. Dian Erata, Padangpanjang
JB78)	1602		R. Paksi, Bandung
JB79)	1602	0.25	R. Swadaya Cempaka 23, Karawang

SW	kHz	kW	Station
NT09)	2960	0.3	RPDT2 Manggarai, Ruteng: 2145-2300, 0900-1400
SB02)	3232	10	RRI Bukittinggi: 2200-0300, 1000-1600 irr.

SW	kHz	kW	Station
GO01)	3267	10	RRI Gorontalo: 2100-0015, 0800-1400
KH01)	3325	10	RRI Palangkaraya: 2200-0200, 0800-1430
MU01)	3345	10	RRI Ternate: 2000-0030, 0750-1400
NT01)	3385		RRI Kupang: 0900-1400
NT06)	3579		RSPK Ngada:0900-1330
PA02)	3905	10	RRI Merauke: 2000-2200, 0700-1115 irr.
SH01)	3960	10	RRI Palu: 2030-0100, 0830-1600
KB01)	3976		RRI Pontianak: 2200-0030, 1000-1600
SG01)	4000	5	RRI Kendari: 2030-0100, 0750-1530
PA03)	4605	1	RRI Serui: 2000-2315, 0845-1400
SL01)	4750	20	RRI Makassar: 2055-0000, 0745-1555
PA07)	4790		RRI Fak-Fak: 2100-2230, 0700-1400
PA06)	4870		RRI Wamena: 2015-2315, 0800-1400 irr.
PA04)	4871	10	RRI Sorong: 2050-2300, 0800-1115 irr.
PA05)	4920		RRI Biak: 2000-2400, 0800-1500 irr.
JA01)	4925	10	RRI Jambi: 2200-0205, 0900-1400v irr.
PA07)	7115		RRI Fak-Fak: 2230-0400, 0500-0700
SH01)	7235		RRI Palu: 0000-0800
PA09)	7290		RRI Nabire: 0500-0820
JK01)	9525	250	Voice of Indonesia, Jakarta (Cimanggis): 0030-0400, 0800-1300
SL01)	9552	7.5	RRI Makassar: 0000-0800
JK01)	9680	250	RRI Jakarta (Cimanggis): 2200-1600
PA04)	9743	10	RRI Sorong: 0000-0755
JK01)	11785	250	Voice of Indonesia, Jakarta (Cimanggis): alternate frequency.
JK01)	11860	250	RRI Jakarta (Cimanggis): 2200-1600
JK01)	15125	250	RRI Jakarta (Cimanggis): 2200-1300
JK01)	15150	250	Voice of Indonesia, Jakarta (Cimanggis): 1730-2100

HOME SERVICES:
RADIO REPUBLIK INDONESIA (Gov.)
✉ Jl. Medan Merdeka Barat 4-5, Jakarta 10110, or Tromolpos 1157 (or Kotak Pos 356), Jakarta 10001 ☎ +62 21 3842083 🖷 +62 21 3457132 **Web:** www.rri-online.com
Email: rri@rri-online.com
National Station: Jakarta JK01)
Programa 1 (Prosatu): Information and entertainment on 99.85 MHz. **Programa 2 (Produa):** Music and information on 105.0 MHz..**Programa 3 (Protiga):** News and information on 1332, 11860, 15125 kHz, 91.2 MHz: 24 h. N: on the h. **Programa 4 (Proempat):** Culture and sport on 999, 9680 kHz, 92.8 MHz. 24 h. Relays Protiga 1700-2200. **Programa 5 (Prolima):** Classical music on 103.0 MHz. 2200-0200, 0900-1200. At other times between 2200-1600 relays other prgrs.
Voice of Indonesia: on 88.8 MHz. 0030-0400, 0800-1200, 1730-2100.

EXTERNAL SERVICES: The Voice of Indonesia
see International Broadcasting section.

Commercial Stations
Permitted power: 1kW (MW) and 2kW (FM).

Radio Angkatan Bersenjata/Radio Angkatan Udara (Military Stations).
Provincial Gov. Stations: Radio Khusus Pemerintah Daerah Tingkat Satu
District Gov. Stations: Radio Khusus Pemerintah Daerah Tingkat II (Dua). Sometimes "Khusus" (Special) is deleted or "Siaran" (Broadcast) added. "Kabupaten" is occ. used instead of, or as well as, Daerah Tingkat Dua. Both mean "District".
Municipal Gov. Stations: Radio Khusus Pemerintah Daerah Kotamadya. Only intended for particular cities.

Indonesian Station Headings:

RDKDT2	Radio Daerah Kabupaten Daerah Tingkat Dua
RKDT2	Radio Kabupaten Daerah Tingkat Dua
RKPDK	Radio Khusus Pemerintah Daerah Kabupaten
RKPDT1	Radio Khusus Pemerintah Daerah Tingkat Satu
RKPKDT2	Radio Khusus Pemerintah Kabupaten Daerah Tingkat Dua
RPDKDT2	Radio Pemerintah Daerah Kabupaten Daerah Tingkat Dua
RPDT2	Radio Pemerintah Daerah Tingkat Dua
RRI	Radio Republik Indonesia
RSPDT2	Radio Siaran Pemerintah Daerah Tingkat Dua.

Note: There are several other possible station headings which can be determined by using the appropriate letters/words.

Addresses (Jl. = Jalan)
AC00) NANGGROE ACEH DARUSSALAM (State of Aceh)
AC01) Jl. Sultan Iskandar Muda 13, P.O. Box 112, Banda Aceh 23423 - **FM:** 88.5/97.6/99.3/103.0 MHz – **AC02)** RRI Lhokseumawe, P.O. Box 145, Jl. Cik Ditiro 1, Lancang Garam – Lhokseumawe 24352 -**FM:** 94.4/97.9 MHz – **AC03)** Jl. Teuku Umar Km 10, Desa Tonjong, Lho'nga Leupeung 23353 – **AC04)** Takengon – **AC05)** Jl. Veteran 18, Kp. Jawabaru, Kec. Bandasakti, Lhokseumawe 24351 – **AC06)** Jl. Letkol Abdullah Basah 3, Bandar Mutiara, Beureunuen 24173 – **AC07)** Jl. Teuku Cik Ditiro 1, Lhok Sukon – **AC08)** Jl. Mayjen Sutomo 31, Kuala Simpang 24475 – **AC09)** Jl. K.H. Ahmad Dahlan 86, Banda Aceh – **AC10)** Langsa – **AC11)** Jl. Mawar 25, Sigli 24112 – **AC12)** Jl. Ujung Kalak 16, Meulaboh 23613 – **AC13)** Jl.Diponegoro,Sabang, Weh – **AC14)** Jl. Gayo 137, Bireun 24211 – **AC15)** Jl. Rel Kereta Api 14, Lhokseumawe 24310 – **AC16)** Jl. Kreung Pase 12, Geudong – Lhokseumawe 24374 – **AC17)** Jl. Rantau Dusun Jawa, Rantau – Kuala Simpang 24474 – **AC18)** Jl. Diponegoro 53, Sabang, Weh – **AC19)** Jl. Pabrik Padi 43, Bireuen 24201 – **AC20)** Jl. Rantau 19, Langsa – **AC21)** Blangpidie – **AC22)** Lamno
BA00) BALI
BA01) Jl. Hayam Wuruk, Keladis – Denpasar 80233 (Kotak Pos 31,Denpasar 80001) - **FM:** 88.8/93.55/95.0/95.9 MHz – **BA02)** Jl. Gajah Mada 144,Tromolpos 153, Singaraja 81113. **Email**: RRISINGARAJA@wasantara.net.id - **FM:** 93.2/102.0/103.7MHz – **BA03)** Jl.Untung Surapati Gg. Sedap Malam 8, Amlapura 80811 – **BA04)** Jl. Ngurah Rai 141, Negara 82217 – **BA05)** Jl. Hayam Wuruk 78A, Denpasar 80235 – **BA06)** Kompleks Taman Sekar Kav. A-34, Jl. Kartini, Kediri – Tabanan 82113 – **BA07)** Jl. Udayana 45, Negara 82213 – **BA08)** Jl. Merdeka 99, Bangli 80614 – **BA09)** Jl. Batu Tabeh 30, Klungkung 80712 – **BA10)** Sorongga – Gianyar – **BA11)** Jl. Jendral Sudirman 59, Singaraja 81116 – **BA12)** Jl. Jend. A. Yani 123, Singaraja 81116 – **BA13)** Jl. Manik 1, Gianyar - **BA14)** Singaraja
BB00) BANGKA BELITUNG
BB01) Jl. H.O.S. Cokroaminoto 13, Sungai Liat 33211, Bangka - **FM:** 93.0/96.6/97.3 MHz
BE00) BENGKULU
BE01) Jl. Let. Jend. S. Parman 25, Kotak Pos 13, Bengkulu 38227. - **FM:** 90.6/93.0/97.0/105.0 MHz – **BE04)** Jl. D.I. Panjaitan 99, Curup – Bengkulu 39118 – **BE05)** Jl. Hibrida Tiga 30, Bengkulu 38001
BN00) BANTEN
BN01) Jl. Raya Serang Km. 2, Kesambi – Pandeglang 42213 – **BN02)** Jl. Raya Km. 4, Kaduagung Barat – Rangkasbitung 42311 – **BN03)** Tangerang – **BN04)** Jl. Yusuf Martadilaga 55, Pandeglang – **BN06)** Jl. Raya Cipondoh (K.H. Hasyim Ashari) 82, Tangerang 15140 – **BN07)** Wisma Pemda Tangerang, Jl. Sutopo 1, Tangerang – **BN11)** Jl. May. Syafei 66B, Serang – **BN12)** Tangerang – **BN13)** Jl. Putih Derus 6, Rangkasbitung – **BN14)** Jl. K.H. Syam'un 2, Rangkasbitung 42311
GO00) GORONTALO
GO01) Jl. Jenderal Sudirman 30, Gorontalo 96128 - **FM:** 93.6/102.0 MHz – **GO02)** Jl. Teuku Umar 46, Gorontalo 96115
JA00) JAMBI
JA01) Jl. Jendral A. Yani 5, Telanaipura – Jambi 36122 - **FM:** 88.8/98.0/103.7 MHz – **JA02)** Jl. D.R. Rajiman 201, Jambi 36134 – **JA03**)Jl. Sultan Thoha 1, Komplek Airpanas, Muarabulian 36613 – **JA04)** Jl.Gajah Mada, Muarabulian 36610 – **JA05)** Jl. Yos Sudarso 55, Sungai Penuh, Kerinci – **JA07)** Jl. Sisingamangaraja 23, Sungaipenuh – Kerinci 37113 – **JA08)** Jl. Prof. Dr. M. Yamin S.H. 19, Jambi 36135
JB00) JAWA BARAT (West Java)
JB01) Jl. Diponegoro 61, Bandung 40122 (Kotak Pos 1076, Bandung 40001). **Email:** or rribandung@yahoo.com - **FM:** 96.0/97.6 MHz – **JB02)** Jl. Pangrango 30, P.O. Box 232, Bogor 16161.- **FM:** 91.1/92.35/94.25 MHz – **JB03)** Jl. Brigjen Dharsono/By Pass,Cirebon 45132 - **FM:** 93.5/97.6/99.6/107.3 MHz – **JB04)** Jl. P. Geusan Ulun 125, Sumedang – **JB05)** Jl. Ion Martasismata 24, Pamanukan – Subang 41254 – **JB06)** Jl. Pahlawan 313/41, P.O. Box 3, Purwakarta 41115 – **JB07)** Jl. Raya Siliwangi 311, Cicurug – Sukabumi 43159 – **JB08)** Jl. Radio 9, Cirendang – Kuningan – **JB09)** Cileunyi, Lembang-Bandung – **JB10)** Jl. Raya Bojongsari 17, Sawangan – Bogor 16516 – **JB11)** Kuningan – **JB12)** Jl. Pangeran Drajat, Kesambi – Cirebon 45133 – **JB13)** Jl. Pahlawan 78, Arjawinangun – Cirebon – **JB14)** Jl. Cagak Gobras 3, Tasikmalaya – **JB15)** Jl. A. Yani 56, Ciasem, Sukamandi-Subang – **JB16)** Jl. Pala 99, Kompl. Leuwiliang Permai, Leuwiliang - Bogor – **JB17)** Jl. Batulawang 1, Banjar – Ciamis 46133 – **JB18)** Cianjur – **JB19)** Jl. Pramuka 10, Majalengka 45418 – **JB20)** Jl. Adikusumah, Bale Endah, Dayeuh Kolot, Bandung – **JB21)** Jl. Siliwangi 5, Bandung 40132 – **JB22)** Jl. Bojong Tengah 28, Tasikmalaya – **JB23)** Jl. Brawijaya, P.O. Box 12, Kadipaten – Majalengka 45452 – **JB24)** Jl. Siliwangi 103, Pelabuhanratu – Sukabumi 43164 – **JB25)** Jl. Raya Timur 12, Singaparna – Tasikmalaya – **JB26** Jl. Suryakencana 91, Sukabumi 43113 – **JB27)** Gedung Olahraga, Jl. Jendral Akhmad Yani 2, Bekasi – **JB28)** Jl. Raya Barat 98, Banjarsari – Ciamis 46383 – **JB29)** Kompleks Stadion Pajajaran, Jl. Kesehatan 2, Bogor 16161 – **JB30)** Jl. Pembangunan 7, Garut 44151 – **JB31)** Jl. Suroso 46, Cianjur 43214 – **JB32)** Jl. Raya Kedung Halang 2, Waru Jambu – Bogor 16710 – **JB33)** Jl. Raya Jatiwaringin 50, Bekasi 17411 –

JB34) Subang – **JB35)** Jl. Raya Cipaku16, Bogor 16720 – **JB36)** Jl. Babakan 85, Majalaya – Bandung 40382 – **JB37)** Jl. Perintis Kemerdekaan 86, Cibadak – Sukabumi – **JB38)** Jl. Raya Siliwangi 101, Ciawi Gebang – Kuningan 45591 – **JB39)** Jl. Satria 22, Pemeungpeuk – Garut 44175 – **JB40)** Bandung – **JB41)** Jl. Merdeka 92A, Garut – **JB42)** Jl. Manggis I/20, Sukabumi – **JB43)** Jl. Gegerkalong Girang 67, Bandung 40154 – **JB44)** Jl. Ir. H. Juanda 128, Ciamis 46211 – **JB45)** Jl. Pramuka 653, Pangandaran – Ciamis – **JB46)** Jl. Raya Tipar 16, Sukabumi – **JB47)** Jl. Cendana 70, Bekasi 17100 – **JB48)** Jl. Raya Bandung Km. 15, Ciranjang – Cianjur 43282 – **JB49)** Jl. Dadaha 17, Tasikmalaya – **JB50)** Jl. Ky. Dulngali 6, Losali – Cirebon – **JB51)** Jl. R.E. Abdullah 3, Gunung Batu – Bogor 16610 – **JB52)** Jl. Olahraga 21, Indramayu – **JB53)** Cianjur – **JB54)** Mangunjaya, Tambun - Bekasi – **JB55)** Jl. Kalijaga 14, Cirebon 45110 – **JB56)** Jl. Selabintana 146, P.O. Box 59, Sukabumi – **JB57)** Jl. K.H.A. Dahlan 1, Karawang – **JB58)** Jl. Raya Sukamantri 107, Ciawi – Tasikmalaya – **JB59)** Jl. R.E. Martadinata 155, Kuningan 45514 – **JB60)** Jl. Guntur 154, Garut – **JB61)** Kompleks Pemda Kab. Bogor, Desa Tengah – Cibinong 16914 – **JB62)** Komplek Asrama Haji, Cisalak – Sukabumi – **JB63)** Jl. Cikamiri 7, Cisadea – Bandung – **JB64)** Jl. Ki Hajar Dewantara 69, P.O. Box 15, Karawang – **JB67)** Jl. Tujuh Pahlawan Revolusi (Tuparev) 69, Cirebon – **JB68)** Jl. Raya Timur, Majalengka – **JB69)** Sukabumi – **JB70)** Jl. Olahraga Komplex B.T.N. Lama, Indramayu 45213 – **JB71)** Jl. Sukajadi Belakang 227, Bandung 40153 – **JB72)** Jl. Brigpol. Nasuha 2, Karawang – **JB73)** Jl. Raya Puncak 70, Cipayung – Bogor – **JB74)** Jl.Raya Timur 74, Jatiwangi – Majalengka – **JB75)** Garut – **JB76)** Jl. Siswa 56, Cikampek – Karawang 41373 – **JB77)** Bekasi – **JB78)** Gang Sukarame II/4, Bandung – **JB79)** Jl. Cempaka 5, Karawang

JH00) JAWA TENGAH (Central Java)

JH01) Jl. Ahmad Yani 144-146, Kotak Pos 1307, Semarang 50241. - **FM:** 89.0/90.4/95.3/97.6 MHz – **JH02)** Jl. Abdul Rahman Saleh 51. Kotak Pos 40, Surakarta 57133. - **FM:** 97.2/99.15/101.95/105.5 MHz – **JH03)** Jl. Jendral Sudirman 427, Kotak Pos 5, Purwokerto 53116. **Email:** rripwt@astagamail.com - **FM:** 93.0/98.8/100.0 MHz – **JH04)** Jl. Sunan Ngerang 2A, Juwana – Pati – **JH05)** Jl. Kutoarjo 60, Kebumen 54312 – **JH06)** Jl. Brigjen. Slamet Riyadi, Ungaran – **JH08)** Jl. Margantara Tanjung, P.O. Box 45, Purwokerto 53143 – **JH09)** Jl. Pegadaian 108, Weleri – Kendal 51355 – **JH10)** Jl. Barito 4, Pekalongan 51116 – **JH11)** Ambarawa – **JH12)** Jl. Pamukti Baru 9, Prambanan – Klaten 57454 – **JH13)** Jl. Dr. Cipto 18, Cilacap 53231 – **JH14)** Jl. Kartini 4, Magelang – **JH15)** Jl. Purworejo VI/10, Surakarta – **JH16)** Jl. Jeruk Raya 27, Semarang 50249 – **JH17)** Jl. Mayjen. Sungkono 89, Purbalingga – **JH20)** Jl. Dr. Setia Budi 1, Purworejo 54111 – **JH21)** Jl. K.H. Ahmad Fauzan 1, Jepara 59411 – **JH22)** Jl. Osa Maliki 29, P.O. Box 57, Salatiga – **JH23)** Komplek Perluasan Kota, Jl. Plongkowati, Wonogiri – **JH25)** Jl. Alun-Alun Utara, Blora – **JH26)** Jl. Dieng 1A, Wonosobo 56311 – **JH27)** Jl. Raung 7, Candi Baru – Semarang – **JH28)** Jl. Pang. Diponegoro 18, Majenang – Cilacap 53257 – **JH29)** Jl. Brigjen. Katamso, Perum Sugih Waras No. 1, Pemalang 52531 – **JH30)** Jl. K.H. Agus Salim 22, Surakarta 57147 – **JH31)** Jl. Bhakti 2, Kudus – **JH32)** Jl. Pandanaran 5, Boyolali 57311 – **JH33)** Jl. Gajah Mada 5, Pekalongan 51118 – **JH35)** Jl. Kemuning 30, P.O. Box 48, Salatiga 50724 – **JH36)** Jl. Dr. Wahidin 1, Pati – **JH37)** Slawi – Tegal – **JH38)** Jl. Bhayangkara 49, Surakarta – **JH39)** Jl. R.A. Wirya Atmaja 28, Purwokerto – **JH40)** Jl. Letjend. S. Parman 28, Banjarnegara – **JH41)** Jl. Madugondo 15, Grogol – Sukoharjo 57552 – **JH42)** Semarang – **JH44)** Jl. Overste Isdiman 22, Purbalingga 53313 – **JH45)** Jl. Pahlawan 99, Magelang – **JH46)** Jl. D.I. Panjaitan 3, Surakarta – **JH47)** Jl. Kawi V/1, Semarang – **JH48)** Jl. Yos Sudarso 171, Gombong – Kebumen 54411 – **JH49)** Purbalingga – **JH50)** Jl. Raya Kramat Km. 7, Tegal 52181 – **JH51)** Jl. Jendral Sudirman 16A, Cilacap – **JH52)** Jl. Pemuda 3, P.O. Box 43, Salatiga 50711 – **JH53)** Jl. Veteran 21, Sragen 57211 – **JH55)** Jl. Kanjengen C-308, Kranggan – Temanggung 56271 – **JH56)** Jl. Lintar Solo – Boyolali Km. 12, Boyolali 57373,P.O. Box 17, Kartosuro 57560 – **JH57)** Jl. Wonopringgo 414, Pekalongan – **JH58)** Jl. D.I. Panjaitan 3, Banjarnegara 53415 – **JH59)** Jl. Satria Selatan III/H 262, Semarang – **JH61)** Jl. Pahlawan 134A, Magelang 56116 – **JH62)** Jl. Lawu Timur, P.O. Box 50, Karanganyar – **JH63)** Wonosobo – **JH64)** Jl. Kemuning 3, Purbalingga 53316 – **JH65)** Jl. Pasar Hewan 75, Bumiayu 52273 – **JH66)** Jl. Raya Tegalsari 7, Batang – **JH67)** Jl. Pemuda Pucungrejo, Muntilan – Magelang – **JH68)** Jl. Pesantren 19, Ketanggungan – Brebes 52263 – **JH70)**Jl. Raya Ngadirejo, Ngadirejo – Wonogiri – **JH71)** Salatiga – **JH73)** Jl. Kompleks Kawedanan Lama 296, Banyumas 53192 – **JH74)** Jl. Jenderal Ahmad Yani 32, Temanggung – **JH75)** Jl. Tentara Pelajar 52, Tegal 52122 – **JH76)** Jl. Pancurendang 26, Ajibarang – Banyumas 53163 – **JH77)** Jl. Raya Pedurungan Kidul V/18, Semarang – **JH78)** Jl. Raya Wiradesa, Pekalongan – **JH79)** Wisma Klidanggo Lt. 2, Pemalang – **JH82)** Jl. Kol. Sugiyono 18, P.O. Box 144, Wonogiri 57612 – **JH83)** Jl. Kyai Gembyang 7, Kendal – **JH84)** Jl. Ahmad Yani 186, Batang 51215 – **JH85)** Jl. Raya Sukowati 530, Sragen 57215 – **JH86)** Jl. Raya Delanggu Utara 53, Delanggu – Klaten 57471 – **JH87)** Jl. Pemuda 4, Balaikota, Tegal – **JH88)** Jl. Raya Banjaran 34B, Adiwerna – Tegal 52194 – **JH89)** Jl. Sapen 60, Sukorejo – Kendal 51363 – **JH90)** Jl. Dipokusumo, Purbalingga – **JH91)** Jl. Kapt. Mulyadi 117, Surakarta 57113 – **JH92)** Purwokerto – **JH93)** Jl. Raya Taunan Km. 6, Jepara – **JH94)** Jl. Raya Jepon 147, Blora – **JH95)** Jl. Raya Kramat 1, Kaliwungu – Kendal 51372 – **JH96)** Jl. Kapt. Sudiboyo 46, Lt. 2, Tegal 52113 – **JH97)**Jl. Kol. Sugiyono 288, Jepara 59417 – **JH98)** Jl. D.I. Panjaitan 47, Purwodadi – **JH99)** Jl. Waru 32, Rembang – **JH100)** Jl. Dr. Muwardi 47, Badranasri – Karanganyar 5771 – **JH101)** Jl. Kyai Jebat 1, Demak – **JH102)** Jl. Syah Alibahayar Salamah 2, Jatibarang – Brebes 52261 – **JH103)** Jl. Raya Utama Jend. Sudirman 44B, Sukoharjo – **JH104)** Jl. A. Yani 112, Brebes 52212 – **JH105)** Jl. Diponegoro 14, Purwodadi 58100 – **JH106)** Jl. Johar 109, Kudus – **JH107)** Jl. Kartini 34, Temanggung 56216 – **JH108)** Jl. H. Kimar III/5, Semarang 50249 – **JH109)** Jl. Pemuda 55, Cepu – Blora 58312 – **JH110)** Jl. Pemuda Tengah 56, Kotak Pos 113, Klaten – **JH111)** Komplek Kabupaten Wonosobo, Jl. Merdeka 1, Wonosobo – **JH113)** Jl. Sunan Kudus 194, Kudus – **JH114)** Jl. Sultan Patah 3, Demak – **JH115)** Jl. Bahari 325, Weleri – Kendal 51355 – **JH116)** Jl. Pandanwangi Selatan A88, Semarang

JK00) JAKARTA

JK01) Jl. Medan Merdeka Barat 4-5, Jakarta 10110 (Tromolpos 1157, Jakarta 10001) – **JK02)** Institut Studi Arus Informasi, Jl. Utan Kayu 68H, Jakarta Timur 13120. - **FM**: 89.35 MHz – **JK03)** Komplek Taman Mini Indonesia Indah, Pondok Gede, Jakarta – **JK04)** Jl. Tebet Timur Dalam I-N/249, Jakarta Selatan – **JK05)** Jl. Dakota V/1, Kemayoran, Jakarta 10630 – **JK06)** Jl. Batu Ceper V/52, Jakarta Pusat 10120 – **JK07)** Jl. Letjen. S. Parman 1, Jakarta Barat – **JK08)** Jakarta – **JK09)** Jakarta Selatan – **JK10)** Jl. Matraman 39, Jakarta – **JK11)** Universitas Mercu Buana, Meruya Selatan, Jakarta Barat – **JK12)** Jakarta Utara – **JK13)** Jakarta – **JK14)** Jl. Kebon Baru Utara F No. 19, Tebet, Jakarta 12830

JT00) JAWA TIMUR (East Java)

JT01) Jl. Pemuda 82-90, Kotak Pos 239, Surabaya 60271. **FM:** 89.7/95.2/99.2/106.3 MHz – **JT02)** Jl. Candi Panggung 58, Kotak Pos 78, Mojolangu – Malang 65142. - **FM:** 94.6/95.4/105.1 MHz – **JT03)** Jl. D.I. Panjaitan 61, Jember 68110 (Kotak Pos 116, Jember 68101). - **FM:** 91.1/98.45/104.05 MHz – **JT04)** Jl. Mayjen. Panjaitan 10-12, Madiun 63133. - **FM:** 97.6/99.7/104.0/106.4 MHz – **JT05)** Jl. Urip Sumoharjo 26, Sumenep 69411, Madura. - **FM:** 93.0/98.5 MHz – **JT06)** Jl. Dr. Sutomo 17, Pare – Kediri – **JT07)** Jl. Agus Salim, Lirboyo - Kediri – **JT08)** Jl. Kombes Pol M. Duryat 20, Lamongan 62217 – **JT09)** Jl. Irian Jaya IV/10, Tebu Ireng – Jombang – **JT10)** Komplek Taman Wisata Panataran, Blitar – **JT12)** Jl. Pang. Besar Sudirman 141, Kediri – **JT13)** Gedung GNI, Jl. Mayjen Sungkono 28, Kediri – **JT15)** Jl. Raya Kalianget 288, Situbondo – **JT16)** Jl. Pahlawan 110, Surabaya – **JT17)** Jl. Trunojoyo 222, Pamekasan 69316 – **JT18)** Pasuruan – **JT19)** Jl. Letjend. Sutoyo 184, Ngawi – **JT20)** Jl. Basuki Rakhmat Timur, Magetan 63314 – **JT21)** Jl. Wijaya Kusuma 3, Mangelo Sooko – Mojokerto 61361 – **JT23)** Jl. Yos Sudarso 173, Sumenep – **JT25)** Jl. K.H. Wakhid Hasyim 133, Jombang 61419 – **JT26)** Jl. Dr. Sutomo 26, Malang 65111 – **JT28)** Jl. Alun-Alun Utara 3, Ponorogo 63413 – **JT29)** Jl. Simolawang I/96, Surabaya – **JT31)** Wisma Sarinadi, Kawasan GOR, Sidoarjo – **JT32)** Mojosari, Mojokerto – **JT33)** Jl. Gatot Subroto 107, Pacitan – **JT34)** Jl. Dharmhusada Indah Blok A75, Surabaya 60285 – **JT35)** Jl. Pamong Praja 3, Pamekasan – **JT36)** Jl. K.H. Wakhid Hasyim 9, Gresik – **JT37)** Jl. Sultan Agung 25-27, Lumajang 67315 – **JT40)** Jl. Veteran 6B, Bondowoso 68211 – **JT41)** Jl. Aipda Karel Sasuit Tubun 15, Gresik 61114 – **JT42)** Jl. Megantoro 83, Nganjuk 64419 – **JT43)** Jl. W.R. Supratman 29, Situbondo – **JT44)** Jl. Hayam Wuruk 169, Probolinggo 67281 – **JT45)** Jl. Raden Patah 19, Jombang 61413 – **JT46)** Jl. Jagalan II/4, Kedok – Malang – **JT47)** Jl. Joyoboyo 77, Kediri 64132 – **JT48)** Jl. Panglima Sudirman 21, Kepanjen – Malang 65163 – **JT49)** Jl. K.H.A. Dahlan 28, Trenggalek 66315 – **JT50)** Jl. Gentengkali 33, Surabaya – **JT51)** Kompleks Manyar Indah Plaza, Jl. Ngagel Jaya Selatan, Surabaya – **JT52)** Jl. Teuku Umar 12, Ngawi – **JT53)** Jl. Ngagel Jaya Utara IV/21, Surabaya 60283 – **JT54)** Jl. Sidoluhur 2A, Ponorogo 63410 – **JT55)** Jl. Kahuripan 91, Malang 65119 – **JT57)** Jl. Amir Hamzah 18, Surabaya 60241 – **JT58)** Jl Panglima Sudirman 72, Surabaya 60272 – **JT59)** Jl. Teluk Aru 68, Surabaya 60165 – **JT60)** Jl. Mondoroko 2, Singosari – Malang 65153 – **JT61)** Jl. Letnan Karsono 47, Bondowoso – **JT62)** Jl. AKBP M. Suroko 11, Bojonegoro 62111 – **JT63)** Jl. Jember 17, Genteng – Banyuwangi 68465 – **JT65)** Jl. Dr. Cipto, Sumenep 69410 – **JT66)** Jl. Adityawarman 81, Surabaya 60242 – **JT68)** Jl. Pesanggrahan V Taman, Madiun 63131 – **JT70)** Jl. Kusuma Bangsa 4, Surabaya 60241 – **JT71)** Jl. Dr. Sutomo 60, Nganjuk – **JT72)**Jl. Raya Bedahan 17, Babat – Lamongan – **JT73)** Jl. W.R. Supratman 27, Lumajang 67310 – **JT74)** Jl. Timur Alun-Alun, Tulungagung – **JT75)** Humas Gelora 10 Nopember, Jl. Tambaksari, Surabaya 60136 – **JT77)** Jl. Kartini 12, Jember 68137 – **JT78)** Jl. J.A. Suprapto 85, Bojonegoro 62118 – **JT79)** Jl. P.B. Sudirman 14, Situbondo 68416 – **JT80)** Bangkalan – **JT81)** Jl. Jaksa Agung Suprapto 8, Pacitan 63512 – **JT82)** Jl. K.H. Wakhid Hasyim 1, Trenggalek 66311 – **JT83** Jl. Ikan Cakalang 3, Banyuwangi – **JT84)** Jl. P. Sudirman 62, Kraksaan – Probolinggo 67282 –

JT85) Jl. Dr. Wahidin Sudirohujodo 31C, Tuban 63210 – **JT86)** Jl. K.H. Mansyur 65A, Sumenep 69411 – **JT87)** Jl. Prof. Dr. M. Yamin 47, Ponorogo – **JT88)** Jl. Ahmad Yani 112, Wonokromo - Surabaya – **JT89)** Jl. Candian 132, Rogojampi – Banyuwangi 68462 – **JT90)** Jl. Jendral Basuki Rakhmad 15, Kediri 64123 – **JT91)** Jl. K.H. Tohir Saleh 151, P.O. Box 1, Krian – Sidoarjo 61262

KB00) KALIMANTAN BARAT (West Kalimantan)

KB01) Jl. Jendral Sudirman 7, Kotak Pos 6, Pontianak 78111. - **FM:** 90.3/102.0/104.0 MHz – **KB02)** Jl. Raya Sambas Bukitluwing 1, Sambas 79162 – **KB03)** Jl. Raya Bengkayang 72, Bengkayang 79152 – **KB04)** Jl. D. Menambon 738, Mempawah 78912 – **KB05)** Jl. Kelam Akcaya I/18, Sintang 78611 – **KB06)** Jl. Raya Ngabang 72, Ngabang – Pontianak – **KB07)** Jl. Husein Hamzah Pal IX, Ds. Puring, RT 02/01, Pontianak 78121 – **KB08)** Jl. Kom. Yos Sudarso 9, Sanggau 78582 – **KB09)** Jl. Kawak 26, Sekadau 78582 – **KB11)** Jl. Pembangunan RT 003/XIV, Desa Harapan – Pemangkat 79153 – **KB13)** Jl. Pendidikan II, Sungai Pinyuh 78353 – **KB16)** Jl. Jendral Urip, Gg. Kutilang 72, Pontianak 78111

KH00) KALIMANTAN TENGAH (Central Kalimantan)

KH01) Jl. M. Husni Thamrin 1, Palangkaraya 73112. - **FM:** 89.4/92.1/93.0 MHz – **KH02** Jl. Merdeka Raya 21, Buntok 73711 – **KH03)** Jl. Pelita 1, Tamiang Layang 73611 – **KH04)** Jl. Jendral Ahmad Yani Kompl. Nusa Indah 118, Sampit 74322 – **KH05** Jl. H. Abdul Syukur 23, Pangkalan Bun 74114 – **KH06)** Jl. Jend. A. Yani, Kuala Kapuas – **KH07)** Jl. M.T. Haryono I/32, Sampit 74322 – **KH08)** Jl. Pongsongteleng 47, Ampah 73652 – **KH09)** Jl. Jend. Ahmad Yani 23, Palangkaraya 73111 – **KH10)** Jl. Ahmad Yani 45, Pangkalan Bun 74113 – **KH11)** Jl. Merak 34, Muarateweh 73810 – **KH12)** Jl. Teratai 20, Kuala Kapuas 73514 – **KH13)** Jl. Haji Ikap 47, Palangkaraya 73111 – **KH14)** Jl. Pangeran Diponegoro 22T, Palangkaraya 73111 – **KH15)** Muarateweh

KR00) KEPULAUAN RIAU (Riau Archipelago)

KR01) Jl. Ahmad Yani, Kotak Pos 8, Tanjung Pinang 29133, Bintan. - **FM:** 96.5/97.6 MHz – **KR02)** RRI Natuna, Ranai, Bunguran Timur, Pulau Natuna Besar 29183. - **FM:** 90.0/104.1 MHz – **KR03)** Jl. Pemuda, Tanjung Pinang 29110

KS00) KALIMANTAN SELATAN (South Kalimantan)

KS01) Jl. Jenderal A. Yani Km. 3.5 No. 234, Kotak Pos 117, Banjarmasin 70234. - **FM:** 95.65/97.75/105.4 MHz – **KS02)** Jl. H. Sibli Imansyah 3, Barabai 71314 – **KS03)** Jl. Brigjend. Hasan Basri 15, Rantau – Tapin 71111 – **KS04)** Jl. Abdul Muis Ridhani 5, Barabai 71312 – **KS05)** Banjarmasin – **KS06)** Jl. Pahlawan 33, Kandangan 71211 – **KS07)** Jl. Bali RT14 23B, Banjarmasin 70114 – **KS08)** Jl. Manggis 31, Banjarmasin 70235 – **KS09)** Jl. Raya Batulicin 43, Batulicin 72171 – **KS10)** Jl. Brigjen. H. Hasan Basry 56/58, Rantau 71111 – **KS11)** Banjarmasin – **KS12)** Jl. Candi Agung 88-89, Amuntai 71418 – **KS13)** Kotabaru – **KS14)** Jl. Kapten Piere Tendean 50, Banjarmasin 70231 – **KS15)** Jl. Kemakmuran 8, Peleihari – Tanah Laut – **KS16)** Jl. H. Abdul Wahab Syahrani 90, Kandangan 71213 – **KS18)** Jl. Brigjen. H. Hasan Basry Kayu Tangi, Banjarmasin 70124 – **KS19)** Jl. Barintik 35, P.O. Box 48, Martapura 70613 – **KS20)** Jl. Kayutangi II Jalur I/88, Banjarmasin 70124 – **KS21)** Jl. Jend. A. Yani, Pesayangan Utara – Martapura 70619

KT00) KALIMANTAN TIMUR (East Kalimantan)

KT01) Jl. Moh. Yamin 8, P.O. Box 45, Samarinda 75110. - **FM:** 88.8/93.5/96.9/97.9 MHz – **KT02)** Jl. Mulawarman 66, Tenggarong – **KT03)** Jl. Jend. A. Yani 82, Balikpapan 76123 – **KT04)** Jl. A. Yani 50, Balikpapan 76123 – **KT05)** Jl Anggur 33, Samarinda 75123 - **KT06)** Balikpapan. **FM:** 99.9 MHz

LA00) LAMPUNG

LA01) Jl. Gatot Subroto 26, Kotak Pos 24, Pahoman – Bandar Lampung 35213. - **FM:** 90.9/93.0/98.0 MHz – **LA02)** Jl. Veteran 475, Purwodadi – Trimurjo 34114 – **LA05)** Jl. Ir. Sukarno 278, Sukadana 34194 – **LA06)** Jl. Raya Simpang Agung 58, Terbanggi Besar – Lampung Tengah – **LA07)** Jl. Proklamator Raya 163, Bandar Jaya – Lampung Tengah 34162 – **LA08)** Jl. Teuku Umar 65A, Rajabasa – Bandar Lampung 35144 – **LA09)** Jl. Batu Tegi 40, Talangpadang 35377 – **LA10)** Jl. Jend. Sudirman 14A, Metro 34114 – **LA12)** Jl. Raya Bakauheni 177, Kota Dalam – Lampung Selatan – **LA14)** Jl. Raden Intan 188, Wonodadi – Gadingrejo 35372 – **LA15)** Jl. Raden Intan Way Mangaku 54, Liwa 34573 – **LA16)** Jl. Raya Sribawono Panjang 576, Sribawono – Labuhan Maringgai 34198 – **LA17)** Jl. Raya Hamka 576, Sidomulyo – Kalianda – **LA18)** Jl. Pahlawan 6, Kotabumi 34511 – **LA19)** Jl. Indra Bangsawan 188, Kalianda 35513 – **LA20)** Jl. Tanggamus 69, Gisting – **LA21)** Jl. Raya Lintas Timur 148, Unit II, Tulang Bawang – **LA23)** Jl. Indra Bangsawan, Kalianda 35511

MA00) MALUKU (Moluccas)

MA01) Jl. Jendral Akhmad Yani 1, Ambon 97124. - **FM:** 90.3/98.4/105.0/107.3 MHz – **MA02)** Jl. Sukarno-Hatta, Kec. Wat Deh – Tual 97661, Pulau Kai. - **FM:** 93.2/97.8 MHz – **MA04)** Jl. Sirimau 54, Sonya Atas 97125, Ambon

MU00) MALUKU UTARA (North Moluccas)

MU01) Jl. Sultan Khairun, Kedaton, Ternate 97720. - **FM:** 93.5/102.0/103.5 MHz

NB00) NUSA TENGGARA BARAT (West Nusa Tenggara)

NB01) Jl. Langko 83, P.O. Box 2, Ampenan – Mataram 83114, Lombok. - **FM:** 89.1/91.8/93.5/97.2/104.0 MHz – **NB02)** Jl. Gajah Mada 4, Praya 83511 – **NB03)** Jl. Jend. Sudirman 10, Pancor – Selong 83611, Lombok – **NB04)** Jl. R.A. Kartini 11, Sumbawa Besar 84310, Sumbawa – **NB05)** Jl. Pahlawan 70, Pancor - Selong, Lombok – **NB06)** Jl. Koperasi (KLP Sinar Rinjani), Aikmel 83653, Lombok – **NB07)** Jl. Swara Mahardika 3, Panjang Timur – Mataram 83121, Lombok – **NB08)** Jl. Prof. Muh. Yamin S.H. 3, Selong 83612, Lombok – **NB09)** Jl. Miru 72, Cakranegara – Mataram 83511, Lombok - **NB10)** Selong, Lombok

NT00) NUSA TENGGARA TIMUR (East Nusa Tenggara)

NT01) Jl. Tompello 8, Kupang 85225, Timor. - **FM:** 90.6/93.5/102.0 MHz – **NT02)** Waikabubak, Sumba – **NT03)** Jl. Nusa Indah 21, Oepura – Kupang 85117, Timor – **NT04)** Jl. Untung Suropati 2B, Kupang 85119, Timor – **NT05)** Jl. Basuki Rahmat 2, Atambua 85711, Timor – **NT06)** Jl. Sukarno-Hatta, Bajawa, Flores – **NT07)** Jl. Panglima Sudirman, Ende, Flores. - **FM:** 103.5 MHz – **NT08)** Jl. Palapa 17, Kupang 85111, Timor – **NT09)** Ruteng, Flores – **NT10)** Soe, Timor

PA00) PAPUA (formerly Irian Jaya)

PA01) Jl. Tasangkapura 23, Kotak Pos 1077, Jayapura 99200. - **FM:** 90.0/93.6 MHz – **PA02)** Jl. Jendral A. Yani, Mopa Baru – Merauke 99611 (Kotak Pos 11, Merauke 99601). - **FM:** 90.0/105.0 MHz – **PA03)** Jl. Pattimura, Serui 98213. - **FM:** 97.5 MHz – **PA04)** Jl. Jendral Ahmad Yani 44, KLA Demak II, Kotak Pos 146, Sorong 98414. **FM:** 96.7 MHz – **PA05)** Jl. Majapahit, Kotakpos 505, Biak 98117.- **FM:** 93.7/97.8/107.6 MHz – **PA06)** Jl. Jendral A. Yani 14, Wamena 99511 (Kotak Pos 10, Wamena 99501). - **FM:** 93.5/97.8 MHz – **PA07)** Jl. Kapt. P. Tendean, Kotak Pos 154, Fak-Fak 98612 . - **FM:** 93.3 Mhz – **PA08** Jl. Merdeka 68, Manokwari 98311. - **FM:** 92.4/97.8 MHz – **PA09)** Jl. Merdeka 74, Nabire 98811 (Kotak Pos 110, Nabire 98801). - **FM:** 96.3/98.1 MHz – **PA10)** Jayapura – **PA11)** Jayapura

RI00) RIAU

RI01) Jl. Jend. Sudirman 322, Kotak Pos 51, Pekanbaru 28113. - **FM:** 88.0/91.2 MHz – **RI02)** Jl. Putri Nilam 51, Sukajadi – Pekanbaru 28128 – **RI03)** Jl. Jend. Sudirman 674, Bagan Batu – Bengkalis – **RI04)** Jl. Sultan Komplek Taman Rekreasi Danau Raja, Rengat – **RI05)** Jl. Pertanian 90/06, Duri, Mandau – Bengkalis 28884 – **RI06)** Jl. Jendral Ahmad Yani 74, Bengkalis – **RI07)** Jl. Gerilya 8 Hulu, Tembilahan – **RI08)** Jl. Prof. M. Yamin S.H., P.O. Box 21, Bangkinang 28412 – **RI09)** Jl. Teratai 17, Pekanbaru – **RI10)** Jl. Veteran 5, Tembilahan 29211

SB00) SUMATERA BARAT (West Sumatra)

SB01) Jl. Jendral Sudirman 12, Kotak Pos 77, Padang 25124. - **FM:** 90.9/93.5/103.7 MHz – **SB02)** Jl.Prof. Muhammad Yamin 199, Kotak Pos 3, Aurkuning – Bukittinggi 26131. - **FM:** 93.2/97.2/107.0 MHz – **SB03)** Jl. Jend. Sudirman 18, Payakumbuh 26211 – **SB04)** Jl. Sisingamangaraja 1, Padang 25122 – **SB05)** Lubuk Alang – **SB06)** Jl. Limo Singke Baringin, Gando Sulit Air – Solok – **SB07)** Jl. Pontianak 22, UKT – Padang 25135 – **SB08)** Jl. W.R. Mongonsidi 4B, Lantai 2, Padang 25117 – **SB09)** Jl. Cindurmato 140, Solok 27310 – **SB10)** Jl. Simpurut 34, Batusangkar 27211 – **SB11)** Jl. Jend. Sudirman 203, P.O. Box 145, Pariaman 25518 – **SB12)** Jl. Prof. M. Yamin S.H. 4, Padangpanjang 27116 – **SB14)** Jl. Pancasila (Sukarno-Hatta) 18, Padangpanjang 27115

SG00) SULAWESI TENGGARA (South-East Celebes)

SG01) Jl. Laute Mandonga 44, Kotak Pos 7, Kendari 93111. - **FM:** 91.2/103.0/107.3 MHz – **SG02)** Kendari – **SG03)** Kendari – **SG04)** Bau-Bau, Buton – **SG05)** Kolaka

SH00) SULAWESI TENGAH (Central Celebes)

SH01) Jl. R.A. Kartini 39, Palu 94112. - **FM:** 90.6/93.0/105.0 MHz – **SH02)** Jl. Bakuku 1, Palu Barat 94226 – **SH03)** Jl. Palu 106, Donggala 94112 – **SH04)** Jl. Sutoyo Siswomiharjo 44, Palu 94111 – **SH05)** Jl. Magamu 33, Toli-Toli 94514 – **SH06)** Jl. Pulau Kalimantan 45, Poso 94610 – **SH07)** Jl. Sarikaya 3, Palu 94112 – **SH08)** Jl. Saputan Raya 117, Toli-Toli – **SH09)** Jl. Jend. Sudirman 128, Luwuk – **SH10)** Jl. Setia Budi 20A, Palu 94111

SL00) SULAWESI SELATAN (South Sulawesi)

SL01) Jl. Riburane 3, Kotak Pos 103, Makassar 90111.- **FM:** 90.75/97.6/99.15 MHz – **SL02)** Jl. Sungai Limboto 42, Makassar 90114 – **SL03)** Jl. Ujung Lr. 51, Makassar 90155 – **SL04)** Jl. Bandang 9 Lr. II, Pinrang 91211 – **SL05)** Jl. Ratulangi 17, Rantepao 91831 – **SL06)** Jl. Poros Cabenge 1, Watansoppeng – **SL07)** Jl. Buru 34, P.O. Box 1479, Makassar 90171 – **SL08)** Jl. Abubakar Lambogo 11, Enrekang 91711 – **SL09)** Jl. Manggis 16, Makassar 90112 – **SL10)** Jl. Mesjid Raya 100, Sengkang – Wayo 90914 – **SL11)** Jl. Andi Naboang 1, Pangkajene – **SL12)** Jl. Buru 28, Kotak Pos 45, Makassar 90171 – **SL13)** Sinjai – **SL14)** Jl. Brawijaya 2, Wonomulyo – Polmas 91352 – **SL15)** Jl. Gelatik 2, Kel. Pallanting, Bantaeng 92411 – **SL16)** Jl. Mangga 1, Palopo 91921 – **SL17)** Jl. Pasar Sentral 48, Mamuju – **SL18)** Jl. Sultan Hasanuddin 94, Pangkep – **SL19)** Jl. Mannennungeng Kav. 33, Palopo 91922 – **SL20)** Jl. M.H. Thamrin 45, Watampone 92712

SS00) SUMATERA SELATAN (South Sumatra)

SS01) Jl. Radio 2 Km. 4, Palembang 30128. - **FM:** 88.9/91.8/93.1/ 97.2 MHz – **SS02)** Jl. Raya Betung 281, Betung – Musi Banyuasin – **SS03)** Jl. Kapasan 112, Belitang – OKU 32182 – **SS04)** Jl. Simpang Tiga Tanjung Seteko, Indralaya – OKI 30662 – **SS05)** Jl. Letjen. R. Suprapto 10, Sukorejo, Pagar Alam – Lahat – **SS06)** Jl. Cut Nyak Din 3, Baturaja – OKU 32111 – **SS07)** Jl. Letjen. Bambang Sutoyo 113, RT 13A, 3 Ilir, Palembang 30116 – **SS08)** Pagar Alam - Lahat – **SS09)** Jl. Dr. M. Isa 38, 8 Ilir, Palembang 30114 – **SS11)** Jl. Pramuka I/15, Muara Enim – **SS12)** Jl. D.I. Panjaitan 3/41, Plaju – Palembang 30265 – **SS13)** Jl. Lintas Timur Km. 135, Tugumulyo, Pembantu Lempuing – OKI 30657 – **SS14)** Jl. Jend. Sudirman 182/IV, Prabumulih Barat 31123 – **SS15)** Jl. K.H.A. Azhari 136, 12 Ulu, Palembang 30262 – **SS17)** Jl. Mayor Iskandar 427, Baturaja – **SS18)** Jl. Mayor Ruslan III/30A, Pasar Lama – Lahat 31413 – **SS19)** Jl. Sakura 103, RT 04, Bedilan – Belitang 32182 – **SS23)** Jl. Raya Bandar Agung 4, Bandar Agung – Lahat 31414 – **SS24)** Jl. Kol. Wahid Udin 565, Lingkungan 7, Sekayu – Musi Banyuasin

ST00) SULAWESI UTARA (North Celebes)

ST01) Jl. Radio 1, Kotak Pos 1110, Tikala Ares, Manado 95124. - **FM:** 89.1/97.2/102.0 MHz – **ST02)** Jl. Teuku Umar 155, Kotamobagu

SU00) SUMATERA UTARA (North Sumatra)

SU01) Jl. Letkol. Martinus Lubis 5, Medan 20232. - **FM:** 88.0/90.6/ 92.35/95.1/97.8 MHz – **SU02)** RRI Sibolga, Jl. Ade Irma Suryani Nasution 11, Sibolga 22513. - **FM:** 93.0/98.1 MHz – **SU03)** Jl. Dr. F.L. Tobing 59, Sidikalang 22212 – **SU04)** Jl. M.T. Haryono 64, Tanjungbalai 21311 – **SU05)** Jl. Cirebon 3, Belawan – Medan 20412 – **SU06)** Jl. Galang 9, Lubukpakam 20510 – **SU07)** Jl. Brig. Jendral Katamso 43, Lubukpakam – Medan – **SU08)** Jl. Jenderal Sudirman, Tebingtinggi – **SU09)** Jl. Diponegoro 69, Gunungsitoli, Nias – **SU10)** Jl. Imam Bonjol 16, Tebingtinggi 20610 – **SU11)** Jl. Iskandar Muda 117A, Medan 20119 – **SU12)** Jl. Deli Gg. Kereta Api 6, Perbaungan – Deli Serdang 20586 – **SU13)** Kisaran – **SU14)** Jl. Cokroaminoto 171, Kisaran 21216 – **SU15)** Jl. Ismail 5A, Binjai – **SU16)** Medan – **SU18)** Jl. W.R. Supratman 37, Rantau Prapat – **SU19)** Jl. Merdeka 1, P.O. Box 25, Pematang Siantar – **SU20)** Jl. Pemuda, Gg. Singadua 29A, Tanjungpura – Langkat 20853 – **SU21)** Jl. Raya Medan 52, Tebingtinggi 20610 – **SU22)** Jl. Hasanudin 35, Binjai 20713 – **SU23)** Jl. Tenggiri 13, Sibolga 22510 – **SU24)** Jl. Palembang 36, Binjai 20721 – **SU25)** Jl. Hokki 21, Medan 20217 – **SU26)** Jl. Letjend. Suprapto 101, Sibolga 22351 – **SU27)** Jl. Beringin 1, Tanjung Gading – Asahan 21257 – **SU28)** Jl. Kol. Liberti Malau, Pasar Baru – Tarutung – **SU29)** Jl. Merdeka, Pematang Siantar – **SU30)** Jl. Jend. Sudirman 35, Kabanjahe 22113 – **SU32)** Tanjung Balai – **SU33)** Kisaran – **SU34)** Komplek Monumen D.I. Panjaitan 1, P.O. Box 4, Balige – **SU35)** Tebingtinggi – **SU36)** Jl. Kapten Mokhtar Basri 3, Medan – **SU37)** Jl. Besar Sumberpadi, Limapuluh 21255 – **SU38)** Jl. Kejora 24, Brastagi – **SU39)** Jl. Sisingamangaraja 188, Balige 22316 – **SU40)** Jl. Waja 18, Kisaran 21216 – **SU41)** Jl. Besar 159, Dolok Masihul – Deli Serdang – **SU42)** Jl. Veteran, Gg. Kembang 2, Kabanjahe 22113 – **SU43)** Jl. Seram Atas 113A, Banten – Pematang Siantar 21111 – **SU44)** Jl. Kamboja 1, Padangsidempuan 22730 – **SU46)** Jl. Simbolon 5, Pematang Siantar 21115

YG00) DAERAH ISTIMEWA YOGYAKARTA (Yogyakarta Special Region)

YG01) Jl. Ahmad Jazuli 4, Tromolpos 18, Kotabaru – Yogyakarta 55224. **Email:** rri-yk@yogya.wasantara.net.id - **FM:** 91.1/101.2/102.5/102.9 MHz – **YG02)** Jl. K.H. Agus Salim 119, Ketek – Wonosari, Gunung Kidul – **YG03)** Sidokarto - Sleman – **YG04)** Jl. Tamtama 3, Wates – **YG05)** Jl. Jagalan 36, Yogyakarta – **YG06)** Jl. K.H.A.Dahlan 3, P.O.Box 105, Yogyakarta.

FM: A large number of FM stations operate throughout the country. A new FM freq. plan was phased in beginning May 2004. See address list for RRI FM freqs.

Jakarta FM: 87.6 Antarnusa Jaya – 88.0 Mustang Utama – 88.4 Arief Rahman Hakim – 89.2 Metro Jaya Kartika – 90.0 Elshinta – 90.4 Muara Abdi Nusa – 90.8 Suara Gema Pembangunan Utama – 91.6 Indika Millenia – 92.0 Sonora – 92.4 Primaswara Adi Spirit Semesta – 93.2 Merpati Dharmawangsa – 93.6 Gema Wargakarya Satnawa, Bekasi – 93.9 Swara Mersidiona, Tangerang – 94.3 Gardia Asia Bumi – 94.7 Agustina Yunior – 95.1 Kirana Indah Suara – **JK14)** 95.5 Assyafi'yah – 95.9 Smart Media Utama – 96.3 Pelita Kasih – 96.7 Swara Rhadana Dunia – 97.1 Suara Monalisa – 97.5 Safari Bina Budaya – 97.9 Kayumanis – 98.3 Cakrawala Gita Swara – 98.7 Attahiriyah – 99.1 Delta Insani – 99.5 Jati Yaski Mandiri, Tangerang – 99.9 Draba – 100.3 Elgangga, Bekasi – 100.6 Bahana Sanada Dunia, Tangerang – 101.0 Suara Irama Indah – 101.4 Suara Kejayaan – 101.0 Terik Matahari Bhn Pembangunan – 102.2 Prambors – 102.6 Camajaya Surya Nada – 103.4 Taman Mini – 103.8 Pesona Gita Anindita – 104.2 Media Suara Trisakti – 104.6 Trijaya Sakti – 105.4 Niaga Chakti Bhudi Bhakti – 105.8 Ramako Jaya Raya – 106.2 Bergaya Nyanyian Irama Sejati, Tangerang – 106.6 Sabda Sosok Sohor – 107.0 Nada Komunikasi Utama, Bekasi – 107.3 Suara Tunggal Angkasa Raya, Tangerang.

Denpasar (Bali) FM: 89.4 Gema Sunari Indah – 91.8 Flamboyant Bali Indah – 94.5 Citra Dharma Bali Satya – 97.7 Gema Merdeka – 98.5 Plus – 99.3 Balina Citra – 102.0 Surya Permai – 102.8 Pinguin – 103.6 Menara – 104.4 Aneka Rama – 105.2 Suara Denpasar Chakti – 106.0 Swara Kreasi Utama, Kuta..

IRAN

L.T: UTC +3½h (21 Mar-22 Sept: UTC +4½h) — **Pop:** 66m — **Pr.L:** Farsi (Persian) — **E.C:** 50Hz, 230V — **ITU:** IRN

ISLAMIC REPUBLIC OF IRAN BROADCASTING (IRIB)

✉ P. O. Box 19395-333, Tehran. (Int. Tech. Affairs: P.O. Box 15875-4344, Tehran) ☎ +98 21 2040097 🖷 +98 21 2045056
Web: www.irib.com/radio **Email:** plninfseda@irib.com
L.P: Pres: Dr. Ali Larijani. Vice Pres. Admin. & Financial Affairs: Ali Kordan.

MW

Prov.& Location	kHz	kW	N	Prov.& Location	kHz	kW	N
3 Azarshahr	531	500	R	15 Mahshar	1080	750	R/E
24 Iranshahr	531	600	S/E	23 Biarjmand	1089	-	R
29 Mashhad	540	200	S	24 Zabol	1098	100	E
13 Sirjan	549	400	S	15 Sabzevar	1107	10	R
25 Gheslagh	558	1000	F	26 Ardekan	1116	200	R
15 Mahshahr	576	750	R/E	30 Nehbandan	1125	10	R
25 Tehran	585	600	Q	28 Bojnurd	1134	50	R
7 Shiraz	594	400	R	16 Yasuj	1143	50	S 3
24 Zahedan	603	100	R	Tabriz	1152	100	F
14 Qasr-e-Shirin	612	600	E	14 Qasr-e-Shirin	1161	600	E
30 Birjand	621	20	R	15 Abadan	1169v	750	S
3 Bonab	639	400	E	23 Semnan	1170	50	S
5 Shahr-e-Kord	648	10	R	9 Gonbad	1179	50	S
24 Zahedan	657	100	S	25 Tehran	1188	300	P
15 Shushtar	666	-	S	1 Moghan	1197	50	R
10 Hamadan	675	50	R	19 Azna	1206	50	S
29 Mashhad	684	100	R	20 Chalus	1215	50	R
11 Bandar-e-Lengeh	693	100	R	13 Kerman	1224	400	E
4 Bushehr	702	500	S	7 Abadeh	1233	50	R
8 Kiashahr	702	500	E	11 Bandar Abbas	1233	-	S
15 Ahwaz	711	200	R/E	27 Zanjan	1242	50	S
5 Mahidasht	720	750	R/E	8 Kiashahr	1251	100	S
29 Tayebad	720	400	R/E	6 Khur	1260	10	S
4 Dayyer	738	-	R	1 Khalkhal	1269	50	R
9 Gonbad	747	150	R	14 Kermanshah	1278	100	R
8 Rasht	756	100	S/E	7 Lar	1287	100	R
24 Chah Bahar	765	600	E	21 Qazvin	1296	50	S
19 Arak	774	100	R	24 Zahedan	1296	-	R
24 Iranshahr	783	150	R	4 Bushehr	1305	50	R
27 Zanjan	792	50	R	1 Ardabil	1314	10	R
29 Kashmar	801	50	S	3 Jolfa	1323	50	R
18 Khorramabad	810	100	S	25 Tehran	1332	300	T
20 Sari	819	30	R	13 Bam	1341	10	S
26 Tabas	828	50	R	15 Shushtar*	1350	600	R
6 Isfahan	837	300	R	7 Lar	1359	50	S
3 Mianeh	846	10	S	20 Sari	1368	20	S
14 Qasr-e-Shirin	864	50	R	24 Chabahar	1377	10	S
2 Mahabad	882	60	R	14 Paveh	1377	10	R
16 Yasuj	891	50	R	11 Hajiabad	1395	50	S
25 Tehran	900	600	S	8 Kiashahr	1404	500	E
7 Lar	909	50	S	7 Estahban	1413	-	R
13 Jiroft	918	50	R	14 Kermanshah	1422	100	S
18 Dorud	927	10	S	6 Isfahan	1430v	200	S
2 Urumiyeh	936	50	R	13 Kerman	1431	-	S
17 Dehgolan	945	100	R	9 Bandar-e-Torkamen	1449	400	E
30 Birjand	963	50	S	2 Khoy	1458	10	S
12 Ilam	972	100	R	22 Qom	1467	10	R
10 Hamadan	981	100	S	17 Marivan	1476v	10	R
7 Shiraz	990	400	S	7 Jahrom	1485	10	R
17 Baneh	999	50	R	15 Izeh	1485	-	R
23 Semnan	1008	50	R	2 Maku	1494	20	S
3 Tabriz	1026	100	R	4 Bushehr	1503	500	S
26 Yazd	1035	50	S	1 Ardabil	1512	50	S
12 Dehloran	1044	50	S	8 Kiashahr	1521	100	F
18 Khorramabad	1053	100	R	26 Yazd	1530	10	S
13 Kerman	1062	50	R	9 Gorgan	1539	10	R
22 Qom	1071	100	M	20 Larijan	1548	10	R

Prov.& Location	kHz	kW	N	Prov.& Location	kHz	kW	N
17 Sanandaj	1548	10	S	30 Ghaen	1575	10	S
30 Ferdows	1548	10	S	2 Maku	1584	10	R
16 Gach Saran	1548	-	S	15 Ahwaz	1602	-	R
24 Zabol	1557	50	S	7 Kazerun	1602	-	S
11 Bandar Abbas	1566	100	S	26 Bahabad	1602	-	S

*inactive

Capitals/Provinces: 1) Ardabil/Ardabil **2)** Urumiyeh(ex-Rezayeh)/ West Azerbayjan **3)** Tabriz/East Azerbayjan **4)** Bushehr/Bushehr **5)** Shahr-e-Kord/Bakhtiari **6)** Isfahan/Isfahan **7)** Shiraz/Fars **8)** Rasht/ Gilan **9)** Gorgan/Golestan **10)** Hamadan/Hamadan **11)** Bandar Abbas/ Hormozgan **12)** Ilam/Ilam **13)** Kerman/ Kerman **14)** Kermanshah/ Kermanshah **15)** Ahwaz/Khozestan **16)** Yasuj/ Boyerahmad **17)** Sanandaj/ Kordestan **18)** Khorramabad/Lorestan **19)** Arak/Markazi **20)** Sari/ Mazandaran **21)** Qazvin/Qazvin **22)** Qom/Qom **23)** Semnan/Semnan **24)** Zahedan/ Systan & Baluchestan **25)** Tehran/Tehran **26)** Yazd/ Yazd **27)** Zanjan/ Zanjan **28)** Bojnurd/North Khorasan **29)** Mashhad/ Razavi Khorasan **30)** Birjand/South Khorasan.

Networks:

S=Sarasarye (Nationwide): 24h on **MW** + **FM:** 88/88.1/88.5/88.8/89/89.3/90.4/90.8/92/92.3/92.9/93/93.2/93.4/93 .5/93.7/93.9/94/94.8/94.9/96/96.5/96.7/97/97.1/97.5/97.7/98/98.1/ 98.5/98.6/99.4/99.6/99.7/100/100.1/100.7/101/101.1/101.2/101.5/ 101.9/103.4/104.2/104.3/105.9/107.5MHz. Also rel. on SW. **N:** 0230, 0330, 0430, 0530, 0630, 0730, 0830, 1030, 1330, 1530, 1730, 1830, 1930.

R=Regional (provincial) stations. There are studios in 39 centres producing prgrs in Farsi and local languages, including some locally produced Ext. Sce. prgrs. These st's also relay Sarasarye network at night. **D.Prgr**: usually between 0230-1630 exc. Tehran City and Qom prgr's, which are 24 hrs. **Regional N**: usually at 1330, 1430, 1530. **FM freq's**: 88.1/89.7/90.5/91.2/91.5/91.7/92.4/93.2/93.6/94.2/ 94.4/95/96/96.3/96.5/96.8/97/97.1/97.3/98.8/99/99.7/100/100.9/ 101.1/102/102.9/104.3/105.6/105.7/106.9/108 MHz.

T=Tehran City Prgr. 24h on **MW** 1332 kHz & **FM** 93/93.4/95/98.5/ 101.1MHz.

F=R. Farhang (cultural): 24h on **MW** 558/1152/1521 kHz + **FM** 88.3/ 89/89.8/90.1/90.2/91.1/92/92.1/92.9/93.1/93.4/93.7/94/94.2/94.3/ 95.6/95.9/96/97/97.5/97.7/97.9/100/100.1/100.2/101.1/101.2/101. 4/101.5/102.2/102.4/102.5/102.6/103.3/106.5/106.7/107.5 MHz.

Q=R. Quran: 24h on **MW** 585 kHz.

M=R. Ma'aref (Presentation): 24h on **MW** 1071kHz & **FM** 107.1MHz.

P=R. Payam (actualities): 24h on **MW** 1188kHz + **FM** 104.7MHz.

E=External service

R. Javan (Youth): 24h. **FM**: 88.3/91.7MHz.

R. Varzesh (Sports): 2230-1930. **FM**: 102.5MHz.

R. Salamat (Health R): 0630-1030. **FM:** 88/88.1/89.4/89.8/92/92.1/ 92.5/92.7/93.4/93.7/93.8/94/94.2/94.6/95.5/96/96.5/98.4/99.1/99.2 /99.4/99.8/100/102.1/103.1/103.3/105.6/106.5/106.6/106.8/107.1/ 107.2/107.3/107.4/107.7MHz.

R. Sahar (special night programmes during Ramadan).

Foreign Language Prgr's on Tehran 100.7MHz: **Arabic:** 0330-0730, 0930-1130, 1700-2130. **Armenian:** 1530-1630. **Bengali:** 1430-1530. **English:** 0030-0130, 1130-1230. **French:** 2230-2330. **Persian** (V. of Ashena): 2130-2230, 0230-0330. **Pushtu:** 1230-1330. **Urdu:** 1330-1430. **Serbian/Croatian:** 1630-1700. **Spanish:** 0130-0230. On 106.7MHz: **English:** 2130-2230, 2030-2130. **Russian:** 1930-2030. **External Service prgr's in other provinces on FM**: 88.6/96.7/99.3 MHz.

ANN: S: "Inja Tehran ast, shabakeye Sarasarye, Sedaye Jomhuriye Islamiye Iran". Farhang: "Inja Tehran ast, Sedaye Jomhuriye Islamiye Iran, shabakeye sarasarye Farhang". M: "Inja Qom ast, shabakeye Ma'aref, Sedaye Jomhuriye Islamiye Iran". Q: "Radio Qur'an". R: "Inja (capital) ast, Sedaye Jomhuriye Islamiye Iran, shabakeye/markazye (province)."

EXTERNAL SERVICE: Voice of the Islamic Republic of Iran see International Radio section.

IRAQ

L.T: UTC +3h (1 Apr-1 Oct UTC +4h) — **Pop:** 25m — **Pr.L:** Arabic, Kurdish, Assyrian, Turkoman — **E.C:** 50Hz, 230V — **ITU:** IRQ

IRAQI COMMUNICATIONS AND MEDIA COMMISSION

The CPA Media Regulation Office, Convention Center, 3rd floor, Baghdad ☎ (MCI) 001 703 270 0405 **Web:** www.iraqicmc.org **Email:** broadcast-licence@baghdadforum.com

RADIO OF THE REPUBLIC OF IRAQ

(operated by the Iraqi Media Network)

L.P: Jalal al-Mashta, DG. Shamin Rassam, Dir. FM.

MW: Baghdad 603*/675/1026*kHz. **FM:** 98.3MHz. *inactive

D.Prgr in Arabic: 24h on FM exc. in **English**: Sat-Thurs 1130-1220. **IS:** Soft chirps of a mechanical nightingale. **ANN:** A: "Idha'at al-jumhuriyat al-Iraq min Baghdad", E: "This is Radio Iraq from Baghdad". FM and 675kHz: "Idha'at FM min Baghdad".

INFORMATION RADIO (American forces)

MW: No. Iraq 756kHz.**ANN:** "Huna Idha'at Radio Ma'alumat".

RADIO NAHRAIN (TWO RIVERS)

(operated by Coalition Provisional Authority)

MW: Basra 909kHz 20kW. **FM:** Basra 94.6/100.4MHz, unk. location 96.0MHz. **ANN:** "Huna Radio Nahrain".

RADIO AS-SALAM (PEACE)

L.P: Ali al-Ansari, Dir.

MW: Baghdad 1053kHz. **FM:** Baghdad 92/106MHz.

D.Prgr in Arabic: 0700-1700. **ANN:** "Idha'at as-Salam min Baghdad".

RADIO BILAD ("LANDS")

MW: 999kHz. **D.Prgr:** Koran recitations 0500-1300. **ANN:** "Idha'at al-Bilad min Baghdad".

RADIO DAR AS-SALAM (HAVEN OF PEACE)

(operated by Iraqi Islamic Party)

Web: www. darusalam.org **Email:** Radio@darusalam.org

MW: 1152kHz. **FM:** 91MHz. **D.Prgr** in Arabic: 0500-1800. **ANN:** "Idha'at-il Dar as-Salam min Baghdad, Sowt-il Hezb-il Islamiayh Iraqi".

RADIO VOICE OF IRAQ

(operated by Imam Al-Shirazi International Association)

P.O. Box 74143, Baghdad ☎ + 964 1 5210957

Web: www.voiraq.com **Email:** admin@voiraq.com

MW: Baghdad 1179kHz. **D.Prgr** in Arabic: 0400-1800 exc. **English:** 1210-1300, Turkmen 1500-1530. **ANN:** "Idha'at Sowt-il Iraq min Baghdad", "This is the Voice of Iraq from Baghdad".

RADIO AL-MUSTAQBAL (FUTURE)

(supports Iraqi National Accord)

☎ + 964 7901 391549 **Web:** www.wifaq.org

Email: baghdadwifaq@hotmail.com

MW: Baghdad 1305kHz. **FM:** Baghdad 95.5MHz. **D.Prgr** in Arabic: 0500-1700. **ANN:** "Idha'at al-Mustaqbal min Baghdad, Sawt al-Wifaq al-Watani al-Iraqi".

VOICE OF THE WORKER-COMMUNIST PARTY OF IRAQ

Web: www.wpiraq.org **Email:** forward_wcpi@yahoo.com

MW: 1413kHz. **D.Prgr in Arabic/Kurdish:** 0600-1300.

ANN: "Huna al-Hizb al-Shiyouii al o'Maaly al-Iraqi min Baghdad."

RADIO SHRARA

Web: www.atranaya.org **Email:** app@atranaya.org

MW: Baghdad 1588kHz 0.1kW. **FM:** Dohuk 94MHz.

D.Prgr in Assyrian and Arabic: 0600-0900, 1400-1700.

RADIO ASHUR

(operated by Assyrian Democratic Movement (ZOWAA))

Web: www.zowaa.org **Email:** info@sowaa.org **FM:** Baghdad 99.4MHz. **D.Prgr** in Assyrian/Arabic: 0600-1700. **ANN:** Assyrian: "Pres Qalo Ashur men Baghdad". Arabic: "Radio Ashur min Baghdad".

RADIO DIJLA (TIGRIS)

Web: www.radiodijla.com **L.P:** Founder: Dr. Ahmad al-Rikabi.

FM: Baghdad 89.5MHz. **D.Prgr** in Arabic: 0500-2400. **ANN:** "Radio Dijla min Baghdad".

RADIO DIYALA - IRAQI MEDIA NETWORK

FM: Baquba 94.8MHz. **D.Prgr** in Arabic: 0400-2100. **ANN:** "Huna Shabakat ale'laam al-Iraqi, Idha'at al-Diyala".

HOT FM

FM: Baghdad 104.1MHz. **D.Prgr** in English/Arabic: 24h.

RADIO SHAFAQ (TWILIGHT)

FM: Baghdad 101.2MHz. **D.Prgr** in Arabic/Kurdish: 0600-0900, 1400-1700.

RADIO FREEDOM

(operated by Patriotic Union of Kurdistan)

1634 Eye St. N.W, Suite 210, Washington D.C. 20006, USA ☎ +1-202-637 2496 📠 +1-202-637 2723 **Web:** www.puk.org **Email:** puk@puk.org

FM: Baghdad 97.5MHz. **D.Prgr** in Arabic/Kurdish: 0500-2000. **ANN:** "Huna Idha'at al-Hurriyah min Baghdad".

VOICE OF IRAQI KURDISTAN

(operated by Kurdistan Democratic Party)
✉ KDP Press Office, P.O. Box 4912, London SE15 4EW, UK ☎ +44 207 498 26 64 🖷 +44 207 498 25 31 **Web:** www.kdp.pp.se **Email:** party@kdp.se
SW: Salah al Deen 6340v kHz (alt. fq 4085kHz).
FM: Salah el Deen 91.4MHz, Arbil 91.5MHz, Dohuk 93.3MHz.
D.Prgr in Sorani Kurdish/Arabic: 0400-1930. **ANN:** K: "Era Dengi Kurdistani Iraka". A: "Huna Sawt al-Kurdistan al-Iraqa".

VOICE OF THE PEOPLE OF KURDISTAN

(operated by Patriotic Union of Kurdistan)
✉ 1634 Eye St. N.W, Suite 210, Washington D.C. 20006, USA ☎ +1-202-637 2496 🖷+1-202-637 2723 **Email:** puk@puk.org **Web:** www.aha.ru/~said/dang.htm
MW: Sulaimaniyah 1206kHz. **SW**: Sulaimaniyah 4025v kHz.
D.Prgr in Sorani Kurdish/Arabic: 0300-0600, 1700-2200.
ANN: Kurdish: "Era Dengi Gelli Kurdistana". Arabic: "Huna Idha'at Sawt as-Sha'ab Kurdistan, sawt al-Ittihadi al-Watani al-Kurdistani".

VOICE OF INDEPENDENCE

(operated by Conservative Party of Kurdistan)
SW: 4160v kHz. **D.Prgr** in Arabic/Kurdish: 0400-0600, 1600-1800.
ANN: Arabic: "Huna sawt al-Istiqlal, Idha'at al-Hizb al-Muhafidhin al-Kurdistani." Kurdish: "Era Dengi Sarbakhoye, Izgay Parti Parezgani Kurdistan".

VOICE OF IRAQI TURKMEN RADIO

(operated by Iraqi Turkoman Front)
Web: www.turkmenfront.org **Email:** info@turkmenfront.Org
D.Prgr: 18 hrs. in Turkoman. Tr's in Kirkuk, Mosul and Talla'far, fq's not known. One hour a day on 1206/4025kHz via Voice of the People of Kurdistan.**ANN:** "Burasi Iraq Türkmen Sesi Radyosu".

VOICE OF KOMAL (operated by Kurdistan Islamic Group)

MW: Kirkuk 1341kHz. **D.Prgr** in Arabic/Kurdish/Turkish.

RADIO SAWA (BBG)

MW: via Kuwait 1548kHz 600kW.
FM: Sulaimaniayh 88MHz, Baghdad 100.4MHz, Arbil 100.5MHz, Mosul 106.6MHz, Basra 107MHz.
D.Prgr in Arabic: 24h. For details see International Radio section.

RADIO FREE IRAQ (Iraqi Sce. of R. Free Europe/R. Liberty)

MW: via Kuwait 1593kHz 150kW. **FM:** Baghdad 102.4MHz, Erbil 104.5MHz. For SW frequencies and more details see International Radio section.

OTHER STATIONS:
American Forces Network: Baghdad 92.3/107.7MHz, Balad 107.3MHz, Falluja 105.1MHz, Kirkuk 100.1/107.3MHz, Mosul 105.1MHz, Qayyarah 93.3MHz, Ramadi 93.3/107.3MHz, Sinjar 107.9MHz, Tallil 100.1/107.3MHz, Al-Taqaddum 107.1MHz, Tikrit 93.3MHz (powers 0.1–1kW) – **BBC World Sce**: Arabic: Al-Amara/Al-Kut 89MHz, Baghdad 89MHz, Basra 90MHz, Kirkuk 92.6MHz, Irbil/Mosul 96MHz, Al-Nasiriya 100MHz. English: Baghdad 98MHz, Basra 88MHz – **BFBS**: R. One: Al-Amara/Basra/Shaibah/ Umm-Qasr 106.5MHz, Baghdad 106.9MHz. R. Two: Al-Amara 87.5MHz, Basra/Shaibah/ Umm-Qasr 102.1MHz. Gurkha R: Shaibah 104MHz. – **Guven R. (Turkish Army):** No. Iraq 96.3MHz. – **MBC:** Baghdad 88.6MHz (for further details see UAE). – **R. France Int**: Baghdad 93.5MHz. – **RMC Moyen-Orient**: Baghdad/Mosul 88MHz, Basra 88.8MHz. – **R. Babil,** Al-Hilla: 1071kHz. – **Al-Ghadeer R,** Najaf: 96.1MHz. – **Al-Huda Islamic R,** Karbala: 89.7MHz. – **Al-Nakheel R,** Basra: 93.3MHz. – **R. Karbala FM,** Karbala: 92.8MHz.
R. Kull al-Iraq (All of Iraq), Nasiriyah: 610kHz 0.5kW. – **Radio Azadi** (Communist Party of Iraqi Kurdistan): fq. unknown. – **Voice of Fadhilah,** Najaf: 1008kHz. – **Voice of Snunu,** Al-Sinjar: fq. unknown. – **Yekgirtu R,** Dohuk: fq. unknown.

IRELAND

L.T: UTC (27 Mar-30 Oct: UTC +1h) — **Pop:** 3.6 million — **Pr.L:** Irish, English — **E.C:** 50Hz, 220V — **ITU**: IRL.

RAIDIÓ TEILIFÍS ÉIREANN (Statutory Corporation)

✉ Donnybrook, Dublin 4 ☎ +353 1 208 3111 🖷 +353 1 208 3080 **Web:** www.rte.ie. **2FM Web:** www.2fm.ie.
L.P: Chmn: Patrick J Wright. DG: Cathal Goan. Ch.Financial Offr.: Conor Hayes. MD TV: Noel Curran. MD Radio: Adrian Moynes. MD News: Ed Mulhall. Comm. Dir: Geraldine O'Leary. Dir Comm: Bride Rosney
Raidió Na Gaeltachta: Casla, Conamara, Co Galway. ☎ +353 91 506677 🖷 +353 91 506666 **Email:** rnag@rte.ie **Web:** www.rte.ie/rnag
RTE Lyric FM: Cornmarket Square, Limerick ☎ +353 61 207300 🖷 +353 61 207390 **Email:** lyric@rte.ie **Web:** www.lyricfm.ie
Publication: RTE Guide **Email:** rteguide@rte.ie

Networks:1=R1, 2=2FM, 3=Raidió Na Gaeltachta, 4=Lyric FM. 5=LW

LW/MW	kHz	kW	N	MW	kHz	kW	N
Clarkestown	252	500	1	Cork	729	10	1
Tullamore	567	500	1				

FM (MHz)	1	2	3	4	kW
Achill	89.3	91.5	93.7	98.9	2
Aranmore	89.6	91.8	94.0	99.2	3
Ballybofey	89.7	91.9	94.1	99.3	1
Bantry	88.7	90.9	93.1	98.3	1
Cahirciveen	89.5	91.7	93.9	99.1	2
Casla	88.4	90.6	92.8	98.0	2
Castlebar	89.8	92.0	94.2	99.4	3
Castletownbere	88.3	90.5	92.7	97.9	1
Clermont Carn	95.2	97.0	102.7	87.8	40
Clifden	89.5	91.7	93.9	99.1	3
Clonmel	88.3	90.5	92.7	97.9	1
Cnoc an Oir	89.2	91.4	93.6	98.8	1
Cork (Spur Hill)	89.2	91.4	93.6	98.8	5
Crosshaven	88.2	90.4	92.6	97.8	3
Dungarvan	88.5	90.7	92.9	98.1	3
Fanad	89.8	92.0	94.2	99.4	4
Greystones	89.5	91.7	93.9	99.1	1
Holywell Hill	89.2	91.4	93.6	98.8	2
Kippure	89.1	91.3	93.5	98.7	40
Knockmoyle	88.4	90.6	92.8	98.0	1
Limerick City	89.4	91.6	93.8	99.0	2.5
Maghera	88.8	91.0	93.2	98.4	160
Malin	89.9	91.1	93.3	98.5	1
Monaghan	89.9	91.1	93.3	98.5	3
Moville	88.3	90.5	92.7	97.9	10
Mt. Leinster	89.6	91.8	94.0	99.2	100
Mullaghanish	90.0	92.2	94.4	99.6	160
Suir Valley	89.0	91.2	93.4	98.6	3
Three Rock	88.5	90.7	92.9	96.7	10
Truskmore	88.2	90.4	92.6	97.8	80

+ 9 relays below 1kW.
1) RTE Radio 1: 24h in English & Irish on LW, MW, FM, satellite and internet. **N. in English:** on the h 0600-0100 + 0630, 0730W, 0830MF, 1830 – **2) 2FM:** 24h in English on FM, satellite and internet. **N:** on the h – **3) Raidió Na Gaeltachta**: 24h in Irish Gaelic on FM, satellite and internet – **4) Lyric FM**: 24h on FM, satellite and internet.

BROADCASTING COMMISSION OF IRELAND (BCI)

✉ 2-5 Warrington Place, Dublin 2 ☎ +353 1 676 0966 🖷 +353 1 676 0948 **Email:** info@bci.ie **Web:** www.bci.ie **L.P:** Chief Exec: Michael O'Keeffe. Dep Ch Exec & Dir Broadcasting: Celene Craig.
Responsible for regulation of commercial broadcasting in the Irish Republic. Full list of licensed stations can be found at **Web**: www.bci.ie/l_station.html

TODAY FM (Comm.)

✉ Today FM House, 124 Upper Abbey Str, Dublin 1 ☎ + 353 1 804 9000 🖷 + 353 1 804 9099. **Web:** www.todayfm.com
L.P: CEO Willy O'Reilly. Prog Mgr: Tom Hardy.

FM	MHz	kW	FM	MHz	kW
Crosshaven	100.0	3	Holywell Hill	101.0	2
Truskmore	100.0	80	Spur Hill, Cork	101.0	5
Castletownbere	100.1	1	Knockanore	101.0	1
Clonmel	100.1	1	Achill	101.1	2
Moville	100.1	3	Woodcock Hill	101.2	2.5
Knockmoyle	100.2	1	Cahirciveen	101.3	2
Casla	100.2	2	Clifden	101.3	3
Dungarvan	100.3	3	Aranmore	101.4	3
Three Rock	100.3	10	Mt. Leinster	101.4	100
Maghera	100.6	160	Ballybofey	101.5	1
Malin	100.7	1	Castlebar	101.6	3
Monaghan	100.7	3	Fanad	101.6	4
Suir Valley	100.8	3	Mullaghanish	101.8	160
Kippure	100.9	40	Clermont Carn	105.5	40

D.Prgr:24h. **N:** on the h, also on the half h at peak times.

LOCAL STATIONS

	MHz	kW (ERP)	Name, tr. location
10)	87.9	2	Highland R, Black Mtn
18)	94.8	2	Northern Sound, Slieve Glah
2)	95.0	5	Limerick Live 95 FM, Woodcock Hill
16)	95.1	10	WLR FM, West Waterford
10)	95.2	1	Highland R, Arran Mor
4)	95.5	1	LM FM, Saggart
7)	95.5	1	Clare FM, Ennis

	MHz	kW (ERP)	Name, tr. location
3)	95.6	2	South East R, Wexford
4)	95.8	10	LM FM, Mt. Oriel
17)	95.8	5	Cork's 96 FM, Nowen Hill
7)	95.9	1	Clare FM, Woodcock Hill
5)	96.1	5	MWR FM,Kiltimagh
20)	96.2	3	R. Kerry, Cahirciveen
1)	96.2	5	East Coast FM, Bray
18)	96.3	5	Northern Sound, Monaghan
7)	96.4	5	Clare FM, Maghera
17)	96.4	1	Cork's 96 FM, Holly Hill
8)	96.6	5	KCLR 96 FM, Johns Well
9)	96.8	5	Galway Bay FM, Knockroe
20)	97.0	20	R. Kerry, Mullaghanish
11)	97.1	1.5	Tipp FM, Scrouthea
5)	97.1	5	MWR FM, Achill
12)	97.3	2.5	Kfm, Kileshin
9)	97.4	1	Galway Bay FM, Balinasloe
16)	97.5	10	WLR FM, East Waterford
20)	97.6	1	R. Kerry, Knockanore
12)	97.6	1	Kfm, Red Gap
13)	98.1	4.6	98 FM, Three Rock
1)	99.9	5	East Coast FM, Red Gap
24)	102.0	6.3	Beat 102-103 FM, Mount Leinster
24)	102.2	3	Beat 102-103 FM, West Waterford
26)	102.2	5	Q 102, Three Rock
24)	102.4	5	Beat 102-103 FM, Clonmel
21)	102.5	5	Ocean FM, Truskmore
17)	102.6	1	103FM County Sound North, Cork City
24)	102.8	5	Beat 102-103 FM, East Waterford
1)	102.9	7.9	East Coast FM, Ballyguille
1)	102.9	1	East Coast FM, Baltinglass
22)	103.2	0.25	Anna Livia FM, Three Rock
10)	103.3	5	Highland R, Scalp Mountain
17)	103.3	5	103 FM County Sound West, Nowen Hill
6)	103.5	1.3	Midlands Radio 3, Sliabh Bloom
17)	103.7	2.5	103 FM County Sound North, Mt. Hillary
25)	103.8	5	Spin 103.8, Three Rock
11)	103.9	1.6	Tipp FM, Kilduff
14)	104.1	2.5	Shannonside 104FM, Sliabh Bawn
15)	104.4	10	FM 104, Three Rock
28)	104.5	5	Red FM, WCork (Nowen Hill)
19)	104.8	5	Tipperary Mid-West R, Dangandargan
28)	104.9	2	Red FM, Bandon
21)	105.0	5	Ocean FM, Oughdarnid
30)	105.0	2	Inishowen Community R, Malin
28)	105.7	2.5	Red FM, North Cork
29)	106.0	10	Newstalk 106 FM, Three Rock
28)	106.1	2	Red FM, Knocknaheeny
23)	106.4	2	Raidió Na Life, Three Rock
27)	106.8	5	106.8FM Dublin's Country, Three Rock

+ 80 additional tr's of less than 1kW

Addresses and other information:
1) Radio Centre, Killarney Rd, Bray, Co Wicklow.**Email:** mail@eastcoast.fm **Web:** www.eastcoast.fm – **2)** Radio House, Dock Rd, Limerick. **Email**: mail@live95fm.ie **Web:** www.live95fm.ie – **3)** Custom House Quay, Wexford Town, Co Wexford. **Email:** info@southeastradio.ie **Web**: www.southeastradio.ie – **4)** Broadcasting House, Rathmullen Road, Drogheda, Co Louth. **Email:** info@lmfm.ie **Web:** www.lmfm.ie – **5)** Clare Str, Ballyhaunis, Co Mayo. **Email:** info@mnwr.ie **Web:** www.mnwr.ie – **6)** The Mall, William Street, Tullamore, Co Offaly. **Email:** goodcompany@midlandsradio.fm **Web:** www.midlandsradio.fm – **7)** Abbeyfield Centre, Francis Str, Ennis, Co Clare. **Email:** info@clarefm.ie **Web:** www.clarefm.ie – **8)** The Broadcast Centre,Carlow Rd, Kilkenny. **Email:** info@kclr96fm.ie **Web**: www.kclr96fm.ie –**9)** Unit 13, Sandy Rd, Galway. **Email:** info@galwaybayfm.ie **Web:** www.galwaybayfm.ie.net –**10)** Pine Hill, Letterkenny, Co Donegal. **Email:** enquries@highlandradio.com **Web**: www.highlandradio.com – **11)** Davis Road, Clonmel, Co. Tipperary. **Email:** sales@tippfm.com **Web**: www.tippfm.com – **12)** KFM Broadcasting Centre, M7 Business Park,Newhall, Naas, Co Kildare. **Email:** info@kfmradio.com **Web**: www.kfmradio.com – **13)** South Block, The Malt House, Grand Canal Quay, Dublin 2. **Email:** online@98fm.ie **Web:** www.98fm.ie – **14)** Unit 8 Mater Tech Business Park, Athlone Rd, Longford. **Email**: info@shannonside.ie **Web**:www.shannonside.com – **15)** Hume House, Pembroke Rd, Ballsbridge, Dublin 4. **Email:** sales@fm104.ie **Web:** www.fm104.ie – **16)** Broadcast Centre, Ardkeen, Dunmore Rd, Waterford. **Email:** reception@wlr.com **Web:** www.wlrfm.com – **17)** County Sound, Broadcasting House, Patrick's Place, Cork. **Email:** info@96fm.ie **Web:** www.96fm.ie – **18)** Dawson Street, Monaghan & 26A Bridge St.,Cavan. **Email:** info@norththernsound.ie **Web**:www.northernsound.ie – **19)** St. Michael's St,Tipperary. **Email:** tippmidwest@radio.fm **Web**: www.tipperarymidwestradio.com – **20)** Main St, Tralee, Co Kerry. **Email:** elma@radiokerry.ie **Web**: www.radiokerry.ie – **21)** Ocean FM Broadcasting Centre, North West Business Park, Collooney, Co Sligo. **Email**: sales@oceanfm.ie **Web**: www.oceanfm.ie –**22)** Docklands Innovation Park, Unit 6, Eastwall Rd, Dublin 3. **Email:** info@annaliviafm.com **Web:** www.annalivia.com –**23)** 7 Cearnog Mhuirfean, Baile Atha Cliath 2. **Email**: Rnl106@iol.ie **Web**: www.rnl106.ie (Irish language st) – **24)** Broadcasting Centre, Ardkeen, Dunmore Rd, Waterford. **Email**: info@beat102103.com **Web**: www.beat102103.com – **25)** 73 North Wall Quay, Dublin 1. **Email:** info@spin1038.com **Web: www**.spin1038.com – **26)** Glenageary Office Park, Glenageary, Co Dublin. **Web:** www.q102fm.ie – **27)** Radio Centre, Killarney Rd, Bray, Co Wicklow. **Email:** info@dublins1068.com **Web:** www.dublins1068.com – **28)** 1 University Technology Centre, Bishoptown, Cork. **Email:** info@redfm.ie **Web:** www.redfm.ie – **29)** Warrington House, Mount Street Crescent, Dublin 2. **Email:** info@newstalk106.ie **Web:** www. newstalk106.ie –**30)** Inishowan Community Radio, Carndonagh, Inishowen, Co Donegal. **Email:** studio@icrfm.ie **Web:** www.icrfm.ie

Community/special interest st's: 18 sts in operation at October 2004
Hospital/Institutions: 6 stations in operation

ISRAEL

L.T: UTC +2h (DST usually April-Sept: UTC +3h). — **Pop:** 6.8 million — **Pr.L:** Hebrew, Arabic — **E.C:** 50Hz, 230V — **ITU:** ISR

ISRAEL BROADCASTING AUTHORITY

P.O. Box 28080, Jerusalem 91280 ☎ +972 2 501555 🖷 +972 2 5015521 **Email:** davidg@iba.org.il **Web:** www.iba.org.il
Visiting-address: 161 Jaffa Road, Jerusalem.
L.P: DG: Yosef Barel. Spokesman Email: dover@iba.org.il Dep.DG: Yair Aloni. Transmission Manager: David Gombosh

KOL ISRAEL – THE VOICE OF ISRAEL

Main Studios: Heleni Hamalka 21, Jerusalem 91010 ☎ +972 2 5302222 🖷 +972 2 5383173 **News & current affairs studios:** Torah Me'Zion 15, Romema, Jerusalem ☎ +972 2 5383311 🖷 +972 2 5383173 **Email:** englishradio@iba.org.il **Web:** www.iba.org.il.
L.P: Dir. & PD: Yonatan Ben-Menachem. Dir. of Engineering: Moshe Rozendorn Liaison & Coordination: R. Kohanowski. +972 2 5313228 +972 2 5313376 English Dept:☎ +972 2 5302200. 🖷 +972 2 5302424. Independently produced **Web**: www.israelradio.org.

MW	kHz	kW	Prgr.	Times
Yavne	531	50	A	24h
Yavne	657	200	B	24h
Zefat	846	1	B	24h
Shear-Yashuv	882	10	B	24h
Eilat	927	1	B	24h
Akko	927	50	B	24h
Yavne	954	50	B	0500-2200
Yavne	1026	50	D	24h
Jerusalem	1080	5	B	24h
Akko	1206	50	D	24h
Jerusalem	1458	10	A	24h
Eilat	1458	10	A	24h
Akko	1575	10	R	0400-2205

FM (MHz)	A	B	C	D	M	X	R
Upper Galilee	102.8	100.5	97.7	-	95.7	-	94.4
Zefat	100.7	92.0	88.1	99.3	98.5	87.6	
Beit Shean	-	102.0	99.5	-	95.2	-	-
Haifa	97.2	95.5	105.5	92.4	100.2	89.5	93.7
	-	103.7	-	-	-	88.0	-
Tel Aviv	100.7	95.0	97.8	90.3	94.4	88.0	101.2
	-	95.5	89.7	91.3	-	-	-
Jerusalem	98.4	95.0	97.8	88.8	91.3	88.0	101.3
	-	95.5	-	90.3	-	-	88.2
Beer Sheva	100.7	103.3	106.9	93.3	90.2	88.0	107.3
	-	106.2	-	94.4	-	-	-
N.Negev	-	104.1	104.3	-	87.6	-	-
	-	95.0	-	-	-	-	-
Aravah Valley	-	95.5	89.5	-	92.4	-	-
Eilat	-	90.7	100.5	-	97.0	-	-

Prgrs: A Reshet Alef(Hebrew) cultural programming 24hrs except times listed in Reshet Moreshet below. General talk-and cultural programs. **N.** in Hebrew: rel of Prgr. B – **B "Reshet Bet"** (Hebrew): 24h. News, current affairs and sport. **N:** on the h – **C "Reshet**

Gimel".(Hebrew) 24h Israeli popular music. **N:** rel. Prgr. B – **D "Reshet Dalet"** (Arabic). 24 h – **X "88 FM"** (Hebrew). 0358-2305. **N:** as Prgr. B. Music, Traffic Reports & Financial news – **R REQA (aka REKA)"Reshet Qlita v'Aliya"**, the immigrants network, 0430-2200 in Russian, Amharic, French, Yiddish, Ladino, Romanian, Spanish,. Moghrabi, Bukharian, Georgian and Hungarian. English 0430-0445, 1030-1045 & 1830-1845 – **M Voice of Music. "Kol Ha Musica"** (Hebrew) 0400-2205 in stereo. Classical music and drama – **"Reshet Moreshet"** (Heritage Network). Religious programming in Hebrew on Reshet Alef's network. Sun-Thurs 1400-2200, Fri 0600-1500, sat 1900-2200 – **Overseas service "Reshet Hei"** is relayed on Jerusalem on 88.2 MHz 1500-2100 (otherwise REQA) – **Local education prgrs "Kol Limudi"** are transmitted on 106.0 MHz in Holon, Tiberias, Beer Sheva, Haifa, Bet El and more lowpowered transmitters in colleges around Israel.

EXTERNAL SERVICES: Israel Radio International, Kol Israel see International Broadcasting section.

GALEI TZAHAL (Israel Defence Forces Radio)

✉ Military Post Office Box 01005. ☎+972 3 5126662 **Web:** www.glz.co.il **Email:** glz@galatz.co.il
L.P: Commander: Colonel Avi Bnayahu.

MW	kHz	kW	MW	kHz	kW
Beersheba	1224	20	Hivan	1368	20
Ramle	1287	100	Pilon(Zefat)	1368	50
Eilat	1305	10	Rama	1404	20

FM (MHz)	GT	GG	FM (MHz)	GT	GG
Eilat	104.0	106.4	Mitzpe Ramon	100.7	-
Haifa	102.3	106.4	Nebi Yesha	93.9	-
Jerusalem	96.6	-	Smadar	99.8	-
Kiryat Shmona	104.1	-	Tel Aviv	104.0	91.8
Mishmar HaNegev	99.8	102.3			

Main Prgr (GT=Galei Tzahal): 24h. **N:** on the h
GG=Galgalatz (traffic reports and music): 24h
ANN: Main Prgr: "Galei Tzahal, Shidure Tsva Hagana Le'Yisrael".
SW: 6973kHz, 10kW, 1900-0400, 15785 0400-1900. Relay of Main program, target Eu.

RADIO A'SHAMS (THE SUN)

Nazareth-Ein Hahoresh area.
☎+972 4 6084101. 🖷 +972 4 6083101.**Web:** www.ashams.com
L.P: Dir.: Suhi Kram.
FM(MHz): 98.1 & 101.0. All in Arabic. Broadcasting to the Arabic community in Israel.

RADIO SAWA

Web: www.radiosawa.com. **Email:** comment@radiosawa.com
FM(MHz): Bethlehem/Ramallah: 94.2
D. Prgr: 24 h in Arabic (see USA entry for full details)

Regional Commercial Radio (all in Hebrew) **FM**(MHz):
R. Darom (South Radio), Beersheva: 97.0. Local relays 96.0. **Web**: www.9697.fm
R.Haifa , Haifa: 107.5, 92.7 MHz. **Web:**www.1075fm.co.il
R. Jersualem, Jersualem: 101.0MHz, Bet Shemesh 89.5. **Web**: 101fm.tapuz.co.il
Kol Ha Yam Ha Adom (V. of the Red Sea) ✉ P.O. Box 2148, 8121 Eilat. ☎ +972 7 340630. 🖷 +972 7 340590. 101.1, 102.0 1kW
R. L'Lo Hafsaka (R. Nonstop), Ramat Gan: 103.0. **Web:** www.103fm.co.il
Pepsi Music Radio, Tel Aviv: 102.0 MHz **Web:** www.102fm.co.il
Bu 99FM, Hertzlia 99.0. **Web:** www.bu99fm.co.il
Radios, Tel Aviv: 100.0. **Web:** www.100fm.co.il
Radio Mix 104.5. North 101.5
Radio Tzafon L'Lo Hafsaka (Northern R. Nonstop) Upper Galilee 101.5, Lower Galilee 104.5
R.Emtza Ha Derech, (Radio Middle of the Road), Tel Aviv: 90.0. **Web:** www,90fm.co.il
Kol Chai, Bene Brak: 93.0, 92.8. **Web:** kolchai.moreshet.co.il
Radio Kol Rega. Galilee 96.0, Tiberias 91.5. **Web**: www.kol-rega.co.il
Radio Lev Hamedena. Rishon Lezion. Shfola 01.0, Ashdod 89.1. **Web**: www.91fm.co.il
Radio 99 ESC, Hertzliyah. 99.0. **Web**: www.99esc.co.il
R. Mashrek, northern Israel. FM 99.1 MHz and MW 756 kHz. **Web:** www.camelnews.org.
Radio Tel Aviv, Tel Aviv. 102.0. **Web**: www.102fm.co.il
For regional FM-stations: see **Web:**www.rashut2.org.il/radio gate.asp

WEST BANK & GAZA STRIP (Palestinian Authority)

L.T: UTC +2h (DST Gaza 15 Apr-21 Oct, West Bank as Israel: UTC +3h) — **Pop:** West Bank 1.5 million, Gaza 1 million — **Pr.L:** Arabic — E.C: 50Hz, 230V — **ITU:** PSE

PALESTINIAN BROADCASTING CORPORATION Voice of Palestine

✉ P.O. Box 984, Al-Bireh, Ramallah, West Bank ☎ +972 22 987903 🖷 +972 22 959891 **Email:** pbcinfo@pbc.gov.ps **Web:** www.pbc.gov.ps
L.P: Chmn: Radwan Abu Ayyash
1st Programme: FM(MHz): Ramallah 90.7 Earlier rep. frequencies: 91.5, 99.4, 100.6 and 104.8 MHz. Current status of these freqs unknown. N. in French: 1330-1340.
2nd Programme: FM(MHz): Gaza 102.0.
D.Prgr. in Arabic: 0400-2300. **N:** on the h. **Local N:** 1100 (exc. Fri).
English: Mon/Wed 1505-1550. **N. in Hebrew:** Mon/Wed 1550.
ANN: "Sawt Filastin".

Private stations FM (MHz):
West Bank: 1) Amwaj Radio, Ramallah, 91.5/99.5 – **2) Aijal Radio**, Ramallah,92.4/103.4 – **3) Radio Sawa**, Ramallah, 94.2 – **4) R. 2000**, Bethlehem, 89.6 – **5) Marah Radio**, Hebron,100.6.
Gaza: 1) Al-Qur'an al-Karim Radio (Holy Koran) Gaza **FM**: 89.6.**D. Prgr**: 0400-1800. All in Arabic – **2) R. Isis** Bethlehem. ☎ +972 2 2774405 **Web**: www.radioisis.net. **Email:** info@radioisis.net **FM**: 95.9 **D.Prgr:** 0700-2200. N in English: 1600, 1800 – **3) Voice of Al-Aqsa** Gaza - **FM:** 106.7 **Web**: www.aqsavoice.com (A) – **4) The Voice of Love and Peace,** Ramallah - **FM**: 94.2 **Web:** www.volpfm.com. **Email**: volp@palnet.com – **5) Radio Gaza FM,** Gaza **FM**: 100.9 **Web**: www.ymnis.com/e/index.htm
Other FM (freqs not known): Al-Hurriyah Radio (Freedom), Alwan Radio (Colours), Al-Shabab Radio (Youth), Al-Umal Radio (Workers) and Al-Manar Radio (Lighthouse)

ITALY

L.T: UTC +1h (27 Mar-30 Oct UTC +2h) — **Pop:** 56 million — **Pr.L:** Italian — **E.C:** 50Hz, 220V — **ITU:** I

RAI-RADIOTELEVISIONE ITALIANA (State Service by Public act to RAI)

✉ Viale Mazzini 14,IT- 00195 Roma ☎ +39 06 38781 🖷 +39 06 3622621 ✉ (Listeners) Centro Corrispondenza, C.P. 320, IT-00100 Roma. ☎ +39 06 3317 2591 🖷 +39 06 3317 1895 **Email:** service@rai.it **Web:** www.rai.it **Tech. Dept.: Rai Teche:** Via Cernaia 33, IT-10121 Torino,Dir.Barbara Scaramucci, **WEB** : www.teche.rai.it **Email** : sisani@rai.it **Rai Way**:Centro Ascolto e Qualità Controllo Servizio RAI Monza, Via Parco Mirabellino 1, IT-20052 Monza. Dir.:Pietro Gaffuri **Web** : www.raiway.rai.it **Email** : qsc2@rai.it **V.:** QSL-card. No Rp.
L.P: Pres.: vacant GM: Flavio Cattaneo, Dir.Reg.Radio: Giuseppe Cereda, Dir.Rai International: Massimo Magliaro.

Regional Centres: Abruzzo: Viale de Amicis 27, IT-65123 Pescara – **Alto Adige:** Piazza Mazzini 23, IT-39100 Bolzano/Bozen – **Basilicata:** Viale del Basento 16, IT-85100 Potenza – **Calabria:** Viale G. Marconi 1,IT- 87100 Cosenza – **Campania:** Via Marconi 9,IT-80125 Napoli – **Emilia-Romagna:** Viale della Fiera 13, IT-40127 Bologna – **Friuli-Venezia-Giulia:** Via Fabio Severo 7, IT-34133 Trieste – **Lazio:** Largo Willy de Luca 4, IT-00188 Roma – **Liguria:** Corso Europa 125, IT-16132 Genova – **Lombardia:** Corso Sempione 27, IT-20145 Milano – **Marche:** Piazza della Repubblica 1,IT- 60121 Ancona – **Molise:** Viale Principe di Piemonte 59, IT-86100 Campobasso – **Piemonte:** Via G.Verdi 16, IT-10124 Torino – **Puglia:** Via Dalmazia 104, IT-70121 Bari – **Sardegna:** Viale Bonaria 124, IT-09125 Cagliari – **Sicilia:** Viale Strasburgo 19, IT-90146 Palermo – **Toscana:** Largo Alcide de Gasperi 1, IT-50136 Firenze – **Trentino:** Via Fratelli Perini 141, IT-38100 Trento – **Umbria:** Via L. Masi 2, IT-06100 Perugia – **Valle d'Aosta:** Via Chambery 36, IT-11100 Aosta – **Veneto:** Palazzo Labia, Campo S. Geremia,Sestiere Cannaregio 275, IT-30131 Venezia.

Home services

LW/MW	kHz	kW	Prgr
Caltanissetta (St.Anna)	189	10	R1 (b.c)
Caltanissetta (St.Anna)	567	20	R1 (b,c)
Bolzano (Monticolo)	657	25	R1 (e)
Napoli (Marcianise)	657	120	R1
Torino (Eremo)	657	50	R1
Potenza	693	20	R1
Trieste (Monte Radio)	819	20	R1 (a)
Taranto	873	1	R1

LW/MW	kHz	kW	Prgr
Milano (Siziano)	900	600	R1
Trapani	936	10	R1
Venezia (Campalto)	936	20	R1 (+a)
Trieste(Monte Radio)	981	10	S
Vibo Valentia (CapoVatic)	999	2	R1
Perugia(Torgiano)	999	20	R1
Rimini (Viserba)	999	20	R1
Pescara (SanSilvestro)	1035	10	R1
Ancona (Montagnolo)	1062	10	R1
Cagliari (Sestu)	1062	25	R1 (d)
Catania (Barriera del Bosco)	1062	2	R1 (c)
Pisa (Coltano)	1062	10	R1
Trento (Villazzano)	1062	2	R1
Roma (Monte Ciocci)	1107	100	R1
Aosta (Gerdaz)	1116	2	R1 (f)
Bari (Ceglie Messapico)	1116	2	R1
Bologna (Budrio)	1116	60	R1
Cuneo (Tetti Pesio)	1116	20	R1
Palermo (Mte Pellegrino)	1116	10	R1 (c)
Messina (Mte Piselli)	1143	10	R1 (c)
Sassari (La Crucca)	1143	10	R1 (d)
La Spezia (Valdellora)	1296	5	R1
Matera	1314	2	R1
Firenze (Terrarossa)	1368	25	R1
Foggia	1431	2	R1
Biella (S.Paolo)	1449	2	R1
Bolzano (Bressanone)	1449	2	R1 (e)
Bolzano (Brunico)	1449	2	R1 (e)
Bolzano (Cortina)	1449	2	R1 (e)
Siena	1449	2	R1
Sondrio	1449	2	R1
Squinzano	1449	50	R1
Vicenza	1485	2	R1
Campobasso	1575	2	R1
Genova (Portofino)	1575	50	R1
Gorizia (Piuma)	1575	2	R1 (a)
Nuoro (S.Onofrio)	1575	1	R1 (d)
Terni (S.Lorenzo)	1584	2	R1

FM (MHz)	R1	R2	R3	R4	GRP	kW
Bertinoro (FC)	90.8	93.4	99.6	89.7		30
Bologna (BO)	89.5	91.7	93.9	93.6		60
Bolzano (BZ)	91.5	93.7	97.1	99.6	95.1	14
Ca' del Vento (PC)	92.1	96.5	98.5	90.6		40
Canepina-Poggio Nibbio (VT)	-	-	93.7	99.4		12
Capo Spartivento (RC)	95.6	97.6	99.7	104.2		10
Col Visentin (BL)	91.1	93.1	95.5	99.4		30
Crotone (KR)	94.9	97.9	99.9	97.4		10
Firenze (FI)	87.8	91.1	98.4	88.0		10
Friscano (PN)	88.4	90.5	94.1			10
Gambarie (RC)	95.3	97.3	99.3			40
		103.9				40
Genova (GE)	89.5	91.9	95.1	104.5		80
Golfo di Policastro (SA)	88.5	90.5	92.5			10
Golfo di Salerno (SA)	95.1	97.1	99.1	92.9		20
Gorizia (GO)	89.5	92.3	94.6	98.3	106.8	10
Martina Franca (TA)	89.1	91.1	93.1	90.3		100
Milano (MI)	90.6	93.7	99.4	102.2	88.3	60
Monte Argentario (GR)	90.1	92.1	94.3	99.6		70
	-	89.0				16
Monte Beigua (SV)	91.5	94.6	98.9	100.1		40
Monte Caccia (BA)	94.6	96.7	99.2	98.2		100
Monte Cammarata (AG)	91.1	95.9	99.9	98.3		100
Monte Canate (PR)	-	95.9	-			24
Monte Cavo (RM)	87.6	91.2	98.4	99.3		80
Monte Conero (AN)	88.3	90.3	92.3	105.2		100
Monte Faito (NA)	94.1	96.1	98.1	91.0		100
Monte Lauro (SR)	94.7	96.7	98.7	89.0		100
Monte Limbara (SS)	88.9	95.3	99.3	106.5		60
Monte Luco (SI)	88.1	92.5	96.2			30
Monte Nerone (PU)	94.7	96.6	98.7	88.1		100
Monte Peglia (TR)	95.7	97.7	99.7	102.1		60
	-	88.3				30
Monte Penice (PV)	94.2	97.4	99.9	88.2		120
	-	103.0				120
Monte Pierfaone (PZ)	88.1	90.1	92.1	91.2		45
Monte Sambuco (PG)	88.6	90.7	93.5			100
	-	100.7	-			100
Monte Scuro (CS)	88.5	90.5	92.5	98.4		30
Monte Serpeddi (CA)	90.7	92.7	96.3	106.5		70
Monte Serra (PI)	88.5	90.5	92.9	88.2		70

FM (MHz)	R1	R2	R3	R4	GRP	kW
Monte Soro (ME)	89.9	91.9	93.9	104.2		30
Monte Subasio (PG)	89.3	91.4	93.5	104.6		30
Monte Venda (PD)	88.1	89.0	89.9	106.8		160
Monte Vergine (AV)	87.9	90.3	92.3	93.1		20
Napoli Camaldoli (NA)	89.3	91.3	93.3	103.9	101.0	12
Nova Siri (MT)			89.5			10
PalermoMtePellegri (PA)	94.9	96.9	98.9	90.3		40
Pescara S. Silvestro (PE)	89.2	94.3	96.4	102.0		70
Pomarico (MT)	88.7	92.7	95.7	98.7		10
Punta Badde Urbara (OR)	91.3	93.3	97.3			70
Roma M. Mario (RM)	89.7	91.7	93.7	100.3		100
Roseto Capo Spulico(CS)	94.4	96.5	98.5			10
Salento Turrisi (LE)	90.7	95.5	97.59	91.0		60
San Cerbone (FI)	95.3	97.3	99.3			12
SanZenodiMontagna(VR)	93.2	96.5	98.5	89.4		10
Selva Piana (BS)	88.4	90.3	92.4			20
Torino Eremo (TO)	92.1	95.6	98.2	101.8	88.2	100
Trapani Erice (TP)	88.4	90.5	92.5	90.8		60
TriesteMteBelvedere(TS)	91.5	93.6	95.8	103.9	88.7	30
Udine (UD)	94.9	97.2	99.8			60
Velletri (RM)	88.7	90.7	92.7			15

+ over 5600 st's below 1kW not mentioned.

D.Prgr:All stations transmit from 0500 to 2300, except for Milano 900kHz, Roma 1107kHz and Napoli 657kHz all 24h.
R1=Radiouno, **R2FM**=Radiodue, **R3FM**=Radiotre, **S**=Special Prgrs.
Regional Prgrs: 0620-0628 Mo/Sat RAI 1; 1110-1127 Mo/Sa RAI 1; Su. 1140-1157. **(a)** 0630-0657,1330-1430 Mo/Sat;1330-1500 Sun "L'ora della Venezia Giulia"(**+a**),1830-1900.Summertime 1h earlier **(b)** 1330-1345, Mo/Sat Arabic service.Summertime 1h earlier. **(c)** Regional service: Sicilia Mo/ Sat.0630-0657.1830-1900.Summertime: 1h earlier. **(d)** Regional service: Sardegna Mo/Sat 0630-0657,1400-1500, 1830-1900.Summertime: 1h earlier. **(f)** Regional service: Valle D'Aosta Mo/Sat 0630-0657,1830-1900.(Bilingual) Summertime 1h earlier. **(e)** Regional service Alto Adige Mo/Sat 0630-0657,1830-1900. Summertime 1h earlier.

SPECIAL PRGRS

ISO Radio: 24h sce. for motorway users on 103.3MHz FM (220 tr's);103,2MHz Milano,Como,Lecco area;103,45MHz, Roma area.
GR Parlamento: 24h sce. Italian Parlament channel. Relay V channel Filodiffusione if no Parliament works. FM (150 tr's of 5kW or less)
Sender Bozen (Bolzano): Prgrs in **German** on FM (46 tr's of 1kW or less) **DPrgr:** 0500 (Sun 0600)-2300. **N.** 0615 (W), 0800 (Sun), 1000 (W), 1100, 1200, 1300, 1700 (W), 1930.
Regional Prgr. in Slovene: Trieste 981kHz 10kW + 103.9MHz 20kW (and 22 additional FM-tr's). **D. Prgr:** 0500 (Sun 0600)-2300. **N:** W 0500, 0700, 0900, 1200, 1300, 1600, 1800; Sun 0700, 1200, 1300, 1800. **N. in German:** 0900 (W).
N. in Arabic (for Mediterranean area): W 1330-1345 on Caltanissetta 189kHz&567kHz .

ANN: Home Sce: "RAI Radiouno", "RAI Radiodue", "RAI Radiotre" as appropriate. Night Prgr: "RAI-Radiotelevisione Italiana stazioni a onda media di Milano kHz 900, di Roma kHz 1107, e di Napoli kHz 657 e stazione ad onda corta di kHz 6060 RAI International Notturno Italiano".

EXTERNAL SERVICE: RAI International
see International Broadcasting section.

R.A.S.
✉ Europaallee 164/A,IT- 39100 Bozen ☎ +39 0471 546666 🖷 +39 0471 200378 **Web:** www.ras..bz.it **Email:** info@ras.bz.it
L.P: Pres: Helmuth Hendrich. MD: Karl Rainer. Dir. Tec: Dr Ing. Georg Plattner. RAS is a public body of the autonomous Region of Southern Tyrol whose purpose is to relay TV and Radio from Germany, Austria and Switzerland to the German-speaking population.

FM (MHz)	RAS 1	RAS 2	RAS 3	kW
Kronplatz	100.7	103.0	104.7	2
Meransen	101.3	103.9	107.3	1
Obervinschgau	100.5	103.0	106.1	0.6
Penegal	103.3	100.3	104.7	2
Perdonig	101.8	104.0	106.0	1
Plose	99.8	102.0	105.6	1
Vinschgau	101.1	102.9	105.0	2

+ 880 low power st's.
RAS 1: rel. OE-3 (Austria)- **RAS-2:** rel. OE-R (Austria)- **RAS-3:** rel. OE-1 (Austria)

DAB: RAI & RAS on Blocks 12A-12DA, 223.936MHz - 229.072MHz. **Consorzio DAB Italia** on block 9D. 208.064MHz

PRIVATE STATIONS
Only sts with MW/SW broadcasts and FM networks are listed. A number of other sts are heard irr. There are approx. 1200 FM sts.

MW kHz	**kW**	**Name, location and h of tr.**
1) 1404v	1	Radio 106, Salvaterra di Casalgrande 0700-1800
2) 1584	7	Radio Studio X, Momigno: 24h
SW kHz	**kW**	**Name, location and h of tr.**
3) 7306	1	R. Europe, Pioltello (USB): 0700-1200v

Addresses and other information
1) Via Ligabue 12, IT- 42010 Salvaterra di Casalgrande (RE) - ☎ +39 0522 996477 🖷 +39 0522 999550 **Web:** www.radio106.it **Email:** info@radio106.it - **FM:** 102,20-105,95Mhz 5kW Relay Popolare Network.. **2)** Via Mammianese 687, IT-51030 Momigno (PT) ☎ +39 0572 694019 🖷 +39 0572 669956 **Web:** www.studiox.it **Email:** info@radiostudiox.it SM: Luca Betti.,MD:Eleonora Pellegrini- **FM:** 87.35 /96,55/105.55MHz 5kW . **V.** by letter. Rp – **3)** P.O.Box 12, IT-20090 Limito (MI) **Web:** www.radioeurope.it **Email:** Radioeurope@iol.it SM: Alex Bertini,PR:Dario Monferini. **V.** by QSL-card.Rp. Dx-Progr.:Play-Dx-News Su.1030.

FM NETWORKS IN MAJOR CITIES (MHz):

Network	To	Mi	Ve	Bo	Ge
1) Circuito Margherita	91.8	92.2		89.8	90.1
2) Company Network	102.1	91.7	90.9	95.3	-
4) Kiss Kiss Network	92.4	97.8	-	101.8	104.9
5) InBlu Radio	89	88.9	94.6	92.3	96
6) Latte Miele	103.5	105.9	106.2	98.7	101.7
7) m2o	90.3	90.3	-	89	
8) Popolare Network	97.6	107.6	93.1	96.2	108
9) Radio Capital	93	93.1	98.5	88.7	93.9
10) Radio Centouno 101	101	101.2	107.3	107.9	105.2
11) Radio Classica	98.7	94	-	-	101.1
3) Radio Cuore	95	95.9	96.2	94.2	98.2
12) Radio Deejay	106.9	99.7	89.3	99.7	96.9
13) Radio RDS	96.2	95.5	99.8	95.7	95.7
14) Radio Italia Anni 60	-	106.3	99.5	102.1	91.3
15) Radio Italia S.M.I	106.6	106.7	103.7	100.6	106.3
16) Radio Maria	107.7	107.9	106.5	90.5	106.6
17) Radio Mater	105.7	95.3	100.1		
18) Radio Montecarlo Italie	105.5	105.5	100.8	101.3	104.2
20) Radio Padania Libera	106.1	103.5	93.8		
21) Radio Radicale	102.8	96.8	104.7	92.8	95.4
23) Radio 105 Network	99.6	99.1	98.8	103.5	99.5
24) Radio 24	105	104.8	89.6	107	90.9
25) RIN Radio Italia Net.	90.9	104.5	95.7	106.5	105.5
26) RTL 102.5	102.5	102.5	102.5	95	102.4
6) Tam Tam Netwok	88.5	-	-	107.6	93.6

Network	Fi	Ro	Na	Ba	Pa
1) Circuito Margherita	96.7	90.7	108	95.2	95.2
2) Company Network	-	100.5	88.4	92.9	-
4) Kiss Kiss Network	93.1	97.2	89	100.8	104
5) InBlu Radio	92.7	96.3	93.4	104	88
6) Latte Miele	104.5	92	101.2	93.5	94.6
7) m2o	105.8	97	98.4	87.6	107.8
8) Popolare Network	93.6	-	-	97.3	
9) Radio Capital	97.6	95.5	104.5	99.5	103.3
10) Radio Centouno 101	95.1	90.1	96.6	107.3	98.4
11) Radio Classica	99.4	89.5	-	-	99.6
3) Radio Cuore	99.1	100	107.2	100.5	89.2
12) Radio Deejay	99.7	101	99.5	88.5	107.5
13) Radio RDS	101.8	103	100.7	89.1	106.6
14) Radio Italia Anni 60	-	88.3	-	89.6	95.8
15) Radio Italia S.M.I	107.6	104.2	96.8	104.3	104.8
16) Radio Maria	89.6	95.1	98.8	103.8	105.4
17) Radio Mater	93.9	93.5	-	95.4	
18) Radio Montecarlo Italie	106.6	106.1	91.6	92	96.6
19) Radio Norba	-	-	92.8	105.5	
21) Radio Radicale	97	88.6	101.8	89.4	92
22) Radio Subasio	94.5	94	100.3		
23) Radio 105 Network	105	96.1	99.7	87.9	105.1
24) Radio 24	103.6	107.9	103.5	88.2	104.5
25) RIN Radio Italia Net.	107.2	98.7	93.5	106.6	93.2
26) RTL 102.5	102.4	102.1	102.6	102.8	102.3
6) Tam Tam Netwok	91.4				

To=Torino, Mi=Milano, Ve=Venezia, Bo=Bologna, Ge=Genova, Fi=Firenze, Ro=Roma, Na=Napoli, Ba=Bari, Pa=Palermo

Addresses and other information
1) Via Marchese di Villabianca 82, 90143 Palermo (PA) ☎ +39 091 302712 🖷 +39 091 8724835 **Web:** www.radiomargherita.com **Email:** info@radiomargherita.com SM: Giuseppe Orobello **V.** by letter. Rp. – **2)** Via Longhin 121, 35129 Padova (PD) ☎ +39 049 8944150 🖷 +39 049 8944112 **Web:** www.companygroup.com **Email:** info@companygroup.com SM: Claudio Rampazzo **V.** by letter. Rp. – **3)** Via Giovanni da Verrazzano 16, Localita Le Melorie, 56038 Ponsacco (PI) ☎ +39 0587 2861 🖷 +39 0587 733861 **Web:** www.mediahit.it/leradio.shtml **Email:** info@mediahit.it SM: Italo Bessi **V.** by letter. Rp. – **4)** Via Sgambati 61, 80131 Napoli (NA) ☎ +39 081 5461212 🖷 +39 081 5467789 **Web:** www.kisskissnetwork.it **Email:** info@kisskissnetwork.it SM: Antonio Niespolo **V.** by letter. Rp. – **5)** Via Aurelia 796, 00165 Roma (RM) ☎ +39 06 6650851 🖷+39 06 66508516 **Web:** www.radioinblu.it **Email:** info@radioinblu.it SM: Dino Boffo. V. by letter. Rp. – **6)** Via G.Dozza 54, 40013 Castelmaggiore (BO) ☎ +39 051 712601 🖷 +39 051 715626 **Web:** www.lattemiele.com **Email:** Redazione.bologna@lattemiele.com SM: Franco Mignani **V.** by QSL-card. .Rp. – **7)** Piazza della Repubblica 23/c 00185 Roma (RM) ☎ +39 06 492311 🖷 +39 06 4453758 **Web:** www.m2o.it **Email:** contatti@m2o.it **V.** by letter. Rp. – **8)** Via U.Ollearo 5, 20155 Milano (MI) ☎ +39 02 392411 🖷 +39 02 39273125 **Web:** www.radiopopolare.it **Email:** Radiopop@radiopopolare.it **SM:** Danilo De Biasio. **V.** by QSL-card. Rp. – **9)** Piazza della Repubblica 23/c, 00185 Roma (RM) ☎ +39 06 494321 🖷 +39 06 44702290 **Web:** www.capital.it **Email:** infoline@capital.it **SM:** Vittorio Zucconi. **V.** by QSL-card. Rp. – **10)** Via Locatelli 1, 20124 Milano (MI) ☎ +39 02 66982551, 🖷 +39 026704900. **Web:** www.radio101.it **Email:** info@radio101.it SM: Gigio D'Ambrosio **V.** by QSL-card. Rp. Re. to PLAY-DX, Via Davanzati 8, 20158 Milano (MI). – **11)** Via M.Burigozzo 5,20122 Milano (MI) ☎+39 02 58219600 🖷 +39 02 58219407 **Web:** www.radioclassica.fm **Email:** radioclassica@class.it SM:Carla Signorile **V.** by letter. Rp. – **12)** Casella Postale 314, 20100 Milano (MI) ☎ +39 02 342522 🖷 +39 02 342888 **Web:** www.deejay.it **Email:** stampa@deejay.it SM: Linus **V.** by QSL-card. Rp..– **13)** Via G.Mazzini 119, 00195 Roma (RM) ☎ +39 06 377051 🖷 +39 06 3725336 **Web:** www.rds.it **Email:** ufficiotecnico@rds.it SM: Stefano Montefusco **V.** by letter. Rp. – **14)** Via Lussimpiccolo 3, 00177 Roma (RM) ☎ +39 010 6196417 🖷 +39 02 70036123 **Web:** www.radioitaliaanni60.it **Email:** info@radioitaliaanni60.it SM: Francesco Nisi V. by letter. Rp. – **15)** Viale Europa 49, 20093 Cologno Monzese (MI) ☎ +39 02 25441 🖷 +39 02 25444220 **Web:** www.radioitalia.it **Email:** info@radioitalia.it SM: Mario Volanti **V.** by letter. Rp. – **16)** Via F.Turati 7, 22036 Erba (CO) ☎ +39 031 610600 🖷 +39 031 611288 **Web:** www.radiomaria.org **Email:** info.ita@radiomaria.org SM: Don Livio Fanzaga **V.** by QSL-card. Rp. – **17)** Via G.Marconi 85, 22036 Arcellasco d'Erba (CO) ☎ +39 031 645214 🖷 +39 031 6490527 **Web:** www.radiomater.com **Email:** info@radiomater.com SM: Don Mario Galbiati **V.** by letter. Rp. – **18)** Via Principe Amedeo 2, 20121 Milano (MI) ☎ +39 02 29001636 🖷 +39 02 6551451 **Web:** www.radiomontecarlo.net **Email:** rmc@radiomontecarlo.net SM: Paolo Del Forno **V.** by QSL-card.Rp. – **19)** Via Foggia 29, 70014 Conversano (BA) ☎ +39 80 4951229 🖷 +39 80 4953079 **Web:** www.radionorba.com **Email:** radionorba@radionorba.it SM: Annamaria Fantasia **V.** by letter. Rp. – **20)** Via C.Bellerio 41, 20161 Milano (MI) ☎ +39 02 66203529 🖷 +39 02 66220964 **Web:** www.radiopadania.net **Email:** direzione@radiopadania.net SM: Pietro Reina **V.** by letter. Rp. – **21)** Centro di Produzione, Via Principe Amedeo 2, 00185 Roma (RM) ☎ +39 06 4880541 🖷 +39 06 4880196 **Web:** www.radioradicale.it **Email:** staff@radioradicale.it SM: Massimo Bordin **V.** by letter. Rp. – **22)** Localita Colle de Bensi, 06081 Assisi (PG) ☎ +39 075 8060 🖷 +39 075 8065419 **Web:** www.radiosubasio.it **Email:** subasio@radiosubasio.it SM: Mario Settimi **V.** by letter. Rp. – **23)** Largo G. Donegani 1, 20121 Milano (MI) ☎ +39 02 6596116 🖷 +39 02 6592272 **Web:** www.105.net **Email:** diretta@105.net SM: Alberto Hazan **V.** QSL-Card. Rp. – **24)** Viale G.Richard 1, 20143 Milano (MI) ☎ +39 02 818761 🖷 +039 02 89155143 **Web:** www.radio24.it **Email:** frequenze@radio24.it SM: Elia Zamboni **V.** by letter. Rp – **25)** Viale G.Richard 1, 20143 Milano (MI) ☎ +39 02 89155339 🖷 +39 02 89155379 **Web:** www.rin.it **Email:** info@rin.it SM: Marco Biondi **V.** QSL-Card. Rp. – **26)** Viale Piemonte 61/63, 20093 Cologno Monzese (MI) ☎ +39 02 250961 🖷 +39 02 25096211 **Web:** www.rtl.it **Email:** qualita@rtl.it SM: Luigi Tornari **V.** QSL-card. Rp.

NEXUS - INTERNATIONAL BROADCASTING ASSOCIATION
See International Broadcasting section.

AMERICAN FORCES NETWORK EUROPE (U.S. Mil.)
Web: www.afneurope.net **Email:** harringtonj@afns.vicenza.army.mil **1st Prgr. Z-106 FM** on 106.0 MHz **Key Stations:** Vicenza (10kW) AFN,C/o Caserma Ederle,Via della Pace 100,IT-36100 Vicenza (VI) ☎+039 0444 397111 V. by letter. NoRp. Livorno(10kW) AFN Livorno,UNIT 31301,Box 64,APO AE,09613,USA. Local pgrm 0500-0800,1000-1200,1400-1700,2000-2200 Mo-Fr. Other st's: Aviano/San Vito (all 5kW), Napoli "LAVA 106" (10kW), PSC 817,Box 31,FPO AE 09622,USA. **Email:** Ask.NSA@nsa.naples.navy.mil /Decimomannu/La Maddalena (all 0.5kW). **2nd Prgr. Power Network** on 107.0MHz **Key Station:** Aviano (10kW) AFN,C/o Base USA, Dept.8.AFBS/ XOOR, IT-33081 Aviano (PN) ☎+039 0434 664284 🖷 +39 0434 664050 V.by letter. No Rp. Other st's:Vicenza/Livorno/Sigonella **Email:** jeffrey.wells@afn.sicily.army.mil/nick.spinelli@afn.lamaddalena.army.mil (all 5kW), Napoli (10kW), San Vito (0.5kW).

IVORY COAST

L.T: UTC — **Pop**: 16m — **Pr.L:** French, Diola, 12 ethnic — **E.C:** 50Hz, 220V — **ITU:** CTI.

CONSEIL NATIONAL DE LA COMMUNICATION ET DE L'AUDIOVISUEL (CNCA)
✉ Abidjan **L.P:** Bailly Djégou Jérôme, President.

RADIODIFFUSION-TÉLÉVISION IVOIRIENNE (RTI)
✉ B.P. 191, Abidjan ☎ +225 20 214800 🖷 +225 20 215038 **Web:** www.rti.ci **Email:** info.rti@rti.ci
L.P: Chairman: Maurice Kouakou. DG: Yacouba Kébé. Adv. for Int. Affairs: Paul Kadio.

MW: Abidjan 1494kHz 20kW, Bondoukou 1242kHz 1kW. (MW tr's rep. inactive).

FM (MHz):

Location	R	2	kW	Location	R	2	kW
Abobo-Abidjan	88.0	92.0	5	Man	96.9	100.2	-
Bouaflé	99.0	102.6	-	Naingbo	93.0	103.0	-
Dabakala	90.7	100.7	-	Niangue	92.7	95.9	-
Dimbokro	99.4	102.9	-	Séguéla	88.7	95.0	-
Divo	87.7	90.8	10	Tiémé	87.9	91.0	5
Grabo	87.9	91.0	0.5	Touba	94.7	101.5	-
Kouakoussikro	89.3	92.4	-	Tengréla	96.3	99.6	-
Koun Fao	94.2	101.0	-				

R. Côte d'Ivoire (R): 0500-2400. **Main N:** 0530, 0615, 0700, 0745, 1245, 1900, 2200. **N. in Vernaculars:** W 1700.
Fréquence Deux (2): 24 hrs. **Main N:** 1330. **Rel. (R):** 0500-0800, 1200-1230, 1900-1930. **English:** 1833-1930. **N:** 1845.
ANN: "R. Côte d'Ivoire" or "Fréquence Deux" - IS: s/on with clock chimes & National Anthem.
Note: most transmitters in the north are occupied by rebel groups.

Other stations:
City FM, Immeuble Alpha Cisse, 01 B.P. 7207, Abidjan: 106.1MHz 0600-2400. **Web**: www.assistweb.net/cityfm
R. Espoir, 06 BP 355, Abidjan: 102.8MHz **Web**: www.cmda.ci
R. Evangile Alliance, Bouaké. **F.PI**: in addition to R. Fréquence Vie relay, own tr's in Abengourou and Yamoussoukro. **Web**: www.christ-web.com/missions/farho/radio.html
R. Femmes Solidarité, Abidjan: 105.6MHz
R. Fréquence Vie, Abidjan: 89.4MHz **Web**: www.geocities.com/projectelva/radioelva.htm
R. Nostalgie, 01 B.P. 157, Abidjan: 101.1MHz
ONUCI FM, Abidjan: 96MHz, Bouaké 95.3MHz – **R. Paix Sanwi**, B.P. 219, Aboisso: 89.2MHz **Web**: www.ci.refer.org/ivoir_ct/med/rps/accueil.htm
R. Rurale (community st's set up by the development agency ACTT): st's are operating in Adzopé, San Pédro, Bin-Houyé, Tengréla & Bouna.

Africa No 1: Abidjan 91.1MHz.
BBC African Sce. in French: Abidjan 94.3MHz.
RFI Afrique: Abidjan, Bouaké & Korogho on 97.6MHz.

JAMAICA

L.T: UTC -5h — **Pop:** 2.7 million — **Pr.L:** English — **E.C:** 50Hz, 110/220V — **ITU:** JMC.

RJR COMMUNICATIONS GROUP (Comm.)
✉ 32 Lyndhurst Road, P.O. Box 23, Kingston 5 ☎ +1 876 926 1100/9 🖷 +1 876 929 7467 **Email:** webmaster@radiojamaica.com **Web:** www.radiojamaica.com.
L.P: Chmn. & MD: J.A. Lester Spaulding. CEN: Carroll Lawrence. Exec. Producer RJR 94: Henry Stennett. Exec. producer FAME FM: Francois St. Juste. Media Services Mgr. (radio): Donald Topping. Publ. Rel. (radio): Norma Brown-Bell.

MW RJR94	kHz	kW
Llandilo (Westmoreland)	550	1.5
Baileys Vale (St. Mary)	580	1.5
Hague (Trelawny)	700	1.5
Innswood (St. Catherine)	720	10
Grove Place (Manchester)	770	1.5

FM	RJR94	FAME	R. 92FM	kW
Broadcasting House	94.1	95.7		1/1
Half Way Tree			105.7	2.5
Coopers Hill	94.5	92.7	91.1	5/5/5
Spur Tree	94.3	98.1	103.3	10/5/10
Coleyville	94.9	95.9		5/5
Mt. Airy (Negril)	94.7	95.3	96.3	5/5/1
German Hill	94.5			3.5
Flower Hill	94.1	95.7	92.1	2.5/3.5/10
Oracabessa	94.3	91.5	100.3	10/10/5
Pt. Antonio	94.7	95.3	96.3	2.5/2.5/5
Cabbage Hill	94.9	95.5		0.5/0.1
Rowlandsfield			92.1	2.5

D.Prgr: 24h.

Other Stations:
Hot 102 - FM Radio, CVM Communication Group, Blaise Industrial Park, 69 Constant Spring Rd, Kingston 10. ☎ +1 876 960 8453. **L.P.:** Chairman: Neville Blythe. President: David McBean. Radio operations: Andrea Wilson-Messam. Prgs/operations mgr.: Tomlin Ellis. - **FM:** Kingston: 102.1, Manchester: 102.3, St. Ann: 102.5, St. Andrew: 102.7, Westmoreland: 102.7, Portland: 102.9 & St. James: 102.9MHz. **Format:** Talk & Hit radio.
Irie - FM, P.O. Box 282, Coconut Grove, Ocho Rios. ☎ +1 876 974 5051. 🖷 +1 876 974 5943. **Web:** www.irie- FM.net. - **FM:** St. Mary 107.1, Kingston: 107.5, Ocho Rios: 107.7, Montego Bay: 107.9MHz **L.P.:** MD Karl Young **Format:** Reggae.
KLAS - FM, 41B Half Way Tree Rd, Kingston 5. ☎ +1 876 929 1344. 🖷 +1 876 906 7604. - **FM:** 89.1/89.5/89.9MHz. **Format:** Rlg.
Kool - FM, 1 Braemar Ave, Kingston 10. ☎ +1 876 978 3974/4037. 🖷 +1 876 978 6080. - **FM:** 97.1/97.3/97.5/97.7/97.9MHz.
Love 101, 12 Carlton Cresent, Kingston 10. ☎ +1 876 968 9596. 🖷 +1 876 968 7545. **L.P.:** GM: Winston Ridgard. - **FM:** 101.1/101.3/101.5/101.7/101.9MHz. **Format:** Rlg.
LYNX - FM, 8 Beckford St., Savanna-la-mar. ☎ +1 876 955 4650/4301. **L.P.:** CEO Roger Allen. - **FM**: 96.5/96.9 MHz.
Mega Jamz, 3 Bradley Av., Kingston 10. ☎ +1 876 968 3430. **L.P.:** CEO Collin Smith. - **FM:** 97.9/98.3 MHz.
Mello - FM, 63 Barnett St, Montego Bay. ☎ +1 876 971 4163. 🖷 +1 876 971 4163. **L.P.**: CEO Al Robinson. Ops. Mgr. Edwin George. - **FM:** 96.1MHz.
Music 99, 6 Bradley Av., Kingston. ☎ +1 876 968 4880. 🖷 +1 876 968 9165. **L.P.:** MD Newton James. - **FM:** 99.1/99.5/99.7/99.9MHz.
Power 106 - FM, 6 Bradley Av., Kingston 10. ☎ +1 876 968 4880. 🖷 +1 876 968 9165. **L.P.**: MD Newton James. - **FM:** 106.1/106.5/106.7/106.9MHz.
Radio Mona, University of the West Indies, Mona, Kingston 7. ☎ +1 876 970 3545/1709. **L.P.:** Mgr: Michael Anthony Cuffe. - **FM:** 93.1/93.3/93.5/93.7.
Roots - FM, 1 Mahoe Drive, Kingston 11. ☎ +1 876 923 6488. 🖷 +1 876 923 6000. - **FM:** Kingston 96.1MHz.
TBC - FM (The Breath of Change), 51 Molynes Rd, Kingston 10. ☎ +1 876 754 5120. - **FM:** Kingston 88.5 MHz. **Format:** Rlg. (Baptist).
VBYZ - FM, 98 Great George Street, Savanna-la-Mar.
Zip 103, 1B Derrymore Road, Kingston. ☎ +1 876 929-2748/6233. 🖷 +1 876 960 0523. **L.P.:** MD Karl Young. - **FM:** 103.1/103.3/103.5/103.7/103.9MHz. **Format:** Techo/dance/alternative.

JAPAN

L.T: UTC +9h — **Pop:** 127,944,200 — **Pr.L:** Japanese — **EC:** 50 & 60Hz, 100V — **ITU:** J

INFORMATION AND COMMUNICATIONS POLICY BUREAU, MINISTRY OF PUBLIC MANAGEMENT, HOME AFFAIRS, POSTS & TELECOMMUNICATIONS (SOUMU SHO)
✉ 1-2, Kasumigaseki 2-chome, Chiyoda-ku, Tokyo 100-8926 ☎ +81 3 5253 5111 **Web:** www.soumu.go.jp **L.P:** Minister: T. Aso.

NIPPON HOSO KYOKAI (NHK) (The Japan Broadcasting Corporation)
✉ 2-1, Jinnan 2-chome, Shibuya-ku, Tokyo 150-8001 ☎ +81 3 3465 1111 **Web:** www.nhk.or.jp
L.P: Chmn. (Board of Governors): H. Suda. Pres: K. Ebisawa, Exec. Vice-Pres: T. Kasai. Gen. MD & Exec. Dir. Gen. Eng: T. Yoshino, Gen.MD: A. Sekine, MD's: H. Yasuoka, G. Hashimoto, N. Miyashita, S. Wazaki, N. Nojima, S. Nakayama, M. Moroboshi, Y. Ideta, C. Narita, H. Ikeda, M. Nishio. **Pub:** NHK Nenkan (Japanese) and NHK Update (English).

STATIONS:

MW	Location & Prgr	Call	kHz	kW
F2)	Morioka 1	QG	531	10
E4)	Nago 1		531	1
F3)	Yamagata 1	JG	540	5
E2)	Miyazaki 1	MG	540	5
E3)	Kitakyushu 1	SK	540	1
A2)	Matsumoto 1		540	1
C6)	Nanao 1		540	1
E4)	Ishigaki 1		540	1
E4)	Okinawa 1	AP	549	10
G1)	Sapporo 1	IK	567	100
E5)	Kagoshima 1	HG	576	10
C2)	Hamamatsu 1	DG	576	1
G2)	Kushiro 1	PG	585	10
A1)	Tokyo 1	AK	594	300
D2)	Okayama 1	KK	603	5
G3)	Obihiro 1	OG	603	5
B1)	Fukuoka 1	LK	612	100
G4)	Asahikawa 1	CG	621	3
B2)	Kyoto 1	OK	621	1
A2)	Iida 1		621	1
E2)	Nobeoka 1		621	1
E6)	Oita 1	IP	639	5
C3)	Shizuoka 2	PB	639	10
C4)	Toyama 1	IG	648	5
B1)	Osaka 1	BK	666	100
G5)	Hakodate 1	VK	675	5
D3)	Yamaguchi 1	UG	675	5
E7)	Nagasaki 1	AG	684	5
A1)	Tokyo 2	AB	693	500
G6)	Kitami 2	KD	702	10
D1)	Hiroshima 2	FB	702	10
C1)	Nagoya 1	CK	729	50
G1)	Sapporo 2	IB	747	500
E8)	Kumamoto 1	GK	756	10
F4)	Akita 2	UB	774	500
C8)	Takayama 1		792	1
G4)	Enbetsu 1		792	1
A3)	Takada 1		792	1
E5)	Naze 1		792	1
A2)	Nagano 1	NK	819	5
B1)	Osaka 2	BB	828	300
A3)	Niigata 1	QK	837	10
G4)	Nayoro 1		837	1
F6)	Koriyama 1		846	5
H1)	Uwajima 1		846	1
E8)	Hitoyoshi 1		846	1
E8)	Kumamoto 2	GB	873	500
C3)	Shizuoka 1	PK	882	10
F1)	Sendai 1	HK	891	20
C1)	Nagoya 2	CB	909	10
A4)	Kofu 1	KG	927	5
C5)	Fukui 1	FG	927	5
G4)	Wakkanai 1		927	1
D2)	Tsuyama 1		927	1
H2)	Tokushima 1	XK	945	5
G7)	Muroran 1	IQ	945	3
B3)	Hikone 1	QP	945	1
E7)	Fukue 1		945	1
F5)	Aomori 1	TG	963	5
H1)	Matsuyama 1	ZK	963	5
E9)	Saga 1	SP	963	5
D4)	Yonago 1		963	1
D3)	Hagi 1		963	1
A2)	Kisofukushima 1		981	1
E7)	Sasebo 1		981	1
H3)	Kochi 1	RK	990	10
F5)	Hachinohe 1		999	1
D1)	Fukuyama 1		999	1
H3)	Nakamura 1		999	1
E1)	Fukuoka 2	LB	1017	50
C4)	Toyama 2	IC	1035	1
H4)	Takamatsu 2	HD	1035	1
F3)	Tsuruoka 2		1035	1
D1)	Hiroshima 1	FK	1071	20
F1)	Sendai 2	HB	1089	10
G3)	Obihiro 2	OC	1125	1
G7)	Muroran 2	IZ	1125	1
D4)	Tottori 2	LC	1125	1
G4)	Nayoro 2		1125	1
D3)	Hagi 2		1125	1
C8)	Takayama 2		1125	1
E4)	Okinawa 2	AD	1125	10
G2)	Kushiro 2	PC	1152	10
H3)	Kochi 2	RB	1152	10
G6)	Kitami 1	KP	1188	10
C6)	Kanazawa 1	JK	1224	10
D5)	Matsue 1	TK	1296	10
F6)	Fukushima 1	FP	1323	1
F2)	Yamada 1		1323	1
E8)	Minamata 1		1341	1
F6)	Iwaki 1		1341	1
H4)	Takamatsu 1	HP	1368	5
D4)	Tottori 1	LG	1368	1
F3)	Tsuruoka 1		1368	1
D3)	Yamaguchi 2	UC	1377	5
E7)	Nagasaki 2	AC	1377	1
F5)	Hachinohe 2		1377	1
F2)	Morioka 2	QC	1386	10
C6)	Kanazawa 2	JB	1386	10
E5)	Kagoshima 2	HC	1386	10
D2)	Okayama 2	KB	1386	5
G5)	Hakodate 2	VB	1467	1
A2)	Nagano 2	NB	1467	1
E6)	Oita 2	ID	1467	1
E2)	Miyazaki 2	MC	1467	1
G4)	Wakkanai 2		1467	1
A2)	Iida 2		1476	1
F4)	Akita 1	UK	1503	10
E8)	Aso 1		1503	1
H1)	Matsuyama 2	ZB	1512	5
F6)	Koriyama 2		1512	1
A2)	Matsumoto 2		1512	1
F3)	Yamagata 2	JC	1521	1
F5)	Aomori 2	TC	1521	1
C2)	Hamamatsu 2	DC	1521	1
C5)	Fukui 2	FC	1521	1
D4)	Yonago 2		1521	1
H3)	Nakamura 2		1521	1
E4)	Ishigaki 2		1521	1
A3)	Niigata 2	QB	1593	10
D5)	Matsue 2	TB	1593	10
G4)	Asahikawa 2	CC	1602	1
A4)	Kofu 2	KC	1602	1
E3)	Kitakyushu 2	SB	1602	1
F6)	Fukushima 2	FD	1602	1
D1)	Fukuyama 2		1602	1
G4)	Enbetsu 2		1602	1
H1)	Uwajima 2		1602	1
E8)	Hitoyoshi 2		1602	1
E2)	Nobeoka 2		1602	1
E5)	Naze 2		1602	1

+ approx 234 st's. St's below 1kW.
1: NHK Radio One, **2:** NHK Radio Two. **Call: JO(call).**

SW	Location & Prgr	kHz	kW	H. of tr
E1)	Fukuoka 1	3259*	0.6	0800-1300
B1)	Osaka 2	3373.5*	0.3	0800-1300
A1)	Tokyo 1	3607.5*	0.9	0800-1300
G1)	Sapporo 1	3970	0.6	1300-1500
C1)	Nagoya 1	3970*	0.3	2000-0030, 0400-1300
B1)	Osaka 2	5428*	0.3	2030-0300, 0500-0730
G1)	Sapporo 1	6005	0.6	2000-0030, 0400-1230
C1)	Nagoya 1	6005*	0.3	0100-0330
E1)	Fukuoka 1	6130*	0.6	2000-0400
A1)	Tokyo 1	6175*	0.9	2000-0030
B1)	Osaka 2	9181*	0.3	0330-0430
G1)	Sapporo 1	9535	0.6	0100-0330
E1)	Fukuoka 1	9535*	0.6	0430-0730
A1)	Tokyo 1	9550*	0.9	0100-0730

*) Upper side band transmission. **1:** NHK Radio One, **2:** NHK Radio Two. These SWs are transmitted from standby/emergency trs.

FM	Location	Call	MHz	kW
A5)	Utsunomiya	BP	80.3	1
A6)	Chiba	MP	80.7	5
C4)	Toyama	IG	81.5	1
A7)	Maebashi	TP	81.6	1
C7)	Tsu	NP	81.8	3
A8)	Yokohama	GP	81.9	5
F3)	Yamagata	JG	82.1	1
C6)	Kanazawa	JK	82.2	1
A3)	Niigata	QK	82.3	1
A1)	Tokyo	AK	82.5	10
C1)	Nagoya	CK	82.5	10
F1)	Sendai	HK	82.5	5
B2)	Kyoto	OK	82.8	1
F2)	Morioka	QG	83.1	1
A9)	Mito	EP	83.2	1
C5)	Fukui	FG	83.4	1
H2)	Tokushima	XK	83.4	1
A3)	Yamato		83.5	1
C8)	Gifu	OP	83.6	1
B3)	Otsu	QP	84.0	1
B4)	Himeji		84.2	1
E5)	Tanegashima		84.4	1
E1)	Fukuoka	LK	84.8	3
E4)	Hirara		85.0	1
A10)	Saitama	LP	85.1	5
G1)	Sapporo	IK	85.2	5
F6)	Fukushima	FP	85.3	1
E8)	Kumamoto	GK	85.4	1
A4)	Kofu	KG	85.6	1
E5)	Kagoshima	HG	85.6	1
D5)	Hamada		85.8	1
F5)	Aomori	TG	86.0	5
H4)	Takamatsu	HP	86.0	1
F4)	Akita	UK	86.7	3
H1)	Matsuyama	ZK	87.7	1
B1)	Osaka	BK	88.1	10
E4)	Okinawa	AP	88.1	1
G4)	Nayoro		88.2	1
D1)	Hiroshima	FK	88.3	1
D2)	Okayama	KK	88.7	1
C3)	Shizuoka	PK	88.8	1
E6)	Oita	IP	88.9	1
G4)	Chikoma		89.1	1
G2)	Nakashibetsu		89.9	1

Call: JO(call)-FM + approx 480 st's.below 1kW

Addresses of regional HQs:
A) Kanto-Koshinetsu area = Tokyo A1): same as NHK general HQ address. **B)** Kinki area = Osaka B1): 1-20, Otemae 4-chome, Chuo-ku, Osaka 540-8501. **C)** Tokai-Hokuriku area = Nagoya C1): 13-3, Higashisakura 1-chome, Higashi-ku, Nagoya 461-8725. **D)** Chugoku area = Hiroshima D1): 11-10, Otemachi 2-chome, Naka-ku, Hiroshima 730-8672. **E)** Kyushu area = Fukuoka E1): 1-10, Ropponmatsu 1-chome, Chuo-ku, Fukuoka 810-8577. **F)** Tohoku area = Sendai F1): 11-1, Nishiki-machi 1-chome, Aoba-ku, Sendai 980-8435. **G)** Hokkaido area = Sapporo G1): 1-1, Odori Nishi, Chuo-ku, Sapporo 060-8703.
H) Shikoku area = Matsuyama H1): 5, Horinouchi, Matsuyama 790-8501.

NHK R. One (General prgr): 24h. **N:** every h (exc Sun 0000). Also exc Fri & Sat at 2030, 2140(exc Sat), 2230, 2330(exc Sat) and exc Sat & Sun at 0430, 1230. **Regional and local prgrs** (the amount of local prgr's varies between the st's): 2055wrp, 2125N/wrp/inf, 2155 wrp/inf, 2210(Fri & Sat)N/wrp, 2215(Sun-Thu)N/wrp, 2240(exc Sat)N/wrp/inf, 2255(Sat)N/wrp/inf, 2355N/wrp/inf, 0055(exc Sun)N/wrp/inf, 0155N/wrp/inf, 0250wrp/inf, 0310N/wrp, 0355(exc Sun)wrp/inf, 0455N/wrp/inf, 0555N/wrp/inf, 0655N/wrp/inf, 0755N/wrp/inf, 0855N/wrp/inf, 0950N/wrp/inf, 1015(Sat & Sun)N/wrp, 1045(exc Sat & Sun)N, 1055(exc Sun)wrp/inf, 1155(exc Sat & Sun) N/wrp/inf, 1255N/wrp/inf, 1355N/wrp. **IS:** Original music played by Celesta. **ANN:** "JO(call), NHK (location) Daiichi Hoso desu". Local ID's with call letters, network & location given by studio st's just before: 2000, 0300, 1000.

NHK R. Two (Educational prgr): 2030-1640 (Sun & Mon 1500). No regular regional and local prgrs. **Foreign language N** (rel. NHK World - R. Japan): **Chinese:** 0400-0410. **Korean:** 0410-0420. **English:** 0500-0515(Sat & Sun: 0500-0510), 1400-1415(Sat & Sun: 1400-1410). **Portuguese:** 0900-0910. **Spanish:** 0910-0920. Weather map: 0010, 0700, 1300 (all 20 mins.) **IS:** Original music played by Celesta. Nat. Anthem at s/on on national holidays & s/off. **ANN:** "JO(call), NHK (location) Daini Hoso desu". Local ID's on certain st's (as 1st Netw) just before 2030, 0030, 0720, 1320 and sign off.

NHK FM Netw: 24h. 1600-2000 relays R. One, **N:** 2200, 0300, 0950(local), 1000, 1400. **ANN:** "JO(call)-FM, NHK (location) FM Hoso desu". Local ID's just before 2000, 0300, 1000.

V: NHK officially has no organised QSL sce. However, many local st's verify by QSL card or letter for DX reports.

INTERNATIONAL SERVICES:
RADIO JAPAN, NHK WORLD NETWORK
See International Broadcasting section

THE NATIONAL ASSOCIATION OF COMMERCIAL BROADCASTERS IN JAPAN (NIPPON MINKAN HOSO RENMEI)
3-23, Kioi-cho, Chiyoda-ku, Tokyo 102-8577 ☎ +81 3 5213 7711 +81 3 5213 7703 **Web:** www.nab.or.jp
L. P: Pres: H. Hieda, Vice-Presidents: H. Inoue, K. Manabe, M. Hirose, K. Murakami, S. Sugaya, J. Matsui, T. Doi, M. Gondo, Exec. Dir: T. Tamagawa. **Pub:** Nippon Minkan Hoso Nenkan (Japanese), Gekkan Minpo (Japanese), Minkan Hoso (Japanese) and NAB Handbook (English) etc.

MW	Call	kHz	kW	ID	Name, location and schedule
1)	CR	558	20d	AMK	AM Kobe, Kobe 2000(Fri & Sat 2030)-1900(Sat 1845)
2)	WN	639	5	STV	Sapporo TV Hoso, Hakodate as 1440kHz
3)	DF	684	5	IBC	Iwate Hoso, Morioka
3)	LO	684	1	IBC	Iwate Hoso, Ofunato
4)	IL	720	1	KBC	Kyushu Asahi Hoso, Kitakyushu
5)	LR	738	5	KNB	Kita Nihon Hoso, Toyama
5)		738	1	KNB	Kita Nihon Hoso, Takaoka
6)	RR	738	10	RBC	Ryukyu Hoso, Naha
7)	JF	765	5	YBS	Yamanashi Hoso, Kofu
8)	PF	765	5	KRY	Yamaguchi Hoso, Shunan
9)	XR	864	10	ROK	R. Okinawa, Naha 2000-1800(Sun 1600)
10)	SO	864	1	SBC	Shin'etsu Hoso, Matsumoto
11)	HE	864	3	HBC	Hokkaido Hoso, Asahikawa
11)	QF	864	3	HBC	Hokkaido Hoso, Muroran
11)		864	1	HBC	Hokkaido Hoso, Enbetsu
12)	PR	864	5d	FBC	Fukui Hoso, Fukui
13)	XN	864	1	CRT	Tochigi Hoso, Nasu as 1530kHz
2)	WS	882	3	STV	Sapporo TV Hoso, Kushiro as 1440kHz
2)		882	1	STV	Sapporo TV Hoso, Esashi as above
11)	HO	900	5	HBC	Hokkaido Hoso, Hakodate
14)	HF	900	5	BSS	San'in Hoso, Yonago: 1800-2055, Sun 1500-1900 (off air Sat)
15)	ZR	900	5	RKC	Kochi Hoso, Kochi
2)	VX	909	5	STV	Sapporo TV Hoso, Abashiri as 1440kHz
16)	EF	918	5	YBC	Yamagata Hoso, Yamagata
16)		918	1	YBC	Yamagata Hoso, Tsuruoka/Yonezawa/Shinjo
8)	PM	918	1	KRY	Yamaguchi Hoso, Shimonoseki
8)	PN	918	1	KRY	Yamaguchi Hoso, Iwakuni
17)	TR	936	5	ABS	Akita Hoso, Akita
18)	NF	936	5	MRT	Miyazaki Hoso, Miyazaki
18)		936	1	MRT	Miyazaki Hoso, Nobeoka/Nichinan/Kobayashi/Takachiho
19)	KR	954S	100	TBS	TBS Radio, Tokyo
20)	NR	1008S	50	ABC	Asahi Hoso, Osaka
21)	AR	1053S	50	CBC	Chubu Nippon Hoso, Nagoya
2)	WM	1071	5	STV	Sapporo TV Hoso, Obihiro as 1440kHz
10)	SR	1098	5	SBC	Shin'etsu Hoso, Nagano
10)	SW	1098	1	SBC	Shin'etsu Hoso, Iida

MW	Call	kHz	kW	ID	Name, location and schedule
22)	MF	1098	1	NBC	Nagasaki Hoso, Sasebo
23)	GF	1098	5	OBS	Oita Hoso, Oita
24)	WO	1098	5	RFC	R. Fukushima, Koriyama
25)	CF	1107	20d	MBC	Minami Nihon Hoso, Kagoshima, 24h
25)		1107	1	MBC	Minami Nihon Hoso, Akune/Oguchi/ Sendai as above
26)	MR	1107	5	MRO	Hokuriku Hoso, Kanazawa
26)		1107	1d	MRO	Hokuriku Hoso, Nanao
27)	AF	1116	5	RNB	Nankai Hoso, Matsuyama
27)	AL	1116	1d	RNB	Nankai Hoso, Niihama
27)	AM	1116	1	RNB	Nankai Hoso, Uwajima
28)	DR	1116	5	BSN	Niigata Hoso, Niigata
29)	QR	1134S	100	NCB	Bunka Hoso, Tokyo
30)	BR	1143	20	KBS	KBS Kyoto, Kyoto
31)	OR	1179S	50	MBS	Mainichi Hoso, Osaka
15)		1197	1	RKC	Kochi Hoso, Nakamura
32)	FO	1197	1	RKB	RKB Mainichi Hoso, Kitakyushu
33)	BF	1197S	10d	RKK	Kumamoto Hoso, Kumamoto
33)		1197	1	RKK	Kumamoto Hoso, Hitoyoshi/Aso/ Goshoura
34)	YF	1197	5	IBS	Ibaraki Hoso, Mito 2045(Sat 2100)-2000(Sat 1930, Sun 1430)
2)	WL	1197	3	STV	Sapporo TV Hoso, Asahikawa (as 1440kHz)
2)		1197	1	STV	Sapporo TV Hoso, Wakkanai/ Nayoro/Enbetsu as 1440kHz
30)	BO	1215	2	KBS	KBS Kyoto, Maizuru
30)	BW	1215	1	KBS	KBS Shiga, Hikone
22)	UR	1233	5	NBC	Nagasaki Hoso, Nagasaki
35)	GR	1233	5d	RAB	Aomori Hoso, Aomori
36)	LF	1242S	100	NBS	Nippon Hoso, Tokyo
37)	IR	1260S	20	TBC	Tohoku Hoso, Sendai
11)	HW	1269	5	HBC	Hokkaido Hoso, Obihiro
11)	FM	1269	1	HBC	Hokkaido Hoso, Esashi
38)	JR	1269	5	JRT	Shikoku Hoso, Tokushima
38)		1269	1	JRT	Shikoku Hoso, Ikeda
32)	FR	1278S	50	RKB	RKB Mainichi Hoso, Fukuoka
11)	HR	1287S	50	HBC	Hokkaido Hoso, Sapporo
39)	UF	1314S	50	OBC	R. Osaka, Osaka
40)	SF	1332S	50		Tokai R. Hoso, Nagoya
41)	ER	1350S	20	RCC	Chugoku Hoso, Hiroshima
11)	TS	1368	1	HBC	Hokkaido Hoso, Wakkanai
1)		1395	1	AMK	AM Kobe, Toyooka as 558kHz
24)	WE	1395	1	RFC	R. Fukushima, Wakamatsu
11)	QL	1404	5	HBC	Hokkaido Hoso, Kushiro
42)	VR	1404	10d	SBS	Shizuoka Hoso, Shizuoka
42)	VO	1404	1d	SBS	Shizuoka Hoso, Hamamatsu
4)	IF	1413S	50	KBC	Kyushu Asahi Hoso, Fukuoka
43)	RF	1422	50d	RF	RF R. Nippon, Yokohama
14)	HL	1431	1	BSS	San'in Hoso, Tottori as 900kHz
14)		1431	1d	BSS	San'in Hoso, Izumo as 900kHz
22)		1431	1	NBC	Nagasaki Hoso, Fukue
24)	WW	1431	1	RFC	R. Fukushima, Iwaki
44)	VF	1431S	5	WBS	Wakayama Hoso, Wakayama
45)	ZF	1431	5	GBS	Gifu Hoso, Gifu: 1500-2000 (off air Mon)
2)	WF	1440S	50	STV	Sapporo TV Hoso, Sapporo
2)		1440	3	STV	Sapporo TV Hoso, Muroran as above
2)		1440	1	STV	Sapporo TV Hoso, Tomakomai as above
11)	QM	1449	5	HBC	Hokkaido Hoso, Abashiri
46)	KF	1449	5	RNC	Nishi Nippon Hoso, Takamatsu (off the air Sun 1630-2030)
46)		1449	1	RNC	Nishi Nippon Hoso, Marugame as above
22a)	UO	1458	1	NBC	Nagasaki Hoso, Saga
24)	WR	1458	1	RFC	R. Fukushima, Fukushima
34)	YL	1458	1	IBS	Ibaraki Hoso, Tsuchiura as 1197kHz
34)		1458	1	IBS	Ibaraki Hoso, Sekijo as above
41)		1458	1	RCC	Chugoku Hoso, Shobara
8)	PL	1485	1	KRY	Yamaguchi Hoso, Hagi
35)	GO	1485	1	RAB	Aomori Hoso, Hachinohe
11)	TL	1494	1	HBC	Hokkaido Hoso, Nayoro
47)	YR	1494S	10	RSK	Sanyo Hoso, Okayama
47)		1494S	1	RSK	Sanyo Hoso, Takahashi
47)		1494	1	RSK	Sanyo Hoso, Tsuyama/Niimi/Bizen/Ochiai
28)	DO	1530	1	BSN	Niigata Hoso, Joetsu
13)	XF	1530	5	CRT	Tochigi Hoso, Utsunomiya 2100-2000(Sun1500)
41)	EO	1530	1	RCC	Chugoku Hoso, Fukuyama
41)		1530	1	RCC	Chugoku Hoso, Mihara

Relay sts below 1kW (approx 125 st's) are not included here.
Call: JO(call). **S:** AM Stereo (C-QUAM System). **Schedule:** 24h, unless otherwise indicated above. Most 24h sts are off the air for 1 to 5 hours until 1900 or 2000 on Sun except particularly mentioned station. All other days a network prgr is aired 1600 or 1800 to 2000 on most sts. Network prgrs also may be broadcast at other times of the day. **ID:** Company initials are usually used as st.identification.

Addresses and other information:
1) R. Kansai Co., Ltd., 5-7, Higashi Kawasaki-cho 1-chome, Chuo-ku, Kobe 650-8580. **Web:** www.amkobe.co.jp – **2)** The Sapporo Television Broadc. Co., Ltd., 1-1, Nishi 8-chome, Kita 1-jo, Chuo-ku, Sapporo 060-8705. **Web:** www.stv.ne.jp – **3)** Iwate Broadc. Co., Ltd., 6-1, Shike-cho, Morioka 020-8566. **Web:** www.ibc.co.jp – **4)** Kyushu Asahi Broadc. Co., Ltd, 1-1, Nagahama 1-chome, Chuo-ku, Fukuoka 810-8571. **Web:** www.kbc.co.jp – **5)** Kita-nihon Broadc. Co., Ltd.,10-18 Ushijima-machi, Toyama 930-8585. **Web:** www.knb.ne.jp – **6)** Ryukyu Broadc. Corp., 3-1, Kumoji 2-chome, Naha 900-8711. **Web:** www.rbc-ryukyu.co.jp – **7)** Yamanashi Broadc. System, 6-10, Kitaguchi 2-chome, Kofu 400-8566. **Web:** www.ybs.ne.jp – **8)** Yamaguchi Broadc. Co., Ltd., Koen-ku, Shunan 745-8686. **Web:** www.kry.co.jp – **9)** R. Okinawa Co., 4-8, Nishi 1-chome, Naha 900-8604. **Web:** www.rokinawa.co.jp – **10)** Shin-etsu Broadc. Co., Ltd., 21-24, Yoshida 1-chome, Nagano 381-8585. **Web:** http://sbc21.co.jp – **11)** Hokkaido Broadc. Co., Ltd., 2, Nishi 5-chome, kita 1-jo, Chuo-ku, Sapporo 060-8501. **Web:** www.hbc.co.jp – **12)** Fukui Broadc. Co., Ltd., 37-1-1 Owada-cho, Fukui 910-8588. **Web:** www.fbc.jp —**13)** Tochigi Broadc. Co., Ltd., 12-11 Honcho, Utsunomiya 320-8601. **Web:** www.crt-radio.co.jp – **14)** Broadc. System of San-in, 1-71, Nishi-Fukubara 1-chome, Yonago 683-8670. **Web:** http://bss.jp – **15)** Kochi Broadc. Co., Ltd., 2-15, Hon-machi 3-chome, Kochi 780-8550. **Web:** www.rkc-kochi.co.jp – **16)** Yamagata Broadc. Co., Ltd., 2-5, Hatago-machi, Yamagata 990-8555. **Web:** www.ybc.co.jp – **17)** Akita Broadc. System, 9-42, Sanno 7-chome, Akita 010-8611. **Web:** www.akita-abs.co.jp – **18)** Miyazaki Broadc. Co., Ltd., 6-7, Nishi 4-chome, Tachibana-dori, Miyazaki 880-8639. **Web:** www.mrt-miyazaki.co.jp – **19)** TBS Radio & Communications, Inc., 3-6, Akasaka 5-chome, Minato-ku, Tokyo 107-8006. **Web:** www.tbs.co.jp – **20)** Asahi Broadc. Corp., 2-48, Oyodominami 2-chome, Kita-ku, Osaka 530-8501. **Web:** www.asahi.co.jp – **21)** Chubu-Nippon Broadc. Co., Ltd., 2-8, Shinsakae 1-chome, Naka-ku, Nagoya 460-8405. **Web:** http://hicbc.com – **22)** Nagasaki Broadc. Co., Ltd., 1-35, Uwamachi, Nagasaki 850-8650. **Web:** www.nbc-nagasaki.co.jp – 22a) Nagasaki Broadc. Co., Ltd. Saga station, 1249, Honjo-machi, Saga 840-0027 Web: www.nbc-saga.jp – **23)** Oita Broadc. System, 1-1, Imazuru 3-chome, Oita 870-8620. **Web:** www.e-obs.com – **24)** R. Fukushima Broadc. Co., Ltd., 13-17, Otamachi, Fukushima 960-8655. **Web:** www.rfc.jp – **25)** Minaminihon Broadc. Co., Ltd., 5-25, Korai-cho, Kagoshima 890-8570. **Web:** www.mbc.co.jp – **26)** Hokuriku Broadc. Co., Ltd., 2-1, Honda-machi 3-chome, Kanazawa 920-8560. **Web:** www.mro.co.jp – **27)** Nankai Broadc. Co., Ltd., 6-24 Dogohimata, Matsuyama 790-8510. **Web:** www.rnb.co.jp – **28)** Broadc. System of Niigata, Inc., 3-18, Kawagishi-cho, Niigata 951-8655. **Web:** www.ohbsn.com – **29)** Nippon Cultural Broadc., Inc., 1-5, Wakaba, Shinjuku-ku, Tokyo 160-8002. **Web:** www.joqr.co.jp – **30)** Kyoto Broadc. System Co., Ltd., Kamichojamachi, Karasumadori, Kamigyo-ku, Kyoto 602-8588. **Web:** www.kbs-kyoto.co.jp – **31)** Mainichi Broadc. System, Inc., 17-1, Chayamachi, Kita-ku, Osaka 530-8304. **Web:** http://mbs.jp – **32)** RKB Mainichi Broadc. Corp., 3-8, Momochihama 2-chome, Sawara-ku, Fukuoka 814-8585. **Web:** www.rkb.ne.jp – **33)** Kumamoto Broadc. Co., Ltd., 30, Yamasaki-machi, Kumamoto 860-8611. **Web:** www.rkk.co.jp – **34)** Ibaraki Broadc. System, 2084 Senba-cho, Mito 310-8505. **Web:** www.ibs-radio.com – **35)** Aomori Broadc. Corp., 8-1, Matsumori 1-chome, Aomori 030-0965. **Web:** www.rab.co.jp – **36)** Nippon Broadc. System, Inc., 4-8, Daiba 2-chome, Minato-ku, Tokyo 137-8686. **Web:** www.jolf.co.jp – **37)** Tohoku Broadc. Co., Ltd., 26-1, Kasumi-cho, Yagiyama, Taihaku-ku, Sendai 982-8668. **Web:** www.tbc-sendai.co.jp – **38)** Shikoku Broadc. Co., Ltd., 5-2, Nakatokushima-cho 2-chome, Tokushima 770-8573. **Web:** www.jrt.co.jp – **39)** Osaka Broadc. Corp., 2-4, Benten 1-chome, Minato-ku, Osaka 552-8501. **Web:** www.obc1314.co.jp – **40)** Tokai Radio Broadc. Co., Ltd., 14-27, Higashisakura 1-chome, Higashi-ku, Nagoya 461-8503. **Web:** www.tokairadio.co.jp – **41)** Chugoku Broadc. Co., Ltd., 21-3, Moto-machi, Naka-ku, Hiroshima 730-8504. **Web:** www.rcc.net – **42)** Shizuoka Broadc. System, 1-1, Toro 3-chome, Shizuoka 422-8680. **Web:** www.digisbs.com – **43)** RF Radio Nippon Co., Ltd., 5-85, Choja-machi, Naka-ku, Yokohama 231-8611. **Web:** www.jorf.co.jp – **44)** Wakayama Broadc. System, 3-3, Minato-hon-machi, Wakayama 640-8577. **Web:** http://wbs.co.jp – **45)** Gifu Broadc. System, 8, Imako-machi, Gifu 500-8588. **Web:** www.zf-web.com – **46)** Nishi-nippon Broadc. Co., Ltd., 8-15, Marunouchi, Takamatsu 760-8575.**Web:** www.rnc.co.jp – **47)** Sanyo Broadc. Co., Ltd., 1-3, Marunouchi 2-chome, Okayama 700-8580. **Web:** www.rsk.co.jp.
V: Most st's verify by QSL-card. Rec acc. Rp.

NIKKEI RADIO BROADCASTING CORPORATION (RADIO NIKKEI)

✉ 9-15, Akasaka 1-chome, Minato-ku, Tokyo 107-8373 ☎ +81 3 3583 8151 🖷 +81 3 3583 7441 **Web:** www.radionikkei.jp

Call	kHz	kW	Prgr	Call	kHz	kW	Prgr
JOZ	3925	50	1	JOZ6	6115	50	2
JOZ4	*3925	10	1	JOZ3	9595	50	1
JOZ5	3945	10	2	JOZ7	9760	50	2
JOZ2	6055	50	1				

There are satellite channels for both prgrs. *) Nemuro; others Nagara(Chiba)

1st Prgr: 2030-1400(Thu 1530, Fri 1500, Sat 1430, Sun 1250) on 3925/ 6055/9595 kHz; as above except 2300-0750 on 3925 kHz (Nemuro). Weather map: 2030.

2nd Prgr: 2300-0900 Fri & Sat only.

IS: Slow tempo chime with Japanese instrument "Koto" at sign on and sign off – **V.** by QSL card. Rp.

COMMERCIAL FM STATIONS

	Call	MHz	kW	Name, location and schedule
1)	QU	76.1	1	FM Iwate, Morioka
2)	LU	76.1	1	FM Fukui, Fukui
3)	DW	76.1	10	Inter FM, Tokyo
4)	FW	76.1	1	Love FM, Fukuoka
5)	SV	76.4	1	R. Berry, Utsunomiya
6)	AW	76.5	10	FM CO-CO-LO, Osaka: 1700-2130 (not Sun)
7)	VV	76.8	1	FM Okayama, Okayama
8)	UV	77.0	1	E-Radio, Otsu
9)	JU	77.1	5	Date FM, Sendai
10)	SU	77.4	1	FM Naka Kyushu, Kumamoto
11)	VU	77.4	0.5	V-air, Matsue
12)	XU	77.5	1	FM Niigata, Niigata
13)		77.6	1	Kiss-FM, Himeji
14)	QV	77.8	10	ZIP FM, Nagoya
15)	NV	77.9	0.5	FM Saga, Saga
16)	GV	78.0	5	BAY-FM, Chiba: 1920-2000 (not Sun)
17)	GU	78.2	1	Hiroshima FM, Hiroshima
18)	YU	78.6	1	FM Kagawa, Takamatsu 24h
19)	RV	78.7	3	CROSS FM, Kitakyushu (Fukuoka)
20)	NU	78.9	3	FM Mie, Tsu
21)	WV	79.0	1	FM Port, Niigata: 1600-2100 (not SS)
22)	KU	79.2	1	K-MIX, Hamamatsu, Shizuoka
23)	UU	79.2	1	FM Yamaguchi, Yamaguchi
24)	HU	79.5	1	Smile-FM, Nagasaki
25)	DV	79.5	5	NACK 5, Saitama
26)	GW	79.5	5	Radio-I, Nagoya
27)	EU	79.7	1	FM Ehime, Matsuyama 2057-1803 (Sun1633)
28)	ZU	79.7	1	FM Nagano, Matsumoto (Nagano)
29)	OV	79.8	1	μ FM, Kagoshima
30)	WU	80.0	1	FM Aomori, Aomori
31)	AU	80.0	10	Tokyo FM, Tokyo
32)	XV	80.0	1	Radio 80, Ogaki (Gifu)
33)	FV	80.2	10	FM 802, Osaka
34)	FU	80.4	5	AIR-G', Sapporo
35)	EV	80.4	1	Boy FM, Yamagata
36)	HV	80.5	1	FM Ishikawa, Kanazawa
37)	CU	80.7	10	FM Aichi, Nagoya
38)	MV	80.7	1	FM Tokushima, Tokushima
39)	DU	80.7	3	FM Fukuoka, Fukuoka
40)	AV	81.3	10	J-WAVE, Tokyo
41)	LV	81.6	0.5	FM Kochi, Kochi
42)	TV	81.8	1	Fukushima FM, Fukushima
43)	PV	82.5	5	FM North Wave, Sapporo
44)	OU	82.7	1	FM Toyama, Toyama
45)	PU	82.8	3	FM Akita, Akita
46)	CV	83.0	1	FM Fuji, Kofu 2000-1800(Sun 1600)
47)	MU	83.2	1	Joy FM, Miyazaki
48)	TU	84.7	5	FM Yokohama, Yokohama
49)	BU	85.1	10	FM Osaka, Osaka, 24h
50)	RU	86.3	1	FM Gunma, Maebashi
12)		86.5	1	FM Niigata, Yamato
11)		86.6	1	V-air, Hamada
51)	IU	87.3	1	FM Okinawa, Naha
52)	JV	88.0	1	FM Oita, Oita
53)	KV	89.4	3	Alpha-Station, Kyoto
13)	IV	89.9	1	Kiss-FM, Kobe

Relay st's below 1kW and the Community sts are not included.

Call JO(call)-FM. Schedule: 24h unless otherwise indicated above. Most 24h sts are off the air for 2 to 5 hours until 1900, 2000 or 2100 on Sun.

Addresses and other information:

1) Iwate FM Broadc. Co., Ltd., 8-17, Morioka-Ekimaedori, Morioka 020-8512. **Web:** www.fmii.co.jp – **2)** Fukui FM Broadc. Co., Ltd., 1-1, Miyuki 1-chome, Fukui 910-8553. **Web:** www.fmfukui.jp – **3)** FM Inter-wave Inc., 5-4, Shibaura 4-chome, Minato-ku, Tokyo 108-8070 - Prgr. in English & foreign languages. A satellite audio service also exists. **Web:** www.interfm.co.jp – **4)** Kyushu International FM Inc., 5-35, Tenjin 2-chome, Chuo-ku, Fukuoka 810-8565. Prgr in English, Chinese and Korean etc. **Web:** www.lovefm.co.jp – **5)** FM Tochigi Co., Ltd., 1-19, Ichijo 3-chome, Utsunomiya 320-8550. **Web:** www.berry. co.jp – **6)** Kansai Intermedia Corp., 14-16, Nanko Kita 1-chome, Suminoe-ku, Osaka 559-8522. Foreign language prgr. in English, Chinese, Korean, etc. **Web:** www.cocolo.co.jp – **7)** Okayama FM Broadc. Co., Ltd., 8-45, Nakasange 1-chome, Okayama 700-0821. **Web:** www.fm-okayama.co.jp – **8)** FM Shiga Co., Ltd., 19-10, Nishinosho, Otsu 520-0818. **Web:** www.e-radio.co.jp – **9)** Sendai FM Broadc., Inc., 10-28, Honcho 2-chome, Aoba-ku, Sendai 980-8420. **Web:** www.datefm.co.jp – **10)** FM Nakakyushu Broadc. Co., Ltd., 5-50, Chibajomachi, Kumamoto 860-0001. **Web:** www.fmk.fm **F.PI** The company will change the station name as FM Kumamoto on Apr. 1, 2005 – **11)** San-in FM Broadc. Co., Ltd., 383, Tono-machi, Matsue 690-8508. **Web:** www.fm-sanin.co.jp – **12)** FM Radio Niigata Co., Ltd., 3-5, Saiwainishi 4-chome, Niigata 950-8581. **Web:** www.fmniigata.com – **13)** Hyogo FM Radio Broadc. Co., Ltd., 5-4 Hatoba-cho, Chuo-ku, Kobe 650-8589. **Web:** www.kiss-fm.co.jp – **14)** FM Nagoya Inc., 20-17, Marunouchi 3-chome, Naka-ku, Nagoya 460-8578. **Web:** http://zip-fm.co.jp – **15)** FM Saga Co., Ltd., 286-5, Fukuro, Honjo-Machi, Saga 840-0023. **Web:** www.fmsaga.co.jp – **16)** FM Sound Chiba Co., Ltd., 11-1, Chuo 1-chome, Chuo-ku, Chiba 260-8625. **Web:** www.bayfm.co.jp – **17)** Hiroshima FM Broadc. Co., Ltd., 8-2, Minamimachi 1-chome, Minami-ku, Hiroshima 734-8511. **Web:** http://hfmweb.jp – **18)** FM Kagawa Broadc. Co., Ltd., 4-23, Saiho-cho 1-chome, Takamatsu 760-8584. **Web:** www.fmkagawa.co.jp – **19)** FM Kyushu Co., Ltd., 9-11, Furusenba-machi, Kokurakita-ku, Kitakyushu 802-8570. **Web:** www.crossfm.co.jp – **20)** Mie FM Broadc. Co., Ltd., 1043-1, Yakio, Kannonji-cho, Tsu 514-8505. **Web:** www.fmmie.co.jp – **21)** Niigata Kenmin FM Broadc. Co., Ltd., 1-1, Bandai 2-chome, Niigata 950-8579. **Web:** www.fmport.com – **22)** Shizuoka FM. Broadc. Co., Ltd., 133-24, Tokiwa-cho, Hamamatsu 430-8575. **Web:** www.k-mix.co.jp – **23)** FM Yamaguchi Co., Ltd., 3-31, Midori-cho, Yamaguchi 753-8521. **Web:** www.fmy.co.jp – **24)** FM Nagasaki Co., Ltd., 5-5, Sakae-machi, Nagasaki 850-8550. **Web:** www.smilefm.co.jp – **25)** FM Nack 5 Co. Ltd., 16-2, Tokiwa 4-chome, Urawa-ku, Saitama 330-8579. **Web:** www.nack5.co.jp – **26)** Aichi International Broadc. Co., Ltd., 10-37, Higashisakura 1-chome, Higashi-ku, Nagoya 461-8639. Prgr in English & foreign languages. **Web:** www.radio-i.co.jp – **27)** FM Ehime Broadc. Co., 10-7, Takewara-machi 1-chome, Matsuyama 790-8565. **Web:** www.joeufm.co.jp – **28)** Nagano FM Broadc. Co., Ltd., 13-5, Honjo 1-chome, Matsumoto 390-8520. **Web:** www.fmnagano.co.jp – **29)** FM Kagoshima Co., Ltd., 1-38, Higashisengoku-cho, Kagoshima 892-8579. **Web:** www.myufm.jp – **30)** Aomori FM Broadc. Co., Ltd., 7-19, Tsutsumi-machi 1-chome, Aomori 030-8691. **Web:** www.afb. co.jp – **31)** Tokyo FM Broadc. Co., Ltd., 1-7 Kojimachi, Chiyoda-ku, Tokyo 102-8080. **Web:** www.tfm.co.jp – **32)** Gifu FM Broadc. Co., Ltd., 35-10, Kono 4-chome, Ogaki 503-8580. **Web:** www.radio-80.com – **33)** FM 802 Co., Ltd., Kita 2-6, Tenjinbashi 2-chome, Kita-ku, Osaka 530-8580. **Web:** http://funky802.com – **34)** FM Hokkaido Broadc. Co., Ltd., 1, Nishi 2-chome, kita 1-jo, Chuo-ku, Sapporo 060-8532. **Web:** www.air-g.co.jp – **35)** Yamagata FM Broadc. Co., Ltd., 14-69, Matsuyama 3-chome, Yamagata 990-9543. **Web:** www.boyfm.co.jp – **36)** FM Ishikawa Broadc. Co., Ltd., 1-45, Hikoso-machi 2-chome, Kanazawa 920-8605. **Web:** www.fmishikawa.co.jp – **37)** FM Aichi Broadc. Co., Ltd., 15-18, Chiyoda 2-chome, Naka-ku, Nagoya 460-8388. **Web:** http://fma.co.jp – **38)** FM Tokushima Broadc. Co., 1-6, Saiwai-cho, Tokushima 770-8567. **Web:** www.fm-tokushima.co.jp – **39)** Fukuoka FM Broadc. Co., Ltd., 1-82, Watanabe-dori 2-chome, Chuo-ku, Fukuoka 810-8575. **Web:** http://fmfukuoka.co.jp – **40)** J-WAVE Inc., Roppongi Hills Mori Tower 33F, 10-1, Roppongi 6-chome, Tokyo 106-8088. A satellite audio service also exists. **Web:** www.j-wave.co.jp – **41)** FM Kochi Broadc. Co., Ltd., 3-21, Hon-machi 3-chome, Kochi 780-8532. **Web:** www.fmkochi.com – **42)** FM Fukushima Inc., 6-6, Sakae-machi, Fukushima 960-8031 **Web:** www.fmf.co.jp – **43)** FM North Wave Co., Ltd., 3-1, Nishi 4-chome, Kita 7-jo, Kita-ku, Sapporo 060-8557. **Web:** www.fmnorth.co.jp – **44)** Toyama FM Broadc. Co., Ltd., 2-11, Okuda-machi, Toyama 930-8567. **Web:** www.fmtoyama.co.jp – **45)** FM Akita Broadc. Co.,Ltd., 7-10, Yabase Honcho 3-chome, Akita 010-0973. **Web:** www.fm akita.co.jp **46)** FM Fuji Co., Ltd., 7-23, Marunouchi 2-chome, Kofu 400-8550. **Web:** www.fmfuji.co.jp – **47)** Miyazaki FM Broadc. Co., Ltd., 2-78 Gion, Miyazaki 880-8583. **Web:** www.joyfm.co.jp – **48)** Yokohama FM Broadc. Co., Ltd., 2-1, Minato-Mirai 2-chome, Nishi-ku, Yokohama 220-8110. **Web:** www.fmyokohama.co.jp – **49)** FM Osaka Co., Ltd., 3-1, Minatomachi 1-chome, Naniwa-ku, Osaka 556-8510. **Web:** www.fmosaka.net – **50)** Gunma FM Broadc.

Co., Ltd., 4-8, Wakamiyacho 1-chome, Maebashi 371-8533. **Web:** www.fmgunma.com – **51)** FM Okinawa Broadc. Corp., 40, Kowan, Urasoe, Okinawa 901-2525. **Web:** www.fmokinawa.co.jp – **52)** FM Oita Broadc., Co., Ltd., 17-19, Higashi kasuga-machi, Oita 870-8558. **Web:** www.fmoita.co.jp – **53)** FM Kyoto, Inc., 98, Matsumoto-cho, Kamigamo, Kita-ku, Kyoto 603-8588. **Web:** http://fm-kyoto.jp
V. Most sts verify by QSL card. Rec acc. Rp.

UNIVERSITY BROADCASTING STATION

Hoso Daigaku, 2-11, Wakaba, Mihama-ku, Chiba 261-8586 ☎ +81 43 276 5111 **Web:** www.u-air.ac.jp **Pub:** Textbooks for their students.
FM: JOUD-FM 77.1MHz 10kW Tokyo. 78.8MHz 1kW Maebashi. A satellite channel also exists. **D. Prgr:** 2100-1500. **V.** by QSL card. Rp.

Digital Radio

A digital system has been tested in Tokyo and Osaka by the Digital Radio Promotion Association (DRP) since October 2003. The service is not DAB, but the ISDB-T system (Integrated Services Digital Broadcasting for Terrestrial).

Location	Call	MHz	kW
Tokyo	JOAZ-FM	190.214286	0.80
Osaka	JOBZ-FM	190.214286	0.24

AMERICAN FORCES NETWORK (AFN) (U.S. Mil.)

The network serves the members of the US forces. The sts in Japan broadcast by authority of Commander, US Forces, Japan, in cooperation with the Information and Communications Policy Bureau in Japan. Sts are linked by land line and microwave.
AFN Tokyo, Yokota Air Base, Fussa, Tokyo 197-0001 ☎ +81 42 552 2511 ext 52379 **Email:** afn.eagle810radio@yokota.af.mil or afnews.det10bg@yokota.af.mil **Web:** www.yokota.af.mil/afn
Other sts: **AFN Okinawa** – Okinawa. **Email:** afnokinawa@mcbbutler.usmc.mil – **AFN Misawa** – Misawa, Aomori. **Email:** afn@misawa.af.mil **Web:** www.misawa.af.mil/default.asp?org=associates_afn – **AFN Iwakuni** – Iwakuni, Yamaguchi. **Email:** det13bg@iwakuni.usmc.mil **Web:** www.iwakuni.usmc.mil/afn/newafn.htm – **AFN Sasebo** – Sasebo, Nagasaki. **Email:** afn-marquardt@cfas.navy.mil

MW	kHz	kW	MW	kHz	kW
Okinawa	648	10	Misawa	1575	0.6
Tokyo	810	50	Iwakuni	1575	1
Sasebo	1575	0.25			

FM: Okinawa 89.1MHz 20kW.
D. Prgr: 24h. **N:** on the h. **ANN:** "This is the Armed Forces Radio and Television Service". "This is Eagle 810" for AFN Tokyo. **V.** by QSL card.

JORDAN

L.T: UTC +2h (31 Mar-29 Sept UTC +3h) — **Pop:** 5m — **Pr.L:** Arabic — **E.C:** 50Hz, 230V — **ITU:** JOR

MINISTRY OF INFORMATION AND COMMUNICATIONS TECHNOLOGY (MOICT)

8th Circle, Bayader Wadi Al Seer, P.O. Box 9903, Amman 11191 ☎ +962 6 5859001 🖷 +962 6 5861059 **Web:** www.moict.gov.jo

JORDAN RADIO AND TELEVISION CORPORATION (JRTV)

P.O. Box 909, Amman ☎ +962 6 77311/9 🖷 +962 6 4778578 **Web**: www.jrtv.jo/rj **Email:** rj@jrtv.gov.jo
L.P: DG: Ihsan Ramzi. Dir. Radio: Hashem Khresat. Dir. Eng: Fawzi Saleh. Dir. Eng (Radio): Yousef Al-Areeny. Dir. Int. Rel: Mrs. Fatima Massri. Dir. Arabic Services: Muhammad Sarayrah. Dir. Foreign Services: Haytham Atum.

MW	kHz	kW	Prgr.	Times
Amman	612	200	Arabic	24h
unk. location	693	-	Arabic	24h
Ajlun	801	2000*	Arabic	24h
Amman	855	10	English	0500-2200
unk. location	1035	-	Arabic	24h
Aqaba	1485	5	Arabic	24h
Al Karanah	1494	1000	Arabic	24h

*Running on lower power.

FM	Arabic	English	French	Quran	kW
Ajlun	105.0	90.9	90.0		5
Amman	88.0	96.3		93.1	3/120/10
	99.0				0.6
Aqaba	105.4			91.5	3
Irbid	95.4			91.5	0.5

Main Arabic sce: 24h. **N:** on the h. (not 0400, 1100 Fri, 1300, 1700). Jordanian Armed Forces R: 1300-1500. Also relayed on SW. **English prgr:** 0400-2400. **N:** 0500, 0800, 1000 (not Fri), 1100MF, 1200, 1400, 1600, 1700, 1900, 2000, 2100. **French:** 1600-2400. **Quran Prgr:** 0500-2200.
ANN: Arabic: "Huna Amman, Idha'atu-l-Mamlakah al-Urdoniyah al-Hashemiyah". Armed forces R: "Idha'at Al-Quwaat Al-Musalah al-Urdoniyah, al-Gayish al-Arabi". E: "This is R. Jordan broadcastng from Amman".

EXTERNAL SERVICES: R. Jordan

see International Radio section.

RADIO FANN (operated by the Jordan Armed Forces)

Amman **Web:** www.radiofann.com **Email:** requests@radiofann.com **L.P:** Dir: Nadine Querish.
FM(MHz): Aqaba 91.1, Irbid 91.3, Ajlun-Karak 94.3, Tafileh 94.7, Amman 104.2, Petra/Azraq 105.4. **D.Prgr:** 24h in **Arabic.**

Other stations:
MBC FM: Amman 106.7MHz. See main entry under UAE.
R. Orient, Deir al-Acher: 88.3MHz. See main entry under France.
R. Sawa: Amman 98.1MHz, Ajlun 107.4MHz. Main entry under USA.
BBC Arabic Sce: Amman 103.1MHz 5kW, Ajlun 89.1MHz.
R. Monte-Carlo Moyen-Orient: Amman 97.4MHz, Ajlun 106.2MHz.

KAZAKHSTAN

L.T: UTC +5h (West Kazakhstan: +4h; East Kazakhstan: +6h); 27 Mar - 30 Oct 2005: UTC +5/6/7h — **Pop:** 16,8 million — **Pr.L:** Kazakh, Russian — **E.C:** 50Hz, 220V — **ITU:** KAZ

QAZAQSTANNYNG TELEDIDARY ZHÄNE RADIOSY RESPUBLIKALYQ KORORATSIYASYNYNG (Republican Corp. "TV and Radio Kazakhstan", Gov.)

Almaty broadcasting house: Zheltoqsan köshesi 175a, 480013 Almaty. ☎ +7 3272 635629. 🖷 +7 3272 631968.
Astana broadcasting house: Moskva köshesi 49, 473032 Astana. ☎ +7 3172 327153. 🖷 +7 3172 327153. **Email:** teleradio@nursat.kz.
L.P: Gen. Dir: Torekhan Daniyarov.

MW	kHz	kW	MW	kHz	kW
Almaty	1098	150	Almaty	**1341	30
Abay	*1188	-	Qyzylorda	*1440	-
Astana	*1197	-			

*) carries BBC prgr's after c/d;**) also carries VOA/RFE-RL prgr's

FM (MHz)	QR	ShR		QR	ShR
Almaty	101.0	106.5	Ösqemen	101.4	-
Astana	106.4	101.4	Qyzyorda	102.0	-
Pavlodar	103.0		Taraz	101.0	-

+ nationwide OIRT FM network. The CCIR FM network for both prgr's is due to be expanded.
D.PRGR: Qazaq Radiosy (QR) in Kazakh, Russian 0100-1800 (joint prgr from Almaty and Astana studios). – **Shalqar Radiosy (ShR)** in Kazkh: 0000-1800.

REGIONAL SERVICES (Gov.)

Regional state broadcasting companies (OTRK = oblysynyn teleradio kompaniyasy) serve the 14 Kazakh provinces. These companies are broadcasting on own frequencies (mostly OIRT FM) at various times in Kazakh and numerous languages of ethnic minorities (Russian, German, Ukrainian, etc).

Manghqystau OTRK: 24 mkrn. TS, 466200 Aqtau. - **Aqtöbe OTRK:** 50 let Oktyabrya köshesi 54, 463022 Aqtöbe. - **Atyrau OTRK:** P.O.Box 4, 465027 Atyrau. – **Onghtüstik Qazaqstan OTRK:** Nekrasov köshesi 15, 486024 Shymkent. – **Zhambyl OTRK:** Kumzhat köshesi, 484000 Taraz. - **Qaraghandy OTRK:** Voinov-Internatsionalistov köshesi 14, 470061 Qaraghandy: in Kazakh, Russian on 747kHz (20kW). Also relays RFE-RL. Email: kartv@tv.krg.kz. – **Aqmola OTRK:** Pushkin köshesi 54, 458000 Qostanay. Email: otrk@mail.kst.kz – **Kökshetau OTRK:** Sovetskaya köshesi 141, 475000 Kökshetau. – **Pavlodar OTRK:** P.O.Box 332, 637002 Pavlodar. On 100.5MHz & FM network. - **Semey OTRK:** Shugayev köshesi 157, 490018 Semey. – **Soltüstik Qazaqstan OTRK:** Proletarskaya köshesi 1, 642000 Petropavl. – **Batys Qazaqstan OTRK:** Lenin dangyla 204, 417000 Oral. – **Shyghyz Qazaqstan OTRK:** Stakhanov köshesi 70, 492018 Ösqemen: 0100-0400, 1500-1800 in Russian, Kazakh on 1071kHz (100 kW). Email: vktrk@ukg.kz. Also relays R.Rossii & R.Mayak from Russia, and RFE-RL (USA).

OTHER STATIONS

FM	MHz	kW	Location	Station
12)	66.26		Qaraghandy	R. Terra
A)	66.80	4	Shymkent	BBC
18)	68.27	-	Aqtöbe	R. Rifma
17)	69.38	4	Qostanay	R. Bars
A)	70.19	0.1	Shymkent	RFE-RL
28)	70.28		Lísakovsk	R. Rauan
15A)	70.58		Temirtaú	R. 102
B)	71.21	1	Semey	RFE-RL
9)	71.33	-	Balqash	R. dlya vsekh
7)	71.51	-	Almaty	R. 31
27)	71.93	-	Pavlodar	R. Irbis
25)	72.77	-	Semey	R. Bekzat
26)	72.80	-	Petropavl	R. Kamerton
23)	72.83	-	Aqtöbe	R. Retro
35)	72.98	-	Ösqemen	R. Lira
36)	73.31	-	Aqtöbe	R. Maks
14)	73.76	-	Ösqemen	R. Miks
8)	91.75	-	Almaty	R. Retro-Karavan
1)	100.2	0.1	Qostanay	Europa+ Kazakhstan
2)	100.5	-	Ösqemen	Russkoye R.
1)	100.5	0.25	Lísakovsk	Europa+ Kazakhstan
16)	100.6	0.1	Oral	R. Talap
2)	100.6	-	Aqtöbe	Russkoye R.
13)	101.2	-	Qaraghandy	R. Teks
32)	101.2	-	Shymkent	R. UMAX
1)	101.4	0.1	Kachíry	Europa+ Kazakhstan
29)	101.4	-	Aqtöbe	Aqtöbe Radio
34)	101.5	-	Qostanay	Novoye R KN
1)	101.5	0.1	Zyryanovsk	Europa+ Kazakhstan
3A)	101.6	0.5	Petropavl	NS Radio
2)	101.7	-	Shymkent	Russkoye R.
1)	101.8	0.1	Ösqemen	Europa+ Kazakhstan
2)	102.0	-	Kökshetaú	Russkoye R.
1)	102.0	0.1	Zhezqazghan	Europa+ Kazakhstan
15B)	102.0	-	Temirtaú	R. DV-Temirtau
1)	102.0	0.1	Taldyqorghan	Europa+ Kazakhstan
30)	102.1	-	Aqtaú	R. RIF
6)	102.2	-	Almaty	R. Shakhar
2)	102.2	-	Oral	Russkoye R.
2)	102.6	-	Stepnogorsk	Russkoye R.
3A)	102.7	0.1	Lenínogorsk	NS Radio
3A)	102.6	0.25	Balqash	NS Radio
2)	102.8	-	Qaraghandy	Russkoye R.
2)	102.8	-	Qyzylorda	Russkoye R.
10)	102.8	-	Almaty	Hit FM Khabar
2)	103.0	-	Qostanay	Russkoye R.
1)	103.0	0.1	Atbasar	Europa+ Kazakhstan
22)	103.1	-	Aqtöbe	R. Tolkyn
1)	103.1	0.1	Lenínogorsk	Europa+ Kazakhstan
11)	103.2	-	Astana	R. Tsesna
1)	103.2	-	Aqsay	Europa+ Kazakhstan
19A)	103.3	-	Rúdnyy	R. Sana
3A)	103.3	0.1	Zyryanovsk	NS Radio
1)	103.5	0.1	Shymkent	Europa+ Kazakhstan
7)	103.5	-	Almaty	R. 31
2)	103.6	-	Taldyqorghan	Russkoye R.
1)	103.6	0.1	Arqalyq	Europa+ Kazakhstan
1)	103.6	0.1	Petropavl	Europa+ Kazakhstan
1)	103.6	0.1	Qyzylorda	Europa+ Kazakhstan
25)	103.6		Atyraú	R. Atyraú-Tandem
3A)	103.7	0.25	Zhezqazghan	NS Radio
)	103.8	0.5	Aqtaú	TOO Batys
3A)	103.9	0.5	Taraz	NS Radio
2)	103.9	0.25	Semey	Russkoye R.
5)	104.0	-	Almaty	Nashe Radio
1)	104.0	0.1	Qaraghandy	Europa+ Kazakhstan
21)	104.0	-	Zyryanovsk	R. SKAD
2)	104.1	-	Astana	Russkoye R.
1)	104.2	-	Kökshetaú	Europa+ Kazakhstan
33)	104.2	0.25	Türkistan	TOO Ayna
3A)	104.2	0.25	Ekibastuz	NS Radio
1)	104.3	0.1	Stepnogorsk	Europa+ Kazakhstan
31)	104.6	-	Aqtaú	Aqtau-Tandem
3A)	104.6	0.5	Oral	NS Radio
3A)	104.6	0.25	Lisakovsk	NS Radio
24)	104.7	-	Aqtöbe	R. Tandem
2)	104.7	-	Almaty	Russkoye R.
1)	105.0	1	Astana	Europa+ Kazakhstan
3A)	105.0	0.25	Aqsay	NS Radio
3A)	105.0	0.25	Semey	NS Radio
2)	105.1		Balqash	Russkoye R.
1)	105.1	0.25	Türkistan	Europa+ Kazakhstan
1)	105.2	0.25	Ekibastuz	Europa+ Kazakhstan
1)	105.2	0.1	Taraz	Europa+ Kazakhstan
2)	105.2	-	Atyraú	Russkoye R.
2)	105.2	-	Arqalyq	Russkoye R.
2)	105.2	-	Zhezqazghan	Russkoye R.
2)	105.2	-	Petropavl	Russkoye R.
2)	105.4	-	Aqtaú	Russkoye R.
4)	105.4	-	Almaty	Avtoradio
3A)	105.4	0.1	Taldyqorghan	NS Radio
3A)	105.6	-	Qaraghandy	NS Radio
18)	105.7	-	Aqtöbe	R. Rifma
3A)	105.7	0.25	Kökshetaú	NS Radio
1)	105.8	0.25	Semey	Europa+ Kazakhstan
3A)	105.9	-	Astana	R. NS
3A)	105.9	-	Shymkent	R. NS
3B)	106.0	-	Almaty	Ekho Moskvy
2)	106.2	-	Pavlodar	Russkoye R.
2)	106.4	-	Taraz	Russkoye R.
1)	106.5	0.1	Oral	Europa+ Kazakhstan
1)	106.8	0.1	Atyraú	Europa+ Kazakhstan
1)	106.8	-	Aqtöbe	Europa+ Kazakhstan
19B)	106.9	-	Rúdnyy	Rúdnyy daúysy
1)	107.0	1	Almaty	Europa+ Kazakhstan
3A)	107.0	0.5	Qostanay	NS Radio
1)	107.0	0.1	Aqtaú	Europa+ Kazakhstan
20)	107.0	-	Semey	R. 7
12)	107.0	-	Qaraghandy	R. Terra
3A)	107.0	-	Ösqemen	NS Radio
3A)	107.7	0.5	Qyzylorda	NS Radio
3A)	107.9	0.5	Atyraú	NS Radio

Addresses & other information:
1) Respublik alana 13, 480013 Almaty. Email: europa_plus_radio@kaznet.kz – **2)** Respublik alana 13, 480013 Almaty. Email: rosradio_office@nursat.kz – **3A,B)** P.O.Box 93, 480036 Almaty. Email: radio@root.nsgroup.asdc.kz – **4)** Zheltoqsan kösh. 177a, 480012 Almaty. Email: avtoradio@kaznet.kz – **5)** 480000 Almaty. Email: 104@nashe.kz – **6)** Bogenbay batyr kösh. 156, 480083 Almaty. Email: shahar@lorton.com – **7)** Abay kösh. 76/109, 480008 Almaty. Email: radio31@kaznet.kz – **8)** Respublik alana 13, 480013 Almaty. Email: radio@ktk.caravan.kz – **9)** Karamende-bi köshesi 13, 473210 Balqash. – **10)** Respublik alana 13, 480013 Almaty. Email: radiokhabar@banknet.kz – **11)** Serov kösh. 5, 473037 Astana. Email: astv@keter.kz – **12)** P.O.Box 197, 470061 Qaraghandy. Email: terra@mail.krg.kz – **13)** Panfilov kösh. 30, 470077 Qaraghandy. Email: tex@sys-pro.com – **14)** P.O.Box 3166, 492022 Ösqemen. Email: rmix@sigma-east.com – **15A,B)** Mir kösh. 55/1-3-29, 472300 Temirtau. Email: tkt@temirtau.kz – **16)** Pochitalin kösh. 124, 417000 Oral. Email: talap@nursat.kz – **17)** Lenin kösh. 124, 458003 Qostanay. Email: info@alau.com – **18)** P.O.Box 107, 463000 Aqtöbe. Email: rifma@kaznet.kz – **19A,B)** Korchagín kösh. 76, 459120 Rudnyy. Email: sanatv@mail.ru – **20)** 490000 Semey. – **21)** Sovetskaya köshesi 31, 493730 Zyryanovsk. Email: info@alsiscad.com – **22)** 463000 Aqtöbe. – **23)** 463000 Aqtöbe. – **24)** 463000 Aqtöbe. – **25)** Atyraú. – **26)** Pervomayskaya kösh. 69, 643000 Petropavlovsk. – **27)** P.O.Box 332, 637002 Pavlodar. Email: inbox@irbistv.kz – **28)** Uzel telekommunikatsii, 459335 Lisakovsk. – **29)** Maresyev kösh. 2a, 463000 Aqtöbe. Email: aktoberadio@inbox.ru – **30)** 2-mkr, KAZKOR building, 466200 Aqtaú. Email: rostmistroff@atis.kz – **31)** 3-mkr 73, 466200 Aqtaú. Email: tandem@atis.kz – **32)** Tauke-Khana alana 12a, Shymkent. Email: umaks@novicom.kz – **33)** Türkistan. – **34)** 458000 Qostanay. – **35)** 492022 Ösqemen. – **36)** 463000 Aqtöbe. – **A)** BBC relay (cf. UK) – **B)** RFE-RL relay (cf. USA) – **C)** VOA relay (cf. USA).

KENYA

L.T: UTC +3h — **Pop:** 31million — **Pr.L:** English, Swahili, Kikuyu, Luhya, Luo, Kalenjin, Somali, others — **E.C:** 50Hz, 240V — **ITU:** KEN

COMMUNICATIONS COMMISSION OF KENYA (CCK)
(Regulatory authority for telecommunications and the electronic media)
✉ P. O. Box 14448, Nairobi ☎ +254 20 240165/173 🖷 +254 20 252547 **Web:** www.cck.go.ke **Email:** info@cck.go.ke

KENYA BROADCASTING CORPORATION (KBC)
✉ P.O. Box 30456, Harry Thuku Rd, Nairobi 00100 ☎ +254 20 334567/223757 🖷 +254 20 220675 **Web:** www.kbc.co.ke **Email:** kbc@swiftkenya.com **Local** ✉ Box 799, Nyeri - Box 1585,

Nakuru - Box 1327, Meru - Box 3287, Kibirichia - Box 90200, Mombasa - Box 844, Kisumu - Box 38, Maralal.
L.P: Chairman: James Kangwana. MD: Wachira Waruru. Deputy MD: Dr. Lewis Odhiambo.

MW	kHz	kW	Netw.	MW	kHz	kW	Netw.
Voi	540	100	S	Malindi	927	100	S
Kapsimotwa+	558	20	W	Nyamninia+	954	100	E
Garissa	567	50	S	Voi	981	100	E
Ngong++	612	100	S	Malindi	1044*	100	E
Garissa	639	50	E	Maralal	1107	100	S
Marsabit	675	50	S	Kitale	1134	50	E
Marania+++	702	100	S	Wajir	1152	50	S
Ngong++	747	100	E	Marsabit	1233	50	E
Nyamninia+	846	100	S	Ngong++	1269	20	C
Kitale	882	50	S	Wajir	1305	50	E
Marania+++	900	100	E	Maralal	1386	100	E

+) near Kisumu, ++) near Nairobi, +++) near Meru. *= inactive

SW: Langata (Nairobi) (G.C: 01S21 036E47) 4915kHz 10kW, MF 0300-0700, 1300-1905 (rel. North Eastern Sce).

FM:

Site	S	E	N	C	W	Metro	Coro	Pwani
Nairobi	89.3	97.3	89.5	89.9	-	-	91.9	-
Limuru	92.9	95.6	-	-	-	101.9	99.5	-
Malindi	90.3	93.6	-	-	-	-	-	-
Nyambene	90.5	103.5	-	-	-	-	-	-
Nyeri	87.6	100.7	-	-	-	97.0	102.3	-
Mombasa	100.8	104.4	-	-	-	89.1	-	103.0
Timboroa	88.6	91.5	-	-	-	-	-	-
Nakuru	-	-	-	-	-	94.4	-	-
Eldoret	-	-	-	-	-	98.0	-	-
Kapsimotwa	-	-	-	-	-	100.9	-	-
Kisumu	-	-	-	-	100.2	-	-	-

Networks (from Nairobi studios unless stated):
S=Swahili Sce: 0200-2110 on MW and FM as above. Rel. China Radio International 1400-1430.
E=English Sce: 0200-2110 on MW and FM. Rel. China Radio International 1430-1500. **N:** Main bulletins at 0400, 0600, 1000, 1300, 1600, 1800. Headlines on the hour at most other times.
N=(North) Eastern Sce. in Somali, Borana, Burji, Rendile and Turkana: MF 0300-0700, 1300-1905 on SW and FM.
C=Central Sce. in Kiembu, Kikamba, Kimasai and Kimeru: Mon-Sat 0200-0700, 1400-2010 on MW and FM.
W=Western Sce. from Kisumu studios in Kalenjin, Kisii, Kuria, Luhya, Luo, Pokot, Suba and Teso: MF 0300-2005, SS 0900-2005 on MW and FM.
Metro FM in English/Swahili: 24h entertainment service on FM.
Coro FM in Kikuyu.
Pwani FM from Mombasa studios in Swahili/English/Arabic: P.O. Box 82006, Mombasa.
ANN: E: "This is KBC, Nairobi". S: "Hii ni KBC, Nairobi". **IS:** Flute & drum melody. National Anthem at s/on and s/off.

NATIONAL INDEPENDENT NETWORKS:

R. Citizen in Swahili/English (parent company is Royal Media Services Ltd): Maalim Juma Rd, (P.O. Box 7468), Nairobi 00300 ☎ +254 20 2721415/2721416, 2735062 (studio) 🖷 +254 20 2724220/2724211 **Email:** citizen@clubinternetk.com **L.P:** Owner: Samuel K. Macharia. Editor-in-chief: Herman Igambi. **FM:** Nairobi 106.7MHz, Kisumu 97.6MHz, Meru 94.3MHz, Mombasa 97.3MHz, Nakuru 100.5MHz, Nyeri 104.3MHz, Voi 91.8MHz, Western Kenya 90.4 & 94.5MHz. Royal Media Services Ltd also operates Inooro FM and R. Ramogi - see below.
Kiss 100 in English/Swahili (parent company is Radio Africa Ltd): Lion Place (3rd flr), Waiyaki Way, Westlands (P.O. Box 74497), Nairobi ☎ +254 20 4447403/4447409/4447411, 4244100 (studio) 🖷 +254 20 4447410 **Web:** www.kissfm.co.ke **Email:** info@kissfm.co.ke **L.P:** Chairman: Kiprono Kittony. MD: Patrick Quarcoo **FM:** Nairobi 100.3MHz, Eldoret 89.2MHz, Kisumu 92.6MHz, Mombasa 88.5MHz, Nakuru 98.1MHz. **F.PI:** Separate st. in Nairobi on 105.2MHz possibly to be called Soul FM.
Nation FM in English/Swahili (parent company is Nation Media Group Ltd): Nation Centre, Kimathi St (P.O. Box 49010), Nairobi 00100 ☎ +254 20 3208 8000 🖷 +254 20 213946 **Web:** www.nation-media.com/nationfm/home.asp **L.P:** CEO Nation Media Group: Wilfred D. Kiboro. MD Broadcasting Division: Cyrille Nabutola. PD: Phil Matthews. Tech Mgr: Yuvenalis Ayunga **FM:** Nairobi 96.4MHz, Eldoret 102.9MHz, Kisumu 102.1MHz, Mombasa 101.3MHz, Nakuru 97.6MHz, Nyeri 104.8MHz.

OTHER STATIONS IN NAIROBI:
Biblia Husema Broadcasting (Christian): P.O. Box 45019, Nairobi. **FM:** 90.9MHz and 96.9MHz – **Capital FM** (in English): Lonrho House (19th flr), Standard St (P.O. Box 74933), Nairobi. **Web:** www.capitalfm.co.ke **Email:** info@capitalfm.co.ke **FM:** 98.4MHz – **East Africa R.** (in English/Swahili - relay of station in Dar es Salaam, Tanzania): **FM:** 94.7MHz – **East FM** (Asian): Ellies Bldg (1st flr), Baricho Road, (P.O. Box 32364), Nairobi-Ngara. **Web:** www.eastfm.com **Email:** info@eastfm.com **FM:** 106.0MHz – **Family FM** (Christian). **Web:** www.familykenya.com/familyfm **Email**: info@familykenya.com **FM:** Nairobi 103.9MHz, Mombasa 97.9MHz, Nakuru 102.1MHz – **Hope FM** (Christian): Nairobi Pentecostal Church, P.O. Box 42254, Nairobi. **FM:** 93.3MHz. Also rel. The Voice (UK) – **Inooro FM** (owned by R. Citizen - see above): All prgr in Kikuyu. **FM:** Nairobi 99.2MHz, Nakuru 89.8MHz, Nyeri 97.8MHz – **Iqra FM** (Islamic programming in English, Somali, Swahili, Urdu): Bandari Plaza (7th flr), Woodvale Grove, Westlands (P.O. Box 45163), Nairobi. **Email:** iqrafm@bidii.com **FM:** 95.1MHz – **Kameme FM** (mainly in Kikuyu): Longonot Place (3rd flr), Kijabe St, (P.O. Box 49640), Nairobi 00100. **Web:** www.kameme.com **Email:** rreach@kamemefm.com **FM:** Nairobi 101.1MHz, Nyeri 92.3MHz. Also rel. BBC – **R. Ramogi** (owned by R. Citizen - see above): All prgr in Luo. **FM:** Nairobi 107.1MHz, Kisumu 107.6MHz, Nakuru 95.4MHz – **Sound Asia:** View Park Towers (21st flr), Monrovia St, (P.O. Box 12505), Nairobi. **Email:** soundasia@iconnect.co.ke **FM:** Nairobi 88.0MHz, Mombasa 89.9MHz – **R. Waumini** (Catholic Church): Sarit Centre, Thika Rd, P.O. Box 1373, Nairobi 00606. **Email:** radiowaumini@wananchi.com **FM:** 88.5MHz 4kW.

OTHER STATIONS IN MOMBASA:
Baraka FM (Christian: operated by FEBA): P.O. Box 87751, Mombasa. **FM:** 95.5MHz – **Pulse FM:** 91.5MHz – **Shakey FM:** 106.6MHz.

RELAYS OF INTERNATIONAL STATIONS:

BBC African Service (English/Swahili): Nairobi 93.7MHz, Mombasa 93.9MHz, Kisumu 88.2MHz. Also rel. at times via Kameme FM (see above). **F.PI:** Relays elsewhere.
Voice of America (English/Swahili): Nairobi 107.5MHz.
Radio France Int. (French/English): Mombasa 105.5MHz.

KIRIBATI

L.T: UTC +12h — **Pop:** 94,000 — **Radios:** 6,050 — **PrL**: I-Kiribati, English — **E.C:** 50Hz, 240V — **ITU:** KIR

RADIO KIRIBATI (A division of the Broadcasting and Publications Authority)

P.O. Box 78, Bairiki, Tarawa ☎ +686 21187 🖷 +686 21096 **Email:** bpa@tskl.net.ki **L.P:** Mgr: Bill Reiher. Prgr. Organiser: Atiota Bauro. Engineer: Tooto Kabwebwenibeia.
MW: 846kHz 10kW.
SW: Tarawa (G.C: 01N21 172E56): 9825kHz 1kW. Inactive.
FM: 99MHz 0.1kW
D.Prgr in I-kiribati (90%)/English (10%): 1800-2000, 0000-0130, 0530-0930. **N. in English:** 0600 (rel. BBC). Also relays R. Australia.
ANN: "This is Radio Kiribati, the national broadcasting service of Kiribati in the Central Pacific". "Aio Bwanaan Kiribati te botaki ni kanako bwanaa i bukin Kiribati i nukan te Betebeke". **V.** by QSL-card. Enclose US$1 for postage. IRC's not acc.

KOREA (North, DPR)

L.T: UTC +9h — **Pop:** 26 million —**Pr.L:** Korean — **E.C:** 60Hz, 100/200/220V — **ITU:** KRE

THE RADIO AND TELEVISION BROADCASTING COMMITEE OF THE DEMOCRATIC PEOPLE'S REPUBLIC OF KOREA

Jonsung-dong, Moranbong District, Pyongyang ☎ +850 2 816035. **L.P:** Chairman: Cha Sung Su.

KOREAN CENTRAL BROADCASTING STATION (Joson Jung-ang Pangsong)

Jonsung-dong, Moranbong District, Pyongyang ☎ +050 2 812301.

MW	kHz	kW	Prgr	MW	kHz	kW	Prgr
Chongjin	702	50	C/R	Hyesan	765	50	C/R
Wiwon*	720	500	C/R	Kaesong	810	50	C/R

MW	kHz	kW	Prgr	MW	kHz	kW	Prgr
Pyongyang	819	500	C	Hamhung	999	250	C/R
Sinuiju	864	250	C/R	Haeju	1080	1500	C/R
Wonsan	882	250	C/R	Pyongyang	1368	2	E
Hwangju+	927	50	C/R				

*= Kanggye, += Sariwon, C = Central Broadcast from Pyongyang, R = Regional Sce, E = rel. Ext. Sce.

SW: (all freqs variable):

	kHz	Prgr		kHz	Prgr
Sariwon	2350	C/R	Kanggye	3960	C/R
Pyongyang	2850	C	Wonsan	3970	C/R
Hamhung	3220	C/R	Kanggye	6100	C
Pyongsong	3350	C/R	Pyongyang	9665	C
Hyesan	3920	C/R	Kanggye	11680	C
Chongjin	3940	C/R			

FM: Kaesong 102.3MHz.

D.Prgr in Korean: 2000-1800 on all freqs exc. 6100 (2000-0630 & 1330-1800). **N:** 2100, 2200, 0100, 0300, 0600, 0800, 1100, 1200, 1300. Regional Prgrs: W0500-0600. Rel. Pyongyang Broadc. St: 1500-1800 on 702/720/864kHz. 1500-2000 on 102.3MHz. 1800-2000 on 3220/3940/3970kHz.
ANN: "Joson Jung-ang Pangsong-imnida". Reg. Prgrs: "(location) Pangsong-imnida". **IS:** Song of General Kim Il Sung. Opening & closing music: Nat. Anthem. **V:** not verified.

PYONGYANG BROADCASTING STATION (Pyongyang Pangsong)

✉ Pyongyang.

MW	kHz	kW	Prgr		kHz	kW	Prgr
Chongjin	621	500	P/E	Sepo	729	50	P
Kangnam*	657	1500	P	Hwadae	801	500	P
Samgo	684	250	P	Sangwon	855	500	P

P = Pyongyang Broadc. St, E = Ext. Sce.*) Key st. serving Pyongyang area.

SW (all freqs variable): Pyongyang 3250/3320/6250kHz, Kanggye 6400kHz.

FM: Pyongyang 89.1, 89.5, 90.3 , 91.1, 91.9, 92.9, 95.1, 95.9 , 96.7, 97.3, 99.5, 101.1, 101.9, 104.5, 106.5, 107.3MHz - Kaesong 90.7, 91.4, 91.9, 98.2, 104.1, 104.5, 104.9, 105.9, 107.1MHz

D.Prgr. in Korean: 2100-2030 on 657/729/801/855kHz; 2100-1800 on 684/6400kHz; 2100-1900 on 801/3320/6250kHz; 0000-0700 on 621/3250kHz; 1300-2030 on 3250kHz; 1300-1800 on 621 kHz. **N:** 2200, 2300, 0100, 0300, 0600, 0800, 1100, 1200, 1300. **ANN:** "Pyongyang Pangsong-imnida". **IS:** Song of General Kim Il Sung. Opening & closing music: Nat. Anthem. **V:** not verified.

EXTERNAL SERVICES: Voice of Korea
See International Broadcasting section

PYONGYANG FM BROADCASTING STATION (Pyongyang FM Pangsong)

Station	MHz	kW		MHz	kW
Pyongsong	90.1	2	Komdok	102.1	1
Kaesong	92.5	2	Sariwon	103.0	2
Kanggye	93.3	5	Haeju	103.7	10
Hyesan	93.8	2	Pyongyang	105.2	20
Wongsan	95.1	5	Chongjin	105.5	10
Heaju	97.8	10	Hamhung	106.1	20
Sinuiju	101.3	5	Nampo	107.2	2

D.Prgr: 0700-2000, 2100-2400 (National holidays: 2100-2030) (music, drama and novel).
ANN: "Pyongyang FM Pangsong-imnida". **IS:** Song of General Kim Jong Il. Opening music: Pyongyang Is My Heart.

PYONGYANG BRANCH OF THE NATIONAL DEMOCRATIC FRONT OF SOUTH KOREA

✉ Pyongyang.
MW: Haeju 1053kHz 1500kW.
SW: Pyongyang 4450kHz, Wonsan 3480kHz, Haeju 4557kHz.
D.Prgr: 2200-0400, 0800-1400. Rel. Korean Central Broadc. Station.
ANN: "Yeogineun Hanguk Minzok Minju Jeonseon Pyongyang Jibuimnida". **IS:** We Are One.

KOREA (South, Rep.)

L.T: UTC +9h — **Pop:** 47 million — **Pr.L:** Korean — **E.C:** 60Hz, 110/220V — **ITU:** KOR

KOREAN BROADCASTING SYSTEM (KBS) (Hanguk Bangsong Gongsa) (Public Corporation)

✉18, Yeouido-dong, Yeongdeungpo-gu, Seoul 150-790 ☎ +82 2 781 1000 🖷 +82 2 761 2499 **Web:** www.kbs.co.kr
L.P: Pres & CEO: Jung, Yun Joo. Exec.Vice Pres: An, Dong Soo. Man. Dir.(Prog.): Lee, Won Kun. Man. Dir.(N. & Sports): Kim, Hong. Man. Dir.(R.): Cho, Won Suck. Man. Dir.(International): Nam, Sun Hyun. Man. Dir.(Broadc.Engineering): Hong, Soo Wan. Man. Dir.(Administration): Jung, Tae Jin. Dir. Int. Rel. Div: Choi, Choon Ae.
MW: N1 = KBS R. One, N2 = KBS R. Two, N3 = KBS R. Three, L1 = First Liberty Prgr, L2 = Second Liberty Prgr, E = also used for Ext. sce., N = Netw. or local st. area, *) Key st, + = Regional key St, 2 = rel N2 exc. for local prgrs, 3 = rel N3 (other local st take N1), Call: HL(call).

N	Location	Call	kHz	kW
9)	Jangsu	-	540	1
13)	Jeomchon	-	540	1
8)	Hongseong	-	540	10
10)	Jangheung	-	540	1
13)	Daegu+2	QH	558	250
9)	Jeonju+	KF	567	100
12)	Suncheon 3	-	576	1
14)	Yeongju	-	594	10
N2)	Namyang*	SA	603	500
4)	Taebaek	-	621	10
19)	Seogwipo	-	621	10
6)	Yeongdong	-	621	1
3)	Inje	-	630	5
12)	Yeosu	-	630	10
N3)	Gaebong*	KC	639	50
10)	Boseong	-	648	1
3)	Chuncheon+	KM	657	50
9)	Jeonju 3	-	675	10
N1)	Sorae*	KA	711	500
13)	Daegu+	KG	738	100
10)	Gwangju+	KH	747	100
N1)	Yeoju*	-	756	100
5)	Yeongwol	-	783	10
3)	Yanggu	-	846	5
4)	Gangneung+	KR	864	100
8)	Daejeon+	KI	882	20
2)	Busan+	KB	891	250
13)	Gumi	-	909	10
N1)	Yeoncheon*	-	918	50
8)	Buyeo	-	927	10
18)	Hadong	-	927	1
5)	Hongcheon	-	927	1
16)	Changwon 3	-	936	10
6)	Boeun	-	945	10
19)	Jeju+	KS	963	10
14)	Andong+	CR	963	10
L1)	Dangjin*	CA	972	1500
4)	Gangneung 3	-	1008	50
3)	Hwacheon	-	1026	1
18)	Geochang	-	1026	1
15)	Pohang+	CP	1035	10
4)	Samcheok	-	1044	10
7)	Jecheon	-	1044	10
6)	Cheongju+	KQ	1062	50
7)	Chungju+	CH	1089	10
18)	Jinju+	CJ	1098	20
L1)	Hwaseong*	-	1134	500
5)	Wonju+	CW	1152	10
L2E)	Gimje*	SR	1170	500
5)	Jeongseon	-	1206	1
14)	Cheongsong	-	1206	1
10)	Gwangju 3	-	1224	20
5)	Pyeongchang	-	1233	1
14)	Yeongyang	-	1233	1
9)	Namwon	-	1260	10
N1)	Yangju	-	1269	10
9)	Gurye	-	1269	1
16)	Hapcheon	-	1278	1
15)	Uljin	-	1305	10
10)	Yeonggwang	-	1323	1
15)	Ulleung	-	1323	1
N1)	Gimpo*	-	1341	10

N	Location	Call	kHz	kW
9)	Muju	-	1368	1
N1)	Cheorwon*	-	1395	10
17)	Ulsan+	QB	1449	10
18)	Hamyang	-	1458	1
14)	Bonghwa	-	1458	1
11)	Mokpo+	KN	1467	50
12)	Goheung	-	1485	1
8)	Gongju	-	1485	1
13)	Gimcheon	-	1503	1
19)	Gosan	-	1539	1
7)	Danyang	-	1584	1
18)	Sancheong	-	1584	1
8)	Geumsan	-	1584	1
5)	Sabuk	-	1602	1

NB: Liberty sts and FM-sts do not use call letters (even if assigned). Other sts without call letters use the calls from their regional key sts.

SW: Hwaseong (G.C: 37N13 126E47)

kHz	kW	Prgr.
3930	10	N1
6135	10	L2 + R. Korea Int.
6015	100	L1

FM: (MHz) Reg = region in MW section. I-Standard FM(R. One); II-KBS FM One; III a = FM Two, b = R. Two. *) are also SCA (R. Three).

Reg.	Location	I	II	III	kW
1)	Namsan		93.1	89.1a/106.1b	-/10/10/10
1)	Gwanaksan	97.3*			10
1)	Yongmunsan	90.3*			1
2)	Yeongdo	103.7	92.7	97.1b	3/5/3
3)	Hwaaksan	99.5*	91.1	98.7b	5/5/3
4)	Gwaebangsan	98.9*	89.1	102.1b	1/5/5
5)	Baegunsan	97.1	89.5		1/3
5)	Taegisan	95.5*			1
4)	Hambaeksan	93.7*	97.3		1/3
6)	Sikchangsan		102.1		-/3
8)	Sikchangsan			100.9b	-/-/3
6)	Heukseongsan	89.9*			1
6)	Uamsan	89.3	94.1		1/1
6)	Gayeopsan			90.9b	-/-/3
7)	Gayeopsan	92.1*	100.3		1/3
8)	Gyeryongsan	94.7*	98.5		1/5
9)	Moaksan	96.9*	100.7	92.9b	5/5/?
9)	Nogodan	88.3*	104.5		1/3
10)	Mudeungsan	90.5*	92.3	95.5b	5/5/3
11)	Yangulsan		98.3		-/1
11)	Daedunsan	105.9			1
12)	Suncheon			102.7b	-/-/3
12)	Mangunsan	95.7*	94.5		1/3
13)	Palgongsan	101.3*	89.7	102.3b	5/5/3
14)	Ilwolsan	90.5*			1
14)	Hakkasan		88.1		-/3
15)	Johangsan	95.9*	93.5		1/3
16)	Bulmosan	91.7*	93.9	106.1b	1/1/3
17)	Muryongsan	90.7*	101.9		1/3
18)	Gamaksan		92.1		-/3
18)	Mangjinsan	90.3	89.3		1/1
19)	Gyeonwolak	99.1*	96.3	91.9b	5/3/3
19)	Sammaebong		99.9	89.7b	-/3/1

+ low power relay st.

KBS R. One (KBS Je-il Radio, HLKA): 0300-0100 on 3930kHz, others 24h. Non-commercial nationwide news sce. Key freq's 711/756/3930kHz, 90.3/97.3MHz. Also rel. by Standard FM St's and most reg. st's. Reg. st's may broadcast local prgr's at designated times. **N:** hourly 2000-1600 except 1100(W). Local N: 2205(Sun), 2210(W), 0000(Sun), 0005(w), 0310(Sun), 0315(W), 0605, 0805(Mon-Fri), 0900(Sun), 0905(W).

KBS R. Two (KBS Je-i Radio, Happy FM, HLSA): 2000-1800 (558kHz to 1500). Commercial. Key freq's 603kHz/106.1MHz. Reg. st's may broadcast local prgr's at designated times. **N:** hourly 2000-1200. Local N: 2300, 0400, 0700, 1200. Liberty prgr 1700-1800.

KBS R. Three (KBS Je-sam Radio, Sarang-ui Sori Bangsong, HLKC): 2100-1800. Non-commercial sce. **N:** 0000(W), 0100(W), 0300(W), 0800(Mon-Fri).

LIBERTY Prgr. (Sahoe Gyoyuk Bangsong)(Social educ. sce.): A sce. for ethnic Koreans living outside of the Rep. of Korea. Two separate sce's + prgr's on KBS R. Two and R. Three.

First Liberty Prgr. (Sahoe Gyoyuk Je-il Bangsong, HLCA): 0400-2400 on 972/1134/6015kHz, 1500-1800 on 558kHz. **N:** 0400, 0500, 0600(W), 0800, 0900, 1100, 1200, 1500, 2300(Sun-Thu).

Second Liberty Prgr. (Sahoe Gyoyuk Je-i Bangsong, HLSR): 1000-0400 on 1170kHz, 1100-2400 on 6135kHz. Relay First Liberty Prgr 1400-2400 and takes R. Korea Int. until 1400.

KBS FM One (KBS Je-il FM Bangsong, HLKA-FM): 24h. Mainly Korean traditional and western classical music.

KBS FM Two (KBS Je-i FM Bangsong. Cool FM, HLKC-FM): 24h. Mainly Korean and western popular and light classical music.

NB: Regional FM One st's relay FM Two 2100-2200.

ANN: N1: "AM Chilbaek-sib-il(711) kHz, FM Gusib-chil-jeom-sam(97.3) MHz, Je-il Radiomnida. HLKA". N2: "KBS Je-i Radiomnida". N3: "AM Yukbeak-samsib-gu(639) kHz, KBS Je-sam Radio, Sarang-ui Sori Bangsong-imnida. HLKC". Liberty prgr: "Pyeonghwa-ro Hana-ro Tongil-ro, KBS Sahoe Gyoyuk Bangsong-imnida".

Addresses of regional key stations:
2) 63, Namcheon-dong, Suyeong-gu, Busan 608-790 – **3)** 86-1, Nagwon-dong, Chuncheon-si, Gangwon-do 200-100 – **4)** 62-5, Yonggang-dong, Gangneung-si, Gangwon-do 210-070 – **5)** 79-1, Won-dong, Wonju-si, Gangwon-do 220-060 – **6)** 417, Gaesin-dong, Cheongju-si, Chungcheongbuk-do 361-790 – **7)** 417, Munhwa-dong, Chungju-si, Chungcheongbuk-do 380-790 – **8)** 300, Mannyeon-dong, Seo-gu, Daejeon 302-790 – **9)** 523-3, Geumam 2-dong, Deokchin-gu, Jeonju-si, Jeollabuk-do 560-790 – **10)**1206-1, Chipyeong-dong, Seo-gu, Gwangju 502-270 – **11)** 1188-3, Yongdang 1-dong, Mokpo-si, Jeollanam-do 530-360 – **12)** 91-3, Seokhyeon-dong, Suncheon-si, Jeollanam-do 540-100 – **13)** 245, Beomeo 4-dong, Suseong-gu, Daegu 706-790 – **14)** 666, Taehwa-dong, Andong-si, Gyeongsangbuk-do 760-790 – **15)** 655, Sangdo-dong, Nam-gu, Pohang-si, Gyeongsangbuk-do 790-790 – **16)** 97-1, Sinwol-dong, Changwon-si, Gyeongsangnam-do 641-790 – **17)** 416-7, Dal-dong, Nam-gu, Ulsan 680-790 – **18)** 13-22, Sinan-dong, Jinju-si, Gyeongsangnam-do 660-790 – **19)** 302-3, Yeon-dong, Jeju-si, Jeju 690-170.

Local identifications: Within local prgrs. **N1**: just before the h. at 2000, 2200(Sun), 2300, 0000(W), 0200, 0300, 0500, 0700(Mon-Fri), 0800, 0900(Sun), 1000(W), 1100(Sun), 1300, 1400, 1500(Sun), 1600. **N2**: just before the h. 2000-1700. **N3**: just before the h. 2100-1700. **FM One**: just before the h. at 2000-2200, 0000, 0200, 0300, 0500, 0700-0900, 1100, 1300, 1500, 1600, 1800. **FM Two**: just before the h.

EXTERNAL SERVICES: Radio Korea International
See International Broadcasting section

KOREA EDUCATIONAL BROADCASTING SYSTEM (EBS)

(Gyoyuk Bangsong) (Public Corporation)
✉ 92-6, Umyeon-dong, Seocho-gu, Seoul 137-791 ☎ +82 2 522 8039 🖷 +82 2 598 9530 **Web:** www.ebs.co.kr
Call letters HLQL used for all the stations.

Sce. area	Tr. location	MHz	kW
Chungju	Gayeopsan	104.1	5
Changwon	Bulmosan	104.3	5
Seoul	Gwanaksan	104.5	5
Jinju	Gamaksan	104.7	3
Gangneung	Gwaebangsan	104.9	3
Wonju	Baegunsan	104.9	3
Seogwipo	Sammaebang	104.9	3
Daegu	Palgongsan	105.1	5
Gwangju	Mudeungsan	105.3	5
Daejeon	Gyeryongsan	105.7	5
Ulsan	Muryongsan	105.9	3
Yeosu	Mangunsan	106.3	1
Chuncheon	Hwaaksan	106.5	5
Pohang	Johangsan	106.7	3
Jeonju	Moaksan	106.9	5
Taebaek	Hambaeksan	107.1	3
Jeju	Gyeonwolak	107.3	3
Namwom	Nogodan	107.5	3
Andong	Hakkasan	107.7	3
Busan	Yeongdo	107.7	3
Cheongju	Sikjangsan	107.9	3

+ low power relay st's.
D.Prgr: 2000-1700
ANN: "EBS, Gyoyuk Bangsong-imnida"

GUGAK FM BROADCASTING SYSTEM
(Gugak Bangsong) (Public Corporation)
✉ 700, Seocho-dong, Seocho-gu, Seoul 137-070 ☎ +82 2 581 9910 **Web:** www.gugakfm.co.kr
Stations: Seoul HLQA-FM 99.1MHz 5kW: 2000-1800, Namwon 95.9MHz 1kW: 2000-1800. **ANN:** "Gugak Bangsong-imnida."

MUNHWA BROADCASTING CORP. (MBC)
(Munhwa Pangsong) Nationwide commercial network
31, Yeouido-dong, Yeongdeungpo-gu, Seoul 150-728
☎ +82 2 784 2000 **Web:** www.imbc.com
MW: Call: HL(call).

	Call	kHz	kW	St. and h. of tr.
1)	CQ	765	10	Daejeon MBC: 24h.
2)	AJ	774	10	Jeju MBC: 24h.
3)	AN	774	10	Chuncheon MBC: 24h.
4)	CT	810	20	Daegu MBC: 24h.
5)	CN	819	20	Gwangju MBC: 24h.
6)	AU	846	10	Ulsan MBC: 24h.
7)	CX	855	10	Jeonju MBC: 24h.
8)	KV	900	50	Seoul MBC: 24h.
9)	AP	990	10	Masan MBC: 24h.
10)	AW	1017	10	Andong MBC: 24h.
11)	AT	1080	10	Yeosu MBC: 24h.
12)	AV	1107	10	Pohang MBC: 24h.
13)	KU	1161	20	Busan MBC: 24h.
14)	AK	1215	10	Jinju MBC: 24h.
15)	SB	1242	10	Wonju MBC: 24h.
16)	AF	1287	10	Gangneung MBC: 24h.
17)	AX	1287	10	Cheongju MBC: 24h.
18)	AO	1332	10	Chungju MBC: 24h.
19)	AQ	1350	10	Samcheok MBC: 24h.
20)	AM	1386	10	Mokpo MBC: 24h.

FM:

	Location	Music FM		Standard FM	
	Studio (Transmitter)	MHz	kW	MHz	kW
8)	Seoul	91.9	10	95.9	10
13)	Busan	88.9	5	95.9	3
4)	Daegu	95.3	5	96.5	5
5)	Gwangju	91.5	5	93.9	5
	Gwangju	95.1	3		
1)	Daejeon	97.5	5	92.5	1
7)	Jeonju	99.1	5	94.3	2
	Jeonju(Namwon)			101.7	3
9)	Masan	100.5	1	98.9	3
3)	Chuncheon	94.5	1	92.3	4
17)	Cheongju	99.7	1	107.1	1
2)	Jeju	90.1	3	97.9	1
	Jeju(Seogwipo)	102.9	3	97.1	1
6)	Ulsan	98.7	3	97.5	1
16)	Gangneung	94.3	5	96.3	3
14)	Jinju	97.7	1	91.1	3
	Jinju	96.1	3	93.5	1
20)	Mokpo	102.3	1	89.1	2
11)	Yeosu	98.3	2	100.7	1
10)	Andong	91.3	3	100.1	3
15)	Wonju	98.9	3	92.7	1
	Wonju			102.5	
18)	Chungju	88.7	3	96.1	1
19)	Samcheok	98.1	3	101.5	1
	Samcheok	99.9	1	93.1	1
12)	Pohang	97.9	3	100.7	3
	Pohang(Uljin)	94.9	1	102.7	1

+low power rel. st's.

NB: Standard FM St's simulcast with the MW St in the same city. A seperate sce. is provided to the Music FM St's. All regional st's broadcast a combination of a feed from Seoul and their own local prgrs. Standard FM st's follow the same schedule as their corresponding MW outlet. Music FM of Seoul MBC sched: 24h.
ANN: "(freq. and location) Munhwa Bangsong-imnida. (call letters)" or "Munhwa Bangsong-imnida" or "MBC". Seoul: "Jungpa Gubaek (900)kHz, Pyojun FM Gushib-o-jeom-gu (95.9)MHz Munhwa Bangsong-imnida"

Addresses and other information Add "(location) Munhwa Broadc. Corp." to addr.
1) 4-5, Doryong-dong, Yuseong-gu, Daejeon 305-740. **Web:** www.tjmbc.co.kr – **2)** 321-22, Yeon-dong, Jeju-si, Jeju-do 690-170. **Web:** www.jejumbc.co.kr – **3)** 238-3, Samcheon-dong, Chuncheon-si, Gangwon-do 200-200. **Web:** www.chmbc.co.kr – **4)** 1, Beomeo-dong, Suseong-gu, Daegu 706-728. **Web:** www.tgmbc.co.kr – **5)** 300, Wolsan-dong, Nam-gu, Gwangju 503-728. **Web:** www.kjmbc.co.kr – **6)** 409-1, Hakseong-dong, Jung-gu, Ulsan 681-728. **Web:** www.ulsanmbc.co.kr – **7)** 151-9, Junghwasan-dong 2-ga, Wansan-gu, Jeonju-si, Jeollabuk-do 560-728. **Web:** www.jmbc.co.kr – **8)** National addr. – **9)** 525-1, Yangdeok-dong, Hoewon-gu, Masan-si, Gyeongsangnam-do 630-490. **Web:** www.masanmbc.co.kr – **10)** 709-1, Taehwa-dong, Andong-si, Gyeongsangbuk-do 760-290. **Web:** www.andongmbc.co.kr – **11)**101-1, Munsu-dong, Yeosu-si, Jeollanam-do 550-728. **Web:** www.ysmbc.co.kr – **12)** 907-4, Daejam-dong, Pohang-si, Gyeongsangbuk-do 790-728. **Web:** www.phmbc.co.kr – **13)** 316-2, Millak-dong, Suyeong-gu. Busan 613-728. **Web:** www.busanmbc.co.kr – **14)** 47, Pyeongan-dong, Jinju-si, Gyeongsangnam-do 660-728. **Web:** www.jinjumbc.co.kr – **15)**1023-70, Hakseong 1-dong, Wonju-si, Gangwon-do 220-031. **Web:** www.wjmbc.co.kr – **16)** 1091-6, Ponam 2-dong, Gangneung-si, Gangwon-do 210-112. **Web:** www.gnmbc.co.kr – **17)** 261-30, Uam-dong, Sangdang-gu, Cheongju-si, Chungcheongbuk-do 360-728. **Web:** www.mbccj.co.kr – **18)** 680, Hoam-dong, Chungju-si, Chungcheongbuk-do 380-130. **Web:** www.cjmbc.co.kr – **19)** 111, Galcheon-dong, Samcheok-si, Gangwon-do 245-090. **Web:** www.scmbc.co.kr – **20)** 1096-1, Yongdang-dong, Mokpo-si, Jeollanam-do 530-728. **Web:** www.mokpombc.co.kr

CHRISTIAN BROADCASTING SYSTEM (CBS)
(Gidokkyo Bangsong)
MW: Call: HL(call).

	Call	kHz	kW	St.and h.of tr.
1)	KY	837	50	*CBS Seoul: 24h.
2)	CL	999	10	CBS Gwangju: 2000-1600.
3)	KT	1251	10	CBS Daegu: 2000-1600.
4)	CM	1314	10	CBS Jeonbuk: 2000-1600.
5)	KP	1404	10	CBS Busan: 2000-1600.

FM:
1) CBS-FM Seoul HLKY-FM 93.9MHz 7kW 24h(Music FM).
1) CBS Seoul HLKY-SFM 98.1MHz 10kW 24h.
2) CBS Gwangju HLCL-SFM 103.1MHz 5kW 2000-1600.
3) CBS Jeonnam HLCL-FM 102.1MHz 2kW 2000-1600.
4) CBS Daeju HLKT-SFM 103.1MHz 5kW 2000-1600.
5) CBS Jeonbuk HLCM-SFM 103.7MHz 5kW 2000-1600.
6) CBS Busan HLKP-SFM 102.9MHz 5kW 2000-1600.
7) CBS Cheongju HLAC-FM 91.5MHz 3kW 2000-1600.
8) CBS Chuncheon HLDC-FM 93.7MHz 3kW 2000-1600.
9) CBS Daejeon HLDX-FM 91.7MHz 5kW 2000-1600.
10) CBS Pohang HLCB-FM 91.5MHz 3kW 2000-1600.
11) CBS Gyeongnam HLCC-FM 106.9MHz 5kW 2000-1600.
12) CBS Jeju HLKO-FM 93.3MHz 3kW 2000-1600.
12) CBS Jeju (Seogwipo relay st) 90.9MHz 1kW 2000-1600.
13) CBS Yeongdong HLCO-FM 91.5MHz 3kW 2000-1600.
14) CBS Ulsan HLKP-FM 100.3MHz 1kW 2000-1600.
+low power relay st's.

Adresses and other information:
1) 917-1, Mok-dong, Yangcheon-gu, Seoul 158-701 ☎ +82 2 650 7000. **Web:** www.cbs.co.kr **ANN:** "Jeongjikhan Sesang-eul Gakkuneun AM Palbaek-samsip-chil(837) kHz, Pyojun FM Gusip-pal-jeom-il(98.1) MHz, CBS-mnida. HLKY." – **2)** 721-2, Geumho-dong, Seo-gu, Gwangju 506-154 ☎ +82 62 376 8500 – **3)** 117-5, Maegok-dong, Suncheon-si, Jeollanam-do 540-947 ☎ +82 61 902 1000 – **4)** 3-7, Chimsan 2-dong, Buk-ku, Daegu 702-703 ☎ +82 53 426 8001 – **5)** 114-8, Daga-dong, Wansan-gu, Jeollabuk-do 560-053 ☎ +82 63 281 0430 – **6)** 1155-2, Beomchon 4-dong, Busanjin-gu, Busan 614-024 ☎ +82 51 636 0050 – **7)** 1010, Sugok-dong, Heungdeok-gu, Cheongju-si, Chungcheongbuk-do 361-150 ☎ +82 43 292 4100 – **8)** 174-3, Ungyo-dong, Chuncheon-si, Gangwon-do 200-080 ☎ +82 33 255 2001 – **9)** 1-13, Munhwa-dong, Jung-gu, Daejeon 301-130 ☎ +82 42 259 8888 – **10)** 640-7, Daedo-dong, Nam-gu, Pohang-si, Gyeongsangbuk-do 790-824 ☎ +82 54 277 5500 – **11)** 323-3, Sanho-dong, Happo-gu, Masan-si, Gyeongsangnam-do 630-811 ☎ +82 55 224 5600 – **12)** 271, Yeon-dong, Jeju-si, Jeju-do 690-813 ☎ +82 64 744 0933 – **13)** 935-1, Gyo 1-dong, Gangneung-si, Gangwon-do 210-923 ☎ +82 33 642 9131 – **14)** 186-11, Sinjeong 3-dong, Nam-gu, Ulsan 680-822 ☎ +82 52 256 3333.
ANN: St's 2)-8): "Jeongjikhan Sesang-eul Kakkuneun (freq.), CBS (location) Bangsong-imnida. (call letters)" or "Maeumgwa Maeumi Mannaneun Bangsong, (freq.), CBS (location) Bangsong-imnida. (call letters)"
F.PI: Relay st's in Chungju, Wonju, Andong.

SEOUL BROADCASTING SYSTEM (SBS)
920 Mok-dong, Yangcheon-gu, Seoul 158-725. ☎ +82 2 2061 0006. +82 2 2113 3169 **Web:** www.sbs.co.kr
MW: HLSQ Goyang (near Seoul) 792kHz 50kW (AM stereo; C-QUAM System). **D.Prgr:** 24h.
Standard FM(Love FM): 103.5MHz HLSQ-SFM 10kW: 24h.
Music FM (Power FM): 107.7MHz HLSQ-FM 10kW: 24h.
ANN: "AM Chilbaek-gusib-i(792) kHz, FM Baek-sam-jeom-o(103.5) MHz, SBS Love FM-imnida. HLSQ", "FM Baek-chil-jeom-chil(107.7) MHz, Yeoreobune SBS Power FM-imnida. HLSQ"

FAR EAST BROADCASTING CO., KOREA (Rlg.)

MW:		kHz	kW
1)	HLKX, Seoul	1188	100
2)	HLAZ, Jeju	1566	250/100
FM:		**MHz**	**kW**
1)	HLKX-SFM, Seoul	106.9	5
3)	HLAD-FM, Daejeon	93.3	5
4)	HLDD-FM, Changwon	98.1	5
5)	HLDY-FM, Yeongdong	90.1	3
6)	HLKW-FM, Mokpo	100.5	1
7)	HLDZ-FM, Pohang	90.3	3
8)	HLQR-FM, Ulsan	107.3	3

+ low power relay st's.

Addresses and other information

1) Far East Broadc. Co.(Geukdong Bangsong), P.O. Box 88, Mapo, Seoul 121-707. ☎ +82 2 320 0114; 🖷 +82 2 320 0229 **Web:** www.febc.or.kr **D.Prgr:** 1900-1700. Korean: 1900-1100(Stangdard FM: 1900-1700). **English:** 1100-1230(1188kHz). **Chinese:** 1230-1700(1188kHz). **ANN:** Korean "Jungpa Cheonbaek-palsip-pal(1188) kHz, Pyojun FM Paeng-nyuk-jeom-gu(106.9) MHz, Areumdaun Chanyanggwa Gibbeun Sosigeul Jeonhaneun Geukdong Bangsong-imnida.". English: "This is HLKX Radio broadcasting with 100,000 watts of power on 1188kHz" **Fl:** by contributions & free will offerings. – **2)** Jeju Geukdong Bangsong, 2761, Hagwi-ri, Aewol-up, Bukjeju-gun, Jeju-do 695-750. ☎ +82 64 799 8100 **D.Prgr:** 1900-1800. **Korean:** 1900-1100. **Chinese:** 1100-1230, 1345-1730. **Japanese:** 1230-1345. **Russian:** 1730-1800. – **3)** Daejeon Geukdong Bangsong, 233-15, Chijok-dong, Yuseong-gu, Daejeon 305-711. ☎ +82 42 828 9330. **D.Prgr:** 24h. – **4)** Changwon Geukdong Bangsong, 117, Jungang-dong, Changwon-si, Gyeongsangnam-do 641-030. ☎ +82 55 269 9810 **D.Prgr:** 24h. – **5)** Yeongdong Geukdong Bangsong, 500-1, Jangsa-dong, Sokcho-si, Sokcho-si, Gangwon-do 217-130. ☎ +82 33 638 9000 **D.Prgr:** 1900-1700. – **6)** 878-9, Sang-dong, Mokpo-si, Jeollanam-do 530-822. ☎ +82(61)284 9000 **D.Prgr:** 1900-1700. – **7)** 164-11, Daedo-dong, Nam-gu, Pohang-si, Gyeongsangnam-do. ☎ +82 54 275 3000 **D.Prgr:** 24h. – **8)** 459-7, Yaeum 2-dong, Nam-gu, Ulsan-si. ☎ +82 52 256 2000 **D.Prgr:** 24h.

PYEONGHWA BROADCASTING CORP. (PBC)

(Pyeonghwa Bangsong) Endowment by the Catholic Church.
Stations:
1) Seoul HLQP-FM 105.3MHz 5kW: 1957-1702.
2) Gwangju HLDL-FM 99.9MHz 5kW, 99.5MHz 1kW(rel. st. in Yeosu): 1957-1702.
3) Deagu HLDK-FM 93.1MHz 3kW, 96.9MHz(rel. st. in Pohang), 100.7MHz(rel. st. in Andong): 1957-1702.
4) Busan HLDW-FM 101.1MHz 3kW: 1957-1702.
5) Daejeon HLQO-FM 106.3MHz 3kW: 1957-1702.

Addresses

1) 2-3, Jeo-dong 1-ga, Jung-gu, Seoul 100-031 ☎ +82 2 270 2114 🖷: +82 2 278 4972. **Web:** www.pbc.co.kr **ANN:** "Saengmyeng Sarang, FM Baeg-o-jeom-sam(105.3) MHz, Gibbeun Sosik, Balgeun Sesang, PBC Pyeonghwa Bangsong-imnida. HLQP." – **2)** 3-5, Geumnam-ro 3-ga, Dong-gu, Gwangju 501-023 – **3)** 71, Gyesan-dong 2-ga, Jung-gu, Daegu 700-082 – **4)** 81-1, Daecheong-dong 4-ga, Jung-gu, Busan 600-094 – **5)** 189, Daeheung-dong, Jung-gu, Daejeon 301-802. ☎ +82 42 250 3200.

BUDDHIST BROADCASTING SYSTEM (BBS)

(Bulgyo Bangsong) Owned and operated by the Buddhists.
Stations:
1) Seoul HLSG-FM 101.9MHz 5kW: 2000-1700.
2) Gwangju HLDB-FM 89.7MHz 3kW: 2000-1700.
3) Busan HLDA-FM 89.9MHz 3kW: 2000-1700.
4) Daegu HLDI-FM 94.5MHz 3kW, 105.5MHz(rel. st. in Pohang), 97.7MHz(rel. st. in Andong):: 2000-1700.
5) Cheongju HLDJ-FM 96.7MHz 3kW: 2000-1700.
6) Chuncheon HLQM-FM 100.1MHz 3kW: 2000-1700.

Addresses

1) Dabo Building; 140, Mapo-dong, Mapo-gu, Seoul 121-050 ☎ +82 2 704 5114 🖷 +82 2 705 5229 **Web:** www.bbsfm.co.kr – **2)** Daesaeng Bldg, 78-2, Im-dong, Buk-gu, Gwangju. 500-010 ☎ +82 62 520 1114 – **3)** Bosaeng Bldg, 833-13, Beomil 2-dong, Dong-gu, Busan 601-060 ☎ +82 51 520 5114 – **4)** Jingak Hoegwan, 156-1, Daebong-dong, Jung-gu, Daegu 700-430 ☎ +82 53 427 5114 – **5)** 1646, Yongam-dong, Sangdang-gu, Cheongju-si, Chungcheongbuk-do 360-181 ☎ +82 43 294 5114 – **6)** 4-1, Yoseon-dong, Chuncheon-si, Gangwon-do 200-030 ☎ +82 33 250 2114. **ANN:** 1) "FM Baeg-il-jeom-gu (101.9) MHz, BBS Bulgyo Bangsong-imnida. HLSG."

TRAFFIC BROADCASTING SYSTEM (TBS)

(Gyotong Bangsong)
Municipal Station. This station is operated by the Seoul Municipal Traffic Broadcast Headquarters to provide traffic information and education to the citizens of Seoul and surroundings.
🖃 3-8, Yejang-dong, Jung-gu, Seoul ☎ +82 2 311 5114 🖷 +82 2 311 5219
Web: http://tbs.seoul.kr
Station: HLST-FM 95.1MHz 5kW: 24h.
ANN: "FM Gusib-o-jeom-il(95.1) MHz, TBS Gyotong Bangsong-imnida"

TRAFFIC BROADCASTING NETWORK (TBN)

(Gyotong Bangsong)
🖃 171, Sindang-dong, Jung-gu, Seoul 100-789 ☎ +82 2 2230 6114 🖷 +82 2 2230 6269 **Web:** www.tbn.or.kr
Stations:
1) Busan 94.9MHz HLDN-FM 3kW: 2100-1700.
2) Gwangju 97.3MHz HLDM-FM 3kW: 2100-1700.
3) Daejeon 102.9MHz HLDT-FM 3kW: 2100-1700.
4) Daegu 103.9MHz HLDU-FM 3kW: 2100-1700.
5) Incheon 100.5MHz HLSU-FM 1kW: 2100-1700.
6) Gangwon(Wonju) 105.9MHz HLSV-FM 3kW: 2100-1700.
6) Gangwon(Chuncheon) 103.7MHz 3kW: 2100-1700.
6) Gangwon(Gangneung) 105.5MHz 1kW: 2100-1700.
7) Jeonju 102.7MHz HLCM-FM 1kW: 2100-1700.
+ low power relay st's.

Addresses and other information

1) 580-8, Daeyeon 3-dong, Nam-gu, Busan 608-023 ☎ +82 51 6105 114 **ANN:** "FM Gusib-sa-jeom-gu(94.9) MHz, Busan Gyotong Bangsong-imnida. HLDN-FM" – **2)** 665-2, Ssangam-dong, Gwangsan-gu, Gwangju 506-303 ☎ +82 62 9701 114 **ANN:** "FM Gusib-chil-jeom-sam(97.3) MHz, Gwangju Gyotong Bangsong-imnida. HLDM" – **3)** 152-7, Nae-dong, Seo-gu, Daejeon 302-181 ☎ +82 42 6001 114 **ANN:** "FM Baeg-i-jeom-gu(102.9) MHz, Dallineun Radio Daejeon Gyotong Bangsong-imnida." – **4)** 1679-2, Daemyeong-dong, Nam-gu, Daegu 705-031 ☎ +82 53 6060 114 **ANN:** "FM Baek-sam-jeom-gu(103.9) MHz, Daegu Gyotong Bangsong-imnida. HLDU-FM"– **5)** 401-74, Hagik-dong, Nam-gu, Incheon 402-865 ☎ +82 32 4531 114 **ANN:** "FM Baek-jeom-o(100.5) MHz, TBN Incheon Gyotong Bangsong-imnida. HLSU" – **6)** 1400, Bangok-dong, Wonju-si, Gangwon-do ☎ +82 33 7490 114 **ANN:** "Haengbogui Giljabi, Ggumi Inneun Bangsong, FM Baeg-o-jeom-gu(105.9) MHz, Gangwon Gyotong Bangsong-imnida." – **7)** 410-1, Jinbuk-dong, Deokjin-gu, Jeonju 561-162. ☎ +82 63 2593 114 **ANN:** "FM Baeg-i-jeom-chil(102.7) MHz, TBN Jeonju Gyotong Bangsong-imnida. HLCM"

PUSAN BROADCASTING CORP. (PSB)

(Busan Bangsong)
🖃 603-8, Yeonsan-4-dong, Yeonje-gu, Busan 611-084 ☎ +82 1 850 9000 **Web:** www.psb.co.kr **Station:** HLDG-FM 99.9MHz 3kW: 24h. **ANN:** "Guship-gu-jeom-gu (99.9) MHz, PSB-FM Bluewavemnida.HLDG."

TAEGU BROADCASTING CORPORATION (TBC)

(Daegu Bangsong)
🖃 201-9, Tusan-dong, Susong-gu, Daegu 760-080 ☎ +82 53 760 1900 **Web:** www.tbc.co.kr
Station: HLDE-FM(Dream FM) 99.3MHz 5kW: 24h. Relay station: Pohang 99.7MHz. **ANN:** "HLDE-FM TBC Dream FM-imnida."

KWANGJU BROADCASTING CO., LTD. (KBC)

(Gwangju Bangsong)
🖃 114-14, So-dong, Nam-gu, Gwangju 503-010 ☎ +82 62 650 3114 **Web:** www.ikbc.co.kr **Station:** HLDH-FM(MY FM) 101.1MHz 5kW: 24h. Relay station: Yeosu 96.7MHz.

TAEJON BROADCASTING CO., LTD. (TJB)

(Daejeon Bangsong)
🖃 122-1, Hyo-dong, Tong-gu, Daejeon 300-722 ☎ +82 42 281 1101 **Web:** www.tjb.co.kr
Station: HLDF-FM(Power FM) 95.7MHz 5kW: 24h Relay station: Seosan 96.5MHz **ANN:** "Gusib-o-jeom-chil(95.7), Gusim-nyuk-jeom-o(96.5) MHz, TJB Power FM-imnida. HLDF"

JEONJU TELEVISION CORPORATION (JTV)

(Jeonju Bangsong)
🖃 656-3, Seonosong-dong, Deokjin-gu, Jeonju-si, Jeollabuk-do 561-090 ☎ +82 63 250 5241 **Web:** www.jtv.co.kr
Station: HLDQ-FM(Magic FM) 90.1MHz 5kW: 24h.
ANN: "FM Gusib-jeom-il(90.1) MHz, JTV Magic FM-imnida. HLDQ"

CHEONGJU BROADCASTING CORPORATION (CJB)

(Cheongju Bangsong)

✉ 12-16, Sajik 2-dong, Hongdeok-gu, Cheongju-si, Chungcheongbuk-do 361-102 ☎ +82 43 265 7000 **Web:** www.cjb.co.kr
Station: HLDI-FM(Joy FM) 101.5MHz 5kW: 24h.
ANN: "FM Baeg-il-jeom-o(101.5) MHz, CJB Joy FM-imnida. HLDI"

ULSAN BROADCASTING CORPORATION (UBC)
(Jeonju Bangsong)
✉ 1521-1, Samsan-dong, Nam-gu, Ulsan 680-732 ☎ +82 52 228 6000 **Web:** www.ubc.co.kr
Station: HLDP-FM(Green FM) 92.3MHz 5kW: 24h.
ANN: "Gusib-i-jeom-sam(92.3) MHz, UBC Green FM Bangsong-imnida. HLDP"

JEJU FREE INTERNATIONAL CITY BROADCASTING. SYSTEM (JIBS) (Jeju Bangsong)
✉ 2750, Ora 3-dong, Jeju-si, Jeju-do 690-163 ☎ +82 64 740 7800 **Web:** www.jibstv.com
Station: HLQC-FM(Power FM) 101.5MHz 3kW: 24h. Relay station: Seogwipo 98.5MHz.

GANGWON TELEVISION BROADCASTING CO., LTD (GTB)
(Gangwon Minbang)
✉ 632-2, Janghak-ri, Dong-myeon, Chuncheon-si, Gangwon-do 200-853 ☎ +82 33 248 5000 **Web:** www.igtb.co.kr
Station: HLCG-FM(Fresh FM) 105.1MHz: 24h. Relay station: Gangneung 106.1MHz.
ANN: "Chuncheon Baeg-o-jeom-il(105.1) MHz, Gangneung Baeng-ryuk-jeom-il(106.1) MHz, GTB Fresh FM, HLCG"

KYONGGI BROADCASTING CO. (KFM)
(Gyeonggi Bangsong)
✉ 961-17, Yeongtong-dong, Yeongtong-gu, Suwon-si, Gyeonggi-do 443-810 ☎ +82 31 210 0999 **Web:** www.kfm.co.kr
Station: HLDS-FM 99.9MHz 5kW: 2000-1900.
ANN: "FM Gusib-gu-jeom-gu(99.9) MHz, Gyeonggi Bangsong-imnida. HLDS"

KYUNG-IN BROADCASTING LTD. (iTV-iFM)
(Gyeongin Bangsong)
✉ 587-46, Hagik-dong, Nam-gu, Incheon 402-773 ☎ +82 32 830 0907 **Web:** www.itv.co.kr
Station: HLDO-FM 90.7MHz 1kW: 24h
ANN: "iTV-iFM"

WONBUDDHISM BROADCASTING SYSTEM (WBS)
(Woneum Bangsong)
✉ **1)** 344, Sinyeongdong, Iksan-si, Jeollabuk-do 570-754 ☎ +82 63 850 3166 **Web:** www.wbsfm.com – **2)** 1-3, Heukseok 1-dong, Dongjak-gu, Seoul 156-856 ☎ +82 2 2102 7700 – **3)** 38-6, Sinchang-dong 1-ga, Jung-gu, Busan 600-061 ☎ +82 51 247 3844.
Stations:
1) Iksan HLDV-FM 97.9MHz 3kW: 2000-1700.
2) Seoul HLQK-FM 89.7MHz 1kW: 2000-1700.
3) Busan HLQJ-FM 104.9MHz 3kW: 2000-1700.
ANN: 1) "FM Gusib-chil-jeom-gu(97.9) MHz, WBS Woneum Bangsong-imnida. HLDV", **2)** FM Palsib-gu-jeom-chil(89.7) MHz, WBS Woneum Bangsong-imnida. HLQK", **3)** "FM Baeg-sa-jeom-gu(104.9) MHz, WBS Busan Woneum Bangsong-imnida. HLQJ"

KOREA INTERNATIONAL BROADCASTING FOUNDATION (Arirang FM)
✉ Arirang Tower, 1467-80, Seocho-dong, Seocho-gu, Seoul 137-878 ☎ +82 2 3475 5000 **Web:** www.arirangtv.com
Station: Jeju 88.7MHz: 2100-1700 in English. Relay station: Seogwipo 88.1MHz. **ANN:** "You're listening to Arirang FM"

ARMED FORCES BROADCASTING SYSTEM
(Gukkun Bangsong)
✉ San 2, Yongsan-dong 2-ga, Yongsan-gu, Seoul 140-022
Web: http://kookbang.dema.mil.kr:7070/service/WebCast.jsp
Stations: FM (operated by KBS): Hwaaksan HLSE-FM 96.7MHz 5kW, Yongmunsan 101.1MHz 3kW, Gwaebangsan 92.5MHz 3kW + 4 low power st's.
D.Prgr: 24h. Own prgr's 2100-1305, other times relay KBS R. One (HLKA). Prgr's for soldiers located near the demilitarized zone. Also 0805-0900(Sun) via KBS R. One network & 0340-0400 on 1170kHz (KBS Second Liberty Prgr).
ANN: "Jeolmeumi Inneun Bangsong, Huimang-i Neomchineun Bangsong, Yeoreobune Gukkun Bangsong-imnida".

AMERICAN FORCES NETWORK KOREA (AFN)
✉ As below ☎ +82 2 7914 6495/6 **Web:** afnkorea.com

Stations	**MW(kHz)**	**kW**	**FM(MHz)**	**kW**
1) Seoul/Yongsan	1530	5	102.7	5
2) Munsan/Western Corridor	576	5	88.5	0.05
3) Daegu/Camp Walker	1080	5	88.5	1
4) Busan/Camp Hialeah	1260+	5	88.1	0.25
Chuncheon/Camp Page	1044		88.5	0.1
Uijeongbu/Camp Red Cloud	1161	0.25	88.5	0.1
5) Dongducheon/Camp Casey	1197+	1	88.3	0.25
Chuncheon/Camp Page	1260 F.Pl	1	88.5	0.1
6) Songtan/Osan Air Base	1359*	1	88.5	0.05
7) Pyeongtaek/Camp Humphroys	1440+	1	88.3	0.05
8) Gunsan/Gunsan Air Base	1440	1	88.5	0.25
Wonju/Camp Long	1440	0.25	88.3	0.05
Waegwan/Camp Carrol	1440	0.25		
2) Munsan/Western Corridor	1440 F.Pl	5	88.5	0.05
Pohang/Camp Libby	1512	0.25		
Jinhae/Naval St.	1512	0.25	88.5	0.05
Kotar Range	1512			

Low power: 1512kHz (Jeju-do Sangdong); 88.5MHz Gwangju Air Base.
+= local prgr's 2005-0000 Mon-Fri; otherwise rel.1).
*= local prgr's 2005-0000 & 0605-0900 Mon-Fri; otherwise rel.1).
D.Prgr: 24h (MW/FM separate prgr's). N. on the h. Formal sign on at 1505.
ANN: AM: "American Forces Network Korea", FM (Seoul): "This is Eagle FM"
Addresses
1) Headquarters, American Forces Network Korea, Unit #15324, APO AP 96205-0097, USA ☎ +82(2) 7914 6495. Commanding Officer: LTC Chad C. Starr – **2)** Unit #15325, APO AP 96251-0098, USA – **3)** Unit #15029, APO AP 96218-0186, USA – **4)** Unit #15184. APO AP 96259-0274, USA – **5)** Unit #15116, APO AP 96224-0380, USA – **6)** Unit #2034. APO AP 96278-5000, USA – **7)** Unit #15473. APO AP 96271-0543, USA – **8)** Unit #2011, APO AP 96264-5000, USA.

KUWAIT

L.T: UTC +3h — **Pop:** 2m — **Pr.L:** Arabic — **E.C:** 50Hz, 240V — **ITU:** KWT

MINISTRY OF INFORMATION
✉ P.O. Box 193, 13002 Safat ☎ +965 2415301 🖷 +965 2434511 **Web:** www.moinfo.gov.kw **Email:** info@media.gov.kw

RADIO OF THE STATE OF KUWAIT
✉ P.O. Box 967, 13010 Safat ☎ +0 965 2436193 🖷 +0 965 2415498/2415946 **Web:** www.radiokuwait.org
Email: kwtfreq@ncc.moc.kw

MW kHz	**kW**	**Prgr.**	**Times**
540	600	Main	24h
630	10	Quran	24h
963	20	Main	1200-1600, 2100-0500
		Multi	0500-1200, 1600-2100
1134	10	Main	24h
1269	100	Music	24h
1341	10	Quran	0200-0700, 1700-2300
		2nd A	0700-1700

F.Pl: tr's on 1485 and 1602kHz.

FM MHz	**kW**	**Prgr.**	**Times**
87.9		Arabic Music	24h
89.5		Main Arabic	24h
92.5	5	Easy FM	24h
93.3	-	Holy Quran	24h
95.0	-	FM International	24h
96.3	-	Main Arabic	1200-1600, 2100-0500
		Multilingual	0500-1200, 1600-2100
97.5	2	Holy Quran	0200-0700, 1700-0200
		2nd Arabic	0700-1700
98.9	20	Arabic Music	24h
99.7	-	Super Station	24h
100.5	-	TV sound (Prgr. 1/4)	24h
103.7	-	2nd Arabic Music	24h
105.9	-	Arabic Music	24h

Main Arabic Prgr: 24hrs. Also relayed on SW. **N:** 0300, 0400, 0500, 0730, 1000, 1300, 1500, 1900, 2100, 2200.
2nd Arabic Prgr: 0700-1700.
Arabic Music (Classical) Prgr: 24hrs.
2nd Arabic Music (Modern) Prgr: 24hrs.

Multilingual prgr: English 0500-0800, 1800-2100, Persian 0800-1000, Filipino 1000-1200, Urdu 1600-1800.
Quran prgr: 24hrs.
"Easy FM" in English: 24hrs.
"FM Super Station" in English: 24hrs.
"FM International" in English: 24hrs.
ANN: A: "Idha'at al-Dawlat Al Kuwait". E: "This is Radio Kuwait".
IS: old Kuwaiti tune on clarinet.

R. Kuwait on shortwave & VOA/FRRFE-RLelay station: (MW: 1593kHz 150kW 1400-0700). SW: see International Radio section.

Other stations:
AFN: Al-Jabber/Camp Doha 104.3/107.9MHz 50W/5kW.
BBC Arabic Sce, Kuwait City 90.1MHz 0300-2115.
MBC: 91.4MHz. See main entry under UAE.
R. Monte Carlo Moyen-Orient: 107.3MHz.
R. Sawa, Kuwait City MW: 1548kHz 600kW 24h, FM: 95.7MHz 24h.
VOA in English: 96.9MHz. See main entry under USA.

KYRGYZSTAN

L.T: UTC +5h (27 Mar - 30 Oct 2005: UTC +6h) — **Pop:** 4,9m — **Pr.L:** Kyrgyz, Russian, German, Uzbek — **E.C:** 50Hz, 220V — **ITU:** KGZ.

KYRGYZ RESPUBLIKANYN ULUTTUK TELERADIO-BERÜÜ KORPORATSIYASY
(Kyrgyz National Broadcasting Corp., Gov.)
Jash Gvardiya blvd. 59, 720010 Bishkek. ☎ +996 312 656639. Fax +996 312 257930. **Email:** rkaktr@elcat.kg **Web:** www.ktr.kg
L.P: Pres: Toktosh Aytikeyeva

MW/SW	kHz	kW	Prgr.
Bishkek	1287	150	KGR1
Cholpon-Ata	1404	1	KGR1
Haidarkan	1404	7	KGR1
Jojomel	1404	20	KGR1
Naryn	1404	7	KGR1
Orgochor	1404	-	KGR1
Bishkek	4010	100	KGR1
Bishkek	4795	15	KGR1

FM (MHz)	KGR1	KGR2	kW
Alaikuu	-	69.08	17
Arstanbap	70.07	71.93	17
Bishkek	67.94	66.38	17
Bishkek	104.1	106.9	1
Gulcha	-	69.68	17
Jalal-Abad	72.20	70.64	17
Karakol	66.26	67.28	17
Kara-Kul	68.66	66.86	17
Kazarman	69.95	71.69	17
Kemin		67.04	17
Narin	70.82	72.38	17
Osh	69.92	71.69	17
Suluktu	72.44	70.88	17
Talas	70.40	72.08	17

D.PRGR: KGR1 (Kyrgyz radiosu): 0000-1900 in Kyrgyz, Russian. **N. English:** MF 0115-0120 & 0315-0320. For ethnic minorities: German MF 1410-1420, Dungan Wed 1210-1230, Korean Wed 1545-1600, Tatar Fri 1345-1400, Uighur Mon 1420-1450, Uzbek MF 0910-0915. – **KGR2 ("XXI kylym" radiosu):** 0100-1900 in Kyrgyz, Russian. **N. English:** MF 0150-0200.

OTHER STATIONS

MW	kHz	kW	Location	Station
19)	576	40	Osh	R. DDD
3,B)	1323	30	Bishkek	R. Piramida/RFE-RL
20)	1467	75	Bishkek	R. Extol
FM	**MHz**	**kW**	**Location**	**Station**
14)	66.38	0.1	Chon-Dyobyo	R. Tenir Too
15)	70.24	-	Karakol	R. LW
3)	70.24	-	Bishkek	R. Piramida
12)	87.5	-	Bishkek	R. Retro
13)	89.0	-	Bishkek	Love R.
21)	91.5	-	Bishkek	AFN
7)	100.5	0.25	Bishkek	R. O'key
9)	100.9	0.5	Bishkek	Avtoradio
8)	101.1	0.25	Bishkek	Ekho Moskvy
1A)	101.6	0.5	Osh	Europa+ Kyrgyzstan
1A)	101.7	0.9	Bishkek	Europa+ Kyrgyzstan
15)	101.8	0.1	Karakol	R. LW
14)	102.0	0.1	Naryn	R. Tenir Too
2)	102.0	0.3	Bishkek	R. Almaz
2)	102.0	0.2	Osh	R. Almaz
1B)	102.5	1	Bishkek	Russkoye R.
10)	102.9	0.7	Bishkek	R. Manas FM
3)	103.2	1	Osh	R. Piramida
3)	103.2	0.1	Vostochnaya	R. Piramida
A)	103.2	0.2	Bishkek	RFI
1B)	103.2	1	Cholpon-Ata	Russkoye R.
1A)	103.8	0.5	Osh	Europa+ Kyrgyzstan
17)	105.0	-	Batken	R. Salam
3)	105.0	1	Bishkek	R. Piramida
2)	105.5	0.05	Naryn	R. Almaz
6)	105.6	0.25	Bishkek	Hit FM
4)	106.0	0.2	Bishkek	R. Maks
18)	106.3	0.1	Kara-Balta	R. Tatina
1C)	106.5	0.25	Bishkek	Kyrgyzstan obondoru
1A)	107.1	0.5	Vostochnaya	Europa+ Kyrgyzstan
5)	107.4	0.5	Bishkek	R. VOSST
16)	103.0	-	Chui-Tokmok	R. Burana
11)	107.8	0.3	Bishkek	R. Shanson

Addresses & other information:
1A,B,C) Almaty Str. 4b, 720082 Bishkek. Email: office@europa.kg. Email 1B) rusradio@europa.kg; 1C) obon@europa.kg – **2)** A.Chuikov str. 133a, 720040 Bishkek. Email: almaz@kyrnet.kg – **3)** Dzhantoshev str. 70, 720005 Bishkek. Email: pyramid@mail.elcat.kg – **4)** Chuy pr. 315, 720000 Bishkek. Email: radiomax@elcat.kg – **5)** 7 mkr 46a, 720000 Bishkek. Email: trkvosst@imfiko.bishkek.su – **6)** Chuy pr. 36, 720065 Bishkek. Email: hitfm@mail.ru – **7)** Almaty Str. 6, 720082 Bishkek. Email: okradio@elcat.kg – **8)** Chuy pr. 207, 720032 Bishkek. Email: echo@elcat.kg – **9)** Akhunbaev str. 119-a, Bishkek. Email: autoradio@elcat.kg – **10)** Mir pr. 56, 720044 Bishkek. Email: manasfm@manas.kg – **11)** Bishkek. Email: shanson@infotel.kg – **12)** Bishkek. Email: timskar@hotmail.kg – **13)** Ibraimov Str. 24, 720031 Bishkek. Email: bishkek@maximum.ru – **14)** Lenin Str. 98, 722600 Naryn. Email: tenir-too@hotmail.kg – **15)** Gebze Str. 120, 722360 Karakol. Email: lw@pari.issyk-kul.kg – **16)** Chiu-Tokmok. Email: burana@ktnet.kg – **17)** Hojaev Str. 22a, 715400 Batken. Email: rs@osh.kg – **18)** Gvardeyskaya Str. 18, 722030 Kara-Balta. Email: tatina@infotel.kg – **19)** Kurmanjan Datka Str. 224, Osh. Email: trk_ddd@mail.ru – **20)** Bishkek. Rel. TWR prgr's in Central Asian languages and Russian on 1467kHz. – **21)** AFN Bishkek, Ganci Air Base, APO AE 09807, USA. – **A)** Rel. RFI Cf. France. **B)** Rel. RFE-RL ("R. Azattyk") in Kyrgyz: 0100-0300, 1300-1330, 1400-1430, 1500-1600; Russian ("R. Svoboda"): 0200-0300, 1330-1400, 1700-1800 (cf. USA).

LAOS

L.T: UTC +7h — **Pop:** 5.6 million — **Pr.L:** Lao Soung, Lao Theung — **E.C:** 50Hz, 230V — **ITU:** LAO

RADIO NATIONALE LAO (Gov.)
B. P. 310, Vientiane ☎ +856 21 212432 Fax +856 21 212430. **Web**: www.lnr.or.la.
L.P: DG: Bounthan Inthaxay. Dep. DG: Keungkham Vilayasith. Tech. Dir: D. Sisombath.
City and Provincial sce's: These are operated by the local governments and are not part R. Nationale Lao. Sisavangvong Rd, Luang Prabang - Route 13 South, Pakse, Champassak Province - Manthatulat Road, Vientiane.

MW:

Location	kHz	kW	S	H. of tr.
Vientiane	567	200	N	2200-0830, 0930-1500
Khantabouly, S	585	20	P	2200(?)-1305
Vientiane	640	1	C	2330-1000
Luang Prabang	705	2.5	P	2200-0800, 1025-1500
Muang Hay, O	800	1	P	2300-0200, 1100-1400 u)
Houa Phan	1000	–	P	1255-1425 u)
Vientiane	1030	10	I	2330-0030, 0500-0630, 1130-1400x)
Phonsavan, XK	1215	1	P	2230-0100, 1000-1300 (r. inactive)
Pakse, Ch	1370	10	P	2155-1400 u)

SW:

Location	kHz	kW	S	H. of tr.
Sam Neua, HP	4649v	1	P	2300-0130, 1000-1230
Vientiane	6130	50	N	2200-0830, 0930-1500

S=Sce., N=National, P=Provincial, C=City, I=International

Ch=Champassak prov. HP=Houa Phan prov. O=Oudomxay prov. S=Savannakhet prov. XK=Xiang Khouang prov. u) not recently confirmed, may be inactive or on new freq. x) confirmed inactive May 2003. Reg. st's usually rel. national news at 0000, 0500, 1200.

FM: Vientiane 103.7MHz 20kW: 2300-1500 FM sce. 105.5 2330-1700 City FM sce. 97.25MHz 2330-1400 rel. Int'l Sce, at other times Lao FM sce. Luang Prabang: 103.5MHz 100W. Sam Neua, HP: 102.75MHz 100W (ann. freq.): As 4640kHz. Pakse, Ch: 100.0MHz: 2nd prgr. Sayaboury: 100W, unknown freq. Muang Khong, C: 97.2MHz. Attapeu: unknown freq. Luang Namtha prov: 1kW, unknown freq.
National Sce: N: 2300, 0000, 0500, 1200, 1400. **Hmong:** 2200-2230, 0630-0700. **Khmu:** 2230-2300, 0700-0730. **English/French LL:** Mon-Sat 1300-1330.
ANN: "Thini Sathani Vitthayou Krachaisiang Hengsat". Sam Neua: "Thini Vitthayou Krachaisiang Houa Phan, krachaisiang chak Muang Sam Neua".
IS: Music on Khéne (mouth organ) & Solo (bamboo instrument).

External Services: see International Broadcasting section.

LATVIA

L.T: UTC +2h (27 Mar - 30 Oct 2005: UTC +3h) — **Pop:** 2.5 million — **Pr.L:** Latvian, Russian — **E.C:** 50Hz, 220V — **ITU:** LVA

NACIONALA RADIO UN TELEVIZIJAS PADOME

Smilšu iela 1/3, 1939 Riga. ☎ +371 7221848. +371 7220448.
Email: tvcounc@mailbox.riga.lv **Web:** www.nrtp.lv
L.P: Chmn: Imants Rakins.
NOTES: NRTP is the regulatory authority for broadcasting.

LATVIJAS RADIO (Pub.)

Doma laukums 8, 1505 Riga. ☎ +371 7206722. +371 7206709.
Email: radio@radio.org.lv. **Web:** www.radio.org.lv
L.P: Dir. Gen: Dzintris Kolats.

FM (MHz)	**FM1**	**FM2**	**FM3**	**FM4**	**kW**
Aluksne	106.8	-	-	-	3.5
Cesvaine	102.5	105.0	103.5	-	20/20/5
Daugavpils	106.1	100.7	90.6	104.0	6.5/10/3.2
Dundaga	91.1	106.7	-	-	4
Kuldiga	95.9	101.3	92.0	-	10/18
Lielauce	99.6	-	-	-	1
Liepaja	107.1	101.0	104.6	97.9	10/10/1/5
Rezekne	104.2	101.0	101.8	107.5	20/20/20/5
Riga	90.7	91.5	103.7	107.7	15/3.5/5/6.3
Valmiera	104.0	101.5	87.6	-	18
Ventspils	99.2	103.0	89.8	95.3	0.3/0.3/0.3/1
Viesite	107.6	-	-	-	5
Vitrupe	105.5	-	-	-	1.6

D.PRGR: Prgr 1 (Latvijas Radio Viens): 24h on FM1 tx's. – **Prgr 2 (Latvijas Radio Divi):** 24h on FM2 tx's. – **Prgr 3 (Klasika)** 24h on FM3 tr's. The FM3 network also carries live broadcasts from parliament (exc. Riga 103.7), in Riga on 96.2MHz. – **Prgr 4 (Doma laukums/Domskaya ploshchad):** 24h on FM4 tx's in Russian, Latvian.

OTHER STATIONS

MW	**kHz**	**kW**	**Location**	**Station**
29)	945	2.7	Riga	R. Nord

FM	**MHz**	**ERP**	**Location**	**Station**
2)	87.9	2	Madona	Star FM
2)	88.1	1	Selpils	Star FM
3)	88.4	2.2	Liepaja	Kurzemes R.
17)	88.4	1	Gulbene	European Hit R.
8)	88.6	1	Jelgava	Gold FM
1C)	89.2	2.8	Riga	R. SWH Rock
4)	89.9	0.5	Sigulda	R. Sigulda
5)	90.3	0.5	Mazsalaca	R. Mazsalaca
12)	90.8	1	Ventspils	Kristigais R.
2)	91.0	2.2	Liepaja	Star FM
6)	91.4	1	Rezekne	R. EF-EI
17)	91.6	1	Viški	European Hit R.
2)	91.9	2	Rezekne	Star FM
3)	92.4	1.3	Tukums	Kurzemes R.
1A)	94.7	1.4	Saldus	R. SWH
17)	96.1	1.2	Liepaja	European Hit R.
28)	96.2	5	Riga	R. NABA
12)	98.5	3.3	Kuldiga	Kristigais R.
26)	99.0	2	Jurmala	R. Jurmala
17)	99.1	0.7	Cesis	European Hit R.
20A)	99.4	0.6	Daugavpils	R. Daugavai
7)	100.0	2.5	Riga	R. PIK
1A)	100.1	0.4	Kuldiga	R. SWH
1A)	100.3	5	Cesvaine	R. SWH
A)	100.5	0.9	Riga	BBC World Service
12)	100.6	0.6	Grobina	Kristigais R.
9)	100.9	0.4	Cesis	R. Saules Iela
25)	101.0	2.5	Iecava	Capital FM
1A)	101.2	1.4	Jekabpils	R. SWH
11)	101.6	2.5	Daugavpils	Alise Plus
12)	101.8	4.6	Riga	Kristigais R.
13)	102.0	1	Madona	Madonas R.
1A)	102.2	4	Talsi	R. SWH
14)	102.4	0.8	Valmiera	R. Imanta
15)	102.7	9.1	Riga	R. Mix FM
12)	102.8	1	Jekabpils	Kristigais R.
18)	103.0	0.8	Limbazi	R. Tris
18)	103.1	0.8	Smiltene	R. Tris
16)	103.2	0.2	Riga	Europa+ (R. Nova)
2)	103.2	5	Svente	Star FM
20)	103.4	0.8	Valmiera	R. Tris
2)	103.8	8	Kuldiga	Star FM
17)	104.3	4.6	Riga	European Hit R.
18)	104.7	1	Cesis	R. Tris
12)	104.7	0.9	Talsi	Kristigais R.
2)	105.0	1.6	Pope	Star FM
1A)	105.1	4.5	Liepaja	R. SWH
17)	105.1	1.3	Rezekne	European Hit R.
1A)	105.2	2.2	Daugavpils	R. SWH
1A)	105.2	20	Riga	R. SWH
1A)	105.4	1	Ventspils	R. SWH
27)	105.5	0.1	Rezekne	Europa+ (R. Latgalei)
1B)	105.7	4.5	Riga	R. SWH Pluss
19)	105.8	1	Liepaja	Rietumu R. 105.8
12)	105.9	4	Cesvaine	Kristigais R.
2)	106.2	5	Riga	Star FM
3)	106.4	10	Kuldiga	Kurzemes R.
1A)	106.5	4.6	Valmiera	R. SWH
1A)	106.5	4	Rezekne	R. SWH
10)	106.6	1	Bauska	R. Zemgale
21)	107.0	0.9	Jekabpils	R. 1 Jekabpils
23)	107.2	4.6	Riga	R. Skonto
20B)	107.2	2.5	Daugavpils	Europa+ (R. Maksimums)
17)	107.4	1	Kuldiga	European Hit R.
2)	107.4	2	Valmiera	Star FM
22)	107.6	1.6	Liepaja	R. Liepaja
3)	107.9	1	Ventspils	Kurzemes R.
24)	107.9	0.5	Saldus	Saldus R.

Addresses & other information:
1A,B,C) Skanstes iela 13, 1013 Riga. Email: radio@radioswh.lv. 1B) in Russian. Email: swhplus@radioswh.lv – **2)** Zakusalas krastmala 3, 1509 Riga. Email: info@starfm.lv – **3)** Pilsetas laukums 4, 3300 Kuldiga. Email: studija@kurzemesradio.lv – **4)** L.Paegles iela 3, 2150 Sigulda. Email: sigulda.fm@delfi.lv – **5)** Avotu iela 13, 4215 Mazsalaca. Email: rm@mauer.lv – **6)** Atbrivošanas aleja 98, 4600 Rezekne. Email: info@efeipro.lv. In Russian & Latvian. – **7)** Brivibas iela 30, 1050 Riga. Email: mail@pik.lv – **8)** L.Nometnu iela 62, 1002 Riga. Email: jr@valsts.lv – **9)** Meness iela 10, 4101 Cesis. Email: saulesiela@hotmail.lv – **10)** Grafa laukums 6, 3913 Iecava. Email: top@radiozemgalei.lv – **11)** Raina iela 28, 5403 Daugavpils. Email: alise_plus@daugavpils.apollo.lv. In Russian & Latvian. – **12)** Lacpleša iela 37, 1011 Riga. Email: lkr@lkr.lv. In Latvian & Russian. – **13)** Saieta laukums 1, 4800 Madona. – **14)** Terbatas iela 1, 4201 Valmiera. – **15)** K.Valdemara iela 8, 1010 Riga. Email: radio@mixfm.lv. In Russian. – **16)** Azenes iela 22a, 1081 Riga. Email: radio@103.2fm.lv. In Russian. Rel. Europa+ from Russia. – **17)** Elijas iela 17, 1050 Riga. Email: radio@superfm.lv – **18)** Valnu iela 13, 4101 Cesis. Email: radio@radio3.lv – **19)** Peldu iela 5, 3400 Liepaja. Email: info@rietumuradio.lv – **20A,B)** S.Mihoelsa iela 9, 5400 Daugavpils. In Russian & Latvian. Email: 20B) radiomax@mbox.latg.lv. Rel. Europa+ from Russia. – **21)** Brivibas iela 116, 5200 Jekabpils. Email: reklama@radio1.lv. In Latvian & Russian. – **22)** Klaipedas iela 19/21, 3401 Liepaja. Email: info@radioliepaja.lv – **23)** Elizabetes iela 75, 1011 Riga. Email: reklama@radioskonto.lv – **24)** Brivibas iela 16, 3801 Saldus. Email: radio@saldus.lv – **25)** L.Nometnu iela 62, 1002 Riga. Email: info@capitalfm.lv – **26)** Brivibas iela 30, 1050 Riga. – **27)** Latgales iela 20, 4600 Rezekne. Email: radio.latgalei@ rezekne.lv. In Russian. Rel. Europa+ from Russia. – **28)** Doma laukums 8, 1505 Riga. Email: naba@radionaba.lv. Shares tx with Latvijas Radio's live transmissions from parliament. – **29)** Ulbrokas Raidstacija 21, 2130 Ulbroka. Email: tesug@parks.lv – **A)** Relay BBCWS (cf. UK).

LEBANON

L.T: UTC +2h (27 Mar-30 Oct UTC +3h) — **Pop:** 3.6 million — **Pr.L:** Arabic, French, English, Armenian — **E.C:** 50Hz, 110/220V — **ITU:** LBN

MINISTRY OF INFORMATION

✉ Hamra, Beirut ☎ +961 1 754400 **Web:** www.ministryinfo.gov.lb

RADIO LEBANON

✉ Rue Lyon, Sanayeh, P.O. Box 4848, Beirut ☎ +961 1 743531 **Web:** www.libanvision.com/radio-liban96.2.htm **Email:** mykee@cyberia.net.lb

L.P: Dir: M. Sobhi Eid. Tech. Dir: Nazih Chahine. Chief, Prgr. Dept: Waheed Jalal. Chief, Public Rel: Faouzi Fehmy.
MW: Hamat 837kHz 1000kW (rep. using 10kW standby tr. at Amchit).
FM: Beirut 96.2MHz.
1st Prgr. in Arabic: 0330-2330 on MW. **2nd Prgr. in French/English/Armenian**: 24h on 96.2MHz. **Rel. R. France Int:** 13h daily. **ANN:** A: "Iza'at Loubnan min Beirut". F: "Ici Radio Liban émettant de Beyrouth" **IS:** Opening notes from the Lebanese National anthem played on guitar.

OTHER STATIONS

FM	MHz	Name	FM	MHz	Name
15)	87.5	Vo Charity	13)	97.4	Voice of Faith
21)	87.8	R. Nostalgie	26)	97.4	R. Strike
4)	88.5	R. Orient	26)	97.6	R. Strike
14)	89.1	Holy Quran R	12)	98.0	Voice of Tomorrow
8)	89.2	Nat. Broadc. Netw.	7)	98.5	Jabal Loubnan
17)	90.0	Kiss FM, Aajaltoun	5)	99.0	RML
14)	90.1	Holy Quran R.	13)	99.3	Voice of Faith, Beit Meri
13)	90.3	Voice of Faith	16)	99.7	Fame FM
18)	90.6	R. Light FM	24)	100.4	R. Lebanon Star
17)	91.0	Kiss FM, Achrafieh	25)	101.1	R. Scope
9)	91.3	The Call of Islam	23)	101.8	R. Delta
3)	92.0	R. of the Light	10)	102.5	R. Free Lebanon
28)	92.7	France FM La Une	22)	103.2	Pax R.
1)	93.4	Voice of Lebanon	2)	103.9	Voice of the People
6)	94.0	Radio One	20)	104.6	Mix FM, Achrafieh
14)	94.1	Holy Quran R	12)	105.1	Voice of Tomorrow
6)	94.5	Radio One	6)	105.3	Radio One
11)	94.8	R. Van	15)	106.0	Voice of Charity
4)	95.1	RML, Farya Mzaar	27)	106.7	Sound of Music
13)	95.5	Voice of Faith	19)	107.4	Master Broadc. Station
3)	95.9	R. of the Light	15)	107.5	Voice of Charity
12)	96.9	Voice of Tomorrow			

Note: the stations have been allocated 400 kHz frequency range, of which the centre freq. is listed above. In many cases the transmitters from various sites are placed on both upper and lower limits of this range.

Addresses & other information
1) P.O. Box 165271, Ashrafieh, Bachir el Gemayel Ave, Beirut ☎ +961 1 323458 🖷 +961 1 219290 **Web**: www.vdl.com.lb **Email**: info@vdl.com.lb **D.Prgr**: 0350-2330. Also rel. RCI & RFI. **N: French:** 0800, 1300, 1715. **English:** 0900, 1200, 1700. **ANN:** A: "Huna Saout Loubnan". F: "Ici La Voix du Liban". E: "This is the Voice of Lebanon" **IS:** Opens with River Kwai March and Lebanese National Anthem. Closes with River Kwai March and Kataëb Party Anthem. – **2)** Jabal el Arab St, Wata el Mousaitbeh, P.O.Box 14/5425, Beirut ☎ +961 1 311480 🖷 +961 1 313605 **D.Prgr**: 0400-2300 in **Arabic**. **ANN:** "Saout al Shaab". – **3)** Al-Nour Bldg, Abdel Nour St, Haret Hreïk, P.O.Box 25-197, Ghbeiry, Beirut ☎ +961 1 543555 **Web**: www.alnour.net **Email**: info@al-nour.net **D.Prgr**: 0400-2230. **ANN:** " Izaat Al Noor". – **4)** Annajah Centre, Mar Elias St, Karakol Druz, P.O.Box 11-6362, Beirut ☎ +961 1 646698/9 🖷 + 961 1 869772/3 **Web**: futuretvnetwork.com/radioorient **Email**: radioorient@future.com.lb **ANN:** "Idha'at as-Shark min Beirut". – **5)** Mont Liban Bldg, Ave. Fouad Chehab, Fassouh, P.O. Box 16-6000, Achrafieh, Beirut ☎ +961 1 217000 🖷 +961 1 215215 **Web**: www.rml.com.lb **Email**: rml@rml.com.lb **D.Prgr**: 24h in **English**. – **6)** Zakhem Bldg, Beit Meri El Metn ☎ +961 4 872000 🖷 +961 4 972818 **D.Prgr:** 0400-2300 in **English**. **Web:** www.radioonev5.com **Email:** radio1@radioonc.com.lb **7)** Mont Liban Bldg, Avo. Fouad Chohab, Fassouh, P.O.Box 16-6000, Achrafieh, Beirut ☎ +961 1 202500 🖷 +961 1 215215. – **8)** Adnan Al Hakim St, Block A, P.O.Box 13-6633, Chouran, Beirut ☎ +961 1 841020 🖷 +961 1 841029 **Web**: www.nbn.com.lb **Email**: nbnradio@nbn.com.lb – **9)** Shaykh Ahmad Iskandarani Centre, Bourj Abi Haidar, Beirut. – **10)** Kebbe Bldg, Adonis, Zouk Mosbeh, P.O.Box 110, Zouk Mekhael, Jounieh ☎ +961 9 225577 🖷 +961 9 215868 **Web**: www.rll.com.lb **Email**: info@rll.com.lb **D.Prgr**: 0340-2300. **ANN:** "Iza'at Loubnan al Horr". – **11)** 2nd floor, Shaghzoyan Centre, Borj Hammoud, P.O. Box 80-860, Beirut ☎ +961 1 267657 🖷 +961 1 241272. **D.Prgr**: 24h in **Armenian**. – **12)** 2nd floor, Disco Samir Bldg, Zalka Rd, El Metn ☎ +961 4 710200 🖷 +961 4 710300 **Web**: www.sawtelghad.com **Email**: info@sawtelghad.com **ANN:** "Saout al Ghad". – **13)** Near Riyad el Solh Palace, Bir Hassan, P.O. Box 83/25, Ghbeiri, Beirut ☎ +961 1 822413 🖷 +961 1 601062 **D.Prgr**: 0430-2400. – **14)** Dar al Fatwa, P.O. Box 14-5380, Al Mazraa-Beirut 28031105 ☎ +961 1 794700 🖷 +961 1 795700 **Web**: www.darfatwa.gov.lb **Email**: quran@cyberia.net.lb **ANN:** "Dar Al Fatwa, Izaat al-Quran al-Kareem min Loubnan". – **15)** Couvent St. Jean, Fouad Chehab St, P.O. Box 850, Jounieh ☎ +961 9 918090 🖷 +961 9 930272 **D.Prgr**: 24h in **Arabic/French/English/others**. Also rel. Vatican R. Relayed on SW by Vatican R. 0530-0555. **Ann**: "Sowt Al-Mahaba". – **16)** 3rd floor, La Perla Centre, Sabra Highway, Jounieh, or P.O. Box 166771, Achrafieh, Beirut ☎/🖷 +961 9 644995 **Web**: www. famefm.com **Email**: famefm@famefm.com – **17)** Mar Mikhaël, Achrafieh, Beirut ☎ +961 3 708811 🖷 +961 1 583749 **D.Prgr**: 24h in **French/English**. – **18)** 8th floor, Mansour Bldg, Independence St, Sassine Square, Achrafieh, Beirut ☎/🖷+961 1 202215 **Web**: www.radiolightfm.com **Email**: lightfm@radiolightfm.com **D.Prgr**: 0500-2200 in **English/French**. – **19)** St. Paul bldg, facing La Cite, Jounieh ☎ +961 3 314123 🖷 +961 9 635933 – **20)** Alfred Naccache Ave, P.O. Box 166-815, Achrafieh, Beirut ☎ +961 1 333288 🖷 +961 1 217788 **Web**: www.mixfm.com.lb **Email**: info@mixfm.com.lb **D.Prgr**: 24h in **English**. – **21)** Mont Liban Bldg, Ave. Fouad Chehab, Fassouh, P.O.Box 16-6000, Achrafieh, Beirut ☎ +961 1 328000 🖷 +961 1 423121 **Web**: www.nostalgie.com.lb **Email**: nostalgie@nostalgie.com.lb **D.Prgr**: 24h in **French**. – **22)** P.O. Box 116-5104, Beirut ☎/🖷+961 1 330104 **D.Prgr**: 24h in **English**. – **23)** Kahalé Bldg, Old St, P.O.Box 1306, Beit Meri el Metn ☎ +961 4 972324 🖷 +961 4 870884 **Web**: www.4com.net.lb/delta – **24)** 1st floor, Nehme Bldg, Sin el Fil main rd, Hayek ☎ +961 4 971320 🖷 +961 4 871444 **ANN:** "Noujoum Loubnan". – **25)** facing Tal-Shiha Hospital, Tal-Shiha, Zahlé ☎ +961 8 806200 🖷 +961 8 822730 **D.Prgr**: 0400-2200 in **Arabic**. – **26)** 2nd floor, Abi Jaber Bldg, Al Saideh St, Sin El-Fil, Beirut ☎ +961 1 510517 🖷 +961 1 510519 **Web**: www.radiostrike.com **Email**: radiostrike@radiostrike.com **D.Prgr**: 0600-2200 in **Arabic**. – **27)** Centre Nasrallah, Rue Al-Anwar, Jdeideh, P.O. Box 90-1119, Beirut ☎ +961 1 878819 🖷 +961 1 602222 **Web**: www.sawtelmousika.com **Email**: info@sawtelmousika.com **D.Prgr**: 0430-2400 in **Arabic**. **ANN:** "Saout al Moussika" – **28)** 8th floor, Mansour Bldg, Independence St, Sassine Square, Achrafieh, Beirut ☎ +961 4 872000 🖷 +961 1 331039 **Email**: francefm@hotmail.com **D.Prgr**: 24h in **French**.

LESOTHO

L.T: UTC +2h — **Pop:** 2.2 million — **Pr.L:** Sesotho, English — **E.C:** 50Hz, 220V — **ITU:** LSO

MINISTRY OF COMMUNICATIONS

✉ P.O. Box 36, Maseru 100 ☎+266 323561 🖷 +266 310264 **L.P:** Dr. M. Khatletla, Minister. **Web:** www.lesotho.gov.ls/mninfor.htm

LESOTHO NATIONAL BROADCASTING SERVICE (LNBS)

✉ P. O. Box 552,Lerotholi Str, Opposite Royal Palace, Maseru 100 ☎/🖷+266 22 323371 **Web**: www.radiolesotho.co.ls
L.P: Dir. of Broadc: Mr. Lebohang Dada Mokasa. CE: Mr. Motlatsi Monyane. Principal Tech. Officer: 'Masekoala Ratia.
STATION: Maseru (Lancer's Gap, G.C: 29S19 027E32).
MW: 891kHz 100kW
SW: 4800kHz 100kW (inactive).
FM:

Location	MHz	kW	Location	MHz	kW
Mohale's Hoek	90.0	1	Semonkong	98.9	0.25
Maseru	93.3	1	Maseru	99.8	1
Leribe	96.0	1	Quthing	102.4	1
Thaba-Tseka	96.8	1	Mokhotlong	103.6	0.25
Mafeteng	97.2	1			

D.Prgr in Sesotho/English: 24h. **N. in English:** 0500, 1130, 1600.
ANN: E: "This is Radio Lesotho" or "This is the Lesotho National Broadcasting Service, Maseru". Sesotho: "Se-ea-le-moea sa Lesotho, Maseru". **IS:** National Anthem at s/on and s/off.

Other stations:
Family R, Maseru. **MW**: 1197kHz 100kW. **D.Prgr:** English 1600-1900, 2000-2200, Portuguese 1900-2000. For further details see International Radio section (USA).
Catholic R. FM, 103.3MHz.
Joy R, Private Bag A68, Maseru 100. **Web:** www.joyfm.co.ls **FM:**

106.9MHz 1kW. Also rel. VOA. **F.PI**: tr's in Mafeteng and Maputsoe.
Khotso FM, Maseru: 106.1MHz. **Web:** www.desk.nl/~gris/public/RTL2000/IEMS/KFM
Maseru 100, Maseru: 100MHz. Also rel. VOA.
MoAfrika FM, Maseru: 97MHz.
People's Choice FM, Development House, Block D, Floor 9, Kingsway Str, Maseru. **FM**: 95.6MHz. **Web**: www.pcfm.co.ls
BBC African Sce: Maseru 90.2MHz.
RFI Afrique: Maseru 96.5MHz in French/English.

LIBERIA

L.T: UTC — **Pop:** 3.2 million — **Pr.L:** English, 18 ethnic — **E.C:** 60Hz, 120V — **ITU:** LBR

MINISTRY OF INFORMATION

✉ 110 U.N. Drive, P.O. Box 10-9021, 1000 Monrovia 10, Liberia
L.P: Jacob Hina, Dir. of Broadcast Division.

LIBERIA BROADCASTING SYSTEM (LBS)

✉ P.O. Box 10-594, 1000 Monrovia 10 ☎ +231 224984/221036/222758/222647 📠 +231 228042
FM: R. Liberia: 91.7MHz 5kW, 99.9MHz 1kW.
D.Prgr: FM 0455-1005 & 1200-2400, Sat 0450-2400, Sun 0650-2400 (91.7 also rel. BBC African Sce).

RADIO ELWA (Rlg.)

✉ Radio ELWA, Box 192, Monrovia ☎ +231 000 330745
Web: www.radioelwa.org **L.P:** GM: Moses T. Nyantee
FM: Monrovia 94.5MHz 0.25kW – **SW:** Monrovia 4760kHz 1kW.
D.Prgr: 0600-1200, 1730-2230 in English/Vernaculars.

RADIO VERITAS (Rlg.)

✉ P.O. Box 3569, Monrovia ☎ +231 221658/226979. **L.P:** Stn. Mgr: Ledger Hood.
SW: Monrovia 10kW: 0600-1700 on 6090kHz, 1700-2300 on 5470kHz (inactive). **FM:** 97.8MHz 5kW.
D.Prgr: 0600-2300 in English/Vernaculars. Also rel. VOA.
ANN: "This is R. Veritas, the Voice of Truth".

WORD BROADCASTING (Rlg.)

✉ c/o Morgan Freeman, 5400 Minors Lane, Louisville KY 40219, USA. ☎ +1 502 9681220. **Web**: www.wjiesw.com
Email: morgan@wjiesw.org **FM:** Monrovia 102.1MHz.
F.PI: shortwave transmissions from Monrovia.

Other stations:
R. LIJ (Liberia Institute of Journalism) ✉ Corner of Broad and Johnson Streets, Kashour Building, Second Floor, P.O. Box 2314, Monrovia ☎ +231 227327 **Web:** www.radiolij.org **Email:** info@radiolij.org **L.P:** Vinicius Hodges, Dir. **FM:** 96.6MHz.
R. Monrovia 98 FM ✉ P.O. Box 10-3501, Monrovia ☎ +231 225301 📠 +231 222743 - **FM:** 98MHz 1.35kW **D.Prgr**: 0600-2400. **N:** rel. VOA.
DC 101.1 FM ✉ Ducor Broadc. Corp, P.O. Box 1312, Monrovia. **L.P:** Stn. Mgr: Martin Browne. **FM:** 101.1MHz **D.Prgr:** 0600-2400 (also rel. BBC African Sce).
Stone FM: 105MHz.
RFI Afrique: Monrovia 106MHz in French/English.
F.PI: reactivation of Star Radio on shortwave.

LIBYA

L.T: UTC +2h — **Pop:** 7.5 million — **Pr.L:** Arabic — **E.C:** 50Hz, 127/230V — **ITU:** LBY

LIBYAN JAMAHIRIYA BROADCASTING CORPORATION (The Great Socialist People's Libyan Arab Jamahiriyah Broadcasting Corporation)

✉ P.O. Box 9333 (**Ext. Sce:** Box 4677), Soug al Jama, Tripoli ☎ +218 21 603191/5. **Benghazi** local radio station📠 +218 61 9092203. **Misurata** local radio station 📠 +218 51 618930 **Sabha** local radio station ☎ +218 71 629453 **Sirt** local radio station 📠 +218 54 62002 **Tripoli** local radio station 📠 +218 21 4447888. **Al Baida** local radio station ☎ +218 84 2400. Sabha local radio station ☎+218 71 629453. **Web:** www.ljbc.net.

MW	kHz	kW	N
Tobruk	648	300	V
Benghazi	675	100	H
Ghadames	711	50	V
Jefren	711	50	V
Sabha	711	50	V+L
Sirt	792	20	H
Sabha	828	300	H
Ghiagboub	909	20	H
Kufra	909	10	H
Sirt	972	50	H
Tripoli	1053	50	H
Al Beida	1125	500	H
Tripoli	1251	500	V
Tripoli	1404	20	Q
Misurata	1449	500	H+V
Brak	1485	1	Q/F

Networks: H=Home Sce, V=V. of Africa, Q=Holy Quran Prgr, F=Foreign Language Prgr, E=Ext. Sce. L= Local R.

FM(MHz)	Location	Network
87.9	Al Beida	H
89.3	Benghazi	L
91.9	Tripoli	H
94.0	Tripoli	L
95.6	Tripoli	H
96.0	Tripoli	H
98.0	Tobruk	H
98.8	Benghazi	Q
101.3	Tripoli	L
103.4	Tripoli	L
104.0	Tripoli	Q
105.5	Misurata	Q
106.6	Tripoli	Q
107.0	Tripoli	Q

(These sts have been monitored from Italy. No info. available from LJBC)

Home Service: 0530-2350. **N:** 0600, 0900, 1200, 1330, 1600, 1700, 1900, 2130, 2300. **Voice of Africa:** 1000-0330 in Arabic, but short newscast in English & French (15 mins) irregularly – **Holy Quran Prgr:** 0500v-1900v on 1404kHz, 0500v-1400 on 1485kHz.
Foreign Language Prgr: French 1400-1600, **English** 1600-1800.All programs on FM & 1485 kHz.
Tripoli Radio of the Arabs on 104.0MHz: 0700-1100 & 1600-1800.

ANN: H: "Idha'at al jamahiriya al-'arrabiya al-libyya ash-sha'abiyya al-sitirakkiya". V: "Idha'at saout al-watan al'arabbiy al-Kabir".
IS: Prgrs open and close with National Anthem **V.** by QSL-card.

EXTERNAL SERVICE: **Voice of Africa**
see International Broadcasting section

LIECHTENSTEIN

L.T: UTC +1h (27 Mar-30 Oct: UTC +2h) — **Pop:** 31,000 — **Pr.L:** Allemanian (German dialect), German — **E.C:** 50Hz, 220V — **ITU:** LIE

LIECHTENSTEINISCHER RUNDFUNK (Pub.)

✉ Dorfstr. 24, 9495 Triesen, Fürstentum Liechenstein ☎ +423 399 1313 📠 +423 399 1399 **Email:** admin@radiol.li **Web:** www.radiol.li
L.P: Super. Mario Aldrovandi.
FM: Vaduz 96.9MHz 0.8kW, Buchs 96.9 MHz, Sargans 96.9 MHz 0.2kW, Bregenz & Feldkirch 106.1MHz 0.25kW.
D.PRGR: Radio Liechtenstein24h music & information **V.** by letter. Rp.

LITHUANIA

L.T: UTC +2h (27 Mar - 30 Oct: UTC +3h) — **Pop:** 3.7 million — **Pr.L:** Lithuanian, Polish, Russian — **E.C:** 50Hz, 220V — **ITU:** LTU

LIETUVOS RADIJO IR TELEVIZIJOS KOMISIJA

✉ Vytenio g. 6/23, 03113 Vilnius. ☎ +370 5 2330660. 📠 +370 5 264 7125. **Email:** lrtk@rtk.lt **Web:** www.rtk.lt
L.P: Chmn: Jonas Liniauskas
NOTES: LRTK is the regulatory authority for broadcasting.

LIETUVOS RADIJAS (Pub.)

✉ S.Konarskio g. 49, 03123 Vilnius. ☎ +370 5 2363209. 📠 +370 5 2363208. **Email:** lrt@lrt.lt **Web:** www.lrt.lt
L.P: Dir: Rimgaudas Gelezevicius.

MW	kHz	kW	Station
Sitkunai	666	500	LR1

FM (MHz)	LR1	LR2	kW
Alytus	104.6	102.8	0.5
Anykščiai	101.9	106.5	17.4/4
Birzai	100.8	87.5	10/5
Bubiai	100.9	103.4	1.3/10
Dieveniškes*	-	107.6	2
Druskininkai	102.3	103.7	5
Ignalina	92.3	99.6	1/2
Juragiai	102.1	96.2	20/10
Kalvarija*	-	104.8	2
Klaipeda	102.8	105.3	17
Mazeikiai	93.3	101.8	5/0.5
Nida	106.8	103.3	0.5
Pazagieniai	107.5	105.3	1.5

MW	kHz	kW	Station
Plunge	88.0	105.0	1/2
Skuodas	99.3	103.5	0.7/4
Taurage	98.8	107.4	4/1
Telsiai*	93.0	107.0	-
Vilnius	102.6	105.1	5
Visaginas	102.9	100.4	11

*) FPl.

D.PRGR: LR1 (Pirmoji programa): 24h in on FM, 0300-2000 on MW. Russian: 1430-1500. R. Vilnius in **English:** 1900-1930. – **LR2 (Klasika):** 0400-2200. For ethnic minorities: 1500-1530 Belarusian (Tue/Sat), Russian (Wed-Fri, Sun), Yiddish (Mon); Polish: 1530-1600.

EXTERNAL SERVICE: Radio Vilnius
See International Radio section

OTHER STATIONS

MW	kHz	kW	Location	Station
33A)	612	100	Vilnius	Baltijos bangu radijas
33B)	1386	500	Sitkunai	Relays (RBWI)
33B)	1557	150	Sitkunai	Relays (RBWI)

FM	MHz	ERP	Location	Station
3A)	67.52	0.9	Klaipeda	Radiocentras
3A)	67.55	1	Pazagieniai	Radiocentras
3A)	67.67	1.4	Juragiai	Radiocentras
3A)	67.94	4	Vilnius	Radiocentras
10)	70.04	0.12	Alytus	FM 99
5A)	70.22	0.25	Kaunas	Pukas
3B)	88.2	3.2	Bubiai	RC2
7)	88.7	1.6	Palanga	FM Palanga
5B)	90.1	2	Klaipeda	Pukas 2
3C)	90.6	2.3	Klaipeda	Russkoje R. Baltija
1B)	90.7	0.5	Raseiniai	M-1 Plius
3A)	91.2	4	Tryškiai	Radiocentras
3B)	91.6	2	Skuodas	RC2
28)	91.8	2	Šiauliai*	Marijos radijas
3B)	92.1	0.7	Nida	RC2
26)	92.2	3.5	Bubiai	Relax FM
5B)	92.4	3.2	Kaunas	Pukas 2
3B)	92.5	4.5	Klaipeda	RC2
3B)	92.7	5	Mazeikiai	RC2
1A)	92.8	1	Kedainai*	M-1
6)	93.4	2.5	Marijampole	Ziniu radijas
5A)	94.0	2.5	Alytus	Pukas
5A)	94.2	5	Raseiniai	Pukas
30)	94.2		Videniškiai	Videniškiu radijas
4B)	94.4	0.6	Palanga*	European Hit R.
32)	94.4		Utena	Victoria FM
5A)	94.6	2	Ukmerge	Pukas
5A)	94.8	3.2	Marijampole	Pukas
14A)	94.9	2	Klaipeda	Laluna
27)	94.9	0.1	Vilnius	Uzupio radijas
6)	95.3	0.6	Alytus	Ziniu radijas
22)	95.4	4	Teliai	Zemaitijos radijas
A)	95.5	3.2	Vilnius	BBC World Service
5A)	95.7	2	Šiauliai	Pukas
5A)	95.8	0.6	Utena	Pukas
23)	95.9	2	Vilnius	Power Hit R.
6)	96.0	2	Birzai	Ziniu radijas
6)	96.4	2	Mazeikiai	Ziniu radijas
8)	96.4	1.4	Vilnius	A2
1B)	96.5	0.5	Taurage	M-1 Plius
9)	96.6	1	Panevezys	Pulsas
23)	96.7	2.5	Klaipeda	Power Hit R.
	96.8	0.5	Vilnius	[Testtone]
6)	97.0	0.9	Šiauliai	Ziniu radijas
6)	97.3	0.6	Vilnius	Ziniu radijas
5B)	97.4	1	Šiauliai	Pukas 2
1B)	97.6	4	Juragiai	M-1 Plius
3A)	97.7	2	Plunge	Radiocentras
1B)	98.3	3	Klaipeda	M-1 Plius
B)	98.3	0.5	Vilnius	RFI
1B)	98.7	3	Utena	M-1 Plius
3B)	99.0	0.6	Ignalina	RC2
10)	99.0	3.1	Alytus	FM 99
29)	99.0	0.3	Klaipeda	Vox Maris
3B)	99.1	0.3	Pazagieniai	RC2
11)	99.3	0.4	Vilnius	Spiritus Movens
3A)	99.5	0.5	Ukmerge	Radiocentras
4A)	99.7	1	Vilnius	Super FM
20)	99.8	3.2	Klaipeda	Kelyje
3A)	99.9	3	Raseiniai	Radiocentras
6)	100.0	0.3	Druskininkai	Ziniu radijas
3B)	100.1	12.6	Vilnius	RC2
1B)	100.2	1	Pazagieniai	M-1 Plius
12)	100.2	0.9	Marijampole	Kapsai
3C)	100.4	4	Kaunas	Russkoje R. Baltija
13)	100.4	4	Mazeikiai	Mazeikiu aidas
1B)	100.5	2	Bubiai	M-1 Plius
6)	100.6	0.6	Ukmerge	Ziniu radijas
3B)	100.8	1	Marijampole	RC2
14B)	100.8	1.3	Klaipeda	Raduga
5B)	100.9	1.1	Vilnius	Pukas 2
3A)	101.0	2	Utena	Radiocentras
3A)	101.1	2	Alytus	Radiocentras
3A)	101.3	1	Jonava	Radiocentras
3A)	101.4	4	Pazagieniai	Radiocentras
3A)	101.5	3.5	Vilnius	Radiocentras
3A)	101.5	2.5	Klaipeda	Radiocentras
31)	101.5		Utena	Indros radijas
3A)	101.6	2	Druskininkai	Radiocentras
5A)	101.6	1.6	Taurage	Pukas
3A)	101.7	3.2	Bubiai	Radiocentras
3A)	101.8	2	Marijampole	Radiocentras
25)	101.9	0.16	Vilnius	Geras FM
5A)	102.0	1	Visaginas	Pukas
6)	102.2	1.6	Klaipeda	Ziniu radijas
5A)	102.3	0.5	Panevezys	Pukas
15)	102.5	3.4	Bubiai	Saules radijas
23)	102.5	0.1	Kaunas	Power Hit R.
5A)	102.6	1	Skuodas	Pukas
3A)	102.7	1.5	Taurage	Radiocentras
3A)	102.7	1	Ignalina	Radiocentras
16)	102.9	4	Juragiai	Tau
2)	103.0	3	Pazagieniai	Lietus
2)	103.0	1.1	Tryškiai	Lietus
2)	103.1	1.7	Taurage	Lietus
2)	103.1	2	Vilnius	Lietus
2)	103.3	2	Alytus	Lietus
2)	103.3	2	Birzai	Lietus
2)	103.4	1.2	Utena	Lietus
2)	103.5	3.4	Juragiai	Lietus
2)	103.7	1.2	Klaipeda	Lietus
3C)	103.7	0.3	Panevezys	Russkoje R. Baltija
6)	103.7	1.1	Visaginas	Ziniu radijas
17)	103.8	4	Vilnius	Znad Wilii
2)	103.9	2.2	Bubiai	Lietus
4B)	103.9	0.3	Marijampole	European Hit R.
3B)	104.1	20	Juragiai	RC2
4B)	104.1	3.2	Klaipeda	European Hit R.
1B)	104.3	3.2	Marijampole	M-1 Plius
4B)	104.3	1.8	Šiauliai	European Hit R.
26)	104.3	0.5	Vilnius	Relax FM
6)	104.4	2.2	Utena	Ziniu radijas
4B)	104.5	4	Juragiai	European Hit R.
24)	104.5	0.2	Plunge	Spindulys
4B)	104.7	1	Vilnius	European Hit R.
4B)	104.8	1.1	Pazagieniai	European Hit R.
6)	104.8	2.5	Taurage	Ziniu radijas
6)	104.9	1	Kaunas	Ziniu radijas
3B)	105.2	1.3	Raseiniai	RC2
3B)	105.4	10	Visaginas	RC2
18)	105.4	4	Kaunas	KF 105.4
3A)	105.5	2	Birzai	Radiocentras
3C)	105.6	0.7	Vilnius	Russkoje R. Baltija
19)	105.6	0.3	Mazeikiai	Ventus
3B)	105.7	2	Taurage	RC2
3C)	105.8	4.2	Šiauliai	Russkoje R. Baltija
1A)	105.9	3.2	Ignalina	M-1
20)	105.9	1	Kaunas	Kelyje
1A)	106.0	2	Alytus	M-1
1A)	106.0	2	Pazagieniai	M-1
1A)	106.0	2	Tryškiai	M-1
28)	106.0	0.3	Klaipeda*	Marijos radijas
1A)	106.2	1.6	Taurage	M-1
1B)	106.2	2.5	Vilnius	M-1 Plius
1A)	106.3	2.5	Bubiai	M-1
1A)	106.3	2	Utena	M-1
1A)	106.3	2.5	Marijampole	M-1
1A)	106.4	2	Raseiniai	M-1
1A)	106.5	2.5	Klaipeda	M-1
1A)	106.6	2.5	Juragiai	M-1
3B)	106.7	2	Laukuva	RC2

FM	MHz	ERP	Location	Station
1A)	106.8	1	Vilnius	M-1
21)	106.9	0.8	Pazagieniai	Aukštaitijos radijas
3A)	107.1	2.5	Juragiai	Radiocentras
5A)	107.1	1	Varena*	Pukas
5A)	107.3	1	Vilnius	Pukas
9)	107.3	3.2	Birzai	Pulsas
3B)	107.6	0.2	Druskininkai	RC2
5A)	107.6	4	Kaunas	Pukas
20)	107.7	0.6	Vilnius	Kelyje
5A)	107.8	3.2	Klaipeda	Pukas
6)	107.9	1.2	Panevezys	Ziniu radijas

+ 12 sts of less than 0.1kW *) F.Pl

Addresses & other information:

1A,B) Laisves pr. 60, 05120 Vilnius. Email: 1A) m-1@m-1.fm, 1B) pliusas@pliusas.fm – **2)** Laisves pr. 60, 05120 Vilnius. Email: lietus@lietus.fm **3A,B,C)** Laisves pr. 60, 05120 Vilnius. Email: 3A) programa@rc.lt; 3B) info@rc2.lt; 3C) Rel. Russkoye R. (cf. Russia) rusradio@rc.lt – **4A,B)** Naugarduko g. 91, 03202 Vilnius. Email: info@ehr.lt – **5A,B)** Ringuvos g. 61, 45243 Kaunas. Email: radio@pukas.lt – **6)** Laisves pr. 60, 05120 Vilnius. Email: biuras@ziniur.lt – **7)** Vanagupes g. 15, 00169 Palanga. – **8)** S.Staneviciaus g. 60-18, 07117 Vilnius. Email: a2@a2.lt – **9)** Respublikos g. 28, 35174 Panevezys. Email: pulsas@elektra.lt – **10)** Rotušes a. 2a, 62141 Alytus. Email: fm99@fm99.lt – **11)** Laisves pr. 60, 05120 Vilnius.. Email: jazz_fm@takas.lt – **12)** P. Armino g. 71, 68127 Marijampole. Email: kapsai@delfi.lt – **13)** Sodu g. 13-93, 89116 Mazeikiai. Email: info@mazeikiuaidas.lt – **14A,B)** Taikos pr. 81, 94114 Klaipeda. Email: 15A) laluna@laluna.lt, 15B) (in Russian): raduga@raduga.lt – **15)** Aušros al. 64, 76235 Šiauliai. Email: info@saulesradijas.lt – **16)** Draugystes g. 19, 51230 Kaunas. Email: info@tau.lt – **17)** Laisves pr. 60, 05120 Vilnius. In Polish. Email: radio@znadwilii.lt – **18)** Radastu g. 2, 44164 Kaunas. Email: info@kaunoradijas.lt – **19)** Montuotoju g. 2, 89101 Mazeikiai. Email: admin@ventus.lt – **20)** Savanoriu pr. 151, 50174 Kaunas. Email: kelyje@takas.lt – **21)** Laisves a. 1, 35175 Panevezys. Email: ar@laineta.lt – **22)** Mazeikiu g. 18, 87101 Telšiai. Email: zemaitijos@radijas.lt – **23)** Nemencines pl. 4, 10102 Vilnius. Email: info@powerhitradio.lt – **24)** Senamieščio a. 3, 90162 Plunge. Email: rs.spindulys@takas.lt – **25)** Gariunu g. 49, 02242 Vilnius. Email: geruda@takas.lt – **26)** Fabioniškiu g. 31-12, 07120 Vilnius. Email: info@relaxfm.lt – **27)** Uzupio g. 40, 01203 Vilnius. Email: radijas@tores.lt – **28)** M.Daukšos g. 21, 44282 Kaunas. Email: direktorius@marijosradijas.lt – **29)** Turgaus g./Teatro a. 1, 91247 Klaipeda. Email: Email: vox@vox.lt – **30)** Videniškiai, 33031 Moletu r. Email: videniskiupm@is.lt – **31)** Maironio g. 12, 28143 Utena. – **32)** Jasoniu k. 5-9, 28103 Utenos r. Email: vygan@one.lt – **33A,B)** P.d. 3245, 02002 Vilnius. Email: radio@balticwaves.cjb.net. On 612: 0400-0600 RFE-RL, 0800-0900 Voice of Russia "Russian Int'l R."*, 0900-1600 Voice of Russia "Radiokanal Sodruzhestvo"*, 1600-2200 RFE-RL, 2200-2230 R.Polonia (all in Belarusian exc. * in Russian). Relays on 1386/1557 kHz: see International Radio section. **A)** Rel. BBCWS (cf. UK) **B)** Rel. RFI (cf. France).

DAB: Ch 13A 230.784MHz, 0.5kW, LRTC, Vilnius

LORD HOWE ISLAND (Australian)

L.T: UTC +10½h (31 Oct-27 Mar: UTC +11h) — **Pop:** 270 — **Pr.L:** English — **E.C:** 50Hz, 240V. — **ITU:** AUS (**WRTH:** LHW)

RADIO LORD HOWE ISLAND

✉ P O Box 5, Lord Howe Island, NSW 2898, Australia ☎ +61 (02) 656 32123 **L.P:** SM: Gary Millman,

AM: 1494kHz 0.1kW (reported relaying 4QR 621kHz). **FM:** Signal Point 101.0MHz 30W.

D.Prgr: Thurs 1830-2400. Other times vary seasonally. Rel. 2JJJ when no local announcer available. **V.** by letter. Rp.

LUXEMBOURG

L.T: UTC +1h (27 Mar-30 Oct: UTC +2h) — **Pop:** 400,000 — **Pr.L:** Luxembourgish, French, German — **E.C:** 50Hz, 110/220V — **ITU:** LUX

CLT-UFA (Comm.)

✉ 45 blvd. Pierre Frieden, L-1543 Luxembourg ☎ +352 4214 22175 🖷 +352 4214 22756 **Web:** www.clt-ufa.com

L.P: Pres:Alain Berwick. Exec. VP (Radio): Jean-Michel Kerotraon. Exec. VP (Gen. Affairs): Dan Brendt.

Luxembourg Sce: RTL Radio Lëtzebuerg: ☎ +352 4214 23 🖷 +352 4214 22737 **Web:** www.rtl.lu

German Sce: RTL Radio – die Grössten Oldies: ☎ +352 4214 23500 🖷 +352 4214 22738 **Web:** www.rtlradio.de **L.P:** PD: Holger Richter.

French Sce: RTL: 22 rue Bayard, F-75008 Paris ☎ +33 (1) 4070 4070 🖷 +33 (1) 4070 4272. **RTL2:** ☎+33 (1) 4070 4000 🖷 +33 (1) 4070 4350 **Web:** www.rtl2.fr — **L.P:** CEO: Jacques Rigaud. VP & PD: Philippe Labro. Prgr. Mgr RTL2: Frédéric Jouve.

LW/MW: Junglinster 234kHz 2000kW, Marnach 1440kHz 300kW; via 1440 kHz also relay of China Radio International (2000-2400 CET)

FM: Marnach 88.9/97.0/107.0MHz 100kW, 92.5MHz 50kW. Dudelange 93.3MHz 100kW. Also FM relays in France & Germany.

RTL Radio Lëtzebuerg in English/German/Luxembourgish: 24h on 92.5MHz (2000-0500 rel. German Sce.)

RTL: 24h on 234kHz + FM network in France.

RTL2: 24h on FM network in France

RTL Radio – die Grössten Oldies: 24h on 93.3 and 97.0MHz + 1440 kHz 0500-2000 + satellite and via tr's in Germany.

OTHER STATIONS

Den Neie Radio, P.O. Box 1522, L-1015 Luxembourg. **Web:** http://www.dnr.lu/ 102.9/ 104.2/107.7MHz – **Eldoradio,** B.P. 1344, L-1013 Luxembourg. **Web:** eldoradio.lu 24h on 105.0/107.2MHz. – **Honnert.7** (non-comm.), **b.p. 1833, L-1018 Luxembourg**. **Web:** www.100komma7.lu 100.7MHz – **R. Ara,** 2 rue de la Boucherie, L-1247 Luxembourg. **Web:** www.ara.lu 103.3/105.2MHz – **R. Latina,** 2 rue Astrid, L-1143 Luxembourg: 101.2/103.1MHz – **R. LRB,** B.P. 8, L-3201 Bettembourg. **Web:** www.lrb.lu 24h on 103.9MHz – **Radio WAKY Power FM 107,** P. O. Box 70, L-5801 Hesperange, Luxembourg: 24h on 107.0MHz in English & Luxembourgish – **Sunshine Radio,** 29 ave. de la Financerie, L-1510 Luxembourg: 24h on 102.2MHz in English & Luxembourgish.

MACAU (China, SAR)

L.T: UTC +8h — **Pop:** 446,000 — **Pr.L:** Portuguese, Cantonese — **E.C:** 50Hz, 220V — **ITU:** MAC

TELEDIFUSAO DE MACAU, SARL (Priv. Comm.)

✉ Avenida Dr. Rodrigo Rodrigues, No. 223-225, Edif. "Nam Kwong" 7 Andar, Macau ☎ +853 335888 🖷 +853 343199 **Email:** rmacau@tdm.com.mo, **Web:** www.tdm.com.mo

D.Prgr in **Portuguese** 24h: 98.0MHz 2.5kW, in **Cantonese** 24h: 100.7MHz 2.5kW.

RADIO VILAVERDE LDA (Priv. Comm.)

✉ Hipodromo da Taipa, Macau ☎ +853 820338, 🖷 +853 820337.

D.Prgr in **Cantonese** and **Portuguese** 24h: 738kHz 10kW.

MACEDONIA

L.T: UTC +1h (27 Mar-30 Oct: UTC +2h) — **Pop:** 2.1 million — **Pr.L:** Macedonian — **E.C:** 50Hz, 220V — **ITU:** MKD

REPUBLIKA MACEDONIJA SOVET ZA RADIODIFUZIJA (Regulatory Authority)

✉ Ilindenska No. 9, 1000 Skopje ☎ +389 2 3129084 🖷 +389 2 3130211 **Web:** www.srd.org.mk **Email:** sovet@srd.org.mk. Responsible for regulation of commercial broadcasting.

MAKEDONSKA RADIO-TELEVIZIJA (MRT)

✉ Goce Delcev bb, 1000 Skopje ☎ +389 2 3112200 🖷 +389 2 3111821 **Web:** www.mr.com.mk, www.kanal103.com.mk **Email:** info@mr.com.mk/radiomakedonija@mr.com.mk & kanal 103@mol. com.mk

L.P: DG: Aton Seredin

Public Broadcasting Service with local area coverage:

	MW (kHz)	FM (MHz)	Location	kW
1)	567	95.9	Strumica	10
2)	639	96.6†	Stip	1
3)	720	92.3	Veles	1
4)	810	97.3	Skopje	1200
5)	936	102.9	Gevgelija	10
6)	945	89.0	Kumanovo	2
7)	1197	102.7	Kriva Palanka	1
8)	1242	89.0‡	Ohrid	10
	1314	92.4	Skopje 2	5
9)	1323	101.5	Bitola	10
10)	1323	95.2	Delcevo	10
11)	1323	94.9	Gostivar	10

MW (kHz)	FM (MHz)	Location	kW
12) 1431	94.9	Probistip	1
13) 1485	88.2	Berovo	1
15) 1485	88.2	Kicevo	1
16) 1521	98.4	M. Brod	1
17) 1584	103.6	Radovis	1
14) 1602	94.4	Debar	1
18 1602	89.7	Resen	1

†also on 99.2MHz. ‡also on 98.8MHz. Radio Macedonia leases the transmitter on 810 kHz to Deutsche Welle, Germany for programs in Albanian, Bulgarian, Greek and Serbian.

Macedonian Radio consists of Radio Skopje (MR1) 24h, 2nd Program (MR2) 24h, Radio Kultura (MR3) 1930-2400, Radio for Nationalities and Kanal 103 (103.0 MHz) 24h.

Addresses & other information

1) Boro Jhoni br. 10, 2400 Strumica – **2)** Josif Kovacev bb, P.F. 136, 2000 Stip. **Email**: radiostip@mail.com – **3)** Sevki Sali 4, 1400 Veles – **4)** see MRT.– **5)** Marsal Tito 144, 1480 Gevgelija – **6)** 11 Oktomvri 1, 1300 Kumanovo – **7)** Marsal Tito bb, 1330 Kriva Palanka – **8)** Sveti Kliment Ohridski 2, 6000 Ohrid – **9)** Tomaki Dimitrovski 7, 7000 Bitola – **10)** Metodi Mitevski-Brico 38, 2320 Delcevo – **11)** ul. Nikola Parapumov bb., Gostivar – **12)** Cvetko Tonev bb., 2210 Probistip – **13)** Marshal Tito 68, 2330, Berovo – **14)** ul.Veljko Vlahovic br. 13, Debar – **15)** Aleksandar Makedonski 72, 6250 Kicevo – **16)** Partizanska 12, 6630 Makedonski Brod – **17)** Ilindenska bb., 2420 Radovis – **18)** 29 Noemvri 25, 6310 Resen.

Main stations on FM:

FM (MHz)	MR1	MR2	MR3	kW
Belasica	91.5	97.8		10
Boskija	95.3	98.1		10
Crn Vrv	97.3	94.1		10
Golak		87.9		10
Pelister	92.3	96.1	102.6	20
Mali Vlaj	93.3	91.0	98.9	10
Sveti Erazmo	89.9	10		
Turtel	93.3	90.5		50
Vodno	98.9	92.4	87.8	10

+ more than 100 st's less than 10kW.

FM stations in the Skopje area (MHz):

88.4 Radio Vat, Skopje **Web:** www.soros.org.mk/radiovat.
89.1 Radio Star FM/Radio Top FM, Skopje. Time sharing.**Web:** www.geocities.com/hristo /www.topfm.com.mk/
89.7 Kanal 77, Stip **Web:** www.kanal77.com.mk
90.3 Grom Radio, Skopje **Web:** www.grom.com.mk
90.8 Radio Klasik FM, Skopje **Web:** www.klasikfm.com.mk
92.4/92.9 MJ Radio, Skopje **Web:** www.mjradio.com.mk
94.1 MR2, Skopje **Web:** www.mr.com.mk
94.7 MR3, Skopje. **Web:** www.mr.com.mk
95.5 Radio Antenna 5, Skopje **Web:** www.antenna5.com.mk
96.0 Radio Ravel, Skopje **Web:** www.radioravel.com.mk
96.8 Radio Fortuna, Skopje/MR1. **Web:** www.radiofortuna.com.mk
97.3 MR1, Skopje. **Web:** www.mr.com.mk
98.1 Mega Radio, Skopje **Web:** www.megaradio.com.mk
98.9 MR1, Skopje **Web:** www.mr.com.mk
99.4 Radio Ros, Skopje **Web:** www.radioros.com.mk
99.9 Radio Arachina, Arachinovo **Web:** www.arachina.com.mk
100.8 Jazz Radio, Skopje
102.4 Noma Radio, Skopje **Web:** www.radionoma.com.mk
103.0 Kanal 103, Skopje. **Web:** www.kanal103.com.mk
103.4 Radio Uno, Skopje **Web:** www.unoradio.cjb.net
104.4 Folk Radio, Skopje
105.2 R Buba Mara,Skopje **Web:** www.radiobubamara.com.mk
107.4 Kanal 4, Skopje. Time sharing **Web:** www.kanal4.com.mk
Note: max. ERP power for FM stations 0.5kW.

Local Private Stations: There are approx. 60 private local radio stations in Macedonia on FM. Most of them relay MR for part of the day.

RFI Radio France Internationale: FM(MHz): Skopje 91.3 1 kW **D.Prgr:** 24 h

BFBS Balkans (UK Mil.): Web: www.bfbs.com **FM**(MHz): BFBS Radio 1: Petrovec 105.8, BFBS Radio 2: Petrovec 106.9, Skopje 106.9. All transmitters 0.3 kW. **D.Prgr:** 24h

MADAGASCAR

L.T: UTC +3h — **Pop:** 14.5 million — **Pr.L:** Malagasy, French — **E.C:** 50Hz, 220V — **ITU:** MDG

RADIO NASIONALY MALAGASY (RNM) (Pub.)

✉ BP 4422, Anosy, 101 Antananarivo. ☎ +261 20 2221745. 🖷 +261 20 2232715. **Email**: mmdir@dts.mg **Web**: takelaka.dts.mg/radmad

L.P: Dir: Félix Malazarivo

MW	kHz	kW	H. of tr.
Antananarivo	630	150	1500-1900 (SS 2100)
Antananarivo	1394	4	0300-1500
SW	**kHz**	**kW**	**H. of tr.**
Antananarivo	3288	10	0300-0500, 1500-1900 (SS 2100)
Antananarivo	5010	100	0300-0500, 1500-1900 (SS 2100)
Antananarivo	6135	30	0500-1500
Antananarivo	7105	20	0500-1500
Antananarivo	9690	10	0500-1500

FM: Antananarivo 99.2MHz (0.5kW) & relay tx's

D.PRGR: 0300-1900 (SS 2100) in Malagasy & French.

ANN: Malagasy: "Radio Madagasikara"; French: "Radio Nationale Malgache"

OTHER STATIONS

SW	kHz	kW	Location	Station
15)	3215	50	Tanarive	R. Feon'ny Filazantsara

FM	MHz	kW	Location	Station
3)	88.8	-	Antananarivo	R. Fahazavana
A)	89.2	-	Antananarivo	BBCWS
4)	90.0	-	Antananarivo	R. Korail
1C)	92.0	-	Antananarivo	Alliance FM (RFI)
2)	93.4	-	Ivato	R. Don Bosco
1A)	94.4	-	Antananarivo	R. Tana
5)	95.4	-	Antananarivo	MBS Radio
6)	96.8	-	Antananarivo	R. Fanamby
7)	97.6	-	Antananarivo	R. Antsiva
1C)	98.0	-	Antsiranana	Alliance FM (RFI)
14)	98.2	-	Antananarivo	R. Ravinala
11)	100.0	-	Antananarivo	R. Tsioka Vao
1B)	102.0	-	Antananarivo	RTA
12)	104.0	-	Antananarivo	R. Mamalifaly
8)	105.0	-	Antananarivo	R. Fy
9)	105.2	-	Antananarivo	Ma FM
10)	106.0	-	Antananarivo	R. Lazan'Iarivo
13)	107.4	-	Antananarivo	R. FMFOI

N.B. Unlicensed stn's is operating in many parts of the country.

Addresses & other information:

1A-C) BP 7547, Ampesiloha, 101 Ananarivo. 1A) in Malagasy, 1B) in French, 1C) rel. RFI from France. RFI is available on FM in many cities. – **2)** BP 60, 105 Ivato. Email: rdb@dts.mg – **3)** BP 623, 101 Antananarivo. Email: fahazavana@dts.mg – **4)** Rue Dr Ralarosy, 101 Antananarivo. – **5)** BP 11137, Anosipatrana, Antananarivo. Email: adm@mbs.mg. Relay tx's not listed. – **6)** Antananarivo. – **7)** Lot VX 28 Aravadrova, 101 Antananarivo. – **8)** Lot III B 66, Ampasambazaha, Miarinarivo, Itasy. Email: smc@malagasy.com – **9)** BP 1414, Ankorondrano, 101 Antananarivo. Email: ma-fm@matv.mg – **10)** Lot VA 49, Atsimon, Andafiavaratra, 101 Antananarivo. Email: rli@simicro.mg – **11)** BP 315, Tana. – **12)** Antananarivo. – **13)** Rue Docteur Ralarosy, 101 Antananarivo. – **14)** Antananarivo. – **15)** BP 1741, 101 Antananarivo. Email: flm@wanadoo.mg. In Malagasy: 1630-1700. Tx is leased for R.Nederland Wereldomroep. **A)** Rel. BBCWS (cf. United Kingdom).

MADEIRA (Portuguese)

L.T: UTC (27 Mar-30 Oct: UTC +1h) — **Pop:** 300,000 — **Pr.L.:** Portuguese — **E.C:** 50Hz, 220/380V — **ITU:** MDR

ANACOM-Autoridade Nacional de Comunicações, Delegação da Madeira.

✉ Rua do Vale das Neves, 19, São Gonçalo, 9050-332 FUNCHAL, ☎ +351-291 79 22 00, 🖷+351-291-79 35 30.

RADIODIFUSÃO PORTUGUESA Centro Regional da RDP-Madeira

✉ Rua Tenente Coronel Sarmento, 15, 9000-020 FUNCHAL ☎ +351-291 22 91 55 🖷 +351-291 23 07 53 **Email:** rdpmadeira@rdp.pt

L.P: Dir: Tito de Freitas **Web:** www.rdp.pt.

MW (Antena 1 Madeira):

Location	kHz	kW	Location	kHz	kW
Porto Santo **	531	10	Ponta do Pargo*	1125	1
Pico do Areeiro*	603	10	Senhora do Monte*	1332	1

*Madeira island **Porto Santo island

FM (MHz)	Ant. 1	Ant.2	Ant. 3	kW
Achada da Cruz	104.3		105.0	0.8
Cabo Girão	96.7	99.4	94.8	1/3/1
Caniço	101.6	99.0	89.3	0.5
Encumeada	93.1		90.8	0.06

FM (MHz)	Ant. 1	Ant.2	Ant. 3	kW
Gaula	98.5	106.3	91.3	1/0.7/1
Monte	104.6	102.4	89.8	1/1/0.7
Paúl da Serra	101.9		93.3	1
Pico do Areeiro	95.5		94.1	13/15
Pico do Facho	93.1		90.8	0.03
Ponta do Pargo	90.2		94.6	1
Porto Santo	100.5	103.3	96.5	10
Ribeira Brava	105.6		103.1	1
Santa Clara	104.6	102.4	89.8	

D.Prgr: all networks 24 h. Antena 1 of RDP Madeira provides regional progrs. M-F 0700-2000, Sat 0800-1800 & Sun 0900-1800 LT; Antena 2 relays Lisboa 24 h; Antena 3 carries regional progrs. M-F 0700-1900, Sat 0100-0400 & 1000-2200, Sun 0100-0400 & 1000-2400 LT; other times relays Antena 3 Lisboa.
DAB: RDP has 6 T-DAB transmitters at Cabo Girão, Gaula, Monte, Pico do Facho, Pico do Areeiro and Monte, all in Madeira island and in Porto Santo, all broadcasting Antena 1, 2, 3 , RDP África and RDP Internacional on 225.648 MHz, ch. 12, block B.
V. by QSL-card via RDP Lisboa.

PEF – POSTO EMISSOR DE RADIODIFUSAO DO FUNCHAL (Priv., comm.)
✉ Rua Ponte de São Lázaro 3, 9000-027 FUNCHAL ☎ +351-291 23 03 93. 🖷 +351-291 22 17 97
MW: Funchal 1530kHz 10kW, Santana 1017kHz 1kW.
FM: Funchal 92.0MHz 2kW.
D.Prgr: 24h. Relays R.Renascença, Lisboa, at certain times.

Local stations (FM only) (Priv, comm.)

	Island	Station & location	MHz	(kW)
4)	Madeira	R. Jornal da Madeira, Funchal	88.8	1
9)	Madeira	R. São Vicente, São Vicente	89.2	0.5
3)	Madeira	R. Zarco, Machico	89.6	1
7)	Pto Santo	R. Praia, Porto Santo	91.6	0.5
8)	Madeira	R. Santana, Santana	92.5	0.5
3)	Madeira	R. Palmeira, Santa Cruz	96.1	0.5
3)	Madeira	R. Brava, Ribeira Brava	98.4	0.5
1)	Madeira	R. Calheta, Calheta	98.8	0.5
5)	Madeira	R. Notícias/TSF, Funchal	100.0	2
2)	Madeira	R. Popular, Câmara de Lobos	101.0	2
6)	Madeira	R. Porto Moniz, Porto Moniz	102.9	0.5
3)	Madeira	R. Sol, Ponta do Sol	103.7	0.5
3)	Madeira	R.Club da Madeira, Funchal	106.8	0.4

+ five 50 watt repeaters used by certain stns.

Addresses and other information (add +351to tel/fax nos): **1)** Edifício Ondaparque, 9370-133 Calheta, ☎ 291-82 01 36, 🖷 291-82 01 38, – **2)** (unknown addr.) – **3)** Av. dos Estados Unidos da América, 146-150, 9000-090 Funchal, ☎291-76 4124, 🖷 291-76 63 92, – **4)** Rua Dr. Fernão de Ornelas, 35-r/c, 9000 Funchal **Email** radio@jornaldamadeira.pt **Web** www.jornaldamadeira.pt – **5)** Rua Fernão de Ornelas, 56-3°, 9050-021 Funchal, ☎ 291-20 23 94/5/6, 🖷 291-20 23 87; relays TSF Lisboa – **6)** 9240 São Vicente, ☎291-84 21 35, 🖷291-84 26 66, – **7)** Rua Goulart de Medeiros, 1, 9400 Porto Santo, ☎ 291-98 01 30, 🖷 291-982484, – **8)** Rua da Igreja, 8-3°, 9325-031 Estreito de Câmara de Lobos ☎ 291-94 75 73, 🖷 291-94 87 94, – **9)** Bombeiros Voluntários de São Vicente e Porto Moniz, Vila de São Vicente, 9240 São Vicente, ☎291-84 26 94 & 291-84 26 61, 🖷 291-84 23 93

MALAWI

L.T: UTC +2h — **Pop:** 10.5 million — **Pr.L:** Chichewa, English — **E.C:** 50Hz, 230V — **ITU:** MWI

MALAWI COMMUNICATIONS REGULATORY AUTHORITY (MACRA)
✉ Salmon Amour Rd, Private Bag 261, Blantyre ☎ +265 1 623611 🖷 +265 1 623890 **L.P:** DG: Evans Namanja. Dir. of Broadc: James Chimera. **Web:** www.macra.org.mw **Email:** dg-macra@malawi.net

MALAWI BROADCASTING CORPORATION (MBC)
✉ Private Bag 30133, Chichiri, Blantyre 3
☎ + 265 1 671222/675587/671343 🖷 +265 1 671257/671353
Web: www.mbcradios.com **Email:** dgmbc@malawi.net
L.P: DG: Owen Maunde. Dir. of N. & Current Affairs: Maxwell Kasinja. Dir. of Eng: Joseph Chikagwa. Contr. of Prgrs: Joshua Kambwiri (R.1), Martin Chilimampunga (R.2). Contr. of Tr's: Abraham Nsapato

MW:

Location	kHz	kW	Location	kHz	kW
Mangochi	540	10	Bangula	810	10
Karonga	558	10	Nkhota Kota	1107	1
Lilongwe	594	30	Chitipa	1404	10
Ekwendeni	675	50	Matiya	1422	10
Blantyre	756	25			

SW: Limbe (G.C: 15S42 035E02): 3380/7130kHz 50kW (inactive).

FM	R1	R2
Blantyre	95.4	92.2
Chitipa	90.7	100.5
Lilongwe	94.7	91.5
Livingstonia	90.1	104.5
Karonga	95.5	98.7
Mzuzu	97.8	91.3
Ntchisi	100.5	92.4
Zomba	94.1	96.8

MBC Radio 1 in English/Chichewa/Vernaculars on MW/FM: 0253-2200. **N. in English:** 0300, 0500W, 0600Sun, 0700W, 0800Sun, 0900W, 1000Sun, 1030MF, 1100SS, 1200MF, 1400MF, 1600, 1800, 2000W, 2100, 2200.
MBC Radio 2 in English/Chichewa on FM: 24h.
ANN: E: R1: "MBC Radio 1", R2: "Radio 2 FM". Chichewa: "Kuno ndi ku ya MBC". **IS:** 0253 Cock crow and rapid drum beat.

TRANS WORLD RADIO MALAWI (Rlg.)
Web: www.twrafrica.org/Programmes-1/blantyrefm.asp
SW: Lilongwe 4870kHz 1kW.
FM: Blantyre 89.1MHz, Mvera 91.1MHz, Dedza 96.4MHz, Zomba 106.4MHz, Lilongwe 106.5MHz. **D.Prgr:** 24h in English/Chichewa

Other Stations:
R. ABC, P.O. Box 128, Lilongwe: 88.3MHz. **Web:** www.africanbiblecolleges.com/malawi/radio – **Capital R**, Private Bag 437, Blantyre 3 ☎ +265 1 620858 🖷 +265 1 623280 **Web:** www.capitalradiomalawi.com **Email:** capitalfm@ africa-online.net - **FM:** Blantyre/Lilongwe/Zomba/Dedza/Mulanje/ Salima 102.5MHz (Also rel. BBC & VOA) – **FM 101 Power:** Mangochi 93.1MHz, Lilongwe 100.8MHz, Blantyre/Chitipa 101MHz. **Web:** www.fm101.malawi.net **Email:** fm101@malawi.net – **Joy FM**,Blantyre 89.6MHz. – **MIJ FM**, Blantyre: 90.3MHz. – **R. Maria Malawi** (Rlg.), P.O. Box 406, Mangochi. **In Chichewa/ Yao:** Mangochi 88.5Mhz 1kW, Dowa 94MHz 1kW, Blantyre 99.2MHz 1kW, Zomba 99.4MHz 2kW, Dedza 99.7MHz 2kW, Balaka 104MHz. **Web:** www.radiomaria.mw **Email:** radiomaria@malawi.net
BBC African Sce: Mzuzu 87.9MHz, Lilongwe 98MHz, Blantyre 98.1MHz

MALAYSIA

L.T: UTC +8h — **Pop:** 23 million — **Pr.L:** Bahasa Malaysia (Malay), English, Chinese. In West Malaysia also Tamil, East Malaysia also 12 local languages or dialects — **E.C:** 50Hz, 240V — **ITU:** MLA

WEST MALAYSIA

RADIO TELEVISION MALAYSIA – RTM (Gov.)
✉ Dept. of Broadcasting, Angkasapuri, Bukit Putra, 50614 Kuala Lumpur ☎ +60 322825333 🖷 +60 322824735. Web: www.rtm.net.my Email: rtm@asiaconnect.com.my.
L.P: DG: Alimusa Sulaiman. MD (Radio): Ms Adilah Shek Omar. Dep. Dir. of Eng. (Broadc.): Mrs Aminah Din. Head of Int. Rel: Ms Mazura Mansur.

MW:

Location	kHz	kW	Sce, h. of tr.
Gerik	657	20	RM Perak: ?2200-?1600
Mersing	1055	20	RM Johor (RMJ): 2350-0800
Gerik	1089	20	R5 (Chinese): 2200-1600
Mersing	1310	20	R6 (Tamil): 2350-0800

SW: Kajang (G.C: 03N01 101E46): 9 x 100kW, 1 x 50kW.

kHz	kW	Sce.	H. of tr.	kHz	kW	Sce.	H. of tr.
4845v	100	R6	r	7295	100	R4	24h
5965v	100	R1	24h	6175	100	VOI	1400-1700
6025	100	+	0400-1700*	9750	100	VOI	1400-1700

r) rep. inactive +) 0200-0500 R8, 0500-1400 R7, 1400-1700 VOI.

FM (MHz, TRP)

Area	Site	1	2	4	5	6	kW
Alor Setar	a	94.9	100.5	98.7	101.3	96.7	5

Area	Site	1	2	4	5	6	kW
Balik Pulau	t	99.5	93.9	90.1	92.1	98.9	-
Baling	b	88.7	89.7	91.7	92.5	93.3	1
Besut	c	94.3	98.8	97.0	97.8	95.3	0.1
Cameron	d	89.1	93.1	101.1	103.5	104.3	0.1
Dungun	e	95.9	96.9	98.9	99.7	100.7	1
Ipoh	f	88.3	90.9+	90.1	92.1	98.9	0.5+1
Jeli	g	88.4	89.2	90.8	91.6	92.4	0.1
Jerantut	h	88.1	93.5	89.9	90.7	91.9	0.1
Johor Bahru	i	106.7	105.7	102.9	104.9	101.1	0.5
Kota Bharu	j	101.1	101.9	104.7	105.7	106.7	1
KL1	k	87.7	88.5	90.3	89.3	92.3	1
KL2	l	98.3	95.3+	100.1	106.7	96.3	1+5
KT	m	92.5	91.7	89.7	90.5	87.9	1
Kuantan	n	107.9	107.1	105.3	106.1	103.3	1
Machang	o	95.5	96.5	98.5	99.3	100.9	2
Melaka	p	93.6	96.6+	97.4	100.4	103.3	0.5+1
Mersing	q	90.1	90.9	92.9	89.1	88.3	1
Seremban	r	87.9	91.7	88.7	89.7	90.5	0.1
Sik	u	99.5	102.7	105.9	106.7	107.5	1
Taiping	s	103.3	107.2	105.3	106.1	107.9	0.1

1-6=Channel 1-6. **Radio 7/8/VOI:** Cameron Highlands 105.1MHz, KL1 91.1MHz, KL2 102.5MHz. **Channel RIMA:** KL1 93.9MHz.
KL1= Kuala Lumpur. KL2=KL/Selangor/Pahang (West). KT=Kuala Terengganu. Cameron Highlands possibly F.Pl.
Sites: a) Gunung Jerai, b) Bukit Palong, c) Bukit Bintang, d) Gunung Berinchang, e) Bukit Bauk, f) Bukit Keledang, g) Bukit Tangki Air, h) Bukit Istana, i) Gunung Pulai, j) Telipot, k) Menara KL (Bukit Nanas), l) Gunung Ulu Kali, m) Bukit Besar, n) Bukit Pelindung, o) Bukit Bakar, p) Gunung Ledang (Mt Ophir), q) Bukit Tinggi, r) Bukit Telapa Burok, s) Bukit Larut (Maxwell Hill) t) Bukit Genting (Penang).

RTM national services
(1) Radio 1 (Radio Satu): 24h General Sce in Malay. **(2) Radio Muzik:** 24h Music presented in Malay. **(4) Radio 4:** 24h General Sce in English. **(5) Radio 5 (Radio Lima / Di Wu Tai):** 24h General Sce in Chinese (Mandarin exc. news at 0200 in Hakka, 0500 Cantonese, 0700 Hakka & 1300 Chaozhou. **(6) Radio 6:** 24h General Sce in Tamil. **Radio 7 (Radio Tujuh):** 0700-1300 Orang Asli languages. **Radio 8 (Radio Lapan):** 0400-0700 information Sce. in Malay. **VOI, Voice of Islam (Suara Islam):** Rlg. prgr's 1400-1700. **Channel RIMA (Saluran RIMA, Radio Irama Melayu Asli):** Malay music prgr. 0400-1600. **V.** occasionally by letter or Email.
RTM regional services in West Malaysia.
Most sces. operate 2200-1600 in Malay (exceptions include Langkawi, which carries local & tourist information in English).
Refer to the above lists for tr sites and powers.
Johor: RTM Johor Bahru, Karung Berkunci 716, 80990 Johor Bahru, Johor. **Web**: www.rtmjb.net.my **Email**: rmjb@rtmjb.net.my.
State sce. On1055kHz, 92.1MHz q, 101.9MHz i, 105.3MHz p. Johor Bahru city sce: **FMJB 107.5** on 107.5MHz p.
Kedah: RTM Alor Setar, Kompleks Penerangan dan Penyiaran Sultan Abdul Halim, KM 3, Jalan Kuala Kedah, 05400 Alor Setar, Kedah. **Email**: rtmas@rtm.net.my. On 88.5MHz Selama-Bandar Baharu (site Bukit Sungai Kecil Hilir), 90.5MHz b, 97.5MHz a, 105.1MHz u,105.7MHz Gunung Raya, 107.0MHz Kuah.
Kelantan: RTM Kota Bharu, Peti Surat 143, 15720 Kota Bharu, Kelantan. **Email**: rtmkb@rtm.net.my. On 88.1MHz Paloh, 97.3MHz o, 102.9MHz j, 89.1MHz Gua Musang, 90.0MHz Jeli, 88.9MHz Taman Wangi, 107.1MHz Bukit Bintang.
Kuala Lumpur: On 97.2MHz k. **Web**: www.rtm.net.my/rmkl
Langkawi (Kedah): RTM Langkawi, Tingkat 2, Bangunan Tabung Haji, Jalan Padang Mat Sirat, 07000 Kuah, Langkawi. On 87.0MHz (?) Kuah, 104.8MHz Gunung Raya. **English:** 0100-0400, 0700-1000. Malay/English 1300-1600.
Melaka: RTM Melaka, Jalan Taming Sari, 75614 Melaka. **Web**: media.unitele.edu.my/rmm **Email**: rtmmlk@rtm.net.my On 102.3MHz
Negeri Sembilan: RTM Seremban, Jalan Raja Ali, 71000 Seremban, Negeri Sembilan. On 107.9MHz Seremban, 92.5MHz Bukit Telapa Buruk, 96.3MHz Gemencheh, 101.3MHz Port Dickson, 95.7MHz Tampin.
Pahang: RTM Kuantan, Peti Surat 152, 25710 Kuantan, Pahang. **Email**: rtmktn@rtm.net.my. On 104.1MHz n, 107.5MHz l, 100.3MHz Cameron Higlands, 92.7MHz Jerantut, 92.0MHz Maran, 91.9 Rompin.
Perak: RTM Ipoh, Jalan Dairy, 31400 Ipoh, Perak. **Email**: rtmipoh@rtm.net.my. On 657kHz, 95.6MHz f, 97.3MHz Changkat Rembian, 94.7MHz Cameron Highlands, 104.1MHz Taiping.
Perlis: RTM Kangar, Tingkat 6, Bangunan KWSP, Jalan Bukit Lagi, 01000 Kangar, Perlis. **Email**: rtmkgr@rtm.net.my. On 102.9MHz Pauh.
Pulau Pinang (Penang): RTM Pulau Pinang, Jalan Burmah, Peti Surat 433, 10350 Pulau Pinang. **Email**: rtmpp@rtm.net.my. On 90.9MHz t, 93.9MHz a, 95.7MHz Bukit Penara.
Selangor: RTM Shah Alam, Bangunan Sultan Salehudin Abdul Aziz Shah, 40000 Shah Alam, Selangor. **Web**: www.mmu.edu.my/rms/indexnew.html. On 100.9MHz l.
Terengganu: RTM Kuala Terengganu, Peti Surat 63, 20914 Kuala Terengganu, Terengganu. **Web**: www.rtm.net.my/rmkt **Email**: rtmkt@rtm.net.my. On 88.7MHz m, 96.2MHz c, 97.7MHz e.

EXTERNAL SERVICE: RTM OVERSEAS SERVICE
see International Broadcasting section.

RADIO LEBUHRAYA SDN. BHD. (THR.FM) (Comm.)
✉ 20th Flr, Plaza Berjaya, 12 Jalan Imbi, 55100 Kuala Lumpur
☎ +60 (3) 2433088 **Web**: www.thr.fm

Coverage Area	MHz	Coverage Area	MHz
Kota Bharu	88.1	Negeri Sembilan	101.5
Kuantan	88.8	No. Perak (Taiping)	102.1
Ce. Perak (Ipoh)	97.9	Kedah (Alor Setar)	102.4
K. Lumpur/Selangor	99.3	Johor	103.7
So. Penang	99.3	Kuala Terengganu	106.8
Melaka	99.7		

D.Prgr: Music and traffic information in Malay, Tamil (west coast) or Malay (east coast): 24h.

SUARA JOHOR (Comm.)
✉ Bukit Pelangi, Jalan Pasir Pelangi, 80050 Johor Bahru, Johor
☎ +60 73316104 **Web**: www.best104.fm
BEST 104: Melaka & Segamat 94.8MHz, Johor Bahru 104.1MHz, Kuala Lumpur/Selangor 104.1MHz, Mersing 102.5MHz.
D.Prgr: 2200-1700 (Malay & English music).

AMP RADIO NETWORKS SDN. BHD. (ASTRO) (Comm.)
✉ All Asia Broadcast Centre, Technology Park Malaysia, Bukit Jalil, 57000 Kuala Lumpur **Web**: www.astro.com.my/radio

FM (MHz)	MY	ERA	L&E	Mix	Hitz	Sin	Var
Alor Setar	99.7	103.6	104.4	91.0	92.8	97.1	106.5
Ipoh	100.6	103.7	101.5	94.3	92.7	96.1	98.5
Johor Bahru	95.4	104.5	94.6	99.1	97.6	87.8	-
Kemaman		98.6					
Kota Bharu	102.3	103.3	104.3	94.6	92.8	93.8	-
K. Terengganu	101.2	102.8	105.9	94.8	98.3	97.5	104.0
KL/Selangor	101.8	103.3	105.7	94.5	92.9	96.7	103.0
Kuantan	101.1	98.0	104.7	94.1	93.2	97.2	100.0
Melaka	106.4	90.3	92.2	91.1	93.0	96.0	107.3
Seremban	100.6	103.6	104.6	94.2	95.0	96.9	97.9
Taiping	100.2	95.2	89.3	91.3	93.6	96.4	104.9

Prgrs: MY FM: Music channel in Mandarin & Cantonese. **ERA:** Contemporary Malaysian music channel in Malay. **Light & Easy:** Easy listening music presented in English. **Mix FM:** Music and variety in English. **Hitz.fm:** Top 40 presented in English. **Sinar FM:** Malay. **Varia FM:** Testing at editorial deadline.

STAR RFM SDN. BHD. (Comm.)
✉ 19th Floor, Bangunan AMDB, 1, Jalan Lumut, 50400 Kuala Lumpur ☎ +60 340481988 🖷 +60 340439988 **Web**: www.redi988.net/ www.red1049.com **Email**: rfm988@silicon.net.my

FM (MHz)	Red	Redi	FM (MHz)	Red	Redi
Alor Setar	98.1	96.1	Melaka	98.9	98.2
Ipoh	106.4	99.8	Penang	107.6	94.5
Johor Bahru	92.8	99.9	Seremban	106.0	93.3
KL/Selangor	104.9	98.8	Taiping	98.2	101.0
Kuantan	91.6	90.4			

Red: In English. **988** (jiu ba ba): In Mandarin & Chinese dialects.

WAFM
✉ No.7, Jalan Jurubina U1/18, Hicom-Glenmarie Industrial Park, 40000 Shah Alam, Selangor Darul Ehsan.
WAfm: Kuala Lumpur 97.6MHz, Alor Setar 88.2MHz, Ipoh 104.5MHz, Johor Bahru 90.1MHz.

HUSA NETWORK SDN. BHD. (Comm.)
✉ 4213C Tingkat 2, Lot 51 & 52, Seksyen 27, Jalan Kebun Sultan, 15350 Kota Bharu, Kelantan ☎ +60 97436661 🖷 +60 97436664 **Web**: www.manis.fm
Manis FM (Sweet FM): Kelantan 90.6MHz, Pahang 95.1MHz Terengganu 102.0MHz. ?2200-1600 in Malay.

INSTITUT KEFAHAMAN ISLAM MALAYSIA (Rlg.)
✉ No 2, Langgak Tunku, Off Jalan Duta, 50480 Kuala Lumpur
☎ +60 362046200 🖷 +60 362014189 **Web**: www.ikim.gov.my/f_ikimfm.html

Area	MHz	Area	MHz
Alor Setar	89.0	Kuala Terengganu	100.2
Ipoh	102.7	Kuantan	89.5

Area	MHz	Area	MHz
Johor Bahru	106.2	Melaka	89.5
Klang Valley (KL)	91.5	Negeri Sembilan	102.7
Kota Bharu	89.9		

Radio Ikim (IKIM.FM): 24h.

University stations:

PUTRA FM

🖃 Tingkat 2 Jabatan Komunikasi, Fakulti Bahasa Moden dan Komunikasi, Universiti Putra Malaysia, 43400 UPM Serdang, Selangor.
Station: 90.7 MHz 1 kW: Mon-Fri 0400-1600

RADIO UiTM (UFM)

🖃 Level 13, Menara Ilmu Universiti Teknologi MARA, 40450 Bandaraya Shah Alam, Selangor.
Station: 93.9MHz 1 kW.

EAST MALAYSIA

RADIO TELEVISION MALAYSIA SABAH (Gov.)

🖃 2.4km, Tuaran Road, Beg Berkunci 2022, 88614 Kota Kinabalu ☎ +60 88213444 🖷 +60 88223493 **Web**: www.p.sabah.gov.my/rtm **Email**: rtmkk@rtm.net.my
Addresses of local st's: 🖃 Tingkat 6, Wisma Persekutuan, W.D.T. 52, 90500 Sandakan - Peti Surat 606, 91008 Tawau.
L.P: Dir. Broadcasting: Jumat Engson. Dir. Tech. (Radio): Abdul Jalani bin Mahmud. Dir. Prgr: Tuan HJ. Mahat Jamal.

Radio Television Malaysia Labuan

🖃 5004 Tanjung Taras, Peti Surat 299, 87008 WP Labuan ☎ +60 87415677 🖷 +60 87416658 **Email**: radiowpl@tm.net.my
Stations: KK=Kota Kinabalu (tr's at Kampung Laya-Laya, near Tuaran, G.C: 116.14E/06.12N. 1475kHz tr. in separate section of site).

MW	kHz	kW	Netw.	H. of tr.
Tenom	565	10	N	0230-1040
KK	603	20	N	0230-1040
Lahad Datu	675	10	N	0230-1000
KK	690	20	B	0320v-1330
Tawau	750	10	NL	2145-1100
Tenom	777	10	B	0320v-1330
Sandakan	783	10	NL	2155-1000
Kudat	801	10	N	2130-1600
Lahad Datu	828	10	B	0330-1000
Tawau	927	10	B	inactive
Kudat	1197	10	B	2030-1400
KK	1475d	700	SM	1030-1300
KK	5980v	10	B	0325v-1330

FM (MHz)	NS	Blue	R1	R2	R4	R5	kW
Sandakan a	92.9	96.1	91.1	92.1	94.3	95.1	1
Lahad Datu b	89.7	92.6	87.9	88.7	90.5	91.7	1
Sipitang c	97.9	102.9	95.5	96.5	99.1	99.9	1
Kudat d	95.9	98.9	94.1	94.9	96.7	98.1	1
Tawau e	95.7	99.3	93.9	94.7	97.1	98.1	1
Tenom f	90.3	93.1	88.5	89.3	91.7	92.3	1
Layang-L. g	104.5	107.1	99.5	100.3	105.3	106.3	1
K. Kinabalu h	89.9	92.7	88.1	88.9	90.7	91.9	1
FELDA S. i	104.1	106.7	99.9	102.9	104.9	105.7	0.1
Gadong	89.3	92.6	88.0	88.9	90.7	91.6	0.1
Kota Belud j	101.5	104.1	99.9	100.7	102.5	103.3	0.1
Labuan k	91.5	95.0	88.3	89.1	92.5	93.3	F.PI?

Tr. locations: a) Bukit Trig, b) Gunung Silam, c) Bukit Tampulagus, d) Bukit Kelapa, e) Gunung Andrassy, f) Bukit Sigapon, g) Layang-Layang, Mount Kinabalu, h) Kota Kinabalu, Bukit Lawa Mandau, i) FELDA Sahabat, j) Bukit Pompod, k) Bukit Timbalai. Tr. powers are TRP.
National networks: R1, R2, R4, R5: see West Malaysia above.
Provincial networks: NS=R. Malaysia Sabah "Nasional" in Malay 24h. **Reg. N:** 2200, 2330, 0400, 0530, 0830, 1400. **Blue**=Blue Network (Rangkaian Biru) in **English** 0230-0730 & 1430-1900 (Sat - 1630), Mandarin 0000-0230 (exc. Hakka 0000-0010), Bajau 1900-2100 & 1000-1200, Dusun 2200-2300, 1200-1315, Kadazan 2300-2400 & 0730-1000, Murut 2100-2200 & 1315-1430. **N. (English):** 0510, 1430. **SM**=Suara Malaysia (Overseas Sce) in Tagalog to the Philippines 1030-1300 from studios in Kota Kinabalu, also on 94.7MHz (studio link to MW tr).
Local Sce's: Labuan on 103.7MHz 0.1kW: 2145-1200 incl. **English** 0100-0300 – Tawau on 747kHz, 92.9MHz: 2145-0100, 0400-1100 – Sandakan on 783kHz, 100.2MHz: 2155-0100, 0600-1000.
ANN: Rangkaian Nasional (Malay): "Inilah Radio Malaysia Sabah siaran Bahasa Malaysia", (English): "This is Radio Malaysia Sabah", (Chinese): "Zhe shi Shaba Malaixiya Guangbo Diantai". Blue Netw. (Malay): "Inilah Radio Malaysia Sabah siaran berbagai bahasa".

RADIO TELEVISION MALAYSIA SARAWAK (Gov.)

🖃 Broadcasting House, Jalan P. Ramlee, 93614 Kuching ☎ +60 82248422 🖷 +60 82241914 **Email**: rtmkuc@rtm.net.my.
Addreses of local st's: Bangunan Penyiaran, 98700 Limbang – Bangunan Penyiaran, Jalan Brighton, 98000 Miri – Bangunan Penyiaran, 96009 Sibu – Bangunan Penyiaran, 95000 Sri Aman.
Stations: Kuching (Stapok, G.C: 110.20E/01.33N), Sibu (G.C: 111.49E/02.18N), Limbang (Kampung Sungai Poyoh, G.C: 115.00E/04.45N), Miri (G.C: 113.59E/04.23N), Sri Aman (G.C: 111.28E/01.13N).

Location	kHz	kW	Netw.	Location	kHz	kW	Netw.
Kuching	549	20	Y	Sri Aman	1044	20	Y+L
Miri	576	20	Y+L	Sibu	1062	20	G+L
Sibu	621	20	R+L	Sri Aman	1161	20	G+L
Limbang	648	20	Y+L	Miri	1206	20	G+L
Kuching	729	20	B	Kuching	4895	10	Y
Miri	819	20	R+L	Kuching	5030	10	B
Kuching	846	10	G	Sibu	6050	10	G
Limbang	873	20	R+L	Kuching	7130	10	Y
Sibu	909	20	Y+L	Kuching	7270	100/10	G/B
Kuching	954	10	R				

FM (MHz)	Y	Red	R1	R2	R4	R5	kW
Belaga	105.4	107.8	103.8	104.6	106.2	107.0	0.1
Betong a	94.4	97.8	92.8	93.6	95.2	96.0	0.1
Bintulu b	93.7	100.5	87.9	90.3	98.5	99.3	1
Bintulu c	94.7	96.7	-	-	-	-	1
Dalat	-	-	96.9	-	-	-	
Stapong d	95.1	101.1	93.3	94.1	95.9	97.1	1
Kapit e	92.7	89.9	90.7	91.9	88.1	88.9	0.1
Kuching f	88.9	91.9	92.9	88.1	89.9	90.7	1
Lambir Hills g	88.1	90.7	91.9	92.7	88.9	89.9	1
Lawas h	97.5	100.5	94.7	96.7	98.5	99.3	0.1
Limbang i	101.5	104.1	97.1	98.1	102.3	103.3	1
Marudi o	-	-	97.9	-	-	-	
Miri	100.3	106.3	107.1	99.3	104.5	105.3	0.1
Mukah	89.9	92.3	88.3	89.1	90.7	91.5	0.5
Sarikei n	91.5	89.2	87.9	90.3	92.3	93.6	
Serian j	94.8	97.2	98.0	94.0	95.6	96.4	0.5
Sibu k	101.5	104.1	95.5	98.5	102.5	103.3	0.1
Sri Aman l	100.3	106.3	107.3	98.9	92.3	105.3	1
Limbang m	100.0	107.7	95.3	99.2	106.0	106.8	0.1

Y=Yellow Network. Bintulu also Green Network on 97.5MHz. All powers are TRP. Ann. additional freq's: Kuching 101.3MHz (Iban/Bidayuh sce.), Sibu 87.6MHz (local sce's).
Tr. sites: a) Off. Spaoh b) Bukit Setiam c) Bukit Nyabau d) Bukit Singgalang e) Bukit Kapit f) Gunung Serapi g) Bukit Lambir h) Bukit Tiong i) Bukit Mas j) Bukit Ampangan k) Bukit Lima l) Bukit Temunduk m) Bukit Sagan Rudang, n) Bukit Kayu Malam, o) Bukit Dabei.
National networks: R1, R2, R4, R5: see West Malaysia above.
Provincial networks: Yellow Network (Rangkaian Nasional) in Malay 24h on FM, 2100-1600 on MW. MF 0706-0800 networked local studio prgr's. **N.** (provincial): 2200, 0400, 1000, 1400. **Red Network** 2200-1600, in Chinese: 2200-0100, 0700-1300; English: 0100-0700, 1300-1600. FM tr's relay Rangkaian Nasional overnight. Educational prg's during school terms: W within 0100-0400 period on MW/SW. **N.** (provincial): English 0400, 0530, 1400; Chinese 0000, 0701, 1000, 1245; Hakka 1030; Hokkien 1045. **Green Network** 2200-0100 (Sun 0600), 0400 0600, 0800-1500, in Iban exc. 0500-0600, 0800-1000 in Kayan/Kenyah. **Blue Network** in Bidayuh 2200-2400 (Sun 0200), 0400-0600, 1000-1500. NB: Iban and Bidayuh prgr's appear to have been consolidated into a single programming stream, using Iban 2200-0100, Bidayuh 0100-0400, Iban 0400-0700, Bidayuh 0700-? etc. Educational prgr's during school terms: W within 0100-0300 period, also on 1062/6050kHz.
Local sce's: Local prgr's in Malay generally are carried in the 0100-0400 and 0600-1000 periods. Chinese is carried 2330-0100. Iban refers to Iban and/or Orang Ulu languages. **Limbang:** 648kHz in Malay 0830-1000. 873kHz in Bisaya (?) 1000-1100, Sun 0200-0300, in Lun Bawang (Murut) 1000-1000. **Miri:** 576kHz, 94.7MHz in Malay 0100-0400v, 0830-1000. 819kHz, 96.7MHz in Chinese 0330-0500. 1206kHz, 97.5MHz in Iban 0600-0800. **Sibu:** 909kHz in Malay 0100-0400v, 0830-1000. 621kHz in Chinese 0330-0500. 1062kHz in Iban 2300-2400, 1000-1100 from Sibu, 0900-100 from Sri Aman. **Sri Aman:** 1044 in Malay 0100-0400v, 0830-1000. 1161kHz in Iban 0900-1100.

SW: (approximate sched's):
4895kHz 2200-0100, 0800-1557. **5030kHz** 2200-2400 (Sun 0100), 1000-1500 (r. inactive). **6050kHz** 2200-0100 Iban (Kuching), 0100-0300 Malay (local), 0300-0600 Iban (local), 0600-0900 Chinese (local), 0900-1100 Malay (local). **7130kHz** Sun 2330-0200, D0400-

0600 (new schedule possibly D2100-1600), also educational prgr's W0100-0300 during school terms. **7270kHz** 2200-1500?. NB: The above schedule information is largely based on monitoring. Frequent changes were reported for the SW sce's in 2004.
ANN: Kuching: (Malay) "Inilah R. Malaysia Sarawak"; (Chinese): "Zhe shi Shalayue Malaixiya Guangbo Diantai". Limbang (Malay): "R. Malaysia Sarawak, siaran dari Limbang". Miri: (Malay) "R. Malaysia Sarawak, Saluran Miri"; (Chinese) "Meili Shalayue Malaixiya Guangbo Diantai". Sibu (Chinese): "Shiwu Shalayue Malaixiya Guangbo Diantai". **IS:** A musical phrase (played on a native instrument, the Sape), alternating between A and F.

WAFM (Comm.)
Kota Kinabalu area on 87.7MHz, Kuching area on 94.3MHz. See WAFM under West Malaysia above for details.

RADIO IKIM (Rlg.)
Kota Kinabalu area (Bukit Kokol): 93.9MHz. Kuching area (pending): 98.8MHz. See Institut Kefahaman Islam Malaysia under West Malaysia above for details.

AMP RADIO NETWORKS SDN. BHD. (ASTRO) (Comm.)
Kota Kinabalu tr site: Bukit Kokol. Kuching tr site: Muara Tabuan.

FM (MHz)	MY	ERA	L&E	Mix	Hitz
Kota Kinabalu	104.0	102.4	103.2	101.6	100.8
Kuching	96.9	96.1	100.1	97.7	95.3

See under West Malaysia above for other details.

KRISTAL HARTA SDN. BHD. (CATS RADIO) (Comm.)
5th Floor, Wisma Ting Pek Khiing, No.1 Jalan Padungan, 93100 Kuching, Sarawak **Web**: www.catsfm.com.my

FM	Tr. location	MHz	FM	Tr. location	MHz
Bintulu	Bukit Nyabau	88.3	Mukah	Mukah	97.9
Kuching	Gunung Serapi	99.3	Sarikei	Bt. K. Malam	96.7
Limbang	Bukit Mas	88.7	Sibu	Bukit Lima	88.4
Miri	Miri	93.3	Sibu	?	99.9

Prgr.: 24h in Chinese (0200-0500, 1100-1300), English (0000-0200, 0700-1000, 1600-1800), Iban (1000-1100) and Malay (0500-0700, 1300-1600, 1800-2400).

MALDIVES

L.T: UTC +5h — **Pop:** 311,000 — **Pr.L:** Dhivehi (Maldivian) — **E.C:** 50Hz, 230V — **ITU:** MLD

VOICE OF MALDIVES (Gov.)
"Moonlight Higun", Male 20-06 ☎ +960 325577 🖷 +960 328357.
L.P: DG (Broadc.): Ibrahim Manik. DG (Eng): Maizan Ahmad Maniku.
MW: 1449kHz 10kW (standby tr: 1458kHz 5kW).
FM: 103.8MHz 20W. **F.PI:** 89.0 & 99.0MHz 1kW.
SW: Transmissions ceased.
D.Prgr. on 1449kHz: 0025-1000, 1200-1740 (during Ramadan st. operates 0025-1800 continuously). **N:** 0200, 0900, 1200, 1400, 1700.
English: 1200-1400. **N:** 1300.
R. Eke on 103.8MHz: 1745-0020. **N:** 1700

ANN: MW: "Mee Dhivehi Raajjeyge Adu" **V.** by QSL-card.
F.PI: 10kW SW-tr. Regular SW sce (possibly in 11MHz band).

MALI

L.T: UTC — **Pop:** 11 million — **Pr.L:** French (official), Bambara, Peuls, Sonrhai, Sarakolé, Bobo etc. — **E.C:** 50Hz, 220V — **ITU:** MLI

CONSEIL SUPÉRIEUR DE LA COMMUNICATION (CSC)
B.P. 116, Bamako ☎ +223 21 2647 🖷 +223 21 8319

OFFICE DE RADIODIFFUSION TÉLÉVISION DU MALI (ORTM)
B.P. 171, Bamako ☎ +223 21 2019/2474/4521/4727 🖷 +223 21 4205 **Web:** www.ortm.net **Email**: ortm@ortm.net
L.P: DG: Sidiki Konate. DG Adj: Nouhoum Traore. Dir. Radio: Seydou Baba Traore. Dir. Rural Radio: Mme Gnouma Keita. Dir. Research & New Tech.: Gaoussou Singare.
MW: Bamako (Kati) 540kHz 50kW
SW: Bamako (Kati, G,C; 12N39 008W01) 2x50kW, 3x100kW

kHz	Times	kHz	Times
4784v*	0555-0800, 1800-0000	7285	0800-1800
4835	0555-0800, 1800-0000	9635	0800-1800
5995	0555-0800, 1800-0000	11960	0800-1800

*irreg.

FM: National Radio (Radio Mali)

Location	MHz	kW
Bamako	92.0	1

+ 47 transmitters of 0.5/0.25kW

Regional Radio(Chaîne 2)

Location	MHz	kW	Location	MHz	kW
Mopti	94.4	10	Ségou	96.8	1
Bamako	95.2	1	Sikasso	98.3	1
Kayes	95.4	10			

National R. (Radio Mali) in French/Arabic/English/Bambara/Vernaculars: MW, SW & FM. **D.Prgr:** 0555-2400. **N. in English:** Sat 1905-1920.
Regional R. (Chaîne 2) on FM only: **D.Prgr:** 0800-1945.
ANN: "Vous écoutez l'office de Radiodiffusion-Télévision Malienne émettant de Bamako". E: "This is Bamako, Mali Radio Telecommunications". **IS:** Guitar.
R. Rurale on FM in Kayes 89.1MHz, Kolondieba 93.7Mhz, Koutiala and Macina.

Other FM Stations in Bamako:
R. Patriote FM 88.1MHz – **R. Canal 2000** 90.7MHz. **Web:** membres.lycos.fr/canal2000 **Email:** canal2000@spider.toolnet.org – **R.Mirador** 91.1MHz – **La Voix de la Verité** 91.5MHz – **Fréquence 3** 93.8MHz – **R. Tabalé** 94.3MHz. **Email:** tabale@malinet.ml – **R. Guintan** 94.7MHz – **R. Benkan** 97.1MHz – **R.Liberté** 97.7MHz – **R. Bamankan** 100.3MHz – **R. Klédu** FM 101.2MHz – **R Jakafo** 100.7MHz – **R. Kayira FM** 104.4MHz – **R. Voix de l'Islam** 107.4MHz.
RFI Afrique: 98.5MHz. Also relayed partly by regional stations on 91.8/92.6/93.1/95.7/97.7/97.9/98.2/104/105.3/105.9/107.5/107.8MHz.
Africa No. 1: 102MHz (see main entry under Gabon).
BBC African Service: 88.9MHz.

CHINA RADIO INTERNATIONAL RELAY STATION:
see International Radio section.

MALTA

L.T: UTC +1h (27 Mar-30 Oct: UTC +2h) — **Pop:** 395,000 — **Pr.L:** English, Maltese — **E.C:** 50Hz, 240V — **ITU:** MLT

MALTA BROADCASTING AUTHORITY (Regulatory Authority)
11 Mile-end Rd, Hamrun ☎ +356 21247908, 21221281 🖷 +356 21240855 **Email:** info@ba-malta.org **Web:** www.ba-malta.org **L.P:** Chairman: Chief Justice Emeritus, Joseph Said Pullicino, Chief Exec: Dr. Kevin Aquilina

PUBLIC BROADCASTING SERVICES LTD
75, St. Luke's Road, Gwardamangia MSD 09 ☎ +356 21225051 🖷 +356 21244601 **Email:** info@pbs.com.mt **Web:** www.pbs.com.mt.
L.P: Head of Radio: S. Cristina. CE: A. Psaila Exec Engineer: Costantino Abela (cabela@pbs.com.mt)
MW: Bizbizja 999kHz 5kW
FM: 91.7Mhz 2kW, 93.7MHz 5kW, 107.5 25W
R. MALTA: 24h on 999kHz, 93.7MHz, 107.5MHz **N:** 0600, 0700, 0900, 1100, 1400, 1700, 2130. Also streaming on web.
R. BRONJA: 24h on 91.7MHz (F.P. night relay of Sicilian private station)
R. 10-66: 106.6MHz (mono - also parliamentary sessions)

COMMERCIAL STATIONS:
BAY, St. George's bay, St. Julians STJ02 ☎ +356 21373813. 🖷 +356 21376113 **Email:** 897@bay.com.mt **Web:** www.bay.com.mt. - **FM:** 89.7MHz 2kW. **LP**: News Ed: Robert Francalanza. Also streaming on web on www.di-ve.com – **CALYPSO FM,** Oasis Buildings, Mons. P. Pace Street, Victoria, VCT 106 Gozo. ☎ +356 21563000 🖷 +356 21563560. **Email:** info@calypso102.com **Web:** www.calypso102.com - **FM:** 102.3MHz 2kW. **LP**: Exec chairman: Paul Portelli. MD: Johann Grech. News dir: Pierre J. Mejlak. Technical dir: Sam Mifsud. Format: news, educational, entertainment. Also streaming on web – **CAMPUS FM,** University Broadcasting Services, Old Humanities Bldg, University of Malta, Tal-Qroqq Msida MSD 06. ☎ +356 21333313. 🖷 +356 21314485 **Email:** campusfm@um.edu.mt **Web:** http://campusfm.um.edu.mt - **FM:** 103.7MHz 2kW. **LP**: Station Coordinator: Vicky Spiteri. Also relay of BBC WS. Also streaming on web – **CAPITAL.,** Mediacoop Ltd., 149 Triq L-Arcisqof, Valletta ☎ +356 21 233078; +356 21 23737. 🖷 +356 21 239701. **Email:** capital@maltanet.net **Web:** www.capitalradio.com.mt. - **FM:** 88.7MHz 2kW. **LP**: Executive Chairperson: Louis Borg. Sttn Mangr: John Mallia; Prgr Contr: Renald Bugeja. Also streaming on web on www.di-ve.com – **A3FM,** The Blues Complex, Triq il-Pijunieri, Bugibba. ☎ +356 21578022

🖷 +356 21581224 - **FM:** 101.8MHz 2kW. **Web:** www.a3fm.com.mt Also streaming on web – **R. 101**, Triq Sant'Andrija, San Gwann SGN05. ☎ +356 21345101 🖷 +356 21373113. **Email:** info@nettelevision.cjb.net **Email:** www.radio101.com.mt/ - **FM:** 101.0MHz 2kW, 95.5MHz 300W. **LP** Head of News: John Zammit. Also streaming on web. (Operated by Maltese Nationalist Party's) – **RTK, MEDIA CENTRE,** Archdiocese of Malta and Diocese of Ghawdex, Triq Nazzjonali, Blata-Badja HMR02 ☎ +356 2569 9100 / +356 2569 9158. 🖷 +356 2569 9151 - +356 2569 9160 **Email:** info@rtk.org.mt **Web:** www.rtk.org.mt - **FM:** 103.0MHz 2kW, Ghawdex 97.8MHz 400W, Malta 97.6MHz 400W. **LP**: Exec chairman: Fr. Nicholas Cachia. MD Jeffrey Calafato (jcalafato@mediacentre.org.mt). Prgr dir: Tonio Bonello. Tech dir: George Pollacco (gpollacco@rtk.org.mt). Marketing mngr: Sylvana Magro. Format: news, educational, entertainment. Also streaming on web. – **SMASH,** 4 Thistle Lane, Paola PLA 19. ☎ +356 21667777. 🖷 +356 21697830 **Email:** smash@vol.net.mt **Web:** www.smashmalta.com. - **FM:** 104.6MHz 2kW (RDS).**LP**: News Ed: Jesmond Saliba. Also streaming on web. – **SUPER ONE** A28b, Qasam Industrijali, Marsa. ☎ +356 21235315. 🖷 +356 21240717. **Email:** radio@super1.com **Web:** www.super1.com. - **FM:** 92.7MHz 2kW, 88.3MHz 200W, 88.0MHz 25W. **LP**: Head of News: Evarist Saliba. Also streaming on web. (Operated by Maltese Labour Party) – **XFM,** Grima Communications Ltd;, Ivy 2, 16, Triq il-Mediterran, The Village St. Julians. ☎ +356 21376385. 🖷 +356 21378167. **Email:** news@xfmmalta.com **Web:** www.xfmmalta.com. - **FM:** 100.2MHz 2kW

Community Stations: 40 stations with temporary licences for up to 2 years and powers of 2-5 Watts:

MARSHALL ISLANDS

L.T: UTC +12h — **Pop:** 71,000 — **Pr.L:** English, Marshallese — **E.C:** 60Hz, 110/220V — **ITU:** MHL

MARSHALL ISLANDS BROADCASTING CO. (Gov. Comm.)

✉ P.O. Box 19, Majuro 96960 96960 ☎ +692 (29) 3240 🖷 +692 (29) 3413 **L.P:** Chief Info Specialist: Billy Sawej.
MW: V7AD 1098kHz 25kW **FM:** 97.9MHz. **D Prgr:** 1900(Sun 2000)-1000 **V.** by letter. **ANN:** "Radio Majuro".

MICRONESIA HEATWAVE (Comm.)

✉ P.O. Box 1, Majuro 96960 ☎ +692 625 3250.
L.P: SM: Arden Sorimle **MW:** V7RR 1557kHz 10kW.
D.Prgr: 24h (mostly pop music with no ann.).

V7AA (Rlg.)

✉ P.O. Drawer H, Majuro 96960-1008 ☎ +692 (625) 3141 🖷 +692 (625) 4690 **FM:** 96.3MHz

CENTRAL PACIFIC NETWORK (AFRTS – U.S. Mil.)

✉ Box 23, APO San Francisco, CA 96555, USA **Web:** www.dtic.mil/armylink/abs
MW: Kwajalein 1224kHz 1kW. Format: National Public Radio/CNN/variety **FM:** 99.9/101.1/102.1MHz 1kW.
D.Prgr: 24h (on FM: 1 automated and 2 satellite-fed sces, local programming on 101.1MHz.). **N:** hourly via satellite **ANN:** "AFN Kwajalein"

MARTINIQUE (French)

L.T: UTC -4h — **Pop:** 418,000 — **Pr.L:** French, Créole Patois — **E.C:** 50Hz, 220V — **ITU:** MR.

RADIO MARTINIQUE

✉ B.P. 662, F-97263 Fort de France. ☎ +596 595200 **L.P:** Dir: Fred Jouhoud. CE: Jean Claude Arrivé.
FM: Fort-de-France 92.0/94.5 MHz, Morne-Rouge 94.3 MHz, Marin 93.2 MHz, Trinité 94.0 MHz, Macouba 92.0 MHz, St-Pierre 94.0 MHz.
D.Prgr: 0800-0400. **N:** 1000, 1030, 2000, 2300 + rel. France-Inter.
IS: Piano **V.** by QSL-card.

RCI – RADIO CARAÏBES INTERNATIONAL MARTINIQUE (Comm.)

✉ 2 Boulevard de la Marne, F-97200 Fort de France. ☎ +596 639870. 🖷 +596 632659. **Web:** www.fwinet.com/rci
L.P: Dir: Yann Duval. Editor-in-Chief: Jean Philippe Ludon (**Email:** 100444.2371@compuserve.com). CE: Daniel Toussaint
FM: 91.2/88.5/98.7/104.6MHz.
D.Prgr: 24h. **N:** on the h. (rel. Europe 1) **V.** by letter. Rp.

R. France Internationale: rel. via R. Intertropical 99.9MHz, R. 105 Canal Antilles 105.0MHz & R. AS 106.2MHz.

Other stations: approx. 40 FM st's are operating.

MAURITANIA

L.T: UTC — **Pop:** 2.7 million — **Pr.L:** Arabic, French, Poular, Soninké, Wolof — **E.C:** 50Hz, 220V — **ITU:** MTN

MINISTÈRE DE LA COMMUNICATION

✉ Immeuble Sonimex, Route du Ksar, Nouakchott ☎ 222 257220 🖷 222 257488 **Web:** www.mauritania.mr

RADIO MAURITANIE (RM)

✉ Av. Gamal Abdel Nasser, B.P. 200, Nouakchott ☎ +222 252164/252679/252101 🖷 +222 251264. **Email:** rm@mauritania.mr
L.P: DG: Sidi Brahim Ould Hamdinou.
MW: Nouakchott 783kHz 50kW.
SW: Nouakchott (G.C: 18N07 015W57): 4845/7245kHz 100kW.
FM: Nouakchott 98.01MHz 2kW, Nouadhibou 94.7MHz + 98.0MHz (local st.), Néma 98.5MHz, Aïoun 94.7MHz, Kiffa 96.7MHz, Akjoujt 98.7MHz, Aleg 96.1MHz 1kW + 90.8MHz 1kW (local st.), Atar 98.5MHz, Kaedi 98.3MHz, Rosso 96.7MHz + 98.0MHz (local st.), Sélibabi 97.7MHz, Tidjikja 98.5MHz, Zouérate 96.7MHz, Barkéol 100MHz. Where no power level is shown, st's are 0.1kW.
D.Prgr Arabic/French/Vernaculars: Sat-Thurs 0630-0100 on FM, 0830-1600 & 1800-0100 on 783kHz, D 0630-0830, 1700-0100 on 4845kHz, 0830-1700 on 7245kHz. Fri 0830-0100 on 783kHz + all FM.
N: Sat-Thurs **Arabic:** 0700, 1100(not Fri), 1200, 1300, 1500(not Fri), 1600(Fri), 2200, 2400. **French:** 1330(Fri), 1430, 1900.
ANN: A: "Huna Nouakchott, Idha'at al-Gumhuriyati al-Islamiyya al-Mauritaniaya". F: "Ici Nouakchott, R. Mauritanie émettant de Nouakchott".**IS:** Mauritanian guitar.

RFI Afrique: Nouakchott 93.3MHz.

MAURITIUS

L.T: UTC +4h — **Pop:** 1.2 million — **Pr.L:** English, French, 6 Indian languages, Chinese — **E.C:** 50Hz, 240V — **ITU:** MAU (Rodrigues: ROD)

MAURITIUS BROADCASTING CORPORATION (Part-comm.)

✉ 1, Louis Pasteur Street, Forest Side ☎ +230 6021200 🖷 +230 6757332 **Web:** http://mbc.intnet.mu/radio.main.htm **Email:** mbc@intnet.mu
L.P: MD M. Chellapermal, CE Radio: C Mootoosamy.
MW: RM1, R.Maurice (Malherbes) 684 kHz 10 kW, **RM2, R.Mauritius** (Malherbes) 819kHz 10kW, **Radio Rodrigues** (Citronelle) 1206kHz 1kW.
FM (MHz):

Station	Location	MHz	kW
Kool FM	Signal Mt.	91.7	0.5
Kool FM	Malherbes	97.3	1.0
Kool FM	Jurançon	89.3	0.5
Taal FM	Signal Mt.	98.2	0.5
Taal FM	Malherbes	94.0	1
Taal FM	Jurançon	95.6	0.5
World Hit Radio	Signal Mt.	94.9	0.5
World Hit Radio	Malherbes	90.8	1
World Hit Radio	Jurançon	92.4	0.5

RM1, R. Maurice on 684kHz: 24h in French. Relay of KOOL FM during daytime and France Inter during local nighttime. N on the hour.
English: 0500-0515. Relay of DW in English 0730-0800.
RM2, R. Mauritius on 819kHz: 24h. All programs in Indian languages.
R. Rodrigues on 1206kHz (Mont Malartic). Relay of RM1 684 kHz. Local slot 1400-1415.
✉Mont Venus, Rodrigues. ☎+230 95 8311710. 🖷 +230 958311784.
FM(MHz): 97.3 0.5 kW 24h. **ANN:** E: "This is the Mauritius Broadcasting Corporation". F: "Ici MBC".

BBC WORLD SERVICE: Bigara 1575kHz 2 kW 24h

Private stations
RADIO PLUS
✉ Labourdonnais Street, Port-Louis
FM (MHz): Centre 87.7, North 88.6, South 98.9

RADIO ONE
✉Brown Sequard Street, Port-Louis
FM (MHz): Centre 100.8, North 101.7, South 102.4
TOP FM-SKYWAVE
FM (MHz): Centre 104.4, North 105.7, South 106.0

MAYOTTE (French)

L.T: UTC +3h — **Pop:** 163,000 — **Radios:** 50,000 — **Pr.L:** French, Mahorian — **E.C:** 50Hz, 220V — **ITU:** MYT

RADIO-TÉLÉVISION FRANÇAISE D'OUTRE-MER (RFO-MAYOTTE) Radio Mayotte
✉ B.P. 103, Rue de jardins, FR-97600 Mamoudzou, Ile de Mayotte ☎ + 269 601017 🖷 +269 601852 **Web:** www.rfo.fr/mayotte
L.P: DG: Georges Chow-Toun.
MW: Pamandzi 1458kHz 5 kW **FM:** Dzaoudzi 91MHz 100W, Lima Combani 92MHz 500W **D.Prgr:** Mon-Sat 1030-2400, Sun 0830-2400 N.in Mahorian:1630.
ANN: "Vous êtes à l'écoutee de RFO-Mayotte".
IS: Melody on guitar **V.** by letter.

Europe 2: Boueni 90.2MHz, Mamoudzou 99.1MHz, Pamandzi 97.7MHz

MEXICO

L.T: UTC -6h (DST*: UTC -5h) exc. Baja California Sur, Chihuahua, Nayarit Sonora, Sinaloa: UTC -7h (DST* exc. Sonora: UTC -6h), Baja California Norte: UTC -8h (DST*: UTC -7h) *DST: 3 Apr-30 Oct — **Pop:** 103 million — **Pr.L:** Spanish — **E.C:** 60Hz, 127V — **ITU:** MEX

SECRETARIA DE COMUNICACIONES
Dirección General de Telecomunicaciones
✉ Xola y Av.Universidad, Cuerpo C, P1, Col.Narvarte, 03028 México, D.F. ☎ +52 5530 9109.

DIRECCION GENERAL DE SISTEMA DE RADIO
Departamento de Asignación de Frecuencias
✉ Xola y Av.Universidad, Cuerpo C. P1, Col.Narvarte, 03028 México, D.F. ☎ +52 5538 3063.

MW: Call XE–,
° = also on SW, * = inactive, (r) = repeater, v = varying fq, d = daytime operation. The letters preceding the st.number indicate the State. Addresses are listed by State in alphabetical order.

Call	kHz	kW	Name and h. of tr.
BC19) SURF	540	25	Oldies 540, Tijuana: 24h
CH15) TX	540	1/0.25	La Ranchera de Paquime, Nuevo Casas Grandes: 1200-0400
CS22) MIT	540	5/1	LV de BalunCanán, Comitán: 1100-0700
NL01) WA	540	0.5	W Radio, Monterrey: 24h (rel: XEW 900 kHz)
SL01) WA	540	150	W Radio, San Luis Potosí: 24h (rel: XEW 900 kHz)
SN13) HS	540	5/0.2	La Norteñita, Los Mochis: 24h
CH01) PL	550	5/0.15	La Super Estación, Cd. Cuauhtémoc: 24h
GR01) ACD	550	1/0.25	R. Sensación, Acapulco: 1200-0600
JL23) ZK	550	1/0.25	Poder 55, Tepatitlán: 1200-0300
NA14) TNC	550	5/0.15	R. Nayarit, Tepic:1300-0600
OX01) HLL	550	1.5/0.25	R. Mar, Salina Cruz: 1200-0500
VE01) KL	550	5/0.25	Romántica 550, Jalapa: 1300-0400
YU01) QW	550	5/0.35	QW La Poderosa, Mérida: 1130-0100
CO07) GIK	560	5/0.5	Acerera, Monclova: 1200-0600
CS06) IN	560	2/0.25	LV del Valle, Cintalapa: 1100-0500
DF01) OC	560	5/0.5	R. Chapultepec, México: 1100-0700
DG05) SRD	560	5/0.25	La Que Suave, Santiago Papasquiaro: 1200-0400
JL33) MZA	560	10/1	La Buena Onda del Pacífico, Cihuatlán: 1200-0500
QR13) QAA	560	1/0.5	La Poderosa, Chetumal
SO37) YO	560	1/0.5	R. Lobo/R. 5-60, Huatabampo: 1300-0500
ZC12) XZ	560	10/0.25	La Z, Zacatecas: 1100-0800
CO01) TJ	570	1/0.25	La Invasora/R. Alegría, Torreón: 1200-0400
JL29) KZX	570	5/0.5	Tejano KZK, Cd.Guzmán: 1200-0600
MI01) LQ	570	2/1.7	R. Fórmula, Primera Cadena Nacional, Morelia: (rel: XERFR 970 kHz)
NL02) BJB	570	5/0.5	La Estación del Barrilito/R. Alegría, Monterrey: 1100-0600
OX02) OA	570	5/0.25	R. Mexicana, Oaxaca: 1200-0400
PU13) VJP	570	5/1	R. Xicotepec, Xicotepec de Juárez: 1100-0300
SO26) UK	570	25/0.25	U-K, Caborca: 1400-0600
TB01) VX	570	10/1	R. Fórmula/La Grande de Tabasco, Villahermosa: 1000-0600
YU09) ME	570	2.5	Radio Valladolid "La Poderosa de Oriente", Valladolid: 1200-0400
CH08) FI	580	5/0.7	R. Mexicana, Chihuahua: 24h
CO02) MU	580	5/2.5	La Rancherita del Aire, Piedras Negras: 24h
CS01) UE	580	1/0.25	Imperio, Tuxtla Gutiérrez: 1100-0600
JL02) AV	580	10/1	Canal 58/R. Guadalajara, Guadalajara: 1200-0700
QE08) UAQ	580	0.25	R. Universidad, Querétaro: 1200-0600
QR01) YI	580	1/0.25	Mix AM, Cancún: 1100-0600 (rel: XHYI 93.1)
SO06) HO	580	1/0.25	R. 13/La Fuerza de la Palabra, Cd.Obregón (rel: XEDA 1290 kHz))
TM01) BJ	580	1/0.2	La Ranchera, Cd.Victoria: 1200-0600
VE02) DZ	580	1/0.5	Canal 58, Córdoba: 1230-0430
CS02) ZZZ	590	5/1	R. Z, Tapachula: 1100-0500
DF02) PH	590	25/10	Tuya 590, México: 24h
DG01) E	590	1	R. Fiesta Mexicana, Durango: 24h
GJ10) GTO	590	1/0.25	La Nueva R. Cañon, León: 1200-0100
JL31) CJU	590	10/1	La Explosiva, Puerto Vallarta
SO01) XA	590	1	Exa, Hermosillo: 1300-0800 (rel: XHBH 98.5)
TM02) FD	590	5/0.5	La Consentida, Reynosa: 1100-0500
VE17) OM	590	1	R. Fórmula, Coatzacoalcos: 24h
CO01) DN	600	1	La Mexicana, Torreón: 1200-0500
CS10) OB	600	5/0.5	La Máquina Musical, Pichucalco: 1100-0500
CS24) OCH	600	10/1	Quién Radio, Ococingo
GR03) BB	600	5/1	La Comadre, Acapulco: 1200-0400
JL36) LAZ	600	10	La Z, Cd.Guzmán: 1200-0600
MI02) TA	600	1	R. Fórmula, Zitácuaro: 1200-0600 (SS-0400)
NL03) MN	600	1/0.5	La Regiomontaña, Monterrey: 24h
SL16) CV	600	5/1	La Gran Compañía, Cd.Valles: 1200-0500
SN20) HW	600	5/1	La Estación del Poder, Rosario: 1200-0700
YU02) Z	600	20/1	R. Fórmula,Tercera Cadena Nacional, Mérida (rel: XEAI 1470 kHz)
CO03) BX	610	5/0.5	La B-X, Sabinas: 1100-0500
CO26) SAC	610	1	R. Lobo, Saltillo: 1200-0600
MI03) UF	610	10/1	Stereo Mía, Uruapan: 24h
OX03) KZ	610	1/0.5	LV del Istmo, Tehuantepec: 1200-0600
SN02) GS	610	1/0.5	La Ley, Guasave: 1230-0600
VE01) JA	610	1/0.5	Mundo 610, Jalapa: 1200-0500
ZC01) EL	610	5/0.1	Super Canal 610/La L, Fresnillo: 1200-0600
BC09) SS	620	5	La Tropical, Ensenada
CH03) BU	620	5/1	La Norteñita, Chihuahua: 1200-0700
DF03) NK	620	50/10	R. 6-20, México: 24h
DG02) CK	620	1/0.5	Digital 620, Durango: 1200-0500
NA01) OO	620	5/1	R. Triunfadora, Tepic: 24h
QR14) KX	620	1/0.25	R. Cultural de la Zona Maya, Felipe Carillo Puerto
SL14) WZ	620	2.5/0.5	R. 6-20, San Luis Potosí: 1200-0400
TB05) HGR	620	2.5/0.1	R. Fórmula 620, Villahermosa: 1200-0600
TM30) GH	620	1/0.25	Bonita, Reynosa: 24h
GR27) JR	630	5	Coral 630, Zihuatanejo
JL02) JB	630	10/0.5	Radiarte 630, Guadalajara: 1300-0700
NL03) FB	630	50	La Nueva F-B Romántica, Monterrey: 24h
QR08) CCQ	630	1/0.5	La Nueva Coqueta, Cancún: 1200-0300 (rel: XHCCQ 91.5)
SN03) OPE	630	5/0.25	Exa, Mazatlán: 24h (rel:XHOPE 89.3)
SO02) FX	630	2/0.25	R. 6-30, Guaymas: 24h
TM27) ERO	630	1/0.15	R. Tamaulipas, Altamira: 1200-0400
VE03) FU	630	10/0.75	LV Amiga de AM, Cosamaloapan: 1200-0400
CH27) JUA	640	1d	La Caliente, Cd.Juárez: 1200-0200
CH29) HHI	640	10/1	R. Uno, Hidalgo del Parral: 24h
CS03) WM	640	5/1	R. 6-40, San Cristóbal de las Casas: 1200-0300
HG04) NQ	640	50	La N-Q/R. 6-40, Tulancingo: 1100-0600
OX26) HDL	640	1d	XEHDL, Huajuapán de León
TM19) TAM	640	1/0.25	La Poderosa, Cd.Victoria: 24h
CO33) RCG	650	0.5d	XERCG, Cd. Acuña
GR21) CHH	650	5/0.25	La Explosiva, Chilpancingo: 1200-0300
JL03) EJ	650	10/0.5	R. Paraíso, Puerto Vallarta: 24h
MI04) ZM	650	5/1	La Zamorana, Zamora: 1200-0600
OX12) PX	650	5/0.2	La Voz del Ángel, Puerto Ángel: 1200-0200
SN04) TNT	650	2/0.1	65 La Ley, Los Mochis: 24h
SO29) VSS	650	2.5/0.1	R. 13/La Fuerza de la Palabra, Hermosillo (rel XEDA 1290 kHz)
TB15) VILL	650	1/0.5	R. Felicidad, Villahermosa. 24h
YU03) VG	650	1	Éxtasis, Mérida: 1200-0400 (rel: XHVG 94.5)
AG01) EY	660	50	La Consentida, Aguascalientes: 24h
BS06) SJC	660	25/0.25	La Tremenda, San José del Cabo: 1200-0600
CH04) ACB	660	5/1	Radio 6-60, Cd.Delicias: 1200-0600
DF04) DTL	660	50	XEDTL -60, México: 1200-0800

Call	kHz	kW	Name and h. of tr.
DG01) WX	660	1/0.5	R. Fórmula, Durango: 1200-0600
NL02) FZ	660	10/0.25	Noti-Radio 6-60, Monterrey: 24h
OX04) YG	660	1/0.5	R. Fiesta Mexicana, Matías Romero: 1200-0100
QR09) CPR	660	1	R. Chan Santa Cruz-LV de los Mayas, Félipe Carillo Puerto
TM20) AR	660	5/1	La Mexicana, Tampico: 24h
CO04) TOR	670	5/0.25	R. Ranchita, Torreón: 1200-0600
JL01) IS	670	5/0.25	La Rancherita Consentida, Cd.Guzmán: 1200-0600
QE01) QG	670	1/0.1	R. Lobo, Querétaro: 24h
VE38) SIC	670	5d	R. ACIR, Córdoba: 24h
CH08) FO	680	1/0.25	Energía 6-80, Chihuahua: 1200-0100
CS04) KQ	680	5/0.5	R. Mexicana, Tapachula: 1100-0400
GJ25) LG	680	10/5	LG, La Grande, León: 24h
GR15) CHG	680	1	Fiesta Mexicana, Chilpancingo: 1200-0600
OX27) OAX	680	5	Aro AM, Oaxaca
PU01) FJ	680	1/0.1	La Consentida, Teziutlán: 1200-0400
SN05) ORO	680	1/0.5	La Tremenda, Guasave: 1200-0600
SO35) SON	680	1	R. ACIR, Hermosillo: 24h
YU03) PY	680	2.5/1	Foro 6-80, Mérida
BC01) TRA	690	77.5	Extra Sports, Tijuana: 24h (English, rel: KXTA, Los Angeles, CA)
CL03) CS	690	5/1	La Z/La Grande de Manzanillo, Manzanillo: 24h
DF08) N	690	50/5	La 69, México: 24h
MI10) XL	690	1.5/0.5	La Ley, Pátzcuaro: 1200-0400
NL04) RG	690	10/1	La Deportiva 6-90/La R-G, Monterrey: 1200-0700
SN19) ST	690	10/0.25	La Invasora, Mazatlán: 1300-0500
VE07) AFA	690	2/0.25	La Más Picuda, Coatzacoalcos: 24h
ZC03) MA	690	50/1	M-A/La Madre de Todas, Fresnillo: 1200-0600
CA09) PUJ	700	5	LV del Corazón de la Selva, X'pujil: 1100-1600, 2000-0000
CH25) GD	700	1/0.25	La Poderosa, Hidalgo del Parral: 1200-0600
JL04) DKR	700	1	R. Red, Guadalajara: 24h (rel: XERED 1110kHz)
MI02) LX	700	5	R. Mexicana, Zitácuaro: 1200-0600 (SS-0400)
VE02) VC	700	2.5/0.1	Canal 70, Córdoba: 1300-0100
CH05) DP	710	10/1	La Ranchera de Cuauhtémoc, Cd.Cuauhtémoc: 2300-0700
CL01) RL	710	1/0.25	La R-L de Colima, Colima: 1100-0600
CO04) LZ	710	5/0.25	La Z, Torreón: 1200-0600 (rel: XHLZ 103.5)
CS05) ON	710	4.5/1	R. Mexicana, Tuxtla Gutiérrez: 24h
DF04) MP	710	10/1	R. 7-10, Mexico: 24h
GR03) MAR	710	1	R. Inolvidable, Acapulco: 1200-0300
NA02) RK	710	1	R. Korita, Tepic: 1200-0800
OX05) RPO	710	5/0.5	R. Variedades, Oaxaca: 24h
SL10) SMR	710	1/0.25	R. Fórmula, San Luis Potosí: 24h
SN01) BL	710	5/1	La Poderosa, Culiacán: 24h
SO03) PS	710	1/0.25	La Super Grupera, Empalme: 1300-0700
TM10) OLA	710	1/0.25	R. Ola, Tampico: 1200-0400
YU01) YK	710	5/0.25	R. Familiar, Mérida: 1200-0400
CO19) DE	720	5/0.25	R. Fórmula, Primera Cadena Nacional, Saltillo (rel: XERFR 970 kHz)
JL05) QZ	720	1/0.25	La Máquina Musical, San Juan de los Lagos: 1300-0100
QR05) CPQ	720	2d	Ritmo 720, Félipe Carillo Puerto: 1300-0100
SN19) VU	720	1/0.5	La Poderosa, Mazatlán: 1300-0700
VE37) AVR	720	25/0.25	R. Fórmula, Primera Cadena Nacional, Veracruz (rel: XERFR 970 kHz)
BC21) EBC	730	5	R. Felicidad, Ensenada: 24h
BS07) LBC	730	10d	XELBC, Loreto
CO05) PQ	730	1	La 73/La Sabrosita, Cd.Muzquiz: 1200-0400
CS14) VF	730	10/5	R. Villaflores, Villaflores: 1200-0400
DF06) X	730	100	Estado W, México: 24h
JL30) GDL	730	3.5/0.5	La Explosiva, Zapotlanejo: 1300-0100
YU10) PET	730	10d	LV de los Mayas, Peto: 1100-0100, Sun 1300-2200
AG05) LZ	740	1/0.5	El Planeta, Aguascalientes: 1200-0600
CO28) QN	740	10/1	R. Fórmula 7-40, Torreón: 1200-0600 (rel: XERFR 970 kHz)
GJ04) OF	740	5/1	Romántica 7-40, Cortázar: 1200-0600
JL25) VAY	740	1	Bonita, Puerto Vallarta: 1200-0600
QR11) CAQ	740	1	R. Fórmula, Cancún: 24h (rel: XERFR 970 kHz)
SN18) CW	740	5/1	La Z, Los Mochis: 1200-0400
TB02) KV	740	5/1	Stereo Vida, Villahermosa: 24h
VE29) GF	740	2/1	R. Fiesta 740 AM, Gutiérrez Zamora: 1200-0300
CH21) OH	750	1/0.75	La Chiquita, Camargo: 24h
DG03) DGO	750	5/0.5	R. Capital, Durango: 1100-0500
GR01) KOK	750	5/0.25	R. Fórmula, Acapulco: 24h (rel: XERFR 970 kHz)
MI29) URM	750	10/1	Fiesta Mexicana, Uruapán: 24h
NA09) JMN	750	5d	LV de los Cuatro Pueblos, Jesús María: 1200-2000
OX06) CORO	750	1/0.1	Arco Iris 750, Loma Bonita: 1200-0400
SL17) RASA	750	1/0.1	XERASA, San Luis Potosí: 24h (rel: XENK 620kHz)
SN23) CSI	750	1/0.25	R. Mexicana, Culiacán: 24h
VE31) TI	750	10/0.25	R. Fiesta, La Más Picuda, Tempoal: 1200-0400
CS07) RA	760	8/1	R. Chiapas, San Cristóbal las Casas
DF07) ABC	760	70/5	ABC Radio, México: 24h
JL15) ZZ	760	10/0.25	La Ke Buena/Gallito, Guadalajara: 1230-0600
SL10) EQ	760	0.25d	La Pantera, San Luis Potosí: 1200-0100
SO07) EB	760	5/0.25	La Comadre, Cd.Obregón: 1200-0800
SO17) NY	760	5/0.1	R. Geny, Nogales: 24h
YU01) YW	760	5/0.5	Mexicanísima, Mérida: 1200-0600
CH07) HB	770	1/0.25	La Rancherita, Hidalgo del Parral: 1300-0100
GR20) SUR	770	5/1	La Más Bonita, Chilapa: 1200-0200
MI05) ML	770	1/0.1	La Ranchera, Apatzingán: 1200-0500
NL07) ACH	770	5/0.2	R. Fórmula, Monterrey: 1200-0000
OX28) MRO	770	1d	XEMRO, Matias Romero
OX29) HUA	770	1d	XEHUA, Sta Cruz Huatulco
SN04) JJR	770	1/0.1	La Ke Guapa, Los Mochis: 1300-0700
VE09) QRV	770	5/0.5	R. Costenita, Veracruz: 1200-0600
ZC01) IH	770	10/1	La Unica, Fresnillo: 1200-0600
CO31) MF	780	5/0.5	R. Nostalgia, Monclova: 24h
CS02) TS	°780	5/0.5	R. Tapachula, Tapachula: 1100-0500
GJ04) ZN	780	5/1	Stereo Digital, Celaya: 1200-0100
GR04) XY	780	2.5/1	LV del Balsas, Cd.Altamirano: 1200-0430
JL07) LD	780	10/0.5	R. Costa, Autlán: 1200-0500
OX15) GLO	780	5d	LV de la Sierra Juárez, Guelato de Juárez: 1200-0130
TM20) MTS	780	1/0.25	R. Fórmula, Tampico: 1200-0600
TM25) SFT	780	5/1	La Triple T/La Caliente, San Fernando: 1200-0600
AG03) BI	790	20/2	R. B-I, Aguascalientes: 24h
BC06) SU	790	1/0.25	R. 790, Mexicali: 1400-0200
BS01) NT	790	5/0.75	R. La Paz, La Paz: 1300-0700
CH02) RPC	790	5/0.4	R. Ranchito, Chihuahua: 24h
CO01) GZ	790	1/0.25	La Pantera, Torreón: 1200-0500
DF08) RC	790	50/1	Formato 21, México: 24h
JL34) GAJ	790	1d	R. Fórmula, Primera Cadena Nacional, Guadalajara (rel: XERFR 970)
TB03) VA	790	25/5	La Emisora del Hogar, Villahermosa: 1000-0600
TM03) FE	790	1/0.5	La Pura Ley, Nuevo Laredo: 1230-0600
VE11) COV	790	1/0.5	R. Lobo, Poza Rica: 1200-0600
YU06) UP	790	2.5/1	Candela, Tizimín: 1200-0500
BC03) SPM	800	0.5	ESPN Radio 800, Tijuana: 1300-0800
CH12) ROK	800	50	R. Cañon Láser, Cd.Juárez: 24h
CO29) ZR	800	2/0.25	La Formula, Zaragoza: 1200-0400
CS13) UI	800	5/1	R. Comitán, Comitán: 1200-0400
GJ19) GX	800	5/1	Fiesta Mexicana, San Luis de la Paz: 1300-0300
GR09) ZV	800	3d	LV de la Montaña, Tlapa de Comonfort: 1200-0100 (SS -2000)
JL27) AN	800	1/0.25	R. Alegría, Ocotlán: 24h
NL10) DD	800	10	La Doble D/La Pezada, Montemorelos: 24h
VE09) QT	800	5	La Poderosa, Veracruz: 1200-0600
CA12) IC	810	0.1	XEIC, Campeche
CH09) SB	810	1d	R. Mexicana, Santa Bárbara: 1100-0200
CL05) MAX	810	3/0.25	Radiomax, Tecomán: 1100-0400
CO06) IM	810	1/0.5	Bonita, Saltillo: 1200-0600
CS04) OE	810	1/0.15	R. Èxitos, Tapachula: 1100-0400
GJ12) EMM	810	1/0.5	R. Salmantina, Salamanca: 1300-0400
GR01) AGR	810	1/0.15	Éxtasis Digital, Acapulco: 24h
NA03) UX	810	10/0.25	La Tremenda, Tepic: 1300-0100
QR04) RB	810	5/0.15	Sol Estéreo, Cozumel: 24h (rel: XHRB 89.9)
SO04) RSV	810	5/0.25	R. Alegría, Cd.Obregón: 1300-0200
TM04) RI	810	1/0.1	R. Rey, Reynosa: 24h
TM05) FW	810	50/1	R. Estrella, Tampico: 1200-0400
TX01) HT	810	2.5/1	R. Huamantla, Huamantla: 1200-0600
YU03) MQ	810	2/0.25	R. Fórmula, Segunda Cadena Nacional, Mérida (rel: XERFR 970 kHz)
ZC05) ZC	810	1/0.25	R. Felicidad, Río Grande: 1200-0500
BC07) MVS	820	3/0.5	Zona 820, Mexicali: 24h
CA01) ESC	820	0.75d	R. Escárcega, Escárcega: 1200-2400
DG01) DRD	820	1/0.5	Energy, Durango: 1200-0600
GR17) GRC	820	1d	R. Guerrero, Coyuca de Catalán
JL15) BA	820	10/0.1	La Consentida, Guadalajara: 24h
OX23) YN	820	1/0.5	Sonido 820, Oaxaca: 1200-0600
SL19) BM	820	1	La Ranchera, La Mera, San Luis Potosí: 24h
SN14) UDO	820	1/0.25	R. Universidad de Occidente, Los Mochis: 1300-0500
TB09) ZQ	820	5/0.25	R. Futurama, Villahermosa: 1200-0130
VE02) KG	820	2.5/0.1	Golden Hits, Córdoba: 1300-0100

Call	kHz	kW	Name and h. of tr.
CO15) IK	830	5	La Norteñita, Piedras Negras: 1100-0600
DF19) ITE	830	10	R. Capital, México: 24h
MI06) PUR	830	5d	LV de los Purépechas, Cheran: 1300-0020
NL13) LN	830	3/0.25	La Super Llegadora, Linares: 1200-0600
OX20) TLX	830	1/0.25	R. Tlaxiaco, Tlaxiaco: 1200-0400
SN12) VQ	830	5/1	La Superestación/La Grande, Culiacán: 1300-0200
ZC12) LK	830	10/0.5	La L-K, Zacatecas: 1200-0700
CA10) CUC	840	0.5	Casa de la Cultura de Campeche, Campeche
CS01) IO	840	10/1	La Ranchera, Tuxtla Gutiérrez: 1200-0500
GJ04) FG	840	5/0.5	La Pachanga, Celaya: 1200-0600
JL16) XXX	840	5/1	Fiesta Mexicana/Fiesta Digital, Tamazula: 1200-0600
NA02) TEY	840	1/0.25	R. Sensación, Tepic: 1300-0500
TM18) MY	840	1d	La Cañerita, Cd.Mante: 1200-0100
VE18) PV	840	2.5/0.1	La Fiera Tropical, Papantla: 1200-0600
BC04) ZF	850	0.5d	Éxtasis, Mexicali: 1300-0100
CH03) M	850	5/1	R. Exitos, Chihuahua: 1200-0500
JL08) MIA	850	5/1	Bonita, Guadalajara: 1200-0600
QE02) JAQ	850	4/1	R. Felicidad, Jalpan: 1200-0600
SO05) US	850	1/0.2	R. Universidad de Sonora, Hermosillo: 1200-0620
VE04) TQ	850	10	La Q Internacional, Orizaba: 1300-0900
AG05) PLA	860	5/1	R. Mexicana, Aguascalientes: 1100-0600
BC05) MO	860	5	R. 86/La Poderosa AM Estéreo, Tijuana: 24h
CH33) ZOL	860	1/0.5	R. Noticias 860, Cd.Juárez: 24h
CL02) AL	860	5/0.1	R. Mundo, Manzanillo: 1100-0700
CS08) DB	860	5/0.25	Canal 86, Tonalá: 1100-0500
DF10) UN	860	50/10	R. UNAM-Universidad Nacional Autónoma de México, México: 1300-0700
DG03) DU	860	5/0.5	D-U la que le gusta, Durango: 1100-0500
NL04) NL	860	5/2	R. Recuerdo, Monterrey: 1200-0600
QR06) CTL	860	5	R. Chetumal, Chetumal: 2300-0700
QR07) CCM	860	5	R. Caribe, Cancún: 1100-0500 (rel: XHCBJ 106.7)
SN07) NW	860	1/0.25	La Radio de la Ciudad, Culiacán: 1300-0600
TB04) ZX	860	1/0.15	La Comadre, Tenosique: 1200-0200
TM05) TW	860	1/0.25	R. Fiesta/La Sabrosona, Tampico: 1200-0100
YU01) RRF	860	5/0.5	R. Felicidad, Mérida: 1200-0200
CH18) TAR	870	10d	LV de la Sierra Tarahumara, Guachochi: 1200-0000
GJ05) AMO	870	1/0.5	AMO 870, Irapuato: 1200-0600
GR14) GRO	870	1	R. Guerrero, Acapulco: 1200-0700
MI01) LY	870	1/0.1	R. Moderna, Morelia: 1200-0300
OX07) ACC	870	5/0.25	LV del Puerto, Puerto Escondido: 1300-0100
PU06) NG	870	1/0.1	R. Nueva Generación, Huauchinango: 24h
SN19) FIL	870	1/0.25	R. Fórmula, Mazatlán: 1300-0700 (rel: XERFR 970kHz)
CH08) V	880	5/0.25	R. Fórmula, Primera Cadena Nacional, Chihuahua: (rel: XERFR 970 kHz)
CO16) TC	880	10/0.1	Estéreo Mayrán, Torreón: 1200-0600
GR10) IG	880	1/0.1	RCN La Grande de Iguala, Iguala: 1200-0600
JL09) AAA	880	20/1	R. 8-80/La Triple A, Guadalajara: 24h
SL04) EM	880	1d	La EM Mexicana, Río Verde: 1300-0100
SN18) PNK	880	10/2	Canal 88/Superestación, Los Mochis: 1100-0600
TB10) QQQ	880	10/0.5	Super Q, Villahermosa: 1100-0500
VE19) YV	880	1d	La Invasora, Córdoba: 1200-0100
CS18) FRT	890	20/1	R. Frontera, Comitán: 1100-0500
GJ11) AK	890	5/0.5	R. Consentida, Acámbaro: 1200-0400
NA02) PNA	890	1/0.25	R. Joya, Tepic: 1300-0500
OX19) POR	890	1/0.5	La Explosiva, Putla de Guerrero: 1200-0130
SN01) NZ	890	10/1	La Sinaloense, Culiacán: 24h
VE24) BY	890	1/0.25	La Consentida, Tuxpam: 1200-0400
ZC06) PC	890	5/1	Sonido Estrella, Zacatecas: 24h
ZC09) YQ	890	5/1	R. Fresnillo, Fresnillo: 1200-0700
CH31) DT	900	1d	La Reina, Cd.Cuahtémoc: 1300-0100
CS04) TAK	900	1/0.75	La K-900, Tapachula: 1100-0100
DF06) W	900	250	W Radio, México: 24h
VE05) WB	900	50	W Radio, Veracruz (rel: XEW 900 kHz)
NL05) OK	900	10/2.5	R. ACIR, Monterrey: 24h
BC06) AO	910	1/0.25	R. Mexicana, Mexicali: 24h
GJ06) ACN	910	5/0.1	R. Uno, León: 24h (rel: XEDF 1500 kHz)
NA01) NAY	910	10/1	La Buena Onda del Pacífico, Nuevo Vallarta: 24h
PU02) UL	910	10/0.5	R. Impacto, Teziutlán: 1200-0400
TB06) ACM	910	5/0.1	R. Exitos, Cárdenas: 1200-0600
CA11) TEB	920	1.5/0.5	R. Mar, Campeche: 1200-0600
CH03) QD	920	1/0.25	R. Noticias 920, Chihuahua: 1200-0700
CO04) RCA	920	5/0.2	La Joya, Torreón: 24h
CO08) MJ	920	1/0.25	La Coqueta, Piedras Negras: 1200-0500
CS05) VV	920	10/0.5	R. Diversión, Tuxtla Gutiérrez: 1200-0600
GJ07) RE	920	5/1	La Comadre/Salvatierra, Celaya: 1300-0130
JL15) LT	920	10/0.25	Oasis 920, Guadalajara: 24h Prgrs: R. María México
MI27) LCM	920	1	R. Mexicana, Cd.Lázaro Cárdenas: 24h
OX24) PNX	920	1/0.15	R. Costa, Pinotepa Nacional: 1200-0600
PU14) ZAR	920	1	Inolvidable 920, Puebla: 24h
SN08) CQ	920	5/0.5	C-Q/La Ranchera de Culiacán, Culiacán: 24h
SO01) HQ	920	5/1	La Mejor, Hermosillo: 1200-0700
BS08) RLA	930	1d	XERLA, Santa Rosalía
CL01) TTT	930	1	La Rocola, Colima: 1200-0400
CO17) SHT	930	1/0.25	Digital 930, Saltillo: 1200-0200
CS12) MK	930	5/0.5	R. Mexicana, Huixtla: 1100-0100
HG02) CY	930	2/1	Banda 930, Huejutla: 1200-0200
MI16) ZU	930	1	Sonido ZU Poder Musical, Zacapu: 1200-0400
OX17) TLA	930	5d	LV de la Mixteca, Tlaxiaco: 1200-0000
VE06) U	930	10/1	La U de Veracruz, Veracruz: 1130-0700
YU07) UL	930	2.5/0.2	R. Fórmula, Primera Cadena Nacional, Progreso: 1200-0500 (rel: XERFR 970 kHz)
ZC03) QS	930	10/1	Romance en Radio, Fresnillo: 24h (rel: XEL 1260 kHz 0500-1600)
BC07) WV	940	1/0.1	Fiesta Mexicana, Mexicali: 24h
DF06) Q	940	50	Besame 9-40, México: 24h
CS17) REC	940	1d	R. Fiesta, Reforma: 1200-2400
JL20) HE	940	1d	LV 9-40, Atotonilco: 1300-0100
TM07) RKS	940	1d	La Poderosa, Reynosa: 1200-0400
CO09) YJ	940	15	La Y-J Mexicana, Sabinas: 24h
AG05) CAA	950	1/0.5	Azul 95, Aguascalientes: 1200-0600
BC08) KAM	950	17/5	R. Fórmula Californias, Tijuana: 24h
CA02) MAB	950	1/0.25	Canal Internacional, Cd.del Carmen: 1200-0400
CH08) FA	950	1/0.25	R. Rama/R Amor, Chihuahua: 24h
CS01) TUG	950	1/0.25	Dimensión 9-50, Tuxtla Gutiérrez: 1200-0600
GJ24) CEL	950	5/1	R. Lobo, Cortazar: 24h
GR02) ACA	950	5	R. ACIR, Acapulco: 24h
JL22) MEX	950	5/0.5	La Mexicana, Cd.Guzmán: 1200-0600
NA07) ZE	950	2.5/1	La Invasora, Santiago Ixcuintla: 1200-0200
NL06) RN	950	5/1	R. Naranjera, Monterey: 1150-0600
OX16) OJN	950	5d	LV de la Chinantla, San Lúcas Ojitlán: 1400-2200
SN18) ORF	950	5/0.5	R. Amor, Los Mochis: 1200-0700
SO12) PB	950	10/0.1	La Grande, Hermosillo: 1300-0800
TM20) TO	950	1	Romántica, Tampico: 24h
CH11) FAMA	960	1/0.1	R. 960 La Fama, Cd.Camargo: 1300-0400
CO10) KS	960	1/0.1	Super Mix, Saltillo: 1100-0600
CS04) TAP	960	5/0.15	Imperio, Tapachula: 1100-0100
GR05) UQ	960	1/0.5	R. Variedades, Zihuatanejo: 1200-0300
GR12) XC	960	1	Super Mil, Taxco: 1200-0500
JL10) HK	960	10/5	LV de Guadalajara, Guadalajara: 24h
MI07) MM	960	1	La Grupera, Morelia: 24h
QR02) ROO	960	5/0.5	La Voz de Quintana Roo, Chetumal: 1200-0500
SL03) CZ	960	1/0.25	Perfil 9-60, San Luis Potosí: 24h
SO07) IQ	960	1/0.5	R. ACIR, Cd.Obregón: 24h
TM08) K	960	5/1	La Estación Grande de Nuevo, Laredo: 1155-0400
VE07) GB	960	1/0.5	Romántica, Coatzacoalcos: 24h
VE08) OZ	960	1/0.25	Satélite, Jalapa: 1200-0600
CH30) J	970	50/5	La J Mexicana, Cd.Juárez: 24h
DF11) RFR	970	100	R. Fórmula, Primera Cadena Nacional, México: 24h
GJ08) UG	970	1	R. Universidad de Guanajuato, Guanajuato: 1300-0200
MI08) CJ	970	1/0.25	R. Apatzingán, Apatzingán: 1200-0400
SN10) VOX	970	10/1	R. Mujer, Mazatlán: 24h
SO08) EZ	970	5/0.25	La Super Z, Caborca: 1400-0600
TB05) VT	970	10/1	La Primera Estación de Tabasco, Villahermosa: 24h
TM09) O	970	1	R. Gallito, Matamoros: 1200-0600
YU03) MH	970	5/0.5	Candela Tropicaliente, Mérida: 1200-0500
ZC12) ZAZ	970	10/0.5	De Mil Amores 9-70, Zacatecas: 24h
CH24) JK	980	1	La Comadre, Cd.Delicias: 1300-0500
CO12) NR	980	5/0.5	R. 980, Nueva Rosita: 1155-0600
MI09) LC	980	10/0.2	Dual Stereo, La Piedad: 1230-0500
NA04) XT	980	1	R. Fiesta, Tepic: 1300-0700
SL06) FF	980	1/0.25	La Norteña, Matehuala: 1200-0400
SO09) FQ	980	1/0.5	LV de la Ciudad del Cobre, Cananea: 1200-0700
SO10) KE	980	1/0.25	KE-98 Acción Digital, Navojoa: 24h
TM10) TU	980	10/1	R Tampico, Tampico: 1200-0600
VE03) QO	980	5	R. Romance, Cosamaloapan: 1200-0400
BC04) CL	990	5/3	Rocola 990, Mexicali: 24h
BS02) HZ	990	5/0.25	R. 9-90, La Paz: 1300-0700
CH13) ER	990	5/0.25	R. Lobo, Cd.Cuauhtémoc: 1300-0600
CS09) TG	990	10	La Grande del Sureste, Tuxtla Gutiérrez: 24h
JL01) BC	990	1/0.1	La Buena Onda, Cd.Guzmán: 1200-0600

Call	kHz	kW	Name and h. of tr.
MI01) ATM	990	1	A Toda Máquina, Morelia: 1200-0900
NL04) T	990	50	La T Grande, Monterrey: 24h
OX08) IU	990	1	Estéreo Cristal, Oaxaca: 1200-0600
VE15) ID	990	10/1	R. Álamo, Àlamo: 1200-0400
YU04) UM	990	1/0.25	Candela Valladolid, Valladolid: 24h
ZC10) FP	990	10/1	R. Alegría, Jalpa: 24h
CH33) FV	1000	5/1	La Rancherita, Cd.Juárez: 1200-0300
CH29) HPC	1000	1/0.5	R. Mil, Hidalgo del Parral
CS02) TAC	1000	5/1	Audio Mil de Chiapas, Tapachula: 1200-0400
DF02) OY	°1000	50/20	R. Mil "Tradición y Excelencia en Radio", México: 24h
GJ23) RZ	1000	1/0.5	Bonita, León: 1200-0600
SN11) MIL	1000	1/0.25	La Comadre, Los Mochis: 1200-0700
SN24) MMS	1000	1	Inolvidable, Mazatlán: 1300-0700
TM24) NLT	1000	1/0.1	Laredo Radio, Nuevo Laredo: 1200-0600
VE30) CSV	1000	1	La Tremenda, Coatzacoales: 1200-0600
YU01) MYL	1000	5/0.25	Juvemil, Mérida: 1200-0400
BC22) DX	1010	1/0.5	R. Variedades, Ensenada: 1400-0800
CH14) LO	1010	5/0.5	R. Lobo Latino, Chihuahua: 1200-0600
CO01) VK	1010	5/1	La Ke Buena, Torreón: 1200-0500
CO13) KD	1010	1/0.25	K de Oro, Cd.Acuña: 1200-0600
HG11) HGO	1010	1d	R. Hidalgo, Huejutla
JL15) HL	1010	50/5	W Radio 1010, Guadalajara: 24h (rel: XEW 900 kHz)
MI32) TUMI	1010	5d	LV de la Sierra Oriente, Tuxpán: 1200-2330
PU19) PA	1010	10/1	La Prendida, Puebla: 24h
SN12) WS	1010	5/0.5	Inolvidable, Culiacán: 1300-0500
SO11) XN	1010	2.5/0.5	R. Ures, Ures: 1300-0500
VE09) FM	1010	1/0.5	La Máquina Tropical, Veracruz: 1200-0600
CL09) VE	1020	1	La Comadre, Colima: 1200-0400
NA02) PIC	1020	1	R. Hits, Tepic: 24h
OX14) OU	1020	2.5/1	Sensación Estéreo, Huajuapan de León: 1300-0100
QE06) KH	1020	2.5/0.5	R. Centro, Querétaro: 24h
QR03) WO	1020	1/0.1	Sol Estéreo Frontera, Chetumal: 1200-0400
VE14) PR	1020	5/0.5	Estéreo Vida, Poza Rica: 1200-0600
BC09) SDD	1030	5	La Tremenda, Ensenada: 1400-0800
CA05) BCC	1030	1/0.25	La Gaviota Musical, Cd.del Carmen: 1200-0500
CH32) YC	1030	5/0.5	R. Fórmula, Cd.Juárez: 24h
CS15) VFS	1030	10/0.25	LV de la Frontera Sur, Las Margaritas: 1200-0030 (SS -0000)
DF08) QR	1030	50/5	R. Centro, México: 24h
GR01) VP	1030	1/0.5	La Estación del Puerto, Acapulco: 1200-0200
JL11) LJ	1030	5/1	La Ke Buena, Lagos de Moreno: 1300-0400
MI24) GQ	1030	1d	R. Variedades, Los Reyes: 1200-0200
OX13) TEKA	1030	1/0.5	R. Teca, Ixtepec: 1200-0200
QR12) NKA	1030	2.5d	LV del Gran Pueblo, Félipe Carillo Puerto: 1200-1700
SL07) IE	1030	5/0.15	Stereo 1030 AM, Matehuala: 1155-0405
SN13) MPM	1030	10/1	R. Fama/El Fuerte, Los Mochis: 1300-0700
TM10) PAV	1030	1/0.5	W Radio, Tampico: 1200-0600
CH08) HES	1040	5/0.25	R. Luz, Chihuahua: 24h
CS27) PLE	1040	5d	R. Palanque, Palenque
GJ26) SAG	1040	1/0.25	Tu Radio 1040, Irapuato: 1300-0100
JL09) BBB	1040	10/1	R. Mujer, Guadalajara: 24h
ME05) CH	1040	10	R. Capital, Toluca: 1100-0500
SO42) GYS	1040	1/0.25	Super Banda, Guaymas: 24h
VE01) GR	1040	2.5/1	R. Favorita, Jalapa: 1300-0100
AG06) DC	1050	25/1	Satélite, Aguascalientes: 1200-0400
BC06) D	1050	10/1	W Radio, Mexicali: 24h
BS05) BCS	1050	10/1	R. Cultural Surcalifornia, La Paz: 1300-0500
CO23) VUC	1050	1d	La Norteñita, Allende: 1200-0200
GR19) ZUM	1050	2.5/0.5	La Invasora, Chilpancingo: 1200-0400
MI29) IP	1050	1/0.5	Fiesta Mexicana, Uruapán: 24h
NL08) G	1050	100	La Ranchera de Monterrey, Monterrey: 24h
QR10) QOO	1050	35/2.5	R. Pirata, Cancún: 24h
TB03) TAB	1050	10/5	R. Tabasco, Villahermosa: 1200-0400
VE25) JF	1050	5d	R. Sensación, Tierra Blanca: 1200-0200
DF12) EP	°1060	100/20	R. Educación, México: 24h
CA02) IT	1070	1/0.25	R. Interactiva, Cd.del Carmen: 1200-0400
CS01) RPR	1070	1/0.5	Retro, Tuxtla Gutiérrez
GR03) AGS	1070	1/0.2	Bonita, Acapulco
JL12) SP	1070	5/1	R. Juventud Unica, Guadalajara: 24h
PU03) GY	1070	1/0.25	R. Lobo, Tehuacán: 1200-0700
SL02) EI	1070	1/0.25	Momentos 10-70, San Luis Potosí: 24h
SL13) ANT	1070	5d	LV de las Huastecas, Tancanhuitz de Santos: 1200-0200
SO18) OBS	1070	1/0.25	La Norteña 1070, Cd.Obregón: 24h
VE10) MI	1070	1/0.1	La Poderosa, Minatitlán: 1100-0600
BS09) PAB	1080	1/0.25	R. Celebridad, La Paz
CL04) UU	1080	1/0.5	R. Variedades, Colima: 1200-0600
GJ05) CN	1080	1/0.5	Fuerza 1080, Irapuato: 1200-0600
JL32) JLV	1080	5d	Sistema Jalisciense, Puerto Vallarta
ME07) TUL	1080	5/0.25	Sistema XEGEM "R. Mexiquense", Tultitlán: 1200-0600 (rel: XEGEM 1600 kHz)
SO31) DY	1080	1/0.25	R. Gallo, San LuisRíoColorado: 1200-0700
VE11) XK	1080	10/0.25	1080 R. Mundo, Poza Rica: 1200-0600
BC11) PRS	1090	50	The Mighty 1090, Rosarito: 24h
JL13) LB	1090	5/1	Tremenda 10-90, La Barca: 1200-0200
NL04) AU	1090	5/0.25	Que Buena, Monterrey: 1200-0600
PU16) HR	1090	5/1	La HR/R. ACIR, Puebla: 24h
QE07) XE	1090	2.5/1	R. Fórmula, Primera Cadena Nacional, Querétaro: 24h (rel: XERFR 970 kHz)
TM11) WL	1090	1d	La Romantica, Nuevo Laredo: 1200-0200
VE12) MCA	1090	10/0.5	MCA 1090, Pánuco: 1200-0600
VE13) IL	1090	1/0.5	La Grupera 1090, Veracruz: 24h
YU01) FC	1090	10/0.25	Frequencia Cordial, Mérida: 1200-0400
BS10) BAC	1100	1d	XEBAC, Bahía Asunción
GJ09) BV	1100	5/1	R. Alegría, Moroleón: 1200-0600
GR24) GRM	1100	1d	R. Guerrero, Ometepec
QR15) CAN	1100	4d	R. Mundo Maya Turquesa, Cancún
SL15) PO	1100	1/0.25	R. ACIR, San Luis Potosí: 24h
SO43) NAS	1100	1/0.5	Radiante 1100, Navojoa: 24h
ZC11) TGO	1100	5/0.5	R. Alegría Digital, Tlaltenango: 1200-0400
CH03) ES	1110	1/0.5	La Radio Viva, Chihuahua: 1300-0500
CH33) WR	1110	1/0.5	Classics 11-10, Cd.Juárez: 1200-0200
CO33) PU	1110	0.25d	Patronato Cultural Monclova, Monclova
DF08) RED	1110	50	R. Red, México: 24h
GJ25) LEO	1110	5/1	La Rancherita, León: 1300-0100
JL35) PVJ	1110	1/0.2	Energía Vallarta La Líder, Puerto Vallarta: 1200-0600
OX22) TED	1110	0.5d	XETED, Teotitlán de Flores Magon
OX30) TUX	1110	0.5d	XETUX, Tuxtepec
SO32) VS	1110	1/0.25	Maxima, Hermosillo: 24h
TM02) OQ	1110	1d	Dimensión Gape 1110, Reynosa: 1300-0100
BC07) MX	1120	1	MVS Noticias, Mexicali: 1400-0800
JL14) UNO	1120	1/0.5	R. Uno, Guadalajara: 24h
OX09) ZB	1120	2/0.25	R. Oro, Oaxaca: 1200-0300
PU16) POP	1120	1/0.1	La Preciosa, Puebla: 24h
QE04) GV	1120	1/0.5	R. ACIR, Querétaro: 24h
SL05) TR	1120	1/0.5	R. Panorámica, Cd.Valles: 1200-0200
TB17) TQE	1120	5/0.5	XETQE, Tenosique (rel: XETVH 1230 kHz)
YU08) RUY	1120	1/0.25	R. Universidad, Mérida: 1200-0600
ME02) TOL	1130	10/5	R. Lobo, Toluca: 24h
MI11) FN	1130	1/0.1	R. Moderna, Uruapan: (rel: XHFN 91.1)
NA05) LUP	1130	1d	R. Lupita, Las Varas: 1300-0100
SN27) MOS	1130	1/0.25	Banda Sonora, Los Mochis: 24h
SO36) HN	1130	1d	Rockola, Nogales: 1200-0200
SO44) ETCH	1130	5d	LV de los Tres Ríos, Etchojoa: 1200-2000
VE08) ZL	1130	10/1	La Grupera, Jalapa: 1200-0400
CS28) TEC	1140	2.5d	XETEC, Tecpatan
GJ23) XF	1140	5/1	La Grupera, León: 24h
HG12) PEC	1140	1d	XEPEC, San Bartolo Tutotepec
MI22) LIA	1140	1d	La Tremenda, Morelia: 1200-0400
NL02) MR	1140	50	M-R 140 AM, Música Romántica, Monterrey: 24h
PU04) TE	1140	5/0.1	1140 Punto Digital, Tehuacán: 1300-0100
SO39) SOS	1140	10	R. Uno, Agua Prieta: 24h
BC06) RM	1150	1	R. Fórmula, Mexicali: 24h
CH16) JS	1150	1/0.5	JS Digital, Hidalgo del Parral: 1245-0500
CO14) BF	1150	1/0.25	La Tremenda, San Pedro: 1200-0100
DF08) CMQ	1150	20/10	El Fonógrafo/Canal 115, México: 24h
JL06) AD	1150	20/0.5	R. Metrópoli, Guadalajara: 24h
OX10) XP	1150	10/1	La Super Buena, Tuxtepec: 1200-0100
QE10) QUE	1150	1	R. Querétaro, Querétaro: 1200-0600
SN16) UAS	1150	10/0.15	R. Universidad, Culiacán: 1300-0200
SO22) SO	1150	5/0.3	La Coqueta, Cd.Obregón: 1200-0800
TB07) RTM	1150	5/1	Zonido Zeta, Macuspana: 1200-0500
VE43) TVR	1150	1.5/0.5	La Nueva Azul, Tuxpam: 1100-0500
GJ11) VW	1160	2.5/0.5	R. Sensación, Acámbaro: 1300-0130
MI12) IW	1160	1/0.1	Canal Juvenil, Uruapan: 1300-0400
SL12) GI	1160	1/0.1	Reyna de las Huastecas, Tamazunchale: 1200-0200
VE16) BE	1160	5/0.25	Imversa Radio, Perote: 1200-0300
AG03) UVA	1170	10/1	La Rancherita, Aguascalientes: 24h
CO11) MDA	1170	1/0.5	La Ley 11-70, Monclova: 1300-0600
JL19) JTF	1170	1/0.1	Prisma Musical, Zacoalco de Torres: 1300-0100
ME01) RLK	1170	1/0.25	Super Stereo Miled, Atlacomulco: 24h
PU05) CD	1170	10/0.5	XECD 1170 R. De Verdad, Puebla: 1200-0600
SO33) IB	1170	1	Super Banda/Punto de Vista, Caborca: 1300-0700
SO35) FEM	1170	5/1	R. Felicidad, Hermosillo: 1200-0600

Call	kHz	kW	Name and h. of tr.
TM07) RT	1170	5d	Voz 1170, Reynosa: 1200-0200
VE46) ZS	1170	2.5/1	R. Hit, Coatzacoalcos: 1200-0600
BS05) UBS	1180	10d	R. Universidad Autonoma de Baja California Sur, La Paz
CH35) DCH	1180	1/0.25	Romántica 11-80, Cd.Delicias: 1200-0600
DF14) FR	1180	10	R. Felicidad, México: 24h
GJ05) YA	1180	1	La Picosa, Irapuato: 1200-0600
OX11) AH	1180	0.5	R. Hit, Juchitán: 1130-0630
VE34) GN	1180	10/1	La Gigante, Piedras Negras: 1200-0600
BC07) MBC	1190	0.5/0.1	R. Hablada, Mexicali: 1400-0800
CH30) PZ	1190	5/0.1	R. Norteña, Cd.Juárez: 1200-0200
JL15) WK	1190	50/10	La W de Guadalajara, Guadalajara: 24h
MI13) SOL	1190	2.5/0.5	R. Sol, Cd.Hidalgo: 1200-0400
MO01) JPA	1190	5/0.5	La Grande/Red W, Cuernavaca: 1200-0600
NL08) CT	1190	10/0.1	Morena, Monterrey: 1200-0800
TB12) RV	1190	10/0.5	R. Villa, Villahermosa: 1100-0500
TM20) TOT	1190	5/0.5	Éxtasis Digital, Tampico: 1200-0600
VE32) PP	1190	5/0.25	La Comadre, Orizaba: 1200-0600
AG06) AGA	1200	1	La Bonita, Aguascalientes: 1200-0400
BS11) PAS	1200	1d	XEPAS, Punta Abrejos
GJ27) ITC	1200	0.25	R. Tecnológico, Celaya
ME02) QY	1200	1/0.5	Inolvidable 1200 AM, Toluca: 24h
MI14) ZI	1200	1d	Canal Festivo 120, Zacapu: 1200-0100
SN06) WT	1200	1/0.25	La Buenísima, Culiacán: 1200-0300
SO29) YF	1200	1/0.25	R. Fórmula, Primera Cadena Nacional, Hermosillo (rel: XERFR 970 kHz)
VE11) PW	1200	1/0.3	Tu Música, Poza Rica: 1200-0600
CL07) BCO	1210	50/5	La Poderosa Voz de Colima, Colima: 24h
CS26) COPA	1210	5d	LV de los Vientos, Copainalá: 1230-2230
PU16) PUE	1210	5/1	Méxicana 1210, Puebla: 1200-0600
VE27) BD	1210	10/0.25	R. Centro, Jalapa: 1200-0600
VE33) VZ	1210	5/1	R. La Veraz, Acayacan: 1200-0600
CO32) SAL	1220	2.5d	R. Universidad, Saltillo
DF04) B	1220	100	La B Grande, México: 24h
JL34) DKN	1220	1/0.25	R. Fórmula, Guadalajara: 24h
MI30) LP	1230	1	R. Pía, La Piedad: 1300-0300
PU20) TCP	1230	1	La Romántica, Tehuacan
SN12) EX	1230	1/0.25	R. Fórmula, Culiacán: 24h
TB11) TVH	1230	20/1	La Morena, Villahermosa
CH12) WG	1240	1	R. Amor, Cd.Juárez: 1200-0600
CH17) BN	1240	1/0.25	Radiola, Cd.Delicias: 1300-0400
CO15) VM	1240	1	La Estación del Amor, Piedras Negras: 1100-0600
CS01) LM	1240	1	R. Capital, Tuxtla Gutiérrez: 1200-0500
HG08) RD	1240	1	R. Lobo, Pachuca: 1200-0500
MI15) RPA	1240	5/0.5	R. Ranchito, Morelia: 1200-0500
NA06) SI	1240	2.5/1	R. Felicidad, Santiago Ixcuintla: 1300-0500
NL04) IZ	1240	1	R. Fórmula,Tercera Cadena Nacional, Monterrey (rel: XEAI 1470 kHz)
OX25) CE	1240	2.5/1	R. Hit 12-40, Oaxaca: 1130-0600
SO36) CG	1240	1	R. Mexicana, Nogales: 1300-0700
SO14) BQ	1240	1	Estelar 12-40/R. Mexicana, Guaymas: 1300-0500
TM10) S	1240	1/0.25	La Tamaulipeca, Tampico: 1200-0400
VE04) OV	1240	2.5/0.5	La Picosa, Orizaba: 1200-0700
CH19) AT	1250	5/0.25	R. Imagen, Hidalgo del Parral: 1200-0500
CO03) SC	1250	1/0.5	R. 1250, Sabinas: 1300-0100
CO30) SJ	1250	5/0.5	R. Saltillo, Saltillo: 24h
CS11) MG	1250	5/0.25	Máxima 1250/La R.Impresionante, Arriaga: 1200-0400
GR06) PI	1250	2.5/0.5	La Consentida, Chilpancingo: 1200-0200
JL26) DK	1250	10/1	DK 12-50, Guadalajara: 1200-0600
ME07) TEJ	1250	1/0.25	Sistema XEGEM "R. Mexiquense", Tejupilco: 1200-0600 (rel: XEGEM 1600 kHz)
PU17) ZT	1250	5/0.5	R. Tribuna 12-50, Puebla: 24h
QE07) JX	1250	5/0.1	R. Fórmula, Segunda Cadena Nacjonal, Querétaro: 24h (rel: XEDF 1500 kHz)
SO32) DL	1250	5/0.5	R. 13/Fuerza de la Palabra, Hermosillo (rel: XEDA 1290 kHz)
VE21) TF	1250	1	La Jarocha, Veracruz: 1130-0600
AG03) RO	1260	5/2.5	R. Recuerdo, Aguascalientes: 24h
CH20) OG	1260	5/0.15	R. Ranchito, Ojinaga. 1200-0400
CO31) WGR	1260	5/0.25	Estéreo Vida, Monclova: 24h
DF14) L	1260	50/10	R. ACIR, México: 24h
GJ13) ZH	1260	1/0.25	La Estación que es Escucha, Salamanca: 1300-0500
JL24) JY	1260	10/1	R. Ambiente, Autlán: 1200-0300
MI04) QL	1260	1	Sonido Brillante, Zamora: 1200-0600
NL13) R	1260	1/0.25	R. Linares, Linares: 1200-0400
OX18) JAM	1260	5d	LV de la Costa Chica, Santiago Jamiltepec: 1200-0000
SL16) XR	1260	5/1	R. Mensajera, Cd.Valles: 1200-0300
SN26) SA	1260	5/0.5	La Sabrosita/La Mejor, Culiacán: 24h
SO15) MW	1260	1/0.25	R. San Luis, San Luis Río Colorado: 24h
VE22) MTV	1260	1	R. Lobo de Mina, Minatitlán: 1200-0100
VE48) TBV	1260	1	La Poderosa, Tierra Blanca: 1200-0500
BC12) AZ	1270	0.5	R. Zeta 13, Tijuana: 24h
CO04) WN	1270	05/0.15	El Fonógrafo del Recuerdo, Torreón: 1200-0600
DG04) HD	1270	1.5/0.5	Universidad Juárez del Estado de Durango, Durango
GJ01) RPL	1270	10/0.15	La Poderosa, León: 24h
HG05) QH	1270	1/0.1	R. Sinfonía, Ixmiquilpán: 1200-0100
OX09) AX	1270	5/0.5	Tu Frecuencia 1080, Oaxaca: 1100-0600
SO16) GL	1270	1/0.5	Digital 12-70, Navojoa: 1200-0700
TB16) VHT	1270	1	Romántica 12-70, Villahermosa: 24h
TM10) RRT	1270	5/0.5	Solar 1270, Cd.Madero: 24h
VE20) RRR	1270	1/0.25	La Invasora 12-70, Poza Rica: 1200-0300
CA03) CAM	1280	2.5/1	Mix, Campeche: 1155-0500
CH03) BW	1280	1/0.5	La Pantera, Chihuahua: 24h
CS12) KY	1280	1/0.1	LV de la Costa de Chiapas, Huixtla: 1100-0300
GJ14) SQ	1280	2.5/0.15	R. San Miguel. San Miguel de Allende: 1200-0400
JL28) BON	1280	10/0.5	R. Fórmula,Tercera Cadena Nacional, Guadalajara (rel: XEAI 1470 kHz)
NL04) AW	1280	10/1	Teleradio, Monterrey: 24h
PU18) EG	1280	1/0.5	R. Fórmula Puebla, Puebla: 24h
TM12) TUT	1280	1	R. Tamaulipas, Tula: 1200-0400
VE38) AG	1280	2/1	R. Cafetal, Córdoba: 24h
BC20) QIN	1290	2.5	LV de las Montañas/LV del Valle, San Quintín: 1400-0300 (Sun -2200)
CA04) TH	1290	0.25d	R. Palizada, Palizada: 1200-2400
DF09) DA	1290	25/1	R. 13/La Fuerza de la Palabra, México: 24h
GJ03) FAC	1290	5/0.25	La Mera Mera, Salvatierra: 1230-0130
MI17) IX	1290	1/0.5	Enlace Digital 12-90, Sahuayo: 1300-0200
SL04) IY	1290	1d	Espectacular 12-90, Río Verde: 1200-0200
SN10) NX	1290	10/1	Fiesta Mexicana, Mazatlán: 24h
SO18) AP	v1290	1/0.25	Romántica 1290, Cd.Obregón: 24h
CH22) SW	1300	1/0.5	R. Madera, Cd.Madera: 1300-0400
CH30) P	1300	50	R. 13/R. Centro, Cd.Juárez: 24h
GJ15) XV	1300	10/0.75	R. Capital, León: 1200-2400 (rel: XHXV 88.9)
HG13) AWL	1300	1/0.25	R. Jacala,Jacala
MI07) KW	1300	1	Bonita, Morelia: 1200-0400
SN15) JL	1300	1/0.25	La 130, La Ley, Guamuchil: 1200-0500
SO13) XW	1300	1/0.1	Estéreo Vida, Nogales: 1300-0700
TM13) LE	1300	1/0.15	R. 13, Tampico: 1200-0600
VE23) HU	1300	1/0.1	R. Tropical, Martinez de la Torre: 1200-0600
BC13) C	1310	1	R. Enciso, Tijuana: 24h
BS12) BTS	1310	1d	XEBTS, Bahía de Tortugas
BS13) LPZ	1310	10	R. Variedades, La Paz
CH23) RU	1310	1/0.25	R. Universidad, Chihuahua
GR07) HJ	1310	0.25	R. Petatlán, Petatlán: 1200-0100
GR23) GRT	1310	1d	Jaguar 1310, Taxco: 1200-0400
JL06) TIA	1310	10/0.25	Alma de México, Guadalajara: 24h
NL02) VB	1310	5/0.1	R. 13, Monterrey: 1200-0600
PU14) HIT	1310	5/1	R. Felicidad, Puebla: 24h
QE06) HY	1310	1/0.25	13-10 La Jefa, Querétaro: 1200-0600
SO19) FH	1310	1/0.1	R. Plan de Agua Prieta, Agua Prieta: 1400-0300
TM14) AM	1310	5/0.25	La M Grande, Matamoros: 24h
VE06) HV	1310	2.5/1	HV 1310 AM, Veracruz: 1200-0700
VE44) TRC	1310	1	R. Gazeta de la Tierra Norte, Tepetzintla
AG07) NM	1320	0.25	Expresión Total, Aguascalientes
BS03) SR	1320	1/0.25	R. Cachanía, Santa Rosalia: 1200-0600
CH06) JZ	1320	5/0.25	La Campera, Cd.Jimenez: 1300-0200
CO25) CPN	1320	10/0.1	La Mexicana 1320, Piedras Negras: 24h
DF20) D	1320	20	R. Bienestar/Monitor, México: 24h
MI18) NI	1320	20/0.5	Mix, Uruapán: 24h
OX10) UH	1320	5/1	La Consentida, Tuxtepec: 1200-0400
SN03) RJ	1320	5/0.5	La Ranchera, Mazatlán: 24h
TB16) FRO	1320	2.5/1	Fiesta Mexicana, Villahermosa: 1200-0100
CL08) MAC	1330	0.5	La Poderosa, Manzanillo: 1100-0600
CO18) WQ	1330	4/0.25	La Superestación, Monclova: 24h
CO27) AJ	1330	2/0.25	La Imagen de la R en Satillo, Saltillo: 24h
GJ16) BO	1330	5/0.2	R. Variedades, Irapuato: 1030-0600
PU07) EV	1330	1d	R. Festival, Izúcar de Matamoros: 1200-0600
TM10) RP	1330	1/0.1	Èxtasis Digital, Cd.Madero: 1200-0600
VE23) HTY	1330	2.5/1	Inolvidable, Martínez de la Torre: 1200-0600
BC24) AA	1340	1	La Caliente, Mexicali: 24h
CH20) RCH	1340	0.25/0.1	La Pantera, Ojinaga: 1400-0200
CO13) DH	1340	1	La Tremenda Tropical, Cd.Acuña: 1200-0800
GR03) CI	1340	1	Romántica 1340, Acapulco: 1200-1000
HG03) QB	1340	1	La Divertida, Tulancingo: 1200-0600

Call	kHz	kW	Name and h. of tr.
JL26) DKT	1340	5/1	R. Ranchito, Guadalajara: 1200-0600
MI05) APM	1340	1	Candela, Apatzingán: 1200-0300
MI19) CR	1340	1	Stereo Mía, Morelia: 1200-0300
MO01) ASM	1340	5/1	Romántica 13-40, Cuernavaca: 1200-0600
NL02) NV	1340	1	La Sabrosita, Monterrey: 24h
PU08) LU	1340	5/0.25	R. Esmeralda, Cd.Serdán: 1300-0100
SL02) SL	1340	2	Cancionero 13-40, San Luis Potosí: 1200-0600
SN17) QE	1340	1d	La Perla Camaronera, Escuinapa
SO40) OS	1340	1	La Super Tremenda, Cd.Obregón: 1300-0500
TB08) YR	1340	1	R. 13, Teapa
TM01) RPV	1340	1	R. Festival, Cd.Victoria: 1300-0200
TM14) MT	1340	1	Magia 13-40, Matamoros: 1200-0300
TM15) BK	1340	5/1	Super Grupera, Nuevo Laredo: 1155-0600 (Sat -0800, Sun -0200)
CO04) TB	1350	5/0.5	R. Laguna, Torreón: 24h
CS16) CAH	1350	5/1	La Popular 13-50, Cacahoatán: 1100-0700
DF04) QK	1350	5/1	La R. de los Ciudadanos, México: 24h
PU15) CTZ	1350	5d	LV de la Sierra Norte, Cuetzalán: 1200-0100
SO15) LBL	1350	6/1	R. Centro, San Luis Río Colorado: 1300-0100 (cfr 1570)
SO20) TM	1350	1	El Heraldo de la Frontera, Naco: 1300-0200
TM16) ZD	1350	1/0.25	La Doña de la Frontera, Camargo: 1200-0400
CH02) DI	1360	1/0.4	Éxtasis Digital, Chihuahua: 24h
CS09) UD	1360	5/0.5	La U de Tuxtla, Tuxtla Gutiérrez: 1100-0700
GJ07) Y	1360	1/0.25	La Grupera, Celaya: 1100-0600
GR08) KF	1360	1/0.5	Stereomil 1360, La K-F, Iguala: 1155-0500
VE26) DQ	1360	1/0.15	La Comadre, San Andrés Tuxtla: 1200-0600
VE42) ZON	1360	5d	LV de la Sierra de Zongolica, Zongolica: 1300-0000
ZC08) XM	1360	1	R. Jerez, Jerez de García Salinas: 1200-0400
AG04) UAA	1370	5/1	R. Universidad, Aguascalientes
BC06) HG	1370	1/0.5	R. Norteña, Mexicali: 1400-0200
CA06) A	1370	5/1	El Eco de las Murallas, Campeche: 1200-0600
DG07) RPU	1370	1/0.25	Sonido Z, Durango: 24h
GJ17) JE	1370	5/1.5	R. Reyna, Dolores Hidalgo: 1200-0600
JL08) PJ	1370	10/1	Super Deportiva, Guadalajara: 24h
MI20) SV	1370	1/0.5	R. Universidad, Morelia
NL14) MON	1370	10	R. Fórmula, Monterrey: 1200-0600 (rel: XEDF 1500 kHz)
SO36) HF	1370	5	R. Fórmula, Nogales: 1400-0800
TM17) GNK	1370	5d	R. Mexicana, Nuevo Laredo: 1200-0200
CO01) RS	1380	1/0.25	Romántica 1380, Torreón: 1300-0500
CO20) VD	1380	1/0.1	La V-D, Allende: 1200-0400
DF13) CO	1380	50/5	Romántica 13-80, México: 24h
TM01) GW	1380	5/0.15	Expansión W, Cd.Victoria: 1200-0400
VE27) TP	1380	10/1	R. Sensación. Jalapa: 1300-0100
BC14) KT	1390	5/0.1	La Súper Estación, Tecate: 24h
CL06) TY	1390	5/0.2	La Mexicana, Tecomán: 1100-0300
GJ06) RW	1390	10/0.25	R. Formula, Primera Cadena Nacional, León (rel: XERFR 970 kHz)
HG06) ZG	1390	0.5d	R. Mezquital y Huasteca Hidalguense, Ixmiquilpán: 1300-0100
MO03) CTA	1390	1/0.25	R. Cuautla, Cuautla: (rel.XHVAC 102.9)
SO21) QC	1390	5/0.15	LV de Pto Penasco "Rocky Point", Pto Peñasco: 1200-0100
TM18) XO	1390	5/0.1	La Super Buena, Cd.Mante: 1200-0600
TM02) OR	1390	1	Mix 13-90, Reynosa: 1230-0600
VE24) TL	1390	5/1	LV de la Huasteca, Tuxpan: 1200-0600
AG02) AC	1400	5/1	La Ke Buena, Aguascalientes: 24h
BC15) PF	1400	1	La Rancherita, Ensenada: 24h
GR01) KJ	1400	1	La Rancherita, Acapulco: 1200-0400
ME03) XI	1400	2.5/1	La I de Ixtapan, Ixtapan de la Sal: 1200-0600
MI21) OJ	1400	5/1	R. Horizonte, Cd.Lázaro Cárdenas: 1200-0400
MI22) I	1400	1	R. Morelia, Morelia: 24h
NA08) LH	1400	1/0.25	La Gardenia Musical, Acaponeta: 1300-0100
NL09) SH	1400	1	R. Sabinas, Cd.Sabinas: 1200-0600
OX21) UBJ	1400	1	R. Universidad Benito Juárez, Oaxaca
PU09) FS	1400	1/0.25	R. Matamoros, Izúcar de Matamoros: 24h
QE03) VI	1400	1	Fantasía 99-1, San Juan del Río: 1200-0400 (rel: XHVI 99.1)
SL06) WU	1400	0.5	La Poderosa, Matehuala: 1300-0100
SO23) AB	1400	1/0.5	R. Santa Ana, Santa Ana: 1400-0500
CA13) CUA	1410	1/0.25	R. Universidad, Campeche
CO01) YD	1410	1/0.1	Super Banda, Torreón: 1200-0400
DF02) BS	1410	25/10	R. Sinfonola, México: 24h
GR25) ZHO	1410	2/1	R. Fama, Zihuatanejo
JL17) KB	1410	25/10	Canal 14-10, Guadalajara: 24h
SL11) IR	1410	5/0.5	Estelar 14-10, Cd.Valles: 24h
SN13) CF	1410	10/0.5	La Mexicana, Los Mochis: 1300-0700
TM11) AS	1410	5/0.25	La Tamaulipeca, Nuevo Laredo: 24h
BC16) XX	1420	2	R. Mexicana 14-20/Doble X, Tijuana: 24h
CH33) F	1420	5/0.5	Línea 1420, Cd.Juárez: 24h
GJ05) WE	1420	10/1	La Estación Familiar, Irapuato: 1100-0500
HG08) PK	1420	1	Inolvidable, Pachuca: 1200-0600
JL18) KMX	1420	1d	La Super X, Sayula: 1200-2400
MO01) WF	1420	1	R. Mexicana, Cuernavaca: 24h
NL03) H	1420	5/1	R. Tremenda, Monterrey: 24h
PU03) WJ	1420	2.5/0.25	R. Popular, Tehuacán: 1200-0600
TM21) EW	1420	1	R. Fórmula, Matamoros: 1155-0600
VE10) AFQ	1420	1d	Mariachi Stereo, Minatitlan: 1200-0300
CA06) RAC	1430	1/0.25	La Número Uno de Campeche, Campeche: 1200-0600
CL09) COC	1430	1	La ACIR, Colima: 1200-0400
OX33) CA	1430	1/0.2	R. Éxitos, Ixtepec
SO24) OX	1430	5/1	Doble Impacto/O-Equis, Cd.Obregón: 24h
TM22) WD	1430	2/0.15	Poder de la Radio, Cd.Miguel Alemán: 1155-0400
TX02) TT	1430	5/0.1	R. Tlaxcala, Tlaxcala: 1200-0600
VE06) LL	1430	5/1	R. Onda, Veracruz: 1130-0700
BS04) VSD	1440	5/0.5	La Señal del Progreso, Cd. Constitución: 1300-0700
DF16) EST	1440	25/1	La 14-40, La Reina del Hogar, México: 24h
JL09) CCC	1440	10/1	Estadio 1440, Guadalajara: 1300-0700
TB13) NAC	1440	1d	LV de los Chontales, Nacajuca
CH26) ARE	1450	1/0.25	R. Pegüis, Ojinaga: 1200-0500
CO01) BP	1450	1	Bonita, Torreón: 1200-0500
GR11) RY	1450	2/1	LV del Sur, Arcelia: 1200-0300
JL21) ED	1450	1/0.25	ED Contigo, Ameca: 1200-0400
MI17) GC	1450	1	R. Impacto, Sahuayo: 1300-0100
NA10) TD	1450	1/0.25	Su Favorita, Tecuala: 1200-2400
NL04) JM	1450	1	1450 Bombazo Vallenato, Monterrey: 1200-0600
OX32) PNO	1450	0.5d	XEPNO, Santiago Pinotepa Nacional
QE05) NA	1450	10	R. Alegría, Querétaro: 1200-0600
SN18) CU	1450	10/1	La Rancherita, Los Mochis: 24h
SO25) DJ	1450	0.5	R. Clave, Magdalena: 1300-0300
TM18) CM	1450	1/0.25	R. Festival, Cd.Mante: 1200-0400
TM29) VH	1450	1	Activa 14-50, Matamoros: 1200-0600
VE20) JD	1450	1	R. Mundo 14-50, Poza Rica: 24h
VE22) KM	1450	1	R. Mina/Onda 14-50, Minatitlán: 1100-0500
GR14) GRA	1460	10/0.5	R. Guerrero, Acapulco: 1200-0600
OX05) KC	1460	5/0.5	Estéreo Exitos, Oaxaca: 1200-0600
SL08) XQ	1460	0.25	R. Universidad, San Luis Potosí
SO15) CB	1460	6.5/1	R. Ranchito, San Luis Río Colorado: 1300-0700
SO40) HX	1460	1/0.25	R. Fama 14-60, Cd.Obregón: 1200-0400
VE08) JH	1460	1/0.1	Inolvidable, Jalapa: 24h
BC05) RCN	1470	10/5	R. Hispaña, Tijuana: 1300-0800
CA08) BAL	1470	2.5/0.5	R. Voz Maya de México, Bécal: 1200-0600
DF11) AI	1470	50/15	R. Fórmula, Tercera Cadena Nacional, México: 24h
DG03) CAV	1470	5/0.25	Estéreo Imagen, Durango: 1200-0500
HG07) IND	1470	1/0.5	LV Sierra Hidalguense, Tlanchinol: 1200-0200
SN21) ACE	1470	1/0.1	Magia Digital, Mazatlán: 24h
TM23) HI	1470	10/0.25	Heraldo Int., Cd.Miguel Alemán: 1155-0500
CO21) XU	1480	1/0.1	La Poderosa, Monclova: 1200-0600
CH28) HM	1480	1/0.5	R. Alegría/H-M, Cd.Delicias: 1300-0300
HG10) CARH	1480	2.5d	LV del Pueblo Hña-hñu, Cardonal: 1300-2300
JL10) ZJ	1480	20/5	XEZJ El 1480 AM, Guadalajara: 24h
NL04) TDK	1480	10/0.5	Tancherita y Regional, Monterrey: 1200-0600
SO10) NS	1480	5/1	R. 14-80, Navojoa: 1200-0700
TM28) VIC	1480	2.5/0.1	R. Tamaulipas, Cd.Victoria: 1200-0800
AG03) YZ	1490	5/2.5	La Poderosa, Aguascalientes: 24h (rel: XHYZ 107.7)
CH10) CJC	1490	1	R. Net, Cd.Juárez: 1200-0400
MI04) GT	1490	5/1	R. Alegría, Zamora: 1200-0600
MI23) KN	1490	2.5/1	R. Variedades, Huetamo: 1200-0300
NA11) SK	1490	2.5/0.2	La Super K, Cd.Ruiz: 1200-0300
SO03) DR	1490	1/0.25	Digital 99, Empalme: 1100-0700 (rel: XHDR 99.5)
SO27) AQ	1490	1	La AQ, Agua Prieta: 1500-0600
TM29) MS	1490	1	R. Mexicana, Matamoros: 24h
VE28) YT	1490	1	R. Teocelo, Teocelo: 1200-0200
CO22) JQ	1500	0.4d	La Explosiva, Parras: 1100-0100
DF11) DF	1500	50/5	R. Fórmula, Segunda Cadena Nacional, México: 24h
GJ20) FL	1500	1/0.5	La FL, Guanajuato: 1300-0300
HG09) HUI	1510	0.25d	R. Huichapan, Huichapan
NL11) QI	1510	50d	La Sultana, Monterrey: 24h
VE45) JPM	1510	0.5	R. Veracruz, La Antigua Veracruz: 1200-0300
CH30) JCC	1520	5	Bonita, Cd.Juárez: 24h
ME07) ATL	1520	1/0.25	Sistema XEGEM "R. Mexiquense", Atlacomulco: 1200-0600 (rel: XEGEM 1600 kHz)

Call	kHz	kW	Name and h. of tr.
MO02) ART	1520	2	La Señal de las Estrellas, Jojutla: 1200-0400
SO15) EH	1520	1	R. Exitos, San Luis Río Colorado: 1200-0600
TM18) YP	1520	1d	La Juvenil, El Limón: 1150-0100
VE35) VO	1520	1d	La Furia, San Rafael: 1300-0100
DF13) UR	1530	50/1	La Positiva, México: 24h
GJ21) SD	1530	10/0.1	La Ley, Silao: 1300-0400
GJ07) NC	1540	1/0.25	Inolvidable 15-40, Celaya: 24h
NL04) STN	1540	0.5/0.1	R. Red, Monterrey: 24h (rel: XERED 1110 kHz)
PU12) RTP	1540	2.5/1	R. Impacto Estéreo Digital, San Martín Texmelucán: 1200-0600
SO29) HOS	1540	5	La Poderosa, Hermosillo: 24h
BC03) BG	1550	10/1	R. 15-50/La B-G, Tijuana: 24h
ME04) XOO	1550	1	La O de Oro, El Oro
MI26) REL	1550	1	R. Michoacán, Morelia
TM11) NU	1550	5/0.25	La Rancherita, Nuevo Laredo: 24h
VE36) RUV	1550	10	R. Universidad Veracruzana, Jalapa: 1100-0700
CA07) SE	1560	5d	LV de Campeche, Champotón: 1200-2400
CH33) JPV	1560	1d	La Nueva Radio Viva, Cd. Juárez: 1200-0200
CS29) CHZ	1560	20/0.15	R. Lagarto, Chiapa de Corzo
DF20) INFO	1560	50/10	R. Monitor, México: 24h
GJ12) MAS	1560	1/0.25	Más 1560, Salamanca: 1200-0500
MI25) LAC	1560	5/1	R. Azul, Cd.Lázaro Cárdenas: 1100-0600
NA12) RIO	1560	5d	La Poderosa, Ixtlán del Río: 1300-0100
OX22) HUO	1560	5d	XEHUO, Huantla de Jiménez
SL09) ZW	1560	1d	R. Diversión, Cerritos
CO24) RF	1570	100	La Poderosa, Cd.Acuña: 24h
SO15) LBL	1570	6/1	R. Centro, San Luis Río Colorado: 1300-0100 (cfr 1350)
GJ07) AF	1580	1/0.5	R. Felicidad, Apaseo el Grande: 1200-0800
GR13) LI	1580	1/0.25	LV del Sur, Chilpancingo: 1200-0400
ME06) VAB	1580	1	Super Stereo Miled, Valle del Bravo: 24h
SO35) DM	1580	50	La Grande de Sonora, Hermosillo: 1300-0700
BC10) HC	1590	1	R. Bahía, Ensenada: 1400-0700
CH24) BZ	1590	1/0.25	Inolvidable, Cd.Delicias: 24h
DF14) VOZ	1590	50/10	Bonita AM, México: 24h
GJ26) IRG	1590	1	La Campirana, Irapuato
VE39) PT	1590	1/0.1	R. Misantla, Misantla: 1200-0200
YU12)	1590	10d	Valladolid (CP)
CO13) AE	1600	1	Texano Hits, Cd.Acuña: 1300-0700
GR26) TPA	1600	1d	R. Guerrero, Tlapa de Comonfort
ME07) GEM	1600	25/0.25	Sistema XEGEM "R. Mexiquense", Metepec: 1200-0600
ME08) UACH	1610	0.25d	R. Universidad Autónoma de Chapingo, Chapingo: 1800-0200
BC25) UT	1630	10/1	R. Universidad, Mexicali: 1400-0600
BC02) KTT	1700	10	La Romantica, Tecate

SW:

Sts denoted with a (*) are reported to be inactive, but may occasionally be reactivated for variable periods of time.

Call	kHz	kW	Name and h. of tr.
VE40) JN	v2390	0.5	R. Huayacocotla, Veracruz: Mon-Sat1200-1600, 2100-0100
DF18) RTA	4810	0.5	XERTA R. Transcontinental, México
DF02) OI	6010	1	R. Mil Onda Corta, México
SL08) XQ	6045	0.25	R. Universidad, San Luis Potosí: M-F 1200-0400, SS 1200-0000
YU03) QM	6105	0.25	Candela FM, Mérida: irr (rel: XHMH 95.3)
CS02) TS	6120	1	R. Tapachula, Tapachula (F.Pl.)
DF12) PPM	6185	10	R. Educación, México: 0000-0600 (0600-1200 rel: XEEP 1060 kHz)
DF10) YU	v9598	1	R.UNAM-Universidad Nacional Autónoma de México, México (nom 9600 kHz)

State abbreviations: AG = Aguascalientes; BC = Baja California; BS = Baja California Sur; CA = Campeche; CH = Chihuahua; CL = Colima; CO = Coahuila; CS = Chiapas; DF = Distrito Federal; DG = Durango; GJ = Guanajuato; GR = Guerrero; HG = Hidalgo; ME = Estado de México; MI = Michoacán; MO = Morelos; NA = Nayarit; NL = Nuevo León; OX = Oaxaca; PU = Puebla; QE = Querétaro; QR = Quintana Roo; SL = San Luis Potosí; SN = Sinaloa; SO = Sonora; TB = Tabasco; TM = Tamaulipas; TX = Tlaxcala; VE = Veracruz; YU = Yucatán; ZC = Zacatecas.

N.B: These abbreviations are not officially recognized by the Mexican Post Office. Letters should therefore carry the abbreviations in brackets or full State name.

Addresses and other information:

AG00) AGUASCALIENTES (Ags.)

AG01) Av. Universidad N° 1001, Desp. 614, Edif.Torre Plaza Bosques, 20127 Aguascalientes. – **AG02)** Av.Las Americas y Valparaíso, Fracc.La Fuente, 20000 Aguascalientes. – **AG03)** Morelos 222, Col. Centro, 20000 Aguascalientes. **Web:** www.radiogrupo.com.mx – **AG04)** Universidad Autónoma de Aguascalientes, Av.Universidad 940, 20127 Aguascalientes. – **AG05)** Madero 333-501, Col.Centro, 20000 Aguascalientes. – **AG06)** San Miguel 117-A, Col.Salud, 20240 Aguascalientes. ☎+52 (449) 9182370 🖷+52 (449) 9182371 – **AG07)** Av.Adolfo López Mateos 426 Pnte, 20000 Aguascalientes. **Web:** http://ags.infosel.com.mx/ryta

BC00) BAJA CALIFORNIA (B.C.)

BC01) Ap.100, 22000 Tijuana (or: c/o Noble Broadcasting of San Diego, 4891 Pacific Highway, San Diego, CA 92110, USA). **Web:** xtrasports.com/ – **BC02)** Blvd.Benito Juárez 500, Local 2-B, Plaza Cuchuma, 21450 Tecate. – **BC03)** Av.de los Olivos 3401, Fracc.Cubillas, 22410 Tijuana. – **BC04)** Pasaje Vallarta 1128 Altos, Centro Cívico, 21010 Mexicali (or: Box 1014, Calexico, CA 92231, USA). – **BC05)** Gral.Manuel Márquez de León 950, Zona Río, 22320 Tijuana (or: 713 Broadway, Suite "F", Chula Vista, CA 91910, USA). – **BC06)** Av.Calafia 519, Centro Cívico, 21000 Mexicali. – **BC07)** Francisco L.Montejano 2200, Fracc.Fovisste, 21030 Mexicali. (or: P.O.Box 872125, Calexico, CA 92232, USA). ☎ +52 6556 0600. 🖷 +52 6556 0662. **Web:** www.mvs.com.mx – **BC08)** CarR. Escenica Tijuana-Ensenada km 22.5, 22440 Tijuana. – **BC09)** Calle 3a N° 1323-15, Plaza Elva, 22800 Ensenada. – **BC10)** Ap.777, 22800 Ensenada. – **BC11)** Blvd.Agua Caliente 10535-506, Fracc.Chapultepec. 22420 Tijuana (or: Box 5413, Chula Vista, CA 91912, USA). – **BC12)** Baja California 1310, Zona Norte, 22100 Tijuana (or: Box 430233, San Ysidro, CA 92073, USA). – **BC13)** Ap.23, 22000 Tijuana. – **BC14)** Ap.19, 21400 Tecate. – **BC15)** Ap.123, 22800 Ensenada. – **BC16)** Carlos Robirosa 3110, Fracc.Aviación, 22420 Tijuana. – **BC19)** Blvd.Lázaro Cárdenas 10183, Desp.201, 22450 Tijuana – **BC20)** Calle Octava n° 139, Fracc. Cd. San Quintín, 22930 San Quintín. ☎ +52 6165 2023. Prgrs. in Sp., Mixteco, Triqui and Zapateco. – **BC21)** Calle 16, N° 159, Centro, 22800 Ensenada. – **BC22)** Ap.526, 22800 Ensenada. **Web:** www.bajanet.com.mx/cbc/ – **BC23)** Lázaro Cárdenas, Esq.Colegio Militar, Centro Comercio, Villa Fontana, Loc 33 y 34, 21180 Mexicali. – **BC24)** Av. de los Héroes y Pioneros 601, Centro Cívico, 21000 Mexicali. – **BC25)** Edif.Rectoria, Av.Alvaro Obregón y Calle Julián Carillo s/n, Col.Nueva, 21100 Mexicali (or: UABC Radio, 233 Paulin Avenue, P O Box MSC 5163, Calexico, CA 92231-2646, USA). **Web:** www.uabc.mx/RadioU/radio.htm - **FM** 104.1.

BS00) BAJA CALIFORNIA SUR (B.C.S.)

BS01) Ap.105, 23010 La Paz. – **BS02)** Hidalgo 314-B, Centro, 23000 La Paz. – **BS03)** Av.Las Flores 1, 23920 Santa Rosalía. – **BS04)** Ap.279, 23600 Cd.Constitución. – **BS05)** Ap.19-B, 23010 La Paz. – **BS06)** Blvd.Mauricio Castro, Dorada's Plaza 4, 23400 San José del Cabo. – **BS07)** 23880 Loreto. – **BS08)** Av. de Las Flores 1, 23920 Santa Rosalía. – **BS09)** 23010 La Paz. – **BS10)** 23960 Bahía Asunción. – **BS11)** 23970 Punta Abreojos. – **BS12)** 23950 Bahía de Tortugas. – **BS13)** 23010 La Paz.

CA00) CAMPECHE (Camp.)

CA01) Calle 44 y 21 s/n, 24350 Escárcega. – **CA02)** Calle 22 N° 131, 24100 Cd.del Carmen. – **CA03)** Av.Luis Álvarez Barret 11, 24000 Campeche. – **CA04)** Ap.22, 24200 Palizada. – **CA05)** Calle 32 N° 23-2 P.B., Centro, 24100 Cd.del Carmen. – **CA06)** Tamaulipas 15, Col.Santa Ana, 24050 Campeche. – **CA07)** CarR. Cd.del Carmen-Champotón km 1, 24400 Champotón. – **CA08)** Ap.1, 24930 Bécal. – **CA09)** Domicilio Conocido, 24640 X'pujil - Prgrs. in Sp., Maya and Chol. – **CA10)** 24000 Campeche. – **CA11)** Prol.Calle 53, Esq.Av.16 de Septiembre s/n, 24000 Campeche. – **CA12)** Instituto Campechano, 24000 Campeche. – **CA13)** Universidad Autónoma de Campeche, 24000 Campeche.

CH00) CHIHUAHUA (Chih.)

CH01) Calle Agustín Melgar 473, 31500 Cd.Cuauhtémoc. – **CH02)** Libertad 1306, 31000 Chihuahua. – **CH03)** Calle Novena 513, 31000 Chihuahua. – **CH04)** Calle 4a Poniente 606, 33000 Cd.Delicias. – **CH05)** Calle 2A N° 437 (or: Ap.271), 31500 Cd.Cuauhtémoc. – **CH06)** Allende 613, 33980 Cd.Jiménez. – **CH07)** Plaza Crystal, Local 64 P3, 33800 Hidalgo del Parral. **Email:** larancherita@red-sat.com.mx – **CH08)** Julián Carrillo 705-A, 31000 Chihuahua. – **CH09)** Coronado 71, 33580 Santa Bárbara. – **CH10)** José Borunda 1178 Oriente, 32030 Cd.Juárez. **Web:** www.radionet1490.com – **CH11)** Gonzáles Ortega 1130, Centro, 33700 Cd.Camargo. ☎ +52 (648) 462 0527 🖷 +52 (648) 462 3333 –**CH12)** Av.Insurgentes 2127, Col.Ex-Hipódromo, 32330 Cd. Juárez.**Email:** readiocanon800@latinmail.com – **CH13)** Ap.1771, 31500 Cd.Cuauhtémoc. – **CH14)** Cuauhtémoc 2000, Col.Centro, 31020 Chihuahua. – **CH15)** Jesús Urueta 504, 31700 Nuevo Casas Grandes. ☎ +52 (636) 694 0083. – **CH16)** Ap.125, 33800 Hidalgo del Parral. – **CH17)** Ap.222, 33000 Cd.Delicias. – **CH18)** Domicilio Conocido, 33180 Guachochi. ☎/🖷 +52 1543 0168 –Prgrs. in Sp., Tarahumara, Tepehuáno and Guarijío. – **CH19)** Ap.122, 33800 Hidalgo del Parral. – **CH20)** Calle de la Paz 602, 32000 Ojinaga. – **CH21)** Av.Mariano Negrete 8, Fracc. Los Pinos, 33700 Cd.Camargo. ☎+52 (648) 462 1316 – **CH22)** Calle 3a N° 1204, 31940 Cd.Madero. – **CH23)** Universidad de Chihuahua, 31000 Chihuahua. – **CH24)** Ap.250, 33000 Cd.Delicias. – **CH25)** Ap.190, 33800 Hidalgo del Parral. – **CH26)** Juárez y 2a 201, 32881 Ojinaga (or: Box 276, Presido, TX 79845, USA). – **CH27)** Priv.Agustín Lara 3, Zona 5, 32000

Cd.Juárez. – **CH28)** Av.del Parque Sur 6, 33000 Cd.Delicias. – **CH29)** Blvd.Ortíz Mena 54, P3, 33800 Hidalgo del Parral. – **CH30)** Av. Vicente Guerrero 2329, Col.Partido Romero, 32280 Cd.Juárez. – **CH31)** Agustín Melgar 602, Niños Heroes, 31500 Cd.Cuauhtémoc. – **CH32)** José Borunda 1178, Col.Partido Romero, 32030 Cd.Juárez. – **CH33)** 16 de Septiembre 337, Col.Centro, 32000 Cd.Juárez (or: Box 17718, El Paso, TX 79917-7718, USA). ☎+52 (656) 614 2869 – **CH35)** Calle 2a Norte N° 309, Interior 107, Col.Centro, 33000 Cd.Delicias.

CL00 COLIMA (Col.)

CL01) Calzada la Armonía 270, 28020 Colima. ☎+52 (3) 313 1940. 🖷+52 (3) 313 1500. **Web:** www.radiolevy.com/xetttinfo.htm **Email:** grlevy@col1.telmex.net.mx – **CL02)** Av.México 51-A, Esq.Juárez, 28200 Manzanillo. – **CL03)** Ingenieros 14, Esq.Av.México, 28200 Manzanillo. – **CL04)** Ignacio Sandoval 13, 28000 Colima. – **CL05)** Allende 408-102, 28100 Tecomán. ☎+52 (3) 324 1950. 🖷+52 (3) 324 1616. **Web:** radiolevy.com/xemaxinfo.htm **Email:** grlevy@prodigy. net.mx – **CL06)** Av.Antonio Leaño del Castillo 663, 28160Tecomán. – **CL07)** Ap.2-1690, Suc.A, 28950 Colima. – **CL08)** Lote 4, Manzana B, Parque Industrial Fondeport, 28200 Manzanillo. – **CL09)** Av.Félipe Sevilla del Río 585, Col.Jardines Cista Hermosa, 28017 Colima.

CO00) COAHUILA (Coah.)

CO01) Blvd.González de la Vega 195, 27000 Torreón. – **CO02)** Ap.3, 26000 Piedras Negras (or: Box 196, Eagle Pass, TX 78853-0196, USA). **Web:** www.larancherita.com.mx - **Email:** xemu@larancherita.com. mx – **CO03)** Ap.60, 26700 Sabinas. – **CO04)** Priv.Eulogio Ortiz y Pamanes, Col.Ampl.Los Angeles, 27140 Torreón. – **CO05)** Ap.71, 26340 Cd.Múzquiz. – **CO06)** Piedras Negras 1812, 25280 Saltillo. – **CO07)** De la Fuente 223 Pte, 25700 Monclova. **Email:** – **CO08)** Rassini 617, Col.Bravo, 26000 Piedras Negras. – **CO09)** Zaragoza Pte 1270, Del Valle, 26788 Sabinas. ☎ +52 (861) 614 1200 – **CO10)** Gral.Manuel Pérez Trevino 839, Pte Interior, Centro, 25000 Saltillo. ☎+52 (01-8) 414 8149. **Web:** xeksradio.com.mx/set-b01.html **Email:** xeks@infosel. com – **CO11)** Venustiano Carranza 612-2 Ote, 25700 Monclova. – **CO12)** Pte Carranza 1000, Col.Comercial, 26850 Nueva Rosita. – **CO13)** Ap.10, 26200 Cd.Acuña. – **CO14)** Ap.78, 27000 San Pedro. – **CO15)** Av. Carranza 1104, Col.Roma, 26000 Piedras Negras (or: Box 1261, Eagle Pass, TX 78852, USA). – **CO16)** Acuña 276 Sur, P2, 27000 Torreón. – **CO17)** América Latina y Alaska s/n, Col.Virreyes, 25230 Saltillo. – **CO18)** De la Fuente 304 Ote, 25700 Monclova. – **CO19)** Av.Universidad 205, Esq.Monclova, Col.República, 25280 Saltillo. – **CO20)** Juárez 1400 Sur, 26530 Allende. – **CO21)** Pte Carranza CarR. 4 Ciénegas, 25700 Monclova. – **CO22)** Fco.I.Madero 501 Pte, 27980 Parras. – **CO23)** Juárez 118 Norte, 26539 Allende. – **CO24)** Hidalgo 349 Pte, 26200 Cd.Acuña. – **CO25)** Lerdo 1612, Col.Nísperos, 26020 Piedras Negras. – **CO26)** Chihuahua 151, P1, Col.Reública, 25280 Saltillo. – **CO27)** Av. Universidad 1035, Col.Universidad, 25260 Saltillo. ☎+52 (844) 438 8108 **Email:** 1330radio@mail.com– **CO28)** Av.Morelos 1320-204, Edif.Monterrey, 27000 Torreón. – **CO29)** 505 Sur Alto, Ap 26850, 26450 Zaragoza. – **CO30)** Ap.27, 25230 Saltillo. – **CO31)** Puebla y Washington, Col Guadalupe, 25750 Monclova. – **CO32)** Universidad Autónoma Agraria, "Antonio Narro", Buenavista, 25315 Saltillo. – **CO33)** 26200 Cd. Acuña.

CS00 CHIAPAS (Chis.)

CS01) Ap.59, 29000 Tuxtla Gutiérrez. – **CS02)** 7a Oriente N° 42, 30700 Tapachula. **Web:** www.radionucleo.com – **CS03)** Ap.74, 29250 San Cristóbal de las Casas. – **CS04)** Ap.76 (or: 1a Av.Sur N° 2), 30700 Tapachula. – **CS05)** Av.Central Pte 554-4, 29000 Tuxtla Gutiérrez. – **CS06)** Ap.60, 30400 Cintalapa. – **CS07)** 29200 San Cristóbal las Casas. – **CS08)** CrR. Tonalá-Arriaga 1500, 30500 Tonalá. – **CS09)** Blvd.Belisario Domínguez 4820, 29000 Tuxtla Gutiérrez. – **CS10)** CarR. Pichucalco-Teapa km 2, 29520 Pichucalco. – **CS11)** Ap.28, 30450 Arriaga. – **CS12)** Av.Central Norte 8, 30640 Huixtla. – **CS13)** 2a Norte N° 2, 30000 Comitán. – **CS14)** 1a Av.Norte Pte N° 53, 30470 Villaflores. – **CS15)** 14 Sur-Poniente s/n, Barrio San Sebastián, 30180 Las Margaritas. ☎/🖷 +52 9636 0358. Prgrs. in Sp., Tojobal, Mame, Tzeltal and Tzotzil. – **CS16)** Km 1.5 CarR. Cacahoatán-Unión Juárez, Ejido Rosario Ixtal, 30890 Cacahoatán. – **CS17)** CarR. Boca del Limón km 2.5, 29500 Reforma. – **CS18)** Primera Calle Norte Pte 7, 30000 Comitán. – **CS22)** Av.Chichimá 405, 30000 Comitán. – **CS24)** Gobierno del Estado de Chiapas, 29950 Ococingo. – **CS26)** Primera Oriente s/n, Barrio Siete Hescos, 29650 Copainalá. ☎/🖷 +52 9661 0051.PrgR. in Sp., Zoque and Tzotzil. – **CS27)** 29960 Palenque (belongs to Gobierno del Estado de Chiapas). – **CS28)** 29610 Tecpatan (belongs to Gobierno del Estado de Chiapas). –**CS29)** Km 14 Libramiento Norte, 29160 Chiapa de Corzo.

DF00) DISTRITO FEDERAL (D.F.)

DF01) Radio Chapultepec, Av.Chapultepec 473, P7, Col.Juárez, 06600 México. ☎+52 (55) 5211 6738 – **Web:** www.radiochapultepec.com.mx **Email:** info@radiochapultepec.com.mx – **DF02)** NRM Comunicaciónes, Prolongación Paseo de la Reforma 115, Col.Paseo de las Lomas, 01330 México. ☎ +52 (55) 5322 1700. 🖷 +52 (55) 5663 0739. **Web:** www.nrm.com.mx – Stereo Cien 100.1: Darwin 68, P8, Col. Anzures, 11590 México. ☎+52 (55) 5545 6339. – **Radio Mil sw:** Ap.21-1000, 04021 México. **Email:** radiomil@nrm.com.mx – **DF03)** Radiodifusoras Asociadas, Durango 341, Planta Baja, Col.Roma, 06700 México. ☎ +52 (55) 5553 4620, 🖷 +52 (55) 5286 2774 – **Web:** www.rasa.com.mx/ **Email:** info@rasa.com.mx – **DF04)** Instituto Mexicano de la Radio, Real de Mayorazgo 83, Barrio Xoco, 03330 México. ☎ +52 (55) 5628 1700. 🖷+52 (55) 5628 1693. **Web:** www.imer.gob.mx Órbita-FM: www.orbita.com.mx – **Radio México Internacional,** Ap.21-300, 04021 México. ☎+52 (55) 5628 1720. 🖷 +52 (55) 5628 1710. – See also International Broadcasting section. – **DF06)** Televisa Radio, Calzada de Tlalpan 3000, Col. Espartaco, 04870 México. ☎ +52 (55) 5327 2000. 🖷+52 (55) 5679 7996. **Web:** www.televisa.com.mx/radio – www.wradio.com.mx **DF07)** México Radio, Gómez Farias 51, Col.San Rafael, 06470 México. ☎ +52 (55) 5705 6746, 5705 2275. 🖷+52 (55) 5535 0295. **Web:** www.abcradio.com.mx or www.760.com.mx – **DF08)** Grupo Radio Centro, Av.Constituyentes 1154, Col.Lomas Altas, 11590 México. ☎+52 (55) 5728 4800-10. **Web:** www.radiocentro.com.mx – **DF09)** Radio S.A., Rodolfo Emerson 408, Col.Chapultepec Morales, 11570 México. ☎ +52 (55) 5203 5577. 🖷 +52 (55) 5545 2078. – **DF10)** Universidad Nacional Autónoma de México, Adolfo Prieto 133, Col.del Valle, 03100 México. ☎ +52 (55) 5523 2633. **Web:** www.unam.mx/radiounam **Email:** radiounam@www.unam.mx – **DF11)** Organización R. Fórmula, Av.Universidad 1873, Col.Del Valle, 03100 México. ☎ +52 (55) 5279 2207. **Web:** www.radioformula.com.mx **Email:** radioformula@supernet.com.mx – **DF12)** Radio Educación, Ángel Urraza 622, Col.del Valle, 03100 México. ☎ +52 (55) 5559 6169. 🖷+52 (559) 5575 6566. **Radio Educación sw:** Ap.21-465, 04021 México. **Web:** www.radioeducacion.edu.mx – **DF13)** Radiorama, Paseo de la Reforma 56, P1, Col.Juárez, 06000 México. ☎ +52 (55) 5566 0299. 5566 0471. 🖷 +52 (55) 5566 1454. **Web:** www.radiorama.com.mx – **DF14)** Grupo ACIR, Pirineos 770, Lomas de Chapultepec, 11000 México. ☎ +52 (55) 5201 1700. 🖷 +52 (55) 5540 4106. – **DF15)** Grupo ACIR, Blvd.de los Virreyes 1030, Lomas de Chapultepec, 11000 México. ☎ +52 (55) 5520 1956. – **DF16)** Grupo 7 División Radio, Montecito 59, Col.Nápoles, 03810 México. ☎ +52 (55) 5669 1421, 5669. 🖷 +52 (55) 5569 0047. **Web:** www.grupsiete.com.mx **Email:** cambio@spin.com.mx – **DF17)** MVS Radio, Mariano Escobedo 532, Anzures, 11300 México. ☎ +52 (55) 5263 2100. 🖷+52 (55) 5203 4574. **Web:** www.mvsradio.com.mx – **DF18)** Radio Transcontinental de América, Plaza de San Juan 5, P1, Desp. 2, Esquina con Ayuntamiento, Centro, 06070 México (or: Ap.653, 06002 México). ☎ +52 (55) 5518 4938. **Web:** www.misionradio.com **E** xerta@radiodifusion.com – **DF19)** Imagen Telecomunicaciones, Prado Sur 150, Col. Lomas de Chapultepec, 11000 México. ☎ +52 (55) 9000. **Web:** www.imagen.com.mx Radio 9-85 FM: www.985.com.mx – **DF20)** Info-Red, La Presa 212, San Jerónimo Lidice, 10200 México. ☎+52 (55) 5329 1100 🖷+52 (55) 5681 5000. **DF21)** Universidad Ibero-Americana, Av.Prol.Paseo de la Reforma 880, Col.Lomas de Santa Fe, México 01210 ☎+52 (55) 5267 4239. **DF22)** Instituto Politécnico Nacional, Av.Santa Ana 1000, San Fco.Culhuacán, México 04260. ☎+52 (55) 5624 2012. **Web:** www.radioipn.xs3.com

DG00) DURANGO (Dgo.)

DG01) Manuel Rangel 100, P3, 34270 Durango. – **DG02)** Av.20 de Noviembre 1918 Ote, Col.Guillermina, 34270 Durango. – **DG03)** Negrete 405-B Oriente, 34270 Durango. – **DG04)** Universidad Juárez del Estado de Durango, 34270 Durango. – **DG05)** Fco.I.Madero y Heroico Colegio Militar s/n, 34600 Santiago Papasquiaro. – **DG07)** Capitán de Ibarra 1203, Farcc.del Lago, 34080 Durango. – **DG08)** Blvd.González de la Vega 195, Sur Zona Industrial, 35000 Gómez Palacio.

GJ00) GUANAJUATO (Gto.)

GJ01) Cañada 310, Esq.Roca, Col. Jardines de Moral, 37160 León. – **GJ02)** Ap.301, 37160 León. – **GJ03)** Morelos 704, Centro, 38900 Salvatierra. – **GJ04)** Blvd.López Mateos Ote 1117, 38070 Celaya. **Email:** telradio@mail.mindvox.ciateg.mx – **GJ05)** Morelos 110, 36500 Irapuato. **Web:** www.intercon.net.mx/radio **Email:** radiogpo@intercon.net.mx – **GJ06)** Blvd.Mariano Escobedo Pte 4206, Col.Flores Magón, 37350 León. – **GJ07)** Privada Renovación 135, Fracc. Suárez Irigoyen, 38090 Celaya. – **GJ08)** Palacio Federal, Casa de Moneda, Sopeña 1m, P2, 36000 Guanajuato. **Web:** http://radioug.ugto.mx – **GJ09)** Elodia Ledezma 658, 38890 Moroleón. – **GJ10)** Av. Roma 910, Col. Andrade, 37370 León. **FM:** 95.9. – **GJ11)** Allende 17, 38600 Acámbaro. – **GJ12)** Ap.300, 36700 Salamanca. – **GJ13)** Ap.24, 36700 Salamanca. – **GJ14)** Calle Solano 4, 37700 San Miguel de Allende. – **GJ15)** Ap.13, 37000 León. – **GJ16)** Ap.72, 36500 Irapuato. – **GJ17)** Ap.43, 37800 Dolores Hidalgo. – **GJ19)** Ap.67, 37900 San Luis de la Paz. – **GJ20)** Municipio Libre 8, 36080 Guanajuato. – **GJ21)** Ap.60, 36100 Silao. – **GJ22)** Ap.528, 38000 Celaya. – **GJ23)** Ap.311, 37530 León. **Email:** acir_leon@infosel.net.mx – **GJ24)** PrivadaVenustiano Carranza 119, P1, 38000 Celaya. – **GJ25)** Ap.642, 37160 León. – **GJ26)** Av.Guerrero y Francisco Sarabia, Centro Plaza Magna, Local 3-B, 36500 Irapuato. – **GJ27)** Av.Tecnológico 310, 38000 Celaya.

GR00) GUERRERO (Gro.)

GR01) Calle de la Paz 190, P2, Edif.Nick, 39300 Acapulco. – **GR02)** Ap.60, 39390 Acapulco. – **GR03)** Av.La Suiza 19, Fracc.Las Playas, 39390

Acapulco. – **GR04)** Fray Bautista Moya 410, Centro, 40660 Cd.Altamirano. – **GR05)** Paseo del Limón, Lote 4 Manzana 14, Col.Limón, 40880 Zihuatanejo. – **GR06)** Miguel Alemán 2-4, Centro, 39000 Chilpancingo. – **GR07)** Ap.31, 40830 Petatlán. – **GR08)** Juan N.Álvarez 3 Altos, 40000 Iguala. – **GR09)** CarR. Tlapa-Chilapa km 1, 41300 Tlapa de Comonfort. ☎ +52 7476 0156. Prgrs. in Sp., Náhuatl, Mixteco and Tlapaneco. – **GR10)** Av. Bandera Nacional 51-A, P1, (or: Ap.52) 40000 Iguala. – **GR11)** Entronque CarR. Igualada-Cd.Altamirano, 40500 Arcelia. – **GR12)** Cerro de la Bermeja s/n, Taxco de Juan Ruíz de Akarcón, 40200 Taxco. – **GR13)** Ap.40, 39000 Chilpancingo. – **GR14)** Monteblanco 37, Fracc.Hornos-Insurgentes, 39350 Acapulco. – **GR15)** Av.Del Sur 14, Col.Margarita Viguri, 39000 Chilpancingo. – **GR17)** 40700 Coyoca de Catalán. – **GR19)** Morelos 6-3, 39000 Chilpancingo. – **GR20)** Calle 5 Sur 305, 41100 Chilapa. – **GR21)** Av.Guerrero 10-B, P1, Desp.2, Centro, 39000 Chilpancingo. **Web**: www.pmp.com.mx/radio.html – **GR23)** 40200 Taxco. – **GR24)** 41700 Omtepec (belongs to Gobierno del Estado de Guerrero). – **GR25)** 40880 Zihuatanejo. – **GR26)** 41300 Tlapa de Comonfort (belongs to Gobierno del Estado de Guerrero). **GR27)** Paseo de la Boquita 45, Entre Paseo del Palmar y Paseo del Diamante, 40880 Zihuatanejo. ☎+52 (755) 554 9520.

HG00 HIDALGO (Hgo.)

HG01) Ap.123, 42000 Pachuca. – **HG02)** Ap.35, 43000 Huejutla. – **HG03)** Hidalgo Ote.209, 43600 Tulancingo. – **HG04)** Plaza Constitución y Manuel F. Soto (or: Ap.96), 43600 Tulancingo. – **HG05)** CarR. a Cardonal km 2.689, Barrio San Nicolás, 42300 Ixmiquilpán. – **HG06)** Félipe Ángeles s/n, 42300 Ixmiquilpán. – **HG07)** 43150 Tlanchinol. – **HG08)** Ap.123, 42000 Pachuc. **Email:** acirpachuca@netpac.net.mx – **HG09)** Chávez Macotela 7A, 42400 Huichapan. – **HG10)** Domicilio Conocido, 42370 Cardonal. Prgrs. in Sp., Otomí and Náhuatl. – **HG11)** Radio y Televisión de Hidalgo, 43000 Huejutla. – **HG12)** Radio y Televisión de Hidalgo, 43440 San Bartolo Tutotepec. – **HG13)** Radio y Televisión de Hidalgo, 42200 Jacala.

JL00) JALISCO (Jal.)

JL01) Hidalgo 158, Centro, 49000 Cd.Guzmán. – **JL02)** Constituyentes 21, Casa de la Cultura Jalisciense, Col.Centro, 44100 Guadalajara. ☎+52 (3) 650 0101 - 🖷+52 (3) 619 1758 – **JL03)** Paseo de las Gaviotas 198, Fracc.Las Gaviotas, 48328 Puerto Vallarta. – **JL04)** Lorenzana 884, 45040 Guadalajara. – **JL05)** CarR. Tampico-Barra de Navidad km 695, 47000 San Juan de los Lagos. – **JL06)** Av.México 3150, Activa de Centro SA de CV, 44670 Guadalajara. – **JL07)** Ap.7, 48900 Autlán. – **JL08)** Av.Lázaro Cárdenas 2820, Jardines del Bosque, 44520 Guadalajara. – **JL09)** Av.Mariano Otero 3405, Fracc.Verde Valle, 45060 Guadalajara. – **JL10)** Vidrio 2056, 44100 Guadalajara. – **JL11)** Constituyentes 262, 47400 Lagos de Moreno. – **JL12)** Pablo Casal 567, Prados Providencia, 44670 Guadalajara. – **JL13)** Km 6.5 CarR. La Barca-Guadalajara, 47910 La Barca. – **JL14)** Hidalgo 2055, Sector Hidalgo, 44500 Guadalajara. **Email:** xkguad@mail.udg – **JL15)** Televisa Radio, Rubén Dario 158, Circunvalación vallarta, 44680 Guadalajara. **Radio María México-address**: Av. Cruz del Sur 3195, P3, Lomas de Victória, 44580 Tlaquepaque, Jalisco – **JL16)** Portal Hidalgo 13, Int.10, Centro, 49650 Tamazula. – **JL17)** 16 de Septiembre 426, P2, 44100 Guadalajara. – **JL18)** Ap.36, 49300 Sayula. – **JL19)** Fco.I.Madero 77, 45750 Zacoalco de Torres. – **JL20)** Centro Comercial del Valle de Atotonilco, Local 17, Centro, 47750 Atotonilco. ☎+52 (391) 917 1358. – **JL21)** Ap.16, 46600 Ameca. – **JL22)** Primero de Mayo 126-8, 49000 Cd.Guzmán. – **JL23)** Lerdo de Tejada 184, 47600 Tepatitlán. – **JL24)** Ap.5, 48900 Autlán. – **JL25)** Paseo de las Gaviotas, 48328 Puerto Vallarta. – **JL26)** Av.Lázaro Cárdenas 3126, Col.Chapalita, 45040 Guadalajara. – **JL27)** Monterrey 190, Fracc.Camino Real, 47820 Ocotlán. – **JL28)** Av.México 3370, Plaza Bonita, Local Subanda P, 45120 Guadalajara. – **JL29)** Montezuma 68, 49000 Cd.Guzmán. – **JL30)** Alvaro Obregón 96, Loma Dorada, 45430 Zapotlanejo. – **JL31)** Blvd.Francisco Medina Asencio km 7.5, Plaza Marina Local 101, Col.Marina Vallarta, 48300 Puerto Vallarta. – **JL32)** Oceano Pacífico 201, Palmar de Aramara, 48300 Puerto Vallarta – **JL33)** Av.México 3150, 44670 Guadalajara. **Web:** www.unidifusion.com.mx – **JL34)** Av.Niños Héroes 1550-510, Edif.Plaza Tolsá, Col.Moderna, 44100 Guadalajara. ☎ +52 (33) 3610 4117 – **JL35)** Honduras 309 Int 161, Hotel Paloma del Mar, Col.5 de Diciembre, 48350 Puerto Vallarta. – **JL36)** Moctezuma 69, Centro, 49000 Cd.Guzmán. ☎+52 (341) 412 5710.

ME00) ESTADO DE MÉXICO (Edo.Méx.)

ME01) CarR. Panamericana km 24, 50450 Atlacomulco. – **ME02)** Paseo Tollocan Pnte 300, Col.Universidad, 50130 Toluca. (or: Calle Tetitla N° 23, Col.Toriella Guerra, Delegación Tialpán, 14050 Mécico, DF) – **ME03)** José María Morelos 948, 51900 Ixtapan de la Sal. – **ME04)** Independencia 19, 50600 El Oro. – **ME05)** Ernesto Monroy, Lote 7 Manzana 3, parque Industrial Exportec II, 50200 Toluca. ☎+52 (722) 273 1754 🖷+52 (722) 276 0700 – **ME06)** Independencia 506, 51200 Valle del Bravo. – **ME07)** Av.Estado de México Km 1,5, Col. La Virgen, 52140 Metepec. – **ME08)** CarR. México-Texcoco km 38.5, 56235 Chapingo. ☎ +52 (595) 952 1610.

MI00) MICHOACÁN (Mich.)

MI01) Aqua 78, Col.Prados del Campestre, 58297 Morelia. – **MI02)** Ap.50, 61500 Zitácuaro. – **MI03)** Ap.61, 60100 Uruapan. – **MI04)** Av.5 de Mayo 501 Sur, Jardines de Catedral, 59670 Zamora. – **MI05)** Av.Constitución de 1814 Norte 10 Altos, 60600 Apatzingán. – **MI06)** Domicilio Conocido, Predio INI, 60270 Cheran. ☎/🖷 +52 4594 2005. Prgrs. in Sp. and Purépecha. – **MI07)** Laguna de Parras 630, Col.Ventura Puente, 58020 Morelia. – **MI08)** Av.Constitución de 1814 Norte 2 Altos, 60600 Apatzingán. – **MI09)** Ap.10, 59300 La Piedad. – **MI10)** Ap.244, 61600 Pátzcuaro. – **MI11)** Ap.132, 60000 Uruapan. Email: moderna@mail.com-puscp.com – **MI12)** Mazatlán 30, 60050 Uruapan. – **MI13)** Plaza Hidalgo 3-B, 61100 Cd.Hidalgo. – **MI14)** Ap.65, 58600 Zacapu. – **MI15)** Av.Madero Pte 644, 58000 Morelia. – **MI16)** Ap.50, 58600 Zacapu. – **MI17)** Ap.60, 59000 Sahuayo. – **MI18)** Venezuela 116, Col.Ángeles, 60160 Uruapan. – **MI19)** Ap.275, 58020 Morelia. – **MI20)** Universidad de San Nicolás, 58000 Morelia. – **MI21)** Av.Río Balsas 7, 60950 Cd.Lázaro Cárdenas. – **MI22)** 20 de Noviembre 358, 58000 Morelia. – **MI23)** Madero Norte 15, 61940 Huetamo. – **MI24)** Mariano Jiménez Norte 8-1, Centro, 60300 Los Reyes. – **MI25)** Ap.430, 60950 Cd.Lázaro Cárdenas. – **MI26)** 58000 Morelia. – **MI27)** CarR. Lázaro Cárdenas-La Mira, 5 de Mayo, 60990 Lázaro Cárdenas. – **MI29)** Macarena 32, Inhuambo, 60130 Uruapan. – **MI30)** Ap.73, 59300 La Piedad. – **MI32)** CarR. Federal N° 15 Morelia-Zitácuaro km 125.6, 61420 Tuxpán. Prgrs. in Sp., Mazahua, Otomí and Matlatzinca.

MO00) MORELOS (MoR.)

MO01) Av.Morelos 309, Col.Centro, 62000 Cuernavaca. ☎+52 (777) 312 8872. 🖷+52 (777) 312 4388 – **MO02)** Plaza Yuliana, P2, 62900 Jojutla. ☎+52 (734) 342 1778. 🖷+52 (734) 342 1777 – **MO03)** 62746 Cuautla (alt.address: Hidalgo 105, 62220 Ocotepec, Cuernavaca).

NA00) NAYARIT (Nay.)

NA01) Puebla 64, Sur Centro, 63060 Tepic. – **NA02)** Insurgentes 1046 Pte, Col.El Rodeo, 63060 Tepic. – **NA03)** Av.Juarez N° 160 Ote, Col.Centro, 63000 Tepic. – **NA04)** Durango 349 Sur, Col.Fray Junipero Serra, 63000 Tepic. – **NA05)** López Mateos 61, 63715 Las Varas. – **NA06)** P. Sánchez 87 (or: Ap.22), 63310 Santiago Ixcuintla. – **NA07)** Amado Nervo 106-B Ote, (or: Ap.4), 63310 Santiago Ixcuintla. – **NA08)** Carr.INT.méxico-Nogales. Km 1042, (or: Ap.49), 63440 Acaponeta. – **NA09)** Domicilio Conocido, 63530 Jesús María. ☎ +52 3233 1170. Prgrs. in Sp., Cora, Huichol, Tepehuáno and Náhuatl. – **NA10)** Ap.7, 63440 Tecuala. – **NA11)** Puebla 3, 63600 Cd.Ruíz. – **NA12)** Av.Hidalgo 117 Ote, (or: Ap.33), 63940 Ixtlán del Río.

NL00) NUEVO LEÓN (N.L.)

NL01) CarR. a Verde km 6.5, Col.Juárez, 78000 San Luis Potosí, S.L.P. – **NL02)** Ap.2747, 64700 Monterrey. – **NL03)** Juan Ignacio Ramón 506 Oriente, P20, Edif. Latino, 64000 Monterrey. – **NL04)** Paricutín Sur 316, Col.Roma, (or: Ap.203) 64700 Monterrey. – **NL05)** Calle Monterrey 698, Esq.Cerralvo, Col.Libertad, 64130 Cd. Guadalupe. – **NL06)** Privada Rhin 647, 64000 Monterrey. – **NL07)** Quintana Roo 1122, Col.Nuevo Repueblo, 64000 Monterrey. – **NL08)** Ap.118, 64000 Monterrey. – **NL09)** Ap.38, 65290 Cd.Sabinas Hidalgo. – **NL10)** Ap.45, 67500 Montemorelos. – **NL11)** Av. San Francisco y Loma Grande, Col.Loma Grande, 64000 Monterrey. ☎+52 (81) 8347 6573 – **NL12)** Ap.62, 67701 Linares. – **NL13)** Ap.81, 67701 Linares. – **NL14)** Juan Ignacio Ramón 506 Ote, P28, Edif.Latino, 64000 Monterrey.

OX00) OAXACA (Oax.)

OX01) M.Ávila Camacho 514, P3, 70600 Salina Cruz. – **OX02)** Ap.175, 68000 Oaxaca. ☎ +52 9515 2134. 🖷+52 9513 5740. – **OX03)** Ap.21, 70760 Tehuantepec. – **OX04)** Áquiles Serdán y Mina, 70301 Matías Romero. – **OX05)** Netzahualcóyotl 216, Col. Reforma, 68050 Oaxaca. ☎ +52 951 39653, 39654. – **OX06)** CarR. Cd.Ale´man a sayula km 27, 68400 Loma Bonita. – **OX07)** CarR. Puerto Escondido-Pochutla km 143, 71980 Puerto Escondido. – **OX08)** Jazmines 907, 68000 Oaxaca. ☎ +52 9513 4344. – **OX09)** Gómez Farias 113, 68000 Oaxaca. ☎ +52 951 57899. 🖷+52 9515 8811. – **OX10)** Abasolo 37, Centro, 68300 Tuxtepec. – **OX11)** Ap.60, 70030 Juchitán. – **OX12)** Ap.35, 70900 Puerto Angel. – **OX13)** CarR. Cristóbal Colón km 819.5, 70030 Juchitán. ☎ +52 9711 1233. – **OX14)** Ap.48, 69000 Huajuapan de León. – **OX15)** Lázaro Cardenas s/n, 68770 Guelato de Juárez. ☎ +52 9553 6011 –Prgrs. in Sp., Zapoteco, Mixe and Chinanteco. – **OX16)** Domicilio Conocido, 68470 San Lúcas Ojitlán. ☎ +52 2877 6063 –Prgrs. in Sp., Mazateco, Cuicateco and Chinanteco. – **OX17)** CarR. Yucudaa km 54.5, 69899 Tlaxiaco. ☎/🖷 +52 955 20240. Prgrs. in Sp., Mixteco and Triqui –**OX18)** Plaza de la Constitución y Negrete s/n, 71700 Santiago Jamiltepec. ☎ +52 9582 8059. Prgrs. in Sp., Mixteco, Amuzgo and Chatino. – **OX19)** Morelos 6-2, 71000 Putla de Guerrero. ☎/🖷 +52 (953) 533 0000 – **OX20)** José Inés Dávila 2, Centro, 69800 Tlaxiaco. – **OX21)** Universidad AutónomaBenito Juárez, 68000 Oaxaca. – **OX22)** 68540 Teotitlán de Flores Magon. – **OX23)** Macedonio Alcala 915, 68000 Oaxaca. – **OX24)** Av.Alfonso Perez Gasca 504, 71600 Pinotepa Nacional. – **OX25)** Valerio Trujano 708, 68000 Oaxaca. ☎ +52 9514 0653. – **OX26)** 69000 Huajuapán de León (belongs to Gobierno del Estado de Oaxaca). – **OX27)** Corporación Oaxaqueña de Radio y Televisión, Madero s/n, Centro Cultural, 68000 Oaxaca. – **OX28)** 70300 Matías Romero (belongs to Gobierno del Estado de Oaxaca). – **OX29)** 70989 Sta Cruz Huatulco (belongs to Gobierno del Estado de Oaxaca). – **OX30)** 68300 Tuxtepec (belongs to Gobierno del Estado de Oaxaca). – **OX31)** 68500 Huautla de

Jiménez. – **OX32)** 71600 Santiago Pinotepa Nacional. – **OX33)** CarR. Ixtepec-Juchitán km 2, 70110 Ixtepec. ☎ +52 9713 0048.

PU00) PUEBLA (Pue.)

PU01) Allende 507, 73800 Teziutlán. – **PU02)** Ap.176, 73800 Teziutlán. – **PU03)** Ap.84, 75700 Tehuacán. ☎ +52 2382 3240. 🖷 +52 2382 0777. – **PU04)** Primera Norte 101-103, Desp.6, 75700 Tehuacán. ☎ +52 2382 4452. 🖷 +52 2382 1093. – **PU05)** Teziutlán Sur 17, Col. La Paz, 72160 Puebla. ☎ +52 2230 3499. 🖷 +52 2249 4199. **Web:** www.radiooro. com **Email:** Organización@radiooro.com – **PU06)** Ap.54, 73160 Huauchinango. – **PU07)** Ap.49, 74400 Izúcar de Matamoros. ☎ +52 2436 1026. – **PU08)** Prol.Manuel M.Flores s/n, 75520 Cd.Serdán. – **PU09)** Zaragoza 31-A, Centro, 74400 Izucár de Matamoros. ☎ +52 2436 0594. 🖷 +52 2436 1325. – **PU12)** Ap.4, 74000 San Martín Texmelucan. ☎ +52 2484 0520. 🖷 +52 2484 4040. – **PU13)** Plaza de la Constitución 102, altos 1, 73080 Xicotepec de Juárez. – **PU14)** Av.15 Pte.1306, Col.Santiago, Santiago, 72000 Puebla. ☎ +52 2243 0100. 🖷 +52 2237 0738. – **PU15)** Miguel Alvarado 45, 73560 Cuetzalán. ☎ +52 2331 0382. Prgrs. in Sp., Náhuatl and Totonaco. – **PU16)** Av.15 de Mayo 2939, Frac.Las Hadas, 72070 Puebla. ☎ +52 2249 6840. 🖷 +52 2249 6830. **Email:** acir@giga.com – **PU17)** 3 Sur N° 107, P3, 72000 Puebla. ☎ +52 2232 8000. **Web:** www.radiotribuna.com **Email:** general@radiotribuna.com – **PU18)** San Martín Texmelucan 57, Col.La Paz, 72160 Puebla. ☎ +52 2242 0911. 🖷 +52 2242 3322. – **PU19)** Privada 7-B Sur 4105, Col.Gabriel Pastor, 72420 Puebla. ☎ +52 2230 5049 **Email:** xepa@mail.computime.com.mx – **PU20)** 1 Sur 108, Desp.307, Col.Centro, 75700 Tehuacan.

QE00) QUERÉTARO (Qro.)

QE01) Fray Sebastián de Aparicio 28, Col.Cimatario, 76030 Querétaro. ☎ +52 42 241491. 🖷 +52 42 241490. – **QE02)** CarR. San Juan del Rio-Xilitla km 181, Col.San José, 76340 Jalpan. **QE03)** Av.Juárez 38 Pte, 76800 San Juan del Río. ☎ +52 4272 2664. 🖷 +52 4272 0588. – **QE04)** Paseo del Prado 102, Desp. 401, Fracc.del Prado, 76030 Querétaro. ☎ +52 4216 5556. 🖷 +52 4216 5555. – **QE05)** Ap 64, 76000 Querétaro. ☎ +52 4216 9030. 🖷 +52 4216 7766. – **QE06)** Av.Carrizal 28-F2, Fracc.Ampliación Carrizal, 76030 Querétaro. **Email:** rrdir@rR. com.mx - **Web:** www.rR. com.mx – ☎ +52 4215 0333. 🖷 +52 4215 2590. – **QE07)** Av.Tecnológico Sur 2, Local 106, Col.Niños Héroes, 76010 Querétaro. ☎ +52 4215 2236. – **QE08)** Centro Universitario, 76010 Querétaro. **Email:** radiouaq@sunserveR. uaq.mx **Web:** www.uaq.mx/servicios/cultural/radio.html – **QE09)** Av.Tecnológico 100, Desp.306-307, Edif.Tec 100, 76000 Querétaro. – **QE10)** Luis Pasteur 6 Norte, Col.Centro, 76000 Querétaro. **Email:** radiogro@grol.telmex.net.mx –**Web:** http://members.xoom.com/ RadioQro

QR00) QUINTANA ROO (Q.Roo.)

QR01) Ap.506, 77500 Cancún. ☎+52 (988) 9884 1068 – **QR02)** Ap.96, 77010 Chetumal. – **QR03)** Prol.Av.Heroes 680, 77000 Chetumal. – **QR04)** Ap.299, 77600 Cozumel. ☎+52 (987) 9872 0948 – **QR05)** Ap.13, 77200 Félipe Carillo Puerto. – **QR06)** Av.Miguel Hidalgo 201, 77000 Chetumal. – **QR07)** Av.Uxmal s/n, 77500 Cancún. – **QR08)** Región 92, Manzana 62, Lotes 21-23, Z-7, 77500 Cancún. ☎+52 (988) 9888 7163 – **QR09)** Av.Lázaro Cárdenas 46, 77200 Félipe Carillo Puerto. – **QR10)** Av.Náder 25, SM2 Mzna 13, Desp.401, 77500 Cancún. ☎+52 (988) 9887 4550. **Web:** www.radiopirata.com – **QR11)** Nader 27, Desp.1043, 77500 Cancún. ☎+52 (988) 9887 6660 –**QR12)** CarR. Carillo Puerto-Cancún km 1, Col. Emiliano Zapata, 77229 Félipe Carillo Puerto. Prgrs. in Sp. And Maya. – **QR13)** Calle 22 de Enero 48, Esq. 5 de Mayo, Centro, 77000 Chetumal. – **QR14)** Patronato Prodifusora Cultural de la Zona Maya, 77200 Felipe Carillo Puerto. – **QR15)** 77500 Cancún.

SL00) SAN LUIS POTOSÍ (S.L.P.)

SL01) CarR. a Verde km 6.5, Col.Juárez, 78000 San Luis Potosí. – **SL02)** Capitan Caldera 315, Col.Tequisquiapan, 78250 San Luis Potosí. – **SL03)** Los Bravo 445 Altos, 78000 San Luis Potosí. – **SL04)** Hidalgo 7-A, 79600 Río Verde. – **SL05)** Ap.160, 79050 Cd.Valles. – **SL06)** Ap.80, 78700 Matehuala. – **SL07)** Ap.18, 78700 Matehuala. – **SL08)** General Mariano Arista 245, Centro Hist´rico, 78000 San Luis Potosí. ☎+52 (444) 4826-13-48. **Web:** uaslp.mx/rtu – **SL09)** Martín de Turubiartes 500, 79400 Cerritos. – **SL10)** Av.Himno Nacional 1951, Fracc.Tangamanga, 78269 San Luis Potosí. – **SL11)** Av.Hidalgo 1, Zona Centro, 79000 Cd.Valles. – **SL12)** Privada Pemex 3. Barrio San Rafael, 79960 Tamazunchale. – **SL13)** Josefa Oríz de Domínguez s/n, 79800 Tancanhuitz de Santos. ☎ +52 1367 0264.Prgrs. in Sp., Náhuatl, Pame and Huasteco. – **SL14)** Fausto Nieto 220, 78000 San Luis Potosí. – **SL15)** Venustiano Carranza 460, 78000 San Luis Potosí. – **SL16)** Londres y atenas s/n, Fracc.Lomas, 79090 Cd.Valles. – **SL17)** Carranza 1408-interior, 78250 San Luis Potosí. – **SL19)** Capitan Caldera 420, Col.Tequisquiapan, 78250 San Luis Potosí. **Email:** oet@infosel.net.mx

SN00) SINALOA (Sin.)

SN01) Av.Lazaro Cardenas 750 sur altos, Local I-1, Plaza Palacio, 80129 Culiacán. – **SN02)** Ap.61, 81000 Guasave. – **SN03)** Av.Juan Carrasco y Pequeira, Local 5-D, Plaza Las Américas, 82010 Mazatlán. – **SN04)** Sinaloa 442 Pte, 81200 Los Mochis. ☎+52 6812 7879. **Web:** www.promored.com.mx –**SN05)** Ap.68, 81000 Guasave. – **SN06)** Av.Álvaro Obregón 24 Sur, L-50, Centro, 80000 Culiacán. – **SN07)** Malecon y Bravo, 80000 Culiacán. – **SN08)** Ap.233, 80000 Culiacán. – **SN10)** Ap.148, 82000 Mazatlán. – **SN11)** Antonio Rosales 223 Norte, 81200 Los Mochis. – **SN12)** Av.Álvaro Obregón 650-1 Norte, 80000 Culiacán. – **SN13)** Aquiles Serdán 860 Pte, 81200 Los Mochis. – **SN14)** Universidad de Occidente, Blvd.Macario Gaxiola y CarR. Internacional, 81200 Los Mochis. – **SN15)** Blvd Antonio Rosales 509 Ote, Col.Morelos, 81460 Guamuchil. – **SN16)** Universidad de Sinaloa, Rosales 284 Pte, 80000 Culiacán. – **SN17)** Hidalgo 408, 82400 Escuinapa. – **SN18)** Hidalgo 755 Pte, 81200 Los Mochis. **Web:** oirmochis.com.mx/ – **SN19)** Av.Miguel Aleman 619 Ote, 82000 Mazatlán. – **SN20)** Ap.35, 82800 Rosario. – **SN21)** Av.Del Mar 548, 82000 Mazatlán. – **SN23)** Insurgentes 334 Sur, Centro Sinaloa, 80129 Culiacán. – **SN24)** Av.del Mar 80, 82010 Mazatlán. – **SN26)** Ap.113, 80129 Culiacán. – **SN27)** Sinaloa 442 Pte, Col.Centro, 81200 Los Mochis.

SO00) SONORA (Son.)

SO01) Yáñez 5, entre Zacatecas y San Luis Potosí, 83000 Hermosillo. ☎+52 (6) 215 1522 – **SO02)** Ap.630, 85480 Guaymas. – **SO03)** Calle 19 N° 81, entre 15 y 16, Centro, 85400 Guaymas (tx-site Empalme). – **SO04)** Durango 901 Sur Altos, 85160 Cd.Obregón. ☎ +52 6416 3878. – **SO05)** Ap.1817, 83000 Hermosillo. – **SO06)** Blvd.Rodolfo Elias Calles 252 Ote, 85000 Cd.Obregón. – **SO07)** Sinaloa Sur N° 408, 85000 Cd.Obregón. – **SO08)** Obregón Este 184, Col.Centro, 83600 Caborca. – **SO09)** Av.Juárez y 11ª Este 226, 84620 Cananea. – **SO10)** Ap.226, 85800 Navojoa. – **SO11)** Ap.6, 84900 Ures. – **SO12)** Heriberto Aja 96, 83000 Hermosillo. – **SO13)** Vasquez 127, P.P.A, Local 1, Col.Fundo Legal, 84000 Nogales. ☎+52 (631) 312 0960 – **SO14)** Ap.371, 85400 Guaymas. – **SO15)** Ap.4, 83400 San Luis Río Colorado. ☎ +52 6534 1901. – **SO16)** Av.Morelos y Ramón Corona s/n, Col.Constitución, 85830 Navojoa. – **SO17)** Ap.256, 84000 Nogales (or: Box 1472, Nogales, AZ 85628, USA). – **SO18)** Guerrero y California, Plaza Tutuli, Local E17, 85000 Cd.Obregón. – **SO19)** Ap.28, 84200 Agua Prieta. – **SO20)** Ap.7, 84180 Naco. – **SO21)** Ap.66, 83550 Pto Peñasco. – **SO22)** Allende 914 Oriente, Esq.con Sinaloa, 85000 Cd. Obregón. ☎+52 (644) 413 0607 – **SO23)** Ap.44, 84600 Santa Ana. – **SO24)** Ap.158, 85000 Cd.Obregón. – **SO25)** Ap.63, 84160 Magdalena. – **SO26)** Morelos y Calle Obregón, 83600 Caborca. – **SO27)** Ap.28, 84200 Agua Prieta. – **SO29)** Blvd Navarrete 38, Local 2, Col.Valle Hermoso, 83209 Hermosillo. ☎ +52 (662) 215 4900 🖷+52 (662) 215 4940. – **SO31)** Ap.148, 21960 Cd. Morelos, BC - (transmitter site: San Luís Colorado, Sonora). – **SO32)** Heriberto Aja 96 y Nayarit, 83000 Hermosillo. – **SO33)** Av.13 de Julio 5, 83600 Caborca. – **SO35)** Ap.285, 83000 Hermosillo. – **SO36)** Ap.199, 84000 Nogales. – **SO37)** Juarez 33 Ote, 85900 Huatabampo. – **SO39)** Calle Internacional y Av.5 Int. 8-C, 84200 Agua Prieta. ☎ +52 6338 2017. – **SO40)** Veracruz 230 Sur Altos, 85000 Cd.Obregón. – **SO42)** Edif.Leo, Abelardo Rodríguez 180, Desp.45, Col.Centro, 85400 Guaymas. – **SO43)** Blvd.Obregon y Plaza 5 de Mayo, Edif.Plaza, Local 14 altos, 85800 Navojoa. ☎+52 (6) 422 2999 – **SO44)** CarR. a Novojoa km 27, 85280 Etchojoa. ☎ +52 6425 0043. 🖷 +52 6425 0045. Prgrs. in Sp., Mayo, Yaqui and Guarijío.

TB00) TABASCO (Tab.)

TB01) Paseo de la Ceiba 102, P1, Col.3 de Mayo, 86190 Villahermosa. – **TB02)** J.Alvarez 301, 86000 Villahermosa. – **TB03)** Paseo Usumacinta y Ayuntamiento, 86100 Villahermosa. – **TB04)** Calle 28 N° 117, 86900 Tenosique. – **TB05)** Rosendo Taracena s/n, Local 97, 86030 Villahermosa. ☎ +52 9315 2 2223. – **TB06)** Leandro Adriano y Rogelio Ruiz Rojas, 86500 Cárdenas. – **TB07)** Abasolo esquina Carlos Pellicer Cámara, Local B, 86700 Macuspana. ☎ +52 9302 2644. – **TB08)** José Julián Dueñas 201, Parque Hidalgo, 86800 Teapa. – **TB09)** Av.Méndez 1407, P1, Col.Nueva Villahermosa, 86070 Villahermosa. – **TB10)** José Martí 101-107, 86000 Villahermosa. – **TB11)** Prolongación 27 de Febrero 1001, Col.F.Galaxias, 86035 Villahermosa. ☎+52 (993) 316 3317 – **TB12)** Sánchez Mármol 408, 86000 Villahermosa. – **TB13)** 86220 Nacajuca. – **TB15)** Calle de la Ceiba 102-3, Primero de Mayo, 86190 Villahermosa. – **TB16)** Constitución 1011, Centro, 86000 Villahermosa. – **TB17)** 86900 Tenosique (belongs to Gobierno del Estado de Tabasco).

TM00) TAMAULIPAS (Tamps.)

TM01) Gaspar de la Garza 170 Sur, 87000 Cd.Victoria. – **TM02)** Ap.134, 88500 Reynosa. – **TM03)** Ap.4, 88000 Nuevo Laredo. – **TM04)** Ap.246, 88500 Reynosa. – **TM05)** Ap.797, 89160 Tampico. – **TM06)** Ap.79, 89901 Cd.Mante. – **TM07)** Ap.241, 88560 Reynosa. – **TM08)** Ap.99, 88000 Nuevo Laredo (or: Box 87, Laredo, TX 78040, USA). – **TM09)** Ap.735, 87300 Matamoros (or: Box 1708, Brownsville, TX 78522, USA). – **TM10)** Valentín Gómez Farías, 89150 Tampico. – **TM11)** Gonzales y Mendoza 3848, Col.Centro, 88000 Nuevo Laredo (or: 1510 Calle del Norte, Suite 2, Laredo, TX 78041, USA). **Email:** xe2xpk@nld.bravo.net – **TM12)** Diego Acuña, 87900 Cd.Tula. – **TM13)** Aquiles Seldan 119 Sur, 89000 Tampico. – **TM14)** Ap.540, 87300 Matamoros. – **TM15)** Ap.232, 88000 Nuevo Laredo. – **TM16)** Ap.20, 88440 Cd.Camargo. – **TM17)** Ap.110, 88000 Nuevo Laredo. – **TM18)** Av.Juárez 703 Ote, 89800 Cd.Mante. – **TM19)** Calle 9 y 10, Blvd.P.Balboa 805-6, 87000 Cd.Victoria. – **TM20)** Benito Juárez 506-A, Col.Tolteca, 89160 Tampico. **Email:** mexicana660tampico@terra.com – **TM21)** Av.Cuauhtémoc y Calle 12, Col.San Francisco, 87350 Matamoros.

☎ +52 8812 0202. – **TM22)** Ap.13, 83000 Cd.Miguel Alemán. – **TM23)** Ap.1, 83000 Cd.Miguel Alemán. – **TM24)** Morelos 2513, Juarez, 88209 Nuevo Laredo. – **TM25)** Zaragoza 85, 87600 San Fernando. – **TM27)** Altamira Calle Principal de Estereos, CarR. Tampico-Gonzalez, 89600 Altamira. – **TM28)** Calle 8 y Cuauthémoc 125, Col.Pedro Sosa, 87120 Cd. Victoria. – **TM29)** Ap.134, 87300 Matamoros. – **TM30)** Lázaro Cárdenas 210, Local 19,20 y 21, Col.Centro, 88500 Reynosa.

TX00) TLAXCALA (Tlax.)
TX01) Av.Juárez Norte 203, 90500 Huamantla. – **TX02)** Calle Uno 420, 90070 Tlaxcala.

VE00) VERACRUZ (VeR.)
VE01) Plaza Crystal, Loc.26, 91150 Jalapa. – **VE02)** Av.Tres 425, 94500 Córdoba. **Web:** www.rogsa.com.mx – **VE03)** Ap.18, 95400 Cosamaloapan. – **VE04)** Av.Oriente 6 No 261-210, 94300 Orizaba. – **VE05)** (See DF06). – **VE06)** Melchor Ocampo 119, P7, Edif.Pazos, 91700 Veracruz. – **VE07)** Av.Hidalgo 1117-A Altos, 96400 Coatzacoalcos. – **VE08)** CarR. Jalapa-Veracruz 200, 91190 Jalapa. – **VE09)** Bwnhamin Franklin 4, 91700 Veracruz. – **VE10)** Juárez 100, 96700 Minatitlán. – **VE11)** Blvd.Adolfo Ruiz y Heriberto Kehoe, Obrera, 93260 Poza Rica. – **VE12)** Ignacio de la Llave 38, 92000 Pánuco. – **VE13)** Av.Salvador Díaz Mirón 2625, Esq.Heroico, Col.Militar, 91700 Veracruz. – **VE14)** Ap.4, 93300 Poza Rica. – **VE15)** Esq.Comunicación, Gabino Gonzales, 92730 Álamo. – **VE16)** Humboldt Sur 36, 91270 Perote. – **VE17)** Zaragoza 300, Local 14, Galería Margón, 96400 Coatzacoalcos. – **VE18)** Av.González Ortega 200, Centro, 93400 Papantla. – **VE19)** Av.1 N° 211, Centro, 94500 Córdoba. – **VE20)** Ap.4, 93300 Poza Rica. – **VE21)** Bravo 1103 N° 201, 91700 Veracruz. – **VE22)** Eulalio Vela 15, 96700 Minatitlán. – **VE23)** Ap.80 (or: Pedro Belli 229), 93600 Martinez de la Torre. ☎+52 (232) 324 0084 – **VE24)** Av.Juárez 13, P4, 92800 Tuxpam. – **VE25)** Libertad y Morelos 301, 95100 Tierra Blanca. – **VE26)** Constitución 7, 95700 San Andrés Tuxtla. – **VE27)** Plaza Crystal, Loc.20, 91150 Jalapa. – **VE28)** Ap.15, 91615 Teocelo. – **VE29)** Av.Manuel Avila Camacho 11, Col.Centro, 93550 Gutiérrez Zamora. – **VE30)** Ursulo Galván 403, Esq.A.Serdán, 96480 Coatzacoales. – **VE31)** Ap.1, 92060 Tempoal. – **VE32)** Sur 31 N° 336, 94300 Orizaba. – **VE33)** Ap.26, 96000 Acayucan. – **VE34)** Av.Libertad 201, 95220 Piedras Negras. – **VE35)** CarR. Nacional 38, 93620 San Rafael. – **VE36)** Universidad Veracruzana, Ap.629, 91000 Jalapa. – **VE37)** Zamora 364-Altos, Centro, 91700 Veracruz. ☎ +52 2931 7494. – **VE38)** Calle 8 N° 119, Entre Av. 1 y 3, 94500 Córdoda. – **VE39)** Zaragoza 105, 93820 Misantla. – **VE40)** Ap.13, 92600 Huayacocotla - Prgrs in Sp., Otomi, Nahua and Tepehua. **Web:** www.sjsocial.org/ Radio/huarad.html/ – **VE41)** Fernando Siliceo 801, 91970 Veracruz. – **VE42)** Callejón de las Animas s/n, 95000 Zongolica. ☎ +52 2732 6256. Prgrs. in Sp. And Maya. – **VE43)** Banderas 4, 92800 Tuxpam. – **VE44)** 92530 Tepetzintla. – **VE45)** 91687 La Antigua Veracruz. – **VE46)** Av.Vicente Guerrero Sur 202, 96400 Coatzacoalcos. – **VE48)** CarR. Federal a Cd.Alemán km 38.5, Col.Pemex, 95180 Tierra Blanca.

YU00) YUCATÁN (Yuc.)
YU01) Calle 62 N° 465, Entre 53 y 55, 97000 Mérida. – **YU02)** Ap.152, 97001 Mérida. – **YU03)** Ap.217, 97001 Mérida. (XEQM-6105 rel XHMH 95.3 "Candela FM" and also XEMH 970 kHz) – **YU04)** Km 1 CarR. Valladolid-Carillo Puerto, 97780 Valladolid. ☎+52 (985) 9856 2101 – **YU05)** Calle 56 N° 447, 97000 Mérida. – **YU06)** Ap.5, 97700 Tizimín. – **YU07)** Ap.78, 97320 Progreso. – **YU08)** Universidad Autonoma de Yucatán, Ap.63-B, 97000 Mérida. – **YU09)** Calle 42 N° 194-A, Entre 35 y 37, 97000 Valladolid. – **YU10)** Domicilio Conocido, 97930 Peto. ☎/🖷 +52 9976 0140. Prgrs. in Sp. And Maya. – **YU11)** Calle 60 N° 451, Entre 49 y 51, 97000 Mérida. – **YU12)** 97780 Valladolid.

ZC00) ZACATECAS (Zac.)
ZC01) CarR. Panamericana km 724.6, 99030 Fresnillo. **Email:** xeelxeih@logicnet.com.mx – **ZC03)** Av.Hidalgo 316, P1, Centro, 99000 Fresnillo. **Email:** gpb15@gauss.logicnet.com.mx – **ZC05)** DR. Gilberto Delgadillo 18-3, 98400 Río Grande. – **ZC06)** Radio S.A.Julián Aguirre 110, Col.Lomas de la Soledad, 98040 Zacatecas. ☎ +52 4922 2612. – **ZC08)** Ap.198, 99300 Jerez de García Salinas. – **ZC09)** Ap.324, 99000 Fresnillo. – **ZC10)** Ocampo 22, Centro, 99600 Jalpa. – **ZC11)** Josefa Ortiz de Dominguez 51, P3, 99700 Tlaltenango. – **ZC12)** Juan de Tolosa 402, Col.Sierra de Alica, 98000 Zacatecas.

FM in México City: DF08) 88.1 Red FM – DF14) 88.9 Azul 89 – DF02) 89.7 Oye 89.7 – DF19) 90.5 Imagen – DF21) 90.9 Ibero – DF08) 91.3 Alfa – DF08) 92.1 Universal – DF06) 92.9 La Ke Buena – DF08) 93.7 Stereo Joya – DF04) 94.5 Opus 94 – DF14) 95.3 La Nuova Amor – DF22) 95.7 El Politécnico en Radio – DF10) 96.1 UNAM – DF06) 96.9 W Radio – DF08) 97.7 Stereo 97 – DF19) Reporte 98.5 – DF14) 99.3 Digital 99 – DF02) 100.1 Stereo Cien – DF02) 100.9 Sabrosita – DF06) 101.7 Vox – DF17) 102.5 MVS 102.5/Monitor MVS – DF11) 103.3 Fórmula 103 – DF11) 104.1 Uno – DF17) 104.9 Exa-FM – DF04) 105.7 Órbita – DF14) 106.5 Mix 106 – DF08) 107.3 La Z – DF04) 107.9 Horizonte 108.

MICRONESIA

L.T: Chuuk, Yap: UTC +10h; Kosrae, Pohnpei: UTC +11h — **Pop:** 135,000 — **Radios:** 70,000 — **Pr.L:** Yapese, Trukese, Ponapean, Kosraean, English — **E.C:** 60Hz, 110/220V — **ITU:** FSM

FEDERATED STATES OF MICRONESIA BROADCASTING SERVICE (Gov.)

✉ P.O. Box 34, Palikir Station, Pohnpei FSM 96941, Eastern Caroline Islands ☎ +691 320 2548 🖷 +691 320 4356.
L.P: Special Asst. to Pres. for Information Office: Mrs. Terry Gamabruw. ABU Liaison Officer: Terry G. Thinom. ABU Tech. Liaison Officer: Elieser Rospel.

FSM BROADCASTING ASSOCIATION (FSMBA)

✉ P.O. Box JT, Weno, Chuuk State, FSM 96942 ☎ +691 330 4252 🖷 +691 330 2233

MW	Call	kHz	kW	H.of tr.*
1)	V6A	1350	1	
2)	V6AH	1449	10	24hr
3)	V6AI	1494	10	2000-1400
4)	V6AJ	1503	1	1800-1200
5)	V6AK	1593	5	2000-1400

*) all st's operate 24h during adverse weather conditions.
FM: 6) V6AF 104.0MHz

Addresses and other information
1) Moen, Chuuk State, FSM 96942. Rlg. (Baptist) – **2)** P .O. Box 1086, Kolonia, Pohnpei State, FSM 96941 ☎ +691 320 2296 🖷 +691 320 5212 **Web:** http://www.fm/ppbc/ **ANN:** "Met Station V6AH nan Pohnpei" CE: Hirosy Santos – **3)** P.O. Box 117, Colonia, Yap State, FSM 96943 ☎ +691 350 2174 🖷 +691 350 4426 **ANN:** "Pary e radio station V6AI nu Waab" – **4)** P.O. Box 147, Tofol, Kosrae State, FSM 96944 ☎ +691 370 3040 🖷 +691 370 3880 **ANN:** "Painge station V6AJ, fwin an Kosrae" – **5)** P.O Box 189, Weno, Chuuk State 96942 ☎ +691 330 2593 🖷 +691 330 2777 **ANN:** "Ach nenien appio V6AK lon Chuuk" – **6)** Pohnpei. ✉ Calvary Christian Academy, WWNTBM, P.O. Box 725, Kings Mountain, NC 28086.

MOLDOVA

L.T: UTC +2h (27 Mar - 30 Oct 2005: UTC +3h) — **Pop:** 4.4 million — **Pr.L:** Moldovan (Romanian), Russian, Gagauz — **E.C:** 50Hz, 220V — **ITU:** MDA

CONSILIUL COORDONATOR AL AUDIOVIZUALULUI (Coordinating Audio-Visual Council)

✉ str. Mihai Eminescu 28, 2012 Chisinau. ☎ +373 22 277551. 🖷 +373 22 277471. **Email:** cca_moldova@mtc.md
L.P: Chmn: Ion Mihailo
CCA is the regulatory & licensing authority.

RADIODIFUZIUNII NATIONALE (Pub.)

✉ str. Miorita 1, 2028 Chisinau. ☎ +373 22 721388. 🖷 +373 22 723537. **Email:** info@trm.md **Web:** www.trm.md
L.P: Dir: Sergiu Batog

MW	kHz	kW		kHz	kW
Chisinau	873	75	Edinet	1494	20
Cahul	1494	30			
FM	**MHz**	**kW**		**MHz**	**kW**
Cahul	100.7	4	Soroca	105.8	0.4
Causeni	71.24	4	Straseni	72.02	4
Cimislia	103.5	3	Straseni	100.5	4
Edinet	70.31*	4	Trifesti	103.3	4
Mândrestii-Noi	66.68	4	Ungheni	68.00	4
Mândrestii-Noi	104.9	4	Ungheni	102.0	-

*) incl. RFE-RL 1600-2200 (see below)
D.PRGR: Radio Moldova 0400-2200 in Moldovan, Russian. For ethnic minorities: 1830-1900 Polish (Mon), Ukrainian (Thu), Bulgarian (Fri).

OTHER STATIONS

FM	MHz	kW	Location	Station
1)	67.58	4	Straseni	Antena C
A)	68.48	4	Straseni	BBC
A)	69.14	4	Cahul	BBC
2)	69.44	0.1	Chisinau	R. Micul Samaritean
B)	69.53	4	Ungheni	RFE-RL
6)	71.00	0.1	Chisinau	Europa Plus Moldova

FM	MHz	kW	Location	Station
2)	71.39	1	Drochia	R. Micul Samaritean
10)	72.71	0.1	Chisinau	R. 7
16)	87.6	0.2	Chisinau	R. Chanson
21)	88.6	0.3	Chisinau	Prosto R.
22)	89.1	0.4	Chisinau	R. Retro
23)	90.7	-	Chisinau	R. Melodia
18)	92.1	0.3	Chisinau	Dinamit FM
11)	99.9	-	Glodeni	Vocea Basarabiei
14)	100.1	2	Chisinau	R. Maksimum
2)	100.7	5	Balti	R. Micul Samaritean
5)	100.9	0.1	Chisinau	Kiss FM
9)	101.3	2	Chisinau	Nase Radio
5)	101.3	-	Hâncesti	Kiss FM
23)	101.5	0.05	Balti	R. Melodia
A)	101.5	1	Causeni	BBC
12)	101.7	0.1	Chisinau	Hit FM
12)	101.7	-	Drochia	Hit FM
2)	102.0	0.5	Causeni	R. Micul Samaritean
8)	102.1	1	Comrat°	Teleradio Gagauzia
1)	102.3	3	Chisinau	Antena C
15)	102.7	0.25	Chisinau	Inforadio
20)	102.7	0.03	Vulcanesti°	X-Stream
1)	102.9	4	Balti	Antena C
7A)	103.0	0.1	Causeni	Russkoie Radio
13)	103.2	0.1	Chisinau	Avtoradio
2)	103.2	1	Ciadâr-Lunga°	R.Micul Samaritean
19)	103.5	1	Balti	R. 103.5 FM
8)	103.6	0.1	Vulcanesti°	Teleradio Gagauzia
7A)	103.7	1	Chisinau	Russkoie Radio
12)	103.8	-	Stefan Voda	Hit FM
2)	103.8	2	Edinet	R. Micul Samaritean
10)	104.0	0.6	Tighina	R. 7
2)	104.1	1	Chisinau	R. Micul Samaritean
12)	104.5	4	Ungheni	Hit FM
12)	104.6	1	Ciadâr-Lunga°	Hit FM
7B)	104.7	1	Chisinau	Russkoie Radio 2
12)	104.7	-	Rezina	Hit FM
24)	105.0	0.15	Basarabeasca	Bas-Hit FM
12)	105.2	1	Cahul	Hit FM
10)	105.2	0.1	Chisinau	R. 7
2)	105.4	2	Rezina	R. Micul Samaritean
7B)	105.5	5	Comrat°	Russkoie R. 2
12)	105.6	-	Cimislia	Hit FM
11)	105.7	1	Nisporeni	Vocea Basarabiei
4)	105.9	0.1	Chisinau	R. Nova
7A)	106.2	0.1	Balti	Russkoie Radio
6)	106.4	0.1	Chisinau	Europa Plus Moldova
12)	106.5	0.1	Criuleni	Hit FM
12)	106.6	1	Comrat°	Hit FM
3)	106.8	1	Causeni	Pro FM
3)	106.9	0.1	Chisinau	Pro FM
12)	106.9	0.1	Leovo	Hit FM
2)	107.0	4	Ungheni	R. Micul Samaritean
B)	107.3	1	Chisinau	RFI
12)	107.3	0.1	Ocnita	Hit FM
12)	107.6	1	Balti	Hit FM
2)	107.7	1	Cahul	R. Micul Samaritean
17)	107.9	0.1	Chisinau	Serebriannii Dojdi
12)	107.9		Edinet	Hit FM

°) Gagauz-Yeri (autonomous district)

Addresses & other information:

1) str. Veronica Micle 10, 2012 Chisinau. Own prgr's & rebroadcasts of RFE/RL, DW, BBC. Email: antenac@cni.md – **2)** str. Bucuresti 68, 2012 Chisinau. – **3)** bd. Stefan cel Mare 162, 2004 Chisinau. Rel. Pro FM, Bucuresti (cf. Romania). Email: sales@protv.md – **4)** str. Bucuresti 68, cam. 724, 2012 Chisinau. Email: nova@novaradio.com – **5)** sos. Hancesti 53, birou 500, 2028 Chisinau. Own prgr's and rel. Kiss FM, Romania. Email: office@rcontact.mnc.md – **6)** str. Alecu Russo 1, et. 16, 2068 Chisinau. Email: europlus@dnt.md. Rel. Europa Plus from Russia. – **7A,B)** sos. Hancesti 59/1, 2028 Chisinau. Rel. Russkoye R. resp. Russkoye R. 2 from Russia. Email: a@polidisc.moldova.su – **8)** str. Lenin 164, 3805 Comrat. Own prgr's in Gagauz, Russian and relay TRT (cf. Turkey). – **9)** str. Grenoble, 193, et.9, 74, 2043 Chisinau. Email: hitfm@dixi.net.md. Rel. Nashe R. from Russia. – **10)** str. Grenoble 193, 2043 Chisinau. Rel. R. 7 from Russia. Email: nostalgie@nache.mldnet.com – **11)** str. Alexandru cel Bun 96, 6401 Nisporeni. Email: gvest@iatp.md – **12)** str. Sciusev 93, 2012 Chisinau. Rel. Hit FM from Russia. Email: hitfm@dixi.net.md – **13)** bd. Stefan cel Mare 180, et. 14, 2004 Chisinau. Email: sales@auto.radio.md – **14)** str. Grenoble 193, 2043 Chisinau. Rel. R. Maksimum from Russia. Email: kishinev@maximum.ru – **15)** Chisinau. Own prgr's and rel. Ekho Moskvy from Russia. Email: inforadio2001@yahoo.com – **16)** Chisinau. Rel. R. Shanson from Russia. – **17)** sos. Hancesti 59/1, 2028 Chisinau. Rel. Serebryanyy dozhd from Russia. Email: silver@silver.net.md – **18)** Chisinau. Rel. Dinamit FM from Russia. – **19)** str. Independentei 3, 3100 Balti. – **20)** Vulcanesti. – **21)** Chisinau. Rel. Prosto R. from Ukraine. – **22)** Chisinau. Rel. R. Retro from Russia.– **23)** Chisinau. Rel. R. Melodia from Ukraine (in Ukrainian, Russian). – **24)** Basarabeasca. – **A)** CP 86, 2012 Chisinau. Relays BBC in E, Romanian, Russian, Ukrainian. – **B)** Rel. RFE-RL in Romanian ("R. Europa Libera"): 1600-1630, 1900-2000; in Russian ("R. Svoboda"): 1630-1700, 1800-1900, 2000-2200.

TRANSDNIESTER (Pridnestrovye/Transnistria)
(Self-proclaimed, self-governed territory)

RADIO PMR (Gov.)

✉ ul. Rozy Lyuksemburg 10, 3300 Tiraspol. ☎ +373 533 35570. 🖷 +373 533 32245. **Email:** radiopmr@inbox.ru **Web:** www.president-pmr.org/radio

L.P: Dir: Arkady D. Shablenko.

MW	kHz	kW	Hour of tr.
Maiac	549	150	0500-0530, 1700-1730

FM	MHz	kW		MHz	kW
Tiraspol	74.00	0.2	Maiac	100.6	1
Voroncovo	100.6	1	Camenca	106.0	1
Tiraspol	100.7	0.2			

D.PRGR: 24h on FM in Russian, Ukrainian, Moldovan. Own prgr's and rel. R.Mayak (cf. Russia). On MW: 0500-0530, 1700-1730 in Russian.

EXTERNAL SERVICE: R. PMR (DMR)
See International Broadcasting section

OTHER STATIONS

FM	MHz	kW	Location	Station
2)	101.1	-	Tiraspol	Hit FM
A)	102.6	0.1	Tiraspol	R. Rossii
A)	104.6	0.1	Slobodzia	R. Rossii
B)	105.8	0.1	Slobodzia	R. Mayak
1)	107.7	1	Maiac	R. Inter FM

Addresses & other information:

1) ul. K.Libnikhta 1/2, 3300 Tiraspol. Email: reklama@inter-fm.idknet.com – **2)** see Hit FM Chisinau (station 10). – **A)** Rel. R.Rossii (cf. Russia).– **B)** Rel. R.Mayak (cf. Russia).

MONACO

L.T: UTC +1h (27 Mar-30 Oct: UTC+2h) — **Pop:** 33,000 — **Pr.L:** French — **E.C:** 50Hz, 220V — **ITU:** MCO

MONTE CARLO RADIODIFFUSION (Comm)

✉ 10 Quai Antoine 1er, MC-98000 Monaco ☎ +377 97974799 🖷 +377 97974707. **Web:** www.mcr.mc
Email: mcradiodiffusion@mcr.mc

MW	kHz	kW	Prgr.
Roumoules (France)	1467	1000	TWR , Vatican Radio
Col de la Madone (France)	1467	40	inactive
Col de la Madone (France)	702	200	inactive

RMC INFO (Comm.)

✉ HQ: 12 Rue d'Oradour sur Glane, FR-75015 Paris,France. ☎ +331 71191191 🖷 +331 71191190 **Web:** www.rmcinfo.fr
Email: technique@rmcinfo.fr
L.P: Pres: Alain Weill, MD: Etienne Combet, CE: Bernard Poizat.
LW: Roumoules (France) 216kHz 1400kW, RMC INFO 0400-0005
FM: Monaco 98,5MHz 10kW; Mt Agel 98,8MHz 50kW V.by QSL-card. Rp.

RADIO MONTE CARLO ITALIE(Comm)

✉ 8 Quai Antoine 1er, MC-98000 Monaco ☎ +377 97976666 🖷 +377 97708661 **Web:** www.radiomontecarlo.net **Email:** rmc@radiomontecarlo.net **FM:** Monaco 106,8MHz 10kW; Mont Agel 107,3MHz 50kW **V.**by QSL-card. Rp.

RIVIERA RADIO (Comm)

✉ 10 Quai Antoine 1er, MC-98000 Monaco ☎ +377 97979494 🖷 +377 97979495 **Web:** www.rivieraradio.mc **Email:** info@rivieraradio.mc
L.P.: MD: Paul Kavanagh.
FM: Monaco 106.3MHz 10kW; Mt Agel 106.5MHz 50kW
D.Prgr. in English: 24h , 1900-0300 Monte Carlo Nights. **Rel. BBCWS** every hour 0600-1900

Other Stations FM (all sces. 24h)

Location	MHz	kW	Prgr.
Monaco	93,8	1	Nostalgie FM
Monaco	98.2	0.5	MC one
Monaco	102.9	1	R. Classique
Mont Agel	90.3	50	MFM
Mont Agel	93.5	50	Nostalgie FM
Mont Agel	95.4	5	R. Maria (Italian/French)
Mont Agel	102.7	50	R.Classique

Religious stations over RMC Info on 216 kHz and FM. (all F). **1) Radio Evangile** 0340-0355 (Mo-Sa) 0330-0400 (Sun) ✉ BP 1 FR-26101 Romans Sur Isère ☎ +334 75021010 🖷+334 75021421 **Web:** www.radio-evangile.com **Email** : radioevangile@wanadoo.fr V. by QSL card. – **2) Radio Réveil** 0328-0340 (Tu, Th) ✉ Les Chapons 4 CH-20022 Bevais ☎. +413 28470610 🖷 +413 28470615 **Web:** www.paroles.ch **Email**: contact@paroles.ch – **3) Christ Vous Appelle** 0328-0340 (Mo,We,Fr) ✉ BP 2017 FR-06101 Nice Cedex 2 **Web:** www.cvamm.com **Email**: secretariat@cvamm.com

EXTERNAL SERVICES: Trans World Radio Europe see International broadcasting section

MONGOLIA

L.T: UTC +8h (West Mongolia: +7h; East Mongolia: +9h); 26 Mar-24 Sep: UTC +8/9/10h — **Pop:** 2.7 million — **Pr.L:** Mongolian — **E.C:** 50Hz, 220V — **ITU:** MNG

MONGOLIIN RADIO (Pub.)

✉ Huvisgalyn zam 3, Ulaanbaatar 11. ☎ +976 11 327900. 🖷 +976 11 327234. **Email:** mr@mongol.net **Web:** n/a
L.P: Head: Biligt Bayanmunkhyin.

LW/MW	kHz	kW	P	MW	kHz	kW	P
Ulaanbaatar	164	500	1	Altay	227	75	1
Choibalsan	209	75	1	Mörön	882	75	1
Dalanzadgad	209	75	1	Ulaanbaatar	990	500	F
Ulgii	209	30	1				
SW	**kHz**	**kW**	**P**	**SW**	**kHz**	**kW**	**P**
Altay	4830	10	2	Ulaanbaatar	7260	50	2
Mörön	4895	10	2				

FM (MHz)	MR1	MR2	kW
Ulaanbaatar	106.0	100.9	-

+ FM tx's in other parts of the country.
D.PRGR: MR1 (Mongoliin Radio): 2200-1600. – **MR2 (Höh tenger):** 2200-1600. N. Russian: 0750-0800 on FM (Mon/Wed/Fri also on SW).
EXTERNAL SERVICE: Voice of Mongolia (F) - see International Radio section.

OTHER STATIONS:

FM	MHz	kW	Location	Station
11)	93.0	0.05	Erdenet	Avtoradio
8)	100.1		Ulaanbaatar	R. Elgen Nutag
12)	100.4	0.05	Erdenet	Nomyn FM
9)	100.5	1	Ulaanbaatar	R. Miniy Mongol
10)	101.7	-	Ulaanbaatar	R. Höh Mongol
2)	102.5	-	Ulaanbaatar	R. Ulaanbaatar
A)	103.1	-	Ulaanbaatar	BBC Relay
3)	104.0	-	Ulaanbaatar	R. Salhi
7)	104.5	-	Ulaanbaatar	R. Erh Chölöö
4)	105.0	-	Ulaanbaatar	Ger Büüliin R.
1)	105.5	-	Ulaanbaatar	Inforadio
B)	106.6	1	Ulaanbaatar	VOA Relay
6)	107.0	-	Ulaanbaatar	Shine Zuuny R.
5)	107.5	-	Ulaanbaatar	Shine Dolgion R.

Addresses & other information:
1) Ulaanbaatar. Email: support@inforadio.mn – **2)** Ulaanbaatar. – **3)** Ulaanbaatar. – **4)** Ulaanbaatar. Email: windfm@mongol.net – **5)** Ulaanbaatar. – **6)** Ulaanbaatar. – **7)** Ulaanbaatar. – **8)** Ulaanbaatar. – **9)** Ulaanbaatar. – **10)** Ulaanbaatar. – **11)** Erdenet. Rel. Avtoradio from Russia. – **10)** Erdenet.

MONTSERRAT (British)

L.T: UTC -4h — **Pop:** 5,000 — **Pr.L:** English — **E.C:** 60Hz, 220V — **ITU:** MSR

RADIO MONTSERRAT (Gov. Comm.)

✉ P.O. Box 51, Sweeneys. ☎ +1 664 491 2885/6349/7242. 🖷 +1 664 491 9250. **Web:** www.zjb.gov/ms. **Email:** radmon@candw.ag.
L.P: SM: Herman Sargeant. Technician: Ivor Grenaway.
FM: 91.9 (Southern Island: 0.15kW) and 95.5MHz (Silver Hills 5kW)
D.Prgr: 24h. BBC relay at night 0400-0930.
ANN: "ZJB Radio Montserrat, the Voice of Montserrat".

FAMILY RADIO NETWORK:

✉ P.O Box 350, Baker Hill. ☎ +1 664 491 7331
FM: 89.9/90.9MHz. (Relay Antigua).

GEM RADIO NETWORK:

FM: 93.9/94.5MHz. (Relay Trinidad).

MOROCCO

L.T: UTC — **Pop:** 30.6 million — **Radios:** 5,100,000 — **Pr.L:** Arabic, French, Spanish, English, Berber languages, Hassania — **E.C:** 50Hz, 127/220V — **ITU:** MRC

AGENCE NATIONALE DE RÉGLEMENTATION DES TÉLÉCOMMUNICATIONS (ANRT)

ANRT is the authority that supervises activities in radio & telecom.
✉ BP 2939, Rabat, Hay Ryad ☎+212 3 771 8600 **Web:** www.anrt.net.ma
L.P: DG: Mostafa Terrab.

RADIODIFFUSION-TÉLÉVISION MAROCAINE (RTM)

✉ 1, Rue El Brihi (or B.P. 1042), 10000 Rabat ☎ +212 3 7766880 🖷+212 3 7766888 **Web:** www.rtm.ma. **Regional** ✉ B.P. 459, Laayoune
L.P: DG: Mohamed Tricha, Dir. Radio: Abderrahman Achour.

LW/MW	kHz	kW	N	LW/MW	kHz	Kw	N
Azilal	207	400	A	Safi	909	20	B
Tahadart	540	300	A/R	Agadir	936	100	C
Tanger	540	300	A/R	Tanger	999	300	A/R
Oujda	594	50	A/R	Rabat	1026	1	B
Sebaa-Aioun	612	300	A/R	Sebaa-Aioun	1044	300	C
Sebaa-Aioun	702	140	C	Beni Makada	1053	10	A/R
Dakhla	711	300	A/R	Quarzazate	1116	5	C
Sidi-Bennour	711	7.5	A	Agadir	1197	50	C
Agadir	774	600	A/R	Marrakech	1233	600	A/R
Rabat	819	25	A	Safi	1323	5	B
Oujda	828	50	A/R	Casablanca	1485	1	C
Laâyoune	864	7.5	A	Marrakech	1593	1	A/C/R
Errachidia	864	7.5	A				

FM (MHz)	Prgr. A	Prgr. B	Prgr.C	kW
Azrou	90.5		7	
Boujdour	88.9		10	
Dakhla	93.0		12	
El Houceima	105.7		92.1	7.5
Tanger	88.7		91.8	20
Casablanca	96.0		90.0	39
Khénifra	89.3		5	
Laayoune	97.5		94.2	10
Marrakech	91.7	98.8	31	
Oujda	101.9/89.8	93.4	10	
Rabat	92.1/89.2		87.9	39/5/39
Tetouan	90.6	100.2	12	
Tata	88.2		99.9	10
Fès. Meknès	98.4/101.9		95.1	10

Netw. A in Arabic: 0500-0100. **N:** on the h.
Regional Prgrs (exc.Sun): **Tetouan,** 30, Avenue Mohammed V, Tetouan: 0800-1200 in Arabic and Rifain dialect on 1053kHz. **Tangier,** 33, Avenue Amir Moulay Abdallah, Tanger: 1500-1600 & 1620-1800 on 1053kHz. **Oujda,** Avenue Omar Errifi, Oujda: 1200-1300 & 1330-1500 on 594kHz. Sidi-Bennour: 0900-1300 exc. Sun. and Wed.**Marrakech,** 40, Avenue Yugoslavie, Marrakech: 1500-1600 & 1620-1800 on 540kHz. **Casablanca,** Ain Chock, Casablanca: 1500-1600 & 1620-1800 on 96.0 MHz. **Agadir,** Avenue Hassan II, Agadir: Mo 0900-1200 in Arabic, 2000-2400 in Tachelhit dialect. Tues.-Sat. 0900-1300 2 h Arabic + 2 h Tachelhit dialect on 936kHz. **Laayoune:** 2030-0200. Fri/Sat 2300-2400 in **Spanish** on 711kHz. **Dhakla,** 21, Avenue Imili, Dakhla on 999kHz: 1500-1600.
Int. Netw. B, Chaine Inter : 0600-0100. **English:** W 1000-1200, Sun 1400-1500v. **Spanish:** 0900-1000. **N:** 0915, 0930. Other times in **French.**
Netw. C in Dialects(Berber/Arabic): 1200-2400 (incl. relays of Netw. A 0600-1200).
ANN: Arabic: "Huna Ribat, idha'atu-l-mamlaka al Maghribiyya". French: "Ici Rabat, Radiodiffusion Télévision Marocaine". Berber:

"Dahab Rbad Lidaa Attalfaza Li mamlaka Lmaghrib". **V.** by QSL-card. Rec.acc. Rp.

EXTERNAL SERVICES: Radiodiffusion Télévison Marocaine see International Broadcasting section.

RADIO MEDITERRANÉE INTERNATIONALE (Gov. Comm.)

3, rue Emsallah , 9000 Tanger (B.P. 2055, Tanger) ☎ +212 9 936363 🖷 +212 9 935755 **Web:** www.medi1.com **Email:** medi1@medi1.com (**in France:** 78 av.Raymond Poincaré, 75116 Paris)
LW: Nador 171 kHz 2000kW.
SW: see international section.
FM (MHz):Agadir 104.6, Casablanca 99.6, Essaouira 94.6, Fès 101.4, Laayoune 101.0, Marrakech 105.3, Meknes 105.5, Nador 94.0/99.9, Meknes 105.5, Oujda 102.9, Rabat 97.5, Tanger 95.6, Tetouan 103.7MHz
D.Prgr. in French/Arabic: 0500-0100. **N. in French:** 0630, 0730, 0830, 1230, 1700, 1930, 2200. **N. in Arabic:** 0600, 0700, 0800, 1200, 2000, 2300 **ANN:** "Médi 1" **V.** by letter

RADIO SAWA MOROCCO

Web: www.ibb.gov/radiosawa. **Email**: comment@radiosawa.com FM(MHz): Rabat & Agadir 101.0 – Casablanca 101.5 – Tangier 101.8. D.Prgr: 24 h. (see USA for full details). All in Arabic.

VOICE OF AMERICA RELAY STATION

see International Broadcasting section.

CEUTA (Spanish)

L.T: UTC +1h (27 Mar-30 Oct: UTC +2h) — **Pop:** 76,000 — **Pr.L:** Spanish — **E.C:** 50Hz, 220V — **ITU:** E

RADIO NACIONAL DE ESPAÑA, S.A.

Real 90, E-51001 Ceuta ☎ +34 (956) 524858 🖷 +34 (956) 519067
FM: RNE-1 97.2,105.2 MHz, Radio Clasica 100.8, RNE-3 106.8. Power 1 kW.

SOCIEDAD ESPANOLA DE RADIODIFUSIÓN RADIO OLÉ-COSTA DEL ESTRECHO-CEUTA

José Antonio 7, E-11201 Algeciras ☎ +34 (956) 511820 🖷 +34 (956) 516820. **Web:** www.cherrytel.com/cadenaser
MW: 1584kHz 5kW 24h (SER). Local programs until 1830 then relay of Radiolé network **FM:** 96.2 MHz Radio Ceúta..

COPE CEUTA (Comm.)

Sargento Mena 8,1°izq, E-11701Ceuta ☎ +34(956)511122 🖷 +34 (956) 517603 **FM:** 89.8 MHz Cope Ceuta/Cadena 100

OCR (Comm.)

Grupos Alfa 4,3°nz, E-11701Ceuta ☎ +34 956 617886 🖷 +34 956 517004
FM:101.4 MHz Onda Cero Radio 3kW.

MELLILLA (Spanish)

L.T: UTC +1h (27 Mar-30 Oct: UTC +2h) — **Pop:** 66,000 — **Pr.L:** Spanish — **E.C:** 50Hz, 220V — **ITU:** E

RADIO NACIONAL DE ESPAÑA, S.A.

Altos de la Vía 3, E-52006 Melilla ☎ +34 956 681907. 🖷 +34 956 687332 **L.P:** Dir: Pedro A.Medina Barrenechea.
MW: 972kHz 20 kW (RNE1)
FM (0.3kW): 97.7 MHz (R1), 105.3MHz (R2), 107.6MHz (R3).

SOCIEDAD ESPANOLA DE RADIODIFUSIÓN R. MELILLA (Comm.)

Muelle Ribera s/n, E-52005 Melilla ☎ +34 956 681708 🖷 +34 956 681753 **L.P:** Dir: Gaspar Diaz Cerdá.
MW: EAJ21 1485kHz 5 kW 24h(SER)
FM (MHz): 96.3 Cadena 40 Melilla, 101.1 Dial Melilla

OCR: General Mola 26 E-29804 Melilla.
FM (MHz): 89.6 Onda Cero Radio, 96.3 Los 40 Principales, 98.4 Europa FM.

WESTERN SAHARA

L.T: UTC — **Pop:** 270,000 — **Pr.L:** Arabic, Spanish — **E.C:** 50Hz, 220V — **ITU:** AOE

RADIO NACIONAL DE LA R.A.S.D.: see under Algeria

MOZAMBIQUE

L.T: UTC +2h — **Pop:** 19 million — **Pr.L:** Portuguese, 20 ethnic languages — **E.C:** 50Hz, 220V — **ITU:** MOZ

MINISTÉRIO DOS TRANSPORTES E COMUNICAÇÕES

Av. Mártires de Inhaminga 336, C.P. 276, Maputo ☎ +258-1-430152/5, 420223 🖷 +258-1-431028 **Web:** www.mtc.gov.mz

RÁDIO MOÇAMBIQUE (RM)

Rua da Rádio n.° 2, C.P. 2000, Maputo ☎ +258 1 431687 🖷 +258 1 321816 **Web:** www.teledata.mz/radiomocambique
Email: caprimoe@zebra.uem.mz
L.P: Chmn: Dr. Manuel Fernando Veterano. TD: Luis Loforte. Int. Rel. Dir:Ms Maria Cremilda Massingue. Fin. Dir: Arlindo Piedade de Sousa
MW:

P	Location	kHz	kW	N	P	Location	kHz	kW	N
1)	Maputo	738	50	N	1)	Maputo	1008	50	M
3)	Nampula	765	50	EP	4)	Chimoio	1026	50	EP
10)	Xai-Xai	810	50	EP	7)	Quelimane	1179	50	EP
2)	Beira	873	50	EP	5)	Inhambane	1206	50	EP
1)	Maputo*	918v	50	C	8)	Pemba	1224	50	EP
9)	Tete	963	50	EP	6)	Lichinga	1260	50	EP

*rep. inactive
FM:

P	Location	MHz	kW	N	P	Location	MHz	kW	N
10)	Xai-Xai	87.8	-	N	1)	Maputo	97.9	5	C
9)	Tete	90.7	-	N	9)	Tete	100.7	-	EP
10)	Xai-Xai	90.9	-	EP	6)	Lichinga	101.7	-	N
2)	Beira	91.6	-	N	1)	Maputo	102.3	-	M
7)	Quelimane	92.1	10	N	4)	Chimoio	102.5	-	EP
1)	Maputo	92.3	10	N	5)	Inhambane	105.1	-	EP
1)	Maputo	93.1	-	D	2)	Beira	105.2	-	C
3)	Nampula	95.1	-	N	3)	Nampula	105.5	0.25	EP
8)	Pemba	95.3	-	N	1)	Maputo	105.9	-	E

Antena Nacional (N) in Portuguese: 24h.
R. Cidade (C) in Portuguese: 24h. Also rel. BBC.
RM Desporto (D) in Portuguese: 0300-2200.
Maputo Corridor R. (E) in English: 1000-2200.
Emissão Provincial (EP) in Portuguese and Vernaculars: Mostly provincial programmes on MW/FM 0250-2200. Also rel. N network News at 1600 and 2130 and "RM Jornal" at 1030-1100 & 1730-1800.
1) Rádio Provincial de Maputo – **2)** EP de Sofala, C.P. 1942, Beira – **3)** EP de Nampula, C.P. 93, Nampula – **4)** EP de Manica, C.P. 390, Chimoio – **5)** EP de Inhambane, C.P. 196, Imhambane – **6)** EP do Niassa, C.P. 171, Lichinga – **7)** EP de Zambézia, C.P. 333, Quelimane – **8)** EP de Cabo Delgado, C.P. 45, Pemba – **9)** EP de Tete, C.P. 384, Tete – **10)** EP da Gaza, C.P. 130, Xai-Xai.
ANN: "Rádio Moçambique, Antena Nacional", "Emissão Provincial de (province)". **IS:** Mbira (indigenous xylophone) Opens and closes with National Anthem.

Other stations:
R. Capital: Maputo 90.7MHz (rel. Trans World Radio) – **R. Maria Moçambique**, Paróquia Sagrada Familia, Rua da Igreja 156/A, Machava Centro-Matola **Web:** www.salesianos.com/rma/rm.html **Email:** info.moz@radiomaria.org **D.Prgr** in Portuguese and vernaculars on FM: Matola 103.1MHz, Villankulo/Xai Xai 102MHz, Chokwe 101.4MHz, Quissico 106.4MHz, Maxixe 104.2MHz, Nova Mambone 104MHz – **R. Miramar**: Maputo 101.4MHz – **R. N'tyana:** Maputo 93.5MHz – **Rádio-Televisão Klint**: Maputo 88.3MHz – **R. Terra Verde:** Maputo 98.5MHz – **BBC African Service:** Maputo 95.5MHz 1kW, Beira/Nampula 91.6MHz in English/Portuguese – **RDP África**: Beira 94.8MHz, Maputo 89.2MHz, Nampula 91.9MHz, Quelimane 89MHz (all 50kW) – **RFI Afrique**: Maputo 105MHz 1kW in French/English/Portuguese, Nampula (R. Encontro) 101.9MHz and Beira (R. Pax) 103MHz in Portuguese.

MYANMAR

L.T: UTC + 6½h — **Pop:** 42 million — **Pr.L:** Myanmar (Bamar, Burmese), English. Major minority languages: Kachin, Kayah, Kayin (Po & Sakaw), Chin, Mon, Rakhine, Shan — **E.C:** 50Hz, 230V — **ITU:** BRM

MYANMAR RADIO AND TELEVISION, MRTV (Gov.) RADIO MYANMAR

Pyay Rd, Kamayut-11041, Yangon (**Postal** GPO Box 1432, Yangon-11181). ☎ +95 1 532814. 🖷 +95 1 525428.

L.P: DG: U Khin Maung Htay. Dir. (Broadc.): U Ko Ko Htway. CE: U Tin Wan. Dir (TV): U Phone Myint.
STATION: Yangon (Yegu: G.C: 16N52 096E10).
MW:

kHz	kW	P	Times
576	200	M	0030-0245 (SS 0830), 0330-0830, 0930-1600

SW:

kHz	kW	P	Times
5040v	50	Mi	0930-1530 (occ. to 1300, 1430 or 1600)
5986	50	M	0930-1600
7185	50	M	0030-0245 (SS 0300)
9731	50	M	0330 (SS 0245)-0830

FM: Yangon 104.0MHz 0.5kW.
P=Prgr: M=Main Prgr. in Bamar, English. Mi=Minorities Prgr. in several minority languages, after 1330 educational services, incl. segments in E, F. **English** (in Main Prgr): 0200-0245 (SS -0300), 0700-0830, 1430-1600.
N: 0100, 0130, 0200, 0220, 0235 , 0325, 0410, 0455, 0510, 0630, 0700, 0720, 0735, 0945, 1200, 1230, 1330, 1515.
ANN: (0030: "Min Ga La Nan Net Khinn Bar Shin") "Thaw Ta Shin Myar Min Ga Lar Ah Paung Ne Pyayt Son Bar Zay Lo Hnoke Khun Hset Tha Ga Ra Wa Pyu Laik Par Dae Shin". E: "This is Myanmar R, Yangon" **IS:** Myanma Orchestral Music.

CITY FM (FM-89)
Yangon City Development Committee, City Hall, Yangon.
FM: 89MHz. **D.Prgr:** 0130-0530, 0730-1130.

DEFENCE FORCES BROADCASTING UNIT (Mil.)
Taunggyi, Shan State
SW: 5770kHz 10kW.
D.Prgr. in Bamar and minority languages: 0130-0430, 0630-0930, 1330-1630.

MYAWADDY RADIO STATION (Mil.)
MW: 1440kHz. Current activity unconfirmed.

NAMIBIA

L.T: UTC +1h (5 Sept-6 Apr: UTC +2h) — **Pop:** 1.8 million — **Pr.L:** English (official), Afrikaans, German, Owambo, Kwanyama, Herero, Setswana, Damara, Nama, Kwangali — **E.C:** 50Hz, 220V — **ITU:** NMB

NAMIBIAN COMMUNICATIONS COMMISSION (NCC)
119 Independence Ave, 2nd floor, SWACO House, Private Bag 13309, Windhoek ☎ +264 61 222666 🖷 + 264 61 222790
Web: www.ncc.org.na

NAMIBIAN BROADCASTING CORPORATION (NBC)
P.O. Box 321, Windhoek 9000 ☎ +264 61 291 9111/3111 🖷 + 264 61 217760/216209 **Web**: www.nbc.com.na
L.P: DG: Jerry Munjama. Contr. Radio: Penny Uukunde. Sen. Contr. Personnel & Admin: Vitura Kavari. Contr. Mktg: Jaap Blaauw. Contr. Tech. Sces: Rector Mutelo. Tech. GM: Ruben Prinz. Transm. Mgr: Mbeno Murangi.
SW: Windhoek (G.C: 22S33 017E13): 2 x 100kW.

kHz	Prgr.	H. of tr.	kHz	Prgr.	H. of tr.
6060	2	24h	6175	1	24h

(6060kHz rep. inactive, 6175kHz irregular).
SW Sce. 1 in Afrikaans/German, SW Sce. 2 in English/Vernaculars. Both SW services relay National Sce (in English) at times; e.g. news at 0600.
FM: 31 medium & low power st's.
National Sce. in English: 24hrs. Windhoek 91.7MHz, Klein 92.6MHz & on 19 other FM tr's. Also rel. **BBC African Sce & RFI Afrique** in English. Relayed on all freq's 2100-0500 – **Afrikaans Sce:** MF 0900-1600 & 1700-2000, SS 0600-2000. Windhoek 88.6MHz, Klein Windhoek 89.5Mhz & 20 other FM-tr's – **German Sce:** MF 0900-1600 & 1700-2000, SS 0500-2000. Windhoek 95.8MHz & on 13 other FM-tr's –**Oshiwambo Sce in Ovambo/Kwanyama:** 0900 (SS 0500)-2200 on FM Windhoek 98.2MHz & on 9 other FM tr's. At other times rel. National Sce – **Otjiherero Sce in Herero/Setswana:** MF 0900-1600 & 1700-2000, SS 0500-2000. Windhoek 101.7MHz & 6 other FM tr's – **Damara/Nama Sce:** MF 0900-1600 & 1700-2000, SS 0500-2000. Windhoek 105.3MHz & on 17 other FM tr's – **Rukavango Sce in Kwangali:** 0900 (Sat/Sun 0500)-2000 on 7 FM-tr's. – **R. Opuwo** – **San R.**
ANN: National Sce: "National Radio". On all NBC transmitters overnight: "Here is the National Sce. of the NBC Nationwide"..G: "Hier ist das Deutsche Hörfunkprogramm der NBC". Damara/Nam: "Nes ge Damara/Nama Gowab loabas NBC's disa". A: "Dit is die Afrikaanse diens van die NBC". Otjiher: "Indji oradio ja Namibia morupa rueraka Otjiherero"
IS: at s/on: National Anthem with choir/orchestra.

OTHER STATIONS:
R. 99 P.O. Box 11849, Windhoek ☎ +264 61 223634/225182 🖷 +264 61 230964 - **FM:** Windhoek 99MHz, Walvis Bay & Swakopmund 96.5, Tsumeb 101.7, Oshakati & Ondangwa 104.5, Otjiwarango 99.9MHz. Also rel. VOA.
Kanaal 7 (rlg.), Windhoek: 102.3MHz + 18 FM fq's. **Web:** www.k7.com.na **Email:** channel7@k7.com.na
R. Energy P.O. Box 11720, Windhoek ☎ +264 61 223863 🖷 +264 61 230964 **Web:** www.energy100fm.com **Email:** studio@energy100fm.com - **FM:** Windhoek 100MHz 0.5kW, Oshakati 100.9MHz 2kW, Walvis Bay 88.8MHz 0.1kW.
R. Cosmos, Windhoek. Mainly in Afrikaans on 94.1MHz.
R. Kudu, Windhoek. In English. **Web:** www.radiokudu.com.na **Email:** radiokudu@radiokudu.com.na - **FM:** Windhoek 103.5MHz, Grootfontein 95.5MHz, Swakopmund 94.3MHz, Walvis Bay 93.3MHz, Lüderitz 94.7MHz, Otjiwarongo 92.3MHz, Gobabis/Keetmanshoop 95.6MHz.
Omulunga R. in Oshiwambo. - **FM:** Oshakati 102.3MHz, Walvis Bay/Swakopmund/Henties Bay/Arandis 104.7MHz, Windhoek 100.9MHz
R. Wave, P.O. Box 9953, Eros, Windhoek. ☎ +264 61 242350 🖷 +264 61 242322 **Web:** www.radiowave.com.na **Email:** radiowave@radiowave.com.na - **FM:** Central Namibia 87.8MHz 3kW, Grootfontein 88.9MHz 100W, Luderitz 90.6MHz 100W, Henties Bay/Swakopmund/Rossing 91.1MHz 250W, Walvis Bay 91.9MHz 100W, Keetmanshoop 92.4MHz 100W, Tsumeb 95.8MHz 100W, Windhoek 96.7MHz 2kW, Otjiwarongo 100.9MHz 100W, Katima Mulilo 104.5MHz 100W, Rundu 105.4MHz 350W, Oshakati 106.8MHz 350W, Ondangwa 350 W

NAURU

L.T: UTC +12h — **Pop:** 12,000 — **Pr.L:** English, Nauruan — **E.C:** 50Hz, 110/240V — **ITU:** NRU

NAURU BROADCASTING SERVICE (Gov.)
P O Box 429, Rep. of Nauru, Ce. Pacific ☎ +674 555 6066 🖷 +674 4443195.
L.P: SM: Miss Rin Tsitisi. TD: Malcom Aroi.
Email: radionaurufm@hotmail.com
MW: 1323kHz 1kW. **FM:** 88.8MHz. **D.PRGR:** 1900-1130. Relays R Australia **V.** by letter.

NEPAL

L.T: UTC +5¾h — **Pop:** 25.3 million — **Pr.L:** Nepali, English — **E.C:** 50Hz, 220V — **ITU:** NPL

RADIO NEPAL (Semi-Gov, Comm.)
Radio Broadcasting Service, P.O. Box 634, Singha Durbar, Kathmandu ☎ +977 (1) 233910 or 225467 🖷 +977 (1) 221952 **Web:** www.radionepal.org **Email:** radio@engg.wlink.com.np
L.P: Exec. Dir: Shailendra Raj Sharma. Dep. Exec. Dir: M. P. Adhikari.

MW	kHz	kW	MW	kHz	kW
Surkhet	576	100	Kathmandu	792	100
Dhankuta	648	100	Dipayal	810	10
Pokhara	684	100	Bardibas	1143	10

SW: Khumaltar (G.C: 27N42 085E12): 3 x 100kW.
kHz: 3230 (winter-inactive), 5005, 7165 (summer-inactive)
FM: Radio Nepal FM-Kathmandu: 6h daily on Khumaltar 100MHz 1kW.
D.Prgr on MW/SW: 2345-0515 (Sat & public holidays -0715) & 0715-1715. **N. in Nepali 0015 hrs** and on the hour, main News at 0115, 0715, 1315; **in English:** 0215, 0815, 1415; **in Hindi**: 1615.
Variation at Regional Centers: 0345-0515 & 1220-1245.
ANN: Nepali: "Yo Radio Nepal Ho"
IS: Instruments used are conch shell, violin, piano and jal tarang. **V.** by QSL-card.

R. SAGARMATHA (Community)
Kathmandu.
BBC RELAY: Surkhet 576 kHz 1630-1700 World Service, 1700-1730 Hindi, 1730-1800 World Service daily.
R.Sagarmatha 102.4 MHz 0.1kW, Nepali 1500-1530 daily.

OTHER STATIONS: **Kantipur FM** 96.1MHz, **Hits FM** 91.2MHz, **Shakti Radio** 94.0MHz, **Radio Sagarmartha** 102.4MHz, **KATH** 97.9MHz, **Classic FM** 100MHz, **MetroFM** 106.7MHz
F.Pl: Shree Bhaktapur FM

BFBS: Gurkha Radio, Kathmandu MF 0900-1100. English 92.1MHz, Nepali 99.6MHz

NETHERLANDS

L.T: UTC +1h (27 Mar-30 Oct: UTC +2h) — **Pop:** 16 million — **Pr.L:** Dutch — **E.C:** 50Hz, 230V — **ITU:** HOL

NEDERLANDSE OMROEP STICHTING (NOS)

✉ Sumatralaan 45, 1217 GP Hilversum; Postbus 26600, 1202 JT Hilversum ☎ +31 (35) 6779222 🖷 +31 (35) 6772649
Email: publieksreacties@rtv.nos.nl

NEDERLANDSE PROGRAMMA STICHTING (NPS)

✉ P.O. Box 29000, 1202 MA Hilversum ☎ +31 (35) 6779333 🖷 +31 (35) 6774959 **Email:** publiek@nps.nl **Web:** www.omroep.nl (for all national public broadcasters) **L.P:** Dir: W.J.M. van Beusekom
Dutch national public prgrs are provided by the **NOS**, **NPS** and the following broadcasting organisations: **AVRO, BNN, EO, KRO, NCRV,TROS, VARA, and VPRO.**

MW:

Location	kHz	kW	Prgr.
Flevoland	747	400	747 AM
Hulsberg	1251	10	747 AM

747 AM: ✉ Postbus 26444, 1202JJ Hilversum ☎ +31 (35) 6772264
Web: www.omroep.nl/747am/

FM:

Location	Radio 1	Radio 2	3FM	Radio 4	kW
Amsterdam	98.6	92.3	96.5	94.5	0.04
Arnhem	98.6	92.9	96.5	92.1	0.1
Eys	-	97.2	-	-	10
Goes	104.4	94.4	99.8	95.0	15
Hulsberg	105.3	93.4	103.9	98.7	10
Hulst	-	107.1	-	-	0.1
Loon op Zand	-	-	-	98.2	40
Lopik	98.9	92.6	96.8	94.3	100
Markelo	98.4	104.6	96.2	91.4	100
Philippine	-	97.8	-	-	50
Roermond	104.8	88.2	90.9	94.5	100
Rotterdam	98.6	92.9	97.1	94.7	0.1/10
Smilde	91.8	88.0	88.6	94.8	100
Wieringermeer	95.0	92.9	97.1	101.6	25/50

ANN: "Dit is de VARA..", "Dit is de VPRO..". etc. **V:** by QSL-card.

Regional stations

	Mhz	kW	Location	Station
2)	87.6	5	Mierlo	Omroep Brabant
4)	87.9	16	Goes	Omroep Zeeland
9)	88.9	10	Amsterdam	Radio Noord-Holland
6)	89.1	5	Megen	Radio Gelderland
13)	89.3	10	Rotterdam	Radio West
10)	89.4	10	De Lutte	Radio Oost
12)	89.8	25	Lelystad	Radio Flevoland
3)	89.9	-	Vlieland	Omrop Fryslân (F.Pl.)
6)	90.4	10	Ruurlo	Radio Gelderland
5)	90.8	4	Smilde	Radio Drenthe
2)	91.0	10	Roosendaal	Omroep Brabant
2)	91.9	2	Loon op Zand	Omroep Brabant
3)	92.2	100	Smilde	Omrop Fryslân
7)	93.1	4	Lopik	Radio M
11)	93.4	10	Rotterdam	Radio Rijnmond
9)	93.9	10	Wieringermeer	Radio Noord-Holland
1)	95.3	10	Hulsberg	L1 Radio
10)	95.6	5	Markelo	Radio Oost
2)	95.8	5	Megen	Omroep Brabant
8)	97.5	15	Hoogezand	Radio Noord
7)	97.9	1	Rhenen	Radio M
10)	99.4	25	Zwolle	Radio Oost
3)	99.7	-	Terschelling	Omrop Fryslân (F.Pl.)
1)	100.3	100	Roermond	L1 Radio
6)	103.5	20	Ughelen	Radio Gelderland

+5 low-power relays

1) Postbus 31, 6200 AA Maastricht ☎ +31 (43) 3467777 🖷 +31 (43) 3467715 **Email:** redactie@L1.nl **Web:** www.l1.nl – **2)** Postbus 108, 5600 AC Eindhoven ☎ +31 (40) 2949494 🖷 +31 (40) 2949320 **Web:** www.omroepbrabant.nl – **3)** Postbus 7600, 8903 JP Leeuwarden ☎ +31 (58) 299 7799 🖷 +31 (58) 2997778 **Email:** direksje@omropfryslan.nl **Web:** www.omroepfryslan.nl – **4)** Postbus 1090, 4388 ZH Oost-Souburg ☎ +31 (118) 499900 🖷 +31 (118) 499929 **Web:** www.omroepzeeland.nl – **5)** Postbus 999, 9400 AZ Assen ☎ +31 (592) 338080 🖷 +31 (592) 331048 **Email:** redactie@rtvdrenthe.nl – **6)** Postbus 747, 6800 AS Arnhem ☎ +31 (26) 3713713 🖷 +31 (26) 3713710 **Email:** rtv@omroepgelderland.nl **Web:** www.omroepgelderland.nl – **7)** Postbus 1012, 3500 BA Utrecht ☎ +31 (30) 8500600 🖷 +31 (30) 8500601 **Email:** info@radiom.nl **Web:** www.rtvutrecht.nl – **8)** Postbus 30101, 9700 RP Groningen ☎ +31 (50) 3199999 🖷 +31 (50) 3185147 **Email:** radio@rtvnoord.nl – **9)** Postbus 9823, 1006 AM Amsterdam ☎ +31(20) 8505050 🖷 +31 (20) 8505850. **Email:** info@rtvnh.nl **Web:** www.rtvnh.nl – **10)** Hazenweg 25, 7556 BM Hengelo (Ov) ☎ +31 (74) 2456456 🖷 +31 (74) 2437148 **Email:** info@rtvoost.nl **Web:** www.rtvoost.nl – **11)** Postbus 1515, 3000 BM Rotterdam ☎ +31 (10) 4400600 🖷 +31 (10) 4400698 **Email:** info@rijnmond.nl **Web:** www.rijnmond.nl – **12)** Postbus 567, 8200 AN Lelystad ☎ +31 (320) 285085 🖷 +31 (320) 285099 **Email:** rtv@omroepflevoland.nl **Web:** www.omroepflevoland.nl – **13)** Postbus 24025, 2490 AA Den Haag ☎ +31 (70) 3078888 🖷 +31 (70) 3078844 **Email:** west@rtvwest.nl

Public local stations in major cities
Amsterdam 96.1 FUN X, 99.4 Wereld FM, 105.2 Radio Zuid Oost, 106.8 Stads FM, 107.9 Caribbean FM
Den Haag 92.0 Stadsradio Den Haag, 98.4 FUN X
Rotterdam 91.8 FUN X, 93.9 Stadsradio Rotterdam
Utrecht 96.1 FUN X, 107.7 Stadsradio Utrecht
Note: FUN X is an initiative of SALTO Omroep Amsterdam, Slor Rotterdam, Stadsomroep Den Haag and Omroep RTV Utrecht.
± 340 local stations.

Commercial stations

MW	kHz	kW	Location	Station
2)	675	100	Lopik	Arrow Rock Radio
14)	891	20	Hulsberg	Radio 538
16)	1008	400	Flevoland	Radio 10 Gold*

*200kW nighttime

FM	Mhz	kW	Location	Station
20)	87.6	1	Enschede	Rebecca FM Classic Rock
28)	87.6	43	Smilde	Yorin FM
28)	87.7	50	Lelystad	Yorin FM
23)	87.8	1	Arnhem	RTL FM
28)	87.8	1	Utrecht	Yorin FM
28)	87.9	2	Den Bosch	Yorin FM
28)	88.1	4	Hilversum	Yorin FM
23)	88.2	1	Ugchelen	RTL FM
9)	88.4	30	Roosendaall	D&T Radio
3)	88.6	20	Mierlo	BNR Nieuwsradio
8)	88.7	1	Apeldoorn	HOT Radio
15)	88.9	1	Den Bosch	Radio 8 FM
23)	89.0	2	Lochem	RTL FM
5)	89.1	1	Groningen	Freez FM
20)	89.2	3	Zwolle	Rebecca FM Classic Rock
23)	89.5	10	Alkmaar	RTL FM
23)	89.5	10	Utrecht	RTL FM
8)	89.6	2	Huissen	HOT Radio
3)	89.6	5	Smilde	BNR Nieuwsradio
2)	89.7	1	Breda	Arrow 90.7FM
2)	89.7	1	Eindhoven	Arrow 90.7FM
20)	89.9	1	Emmen	Rebecca FM Classic Rock
23)	90.0	1	Breskens	RTL FM
23)	90.0	20	Loon op Zand	RTL FM
9)	90.1	3	Den Helder	ID&T Radio
23)	90.2	50	Roosendaal	RTL FM
27)	90.3	1	Eindhoven	XFM
2)	90.3	5	Groningen	Arrow 90.7FM (F.Pl.)
2)	90.4	10	Hoorn	Arrow 90.7FM
27)	90.5	3	Helmond	XFM
2)	90.5	10	Rotterdam	Arrow 90.7FM
2)	90.5	20	Smilde	Arrow 90.7FM
2)	90.7	4	Enschede	Arrow 90.7FM
2)	90.7	100	Lopik	Arrow 90.7FM
2)	90.8	2	Terneuzen	Arrow 90.7FM (F.Pl.)
9)	91.0	10	Irnsum	ID&T Radio
9)	91.0	1	Markelo	ID&T Radio
9)	91.1	40	Hilversum	ID&T Radio
28)	91.1	1	Maastricht	Yorin FM
9)	91.2	1.5	Leeuwardenl	D&T Radio (F.Pl.)
18)	91.3	1	Hoogezand	Simone FM
3)	91.3	10	Rotterdam	BNR Nieuwsradio

FM	Mhz	kW	Location	Station
3)	91.3	1	Tilburg	BNR Nieuwsradio
3)	91.5	2	Breda	BNR Nieuwsradio
3)	91.5	4	Driewegen	BNR Nieuwsradio
3)	91.5	10	Eys	BNR Nieuwsradio
19)	91.6	5	Haarlem	Radio Veronica
23)	92.1	10	Hulsberg	RTL FM
12)	92.4	2	Oude Polder	Maximaal FM
18)	92.9	1	Groningen	Simone FM
28)	93.0	10	Oude Polder	Yorin FM
9)	93.1	1	Emmen	ID&T Radio
26)	93.2	20	Irnsum	Waterstad FM
25)	93.3	1	Amsterdam	Ujala Radio
28)	93.3	1	Breskens	Yorin FM
8)	93.3	1	Hengelo	HOT Radio
8)	93.5	4	Lochem	HOT Radio
29)	93.6	2	Amsterdam	Wild FM (F.Pl.)
22)	93.6	5	Eindhoven	Royaal FM
9)	93.6	10	Zwolle	ID&T Radio
9)	93.7	5	Enschede	ID&T Radio
9)	93.7	2	Groningen	ID&T Radio
23)	93.8	1	Haarlem	RTL FM
9)	93.8	10	Megen	ID&T Radio
15)	93.9	2	Roosendaal	Radio 8 FM
19)	94.0	1	Emmen	Radio Veronica
27)	94.1	1	Den Bosch	XFM
5)	94.1	2	Tjerkgaast	Freez FM
10)	94.2	1	Nijmegen	Keizerstad FM
11)	94.9	1	Amsterdam	Magic FM
23)	94.9	5	Mierlo	RTL FM
23)	95.0	1	Amersfoort	RTL FM (F.Pl.)
23)	95.0	2	Nijmegen	RTL FM
9)	95.2	25	Alphen aan de Rijnl	D&T Radio
3)	95.3	20	Zwolle	BNR Nieuwsradio
3)	95.4	1	Emmen	BNR Nieuwsradio
28)	95.4	10	Gilze	Yorin FM
10)	95.5	1	Duiven	Keizerstad FM
3)	95.5	30	Tjerkgaast	BNR Nieuwsradio
6)	95.6	1	Rijswijk	Fresh FM
6)	95.7	10	Amsterdam	Fresh FM
20)	95.7	1	Meppel	Rebecca FM Classic Rock
6)	95.9	3	Alphen aan de Rijn	Fresh FM
10)	96.0	1	Ede	Keizerstad FM
29)	96.3	1	Alkmaar	Wild FM (F.Pl.)
19)	96.3	20	Loon op Zand	Radio Veronica
19)	96.6	2	Goes	Radio Veronica
5)	96.6	1	Leeuwarden	Freez FM
19)	97.1	1	Vlissingen	Radio Veronica
23)	97.6	1	Hengelo	RTL FM (F.Pl.)
4)	97.6	20	Rotterdam	City FM
19)	97.7	10	Arnhem	Radio Veronica
17)	97.7	5	Kerkrade	Radio Limburg 97 FM
19)	97.7	4	Mierlo	Radio Veronica
19)	97.8	5	Lopik	Radio Veronica
8)	97.9	2	Sneek	HOT Radio (F.Pl.)
4)	98.0	10	Amsterdam	City FM
4)	98.3	5	Alkmaar	City FM
20)	98.5	2	Groningen	Rebecca FM Classic Rock
20)	98.7	20	Smilde	Rebecca FM Classic Rock
23)	99.1	10	Enschede	RTL FM
23)	99.1	4	Groningen	RTL FM
23)	99.1	5	Tjerkgaast	RTL FM
9)	99.2	5	Vlissingen	ID&T Radio
7)	99.4	2	Den Haag	Hofstad Radio
9)	99.4	20	Mierlo	ID&T Radio
3)	99.6	2	Dordrecht	BNR Nieuwsradio
9)	99.6	10	Hoorn	ID&T Radio
9)	99.6	10	Smilde	ID&T Radio
3)	99.9	1	Dedemsvaart	BNR Nieuwsradio
3)	99.9	3	Ugchelen	BNR Nieuwsradio
3)	99.9	50	Wormer	BNR Nieuwsradio
3)	100.1	100	Lopik	BNR Nieuwsradio
3)	100.2	10	Lochem	BNR Nieuwsradio
3)	100.2	2	Nijmegen	BNR Nieuwsradio
13)	100.4	10	Lichtenvoorde	Noordzee 100.7 FM
13)	100.4	10	Oude Polder	Noordzee 100.7 FM
13)	100.4	5	Roosendaal	Noordzee 100.7 FM
13)	100.4	5	Rotterdam	Noordzee 100.7 FM
13)	100.4	100	Smilde	Noordzee 100.7 FM
13)	100.5	5	Wieringermeer	Noordzee 100.7 FM
13)	100.7	10	Breskens	Noordzee 100.7 FM
13)	100.7	10	Doetinchem	Noordzee 100.7 FM
13)	100.7	10	Enschede	Noordzee 100.7 FM
13)	100.7	100	Lopik	Noordzee 100.7 FM
24)	101.0	100	Smilde	Sky Radio 101 FM
24)	101.1	10	Nijmegen	Sky Radio 101 FM
24)	101.2	2	Boxtel	Sky Radio 101 FM (F.Pl.)
24)	101.2	10	Hengelo	Sky Radio 101 FM
24)	101.2	200	Hilversum	Sky Radio 101 FM
24)	101.2	20	Terneuzen	Sky Radio 101 FM (F.Pl.)
24)	101.3	5	Roosendaal	Sky Radio 101 FM
24)	101.4	10	Deventer	Sky Radio 101 FM
24)	101.5	1	Arnhem	Sky Radio 101 FM
24)	101.5	5	Den Bosch	Sky Radio 101 FM
24)	101.5	1	Lopik	Sky Radio 101 FM
24)	101.5	10	Rotterdam	Sky Radio 101 FM
24)	101.6	5	Breda	Sky Radio 101 FM
24)	101.6	5	Eindhoven	Sky Radio 101 FM
24)	101.6	2.5	Roermond	Sky Radio 101 FM
18)	101.7	1	Emmen	Simone FM
24)	101.8	2	Tilburg	Sky Radio 101 FM
24)	101.9	50	Goes	Sky Radio 101 FM
8)	101.9	1	Ruurlo	HOT Radio
14)	102.1	100	Hilversum	Radio 538
14)	102.2	10	Groningen	Radio 538
1)	102.2	1	Rotterdam	Radio Amor FM
14)	102.3	20	Alkmaar	Radio 538
14)	102.3	100	De Mortel	Radio 538
14)	102.3	10	Lochem	Radio 538
14)	102.3	1	Roermond	Radio 538
14)	102.4	1	Arnhem	Radio 538
14)	102.4	20	Oude Polder	Radio 538
14)	102.5	1	Tilburg	Radio 538
14)	102.5	50	Tjerkgaast	Radio 538
14)	102.5	1	Utrecht	Radio 538
14)	102.6	5	Enschede	Radio 538
14)	102.6	2	Nijmegen	Radio 538
14)	102.7	10	Emmen	Radio 538
14)	102.7	100	Rotterdam	Radio 538
19)	102.9	50	Tjerkgaast	Radio Veronica (F.Pl.)
19)	103.0	50	Lelystad	Radio Veronica
19)	103.1	5	De Lutte	Radio Veronica
19)	103.1	10	Markelo	Radio Veronica
19)	103.1	5	Megen	Radio Veronica
19)	103.2	50	Rotterdam	Radio Veronica
19)	103.2	25	Smilde	Radio Veronica
19)	103.3	2	Roosendaal	Radio Veronica
19)	103.3	1	Terneuzen	Radio Veronica
19)	103.4	3	Groningen	Radio Veronica
28)	103.6	6	Amsterdam	Yorin FM
15)	103.6	2	Tilburg	Radio 8 FM
28)	103.8	5	Emmen	Yorin FM
28)	103.8	20	Rotterdam	Yorin FM
28)	103.8	10	Tjerkgaast	Yorin FM
28)	103.9	1	Lichtenvoorde	Yorin FM (F.Pl.)
28)	104.1	50	Arnhem	Yorin FM
11)	104.2	5	Alkmaar	Magic FM (F.Pl.)
23)	104.4	50	Hilversum	RTL FM
23)	104.6	100	Rotterdam	RTL FM

+ 51 stations below 1kW

1) Spartapark-Oost 13-15, 3027 VX Rotterdam ☎ +31 (10) 2440929 📠 +31 (10) 2447248 **Email:** info@amorfm.nl **Web:** www.amorfm.nl – **2)** Postbus 116, 2501 CC Den Haag ☎ +31 (70) 3632727 📠 +31 (70) 3653511 **Email:** info@arrow.nl **Web:** www.arrow.nl – **3)** Postbus 651, 1000 AR Amsterdam ☎ +31 (20) 5158515 📠 +31 (20) 5898755 **Email:** operations@bn.nl **Web:** www.bn.nl – **4)** Postbus 12983, 1100 AZ Amsterdam ☎ +31 (20) 5849983 📠 +31 (20) 5849980 **Web:** www.cityfm.nl – **5)** Postbus 7593, 8903 JN Leeuwarden. ☎ +31 (58) 2553464 📠 +31 (58) 2553465 **Email:** info@freez.fm **Web:** www.freez.fm – **6)** Darwinstraat 20, 2722 PX Zoetermeer ☎ +31 (79) 3434491 📠 +31 (79) 3434492 **Web:** www.fresh.fm – **7)** Postbus 82087 2508 EB Den Haag ☎ +31 09004637823 📠 +31 084 8743054 **Email:** info@hofstadradio.net **Web:** www.hofstadradio.nl – **8)** Postbus 700, 7550 AS Hengelo ☎ +31 (74) 2509090. 📠 +31 (74) 2509099. – **9)** Rhoneweg 54, 1043 AH Amsterdam **Email:** radio@id-t.com **Web:** www.id-t.com – **10)** Postbus 22, 6660 AA Elst ☎ +31 (481) 370378 📠 +31 (481) 377508 **Email:** info@keizerstad.nl **Web:** www.keizerstad.fm – **11)** Postbus 15350, 1001 MJ Amsterdam ☎ +31 (20) 4203536 **Email:** info@magicfm.nl **Web:** www.magicfm.nl – **12)** Postbus 36, 4450 AA Heinkenszand ☎ 0900 5105100 📠 +31 (113) 567670 **Email:** info@maximaal.nl **Web:** www.maximaal.nl – **13)** Postbus 102, 1200 AC Hilversum ☎ +31 (35) 655 2 655 📠 +31 (35) 655 2 656 **Email:** info@noordzeefm.nl **Web:** www.noordzeefm.nl – **14)** Postbus 2538, 1200

CM Hilversum ☎ +31 (35) 5385538 🖷 +31 (35) 6283538 **Web:** www.radio538.nl – **15)** Postbus 8, 5201 AA Den Bosch ☎ +31 (73) 6312003 🖷 +31 (73) 6313311 **Email:** info@radio8fm.nl **Web:** www.radio8fm.nl – **16)** Postbus 102, 1200 AC Hilversum **Web:** www.radio10gold.nl – **17)** Postbus 1111, 6201 BC Maastricht ☎ +31 (045) 3215566 🖷 +31 (045) 3216677 – **18)** Hoogveen 2, 9501 XK Stadskanaal ☎ +31 (599) 312183 🖷 +31 (599) 312187 **Email:** info@simone.nl **Web:** www.radiosimone.nl – **19)** Postbus 1007, 1400 BA Hilversum ☎ +31 (35) 5277555 🖷 +31 (35) 5277557 **Web:** www.radioveronica.nl – **20)** Postbus 1058, 7940 KB Meppel ☎ +31 (522) 242624 **Web:** www.rebecca.nl 🖷 +31 (522) 252485. – **21)** Postbus 77, 9640 AB Veendam ☎ +31 (598) 633055 🖷 +31 (598) 633308 **Email:** info@touchradio.nl **Web:** www.touchradio.nl – **22)** Dukaathof 3, 5551 VG Valkenswaard ☎ +31 (40) 2017283 🖷 +31 (40) 2040066 **Email:** redactie@royaal.fm **Web:** www.royaal.fm – **23)** Postbus 15016, 1200 TV Hilversum ☎ +31 (35) 6718300 🖷 +31 (35) 671830 **Web:** www.rtl.nl – **24)** Naarderpoort 2, 1411 MA Naarden ☎ +31 (35) 6991050 **Email:** Skyradio@skyradio.nl **Web:** www.skyradio.nl – **25)** Postbus Hoogoord 191 A, 1102 CK Amsterdam ☎ +31 (20) 4090807 🖷 +31 20 4510179 **Email:** radio@ujala.nl. – **26)** Postbus 248, 8600 AE Sneek ☎ +31 (515) 432360 🖷 +31 (515) 432 986 **Email:** info@waterstadfm.nl **Web:** www.waterstadfm.nl – **27)** Postbus 170, 5660 AD Geldrop ☎ +31 (40) 2233303 🖷 +31 (40) 2960610 **Web:** www.xfm.nl – **28)** Postbus 15016, 1200 TV Hilversum ☎ +31 (35) 6718300 🖷 +31 (35) 6718380 **Web:** www.rtl.nl – **29)** Gyroscoopweg 144, 1042 AZ Amsterdam **Web:** www.wildfm.nl

Other stations

MW	kHz	kW	Location	Station
1)	1116	0.5	Bloemendaal	Radio Bloemendaal
2)	1485	1	Rijswijk	Haagstad Radio
3)	1602	1	Stiens	Radio Waddenzee (F.Pl.)
FM	**MHz**	**kW**	**Location**	**Station**
5)	87.7	0.05	Maastricht	BFBS
4)	89.2	1	Brunssum	AFN
5)	90.2	0.05	Brunssum	BFBS
4)	91.6	0.1	Erp	AFN
6)	96.9	1.6	Brunssum	CFN/RFC
6)	99.7	0.5	Brunssum	CFN/RFC

1) Vijverweg 14, 2061GX Bloemendaal ☎ +31 23 5250471 **Email:** bureau@radiobloemendaal.nl **Web:** www.radiobloemendaal.nl **D.Prgr:** Sun & christian holidays 0800-2000 & tuesdays 1100-1130v. **V:** by QSL-card. – **2)** Beeklaan 402A, 2562 BH Den Haag ☎ +31 70 3644690 🖷 +31 70 3465318 GM: Mrs Mila Kishoendajal D.Prgr: 24h. **Email:** receptie@haagstadradio.nl **Web:** www.haagstadradio.nl **D.Prgr:** Hindi and Dutch **V:** by QSL-card; Reception reports to: jhwijnants@wanadoo.nl – **3)** Postbus 24, 8860 AA Harlingen ☎ +31 06 28580161 🖷 +31 84 7248432 **Email:** info@radiowaddenzee.nl **Web:** www.radiowaddenzee.nl **D.Prgr:** 06.00-18.00 for tourists – **4) Email:** spannb@afn.shape.army.mil www.afneurope.army.mil/shape/ **D.Prgr:** 24h relay AFN SHAPE (Belgium) – **5) D.Prgr:** Relays BFBS 1 prgrs Germany – **6) D.Prgr:** 24h CFN/RFC ☎ +31 45 5263791 🖷 +31 45 5263792 **Email:** mail@cfnradio.com **Web:** www.cfnradio.com

EXTERNAL SERVICE:
RADIO NEDERLAND WERELDOMROEP (RNW)
See International Broadcasting Section

NETHERLANDS ANTILLES

L.T: UTC-4h — **Pop:** 212,000 — **Pr.L:** Dutch (official), Papiamento (Leeward Antilles), English (Windward Antilles), Spanish — **E.C:** 50 + 60Hz, 127/220V — **ITU:** ATN

LANDSRADIO (Telecommunication Administration)

✉ Schouwburgweg 22, P.O. Box 103, Curaçao ☎ +599 (9) 631111

MW, Call	kHz	kW	Station, location
1) PJB	800	100	TWR, Bonaire
2) PJZ-86	860	10	R. Curom, Willemstad
4) PJL-3	1100	0.25	R. Caribe, Willemstad
5) PJE-3	1120	1	R. Statia, St. Eustasius
6) PJD-2	1300	1	The Voice of St. Maarten, Philipsburg

FM	MHz	kW	Station, location
17)	90.7	-	Tropical 90.7, Willemstad
27)	91.5		St. Eustatius Broadcasting Foundation, St. Eustatius
24)	91.9	-	Island 92, Simpson Bay, St. Maarten
8)	92.3	5	R. Merkadeo, Willemstad
21)	92.7	-	R. Edukativo, Deltha 92, Willemstad
9)	93.9	20	R. Korsou FM, Willemstad
7)	93.9	1	Voice of Saba, Saba
10)	94.7	1	Voz di Bonaire, Bonaire
25)	94.7	-	Mix 94.7, Philipsburg, St. Maarten
2)	95.7	4	Mi 95Z FM, Willemstad
11)	97.1	5	Ritmo FM, Bonaire
22)	97.3	-	Dolfijn FM, Willemstad
2	97.5		Dolfijn FM, Bonaire
22)	97.5		Dolfijn FM, St. Maarten
18)	97.9	0.5	Easy 97.9 FM, Willemstad
20)	98.3	-	Family Radio Network, Saba
12)	98.7	2.5	R. Semiya, Willemstad
19)	99.9	-	R. Soualiga,Choice FM, St. Maarten
15)	100.3	-	Hit 100.3, Willemstad
26)	101.1	-	Laser 101, St. Maarten
10)	101.1	0.4	Mega FM, Bonaire
9)	101.1	5	Laser 101, Willemstad
3)	101.9	5	R. Hoyer 1, Willemstad
6)	102.7	3.5	The Voice of St. Maarten, Philipsburg, St. Maarten
13)	103.1	-	Trosparadise, Willemstad
18)	103.9	-	Radio One FM, Willemstad
3)	105.1	5	R. Hoyer 2, Willemstad
28)	105.5		SBN, St. Maarten
23)	107.1	-	Radio Direkt, Willemstad
14)	107.9	1	R. Exito, Willemstad
16)	107.9	1	Gem Radio Network, Philipsburg, St Maarten

Addresses and other information

All st's comm. exc. **1)** (see separate listing under Trans World R.) – **2)** R. Curom, Roodeweg 64, P.O. Box 2169, Willemstad, Curaçao. ☎ +599 9 626586 🖷 +599 9 625796. Dir. & GM: Orlando Cuales. CE: C. Siegenthaler. 1000-0400 in Papiamento. Separate music prgrs. ("Mi FM") on 95.7MHz. **V.** by letter. **Web:** www.curom.com. – **3)** Plasa Horacio Hoyer 21, Willemstad, Curaçao. ☎ +599 9 461 1678. 🖷 +599 9 461 6528. **Email:** hoyer1@radiohoyer.com **Web:** www.radiohoyer.com MD: Ms. Helen Hoyer. W,Sun: 1000-0400. R. Hoyer 1 in Papiamento, R. Hoyer 2 in Dutch. – **4)** Ledaweg 35, Brievengat, Willemstad, Curaçao. ☎ +599 9 736 9564. 🖷 +599 9 369 569. DG: C.R. Heilegger. TD: G.A. Heilegger. 1000(Sun 1200)-0400. Papiamento: W 1000-1700, 1900-2200, 0100-0400. Sun 1400-1700, 1830-2200, 2300-0400. **N:** 1615W, 1700W. Spanish: W 1700-1900, 2200-0100. Sun 1700-1830. **N:** 1700W, 1800W (VOA), 1815Sun 2200W, 0015W. English (rlg. prgr's): Sun 1200-1400, 2200-2300. **V.** by letter. Rec. acc. – **5)** St. Eustasius Broadc. N.V., Korthals Weg, St. Eustasius. ☎ +599 3 82262. – **6)** "The Voice of St. Maarten" Plaza 21 Shopping Centre, P.O. Box 366, Philipsburg, St. Maarten. ☎ +599 5 5422580, 5422764. 🖷 +599 5 5424905, 5425531 GM/Dir: Donald R. Hughes. MW: 0930-0600(Mon 0400). **N**: 1030, 1700, 0000. FM: 0930-0400. **N**: 1200, 1800, 0000. – **7)** P.O.Box 1, The Bottom, Saba. 🖷 +599 5 63213. Owner: Max Nicholson **Web:** www.manelli.com/saba/ – **8)** Generaalsweg 50, Willemstad, Curaçao. ☎ +599 9 376115. 🖷 +599 9 374514. Dir: E. Leito. 1000-0400 in Papiamento. – **9)** Bataljonweg 7, Willemstad, Curaçao. ☎ +599 9 7373012. 🖷 +599 9 7372888. Dir: J.P.C. Oosterhof. PD: Alan H. Evertsz. 24h. **Web:** www.korsou.com Separate prgrs ("Laser 101") on 101.1 MHz. 24h. **N.** in Dutch: 1000, 1600, 2100. **N.** in Papiamento: 2200. English: Tues 0000. Portuguese: Wed 2330. Sranan Tongo: Fri 0000. Relaying Radio Nederland Wereldomroep at 09.30 – **10)** P. O. Box 325, Kralendijk, Bonaire. ☎ +599 7 175947. 🖷 +599 8 5000. Dir: Edsel Jesurun Jr. & Irwin E. Halley. **Web:** www.megafm.com www.geocities.com/vozdibonaire.htm **Email:** vozdibon@bonairenet.com – **11)** Kaya Gob. N. Debrot 2, Kralendijk, Bonaire. ☎ +599 7 7220 (offices), 8273 (studios). 🖷 +599 7 8220. Dir: F. Piloto. 1000-0400 in Papiamento and Dutch. **N:** 2200. **N:** in Dutch: 1900, 2000. – **12)** Klipstraat 9-K, Willemstad, Curaçao. ☎ +599 9 462 4000. 🖷 +599 9 64 8390. Dir: Ferris Thode. 1000-0400 in Papiamento. – **13)** Village Riffort, Willemstad, Curaçao. ☎ +599 9 4628103. 🖷 +599 9 4619103 **Web:** www.trosparadise.nl MD: Jacques Visser. 1000-0400. Dutch: 1000-1300. **N.** & tourist information: Dutch: 1430, 1630, 1830, 2030, 0030. English: hourly 1300-2300. Spanish: 1530. Portuguese: 1330. – **14)** Julianaplein 39-A, Willemstad, Curaçao. ☎ +599 9 462 5577. 🖷 +599 9 4625580. Dir: Donny Hernandez. 24h in Papiamento. – **15)** Compleho Deportivo Casa Grandi Z/N Willemstad. ☎ +599 9 7473333/7676103. 🖷 +599 9 7471003. Manager: Elmer Cijntje Email: hit100.3fm@cura.net **Web:** www.radiohitfm.com – **16)** Relays prgrs from Trinidad. – **17)** Salinja Galleries, Unit B 101-103, Willemstad. ☎ +599 9 652467. 🖷 +599 9 652470. Dir: Dwight Rudolphina. – **18)** Arikokweg 19A, Willemstad. ☎ +599 9 462 3162. 🖷 +599 9 462 8712. Info line: +599 9 462 3611. **Email:** radio@easyfm.com . **Web:** easyfm.com. Dir: Kevin Carthy. 24h. – **19)** Philipsburg, St Maarten ☎ +599 5 422049. 🖷 +599 5 425791 **Web:** www.sxmradio.com/choicefm.html – **20)** W1102, 1 Independence Drive, St John's, Antigua. – **21)** Suffisantweg 16, Willemstad ☎ +599 9 888 0120. – **22)** Berg Altena 54, Willemstad ☎ +599 9 4659975 🖷 +599 9 4619975 **Email:** info@dolfijnfm.com **Web:** www.dolfijnfm.com – **23)**

F.D Rooseveltweg 214, Tesoro Building, Willemstad ☎ +599 9 8885107 **Email:** studio@direct107.com **Web:** www.direct107.com – **24)** Caribbean Broadcasting System NV, Simpson Bay, St. Maarten ☎ 599 544337 🖷 +599 5443319 **Email:** info@island92.com **Web:** www.island92.com – **25)** Lighthouse Broadcasting Network, 7 Brooks Towers, Suites 5A and 5B, Philipsburg ☎+599 5425773 🖷 +599 542 5778 **Web:** www.mix947fm.com – **26) Web**: www.laser101.fm – **27)** Relaying programs of Radio Nederland Wereldomroep 11.00-11.30, 19.30 and mo.-fr. 23.00-00.00, Sundays 14.00-18.00 – **28)** relaying programs of Radio Nederland Wereldomroep.

TRANS WORLD RADIO (Cult. Educ. Rlg.)
RADIO NEDERLAND RELAY STATION:
see International Broadcasting section.

NEW CALEDONIA (French)

L.T: UTC +11h — **Pop:** 205,000 — **Pr.L:** French, 33 Melanesian-Polynesian dialects — **E.C:** 50Hz, 220V — **ITU:** NCL

RADIO NOUVELLE CALEDONIE

✉ Mt Coffyn, B.P. G3, Noumea ☎ +687 274327 🖷 +687 281252 **Web:** www.rfo.fr/ncaledonie/nc.htm
L.P: Reg. Dir: Wallés Kotra. PD: Louis Palmieri.
MW: 666kHz 20kW **FM:** Noumea 89.0MHz, 90.0MHz, Touho 88.0MHz, Canala 90.0MHz, Hienghene 90.0MHz, Kone 90.0MHz, Poya 90.5MHz, Bourail 91.0MHz, Houailou 91.0MHz, Thio 91.0MHz, Fayaoue 89.5MHz, We 91.5MHz, Tadine 91.5MHz, Ouaco 88.0MHz, Kouaoua 88.5MHz, Aoupinie 89.0MHz, Pouebo 89.0MHz, Poum 90.0MHz, Koumac 91.0MHz, Noumea 89.0MHz, 90.0MHz, Mount Dore 91.0MHz, Port Boise 88.0MHz, Point Ita 89.0MHz, Deete Kari 89.5MHz, Yate 90.0MHz
D.PRGR: 24h in French. **Rel. France-Inter:** 1100-1900.
ANN: "Bonjour, vous êtes à l'ecoute de Radio Nouvelle Caledonie". **France-Inter** is relayed 24h on 90.2MHz in Noumea.

NOUMEA RADIO JOKER 2000 (N.R.J. 2000),
✉ 41/43 rue Sebastopol, B.P. 179, Noumea ☎ +687 272584 🖷 +687 281627 **Web:** www.nrj.nc
FM: Noumea 93.5MHz - 24h.

RADIO RYTHME BLEU (RRB),
✉ B.P. 578 Noumea ☎ +687 254646 🖷 +687 284928
FM: Noumea 100.4MHz, Canala 98.0MHz, Hienghene 98.0MHz, Kone 98.0MHz, Thio 99.0MHz, Bourail 99.0MHz, Houailou 99.0MHz, Touho 100.0MHz, We 102.5MHz, Tadine 102.5MHz, Fayaoue 103.5MHz, Poum 98.0MHz, Koumac 99.0MHz, Wala 100.0MHz, Ouaco 100.0MHz, Aoupine 101.0MHz, Pouebo 101.0MHz, Dumbea 98.0MHz, Mount Dore 100.0MHz, Vao 97.0MHz, Yate 98.0MHz

RADIO DJIDO
✉ 29 rue Mar Juin Ht Mgta, B.P. 1671, Noumea ☎ +687 253515 🖷 +687 253433
FM: Noumea 97.4 MHz - 24h. Touho 96.0MHz, Canala 102.0MHz, Hienghene 102.0MHz, Kone 102.0MHz, Bourail 103.0MHz, Thio 103.0MHz, Houailou 103.0MHz, Fayaoue 96.5MHz, We 98.5MHz, Tadine 98.5MHz, Wala 96.0MHz, Ouaco 96.0MHz, Aoupinie 97.0MHz, Pouebo 97.0MHz, Poum 102.0MHz, Koumac 103.0MHz , Mount Dore 96.0MHz, Dumbea 102.0MHz, Port Boise 96.0MHz, Yate 102.0MHz, Vao 102.0MHz

Other FM stations:
Radio Alizes, ✉ BP 2557, Noumea ☎ +687 47 3048
Radio Baie des Tortues, ✉ BP 241, Bourail ☎ +687 25 4500, Bourail
Radio Cote Est, ✉ BP 123, Poindimie ☎ +687 27 3242.
Radio France International - **FM:** Noumea 93.0MHz
Radio Oceane FM, ✉ 1 Avenue d'Auteuil Lotissement FSH Koutio, 98835 Dumbea - **FM:** 95.0 MHz

NEW ZEALAND

L.T: UTC +12h (5 Oct-20 Mar: UTC +13h) — **Pop:** 3.9 million — **Pr.L:** English, Maori — **E.C:** 50Hz, 230V — **ITU:** NZL

RADIO NEW ZEALAND (State-owned enterprise)

✉ P.O. Box 123, Wellington ☎ +64 04 474 1999 🖷 +64 04 474 1730 **Web:** www.radionz.co.nz
L.P: Chief Exec: Sharon Crosbie; Infrastructure Mgr: Matthew Finn; Transmission Mgr; Gary Fowles.
Networks: Concert FM, Parliamentary Broadcasting Service and National Radio.
National Radio Net: 24h. **N:** On the hour every hour except 0700 & 1500, plus 0030, 1830, 1930 & 2030.
Concert FM: 24h N: relays of National Radio at 1800, 1900, 2000, 2100, 0000, 0100, 0300, 0500, 0600 & 1100

RADIO NEW ZEALAND INTERNATIONAL

See international broadcasting section.

MW & FM station codes
Key: #) = Rel. A = Access Radio (mostly cultural, ethnic and minority group programs), C = Concert FM, F = Southern Star (rlg.), G = R. Rhema (rlg.), H = Community Network (local breakfast shows, otherwise automated with local news, weather, advertisements until 1200 UTC, then fully networked till 1800 UTC), M = ZM Net, N = National Radio, P = Private, S = Radio Sport (carries live audio feeds of US sports stations over-night), T = R. Pacific (all talk). B = Parliamentary Broadcasting Service (only when Parliament is sitting, otherwise carries "Southern Star" network), Z = Classic Hits (local days, networked over night), D = News-Talk ZB (local days, networked over night). SH = Share Time

MW (NB: RNZ & private st's both shown in list)

MW	Call	kHz	kW	N	Name and location
166)		531	5	P	531 PI, Auckland
33)		531	2	P	Solid Gold AM, Alexandra.
42)	1XC	540	5	G	R. Rhema, Tauranga
42)	2XV	540	2	G	R. Rhema, New Plymouth
42)	2XC	549	5	G	R. Rhema, Gisborne
28)		549	1	S	R. Sport, Nelson
42)		549	2	G	R. Rhema, Kaitaia
28)		558	5	S	R. Sport, Invercargill
2)	2YA	567	100	N	National R, Wellington
42)	1XLR	576	2	F	Southern Star, Hamilton
46)	2XR	585	2	P	R. Ngati Porou, Ruatoria
42)		585		G	R. Rhema, Blenheim (**F.PI.**)
42)	3XL	594	5	G	R. Rhema, Timaru
42)		594	2	G	R. Rhema, Wanganui
41)		603	5	P	R. Waatea, Auckland
42)	3XG	612	2	G	R. Rhema, Christchurch
42)	4XG	621	2	G	R. Rhema, Dunedin
42)		621	2	G	R. Rhema, Whangarei
2)	2YZ	630	10	N	National R, Napier
2)	4YW	639	2	N	National R, Alexandra
2)	2YC	657	50	B	Parl. Broadc. Wellington. SH
42)		657	50	F	Southern Star, Wellington. SH
2)	3YA	675	10	N	National R, Christchurch
28)		693	5	S	R. Sport, Dunedin
56)	1XP	702	10	T	R. Pacific, Auckland
10)		702		D	Newstalk ZB, Rotorua
79)	2XP	711	5	T	R. Pacific, Wellington
2)	4YZ	720	10	N	National R, Invercargill
2)	1YP	729	2	N	National R, Tokoroa
126)	4XX	729	0.9	P	Ranfurly R, Ranfurly
28)		729	2.5	S	R. Sport, Whangarei
56)		738	5	T	R Pacific, Christchurch
2)	1YA	756	10	N	National R, Auckland
124)	2XT	765	2.5	P	R. Kahungunu, Napier
28)		774	5	S	R. Sport, New Plymouth
139)	2YB	783	10	A	Access R, Wellington
175)	2YB	783	10	P	Samoan Capital R, Wellington
28)	1XSR	792	5	S	R. Sport, Hamilton
42)	2XL	801	1	G	R. Rhema, Nelson
2)	4YA	810	10	N	National R, Dunedin
2)	1YZ	819	10	N	National R, Rotorua
43)	2XS	828	2	P	Magic 828, Palmerston North
2)	1YX	837	2	N	National R, Whangarei
2)	1YX	837	2	N	National R, Kaitaia
12)	2ZD	846	2	D	Newstalk ZB, Masterton
28)		846	2	S	R Sport, Masterton SH
42)	1XH	855	2	G	R. Rhema, Hamilton
3)	4ZA	864	10	D	Newstalk ZB, Invercargill
13)	3ZE	873	1	D	Newstalk ZB, Ashburton
2)	1YC	882	10	B	Parl. Broadc. Auckland. SH
42)		882	10	F	Southern Star, Auckland. SH
44)	2XW	891	5	P	The Breeze, Wellington
42)		900		G	R. Rhema, Kaikohe (**FPI**)
2)	4YC	900	10	B	Parl. Broadc. Dunedin
42)		900	10	F	Southern Star, Dunedin, SH
2)	2XD	909	5	B	Parl. Broadc. Napier
42)		909	5	F	Southern Star, Napier, SH
2)	3YT	918	2	N	National R, Timaru
14)	2ZA	927	2	D	Newstalk ZB, Palmerston No.
143)		936	1	P	New Supremo 936, Waiuku (Mandarin)
15)	2ZG	945	2	D	Newstalk ZB, Gisborne. SH
28)		945	2	S	Radio Sport, Gisborne. SH

MW	Call	kHz	kW	N	Name and location
56)	1XW	954	2	T	R. Pacific, Hamilton
87)		954	0.8	P	Puketapu R, Palmerston FPL: 1251kHz
2)	3YC	963	10	B	Parl. Broadc. Christchurch. SH
42)		963	10	F	Southern Star,Christchurch SH
42)	2XG	972	5	G	R. Rhema, Wellington
2)	1YE	981	2	N	National R, Kaikohe
34)		990	1	P	Ace Broadc. BBC Mandarin/ Cantonese Svce, Auckland
91)		990	1	P	Fifeshire Classics, Nelson
38)		999	1.5	A	Sounz AM, Palmerston North
16)	1ZD	1008	10	D	Newstalk ZB, Tauranga
28)		1017	2	P	R. Hauraki, Christchurch
11)	1ZN	1026	2	Z	R. Northland, Whangarei
11)	1ZK	1026	2	Z	R. Northland, Kaitaia
28)	4XSR	1026	1	S	Radio Sport, Invercargill. SH
42)		1026	1	F	Southern Star, Invercargill. SH
27)	2ZB	1035	20	D	Newstalk ZB, Wellington
5)	4ZB	1044	10	D	Newstalk ZB, Dunedin
17)	2ZP	1053	2	D	Newstalk ZB, New Plymouth
28)		1062	1	S	R. Sport, Wanganui
2)	2YE	1071	2	N	National R, Masterton
56)		1071			Radio Pacific, Ashburton
28)	1ZB	1080	10	D	Newstalk 1ZB, Auckland
28)		1089	2.5	S	R. Sport, Palmerston North
6)	3ZB	1098	10	D	Newstalk ZB, Christchurch
2)	2YX	1116	2	N	National R, Nelson
28)		1125	0.2	Z	R. Hauraki, Dunedin
28)		1125	1	S	R. Sport, Napier
2)	4YQ	1134	2	N	National R, Queenstown
2)	1YW	1143	2	N	National R, Hamilton
20)	3ZC	1152	2	D	Newstalk ZB,Timaru
70)	2XM	1161	5	P	Te Upoko o Te Ika, Wellington
30)	1ZW	1170	0.4	H	V. of Waitomo, Te Kuiti
137)		1179	5	P	Ruia Mai, Auckland (FPL: silent)
2)	1YR	1188	0.4	N	National R, Rotorua
21)	2ZW	1197	2	H	River City R, Wanganui
40)	4XO	1206	2	P	R. Otago, Dunedin
130)	1XHC	1206	0.5	A	Access Community R,Hamilton
11)	1ZE	1215	2	Z	Classic Hits, Kaikohe
47)	4XF	1224	2	P	R. Foveaux, Invercargill
33)		1233	2	P	Solid Gold AM, Wellington
48)	1XX	1242	2	P	1 Double X, Whakatane
48)	1XX	1242	0.1	P	1 Double X, Galatea
42)	1XG	1251	5	G	R. Rhema, Auckland
87)		1251	0.8	P	Puketapu R, Palmerston FPL: 2kW
42)	3XA	1260	2	P	"Lite FM", Christchurch
18)	2ZT	1269	0.4	Z	Classic Hits, Takaka
4)	2ZC	1278	2	D	Newstalk ZB, Napier
7)	3ZW	1287	2	H	Scenicland FM, Westport
19)	1ZH	1296	2.5	D	Newstalk ZB, Hamilton
50)	4XD	1305	2	P	R. Dunedin, Dunedin
2)	2YW	1314	2	N	National R, Gisborne
28)		1332	10	S	R. Sport, Auckland
18)	2ZN	1341	2	D	Newstalk ZB, Nelson
28)		1350	1	S	R. Sport, Rotorua
40)	4XC	1359	1	P	Resort R, Queenstown
52)	1XT	1368	1	P	Village R, Tauranga Suns only 2100-0500
28)	2XX	1377	2	P	R. Sport, Levin
162)		1386	10	P	R. Tarana, Auckland
188)		1386	5	P	R. Korea, Auckland
189)		1386	5	P	Chinese Life Comm. R., Auckland
23)	4ZW	1395	2	D	Newstalk ZB, Oamaru
42)	4XL	1404	2.5	G	R. Rhema, Invercargill
24)	1ZO	1413	2	H	R. Forestland, Tokoroa
108)	3XP	1413	0.1	P	R. Ferrymead, Christchurch Sun. 2100-0600
94)	3XP	1413	0.1	P	Nga Hou E Wha, Christchurch
60)	2XKC	1431	2	A	R. Kidnappers, Hastings
112)	1XK	1440	0.2	P	Te Reo o Tauranga Moana, Tauranga
125)		1440	0.1	P	Goldrush 14-40, Lawrence
2)	2YM	1449	2	N	National R, Palmerston North
2)	3YW	1458	0.4	N	National R, Westport
105)	1XD	1476	5	P	BBC World Service, Auckland Airport
28)		1494	2.5	S	R. Sport, Timaru
28)		1503	2.5	S	R. Sport, Christchurch
28)		1503	5	S	R. Sport, Wellington
25)	1ZU	1512	1	H	King Country R, Taumarunui
9)		1512	0.3	A	Coast Access R., Waikanae
35)		1521		P	"Classic Good time Oldies", Tauranga
2)	2YP	1530	2	N	National R, New Plymouth
153)		1530	1/0.3	P	"Coast 15-30", Hastings
26)	2ZE	1539	1	S	R. Sport, Blenheim
89)	1XN	1548	0.99	P	Classic Country, Rotorua
31)	2ZH	1557	2	D	Newstalk ZB, Hawera
113)	4XS	1575	2.5	A	Hills AM, Dunedin
26)	2ZF	1584	0.4	H	R. Marlborough, Picton
37)		1593	2	A	R. Asia Pacific, Auckland
39)		1593	2	P	R. Samoa, Auckland
28)		1593	2	P	i1593 AM, Christchurch
57)	2XA	1602	2.5	P	R. Reading Sce, Levin (relays Nat. R. overnight)

SW	Call	kHz	kW	N	Name and location
57)	ZLXA	3935	1	P	R. Reading Service, Levin (relay 1602kHz 24hrs)
57)	ZLXA	5960	1	P	R. Reading Service, Levin (inactive)
57)	ZLXA	7290	1	P	R. Reading Service (inactive)

FM: (NB: RNZ & private stations both shown in list)

	MHz	kW	N	Name, location & h. of tr.
137)	88.6	1	P	Mai FM, Auckland Sky Tower
68)	88.6		P	88Country, Christchurch
2)	89.0		C	Concert FM, Horokaka (Lower Northland)
138)	89.0		P	Coromandel FM, Paeroa
81)	89.0		P	The Generator, Waikato University, Hamilton
28)	89.0		P	Radio Hauraki, Tauranga
71)	89.0	1	P	Pumanawa 89FM, Rotorua
2)	89.0	40	C	Concert FM, Palmerston North
91)	89.0		P	The Edge, Nelson
64)	89.0		P	The Edge, Christchurch
2)	89.0		N	National R., Tekapo (Community owned)
42)	89.0		G	R. Rhema/Southern Star, Wanaka
138)	89.1		P	Coromandel FM, Coromandel
66)	89.1		P	The Edge, Taupo
33)	89.1		T	R. Pacific, Hokitika
6)	89.2		M	91ZM-FM, Sumner # 91.3
82)	89.2		P	The Rhythm 89.2FM, Waihi Beach
33)	89.2		P	Solid Gold FM, Thames/Hauraki Plains
58)	89.2		T	R. Pacific, Taranaki
47)	89.2		P	Foveaux R, Hedgehope (Invercargill)
83)	89.3		P	89FM, Gisborne
28)	89.4	40	T	Newstalk ZB, Auckland
28)	89.4		S	R. Sport, Upper Hutt
5)	89.4	3	Z	Classic Hits 89FM, Dunedin (Mount Cargill)
193)	89.5		P	Ski-FM, Central Plateau (Taumaranui)
4)	89.5		Z	Classic Hits 89.5FM, Hawkes Bay (Napier)
42)	89.5		G	R. Rhema, Cromwell
59)	89.6	10	P	KCC FM, Hikurangi
2)	89.7	40	C	Concert FM, Christchurch
180)	89.7	3	P	Coast FM, Grey Valley # 96.5
2)	89.7		N	National R., Chatham Is.(Community owned)
19)	89.8		M	ZM-FM, Hamilton/Tauranga
193)	89.8		P	Ski FM, Taihape
28)	89.8		Z	Classic Hits 90FM, Nelson
194)	89.9		P	Rodney Times FM, Orewa # 96.6
33)	89.9		P	The Edge, Gisborne
64)	89.9		P	R. Pacific, Mt. Studholme (Timaru)
17)	90.0	3	Z	Classic Hits 90FM, New Plymouth
28)	90.0		P	Radio Sport, Greymouth (alt. 99.0 FM)
2)	90.0		C	Concert FM, Hedgehope (Invercargill)
27)	90.1		Z	Classic Hits Wairarapa, Masterton
128)	90.1		P	Son FM, Wairoa (Hawkes Bay)
33)	90.1		T	R. Pacific, Mount Rochcroft (Westport)
33)	90.2		T	The Rock, Auckland Sky Tower
28)	90.2		S	R. Sport, Taupo
53)	90.2		P	2XX FM, Forest Heights
109)	90.2		P	More FM, Akaroa Peninsula (private relay)
40)	90.2		P	Solid Gold FM, Mount Cargill (Dunedin)
2)	90.3		C	Concert FM, Tihiotonga, Rotorua
28)	90.3		P	Easy Listening i90.3FM, Hawkes Bay
180)	90.3	3	P	Coast FM, Reefton # 96.5
42)	90.4		G	R. Rhema, Kaikohe/Bay of Islands
28)	90.4		P	Classic Hits, Motueka # 89.8
28)	90.4		Z	Classic Hits 90 FM, Te Anau
48)	90.5	10	P	1XX-FM, Whakatane
28)	90.5		Z	Classic Hits Scenicland FM, South Westland
190)	90.6		P	The Beach FM, Waiheke Island, Hauraki Gulf
97)	90.6		P	Raukawa FM, South Waikato # 95.7
14)	90.6	40	M	91ZM-FM Palmerston North
93)	90.8		P	Tautoko FM, Mangamuka (Northland) # 92.8
17)	90.8	3	Z	Classic Hits 90FM, Taranaki # 90.0
176)	90.8		P	The Rock, Hedgehope (Invercargill)
15)	90.9		H	Classic Hits ZG-FM, Gisborne
2)	90.9	50	M	91ZM-FM Wellington
28)	90.9		Z	Classic Hits Scenicland FM, Westport # 1287AM
28)	91.0	50	M	91ZM, Auckland
28)	91.0		S	R. Sport, Tauranga
23)	91.0		H	R. Waitaki, Pukeuri (Oamaru) # 1395AM
155)	91.1		P	Mercury FM, Tairua/Pauanui # 96.6
67)	91.1		P	Solid Gold FM, Rotorua
33)	91.1		P	The Chill, Taupo
2)	91.1	3	C	Concert FM, Napier (Hawkes Bay)

FM	MHz	kW	N	Name, location & h. of tr.
94)	91.1		P	Tahu FM, Kaikoura # 90.5
28)	91.1		Z	Classic Hits Scenicland FM, Greymouth
42)	91.1		G	Life fm, Cromwell
59)	91.2		P	KCC FM, Kaitaia
123)	91.2		P	Awa FM, Ruapehu # 100.0
78)	91.2		P	Port FM, Omarama # 97.9
42)	91.2		G	Life FM, Te Anau
6)	91.3	40	M	91ZM-FM Christchurch (Otematata)
2)	91.4	40	C	Concert FM, Mount Te Aroha (Waikato)
42)	91.4		G	Radio Rhema, Wharite (Manawatu)
2)	91.4	3	C	Concert FM, Grampians (Nelson)
2)	91.4		N	National Radio, Wanaka (Community owned)
59)	91.5		P	The Edge, Whangarei
59)	91.6		P	Magic 91.5 FM, Kerikeri
2)	91.6	3	C	Concert FM, Mt. Taranaki (New Plymouth)
146)	91.7		P	Channel Z, Wellington
151)	91.7		P	Turanganui a Kiwa, Gisborne
109)	91.8		P	More FM, Auckland Sky Tower
40)	91.8		P	The Edge, Mount Cargill (Dunedin)
181)	91.9		P	Whangamata FM, Coromandel
145)	91.9		P	Maniapoto FM, Okahukura (Benneydale) # 99.6
63)	91.9		P	Solid Gold FM, Hawkes Bay
53)	91.9		P	The Rock, Kapiti Coast
104)	91.9		P	Blue Skies FM, Alexandra # 99.9
109)	92.0		P	More FM, Hamilton
142)	92.0		P	Q 92 FM, Queenstown
2)	92.0		N	National R., Milford Sound (Community owned)
2)	92.0		N	National R., Te Anau (Community owned)
91)	92.0	3	P	Fifeshire FM, Takaka # 93.0
96)	92.1	34.5	P	More FM Christchurch
144)	92.1		P	R. Weka, Waitangi, Chatham Islands
80)	92.2	1	P	Nga Iwi FM, Thames/Waikino
43)	92.2		P	XS-FM, Palmerston North
195)	92.2		P	Radio Wanaka, 92.2 FM, Wanaka
42)	92.3		G	R. Rhema, Greymouth
8)	92.3		P	The Heat, Timaru
59)	92.4	10	P	KCC FM Hobson # 1KCC 89.3
58)	92.4	1	P	Energy FM, Opunake (Taranaki)# 93.2
157)	92.4		P	Hokonui Gold, Forest Hills (Invercargill) # 94.8
42)	92.5		P	Life fm, Gisborne # 99.8
65)	92.5		P	Solid Gold FM, Tauranga
2)	92.5	40	C	Concert FM, Wellington
28)	92.5		Z	Classic Hits FM, Ashburton
2)	92.6	40	C	Concert FM Auckland
200)	92.6		P	The Mulcher FM, Hawera
2)	92.6		N	National Radio, Twizel (Community Owned)
2)	92.6	25	C	Concert FM Dunedin
42)	92.6		G	Life fm, Gore
67)	92.7		P	The Rock, Rotorua
145)	92.7		P	Maniapoto FM, Pio Pio # 99.6
63)	92.7	2.5	P	Hot 93FM Hastings
28)	92.7		S	R. Sport, Kapiti Coast
78)	92.7		P	Port FM, Otematata # 97.9
42)	92.7		G	R. Rhema, Alexandra
141)	92.9		P	Big River FM, Ruawai # 96.2
48)	92.9		P	Kiwi-FM/1XXX-FM, Te Puke # 90.5
64)	92.9	40	P	Sold Gold FM Christchurch
103)	93.0		P	The Rock 93FM, Hamilton
42)	93.0		G	R. Rhema, Opunake
43)	93.0		P	Manawatu's 'The Edge', Palmerston North
91)	93.0	3	P	Fifeshire FM, Nelson
11)	93.1		Z	93ZM-FM, Whangarei
28)	93.1		Z	Classic Hits FM, Hokitika # 91.1
58)	93.2	3	P	Energy FM, New Plymouth
78)	93.2		P	Port FM, Mt Studholme (Sth Canterbury)
28)	93.2		P	Radio Hauraki, Invercargill (Southland)
46)	93.3		P	R. Ngati Porou, Gisborne
90)	93.4	25	P	Coastline FM Tauranga
33)	93.4		P	Solid Gold FM, Auckland
40)	93.4		P	The Rock, Mount Cargill (Dunedin)
42)	93.5	1	G	R. Rhema, Rotorua
123)	93.5		P	Awa FM, Taumarunui # 100.0
148)	93.5		P	Central FM, Waipukurau (Hawkes Bay)
42)	93.5		G	Life fm, Hawkes Bay
116)	93.5		P	Kapiti's Beach FM, Paraparaumu
33)	93.5		P	Solid Gold FM, Alexandra (Central Otago)
178)	93.6		P	George FM, Queenstown # 96.8
59)	93.7		P	Magic 91.5 FM, Bay of Islands
64)	93.7		T	The Rock, Christchurch
78)	93.7		P	Port FM, Twizel # 97.9
146)	93.8		P	Channel Z, Auckland
103)	93.8		P	Solid Gold FM, Hamilton
43)	93.8	5	P	R. Pacific, Wharite (Palmerston North)
45)	93.8		P	Solid Gold FM, Wairarapa
33)	93.9		T	Radio Pacific, Greymouth

FM	MHz	kW	N	Name, location & h. of tr.
42)	93.9		G	Life fm, Timaru
59)	94.0		T	R. Pacific, Whangarei
58)	94.0		P	The Edge, Pukeiti (Taranaki)
2)	94.0		N	National Radio, Te Kuiti (Community owned)
176)	94.0		T	R. Pacific, Hedgehope (Invercargill)
138)	94.1		P	Coromandel FM, Matarangi
33)	94.1		P	The Edge, Gisborne
91)	94.1		P	Fifeshire FM, Murchison
128)	94.1		P	Son FM, Wairoa (Hawkes Bay) # 90.1
109)	94.2		P	The Edge, Auckland Sky Tower
65)	94.2		P	The Rock, Tauranga
28)	94.3		P	Radio Hauraki, Rotorua
124)	94.3		P	Kahungunu, Taradale, Napier # 765
66)	94.3		P	The Rock, Taupo
42)	94.3		G	R. Rhema, Te Anau
40)	94.3		P	Radio Central, Cromwell
114)	94.4	1	P	TeReo Irirangi o Te Hika o Te Ika, Kaitaia
193)	94.4		P	Ski FM, Whakapapa (ski season only)
33)	94.4		P	Solid Gold FM, Wanganui
74)	94.5		P	Sounds FM, Picton
64)	94.5	2.3	P	The Breeze (ex Lite FM),Christchurch
42)	94.6	80	G	Life fm, Waikato/Bay of Plenty # 99.8
91)	94.6		P	The Rock, Nelson
33)	94.6		P	Solid Gold FM, Wharite (Manawatu)
146)	94.7		P	Channel Z, Mt Fitzherbert, Hutt Valley # 91.7
42)	94.7		G	Life fm, Timaru # 99.8
33)	94.8		T	R. Pacific, Gisborne
59)	94.8		T	R. Pacific, Bay of Islands
157)	94.8		P	Hokonui Gold, High Peak, Gore
187)	94.8		P	4XX Kingston
156)	94.9		P	Atiawa Toa FM, Hutt Valley #96.9
42)	94.9		G	R. Rhema, Westport
165)	94.9	1	P	Fox FM, Ashburton # 98.9
69)	95.0	10	P	bFM, Auckland Sky Tower
16)	95.0		Z	Classic Hits 95 BOP FM, Tauranga
78)	95.0		P	Port FM, Fairlie # 97.9
94)	95.0		P	Tahu FM, Dunedin # 90.5
56)	95.1		P	Easy Listening I-95FM, Rotorua
98)	95.1		P	Tuwharetoa FM, Taumarunui # 97.2
63)	95.1		P	The Rock, Hawkes Bay
53)	95.1		P	Horowhenua's 95FM, Levin
59)	95.2		T	R. Pacific, Kaitaia (Northland)
40)	95.2		P	The Edge, Queenstown
2)	95.3		C	Concert FM, Whakatane
196)	95.4		P	Red FM, Auckland
43)	95.4		P	The Rock, Wharite (Manawatu)
135)	95.4		P	Fresh FM, Nelson # 99.4
2)	95.4		C	Concert FM, Wanaka
151)	95.5		P	Turanganui a Kiwa, Wharekopae (Gisborne)
2)	95.5		N	National R., Paparoa(Greymouth)
64)	95.5		P	The Edge, Timaru (Mount Horrible)
59)	95.6		T	R. Pacific, Kaikohe (Central Northland)
58)	95.6		P	The Rock 95.6FM, Taranaki
5)	95.6		M	96ZM-FM, Hedgehope (Invercargill)
42)	95.7		G	Life fm, Masterton
198)	95.7		P	The Generator!, Tawa, Wellington
165)	95.7		P	The Fox Gold, Ashburton
28)	95.7		Z	ZM-FM, Kurow
150)	95.8	2	P	Peak FM, Raetihi/Ohakune #99.4
197)	95.8		P	Real Good Life RGL-FM, Manukau # 936AM
28)	95.9		T	Newstalk ZB, Taupo
28)	95.9	3	Z	96ZM-FM, Hawkes Bay
33)	95.9		T	R. Pacific, Alexandra
2)	96.0		C	Concert FM, Kaitaia
28)	96.0		P	Classic Hits Radio Northland 96FM, Whangarei
28)	96.0		P	Hauraki FM, Hamilton
33)	96.0		T	Radio Pacific, Wanganui
40)	96.0		P	The Edge, Oamaru
28)	96.1		P	Flava FM, Auckland
65)	96.1		T	R. Pacific Tauranga
49)	96.1		P	Easy FM, Blenheim
61)	96.1		P	G-FM, The Switch, Christchurch Polytechnic
141)	96.2		P	Big River FM, Dargaville
138)	96.2	1	P	Coromandel FM, Thames
133)	96.2	1	P	Gisborne City 96FM, Gisborne
91)	96.2		T	R. Pacific, Nelson
84)	96.3		P	Tainui FM, Kawhia # 95.4
42)	96.3		G	Life fm, Palmerston North (Manawatu)
79)	96.3		P	The Rock, Wellington
20)	96.3		Z	Classic Hits Caroline 3ZC 99FM, Timaru # 98.7
64)	96.3		P	Radio Pacific, Otematata
121)	96.4		P	Radio Ngati Hine, Kaikohe #99.5
1)	96.4		P	WCR Waihi Community Radio (relays National Radio 9pm-9am)
58)	96.4		P	Energy FM, Oakura (Taranaki)

FM	MHz	kW	N	Name, location & h. of tr.
55)	96.4		A	Heritage Radio, Oamaru
120)	96.4		A	R. Southland, Forest Hills (Invercargill)
84)	96.5		P	Tainui FM, Pukekohe # 95.4
145)	96.5		P	Maniapoto FM, Te Awamutu/Waipa # 99.6
180)	96.5		P	Coast FM, Mount Rochcroft (Westport)
194)	96.6		P	Rodney Times FM, Orewa # 89.9
193)	96.6		P	Ski FM, Ohakune/Raetihi/Turoa (ski season only)
129)	96.6		P	Raglan Community R. Raglan
—)	96.6		P	MacKenzie FM, Twizel
40)	96.6		T	R. Pacific, Mount Cargill (Dunedin)
199)	96.7		P	Mai FM, Rotorua
148)	96.7		P	Central FM, Tourere (Hawkes Bay)
122)	96.7		P	Whitestone FM, Kurow # 100.0
142)	96.7		P	Q 92 FM, Alexandra/Cromwell
92)	96.8		P	Sunshine FM, Kaitaia
178)	96.8		P	George FM, Auckland
40)	96.8		P	Solid Gold FM, Omarama/Kurow
142)	96.8		P	Studio 96.8FM, Queenstown
159)	96.9		P	Sun 98FM, Te Reo Irirangi o Te Manuka
28)	96.9		Z	Classic Hits Marlborough, Blenheim # 1584AM
61)	96.9	3.5	A	Plains FM, Christchurch
28)	97.0	50	T	NewsTalk ZB, Hamilton # 1296AM
—)	97.0		P	Hot Country FM, Feilding
18)	97.0	1	Z	97 ZM-FM, Grampians (Nelson)
195)	97.0		P	Wanaka Rox, Wanaka
180)	97.1	3	P	Coast FM, Greymouth # 96.5
40)	97.1		P	Solid Gold FM, Timaru # 90.2
119)	97.2		P	Te Reo Irirangi o te Ika Whenua,Murupara
2)	97.2		C	Concert FM, Whakapunake, Gisborne
98)	97.2		P	Tuwharetoa FM, Mt Pihanga, Turangi
28)	97.2	1	P	Radio Hauraki, Taranaki
176)	97.2		P	The Edge, Hedgehope (Invercargill)
53)	97.3		P	The Edge, Kapiti Coast
28)	97.3		Z	Classic Hits Scenicland FM, Reefton # 1287
2)	97.3		P	National Radio, Omarama (Community owned)
28)	97.4	40	M	Classic Hits 97FM Auckland
62)	97.4		P	Blowhole FM, Tauranga
40)	97.4	1.2	P	4XO-FM, Mount Cargill (Dunedin) # 1206AM
86)	97.5		P	Classic Rock Beach FM, Whitianga
138)	97.5		P	Coromandel FM, Waihi
63)	97.5		T	R. Pacific, Napier
79)	97.5		P	The Edge, Wellington
79)	97.5		P	The Edge, Upper Hutt (synchronisation trial)
2)	97.5		C	Concert FM, Alexandra
77)	97.6	0.8	P	Kaitaia Country R., Kaitaia
91)	97.6		T	R. Pacific, Nelson
40)	97.6		P	Solid Gold FM, Queenstown
48)	97.7		P	Bayrock, Whakatane #99.3
6)	97.7	7.5	Z	Classic Hits 98FM, Christchurch
132)	97.8		P	Mai FM, Whangarei
103)	97.8		P	The Edge, Hamilton
14)	97.8		Z	Classic Hits 97.8 FM, Palmerston North
142)	97.8		P	Q92FM, Wanaka
33)	97.9		P	Solid Gold FM, Whangamata
78)	97.9		P	Port FM, Mount Horrible (Sth Canterbury)
176)	98.0		P	Solid Gold FM, Hedgehope (Invercargill)
46)	98.1		P	R. Ngati Porou, Ruatoria # 585AM
45)	98.1		T	R. Pacific, Masterton
28)	98.2		P	Easy Listening i98FM Auckland
2)	98.2		N	National R., Takaka/Golden Bay (Community owned)
96)	98.2		P	More FM, Mount Cargill (Dunedin)
10)	98.3		P	98ZM Rotorua
63)	98.3		P	Hawkes Bay's The Edge, Napier
107)	98.3		P	Radio Wai, Greymouth
2)	98.4		C	Concert FM, Hikurangi (Northland)
159)	98.4		P	Sun 98FM, Te Reo Irirangi o Te Manuka, Whakatane # 96.9
23)	98.4		P	Radio Waitaki, Oamaru
2)	98.4		C	Concert FM, Queenstown
146)	98.5		P	Channel Z, Porirua (Wellington) # 91.7
49)	98.5		P	Easy FM, Picton
118)	98.5		P	Radio Twizel, Twizel
28)	98.6	40	Z	Classic Hits ZH-FM, Hamilton
91)	98.6		P	Solid Gold FM, Nelson
103)	98.6		P	The Edge, Wanaka
42)	98.7		G	Life FM, Whangarei
28)	98.7		Z	Classic Hits Caroline 3ZC 99FM, South Canterbury
2)	98.8		C	Concert FM, Russell (Bay of Islands)
28)	98.8		P	ZM-FM, Mount Egmont (New Plymouth)
3)	98.8	5	Z	Classic Hits ZA-FM, Hedgehope (Invercargill)
28)	98.9		P	Radio Hauraki, Gisborne (Franchise)
28)	99.0	40	P	Hauraki 99FM, Auckland
28)	99.0		P	Easy Listening i99FM, Tauranga
51)	99.1		P	Jukebox Radio, Waipu, Northland
71)	99.1		P	The Pulse, Rotorua
42)	99.1	3.6	G	R. Rhema, Mt.Erin (Hawkes Bay)
152)	99.1	1.5	P	Heartbeat 99FM, Taumarunui
99)	99.1		P	R. Foxton 2XXP, Foxton
28)	99.1		S	Newstalk ZB, West Coast (Greymouth)
140)	99.1	1	P	Rush99 FM, Lawrence
2)	99.2	2.5	C	Concert FM, Masterton
42)	99.2		G	Life fm, Porirua FPl
40)	99.2		P	Resort R., Queenstown # 1359AM
103)	99.3		P	The Breeze 99.3FM, Hamilton
35)	99.3		P	The Qube, Te Puke
48)	99.3		P	Bayrock, Ohope (Whakatane)
2)	99.3		N	Concert FM, Blenheim
146)	99.3		P	Channel Z, Christchurch
150)	99.4	1	P	Peak FM, Taihape
148)	99.4		P	Central FM, Dannevirke (Hawkes Bay)
135)	99.4		P	Fresh FM, Nelson/Motueka/Takaka
40)	99.4		P	Radio Central, Wanaka # 1179
42)	99.5		G	Life fm, South Taranaki FPl
180)	99.5	3	P	Coast FM, Hokitika # 96.5
2)	99.5		C	Concert FM, Mount Studholme (Timaru)
80)	99.5	1	P	Nga Iwi FM, Paeroa # 92.2
42)	99.6		G	R. Rhema, Tokoroa
145)	99.6		P	Maniapoto FM, Te Kuiti
95)	99.6		P	More FM, Kapiti Coast
42)	99.6		G	R. Rhema, Tapanui, Southland
94)	99.6		P	Tahu FM, Invercargill
83)	99.7		Z	99.7 ZM-FM, Gisborne (Franchise)
28)	99.7		Z	96ZM, Wairoa, Hawkes Bay # 95.9
42)	99.8		G	Life fm, Auckland
65)	99.8		P	The Edge, Tauranga
67)	99.9		P	The Edge, Rotorua
28)	99.9		P	Classic Hits King Country Radio, Taumarunui
66)	99.9		P	Solid Gold FM, Taupo
28)	99.9		P	Radio Hauraki , Hawkes Bay
104)	99.9		P	Blue Skies FM, Cromwell # 91.9
59)	100.0		P	The Edge, Kaikohe/Bay of Islands # 91.5
103)	100.0		P	Radio Pacific, Hamilton # 954AM
123)	100.0		P	Awa 100 FM, Wanganui
95)	100.0	50	P	More FM, Wellington
122)	100.0		P	Whitestone Gold 100FM, Oamaru
40)	100.0		P	Resort R., Queenstown # 1359AM
42)	100.0		G	Life fm, Invercargill FPl
36)	100.3		A	Niu-FM, Whangarei
33)	100.6		p	RadioWorks unconfirmed format, Skytower, Auckland FPl.
36)	100.7		A	Niu-FM, Wellington # 103.7
36)	100.9		A	Niu-FM Christchurch # 104.1
2)	101.0	1	N	National Radio, Mount Te Aroha, Waikato/Bay of Plenty
2)	101.0	1	N	National Radio, Wharite, Manawatu
2)	101.0		N	National Radio, Grampians (Nelson) FPl.
2)	101.2		N	National Radio, New Plymouth (Taranaki)
2)	101.2		N	National Radio, Invercargill (Southland)
2)	101.3	1	N	National Radio, Mount Kau Kau, Wellington
2)	101.4		N	National Radio, Sky Tower, Auckland
2)	101.4		N	National Radio, Highcliff, Dunedin
2)	101.5		N	National Radio, Napier
2)	101.5		N	National Radio, Kapiti Coast
2)	101.7	1	N	National Radio, Sugarloaf, Christchurch
36)	103.4		A	Niu-FM, Waikato (Hamilton) # 103.8
36)	103.7		A	Niu-FM, Wellington # 100.7
36)	103.8		A	Niu-FM, Auckland
36)	103.8		A	Niu-FM, Dunedin
36)	104.1		A	Niu-FM, Christchurch # 100.9
36)	104.2		A	Niu-FM, Tokoroa
2)	104.3		N	National Radio, Parahaki, Whangarei FPl.
183)	104.6		A	Planet FM, Access Community Radio, Auckland
2)	104.7		N	National Radio, Acacia Bay, Taupo
9)	104.9		A	Coast Access FM, Levin/Kapiti
160)	105.4		P	Coast FM, Auckland
64)	106.5		P	The Breeze (ex Lite FM), Dunsandel # 94.5
2)	106.7		N	National Radio, Otematata (Community owned)
42)	106.7		G	Life fm, Nelson

Note: Excluded from this listing are 85 sts of less than 1kW and a growing number of local low-powered FM 'micro-broadcasters' in the'guardband' frequency ranges 88.0 to 88.7 and 106.7-107.8MHz. Please refer to Internet www.radiodx.com

Tourist Information FM
FM radio provides visitors travelling throughout New Zealand with information on the history and culture of an area, the availability of local services, accommodation and activities 24 hours a day. A blue road sign tells visitors they are in a broadcast area with transmissions in English on 88.2 FM, German language on 100.4 FM and Japanese on 100.8 FM. Address: P.O.Box 47-376, Auckland

Private Organisations & Station Addresses
INDEPENDENT BROADCASTERS ASSOC. INC.
P.O. Box 3762, Auckland ☎ +64 (9) 378 0788 🖷 +64 (9) 378 8180 **L.P:** Exec. Dir: Brent Impey. Secr: Janine Bliss.

THE RADIO NETWORK OF NEW ZEALAND (Privately-owned company)
54 Cook Street, Private Bag 92198, Auckland ☎ +64 (9) 373 0000 🖷 +64 (9) 367 4650
L.P: CEO: John McElhinney **Email:** johnm@ radionetwork.co.nz Networks: Radio Sport, ZM-FM, Newstalk ZB, Radio Hauraki, Easy Listening i , Jammin' Oldies.
N: Independent Radio & Sports (owned by TRN).
COMMUNITY RADIO NETWORK NEW ZEALAND (Subsidiary of The Radio Network of N.Z.)
P.O Box 952, Taupo ☎ +64 (7) 378 2600 🖷 +64 (7) 378 7295 G.M. Brian Jenning **Email:** brianj@crn.co.nz Network: Classic Hits
CANWEST RADIOWORKS (Privately-owned company)
Private Bag, Ponsonby, Auckland ☎ +64 (9) 375 7171 🖷 +64 (9) 376 0668 **L.P:** CEO. Dir: Brent Impey. COO: Sussan Turner. Networks: Radio Pacific, The Edge, The Rock, Solid Gold, Channel Z, More FM, The Breeze, plus 22 local stations.

Station addresses:
1) P.O. Box 136, Waihi. – **2)** P.O. Box 123, Wellington. – **3)** P.O. Box 802, Invercargill. **Email:** leep@radionetwork.co.nz – **4)** P.O. Box 241, Napier. **Email:** philips@radionetwork.co.nz – **5)** P.O. Box 888, Dunedin. **Email:** philh@radionetwork.co.nz – **6)** P.O. Box 1484, Christchurch. – **7)** P.O. Box 378, Greymouth. **Email:** radios@minidata.co.nz – **8)** 9 George Street Timaru – **9)** c/o 3 Horopito Place, Kapiti. – **10)** P.O. Box 1147, Rotorua. **Email:** lynm@radionetwork.co.nz – **11)** P.O. Box 845, Whangarei. **Email:** murraym@radionetwork.co.nz – **12)** P.O. Box 220, Masterton. **Email:** mark.roughton@xtra.co.nz – **13)** P.O. Box 465, Ashburton. Email: zefm@xtra.co.nz – **14)** P.O. Box 1045, Palmerston North. **Email:** megb@radionetwork.co.nz – **15)** P.O. Box 1040, Gisborne. **Email:** zgfm@xtra.co.nz – **16)** P.O. Box 642, Tauranga. **Email:** gregr@radionetwork.co.nz – **17)** P.O. Box 141, New Plymouth. **Email:** richardw@radionetwork.co.nz – **18)** P.O. Box 43, Nelson. – **19)** P.O. Box 489, Hamilton. **Email:** kevinw@radionetwork.co.nz – **20)** P.O. Box 275, Timaru. **Email:** gaz99fm@xtra.co.nz – **21)** P.O. Box 632, Wanganui. **Email:** richard-l@rivercityfm.co.nz – **22)** P.O. Box 740, Taupo. **Email:** nigeln@crn.co.nz – **23)** P.O. Box 426, Oamaru. **Email:** dan.lewis@radiowaitaki.com – **24)** P.O. Box 272, Tokoroa..**Email:** radioforestland@xtra.co.nz – **25)** P.O. Box 383, Taumarunui. **Email:** k.c.radio@xtra.co.nz – **26)** P.O. Box 225, Blenheim. **Email:** gapgolf@hotmail.co.nz – **27)** P.O. Box 300, Wellington. – **28)** The Radio Network, Private Bag 92-198, Auckland. – **29)** P. O. Box 116, Lake Tekapo – **30)** P.O. Box 276, Te Kuiti. **Email:** radioforestland@xtra.co.nz – **31)** P.O. Box 341, Hawera. – **32)** P.O. Box 1991, Wellington.. – **33)** P.O. Box 47-560, Ponsonby, Auckland. – **34)** 491 Pakuranga Rd, Howick, Auckland. **Email:** ericliu@am990.co.nz – **35)** State Insurance Building, Floor 2, Spring Street, Tauranga. SM: Kev Stanton. Operated by NZ School of Radio Limited – **36)** P.O. Box 99-582, Newmarket, Auckland – **37)** 11 Nikau St, Eden Tce, Auckland.. – **38)** P. O. Box 1206, Palmerston North. – **39)** Box 200-105, Papatoetoe Central, Auckland. **Email:** studio@radiosamoa.co.nz – **40)** Private Bag 1957, Dunedin. – **41)** 31 Calthorp Close, Mangere, Auckland **Email:** waatea@ihug.co.nz – **42)** Private Bag 92-636, Auckland. NB: There are regional ad streams. – **43)** P.O. Box 446, Palmerston North. – **44)** P.O. Box 11-441, Wellington. – **45)** P.O. Box 881, Masterton. – **46)** P.O. Box 226, Ruatoria **Email:** reception@radiongatiporou.co.nz – **47)** P.O. Box 1740, Invercargill. – **48)** P.O. Box 383, Whakatane. – **49)** Seymour Str, Blenheim. – **50)** Otago R. Assoc., P.O. Box 404, Dunedin. – **51)** South Road, RD2 Waipu 0254. – **52)** P.O. Box 597, Tauranga. Station is completely voluntary and operates under the auspices of the Tauranga District Museum as part of the Historic Village complex. – **53)** P.O. Box 132, Paraparaumu. – **55)** c/o 15 Weaver St, Oamaru – **56)** 1140 Fenton Str, Rotorua – **57)** NZ R. for the Print Disabled Inc, P.O. Box 360, Levin. Hours: Sun to Thurs 2000-1000, Fri 2000-Sat 0500, Sun 0130-0900, other times relays National Radio. Operated by volunteers. St. Mgr. Ash Bell. Chief Exec. Allen J. Little ZL2GB. **Email:** nzrpd@xtra.co.nz . Prgr. Supervisor/QSL Mgr: Brian Stokoe. V. by QSL-card. Rp or SAE req. FPI: stations in other main centres. – **58)** P.O. Box 869, New Plymouth. – **59)** P.O. Box 100, Whangarei. – **60)** Box 680, Hastings. – **61)** Canterbury Communications Trust, P.O. Box 22297, Christchurch. – **62)** P.O. Box 13341, Tauranga – **63)** P.O. Box 193, Hastings. – **64)** Private Bag 4750, Christchurch. – **65)** P.O. Box 13344, Tauranga. – **66)** P.O. Box 393, Taupo. – **67)** P.O. Box 92, Rotorua. – **68)** 590A Colombo Str, Christchurch. – **69)** Private Bag 92019, Auckland. – **70)** 128 Featherston Str, Wellington. – **71)** P.O. Box 883, Rotorua. – **72)** Private Bag, Palmerston North. – **74)** P.O. Box 930, Blenheim. – **75)** Otago Univ. Students Assoc., P.O. Box 1436, Dunedin. – **76)** Canterbury Univ. Students Assoc., Ilam Rd., Ilam, Christchurch. – **77)** P.O. Box 81, Kaitaia. – **78)** P.O. Box 635, Timaru. – **79)** P.O. Box 11-850, Wellington. – **80)** P.O. Box 135, Paeroa. – **81)** Hillcrest Rd, Hamilton. – **82)** 7 The Crescent, Waihi Beach. – **83)** P.O. Box 230, Gisborne. – **84)** P.O. Box 208, Ngaruawahia. – **85)** 605 Port Road, Whangamata. – **86)** Whitianga. – **87)** 114 Ronaldsay St, Palmerston **Email:** salmcc@xtra.co.nz. – **88)** 107 Great North Road, Auckland. – **89)** – P.O. Box 1007, Rotorua. – **90)** P.O. Box 2429, Tauranga. – **91)** P.O. Box 907, Nelson. – **92)** 61 Commerce Str, Kaitaia. – **93)** Main Road, Mangamuka Bridge, RD2 Okaihau – **94)** Box 13-469, Christchurch. – **95)** P.O. Box 27-000, Wellington. – **96)** P.O. Box 25-209, Christchurch. – **97)** P.O. Box 842, Tokoroa. – **98)** P.O. Box 198, Town Centre, Turangi. – **99)** 55 Main St., Foxton. – **100)** 12 Bell Street, New Plymouth. – **102)** Box 920. Wanganui. –**103)** P.O.Box 19-293, Hamilton. – **104)** 22 Centennial Ave, Cromwell. – **105)** Box 1434, Auckland. – **106)** Box 105, Napier. – **107)** 80A Mackay Str, Greymouth – **108)** 269 Bridal Path Rd., Christchurch. – **109)** P.O. Box 8880, Auckland. – **110)** P.O. Box 5609, Wellington. – **111)** c/o NZ Post, Kingston. – **112)** P.O. Box 382, Tauranga. – **113)** P.O. Box 2142, South Dunedin. – **114)** P.O. Box 458, Kaitaia. – **115)** Box 680. Hastings. – **116)** P.O. Box 1445, Paraparaumu Beach. – **117)** P.O. Box 354, Nelson. – **118)** Market Place, Twizel. – **119)** P.O. Box 98, Murupara. – **120)** Box 1, Invercargill. – **121)** P.O. Box 1127, Whangarei. – **122)** Box 12, Oamaru. – **123)** P.O. Box 430, Wanganui. – **124)** P.O. Box 7010, Taradale. – **125)** 7 Maryport Str, Lawrence. Some local otherwise relays ZB-FM, 89.4MHz. **Email:** GoldRush.Radio@xtra.co.nz . – **126)** 3 Charlemont St., Ranfurly. **Email:** diack@xtra.co.nz). – **127)** 1 Gordon Rd, Mosgiel. – **128)** P.O. Box 427, Wairoa. – **129)** 42 Norrie Str, Raglan. – **130)** P.O. Box 15-213, Hamilton. – **131)** Box 9540, Hamilton. – **132)** Unit 3, Level 1, Cnr Cameron Str & Quality Str, Whangarei – **133)** Box 230, Gisborne. – **134)** Box 1131, Taupo. – **135)** 1 Haven Road, Nelson – **136)** P.O. Box 92, Auckland. – **137)** P.O. Box 68-886, Newton, Auckland. – **138)** Box 962, Thames. – **139)** Box 9073, Wellington. – **140)** c/o Roy Gillions, 24 Ross Str, Lawrence. – **141)** Box 199, Dargaville. – **142)** The Station, Shotover Str, Queenstown. – **143)** P O Box 12743, Penrose, Auckland – **144)** Box 92, Waitangi, Chatham Islands. – **145)** P.O. Box 416, Te Kuiti. – **146)** P.O. Box 8822 Symonds St, Auckland. – **147)** 12 John Str, Balclutha. – **148)** Northumberland Str, Waipukurau. – **149)** Box 4232, New Plymouth – **150)** 20 Goldfinch Str, Ohakune. – **151)** P.O. Box 847, Gisborne. – **152)** P.O. Box 77, Taumarunui. – **153)** P.O. Box 241, Napier. GM: Philip Stephens. **Email**: – **154)** P.O. Box 9969, Wellington. – **155)** P.O. Box 16, Whitianga. – **156)** Box 36-111, Moera, Lower Hutt. – **157)** Box 292, Gore. – **158)** P.O. Box 4422, Palmerston North – **159)** P.O. Box 2090, Whakatane. – **160)** Private Bag 92198, Auckland – **162)** Box 68-100, Newton, Auckland. **Email:** tarana@titan.com – **163)** Box 8379, Christchurch. – **164)** P.O. Box 202, New Plymouth. – **165)** P.O. Box 521, Ashburton – **166)** Box 11-320, Ellerslie. Auckland – **169)** P.O. Box 68-393, Auckland. – **175)** Bowen House, 32 Bowen Str, Wellington. – **176)** P.O. Box 17400, Invercargill – **177)** c/o Market Place, Twizel. – **178)** P.O Box 331-216, Takapuna, Auckland. – **179)** 96 Queen Str, Masterton. – **180)** c/o West Coast News, P.O. Box 249, Westport. – **181)** 708 Port Road, Whangamata. – **182)** 79 Vogel Str, Woodville. – **183)** P.O. Box 5609, Wellesley Str, Auckland. – **184)** P.O. Box 5026, Rotorua. – **186)** 590A Colombo St, Christchurch. – **187)** c/o NZ Post, Kingston. – **188)** Box 300, Westpark Village, Auckland**. Email:** hibs@ihug.co.nz – **189)** Box 10-289, Auckland – **190)** P.O. Box 23, Claris, Great Barrier Island – **193)** Private Bag, Ohakune – **194)** P.O. Box 79, Orewa, Hibiscus Coast – **195)** P.O. Box 2, Wanaka – **196)** P.O. Box 100-430, NSMC Auckland – **197)** PO Box 12743, Penrose, Auckland – **198)** P. O Box 56-063 Tawa, Wellington – **199)** P. O Box 981, Rotorua – **200)** PO Box 151, Hawera.

NICARAGUA

L.T: UTC -6h — **Pop:** 6 million — **Radios:** 925,000 — **Pr.L:** Spanish — **E.C:** 60Hz, 120V — **ITU:** NCG

DIRECCION DE TELECOMUNICACIONES
Ap. 232, Managua ☎ +505 2 632171, 632181.

ASOCIACION NICARAGUENSE DE RADIODIFUSION (ANIR)
c/o R. Ya, Ap. 1787, Managua ☎ +505 2 785600.

CAMARA NICARAGUENSE DE RADIODIFUSION
c/o R. Corporación, Ap. 2442, Managua ☎ +505 2 443824.

MW: Call YN–, * = inactive, (r) = repeater, v = varying fq.

	Call	kHz	kW	Name and h. of tr.
1)	OW	540	25	R. Corporación, Managua 0900-0600
2)	CH	550	10	R. 19 de Julio "la 19", Chinandega: 1000-0200
60)		560	30	R. 5-60 "La Poderosa", Managua
50)		570	5	R. 5-70, Chinandega: 1030-0250
47)	EA	580	1	R. 5-80, Managua 1000-0400
3)	LD	600	10	La Nueva Ya, Managua: 1000-0600, SS 24h.

	Call	kHz	kW	Name and h. of tr.
4)	N	620	50	R. Nicaragua, Managua: 0955-0600
4)	LN	640	10	R. Ranchera "La Mera, Mera", Managua:1000-
5)	RI	650	12	R. Septentrión, Matagalpa: 1100-0100
6)	RD	650	10/8	R. Diriangén "La Super D", Granada: 0950-2300
52)	RC	670		R. Caribe, Puerto Cabezas
7)	AM	680	10/2	R. La Primerísima, Managua: 1000-0400
53)	RH	690	10/5	R. Hermanos, Matagalpa: 1000-0400
8)	MM	700	10	R. Managua, Managua: 1000-2400
9)	RC	720	10	R. Católica, Managua: 1100-0355
10)	NS	730	10	R. Segovia, Ocotal: 1100-0200
11)	RS	740	50	R. Sandino "La S Grande", Managua: 1025-0400
54)		*760	10	Ultravisión de Nicaragua, Managua
17)	AD	780	1	R. Deportes, Managua
51)		800	1	R. 800, Managua: 1000-0500
13)	OL	820	20	R. Ondas de Luz, Managua: 1000-0400
14)	RZ	v830	10	R. Zinica "Alegre Corazón Costeño", Bluefields
15)	NR	840	5	R. Noticias, Managua: 1030-0200
54)		*860	5	Ultravisión de Nicaragua, Managua
16)	CD	870	10	R. Centro, Juigalpa: 1000-0200
17)	AT	880	10	R. El Pensamiento, Managua: 1200-0600
18)	RT	900	5	R. Tiempo, Managua: 1050-0400
55)		910	5	R. Jinotega, Jinotega
19)	W	920	10	R. Mundial, Managua: 1100-0400
12)	CC	950	2.5	R. Rumbos de Rivas, Rivas: 1000-2400
56)		960	2.5	LV del Trópico Húmedo, San Carlos: 1000-0300
45)	VA	980	1	R. Redención Internacional, Managua: 1200-0400
20)	FF	1000	10	R. Mil, Managua: 1200-2400
21)	HG	1010	5	R. LV del Pinar, Ocotal: 1100-0400
22)	LL	1030	2	R. Masaya, Masaya
23)	VJ	1040	2	LV de Jinotega, Jinotega
24)	JJ	1060	1	R. Juvenil, Managua
25)		1060	1	LV del Atlántico, Bluefields
61)	LC	1080		R. 15 de Septiembre, Managua
57)	AI	1090	5	R. Alma Latina, Estelí: 1100-0400
26)	MT	1110	1	R. Momotombo, La Paz Centro
27)	CP	1120	5	R. CEPAD "El Arco Iris Del Amor", Managua: 1100-0100
29)	UW	1150	5	R. Darío, León: 1000-0300
30)	HM	1160	1	R. Satélite, Estelí
58)		1170	5	R. Máxima, Masaya
45)	VA	1220	1	R. América, Managua: 1200-0400
31)	MNG	1230	5	R. Manantial, Nueva Guinea: 1000-0300
59)		1240	1	R. Restauración, Managua
32)	CR	1250	2.5	Cadena Radial Samaritano, Condega: 1000-0400
33)	RA	1270	3	R. Amistad, Matagalpa
34)	R	1300	1	Canal 130 AM, Managua: 1200-2330
35)	SC	1310	10/1	R. San Cristóbal, Chinandega: 1000-0200
37)	GA	1330	5	R. Matagalpa, Matagalpa: 1100-0500
36)	OS	1340	1	R. Ondas Sonoras, Managua
46)	GF	1350	1	R. Ondas del Sur, Jinotepe
38)	RE	1370	1	R. Somoto, Somoto
62)	RG	1400	10	R. María, Managua
39)	RA	1410	3/1	La Estación de la Amistad, León: 1000-0200
40)	LE	1430	5	R. Liberación "La Tayacana", Estelí: 1100-0300
41)	RM	1440	25	R. Maranatha, Managua: 1000-0500
42)	RY	1470	1	R. Yarrince, Boaco
43)	PT	1500	1	R. Minuto, Managua
44)	RF	*1520	1	R. Flash, Managua
28)	RST	1530	0.5	LV de Sta Teresa, Sta Teresa: 1400-0200
45)	CN	1560	5	R. América, Managua: 1600-0200

SW:

	Call	kHz	kW	Name and h. of tr.
49)	PMK	5770	1	R. Miskut, Puerto Cabezas: 1200-2400

Addresses and other information:
1) Ap. 2442 (or: Ciudad Jardín, Casa Q-20), Managua.**Email:** rc540@ns.tmx.com.ni – **Web:** www.rc540.com.ni – **2)** Ap. 12 (or: Frente Iglesia Guadalupe), Chinandega. – **3)** Ap. 1787 (or: Frente a la Universidad Centroamericana), Managua. **Web:** www.nuevaya.com.ni – **4)** Ap. 4665 (or: Contiguo a TELCOR, Villa Fontana), Managua. **Web:** www.radionicaragua.com.ni – **5)** Frente a la Catedral, Matagalpa. – **6)** Piedra Bocona. ½ cuadra abajo, Granada. – **7)** Ap. 4003 (or: Bolonia, Teatro Cabrera 2, 2 cuadras abajo, 3 cuadras al sur), Managua. – **8)** Ap. 700 (or: Del Zumen, 1 cuadra abajo, 2 cuadras al sur), Managua. – **9)** Ap. 2183 (or: Altamira D'Este N° 621, Etapa III), Managua **Email:** catolica@ibw.com.ni – **10)** Detras de la Iglesia la Asunción, Ocotal. **Web:** - **FM:** 97.3. – **11)** Ap. 4776 (or: Paseo Tiscapa este, Contiguo al Restaurante Mirador), Managua.**Web:** www.lasandino.com.ni – **12)** Carr. a San Jorge, Rivas. ☎/🖷 +505 453 3202. **Email:** radiorumbos - **FM:** 105.7 – **13)** Ap. 607 (or: Barrio Largaespada), Managua. ☎+505 222 2250. **Email:** ondaluz@ibw.com.ni – **14)** Ap. 06 (or: Barrio Central), Bluefields. ☎+505 822 2771. **Email:** rzinica@ibw.com.ni – **15)** Ap. A-150 (Ciudad Jardín, Casa N-10), Managua. – **16)** Caracoles negros, Juigalpa. ☎/🖷 +505 812 2660. – **17)** Altamira N° 73, Managua. **Email:** 🖷 +505 278 1633. – **18)** Ap. 2776 (or: Col. Los Robles, Repto. Pancasán N° 217, Etapa VII), Managua. – **19)** Ap. 3170 (or: Repto. Loma Verde, Casa 5, Munich 4 cuadras Al Lago, 1 cuadra abajo), Managua. – **20)** Colonial Los Robles, IV Etapa, N° 70, Managua. – **21)** Parroquita Asunción, 1 cuadra al norte, Ocotal. - **FM:** 100.9. – **22)** Teatro Masaya 1½ cuadras al oeste N° 135, Masaya. – **23)** Cine Betty, 2½ cuadras al norte, Jinotega. – **24)** Col. Los Robles del gimnasio Atlas, 1 cuadra al sur, Managua. - **FM:** 101.5. – **25)** Frente al Palacio Municipal, Barrio Beholdeen, Bluefields. – **26)** Del Puerto del Mct, 1 cuadra abajo, ½ cuatra norte, León. – **27)** Ap. 3091 (or: Del Portón Cementerio General 1 cuadra al norte), Managua – (Owned and operated by CEPAD – Consejo Evangélicas Pro Alianza Denominacional) – **Web:** www.cepad.org.ni/radio_cepad.html – **28)** Entrada II Calle, ½ cuadra abajo, Sta Teresa. ☎ +505 412 3683. – **29)** Residencial Posada del Sol, Casa N° 93, León. – **30)** Esquina Sur-Oeste de la Escuela Nexo, 25 vrs al Río, Estelí. – **31)** TELCOR, 1½ cuadras este, Nueva Guinea. – **32)** Instituto Bíblico Samaria, Calle Principal, Condega. ☎/🖷 +505 752 2287. – **33)** Detrás de la Iglesia San José, Matagalpa. – **34)** Ap. E-2 (or: Carr. a Masaya km 12¾, 450 m al este), Managua. – **35)** Ap. 59 (or: Cine Nela 75 vrs norte), Chinandega. – **36)** Cine Blanco 5 cuadras al norte, ½ cuadra al este, Casa 1112, Managua. – **37)** Del Teatro Matagalpa, 40 vrs al este, Matagalpa. ☎ +505 612 3802. 🖷 +505 612 5182. – **38)** Madriz, Somoto. – **39)** Unan 1½ cuadra al norte, León. – **40)** Shell, 1 cuadra al norte, Estelí. – **41)** Ap. 2434 (or: Semáforo de Metrocentro, 1 cuadra al sur, ½ cuadra abajo, Casa 41), Managua. – **42)** Casa del Finquero, 20 vrs al este, Boaco. – **43)** Ap. 2442 (or: Cd. Jardín Q-31), Managua. – **44)** Cd. Jardín S-24, Managua. – **45)** Calle Edgar Lang, Managua. ☎+505 244 2068 🖷+505 277 1463. **Email:** maugepc8@cablenet.com.ni – **46)** BANIC, 2½ cuadras al oeste, Jinotepe. **Web:** – **47)** Col. del Periodista, Casa N° 128, Managua. – **48)** Ap. 88 (or: Suc. 14 de Septiembre), Managua. – **49)** Barrio Pancasan, Puerto Cabezas. ☎ +505 282 2323. - **FM:** 104.0. – **50)** Frente a la Iglesia de Guadalupe, Chinandega. – **51)** Plaza El Sol, 2 cuadras al sur, 5 cuadras al este N° 35, Managua. – **52)** Barrio 19 de Julio, Puerto Cabezas. – **53)** De Banexpo, ½ cuadra al este, Matagalpa. ☎ +505 612 2964.🖷 +505 612 2792. - **FM:** 92.3. – **54)** Iglesia El Carmen, 1 cuadra al norte, Managua. – **55)** Del Silais 75 vrs al este, Jinotega. – **56)** Costado Norte de la Iglesia Católica, San Carlos. ☎+505 283 0351. – **57)** Esquina Norte de Hospital Adb, 2 cuadras al norte, 3½ cuadras este, Estelí. – **58)** Carr. a Managua km 24½, Masaya. – **59)** Montoya 5 cuadras al lago, ½ cuadra abajo, Managua. – **60)** Shell Ciudad Jardin, 5 cuadras al lago, 20 varas arriba Edif. Radio 560 La Poderosa, Managua. ☎+505 240 0544. – **61)** Bello Horizonte, De La Rotonda, 5 cuadras al sur, 1 cuadra abajo, Managua. – **62)** Iglesia San Francisco, 1½ cuadra del este, Managua. ☎+505 268 9034. **Web:** www.radiomaria.org/nicaragua **Email:** info.nic@radiomaria.org

FM in Managua: 88.7 R.Nicaragua – 89.1 Exitos – 89.5 Canal 21 – 90.5 Ya – 91.7 Estéreo Amante – 92.1 Estación X – 92.7 La Bonita – 93.1 Estéreo Linda – 93.5 Eco – 93.9 La Tigre – 94.3 Ondas de Luz – 94.7 Mujer – 95.5 Horizonte – 95.9 Amor – 96.3 La Gran Cadena – 96.7 Flash – 97.1 Corporación – 98.3 Estéreo Variedades – 99.1 Stereo La Grande – 99.5 Universidad – 99.9 Pirata – 100.7 Omega – 101.1 Güegüense – 101.5 Juvenil – 102.3 Universidad – 103.1 Bautista – 103.5 Maranatha – 103.9 Titania Estéreo – 104.3 Estrella del Mar – 106.7 Minuto – 107.1 Sol – 107.5 Sandino – 107.9 Restauración.

NIGER

L.T: UTC +1h — **Pop:** 10 million — **Pr.L:** French (official), Hausa, Zarma, Tamashek, Fulfulde, Kanouri etc. — **E.C:** 50Hz, 220V — **ITU:** NGR

CONSEIL SUPÉRIEUR DE LA COMMUNICATION

✉ Plateau I, Niamey ☎ +227 722356 🖷 +227 722667

LA VOIX DU SAHEL – OFFICE DE RADIODIFFUSION DU NIGER (ORTN)

✉ Maison de la Radio, B.P. 309, Niamey ☎ +227 722272 🖷 +227 722548 **L.P:** DG: Adamou Mahamadou. Dir. R: A.Khamed. TD: Y.A.Tidjani. Dir. Admin: Y.Ibrahim. Editor-in-Chief: Adamou Oumarou.

MW	kHz	kW	MW	kHz	kW
Niamey	1125	20	Difa	1484	0.1
Tahoua	1215	0.1	Niamey	1575	1
Meninsoroua	1332	20			

SW: Niamey (G.C: 13N30 002E06) 9705v kHz 100kW (irr).
FM: Niamey 91.3/93.6MHz + 13 relay st's.
D.Prgr in French/Vernaculars: 0500-2300. **N. in French:** 0545, 1200, 1900. **N. in English:** 2000 (Sun).
ANN: "Ici la Voix du Sahel".

Other stations:
R. Anfani FM, B.P. 2096, Niamey - **FM:** Niamey/Zinder/Maradi/Diffa 100MHz 1.5kW. Also rel. DW & VOA. **Email:** anfani@intnet.ne – **Radio & Musique**, Immeuble Sonara II, B.P. 420, Niamey: 104.5MHz 1kW. Also rel. BBC African Sce in French/Hausa/English. – **R. Saraounia**, Quartier Grand Marché, B.P. 13707, Niamey: 102.1MHz. **Tambara FM**, Rue de Petit Marché, B.P. 13294, Niamey: 107MHz 0.5kW. – **Ténére FM**, Rue de Copro, B.P: 13600, Niamey: 98MHz 1kW. **Email:** tenerefm@intnet.ne – **La Voix de l'Hemicycle,** Assemblée Nationale, B.P. 12234, Niamey: 95.1MHz.
R. Rurale stations on FM in Agadez, Bankilaré, Diffa, Dosso, Gaya, Maradi, Niamey, Tahoua, Tillabéri, Zinder.
BBC African Sce: 100.4MHz.
RFI Afrique: Niamey/Maradi/Zinder 96.2MHz.
Africa No. 1: Niamey 103MHz (see main entry under Gabon).

NIGERIA

L.T: UTC +1h — **Pop**: 127 million — **Pr.L**: English, Yoruba, Hausa, Igbo — **E.C**: 50Hz, 230V — **ITU**: NIG

NATIONAL BROADCASTING COMMISSION (NBC)

Plot 897, Ibrahim Taiwo Rd, Asokoro District, P.O. Box 5747, Abuja ☎+234 9 3147521 🖷+234 9 3147522 **Web:** www.nbc-nig.org **Email:** infonbc@nbc-nig.org **L.P:** Chief Public Affairs Officer, Ahmed Abdulkadir.

MW	Location	kHz	kW	MW	Location	kHz	kW
19)	Akure	531	50	3)	Enugu	828	25
17)	Sokoto	540	50	21)	Azare	846	10
14)	Tukun Tawa	549	50	8)	Kafanchan	882	25
23)	Calabar	558	50	34)	Osu	891	-
4)	Alaho	567	50	18)	Abeokuta	900	25
13)	Owerri	567	50	2)	Fwagwa Lada	909	50
40)	Gusau	567	-	10)	Makurdi	918	50
4)	Moniya	576	25	20)	Ikeja	918	50
6)	Abakaliki	585	50	27)	Birnin Kebbi	945	10
5)	Jaji	594	100	25)	Katsina	972	25
9)	Maiduguri	603	50	35)	Otite	972	10
16)	Ilorin	612	50	20)	Ikeja	990	10
28)	Akwa	621	20	21)	Bauchi	990	50
22)	Port Harcourt	630	50	34)	Iree	1008	10
8)	Katabu	638	25	11)	Yola	1017	10
4)	Ibadan	657	100	33)	Dutse	1026	25
7)	Benin City	666	50	6)	Onitsha	1062	10
15)	Ojeowode	675	25	1)	Sogunle	1089	20
30)	Damaturu	684	50	5)	Jaji	1107	25
35)	Ochaja	693	10	7)	Hievbe	1125	-
31)	Wukari	702	25	23)	Ugaga	1134	10
13)	Owerri	720	50	12)	Bida	1143	10
14)	Jogana	729	25	18)	Abeokuta	1170	25
9)	Damagun	756	25	24)	Jos	1224	50
15)	Ibadan	756	100	31)	Jalingo	1269	10
12)	Minna	756	50	34)	Iwo	1359	10
31)	Wukari	774	10	8)	Zaria	1359	25
35)	Okene	783	50	35)	Egbe	1395	10
15)	Gambari	792	25	26)	Abak	1395	10
30)	Damaturu	801	20	11)	Gombe	1404	10
27)	Zuru	801	1	39)	Yola	1440	50

	SW	kHz	kW		SW	kHz	kW
1)	Lagos	3326	50	5)	Kaduna	6090	50
5)	Kaduna	4770	50	2)	Abuja	7275	100*
4)	Ibadan	6050	50				

*inactive

FM (MHz): **1)** 92.9/97.6 **2)** 93.5 **3)** 92.85 **4)** 93.7 **5)** 96.1 **6)** 96.1 **7)** 95.8 **8)** 90.8 **9)** 95.3 **10)** 95.0 **11)** 95.8 **12)** 91.2 **13)** 94.4 **14)** 89.3 **15)** 98.5 **16)** 99.0 **17)** 96.4 **18)** 91.4 **19)** 96.5 **20)** 107.5 **21)** 94.5 **22)** 99.1 **23)** 92.7 **24)** 90.5 **26)** 90.5 **28)** 88.5 **29)** 88.6/97.9 **31)** 90.6 **32)** 88.1 **34)** 89.5 **35)** 94.0 **36)** 97.1 **37)** 91.5 **38)** 97.3 **39)** 96.8 **41)** 98.1

FEDERAL RADIO CORPORATION OF NIGERIA (FRCN)

Herbert Macauley Way, Area 10, Garki, Abuja, Federal Capital Territory ☎ +234 9 2341103 🖷 +234 9 2346486
Web: www.nigeria.gov.ng/ministryinformation/frcn.htm
Email: frcnmkt@alpha.linkserve.com **LP:** DG: Eddie Iroh. Dir. Eng. Sces: Ibrahim Abdullahi. Dir. Prgr: Tolu Fatoyinbo.
1) FRCN Lagos, Broadcasting House, P.M.B. 12504, Ikoyi, Lagos, Lagos State. ☎+234 1 2690301-5. **L.P:** Exec. Dir: Prince Atilade Atoyebi. **R. Nigeria 1 (RN-1)** in English: 0425-2305 on 1089/3326kHz. **N**: On the h. NB: Nigerian N. from Lagos or Abuja at 0600, 1500 & 2100 is relayed by all FRCN stations and most state stations. **ANN:** "This is R. Nigeria, Lagos". **RN-2 Metro FM** in English: 0500-2300 on 97.6MHz 20kW. **N**: on the half h. **ANN:** "Metro FM 97.6". **R. Nigeria 3** in Pidgin/English/Yoruba/Hausa/ Igbo on 92.9MHz 20kW: 0430-2300. **ANN:** "The Sunshine Station".
2) FRCN Abuja, Broadcasting House, Gwangwalada, P.M.B. 71, Abuja, Federal Capital Territory ☎+234 9 8821040 **L.P:** Exec. Dir: Shuaibu Ibrahim. **D.Prgr:** 0430-2305 in English/Hausa/Igbo/Yoruba and others. Local **N.** in English 0500, 1700. **ANN:** "The Capital Radio, the Voice of Unity".
3) FRCN Enugu, Broadcasting House, Onitsha Rd, P.M.B. 1051, Enugu, Enugu State ☎ +234 42 254400 🖷+ 234 42 254173 **L.P:** Exec. Dir: Eddy Agwuegbo. 0430-2305 in English/Igbo/Tiv/Efik/Izon.
4) FRCN Ibadan, Broadcasting House, Oba Adebimpe Rd, P.M.B. 5003, Ibadan, Oyo State ☎ +234 2 2414093 🖷 + 234 2 2413930 **L.P:** Exec. Dir: Princess Banke Ademola. **D.Prgr:** 0430-2305 in English/Yoruba/Edo/Igala/Urhobo. **ANN:** "R. Nigeria Ibadan, Station with distinction".
5) FRCN Kaduna, No. 7 Yakubu Gowon Way, P.O.Box 250, Kaduna, Kaduna State ☎+234 62 235390 🖷 + 234 62 245392 **L.P:** Shehu A. Muhammad, Chief Tech. Officer. Ch. 1 in Hausa: 0430-2305 on 594/6090kHz. Ch. 2 in English/Hausa/Fulfulde/Kanuri/Nupe: 0430-2305 on 1107/4770kHz. **N.** on the h. English N. (both ch's): 1100, 1600, 1700. Ch. 3 in English: 0430-2305 on 96.1MHz. **ANN:** "This is R. Nigeria, Kaduna".

Further federal FM stations (MHz): Abakaliki 101.5, Abeokuta 94.5, Akure 102.5, Asaba 104.5, Awka 102.5, Bauchi 98.5, Benin 101.5, Benue, Makurdi 103.5, Birnin-Kebbi 103.5, Borno, Maiduguri 102.5, Calabar 99.5, Damaturu 104.5, Dutse 100.5, Ado-Ekiti 104.5, Gombe 103.5, Gusau 102.5, Kano 103.5, Kastina 104.5, Ilorin 103.3, Jalingo 100.5, Jos 101.5, Lafia 102.5, Lokoja 101.5, Minna 100.5, Osogbo 93.5, Owerri 100.5, Port-Harcourt 98.5, Sokoto 101.5, Umuahia103.5, Uyo 104, Yenogoa 101.5, Yola 101.5.

State radio stations:
6) Enugu State Broadc. Service (ESBS), Broadcasting House, Independence Layout, P.M.B. 01600, Enugu, Enugu State. MD: Charlie Nnaji - 0430-2300 in English/Igbo/Igala. N: on the h. Ann: "Second to None". Prgr. 2 on FM ("Sunrise 96"): 0500-2100 – **7)** Edo State Broadc. Sce, P.M.B. 1012, Aduwawa, Benin City, Edo State - GM: Rev. Tunde Ebosojie. 0400-2305 in English + 12 local languages. N: 0530, 0600, 1200, 1500, 2100. Ann: "The Star Station" – **8)** Kaduna State Media Corp, Wurno Close, P.M.B. 2013, Kaduna, Kaduna State - MD: Alhaji Zubairu Idris Abdur-Ra'uf. 0430-2315 in English/Hausa. Ann: "Capital Sound" – **9)** Borno Radio & TV Corp., P.M.B. 1020, Maiduguri, Borno State - GM: Alh. Usman Uma. 0400-2305 in English/Hausa/Kanuri/Marghi/Suwa/Babur-Bura. Ann: "People's Channel" – **10)** R. Benue, P.M.B. 102202, Makurdi, Benue State - GM: Maria Ode - Prgr. 1: 0430-2305 in English/Tiv/Idoma/Igede/others. Prgr. 2 on FM: 0500-2105. N: 0800, 1100, 1600. Ann: "This is R. Benue, Makurdi" – **11)** Adamawa Broadc. Corp. (ABC), P.M.B. 2123, Yola, Adamawa State - Prgr. Mgr: Michael Midallah. 0430-2300 in English/Hausa + 6 Nigerian languages. N: on the h + 0530, 1445. Ann: "This is GBC Yola, your No. 1 Radio Station". – **12)** Niger State Media Broad. Corp (Crystal R.), Radio House, Ibrahim Babangida St, P.M.B. 88, Minna, Niger State - GM: Alh. Ibrahim Abdulmalik. 0430-2330 in English/Hausa/Nupe/Gwari. Also rel. VOA. Ann: "The station you can depend" – **13)** Imo Broadc. Corp, Ebu Rd, P.O. Box 329, Owerri, Imo State - CEO: Azie Nzeribe. Prgr. 1: 0425-2305 on MW. Prgr. 2: 0440-2305 on FM. English: 0430-0630, 1100-1830, 2100-2300 (Sat/Sun 0100), other times Igbo. N. 0500, 0530, 1100, 1300, 1400, 1600, 1700, 2100, 2200, 2300. Rel. R. Nigeria: 0600, 1200, 1500. Other times in Igbo. Ann: "The clear voice east of Niger". – **14)** Kano State Broadc. Corp, Gidan Bello Dandago, P.M.B. 3014, Kano, Kano State - CEO: Alh. Halihu Ahmed Getso. Prgr. 1 on MW: 0430-2320. Prgr. 2: on FM: 0550-2320 in English/Hausa. Ann: "Radio Kano" – **15)** Broadc. Corp. of Oyo State, P.M.B. 1, Akodi Post Office, Ibadan, Oyo State - GM: Mrs. Subuola Oguntunde. Prgr. 1: 0400-2200 in English/Yoruba. Prgr 2: on FM: 0700-2100. Ann: "R. O-y-o" – **16)** Kwara State Broadc. Corp, Akpata Yakuba, P.M.B. 1345, Ilorin, Kwara State - GM: Alhaja Mairo Mustapha. 0400-2305 in English/Yoruba/Nupe/Batunu/Hausa. N. in English: 0530, 0700, 1200, 1400, 1500, 1700, 2000. Ann: "Heartbeat of the Midland" – **17)** Sokoto State Broadc. Corp, Moliba Adamawa Rd, Tudua Wada, P.M.B. 2156, Sokoto, Sokoto State - CEO: Sani Yahaya. 0430-2315 in English/Hausa. **N**: 1100, 1430, 1900. Ann: "Rima Radio" – **18)** Ogun State Broadc. Corp, Ibara Housing Estate, P.M.B. 2084, Abeokuta, Ogun State - CEO: Akin Majiyagbe. OGBC1 on MW, OGBC2 on FM: 0400-2400 in English/Yoruba. Ann: "Nation's Model Station" **19)** Undo State Radio Corp, Broadcasting House, Oba-Ile, P.M.B. 709, Akure, Ondo State - MD: Ade Ayeni. 0400-2300 in English/Igbo/Igala. Ann: "The Sunshine Station" – **20)** Lagos State Broadc. Corp, Obafemi Awolowo Way, P.M.B. 21035, Ikeja, Lagos State. CE: Lekan Ogunbanwo. 0430-0005 in English/Yoruba. Ann: "NBC" – **21)** Bauchi Radio Corp, Broadc. House, Ahmadu Bello Way, P.M.B. 0133, Bauchi, Bauchi State - MD: Alh. Sani Ahmed. Prgr 1: 0430-2300 on MW, Prgr. 2: 0500-1700 (F.Pl: 24h.) on FM in

English/Hausa/Fulfulde – **22)** Rivers State Broadc. Corp, 4 Degema St, P.M.B. 5170, Port Harcourt, Rivers State - GM: Mike Oku. Prgr. 1: 0450-2310 on MW, Prgr. 2: 0450-2310 on FM in English/Pidgin & local languages. Ann: "No. 1 in Africa" – **23)** Cross River State Broadc. Corp. (CRBC), No. 8 IBB Way, P.M.B. 1035, Calabar, Cross River State. CEO: Patrick Ogar. 0430-2315 in English/Efik/ Ejagham/Bekwara. N: on the h. Ann: "House on the Hill" – **24)** Plateau Radio & TV Corp. (PRTVC), 5 Joseph Gomwalk Rd, P.M.B. 2043, Jos, Plateau State - CEO: Joseph Ari. Ch. 1 on MW: 0500-2300, Ch. 2 on FM: 0500-2300 in English/Hausa & other local languages. Ann: "This is Radio Plateau 1 AM", "This is Radio Plateau 2, 90.5 FM Stereo" – **25)** Katsina State Radio & TV Sces (KSRTV), Former SDP State Headquarters, Batsari Rd, P.M.B. 2163, Katsina, Katsina State - MD: Musa Muhammad Kankara. 0430-2300 in English/Hausa/Fulfulde. N. in English: 0530, 0600, 1100, 1400, 1500, 1800, 2100. Ann: "This is Katsina State R." – **26)** Akwa Ibom Broadc. Corp, 205 Aka Rd, P.M.B. 1122, Uyo, Akwa Ibom State - CEO: Ini Usen. 0500-2300 in English/Pidgin & local languages – **27)** R. Kebbi, km 9 Kalgo Rd, Birnin Kebbi, Kebbi State - CEO: Ibrahim Bello Ribah. 0500-2300 in English/Hausa/Dakarchi/Zabarmanci – **28)** Anambra Broadc. Sce (ABS), off Arroma Junction, P.M.B. 5070, Awka, Anambra State - MD: Ikechukwu Abana. 0500-2300 in English/Igbo – **29)** Delta State Broadc. Sce, Broadc. House P.M.B. 5032, Asaba, Delta State - GM: Oritsejafor Idowu. 0500-2300 in English/local languages. Ann: "The Rainbow Station" – **30)** Yobe Broadc. Corp, km 6 Gujba Rd, P.M.B. 1044, Damaturu, Yobe State - GM: Alh. Muhammed A. Gaba. 0500-2300 in English/Hausa/Fulfulde/ Bole/Kanuri – **31)** Taraba State Broadc. Sces, Broadc. House, adjacent Gen. Sani Abacha State Secretariat, P.M.B. 1038, Jalingo, Taraba State - GM: Mal. Hussein Modibbo. 0500-2300 in English/Hausa/Fulfulde/ Jukun/Mumuye. Ann: "The Voice of Unity" – **32)** Broadc. Corp. of Abia State (BCAS), Broadc. House, Government Station Layout, B.M.P. 7276, Umuahia, Abia State - DG: Chuzi P. Iboko. 0500-2300 in English/Igbo. Ann: "The Station Born to Lead" – **33)** Jigawa Broadc. Corp, Broadc. House, Kiyawa Rd, P.M.B. 7032, Dutse, Jigawa State. Administrator: Alh. Adamu Abubakar. 0500-2205 – **34)** Osun State Broadc. Corp, Studio 1, Ita-Akogun St, P.M.B. 4425, Osogbo, Osun State - GM: Mr. Adegbayibi. 0500-2300 in English/Hausa/Fulfulde. Ann: "Station of the Living Spring" – **35)** Kogi State Broadc. Corp, 1 Danladi Zakari Rd, P.M.B. 1095 GRA, Lokoja, Kogi State - CEO: Alh. Abu Onaji. 0500-2300 in English/Igala/Ebira/Yoruba. Ann: "R. Kogi, Station for the People" – **36)** Nasawara Broadc. Sce (NBS), Tudun K. Nasarawa auri, Makurdi Rd, P.M.B. 97, Lafia, Nasarawa State - CEO: Alh. Dalhatu Abdullahi Bawa. 24h in English & local languages. Ann: "NBS-FM" – **37)** Broadc. Sce of Ekiti State, Old Ado Ekiti Local Government Secretariat, Okeyinmi, P.M.B. 5343, Ado, Ekiti State - GM: Olajide Olusola. Voice of Ekiti on MW, freq. not known. – **38)** Bayelsa State Broadc. Corp, P.M.B. 56, Ekeki, Yenagoa, Bayelsa State - DG: Comish Ekiye. "Glory FM" in English/Pidgin & local languages. – **39)** Gombe State Broadc. Sce, Buhari Estate Rd, GRA, Gombe, Gombe State - GM: Ibrahim Maikudi Tadu. 0500-2300 English/Hausa/Fulfulde – **40)** Zamfara State R, Mall. Yahaya Secretariat, Off Zaria Road, P.M.B. 01007, Gusau, Zamfara State - CEO: Mamman Maru – **41)** Ebonyi Broadcasting Service (EBBS), Ministry of Information Building, Government House Annex, Abakaliki, Ebonyi State.

Other stations:
Choice FM, 103.5MHz – **Cool FM**, PMB 10096, Victoria Island, Lagos: 96.9MHz. **Web:** www.coolfm.us **Email:** info@coolfm.nu – **Eko-FM**, Lagos: 89.75MHz. **Web:** ekofm.com – **Independent Radio**, Benin City: 92.3MHz. Also rel. VOA – **R. Jeremi,** No. 54, Effurun/Sapele Rd, Eco Bank Building (5th Floor), Effurun-Uvwie LGA, Warri: 95.1MHz. – **Minaj Radio**, Radiovision Plaza, Minaj Drive, Obosi: 88.5MHz. – **Daar Communications**, 1 AIT Road, Off Lagos-Abeokuta Expressway, Alagbado, Lagos. **Ray Power 1:** Lagos/Abuja 100.5MHz. **Ray Power 2:** Lagos/Kano 106.5MHz + relays in other towns (Incl. rel. of BBC African Sce in English/Hausa). – **Rhythm FM**, 17A Commercial Ave, Yaba, Lagos: 93.7MHz. – **Star FM**, MITV Plaza, Ikeja Central Business District, Obafemi Awolowo Way, Alausa, Ikeja, Lagos: 101.5MHz 10/40kW. **Web:** www.murhi-international.com/starfm.htm **Email:** mitv@murhi-international.com

EXTERNAL SERVICE: VOICE OF NIGERIA
see International Radio section.

NIUE

L.T: UTC -11h — **Pop:** 2,000 — **Radios:** 1,000 (est.) — **Pr.L:** Niuean, English — **E.C:** 50Hz, 230V — **ITU:** NIU

BROADCASTING CORPORATION OF NIUE (BCN)
✉ P.O. Box 68, Alofi, Niue Isl ☎ +683 4026 ℻ +683 4217 **Email:** sunshine@mail.gov.nu
L.P: Chmn: Hunukitama. GM: Shona Pitt. CE: Trevor Tiakia.
FM: 91.0MHz 0.5kW, 102.0MHz, 0.1kW.
D.Prgr: 1730-2000, 2230-0030, 0500-0830. **N:** on the h.
ANN: "This is Radio Sunshine". **V.** by letter.

NORFOLK ISLAND (Australian)

L.T: UTC +11½h — **Pop:** 2,000 — **Pr.L:** English, Pitcairn Norfolk — **E.C:** 50Hz, 220V — **ITU:** NFK

NORFOLK ISLAND BROADCASTING SCE. (Gov.)
✉ New Cascade Road, Norfolk Island 2899, Australia ☎ +6723 22137 ℻ +6723 23298 **Email:** 2niradio@ni.net.nf **Web:** http://vl2ni.nf **L.P:** Broadc. Mgr: Margaret Meadows.
MW: 1566kHz 0.1kW.
FM: 89.9/93.9/95.9MHz 0.25kW.
Local Svc: R. VL2NI - 1566kHz & 89.9MHz daytime. Overnight Rel: ABC Regional R. on 1566kHz, & Triple J on 89.9MHz. **Rel. ABC Regional R: 24h** on 95.9MHz. **Rel. ABC Fine Music:** 24h on 93.9MHz. **Rel. Red FM: 24h** on 88.9MHz.

NORTHERN MARIANA ISLANDS (U.S. Commonwealth)

L.T: UTC +10h — **Pop:** 75,000 — **Pr.L:** English, Chamorro, Carolinian, Filipino — **E.C:** 60Hz, 110V — **ITU:** MRA

INTER ISLAND COMMUNICATIONS INC. (Comm).
✉ P.O. Box 914, Saipan, CM 96950 ☎ +670 234 7239 ℻ +670 234 0447 **Web:** www.itecnmi.com/news **L.P:** GM: Hans W. Mickelson. PD: Ken Warnick. CE: Angel Ocampo. N. Dir: Ken Phillips
MW: Chalan Kiya: KCNM 1080kHz 10kW (country, local)
FM: KCNM-FM 101.1MHz 3.2kW (islands music) KZMI 103.9MHz 3.2kW (stereo).
D.Prgr: 24h. **N:** KCNM: AP Network N. on the h, **ANN:** "KCNM (or) KZMI, Your Music Station". **V.** by QSL-card & letter.

SORENSEN PACIFIC BROADCASTING INC. (Comm.)
PPP 415, Box 10-000, Saipan 96950 ☎ +670 235 7996 ℻ +670 235 7998 **Web:** www.radiopacific.com **Email:** cdancoe@sbpguam.com
L.P: SM: Curtis Dancoe
FM: KPXP 99.5MHz 6.5kW. KRSI 97.9Mhz 4.5kW
ANN: "Power 99" "The Rock", "Saipan's Roots, Rock and Reggae Station"
NORTHERN MARIANAS COLLEGE
✉ P O Box 1250, Saipan 96950
FM: KRNM Chalan Kanoa 88.1MHz 1.8kW
KWAW
✉ Boon Bldg., 1270 N. Marine Dr., Tamuning, Guam 96911
FM: Garapan 100.3MHz 2.5kW

EXTERNAL SERVICES: Christian Science Publishing Society
See International Broadcasting section

NORWAY

L.T: UTC +1h (27 Mar-30 Oct: UTC +2h) — **Pop:** 4.6 million — **Pr.L:** Norwegian — **EC:** 50Hz, 230V — **ITU:** NOR

POST OG TELETILSYNET
Norwegian Post and Telecommunications Authority
✉ Postboks 447-Sentrum, N-0104 Oslo ☎ +47 22824600 ℻ +47 22824640 **Web:** www.npt.no.

NORKRING (transmission provider)
✉ Telenor Broadcast, Snarøyveien 30, N-1331 Fornebu ☎ +47 67892000 ℻ +47 67893614 **Web:** www.norkring.no

NORSK RIKSKRINGKASTING AS
✉ N-0340 Oslo ☎ +47 23047000 ℻ +47 23047575. **Inf.Dpt:** +47 81565900 ℻Inf.Dpt: +47 75122777 **Email:** info@nrk.no **Web:** www.nrk.no
L.P: DG: John G Bernander.

LW/MW	kHz	kW	LW/MW	kHz	kW
Ingøy	153*	100	Røst	675*	20
Vigra	630*	100	Kvitsøy	1314	1200

*Carries regional prgrs in addition to Europakanalen.

FM	P1	P2	P3	Kanal24+	kW
Alta	89.7b	94.6Þ	91.3	101.0	3.5

FM	P1	P2	P3	Kanal24+	kW
Bagn	91.7h	95.3	88.0	102.1*	35/7*
Bangsberget	90.4h				4.1
Bergen	89.1d	94.8	99.0	102.5	46
Bjerkreim	94.2i	98.7	91.8	101.0*	60/6*
Bokn	93.5i	97.3	91.1	90.3	120
Bremanger	93.6j	98.1	91.3	103.4*	46/9.2*
Dikkevikfjell	87.8b	93.4Þ	95.0		1.4
Fauske		91.3			1
Førde	92.8j	88.7	97.1	102.0*	12/2.4*
Gamlemsveten	91.9e	96.3	90.0	102.8	50
Gausta	89.5m	96.4	99.7	103.1*	55/5.5*
	101.1a				6.7
Greipstad	88.8k	92.5	97.0	100.1	57.5
Grong	91.9g	96.6	88.9	102.0*	95/9.5*
Gulen	88.0j	94.5	97.6	101.4*	39/7.8*
Hadsel	92.4f	99.3	94.5	101.4*	30/6*
Halden	94.8p	89.1	101.5		72.5
	94.1o				75
Hammerfest	96.6b	87.7Þ	93.6	102.8*	24/4.2*
Hasvik	90.1b	99.0Þ	94.9		2
Hemnes	88.5f	99.8	96.1	104.2*	36/7.2*
Hestmannen	97.0f	90.7	93.5		1.2
Hovdefjell	87.8k	93.7	96.0	103.6*	25/5*
Hvitingen	91.7o				2.76
Iskuras	88.7b	96.1Þ	92.0		2.2
Jetta	95.9h	99.5	91.1	101.6*	85/8.5*
Kappfjell	95.5f	99.4	93.4		1.3
Karasjok	87.9b	94.7Þ			1.5
Kautokeino	90.3b	93.8Þ	99.2		35
Kistefjell	91.8n	95.7Þ	99.8	103.1*	44/4.4*
Kongsberg	91.3a	95.5	97.8*	102.5	60/30*
Kongsvinger	89.8c	93.9	96.1	107.2*	33/6.6*
	98.9q				11
Kopparen	88.3l	94.5	96.0	102.4*	40/8*
Lyngdal	97.6k	88.3	95.0	102.0*	50/10*
Lyngen	93.3n	97.5Þ			4.2
Lønahorgi	93.3d	88.3	96.7	100.6*	48/4.8*
Melhus	92.4l	97.2	99.1	101.1*	60/2.4*
Mosvik	90.9g	98.4	93.4		33
Narvik	88.8f	98.9Þ	91.1	101.1*	90/9*
Nordfjordeid	89.4j	99.3	92.3	101.2*	12/2.4
Nordhue	87.6c	97.1*	92.5	106.5	70/60*
Nordkapp	89.2b	95.4Þ	98.2	102.5*	15/3*
Oslo	88.7q	100.0	93.5	103.9	90
Reinsfjell	89.1e	95.1	90.7	103.9*	24/2.4*
Salten	93.3f	95.5	89.8	100.4*	48/9.8*
Skien	88.2m	92.3	100.4	105.2	80
	90.3o				7.25
Sogndal	91.5j	95.1	98.7	103.9*	25/2.4*
Steigen	90.3f	97.8Þ	93.9	102.1*	102/106/107/7*
Stord	96.0d	99.6	92.6	101.8*	60/6*
Store Jekkir	99.9b	97.3Þ	90.9	103.3	1.2/1.16/1.13/1.2
Tana	92.5b	97.0Þ	91.1		24
Trolltind	88.2n	94.0Þ	90.5	101.7*	50/5*
Tron	98.3c	88.6	94.3	102.5*	24/4.8*
Varanger	88.1b	91.8Þ	102.9	105.8*	30/6*
Vega	89.3f	95.2	98.2	102.8*	55/5.5*
Åndalsnes		99.9			2.2

+ more than 1800 low power tr's less than 1 kW +) Private comm. st. (see below) Þ) carries Sámi Radio a-q) refers to regional programmes listed below.

FM	AN	Stor	AK	MP3
Alta	90.8		93.4	96.3
Bangsberget	88.4		89.3	93.2
Bergen	93.8	97.1	98.2	95.4
Bodø	94.8		90.9	97.2
Bokn	95.6		90.0	92.2
Fredrikstad	90.7		95.7	87.6
Kristiansand	94.0		98.6	95.7
Oslo	93.0	90.5	91.9	97.0
Porsgrunn	95.8		97.4	90.8
Stavanger	93.0		99.3	96.6
Tromsø	89.8		94.4	96.8
Trondheim	94.9	97.9	96.3	92.7
Vadsø	90.7		88.8	92.2

Transmitter powers 40W-3kW, typically 50-200W.

P1: ✉ N-7005 Trondheim ☎ +47 73881400 🖷 +47 73881809. 24h on FM and DAB. **N:** MF on the h. also 0530, 0630, 0730, 1130, 1530, 1630. Sat on the h. also 0630, 1130. Sun on the h. Regional Prgrs: see below.

P2: ✉ N-0340 Oslo ☎ +47 23048649 🖷 +47 23047480. 24h cultural prgr. on FM and DAB. **N:** MF on the hour 0500-2300 except 1800, 1900 and 2000. Also 0530, 0630, 0730, 1130, 1530. Sat: on the h. 0500-2300 except 0900, 1200, 1800, 1900, 2000. Also 0630, 1130, 1530. Sun: on the h. 0500-2300 except 1200, 1300, 1600, 1800, 1900. Also 1530. Regional Prgr: Rly regional newsbulletins MF //P1 at 0640-0642.

P3: ✉ N-7005 Trondheim ☎ +47 73881600 🖷 +47 73881609. 24h youth prgr. on FM and DAB. Rly P1 2300-0500. **N:** MF on the h. 0500-1500, also 0530, 0630, 0730. Sat: on the h. except 1600, 1800, 2000, 2100, 2200. Sun: on the h. except 2200.

Sámi NRK Sámiradio (special programmes in Lappish): ✉ Postboks 183, N-9730 Karasjok ☎ +47 78469200 🖷 +47 78469223. D.Prgr: P1: Sun 2130-2200 (in Norwegian). P2: MF 1230-1300. Additional programmes on P2 in northern Norway (marked Þ in the frequencytable) plus 90.1 MHz (122W) in Oslo: MF 0600-0800, 1300-1630, (Fri also1200-1230, 1630-1700), Sat/sun 1700-1800.

AK: NRK Alltid Klassisk: ✉ N-0340 Oslo ☎ +47 23047882 🖷 +47 23048575. 24h FM and DAB. Classical music channel. Some rly P2.

AN: NRK Alltid Nyheter): ✉ N-0340 Oslo ☎ +47 23042612 🖷 +47 23045141. 24h rolling newsservice on FM and DAB. Rly BBC World Service most of the day Sat/Sun and 2100-0500 weekdays.

Stor: NRK Storting: ✉ N-0340 Oslo ☎ +47 23048444. Broadcast all meetings at the Norwegian parliament on FM and DAB. Rly P2.

MP3: NRK MPETRE: ✉ N-7005 Trondheim ☎ +47 73881600 🖷 +47 73881609. 24h teenager channel based on techno/dance music on FM and DAB. Some rly of P3.

EK: NRK Europakanalen: ✉ N-0340 Oslo: Broadcast on LW/MW a mixture of P1 (incl. some Østlandssendingen regional slots) and P2, plus exclusive weather forecasts MF 0445, 1103, 1350, 1650, 2105. Sat 0445, 1103, 1350, 2105. Sat 0603, 1350, 2105. Note that except 1314 kHz, the remaining net of LW/MW carries regional P1-programmes in addition to Europakanalen.

NRK REGIONAL SERVICES:

On P1. D.Prgr: MF 0503-0530, 0540-0600, 0603-0630, 0640-0650, 0654-0700, 0705-0718, 0725-0730, 0737-0800, 0803-0805, 0903-0905, 1003-1100, 1103-1130, 1203-1205, 1303-1305, 1403-1405, 1503-1530, 1533-1600, 1603-1630, 1703-1705. Sat: 0705-0707, 0803-0805, 0903-0905, 1003-1008, 1103-1108.

Also in // on P2 MF 0640-0642.

a) NRK Buskerud, Postboks 7030, N-3007 Drammen: 91.3/101.1MHz. – **b)** NRK Troms og Finnmark, Postboks 613, N-9811 Vadsø: **153kHz**, 87.9/88.1/88.7/89.2/89.790.1//90.3/92.5/96.6/99.9MHz. Shared prg with Troms and Nordland 1003-1130, and with Troms 1507-1630. – **c+h)** NRK Hedmark og Oppland, Postboks 273, N-2626 Lillehammer: 90.4/91.7/95.9MHz and Postboks 216, N-2402 Elverum: 87.6/89.8/98.3MHz. Separate news hourly, remaining programmes shared – **d)** NRK Hordaland, Postboks 7777, N-5020 Bergen: 89.1/93.3/ 96.0MHz. – **e)** NRK Møre og Romsdal, Postboks 1311 Sentrum, N-6001 Ålesund: **630kHz**, 89.1/91.9MHz. – **f)** NRK Nordland, Postboks 303, N-8001 Bodø: **675kHz**, 88.5/88.8/89.3/90.3/92.4/93.3/95.5/97.0MHz. Shared prg with Finnmark and Troms 1003-1130. – **g+l)** NRK Trøndelag, Postboks 2250, 7005 Trondheim: 88.3/92.4MHz and Postboks 2055, N-7707 Steinkjer: 90.9/91.9MHz. Some separate newsbulletins, remaining programmes shared– **i)** NRK Rogaland, Postboks 614 Madla, N-4090 Hafrsfjord: 93.5/94.2MHz. – **j)** NRK Sogn og Fjordane, Postboks 100, N-6801 Førde: 88.0/89.4/91.5/92.8/93.6MHz. – **k)** NRK Sørlandet, Postboks 2000-Posebyen, N-4668 Kristiansand: 87.8/88.8/97.6MHz.– **m)** NRK Telemark, Postboks 284, N-3901 Porsgrunn: 88.2/89.5MHz. – **n)** NRK Troms og Finnmark, Postboks 1153, N-9261 Tromsø: 88.2/91.8/93.3MHz. Shared prg with Finnmark and Nordland 1003-1130, and with Finnmark 1507-1630. – **o)** NRK Vestfold, Postboks 700, N-3101 Tønsberg: 90.3/91.7/94.1MHz. – **p)** NRK Østfold, Postboks 1138, N-1631 Gamle Fredrikstad: 94.8MHz. – **q)** NRK Østlandssendingen, Postboks 4555 Torshov, N-0404 Oslo: 88.7/98.9MHz.

V. Reception reports on long- and MW-trs must be on reg. transmissions to be verified.

ANN: 1st Prgr: "P1". 2nd Prgr: "P2". 3rd Prgr: "Petre". Lappish: "Datlae Sáméradio, Kárássjagás".

KANAL 24 (Comm.)

✉ P.O.Box 144, N-1601 Fredrikstad. ☎ +47 69707600 🖷 +47 69707601 **Web:** www.kanal24.no **L.P:** MD: Jan Erik Pedersen. **FM:** See frequency table above. D.Prgr: 24h **N:** M-F: on the h. 0500-2300, also 0630, 0730, 1430, 1530. Sat: on the h. 0800-1500. Sun: on the h. 1100-2000.

P4 – RADIO HELE NORGE (Comm.)

✉ Serviceboks, N-2626 Lillehammer ☎ +47 61248444 🖷 +47 61248445 **Web:** www.p4.no **L.P:** MD: Kalle Lisberg **FM:** Main frequencies MHz: Bjerkreim: 88.5 1 kW, Kistefjell: 89.4 4 kW, Steigen: 91.5 10 kW, Vega: 94.1 2 kW, Ski: 94.5 1 kW, Nordhue: 95.0 5 kW, Horta: 95.6 1.1 kW, Hammerfest: 96.8 7 kW, Hadsel: 97.3

5 kW, Førde: 98.4 4 kW, Hemnes: 98.6 5 kW, Sogndal: 99.9 5 kW, Varanger: 102.8 8 kW, Bokn: 102.8 120 kW, Mosvik: 103.8 33 kW, Greipstad: 104.9 38 kW, Tron: 105.8 6 kW, Halden: 106.1 72.5 kW. + 102 transmitters below 1 kW.
D.Prgr: 24h on FM and DAB. **N:** M-F: on the h. 0500-2300, also 0530, 0630, 0730, 1430, 1530, 1630. Sat-Sun: on the h. 0700-2300.

LOCAL FM STATIONS
Around 300 low power FM commercial st's are in operation, some sharing frequencies. Many of them organised through Lokalradioforbundet
Web: www.lokalradioforbundet.no.
RADIO 1 NORGE (Comm.),
✉ Postboks 4731 Nydalen, N-0421 Oslo ☎ +47 22023300 🖷 +47 22952202 **Web:** www.radio1.no
Network of stns. in Oslo, Bergen, Trondheim and Stavanger.
NRJ NORGE (Comm.),
✉ Trondheimsveien 184, N-0570 Oslo ☎ +47 22797500 🖷 +47 22797501 **Web:** www.nrj.no
Network of stns. in Oslo, Bergen, Trondheim, Stavanger and Romerike.
Jærradioen (Comm.),
✉ Postboks 10, N-4301 Sandnes ☎ +47 51979200 🖷 +47 51979256 **Web:** www.jaerradioen.no
Major shareholder in 6 stations around the country with networked programmes.

AFRTS (U.S. Mil.)
FM: Lifjell 101.5MHz (Stavanger). D.Prgr: 24h rly AFN Europe.

Satellite: Most NRK-channels, radio and TV (incl some regional) Kanal 24 and P4 are available through satellite.
Internet: Most stations provide webstreams and/or on-demand audio services.
DAB: One DAB-multiplex (12D) covering parts of Norway. Includes all NRK-channels, P4 and Radio 5 (a DAB-only commercial channel). Regional DAB-multiplex (12C) for southeastern Norway. Includes NRK Østfold, Østlandssendinga, Buskerud, Vestfold, Telemark and NRK Stortinget.

SVALBARD (SPITSBERGEN) (Norwegian Territory)
L.T: UTC +1h — **Pr.L:** Norwegian — **E.C:** a/c 50, 230V.

FM	P1	P2	P3	K24	P4	ERP
Hjorthamnfjell					103.0	63W
Isfjord Radio	89.7	93.6	97.3			50W
Longyearbyen	88.8	94.5	98.3	104.0*		45W/13W*
Ny-Ålesund	91.3	94.8				120W
Svea	89.1	92.0				25W

MW:
Longyearbyen (G.C: 25.24E/78.14N): 1485kHz 1kW. (P1)
D.Prgr: 24 h. Rly NRK Europakanalen (incl. regional prgrs NRK Troms).

OMAN

L.T: UTC +4h — **Pop:** 2.6 million — **Pr.L:** Arabic — **E.C:** 50Hz, 240V — **ITU:** OMA

MINISTRY OF INFORMATION
Web: www.omanet.om **Email:** omanet@omantel.net.om

RADIO SULTANATE OF OMAN
✉ Ministry of Information, P.O. Box 600, 113 Muscat. ☎ +968 603888 🖷 +968 604629. **Web:** www.oman-radio.gov.om **Email:** feedback_rd@oman-radio.gov.om
L.P: DG: Ibrahim Al Yahmadi. DG Eng.: Mohd Salim Al Marhouby. Dir. R. Studios: M A Alghassani. Dir. Frq.: Salim Al-Nomani. Dir. Trs: Abdullah Saif Al-Nabhani.

MW	kHz	kW	MW	kHz	kW
Haima	576	100	Seeb	1242v	200
Salahah	738	100			

FM:

Station	MHz	Station	MHz	Station	MHz
Sumail	87.8	Al-Ghashb	88.5	Qurum	89.0
Al-Hajer	87.8	Sh'm	88.6	Sicq	89.2
Ja'alan Bani	88.1	Al-Rustaq	88.7	Al-Awabi	89.3
Al-Ghubrah	88.2	Fanja	88.7	Hatta Mts	89.3
Riyam	88.5	Al-Saaidi	89.0	Quriyat	89.5
Nizwa Main	88.5	Heibi	89.0	Al-Ansab	89.5

Station	MHz	Station	MHz	Station	MHz
Butain	89.8	Al-Shurah	93.2	Al-Aabla	97.8
Al-Hamra	89.9	Ibra	93.2	Al-Taher	99.1
Ruwi Murtafat	90.4	Tiwi	93.5	Ibri	99.1
Salalah	90.4	Bi Thaat	93.8	Tibat	99.2
Wad	90.5	Kumzar	94.0	Mazraa al-Hadri	99.4
Samad	90.7	Al-Ain	94.1	City	100.5
Yamit	90.8	Mazrah	94.1	Al-Qalaat	100.5
Tawi al-nawa	90.9	M'zara	94.2	Wadi Dimah	100.6
Tanuf	91.2	Bidbid	94.4	Lima	100.6
Dhank	91.2	Sabt	94.4	Amirat	101.2
Wadi Dima	91.3	Sital	94.5	Hulm	101.2
Thumrait	91.3	Sultan Qaboos	94.6	Shinas	101.5
Badaa	91.5	Wadi Bani Omar	94.7	Maqal	101.7
Hawraa Mts	91.5	Mazbar	95.3	Qantab	101.8
Khasab	91.5	Wadi Sahtan	95.3	Al-Jinah	102.2
Barkah	91.7	Al-Hujirat	95.8	Khur al-Juramah	103.3
Al-Badiaah	92.0	Saifah	96.1	Qadi	103.4
Maskan	92.0	Yakka	96.1	Saham Main	103.7
Wadi Rajmaa	92.0	Yanqul	96.4	Daba	103.8
Qumiraa	92.2	Harat Mts	96.5	Al-Jafnen	103.9
Tahwat	92.3	Al-Waqba	96.7	Al-Wasat	104.0
Al-Khafdi	92.5	Qahwi Mts	97.0	Rawtha Lima	104.0
Al-Qhudhift	92.5	Al-Buraimi	97.1	Al-Bustan	104.2
Wadi Mahram	92.6	Sur	97.2	Al-Filaj	105.7
Barkha	92.8	Madha	97.4	Thouyan	107.2
Al-Gafat	93.0	Ajran	97.5	Bahla	107.3
Siyyah	93.1	Sidab	97.8	Fl'm	107.4
Al Fi	93.1				

Arabic: 24 hrs on MW & FM. **N:** 0300, 0700 (Fri 0830), 1300, 1600, 1700, 1900, 2000. **English:** 0300-1800 on Muscat/Salalah 90.4MHz, Thumrait 91.3MHz. **Al-Shabab channel** on: Muscat/Salalah/ Thamrat/Taqa/Murbat/Sadah 100MHz, Al-Batina region 91.7/101.5/ 103.6MHz, A'Dakhlia region/Al-Wusta/Al A'Sharqia 98.8MHz, Dhank 91.2MHz, Dhalkot/Rakhuot 94.5MHz.
ANN: A: "Idha'atul Saltanat al-Oman min Muscat." E: "This is the English Service of Radio Sultanate of Oman from Muscat".

Other stations:
BBC World Sce in English: Salalah 93.5MHz.
F.PI: licensing of private broadcasting stations

EXTERNAL SERVICES:
Radio Sultanate of Oman (shortwave broadcasts)
BBC Eastern Relay Station
see International Broadcasting section

PAKISTAN

L.T: UTC +5h — **Pop:** 144 million — **Pr.L:** Urdu, Punjabi, Sindhi, Pushto, Balochi, English — **E.C:** 50Hz, 230V — **ITU:** PAK

PAKISTAN ELECTRONIC MEDIA REGULATORY AUTHORITY (PEMRA)
✉ Green Trust Tower, 6th Floor F-6, Jinnah Ave, Blue Area, Islamabad **Web**: www.pemra.gov.pk
L.P: Chairman: Mian Muhammad Javed.
PEMRA is responsible for licensing stations.

PAKISTAN BROADCASTING CORP. (PBC) (Gov.) RADIO PAKISTAN
✉ Broadcasting House, Constitution Avenue, Islamabad 44000 ☎ +92 519214278 🖷 +92 519223827 **Web**: www.radio.gov.pk
L.P: DG: Tarique Imam. Dir. News: Raza ur Rehman Jaffri. Dir. Prgrs: Faqir Hussain Sahir. Dir. Eng: Zulfiqar Ahmad. Head of Training & Overseas Liaison (CBA Liaison): Mujtaba Aamer.

MW	kHz	kW	R	H. of tr.
Peshawar	540	300	N	0045-0405, 0600-1805
Khuzdar	567	300	B	1155-1808, CA1
Islamabad	585	1000	F	0045-0605, 0800-1900
Karachi-II (Landhi)	612	10	S	0215-0700, 0900-1645
Lahore-I	630	100	F	0045-0405 (Fri 0820), 0800 (Fri 1000)-1900
Karachi (Landhi)	639	100	S	CA
Peshawar II	729	100	N	1230-1705
Quetta-I (Pishin)	756	150	B	0045-0805, 1000-1810
Karachi-I	828	100	S	0045-0405, 0600-1900
Quetta-II	855	10	B	0200-0400, 0600-1810, CA
Khairpur	927	100	S	0045-0605, 1000-1808

MW	kHz	kW	R	H. of tr.
Hyderabad-I	1008	120	S	0045-0405, 0600-1808
Multan	1035	120	P	0045-0405, 0600-1808
Lahore-II	1080	50	P	1230-1705, CA
Hyderabad-II	1098	50	S	1230-1705, CA
Rawalpindi	1152	100	P	0045-0405, 0600-1808
Loralai	1251	10	B	1145-1615, CA1
Larkana	1305	10	S	F.Pl.
Bahawalpur	1341	10	P	0850-1808, CA1
Dera Ismail Khan	1404	10	N	0855-1600, CA1
Zhob	1449	10	B	1155-1600, CA1
Faisalabad	1476	10	P	0045-0820
Gilgit	1512	10	N	1000-1700
Skardu	1557	10	N	1000-1700
Turbat	1584	0.25	B	1300-1810, CA1
Sibi	1584	0.25	B	0755-1108
Chitral	1584	0.25	N	1050-1515
Abbottabad	1602	0.25	N	0845-1415

SW: Islamabad (Rawat, G.G: 33N27 073E12).

Location	kHz	kW	Times
Islamabad	4955	100	1350-1400, 1420-1428 (BS)
Islamabad	4955	100	1615-1700 Aaina prgr.
Quetta	5027v	10	0044-0405 (Fri 0345), 1200-1810
Islamabad	5050	100	0045-0215 Haya Allal Falah prgr.
Islamabad	5080	100	1300-1800 (CA)
Islamabad	6225	100	0200-0400 (CA)
Islamabad	7105	100	1230-1330 Kashmiri sce.
Quetta	7155	10	0600-1145 (Fri. 0400-0820, 1000-1145)
Islamabad	7225	100	0430-0515, 0530-0615 (BS)
Peshawar	7320	10	1100-1400 Chitrali sce.
Islamabad	9340	100	0600-0900 (R), 0900-1115 (Islamabad)

(BS): Balti & Sheena Sce's. (CA): News & Current Affairs prgr. (R): 0707-0800 & 0807-0900 Rawalpindi prgr. Freq's are subject to seasonal variations.

FM	MHz	kW	R	H. of tr.
Rawalpindi	98	2	L	
Larkana	101	1	S	0350-1904, CA
Rawalpindi	102	–	P	0300-1030
Islamabad	104	–	F	1245-1730

R=Region: N=No. We. Frontier Province & Northern tribal areas, F=Federal District of Islamabad, P=Punjab, S=Sindh, B=Balochistan.
D.Prgr: as above in Urdu, English and regional languages. The local st' have local prgr's at various times, otherwise rel. Islamabad. Local IDs are usually heard at sign on/off. **N. in English** (National): 0300, 0500, 0800, 1100, 1300, 1600. **CA:** News & Current Affairs prgr from Islamabad: 0200-0400, 1300-1800 in Urdu & English. CA1 st's only take the 0200-0400 slot.
F.Pl: MW: Turbat to 100kW. Abbottabad to 10kW. 100kW at Peshawar, Lahore and Quetta. St's in Gwadar, Umerkot. SW: 1x100kW to be added at Rawat. FM: Mirpur.

FM101: ✉ Broadcasting House, 303 Peshawar Road, Rawalpindi. Operating 24h on 101MHz from Faisalabad, Hyderabad, Islamabad, Karachi, Lahore, Peshawar, Quetta and Sialkot (all 2kW exc. Karachi 5kW). Information and entertainment channel. Also rebrodcasts R. Aap ki Dunya from V. of America (see USA) mornings and evenings.

EXTERNAL SERVICES: Radio Pakistan
See International Broadcasting section.

AZAD KASHMIR RADIO (AKR) (Gov.)

✉ Broadcasting House, Muzaffarabad (AJK) 13100, via Pakistan.
L.P: Dep. Controller (Eng): Syed Ahmed.
Stations: Muzaffarabad 792kHz 150kW. Mirpur 936kHz 100kW. Rawalpindi (G.C: 73.03E/33.37N) 4790kHz 10kW. Islamabad (Rawat) 4790/7145/7265kHz 100kW.
D.Prgr: Muzaffarabad channel: 0045-0445 & 1000-1808 on 792kHz. Rawalpindi-III channel: 4790kHz 100kW: 0040-0215 & 1445-1810, 10kW: 0230-0430, 1230-1330, 1345-1430. 7265kHz 100kW: 0900-1215. Prgr's of both channels also contain R. Pakistan relays.
ANN: 792kHz: "Yeh Azad Kashmir Radio Muzaffarabad Hay". Other freqs: "Yeh Azad Kashmir Radio Trarkhal Hay".**IS:** Azad Kashmir anthem at open and close.

OTHER STATIONS:
Apna Karachi: Karachi 107MHz – **Awaz 105:** Gujrat 105MHz– **Campus Radio**: Islamabad 90.6MHz, Lahore 104.6, Peshawar 107MHz – **Capital FM:** Islamabad 100MHz – **City FM:** Islamabad, Lahore, Karachi, Faisalabad 89MHz – **FM-100:** Karachi 100MHz – **Lakki FM:** Lakki Marwat 88MHz – **PK100:** Lahore 100.0MHz – **PKLIVE:** Lahore 101.3MHz – **Power FM:** Islamabad 99MHz – **Radioactive96:** Karachi 96MHz – **Radio Buraq:** Peshawar, Sialkot, Mardan 104MHz – **Sachal FM:** Karachi, Lahore, Faisalabad, Multan 103MHz, Hyderabad 105MHz – **Soundwave:** Nooriabad 91MHz – **Sunrise FM**: Hasanabdal 97MHz.
Under construction: Islamabad 106.2MHz, Karachi 106.2MHz, Lahore 106.2MHz, Gujranwala 105MHz, Bahawalpur 102.2, Tando Adam 92MHz, Khairpur 93MHz, Ubaro 94MHz, Hub Chowki 91MHz, Muridkee 91MHz, Gawadar 91MHz, Sukkur 106.2MHz, Vehari 99MHz, Abbotabad 99MHz, Sheikhupura 105MHz. – A large increase in the number of FM stations is under way

PALAU

L.T: UTC +9h — **Pop:** 19,000 — **Pr.L:** Palauan, English — **E.C:** 60Hz, 115/230V — **ITU:** PLW

T8AA BROADCASTING STATION

✉ Box 279, Koror State, Republic of Palau 96940 ☎ +680 488 2417 🖷 +680 488 1932. **L.P:** SM: Salustiano Albert.
MW: T8AA Malakal Island 1584kHz 5kW.
D.Prgr: 0300-1500 (SS -1400). Occ. relays R Australia **N:** on the h.
ANN: "Voice of Palau".

BBC World Service: FM: Bamako 88.9MHz

WWFM

✉ PNCC P O Box 99, Koror 96940 ☎+680 488 1424 🖷 +688 587 1888 **Web:** http://www.brouhaha.net/palau/wwfm.html **Email:** wwfm@palaunet.com
FM: Koror 89.5MHz

INTERNATIONAL SERVICES: T8BZ (Rlg.)

See International Broadcasting section.

PANAMA

L.T: UTC -5h — **Pop:** 3.1 million — **Pr.L:** Spanish — **E.C:** 60Hz, 110V — **ITU:** PNR

DIRECCION NACIONAL DE MEDIOS DE COMUNICACION SOCIAL

✉ Ap. 1628, Panamá 1 ☎ + 507 227300.

ASOCIACION PANAMEÑA DE RADIODIFUSIÓN

✉ Ap. 55-1326, Panamá

MW: Call HO–, * = inactive, (r) = repeater, v = varying fq.

	Call	kHz	kW	Name and h. of tr.
PA01)	U23	540	10	R. Mía, David (r: 650) 24h
PA02)	PU	540	10	R. 540 AM, Panamá: 1000-0400
PA03)	H2	560	1	RPC Radio, Colón (r: 610)
PA04)	S	570	5	R. Soberana, Panamá 1000-0300
PA03)	H4	580	10	RPC Radio, David (r: 610)
PA03)	H3	590	10	RPC Radio, Chitré (r: 610)
PA03)	HM	610	10	RPC Radio, Panamá: 24h
HE01)	J35	630	1	R. Provincias, Chitré
PA05)		630	1	R. Capital, Panamá
CN01)	K22	640	2.5	R.CPR, Colón
PA14)		640	2.5	Caracol, La Palma
PA01)	S22	650	5	R. Mía "Cadena Nacional", Panamá: 24h
PA03)	F33	660	1	RPC Radio, Bocas del Toro (r: 610) 24h
PA09)		660	5	La Nueva Exitosa, Sabana Grande (r: 930) 24h
PA06)	LY	670	5	R. Hogar, Panamá: 0955-0300
DA01)		680	5	Voz Sin Fronteras, Metetí: 1000-2400
CH02)	F32	680	5	Súper Z Stereo, David
VE01)	R43	690	10	R. Veraguas, Santiago: 1000-0300
PA18)		690	5	R. Evangelio Vivo, Panamá
PA08)	Q51	710	10	KW Continente, Panamá: 24h
BT01)	B52	710	5	Ondas del Caribe, Bocas del Toro: 1000-0400
HE04)	B50	720	10	R. República, Chitré: 1100-0300
CH03)	N26	740	5	R. Cristal, David
PA37)	R44	740	2.6	La Exitosa de Chorrera, La Chorrera: 24h
HE07)		750	5	R. Inolvidable, Chitré: 1000-2300
PA10)	XO	760	5	LV del Istmo, Panamá: 1145-0300
HE05)	L83	*770	10	R. Nacional Herrera, Chitré: 1100-0100
CH04)	B55	780	10	R. Chiriquí, David: 1100-2300
PA14)		790	6	Caracol, Santiago
CE02)		800	3	Tropical 800, Las Tablas
PA11)	G	810	1	R. 10, Panamá
CH05)	F28	820	3	R. Ritmo Chiriquí, David: 1100-0400
LS01)	R56	830	5	R. Península, Macaracas

	Call	kHz	kW	Name and h. of tr
PA12)	L80	840	10	R. Nacional, Panamá: 24h
PA09)	T61	850	5	La Exitosa de Chiriquí, David (r: 930) 24h
PA09)		*850	1	La Exitosa de Colón, Colón
HE03)	L55	860	10	R. Reforma, Chitré 1030-0400
PA13)	HO	v870	5.5	R. Libre, Panamá: 24h
CN02)	B51	880	1	R. Visión Panamá, Colón
PA14)		880	2.5	Caracol, Bocas del Toro
PA14)		880	2.5	Caracol, Chiriquí
HE02)	Q62	890	5	R. Ritmo Stereo, Chitré.
PA14)	HA	900	10	Caracol, Panamá
CH12)	L81	*910	10	R. Nacional, David
CN03)	L85	*910	3	R. Nacional, Colón
PA12)		*910	10	R. Nacional, Darién
PA01)	S56	920	5	R. Mía de Los Santos, Los Santos (r: 650): 24h
PA09)	R46	930	10	La Nueva Exitosa de Panamá, Panamá: 24h
CH06)	K85	930	2	Mi Preferida Estéreo, Pto Armuelles: 1000 (SS 1200)-0400
CE04)	L84	950	3	R. Nacional, Penonomé
PA14)		950	2.5	Caracol, Las Mercedes, Colón
CH07)	M33	960	1	CHT Stereo Digital, David
CE02)	S97	970	3	Ondas Centrales, Santiago: W 1000-0300, Sun 1300-2400
PA01)		980	1	R. Mía, Bocas del Toro (r: 650) 24h
PA15)		990	5	R. Impacto, Panamá (Prgr: Filadelfia Radio)
CE01)	K36	1000	10	R. Poderosa "La Fuerte", Aguadulce: 1000-0500
BT03)	L86	*1010	3	R. Nacional, Bocas del Toro
PA16)		1020	5	R. Ancón, Panamá: 1000-0400
LS02)	J2	1040	2.5	Ondas del Canajagua, Las Tablas: 1000-0200
PA35)		1040	3	LV del Mamoni, Panamá
CN04)		*1050	3	Caribe Stereo, Colón
PA39)	J60	1060	3.5	R. LV de Panamá "La Auténtica", Panamá: 1100-0300
CE02)		1070	3	Radio Estéreo Mi Favorita, Penonomé: 1030-0300
LS04)		*1070	10	R. Nacional, Los Santos
PA07)	J24	1080	5	CNB, Panamá: 24h
PA07)		1080	5	CNB, Chiriquí
VE04)	L82	*1090	10	R. Urracá Civilista, Santiago W 1000-0100, Sun 1100-1800
PA08)	M92	1100	5	R. Sabrosa, Panamá
PA25)		1110		LV Podrosa, Los Santos (CP)
PA19)	M21	1120	5	R. Sonora, Panamá: 1030-0300
PA25		1120		LV Poderosa, Colón (CP)
CE03)	U80	1130	2.5	R. Sensación, Aguadulce
PA25)		1130		LV Poderosa, Chiriquí (CP)
PA20)	B49	1140	5	R. Panamericana, Panamá: 1100-0500
PA07)		1150	5	Ecos de Pedasí, Pedasí
CH08)	C20	1160	5	Ondas Chiricanas, David
PA17)	WK	1160	10	R. Metrópolis, Panamá
PA07)		1160	5	Ecos de Pedasí, Pedasí (F.PI 1150 kHz)
VE03)	U	1180	10	R. Belén, Santiago: 1100-0200
PA21)		1180	10	China Visión Panamá, Panamá
PA11)	E91	1210	1	R. El Mundo, Panamá
CH09)	M56	1240	1	Faro de David, David
CE05)	LY	1250	5	R. Hogar, Penonomé: 0955-0300
PA22)	J22	1270	3	R. Tipy Q, Panamá
PA23)	S23	1290	10	RCM Noticias, Panamá (R. Cadena Milenium)
PA23		1290	10	RCM Noticias, David (r: 1290)
PA23)		1290	10	RCM Noticias, Guararé (r: 1290)
CH10)	I417	1300	5	R. Bahá'í, Boca del Monte: 1045-2300
PA24)		1310	12	R. María, Panamá
PA25)		1330	5	LV Poderosa, Panamá
LS05)		1340	2.5	R. Tipical, Las Tablas
PA36)	Z38	1350	5	R. Integridad, Panamá
CH11)	B64	1370	1	R. Sitrachilco, Pto Armuelles: 1000-0200
PA26)		1380	10	R. América, Panamá: 1130-0400
PA07)		1390	6	R. Mundo Internacional, Colón
PA27)	T40	1400	10	Digital Radio Luz, La Chorrera
LS03)	H779	1410	5	R. Mensabé, Las Tablas: 1000-0300
PA28)		1430	7.5	R. Kids, Panamá
PA29)		1450	5	R. Melodía, Panamá: 1000-0330
BT02)	D42	1460	0,5	LV de Almirante, Bocas del Toro: 1400-0400
PA30)		1470	5	R. La Primerísima, Panamá Prgr: "LV de China"
PA31)	A95	v1510	5	Hosanna R, Panamá: 24h
PA32)		1530	3	R. Avivamiento, Panamá
PA33		1560	10	R. Adventista de Panamá, Panamá: 1000-0300
PA34)		1580	1	Resplandor Estéreo, Panamá

Province abbreviations: (Provincias) BT = Bocas del Toro, CE = Coclé, CH = Chiriquí, CN = Colón, DA = Darién, HE = Herrera, LS = Los Santos, PA = Panamá, VE = Veraguas.
N.B: These abbreviations are not recognized by the Post Office. Letters should therefore carry the full name.

Addresses and other information:

BT00) BOCAS DEL TORO
BT01) Finca 13, Empalme, Changuinola ☎+507 758 6087 - **FM:** 90.1. – **BT02)** Calle 6 y Av. N. Almirante. – **BT03)** Av. Central, Bocas del Toro.

CE00) COCLÉ
CE01) Ap. 090 (or: Vía al Puerto), Aguadulce **Email:** r.poderosa@cwpanamá.net ☎ +507 997 4156 🖷 +507 997 4157 - **FM:** 99.9. – **CE02)** Av. Juan Demóstenes Arosemena, Galerías Aro, Penonomé. **Email:** darfer@cwpanama.net ☎+507 997 7167. 🖷+507 997 1386. - **FM:** 91.7. – **CE03)** Calle Pablo Arosemena, Pueblo Nuevo, Aguadulce ☎/🖷+507 997 6280 **Web**: www.plateadas.com/sensacion - **FM:** 103.7. – **CE04)** Villa Inter-americana, Penonomé. – **CE05)** La Esperanza, Penonomé ☎+507 997 8929. 🖷+507 997 7340.

CH00) CHIRIQUÍ
CH02) Calle D.Norte, Doleguita, David ☎+507 774 3352 - **FM:** 101.7 – **CH03)** Ap. 540 (or: Av. 8 y Calle A Norte, Barrio Bolívar), David ☎+507 774 3852 **Web**: - **FM:** 98.1 – **CH04)** Ap. 43 (or: Calle Central), David **Web: Email:** rguerra@chiriqui.com ☎+507 775 2822 - **FM:** 107.1 – **CH05)** Av. D.Noreste, Medio Oeste, David ☎+507 774 3352 🖷+507 774 0512 - **FM:** 93.1 – **CH06)** Ap. 44 (or: Barriada San José), Puerto Armuelles ☎+507 770 7408 - **FM:** 105.3– **CH07)** Calle Central, David ☎+507 774 0755 🖷+507 774 8081 - **FM:** 107.9 – **CH08)** Ap. 172 (or: Calle Elisandro Calvo, Doleguita), David ☎+507 775 2742 - **FM:** 100.1 – **CH09)** Av.Estudiante, Calle 4 final, Edif.Hermanos Pinzón, David – **CH10)** Ap. 1187, David. 🖷+507 726 5004. – **CH11)** Principal, Barriada Santa Fe, Puerto Armuelles ☎+507 770 744 🖷+507 770 7217 – **CH12)** Av. Primera Oeste, David.

CN00) COLÓN
CN01) Calle 2da detras de Panamá All Brown, Colón ☎+507 441 1300 - **FM:** 101.5+103.5 – **CN02)** Calle 1 Paseo Washington, Colón ☎+507 433 1035 - **FM:** 105.3 – **CN03)** Av. Bolívar, Calle 9, Colón – **CN04)** Calle 5 Av. Amador Guerrero, Colón **Email:** caribestereo@hotmail.com ☎+507 441 4050 🖷+507 441 4052 - **FM:** 95.5.

DA00) DARIÉN
DA01) Calle Principal de Metetí, Metetí. (or: Ap. 87-0871 Panamá 7) ☎/🖷+507 299 6346 **Email:** vozst@cwp.net.pa - **FM:** 100.1

HE00) HERRERA
HE01) Ap. 423 (or: Urb.Las Mercedes), Chitré ☎+507 996 4127 🖷+507 996 2668 – **HE02)** Paseo Enrique Geenzier, Chitré ☎+507 996 2061 - **FM:** 97.5 – **HE03)** Ap. 194, Chitré **Web:** ☎+507 996 4223 - **FM:** 98.5 – **HE04)** Ap. 191, Chitré ☎+507 994 4627 -**FM:** 103.3. – **HE05)** Av. Pérez, Chitré. – **HE07)** Ap. 375 (or: Calle Francisco Audia), Chitré. ☎+507 996 5302.

LS00) LOS SANTOS
LS01) Calle Central, Macaracas - **FM:** 93.7 – **LS02)** Ap. 10 (or: Av. Belisario Porras, final), Las Tablas **Email:** rocavi@cwp.net.pa ☎+507 994 6674 🖷+507 994 8133 – **LS03)** Ap. 20 (or: Av. Agustín Cano Castillero), Las Tablas ☎ +507 994 6606 🖷 +507 994 8477. – **LS04)** Los Santos. – **LS05)** Los Cerritos, Las Tablas.

PA00) PANAMÁ
PA01) Ap. 5117, Panamá 5. **Web:** www.raiomia.com **Email:** mia@sinfo.net ☎ +507 227 2700 🖷 +507 227 2523. – **PA02)** Parque Lefebre, Edif.Sta Elena Torre II, Ofc.11, Panamá. ☎ +507 222 0500 **Email:** radio540@sinfo.net **Web:** www.sinfo.net/radio540 – **PA03)** Ap. 1795 (or: Edif.Vista Mar, Calle 50, P6), Panamá 1. ☎+507 210 6969 **Web:** www.rpcradio.com **Email:** rpcradio@medcom.com.pa – **PA04)** Ap. 6-2323, El Dorado (or: Calle 63B, Casa N° 2), Panamá ☎+507 236 1940 **Web:** www.radio-soberana.com – **PA05)** Edif. Orion, P8, Via España frente al PIEX, Panamá. ☎+507 263 0183 – **PA06)** Ap. 102 (or: San Francisco de la Caleta, via Cincuentario y Av. José Matilde Pérez), Panamá 9-A ☎ +507 270 0141 🖷 +507 270 0145 **Email:** rhogas@cableonda.net **Web:** www.sinfo.net/rhogar **PA07)** Radio Hit SA, Calle 50 y 77 San Francisco 35, Panamá **Web:** http://estereobahia.com **PA08)** Ap. 87-1324, Panamá 7 (or: Vía Argentina, Edif. Carillón, Panamá) **Web:** www.kwcntinente.com **Email:** kwcontinente@cableonda.net ☎+507 223 8846 🖷+507 264 6230. – **PA09)** Ap. 7462, Panamá 5 **Web:** www.sinfo.net/exitosa ☎ +507 225 2052 🖷 +507 225 7252 – **PA10)** Ap. 6-1192, (or: 66 Oeste N° 641) El Dorado, Panamá. **Email:** atrd@panama.c-com.net ☎ +507 229 3989 🖷 +507 261 3366. – **PA11)** La Gloria 31-B Bethania, Panamá. – **PA12)** Ap. 4950 (or: Edif.Dorchester, P5), Panamá 5 ☎+507 269 6594 🖷+507 269 5910. – **PA13)** Edif. Dorchester, Vía España, Panamá 4. ☎+507 264 5239 – **PA14)** Calle 54 Obarrio, detras de la Agencia de Autos Jaguar, Panamá ☎ +507 263 0180. – **PA15)** Río Abajo, Calle 13, Panamá ☎+507 221 0110. Filadelfia Radio: Filadelfia Eglesia, Plaza El Conquistador, Local 61, Vía Domingo Diaz, Panamá. – **PA16)** Calle Cuba y Calle 37, Panamá. 🖷+507 225 0025. – **PA17)** Vía España y Calle 45, Edif. El Conquistador PB, Panamá **Web:** www.sinfo.net/radiometropolis/ **Email:** radiometropolis@hotmail.com 🖷+507 212 0112– **PA18)**

Condomino Dorado N° 2, Ofc. 10A, Vía Ricardo J. Alfaro, Panamá – **PA19)** Ap. 87-1165 (or: Calle 63 Oeste N° E-21, Urb. Los Angeles), Panamá 7 ☎/🖷 +507 236 3065. – **PA20)** Ap. 6956 (or: Vía José Agustín Arango), Panamá 5. – **PA21)** Sun Tower Mall, Av. Ricardo J.Alfaro, Panamá ☎+507 236 5363. 🖷+507 236 9810. – **PA22)** Calle 45, Edif. Conquistador, Bella Vista, P2, Panamá ☎+507 269 4226. – **PA23)** Ap. 6-8868, El Dorado, Panamá ☎+507 236 9465 🖷+507 360 0831. – **PA24)** Ap. 6- 4509, El Dorado, (or: Calle Betin Portobelo, entre Av. 7a norte y Calle 67,) Panamá **Web:** www.radiomariapanama.org **Email:** info.pan@radiomaria.org ☎+507 261 0449 🖷+507 261 1535 – **PA25)** Iglesia Internacional del Evagélico Cuadrangular, Los Andes N° 2, Panamá. – **PA26)** Vía José Agustín Arango, Panamá. – **PA27)** Ap. 473, La Chorrera. – **PA28)** Río Abajo, Panamá. – **PA29)** Ap. 87-3541 (or: Vía Fernández de Córdoba, Jardin Cosita Buena), Panamá 7 **Email:** lizbethcardenas@hotmail.com ☎+507 229 1504 🖷+507 229 4850. – **PA30)** Edif.La Marqueta, Vía Porras, Panamá. **Email:** rlprimerisima@latinol.com ☎ +507 226 6476. **Web:** www.sinfo.net/laprimerisima – **PA31)** Ap. 6-8229 (or: Calle Erick del Valle y Vía Argentina, Edif. Vicky 2), El Dorado, Panamá **Web:** www.hosanna.pma.org/sradio.htm – **PA32)** Av. Ernesto T. Lefevre, Panamá. – **PA33)** Ap. 3244, Panamá 3 (or: Carrasquilla, Calle 2da N° 39, Panamá) ☎ +507 214 6430 🖷 +507 263 4255 **Web:** www.tagnet.org/radioadvpma **Email:** celes@usa.com - Ids: "Radio Adventista - La Voz de la Esperanza" – **PA34)** Sky Phone S.A., Cerro Peñon, Panamá. – **PA35)** Av. José Agustin Arango N° 5013, Panamá. – **PA36)** Ap. 0860-00356, Panamá. **PA37)** Av. Las Américas, La Chorrera. – **PA39)** Vía España y Calle 45, Edif. El Conquistador, PB, Panamá **Email:** vozdepanama@hotmail.com

VE00) VERAGUAS

VE01) Ap. 48 (or: Calle 9 y vía Panamericana), Santiago ☎/🖷+507 958 7060 **Email:** radioveraguas@cerco.net - **FM:** 102.1. – **VE02)** Ap. 131, Santiago. – **VE03)** Ap. 286 (or: Calle 10), Santiago ☎ +507 998 1655 🖷 +507 998 5580. – **VE04)** Barriada Urracá, MIDA Central, Santiago.

FM in Panamá City: 88.1 Diez – 88.5 FM Estéreo – 88.9 RCM Noticias – 89.3 RM Stereo – 89.9 Estéreo 89 – 90.5 Super Q – 90.9 RPC Radio – 91.3 40 Principales – 91.7 Estéreo Bahía – 92.1 Super Estación – 92.5 BB Estéreo – 92.9 Tropical – 93.5 Metrópolis – 93.9 María – 94.5 Caracol – 94.9 Hosanna – 95.3 La Nueva Exitosa – 95.9 KW Continente – 96.3 Estéreo Selecta – 96.7 Power 96.7 – 97.1 Caliente Panamá –97.5 WAO 97.5 – 97.9 Mix – 98.3 La Mega – 98.9 Ultra Estéreo – 99.3 FM99 – 99.7 Tropic Q – 100.1 Antena 8 – 100.5 Fabulosa – 101.1 Estéreo Azul – 101.5 Economía – 101.9 Nacional – 102.1 Lo Nuestro – 102.5 FM Corazón – 103.1 FM Latina – 103.5 Quiubo Estéreo – 103.9 Mil – 104.3 Amor – 104.7 La Típica – 105.1 Estéreo Vida – 105.7 Estéreo Bahía – 106.1 Sol – 106.7 Rocks & Pops – 107.3 Omega Stereo – 107.9 Estéreo Universidad.

PAPUA NEW GUINEA

L.T: UTC +10h — **Pop:** 5.04 million — **Radios:** 234,000 — **Pr.L:** English, Melanesian Pidgin, Hiri Motu + 30 ethnic languages — **E.C:** 50Hz, 240V — **ITU:** PNG

PAPUA NEW GUINEA NATIONAL BROADCASTING CORPORATION

✉ P.O. Box 1359, Boroko, N.C.D ☎ +675 323 3022 🖷 +675 323 0404 **Email:** pom@nbc.com.pg **Web:** www.nbc.com.pg

L.P: MD & Chief Exec: Dr. Kristoffa Ninkama, Mgr Eng Tech: Isaac Marinjembi, Mgr Network Ops: Demas Totil

Stations: N=Karai Sce. (National), P=Kundu Sce. (Provincial).

MW	kHz	kW	N	Station & h. of tr.
1)	585	10	N	Karai Radio, Port Moresby: 1930-1400
1)	675	10	N	Lae: 1930-1400
1)	675	10	N	Wewak: 1930-1400
1)	810	10	N	Rabaul: 1930-1400
1)	864	10	N	Madang: 1930-1400
1)	900	10	N	Goroka: 0700-1200
17)	1107	2	N	Alotau: 1930-1400
19)	1494	10	N	Wabag:MF 1930-1200
8)	1593	10	N	Vanimo: MF 1930-1200
SW	**kHz**	**kW**	**N**	**Station & h. of tr.**
19)	2410	10	P	R. Enga: 2000-2200, 0800-1200v
8)	3205	10	P	R. West Sepik: 2000-2200, 0800-1200v
9)	3220	10	P	R. Morobe: 2000-2200, 0800-1200v
2)	3235	10	P	R. West New Britain: 2000-2200, 0800-1300v
10)	3245	10	P	R. Gulf: 2000-2200, 0800-1300
11)	3260	10	P	R. Madang: 2000-2200, 0800-1200
12)	3275	10	P	R. Southern Highlands: 2000-2200, 0800-1300
13)	3290	10	N	R. Central: 2000-2200, 0800-1200v
14)	3305	10	P	R. Western: 2000-2200, 0800-1200v
SW	**kHz**	**kW**	**N**	**Station & h. of tr.**
18)	3315	10	P	R. Manus: 2000-2200, 0800-1200v
15)	3325	10	P	R. North Solomons: 2000-2200, 0800-1200v
16)	3335*	10	P	R. East Sepik: 2000-2200, 0800-1200
7)	3345	10	P	R. Oro: 2000-2200, 0800-1200v
3)	3355	10	P	R. Simbu: 2000-2200, 0800-1200v
17)	3365	10	P	R. Milne Bay: 2000-2200, 0730-1200
6)	3375	10	P	R. Western Highlands: 2000-2200, 0800-1200v
20)	3385	10	P	R. East New Britain: 1900-2200, 0800-1200
4)	3395	10	P	R. Eastern Highlands: 2000-2200, 0800-1200
5)	3905	10	P	R. New Ireland: 2000-2200, 0800-1200
1)	4890	100	N	Port Moresby: 0730-1200 1900-2200
6)	5965*	10	N	NBC Mt. Hagen: MF 2200-0700
17)	6040*	10	N	NBC Alotau: MF 2200-0700
14)	6080*	10	N	NBC Daru: MF 2200-0700
16)	6140*	10	N	NBC Wewak: MF 2200-0700
1)	9520*	100	N	Port Moresby: 2200-0700
1)	9675	100	N	Port Moresby: 2200-0730
1)	11880*	10	N	Port Moresby: 2200-0700
FM	**MHz**	**kW**	**N**	**Station**
13)	89.9	1	P	R. Central, Boroko
20)	98.3	1	P	R. East New Britain, Kokopo
20)	101.3	0.3	P	R. East New Britain, Palmalmal
20)	103.3	1	P	R. East New Britain, Rabaul/Kokopo
20)	104.3	0.2	P	R. East New Britain, Malmaluan
9)	105.1	1	P	R. Morobe, Lae

*** = inactive. (N.B:** a number of SW operations are irregular)

Kundu (Provincial) Stations

2) P.O. Box 415, Kimbe. Mgr: Valuka Lowa. **ANN:** "Maus bilong Tavur" – **3)** P.O. Box 228, Kundiawa. Actng Mgr: John Bare. **ANN:** "Karai bilong Manbu" – **4)** P.O. Box 311, Goroka. Actg Mgr: Lucy Baru. **ANN:** "Karai bilong Kumul" – **5)** P.O. Box 140, Kavieng. Mgr: Tonko Nonao. **ANN:** "Maus bilong Mai Mai" – **6)** P.O. Box 811, Mount Hagen. Mgr: Anna Pundia. **FM:** 90.5MHz. **ANN:** "Neck bilong Tarangau" – **7)** P.O. Box 137, Popondetta. Mgr: Gerald Didymus. **ANN:** "Voice of Oro" – **8)** P.O. Box 37, Vanimo. Mgr: Leone Ramram **ANN:** "Maus bilong Sundaun" – **9)** P.O. Box 1262, Lae. Mgr: Meck Muruk. **ANN:** "Maus bilong Kundu" – **10)** P.O. Box 36, Kerema. Mgr: Timothy Akia. **ANN:** "Voice of the Seagull" – **11)** P.O. Box 2036, Madang. Provincial Prgr. Mgr: Geo Gedabing. **ANN:** "Maus bilong Garamut" – **12)** P.O. Box 104, Mendi. Mgr: Andrew Meles. **ANN:** "Karai bilong Muruk" – **13)** P.O. Box 1359, Boroko. Mgr: Akuss Matiki. **ANN:** "Kibi ena Gadona" – **14)** P.O. Box 23, Daru. Mgr: Theothilus Beu. **ANN:** "Voice of the Sunrise" – **15)** P.O. Box 35, Kieta. Mgr: Alausis Rumina. **ANN:** "Maus bilong Sunkamap" – **16)** P.O. Box 53, Wewak. Mgr: Andrew Lunge. **ANN:** "Nek bilong Sepik" – **17)** P.O. Box 111, Alotau. Mgr: Trevor Webumo. **ANN:** "Voice of Kula" – **18)** P.O. Box 593, Lorengau. Mgr: John Mandrakamu. **ANN:** "Maus bilong Chauka" – **19)** P.O. Box 196, Wabag. Mgr: Matthew Gole. **ANN:** "Karai bilong Miok" – **20)** P.O. Box 393, Rabaul **V.** Most st's verify direct.

KARAI RADIO

MHz	Station	kHz	MHz	Station	kHz
90.4	Madang	0.05	90.7	Rabaul; Port Moresby	1.0
90.5	Popendetta	0.05	90.8	Wewak	0.05
90.6	Mount Hagen	0.3			

Addr. & L.P: see **NBC** above. **N. in English:** 2000W, 2045, 2145W, 2245Sun, 0230, 0330 (not. Sat), 0600MF, 0800 (not Sat), 0900, 1100, 1300. **V.** by QSL-card. Rp. Specific prgr. details, time, frequency, date req. for verifications.

Commercial & other stations:

KALANG RADIO (FM 100)

✉ P.O. Box 1534, Pt. Moresby ☎ +675 3259796 🖷 +675 3251747 **Web:** www.tiare.net.pg **L.P:** MD: John Malisa. **CE:** V. Kuppusamy **FM:** Port Moresby 100.4MHz, 1.0kW + 10 low-power relays

NAU FM & YUMI FM (Comm.)

✉ P.O. Box 744, Pt. Moresby, NCD ☎ +675 3201996 🖷 +675 3201995 **Web:** www.pngvillage.com/radio/naufm/nauhome.shtml & www.pngvillage.com/radio/yumifm/yumihome.shtml

Email: pngvillage@naufm.com.pg

L.P: GM (Nau FM): Mark Rogers. GM (Yumi FM): Justin Kili

Yumi FM: Port Moresby 93.1MHz, 1.0kW + 8 low-power relays

Nau FM: Port Moresby 96.5MHz, 1.0kW + 10 low-power relays

D.Prgr: 24h (Nau FM for young people, Yumi FM for older audience).

PAPUA NEW GUINEA CHRISTIAN BROADCASTING NETWORK

✉ Nambawan Finance Building, Waigani, Port Moresby., (Joint venture between HCJB and Evangelical Bible Missions through Life Radio Ministries, Griffin, GA). **LP:** Interim MD: Andrew Ogil

FM: Port Moresby 93.9MHz 5kW; Lae 106.9MHz **FPI:** SW 100kW. **ANN:** "Wantok Radio Light"

UCB PACIFIC PARTNERS (PNG)

✉ P O Box 556, Wewak ☎ +675 (856) 1232 **LP:** Bill Chambers **Email:** laif.fmpng@juno.com **Web:** www.pacificpartners.org

F.M: Laif FM, Wewak 98.0MHz 1kW, and 102.0MHz 4kW (different programs) **D.Prgr:** local Pijin & English

F.PI: FM stations in Goroko, Madang & Port Moresby.

CATHOLIC RADIO NETWORK

SW: Vanimo 4960kHz 1kW.

FM: Rabaul/Malmaluan 91.3MHz 0.5kW; Aitape 92.9MHz 0.3kW; Port Moresby 103.5MHz 0.5kW; Vanimo 91.5MHz 0.3kW; Trinity FM, Mount Hagen 98.1MHz 0.3kW. **D.Prgr:** 24 hours Christian

BIBLE BROADCASTING NETWORK

FM: Mount Hagen 92.5MHz 0.5kW.

FPI: SW broadcasts **Ann**: Krai bilong Baibel Broadcasting Network

UNIVERSITY OF PAPUA NEW GUINEA

✉ Radio UPNG, PO Box 320, University, National Capital District. ☎🖷: +675 3267191. **Email:** Sorariba.n@upng.ac.pg.

FM: 98.5MHz 0.02kW

Other FM:

ERE' ERE BEREINA Bereina 99.5MHz 0.01kW – **FM MOROBE** Lae 94.7MHz 0.5kW Email: fmmorobe@global.net.pg – **PARADISE FM** Boroko 89.1MHz 0.02kW, 105.1MHz 0.02kW – **FM LIGHT** Port Moresby 93.9MHz 1.0kW – **FM Central** Port Moresby 89.9MHz ✉ P O Box 333, Port Moresby D.Prgr: Motu and English 24hrs – **BBC WORLD SERVICE** Port Moresby 106.7MHz 0.1kW – **CDI FM Kikori** Gobo 90.0MHz 0.02kW; Kikori 92.3MHz 0.5kW; Moro 98.3MHz 0.02KwCDI Foundation, ✉ P O Box 383, Port Moresby Web: www.cdi.org.pg/cdifm.html **RED FM** Gobo 98.0MHz, Moro 98.0MHz – **PIAM TOWN RADIO** Porgera 88.7MHz 0.1kW

PARAGUAY

L.T: UTC -4h (5 Sep-6 Apr: UTC -3h) — **Pop:** 5.5 million — **Pr.L:** Spanish, Guaraní — **E.C:** 50Hz, 220V — **ITU:** PRG

COMISIÓN NACIONAL DE TELECOMUNICACIONES (CONATEL)

Offices: Avenida Yegros 437, Asunción. ☎ +595 21 440 020 **Web:** www.conatel.com.py **L.P:** Pres: Ing. Victor A. Bogado González.

MW: ° = also on SW, * = inactive, v = varying freq.

	Call	kHz	kW	Name, location and h. of tr.
10)	ZP16	550	20/12	R.Parque, Ciudad del Este
1)	ZP15	570	1	R. LV del Amambay, Pedro Juan Caballero: 0930 (Sun 1000)-0100
2)	ZP15	570	1	R. S. Roque González de Sta. Cruz, Ayolas 0830-0200
3)	ZP32	590	5	R. Ycuámandyyú, Villa de S. Pedro: 0900-0200
4)	ZP30	610	10/1	R. ZP30, LV del Chaco Paraguayo, Filadelfia: 0900-0200
5)	ZP40	v620	10	R. Ñasaindý, San Estanislao (r. 619-616.6v)
6)	ZP19	v640	8	R. Caaguazú, Coronel Oviedo:0830-0300
7)	ZP4	650	15	R. Uno, Asunción: 0900 (Sun 0930)-0400 (SS 0300)
8)	ZP26	660	6/10	R. Itapirú, Cd. del Este: 0800-0100
9)	ZP11	680	10/1	R. Caritas, Asunción: 0900-0400
11)	ZP12	v700	10	R. Carlos Antonio López, "LV del Ñeembucú", Pilar: 0900-0200 (r. 699.6)
12)	ZP17	720	25	R. Pa'i Puku, Teniente Irala Férnandez
13)	ZP7	730	50/5	R. Cardinal, Asunción: 24h.
15)	ZP42	750	1	LV de la Policía Nacional, Asunción: 0900-0200
16)	ZP70	780	30	R. Primero de Marzo, Asunción: 0830-0400
17)	ZP27	800	5/3	R. Mbaracayú, Saltos del Guairá: 0900-0300
18)	ZP6	v°840	5	R. Guairá, Villarrica: 0900-2400 (r. 835)
19)	ZP28	v860	25	LV de la Cordillera, Caacupé: 0900 (Sat/Sun 1000)-0400
20)	ZP33	v890	5	R. Tres de Febrero, Itá: 0900-0300 (r 885)
21)	ZP1	°920	10/100	R. Nal. del Paraguay, Asunción: 24h
22)	ZP9	970	10	R. 9-70 AM, Asunción: 0900-0400
23)	ZP31	980	5	R. Mburucuyú, Pedro Juan Caballero: 0900-0300
24)	ZP36	1000	5/1	R. Mil, San Antonio: 0900-0100
25)	ZP14	1020	25/10	R. Ñandutí, Asunción: 24h.
26)	ZP43	1040	5	R. Arapisandú, San Ignacio: 0900-0200
27)	ZP13	v1060	3	R. Boquerón, Alberdi: 1000-0300 (r. 1060.5)
28)	ZP25	1080	10	Radiodif. Nanawa, Luque: 0800 (Sun 0900)-0300
29)	ZP71	1100	5	R. Nu Vera, Capitán Bado: 0900-0200
30)	ZP24	1120	10	R. Nuevo Mundo, San Lorenzo: 0900-0200
31)	ZP22	1140	5/3	R. Panambí Verá, Villarrica: 0900-0200
32)	ZP72	1160	10	R. Antena 2, Asunción
33)	ZP52	1180	5/1	R. Coronel Oviedo – RCO-AM, Coronel Oviedo: 0900-0100
47)	ZP45	1190		LV de la Libertad, Henendarias
34)	ZP44	1200	10	R. Libre, Fernando de la Mora
35)	ZP21	1230	3	R. Oriental, 'La radio del Pueblo', Caaguazú: 0800-0300
36)	ZP3	1250	1	R. Libertad,. 0900-0600
37)	ZP34	1260	1	R. Cultura, Villarrica
38)	ZP53	1280	20	R. LV del Este, Cd. del Este
46)		1330	5	R. Chaco Boreal, Asunción
39)	ZP37	1360	1	R. Yby Ya'u, Ybu Ya'u: 0900-0300
40)	ZP8	1380	1	R. Concepción, "LV del Norte": 0930-0100
41)	ZP35	1410	2	La Voz de Misiones, S. Juan Bautista: 1000-0130 (n. 1430)
42)	ZP42	1417	5	R. Güyrá Campana, Horqueta (n. 1420)
43)	ZP23	1480	1	R. Mariscal Francisco Solano López, Bella Vista Norte: 1000-0100
44)	ZP20°	1480	5	R. América, Ñemby: 24h
49)		1570		R. Oriental AM 1570, Caaguazú
45)		*1590	0.2	R. Villeta, Villeta: 24h
48)		1610	0.1	R. Colegio Tecnico Municipal: W.: 1000-2000

SW: * = inactive, v = varying freq.

	Call	kHz	kW	Name, location and h. of tr.
18)	A6	*5975	1	R. Guairá, Villarrica
21)	A1	*6025	0.7	R. Nal. del Paraguay, Asunción
4)		6884		LV del Chaco Paraguayo, Chaco (feeder)
44)		7370	1	R. América, Ñemby: 24h
48)		7371	0.05	R. Colegio Tecnico Municipal: W.: 1000-2000
21)	A1	9735	100	R. Nal. del Paraguay, Asunción
44)		9905	0.2	R. América, Villeta: 24h
44)		*9983	0.2	R. América, Villeta
44)		15483	0.2	R. América, Villeta: 24h

Addresses and other information

1)14 de Mayo 485, Pedro Juan Caballero. – **2)** 7ma y 2da Proyectadas, Ayolas. **Email:** sanroque@itacom.com.py – **3)** Ruta 11 Juana M. de Lara, Villa de San Pedro. – **4)** Av. Trebol 137E, Filadelfia, Chaco (✉ Casilla 984, Asunción) **Web:** www.zp30.com.py ☎ +595 491 32031/32330. 🖷 +595 491 32501. – Prgrs in Sp. (62 %), German (20 %). 4 ethnic languages: 1000-1030, 1630-1700 , 2230-2315. Operated by Mennonite Mission. – **5)** Mariscal López y B. Caballero, San Estanislao, San Pedro **Web.:** www.rednace.org.py **Email:** lauda@pla.net.py. – **6)** Ruta Mcal. Estigarribia Km 131, Coronel Oviedo☎🖷 +595 21 202251. – **7)** Av. Mariscal López 2948 c/MacArthur, Asunción ☎ +595 21 612 151, 612 994 **Web:** www.mm.com.py/radiouno/ – **8)** Av. Coronel Sánches 3800, Cd. del Este **Web:** www.radioitapiru.com - **FM:** 96.1. – **9)** Kubichek 661 y Azara, (✉ Cas. 1313), Asunción. **Email:** caritas@conexion.com.py +595 21 213 570 🖷+595 21 204 161. – **10)** Ciudad del Este. – **11)** Alberdi 998, Pilar. – **12)** Km. 389 de la Ruta Transchaco, Teniente Irala Fernández, Chaco. **Web:** www.radiopaipuku.org.py/ – **13)** Calles Comendador Nicalás Bó y Guaranies, Lambaré. (✉ Cas. 247, Asunción) **Web:** www.cardinal.com.py – **FM:** 92.3– **15)** Comandancia de la Policia Nacional, El Paraguayo Independiente c/Chile, Asunción. ☎ +595 21 492 515. – **16)** Av. Perón y Concepción Prieto Yegros (✉ Cas. 1456), Asunción **Web:** www.780am.com.py - **FM:** Asunción 97.1 + Chaco 96.9 "R. Mariscal Estigarríbia". – **17)** Defensa Nacional y Av. Paraguay, Saltos del Guairá. – **18)** Pte. Franco 788 y Alejo Garcia, Villarrica ☎🖷 +595 541 42130/42385. **E.mail:** guaira@rieder.net.py – **Guaraní:** 2100-2300. - **FM:** 103.5. – **19)** Dr. Venancio Pino y 3ra. Proyectada, Caacupé. – **20)** Av. Enrique Doldán Ibieta y Presidente Franco, Itá. ☎ +595 24 2543. - **Guaraní:** 0900-1000, 1330-1430, 1800-1845. – **21)** Av. Blas Garay 241 c/Iturbe, Asunción. – **22)** Av. Rodriguez de Francia 343, Asunción. +595 21 450 281– **23)** Villa María Victoria, Fracción San Jorge, Pedro Juan Caballero **Web:** www.infonet.com.py/holding/mburu/mburu.htm – **24)** Av. 25 de Mayo 1164 c/Brasil, Asuncion. **Web:** www.milnoticias@hotmail.com – **Guaraní:** 0900-1030, 1730-1830. – **25)** Choferes del Chaco 1194, Asunción ☎ +595 21 604 308 🖷 +595 21 606074 **Web:** www.holdingderadio.com.py – **26)** Av. Mariscal López y Capitan del Puerto, San Ignacio (Misiones). – **27)** Av. Mariscal López 379, Alberdi. – **28)** Av. General Aquino y José Bonifacio Km. 14, Luque. – **29)** Estrella c/4 de Enero, Capitán Bado, Amambay. +595 37 262 – **30)** Coronel Romero y de Las Residentes, San Lorenzo. (Asunción: General Díaz 488, Ofic. 34.) ☎ +595 21 582424. 🖷 +595 21 586258. - **Guaraní:** 0900-1000, 1700-1800. – **31)** General Caballero 650, Villarrica. – **FM:** 94.7 – **32)** Estados Unidos 2019, Asunción. – **33)** Av. Mariscal Estigarribia 304 casi Yrendague, Coronel Oviedo **Email:** rco@telesurf.com.py ☎🖷 +595 521 202579. - **Guaraní:** 50 % of the programming. - **FM:** 91.9 FM del Sol". – **34)** Av. Zabala-Cué 1615, Fernando de la Mora **Web:** www.highway.com.py/libre.ram **Email:** rlibre@highway.com.py – reception reports to: Dr. Benjamin Frenández Bogado. – **35)** Mariscal López 450 entre Walter Insfrán y San Lorenzo, Caaguazú. 🖷+595 522 42790. – **36)** Capitán Lombardo 174 y Av. Artigas, Asunción. – **37)** Angostura y Olimpio, Bo. Ybarotu, Villarrica. – **38)** Km. 213 Ruta 7a, Caaguazú. +595 61 512 583 **Email:** lavozam@hotmail.com – **39)** Ruta V, Ybu Ya'u. – **40)** Panchito López 241 entre Prof.Cabral y Screiber, (Cas. 78), Concepción ☎ +595 31 42254 🖷 +595 31 40919. – Prgrs. in **Spanish & Guaraní**. – **41)** Coronel Alfredo A. Ramos esq. San Juan, San Juan Bautista, Misiones. – **42)** José Luís Arbues c/Ruta 5, Horqueta. – **43)** Calle Iturbe 146, Bella Vista Norte.- **FM:** 92.5 – **44)** Cas. 2220, Asunción **Web:** www.radiodifusionamerica.com.py **Email:** radioamerica@lycos.com ☎ +595 21 960 228. 🖷+595 21 963 149. – **45)** Cas. 2220, Asunción. – **46)** Edif. La Opinion, Av. Boggiana 6950 3° piso, Fernando de la Mora. +595 21 213 936 – **47)** Juan E.O´Leary 152, 1a piso, Oficina 5, Hernendarias. – **48)** Santa Rosa de Lima, Ñemby – Rpt.: to Orlando Torres, RCTMSRL, Santa Rosa de Lima, Ñemby. **Email:** ctmsrl@hotmail.com.py. – **49)** Mcal. López 450, Caaguazú.

FM in Metro Asunción: 87.9 LV de San Juan María Viani – 88.3 R.Ñemby – 89.1 Conquistador – 89.5 RRB – 90.7 Ysapy – 91.1 La Estacion – 91.5 R. Top – 91.9 R. Comunitaria GBS – 13) 92.3 – 92.7 R. Atake – 93.1 FM Florida – 93.3 R. Luque – 93.5 R.Rebelde – 93.9 FM Universal – 94.3 R. Fernando de la Mora – 21) 95.1 – 25) 95.5 Rock & Pop – 96.5 R.Disney – 97.1 FM – 97.9 R.Nuevo Tiempo FM – 98.5 Yacyretá – 99.1 City – 100.1 R. Canal 100 – 100.5 FM Arpa –100.9 Monte Carlo – 101.3 R. San Pablo – 101.5 R.Universitaria– 102.1 Obedira FM – 102.7 Aspen Classic FM – 103.1 R. Laser – 103.7 R.Lambaré – 104.1 R.Planeta – 105.1 R.Venus – 106.1 FM Paraguay – 107.3 R.Maria – 25) 107.7 FM Concert.

PERU

L.T: UTC -5h (Su: UTC -4h) — **Pop:** 27 million— **Pr.L:** Spanish, Quechua, Aymara — **E.C:** 60Hz, 220V — **ITU:** PRU

MINISTERIO DE TRANSPORTES, COMUNICACIONES, VIVIENDA Y CONSTRUCCION

Dirección General de Telecomunicaciones.
✉ Av. 28 de Julio 800, Lima 1 ☎ +51 1 433 7800, 433 1212, 433 0570 **Web:** www.mtc.gob.pe **Email:** dgt@mtcgob.pe
L.P: Dir. de Telecomunicaciones: Ing. Carlos A. Romero Sanjinés. Dir. Freq. Div: Ing. José Villa Gamboa.

ASOCIACION DE RADIO Y TELEVISION DEL PERU (ARTV)

✉ Jr. Manuel Corpancho 208, Santa Beatriz, Lima ☎ +51 1 433 3908, 433 3953.
L.P: Pres: Humberto Maldonado Balbín. Dir: Daniel Linares Bazan.

INSTITUTO NACIONAL DE COMUNICACION SOCIAL

✉ Jr. de la Unión 264, Lima **L.P:** Hernán Valdizán C. Dir. Bc: Sra. Clarisa P. de Olivera.

UNION DE RADIOEMISORAS DE PROVINCIAS DEL PERU (UNRAP)

✉ Mariano Carranza 754, Santa Beatriz, Lima 1.

MW: ° = also on SW, * = inactive, v = varying freq., r = reported

	Call	kHz	kW	Name and h. of tr.
LI01)	OBX4E	540	1	R.Inca del Perú, Lima: 24h
LL01)	OCX2D	540	1	R.San Antonio, Trujillo
LI02)	OBZ4L	v560	2	R.Oriente, Lima: 1000-0500 (Sun 1100-2300)(r: 559-564)
JU01)		560	1	R.Mover de Dios, Huancayo
LI01)	OBX4E	540	12	R. Inca del Perú, Lima: 24h
LL01)	OCX2D	540	1	R. San Antonio, Trujillo: 0900 (Sun 1100)-0500 LA01) 560 Radiomar, Chiclayo
PI01)	OBU1F	560	1	R.OBU1F, Coscomba
LA02)	OAU1M	570	1	R. Univ. Nal. Pedro Ruiz Gallo, Lambayeque
CA01)	OAX2E	°580	10	R. Marañón, Jaén: 1000-0400 (Sat 1000-0200, Sun 1100-1800)
LL02)	OCY2L	580	1	R. El Sol, La Esperanza
LI03)	OAX4M	580		R. Maria, Lima: 1100-0400
AR01)		590		R.del Sur, Arequipa
AR02)	OCX6V	590	1	R.Catedral, Miraflores, Arequipa
CU01)	OAU7A	600	1	R.Tropicana, Cusco
LL03)	OBX2B	600	1	R.Star, Trujillo: 24h
LI04)	OBZ4W°	*600	10	R.Cora, Lima: 24h
PI02)	OBU1E	610	1	R.Santa Rosa, Sullana
LL04)	OAX2N	620	0.4	R.Chepen, Chepen
LI05)	OBU4B	620	10	R.del Sur, San Isidro
CU02)	OAU7N	630	1	R.Univ.Nal.San Antonio Abad, Cusco
PI03)	OBU1A	630	1	R.OBU1A, Piura
LA03)	OAU1Y	640	1	R.La Luz, José Leonardo Ortiz
LI06)	OAZ4K	°640	10	R.Pacifico, Lima: 1030-0430
PU01)	OBX7B	640	10	R.Onda Azul, Puno: 0900-0300
CA02)	OBU2P	650	1.5	R.Estación Universal, Huambos
LL05)	OAX2N	650	1	R.Reginal del Norte, Trujillo: 1100-0500
JU02)	OCX4L	660	1	R.Chinchaycocha, Junin
LA04)	OCX1U	660	5	R. J.H.C., Chiclayo: 1000-0500
LI07)	OCX4R	660	10	La Inolviable 660 AM, Lima: 1100-0700
PU02)	OAX7H	670	10	R.Nacional del Perú, Puno
CA03)	OCY2Y	680	5	R.San Luis, Jaén
CU03)		*680		CP, Cusco
IC01)	OAX5E	680	5	Emisora del Pacifico, Ica: 1100-0600
LL06)	OBX2L	680	0.5	R.Amauta, Chócope: 1100-0500
LI089	OBX4A	680	20	R.Tigre, San Isidro
AR03)	OBX6Q	690	0.5	R.Comercial, La Joya
LA05)	OCX1W	690	1	CPN Radio, Chiclayo (r.: 1470)
LA07)	OCX1T	693	1.5	R.Horizonte, Chiclayo (n.f.: 770)
CU04)	OBU7K	700	1	R.Teleducional, Maras
JU03)	OBU4J	700	1	R. La Luz, Huancayo
LL07)	OCY2H	700	1	R.Sausal Superior, Sausal
LI09)	OBZ4H	700	1	R.Aeropuerto, San Miguel
PI04)	OBX1U	700	10	R.Cutivalú "LV del Desierti", Castilla: 1030-0100 (Sun.1100-0100)
AR04)	OAU6L	710	1	R.Amor, Arequipa
IC02)	OBX5Q	710	5	R.Programas del Perú (r.: 730), Ica
MD01)	OCX7I	710	10	R.Ncional del Peru, Puerto Maldonado
CU05)	OBU7D	720	1	R.Alegria, Wanchaq
JU04)	OAU4E	720	10	R.Sideral, La Oroya
LL08)	OAX2J	720	25	R.Nacional del Perú, Trujillo
LA06)	OAU1Q	720	1	R.Frecuencia Oceánica, Lambayque: 1030-0500
PU04)	OAZ7S	730	10	LV de la Esperanza, Juliaca: 0800-1400, 2100-0200 (rel.: 780)
CA05)		730	5	R.Maria, Cajamarca
LI10)	OAX4G	730	50	R.Programas del Peru (rel.: RPP), San Isidro: 24h
PI05)	OAX1D	730	10	R.del Pacifico, Piura: 1100-0500
AR05)	OAX6C	°740	10	R.Continental, Arequipa: 0900-0300
CU06)	OBU7C	740	1	Rede Latino, Cusco
LL09)	OCX2X	740	1	R.El Puerto, Pascamayo
CA06)	OBX2R	*750	3	R.Oriental, Jaén
PA01)	OCX4X	°750	5	R.Altura, Cerro de Pasco: 1000-0400
LL01)	OBX2K	760	0.5	R.Andino, Otuzco
LI11)	OBZ4X	760	10	Radiomar, Chorillos: 24h
AR06)	OBX6H	770	5	Radiomar, Uchumayo
LA07)	OCX1T	770	1.5	R.Horizonte, Chiclayo (r.: 693)
LO01)	OAX8M	°770	5	LV de la Selva, Iquitos:1000-0300 (Sun 1100-1700)
PU03)	OAU7D	770	2.5	R.OAU7D, Macusani
CA07)		780	1	R.Coremarca, Bambamarca: 24h
LI12)	OAX4X	780	3	R.Victoria,Lima: 24h
PU04)	OAZ7S	780	10	LV de la Esperanza, Juliaca: 0800-1400, 2100-0200 (nom: 730)
TU01)	OAX1K	780	10	R.Nacional del Perú, Tumbes
CU07)	OAZ7H	790	5	R.Armonia, Wanchaq
LL11)	OAX2I	790	10	R.Programas del Perú, Trujillo: 24h
AR07)	OBX6A	800	0.3	R.Porteña, Arequipa
IC03)	OBX5B	*800	1	R.Maria, Ica (F.Pl.)
JU05)	OBU4D	800	1	Emp. de Communicaciones Vida, Huancayo
LI13)	OAU4H	800	0.5	R.La Luz, Huaral
PI06)	OCX1P	800	1	Telecom de Norte, Piura
LL12)	OAU2G	810	1	R.Apocali, Trujillo
PU05)	OAX7V	810	10	R.Programas del Perú, Juliaca: 24h
AR08)	OCX6J	820	1	R.Paraiso, Camaná
CA43)	OBX2J	820	0.5	R.Nuevo Continene, Cajamarca (r: 1560)
LI14)	OAX4O	820	20	R.Libertad, Lima: 24h
CU08)	OAZ7U	830	1	R.Inti Raymi, Santiago: 24h
HU01)	OAX3Y	830	1	R.La Selva, Rupa-Rupa (n.f.: 1280)
JU06)	OAU4C	830	1	CPN Radio, El Tambo (rel.: CPN 1470)
LI 13)	OCX2Y	830	1	CPN Radio, Trujillo (rel.: CPN 1470)
TA02)	OAX6D	830	10	R.Nacional del Perú, Tacna
AN01)	OAX3S	840	1	R.Casma, Casma: 1100-0300
AR01)	OBX6Y	840	1	R.Azul, Arequipa: 24h
CA08)	OAU2E	°840	1	R.Frequencia, San Ignacio (r.: 1577)

	Call	kHz	kW	Name and h. of tr.
PI07)	OCX1N	840	1	CPN Radio, Piura (rel.: CPN 1470)
CU09)	OAU7J	850	1	R.Quispicanchi, Urcos
LL14)	OCX2F	850	1	R.Selecta, Virú
LI15)	OAX4A	*850	40	R.Nacional del Perú, Lima
PU36)	OBU7Z	850		Instituto de Desarrollo, Puno
AY01)	OAU5Q	860	5	R.Educativo Macedonia, Ayacucho
CA09)	OAU2J	860		CPN Radio, Cajamarca (rel.: CPN 1470)
PI08)	OCX1M	860	3	R.Nuevo Norte, Sullana
AR10)	OCX6F	870	1	R.TV Impacto, Arequipa
CU10)	OCX7R	870	1	R.Mundo, Wanchaq: 0900-1000
JU34)	OCX4D	°870	2.5	R.Huancayo, Huancayo: 24h
LA08)	OBX1F	870	10	R.Programas del Perú, Chiclayo: 24h
PU06)	OAU7O	870	5	R.Libertad, Puno
PI09)	OAU1G	879	1	R.San Pedro Chanel, Sullana
LL15)	OAX2P	880	1	R.Sintonia, Trujillo: 0900-0300
LI16)	OBZ4N	°880	10	R.Union, Lima: 24h
CA10)	OAU2N	890	1	R.Libertad, Cajamarca: 1000-0400
PU07)	OBX7S	890	1	R.Bahá'í del Lago Titicaca, Chiucuito: 0900-0200
AR11)	OBX6K	900	1	R.Nevada, Uchumayo: 24h
CA11)	OAU2Q	900	1	R.Nor Oriental, Jaén
CU11)	OAU7I	900	1	R.Frecuencia Telerad, Cusco
HU02)	OAX3E	900		R.Ribereña, Aucaycu: 1000-0500
LA09)	OCX1D	900	1	R.Sensacional, Ferreñafe: 1000-0300
LI17)	OBX4X	°900	10	R.Canal N, Lima: 0900-0500
AY02)	OAU5M	910	1	R.Lider, Ayacucho
PU08)	OAU7G	910	1	R.Vision de Altiplano, Juliaca
CU12)	OCX7M	920	1	R.Programas del Perú, Cusco: 24h
IC04)	OCX5C	920	0.1	R.Stelar, Chinca Alta
JU07)	OAU4D	920	1	R.Super AM, Sta. Rosa de Sacco: 1000-0400, Sun 1100-0200
LL16)	OBX2S	920	1	R.Ollantay, Virú
PI10)	OBX1J	920	10	R.Programas del Peru, Piura: 24h
SM01)	OAX9V	°920	1	R.Marginal, Tocache
TA03)	OAU6G	920	1	R.La Heróica, Tacna
AR12)	OBX6T	930	2.5	R.Yaravi, Arequipa: 0900-0500
LL17)	OCX2V	930	1	R.Inti, Chepén: 1000-0300
LA10)	OAU1X	930	1	R.La Favorita, Olmos
LI18)	OAX4E	930	5	R.Modern – "R.Papa", Lima: 24h
PU09)		930		R.Colca, Juliaca
CU13)	OBX7L	940	1	R.Willkamayu, Wanchaq: 24h
JU08)	OBU4E	940	1	R.Comericial, Jauja
LL18)	OAY2F	940	1	R.Wipimsa – "Waicocha Radio", Huamachuco: 0900-0400
AN02)	OBX3S	950	1	R.Programas del Perú, Chimbote
AY03)	OAU5K	950	1	R.La Luz, Ayacucho
CA12)	OBX2G	°950	1	R.Cutervo, Cutervo
PU10)	OAZ7T	950	10	R.Instituto Comunicacion Pututo, Puno
SM02)	OBX9L	950	1	R.Estacón Láser, Rioja
AR13)	OBX6S	*960	12	R.Hispania, Mariano Melgar
CU14)		960	1	R.Concierto Santa Monica, Espinar
JU09)	OCY4V	960	1	R.Constelación, Huancayo: 1100-0400
LA11)	OBX1Y	v960	3	R.WST, Chiclayo: 0900-0400 (r: on 958)
LI19)	OAX4D	960	10	R.Panamericana, Lima: 24h
LO02)	OBX8H	960	1	R.Diez, Iquitos
AN03)	OAU3B	970	1	R.Huaraz, Huaraz
CA13)	OAU2K	*970	1	R.Lider del Norte, Cajamarca
CU15)	OAU7A	970	1	R.Tropicana, Wanchaq
IC05)	OBX5A	970	1	R.Comericial Sonora, Ica: 1100-0500
PI11)	OBX1V	970	1	R.La Capullana, Sullana: 1100-0100
PU11)	OBU7B	970	1	R.Virgin de Copacabana, Juliaca
AR14)	OAU6F	980	1	R.Universidad, Arequipa: 1000-0100
AY04)	OAU5O	980	1	R.OAU5O, Querobamba
JU10)	OBU4H	980	1	R.OBU4H, Huancayo
LA12)	OAU1N	980	1	Radio y Sonido, Lambayque
CA14)	OBX2M	990	0.5	R.Contumaza, Contumaza: 1100-0400
LI20)	OBX4J	990	10	R.Disco, Miraflores:1000-0500
LO03)	OBX8E	990	1	R.Programas del Perú, Iquitos
PI12)	OBU1C	990	1	R.OBU1C, Sechuar
TA04)	OAX6K	990	10	R.Continental, Tacna
AR15)	OBX6R	1000	1	R.Endesa, Paucarpata
CA41)	OAU2P	°1000	2	R.Bambamarca, Bambamarca: 1000-0300 (n.f.: 1530)
CU16)	OAZ7P	1000	2	R.Prensa el Dia, Cusco
HA01)	OBX5W	1000	1	R.Lircay, Lircay
LA13)	OAU1P	1000	1	R.California, Lambayque
PA07)		1000		R.LV de Campesino, Paucartambo
PI36)		°1000	0.5	R.Huarmaca, Huarmaca: 1200-0100
AP01)	OAU5G	1010	1	R.Amistad,Abancay
CA15)	OBX2P	1010	1.5	R.San Francisco, Cajamarca
PI13)		1010		R.LV de las Huaringas, Huancabamba
PU35)	OAX7F	1010	1	R.Ayaviri "LV Melgar", Ayaviri: 0930-0300
TU02)	OBZ1C	1010	1	R.Sonora, Tumbes
AN06)	OBX3U	*1020	1	R.Nacional, Chimbote
CU17	OBU7O	1020	1	R.Informes, Sivuani
JU11)	OBU4F	1020	1	R.Cristo Vivea, Huancayo
PI14)	OBU1D	1020	1	R.La Luz, Piura
TA05)	OAU6J	1020	1	R.Internacional, Tacna
AR16)	OCX6L	1030	1	R.San Luis, Arequipa
CU18)	OCX7O	1030	1	R.HG-AM, Cusco
LL19)		1030	3	R.Imperio, Huamachuco
PU12)	OAX7N	1030	1	R.LV del Altiplano, Puno: 1000-0400
CA16)	OBX2O	1040	1	R.Nor Oriente, Jaén
CU19)	OAU7H	1040	1	Multimedio Sistena de R., Espinar
IC06)	OBX5U	1040	1	R.Andina del Pacifico, Ica
LI21)	OBX4O	1040	10	R.Em. Nor-Oriente, Miraflores (ex. R.Exito)
PI15)	OAZ1D	1040	1	R.Alas Peruanas, Piura
AR17)	OBX6D	°1050	1	R.Bethel, Arequipa
JU12)	OBZ4J	1050	1	R.Bolognesi, Huancayo
LL20)	OCX2B	1050	1	R.Maria, Chepén
LO04)	OBX8F	1050	1	CPN Radio, Iquitos (rel.: CPN 1470)
CA52)		1050	1	R.Campesina, Cajamarca
PU13)	OAZ7Q	1050	1	R.San Augistín, Juliaca
CA17)	OCY2O	v1060	5	R.Sudamerica, Cutervo: 1130-0300, Sun 1200-2300
CU20)	OAU7U	1060		R.OAU7U, Cusco
LI22)	OCY4D	1060	1	R.Mil Sesenta, Lima: 1000-0600
MO02)	1060			R.La Luz, Ilo
TU03)	OAU1C	1060	5	CPN Radio, Tumbes (rel.: CPN 1470)
AR18)	OAU6K	1070	1	R.Trinidad, Arequipa: 1000-0200
IC07)	OAX5A	1070	0.2	R.San Juan, San Juan de Marcona
JU13)	OBX4G	1070	1	R.Visión, San Ramón
LA14)	OAU1J	1070	1	R.Vida, Chiclayo
SM03)	OBX9J	1070	3	R.Andes, Tarapoto
CA18)	OAU2L	1080	1	R.Andes, Cajamarca
CU21)	OAX7S	1080	2.2	R.Salkantay, CuscO: 0900-0400, Sun 1000-0200
LI23)	OAU4I	1080	10	R.La Luz, Lima // 1340: 24h
MO03)	OCX6X	1080	1	R.Futura, Ilo
PI16)	OBX1D	v1080	1.5	R.San Miguel, Piura: 0900-0600
AR19)	OBX6X	1090	1	R.Amistad, Arequipa
AY05)	OAU5F	1090	1	R.Apoyo El Agrario, Aucara
CA19)	OBX2A	1090	1	R.Cajabamba, Cajabamba: 0900-0500
JU14)	OCY4G	1100	1	Sonorama Radio, Huancayo: 1100-0300
LA15)	OBX1L	*1100	1	R.Star, Chiclayo
LI24)	OAZ4W	1100	1	R. Programas del Perú, Lima
LI25)	OCX4S	1100		R.Imperial "LV de la Provincia", Cañete: 0900-0300
PI39)		1100	1	R.Altura, Huarmaca: 1000-0200
PU15)	OBX7Z	°1100	1	R.LTC, Juliaca
SM04)	OAX9J	1100	0.5	R.Lamas, Lamas
AN06)	OBX3B	1110	1	R.Heroica, Huaraz
CA20)	OCX2U	°1110	1	R.Jaén, Jaén: 1030-0600
CU22)	OCX7T	1110	5	R.Comer, Cusco: 0900-0100, Sun 0900-1600
LI26)	OAU4J	1110	1	R.Sonora, Los Olivios: 1000-0400
MO04)	OCX6P	1110	1	R.Austral, Ilo
PI17)	OCX1R	1110	0.5	R.Centro Popular, La Union: 1000-0500
AR20)	OCX6U	1120	1	R.Municipal, Cerro Colorado
AY06)	OAU5H	1120	1	R.Quispillaccta, Ayacucho: 0900-1400, 2100-0100
LL21)	OBX2I	1120	1.5	R.Dinamica, Trujillo: 0900-2400
LO05)	OAX8A	1120	5	R.Nacional del Perú, Iquitos
AP02)	OAU5A	1130	1	R.Armonia, Abancay (r.: 1587)
CA21)	OAX2V	1130	1.2	R.Los Andes, Cjamarca
JU15)	OAZ4S	°1130		R.Chanchamayo, Chanchamayo: 1000-0300
LI27)	OAX4N	1130	2.6	R.Bacán, Lince
PU16)	OAU7B	1130	1	R.San Gabriel, Juliaca
SM05)	OAX9Q	°1130	3	R.San Martin, Tarapoto
AN07)	OAX3R	1140	1	R.Bahia, Chimbote: 1000-0200 (Sun 2200)
AR21)	OAX6L	°1140	1	R.Concordia, Arequipa (rel.: CPN 1470)
IC02)	OAX5W	1140	0.5	R.Chinchaysuyo, Chinca Alta
JU16)	OCY4C	1140	1	R.Programas del Perú, Pilcomayo
LA16)	OAU1T	1140		R.Fraternal, Ferreñafe
PI18)	OBX1W	1140	1.5	R.Piura, Piura
CA22)	OCY2E	1150	0.5	R.Chasqui Llacta, San Marcos: 1030-2200
CU23)	OCX7Q	1150	2.5	R.Universal, Wanchaq: 1000-2400
LO06)	OAX8D	°*1150	10	R.Loreto, Iquitos
PA02)	OBU4K	°1150	5	R.Mineria, Cerro de Pasco

	Call	kHz	kW	Name and h. of tr.
PU17)	OAU7K	1150	2.5	R.Lider, Juliaca
AY07)	OBX5O	°1160	1	R.Huanta 2000, Huanta: 1030-0130 (r 1390)
CA23)	OAU2T	1160	1	R.OAU2T, Chota
IC18)	OBX5M	1160	1	R.Luren, Ica
LL22)	OAX2C	°1160	0.3	R.Libertad, Trujillo: 1100-0400
LA17)	OCX1S	1160	1	Radiales Nor Oriental del Marañon, Chiclayo
LI28)	OAX4C	1160	5	R.1160 Noticias, Lima: 24h
MD02)	OCX7Z	1160	1	R.del Sur, Puerto Maldonado
MO05)	OBX6G	1160	1	R.Nacional del Perú, Moquegua
SM06)	OAX9A	1160	1	R.Imagen, Tarapoto
AN08)	OAZ3K	*1170	1	R.Nor Peruano Chimbote
AR22)	OBX6L	1170	10	R.Programas del Perú, Arequipa
CA24)	OAU2M	1170	1	R.Layzon, Cajamarca
CU24)		1170		R.Bethel, Cusco
JU17)	OCX4Y	°1170	1	R.COSAT, Satipo: 1100-0200
LO07)	OBX8M	1170	1	R.La Luz, Iquitos
PI19)	OCX1B	1170	1	R.San Juan, Talara
PU18)	OCX7Y	1170	0.5	R.Constelación, Puno: 0900-0300
CA25)		1180	1	R.La Luz, Jaen
JU18)	OCY4Z	1180	1	R.Libertad "R.RLJ", Junin: 24h
LL23)	OCX2A	1180	1	R.America, Quiruvilca
PI20)	OAZ1C	1180	1	R.Chulucanas, Chulucanas
AN09)	OBX3D	°1190	5	R.Ancash, Huaraz: 24h
AR23)	OCX6G	1190	1.5	R.Encuentro, Yanahuara: 1100-0400
CU25)	OAX7B	°1190	2	R.Twantinsuyo, Cusco: 1000-0300
LA18)	OAX1E	°1190	10	R.Chiclayo, Chiclayo
AP03)	OBX5X	1200	1	R.Comercial, Abancay
CA26)	OAU2A	1200	1	Frecuencia Pedagogica, Cajamarca
JU19)	OAU4G	1200	3	R.Andes, Huancayo
LI29)	OAX4B	1200	3	R.Cadena, Lima: 1000-0500
PU19)	OCX7S	1200	1	R.Cultura, Juliaca
TA06)		1200		R.La Luz, Tacna
UC01)		1200		R.La Luz, Pucallapa
CU26)	OAX7M	°1210	1	R.Quillabamba, Santa Ana: 1000-0300
JU20)	OCY4T	1210	1	R.Galaxia, Satipo
LL24)	OAX2Q	1210	1	R.Universo, Trujillo: 24h
PI21)		1210	1	R.Municipalidad, Aybaca
AR24)	OAX6X	°1220	4	R.Melodia, Arequipa: 24h
IC09)	OAU5N	1220	1	R.La Luz, Ica
LA19)	OCX1X	1220	3	R.Gran Plaza, Chiclayo: 0900-0400
JU21)	OBZ4Y	1230	1	R.Selleciones, Tarma: 1100-0200 (Sun 1800)
LL25)	OAX2T	1230	1	R.Albújar, Guadalupa: 1200-0400
LL27)	OBX2C	1230	1	R.Otuzco, Otuzco
MD03)	OBX7J	°1230	0.5	R.Madre de Dios, Puerto Maldonado: 1030-0200
PA03)	OBX4Z	°*1230	1	R.LV de Oxapampa, Oxapampa
PU20)	OAU7V	1230	1	R.OAU7V, Juliaca
AN10)	OAU3C	1240	1	R.La Luz, Chimbote
AR25)	OAU6D	1240	5	R.Lider, Arequipa
CU27)	OBX7M	1240		R.Túpac Amaru, Sicuani: 1000-0100
JU22)	OAU4V	1240	10	R.Cumbre, Chilca: 24h
LL26)	OAU2Y	°1240	1	R.Bolivar, Bolivar
PI22)	OCX1C	1240	1	R.Sechura, Sechura
CA27)	OAU2V	1250	1	HGV, Santa Cruz
CU28)	OBX7A	1250	3	R.Solar, Cusco: 1000-0500
LI30)	OAX4L	1250	5	R.Miraflores, Miraflores: 1100-0500
PI23)	OBZ1B	1250	1	R.B.N.S., Talara Alta
UC02)	OAX8P	°1250	1	R.Pucallapa, Pucallapa: 1030-0500
AN11)		1260		R.Periodico, Chimbote
AR26)	OBX6D	1260	1	R.Mundial, Arequipa
AT08)	OBX5S	*1260	0.3	R.Nacional del Perú, Ayacucho
CA50)		1260	1	R.Ebenezer, Bambamarca: 1100-2300
CU29)	OAU7K	1260		R.Stereo Nevada, Espinar
HU04)	1260		1	R.La Luz, Huanuco
LA20)	OCX1O	1260	1	R.Nor Puruana, Chiclayo
LA21)	OAZ1A	1260	1	R.Ferrañafe, Ferrañafe
CU30)	OAU7S	1270	2	R.Horizonte, Cusco
JU23)	OBZ4T	1270	0.4	R.La Merced, Chanchamayo: 1100-1900, 2200-0200 (Sun 1200-1900)
LL28)	OCX2Z	1270	1	R.Estacion Latina, Cepén: 1000-0400
LI31)	OAZ4H	1270	0.4	R.Huacho, Huacho
LO08)	OAX8T	°1270	1	R.Eco, Iquitos: 0900-0400
PI24)	OAU1S	1270	1	R.Nor Paita, Paita
LA22)	OAU1R	v1276	1	R.Gotas del Oro, Urrunaga: 0900-0500, Sun. 1100-0200 (n.f.: 1280)
AN12)	OBX3C	*1280		R.Alopesa, Chimbote
AR27)	OBX6P	1280	0.5	R.Fénix, Camaná
CA28)	OBX2F	°1280	1	R.Moderna, Cajamarca: 1000-0400 (Sun 0300)
HU01)	OAX3Y	1280	1	R.La Selva, Rupa-Rupa (r: 830)

	Call	kHz	kW	Name and h. of tr.
LA22)	OAU1R	1280	1	R.Gotas del Oro, Urrunaga: 0900-0500, Sun. 1100-0200 (r: 1276)
AM02)	OAX9N	*1290	10	R.Nor Oriental, Bagua Grande
AR28)	OCX6B	1290	1	R.Trebol, Mariano Melgar
LL29)		°1290		R.TV Sonorama, Trujillo
LI32)	OBU4Q	1290	1	S & RD, Hualmay
TU04)	OCX1Q	1290	1	R.Programas del Perú, Tumbes: 24h
AN13	OAX3O	1300	0.5	R.Huascarán, Independencia: 1100-0300
CA29)	OAU2I	1300	1	R.Paraiso, Cajabamba
CU31)	OAX7P	1300	5	R.Misercordia, Cusco: 1200-2130
JU25)	OAZ4B	°v1300	1	R.Andina, Huancayo: 0900-1400, Sun 1000-0300
LA23)	OAU1U	1300	1	R.Frecuencia Lider, Morrop
LI33)	OAX4S	°1300	5	R.Comas, Comas: 1000-0500
PU21)	OAX7X	°1300	0.3	R.Juliaca, Juliaca: 0900-0300 (Sun 2300)
SM08)		1300		R.La Luz, Tarapoto
TA07)	OAX6P	1300	0.4	R.Comercial Latina, Tacna (rel.: RPP 730)
UC03)	OAZ8B	1300		R.Nuevo Mundo, Pucallapa: 24h
AR29)	OAU6N	1310	1	R.MCV, Paucarpata
CA30)	OBX2D	°1310	1	R.Chota, Chota: 1130-0300
LI34)	OBX4L	1310	1	R.Irvisa, Huacho
LO09)	OBX8L	°1310	1	R.Vision Amazonia, Iquitos
AN14)	OAX3U	*1320	1	R.Miramar, Chimbote
AP04)	OAU5C	1320	1	R.Perú, Abancay
JU26)	OBU4I	°1320	1	R.Majestad, Huancayo
LL30)	OBX2Q	1320	1	R.Frecuencia Popular, Chepén: 0900-0500
LI15)	OAX4A	1320	10	R.Nacional del Perú (R.La Cronica), Lima
PU22)	OAU7W	1320	3	R.Peru, Juliaca
AR30)	OVX6E	1330	1	R.Ondas del Misti, Mariano Melgar
AY09)	OAU5L	1330	0.5	R.San Juan. San Juan Bautista
CU32)	OCX7K	1330	1	R.San Miguel, Wanchaq: 0900-0300, Sun 1100-0200
LA25)	OAU1A	1330	1	R.Dos Mil, Chiclayo: 1000-0400
AR31)		1340		R.Comercial, Molendo
CA31)	OAU2S	1340	1	R.Shalom, Cajamarca
IC11)	OAX5D	1340	0.5	R.Chinca, Chinca Alta
JU27)	OAU4N	1340	1	R.Jauja, Jauja: 0900-0300
LI35)	OAU4Q	1340	5.5	R.Colonial, Pucasana
LI36)	OAZ4M	1340	0.2	R,Huaral, Huaral
PU23)		1340		R.Comercial Sudamericana, Juliaca
CU33)	OBU7E	1350	1	R.Lider, Cusco
LA26)	OAU1H	1350	1	R.Capimag, Chiclayo
MO06)	OBX6F	1350	1	R.Ilo, Ilo: 24h
UC04)	OBX8D	1350		R.Super, Pucallpa: 1030-0500
HU05)	OAX3N	°v1352	1	R.Ondas del Huallaga, Huanuco: 0930-(Sun 1100)-0300 (n.f.: 1350)
AN16)	OAU3A	1360	0.2	R.Intercontinental, Yungay
AR32)	OCX6T	1360	1	R.Luza, Paucarpata
CA32)	OCY2I	1360	5	R.Santa Monica, Chota: 1100-0100
CU34)	OAX7R	°v1360	2.5	R.Sicuani, Sicuani: 0900-0300 (r: v1362)
IC12)	OBZ5Z	1360	1	R.Cruz del Sur, Palpa: 1030-0300
JU28)	OAU4O	1360	1	R.Hecaburt, Tarma
LL31)	OBX2N	1360	1	R.Super Uno, Santiago de Cao
PI25)	OBZ1A	1360	1	R.del Norte, Sullana
PU24)	OUA7L	1360	2.5	R.Continente, Juliaca
AP05)	OCX5A	1370	1	R.Sudamericana, Abanacy
CA51)		v1370		R.S. Miguel Arcangel, S.Migeul de Pallaques: 1100-0200
CU35)	OAZ7J	°1370	1	R.Santa Monica, Wanchaq: 0900-0300
LA27)	OAU1W	1371	1	R.OAU1W, Chiclayo
LI37)	OAZ4O	1370	0.5	R.Tres de Octubre (R.Cosmos), Huacho
MO07)	OAX6T	1370		R.Moquegua, Moquegua: 0930-0500
SM09)	OBX9A	1370		R.Palmera: 1100-0500
AR33)	OAX6O	1380	2.5	R.San Martin, Arequipa: 1000-0130
CA33)	OAX2W	°1380	1	R.Atahualpa, Cajamarca: 1100-0500
LI38)	OCY4U	1380	1	R.ABC, Lima: 1000-0300
PI26)	OBZ1D	1380	1	R.Bellavista, Bellavista
HU06)	OBX3I	v1382	1	R.Pilco Mozo, Huanucio (n.f.: 1380)
AR34)		1390		R.Neptuno, Mollendo
AY07)	OBX5O	°1160	1	R.Huanta 2000, Huanta: 1030-0130 (n.f.: 1160)
CU36)	OAU7T	1390	1	R.Enlace, Kunturkanki
LL32)	OAU2Z	1390	1	R.La Luz, Trujillo
LA28)	OAU1V	1390	1	R.Tropical, Morrop
PU25)	OCX7U	1390	1	R.Cultura, Yunguy
AR35)	OAX6J	1400	0.5	R.Landa, Arequipa
CA34)	OAU2H	1400	1	R.OAU2H, Cajamarca
CU37)	OAX7I	°1400	1	R.La Hora, Cuzco: 1000-0200 (Sun 1100-1700)
IC13)	OCX5B	1400	1	R.Interandina, Pisco: 24h
JU30)	OBX4H	1400	1	R.Selecciones, Tarma

	Call	kHz	kW	Name and h. of tr.
LI39)	OBX4W	1400	2.5	R.Callao, Lima: 1100-0500
PI27)	OCX1A	1400	1	R.MDY, Talara Alta: 1000-0600
LL33)	OAX2Y	1410	1	R.Heróica, Trujillo: 0900-0600
LA29)		1410		R.Olmos, Olomos
LI40)	OBZ4V	1410	1	R.Universal, Santa Maria. 1000-0600
TU05)	OBU1H	1410	1	R.La Luz, Tumbes
UC05)	OBX8I	1410		Dif.Comercial, Pucallapa
CA04)	OAU2R	1415		R.Cajamarca, Cajamarca: 0800-0200, SS 0800-0300 (n.f.: 1420)
CA38)	OBX2U	1420	5	R.Ilucan, Cutervo (r.: 1476)
CU38)	OBU7L	1420		R.OBU7L, Yanaoca
LI41)	OBZ4G	1420	1	R.San Isidro, Lima
LO10)	OAZ8Z	°1420	1	R.Oriente, Yurimaguas
PI28)	OCX1H	1426	0.2	R.San Jose, La Union: 0900-0100 (n.f. 1420)
AM03)	OBX9H	1430	1	R.Utcubamba, Bagua Grande
AN17)	OBX3E	1430	1	R.Huarmey, Huarmey
AN18)	OAZ3H	*1430	1	R.Chavin, Chimbote
CU39)	OAZ7M	1430	1	CPN Radio, Cusco (r: CPN 1470)
JU31)	OAZ4V	1430	0.5	R.Universal, El Tambo: 1100-0500
LL34)	OBX2T	1430	1	R.Santa Bárbara, Ascope
LI42)		1430		R.Forestal, San Vincente de Cañete
PU27)		1430		R.Red, Andina
TA08)	OAU6M	1430	1	R.Lider, Tacna
AN19)	OAZ3O	°1440	1	R.LV de Pomebamba, Pomebamba
AR36)	OAX6R	1440	1	R.El Tiempo, Cayma: 1000-0300
CA35)	OAU2O	1440	1	R.Frecuencia VH, Celendin: 1100-2300
CU40)	OAU7M	1440	1	R.Satelite, Sicuani
LA30)	OBX1T	1440	2	R.Cooperativa Tumán, Chiclayo: 1100-0300
LI43)	OAX4K	1441	1	R.Imperial, Lima (n.f.: 1440)
CU41)	OCX7W	1450	1	R.Santa Rosa, Santa Ana
LL35)	OCX2J	1450	1.5	R.San Juan, Trujillo: 1000-0400
LI44)	OBX4K	1450	1	R.Fortaleza, Barranca
CA36)	OAU2W	°1453	1	R.San Miguel, San Miguel: 0900-0200 (n.f.: 1450)
PI29)	OAX1V	1457	1	R.Sullana "LV de Chira", Sullana (n.f. 1460)
AN20)	OBX3A	*1460	1	R.Chimu, Chimbote
AR37)	OBX6C	1460	1	R.Bahia, Mollendo
CA37)	OBU2E	1460	1	R.Comercial, Jaén
CU42)	OBU7M	1460		R.OBU7M, Marcapata
IC14)	OAX5K	1460	2.5	R.Internacional, Pisco
JU32)	OCY4I	1460	0.5	R.Imperial, Junin
JU33)	OAZ4F	°1460	1	R.La Oroya, La Oroya: 1000-0500
LL36)	OBX2Y	1460	1	R.Estelar, Guadalupe: 1000-0600
PI29)	OAX1V	1460	1	R.Sullana "LV de Chira", Sullana (r. 457)
PU28)	OAX7W	°1460	10	R.El Sol de los Andes, Juliaca: 0900-0200
SM10)	OBX9B	1460	1	R.Frecuencia popular, Rioja: 1000-0500
AR38)	OAU6E	1470	1	R.del Sur, Arequipa
CU43)	OAX7G	°1470	1	R.Cusco, Cusco: 1000-0300
LL37)	OCX2G	1470	1	R.Occidenta, Quiruvilca
LI45)	OAU4B	1470	20	CPN Radio, Lima: 24h
TA09)	OAX6M	°1470	0.8	R.Tacna, Tacna: 0900-0500
CU44)	AOZ7G	1475	1	R.Espinar, Yauri (n.f.: 1480)
CA38)	OBX2U	1476	5	R.Ilucan, Cutervo: 1100-0300 (Sun: 1030-2300) (n.f.: 1420)
CA44)	OBU2H	°1480	0.5	R.San Lorenzo, Socota (r.: 1584)
JU35)	OAU4A	1480	1	R.Laser, Santa Rosa de Sacco
LL38)	OCX2C	1480	0.6	R.Comercial, Virú
JU35)	OAU4A	1480	1	R.Laser, Santa Rosa de Sacco
LL38)	OCX2C	1480	0.6	R.Comercial, Virú
LI46)	OCX4V	1480	1	R.K´ler, Paramonga
PI30)	OCX1L	1480	1	R.Supercontinental, Chulucanas: 1100-0500
AR39)	OAX6Q	1490	1.3	R.Minuto, Cerro Colorado
CU45)	OBU7I	1490		R.Chaski, Maras: 1100-2300
IC15)	OAX5N	1490	0.3	R.Nazca, Nazca
LA31)	OAX1L	°v1490	1	R.Imperio, Chiclayo: 0845-0500
LO11)	OAX8F	°1490	1	R.Atlantida, Iquitos
PA04)	OBU4N	1490	1	R.La Luz, Cerro de Pasco
PU29)	OCX7P	1490	1	R.Emisora Frontera, Puno
CA39)		1500		R.San Pedro, San Pablo
CU46)	OCX7G	1500	1	R.Chancis, Sicuani
HU07)	OBX3J	°1500	1/3	R.Luz y Sonido, Huanuco: 0900-0300
JU36)	OAU4W	1500	1	R.Wanka, Huancayo: 1000-0500
LL39)	OBX2X	1500	1	R.Comercial, Trujillo. 0845-0300
LI47)	OBX4I	°v1500	10	R.Santa Rosa, Lima: 24h
TA10)	OAU6B	1500	1	R.Bulevar, Tacna: 1100-0100
AR40)	OCX6Q	v1510	1	R.Alegria, Arequipa: 0900-0200
CA40	OCX2O	1510		R.Inca, Los Baños del Inca (r.: 1517)
CU47)	OBX7P	1510	1	R.El Sur, Wanchaq
IC16)	OAX5F	1510	1	R.LV Huamanga, Nazca: 24h
JU37)	OCX4J	°1510	1	R.Tarma, Tarma: 1000-0500
LL40)	OAU2U	°1510	2.5	R.Virgin, Huamachuco (ex.R.Los Andes)
LA32)	OBU1B	1510	1	R.OBU1B, Olmos
LI48)	OAU4M	1510	1	R.Flores de Campo, Barranca
TU06)	OCX1V	1510	1	R.Tumbes, Tumbes
UC06)	OBX8K	1510	1	R.Centro de los Medios, Sepahua
CA40)	OCX2O	1517	1	R.Inca, Los Baños del Inca: 0800-0300 (n.f.: 1510)
CU48)		1520		R.Fuentes Mollo, Espinar
HO02)	OAU5J	1520	1	R.Virgin de Carmen, Huancavelica
LA33)	OAX1C	1520	1	R.Delcar, Chiclayo
PU30)	OAU7Y	1520	5	R.OAU7Y, Juliaca
SM11)	OAX9X	1520	1	R.Vision, Janjui (r.: 1545)
AN21)	OBX3H	1530	1	CPN Radio, Chimbote (rel.: CPN 1470)
CA41)	OAU2P	°1530	2	R.Bambamarca, Bambamarca: 1000-0300 (r: 1000)
CU49)	OAZ7F	1530	0.5	R.dif. Espinar, Yauri (R.Confraternidad)
CU50)		°1530		R.Ondas del Sur Oriente, Quillabamba
IC17)		1530		R.Universidad, San Juan Bautista
JU38)	OBZ4S	1530	1	R.15-15, Huancayo: 1000-0600
LI49)	OBU4C	°1530	10	R.Milena, Lima
PI31)	OCX1Y	1530	1	R.Leomar, Bellavista
AR41)	OAU6A	1540	1	R.M–U, Arequipa: 24h
CU51)	OCX7V	1540	1	R.Los Andes, Cusco
LL41)	OAU2X	1540	1	R.Espacial, Otuzco
LL42)	OBU2A	1540	2	R.Mundial AM, Trujillo
LI50)	OBZ4U	*1540	1	R.Barranca, Barranca
PA05)	OBX4N	*1540	0.3	R.Corporacion, Cerro de Pasco
TU07)	OBX1B	1540	1	R.LV de la Frontera, Tumbes
SM11)	OAX9X	1545	1	R.Vision, Janjui (n.f.: 1520)
AN22)	OAU3D	*1550	1	R.Cruz, Chimbote
AY10)	OBX5J	1550	1	R.San Cristobal, Carmen Alto (R.Maria)
CA42)	OCX2R	1550	1	R.OCX2R, Chota
LA34)	OAX1D	1550	1	R.Superior, Monsefú: 1100-0400
LI51)	OBX4P	1550	1	R.Independencia, Lima: 0900-0500
PU31)	OCX7A	*1550	1	R.Cultura, Puno
AR42)	OCX6N	1560	1	R.La Union, Arequipa
CA43)	OBX2J	1560	0.5	R.Nuvo Continente, Cajamarca: 1000-0300 (n.f.: 820)
CU52)	OAZ7N	1560	1	R.Maria, Wanchaq
HU39)	OBU4G	1560	1	R.San Sebastian, Yauyos
CA44)	OBU2H	°1564	0.5	R.San Lorenzo, Socota (n.f.: 1480)
AN23)	OBX3N	1570	1	R.Chasquie, Yungay
AR43)	OCX6I	1570	1	R.Willy, Uraca
HU08)	OBX3M	1570	1	R.San Martin, Huanuco
PI32)	OCX1Z	1570	1	R.La Nueva Esperanza, Tambo Grande
PU32)	OAU7Z	1570	1	Em.Comercial Oriunda Eco, Juliaca
CA08)	OAU2E	°1577	1	R.Frecuencia, San Ignacio: 1200-2300 (n.f.: 840)
CU53)	OBX7Q	1584	0.5	R.El Triunfo, Cusco (r: 1584)
JU40)	OAU4P	1580	1	R.San Juan, Tarma: 1030-0230 (Sun: 1100-2100)
LA36)	OBX1M	1580	3/1	R.Naylamp, Lambayeque: 1000-0200
SM12)		1580	1	R.Central, Bellavista: 1100-0300
CU53)	OBX7Q	1584	0.5	R.El Triunfo, Cusco (n.f.:1580)
AR44)	OCX6S	1590	1	R.Mundo, Arequipa
AP02)	OAU5A	1587	1	R.Armonia, Abancay: 1030-0300 (n.f.1130)
AR44)	OCX6S	1590	1	R.Mundo, Arequipa
LL43)	OBU2C	1590	1	Agro Radio, Trujillo
LI52)	OAZ4Z	1590	2	R.Agricultura "La Peruanísima" Lima: 1100-0400
PU33)	OAU7C	1590	1	R.Publicidad Lider, Juliaca
CA45)	OCY2D	1600	1	R.Internacional, San Pablo: 1000-1700, 2100-0300
AP09)		1610		R.Haquira, Haquira (r.)
AR45)	OAU6O	1610	0.5	R.Flor de los Andes, José Luis Bustamente y Rivero (R.El Sabor, Arequipa)
LL45)		1610		R.Carabamba, Julcánn (r.)

SW:

	Call	kHz	kW	Name and h. of tr.
HU09)		v3173		R.Municipal, Distrito de Panao
PU28)	OBX72	3230	1	R.El Sol de Los Andes, Juliaca (irr.)
HU07)	OAW3A	v3235	1	R.Luz y Sonido, Huánuco: 0900-0200
CA38)	OAW2B	*3280	1	R.Ilucan, Cutervo (**F.PL**) (rp. 5678)
LA07)	OAZ1F	*3290	1	R.Horizonte, Chiclayo (**F.PL**) (r: 4534)
CA46)	OAW2D	*3320	1	R.Sudamérica, Cutervo (**F.PL**) (r: 5620)
HU05)	OAX3Q	v3330	5	R.Ondas del Huallaga, Huánuco (irr.)
CA41)	OAW2C	*3350	1	R.Bambamarca, Bambamarca (**F.PL**) (r: 4426)

	Call	kHz	kW	Name and h. of tr.
LO10)		*3350	5	R.Oriente, Yurimaguas (**F.PL**)
PI33)	OAW1A	*3370	1	R.Huancabamba, Huancabamba (**F.PL**) (r: 6536)
AR46)	OAW6B	3375	1	R.San Antonio, Callalli (irr.)
CA12)	OAX2R	*3390	1	R.Cutervo, Cutervo (**F.PL**)
LI53)	OAU4L	*3395	1	R.Internacional, Comas
LA31)		4386	0.5	R.Imperio, Chiclayo: 0845-0500
CA41)	OAW2C	v4427	1	R.Bambamarca, Bambamarca: 2200-0300 (n.f.: 3350)
LA36)		v4435	0.5	R.Nyalamp, Lambayeque (irr)
CA48)		4461	1	R.Nor Andina, Celendin (irr.)
CA35)		4485	1	R.Frecuencia VH, Celendin (2300-0300)
LA07)		*4534	0.5	R.Horizonte, Chiclayo
PI13)		*4750		R.San Francisco Solano, Sondor
AY07)	OAZ5B	v4751	0.5	R.Huanta 2000, Huanta (n.f.: 4755)
AY07)	OAZ5B	*4755	0.5	R.Huanta 2000, Huanta (r: 4751)
LI01)	OCX4W	*4770	5	R.Inca del Peru, Lince
JU37)	OCX4W	4775	0.4	R.Tarma, Tarma: 1000-0500
CA47)	OAX2L	4781	1	R.Satelite, Santa Cruz: 2300-0300
LO11)	OAX8J	4790	1	R.Atlantida, Iquitos :0900(Sun. 1000)-0500
LO01)	OAX8R	4824	10	LV de la Selva, Iquitos: 0950-0300, Sun: 1100-1700
CU34)	OAX7T	v4826	0.3	R.Sicuani "LV de Canchis", Sicuani: 1000-0300 (n.f.:4835)
CA01)	OCX2E	4835	1	R.Marañon, Jaen: 1000-0300, Sun: 1000-0200
CU34)	OAX7T	*4835	0.3	R.Sicuani "LV de Canchis", Sicuani: 1000-0300 (r: 4826)
CU37)	OAZ7A	4856	1	R.La Hora, Cusco: 1000-1500, 1700-0100 Sun 1100-1700 (n.f.: 4855)
LI33)	OAW4A	v4880	1	R.Comas, Lima: 1000-0430
HA02)	OAX5X	4886	0.8	R.Virgin del Carmen, Huancavelica: 1400-0100 (n.f.: 4885)
AY12)	OAZ5C	4899	1	R.Huanta, Huanta (n.f.: 4890)
AR48)		4890	1	R.Macedonia, Arequipa (irr.)
CA30)	OAZ2B	v4890	1	R.Chota, Chota: 1100-0300v
JU33)	OAZ4G	4905	1	R.La Oroya, La Oroya: 1000-0500
LI04)	OAZ4N	v*4915	10	R.Cora, Lima: 1030-1500, 2300-0500
CU32)		4930		R.San Miguel, Cusco (r)
PI13)	OAW1B	*4930	1	R.LV de Huarinjas, Huancabamba (**F.PL**) (r: 6820)
UC07)	OAW8A	4940	1	R.San Antonio, Villa Atalaya
MD03)	OBX7I	4950	5	R.Madre de Dios, Puerto Maldonado: 1000(Sun: 1100)-0200
AY13)	OAX5S	4955	5	R.Cultural Amauta, Huanta: 1000-1400, 2100-0100
CU32)	OAZ7B	4965	1	R.Santa Monica, Wanchaq
LI06)	OAZ4X	v4975	5	R.Pacifico, Lima: 1030-1400, 2300-0100v
PI13)	OAW1B	*4980		LV de las Huarinjas, Huancabamba (r: 6820)
AN09)	OAZ3B	4992	5	R.Ancash, Huaraz: 24h (n.f.: 4990)(irr.)
CA20)	OAX2S	v4996	2	R.Andina, Huancayo: 2100-0400 (Sun 0300)(n.f.:4995)
PU15)	OAW7E	5005	1	R.LTC, Juliaca: 1100-1300, 0000-0200, Sun: 1100-1900
PA01)	OBZ4B	5014	1	R.Altura, Cerro de Pasco: 1000-0430 (n.f.: 5010)
AM04)	OBX9K	v5020	5	R.Horizonte, Chachapoyas: 1100-0200
CU36)	OAX7Q	5025	5	R.Quillabamba, Quillabamba: 1000-0300
LL40)	OAZ2A	v5030	5	R.Virgin, Huamachuco (ex. R.Los Andes)
JU18)	OCY4Y	5039	1	R.Libertad, Junín (irr.)
CU50)		5119	1	R.Ondas del Sur Oriente, Quillabamba
PI36)		5385	0.3	R.Huarmaca, Huarmaca(irr.)
LL26)		5460		R.LV Bolivar, Bolivar: 2200-0300
AM09)	OBX1M	5470	0.5	R.San Nicolas, Rodriguez de Mendoza
AM06)		5487		Reina de la Selva, Chachapoyas
CA36)		*5500		R.San Miguel, San Miguel
CA38)		5678		R.Ilucan, Cutervo: 1100-0300
CA08)	OAW2E	v5700	0.1	R.Frecuencia, San Ignacio (n.f.: 4870)
AR24)	OBX6I	v5939	1	R.Melodia, Arequipa: 24h
AR17)	OAX6A	5949	1	R.Bethel, Arequipa (n.f.: 4950)
CU45)	OBW7B	v5980	5	R.Chasqui, Cusco: 100-2300, 0000-0200
LI12)	OAX4Q	v6020	3	R.Victoria, Lima: 24h
LI47)	OCY4H	v6047	10	R.Santa Rosa, Lima (irr.)
LI16)	OBZ4O	v6115	10	R.Union, Lima: 24h
AR21)	OBX6B	*6141		R.Concordia, Arequipa (n.f.: 6150)
LI49)	OAW4C	6160	10	R.Milenia, Lima (**F.PL.**)
CU25)	OAX7C	6173	1	R.Tawantinsuyo, Cusco: 1000-0300 (n.f.: 6175)

	Call	kHz	kW	Name and h. of tr.
LO10)	OAX8I	6188	1	R.Oriente, Yurimaguas: 1000-0200 (n.f.: 6190)
CU43)	OAX7A	6193	1	R.Cusco, Cusco: 1000-0300, Sun: 1100-0200 (n.f.: 6195)
AP07)	OBX5I	6277	0.4	R.Apurimac, Abancay: 1000-0200, Sun: 100-2300 (n.f.: 4830)
CA53)		6329		R.LV de Faique
CU54)	OAW7A	6520		R.Paucartambu, Paucartambo (nf 3200)
PI33)	OAW1A	6536	1	R.Huancabamba, do (R.La Ponderosa) (n.f.: 3370)
PI37)		6560		Estacion Dos, Huancabamba (irr.)
PI35)	OAW1C	6674		R.Super Sencacion, Huancabamba (n.f.: 4840)
LA37)		v6724		R.Cielo, Chiclayo (irr)
SM14)		6798	1	R.Ondas del Rio Mayo, Nueva Cajamarca
PI13)	OAW1B	6820		LV de las Huarinjas, Huancabamba: 1045-0200 (n.f.: 4930)
PI40)		6895		R.San Miguel, San Miguel de El Faique
PI38)		v6957		R.LV de Campesino, Huarmaca
TA09)	OAX6H	v9505	0.2	R.Tacna, Tacna: 0900-0500 (irr.)
LI06)	OBZ4A	*9675	7.5	R.Pacifico, Lima: 1400-2300
LI12)	OCX4C	v9722	1	R.Victoria, Lima

Addresses and other information:
(Names of **departamentos** should be added to address info, main capitals excluded).

AM00 (AMAZONAS):
AM01) CP – Av. Circunvalacion 1336, Bagua Grande. – **AM02)** Simón Bolívar 433, Bagua Grande. – **AM03)** Jr. F. Villareal 400, Utcubamba – **FM** 96.9. – **AM04)** Jr. Amazonas 1717 (Ap. 69), Chachapoyas. +51 4177 7793. +51 4175 7004. - **FM:** 99.9. – **AM05)**) Jr. Huayabamba 513, San Nicolas, Prov. Rodríguez de Mendoza. **AM06)** Jr. Ayacucho 944, Plaza Mayor, Chachapoyas. +51 4177 7203/4177 8172 +54 4177 7989 **Web:** www.reinadelselva.com.pe - **email:** joreno@terra.com.pe – **FM:** 102.5 – **AM07)** Jr. Amazonas 315, Aramango, Prov. de Bagua. – **AM08)** Calle San Martín, cuadra 16, Sector El Libertador, Bagua Grande, Prov. de Utcubamba. – **AM09)** Pasaje Hilario López 111, entrada del "Hotel Grández", San Nicolas, Prov Rodriguez de Mendoza – **FM:** 98.5.

AN00 (ANCASH):
AN01) Av. Nepeña Mza. 8-C, Lote 3, Casma. +51 4371 1266. - **FM:** 92.5. – **AN02)** Av. Francisco Pizzarro, Chimbote. - **FM:** 95.5. – **AN03)** Jr. 13 de Deciembre, Huaraz. – **AN04)** Urb. el Trapecio 2da etapa, MZ. G, Lote 18, Chimbote – **FM:** 97.5 – **AN05)** Manzana 8 Lote Ind. Primero de Mayo, Chimbote. - **FM:** 105.1. – **AN06)** Av. Mariscal Luzuriaga 1239, Huaraz. – **AN07)** Pasaje los Jardines 129, Chimbote. +51 4332 2391. – **AN08)** Zona Denominada Alto Peru, Chimbote. - **FM**: 104.3. – **AN09)** Av. Francisco Araos 146, Huaraz. **Web:** invierteenhuaraz.com.pe/radioancash/default.asp +54 4372 1359. - **FM:** 101.3. – **AN10)** Jr. Elias Aguire 238 Of. 204, Chimbote.- +51 4376 6940. – **AN11)** Calle Ramon Castilla MZ.J, Lote 11, Chimbote – **AN12)** Av. Leoncio Prado 660, Chimbote. - **FM**: 89.9. – **AN13)** Jr. San Martin 655, Huaraz. - **FM:** 104.5. – **AN14)** Av. San pedro 246, Chimbote +54 4332 2279/4334 3448. - **FM**: 106.7. – **AN15)** Av. Pardo 6788 – AA.HH., 1° de Mayo, Chimbote. – **AN16)** Casero el Rayan, Yungay. – **AN17)** Av. Cabo Alberto Reyes 281, Huarmey - **FM:** 89.7. – **AN18)** Urb. San Juan ZN 5, Chimbote – **FM:** 92.3. – **AN20)** Prolongación Javier Pardo (2da etapa), Villa Maria, Chimbote. – **AN21)** Calle Aviación 298, Chimbote. - **FM**: 103.5. – **AN22)** Jr. Alfonso Ugarte 627 4° piso, Chimbote. – **AN23)** Barrio Lucmapampa, Yungay. – **AN24)** Plaza de Armas S/N, Chiquian.

AP00 (APURIMAC):
AP01) Av. Seoane s/n, Abancay. – **AP02)** Jr. Cusco 319, Abancay. - **FM:** 92.1. – **AP03)** Av. Nuñez 401, Abancay. – **AP04)** Jr. Cusco 206, Abancay. – **AP05)** Av. Seoane 200, Region Inca, Abancay. - **FM:** 103.3 "Sudamericana". – **AP06)** Jr. Apurimac s/n, Chincheros. - **AP07)** Jr. Cuzco 206, Abancay. - **FM:** 104.5. – **AP08)** Guillermo Cáceres Tresierra 381, Andahuaylas. +51 8372 1511 - **FM:** 94.9. – **AP09)** Haquira, Dis. de Haquira, Prov. de Cotabambas

AR00 (AREQUIPA):
AR01) Calle San Juan de Dios 210, Arequipa – **FM:** 89.5. – **AR02)** Av. Goyeneche 818, Miraflores, Arequipa. – **AR03)** Lote 64-5-C Km 48 Panamericana Sur, La Joya. – **AR04)** Cl. Dean Valdivia 418, Of.25, Urb. Cercado, Arequipa +51 5480 7362. – **AR05)** Av. Independencia 56, Arequipa +51 5422 4109 - **FM:** 93.5. – **AR06)** Cruco Ferroc, Puno Variante, Uchumayo. – **AR07)** Calle Alto de la Luna 334, Arequipa. – **AR08)** Calle Samuel Pastor s/n, Camaná. - **FM:** 100.1. – **AR09)** Calle Francia 120, Urb. Satélite Chico-Paucarpata, Arequipa. +51 54 424237, 236086, 457806. – **Quechua:** Sun 0830-1030. - **FM:** 103.5. – **AR10)** Av. La Paz 504, Cercado Arequipa, Arequipa. – **AR11)** Av. Victor A. Belaúnde

C-8, Umacollo, Arequipa. +51 5425 5888. +51 5425 1822. – **English:** 1900. - **FM:** 97.1. – **AR12)** Los Robles 139, Urb. Orranta (Ap. 17061), Arequipa. +51 5421 3172. – **Quechua:** 2h per day. - **FM:** 106.3. – **AR13)** Calle Consuelo 404, Depto. A, Arequipa. +51 5421 9928. - **FM:** 98.5 in Majes, 102.1 in Tacna. – **AR14)** Av. Independencia s/n, Ciudad Universitaria (Cas. 23), Arequipa. +51 5428 7771. – **AR15)** At. 200 Millas La Pina, Paucarpata. – **AR16)** Calle Santa Martha 304, Arequipa. - **FM**: 107.7. – **AR17)** Av. Union 225, Arequipa. – **AR18)** Urb. Chapi Chico, Mz. A, Lt. 4, Miraflores, Arequipa. +51 5420 4847/5466 796. – **Quechua:** 1000-1200. – **AR19)** Av. Independencia 905, Arequipa +51 5420 1904. – **AR20)** Calle Mariano Melgar 500, Cerro Colorado, Prov. de Arequipa. – **AR21)** Av.La Paz 512, Arequipa +51 5444 6053. - **FM:** 95.8. – **AR22)** Av. La Paz 511 "A", Of. 312 – 3er piso, Arequipa +51 5428 7821. – **AR23)** Calle Leticia 218 +51 5420 5550. – **AR24)** Calle San Camilo 501 A, Arequipa +51 5420 4420 +51 5420 4420 - **FM:** 104.3. – **AR25)** Av. Independencia 1819, Arequipa +51 5428 6438. – **AR26)** Calle Pierola 209, Of. 205, Arequipa. – **AR27)** Esq. Av. Lima y Bolognesi, Camaná. – **AR28)** Parque Azángaro 150, Miraflores, Arequipa. – **AR29)** Jr. Benavides 405, Urb. Selva Alegre, Arequipa. – **AR30)** Av. República de Chile 123, Mariano Melgar, Prov. de Arequipa. – **AR31)** Calle Cesar Vallejo 107, Mollendo. – **AR32)** Zona Rural Huayracpampa, Paucarpata, Prov. de Arequipa. – **AR33)** Calle Deán Valdivia, Of-221 (56), Arequipa **Email:** dominico@terre.com. +51 5421 3301. +51 5428 8229. - **FM:** 97.7. – **AR34)** Calle Tupac Amaru A-18, Urb. Miramar, Mollendo. – **AR35)** Sucre 409, Arequipa. – **AR36)** Santa Martha 310, Arequipa. +51 54 244421. – **AR37)** C.Baca Flor 410, (Cas.) 128, Mollendo +51 5453 2521 – **FM:** 101.5. – **AR38)** Av. Independencia 935, Urb. Municipal, Arequipa. – **AR39)** Santo Domingo 113 , Galerias Gamesa Of .700, Arequipa, (Ap. 2330) +51 5421 4997 **Email:** radiominuto@terra.com.pe - **FM:** 99.9. – **AR40)** Centro Comercial Independencia, Av. Independencia 403-A, Ofic. 433, 4° piso, Arequipa. – **AR41)** Av. Brasil 612, Distrito de Alto Selva Alegre, Arequipa. +51 5426 4319, 204360, 940516. – **Quechua:** 2000-2100. – **AR42)** Alto Siguas s/n, Arequipa +51 5428 0414. – **AR43)** Av. Progreso 58, Corire, Uraca, Prov. de Castilla - **FM:** 97.9. – **AR44)** Calle Castilla 39, Urb. Municipal, Arequipa. – **AR45)** Urb. Mi Perú MZ G Lote 3, Jose Luis Bustamente y Rivero, Prov. de Arequipa. – **AR46)** Parroquia San Antonio de Padua, Plaza Principal s/n, Callalli, Prov. de Caylloma. **Email**: rsan_antonio14@hotmail.com - **FM:** 94.5. – **AR47)** Calle Puno 820, Miraflores, Arequipa. – **AR48)** Casilla 1677, Arequipa. – **AR49)** Sucre 409, Arequipa (Apartado Postal 105, Serpost, Cercado, Arequipa). **Web:** www.radziovosdasalvacion.100megas.com

AY00 (AYACUCHO):

AY01) Av. Los Rosales 199, Urb. Jardin, Ayacucho - **FM:** 93.3. – **AY02)** Calle Nazareno 108H, Ayacuco. – **AY03)** Jr. Prolongación Bellidon 170, Ayacucho. – **AY04)** Calle Huascarn 667, Querobamba, Prov. de Sucre - **FM:** 100.5. – **AY05)** Plaza Mayor Felipe Guzman Poma, Aucara, Prov. de Lucanas. – **AY06)** Jr. Chorro 274, Ayacucho. **Email**: aba-ay@wayna.rcp.net.pe +51 6483 6042. Prgr. mainly in **Quechua**. – **AY07)** Jr. Gervasio Santillana 455, Huanta +51 6683 2105 - **FM**: 92.7. – **AY08)** Jr. Piura s/n, Ayacucho. – **AY09)** Jr. Arica 105, San Juan Bautista, Huamanga. – **AY10)** Local de Obispado, Carmen Alto, Prov. de Huamanga – **FM:** 106.7. – **AY11)** Calle Nazareno 108, Ayacucho. – **AY12)** Jr. Ayacucho 474, Huanta (Cas. 43). - **FM:** 98.3. – **AY13)** Jr. Cahuide 278, Huanta (Cas. 24) +51 6683 2153 **Email**: arca@terra.com.pe - **FM:** 99.9.

CA00 (CAJAMARCA):

CA01) Jr. Francisco de Orellana 343 (Apt 50), Jaén. **Web:** www.radiomaranon.org.pe +51 7673 1147. - **FM:** 96.1. – **CA02)** Jr. 24 de Junio 189, Huambos, Chota. – **CA03)** Km 5 Carretera Jaen-San Ignacio, Jaen - **FM:** 90.9. – **CA04)** Jr. Revilla Peréz 194, Cajamarca +51 7682 9067 - **FM:** 105.1. – **CA05)** Predio Coliga, Cajamarca. – **CA06)** Av. Mesones Muro 157, Jaén. – **CA07)** Jr. 28 de Julio 660, Bambamarca. **Email**: coremarca@latinmail.com +51 76 843169. - **FM:** 101.1. – **CA08)** Jr. Villanueva Pinillos 330, San Ignacio. +51 7471 6100 - **FM:** 96.3. – **CA09)** Jr.Amazons 725, Cajamarca – **FM:** 99.3. – **CA10)** Jr.Mejillones 293 Cajamarca. +51 4482 6251. +51 7683 0238. – **CA11)** Calle Zurumilla 1328, Jaén. - **FM:** 94.9. – **CA12)** Calle La Merced y Calle Comercio, Cutervo. – **CA13)** Jr. Huánuco 2367, Cajamarca. +51 7682 3363. - **FM:** 90.3. – **CA14)** Jr. David León 601, Contumazá. – **CA15)** Jr. 2 de Mayo 271, Cajamarca +51 7682 8602 – **FM:** 91.9. – **CA16)** Calle Bolívar 1020, Jaén. – **CA17)** Jr. Ramón Castilla 491, Cutervo. +51 7673 7090 - **FM:** 97.7. – **CA18)** Av. Arequipa 101, Cajamarca. - **FM:** 96.1. – **CA19)** Jr. Lara s/n, Cajabamba. – **CA20)** Jr. Mariscal Castilla 439, Prov. de Jaén. - **FM:** 96.7. – **CA21)** Av. San Martin De Porres s/n, Cajamarca +51 7682 8566. - **FM:** 101.3. – **CA22)** Jr. Leoncio Prado 330, San Marcos. +51 4485 8083. – **CA23)** Av. Inca Garcilaso de la Vega 473, Chota. – **CA24)** Jr. Sullana 212, Cajamarca. – **CA25)** Zona Baja s/n, Jaèn – **FM:** 105.7. – **CA26)** Av. El Maestro 290, Cajamarca. – **CA27)** Jr. Simon Bolivar 280, Santa Cruz. – **CA28)** Jr. 2 de Mayo 484, Cajamarca. – **CA29)** Jr. Silva 673, Cajabamba. – **CA30)** Jr. Anaximandro 690 (Ap. 14), Chota. +51 7684 1240. – **CA31)** Jr. Cajamarca s/n, Cajamarca. – **CA32)** Jr. 30 de Agosto 641, Chota. **Email**: rsantamonica@terra.com.pe +51 7684 1477. +51 7684 1132. - **FM:** 95.7. – **CA33)** Juan XXIII s/n (Plaza Bolognesi), Cajamarca. - **FM:** 89.9. – **CA34)** Jr 5 Escuinos 563, Cajamarca +51 7682 3041. – **CA35)** Jr. Dos de Mayo No 673, Celendín. +51 7685 5149 - **FM:** 95.7. – **CA36)** Jr. Alfonso Ugarte 758, San Miguel de Pallaques. - **FM:** 97.9. – **CA37)** Calle Libertad 430, Jaén. – **CA38)** Ca. Lima 228, Cutervo. +51 7673 7010. +51 7673 7269. - **FM:** 96.1. – **CA39)** Av. Bolognesi 532, San Pablo. – **CA40)** Jr. Pachacutec 433, Los Baños del Inca +51 7680 1408. – **CA41)** Jr. Jorge Chávez 416, Bambamarca. +51 4484 3260. +51 4484 3078. - **FM:** 100.5 "Stereo Líder". – **CA42)** Jr. Michael Bastidas 352, Chota. – **CA43)** Amazonas 655, Cajamarca. – **CA44)** Jr. Castro Alfaro s/n, Socota, Cutervo, Prov. de Cutervo. – **CA45)** Av. Bolognesi 532, San Pablo, Prov. de San Pablo. - **FM:** 100.7. – **CA46)** Jr. Ramón Castilla 491, tercer piso, Plaza de Armas, Cutervo. +51 7673 6090, 737443. - **FM:** 97.7. – **CA47)** Jr. Cutervo 543, Santa Cruz +51 7684 4068. – **CA48)** Jr. José Gálvez 602, Celendin. – **CA49)** Jr. Bolognesi 1300, Barrio La Almeda, Sector Los Delfines, Cajabamba, Prov. de Cajabamba – **CA50)** Jr. Los Libertadores 250, Bambamarca. – **CA51)** Jirón Bolivar 354, San Miguel de Pallaques, Prov. de San Miguel. – **CA52)** Av. Los Héroes 630, Cajamarca. – **CA53)** Dis. de Faique.

CU00 (CUSCO):

CU01) Urb. Barrio los Periodistas F3, Cusco. – **CU02)** Ciudad Universitaria de Perayoc, Sotano del Pabellón "C", Cusco. – **CU03)** Av.Ejercito 164, Cusco. – **CU04)** Av.Charcahuaylla s/n, Distrito Maras, Prov. Urubamba - **FM:** 91.7. – **CU05)** Tres Cruces de Oro 205, Cusco. – **CU06)** Jr. Hipolito Unanue M4, Urb. Industrial, Cusco. – **CU07)** Diagonal Angamos 2300, Cusco. +54 8424 1806 – **CU08)** Calle Inca 650, Santiago, Cusco. +51 8422 8649. – **Quechua:** 2 hours: 1100, 1500. – **CU09)** Urb. Vista Alegre s/n, Urcos, Prov. Quispicanchi - **FM:** 101.5. – **CU10)** Cl. Daniel A. Carrioón 602, Cusco +51 8422 4371. – **CU11)** Calle Marquez 219, Cusco. – **CU12)** Calle "C" 13, Urb. Jardin, Cusco. – **CU13)** Jr. Infancia 527, Wanchaq +51 8424 6391. – **CU14)** Calle Nueve de Diciembre s/n, Espinar -**FM:** 103.9. – **CU15)** Asoc.. Pro-Vivendi el Periodista Lt. B-13, Wanchaq. – **CU16)** Portal de Carnes 260, Cusco. – **CU17)** Calle Sucre 107, Sicuaní. – **CU18)** Jr. Ricardo Palma Mz.L-1, Urb. Santa Monica, Cusco +51 8424 6201 - **FM:** 100.7. – **CU19)** Calle Anta s/n, Antanampa, Espinar - **FM:** 98.9. – **CU20)** Jr.Juan Espinoza Medrano P-13, Urb. Rosas Pata, Cusco. – **CU21)** Cl. Triunfo 201, Cusco +51 8423 6020 - **FM:** 92.7. – **CU22)** Lote E-11, Urb. Bancopata, Cusco. - **FM:** 100.1. – **CU23)** Jr. Santos Chocano Lloque, Bloque G-11, Urb. Santa Monica, Wanchaq +51 8422 6765. - **FM:** 103.3. – **CU24)** Calle Meloc 417, Cusco. – **CU25)** Av. El Sol 830, Cusco +51 8422 8411 - **FM:** 91.3. – **CU26)** Av. Ricardo Palma 442 (Ap. 76), Quillabamba. – **Quechua:** 1300-1430, 2100-0100 +51 8428 1002 - **FM:** 91.9. – **CU27)** Av. Manuel Callo Cevallos 111, Sicuani. – **CU28)** Pasaje Constancia 102, Of. 410, Wanchaq. – **CU29)** Jr. 22 de Febrero 104, Espinar. +51 8430 1045. – **CU30)** Jr. José Olaya Mz H-9, Urb. Bancopata, Cusco +51 8425 2591. – **CU31)** Calle Sacsaywaman K-10, Urb. Manuel Prado, Cusco - **FM:** 104.1. – **CU32)** Av. Huayna Capac 146, Wanchaq +51 8422 5160. – **CU33)** Calle Bélen 306, Cusco. –**CU34)** Jr. 2 de Mayo 206, Sicuani. **Email**: cecesda@terra.com.pe +51 8435 1136. – **Quechua:** 0930-1100, 2300-0300. - **FM:** 91.1. – **CU35)** Urb. Marcavalle, P-20, Wanchaq. +51 8422 5357 +51 8422 6555 - **FM:** 93.9. – **CU36)** Plaza de Armas s/n, El Descanso, Kunturkanki Canas, Prov. de Canas. – **CU37)** Av. Garcilazo 185, Cusco. +51 8421 1371/8422 8008 – Rpt. to Carlos Gamarra Moscoso, Av. Garcilazo 411, Wanchác. – **CU38)** Av.Tupac Amaru s/n, Yanaoca, Prov. de Canas. – **CU39)** Jr. Matara 526, Cusco - **FM:** 106.5 – **CU40)** Pasaje San Pablo 142, Sicuani - **FM:** 97.7. – **CU41)** Jr. Independencia 143 Piso 2, Quillabamba. – **CU42)** Plaza de Armas s/n, Marcapata, Provincia de Quispicanchi. – **CU43)** Calle Saphi 601, Cusco. +51 8422 5851 - **FM:** 90.1. – **CU44)** Av. El Sol 230, Yauri, Prov. de Espinar - **FM:** 103.1. – **CU45)** Alameda Pachacutec B-5, Urb. Bancapata (Apt. 713), Cusco. +51 8422 5052. – **CU46)** Calle Sucre s/n, Sicuani. +51 8435 1323. – **CU47)** Huayna Capac 154, Wanchaq - **FM:** 100.1. – **CU48)** Av. Panamericana 105, Yuari, Provincia de Espinar. – **CU49)** Av. Cusco s/n, Yauri, Provincia de Espinar. – **CU50)** Jr. Ricardo Palma 516, Quillabamba - **FM: 96.5**. – **CU51)** Cl. Choquechaca 152, Cusco +51 8480 2444 – **CU52)** Calle Heladeros 220, Wanchaq - **FM:** 102.1. – **CU53)** Calle Siete Angelitos 715, San Blas, Cusco. +51 8423 3101. +51 8423 1881. - **FM:** 93.3. – **CU54)** Plaza de Armas 124, Paucartambo. - **FM:** 104.5.

HA00 (HUANCAVELICA):

HA01) Puno 110, Lircay, Prov. de Angaraes. – **HA02)** Plaza Bolognesi 142, Cercado, (Ap. 92), Huancavelica. **Email:** jlopez–alvarado@hotmail.com +51 6775 1257 - **FM**: 105.3.

HU00 (HUANUCO):

HU01) Av. Raymondi 432, Tingo María +51 6256 2024. – **HU02)** Malecón Huallaga 1038, Aucayacu, José Crespo y Castillo. – **HU03)** MZ F, LT 8, Urb. Leoncio Prado, Huanuco. – **HU04)** Jr.Leoncio 163F, Huánuco. +51 6251 6360. – **HU05)** Jr. Leoncio Prado 723 (Cas. 343), Huánuco. +51 6251 1525. +51 6251 2428. – Prgr. in **Sp. & Quechua**. - **FM:** 88.9. – **HU06)** Ruben Dario 128, Zona Cerro Paucarbamvilla, Distrito Amarilis,

Huánuco +51 6251 2428. – **HU07)** Jr. Dos de Mayo 1286, Of. 308, Huánuco. **Email**: rpemac@yahoo.com +51 6251 8500. +51 6251 1985. – **Quechua:** 1000-1200, 2300-0200. - **FM:** 105.7. – **HU08)** Jr. Aguilar 744-746, Huánuco - **FM:** 100.1. – **HU09)** Jr. Bolognesi 175, Distrito de Panao, Provincia de Pachitea. - **FM**: 95.3.

IC00 (ICA):

IC01) Conde de Neiva 125, Ica. – **IC02)** Av. Ayacucho Esq. Grau s/n, Ica +51 5623 1956 - **FM:** 105.3. – **IC03)** Av. Conde de Neiva, Urb. Luren, Ica. - **FM:** 90.7. – **IC04)** Av. San Martín 305, 2° piso, Chincha Alta, Prov. de Chinca. - **FM:** 89.7. – **IC05)** Calle Cajamarca 195, Ica. - **FM:** 103.3. – **IC06)** Av. Arenales 1370, Ica. - **FM:** 98.7. – **IC07)** s/n Mz. A21. Urb. aa.Hh. Tupac Amaru, San Juan de Marcona +51 5652 5268. – **IC08)** Jr. Mauytua 189 (Ap. 54), Chincha Alta, Prov. de Chinca. – **IC09)** Av. Arenales 589, Ica. - +51 5680 8460. – **IC10)** Calle L, 204 – Urb. San Miguel, Ica. – **IC11)** Camino a San Juan, Chincha Alta, Prov. Chincha. – **IC12)** Los Portales de Escribanos 167, Plaza de Armas, Palpa. - **FM:** 101.7. – **IC13)** Calle San Francisco, Pisco. +51 5653 3150. - **FM:** 96.5 "Paracas". – **IC14)** Av. 8 de Septiembre s/n (Cas. 24), Pisco. – **IC15)** San Martín 120, Urb. Pencal, Nazca. – **IC16)** Av. los Incas 117-119 (. 57), Nazca. – **IC17)** MZ 1, LT. 1, Urb. Los Viñedos, San Juan Bautista. – **IC18)** Jr. Zarumilla 360, Ica +51 5622 1776 +51 5623 5321 – **FM:** 106.5

JU00 (JUNIN):

JU01) Pasaje Banchero Rossi 142, Huancayo. – **JU02)** Jr.Grau 642, Junin. – **JU03)** Jr. Lima 354, Edif. Marakami 7 piso, Huancayo - +51 6423 1935 – **FM:** 101.7. – **JU04)** Av.Tayacaja 324, Of. 202, La Oroya. – **JU05)** Av. Jorge Chavez 851, Anexo Zaños Grande, El Tambo. – **JU06)** Calle Ancash 543, Of. 208, Huancayo. - **FM:** 103.1. – **JU07)** Av. Las Palmeras 285,La oroya +51 6439 1595. – **JU08)** Jr. Acolla 935, Jauja. – **JU09)** Av. Calmell del Solar 469-481, Sn. Carlos Hye, Huancayo. +51 6420 0383. – **Quechua & English:** 1h daily. - **FM:** 104.5. – **JU10)** Jr.Huancas 251, A San Carlos, Huancayo. – **JU11)** Esquina Prolongación Pachitea 136 y Pasaje Andaluz 106 4° piso, Huancayo. – **JU12)** Jr. Lima 400, 2° piso, Huancayo. - **FM:** 92.9. – **JU13)** Calle Mercado 194, San Ramón. – **JU14)** Calle Real 270, El Tambo, Huancayo. +51 6424 5396. +51 6425 3921. - **FM:** 96.7 "R. Futura". – **JU15)** Jr. Tarma 545, La Merced. +51 6453 1068. +51 6453 1304. - **FM:** 105.7. – **JU16)** Paseo La Breña 174 2 piso Of 202, Huancayo +51 6421 9990. - **FM:** 89.7. – **JU17)** Jr. Manuel Prado 459, Satipo. – **JU18)** Jr. Cerro de Pasco 582, (Ap. 2), Junín. +51 6434 4026. - **FM:** 97.7. – **JU19)** Av. Ayacucho 7300, Huancayo - **FM:** 105.7. – **JU20)** Av. Manuel Prado 239, Satipo. – **JU21)** Jr. Moquegua 648, Tarma – **JU22)** Jr. Ancash 555, Chilca. (Apt. 245, Huancayo). **Email**: radiocumbre@terra.com.pe +51 6421 8080. +51 6423 9189. - **FM:** 98.5. – **JU23)** Jr. Junín 163, La Merced. – **JU24)** Jr. Dario Leon 198, 4° piso, La Oroya. – **JU25)** Calle Real 175, Chilca, Huancayo +51 6423 1123. – **JU26)** Calle Real 420, Of. 302, Chilca. – **JU27)** Jr. Junin , 2° piso, Jauja. +51 6436 2428. +51 6436 1850. – **JU28)** Jr. Jauja 494, Tarma. – **JU29)** Pasaje Andalz 175, Huancayo. – **JU30)** Jr. Moquegua 642, Tarma +51 6432 1864. – **JU31)** Av. Jose Carlos Mariátegui 699, Urb Tambo, Huancayo. +51 6424 1941. +51 6425 2840. - **FM**: 102.5. – **JU32)** Jr. Cerro de Pasca 582, Junin. – **JU33)** Calle Lima 190, 3° piso, Of. 3, La Oroya. **Email**: radiolaoroya@terra.com.pe +51 6439 1401. +51 6439 1748. - **FM:** 100.1. – **JU34)** Calle Real 517, Of. 403, Huancayo +51 6421 9901. - **FM:** 104.3. – **JU35)** Av. Arevaldo 484, Anexo Chuccus, Santa Rosa de Sacco, Prov. de Yauli. – **JU36)** Paseo La Breña 125-133, Tercer Piso No 109, Huancayo. - **FM:** 107.1. – **JU37)** Jr. Molino del Amo 167 (Cas.167), Tarma. +51 6432 1510. +51 6432 1167. **Email:** radiotarma@terra.com.pe - **FM:** 99.3 & 101.7 "R. Tropicana" in La Merced. – **JU38)** Av. Huancavelica 430, 2° piso (Ap. 230), Huancayo +51 6423 3640. - **FM:** 88.9. – **JU39)** Jr. Arequipa 572, Yauyos - **FM:** 98.3. – **JU40)** Jr. Huancavelica 498, 2° piso, Tarma. – **JU41)** Brasilia 200, Huancayo. – **JU42)** Jr. Tarma 551, La Merced. +51 6453 1068. +51 6453 1304. - **FM:** 105.7. – **JU43)** H.Zevallos Gomez 231, La Oroya

LA00 (LAMBAYEQUE):

LA01) Km. 4 de la Carretera Pimentel, Chiclayo - **FM:** 105.1. – **LA02)** Calle Juan XXXIII 391 (Ciudad Universitaria), Lambayeque. – **LA03)** Calle Incanato 390, José Leonardo Ortiz. – **LA04)** Juan Guglievan 984, Chiclayo. – **Quechua:** Sun. 0600-1100. - **FM:** 107.7. – **LA05)** Zona Santa Isabel, Chiclayo - **FM:** 102.3. – **LA06)** Alfonso Ugarte 505, Distrito San José, Prov. de Lambayeque. (Ap. 67, Correo Central, Chiclayo). - **FM:** 103.3. – **LA07)** Jr. Incanato 387, Altos, Distrito José Leonardo Ortiz, Chiclayo. – **LA08)** Calle San José 462, Of. 207, Chiclayo +51 7420 4786 - **FM:** 102.9. – **LA09)** Jr. Nicanor Carmona 177, Ferreñafe. – **LA10)** Calle Santa Cecilia s/n, Olmos, Prov. Lambayeque. – **LA11)** Av. Pedro Ruiz 1123, 3° piso, Chiclayo - **FM:** 100.5. – **LA12)** Calle 28 de Julio 440, San José, Provincia de Lambayeque. – **LA13)**Ca Antonio Monsalve Baca 204. P.J.Santa, Lambayeque +51 7428 3562 - **FM:** 97.7. – **LA14)** Calle Arica 1247, Chiclayo +51 7420 8523 – **LA15)** Av. Saenz Peña 1046, Chiclayo - **FM:** 98.3. – **LA16)** Av. Tupac Amaru 532, Ferreñafe. – **LA17)** Calle San José 1084, Chiclayo. – **LA18)** Calle F. Villareal y A. Arguedas s/n, Chiclayo - **FM:** 94.1. – **LA19)** Av. Miguel Grau 350, Oficina 222, Chiclayo +51 7423 6363. – **LA20)** Calle Las Violetas s/n, Chiclayo - **FM:** 94.9. – **LA21)** Calle Francisco Gonzales Burgán 717, Ferreñafe +51 7428 6351. – **LA22)** Calle 1 de Mayo 278, Urrunaga, Provincia de Chiclayo. – **LA23)** Caserio Tranca Falupe, Morrope, Prov. Lambayeque. – **LA24)** Jr. San Francisco 239, Olmos, Prov. de Lambayeque. – **LA25)** Nicolás de Pierola 335, Distrito de José Leonardo Ortiz, Pro. de Chiclayo. - **FM:** 107.7. – **LA26)** Calle Justicia 102, Urb. Tupac Amaru, Chiclayo. – **LA27)** Av. Balta 1144, Chiclayo. – **LA28)** Av.Los Incas 946, Morrope, Prov. de Lambayeque. – **LA29)** Calle San José 148, Olmos, Prov. de Lambayequea. – **LA30)** Av. el Tren s/n, Chiclayo. – **LA31)** Av. Pedro Ruiz 1250, Urb. San Juan, Chiclayo. +51 7422 9494. – **LA32)** Calle Tarata s/n, Olmos, Prov. de Lambayque. – **LA33)** Av. Balta, 2° piso Of. 205, Chiclayo. – **LA34)** Av. Mariscal. Castilla 859, Monsefú, Prov. de Chiclayo. – **LA35)** Calle San Marrtin 322, Olmos, Prov. de Lambayeque. – **LA36)** Av. Andrés Avelino Cáceres 800, Lambayeque. **Emai:** naylamp@llampallec.rep.net.pe +51 7428 3353 - **FM:** 96.1. – **LA37)** Chiclayo.

LI00 (LIMA):

LI01) Josto Pastor Dávila 197, Chorillos +51 1251 2596/1251 2595. – **LI02)** Av Iquitos 737. La Victoria, Lima . – **LI03)** Calle Mama Ocllo, 2058 Lince, Lima **Web:** www.radiomariaperu.org +51 1265 1723/1470 7766. +51 1470 9140. – 15 FM repeater stations. – **LI04)** Av. 28 de Julio 1004, Piso 4, La Victoria +51 1330 9654/1335 0171. – **LI05)** Calle Miguel Dasso 144, Of. 2A, San Isidro, Lima. – **LI06)** Av. Guzman Blanco 465, 7° piso, (Ap. 4236) Lima 1. **Web:** www.grupopacifico.org **Email:** grupapacifico-municartv@hotmail.com. – **LI07)** Av. Javier Prado Este 309, Of.1001, San Isidro +51 1251 2596/1251 2595. – **LI08)** Av. Amador Merino Reyna 295, Of. 801, San Isidro – Prgr. in **Quechua** 4h./day. – **LI09)** Av. La Marina 3099, San Miguel +51 1578 5723. – **LI10)** Av. Paseo de la República 3866, 2° piso, San Isidro. +51 1215 0200. **Web:** www.rpp.com.pe – **LI11)** Justo Pastor Dávila 197, Chorillos. +51 1425 5151. +51 1467 5557.**Email:** radiomarplus@radiomar.com.pe – Signal downlinked to 76 repeaters. – **LI12)** Av. Arica 254, Breña +51 1336 5448. +51 1 336 8308. – **LI13)** Av. Andrés Mármol Castellanos 230, Huaral – **FM:** 104.1 – **LI14)** Av. Salaverry 1082, Jesús Maria. **Email:** r.libertad@terra.com.pe +51 1266 0777. +51 1471 5319. – **LI15)** Av. Petit Thouars 447 Santa Beatriz, Lima. **Web:** www.radionacional.com.pe +511433 8956. – **LI16)** Av. José Pardo 138, Edifico Neptuno, Piso 16, Miraflores +51 1445 8549 +51 1445 8901. – **LI17)** Av. Madrid 181, Miraflores, Lima 18 +51 1330 0713 **Web:** www.elcomercioperu.com.pe. **Email:** info@canaln.com.pe. – **LI18)** Esq. Av. Argentina y Nicolás Dueñas 813, Lima 1. **Email:** correomoderna@hotmail.com – **LI19)** Paseo Parodi 340, San Isidro. **Web:** www.radiopanamericana.com **Email:** radio@panamericana.com.pe +51 1422 6787. +51 1422 1223. – Satellite signal downlinked by 60 FM repeaters. – **LI20)** Ignacio Merino 230, Miraflores. – **LI21)** Calle Porta 130, Miraflores. – – **LI22)** Av. Colonial 1512, Lima. – **LI23)** Jr. Huancayo 288, Of. 701, Lima. **Web:** www.radio-laluz.com +51 1433 4599. – **LI24)** Alejandro Tirado 217, Of. 505, Lima. – **LI25)** 2 de Mayo 573, Imperial +51 1284 8052. –**LI26)** Calle Gerardo Unger 6347, Urb. Santa Luisa, Los Olivos. – **LI27)** Jr.Bernardo Alcedo 375, Lince, Lima 14. **Web:** radiobacan.com **Email:** bacan@radiobacan.com +51 1471 3908 – **LI28)** Jr. Orbegozo 140, Breña. **Email:** 1160radionoticias@popamericana.com – **LI29)** Cl. Los Angeles 429, Miraflores +51 1422 0905. – **LI30)** Av. Manco Cápac 495, Of. 401, Miraflores. +51 1444 1773/1444 0966/1445 0126 +51 1445 0126. – **LI31)** Jr. Echenique 140, Huacho. – **LI32)** Mz. L, Lt. 7, Urb. La Esperanza, Hualmay. – **LI33)** Av. Estados Unidos 327, Urb. Huaquillay, Comas. **Web:** www.radiocomas.com **Email**: rtcomas@.terra.com.pe +51 1525 0859 +511525 0094. - **FM:** 101.7. – **LI34)** Jr. Atahualpa 148, 5° piso, Huacho. – **LI35)** Km. 58.5 Panamericana Sur, Pucasana, Prov. de Lima. – **LI36)** Calle Cahuas 447 (Cas. 66), Huaral. – **LI37)** Av. Grau 538, Huacho. – **LI38)** Calle Los Heliotropos 276, Santa Maria de Chosica. – **LI39)** Calle Juan del Carpo 140-144 2° piso, San Isidro. **Email:** radiocallao@hotmail.com – **LI40)** Ausejo Salas 153, Huacho. +51 1323 1976. - **FM:** 101.7. – **LI41)** Av. Petit Thouars 1806, Lince, Lima. – **LI42)** Jr. Independencia 349. San Vincente de Cañete. – **LI43)** Av. Separadora Industrial s/n, Villa El Salvador +51 1291 3012. – **LI44)** Alfonso Ugarte 149, Barranca +51 1235 4238. – **LI45)** Cadena Peruana de Noticias, Gral. Salaverry 152–156, Miraflores. **Email:** publicidid@gestion.com.pe **Web:** www.cpnradio.com.pe +51 1447 1789. +51 1447 6763, 1447 6569. **NB:** CPN operates a network of FM and AM stations all over the country. – **LI46)** Av. Recreo 317, Altos, Paramonga. – **LI47)** Jr. Carmaná 170, El Cercado (Apt. 4451San Miguel), El Cercado. **Web:** www.radiosantarosa.com,/ **Email:** radiosantarosa@terra.com.pe +51 1427 7488 +51 1426 6587. – **Quechua:** 1300. **English:** 0130. – **LI48)** MZ G-17, Urb. El Olivar, Barranca. – **LI49)** Av.Arnaldo Márquez 1944 Jesús Maria, Lima 11. **Web:** www.radiomilenia.com.pe **Email:** milenia@radiomilenia.com.pe – **LI50)** Plaza de Armas 132, Barranca +51 1235 2301. - **FM:** 99.1. – **LI51)** Jr. Yahuar Huaca 108, Urb. Tahuantinsuyo, Independencia +51 1526 0469. – **LI52)** Av. Alfonso Ugarte 1428, Of. 202, Breña (Cas.11-0625), Lima +51 1424 6677 11). **Email:** radioagriculturadelperu@yahoo.com. – **LI53)** Calle las Gardeniaa MZ E3, LT.8, Urv La Alborada, Comas.

LL00 (LA LIBERTAD):
LL01) Jr. Trujillo 597, Otuzco +51 4443-6007. – **LL02)** Jr. Benito Juarez 1753, La Esperanza. – **LL03)** Calle Opalo 298 2° piso-A, Urb. Sta.Ines, Trujillo. +51 4420 2156. - **FM:** 98.3. – **LL04)** Calle Lima 599, Chepén. – **LL05)** San Martín 472, Trujillo. +51 4425 1792, 252974. – **LL06)** Av. Los Incas s/n, Anexo Facala, Chócope, Prov. de Ascope. - **FM:** 102.5. – **LL07)** Calle Junín 23, Sausal, Prov. de Ascope. – **LL08)** Francisco Pizarro 532, Of. 205, Trujillo. – **LL09)** Jr. Ayacucho 65, Pacasmayo, Prov. Pacasmayo. – **LL10)** Jr. Trujillo 597, Otuzco. – **LL11)** Jr. Marcelo Corne 224, Urb. San Andrés, Trujillo. +51 4429 4050 - **FM:** 90.9. – **LL12)** Av. V. Belaunde MZ.L lote 15, Urb. Santo Dominguito, Trujillo. – **LL13)** Jr. Francisco Pizarro 208, Of. 302,.Trujillo. +51 4424 2666 - **FM:** 107.5. – **LL14)** Av. Grau s/n, Virú. – **LL15)** Av. del Ejercito 717, Trujillo. – **LL16)** Alfonso Ugarte 222, Virú - **FM:** 102.3. – **LL17)** Calle Trujillo 699-A, Chepén. – **LL18)** Pasaje Educación 220, Huamachuco, Prov. de Trujillo. +51 4422 1222. – **LL19)** Jr.Baltan 252, Huamachuco. – **LL20)** Jr. Atahualpa 795, Chepén +51 4456 2038 - **FM:** 92.7. – **LL21)** Mz.B-1 2-A, Urb. La Libertad, Trujillo. +51 4421 7885. – **LL22)** Zepita 452, Trujillo. +51 4424 9326, 233644. +51 4425 2970. – **LL23)** Jr. Progreso 121, Quiruvilca – **LL24)** Bolívar 780 (Cas. 1029), Trujillo. +51 4423 3981. – **LL25)** Victoria 229, Guadalupe, Prov. de Pacasmayo. – **LL26)** Jr. Caceres s/n, Bolívar, Prov. de Bolívar. +51 4423 0277/4423 0299. – **LL27)** Calle Grau s/n, Otuzco. – **LL28)** Jr. Progreso 759, Chepén - **FM:** 98.7. – **LL29)** Jr. Bolivar 989, Of. 401, Trujillo. – **LL30)** Urb. El Recodo s/n L-17, Chepén. +51 4456 2522. - **FM:** 100.3. – **LL31)** Ca. Camal 13, Cartavio, Prov.de Ascope +51 4443 2448. – **LL32)** Mercado La Hermelinda Puesto C 288 – seccion abarrotes, Trujillo. +51 4480 3207. – **LL33)** Jr. Gamarra 713, Of. 405, Trujillo. +51 4424 6211. – **LL34)** Ascope. – **LL35)** Pasaje San Martin 300, Urb. Alto Mochica, (Ap. 352) Trujillo. +51 4426 3592. – **LL36)** Calle Victoria 310, Guadalupe, Prov. de Pacasmayo - **FM: 91.3**. – **LL37)** Jr. Trujillo 281, Quiruvilca. – **LL38)** Jr. Grau s/n, Virú. – **LL39)** Sebastian Barranca 469, Urb. Chimú, Trujillo. – **LL40)** Pasaje Monseñor Damián Nicolau 108, Huamachuco **Email:** radiolosandes@starmedia.com - **FM:** 103.1. – **LL41)** Calle Bolívar 130, Otuzco. – **LL42)** Jr. Ayacucho 459, 5° piso Of. 901, Trujillo +51 4425 7431 - **FM:** 96.9. – **LL43)** Av. Perú 608, Trujillo. – **LL44)** Jr. Zepita 450, Trujillo. – **LL45)** Carabamba, Prov.Julcánn.

LO00 (LORETO):
LO01) Calle Abtao 255 (Ap 207), Iquitos. +51 6526 5244 +51 6526 5244. - **FM:** 93.9. – **LO02)**Jr. Elias Agurrie 857, Iquitos. - **FM:** 104.5. – **LO03)** Prolong. Perú s/n, Cuadra 19, Iquitos. - **FM:** 98.9. – **LO04)** Jr. Lima 821, Iquitos. - **FM:** 90.1. – **LO05)** Av.Antonio Raymondi 331, Iquitos. – **LO06)** Arica 228, Iquitos. +51 6523 3302 **Email:** radioloreto@yahoo.es - **FM:** 103.5. – **LO07)** Plaza de Armas s/n, Iquitos. – **LO08)** Jr. Prospéro 645 Iquitos (Cas 174). - **FM:** 105.9. – **LO09)** Av. Abelardo Quiñones km. 4.5 Carretera a Nauta, Iquitos. – **LO10)** Jr. Progreso 112, Yurimaguas. **Email:** vicariatoyms@terra.com.pe +51 6535 1611. - **FM:** 99.5. – **LO11)** Av. Mariscal Cáceres 1037 (Ap. 786), Iquitos. (Reports to: Pablo Rojas Bordales, Jr. Bermúdez 445), Iquitos +51 6580 7556. – **LO12)** Av. Alfredo Vargas Guarra 440, Contama, Prov. de Ucayali.

MD00 (MADRE DE DIOS):
MD01) Jr. Guillermo Billingurst 406 PTO, Puerto Maldonado - **FM:** 101.3. – **MD02)** Nueva Plaza de Armas 200, Puerto Maldonado - **FM:** 100.5. – **MD03)** Jr. Daniel A. Carrion 387, Puerto Maldonado +51 8257 1050 - **FM:** 92.5.

MO00 (MOQUEGUA):
MO01) Edifico S-27 Barrio Azul Asiento Minero, Ilabaya, Prov. de Jorge Basadre - **FM:** 101.1. – **MO02)** Jr. Callao s/n, Ilo. - **MO03** Alto Ilo, Sector Arenal G-6, Ilo - **FM:** 96.7. – **MO04)** Mz. E lote 48 P, Joven J.F. Kennedy, Ilo. – **MO05)** Jr. Tarapaca 260, Moquegua. – **MO06)** Jr. Moquegua 123, 5° piso, Ilo. +51 5378 1313. - **FM:** 105.5. – **MO07)** Jr. Ayacucho 639 (Ap. 22), Moquegua +51 5376 1542. - **FM:** 105.3.

PA00 (PASCO):
PA01) Pasaje Tarma 127, Cerro de Pasco +51 6372 2398 - **FM:** 97.7. – **PA02)** Jr. Puno s/n, Chaupimarca - **FM:** 102.5. – **PA03)** Jr. Mullembruck 468, Urb. Cercado, Oxapampa. +51 6376 2689. – **German:** 0300-0400 - **FM:** 101.5. – **PA04)** Zona Denominada Principal, Chaupimarca. – **PA05)** San Cristobal 340, Cerro de Pasco. – **PA06)** Jr.Huamachuco 221, Caupimarcan – **PA07)** Av. Cerro de Pasco, Barrio Arriba, Paucartambo

PI00 (PIURA):
PI01) AAHH.Alm. Grau MZ C, Lt 21, Sector Coscomba, Piura. – **PI02)** Calle Santa Ana 471, Urb. Santa Rosa, Sullana. – **PI03)** Calle Libertad 546, 2° piso, Piura. – **PI04)** Jr. San Ignacio de Loyola 300, Dist. Castilla (Cas. 165), Piura. **Web:** www.radiocutivalu.org/ **Email:** cutivalu@cipca.org.pe +51 7334 2802. +51 7334 2965 - **FM:** 100.5. – **PI05)** Ica 419, Of. 206, Piura. - **FM:** 92.1. – **PI06)** Santa Maria C., Piura - **FM:** 94.5. – **PI07)** Jr. Cusco 750, Piura. - **FM:** 90.7. – **PI08)** Ugarteche 490, Sullana - **FM:** 99.3. – **PI09)** Calle Santa Teresa Cdra. 8 s/n, Urb. Santa Rosa, Sullana. **Web:** www.chanel.edu.pe/serviciosl.php +51 73 504760/501468. +51 7350 1382. – **PI10)** Calle Tacna 260 4 piso, (frente al banco de la nación), Piura +51 7330 3369/3395 – **FM:** 103.3 – **PI11)** Esquina Grau y Piura 1084, Sullana. - **FM:** 95.7. – **PI12)** Jr. Cesar Pinglo 345, Sechura. – **PI13)** Barrio El Altillo s/n, Huancabamba. – Re. to Correo Central, Huancabamba. – **PI14)** Av.Sánches Cerro 582 2do Piso, Piura. +51 7330 4221 - **FM:** 107.9 – **PI15)** Calle Cusco 670, Piura. – **PI16)** Zona Industrial III Mz. O, lote 10, Piura. – **PI17)** Calle Unión 515, La Unión +51 7337 4106. – **PI18)** Jr. Callao 318, P. 2, Piura - **FM:** 101.9. – **PI19)** Urb. Aproviser A2-1, Pariñas, Prov. de Talara - **FM:** 98.1. – **PI20)** Cl. Lambayeque 1005, Chulucanas +51 7337 8627. – **PI21)** Jr. Bolognesi Cuadra 1, Ayabaca. – **PI22)** Calle San Martín 354, Sechura. – **PI23)** Calle 8 s/n, Talara Alta, Talara – **PI24)** Mz. E 8, Fonavi I Etapa, Paita +51 7361 1885 - **FM:** 102.9. – **PI25)** Jr. Leoncio Prado 425, Sullana. – **PI26)** Madre de Dios 258, Sullana +51 7350 5026 – **PI27)** Jr. Las Azucenas Urb. El Milagro, Talara Alta, Talara +51 7449 5431. – **PI28)** Calle Tumbes 641, La Unión. – **PI29)** Jr. Sucre 556, Sullana. – **PI30)** Maria Prado de Bellido 500, Chulucanas, Prov. Morropón +51 7337 8740. – **PI31)** Calle Cajamarca 485, Bellavista, Prov. de Sullana - **FM:** 107.5. – **PI32)** Av. Grau Cuadra 5, Cruceta San Lorenzo, Tambo Grande, Prov. de Piura – **PI33)** Calle Ayabaca, Barrio La Villa, Huancabamba. – **PI34)** Calle San Miguel 207, Distrito de Sondor, Región Grau, Prov. de Huancabamba – **FM:** 89.1. – **PI35)** Av. Ramon Castilla 254, Huancabamba +51 7347 3369. – **PI36)** Jr. 9 de Octubre 110 frente al Parque Leoncio Prado, Huarmaca, Prov. de Huancabamba. – **PI37)** Av. Quiles Escala s/n, Barrio San Francisco, Huancabamba. – **PI38)** Av. San Francisco Assisi s/n, Huarmaca, Prov. de Huancabamba. – **PI39)** Prolongación San Martin s/n, Huarmaca. – **PI40)** Av. Piura 2000, Pampa Alegra, Distrito de El Faique. Prov. de Huancabamba.

PU00 (PUNO):
PU01) Jr. Conde Lemos 226 (Cas. 210), Puno. +51 5135 1562. +51 5135 2233. – **Quechua & Aymara:** 6h daily. - **FM:** 95.7 "Stereo Azul". – **PU02)** Jr. Arequipa 385, Puno. – **PU03)** Plaza 28 de julio s/n, Macusani, Prov. de Carabaya. - **FM:** 90.5. – **PU04)** Jr. 7 de Juino 580, Juliaca. – **PU05)** Calle San Román 116, Juliaca +51 5132 5357. - **FM:** 89.5. – **PU06)** Simon Bolivar 442, Puno. – **PU07)** Av. Panamericana 940, Chucuito (299, Puno), Prov. de Puno – **Aymara & Quechua** 0900-1400, 1900-0100. – **PU08)** Jr. Altiplano 206, Urb. La Pampilla, Juliaca. - **FM:** 107.9. – **PU09))** Calle Mariano Melgar 1322, Juliaca. **Web:** www.radiondaazul.com – **PU10)** Jr. Deustua 901, Puno. - **FM:** 101.7. – **PU11)** Hipolito Unanue 240, Juliaca. – **PU12)** Carlos B.Oquendo 290 (Ap. 130), Puno. – **PU13)** Calle Mariano Pandía 166, 2° piso, Juliaca. – **PU14)** Jr. Lambayeque 520, Puno. – **PU15)** Jr. Unión 242, Juliaca. **Email:** radioltcj@latinmail.com +51 5132 2452. +51 5136 9450. - **FM:** 102.7. **Quechua & Aymara:** 1000-1100, 1800-1900. – **PU16)** Av. El Maestro 1140, Juliaca - **FM:** 88.9. – **PU17)** Av. El Maestro 950, Juliaca. – **PU18)** Jr. Piura 167, Puno. +51 5135 3680. – **Aymara & Quechua:** 0900-1100. – **PU19)** Jr. Union 229, 3° piso, Juliaca. – **PU20)** Jr. Apurimac 1316, Barrio Manco Capac, Juliaca. – **PU21)** Ramon Castilla 949, Juliaca +51 5132 7143/5132 1372. - **FM:** 90.1. – **PU22)** Jr. Apurimac 644, Juliaca +51 5132 5733. – **PU23)** Jr. 2 de Mayo 790, Juliaca. – **PU24)** Jr. Ricardo Palma 111, Juliaca +51 5132 7208. – **PU25)** Jr. San Martin 134, Yunguyo. – **PU27)** Jr. Chachani 220, Juliaca. – **PU28)** Jr. 2 de Mayo 2578, Juliaca +51 5133 6103/5132 1115. – **Aymara & Quechua:** 0900-1100, 1900-2100. - **FM:** 104.5 "El Sol de los Andes FM". – **PU29)** Av. Titicaca 160 Int. C, Puno. – **PU30)** Av. El Maestro 1140, Barrio Tupac Amaru, Juliaca. – **PU31)** Jr. Teodoro Valcarcel 134 (Cas. 340), Puno. – **PU32)** Guillermo Briceño Rosa Medina 262, Juliaca. – **PU33)** Nicolas de Pierola 432, Juliaca. - **FM:** 107.3. – **PU34)** Jr. 7. de Junio 580, Juliaca. – **PU35)** Jr, Acora 222, Puno.

SM00 (SAN MARTIN):
SM01) Jr. San Martín 257, Tocache +51 4255 1031. – **SM02)** Jr. Santo Toribio 1252, Rioja. – **SM03)** Av. Compagñón 410, Tarapoto. – **SM04)** San Martín 317, Lamas. – **SM05)** Jr. Progreso 225 Altos, Tarapoto +51 4252 2459/4252 7709 - **FM:** 97.5. – **SM06)** Jr. San Martín Cuadra 3 s/n, Tarapoto. - **FM:** 102.3. – **SM08)** Jr. Bolognesi 180 Altos, Tarapoto. – **SM09)** Cl. Bolognesi s/n, Bellavista. +51 4254 4170. +51 4254 4135. - **FM:** 95.1. – **SM10)** Jr. San Martín 1188, Rioja. +51 4256 0212-3071.— **FM:** 92.3. – **SM11)** Peña Meza 467, Juanjuí. – **SM12)** Jr. Progreso 389, Bellavista. +51 4254 4179. – **SM13)** Tocacha, Prov. de Tocache. - **FM:** 96.1. – **14)** Jr.Huallaga 348, Nueva Cajamarca, Rioja.

TA00 (TACNA)
TA02) Prolong. Unanue 1041 (Cas. 113), Tacna. - **FM:** 99.9. – **TA03)** Av. Varela 705, Tacna. – **TA04)** Jr. Sir Jones s/n (Cas. 281), Tacna. – **TA05)** Arias y Araguez 584, Tacna. – **TA06)** Calle Candarave 645, Urb. Bacigalupo, Tacna. – **TA07)** Urb. Jorge Chavez 9 (Ap. 115), Tacna. - **FM:** 89.5. – **TA08)** Av. Internacional 484, Tacna +51 5280 4100/5280 4051 - **FM:** 106.7. – **TA09)** Aniceto Ibarra 436 (Cas. 370), Tacna. +51 5271 4871. +51 5272 3745. **Web:** radiotacna.com - **FM:** 104.3. – **TA10)** Av. San Martín de Porras 209, Natividad, Tacna. **Email:** radiobulevar@hotmail.com +51 5284 8537.

TU00 (TUMBES):
TU01) Pza. Alipio Rosales s/n, Tumbes. – **TU02)** Calle Tarapaca 163, Tumbes. – **TU03)** Av. del Ejercito, cuadra 5, Tumbes - **FM:** 91.1. – **TU04)** Panamericana Norte Km. 1321, Tumbes. - **FM:** 100.5. – **TU05)** Calle

Huáscar 502 3er Piso, Tumbes. +51 7252 7002. – **TU06)** Jr. Bolívar 117, Tumbes. +51 7252 3003. – **TU07)** Jr. Piura 1010, Tumbes.

UC00 (UCAYALI):

UC01) Calle Diego de Almagro s/n, Pucallpa. – **UC02)** Jr. Inmaculada 667, (Cas. 263), Pucallpa +51 6157 8615/6159 3450- **FM:** 89.1. – **UC03)** Av. 9 de Diciembre 646, Pucallpa. - **FM:** 102.5. – **UC04)** Jr. Coronel. Portillo 448-A, Pucallpa. +51 6157 3876. +51 6157 1540. - **FM:** 103.3. – **UC05)** Zona San Fernando, Callería, Pucallpa. – **UC06)** Calle Padre Francisco Alvares s/n, Sephua, Prov. de Atalaya - **FM:** 95.5. – **UC07)** Jr. Iquitos 499, Villa Atalaya, Distrito de Raymondi, Prov. de Atalaya. +51 6146 1240 - **FM:** 93.5.

FM in Lima: 87.9 R.Onda Sur – 88.3 Telestereo 88 – 88.9 Ke-Buena – 89.7 Emisoras Perúanos – 90.1 Iglesia Independiente – 90.5 CPN Radio – 90.9 R.Superior – 91.1 R.San Borja – 91.5 LV del Sur – 91.5 R.Planicie – 91.9 Okey – 92.5 R.Studio 92 – 93.1 R.Ritmo – 93.7 R.La Inolvidable – 94.3 R.America – 94.9 R. "A" – 95.5 R.Z "Solo rock & Pop" – 96.1 R.Miraflores – 96.7 R.Corazon – 97.3 R.Moda – 97.7 R.Comas – 97.7 R.Maria – 97.7 Canto Grande – 97.7 Publicidad Odeese1 – 98.1 R.Once Sesenta – 98.5 R.Turbo Laser – 98.7 R.La Caribeña – 99.1 Doble Nueve – 99.5 Imparcial II – 99.7 Codigo 99 – 100.1 Stéreo 100 – 100.5 R.Chasqui – 100.7 R.Poder – 101.1 R.Panamericana – 101.5 R.Super FM – 101.7 R.Comas – 102.1 R.Oxigeno – 102.5 R.Stereo Villa – 102.7 Filharmonía – 103.3 Unión FM – 103.5 Produccion JR – 103.5 R.Nuevo – 103.9 R.Nacional – 104.3 Impacto Andino – 104.3 Turbo Stereo – 104.7 Viva FM – 105.1 R.Santa Rosa – 105.5 Fiesta – R.Stereo Olivos – 106.3 Radiomar Plus – 106.7 R.Peru – 107.1 R.Inca del Peru – 107.7 R. Planeta

PHILIPPINES

L.T: UTC +8h — **Pop:** 79 million — **Pr.L:** Pilipino (Tagalog), English, Cebuano, Ilocano, Hiligaynon, Bicol — **E.C:** 60Hz, 220V — **ITU:** PHL

NATIONAL TELECOMMUNICATIONS COMMISSION (NTC) (Dept. of Transportation and Communications).

✉ NTC Bldg., BIR Road, East Triangle, Diliman, Quezon City 1104. ☎ +63 9254651 or 9267722 **Web**: www.ntc.gov.ph.

L.P: Commissioner: Retired Gen. Eliseo M. Rio Jr. Deputy Commissioners: Armi Jane R. Borje, Kathleen Heceta. Chief Broadcast Sce. Dept: Carlos D. Saliuan Jr.

KAPISANAN NG MGA BRODKASTER NG PILIPINAS (KBP) (Assoc. of Broadcasters of the Philippines).

✉ 6th Flr, LTA Bldg, 118 Perea Str, Legaspi Village, Makati C, 1226 NCR ☎ +63 2815 1990/1/2 🖷 +63 (2) 815 1989. **Web**: www.kbp.org.ph

L.P: Chmn: Joselito G. Yabut. Pres: Ruperto S. Nicdao, Jr. Chmn. Metro-Manila Chapter: Mario Garcia. Most st's are KBP members.

PHILIPPINE FEDERATION OF CATHOLIC BROADCASTERS

✉ 2307 Pedro Gil Str, Santa Ana, Manila 2802 or P.O. Box 3169, Manila 1099.

L.P: Pres: His Excellency Most Rev. Jesus Y. Varela. Chmn: Fr. James B. Reuter, S.J. (14 member st's).

GENERAL NOTES:

Station identifications: Generally, station IDs are given on the h. and half h. The English alphabet is used for the call letters, while the freq. is usually expressed in Spanish- or English-language numerals. Extensive st. details are included in sign on and sign off ann's.

Callsign assignments: DU = Shortwave only; DW = Luzon; DX = Mindanao and Sulu; DY = Visayas and Palawan; DZ = Luzon.

Administrative divisions: Level 1: regions, 2: provinces, cities (C.), 3: municipalities, 4: barangays (brgy.). The National Capital Region (NCR) is also known as Metropolitan Manila or Metro-Manila.

NB: Cities may be referred to with or without "City", e.g. Baguio City or Baguio, Naga City or Naga, except that Quezon City is **always** referred to by its full name.

MW:

H. of tr: Mostly 2100-1600. CP=Construction permit.

	Call	kHz	kW	Net
73)	(CP)	531	5	
67)	DXGH	531	5	dz
118)	DYDW	531	10	
47)	DZBR	531	5	
83)	DYRB	540	10	
54)	DZWT	540	10	
16)	DXHM	549	5	
84)	DZXL	558	50	
67)	DXCH	567	5	dz
76)	DWRB	567	10	
76)	DWRM	567	10	
73)	DXMF	576	10	bo
76)	DYMR	576	10	
76)	DZMQ	576	5	
17)	DZSH	576	5	dz
16)	DXCP	585	5	
76)	DYLL	585	1	
16)	DXDB	594	5	
60)	DYWR	594	10	bo
36)	DZBB	594	20	
10)	DZLL	603	10	
84)	DXPR	603	5	
22)	DZVV	603	5	bo
68)	(CP)	612	5	
75)	DWSP	612	5	dz
84)	DYHP	612	10	
84)	DXDC	621	10	ag
76)	DZVC	621	1	
85)	DZTG	621	5	
13)	DYAG	630	5	
2)	DZMM	630	50	
88)	(CP)	639	5	
84)	DXKR	639	5	
85)	DZRL	639	1	
117)	DWPS	648	5	
67)	DWRH	648	10	
84)	DXMB	648	5	
50)	DYXR	648	5	ak
77)	DWRN	657	5	
16)	DXDD	657	5	
76)	DYES	657	1	
84)	DYVR	657	5	ag
98)	DZLU	657	1	
76)	DXRP	666	10	
50)	DZRH	666	50	
42)	DWLW	675	5	
103)	DXGD	675	1	
85)	DYKC	675	5	
42)	DWGW	684	1	
43)	DWJJ	684	5	
50)	DYEZ	684	10	ak
33)	DZCV	684	5	
84)	DXBC	693	10	ag
85)	DXDX	693	1	
50)	DYKH	693	1	dz
50)	DYPH	693	10	dz
106)	DZTP	693	10	
31)	DZAS	702	50	
84)	DXIC	711	5	ag
58)	DXRD	711	5	an
29)	DYBR	711	5	
71)	DZLW	711	10	
60)	DZVR	711	5	bo
58)	DZYI	711	5	an
50)	DYOK	720	10	ak
7)	DZJO	720	5	
60)	DZSO	720	5	bo
76)	DWPE	729	10	
84)	DXMY	729	5	
70)	DXOR	729	5	
72)	DZGB	729	5	
76)	DZRB	738	60	
62)	DXND	747	5	
84)	DYHB	747	10	
50)	DZJC	747	10	ak
76)	DWRS	756	10	
9)	DWHL	756	1	
42)	DWNW	756	5	
82)	DXJM	756	2	
83)	DXGS	765	5	
58)	DYAR	765	5	an
68)	DYPR	765	10	
58)	DZYT	765	5	an
41)	DWWW	774	25	
76)	DXSM	774	1	
76)	DXSO	774	10	
84)	DYRI	774	10	ag
94)	DXRA	783	10	
51)	DYME	783	5	
75)	DZNL	783	5	ak
95)	DWES	792	5	
38)	DWGV	792	5	
76)	DXBN	792	10	
73)	DXPD	792	5	bo
66)	DYRR	792	5	
39)	DWFA	801	5	
58)	DXBL	801	1	
22)	DXES	801	5	bo
16)	DYKA	801	5	
35)	DYWC	801	5	
60)	DZNC	801	10	bo
90)	DZRJ	810	10	
114)	DWMG	819	1	
58)	DWRI	819	5	an
101)	DXSC	819	1	
53)	DXUM	819	10	uk
50)	DYVL	819	10	ak
39)	DWZR	828	5	
84)	DXCC	828	10	ag
46)	DYER	828	10	
88)	DZTC	828	1	
17)	(CP)	837	5	
58)	DXRE	837	5	an
22)	DYFM	837	10	bo
30)	DZXE	837	5	
78)	(CP)	846	5	
87)	DZRV	846	50	
67)	DXGO	855	10	ak
42)	DXWG	855	1	
17)	DXZH	855	5	dz
33)	DZGE	855	10	
58)	DWSI	864	5	an
97)	DYHH	864	10	
58)	DZSP	864	5	an
16)	DZWM	864	5	
76)	DXJS	873	10	
58)	DXRB	873	5	an
58)	DXRT	873	5	
1)	DZPA	873	5	
33)	DZRC	873	5	
3)	DWIZ	882	50	
62)	DXMS	882	10	
76)	DXRG	882	1	
76)	DYOG	882	10	
12)	DWAR	891	5	
59)	DYSR	891	10	uk
73)	DZGR	891	5	
63)	DWNE	900	5	
99)	DXIP	900	5	
84)	DXRZ	900	5	ag
22)	DYOW	900	5	bo
115)	DYLA	909	5	
91)	DYSP	909	5	su
16)	DZEA	909	5	
76)	DZSR	918	10	
122)	DWBS	927	10	
64)	DXDA	927	5	
84)	DXMD	927	5	ag
103)	DXMM	927	5	
73)	DZLG	927	5	bo
40)	DWIM	936	5	
111)	DXDN	936	5	uk
76)	DXIM	936	10	
84)	DYCC	936	1	
85)	DYKW	936	1	
82)	DZXT	936	1	
116)	DXDV	945	10	uk
58)	DXRO	945	5	an
4)	DYRO	945	5	
76)	DWFB	954	10	
110)	DYMM	954	5	
93)	DZAL	954	5	
20)	DZEM	954	40	
58)	DXYZ	963	5	an
73)	DYMF	963	10	bo
16)	DZNS	963	5	
76)	DWFR	972	5	
45)	DWTI	972	5	
17)	DXKH	972	5	dz
17)	DYSM	972	1	ak

Call	kHz	kW	Net	Call	kHz	kW	Net
75) DWMT	981	5	dz	86) DZRS	1179	1	
22) DXBR	981	10	bo	60) DXIF	1188	10	bo
84) DXDR	981	5	ag	22) DXLX	1188	5	bo
88) DXOW	981	10		2) DYRV	1188	1	
42) DYBQ	981	10		82) DZLT	1188	5	
58) DZRD	981	5	an	114) DZXO	1188	5	
107) DWRT	990	15		12) (CP)	1197	10	
91) DXBM	990	5		98) DWBA	1197	5	
67) DYTH	990	5	dz	31) DXFE	1197	5	
67) DZMT	990	5	dz	4) DYRH	1197	5	
45) DWMI	999	5		6) DWAN	1206	10	
84) DXHP	999	1		84) DXRS	1206	5	ag
76) DXDC	999	1		50) (CP)	1215	5	
91) DYSS	999	5		118) DYRF	1215	10	
76) DZEQ	999	5		76) DWBF	1224	5	
16) DWBS	1008	5		50) DWSR	1224	5	
102) DWGO	1008	5		28) DXED	1224	10	
85) DXXX	1008	10		76) DZAG	1224	10	
42) DWDW	1017	10		87) DWRV	1233	5	
76) DWLC	1017	10		31) DYVS	1233	5	
44) DXRR	1017	10		32) DWBL	1242	20	
16) DXSN	1017	5		105) DXSY	1242	5	
4) DYRP	1017	10		27) DXZB	1242	5	
73) DXMC	1026	5	bo	50) DXPH	1251	5	
111) DXMI	1026	1		42) DYRG	1251	1	
58) DZAR	1026	10	an	72) DZMS	1251	2.5	
88) DYRL	1035	10		49) DWMC	1260	5	
111) DYUM	1035	5/2.5		50) DXRF	1260	5	dz
22) DZWX	1035	5	bo	97) DYDD	1260	10	
88) DXCO	1044	5		28) DZEL	1260	5	
81) DXLL	1044	5	uk	91) DWRC	1269	10	
96) DXML	1044	1		22) DYWB	1269	10	bo
17) DYMS	1044	5	ak	60) DZVX	1269	5	bo
60) DZNG	1044	10	bo	42) DXAM	1278	10	
85) DXKD	1053	10		76) DZRM	1278	10	
112) DYSA	1053	5		91) DXRC	1287	5	su
31) DXKI	1062	5		50) DZZH	1287	5	dz
28) DZEC	1062	40		4) DWLQ	1296	5	
85) DXKT	1071	5		4) DWPR	1296	5	
110) DYXT	1071	1		2) DXAB	1296	10	
123) DZSL	1071			42) DYJJ	1296	5	
16) DWAM	1080	1		50) (CP)	1305	10	
28) DWIN	1080	5		28) DYFX	1305	10	
83) DWRL	1080	5		25) DWXI	1314	10	
85) DXKS	1080	1		57) DXAD	1323	5	
34) DXRH	1080	5		36) DYSI	1323	10	su
67) DYBH	1080	5	dz	76) DZRK	1323	0.25	
111) DXCM	1089	10	uk	58) DWAY	1332	5	an
39) DYHR	1089	1		85) DZKI	1332	1	
23) DWAD	1098	10		91) DXRL	1341	10	
58) DXCL	1098	5	an	36) DXXY	1350	5	
61) DWDY	1107	10		48) DZXQ	1350	10	
91) DXBB	1107	5		76) DYSL	1359	1	
73) DYIN	1107	5	bo	77) DZYR	1359	5	
8) DZOM	1107	1		58) DWTT	1368	5	
31) DXAS	1116	5		85) DXKO	1368	10	
104) DYTR	1116	10		85) DZBS	1368	2.5	
113) DZLB	1116	5		15) DZRA	1368	1	
31) DWAS	1125	5		50) (CP)	1377		
69) DXGL	1125	10		85) DXKP	1377	10	
91) DXGM	1125	5	su	78) (CP)	1386	10	
22) DZWN	1125	10	bo	55) DXCR	1386	10	
26) DWDD	1134	10		16) DYVW	1386	5	
95) DWJS	1134	5		17) DYRC	1395	10	dz
111) DXMV	1134	5	uk	16) DZVT	1395	5	
79) DXOS	1134			85) DYKB	1404	1	
77) DYRM	1134	1		91) DWRA	1413	5	
76) DWBT	1134	1		121) DXBZ	1413	10	
16) DYAF	1143	5		33) DYXW	1413	5	
51) DYCM	1152	5		109) DWBC	1422	10	
75) DWCM	1161	10		18) DXMU	1422	5	
111) DXDS	1161	1	uk	11) DYZD	1422	5	
84) DYKR	1161	5		119) DZOR	1422	1	
11) DYRD	1161	5		89) DYRS	1431	5	
72) DZMD	1161	5		50) DWDH	1440	10	dz
76) DXMR	1170	10		100) DXSI	1440	0.01	
65) DZCA	1170	10		52) DXSA	1449	5	
91) DXRC	1179		su	19) DYAC	1449	5	
91) DXYK	1179	5		31) DWRF	1458	10	
36) DYCX	1179	5	su	97) DYZZ	1458	10	

Call	kHz	kW	Net	Call	kHz	kW	Net
120) DZJV	1458	10		77) DZYM	1539	5	
87) DWVR	1467	1		36) DZSD	1548	10	su
16) DXVP	1467	5	su	16) DYDM	1548	5	
50) (CP)	1476	5		43) DZKV	1548	5	
92) DWRB	1476	1		5) DXID	1566	10	
90) DXRJ	1476	10		74) DZHH	1566	10	
88) DZYA	1476	1		21) DXJR	1575	10	
67) DYDH	1485	5	dz	4) DYAY	1584	10	
108) DWSS	1494	10		24) DWBR	1584	1	
83) DXOC	1494	5		124) DXFM	1593	-	
36) DYBB	1503	5	su	113) DZUP	1602	10	
2) DYAB	1512	10		37) DWGI	1674	0.01	
50) (CP)	1530	5		56) DZBF	1674	1	
14) DZME	1530	10					

SW:

	Call	Location	kHz	kW	H. of tr.
76)	DUR2	Marulas, Valenzuela	9580v	0.25	0000-0930v

Operated by PBS, Philippine Broadc. Sce, this tr. relays various PBS AM and FM sce's. Tr. G.C: 14.41N/120.59E.

Prgr. networks: ag=Radyo Agong – ak=Aksyon Radyo – an=Angel Radyo (key: 1026kHz) – bo=Bombo Radyo – dz=DZRH (key: 666kHz) – su=Super Radyo – uk=Radyo Ukay.
Web URLs for broadc. networks: FEBC: www.febc.org – R. Mindanao Netw: www.rmn.com.ph – R. Ukay: www.umbn.com.ph – Manila Broadc. Co: www.mbcradio.net – Aksyon R: www.aksyon-radyo.com – PBS: www.pbs.gov.ph.

FM: A large number of FM stations are operating throughout the country.
Manila FM: – 88.3 DWCT-FM "City Lite" – 89.1 DZMZ "Wave 89.1" – 89.9 DWTM "Magic 89.9" – 90.7 DZMB "Love Radio" – 91.5 DWKY "K-91" – 92.3 DZRU "Joey at Rhythms 92.3" – 93.1 DWRX "RX 93.1" – 93.9 DWKC – 94.7 DWLL "Mellow Touch" – 95.5 DWDM "DM 95.5" – 96.3 DWRK "W-Rock" – 97.1 DWLS "WLS Campus Radio" – 97.9 DWQZ "Home Radio" – 98.7 DZFE "FEBC/The Master's Touch" – 99.5 DWRT-FM "RT" – 100.3 DZRJ "The Hive" – 101.1 ?DWKS-FM (DWST) "MBC/Yes FM" – 101.9 DWRR "ABS-CBN/Music for Life" – 102.7 DWSM "Star" – 103.5 DWCS "K-Light" – 104.3 DWBR "Business Radio" – 105.1 DWBM "Marenco Broadcasting Network" – 105.9 DWLA "WLA" – 106.7 DWET "ABC Radio" – 107.5 DWNU "New 107".

Addresses
For each entry the company name is followed by the call letters (in alphabetical order) and addresses of the sts owned by the company. When contacting a st, use "Radio Station" + the call letters as st name.
1) Abra Community Btcg. Corp. DZPA, Samora & Rizal Sts, Bangued, 2800 Abra – **2)** ABS-CBN Broadc. Corp. DXAB, KM-4, Shine Hills, Matina, Davao C, 8000 Davao del Sur. DYAB, P. del Rosario cor. Lion Kilat Str, Cebu C, 6000 Cebu. DYRV, Catbalogan, 6700 Samar. DZMM, Chronicle Bldg, Mother Ignacia St. cor. Sgt Esguerra Ave, Quezon C – **3)** Aliw Broadc. Corp. DWIZ, 5th Floor, Dominga Bldg, 2113 Pasong Tamo, Makati C, 1231 NCR – **4)** Allied Broadc. Center, Inc. DWLQ, Happy Valley Str, Ibabang Dupay, Lucena C, 4301 Quezon Province. DWPR, A.B. Fernandez Ave, Bolosan District, Dagupan C, 2400 Pangasinan. DYAY, Minglanilla, 6046 Cebu. DYRH, JTL Bldg, North Drive, Bacolod C, 6100 Negros Occidental. DYRO, Arnaldo Blvd, Roxas C, 5800 Capiz. DYRP, Bo. Alalasad, Iloilo C, 5000 Iloilo – **5)** Association of Islamic Dev't. Cooperative. DXID, Banale Dist, Pagadian C, 7016 Zamboanga del Sur – **6)** Banahaw Broadc. Corp. DWAN, Broadcast City Complex, Capitol Hills, Diliman, Quezon C, 1104 NCR – **7)** Bayanihan Broadc. Corp. DZJO, 120 J. Arellano Str, San Juan, NCR – **8)** Ben Viduya (OMARCO). DZOM, Calapan C, 5200 Mindoro Oriental – **9)** Beta Broadc. Syst. DWHL, 8 Kessing Str, Olongapo C, 2200 Zambales – **10)** Bicol Broadc. Syst. DZLL, BBS Bldg, Balatas Str, Naga C, 4400 Camarines Sur – **11)** Bohol Chronicle Radio Corp. DYRD, Dejaresco Bldg, Tagbilaran C, 6300 Bohol. DYZD, Ubay, 6315 Bohol – **12)** Caceres Broadc. Corp. DWAR, Diversion Rd. Tabuco, Naga C, 4400 Camarines Sur. CP 1197kHz, Daet, 4600 Camarines Norte – **13)** Cadiz Radio & TV Netw. DYAG, Cadiz C, 6121 Negros Occidental – **14)** Capitol Broadc. Center. DZME, Capitol Broadc. Center, 317 Roosevelt Ave, San Francisco del Montc, Quczon C – **15)** Catanduanes State College. DZRA, Virac, 4800 Catanduanes – **16)** Catholic Welfare Org. DWAM, Basilican Site, Batangas C, 4200 Batangas. DWBS, Sto. Domingo, 4508 Albay. DXCP, Lagao, Gen. Santos C, 9500 South Cotabato. DXDB, Clergy House, Malaybalay C, 8700 Bukidnon. DXDD, Ozamis C, 7200 Misamis Occidental. DXHM, Clergy House, Madong, Oriental Mindoro. DXSN, 55 Magallanes, Surigao C, 8400 Surigao del Norte. DXVP, Zamboanga C, 7000 Zamboanga del Sur. DYAF, Bacolod C, 6100 Negros

Occidental. DYDM, Maasin C, 6600 Southern Leyte. DYKA, San Jose, 5700 Antique. DYVW, Clergy House, Borongan, 6800 Eastern Samar. DZEA, Brgy. Nalbo, Laoag C, 2900 Ilocos Norte, DZNS, Vigan, 2700 Ilocos Sur. DZVT, Brgy. Labangan, San Jose, 5100 Mindoro Occidental. DZWM, Lucap, Alaminos, 2404 Pangasinan – **17)** Cebu Broadc. Co. DXKH, Cagayan de Oro C, 9000 Misamis Oriental. DXZH, Zamboanga C, 7000 Zamboanga del Sur. DYMS, San Bartolome Str, Catbalogan, 6700 Samar. DYRC, 5 Centrum F. Osmeña, Bo. Tangue, Talisay C, 6045 Cebu. DYSM, Brgy. Cawayan, Catarman, 6400 Northern Samar. DZSH, Tuguegarao, 3500 Cagayan. CP 837kHz, Cauayan, 3305 Isabela – **18)** Central Mindanao University. DXMU, Musuan, 8710 Bukidnon – **19)** Central Visayas College of Agriculture. DYAC, VISCA Baybay, 6521 Leyte – **20)** Christian Era Broadc. Sce. DZEM, Maligaya Bldg 2, 887 EDSA, Quezon C – **21)** COC Broadc. Netw. DXJR, Cagayan de Oro College, Max Suniel St, Carmen, Cagayan de Oro C, 9000 Misamis Oriental – **22)** Consolidated Broadc. Syst, Inc. DXBR, Bombo R. Broadc. Center, Aruj Ville Subd, Brgy. Libertad, Butuan C, 8600 Agusan del Norte. DXES Bombo R. Broadc. Center, Brgy. Bula, Gen. Santos C, 9500 South Cotabato. DXLX, Tambo, Brgy. Hinaplon, Iligan C, 9200 Lanao del Norte. DYFM, Sky City Tower, Mapa Str, Jaro, Iloilo C, 5000 Iloilo. DYOW, Bombo R. Broadc. Center, Arnaldo Blvd, Roxas C, 5800 Capiz. DYWB, CBS Dev. Corp. Bldg, Lacson Str, Mandalagan, Bacolod C, 6100 Negros Occidental. DZVV, Brgy. Tamag, Vigan, 2700 Ilocos Sur. DZWN, Bombo R. Broadc. Center, Maramba Bankers' Village, Bonuan Catacdang, 2400 Dagupan C, Pangasinan. DZWX, Bombo R. Broadc. Center, 14 Lourdes Subdivision, Baguio C, 2600 Benguet – **23)** Crusaders Broadc. Syst. DWAD, 209 E. de la Paz Str, Mandaluyong C, NCR – **24)** Dawnbreaker's Foundation. DWBR, Radyo Bahay, Bulac, Talavera, 3114 Nueva Ecija or P. O.Box 27, San José City 3121 – **25)** Delta Broadc. Syst. DWXI, Mathew Str, Multinational Village, Parañaque C, 1708 NCR – **26)** Dept. of National Defense. DWDD, Camp Aguinaldo, Quezon C, 1110 NCR – **27)** DXZB/TV13 Cooperative, Inc. DXZB, Zamboanga C, 7000 Zamboanga del Sur – **28)** Eagle Broadc. Corp. DWIN, Bo. Lucao, Dagupan C, 2400 Pangasinan. DXED, Cabiguio Ave, Davao C, 8000 Davao del Sur. DYFX, Leyden Bldg, F. Ramos Str, Cebu C, 6000 Cebu. DZEC, R Aguila, Maligaya Bldg II, 887 EDSA, Quezon C. DZEL, Bo. Mayao, Lucena C, 4301 Quezon Province – **29)** East Visayan Broadc. DYBR, Sagcahan Rd, P.O. Box 80, Tacloban C, 6500 Leyte – **30)** Fairwaves Broadc. Netw. DZXE, Mira Hills, Vigan, 2700 Ilocos Sur – **31)** Far East Broadc. Co. DWAS, P.O. Box 78, Arimbay, Legaspi C, 4500 Albay. DWRF, P.O. Box 3222, Amungan, Iba, 2201 Zambales. DXAS, P.O. Box 349, Tugbungan, Zamboanga C, 7000 Zamboanga del Sur. DXFE, P.O. Box 81103, Davao C, 8000 Davao del Sur. DXKI, P.O. Box 8004, Koronadal C, 9506 South Cotabato. DYVS, P.O. Box 393, Km. 7, Pahanocoy, Bacolod C, 6100 Negros Occidental. DZAS, P.O. Box 1, Valenzuela C, 0560 NCR – **32)** FBS Radio Netw. DWBL, 18th Flr, Philcomcen Bldg, Ortigas Ave, Pasig C, NCR – **33)** Filipinas Broadc. Netw. DYXW, Baruyan, San Jose, Tacloban C, 6500 Leyte. DZCV, Ugac Norte, Tuguegarao, 3500 Cagayan. DZGE, Nordia Resort Baras, Canaman, Naga C, 4400 Camarines Sur. DZRC, Capt. Aquendes Drive, Legaspi C, 4500 Albay – **34)** First United Broadc. Corp. DXRH, Zamboanga C, 7000 Zamboanga del Sur – **35)** Franciscan Broadc. Corp. DYWC, Chancery, Dumaguete Cathedral, Dumaguete C, 6200 Negros Oriental – **36)** GMA Netw, Inc. DZSD, Dagupan C, 2400 Pangasinan. DXXY, Dipolog C, Zamboanga del Norte. DYBB, 2nd Flr, Oscar R. Arcenas Bldg, Roxas Av, Roxas C, 5800 Capiz. DYCX, Bacolod C, 6100 Negros Occidental. DYSI, Phase V Alta Tierra Village, Jaro, Iloilo C, 5000 Iloilo. DZBB, GMA Netw. Center, EDSA corner Timog Avenue, Diliman, 1103 Quezon C – **37)** Guzman Institute of Tech. DWGI, Sta. Cruz, Manila, NCR – **38)** GV Broadc. Syst. DWGV, Angeles C, 2009 Pampanga – **39)** Hypersonic Broadc. Center. DWFA, Sorsogon C, 4700 Sorsogon. DWZR, Zoom Radio, Penaranda Str, Legaspi C, 4500 Albay. DYHR, Calbayog C, 6710 W. Samar – **40)** Insular Broadc. Syst. DWIM, Brgy. Bayanihan, Calapan, 5200 Mindoro Oriental – **41)** Interactive Broadcast Media, Inc. DWWW, 23 E. Rodriguez Sr. Blvd, Quezon C – **42)** Intercontinental Broadc. Corp. DWDW, R. Tambuyoc, Tambac District, Dagupan C, 2400 Pangasinan. DWGW, Penaranda Str, Legaspi C, 4500 Albay. DWLW, Brgy. Nangalisan, Laoag C, 2900 Ilocos Norte. DWNW, Panganiban Str, Naga C, 4400 Camarines Sur. DXAM, Maramag, 8714 Bukidnon. DXWG, Iligan C, 9200 Lanao del Norte. DYBQ, 4/F UEC Bldg, Mapa Str, Iloilo C, 5000 Iloilo. DYJJ, Roxas Ave, Roxas C, 5800 Capiz. DYRG, Tunting Reyes Str, Kalibo, 5600 Aklan – **43)** Kaissar Broadc. Netw. DWJJ, Araullo University, Bitas, Cabanatuan C, 3100 Nueva Ecija. DZKV, Lipa C, 4217 Batangas – **44)** Kalayaan Broadc. Syst. DXRR, Bug-ac, Matina, Davao C, 8000 Davao del Sur – **45)** Katigbak Enterprises. DWMI, Calapan, 5200 Mindoro Oriental. DWTI, Ibabang Dupay, Lucena C, 4301 Quezon Province – **46)** Katigbak Entertainment. DYER, Puerto Princesa C, 5300 Palawan – **47)** Kumintang Broadc. Syst. DZBR, R. Balisong, KBS Bldg, Capitol Hills, Batangas C, 4200 Batangas – **48)** Mabuhay Broadc. Syst., Inc. DZXQ, Centerpoint Condominium, Dona Julia Vargas Ave., Ortigas Center, Pasig C – **49)** Magiliw Community Broadc. Co. DWMC, Tomana, Rosales, 2441 Pangasinan – **50)** Manila Broadc. Co. DWDH, Lucao District, Dagupan C, 2400 Pangasinan. DWSR, Lucena C, 4301 Quezon Province. DXPH, Prosperidad, 8500 Agusan del Sur. DXRF, Davao C, 8000 Davao del Sur. DYEZ, Wilrose Building, Burgos Str, Bacolod C, 6100 Negros Occidental. DYKH, Kalibo, 5600 Aklan. DYOK, 2nd flr. Overton Bldg. Rizal Str, Bgy. Benedicto Jaro, Iloilo C, 5000 Iloilo. DYPH, Puerto Princesa C, 5300 Palawan. DYVL, J. Romualdez corner Real Streets, Tacloban C, 6500 Leyte. DYXR, 3rd Floor, Cinco Centrum Building, Fuente Osmeña Blvd, Cebu C, 6000 Cebu. DZJC, Brgy. 29, Rizal Street, St. Joseph District, Laoag C, 2900 Ilocos Norte. DZRH, 4/F, FJE Bldg, 105 Esteban Str, Legaspi Village, Makati C, 1229 NCR. DZZH, Cabit-an, Sorsogon C, 4700 Sorsogon. CP 1377kHz, Bogo, 6010 Cebu. CP 1530kHz, Ozamis C, 7200 Misamis Occidental. CP 1476kHz, Santiago C, 3311 Isabela. CP 1305kHz, Legaspi C, 4500 Albay. CP 1215kHz, Koronadal C, 9506 South Cotabato – **51)** Masbate Community Broadc. Co. DYCM, Bogo, 6010 Cebu. DYME, Tugbo Str, Masbate C, 5400 Masbate – **52)** Mindanao Broadc. Co, Inc. DXSA, Marawi C, 9700 Lanao del Sur – **53)** Mt. Apo Science Foundation. DXUM, UM Matina Campus, Ma-a, Davao C, 8000 Davao del Sur – **54)** Mt. Province Broadc. Corp. DZWT, P.O. Box 156, Baguio C, 2600 Benguet – **55)** Mt. View College. DXCR, MVC, Valencia, 8709 Bukidnon – **56)** Municipality of Marikina. DZBF, R. Marikina, Second Floor, City Hall, Marikina C, NCR – **57)** Muslim Mindanao Dev. Multi-Purpose Coop. DXAD, Marawi C, 9700 Lanao del Sur – **58)** Nation Broadc. Corp. DWAY, Cabanatuan C, 3100 Nueva Ecija. DWRI, Laoag C, 2900 Ilocos Norte. DWSI, North Eastern Foundation College, Santiago, 3311 Isabela. DWTT, Tarlac C, 2300 Tarlac. DXBL, Mangagoy, Bislig C, 8311 Surigao del Sur. DXCL, Cagayan de Oro C, 9000 Misamis Oriental. DXRB, NBC Bldg, B. Libertad, Butuan C, 8600 Agusan del Norte. DXRD, NBC Bldg. Florentino Torres, Davao C, 8000 Davao del Sur. DXRE, Lagao, Gen. Santos C, 9500 South Cotabato. DXRO, Don Roman Vilo Str, Cotabato C, 9600 Maguindanao. DXRT, Jolo, 7400 Sulu. DXYZ, NBC Bldg, San Jose, Baliwasan, Zamboanga C, 7000 Zamboanga del Sur. DYAR, Ybanez Bldg, Fuente Osmena, Cebu C, 6000 Cebu. DZAR, 3/F Jacinta Bldg II, Edsa-Guadalupe, Makati C, 1212 NCR. DZRD, NBC Comp. Banuan Guesset, Dagupan C, 2400 Pangasinan. DZSP, San Pablo C, 4000 Laguna. DZYI, Capitol site, Ilagan, 3300 Isabela. DZYT, Cagayan Teachers College, Tuguegarao, 3500 Cagayan – **59)** National Council of Churches in the Philippines. DYSR, Camp Seasite Banilad, Dumaguete C, 6200 Negros Oriental – **60)** Newsounds Broadc. Netw. DXIF, Bombo R. Broadc. Center, Corrales Ave, Cagayan de Oro C, 9000 Misamis Oriental. DYWR, Bombo R. Broadc. Center, Sto. Nino cor. Imelda Ave, Tacloban C, 6500 Leyte. DZNC, Bombo R. Broadc. Center, Barrio Menante II, Cauayan, 3305 Isabela. DZNG, Bombo R. Broadc. Center, Diversion Road, Brgy. Tabuko, Naga C, 4400 Camarines Sur. DZSO, Pennsylvania Ave, San Fernando C, 2500 La Union . DZVR, Brgy. 48 K, Kabungaan Airport Ave, Laoag C, 2900 Ilocos Norte. DZVX, J. Pimentel Str, Daet, 4600 Camarines Norte – **61)** Northeastern Broadc. Sce. DWDY, Ground Floor, Isabela Hotel, Mirante Uno, Cauayan, 3305 Isabela – **62)** Notre Dame Broadc. Corp. DXMS, Sinsuat Ave, Cotabato C, 9600 Maguindanao. DXND, Quezon Blvd, Kidapawan C, 9400 North Cotabato – **63)** Nueva Ecija Provincial Gov. DWNE, Cabanatuan C, 3100 Nueva Ecija – **64)** Office of the Governor, Prov. of Agusan del Sur. DXDA, San Francisco, 8501 Agusan del Sur – **65)** Office of the Civil Defense. DZCA, Agham Rd. Science Garden, Pag-asa Planetarium, NCR – **66)** Ormoc Broadc. Co. DYRR, Bantique, Ormoc C, 6541 Leyte – **67)** Pacific Broadc. Syst. DWRH, Santiago C, 3311 Isabela.. DXCH, Cotabato C, 9600 Maguindanao. DXGH, Gen. Santos C, 9500 South Cotabato. DXGO, MBC Compound, Brgy. Duterte, R. Castillo Str, Agdao, Davao C, 8000 Davao del Sur. DYBH, Bacolod C, 6100 Negros Occidental. DYDH, Iloilo C, 5000 Iloilo. DYTH, Tacloban C, 6500 Leyte. DZMT, Laoag C, 2900 Ilocos Norte – **68)** Palawan Broadc. Corp. DYPR, Rey Olivar Bldg. Mabini St. Puerto Princesa C, 5300 Palawan. CP 612kHz, Taytay, 5312 Palawan – **69)** PEC Broadc. Corp. DXGL, Butuan C, 8600 Agusan del Norte – **70)** Pedro N. Roa Broadc. DXOR, Don A. Velez Str, Cagayan de Oro C, 9000 Misamis Oriental – **71)** Penafrancia Broadc. Corp. DZLW, Naga C, 4400 Camarines Sur – **72)** People's Broadc. Netw. DZGB, Imperial Court, Legaspi C, 4500 Albay. DZMD, Vinzons Ave, Daet, 4600 Camarines Norte. DZMS, Balobo Str, Sorsogon C, 4700 Sorsogon – **73)** People's Broadc. Sce. DXMC, Bombo R. Broadc. Center, General Santos Drive, Koronadal C, 9506 South Cotabato. DXMF, Bombo R. Broadc. Center, San Pedro Str, Davao C, 8000 Davao del Sur. DXPD, Bombo R. Broadc. Center, North Diversion Road, Brgy. Banale, Pagadian C, 7016 Zamboanga del Sur. DYIN, Bombo Radyo Broadcast Center, Oyo Torong Str, cor. C. Laserna Ext. Str, Kalibo, 5600 Aklan. DYMF, 87-A. Borromeo Str, Cebu C, 6000 Cebu. DZGR, Bombo R. Broadc. Center, Población Bagumbayan, Tuguegarao, 3500 Cagayan. DZLG, Bombo R. Broadc. Center, Tahao Road near Central City, Subdivision Gate, Legaspi C, 4500 Albay. CP 531kHz, Puerto Princesa C, 5300 Palawan – **74)** Philippine Air Force. DZHH, Villamor Air Base, Pasay C, 1309 NCR – **75)** Philippine Broadc. Corp. DWCM, Caranglaan District, Dagupan C, 2400 Pangasinan. DWMT, Naga C, 4400 Camarines Sur. DWSP, Tuding, Itogon, 2604 Benguet. DZNL, Brgy. Pagdalagan, San Fernando C, 2500 La Union – **76)** Philippine Broadc. Sce. DWFB, Mariano Marcos University, Laoag C, 2900 Ilocos Norte. DWFR, Multipurpose Bldg, Provincial Capitol Compound, Bontoc, 2616 Mountain Province. DWLC, Perez Park, Lucena C, 4301 Quezon Province. DWPE, Caritan, CSU Campus, Tuguegarao, 3500 Cagayan.

DWRB, City Civic Center, Taal Ave, Naga C, 4400 Camarines Sur. DWRM, City Hall Compound, Puerto Princesa C, 5300 Palawan. DWRS, Poblacion, Tayug, 2445 Pangasinan. DXBN, City Hall Compound, Brgy. Doongan, Butuan C, 8600 Agusan del Norte. DXDC, Tubig Boh, Bongao, 7500 Tawi-Tawi. DXIM, A. Velez Str, Cagayan de Oro C, 9000 Misamis Oriental. DXJS, Capitol Hills, Tandag, 8300 Surigao del Sur. DXMR, Baliwasan Chico, Zamboanga C, 7000 Zamboanga del Sur. DXRG, Dugenio Str, Gingoog C, 9014 Misamis Oriental. DXRP, Rm 5, PTA Bldg, Magsaysay Park, Davao C, 8000 Davao del Sur. DXSM, Camp Asturias, Jolo, 7400 Sulu. DXSO, Satellite Office, MSU Campus, Marawi C, 9700 Lanao del Sur.DYES, Capitol Compd, Borongan, 6800 Eastern Samar. DYLL, PNRC Youth Center Bldg, Bonifacio Drive, Iloilo C, 5000 Iloilo. DYMR, CSCST Compound, M.J. Cuenca Ave, Cebu C, 6000 Cebu. DYOG, City Hall Compound, Calbayog C, 6710 W. Samar. DYSL, SLSAT Campus, Sogod, 6606 Southern Leyte. DZAG, Don Mariano Marcos Memorial State University, Agoo, 2504 La Union. DZEQ, Polo Field, Pacdal Circle, Baguio C, 2600 Benguet. DZMQ, Tondaligan Beach, Dagupan C, 2400 Pangasinan. DWBT, San Antonio, Basco, 3900 Batanes. DZRB, Philippine Information Agency Bldg., Visayas Ave., Del Monte, Quezon C, 1105 NCR . DZRK, Capitol Compound, Tabuk, 3800 Kalinga. DZRM and DZSR as DZRB. DZVC Virac, State College Campus, 4800 Catanduanes – **77)** Philippine Radio Corp. DWRN, Manipit Rd, Queborac Bagumbayan, Naga C, 4400 Camarines Sur. DYRM, Bo. Calindangan, Dumaguete C, 6200 Negros Oriental. DZYM, Puerto Gallenero, Pag-asa, San Jose, 5100 Mindoro Occidental. DZYR, San Fernando C, 2500 La Union – **78)** Prime Broadc. Netw. 846kHz, Cebu C, 6000 Cebu. 1386kHz, NCR – **79)** Public Affairs Sce, Armed Forces of the Philippines. DXOS, Basilan Island, Basilan – **81)** R.T. Broadc. Specialists Philippines. DXLL, Campaner Str, Zamboanga C, 7000 Zamboanga del Sur – **82)** Radio Corp. of the Philippines. DXJM, J & M Bldg, Butuan C, 8600 Agusan del Norte. DZLT, Bo. Ibabang Dupay, Lucena C, 4301 Quezon Province. DZXT, MacArthur H-way, Tarlac C, 2300Tarlac – **83)** Radio, Inc. DWRL, Brgy. Bitano, PNR Site, Legaspi C, 4500 Albay. DXGS, Sampaloc Str, Gen. Santos C, 9500 South Cotabato. DXOC, Manabay, Ozamis C, 7200 Misamis Occidental. DYRB, Gorodo Ave, Cebu C, 6000 Cebu – **84)** Radio Mindanao Netw. DXBC, Montilla Blvd, Butuan C, 8600 Agusan del Norte. DXCC, Canoy Bldg. Don Apolinar Velez Str, Cagayan de Oro C, 9000 Misamis Oriental. DXDC, San Vincente Bldg, cor. Anda & Bonifacio Sts, Davao C, 8000 Davao del Sur. DXDR, Bo. Mario Turno, Dipolog C, 7100 Zamboanga del Norte. DXHP, Flomencia Bldg. P. Castillo Mangagoy, Bislig C, 8311 Surigao del Sur. DXIC, Pafs Mejia Bldg, Roxas Str. cor Aguinaldo Str, Iligan C, 9200 Lanao del Norte. DXKR, Gen. Santos Drive, Koronadal C, 9506 South Cotabato. DXMB, Fortich Str, Malaybalay C, 8700 Bukidnon. DXMD, Bo. Obrero National Highway, Gen. Santos C, 9500 South Cotabato. DXMY, Esteros Brgy, RH #10, Cotabato C, 9600 Maguindanao. DXPR, Consolacion Str, Balangayan Dist, Pagadian C, 7016 Zamboanga del Sur. DXRS, Bldg. Km. 1 Surigao C, 8400 Surigao del Norte. DXRZ, Zamaveco Bldg, Pilar Str, Zamboanga C, 7000 Zamboanga del Sur. DYCC, Brgy. Obrero, Calbayog C, 6710 W. Samar. DYHB, 17th Lacson Str, Bacolod C, 6100 Negros Occidental. DYHP, 2nd Flr, Gold Palace Bldg, 168 Osmeña Blvd, Cebu C, 6000 Cebu. DYKR, C. Laserna Str, Kalibo, 5600 Aklan. DYRI, 3rd Flr, MJM Bldg. cor Ledesma & Quezon Sts, Iloilo C, 5000 Iloilo. DYVR, Punta, Tabuc, Roxas C, 5800 Capiz. DZXL, 15/F, Philcomcen Bldg, Ortigas Ave, Pasig C, NCR – **85)** Radio Philippines Netw. DXDX, Acharon Blvd, Gen. Santos C, 9500 South Cotabato. DXKD, Revolacion Str, Dipolog C, 7100 Zamboanga del Norte. DXKO, Gusa, Cagayan de Oro C, 9000 Misamis Oriental. DXKP, Araulio Str, Pagadian C, 7016 Zamboanga del Sur. DXKS, Capitol Rd, Surigao C, 8400 Surigao del Norte. DXKT, Bolton Ext, Davao C, 8000 Davao del Sur. DXXX, Veterano Str, San Jose, Zamboanga del Sur. DYKB, Bo. Sumag, Bacolod C, 6100 Negros Occidental. DYKC, Mandaue C, 6014 Cebu. DYKW, Cagamayan, Binalbagan, 6107 Negros Occidental. DZBS, Agrix Supermarket cor. Magsaysay Ave. & Bakawkan, Baguio C, 2600 Benguet. DZKI, Iriga C, 4431 Camarines Sur. DZRL, Bo. Kawayan, Batac, 2906 Ilocos Norte. DZTG, 46 Rizal Str, Tuguegarao, 3500 Cagayan – **86)** Radio Sorsogon Netw, Inc. DZRS, Don Luis Lee Bldg, Plaza Bonifacio, Sorsogon C, 4700 Sorsogon – **87)** Radio Veritas Global Broadc. Syst. DWRV, Bayombong, 3700 Nueva Vizcaya. DWVR, San Jose C, 3121 Nueva Ecija. DZRV, R. Veritas, 20th Floor, "The Centerpoint", Doña Juliana Vargas Ave/Corner Garnet Str,Ortigas Complex, Pasig, 1600, M.M – **88)** Radyo Pilipino Corp. DXCO, Atco Bldg, Capistrano & Gomez Str, Cagayan de Oro C, 9000 Misamis Oriental. DXOW, Mapa, Davao C, 8000 Davao del Sur. DYRL, Camaroli Ave, Lupit Subd, Bacolod C, 6100 Negros Occidental. DZTC, Mariposa Bldg. E. Tanedo Str, Tarlac C, 2300 Tarlac. DZYA, 2/F Tanglao Bldg, Balibago, Angeles C, 2009 Pampanga. 639kHz, Surigao C, 8400 Surigao del Norte – **89)** Ragde, Vicente & Sons. DYRS, Ragde Comp, San Carlos C, 6127 Negros Occidental – **90)** Rajah Broadc. Netw. DXRJ, R. Asenso, RJ Clubhouse, Sta. Filomena, Iligan C, 9200 Lanao del Norte. DZRJ, J&T Bldg, 3894 Ramon Magsaysay Blvd, Santa Mesa, Manila, 1016 NCR – **91)** Republic Broadc. Syst. DWRA, Baguio C, 2600 Benguet. DWRC, San Nicolas, 2901 Ilocos Norte. DXBB, Gen. Santos C, 9500 South Cotabato. DXBM, Cotabato C, 9600 Maguindanao. DXGM, Davao C, 8000 Davao del Sur. DXRC, Zamboanga C, 7000 Zamboanga del Sur. DXRL (r. as DXRC, 1179kHz), 3/F Carisma Bldg., General Santos Drive, Koronadal C, 9506 South Cotabato. DXYK, Butuan C, 8600 Agusan del Norte. DYSP, Puerto Princesa C, 5300 Palawan. DYSS, Barrio Mambaling, Cebu C, 6000 Cebu – **92)** Ribbon Broadc. Netw. DWRB, 5/F, LCC Bldg, Lipa C, 4217 Batangas – **93)** Rinconada Broadc. Corp. DZAL, UNEP Compound, San Roque, Iriga C, 4431 Camarines Sur – **94)** RMC Broadc. Co, Inc. DXRA, Madapo Hills, Davao C, 8000 Davao del Sur – **95)** Rolin Broadc. Enterprises. DWES, Narra, 5303 Palawan. DWJS, Roxas, 5308 Palawan – **96)** Rural Electrification Corp. DXML, Digos C, 8002 Davao del Sur – **97)** Siam Broadc. Netw. Corp. DYDD, Lapu-Lapu C, 6015 Cebu. DYHH, Bogo, 6010 Cebu. DYZZ, Guihulngan, 6214 Negros Oriental – **98)** Satellite Broadc. Corp. DWBA, Bangued, 2800 Abra. DZLU, NLTI Bldg, San Fernando C, 2500 La Union – **99)** Southern Broadc. Netw. DXIP, Bangkal, Davao C, 8000 Davao del Sur – **100)** Southern Institute of Tech. DXSI, Cagayan de Oro C, 9000 Misamis Oriental – **101)** Southern Philippines Mass Comm. DXSC, Camp Navarro, Calarian, Zamboanga C, 7000 Zamboanga del Sur – **102)** Subic Broadc. Corp. DWGO, 1 Kasarinlan Rd, Olongapo, 2200 Zambales – **103)** Sulu Tawi-Tawi Broadc. Foundation. DXGD, Bongao, 7500 Tawi-Tawi. DXMM, Jolo, 7400 Sulu – **104)** Tagbilaran Broadc. Corp. DYTR, Dampas, Tagbilaran C, 6300 Bohol – **105)** Times Broadc. Corp. DXSY, Mariano Marcos, Ozamis C, 7200 Misamis Occidental – **106)** Tirad Pass R/TV Broadc. Netw. DZTP, Candon, 2710 Ilocos Sur – **107)** Trans-Radio Broadc. Corp. DWRT, Suite 608, Pacific Bank Bldg, Ayala Avenue, Makati, NCR – **108)** Ultrasonic Broadc. Syst. DWSS, 18 Flr, Strata 200Bldg, Emerald Ave, Pasig C, NCR – **109)** United Broadc. Netw. DWBC, Bo. Ugong del Norte, Quezon C, 1110 NCR – **110)** Universal Broadc. Syst. DYMM, Sunshine Village, Esperos Str, Tacloban C, 6500 Leyte. DYXT, Luna Str, Tagbilaran C, 6300 Bohol – **111)** University of Mindanao. DXCM, UM School Compound, Cotabato C, 9600 Maguindanao. DXDN, UM Tagum School Compund, Tagum C, 8100 Davao del Norte. DXDS, Cor. P. Reyes and Palima Gil Streets, Davao C, 8000 Davao del Sur. DXMI, Iligan C, 9200 Lanao del Norte. DXMV, Mt. Kitangcad Cor. Kanlaon Street, Valencia, 8709 Bukidnon. DYUM, Ormoc C, 6541 Leyte – **112)** University of San Agustin. DYSA, 2/F Univ. of S. Agustin, Gen. Luna Str, Iloilo C, 5901 Iloilo – **113)** University of the Philippines. DZLB, UP Los Banos College, 4031 Laguna. DZUP, UP Diliman, Quezon C, 1104 NCR – **114)** Vanguard Radio Netw. DWMG, Solano, 3709 Nueva Vizcaya. DZXO, Ground Floor Diego Building, National Highway, Cabanatuan C, 3100 Nueva Ecija – **115)** Visayas Mindanao Confederation of Trade Unions. DYLA, Alu-Vimcontu Welfare Center, Cebu C, 6000 Cebu – **116)** Vismin Radio & TV Broadc. Net. DXDV, Baan, Butuan C, 8600 Agusan del Norte – **117)** Western Philippines Broadc. Corp. DWPS, Puerto Princesa C, 5300 Palawan – **118)** Word Broadc. Corp. DYDW, Radio Diwa, Burayan, San José, Tacloban C, 6500 Leyte. DYRF, Pelaez Str, Cebu C, 6000 Cebu – **119)** Zambales Btcg. & Devt. Corp. DZOR, 1683 Rizal Ave, Olongapo C, 2200 Zambales – **120)** ZOE Broadc. Netw. DZJV, Calamba, 4027 Laguna – **121)** Baganian Broadc. Corp. DXBZ, Dumalinao, 7015 Zamboanga del Sur – **122)** Solid North Broadcasting. DWBS, Radyo Commando, Vigan, 2700 Ilocos Sur – **123)** Talisay, Camarines Norte – **124)** MPG Broadcasters Asia, DXFM, Radyo Ranaw, Marawi C, 9700 Lanao del Sur.

INTERNATIONAL SERVICES
Radyo Pilipinas
Radio Veritas Asia
FEBC International Service
VOA/IBB
see International Broadcasting section.

POLAND

L.T: UTC +1h (27 Mar - 30 Oct 2005: UTC+2h) — **Pop:** 38,5 million — **Pr.L:** Polish — **E.C:** 50Hz, 230V — **ITU:** POL

KRAJOWA RADA RADIOFONII I TELEWIZJI

Skwer Ksiedza Kardynala Stefana Wyszynskiego Prymasa Polski 9, 01-015 Warszawa. ☎ +48 22 5973000. Fax +48 22 5973180. **Email:** krrit@krrit.gov.pl **Web:** www.krrit.gov.pl
L.P: Chwmn: Danuta Waniek.
NOTES: KRRiT is the regulatory authority for broadcasting.

POLSKIE RADIO S.A. (Pub.)

al. Niepodleglosci 77/85, 00-977 Warszawa. ☎ +48 22 6459212. Fax +48 22 6453993. **Email:** polskie.radio@radio.com.pl **Web:** www.radio.com.pl
L.P: Chmn: Andrzej Siezieniewski.

LW	**kHz**	**kW**	**Prgr.**
Raszyn	198	200	PR R. Parlament/PR1
Solec Kujawski	225	1000	PR1

FM (MHz)	**PR1**	**PR2**	**PR3**	**PR4**	**Reg***	**kW**
Bialystok	106.4	92.3	96.0	91.1	99.4a	1/30/30/30/30

FM (MHz)	PR1	PR2	PR3	PR4	Reg*	kW
Biala Podlaska	-	-	-	-	93.1i	1
Bialogard	-	98.2	101.5	106.0	98.7n	15/15/10/15
	-	-	-	-	92.5f	15
Bielsko-Biala	-	-	-	104.5	-	0.1
Bogatynia	102.8	-	-	92.8	89.0p	1
Brzeg	-	-	-	-	88.0l	1
Bydgoszcz	-	97.6	102.1	106.5	100.1b	120/120/60/120
Chrzelice	94.5	88.3	90.3	-	103.2l	10/60/60/60
Czestochowa	89.5	90.6	91.7	87.5	98.4d	10/60/60/10/60
Deblin	105.1	-	-	88.7	103.1i	10
Elblag	101.2	-	-	-	-	0.1
Gdansk	89.5	95.7	99.9	93.4	103.7c	0.1/120/120/1
Gdynia	97.2	-	-	-	-	0.1
Glubczyce	-	-	-	-	94.8l	1
Gniezno**	-	-	-	94.1	-	-
Gologóra	-	93.8	97.4	107.9	103.1f	60
Gorzów	105.4	-	-	-	95.6q	1
Grudziadz	99.6	-	-	-	-	0.1
Grybów**	-	-	-	-	97.4g	0.2
Gyzicko	97.1	-	94.4	92.6	99.6k	1/10/10/10
G.Jawor	-	-	-	-	99.5m	5
Ilawa	104.8	-	-	-	-	-
Jaroslaw	100.0	-	-	-	-	1
Jelenia Góra	-	92.5	94.0	-	96.7p	10/10/1
Jemiolów	-	89.0	94.1	105.0	103.0q	60/60/60/120
Kalisz	100.0	95.6	102.5	94.2	91.1j	1/10/10/10/10
Katowice	97.9	92.3	99.7	-	102.2d	60
Kazimierz Dolny	-	-	-	-	99.6i	1
Kedzierzyn-K.	101.8	-	-	97.3	-	0.1
Kielce	102.7	92.3	96.2	87.6	101.4e	0.1/60/60/10/60
Klodzko	-	-	89.2	97.6	96.0p	10
Kluczbork	-	-	-	-	96.3l	10
Kolobrzeg	87.9	-	-	-	-	0.5
Konin	95.0	87.7	103.3	-	91.9j	1/30/30/30
Kraków	104.8	89.4	99.4	-	101.6g	1/60/60/60
Krynica	106.4	-	-	-	102.1g	1
Kudowa Zdrój	-	-	-	-	98.0p	0.1
Lebork	100.5	-	-	107.5	101.1c	10
Legnica	105.3	-	-	-	-	2
Lezajsk	-	96.8	98.9	-	102.9m	5
Lobez	-	-	-	-	88.1f	10
Lódz	107.3	91.4	103.8	107.8	99.2h	1/2/2/30/10
Losice	-	-	90.5	88.3	103.4o	30/30/120
Lowicz	-	-	-	101.6	-	10
Lubaczów	-	88.4	96.0	-	-	10
Luban	-	99.0	91.5	-	103.6p	10/60/60
Lublin	91.8	-	-	99.0	89.9i	0.1
Makarki	-	-	-	-	104.1a	1
Nowy Sacz	99.1	88.0	94.7	-	90.0g	0.5/10/2.5/2.5
Nowy Targ	-	90.4	-	93.4	87.6g	5
Olesno	-	-	-	-	89.1l	1
Olsztyn	97.3	93.0	99.1	-	103.2k	0.1/30/120/120
Olsztyn (Miesto)**	-	-	-	-	102.2k	0.1
Opole	94.5	-	-	-	101.2l	1
Ostroleka	-	96.3	98.5	-	100.8o	0.3
Ostrów Maz.	-	-	-	-	87.6o	1
Paczków	-	-	-	-	92.6l	1
Piaski	-	90.8	104.2	-	102.2i	30/90/90
Plock	-	-	96.1	92.2	101.8o	60
Piotrków Tryb.**	-	-	-	-	89.9	-
Polkowice	95.7	-	-	-	-	2
Pniewy**	-	-	-	107.7	-	5
Poznan	89.1	-	-	-	102.7j	0.1/0.4
Przasnysz**	-	-	-	105.9	-	5
Przemysl	100.0	87.8	99.6	-	102.0m	1/1/1/10
Przysucha	92.0	-	-	-	-	-
Racibórz	-	-	-	-	97.0d	1
Radom	100.3	-	-	104.6	89.1o	1
Rzeszów	105.8	-	-	91.5	-	0.1
Ryki	105.1	-	-	-	-	-
Slupsk	104.3	-	-	106.8	105.3f	2.8/5/1
Srem	-	92.3	96.4	-	101.9j	120
Sucha Góra	-	88.0	92.0	-	90.5m	120
Stalowa Wola	98.3	-	-	97.7	-	0.1
Strzelce Op.	-	-	-	-	105.1l	1
Suwalki	105.5	92.0	96.6	-	98.6a	20/30/30/30
Swinoujscie	107.7	-	-	-	106.3n	10
Szczecin	96.3	100.3	102.3	-	92.0n	0.1/60/60/60
Tarnów	-	88.6	-	91.1	100.0g	10
Trzebnica	87.7	-	-	-	89.8p	10
Wagrowiec**	-	-	101.3	-	98.3j	30
Walbryzch	-	-	99.8	87.9	95.5p	5
Walcz	-	101.9	90.9	-	103.6j	30/30/60
	-	-	-	-	88.1f	3
Warszawa	92.0	102.4	98.8	104.9	101.0o	0.1/10/10/0.1/10
Wisla	-	91.5	100.8	-	103.0d	1/10/10
Wlodawa	-	-	-	-	102.5i	10
Wojsk	-	-	-	-	107.0c	10
Wroclaw	-	98.8	100.2	107.5	102.3p	40/40/1/40
Wroclawek	93.9	-	-	-	100.3b	1
Zagan	101.2	-	-	-	-	-
Zamosc	105.7	-	91.3	87.6	103.2i	1/30/30/30
Zakopane	-	92.8	98.2	-	100.0g	10
Zary**	-	-	-	-	96.5q	1
Zielona Góra	104.0	-	-	-	97.1q	2/1

*) See below. **) F.Pl

D.PRGR: PR1 (Jedynka): 24h. – **PR2 (Dwójka):** 24h – **PR3 (Trójka):** 24h. – **PR4 (R. BIS):** 24h. – **PR R.Parlament:** 0700-1700 on 198kHz (live coverage from Polish Parliament), carries PR1 as filler.

EXTERNAL SERVICE: R. Polonia. See International Radio section.

POLSKIE RADIO S.A. REGIONAL STATIONS (Pub.)

D.PRGR: All stations broadcast 24h.

a) PR R.Bialystok: ul. Swierkowa 1, 15-328 Bialystok. Email: radiobia@radio bialystok.pl. - **b) PR Pomorza i Kujaw**: ul. Gdanska 48-50, 85-006 Bydgoszcz. Email: radio@radiopik.bydgoszcz.pl. - **c) PR R.Gdansk:** ul. Grunwaldzka 18, 80-006 Gdansk. Email: poczta@radio.gdansk.pl. - **d) PR R.Katowice:** ul. Ligonia 29, 40-953 Katowice. Email: sekretariat@radio.katowice.pl. - **e) PR R.Kielce:** ul. Radiowa 4, 25-317 Kielce. Email: radio@radio.kielce.com.pl. - **f) PR R.Koszalin:** ul. Pilsudskiego 43-49, 75-502 Koszalin. Email: radio@radio.koszalin.pl. - **g) PR R.Kraków:** al. Slowackiego 22, 30-007 Kraków. Email: radio@radio-krakow.pl. - **h) PR Lódz:** ul. Narutowicza 130, 90-146 Lódz. Email: miejska@radiolodz.pl. - **i) PR R.Lublin:** ul. Obronców Pokoju 2, 20-030 Lublin. Email: poczta@radio.lublin.pl. **j) PR R.Merkury:** ul. Berwinskiego 5, 60-765 Poznan. Email: office@radio-merkury.poznan.pl. - **k) PR R.Olsztyn:** ul. Radiowa 24, 10-206 Olsztyn. Email: radio@ro.com.pl. - **l) PR Pro FM:** ul. Strzelców Bytomskich 8, 45-084 Opole. Email: pro_fm@radio.opole.pl. - **m) PR R.Rzeszów:** ul. Zamkowa 3, 35-032 Rzeszów. Email: radiorz@radio.rzeszow.pl. - **n) PR R.Szczecin:** ul. Niedzialkowskiego 24, 71-410 Szczecin. Email: sekretariat@radio.szczecin.pl. - **o) PR R.Dla Ciebe:** ul. Mysliwiecka 3/5/7, 00-977 Warszawa. Email: radio@rdc.pl. - **p) PR R.Wroclaw:** ul. Karkonoska 8-10, 53-015 Wroclaw. Email: radio@prw.pl. - **q) PR R.Zachód:** ul. Kukulcza 1, 65-472 Zielona Góra. Email: radio@radio.zachod.pl.

OTHER STATIONS

MW	kHz	kW	Location	Station
73)	963	0.1	Lipsko	Twoje R. Lipsko
74)	1062	0.1	Cmolas	Twoje R. Cmolas
75)	1062	1	Pulawy	Twoje R. Pulawy
FM	**MHz**	**kW**	**Location**	**Station**
3)	87.7	3	Miedzyzdroje	R. Maryja
3)	87.8	1	Biala Podlaska	R. Maryja
4)	87.9	25	Lublin	R. Plus Lublin
3)	87.9	10	Lódz	R. Maryja
1)	88.2	120	Kielce	R. RMF FM
2)	88.3	60	Zielona Góra	R. ZET
58)	88.3	1	Krynica	R. RDN Malopolska
3)	88.3	1	Kutno	R. Maryja
3)	88.4	10	Bielsko-Biala	R. Maryja
8)	88.4	5	Poznan	R. Zlote Przeboje 88.4 FM
3)	88.5	10	Slupsk	R. Maryja
61)	88.6	1	Skierniewice	R. RSC
7)	88.6	1	Bialystok	R. WAWa
2)	88.7	1	Koszalin	R. ZET
35)	88.8	1	Torun	R. Gra
47)	88.8	1	Lomza	R. Lomza
3)	88.9	2	Gdansk	R. Maryja
3)	88.9	120	Wroclaw	R. Maryja
4)	88.9	15	Szczecin	R. Plus Szczecin
3)	89.0	1	Warszawa	R. Maryja
39)	89.2	1	Bialystok	R. Jard
1)	89.3	60	Koszalin	R. RMF FM
1)	89.3	30	Lublin	R. RMF FM
2)	89.4	60	Luban	R. ZET

FM	MHz	kW	Location	Station
3)	89.4	2	Stargard Szczec.	R. Maryja
4)	89.5	10	Gniezno	R. Plus Gniezno
22)	89.5	1	Sanok	R. Bieszczady
8)	89.8	1	Szczecin	R. Zlote Przb. Na Fali 89.8
3)	89.8	1	Mielec	R. Maryja
30)	89.8	1	Poznan	R. Emaus
19)	90.0	1	Wodzislaw Slaski	R. 90
13)	90.1	10	Zamosc	Katolickie R. Zamosc
2)	90.1	2	Lódz	R. ZET
43)	90.2	1	Kolobrzeg	R. Kolobrzeg
3)	90.2	2	Kamiensk	R. Maryja
3)	90.3	1	Zielona Góra	R. Maryja
8)	90.4	1	Wroclaw	R. Zlote Przeboje Kolor
3)	90.6	5	Kraków	R. Maryja
4)	90.7	2	Gryfice	R. Plus Gryfice
4)	90.7	5	Radom	R. Plus Radom
1)	91.0	120	Warszawa	R. RMF FM
8)	91.2	1	Katowice	R. Zlote Przeboje Karolina
1)	91.3	10	Lobez	R. RMF FM
38)	91.4	1	Pelplin	R. Glos
71)	91.5	1	Slupsk	R. Vigor FM
1)	91.5	30	Ostroleka	R. RMF FM
2)	91.6	10	Ryki	R. ZET
4)	91.7	1	Zielona Góra	R. Plus Zielona Góra
2)	91.8	10	Swinoujscie	R. ZET
1)	91.9	30	Siedlce	R. RMF FM
59)	92.0	10	Wroclaw	R. Rodzina
8)	92.1	1	Bydgoszcz	R. Zlote Przeboje Elita
2)	92.2	10	Opole	R. ZET
49)	92.3	1	Pszczyna	R. Mega FM
8)	92.5	1	Kraków	R. Zlote Przeboje Wanda
67)	92.6	1	Sepólno Kraj.	R. Weekend
3)	92.7	10	Lebork	R. Maryja
8)	92.8	1	Opole	R. Zlote Przeboje O!LE
1)	92.9	10	Wroclaw	R. RMF FM
2)	92.9	10	Gryfice	R. ZET
1)	93.0	60	Katowice	R. RMF FM
5A)	93.0	10	Poznan	R. Eska Poznan
3)	93.1	1	Krynica	R. Maryja
4)	93.2	10	Swieradów-Zd.	R. Plus Legnica
1)	93.3	120	Bydgoszcz	R. RMF FM
1)	93.5	10	Lódz	R. RMF FM
2)	93.6	120	Wroclaw	R. ZET
9)	93.7	1	Kraków	Radiostacja
1)	93.8	60	Luban	R. RMF FM
5A)	93.8	10	Gorzów Wlkp.	R. Eska Gorzów
4)	93.8	1	Kutno	R. Plus Miedzy Lodzia i W.
54)	93.9	1	Kedzierzyn-Kozle	R. Park FM
27)	94.1	1	Elblag	R. El
1)	94.3	60	Plock	R. RMF FM
3)	94.3	1	Racibórz	R. Maryja
8)	94.4	10	Zary	R. Zlote Przeboje 98.1 FM
3)	94.4	1	Tarnobrzeg	R. Maryja
5A)	94.4	1	Bydgoszcz	R. Eska Bydgoszcz
23)	94.5	1	Grodzisk Maz.	R. Bogoria
3)	94.5	1	Ustrzyki Dolne	R. Maryja
1)	94.6	120	Poznan	R. RMF FM
5B)	94.6	1.5	Gdansk	R. Hit FM
36)	94.7	10	Czestochowa	R. Fiat
4)	94.7	1	Rawa Maz.	R. Plus Miedzy Lodzia i W.
1)	94.8	30	Zagan	R. RMF FM
4)	94.9	1	Jelenia Góra	R. Plus Legnica
25)	94.9	1	Oswiecim	R. CCM
31)	94.9	1	Sochaczew	R. Fama Sochaczew
2)	95.0	20	Lezajsk	R. ZET
3)	95.0	3	Szczecinek	R. Maryja
1)	95.1	1	Suwalki	R. RMF FM
2)	95.2	60	Szczecin	R. ZET
3)	95.2	1	Luban	R. Maryja
3)	95.2	1	Sieradz	R. Maryja
1)	95.3	60	Olsztyn	R. RMF FM
1)	95.3	60	Opole	R. RMF FM
1)	95.4	10	Tarnów	R. RMF FM
3)	95.4	5	Skierniewice	R. Maryja
3)	95.4	1	Gniezno	R. Maryja
2)	95.6	120	Bydgoszcz	R. ZET
8)	95.6	1	Lublin	R. Zlote Przeboje Puls
2)	95.7	10	Wisla	R. ZET
3)	95.8	1	Hrubieszów	R. Maryja
56)	95.9	1	Koszalin	R. Pólnoc
65)	95.9	1	Olsztyn	R. UWM FM
53)	96.0	1	Lódz	R. Parada
1)	96.0	60	Kraków	R. RMF FM
1)	96.1	1	Legnica	R. RMF FM
4)	96.2	2	Zabrze	R. Plus Gliwice
1)	96.4	15	Bialogard	R. RMF FM
5A)	96.4	1	Gdansk	R. Eska Nord
42)	96.5	10	Warszawa	R. Józef 96.5 FM
3)	96.5	10	Zamosc	R. Maryja
1)	96.6	30	Walcz	R. RMF FM
2)	96.6	10	Lebork	R. ZET
64)	96.7	3	Torun	R. Torun 96.7 Gold FM
72)	96.7	2	Kraków	RMF Maxxx Kraków
3)	96.9	7.5	Ilawa	R. Maryja
2)	97.0	30	Poznan	R. ZET
3)	97.0	1	Lublin	R. Maryja
1)	97.1	10	Radomsko	R. RMF FM
2)	97.2	1	Walbrzych	R. ZET
2)	97.3	60	Plock	R. ZET
33)	97.3	1	Zamosc	R. FAN FM Zamosc
5A)	97.7	1	Kraków	R. Eska Kraków
2)	97.8	2.5	Szczawnica	R. ZET
2)	97.9	60	Walcz	R. ZET
1)	98.0	10	Kalisz	R. RMF FM
48)	98.1	2	Tarnów	R. Maks
4)	98.1	1	Mszczonów	R. Plus Miedzy Lodzia i W.
34)	98.2	1	Przemysl	R. Fara
1)	98.4	120	Gdansk	R. RMF FM
28)	98.5	1	Leszno	R. Elka
3)	98.8	10	Gorzów Wlkp.	R. Maryja
1)	98.9	30	Konin	R. RMF FM
5A)	99.0	1	Szczecinek	R. Eska Szczecinek
67)	99.3	1	Chojnice	R. Weekend
70)	99.4	30	Poznan	R. RMI FM
71)	99.7	1	Koszalin	R. Vigor FM
3)	100.0	5	Zielona Góra	R. Maryja
8)	100.1	1	Warszawa	R. Zlote Przeboje Pogoda
1)	100.1	120	Krosno	R. RMF FM
1)	100.2	120	Bialystok	R. RMF FM
66)	100.3	1	Racibórz	R. Vanessa
3)	100.3	1	Bogatynia	R. Maryja
3)	100.4	10	Ostróda	R. Maryja
3)	100.4	10	Ostrów Maz.	R. Maryja
4)	100.4	2	Lódz	R. Plus Lódz
3)	100.4	1	Nysa	R. Maryja
3)	100.5	1	Jelenia Góra	R. Maryja
3)	100.6	10	Torun	R. Maryja
40)	100.6	60	Czestochowa	R. Jasna Góra / R. Maryja
3)	100.6	10	Krosno	R. Maryja
3)	100.6	10	Glogów	R. Maryja
4)	100.7	10	Gorzów Wlkp.	R. Plus Gorzów
3)	100.7	5	Rabka	R. Maryja
2)	100.7	2	Zamosc	R. ZET
1)	100.8	10	Jelenia Góra	R. RMF FM
32)	100.8	1	Kielce	R. Fama Kielce
3)	100.9	1	Wloclawek	R. Maryja
41)	101.0	1	Kraków	R. Jazz
5A)	101.1	2	Kalisz	R. Eska Ostrów-Kalisz
24)	101.1	5	Walbrzych	R. BRW 101.1 FM
1)	101.1	30	Solina	R. RMF FM
3)	101.1	10	Zlotów	R. Maryja
3)	101.2	10	Zagan	R. Maryja
1)	101.2	10	Swinoujscie	R. RMF FM
58)	101.2	1	Nowy Sacz	R. RDN Malopolska
8)	101.3	1	Pabianice	R. Zlote Przeboje 101.3 FM
55)	101.3	1	Kraków	R. Planeta Kraków
3)	101.3	1	Lomza	R. Maryja
3)	101.4	10	Czersk	R. Maryja
2)	101.4	30	Suwalki	R. ZET
3)	101.6	10	Pisz	R. Maryja
1)	101.6	10	Klodzko	R. RMF FM
3)	101.6	1	Szczecin	R. Maryja
62)	101.7	1	Kepno	R. Sud
46)	101.7	120	Siedlce	Katolickie R. Podlasie
4)	101.7	120	Gdansk	R. Plus Gdansk
1)	101.8	60	Lezajsk	R. RMF FM
1)	101.8	10	Zakopane	R. RMF FM
3)	102.0	10	Bielsk Podl.	R. Maryja
1)	102.0	10	Gizycko	R. RMF FM
5A)	102.0	1	Leszno	R. Eska Leszno

FM	MHz	kW	Location	Station
3)	102.3	10	Lubaczów	R. Maryja
3)	102.4	1	Kartuzy	R. Maryja
57)	102.4	1	Mielec	R. Puls FM
18)	102.6	1	Elk	R. 5 Elk
4)	102.6	1	Koszalin	R. Plus Koszalin
3)	102.6	10	Tarnów	R. Maryja
4)	102.6	20	Polkowice	R. Plus Legnica
51)	102.7	1	Skierniewice	R. Niepokalanów
4)	102.7	5	Rabka	R. Plus Kraków
2)	102.8	3	Ostroleka	R. ZET
3)	102.8	1	Chelm	R. Maryja
2)	102.8	1	Katowice	R. ZET
1)	102.9	5	Walbrzych	R. RMF FM
69)	102.9	1	Slupca	Wielkopolskie R. Warta
6)	102.9	1	Kraków	R. TOK FM
3)	102.9	10	Gryfice	R. Maryja
71)	102.9	1	Lebork	R. Vigor FM
8)	103.0	2	Gdansk	R. Zlote Przeboje Trefl
44)	103.0	1	Warszawa	R. Kolor 103 FM
2)	103.1	30	Solina	R. ZET
60)	103.1	1	Kalisz	R. Rodzina / R. Maryja
1)	103.2	10	Szczawnica	R. RMF FM
4)	103.3	1	Bialystok	R. Plus Bialystok
2)	103.4	60	Czestochowa	R. ZET
1)	103.4	5	Lebork	R. RMF FM
1)	103.4	10	Przemysl	R. RMF FM
4)	103.5	5	Lowicz	R. Plus Miedzy Lodzia i W.
10)	103.5	1	Bydgoszcz	R. Blue FM Bydgoszcz
58)	103.6	30	Tarnów	R. RDN Malopolska
50)	103.6	10	Lomza	R. Nadzieja
5A)	103.6	1	Lublin	R. Eska Lublin
3)	103.7	3	Katowice	R. Maryja
2)	103.8	10	Klodzko	R. ZET
10)	103.8	1	Kraków	R. Blue FM Kraków
12)	103.8	10	Rzeszów	Kat. R. Rzeszów VIA
45)	103.9	1	Ciechanów	Kat. R. Ciechanów
3)	104.0	10	Swiecie	R. Maryja
2)	104.0	10	Gizycko	R. ZET
2)	104.1	60	Kraków	R. ZET
16)	104.1	5	Pila	R. 100
3)	104.2	10	Elblag	R. Maryja
2)	104.2	10	Bialogard	R. ZET
2)	104.2	1	Jelenia Góra	R. ZET
45)	104.3	1	Plock	Kat. R. Plock
4)	104.3	1	Lipiany	R. Plus Lipiany
3)	104.4	1	Stalowa Wola	R. Maryja
2)	104.4	10	Kalisz	R. ZET
3)	104.5	10	Wlodawa	R. Maryja
3)	104.5	5	Wielen	R. Maryja
34)	104.5	1	Krosno	R. Fara
3)	104.6	2	Opole	R. Maryja
5A)	104.6	1	Torun	R. Eska Torun
3)	104.7	120	Bialystok	R. Maryja
3)	104.7	10	Lobez	R. Maryja
15)	104.7	2	Sieradz	Nasze R.
5A)	104.9	60	Wroclaw	R. Eska Wroclaw
22)	104.9	10	Krosno	R. Bieszczady
11)	104.9	1	Chelm	Bon Ton R.
1)	104.9	1	Koszalin	R. RMF FM
2)	105.0	120	Gdansk	R. ZET
3)	105.1	1	Przemysl	R. Maryja
3)	105.1	30	Konin	R. Maryja
3)	105.1	10	Elk	R. Maryja
20)	105.2	1	Zakopane	R. Alex
3)	105.2	5	Wielun	R. Maryja
2)	105.3	60	Kielce	R. ZET
2)	105.3	30	Koszalin	R. ZET
3)	105.3	1	Plonsk	R. Maryja
2)	105.4	30	Siedlce	R. ZET
68)	105.4	8	Poznan	Rock R. Wielkopolska
3)	105.6	1	Kalisz	R. Maryja
7)	105.6	1	Gdynia	R. WAWa
5A)	105.6	1	Pila	R. Eska Pila
5A)	105.6	2	Warszawa	R. Eska Warszawa
2)	105.7	20	Olsztyn	R. ZET
14)	105.8	5	Jelenia Góra	Muzyczne R.
1)	105.9	60	Czestochowa	R. RMF FM
10)	106.1	10	Wroclaw	R. Blue FM Wroclaw
4)	106.1	10	Kraków	R. Plus Kraków
3)	106.2	10	Lidzbark Warm.	R. Maryja
8)	106.2	1	Jelenia Góra	R. Zlote Przeboje 106.2 FM
3)	106.3	60	Plock	R. Maryja
3)	106.3	5	Klodzko	R. Maryja
2)	106.3	10	Zakopane	R. ZET
3)	106.3	20	Lezajsk	R. Maryja
1)	106.4	60	Zielona Góra	R. RMF FM
26)	106.4	10	Kalisz	R. Centrum Kalisz
37)	106.4	1	Zabrze	R. Flash
1)	106.5	10	Elk	R. RMF FM
63)	106.5	5	Kielce	R. Tak
5A)	106.5	1	Zlocieniec	R. Eska Szczecinek
10)	106.6	10	Opole	R. Blue FM Wroclaw
21)	106.7	1	Bielsko-Biala	R. Bielsko
52)	106.7	2	Ostroleka	R. Oko
5A)	106.7	3	Gdynia	R. Eska Nord
1)	106.7	60	Szczecin	R. RMF FM
14)	106.7	5	Swieradów-Zd.	Muzyczne R.
3)	106.8	120	Poznan	R. Maryja
48)	106.8	1	Bochnia	R. Maks
5A)	106.9	10	Radom	R. Eska Radom
3)	107.0	5	Czestochowa	R. Maryja
7)	107.0	1	Kraków	R. WAWa
2)	107.0	120	Lublin	R. ZET
2)	107.1	30	Konin	R. ZET
3)	107.2	120	Kielce	R. Maryja
2)	107.3	120	Bialystok	R. ZET
2)	107.4	30	Krosno	R. ZET
3)	107.4	2.5	Walbrzych	R. Maryja
17)	107.4	1	Poznan	R. 107.4 Gold FM
3)	107.4	3	Koszalin	R. Maryja
2)	107.5	10	Warszawa	R. ZET
29)	107.6	60	Katowice	R. eM
1)	107.7	15	Zamosc	R. RMF FM
3)	107.7	10	Siedlce	R. Maryja
3)	107.7	20	Olsztyn	R. Maryja
2)	107.8	10	Tarnów	R. ZET
4)	107.9	1	Kielce	R. Plus Kielce
3)	107.9	20	Suwalki	R. Maryja
3)	107.9	10	Ryki	R. Maryja
4)	107.9	10	Opole	R. Plus Opole
2)	107.9	10	Przemysl	R. ZET

NB. Tx's below 1kW not mentioned.

Addresses & other information:

1) al. Waszyngtona 1, 30-204 Kraków. Email: redakja@rmf.fm – **2)** ul. Zurawia 8, 00-503 Warszawa. Email: radiozet@radiozet.com.pl – **3)** ul. Zwirki i Wigury 80, 87-100 Torun. Email: radio@radiomaryja.pl – **4)** ul. Zakopianska 86, 30-418 Kraków. Email: radio@radioplus.com.pl. Addresses of local outlets not listed. – **5A,B)** ul. Senatorska 13/15, 00-075 Warszawa. Email: skrzynka@radioeska.com.pl. Addresses of local outlets not listed. – **6)** ul. Czerska 14, 00-732 Warszawa. Email: tokfm@tokfm.com.pl – **7)** ul. Senatorska 12, 00-082 Warszawa. Email: radio@wawa.com.pl – **8)** ul. Czerska 14, 00-732 Warszawa. Addresses of local outlets not listed. – **9)** ul. Piekna 66A, 00-672 Warszawa. – **10)** ul. Grabiszynska 241E, 52-402 Wroclaw. – **11)** ul. Wojslawicka 7, 22-100 Chelm. – **12)** ul. Zamkowa 4, 35-032 Rzeszów. – **13)** ul. Hetmana J. Zamoyskiego 1, 22-400 Zamosc. – **14)** pl. Ks. K. Wyszynskiego 45, 58-500 Jelenia Góra. – **15)** ul. Rynek 14, 98-200 Sieradz. – **16)** ul. Roosevelta 39, 64-920 Pila. – **17)** ul. Piekary 14/15, 61-823 Poznan. – **18)** ul. Bulwarowa 5, 16-400 Suwalki. – **19)** Os. Dabrówki 1b, 44-286 Wodzislaw Sl. – **20)** ul. Smrekowa 26A, 34-500 Zakopane. – **21)** ul. Olszówka 62, 43-300 Bielsko-Biala. – **22)** ul. Zapolskiej 30, 38-500 Sanok. – **23)** ul. Kilinskiego 14, 05-825 Grodzisk Mazowiecki. – **24)** ul. Lipowa 17, 58-310 Szczawno Zdrój. – **25)** ul. Jana Pawla II 2, 44-100 Gliwice. – **26)** ul. Lazienna 6, 62-800 Kalisz. – **27)** ul. 1-go Maja 2, 82-300 Elblag. – **28)** ul. Spóldzielcza 6, 64-100 Leszno. – **29)** ul. Jordana 39, 40-953 Katowice. – **30)** ul. Zielona 2, 61-851 Poznan. – **31)** ul. Narutowicza 1/1, 96-500 Sochaczew. – **32)** ul. Piotrkowska 12/522, 25-510 Kielce. – **33)** ul. Zeromskiego 26, 22-400 Zamosc. – **34)** pl. Katedralny 4, 37-700 Przemysl. – **35)** ul. Chrobrego 75, 88-100 Inowroclaw. – **36)** al. Najswietszej Marii Panny 54, 42-200 Czestochowa. – **37)** ul. Zbozowa 42B, 40-659 Katowice. – **38)** ul. Biskupa Dominika 11, 83-130 Pelplin. – **39)** ul. Rzemieslnicza 4A, 15-703 Bialystok. – **40)** ul. O. Augustyna Kordeckiego 2, 42-225 Czestochowa. – **41)** ul. Krzywickiego 34/318, 02-078 Warszawa. – **42)** ul. Miodowa 17/19, 00-246 Warszawa. – **43)** ul. Janusza Korczaka 2, 78-100 Kolobrzeg. – **44)** ul. Narbutta 41/43, 02-536 Warszawa. – **45)** ul. Tumska 3, 09-400 Plock. – **46)** ul. Pilsudskiego 62, 08-110 Siedlce. – **47)** ul. Pilsudskiego 11A, 18-404 Lomza. – **48)** ul. Nowy Swiat 3, 33-100 Tarnów. – **49)** ul. Kilinskiego 5, 43-200 Pszczyna. – **50)** ul. Sadowa 3, 18-

400 Lomza. – **51)** ul. Zakroczymska 1, 00-225 Warszawa. – **52)** ul. Boguslawskiego 23, 07-410 Ostroleka. – **53)** ul. Pilsudskiego 141, 92-318 Lódz. – **54)** ul. Piastowska 1, 47-200 Kedzierzyn-Kozle. – **55)** ul. Zbozowa 42B, 40-659 Katowice. – **56)** ul. Mieszka I-go 30, 75-132 Koszalin. – **57)** ul. Solskiego 10, 39-300 Mielec. – **58)** ul. Moscickiego 9, 33-100 Tarnów. – **59)** ul. Katedralna 13/15, 50-328 Wroclaw. – **60)** ul. Widok 80/82, 62-810 Kalisz. – **61)** ul. Wita Stwosza 2/4, 96-100 Skierniewice. – **62)** ul. Jankowy 55, 63-600 Kepno. – **63)** ul. Wesola 47/49, 25-363 Kielce. – **64)** ul. Szosa Lubicka 2/18, 87-100 Torun. – **65)** ul. Kanafojskiego 1/14, 10-724 Olsztyn. – **66)** ul. Batorego 5, 47-400 Racibórz. – **67)** ul. Jana Pawla II 1B, 89-804 Chojnice. – **68)** ul. Powstanców Wlkp. 4A, 63-100 Srem. – **69)** ul. Przemyslowa 7, 62-400 Slupca. – **70)** ul. Mickiewicza 28, 60-836 Poznan. – **71)** ul. Armii Krajowej 38, 76-200 Slupsk. – **72)** ul. Rynek 18, 32-100 Proszowice. – **73)** ul. Ilzecka 6a, 27-300 Lipsko. Own prgr: 0600-0700&1700-1800, relay PR R. Kielce at other times. – **74)** 36-105 Cmolas. Own prgr: 0600-0700&1700-1800, relay PR R. Rzeszów at other times. – **85)** Pulawy. Own prgr: 0600-0700&1700-1800, relay PR R. Lublin at other times.

DAB: Ch 10B 211.648MHz, TP EmiTel, Warszawa

PORTUGAL

L.T: UTC (27 Mar-30 Oct: UTC +1h) — **Pop:** 10.5 million — **Pr.L:** Portuguese — **E.C:** 50Hz, 220V — **ITU:** POR

ANACOM – Autoridade Nacional de Comunicações.

✉ HQ: Avenida José Malhoa, 12, 1099-017 Lisboa ☎+351 21 721 10 00 🖷 +351 21 721 10 06 **Email:** info@anacom.pt
Web: www.anacom.pt
Government body responsible for licensing & monitoring radio & TV transmissions, broadcasting or other, except military

APR - Associação Portuguesa de Radiodifusão (Assoc. of Portuguese Broadcasters)

✉ Av. das Descobertas, 17, 1400-091 Lisboa, ☎+351-21-301 69 99, 301 54 53/9 🖷 +351-21 301 65 36, **Email:**: apr@apradiofusao.pt, **Web:**: www.apradiodifusao.pt.

RTP-Rádio e Televisão de Portugal, SGPS (incorporates the RDP and the RTP [TV])

✉ Av. Marechal Gomes da Costa, 37, 1849-020 Lisboa
Web: www.rtp.pt. **LP:** Chmn: Almerindo da Silva Marques.

RDP - RADIODIFUSÃO PORTUGUESA (public, non-comm.)

✉ Av. Marechal Gomes da Costa, 37, 1849-030 Lisboa
☎ +351-21 382 00 00 🖷 +351-21-382 00 98) **Email:** rdp@rdp.pt
Web: www.rdp.pt *or* directly at http://programas.rtp.pt/EPG/radio
Antena 1/Antena 2/Antena 3/RDP Africa:
☎ +351 21 382 00 00. Antena 1 🖷 +351-21-382 00 70 🖷+351-21-382 00 05, Antena 2 ☎+351-21-382 02 82 🖷 +351-21-382 01 99, Antena 3 +351-21-382 02 02, ☎+351-21-382 00 17, RDP África ☎ +351-21-382 02 12🖷 +351-21 382 00 81. **News Dept:** ☎ +351-21 382 00 02 🖷 +351-21 382 01 83.
L.P: Chmn.: Almerindo da Silva Marques, Vice-Chmn: Ponce de Leão, TD: Francisco Mascarenhas, Head of Legal Dept.: Rosa Simões, Dir. of Antena 1:António Luís Marinho, Dir. of Antena 2: João Pereira Bastos, Dir. of Antena 3: António Luís Marinho, Dir. of RDP África: David Borges, Dir. of News: Luís Marinho, Dir. of Finance: Augusto Teixeira Bastos, Dir. of Computing: Vítor Pombal, Reg. Dir (RDP Norte, Porto): José Alberto Lemos, Reg. Dir (RDP Centro, Coimbra): José Manuel Portugal, Reg. Dir (RDP Sul, Faro): Feliciano Estêvão, Reg. Dir. Açores & Madeira: see respective entries, Dir. RDPi (RDP Internacional): see International Radio section.

MW

Antena 1	kHz	kW	Antena 1	kHz	kW
Chaves	630	2	Covilhã	666	10
Miranda do Douro	630	2	Castanheira do Ribatejo*	666	10
Montemor-o Velho	630	10	Valença	666	10
Bragança	666	2	Vila Real	666	10
Viseu	666	10	Mirandela	720	10
Castelo Branco	720	10	Canidelo (Porto)	720	10
Elvas	720	10	Lamego	756	2
Faro	720	10	Portalegre	1287	2
Guarda	720	10			

*) north of Lisbon; also known as "CEN" (Centro Emissor Nacional)

FM (MHz)

Location	1	2	3	kW
Alcoutim S	88.9	91.5	101.9	0.2
Arestal (Aveiro)C	106.7	95.2		0.5
Bornes N	92.8	91.1	102.1	10
Braga (Sameiro)N	91.3	88.0	103.0	10/2/10
Bragança N	96.4	98.2	104.2	9
Castelo Branco C	89.9	94.9	104.3	0.5
Coimbra C	94.9			4
Elvas (V^{a}Boim)	103.8	98.3	101.6	5.4
Faro (S.Miguel) S	97.6	93.4	100.7	10
Gardunha C	96.4	93.9	101.3	10
Grândola	99.2	90.6	103.6	10
Guarda C	94.7	88.4	100.6	6.4
Janas (Sintra)	96.9	96.0	103.8	0.2
Leiria C	98.7	104.2	106.4	1
Lisboa (Banática)	99.4	88.9		1
Lisboa (Monsanto)	95.7	94.4	100.3	36/36/32
Lousã C	87.9	89.3	102.2	34/34/39
Manteigas B	104.8	91.6	100.3	0.5
Marão N	95.2	99.8	101.5	9
Marofa C	97.2	93.4	104.6	20/20/10
Mendro	87.7	91.1	102.4	20/20/44
Mértola	90.9	92.2	100.1	0.4
Minhéu N	94.9	88.0	104.7	10
Miranda do Douro N	90.3	95.7	98.9	0.05
Moledo N	102.9	88.0	92.3	0.5
Monchique S	88.9	91.5	101.9	25
Montejunto	98.3	88.7	105.2	10
Montargil	93.6	99.6	105.0	3
Muro N	88.3	94.6	102.0	10
Pena C	104.5	106.8	107.9	0.1
Portalegre	97.9	92.9	102.8	10
Porto N	96.7	92.5	100.4	44/44/50
Santarém	98.8			0.4
Santiago do Cacém			101.2	10
S. Domingos N	87.9	89.3	103.7	0.2
Tróia (Setúbal)	106.7	99.7	107.9	0.07
Valença N	98.2	89.6	104.0	10
Viseu C	88.2	97.5	101.8	0.5/0.5/0.7

#) also RDP África 101.5 4kW ERP
D.Prgrs: 24h. 1=Antena 1 (general prgrs, sport), 2=Antena 2 (serious music, culture), 3=Antena 3 (pop/rock music), RDP Africa (general prgrs aimed at the Portuguese-speaking African community in the greater Lisbon area. **C, N, S**: carry reg. prgrs. M-F 1400-1500 LT on VHF-FM only.

RDP Reg. Centres, mainland:
N=RDP Norte: Rua Cândido dos Reis, 74, 4050-151 Porto, ☎+351-22 339 99 00, 🖷+351-22 339 99 02. Dir. José Alberto Lemos
C=RDP CeNtro: Rua Dr. José Alberto Reis, 74, 3000-232 Coimbra, ☎+351-23 979 89 00 🖷 +351-239 72 42 53 Dir. José Manuel Portugal **Email:** rdpcentro@rdp.pt
S=RDP Sul: Campo Senhora da Saúde, 8001-904 Faro ☎ +351-289 89 68 69 🖷+351-289 80 21 92 **Email:** rdpsul@rdp.pt. Dir. Feliciano Estevão.
RDP Reg. Centres in the autonomous regions of Açores and Madeira: Ponta Delgada (Açores) and Funchal (Madeira) (see respective entries).
RDP abroad: RDP FM tr's in Cape Verde, Guinea-Bissau, São Tomé e Príncipe, Mozambique, all relaying RDP África, in Timor, relaying RDPi and airing a local prgr, and in Bosnia for the Portuguese peace keeping force (see respective country entries). **RDP África:** ✉ Av. Eng^o Duarte Pacheco, 26, 1070-10 Lisboa. LP: Dir: David Borges, Email rdpafrica@rdp.pt.

DAB: 27 T-DAB transmitters on 225.648 MHz, ch. 12, block B, covering mainland's western & southern areas & carrying Antena 1, 2, 3, RDP África and RDP Internacional.
Web Radio: Audio feeds at www.rdp.pt Antena 1, 2 & 3 and RDP-África, RDP-Norte, RDP-Centro, RDP-Sul, RDP-Madeira and RDP-Açores in Windows Media Player.
SATELLITE: Europe, N. Africa & Mid. East: Hot Bird 4 (13° E), Transponder 111 (10.72288 GHz), Ku Band, H. Pol., FEC: ¾, SyR: 29.9 Ms/s, RDPi: PID 1230 (stereo), RDP Antena 1: PID 1235. 24h. **Africa:** Intelsat 907 (332.5° W), Transponder 22/22 (3.8565GHz), C Band, Right Circ. Pol. , Symbol Rate 6,26175. RDP África M-F 0400-2400, Sat/Sun 0600-2300 on 3856.6 MHz (co-ch with RTPi). RDP Antena 1 aired during the remaining hrs. RDP Internacional stereo aired on 3830 MHz (co-ch with RTP África). **Asia & Oceania:** Asiasat 2 (100.5° E), "European Bouquet", Transponder 10B (4GHz), C Band, Horiz. Pol. on 28.125 Ms/s, FEC ¾. RDP Internacional stereo on the audio ch. 704 (co-ch with RTPi), RDP Antena 1 aired on the audio ch. 705 on ch. (co-ch with RTP-I). **N.America & Hawaii:** AMC-4 (101° W), Transponder K16 (12169 MHz), Ku Band, H. Pol., SyR 3.003 Ms/s,

FEC ¾. RDP Internacional audio 2 PID: 35 (stereo). **The Americas**: Intelsat 805 (55.5° W), Transponder 16/16 (4080 MHz), C Band, V. Pol., SyR 4.3404 Ms/s, FEC ¾. RDP Internacional: PID 1230 stereo.

RÁDIO COMERCIAL, S.A. (priv., comm.)
✉ Rua Sampaio e Pina, 24-26, 1099-044 Lisboa ☎ +351-21 382 15 00 🖷 +351-21 382 15 09 **Email:** marketing@radiocomercial.iol.pt, Northern office: Rua Tenente Valadim, 181, 4100 Porto ☎ +351-22 605 75 00. **Web:** www.radiocomercial.iol.pt

MW	kHz	kW		kHz	kW
Faro	558*	10	Miramar (Porto)	1170*	10
Miramar	783	10	Vila Real	1170*	10
Castelo Branco	828*	1	Valença	1170*	10
Covilhã	828*	1	Guarda	828*	1
Montemor-o-Velho	828*	1	Viseu	828*	1
Porto Alto	1035	100°			

*) inactive.°) nominal 120 kW (2x25kW reserve)
D.Prgr.: 24 h **ANN.:** "Rádio Nacional" or "Nacional"

FM	MHz	kW		MHz	kW
Alcácer do Sal	92.3	6	Fóia (Monchique)	88.1	
Braga	99.2	5	Lamego	88.7	
Bragança	93.9		Montejunto	99.8	
Chaves	91.9		Monsanto (Lisboa)	97.4	100
Lousã	90.8		São Mamede	98.9	6
Mendro (Évora)	92		Porto	97.7	40
São Miguel (Faro)	96.1	5	Valença	99	5
Gardunha	98.2		Vila Real	88.9	
Guarda	96.1				

D.Prgr: 24h. **ANN.:** Rádio Comercial.
Note: MW & VHF-FM carry separate prgrs.

RÁDIO RENASCENÇA – Emissora Católica Portuguesa (rlg/comm)
✉ Rua Capelo, 5, 1200-087 Lisboa ☎ +351-21 323 92 00 🖷 +351 +351-21 323 92 20, **Email:** info@rr.pt, **PR**: rp@rr.pt. **L.P**: News Dir.: Dr. Francisco Sarsfield Cabral, PD (for R.Renascença): Rui Pêgo, PD (for RFM): Dr. António Mendes. **Web:** www.rr.pt *and* www.rfm.pt

MW

Canal 1	kHz	kW	Canal 1	kHz	kW
Braga	576L	10	Coimbra	981	10
Muge	594	100	Guarda	981	1
Vila Moura	891	20	Chaves	1251L	10
Evora	927L	1	Valongo	1251L	10
Seixal	963L	10	Castelo Branco	1251	1
Bragança	981	1	Viseu	1251L	10
Vila Real	981	1			

FM MHz	Canal 1	"RFM"	kW
Aveiro	102.5		200
Arrabida	105.8	89.9	10/12
Bornes	89.6	101.1	10
Braga	101.1	89.7	10/1
Bragança	105.7	99.5	10
Elvas	102.3		100
Elvas	99.8	L	1
Fóia	98.6	104.9	12
Gardunha	103.4	99.5	10
Guarda	90.2	104.0	1
Lamego	98.6	106.2	12
Leiria	95.1	L	10
Lisboa	103.4	93.2	50
Lousã	106.0	91.7	50/56
Marofa	94.2	103.0	16/10
Mendro	96.5	100.9	50
Minhéu	89.8	102.6	10
Montejunto	90.2	106.8	10
Muro	103.4	90.4	10/20
São Mamede	95.3	101.1	10
São Miguel	103.8	89.6	10
Valença	100.0	95.4	10
V.N.de Gaia	93.7	104.1	50
Viseu		103.7	1

Canal 1 = ch. 1. "RFM" = Renascença FM. L=includes local prgrs. **D.Prgr**.: 24 h. **ANN.:** "Canal Um da Renascença." "Escutam a RFM." **Stn IDs** during local prgrs: Seixal (Lisboa) "Voz de Lisboa", Porto "Centro de Produção do Porto", Braga "Renascença Braga", Viseu "Renascença viseu", Leiria "Renascença Leiria", Elvas "Renascença Elvas", Évora "Renascença Évora" and Chaves "Renascença Chaves." **Times of local prgrs on MW**: Voz de Lisboa 963 kHz M-F 1300-2130, Sat 1200-2200, Sun 1400-2200; "Renascença Braga" 576 kHz M-F 1800-1800, Sat 0900-1400, Sun 1300-1400; "Renascença Viseu" 1251 kHz M-F 1300-1700, Sun 1400-1600; "Renascença Évora" 927 kHz M-F 1300-1700, Sat 1300-1700; "Renascença Chaves" 1251 kHz M-F 1300-1400.

Regional FM networks:
Northern network
Radiopress – Comunicação e Radiodifusão, Ld^a^
✉ Edifício "Altejo", Rua 3 – 3º piso, sala 301, Matinha, 1900-823 Lisboa, ☎ +351-21 861 25 00, 🖷 +351- 21 861 25 07/8. LP: Chmn.: Dr. Henrique Manuel Granadeiro, TD: Jaime Silva, Comm. Dir.: Hernâni Gomes. Northern office & Radiopress HQ: ✉ Rua Gonçalo Cristóvão, 195, 4000-269 Porto, ☎ +351-22 206 28 00 🖷 +351-22 206 28 03 **Email:**: tsf@tsf.pt **Web:**: www.tsf.sapo.pt
Station Name: "TSF" (priv., comm.)

FM	MHz	kW	FM	MHz	kW
Pena (Vouzela)	102.5	0.1	Guarda	106.6	10
Bornes	103.2	10	Minhéu	106.7	10
Gardunha	105.1	10	Braga	106.9	10
Valongo (Porto)	105.3	50	Bragança	107.0	10
Marofa	105.4	10	Lousã	107.4	50
Valença	105.7	10	Marão	107.6	10
Muro	106.5	10			

NB: the whole netw. relays key stn TSF 89.5MHz Lisboa (cf. local FM stns list).TSF is also available on mainland south during most of the day via **R. Jovem** 105.4MHz 5kW Évora and **R. Santa Maria** 90.9MHz 2kW Faro (Algarve), in the Açores via **R.Comercial dos Açores-TSF** 99.4MHz 3kW Ponta Delgada (São Miguel isl.) & **R.Canal** 100.5MHz 0.5kW (São Jorge isl.) and in Madeira via **R.Notícias-TSF** 100.0MHz 2kW Funchal. **Format:** mainly news. **D.Prgr.:** 24h.

Southern network
Licensee: Rádio Regional de Lisboa, S.A.
✉ see R.Comercial.
Station name: RCP, "Rádio Clube Português" (priv., comm.)

FM	MHz	kW	FM	MHz	kW
Aveiro	94.4	2	Monsanto (Lisboa)	104.3	100
Coimbra	98.4	5	SMamede (Ptlgr)	106.7	10
Mendro (Évora)	106.4	50	Maia (Porto)	100.8	1.5
São Miguel (Faro)	106.1	10	Fóia (Monchique)	107.1	10
Figueiró dos Vinhos	97.5	1	Vila Real	97.4	1
Grândola	107.5	10	Matosinhos	89.5	1.5
Montejunto	96.4	10	Vale de Cambra	101.0	0.5

Format: music stn, mainly oldies. **N:** very short bulletins every h on the h. **D.Prgr:** 24 h. **ANN.:** Rádio Clube Português.

Local Stations: (all priv. & comm.)
RADIO ALTITUDE
✉Rua Batalha Reis, 6300 GUARDA ☎ +351-271-22 19 95 🖷 +351-271 22 14 92, **Email:** radioaltitude@netvisao.pt
Web: www.altitude.fm **L.P**: Dir: Rui Isidro
MW: 1584kHz 1kW 24 h. **FM:** 90.9 MHz 2 kW 24h.. **Reg. News** : 0730, 0830, 1030, 1130, 1230, 1730, 1830 LT; relays TSF stn news bulletins every h on the h 0700-2000 LT. **ANN.:** Rádio Altitude.

Other FM stations:

	MHz	kW	Station, location
81)	88.2	2	R.Ateneu, Vila Franca de Xira
72)	88.5	2	R.Guadalupe, Serpa
74)	88.6	2	R.Jornal de Setúbal, Setúbal
80)	88.6	2	R.Foz do Ave, Vila do Conde
61)	88.9	2	R.São Mamede, Portalegre
63)	89.0	2	R.Mar, Póvoa de Varzim
82)	89.1	2	R.Lezíria, Vila Franca de Xira
9)	89.2	2	R.Club de Amarante, Amarante
56)	89.3	2	R.Praia, Zambujeira do Mar
48)	89.5	5	TSF, Lisboa (No. Network key stn)
1)	89.7	2	R.Antena Livre, Abrantes
25)	90.0	5	Mega FM, Coimbra (cf.R.Renascença)
66)	90.0	5	VOX X, Porto
46)	90.4	5	R.Paris-Lisboa, Lisboa (relays RFI prgrs)
78)	90.5	2	R.Cidade de Tomar, Tomar
36)	90.6	2	Mega FM, Gondomar (cf. R.Renascença)
79)	90.8	2	R.Geice, Viana do Castelo
17)	91.4	2	R.Íris FM, Benavente
47)	91.6	5	VOX X, Lisboa
59)	91.8	2	R.Club de Penafiel, Penafiel
12)	91.9	2	R.Local de Barcelos, Barcelos
22)	92.0	2	R.Beira Interior, Castelo Branco
99)	92.0	2	RNA-R.Nova Antena, Loures
34)	92.1	2	R.Maiorca, Figueira da Foz
75)	92.4	2	RACAL, Silves
97)	92.4	5	Mega FM, Lisboa (cf.R.Renascença)

	MHz	kW	Station and location
8)	92.7	2	ERA FM-Emissora Reg. de Amarante, Amarante
68)	92.7	2	R.Piranha, Santarém
52)	92.8	2	Horizonte Tejo, Bobadela
19)	92.9	2	RTM-R. e TV do Minho, Braga
44)	93.0	2	Central FM, Leiria
4)	93.9	2	R.Mirasado, Alcácer do Sal
41)	94.0	2	R.Douro, Sul Lamego
43)	94.0	2	R.94 FM, Leiria
84)	94.0	2	R.Cidade Hoje, Vila Nova de Famalicão
30)	94.1	2	Diana FM, Évora
29)	94.5	2	R.Despertar, Estremoz
28)	94.7	2	A Voz do Sorraia, Coruche
64)	94.8	5	R.Festival, Porto
94)	94.8	2	R.Gilão, Tavira
95)	95.8	2	R.Fundação, Guimarães
60)	95.8	2	R.Tempos Livres, Ponte de Sor
38)	96.0	2	R.Fundação, Guimarães
67)	96.1	2	R.Onda Viva, Póvoa de Varzim
14)	96.2	2	Metropolitana FM, Barreiro
11)	96.5	2	R. Aveiro FM, Aveiro
45)	96.6	5	"Best Rock" FM (cf. R.Comercial), Lisboa
96)	96.7	2	R.Tágide, Abrantes
76)	96.9	2	R.Horizonte-Algarve, Tavira
40)	97.0	2	R.Club de Lamego, Lamego
24)	97.5	2	R.Urbana, Castelo Branco
2)	97.7	2	R.Tágide, Abrantes
70)	97.7	2	2000 FM, Santarém
6)	97.8	2	R.Voz de Almada, Almada
39)	98.0	2	R.Santiago, Guimarães
77)	98.0	2	R.Hertz, Tomar
21)	98.1	3	R.Marginal, Cascais
26)	98.4	5	R. "A5" (cf. RCP), Coimbra
65)	98.9	5	R.Nova, Porto
73)	98.9	2	R.Azul, Setúbal
33)	99.1	2	R.Club Foz do Mondego, Figueira da Foz
3)	99.3	2	R.Soberania, Águeda
5)	99.3	2	Nacional FM, Alcanena
49)	99.7	2	R.Club de Loulé, Loulé
93)	100.1	2	R.Terra Verde, Paredes
62)	100.5	2	R.Portalegre, Portalegre
91)	100.6	2	R.Voz de Setúbal, Setúbal
7)	100.8	2	R.Capital, Almada
58)	101.1	2	R.Nova Era, Paredes
42)	101.3	2	R.Liz, Leiria
55)	101.3	2	RNA-R.Nova, Antena Montemor-o-Novo
87)	101.3	2	R.Nova Era, Vila Nova deGaia
15)	101.4	2	R.Pax, Beja
69)	101.7	2	R.Pernes, Santarém
23)	101.8	2	R.Juventude, Castelo Branco
51)	101.9	2	Estação Orbital, Loures
85)	102.1	2	R.Gaia FM, Vila Nova de Gaia
86)	102.2	2	PAL FM, Palmela (incl. prg in Russian)
35)	102.7	2	R.Club de Gondomar, Gondomar
71)	102.7	2	Antena Miróbriga, Santiago do Cacém
88)	102.8	2	R.Viriato, Viseu
13)	103.0	2	R.Margem Sul, Barreiro
20)	103.0	2	R.Nova Cantanhede, Cantanhede
50)	103.1	2	Total FM, Loulé
32)	103.2	2	R.Telefonia do Alentejo, Évora
57)	103.7	2	ABC Rádio, Ourém
16)	104.5	2	R.Voz da Planície, Beja
92)	104.6	2	R.Linear, Vila do Conde
83)	105.0	2	Digital FM, Vila Nova de Famalição
98)	105.4	2	R.Jovem (relays TSF Lisboa), Évora
31)	105.5	2	RCI, Viseu
10)	105.6	2	R.Moliceiro (cf. RCP), Aveiro
37)	105.8	2	R."F", Guarda
18)	106.0	2	R.Antena Minho, Braga
90)	106.4	2	R."Noar", Viseu
54)	107.1	2	R.Voz de Mangualde, Mangualde
27)	107.9	2	R.Universidade de Coimbra, Coimbra

+ over 200 stns of less than 2 kW. Power in kW are ERP.

Foreign lang. prgrs.: a few stns air prgrs, usually in Russian & mainly for the Russian, Ukrainian & Moldavian immigrants, as well as in Indian langs. for the Indian community, viz. in the capital region.

Addresses and other information:
Many stns have websites and may also be available through the internet; most, if not all, have an e-mail address. Country codes must be added to tel. & fax nrs.

1) Rua General Umberto Delgado, Edifício Mira Rio, 2200 Abrantes ☎ 241-360170/1 ℻ 241-360179 **Email:** antenalivre@clix.pt, mediaon@mail.telepac.pt – **2)** Estrada Nacional 118, 1010 – 1º, 2200 Tramagal ☎ 241-897192 ℻ 241-897859 – **3)** Rua José Lucena, 120-3º, 3750-157 Águeda ☎ 234-602133 ℻ 241-624334 – **4)** Rua da Fábrica, Convento dos Frades, 7580-122 Alcácer do Sal☎ 265-622981 ℻ 265-622479 – **5)** Rua João Baptista Vassalo, 6, 2380 Alcanena ☎ 249-881219 ℻ 249-881824 **Email:** comerciais@radionacional.pt, internet@radionacional.iol.pt – **6)** Rua Viriato, 25-6º, S.Sebastião da Pedreira, 1050-234 Lisboa ☎ 21-3112050 ℻ 21-3192059 **Email:** radar@netcabo.pt **Web:**: oscar.pt/voz-de-almada – **7)** Rua Torcato José Clavine, 17-D-piso 02, Pragal, 2800-526 Almada ☎ 21-2721380 ℻ 21-2740781 – **8)** Edifício Santa Luzia, 4600 Amarante, ☎ 255-420480/9 ℻ 244-431723 – **9)** Edifício Pássaro de Fogo, r/c, 4600 Amarante, ☎ 255-410150/5 ℻ 255-426273 **Email:** clubfm@iol.pt – **10)** (cf. R.Comercial), **11)** Av. Dr. Lourenço Peixinho, 15-1º G, 3800 Aveiro ☎ 234-424601 ℻ 234-428965 **Email:** regional@mail.telepac.pt – **12)** Centro Comercial Bolívar, lojas 45-49, 4750 Barcelos ☎ 253-823600/1 ℻ 253-823531 **Email:** mail@rb.fm, geral@rb.fm **Web:** www.rn.fm – **13)** (cf. R.Comercial) – **14)** Rua Oliveira ao Carmo, 8, 1200-309 Lisboa – **15)** Rua de Ângola, Torre C-11º, 7800 Beja ☎ 284-323859 ℻ 284-326312 **Email:** radio@radiopax.com **Web:** www.radiopax.com – **16)** Rua da Misericórdia, 4, 7800-285 Beja ☎ 284-321330 ℻ 284-321446 **Email:** vozplanicie@mail.telepac.pt – **17)** Rua dos Operários Agrícolas, 2135 Samora Correia, ☎ 263-654840 ℻ 263-655567**Email:** irisfm@mail.telepac.pt **Web:** www.irisfm.pt – **18)** Praceta do Magistério, 36, 4700-222 Braga ☎ 253-309560 ℻ 253-309569 **Email:** ram@nordenet.pt, info@antena-minho.pt **Web:** www.antena-minho.pt – **19)** Rua Prof. Machado Vilela, 110-9º e 11º, 4710-423 Braga ☎ 253-616135 ℻ 253-615192 **Email:** rtm@rtm.pt, rtm@bragatel.pt **Web:** www.rtm.pt **20)** Largo dos Combatentes da Grande Guerra, Edifício Rossio – sala 26, 3060 Cantanhede ☎ 231-420009 ℻ 231-429011 – **21)** Quinta da Torre d'Aguilha, São Domingos de Rana, 2775 Parede ☎ 21-4451241 ℻ 21-4451383 – **22)** Av. 1º de Maio, 39 – 1º dtº, 6000-909 Castelo Branco, ☎ 272-328726 ℻ 272-320488 **Email:** rbimagem@iol.pt – **23)** Rua Prof. Hugo correia Pardal, Edifício Plátano-loja "A", 6000-267 Castelo Branco ☎ 272-341758 ℻ 272-347660 **Email:** juventudefm@ip.pt, radiojuventude@netsigma.pt **Web:** www.radiojuventude.com – **24)** Rua Cadetes de Toledo, lote 5-1º esqº, 6000 Castelo Branco ☎ 272-347676 ℻ 272-328670 **Email:** radiourbana@portugalmail.com– **25)** (see R.Renascença) **Format:** music stn **LP**: PD Dr. Nelson Ribeiro **Web:** www.mega.fm – **26)** (cf. R.Club Português) – **27)** Rua Padre Anónio Vieira, Apartado 1178, 3000 Coimbra **28**) Rua do Couço, 29-r/c frt, 2100 Coruche ☎ 243-617436/0 ℻ 243-617100 **Email:** radiovozsorraia@mail.telepac.pt – **29)** Rua Serpa Pinto, 22-24 7100-452 Estremoz ☎ 268-339454 ℻ 268-339456 – **30)** Rua da República, Maré, EE08, 7000-500 Évora ☎ 266-742282 ℻ 266-700333 **Email:** dianaev@mail.telepac.pt, radiodiana@netc.pt – **31)** Rua do Muro, 14-1º, 7000 Évora ☎ 266-750180 ℻ 266-750181 – **32)** Apartado 2037, 7000 Évora ☎ 266-703144 ℻ 266-741252 **Email:** telefonia@mail.telepac.pt **Web:** www.diariodosul.com.pt – **33)** Rua da Alegria, Edifício Atlântico, 3081-501 Figueira da Foz, ☎ 233-425173 ℻ 233-426895 **Email:** geral@rcfm@mail.telepac.pt **Web:** www.rcfm.web.pt – **34)** Rua Poeta João de Lemos 6, Maioca, 3080-476 Maiorca ☎ 233-930500 ℻ 233-930499 **Email:** maiorcafm@iol.pt – **35)** Rua Torcato José Clavine, 17-D, piso 02, Pragal, 2804-526 Almada ☎ 21-2740765 ℻ 21-2740781 – **36)** (cf. R.Renascença) (cf. nº 25) – **37)** Sua Soeiro Viegas, 2-B, 6300-758 Guarda ☎ 271-221468 ℻ 271-221482 **Email:** radiof@radiof.com **Web:** www.radiof.com – **38)** Rua Arquitecto Mário Cardoso, 253-C, Guimarães "Palace"-Atouguia, 4800 Guimarães ☎ 253-420520 ℻ 253-420529 – **39)** Praceta de Santiago, 31, 4800 Guimarães ☎ 253-421700 ℻ 253-421709 – **40)** Urbanização da Urtigosa, Bloco 6, 5100 Lamego ☎ 254-609300/1 ℻ 254-609309 **Email:** rclamego@mail.telepac.pt **Web:** www.rclamego.com – **41)** Rua Fausto Guedes Teixeira, Bloco 1, 5100 Lamego ☎ 254-611550/1 ℻ 254-614505 **Email:** radiodourosul@clix.pt **Web:** www.radiodourosul.web.pt – **42)** 2400 Leiria ☎ 244-817700 ℻ 244-813951 **Email:** radio.liz.fm@portugalmail.pt **Web** www.lizfm.com – **43)** Av. dos Combatentes da Grande Guerra, Edifício Lis – 10º, 2400-801 Leiria, ☎ 244-860090 ℻ 244-860098 **Email:** geral@radio94fm.pt **Web:** www.radio94fm.pt – **44)** Av. Dr. Francisco Sá Carneiro, Quinta da Cascalheira, 8 – loja 1, 2400-754 Leiria ☎ 244-850093 ℻ 244-850098 **Email:** radio@radiocentralfm.pt **Web:** www.radiocentralfm.pt – **45)** (cf. R.Comercial), – **46)** Rua Latino Coelho, 50 – 1º, 1050 Lisboa ☎ 21-3522619 ℻ 21-3526220 **Email:** rpl@rpl.fm **Web:** www.rpl.fm **Relay RFI in French** M-F 1300-1310 & 1900-2400, Tues 0000-0700, Fri 1900-Mon 0700 – **47)** Rua Sacadura Cabral, 31 – 1º F, 2775-626 Carcavelos ☎ 21-4583333 ℻ 21-4570948 **Email:** voxx@net.sapo.pt – **48)** (cf. Northern Network) **49)** Av. João Meireles, Edifício Átrio, Esc. A1, 8125 Vilamoura – **50)** Sítio do Troto, 8135-030 Almancil ☎ 289-397666 ℻ 289-397110 **Email:** radiototal@mail.telepac.pt, totalfm@totalfm.pt **Web:** www.totalfm.pt – **51)** Travessa do Olival, 6, 2685 Sacavém ☎ 21-9401019 & 21-9427750 ℻ 21-9427757 **Email:** orbital@orbital.pt, estacaoorbital@ mail.telepac.pt

Web: www.orbital.pt – **52)** Travessa da Boa Vista, lote 20 –r/c, 2685-027 Bobadela ☎ 21-9553113 & 21-9555664 ⎙ 21-9558465 **Email:** rht@rht.pt **Web:** www.radiohorizonte.net – **53)** Rua Correia Garção, 11, 2675 Odivelas ☎ 21-9388833 & 21-9387107 ⎙ 21-9387131 – **54)** Av. D. Henrique, Bloco 4 – B – r/c, 3531 Mangualde ☎ 232-612363 ⎙ 232-611490 – **55)** Rua Francisco José Mareco, lote 28, 7050 Montemor-o-Novo ☎ 266-899100 ⎙ 266-899112 – **56)** Rua da Saudade, Zambujeira do Mar, 7630 Odemira ☎ 283-959004 – **57)** Av. D. Nuno Álvares Pereira, 206 – 2º dtº, 2490 Ourém ☎ 249-544555 ⎙ 249-544111 – **58)** Rua das Camélias, 134-B, 4401 Vila Nova de Gaia ☎ 22-3770180 ⎙ 22-3759675 – **59)** Rua Alfredo Pereira, 14-2º, 4560 Penafiel ☎ 255-710040 ⎙ 255-710049 **Email:** info.mail@radioclube-penafiel.pt **Web:** www.radioclube-penafiel.pt – **60)** Rua Movimento das Forças Armadas, 17, 7400 Ponte de Sor ☎ 242-204054 ⎙ 242-206302 – **61)** Av. Francisco Fino, 18-A, Zona Industrial, 7300-053 Portalegre ☎ 245-301140 ⎙ 245-301145 – **62)** Av. de Santo António, Edifício Régio 1, Aier "B", 7300-901 Portalegre ☎ 245-300550 ⎙ 245-331630 **Email:** radioportalegre@radioportalegre.pt **Web:** www.radioportalegre.pt – **63)** Av. Cidade de Montegeron, 169-r/c, 4490-402 Póvoa de Varzim ☎ 252-690140 ⎙ 252-690149 **Email:** radiomar@radiomar.com – **64)** Rua da Alegria, 582-9º esqº/frt, 4000 Porto ☎ 22-5101008 ⎙ 22-5700177 – **65)** R. João de Deus Barros, 265, Foz do Douro, 4100 Porto ☎ 22-6101390/5 ⎙ 22-6101420 **Email:** nova@esoterica.pt, nova@publico.pt, info@radionova.fm **Web:** www.radionova.fm – **66)** (see VOXX, nº 47) – **67)** Praça dos Combatentes, 15, 4490 Póvoa de Varzim ☎, 252-613686 ⎙ 252-613898 **Email:** radioondaviva@clix.pt – **68)** Travessa Padre António Fernandes, 3, 2000 Santarém ☎ 243-333030 ⎙ 243-333324 – **69)** Rua da Fé, 1, 2035 Pernes & R. Pedro de Santarém, 10-3º dtº, 2000 Santarém ☎ 243-332922 & 243-332004 ⎙ 243-440112 **Email:** radiopernes@mail.telepac.pt – **70)** Rua Pedro de Santarém, 10-3º dtº, 2000 Santarém ☎ 243-321175 ⎙ 243-332998 – **71)** Rua Condes de Avillez, 19-21, Apartado 45, 7540 Santiago do Cacém ☎ 269-829920/8 **Email:** antenamirobriga@mail.telepac.pt **Web:** www.antenamirobriga.pt – **72)** Rua Eduardo Fernandes Oliveira, 7, 7830 Serpa – **73) & 74)** Rua Dr. António Rodrigues Manito, 58 – r/c "B", 2900-061 Setúbal ☎ 265-08 90 52 ⎙ 265-237437 **Email:** radioazul98.9@sapo.pt, radioazul_setubal@hotmail.com – **75)** Rua Conselheiro Magalhães Barros, 8300-129 Silves, ☎ 282-440100 ⎙ 282-440102 **Email:** radioracal@clix.pt **Web:** www.racal-clube.pt – **76)** Quinta de São Pedro, E.N. 125, 8800-902 Tavira ☎ 281-320240 ⎙ 281-325523 **Email:** 96.9@radiohorintewebside.pt **Web:** www.radiohorizonte.com – **77)** Rua de Coimbra, 4-r/c esqº, 2300-471 Tomar ☎ 249-323120 ⎙ 249-316995 **Email:** radiohertz@radiohertz.pt – **78)** Praça da República, 2, 2301 Tomar ☎ 249-310010 ⎙ 249-310016 – **79)** Praça 1º de Maio, 6-traseiras, 490-534 Viana do Castelo ☎ 258-800400 ⎙ 258-800409 **Email:** rgeice@mail.telepac.pt – **80)** Av. Dr. João Canavarro, 305-4º, sala 4.5-Edifício Alameda dos Descobrimentos, 4480 Vila do Conde ☎ 252-632896 ⎙ 252-689185 – **81)** Edifício Torre, Porto Alto, 2135 Samora Correia ☎ 263-650394 ⎙ 263-271933 **Email:** nova.ateneu@oninet.pt – **82)** Praça Marquês de Pombal, 2-7º,2600 Vila Franca de Xira ☎ 263-200600 ⎙ 263-200607 **Email:** geral@leziriafm.com - **83)** Rua 8 de Dezembro, 214, 4760 Vila Nova de Famalicão ☎ 252-30 81 40/8 ⎙ 252-308149 **Email:** comercial@opiniaopublica.pt– **84)** Edifício Vilarminda, loja 204, Rorigo, 4762 Vila Nova de Famalicão ☎ 252-374654 ⎙ 252-372888 – **85)** Av. da República, 1622-7º, Salas 19 e 20, 4430-193 Vila Nova de Gaia ☎ 22-3770840 ⎙ 22-3701005 **Email:** gaia.fm2002@netcabo.pt – **86)** Largo de São João, 17, 2950-248 Palmela ☎ 21-2338310 ⎙ 21-2338315 **Email:** palfm.geral@radiopal.pt **Web:** www.palfm.com, **Russian** Sat 1800-1900 – **87)** Rua das Camélias, 134-B, 4401 Vila Nova de Gaia ☎ 22-3770180 ⎙ 22-3759675 **Email:** novaera@mail.telepac.pt, geral@radionovaera.pt – **88)** Complexo Conventuris-press, Orgens, 3500 Viseu ☎ 232-410410 ⎙ 232-410418 **Email:** inforadio@viriatofm.com **Web:** www.viriatofm.com – **89)** Rua Luís Ferreira, 58-3º "C", Comercial "Ecovil", 3510-110 Viseu ☎ 232-423411/2 ⎙ 232-410418 – **90)** Av. 5 de Outubro, 87-2º, 3500 Viseu, ☎ 232-426959, ⎙ 232-425432 – **91)** Rua Nossa Srª do Amparo, 15 – 3º "A", 2900-144 Setúbal, ☎ 265-23 64 45 ⎙ 265-23 74 37 **Email:** radio-lda@clix.pt – **92)** Rua das Donas,4480 Vila do Conde ☎ 252-64 24 26 ⎙ 252-64 2303 **Email:** radiolinear@clix.pt – **93)** Rua das Camélias, 134-B, 4401 Vila Nova de Gaia ☎ 22-377 01 80 ⎙ 22-375 96 75 – **94)** Largo Santana, 1, 8800-902 Tavira ☎ 281-32 02 40 ⎙ 281-32 55 23 **Email:** ragil@mail.telepac.pt **Web:** www.radiogilao.sdv.pt – **95)** Rua Arqº Mário Cardoso, 411- r/c, Guimarães Palace - Atouguia, 4800 Guimarães ☎ 253-42 05 20 ⎙ 253-42 05 29 **Email:** geral@radiofundacao.net, fundacao-fm@iol.pt **Web:** www.radiofundacao.net – **96)** EN nº 118, 1010 - 1º, 2200 Tramagal ☎ 241-89 71 92 ⎙ 241-89 78 59 **Email:** radio.tagide@clix.pt – **97)** (cf. R.Renascença) (cf. nº 25) – **98)** Rua do Muro, 14 – 1º, 7000 Évora, ☎ 266-75 01 80 ⎙ 266-75 01 81 (cf. TSF, No Network) – **99)** Praceta Terras da Mina, lote 4 - lojas dtª e esqª, 2620-486 Ramada, ☎ 21-933 22 11 ⎙ 21-933 22 44 **Email:** rna@mail.telepac.pt **Web:** www.rna.pt

Other Stations (mil.):
CINCSOUTHLANT-Commander-in-Chief South Atlantic Area / **CINCIBERLANT**-Commander-in-Chief Iberian Atlantic Area: ✉ 2780 OEIRAS, ☎. PR: +351-21 440 41 06 - **FM** 88.4 MHz 0.1kW ERP. **D. Prgr.:** AFN in English.

EXTERNAL SERVICES:
RDPi (RDP Internacional) / Rádio Portugal
see International Broadcasting section
Pro-funk GmBH owns & operates Deutsche Welle relay stn Sines.
see International Broadcasting Section

PUERTO RICO (U.S. associated)

L.T: UTC -4h — **Pop:** 4 million — **Pr.L:** Spanish, English — **E.C:** 60Hz, 120V — **ITU:** PTR

BROADCASTERS ASSOCIATION OF PUERTO RICO
✉ Suite 212, Cobians Plaza, 1607 Ave. Ponce de León, San Juan 00926

MW:
Most sts broadcast in Spanish only. °=English or mainly English, d=directional antenna.

	Call	kHz	kW	Name and h. of tr.
1)	WPAB	550	5	Cadena R. Puerto Rico, Ponce: 24h
2)	WKAQ	580	10	R. Reloj, San Juan: 24h
3)	WAEL	600	5	R. 600, Mayagüez: 0830-0400
4)	WEXS	610	0.25/1	X-61, Patillas
5)	WUNO	630	5	NotiUno, San Juan: 24h
6)	WAPA	680	10	Cadena WAPA "Guapa", San Juan: 24h
	WAPA	680	0.4/0.4	Arecibo (synchr. WAPA)
7)	WKJB	710	10/0.75	KJB, Mayagüez: 0915-0400
8)	WIAC	740	10	Cadena R. Puerto Rico, San Juan: 24h
8)	WIAC	740	0.5/0.1	Cadena R. Puerto Rico, Ponce (synchr)
9)	WORA	760	5	NotiUno, Mayagüez
10)	WKVM	810	50	AM-81, San Juan: 0900-0500
11)	WXEW	840	5	NotiUno/R. Victoria, Yabucoa: 0830-0300
12)	WABA	850	5/1	Waba "La Grande", Aguadilla: 24h
13)	WQBS	870	5	La Gran Cadena QBS, San Juan: 0800-0300
14)	WYKO	880	1/0.5	La Poderosa 880, Sabana Grande: 0900-0400
15)	WFAB	890	0.25	WFAB, Ceiba
16)	WPRP	910	4.2	NotiUno, Ponce: 24h
17)	WYAC	930	2.5	Cadena R. Puerto Rico, Cabo Rojo: 24h
18)	WIPR	940	10	WIPR R. Dif de Puerto Rico, San Juan: 24h
19)	WCHQ	960	1/1.7	Quebradillas
20)	WPRA	990	1	R. Mil, Mayagüez: 0900-0400
21)	WOQI	1020	1	R. Coquí/Gigante, Adjuntas: 0900-0200
22)	WOSO	°1030	10	El Oso, San Juan: 24h
23)	WZNA	1040	5/0.2	Zona 1040/Super Kadena Noticias, Moca
24)	WCGB	1060	5/0.5	Iniciativa Mil 60, Juana Díaz: 0900-0300
25)	WMIA	1070	2.5	WMIA/R. Arecibo, Arecibo: 0925-0400 (Sun -0200)
26)	WLEY	1080	0.25	Motivos 1080, Cayey: 24h
27)	WSOL	1090	0.5/0.7	R. Sol, San Germán: 0930 (Sun 1000)-0400
28)	WVJP	1110	2.5/0.5	R. Caguas/Criolla, Caguas: 24h
29)	WMSW	1120	2.6/5	R. Once/La Gran W, Hatillo: 1000-0200
30)	WOIZ	1130	0.2/0.7	R. Antillas, Guayanilla: 0900-0200
31)	WQII	1140	10	Once Q, San Juan: 24h
32)	WBQN	1160	5/2.5	Super Borinquén, Barceloneta-Manatí: 1100-0200
33)	WLEO	1170	0.2	Zona Metro del Sur, Ponce: 24h
34)	WBMJ	°1190	10/5	WBMJ Rock Radio Network "La Roca", San Juan: 24h
35)	WGDL	1200	1	R. Grito/La Radioemisora Lareña, Lares
36)	WHOY	1210	5	R. Hoy, Salinas: 0900-0200
37)	WNIK	1230	1	R. Unica, Arecibo: 24h
38)	WALO	1240	1/5	R. Oriental/Cadena R. Puerto Rico, Humacao: 24h
39)	WJIT	1250	0.25/1	R. Hit, Sabana
40)	WISO	1260	2.5	R. Wiso/Cadena WAPA, Ponce: 1000-0300
40)	WISO	1260	2.5/0.8	R. Wiso/Cadena WAPA, Aguadilla (synchr)
41)	WCMN	1280	5/1	NotiUno/R. Centro, Arecibo: 24h
42)	WTIL	1300	1	R. Util/Cadena R. Puerto Rico, Mayagüez: 24h
43)	WSKN	1320	5/2.3	Super Kadena Noticias, San Juan: 24h
44)	WENA	1330	2/1.5	La Buena del Sur, Yauco: 24h
45)	WWNA	1340	0.95	R. Tiempo/R. Una, Aguadilla: 0900-0300
46)	WEGA	1350	2.5	R. Las Vegas, Vega Baja: 1000-0200
47)	WCHQ	1360	5/1	C-H-Q, Camuy: 24h
48)	WIVV	°1370	5/2.5	WIVV Rock Radio Network "La Roca", Viequez Isl: 24h (r: 1190 kHz)
49)	WOLA	1380	1	R. Prócer, Barranquitas: 0900-0200
50)	WISA	1390	1	Cadena Radio Puerto Rico, Isabela: 24h
51)	WIDA	1400	1	R. Vida, Carolina: 24h

	Call	kHz	kW	Name and h. of tr.
52)	WRSS	1410	1	R. Progreso, San Sebastián: 24h
53)	WUKQ	1420	1	R. Universidad Católica, Ponce: 0900-0200 (0200-0900 rel. R. Reloj 580 kHz)
54)	WNEL	1430	5	NotiUno/ R. Tiempo, Caguas: 24h
55)	WCPR	1450	1	R. Coamo, Coamo: 1000-0200
56)	WRRE	1460	0.5	R. La Fabulosa, Juncos
57)	WLRP	1460	0.5	R. Raíces, San Sebastián: 0900-0400
58)	WKCK	1470	1/2.5d	R. Cumbre, Orocovis: 0900-0200
59)	WMDD	1480	5	R. Tropical 14-80, Fajardo: 24h
60)	WDEP	1490	3.6/0.8	Super Kadena Noticias "La Isla", Ponce
61)	WMNT	1500	1/0.25	R. Atenas, Manatí: 0900-0200
62)	WSQD	1510	1	R. Voz, Lajas
63)	WVOZ	1520	25/10	R. Voz, San Juan: 24h (CP 25/25 kW)
64)	WUPR	1530	1/0.25	Exitos 15-30, Utuado: 1000-0300
65)	WIBS	1540	1d	R. Caribe/Cadena R. Puerto Rico, Guayama
66)	WKFE	1550	0.25	R. Café, Yauco: 24h
67)	WRSJ	1560	5	WRSJ, Bayamón: 24h
68)	WPPC	1570	1/0.1	R. Felicidad, Peñuelas: 1000-2400
69)	WEKO	1580	5/2.5	R. Voz, Morovis: 24h
70)	WXRF	1590	1	R. Voz/R. 15-90, Guayama: 24h
71)	WLUZ	1600	5	R. Luz/Romántica 1600, Bayamón: 1100-0400
72)	WGIT	1660	10/1	Gigante 16-60, Canóvanas: 24h

Addresses and other information:
1) Box 7243, Ponce 00732-7243 ☎+1 787 8405550 🖷+1 7878407077 **Web:** www.wpabradio.com/index.html **Email:** pab@coqui.net - **FM:** WOQI 93.3, WIOC 105. 1, WOYE 94. 1 Mayagüez. – **2)** Box 364668, San Juan 00936-4668 ☎+1 7877585800 🖷+1 7877565220 **Web:** www.wkaqradio.com - **FM:** 104.7 KQ-105 La Primera. – **3)** Box 1370, Mayagüez 00681-1370 **Web**: www.radio600am.com - **FM:** WAEL-FM 96.1 Maricao. – **4)** Box 640, Patillas 00723-0640. – **5)** Box 363222, San Juan 00936-3222. **Web:** www.notiuno.com - **FM:** WFID 97.7 Río Piedras. – **6)** Urb. Baldrich, 134 Domenech Ave, Hato Rey 00918-3502. – **7)** Box 1293, Mayagüez 00709-1293. **Web:** http://home.coqui.net/bechara/ kjb.htm - **FM**: WKJB-FM 99.1. – **8)** Box 9023916, San Juan 00902-3916. **Web:** www.radiopr740.com - **FM:** 102.5. – **9)** Box 43, Mayagüez 00681-0043. – **10)** Urb. Roosevelt, 415 Calle Carbonell, Hato Rey 00918-2866. - **FM:** WORO 92.5 Corozal. – **11)** Box 840, Yabucoa 00767-0840. **Web:** www.radiovictoria.com – **12)** 6 Calle Munoz Rivera St., Aguadilla 00603-5154. **Web:** www.waba.850.com – **13)** Urb. San Francisco, 129 Ave de Diego, San Francisco, San Juan 00927-6310. – **14)** 63 Calle Comercio, Yauco 00698-3541. – **15)** Box 1231, Juncos 00777-1231. – **16)** Box 7771, Ponce 00732-7771. – **17)** Box 681, Cabo Rojo 00623-0681. - **FM:** WMIO 102.3. – **18)** Box 190909, Hato Rey 00918-0909 ☎+1 787 7660505 🖷+1 787 2507694 **Web**: www.wipr.com/wipradio.htm - **FM**: 91.3 Allegeo. – **19)** Box 1115, Isabela 00662-1115. – **20)** Box 1293, Mayagüez 00681-1293 **Web**: http://home.coqui.net/bechara/wpra.htm – **21)** Box 982, Adjuntas 00601-0982. ☎+1 787 829 1453. 🖷+1 787 829 1453. **Email**: coki@coqui.net – **22)** Box 9023940, San Juan 00902-3940. **Web:** www.woso.com – **23)** Box 7, Moca 00676-0007. **Web**: www.zona1040.com – **24)** Box 248, Juana Díaz 00795-0248. – **25)** Box 1055, Arecibo 00613-1055. – **26)** Box 1186, Cayey 00737-1186. – **27)** Box 442, San Germán 00683-0442. – **28)** Box 207, Caguas 00726-0207. - **FM:** 103.3 Criolla. – **29)** 550 Calle Truncado, Hatillo 00659-2712. – **30)** Box 561130, Guayanilla 00656-1130. ☎+1 787 835 1130. 🖷+1 787 835 3130. **Email**: radioantillas@yahoo.com – **31)** Cobian's Plaza, Santurce 00909-1820 (or: Box 363779, Hato Rey 00936-3779). – **32)** Box 1625 (or: Calle 16 H-6 Urb. Flamboyán), Manatí 00674-1625. ☎+1 787 854 2450. 🖷+1 787 854 3738 – **33)** Box 7213, Ponce 00732-7213. - **FM:** WZAR 101.9. – **34)** Box 367000, San Juan 00936-7000 (or: Av. Ponce de León N° 1409, P4, Santurce 00907). (Parallel with 48). ☎+1 787 724 1190. 🖷+1 787 722 5395. **Web:** www.wbmjwivv.org **Email:** radio@cem.wbmj.org – **35)** Box 487, Caguas 00726-0487. – **36)** Box 1148, Salinas 00751-1148. ☎+1 787 824 3420. 🖷+1 787 824 8054. **Email:** whoyam@coqui.net – **37)** Box 556, Arecibo 00613-0556. - **FM:** 106.5. – **38)** Box 1240, Humacao 00792. **Web:** http://walo.coqui.net – **39)** Box 316, Coamo 00769-0316. – **40)** Box 7251, Ponce 00732-7251. – **41)** Box 436, Arecibo 00613-0436. - **FM:** 107.3. – **42)** Box 1360, Mayagüez 00681-1360. – **43)** Box 363222, San Juan 00936-3222. **Web:** http://superkadena.spiderlink.net – **44)** Box 1338, Yauco 00698-1338. – **45)** Box 7, Moca 00676-0007. **Web:** www.inc.com/users/ncn.html – **46)** Box 1488, Vega Baja 00694-1488. **Web:** www.wegabaja.com – **47)** Box 629, Camuy 00627-0629. - **FM:** WCHQ-FM 102.9. – **48)** Address, **Web** and **Email:** As 34). – **49)** Box 189, Barranquitas 00794-0189. – **50)** Box 750, Isabela 00662-0750. - **FM:** WKSA 101.5. – **51)** Box 188, Carolina 00986-0188. **Web:** www.radiovida.com - **FM:** 90.5. – **52)** Box 1410, San Sebastián 00685-1410. – **53)** Box 529, Stn 6, Catholic University of Puerto Rico, Ponce 00732-0529. - **FM:** 88.9+91.1. – **54)** Box 487, Caguas 00726-0487. ☎+1 787 744 3131. 🖷+1 787 743 0252. **Email**: buzoncadena@hotmail.com - **FM:** WPRM 98.5 San Juan. – **55)** Box 1863, Coamo 00769-1863. ☎+1 787 825 7061 🖷+1 787 825 1905. **Web:** http://attila.stevens-tech.edu/wcpr – **56)** Box 1460, Juncos 00777-1460. – **57)** Box 1670, San Sebastián 00685-1670. – **58)** 10 Calle Pedro Arroyo, Orocovis 00720-2202. – **59)** Box 948, Fajardo 00738-0948. - **FM:** WDOY 96.5. – **60)** Box 7213, Ponce 00732-7213. – **61)** Box 6, Manatí 00674-0006 – **Web:** www.radioatenas.com **Email**: radio@atenas.com – **62)** Box 593, Lajas 00667-0593. – **63)** Calle Barin 1554, San Juan 00927-6113. - **FM:** 107.7 Carolina. – **64)** Box 868, Utuado 00641-0868. – **65)** Box 1540, Guayama 00785-1540. – **66)** Box 324, Yauco 00698-0324. – **67)** Box 4036, Carolina 00984-4036. **Web:** www.fuentedeaguaviva.org – **68)** Box 9064, Ponce 00732-9064 (or: 1896 Av. Las Américas, Ponce 00728-1818) ☎/🖷+1 787 840 7105. **Email:** radiofelicidad@yahoo.com – **69)** Urb. Floral Park, 155 Ave. San António, Hato Rey 00917-3910. – **70)** Urb. Caribe, 1603 Ave. Ponce de León, N° 102, San Juan 00926-2714. – **71)** Box 9394, Santurce 00908-9394. ☎+1 787 729 1600. 🖷+1 787 723 8685. – **72)** Box 7, Moca 00676-0007. **Email:** wuna@centennial pr.net

AFRTS
✉ Naval Media Center, 2713 Mitscher Road SW, Washington, DC 20373-5819, USA. **Web**: www.afrts.osd.mil/afnonradio
MW: AFCN 1200kHz 0.25kW, Roosevelt Roads
SW:AFCN 7507kHz USB, Roosevelt Roads
FM: AFCN 101.5MHz 1kW, Roosevelt Roads. 93.1MHz 0.25kW, Sabana Seca. 90.5MHz 0.20kW, Aguadilla. 91.1MHz 0.20kW, unk.

QATAR

L.T: UTC +3h — **Pop:** 610,000 — **Pr.L:** Arabic — **E.C:** 50Hz, 240V — **ITU:** QAT

MINISTRY OF INFORMATION & CULTURE
✉ P.O. Box 3939, Doha ☎ +974 831447 **L.P:** Minister of Inf: Dr.Hamad Abdul Aziz Al Kawari.

QATAR BROADCASTING SERVICE
✉ P.O. Box 1414, Doha ☎ +974 894444 (SW:+974 864111) 🖷 +974 882888 **L.P:** Vice-Chairman for Radio & TV Corp: Abdul Rahman Saif Al-Mahmadi (☎+974 864823). Dir. of Broadc: Mubarak Jaham Al-Kawari (☎ +974 864822).

MW	kHz	kW	Prgr.	H. of tr.
Al Khaisah	675	50	A	0245-2130
Al Arish	954	1500	A	0245-2130
Al Khaisah	999	50	Q/S/U	0245-0700, 1300-1900
Al Khaisah	1233	100	E/F	0300-1000, 1300-1900
Doha	1602	1	Q/S/U	0245-0700, 1300-1900

FM (MHz): Al-Jumailiyah 90.8MHz 40kW (A), Al-Jumailiyah 92.6 MHz 20kW (A), Umm Said 93.4 (A), Al Kohr 97.6 (A), Markhiyah 102.0 (A), Al Ruwais 104.0 (A).
Arabic Prgr. (A): 0245-2130 (954 kHz 24 h). **English Prgr. (E):** 0300 - 2130 on FM Doha 97.5 (10 kW), 102.6 MHz (20 kW) & 1233 kHz. **N:** 0330, 1000, 1700. **French Prgr. (F):** Al Jumaliyah 100.8 0400-0700. **Sha'abi Prgr. (S):** 1300-1600 (Folklore prgrs. in local dialect). **Urdu Prgr. (U):** 1600-1900. **Qur'an Prgr. (Q):** 0245-0700. Music Prgr. (M): 1800-2100.

EXTERNAL SERVICE: Qatar Broadcasting Service see International Broadcasting section.

FM Stations (MHz):
RFI AFRIQUE/RFI MUSIQUE, Doha, 107.7, 24h – **BBC ARABIC SERVICE, Doha,** 107.4, 24h in Arabic and English – **RADIO MONTE CARLO, Doha,** 93.4, Arabic and French – **MIDDLE EAST BROADCASTING COMPANY, Doha,** Markhiyah 92.0, 24 h in Arabic – **RADIO SAWA, Doha, Web:** www.radiosawa.com **Email:** comment@radiosawa.com 92.6, 24h in Arabic (see USA entry for full details) – **AFN Qatar,** Al Udeid Air Base 107.5, 24h

RÉUNION (French)

L.T: UTC +4h — **Pop:** 780,000 — **Pr.L:** French — **E.C:** 50Hz, 220V — **ITU:** REU

RADIO REUNION
✉ 1 rue Jean-Chatel, FR-97716 St. Denis Messag Cédex 9 ☎ +262 406767 🖷 +262 216484 **Email:** ambassadeur.reunion@rfo.fr **Web:** www.rfo.fr **L.P:** Directrice Regional: Dominique Richard
MW: St. Pierre 666kHz 20kW. Saint André on 729kHz 20kW

FM	MHz	FM	MHz
Sainte-Rose	87.9	Saint-Joseph	90.7
Saint-Pierre	89.0	Salazie	90.8
Saint-Denis	89.2	Le Port	92.6
Piton Textor	89.6	Saint-Phillipe	92.6
Saint-Benoît	89.6	Cilaos	93.5
Sainte-Suzanne	90.0	Saint-Denis Montagne	96.6
Saint-Leu	90.7		

D.Prgr: 24h. During nighttime 2200-0500 relay of RFI.
ANN: "Société Nationale de Radio-Télévision Française d'Outre Mer, Station de la Réunion". **IS:** "Séga & Maloya" (Réunion Folklore).

RADIO ARC-EN-CIEL
✉ 18 bis rue Montreuil (B.P .382), FR-97467 St-Denis ☎ +262201082 **Web:** http://perso.wanadoo.fr/radio-arc-en-ciel
Email: radio-arc-en-ciel-reunion@wanadoo.fr

FM	MHz	FM	MHz
St.Joseph	89.3	St. Giles	95.6
Le Pont	89.6	Montagne	103.4
St. Denis	91.3	St. Benoit	105.2C
St. Pierre	94.7	St. Leu	106.3

R. VIE
✉ B.P. 772, 97476 Saint Denis Cedex. **FM**: 105.5MHz 24h.

Over 40 low-power private & commercial st's broadcast locally on FM. See **Web:**www.outremer.com/440-Radio/440.40-Radio-01.html

BBC African Service relayed by Radio Kanal West Réunion 97.0, East Réunion 98.1 and South Reunion 98.4 MHz
France Inter: 98.8MHz + 7 relay st's.
R Kanla Ocean Indien: 97.0 (west), 98.1 (east), 98.4 (south) (includes relays of BBC World Service).

ROMANIA

L.T: UTC +2h (27 Mar - 30 Oct 2005: UTC +3h) — **Pop:** 21.5 million — **Pr.L:** Romanian, Hungarian, German — **E.C:** 50Hz, 230V — **ITU:** ROU

SOCIETATEA ROMÂNA DE RADIODIFUZIUNE (Pub.)
✉ Str. Berthelot nr. 60-64, 010105 Bucuresti. ☎ +40 21 3031777. 🖷 +40 21 3031726. **Email:** mesaje@rornet.ro **Web:** www.srr.ro
L.P: DG: Dragos Stefan Seuleanu.

LW/MW	kHz	kW	P
Brasov (Bod)	153	600	1
Petrosani	531	14	AS/1
Târgu Jiu	558	400	1 (0400-2000)
Brasov (Bod)	567	50	1
Satu Mare	567	50	1
Botosani	603	50	1
Bucuresti (Herastrau)	603	50	AS/1
Oradea	603	14	1
Turnu Severin	603	14	1
Timisoara (Ortisoara)	630	400	R/1
Voinesti	630	400	AS/1
Sighetul Marmatiei	711	50	1 (0300-2200)
Baia Mare	720	7	1
Isaccea	720	14	1
Sinaia	720	14	1
Lugoj (Boldur)	756	400	1 (0600-2200)/VOA°
Bucuresti (Tâncâbesti)	855	1500	1
Cluj (Alba Iulia)	909	400	R/MG
Timisoara	909	50	1/MG
Constanta (Valu lui Traian)	909	14	R
Miercurea Ciuc	945	14	1
Iasi (Uricani)	1053	1000	R (0400-2000)
Cluj (Alba Iulia)	1152	950	1 (0300-2200)
Bacau (Galbeni)	1179	200	1
Resita (Vascau)	1179	7	1
Brasov (Bod)	1197	14	R/MG/L (0400-2000)
Constanta	1314	14	AS/1
Craiova	1314	7	R/1
Timisoara	1314	30	AS/1
Târgu Mures	1323	7	R/MG (0400-2000)
Galati	1332	50	1
Sighetul Marmatiei	1404	50	R/L
Rm. Vâlcea (Olanesti)	1422	7	1
Constanta (Agigea)	1458	50	1
Mahmudia	1530	14	AS/1
Radauti (Sâveni)	1530	14	1
Miercurea Ciuc (Harghita)	1593	14	R/MG (0400-2000)
Ion Corvin	1593	14	1
Oradea	1593	20	R/MG
Sibiu	1593	20	R/MG/L

NOTE: All tx's are on the air 24h (except where stated), relaying R.România Actualitati at nighttime. °) Relay VOA: see International Radio section under USA; R=Regional prgr's, L=Local prgr's

FM (MHz)	RR1	RR2	RR4	kW
Alexandria	91.8	89.7	-	10
Arad (Siria)	103.8	106.8	-	10
Bacau (Turn)	98.8	101.8	-	10
Baia Mare (Mogosa)	102.5	100.1	-	-
Baile Herculane	97.3	-	-	0.05
Bicaz	87.7	-	-	0.1
Bârlad	103.9	102.8	-	-
Bechet (Dabuleni)	99.1	-	-	2
Bihor	91.0	105.8	-	10
Bistrita (Heniu)	103.9	**72.44	-	30/15
Borsec	-	98.4	-	-
Botosani (Sâveni)	106.0	100.8	-	10
Bran	103.7	-	-	-
Brasov	102.5	105.0	-	1
Bucuresti (Herastrau)	105.3	101.3	104.8	10
Buzau (Dealul Istrita)	100.3	103.7	-	2
Calafat (Plenita)	95.5	101.1	-	10
Calarasi (Baneasa)	*106.6	*105.2	-	10
Câmpulung M. (Rarau)	96.0	98.7	-	5
Cluj-Napoca (Feleacu)	88.8	101.0	-	10
Comanesti (Laposi)	104.7	101.4	-	5
Constanta (Techirghiol)	102.7	**67.79	-	-/52
Craiova	88.7	-	-	10
Deva (Magura Boiu)	103.4	105.0	-	4
Faget	89.8	-	-	5
Focsani (Magura Odob.)	102.5	101.0	-	60
Galati (Vacareni)	106.4	101.6	-	-
Gheorgheni (Suseni)	103.4	106.8	-	-
Giurghiu	104.6	102.6	-	2
Iasi (Pietrarie)	101.1	103.1	-	10
Lehliu Gara	106.2	-	-	-
Moldova Noua	*105.1	-	-	2
Negresti-Oas	89.4	-	-	2
Novaci (Cerbu)	92.9	89.5	-	10
Oradea	104.1	96.1	-	-
Petrosani (Parâng)	88.1	90.6	-	10
Piatra Neamt	103.6	100.3	-	-
Ploesti (Sinaia, Bucegi)	102.2	104.1	97.6	10
Resita (Semenic)	*102.5	**66.44	-	100/40
Rm. Vâlcea (Cozia)	103.4	102.5	-	5
Sibiu (Paltinis)	101.8	103.7	-	-
Sighetul Marmatiei	106.2	-	-	2
Slobozia	96.3	-	-	2
Suceava (Mihoveni)	99.6	101.6	-	5
Sulina	101.9	-	-	2
Târgu Mures	93.6	104.9	-	-
Timisoara (Urseni)	106.4	100.7	-	10
Toplita	*101.0	-	-	-
Tulcea	99.4	105.4	-	-
Tulcea (Topolog)	105.0	103.0	-	-
Turnu Severin (Balota)	91.4	105.8	-	-
Varatec	91.2	100.8	-	10
Vaslui	106.1	102.4	-	2
Vatra Dornei	100.7	107.7	-	1
Zalau (Mezes)	88.1	105.0	-	15

*) in preparation; **) to move to CCIR FM

D.PRGR: R. România Actualitati (RR1): 24h. – **R. România Cultural (RR2):** 0600-2200. – **R. 3 România Tineret (RR3):** 24h, only webcasting: radio3net.ro. – **R. România Muzical "George Enescu" (RR4):** 24h. – "**Program Maghiar-German" (MG):** W 1200-1300 German & 1300-1400 Hungarian; Sun 0800-0820 Hungarian & 0820-0830 German. – **"Antena Satelor" (AS):** 0400-0700, 1700-2000 (this service is currently being expanded).
EXTERNAL SERVICE: Radio Romania International.
See International Radio section.

R. ROMÂNIA REGIONAL STATIONS (Pub.)
R. Bucuresti: Str. Berthlot nr. 60-64, 010105 Bucuresti. Email: radiobucuresti@srr.ro. Local service **"Antena Bucurestilor"** 24h on 98.3MHz (Bucuresti). Suburban service **"R. Snagov"** 24h on 91.2MHz (Snagov), mostly rel. R. Bucuresti.

R. Cluj: Str. Donath nr. 160, 400293 Cluj-Napoca. Email: office@radiocluj.ro. 0400-2200 on 95.6MHz (Cluj), 0400-2100 on 909 (Cluj)/1404(Sighetul M.)/1593kHz (Oradea & Sibiu). Hungarian ("Kolozsvári Rádió"): 0600 (Sun 0730)-0800, Sun 1200-1600, W 1300-1600 (Sat 1630), Mon 1900-2000, Tue-Fri 1900-1930. Local studio: Str. Brutarilor nr. 3, 550251 Sibiu. Own prgr **"Antena Sibiului"** on 1593kHz: 1700-1900, other times rel. R. Cluj. Local studio: Sighetul Marmatiei. Own prgr on 1404kHz: 1700-1900, other times rel. R. Cluj.
R. Constanta: Vila nr. 1, 900001 Mamaia. Email: rcast@rdsct.ro. 0400-2000 on 909kHz (in part) & 100.1 (Constanta), 105.4MHz (Tulcea) (June-August on MW only). Multilingual tourist service (Romanian, English, French, German, Russian) **"R. Vacanta"** (1 June - 1 Sep): 0400-2000 on 100.1/105.4MHz. Email: radio.vacanta@rdsct.ro. NB. R.Vacanta may return to a MW freq. in summer 2005.
R. Iasi: Str. Catargi Lascar nr. 44, 700107 Iasi. Email: secretariat@radioiasi.ro. 0400-2000 on 1053kHz & 90.8 (Rarau), 96.3MHz (Iasi).
R. Oltenia Craiova: Str. Stirbei Voda nr. 3, 200352 Craiova. Email: office@radio.oltenia.ro. 0400-2000 on 1314kHz & 102.9 (Craiova), 105.0MHz (Târgu Jiu).
R. Resita: Str. Maior Petru nr. 71, 320111 Resita. Email: secretariat@radio-resita.ro. On 105.6 MHz. German: Tue 1220-1240.
R. Târgu Mures: Bd. 1 Decembrie 1918 nr. 109, 540445 Târgu Mures. ☎+40 265 269103. Email: office@radiomures.ro. 0400-2000 on 1197 (Brasov)/1323(Târgu Mures)/1593kHz (Miercurea Ciuc), 0400-2200 on 98.4 (Toplita), 98.9 (Harghita), 102.9MHz (Târgu Mures). Hungarian ("Marosvásárhelyi Rádió"): MF 0900-1600, Sat 0600-0900 & 1200-1600, Sun 0800-1600. German ("R. Neumarkt") on MW: W 1900-2000, Sun 0830-0930. Local studio: Bd. Eroilor nr. 29, 507246 Brasov. Email: antenabv@rdsbv.ro. Own prgr **"Antena Brasovului"** on 1197kHz: Mon-Fri 0600-0700 & 1600-1700, Sat 0900-1100, Sun 0700-0800, other times rel. R.Târgu Mures.
R. Timisoara: Str. Pestalozzi nr. 14A, 300115 Timisoara. Email: secretariat@radiotimisoara.ro. 0400-2000 on 630kHz & 91.3 (Timisoara), 95.9 (Deva), 105.3MHz (Arad). German ("R. Temeswar"): 1100-1200, Hungarian ("Temesvári Rádió"): 1200-1300, Serbian: 1300-1400. Bulgarian: Sun 1400-1430, Czech: Sun 1430-1500, Slovak: Sun 1500-1630 (exc. 1st Sun -1620), Ukrainian 1st Sun 1620-1700.
NB: All reg. stn's relay news from national networks at certain times.

OTHER STATIONS

MW	kHz	kW	Location	Station
3)	1485	1	Botosani*	Favorit FM
10)	1485	1	Oradea*	R. Maria
8)	1584	1	Bacau*	Aurora FM
8)	1584	1	Galati*	Aurora FM
3)	1584	1	Iasi*	Favorit FM
9)	1584	1	Craiova*	Micul Samaritean
9)	1584	1	Fagaras*	Micul Samaritean
9)	1584	1	Radauti*	Micul Samaritean
9)	1584	1	Sânnicolau Mare*	Micul Samaritean
9)	1584	1	Tulcea*	Micul Samaritean
9)	1602	1	Piatra Neamt*	Micul Samaritean
8)	1602	1	Focsani*	Aurora FM
8)	1602	1	Iasi*	Aurora FM
3)	1602	1	Bistrita*	Favorit FM
11)	1602	1	Arad	R. CNM
12)	1602	1**	Slobozia	R. Sud Est

*) in preparation; **) run with reduced power

FM	MHz	kW	Location	Station
1)	88.2	4.8	Botosani	Europa FM
2A)	88.4	10	Varatec	Info Pro
2A)	88.5	100	Semenic	Info Pro
17)	88.9	10	Tulcea	Romantic FM
2A)	89.1	10	Târgu Mures	Info Pro
1)	89.3	4.7	Arad	Europa FM
1)	90.0	4.6	Bistrita	Europa FM
2A)	90.0	60	Magura Odobesti	Info Pro
5)	90.2	10	Calafat*	R. Galaxy
1)	90.5	4.7	Baia Mare	Europa FM
1)	90.7	4.2	Târgu Mures	Europa FM
2A)	91.3	10	Urseni	Info Pro
2A)	91.4	60	Suseni	Info Pro
2A)	91.8	10	Turn	Info Pro
2A)	92.0	60	Vacareni	Info Pro
1)	92.1	4.5	Petrosani	Europa FM
2A)	92.4	60	Paltinis	Info Pro
1)	93.2	4.8	Oradea	Europa FM
1)	93.4	10	Alexandria*	Europa FM
2A)	93.9	30	Baneasa	Info Pro
2A)	94.3	30	Cozia	Info Pro
4)	94.8	5	Faget*	R. DEEA
2A)	95.7	30	Bârlad	Info Pro
2A)	95.9	30	Magura Boiu	Info Pro
2A)	96.2	60	Techirghiol	Info Pro
2A)	96.7	10	Saveni	Info Pro
6)	97.2	30	Turnu Magurele*	R. Global
2A)	97.9	10	Bucuresti	Info Pro
2A)	98.5	10	Parâng	Info Pro
2A)	98.5	30	Laposi	Info Pro
2A)	99.2	100	Pietrarie	Info Pro
1)	99.5	4.9	Calarasi	Europa FM
2A)	99.6	100	Sinaia (Bucegi)	Info Pro
2A)	100.7	100	Carbu	Info Pro
2A)	101.6	10	Mezes	Info Pro
1)	102.7	5	Mezes	Europa FM
1)	103.4	9.5	Galati	Europa FM
2A)	103.4	30	Mihoveni	Info Pro
1)	104.2	4.7	Gheorgheni	Europa FM
1)	104.2	4.4	Bacau	Europa FM
1)	104.4	5	Timisoara	Europa FM
2A)	104.5	30	Feleac	Info Pro
2A)	104.8	30	Rarau	Info Pro
1)	105.1	4.6	Piatra Neamt	Europa FM
2A)	105.3	60	Siria	Info Pro
2A)	105.3	60	Mogosa	Info Pro
1)	105.5	7.6	Suceava	Europa FM
2A)	105.5	30	Craiova	Info Pro
1)	105.8	7.6	Focsani	Europa FM
1)	106.1	5.2	Constanta	Europa FM
1)	106.2	4.9	Sibiu	Europa FM
1)	106.2	4.8	Bârlad	Europa FM
1)	106.3	5.1	Comanesti	Europa FM
1)	106.5	5.1	Iasi	Europa FM
1)	106.6	11.7	Feleac	Europa FM
1)	106.7	23.4	Bucuresti	Europa FM
1)	107.0	30	Dealul Istrita	Europa FM
1)	107.1	5.1	Târgu Jiu	Europa FM
1)	107.4	5	Tulcea	Europa FM
1)	107.5	5	Resita	Europa FM
2A)	107.6	60	Oradea	Info Pro
1)	107.7	4.8	Magura Boiu	Europa FM
2A)	107.8	30	Heniu	Info Pro
2A)	107.9	60	Bigor (Curcubata)	Info Pro
7)	107.9	10	Tulcea*	R. XXI
2A)	107.9	30	Balota	Info Pro

NB. FM tx's below 4kW not mentioned. *) in preparation

Addresses & other information:
1) Intr. Camil Petrescu, sector 1, 010541 Bucuresti. Email: europafm@europafm.ro – **2A,B)** Bd. Pache Protopopescu nr. 109, 021409 Bucuresti. Email: 1A) infopro@infopro.ro; 1B) profm@profm.ro – **3)** Str. Ianus Pannonius nr. 25A, 410150 Oradea. – **4)** Bd. Republicii nr. 1, 601018 Onesti. Email: deea.sediu@xnet.ro. – **5)** Calafat. – **6)** Bucuresti. – **7)** Calea Victoriei nr. 224, 010099 Bucuresti. Email: radio21@radio21.ro. – **8)** Bucuresti. – **9)** Str. Nicolae Teclu nr. 37, 550200 Sibiu. Email: florin@littlesamaritan.org – **10)** Oradea. –**11)** Str. Poetului nr. 24, 310369 Arad. Email: contact@radiocnm.com. – **12)** Str. Alexandru Odobescu nr. 12, 920025 Slobozia. Email: rse@radiosudest.ro.

RUSSIA

L.T: Moscow: UTC +3h (27 Mar - 30 Oct 2005: UTC +4h)); See Reg. Services section for other zones — **Pop:** 146 million — **Pr.L:** Russian, numerous minority languages — **E.C:** 50Hz, 220V — **ITU:** RUS

VSEROSSIYSKAYA GOSUDARSTVENNAYA TELERADIOKOMPANIYA (VGTRK, Gov.)

✉ Leningradskiy pr. 22/2, 125124 Moskva. ☎ +7 095 2348600. 🖷 +7 095 2142347. **Email:** vgtrk2@space.ru **Web:** www.vgtrk.com
L.P: Chmn: Oleg Dobrodeyev.
VGTRK is the national state broadcasting company of the Russian Federation. This state enterprise is the administrative parent company of the national radio networks R. Rossii, R. Mayak, R. Yunost, R. Orfey, R. Kultura (the regional state broadcasting companies, see Regional secton):

GRK "RADIO ROSSII"

✉ Yamskogo polya 5-ya ul. 19/21, 125124 Moskva. ☎ +7 095 2140730. 🖷 +7 095 2145366. **Email:** direction@radiorus.ru **Web:** www.radiorus.ru **L.P:** Gen Dir: Aleksey V. Abakumov.

GRK "MAYAK"
🖃 ul. Pyatnitskaya 25, 115326 Moskva. ☎ +7 095 9506767. 🖷+7 095 9594207. **Email:** inform@radiomayak.ru **Web:** www.radiomayak.ru **L.P:** Chmn: Sergey V. Kurokhtin. Dir radio channel "R. Mayak 24": Darya Sergeyeva, Dir radio channel "R. Yunost": Igor Mushastikov.

RADIO ORFEY
🖃 ul. M. Nikitskaya 24, 123995 Moskva. ☎ +7 095 2906302. 🖷 +7 095 2901916. **Email:** orphei@starnet.ru **Web:** www.mmv.ru/orphei **L.P:** Gen. Dir: Olga A. Gromova.

GTRK "KULTURA"
🖃 ul. M. Nikitskaya 24, 123995 Moskva. ☎ +7 095 7805609. 🖷 +7 095 2900964. **Email:** radio@tv-culture.ru **Web:** www.cultradio.ru **L.P:** Gen Dir: Aleksandr Ponomarev.

HOME SERVICES (Gov.)
Abbreviations: RR = R. Rossii - RM = R. Mayak - RY = R. Yunost - RO = R. Orfey - Reg = Regional prgr's - GR = Golos Rossii (Foreign service prgr's) - RChS = Prgr "R. Chechnya Svobodnaya" - Rg = Region - Geographical location (acc. to Russian administrative division): E = European part of Russia - S = Siberia - FE = Russian Far East.

LW/MW

Rg	Location	kHz	kW	Hour of tr.	Prgr.
MO	Taldom, E	153	300	0300-2200	RY
KH	Komsomolsk, FE	153	1200	2000-1600	RR
BA	Yazykovo, E	162	150	0100-2000	Reg
TM	Norilsk, S	162	150	2200-2100	RR,RM,Reg
KA	Bolshakovo, E	171	600	0400-2100	RR
KD	Tbilisskaya, E	171	1200	0300-2100	RChS
NS	Oyash, S	171	500	2200-1800	RR, Reg
RS	Yakutsk, FE	171	150	2000-1600	RR, Reg
CH	Chita, S	180	150	2100-1600	RR, Reg
KM	Yelizovo, FE	180	150	1800-1400	RR, Reg
AM	Belogorsk, FE	189	1200	2000-1600	RR, Reg
BA	Ufa, E	198	150	0100-2000	RM
MO	Noginsk, E	198	150	0300-2200	RM
SP	Olgino, E	198	150	0100-2300	RM
AM	Tynda, FE	207	150	2100-1600	RM
YV	Birobidzhan, FE	216	30	2000-1600	RR, Reg
KN	Krasnoyarsk, S	216	150	2200-1800	RR, Reg
KY	Surgut, S	225	1000	0000-2000	RR, Reg
IR	Angarsk, S	234	250	2200-1800	RR, Reg
MA	Arman, FE	234	1000	1800-1400	RR, Reg
PM	Razdolnoye, FE	243	500	2000-1600	RR, Reg
TS	Kazan, E	252	150	0200-2200	RR, Reg
CH	Chita, S	261	600	2000-1600	RM
MO	Taldom, E	261	2500	0200-2200	RR
OB	Orenburg, E	270	50	0000-2000	RR, Reg
NS	Novosibirsk, S	270	150	0000-2000	RR, Reg
BU	Selenginsk, S	279	150	2200-1800	RR, Reg
SV	Yekaterinburg, E	279	150	0000-2000	RR, Reg
RA	Gorno-Altaysk, S	279	50	2200-1800	RR, Reg
SL	Yu-Sakhalinsk, FE	279	1000	1800-1400	RR, Reg
CV	Cheboksary, E	531	30	0300-2200	RM, Reg
OB	Orenburg, E	540	50	0100-2000	RM
MO	Kurovskaya, E	549	500	0300-2200	RM
AM	Svobodnyy, FE	549	150	2100-1600	RM
RS	Yakutsk, FE	549	50	2100-1600	RM
RO	Novocherkassk, E	549	50	0300-2200	RM
KO	Syktyvkar, E	549	150	0300-2200	RM
KA	Kaliningrad, E	549	50	0200-2100	RM
MA	Magadan, FE	549	25	1900-1600	RM
SP	Krasnyy Bor, E	549	1200	0100-2300	RM
PM	Tavrichanka, FE	549	500	1900-1600	RM
VG	Volgograd, E	567	1000	0200-2200	RR, Reg
RT	Kyzyl, S	567	150	2200-1800	RR, Reg
AS	Astrakhan, E	576	50	0400-2300	RM
NS	Oyash, S	576	1000	0000-1900	RM
KH	Khabarovsk, FE	576	150	2000-1500	RM
KM	Petropavlovsk-K., FE	576	150	1800-1300	RM
IR	Angarsk, S	576	250	2200-1700	RM
AM	Belogorsk, FE	585	1200	… (*) …	GR
PR	Perm, E	585	150	0000-2000	RR, Reg
KY	Surgut, S	594	1000	0100-2000	RM
KN	Krasnoyarsk, S	594	150	2300-1800	RM
SO	Vladikavkaz, E	594	25	0300-2200	RM, Reg
UD	Izhevsk, E	594	40	0200-2200	RR, Reg
AM	Skovorodino, FE	603	30	2100-1600	RM
AM	Belogorsk, FE	603	30	2100-1600	RM
TM	Norilsk, S	612	25	2300-1800	RM
MO	Kurkino, E	612	40	0300-2200	GR, Relays
KT	Petrozavodsk, E	612	150	0300-2200	RM
KH	Khabarovsk, FE	621	50	2000-1600	RR, Reg
KO	Syktyvkar, E	621	50	0200-2200	RR, Reg
DA	Makhachkala, E	621	50	0200-2200	RR, Reg
DA	Kochubey, E	621	5	0200-2200	RR, Reg
KH	Komsomolsk, FE	630	500	… (*) …	GR
SR	Saratov, E	630	42	0300-2200	RM
OM	Omsk, S	639	75	0000-2000	RR, Reg
PM	Razdolnoye, FE	648	1000	… (*) …	GR
MU	Murmansk, E	657	150	0200-2200	RR
CC	Alpatovo, E	657	100	0200-2200	RR, RChS
KH	Komsomolsk, FE	666	150	2000-1500	RM
AM	Tynda, FE	666	150	2000-1600	RR, Reg
KD	Sochi, E	666	25	0300-2200	RM
CK	Anadyr, FE	693	25	1800-1400	RR, Reg
BA	Ufa, E	693	150	0000-2000	RR
IR	Bratsk, S	702	7	2200-1700	RM
NE	Naryan-Mar, E	711	7	0200-2200	RR, Reg
KH	Okhotsk, FE	711	5	2000-1600	RR, Reg
KH	Nikolayevsk, FE	711	5	2000-1600	RR
SL	Yu-Sakhalinsk, FE	720	1000	1900-1100	RM, GR
KK	Palana, FE	738	25	1800-1400	RR, Reg
CB	Chelyabinsk, E	738	40	0000-2000	Reg, RR/RM
KT	Petrozavodsk, E	765	150	0200-2200	RR, Reg
VN	Voronezh, E	774	30	0300-2200	RM, Reg
SL	Aleksandrovsk, FE	792	50	1800-1400	RR, Reg
RK	Abakan, S	792	25	2200-1800	RR, Reg
AS	Astrakhan, E	792	50	various	Reg
CH	Chita, S	801	1200	1100-1500	GR
VG	Volgograd, E	810	500	0400-2300	RM
SV	Yekaterinburg, E	810	50	0100-2200	RM
PM	Razdolnoye, FE	810	150	2200-1800	RR, Reg
NN	Nizhniy Novgorod, E	828	50	0200-2200	RR, Reg
RT	Kyzyl, S	828	150	2300-1800	RM
KX	Elista, E	846	42	0200-2200	RR, Reg
MO	Noginsk, E	846	150	various	Reg
PR	Perm, E	846	10	0100-2000	RY
PZ	Kamenka, E	855	50	0200-2200	RR, Reg
MO	Elektrostal, E	873	1250	0200-2200	RR
SP	Olgino, E	873	150	0200-2200	RR, Reg
SA	Novosemeykino, E	873	1200	0200-2200	RR
KA	Kaliningrad, E	873	50	0300-2200	RR, Reg
KH	Khabarovsk, FE	873	300	2000-1600	RM
ST	Stavropol, E	882	30	0300-2200	RM, Reg
KT	Petrozavodsk, E	891	50	0300-2200	RY
TY	Tyumen, S	891	50	0100-2000	RM, Reg
ME	Sovetskiy, E	900	20	0300-2200	RM, Reg
AR	Arkhangelsk, E	918	150	0200-2200	RR, Reg
DA	Makhachkala, E	918	50	0300-2200	RM, Reg
KG	Shumikha, S	918	5	0100-2000	RM
KG	Makushino, S	918	5	0100-2000	RM
KG	Shadrinsk, S	918	7	0100-2000	RM
KN	Krasnoyarsk, S	936	5	2200-1800	RY
OB	Matveyevka, E	936	5	0000-2000	RR, Reg
RO	Novocherkassk, E	945	40	0200-2200	RR, Reg
BU	Zakamensk, S	963	25	2200-1800	RR, Reg
BU	Guzinoozersk, S	963	1	2200-1800	RR, Reg
SL	Yuzhno-Kurilsk, FE	972	0.2	1900-1400	RM
CB	Yuryuzan, E	990	1	0100-2000	RM
YV	Birobidzhan, FE	999	7	2000-1800	RM, Reg
KH	Khabarovsk, FE	1008	25	2000-1600	RY
KD	Tuapse, E	1008	5	0300-2200	RM
KM	Petropavlovsk-K., FE	1008	50	1800-1400	RY, Reg
AR	Porog, E	1026	5	0300-2200	RM
AR	Urdoma, E	1026	5	0300-2200	RM
AR	Nyandoma, E	1026	5	0300-2200	RM
NS	Oyash, S	1026	1000	… (*) …	GR
OB	Orenburg, E	1053	50	various	Reg
KM	Ust-Kamchatsk, FE	1062	1	1800-1300	RM
AM	Zeya, FE	1071	7	2100-1600	RM
IR	Angarsk, S	1080	1000	1200-1400	GR
MD	Kovylkino, E	1080	100	0200-2200	RR, Reg
KD	Tbilisskaya, E	1089	1200	0200-2200	RR, Reg, GR
KK	Tilichiki, FE	1089	5	1800-1400	RR, Reg
VO	Nikolsk, E	1098	5	0200-2200	RR, Reg
VO	Chagoda, E	1098	7	0200-2200	RR, Reg
SA	Samara, E	1107	150	various	Reg
KA	Bolshakovo, E	1116	75	various	Reg
KD	Sochi, E	1116	30	0200-2200	RR, Reg
SP	Olgino, E	1125	150	0300-2100	RO
MD	Kovylkino, E	1134	25	0300-2200	RM

Rg	Location	kHz	kW	H. of tr.	Prgr.
BR	Shvedchiki, E	1134	7	0300-2200	RM
RO	Volgodonsk, E	1134	5	0200-2200	RR, Reg
RO	Salsk, E	1134	5	0200-2200	RR, Reg
MU	Murmansk, E	1134	75	0300-2200	RM
RO	Veshenskaya, E	1134	5	0200-2200	RR, Reg
IR	Tayshet, S	1143	7	2200-1700	RM
SA	Mekhzavod, E	1143	150	0300-2200	RM
KA	Bolshakovo, E	1143	150	0200-2100	RM, GR
KH	Komsomolsk, FE	1152	50	2000-1600	RR, Reg
KY	Khanty-Mansiysk, S	1152	20	0000-2000	RR, Reg
MO	Kupavna, E	1152	150	0300-2100	RO
VG	Volgograd, E	1161	75	0300-2100	RO
KD	Tbilisskaya, E	1170	1200	... (*) ...	GR
CH	Mogocha, S	1197	0,2	2000-1600	RR, Reg
KY	Berezovo, S	1197	5	0000-2000	RR, Reg
CH	Ulety, S	1197	0.2	2000-1600	RR, Reg
CH	Nerchinsk, S	1197	0.2	2000-1600	RR, Reg
CH	Chernyshevsk, S	1197	0.2	0000-2000	RR, Reg
SR	Balakovo, E	1197	5	0200-2200	RR, Reg
SR	Balashov, E	1197	5	0200-2200	RR, Reg
SR	Yershov, E	1197	5	0200-2200	RR, Reg
AR	Plesetsk, E	1206	5	0300-2200	RM
IN	Nazran, E	1206	1	0300-2200	RM
KA	Bolshakovo, E	1215	1200	... (*) ...	GR
UD	Izhevsk, E	1251	7	0300-2200	RY
ST	Neftekumsk, E	1251	1	0300-2200	RM, Reg
ST	Letnyaya Stavka, E	1251	5	0300-2200	RM, Reg
KC	Cherkessk, E	1251	7	0300-2200	RM, Reg
PM	Ussuriysk, FE	1251	600	... (*) ...	GR
VG	Dubovka, E	1278	50	0200-2200	RY
SR	Balashov, E	1278	5	0200-2200	RY
SR	Saratov, E	1278	30	0200-2200	RY
UD	Balezino, E	1278	5	0200-2200	RY
SR	Yershov, E	1278	5	0200-2200	RY
RO	Novocherkassk, E	1278	50	0200-2200	RY
BU	Bagdarin, S	1278	5	2200-1800	RR
BU	Severobaykalsk, S	1278	7	2200-1800	RR, Reg
SR	Balakovo, E	1278	5	0200-2200	RY
KO	Syktyvkar, E	1287	10	0200-2200	RY
RT	Chadan, S	1287	7	2200-1800	RR, Reg
RT	Shagonar, S	1287	7	2200-1800	RR, Reg
BA	Yazykovo, E	1287	50	0200-2200	RY
KL	Sukhinichi, E	1287	5	0200-2200	RY
BU	Kyakhta, S	1287	5	2200-1800	RR, Reg
SV	Serov, E	1305	7	0100-2000	RM
IR	Ust-Kut, S	1305	7	2200-1700	RM
OB	Pleshanovo, E	1314	1	0000-2000	RR, Reg
RA	Ust-Kan, S	1350	5	2200-1800	RR, Reg
RA	Ust-Ulagan, S	1350	5	2200-1800	RR, Reg
PR	Perm, E	1359	50	0100-2000	RM
RA	Shebalino, S	1359	1	2300-1800	RM
RA	Onguday, S	1359	5	2300-1800	RM
RA	Choya, S	1359	1	2300-1800	RM
IR	Ust-Ilimsk, S	1359	7	2200-1700	RM
SV	Yekaterinburg, E	1377	50	0100-2000	RY
PM	Tavrichanka, FE	1377	75	2000-1500	RY
SL	Okha, FE	1377	5	1900-1400	RM
KA	Bolshakovo, E	§1386	1200	1200-1800	GR
KL	Obninsk, E	1386	5	0300-2200	RY
YA	Lyubim, E	1395	1	0200-2200	RY
YA	Volga, E	1395	5	0200-2200	RY
YA	Dubki, E	1395	1	0200-2200	RY
OB	Buguruslan, E	1395	5	0000-2000	RR, Reg
RS	Sangar, FE	1413		2000-1600	RR
ST	Stavropol, E	1413	30	0200-2200	RY
CH	Kuanda, S	1422	5	0000-2000	RR
RA	Kosh-Agach, S	1440	5	2200-1800	RR, Reg
RA	Ust-Koksa, S	1440	5	2200-1800	RR, Reg
MU	Kirovsk, E	1449	5	0300-2200	RM
MU	Umba, E	1449	7	0300-2200	RM
OL	Livny, E	1449	5	0200-2200	RR, Reg
BR	Unecha, E	1449	7	0300-2200	RM
MU	Monchegorsk, E	1449	42	0300-2200	RM
MU	Kandalaksha, E	1449	1	0300-2200	RM
MU	Ostrovnoy, E	1449	7	0300-2200	RM
MU	Nikel, E	1449	1	0300-2200	RM
BE	Valuyki, E	1458	5	0300-2200	RY
KP	Kudymkar	1458	7	0000-2000	RR, Reg
RA	Onguday, S	1476	20	2200-1800	RR, Reg
RS	Cherskiy, FE	1485	1	2100-1600	RM
RS	Olekminsk, FE	1485	0.2	2000-1600	RR
TY	Tyumen, S	1485	1	0000-2000	RR
RS	Solnechnyy, FE	1485	2	2100-1600	RM
KK	Kamenskoye, FE	1485	1	1800-1400	RR, Reg
YN	Krasnoselkup, S	1485	1	0000-2000	RR
YN	Gazsale, S	1485	1	0000-2000	RR
PR	Oktyabrskiy, E	1485	1	0000-2000	RR
RS	Batagay, FE	1485	1	2000-1600	RR
SP	Krasnyy Bor, E	1494	600	... (*) ...	GR, Relays
IR	Magistralnyy, S	1503	1	2200-1800	RR, Reg
YN	Salekhard, S	1503	5	0100-2000	RM
CV	Ibresi, E	1512	7	0200-0000	RY, Reg
PR	Chaykovskiy, E	1512	5	0000-2000	RR, Reg
KN	Boguchany, S	1521	5	2200-1800	RR
TS	Kazan, E	1521	20	0300-2200	RM
MU	Zapolyarnyy, E	1521	7	0300-2200	RM
CH	Krasnyy Chikoy, S	1530	5	2100-1600	RM
KD	Sochi, E	1539	5	0300-2200	RY
SL	Aleksandrovsk, FE	1548	10	1900-1400	RM
SL	Yu-Sakhalinsk, FE	1575	30	2000-1500	RY, Reg
KM	Klyuchi, FE	1584	1	1800-1400	RR, Reg
KK	Tigil, FE	1584	1	1800-1400	RR, Reg
RS	Ust-Nera, FE	1584	1	2100-1600	RM
RS	Khandyra, FE	1584	0.2	2000-1600	RR
RS	Aykhal, FE	1584	5	2100-1600	RM
BU	Taksimo, S	1584	1	2200-1800	RR
DA	Khunzakh, E	1584	7	0200-2200	RR
RS	Belk.Gora, FE	1584	0.2	2000-1600	RR
IR	Irkutsk, S	1593	50	2300-1700	RY
TY	Tyumen, S	1602	1	0100-2000	RY
BU	Novoilinsk, S	1602	1	2200-1800	RR
SL	Severo-Kurilsk, FE	1602	1	1900-1400	RM
BU	Ust-Barguzin, S	1602	1	2200-1800	RR
KP	Gayny, E	1602	5	0000-2000	RR, Reg
SL	Kurilsk, FE	1602	1	1900-1400	RM
KH	Chumikan, FE	1602	0.2	2000-1600	RR

(*) See International Radio section; §) Tx will be closed down on 1 November 2007.

Shortwaves

Rg	Location	kHz	kW	Hour of tr.	Prgr
BU	Selenga, S	4795	50	2200-1800	RR, Reg
MO	Moskva, E	**5895	250	1830-2200	RR
MO	Moskva, E	**5925	250	0200-0500	RR
MU	Monchegorsk, E	5930	50	0200-2200	RR
MA	Arman, FE	+5935	100	1800-0900	RR
MA	Arman, FE	++5940	100	1900-1500	RR
KD	Tbiliskaya, E	6005	100	1800-1900	R. Nalch./R. Cherk.
PR	Perm, E	6030	5	0100-1600	RR, Reg
RS	Yakutsk	++6060	5	2000-1600	RR, Reg
MA	Arman, FE	+6075	100	0930-1400	RR
KN	Krasnoyarsk, S	6085	50	2200-1800	RR, Reg
RT	Kyzyl, S	6100	5	2200-1800	RR, Reg
RS	Yakutsk, FE	+6150	50	2000-1600	RR, Reg
PR	Perm, E	++6150	5	0100-1600	RR, Reg
AR	Arkhangelsk, E	6160	40	0200-2200	RR, Reg
RS	Yakutsk, FE	7140	50	2000-1600	RR, Reg
RS	Yakutsk, FE	7200	100	2000-1600	RR, Reg
MO	Moskva, E	**7310	250	1530-1800	RR
MA	Arman, FE	7320	100	2000-1400	RR
RS	Yakutsk, FE	7345	50	2000-1600	RR, Reg
KM	Razdolnoye, FE	°9480	100	0740-0800	R/S Tihkiy Okean
PR	Perm, E	11650	5	1600-2000	RR, Reg
SL	Yu-Sakhal., FE	$11840	15	1800-1400	RR, Reg
SA	Samara, E	11915	200	0900-1000	Tatarstan dulk.
KM	Yelizovo, FE	11975	200	0000-0100	Kamchatka ryb.
MO	Moskva, E	**12075	250	0530-0800	RR
SA	Samara, E	15105	200	0500-0600	Tatarstan dulk.
SA	Samara, E	15105	200	0700-0800	Tatarstan dulk.
MO	Moskva, E	**17600	250	0830-1500	RR

+) winter only; ++) summer only (note: schedule always refers to winter time); °) preliminary service; $) USB

NOTE: **) These SW frequencies of R. Rossii are preliminary and subject to change/expand, depending on the plans of VGTRK.

D.PRGR: The national programmes **Radio Rossii (RR), Radio Mayak (RM), Radio Yunost (RY)** are produced around the clock in the Moscow studios in order to serve listeners in the numerous timezones of the Russian Federation. The FM & MW/LW transmitters in each zone are (with some exceptions) usually operating between early morning and 0100/0200 local time. R. Rossii is broadcast in a European edition (0000-2000) and in 4 time-shifted versions: "Dubl 4" via tx's in the region between Volga and the Urals; "Dubl 3" for We.Siberia: 2200-1800, "Dubl 2" for Ea.Siberia: 2000-1600, "Dubl 1" for the Russian Far East: 1800-1400. FM:

All national channels are broadcast over a large network of FM tx's, usually in the OIRT FM band (66-74 MHz). **Radio Mayak 24** ("metropolitan edition" of R. Mayak): 24h via CCIR FM tx's. **Radio Orfey (RO):** 0300-2100. **Radio Kultura (RK):** 24h on CCIR FM. **Radio Chechnya Svobodnaya (RChS):** ✉ ul. Pyatnitskaya 25, 115326 Moskva. Email: info@chechnyafree.ru **Web:** www.chechnyafree.ru. 0300-2100 in Russian (exc. Chechen W 1200-1210 & 1600-1610) for listeners in Chechnya on Tbilisskaya 171, Alpatovo 657kHz & FM tx's in Chechnya.

REGIONAL SERVICES (Gov.)
Regional state broadcasting companies (GTRK - gosudarstvennaya teleradiokompaniya) are providing the regional services in each of the 89 regions of the Russian Federation. These prgr's are broadcast for a few hours a day on tx's shared with national services, usually R. Rossii. The prgr's are embedded in newscasts from R. Rossii (RR); these RR newscasts are even relayed if the tx's are shared with other networks. There is also an opt-out for local advertisments on RR or RM frequencies. All GTRKs have regional services on FM, some also on AM. Many GTRKs have additional, full-time regional outlets on seperate frequencies, see below.
NOTE: Several regions are planned to merge and form new provinces. Local Time: [+3] - differences in hours to UTC (winter)
AB) Aginskiy Buryatskiy avt. okrug [+9]: Aginskaya Buryatskaya GTRK, ul. Bazara Rinchino 7, 687000 Aginskoye. Email: abgtrk@aginsk.chita.ru **Reg:** On Aginskoye 70.07MHz in Buryat, Russian: Mon 2230-2320, Tue/Fri 2300-2330, Wed/Thu 2300-2345, Tue/Wed 0410-0500, Sat 2300-2400, 0300-0400. Tr also relays Chitinskaya GTRK, Chita CH. [NB: AB is subordinated to region CH]
AD) Respublika Adygeya [+3]: GTRK "Adygeya", ul. Zhukovskogo 24, 352700 Maykop. Email: trkra@maykop.ru **Reg:** On Tbilisskaya 1089kHz (KD) + (MHz) Maykop 69.08, Koshekhabl 71.93, Takhtamukay 73.76 in Adyghian, Russian: W 0510-0600, 1310-1400. Tr's also relay GTRK "Kuban", Krasnodar KD. Channel "Adygeya+" on 67.88MHz: 24h.
AK) Altayskiy kray [+6]: GTRK "Altay", Zmeinogorskiy trakt 27a, 656020 Barnaul. Email: gtrk@ab.ru. **Reg:** On Gorno-Altaysk (RA) 279kHz + (MHz) Gornyak 66.59, Slavgorod 66.59, Mikhaylovka 66.59, Tselinnoye 66.74, Blagoveshchenka 66.95, Mamontovo 67.16, Ust-Kalmanka 67.85, Zmeinogorsk 68.15, B.Istok 68.27, Pankrushikha 68.36, Barnaul 68.60, Zarinsk 69.53, Rubtsovsk 69.68, Kamen-na-Obi 70.31, Shipunovo 70.35, Biysk 70.40 (also via tr's in region RA): MF 0100-0200, 0410-0500, 1300-1400; Sat 0200-0500; Sun 0500-0600. Channel "Heart FM" on 69.80MHz: 24h.
AM) Amurskaya oblast [+9]: GTRK "Amur", per. Svyatitelya Innokentiya 15, 675000 Blagoveshchensk. Email: vesty@tsl.ru **Reg:** On Belogorsk 189, Tynda 666kHz + (MHz) Skovorodino 67.22, Belogorsk 67.82, Progress 68.36, Shimanovsk 68.72, Svobodnyy 69.92, Blagoveshchensk 72.86: MF 2000-0000, 0300-0400, 0900-1000; Sat 2200-2300; Sun 0010-0100.
AR) Arkhangelskaya oblast [+3]: GTRK "Pomorye", ul. Popova 2, 163061 Arkhangelsk. Email: pomorie@atnet.ru. **Reg:** "R. Pomorya" on Arkhangelsk 918/6160kHz + (MHz) Arkhangelsk 66.08, Urdoma 66.38, Nyandoma 67.31, Karpogory 67.76, Plesetsk 69.23, Vazhskiy 69.56, Pogost 69.92, Pogor 70.19 (also via tr's in region NE): W 0400-0500, 1500-1600 (Sat 1510); Sun 0500-0600.
AS) Astrakhanskaya oblast [+3]: GTRK "Lotos", ul. Molodoy Gvardii 17, 414000 Astrakhan. Email: tvlotos@astranet.ru. **Reg:** On Astrakhan 792kHz + (MHz) Astrakhan 66.02, Chernyy Yar 69.98, Tambovka 70.16: MF 0320-0400, 0410-0500, 0910-1000, 1500-1520; Sat 0510-0600; Sun 0910-1000, 1520-1600.
BA) Resp. Bashkortostan [+5]: GTRK "Bashkortostan", ul. Gafuri 9/1, 450076 Ufa. Email: gtrk@bashinform.ru. **Reg:** "R. Bashkortostana" on (MHz) Neftekamsk 66.47, Mesyagutovo 66.86, Salavat 67.04, Baymak 67.16, Ufa 68.24, Belebey 70.61, Burayevo 71.90, Beloretsk 72.05 in Bashkir, Russian. Channel "R. Yuldash" on Ufa 162kHz + (MHz) Ufa 66.68, Mesyagutovo 68.60, Salavat 68.99, Baymak 69.20, Burayevo 70.04, Beloretsk 70.31, Belebey 72.20, Ufa 105.5 in Bashkir, Tatar: 0200-2000; Channel "R. Sputnik FM" on Ufa 107.0 in Russian.
BE) Belgorodskaya oblast [+3]: Belgorodskaya GTRK, ul. Frunze 60, 308000 Belgorod. Email: trcbg@belgtts.ru. **Reg:** On (MHz) Stroitel 66.17, Valuyki 66.80, Rakitnoye 68.39, Belgorod 70.16, Prokhorovka 70.76, Staryy Oskol 71.09, Borisovka 71.30: MF 0310-0400, 0510-0600, 1610-1700; Sat 0510-0600, 0710-0800, 1110-1200; Sun 0510-0600.
BR) Bryanskaya oblast [+3]: GTRK "Bryansk", ul. Stanke Dimitrova 77, 241033 Bryansk. Email: tvrc@online.bryansk.ru. **Reg:** On (MHz) Bryansk 67.58, Shvedchiki 70.04, Unecha 70.55, Trubchevsk 73.94: 0410-0500, 1120-1200, 1510-1600.
BU) Respublika Buryatiya [+8]: Buryatskaya GTRK, ul. Erbanova 7, 670000 Ulan-Ude. Email: office@bgtrk.ru. **Reg:** On Ulan-Ude 279, Zakamensk 963, Kyakhta 1278, Taksimo 1584, Selenga 4795kHz + (MHz) Severobaykalsk 66.30, Zakamensk 66.68, Ulan-Ude 69.74 in Buryat, Russian: 2200-0500, 1100-1200.
CB) Chelyabinskaya oblast [+5]: Chelyabinskaya GTRK, ul. Ordzhonikidze 54b, 454000 Chelyabinsk. Email: radio@cheltv.ru. **Reg:** On Chelyabinsk 738kHz + (MHz) Kartaly 66.65, Kyshtym 67.13, Yuryuzan 67.25, Stepnoye 68.36, Novoburino 70.82, Zlatoust 71.69, Magnitogorsk 71.81: MF 0100-0300, 0500-0600, 0710-0900, 1210-1400; Sat/Sun 0300-0400. Channel "Studiya 1": 0300-1900 on Chelyabinsk 738kHz + (MHz) Miass 65.90, Yuryuzan 68.03, Chelyabinsk 71.96, Zlatoust 72.47.
CC) Chechenskaya respublika [+3]: Chechenskaya GTRK, ul. Lenina 5, 366900 Gudermes. **Reg:** 0410-0500, 1110-1200, 1510-1600 on Groznyy 67.37/103.6MHz in Chechen, Russian.
CH) Chitinskaya oblast [+9]: Chitinskaya GTRK, ul. Kostyushko-Grigorovicha 27, 672090 Chita. Email: gnchrtv@mail.ru. **Reg:** On Kruchina 180, Mogocha/Nerchinsk/Ulety/Chernyshevsk 1197kHz + (MHz) Petrovsk-Zabaykalskiy 66.14, Chita 66.32, Khilok 68.09, Khada-Bulak 69.56, Kholbon 69.80, Orlovskiy 70.07, Krasnokamensk 70.67 in Russian, Buryat: 1959-2003, MF 2110-2200, D 2210-2300, MF 1000-1100, 1120-1200, Wed/Fri 1210-1300, Sat/Sun 2320-2400, 0010-0100, 0110-0200.
CK) Chukotskiy avt. okrug [+12]: GTRK "Chukotka", ul. Lenina 18, 686710 Anadyr. Email: gtrk@anadyr.ru. **Reg:** On Anadyr 693kHz + (MHz) 100.5 (6 tr's), 101.6 (6 tr's), 102.8 (2 tr's), 104.7 (Andayr & 7 tr's) in Chukchi, Eskimo, Russian: 1825-1900, MF 1940-2000, 2015-2100, Sat 2115-2145, Thu 0115-0145, MF 0700-0800, Mon/Wed/Fri 0815-0900. Tr's also relay GTRK "Magadan", Magadan MA. (NB: CK is subordinated to region MA)
CV) Chuvashskaya respublika - Chavash [+3]: GTRK "Chuvashiya", ul. Nikolayeva 10, 428020 Cheboksary. Email: gtrk@tvr.chtts.ru. **Reg:** On Cheboksary 531, Ibresi 1512kHz + (MHz) Cheboksary 67.04, Ibresi 72.41 in Chuvash, Russian: MF 0310-0400, 0910-1000, 1500-1610; Sat 0310-0500, 0800-0825, 1400-1710; Sun 0400-0600. Channel "Vashe R." on 67.82MHz: 0200-2200.
DA) Respublika Dagestan [+3]: GTRK "Dagestan", ul. Magomeda Gadzhieva 182, 367032 Makhachkala. Email: gtrk-rd@datacom.ru **Reg:** On Makhachkala/Kochubey 621kHz + (MHz) Kochubey 67.04, Makhachkala 68.87, Gergebil 69.95. Russian: D 0340-0400, Sat 0800-0900 & 1215-1300, Sun 0525-0600 & 0820-0900, Wed 0815-0900, 1500-1540/1600. Other times in various minority languages.
EV) Evenkiyskiy avt. okrug [+7]: Evenkiyskaya GTRK "Kheglen", ul. 50 let Oktyabrya 28, 663370 Tura. **Reg:** In Evenki, Russian: D 0100-0200, 0500-0515. (NB: EV is subordinated to region KN)
IN) Ingushskaya respublika [+3]: GTRK "Ingushetiya", ul. Moskovskaya 33, 247520 Nazran. **Reg:** On Nazran 1206 kHz in Ingush, Russian.
IR) Irkutskaya oblast [+8]: Irkutskaya GTRK, ul. Gorkogo 15, 664003 Irkutsk. Email: igtrk@irmail.ru. **Reg:** On Angarsk 234kHz + (MHz) Zhmurovo 66.32, Zheleznogorsk 66.56, Ulkan 66.62, Tulun 66.74, Ust-Ilimsk 66.80, Chuna 67.10, Tayshet 69.80, Nizhneudinsk 70.04, Bratsk 70.28, Irkutsk 70.31, Ust-Kut 70.64, Zima 72.14, Ust-Ordynskiy 107.8: 2110-2200, 2210-2310; Fri 2300-2310; Sun 0000-0130; Sat 0100-0200; MF 0300-0310, 1000-1100. Ust-Ordynskiy okrug prgr: W0010-0040 in Buryat, Russian.
IV) Ivanovskaya oblast [+3]: GTRK "Ivteleradio", ul. Teatralnaya 31, 153647 Ivanovo. Email: admin@ivanovo-tv.ru. **Reg:** On (MHz) Rodniki 70.13, Ivanovo 71.21: MF 0330-0400, 1110-1200, 1510-1600; SS 0610-0700, 1110-1200, 1425-1500. Channel "Ivanovo 104,2"on 104.2MHz: 24h.
KA) Kaliningradskaya oblast [+2]: GTRK "Yantar", ul. Klinicheskaya 19, 236016 Kaliningrad. Email: tv-rv@baltnet.ru. **Reg:** On Bolshakovo 1116kHz + (MHz) Veselovka 65.90, Kaliningrad 66.02/102.5: MF 0510-0700, 1500-1520; Sat 0610-0700, 1300-1400; Sun 0600-1100, 1300-1500. Channel "Baltiyskaya volna" on Kaliningrad 102.5MHz: W 0500 (Sat 0600)-2100; Sun 0100-2200.
KB) Kabardino-Balkarskaya respublika [+3]: GTRK "Kabbalkteleradio", pr. Lenina 3, 360000 Nalchik. Email: tvkbr@mail.ru. **Reg:** On (MHz) Samarkovo 66.62, Nalchik 70.52 in Kabardino-Circassian, Balkar, Russian: 0400-0700, 1400-1600.
KC) Karachayevo-Cherkesskaya respublika [+3]: GTRK "Karachayevo-Cherkesiya", ul. Krasnoarmeyskaya 51, 357100 Cherkessk. Email: vgtrk@khakasnet.ru. **Reg:** On Cherkessk 1251kHz + (MHz) Adyge-Khabl 68.66, Cherkessk 70.31, V.Mara 71.06, in Abaza, Circassian, Karachay, Nogay, Russian: 0330-0400, 0615-0700, 0715-0800 (Tue-Sun), 0815-0900 (Thu/Fri), 1300-1400, 1415-1500 (Mon/Fri), 1645-1745 (Mon/Wed).
KD) Krasnodarskiy kray [+3]: GTRK "Kuban", ul. Radio 5, 350038 Krasnodar. Email: root@gtrc.kuban.ru. **Reg:** "Radiostantsiya Kuban" on Tbilisskaya 1089, Sochi 1116kHz + (MHz) Tbilisskaya 66.20, Novorossiysk 67.97, Kanevskaya 68.36, Krasnyy Kut 70.43, Psebay 70.43, Krasnodar 71.81, Sochi 71.93 (also via tr's in region AD): MF 0410-0500, 0710-0800, 1510-1600; Sun 0910-1000. – Sochinskaya GTRK: ul. Teatralnaya 11a, 354000 Sochi. Email: sgtrk@sochi.ru. **Reg:** On Sochi 71.93MHz: MF 1045-1100, 1600-1615, Tue-Sat 0445-0500, Sat 1200-1300.
KE) Komerovskaya oblast [+7]: GTRK "Kuzbass", ul. Krasnoarmeyskaya 137a, 650099 Kemorovo. Email: admin@gtrk.kuzbass.net. **Reg:** On (MHz) Yugra 66.11, Novokuznetsk 66.20, Kemerovo 66.56, Klyuchevaya 67.04, Leninsk-Kuznetskiy 69.71, Tashtagol 69.80, Anzhevo-Sudzhensk 70.40, Mezhdurechensk 70.64: MF 0000-0100, 0510-0600, 1120-1200; Tue-Thur 1300-1500; Sat 0100-0200, 1000-1100. Channel "Kuzbass-FM" on Kemerovo 102.3MHz: 24h.
KG) Kurganskaya oblast [+5]: Kurganskaya GTRK, ul. Sovetskaya 105,

640018 Kurgan. Email: report@kurgan.isp.ru. **Reg:** On (MHz) Shumikha 66.89, Makushino 68.48, Shadrinsk 69.23, Kurgan 71.87: W 0315-0330 & 0410-0440, MF 1300-1400.

KH) Khabarovskiy kray [+10]: GTRK "Dalnevostochnaya", ul. Lenina 4, 682632 Khabarovsk. Email: main@dvtrk.khv.ru. **Reg:** On Khabarovsk 621, Okhotsk 711, Komsomolsk-na-Amure 1152kHz + (MHz) Ayan 68.00, Chumikan 68.12, Komsomolsk 68.72, Okhotsk 69.32, Glebovo 69.47, Vyazemskiy 69.83, Bikin 69.92, Chegdomyn 70.16, Khabarovsk 72.80 (also via tr's in region YV): schedule not available. Channel "R. 101.8" on Khabarovsk 101.8MHz: 24h.

KK) Koryakskiy avt. okrug [+12]: Koryakskaya GTRK "Palana", ul. Obukhova 4, 684620 Palana. Email: palana_tv@svyaz.kamchatka.ru. **Reg:** On Palana 738, Tilichiki 1089, Tigil 1584, Palana 4520kHz in Koryak, Russian: D 2000-2030, Tue-Thu 2145-2200, Tue-Wed 0115-0145, Sat 0700-0800. Tr's also relay GTRK "Kamchatka", Petropavlovsk-Kam. KM. (NB: KK is subordinated to region KM)

KL) Kaluzhskaya oblast [+3]: GTRK "Kaluga", Pole Svobody 40a, 248021 Kaluga. Email: gtrk@kaluga.ru. **Reg:** On (MHz) Kaluga 66.23, Sukhinichi 69.62: MF 0410-0500, 1500-1600; Sat 1100-1200.

KM) Kamchatskaya oblast [+12]: GTRK "Kamchatka", ul. Sovetskaya 62, 683000 Petropavlovsk-Kamchatskiy. Email: gtrkbuh@mail.iks.ru. **Reg:** On Yelizovo 180, Klyuchi 1584kHz + Petropavlovsk 69.68MHz (also via tr's in region KK): W1830-2000 (Sat 1900), Sat/Sun 2030-2100, Fri 0000-0100, MF 0720-0800.

KN) Krasnoyarskiy kray [+7]: Krasnoyarskaya GTRK "Tsentr Rossii", ul. Mechnikova 44a, 660028 Krasnoyarsk. Email: new@public.krasnet.ru **Reg:** On Krasnoyarsk 216/6085kHz + (MHz) Dikson 66.13, Dudinka 66.25, Balakhta 66.32, B.Uluy 67.40, Krasnoyarsk 68.09, Solyanka 68.84, Novomikhaylovka 69.23, Uzhur 69.56, Shira 70.16, Achinsk 70.52, Tyukhtet 71.42, Yeniseysk 72.74 (also via tr's in regions EV and TM): MF 2310-0100, 1110-1300; Sat/Sun 0000-0400.

KO) Resp. Komi [+3]: GTRK "Komi gor", Oktyabrskiy pr. 164, 167610 Syktyvkar. Email: komigor@online.ru. **Reg:** On Syktyvkar 621kHz + (MHz) Yarashyu 65.90, Priuralsk 66.35, Ukhta 66.44, Vorkuta 66.60, Syktyvkar 66.80, Pechora 66.92, Ust-Tsilma 67.10, Sludka 67.16, Kadzherom 68.30, N.Odes 68.36, Troitsko-Pechorsk 68.60, Shoshka 68.72, Aykino 68.78, Kartayel 68.93, Shchelyabozh 68.93, Trakt 68.96, Meshchura 69.02, Mordino 69.05, Inta 69.08, Krasnobor 69.11, Okunevo 69.20, Usogorsk 69.56, Koygorodok 69.74, Myyeldino 69.83, Ust-Kulom 70.16, Petrun 70.28, Vetyu 70.40, Voyvozh 70.64, Vuktyl 71.06, Kuratovo 71.09, B.Pyssa 71.15, Usinsk 73.31, Vekshor 73.31 in Komi, Russian: MF 0310-0500, 1100-1110, 1510-1600; Sat/Sun 0400-0500.

KP) Komi-Permaytskiy avt. okrug [+3]: see PR Permskiy kray.

KS) Kostromskaya oblast [+3]: Kostromskaya GTRK, ul. Nikitskaya 10, 156005 Kostroma. Email: gtrk@gtrk.kmtn.ru. **Reg:** On (MHz) Bogovarovo 66.20, Vokhma 66.98, Kostroma 69.86, Galich 66.74, Sharya 67.10, Ostrovskoye 72.26, Pavino 73.10, Chukhloma 73.64, Pyshchug 73.88: MF 0400-0500, Sun-Fri 1600-1710, Sat/Sun 0600-0700.

KT) Respublika Kareliya (Karjalan tasavalta) [+3]: GTRK "Kareliya", ul. Pirogova 2, 185630 Petrozavodsk. Email: gtrk@onego.ru. **Reg:** On Pedaselga 765kHz + (MHz) Nadvoitsy 66.29, Sortavala 67.13, Naystenyarvi 69.80, Loukhi 70.07, Kostomuksha 70.28, Petrozavodsk 70.52, Muyezerskiy 72.17, Medvezhyegorsk 72.47 in Russian, Finnish, Karelian, Vepsian: MF 0410-0500, 0510-0610, 1210-1300, 1510-1600; Sat 0510-0600, 0610-0700, 0710-0800, 1210-1300, 1510-1600; Sun 0610-0700, 0810-0900, 1110-1200, 1410-1500.

KU) Kurskaya oblast [+3]: GTRK "Kursk", ul. Sovetskaya 32, 305016 Kursk. Email: vvo@vit.kursk.ru. **Reg:** On (MHz) Kursk 69.71, Kshenskiy 72.41: W 0300-0400, 1500-1600, Sun 0400-0500, 0800-0900.

KV) Kirovskaya oblast [+3]: GTRK "Vyatka", ul. Uritskogo 34, 610002 Kirov. Email: office@kgtrk.vyatka.ru. **Reg:** On (MHz) Vyatskiye Polyarny 66.35, Kirov 66.92, Kirs 66.86, Klyuchi 67.91, Pinyug 70.55, Shmelevo 70.73, Urzhum 71.06, Omutninsk 71.33, Sanchursk 73.28: MF 0310-0400, 0910-1000, 1510-1600; Sat/Sun 0510-0600, 1510-1600. Channel "Vyatka region" on 66.47/101.4MHz: 24h.

KX) Respublika Kalmykiya-Khalmg Tangch [+3]: Kalmykskaya GTRK, ul. M. Gorkogo 34, 358000 Elista. Email: tele@elista.ru. **Reg:** On Elista 846kHz + (MHz) Sadovoye 66.95, Elista 67.28, Utta 68.24, Ulan-Kholl 69.59 in Kalmyk, Russian: W 0320-0400, 0410-0500, MF 1600-1700, Mon 1200-1210, Tues-Fri 1100-1120, Sat 1100-1200, 1700-1800.

KY) Khanty-Mansiyskiy avt. okrug [+5]: Khanty-Mansiyskaya GTRK "Yugoriya", ul. Mira 7, 626200 Khanty-Mansiysk. Email: yugoriya@hmansy.wsnet.ru. **Reg:** "R. Yugry" on Surgut 225kHz + (MHz) Khanty-Mansiysk 66.08, Beloyarskiy 67.22, Langepas 67.28, Surgut 68.84, Nyagan 70.82, Beryozovo 71.42, Kogalym 71.30, Yugorsk 71.78, Nizhnevartovsk 72.56 in Khanti, Mansi, Russian: Tue-Fri 0200-0230, Mon 0210-0230, W 0800-0900, Sat 0400-0500. FM tr's also relay GTRK "Region-Tyumen", TY. (NB: KY is subordinated to region TY)

LI) Lipetskaya oblast [+3]: GTRK "Lipetsk", pl. Plekhanova 1, 398050 Lipetsk. Email: glavred@ltr.lipetsk.ru. **Reg:** On (MHz) Lipetsk 66.53, Izmalkovo 73.79, Terbuny 101.9, Ploty 102.6, Usman 104.0, Volovo 104.4: 0320-0500, 1520-1600.

MA) Magadanskaya oblast [+11]: GTRK "Magadan", ul. Kommuny 8/12, 685024 Magadan. Email: center@gtrvk.magadan.su. **Reg:** On Arman 234kHz : D 0010-0100, MF 2000-2100 & 0115-0200 & 0320-0400 & 0720-0800, Sat/Sun 2020-2100, Sat 0111-0120(0200). Local prgr on 105.0MHz.

MD) Respublika Mordoviya [+3]: GTRK "Mordoviya", ul. Dokuchayeva 29, 430000 Saransk. Email: gtrk@whrm.moris.ru. **Reg:** On Kovylkino 1080kHz + (MHz) Tengushevo 66.35, Saransk 66.68, Dubenki 67.28, B.Ignatovo 67.34, Ruzayevka 67.46, Yavas 67.67, Umet 68.33, B.Berezniki 68.42, Torbeyevo 68.69, Chamzinka 68.75, Kovylkino 69.14, Ardatov 69.53, St.Shaygovo 69.65, Insar 71.03, Romodanovo 71.12, Atyuryevo 71.33 in Mordvin, Russian: MF 0040-0500, 0900-1100, 1520-1600, Sat 1300-1400, Sun 0400-0500, 1400-1500.

ME) Respublika Mariy El [+3]: GTRK "Mariy-El", ul. Osipenko 50, 424014 Yoshkar-Ola. Email: gtrk@mari.infotel.ru. **Reg:** On Sovietskiy 900kHz + (MHz) Yoshkar-Ola 70.34, Sovetskiy 71.21, Kozmodemyansk 72.20 in Mari, Russian: W 0310-0400, D 0410-0500 (Sun 0600), MF 1500-1600, Mon, Sat 1610-1700, Sun 1410-1600.

MO) Moskva & Moskovskaya oblast [+3]: GRK "R. Podmoskovya", ul. Korolyova 13, 129515 Moskva. Email: onekishev@gtrk.m5.ru. **Reg:** On Noginsk 846kHz + (MHz) Chekhov 65.90, Moskva 66.44, Serebryanyye Prudy 67.67, Kolomna 67.70, Ruza 67.73, Lukhovitsy 69.98, Klin 70.43, Zosimova Pustyn 70.49, Ramenskoye 70.76, Solechnogorsk 70.82, Taldom 100.2, Stupino 100.3, Istra 100.7, Sergiyev Posad 100.7, Podolsk 100.8, Mozhaysk 101.6, Orekhovo-Zuyevo 102.1, Dmitrov 102.8, Voskressensk 102.8, Serpukhov 104.0, Pavlovskiy Posad 104.5, Noginsk 107.3: 0300-0400 (Sat/Sun not on 66.44MHz); MF 0800-0900; Fri/Sat 1400-1500; Mon-Thu 1600-1700; Sun 1000-1100.

MU) Murmanskaya oblast [+3]: GTRK "Murman", per. Rusanova 7, 183032 Murmansk. Email: radio@tvmurman.com. **Reg:** On (MHz) Murmansk 67.22/103.5, Kandalaksha 67.70, Zapolyarnyy 69.74, Kirovsk 70.34: 0400-0500, 0800-0810, 0910-1010, 1510-1600, 1610-1700.

NE) Nenetskiy avt. okrug [+3]: Nenetskaya GTRK "Zapolyarye", ul. Smidovicha 19, 164700 Naryan-Mar. Email: choom@atnet.ru. **Reg:** On Naryan-Mar 711kHz + 66.20MHz: 0330-0400 in Nenets, Russian. Tr's also relay GTRK "Pomorye", Arkhangelsk AR. (NB: NE is subordinated to region AR)

NN) Nizhegorodskaya oblast [+3]: Nizhegorodskaya OGTRK, ul. Belinskogo 9a, 603600 Nizhniy Novgorod. Email: ntr@nts.ru. **Reg:** On (MHz) Sergach 67.16, N.Novgorod 67.94, Arzamas 69.95, Krasnyye Baki 70.64, Vyksa 71.09, Shakhunya 71.69, Lukoyanov 72.50: MF 0320-0350, 0410-0500 0800-0810, 1520-1600, Sat 0510-0520, 1010-1100, 1120-1200, 1210-1300.

NO) Novgorodskaya oblast [+3]: GTRK "Slaviya", ul. B.Moskovskaya 106, 173620 Novgorod Velikiy. Email: radio@slavia.natm.ru. **Reg:** "R. Slaviya" on (MHz) Borovichi 69.02, Zaluchye 71.93, Novgorod 71.39: MF 0310-0330, 0410-0500, 0910-1000, 1310-1400, 1510-1600; Sat 0510-0600.

NS) Novosibirskaya oblast [+6]: GTRK "Novosibirsk", ul. Rimskogo-Korsakova 9, 630048 Novosibirsk. Email: gtrknsk@drbit.ru. **Reg:** On Novosibirsk 270kHz (in part) + (MHz) Chulym 66.35, Vengerovo 66.35, Severnoye 66.50, Ust-Tarka 66.62, Suzun 66.68, Ordynskoye 66.74, Kargat 66.89, Kyshtovka 66.98, Chistoozernoye 67.04, Dovolnoye 67.28, Proletarskiy 67.52, Novosibirsk 67.88, Bagan 68.36, Ubinskoye 68.63, Kyshovka 68.84, Karasuk 68.93, Osinovskiy 68.93, Zdvinsk 68.96, Maslyanino 69.05, Kuybyshev 69.68, Kochki 69.95, Krasnozerskoye 69.95, Cherepanovo 70.10, Moshkovo 70.22, Tatarsk 71.60, Kisilevka 71.66, Beloye 72.08: Sun-Fri 0010-0100, 0110-0200, 0210-0300, 0500-0510, 0710-0900, 1110-1400.

OB) Orenburgskaya oblast [+5]: GTRK "Orenburg", per. Televizionnyy 3, 460024 Orenburg. Email: gtrc@public.orenburg.ru. **Reg:** On Orenburg 270, Matveyevka 936, Pleshanovo 1314, Buguruslan 1395kHz + (MHz) Orenburg 66.02, Buzuluk 66.62, Orsk 66.92, Yasnyy 69.71, Kuvandyk 70.04 in Russian, Chuvash, Tatar: 0110-0300, 0700-0810, 1400-1410, 1600-1610. Channel "R. Menovoy dvor" on Orenburg 1053kHz.

OL) Orlovskaya oblast [+3]: Orlovskaya GTRK, ul. 7 noyabrya 43, 302028 Oryol. Email: post@ogtrk.oryol.ru. **Reg:** On Livny 1449kHz + (MHz) Livny 67.19, Oryol 70.3. Channel "R. Ekspress" on (MHz) Oryol 100.4, Livny 100.8MHz: 0500-2100.

OM) Omskaya oblast [+6]: GTRK "Irtysh", pr. Mira 2, 644050 Omsk. Email: gtrk@dionis.omskelecom.ru. **Reg:** On Omsk 639kHz + (MHz) Isilkul 66.50, Ust-Ishim 67.04, Nazyvayevsk 67.28, Tara 68.39, Khutora 70.43, Cherlak 71.06: D 0100-0200, Sat/Sun 0400-0600, D 1300-1400.

PM) Primorskiy kray [+10]: Tikhookeanskaya GTRK "Vladivostok", ul. Uborevicha 20a, 690091 Vladivostok. Email: ptr@ptr-vlad.ru. **Reg:** On Razdolnoye 243kHz + (MHz) Nakhodka 66.74, Arsenyev 68.60, Dalnerechensk 69.32, Dalnegorsk 70.04, Novozhatkovo 70.64, Vladivostok 71.84, Chkalovka 72.08: MF 2000-0200, 0300-0400, 0800-0900; Sat 2100-0300; Sun 2100-2400.

PR) Permskiy kray [+5]: Permskaya GTRK "T-7", ul. Tekhnicheskaya 7, 614070 Perm. Email: main@t7.ru. **Reg**: On Perm 585kHz + (MHz) Perm 66.02, Kungur 66.65, Barda 67.10, Ilyinskiy 68.93, Uinskoye 69.38, Karagay

69.53, Chusovoy 70.67, Krasnovishersk 71.33, Berezniki 71.87 (also via tr's in region KP): MF 0210-0300, 0310-0400, 1310-1400; Wed 1610-1700; Sat 0210-0300, 0810-0900; Sun 0410-0500. Channel "R. Alfa" on Perm 104.1MHz: 24h. – GTRK "Komi Permyatskaya", ul. Volodarskogo 18, 617240 Kudymkar. Email: kudym-osh@permonline.ru. **Reg:** On Kudymkar 1458, Gayny 1602kHz + (MHz) Kudymkar 67.19, Gayny 67.34, Ust-Chernaya 68.84, Kosa 73.10 in Komi, Russian: MF 0230-0300, 1410-1500; Sat 0200-0300; Sun 0230-0300. Tx's also relay GTRK "T-7". NB. Permskiy kray is a merger of Permskaya oblast & Komi-Permaytskiy avt. okrug (to be established December 2005).

PS) Pskovskaya oblast [+3]: GTRK "Pskov", ul. Nekrasova 50, 180000 Pskov. Email: tv-pskov@ellink.ru. **Reg:** On (MHz) Pskov 66.05, Trutnevo 67.34, Novosokolniki 67.94, Dedovichi 69.86, Glubokoye 71.27: MF 0410-0500, 1610-1700, Sat 0610-0900, Thurs, Fri 1510-1600. Channel "R. Pilot" on Velikiye Luki 67.25, Pskov 71.99MHz.

PZ) Penzenskaya oblast [+3]: Penzenskaya GTRK, ul. Lermontova 39, 440602 Penza. Email: tvpenza@penza.com.ru. **Reg:** On Kamenka 855kHz + (MHz) Pachelma 66.80, Meshcherskoye 66.84, Blagodatka 69.08, Penza 70.67: W 0400-0500, 0800-0810, 1510-1600.

RA) Respublika Altay [+7]: GTRK "Gornyy Altay", ul. Choros-Gurkina 38, 659700 Gorno-Altaysk. Email: info@gtrk.gorny.ru. **Reg:** On Gorno-Altaysk 279, Ust-Kan/Ust-Ulagan 1350, Ust-Koksa 1440, Unguday 1476kHz + (MHz) Tashanta 67.10, Gorno-Altaysk 67.22, Onguday 71.66, Tiyakhty 71.66 in Altai, Russian: MF 2310-2400, 1110-1200. Tr's also relay GTRK "Altay", Barnaul AK.

RK) Respublika Khakasiya [+7]: GTRK Respubliki Khakasiya, ul. Vyatkina 12, 662000 Abakan. Email: vgtrk@mtk.khakasnet.ru. **Reg:** On Abakan 792kHz + (MHz) Abaza 66.02, Abakan 66.89, Kopyevo 68.00, Tashtyp 71.00, Askiz 72.59, Cheremushki 73.01, Sorsk 73.19, Beya 73.61 in Khakass, Russian: MF 0010-0100 & 1120-1200, Sat 0110-0200 & 0320-0400, Sun 0320-0400.

RO) Rostovskaya oblast [+3]: GTRK "Don-TR", ul. 1-ya Barrikadnaya 18, 344101 Rostov-na-Donu. Email: dontr@rost.ru. **Reg:** On Novocherkassk 945, Salsk/Volgodonsk/Veshenskaya 1134kHz + (MHz) Salsk 66.86, Morozovsk 67.07, Volgodonsk 70.13, Kamensk 70.28, Veshenskaya 70.67, Rostov-na-Donu 72.95: MF 0410-0500, 0710-0800, 1310-1400, 1510-1600, 1610-1700; Sat/Sun 0500-0700, Sun 1510-1600.

RS) Respublika Sakha (Yakutiya) [+9]: NVK "Sakha", ul. Ordzhonikidze 48, 677007 Yakutsk. Email: nbc@nbcsakha.ru. **Reg:** On Yakutsk 171/6060(su)6150(wi)/7140/7200/7345kHz + (MHz) Neryungri 66.68, Aldan 69.38, Yakutsk 70.40/106.5 in Yakut, Russian: MF 2120-2300; Tue-Fri 0410-0500; MF 0910-1010, 1200-1300; Sat/Sun 2210-2300, 2310-2400; Sun 0310-0400; Sat/Sun 0410-0455.

RT) Respublika Tyva [+7]: GTRK "Tyva", ul. Gornaya 31, 667003 Kyzyl. Email: tv@tuva.ru. **Reg:** On Kyzyl 567, Shagonar/Chadan 1287, Kyzyl 6100kHz + (MHz) Kyzyl 67.10, Shagonar 70.64 in Tuvinian, Russian: 0010-0100, 0110-0200, 1310-1400.

RY) Ryazanskaya oblast [+3]: GTRK "Oka", ul. Skomoroshinskaya 20, 390006 Ryazan. Email: okatv@org.etr.ru. **Reg:** On (MHz) Kadom 68.03, Ryazan 69.32, Yermish 69.35, Mosolovo 71.66: MF 0400-0500, Mon-Thurs 1510 (Mon 1500)-1600; Sat 0500-0600.

SA) Samarskaya oblast [+4]: GTRK "Samara", ul. Sovetskoy Armii 205, 443011 Samara. Email: office@tvsam.samara.ru. **Reg:** On (MHz) Sergiyevsk 66.71, Zhigulevsk 67.31, Samara 70.31, B. Glushitsa 71.15: MF 0300-0400, 1400-1500; Sat/Sun 0600-0800.

SL) Sakhalinskaya oblast [+10]: GTRK "Sakhalin", ul. Komsomolskaya 209, 693000 Yuzhno-Sakhalinsk. Email: romanov@gtrk.sakhalin.su. **Reg:** On Vestochka 279, Aleksandrovsk-Sakhalinskiy 792, Yuzhno-Sakhalinsk 11840kHz (parttime, USB) + (MHz) Smirnykh 68.69, Okha 69.20, Aleksandrovsk-Sakhalinskiy 69.44, Gornozavodsk 69.50, Nogliki 69.56, Poronaysk 69.92, Tomari 70.16, Uglegorsk 70.40, Shebunino 71.63, Korsakov 72.29, Nevelsk 101.7, Dolinsk 102.0, Kholmsk 104.8, Yuzhno-Sakhalinsk 106.0: 2000-2100, 0210-0300, 0800-0815, 1120-1210. Local prgr on Yuzhno-Sakhalinsk 106.0MHz: 2000-1600.

SM) Smolenskaya oblast [+3]: GTRK "Smolensk", ul. Nakhimova 1, 214025 Smolensk. Email: tvsmol@sci.smolensk.ru. **Reg:** On (MHz) Smolensk 68.54, Smogiri 68.96, Vyazma 69.20, Roslavl 70.91: W 0410-0500, MF 1510-1600; Sat 1200-1400.

SO) Respublika Severnaya Osetiya - Alaniya [+3]: GTRK "Alaniya", Osetinskaya gorka 2, 362007 Vladikavkaz. Email: radio@osetia.ru. **Reg:** On Vladikavkaz 594kHz + (MHz) Vladikavkaz 71.24, Mozdok 71.78 in Ossetic, Russian: W 0430-0500 & 0525-0600 (Mon 0545), Sun 0800-0900 & 1000-1200, Sat 0945-1100, Wed 1300-1400, MF 1500-1540/1600.

SP) Sankt Peterburg & Leningradskaya oblast [+3]: TRK "Peterburg", ul. Chapygina 6, 197376 Sankt-Peterburg. Email: admin@spbtv.ru **Reg:** "Radio Peterburg" on (MHz) Kingisepp 66.59, Vyborg 67.79, Tikhvin 68.63, Budogoshch 69.26, St.Peterburg 69.47, Priozersk 70.82, Luga 70.88, Podporozhye 71.06, Yefimovskiy 72.05MHz: 0300-2100.

SR) Saratovskaya oblast [+3]: GTRK "Saratov", 2-ya Sadovaya 7, 410004 Saratov. Email: radio@tv.saratov.ru **Reg:** On Balakovo/Balashov/Yershov 1197kHz + (MHz) Perelyub 66.44, Yershov 66.48, Aleksandrov Gay 69.68, Balashov 70.16, Balakovo 70.52, Saratov 71.09: D 0410-0500, MF1510-1600.

ST) Stavropolskiy kray [+3]: Stavropolskaya GTRK, ul. Artema 35a, 355000 Stavropol. Email: vice@stavtvradio.ru. **Reg:** "R. Rus" on Stavropol 882kHz + (MHz) Ipatovo 66.77, Pyatigorsk 68.96, Stavropol 69.53, Neftekumsk 70.01: MF 0400-0500; SS 0600-0700; D 1500-1600. Channel "R. Rus" on Stavropol 73.10MHz: 0300-2100.

SV) Sverdlovskaya oblast [+5]: Sverdlovskaya GTRK, ul. Lunacharskogo 212, 620219 Yekaterinburg. Email: admin@sgtrk.e-burg.ru. **Reg:** "R. Ural" on Yekaterinburg 279kHz + (MHz) Talitsa 65.93, Alapayevsk 66.50, Zaykovo 66.83, Nizhniye Sergi 67.01, Ivdel 67.76, Rezh 69.17, Bisert 69.20, Baranchinskiy 69.29, Serov 69.65, Andronovo 70.16, Afanasyevskoye 70.43, Azanka 70.43, Yekaterinburg 71.06, Pyshma 71.24, Kamyshlov 72.53: MF 0110-0300, 0910-1000, 1310-1400; Sat 0410-0720; Sun 0410-0700.

TA) Tambovskaya oblast [+3]: Tambovskaya GTRK, ul. Michurinskaya 8a, 392720 Tambov. Email: tgtrk@mtts-tambov.ru. **Reg:** On Tambov 71.00MHz: W 0359-0400, 1510-1600, MF 0400-0510, Sat 0459-0500, 0510-0610, 0700-0720, 1710-1810.

TL) Tulskaya oblast [+3]: GTRK "Tula", Staronikitskaya ul. 1, 300600 Tula. Email: tvtula@tula.net. **Reg:** On (MHz) Efremov 66.92, Tula 71.15, Novomoskovsk 72.35, Suvorov 102.4: MF 0400-0600, Sat 0500-0600, D 1500-1600.

TM) Taymyrskiy (Dolgano-Nenetskiy) avt. okrug [+7]: GTRK "Taymyr", ul. Gorgogo 15, 647000 Dudinka. Email: gtrktaimyr@dudinka.krasnet.ru. **Reg:** On Norilsk 162kHz + 69.68/104.0MHz in Nenets, Russian: MF 0030-0100, 0610-0700, 1210-1300, Sat/Sun 0510-0600. Tr's also relay GTRK "Tsentr Rossii", Krasnoyarsk KN. (NB: TM is subordinated to region KN)

TO) Tomskaya oblast [+6]: GTRK "Tomsk", ul. Pushkina 19, 634003 Tomsk ul Yakovleva 5, 634050 Tomsk. Email: adm@gtrk.tsu.ru. **Reg:** On Oyash (NS) 171kHz + (MHz) Aleksandrovskoye 66.02, Kozhevnikovo 67.01, Tomsk 67.22, Krivosheino 67.31, Malinovka 68.39, Parabel 68.45, Kolpashevo 68.87, Strezhevoy 66.78, St.Yuvala 68.15, Strezhevoy 68.51, Teguldet 68.60, Koplashevo 68.87, Podgornoye 69.20, Belyy Yar 69.56, Bakchar 70.01, Kargasok 71.42, Asino 71.57, Molchanovo 71.84, Krasnyy Yar 72.17, Chilino 72.20, Zyryanskoye 73.01, Volodino 73.40: MF 0010-0100, 0110-0200, 0500-0600, 1110-1200, 1310-1400; Sat 0110-0200, 0310-0400; Sun 0510-0600.

TS) Respublika Tatarstan [+3]: GTRK "Tatarstan", ul. M. Gorkogo 15, 420015 Kazan. Email: root@gtrkrt.kazan.su. **Reg:** "Tatarstan radiosi"/"R.Tatarstana" on Kazan 252kHz + (MHz) sovkhoz im. Kirova 67.28, Kazan 68.48, Naberezhnyye Chelny 67.01, Bavly 68.45, Leninogorsk 68.63, Tetyushi 69.95, Bilyarsk 70.13, Aktanysh 70.22, Nurlat 70.46, Buinsk 70.61, Cheremshan 72.14, Nizhnekamensk 72.29, A.Saplyk 72.29, Almetyevsk 103.9, Agryz 106.4 in Tatar, Russian: MF 0300-0400, MF 0510-0600, Tue-Fri 0910-1010, Tue/Thu/Fri 1110-1200, MF 1310-1400, MF 1410-1500, MF 1610-1800; Sat 0300-1130; Sun 0300-1200. – TRK "Novyy vek", ul. M. Gorkogo 15, 420015 Kazan. **Reg:** Channel "Yana gasir radiosi"/"R. Novyy vek" on (MHz) Kazan 91.5, Zelenodolsk 100.9, Bilyarsk 101.4, Leninogorsk 102.1, Shemordan 102.3, Nizhnekamsk 102.6, Bogatye Saby 103.9, Kaybitsy 105.0, Absalyamovo 105.4, Nab. Chelny 105.5, Novosheshminsk 107.0, Menzilinsk 107.3.

TV) Tverskaya oblast [+3]: GTRK "Tver", ul. Vagzhanova 9, 170000 Tver. Email: gtrktver@chat.ru. **Reg:** On (MHz) Kashin 66.95, Andriyanovo 68.48, Selizharovo 69.68, Maksatikha 71.24: MF 0410-0500, 0510-0530 & 1520-1600, Thu 1610-1700, Sat/Sun 0610-0700.

TY) Tyumenskaya oblast [+5]: GTRK "Region-Tyumen", ul. Permyakova 6, 625013 Tyumen. Email: gtrk@regtum.da.ru. **Reg:** On Tyumen 1485kHz + (MHz) Gagarino 66.89, Masali 68.96, Tobolsk 71.90, Tyumen 71.66, Shabanovo 72.17 (also via tr's in region KY): MF 0110-0200, 0230-0300, 0600-0610, 1000-1010, 1400-1410, Sat/Sun 0300-0500; Sat 1300-1400; Sun 0700-0800.

UB) Ust-Ordynskiy Buryatskiy avt. okrug [+8]: Ust-Ordynskaya okruzhnaya radioredaktsiya GTRK "Irkutsk", ul. Kalinina 10, 666110 Ust-Ordynskiy. **Reg:** On Ust-Ordynskiy 107.8MHz in Buryat (Tue/Sat), Russian (other days): 0010-0040. (NB: UB is subordinated to region IR)

UD) Udmurtskaya respublika [+4]: GTRK "Udmurtiya", ul. Komunarov 216, 426004 Izhevsk. Email: admin@udmtv.udm.ru. **Reg:** On Izhevsk 594kHz + (MHz) Izhevsk 68.06, Balezino 70.94 in Udmurt, Russian, Tatar, Mari: 0300-0500, 0910-1000, 1510-1800.

UL) Ulyanovskaya oblast [+3]: GTRK "Volga", ul. Simbirskaya 5, 432030 Ulyanovsk. Email: volga@mv.ru. **Reg:** On (MHz) Novospasskoye 67.07, Dimitrovgrad 67.19, Vochkayma 70.40, Ulyanovsk 71.00: 0310-0400, 0610-0700W, 1010-1100, 1510-1600.

VG) Volgogradskaya oblast [+3]: GTRK "Volgograd-TRV", ul. Mira 9, 400066 Volgograd. Email: vlg@trk.tsaritsyn.ru. **Reg:** On Volgograd 567kHz + (MHz) Mikhaylovka 66.83, Kamyshin 69.14, Chilekovo 69.44, Volgograd 70.43, Kletskiy 70.94, Surovikino 71.00: MF 0410-0500, 0910-1000, 1510-1600; Sat 0510-0600; Sun 0710-0800.

VL) Vladimirskaya oblast [+3]: GTRK "Vladimir", ul. Bol. Moskovskaya 62, 600000 Vladimir. Email: main@vladtv.elcom.ru. **Reg:** On (MHz) Murom 66.32, Petushki 66.70, Aleksandrov 67.67, Suzdal 68.72, Gorokhovets 69.08, Sudogda 69.47, Melenki 70.25, Vyazniki 70.28, Sobinka 70.61, Kolchugino 73.55, Gus-Khrustalnyy 103.1: MF 0410-0500, 0910-1000, 1610-1700; Sat/Sun 0510-0600, 0710-0800.
VN) Voronezhskaya oblast [+3]: Voronezhskaya GTRK, ul. Karl Marksa 114, 394625 Voronezh. Email: tv@vgtv.vrn.ru. **Reg:** On Somovo 774kHz + (MHz) Bobrov 67.04, Borisoglebsk 70.82, Boguchar 71.90, Voronezh 72.11: MF 0410-0500, 0910-1000, 1710-1800; Sat/Sun 0810-0900, 0910-1000.
VO) Vologodskaya oblast [+3]: Vologda-GTRK, ul. Lomonosova 31, 162610 Cherepovets. Email: vtv@cherepovets.ru. **Reg:** On Chagoda/Nikolsk 1098kHz + (MHz) Cherepovets 66.38, Sludno 66.77, Yakutino 66.86, Ozerki 66.86, Syamzha 67.88, Nyuksenitsa 68.03, Vologda 69.05, Totma 69.71, Lipin Bor 69.65, Kurilovo 70.07: MF 0410-0500, Mon/Fri 1500-1600, Tue-Thu 1510-1600, Sat/Sun 0600-0700.
YA) Yaroslavskaya oblast [+3]: GTRK "Yaroslaviya", ul. Bogdanovicha 20, 150014 Yaroslavl. Email: gtrk@yaroslavl.ru. **Reg:** On (MHz) Dubki 68.66, Volga 70.88: MF 0400-0500, 1500-1600, Sat/Sun 0500-0600, 1400-1500.
YN) Yamalo-Nenetskiy avt. okrug [+5]: OGTRK "Yamal-Region", ul. Lambinykh 3, 626600 Salekhard. Email: gk@yamalinfo.ru. **Reg:** On Salekhard 603kHz + (MHz) Muzhi 68.90, Nadym 71.78, Salekhard 71.99/100.6: W 0200-0215, MF 0800-0900 & 1000-1010, Mon-Thu 1415-1445; Sat 1100-1200, 1300-1400. Tr's also relay GTRK "Region-Tyumen", Tyumen TY. (NB: YN is subordinated to region TY)
YV) Yevreyskaya avt. oblast [+10]: GTRK "Bira", ul. Sovetskaya 13, 682290 Birobidzhan. Email: gtrkbira@on-line.jar.ru. **Reg:** On (MHz) Birobidzhan 67.88, Bidzhan 70.07 in Yiddish, Russian: Mon 2115-, Sun 2145-, Sat 2315-2400, 0140-0300, Wed 0515, Fri 0950, and others. Tr's also relay GTRK "Dalnevostochnaya", Khabarovsk KH. Channel "R.St. Tykhonkaya" on Birobidzhan 999kHz.

SPECIAL SW PRGR'S PRODUCED BY REGIONAL STUDIOS
1) "Kabardino-Balkarskoye Radio"
Produced by GTRK "Kabbalkteleradio" (see region KB): 1800-1830 on Tbilisskaya 6005kHz (100kW) for expatriots in the Middle East.
2) "Karachayevo-Cherkesskoye Radio"
Produced by GTRK "Karachayevo-Cherkesiya" (see region KC): 1830-1900 on Tbilisskaya 6005kHz (100kW) for expatriots in the Middle East.
3) "Kamchatka rybatskaya"
Produced by GTRK "Kamchatka" (see region KM): 0000-0100 on Yelizovo 11975kHz (200kW) for fishermen (Sea of Okhotsk/Bering Sea).
4) "Radiostantsiya Tikhiy Okean"
Produced by GTRK "Vladivostok" (see region PM): 0740-0800 on Razdolnoye 9480kHz (100kW) & Vladivostok 810kHz for fishermen (Sea of Okhotsk/Bering Sea). NB. Preliminary schedule (tests Oct.2004)
5) "Tatarstan dulkynynda"(Na volne Tatarstana)
Produced by TRK "Novyy vek" (see region TS): 0500-0600 towards Russian Far East & 0700-0800 towards Urals and We.Siberia on 15105 (200kW), 0900-1000 towards We.Russia on 11915kHz (100kW) & Kazan 252kHz. In Tatar, Russian for Tatar listeners outside of Tatarstan. SW tx's: Samara; freqs subject to seasonal changes. V: QSL-card (reception reports: c/o Ildus Ibatullin, P.O.Box 134, 420136 Kazan).

EXTERNAL SERVICE: Voice of Russia
- see International Radio section.

OTHER STATIONS: LW & MW

	kHz	kW	Location	Station
1)	270	150	Novosibirsk, S	R. Slovo
16)	531	5	Yu-Sakhalinsk, FE	Avtoradio
A)	612	20	Moskva, E	Relay Services
3)	612	20	Moskva, E	Narodnoye R.
2)	612	10	Vladivostok, FE	R. VBC
B)	666	10	Yekaterinburg, E	BBC Relay
14)	675	40	Razdolnoye, FE	R. Radonezh
3)	675	250	Oyash, S	Narodnoye R.
5)	684	10	Nakhodka, FE	R. Nakhodka
4)	684	10	St.Peterburg, E	NERS (Relays)
D)	693	20	Moskva, E	DW Relay
8)	711	0.2	Abakan, S	Avtoradio
7)	711	7	Khabarovsk, FE	R. Vostok Rossii
3)	729	50	Samara, E	Narodnoye R. (cf.1107)
G)	738	5	Moskva, E	WRN Relay
9)	738	50	Vladivostok, FE	R. Novaya volna
7)	765	5	Bikin, FE	R. Vostok Rossii
11)	783	75	Vladivostok, FE	Russkoye R. Lemma
12)	810	10	Krasnoyarsk, S	Avtoradio-Krasnoyarsk
F)	810	20	Kurkino, E	VOA Relay
13)	828	10	St.Peterburg, E	Eldoradio
14)	846	150	Noginsk, E	R. Radonezh
28)	855	20	Petropavlovsk-K., FE	R. 3
29)	864	25	Blagoveshchensk, FE	R. Shanson
15)	909	10	Yekaterinburg, E	Studiya Gorod (RFE-RL)
47)	918	75	Moskva, E	R. Svobodnaya Rossiya
2)	936	5	Dalnegorsk, FE	R. VBC
17)	963	5	Moskva, E	Radiotserkov
18)	990	15	Moskva, E	R. Slavyanka
E)	1044	40	Moskva, E	RFE-RL Relay
20)	1053	10	Krasnoyarsk, S	R. Shanson
14)	1053	50	Orenburg, E	R. Radonezh
46)	1053	25	Belogorsk, FE	R. Plyus
19)	1053	10	St.Peterburg, E	R. Mariya
22)	1089	20	St.Peterburg, E	R. Teos
21)	1098	10	Moskva, E	R. Vatanym
23)	1098	75	Vladivostok, FE	R. Vladivostok
3)	1107	150	Samara, E	Narodnoye R. (F.Pl)
25)	1116	5	Moskva, E	KhrTserkObshchKanal
26)	1134	7	Khabarovsk, FE	Avtoradio
22)	1134	20	Kurkino, E	R. Teos
D)	1188	10	St.Peterburg, E	DW Relay
35)	1188	5	Samara, E	R. XXI vek
27)	1188	10	Khabarovsk, FE	Radiotserkov
24)	1224	30	Elista, E	R. Ura
32)	1224	10	Khabarovsk, FE	Ekho Moskvy
28)	1233	20	Yelizovo, FE	R. 3
30)	1242	2	Angarsk, S	R. Avtos/ORR
14)	1260	10	Yekaterinburg, E	R. Radonezh
B)	1260	10	Moskva, E	BBC Relay
B)	1260	10	St.Peterburg	BBC Relay
7)	1269	10	Komsomolsk, FE	R. Vostok Rossii
31)	1269	5	Ussuriysk, FE	R. Ussuri
14)	1287	75	Novosibirsk, S	R. Radonezh
48)	1296	5	Irkutsk, S	Ekho Moskva
50)	1296	10	Vladivostok, FE	Ekho Moskvy
6)	1305	100	Kupavna, E	R. Druzhba
33)	1323	10	St.Peterburg, E	R. Grad Petrov
34)	1332	10	Irkutsk, S	Nashe vremya na MV
49)	1359	75	Moskva, E	Nash soyuz (F.pl)
E)	1386	50	Khabarovsk, FE	RFE-RL/VOA Relay
36)	1395	10	Krasnoyarsk, S	Ekho Moskvy
10)	1413	7	Khabarovsk, FE	Russkoye Radio
C)	1440	10	St.Peterburg, E	RFI Relay
C)	1440	10	Moskva, E	RFI Relay
38)	1476	75	Vladivostok, FE	Studiya O'key
45)	1503	5	Ussuriysk, FE	Ekho Moskvy
40)	1503	20	Moskva, E	R. Sadko
39)	1503	20	Moskva, E	R. Tsentr
41)	1557	10	Vladivostok, FE	R. Shanson/Radiotserk.
37)	1557	5	Irkutsk, S	Inta R.
42)	1575	0.2	Usolye-Sibirskoye, S	Ekho Usolya
43)	1584	5	Nakhodka, FE	R. Svob. Nakhodka
44)	1602	1	Zheleznogorsk-Ilimsk, S	R. Shanson

Addresses and other information:
1) ul. Kirova 3, 630011 Novosibirsk. Tr shared with R. Rossii/GTRK "Novosibirsk". Email: rslovo@mail.ru – **2)** ul. Uborevicha 20a, 690091 Vladivostok. Email: info@radiovbc.ru – **3)** ul. Pyatnitskaya 25, 115326 Mosva. Email: nr@narodinfo.ru – **4)** St.Peterburg. Email: nerrs@mail.admiral.ru – **5)** ul. Pirogova 17, 692000 Nakhodka. Email: info@radio.nakhodka.ru – **6)** ul.Akademika Koroleva 12, 127427 Moskva. – **7)** ul. Lenina 4, 680000 Khabarovsk. Email: radio@erussia.khv.ru – **8)** P.O.Box 245, 662617 Abakan. – **9)** ul. Pogranichnaya 2, 690008 Vladivostok. Email: info@newwave.ru – **10)** ul. Zaparina 82, 680000 Khabarovsk. Email: radio@rusradio.khv.ru – **11)** ul. Stelnikova 3a, 690000 Vladivostok. Email: lemma@vtc.ru Rel. Russkoye R. – **12)** ul. Kirova 19, 660049 Krasnoyarsk. Email: radio@kr.ru – **13)** P.O.Box 92, 194100 St.Peterburg. Email: eldoradio@mail.com – **14)** ul. Pyatnitskaya 25, 113326 Moskva: 1700-2000 on 612/684/846/1053/1260/1287kHz; 1000-1300 on 675kHz. Email: radonezh@radonezh.ru – **15)** pr. Lenina 24a-449, 620038 Yekaterinburg. Email: info@gorodfm.ru – **16)** ul. Komsomolskaya 209, 693000 Yuzhno-Sakhalinsk. Email: gtrk@sakhalin.ru – **17)** P.O.Box 106, 121019 Moskva. Email: radio@radiotserkov.ru – **18)** Bumazhnyy per. 14, 101160 Moskva. – **19)** P.O.Box 732, 190068 St.Peterburg. Email: mail@radiomaria.ru – **20)** P.O.Box 6119, 660017 Krasnoyarsk. Email: ncity@vsptus.ru. Rel. Nashe Vremya na Militseyskoy volne, Moskva. – **21)** ul. Bolshaya Dmitrovka 9, 125009 Moskva. – **22)** P.O.Box 110, 190000 St.Peterburg. Email: radio@teos.org.ru – **23)** ul. Vs. Sibirtseva 15, 690078 Vladivostok. Email: r1098@mail.primorye.ru – **24)** Elista. – **25)** P.O.Box 73, 127422 Moskva. – **26)** ul. Lenina 75, 680013 Khabarovsk. Email: air@avtoradio.khr.ru. Rel. Avtoradio, Moskva. – **27)** P.O.Box 2128, 680030 Khabarovsk. Relays a.o. FEBC. **28)** ul. Lukashevskogo 5, 683025 Petropavlovsk-Kamchatskiy. – **29)** Blagoveshchensk. Rel. R. Shanson. – **30)** P.O.Box 3485, 665839 Angarsk. Email: radio@avtos.com. Own prgr's: 2300-1400, rel. ORR from Moscow: 1400-2300. – **31)** ul. Kirova 28, 692525 Ussuriysk. – **32)** ul. Lenina 69, 680013 Khabarovsk. Email:

radio@olimp.khv.ru. Rel. of Ekho Moskvy, Moscow. – **33)** nab. L. Shmidta 39, 199034 St.Peterburg. – **34)** P.O.Box 3, 664000 Irkutsk. Email: info@volna.irnet.ru. Rel. Nashe Vremya na Militseyskoy volne, Moskva: 2300-1500. – **35)** Samara. – **36)** ul. Mechnikova 44a, 660028 Krasnoyarsk (GTRK "Tsentr Rossii"). Rel. Ekho Moskvy, Moskva. Email: new@public.krasnet.ru – **37)** ul. Akademicheskaya 5a, 664000 Irkutsk. Email: intaradio@front.ru – **38)** ul. Aleutskaya 45a, 690009 Vladivostok. Email: reklama@ok.vl.ru – **39)** ul. Nikolskaya 7, 103012 Moskva. Email: radio@radiocenter.net – **40)** ul. Malaya Nikitskaya 24, 121810 Moskva. – **41)** ul. Pologaya 72, 690090 Vladivostok. Rel. R. Shanson, Moskva. Email: info@radiovbc.ru – **42)** ul. Krasnoarmeyskaya 24, 665470 Usolye-Sirbirskoye. **43)** ul. Sportivnaya 6, 692000 Nakhodka. – **44)** P.O.Box 10, 665680 Zheleznogorsk-Illimskiy. Rel. R. Shanson, Moskva. – **45)** ul. Kirova 28, 692500 Ussuriysk. Rel. Ekho Moskvy, Moskva. – **46)** ul. Nagornaya 9, 675000 Blagoveshchensk. Email: mail@radioplus.ru – **47)** ul. Pyatnitskaya 25, 115326 Moskva. – **48)** ul. Bogdana Khmesnitskogo 36, 664003, Irkutsk. Email: echo@asbaikaltv.ru. Rel. Ekho Moskvy, Moskva. – **49)** Moskva. Licensed since 2003. – **49)** Vladivostok. – **A)** Various relay services incl. Golos Rossii (for listeners in Moscow). – **B)** Rel. BBC (cf. UK). – **C)** Rel. RFI (cf. France). – **D)** Rel. DW (cf. Germany). – **E)** Rel. RFE-RL (cf. USA). – **F)** Rel. VOA (cf. USA).

FM

There are about 2000 commercial radio stations on FM in Russia. Most tx's carry a relay of one of the nationwide networks (with opt-outs for local advertisments) which include:

Avtoradio (Web: www.avtoradio.ru), **Dinamit FM** (Web: www.dinamitfm.ru), **Ekho Moskvy** (www.echo.msk.ru), **Hit-FM** (Web: www.hitfm.ru), **R.Energiya** (Web: www.energyfm.ru), **R.Maksimum** (Web: www.maximum.ru), **Kanal Melodiya** (Web: www.melodia.ru), **Love R.** (Web: www.loveradio.ru) , **Nashe R.** (Web: www.nashe.ru), **ORR** (Web: www.orr-radio.ru), **R.Retro** (Web: www.radioretro.ru), **R.Shanson** (Web: www.chanson.ru), **Russkoye R. & Russkoye R. 2** (Web: www.rusradio.ru & www.rusradio2.ru), **R. Troyka** (Web: www.radiotroyka.ru), **Serebryanyy dozhd** (Web: www.silver.ru), **Yevropa plyus** (Web: www.europaplus.ru), **R.7** (Web: www.radio7.ru).

FM	MHz	kW	Location	Station
TO11)	65.93	1	Seversk	R. SV
RO05)	65.96	1	Rostov-na-Donu	R. Aleks
MO21)	66.02	2	Moskva	Love Radio
AK06)	66.08	1	Barnaul	Molodyozhnyy kanal
RK01)	66.11	1	Abakan	R. MIG
IV05)	66.11	1	Ivanovo	R. Retro
PR03)	66.20	1	Berezniki	Avtoradio Perm
TS20)	66.23	1	Nab.Chelny	Kanal Melodiya
CV05)	66.26	1	Cheboksary	R. Miks
AK10)	66.29	1	Biysk	R. Rif
ST07)	66.41	1	Pyatigorsk	R. Sfera
RO16)	66.41	1	Azov	Avtoradio
AR06)	66.41	1	Plesetsk	ORR
BU04)	66.53	1	Ulan-Ude	Puls-Radio
TL02)	66.62	1	Tula	R. Vizavi
SV17)	66.62	1	Yekaterinburg	Russkoye R. 2
BE03)	66.68	1	Belgorod	R. Shanson
CB03)	66.74	1	Chelyabinsk	Intervolna
VO12)	66.77	4	Babayevo	Babayevskoye Radio
OB03)	66.80	1	Orenburg	Hit FM
TS03)	66.80	2	Kazan	R. Passazh
PS01)	66.83	1	Pskov	Nord-Vest R.
TO05)	66.83	1	Tomsk	R. Svobodnyy Stil
MO03)	66.86	7.5	Moskva	R. Maksimum
SL01)	66.86	1	Yuzhno-Sakhalinsk	R. Retro
TO03)	66.92	1	Teguldet	Nashe R.
KD24)	66.92	1	Lazarevskaya	Mayak Kubani
TA07)	67.01	1	Morshansk	Kanal Melodiya
TY06)	67.04	1	Tyumen	R. Shanson
RO06)	67.10	1	Rostov-na-Donu	R. Shanson
PR03)	67.10	1	Solikalamsk	Avtoradio Perm
KG02)	67.13	1	Kurgan	Russkoye R.
VO01)	67.16	4	Cherepovets	R. Transmit
ST03)	67.19	1	Stavropol	R. Provintsiya
SR05)	67.19	1	Saratov	Hit FM
RO26)	67.22	1	Gukovo	Nika-TR
TS29)	67.25	1	Almetyevsk	R. Mirazh
IR02)	67.34	1	Irkutsk	R. Shanson
NN20)	67.37	1	N.Novgorod	Govorit Arzamas
NN19)	67.43	1	N.Novgorod	Govorit Semenov
BA03)	67.46	2	Ufa	Ekho Moskvy
SV03)	67.46	1	Yekaterinburg	Kanal Melodiya
SL03)	67.46	1	Kholmsk	Yevropa plyus
RO24)	67.58	1	Taganrog	R. Universitet
PS02)	67.58	1	Pskov	R. Sedmoye nebo
TO03)	67.61	1	Tomsk	Nashe R.
SA04)	67.61	1	Samara	R. Megapolis
VG08)	67.61	1	Mikhaylovka	R. Aprel
AK08)	67.64	1	Barnaul	R. Universitet
TO03)	67.64	1	Padoga	Nashe R.
KY04)	67.64	1	Khanty-Mansiysk	R. Yugra
ST16)	67.67	1	Nevinnomyssk	Khit-Kontakt
KN03)	67.67	1	Abakan	Avto-Radio Krasnoyarsk
CB14)	67.70	1	Magnitogorsk	Yevropa plyus
VN03)	67.70	1	Voronezh	R. Maksimum
AK13)	67.73	1	Smolenskoye	Novaya volna
TO03)	67.79	1	Kolpashevo	Nashe R.
KL07)	67.79	1	Obninsk	Serebryanyy dozhd
TS14)	67.79	1	Nab.Chelny	R. Kunel
TO10)	67.79	1	Kozhevnikovo	Russkoye R.
KV04)	67.91	1	Vyatskiye Polyarny	R. Mariya
SV23)	67.94	1	Serov	R. Serova
MO04)	68.00	1	Moskva	Avtoradio
BU05)	68.00	1	Ulan-Ude	Russkoye R. 2
RO03)	68.00	1	Rostov-na-Donu	Nashe R.
PZ01)	68.09	1	Penza	Yevropa plyus
SA22)	68.09	1	Tolyatti	Russkoye R. 2
KN03)	68.15	1	Minusinsk	Avto-Radio Krasnoyarsk
KD03)	68.15	1	Krasnodar	Ekho Moskvy
TM01)	68.18	1	Norilsk	Nago-Radio
MU07)	68.21	1	Murmansk	ORR
SP03)	68.24	1	St.Peterburg	Love Radio St.Peterburg
MO05)	68.30	2.5	Moskva	Radio-1
KA02)	68.36	2	Kaliningrad	Russkoye R.
KL05)	68.36	1	Obninsk	R. Reyting
TS15)	68.36	1	Nab.Chelny	Formula Da
SV04)	68.39	2	Yekaterinburg	R. Si
KG01)	68.39	1	Kurgan	Yevropa plyus
NS03)	68.48	1	Novosibirsk	R. Sibiri
KU04)	68.48	1	Kursk	Hit FM
SA05)	68.51	1	Samara	Ekho Moskvy
KN03)	68.51	1	Achinsk	Avto-Radio Krasnoyarsk
AK09)	68.51	1	Rubtsovsk	Russkoye R.
VN04)	68.57	1	Voronezh	Kanal Melodiya
CB29)	68.57	1	Magnitogorsk	R. Magnit
SR01)	68.60	2	Saratov	Yevropa plyus
OM02)	68.60	4	Omsk	Russkoye R.
IR09)	68.63	1	Bratsk	Golos Angary
YN04)	68.63	1	Nadym	Kanal Melodiya
RO08)	68.63	1	Rostov-na-Donu	R. Oktava
KE01)	68.66	1	Kemerovo	Yevropa plyus
SP04)	68.66	3	St.Peterburg	R. Khit 90i6
UD02)	68.84	4	Izhevsk	Russkoye R.
NS16)	68.84	1	Iskitim	R. NTN
KA12)	68.84	1	Kaliningrad	Kolledzh Radio
CV04)	68.90	1	Cheboksary	Otkrytoye Radio
RO09)	68.90	1	Rostov-na-Donu	R. Novaya provintsiya
KN01)	68.90	4	Krasnoyarsk	Yevropa plyus
KD10)	68.90	1	Sochi	R. Retro
SV25)	68.90	1	Kamensk-Uralskiy	R. Kamensk
TM02)	68.93	1	Norilsk	R. Polyus
TS27)	68.96	1	Almetyevsk	Avtoradio
TA01)	69.02	1	Tambov	Hit FM
TL03)	69.02	1	Tula	R. Retro
SV05)	69.02	1	Yekaterinburg	Avtoradio
SP05)	69.05	3	St.Peterburg	Nevskaya volna
KG05)	69.08	4	Kurgan	Hit FM
TO03)	69.08	1	Belyy Yar	Nashe R.
AK01)	69.11	1	Barnaul	Yevropa plyus
LI07)	69.14	4	Lipetsk	ORR
TO03)	69.17	1	Krivosheino	Nashe R.
KO09)	69.17	1	Vuktyl	Kanal Melodiya
BE13)	69.23	1	Staryy Oskol	Avtoradio
CH02)	69.23	1	Chita	Russkoye R.
OB08)	69.26	1	Orenburg	Ekho Moskvy
CB02)	69.26	4	Yuryuzan	Russkoye R.
MO06)	69.26	15	Moskva	Russkoye R. 2
IV02)	69.29	1	Ivanovo	Russkoye R.
AR03)	69.32	1	Arkhangelsk	R. Shanson
ME01)	69.38	2	Yoshkar-Ola	Yevropa plyus
SO03)	69.38	1	Vladikavkaz	R. OS
KO05)	69.38	1	Ukhta	Kanal Melodiya
RO11)	69.44	1	Rostov-na-Donu	Ekho Moskvy
RK04)	69.50	1	Chernogorsk	R Panorama
TO06)	69.50	1	Asino	R. Sibir
IR10)	69.51	2	Shelekhov	Ekho Moskvy
MO31)	69.53	1	Serpukhov	R. Serpukhova
KY21)	69.59	1	Surgut	R. Figaro
VG01)	69.59	2	Volgograd	Yevropa plyus
SP28)	69.62	1	Luga	R. Miks

FM	MHz	kW	Location	Station
VO01)	69.62	1	Velikiye Ustyug	R. Transmit
NN18)	69.68	1	N.Novgorod	Govorit Balakhna
RO25)	69.68	1	Novocherkassk	R. N
BA04)	69.68	1	Ufa	Pervyy kanal
TS16)	69.71	1	Nab.Chelny	R. Retro
UL03)	69.74	1	Ulyanovsk	Kanal Melodiya
YA08)	69.74	1	Rybinsk	Yevropa plyus
VO11)	69.77	5	Cherepovets	R. Shanson
TO03)	69.79	1	Kozhevnikovo	Nashe R.
TO07)	69.80	1	Tomsk	Serebryanyy dozhd
TO03)	69.80	1	Strezhevoy	Nashe R.
MO01)	69.80	15	Moskva	Yevropa plyus
UD06)	69.83	1	Balezino	R. Retro
TA02)	69.86	4	Tambov	Top-Radio
RO17)	69.89	1	Azov	R. Telekom
KY05)	69.89	1	Nyagan	Ekho Moskvy
OB09)	69.92	1	Orenburg	R. Retro
KY03)	70.01	1	Surgut	R. Maksimum
RK03)	70.01	1	Sayanogorsk	R. Sibir
AR04)	70.04	1	Arkhangelsk	Avto-Radio
VO02)	70.04	1	Vologda	Russkoye R.
PR03)	70.04	4	Perm	Avtoradio Perm
MD03)	70.07	1	Saransk	R. Shanson
KE07)	70.07	1	Novokuznetsk	Apeks-Radio
TO03)	70.10	1	Zyryanskoye	Nashe R.
TV03)	70.13	1	Tver	R. Retro
KH03)	70.13	1	Komsomolsk-na-A.	R. Retro
NN03)	70.16	1	N.Novgorod	R. Randevu
MO07)	70.19	1	Balashika	R. Ultra
TO04)	70.19	2	Tomsk	R. Shanson
TO03)	70.22	1	Aleksandrovskoye	Nashe R.
UL05)	70.25	1	Ulyanovsk	Ekho Moskvy
VN12)	70.25	1	Voronezh	Serebryanyy dozhd
KH01)	70.28	4	Khabarovsk	Yevropa plyus
KD25)	70.31	1	Gelendzhik	ORR
AK14)	70.31	4	Kamen-na-Obi	Mayak Pobedy
KY07)	70.37	1	Yugorsk	R. Nord
KG03)	70.43	1	Kurgan	Ekho Moskvy
BU01)	70.43	1	Ulan-Ude	Yevropa plyus
SV06)	70.52	1	Yekaterinburg	Hit FM
AK05)	70.52	1	Barnaul	R. Uniton
MU04)	70.52	1	Murmansk	Hit FM
OM05)	70.55	1	Omsk	Ekho Moskvy
VN14)	70.58	4	Bobrov	R. Region
NO03)	70.61	4	Novgorod V.	Kanal Melodiya
MO32)	70.64	1	Moskva	R. Dacha
CB28)	70.64	1	Verkhniy Ufaley	R. Ufaleya
SA16)	70.64	1	Tolyatti	R. Avgust
BE12)	70.67	1	Staryy Oskol	R. Oskol
BR03)	70.67	1	Bryansk	R. Shanson
CB06)	70.70	1	Chelyabinsk	Russkoye R. 2
VO03)	70.70	1	Vologda	R. Premier
KD25)	70.70	1	Lazorevskiy	ORR
KE03)	70.73	1	Kemerovo	Ekho Moskvy
LI05)	70.73	1	Lipetsk	Otkrytoye Radio
KX01)	70.73	1	Elista	R. Lebediya
OB11)	70.82	1	Buzuluk	Yevropa plyus
PR04)	70.82	4	Perm	R. Maksimum
KV03)	70.85	1	Kirov	Hit FM
TY03)	70.88	1	Tyumen	R. 7
NS04)	70.88	2	Novosibirsk	R. Yuniton
TO08)	70.91	1	Tomsk	R. Retro
KG07)	70.94	1	Kurgan	Russkoye R. 2
VO01)	70.94	1	Totma	R. Transmit
BA14)	70.97	1	Kumertau	Otkrytoye Radio ARIS
KS01)	71.00	1	Kostroma	Hit FM
CB16)	71.03	1	Magnitogorsk	R. Lyuks
SM03)	71.09	4	Smolensk	R. Vesna
ST08)	71.09	5	Pyatigorsk	Hit FM
ST15)	71.09	1	Yessentuki	Hit FM
VN14)	71.12	4	Boguchar	R. Region
KU03)	71.18	1	Kursk	R. Retro
KO11)	71.18	1	Inta	Kanal Melodiya
SP07)	71.24	15	St.Peterburg	R. Baltika
SA01)	71.27	1	Samara	Yevropa plyus
OL05)	71.27	1	Oryol	R. Retro
BA05)	71.30	1	Ufa	R. Retro
MO02)	71.30	10	Moskva	Russkoye R.
RS01)	71.30	1	Yakutsk	R. Viktoriya
MA01)	71.36	1	Magadan	Novaya zhizn
KY09)	71.42	1	Surgut	Surgutinform
BA12)	71.45	1	Oktyabrskiy	KRK Yevropa
KB01)	71.45	1	Nalchik	Yevropa plyus
PZ03)	71.45	5	Penza	R. Premyer 71.45
AR06)	71.48	1	Arkhangelsk	ORR

FM	MHz	kW	Location	Station
CB17)	71.51	1	Ozersk	Volna
SM01)	71.55	1	Smolensk	Yevropa plyus
AK04)	71.57	1	Barnaul	R. Stolitsa
YA09)	71.66	4	Yaroslavl	ORR
SA06)	71.66	1	Samara	Serebryanyy dozhd
SP08)	71.66	15	St.Peterburg	R. Retro
UD02)	71.72	4	Balezino	Russkoye R.
KL03)	71.72	4	Kaluga	R. Shanson
KA04)	71.75	1	Bolshakovo	R. Baltik plyus
UL02)	71.78	1	Ulyanovsk	Russkoye R.
KY10)	71.78	1	Nizhnevartovsk	R. Samotlor
PR10)	71.78	1	Perm	ORR
KV07)	71.84	1	Kirov	Relaks-Radio
KO10)	71.93	1	Vorkuta	Kanal Melodiya
KO07)	71.93	1	Usinsk	Kanal Melodiya
KY11)	71.93	1	Surgut	Russkoye R.
TO06)	71.96	1	Tomsk	R. Sibir
IV08)	71.99	4	Rodniki	Russkoye R. 2
UD03)	72.02	1	Izhevsk	R. Adam
OB04)	72.11	1	Orenburg	Avtoradio
KA04)	72.11	1	Kaliningrad	R. Baltik plyus
KD24)	72.14	1	Gelendzhik	Mayak Kubani
SP09)	72.14	5	St.Peterburg	Nashe R.
SA16)	72.17	1	Dimitrovgrad	R. Avgust
KY12)	72.17	1	Kogalym	R. Alyans
BR02)	72.26	1	Bryansk	Russkoye R.
AS01)	72.26	1	Astrakhan	Yevropa plyus
AR02)	72.26	1	Arkhangelsk	Yevropa plyus
YA02)	72.26	1	Yaroslavl	Russkoye R. 2
CH04)	72.29	1	Chita	Popularnoye Radio
KD02)	72.32	1	Krasnodar	Yevropa plyus
VN14)	72.38	4	Borisoglebsk	R. Region
NN09)	72.41	1	N.Novgorod	Avtoradio
ST02)	72.41	1	Stavropol	Russkoye R.
TY05)	72.44	2	Tyumen	Ekho Moskvy
KV06)	72.44	1	Kirov	R. Shanson
PR05)	72.44	1	Perm	R.7
NS01)	72.44	2	Novosibirsk	Yevropa plyus
KN04)	72.50	1	Krasnoyarsk	Hit FM
CB18)	72.59	1	Magnitogorsk	Russkoye R.
KG04)	72.65	1	Kurgan	Avtoradio
SP01)	72.68	4	St.Peterburg	Yevropa plyus
AK07)	72.68	1	Barnaul	Russkiy Vityaz
TL10)	72.71	1	Tula	Kanal Melodiya
KY13)	72.71	1	Surgut	R. Geleum
CB30)	72.74	4	Chelyabinsk	R. Shanson
TO03)	72.77	1	Bakchar	Nashe R.
UD01)	72.80	1	Izhevsk	Yevropa plyus
PR03)	72.80	1	Ochyor	Avtoradio Perm
SP24)	72.80	1	Vyborg	R. Retro
LI01)	72.80	4	Lipetsk	Yevropa plyus
SA02)	72.83	1	Samara	Russkoye R.
VL03)	72.83	1	Vladimir	R. Shanson
YN10)	72.86	1	Noyabrsk	R. Noyabrsk
KC01)	72.89	1	Cherkessk	Russkoye R.
PR03)	72.89	1	Krasnovishersk	Avtoradio Perm
SR10)	72.92	1	Balakovo	R. Ekspress
MO08)	72.92	15	Moskva	R. Retro
VN01)	72.95	1	Voronezh	Yevropa plyus
TV06)	72.98	1	Belyy	ORR
VO01)	72.98	4	Vologda	R. Transmit
NN01)	73.01	2	N.Novgorod	Yevropa plyus
OB13)	73.10	1	Orsk	Russkoye R.
SP10)	73.10	15	St.Peterburg	R. Vertikal
YA04)	73.13	1	Yaroslavl	R. Elis
RY03)	73.13	1	Ryazan	ORR
RO20)	73.13	1	Volgodonsk	R. Retro
NS05)	73.16	1	Novosibirsk	Studiya ENN
NN17)	73.16	1	Sarov	R. Ekspress
OM03)	73.16	1	Omsk	R. Alternativa
OB01)	73.16	1	Orenburg	Yevropa plyus
KV02)	73.19	1	Kirov	Russkoye R.
UL04)	73.19	1	Ulyanovsk	R. Shanson
VL01)	73.25	1	Vladimir	Yevropa plyus
KL02)	73.25	1	Kaluga	Russkoye R. 2
KN02)	73.28	1	Krasnoyarsk	Russkoye R.
AK11)	73.28	1	Biysk	Russkoye R.
TS04)	73.28	1	Kazan	R. Dulkin
TM03)	73.28	1	Norilsk	Russkoye R.
BE11)	73.31	1	Gubkin	Volna Gubkina
TV06)	73.34	1	Zharkovskiy	ORR
KY14)	73.37	1	Nizhnevartovsk	Avtoradio
UL07)	73.37	1	Dimitrovgrad	Yevropa plyus
ST09)	73.40	1	Pyatigorsk	R. Provintsiya
MO09)	73.40	5	Moskva	R. 7

FM	MHz	kW	Location	Station
NO01)	73.40	5	Novgorod V.	Yevropa plyus
UD04)	73.40	4	Izhevsk	Avtoradio
SR03)	73.43	1	Saratov	R. S
NN11)	73.43	1	N.Novgorod	Kanal Melodiya
VN06)	73.43	1	Borisoglebsk	ORR
DA01)	73.49	1	Makhachkala	Yevropa plyus
KU05)	73.49	1	Kursk	R. Kurs
AD01)	73.52	1	Maykop	R. Zebra
TS21)	73.52	4	Nab.Chelny	R. Vtoroye dykhanie
TY07)	73.55	1	Tyumen	Avtoradio
VN02)	73.55	1	Voronezh	Russkoye R.
VN06)	73.58	1	Boguchar	ORR
NS06)	73.58	1	Novosibirsk	R. Novosibirsk
TA03)	73.61	2	Tambov	Ekho Moskvy
TV04)	73.61	1	Tver	R. Pilot
SA07)	73.61	1	Samara	R. Samara-Maksimum
OL02)	73.61	1	Oryol	Russkoye R.
RO21)	73.61	1	Volgodonsk	Hit FM
AM02)	73.64	1	Blagoveshchensk	Russkoye R.
ST04)	73.64	5	Stavropol	R. Retro
CV02)	73.67	1	Cheboksary	Russkoye R.
VG03)	73.67	1	Volgograd	R. Novaya volna
NN04)	73.70	1	N.Novgorod	Feliks-Radio
VN06)	73.76	1	Bobrov	ORR
IR06)	73.76	1	Irkutsk	Russkoye R.
RO10)	73.76	1	Rostov-na-Donu	R. 7
AK12)	73.79	1	Biysk	Yevropa plyus
SP11)	73.82	4	St.Peterburg	R. Maksimum
MO10)	73.82	10	Moskva	Ekho Moskvy
SA07)	73.88	1	Tolyatti	R. Samara-Maksimum
YN01)	73.88	1	Novyy Urengoy	Mig-Inform
MD01)	73.88	1	Saransk	Yevropa plyus
BE10)	73.88	1	Staryy Oskol	S-Radio
VL04)	73.91	1	Vladimir	Nashe R.
KY04)	73.94	1	Nizhnevartovsk	R. Yugra
YA01)	73.94	1	Yaroslavl	Yevropa plyus
NN30)	73.94	1	Sarov	ORR
OB10)	73.94	1	Orenburg	N-Radio
OM01)	73.94	1	Omsk	R. Shanson
TS06)	73.97	1	Kazan	R. Kuray
TY10)	73.97	1	Tyumen	Dinamit FM
CB05)	73.97	1	Chelyabinsk	Ekho Moskvy
KU06)	73.97	1	Kursk	Kanal Melodiya
KV04)	73.97	1	Kirov	R. Mariya
MO25)	87.5	1	Moskva	R. Arsenal
SP29)	87.5	2.5	St.Peterburg	Dorozhnoye R.
AM02)	87.7	1	Blagoveshchensk	Russkoye R.
SP08)	88.0	1	St.Peterburg	R. Retro FM
PR11)	88.0	1	Perm	Hit FM
MO11)	88.0	1	Moskva	DO-Radio
MO08)	88.3	1	Moskva	R. Retro
SP12)	88.4	2	St.Peterburg	Avtoradio
MO12)	88.7	1	Balashika	R. Disko
SP30)	88.9	5	St.Peterburg	Klassika Peterburg
MO24)	89.1	1	Moskva	R. Jazz
MO28)	89.5	1	Moskva	Megapolis FM
MO27)	89.9	1	Moskva	R. Kuranty
SP13)	90.1	1	St.Peterburg	R. Eremitazh
SV07)	90.2	1	Yekaterinburg	R. SK
MO04)	90.3	5	Moskva	Avtoradio
NN16)	90.6	1	N.Novgorod	Dinamit FM
SA08)	90.6	1	Samara	R. Shanson
SP04)	90.6	1	St.Peterburg	R. Khit 90i6
MO26)	90.8	1	Moskva	R. Sport FM
SV08)	90.8	1	Yekaterinburg	R. Maksimum
SA15)	91.0	1	Samara	R. 7
SP10)	91.1	5	St.Peterburg	Kanal Melodiya
PR06)	91.2	1	Perm	Ekho Moskvy
MO10)	91.2	1	Moskva	Ekho Moskvy
SV09)	91.4	1	Yekaterinburg	Ekho Moskvy
SP14)	91.5	10	St.Peterburg	Ekho Moskvy
MO33)	92.8	1	Moskva	R. Karnaval
MO32)	92.4	1	Moskva	R. Dacha
NS15)	96.2	1	Novosibirsk	R. Start
MO34)	96.4	1	Moskva	Smeshnoye R.
CB07)	96.4	1	Chelyabinsk	R. Retro
SA03)	98.6	1	Samara	Avtoradio
NS07)	98.7	1	Novosibirsk	Avtoradio
CB05)	99.5	1	Chelyabinsk	Ekho Moskvy
MO35)	90.0	1	Moskva	R. Russkiye pesni
TY07)	100.0	1	Tyumen	Avtoradio
KD25)	100.0	1	Otradnaya	ORR
PR07)	100.0	5	Perm	Nashe R.
VG04)	100.0	1	Volgograd	R. Vedo
NN05)	100.0	1	N.Novgorod	R. 7
KA06)	100.1	1	Kaliningrad	R. Shok
PZ04)	100.1	1	Kuznetsk	Serebryanyy dozhd
MO13)	100.1	5	Moskva	Serebryanyy dozhd
RO04)	100.1	1	Rostov-na-Donu	Hit FM
KL07)	100.2	1	Obninsk	Serebryanyy dozhd
VO04)	100.2	1	Vologda	Yevropa plyus
MU05)	100.2	1	Murmansk	Neru+
OB12)	100.2	1	Buzuluk	Avtoradio
RO18)	100.3	1	Volgodonsk	Yevropa plyus
VN01)	100.3	1	Voronezh	Yevropa plyus
SA02)	100.3	1	Samara	Russkoye R.
KN05)	100.3	5	Krasnoyarsk	R. Gorod
KO01)	100.3	1	Syktyvkar	Yevropa plyus
BR01)	100.3	1	Bryansk	Yevropa plyus
SV10)	100.4	1	Yekaterinburg	Nashe R.
NO03)	100.4	1	Novgorod V.	Kanal Melodiya
NN06)	100.4	4	N.Novgorod	Serebryanyy dozhd
KT01)	100.4	1	Petrozavodsk	Yevropa plyus
CB02)	100.4	1	Chelyabinsk	Russkoye R.
KA04)	100.4	1	Bolshakovo	R. Baltik plyus
ST08)	100.4	5	Pyatigorsk	Hit FM
KY15)	100.4	1	Langepas	R. Prostor S
SP01)	100.5	5	St.Peterburg	Yevropa plyus
CB19)	100.5	1	Magnitogorsk	R. Lyuks
SV18)	100.5	1	Nizhniy Tagil	Ekho Moskvy
CK02)	100.5	1	Anadyr	R. Maksimum
TS12)	100.5	1	Kazan	Tatar Radiosi
MO07)	100.5	5	Balashika	R. Ultra
KY16)	100.5	1	Kogalym	Russkoye R.
UD02)	100.5	1	Izhevsk	Russkoye R.
KE07)	100.5	4	Novokuznetsk	Apeks-Radio
VL01)	100.5	1	Kovrov	Yevropa plyus
VL05)	100.6	1	Kolchugino	R. Stil
TV02)	100.6	1	Tver	Russkoye R.
TY08)	100.6	1	Tyumen	R. Siti
VG01)	100.6	4	Volgograd	Yevropa plyus
YA04)	100.6	1	Yaroslavl	R. Elis
DA03)	100.7	1	Makhachkala	R. Priboy
RS03)	100.7	1	Yakutsk	R. RIM
PR08)	100.7	5	Perm	Music Radio
RO11)	100.7	1	Rostov-na-Donu	Ekho Moskvy
NS04)	100.7	3	Novosibirsk	R. Yuniton
RY04)	100.7	1	Ryazan	Ekho Moskvy
KN06)	100.8	1	Krasnoyarsk	Russkaya volna
MO29)	100.8	1	Podolsk	R. Podolska
MO36)	100.9	5	Moskva	R. Klassik
BA15)	100.9	1	Steplitamak	Yevropa plyus
IR08)	100.9	1	Irkutsk	Dinamit FM
KL06)	100.9	1	Obninsk	Russkoye R.
SP15)	100.9	10	St.Peterburg	R. Russkiy Shanson
KD04)	100.9	1	Anapa	R. ROKS-Region
KA03)	100.9	1	Kaliningrad	R. BAS
LI02)	100.9	1	Lipetsk	Russkoye R.
NN07)	100.9	5	N.Novgorod	Nashe R.
ST09)	100.9	1	Pyatigorsk	R. Provintsiya
BE07)	100.9	1	Belgorod	R. Retro
KD26)	100.9	1	Kushchevskaya	R. Troyka
SA07)	100.9	1	Syzran	R. Samara-Maksimum
TY09)	101.0	1	Tyumen	R. Shanson
TS24)	101.0	1	Bugulma	Russkoye R.
SA09)	101.0	1	Samara	Kanal Melodiya
KD24)	101.0	1	Otradnaya	Mayak Kubani
SV19)	101.0	1	Nizhniy Tagil	R. Shanson
MU01)	101.0	1	Murmansk	Yevropa plyus
TM04)	101.0	1	Norilsk	R. Planeta
SP25)	101.0	1	Vyborg	R. Sputnik
TS26)	101.0	1	Almetyevsk	Russkoye R.
KG07)	101.1	1	Kurgan	Russkoye R. 2
VL05)	101.1	1	Gus-Khrustalnyy	R. Stil
YA05)	101.1	1	Yaroslavl	Hit FM
KD11)	101.1	1	Sochi	Avtoradio
VN05)	101.1	1	Voronezh	Serebryanyy dozhd
MO14)	101.2	10	Moskva	Dinamit FM
RO12)	101.2	1	Rostov-na-Donu	Oversan-Radio
SA07)	101.2	1	Tolyatti	R. Samara-Maksimum
YN03)	101.2	1	Salekhard	Salekhardskiy videokanal
SV01)	101.2	5	Yekaterinburg	Yevropa plyus
NO02)	101.2	4	Novgorod V.	Russkoye R.
VO09)	101.2	1	Cherepovets	R. Retro
VL07)	101.3	1	Vladimir	R. Retro
KY17)	101.3	1	Surgut	Nashe R.
LI01)	101.3	1	Lipetsk	Yevropa plyus
KN07)	101.3	1	Krasnoyarsk	Avtoradio
MD02)	101.3	1	Saransk	Russkoye R.
KA07)	101.3	5	Kaliningrad	Nashe R.

FM	MHz	kW	Location	Station
OB08)	101.3	1	Orenburg	Ekho Moskvy
TS13)	101.3	1	Kazan	R. Retro
TL09)	101.4	1	Tula	R. Maksimum
IR11)	101.4	1	Angarsk	R. Avtos
NN08)	101.4	1	N.Novgorod	Hit FM
NS14)	101.4	2	Novosibirsk	R. Novosibirsk
SP16)	101.4	10	St.Peterburg	Eldoradio
BA13)	101.4	1	Steplitamak	R. Troyka
SV05)	101.5	1	Nizhniy Tagil	Avtoradio
NO04)	101.5	1	Malaya Vishera	Dinamit FM
KG06)	101.5	1	Kurgan	R. Shanson
KE09)	101.5	1	Novokuznetsk	Ekho Moskvy
SA14)	101.5	5	Samara	R Nostalzhi
KD04)	101.5	1	Maykop	R. ROKS-Region
PR09)	101.5	1	Perm	R Nostalzhi
TS18)	101.5	1	Nab.Chelny	Kanal Melodiya
DA04)	101.5	1	Makhachkala	Hit FM
BR02)	101.5	1	Bryansk	Russkoye R.
AR03)	101.6	1	Arkhangelsk	R. Shanson
KY02)	101.6	1	Khanty-Mansiysk	Hit FM
CB01)	101.6	1	Chelyabinsk	Yevropa plyus
TY04)	101.6	1	Megion	R. Krasnaya Armiya
VN06)	101.6	2.5	Voronezh	ORR
VO10)	101.6	1	Cherepovets	Yevropa plyus
RO13)	101.6	1	Rostov-na-Donu	R. Rostova
CK01)	101.6	1	Anadyr	R. Purga
BA04)	101.6	1	Ufa	Pervyy kanal
RO19)	101.7	1	Volgodonsk	Russkoye R.
KN08)	101.7	1	Krasnoyarsk	R. Shanson
SP05)	101.7	1	Kingisepp	Studio FM
AS04)	101.7	1	Astrakhan	Otkrytoye Radio
UL01)	101.7	1	Ulyanovsk	Yevropa plyus
KH05)	101.7	1	Komsomolsk-na-A.	Russkoye R.
PM01)	101.7	5	Vladivostok	R. VBC
KD04)	101.7	1	Temryuk	R. ROKS-Region
MO15)	101.7	5	Moskva	Nashe R.
IR01)	101.7	1	Irkutsk	Ekho Moskvy
SA07)	101.8	1	Chapayevsk	R. Samara-Maksimum
TV01)	101.8	1	Tver	Yevropa plyus
YN02)	101.8	1	Salekhard	Yevropa plyus
ST02)	101.8	1	Stavropol	Russkoye R.
KO02)	101.8	1	Syktyvkar	Russkoye R.
KD01)	101.8	1	Krasnodar	Russkoye R.
UD05)	101.8	1	Izhevsk	R. Shanson
OB05)	101.8	1	Orenburg	Nashe R.
PZ02)	101.8	1	Penza	Russkoye R.
TY02)	101.8	1	Tyumen	Yevropa plyus
KE05)	101.8	1	Kemerovo	Dinamit FM
KA05)	101.8	1	Kaliningrad	O'Key Radio
AD02)	101.8	1	Maykop	Russkoye R.
KY18)	101.9	3	Surgut	R. 7
KD04)	101.9	1	Gelendzhik	R. ROKS-Region
KD21)	101.9	5	Sochi	R. Nika
DA02)	101.9	1	Makhachkala	Russkoye R.
KA08)	101.9	2.5	Bolshakovo	R. Massiv
AK06)	101.9	1	Barnaul	Molodyozhnyy kanal
TL04)	101.9	5	Tula	Nashe R.
RO23)	101.9	1	Taganrog	R. TVS
TS17)	101.9	1	Nab.Chelny	Yevropa plyus
OM01)	101.9	1	Omsk	Yevropa plyus
NN09)	101.9	5	N.Novgorod	Avtoradio
YN05)	101.9	1	Nadym	Ekho Moskvy
KD22)	101.9	1	Novorossiysk	Yevropa plyus
SO01)	102.0	1	Vladikavkaz	Yevropa plyus
NE01)	102.0	1	Naryan-Mar	Serebryanyy dozhd
CH03)	102.0	1	Chita	R. Maksimum
KG04)	102.0	1	Kurgan	Avtoradio
KD25)	102.0	1	Kanevskaya	ORR
RY05)	102.0	1	Ryazan	Avtoradio
PR10)	102.0	1	Perm	ORR
TM01)	102.0	1	Norilsk	Nago-Radio
OB14)	102.0	1	Orsk	Nashe R.
OB16)	102.0	1	Novotroitsk	Serebryanyy dozhd
SP17)	102.0	10	St.Peterburg	R. ROKS
SV11)	102.0	1	Yekaterinburg	Dinamit FM
MU08)	102.0	1	Murmansk	Ekho Moskvy
CV03)	102.0	1	Cheboksary	Mestnoye Khit Radio
MU13)	102.0	1	Apatity	Serebryanyy dozhd
VG03)	102.0	5	Volgograd	R. Novaya volna
SM01)	102.0	1	Smolensk	Yevropa plyus
CB20)	102.0	1	Magnitogorsk	Yevropa plyus
KD24)	102.1	1	Arkhipo-Osipovka	Mayak Kubani
SA10)	102.1	1	Samara	Nashe R.
VO07)	102.1	1	Cherepovets	Russkoye R.
IR12)	102.1	1	Bratsk	Yevropa plyus
MO16)	102.1	5	Moskva	R. Monte-Karlo
TO02)	102.1	1	Tomsk	Russkoye R.
PS01)	102.1	1	Pskov	Nord-Vest R
KL02)	102.1	1	Kaluga	Russkoye R.
SR03)	102.1	1	Saratov	R. Tango
UL03)	102.1	1	Ulyanovsk	R. 2x2
IR03)	102.1	1	Irkutsk	Hit FM
KU07)	102.1	1	Kursk	Nashe R.
SV05)	102.2	1	Kamensk-Uralskiy	Avtoradio
KV01)	102.2	1	Kirov	Yevropa plyus
RO01)	102.2	1	Rostov-na-Donu	Yevropa plyus
AS02)	102.2	1	Astrakhan	Russkoye R.
KD02)	102.2	1	Krasnodar	Yevropa plyus
KB01)	102.2	1	Nalchik	Serebryanyy dozhd
BE04)	102.2	1	Belgorod	Nashe R.
OB04)	102.3	1	Orenburg	Avtoradio
YN08)	102.3	1	Novyy Urengoy	Ekho Moskvy
KD17)	102.3	1	Armavir	R. Maksimum
KH02)	102.3	1	Khabarovsk	R. Maksimum
SA16)	102.3	1	Tolyatti	R. Avgust
OL03)	102.3	1	Oryol	Serebryanyy dozhd
UD06)	102.4	1	Izhevsk	R. Retro
KD24)	102.4	1	Yeysk	Mayak Kubani
AK05)	102.4	1	Barnaul	R. Uniton
DA01)	102.4	1	Makhachkala	Yevropa plyus
VL05)	102.4	1	Vladimir	R. Stil
NN10)	102.4	1	N.Novgorod	R. Maksimum
VG08)	102.4	1	Volgograd	R. Aprel
KD04)	102.4	1	Novorossiysk	R. ROKS-Region
TS07)	102.4	1	Kazan	R. Nastroyeniye
SP05)	102.4	10	St.Peterburg	Studio FM
YN06)	102.5	1	Nadym	Yevropa plyus
SL01)	102.5	1	Yuzhno-Sakhalinsk	Yevropa plyus
MA01)	102.5	1	Magadan	Novaya zhizn
BA14)	102.5	1	Kumertau	Otkrytoye Radio ARIS
MU04)	102.5	1	Murmansk	Hit FM
SV05)	102.5	1	Yekaterinburg	Avtoradio
OM06)	102.5	1	Omsk	R. Maksimum
KD12)	102.5	4	Sochi	Hit FM
CV01)	102.5	1	Cheboksary	Yevropa plyus
BA06)	102.5	1	Ufa	R. Bulgar
IV04)	102.5	1	Ivanovo	R. Pyatyy etazh
TY01)	102.5	1	Tyumen	Russkoye R.
MO17)	102.5	5	Balashika	Pervoye Popularnoye R.
CB32)	102.5	1	Magnitogorsk	R. Shanson
KY11)	102.5	1	Surgut	Russkoye R.
SR04)	102.6	4	Saratov	R. 7
CB17)	102.6	1	Ozersk	Volna
YA02)	102.6	1	Yaroslavl	Russkoye R.
NS08)	102.6	1	Novosibirsk	R. Shanson
KL01)	102.6	1	Kaluga	Yevropa plyus
CH01)	102.6	1	Chita	R. Shanson
RO25)	102.6	1	Novocherkassk	R. N
KE04)	102.6	1	Novokuznetsk	R. Shanson
BR06)	102.6	1	Bryansk	Avtoradio
KD28)	102.7	5	Krasnodar	Mayak Kubani
PR03)	102.7	5	Perm	Avtoradio Perm
TL03)	102.7	1	Tula	R. Retro
SA17)	102.7	1	Tolyatti	Yevropa plyus
TV04)	102.7	1	Tver	R. Pilot
KG02)	102.7	1	Kurgan	Russkoye R.
MU10)	102.7	1	Murmansk	R. Shanson
AS01)	102.7	1	Astrakhan	Yevropa plyus
BE02)	102.7	1	Belgorod	Russkoye R.
CB02)	102.7	1	Zlatoust	Russkoye R.
OB15)	102.8	1	Orsk	Yevropa plyus
VN07)	102.8	1	Voronezh	R. Shanson
SO05)	102.8	1	Vladikavkaz	Ekho Moskvy
KN03)	102.8	5	Krasnoyarsk	Avto-Radio Krasnoyarsk
SP11)	102.8	10	St.Peterburg	R. Maksimum
TS08)	102.8	1	Kazan	BIM-Radio
PZ05)	102.8	1	Penza	Kanal Melodiya
KE01)	102.8	1	Kemerovo	Yevropa plyus
TY04)	102.8	1	Novyy Urengoy	R. Krasnaya Armiya
BU03)	102.8	1	Ulan-Ude	Ekho Moskvy
AR02)	102.8	1	Arkhangelsk	Yevropa plyus
KD27)	102.8	1	Anapa	Kanal Melodiya
CB03)	102.9	1	Chelyabinsk	R. Nashego Goroda
MU14)	102.9	1	Monchegorsk	R. Troyka
NN02)	102.9	4	N.Novgorod	Russkoye R.
KO06)	102.9	1	Ukhta	R. Maksimum
VL01)	102.9	1	Vladimir	Yevropa plyus
SA05)	102.9	1	Samara	Ekho Moskvy
KA09)	102.9	1	Kaliningrad	Miks FM
TA04)	102.9	1	Tambov	R. Roks

FM	MHz	kW	Location	Station
KV04)	102.9	1	Kirov	R. Mariya
AK02)	102.9	1	Barnaul	Russkoye R.
OB03)	103.0	1	Orenburg	Hit FM
CB21)	103.0	1	Magnitogorsk	MRC
UD01)	103.0	1	Izhevsk	Yevropa plyus
OL04)	103.0	1	Oryol	R. Troyka
BA07)	103.0	1	Ufa	R. Roksana
SV21)	103.0	1	Nizhniy Tagil	Ekoradio
YN10)	103.0	1	Noyabrsk	R. Noyabrsk
TM05)	103.0	1	Norilsk	R. Delta
TS25)	103.0	1	Bugulma	R. Nostalzhi
MO18)	103.0	5	Balashika	R. Shanson
RO03)	103.0	1	Rostov-na-Donu	Nashe R.
SR03)	103.0	1	Saratov	R. Tango
KD25)	103.0	1	Arkhipo-Osipovka	ORR
VO08)	103.0	1	Cherepovets	R. Troyka
MU09)	103.0	1	Murmansk	Nashe R.
TY03)	103.1	1	Tyumen	R. 7
RS01)	103.1	1	Yakutsk	R. Viktoriya
IR04)	103.1	1	Angarsk	Nashe R.
BE09)	103.1	1	Staryy Oskol	Yevropa plyus
LI04)	103.1	1	Lipetsk	R. Armans
KH03)	103.1	1	Khabarovsk	R. Maksimum
MU12)	103.1	1	Apatity	Dinamit FM
KD13)	103.1	1	Sochi	Russkoye R.
VG05)	103.1	1	Volgograd	R. Shanson
ST10)	103.1	1	Pyatigorsk	Russkoye R.
SP05)	103.1	5	Vyborg	Studio FM
PR04)	103.2	5	Perm	R. Maksimum
KD05)	103.2	1	Krasnodar	Avtoradio
NS01)	103.2	3	Novosibirsk	Yevropa plyus
SV12)	103.2	1	Yekaterinburg	R. Shanson
RY01)	103.2	1	Ryazan	Yevropa plyus
SA18)	103.2	1	Tolyatti	R. SV
TA07)	103.2	1	Morshansk	Kanal Melodiya
BE05)	103.2	1	Belgorod	Russkoye R. 2
IR15)	103.2	1	Ust-Illimsk	Russkoye R.
VO05)	103.2	1	Vologda	R. Retro
RO16)	103.3	1	Azov	Avtoradio
YA06)	103.3	1	Yaroslavl	Kanal Melodiya
TL02)	103.3	1	Tula	R. Vizavi
KD24)	103.3	1	Tbilisskaya	Mayak Kubani
BU04)	103.3	1	Ulan-Ude	Puls-Radio
AM01)	103.3	1	Blagoveshchensk	R. Manhattan
KY20)	103.3	1	Surgut	Avtoradio
CH04)	103.3	1	Chita	Popularnoye Radio
TY04)	103.3	1	Nadym	R. Krasnaya Armiya
TS11)	103.3	1	Kazan	Puls-Radio
KD24)	103.3	1	Krasnaya Polyana	Mayak Kubani
KE06)	103.3	1	Kemerovo	R. Shanson
KD28)	103.4	1	Tuapse	Mayak Kubani
NN03)	103.4	5	N.Novgorod	R. Randevu
VL02)	103.4	1	Vladimir	Russkoye R.
KV05)	103.4	1	Kirov	Hit FM
VN08)	103.4	1	Voronezh	R. 101-BISS
TO01)	103.4	1	Tomsk	Yevropa plyus
SP18)	103.4	20	St.Peterburg	Dinamit FM
TA05)	103.4	4	Tambov	Hit FM
TS28)	103.4	1	Almetyevsk	R. Shanson
CB27)	103.5	1	Chelyabinsk	Nashe R.
OM07)	103.5	1	Omsk	R. 3
KM03)	103.5	1	Petropavlovsk-Kam.	Ekho Moskvy
SV24)	103.5	1	Kamensk-Uralskiy	R. Gong
SM02)	103.5	1	Smolensk	Russkoye R.
SR01)	103.5	1	Saratov	Yevropa plyus
BA08)	103.5	1	Ufa	Sport FM
TY04)	103.5	1	Nyagan	R. Krasnaya Armiya
KT04)	103.5	5	Petrozavodsk	Kanal Melodiya
KO04)	103.5	1	Ukhta	Yevropa plyus
BR04)	103.5	1	Bryansk	Nashe R.
CB22)	103.6	1	Magnitogorsk	Radiostudiya HTM
IV03)	103.6	1	Ivanovo	Nashe R.
ST01)	103.6	1	Stavropol	Yevropa plyus
KE10)	103.6	1	Yugra	Avtoradio
BE01)	103.6	1	Belgorod	Yevropa plyus
KL04)	103.6	1	Kaluga	Hit FM
SA11)	103.6	5	Samara	R. Megapolis
TS21)	103.6	4	Nab.Chelny	R. Vtoroye dykhanie
SR02)	103.7	1	Balakovo	Russkoye R.
OB01)	103.7	1	Orenburg	Yevropa plyus
SV04)	103.7	5	Yekaterinburg	R. Si
MO03)	103.7	10	Moskva	R. Maksimum
RK03)	103.7	1	Sayanogorsk	R. Sibir
KH04)	103.7	2	Khabarovsk	Nashe R.
NO01)	103.7	5	Novgorod V.	Yevropa plyus
KG05)	103.7	4	Kurgan	Hit FM
KD06)	103.7	1	Krasnodar	R. 7
RO10)	103.7	1	Rostov-na-Donu	R. 7
KU05)	103.7	1	Kursk	R. Kurs
RO22)	103.8	1	Volgodonsk	Nashe R.
IR05)	103.8	5	Irkutsk	Yevropa plyus
KY29)	103.8	1	Raduzhnyy	Russkoye R.
AR01)	103.8	1	Arkhangelsk	Russkoye R.
ME02)	103.8	1	Yoshkar-Ola	Puls Radio
KY21)	103.8	1	Surgut	R. Figaro
KO03)	103.8	1	Syktyvkar	R. 7
PZ01)	103.8	5	Penza	Yevropa plyus
TY04)	103.8	1	Salekhard	R. Krasnaya Armiya
CB02)	103.8	1	Miass	Russkoye R.
UD07)	103.8	4	Izhevsk	Nashe R.
ST11)	103.8	1	Pyatigorsk	Yevropa plyus
KA13)	103.8	1	Sovetsk	R. Ekspress
KN01)	103.8	1	Krasnoyarsk	Yevropa plyus
NS09)	103.9	1	Novosibirsk	Nashe R.
KA10)	103.9	1	Kaliningrad	Hit FM
RO26)	103.9	1	Gukovo	Nika-TR
TA06)	103.9	1	Tambov	ORR
NN01)	103.9	1	N.Novgorod	Yevropa plyus
AK03)	103.9	1	Barnaul	Rok Radio
KV02)	103.9	1	Kirov	Russkoye R.
KD14)	104.0	1	Novorossiysk	Novaya Rossiya
KY22)	104.0	1	Nizhnevartovsk	Yevropa plyus
VG06)	104.0	1	Volgograd	Ekho Moskvy
BA05)	104.0	1	Ufa	R. Retro
KY24)	104.0	1	Kogalym	Yevropa plyus
TS09)	104.0	1	Kazan	R. Volga
SP19)	104.0	10	St.Peterburg	Nashe R.
KY23)	104.0	1	Yugorsk	Yevropa plyus
MO32)	104.0	1	Serpukhov	R. Revyu
KD24)	104.0	1	Novopokrovskaya	Mayak Kubani
SA14)	104.0	1	Tolyatti	R. Nostalzhi
IR13)	104.1	1	Bratsk	Russkoye R.
OB17)	104.1	1	Buguruslan	Nashe R.
SV27)	104.1	1	Karpinsk	R. Kray
SL04)	104.1	1	Korsakov	Yevropa plyus
RO15)	104.1	1	Rostov-na-Donu	Otkrytoye Radio
KU01)	104.1	1	Kursk	Yevropa plyus
KV08)	104.1	1	Kirov	Planeta Si
CB08)	104.1	1	Chelyabinsk	Russkoye R. 2
PM02)	104.2	5	Vladivostok	R. Novaya volna
ST15)	104.2	1	Yessentuki	Hit FM
KY01)	104.2	1	Khanty-Mansiysk	Russkoye R.
IV05)	104.2	1	Ivanovo	R. Retro Ivanovo
RK02)	104.2	1	Abakan	Nashe R.
MA02)	104.2	1	Magadan	Russkoye R.
KD07)	104.2	1	Krasnodar	R. Retro
CB23)	104.2	1	Magnitogorsk	R. Senator
KY25)	104.2	1	Surgut	Radio-88
MO19)	104.2	10	Moskva	R. Energiya
UL06)	104.2	1	Ulyanovsk	ORR
OB06)	104.2	1	Orenburg	Serebryanyy dozhd
BE03)	104.2	1	Belgorod	R. Shanson
SA07)	104.3	1	Samara	R. Samara-Maksimum
VN02)	104.3	1	Voronezh	Russkoye R.
KE14)	104.3	1	Kemerovo	R. Flora
SR06)	104.3	3	Saratov	Avtoradio
KE11)	104.4	1	Novokuznetsk	Yevropa plyus
KA09)	104.4	4	Sovetsk	Miks FM
SP20)	104.4	5	St.Peterburg	R. Shanson
KD15)	104.4	5	Sochi	Yevropa plyus
OM03)	104.4	1	Omsk	R. Alternativa
TL05)	104.4	5	Tula	V.O.T. Radio
AK04)	104.4	1	Barnaul	R. Stolitsa
VO01)	104.4	1	Vologda	R. Transmit
AM04)	104.4	1	Blagoveshchensk	R. Ekspress
VG07)	104.5	5	Volgograd	R. Maksikum
KM01)	104.5	1	Petropavlovsk-Kam.	R. Tri
SV13)	104.5	1	Yekaterinburg	R. 7
MU03)	104.5	1	Murmansk	Power FM
UD03)	104.5	1	Izhevsk	R. Adam
YA03)	104.5	1	Yaroslavl	R. Shanson
SL02)	104.5	1	Yuzhno-Sakhalinsk	R Nostalzhi
KA01)	104.5	1	Kaliningrad	Yevropa plyus
BA02)	104.5	1	Ufa	Russkoye R.
KY26)	104.5	1	Langepas	Yevropa plyus
ME01)	104.5	1	Yoshkar-Ola	Yevropa plyus
NN04)	104.5	1	N.Novgorod	Feliks-Radio
KD24)	104.5	1	Kanevskaya	Mayak Kubani
SO02)	104.5	1	Vladikavkaz	Russkoye R. 2
KL05)	104.5	1	Obninsk	R. Reyting

FM	MHz	kW	Location	Station
CB09)	104.5	1	Chelyabinsk	R. Olimp
RS01)	104.5	1	Yakutsk	R. Viktoriya
KA09)	104.6	1	Chernyakhovsk	Miks FM
RO07)	104.6	1	Rostov-na-Donu	Dinamit FM
TY04)	104.6	1	Tyumen	R. Krasnaya Armiya
LI03)	104.6	5	Lipetsk	R. Shanson
TO06)	104.6	1	Tomsk	R. Sibir
PS03)	104.6	1	Pskov	Russkoye R.
ST12)	104.6	1	Pyatigorsk	Ekho Moskvy
KU08)	104.6	1	Kursk	Avtoradio
KN04)	104.6	1	Krasnoyarsk	Hit FM
VO01)	104.6	1	Cherepovets	R. Transmit
KY27)	104.7	1	Nizhnevartovsk	Avtoradio
SV26)	104.7	1	Kamensk-Uralskiy	R. Kamensk
BE06)	104.7	1	Belgorod	Hit FM
KT02)	104.7	1	Petrozavodsk	Russkoye R.
AR05)	104.7	5	Arkhangelsk	Nashe R.
CB24)	104.7	1	Zlatoust	Yevropa plyus
TS03)	104.7	1	Kazan	R. Passazh
KD19)	104.7	1	Krasnodar	Nashe R.
YN07)	104.7	1	Gubkinskiy	Ekho Moskvy
MO09)	104.7	7.5	Moskva	R. 7
PR01)	104.7	1	Perm	Yevropa plyus
OL01)	104.8	1	Oryol	Hit FM
OB07)	104.8	1	Orenburg	R. Retro
SP07)	104.8	4	St.Peterburg	R. Baltika
SA19)	104.8	1	Tolyatti	Serebryanyy dozhd
VL04)	104.8	1	Vladimir	Nashe R.
SR07)	104.8	1	Saratov	R. Maksimum
SA12)	104.8	1	Samara	Hit FM
MU15)	104.8	1	Monchegorsk	R. Shanson
TS22)	104.8	1	Nab.Chelny	Russkoye R.
KE02)	104.8	1	Kemerovo	Russkoye R.
NN12)	104.9	1	N.Novgorod	Nizhegorodskaya Volna
AK01)	104.9	1	Barnaul	Yevropa plyus
KD24)	104.9	1	Novorossiysk	Mayak Kubani
CB10)	104.9	1	Chelyabinsk	L-Radio
VO02)	104.9	1	Vologda	Russkoye R.
MO30)	104.9	1	Noginsk	R. Noginska
TL01)	104.9	1	Tula	Yevropa plyus
SO04)	104.9	1	Vladikavkaz	R. MSS
TM02)	105.0	1	Norilsk	R. Polyus
KD24)	105.0	1	Shedok or Psbay	Mayak Kubani
OM08)	105.0	1	Omsk	Nashe R.
KE12)	105.0	1	Novokuznetsk	Hit FM
AS05)	105.0	1	Astrakhan	R. Retro
KY04)	105.0	1	Surgut	R. Yugra
SV14)	105.0	1	Yekaterinburg	R. Pilot
BA09)	105.0	1	Ufa	Hit FM
MU05)	105.0	1	Murmansk	Neru+
RS04)	105.0	1	Neryungri	Russkoye R. 2
RY06)	105.0	1	Ryazan	R. 7
YA01)	105.1	1	Yaroslavl	Yevropa plyus
CB25)	105.1	1	Miass	Yevropa plyus
RO02)	105.1	1	Rostov-na-Donu	Russkoye R.
ST05)	105.1	1	Stavropol	Ekho Moskvy
TS31)	105.1	1	Nizhnekamsk	R. Neftekhim
VL05)	105.1	1	Kovrov	R. Stil
AM03)	105.1	1	Blagoveshchensk	Yevropa plyus
KA04)	105.2	1	Kaliningrad	R. Baltik plyus
YN09)	105.2	1	Novyy Urengoy	Yevropa plyus
CH02)	105.2	1	Chita	Russkoye R.
KD16)	105.2	1	Sochi	Nashe R.
MO20)	105.2	5	Moskva	R. Troyka
CB26)	105.2	1	Magnitogorsk	MaX-Radio
NS02)	105.2	1	Novosibirsk	Russkoye R.
KD04)	105.2	5	Krasnodar	R. ROKS-Region
SO06)	105.3	1	Vladikavkaz	R. IR
TS05)	105.3	1	Kazan	Avtoradio
SP03)	105.3	1	St.Peterburg	Love Radio St.Peterburg
TY04)	105.3	1	Khanty-Mansiysk	R. Krasnaya Armiya
TL06)	105.3	1	Tula	Top Radio
TY04)	105.3	1	Noyabrsk	R. Krasnaya Armiya
IR14)	105.3	1	Bratsk	Golos Angary
SR02)	105.3	1	Saratov	Russkoye R.
OB10)	105.3	1	Orenburg	N-Radio
UD08)	105.3	1	Izhevsk	Ekho Moskvy
KE08)	105.3	1	Kemerovo	Avtoradio
AR06)	105.4	1	Arkhangelsk	ORR
RY02)	105.4	1	Ryazan	Russkoye R.
KY06)	105.4	1	Nyagan	Dinamit FM
KU02)	105.4	1	Kursk	Russkoye R.
KD28)	105.4	1	Armavir	Mayak Kubani
KM02)	105.5	1	Petropavlovsk-Kam.	R. SV
KE13)	105.5	1	Novokuznetsk	Russkoye R.
TV05)	105.5	1	Tver	Nashe R.
SV20)	105.5	1	Nizhniy Tagil	Yevropa plyus
KG01)	105.5	1	Kurgan	Yevropa plyus
AS03)	105.5	1	Astrakhan	Hit FM
KB02)	105.5	1	Nalchik	Russkoye R.
MU02)	105.5	4	Murmansk	Russkoye R.
KD24)	105.6	1	Primorsko-Akhtarsk	Mayak Kubani
SM04)	105.6	1	Smolensk	Hit FM
SP27)	105.6	1	Kingisepp	Yamburg Blues
IR02)	105.6	1	Angarsk	R. Shanson
YA07)	105.6	1	Yaroslavl	Avtoradio
TY05)	105.6	1	Tyumen	Ekho Moskvy
KH01)	105.6	1	Khabarovsk	Yevropa plyus
VG02)	105.6	1	Volgograd	Russkoye R.
SA20)	105.7	1	Tolyatti	Russkoye R.
RS02)	105.7	1	Yakutsk	STV-Radio
TV07)	105.7	1	Vyshniy Volochek	Kanal Melodiya
SV22)	105.7	1	Serov	Yevropa plyus
MO02)	105.7	4	Moskva	Russkoye R.
MU11)	105.7	1	Apatity	Ekho Moskvy
NS10)	105.7	2	Novosibirsk	R. 2
OM02)	105.7	1	Omsk	Russkoye R.
VO06)	105.7	1	Vologda	Ekho Moskvy
SV02)	105.7	1	Yekaterinburg	Russkoye R.
KT03)	105.7	1	Petrozavodsk	Nashe R.
KD28)	105.7	1	Sochi	Mayak Kubani
VN09)	105.7	1	Voronezh	Ekho Moskvy
ST13)	105.8	1	Pyatigorsk	Dinamit FM
SR08)	105.8	1	Saratov	Ekho Moskvy
KD25)	105.8	1	Krasnaya Polyana	ORR
KN02)	105.8	1	Krasnoyarsk	Russkoye R.
KS02)	105.8	1	Kostroma	RDV-FM
CB11)	105.9	1	Chelyabinsk	Hit FM
RO16)	105.9	1	Zverevo	Avtoradio
NN13)	105.9	1	N.Novgorod	R. Retro
RY07)	105.9	1	Ryazan	R. Shanson
KY19)	105.9	1	Surgut	Yevropa plyus
SP21)	105.9	1	St.Peterburg	R. Sputnik
SP26)	106.0	1	Vyborg	Yevropa plyus
TS19)	106.0	1	Nab.Chelny	Hit FM
BU06)	106.0	1	Ulan-Ude	Avtoradio
KD23)	106.0	1	Krasnodar	R. Maksimum
TM06)	106.0	1	Norilsk	R. Severnyy gorod
VL01)	106.0	1	Gus-Khrustalnyy	Yevropa plyus
BA01)	106.0	1	Ufa	Yevropa plyus
IV01)	106.0	1	Ivanovo	Yevropa plyus
TY04)	106.0	1	Kogalym	R. Krasnaya Armiya
TO03)	106.1	1	Tomsk	Nashe R.
VN03)	106.1	1	Voronezh	R. Maksimum
SA01)	106.1	1	Samara	Yevropa plyus
UD04)	106.1	1	Izhevsk	Avtoradio
PR02)	106.2	5	Perm	Russkoye R.
MO01)	106.2	10	Moskva	Yevropa plyus
ST06)	106.2	1	Stavropol	Hit FM
OM04)	106.2	1	Omsk	Avtoradio
LI06)	106.2	1	Lipetsk	R. 7
NS12)	106.2	1	Novosibirsk	R. OTS
SV06)	106.2	4	Yekaterinburg	Hit FM
SP22)	106.3	5	St.Peterburg	R. Rekord
VL05)	106.3	1	Murom	R. Stil
CB12)	106.3	1	Chelyabinsk	Serebryanyy dozhd
BA12)	106.3	1	Oktyabrskiy	Yevropa plyus
VL01)	106.3	1	Murom	Yevropa plyus
KY28)	106.3	1	Nizhnevartovsk	Russkoye R.
SO02)	106.3	1	Vladikavkaz	Russkoye R.
TS10)	106.3	1	Kazan	R. Datt-Dzhin
NN14)	106.4	1	N.Novgorod	ORR
TL08)	106.4	1	Tula	Avtoradio
IR06)	106.4	1	Angarsk	Russkoye R.
KA11)	106.4	1	Kaliningrad	Kanal Melodiya
KY03)	106.4	1	Surgut	R. Maksimum
AR04)	106.4	1	Arkhangelsk	Avto-Radio
BA10)	106.5	1	Ufa	Russkoye R. 2
MU07)	106.5	1	Murmansk	ORR
MO21)	106.6	5	Moskva	Love Radio
KN09)	106.6	1	Krasnoyarsk	R. Maksimum
SA13)	106.6	3	Samara	R. SOK
KY04)	106.6	1	Khanty-Mansiysk	R. Yugra
TS23)	106.7	1	Bugulma	Vashe Radio
NS03)	106.7	1	Novosibirsk	R. Sibiri
KU04)	106.7	1	Kursk	Hit FM
RY03)	106.7	1	Ryazan	ORR
IV07)	106.7	4	Ivanovo	R. 7
KD24)	106.7	1	Temryuk	Mayak Kubani
KD08)	106.8	1	Krasnodar	Hit FM

FM	MHz	kW	Location	Station
TS01)	106.8	1	Kazan	Yevropa plyus
VL06)	106.9	1	Vladimir	ORR
NN15)	106.9	1	N.Novgorod	R. Shanson
VO03)	106.9	1	Vologda	R. Premier
KO08)	106.9	1	Usinsk	Serebryanyy dozhd
UD02)	107.0	1	Izhevsk	Russkoye R. 2
SV15)	107.0	1	Yekaterinburg	Avtoradio
MO06)	107.0	5	Moskva	Russkoye R. 2
TO09)	107.1	1	Tomsk	Daydzhest-FM
PS02)	107.1	1	Pskov	R. Sedmoye nebo
IV06)	107.1	1	Ivanovo	R. Most
IR07)	107.1	1	Irkutsk	Avtoradio
ST14)	107.2	1	Pyatigorsk	R. Sfera
OB02)	107.2	1	Orenburg	Russkoye R.
KD18)	107.2	1	Armavir	Yevropa plyus
MD03)	107.2	1	Saransk	eMSi-Radio
TS02)	107.3	1	Kazan	Russkoye R.
CB13)	107.3	1	Chelyabinsk	Dinamit FM
SR09)	107.3	1	Saratov	Nashe R.
VN13)	107.4	1	Rossosh	Russkoye R.
KD20)	107.4	1	Novorossiysk	Nashe R.
MO22)	107.4	10	Moskva	Hit FM
SP23)	107.4	10	St.Peterburg	R. Leningrad
TS30)	107.5	1	Nizhnekamsk	Serebryanyy dozhd
BU02)	107.5	1	Ulan-Ude	Russkoye R.
BA11)	107.5	1	Ufa	R. Maksimum
KC02)	107.5	1	Karachayevsk	ORR
TL07)	107.5	1	Tula	R. Shanson
SV16)	107.6	1	Yekaterinburg	R. Yekaterinburg
BR05)	107.6	2	Bryansk	Chistyye klyuchi
TY04)	107.6	1	Langepas	R. Krasnaya Armiya
TY04)	107.6	1	Ishim	R. Krasnaya Armiya
UL02)	107.6	1	Ulyanovsk	Russkoye R. 2
VN11)	107.6	3	Voronezh	Hit FM
KD09)	107.7	1	Krasnodar	R. 107
PM03)	107.7	1	Vladivostok	Studiya O'Key
NS11)	107.7	1	Novosibirsk	Ekho Moskvy
BE08)	107.7	1	Belgorod	Avtoradio
MO23)	107.8	4	Moskva	Militseyskaya volna
SP02)	107.8	5	St.Peterburg	Russkoye R.
KD25)	107.8	1	Novorossiysk	ORR
SA21)	107.9	1	Tolyatti	Ekho Moskvy
TY04)	107.9	1	Tobolsk	R. Krasnaya Armiya

NB. Tx's below 1kW not listed.

Addresses and other information (listed by province):

AD) Resp. Adygeya: AD01) ul. Lenina 54-83, 352700 Maykop. AD02) Maykop.

AK) Altayskiy kray: AK01) ul. Pionerov 2, 656099 Barnaul. AK02) ul. Chkalova 57a, 656099 Barnaul. AK03) ul. Papanintsev 105, 656009 Barnaul. AK04) P.O.Box 4264, 656011 Barnaul. AK05) Zmeinogorskiy trakt 29a, 656045 Barnaul. AK06) P.O.Box 3157, 656099 Barnaul. AK07) Zmeinogorskiy trakt 29, 656045 Barnaul. AK08) Barnaul. AK09) ul. Oktyabrskaya 105, 658204 Rubtsovsk. AK10) P.O.Box 419, 659322 Biysk. AK11) P.O.Box 120, 659300 Biysk. AK12) P.O.Box 120, 659300 Biysk. AK13) ul. A. Soboleva 11, 659600 s. Smolenskoye. AK14) ul. Pushkina 14, 658710 Kamen-na-Obi.

AM) Amurskaya oblast: AM01) P.O.Box 227, 675000 Blagoveshchensk. AM02) P.O.Box 227, 675000 Blagoveshchensk. AM03) ul. Nagornaya 9, 675000 Blagoveshchensk. AM04) ul. Gorkogo 224, 675000 Blagoveshchensk.

AR) Arkhangelskaya oblast: AR01) pr. Troitskiy 52, ofis 13, 163061 Arkhangelsk. AR02) pl. Lenina 4, ofis 2202, 163061 Arkhangelsk. AR03) pr. Troitskiy 52, 163061 Arkhangelsk. AR04) Obvodnyy kanal 4, 163060 Arkhangelsk. AR05) pr. Troitskiy 52, ofis 1313, 163061 Arkhangelsk. AR06) Arkhangelsk.

AS) Astrakhanskaya oblast: AS01) ul. 1-ya Perevoznaya 106, 414052 Astrakhan. AS02) P.O.Box 404, 414000 Astrakhan. AS03) ul. Volodarskogo 14, 414000 Astrakhan. AS04) Astrakhan AS05) Astrakhan.

BA) Respublika Bashkortostan: BA01) ul. 50 let Oktyabrya 30, ofis 1, 450005 Ufa. BA02) ul. Mengazheva 160, 450005 Ufa. BA03) ul. Mingazheva 160, 450005 Ufa. BA04) ul. Mendeleyeva 213-77, 450071 Ufa. BA05) P.O.Box 266, 450098 Ufa. BA06) ul. Sotsialisticheskaya 11, 450000 Ufa. BA07) pr. Oktyabrya 71/3, ofis 53, Ufa 54. BA08) Ufa. BA09) P.O.Box 1135, 450000 Ufa. BA10) Ufa. BA11) P.O.Box 85, 450080 Ufa. BA12) ul. Gubkina 3-7, Oktyabrskiy. BA13) Steplitamak. BA14) P.O.Box 51, 453350 Kumertau. BA15) ul. Khudayberdina 17, 453124 Steplitamak.

BE) Belgorodskaya oblast: BE01) ul. Michurina 56, 308007 Belgorod. BE02) ul. Frunze 100, 308000 Belgorod. BE03) ul. Frunze 100, 308800 Belgorod. BE04) ul. Pushkina 49-a, 308820 Belgorod. BE05) ul. Frunze 100, 308800 Belgorod. BE06) ul. Korolyova 2, 308007 Belgorod. BE07) Belgorod. BE08) ul. B. Khmeltnitskogo 131, komn. 509, 308860 Belgorod. BE09) Staryy Oskol. BE10) mikrorayon "Solnechnyy", 309530 St.Oskol. BE11) ul. Dzerzhinskogo 17, 309510 Gubkin. BE12) ul. Revolyutsionnaya 42, St. Oskol. BE13) Staryy Oskol.

BR) Bryanskaya oblast: BR01) ul. Krasnoarmeyskaya 103, ofis 805, 241037 Bryansk BR02) Bryansk. BR03) ul. Romanshina 34/1-293, 241011 Bryansk. BR04) Bryansk. BR05) P.O.Box 32, 241000 Bryansk. BR06) Bryansk.

BU) Respublika Buryatiya: BU01) ul. Borisevicha 7a, 670000 Ulan-Ude. BU02) ul. Borisevicha 7a, 670000 Ulan-Ude. BU03) P.O.Box 4059, 670017 Ulan-Ude. BU04) ul. Tereshkovoy 3, 670031 Ulan-Ude. BU05) Ulan-Ude. BU06) Ulan-Ude.

CB) Chelyabinskaya oblast: CB01) pr. Pobedy 290, kom. 306, 454106 Chelyabinsk. CB02) P.O.Box 8091, 454080 Chelyabinsk. CB03) ul. Ordzhonikidze 41, 454091 Chelyabinsk. CB05) ul. Stepana Razina 1, 454000 Chelyabinsk. CB06) P.O.Box 13758, 454048 Chelyabinsk.CB07) pr. Pobedy 290, of. 904, 454138 Chelyabinsk. CB08) ul. Stepana Razina 1, 454000 Chelyabinsk. CB09) ul. Tsvillinga 46a, 454090 Chelyabinsk. CB10) ul. Griboyedova 57a, 454007 Chelyabinsk. CB11) P.O.Box 8091, 454080 Chelyabinsk. CB12) Chelyabinsk. CB13) ul. Ordzhonikidze 54b, 454000 Chelyabinsk. CB14) ul. Domenshchikov 14, 455049 Magnitogorsk. CB16) ul. Lesoparkovaya 94-90, 455025 Magnitogorsk. CB17) ul. Sverdlova 31-5, 456780 Ozersk. CB18) ul. Sov. Armii 3-15, 455036 Magnitogorsk. CB19) ul. Yeniseyskaya 133, 455025 Magnitogorsk. CB20) ul. Domenshchikov 14, 455049 Magnitogorsk. CB21) ul. Sov. Armii 3-15, 455036 Magnitogorsk. CB22) pr. Lenina 60-21, 455028 Magnitogorsk. CB23) ul. Sov. Armii 3-15, 455036 Magnitogorsk. CB24) ul. Shishkina 15, 456217 Zlatoust. CB25) Miass. CB26) Magnitogorsk. CB27) ul. Tsvillinga 54, 454000 Chelyabinsk. CB28) ul. Lenina 188, 456800 Verkhniy Ufaley. CB29) pr. K.Marksa 65, 455028 Magnitogorsk. CB30) Chelyabinsk. CB32) Magnitogorsk.

CH) Chitinskaya oblast: CH01) Chita. CH02) Chita. CH03) ul. Leningradskaya 78, 672090 Chita. CH04) P.O.Box 479, 672012 Chita.

CK) Chukotskaya avt. okrug: CK01) Anadyr. CK02) Anadyr.

CV) Chavashskaya respublika: CV01) P.O.Box 28, 428017 Cheboksary. CV02) P.O.Box 48, 428017 Cheboksary. CV03) ul. Nikolayeva 12, 428020 Cheboksary.CV04) ul. Lenina 30, 428003 Cheboksary. CV05) Chernogryazkiy proyezd 7, 428000 Cheboksary.

DA) Respublika Dagestan: DA01) ul. Chernyshevskogo 115, 376020 Makhachkala. DA02) Makhachkala. DA03) Makhachkala. DA04) Makhachkala.

IR) Irkutskaya oblast: IR01) Irkutsk. IR02) Irkutsk. IR03) P.O.Box 2882, 664009 Irkutsk. IR04) ul. Gorkogo 19, 664003 Irkutsk. IR05) P.O.Box 35, 666020 Shelekhov. IR06) P.O.Box 3471, 665839 Angarsk. IR06) Irkutsk. IR07) P.O.Box 229, 664003 Irkutsk. IR08) Irkutsk.
IR09) P.O.Box 2219, 665730 Bratsk. IR10) P.O.Box 35, 666020 Shelekhov. IR11) P.O.Box 3471, 665839 Angarsk. IR12) Bratsk. IR13) Bratsk. IR14) P.O.Box 765, 665709 Bratsk. IR15) Ust-Illimsk.

IV) Ivanovskaya oblast: IV01) ul. Stankostroiteley 1, 153000 Ivanovo. IV02) P.O.Box 251, 153012 Ivanovo. IV03) P.O.Box 373, 153025 Ivanovo. IV04) P.O.Box 251, 153012 Ivanovo. IV05) ul. Stankostroiteley 1-91, 153032 Ivanovo. IV06) Ivanovo. IV07) Ivanovo. IV08) Ivanovo.

KA) Kaliningradskaya oblast: KA01) ul. Narvskaya 37/39, 236000 Kaliningrad. KA02) ul. Narvskaya 37/39, 236000 Kaliningrad. KA03) P.O.Box 517, 236029 Kaliningrad. KA04) Sovetskiy pr. 43, 236000 Kaliningrad. KA05) Kaliningrad. KA06) ul. Karla Marksa 18, 236000 Kaliningrad. KA07) Kaliningrad. KA08) Sovetsk. KA09) Kaliningrad KA10) Kaliningrad. KA11) Kaliningrad. KA12) Kaliningrad. KA13) Sovetsk.

KB) Kabardino-Balkarskaya respublika: KB01) pr. Lenina 2, kab.2, 360030 Nalchik. KB01) pr. Lenina 2, kab.2, 360030 Nalchik. KB02) Nalchik.

KC) Karachayevo-Cherkesskaya respublika: KC01) Cherkessk. KC02) Karachayevsk.

KD) Krasnodarskiy kray:
KD01) ul. Korolenko 2, ofis 97, 350038 Krasnodar. KD02) ul. Starokubanskaya 118, 350058 Krasnodar. KD03) P.O.Box 171, 350020 Krasnodar. KD04) ul. Krasnaya 109, 350076 Krasnodar. KD05) P.O.Box 171, 350020 Krasnodar. KD06) P.O.Box 150, 360000 Krasnodar. KD07) ul. Krasnaya 106, 350610 Krasnodar. KD08) ul. Lenina 23, 350063 Krasnodar. KD09) ul. Rashpilevskaya 106, 350048 Krasnodar. KD10) Sochi. KD11) Sochi. KD12) P.O.Box 1288, 354000 Sochi. KD13) P.O.Box 1288, 354000 Sochi. KD14) ul. Revolutsii 1905g. 19, 353900 Novorossiysk. KD15) Sochi. KD16) Sochi. KD17) ul. Lunacharkogo 155a, 352905 Armavir. KD18) Armavir. KD19) ul. Kopolenko 2, ofis 97, 350038 Krasnodar. KD20) ul. Rubina 12, Novorosiysk. KD21) ul. Tonnelnaya 16, 345000 Sochi. KD22) ul. Ledneva 9, 353900 Novorossiysk. KD23) P.O.Box 54, 350048 Krasnodar. KD24) ul. Korolenko 2/1, 350038 Krasnodar. KD25) Novorossiysk. KD25) Gelendzhik. KD26) Kushchevskaya. KD27) Anapa.

KE) Kemerovskaya oblast: KE01) ul. Dzerzhinskogo 2, 650009 Kemerovo. KE02) ul. Sportivnaya 28, 650040 Kemerovo. KE03) Kuznetskiy pr. 83-a, 650055 Kemerovo. KE04) Novokuznetsk. KE05) ul. Sportivnaya 28, 650040 Kemerovo. KE06) Kuznetskiy pr. 83-a, 650055 Kemerovo. KE07) pr. Metallurgov 18, 654000 Novokuznetsk. KE08) Kemerovo. KE09) Novokuznetsk. KE10) Yugra. KE11) Novokuznetsk. KE12) Novokuznetsk.

KE13) Novokuznetsk. KE14) Kemerovo.
KG) Kurganskaya oblast: KG01) ul. Krasina 41, 640020 Kurgan. KG02) ul. Krasina 41, 640020 Kurgan. KG03) Kurgan. KG04) Kurgan. KG05) Kurgan. KG06) Kurgan. KG07) Kurgan.
KH) Khabarovskiy kray: KH01) ul. Zaparina 82-48, 680000 Khabarovsk. KH02) Khabarovsk. KH03) ul. Lenina 69, 680013 Khabarovsk. KH03) Oktyabrskiy pr. 46, 681021 Komsomolsk-na-Amure. KH04) Khabarovsk. KH05) ul. Kirova 2, 681016 Komsomolsk-na-Amure.
KL) Kaluzhskaya oblast: KL01) ul. Pukhova 27/25, ofis 14a, 248010 Kaluga. KL02) ul. Pukhova 27/25, ofis 14a, 248010 Kaluga. KL02) Kaluga. KL03) ul. Pukhova 52, 248010 Kaluga. KL04) Kaluga. KL05) pr. Lenina 127, kom. 408, 249020 Obninsk. KL06) Obninsk. KL07) Obninsk.
KM) Kamchatskaya oblast: KM01) ul. Lukashevskogo 5, 683025 Petropavlovsk-Kamchatskiy. KM02) Petropavlovsk-Kamchatskiy. KM03) ul. Klyuchevskaya 56, Petropavlovsk-Kamchatskiy.
KN) Krasnoyarskiy kray: KN01) ul. Mate Zalke 24, 660018 Krasnoyarsk. KN02) P.O.Box 6180, 660017 Krasnoyarsk. KN03) ul. Kirova 19, ofis 211, 660049 Krasnoyarsk. KN04) ul. Diktatury Proletariata 3, 660017 Krasnoyarsk. KN05) ul. Botkina 61, 660100 Krasnoyarsk. KN07) P.O.Box 6180, 660017 Krasnoyarsk. KN08) Krasnoyarsk. KN09) ul. Mechnikova 44a, 660028 Krasnoyarsk.
KO) Respublika Komi: KO01) ul. Internatsionalnaya 108a, 167000 Syktyvkar. KO02) ul. D.Kalikovoy 27a, 167000 Syktyvkar. KO03) Syktyvkar. KO04) ul. Internatsionalnaya 108a, 167000 Syktyvkar. KO05) Ukhta. KO06) ul. 30 let Oktyabrya 4, 169300 Ukhta. KO07) Usinsk. KO08) Usinsk. KO09) Vuktyl. KO10) Vorkuta. KO11) Inta.
KS) Kostromskaya oblast: KS01) ul. Ivana Susanina 48/76, 156005 Kostroma. KS02) Kostroma.
KT) Respublika Kareliya: KT01) P.O.Box 95, 185035 Petrozavodsk. KT02) nab. Gyullinga 11, 183005 Petrozavodsk. KT03) ul. Titova 11, 185035 Petrozavodsk. KT04) P.O.Box 387, 185035 Petrozavodsk.
KU) Kurskaya oblast: KU01) ul. Dimitrova 78, komn. 501, 305004 Kursk. KU02) Kursk. KU03) ul. K.Marksa 58, 305029 Kursk. KU04) P.O.Box 314, 305290 Kursk. KU05) P.O.Box 200, 305016 Kursk. KU06) ul. Dimitrova 78, komn. 501, 305004 Kursk. KU07) ul. K.Marksa 58, 305029 Kursk. KU08) Kursk.
KV) Kirovskaya oblast: KV01) ul. K.Marksa 127, ofis 316, 610027 Kirov. KV02) ul. K.Marksa 99, 610000 Kirov. KV03) ul. Gaydara, 610011 Kirov. KV04) ul. Molodoy gvardii 436, komn. 102, 610000 Kirov. KV06) ul. K.Marksa 99, 610027 Kirov. KV07) P.O.Box 2728, 610031 Kirov. KV08) Kirov.
KX) Respublika Kalmykiya-Khalmg Tangch: KX01) ul. Lenina 249-505, 358000 Elista.
KY) Khanty-Mansiyskiy avt. okrug: KY01) Khanty-Mansiysk. KY02) Khanty-Mansiysk. KY03) ul. Kukuyevitskogo 6, 628416 Surgut. KY04) ul. Gagarina 4, 628011 Khanty-Mansiysk. KY05) Nyagan. KY06) Nyagan. KY07) ul. Lenina 18, Yugorsk. KY10) ul. Mira 62a, 626440 Nizhnevartovsk. KY11) ul. Energetikov 14, 626400 Surgut. KY12) ul. Druzhby Narodov 15, 626481 Kogalym. KY13) P.O.Box 89, 626400 Surgut. KY14) ul. Lenina 5a, ofis 200, 626440 Nizhnevartovsk. KY15) ul. Lenina 23a, 626449 Langepas. KY16) Kogalym. KY17) ul. Mayakovskogo 12a, Surgut. KY18) ul. Mayakovskogo 16, 626400 Surgut. KY19) Surgut. KY20) Surgut. KY21) ul. Energetikov 14, 626400 Surgut. KY22) ul. Mira 62a, 626440 Nizhnevartovsk. KY23) ul. Lenina 18, Yugorsk. KY24) ul. Molodezhnaya 6, 626481 Kogalym. KY25) ul. Profsoyuzov 37, 626400 Surgut. KY26) Langepas. KY27) ul. Lenina 5a, ofis 200, 626440 Nizhnevartovsk. KY28) Nizhnevartovsk. KY29) Raduzhnyy.
LI) Lipetskaya oblast: LI01) pl. Pobedy 8, 398001 Lipetsk. LI02) Lipetsk. LI03) 9 mikrorayon 2-9, 398042 Lipetsk. LI04) ul. Lenina 42, 398020 Lipetsk. LI05) Lipetsk. LI06) ul. 9 Maya 14-65, 398017 Lipetsk. LI07) Lipetsk.
MA) Magadanskaya oblast: MA01) pr. K.Marksa 67, 685000 Magadan. MA02) Magadan.
MD) Respublika Mordoviya: MD01) ul. Sovetskaya 22, 430000 Saransk. MD02) Saransk. MD03) P.O.Box 49, 430034 Saransk. MD03) P.O.Box 49, 430034 Saransk.
ME) Respublika Mariy-El: ME01) ul. Mashinostroiteley 2-a, 424000 Yoshkar-Ola. ME02) ul. Sovetskaya 138, 424000 Yoshkar-Ola.
MO) Moskovskaya oblast: MO01) Moskva. MO02) ul. Akademika Korolyova 15, 127427 Moskva. MO03) ul. Tverskaya 16/2, 103829 Moskva. MO04) per. Sivtsev Brazhek 34, 121019 Moskva. MO05) Stolovyy per.6, 121836 Moskva. MO06) Moskva. MO07) ul. Shabolovka 37, Moskva. MO08) ul. Akademika Korolyova 19, 127427 Moskva. MO09) ul. Demyana Bednogo 24, 123308 Moskva. MO10) ul. Noviy Arbat 11, 121809 Moskva. MO11) Moskva. MO12) ul. Ak. Korolyova 19, 127427 Moskva. MO13) ul. D.Bednogo 24, 123308 Moskva. MO14) ul. Pyatnitskaya 25, 115326 Moskva. MO15) ul. Profsoyuznaya 84/32, 117485 Moskva. MO16) ul. Kazakova 16, 103064 Moskva. MO17) ul. Pyatnitskaya 25, 115326 Moskva. MO18) ul. Novyy Arbat 21, 121019 Moskva. MO19) ul. Pyatnitskaya 25, 115326 Moskva. MO20) ul. Kazakova 16, 103064 Moskva. MO21) Leningradskiy pr. 30/2, 125040 Moskva. MO22) ul. B.Lubyanka 24/15, 101000 Moskva. MO23) 3-iy Golutvinskiy per. 10/8, 117049 Moskva. MO24) Moskva. MO25) Moskva. MO26) Moskva. MO27) Moskva. MO28) Moskva. MO29) Podolsk. MO30) ul. Sovetskaya 42, 142400 Noginsk. MO31) ul. Voroshilova 126a, 142200 Serpukhov. MO32) ul. Voroshilova 109/6, 142203 Serpukhov. MO32) Moskva. MO33) Moskva. MO34) Moskva. MO35) Moskva. MO36) Moskva.
MU) Murmanskaya oblast: MU01) pr. Lenina 82, ofis 1109, 183038 Murmansk. MU02) Murmansk. MU03) pr. Lenina 12, ofis 612, 183032 Murmansk. MU04) P.O.Box 647, 183038 Murmansk. MU05) ul. Papanina 14, Murmansk. MU07) Murmansk. MU08) pr. Lenina 3, 183032 Murmansk. MU09) Murmansk. MU10) Murmansk. MU11) Apatity. MU12) Apatity. MU13) Apatity. MU14) P.O.Box 20, 184280 Monchegorsk. MU15) Monchegorsk.
NE) Nenetskiy avt. okrug: NE01) Naryan-Mar.
NN) Nizhegorodskaya oblast: NN01) ul. Belinskogo 9a, 603600 N.Novgorod. NN02) P.O.Box "Russkoye Radio", 603000 N.Novgorod. NN03) ul. Belinskogo 9a, 603600 N.Novgorod. NN04) P.O.Box 76, 603076 N.Novgorod. NN05) N.Novgorod. NN06) ul. Fruktovaya 7/3-56, 603120 N.Novgorod. NN07) ul. Belinskogo 9a, 603600 N.Novgorod. NN08) Okskiy syezd 8, 603022 N.Novgorod. NN09) ul. B. Pecherskaya 33-1, 603155 N.Novgorod. NN10) Okskiy syezd 8, 603022 N.Novgorod. NN11) ul. Lunacharskogo 106, 607450 Bor. NN12) N.Novgorod. NN13) Okskiy syezd 8, 603022 N.Novgorod. NN14) N.Novgorod. NN15) P.O.Box "Russkoye Radio", 603000 N.Novgorod. NN16) Okskiy syezd 8, 603022 N.Novgorod. NN17) pr. Mira 29, 607190 Sarov. NN18) pl. M.Gorkogo, Dom svyazi, 603000 N.Novgorod. NN19) pl. M.Gorkogo, Dom svyazi, 603000 N.Novgorod. NN20) pl. M.Gorkogo, Dom svyazi, 603000 N.Novgorod. NN30) Sarov.
NO) Novgorodskaya oblast: NO01) nab. A.Nevskogo 22/2, 173000 V.Novgorod. NO02) ul. Bol.Moskovskaya 106, 173020 V.Novgorod. NO03) ul. Bol.Moskovskaya 106, 173020 V.Novgorod. NO04) Malaya Vishera.
NS) Novosibirskaya oblast: NS01) P.O.Box 296, 630090 Novosibirsk. NS02) Novosibirsk. NS03) ul. Vertkovskaya 10, 630048 Novosibirsk. NS04) ul. Rimskogo-Korsakova 9, 630048 Novosibirsk. NS05) ul. Kamenskaya 1, 630099 Novosibirsk. NS06) pr. Karla Marksa 1, 630064 Novosibirsk. NS07) Novosibirsk. NS08) ul. Gorskaya 16, 630032 Novosibirsk. NS09) ul. Nemirovicha-Danchenko 122, 630087 Novosibirsk. NS10) P.O.Box 304, 630090 Novosibirsk. NS11) Novosibirsk. NS12) Novosibirsk. NS14) pr. Karla Marksa 1, 630064 Novosibirsk. NS15) Novosibirsk. NS16) Iskitim.
OB) Orenburgskaya oblast: OB01) ul. Kiselyova 36, 460024 Orenburg. OB02) Orenburg. OB03) ul. Sovetskaya 31, 460014 Orenburg. OB04) pr. Pobedy 24, 460018 Orenburg. OB05) Orenburg. OB06) Orenburg. OB07) Orenburg. OB08) Orenburg. OB09) Orenburg. OB10) ul. Shevchenko 251, 460026 Orenburg. OB11) Buzuluk. OB12) Buzuluk. OB13) P.O.Box 80, 462419 Orsk. OB14) Orsk. OB15) P.O.Box 95, 462419 Orsk. OB16) ul. Sovetskaya 104a-28, 462351 Novotroitsk. OB17) Buguruslan.
OL) Orlovskaya oblast: OL01) ul. Gorkogo 45, 302000 Oryol. OL02) ul. Gorkogo 45, 302000 Oryol. OL03) P.O.Box 38, 302020 Oryol. OL04) ul. Komsomolskaya 193-41, 302016 Oryol. OL05) Oryol.
OM) Omskaya oblast: OM01) ul. Uchebnaya 83, 644024 Omsk. OM01) ul. Uchebnaya 83, 644024 Omsk. OM02) ul. Uchebnaya 83, 644024 Omsk. OM03) P.O.Box 483, 644050 Omsk. OM04) Omsk. OM05) ul. K.Libknekhta 35-110, 644099 Omsk. OM06) ul. Barrikadnaya 20, 644099 Omsk. OM07) P.O.Box 938, 644046 Omsk. OM08) Omsk.
PM) Primorskiy kray: PM01) ul. Uborevicha 20a, 690091 Vladivostok. PM02) ul. Pogranichnaya 2, 690008 Vladivostok. PM03) Vladivostok.
PR) Permskaya oblast: PR01) ul. Karla Marksa 4a, 614000 Perm. PR02) bul. Gagarina 80a, 614077 Perm. PR03) bul. Gagarina 80, 614077 Perm. PR04) ul. Gorkogo 18, 614600 Perm. PR05) ul. Gazety Zvezda 24a, 614000 Perm. PR06) Perm. PR07) ul. Krasnova 1, Perm. PR08) ul. Gorkogo 18, 614600 Perm. PR10) Perm. PR10) Perm. PR11) Perm.
PS) Pskovskaya oblast: PS01) P.O.Box 10, 180000 Pskov. PS02) Rizhskiy pr. 71, 180024 Pskov. PS03) ul. Ya. Fabritsiusa 5-a, ofis 17, 180017 Pskov.
PZ) Penzenskaya oblast: PZ01) ul. Mira 1a, 440121 Penza. PZ02) ul. Mira 1a, 440121 Penza. PZ03) ul. Pushkina 2, ofis 609, 440600 Penza. PZ04) ul. Lenina 248, 442500 Kuznetsk. PZ05) Penza.
RY) Ryazanskaya oblast: RY01) ul. Televizionnaya 4, 390011 Ryazan. RY02) ul. Televizionnaya 4, 390011 Ryazan. RY03) P.O.Box 16, 390000 Ryazan. RY04) ul. Televizionnaya 6, 390011 Ryazan. RY05) Ryazan. RY06) Ryazan. RY07) Ryazan.
RK) Respublika Khakasiya: RK01) P.O.Box 105, 662617 Abakan. RK02) Abakan. RK03) P.O.Box 1, 662617 Sayanogorsk. RK04) ul. Pushkina 7, 662620 Chernogorsk.
RO) Rostovskaya oblast: RO01) ul. Chistopolskaya 13-65, 344037 Rostov. RO02) pl. Tolstogo 8, 344037 Rostov. RO03) pl. Narodnogo Opolcheniya 2, 344017 Rostov. RO04) pr. Budennovskiy 81, 344011 Rostov. RO05) Rostov-na-Donu. RO06) pr. Budennovskiy 50, 344007 Rostov. RO07) pr. Budennovskiy 50, 344007 Rostov. RO08) pr. Balkanovskiy 25, 346428 Novocherkassk. RO09) ul. Krasnoarmeyskaya 136, 344007 Rostov. RO10) pr. Sholokhova 272v, 344009 Rostov. RO11) pr. Budennovskiy 50, 344007 Rostov. RO12) ul. Lermontovskaya 75, 344011 Rostov. RO13) ul. Bolshaya

Sadovaya 82, ofis 1, 344007 Rostov. RO15) ul. Sodruzhestva 37-73, 344103 Rostov. RO16) ul. Privokzalnaya 10, 346740 Azov. RO17) ul. Promyshlennaya 5, 346740 Azov. RO18) P.O.Box 92, 347340 Rostov. RO19) ul. Volgodonskaya 2b, 347340 Volgodonsk. RO20) P.O.Box 92, 347340 Rostov. RO21) ul. Volgodonskaya 2b, 347340 Rostov. RO22) Volgodonsk. RO23) ul. Oktyarbrskaya 37, Taganrog. RO24) Nekrasovskiy per. 44, 347928 Taganrog. RO25) pr. Yermaka 106-517, 346407 Novocherkassk. RO26) ul. Betonnaya 1, 346340 Gukovo-8.

RS) Respublika Sakha (Yakutiya): RS01) pr. Lenina 14-15, 677000 Yakutsk. RS02) ul. Dzerzhinskogo 13, kab 229, 677000 Yakutsk. RS03) Yakutsk. RS04) Neryungri.

SA) Samarskaya oblast: SA01) ul. Rabochaya 7, 443010 Samara. SA02) Samara. SA03) Samara. SA04) ul. Aerodromnaya 13, 443070 Samara. SA05) ul. Sovetskoy Armii 217a, 443011 Samara. SA06) pr. K.Marksa 201, ofis 89a, 443080 Samara. SA07) ul. Novo-Sadovaya 3, ofis 702, 443002 Samara. SA08) Samara. SA09) ul. Novo-Sadovaya 3, ofis 702, 443002 Samara. SA10) ul. Tashkentskaya 139, 443095 Samara. SA11) ul. Aerodromnaya 13, 443070 Samara. SA12) P.O.Box 1003, 443068 Samara. SA13) pr. K.Marksa 201, ofis 89a, 443080 Samara. SA14) ul. Kuybysheva 96, 443011 Samara. SA15) Samara. SA16) ul. Ushakova 57, 445020 Tolyatti. SA17) ul. Rabochaya 7, 443010 Samara. SA18) Tolyatti. SA19) Tolyatti. SA20) ul. Yubileynaya 6-225, 445029 Tolyatti. SA21) Tolyatti. SA22) ul. Rabochnaya 7, 443010 Samara.

SL) Sakhalinskaya oblast: SL01) ul. Komsomolskaya 213-a, 693016 Yuzhno-Sakhalinsk. SL02) Yuzhno-Sakhalinsk. SL03) Kholmsk. SL04) Yuzhno-Sakhalinsk.

SM) Smolenskaya oblast: SM01) P.O.Box 185, 214000 Smolensk.SM02) ul. Isakovskogo 5, 214014 Smolensk. SM03) P.O.Box 41, 214004 Smolensk. SM04) Smolensk.

SO) Resp. Severnaya Osetiya - Alaniya: SO01) ul. Tkhapsayeva 4, 362040 Vladikavkaz. SO02) Vladikavkaz. SO03) Vladikavkaz. SO04) Vladikavkaz. SO05) Vladikavkaz. SO06) Osetinskaya gorka 2, 362007 Vladikavkaz.

SP) Leningradskaya oblast: SP01) ul. Prof. Popova 47, 197346 St.Petersburg. SP02) P.O.Box 63, 199048 St.Petersburg. SP03) nab. reki Fontanki 46, 191095 St.Petersburg. SP04) ul. Shevchenko 27, 199406 St.Peterburg. SP05) aleya Smolnogo 3, 193311 St.Petersburg. SP05) aleya Smolnogo 3, 193311 St.Petersburg. SP06) St.Peterburg. SP07) Kamenoostrovskiy pr. 67, 197022 St.Petersburg. SP08) St.Peterburg. SP09) ul. Malaya Posadskaya 8, 197046 St.Petersburg. SP10) Konnogvardeyskiy bul. 5, 190000 St.Petersburg. SP10) Konnogvardeyskiy bul. 5, 190000 St.Petersburg. SP11) ul. Mokhovaya 17, of. 18, 191028 St.Petersburg. SP12) ul. Italyanskaya 21, 191011 St.Petersburg. SP13) per. Krapivny 5, ofice 205, 194044 St.Petersburg. SP14) pr. Institutskiy 7, 194021 St.Petersburg. SP15) ul. Sestrovetskaya 8, 197183 St.Peterburg. SP16) P.O.Box 92, 194100 St.Petersburg. SP17) Litovskiy pr. 59, 191040 St.Petersburg. SP18) St.Peterburg. SP19) ul. Malaya Posadskaya 8, 197046 St.Petersburg. SP20) St.Peterburg. SP21) Liteynyy pr. 41, komn.11N, 191028 St.Petersburg. SP22) pr. Stachek 105, 198303 St.Petersburg. SP23) P.O.Box 107-l4, 197022 St.Petersburg. SP24) nab. 40-letiya Komsomola 5, 188900 Vyborg. SP25) P.O.Box 55, 188900 Vyborg. SP26) nab. 40-letiya Komsomola 5, 188880 St.Petersburg. SP27) ul. B. Sovietskaya 24, 188450 Kingisepp. SP28) P.O.Box 26, 188260 Luga. SP29) St.Peterburg. SP30) St.Peterburg.

SR) Saratovskaya oblast: SR01) ul. Moskovskaya 35-424, 410031 Saratov. SR02) ul. Shelkovichnaya 37/45, 410017 Saratov. SR03) P.O.Box 789, 410019 Saratov. SR04) Ilyinskiy pr. 6, 410017 Saratov. SR05) P.O.Box 4111, 410026 Saratov. SR06) P.O.Box 4111, 410026 Saratov. SR07) ul. Tankistov 37, 410019 Saratov. SR08) P.O.Box 1334, 410054 Saratov. SR09) Saratov. SR10) P.O.Box 24, 4138024 Balakovo.

ST) Stavropolskiy kray: ST01) ul. Kominterna 21, 355000 Stavropol. ST02) ul. Lenina 282, 355000 Stavropol. ST03) Stavropol. ST04) ul. Kominterna 21, 355000 Stavropol. ST05) ul. Tukhachevskogo 7/2-29, 355040 Stavropol. ST06) ul. Lenina 282-19, 355000 Stavropol. ST07) pl. Lenina, Dom Sovetov, komn.111, 357530 Pyatigorsk. ST08) ul. Zavodskaya, 357562 Pyatigorsk. ST09) P.O.Box 164, 357500 Pyatigorsk. ST10) ul. Dzerzhinskogo 57, ofis 1201, 357500 Pyatigorsk. ST11) Pyatigorsk. ST12) Pyatigorsk. ST13) ul. Dzerzhinskogo 57, ofis 1201, 357500 Pyatigorsk. ST14) Pyatigorsk. ST15) ul. Pyatigorskaya 143, 357600 Yessentuki. ST16) ul. Gagarina 95, 357030 Nevinnomyssk.

SV) Sverdlovskaya oblast: SV01) ul. Zavodskaya 12, 620028 Yekaterinburg. SV02) P.O.Box 751, 620063 Yekaterinburg. SV03) pr. Lenina 41, 620151 Yekaterinburg. SV04) pr. Lenina 41, 620151 Yekaterinburg. SV05) P.O.Box 311, 620151 Yekaterinburg. SV06) P.O.Box 11, 620078 Yekaterinburg. SV07) ul. Repina 15, 620109 Yekaterinburg. SV08) ul. Malysheva 31, 620014 Yekaterinburg. SV09) ul. Lenina 41-404, 620075 Yekaterinburg. SV10) pr. Lenina 41, 620219 Yekaterinburg. SV11) P.O.Box 751, 620063 Yekaterinburg. SV12) ul. Belinskogo 56, 620086 Yekaterinburg. SV13) pr. Lenina 41, 620151 Yekaterinburg. SV14) pr. Lenina 41, 620151 Yekaterinburg. SV15) P.O.Box 69, 620075 Yekaterinburg. SV16) pr. Lenina 24, kom. 449, 620014 Yekaterinburg. SV17) P.O.Box 751, 620063 Yekaterinburg. SV18) Nizhniy Tagil. SV19) pr. Lenina 28a, 6220001 Nizhniy Tagil. SV20) ul. Oktyabrskoy revolutsii 66, 622036 Nizh. Tagil. SV21) ul. Beregovaya-Krasnokamenskaya 31a, 622042 Nizhniy Tagil. SV22) Serov. SV23) ul. Lunacharskogo 94, 624440 Serov. SV24) ul. Lermontova 50a, 623414 Kamensk-Uralskiy. SV25) ul. K.Marksa 52a, 623401 Kamensk-Uralskiy.

TA) Tambovskaya oblast: TA01) ul. Sovetskaya 187a, 392000 Tambov. TA02) ul. Michurinskaya 121, 392018 Tambov. TA03) ul. Michurinskaya 121, 392018 Tambov. TA04) ul. Senko 9, ofis 2, 392000 Tambov. TA05) ul. Sovetskaya 187a, 392000 Tambov. TA06) Tambov. TA07) ul. Lenina 330a, 393927 Ustye.

TL) Tulskaya oblast: TL01) P.O.Box 2534, 300026 Tula. TL02) ul. Turgenevskaya 50, 300000 Tula. TL03) P.O.Box 2534, 300026 Tula. TL04) P.O.Box 1551, 300000 Tula. TL05) P.O.Box 461, 300000 Tula. TL06) Krasnoarmeyskiy pr. 14, 300041 Tula. TL07) ul. F.Engelsa 62, 300000 Tula. TL08) P.O.Box 1360, 300041 Tula. TL09) ul. Lenina 77, 300000 Tula. TL10) Tula.

TM) Taymyrskiy (Dolgano-Nenetskiy) avt. okrug: TM01) ul. Nansena 26-3, 663300 Norilsk. TM02) P.O.Box 1180, 633300 Norilsk. TM03) Norilsk. TM04) Norilsk. TM05) Norilsk. TM06) Norilsk.

TO) Tomskaya oblast: TO01) ul. Voykova 84-b-34, 634009 Tomsk. TO02) ul. Bolnichnaya 9, 634003 Tomsk. TO04) ul. Bolnichnaya 9, 634003 Tomsk. TO05) per. Mariinskiy 10, 634000 Tomsk. TO06) ul. Bolnichnaya 8, 634053 Tomsk. TO07) ul. Gertsena 72, 634002 Tomsk. TO08) ul. Voykova 84-b-34, 634009 Tomsk. TO09) ul. Gertsena 72, 634002 Tomsk. TO10) Kozhevnikovo. TO11) pr. Kommunisticheskiy 42, 636070 Seversk.

TS) Respublika Tatarstan: TS01) ul. Yershova 31-a, ofis 516, 420045 Kazan. TS02) P.O.Box 233, 420043 Kazan. TS03) P.O.Box 122, 420503 Kazan. TS04) ul. Dekabristov 1, 420066 Kazan. TS05) ul. Dekabristov 1, 420066 Kazan. TS06) ul. Lyadova 5-10, 420036 Kazan. TS07) ul. Troitskiy les 29, 420029 Kazan. TS08) P.O.Box 38, 420036 Kazan. TS09) P.O.Box 353, 420530 Kazan. TS10) Kazan. TS11) ul. Dekabristov 2, 420069 Kazan. TS12) ul. Chistopolskaya 5, 420066 Kazan. TS13) ul. Sultan-Galeyeva 1, kom. 211, 420015 Kazan. TS14) pr. Khasana Tufana 23, 423805 Nab. Chelny. TS15) b-r Yunykh lenintsev 12-128, 423838 Nab. Chelny. TS16) pr. Naberezhnochelninskiy 80, 423822 Nab. Chelny. TS17) P.O.Box 16, 423822 Nab. Chelny. TS19) Nab.Chelny. TS20) Nab.Chelny. TS21) P.O.Box 83, 423810 Nab. Chelny. TS22) pr. Naberezhnochelninskiy 80, 423822 Nab. Chelny. TS23) Bugulma. TS24) Bugulma. TS25) Bugulma. TS26) Almetyevsk. TS27) Almetyevsk. TS28) ul. Shevchenko 25, 423461 Almetyevsk. TS29) P.O.Box 252, 423400 Almetyevsk. TS30) Nizhnekamsk. TS31) 423550 Nizhnekamsk.

TV) Tverskaya oblast: TV01) Smolenskiy per. 29, 170000 Tver. TV02) Smolenskiy per. 29, 170000 Tver. TV03) Smolenskiy per. 29, 170000 Tver. TV04) ul. Semenovskaya 22, 170000 Tver. TV05) Tver. TV06) Tver. TV07) Vyshniy Volochek.

TY) Tyumenskaya oblast: TY01) Tyumen. TY02) ul. Permyakova 3a, 625013 Tyumen. TY03) ul. Tekstilnaya 1, 625012 Tyumen. TY04) ul. Respubliki 211a, 625019 Tyumen. TY04) ul. Respubliki 211a, 625019 Tyumen. TY05) ul. Permyakova 3a, 625000 Tyumen. TY06) ul. Permyakova 3a, 625013 Tyumen. TY07) ul. Permyakova 6, 625016 Tyumen. TY08) ul. Permyakova 5, 625013 Tyumen. TY09) Tyumen. TY10) ul. Respubliki 211a, 625019 Tyumen.

UD) Udmurtskaya respublika: UD01) P.O.Box 5037, Izhevsk. UD02) Izhevsk. UD02) Izhevsk. UD02) Izhevsk. UD03) ul. Pushkinskaya 268, 426008 Izhevsk. UD04) ul. Ukhtomskaya 24, 426009 Izhevsk. UD05) Izhevsk. UD06) Balezino. UD07) Izhevsk. UD08) ul. Azina 4, 426010 Izhevsk.

UL) Ulyanovskaya oblast: UL01) P.O.Box 9911, 432021 Ulyanovsk. UL02) P.O.Box 9911, 432021 Ulyanovsk. UL03) P.O.Box 99, 432601 Ulyanovsk. UL03) P.O.Box 99, 432601 Ulyanovsk. UL04) P.O.Box 55, 432601 Ulyanovsk. UL05) pr. Leninskogo Komsomola 41, 423067 Ulyanovsk. UL06) P.O.Box 99, 432601 Ulyanovsk. UL07) Dimitrovgrad.

VG) Volgogradskaya obl: VG01) ul. Parkhomenko 47b, 450050 Volgograd. VG02) ul. Komsomolskaya 8, 400131 Volgograd. VG03) ul. Komsomolskaya 8, 400066 Volgograd. VG04) ul. Krasnoznamenskaya 15a, 400131 Volgograd. VG05) ul. Raboche-Krestyanskaya 30, 400074 Volgograd. VG06) ul. Raboche-Krestyanskaya 45, 400074 Volgograd. VG07) P.O.Box 37, 400037 Volgograd. VG08) Mikhaylovka.

VL) Vladimirskaya obl: VL01) pr. Lenina 1, 600001 Vladimir. VL02) P.O.Box 132, 600001 Vladimir. VL03) ul. Grazhdanskaya 1, 600008 Vladimir. VL04) ul. Mira 34a, 600017 Vladimir. VL05) P.O.Box 32, 600001 Vladimir. VL06) Vladimir. VL07) Vladimir.

VN) Voronezhskaya obl: VN01) ul. Ordzhonikidze 25, 394636 Voronezh. VN02) P.O.Box 200, 394000 Voronezh. VN03) ul. Nikitskaya 42, komn.303, 394026 Voronezh. VN03) pr. Revolutsii 1a, 394000 Voronezh. VN04) P.O.Box 28, 394000 Voronezh. VN05) Voronezh. VN06) Voronezh. VN07) ul. Kirova 4, 394018 Voronezh. VN08) Moskovskiy pr. 4, 394030 Voronezh. VN09) Voronezh. VN11) Voronezh. VN12) Moskovskiy pr. 97, 394083 Voronezh. VN13) Rossosh. VN14) Voronezh.

VO) Vologodskaya obl: VO01) ul. Lomonosova 31, 162010 Cherepovets. VO02) ul. Batyushkova 7, 160001 Vologda. VO03) ul. Kozlenskaya 35, kab. 415, 160000 Vologda. VO04) ul. Shchetinina 13, 162002 Vologda. VO05) ul. Shchetinina 13, 162002 Vologda. VO06) Vologda. VO07) ul. Lomonosova 31, 162010 Cherepovets. VO08) ul. Lomonosova 31, 162010 Cherepovets. VO09) ul. Lomonosova 31, 162010 Cherepovets. VO10) ul. Lomonosova 31, 162010 Cherepovets. VO11) ul. Lomonosova 31, 162010 Cherepovets. VO12) ul. K.Marksa 41, 162450 Babayevo.
YA) Yaroslavskaya obl: YA01) ul. Chkalova 2, ofis 912, 150000 Yaroslavl. YA02) ul. Sovetskaya 78, 150000 Yaroslavl. YA02) ul. Lekarskaya 1-1, 150002 Yaroslavl. YA03) Yaroslavl. YA04) ul. Respublikanskaya 78, 150000 Yaroslavl. YA05) ul. B.Oktyabrskaya 87, ofis 145, 150049 Yaroslavl. YA06) ul. Andropova 21, 150000 Yaroslavl. YA07) ul. Svobody 46/39, 150000 Yaroslavl. YA08) ul. Krestovaya 92, 152934 Rybinsk. YA09) Yaroslavl.
YN) Yamalo-Nenetskiy avt. okr: YN01) ul. Molodedzhnaya 17a, 626718 Novyy Urengoy. YN02) Salekhard. YN03) Salekhard. YN04) Nadym.YN05) Nadym. YN06) Nadym. YN07) Gubkinskiy. YN08) Novyy Urengoy. YN09) Novyy Urengoy. YN10) ul. Lenina 47-301, 626726 Noyabrsk-7.

RWANDA

L.T: UTC +2h — **Pop:** 7.3 million — **Pr.L:** Kinyarwanda, Swahili, French, English — **E.C:** 50Hz, 230V — **ITU:** RRW

OFFICE RWANDAIS D'INFORMATION (ORINFOR)
✉ B.P. 83, Kigali ☎ +250 575735 🖷 +250 576539 **Web:** www.orinfor.gov.rw

RADIODIFFUSION DE LA REPUBLIQUE RWANDAISE
✉ B.P. 83, Kigali ☎ +250 76665/76180 🖷 +250 76182/76185
L.P: Dir. Broadc: Mweusi Karake. Dir Prgrs: Louise Kayibanda. Ag. Ch.Editor: Faustin Karangira, Ch.Tech: Charles Nahayo.
SW: Kigali (G.C: 01S58 030E04): 6055kHz 50kW. Relays of Chaîne I/II.
FM: Chaîne I: 89.9/96.5/99.3/100.4/100.7MHz. **Chaîne II:** 90.6/90.7/101.1/106.1MHz.
D.Prgr in Kinyarwanda/Swahili/French: D 0255-0600, 0900-2100, Sun 0255-2100. **English**: Thurs 2000-2045. **N. in English:** 0515, 1830
ANN: F: "Vous écoutez Radio Rwanda émettant de Kigali".

Other stations:
R. Communautaire: Cyangugu 92.9MHz, Butare & Gisenyi: fq. unk. – **R. Contact:** freq. unk. – **R. Flash FM:** 89.2MHz – **R. Izuba,** Kigungo: 100MHz – **R. Maria Rwanda:** Gitarama 93.3MHz – **R. 10 FM:** 90.2MHz – **R. de l'Université Nationale du Rwanda:** freq. unk. – **Adventist World R:** 106.4MHz – **BBC African Sce:** Kigali 93.9MHz – **Deutsche Welle:** Kigali 96MHz 2kW – **Voice of America:** Kigali 104.3MHz.

DEUTSCHE WELLE RELAY STATION
see International Radio section.

SAMOA

L.T: UTC -11h — **Pop:** 197,000 — **Pr.L:** Samoan, English — **E.C:** 50Hz, 230/410V — **ITU:** SMO

SAMOAN BROADCASTING SERVICE - 2AP (Gov. Comm.)
✉ P.O. Box 1868, Mulinu'u, Apia ☎ +685 21420 🖷 +685 21072 **Web** www.samoa.net.ws/govtsamoapress/2AP_broadcasting
L.P: DG: Kolotita Stowers Ah Kau. CE: Lua Nafoi. Chief Technical Officer: C. Warren
MW: Apia 540/747kHz 10kW.
Samoan/English: 1700 (Sun 2200)-1000 on 540kHz Educational broadcasts 1930-2030 and Parliament on 747kHz. **World N**: 1800W, 1900W, 1930W. **Local N**: 1630W, 1730W, 1830W, 0730W.
ANN: E: "SBC Radio 1 (540kHz)" "SBC Radio 2". **IS**: Gong **V**. by card.

RADIO POLYNESIA LTD. (Comm.)
✉ P.O. Box 762, Apia ☎ +685 25149 🖷 +685 25147 **Web:** www.fmradio.ws **Email:** info@fmradio.ws **LP:** CEO: Corey Keil
FM: Talofa FM 96.1 & 99MHz, Majik FM 98.1MHz, K-Lite FM 101.1MHz **D.Prgr:** 24h

GRACELAND BROADCASTING NETWORK (Rlg.)
✉ Levili ☎ +685 20 107 🖷 +685 25 487 **Web:** www.angelfire.com/fm/gbn/gbn.htm **Email:** mailto:gbn@post.com
FM: "Laufou FM" Apia/Upoulu Is 90.9MHz, Apia 106.9MHz, Savai'I 94.9MHz. **D.Prgr:** Sun 1800-1100 (gospel music).

SAMOA (American)

L.T: UTC -11h — **Pop:** 67,000 — **Pr.L:** Samoan, English — **E.C:** 60Hz, 120V — **ITU:** SMA

WVUV
✉ Box 4894, Pago Pago, AS 96799, USA ☎ +684 688 7397
MW: Leone, Tutuila 648kHz 10kW 24h. (currently low power)

SAMOA BROADCASTING SYSTEM
✉ Box 793, Pago Pago 96799 ☎ +684 633 7000 🖷 +684 633 5727 **Web:** www.ksbsfm.com **Email:** ksbsfm@samoanet.com
FM: KSBS-FM 92.1MHz, 15kW 18h

ASIA PACIFIC MEDIA MINISTRIES
✉ 2108 West Springfield Avenue, Champaign, IL 61821, USA **Web:** www.wbgl.org **L.P:** Vickie Haleck, Acting Station Manager
MW: KJAL 585kHz 5kW

SHOWERS OF BLESSINGS RADIO
✉ P.O. Box 997777, Pago Pago, American Samoa 96799 ☎ +684 699 8123 🖷 +684 699 8126 **Web:** www.knwj.com **Email:** info@knwj.com
FM: KNWJ Leone 93.9MHz & 104.7MHz. 0.28kW

SOUTH SEAS BROADCASTING, INC.,
✉ P O Box 6758, Pago Pago, AS 96799 ☎ +684-633-4493 **Web:** www.khjradio.com/93khj_001.htm **Email:** 93khj@samoatelco.com
FM: KKHJ 93.1MHz 1.1kW **D.Prgr:** 24hrs

PACIFC ISLANDS BIBLE SCHOOL
✉ P O Box 1268, Pago Pago 96799 **FM:** KULA Ili'Ili 95.1MHz 0.1kW

SAN MARINO

L.T. UTC +1h (27 Mar-30 Oct: UTC +2h) — **Pop.** 29,000 — **Pr.L:** Italian — **ITU:** SMR

RADIO SAN MARINO NETWORK (Priv.)
✉ Via 4 Giugno 21, RSM-47899 Serravalle, Repubblica di San Marino. ☎ +378 0549 901777. 🖷 +378 0549 969071. **Email:** redazione@radiosanmarino.sm **Web:** www.radiosanmarino.sm
L.P: Dir. C. Piombini
FM: 98,9 MHz 5kW. **D.Prgr:** 24h **V.:** by QSL-card. Rp.

SAN MARINO RTV (Gov.)
✉ Viale J.F.Kennedy 13, RSM-47890.Repubblica di San Marino. ☎ +378 0549 882000. 🖷 +378 0549 882840. **Email:** redazione@sanmarinortv.sm **Web:** www.sanmarinortv.sm
L.P: Dir. D. Guerra. Prgr.Dir.: P.Cesetti
FM: 102.7MHz 30kW. **D.Prgr:** 24h
FM: 103.2MHz 30kW. **D.Prgr:** 24h. **San Marino Classic** (started 23 june 2004) Also carry Gov meetings, live service.
F.Pl. no plans to start on mw band, assigned freq. 711 kHz.
V.: by QSL-card. Rp.

SÃO TOMÉ E PRÍNCIPE

L.T: UTC — **Pop:** 165,000 — **Pr.L:** Portuguese, Foro — **E.C:** 50Hz, 220V — **ITU:** STP

RÁDIO NACIONAL DE SÃO TOMÉ E PRÍNCIPE (RNSTP)
✉ Avenida Marginal 12 de Julho, C.P. 44, São Tomé ☎ +239 222875 🖷 +239 223293 **Web:** radionacional.st **Email:** Rnstp04@cstome.net
L.P: Dir: Artur Meneses de Pinho. CE: Felisberto Garcia.
MW: Pinheira (G.C: 06.46E/00.18N): 945kHz 20kW.
FM: 89.7/95.4/99.3MHz.
D.Prgr: 24h in Portuguese. **N:** 0700, 1300, 1630, 1930.
ANN: "Aqui São Tomé, Capital da República Democratica de S. Tomé e Príncipe, transmite a Rádio Nacional". **IS:** 1 note Gong, guitar.

RDP África: São Tomé 92.8MHz 3kW, Príncipe 101.9MHz 0.07kW.
RFI Afrique: 102.8MHz in French/Portuguese.
VOA Music Mix: Pinheira 105.5MHz 0.2kW in English/Portuguese.

VOICE OF AMERICA RELAY STATION
MW 1530kHz 600kW 0300-0630, 1600-2200 & SW.
for further details see International Radio section.

SAUDI ARABIA

L.T: UTC +3h — **Pop:** 23m — **Pr.L:** Arabic — **E.C:** 60Hz, 127/220V — **ITU:** ARS

MINISTRY OF CULTURE & INFORMATION

✉ Nasseriya St, Riyadh 11161 ☎ +966 1 4014440 🖷 +966 1 4023570 **Web:** www.saudinf.com **Email**: sair@saudinf.com
L.P: Minister of Culture & Inf: H.E. Dr. Fouad Al-Farsy. Actg. Asst. Dep. Minister for Eng. Affairs: Mohamed Sahli.

BROADCASTING SERVICE OF THE KINGDOM OF SAUDI ARABIA (BSKSA)

✉ P.O. Box 61718, Riyadh 11575 ☎ +966 1 4425170 🖷 +966 1 4041692 **Web:** www.saudiradio.net

MW	kHz	kW	H. of Tr. & Prgr.
Qurayyat	549	2000	0300-2300 (A)
Gizan	549	1	0300-2300 (A)
Rafha	549	20	0300-2300 (A)
Jeddah	558	1	as Dammam 1098kHz
Abha	567	5	24h (H)
Afif	567	15	24h (H)
Gizan	567	1	24h (H)
Riyadh	585	1200	0300-2300 (A)
Duba	594	2000	0300-1500 (A/P)
Hail	612	5	24h (H)
Khamasin	612	15	24h (H)
Gizan	630	20	0300-2200 (A2)
Najran	630	10	0300-2200 (A2)
Jeddah	648	2000	0300-2300 (A)
Rafha	657	20	24h (H)
Abha	675	5	0300-1500 (A), 1500-2200 (A2)
Afif	675	20	0300-2300 (A)
Riyadh	684	10	0300-2200 (A2)
Jeddah	684	50	0300-2200 (A2)
Tabuk	693	20	24h (H)
Duba	702	40	0300-2200 (A2)
Najran	747	1	0300-2200 (A2)
Qurayyat	765	10	24h (H)
Khamasin	765	20	24h (H)
Dammam	783	100	0300-2200 (A2)
Jeddah	792	50	24h (H)
Hafral Baten	810	20	0300-2200 (A2)
Medinah	828	20	0300-2300 (A)
Buraida	846	20	24h (H)
Dammam	855	100	24h (H)
Qassim	873	10	24h (H)
Dammam	882	100	24h (H)
Qurayyat	900	1000	0300-2300 (A)
Aflaj	927	20	0300-2200 (A2)
Riyadh	936	-	24h (H)
Hail	945	5	0300-2300 (A)
Madinah	981	20	24h (H)
Tabuk	999	20	24h (H)
Madinah	1017	20	24h (P)
Taif	1080	20	0300-2200 (A2)
Qurayyat	1089	10	0300-2200 (A2)
Dammam	1098	5	0500-0800 (M), 0800-1300 (F) 1300-1400 (M), 1400-2100 (F)
Shaqra	1116	20	0300-2200 (A2)
Hafrul Baten	1215	20	0300-2300 (A)
Makkah	1287	5	24h (H)
Taif	1305	1	0300-2200 (A2)
Riyadh	1422	20	as Dammam 1098kHz
Dammam	1440	1600	0300-2300 (A)
Unk. location	1467	-	24h (H)
Jeddah	1485	1	1500-2100 (F)
Jeddah	1512	1000	0100-0300 (Cl), 1300-2100 (H)
Duba	1521	2000	0300-0600, 1500-2300 (A)

FM(MHz): Riyadh 91.2 (A/Cl), 97.7 (M/F), 100.0 (H) – Jeddah 93.2 (A/Cl), 98.0 (M/F) – Dammam 90.0 (A/Cl), 92.8 (H) – Madinah 93.6 (A/Cl), 96.8 (H) – Al-Baha 91.5 (H) – Buraydah 93.2 (A/Cl) + numerous low power stations under 10 kW for local coverage.
General Prgr. (A) in Arabic: 0300-2300 incl. Call of Islam 1500-1700. **N:** 0400, 0600, 0800, 1030, 1130, 1300 (local), 1430, 1630, 1800, 2000, 2230.
Call of Islam (Cl): 0100-1700.
Holy Quran (H) prgr: 24h incl. Call of Islam 0100-0300.
Second Arabic (A2) Prgr: 0300-2200. **N:** 0330, 0500, 0700, 0900, 1000, 1130 (rel. Gen. Prgr), 1400, 1500, 1700, 1900, 2030. **Call of Islam:** 0200, 1630.
Foreign Language (F) Prgrs: English: 1000-1300, 1600-2100. **N:** 1830, 2045. **French:** 0800-1000, 1400-1600.
Music (M) prgr: 24h.
Pilgrimage (P) Enlightment Radio: 24h during two months of the "Haj" season in Arabic/English/French/Persian/Turkish/Hausa/Indonesian/Urdu on MW and on FM 94.2/101MHz in Mina/Arafat/Muzdalifah.
ANN: Arabic: "Ithaat'il-Mamlakah al-Arabiyah al-Saudiyah min ar-Riyadh" Cl: "Nida ul-Islam". E: "This is the Broadcasting Sce. of the Kingdom of Saudi Arabia".
IS: 'Ud' (oriental lute). Opens and closes with National Anthem.

EXTERNAL SERVICE: BSKSA
see International Broadcasting section.

SAUDI ARAMCO RADIO

Serving the staff of Saudi Aramco Co.
✉ P.O.Box 5000, Dhahran 31311 ☎ +966 3 8720115 🖷 + 966 3 8738190 **Web:** www.saudiaramco.com
Email: webmaster@aramco.com.sa
L.P: Supervisor, Radio & Media Services: Ibrahim A. Al-Arfaj.
Studio 1 (pop and country music): Udhailiyah 88.8MHz, Dhahran 91.4MHz, Safaniyah/ Tanajib/Haradh 103.8MHz – **Studio 2** (easy listening and classical music): Udhailiyah 91.9MHz, Dhahran 101.4MHz, Safaniyah/Tanajib/Haradh 107.9MHz. **D.Prgr:** 24h.

American Forces Network: 93.7/100.7/103.9/107.8MHz.
British Forces Broadc. Sce, Al Kharj: 96.2MHz.
MBC FM (MHz): Al Jouf 88, Al Khafji 91.4, Tabuk 97.4, Arar/Yanbu 100.9, Al Zulfi 101, Al Baha 101.5, Dammam/Najran 101.9, Al Qasim/Riaydh 102, Al Hofuf/Al Jubail 102.2, Abha 102.3, Hail/Jeddah/Medina 103, Al Namas 103.2, Taif 103.3.
See main entry under UAE.

SENEGAL

L.T: UTC — **Pop:** 10m — **Pr.L:** French, Wolof, Mandinga, Soninké, Pular, others — **E.C:** 50Hz, 230V — **ITU:** SEN

HAUT CONSEIL DE L'AUDIOVISUEL (HCA)

✉ B.P. 4027, Dakar ☎ +221 8234784 🖷 +221 8234785

RADIODIFFUSION TÉLÉVISION SÉNÉGALAISE (RTS)

✉ Triangle Sud x Avenue El-Hadj Malick SY, B.P. 1765, Dakar ☎ +221 8491212 🖷 +221 8223490 **Web:** www.rts.sn
L.P: DG: Abdou Khoudoss Niang. Dir. Radio: Pèdre Dniaye. Dir: New Tech. & Development: Papa Abdou Diallo.

MW	kHz	kW	Sce
Matam (St.-Louis region)	965	1	R

FM	N	I	R	D	kW
Bakel			107.3		2/0.5
Dakar	95.7	92.5		94.5	2/0.5
Diourbel	97.6	96.6	101.0		2/0.1
Fatick	95.7		92.8		2/0.5
Goudiry			91.1		0.5/0.1
Kaolack	103.0	107.0	97.9		5/2/1
Kédougou		97.7	100.0		2
Kolda	100.0	102.0	92.2		2/1
Linguère			89.0		5/1
Louga	95.0	101.8	88.7		5/2
Ndioum		98.4	92.7		5/2/1
Ourossogui	96.5	89.1	105.3		5/2
Podor			100.6		0.25
Richard Toll			89.6		0.1
Saint-Louis	91.9	90.1	96.3		5/1
Tamba	102.0	88.1	92.0		5/2
Thiès	96.9	94.9	100.6		5/2
Touba			99.3		
Vélingara		89.1	92.2		2/1
Ziguinchor	95.2	100.2	98.9		5/1

N=Chaîne Nationale: 24h in French, Wolof and other nat. languages. **I=R. Sénégal Internationale:** 24h in French,.Arabic, Portuguese and other national languages. **D=Dakar FM**: 24hrs on 94.5MHz in French. **R=Chaîne Régionale ():** 0600-2400. Kaolack 9h, Saint-Louis

18h, Tambacounda 10½h, Ziguinchor 10½h regional services per day. **Regional Centres:** Diourbel – Fatick – B.P 321, Kaolack – Kolda – Louga – La Voix du Nord, B.P. 376, Saint-Louis – Tamba – Thiès – Rue de Général de Gaulle, B.P. 173, Ziguinchor.
ANN: N: "Radiodiffusion Télévision du Sénégal émettant de Dakar". I: "Radio Sénégal Internationale". **IS:** Melody on "Cora" (local harp).

SUD FM
✉ Immeuble Fahd, Bld. Djily Mbaye x rue Macodou Ndiaye (5ème étage), Dakar ☎ +221 8225393/8224205 🖷 +221 8225290 **Web:** www.sudonline.sn **Email:** info@sudonline.sn

FM	MHz	kW	FM	MHz	kW
Unk. location	91.7	-	Kolda	95.4	0.4
Banjul (GMB)	92.1	-	Ziguinchor	95.6	2
St.-Louis/Louga	93.2	2	Malam	98.4	0.2
Kaolack	94.6	2	Dakar	98.5	3
Diourbel	94.6	2	Thiès	102.2	0.2

Other stations:
Diamono FM, Dakar 100.8MHz – **R.Dunyaa**, B.P. 1656, Dakar. **Email:** Dunya@telecomplus.sn **FM:** Dakar 88.9MHz 3kW, Ziguinchor 92.4MHz, Tambacounda 95.3MHz, Kaolack 105MHz, Richard Toll 106.1MHz, Saint-Louis 106.3MHz. Also rel. BBC African Sce. in French/English – **Energie FM**, 72 Route du front de Terre, Dakar: 106.1MHz – **Fagarou FM,** Dakar: 98.2MHz – **R. Fass FM,** Thiès: 96.5MHz – **R. Futurs Medias (RFM),** Immeuble Elimane N'Dour, Rue 15 X Corniche, Dakar: 94MHz. **Web:** www.futursmedias.net **Email:** info@futursmedias.net – **Lamp Fall FM (R. Xarnu Bi):** Dakar 101.7MHz, Touba 97.4MHz. **Web:** www.africatel.sn/Fenetre/Accueil.php **Email:** lamp.fall@africatel.sn – **R. Municipale de Dakar (RMD):** 95.5MHz – **R. Nostalgie:** Dakar 90.3MHz 2.5kW. **Web:** www.metissacana.sn/ nostalgie – **R. Oxy-Jeunes (ROJ)**, c/o Fojes, B.P. 18303, Pikine: 103,4MHz. **Email:** oxyjeune@telecomplus.sn – **La Sept FM**, 71 Ave. Peytavin, B.P. 11357, Dakar. **Email:** Comsept@telecomplus.sn **L.P**: Youssou N'Dour, Owner. **FM:** Dakar 98.5MHz, Kaolack 94.6MHz, Louga 93.2MHz, St.-Louis 93.2MHz, Thiès 98.5MHz – **Sokhna FM,** Dakar: 99.9MHz. – **Temoin FM,** Gibraltar II villa n° 310, B.P. 384, Dakar: 107MHz – **R. Teranga,** Place Faidherbe, B.P. 119, St-Louis: 99.7MHz – **Walf FM:** Dakar 99.1MHz 2kW, Kaolack 101.4MHz 0.5kW. **Web:** www.walf.sn/radio

Rural radios: Niani FM, Koupentoum: 92.8MHz 0.25kW – Jiida FM, Bakel: 88MHz 0.25kW – R. Tim-Timol, Matam: 91.9MHz 1kW – R. La Côtière, Joal: 97MHz 0.25kW – Jéeri FM, Keur Momar Sarr: 97MHz 0.25kW – R. Penc Mi, Fissel: 90.6MHz 1kW – R. Awagna, Bignona: 99.4MHz 0.25kW – Ndef Leng FM, Dakar: 93.4MHz 0.25kW – Manooré FM, Dakar: 89.4MHz – Afia FM, Dakar: 93MHz.

Africa No. 1: Dakar 102.0MHz (see main entry under Gabon).
BBC African Sce: Dakar 105.6MHz in French.
RFI Afrique: Dakar 92.0MHz, Kaolack 91.5MHz, Saint-Louis 99.7MHz, Ziguinchor 87.6MHz.

SERBIA & MONTENEGRO

L.T: UTC +1h (27 Mar-30 Oct: UTC +2h) — **Pop:** 10.7 million — **Pr.L:** Serbian — **E.C:** 50Hz, 220V — **ITU:** SCG

UDRUZENJE RADIOTELEVIZIJE SRBIJE I CRNE GORE d.O.O.
✉ Beogradska 70, 11000 Beograd ☎ +381 11 433-718, 434-688 🖷 +381 11 434-023, 437-280 **Email:** yrtcoord@eunet.yu
L.P: MD: Ms. Vjera Nikolic.
Udruzenje Radiotelevizije Srbije i Crne Gore comprises Radio-televizija Srbije, Radiotelevizija Crne Gore, and the External Service

SERBIA

RADIO TELEVIZIJA SRBIJE
✉ Takovska 10, 11000 Beograd ☎ +381 11 321-2000 **Email:** rtstv@rts.co.yu **Web:** www.rts.co.yu
L.P: DG: Aleksandar Tijanic
R. Beograd: Hilendarska 2, 11000 Beograd ☎ +381 11 324 8888
L.P: Dir: Slobodan Divjak
MW:

Location	kHz	kW	Location	kHz	kW
Bosilegrad 1	675	5d	Nis	711	10a
Aleksinac	684	200d	Medvedja	765	1d
Negotin	693	5d	Kladovo	999	1b
Beograd 2/3	1008	1	Pirot	1485	1a
Novi Pazar	1062	1a	Priboj	1485	1a
Vranje	1296	10d	Tutin	1485	1a
Jagodina	1440	10d	Beograd202	1503	1
Crna Trava	1485	1d	Leskovac	1602	1a
Kladovo	1485	1a	Negotin	1602	1e

a) Beograd 1 + reg. prgr b) rel. Beograd 2/3 d) rel. Beograd 1 e) rel. Beograd 2/3 + reg. prgr

FM (MHz)	I	II/III	IV	L	kW
Avala	95.3	97.6	104.0	101.4	80
Besna Kobila	91.7	95.3	105.6		15
Crni Vrh	89.7	99.3	101.0		25
Crveni Cot	94.5	96.5	101.8	103.2	80
Deli Jovan	87.7	94.9			2
Jastrebac	96.9	89.3	103.5	106.0	100
Kopaonik	93.7	90.9	102.1		50/25
Mokra Gora	91.5	100.1	103.2		15
Nis	99.5			97.9	3.5/0.7
Ovcar	88.1	90.1	101.6		25
Pirot	91.3	98.5			1
Tornik	90.6	97.5	100.2		15
Tupiznica	92.5	96.1	100.4	105.3	40
Vrsac	95.7				30

L) local st's. Additional low power st's not mentioned.
R. Beograd 1: 24h. **N:** W 0303, 0330, 0400, 0430, 0500, 0540, 0700, 0800, 0900, 1000, 1100, 1200, 1300, 1400, 1600, 1700, 1830, 2100, 2200, 2300; Sun 0430, 0500, 0530, 0600, 0700, 0800, 0900, 1000, 1100, 1200, 1400, 1600, 1830, 2000, 2200, 2300. – **R. Beograd 2:** W 0400-1900 (Sun 0600-1900). **N:** W 1130, 1230, 1330, 1500, 1600, 1850. Sun 0630, 0730, 0930, 1055, 1130, 1330, 1730, 1850 – **R. Beograd 3:** 1900-2300 (Serious prgr.) – **R. Beograd 202:** 0400-2400 on 1503kHz, 104.0MHz + FM IV (0000-0400 rel. R. Beograd 1) – **Stereorama:** 0700-1700SS on FM IV. Other times rel. Beograd 202 – **Music R. 101,** Beograd: 24h on 98.5MHz + FM L – **R. B-92,** Beograd: 24h on 92.5MHz 1kW – **R. Politika:** Makedonska 29, 11000 Beograd - 24h on 105.2MHz 3kW + Rudnik 91.5MHz 6kW. – **Ju Radio:** Hilandarska 2, 11000 Beograd – 24h on 100.4MHz 1kW + Rudnik 96.3MHz (operated by Int. R. of Serbia & Montenegro) – **R. Index,** Beograd: 24h on 99.8MHz 1kW. **Web:** www.indexradio.com
Local stations

MW/FM	kHz	kW	MHz	MW/FM	kHz	kW	MHz
Uzice	531	10	92.0	Vrnjacka Banja	1170	1	93.2
Vranje	531	1	96.5	Majdanpek	1206	1	96.7
Soko Banja	-	-	90.5	Mladenovac	-	-	90.8
Lazarevac	-	-	100.9	Kraljevo	-	-	106.6
Krusevac	-	-	92.2	Loznica	-	-	104.8
Arandjelovac	-	-	98.9	Zajecar	-	-	98.1
Smederevo	-	-	96.1	Valjevo	1368	10	88.6
Bor	-	-	93.2	Kladovo	1458	1	89.9
Cacak	981	10	92.8	Priboj	1485	1	87.6
Pozarevac	990	1	90.1	Smed. Palanka	-	-	88.3
Kragujevac	-	-	106.8	Prijepolje	1584	1	95.9
Jagodina	1062	10	97.3	Leskovac	1602	1	99.0
Novi Pazar	1062	1	90.0				

Local/Private FM stations in Beograd:
Studio "B", P.O. Box 10, 11001 Beograd, Masarikova 5. **Prgr. 1** 100.8MHz: 24h. **Prgr. 2** 94.9: 24h. **Prgr. 3** 99.1MHz 1700-2200 – **R. "Pingvin":** Autoput 2, 11070 N. Beograd: 24h on 90.9MHz 1kW

FM	MHz	FM	MHz	FM	MHz
Art R	87.9	BGD1	95.3	Obrenovac	102.4
Glas Roma	88.3	R.JAT	95.7	Sremcica	102.9
R.Sajam	88.5	Naksi	96.9	Suton	103.3
BGD 1	88.9	BGD 2/3	97.6	R24	103.6
Top FM	89.2	Akademac	98.0	BGD 202	104.0
Bonton	89.4	Golf	98.2	Novosti	104.4
Interspeed	89.8	Radio 202	98.5	RadioS	104.7
Pingvin	90.9	Spektar	98.8	Politika	105.2
Pink	91.3	Studio B3	99.1	Alfa X R.	105.5
Stenka	91.8	Bumbum R.	99.5	Haos R.	105.9
B-92	92.5	R.Indeks	99.8	TDI	106.2
Perper	92.8	Viva FM	100.1	R. City	106.5
MIP	93.5	R. YU	100.4	Sport FM	106.9
Sky R.	93.9	Studio B1	100.8	R. Roda	107.9
OK R.	94.3	BGD 101	101.4		
Studio B2	94.9	Kosava	102.2		

Other local stations on FM: Bajina Basta 87.6 – R. Nemanja, Cuprija 87.6 – R. Srpski Venac, Bujanovci 88.5 – Kosjeric 88.5 – R. Dabar, Pozarevac 88.8 – R. M, Cacak 88.9 – R. 34, Kragujevac 88.9 – Gornij Milanovac 88.9 – R. 34, Kragujevac 88.9 – R. Zanuki, Pirot 88.9 – Glas Crkve, Valjevo 90.0 – R. Rec Naroda, Pozarevac 90.1 – R. Osa, Pirot 90.3 – Velika Plana 90.4 –

R. Luna, Karan 91.2 – OK Studio, Krusevac 91.3 – R. Politika, Rudnik 91.5 – R. Sunce, Arandjelovac 91.9 – R. Jagodina 2 91.9 – R. Elektronik, Knjazevac 92.1 – R. Ivanjica 92.4 – R. Ub 93.1 – R. Bum 93, Pozarevac 93.4 – R. Bubamara, Svrljig 93.5 – R. Patak, Valjevo 93.9 – R. Papagaj, Gornji Milanovac 94.3 – Knjazevac 94.5 – R. Maestral, Vranje 95.5 – R. Belami, Nis 95.6 – R. M 31, Uzice 95.6 – Pirot 95.8 – R. 48, Trstenik 95.8 – R. Kis, Vranje 95.9 – R. Maki, Jagodina 96.5 – R. S, Smederevo 97.7 – Paracin 97.8 – R. Caribrod 98.0 – Studio M, Cacak 98.3 – R. Trstenik 99.1 – R. B 90, Negotin 99.6 – R. DEN, Gornji Milanovac 99.8 – R. Duga Sky, Pozarevac 100.2 – R. Sabor, Cuprija 100.6 – Nezavisni RTV, Aleksinac 101.3 – R. 016, Leskovac 101.6 – R. Resava, Svilajnac 101.9 – R. Globus, Kraljevo 102.5 – R. Fast, Nis 102.7 – R. Golub, Valjevo 102.8 – Sremcica 102.9 – R. As, Sabac 103.7 – R. Sunce, Nis 106.1 – Djerdan R. Valjevo 104.5 – R. Mars, Valjevo 106.2 – Omea Radio, Loznica 107.0 – R. Melos, Kraljevo 107.1 – R. Lastavica, Krusevac 107.2 – R. Herc, Petrovac na Mlavi 107.3 – R. F, Leskovac 107.4 – R. Lotel, Loznica 107.4 – Cuprija 107.8.

KOSOVO (Territory under UN mandate)

RADIO TELEVIZIONE KOSOVËS (RTK)

Public Service broadcaster under UN auspices.
✉ Mother Teresa bb, 38000 Pristina, Kosovo. ☎ +381 38 225566 🖷 +381 38 249074 **Web:** www.radio-kosova.com/**Web**: www. blueskylive.com

Radio Kosova (RTK radio ch. 1)
L.P: Dir. Radio Kosova: Avni Spahiu, Dep. Dir: Milazim Avdiu.

MW	kHz	kW	MW	kHz	kW
Pristina	549	10	Prizren	1377	50†
Drenas	1413	1000†			

†under construction

FM	MHz	kW	FM	MHz	kW
Cërnusha	87.6	0.5	Pristina	91.9	0.5
Maja e gjelbërt	88.5	0.5	Goleshi	95.7	5
Zatriqi	88.9	0.5			

D. Prgr: 24h in Albanian. Turkish 19.30-20.30 (UTC)

Radio Blue Sky (RTK radio ch. 2)

FM	MHz	kW	FM	MHz	kW
Maja e gjelbërt	90.5	0.5	Pristina	93.3	0.5
Cërnusha	91.5	0.5	Goleshi	97.7	5
Zatriqi	92.4	0.5			

D. Prgr: 24h in Albanian and Serbian
F.pl.: FM outlets in Mitrovica (87.6, 105.1 and 107.9 MHz).

Private stations operating Kosovo-wide:
Radiotelevizioni 21 (Comm.)
✉ Media House, Annex, 2nd Floor, 38000 Pristina, Kosovo. **Email**: office@radio21.net **Web**: www.radio21.net
FM: Goleshi 102.8MHz, Zatriqi 103.9MHz, Maja e gjelbërt 94.8MHz
D. Prgr: 24h music, sports, cultural and youth programmes in Albanian.
Radio Dukagjini, (Comm.)
FM: Goleshi 99.7MHz, Zatriqi 94.5MHz, Maja e gjelbërt 92.7MHz

Local private stations, mainly commercial
More than 80 stations licensed in the five regions. Normally licensed for low-power (50W ERP) for stations operating for ethnic enclaves only or 1000W ERP. Most stations licensed for 1000W operate with a power of 100-300W.

KFOR: Stations operated by the various national forces which make up the KFOR International Force will be broadcasting on FM, on transmitters ranging from 50W to 1kW. These broadcasts depend on the compostion of forces in the region and, in some cases, on the enthusiasm of individual troops.

Other stations:
Deutsche Welle 88.6MHz, 1000W, Pristina (also in Albanian, Serbian)
IBB 96.2MHz, 1000W, Pristina (VoA, RFE in Albanian, Serbian)
BBC World Service 98.6MHz, 5000W, Goles
Radio France International 89.6 & 101.0MHz, 1000W, Mitrovica & Pristina
War Child Program 104.5MHz, 1000W, Berisa

VOJVODINA (Autonomous Province)

RADIO TELEVIZIJA NOVI SAD

✉ Zarka Zrenjanina 3, 21000 Novi Sad ☎ +381 21 611588 🖷 +381 21 26624 **Email:** rtsrns@eunet.yu **Web:** radionovisad.co.yu

MW	kHz	kW	Notes
Sombor	837	10	(in Hungarian)
Novi Sad	1107	100	(r. Beograd 1)
Novi Sad	1269	1	(in Serbian)

FM (MHz)	I	II	M	kW
Novi Sad	87.7	90.5	97.2	50/50/10
Subotica	99.3	92.5		10/10
Vrsac	99.6		91.7(f)	10

I) in Serbian, II) in Hungarian, M) prgrs for national minorities: Romanian (f), Rossinian, Slovak.
R. Novi Sad 1: 24h in Serbian **R. Novi Sad 2:** 0400-2305 in Hungarian, Romanian, Rossinian. Slovak.

Local stations

MW/FM	kHz	kW	MHz	MW/FM	kHz	kW	MHz
Sombor	666	10	90.9	Beocin	1431	0.2	97.8
Stara Pazova	2783	0.2	107.4	Srbobran	1449	2	102.6
Ruma	936	1	102.7	Zrenjanin	-	-	103.6
Temerin	1044	1	93.5	Novi Sad L	1485	2	93.7
Subotica	-	-	91.5	Apatin	1494	0.2	98.7
Kovin	-	-	88.5	Odzaci	1539	0.2	89.7
Backa Topola	1170	0.2	97.8	Stara Pazova 1	-	-	91.5
Backi Petrovac	1224	1	91.4	Backa Palanka	1575	1	99.1
Sid	1323	1	89.1	Pancevo			92.1
Vrbas	-	-	95.5	Indjija			96.0
Kovacica	-	-	93.2	Vrsac	-	-	98.1

Local/private stations on FM: R. Yusaco, Novi Sad 88.6 – R. Santos, Zrenjanin 88.7 – Plavi R., Belegis 89.1 – Kula 89.2 – Kikinda 89.3 – R. Skala, Novi Sad 89.6 – R. 5, Novi Sad 91.0 – Backi Petrovac 91.4 – R. 021, Novi Sad 92.2 – R. M, Sremska Mitrovica 92.3 – R. Spektar, Pancevo 92.8 –R. Skala, Novi Sad 93.7 – Backa Palanka 95.1/99.1 – Vrbas 95.5 – R. Signal, Novi Sad 95.8 –R.Maraton 98.4 - R. Dunav, Novi Sad 98.8 – Futog 99.5 – R. 100, Novi Sad 100.0 – Pan Radio, Novi Sad 100.6 – YU Eco Radio, Subotica 101.1 – R. Spektar, Sombor 101.3 – R. S, Novi Sad 104.4 – R. Safir, Pancevo 104.9 – Becej 105.4 – R. Pink, Novi Sad 107.0 – R. Ritam, Pancevo 107.6MHz.

MONTENEGRO

RADIO TELEVIZIJA CRNE GORE

✉ Cetinjski put bb, 81000 Podgorica ☎ +381 81 41800 **Email:** marketing@rtcg.org **Web:** www.rtcg.org **L.P:** DG: Z. Jokovic

MW:

kHz	kW	Station, Location
882	300	R. Podgorica 1, Podgorica 24h

FM (MHz)	I	II	III	L	kW
Lovcen	94.9	98.0	101.0	89.8	54
Bjelasica	92.1	99.3			54
Velji Grad	89.6	99.7			10
Podgorica	95.5				1
Mozura		93.4	102.6		1
Durmitor	91.3				1
Sudjina Glava	88.0	98.9			10

+ 11 tr. sites less than 1kW.

Local/private stations:
R. Antena M, Podgorica 87.6 + 5 relays – **R. Cetinje** 94.5 + 1 relay – **R. Elmag**, Podgorica 96.0 + 7 relays. – **R .98**, Podgorica 98.0 + 2 relays. – **R. Bar** 92.9 + 1 relay. – **R. Berane** 88.2 + 1 relay. – **R Bijelo**, Polje 105.8 + 1 relay. – **R.Budva** 98.7 + 1 relay. – **R. Corona**, Bar 88.9 +1 relay. – **R. D**, Podgorica 88.6 + 2 relays. – **R. Danilovgrad** 92.9. – **R. Fokus**, Bijelo Polje 93.9. – **R. Free Montenegro**, Podgorica 103.0. – **R. Glas** Plava, Plav 102.9. – **R. Gorica**, Podgorica 93.3. – **R. Herceg** Novi 90.0 +1 relay. – **R. Jupok**, Rozaje 98.7 + 1 relay. – **R. Kotor** 95.3 + 1 relay. – **R. Max**, Danilovgrad 107.5 + 1 relay. – **R. Mir**, Tuzi 106.1 + 1 relay. – **R. Mojkovac** 92.8. – **R. Montena**, Podgorica 105.7 + 5 relays. – **R. Niksic** 88.0 + 2 relays. – **R. Ozon**, Kolasin 97.6. – **R. Panorama**, Pljevlja 89.2. – **R. Pljevlja** 94.8. – **R. Rozaje** 104.4. – **R. Svetigora**, Cetinje 101.0. – **R. Tivat** 88.5. – **R. Ulcinj** 91.3 + 1 relay. – **R. Zeta**, Podgorica 93.8.

FOREIGN SERVICE:
RADIO SERBIA AND MONTENEGRO
see International Broadcasting section

SEYCHELLES

L.T: UTC +4h — **Pop:** 80,000 — **Pr.L:** Creole, English, French — **E.C:** 50Hz, 240V — **ITU:** SEY

MINISTRY OF INFORMATION TECHNOLOGY & COMMUNICATION (MITC)

✉ Telecom Division, P. O. Box 1389, Oceangate House, Room 16, Victoria, Mahé ☎ +248 382039 🖷 +248 225325
Web: www.virtualseychelles.sc/gover/mitc_telecom.htm
Email: telecom@seychelles.sc **L.P:** Dr. George Ah-Thew, Dir.

SEYCHELLES BROADCASTING CORPORATION (SBC)
P.O. Box 321, Hermitage, Mahé ☎ +248 289600 🖷 +248 225641 **Web:** www.sbc.sc **Email:** sbcradtv@seychelles.sc
L.P: MD: Mr. Ibrahim Afif. Prgr. Mgr.(Radio): Ms. Marguerite Hermitte. CE: Mr. Joyvani Chetty.
MW: Victoria 1368kHz 10kW.
FM: Anse Soleil 93.6MHz 0.25kW, Fairyland 93MHz 0.25kW, St.Louis 93.6MHz 1kW, Praslin 100.8MHz 0.03kW.
D.Prgr: **MW** (spoken word): MF 0200-0930 & 1100-1800, SS 0200-1800. **N: English**: 0300, 0600, 0900, 1500. **French**: 0330, 0700, 1300, 1700. **Creole**: 0230, 0500, 0800, 1600.
FM: **Paradise FM** (musical prgr.): 24hrs.
ANN: E: "This is SBC Radio". F: "Ici la Radio SBC". C: "Isi Radyo SBC" **IS:** Instrumental music.

BBC African Sce: St.Louis 106.2MHz 0.5kW.
RFI Afrique: St.Louis 103.8MHz 1kW, Anse Soleil 102.8MHz 0.25kW in French/English.

BBC INDIAN OCEAN RELAY STATION
see International Radio section.

SIERRA LEONE

L.T: UTC — **Pop:** 4.5 million — **Pr.L:** English, Krio, Limba, Mende, Temne, others — **E.C:** 50Hz, 230V — **ITU:** SRL

MINISTRY OF INFORMATION AND BROADCASTING
Youyi Building, Brookfields, Freetown ☎ +232 22 240911 🖷 +232 22 241757 **Web:** www.statehouse-sl.org/ministryinformation.htm **Email:** info@statehouse-sl.org **L.P:** Minister: Prof. S.M. Kaikai.

SIERRA LEONE BROADCASTING SERVICE (SLBS)
New England, Freetown ☎ +232 22 241919 🖷 +232 22 240922 **Web:** www.slbs.tv **Email:** info@slbs.tv
L.P: Ag. DG: Mrs. Gina Banda-Thomas. Ag. Dir. Eng. Sces: A.K.Sheriff.
SW: Goderich (G.C: 13.14W/08.30N): 3316kHz 10kW (inactive).
FM: Freetown 99.9MHz, Bo 96.5MHz, Kenema 93.5MHz, Mile 91 102MHz.
D.Prgr: "Power FM" on SW/FM: 0558-2400. **N. in English:** 0600, 0700, 0800, 2000, 2100, 2200. Rel. BBC: 1700-1800.
ANN: "This is the SLBS in Freetown", "Power FM 99.9".
IS: 5-note chime, military band.

RADIO UNAMSIL (UN Mission in Sierra Leone)
UNAMSIL HQ, Mammy Yoko, P.O. Box 5, Freetown ☎ +232 22 273183/4/5 🖷 +232 22 273189 **Web:** www.un.org/Depts/dpko/missions/unamsil **L.P**: Station Manager: Ms. Sheila Dallas
SW: Freetown 6140v kHz 1kW. **FM:** 103MHz.
D.Prgr: 24h in English/Vernaculars.

Other stations:
Believers Broadcasting Network (BBN) (rlg.), 11 Pademba Rd, Freetown: 93MHz ☎ +232 22 221425 **Email:** bbn93sl@yahoo.co.uk **L.P:** MD: Ransford S.C. Wright – **Citizen FM**, Freetown: 103.7MHz – **R. Democracy**, Freetown: 98.1MHz (also rel. BBC & VOA) – **R. Gbaft**, Freetown: 91MHz – **R. Kiss FM**, Bo: 104MHz. (Also rel. VOA) – **R. Makeni**, Freetown: 88MHz – **R. Maria,** P.O. Box 1, Makeni 101.1MHz 0.5kW – **R. Sefadu:** 90.2MHz – **SKYY FM**, Freetown: 106MHz – **V. of the Handicapped,** Freetown: 96.2MHz (mostly rel. BBC) – **V. of Peninsular Mountains**, Tombo: 96MHz

BBC African Sce: Freetown 94.3MHz.
RFI Afrique: Freetown 89.9MHz in French/English.

SINGAPORE

L.T: UTC +8h — **Pop:** 4.3 million — **Pr.L:** English, Chinese, Malay, Tamil — **E.C:** 50Hz, 230V — **ITU:** SNG

MEDIA DEVELOPMENT AUTHORITY OF SINGAPORE
(Government statutory board)
140 Hill Street, MITA Building #04-01, Singapore 179369
☎ +65 6837 9973 🖷 +65 6336 8023. **Web**: www.mda.gov.sg.
LP: Chairman: Dr. Tan Chin Nam.

MEDIACORP RADIO SINGAPORE PTE LTD
Caldecott Broadcast Centre, Andrew Road, Singapore 299939 ☎ +65 63339888 🖷 +65 62581181 **Web**: www.mediacorpradio.com
L.P: Chmn: Mr. Ho Kwon Ping. MedieCorp Radio Acting CEO: Mr. James Yip. VP Programming & News: Ms. Tan Siew Ping. VP Technology Services: Mr. Asaad Sameer Bagharib. CBA Liaison Officer: Ms. Sandra Chan.
Stations: Main FM tr. centre at Bukit Batok.

	FM MHz	Network	Format	Lang.	H. of tr.
1)	89.7	Ria 89.7FM	CHR	Malay	2200-1800
2)	90.5	Gold 90FM	Gold	English	24h
3)	92.4	Symphony 92FM	Classical	English	2200-1600
4)	93.3	Y.E.S. 93.3FM	AC	Chinese	24h
5)	93.8	NewsRadio 9-3-8 a)	N./Info	English	2200-1600
6)	94.2	Warna 94.2FM	Full sce.	Malay	24h
7)	95.0	Class 95FM	AC	English	24h
8)	95.8	Capital R. 95.8 FM *	N./Info	Chinese	2200-1800
9)	96.3	Int. Channel	***	F, G, Jap.	2300-1600
10)	96.8	Oli 96.8FM	Full sce.	Tamil	24h
11)	97.2	Love 97.2FM **	Easy	Chinese	24h
12)	98.7	Perfect 10 98.7FM	CHR	English	24h

a) rel. RSI in E. D1200-1300 ("The RSI Hour"). *) in Chinese: "Chengshi Pindao". **) in Chinese: "Zui'ai". ***) Japanese, Deutsche Welle in German, R. France Int. in French. Int. Channel sched. on the web: international963.mediacorpradio.com/programmes. F.Pl: Grooves FM on 99.5MHz.
TV Mobile audio is broadcast on 89.3MHz in FM for commuters.

SW: (Kranji, G.C: 01N25 103E44): 6 x 250kW, 1 x 100kW.

Network(s)	kHz	kW	Language	H. of tr.
4), 8) 11)	6000	250	Chinese	2300-1100, 1400-1600
5)	6150	250	English	2300-1100, 1400-1600
10)	7170	100	Tamil	2300-1600
1), 6)	7235	250	Malay	2300-0900, 1200-1600

Beam: 320 deg. to Malaysia. Freq's also used by R. Singapore Int. at other times.

DAB: Two networks using 190.640MHz, block 7B, and 192.352MHz, block 7C.

EXTERNAL SERVICE: Radio Singapore International (RSI)
See International Broadcasting section.

SAFRA RADIO
Operated by the Singapore Armed Forces Recreation Ass.
Defence Technology Towers Tower B, 5 Depot Rd #12-04, Singapore 109681 ☎ +65 6373 1924 🖷 +65 6278 3039 **Web**: power98.com.sg *or* www.fm883.com.sg
Dongli 88.3 FM: 24h in Chinese on 88.3MHz.
Power 98 FM: 24h in English on 98.0MHz.

UNIONWORKS PTE LTD
510 Thomson Rd, #B1-02 SLF Bldg, Singapore 298135. UFM 1003: PO Box 232, Toa Payoh Central, Singapore 913108
☎ +65 6353 6100 **Web**: www.wkrz913.com or www.ufm1003.com
WKRZ91.3 FM: 24h in English.
UFM1003: 24h in Chinese.

BBC FAR EASTERN RELAY STATION
51 Turut Track, Singapore 718930 ☎ +65 6793 7511
FM: Bukit Batok 88.9MHz 4kW: 24h rel. of BBCWS in English.
SW: see International Broadcasting section

SLOVAKIA

L.T: UTC +1h (27 Mar-30 Oct UTC +2h) — **Pop:** 5 million — **Pr.L:** Slovak — **E.C:** 50Hz, 230V — **ITU:** SVK

SLOVENSKY ROZHLAS (SLOVAK RADIO)
Mytna 1, 817 55 Bratislava ☎ + 421 2 57273856
🖷 + 421 2 57273559. **Web:** www.slovakradio.sk. **Email:** informacie@slovakradio.sk **Rock FM Radio Web:** www.rockfmradio.sk. **Email:** rockfm@radiorockfm.sk **L.P:** DG: Jaroslav Reznik. PD: Pavol Sramek. Mus. Dir.: Vlado Franc. CE: Ladislav Ludiak.

LW & MW:	kHz	kW	Prgr.
Rimavská Sobota	567	20	S4 BB
Zilina	567	6	S4 BB
Orava	621	5	S4 BB
Presov	702	40	S4 KE, S5 Ukr+Ruth
Cadca	864	1	S4 BB
Snina (Stakcin)	864	1	S4 KE, S5 Ukr+Ruth
Poprad (Tatry)	900	6	S4 KE
Kosice	927	5	S5 Hung
Nitra	927	25	S5 Hung
Bratislava (city)	1017	5	S5 Hung

LW & MW:	kHz	kW	Prgr.
Rimavská Sobota	1017	25	S5 Hung
Banská Bystrica	1035	14	S4 BB
Nitra (Jarok)	1098	50	S4 BA

FM (MHz)	S1	S2	S3	S4	S5	kW
Banská Bystrica	90.1	102.0	101.5			100/5/100
Banská Stiavnica	99.0		102.6			20
Bardejov	93.5		101.7			10
Borsky Mikulás		102.8		95.6		1
Bratislava	96.6	99.3	89.3	104.4		100/12/10/5
Kosice	96.6		100.3	103.2		80/34/0.1
Kosice (city)		101.3				0.05
Lucenec	98.0	88.2	103.6			10
Modry Kamen	90.9	98.3	103.1	88.5	103.1	1/1/1/10
Námestovo	100.4	88.7	102.4			10
Nitra	91.2		102.2			10/1
N. Mesto n.V.	103.2		100.7			9
Nové Zámky				102.8	94.6	1
Poprad	92.2	96.9	104.3			30
Rim. Sobota				95.0	106.7	1
Roznava	97.3	88.6	105.9	90.0		5/5/1/1
Ruzomberok	103.8	102.1	100.6			8
Snina	91.2			102.2		10
				107.6		10
Stará Lubovna	89.1	102.3	98.9	96.1		10
Sturovo	96.3	106.2	103.7	91.7		10/5/10/10
Trebisov		106.7		89.2	99.7	10
Trencín	95.9	93.3	101.2			5
Trstená				91.9		10
Zilina	97.2	103.5	100.1			20/25/25
Zvolen				92.6		0.1

S1 = Radio Slovensko: 24h (national prgr, news). **S2** = Radio Devín: 24h (cultural prgr). **S3** = Rock FM Radio: 24h (rock, pop and alternative music). N: on the h. **S4** = Radio Regina: 24h (regional prgrs + prgrs for national minorities in Hungarian, Ukrainian, Ruthenian, German, Czech, Polish and Gypsy/Roma + relays of Radio Slovensko – S1).
S4 BA = Radio Regina Bratislava, Mytna 1, 817 55 Bratislava 15. Mon-Fri 0335-2400, Sat 0500-2100, Sun 0700-2100.
S4 BB = Radio Regina Banská Bystrica, L. Sáru 1, 975 68 Banská Bystrica. Mon-Fri 0335-1730, Sat 0500-2030, Sun 0800-1930.
S4 KE = Radio Regina Kosice, Masarykova 7, 041 61 Kosice. Mon-Fri 0400-2030, Sat 0500-2030, Sun 0500-1600.
S5 = Radio Patria – production of prgrs for national minorities in Hungarian, Ukrainian, Ruthenian, German, Czech, Polish, Gypsy/Roma relayed on S4 and S5 transmitters. Address: Slovensky Rozhlas, HRNEV, Moyzesova 7, 040 01 Kosice. **Email:** patria@slovakradio.sk.
Prgrs for minorities (S 5) on Radio Regina: Hungarian: Mon-Fri 0910-1100, 1200-1700, Sat+Sun 0700-1700; Ukrainian and Ruthenian: Mon, Tue, Thu, Fri 1600-1700, Wed 1630-1700, Sat 0800-1100, Sun 0500-0800, 1000-1330. German: Wed 1600-1630; Czech: 1st Wednesday 1820-1850; Gypsy/Roma: Mon 1820-1850, Wed 1630-1700, 2nd Wednesday 1820-1850, Sunday 1730-1800 for Bratislava and western Slovakia; Polish: 3rd Wednesday 1820-1850; Ruthenian: 4th Wednesday 1820-1850.

FOREIGN SERVICE: Radio Slovakia
see International Broadcasting section

MAJOR PRIVATE STATIONS/NETWORKS:

ASOCIÁCIA NEZÁVISLYCH ROZHLASOVYCH STANIC (Association of Independent Radio Stations)
✉ Stúrova 9, 811 02 Bratislava ☎ +421 2 323 065.

FUN RADIO (Comm.)
✉ Leskova 5, 815 25 Bratislava ☎ +421 2 52494601 🖷 +421 2 52495535 **Web:** www.funradio.sk. **L.P:** MD: Miloslava Zemkova. PD: Milan Kralik. Mus. Dir.: Peter Graus. CE: Robert Oravec. **FM:** see list below **D.Prgr:** 24h.

RADIO TWIST (Comm.)
✉ Salviová 1, 830 00 Bratislava ☎ +421 2 43291247 🖷 +421 2 43424908 **Web:** www.twist.sk. **L.P:** DG: Andrej Hryc. MD: Mikulas Curik PD: Lubos Machaj. CE: Frantisek Maron.
FM: see list below **D.Prgr:** 24h

RADIO EXPRES (Comm.)
✉ Lamacská cesta 1, 841 04 Bratislava ☎ +421 2 59308900 🖷 +421 2 59308991 **Web:** www.expres.sk. **FM:** see list below **D.Prgr:** 24h

OKEY RADIO (Comm.)
✉ Seberíniho, 821 03 Bratislava ☎ +421 2 48222101 🖷 +421 2 48222100 **Web:** www.okey.sk **L.P:** DG: Michal Arpas. PD: Branko Cap. Mus. Dir.: Julius Virsik. CE: Gabriel Suchy.
FM: see list below **D.Prgr:** 24h

RADIO LUMEN (Relig.)
✉ Kapitulská 2, 974 01 Banská Bystrica ☎ +421 2 4125739 🖷 +421 2 4125737 **Web:** www.lumen.sk.
L.P: DG: Vladimir Slovak. MD: Stefan Sajgalik. PD: Pavol Katreniak. CE: Jan Kraus. **FM:** see list below **D.Prgr:** 24h

Private FM:

MHz	kW	Station	Location
87.7	80	Fun Radio	Kosice
87.7	10	R. Rebeca	Banská Bystrica
87.9	0.5	R. Twist	Dolny Kubín
88.0	8.5	R. Naj	Nové Mesto nad Váhom
88.4	2	R. Expres	Hlohovec
88.4	1	R. Expres	Ruzomberok
88.5	2	R. Twist	Strázske
89.0	1	R. Expres	Zvolen
89.1	6	R. Duha	Trencín
89.3	1	R. Expres	Rimavská Sobota (F.Pl.)
89.7	1	R. Lumen	Ruzomberok
89.7	0.5	R. Expres	Nitra
89.8	0.5	R. Okey Top	Presov (F.Pl.)
90.7	1	R. Twist	Trstená (F.Pl.)
90.8	10	R. Naj	Trnava
90.8	2	R. Kiks	Presov
91.0	1	R. Expres	Moldava nad Bodvou
91.1	1	R. Twist	Ruzomberok
91.1	0.5	R. Twist	Brezno
91.6	10	Fun Radio	Lucenec
91.8	0.5	R. Hit FM	Trencín (F.Pl.)
92.2	1	Fun Radio	Dubnica nad Váhom
92.6	1	R. Kiks	Levoca
92.7	0.5	R. Expres	Zarnovica
92.7	1	R. Expres	Nové Zámky
92.9	0.5	R. Twist	Prievidza
93.3	1	R. Lumen	Banská Stiavnica
93.6	1	R. Okey	Ruzomberok (F.Pl.)
93.9	1	R. Beta	Lehota pod Vtácnikom
94.2	30	R. Tatry	Poprad
94.3	90	Fun Radio	Bratislava
94.5	13	R. Zet	Zilina
95.0	1	Fun Radio	Liptovsky Mikulás
95.2	10	N - Radio	Nitra
95.2	0.5	R. Expres	Kosice
95.4	0.5	R. Expres	Cadca
95.4	0.5	R. Expres	Martin
95.7	1	R. Expres	Roznava
95.9	10	R. Kiks	Snina
96.0	5	R. Twist	Lucenec
96.1	1	R. Frontinus	Cadca (F.Pl.)
96.4	0.5	R. Hit FM	Partizánske
96.5	0.5	R. Expres	Banská Bystrica
96.5	2	R. Expres	Trstená
96.5	0.5	R. Expres	Zilina
97.0	0.5	R. Expres	Levice
97.0	10	R. Kiks	Michalovce
97.8	10	R. Lumen	Trencín (F.Pl. S2)
98.1	1	R. Lumen	Handlová
98.5	8.8	R. Okey	Nové Mesto nad Váhom
98.6	50	R. Vychod B1	Kosice
98.7	1	R. Max	Nové Zámky
99.2	25	Fun Radio	Zilina
99.4	1	R. Expres	Sturovo
99.5	1	R. Expres	Svit
99.6		R. Twist	Cadca (F.Pl.)
99.7	0.5	R. Expres	Nové Mesto nad Váhom
100.9	30	R. Okey	Poprad
101.1	5	R. Expres	Lucenec
101.4	1	R. Twist	Roznava
101.8	90	R. Twist	Bratislava
102.0	0.5	R. Okey Top	Kosice
102.5	1	R. Expres	Trencín
102.5	1	Fun Radio	Poprad
102.8	1	R. Okey	Zilina
102.9	2	R. Lumen	Strbské Pleso
103.3	2	R. Lumen	Michalovce
103.7	8	R. Flash	Presov
104.0	95	Fun Radio	Banská Bystrica
104.1	1	R. Kiks	Presov
104.2	0.5	R. Kiks	Domasa
104.5	1	R. Hit FM	Prievidza
104.6	0.75	R. Frontinus	Zilina

MHz	kW	Station	Location
104.8	50	R. Okey	Bratislava
104.8	1	R. Twist	Poprad
104.9	2	R. Twist	Martin
105.1	10	R. Twist	Banská Stiavnica
105.2	1	R. Expres	Povazská Bystrica
105.5	10	R. Twist	Trencín
105.7	1	R. Expres	Stará Lubovna
105.8	10	R. Lumen	Námestovo
105.8	1	R. Twist	Presov
106.0	50	R. Okey	Banská Bystrica
106.2	20	R. Expres	Kosice
106.3	3	R. Lumen	Lucenec
106.5	1	R. Expres	Modry Kamen
106.6	3	City Radio B1	Bratislava
106.6	1	R. Twist	Banská Bystrica
106.9	3	R. Rebeca	Zilina (F.Pl.)
107.5	0.5	R. Expres	Prievidza
107.6	5	R. Expres	Bratislava
107.6	2.5	R. Expres	Bratislava
107.7	1	R. Vychod B1	Stará Lubovna

+ over 20 relays of less than 0.5kW

BBC SLOVAKIA (BBC World Service)

✉ Benediktiho 5, 811 05 Bratislava. ☎ +421 2 5727 3580.
Web: www.bbc.co.uk/slovak
Bratislava 93.8MHz 6kW (24h - BBC Slovakia, Learning English and BBC World Service Europe). **Kosice** 103.2MHz 0.1kW, **Banská Bystrica** 105.4MHz 0.1kW (BBC Slovakia + S4 Radio Regina).

SLOVENIA

L.T: UTC +1h (27 Mar-30 Oct: UTC +2h) — **Pop:** 2 million — **Pr.L:** Slovene — **E.C:** 50Hz, 220V — **ITU:** SVN

SLOVENIAN BROADCASTING COUNCIL (ATRP)

✉ Parmova 53, 1000 Ljubljana ☎ +386 (01) 280 4660 **Web:** www.sigov.st/srd/ www.atrp.si **Email:** urst.box@gov.si
The Council defines the principle of frequency allocation and supervises the electronic mass media.

RADIOTELEVIZIJA SLOVENIJA (Gov.)

✉ Kolodvorska ulica 2-4, SI-1550 Ljubljana ☎ +386 61 1311333 🖷 +386 61 1319171 **Web:** www.rtvslo.si **Email**: miha.lampreht@rtvslo.si
L.P: DG: Miha Lampreht.
Regional Centres: RTV Koper-Capodistria, Ulica O.F. 15, 6000 Koper ☎ +386 56685485 🖷 +386 5 6685488. RTV Studio Maribor, Ilichova 33, 2000 Maribor. ☎ +386 2 101244. 🖷 +386 2 101455.

MW	kHz	kW	Prgr.	MW	kHz	kW	Prgr.
Beli Kriz	549	15	K	Dom ale	918	300	1
Maribor	558	10	1/MMR	B. Kri	1170	300	C

C=R. Capodistria in Italian/R. Slovenija International.
K= R. Koper in Slovene
MMR=Muravideki Magyar Radió in Hungarian

FM (MHz)	Slo 1	Slo 2	Slo 3	Reg.
Ajdovšcina-Planina	89.5	98.6		92.3k
Beli Kri	92.0	94.1		104.3k
				97.7c
Bizeljsko	92.7	96.2	101.5	
Boc				90.4m
Breginj	95.7	97.6		
Cerkno-Lajše		90.9		
Crnonelj-Plešivica	89.0	96.5	99.0	
Fara		99.0		
Grahovo	93.5	90.0		
Idrija I		90.9		
Idrija II-Gradišce	88.9	90.0		
Jezersko	87.7	97.2		
Kanin	89.8	91.6	93.8	
Kocevje-Dekliška Gora		92.6		
Kovor	100.7	92.4		
Kozje	89.6			
Kranjska Gora-Brvogi	94.7	96.8		
Krim	88.0	93.5	96.5	
Krvavec	91.8	98.9	102.0	
Kuk	96.4	87.8		100.6k
Kum	94.1	99.9	103.9	
Lendava				103.3h
Mozirje	87.6	94.7	96.2	
Nanos	92.9	95.3	105.7	88.6k
				103.1c
Pec	100.1			
Pecarovci				87.6h
Plešivec	90.0	92.4	101.4	
Pohorje	88.5	96.9	105.3	93.1m
				102.8si
Skalnica				100.3k
Strari trg ob Kolpi	88.6	94.0		
Tinjan	89.3	94.6		107.6k
				103.6c
				98.9si
Trdinov Vrh	90.9	97.6	100.6	
Trenta-Lomovje	89.1	92.2		
Trenta-Skala	94.7	101.1		
Tr ic 2	96.9			
Vogel	93.7	97.6		
Vreme		99.6		

Reg. st's: c=R. Capodistria in Italian, h=R.MMR in Hungarian, k=R. Koper, m= R. Maribor, si= R. Slovenija International.
R. Slovenija 1 Program A: 24h (Mon 2300-Tues 0300 on FM only). **N.** in E & G: 2130 – **R. Slovenija 2 Val 202:** 0500 -2300. Pop + entertainment – **R. Slovenija 3 Programa ARS:** 0600-2400. Serious music, educational – **R. SI, Radio Slovenjia International**, Ilichova ulica 33, SI-2000 Maribor. **Email:**radio.si@rtvslo.si; Music and entertainment channel 24h on **FM(**MHz**):**: Unknown transmitter site 89.2, Celje 91.1 & 98.3, Tinjan 98.9, Ljubljana 102.4, Maribor 102.8. **MW**(kHz): 1170 2300-0500.

RADIO KOPER – CAPODISTRIA

✉ PO Box 117, SI-6000 Koper-Capodistria ☎ +386 5 6685050 🖷 +386 5 6684500 (Slovene Dept.) +386 5 6685440 (Italian Dept.) **Web:** www.rtvslo.si. **Email:** radio.koper@rtvslo.si; ondablu@rtvslo.si
✉ Rejcva ulica 6, Nova Gorica ☎+386 5 3331535 **L.P:** Editor-in-Chief (Slovene): Leon Horvatic. Editor-in-Chief (Italian): Bruno Fonda.
Radio Koper in Slovenian 0500-2300 on 549 kHz + FM Nanos 88.6, Ajdovscina 92.5, Kuk 100.6, Skalnica 100.3, Tinjan 107.6, Koper 96.4 and Beli Kriz 104.3 MHz. Other times rel. Slovenija 1.
Radio Capodistria in Italian: 0500-2300 on 1170kHz + FM Beli Kriz 97.7, Nanos 103.1, Tinjan 103.6.MHz.
2300-0500 relay of Radio SI, Radio Slovenija International.

RADIO MARIBOR

✉ Ilichova ulica 33, SI-2000 Maribor **Email:** radio.maribor@rtvslo.si **FM** (MHz): Boc 90.4, Pohorje 93.1.

MURAVIDEK MAGYAR RADIO

✉ Glavna ulica 120, SI-9220 Lendava **Email:** mmr.studio@rtvslo.si **MW** (kHz): Maribor 558 10 kW. **FM** (MHz): Pecarovci 87.6, Lendava 103.3 **D.Prgr:** 0445-1800. Other times rel. Slovenia 1 on MW and Radio SI on FM

MURSKI VAL

✉ Ul. arhitekta Novaka 13, 9000 Murska Sobota **Email**: radio-murski.val@siol.net
MW (kHz): Nemcavci 648 10 kW. **FM** (MHz): Pecarovci 94.6, 105.7 **D.Prgr:** 24 h. During nighttime a joint night program of Slovenian and local stations is broadcast.

LOCAL & REGIONAL STATIONS

MW:	kHz	Station	Tr. Location
1)	594	Radio Odmev	Cerkno
2)	648	R.Murski Val	Nemcavci
3)	1584	R. Bre ice	Sremic

Addresses & other information:
1) Platiševa ul. 39, SI-5282 Cerkno. **Email**: radio.cerkno@siol.net. – **2)** ul. arhitekta Novaka 13, SI-9000 Murska Sobota. **Email:** radio-murski.val@siol.net – **3)** Trg Izgnancev 12, SI-8250 Bre ice. **Web:** www.radio-brezice.si

Nationwide Private Station
RADIO OGNJIŠCE
✉ Štula 23, p.p. 4863, SI-1210 Ljubljana-Šentvid. **Email:** public@ognjisce.si **Web:** http://radio.ognjisce.si
FM (MHz): Planina-Ajdovšcina 91.2, Tolmin 91.2, Tinjan 91.2, Tolsti vrh 95.7, Radlje ob Dravi 96.5, Kricna gora 96.8, Ilirska Bistrica 97.3, Kalvarija (Maribor) 97.5, Krvavec 104.5, Kum 105.9, Boc 107.3, Sveta gora nad Solkanom 107.5

Private Stations in Major Cities
Ljubljana: 1TR, Trcaška 148, 1371 Logatec: 91.1 MHz, 107.1 MHz. **Email:** radio@1tr.net. **Web:** www.1tr.net – **Gama MM**, Stegne 21c, 1101 Ljubljana: 106.4 MHz. **Email:** info@gamamm.si **Web:** www.gamamm.si – **Poslovni val**, Trcaška 55, 1111 Ljubljana: 88.4 MHz – **Radio Antena 1**, Gregorciceva 5, 1000 Ljubljana: 105.2 MHz. **Email:** rantena1@siol.net

Web: www.radioantena.si – **Radio Dur**, Šmartinska 152g, 1000 Ljubljana: 103.4 MHz, 107.4 MHz – **Radio RGL**, Cesta 24. junija 23, 1231 Ljubljana-Crnuce: 99.5 MHz, 100.2 MHz – **Radio Salomon**, Pot Heroja Trnika 32, 1261 Ljubljana-Dobrunje: 101.6 MHz – **Radio Študent**, Cesta 27.aprila 31, 1000 Ljubljana: 89.3 MHz. **Web:** www.radiostudent.si – **Radio Veseljak**, Pot Heroja Trnika 32, 1261 Ljubljana-Dobrunje: 94.9 – **Slovenski Poslovni Kanal**, Vojkova 78, 1113 Ljubljana: 88.4 MHz. **Email:** uprava@radiospk.si **Web:** www.radiospk.si

Maribor: Radio Brezje, Na Trati 2, 2112 Maribor: 90.8 MHz. **Email:** radio.brezje@siol.net **Web:** www.radiobrezje.si – **Radio Center**, Citna ul 12, 2000 Maribor: 103.7 MHz. **Email:** info@radiocenter.si **Web:** www.radiocenter.si – **Radio City**, Slovenska 35, 2000 Maribor: 100.6 MHz. **Email:** radio@radiocity.si **Web:** www.radiocity.si – **Radio RGL**, Cesta 24. junija 23, 1231 Ljubljana-Crnuce: 104.8 MHz (Boc) – **Radio Klasik**, Vodole 34, 2000 Maribor: 107.9 MHz – **Radio MARŠ-Mariborski Radio Študent**, Gosposvetska 87b, 2000 Maribor: 95.9 MHz, 101.0 MHz. Email: radio.mars@guest.arnes.si **Web:** www2.arnes.si/~mbrmars – **Radio Net FM**, Loška cesta 13, 2000 Maribor: 100.2 MHz. **Email:** glasba@radionet.si **Web:** www.radionet.si – **Radio Plus**, Lackova 76, 2000 Maribor: 106.8 MHz. **Email:** raplus@raplus.com **Web:** www.raplus.com

There are a number of local commercial radio sts on FM, with very low power, not included, see **Web:** www.sigov.si/srd/eng/rae.htm

SOLOMON ISLANDS

L.T: UTC +11h — **Pop:** 480,000 — **Radios:** 45.000 — **Pr.L:** Pidgin, English — **E.C:** 50Hz, 240V — **ITU:** SLM

SOLOMON ISLANDS BROADCASTING CORPORATION (Statutory Authority, Comm.)

✉ **Honiara**: P.O. Box 654, Honiara ☎ +677 20051 🖷 +677 23159 **Gizo**: P. O. Box 78, Gizo, Western Province ☎ +677 60160 **Lata**: P. O. Box 46, Lata, Santa Cruz. ☎ +677 53047 **L.P:** GM: James Kilua. PD: David Palapu. CE:Cornelius Rathamana. Head of N: Dykes Angiki.
Web: www.sibconline.com.sb
MW: Honiara 1035kHz 10kW(d), Gizo 945kHz 10kW, Lata 1386kHz 5kW
SW: (G.C: 09S25 160E03): 5020 & 9545kHz (irreg.) 10kW.
FM: Wantok FM, Honiara 96.3MHz
D.Prgr: local 1900-1130, BBC 1300 - 1900
N. in English: 2000, 2200 (R. Australia), 0130W (local), 0200 (R. Australia), 0500W (local), 0600 (BBC), 0730 (local), 1000 (R. Australia), 1100 (local).
ANN: "This is the SIBC, Radio Hapi Isles". **IS:** Drum and Bamboo Pipes. **V.** by QSL-card. Rp. Re. must contain prgr. details.

UCB PACIFIC PARTNERS (SLM)

✉ Gud Nius Redio, PO Box 1415, Honiara **Email:** solomons@pacificpartners.org **Web:** www.pacificpartners.org
LP: Stn Mgr: David Tuhanuku
FM: Honiara 88.3MHz **DPrgr:** pPiji & English

SOMALIA

L.T: UTC +3h — **Pop:** 7.5 million — **Pr.L:** Somali, Rahanwein (Maay), Arabic, English — **E.C:** 50Hz, 220V — **ITU:** SOM

RADIO MOGADISHU, Voice of the Republic of Somalia

(operated by the Transitional National Government)
SW: 6822v kHz (inactive). **FM:** 98MHz.
ANN: "Halkani waa Raadiyo Muqdisho, Codka Jamhuuriyadda Soomaaliya."

RADIO SHABELE

✉ Global Building 3rd floor, Bakaraha Market 2nd rd, Mogadishu ☎ +252 5 933111 **Web:** www.shabele.com/radio.htm **L.P:** Chairman: Abdimalik Yusuf Moh'oud.
SW: Mogadishu 6960kHz.
FM: Marka 92MHz, Mogadishu 101.5MHz.
D.Prgr: 0400-0600, 1000-2100.

RADIO BANADIR

✉ Tahlil Warsame Building, KM 4, Maka Al Mukarama Rd, Mogadishu ☎ +252 5 944176/960368
Web: www.radiobanadir.com **Email:** rbb@radiobanadir.com
L.P: GM: Ahmad Ali Mahmud.
SW: 7002v kHz (inactive). **FM**: freq. unknown.
D.Prgr in Somali: 1600-1900. **Ann**: "Halkan wa Radio Banadir".

RADIO HORN AFRIK

☎ +252 1 217777 🖷 +252 1 217778 **Web:** www.hornafrik.com
FM: Mogadishu 99.9MHz (also rel. BBC/CNN/Al-Jazeera). Capital Voice: Mogadishu 88.8MHz (also rel. VOA).

RADIO STN (Somali Telemedia Network)

Web: www.stntv.com **Email:** stn@stntv.com **L.P:** Op. Mgr: Abdiqadir Abdi Ali.
FM: Mogadishu 95MHz. **D.Prgr in Somali:** 0300-2100. **N:** 0400.

HOLY KORAN RADIO (IQK)

FM: Mogadishu 102.5MHz. **D.Prgr in Somali:** 0800-2000.

RADIO DMC (Democratic Media Concern)

☎ +252 1 63727/214900/34444 **L.P:** Dir: Abdifatah Muhammad Ibrahim
FM: Baydhabo (Baidoa) 88.8MHz. **N:** 1400 Rahanwein, 1700 Somali.

GALGUDUUD BROADCASTING CORPORATION

FM: Guriceel 101.2MHz: 0800-1100, 1500-1700.

SOMALILAND

(self-declared autonomous state in northwest Somalia)

MINISTRY OF INFORMATION AND NATIONAL GUIDANCE

Web: www.somaliland-gov.com/information.html
L.P: Abdillahi Mohamed Duale, Minister.

RADIO HARGEISA

✉ Ex-Indian Club, Tima-Cadde, near the Main St, Hargeisa **Web:** www.radiosomaliland.com/radiohargeisa.html **Email:** radiohargeysa@yahoo.com **L.P**: Head of English Prgr: Mohamed Abdillahi.
MW/SW: Hargeisa (G.C: 09N33 004E03): 693kHz, 7530v kHz (AM/U) 1kW (irr.).
D.Prgr in Somali: 0330-0600, 0900-1200, 1500-2000. **N:** 0400, 1700, 1850. **English**: 1215, 1915.
ANN: S: "Halkani waa Radio Hargeisa, Odka Jamhuuriyadda Somaliland". E: "This is Radio Hargeisa, the Voice of the Republic of Somaliland"

PUNTLAND

(self-declared autonomous state in northeast Somalia)

MINISTRY OF INFORMATION, TELECOMMUNICATION AND CULTURE

✉ Garowe **L.P:** Abdikarim Ali Mahdi Sultan, Minister.

RADIO GALKAYO

☎ +252 5 446123 **Web:** www.radiogalkayo.com **Email:** Radiogaalkacyo@yahoo.co.uk **L.P:** Dir: Hasan Muhammad Jama. Prgr. Mgr: Mohamod Yasin Issak.
SW: Galkayo (Gaalkacyo) v6890kHz 0.8kW.
FM: Galkayo 79.5MHz.
D.Prgr in Somali: 0400-0600, 1000-1800. **N:** 1630.
ANN: "Halkani waa Rediyo Gaalkacyo, Idaac-adda Dowlad Goboleedka Puntland."

SOMALI BROADCASTING CORPORATION (SBC)

✉ SBC Building, Airport Rd, Bosaso ☎ +252 5 824600
Web: www.sbconline.net **Email:** sbc@sbconline.net
FM: Bosaso 89.0, Qardho 88.7, Garowe 89.2.

RADIO MIDNIMO

☎ +252 5 235612-14 **Email:** radiomidnimo@hotmail.com
L.P: MD: Abdishakur Mire Adam.
FM: Bosaso 97.5MHz. **N. in Somali:** 1030, 1700.

RADIO DALJIR

☎ +252 5 443315 **Web:** www.radiodaljir.com
Email: daljir@radiodaljir.com
FM: Galkayo 90.9/103.9MHz.

R. Garowe: 88.7MHz.
R. Lascaanod: freq. unk. **Web:** www.radiolascaanod.com

SOUTH AFRICA

L.T: UTC +2h — **Pop**: 48 million — **Pr.L:** English, Afrikaans, isiNdebele, isiXhosa, isiZulu, Sepedi, Sesotho, Setswana, siSwati, Tshivenda, Xitsonga — **E.C:** 50Hz, 230V — **ITU**: AFS

SOUTH AFRICAN BROADCASTING CORPORATION (SABC, National Public Service Broadcaster)

✉ Private Bag X1, Auckland Park 2006. ☎ +27 11 714 9111 🖷 +27 11 714 9744 Web: www.sabc.co.za **Regional** PO Box 2551, Cape Town 8000 – PO Box 1588, Durban 4000 – PO Box 563, Bloemfontein 9300 – PO Box 1040, Port Elizabeth 6000 – PO Box 395, Polokwane

0700 – PO Box 2724, Nelspruit 1200 – PO Box 1008, Kimberley 8300. **L.P**: Group C.E.: Peter Matlare. Chief Operating Officer: Solly Mokoetle. Head of Regions: Charlotte Mampane. MD, Technology: Sharoda Rapeti. MD, PBS: Judy Nwokedi. Senior GM, Audience Services: Anton Heunis. MD, PBCS: vacant.
NB: All transmitters belong to SENTECH (the common carrier for broadcasting in South Africa), ✉ Private Bag X06, Honeydew 2040.

HOME SERVICES (Comm.)
MW:

Location	**Service**	**kHz**	**kW**
Meyerton	R.Metro FM	576	50
Komga	Umhlobo Wenene FM	846	100
Ga-Rankuwa	Ikwekwezi FM	1098	50
Welgedacht	Ligwalagwala FM	1287	2
Welgedacht	Ikwekwezi FM	1404	2

Countrywide FM:

Limpopo	**R. Sonder**				
FM (MHz)	**Grense**	**SAFM**	**R. 2000**	**5 FM**	**R. Metro**
Blouberg	102.3	105.9	-	-	-
Hoedspruit	102.0	105.6	98.5	-	-
Louis Trichardt	100.7	104.3	97.2	-	-
Nylstroom	102.9	106.5	-	-	-
Potgietersrus	101.4	105.0	97.9	91.4	106.7
Thabazimbi	101.9	105.5	98.4	-	-
Tzaneen	102.6	106.2	107.7	-	-

NW Province	**R. Sonder**				
FM (MHz)	**Grense**	**SAFM**	**R. 2000**	**5 FM**	**R. Metro**
Christiana	103.6	107.2	-	-	-
Enzelsberg	101.6	105.2	-	-	-
Groot Marico	102.3	105.9	-	-	-
Klerksdorp	101.2	104.8	97.7	-	-
Piet Plessis	102.8	106.4	-	-	-
Pomfret	101.1	104.7	-	-	-
Rustenburg	100.7	104.3	97.2	-	-
Schweize-Reneke		103.1	106.7	99.6	--
Zeerust	102.6	106.2	99.1	-	-

Gauteng	**R. Sonder**				
FM (MHz)	**Grense**	**SAFM**	**R. 2000**	**5 FM**	**R. Metro**
Heidelberg	100.8	104.4	97.3	-	-
Helderkruin	-	-	-	104.0	-
Johannesburg	101.5	105.1	99.7	98.0	96.4
Menlo Park	102.1	105.7	98.6	-	-
Pretoria	101.0	104.6	97.5	89.9	92.4
Sunnyside	-	-	-	103.6	-
Welverdiend	102.0	105.6	98.5	107.3	-

Mpumalanga	**R. Sonder**				
FM (MHz)	**Grense**	**SAFM**	**R. 2000**	**5 FM**	**R. Metro**
Carolina	103.0	106.6	-	-	-
Davel	103.5	107.1	100.0	90.4	-
Dullstroom	100.8	104.4	-	-	-
Lydenburg	102.8	106.4	-	-	-
Middelburg	101.8	105.4	98.3	97.0	100.3
Nelspruit	102.5	106.1	99.0	91.1	-
Piet Retief	102.1	105.7	-	-	-
Sabie	104.2	107.9	-	-	-
Volksrust	102.6	106.2	-	-	-

Northern Cape	**R. Sonder**				
FM (MHz)	**Grense**	**SAFM**	**R. 2000**	**5 FM**	**R. Metro**
Alexander Bay	102.2#	105.8#	98.7	92.2	
Calvinia	101.5	105.1	-	-	-
Carnavon	102.5	106.1	-	-	-
Colesberg	103.8	107.5	-	-	-
De Aar	102.0	105.6	-	-	-
Douglas	102.9	106.5	-	-	-
Faans Grove	103.0	106.6	-	-	-
Garies	100.7#	104.3#	-	-	-
Kimberley	101.0	104.6	97.5	91.0	-
Kuruman Hills	102.4	106.0	-	-	-
Pofadder	102.8	106.4	-	-	-
Prieska	100.8	104.4	-	-	-
Sringbok	101.6	105.2	-	-	-
Upington	101.7	105.3	-	-	-
Victoria West	101.1	104.7	-	-	-
Williston	103.2	-		-	-

Free State	**R. Sonder**				
FM (MHz)	**Grense**	**SAFM**	**R. 2000**	**5 FM**	**R. Metro**
Bethlehem	101.9	105.5	98.4	-	-
Bloemfontein	103.0	106.6	99.5	91.6	98.1
Boesmanskop	101.2	104.8	-	-	-
Ficksburg	103.7	107.3	-	-	-
Kroonstad	103.4	107.0	99.9	93.4	-
Ladybrand	102.1	105.7	-	-	-
Petrus Steyn	102.3	105.9	98.8	-	-
Senekal	101.1	104.7	97.6	-	-
Springfontein	102.6	106.2	99.1	-	-
Theunissen	102.5	106.1	99.0	92.5	-
Witsieshoek	101.3	104.9	-	-	-

Kwazulu Natal	**R. Sonder**				
FM (MHz)	**Grense**	**SAFM**	**R. 2000**	**5 FM**	**R. Metro**
Donnybrook	102.7	106.3	99.2	-	-
Durban	100.8	104.4	97.3	89.9	93.0
Durban North	102.5	106.1	99.0	103.8	107.9
Eshowe	103.4	107.0	99.9		90.3
Glencoe	103.1	106.7	99.6	-	-
Greytown	101.7	105.3	98.2	-	-
Kokstad	101.0	104.6	-	-	-
Ladysmith	101.0	104.6	97.5	-	-
Matatiele	101.5	105.1	-	-	-
Mooi River	102.2	105.8	98.7	-	-
Nongoma	102.9	106.5	99.4	-	89.8
Pietermaritzburg	101.4	105.0	97.9	100.3	-
Port Shepstone	101.3	104.9	97.8	-	-
The Bluff	102.0	105.6	98.5	107.4	-
Ubombo	102.4	106.0	98.9	-	-
Vryheid	101.2	104.8	97.7	-	-

Western Cape	**R. Sonder**				
FM (MHz)	**Grense**	**SAFM**	**R. 2000**	**5 FM**	**R. Metro**
Beaufort West	100.7@	104.3@	-	-	-
Constantiaberg	102.1	105.7	98.6	89.0	-
Ceres	103.7	107.3	-	-	-
Franschhoek	100.7	104.3	97.2	-	-
George	101.7	105.3	98.2	91.7	-
Grabouw	101.7	105.3	-	-	-
Hermanus	100.8	104.4	97.3	-	-
Hex River	102.0	105.6	-	-	-
Hout Bay	100.9	104.5	97.4	87.8	-
Kleinmond	104.2	107.9	-	-	-
Knysna	102.2	105.8	98.7	92.2	-
Ladismith	101.4	105.0	-	-	-
Matjiesfontein	102.8	106.4	-	-	-
Montagu	104.2	107.9	-	-	-
Napier	102.4	106.0	-	-	-
Oudtshoorn	102.6	106.2	99.1	92.6	-
Paarl	101.6	105.2	98.1	88.5	-
Piketberg	101.1	104.7	97.6	-	-
Plettenberg	100.8	104.4	-	-	-
Riversdale	100.9	104.5	-	-	-
Sea Point	103.5	107.1	100.0	90.4	91.7
Simonstown	100.7	104.3	97.2	87.6	-
Stellenbosch	100.9	104.5	97.4	87.8	-
Table Mountain	102.6	106.2	99.1	89.9	88.6
Tygerberg	103.0	106.6	99.5	88.2	93.0
Uniondale	103.4	107.0	-	-	-
Vanrhynsdorp	103.4	107.0	-	-	-
Villiersdorp	103.3	106.9	99.8	-	-

Eastern Cape	**R. Sonder**				
FM (MHz)	**Grense**	**SAFM**	**R. 2000**	**5 FM**	**R. Metro**
Aliwal North	101.7	105.3	-	-	-
Andrieskraal	103.2	106.8	-	-	-
Barkly East	100.9	104.5	-	-	-
Bedford	100.8	104.4	-	-	-
Burgersdorp	103.9	107.6	-	-	-
Butterworth	101.1	104.7	96.7	-	-
Cala	103.4	107.0	-	-	-
Cradock	102.7	106.3	-	-	-
East London	101.6	105.2	98.1	88.5	107.7
Elliot	101.4	105.0	-	-	-
Graaff-Reinet	103.3	106.9	-	-	-
Grahamstown	103.5	107.1	100.0	90.4	
Hankey	101.0	104.6	-	-	-
Kareedouw	102.9	106.5	-	-	-
King Williams Tn		103.0	106.6	-	--
Mount Ayliff	103.2	106.8	99.7	-	-
Noupoort	101.4	105.0	-	-	-
Patensie	101.5	105.0	-	-	-
Parsons Hill (PE)	101.0	104.6	-	-	87.9
Paul Sauer Dam	103.6	107.2	-	-	-

FM (MHz)	Grense	SAFM	R. 2000	5 FM	R. Metro
Port Elizabeth	102.3	105.9	98.8	89.2	100.5
Port St.Johns	103.7	107.3	100.2	-	-
Queenstown	102.2	105.8	98.7	-	-
Suurberg	101.8	105.4	-	-	-
Ugie	102.6	106.2	-	-	-
Umtata	102.0	105.6	98.5	-	-
Willowmore	101.2	104.8	-	-	-

= mono – no RDS, @ = mono RDS

NATIONAL SW SERVICES
SW: Meyerton (G.C: 26S35 028E08): 4 x 100kW tr's + 1 standby tr.

kHz	Sce.	H. of Tr.	kHz	Sce.	H. of Tr.
3320	RSG	1600-0530	9650	RSG	0800-1600
7185	RSG	0530-0800			

RSG=R. Sonder Grense (transmission for Northern Cape region)

SABC PUBLIC BROADCASTING SERVICES (PBS)
Ikwekwezi FM (isiNdebele): ✉ Private Bag X36, Auckland Park 2006 **Web**: www.hal.co.za ☎ +27 11 714 4559 🖷 +27 11 714 3564 – FM: Middelburg 91.8/Kwamlanga 93.8/Menlo Park 93.6MHz + 5 relays and on MW as above.
Lesedi FM (Sesotho): ✉ Private Bag X20707, Bloemfontein 9300 **Web:** www.lesedifm.co.za ☎ +27 51 503 3091 🖷 +27 51 503 3269 – FM: Bloemfontein 89.9/Johannesburg 88.4/Kroonstad 90.3MHz + 17 relays.
Ligwalagwala FM (siSwati): ✉ PO Box 2724, Nelspruit 1200 **Web:** www.hal.co.za ☎ +27 13 759 6613. 🖷 +27 13 755 3865 – FM: Nelspruit 92.5/Pretoria 92.5MHz + 11 relays and on MW as above.
Motsweding FM (Setswana): ✉ Private Bag X2158, Mmabatho 2735 **Web:** www.hal.co.za ☎ +27 18 389 7174. 🖷 +27 18 389 7326 – FM: Mmabatho 88.7/Johannesburg 89.6/Pretoria 91.0/Rustenburg 87.6MHz + 23 relays.
Munghana Lonene FM (Xitsonga): ✉ PO Box 395, Polokwane 0700 **Web:** www.hal.co.za ☎ +27 15 290 0263. 🖷 +27 15 290 0170 – FM: Johannesburg 103.2/Pretoria 95.6/Tzaneen 92.6/Nelspruit 89.4MHz + 4 relays.
Phalaphala FM (Tshivenda): ✉ PO Box 395, Polokwane 0700 **Web**: www.hal.co.za ☎ +27 15 290 0261. 🖷 +27 15 290 0170 – FM: Johannesburg 107.8/Tzaneen 99.1MHz + 8 relays.
Radio Sonder Grense (National service in Afrikaans): ✉ PO Box 91312, Auckland Park 2006. **Web**: www.rsg.co.za ☎ +27 11 714 2701 🖷 +27 11 714 3472 – On FM and SW as above.
Radio X-K (in !Xu and Khwe languages for Khoi San communities in N.Cape): ✉ PO Box 1008, Kimberley 8300 ☎ +27 53 299 0001 🖷 +27 53 299 0003 – FM: Schmidtsdrift 99.4MHz.
SAfm (National service in English): ✉ PO Box 91162, Auckland Park 2006 **Web**: www.safm.co.za ☎ +27 11 714 4442. 🖷 +27 11 714 5829 – On FM as above.
Thobela FM (Sepedi): ✉ PO Box 395, Polokwane 0700 **Web**: www.hal.co.za ☎ +27 15 290 0265 🖷 +27 15 290 0172 – FM: Johannesburg 90.1/Pretoria 87.9/Tzaneen 89.5MHz + 12 relays.
Ukhozi FM (isiZulu): ✉ PO Box 1588, Durban 4000 **Web:** www.ukhozifm.co.za ☎ +27 31 362 5402. 🖷 +27 31 362 5203 – FM: Durban 90.8/ Johannesburg 91.5/Pretoria 102.4MHz + 27 relays.
Umhlobo Wenene FM (isiXhosa): ✉ PO Box 1119, Port Elizabeth 6000 **Web**: www.uwfm.co.za ☎ +27 41 391 1328. 🖷 +27 41 373 2702 – FM: Port Elizabeth 92.3/King Williams Town 93.0/Durban 96.2/Johannesburg 93.2/Cape Town 92.1MHz + 48 relays.

SABS PUBLIC COMMERCIAL BROADCASTING SERVICES (PCBS)
CKI FM/Radio Ciskei: ✉ PO Box 014, Bisho 6505 ☎ +27 40 635 2940 🖷 +27 40 636 4112 – FM: East London 104.1/Bisho 100.3 + 2 relays.
Good Hope FM: ✉ PO Box 2551, Cape Town 8000 ☎ +27 21 430 8276 🖷 +27 21 434 3392. — FM: Cape Town 95.3MHz + 8 relays.
Lotus FM: ✉ Private Bag X1337, Durban 4000 **Web**: www.lotusfm.co.za ☎ +27 31 362 5445 🖷 +27 31 362 5202 – FM: Durban 87.7/Johannesburg 106.8/Pretoria 100.1 + 7 relays.
R.Metro FM: ✉ PO Box 91162, Auckland Park 2006. **Web**: www.metrofm.co.za ☎ +27 11 714 3485 🖷 +27 11 714 4166. – On FM as above, on MW 576 kHz.
R.Sunshine: ✉ Private Bag X2150, Mmabatho 2735 ☎ +27 18 389 7503 🖷 +27 18 389 7156. – FM: Mmabatho 95.0MHz.
R.2000: Web: www.radio2000.co.za ☎ +27 11 714 3313 🖷 +27 11 714 2436. – on FM as above.
5 FM: ✉ PO Box 91555, Auckland Park 2006 **Web**: www.5fm.co.za ☎ +27 11 714 2905 🖷 +27 11 714 5714 – On FM as above.

EXTERNAL SERVICE: Channel Africa
See International Broadcasting section

INDEPENDENT COMMUNICATIONS AUTHORITY OF SOUTH AFRICA (ICASA)
✉ Private Bag X10002, Sandton 2146 ☎ +27 11 321 8200 🖷 +27 11 444 1919 Email: info@icasa.org.za **Web**: www.icasa.org.za
The ICASA is the regulator of telecommunications and the broadcasting sectors in South Africa. It issues licences for commercial and community stations.

OTHER STATIONS (Comm.)
CAPE TALK (Comm.)
✉ Private Bag X567, Vlaeberg 8018 ☎ +27 21 488 1500. 🖷 +27 21 488 1600. **L.P**: M. Wills. Web: www.capetalk.co.za Email: 567@capetalk.co.za – MW: Klipheuwel (Cape Town) 567kHz, 25 kW.
Y-FM (Comm.)
✉ Postnet X31, Saxonwold 2132 ☎ +27 11 880 7070 🖷 +27 11 880 6966. **L.P**: R.Abrahams. Email: yfm@yfm.co.za – FM: Johannesburg 99.2MHz, 5kW.
CLASSIC FM (Comm.)
✉ PO Box 782, Auckland Park 2006. ☎ +27 11 408 5235 🖷 +27 11 408 5249. **L.P**: E.de Vos. Web: www.classicfm.co.za – FM: Johannesburg 102.7MHz
RADIO KFM (Comm.)
✉ Private Bag X945, Cape Town, 8000 ☎ +27 21 418 7000 🖷 +27 21 418 8647 **L.P**: Kevin Savage. Web: www.kfm.co.za Email: info@kfm.co.za – FM: Cape Town 94.5MHz + 23 relays.
RADIO ALGOA (Comm.)
✉ PO Box 5973, Walmer, 6075 ☎ +27 41 505 9497 🖷 +27 41 583 1533 **LP**: M.Vincent. Web: www.radioalgoa.com Email: algoa@radioalgoa.com – FM: Port Elizabeth 95.5MHz + 17 relays.
OFM/RADIO ORANJE (Comm.)
✉ PO Box 7117, Bloemfontein 9300 ☎ +27 51 505 0900 🖷 +27 51 505 0905. **LP**: A.Grobbelaar. Web: www.ofm.co.za Email: albe@ofm.co.za – FM: Bloemfontein 96.2MHz + 16 relays.
HIGHVELD STEREO (Comm.)
✉ PO Box 3438, Rivonia 2128 ☎ +27 11 506 3200 🖷 +27 11 506 3900 **LP**: M.Freid Web: www.highveld.co.za Email: 94.7@highveld.co.za – FM: Johannesburg 94.7MHz + 3 relays.
EAST COAST RADIO (Comm.)
✉ Private Bag X9495, Durban 4000 ☎ +27 31 570 9495 🖷 +27 31 566 3531. **LP**: D.Macleod. Web: www.ecr.co.za – FM: Durban 94.0MHz + 16 relays.
RADIO P4 (Comm.)
✉ PO Box 4995, Durban 4000 ☎ +27 31 310 9900 🖷 +27 31 310 9914. **LP**: Z.Mapipa. FM: Durban 99.5MHz + 2 relays.
✉ PO Box 211, Greenpoint 8051 ☎ +27 21 406 8900 🖷 +27 21 406 8940. **LP**: T.Ntokwana Email: p4@p4radio.com.zr – FM: Cape Town 104.9MHz + 5 relays.
RADIO JACARANDA (Comm.)
✉ PO Box 11961, Centurion 0046 ☎ +27 12 673 9100 🖷 +27 12 657 0105. **LP**: W.Engelbrecht – FM: Pretoria 94.2MHz + 21relays.
702 TALK RADIO (Comm.)
✉ PO Box 5572, Rivonia 2128. Web: www.702.co.za ☎ +27 11 506 3702 🖷 +27 (11) 506 3633 – MW: Ga-Rankuwa 702kHz 100kW
KAYA FM (Comm.)
✉ PO Box 2869, Parklands 2121 Web: www.kayafm.co.za ☎ +27 11 442 5544 🖷 +27 11 442 5570. **LP**: A. Mashiatshidi – FM: 95.9MHz.

Community Stations
Numerous licences issued by ICASA with over 80 stations currently on the air, mainly on FM. The license terms vary from 1 to 4 years.
MW:

	kHz	kW	Station	Location
1)	657	50	R. Pulpit/R.Kansel	Meyerton
2)	1269	2	Chinese Community R.	Midrand
3)	1422	1	New Panhellenic Voice	Bedfordview
4)	1485	1	R. Today	Honeydew
5)	1548	10	R. Islam	Lenasia
6)	1584	0.25	R. 1584	Pretoria

Addresses and other information:
1) PO Box 3436, Pretoria 0001. **Web:** www.radiokansel.co.za *or* www.radiopulpit.co.za ☎ +27 12 334 1200. 🖷 +27 12 333 7251. Relig. prgs in English and Afrikaans.– **2)** PO Box 623, Midrand, Noordwyk 1687 ☎ +27 11 318 1729. 🖷 +27 11 318 1352. Prgs in Chinese. – **3)** PO Box 96404, Brixton 2091 ☎ +27 11 837 2655 🖷 +27 11 830 1380. Prgs in Greek and English. – **4)** PO Box 81014, Auckland Park 2006 ☎ +27 11 482 6767 🖷 +27 11 482 6761. Prgs in English for over 55 age group. – **5)** PO Box 2580, Lenasia 1820 ☎ +27 11 854 7022. 🖷 +27 11 854 7024. Prgs in English. – **6)** Institute for Islamic Services, PO Box 46001, Belle Ombre 0142 **Web:** www.islam.co.za/1584 ☎ +27 12 374 1584 🖷 +27 12 374 2448. Prgs in English.

F.PI: Radio Veritas (See International Broadcasting section) permanently on 729kHz 25kW, Cape Town and 92.7MHz Johannesburg. Currently the station broadcasts on these frequencies once or twice a year under short term temporary licences issued by ICAS.

SPAIN

L.T: UTC +lh (27 Mar-30 Oct: UTC +2h) — **Pop**: 41.9 million — **Pr.L**: Spanish, Catalan, Galician, Basque — **E.C**: 50Hz, 230V — **ITU**: E

MINISTERIO DE FOMENTO
Secretaría General de Comunicaciones
Alcalá 50, Palacio de Comunicaciones, 28071 Madrid.

RADIO NACIONAL DE ESPAÑA (RNE)
Casa de la Radio, Prado del Rey, 28223 Pozuelo de Alarcón
☎ +34 91 346 2030 🖷 +34 91 346 1769 **Web**: www.rne.es

MW: RNE1 and RNE5 Todo Noticias.

	kHz	kW	Net	Rg	Location
AS01)	531	20	RNE5TN	AS	Oviedo°
AN02)	531	10	RNE5TN	AN	Córdoba
GA02)	531	10	RNE5TN	GA	Pontevedra
NA01)	531	10	RNE5TN	NA	Pamplona°
VA01)	558	50	RNE5TN	VA	València°
GA01)	558	20	RNE5TN	GA	A Coruña°
EU02)	558	20	RNE5TN	EU	Donosti-San Sebastián
MU01)	567	50	RNE5TN	MU	Murcia°
AN03)	567	5	RNE5TN	AN	Marbella
CA01)	576	100	RNE5TN	CA	Barcelona°
MA01)	585	600	RNE1	MA	Madrid°
AN01)	603	50	RNE5TN	AN	Sevilla°
CL02)	603	10	RNE5TN	CL	Palencia
CA02)	612	10	RNE1	CA	Lleida
EU01)	612	10	RNE1	EU	Vitoria-Gasteiz°
AN04)	621	10	RNE1	AN	Jaén
BA01)	621	10	RNE1	BA	Palma de Mallorca°
CL03)	621	10	RNE1	CL	Avila
GA01)	639	300	RNE1	GA	A Coruña°
AR01)	639	50	RNE1	AR	Zaragoza°
EU03)	639	50	RNE1	EU	Bilbo-Bilbao
AN05)	639	20	RNE1	AN	Almería
CM03)	639	10	RNE1	CM	Albacete
EX02)	648	10	RNE1	EX	Badajoz
MA01)	657	50	RNE5TN	MA	Madrid°
AN01)	684	600	RNE1	AN	Sevilla°
CM01)	693	20	RNE1	CM	Toledo°
CA03)	693	10	RNE1	CA	Tarragona (rel.of Barcelona)
AS01)	729	100	RNE1	AS	Oviedo°
AN06)	729	20	RNE1	AN	Málaga
RI01)	729	20	RNE1	RI	Logroño°
CL01)	729	10	RNE1	CL	Valladolid°
CM04)	729	10	RNE1	CM	Cuenca
VA02)	729	10	RNE1	VA	Alacant-Alicante
CA01)	738	600	RNE1	CA	Barcelona°
AN07)	747	10	RNE5TN	AN	Cádiz
VA01)	774	100	RNE1	VA	València°
EX01)	774	60	RNE1	EX	Cáceres°
EU02)	774	50	RNE1	EU	Donosti-San Sebastián
GA03)	774	20	RNE1	GA	Ourense
AN08)	774	10	RNE1	AN	Granada
AN09)	774	10	RNE1	AN	La Línea
CL04)	774	10	RNE1	CL	León
CL05)	774	10	RNE1	CL	Soria
CM05)	801	25	RNE1	CM	Ciudad Real
GA04)	801	20	RNE1	GA	Lugo
CA04)	801	10	RNE1	CA	Girona
CL06)	801	10	RNE1	CL	Burgos
CL07)	801	10	RNE1	CL	Zamora
VA03)	801	10	RNE1	VA	Castelló
MU01)	855	300	RNE1	MU	Murcia°
CT01)	855	50	RNE1	CT	Santander°
CA03)	855	20	RNE1	CA	Tarragona
GA02)	855	20	RNE1	GA	Pontevedra
AN10)	855	10	RNE1	AN	Huelva
AR02)	855	10	RNE1	AR	Teruel
CL08)	855	10	RNE1	CL	Ponferrada
CL09)	855	10	RNE1	CL	Salamanca
NA01)	855	10	RNE1	NA	Pamplona-Iruñea°
AN03)	855	5	RNE1	AN	Marbella
CM02)	864	10	RNE1	CM	Socuellamos (rel.of Toledo)
BA01)	909	10	RNE5TN	BA	Palma de Mallorca°
AR01)	936	20	RNE5TN	AR	Zaragoza°
CL01)	936	20	RNE5TN	CL	Valladolid°
VA02)	936	10	RNE5TN	VA	Alacant-Alicante
AN11)	972	5	RNE1	AN	Cabra (rel.of Sevilla)
GA05)	972	2	RNE1	GA	Monforte de Lemos
AN08)	1017	10	RNE5TN	AN	Granada
CL06)	1017	10	RNE5TN	CL	Burgos
AN05)	1098	25	RNE5TN	AN	Almería
GA04)	1098	20	RNE5TN	GA	Lugo
CL03)	1098	10	RNE5TN	CL	Avila
AN10)	1098	5	RNE5TN	AN	Huelva
RI01)	1107	25	RNE5TN	RI	Logroño°
CT01)	1107	20	RNE5TN	CT	Santander°
EX01)	1107	20	RNE5TN	EX	Cáceres°
AR02)	1107	10	RNE5TN	AR	Teruel
CL08)	1107	10	RNE5TN	CL	Ponferrada (rel.of León)
CL05)	1125	10	RNE5TN	CL	Soria
CM01)	1125	10	RNE5TN	CM	Toledo°
EU01)	1125	10	RNE5TN	EU	Vitoria-Gasteiz°
VA03)	1125	10	RNE5TN	VA	Castelló
EX02)	1125	5	RNE5TN	EX	Badajoz
AN06)	1152	20	RNE5TN	AN	Málaga
CA02)	1152	10	RNE5TN	CA	Lleida
CL07)	1152	10	RNE5TN	CL	Zamora
CM03)	1152	10	RNE5TN	CM	Albacete
MU02)	1152	10	RNE5TN	MU	Cartagena
GA03)	1305	25	RNE5TN	GA	Ourense
CM05)	1305	20	RNE5TN	CM	Ciudad Real
EU03)	1305	20	RNE5TN	EU	Bilbo-Bilbao
CL04)	1305	10	RNE5TN	CL	León
CM04)	1314	20	RNE5TN	CM	Cuenca
CA03)	1314	10	RNE5TN	CA	Tarragona
CL09)	1314	10	RNE5TN	CL	Salamanca
MA01)	1359	600		MA	Madrid°° (irr.)
GA06)	1413	20	RNE5TN	GA	Vigo
AN04)	1413	10	RNE5TN	AN	Jaén
CA04)	1413	5	RNE5TN	CA	Girona
AN09)	1503	5	RNE5TN	AN	La Linea (rel.of Cádiz)
GA05)	1503	2	RNE5TN	GA	Monforte de Lemos (rel. Lugo)

°= regional key station °°= night-time transmission, 2000-0600 UTC approx, also RNE3 prgrs.

FM:		RNE1	RNE2	RNE3	RNE4	RNE5	kW
Andalucía							
AN08)	Baza	92.6	97.3	87.8			5
AN02)	Cabra	95.1					1
AN02)	Córdoba					99.8	2
AN08)	Granada	104.2	96.4	94.4		98.5	1
AN01)	Guadalcanal		90.6				5
AN07)	Jerez	103.5	94.5	96.7		106.3	10
AN02)	Lagar de la Cruz	92.2	97.5	98.6			10
AN06)	Málaga		99.2	104.0		92.5	1
AN03)	Marbella					87.6	1
AN06)	Mijas	106.6	98.1	99.8		88.0	10
AN08)	Parapanda	103.0	91.1	93.9			5
AN05)	Pechina	100.9	92.4	94.9		106.7	5
AN10)	Punta Umbria	95.2	92.6	99.0		88.8	5
AN06)	Ronda	106.1					1
AN04)	Sierra Almadén	105.4	90.0	96.0			10
AN08)	Sierra Lújar	96.7	90.4	94.2			5
AN07)	Tajo	105.0	94.0	103.1			5
AN01)	Valencina	91.2	93.7	98.8		90.0	5
Aragon							
AR02)	Alcañiz	89.5					1
AR03)	Arguis	103.9	88.1	101.5		92.8	5
AR03)	Barbastro	89.6					1
AR01)	Caspe	90.2	99.0			103.7	1
AR01)	Cuarte Torrero	104.4				100.0	5
AR03)	Fraga	95.0					1
AR01)	Inogés	89.4					5
AR03)	Jaca					98.7	1
AR02)	Javalambre		90.0	93.9			1
AR01)	La Muela	94.5	90.9	96.3			10
AR02)	Teruel	104.7	89.2	94.5		95.6	1
Asturias							
AS01)	Avilés	100.0					1

FM:		RNE1	RNE2	RNE3	RNE4	RNE5	kW
AS01)	Boal	93.2	97.8	88.2		90.5	1
AS01)	Cangas de Narcea	97.2	99.0	106.2		89.8	1
AS01)	Cangas de Onis	88.8	90.1	95.7		101.7	1
AS01)	Gamoniteiro	102.5	92.2	94.4		104.4	10
AS02)	Gijón	99.2	98.5	102.0		89.9	5
AS01)	Ibias	95.8	98.7	102.9		105.1	1
AS01)	Llanes	106.1				97.3	1
AS01)	Los Oscos	89.7	96.6	105.7		100.0	1
AS01)	Luarca	96.8	93.8	100.3			1
AS01)	Mieres					101.8	1
AS01)	Oviedo	89.4	96.0	90.3			1
AS01)	San Martín	88.3	96.7	100.2		93.3	1
Baleares							
BA01)	Alfabia	90.1	87.9	92.3		104.5	10
BA01)	Ibiza	101.6	104.0	105.7		94.9	1
BA01)	Menorca	94.6	97.1	105.8		100.4	1
BA01)	Pollensa		95.4	97.4			1
Cantabria							
CT03)	Embalse Ebro	89.0	94.0	98.2		101.9	1
CT01)	Liérganes	96.9	93.0	102.9		105.0	10
CT02)	Torrelavega	99.5	97.9	103.4		89.4	1
Catalunya							
CA02)	Alpicat	94.6	89.2	97.8	87.9		10
CA02)	Baquéira	92.2			93.3		1
CA02)	Bosost	94.4					1
CA01)	Collserola	88.3	93.0	98.7	100.8		20
CA01)	Collsuspina	92.2	97.9	103.1	104.7		1
CA01)	Igualada	89.4	90.9	105.1	106.9		1
CA03)	Monte Caro	104.3	96.6	99.6	90.7		5
CA01)	Montserrat	94.3	99.0		103.8		2
CA03)	Musara	106.5	91.5	94.5	88.8		5
CA01)	Sant Pere Ribes		95.2	97.5	106.3		1
CA04)	Rocacorba	93.3	91.1	95.9	106.2		5
CA02)	Soriguera	99.9	103.6	106.4	90.6		1
CA03)	Ulldecona	95.0					5
CA02)	Viella	90.0			102.6		1
Castilla-León							
CL06)	Aranda Duero	90.0	92.7	101.6			1
CL03)	Arenas Pedro	102.4	90.3				1
CL03)	Avila	87.6	92.0	97.8		102.4	1
CL09)	Béjar	99.9	101.6	104.7			1
CL07)	Benavente	87.8	91.3	97.9		100.2	1
CL05)	Burgo de Osma			88.7			1
CL06)	Burgos	93.6	90.3	91.2		106.6	1
CL04)	Castropodame	103.3	93.0	99.9		105.9	5
CL04)	Cerredo		89.0	91.4			1
CL02)	Cervera	88.6	94.8			100.4	1
CL09)	El Cabaco	102.9	92.4	95.4			5
CL02)	Guardo	89.8	105.6			104.0	1
CL04)	León	97.1	91.1	89.3		102.2	1
CL02)	Palencia	91.8	101.0	97.6		88.0	1
CL06)	Pancorbo	89.7	92.0	101.7		104.5	1
CL07)	Pbla Samabria	93.6	103.5	100.3		91.9	1
CL09)	Salamanca	94.5	88.1	91.4		102.2	1
CL10)	Segovia	97.0				91.5	1
CL05)	Soria	89.7	91.5	94.3		104.7	2
CL01)	Valladolid	97.3	93.1	92.2		95.1	5
CL06)	Villadiego		102.3	103.3			1
CL04)	Villafranca		89.7	97.5			1
CL07)	Zamora	101.8	96.7	98.5		88.8	5
Castilla La Mancha							
CM03)	Almansa	91.2	98.6			94.4	1
CM03)	Chincilla	91.8	93.6	99.0		106.3	5
CM05)	Ciudad Real	95.7	92.8	94.1		88.8	1
CM04)	Cuenca	105.6	93.0	92.0		96.1	1
CM06)	Guadalajara	103.7	93.5	96.9		102.1	1
CM05)	La Mancha	101.0	89.8	94.5			10
CM01)	Puertollano	93.1	99.1			101.8	5
CM05)	Socuéllamos	88.4					1
CM07)	Talevera	97.8	105.5	94.7		89.4	5
CM01)	Toledo	102.0	103.9	106.4		99.9	1
Euskadi							
EU03)	Archanda	100,7	90.6	99.2		96.3	5
EU02)	Azcoitia	88.7	104.9	106.9			1
EU02)	Beasain	100.2	98.4	94.9			1
EU02)	Eibar	92.9	98.7	95.9			1
EU02)	Jaizquibel	104.7	90.0	92.1			10
EU02)	Monte Igueldo	87.6	99.5				1
EU03)	Oiz	106.4	105.3	102.1			5
EU01)	San León					93.3	1
EU02)	San Sebastián			98.9		93.3	1
EU03)	Sollube	105.9	93.9	95.4			5
EU02)	Tolosa	101.9	98.8	96.0			1
EU01)	Vitoria-Gasteiz	92.5	96.9	99.5		89.4	1
Extremadura							
EX02)	Badajoz	94.9	90.1	92.2		106.0	1
EX01)	Cáceres	95.1	101.7	93.7		88.2	1
EX02)	Mérida					101.3	1
EX01)	Montánchez	105.3	97.7	99.3			5
EX01)	Plasencia	88.6		93.3		104.4	1
Galicia							
GA02)	Domayo	90.1	92.1	97.4			5
GA04)	Monforte					88.8	1
GA03)	Monte Meda	102.8	91.2	94.3			5
GA01)	Monte Xalo	100.4	91.6	94.5		95.8	10
GA03)	Ourense	100.6	97.2	99.4		95.1	5
GA04)	Páramo	101.7	88.2	99.6		92.8	5
GA02)	Pontevedra					104.3	1
GA07)	Santiago	103.1	98.1	99.0		93.7	5
GA03)	Verin	90.7	98.4	106.4			1
GA06)	Vigo					96.0	5
GA04)	Xistral	89.5					1
Madrid							
MA01)	Navacerrada	104.9	98.8	95.8			30
MA01)	Torrespaña	88.2	96.5	93.2		90.3	10
Murcia							
MU01)	Carrascoy	101.7	98.2	96.0		92.1	5
MU02)	Cartagena	102.9	94.5	97.5		103.5	1
MU01)	Jumilla	89.1	93.1	100.1			1
MU01)	Yecla	88.8	93.4	103.7			1
Navarra							
NA01)	Estella	89.0	101.2			90.9	1
NA01)	Gorramendi	88.3	99.0	100.6		103.9	1
NA01)	Ibañeta	89.6	93.8	103.4		101.9	1
NA01)	Isaba	90.3	95.1	103.0		91.8	1
NA01)	Leire	88.6	90.5	99.6		101.0	1
NA01)	Lesaka	90.6	94.8	97.0		102.2	1
NA01)	Monreal	106.1	97.5	93.0		95.7	5
NA01)	San Miguel	96.7	100.0			102.7	1
NA01)	Tudela	100.9	102.2	91.3		88.3	1
La Rioja							
RI01)	Logroño	95.4	98.2	101.4		97.2	1
RI01)	Moncalvillo	102.0	88.5	94.6		103.3	40
RI01)	Monte Yerga	87.6	106.8	96.5		105.4	1
Comunitat Valenciana							
VA02)	Aitana	104.8	88.6	99.7			10
VA02)	Alcoi	95.8	92.3	91.1			1
VA03)	Benicasim	89.3	90.3	92.8		95.5	5
VA02)	Elda	93.9					1
VA01)	Monduber	97.4	99.3	100.1			5
VA01)	Monte Picayo	89.8	106.6	95.1		88.2	10
VA01)	Ontinyent	100.7		102.4			1
VA02)	Santa Pola	92.5	100.1	94.3		104.2	5
VA04)	Santa Pola					105.8	5
VA01)	Utiel	98.1	96.6			87.9	1
VA02)	Villena	90.7	97.1	101.1			1

RNE1: (MW and FM): 24h. **N:** On the h. Regional prgrs from key station of each region.
RNE2 R.Clásica: (FM): Classical music & cultural prgrs: 24h.
RNE3: (FM): Young people's music prgr: 24h.
RNE4: (FM): Regional network in Catalunya: 24h. in Catalán.
RNE5TN: (MW and FM): 'Todo Noticias'-All news: 24h. Relays RNE1 0100-0700.

Addresses for RNE regional key stns:
AN Andalucia: Edif.RTVE, Parque del Alamillo, 41092 Sevilla – **AR Aragón**: José Luís Albareda 1-3, 50004 Zaragoza – **AS Asturias**: Melquiades Alvarez 9, 33004 Oviedo – **BA Balears**: Aragó 26, 07006 Palma de Mallorca – **CA Catalunya**: Passeig de Grácia 1, 08007 Barcelona – **CL Castilla y León**: García Morato 27-29, 47007 Valladolid – **CM Castilla La Mancha**: Paseo de San Cristóbal s/n, 45002 Toledo – **CT Cantabria**: Polígono de Raos s/n, 39609 Camargo (Santander) – **EU Euskadi**: Plaza de Simón Bolívar 13, 01003 Vitoria-Gasteiz – **EX Extremadura**: Av. Ruta de la Plata 10, 10001 Cáceres – **GA Galicia**: Xardins de Méndez Nuñez s/n, Edif. "A.Terraza", 15006 A Coruña – **MA Madrid**: Casa de la Radio, Prado del Rey, 28223 Pozuelo de Alarcón – **MU Murcia**: Seda s/n, 30008

Murcia – **NA Navarra**: Emilio Arrieta 8, P8, 31002 Pamplona-Iruñea – **RI La Rioja**: Vara de Rey 42, 26002 Logroño – **VA Comunitat Valenciana**: Av.Colóm 13, 46004 València.

EXTERNAL SERVICES: Radio Exterior de España see International Broadcasting section.

OTHER STATIONS
(COM) COM RÀDIO CATALUNYA ONA MITJANA
✉ Travessera de les Corts 131-159, Recinte Martenitat, Pavello Cambo, 08028 Barcelona **Web:** www.comradio.com
(COPE) CADENA DE ONDAS POPULARES ESPANOLAS
✉ Alfonso XI N° 4, 28014 Madrid ☎ +34 91-3090000 🖷 +34 91-5317517 **Web:** www.cope.es.
FM st's ID as Cadena 100.
(CR) CORPORACIO CATALANA DE RADIO I TELEVISIO
✉ Av. Diagonal 477, planta 7a, 08036 Barcelona ☎ +34 93-4444805 🖷 +34 93-4444825 **Web:** www.catradio.es.
Prgrs: Catalunya Radio; Catalunya Cultura; Catalunya Informació; Catalunya Música.
(CSR) CANAL SUR RADIO
✉ Carr.San Juan de Aznalfarache km 1.300, 41920 Sevilla. ☎ +34 95-5607600. 🖷 +34 95-5607845. **Web:** www.cica.es.
Prgrs: Formula 1: (International music and Spanish pop and rock music); Canal Sur Radio: (Andalucian and Spanish music, news and sports).
(D) CADENA DIAL
✉ Gran Vía 32, 28013 Madrid. ☎ +34 91-3470880. 🖷 +34 91-5211753. Belongs SER.
(EFM) EUROPA FM
Bueso Pineda 7, 28043 Madrid. ☎+34 91 4134361. 🖷+34 91 4137175. **Web:** www.europafm.com
(EI) EUSKADI IRRATIA TELEBISTA
✉ Euskadi Gaztea (FM in Euskera and Sp.) Fueros 2, 20005 Donosti-San Sebastián ☎ +34 943-423630 🖷 +34 943-468078.
✉ Euskadi Irratia (MW and FM in Euskera) Fueros 2, 20005 Donosti-San Sebastián ☎ +34 943-423630 🖷 +34 943-468236
Web: www.eitb.com ✉ R.Euskadi (MW and FM in Sp.) Gran Vía 85, 48011 Bilbo-Bilbao ☎ +34 94-4288000 🖷 +34 94-4425172.
✉ R.Vitoria-Gasteiz Irratia (MW and FM in Sp.) Pasaje Postas 32, 01001 Vitoria-Gasteiz ☎+34 945-144500. 🖷 +34 945-133828.
(M80) M-80 RADIO
✉ Gran Vía 32, 28013 Madrid ☎ +34 91-3470798 🖷 +34 91-5228693. Belongs to SER.
(OCR) ONDA CERO RADIO
✉ Calle de Ortega y Gasset 22-24. 28006 Madrid ☎ +34 91-5386300. 🖷 +34 91-5386323 **Web:** www.ondacero.es
Prgrs: Onda Cero Radio; Onda Cero Música; Onda Cero Melodía; Onda 10.
(RG) RADIO GALEGA - RADIO TELEVISION GALICIA
✉ Casa de la Radio, San Marcos, 15820 Santiago de Compostela ☎ +34 981-562323 🖷 +34 981-561150 **Web:** www.crtvg.es.
(RP) RADIO POPULAR - HERRI IRRATIA
✉ Plaza Segrado Corazón 5, 48011 Bilbo-Bilbao **Web:** www.radiopopular,com
✉Garibai 19, 2004 Donosti-San Sebastián **Web:** www.herri-irratia.com
(R9) RADIO TELEVISION VALENCIANA
✉ Av. Blasco Ibañez 134, 46022 València ☎ +34 96-3721011 🖷 +34 96-3728513 **Web:** www.rtvv.es/
(SER) SOCIEDAD ESPANOLA DE RADIODIFUSION
✉ Gran Vía 32, 28013 Madrid ☎ +34 91-3470700 🖷 +34 91-3470709 **Web:** www.cadenaser.es
FM st's ID as Los 40 Principales, Cadena 40.

MW & FM (MHz)

	kHz	kW	Net	Rg	Station and location	FM
CA07)	540	50	OCR	CA	Onda Cero Catal., Barcelona	89.8
CA08)	666	50	SER	CA	R.Barcelona, Barcelona	93.9
MU05)	711	25	COPE	MU	COPE, Murcia	89.7
EU07)	756	10	EI	EU	R.Euskadi, Bilbo-Bilbao	91.7
CA09)	783	50	COPE	CA	R.Miramar, Barcelona	
AN15)	792	50	SER	AN	R.Sevilla, Sevilla	97.1
MA05)	810	20	SER	MA	R.Madrid, Madrid	93.9
EU08)	819	10	EI	EU	R.Euskadi, Donosti-San Seb	96.5
CA13)	828	5	SER	CA	R.Terrassa, Terrassa	95.5
AN16)	837	10	COPE	AN	COPE, Sevilla	99.6
CL15)	837	10	COPE	CL	COPE, Burgos	95.5
BA05)	837	5	COPE	BA	COPE, Eivissa	89.1
GA09)	837	5	COPE	GA	COPE, El Ferrol	88.7
AR05)	873	25	SER	AR	R.Zaragoza, Zaragoza	95.3
GA10)	873	10	SER	GA	R.Galicia, Stgo de Comp.	90.6
CA10)	882	50	COM	CA	COM Ràdio, Barcelona	91.0
VA07)	882	10	COPE	VA	COPE, Alacant-Alicante	95.6
AN17)	882	5	COPE	AN	COPE, Málaga	89.4
AS05)	882	5	COPE	AS	COPE, Gijón	103.6
CL16)	882	5	COPE	CL	COPE, Valladolid	88.5
EU10)	900	10	RP	EU	R.Popular, Bilbo-Bilbao	97.8
AN18)	900	5	COPE	AN	COPE, Granada	88.2
EX05)	900	5	COPE	EX	COPE, Cáceres	88.8
GA11)	900	5	COPE	GA	COPE, Vigo	87.8
MA06)	918	20		MA	R.Intercontinental, Madrid	95.1
MA07)	954	50	OCR	MA	Onda Cero R., Madrid	97.2
EU09)	963	10	EI	EU	R.Euskadi, Vitoria-Gasteiz	90.9
EU11)	990	10	SER	EU	R.Bilbao, Bilbo-Bilbao	89.5
AN19)	990	5	SER	AN	R.Cádiz, Cádiz	89.4
MA08)	999	50	COPE	MA	COPE, Madrid	99.5
CA11)	1008	10	SER	CA	R.Girona, Girona	88.1
EX06)	1008	5	SER	EX	R.Extremadura, Badajoz	96.9
VA08)	1008	5	SER	VA	R.Alacant, Alacant-Alicante	91.0
CA12)	1026	10	SER	CA	R.Reus, Reus	101.4
AS06)	1026	5	SER	AS	R.Asturias, Oviedo	97.5
GA12)	1026	5	SER	GA	R.Vigo, Vigo	99.4
AN20)	1026	5	SER	AN	R.Jaén, Jaén	96.9
AN21)	1026	5	SER	AN	R.Jerez, J. de la Frontera	97.8
CL17)	1026	5	SER	CL	R.Salamanca, Salamanca	96.9
EU12)	1044	10	SER	EU	R.San Sebastián, Donosti-S Se	97.2
CL18)	1044	5	SER	CL	R.Valladolid, Valladolid	90.9
AR06)	1053	25	COPE	AR	COPE, Zaragoza	97.9
VA09)	1053	5	COPE	VA	COPE, Vila-Real	91.7
EU07)	1071	50	EI	EU	Euskadi Irratia, Bilbo-Bilbao	88.9
AN22)	1080	10	SER	AN	R.Granada, Granada	95.4
AR07)	1080	10	SER	AR	R.Huesca, Huesca	96.9
BA06)	1080	5	SER	BA	R.Mallorca, P. de Mallorca	94.1
CM11)	1080	5	OCR	CM	Onda Cero R., Toledo	100.8
GA13)	1080	5	SER	GA	R.Coruña, A Coruña	91.0
CM12)	1116	5	SER	CM	R.Albacete, Albacete	89.6
GA14)	1116	5	SER	GA	R.Pontevedra, Pontevedra	89.1
CL19)	1134	10	COPE	CL	COPE, Salamanca	90.0
AN23)	1134	5	COPE	AN	COPE, Jerez de la Frontera	92.4
BA07)	1134	5	COPE	BA	COPE, Ciutadella	89.6
CL20)	1134	5	COPE	CL	COPE, Astorga	87.6
CM13)	1134	5	COPE	CM	COPE, Puertollano	97.5
NA05)	1134	5	COPE	NA	COPE, Pamplona-Iruñea	87.9
AN24)	1143	5	COPE	AN	COPE, Jaén	88.8
AS07)	1143	5	COPE	AS	COPE, Oviedo	92.8
CA14)	1143	5	COPE	CA	COPE, Reus	89.7
GA15)	1143	5	COPE	GA	COPE, Ourense	92.4
EU08)	1161	50	EI	EU	Euskadi Irratia, Donosti-San S.	94.4
VA10)	1179	50	SER	VA	R.València, València	94.2
RI05)	1179	2	SER	RI	R.Rioja, Logroño	91.7
EU09)	1197	10	EI	EU	Euskadi Irratia, Vitoria-Gasteiz	95.0
AN25)	1215	5	COPE	AN	COPE, Córdoba	87.6
CL21)	1215	5	COPE	CL	COPE, León	97.7
CT05)	1215	5	COPE	CT	COPE, Santander	88.4
MU06)	1215	5	COPE	MU	COPE, Lorca	93.5
EU13)	1224	10	RP	EU	R.Popular, Donosti-San Seb	88.5
AN26)	1224	5	COPE	AN	COPE, Huelva	91.9
AN27)	1224	5	COPE	AN	COPE, Almería	97.1
BA08)	1224	5	COPE	BA	COPE, Palma de Mallorca	97.6
CA15)	1224	5	COPE	CA	COPE, Lleida	96.0
CM14)	1224	5	COPE	CM	COPE, Albacete	95.4
GA16)	1224	5	COPE	GA	COPE, Lugo	90.0
AN28)	1260	5	SER	AN	R.Algeciras, Algeciras	95.7
MU07)	1260	5	SER	MU	R.Murcia, Murcia	91.3
CA16)	1269	10	COPE	CA	COPE, Figueres	89.4
CM15)	1269	10	COPE	CM	COPE, Ciudad Real	93.6
CL22)	1269	5	COPE	CL	COPE, Zamora	94.9
EX07)	1269	5	COPE	EX	COPE, Badajoz	89.1
CA17)	1287	10	SER	CA	R.Lleida, Lleida	92.6
CL23)	1287	5	SER	CL	R.Castilla, Burgos	89.1
GA17)	1287	5	SER	GA	R.Lugo, Lugo	91.8
VA11)	1296	50	COPE	VA	COPE, València	99.0
AN29)	1341	10	OCR	AN	Onda Cero R., Almería	93.8
CL24)	1341	5	SER	CL	R.León, León	88.2
CM16)	1341	5	OCR	CM	Onda Cero R., Ciudad Real	92.1
CL25)	1485	10	SER	CL	R.Zamora, Zamora	89.8
CT06)	1485	10	SER	CT	R.Santander, Santander	90.9
AN30)	1485	6	OCR	AN	Onda Cero R., Antequera	96.3

	kHz	kW	Net	Rg	Station and location	FM
CA18)	1485	5	OCR	CA	Onda Cero R., Vilanova	96.3
VA12)	1485	5	SER	VA	R.Alcoi, Alcoi	96.3
VA13)	1521	5	SER	VA	R.Castelló, Castelló	94.8
VA14)	1539	6	SER	VA	R.Elche-R.Elx, Elx	94.8
CA19)	1539	5	SER	CA	R.Manresa, Manresa	91.7
NA06)	1575	10	SER	NA	R.Pamplona, Pamplona	92.2
AN31)	1575	5	SER	AN	R.Córdoba, Córdoba	96.6
GA18)	1584	5	SER	GA	R.Ourense, Ourense	87.6
VA15)	1584	5	SER	VA	R.Gandia, Gandia	96.5
EU09)	1602	25	EI	EU	R.Vitoria, Vitoria-Gasteiz	104.1
AN32)	1602	5	SER	AN	R.Linares, Linares	94.9
CL26)	1602	5	SER	CL	R.Segovia, Segovia	93.6
MU08)	1602	5	SER	MU	R.Cartagena, Cartagena	102.3
VA16)	1602	5	SER	VA	R.Ontinyent, Ontinyent	95.3

FM
(St's less than 5 kW omitted)

	MHz	kW	Net	Rg	Station, location
CA25)	87.6	20	CR	CA	Catalunya Informació, Soriguera
AN35)	87.7	6	OCR	AN	Onda Cero Melodía, Jerez de Frontera
AN36)	87.9	5	SER	AN	R.Morón, Morón de la Frontera
CA25)	87.9	5	CR	CA	Catalunya Cultura, Collsuspina
CA25)	88.0	25	CR	CA	Catalunya Cultura, La Mussara
AN37)	88.3	5	CSR	AN	Canal Fiesta R., Algeciras
CA25)	88.4	5	CR	CA	Catalunya R., Montcaro
CA25)	88.6	20	CR	CA	Catalunya Música, Soriguera
CA25)	88.9	25	CR	CA	Catalunya Cultura, Rocacorba
EU07)	88.9	20	EI	EU	Euskadi Irratia, Bilbo-Bilbao
MA05)	89.0	20	M80	MA	M80 Madrid, Madrid
CA07)	89.1	8	OCR	CA	R.Salut, Barcelona
VA21)	89.2	8	OCR	VA	Onda Cero R., Alacant-Alicante
NA11)	89.3	6	OCR	NA	Onda Cero R., Pamplona
MU14)	89.4	6	COPE	MU	COPE, Cartagena
AN42)	89.5	20	CSR	AN	Canal Fiesta R., Huelva
AN62)	89.5	14		AN	Antena Médica, Sevilla
BA11)	89.5	8	OCR	BA	Onda 10, Palma de Mallorca
EX11)	89.5	6	OCR	EX	Onda Cero R., Cáceres
CA07)	89.8	10	OCR	CA	Onda Rambla, Barcelona
AN38)	90.1	8	OCR	AN	Onda Cero Música, Málaga
CA25)	90.2	10	CR	CA	Catalunya Cultura, Sant Celoni
AN35)	90.3	6	OCR	AN	Onda Cero R., Jerez de la Frontera
AN63)	90.4	5		AN	Canal Sevilla, Sevilla
EX12)	90.4	5	OCR	EX	Onda Cero Melodía, Mérida
CA08)	90.5	8	M80	CA	M80 Barcelona, Barcelona
CL31)	90.5	5	SER	CL	R.Miranda, Miranda de Ebro
AN39)	90.8	5	SER	AN	R.Puerto, El Puerto de S.M.
EU09)	90.9	20	EI	EU	R.Euskadi, Vitoria
MA11)	91.0	30	EFM	MA	Europa FM, Madrid
AS06)	91.1	6	D	AS	Dial Asturias, Oviedo
EU07)	91.2	20	EI	EU	Euskadi Gaztea, Bilbo-Bilbao
EX13)	91.4	10	SER	EX	R.Plasencia, Plasencia
AN40)	91.4	8	EFM	AN	Europa FM, Córdoba
AN54)	91.4	6	SER	AN	Radiolé, Málaga
CA28)	91.4	5		CA	Ona Música, Barcelona
EU21)	91.5	8	OCR	EU	Onda Cero R., Donosti-San Sebastián
EX14)	91.5	5		EX	R.Guadiana, Badajoz
EU07)	91.7	20	EI	EU	R.Euskadi, Bilbo-Bilbao
MA05)	91.7	10	D	MA	Dial Madrid, Madrid
AN41)	91.7	5	CSR	AN	Canal Sur R., Málaga
CA25)	91.9	80	CR	CA	Catalunya Música, Alpicat
CT11)	91.9	6	OCR	CT	Onda Cero R., Santander
AR11)	92.0	40	SER	AR	Sinfo R.Zaragoza, Zaragoza
CA25)	92.0	20	CR	CA	Catalunya Informació, Collserola
VA11)	92.0	20		VA	LP Radio, València
CM16)	92.1	5	EFM	CM	Europa FM, Ciudad Real
MA12)	92.1	5		MA	R.Sensación, Torrejón de Ardoz
CA25)	92.2	10	CR	CA	Catalunya Música, Falsel
EX15)	92.2	5		EX	R.Guadiana, Mérida
MA05)	92.4	14	SER	MA	Radiolé, Madrid
CA25)	92.5	10	CR	CA	Catalunya Cultura, Colserola
GA21)	92.6	8		GA	R.Voz, A Coruña
CM21)	92.7	6	OCR	CM	Onda Cero R., Albacete
AN22)	92.8	8	SER	AN	R.Granada 2, Granada
CL34)	92.9	6	OCR	CL	Onda Burgos, Burgos
GA22)	93.1	5	OCR	GA	Onda Cero R., Pontevedra
GA13)	93.4	8	SER	GA	R.Coruña 2, A Coruña
CA30)	93.4	5		CA	R.Segre, LLeida
AR05)	93.5	8	SER	AR	R.Zaragoza 2, Zaragoza
CA25)	93.8	10	CR	CA	Catalunya R., Falsel
AN47)	93.8	5	EFM	AN	Europa FM, Almería
AN42)	94.0	20	CSR	AN	Canal Sur R., Huelva
GA23)	94.0	6	OCR	GA	Onda Cero R., Vigo
GA07)	94.1	5		GA	R.Galega, Santiago de Compostela
CA25)	94.3	10	CR	CA	Catalunya R., Flix
CL39)	94.4	5	EFM	CL	Europa FM, Valladolid
EU08)	94.4	20	EI	EU	Euskadi Irratia, Donosti-San Sebastián
CA25)	94.5	5	CR	CA	Catalunya Informació, Collsuspina
EU07)	94.7	20	EI	EU	Euskadi Gaztea, Bilbo-Bilbao
AN15)	94.8	40	M80	AN	M80 Sevilla, Sevilla
CA26)	94.9	10		CA	R.Espanya, Barcelona
EU09)	95.0	20	EI	EU	Euskadi Irratia, Vitoria-Gasteiz
GA24)	95.0	5		GA	R.España, A Coruña
AN43)	95.1	5	CSR	AN	Canal Sur R., Granada
MA17)	95.1	5		MA	R.Inter Economia, Madrid
AS08)	95.2	6	OCR	AS	Onda Cero R., Oviedo
CA31)	95.3	5	OCR	CA	Onda Cero R., Reus
CA25)	95.4	20	CR	CA	Catalunya R., Soriguera
AN44)	95.4	8	OCR	AN	Onda Cero R., Cádiz
AN52)	95.6	8	OCR	AN	Onda Cero Música, Córdoba
AN45)	95.9	40	OCR	AN	Onda Cero R., Sevilla
RI12)	96.0	6	OCR	RI	Onda Cero R., Logroño
VA10)	96.1	10	M80	VA	M80 Valencia, València
AN46)	96.2	20	CSR	AN	Canal Sur R., Cadiz
CL32)	96.2	6	OCR	CL	Onda 10, Salamanca
AN60)	96.2	6	D	AN	Dial Almería, Almería
AN38)	96.3	5	EFM	AN	Europa FM, Antequera
CM24)	96.4	6	M80	CM	M80 Albacete, Albacete
EU08)	96.5	20	EI	EU	R.Euskadi, Donosti-San Sebastián
CA25)	96.5	10	CR	CA	Catalunya Cultura, Montserrat
AS09)	96.5	8	SER	AS	R.Gijón, Gijón
VA22)	96.5	5	R9	VA	R.Nou, Alacant-Alicante
CL35)	96.5	5	OCR	CL	Onda Cero Música, León
CA25)	96.7	25	CR	CA	Catalunya Música, Rocacorba
MU11)	96.7	6	OCR	MU	Onda Cero R., Cartegena
MA16)	96.8	5		MA	R.María España, Madrid
VA23)	96.9	5	OCR	VA	Onda Cero Música, València
CA08)	96.9	5	SER	CA	R.Barcelona 2, Barcelona
CA25)	97.0	80	CR	CA	Catalunya Informació, Alpicat
EX16)	97.0	6		EX	R.Estudio, Cáceres
AR05)	97.1	5	D	AR	Dial Zaragoza, Zaragoza
AN66)	97.2	6		AN	R.Pinomar, Alhaurín de la Torre
MA07)	97.2	5		MA	Top Madrid, Madrid
CA25)	97.3	10	CR	CA	Catalunya R., Montserrat
CA25)	97.3	10	CR	CA	Catalunya Música, Flix
VA25)	97.3	5		VA	Onda Libre R., Monforte del Cid
MA18)	97.6	8	OCR	MA	Onda Cero R., Alcalá de Henares
CL32)	97.6	6	OCR	CL	Onda Cero R., Salamanca
RI11)	97.7	6	COPE	RI	COPE, Logroño
VA11)	97.7	5		VA	97 Punto 7, València
MU15)	97.8	5		MU	Onda del Segura, Molina de Segura
AN48)	97.9	25	CSR	AN	Canal Fiesta R., Jaén
MA13)	98.0	10	OCR	MA	Onda Cero R., Madrid
AN49)	98.1	5	SER	AN	R.Huelva, Huelva
CA25)	98.3	10	CR	CA	Catalunya Informació, Montserrat
CM23)	98.3	5		CM	R.María, Toledo
VA10)	98.4	5	D	VA	Dial Mediterraneo, València
CA25)	98.5	10	CR	CA	Catalunya Informació, Montcaro
CT11)	98.5	6	OCR	CT	Onda Cero Música, Santander
CM22)	98.5	5	OCR	CM	Onda Cero R., Talavera de la Reina
AR05)	98.6	40	M80	AR	M80 Zaragoza, Zaragoza
AN42)	98.6	20	CSR	AN	Canal Sur R., Huelva
CL36)	98.6	6		CL	R.Arlanzón, Burgos
MU12)	98.8	6		MU	R.Voz, Cartagena
BA12)	98.8	5		BA	R.Jove, Palma de Mallorca
VA26)	98.9	5	COPE	VA	COPE, Benidorm
NA12)	99.2	6		NA	R.España, Pamplona
MU13)	99.3	8	OCR	MU	Onda 10, Murcia
CA08)	99.4	10	D	CA	Dial Barcelona, Barcelona
CA25)	99.4	10	CR	CA	Catalunya Informació, Macanet
CL33)	99.4	8	OCR	CL	Onda Cero Música, Valladolid
AN51)	99.5	8	EFM	AN	Europa FM, Granada
CA25)	99.7	5	CR	CA	Catalunya R., Collsuspina
AN19)	99.9	8	D	AN	Dial Bahía, Cádiz
BA13)	99.9	8		BA	R.Daleor Ciutat, Palma de Mallorca
CA09)	100.0	8	COPE	CA	Cadena 100, Barcelona
AN45)	100.3	40	OCR	AN	Onda Cero Música, Sevilla
CA25)	100.3	25	CR	CA	Catalunya R., La Mussara
AN53)	100.3	8		AN	R.Priego, Priego de Córdoba

	MHz	kW	Net	Rg	Station, location
MA19)	100.4	10		MA	Onda Joven Getafe, Getafe
AN54)	100.4	6	SER	AN	R.Málaga, Málaga
EU22)	100.4	5	SER	EU	Cadena 40, Vitoria-Gasteiz
VA10)	100.4	5	SER	VA	R.Valencia 2, Valencia
AR13)	100.5	40	EFM	AR	Europa FM, Zaragoza
CA25)	100.5	5	CR	CA	Catalunya Música, Collsuspina
GA12)	100.6	8	SER	GA	R.Vigo 2, Vigo
AN48)	100.6	5	CSR	AN	Canal Sur R., Jaén
CA25)	100.7	80	CR	CA	Catalunya R., Alpicat
AN55)	100.8	5	CSR	AN	Canal Sur R., Córdoba
CM11)	100.8	5	EFM	CM	Onda 10, Toledo
GA25)	100.9	30	RG	GA	R.Galega, Xesteiras
AN54)	101.1	5	M80	AN	M80 Málaga, Málaga
VA23)	101.2	5	OCR	VA	Onda Cero R., València
AN56)	101.2	5	OCR	AN	Onda Cero R., Huelva
VA22)	101.2	5	R9	VA	R.Nou, Benidorm
MA14)	101.3	100		MA	Telemadrid R., Madrid
AN55)	101.3	60	CSR	AN	Canal Fiesta R., Córdoba
BA14)	101.4	5		BA	Duco 2 Fiesta R., Inca
CA25)	101.5	10	CR	CA	Catalunya Música, Collserola
AN15)	101.5	40	SER	AN	Radiolé, Sevilla
AN67)	101.8	6	SER	AN	R.Almería, Almería
CA09)	102.0	10	COPE	CA	COPE, Barcelona
CA25)	102.2	70	CR	CA	Catalunya R., Rocacorba
AN42)	102.2	30	CSR	AN	Formula 1, Huelva
VA24)	102.2	10	R9	VA	R.Nou, València
GA25)	102.3	40	RG	GA	R.Galega, Domaio
BA06)	102.3	5	M80	BA	M80 Mallorca, Palma de Mallorca
AN68)	102.4	40	D	AN	Dial Sevilla, Sevilla
CA25)	102.4	10	CR	CA	Catalunya Música, Montserrat
AN57)	102.5	70	CSR	AN	Canal Fiesta R., Almería
CA25)	102.5	30	CR	CA	Catalunya Música, Montcaro
AN22)	102.5	8	D	AN	Dial Granada, Granada
AN58)	102.5	5		AN	R.Carolina, La Carolina
EU23)	102.6	15	COPE	EU	Bizkaia Irratia, Bilbo-Bilbao
MA13)	102.7	100	OCR	MA	Onda 10, Madrid
GA26)	102.7	8	OCR	GA	R.Marineda, A Coruña
CA25)	102.8	10	CR	CA	Catalunya R., Collserola
CA25)	102.8	10	CR	CA	Catalunya Cultura, Macanet de la Selva
BA15)	102.8	5	SER	BA	R.Ibiza, Ibiza
VA22)	103.0	10	R9	VA	R.Nou, Aitana
EU24)	103.0	8		EU	R.Eguín, Hernani
AN15)	103.2	28	SER	AN	R.Sevilla 2, Sevilla
EU07)	103.2	20	EI	EU	R.Euskadi, Bilbo-Bilbao
CL37)	103.4	6	OCR	CL	Onda Cero Música, Salamanca
EU08)	103.5	20	EI	EU	Euskadi Gaztea, Donosti-S. Sebastián
VA24)	103.5	10	R9	VA	R.Nou, València
CA28)	103.5	5	CA		Ona Música, Barcelona
MA15)	103.5	5	MA		R.Voz, Madrid
AN55)	103.6	60	CSR	AN	Canal Sur R., Córdoba
VA24)	103.7	5	R9	VA	R.Nou, Castello
AN59)	103.9	60	CSR	AN	Canal Fiesta R., Sevilla
CA25)	103.9	5	CR	CA	Catalunya Música, Sant Celoni
GA25)	103.9	40	RG	GA	R.Galega, Bailadora
MU07)	103.9	8	D	MU	Dial Murcia, Murcia
EU09)	104.1	20	EI	EU	R.Vitoria, Vitoria-Gasteiz
AN60)	104.1	6	SER	AN	Radiolé, Almería
AN43)	104.2	8	CSR	AN	Canal Sur R., Granada
CA08)	104.2	8	SER	CA	Sinfo R., Barcelona
EU07)	104.4	20	EI	EU	Euskadi Irratia, Bilbo-Bilbao
AN42)	104.5	30	CSR	AN	Canal Sur R., Huelva
CA25)	104.5	25	CR	CA	Catalunya Informació, La Mussara
AN41)	104.6	60	CSR	AN	Canal Sur R., Málaga
AN50)	104.8	80	CSR	AN	Canal Sur R., Jerez de la Frontera
GA25)	104.8	40	RG	GA	R.Galega, Monte Meda
AN57)	104.8	5	CSR	AN	Canal Sur R., Almería
AN43)	104.9	60	CSR	AN	Canal Sur R., Granada
EU09)	104.9	8	EI	EU	Euskadi Gaztea, Amurrio
CA27)	105.0	5	CR	CA	Catalunya Cultura, Barcelona
AN59)	105.1	5	CSR	AN	Canal Sur R., Sevilla
GA14)	105.1	5	M80	GA	M80 Pontevedra, Pontevedra
CL33)	105.2	8	OCR	CL	Onda Cero R., Valladolid
MU16)	105.3	10		MU	Onda Regional, Murcia
MA05)	105.4	100	SER	MA	R.Madrid 2, Madrid
CA25)	105.4	40	CR	CA	Catalunya Música, La Mussara
CA25)	105.5	20	CR	CA	Catalunya Cultura, Soriguera
CA25)	105.5	10	CR	CA	Catalunya R., Macanet
CL38)	105.5	6	EFM	CL	Europa FM, Burgos
AR12)	105.8	40	OCR	AR	Onda 10, Zaragoza
AN41)	105.8	8	CSR	AN	Canal Fiesta R., Málaga
MA14)	106.0	30		MA	Telemadrid R., Madrid
BA12)	106.1	8		BA	Somradio., Palma de Mallorca
GA27)	106.1	8		GA	R.Voz, Santiago de Compostela
VA27)	106.4	5		VA	Onda 15, Alcoi
AN64)	106.5	5		AN	Onda San Pablo, Sevilla
VA28)	106.5	5	OCR	VA	Onda Cero Alicante, Alicante
CA29)	106.6	5		CA	R.Estel, Barcelona
AN61)	106.9	50		AN	R.Voz, Sevilla
MA20)	107.0	13		MA	Hit R., Madrid
AN65)	107.1	5		AN	Onda Guadalate, Bornos
MA16)	107.2	5		MA	R.María España, Madrid

Addresses and other information:

AN00) ANDALUCIA

AN01) Edif.RTVE, Parque del Alamillo, 41092 Sevilla. – **AN02)** Góngora 3, 14002 Córdoba. – **AN03)** Av.Ricardo Soriano 11, 29600 Marbella. – **AN04)** Av.de Granada 57, P1, 23001 Jaén. – **AN05)** Hermanos Machado 23, 04004 Almería. – **AN06)** Av.de la Aurora 40, 29006 Málaga. – **AN07)** Av.de Andalucía 67, 11007 Cádiz. – **AN08)** Plaza Carretas 5, 18009 Granada. – **AN09)** Plaza de Europa s/n, 11300 La Línea de la Concepción. – **AN10)** Av.de Martín Alonso Pinzón 1, 21003 Huelva. – **AN11)** Cervantes 11, 14940 Cabra. – **AN15)** Rafael González Abreu 6, 41001 Sevilla. **Email:** radiosevilla@cadenaser.com – **AN16)** Rioja 4, 41001 Sevilla. **Email:** c-sevilla@arrakis.es – **AN17)** Alameda de Colón 6, 29001 Málaga. **Email:** arjona@metrored-online.es – **AN18)** Gran Vía de Colón 28, 18001 Granada. **Email:** copemolina@teleline.es – **AN19)** Paseo Marítimo 1, Edif.Reina Victoria, 11010 Cádiz. **Email:** radiocadiz@unionradio.es – **AN20)** Obispo Aguilar 1, 23001 Jaén. **Email:** radiojaen@ swin.net – **AN21)** Guadalete 12, 11403 Jerez de la Frontera. **Web:** www.radiojerez.com – **AN22)** Santa Paula 2 (or: Ap.158), 18001 Granada. **Web:** www.radiogranada.es **Email:** radiogranada@radiogranada.es – **AN23)** San Agustín 11 (or: Ap.364), 11403 Jerez de la Frontera. **Email:** c-jerez@arrakis.es – **AN24)** Av.Madrid 68, 23008 Jaén. **Email:** c-jaen@arrakis.es – **AN25)** Plaza Cardenal Toledo 4, 14001 Córdoba. **Email:** c-cordoba@arrakis.es – **AN26)** José María Amoz 2, 21001 Huelva. **Email:** c-huelva@arrakis.es – **AN27)** Padre Luque 11-1, 04001 Almería. **Email:** c-almeria@arrakis.es – **AN28)** General Castanos 2, 11201 Algeciras. **Email:** radioalgeciras@unionradio.es – **AN29)** Av.Federico García Lorca 105, 04005 Almería. – **AN30)** San Agustín 4, 29200 Antequera. – **AN31)** García Lovera 3, 14002 Córdoba. **Web:** www.radiocordoba.es –**AN32)** Plaza Ramón y Cajal 8, 23700 Linares. **Email:** radiolinares@unionradio.es – **AN35)** Gaitan 10, 11402 Jerez de la Frontera. – **AN36)** Pozo Nuevo 60-2, 41530 Morón de la Frontera. – **AN37)** Dr.Ramón P.Rodriguez 36, 11203 Algeciras. – **AN38)** Peregrino 3, 29002 Málaga. – **AN39)** Misericordia 10, 11500 Puerto de Santa María. – **AN40)** Manuel Ruiz Maya 8, 14004 Córdoba. – **AN41)** Carr.de Cádiz 307, Av.Velázquez, 29004 Málaga. – **AN42)** Plaza de San Pedro 3 y 4, 21001 Huelva. – **AN43)** Recogidas 24, 18002 Granada. – **AN44)** Plaza de Asdrúbal 16, 11008 Cádiz. – **AN45)** Pabellón Once, Isla de Cartuja, 41092 Sevilla. – **AN46)** Plaza de España 15, 11006 Cádiz. – **AN47)** Plaza San Sebastián, 04003 Almería. – **AN48)** Av.del Ejército Español 6, 23007 Jaén. – **AN49)** Mendez Nuñez 15-5-6, 21001 Huelva. – **AN50)** Corredera 53, 11402 Jerez de la Frontera. – **AN51)** Recogidas 37, 18005 Granada. – **AN52)** Barroso 4-2, 14003 Córdoba. – **AN53)** Av.América 8, Cana 22D, 14800 Priego de Córdoba. – **AN54)** Palestina 1, 29007 Málaga. – **AN55)** Av.del Gran Capitán 2-4, 14008 Córdoba. – **AN56)** Arquitecto Pérez Carasa 14-16, 21001 Huelva. – **AN57)** Residencial Oliveros, 04004 Almería. – **AN58)** Casa Carolina, 23200 La Carolina. – **AN59)** Carr.San Juan de Aznalfarache km 1.300, 41920 Sevilla. – **AN60)** Av.Cabo de Gata 2, 04007 Almería. – **AN61)** Placentines 2, 41004 Sevilla. – **AN62)** Av.de la Borbolla 47, 41013 Sevilla. – **AN63)** Hotel Meliá Comfort M, San Juan de Rivera 2, 41009 Sevilla. – **AN64)** Sierpes 57, 41004 Sevilla. – **AN65)** San Jerónimo 7, 11640 Bornos. – **AN66)** Urb.Pinas de A., 29130 Alhaurín de la Torre. – **AN67)** Av.Mediterranéo s/n, De Laura 2, 04001 Almería. – **AN68)** Rafael Gonzáles Abreu 6, 41001 Sevilla.

AR00) ARAGON

AR01) José Luís Albareda 1-3, 50004 Zaragoza. – **AR02)** Nueva 1, 44001 Teruel. – **AR03)** José Gil Caves 1, 22005 Huesca. – **AR05)** Paseo de la Constitución 21, 50001 Zaragoza. **Email:** radiozaragoza@unionradio.es – **AR06)** Paseo de Sagasta 50 (or: Ap.42), 50006 Zaragoza. **Email:** zaragoza@cadenacope.net – **AR07)** Calle Alcalde Carderera 1, 22080 Huesca. **Web:** www.radiohuesca.com **Email:** rahusa@ctv.es – **AR11)** Coso 46, 50004 Zaragoza. – **AR12)** Paseo Echegaray y Caballero 76, 50003 Zaragoza. – **AR13)** 50001 Zaragoza.

AS00) ASTURIAS

AS01) Melquiades Alvarez 9, 33004 Oviedo. – **AS02)** Plaza del Instituto 3, 33201 Gijón. – **AS05)** Carr.de la Costa 87 (or: Ap.235), 33205 Gijón. – **AS06)** Asturias 19, Bajo, 33004 Oviedo. **Web:** www. radioasturias.com –

AS07) Prado Picón 16, 33008 Oviedo. **Web:** www.copeasturias.com **Email:** c-oviedo@arrakis.es – **AS08)** Marques de Sta Cruz 7, 33007 Oviedo. – **AS09)** Jovellanos 1, 33202 Gijón.

BA00) BALEARES

BA01) Aragó 26, 07006 Palma de Mallorca. – **BA05)** Felip II N° 28, 07800 Eivissa. **Email:** c-laspalmas@arrakis.es – **BA06)** Camí Son Moix s/n, 07011 Palma de Mallorca. **Email:** radiomallorca@unionradio.es – **BA07)** Av.Negrete 3, 07760 Ciutadela. **Web:** www.telyse.net/cope-menorca **Email:** cmenorca@telepolis.com – **BA08)** Av.Jaume III N° 18, 07012 Palma de Mallorca. **Email:** c-mallorca@arrakis.es – **BA11)** Forners 7, Edif.Once, 07002 Palma de Mallorca. – **BA12)** Passeig Mallorca 32, 07012 Palma de Mallorca. – **BA13)** Menacor 171, 07007 Palma de Mallorca. – **BA14)** Llorenc Villalonga 25, 07300 Inca. – **BA15)** Av.de la Paz s/n, 07800 Eivissa.

CA00) CATALUNYA

CA01) Passeig de Gràcia 1, 08007 Barcelona. – **CA02)** Carrer Lluis Companys 1, 25003 Lleida. – **CA03)** Rambla Nova 23, 43003 Tarragona. – **CA04)** Gran Vía Jaume I N° 60, 17001 Girona. – **CA07)** Av. Diagonal 441-1, 08036 Barcelona. **Email:** ondacero@ ondacero.es – **CA08)** Casp 6, 08010 Barcelona. **Email:** radiobarcelona@unionradio.es – **CA09)** Diputació 238, 08007 Barcelona. **Web:** www.fm/copebarcelona **Email:** barcelona@cadenacope.net – **CA10)** Travessera de les Corts 131-159, Recinte Martenitat, Pavello Cambo, 08028 Barcelona. **Web:** www.comradio.com – **CA11)** Placa Josep Pla 2, 17001 Girona. **Email:** radiogirona@unionradio.es – **CA12)** Tomàs Bergadà 3, 43204 Reus. **Email:** radioreus@unionradio.es – **CA13)** Gütenberg 3, 08224 Terrassa. FM: R.Club 25. **Web:** www.radioterrassa.com – **CA14)** Llovera 54-56, 43204 Reus. **Email:** reus@cadenacope.net – **CA15)** Acadèmia 17, 25002 Lleida. **Email:** lerida@cadenacope.net – **CA16)** Sant Llatzer 21, 17600 Figueres. **Email:** figueres@cadenacope.net– **CA17)** Vila Antònia 5, 25007 Lleida. **Email:** lleida@cadenaser.com – **CA18)** Libertad 25, 08800 Vilanova i La Geltrú. – **CA19)** Plana de l'Om 2, 08240 Manresa. **Email:** rmanresa@minorisa.es – **CA25)** Av Diagonal 477, planta 7a, 08036 Barcelona. **Email:** correu@catradio.com – **Web:** www.catradio.com – **CA26)** Pau Claris 79, P3, 08010 Barcelona. – **CA27)** Bulidor s/n, Polígnon Industrial 1, 08960 St Just D (Barcelona) – **CA28)** Aragó 390-394, P2, 08013 Barcelona. **Email:** onamusica@onacataluna.com – **CA29)** Av. Diagonal 460, 08006 Barcelona. **Email:** radioestel@radioestel.com – **CA30)** Del Riu 6, 25007 Lleida. – **CA31)** Av.Sant Jordi 25, L3 baixos, 43201 Reus.

CL00) CASTILLA Y LEÓN

CL01) García Morato 27-29, 47007 Valladolid. – **CL02)** Becerro de Bengoa 9, 34002 Palencia. – **CL03)** Santa Clara 2, 05001 Avila. – **CL04)** Ordoño II N° 28, 24001 León. – **CL05)** Campo 5, 42001 Soria. – **CL06)** General Yagüe 34, 09004 Burgos. – **CL07)** Av.de Requejo 21, 49012 Zamora. – **CL08)** Ave María 11, 24400 Ponferrada. – **CL09)** Plaza de Colón 2, 37001 Salamanca. – **CL10)** Paseo Ezequiel Gonzales 24, 40002 Segovia. – **CL15)** Av.del Cid 8, 09005 Burgos. **Email:** informativos.burgos@cadenacope.net – **CL16)** Duque de la Victoria 23, 47001 Valladolid. **Email:** Copevalladolid@copevalladolid.jazztel.es – **CL17)** Arco 16-20 (or: Ap.211), 37002 Salamanca. **Web:** www.radiosalamanca.com – **CL18)** Montero Calvo 7, 47001 Valladolid. **Email:** radiovalladolid@unionradio.es – **CL19)** Sol Oriente 11-15, 37002 Salamanca. – **CL20)** Hermanos La Salle 2, 24700 Astorga. **Web:** www.extremadura.com/ **Email:** cpastorga@jazzfree.com – **CL21)** Lope de Vega 1, 24002 León. **Web:** www.copeleon.com **Email:** c-leon@arrakis.es – **CL22)** Plaza Fernández Duró 3 (or: Ap.42), 49001 Zamora. **Email:** c-zamora@arrakis.es – **CL23)** Venerables 8, 09005 Burgos. **Email:** radiocastilla.redaccion@unionradio.es – **CL24)** Villafranca 6, 24001 León. **Web:** www.radioleon.com **Email:** radioleon@radioleon.com – **CL25)** Calle Santa Ana 6, 49006 Zamora. **Email:** radioz@teleline.es – **CL26)** Plaza Cirilo Rodríguez 2, 40001 Segovia. **Web:** www.radiosegovia.com – **CL31)** Vitoria 24, 09200 Miranda de Ebro. – **CL32)** Bermejeros 14, 37001 Salamanca. – **CL33)** Rastrojo 5, 47014 Valladolid. – **CL34)** Vitoria 29, 09004 Burgos. – **CL35)** Julio del Campo 4-6, 24002 León. – **CL36)** Plaza de los Vadillos 5, 09005 Burgos. – **CL37)** Aliso 2 bajo, 37004 Salamanca. – **CL38)** 09004 Burgos. – **CL39)** Edif.Promecal, c/los Astros s/n, 47009 Valladolid.

CM00) CASTILLA-LA MANCHA

CM01) Paseo de San Cristóbal s/n, 45002 Toledo. – **CM02)** Ramiro Ledesma 8, 13630 Socuéllamos. – **CM03)** Nuestra. Sra. De Araceli 1, Edif.Las Torres, 02002 Albacete. – **CM04)** Radio Nacional de España 2 (or: Ap.18), 16003 Cuenca. – **CM05)** Ronda del Carmen s/n (or: Ap.150), 13002 Ciudad Real. **Email:** emisora.cr.rne@rtve.es – **CM06)** Plaza de Consejo, Centro Civico, 19001 Guadalajara. – **CM07)** Ronda del Canillo 35, 45600 Talavera de la Reina. – **CM11)** Plaza de la Merced 1, 45002 Toledo. – **CM12)** Concepción 25, 02002 Albacete. **Email:** radioalbacete@unionradio.es – **CM13)** Alejandro Prieto 2, 13500 Puertollano. – **CM14)** Tesifonte Gallego 9, 02002 Albacete. **Email:** albacete@cadenacope.net – **CM15)** Pasaje San Isidro 3, 13001 Ciudad Real. **Email:** c.creal@arrakis.es – **CM16)** Av.del Rey Santo 8, Edif.Europa, 13001 Ciudad Real. – **CM21)** Av.de la Estación 5, 02001 Albacete. – **CM22)** Av. del Principe 25, 45600 Talavera de la Reina. – **CM23)** Calle Trinidad 12, 45002 Toledo. **Email:** rtv-diocesana@planalfa.es – **CM24)** 02001 Albacete.

CT00) CANTABRIA

CT01) Polígono de Raos s/n, 39609 Camargo (Santander) – **CT02)** Av.del Besaya 1 (or: Ap.46), 39300 Torrelavega. – **CT05)** Rualasal 5, 39001 Santander. **Email:** c-santander@arrakis.es – **CT06)** Pasaje de la Peña 2, Edif.Simeon 11, 39008 Santander. **Web:** www.radiosantander.com **Email:** informativos@radiosantander.com – **CT11)** Fernandez de Isla 14B, 39008 Santander.

EU00) EUSKADI

EU01) Plaza de Simón Bolívar 13, 01003 Vitoria-Gasteiz. – **EU02)** Paseo de los Fueros 2, 20006 Donosti-San Sebastián. **Email:** emisora.ss.rne@the.es – **EU03)** Licenciado Poza 15, Planta 6, 48011 Bilbo-Bilbao. – **EU07)** Gran Vía 85, 48011 Bilbo-Bilbao. – **EU08)** Larramendi 1, 20006 Donosti-San Sebastián. **Web:** www. eitb.com/euskara/ – **EU09)** Pasaje Postas 32, 01001 Vitoria-Gasteiz. **Web:** www.eitb.com/euskara/ – **EU10)** Alameda Mazarredo 47, 48009 Bilbo-Bilbao. **Web:** www.radiopopular.com – **EU11)** Eplaza 8, 48007 Bilbo-Bilbao. **Email:** radiobilbao@unionradio.es – **EU12)** Av.de la Libertad , 20004 Donosti-San Sebastián. **Email:** radiosansebastian@unionradio.es – **EU13)** Garibai 19, 20004 Donosti-San Sebastián. **Web:** www.herri-irratia.com – **EU21)** Av.de la Libertad 17, 20004 -Donosti-San Sebastián. – **EU22)** General Alava 10-6 Depto 9, 01005 Vitoria-Gasteiz. – **EU23)** Fontecha y Salazar 9-5, 48007 Bilbo-Bilbao. – **EU24)** Eziago Poligonoa 10B, 20120 Hernani.

EX00) EXTREMADURA

EX01) Av.Ruta de la Plata 10, 10001 Cáceres. – **EX02)** Plaza de España 5, 06002 Badajoz. – **EX05)** Sánchez Herrero 2, 10002 Cáceres. **Email:** c-caceres@arrakis.es – **EX06)** Ramón Albarrán 2, 06002 Badajoz. **Email:** radioextremadura@unionradio.es – **EX07)** Menacho 12, 06001 Badajoz. **Web:** www.extremadura.com/noticias/cope/cope.html **Email:** c-badajoz@arrakis.es – **EX11)** Av.de España 9-6, 10004 Cáceres. – **EX12)** Av.de Portugal s/n, Ctro Comercial El Foro, 06800 Mérida. – **EX13)** Santa Isabel 4, 10600 Plasencia. – **EX14)** Felipe Checa 15, 06001 Badajoz. – **EX15)** Plaza Santa María 2, 06800 Mérida. – **EX16)** Luis Alvarez Lancero 8, 10001 Cáceres.

GA00) GALICIA

GA01) Xardins de Méndes Nuñez s/n, Edif. "A.Terraza" (or: Ap.199), 15006 A Coruña. – **GA02)** Lepanto 7, 36001 Pontevedra. – **GA03)** Rua de Progreso 115 (or: Ap.268), 32003 Ourense. – **GA04)** Ourense 59-63 (or: Ap.73), 27004 Lugo. – **GA05)** Plaza de España 4, 27400 Monforte de Lemos. – **GA06)** Av.García Barbón 36, 36201 Vigo. – **GA07)** San Marcos s/n, Edif.TVE, 15780 Santiago de Compostela. – **GA09)** Plaza de España 5-6, 15403 El Ferrol. **Email:** c-ferrol@arrakis.es – **GA10)** San Pedro de Mezonzo 3 (or: Ap 469), 15701 Santiago de Compostela. **Email:** radiogalicia@unionradio.es – **GA11)** Principe 57, 36202 Vigo. **Email:** vigo@cadenacope.net – **GA12)** Policarpo Sanz 36, 36202 Vigo. **Web:** www.radiovigo.com – **GA13)** Plaza de Ourense 3, 15004 A Coruña. **Web:** www.radiocoruna.es – **GA14)** Daniel de la Sota 5, 36001 Pontevedra. **Email:** ser@radiopontevedra.com – **GA15)** Rua de Progreso 89, 32003 Ourense. **Email:** vegaorense@terra.es – **GA16)** Plaza de España 20, 27001 Lugo. **Email:** direccion.lugo@cadenacope.net – **GA17)** Plaza de Santo Domingo 3, 27001 Lugo. **Web:** www.lugonet.com/radiolugo – **GA18)** Rua do Paseo 30 (or: Ap.1017), 32003 Ourense. **Web:** www.radioorense.com **Email:** cadenaser@radioorense.com – **GA21)** Concepción Arenal 11-13, 15006 A Coruña. – **GA22)** Salvador Moreno 30, 36001 Pontevedra. – **GA23)** Av.García Barbón 104, 36201 Vigo. – **GA24)** Fernández de la Torre 50, 15006 A Coruña. – **GA25)** Casa de la Radio, San Marcos, 15820 Santiago de Compostela. – **GA26)** Ronda D'Outeiro, 15009 A Coruña. – **GA27)** Salguiriños de Arriba 44, bajo, 15890 Santiago de Compostela.

MA00) MADRID

MA01) Casa de la Radio, Prado del Rey, 28223 Pozuelo de Alarcón. – **MA05)** Gran Vía 32, 28013 Madrid. – **MA06)** Modesto Lafuente 42, 28003 Madrid. **Web:** www.radiointer.es.vg – **MA07)** Av. Isla Graciosa 13, 28700 San Sebastián de los Reyes. – **MA08)** Alfonso XI N° 4, 28014 Madrid. **Web:** www.cope.es/cadena/emisora.madrid.asp **Email:** postmaster@cope.es – **MA11)** Bueso Pineda 7, 28043 Madrid. – **MA12)** Ferrocarril 15, 28850 Torrejón de Ardoz. – **MA13)** Calle de Ortega y Gasset 22-24, 28006 Madrid. – **MA14)** Pso del Principe 3, Cd.de lalmagem, 28223 Pozuelo de Alarcón. **Web:** www.telemadrid.com – **MA15)** Cápitan Haya 1, Edif.Eurocentro, 28020 Madrid. – **MA16)** Av.de los Arqueros s/n, 28024 Madrid. **Email:** radiomaria@arsenet.com – **MA17)** Paseo de la Castellana 36-38, 28046 Madrid. **Web:** www.intereconomia.com – **MA18)** Sta Clara 7, 28801 Alcalá de Henares. – **MA19)** Casa de la Juventud, Guadalajara 1, 28901 Getafe. – **MA20)** Av.de Valladolid 63-65, 28008 Madrid.

MU00) MURCIA

MU01) Seda s/n, 30008 Murcia. **Email:** emisora.mu.rne@rtve.es – **MU02)** Paseo Alfonso XIII N° 51, 30203 Cartagena. – **MU05)** Arco de Santo Domingo 2-3, Edif.Fontanar, 30001 Murcia. – **MU06)** Av.Juan Carlos

I N° 67, 30800 Lorca. – **MU07)** Calle Radio Murcia 4, 30001 Murcia. **Email:** radiomurcia@unionradio.es – **MU08)** Real 82, 30201 Cartagena. **Email:** radiocartagena@unionradio.es – **MU11)** Edif.Mediterráneo, Puerta Murcia 11, 30201 Cartagena. – **MU12)** Alameda de San Antón 9, 30280 Cartagena. – **MU13)** Madre de Dios 15, 30004 Murcia. – **MU14)** Mayor 31, 30280 Cartagena. – **MU15)** Pasado de Rosales 1, Ap 293, 30500 Molina de Segura. – **MU16)** Av.Libertad 6, bajo, 30009 Murcia.
NA00) NAVARRA
NA01) R1: Emilio Arrieta 8, P8, 31002 Pamplona-Iruñea; R5: Aoiz 17, 31004 Pamplona-Iruñea. – **NA05)** Amaya 2-B, 31002 Pamplona-Iruñea. **Email:** c-pamplona@arrakis.es – **NA06)** Yangüas y Miranda 17 (or: Ap.71), 31002 Pamplona-Iruñea. **Email:** serpamplona@teleline.es – **NA11)** Plaza del Castillo 43, 31001 Pamplona-Iruñea. – **NA12)** Cortes de Navarra 1, 31002 Pamplona-Iruñea.
RI00) LA RIOJA
RI01) Vara de Rey 42, (or: Ap.247), 26002 Logroño. – **RI05)** Av.de Portugal 12 (or: Ap.149), 26001 Logroño. **Web:** www.radiorioja.es – **RI11)** 26001 Logroño. – **RI12)** Miguel Villanueva 2, Ofc.5, 26001 Logroño.
VA00) CUMUNITAT VALENCIANA
VA01) Av. Colóm 13, 46004 València. – **VA02)** Angel Lozano 18, 03001 Alacant-Alicante. – **VA03)** Passeig de la Ribalta 5, 12001 Castelló. – **VA04)** Juan Carlos I 37, 03202 Elx. – **VA07)** Rambla de Méndez Nuñez 45, 03002 Alacant-Alicante.**Email:** emisora@copealicante.jazztel.es – **VA08)** Calderón de la Barca 26, 03004 Alacant-Alicante. **Email:** alicante@cadenaser.com – **VA09)** Av.Francisco Tàrrega 69, 12540 Vila-Real. **Email:** castellon@cadenacope.net – **VA10)** Don Juan de Austria 3, 46002 València. **Email:** valencia@cadenaser.com – **VA11)** Passatge Dr.Sierra 2, 46004 València. **Email:** emisora@copevalencia.jazztel.es – **VA12)** Doctor Sempere 16B y C, Bajos, 03803 Alcoi. **Email:** radioalcoy@radioalcoy.com – **VA13)** Moyano 5, 12002 Castelló. **Email:** informativos.radiocs@csnet.es – **VA14)** Dr.Caro 45, 03201 Elx. **Web:** www.rtvelche.com – **VA15)** Calle Loreto 38, 46700 Gandia. **Web:** www.radiogandia.net – **VA16)** Ereta 2A (or: Ap.84), 46870 Ontinyent. **Web:** www.radioontinyent.com – **VA21)** Av.Maissonnave 19-21, 03003 Alacant-Alicante. – **VA22)** Av.Aguilera 1, 03007 Alacant-Alicante. – **VA23)** Cirilo Amorós 27, 46004 València. – **VA24)** Av.Blasco Ibañez 136, 46022 València. – **VA25)** Plaza del Progreso 5, 03670 Monforte del Cid. – **VA26)** Vía Emilia Ortuño 5, 03500 Benidorm. – **VA27)** Av.Alicante, 03801 Alcoi. – **VA28)** Paseo Explanada de España 26, 03001 Alicante.

AMERICAN FORCES RADIO & TV SERVICE (Mil.)
ZFM 92.1 MHz, Morón de la Frontera. ✉ Base Aerea USAF, 41530 Morón de la Frontera – **FM102 Navy** 102.5 MHz, Rota. ✉ Base Naval, 11520 Rota. **D.Prgr:** All st's 24h.

SRI LANKA

L.T: UTC +6h — **Pop:** 19 million — **Radios:** 20,000,000 — **Pr.L:** Sinhala, Tamil, English — **E.C:** 50Hz, 230V — **ITU:** CLN.

SRI LANKA BROADCASTING CORPORATION (Public Corporation)

✉ P.O. Box 574, Independence Square, Colombo 7 ☎ +94 1 2696329, 2584673, 2697491 ℻ +94 1 2695488
Email: brzcast@ sri.lanka.net
L.P: Chairman Hudson Samarasinghe DG: N. M. Arachchi Dep. DG (Eng.) Mr. P. S. Panawenna Dep. DG (Finance): N P W Perera. Dir. News: Somapala Perera.Ekala Eng.: Mr Abeydheera.
Home Services:

MW	kHz	kW	Sce.	MW	kHz	kW	Sce.
Ambewela	531	20	B/R	Naho	801	20	
Diyagama	558	20	D	I'periyakulam	855	20	D
Maho	603	10	B	Puttalam	873	400	D*
Weeraketiya	648	20	A	Mahiyangana	1485	1	E
Diyagama	702	20	A	Mahiyangana	1602	1	B
Ratnapura	729	10	A				

*) and Special tr's.
Only 855 & 873 reported active, all others standby.

SW: Ekala (G.C: 07N06 079E54): 10kW
Note: all domestic SW broadcasts on 4870, 4902, 4940, 5020, 6130, 6150 and 6185 were discontinued in September 2004.A limited service may be resumed.

FM (MHz)	**A**	**B**	**C**	**D**	**E**	**F**	**R**
Colombo	98.3	91.2	101.3	105.6	95.6	93.3	-
Deniyaya	99.6	102.6	-	104.8	90.8	92.8	107.2
Haputale	102.0	92.2	-	-	-	96.4	105.4
Hunasgiriya	102.0	92.2	94.2	98.8	89.3	97.6	107.3
Karagahatenna	107.6	95.0	104.5	90.6	99.6	87.9	102.4
Radella	97.0	94.4	91.7	87.5	100.2	106.9	89.7
Tatiyantota		92.2					
Palali (Jaffna)							102.0

A = Sinhala National Sce, **B** = Sri Lanka Commercial Sce, **C** = Tamil Commercial Sce, **D** = Tamil Commercial Sce, **E** = English Sce, **F** = Sports Sce, **R** = Regional Sce.
Nat. Sce. in Sinhala (A): 2300-1600. **Comm. Sce. in Sinhala (B):** 24h. **Comm. Sce. in Tamil (C):** 2300-1700. **Nat. Sce. in Tamil (D):** 2300-1715. **English Sce.(E):** 0000-1700. **Sports Sce. In Sinhala (F):** 0000-0300. **FM. Sce**: 24h.
Regional Sces: Rajarata Sevaya: Anuradhapura, Kandurata Savaya: Kandy, Ruhunu Sevaya: Matara. All 2300-0230 & 1000-1530.
ANN: A: "Me Sri Lanka Guwan Viduli Sansthave Welanda Sevaya". B: "Me Sri Lanka Guwan Viduli Sansthava Swadeshiya Sevaya". C: "Illangar Oliparappu Kootuthapanam Tamil Sevai". D: "This is the Sri Lanka Broadcasting Corporation".

EXTERNAL SERVICE: Radio Sri Lanka/SLBC
see International Broadcasting section.

TNL RADIO (Comm.)
✉: 5B Tower Bldg., Station Rd., Colombo 4 ☎ (+94 (1) 584107, 584871. Comm. Office: 9D Tower Bldg., 25 Station Rd, Colombo 4 ☎ +94 (1) 501681 2 ℻ 94 (1) 501683 **Web**: www.lanka.net/tnl **L.P**: Chmn. & MD: Shan Wickremesinghe. Comm. Dir: Ms. Ishini Wickremesionghe **FM:** Colombo 90.0/101.7MHz 5kW. **D.Prgr**. in English: 24h.

MBC NETWORKS (PVT) Ltd. (Comm.)
✉ 109 wnd Floor Colllettes Bldg., Rt. Hon. D.S. Senanayake Mw., Colombo 8 ✉ +94 (1) 689234-6. Station: Depanama ℻ +94 (1) 851543-5.
Yes FM in English: 24h on Colombo 89.5/101.0MHz and Kandy 88.2MHz all 1kW (stereo).
Sirasa FM in Sinhala (+ P.O. Box 25, Depanama, Pannipitiya): 24h on 88.9/105.9/106.1/106.5MHz all 1kW (stereo).

COLOMBO COMMUNICATIONS (PVT) Ltd. (Comm.)
✉ 2/9 2nd Floor, Liberty Plaza, 250 R.A. de Mel Mw., Colombo 3 ☎ +94 (1) 577924-7, 330718-9. ℻ +94 (1) 577929.
Gold FM in English: 24h on 100.4MHz 1kW (stereo).
Savana in Sinhala: 24h on 99MHz 1kW (stereo).

PULIGALIN KURAL (VOICE OF THE TIGERS)
✉ Puthukudiyiruppu, Mullaitivu district. ☎ +873 762077512. ℻ +873 762077514.
L.P: Head: Anban Javan
Station: Mullaitivu area 98 MHz 5kW. **F.Pl:** relay tx in Batticaloa.
D.Prgr: in Tamil
Note: Ex-clandestine now licensed by the Sri Lankan Government

TRANS WORLD RADIO (Rlg.)
✉ P.O. Box 364, 91 Wijerama Mawatha, Colombo 7 ☎ +94 (1) 685235/6/7 ℻ + 94 (1) 685245. **L.P**: Dir. of Op's: Mark Blosser. CE: Darryl van Dyken. **Prgr.** ✉ Trans World Radio-India, Box 4407, L-15, Green Park, New Delhi 110 016 ☎ +91 (11) 662058 ℻ +91 (11) 686 8049.
L.P: Regional Dir: Dr. N.Emil Jebasingh.
MW: Puttalam 882kHz 400kW.
D.Prgr: see International Broadcasting section.

RADIO JAPAN RELAY STATION
DEUTSCHE WELLE RELAY STATION
VOICE OF AMERICA RELAY STATION
see International Broadcasting section.

ST HELENA (British)

L.T: UTC — **Pop:** 4,000 — **Pr. L:** English — **E.C:** 50Hz, 240V — **ITU:** SHN

RADIO ST HELENA

✉ St Helena News Media Services, Broadway House, Jamestown, Island of St Helena, So. Atlantic Ocean STHL 1ZZ. ☎ +290 4669 ℻ +290 4542 **Email**: radio.sthelena@helanta.sh **Web:** www.sthelena.se
L.P: SM: Ralph H Peters
MW (G.C: 15S55/05W32): 1548 kHz 1kW.
SW: transmissions discontinued.

D.Prgr.: 24h. Relays BBC World Service 1200-1500 MF, 1300-1900 Sat, 22.00-0700 daily, 0700-1800 Sun — **ANN:** "Radio St. Helena" — **IS:** None (discontinued) — **V.** by QSL-card, Rp. (2 IRCs). Email Re. accepted. Rec not returned
F.Pl: Revival of annual global 'RSH Day' on SW.

SAINT FM
St Helena Media Productions Ltd,Jamestown, St Helena, So. Atlantic Ocean STHL 1ZZ. ☎ +290 2660/2488 **Email**: fm@helanta.sh **Web:** www.saint.fm **L.P:** SM: Mike Olsson
FM (MHz): 93.0, 0.25kW, 90.0/91.0/96.0, 0.03kW. Currently testing 90.0; expected fully operational Nov 2004.
D.Prgr.: 24h. — **ANN:** "Saint FM" — **V.** by QSL-card, Rp. (2 IRCs). Email Re. accepted. Rec not returned

ST KITTS & NEVIS

L.T: UTC -4h — **Pop:** 38,000 — **Pr.L:** English — **E.C:** 60Hz, 220V — **ITU:** SCN

ZIZ RADIO (Gov. Comm.)
P.O. Box 331, Springfield, Basseterre, St. Kitts ☎ +1 869 465 2621. 🖷 +1 869 466 2159. **Email:** info@zizonline.com. **Web:** www.zizonline.com.
L.P: GM: Winston McHahon. CEN: Trevor Liburd. Production mgr: Alvah Bradley. Sales & Marketing Mgr.: Deborah Benjamin.
MW: ZIZ 555kHz (10kW) **FM:** 95.9/96.1/96.7/96.9 MHz.
D.Prgr: Radio ZIZ 24h on 555kHz & 95.9/96.1/96.9MHz. **N:** BBC 1100, 2115. Local: 1115, 1615W, 1755, 1855, 1955, 2055, 2155, 2315.
Big Wave 96.7 FM on 96.7MHz.

RADIO PARADISE (Rlg.)
P.O. Box 508, Charlestown, Nevis. ☎ +1 869 469 1994. 🖷 +1 869 469 1723. (**Addr in USA:** P.O. Box A, Santa Ana, CA 92711 ☎ +1 (714) 832 2950 🖷 +1 (714) 730 0661) **L.P:** Dr. Paul F.Crouch. CE: Ben Miller. Head of PR: Rod Henke. Local mgr: Arthur Gilbert.
MW: St. Kitts 820kHz (50kW).
D.Prgr: 24h. Local prgrs: MF 1100-1900, Sat 1100-2100, Sun 1100-2200. Other times: relays audio feed from TBN satellite TV.
ANN: "This is Radio Paradise, 820 on your AM dial, broadcasting from St. Kitts-Nevis".

VOICE OF NEVIS (Comm.)
P.O. Box 195, Charlestown, Nevis ☎ +1 869 469 1616/1700. 🖷 +1 869 469 5329. **Web:** www.vonradio.com. **Email:** vonradio@caribsurf.com **L.P:** SM: Evered Herbert. Mgr. Ops: Almon Dasent
MW: 895kHz (10kW). **D.Prgr:** Mon-Sat 1000-0200, Sun 1130-0200.
ANN: "This is VON Radio on 895 AM".

PRIVATE FM STATIONS
Choice FM: **FM** 103.5MHz
Family Radio Network: **FM** 89.9/98.3 (relay Antigua).
GEM Radio: **FM**: 92.9/93.2MHz (relay Trinidad).
Goodwill Radio, P.O. Box 95, Basseterre, St. Kitts ☎ +1 869 465 7795. 🖷 +1 869 465 9556. **Email:** goodwillradio@caribsurf.com. **Web:** www.goodwillradio.com. **L.P:** SM: Denis Nilsson. CE: Nigel Brown. - **FM**: 103.3 (Nevis) & 104.5 (St. Kitts) MHz. **Format:** Rlg.
Radio One: ☎ +1 869 466 0941. - **FM:** 94.1MHz.
Sugar City Roc. ☎ +1 869 466 1113. **Web:** www.sugarcityrock.com **FM:** 90.3MHz
WINN FM, Newtown Bay Rd, Basseterre, St. Kitts. ☎ +1 869 466 9586. 🖷 +1 869 466 7904. **Email:** info@winnfm.com. **Web:** www.winnfm.com. **L.P:** GM: Clive Bacchus. Dir: Charles Wilkin. - **FM**: 98.9MHz

ST LUCIA

L.T: UTC -4h — **Pop:** 166,000 — **Pr.L:** English, Creole — **E.C:** 50Hz, 220V — **ITU:** LCA

RADIO ST. LUCIA COMPANY LTD. (Gov. Comm.)
Morne Fortune, P.O. Box 660, Castries ☎ +1 758 452 2337/9 🖷 +1 758 453 1578 **Email:** rsl@candw.lc **Web:** www.rslonline.com
L.P: GM & CE: Eliseus Louis. Prgr. Coordinator: Gerggor Deterville. Director of News: Shelton Daniel.
MW: 660kHz (3kW) (inactive). **FM:** 97.3 (North - 3kW), 97.7 (South - 0.2kW), 107.3 (Castries - 0.2kW).
D.Prgr: 24h. **N:** 1030, 1200, 1400, 1500, 1700, 2000, 2100. **N. in Creole:** 1800. **BBC N:** 1100, 1600, 0200. Relay VoA at night on Weekdays and BBC WS at night during weekends. Own programming: 0930-0400. **ANN:** "You are listening to Radio St. Lucia".

RADIO CARIBBEAN INTERNATIONAL (Comm.)
P.O. Box 121, Castries ☎ +1 758 452 2636 🖷 +1 758 452 2637 **Email:** rci@candw.lc
L.P: GM: Pat Gibson. SM: Peter Ephram.
FM: 96.5/99.9/101.1MHz + relay in Dominica. **D.Prgr:** 24h

PRIVATE FM STATIONS
Catholic TV Broadcasting Service, Micoud Str, Castries. ☎ +1 758 452 7050. **FM:** 87.8MHz (rel. TV sound of EWTN, USA).
Hot FM, Morne, Castries. ☎ +1 758 452 6040. 🖷 +1 758 452 1462. **Web:** www.caribbeanhotfm.com. **LP:** Mgr: Patrick Smith. - **FM:** 96.1/105.3MHz.
Praise FM. FM: 94.5MHz. **Format:** Rlg.
Radio 100 Helen FM, P.O. Box 621, Castries. ☎ +1 758 451 7260. 🖷 +1 758 453 1737. - **FM:** 100.1/100.3/103.5MHz.
The Wave, P.O. Box 1146, Castries. ☎ +1 758 451 6400. 🖷 +1 758 452 2633. - **FM:** 93.7/94.5MHz

ST PIERRE ET MIQUELON (French)

L.T: UTC -3h (3 Apr-30 Oct: UTC -2h) — **Pop:** 7,000 — **Pr.L:** French — **E.C:** 50Hz, 220V — **ITU:** SPM

RADIO TÉLÉVISION FRANÇAISE D'OUTRE MER (RFO)
B.P. 4227, F-97500 St. Pierre et Miquelon. ☎ +508 413824. — **L.P:** Dir: Joseph Edern. Dir. Tec: Daniel Beugin. Head of N: Jacques Barret.
MW: St. Pierre 1375kHz 20kW – **FM:** St. Pierre 97.9MHz 10W, 99.9MHz 0.5kW – Miquelon 98.9MHz 50W.
D.Prgr: 0930-0230. **Rel. France-Inter:** 0230-0930. **N (local):** 1000, 1530, 2200. (**Rel. France-Inter:**) 1100, 1200, 1300, 1400, 1800, 1900 **ANN:** "Ici RFO, Station de Saint-Pierre et Miquelon" **IS:** La Marseillaise **V.** by QSL-card. Rec. acc.
R. Atlantique: 102.1MHz (rel. R. France Internationale).

ST VINCENT & THE GRENADINES

L.T: UTC -4h — **Pop:** 122,000 — **Pr.L:** English — **E.C:** 50Hz, 230V — **ITU:** VCT

NATIONAL BROADCASTING CORPORATION RADIO ST. VINCENT AND THE GRENADINES - NBCSVG (Gov. Comm.)
Richmond Hill, PO. Box 705, Kingstown. ☎ +1 784 457 1111 🖷 +1 784 456 2749. **Web:** www.nbcsvg.com.
Email: nbcsvgadmin@nbcsvg.com
L.P: Chmn: Kenneth Browne. GM: Corlita Ollivierre. Dep. GM: Raphael King. PM: Tamare Job. Technical Director: Lynford Byron. N Editor: Lesley De Bique.

MW: 705kHz (10kW) (inactive – but planned to recommence ops. early 2005 from new site on 700 or 710 kHz).
FM: 89.7/90.7/107.5MHz (1kW).
D.Prgr: 0926-0300 (Fri/Sat 0400). **N:** 1130, 1330, 1430, 1630, 1830, 2030, 2230.
Wrp: 1032, 1142, 1250. **ANN:** "NBC Radio".

PRIVATE STATIONS
CCR - Cross Country Radio, PO. Box 1000, Kingstown. ☎ +1 784 458 5555. 🖷 +1 784 456 4117. **L.P.:** SM Carlos Meloni. - **FM:** 88.5/104.3MHz. **Format:** Rlg.
Hitz-FM, St. Vincent Broadcasting Corp., Dorsetshire Hill, P O Box 617, Kingstown. ☎ +1 784 456 1078. 🖷 +1 784 456 1015. - **FM:** 91.5/103.7MHz.
Hot 97FM, 1 Melville Street, Kingstown. ☎ +1 784 452 9797. 🖷 +1 784 456 2462. - **FM:** 93.1/97.1MHz. **Format:** Urban Caribbean.
Nice FM, Bds Company Ltd., Dorsetshire Hill, Kingstown. ☎ +1 784 458 1013. 🖷 +1 784 456 5556. **L.P:** Mgr: Douglas De Freitas. - **FM:** 90.3/96.7/101.3MHz.
Praise FM, Sion Hill, Kingstown. ☎ +1 784 456 1636, 🖷 +1 784 456 1696. **L.P.:** PD Donny Daniel. - **FM:** 95.7/105.7MHz. **Format:** Rlg.
WE-FM, Lower Questelles, PO Box 1346, Kingstown. ☎ +1 784 457 9992/9994/9997. 🖷 +1 784 457 7123/2911. **Email:** wefm@caribsurf.com. **L.P.:** MD Julius Williams. - **FM:** 99.9MHz.

SUDAN

L.T: UTC +3h — **Pop:** 36 million — **Pr.L:** Arabic, Nubian, Ta Bedawie, several southern Sudanic languages — **E.C:** 50Hz, 240V — **ITU:** SDN

MINISTRY OF INFORMATION & COMMUNICATION
Web: www.sudannow.net **L.P:** Al-Zahawi Ibrahim Malek, Minister.

SUDAN RADIO AND TV CORPORATION (SRTC)
✉ P.O. Box 572, Omdurman ☎ +259 11 555684 🖹 +259 11 75907 **Regional** ✉ Box 532, Khartoum; Box 126, Juba.
L.P: DG: Salah al-Din al-Fadhil Usud. DG Eng. & Tech. Sces: Abbas Sidig.
MW:

Location	kHz	kW	Prgr.	Location	kHz	kW	Prgr.
Nyala	540	50	R	Wadi Halfa	873	5	R
El Obeid	639	10	R	Malakal	909	5	R
Kassala	666	10	R	Al-Foula	945	5	R
Khartoum	747	10	K	Khartoum	963	100	G
Port Sudan	747	5	R	Al-Damazin	1026	5	R
Omdurman	765	50	G	Wou	1071	5	R
Al-Fashir	801	5	R	Reiba	1296	600	G
Juba	810	100	*	Al-Gadarif	1485	5	R
Dongola	819	10	R	Kadogli	1602	5	R
Wad Madani	873	10	R				

* F.PI

SW:

Location	kHz	kW	Prgr.	Times
Omdurman	7200	100	G	0400-1900

Rep. also on 15170kHz.
FM: Khartoum 95.0/100.0MHz Prgr G, Khartoum 98.0MHz Prgr T, Khartoum 105.0MHz Prgr H.

Prgrs: G=General Prgr (incl. **National Unity R**. 1000-1200) in Arabic: 24h (exc. 765kHz 0000-1000 and 963kHz 1000-0600). **N:** 0430, 0700, 1300, 1600, 1900, 2000. **H=Holy Quran R:** 24h. **K=Khartoum State R:** 0300-0700, 1300-1900. **T=Two Niles Radio:** 24 h. Incl. relays of Deutsche Welle in English. **R=Regional stations.** Not all the regional stations are confirmed active and some are known to be off the air or on low power because of maintenance problems. Powers listed are the nominal ones. When on air, regional stations carry a mixture of local prgr's and relays of the General Service.
ANN: "Huna Omdurman, Idha'atu-l-gumhuriya as-Sudan"
IS: Sudanese music. **F.PI:** new shortwave transmitters.

RADIO PEACE (Rlg.)
(a joint project by organisations presented on the following web pages: www.persecutionproject.org , www.edmedia.org and blessingsforobedience.homestead.com/home.html)
SW: Southern Sudan 4750kHz 1kW, Nuba Mountains 5895kHz 5kW.
D.Prgr in southern Sudanese languages and some segments in English: 0230-0430, 1600-1800.
ANN: "This is Radio Peace".

Other stations:
BBC African Sce: Khartoum 91MHz, Wad Madani 91.5MHz in Arabic/English.
R. Monte-Carlo Moyen-Orient: Khartoum 93MHz.

SURINAME

L.T: UTC -3h — **Pop:** 460,000 — **Pr.L:** Dutch, English, Sranang Tongo, Sarnami Hindi, Javanese. — **E.C:** 60Hz, 110/115/127/220V — **ITU:** SUR

TELECOMMUNICATE BEDRIJF SURINAME (TELESUR) (Gov.)
✉ P.O. Box 1839, Paramaribo ☎ +597 474242/473944 🖹 +597 404800 **Web:** www.telesur.sr **Email:** telesur@sr.net

STICHTING RADIO-OMROEP SURINAME (SRS)
✉ P.O. Box 271, Paramaribo ☎ +597 498115 🖹 +597 498116 **Email:** radiosrs@sr.net
MW: 725kHz 5kW (inactive)
FM: Paramaribo 96.3MHz 1kW (stereo), 93.1MHz 0.1kW - Coronie, Wageningen, Nickerie, Mesago all 94.7MHz 0.1kW, Albina 105.7MHz 0.1kW.
D.Prgr: 0730-0400 (Sat 0430, Sun 0300). **Sarnami Hindi:** 0730-0830 on all freqs, W 1900-2030 & 2315-2400 on 600kHz + 93.1MHz. **Javanese:** 0830-0930. Other times in Dutch. **N. in Dutch:** W 1000, 1100, 1200, 1730, 2000, 2345, 0100; Sun 1600, 1900, 0000 **ANN:** "Dit is de Stichting Radio Omroep Suriname, de SRS in Paramaribo" **V.** by QSL-folder or letter. Rec. acc.

PRIVATE COMMERCIAL STATIONS

MW	kHz	kW	Name and Location
1)	600	10	R. Paramaribo, Paramaribo
2)	820	1	R. Apintie, Paramaribo
3)	914	3	R. Nickerie, Nieuw Nickerie

SW: 2) 4990 kHz 1 kW.
NB. only FM stn's reported active
FM: Paramaribo: 1) R. Paramaribo (Rapar) 89.7 4 kW, ACME Broadc. Netw. 92.1 1.5kW – **2)** R. Apintie 97.1 1 kW – **4)** Radika NV 98.3 1kW – **5)** R. Sangeet Mala 96.3 1 kW – **6)** R. 10 88.1 2 kW – **7)** Ampies Broadc. Corp. 101.7 2.5 kW, R. Koyeba 104.9 2 kW, R. Garuda 105.7 3.5 kW – **8)** R. Shalom 94.5 1 kW, R. Portjajab 95.3 1.5 kW – **9)** R. Zon 107.5MHz 1kW +5 other stn's below 1kW.
Other areas: 25 stn's below 1kW

Addresses and other information
1) P.O. Box 975, Paramaribo ☎ +597 499995 24h. **Sarnami Hindi:** W 0845-0930, 1500-1600; Mon-Thurs 2100-0100; Fri 2200-0200; Sat 2200-0300; Sun 0845-1330, 1930-2100. **Javanese:** W 0800-0845, 1900-2100. Other times in Dutch. **N. in Dutch:** 1830 **ANN:** "Dit is R.P. Internationaal, the hot one", or "dit is R. Paramaribo, RAPAR N.V. op de 500 meter AM Band en 89.7 FM" – **2)** P.O. Box 595, Paramaribo ☎ +597 400450 🖹 +597 400684 **Web:** www.apintie.sr **Email:** apintie@sr.net 0730-0400 (Sun 0300). **Sarnami Hindi:** W 1900-2030, Sun 1800-1900. **Javanese:** W 2030-2100, Sun 1900-1930. Other times in Dutch. **N. in Dutch:** 1730, 2200 **ANN:** "U luistert naar R. Apintie op AM-FM stereo en special voor het binnenland op de kortegolf in de zestig meter band". **IS:** The beat of the Apintie drum **V.** by letter. – **3)** R. Nickerie, Waterloostraat 3, Nieuw Nickerie ☎ +597 231462. - 0900-0030. **Javanese:** 2100-2230. Other times in Sarnami Hindi **IS:** "Surinam hamara pyara desh" sung by G. Kallasing. – **4)** R. Radika, Indira Ghandiweg 165, Paramaribo ☎ +597 482800, 482910. - 0800-0300 in Sarnami Hindi plus some Dutch. – **5)** R. Sangeet Mala, Indira Gandhiweg 40, Paramaribo ☎ +597 482390, 482392. - 0800-0400 (Sat 0500) in Sarnami Hindi. **N. in Dutch:** 0830, 1830. **N. in Hindi:** 0915, 2300. – **6)** R. 10, Letitia Vriesdelaan 5, Paramaribo ☎ +597 410881, 410887 🖹 +597 410885 **Email:** radio10@cq-link.sr – **7)** Ampies Broadc. Corp., Maystraat 57, Paramaribo ☎ +597 464609 🖹 +597 464680 **Web:** www.abcsuriname.com **Email:** info@abcsuriname@com – **8)** R. Shalom, Malebatrumstraat 10-12 BV, Paramaribo ☎ +597 422630, 424587 🖹 +597 422737 **Email**: shalom@sr.net – **9)** R. Zon, Burenstraat 60, Paramaribo ☎ +597 475261, 420248 🖹 +597 420233.

SWAZILAND

L.T: UTC +2h — **Pop:** 1.1 million — **Pr.L:** English, Siswati — **E.C:** 50Hz, 230V — **ITU:** SWZ

MINISTRY OF PUBLIC SERVICE AND INFORMATION (MOPSI)
✉ P.O Box 170, Mbabane ☎ +268 404 3521 🖹 +268 404 5379/4161 **Web:** www.gov.sz/home.asp?pid=64 **Email:** hrpd@realnet.co.sz
L.P: Themba Msibi, Minister.

SWAZILAND BROADCASTING AND INFORMATION SERVICE (SBIS)
✉ Corner Gwamile & Msakato Str, P.O. Box 338, Mbabane H100 ☎ +268 404 2761/5 🖹 +268 404 2774 **Web:** www.gov.sz/home.asp?pid=65 **Email:** sbisnews@africaonline.co.sz
LP: Dir: Stan David Motsa. Asst. Principal Prgr's Officer: Phesheya Dube. A/Prgr. Coordinator: Austin Dlamini. A/Tr. Engineer: Christopher Motsa.

MW: Sidvokodvo 954kHz 50/30kW (inactive).
FM: 88.5/91.6/93.6/105.2MHz 10kW + 4 low power relays.
R. Swaziland English Channel: D.Prgr 0255-1800 on FM 91.6/93.6MHz. **N:** 0400, 0500, 1600.
R. Swaziland Siswati Channel: D.Prgr 0255-2100 on MW 954kHz and FM88.5/105.2MHz.
ANN: "This is the English sce. of R. Swaziland". Siswati: "Lona ngu Mawakato waka Ngwane".
IS: at s/on, Cilongo (Swazi instrument). English Sce: cock crow, fanfare, spoken ID, instrumental theme. **F.PI**: 100kW tr. on 954kHz.

RADIO CIDADE
✉ P. O. Box 1586, Alberton 1450, South Africa ☎ +27 11 4344333 🖷 +27 11 4344777
MW: Sandlane 1377kHz 50kW.
D.Prgr in Portuguese/English: 1530-0015.
ANN: P: "Rádio Cidade Internacional", E: "You are tuned to Radio Cidade at 1377 on your AM dial".

TWR Swaziland: MW 1170kHz 50kW 1600-2030 & SW.
For further details see International Radio section.

SWEDEN

L.T: UTC +1h (27 Mar-30 Oct: UTC +2h) — Pop: 9 million — **Pr.L:** Swedish — **E.C:** 50Hz, 230V — **ITU:** S

TERACOM
Responsible for distribution of prgrs. produced by Sveriges Radio (Swedish Broadcasting Corporation) and by most of the commercial radio sts and community radio associations.
HQ: Medborgarplatsen 3, Stockholm (✉ Box 17666, SE-118 92 Stockholm) ☎ +46 8 55542000 🖷 +46 8 55542001 **Web:** www.teracom.se
L.P: Pres. & Temporarily MD: Göran Arvedahl. Chmn., Board of Dir: Håkan Tidlund.

PTS: PTS (Post-och telestyrelsen) is the authority that supervises activities in radio, telecom and datacom.
✉ Box 5398, SE-10249 Stockholm ☎ +46 8 6785500
Web: www.pts.se **Email:** pts@pts.se

SVERIGES RADIO AB
(Swedish Broadcasting Corporation) (Public)
HQ: Radiohuset, Oxenstiernsgatan 20, Stockholm (✉SE-10510 Stockholm) ☎+ 46 8 7845000 🖷+ 46 8 7841500 **Web:** www.sr.se
Email: info@sr.se
L.P: Peter Orn, MD.

MW: Sölvesborg 1179kHz 600/300 Kw: carries Home Sce. 1st Prgr. . 0455-0700 (Sat -0900/Sun -0800). Foreign Sce. 1545-2330.

FM (MHz)	1	2	3	4	5	kW
24) Arvidsjaur	89.4	94.2	97.1	100.6		60
20) Bollnäs	88.4	91.7	96	103.8		60
19) Borlänge	89.4	93	97.7	101.3		60
25) Borås	88.5	94.6	97.9	102.9		10
14) Bäckefors	92.7	96.8	99.1	102.2		60
6) Emmaboda	93	96.7	99.7	101.8		60
7)				95.6		60
19) Falun	91.2	94.2	96.5	100.2		30
5) Finnveden	90.1	94.2	99.9	103.4		30
24) Gällivare	88.3	94.9	98.5	100.9		60
20) Gävle	88.1	97.4	99.8	102		60
13) Göteborg	89.3	96.3	99.4	101.9		60
12) Halmstad	87.7	91.2	95.4	97.3		60
10)				102.6		3
11) Helsingborg	89.8	95.7	98.4	103.2		6
20) Hudiksvall	87.6	90.2	93.8	100.7		60
21) Härnosand	88.8	91.1	95.1	100.5		15
10) Hörby	88.8	92.4	97	101.4		60
11)				89.5		5
24) Kalix	91.3	93.6	97.9	102.2		60
9) Karlshamn	90.3	93.4	98.3	100.4		15
9) Karlskrona	89.1	95	97.7	100.7		10
16) Karlstad	90.5	94.2	96.5	103.5		15
24) Kiruna	89.1	92.7	96.4	102.7		60
4) Kisa	90.5	92.5	96.9	103.6		30
23) Lycksele	92.9	95.4	98.7	103.3		60
11) Malmö	87.9	93.3	98	102		6
Malmö Classic	100.6				6	
19) Mora	92.2	96.7	99	101		60
4) Motala	91.1	94	98.2	101.2		20
3) Norrköping	90	93.5	98.7	102.3		60
4)				94.8		60
5) Nässjö	89.6	92.1	99	102.1		60
24) Pajala	90.8	93	95.9	100.2		60
23) Skellefteå	93.8	96.3	100	103.9		60
16) Skövde	88.9	95.1	97.5	100.3		60
21) Sollefteå	89.3	93.5	98.1	101.2		60

FM (MHz)	1	2	3	4	5	kW
1) Stockholm	92.4	96.2	99.3	103.3		60
1) Stockholm		89.6*		93.8		0.9
23) Storuman	87.6	91.2	99	102.5		60
21) Sundsvall	92.7	96.9	99.2	102.8		60
16) Sunne	90.9	94.5	98.5	101.8		60
22) Sveg	90.6	94.9	97.9	102.2		60
22) Tåsjö	89.9	94.7	97.5	100.8		60
23)				88.2		60
14) Uddevalla	89.9	93.1	97.2	103.3		8
2) Uppsala	90.3	93.3	96.6	102.5		20
12) Varberg	90.4	93.6	98.8	103.8		10
8) Visby	87.6	94.1	97.2	100.2		60
6) Vislanda	88	90.6	94.7	101		20
23) Vännäs	88.5	92.1	95.8	103.6		60
7) Västervik	88.3	91.8	96	102.7		60
18) Västerås	90.7	95.8	98	100.5		60
21) Ånge	93.2	95.6	99.6	103.1		60
22)				94.5		60
24) Älvsbyn	90.6	94.5	99.4	102.9		60
17) Örebro	87.9	91.5	99.6	102.8		60
21) Örnsköldsvik	90.8	94.4	97.8	100.1	60	60
22) Östersund	87.9	91.5	94	100.4		60
2) Östhammar	89.1	92.8	95.5	101.6		60
24) Överkalix	88.9	91.7	99	103.2		15

+ 360 low power tr's. A comprehensive list of all sts is available on www.teracom.se
*) Relays Foreign Service & different international radio sts 24h.

First Prgr. (P1) (news & spoken word): MF 0430-0015,SS0455-0030. News:MF 0430, 0500, 0530, 0600, 0630, 0700, 0800, 0900, 1000, 1130, 1300, 1400, 1500, 1545, 1645, 1800, 1900, 2000, 2100, 2200. **Wrp** (incl. forecast for Swedish waters): 0455, 0555, 0655, 1200, 1455, 2050 **Time Signal:** D 1159-1200. **Rel. of 1st programme on SW:** See Foreign Sce. schedule.
Second Prgr (P2): Classical music and jazz prgrs, Sami, Finnish and prgrs for immigrants. **Serious music:** MF 2300-0655, 1000-1500, 1715-0500, Sat 2300-0500, 0600, 0800-1200, 1400-1500, 1700-2300, Sun 2300-0600. 0800-1430, 1700-2300. **Sami:** MF 0655-0730. **Prgrs in Finnish:** MF 0500-0505, 0710-0800, 0600-0800 (Sun), 1500-1600, 1500-1600 (Sun). **N. in Finnish:** 0500, 0730, 1500, 1555. **Prgrs for Immigrants:** D 1600-1700. **Educational Prgrs:** MF 0800-0900. (UR-Utbildningsradion). **P2 local** over Stockholm 96.2 MHz and Malmö Classic 100.6 MHz: MF 0655-1000, 1500-1700, Sat. 1200-1400, 1600-1700, Sun. 0600-0800, 1500-1700.
Third Prgr (P3): light music, entertainment, current affairs, news for under 40s: 24h. **N:** on the hour & 0430,0530,0630,0730,1545.
Fourth Prgr (P4): Regional network 0500-1700. 1700-0500 relay of P4 network from Stockholm(frequencies as above, addresses given below).
Fifth Prgr (P5): Local prgr, R.Stockholm MF0500-2100. Other times relay of P3.
ANN: Nat. Prgr. "Sveriges Radio" and the service e.g. "Sveriges Radio P1".

Digital Radio (DAB): Malmö 2kW, Göteborg 2kW, Stockholm/Nacka 2.5kW, Enköping 2.6kW, Uppsala 1.5kW, Södertälje 2.3kW, Älvsbyn 3.8kW Single frequency network on 225.648 MHz, block 12B with SRX - pop and rock music, SR Klassiskt - classical music, SR P3 Star - for teens, SR P7 Sisuradio - Finnish lang ch., SR C - cultural ch., SR Sverige – multi-cultural ch with world music, SR Favorit – prgrs from Swedish radio's archives plus current affairs and news

Addresses of Regional Centres
1) SR Stockholm, Pipersgatan 45, 107 80 Stockholm. – **2)** SR Uppland, Box 1552, 751 45 Uppsala. – **3)** SR Sörmland, Box 641, 631 08 Eskilstuna. – **4)** SR Östergötland, Box 500, 601 07 Norrköping. – **5)** SR Jönköping, 551 92 Jönköping. – **6)** SR Kronoberg, Box 62, 351 03 Växjö. – **7)** SR Kalmar, 391 83 Kalmar. – **8)** SR Gotland, Box 1324, 621 24 Visby. – **9)** SR Blekinge, Box 305, 371 25 Karlskrona. – **10)** SR Kristianstad, Box 505, 291 25 Kristianstad. – **11)** SR Malmöhus, 211 01 Malmö. – **12)** SR Halland, Box 133, 301 04 Halmstad. – **13)** SR Göteborg, Delsjövägen, 405 13 Göteborg. – **14)** SR Väst, Box 654, 451 24 Uddevalla. – **15)** SR Västmanland, Box 850, 721 22 Västerås. – **16)** SR Skaraborg, 541 24 Skövde. – **17)** SR Värmland, Box 98, 651 03 Karlstad. – **18)** SR Örebro, Västra Bangatan 15, 701 80 Örebro. – **19)** SR Dalarna, Box 123, 791 23 Falun. – **20)** SR Gävleborg, Box 545, 801 07 Gävle. – **21)** SR Västernorrland, 851 79 Sundsvall. – **22)** SR Jämtland, Lingonvägen 7 B, 831 62 Östersund. – **23)** SR Västerbotten,

Mariehemsvägen 4, 906 15 Umeå. – **24)** SR Norrbotten, Nygatan 3, 971 71 Luleå. **25)** SR Sjuhärad, Box 27, 503 05 Borås.
Sameradion, Föreningsgatan 15, 981 23 Kiruna. Responsible for prgrs in Sami.
Information about e-mail addresses, telephone numbers and programmes can be found at **Web:** www.sr.se

EXTERNAL SERVICE: Radio Sweden International & relay on SW of P1 & P4:
see International Broadcasting section

SVERIGES UTBILDNINGSRADIO AB

(Swedish Educational Broadcasting Company) (Non-Comm. Public Broadcasting Service).
✉ UR, Tulegatan 7, 113 95 Stockholm ☎ + 46 8 7840000 (Managing director, administration, pre-school, school programmes, adult education) **Web:** www.ur.se **Email:** kundtjanst@ur.se.
LP: MD:Christina Björk **FM:** See Swedish Radio

COMMERCIAL STATIONS

Location	MHz	kW	Net	Location	MHz	kW	Net
Skellefteå	92.4	3	C	Stockholm	105.5	1	C
Kungälv	92.5	3	E	Luleå	105.6	2	C
Storebro	99.4	2	D	Nyköping	105.7	4	D
Södertälje	100.8	3	C	Göteborg	105.9	1	C
Östersund	104.0	3	C	Jönköping	106.0	5	C
Färjestaden	104.0	3	C	Västerås	106.1	3	C
Uddevalla	104.2	1	A	Lund	106.1	4	A
Oskarström	104.2	1	C	Visby	106.1	6	A
Umeå	104.2	5	C	Stockholm	106.3	1	B
Stockholm	104.3	1	A	Borlänge	106.3	1	C
Växjö	104.3	2	C	Örebro	106.3	2	C
Linköping	104.3	3	D	Karlshamn	106.4	1	C
Karlstad	104.4	5	C	Skövde	106.4	3	A
Visby	104.4	5	C	Varberg	106.5	1	C
Eskilstuna	104.5	3	C	Norrköping	106.5	3	D
Finnveden	104.6	1	D	Uppsala	106.5	4	E
Örebro	104.7	2	A	Gävle	106.7	1	A
Örnsköldsvik	104.8	10	C	Malmö	106.7	1	C
Gävle	104.9	1	C	Mora	106.8	1	A
Trollhättan	105.0	3	C	Gnosjö	106.8	1	C
Stockholm	105.1	1	B	Västerås	106.9	1	A
Hudiksvall	105.1	3	C	Linköping	106.9	3	D
Jönköping	105.1	4	D	Lund	107.0	1	E
Malmö	105.2	1	B	Umeå	107.0	3	A
Gällivare	105.2	10	A	Borås	107.1	1	C
Göteborg	105.3	1	B	Göteborg	107.3	1	E
Uppsala	105.3	4	C	Kristianstad	107.3	1	C
Skellefteå	105.4	2	A	Eskilstuna	107.3	3	A
Färjestaden	105.4	3	D	Helsingborg	107.6	1	C
Karlstad	105.4	5	E	Skövde	107.6	3	C
Borlänge	105.5	1	A	Nyköping	107.7	4	C
Borås	105.5	1	D				

+ 30 sts below 1kW. Note: These sts belong to networks. There are a number of commercial local sts on FM. A comprehensive list can be found on **Web**: www.teracom.se

Addresses and other information:
A) MIX MEGAPOL, 115 78 Stockholm **Web:** www.mixmegapol.com **Email:** info@mixmegapol.com
B) NRJ, P.O. Box 27340, 115 41 Stockholm ☎ +46 8 6589800 **Web**: www.nrj.se **Email**: info@nrj.se
C) RADIO RIX, Box 17820, 118 94 Stockholm ☎ +46 8 56272000 🖷+46 8 56272082 **Web**: www.rixfm.com **Email**: rix@rixfm.com
D) RADIO MATCH, Web: www.radiomatch.se (see Website for ✉)
E) RADIO CITY Kajskjul 107, Frihamnen, 417 07 Göteborg ☎+46 31-7261000. **Email**: info.gbg@radiocity.se and Carlsgatan 44, 211 20 Malmö ☎+46 40 352700.**Web**: radiocity.se

COMMUNITY STATIONS

Närradio is open for any non-commercial organization, whose main activity is other than broadcasting. The organization may obtain a permit for community radio broadcasting by PTS. The transmitters are made available at a nominal fee and built and operated by Teracom. The transmitters have powers of 10-400W and the target is the local community. There are more than 200 transmitters in operation. Frequency range: MHz 88-108 MHz. A few Närradio stations are also broadcasting commercial prgrs. A comprehensive list of Närradio-stations is at **Web**: www.teracom.se

SWITZERLAND

L.T: UTC +1h (27 Mar-30 Oct: UTC +2h) — **Pop:** 7.5 million — **Pr.L:** German, Swiss-German dialects, French, Italian, Rumantsch — **E.C:** 50Hz, 230V — **ITU:** SUI

SWISS BROADCASTING CORPORATION (SBC)

(A non-profit company responsible for radio & tv prgr services).
✉ Schweizerische Radio-und Fernsehgesellschaft (SRG); Société suisse de radiodiffusion et télévision (SSR); Società Svizzera di Radiotelevisione (SSR); Giacomettistrasse 3, Postfach, CH-3000 Bern 15 ☎+41 31 3509111 🖷+41 31 3509256 **Web:** www.srg-ssr.ch
L.P: Pres. SRG: Jean Bernard Münch. DG: Armen Walpen. Secr. Gen: Beat Durrer

GERMAN LANGUAGE NETWORK

Radio der deutschen und der raeto romanischen Schweiz: Schweizer Radio (DRS).
✉ Radiodirektion SR DRS, Novarastrasse 2, Basel ☎ +41 61 365 3484 🖷 +41 61 365 3483 **Web:** www.schweizerradiodrs.ch **Email:** radio@drs.ch
Radio studios SR DRS: Schwarztorstrasse 21 Postfach, 3000 Bern 14 - Novarastrasse 2, Postach 4024 Basel - Brunnenhofstrasse 22, 8057 Zürich - Bahnhofstrasse 88, Postfach, 5001 Aarau - Inseliquai 8, 6005 Luzern - Rorschacherstrasse 150, Postfach 719, 9006 St. Gallen
L.P: MD: Walter Rüegg.
MW: (Musigwälle): Beromünster 531kHz 160kW (0500-2307). FM Cable(MHz): Spiez 87.0, Zurich 106.4, Kriens 107.7. 24 h.
Main transmitters: (for a comprehensive list see **web**: www.broadcast.ch)

FM (MHz)	DRS 1	DRS 2	DRS 3	RR	kW
Bantiger	88.2	93.2	99.3		5
Biel-Magglingen	-	99.7			1
Castel S.Pietro	98.8				10
Celerina	91.9	100.3	106.3	89.1	0.75
Chasseral	103.0		105.3		20
Feschel	88.2	90.3	101.5		1.5
Froburg	96.0	98.7	91.3		1.2
Gebidem	89.4	93.9	103.9		2.4
Glarus	91.4				1
Haute-Nendaz	92.0				2.5
Leucel	88.1				6
Castel S. Pietro	98.8				10
Niederhorn	93.6	97.2	105.8		4.5
Paudo	96.9				2.2
Pfaender(A)	96.3	97.7	107.5		4
Ravoire	102.1				1.9
Rigi	90.9	96.6	103.8		30
Salève(F)	87.8				1
San Salvatore	96.3				17
Säntis	101.5	95.4	105.6		55
Solothurn	89.7	98.0			1.5
St. Chrischona	90.6	99.0	103.6		33
Tarasp	101.3	103.9	95.1	98.7	0.25
Uetilberg	94.6	106.7	105.8		1.6
Valzeina	93.8	102.5	104.3	90.3	0.75

+ many st's less than 1kW. – RR=Rumantsch (see below).

1st Prgr(DRS 1): 24h. **N.** Every full hour. **Local Broadc. in German:** MF 0512-0514, 0532-0537, 0612-0614, 0632-0637, 0712-0714, 1103-1113, 1630-1700.
2nd Prgr(DRS 2): 24h. **N:** 0500, 0800, , 0900, 1000, 1400, 1500, 1600, 1700, 1800, 2100, 2300. N. In English MF 1630-1640. **N. in Rumantsch:** 1820Sun, 1850W
3rd Prgr(DRS3): 24h **N**: Every full hour. **ANN:** "Schweizer Radio DRS 1", "DRS 2" or "DRS 3". **V.** by QSL-card.
Virus: Only via satellite Hot Bird 12399 GHz, DAB and cable 24h.

RUMANTSCH LANGUAGE RADIO (RTR)

✉ R. Rumantsch, Theaterweg 1, CH-7002 Chur ☎ +41 81 2557575 🖷 +41 81 2557500 **Web:** www.rtr.ch
L.P: Dir:Bernard Cathomas.
FM: see RR network (above) **D.Prgr:** MF 0500-2000, 2000-2300 relay DRS3, 2300-0500 relay DRS1, Sat/Sun 0700-2000, 2000-2300 relay DRS3, 2300-0500 relay DRS1. **N**: Every full hour.

FRENCH LANGUAGE NETWORK

Radio Suisse Romande (RSR)
✉ Ave. du Temple 40, CH-1010 Lausanne ☎ +41 21 3181111

🖷 +41 21 6536767 **Web:** www.rsr.ch. **Email:** webmaster@rsr.ch
L.P: MD RSR:Gérard Tschopp. PD's: RSR1: Nicole Tornare. RSR2: Pascal Crittin. RSR3: Jean-Luc Lehmann. Option Musique: Vladimir Louvrier.
RSR, Studio de Genève: ✉ Bd Carl-Vogt 66, 1205 Genève ☎ +41 22 7087111
MW: (Option Musique: 24 h): Sottens 765kHz 600kW, Savièse 1485kHz 1kW.
FM: Salève: 90.8 MHz,1 kW.

FM (MHz)	**RSR 1 La Première**	**RRS 2 Espace 2**	**RSR 3 Coleur 3**	**kW**
Bantiger	95.1			5
Castel S.Pietro	87.8			10
Chasseral	102.3	100.3	104.2	20
Chamossaire	105.1/98.1	95.1	88.6	1
Chaux de Fo.	92.3	96.3	103.4	1.4
Dôle, La	91.2	100.1	105.6	19
Feschel	91.4	96.1	107.4	1.5
Gebidem	90.8			2.4
Gibloux	91.0	92.5	88.6	1.0
Hte Nendaz	94.4	96.5	106.0	2.5
Leucel(F)	102.6	96.2	98.5	6
Montmagny	92.3	92.0	89.1	4
Mt Pélerin	91.6	101.5	90.6	2
Castel S. Pietro	97.8			10
Les Ordons	94.2	99.6	104.8	9
Paudo	105.3			2.8
Premier	94.7	100.8	104.7	10
Ravoire	93.2	106.9	100.5	1.9
Salève(F)	94.9	101.7	104.4	1
San Salvatore	104.0			17
Säntis	99.9			55
Vallée de Joux	99.5	89.6	101.4	1

+ numerous st's less than 1kW.
For details see **web**: www.rsr.ch/frequences)

1st Prgr: 24h. **N:** On the h. (exc. 2100, 2200). Also 0530, 0630, 1130, 2130 - **2nd Prgr:** 24h. **N:** 0500, 0600, 0700, 0800, 1200(M-F), 1600, 1800, 2130, 2300. **N. in Rumantsch:** 2150 - **3rd Prgr:** 24h non-stop music and N. **ANN:** "Radio Suisse Romande". Prgr. 1: "RSR-La Première". Prgr. 2: "RSR-Espace 2". Prgr. 3: "Couleur 3" **V.** by QSL-card.

ITALIAN LANGUAGE NETWORK
Radiotelevisione Svizzera di Lingua Italiana (RTSI)
✉ Casella postale 235, CH-6903 Lugano-Besso ☎ +41 (91) 803 5111 🖷 +41 (91) 803 5355 **Web:** www.rtsi.ch **Email:** info@rtsi.ch
L.P: Dir. Remigio Ratti.
MW (RSI 1): Monte Ceneri-Cima 558kHz 300kW.
Main transmitters: (For a comprehensive list see **web**: www.rtsi.ch/prog/frequenze)

FM (MHz)	**RSI I Rete1**	**RSI 2 Rete 2**	**RSI 3 Rete 3**	**kW**
Celerina	104.3			2
Chasseral	107.3			4
Leucel(F)	97.8			6
Castel S. Pietro	88.8	98.8	104.5	10
Paudo	89.4	93.5	107.4	2.8
Rigi	106.2			30
Salève(F)	97.1			2
S. Salvatore	88.1	91.5	106.0	17
Valzeina	95.8			1.5

+ numerous st's less than 1kW.
RSI-1: 24h. **N:** hourly (not 1200, 1800) + 1130, 1730.
RSI-2: 24h. **N:** 0530, 0630, 0730, 0830, 0930, 1030, 1130, 1200, 1330, 1430, 1530, 1630, 1800, 2200, 2300. Classical music and cultural programs.
RSI-3: 24h. **N**: 0530, 0630, 0730, 0830, 0930, 1330, 1530, 1800, 2130, 2300. Classical music and cultural programs.(Email: rete3@rtsi.ch)
ANN: "R. Svizzera di lingua Italiana Rete Uno", "Rete Due" or "Rete Tre".
There are many local, commercial stations with a power less than 5 kW.
SWR, Südwestrundfunk in Baden-Baden, Germany transmits in Switzerland on the following frequencies (MHz): SWR1 87.9 and 94.0; SWR2 91.4 and 92.0, SWR3 89.5 and 90.1, SWR4 98.3.

DAB: Palette deutschschweiz canal: 12C 227.360 MHz.
Programs: DRS1, DRS2, DRS3, DRS Musigwälle, DRS Virus, Radio Rumantsch, Swiss Pop, Swiss Classic, Swiss Jazz, RSR La Premiere, RSI Rete Uno.**Stations**: Niederhorn 995W, Bantiger 380W, Biel 285W, St Chrischona 285W, Sissach 190W, Grellingen 190W, Solothurn 195W, Baden 380W, Uetliberg 380W, Bachtel 237W, Winterthur 475W.
Palette Suisse Romande canal: 12B 225.648 MHz.
Programs: RSR La Première, RSR Espace 2, RSR Coleur 3, RSR Option Musique, Swiss Pop. Swiss Clöassic, Swiss Jazz, Radio Rumantsch, DRS 1, RSI Rete Uno. **Stations**: Genève TV Tower 285W, Chalavornaire 237W, Fontanezier 380W, Signal de Bougy 147W

INTERNATIONAL SERVICES:
ICRC Radio, United Nations Radio (USA)
see International Broadcasting section

WORLD RADIO GENEVA (Comm.)
✉ WRG-FM SA, 1 passage de la Radio, 1205 Geneva ☎+41 (22) 809 5040 🖷 +41 (22) 809 5045
FM (MHz): Salève (F) 88.4 2 kW.
D.Prgr. in English: 24h. **Music & N:** 0530-0900, 1530-1800

SYRIA

L.T: UTC +2h (1 Apr-1 Oct: UTC +3h) — **Pop:** 17 million — **Pr.L:** Arabic — **E.C:** 50Hz, 220V — **ITU:** SYR

MINISTRY OF INFORMATION
✉ Mezzeh Autostrad, Dar al Ba'th Building, Damascus ☎+963 11 6664600/6664601 🖷 +963 11 6620052 **Web:** www.moi-syria.com **Email:** moi@net.sy

ORGANISME DE LA RADIO-TÉLÉVISION ARABE SYRIENNE (ORTAS)
✉ TV & Broadcast Directorate, Ommayad Square, Damascus ☎ +963 11 33339 🖷 +963 11 333493 **Web:** www.rtv.gov.sy **Email:** radio@rtv.gov.sy **L.P:** DG: Maan Haidar. Dir. Engineering: Adnan Salhah. Dir. Public Rel: Ghassan Shefiab. Dir. Financial Dpt: Samer Shaheen.

MW	**kHz**	**kW**	**Prgr.**	**MW**	**kHz**	**kW**	**Prgr.**
Adra	567	300	1	Al-Hassake	918	200	1
Sarakeb	594	100	1/2	Homs	936	100	1
Sabboura	666	600	1	Deir ez-Zor	954	50	2
Sarakeb	747	100	1	Tartus	1071	100	1/2
Tartus	783	300	1/E	Al-Hassake	1125	200	2/E
Deir ez-Zor	v828	200	1	Sarakeb	1314	50	2
Adra	873	50	2				

FM: El-Swedaa 87.8MHz, Damascus 88.7MHz, Slenfe 88.6MHz (2), Aleppo 89.9MHz (2), Low power tr's: 92/94/100.5/105.5MHz.

Main Prgr (1): 0315-0040. Incl. **R. Palestine** prgr: 1530-1700. **N:** 0415, 0515, 0915, 1115, 1215, 1515, 1615, 1815, 1915, 2115, 0015.
Voice of the People (2): 0400-1600. **N:** 0600, 0800, 0900, 1100, 1400.
ANN: 1: "Idha'atu-l-Jumhuriyya al-Arabiyya as-Suriyya min Dimashq". 2: "Huna Idha'at Sowt as-Sha'ab min Dimashq". R. Palestine: "Idha'at Falasteen min Dimashq".

EXTERNAL SERVICE: R. Damascus
see International Radio section.

Other stations:
R. Gecko (UN), Camp Faouar, Golan: 95.9MHz. **Web:** www.radio-gecko.com
R. Orient, Deir al Acher: 88.3MHz.
F.PI: four commercial FM stations.

TAIWAN (Rep. of China)

L.T: UTC +8h — **Pop:** 23 million — **Pr.L:** Mandarin(Chinese), Amoy, Hakka — **E.C:** 60Hz, 110V — **ITU:** CHN (**WRTH:** TWN)

BROADCASTING CORPORATION OF CHINA (BCC)
(Priv. enterprise under Gov. contract)
✉ 375 Sungchiang Rd, Chungshan Ward, Taipei 104 ☎ + 886 2 2501 9688 🖷 + 886 2 2501 8834 **Web:** www.bcc.com.tw **Email:** pr@bcc.com.tw
L.P: Pres: Lee Ching-ping, Dir.Eng.Dep.: Lee Muh-tsun.

MW: Call: BE

	Call	Location	kHz	kW	Network
10)	G51	Ilan	630	10	I
1)	D34	Taipei	657	20	N
6)	D92	Tainan	711	10	C
4)	D58	Taichung	720	10	N
1)	D57	Taipei	747	10	H
8)	D28	Taitung	819	10	N
4)	D43	Taichung	837	10	C
9)	D27	Hualien	855	10	N
7)	D25	Kaohsiung	864	10	N
2)	G77	Hsinchu	882	10	N
3)	G78	Miaoli	891	10	I/H
6)	D24	Tainan	891	10	N
7)	D79	Kaohsiung	909	10	C
1)	D55	Taipei	954	20	C
8)	D88	Taitung	1008	10	C
2)	D53	Hsinchu	1017	10	C
5)	D26	Chia-i	1035	10	C
1)	D85	Taipei	1062	10	I
4)	D23	Taichung	1062	10	I
11)	D72	Yuli	1116	3.5	N
12)	D68	Puli	1152	1	C
10)	D86	Ilan	1161	10	C
3)	D89	Miaoli	1161	10	C
9)	D32	Hualien	1188	10	C
7)	D52	Kaohsiung	1224	10	L
4)	D77	Taichung	1242	10	L
6)	D47	Tainan	1296	10	N
5)	D63	Chia-i	1350	10	N
11)	D74	Yuli	1386	3.5	C
2)	D87	Hsinchu	1386	3.5	I/H
10)	D65	Ilan	1404	10	N
3)	D54	Miaoli	1413	10	N
8)	D80	Taitung	1413	3.5	I
12)	D67	Puli	1413	1	N
7)	D48	Kaohsiung	1449	10	I
9)	D81	Huanlien	1467	10	I/H
5)	D82	Chia-i	1467	10	I
6)	D78	Tainan	1539	10	I

N=News Netw, C=Country Netw, I=Information Netw, H=Hakka Ch, L=local.

FM:

	Location	P	F	M	L	kW
1)	Taipei	103.3	105.9	96.3		35/10
3)	Huoyenshan	102.9	101.5	96.1		10/0.1
4)	Taichung	102.1	106.9	96.3	103.9	35/10
5)	Chentoshan	103.1	104.3	96.1		10/0.1
7)	Kaohsiung	103.3	105.9	96.3		35/10
8)	Taitung	102.1	106.9	96.3		5/2.5
9)	Hualien	102.1	106.9	96.3		5/2.5
10)	Ilan	102.1	102.9	96.1	103.9	5/2.5
11)	*Yuli	103.3	105.7			2.5/1
12)	*Puli	107.3				0.1

P=Pop Netw, F=Formosa Netw, M=Music Netw, L=local.
*) relay station.

D.Prgr:
News Network: 24h in Mandarin. – **Country Network:** 24h in Amoy. – **Information Network:** 24h in Mandarin and Amoy. – **Hakka Channel:** 2300-1700 in Hakka. – **Pop Network:** 24h in Mandarin. – **Formosa Network:** 24h in Amoy. – **Music Network (Wave radio 96):** 24h in Mandarin.

Addresses of local stations:
2) 3, 9th Flr, 55 Tungkuang Rd, Hsinchu 300. – **3)** 78, Lane 1008, Chungshan Rd, Kaomiao Li, Miaoli 360. – **4)** 35th Flr, 758 Chungming So. Rd, Taichung 402. – **5)** 121 Wufeng So. Rd, Chia-i 600. – **6)** 5, 19th Flr, 248, Sec. 2, Yunghua Rd, Anping, Tainan 708. – **7)** 1, 24th Flr, 91 Chungshan 2nd Rd, Kaohsiung 806. – **8)** 23, Lane 52, Kuilin No. Rd, Taitung 950. – **9)** 25 Shuiyuan Str, Hualien 970. – **10)** 8 Kuchie Rd, Chuangwei Village, Ilan 263. – **11)** Yuli (relay st.). – **12)** Puli (relay st.).

ANN: Mandarin: "Chungkuo Kuangpo Kungssu" or "Chungkuo Kuangpo Kungssu, (location) Kuangpo Tientai", Amoy: "Tiyon Gok Kon Po Kon Sih, (location) Kon Po Den Tai"

DAB: BCC on 220.352MHz, CBS on 220.064MHz, Sound of Taipei, Power 989 and Kao Ping on 211.648MHz, Asia FM, M-Radio and Kiss FM on 213.360MHz, UFO Network on 215.072MHz.

EXTERNAL SERVICES: Radio Taiwan International
see International Broadcasting section

VOICE OF KUANGHUA

P.O.Box 12329, Taipei ☎ +886 2 2603 0429 Fax +886 2 2603 0433
Web: www.kh2000.org.tw

MW:

Location	kHz	kW	Location	kHz	kW
Hsinfeng	711	250	Hsinfeng	981	250
Kuanyin	801	250	Chingshui	1431	10
Kuanyin	846	250			

D.Prgr. in Mandarin: 0655-0105.
ANN: "Hansheng Kuangpo Tientai, Kuanghua chih Sheng."

OTHER PUBLIC & COMMERCIAL STATIONS

Call: BE

MW	Call	Station	Location	kHz	kW
2)	H7	Fu Hsing	Taipei 1	558	1
2)	H2	Fu Hsing	Taipei 2	594	10
2a)	H38	Fu Hsing	Taichung 2	594	5
2b)	H44	Fu Hsing	Kaohsiung 1	594	10
6a)		Taiwan	Tahsi	621	1
6c)		Taiwan	Sungling	630	10
1b)	V59	Cheng Sheng	Taichung 2	657	10
1c)		Cheng Sheng	Peikang	675	1
9)	C22	Han Sheng	Taipei	684	10
9)	C25	Han Sheng	Taoyuan	693	10
9g)	C32	Han Sheng	Tainan	693	10
8b)	P24	Ching Cha	Taichung	702	10
11)	E43	Shih Hsin	Taipei	729	0.5
31)	L2	Taiwan Yuyeh	Penghu	738	100
12)		Sheng Li	Makung	756	1
6b)	V94	Taiwan	Taichung	774	10
13)	V88	Hsien Sheng	Taoyuan	774	10
9d)	C33	Han Sheng	Hualien	792	10
14)	V79	Keelung	Keelung	792	1
7)		Chien kuo	Hsinhua	801	1
15)	V54	Kuo Sheng	Changhua	810	10
1)	V35	Cheng Sheng	Taipei	819	5
8d)	P28	Ching Cha	Kaohsiung	819	10
12)	V56	Sheng Li	Tainan 1	837	1
2b)	H56	Fu Hsing	Kaohsiung 2	846	10
9f)	C38	Han Sheng	Penghu	846	10
1a)	V72	Cheng Sheng	Chia-i	855	1
17)	V24	Min Pen	Taipei 2	855	1
18)	V52	Chung Sheng	Taichung	864	10
19a)		Feng Ming	Penghu	882	1
2)	H3	Fu Hsing	Taipei 1	909	10
9a)	C42	Kuo Kuang	Taipei	936*	5
7)	V85	Chien Kuo	Hsinying	954	10
20)		Yen Sheng	Wuho	954	1
6c)	V84	Taiwan	Chunghsing	963	10
19)	V68	Feng Ming	Kaohsiung 2	981	1
1b)	V58	Cheng Sheng	Taichung 1	990	10
8e)	P38	Ching Cha	Ilan	990	1
8f)	P34	Ching Cha	Hualien	990	10
22)	V92	Tien Nan	Taipei	999	1
1f)	V60	Cheng Sheng	Kaohsiung	1008	1
21a)		Tien Sheng	Yuanli	1026	1
23)	V51	Chung Hua	Sanchung 2	1026	1
3)	V98	Cheng Kung	Kaohsiung	1044	1
20)	V64	Yen Sheng	Hualien 1	1044	5
1d)	V82	Cheng Sheng	Ilan	1062	1
24)	V74	Min Li	Pingtung	1062	5
25)	V96	Tien Sheng	Tainan	1071	1
2)	H5	Fu Hsing	Taipei 1	1089	5
2a)	H34	Fu Hsing	Taichung 2	1089	10
9)	C31	Han Sheng	Yunlin	1089	10
16)	G28	Kaohsiung	Kaohsiung	1089	10
8a)	P26	Ching Cha	Hsinchu	1116	5
8d)	P25	Ching Cha	Kaohsiung	1116	5
9)	C22	Han Sheng	Taipei	1116	10
9)	C30	Han Sheng	Ilan	1116	10
1c)	V36	Cheng Sheng	Yunlin	1125	5
8g)	P40	Ching Cha	Taitung	1125	1
26)	G26	Taipei	Taipei	1134	10
31)	L3	Taiwan Yuyeh	Penghu	1143	100
28)	V70	Hua Sheng	Taipei 1	1152	5
19)	V67	Feng Ming	Kaohsiung 1	1161	1
6a)		Taiwan	Kuanhsi	1170	1
15a)		Kuo Sheng	Erhlin	1179	2.5
6)	V46	Taiwan	Taipei 2	1188	1
12)	V57	Sheng Li	Tainan 2	1188	1
6a)	V62	Taiwan	Hsinchu	1206	10
21a)		Tien Sheng	Pengshan	1215	1

MW	Call	Station	Location	kHz	kW
28)	V71	Hua Sheng	Taipei 2	1224	1
23)		Chung Hua	Juifang	1233	1
20)		Yen Sheng	Hualien 2	1242	1
9c)	C29	Han Sheng	Kaohsiung	1251	10
1a)		Cheng Sheng	Putzu	1260	1
8)	P22	Ching Cha	Taipei	1260	10
1e)	V37	Cheng Sheng	Taitung	1269	1
9f)	C44	Han Sheng	Penghu	1269	10
9b)	C27	Han Sheng	Taichung	1287	10
24)		Min Li	Fangliao	1287	1
17)	V23	Min Pen	Taipei 1	1296	1
8c)	P32	Ching Cha	Tainan	1314	5
21)	V76	Tien Sheng	Chunan	1314	10
6)	V45	Taiwan	Taipei 1	1323	1
6c)		Taiwan	Puli	1332	1
9e)	C36	Han Sheng	Tsoying	1332	10
23)	V50	Chung Hua	Sanchung 1	1350	2.5
9d)	C40	Han Sheng	Hualien	1359	5
27)		Chin Hsi	Kaohsiung	1368	1
1f)		Cheng Sheng	Tafa	1395	10
30)	V78	Yi Shih	Keelung	1404	10
7)		Chien Kuo	Kuanyin	1422	1
4)	E32	Chiao Yu	Taipei	1494	10
4a)	E34	Chiao Yu	Changhua	1494	5
8a)		Ching Cha	Hsinchu	1512	10
31a)		Taiwan Yuyeh	Ilan	1593	3

*= inactive

FM: Call: BE

	Call	MHz	kW		Call	MHz	kW
4f)		88.9	1	4c)		97.3	3
4l)		88.9	1	37)		97.3	3
63)		91.7		60)		97.3	3
10)		92.1	3	38)		97.5	3
32)		92.1	3	67)	N74	97.5	0.75
33a)		92.3	3	39)		97.7	3
38a)		92.3	3	54)		97.9	3
69)		92.5	3	61)		97.9	3
33)		92.7	3	4i)		98.1	3
66)		92.9	3	40)	M23	98.1	3
8d)	P42	93.1	25	38b)		98.3	3
26)	G25	93.1	13	41)		98.3	3
55)		93.3	3	47a)		98.3	3
56)		93.5	3	62)		98.7	3
				72)		98.7	3
34)		93.7	3	41a)	M31	98.9	3
57)		93.7	3	4k)		99.1	4
8)	P41	94.3	10	43)		99.1	3
8f)	P44	94.3	5	4m)		99.3	3
8g)	P45	94.3	5	44)		99.3	2.5
16)	G29	94.3	21	63)		99.3	0.5
8b)	P43	94.5	30	45)	M24	99.5	3
35)		96.7	3	65)		99.5	3
58)		96.9	3	46)		99.7	3
59)		96.9	3	47b)		99.7	3
36)		97.1	3	47)	M30	99.9	3
47c)		97.1	3	4e)		100.1	1
68)	N61	97.1	3	5b)		100.1	30
4f)	E39	100.3	1	8)	P29	104.9	35
4d)		100.5	3	8c)	P31	104.9	3.5
5)	M3	100.7	30	8d)	P32	104.9	25
5a)		100.7	30	8e)	P30	104.9	35
48)	M26	100.7	3	4k)		105.3	4
8f)	P35	101.3	1.5	9)	C39	105.3	3
8g)	P39	101.3	1	50)		105.5	3
9g)	C28	101.3	35	70)		105.5	3
4)	E33	101.7	30	71)		105.7	3
4b)	E36	101.7	30	51)	M29	106.1	3
49)	M27	102.5	3	8g)	P29	106.5	1.5
64)		102.5	3	9)	C24	106.5	35
				73)		106.5	3
4d)	E38	102.9	5	52)	M28	107.1	3
4a)	E35	103.5	30	61)		107.1	3
4g)	E40	103.5	10	9)	C34	107.3	35
4c)	E37	103.7	5	9c)	C37	107.3	3
4h)	E41	103.9	3	29)		107.3	3
32a)		103.9	3	4j)		107.7	3
1)	M22	104.1	3	53)	M25	107.7	3
9)	C26	104.5	35	54)		107.7	3
9d)	C35	104.5	3	2a)	I44	107.8	10

NB: + more than 70 low-powered Community FM st's.

Addresses and other information:

1) Cheng Sheng Broadc. Co, 7th Flr, 1, Lane 66, Sec. 1, Chungching So. Rd, Taipei 100. 24h (exc. Sun 1800-2100) on 819kHz, 24h on 104.1MHz. – **1a)** 17 Chuiyang Rd, Chia-i 600. 24h. – **1b)** 760, Sec. 2, Chunghsing Rd, Tali City, Taichung 412. 1st prgr on 990kHz, 2nd prgr on 657kHz, both 24h. – **1c)** 10 Shuiyuan Rd, Huwei Town, Yunlin 632. – **1d)** 45 Chienchun Rd, Ilan 260. 24h. – **1e)** 21, Lane 380, Hsinsheng Rd, Taitung 950. 24h (Sat 2120-Sun 1500). – **1f)** 838 Chengching Rd, Niaosung Village, Kaohsiung 833. Kaohsiung St. on 1008kHz, Tafa St. on 1395kHz, both 24h. **Web:** www.csbc.com.tw – **2)** Fu Hsing Broadc. Co, 5, Lane 280, Sec. 5, Chungshan No. Rd, Taipei 111 (operated by Dept. of the Interior). 1st Netw. on 558/909/1089kHz, 2nd Netw. on 594kHz, both 24h. 3rd Netw. on 15250kHz 2158-2400, 0328-0530, 1028-1230 for China Mainland. **ANN:** "Fu Hsing Kuangpo Tientai, (location) Tai". – **2a)** 81 Chungtai Rd, Chunshe Li, Nantun, Taichung 408. 1st Netw. on 107.8MHz, 2nd Netw. on 594/1089kHz. – **2b)** 819 Chengching Rd, Niaosung Village, Kaohsiung 833. 1st Netw. on 594kHz, 2nd Netw. on 846kHz. – **3)** Cheng Kung Broadc. St, 63 Chunghua 3rd Rd, Kaohsiung. 24h (exc. Sun 1600-2100). – **4)** Chiao Yu (Educational) Broadc. System, 41 Nanhai Rd, Taipei 100. On MW, FM both 24h. **ANN:** "Chiao Yu chih Sheng, Chiao Yu Kuangpo Tientai". – **4a)** 5-1 Hukang Rd, Changhua 500. – **4b)** 380 Kuangtung 3rd Rd, Kaohsiung 806. – **4c)** 457 Tunghsing Rd, Hualien 970. – **4d)** 30, Lane 76, Shengli Str, Taitung 950. – **4e)** Keelung (relay st.). – **4f)** Yuli (relay st.). – **4g)** Ilan (relay st.). – **4h)** Miaoli (relay st.). – **4i)** Nantou (relay st.). – **4j)** Chia-i (relay st.). – **4k)** Penghu (relay st.). – **4l)** Chinmen (relay st.). – **4m)** Hengchun (relay st.). **Web:** www.ner.gov.tw – **5)** International Community Radio Taipei (ICRT), 2nd Flr, 373 Sungchiang Rd, Taipei 104. 24h in English. N: on the h. – **5a)** Kaohsiung. – **5b)** Taichung. **Web:** www.icrt.com.tw – **6)** Taiwan Broadc. Co, 4th Flr, 89 Shuiyuan Rd, Chungcheng, Taipei 100. 1st prgr on 1323kHz, 2nd prgr on 1188kHz, both 24h (exc. Sun 1805-2100). – **6a)** 2, Lane 506, Kaofeng Rd, Hsinchu 300. 24h. – **6b)** 2309 Tzuli Tuan, Taya Village, Taichung. 24h. – **6c)** 258-1 Fentsao Rd, Tsaotun Town, Nantou 542. 24h. – **7)** Chien Kuo Broadc. St, 78 Chienkuo Rd, Hsinying City, Tainan 730. 24h.– **8)** Ching Cha Broadc. St (Public Radio System), 17 Kuangchou Str, Chungcheng, Taipei 100. 24h on MW/FM. Taipei Traffic Prgr: 24h on 1512kHz + 94.3MHz. – **8a)** 1-1 Chiahsing Rd, Chupei City, Hsinchu 302. Traffic Prgr on 1512kHz. – **8b)** 99 Po-ai Str, Nantun, Taichung 408. Traffic Prgr on 94.3MHz. – **8c)** 85-21, Nanshih, Nanshih Li, Matou Town, Tainan 721. – **8d)** 246 Chungcheng 4th Rd, Kaohsiung 801. Traffic Prgr on 819kHz + 93.1MHz. – **8e)** 110 Wusha Rd, Ilan 260. – **8f)** 21-2 Fuchien Rd, Hualien 970. Traffic Prgr on 94.3MHz. – **8g)** 191-3, Lane 719, Sec. 1, Chunghua Rd, Taitung 950. Traffic Prgr on 94.3MHz. **Web:** www.prs.gov.tw – **9)** Han Sheng Broadc. St (military broadc. st), 5th Flr, 3, Sec. 1, Hsin-i Rd, Chungcheng, Taipei 100. On MW, FM both 24h. – **9a)** Kuo Kuang Broadc. St, 122, Sec. 1, Chungching So. Rd, Taipei 100. – **9b)** 178 Chenhsing Rd, Taichung 401. – **9c)** 246 Chungcheng 4th Rd, Kaohsiung 801. – **9d)** 643 Chungcheng Rd, Hualien 970. – **9e)** 40 Mingte New Village, Tsoying, Kaohsiung 801. – **9f)** Chukuang Ying, Makong, Penghu 880. – **9g)** 139 Fuhsing Rd, Yongkang City, Tainan 710. **Web:** www.voh.com.tw – **10)** Chin Sheng Broadc. St, 25th Flr, 206 Kuanghua 1st Rd, Lingya, Kaohsiung 802. 24h.– **11)** Shih Hsin (World News) Broadc. St, 1, Lane 17, Sec. 1, Mushan Rd, Wenshan Ward, Taipei 116. 2255(Sat 2355)-1600(Sun 1300). – **12)** Sheng Li chih Sheng (Voice of Victory) Broadc. Co, 22, Sec. 1, Chienkang Rd, Tainan 700. 1st Prgr. on 837kHz, 24h (exc. Sun 1600-2130). 2nd Prgr. on 1188kHz, 2130(Sat 2220)-1800(Sun 1600). Makung St. on 756kHz, 2100(Sat 2220)-1800(Sun 1600). **ANN:** "Tainan Sheng Li chih Sheng Kuangpo Tientai". – **13)** Hsien Sheng Broadc. Co, 1, 16th Flr, Lane 505, Chungshan Rd, Taoyuan 330. 24h.– **14)** Keelung Broadc. St, 12th Flr, 13 Chungsu Rd, Keelung 200. 2055-1810(Sun 1710). – **15)** Kuo Sheng Broadc. Co, 35 Wenchuan Rd, Pakuashan, Changhua 500. 24h. – **15a)** 2 Taiping Rd, Erhlin Town, Changhua 526.– **16)** Kaohsiung Broadc. St, 90 Hsinchiang Rd, Kushan, Kaohsiung 804 (operated by Kaohsiung City Council). On 1089kHz, 94.3MHz, both 2150-1600.– **17)** Min Pen Broadc. Co, 6th Flr, 325, Sec. 3, Huanho So. Rd, Taipei 108. 1st Prgr on 1296kHz, 2nd Prgr on 855kHz, both 24h. – **18)** Chung Sheng Broadc. Co, 134 Kuangfu Rd, Taichung 400. 2040-1800.– **19)** Feng Ming Broadc. Co, 492 Chiuju 2nd Rd, Kaohsiung 807. 1st Prgr on 1161kHz, 2nd Prgr on 981kHz, both 24h. – **19a)** Chentieh Hsien, Li 38, Makung, Penghu.– **20)** Yen Sheng Broadc. St, 31, Sec. 1, Nanpin Rd, Tungchang, Chi-an Village, Hualien 973. On 1044, 1242kHz, both 2055(Sat 2200)-1800(Sun 1600).– **21)** Tien Sheng Broadc. St, 285 Kungyi Rd, Chunan Town, Miaoli 350. 24h. – **21a)** 8, Kozhuang, Chungshue Rd, Yuanli Town, Miaoli 358. Yuanli St on 1026kHz, Pengshan St. on 1215kHz, both 24h (exc. Sun 1605-2200). – **22)** Tien Nan Broadc. St, 31, Sec. 2, Hangchou So. Rd, Taipei 106. Golden Ch. on 999kHz. 24h.– **23)** Chung Hua (China) Broadc. Co, 6th Flr, 238 Hoping No. Rd, Sanchung City, Taipei 241. 1st Prgr on 1350kHz, 2nd prgr on 1026kHz, both 24h (exc. Sun 1600-2050). **ANN:** "Chung Hua Kuangpo Tientai Ti I/Erh Tai". Juifang Relay St, on 1233kHz, 2100-

1600. – **24)** Min Li Broadc. St, 57-20 Minsheng Rd, Pingtung 900. 24h. – **25)** Tien Sheng Broadc. St, 11, 15th Flr, 149, Sec. 1, Linsen Rd, Tainan 701. 24h (exc. Sun 1600-2155). – **26)** Taipei Broadc. St, 3rd Flr, 62-2, Sec. 3, Chungshan No. Rd, Taipei 104 (operated by Taipei City Council). AM on 1134kHz, 2300-1600. FM on 93.1MHz, 24h. Indonesian prgr: Sat 1300-1400, Thai prgr: Sat 1400-1500, Tagalog prgr: Sun 1300-1400, Vietnamese prgr: Sun 1400-1500. Relays BBC World Service: D0000-0100, MF1300-1400. – **27)** Chin Hsi Broadc. Co, 12th Flr, 1091 Yucheng Rd, Kushan, Kaohsiung 804. 24h.– **28)** Hua Sheng Broadc. Co, 18 Huasheng Str, Shihlin, Taipei 111. 1st Prgr on 1152kHz, 2nd Prgr on 1224kHz, both 24h. – **29)** Lan Yang FM Broadc. St, 12th Flr, 186, Sec. 3, Chungcheng Rd, Wuchie Village, Ilan. 24h. – **30)** Yi Shih Broadc. St, 75 Paisan Str, Chitu Ward, Keelung 206. 2130(Sat 2145)-1710(Sun 1610). **ANN:** "Keelung Yi Shih Kuangpo Tientai".– **31)** Taiwan Chu Yuyeh (Taiwan Area Fishery) Broadc. St, 5 Yukang No. 2nd Rd, Kaohsiung 806. 24h. Weather rpt. at every h. **ANN:** "Taiwan Chu Yuyeh Kuangpo Tientai". **Web:** www.tpg.gov.tw/a06x04 – **31a)** Ilan (relay st.). – **32)** Fei Tieh (UFO) Broadc. Co (UFO Netw), 25th Flr, 102, Sec. 2, Lossufou Rd, Taipei 100. 24h. **Web:** www.ufo.net.tw – **32a)** Nan Taiwan chih Sheng (Voice of South Taiwan), 20th Flr, 12 Po-ai 3th Rd, Tsoying, Kaohsiung 813. UFO Netw: Taichung, Changhua, Nantou district 89.9MHz, Miaoli 91.3MHz, Yunlin & Chia-i district 90.5MHz, Ilan 89.9MHz, Penghu 89.7MHz, Hualien & Taitung 91.3MHz. – **33)** Yachou (Asia) Broadc. St (Asia FM Netw), 2, 22nd Flr, 102 Chungping Rd, Taoyuan 330. 24h. **Web:** www.asiafm.com.tw – **33a)** Ya Tai Broadc. St, 1, 15th Flr, 307, Tapei Rd, Hsinchu. – **34)** Sheng Tu Broadc. Co, 233 Fentsao Rd, Tsaotun Town, Nantou 542. 24h. – **35)** Huan Yu Broadc. Co (Uni Radio), 3, 6th Flr, 675, Sec. 1, Chingkuo Rd, Hsinchu 300. 24h. **Web:** www.turc967.com.tw – **36)** Ilan chih Sheng (Voice of Ilan) Chung Shan Broadc. Co, 12th Flr, 289-3 Kungcheng Rd, Lotung Town, Ilan 265. 24h. – **37)** Luse Heping Taiwan Wenhua (Greenpeace Taiwan Culture) Broadc. St, 1, 14th Flr, 97, Sec. 4, Chunghsing Rd, Sanchung City, Taipei 241. 24h. **Web:** www.greenpeace.com.tw – **38)** Kuai Le (Happy) Broadc. St (Happy Netw), 3, 8th Flr, 63 Santo 4th Rd, Lingya, Kaohsiung 802. 24h (exc. Sun 1800-2200). – **38a)** Chia-i (Chia Le Broadc St), 1, 16th Flr, 193, Hsiaoya Rd, Chia-i 600. – **38b)** Hualien (Huan Le Broadc St), 1, Lane 120, Tunghsing 2nd Str, Minhsiang Li, Hualien 970. Happy Netw: Taichung 89.5MHz, Taipei 89.3MHz, Penghu 91.3MHz. – **39)** Hao Chia Ting (Family) Broadc. Co, 37th Flr, 789 Chungming So. Rd, Taichung 402. 24h. **Web:** www.family977.com.tw – **40)** Taiwan Chuan Min Broadc. St (News 98), 1, 25th Flr, 100, Sec. 2, Lossufu Rd, Taipei 100. 24h. – **41)** Kang Tu Broadc. St (Best Radio), 1, 34th Flr, 80 Mintsu 1st Rd, Kaohsiung 807. 24h. **Web:** www.bestradio.com.tw – **41a)** Chin Yue Broadc. St (Best 989), 6th Flr, 88, Sec. 2, Chunghsiao East Rd, Chungcheng, Taipei 100. 24h. Haoshih (Best) Netw: Taichung 90.3MHz, Pingtung 89.3MHz, Hualien 93.5MHz. – **43)** Ta Chien Broadc. St (Super FM), 8th Flr, 83 Hsuehshih Rd, Taichung 404. **Web:** www.superfm99-1.com.tw – **44)** Hsin Sheng FM Broadc. St, 1, 19th Flr, 37 Chianchung 1st Rd, Hsinchu 300. – **45)** Shen Nung (Farmer Radio) Broadc. Co, 10th Flr, 234 Peiping Rd, Huwei Town, Yunlin 632. 2050(Sat 2125)-1805(Sun 1605). – **46)** Taipei Ai Yue Broadc. Co, 7th Flr, 47 Tunghsing Rd, Hsin-i, Taipei 110. 24h. **Web:** www.prtmusic.com.tw – **47)** Ta Chung Broadc. Co (Kiss Radio), 2, 34th Flr, 6 Minchuan 2nd Rd, Kaohsiung 806. 24h. **Web:** www.kiss.com.tw – **47a)** Ta Miaoli FM Broadc. St, 3, 16th Flr, 1 Chanchien, Shangmiao Li, Miaoli 360. – **47b)** Nantou Broadc. St, 1A, 37th Flr, 760 Chungming So. Rd, Taichung 402. – **47c)** Tainan Chih Yin Broadc. St, 18th Flr, 1-119 Chunghua Rd, Yongkang City, Tainan 710 – **48)** Taichung Broadc.Co, 21st Flr, 345, Sec. 1, Chungkang Rd, Taichung 403. 24h. **Web:** www.lucky7.com.tw– **49)** Ku Tu Broadc. Co, 1, 15th Flr, 77, Sec. 2, Chunghua East Rd, Tainan 701. 24h. **Web:** www.fm1025.com.tw – **50)** Tung Shan He FM Broadc. St, 13th Flr, 452-5 Chunching Rd, Lotung Town, Ilan 265. – **51)** Chuan Kuo Broadc. Co, 1, 10th Flr, 1-18, Sec. 2, Chungkang Rd, Taichung 407. 24h. **Web:** www.taichungnet.com.tw – **52)** Taoyuan Broadc. St, 9th Flr, 859, Sec. 1, Chunghua Rd, Chungli City, Taoyuan 320. 24h. – **53)** Tung Taiwan Broadc. St, 55 Chunghsing Rd, Hualien 970. 2200-1600. Wuho Relay St 107.7MHz. – **54)** Taipei chih Yin (Sound of Taipei) Broadc. Co, B, 10th Flr, 15-1, Sec. 1, Hanchou So. Rd, Taipei 100. 24h. Relay St: Ilan 97.9MHz, Penghu 90.5MHz. **Web:** www.vot.com.tw – Music St (Hit Fm): Taipei 91.7MHz, Taichung 91.5MHz, Kaohsiung 90.1MHz. **Web:** www.hitfm.com.tw – **55)** Yun Chia Broadc. St, 9th Flr, 617 Chungshan Rd, Chia-i 600. 24h. **Web:** www.fm933.com.tw – **56)** Hsin Kechia Broadc. St, 1, 16th Flr, 411 Huannan Rd, Pingchen City, Taoyuan 324. 24h. – **57)** Pao Tao Kechia Broadc. St, 2, 17th Flr, 91, Sec. 2, Lossufu Rd, Taipei 106. 24h. Taipei & Ilan 93.7MHz, Taoyuan 98.7MHz, Hsinchu & Miaoli 102.5MHz. **Web:** www.taiwanese.com/org/hakradio – **58)** Tien Tien Broadc. St, 42nd Flr, 760 Chungming So. Rd, Taichung 402. 24h. **Web:** www.sky969.com.tw – **59)** Chu Jen (Boss) Broadc. St, 16th Flr, 121-8 Tachang 2nd Rd, Kaohsiung 807. 24h. – **60)** Ai Yu chih Sheng Broadc. St, 7, Lane 828, Sec. 3, Chinma Rd, Changhua 500. 24h. – **61)** Kai Hsuan Broadc. St, 2, 21th Flr, 425 Chunghua Rd, Yungkang City, Tainan 710. 24h. Smile Netw: Kaohsiung on 90.5MHz, Pingtung on 90.9/91.3/92.5MHz, Tainan on 97.9MHz, Chia-I on 107.1MHz. – **62)** Mei Jih Broadc. Co, 1, 7th Flr, 1-67 Wuchuan Rd, Taichung 403. 24h. **Web:** www.fm987.com.tw – **63)** Chin Ma chih Sheng Broadc. St, 8, 10th Flr, 80, Sec. 2, Kuangfu Rd, Sanchung City, Taipei. 2100-1430. – **64)** Pei Tai chih Sheng Broadc. St (East Taiwan Super Netw), 16th Flr, 5, Lane 2, Shen-aokang Rd, Keelung 201. 2300(Sun 0300)-1600. **Web:** w7.dj.net.tw~fm102.5/ – **65)** Lan Yu Broadc. St, 147, Yujen, Hongtou, Lanyu Village, Taitung 952. 0000-1300. – **66)** Cheng Shih Broadc. St, 28th Flr, 758 Chungming So. Rd, Taichung 402. – **67)** IC chih Yin (Sound of IC) Broadc. St, 2, 11th Flr, 287, Sec. 2, Kuangfu Rd, Hsinchu 300. 24h. **Web:** www.ic975.com – **68)** Ta Han chih Yin Broadc. St, 1-1 Hsintung Rd, Toufen Town, Miaoli. 24h. **Web:** 3q4u.com/fm971/ – **69)** Ti Chiu Tsun Broadc. St, 29 Tajong We. Rd, Taichung 407. – **70)** Huan Hsi chih Sheng (Happy Radio) Broadc. St, 1, 6th Flr, 242, Sec. 1, Chungkang Rd, Taichung 402. **Web:** www.happy1055.com.tw – **71)** Tzu Mei Broadc. St (Sister Radio), 4th Flr, 32, Lane 416, Sec. 1, Linsen Rd, Huwei Town, Yunlin 632. 24h. **Web:** www.sister-radio.com/ – **72)** Ching Chun Broadc. St, 3, 14th Flr, 131 Chonghsueh Rd, Tainan 701. – **73)** Chih Nan Broadc. St, 6, 21st Flr, 3 Tzuchiang 3 Rd, Lingya, Kaohsiung 802.

TAJIKISTAN

L.T: UTC +5h — **Pop:** 6,5 million — **Pr.L:** Tajik, Russian — **E.C:** 50Hz, 220V — **ITU:** TJK

KUMITAI DAVLATII TELEVIZION VA RADIOI TOJIKISTON
(State Committee for Television and Radio Broadcasting)
✉ kuchai Chapayev 31, 734025 Dushanbe. ☎ +992 372 276569. 🖷 +992 372 213495. **Email:** n/a **Web:** radio.tojikiston.com
L.P: Chmn: Ubaydullo Rajabov.

LW/MW	**kHz**	**kW**	**Prgr.**
Yangiyul	252	150	TR1
Dushanbe	549	40	TR3
Orzu	702	150	TR1
Khujand	819	15	TR1
Yangiyul	1143	150	TR2, F
Orzu	1161	40	TR3
Dushanbe	1323	7	TR1
SW	**kHz**	**kW**	**Prgr.**
Yangiyul	4635	50	TR1
Yangiyul	7245	100	TR2,1, F
FM (MHz)	**TR1**	**TR3**	**kW**
Dushanbe	70.64	72.20	17
Qurghonteppa	67.88	66.32	17
Khujand	72.56	69.80	17

+ low power tr's. A network of CCIR FM tx's is under constuction.
D.PRGR: TR1 (Radioi Tojikiston) in Tajik: 24h on FM. On MW: 0100-2200. On SW: 1400-1100 on 4635, 1100-1400 on 7245. N. Russian: 0400-0430, 1000-1030. N. Uzbek: 1030-1100. – **TR2 (Payki ajam)** in Tajik, Russian: 0500-1100. Tx's rel. External Service (F) 0100-0500, 1400-1800. – **TR3 (Sadoi Dushanbe)** in Tajik, Russian: 0300-1900.

EXTERNAL SERVICE: R. Tajikistan
See International Radio section

OTHER STATIONS

MW	**kHz**	**kW**	**Location**	**Station**
A)	972	500	Orzu	R. Rossii
B)	1503	7	Dushanbe	R. Mayak/R. Rossii/VoR
FM	**MHz**	**kW**	**Location**	**Station**
C)	103.0		Dushanbe	Russkoye R.
C)	103.7		Dushanbe	Russkoye R. 2
1)	103.7	4	Khujand	R. Tiroz
4)	105.9	-	Isfara	R. Mavchi Ozod
2)	106.0	-	Dushanbe	R. Vatan
D)	106.1	-	Khujand	BBC Relay
D)	106.5	-	Dushanbe	BBC Relay
3)	107.0	-	Dushanbe	R. Aziya FM

Addresses & other information:
1) 33 mikrorayon 73-86, 735716 Khujand. Email: trrktiroz@sugdien.com – **2)** Dushanbe. – **3)** kuchai Bokhtar 35/1, 734002 Dushanbe. Email: info@asiaplus.tajik.net – **4)** Isfara. – **A)** Rel. R.Rossii (cf. Russia) daytime as filler between foreign relays. – **B)** Rel. R.Mayak, R.Rossii, Voice of Russia (cf. Russia). – **C)** Rel. Russkoye R. from Russia. Tx's are provided by a Russian Army garrison (201-st Motorized Infantry Division) in Dushanbe. – **D)** Rel. BBC in Tajik, English, Russian (cf. United Kingdom).

TANZANIA

L.T: UTC +3h — **Pop:** 36m — **Pr.L:** Swahili, English — **E.C:** 50Hz, 230V — **ITU:** TZA

TANZANIA BROADCASTING COMMISSION (TBC)

P.O. Box 1516, Dar es Salaam ☎ +255 22 2116158/2122186 🖷 +255 22 2124812 **Email:** tnwinfo@plancom.go.tz
Web: www.tanzania.go.tz/maelezo/massmedia/broadcastact.html

RADIO TANZANIA - DAR ES SALAAM (RTD)

Dir. of Broadc., Nyerere/Mandera Rd, P. O. Box 9191, Dar es Salaam ☎ +255 51 860760/6 🖷 +255 51 865577 **Email:** radiotanzania@raha.com or radio@ud.co.tz
L.P: Acting Dir. of Broadc: Mrs. Edda Sanga. Contr. of Prgrs: Mrs. Edda Sanga. Ch.News Ed: Edward Kahurananga. CE: Herman Ipwaga.
Networks: S=Swahili Sce, E=English Sce.

MW	kHz	kW	Sce.	MW	kHz	kW	Sce.
Kunduchi+	531	10	S	Mwanza	720	50/10	S
Dodoma	603	100/10	S	Kunduchi+	837	1	S/E†
Mbeya	621	50/10	S	Songea	990	100/10	S
Nachingwea	648	100/10	S	Kunduchi+	1035	10	E
Kunduchi+	657	2 x 50	S	Arusha	1214	50/10	S
Kigoma	711	100/10	S				

+) near Dar es Salaam † (standby tr.)

SW: Dar es Salaam (G.C:06S50 39E14)

kHz	kW	Sce.	Times
5050	10	S	0200-0700, 1300-2100

FM (S): Arusha 91.6MHz, Dar es Salaam 89.9/92.35MHz, Dodoma 87.7MHz, Kigoma 88.4MHz, Lindi 93.5MHz, Mbeya/Masasi/Nachingwea 92.3MHz, Mwanza 89.2MHz, Songea 98.7MHz (PRT): Dar es Salaam 94.6MHz
Swahili service: "Radio Tanzania - Dar es Salaam" at 0200-2100. MW & FM channels may opt out at times to carry regional prgrs. **N:** Main network bulletins at 0400, 0700, 1000, 1300, 1600 (relay of Zanzibar), 1700, 1900 (relay of Zanzibar).
English services: "Radio Tanzania - Powerful, Realistic, Trustworthy (RTD-PRT)" and "City Radio" share the use of 1035 kHz & 94.6MHz at 0200-1915.
ANN: Swahili: "Hii ni Radio Tanzania - Dar es Salaam". **IS:** Celeste.

PRIVATE STATIONS
Clouds FM, P.O. Box 31513, Dar es Salaam. **Email:** clouds@cloudsfm.com - **FM:** Dar es Salaam 88.4MHz 2kW, Arusha 98.6MHz, Mwanza 99.4MHz.
R. Five, P.O. Box 11843, Arusha: 105.7MHz. **Email:** impala@cybernet.co.tz
R. Free Africa, P.O. Box 1732, Mwanza **Web:** www.africaonline.co.tz/rfa **Email:** rfa@africaonline.co.tz. *R. Free Africa* (Swahili service): **MW/FM:** Mwanza 1377kHz 50kW & 89.8MHz (also rel. BBC/VOA/RTD/DW). *Kiss FM* (English service): Mwanza 88.7, Dar es Salaam 89.0, Arusha 89.9MHz, Mbeya 96.4MHz. **Web:** www.kissfmtz.com.
R. Kwizera (rlg.), Ngara Field Office, P.O. Box 154, Ngara **Web:** www.jrs.net/countries/eaf.php?lang=en **Email:** eastern.africa@jrs.net - **FM:** 97.9MHz (in Swahili, also rel. RFI Afrique in English).
R. One, P.O. Box 4374, Dar es Salaam **Web:** www.ippmedia.com/radio1 **Email:** itv@ipp.co.tz **MW/FM:** Dar es Salaam 89.5MHz, Mwanza 87.8/102.7MHz, Dodoma 100.8MHz, Arusha 95.3MHz, Moshi 1323kHz.
R. Sky FM: Dar es Salaam 101.4MHz, Moshi 90.2MHz, Mwanza 94.4MHz, Dodoma 96.1MHz, Arusha 102.1MHz. **Web:** www.skyfm.co.tz **Email:** info@skyfm.co.tz
East Africa R, P.O.Box 4374, Dar es Salaam: 87.8MHz (also relayed on FM in Kampala, Uganda, & Nairobi, Kenya). **Web:** www.eastafricafm.com **Email:** admin@eastafricafm.com
R. Maria Tanzania: P.O. Box 152, Songea: 89.1MHz 0.5kW. **Web:** www.radiomaria.org **Email:** info.tan@radiomaria.org
R. Sauti ya Injili (rlg.), Lutheran R. Centre, P.O. Box 777, Moshi **Web:** www.elct.org/TechServ/Radio **Email:** Redio@elct.org **FM:** Kilimanjaro 92.2MHz, Arusha 96.2MHz, Same 100.4MHz, Usambara 102.6MHz, Kibaya 102.9MHz. **F.Pl:** low power **SW tr.** in Moshi in the 31/41 mb.
Tanzanite R. FM, Arusha: 96.1MHz.
R. Tumaini (rlg.): P.O. Box 9916, Dar es Salaam **FM:** Dar es Salaam 96.3MHz, Kibahe 91.4MHz. **R.Tumaini 2:** Dar es Salaam/Zanzibar: 105.9MHz.

ZANZIBAR & PEMBA (autonomous islands)

VOICE OF TANZANIA - ZANZIBAR

P.O. Box 1178, Zanzibar, Tanzania ☎ +255 54 31088/9 **L.P:** Dir. of Broadc: Yussuf Omar Chunda. CE: Ali Aboud Talib.
MW: Chumbum 585kHz 10kW.
SW: Dole (G.C: 06S05 039E14): 6015/11734kHz 50kW (11734 inactive).
FM: Spice FM, freq. not known.
D.Prgr in Swahili: 0300-0600 on 585 & 6015kHz, 0900-2100 on 585kHz.
N: Local bulletins at 0400, 1200, 1600, 1800, 1900. Relays R.Tanzania from Dar es Salaam at 1000, 1700. **In English:** 1800 (rel. from Spice FM). **Ann:** "Hii ni Sauti ya Tanzania, Zanzibar".

BBC African Sce: Zanzibar 94.1MHz, Pemba 93.5MHz.

THAILAND

L.T: UTC +7h — **Pop:** 61 million — **Pr.L:** Thai — **E.C:** 50Hz, 220V — **ITU:** THA

RADIO AND TELEVISION EXECUTIVE COMMITTEE (RTEC)

Constituted under the Broadcasting and TV Rule 1975, this body consists of 17 representatives from 14 Government agencies. It controls administrative, legal, technical and programming aspects of broadcasting in Thailand.
Programme, Administration and Law Section: Div. of RTEC Works, Gov. Public Rel. Dept, 9 Rama VI Road, Soi 30 Phaya Thai, Bangkok 10400. **Technical Section:** Radio Frequency Management Division, Post & Telegraph Dept, 87 Soi Sai Lom, Phahonyothin Rd, Sam Sen Nai, Phaya Thai Region, Bangkok 10400. ☎ +66 2271-0151 to 0160. 🖷 +66 2271-3514. **NB:** The functions of these bodies are being transferred to a new organisation, see below.

NATIONAL BROADCASTING COMMISSION (NBC)

The regulation of sound and TV broadcasting is to be transferred to this new body, which will have 7 commissioners appointed by the Senate. At the editorial deadline the NBC was not yet functioning due to political controversies.

MW: (RT=R. Thailand)

	kHz	kW	Province +)		kHz	kW	Province +)
RT)	531	25	Maha Sarakham	15)	756	5	Surin
13)	540	5	Bangkok	6)	765	5	Lampang
RT)	549	100	Lampang (E)	2)	765	5	Lop Buri
RT)	549	10	Mukdahan	31)	774	5	Rayong
RT)	558	50	Songkhla (E)	25)	774	5	Udon Thani
RT)	558	10	Kanchanaburi	RT)	783	10	Ranong
10)	567	5	Chaiyaphum	8)	783	5	Kamphaeng Phet
36)	576	5	Bangkok	19)	792	20	Bangkok
8)	585	5	Phrae	29)	801	5	N. Sawan
5)	585	5	Chumphon	2)	801	5	Chiang Rai
34)	594	5	Bangkok	2)	801	5	U. Ratchathani
5)	603	5	Khon Kaen	RT)	810	20	Nong Khai
20)	612	5	Lop Buri	RT)	*810	7	Khon Kaen
17)	612	5	Chiang Mai	RT)	810	10	Kanchanaburi (F.Pl.)
RT)	621	100	Khon Kaen (E)	RT)	810	10	Trang
22)	630	5	Bangkok	RT)	819	10	Bangkok
RT)	639	10	Lamphun	5)	828	5	N. Si Thammarat
RT)	639	20	N. Si Thammarat	8)	828	5	Sukhothai
RT)	648	25	Khon Kaen	13)	*828	20	Rayong
10)	657	5	Bangkok	9)	837	5	Sakon Nakhon
8)	666	5	Tak	RT)	837	10	Pathum Thani
11)	666	5	Surin	RT)	846	10	Phetchabun
4)	675	5	Bangkok	28)	855	5	Prachin Buri
12)	684	5	N. Si Thammarat	RT)	864	10	Tak
13)	684	5	Udon Thani	RT)	864	10	Si Sa Ket
24)	693	5	Saraburi	RT)	864	10	Phatthalung
19)	711	5	Chiang Mai	3)	873	5	Bangkok
RT)	711	20	U. Ratchathani (E)	RT)	891	1000	Saraburi
20)	711	5	Lop Buri	RT)	909	10	Loei
RT)	720	10	Krabi	RT)	909	25	Surin
4)	720	5	Chon Buri	7)	918	10	Chiang Mai
RT)	729	25	N. Ratchasima	RT)	918	10	Bangkok
5)	738	5	Chiang Mai	RT)	927	20	Chanthaburi (E)
5)	738	5	Songkhla	RT)	927	10	Nong Khai
18)	747	5	Bangkok	12)	936	10	Pattani
11)	747	5	Udon Thani	RT)	936	50	N. Sawan (E)
9)	756	5	Narathiwat	2)	945	10	Bangkok

	kHz	kW	Province +)		kHz	kW	Province +)
11)	945	10	Kalasin	10)	1251	10	Roi Et
2)	954	10	Phitsanulok	2)	1251	5	Bangkok
2)	954	10	Chanthaburi	RT)	1260	25	Chiang Rai
RT)	963	50/10	Krabi (E)	17)	1269	10	Songkhla
31)	963	10	Bangkok	21)	1269	10	Bangkok
9)	972	10	Phetchabun	38)	1278	10	Ranong (F.Pl.)
39)	981	10	Pathum Thani	32)	1287	10	Bangkok
RT)	981	25	Mae Hong Son	8)*	1287	10	Uttaradit
RT)	981	20	N. Phanom	5)	1287	10	U. Ratchathani
RT)	981	25	Yala	RT)	1296	10	Pattani
7)	990	10	N. Ratchasima	13)	1305	10	Bangkok
8)	999	10	Chiang Rai	17)	1314	10	Khon Kaen
16)	999	10	Bangkok	2)	1323	10	Chiang Mai
5)	1008	10	N. Ratchasima	2)	1323	10	Surat Thani
2)	1017	10	Prachuap KK	30)	1332	10	Bangkok
RT)	1026	50	Phitsanulok	2)	1332	10	Maha Sarakham
RT)	1026	10	Yala	RT)	1341	20	Loei
6)	1035	10	Bangkok	RT)	1341	25	U. Ratchathani
15)	1044	10	Khon Kaen	RT)	1341	10	Phangnga
12)	1044	10	N. Si Thammarat	23)*	1350	10	Lampang
23)	1053	10	Lampang	5)	1350	10	Trang
22)	1053	10	Bangkok	16)	1350	10	Bangkok
2)	1062	10	Udon Thani	11)	1359	10	Sakhon Nakhon
RT)	1062	10	Phuket	RT)	1368	25	Nan
37)	1071	10	Bangkok (F.Pl.)	RT)	1368	10	Buri Ram
6)	1071	10	Tak	2)	1368	10	N. Pathom
5)	1080	10	Chiang Rai	26)	1377	10	Phitsanulok
5)	1080	10	N. Sawan	RT)	1377	10	Chumphon
5)	1080	10	Yala	40)	1386	10	Bangkok
6)	1089	10	Bangkok	9)	1395	10	Chiang Rai
6)	1089	10	Udon Thani	RT)	1404	25	Songkhla
7)	1098	10	Songkhla	10)	1404	10	Yasothon
RT)	1098	10	Tak	14)	1404	10	Suphan Buri
17)	1107	10	Samut Sakhon	RT)	1422	10	Amnat Charoen
11)	1107	10	Khon Kaen	16)	1422	10	Bangkok
8)	1116	10	Phitsanulok	7)	1422	10	Phitsanulok
RT)	1116	10	Phangnga	2)	1431	10	N. Ratchasima
RT)	1125	25	Chanthaburi	4)	1431	5	Songkhla
RT)	1134	10	Lampang	11)	1440	10	N. Phanom
11)	1134	10	N. Ratchasima	5)	1440	10	Samut Sakhon
1)	1143	10	Bangkok	8)	1449	10	Phichit
18)	1152	10	Chiang Mai	20)	1449	10	Chumphon
18)	1152	10	Khon Kaen	10)	1458	10	Si Sa Ket
27)	1161	20	Bangkok	4)	1458	10	Phuket
4)*	1161	20	N. Phanom	RT)	1467	100	Pathum Thani (E)
4)	1161	10	U. Ratchathani	RT)	1476	50	Lamphun
4)	1170	10	Chanthaburi	RT)	1485	1	Yala (F.Pl.)
4)	1170	10	Phitsanulok	1)	1494	10	Bangkok
25)	1179	10	Bangkok	10)	1503	10	Surat Thani
9)	1179	10	Chiang Rai	RT)	1512	10	Yasothon (F.Pl.)
15)	1188	10	Sakon Nakhon	15)	1512	10	Phayao
8)	1188	10	Phitsanulok	2)	1512	10	Songkhla
14)	1188	10	Sa Kaeo	9)	1512	5	*Uthai Thani
35)	1197	10	Lop Buri	9)	1521	10	Bangkok
RT)	1206	10	Satun	5)	1530	10	Uttaradit
14)	1206	10	Prachuap KK	14)	1530	10	Chanthaburi
15)	1215	10	Phrae	RT)	1539	10	Surat Thani (F.Pl.)
11)	1215	10	U. Ratchathani	33)	1539	10	Kanchanaburi
RT)	1215	50	Surat Thani	24)	1557	10	Phetchabun
2)	1224	10	Chiang Rai	RT)	1557	10	Trat
2)	1224	10	N. Sawan	–)	1575	1000	Ayutthaya
2)	1233	10	Bangkok	RT)	1584	1	*Loei
5)	1233	10	Udon Thani	12)*	1584	1	Phatthalung
8)*	1242	10	Lampang	6)	1593	10	Buri Ram
8)	1242	10	Phetchabun	RT)	1593	10	Ratchaburi
RT)	1242	50	Surat Thani (E)				

*) r. inactive. +) N=Nakhon, U=Ubon, KK=Khiri Khan.

Note: Mobile 1kW units for Army use with no advertisements have been registered for 747, 1242, 1485, 1584, and 1602kHz.

SW	kHz	kW	H. of tr.
30)	6150v	–	reportedly inactive

BANGKOK FM (exc. R. Thailand, freq's in MHz)
87.5 Sathaanii Witthayu Ratthasapha (Parliament R. St.) – 88.5 Sor. Thor. Ror. 1, "FM Max" – 89.0 Yaan Kraw, "Virgin Soft" – 89.5 Rajamangala Institute of Technology, "Sweet Radio" – 90.0 Phon Neung Ror. Or. "Luukthung FM" – 90.5 Wor. Phor. Thor. – 91.0 Sor. Wor. Phor. – 91.5 Yaan Kraw, "Hot Wave" – 92.0 Wor. Sor. Sor. – 93.0 Sor. Thor. Ror. 1, "Cool FM" – 94.0 Thor. Thor. Bor. (Sathaanii Witthayu Thorathat Kongthap Bok, Army TV Station), "Bangkok Radio" – 94.5 Jor. Sor, "Music Box" – 95.0 Or. Sor. Mor. Thor, "Luukthung FM" – 96.0 Ror. Dor. "City Radio" – 96.5 Or. Sor. Mor. Thor, "Business Radio" – 97.5 Or. Sor. Mor. Thor – 98.0 Phon Neung Ror. Or. – 98.5 Neung Por. Nor, "Post Radio" – 99.0 Or. Sor. Mor. Thor, " Sport Radio" – 99.5 Sathaanii Witthayu 9-1-9, "Woman's Wave"/"INN News and talk" – 100.0 Jor. Sor. – 100.5 Or. Sor. Mor. Thor. – 101.0 Sathaanii Witthayu Kong Banchaakaan Thahaan Suungsut (Supreme Command HQ), "101 News Channel" – 101.5 Sathaanii Witthayu Chulaa or "Witthayu Chulaa" or "CU FM" – 102.0 Khor. Sor. Thor. Bor. – 102.5 Thor. Or, "Get 102.5" – 103.0 Jor. Sor. – 103.5 Thor. Thor. Bor, "Modern Love" – 104.0 Or. Sor. – 104.5 Phon Por. Thor. Or. (Kong Phon Thahaan Peun Yai Tosue Akart Yaan, Anti-Aircraft Artillery Division), "Fat Radio" – 105.5 Or. Sor. Mor. Thor, "Eazy FM" – 106.0 Sor. Thor. Ror. 1, "Life FM" – 106.5 Neung Por. Nor, "Green Wave" – 107.0 Or. Sor. Mor. Thor, "Cosmopolitan 107".

OTHER FM STATIONS: A large number of FM sts belonging to R. Thailand or other operators are on air throughout Thailand.

English language prgrs in Bangkok (frequencies carrying substantial content in English): 837kHz R. Thailand, BBC WS relays 2300-2330, 1400-1500 – 918kHz R.Thailand 3rd prgr (English news & features, western light & classical music) – 95.5MHz "Virgin Hitz" – 105.0MHz "Virgin Smooth" (Radio Thailand) – 107.0MHz "Right FM" (Or Sor Mor Thor). 918kHz/107MHz carry BBC WS news most hours on the hour.

GOVERNMENT PUBLIC RELATIONS DEPT. (Gov.)
✉ Soi Aree Samphan, Rama VI Road, Bangkok 10400
☎ +66 2618-2323 🖷 +66 2618-2364/2399 **Web**: www.prd.go.th/prdnew/eng/radio_e/index.html (general info in English), www.prd.go.th/prdnew/thai/media/radiothai.asp (AM/FM station info in Thai). This body operates the NBT radio & TV services (R.Thailand & Television Thailand).**L.P:** DG: Piyasvasti Amranand.

THE NATIONAL BROADCASTING SERVICES OF THAILAND (NBT) – RADIO THAILAND (Sathaanii Witthayu Krachaisiang Haeng Pratheet Thai (Sor. Wor. Thor.)
✉ 236 Vibhavadi Rangsit Superhighway, Din Daeng, Huay Khwang, Bangkok 10320 ☎ +66 2277-8181 🖷 +66 2277-8182 & 2277-5881.
L.P: Exec. Dir. R. Thailand: Dussadee Sinchermsiri. Head of Home Sce: Mrs. Chalermsri Huncharoen. Head World Sce: Mrs. Amporn Samosorn.
D.Prgr: (SWT=Sathaanii Witthayu Krachaisiang Haeng Pratheet Thai)

Prgr. 1 (Khreungkhai Thii Neung or SWT Pheua Khwamruu Sara Lae Borihan Saa Taranaa): 2200-1700 on 891kHz, 92.5MHz (10kW) in Bangkok and in full or in part on most regional AM stations. **N:** On the h. exc. 0500, 0600 & 1100. Also 0530 & 1545 – **Educational Prgr. 2** (SWT Raikarn Song Pheua Karn Seuksaa): 2300-0430, 0700-1700 on 837kHz. Rel. BBC WS **English** to Asia-Pacific 2300v-2330 & 1400-1500, BBC Thai 2330-2400 and 1235-1300. **N:** rel. Prgr. 1. Mostly carries educational prgr's from Ramkhanghaeng University at other times – **News and local service** (SWT Pheua Khaosaan Lae Borikaan Thongthin): 2200-2000 on 819kHz, also in part on many RT regional MW st's. 92.5MHz has separate prgr's at times – **R. Thailand 3rd prgr (NBT-3):** 2200-1700 **English** news, western light music on 918kHz – **FM prgrs:** 88.0MHz (10kW) "R. No Problem", 93.5MHz (10kW) "EFM", 95.5MHz "Virgin Hitz", 97.0MHz (10kW) "Trinity R.", 105.0MHz (10kW) "Virgin Smooth".

EXTERNAL SERVICE: Radio Thailand
see International Broadcasting section.

NATIONAL EDUCATION RADIO (SWT Pheua Karn Seuksaa)
✉ Soi Aree Samphan, Rama VI Rd, Samsen, Phaya Thai, Bangkok 10400.
D.Prgr: 2130-1640 on 1467kHz in the Bangkok area and nationwide on all "E" tr's. Local st's except for one or two h weekly relay Bangkok.

Addresses. of provincial stations:
Most st's can be reached by quoting "Sathaanii Witthayu Sor. Wor. Tor." or "Radio Thailand" and the location given in the freq. list, followed by the phrase "Muang District" and finally the city, which is generally the same as the location. Exceptions are the following: **Lamphun:** the trs are in Lamphun, but the studios are in Chiang Mai. –

Loei 909kHz: located in Dansai district. – **Nong Khai** 927kHz: located in Bung Kan district. – **Phangnga:** The addr. for 1116kHz is Takua Pa District, Phangnga 82110. – **Saraburi:** Studios in Bangkok. The addr. for the 1000kW tr. on 891kHz is Rim Klong Hog Wa, Mu 4, Nong Rong, Nong Khae, Saraburi 18140. – **Tak:** The addr. for 1098kHz is 14 Asia Hwy, Mae Sot District, Tak 63110. – **Yala:** The addr. for 1026kHz is Betong District, Yala 95110, for 981kHz Raman District, Yala 95140.

OTHER STATIONS
GENERAL NOTES: News: All st's are required to relay N. from R. Thailand at 0000 & 1200 daily, each 30 min's, if on the air at that time. **Station IDs:** Both short names, e.g. Wor. Por. Tho, and long names may serve as station identifications, usually preceded by, as appropriate, "Thiinii" ("Here is"), "Thiinii, Sathaanii Witthayu (Krachaisiang)" ("Here is R. St.") or in some instances "Khannani khun rap fang" ("You are now listening to"). Changwat=province. Amphoe=district (dt.). Prgr's are often supplied by separate production companies. **Thai numerals:** 0 = suun, 1 = neung (et), 2 = song, 3 = saam, 4 = sii, 5 = haa, 6 = hok, 7 = jet, 8 = paet, 9 = kao, 10 = sip, 20 = yi sip, 100 = roi, 1000 = phan; thii = number, jut = decimal point.

1) Or. Sor. Mor. Thor. (Ongkarn Suesarn Muanchon Haeng Pratheet Thai, Mass Communications Org. of Thailand, MCOT). 63/1 Rama IX Rd, Huay Khwang, Bangkok 10320 – **2) Thor. Or.** (Thahaan Akart, Royal Thai Airforce). Tor. Or. 01, 1233kHz, Don Muang: 171 Mu 2, Phahonyothin Rd, Khlong Thanon, Sai Mai, Bangkok 10220. Tor. Or. 01, 945kHz, Min Buri: 74 Mu 2, Nimit Mai, Sai Kong Tin, Min Buri, Bangkok 10510. Tor. Or. 06, 1251 kHz: The Empress Hotel, 1091/343 Phetchaburi Tat Mai Road, Charurat, Makassan, Ratcha Thewi, Bangkok 10400. **Regional st's:** Thor. Or. 02: 301 Wing 2, 1st Air Division, Khao Phra Ngam Rd, Lop Buri 15160 – Thor. Or. 03: Wing 1, Mu 3, Nong Phai Lom, Nakhon Ratchasima 30000 – Thor. Or. 04: 305 Mu 4, Wing 4, 3rd Air Division, Takhli District, Nakhon Sawan 60140 – Thor. Or. 05: Wing 53, 4th Air Division, Ko Lak, Prachuap Khiri Khan 77000 – Thor. Or. 7: Surat Thani Airport Entrance, Huatoey, Phunphin District, Surat Thani 84130 – Thor. Or. 08: 38 Mu 14, Ban Nongphai, Chayangkun Rd, Khamyai, Ubon Ratchathani 34000 – Thor. Or. 09: 549 Mu 9, Wing 23, Thahaan Rd, Makkhaeng, Udon Thani 41000 – Thor. Or. 10: Wing 46, 3rd Air Division, Yaek Khok Matum, Phitsanulok - Wangthong Rd, Nai Muang, Phitsanulok 65000 – Thor. Or. 11: 99 Mu 8, Wing 56, Khok Muang, Khlong Hoykhong District, Songkhla 90110 – Thor. Or. 12: Flying Training School, Malaimaen Rd, Kratip, Kamphaeng Saen District, Nakhon Pathom 73180 – Thor. Or. 13: 90 Mu 3, Suthep, Chiang Mai 50200 – Thor. Or. 14: Wapiprathum Rd, Wangnang, Maha Sarakham 44000 – Thor. Or. 15, 141 Mu 1, Buasali, Mae Lao District, Chiang Rai 57250. 1st prgr: 801kHz. 2nd prgr: 1224kHz – Thor. Or. 16: 1049 Tha Chalaep Rd, Talat, Chanthaburi 22000 – **3) Wor. Kor. Thor. Mor.** (Sathaanii Witthayu Krung Theep Mahaanakhon, Bangkok Radio Station), 192 Sarasin Rd, Lumphini Park, Pathum Wan Region, Bangkok 10330 – **4) Sor. Thor. Ror.** (Siang Chaak Thahaan Reua, Voice of the Navy). Sor. Thor. Ror. 2: Phutianan Stadium, Phra Khanong, Bangna District, Bangkok 10260. **Regional st's:** Sor. Thor. Ror. 3: 99/1 Mu 1, Phuket 83000 – Sor. Thor. Ror. 4: 9/9 Thetsaban-Phatthana Rd, Wat Mai, Chanthaburi 22000 – Sor. Thor. Ror. 5: 652 Mu 2, Sattahip District, Chon Buri 20180 – Sor. Thor. Ror. 6: Songkhla Naval Station, Thale Luang Rd, Bo Yang, Songkhla 90000 – Sor. Thor. Ror. 7: Mae Klang River Operation Unit, Nakhon Phanom 48000 – Sor. Thor. Ror. 8: Ban Khlong Mek, Tha Chang, Phrom Phiram District, Phitsanulok 65150 – Sor. Thor. Ror. 9: Ban Thung Sawang, Ubon-Takan Rd, Rai Noi, Ubon Ratchathani 34000 – **5) Wor. Por. Tho.** (Witthayu Prachaam Thin, Local R, Communications Division, Signals Dept, Royal Thai Army). Wor. Por. Tho. 8: Kamphaeng Phet Akkharayothin Camp, Suan Luang, Krathum Baen District, Samut Sakhon 74110. **Regional st's:** Wor. Por. Tho. 2: Kawila Camp, Kongsai, Wat Ket, Chiang Mai 50000 – Wor. Por. Tho. 3: 001 Na Khai Suranari, Phanibut Rd, Pho Klang, Nakhon Ratchasima 30000 – Wor. Por. Tho. 4: Thep Sattri Si Sunthon Camp, Kabang, Thung Song District, Nakhon Si Thammarat 80310 – Wor. Por. Tho. 5: 5 Kanchanawanit Rd, Hat Yai District, Songkhla 90110 – Wor. Por. Tho. 6: Sapphasiti Prasong Camp, Warin Chamrap District, Ubon Ratchathani 34190 – Wor. Por. Tho. 7: Khai Prachak Sinlaprakhom, Thahaan Rd, Mak Khaeng, Udon Thani 41000 –Wor. Por. Tho. 9: Chiraprawat Camp, Na Khai Chiraprawat Rd, Nakhon Sawan 60000 – Wor. Por. Tho. 10: Mengrai Maharat Barracks, Chiang Rai 57000 – Wor. Por. Tho. 12: 140 Kasikonthungsang Rd, Sila, Khon Kaen 40000 – Wor. Por. Tho. 14: Phichai Dap Hak Camp, 13/7 Prachanimit Rd, Tha It, Uttaradit 53000 – Wor. Por. Tho. 15, Khet Udomsak Camp, Wang Mai, Chumphon 86190– Wor. Por. Tho. 16: 35 Sukayang Rd, Sateng, Yala 95000 – Wor. Por. Tho. 17: Trang-Palian Rd, Ban Khuan, Trang 92000 – **6) Neung. Por. Nor.** (Krom Praisanii Thoralek, Post & Telegraph Dept.). Chaengwattana-Thungsonghong Rd, Don Muang, Bangkok 10210. 1035kHz=Phaak Phiset, 1089kHz=Mor. Sor. Thor. **Regional st's:** Bypass Rd, Nai Muang, Buri Ram 31000 – 219 Mu 4, Lampang-Hang Chat Rd, Pong Yang Khok, Hang Chat District, Lampang 52190 – 2/7 T. Nong Luang, Mahat Thai Bamrung Rd, Nong Luang, Tak 63000 – Ban Nong Bu, Rop Muang Rd, Samphrao, Udon Thani 41000 – **7) Sor. Wor. Phor.** (Sathaanii Witthayu Phitaksantirat, Police R. St.). Radio Broadcasting Section, 2nd Communication Division, Directorate of Police Communications, Police Department, Bang Khen Region, Bangkok 10900. **Regional st's:** 40 Mu 1, Chotana Rd, Maesa, Mae Rim District, Chiang Mai 50180 – Sor. Wor. Phor. 2, Suranarai Rd, Cho Ho, Nakhon Ratchasima 30310 – Sor. Wor. Phor. 3, Banphru, Hat Yai District, Songkhla 90250 – Sor. Wor. Phor. 4, Pracha Uthit Rd, Nai Muang, Phitsanulok – **8) Thor. Phor. Saam** (Kongthap Phaak Thii Saam, 3rd Army Area). Headquarters of the 3rd Army Area, Somdet Phra Ekathosarot Camp, Aranyik, Phitsanulok 65000. **Regional st's:** Mengrai Maharat Camp, Chiang Rai 57000 – 236/5 Mu 3, Nakhon Sawan - Kamphaeng Phet Rd, Nakhon Chum, Kamphaeng Phet 62000 – Khalang Nakhon Camp, Nong Krating, Lampang 52000 – Phokun Pha Muang Camp, 166/1 Mu 1, Wat Pa, Lom Sak District, Phetchabun 67110 – 104/1 Mu 5, Ban Krot Ngam, Ban Na, Wachirabarami District, Phichit 66140 – Ban Mai, Ratsadon Uthit Rd, Nai Wiang, Phrae 54000 – Bypass Road, Pak Khwae, Sukhothai 64000 – Charot Withithong Rd, Nam Ruem, Tak 63000 – Phichai Dap Hak Camp, 109 Mu 8, Uttaradit 53000 – **9) Nor. Thor. Phor.** (Nuai Bannachakaan Thahaan Phatthanaa, Armed Forces Development Command, AFDC). Sathaanii Witthayu 9-1-9, Phitsanulok Rd, Dusit Region, Bangkok 10300. **Regional St's:** Sathaanii Witthayu 9-1-4, Suan Sak Kieo Tap Yong, Ban Pong 00, Mae Chan, Mae Chan District, Chiang Rai 57110 – Sathaanii Witthayu 9-1-4, Mu 2 Ban Khao Kiw, Uthai-Thapthan Rd, Sakaekrang, Uthai Thani 61000 – Sathaanii Witthayu 9-1-2, 13 Chan Uthit Rd, Bang Nak, Narathiwat 96000 – Sathaanii Witthayu 9-2-1, 114 Mu 1, Na Saeng, Lom Kao District, Phetchabun 67120 – Sathaanii Witthayu 9-0-9, Ban Rung Phatthana, Sakon Nakhon-Nakhon Phanom Rd, That Naweng, Sakon Nakhon 47000 – **10) Jor. Sor.** (Krom Jaye Thahaan Suesarn, Army Signals Department). Jor. Sor. 1, Rama V Rd, Saphan Daeng, Bangsue, Dusit Region, Bangkok 10300. **Regional st's:** Jor. Sor. 2, Tharathibodi Rd, Thakham, Phunphin District, Surat Thani 84130 – Jor. Sor. 3, Prasert Songkhram Camp, Kongphon Si Rd, Nua Muang, Roi Et 45000 – Jor. Sor. 4, 104 Thetsaban 1 Rd, Nai Muang, Yasothon 35000 – Jor. Sor. 5, 5 Mu 2 Ban Lao, Ban Lao, Chaiyaphum 36000 – Jor. Sor. 6, 1543/23 Srisumang Rd, Muang Tai, Si Sa Ket 33000 – **11) Thor. Phor. Song** (Kongthap Phaak Thii Song, 2nd Army Area). HQ: Suranari Camp, Ratchadamnoen Rd, Nong Phailom, Nakhon Ratchasima 30000. **Regional st's:** Aphai Rd, Nai Muang, Kalasin 46000 – Si Phatcharin Camp, Sila, Khon Kaen 40000 – Phra Yot Muang Khwang Camp, Nakhon Phanom-Sakon Nakhon Rd, Khurukhu, Nakhon Phanom 48000 – Krit Siwara Camp, That Naveng, Sakon Nakhon 47000 – Wirawatyothin Camp, Phakdichumphon Rd, Nok Muang, Surin 32000 – Sapphasiti Prasong Camp, Warin Chamrap District, Ubon Ratchathani 34190 – Yutthasin Prasit Camp, Non Sung Rd, Udon Thani 41330 – **12) Thor. Phor. Sii** (Kongthap Phaak Thii Sii, 4th Army Area). HQ: Wachirahwud Camp, Ratchadamnoen-Pak Nun Rd, Nakhon Si Thammarat 80000. **Regional st's:** Aphai Borirak Rd, Chumphon, King-Ampoe Si Nakharin, Phatthalung 93000 – Senanarong Camp, Kho Hong, Hat Yai District, Songkhla 90110 – Ban Na San District, Surat Thani 84120 – Charoen Pradit Rd, Rusamilae, Pattani 94000 – **13) Yaan Kraw** (4th Cavalry Batallion, Armoured Unit, Royal Guard). HQ: Military Armoured Car School, 1156 Samsen Road, Bangkabrue, Dusit Region, Bangkok 10300. **Regional st:** Mitraphap Rd, Nong Bua Udon Thani 41000 – **14) Thor. Phor. Neung** (Kongthap Phaak Thii Neung, 1st Army Area). HQ: Headquarters of the 1st Army Area, Suan Mitsakawan, Rajchadamnern Nok Ave, Dusit Region, Bangkok 10300. **Regional st's:** 9 Mu 4, Bang Kacha, Chanthaburi 22000 – Phairirayodet Camp, Suwansri Rd, Tha Kasem, Sa Kaeo 27000 – Kao Kuat, Kraw Plub Pla, Ratchaburi 70000 – Ban Sam Liam, Mu 4, Don Pho Thong, Suphan Buri 72000 – **15) Kor. Wor. Sor.** (Kitkarn Witthayu Krachaisiang, Radio & TV Division, Army Signals Dept). HQ: Radio Broadcasting & Television Division, Signals Department, Royal Thai Army, Rama V Rd, Saphan Daeng, Bangsue, Dusit Region, Bangkok 10300. **Regional st's:** Kor. Wor. Sor. 1, Surin-Prasat Rd, Nok Muang, Surin 32000 – Kor. Wor. Sor. 2, Yantarakit Sokon Rd, Sung Men District, Phrae 54130 – Kor. Wor. Sor. 3, 1879 Mu 14, That Choeng Chum, Sakon Nakhon 47000 – Kor. Wor. Sor. 4, 383 Super Highway, Ban Dom, Phayao 56000 – Kor. Wor. Sor. 5, 252 Mitraphap Rd, Ban Phai District, Khon Kaen 40110 – **16) Phon Neung Ror. Or.** (Kong Phon Thii Neung Raksaa Phra Ong, 1st Infantry Division, Royal Guard). Phitsanulok Rd, Dusit Region, Bangkok 10300. 990kHz=Phaak Phiset, 1350kHz=Phaak Pokkati. **ANN.** on 1422kHz also as "Thaam Phon Neung" (1st Infantry Division Dharma) – **17) Mor. Kor.** (Mahaawitthayalai Kasetsart, Kasetsart University). HQ: 50 Phahonyothin Rd, Bang Khen, Chatuchak, Bangkok 10900. Bangkok. Tr. located at Nongkhaem in Samut Sakhon province. **Regional st's:** 301/1 Mu 5, Paphai, Sansai District, Chiang Mai 50210 – 86/8 Maliwan Rd,

Muang Kao, Sitan, Khon Kaen 40000 – 424 Mu 3, Kanchanawanit Rd, Phawong, Songkhla 90100 – **18) Ror. Dor.** (Kromkarn Raksaa Dindaen, Territorial Defence Dept.). HQ: 2 Charoen Krung Rd, Suan Chaochet, Phra Nakhon Region, Bangkok 10200. **Regional st's:** Nong Ho, Chotana Rd, Chang Peuak, Chiang Mai 50000 – Sri Phatcharin Camp, Raat Khaneung Rd, Nai Muang, Khon Kaen 40000 – **19) Wor. Phor. Thor.** (Witthayu Kromkarn Phalang Ngan Thahaan, Defence Energy Dept. R. St.). New Building, Sukhumvit 24, Phra Khanong, Bangkok 10250. **Regional st:** 141/3 Mu 4, Don Kaeo Rd, Chotana, Mae Rim District, Chiang Mai 50180 – **20) Wor. Sor. Por.** (Witthayu Suun Karn Thahaan Peun Yai, Artillery Centre R. St.). 301 Phahonyothin Camp, Artillery Centre, Khao Phra Ngam, Lop Buri 15160. **Regional st:** Khet Udomsak Camp, Wang Mai, Chumphon 86000 – **21) Kho. Sor. Thor. Bor.** (Kromkarn Khon Song Thahaan Bok, Army Transportation Dept.). Army Transportation Broadcasting Station, Transport School Compound, Thahaan Road, Dusit Region, Bangkok 10300 – **22) Mor. Thor. Bor. Sip Et** (Monthon Thahaan Bok Thii Sip Et, 11th Military Circle). 145 Rama V Rd, Dusit Region, Bangkok 10300. **ANN:** "Suan Mitsakawan" – **23) Mor. Thor. Bor. Saam Sip Song** (Monthon Thahaan Bok Thii Saam Sip Song, 32nd Military Circle). Headquarters of the 32nd Army Area, Surasak Montri Camp, Phahonyothin Rd, Phichai, Lampang 52000 – **24) Siang Adison** (Suun Kaan Thahaan Maa, Cavalry Centre, "Voice of Adison Camp"). Saraburi Cavalry Centre, Adison Camp, Mitraphap Rd, Pak Phrieo, Saraburi 18000. **Regional st:** Saraburi-Lom Sak Rd, Nong Khwai, Lom Sak District, Phetchabun 67110 – **25) Sor. Sor. Sor.** (Siang Sam Yot, Crime Supression Division, Royal Thai Police). Section 1, Superintendency 2, Command Division, Crime Suppression Division, Phahonyothin Rd, Bangkok 10900. **Regional st:** 195 Mu 8, Udon-Nong Samrong Rd, Mumon, Udon Thani 41000.**26) Wor. Phon Sii** (Witthayu Kong Phon Thii Sii, 4th Infantry Division). Headquarters of the 4th Infantry Division, Somdet Phra Naresuan Maharat Camp, Phitsanulok 65000 – **27) Wor. Sor. Sor.** (Witthayu Seuksa, Educational Radio). Educational Technology Centre, Si Ayutthaya Rd, Ratcha Thewi, Bangkok 10400 – **28) Mor. Thor. Bor. Sip Song** (Monthon Thahaan Bok Thii Sip Song, "Siang Khai Chakkrapong", 12th Military Circle, "Voice of Chakkrapong Camp"). Chakkrapong Camp, Dong Phra Ram, Prachin Buri 25000 – **29) Mor. Thor. Bor. Thii Saam Sip Et** (Monthon Thahaan Bok Thii Saam Sip Et, 31st Military Circle). Jiraprawat Camp, Nakhon Sawan 60000 – **30) Or. Sor.** (Sathaanii Witthayu Amphon Sathaan, Phraratchawang Dusit, Amphon Sathan Throne Radio Station). Dusit Palace, Ratchawithi Rd, Chitralada, Dusit Region, Bangkok 10303 – **31) Phon Mor. Song** (Sathaanii Witthayu Kong Phan Thahaan Maa Thii Song, 2nd Cavalry Division), Samsen Rd, Bang Krabeu, Dusit Region, Bangkok 10300 Bangkok. **Regional st:** Rayong-Ban Khai Rd, Nam Khok, Rayong 21000 – **32) Sor. Or. Thor.** (Sathaanii Witthayu Krom Utiniyom Witthayaa, Meteorological Department R. St.), 4353 Sukhumvit Rd, Bangna, Bangkok 10260 – **33) Phon Ror. Kao** (Kong Phon Thahaan Raap Thii Kao, 9th Infantry Division), Surasi Camp, Kanchanaburi 71190 – **34) Phon Por. Thor. Or.** (Kong Phon Thahaan Peun Yai Tosue Akart Yaan, Anti-Aircraft Artillery Division), Kiak Kay Junction, Thahaan Road, Bangsue, Dusit Region, Bangkok 10300 – **35) Jor. Tor. Lor.** (Jangwat Thahaan Bok Lop Buri, Lop Buri Army Province). 13th Military Circle, Narai Maharat Rd, Lop Buri 15000 – **36) Tor. Chor. Dor.** (Tamruat Trawen Chaidaen, Border Patrol Police). Bang Khen Police Dept. Club, Vibhavadi-Rangsit Rd, Bang Khen Bangkok 10210 – **37) Sathaanii Witthayu Ratthasapha** (Parliament Radio Station) – **38) Krom Pramong** (Fisheries Dept), Ranong – **39) Mahaawitthayalai Thammasat** (Thammasat University), Faculty of Journalism and Mass Communications, Thammasat University, Prachan Rd, Phra Nakhon Region, Bangkok 10200 – **40) Sathaanii Witthayu Pheua Kaan Kaset** (Agricultural R. St.), Agricultural Radio Section, Phahonyothin Road, Lat Yao, Bang Khen Region, Bangkok 10900

International Relays
Radio Saranrom, Radio Liberty, Voice of America, Radio Farda, BBC – see International Broadcasting section

TOGO

L.T: UTC — **Pop:** 5 million — **Pr.L:** French, Ewé, Kabyè, Kotokoli, Mina — **E.C:** 50Hz, 127(Lomé)/220V — **ITU:** TGO

AUTORITÉ DE RÉGLEMENTATION DES SECTEURS DE POSTES ET DE TÉLÉCOMMUNICATIONS (ARTP)

✉ B.P. 358, Lomé ☎ +228 2218385 🖷 +228 2228612 **Web:** www.artp.tg **Email:** artp@artp.tg

RADIODIFFUSION-TÉLÉVISION TOGOLAISE (RTT)

✉ B.P. 434, Lomé ☎ +228 212493 **L.P:** Dir: Bawa Semedo. CE: Dodzi Soares.
Station: Lomé (G.C: 06N16 001E12)
MW: 1395kHz 20/1kW
SW: 5047v kHz 100kW (running at reduced power).
FM: Agou 88.3MHz, Alédjo 92.7MHz, Dapaong 98.3MHz, Lomé 99.5MHz.
D.Prgr: 0455-0005. **Main N. in French:** 0600, 0700, 1000, 1100, 1230, 1600, 1900, 2200. **N. in English:** 1005, 1945 (varies 1945-2015).
ANN: "Radiodiffusion Togolaise", "Radio Togo", "Radio Lomé". **IS:** Soft tempo chime. National Anthem at s/on & s/off.

RADIO KARA (Regional station)

✉ B.P. 21, Kara ☎ +228 606060 **L.P:** Dir: Kao Pérézi. CE: Tete Anani.
Station: Kara (G.C: 01.09E/09.35N)
MW: 1503kHz 10kW.
FM: Kara 91.5MHz, Dapaong 91.9MHz, Agou 94.5MHz, Alédjo 99.3MHz, Lomé 101.5MHz.
D.Prgr: 0525-0905, 1200-1435, 1625-2105. **N. in French:** 0535, 0700, 0900, 1205, 1300, 1430, 1700, 1930, 2130, 2300.
ANN: "Radiodiffusion Kara".

Other stations:
R. Avenir, 76 Blvd. de la Kara, Quartier Doumassessé, B.P. 20183, Lomé: **FM** 104.3MHz. – **R. Carré-Jeune**, Quartier Adidogomé, B.P. 2550, Lomé: 103.1MHz. – **R. de L'Evangile** (rlg.), Lomé: **FM** 100.3MHz. – **R. Delta Santé,** Aneho: **FM** 106.1MHz. (Also rel. RFI) – **R. Evangile Jésus Vous Aime** (rlg.), Bretelle de Klimamé, B.P. 2313, Lomé **Web:** www.ramer-fm.org **FM:** Lomé 100.2MHz, Agou 104.1MHz – **R. Kanal FM,** Blvd. du 13 Janvier, Immeuble Decor, B.P. 61544, Lomé **Email:** kanalfm@cafe.tg **FM:** Lomé 93.5MHz – **R. Maria Togo** (rlg.), n°155 de la rue 158, Hédzranawoé, B.P. 30162, Lomé **Web:** www.radiomaria.org **Email:** rmariatg@ids.tg **FM:** Dapaong 88.5MHz 0.25kW, Lomé 98.8MHz, Kara 101.5MHz, Kpalimé/Sokodé 104.5MHz – **R. Missionnaire,** Quartier Tomdé Kara, B.P. 170, Kara. **Email:** emc_kara@yahoo.com **FM:** 106.3MHz. **R. Nana FM**, Angle Rues Tanou et Djossi, B.P. 6035, Lomé **Web:** www.mediatogo.org/nanafm **Email:** petdog2@yahoo.fr **FM:** 95.5MHz. Also rel. RFI – **R. Nostalgie**, B.P. 13836, Lomé **Web:** www.netcom.tg/ Nostalgie/nostalgie.html **FM:** 92.5MHz – **Océan FM,** Aneho: **FM** 93.1MHz – **R. Rurale:** Pagouda 88.9MHz, Notsè 100.1MHz, Dapaong 102.5MHz – **Sport FM,** Tokoin Habitat, B.P. 8675, Lomé: **FM** 91.9MHz **Web:** www.radiosportfm.com – **R. Tropik FM**, Quartier Wuiti, B.P. 2276, Lomé **Email:** tropikfm@nomade.fr **FM:** 93.1MHz – **R. Zion** (rlg.), Adidogomé, B.P. 13853, Lomé. **FM:** Lomé 94.3MHz, Kpalimé 102.5MHz – **Africa No 1:** Lomé 102MHz.

BBC African Sce in English/French: Lomé 97.5MHz
RFI Afrique: Lomé 91.5MHz, Aledjo 95.9MHz, Agou 98.3MHz.

TOKELAU

L.T: UTC -10hrs — **Pop:** 1,400 — **Pr.L:** Tokelauan, English — **E.C:** 50Hz, 240V — **ITU:** TOK

RADIO TOKELAU (Gov.)

✉ Public Service Office, Fakaofo, Tokelau **LP:** Acting Mgr: Aleki Silao
FM: Radio Atafu FM, Radio Fakaofo FM, Radio Nukunonu FM. All 0.005kW
D.Prgr: Tokelaun, shipping & weather info, relays of RNZI Tokelaun service

TONGA

L.T: UTC +13h — **Pop:** 104,000 — **Pr.L:** Tongan, English — **E.C:** 50Hz, 240V — **ITU:** TON

TONGA BROADCASTING COMMISSION (Independent Statutory Board, part-comm.)

✉ P.O. Box 36, Nuku'alofa ☎ +676 23295, 23555, 23556, 23863. 🖷 +676 24417
Web: www.tongabroadcasting.com **Email:** a3z-mgt@kalianet.to
L.P: Interim GM: Mrs. 'Elenoa 'Amanaki. Tech Mgr: Sioeli Maka Tohi. Radio & TV News Editor: Miss Nanise Fifita

MW: A3Z 1017kHz 10kW
FM: 90.0MHz 0.1kW (R. Tonga 2).
SW: 5030kHz 1kW (inactive).
R. Tonga 1 on 1017kHz: 1900-1100. **N. in English:** 1800 (BBC), 1900

(ABC), 0000 (ABC or RNZ), 0700 (local), 0715 (ABC).
R. Tonga 2 on 90.0MHz: 1750-1200 **ANN:** "Radio Tonga", "Kool 90 FM", "The Call of the Friendly Isles"

UCB PACIFIC PARTNERS (TGA)
✉ P O Box 478, Nuku'alofa ☎ +676 27 327 **Web:** www.pacificpartners.org **Email:** tonga@pacificpartners.org
L.P: Loni Akolo **FM:** A3R 93.1MHz 0.2kW (mostly music)
D.Prgr: Tongan & English **ANN:** "Letio Faka Kalisitani FM93 'i Tonga" **FPI:** FM sdtation on Vava'u Is

A3V MILLENIUM RADIO
✉ P. O. Box 838, Nuku'alofa ☎ +676 25 891 ℻ +676 24 195
L.P: Sam Vea, Business Manager. **F.M:** 89.1MHz

RADIO NUKU'ALOFA
✉ Pacifc Royale, Nuku'alofa. **FM:** 88.6MHz 24hr

TRINIDAD & TOBAGO

L.T: UTC -4h — **Pop:** 1.3 million — **Pr.L:** English — **E.C:** 60Hz, 115V — **ITU:** TRD

NATIONAL BROADCASTING NETWORK LTD. (Gov. Comm.)
✉ 11a Maraval Rd, PO. Box 665/610, Port of Spain. ☎ +1 868 622 4141. ℻ +1 868 628 6733. **Email:** nbnl@nbn.co.tt.
L.P: Ag. CEO: Dominic Beaubrun. Head of News: Errol Pilgrim. Mgr. (radio): Brenda de Silva.
MW: 610kHz (50kW). **FM:** 91.1/98.9/99.9/100.1MHz.
Radio 610 AM: 24h on MW. N: on the h. (BBC 2000, 0200). Wrp: on the half h – **Radio 91.1:** 91.1MHz (East Indian) – **98.9 YES FM:** 24h on 98.9MHz – **Experience 100 FM:** 24h on 99.9/100.1MHz.

TRINIDAD BROADCASTING COMPANY (Comm.)
✉ P.O. Box 716, Second Floor, Guardian Building, 22-24 St. Vincent St., Port of Spain ☎ +1 868 623 9202/3/6/7. ℻ +1 868 625 1782.
L.P: MD (radio): Brandon Khan.
MW: 730kHz (20kW). **FM:** 95.1/105.1/105.5/106.1/106.5MHz
Inspirational 7-30 AM: 24h on 730kHz. **N:** On the hr. 0600-1900 – **The Best Mix:** 24h on 95.1MHz – **The Vibe City 105:** 24h on 105.1/105.5MHz – **Sangeet:** 24h on 106.1/106.5MHz.

GEM RADIO NETWORK (Comm.)
✉ 3 A Queens Park West, Port of Spain. ☎ +1 868 625 8426. ℻ +1 868 624 3234. **L.P:** Regional GM: Cheryl Chambers.
HOTT 93 in Trinidad & Tobago on 93.1 (Tobago) & 93.5 (Port of Spain) MHz – **GEM Radio:** studios in Trinidad and transmitters in Anguilla, Antigua, Montserrat and St. Kitts – **The Wave:** studios and transmitters in St. Lucia

RADIO TAMBRIN (Comm.)
✉ 3 Picton Street, Scarborough, Tobago. ☎ +1 868 639 3437. ℻ +1 868 660 7357. **Email**: tambrin@tstt.net.tt. **Web**: www.tambrintobago.com
L.P: GM: George Leacock. SM: Garth James.
FM: 92.1MHz

W.E.F.M. (Comm.)
✉ 153 Tragarete Road, Port of Spain. ☎ +1 868 628 9696. ℻ +1 868 622 9387. **Email:** 96WEFM@96.1wefn.com.
L.P: CEO: Johnny Soong. MD: Anthony Chow. Director: Lin On. SM: Robert Dash. PD: Paul Richards.
FM: 96.1MHz. **Format:** Urban Caribbean

HCU COMMINCATIONS GROUP (Comm.)
✉ 1 Mulchan Seuchan Rd, Endeavour, Chaguanas. ☎ +1 868 665 3630. ℻ +1 868 672 1059. **Email:** bollywood@homeviewtnt.com. **Web:** www.homeviewtnt.com/masela101fm.
L.P: Chmn: Mohan Jaikaran. CEO: Marcel Mahabir. SM: Joy Mahabir.
FM: Radio Shakti: 94.1MHz – **Bollywood Masala** 101.1MHz (25kW)
Format: East Indian

C.L. COMMUNICATIONS GROUP (Comm.)
✉ Level 4, Long Circular Mall, Long Circular Road, St. James. Radio 90.5, Suite 5, Valpark Shopping Plaza, Valsayn. ☎ +1 868 622 4124. Radio 90.5: 645 8083. 103FM: 628 9222. ℻ +1 868 622 6693.
Email: radio90fm@homeviewtnt.com, radio97@wow.net, 103fm@homeviewtnt.com, radio104@tstt.net.tt.
FM: Radio 90.5: 90.5MHz (East Indian Station) – **Music Radio 9-7:** 97.1/97.9MHz – **103FM:** 103.1MHz (East Indian station) – **Ebony 104:** 104.1MHz

POWER 102 (Comm.)
✉ 88-90 Abercromby St., Port of Spain. ☎ +1 868 627 6937. **Web:** www.power102fm.com.
L.P.: MD Ingrid Isaac.
FM: 102.5MHz.

I 95.5 FM (Comm.)
✉ 20 St. Claire Rust St., Port of Spain. ☎ +1 868 628 4955. ℻ +1 868 628 0251. **Web:** www.i955fm.com.
L.P.: CEO: Louis Lee Sing. VP Programming: Anthony Lee. VP Marketing: Ian Lee Sing. VP Finance: Charlene Quamina-Vincent.
FM: 95.5/95.7MHz. **Format:** News/talk/current affairs

ISAAC 98.1 (Rlg.)
✉ 115A Woodford Street, Port of Spain ☎ +1 868 628 5454. **Email:** fbnisaac@tst.tt.
L.P.: CEO Margaret Elcock. **FM:** 98.1MHz. **Format:** Rlg./gospel

RADIO TOCO (Community Stn.)
✉ Galera Road, Toco ☎ +1 868 670 0068. **Web:** www.opus.co.tt/toco/Comms.htm **L.P:** CEO: Michael Als
FM: 106.7MHz (1.2kW). (Community Radio for NE Trinidad). Relays VoA 0200-1200

Note: In late 2004 new licenses were issued to: 91.1 Neil Iwer George, 90.1 WACK FM, 92.1 Sidewalk Radio, 94.7 VL Communications, 96.7 Q Corp. Ltd., 97.5 Upward Trend Entertainment Ltd., 99.5 21st Century Entertainment Ltd., 100.5 Wonderland Entertainment Ltd., 101.7 Heritage Communications Ltd., 103.5 United Cinemas Ltd., 104.7 PBCT Ltd., 107.1 Inner City Broadcasting Company Ltd. and 107.7 Marcel Mahabir.

TRISTAN DA CUNHA (British)

L.T: UTC — **Pop:** 313 — **Pr.L:** English — **E.C:** 50Hz, 220V — **ITU:** TRC

TRISTAN BROADCASTING SERVICE (Gov.)
✉ The Administrator, Tristan da Cunha, So. Atlantic via Cape Town, So. Africa – Dir. of Broadc: A. Swain – **FM:** 93.5MHz 0.015kW – **D.Prgr:** Mon/Wed/Fri 1630-1800, Sun 1000-1200.

TUNISIA

L.T: UTC +1h — **Pop:** 10 million — **Pr.L:** Arabic — **E.C:** 50Hz, 115/220 V — **ITU:** TUN

OFFICE NATIONAL DE LA TÉLÉDIFFUSION (ONT)
✉ B.P. 399, 1080 Tunis. **Email**: ont@ati.tn
ONT is responsible for the frequency management of radio and television.

ÉTABLISSEMENT DE LA RADIODIFFUSION-TÉLÉVISION TUNISIENNE (ERTT)
✉ 71, ave. de la Liberté, Tunis 1002 ☎+216 (1) 287300 ℻+216 (1) 785146 **Web:** www.radiotunis.com **Email:** info@radiotunis.com
L.P: DG: Abdelhafidh Herguem. Dir. R. Monastir: Abdelkader Aguir. Dir. Ext. Rel: Mokhtar Rassaâ. (The location of ERTT will change early in 2005.)

MW	kHz	kW	Prgr.	Times
Gafsa	585	350	N	0400-2400
Tunis	630	600	N	24h
Mednine	684	10-	N-	0400-2400
Remada	882	1	N	0400-2400
Tunis	963	200	I	0500 (Mon 0900)-2300
FM (MHz)	**N**	**I**	**Y**	**kW**
Ain Draham	90.3	96.6	5.6	
Biadha	95.0	101.8		40
Gorrâa	89.1	95.4		3.8
Kasserine	89.6	99.2	89.8	49
Ghraba (Sfax)	93.0	99.5	60	
Tunis	88.6	98.2	88.6	1.2
Zaghouan	94.0/92	96.5	96.5	20
Zarzis	93.9	97.2		72.5

National Network in Arabic (N): 24h. **N.** on the h – **Tunis International R. (I): French:** 0500-2300 (Sat 0500-0100). **N:** 0900 (exc. Mon), 1200, 1300, 1400, 1500, 1630, 2130. **English:** 1302-1400. **N:** 1330. **German:** 1402-1500. **N:** 1430 (local), 1435 (rel. Deutsche Welle). **Italian:** 1502-1600. **N:** 1530 - **Youth Radio (Y):** W 0500-0800, 1100-1400, 1700-2300. Sun 0500-2300.

Regional stations : R. Gafsa, Avenue Habib Bourguiba, 2100 Gafsa ☎+ 216 (6) 226461 🖷+ 216 (6) 226 260 - **FM**: 88.3, 89.2, 91.8, 93.5MHz – **R. le Kef,** Rue Mongi Slim, 7100 Le Kef. ☎+ 216 (8) 222392 🖷+ 216 (8) 222395 - **FM**: 88.2, 92.2, 96.8, 102.2MHz. – **R. Monastir,** Rue Farhat Hached, 5019 Monastir ☎+ 216 (3) 462900 🖷 + 216 (3) 460909 . - **FM**: Monastir 106.1, 90.6, Sousse 99.0MHz. – **R. Sfax,** Route de Menzel Chaker Road, 3058 Sfax ☎+ 216 (4) 240 655 🖷+ 216 (4) 245 971. - **FM**: 105.2, 106.6 MHz. – **R. Tataouine**, Cité 7 Novembre, 3263 Tataouine. - **FM**: 87.6, 89.5, 92.2, 96.6,102.6MHz.
ANN: F: "Ici Radio Tunisie Internationale"; Arabic: "Idha'atu-l-gumhuriya at-tunisiyya" **V.** by letter (Re. in E, F to Dir. Gen. des Telecommunications M. Abdessalem Slim. IRC or 1 USD is reuired).

RADIO MOSAÏQUE FM
✉ Immeuble Montplaisir, Tunis. **FM**(MHz): Tunis 94.9
Prgr mainly music. Language mostly French and English.

INTERNATIONAL SERVICES: R. Tunisia International
see International Broadcasting section

TURKEY

L.T: UTC +2h (27 Mar-30 Oct: UTC +3h) — **Pop:** 67 million — **Pr.L:** Turkish — **E.C:** 50Hz, 230V — **ITU:** TUR

HIGH COUNCIL FOR RADIO AND TELEVISION (RTÜK)
✉ Bilkent Plaza B2 Blok, 06530 Bilkent/Ankara ☎ +90 312 2975000 **Web:** www.rtuk.org.tr **Email:** rtuk@rtuk.org.tr

TÜRKIYE RADYO-TELEVIZYON KURUMU (TRT) (Turkish Radio-Television Corporation)
✉ TRT Sitesi A Blok No. 427, ORAN Ankara 06109 ☎ +90 312 4900379 🖷 +90 312 4901109 **Web:** www.trt.net.tr
Email: genel.sekreterlik@trt.net.tr
TRT Radio Dept:TRT Sitesi,Kat:9/B, OR-AN, 06109 Ankara. ☎ +90 (312) 4901797 🖷 +90 (312) 4905636.
Regional addr: TRT Ankara Radyosu, Atatürk Bulvari, Sihhiye, Ankara – TRT Istanbul Radyosu, Harbiye, Istanbul – TRT Izmir Radyosu, Kültür Parki, Izmir – TRT Çukurova Bölge Müdürlügü, 33130 Mersin – TRT Antalya Bolge Mudurlugu, Memur Evleri Tonguc Caddesi 19, 07050 Antalya – TRT Trabzon Bolge Mudurlugu, Ataturk Bulvari 70, 61200 Sogutlu-Akcabat/Trabzon – TRT Diyarbakir Bolge Mudurlugu, Istasyon Caddesi 24, 21100 Diyarbakir – TRT Erzurum Bolge Mudurlugu, Kosk Caddesi 1, 25070 Erzurum.
L.P: DG: Yücel Yener. Dep. DG (Eng.): Haluk Buran. Dep. DG (Prgr.): Bülent Varol. Dep. DG (Admin): Yalçyn Yenyaras. Dep. DG (Finance): Mehmet Bülbül. Legal Advisor: Gülen Turgut. Secr. Gen: Ayhan Karapars. Dep. Gen. Secr: Halid Ertudrul. Int. Tech. Rel: Elif Soyata Arslan.

STATIONS:
LW & MW:

Location	N	kHz	kW	Location	N	kHz	kW
Agri	4	162	1000	Catalca**	4	702	1200
Polatli*	1-R	180	1200	Gaziantep	4+R	765	600
Etimesgut*	4	198	120	Antalya	4+R	891	600
Van	4+R	225	600	Izmir	1+R	927	200
Erzurum	4+R	243	200	Trabzon	4+R	954	300
Denizli	1	558	600	Mudanya**	1+R	1017	1200
Malatya	4+R	594	600	Diyarbakir	4+R	1062	300
Çukurova	4+R	630	300				

*) Ankara,**) Istanbul. **N**=Radyo 1 & 4. R= carries Regional.prgrs.

FM-tr's in main cities:

Location	TRT-1	TRT-FM	TRT-3	TRT-4	kW
Adana	96.7	92.5	89.2		30
Ankara	93.3	88.0	91.2	105.6	30
Bursa	99.6	95.0	97.6		30
Diyarbakir	98.4	95.5	88.4		30
Eskisehir	89.0	96.8	94.4		30
Gaziantep		97.6	95.2		30
Istanbul	95.6	91.4	88.2		30
Izmir	100.5	91.2	88.0	94.7	30
Kayseri	89.4	97.2	99.2		30
Konya	96.4	95.8	92.4	98.6	30

TRT Radyo 1: 0400-2300. **Main N:** 0530, 1100, 1700, 2100. Programmes in Bosnian, Circassian, Kurdish and Arabic: 0430-0500 – **TRT-FM (TRT-2):** 24h. **N:** 0500, 0530, 0700, 0900, 1100, 1300, 1500, 1700, 2100, 2255 – **TRT Radyo 3:** 24h. **N:** 0500, 0700, 1000, 1200, 1500, 1700, 2000, 2255. **N. in English/French/German** (3 min's each): 0703, 1003, 1203, 1503, 1703, 2003. **Tourist Prgrs: English:** 1715SS. **French:** 1515SS. **German:** 2015SS – **TRT Radyo 4:** 24h on FM & 702kHz, 0400-2300 on other MW fq's – **Regional prgr's:** 180/927/1017kHz & 95.6MHz: 1115-1200. 243/630/891/954kHz: 0400-1600. **GAP (South Anatolia Project) R:** 225/594/765/1062kHz & 93.1/96.8MHz: 0400-1600 – **Tourism R:** FM-stereo prgrs in **English, French, German & Greek** for tourists at 0530-1045 & 1630-2000: Ayvalik 101.1, Ankara 100.3, Izmir/Istanbul 101.6, Alanya 88.7, Antalya 92.1/101.6, Fethiye 103.1, Marmaris/Pamukkale 101, Kapadokya 103, Kusadasi 101.9, Nevsehir 103, Bodrum 97.4, Kalkan 105.9MHz (powers 1-30kW). **N:** 0630, 0830, 1030, 1630 & 1930.
ANN: "Burasi TRT-1 (or Radio Bir), Burasi TRT-3 (or Radio Üç)."

EXTERNAL SERVICE: Voice of Turkey
See International Radio section.

PRIVATE RADIO
Main Networks

FM (MHz)	1)	2)	3)	4)	5)	6)	7)	8)
Adana	101.9	87.7	96.2		104.2	106.3	104.4	89.0
Adapazari		98.4	101.6			100.4		
Adiyaman	100.5		99.9		106.0		104.0	
Afyon	94.9		88.8	94.1	91.0	104.6		
Agri			88.8					
Akçaabat		91.4						
Akhisar							104.0	
Aksaray	99.0		92.0		98.0	97.2		
Alanya		98.4	88.8		97.5	89.9	103.8	
Amasya	101.5			103.5	106.0	106.5	104.0	
Ankara	107.4	98.3	90.0	99.9	105.0	89.8	104.0	97.7
Antalya	93.5	98.4	97.6	103.1	97.3	101.2	104.0	88.0
Ardahan			88.8		96.6			
Artvin			88.8				104.0	
Aydin	91.0		94.4	89.9	94.0		104.0	
Ayvalik							104.0	96.5
B. Çekmece	98.4							
Balikesir	88.5	95.5	106.8	89.7	105.5	97.2	104.0	98.0
Bandirma		102.0					104.0	103.4
Bartin	100.0			107.5		98.4	104.0	
Batman			89.0		105.1			
Bayburt	95.0		98.0		105.0		104.0	
Bayramiç	91.0							
Bilecik	100.0		92.4	95.0				
Bingöl	100.5		96.0	97.0	98.0			
Bitlis			88.8		105.0			
Bodrum		94.0					88.3	104.2
Bolu	107.4	98.4			103.5	89.2		97.9
Burdur	104.5		88.8	101.3	105.0	91.0		
Bursa	96.0	98.4	94.7		105.2	88.2	104.0	94.0
Büyükçekmece							104.0	
Çanakkale	105.0	98.4	88.8	105.3	103.3	105.3		97.3
Çankiri	91.1		102.5		105.0			
Çesme							103.9	98.0
Çorum	89.5		97.7	92.2	99.9	91.3		
Datça/Dalaman							104.0	
Denizli	96.8	98.4	88.8	99.0	102.8	103.2		104.2
Diyarbakir			88.8		105.1	98.0	104.0	93.0
Düzce	105.2	98.4		104.5			104.0	97.6
Edirne	91.3	89.3	104.3		104.8	103.0		95.7
Edremit		102.0					104.0	
Elazig	94.1		98.8		105.2	92.4	104.0	
Erdek							104.0	
Erdemli		98.4						
Erzincan	93.8		88.8	97.9	102.5			97.7
Erzurum	94.0		98.0	97.5	95.3	91.5	104.0	97.7
Eskisehir	92.9	97.5	91.8	91.5	93.7	106.3	104.0	96.4
Fethiye		91.5	90.5			99.0		
Gaziantep	103.0	95.6	88.8		105.0	107.0	104.0	93.3
Gebze		98.4						
Gelibolu		98.2						

FM (MHz)	1)	2)	3)	4)	5)	6)	7)	8)
Gerede								97.0
Giresun	93.0		89.6		105.0	99.2	104.0	
Gümüshane	102.0		88.8				104.0	
Göcek		98.4					103.6	
Gölcuk							104.2	
Hakkari			88.8					
Hatay	101.0		96.0	90.8	95.0		104.0	
Hereke							104.2	
Içel				93.5	102.8			
Igdir			88.8					
Inegöl							104.0	
Iskenderun						94.6	104.0	
Isparta	100.0		102.0	90.2	105.0			
Içel	105.3							
Istanbul	107.6	98.4	88.8		105.0	104.6	104.0	97.7
Izmir	96.9	98.4	105.0	106.8	88.3	101.3	104.0	91.5
Izmit							104.2	
K. Maras	94.0	91.5	97.3		90.0	98.2		
Karabük			88.0	99.0				
Karaman	103.9		88.8	99.6				
Kars			88.8					
Kastamonu			89.0	97.0	91.0		104.0	
Kayseri	88.5	96.5	92.5	103.0	104.0	106.7		88.0
Kelkit/Kemer							104.0	
Kilis			88.8	97.0	105.0			
Kirikkale	105.0		88.8					
Kirklareli	107.6		88.8		104.8			
Kirsehir	94.5							
Kocaeli	107.5	98.4	94.2		93.5	97.8		88.4
Konya	102.0	98.3	92.6	97.4	88.1	92.1	104.0	97.7
Kütahya	93.8		88.4		104.5		104.0	95.0
Kusadasi							103.9	
Malatya	96.7	96.8	105.2		106.5	104.6	104.0	91.1
Manavgat							104.0	
Manisa	103.3		99.1		89.5	101.3	104.0	
Mardin			96.5		105.1			
Marmaris		98.4					104.0	97.7
Mersin	95.1	89.4	106.8			103.0	104.0	97.3
Mugla	98.5		93.1	105.3	106.5	89.5		
Mus	97.3		96.5					
M. Kemal Pasa		98.2						
Nevsehir			98.5		105.0			
Nigde	103.0							
Oguzeli							104.0	
Ordu	92.5		102.0	92.0	105.0		104.0	
Osmaniye	101.7		95.3	104.0	93.4	99.9	104.0	
Rize	101.0		106.5		99.8		104.0	
Sakarya	107.6				105.6			104.3
Salihli/Samandagi							104.0	
Samsun	103.0	99.4	97.0	101.5	100.8	94.1	104.4	94.5
Sanliurfa			94.4		105.0	92.0		97.7
Sarayköy		98.4						
Serik							104.0	
Side							104.0	
Siirt			88.8		105.1			
Sincan		98.4						
Sinop			88.8	96.0		101.0	104.0	
Sirnak			93.0					
Sivas	100.1		93.0	90.0	105.2	91.0	104.0	
Sanliurfa	93.5			96.0			104.0	
Talas		96.5						
Tarsus							104.0	
Tekirdag	105.4	98.2	95.5	105.3	98.0			95.5
Tokat	96.5		101.0	88.3	103.0	98.0		
Torbali		98.4						
Trabzon		91.4	92.5		100.8	93.0	104.0	97.4
Usak	99.0		100.5		95.8			
Van	96.0		92.0		105.0	104.6		
Yalova		98.4	88.8				104.0	
Yesilyurt		91.1						
Yozgat	100.4		99.4		105.0	102.0		
Zonguldak	107.0		100.0	101.3	105.0			97.7

Addresses and other Information

1) Akra FM ✉ Bulgurlu Mah, Duhancý Hacý Mehmet Sk. No: 35, Kuçük Çamlýca, 34696 Üsküdar, Istanbul ☎ +90 216 3252265 🖷 +90 216 3277633 **Web:** www.akradyo.net **Email:** akradyo@akradyo.net – **2) Best FM** ✉ Eski Büyükdere Cad. No:29, Kat:8 4, Levent, 34416 Istanbul ☎ +90 212 2824921 🖷 +90 212 2804423 **Web:** www.bestfm.com.tr **Email:** teknik@bestfm.com.tr – **3) Burç FM** ✉ Camlyca Retatbey Sk. 12, 81880 Üsküdar, Istanbul ☎ +90 216 3448560 🖷 +90 216 4433176 **Web:** www.burcfm.com.tr **Email:** burcfm@burcfm.com.tr – **4) Marmara FM** ✉ Emniyet Mah, Kisikli Büyük Çamlica Cad. Dereyolu Sk. No:5 Kat:5, 81180 Kisikli Üsküdar, Istanbul ☎ +90 216 4222700 🖷 +90 216 4222752 **Web:** www.marmarafm.com **Email:** marmarafm@marmarafm.com – **5) Moral FM** ✉ Sanayi Caddesi Bilge Sokak No: 2, 34530 Yenibosna, Istanbul ☎ +90 212 6527666 🖷 +90 212 6527669 **Web:** www.moralfm.com **Email:** moralfm@moralfm.com – **6) Radyo 7** ✉ Otakçilar Cad No: 60, Eyüp, Istanbul ☎ +90 212 5675454 🖷 +90 212 5677797 **Web:** www.radyo7.com **Email:** radyo7@radyo7.com – **7) Radyo D** ✉ Ortaklar Caddesi 17, Mecidiyekoy, 80290 Istanbul ☎ +90 212 4135333 🖷 +90 212 4135350 **Web:** www.radyod.com – **8) Radyo Tatlises** ✉ Ibrahim Karaoglanoglu cad, Dilek sokak No:3, Seyrantepe, Istanbul ☎ +90 212 2830562 🖷 +90 212 2830957

VOICE OF TIGRIS (operated by the Turkish Army)
MW: 1584kHz.
D.Prgr in Kurdish/Turkish: 1200-1800.
ANN: Turkish: "Burasi Dicle'nin Sesi Radyosu", Kurdish:"Dengê Dicle".

AFN INCIRLIK AIR BASE BROADC. STATION
(operated by the US Air Force Broadc. Sce)
☎ +90 322-316-6421 **Web:** www.afrts.osd.mil
Email: AFNI@incirlik.af.mil
MW: 1593kHz. **FM:** 107.1MHz 5W.
D.Prgr: 24h in English.

TURKMENISTAN

L.T: UTC +5h — **Pop:** 4.5 million — **Pr.L:** Turkmen — **E.C:** 50Hz, 220V — **ITU:** TKM

TÜRKMEN RADIOSI (Gov.)
✉ Magtymguly köçesi 89, 744000 Asgabat. ☎ +993 12 251515. 🖷 +993 12 251421. **Email & Web:** n/a.

LW/MW	kHz	kW	Prgr.
Asgabat	279	150	1
Asgabat	576	150	2/3
Asgabat	675	150	1
Türkmenbasy	675	10	2/3
Ekarça	720	1	1
Etrek	720	1	1
Türkmenabat	927	50	1
Serhetabat	1080	5	1
(*)	1125	-	1
Syrtagta	1233	40	1
Türkmenbasy	1476	10	1

*) Unconfirmed location and power.

SW	kHz	kW	Prgr.
Asgabat	**4930	50	2/3
Asgabat	5015	20	1

**) USB with reduced carrier

FM (MHz)	Prgr 1	Prgr 2/3	kW
Asgabat	71.12	69.68	17
Asgabat	103.2	104.4	-
Balkanabat	70.28	72.02	17
Baýramaly	-	70.27	17
Dasoguz	69.32	67.22	17
Tejen	70.52	72.14	17
Türkmenabat	66.95	68.77	17
Türkmenbasy	69.23	67.19	17
Türkmenbasy	103.2	104.4	-

D.PRGR: Prgr 1 (Watan radioýaýlymy): 24h. On SW: 0000-2000. **N. English:** 1500-1515. – **Prgr 2 (Çar tarapdan radioýaýlymy):** 0100-0400, 0700-0900, 1400-1700. **N. English:** 1630-1645. – **Prgr 3 (Miras radioýaýlymy):** 0400-0700, 0900-1400, 1700-2300.

TURKS & CAICOS ISLANDS (British)

L.T: UTC -5h (3Apr-30 Oct: UTC -4h) — **Pop:** 19,000 — **Pr.L:** English — **E.C:** 60Hz, 110/220/440V — **ITU:** TCA

RADIO TURKS & CAICOS (Gov. Comm.)
✉ P.O. Box 69, Grand Turk. ☎ +1 649 946 2007. 🖷 +1 649 946 1705. **Web:** www.turksandcaicos.tc/RTC.
L.P: MD: Lynette Thomas. Head of News: Audley Astwood.

FM: 101.9 (Grand Turk/Salt Cay & South Caicos), 103.9 (North & Middle Caicos), 105.9 and 107.7MHz (Providenciales).
D.Prgr: 24h. Local prgr: 1100-0300; at other times relays country satellite station. On 105.9: "RTC".
ANN: "This is Radio Turks & Caicos on Grand Turk, Turks & Caicos Islands".

RADIO VISION CRISTIANA INTERNACIONAL (Rlg.)
North End, So. Caicos ☎ +1 809 946 3311 or 6601 ℻ +1 809 946 6600. **Web:** www.radiovision.net
L.P: Mgr: Efrain Rivera. CE: Peter Polano.
MW: So. Caicos 530kHz (100kW; reported using 40kW).
D.Prgr. in Spanish: rel. WWRV 1330, NY, USA.
ANN: "R. Visión Cristiana Internacional, transmitiendo para todo el área del Caribe, Sudamérica y la parte sur de los Estados Unidos."

CARIBBEAN CHRISTIAN RADIO (Rlg.)
Operating under license from West Indies Broadcasting Ltd.
P.O. Box 200, Grand Turk ☎℻ +1 809 946 1095 (**in USA:** Box 3, DeLand, FL 32721).
L.P: GM: Reo Stubbs. SM: Buddy Tucker. CE: Jerry Kiefer.
MW: Grand Turk 1020kHz (20kW directional; reported using 5kW).
ANN: "Super Power 1020".

WIV FM RADIO (Comm.)
WIV Building, Leeward Highway, Box 324, Providenciales ☎ +1 888 628 9391. **Web:** www.power925fm.com
L.P.: Kenny Caughlin.
FM: 90.5/92.5/93.9/99.9/101.5/102.5MHz.
Power 92.5 FM: 92.5MHz.
WIV FM Radio: Progressive 90.5, Classic Rock 93.9, Country 99.9, News 101.5, Soft Rock 102.5.
F.pl.: Stations on 90.5/93.9/99.9/101.5/102.5 will be re-launched with new names and new formats.

WDDR Radio (Comm.), Box 262, Providenciales: 88.7MHz (0.25kW).
Life Radio, Communication Network, Basden Hill, So. Caicos: 105.5MHz (0.6kW) & 107.1MHz
KIST (Rlg.), Providenciales: 106.3MHz. Grand Turk: 94.9MHz (2kW)

TUVALU

L.T: UTC +12h — **Pop:** 11,000 — **Pr.L:** English, Tuvaluan — **E.C:** 50Hz, 240V (Funafuti only) — **ITU:** TUV

RADIO TUVALU (Gov.)
Private Mail Bag, Vaiaku, Funafuti ☎ +688 20139 ℻ + 688 20732.
L.P: Broadc. & Inf. Officer: Pusinelli Laafai. Head of Tech. Sces: John Sammons.
MW: Funafuti T2U2 621kHz 5kW **FM:** 100.1MHz
D.Prgr: 24hrs **N. in English:** 1910, 0710. **ANN:** E: "This is Radio Tuvalu" **V.** by letter.

UGANDA

L.T: UTC +3h — **Pop:** 25 million — **Pr.L:** Luganda, Swahili, English — **E.C:** 50Hz, 240V — **ITU:** UGA

UGANDA BROADCASTING COUNCIL
Uganda Communications Commission, 12th Floor, Communications House, Plot 1, Colville St, P.O. Box 7367, Kampala ☎ +256 41 348830/1/5 ℻ +256 41 348832 **Web:** www.ucc.co.ug

RADIO UGANDA
Uganda Broadcasting Agency, P.O. Box 2038, Kampala ☎ +256 41 257256 ℻ + 256 41 257252 **Web:** www.uba.co.ug
L.P: Dir. of Broadc: Vacant. Commissioners: Radio Broadc: Jack Turyamwijuka. Inf. Dr. Justin Okullu-Mura. Ag. Contr. of Prgrs (Radio): Charles Byekwaso. Ag. Principal Eng. (Radio): Yona Hamala.

MW	kHz	kW	Ch.	MW	kHz	kW	Ch.
Mawagga	576	100	Blue	Kampala	909	20	Red
Kampala	639	50	Blue	Kabale	999	100	Blue
Butebo	729	100	Red	Arua	1485t	10	Blue
Bobi	810	100	Red				

t) freq. tentative

SW (G.C: Kampala 00N20 032E36)

kHz	kW	Ch.	Times
4976	10	Red	0300(SS 0345)-0600, 1300(SS 1430)-2105
5026	10	Blue	0300(SS 0345)-0600, 1300(SS 1430)-2105
7110	10	Blue	0600-1200 (SS 0600-1430)
7195	10	Red	0600-1200 (SS 0600-1430)

FM: Kampala 98MHz (Green Channel), 105.7MHz (Blue Channel).

Red Channel in English/Swahili/vernaculars: MF 0300-1200 & 1300-2105, SS 0345-2105. **N. in English:** 0400, 1000, 1700.
Blue Channel in English/vernaculars: MF 0300-1200 & 1300-2105, SS 0345-2105. **N. in English:** 0400.
Green Channel: 0300-2100 on 93.7MHz in Kampala.

Regional stations (MHz): **Kabale** 93.7, **Jinja** 95.7, **Open Gate FM,** Mbale 96.9, **Star FM** 97.3/100, **Mbarara** 97.4, **Mega FM,** Gulu: 98.6, **Fort Portal** 98.8.

ANN: E: "This is Radio Uganda, Kampala". **IS:** Local Xylophone.

Other stations:
V. of Africa, Kampala: 92.3MHz – **African R**: 104.5MHz – **Akabozi ku biri**, Kampala 87.8MHz – **All Karamoja FM,** Moroto: 94.7MHz – **R. Apac,** Media House, Biashara Str, P.O. Box 38, Apac **FM:** Apac 92.9MHz 0.4kW, Odokomit 106.5MHz 0.1kW **Web:** www.interconnection.org/radioapac – **Arua One FM,** Plot 34, Adumi Rd, P.O. Box 572, Arua: 88.7MHz 2kW – **Beat FM,** Kampala: 96.3MHz – **Buddu Broadc. Sce,** Masaka: 98.8MHz – **Bunuyoro Broadc. Sce,** Masindi: 98.2MHz – **Busoga FM,** Jinja: 96MHz – **Campus FM,** Kampala: 106.6MHz – **Capital FM,** P.O. Box 7638, Kampala **FM:** Kampala 91.3MHz, Mbale 90.9, Mbarara 88.7. Also rel. BBC African Sce. – **Central Broadc. Sce,** Bulange Mengo, P.O. Box 12760, Kampala. **FM** 88.8MHz 6kW, 89.2MHz 5kW **Web:** www.cbsfm-buganda.com – **City FM,** Kampala: 98.1MHz – **Continental FM,** Kumi: 94.7MHz – **Dembe FM,** Kampala: 90.4MHz – **Dona Miss FM,** Kampala: 103MHz – **East Africa R**: 99MHz (relay of station in Dar es Salaam, Tanzania) – **R. Hoima,** We. Uganda: 88.6MHz – **Impact FM**, Plot 849-850 Ndeeba (Near BMK), Masaka Rd, Kampala: 102.1MHz 4kW, Masaka 101.5MHz 1kW. Also rel. Christian Voice, Zambia **Web:** www.impact.fm **Email:** impactfm@dehezi.net – **Kibaale Community R:** 91.7MHz – **V. of Kigezi,** Kabale: 89.5MHz. Also rel. VOA – **Kiira FM,** Jinja: 88.6MHz – **R. Kitara,** Masindi: 101.8MHz – **R. Kyoga Veritas,** P.O. Box 641, Soroti: 91.5MHz 1kW. **Email:** socadido@yahoo.co.uk – **R. Lira:** 95.3MHz – **R. Mama,** P.O. Box 7263, Kampala: 101.7MHz **Web:** interconnection.org/umwa/community_radio.html **Email:** umwa@africaonline.co.ug – **R. Maria Uganda**, P.O. Box 9735, Kampala. **FM:** Masaka 101.8MHz 40W, Kampala 103.7MHz 40W, Fort Portal 104.6MHz, Mbarara 105.4MHz, Mbale 106.9MHz. **Web:** www.radiomaria.org **Email:** info.uga@radiomaria.org – **Mbale FM:** 90.1MHz – **Mega FM,** Gulu: 102.1MHz – **Monitor FM,** Plot 29-35, 8th Str, Industrial Area, P. O. Box 12141, Kampala: 93.3MHz **Web:** www.monitor.co.ug **Email:** info@monitor.co.ug – **Nile Broadc. Sce,** Jinja: 89.4MHz – **R. One,** Box 4589, Kampala: 90MHz. Also rel. BBC African Sce. – **Open Gate FM,** Mbale: 103.2MHz – **R. Paidha,** Nebbi, West Nile: 87.8MHz – **Power FM,** Kampala: 104.1MHz – **Prime R,** Kampala: 91.9MHz – **Rhino FM,** Lira: 96.1MHz – **Rock Mamba FM,** Tororo 106.8MHz – **R. Rukungiri:** 96.9MHz – **Sanyu FM,** Katto Plaza, Nkrumah Rd, Kampala: 88.2MHz. Also rel. VOA **Email:** sanyu@sanyufm.com – **R. Sapientia,** Kampala: 94.4MHz **Email:** socom@africaonline.co.ug – **R. Simba,** Box 31564, Kampala: 97.3MHz **Web:** www.simba.fm **Email:** feedback@simba.fm – **Spirit FM,** Mukono: 96.6MHz – **Star FM,** Kampala 100MHz – **Super FM,** Kampala 88.5MHz – **V. of Teso,** Soroti: 88.4MHz – **Top Radio,** Kampala: 89.6MHz. **Web:** www.christian-life.org/media/TOPrad.html – **V. of Toro,** Box 2203, Kampala. **FM**: Kampala 100.5MHz, Fort Portal 101MHz, Mbarara 95MHz, Mubende 97.5MHz. Also rel. VOA – **Touch FM,** Plot 115, Owen Rd, Kamwokya, Kampala: 95.9MHz 1kW **Web:** www.touch.fm **Email:** enquiries@touch.fm – **R. Unity,** Lira: 97.7MHz – **R. Wa,** Lira: 89.8MHz **Email:** cpc@infocom.co.ug – **R. West FM:** Mbarara 102.2MHz, Tooro 91MHz, Kabale & Masaka.

BBC African Sce: Kampala 101.3MHz, Mbale/Mbarara 107.3MHz in English/Swahili/Kinyarwanda.
RFI Afrique: Kampala 93.7MHz in French/English.

UKRAINE

L.T: UTC +2h (27 Mar - 30 Oct 2005: UTC +3h) — **Pop:** 51.3 million — **Pr.L:** Ukrainian, Russian — **E.C:** 50Hz, 220V — **ITU:** UKR

NATSIONALNA RADA UKRAINI ZA PYTAN TELEBACHENNIA I RADIOMOVLENNIA
(National Council for TV and Radio Broadcasting)

✉ vul. Desiatinna 14, 01025 Kyiv. ☎ +380 44 2287575. 🖷 +380 44 22874110. **Email:** tvr@i.com.ua **Web:** www.nradatvr.kiev.ua
L.P: Chmn: Borys Kholod.
NOTES: The Council is the regulatory authority for broadcasting.

NATSIONALNA RADIOKOMPANIIA UKRAINI (Gov.)

✉ vul. Khreschatyk 26, 01001 Kyiv. ☎: +380 44 2262253. 🖷 +380 44 2994225. **Email:** kolinko@nrcu.gov.ua **Web:** www.nrcu.gov.ua.
L.P: Pres: Viktor Nabrusko.

LW/MW	kHz	kW	Prgr.
Kyiv	207	500	UR1
Kyiv	549	150	UR2/3*
Oktiabrske	648	150	UR1, Reg KR
Chernivtsi	657	25	UR3, F**
Uzhhorod	675	25	UR1
Dokuchaievsk	711	50	UR1
Vinnytsia	873	4	Reg VI
Dnipropetrovsk	873	10	Reg DN
Starobilsk	936	3	UR1
Luhansk	1134	5	UR1
Dokuchaievsk	1359	50	Reg DO
Mykolaiv	1377	7	Reg MY
Verkhovyna	1584	1	UR1, Reg IF

*) UR2: 2300-0400, UR3: 0500-0600, 1700-2200. **) 1700-2200 (UR3+F)

Rg	FM (MHz)	UR1*	UR2	UR3	Reg**	kW
CH	Chernihiv	69.47	71.57	-	-	17
CH	Pryluky	71.00	72.56	-	-	17
CH	Kholmy	66.71	68.27	-	-	17
CK	Cherkasy	72.20	70.64	-	101.0	17/17/1
CK	Buky	67.88	66.32	-	-	17
CV	Chernivtsi	69.26	67.19	-	67.97	17
CV	Novodnistrovsk	69.59	68.39	-	-	17
DN	Dnipropetrovsk	68.36	66.74	-	70.37	17
DN	Kryvyi Rih	71.63	69.56	-	-	17
DN	Nikopol	69.38	-	-	-	1
DO	Donetsk	69.77	70.97	-	71.75	17
DO	Donetsk	-	-	-	101.6	1
DO	Mariupol	67.34	69.44	-	-	17
DO	Kramatorsk	69.41	67.28	-	-	17
IF	Ivano-Frankivsk	71.24	72.80	-	-	17
KA	Izium	72.08	70.46	-	-	17
KA	Kharkiv	67.13	67.91	-	69.20	17
KE	Kherson	71.90	70.04	-	100.6	17/17/5
KE	Vasylivka	69.23	67.16	-	-	17
KH	Kirovohrad	66.98	68.84	-	-	17
KM	Khmelnytskyi	67.70	70.46	-	104.6	17/17/1
KM	Kulchiivtsi	70.76	72.89	-	-	17
KM	Volochysk	68.72	-	-	-	17
KR	Kerch	71.66	70.64	-	-	17
KR	Krasnoperekopsk	66.80	68.48	-	-	17
KR	Oktiabrske	66.68	68.24	-	-	17
KR	Sevastopol	67.25	69.35	-	-	17
KR	Sovietske	72.20	70.64	-	-	17
KY	Kyiv	68.61	71.30	72.86	72.08	60
KY	Kyiv	+105.0	+105.0	-	-	1
LU	Luhansk	68.75	70.83	-	103.6	17/17/1
LU	Rovenky	67.73	69.08	-	-	17
LU	Starobilsk	69.65	71.66	-	-	17
LV	Lviv	67.04	68.99	-	-	17
MY	Mykolayiv	69.80	71.78	-	-	17
MY	Pervomaisk	69.92	68.03	-	-	17
OD	Odesa	70.52	72.14	-	-	17
OD	Izmail	72.53	69.38	-	-	1
OD	Kamianske	66.59	68.15	-	-	17
OD	Kotovsk	67.25	69.35	-	-	17
OD	Zhovten	68.99	67.07	-	-	17
PO	Krasnohorivka	66.08	68.60	-	106.8	17/17/1
RI	Antopil	66.73	67.46	-	-	17
SU	Bilopillia	66.50	68.06	-	-	17
SU	Shostka	65.93	67.45	-	-	17
SU	Trostianets	68.75	69.92	-	-	17
TE	Ternopil	69.86	71.75	-	71.03	17/17/1
VI	Vinnytsia	71.69	68.57	-	-	17
VI	Bershad	70.10	71.93	-	-	17
VO	Kovel	66.02	67.73	-	68.48	17/17/1
VO	Lutsk	71.36	72.14	-	107.3	0.1/0.1/1
ZH	Andriivka	71.90	70.04	-	71.12	17
ZH	Olevsk	69.80	71.78	-	-	17
ZH	Zhytomyr	-	-	-	103.4	1
ZK	Uzhhorod	69.53	71.54	-	-	17
ZK	Khust	70.04	71.90	-	-	17
ZK	Rakhiv	70.19	72.71	-	-	8
ZP	Zaporizhia	70.73	72.29	-	103.7	17/17/1
ZP	Komysh-Zoria	68.99	67.07	-	-	17
ZP	Melitopol	68.72	66.14	-	-	17

+ 51 tr's below 1kW. *) Carries reg prgr's (see below); **) separate reg. channels (see below); +) shared by UR1 & UR2.

D.PRGR: UR1 (Persha prohrama): 0330 (SS0400)-2300. – **UR2 (R. Promin):** 24h. – **UR3 (R. Kultura):** 0330 (SS0400)-2300 on Kyiv 549 (evening) & Kyiv 72.86MHz. On Chernivtsi 657kHz: 1700-1900, 1930-2030, 2100-2200. In Ukrainian, exc. Russian: 1400-1500.
"Radio ERA" (programmes produced by TRK "ERA"): On UR1 tr's 0455-0610, 0700-0800, 1000-1030; on UR2 tr's 0430-0700, 1000-1200, 1630-1800. See station 11) under "Other stations".
EXTERNAL SERVICE: R. Ukraine International. See International Radio section.

REGIONAL STATIONS (Gov.)

D.PRGR: (on UR1 freq's): 0445 (SS0410)-0500, 0610-0630, 1340-1400, 1610-1700, 1800-1830. Times may vary for each station. Most regional b'casting companies also run separate regional channels, cf. below. Obl. = oblast (province); ODTRK = oblasne derzhavna teleradiokompania (regional state b'casting company).
CH) Chernihivska obl: Chernihivska ODTRK, pr. Zhovtnevoi revolyutsii 62, 14001 Chernihiv. Email: chernigivodtrk@utel.net.ua. "R. Siver-Tsentr" on FM. – **CK)** Cherkaska obl: Cherkaska ODTRK, vul. B.Vishnevetskoho 35/1, 18001 Cherkasy. Channel "Prima-Radio" (vul. Khreschatyk 195, 18002 Cherkasy): 0600-1800 on 101.0MHz. – **CV)** Chernivetska obl: Chernivetska ODTRK, vul. Holovna 91, 58001 Chernivtsi. Email: chdin-au@unicom.cv.ua. Reg. prgr "R. Bukovyna" on FM. Channel "R. Bukovyna" 1100-1800 on 67.97MHz. – **DN)** Dnipropetrovska obl: Dnipropetrovska ODTRK, vul. Televiziina 3, 49010 Dnipropetrovsk. Email: dneprtrk@a-teleport.com. Reg on FM. Channel "R. Mryia": 0400-2200 on 873kHz. – **DO)** Donetska obl: Donetska OTDRK, vul. Kuibysheva 61, 83016 Donetsk. Email: beta@k61.donetsk.ua. Reg prgr "R. Donechyna" on FM & (in part) 1359kHz (Dokuchaievsk). Channel "R. Tsentr"on 71.75/101.6MHz: 0500-1700. – **IF)** Ivano-Frankivska obl: Ivano-Frankivska ODTRK, vul. Sichovykh striltsiv 30-a, 76000 Ivano-Frankivsk. Email: radio@il.if.ua. Reg prgr on FM & 1584 (Verkhovyna). – **KA)** Kharkivska obl: Kharkivska ODTRK, vul. Chernyshevskoho 22, 310000 Kharkiv. Email: oblradio@vostok.net. Reg prgr on FM. Channel "R. Kharkiv" on 69.20MHz: 0600-1300. – **KE)** Khersonska obl: Khersonska ODTRK, vul. Perekopska 10, 73000 Kherson. Email: ofis@efir.kherson.ua. Reg. prgr on FM. Channel "R.Tavria" on 100.6MHz: 0400-2200. – **KH)** Kirovohradska obl: Kirovohradska ODTRK, pl. Kirova 1, 25022 Kirovohrad. Email: teleradio@host.kr.ua. Reg prgr "R. Skifia-Tsentr" on FM. – **KM)** Khmelnytska obl: Khmelnytska ODTRK, vul. Volodymyrska 92, 29000 Khmelnytskyi. Email: tvradio@rp.km.ua. Channel "R. Podillia Tsentr" on 104.6MHz 0500-2100. – **KR)** Respublika Krym (Crimea): DTRK "Krym", vul. Studentska 14, 95610 Simferopol. Email: tv@tv.crimea.com. Reg. prgr "R. Krym" on FM & 648kHz in Ukrainian, Russian, Krymo-Tatar. – **KY)** Kyivska obl: Kyivska RDTRK, vul. Khreschatyk 5v, 01001 Kyiv. Email: rtv@sl.net.ua. Reg. prgr "Holos Kyeva" on FM. Local prgr "Studia Maidan" on 72.08MHz: 0800-1700. – **LU)** Luhanska obl: Luhanska ODTRK, vul. Demokhina 25, 91000 Luhansk. Email: lgtrk@lep.lg.ua. Reg prgr on FM. Channel "R.Puls FM" on 103.6MHz: 24h. – **LV)** Lvivska obl: Lvivska ODTRK, vul. Kniazia Romana 6, 79005 Lviv. Email: ltv@litech.lviv.ua. Reg. prgr on FM. – **MY)** Mykolaivska obl: Mykolaivska ODTRK, pr. Lenina 24-b, 54029 Mykolaiv. Email: dac@trk.aip.nikolaev.ua. Reg. prgr "Buzka khvylia" in Ukrainian, Russian on FM. Channel "R.Mykolaiv" on 1377kHz: 0500-1700. – **OD)** Odeska obl: Odeska ODTRK, vul Troitska 43-b, 270011 Odesa. Email: odtrk@farlep.net. Reg. prgr "Chornomorskyi maiak" on FM in Ukrainian & Russian, incl. Romanian Sun 1610-1700, Bulgarian/Gagauz Sun 1800-1830. – **PO)** Poltavska obl: Poltavska ODTRK "Ltava", vul. Rozy Liuksemburg 1, 36000 Poltava. Email: radio@pi.net.ua. Reg. prgr "R.Ltava" on FM. Channel "Vashe khyvlia" on 101.8(Poltava)/105.4(Kremenchuk)/106.8MHz (Krasno-horivka): 0500-2300. – **RI)** Rivnenska obl: Rivnenska ODTRK, vul. Kotliarevskoho 20-a, 33028 Rivne. Email: rodtrk@ukrwest.net. Reg. prgr

"R.Krai" on FM. – **SU)** Sumska obl: Sumska ODTRK, vul. Petropavlovska 125, 244021 Sumy. Reg. prgr on FM. – **TE)** Ternopilska obl: Ternopilska ODTRK, bul. Tarasa Shevchenka 17, 46021 Ternopil. Email: admin@odtrk.te.ua. Reg. prgr on FM. Channel "R.Lad" on 71.03MHz. – **VI)** Vinnytska obl: Vinnytska ODTRK, vul. Teatralna 15, 21100 Vinnytsia. vodtrk@vn.ukrpack.net. Reg prgr "Hovoryt Vinnytsia" on FM. Channel "R. Khvylia" on 873kHz: 0500-1000. – **VO)** Volynska obl: Volynska ODTRK, vul. Horkoho 12, 43000 Lutsk. Email: vodtrk@lutsk.ukrpack.net. Channel "R. Lutsk" on 68.48 (Kovel)/107.3MHz (Lutsk): 0500-2100. – **ZH)** Zhytomyrska obl: Zhytomyrska ODTRK, vul. Teatralna 7, 10014 Zhytomyr. Email: wave@impuls.zhitomir.ua. Reg. prgr on FM. Channel "Zhytomyrska khvylia" on 71.12/103.4MHz: 0500-2300. – **ZK)** Zakarpatska obl: Zakarpatska ODTRK, Kyivska nab. 18, 88018 Uzhhorod. Email: petry@karpaty.uzhgorod.ua. Reg. prgr on FM. – **ZP)** Zaporizska obl: Zaporizska ODTRK, vul. Matrosova 24, 69057 Zaporizhia. Email: radio@mail.zp.ua. Reg. prgr in Ukrainian, Russian on FM. Channel "Zaporizhia FM" on 103.7MHz.

OTHER STATIONS

MW	kHz	kW	Location	Station
A)	612	5	Kyiv	BBC Relay
A)	612	5	Kharkiv	BBC Relay
66)	765	75	Petrivka	R. Maiak
35)	1476	20	Sevastopol	R. Bryz

SW	kHz	kW	Location	Station
67)	11980	0.5	Zaporizhia	Dniprovska khvylia

FM	MHz	kW	Location	Station
24)	66.26	1	Lviv	Lvivska khvylia
3A)	67.61	1	Kryvyi Rih	Europa Plus Ukraina
12)	67.82	1	Lviv	R. Lux FM
17)	68.36	5	Odesa	NART-Radio
15)	68.36	1	Makiivka	R. Shanson
4)	69.02	1	Kyiv	GALA-Radio
46)	69.83	1	Kharkiv	R. Nova khvylia
17)	70.37	2	Dnipropetrovsk*	NART-Radio
17)	70.40	1	Kyiv	NART-Radio
35)	72.02	4	Sevastopol	R. Bryz
13)	72.35	4	Chernihiv	R. Melodia
49)	73.64	1	Kyiv	R. Renesans
17)	73.79	1	Kharkiv	NART-Radio
28)	88.5	1	Dnipropetrovsk*	Music R.
11)	88.6	1	Lviv	R. Era FM
47)	90.2	1	Odesa	R. Nova khvylia 90.2FM
26)	90.9	1	Dnipropetrovsk	M-FM
4)	91.0	1	Odesa	GALA-Radio
11)	91.1	1	Simferopol	R. Era FM
65)	91.1	1	Lviv	RadioMan
8)	91.3	1	Vinnytsia*	R. Sharmanka
1)	91.4	1	Odesa	Avto FM-Star FM
23)	95.2	1	Kyiv	Love R.
3A)	95.6	5	Kyiv	Europa Plus Ukraina
11)	96.0	2	Kyiv	R. Era FM
5)	96.4	2	Kyiv	Hit FM Ukraina
49)	96.8	2	Kyiv	R. Renesans
41)	98.0	1	Kyiv	R. Kyiv
16)	98.5	2	Kyiv	Russkoye R. Ukraina
33)	99.0	2	Kyiv	R. Nostalgie 99FM
8)	99.4	1	Donetsk	R. Sharmanka
1)	99.4	2	Kyiv	Avto FM-Star FM
12)	100.0	1	Donetsk	R. Lux FM
4)	100.0	5	Kyiv	GALA-Radio
1)	100.1	1	Mykolaiv	Avto FM-Star FM
4)	100.2	4	Kryvyi Rih	GALA-Radio
4)	100.3	1	Zaporizhia	GALA-Radio
10)	100.3	1	Vinnytsia	Avtoradio-Ukraina
10)	100.4	1	Odesa	Avtoradio-Ukraina
14)	100.4	1	Ivano-Frankivsk	R. NIKO FM
16)	100.4	1	Luhansk	Russkoye R. Ukraina
25)	100.5	1	Donetsk	Mega-Radio
12)	100.5	2	Dnipropetrovsk	R. Lux FM
18)	100.5	2	Kyiv	Narodne Radio
13)	100.6	1	Simferopol	R. Melodia
10)	100.6	1	Chernihiv	Avtoradio-Ukraina
7)	100.7	1	Rivne	Nashe R.
61)	100.8	1	Zaporizhia	R. Univers
24)	100.8	1	Lviv	Lvivska khvylia
5)	100.8	1	Mariupol	Hit FM Ukraina
14)	100.9	1	Vinnytsia	R. NIKO FM
14)	100.9	1	Lutsk	R. NIKO FM
15)	101.0	1	Kryvyi Rih	R. Shanson
5)	101.0	1	Odesa	Hit FM Ukraina
3A)	101.1	1	Kharkiv	Europa Plus Ukraina
16)	101.1	1	Dnipropetrovsk	Russkoye R. Ukraina
13)	101.1	3	Kyiv	R. Melodia
5)	101.2	1	Donetsk	Hit FM Ukraina
2)	101.2	1	Kherson	Dorosle R.
12)	101.3	1	Poltava	R. Lux FM
13)	101.4	1	Rivne	R. Melodia
57)	101.4	1	Sumy	R. SveSweet
29)	101.5	3	Kyiv	Music-Radio 101FM
13)	101.5	1	Dnipropetrovsk	R. Melodia
14)	101.5	1	Ternopil	R. NIKO FM
16)	101.5	1	Krasnohorivka	Russkoye R. Ukraina
12)	101.5	1	Kharkiv	R. Lux FM
14)	101.6	1	Cherkasy	R. NIKO FM
3A)	101.7	1	Kramatorsk	Europa Plus Ukraina
16)	101.7	1	Khmelnytskyi	Russkoye R. Ukraina
6)	101.8	1	Odesa	Kiss FM
62)	101.8	1	Zaporizhia	R. Velykyi Luh
10)	101.8	1	Luhansk	Avtoradio-Ukraina
12)	101.9	1	Kherson	R. Lux FM
15)	101.9	2	Kyiv	R. Shanson
35)	102.0	1	Sevastopol	R. Bryz
5)	102.0	2	Dnipropetrovsk	Hit FM Ukraina
6)	102.1	1	Mykolaiv	Kiss FM
14)	102.1	1	Khmelnytskyi	R. NIKO FM
15)	102.1	1	Donetsk	R. Shanson
37)	102.2	2	Odesa	R. Fil
5)	102.3	1	Poltava	Hit FM Ukraina
63)	102.3	1	Luhansk	R. Voiazh
4)	102.4	1	Uzhhorod	GALA-Radio
6)	102.4	1	Kharkiv	Kiss FM
5)	102.5	1	Kherson*	Hit FM Ukraina
9)	102.5	2	Kyiv	Prosto R.
36)	102.5	1	Tokmak	R. Nostalgie Zaporizhia
13)	102.5	1	Khmelnytskyi	R. Melodia
3A)	102.5	1	Dnipropetrovsk	Europa Plus Ukraina
14)	102.5	4	Lviv	R. NIKO FM
13)	102.6	1	Donetsk	R. Melodia
39)	102.7	1	Odesa	R. Harmonia Svitu
7)	102.7	4	Kryvyi Rih	Nashe R.
7)	102.7	1	Zhytomyr	Nashe R.
13)	102.7	1	Kovel	R. Melodia
10)	102.8	1	Sevastopol	Avtoradio-Ukraina
7)	102.8	1	Mykolaiv	Nashe R.
2)	102.8	1.3	Mariupol	Dorosle R.
7)	102.9	3	Dnipropetrovsk	Nashe R.
14)	103.0	1	Rivne	R. NIKO FM
13)	103.0	1	Kharkiv	R. Melodia
8)	103.0	1	Ivano-Frankivsk	R. Sharmanka
12)	103.1	5	Kyiv	R. Lux FM
3A)	103.1	1	Kherson	Europa Plus Ukraina
7)	103.1	1	Khmelnytskyi	Nashe R.
14)	103.2	1	Kryvyi Rih	R. NIKO FM
18)	103.2	1	Odesa	Narodne Radio
13)	103.2	1	Melitopol	R. Melodia
22)	103.3	1	Dnipropetrovsk	Klasyk Radio
5)	103.4	1	Sumy	Hit FM Ukraina
59)	103.5	1	Ternopil	R. TON
7)	103.5	1	Kremenchuk	Nashe R.
15)	103.6	1	Khmelnytskyi	R. Shanson
50)	103.6	2	Kyiv	R. ROKS Ukraina
8)	103.6	2	Kryvyi Rih	R. Sharmanka
16)	103.7	1	Cherkasy	Russkoye R. Ukraina
5)	103.7	1	Rivne	Hit FM Ukraina
3A)	103.7	1	Simferopol	Europa Plus Ukraina
11)	103.7	1	Kherson	R. Era FM
16)	103.8	1	Kirovohrad*	Russkoye R. Ukraina
27)	103.8	5	Odesa	Moye Radio
12)	103.8	1	Ivano-Frankivsk	R. Lux FM
5)	103.8	1	Zarichne*	Hit FM Ukraina
7)	103.8	1	Poltava	Nashe R.
1)	103.9	1	Lviv	Avto FM-Star FM
15)	103.9	1	Kramatorsk	R. Shanson
16)	103.9	1	Kremenchuk	Russkoye R. Ukraina
14)	103.9	1	Kovel	R. NIKO FM
5)	104.0	1	Luhansk	Hit FM Ukraina
3A)	104.0	1	Mariupol	Europa Plus Ukraina
2)	104.0	2	Kharkiv	Dorosle R.
8)	104.0	2	Kyiv	R. Sharmanka
8)	104.0	1	Dnipropetrovsk	R. Sharmanka
26)	104.1	1	Donetsk	M-FM
12)	104.2	1	Simferopol	R. Lux FM

FM	MHz	kW	Location	Station
20)	104.3	2	Odesa	Armianske R.
26)	104.3	1	Lviv	M-FM
7)	104.3	1	Chernihiv	Nashe R.
43)	104.4	1	Dniprodzerzhynsk	R. MiKomp
13)	104.4	1	Kherson	R. Melodia
16)	104.5	1	Zaporizhia	Russkoye R. Ukraina
7)	104.5	5	Kharkiv	Nashe R.
12)	104.5	1	Ternopol	R. Lux FM
16)	104.5	2	Sevastopol	Russkoye R. Ukraina
64)	104.5	1	Zhytomyr	Radioklub 104.5FM
32)	104.6	2	Kyiv	R. Apelsyn 104.6FM
9)	104.6	1	Mykolaiv	Prosto R.
12)	104.7	1	Lviv	R. Lux FM
16)	104.7	1	Donetsk	Russkoye R. Ukraina
13)	104.7	1	Kryvyi Rih	R. Melodia
5)	104.7	1	Chernihiv	Hit FM Ukraina
3A)	104.8	1	Luhansk	Europa Plus Ukraina
10)	104.8	1	Dnipropetrovsk	Avtoradio-Ukraina
7)	104.8	1	Lutsk	Nashe R.
16)	104.8	1	Kherson	Russkoye R. Ukraina
34)	104.8	1	Simferopol	R. Asol
12)	104.9	1	Zarichne*	R. Lux FM
16)	104.9	1	Odesa	Russkoye R. Ukraina
14)	105.0	1	Chernivtsi	R. NIKO FM
13)	105.0	1	Poltava	R. Melodia
15)	105.1	1	Zaporizhia	R. Shanson
13)	105.1	1	Mykolaiv	R. Melodia
13)	105.1	1	Sumy	R. Melodia
54)	105.1	4	Donetsk	R. Sport FM
2)	105.2	1	Kryvyi Rih	Dorosle R.
12)	105.2	1	Uzhhorod	R. Lux FM
16)	105.3	1	Mariupol	Russkoye R. Ukraina
9)	105.3	3	Odesa	Prosto R.
56)	105.3	1	Severodonetsk	R. STV
15)	105.3	1	Dnipropetrovsk	R. Shanson
2)	105.4	1	Simferopol	Dorosle R.
3A)	105.4	1	Khmelnytskyi	Europa Plus Ukraina
10)	105.4	1	Lviv	Avtoradio-Ukraina
55)	105.5	2	Kyiv	R. Stolytsia
13)	105.5	1	Lutsk	R. Melodia
52)	105.5	1	Luhansk	R. Shanson Luhansk
16)	105.6	1	Sumy	Russkoye R. Ukraina
10)	105.6	1	Kherson	Avtoradio-Ukraina
14)	105.6	1	Zhytomyr	R. NIKO FM
5)	105.6	1	Krasnohorivka	Hit FM Ukraina
16)	105.7	1	Kharkiv	Russkoye R. Ukraina
12)	105.7	1	Kramatorsk	R. Lux FM
40)	105.8	1	Poltava	R. Kvadrat FM
19)	105.8	2	Dnipropetrovsk	Avtoradio-Dnipro
26)	105.8	1	Kirovohrad	M-FM
16)	105.8	1	Yalta	Russkoye R. Ukraina
12)	105.8	1	Mariupol	R. Lux FM
16)	105.9	1	Kryvyi Rih	Russkoye R. Ukraina
10)	106.0	1	Donetsk	Avtoradio-Ukraina
48)	106.0	1	Odesa	R. Odesa-Mama
2)	106.0	2	Kyiv	Dorosle R.
7)	106.0	1	Lviv	Nashe R.
21)	106.0	1	Berdiansk	Azovska khvylia 106.4FM
12)	106.1	1	Cherkasy	R. Lux FM
58)	106.1	1	Ternopil	R. Ternopil 106FM
10)	106.1	1	Kharkiv	Avtoradio-Ukraina
7)	106.1	1	Luhansk	Nashe R.
3A)	106.2	1	Zaporizhia	Europa Plus Ukraina
12)	106.2	1	Kharkiv	R. Lux FM
7)	106.2	1	Kherson	Nashe R.
6)	106.3	1	Melitopol	Kiss FM
14)	106.4	1	Mykolaiv	R. NIKO FM
10)	106.4	1	Ivano-Frankivsk	Avtoradio-Ukraina
60)	106.4	2	Rivne	R. Trek
7)	106.4	1	Vinnytsia	Nashe R.
4)	106.5	1	Luhansk	GALA-Radio
7)	106.5	1	Mariupol	Nashe R.
6)	106.5	2	Kyiv	Kiss FM
42)	106.6	1	Simferopol	R. Lider
5)	106.6	1	Zaporizhia	Hit FM Ukraina
38)	106.6	2	Odesa	R. Glas
15)	106.6	1	Kharkiv	R. Shanson
13)	106.7	1	Kirovohrad	R. Melodia
45)	106.7	1	Lviv	R. Nezalezhnist
6)	106.8	1	Chernihiv	Kiss FM
6)	106.8	3	Dnipropetrovsk	Kiss FM
51)	106.8	1	Kolomyia	R. Saivo
12)	106.8	1	Poltava	R. Lux FM
3A)	106.8	5	Donetsk	Europa Plus Ukraina
5)	106.9	1	Kryvyi Rih	Hit FM Ukraina
53)	106.9	1	Luhansk	R. Skyway
12)	106.9	1	Lutsk	R. Lux FM
2)	107.0	1	Zaporizhia	Dorosle R.
11)	107.0	1	Kharkiv	R. Era FM
5)	107.0	1	Sevastopol	Hit FM Ukraina
2)	107.0	1	Sumy	Dorosle R.
3B)	107.0	2	Kyiv	Europa FM
13)	107.1	1	Zarichne*	R. Melodia
12)	107.1	1	Mykolaiv	R. Lux FM
11)	107.1	1	Luhansk	R. Era FM
8)	107.1	1	Cherkasy	R. Sharmanka
5)	107.1	2	Khmelnytskyi	Hit FM Ukraina
16)	107.2	1	Chernihiv	Russkoye R. Ukraina
4)	107.2	1	Donetsk	GALA-Radio
13)	107.2	1	Lviv	R. Melodia
14)	107.2	1	Uzhhorod	R. NIKO FM
44)	107.3	1	Dnipropetrovsk	R. Mix
10)	107.4	2.5	Kyiv	Avtoradio-Ukraina
4)	107.4	1	Kharkiv	GALA-Radio
3A)	107.4	1	Odesa	Europa Plus Ukraina
11)	107.4	1	Ternopol	R. Era FM
36)	107.5	1	Zaporizhia	R. Nostalgie Zaporizhia
7)	107.6	1	Donetsk	Nashe R.
31)	107.6	1	Kherson	R. 107.6FM
2)	107.7	1	Dnipropetrovsk	Dorosle R.
30)	107.7	1	Chernihiv	R. Unison plius
12)	107.7	1	Zhytomyr	R. Lux FM
4)	107.8	1	Simferopol	GALA-Radio
11)	107.8	1	Mykolaiv	R. Era FM
11)	107.8	1	Vinnytsia	R. Era FM
7)	107.9	1	Kirovohrad	Nashe R.
10)	107.9	1	Sumy	Avtoradio-Ukraina
13)	107.9	1	Zaporizhia	R. Melodia
7)	107.9	5	Kyiv	Nashe R.
7)	107.9	2	Odesa	Nashe R.

NB. Tr's less than 1kW not mentioned. *) Under preparation

Addresses & other information:

1) pl. 10-ho Kvitnia 1, 65009 Odesa. Email: office@starfm.com.ua – **2)** Chervonozorianyi pr. 10, 03037 Kiev. Email: info@vzrosloe.com.ua – **3A,B)** vul. Holosiivska 7, 01039 Kyiv. Email: europa@europaplus.kiev.ua – **4)** P.O.Box 22, 01032 Kyiv. Email: fm100@galaradio.com – **5)** bul. T.Shevchenka 54/1, 01032 Kyiv. Email: radio@hitfm.ua – **6)** bul. T.Shevchenka 54/1, 01032 Kyiv. Email: radio@kissfm.com.ua – **7)** vul. Nahirna 24/1, 04107 Kyiv. Email: radio@nashe.ua – **8)** bul. T.Shevchenka 54/1, 01032 Kyiv. Email: radio@sharmanka.com.ua – **9)** vul. Tereshkovoi 15, 65076 Odesa Email: advertis@prosto.odessa.ua – **10)** P.O. Box 42, 03113 Kyiv. Email: igor.larin@avtoradio.ua – **11)** bul. Verkhovnoy Rady 20, 02100 Kyiv. Email: info@radioera.com.ua – **12)** vul. Tarasivska 9, 01033 Kyiv. Email: radio@lux.fm – **13)** vul. Marshala Timoshenka 2, 04212 Kyiv. Email: radio@melodiya.ua – **14)** vul. Holovna 36, 58000 Chernivtsi. Email: nikofm@nbm.cv.ua – **15)** bul. T.Shevchenka 54/1, 01032 Kyiv. Email: radio@shanson.ua – **16)** bul. T.Shevchenka 54/1, 01032 Kyiv. Email: radio@rusradio.com.ua – **17)** Kyiv. – **18)** bul. Lesi Ukrainki 34, 01133 Kiev. Email: advertis@narodnoeradio.com.ua **19)** pr. Kirova 111b, 49000 Dnipropetrovsk. Email: office@ard.dp.ua – **20)** vul. Mala Arnautska 107, 65007 Odesa. Email: armenia@radio.odessa.ua – **21)** Melitopolska shose 20, 71100 Berdiansk. Email: radio106@gobius.com – **22)** vul. Cheliuskina 1, 49070 Dnipropetrovsk. Email: master@rclassic.dp.ua – **23)** Kyiv. Email: info@loveradio.com.ua – **24)** P.O. Box 9751, 79013 Lviv. Email: lwr@lwr.com.ua – **25)** pr. Illicha 100, 83052 Donetsk. Email: reklama@megaradio.donetsk.ua – **26)** vul. Artema 145a, 83015 Donetsk. Email: mfm@rr.com.ua – **27)** vul. Artyleriyska 1, 65039 Odesa. Email: trav-ka@art.odessa.ua – **28)** Dnipropetrovsk. – **29)** vul. Dorozhytska 10, 01000 Kyiv. Email: inf@musicradio.kiev.ua – **30)** Chernihiv. Email: unison@ok.net.ua – **31)** park Leninskoho Komsomolu, 73000 Kherson. Email: radio@stylefm.kherson.ua – **32)** vul. Pavlivska 29, 01135 Kiev. Email: info@radioapelsin.com.ua – **33)** Kyiv. Email: info@radio-nostal-gie.fm – **34)** vul. Haharina 5, 95026 Simferopol. Email: assol@cris.crimea.ua – **35)** P.O.Box 140, 90011 Savastopol. Email: briz@a-teleport.com – **36)** vul. Serova 12, 69000 Zaporizhia. Email: info@fm.zp.ua – **37)** vul. Kanatna 83, 65107 Odesa. Email: office@radiofil.com.ua – **38)** vul. Kanatna 83, 65107 Odesa. Email: glas@glas.odessa.ua – **39)** vul. Kanatna 98, 65100 Odesa. Email: garmonia@garmoniamira.com.ua – **40)** Poltava. Email: europa@kfm.poltava.ua – **41)** vul. Volodymyrska 70, 01033 Kyiv. Email: info@radio.kiev.fm – **42)** vul. Balaklavska 68, 95048 Simferopol. Email: radio@lider.crimea.com – **43)** Komsomolskyi pr. 15a,

51900 Dniprodzerzhynsk. Email: radio@micomp.dp.ua – **44)** per. Shevchenka 3, 49000 Dnipropetrovsk. Email: office@rmix.dp.ua – **45)** vul. Kn. Romana 12, 79000 Lviv. Email: radio-n@lv.ukrtel.net – **46)** Kharkiv. Email: nw@radioartel.com – **47)** Odesa. – **48)** vul. Mala Arnautska 107, 65007 Odesa. Email: mama@odessa.fm – **49)** bul. T.Shevchenka 54/1, 01032 Kyiv. Email: radio@jazz.com.ua – **50)** vul. Khreschatyk 2, 01001 Kyiv. Email: radio@rocks.com.ua – **51)** Kolomyia. Email: vade@sat.ko.if.ua – **52)** vul. Demokhina 27/62, Luhansk. Email: echo@lep.lg.ua – **53)** vul. Demokhina 25, 91016 Luhansk. Email: skynews@skyway.lg.ua – **54)** vul. Kuybysheva 67, 83000 Donetsk. Email sportfm@skif.net – **55)** vul. Shampylo 23, 04112 Kyiv. Email: efir@radio1055.fm – **56)** vul. Haharina 93, 93400 Severodonetsk. Email: info@stv.lg.ua – **57)** vul. Kirova 25, 40030 Sumy. Email: reclama@vsesweet.com – **58)** vul. Kulchytskoi 3/5, 46001 Ternopil. Email: reklama@rt.ssft.net – **59)** bul. T.Shevchenka 5, 46001 Ternopil. Email: mail@radio-ton.te.ua – **60)** vul. 16-ho Lypnia 38, 33000 Rivne. Email: reklama@radiotrek.rv.ua – **61)** vul. Zhukovskoho 66, 69600 Zaporizhia. Email: radio@zsu.zp.ua – **62)** vul. Matrosova 8a, 69057 Zaporizhia. Email: radio@vlug.zp.ua – **63)** kv. Dymytrova 20, 91009 Luhansk. Email: voyage@lep.lg.ua – **64)** Zhytomyr. Email: club104@com.zt.ua – **65)** Lviv. Email: radioman@lviv.farlep.net – **66)** vul. Mala Arnautska 107, 65007 Odesa. 0300-1900 in Ukrainian, Russian: 0400-2200. Email: mayak@radio.odessa.ua – **67)** Zaporizhia. Sat/Sun 0630-1030 (times vary), mainly relays UR prgr's. – **A)** Rel. BBC (cf. UK).

UNITED ARAB EMIRATES

L.T: UTC +4h — **Pop:** 2.4 million — **Pr.L:** Arabic — **E.C:** 50Hz, 220V — **ITU:** UAE

MINISTRY OF INFORMATION & CULTURE
✉ P.O. Box 17, Abu Dhabi ☎ +971 2 4453000 🖷 +971 2 4452504 **Web:** www.uaeinteract.com **Email:** mininfex@emirates.net.ae

EMIRATES MEDIA
✉ P.O. Box 63, Abu Dhabi ☎ +971 2 4455555 🖷 +971 2 451155 **Web:** www.emi.ae **Email:** adradio@emi.co.ae
L.P: DG: Abdul Wahab al Radhwan. Contr. of Prgrs: Abdul Hadi al Mobarak. CE: Rushdi Hattab. Dir. Foreign Prgrs: Ms. Aida Hamza.

MW	kHz	kW	Prgr.	Times
Sadiyat	729	750	M	0200-2210
Maqtaa	810	50	Q	24 hrs
Al Ain	828	1	M	0200-2210
Al-Dhabbiya	1539v	60	M	0200-2210

Prgrs: M) Main prgr; Q) Holy Quran.

FM: 88.6/94.8/96.7/98/99.3/100.4/104/106MHz.
Main Prgr in Arabic: 0200-2210 on MW & FM. **N:** 0630, 0930, 1230, 1400, 1430.
Holy Quran Sce: 24h on 88.6/94.8/98.0/98.9MHz; 810kHz.
Emirates FM1 in English: 100.4/104MHz.
Emirates FM2 in English: 96.7/99.3/106MHz.
ANN: A: "Idha'atu-l-imarat min Abu Zabiy". E: "Radio One/Two".

EMIRATES RADIO
✉ P.O. Box 1695, Dubai ☎ +971 4 3077302 🖷 +971 4 3373480 **Web:** www.dubaitv.gov.ae **Email:** radio@dubaitv.gov.ae
L.P: Ag. DG: Ahmed Saeed al Gaoud. Contr. Radio: Hassan Ahmed. Contr. of Eng: Abdul Rehman Al Ali.
MW: Dubai

kHz	kW	kHz	kW	kHz	kW
1107	10	1251	50	1476	1500

Arabic AM on MW: 0215-2050.
ANN: A: "Idha'at al-Imarat min Dubai".

RAS AL KHAIMAH BROADCASTING STATION
✉ P.O. Box 141, Ras al Khaimah ☎ +971 7 851151 🖷 +971 7 353441 **MW:** 1152kHz 200kW **FM:** 95.3MHz.
D.Prgr: 0200-2100. **Arabic** exc. **Urdu:** 0830-1000, **Malayalam:** 1000-1100.
ANN: A: "Idha'atu l-Imarat al-Arabiyya al-Muttahhida min Ras al Khaimah".

UMM AL QUWAIN BROADCASTING STATION
✉ Shamal Media Services, P.O. Box 1106, Umm al Quwain ☎ +971 6 5657106 🖷 +971 6 5651806 **Web:** www.shamal.net
UAQ Radio: MW 846kHz 20kW **D.Prgr:** 0200-1900 in Malayalam, Hindi, Filipino. **Web:** www.uaqradio.com
UAQ FM: 97.8MHz in Arabic. **Web:** www.uaqfm.com
HUM FM: 106.2MHz in Hindi/Urdu. **Web:** www.humfm.com
Email: info@humfm.com

RADIO ASIA
✉ P.O. Box 8588, Dubai ☎ +971 4 3491011 🖷 +971 4 342 1387
L.P: GM: Brij Bhalla. **Email:** drsrak@emirates.net.ae
MW: Ras al Khaimah 1575kHz 100kW. **D.Prgr:** 24h in Malayalam.
ANN: "15-75 AM Radio Asia".

ASIANET RADIO
✉ Dubai Media City, Dubai ☎ +971 4 3914151 🖷 +971 4 3918044 **Web:** www.asianetglobal.com **Email:** asianet@emirates.net.ae
L.P: Mgr: Joseph Francis.
FM: Dubai 94.8MHz. **D.Prgr:** 24h in Malayalam.

CHANNEL 4 RADIO NETWORK
✉ P.O. Box 442, Ajman ☎ +971 6 7461444 🖷 +971 6 7461344
R. 4 FM on 89.1MHz in Hindi/English. **Web:** www.radio4fm.com **Email:** info@radio4fm.com
Channel 4 FM on 104.8MHz in English. **Web:** www.channel4fm. com **Email:** info@channel4fm.com **L.P:** Prgr. Controller: Peter Gowers.
Al Rabea FM on 107.8MHz in Arabic. **Web:** www.1078fm.com **Email:** info@1078fm.com

SOWT AL-ASALA/DUBAI 92
(joint project of Emirates Radio and Arabia Radio Network)
FM: Sowt al-Asala 93.9MHz in Arabic. Dubai 92MHz in English.

ARABIAN RADIO NETWORK (ARN)
✉ P.O. Box 502012, Media City 103, Dubai ☎ +971 4 3912000 🖷 +971 4 3912007 **Web:** www.arnonline.com **Email:** admin@arnon-line.com **L.P:** MD: Abdel Latif Al Sayegh.
Al-Arabiya FM: 98.9MHz in Arabic. **Al-Khaleejiya:** 100.9MHz in Arabic. **Dubai Eye:** English 103.8MHz, Arabic 104.4MHz. **Hit FM:** 96.7MHz in Malayalam. **City FM:** 101.6MHz in Hindi.

MIDDLE EAST BROADCASTING CORPORATION (MBC)
✉ Dubai Media City, Dubai 🖷 +971 4 3916683 **Web:** www.mbcfm.fm **Email:** contactus@mbcfm.fm
FM: Dubai freq. not known, Abu Dhabi 98.1MHz. Transmitters also in Bahrain, Jordan, Kuwait, Qatar, Saudi Arabia and Palestine West Bank. **F.PI:** more transmitters in other Arabic countries.

BBG:
R. Sawa: FM: Dubai 90.5MHz, Abu Dhabi 98.7MHz.
R. Farda: MW: Al-Dhabbiya 1170kHz 800kW 24h.
For more details see main entry in Interational Radio section.
F.PI: 800kW transmitter on MW.

BBC World Sce: Abu Dhabi 90.3MHz, Dubai 87.9MHz. MW: Al-Dhabbiya 1314kHz 1000kW 24h. See International Radio section.

Relays via Al-Dhabbiya on shortwave & Emirates Radio shortwave transmissions: see International Radio section.

UNITED KINGDOM

L.T: UTC (27 Mar–30 Oct: UTC +1h) — **Pop:** 59 million — **Pr.L:** English — **E.C:** 50Hz, 230V — **ITU:** G

CROWN DEPENDENCIES
Note: The Channel Islands and the Isle of Man are dependencies of the British Crown and are not part of the United Kingdom. They are included here for editorial convenience.

THE BRITISH BROADCASTING CORPORATION (Pub.)
The BBC is an independent body created by Royal Charter and operates under licence
✉ Broadcasting House, London W1A 1AA ☎ +44 20 7580 4468 🖷 +44 20 8749 7554. **Web:** www.bbc.co.uk
LP: Chairman: Michael Grade; DG: Mark Thompson; Deputy DG: Mark Byford; Dir Radio & Music: Jenny Abramsky; Dir TV: Jana Bennett; Dir BBC People: Stephen Dando; Dir Strategy & Distribution: Carolyn Fairbairn; Dir New Media & Technology: Ashley Highfield; A/Dir Marketing & Communications: Genevieve Lawrence; CEO: John Smith.

LW/MW

Radio 4	kHz	kW	Radio 4	kHz	kW
Burghead	198	50	Newcastle	603	2
Droitwich	198	500	Lisnagarvey	720	10
Westerglen	198	50	Crystal Palace	720	0.75

Radio 4	kHz	kW	Radio 4	kHz	kW
Londonderry	720	0.25	Plymouth	774	1
Redruth	756	2	Redmoss	1449	2
Enniskillen	774	1	Carlisle	1485	1
Radio 5 Live	**kHz**	**kW**	**Radio 5 Live**	**kHz**	**kW**
Barrow	693	1	Clevedon	909	50
Bexhill	693	1	Exeter	909	1
Brighton	693	1	Fareham	909	1
Burghead	693	25	Lisnagarvey	909	10
Droitwich	693	150	Londonderry	909	1
Enniskillen	693	1	Bournemouth	909	0.25
Folkestone	693	1	Moorside Edge	909	200
Postwick	693	10	Redruth	909	2
Redmoss	693	1	Westerglen	909	50
Stagshaw	693	50	Whitehaven	909	1
Start Point	693	50	Tywyn	990	1
Brookmans Park	909	150			

FM (all stereo)

England, Isle of Man, Channel Isl.	R1	R2	R3	R4	kW
Barnstaple	98.1	88.5	90.7	92.9	1
Beacon Hill	98.4	88.7	90.9	93.1	1
Belmont	98.3	88.8	90.9	93.1	16
Bilsdale	98.6	89.0	91.2	93.4	5
Bow Brickhill	98.2	88.6	90.8	93.0	10
Bristol	98.9	89.3	91.5	93.7	1.3
Chatton	99.7	90.1	92.3	94.5	5.6
Crystal Palace	98.5	88.8	91.0	93.2	4
Douglas (I.O.M.)	98.0	88.4	90.6	92.8	11
Guildford	97.7	88.1	90.3	92.5	3
Caversham	99.4	89.8	92.0	94.2	1
Holme Moss	98.9	89.3	91.5	93.7	250
Keighley	98.5	88.9	91.1	93.3	1
Les Platons (C.I.)	97.1	89.6	91.1	94.8	16
Manningtree	97.7	88.1	90.3	92.5	3
Morecambe Bay	99.6	90.0	92.2	94.4	10
North Hessary Tor	97.7	88.1	90.3	92.5	160
Oxford	99.1	89.5	91.7	93.9	46
Pendle Forest	97.8	90.2	92.6	94.6	1
Peterborough	99.7	90.1	92.3	94.5	40
Pontop Pike	98.1	88.5	90.7	92.9	134
Redruth	99.3	89.7	91.9	94.1	25
Ridge Hill	98.2	88.6	90.8	93.0	10
Rowridge	98.2	88.5	90.7	92.9	250
Sandale	97.7	88.1	90.3	92.5	250
Stanton Moor	99.4	89.8	92.0	94.2	1.2
Sutton Coldfield	97.9	88.3	90.5	92.7	250
Swingate (Dover)	99.5	90.0	92.4	94.4	11
Tacolneston	99.3	89.7	91.9	94.1	250
Winter Hill	98.2	88.6	90.8	93.0	4
Woolmoor	99.6	90.2	92.2	94.4	5
Wrotham	98.8*	89.1	91.3	93.5	125*/250

+ 74 low power tr's less than 1kW.

Radio 1: Pop music incl. dance and urban, live concerts, social action campaigns, comedy: 24h. **N:** MF on the half h. 0430-1630 + 1245, 1700, 1745, 1930, 0000. Sat on the half h. 0730-1630, Sun on the half h. 0730-1530 + 2300.
Radio 2: Popular music, entertainment: 24h. **N:** MF on the h (exc. 2000 & 2100 Fri) + 0530, 0630, 0730, 0830. Sat on the h. + 0630, 0730. Sun on the h. (exc. 2000) + 0730.
Radio 3: Classical music, world music, poetry, school prgrs: 24h. **N:** MF 0600, 0700, 0800, 1300, 1800, 1900, 0030; Sat 0900, 1300, 0100. Sun 0900, 1300, 0030.
Radio 4: News, documentaries, drama, entertainment, and cricket on LW in season: 0530-0100 (approx). **N:** 0535, then on the h. (not 1000 Sun, 1100 Sun, 1500 Sat)
Radio 5 Live: News & sport: 24h. **N:** on the h. and half h.

BBC LOCAL RADIO

MW	Station, Location	kHz	kW
1)	BBC Three Counties R., Luton	630	0.2
6)	R. Cornwall, Redruth	630	2
6)	R. Cornwall, Bodmin	657	0.5
37)	R. York, Fulford	666	0.5
11)	BBC Essex, Manningtree	729	0.2
15)	BBC Hereford & Worcester, Worcester	738	0.037
8)	R. Cumbria, Carlisle	756	1
11)	BBC Essex, Chelmsford	765	0.5
18)	R. Kent, Littlebourne	774	0.7
20)	R. Leeds, Farnley	774	0.5
10)	R. Devon, Barnstaple	801	2
8)	R. Cumbria, Barrow	837	1
10)	R. Devon, Plymouth	855	1
19)	R. Lancashire, Preston	855	1
26)	R. Norfolk, Postwick	855	1.5
26)	R. Norfolk, West Lynn	873	0.3
10)	R. Devon, Exeter	990	1
33)	R. Solent, Fareham	999	1
4)	R. Cambridgeshire, Chesterton Fen	1026	0.5
17)	R. Jersey, Trinity	1026	1
31)	R. Sheffield, Sheffield	1035	1
9)	R. Derby, Burnaston Lane	1116	1
14)	R. Guernsey, Rohais	1116	0.5
30)	BBC Southern Counties R., Bexhill	1161	1
1)	BBC Three Counties R., Bedford	1161	0.1
37)	R. York, Scarborough	1260	0.5
36)	R. Wiltshire, Lacock	1332	0.4
33)	R. Solent for Dorset, Bournemouth	1359	0.85
30)	BBC Southern Counties R., Duxhurst	1368	0.5
36)	R. Wiltshire, Swindon	1368	0.1
22)	R. Lincolnshire, Lincoln	1368	2
12)	R. Gloucestershire, Berkeley Heath	1413	0.5
12)	R. Gloucestershire, Bourton-on-the-Water	1413	0.5
8)	R. Cumbria, Whitehaven	1458	0.5
10)	R. Devon, Torquay	1458	2
25)	R. Newcastle, Wrekenton	1458	2
16)	R. Humberside, Hull	1485	2
30)	BBC Southern Counties R., Brighton	1485	1
23)	R Merseyside, Wallasey	1485	2
34)	R. Stoke, Sideway	1503	1
11)	BBC Essex, Southend-on-Sea	1530	0.15
3)	R. Bristol & Somerset Sound, Mangotsfield	1548	5
19)	R. Lancashire, Oxcliffe	1557	0.25
3)	R. Bristol & Somerset Sound, Taunton	1566	0.6
28)	R. Nottingham, Clipstone	1584	1
15)	BBC Hereford & Worcester, Woofferton	1584	0.3
18)	R. Kent, Rusthall	1602	0.25

FM	Station, Location	MHz	kW
31)	R. Sheffield, Sheffield	88.6	0.3
17)	R. Jersey, Les Platons	88.8	3.8
20)	R. Leeds, Holme Moss	92.4	5.6
14)	R. Guernsey, Les Touillets	93.2	1
34)	R. Stoke, Alsagers Bank	94.6	6.1
2)	R. Berkshire, Henley	94.6	0.25
15)	BBC Hereford & Worcester, Ridge Hill	94.7	2
31)	R. Sheffield, Chesterfield	94.7	0.4
7)	BBC Coventry & Warwickshire, Meriden	94.8	2.2
10)	R. Devon, Huntshaw Cross	94.8	0.675
24)	BBC London, Crystal Palace	94.9	4
3)	R. Bristol, Ilchester Crescent	94.9	0.95
22)	R. Lincolnshire, Belmont	94.9	6
30)	BBC Southern Counties R., Newhaven	95.0	0.1
5)	R. Cleveland, Bilsdale	95.0	10
12)	R. Gloucestershire, Stroud	95.0	0.1
13)	BBC GMR, Holme Moss	95.1	5.6
28)	R. Nottingham, Newark	95.1	0.2
26)	R. Norfolk, Stoke Holy Cross	95.1	4
6)	R. Cornwall, Caradon Hill	95.2	4.3
8)	R. Cumbria, Kendal	95.2	0.1
29)	R. Oxford, Beckley	95.2	5.8
11)	BBC Essex, South Benfleet	95.3	1.2
30)	BBC Southern Counties R., Brighton	95.3	1.2
9)	R. Derby, Stanton Moor	95.3	1.2
20)	R. Leeds, Luddenden	95.3	0.083
2)	R. Berkshire, Windsor	95.4	0.5
25)	R. Newcastle, Pontop Pike	95.4	10
1)	BBC Three Counties R., Sandy Heath	95.5	1
3)	R. Bristol, Mendip	95.5	9
19)	R. Lancashire, Hameldon Hill	95.5	1.6
28)	R. Nottingham, Mansfield	95.5	2
35)	R. Suffolk, Lowestoft	95.5	2
37)	R. York, Olivers Mount	95.5	0.25
8)	R. Cumbria, Sandale	95.6	15
38)	BBC WM, Sutton Coldfield	95.6	11
4)	R. Cambridgeshire, Peterborough	95.7	5.1
23)	R Merseyside, Allerton Park	95.8	8
5)	R. Cleveland, Whitby	95.8	0.1
10)	R. Devon, Exeter	95.8	0.4

FM	Station, Location	MHz	kW
35)	R. Suffolk, Aldeburgh	95.9	2
16)	R. Humberside, High Hunsley	95.9	9.6
4)	R. Cambridgeshire, Cambridge	96.0	1
9)	R.Derby, Buxton	96.0	1.5
32)	R. Shropshire, The Wrekin	96.0	4.8
25)	R. Newcastle, Chatton	96.0	5.6
8)	R. Cumbria, Morecambe Bay	96.1	3.2
33)	R. Solent, Rowridge	96.1	10
18)	R. Kent, Wrotham	96.7	8.7
18)	R. Kent, Folkestone	97.6	0.1
1)	BBC Three Counties R., High Wycombe	98.0	0.2
20)	R. Leeds, Keighley	102.7	0.5
10)	R. Devon, North Hessary Tor	103.4	15
11)	BBC Essex, Great Braxted	103.5	12
36)	R. Wiltshire, Salisbury	103.5	1
36)	R. Swindon, Blunsdon	103.6	0.5
27)	R. Northampton, Geddington	103.6	0.8
7)	BBC Coventry & Warwickshire, Lark Stoke	103.7	1.4
37)	R. York, Acklam Wold	103.7	2
25)	R. Newcastle, Hexham	103.7	0.1
1)	BBC Three Counties R., Zouches Farm	103.8	0.5
28)	R. Nottingham, Mapperley Ridge	103.8	1
33)	R. Solent for Dorset, Bincombe Hill	103.8	0.5
6)	R. Cornwall, Redruth	103.9	18
19)	R. Lancashire, Winter Hill	103.9	2
20)	R. Leeds, Beecroft Hill	103.9	0.1
35)	R. Suffolk, Manningtree	103.9	5
15)	BBC Hereford & Worcester, Great Malvern	104.0	2
30)	BBC Southern Counties R., Reigate	104.0	3.8
8)	R. Cumbria, Whitehaven	104.1	1
31)	R. Sheffield, Holme Moss	104.1	4.4
34)	R. Stoke, Stafford	104.1	0.075
2)	R. Berkshire, Hannington	104.1	3
18)	R. Kent, Swingate	104.2	10
27)	R. Northampton, Northampton	104.2	4
36)	R. Wiltshire, Naish Hill	104.3	0.6
10)	R. Devon, Beacon Hill	104.3	1
37)	R. York, Woolmoor	104.3	0.5
2)	R. Berkshire, Reading	104.4	1
26)	R. Norfolk, Great Massingham	104.4	4.2
30)	BBC Southern Counties R., Heathfield	104.5	10
1)	BBC Three Counties R., Bow Brickhill	104.5	2.2
9)	R. Derby, Drum Hill	104.5	5.4
19)	R. Lancashire, Lancaster	104.5	2
13)	BBC GMR, Saddleworth	104.6	0.1
15)	BBC Hereford & Worcester, Kidderminster	104.6	0.5
30)	BBC Southern Counties R., Guildford	104.6	3
3)	R. Bristol, Bath	104.6	0.082
35)	R. Suffolk, Great Barton	104.6	2
12)	R. Gloucestershire, Churchdown Hill	104.7	2
30)	BBC Southern Counties R., Burton Down	104.8	2
21)	R. Leicester, Copt Oak	104.9	8
36)	R. Wiltshire, Marlborough	104.9	0.1

+ 11 low power tr's less than 0.1 kW

Addresses

1) PO Box 3CR, Luton, LU1 5XL. ☎01582 637400 🖷 01582 401467 – **2)** Caversham Park, Peppard Road, Reading, RG4 8TZ ☎0118 9464200 🖷0118 9464555 – **3)** PO Box 194, Bristol, BS99 7QT ☎0117 9741111 🖷0117 9738823; BBC Somerset Sound, Broadcasting House, Park Street, Taunton, TA1 4DA ☎01823 348920 🖷01823 332539 – **4)** PO Box 96, 104 Hills Road, Cambridge. CB2 1LD. ☎01223 259696 🖷01223 589870 – **5)** PO Box 95FM, Broadcasting House, Newport Road, Middlesbrough. TSI 5DG ☎01642 225211– **6)** Phoenix Wharf, Truro. TR1 1UA ☎01872 275421 🖷01872 240679 – **7)** 1 Greyfriars Road, Coventry. CV1 2WR ☎024 76860086 🖷024 76570100 – **8)** Annetwell Street, Carlisle. CA3 8BB ☎01228 592444 🖷01228 640079 – **9)** PO Box 104.5, Derby. DE1 3HL ☎01332 361111 🖷01332 290794 – **10)** Broadcasting House, Seymour Road, Mannamead, Plymouth. PL3 5YQ ☎01752 260323 🖷 01752 234599– **11)** 198 New London Road, PO Box 765, Chelmsford. CM2 9XB ☎01245 616000– **12)** London Road, Gloucester GL1 1SW ☎01452 308585 🖷01452 309491 – **13)** PO Box 951, Oxford Road, Manchester M60 1SD ☎0161 200 2000 🖷0161 228 6110 – **14)** Broadcasting House, Bulwer Ave, St Sampsons, Guernsey. GY2 4LA ☎ 01481 200600 🖷01481 200361 – **15)** Hylton Road, Worcester. WR2 5WW ☎01905 748485 🖷01905 748006 and 43 Broad Street, Hereford. HR4 9HH ☎01432 355252. 🖷01432 536446 – **16)** Queens Court, Queens Gardens, Hull HU1 3RH ☎01482 323232 🖷01482 226409 – **17)** 18 Parade Road, St. Helier, Jersey, JE2 3PL ☎01534 870000– **18)** The Great Hall, Mount Pleasant Road, Tunbridge Wells. TN1 1QQ ☎01892 670000 🖷01892 675644 – **19)** 20-26 Darwen Street, Blackburn BB2 2EA ☎01254 262411 🖷01254 680821 – **20)** 2 St Peters Square, Leeds. LS9 8AH ☎0113 244 2131🖷0113 2420652– **21)** Epic House, Charles Street, Leicester. LE1 3SH ☎0116 251 6688 🖷0116 2511463 – **22)** PO Box 219, Lincoln. LN1 3XY ☎01522 511411 🖷01522 511058 – **23)** 55 Paradise Street, Liverpool. L1 3BP ☎0151 708 5500 🖷0151 7940988– **24)** PO Box 94.9, Marylebone High St., London W1A 6FL ☎020 7224 2424– **25)** Broadcasting Centre, Barrack Road, Newcastle-Upon-Tyne, NE99 1RN ☎0191 2324141– **26)** The Forum, Millennium Plain, Norwich. NR2 1BH ☎01603 617411 633692 – **27)** Broadcasting House, Abington Street, Northampton. NN1 2BH ☎01604 239100 🖷01604 230709 – **28)** London Road, Nottingham. NG2 4UU ☎0115 955 0500 🖷0115 955 0501 – **29)** 269 Banbury Road, Oxford. OX2 7YL ☎08459 311444 🖷08459 311555 – **30)** Broadcasting Centre, Guildford. GU2 5AP ☎01483 306306 🖷01483 304952 and Broadcasting House, 40-42 Queen's Road, Brighton. BN1 3XB– **31)** 54 Shoreham Street, Sheffield. S1 4RS. ☎0114 2731177 🖷0114 2675454 – **32)** 2-4 Boscobel Drive, Shrewsbury. SY1 3TT ☎01743 248484 🖷01743 271702 – **33)** Broadcasting House, 10 Havelock Road, Southampton. SO14 7PW ☎023 8063 2811 🖷023 8033 9648 – **34)** Cheapside, Hanley, Stoke-on-Trent. ST1 1JJ ☎01782 208080 🖷01782 289115– **35)** Broadcasting House, St. Matthew's Street, Ipswich. IP1 3EP ☎01473 250000 🖷01473 210887 – **36)** PO Box 1234, Trowbridge; PO Box 1234, Prospect Place, Swindon, SN51 3RW; PO Box 1234, Salisbury. ☎08459 513366 or 01793 513626 🖷01793 513650 – **37)** 20 Bootham Row, York. YO30 7BR ☎01904 641 351 🖷01904 610937 – **38)** The Mailbox, Birmingham. B1 1RF ☎08453 009956.

D.Prgr: St's generally carry local prgrs from 0600 to 1800/1900, regional prgrs until 2400/0100, then BBC Radio 5 Live overnight.

BBC SCOTLAND

✉ Broadcasting House, Queen Margaret Drive, Glasgow G12 8DG ☎ +44 (0) 141 339 8844 🖷 +44 (0) 141 338 2943

Web: www.bbc.co.uk/scotland

MW R. Scotland: Burghead 810kHz 100kW, Westerglen 100kW, Redmoss 5kW, Dumfries 585kHz 2kW.

FM stereo	1FM	R2	R3	R4	RS/L	kW
Ashkirk	98.7	89.1	91.3	103.9	93.5f	50
Ben Gullipen	98.3	88.7	90.9	104.9	93.1	1
Black Hill	99.5	89.9	92.1	95.8*	94.3	250/200*
Bressay	97.9	88.3	90.5	94.9	92.7ac	43
Clettraval	97.7	88.1	90.3	95.1	92.5d	2
Daliburgh	98.9	89.3	91.5	95.9	93.7d	1
Darvel	99.1	89.5	91.7	104.3	93.9	10
Durris	99.0	89.4	91.6	95.9	93.8a	2.1
Eitshal	99.4	89.8	92.0	95.1	94.2d	2
Forfar	97.9	88.3	90.5	94.9	92.7	17
Fort William	98.9	89.3	91.5	95.9	93.7d	3
Glengorm	99.1	89.5	91.7	96.1	93.9d	5
Keelylang Hill	98.9	89.3	91.5	96.0	93.7ab	41
Kirkton Mailer	98.6	89.0	91.2	94.6	93.4	1
Meldrum	98.3	88.7	90.9	95.3	93.1a	150
Melvaig	98.7	89.1	91.3	95.7	93.5d	50
Oban	98.5	88.9	91.1	95.3	93.3d	3.6
Rosemarkie	99.2	89.6	91.8	103.6	94.0d	20
Rumster Forest	99.7	90.1	92.3	95.6	94.5d	10
Sandale	97.7	88.1	90.3	92.5	94.7e	250
Skriaig	98.1	88.5	90.7	94.8	92.9d	30
So. Knapdale	98.9	89.3	91.5	95.6	93.7	2.2

+ 30 low power tr's less than 1kW.

RS/L=R. Scotland + local news – a) RS: Aberdeen – b) RS: Orkney – c) RS: Shetland – d) RS: Inverness – e) RS: Dumfries – f) RS: Selkirk.

D.Prgr: 0600 (SS 0700)-2400. Relays BBC Radio 5 Live overnight.

Local Services (FM only). Freqs as above.

a) Beachgrove Terrace, Aberdeen AB15 5ZT. M-F: 0654-0700, 0750-0800, 1254-1300, 1654-1700. **Web:** www.bbc.co.uk/aberdeen – b) Commercial Assurance Bldg, Castle Str, Kirkwall, Orkney KW15 1DF: 0730-0800, 1815-1900 – c) Brentham House, Lerwick, Shetland ZE1 0DW: 0730-0800, 1730-1800, 1815-1930 – d) 7 Culduthel Rd, Inverness IV2 4AD M-F: 0654-0700, 0750-0800, 1254-1300, 1654-1700 – e) Elmbank, Lovers Walk, Dumfries DG1 1NZ: M-F: 0654-0700, 0750-0800, 1254-1300, 1654-1700 – f) Old Municipal Bldg, High Street, Selkirk TD7 4BU M-F: 0654-0700, 0750-0800, 1254-1300, 1654-1700.

RADIO NAN GAIDHEAL

✉ 52 Church Street, Stornoway, HS1 2LS ☎ +44 (0) 1851 705000 🖷+44 (0) 1851 704633

MW: Redmoss 990kHz 1kW.

FM	MHz	kW	FM	MHz	kW
Glengorm	103.5	5	Meldrum	104.2	150
Clettraval	103.7	2	Eitshal	104.3	2
So. Knapdale	103.7	2.2	Kirkton Mailer	104.5	1
Forfar	103.7	17	Rumster Forest	104.5	10
Melvaig	103.9	50	Oban	104.6	3.6
Craigkelly	104.1	5	Black Hill	104.7	10
Daliburgh	104.2	1	Skriaig	104.7	30
Fort William	104.2	3	Rosemarkie	104.9	20

+ 14 low power tr's less than 1kW

D.Prgr: Own prgs in Gaelic and relays of BBC R. Scotland.

BBC WALES

Broadcasting House, Llantrisant Rd, Llandaff, Cardiff CF5 2YQ
☎ +44 (0) 29 2032 2000 Fax +44 (0) 29 2055 2973
Email: radio.cymru@bbc.co.uk **Web:** www.bbc.co.uk/wales

FM stereo	R1	R2	R3	R4	kW
Blaenplwyf	98.3	88.7	90.9	104.0	250
Carmel	98.0	88.4	90.6	92.8	2.5
Haverfordwest	98.9	89.3	91.5	104.9	20
Kilvey Hill	99.1	89.5	91.7	94.6	1
Llanddona	99.4	89.8	92.0	103.6	21
Llandrindod Wells	98.7	89.1	91.3	103.8	2.8
Llangollen	98.5	88.9	91.1	93.3	15.6
Wenvoe	99.5	89.9	92.1	94.3	250

FM stereo	R. Wales	R.Cymru	kW
Blaenplwyf	95.3	93.1	250/120
Carmel	95.1	104.6	3/3.2
Haverfordwest	95.9	93.7	20
Kilvey Hill	93.9	104.2	1
Llanddona	94.8	94.2	21/10
Llandrindod Wells		93.5	2.8
Llangollen		104.3	15.6
Wenallt	103.9		2
Wenvoe		96.8	250

+ 42 low power tr's less than 1kW.

MW R. Wales: Forden 882kHz 1kW, Llandrindod Wells 1125kHz 1kW, Penmon 882kHz 10kW, Tywyn 882kHz 5kW, Washford 882kHz 100kW, Wrexham 657kHz 2kW.

BBC NORTHERN IRELAND

Broadcasting House, 25-27 Ormeau Avenue, Belfast BT2 8HQ
☎ +44 (0) 28 9033 8000 Fax +44 (0) 28 9033 8800.
Web: www.bbc.co.uk/northernireland
MW: Enniskillen 873kHz 1kW, Lisnagarvey 1341kHz 100kW.

FM stereo	R1	R2	R3	R4	R.Ulster	kW
Brougher Mountain	99.0	89.4	91.6	95.6	93.8	9.8
Camlough	98.3	88.7	90.9	104.6	93.1	4
Divis	99.7	90.1	92.3	96.0	94.5	250/125
Limavady	99.2	89.6	91.8	94.0	95.4	3.4
Londonderry	98.3	88.7	90.9	94.9	93.1h	31/10

+ 5 low power tr's less than 1kW – h) **R. Foyle** (see below).

R. Ulster: Enniskillen 873kHz 1kW, Lisnagarvey 1341kHz 100kW. 0630 (Sat 0755, Sun 0740)-2400. Other times rel. BBC World Sce.

BBC RADIO FOYLE

8 Northland Rd, Londonderry BT48 7JD ☎ +44 (0) 28 7126 2244
Fax +44 (0) 28 7137 8666
MW: Londonderry 792kHz 1kW **FM:** 93.1MHz 31kW.
D.Prgr: 24h.Own prgs. and relay BBC R. Ulster. Local N. M-F 0730 and hourly 0800-1600.

BBC ASIAN NETWORK

Epic House, Charles Street, Leicester, LE1 3SH ☎ +44 116 2516688, 0121 432 8558 **Email:** asian.network@bbc.co.uk
Web: www.bbc.co.uk/asiannetwork

MW	kHz	kW	MW	kHz	kW
Freemen's Common	837	0.5	Gunthorpe	1449	0.15
Sedgley	828	0.2	Langley Mill	1458	5

D.Prgr: 0500-0000/0030, relay BBC World Sce overnight.

Other Asian Services

MW	kHz	kW	MW	kHz	kW
BBC 3 Counties R.	630d	0.2	R. Derby	1116c	1
R. Leeds	774a	0.7	3 Counties R.	1161d	0.1
R. Lancashire	855a	1	R Cambr.	1449	0.15
R. Sheffield	1035b1	1			

Key: a) Mon-Sat 1900-0100, b) Mon-Fri 1900-0100, c) Mon-Thur 1900-0100, Fri 2100 - 0100, Sat 1800 - 0100, d) Mon-Fri 2100-0100. BBC 3 Counties R covers Beds, Bucks & Herts.

Also: R. Cambridgeshire local Asian prgrs SS 1300-1500; R Leeds local Asian prgr 'Connection' every MF 1800-1900, local Bengali prgr 2000-2100 Tue, own prgrs Sun night; R Sheffield local Asian prgr SS; R Lancashire local Asian prgrs Sun eves. BBC GMR, Manchester 95.1 & 104.6 Sat 2100-0100.

V. BBC does not QSL national domestic services. BBC local stations v. by letter.

CROWN CASTLE UK LTD

P.O. Box 98, Warwick CV34 6TN ☎+44 1926 416000
Fax +44 (1926) 416600 **Email:** sales@crowncastle.co.uk
Web: www.crowncastle.co.uk. CCUK operates all BBC domestic transmitter sites.

EXTERNAL SERVICE: BBC World Service

See International Broadcasting section.

OFFICE OF COMMUNICATIONS (Ofcom) (Regulatory Authority)

Riverside House, 2A Southwoark Bridge Road, London SE1 9HA
☎+44 20 7981 3000 Fax +44 20 7981 3333 **Email:** contact@ofcom.org.uk **Web:** www.ofcom.org.uk **L.P:** Chief Exec: Stephen Carter. Senior Partner (Content): Kip Meek, Senior Partner (Startegy): Ed Richards, Op. Dir: Vic Brashko, Ext. Rel. Dir: Tony Stoller.

COMMERCIAL RADIO COMPANIES ASSOCIATION (CRCA)

77 Shaftesbury Ave, London W1D 5DU ☎+44 (207) 306 2603
Fax +44 (207) 470 0062 **Web:** www.crca.co.uk
CRCA represents commercial radio to Government, Ofcom, Copyright Societies and other organizations concerned with radio.

DIGITAL RADIO (DAB): DAB transmissions are on Band 3. Tests are taking place in London on L-band.

BBC Digital Radio: BBC Radios 1, 1Xtra, 2, 3, 4, 5 Live, 5 Live Sports Extra, 6 Music, BBC 7, BBC Asian Network, BBC World Service and regional services in Scotland, Wales and N.Ireland are in a single frequency network on 225.648MHz.

Digital One: 7 Swallow Place, London W1B 2AG ☎+44 (207) 288 4600 **Web:** www.ukdigitalradio.com. Programming includes: Classic FM, Virgin Radio, talkSPORT, Planet Rock, Core, Life, Oneword, PrimeTime Radio .All prgrs are in a single frequency network for England on 222.064MHz, block 11D, and for Scotland on 223.936MHz

Local multiplexes: Capital Radio Digital Ltd, Cardiff, Kent, South Hampshire, Sussex Coast. **CE Digital Ltd,** Greater London, Birmingham, Manchester. **Emap Digital Radio Ltd,** Central Lancashire, Humberside, Leeds, Liverpool, South Yorkshire, Teesside, Tyne & Wear. **MXR,** North-East England, North-West England, South Wales/Severn Estuary, West Midlands, Yorkshire. **Now Digital Ltd,** Bournemouth, Bristol & Bath, Cambridge, Coventry, Exeter & Torbay, Leicester, Norwich, Nottingham, Peterborough, Reading & Basingstoke, Southend & Chelmsford, Swindon & West Wiltshire, Wolverhampton/Shrewsbury & Telford. **Score Digital Ltd,** Ayr, Dundee & Perth, Edinburgh, Glasgow, Inverness, Northern Ireland. **SW Digital Radio,** Plymouth & Cornwall. **Switchdigital Ltd,** Aberdeen, Central Scotland, Greater London. **The Digital Radio Group Ltd,** Greater London. **TWG – Emap Digital Ltd,** Bradford & Huddersfield, Stoke-on-Trent, Swansea.

NATIONAL COMMERCIAL STATIONS: CLASSIC FM

7 Swallow Place, Oxford Circus, London, W1B 2AG
☎ +44 (0) 20 7343 9000 Fax +44 (0) 20 7344 2700
Email: enquiries@classicfm.com
Web: www.classicfm.com **L.P:** MD & Prg Contr: Roger Lewis.

FM	MHz	kW	FM	MHz	kW
Cumbria	99.9	250	Presely	100.5	7.13
No.Hessary Tor	100.0	160	Crystal Palace	100.6	2
Angus	100.1	10.3	Arfon	100.7	18.75
Sutton Coldfield	100.1	250	Swindon	100.8	0.72
Bath	100.2	0.2	Selkirk	100.9	10
Douglas I.O.M.	100.2	1	Wrotham	100.9	250
Bradford	100.3	0.5	Fenham	101.0	0.05
Pontop Pike	100.3	130	Blaen Plwyf	101.1	10
Rowridge	100.3	250	Holme Moss	101.1	250
Milton Keynes	100.4	10	Darvel	101.3	8
Ridge Hill	100.4	4.8	Oxford	101.3	46
Belmont	100.5	6.4	Swansea	101.3	1
Londonderry	100.5	31	Bristol	101.4	0.2
Meldrum	100.5	150	Inverness	101.4	11

FM	MHz	kW		MHz	kW
Tacolneston	101.5	250	Wenvoe	101.7	250
Redruth	101.5	10	Dover	101.8	5.2
Gt. Ormes Head	101.6	2.5	Morecambe Bay	101.8	6.4
Bilsdale	101.6	2	Brighton	101.9	0.4
Leeds	101.6	0.3	Divis	101.9	250
Black Hill	101.7	250	Peterborough	101.9	40
Sheffield	101.7	0.5			

D.Prgr: 24h. **N:** on the h.

TALKSPORT

18 Hatfields, London, SE1 8DJ ☎+44 (0) 20 7959 7800 Fax +44 (0) 20 7959 7808. **Web:** www.talksport.net **L.P:** Chief Exec: Kelvin Mackenzie. PD: Mike Parry.

MW	kHz	kW	MW	kHz	kW
Brighton	1053	2.2	Brookmans Park	1089	400
Bournemouth	1053	1	Dartford Tunnel	1089	0.004
Droitwich	1053	500	Lisnagarvey	1089	12.5
Dundee	1053	1	Moorside Edge	1089	400
Dumfries	1053	10	Redmoss	1089	2.2
Exeter	1053	1	Redruth	1089	2
Hull	1053	1	Washford	1089	80
Inverness	1053	1	Westerglen	1089	125
Londonderry	1053	1	Boston	1107	1
Plymouth	1053	1	Fareham	1107	1
Postwick	1053	18	Reigate/Crawley	1107	1
Stockton	1053	1	Lydd	1107	2
Tonbridge	1053	4	Torbay	1107	1
Clipstone	1071	1	Wallasey	1107	0.5
Newcastle	1071	1			

D.Prgr: 24h

VIRGIN RADIO

1 Golden Square, London W1F 9DJ ☎+44 (0) 20 7434 1215 Fax +44 (0) 20 7434 1197 **Web:** www.virginradio.co.uk **Email:** reception@virginradio.co.uk **L.P:** Chief Exec: John Pearson. Stn Mgr. Steve Taylor. PD: Paul Jackson.

MW	kHz	kW	MW	kHz	kW
Brighton	1197	1.1	Norwich	1215	1.2
Bournemouth	1197	0.25	Plymouth	1215	1.1
Cambridge	1197	0.2	Washford	1215	100
Gloucester	1197	0.3	Westerglen	1215	100
Hoo (Kent)	1197	2	Redmoss	1215	2.3
Oxford	1197	0.25	Redruth	1215	2
Torbay	1197	1	Manningtree	1233	0.5
Wallasey	1197	0.4	Kings Heath	1233	0.5
Trowell	1197	0.5	Sheffield	1233	0.3
Brookmans Park	1215	125	Reading	1233	0.16
Dartford Tunnel	1215	0.004	Swindon	1233	0.1
Droitwich	1215	105	Boston	1242	2
Fareham	1215	1	Dundee	1242	0.5
Hull	1215	0.32	Sideway	1242	0.5
Lisnagarvey	1215	16	Stockton	1242	1
Moorside Edge	1215	200	Guildford	1260	0.5
Wrekenton	1215	2.2	Lydd	1260	1

D.Prgr: 24h (Rock music). **N:** on the h.
FM: London 105.8MHz 4kW

INDEPENDENT LOCAL RADIO STATIONS

MW kHz	kW	Name or Slogan	Location
175) 558	1	Spectrum R.	London
40) 603	0.1	Capital Gold Kent	Littlebourne
82) 666	0.34	Classic Gold 666/954	Exeter
129) 756	0.63	R. Maldwyn, Magic 756	Newtown
76) 774	0.14	Classic Gold 774	Gloucester
72) 792	0.275	Classic Gold 828/792	Bedford
56) 828	0.12	Magic 828	Leeds
72) 828	0.2	Classic Gold 828/792	Luton
73) 828	0.27	Classic Gold 828	Bournemouth
128) 855	0.15	Sunshine 855.	Ludlow
87) 936	0.18	Classic Gold 936/1161	Naish Hill
126) 936	1	Fresh R.	Hawes
69) 945	0.2	Classic Gold Gem	Derby
41) 945	0.7	Capital Gold 1323/945	Bexhill
103) 954	0.16	Classic Hits	Hereford
82) 954	0.40	Classic Gold 666/954	Torbay
1) 963	0.95	Club Asia	E. London
218) 963	0.2	Asian Sound R.	Haslingden
1) 972	1	Club Asia	W. London
53) 990	0.25	Magic AM	Doncaster
68) 990	0.09	Classic Gold WABC	Wolverhampton
69) 999	0.25	Classic Gold Gem	Nottingham
60) 999	0.8	Magic 999	Preston & Blackpool
180) 999	0.3	Valleys R.	Aberdare
68) 1017	0.63	Classic Gold WABC	Shrewsbury
153) 1026	1.7	Downtown R.	Belfast
155) 1035	0.78	Northsound Two	Aberdeen
160) 1035	0.32	West Sound AM	Ayr
18) 1035	1	Easy R. London	London
161) 1107	1.5	Moray Firth R.	Inverness
180) 1116	1	Valleys R.	Ebbw Vale
13) 1152	23.5	LBC News	London
158) 1152	3.6	Clyde 2	Glasgow
34) 1152	3	Capital Gold 1152	Birmingham
95) 1152	0.83	Classic Gold Amber	Norwich
45) 1152	1.5	Magic 1152	Manchester
61) 1152	1.8	Magic 1152	Newcastle
79) 1152	0.32	Classic Gold 1152	Plymouth
54) 1161	0.35	Magic 1161	Hull
156) 1161	1.4	Tay AM	Dundee
87) 1161	0.16	Classic Gold 936/1161	Swindon
127) 1170	0.58	Swansea Sound	Swansea
59) 1170	0.32	Magic 1170	Stockton
181) 1170	0.2	Signal Two	Stoke-on-Trent
43) 1170	0.12	Capital Gold 1170/1557	Portsmouth
91) 1170	0.28	Classic Gold Amber	Ipswich
40) 1242	0.32	Capital Gold Kent	Maidstone
91) 1251	0.76	Classic Gold Amber	Bury St.Edmunds
151) 1260	0.29	Sabras R.	Leicester
50) 1260	1.6	Classic Gold 1260	Bristol
100) 1260	0.64	Classic Gold Marcher	Wrexham
106) 1278	0.43	Pulse Classic Gold	Bradford
148) 1296	10	R. XL	Birmingham
42) 1305	0.2	Capital Gold 1305/1359	Newport
53) 1305	0.15	Magic AM	Barnsley
217) 1305	0.5	Premier Christian R.	Epsom
217) 1305	0.5	Premier Christian R.	Chingford
41) 1323	0.5	Capital Gold 1323/945	Brighton
88) 1332	0.6	Classic Gold 1332	Peterborough
217) 1332	1	Premier Christian R.	London
84) 1359	0.27	Classic Gold 1359	Coventry
42) 1359	0.2	Capital Gold 1305/1359	Cardiff
92) 1359	0.28	Classic Gold Breeze	Chelmsford
218) 1377	0.08	Asian Sound R.	Ashton Moss
217) 1413	0.5	Premier Christian R.	Heathrow
217) 1413	0.5	Premier Christian R.	Dartford Marshes
126) 1413	0.1	Fresh R.	Skipton
126) 1413	0.04	Fresh R.	Richmond
89) 1431	0.14	Classic Gold 1431/1485	Reading
92) 1431	0.35	Classic Gold Breeze	Southend
126) 1431	0.01	Fresh R.	Ilkley & Settle
167) 1458	125	Sunrise R.	London
37) 1458	5	Capital Gold	Manchester
89) 1485	1	Classic Gold 1431/1485	Newbury
97) 1521	0.64	Classic Gold 1521	Reigate
106) 1530	0.74	Pulse Classic Gold	Huddersfield
103) 1530	0.52	Classic Hits	Worcester
33) 1548	97.5	Capital Gold 1548	London
53) 1548	0.74	Magic AM	Sheffield
52) 1548	1	Magic 1548	Liverpool
159) 1548	2.2	Forth 2	Edinburgh
66) 1557	0.76	Classic Gold 1557 Northants	Northampton
43) 1557	0.5	Capital Gold 1170/1557	Southampton
195) 1566	0.8	County Sound R.	Guildford
156) 1584	0.21	Tay AM	Perth
11) 1584	0.2	London Turkish R.	London

FM MHz	kW	Name or Slogan	Location
219) 95.2	0.2	Kingdom FM	Dunfermline
33) 95.8	4	Capital FM	London
40) 95.9	0.22	Invicta FM	Thanet
40) 96.1	0.225	Invicta FM	Ashford
219) 96.1	0.5	Kingdom FM	Glenrothes
75) 96.1	0.5	SGR Colchester	Colchester
124) 96.2	4	SIBC	Shetland
93) 96.2	2.5	Lantern FM	Huntshaw Cross
67) 96.2	0.2	KMfm	Tonbridge
216) 96.2	1	Mix 96	Aylesbury
224) 96.2	2.6	North Norfolk R.	Stody

FM	MHz	kW	Name or Slogan	Location
188)	96.2	0.1	The Revolution	Oldham
145)	96.2	0.625	Yorkshire Coast R.	Scarborough
169)	96.2	0.1	Kix 96	Coventry
65)	96.2	1	Trent FM	Nottingham
56)	96.3	1	R. Aire	Leeds
86)	96.3	2	GWR FM	Bristol
92)	96.3	1.03	Essex FM	Southend
176)	96.3	0.2	Q96	Paisley
99)	96.3	1.25	Coast FM	Llandudno
36)	96.4	0.2	Century FM	Hexham
82)	96.4	1	Gemini FM	Torbay
153)	96.4	2	Downtown R.	Limavady
34)	96.4	10	BRMB	Birmingham
185)	96.4	1.5	The Wave 96.4	Swansea
91)	96.4	2	SGR-FM	Bury St.Edmunds
195)	96.4	3	96.4 The Eagle	Guildford
156)	96.4	0.8	Tay FM	Perth
181)	96.4	0.25	Signal One	Congleton
163)	96.4	3	CFM	Carlisle
135)	96.4	0.1	KMfm	Folkestone
31)	96.4	0.1	Compass FM	Grimsby
179)	96.5	0.1	R. Wave 96.5	Blackpool
157)	96.5	0.12	South West Sound	Stranraer
153)	96.6	8.2	Downtown R.	Brougher Mountain
115)	96.6	0.1	Vale FM	Blandford
66)	96.6	4	Northants 96	Northampton
26)	96.6	0.2	RNA FM	Arbroath
59)	96.6	8.9	TFM	Bilsdale
174)	96.6	0.4	R. Ceredigion	Lampeter
142)	96.6	0.45	Nevis R.	Fort William
74)	96.6	0.5	Mercury 96.6 FM	St. Albans
161)	96.6	0.45	Moray Firth R./Speysound	Cairngorm
25)	96.6	0.4	Spirit FM	Chichester
160)	96.7	2.2	West FM	Ayr
43)	96.7	0.5	Ocean FM	Winchester
52)	96.7	8.2	R. City	Liverpool
144)	96.7	0.55	City Beat 96.7	Belfast
196)	96.7	3	KL.FM 96.7	King's Lynn
70)	96.7	0.1	Wyvern FM	Kidderminster
161)	96.7	0.1	Moray Firth R./Kinnaird	Fraserburgh
162)	96.8	5	R. Borders	Selkirk
125)	96.8	0.5	Lochbroom FM	Polbain
54)	96.9	9.4	Viking FM	Hull
71)	96.9	0.9	96.9 Chiltern FM	Bedford
155)	96.9	10	Northsound One	Aberdeen
41)	96.9	0.1	Southern FM	Newhaven
181)	96.9	0.2	Signal 1	Stafford
170)	96.9	3.2	The Bay	Morecambe Bay
40)	97.0	0.5	Invicta FM	Dover
82)	97.0	1	Gemini FM	Exeter
142)	97.0	0.25	Nevis R.	Glencoe
79)	97.0	2	Plymouth Sound	Plymouth
157)	97.0	1	South West Sound	Dumfries
84)	97.0	1.8	Mercia FM	Coventry
89)	97.0	0.5	2 Ten FM	Reading
83)	97.1	0.4	Orchard FM	Chedington
61)	97.1	10	Metro FM	Newcastle
121)	97.1	0.3	NECR	Braemar
121)	97.1	0.1	NECR	Turriff
91)	97.1	3.4	SGR-FM	Ipswich
105)	97.1	1	Buzz 97.1	Wirral
191)	97.1	0.275	Delta FM	Haslemere
153)	97.1	0.08	Downtown R.	Larne
228)	97.1	3	R. Carmarthenshire	Carmel
64)	97.2	2	Beacon FM	Wolverhampton
87)	97.2	0.7	GWR FM	Swindon
78)	97.2	0.2	Vibe 101	Bristol
16)	97.2	0.31	97.2 Causeway Coast R.	Coleraine
118)	97.2	0.625	Wessex FM	Dorchester/Weymouth
147)	97.2	0.6	Stray FM	Harrogate
93)	97.3	0.1	Lantern FM	Ilfracombe
13)	97.3	4	LBC	London
159)	97.3	9.8	Forth 1	Edinburgh
161)	97.4	10	Moray Firth R.	Inverness
60)	97.4	2	Rock FM	Preston/Blackpool
154)	97.4	3.2	Cool FM	Belfast
42)	97.4	0.5	Red Dragon FM	Newport
53)	97.4	0.4	Hallam FM	Sheffield
35)	97.4	0.3	Fox FM	Banbury
174)	97.4	0.4	R. Ceredigion	Penwaun
115)	97.4	0.125	Vale FM	Shaftesbury
134)	97.4	0.24	The Beach	Southwold
43)	97.5	0.85	Ocean FM	Portsmouth
106)	97.5	0.5	The Pulse	Bradford
28)	97.5	0.36	Heartland FM	Pitlochry
160)	97.5	0.15	West FM	Girvan
228)	97.5	0.2	Scarlet FM	Llanelli
72)	97.6	1	Chiltern 97.6 FM	Luton
70)	97.6	0.8	Wyvern FM	Hereford
159)	97.6	0.1	Forth 1	Edinburgh
203)	99.8	0.75	2BR	Burnley
58)	100.0	4	Kiss 100 FM	London
101)	100.1	0.2	Lakeland R.	Kendal
12)	100.2	2	Dream 100 FM	Colchester
122)	100.3	20	Real R - Scotland	Black Hill
120)	100.4	5	Smooth FM	Winter Hill
62)	100.5	0.3	South Hams R.	Totnes
36)	100.7	8.9	Century FM	Bilsdale
47)	100.7	11	Heart FM	Sutton Coldfield
62)	100.8	0.1	South Hams R.	Dartmouth
101)	100.8	0.12	Lakeland R.	Windermere
172)	100.8	0.1	Quay West R	Porlock
78)	101.0	40	Vibe 101	Mendip
122)	101.1	10	Real R – Scotland	Edinburgh
178)	101.2	1.65	Waves R.	Peterhead
62)	101.2	1.15	South Hams R.	Soar
57)	101.2	6.26	Q101.2 West	Brougher Mountain
55)	101.4	0.19	Saga 106.6	Drum Hill
197)	101.6	0.1	Delta FM	Alton
67)	101.6	0.4	KMfm	Wrotham
85)	101.7	0.1	Ten 17	Harlow
36)	101.8	10	Century FM	Burnhope
191)	101.8	0.11	Delta FM	Petersfield
121)	101.9	0.22	NECR	Tullich
62)	101.9	0.5	South Hams R.	Ivybridge
222)	102.0	0.25	Dearne FM	Barnsley
130)	102.0	0.1	Peak 107 FM	Matlock
45)	102.0	0.5	Galaxy 102	Manchester
41)	102.0	0.2	Southern FM	Hastings
146)	102.0	1.25	Spire FM	Salisbury
197)	102.0	0.1	Delta FM	Alton
171)	102.0	3	FM 102 -The Bear	Stratford upon Avon
177)	102.0	0.1	Wave 102	Dundee
121)	102.1	1.25	NECR	Inverurie
87)	102.2	0.5	GWR FM	Naish Hill
159)	102.2	0.5	Forth 1	Penicuik
15)	102.2	4	Jazz FM	Croydon
112)	102.2	6.4	Lincs FM	Belmont
194)	102.2	2.5	Pirate FM	Caradon Hill
47)	102.2	1	Galaxy 102.2	Birmingham
163)	102.2	0.815	CFM	Workington
125)	102.2	0.7	Lochbroom FM	Ullapool
73)	102.3	2	2CR FM	Bournemouth
158)	102.3	0.6	Clyde 1	Rothesay
25)	102.3	0.48	Spirit FM	Littlehampton
153)	102.3	0.5	Downtown R.	Ballymena
142)	102.3	0.8	Nevis R.	Fort William
20)	102.4	0.625	Centre FM	Burton
41)	102.4	8.2	Southern FM	Eastbourne
172)	102.4	4	Quay West R.	Minehead
76)	102.4	2	Severn Sound FM	Gloucester
153)	102.4	10	Downtown R.	Londonderry
104)	102.4	3.3	Broadland 102	Stoke Holy Cross
119)	102.4	0.1	Yorkshire Coast R.	Bridlington
182)	102.4	0.1	Wish FM	Wigan
142)	102.4	0.8	Nevis R.	Glenachulish
158)	102.5	15	Clyde 1	Glasgow
106)	102.5	2	The Pulse	Halifax
161a)	102.5	1.2	Moray Firth R./Caithness	Thurso
102)	102.5	20	R. Pembrokeshire	Haverfordwest
163)	102.5	0.1	CFM	Penrith
181)	102.6	4	Signal 1	Stoke-on-Trent
92)	102.6	2	Essex FM	Chelmsford
35)	102.6	9	Fox FM	Oxford
61)	102.6	0.125	Metro R.	Alnwick
83)	102.6	4	Orchard FM	Mendip
121)	102.6	0.3	NECR	Kildrummy
88)	102.7	4	Hereward FM	Peterborough

FM	MHz	kW	Name or Slogan	Location
97)	102.7	3.6	Mercury 102.7 FM	Reigate
40)	102.8	0.1	Invicta FM	Dunkirk
96)	102.8	0.6	RAM FM	Derby
70)	102.8	1	Wyvern FM	Worcester
156)	102.8	5.25	Tay FM	Dundee
194)	102.8	10.2	Pirate FM	Redruth
161)	102.8	1	Moray Firth R./Keith R.	Keith
53)	102.9	0.5	Hallam FM	Barnsley
89)	102.9	4	2 Ten FM	Hannington
19)	102.9	3.14	Q102.9 FM	Londonderry
51)	103.0	4	Key 103	Manchester
98)	103.0	5	Champion FM	Caernarfon
76)	103.0	0.1	Severn Sound FM	Stroud
143)	103.0	4	Isles FM	Stornoway
80)	103.0	1	Q103 FM	Cambridge
82)	103.0	1	Gemini FM	Stockland Hill
155)	103.0	0.174	Northsound One.	Peterhead
208)	103.0	0.1	Your R.	Dumbarton
157)	103.0	0.7	South West Sound	Kirkcudbright
64)	103.1	2.7	Beacon FM.	Shrewsbury
40)	103.1	4	Invicta FM	Maidstone
14)	103.1	0.5	Central FM	Stirling
153)	103.1	2	Downtown R.	Newry
224)	103.2	0.25	North Norfolk R. (2 tr's)	N. Norfolk
42)	103.2	2	Red Dragon FM	Cardiff
43)	103.2	2	Power FM	Southampton
32)	103.2	0.1	Mansfield 103.2	Mansfield
170)	103.2	0.1	The Bay	Kendal
168)	103.2	0.4	Sunrise FM	Bradford
150)	103.2	0.4	Alpha 103.2	Darlington
61)	103.2	0.12	Metro R.	Hexham
121)	103.2	0.3	NECR	Colpy
226)	103.3	0.17	High Peak R.	Buxworth
226)	103.3	0.1	High Peak R.	Hope Valley
214)	103.3	0.05	London Greek R.	London
174)	103.3	5.8	R. Ceredigion	Blaen Plwyf
77)	103.3	2	FM 103.3 Horizon	Milton Keynes
158)	103.3	0.1	Clyde 1	Rosneath
6)	103.3	0.315	Oban FM	Oban
89)	103.4	0.1	2 Ten FM	Henley
187)	103.4	0.1	River FM	Bathgate
53)	103.4	1.6	Hallam FM	Doncaster
153)	103.4	0.2	Downtown R.	Newcastle
100)	103.4	1.4	MFM 103.4	Wrexham
162)	103.4	0.5	R. Borders	Eyemouth
39)	103.4	0.16	Sun FM	Sunderland
163)	103.4	0.4	CFM	Whitehaven
134)	103.4	2	The Beach	Lowestoft
41)	103.5	0.9	Southern FM	Brighton
21)	103.7	4	Channel 103 FM	Jersey
141)	104.7	2.5	Minster FM	York
5)	104.7	1.25	Island FM	Guernsey
186)	104.9	0.64	Imagine FM	Stockport
33)	104.9	2	XFM	London
49)	105.1	2.58	Galaxy 105	Emley Moor
230)	105.2	30	Saga 105.2 FM	Glasgow
227)	105.2	11	Kerrang!	Sutton Coldfield
164)	105.2	10	Wave 105	Solent
123)	105.2	3.2	Real Radio	Carmel
48)	105.3	10	Galaxy 105-106	Burnhope
37)	105.4	5	Century 105.4 FM	Winter Hill
81)	105.4	5	Leicester Sound	Billesdon
219)	105.4	0.1	Kingdom FM	Fife
58)	105.4	4	Magic 105.4	Croydon
123)	105.4	5	Real Radio	Cardiff
94)	105.6	1	Vibe FM	Cambridge
49)	105.6	0.5	Galaxy 105	Bradford
49)	105.6	0.25	Galaxy 105	Sheffield
223)	105.6	0.25	Ivel FM	Yeovil
221)	105.6	0.25	CTR FM	Maidstone
29)	105.6	0.1	Kick FM	Newbury
44)	105.7	10	Beat 106	Edinburgh
22)	105.7	11	Saga 105.7 FM	Sutton Coldfield
123)	105.7	9.4	Real Radio	Presely
48)	105.8	0.15	Galaxy 105-106	Hexham
164)	105.8	0.625	Wave 105	Poole
2)	105.8	4	Virgin R.	London
49)	105.8	9.4	Galaxy 105	Hull
123)	105.9	1	Real Radio	Newport
213)	106.0	0.6	Mid FM	Cookstown
8)	106.0	0.1	KMfm	Canterbury
38)	106.0	8	Century 106	Copt Oak
123)	106.0	1	Real Radio	Swansea
225)	106.0	0.6	Two Lochs R.	Gairloch
94)	106.1	4	Vibe FM	Stoke Holy Cross
44)	106.1	20	Beat 106	Glasgow
46)	106.2	4	Heart FM	London
131)	106.2	2.35	Real Radio	Emley Moor
123)	106.2	0.5	Real Radio	Fishguard
229)	106.2	0.03	Cuillin FM	Isle of Skye
219)	106.3	0.15	Kingdom FM	Fife
30)	106.3	0.5	Bridge FM	Bridgend
27)	106.3	0.12	Dee 106.3	Chester
94)	106.4	20	Vibe FM	Mendelsham
48)	106.4	8.9	Galaxy 105-106	Bilsdale
121)	106.4	0.3	NECR	Cock Bridge
207)	106.4	0.4	Bright 106.4	Haywards Heath
226)	106.4	0.25	High Peak R. (2 tr's)	Buxton/Glossop
206)	106.5	0.5	Argyll FM	Campbeltown
199)	106.6	0.25	Star 106.6	Slough
55)	106.6	10.8	Saga 106.6 FM	Waltham
223)	106.6	0.25	Ivel FM	Chard
225)	106.6	2	Two Lochs R.	Loch Ewe
25)	106.6	0.4	Spirit FM	Midhurst
23)	106.7	0.1	Hertbeat	Stevenage
24)	106.7	0.11	KCR FM	Knowsley
209)	106.8	0.09	Time FM	SE London
135)	106.8	0.1	KMfm	Dover
136)	106.8	0.1	Lite FM	Peterborough
107)	106.8	0.5	Ridings FM	Wakefield
23)	106.9	0.25	Hertbeat FM	Hertford
152)	106.9	0.15	Silk FM	Macclesfield
208)	106.9	0.1	Your R.	Helensburgh
113)	107.0	0.1	Isle of Wight R.	Chillerton Down
4)	107.0	0.1	Oak 107	Loughborough
90)	107.0	0.2	Reading 107	Reading
9)	107.1	0.1	Choice FM	N. London
108)	107.1	0.5	Trax FM	Doncaster
198)	107.1	0.16	Star 107	Ely
206)	107.1	0.625	Argyll FM	Ballygroggan
220)	107.1	0.1	Rugby FM	Rugby
213)	107.2	0.25	Mid FM	Dungannon
117)	107.2	0.1	Win FM	Winchester
184)	107.2	0.1	Wire FM	Warrington
110)	107.2	0.1	Rutland FM	Oakham
137)	107.2	0.1	Juice 107.2	Brighton
204)	107.2	0.1	KMfm	Thanet
192)	107.2	0.66	Star 107.2	Bristol
209)	107.3	0.1	Time FM	SE London
211)	107.4	0.2	Connect FM	Kettering
205)	107.4	0.1	BCR FM	Bridgewater
130)	107.4	0.1	Peak 107 FM	Chesterfield
138)	107.4	0.1	Telford FM	Heath Hill
215)	107.4	0.1	Tower FM	Bolton
114)	107.4	0.1	107.4 The Quay	Portsmouth
140)	107.4	0.1	Mix 107	High Wycombe
102)	107.5	0.1	R. Pembrokeshire	Fishguard
202)	107.5	0.1	Fen R.	Wisbech
200)	107.5	0.1	Star 107.5	Cheltenham
190)	107.5	0.1	Time FM	Romford
7)	107.5	0.1	Sovereign R.	Eastbourne
10)	107.5	0.1	3TR FM	Warminster
17)	107.6	0.1	Juice 107.6	Liverpool
133)	107.6	0.1	Kestrel FM	Basingstoke
116)	107.6	0.1	Fire 107.6 FM	Bournemouth
131)	107.6	0.1	Real Radio	Bradford
201)	107.7	0.1	Star 107.7	Weston Super Mare
210)	107.7	0.1	Dream 107.7	Chelmsford
94)	107.7	0.2	Vibe FM	Peterborough
131)	107.7	0.1	Real Radio	Sheffield
140)	107.7	0.13	Mix 107	Amersham
183)	107.7	0.1	Splash FM	Worthing
3)	107.7	0.1	The Wolf	Wolverhampton
206)	107.7	0.5	Argyll FM	South Knapdale
149)	107.8	0.1	Arrow FM	Hastings
139)	107.8	0.1	Radio Jackie	SW London
212)	107.8	0.1	The Saint	Southampton
189)	107.9	0.2	The Edge	Hamilton

FM MHz	kW	Name or Slogan	Location
109) 107.9	0.1	Fosseway R	Hinckley
111) 107.9	0.1	Trax FM	Worksop
198) 107.9	0.1	Star 107	Cambridge
165) 107.9	0.1	Bath FM	Bath
193) 107.9	0.1	Star 107.9	Stroud
166) 107.9	0.2	Passion 107.9	Oxford
132) 107.9	0.1	Dune FM	Southport
63) 107.9	0.1	KMfm	Medway
173) 107.9	0.1	Home 107.9	Huddersfield

+ 42 relays of less than 0.1kW

H. of tr: Most st's operate 24h. Stations belonging to groups may have shared programming, especially overnight, but local ID's may still be heard (eg. before **N**.on the h.).

MAJOR COMMERCIAL RADIO GROUPS:

CAPITAL RADIO plc
✉ 30 Leicester Square, London WC2H 7LA ☎ +44 20 7766 6000 🖷 +44 20 7766 6100 **Web:** www.capitalradiogroup.com

CHRYSALIS RADIO Ltd
✉ The Chrysalis Building, Bramley Road, London W10 6SP ☎ +44 20 7221 2213 🖷 +44 20 7314 1062 **Web:** www.chrysalis.com

CLASSIC GOLD DIGITAL Ltd
✉ Network Centre, Chiltern Road, Dunstable LU6 1HQ ☎ +44 1582 676200 🖷 +44 1582 676221 **Web:** www.classicgolddigital.com

EMAP PERFORMANCE NETWORK
✉ Mappin House, 4 Winsley Street, London W1N 7AR ☎ +44 20 7436 1515 🖷 +44 20 7312 8227 **Web:** www.emap.com

GWR GROUP plc
✉ One Passage Street, Bristol BS2 0JF ☎ +44 117 900 5316 🖷 +44 117 900 5306 **Web:** www.gwrgroup.com

THE LOCAL RADIO COMPANY Ltd
✉ 11 Duke Street, High Wycombe HP13 6EE ☎ +44 1494 688200 🖷 +44 1494 688201 **Web:** www.thelocalradiocompany.com

SCOTTISH RADIO HOLDINGS plc
✉ Clydebank Business Park, Clydebank, Glasgow G81 2RX ☎ +44 141 565 2200 **Web:** www.srhplc.com

UKRD GROUP Ltd
✉ Carn Brea Studios, Wilson Way, Redruth TR15 3XX ☎ +44 1209 310435 🖷 +44 **Web:** www.ukrd.com

THE WIRELESS GROUP plc
✉ 18 Hatfields, London SE1 8DJ ☎ +44 20 7959 7900 🖷 +44 20 7959 7802

Addresses & other information

1) Asia House, 227-247 Gascoigne Road, Barking, IG11 7LN ☎ 020 8594 6662 🖷 020 8594 3523 **Web:** www.clubasiaonline.com – **2)** 1 Golden Square, London, W1R 9DJ ☎ 020 7434 1215 🖷020 7434 1197 **Web:** www.virginradio.co.uk – **3)** 10th Floor, Mander House Wolverhampton, WV1 3NB ☎ 01902 571070 🖷 01902 571079 **Web:** www.thewolf.co.uk – **4)** 7 Waldron Court, Prince William Road, Loughborough, LE11 5GD ☎ 01509 211711 🖷 01509 246107 **Web:** www.oak107.co.uk – **5)** 12 Westerbrook, St. Sampsons, Guernsey, GY2 4QQ ☎ 01481 242000 🖷 01481 249676 **Web:** www.islandfm.guernsey.net – **6)** 132 George Street, Oban, PA34 5NT ☎ 01631 570057 🖷 01631 570530 **Web:** www.obanfm.org – **7)** 14 St Mary's Walk, Hailsham, BN27 1AF ☎ 01323 442700 🖷01323 442866 **Web:** www.1075sovereignradio.co.uk – **8)** 9 St George's Place, Canterbury, CT1 1UU ☎ 01227 475950 🖷 01227 785106 **Web:** www.kentonline.co.uk/kmfm – **9)** 291-299 Borough High Street, London SE1 1JG ☎ 020 7378 3969 🖷 020 7378 3911 **Web:** www.choicefm.com – **10)** Riverside Studios, Bishopstrow, Warminster BA12 9HQ. ☎ 01985 322222 🖷 01985 211110 **Web:** www.3trfm.com – **11)** 185b High Road, Wood Green, London, N22 6BA ☎ 020 8881 0606 🖷 020 8881 5151 **Web:** www.londonturkishradio.org – **12)** Northgate House, St Peters Street, Colchester, CO1 1HT ☎ 01206 764466 🖷 01206 715102 **Web:** www.dream100.com – **13)** The Chrysalis Building, Bramley Road, London, W10 6SP ☎ 020 7314 7300 🖷 020 7314 7322 **Web:** www.lbc.co.uk – **14)** 201-203 High Street, Falkirk, FK1 1DU ☎ 01324 611164 🖷 01324 611168 **Web:** www.centralfm.co.uk – **15)** 26-27 Castlereagh Street, London, W1H 5DL ☎ 020 7706 4100 🖷 020 7723 9742 **Web:** www.jazzfm.com – **16)** 24 Cloyfin Road, Coleraine, BT52 2NU. ☎ 028 7035 9100 🖷 028 7032 6666 **Web:** www.q972.fm – **17)** 27 Fleet Street, Liverpool, L1 4AR ☎ 0151 707 3107 🖷 0151 707 3109 **Web:** www.juiceliverpool.com – **18)** 43-51 Wembley Hill Road, Wembley, HA9 8AU ☎ 020 8795 1035 🖷 020 8902 9657 **Web:** www.easy1035.com – **19)** Riverview Suite, 87 Rosdowney Road, Londonderry BT47 5SU. ☎ 02871 344449 🖷 02871 311177 **Web:** www.q102.fm – **20)** 5-6 Aldergate, Tamworth, B79 7DJ ☎ 01827 318000 🖷 01827 318002 **Web:** www.centrefm.com – **21)** 6 Tunnell Street, St. Helier, Jersey, JE2 4LU ☎ 01534 888103 🖷 01534 887799 **Web:** www.channel103.com – **22)** 3rd Floor, Crown House, Beaufort Court, 123 Hagley Road, Birmingham B16 8LD. ☎ 0121 452 1057 🖷 0121 452 3222 **Web:** www.saga1057fm.co.uk – **23)** The Pumphouse, Knebworth Park, SG3 6HQ. ☎ 01438 810900 🖷 01438 815100 **Web:** www.hertbeat.com – **24)** Cables Retail Park, Steley Way, Prescot, L34 5NQ. ☎ 0151 2901501 🖷 0151 2901505 **Web:** www.kcr1067.com – **25)** 9/10 Dukes Court, Bognor Road, Chichester, PO19 8FX ☎ 01243 773600 🖷 01243 786464 **Web:** www.spiritfm.net – **26)** Arbroath Infirmary, Rosemount Road, Arbroath, DD11 2AT ☎ 01241 879660 🖷 01241 439664 Web: www.radionorthangus.co.uk – **27)** 2 Chantry Court, Chester CH1 4QN ☎ 01244 391000 🖷 01244 291010 **Web:** www.dee1063.com – **28)** Atholl Curling Rink, Lower Oakfield, Pitlochry, PH16 5HQ ☎ 01796 474040 🖷 01796 474007 **Web:** www.heartlandfm.co.uk – **29)** The Studios, 42 Bone Lane, Newbury RG14 5SD. ☎ 01635 841600 🖷 01635 841010 **Web:** www.kickfm.com – **30)** PO Box 1063, Wyndham Street, Bridgend, CF31 1EY ☎ 01656 647777 🖷 01656 673611 **Web:** www.bridge.fm – **31)** 26a Wellowgate, Grimsby DN32 0RA. ☎ 01472 346666 🖷 01472 508811 **Web:** www.compassfm.co.uk – **32)** The Media Suite, Brunts Business Centre, Samuel Brunts Way, Mansfield, NG18 2AH ☎ 01623 646666 🖷 01623 660606 **Web:** www.mansfield103.co.uk – **33)** 30 Leicester Square, London, WC2H 7LA ☎ 020 7766 6000 🖷 020 7766 6100 **Web:** www.capitalgold.com XFM: www.xfm.co.uk – **34)** 9 Brindleyplace, 4 Oozells Square, Birmingham, B1 2DJ ☎ 0121 245 5000 🖷 0121 245 5245 **Web:** www.capitalgold.com BRMB: **Web:** www.brmb.co.uk – **35)** Brush House, Pony Road, Oxford, OX4 2XR ☎ 01865 871000 🖷 01865 871036 **Web:** www.foxfm.co.uk – **36)** Century House, PO Box 100, Gateshead, NE8 2YY ☎ 0191 477 6666 🖷 0191 477 5660 **Web:** www.centuryfm.co.uk – **37)** Laser House, Waterfront Quay, Salford Quays, Salford M50 3XW ☎ 0161 4000105 🖷 0161 4001105 **Web:** www.capitalgold.com Century FM: **Web:** www.centuryfm.co.uk,– **38)** City Link, Nottingham, NG2 4NG ☎ 0115 9 106100 🖷 0115 9 106105 – **Web:** www.106centuryfm.com – **39)** PO Box 1034, Sunderland, SR5 2YL ☎ 0191 548 1034 🖷 0191 548 7171 **Web:** www.sun-fm.com – **40)** Radio House, John Wilson Business Park, Whitstable CT5 3QX ☎ 01227 772004 🖷 01227 774474 **Web:** www.invictafm.com, www.capitalgold.com – **41)** Radio House, PO Box 2000, Brighton, BN41 2SS ☎ 01273 430111 🖷 01273 430098 **Web:** www.capitalgold.com, www.southerfm.com – **42)** Radio House, Atlantic Wharf, Cardiff Bay, CF10 4DJ ☎ 029 2066 2066 🖷 029 2066 2060 **Web:** www.reddragonfm.co.uk Capital Gold: www.capitalgold.com – **43)** Radio House, Whittle Avenue, Segensworth West, Fareham, PO15 5SH. ☎ 01489 589911 🖷 01489 589453. Ocean FM **Web:** www.oceanfm.com, www.powerfm.com, www.capitalgold.com – **44)** 4 Winds Pavillion, Pacific Quay, Glasgow, G51 1EB ☎ 0141 566 6106 🖷 0141 566 6110 **Web:** www.beat106.com – **45)** 5th floor, The Triangle, Hanging Ditch, Manchester, M4 3TR ☎ 0161 279 0300 🖷 0161 279 0303 **Web:** www.galaxy102.co.uk – **46)** The Chrysalis Building, 13 Bramley Road, London, W10 6SP ☎ 020 7468 1062 🖷 020 7470 1095 **Web:** www.heart1062.co.uk – **47)** 1 The Square, 111 Broad Street, Birmingham, B15 1AS. ☎ 0121 695 0000 🖷 0121 696 1007 **Web:** www.galaxy1022.co.uk Heart FM: www.heartfm.co.uk – **48)** Kingfisher Way, Silverlink Business Park, Wallsend, NE28 9NX ☎ 0191 206 8000 🖷 0191 206 8080 **Web:** www.galaxy1056.co.uk – **49)** 2a Joseph's Well, Hanover Walk, Leeds, LS3 1AB ☎ 0113 213 0105 🖷 0113 213 1055 **Web:** www.galaxy105.co.uk – **50)** 1 Passage Street, Bristol, BS2 0JF ☎ 0117 984 3200 🖷 0117 984 3202 **Web:** www.classicgold.co.uk – **51)** Castle Quay, Castlefield, Manchester, M15 4PR ☎ 0161 288 5000 🖷 0161 288 5001 **Web:** www.key103.com www.manchestersmagic.co.uk – **52)** St Johns Beacon, 1 Houghton Street, Liverpool, L1 1RL ☎ 0151 472 6800 🖷 0151 472 6821 **Web:** www.magic1548.co.uk, www.radiocity.co.uk – **53)** 900 Herries Road, Sheffield, S6 1RH ☎ 0114-2091000 🖷 0114-285 3159 **Web:** www.magicam.co.uk, www.hallamfm.co.uk – **54)** Commercial Road, Hull, HU1 2SG ☎ 01482 325141 🖷 01482 593067 **Web:** Magic FM: www.magic1161.co.uk Viking FM: www.vikingfm.co.uk – **55)** Alder Court, Riverside Retail Park, Nottingham, NG2 1RX ☎0115 986 1066 🖷0115 943 5000 **Web:** www.saga1066fm.co.uk – **56)** PO Box 2000, 51 Burley Road, Leeds, LS3 1LR ☎ 0113 283 5500 🖷 0113 283 5501 **Web:** www.radioaire.co.uk, www.magic828.co.uk – **57)** 42A Market Street, Omagh BT78 1EN ☎028 6632 0777 🖷028 6632 0676 **Web:** www.q101west.fm - **58)** Mappin House, 4 Winsley Street, London W1W 8HF Magic 105.4: ☎ 020 7955 1054 🖷 020 7975 8165 **Web:** www.magic1054.co.uk Kiss 100 FM: ☎ 020 7975 8100 🖷 020 7975 8150 **Web:** www.kiss100.com – **59)** Radio House, Yales Crescent, Thornaby, Stockton-on-Tees, TS17 6AA ☎ 01642 888222 🖷 01642 868288 **Web:** www.tfmradio.co.uk www.magic1170.co.uk– **60)** PO Box 974, Preston, PR1 1XS ☎ 01772 477700 🖷 01772 477701 **Web:** Rock FM: www.rockfm.co.uk Magic 999: www.magic999.com – **61)** Longrigg, Swalwell, Newcastle, NE99 1BB ☎ 0191 420 0971 🖷0191 488 9222 **Web:** www.magic1152.co.uk www.metroradio.co.uk – **62)** Unit 1G, South Hams Business Park, Churchstow, Kingsbridge, TQ7 3QH ☎ 01548 854595 🖷 01548 857345 **Email:** shouthhams@musicradio.com – **63)** Medway House, Ginsbury Close, Strood, Rochester, ME2 4DU ☎ 01634

227808 ℻ 01634 297072 **Web:** www.kentonline.co.uk/kmfm – **64)** 267 Tettenhall Road, Wolverhampton, WV6 0DQ ☎ 01902 461300 ℻ 01902 461299 **Web:** www.musicradio.com, www.classicgold.co.uk – **65)** 29-31 Castle Gate, Nottingham NG1 7AP. ☎ 0115 952 7000 ℻ 0115 912 9333 **Web:** www.musicradio.com – **66)** 19-21 St. Edmund's Road, Northampton, NN1 5DY ☎ 01604 795600 ℻ 01604 795601 **Web:** www.musicradio.com, www.classicgold.co.uk – **67)** 1 East Street, Tonbridge, TN9 1AR ☎ 01732 369200 ℻ 01732 369201 **Web:** www.kentonline.co.uk/kmfm – **68)** 267 Tettenhall Road, Wolverhampton, WV6 0DQ ☎ 01902 461300 ℻ 01902 461299 **Web:** www.classicgold.co.uk – **69)** 29-31 Castle Gate, Nottingham, NG1 7AP ☎ 0115 952 7000 ℻ 0115 912 9302 **Web:** www.musicradio.com, www.classicgold.co.uk – **70)** 5 Barbourne Terrace, Worcester, WR1 3JZ ☎ 01905 612212 ℻ 01905 746637 **Web:** www.musicradio.com – **71)** 55 Goldington Road, Bedford, MK40 3LT ☎ 01234 272400 ℻ 01234 218580 **Web:** www.musicradio.com – **72)** Chiltern Road, Dunstable, LU6 1HQ ☎ 01582 676200 ℻ 01582 676221**Web:** www.classicgold.co.uk Chiltern FM: www.musicradio.com – **73)** 5-7 Southcote Road, Bournemouth, BH1 3LR ☎ 01202 259259 ℻ 01202 255244 **Web:** www.musicradio.com, www.classicgold.co.uk – **74)** Unit 5, The Metro Centre, Dwight Road, Watford WD18 9UD☎ 01923 205470 ℻ 01923 205471 **Web:** www.mercuryfm.co.uk – **75)** Abbeygate Two, 9 Whitewell Road, Colchester, CO2 7DE ☎ 01206 575859 ℻ 01206 216149 **Web:** www.musicradio.com – **76)** Bridge Studios, Eastgate Centre, Gloucester, GL1 1SS ☎ 01452 313200 ℻ 01452 313213 **Web:** www.musicradio.com, www.classicgold.co.uk – **77)** Broadcast Centre, 14 Vincent Avenue, Crownhill, Milton Keynes, MK8 0AB ☎ 01908 269111 ℻ 01908 591619 **Web:** www.musicradio.com – **78)** 26 Passage Street, Bristol BS1 1SE ☎ 0117 9010101 ℻ 0117 9309149 **Web:** www.vibe101.co.uk – **79)** Earl's Acre, Alma Road, Plymouth, PL3 4HX ☎ 01752 275600 ℻ 01752 275605 **Web:** www.musicradio.com, www.classicgold.co.uk – **80)** Enterprise House, The Vision Park, Chivers Way, Histon, Cambridge. CB4 9WW ☎ 01223 235255 ℻ 01223 235161 **Web:** www.musicradio.com – **81)** 6 Dominus Way, Merdian Business Park, Leicester, LE19 1RP ☎ 0116 256 1300 ℻ 0116 256 1303 **Web:** www.musicradio.com – **82)** Hawthorn Hse., Exeter Business Park, Exeter 3QS ☎ 01392 444444 ℻ 01392 354202 **Web:** www.classicgold.co.uk Gemini: www.musicradio.com,– **83)** Haygrove House, Taunton TA3 7BT ☎ 01823 338448 ℻ 01823 368318 **Web:** www.musicradio.com – **84)** Hertford Place, Coventry, CV1 3TT ☎ 02476 868200 ℻ 02476 868202 **Web:** www.musicradio.com, www.classicgold.co.uk – **85)** Latton Bush Centre, Southern Way, Harlow, CM18 7BB ☎ 01279 431017 ℻ 01279 445289 **Web:** www.musicradio.com – **86)** PO Box 2000, Bristol, BS99 7SN ☎ 0117 984 3200 ℻ 0117 984 3202 **Web:** www.musicradio.com – **87)** PO Box 2000, Swindon, SN4 7EX ☎ 01793 842600 ℻ 01793 842602 **Web:** www.musicradio.com, www.classicgold.co.uk – **88)** PO Box 225, Queensgate Centre, Peterborough, PE1 1XJ ☎ 01733 460460 ℻ 01733 281445 **Web:** www.musicradio.com, www.classicgold.co.uk – **89)** PO Box 2020, Reading, RG31 7FG ☎ 0118 9454400 ℻ 0118 9288458 **Web:** www.musicradio.com, www.classicgold.co.uk – **90)** Radio House, Madejski Stadium, Reading RG2 0FN ☎0118 986 2555 ℻0118 945 0809 **Web:** www.reading107fm.com - **91)** Alpha Business Park, 6-12 White House Road, Ipswich IP1 5LT ☎ 01473 461000 ℻ 01473 741200 SGRM ℻ 01473 467549 **Web:** www.classicgold.co.uk – **92)** Radio House, 19/20 Clifftown Road, Southend-on-Sea SS1 1SX ☎ 01702 333711 ℻ 01702 345224 **Web:** www.classicgold.co.uk, www.musicradio.com – **93)** Roundswell Business Park, 2b Lauder Lane, Barnstaple, EX31 3TA ☎ 01271 340340 ℻ 01271 340345 **Web:** www.musicradio.com – **94)** Reflection House, Olding Road, Bury St Edmunds IP33 1SE ☎ 01284 715300 ℻ 01284 715339 **Web:** www.vibefm.co.uk – **95)** St George's Plain, 47-49 Colegate, Norwich, NR3 1DB ☎ 01603 630621 ℻ 01603 666252 **Web:** www.classicgold.co.uk – **96)** 35-36 Irongate, Derby, DE1 3GA ☎ 01332 205599 ℻ 01332 851199 **Web:** www.musicradio.com – **97)** The Stanley Centre, Kelvin Way, Crawley, RH10 9SE ☎ 01293 519161 ℻ 01293 560927 **Web:** www.mercuryfm.co.uk Classic Gold: **Web:** www.classicgold.co.uk – **98)** Llys-y-Dderwen, Parc Menai, Bangor, LL57 4BN ☎ 01248 671888 ℻ 01248 671971 **Web: Web:** www.champion103.co.uk – **99)** PO Box 963, Bangor, LL57 4ZR ☎ 01248 673272 ℻ 01248 671971 **Web:** www.coastfm.musicradio.com – **100)** The Studios, Mold Road, Wrexham, LL11 4AF ☎ 01978 752202 Marcher Gold: ℻ 01978 759701 **Web:** www.classicgold.co.uk MFM ℻ 01978 722209 **Web:** www.mfmradio.co.uk– **101)** Lakeland Food Park, Plumgarths, Crook Road, Kendal, LA8 8QJ ☎01539 737 380 ℻01539 737 390 **Web:** www.lakelandradio.co.uk – **102)** Unit 14, Old School Estate, Station Road, Narbeth SA67 7DU ☎01834 869384 ℻01834 861524 **Web:** www.radiopembrokeshire.com – **103)**, PO Box 262, Worcester WR6 5ZE ☎ 01905 740600 ℻ 01905 740608 **Web:** www.classicgold.co.uk – **104)** St. George's Plain, 47-49 Colegate, Norwich, NR3 1DB ☎ 01603 671167 ℻ 01603 671175 **Web:** www. musicradio.com – **105)** Media House, 130 Claughton Road, Birkenhead, CH41 6EY ☎ 0151 650 1700 ℻ 0151 647 5427 **Web:** www.thebuzz971.co.uk – **106)** Forster Square, Bradford, BD1 5NE ☎ 01274 203040 ℻ 01274 203130 **Web:** www.pulse.co.uk, www.pulseclassicgold.co.uk – **107)** P.O. Box 333, Monckton Road, Wakefield, WF2 7YQ ☎ 01924 367177 ℻ 01924 367133 **Web:** www.ridingsfm.co.uk – **108)** PO Box 444, Doncaster, DN4 5GW ☎ 01302 341166 ℻ 01302 326104 **Web:** www.traxfm.co.uk – **109)** P.O. Box 107, Hinckley, LE10 1WR ☎ 01455 614151 ℻ 01455 616888 **Web:** www.fossewayradio.co.uk – **110)** 40 Melton Road, Oakham LE15 6AY ☎ 01572 757868 ℻ 01572 757744 **Web:** www.rutlandradio.co.uk – **111)** P.O. Box 444, Bridge Street, Worksop, S80 1GP ☎ 01909 500611 ℻ 01909 500445 **Web:** www.traxfm.co.uk – **112)** Witham Park, Waterside South, Lincoln LN5 7JN ☎ 01522 549900 ℻ 01522 549911 **Web:** www.lincsfm.co.uk – **113)** Dodnor Park, Newport, Isle of Wight, PO30 5XE ☎ 01983 822557 ℻ 01983 822109 **Web:** www.iwradio.co.uk – **114)** Flagship Studios, PO Box 1074, Portsmouth PO2 8YG ☎ 023 92 364141 ℻ 023 92 364151 **Web:**www.quayradio.com – **115)** Longmead Studios, Shaftesbury, SP7 8QQ ☎ 01747 855711 ℻ 01747 855722 **Web:** www.valefm.co.uk – **116)** Quadrant Studios, Old Christchurch Road, Bournemouth, BH1 2AD ☎ 01202 318100 ℻ 01202 318110 **Web:** www.fire1076.com – **117)** PO Box 107.2, The Brooks, Winchester SO23 8FT ☎ 01962 841071 ℻ 01962 841079 **Web:** www.winfm.co.uk – **118)** Radio House, Trinity Street, Dorchester, Dorset, DT1 1DJ ☎ 01305 250333 ℻ 01305 250052 **Web:** www.wessexfm.co.uk – **119)** PO Box 1024, Harbour Road, Bridlington, YO15 2YW. ☎ 01262 404 400 ℻ 01262 404 404 **Web:** www.yorkshirecoastradio.com – **120)** World Trade Centre, 8 Exchange Quay, Salford, M5 3EJ ☎ 0161 877 1004 ℻ 0161 877 1005 **Web:** www.smoothfm.com – **121)** The Shed, School Road, Kintore, Inverurie, AB51 0UX ☎ 01467 632909 ℻ 01467 632969 **Web:** www.necr.co.uk – **122)** Parkway Court, Baillieston, Glasgow, G69 6GA ☎ 0141 781 1011 ℻ 0141 781 1112 **Web:** www.readlradiofm.com – **123)** PO Box 6105, Ty-Nant Court, Cardiff CF15 8YF. ☎ 02920 315100 ℻ 02920 315150 **Web:** www.realradiofm.com – **124)** Market Street, Lerwick, Shetland, ZE1 0JN ☎ 01595 695299 ℻ 01595 695696 **Web:** www.sibc.co.uk – **125)** Mill Street Industrial Estate, Ullapool, IV26 2UN ☎ 01854 613131 ℻ 01854 613132 **Web:** www.lochbroomfm.co.uk – **126)** Firth Street, Skipton BD23 2PT ☎ 01756 799991 ℻ 01756 799771 **Web:** www.freshradio.co.uk – **127)** PO Box 1170, Swansea, SA4 3AB ☎ 01792 511170 ℻ 01792 511171 **Web:** www.swanseasound.co.uk – **128)** Unit 11, Burway Trading Estate, Ludlow, SY8 1EN ☎ 01584 873795 ℻ 01584 875900 **Web:** www.sunshine855.com – **129)** The Studios, The Park, Newtown, SY16 2NZ ☎ 01686 623555 ℻ 01686 623666 **Web:** www.magic756.net – **130)** Radio House, Foxwood Road, Chesterfield, S41 9RF ☎ 01246 269107 ℻01246 269933 **Web:** www.peak107.com – **131)** 1 Sterling Court, Tingley, Wakefield WF3 1EL ☎0113 238 1114 ℻0113 238 1191 **Web:** www.realradiofm.com – **132)** The Power Station, Victoria Way, Southport, PR8 1RR ☎ 01704 502500 ℻ 01704 502540 **Web:** www.dunefm.co.uk – **133)** Paddington House, Festival Place, Basingstoke, RG21 7LJ ☎ 01256 694000 ℻ 01256 694111 **Web:** www.kestrelfm.com – **134)** PO Box 103.4, Lowestoft, NR32 2TL ☎ 0845 3451035 ℻ 0845 3451036 **Web:** www.thebeach.co.uk – **135)** 93-95 Sandgate Road, Folkestone, CT20 2BQ ☎ 01303 220303 ℻ 01303 246659 **Web:** www.kentonline.co.uk/kmfm – **136)** 5 Church Street, Peterborough, PE1 1XB ☎ 01733 898106 – ℻ 01733 898107 **Web:** www.litefm.co.uk – **137)** 170 North Street, Brighton, BN1 1EA ☎ 01273 387107 ℻ 07719 273107 **Web:** www.juicebrighton.com – **138)** c/o Shropshire Star, Waterloo Road, Ketley, Telford, TF1 5HU ☎ 01952 280011 ℻ 01952 280010 **Web:** www.telfordfm.co.uk – **139)** 110-112 Tolworth Broadway, Surbiton KT6 7JD ☎ 020 8288 1300 ℻ 020 8288 1312 **Web:** www.radiojackie.com – **140)** 11 Duke Street, High Wycombe, HP13 6EE ☎ 01494 446611 ℻ 01494 445400 **Web:** www.mix107.co.uk – **141)** PO Box 123, Dunnington, York, YO19 5ZX ☎ 01904 488888 ℻ 01904 488811 **Web:** www.minsterfm.co.uk – **142)** Ben Nevis Estate, Claggan, Fort William, PH33 6PR ☎ 01397 700007 ℻ 01397 701007 **Web:** www.nevisradio.co.uk – **143)** PO Box 333, Stornoway, Isle of Lewis, HS1 2PU ☎ 01851 703333 ℻ 01851 703322 **Web:** www.isles.fm – **144)** Lamont Buildings, 50 Stranmills Embankment, Belfast, BT9 5FN ☎ 028 9020 5967 ℻ 028 9020 0023 **Web:** www.citybeat.co.uk – **145)** PO Box 962, Scarborough, YO12 5YX ☎ 01723 500962 ℻ 01723 501050 **Web:** www.yorkshirecoastradio.com – **146)** City Hall Studios, Malthouse Lane, Salisbury SP2 7QQ ☎ 01722 416644 ℻ 01722 416688 **Web:** www.spirefm.co.uk – **147)** The Hamlet, Hornbeam Park Avenue, Harrogate, HG2 8RE ☎ 01423 522972 ℻ 01423 522922 **Web:** www.972strayfm.com – **148)** KMS House, Bradford Street, Birmingham, B12 0JD ☎ 0121 753 5353 ℻ 0121 753 3111 **Web:** www.radioxl.net – **149)** Priory Meadow Centre, Queen Square, Hastings, TN34 1PJ ☎ 01424 461177 ℻ 01424 422 662 **Web:** www.arrowfm.co.uk – **150)** Radio House, 11 Woodland Rd, Darlington, DL3 7BJ ☎ 01325 255552 ℻ 01325 255551 **Web:** www.alpha1032.com – **151)** Radio House, 63 Melton Road, Leicester, LE4 6PN ☎ 0116 261 0666 ℻ 0116 266 7776 **Web:** www.sabrasradio.com – **152)** Radio House, Bridge Street, Macclesfield, SK11 6DJ ☎ 01625 268000 ℻ 01625 269010 **Web:** www.silkfm.com – **153)** Newtownards, Co. Down, BT23 4ES ☎ 028 9181 5555 ℻ 028 9181 8913 **Web:** www.downtown.co.uk – **154)** PO Box 974,

Belfast, BT1 1RT ☎ 028 9181 7181 🖷 028 9181 4974 **Web:** www.coolfm.co.uk – **155**) Abbottswell Road, West Tullos, Aberdeen, AB12 3AJ ☎ 01224 337000 🖷 01224 400003 **Web:** www.northsound1.co.uk – **156**) 6 North Isla Street, Dundee, DD3 7JQ ☎ 01382 200800 🖷 01382 593252 **Web:** www.radiotay.co.uk – **157**) Unit 40, The Loreburne Centre, High Street, Dumfries, DG1 2BD ☎ 01387 250999 🖷 01387 265629 **Web:** www.westsound.co.uk – **158**) Clydebank Business Park, Clydebank, Glasgow, G81 2RX ☎ 0141 565 2200 🖷 0141 565 2265 **Web:** www.clyde1.com – **159**) Forth House, Forth Street, Edinburgh, EH1 3LE ☎ 0131 556 9255 🖷 0131 558 3277 **Web:** www.forthone.com – **160**) Radio House, 54a Holmston Road, Ayr, KA7 3BE ☎ 01292 283662 🖷 01292 283665 **Web:** www.westsound.co.uk – **161**) Scorguie Place, Inverness, IV3 8UJ ☎ 01463 224433 🖷 01463 243224 **Web:** www.mfr.co.uk – **161a**) Neil Gunn Drive, Thurso KW14 7QU ☎01847 890000 **Web:** www.caithnessfm.co.uk – **162**) Tweedside Park, Galashiels, TD1 3TD ☎ 01896 759444 🖷 01896 759494 **Web:** www.radioborders.com – **163**) PO Box 964, Carlisle, CA1 3NG ☎ 01228 818964 🖷 01228 819444 **Web:** www.cfmradio.com – **164**) 5 Manor Court, Barnes Wallis Road, Segensworth East, Fareham PO15 5TH. ☎ 01489 481057 🖷 01489 481100 **Web:** www.wave105.com – **165**) Station House, Ashley Avenue, Lower Weston, Bath, BA1 3DS ☎ 01225 471571 🖷 01225 471681 **Web:** www.bath.fm – **166**) 270 Woodstock Road, Oxford, OX2 7NW ☎ 01865 351980 🖷 01865 351981 **Web:** www.passion1079.com – **167**) Sunrise House, Merrick Road, Southall, UB2 4AU ☎ 020 8574 6666 🖷 020 8813 9800 **Web:** www.sunriseradio.com – **168**) Sunrise House, 30 Chapel Street, Little Germany, Bradford, BD1 5DN ☎ 01274 735043 🖷 01274 728534 **Web:** www.sunriseradio.fm – **169**) Watch Close, Spon Street, Coventry, CV1 3LN ☎ 024 7652 5656 🖷 024 7655 1744 **Web:** www.kix.fm – **170**) PO Box 969, 24 St George's Quay, Lancaster, LA1 3LD ☎ 01524 848747 🖷 01524 848787 **Web:** www.thebay.fm – **171**) Guard House Studios, Banbury Road, Stratford upon Avon, CV37 7HX ☎ 01789 262636 🖷 01789 263102 **Web:** www.thebear.co.uk – **172**) Harbour Studios, The Esplanade, Watchet, TA23 0AJ ☎ 01984 634900 🖷 01984 634811 **Web:** www.quaywest.fm – **173**) Old Stable Block, Lockwood Park, Huddersfield, HD1 3UR ☎ 01484 321107 🖷 01484 311107 **Web:** www.home1079.co.uk – **174**) The Old Welsh School, Alexandra Road, Aberystwyth, SY23 1LF ☎ 01970 627999 🖷 01970 627206 **Web:** www.ceredigionradio.co.uk – **175**) 4 Inchgate Place, London, SW8 3NS ☎ 020 7627 4433 🖷 020 7627 3409 **Web:** www.spectrumradio.net – **176**) 65 Sussex Street, Kinning Park, Glasgow, G41 1DX ☎ 0141 429 9430 🖷 0141 429 9431 **Web:** www.q96.net – **177**) 8 South Tay Street, Dundee, DD1 1PA ☎ 01382 901000 🖷 01382 900999 **Web:** www.wave102.co.uk – **178**) 7 Blackhouse Circle, Blackhouse Industrial Estate, Peterhead AB42 1BW ☎ 01779 491012 🖷 01779 490802 **Web:** www.wavesfm.com – **179**) 965 Mowbray Drive, Blackpool, FY3 7JR ☎ 01253 304965 🖷 01253 301965 **Web:** www.wave965.com – **180**) Festival Church, Festival Park, Ebbw Vale NP23 8XW ☎ 01495 301116 🖷 01495 300710 **Web:** www.valleysradio.co.uk – **181**) 67-73 Stoke Road, Stoke-on-Trent, ST4 2SR ☎ 01782 441 300 🖷 01782 441 341 **Web:** www.signal1.co.uk – **182**) Orrell Lodge, Orrell Road, Orrell, Wigan WN5 8HJ ☎ 01942 761024 🖷 01942 777694 **Web:** www.wishfm.net – **183**) Guildbourne Centre, Worthing BN11 1LZ ☎01903 210772 🖷01903 233271 **Web:** www.splashfm.net **184**) Warrington Business Park, Long Lane, Warrington, WA2 8TX ☎ 01925 445545 🖷 01925 657705 **Web:** www.wirefm.com – **185**) PO Box 964, Swansea, SA4 3AB ☎ 01792 511964 🖷 01792 511965 **Web:** www.thewave.co.uk – **186**) Regent House, Heaton Lane, Stockport, SK4 1BX ☎ 0161 609 1400 🖷 0161 609 1401 **Web:** www.imaginefm.net – **187**) Stadium House, Aldestone Road, Livingston, EH54 7DN ☎01506 420975 🖷01506 420972 **Web:** www.river-fm.com - **188**) PO Box 962, Oldham, OL1 1JF ☎ 0161 621 6500 🖷 0161 621 6521 **Web:** www.revolutiononline.co.uk – **189**) Radio House, Rowantree Avenue, Newhouse Industrial Estate, Motherwell, ML1 5RX ☎ 01698 733107 🖷 01698 733318 **Web:** www.107theedge.co.uk – **190**) Lambourne House, 7 Western Road, Romford, RM1 3LD ☎ 0870 6011075 🖷 0870 240 3286 **Web:** www.timefm.com – **191**) 65 Wey Hill, Haslemere, GU27 1HN ☎ 01428 651971 🖷 01428 658971 **Web:** www.deltaradio.co.uk – **192**) Bristol Evening Post Building, Temple Way, Bristol, BS99 7HD ☎ 0117 910 6600 🖷 0117 925 0941 **Web:** www.star1072.co.uk – **193**) 3 Brunel Mall, London Road, Stroud, GL5 2BP ☎ 01453 767369 🖷 01453 757107 **Web:** www.star1079.co.uk – **194**) Carn Brea Studios, 102 Wilson Way, Redruth, TR15 3XX ☎ 01209 314400 🖷 01209 314345 **Web:** www.piratefm102.co.uk – **195**) Dolphin House, North Street, Guildford, GU1 4AA ☎ 01483 300964 🖷 01483 531612 **Web:** www.ukrd.com, www.964eagle.co.uk – **196**) 18 Blackfriars Street, Kings Lynn, PE30 1NN ☎ 01553 772777 🖷 01553 766453 **Web:** www.klfmradio.co.uk – **197**) Prospect Place, Mill Lane, Alton, GU34 2SY ☎ 01420 544444 🖷 01420 544044 **Web:** www.deltaradio.co.uk – **198**) Radio House, Sturton Street, Cambridge, CB1 2QF ☎ 01223 722300 🖷 01223 577686 **Web:** www.star107.co.uk – **199**) The Observatory Shopping Centre, Slough, SL1 1LH ☎ 01753 551066 🖷 01753 512277 **Web:** www.star1066.co.uk – **200**) West Suite, Arle Court, Cheltenham, GL51 6PN ☎ 01242 699555 🖷 01242 699666 **Web:** www.star1075.co.uk – **201**) 11 Beaconsfield Road, Weston-super-Mare, BS23 1YE ☎ 01934 624455 🖷 01934 629922 **Web:** www.star1077.co.uk – **202**) 5 Church Mews, Wisbech, PE13 1HL ☎ 01945 476465 🖷 01945 476464 **Web:** www.fenradio.co.uk – **203**) IMEX Spaces, Nelson, BB9 7DR ☎ 01282 690000 🖷 01282 690001 **Web:** www.2br.co.uk – **204**) Imperial House, 2-14 High Street, Margate, CT9 1DH ☎ 01843 220222 🖷 01843 299666 **Web:** www.kentonline.co.uk/kmfm – **205**) BCR FM, PO Box 1074, Bridgewater, TA6 4WE ☎ 01278 727700 🖷 01278 727705 **Web:** www.bcrfm.co.uk – **206**) 27-29 Longrow, Campbeltown PA28 6ER. ☎ 01586 551800 🖷 01586 551888 **Email:** argyllradio@hotmail.com – **207**) Unit 34, The Market Place Shopping Centre, Burgess Hill RH15 9NP. ☎ 01444 248127 🖷 01444 248553 **Web:** www.bright1064.com – **208**) Pioneer Park Studios, Unit 3, 80 Castlegreen Street, Dumbarton, G82 1JB. ☎ 01389 734422 🖷 01389 734380 **Web:** www.yourradio.com – **209**) 2-6 Basildon Road, London, SE2 0EW ☎ 020 8311 3112 🖷 020 8312 1930 **Web:** www.timefm.com – **210**) Cater House, High Street, Chelmsford, CM1 1AL ☎ 01245 2594107 🖷 01245 259558 **Web:** www.dream107.com – **211**) Unit 1, Centre 2000, Kettering, NN16 8PU ☎ 01536 412 413 🖷 01536 517 390 **Web:** www.connectfm.com – **212**) St Marys Stadium, Southampton, SO14 5PF ☎ 023 8033 0300 🖷 023 8020 6400 **Web:** www.saintsfc.co.uk – **213**) 2c Park Avenue, Cookstown BT80 8AH ☎028 8675 8696 🖷028 8976 1550 **Web:** www.mid106fm.co.uk – **214**) LGR house, 437 High Road, London, N12 0AP ☎ 020 8349 6950 🖷 020 8349 6950 **Web:** www.lgr.co.uk – **215**) The Mill, Brownlow Way, Gaskell Street, Bolton, BL1 2RA ☎ 01204 387000 🖷 01204 534065 **Web:** www.towerfm.co.uk – **216**) Friars Square Studios, 11 Bourbon Street, Aylesbury HP20 2PZ ☎ 01296 399396 🖷 01296 398988 **Web:** www.mix96.co.uk – **217**) 22 Chapter Street, London, SW1P 4NP ☎ 020 7316 1300 🖷 020 7233 6706 **Web:** www.premier.org.uk – **218**) Globe House, Southall Street, Manchester, M3 1LG ☎ 0161 288 1000 🖷 0161 288 9000 **Web:** asiansoundradio.co.uk – **219**) Haig House, Haig Business Park, Markinch, Fife, KY7 6AQ ☎ 01592 753753 🖷 01592 757788 **Web:** www.kingdomfm.co.uk – **220**) 4-6 Dunsmore Business Centre, Spring Street, Rugby CV21 3HH ☎ 01788 541100 🖷 01788 541070 **Web:** www.rugbyfm.co.uk – **221**) 6-8 Mill Street, Maidstone ME16 6XH ☎ 01622 662500 🖷 01622 662501 **Web:** www.ctrfm.com – **222**) Unit 7 Network Centre, Zenith Park, Whaley Road, Barnsley S75 1HT ☎ 01226 321733 🖷 01226 321755 **Web:** www.dearnefm.co.uk – **223**) The Studios, Middle Street, Yeovil BA20 1DJ ☎ 01935 848488 🖷 01935 848489 **Web:** www.ivelfm.co.uk – **224**) Breck Farm, Stody, Norfolk NR24 2ER ☎ 01263 860808 🖷 01263 860809 **Web:** www.northnorfolkradio.com – **225**) Gairloch IV21 2LR ☎ 0870 7414657 🖷 0870 7414658 **Web:** www.2lr.co.uk – **226**) PO Box 106, High Peak SK23 0QD ☎ 01298 813144 🖷 01298 813388 **Web:** www.highpeakradio.co.uk – **227**) 20 Lionel Street, Birmingham B3 1AQ ☎ 08450 531052 **Web:** www.kerrangradio.co.uk– **228**) Foothold Centre, Stebonheath Terrace, Llanelli SA15 1NE ☎ 01834 869384 🖷 01834 861524 **Web:** www.radiocarmarthenshire.com www.scarletfm.com– **229**) Bridge Road, Portree IV51 9ER ☎ 01478 612921 **Web:** www.cuillinfm.com – **230**) City Park, Alexandra Parade, Glasgow G31 3AU ☎ 0141 5511052 🖷 0141 5511053 **Web:** www.saga1052fm.co.uk.

MANX RADIO (Comm.)
✉ P.O. Box 1368, Douglas, Isle of Man IM99 1SW ☎ +44 1624 682600 🖷 +44 1624 682604 **Email:** postbox@manxradio.com **Web:** www.manxradio.com
L.P: MD: Anthony Pugh; PD: Andy Wint; Dir Tech: Darren Leeming.
MW: 1368kHz Douglas 20kW **FM:** 89.0 Snaefell 4 kW / 97.2 Carnane 11 kW / 103.7 MHz Jurby 20 kW.
D.Prgr: 24h. Separate prgrs on MW: MF 0730-0830, 1730-1800, Sat 1200-1800, Sun 1900-2200.

ENERGY FM (Comm.)
✉ 100 Market Street, Douglas, Isle of Man IM1 2PH ☎ +44 1624 611936 🖷 +44 1624 664699 **Email:** mail@energyfm.net **Web:** www.energyfm.net
FM: 91.2MHz Snaefell 1.2kW, 93.4MHz Jurby 1.2 kW, 98.6MHz Carnane 2kW (+relays on 98.4/105.2) **D.Prgr:** 24h

3FM (Comm.)
✉ Athol Radio Ltd, 45 Victoria Street, Douglas, Isle of Man IM1 2LD ☎ +44 1624 616333
L.P: MD: Matt Howells; **FM:** 104-106 MHz **D.Prgr:** 24h

BRITISH FORCES BROADCASTING SCE.
(a division of Services Sound & Vision Corp.)
✉ SSVC, Narcot Lane, Gerrards Cross, SL9 8TN ☎ +44 (0) 1494

878703 🖷 +44 (0) 1494 870552 **Email:** adminofficer@bfbs.com **Web:** www.bfbs.com
L.P: Contr BFBS: Charles Foster; Dep Contr: Marc Tyley; Man Ed: Alan Phillips; Dir Tech: Simon Shute.

Low power stations at 10 sites in N. Ireland on 1287 kHz; Gurkha services on 1134 kHz (Bramcote & Sandhurst), 1278 kHz (Folkestone), 1287 kHz (Brecon & Maidstone). See under Belize, Brunei, Bosnia, Canada, Croatia, Cyprus, Falkland Islands, Germany, Gibraltar, Iraq, Macedonia Nepal and Saudi Arabia for other services.

GARRISON RADIO

🖃 Naafi Spar, Shute Road, Catterick Garrison, DL9 4AF ☎ 01748 830050 🖷 01748 872424 **Email:** hq@garrisonradio.com **Web:** www.garrisonradio.com
L.P: MD: Mark Page.
Low power services at Catterick, Bulford/Tidworth and Aldershot garrisons on 1287 kHz, plus Colchester garrison on 1350 kHz.

Restricted Service Licences (RSL) Licences are granted for low power special event stations operating for up to 28 days (occ. longer) on MW or FM.

LPAM (Low Power AM stations) There are currently about 70 stations on the air with transmitters of 0.001kW e.r.p. Frequencies are used 1134, 1251, 1278, 1287, 1350, 1386, 1404, 1431, 1449 and 1575 kHz. There is an updated list of these stations at www.dxradio.co.uk/lpam
LPFM (Low Power VHF/FM stations) There are currently about 18 stations on the air, most on 87.7 MHz, with transmitters of typically 50mW.

Community Radio (formerly Access Radio) Small-scale, low-power and non-profit community radio services to serve a particular neighbourhood.
Community Audio Distribution Systems (CADS) pilot scheme in N. Ireland and W. Yorkshire for religious and community services using 27 MHz Citizens Band frequencies.

UNITED STATES OF AMERICA

L.T: See World Time Table — **Pop:** 287 million — **Pr.L:** English — **E.C:** 60Hz, 110V — **ITU:** USA

FEDERAL COMMUNICATIONS COMMISSION (FCC) Govt. licensing agency for broadcast stations

🖃 445 12th Street, SW, Washington, D.C. 20554. ☎ +1 202 418-0190. 🖷 +1 202 418-0232. **Web:** www.fcc.gov **Email:** fccinfo@fcc.gov.
L.P: Chmn: Michael K. Powell. Commissioners: Kathleen Q. Abernathy, Michael J. Copps, Kevin J. Martin, Jonathan S. Adelstein.
The FCC is an independent federal agency composed of commissioners appointed by the President with the consent of the Senate. One of its major activities is the general regulation of broadcasting, visual as well as aural. This regulation may be divided into three phases: 1) The allocation of spectrum space to the different types of broadcast services; 2) consideration of applications to build and operate individual stations; 3) regulation of their operations. Broadcasting is handled by the FCC Mass Media Bureau.

Call letter assignments: International agreement provides for the identification of the country of a radio station by the first letter or first two letters of the station's assigned call signal and for this purpose apportions the alphabet among different nations. USA nations use the initial letters K, N and W exclusively, and part of the A series. For broadcast stations, calls beginning with K are assigned to stations west of the Mississippi River, incl. Guam and No. Marianas Is, while W is assigned to broadcast stations east of the Mississippi, incl. Puerto Rico. Calls consist of four letters, to which FM or TV may be added with a hyphen for FM or TV stations.

A few exceptions with stations east of the Mississippi using a "K" callsign and stations west of the Mississippi using a "W" callsign will be noted. These are old callsigns that were assigned before the geographical division was introduced and are retained by special permission. Similarly some very old callsigns using only three letters may be retained by the stations that once were assigned these callsigns.

Stations: More than 12,700 st's are operating (MW + FM). As of 31 March 2004 there were 4,781 licensed AM sts.

MAJOR NETWORKS PROVIDING AM STATION PROGRAMMING

ABC RADIO NETWORKS, INC

🖃 13725 Montfort Drive, Dallas, TX 75240. ☎ +1 214 991-9200. **ABC, Inc:** 🖃 77 W. 66th Str, New York, NY 10023. **Web:** www.abcradio.com.
LP: Pres. ABC Radio Div: John Hare.
ABC Radio Networks has more than 4,500 affiliate radio sts and broadcasts five full-service news networks, ABC News Radio, Paul Harvey News and Comment, Radio Disney, ESPN Radio, music, talk and information prgrs, 10 ABC Radio 24-hour formats and daily and weekly long and short form prgrs.

CABLE NEWS NETWORK (CNN) (Turner Broadcasting System, Inc.)

🖃 Box 105573, Atlanta, GA 30348. ☎ +1 404 827-1500. 🖷 +1 404 681-6363. **Web:** www.cnn.com or www.cnnradionet.com/PUBLIC
LP: Turner Chmn. & CEO: Philip Kent.
The CNNRadio Network provides news, sports, business and feature reports to affiliate radio sts worldwide. CNNRadio uses the worldwide resources of CNN to bring accurate and timely news. CNNRadio currently has more than 2,000 radio affiliates.

CBS RADIO DIVISION

🖃 51 W. 52nd Str, New York, NY 10019. ☎ +1 212 975-4468.
News, talk and sports prgrs. CBS Radio is owned by Infinity Broadcasting Corp.

CLEAR CHANNEL RADIO

🖃 50 East Rivercenter Blvd, 12th Floor, Covington, KY 41011. ☎ +1 859 655 2267. **Web:** www.clearchannel.com
L.P: Pres. & CEO: John Hogan.
Clear Channel operates approximately 1,225 radio and 37 television sts in the USA. In addition, Clear Channel's Premiere Radio Network syndicates more than 100 prgrs to more than 7,800 radio sts. Premiere reaches 180 million+ listeners a week with its network of top #1 names including Rush Limbaugh, Dr. Laura Schlessinger, Rick Dees, Casey Kasem, Jim Rome, Carson Daly and Art Bell.

JONES RADIO NETWORKS (JRN)

🖃 8200 S. Akron Str, Suite 103, Englewood, CO 80112. ☎ +1 (303) 784-8700. 🖷 +1 303 784-8612 **Web:** www.jonesradio.com
LP: Pres: Ron Hartenbaum.
JRN serves over 5000 radio sts with 24-hour satellite formats, TotalRadio prgrs and consulting services, personality daypart shows, news and talk prgrs, short form features, show prep and research services, including live 24-hour syndicated music formats with over 1,200 affiliated radio sts. American Comedy Network provides hundreds of sts with comedy material. JRN is part of Jones Media Networks of Jones International, Ltd.

NATIONAL PUBLIC RADIO (NPR) (non-comm.)

🖃 635 Massachusetts Ave, NW, Washington, D.C. 20001. ☎ +1 (202) 513-2000. 🖷 +1 202 513-3329. **Web:** www.npr.org.
L.P: Pres. & CEO: Kevin Klose.
News, features. NPR serves an audience of more than 15 million Americans each week via 750 public radio sts and the Internet, and in Europe, Asia, Australia and Africa via NPR Worldwide, to military installations overseas via American Forces Network, and throughout Japan via cable.

USA RADIO NETWORK (USARadio.com, Inc.)

🖃 2290 Springlake Rd, Suite 107, Dallas, TX 75234.
☎ +1 972 484-3900 or +1 800-829-8111. **Web:** www.usaradio.com
LP: CEO & Pres.: Marlin Maddoux.
Produces news, features, sports prgrs. The USA Radio Network serves over 1100 affiliate sts as well as the Armed Forces Radio Network.

WESTWOOD ONE, INC.

🖃 9540 Washington Blvd, Culver City, CA 90232.
☎ +1 310 204-5000. **Web:** www.westwoodone.com.
L.P: Pres. & CEO: Shane Coppola.
Westwood One is America's largest radio network, providing over 150 news, sports, music, talk, entertainment prgrs, features, live events, 24-hour formats and Shadow Broadcast Services including Shadow Traffic, News and Sports and also Metro Broadcast Services. Westwood One serves more than 7,500 radio sts. Westwood One is managed by Infinity Broadcasting Corporation, a wholly owned subsidiary of Viacom Inc.

OTHER NATIONAL ORGANIZATIONS

NATIONAL ASSOCIATION OF BROADCASTERS

✉ 1771 N Str, NW, Washington, DC 20036. ☎ +1 202 429-5300. 🖷 +1 202 775-3520. **Web:** www.nab.org.
L.P: President & CEO: Edward O. Fritts.

NATIONAL ASSOCIATION OF SHORTWAVE BROADCASTERS, INC.

✉ 10400 NW 240th Str, Okeechobee, FL 34972.
☎ +1 863 763-0281 🖷 +1 863 763-1034. **Web:** www.shortwave.org.
LP: Pres: Douglas W. Garlinger. VP: Paul Hunter.

COMMERCIAL STATIONS

Especially in multi-station markets, radio sts concentrate their prgrs to appeal to a given segment of the population or a given listening taste. Many sts devote their entire broadcast day to news and/or talk programs. Others specialize in hit music (adult contemporary, top 40), country music, oldies (e.g. hits of the fifties and sixties), big bands/standards, black (urban contemporary, jazz, rhythm & blues), religious services and inspirational music, classical music, ethnic prgrs.

Today satellites are widely used for the distribution of prgrs. Numerous such networks are in operation. Sts making extensive use of network prgrs may have only one local identification per hour, usually on top of the hour. The former "clear channel" sts today have a protected area extending to 700 miles. Outside this area, the frequencies are also used by other sts. A few sts have been granted temporary licenses for increased powers to combat interference from neighbouring countries. Many daytime sts may now operate after local sunset using low or very low powers.

With the large decrease in AM listening in favour of FM, an increasing number of AM sts go off the air for a longer or shorter period due to economical difficulties. The latest development is that sts on the so-called regional channels, previously limited to 5kW power, may now apply for up to 50kW, limited only by the required protection of other sts. Relaxed ownership rules have allowed groups of co-owned sts to form in larger markets with the group sts often broadcasting from a common studio address.

Digital broadcasting in the AM band is being tested by a number of sts, using the IBOC system. According to this system, digital signals are emitted on both sides of the st's AM signal, so that both AM and digital receivers can recover the st audio. AM listeners may experience the IBOC signal as an increased noise level on the chs adjacent to the nominal channel of the emitting st.

MW:
Explanations

Call: Station call letters. All sts are required to announce their actual call letters and city of licence once per hour as close as possible to the top of the hour. On sts relaying an FM sister st or carrying certain network prgrs other call letters than those listed below may frequently be heard. #) Construction permit for a new st or for a move to this freq. from another freq.
Sta: State of the licensed city of operation. **N.B:** Hawaii and Alaska are listed under separate country headings.
Ant: Type of licence and use of directional antenna. U=Unlimited operation, up to 24h. D=Daytime operation, basically local sunrise to sunset, in many cases also a few additional hours at low or very low power. L=Limited hours, daytime with some extension. The figure after the letter specifies the use of directional antenna. 1=Nondirectional. 2=Directional nights only. 3, 4=Directional day and night. See the North America section of the MW Frequency List by Region for further explanations.
D: Daytime power in kW. **N:** Nighttime power in kW.
Format: The type of prgr dominating the st's transmissions. AC=Adult Contemporary. CHR=Contemporary Hit Radio (Top 40). UC=Urban Contemporary. (d)=days. (n)=Nights. Stereo: Some stations are operating in AM stereo using the Motorola C-QUAM system. St. 525) Gov.
Scope: Due to the large number of sts in operation, the following list has been limited to major sts, operating at 10kW or more during daytime and/or operating at 5kW or more at night. Further sts are included in the North America section of the MW Frequency List by Region.

	Call	Sta	kHz	Ant	D	N	Format
1)	KMEO	CA	540	U4	10	0.5	Spanish: News/talk
2)	WFLF	FL	540	U4	50	50	Talk
3)	KUZZ	CA	550	U4	5	5	C&W
4)	WDUN	GA	550	U2	10	2.5	News/talk/sports
5)	KTRS	MO	550	U2	5	5	News/talk
6)	WGR	NY	550	U2	5	5	Sports
7)	KFYR	ND	550	U2	5	5	News/talk
8)	KOAC	OR	550	U4	5	5	News/talk
9)	KTSA	TX	550	U2	5	5	News/talk
10)	WSAU	WI	550	U4	15	20	News/talk/sports
11)	KSFO	CA	560	U2	5	5	Talk
12)	KLZ	CO	560	U3	5	5	Sports
13)	WIND	IL	560	U4	5	5	Spanish: CHR
14)	WGAN	ME	560	U4	5	5	News/talk
15)	WEBC	MN	560	U4	5	5	Sports
16)	KMON	MT	560	U2	5	5	C&W
17)	WFIL	PA	560	U4	5	5	Religion/talk
18)	WVOC	SC	560	U2	5	5	News/talk
19)	KLVI	TX	560	U2	5	5.4	Talk/sports
20)	KPQ	WA	560	U2	5	5	News/talk
21)	KLAC	CA	570	U2	5	5	Nostalgia
22)	WTBN	FL	570	U4	5	5	Religion
23)	WMCA	NY	570	U3	5	5	Religion
24)	WSYR	NY	570	U4	5	5	News/talk
25)	WWNC	NC	570	U2	5	5	Talk
26)	WKBN	OH	570	U2	5	5	News/talk
27)	WNAX	SD	570	U2	5	5	News/talk/sports
28)	KLIF	TX	570	U4	5	5	Talk
29)	KNRS	UT	570	U4	5	5	Talk
30)	KVI	WA	570	U1	5	5	Talk
31)	KMJ	CA	580	U5	50	5	News/talk
32)	WDBO	FL	580	U2	5	5	News/talk
33)	KIDO	ID	580	U2	5	5	News/talk
34)	WIBW	KS	580	U2	5	5	News/talk/sports
35)	WTAG	MA	580	U4	5	5	News/talk
36)	WTCM	MI	580	U4	15	0.8	News/talk
37)	WHP	PA	580	U2	5	5	News/talk
38)	WCHS	WV	580	U2	5	5	News/talk/sports
39)	WEZE	MA	590	U3	5	5	Religion
40)	WKZO	MI	590	U2	5	5	News/talk
41)	KOMJ	NE	590	U1	5	5	Nostalgia
42)	WGTM	NC	590	U4	5	5	UC: Gospel
43)	KUGN	OR	590	U2	5	5	News/talk
44)	WARM	PA	590	U3	5	5	News/talk
45)	KQNT	WA	590	U1	5	5	News/talk
46)	KOGO	CA	600	U3	5	5	Talk
47)	WBWL	FL	600	U2	5	5	Children's prgrs
48)	WMT	IA	600	U2	5	5	News/talk
49)	WCAO	MD	600	U3	5	5	UC: Gospel
50)	WSJS	NC	600	U4	5	5	News/talk/sports
51)	KSJB	ND	600	U3	5	5	C&W
52)	WREC	TN	600	U4	5	5	News/talk
53)	KROD	TX	600	U2	5	5	News/talk
54)	KFRC	CA	610	U1	5	5	Oldies
55)	WIOD	FL	610	U4	5	5	News/talk
56)	KDAL	MN	610	U2	5	5	Talk
57)	KCSP	MO	610	U1	5	5	Sports
58)	KNML	NM	610	U2	5	5	Sports
59)	WTVN	OH	610	U2	5	5	Talk
60)	KRTA	OR	610	U4	2.5	5	Spanish: Mexican
61)	WIP	PA	610	U3	5	5	Sports
62)	KILT	TX	610	U4	5	5	Sports
63)	KONA	WA	610	U4	5	5	Talk
64)	KTAR	AZ	620	U2	5	5	News/talk
65)	WDAE	FL	620	U2	5	5	Sports
66)	WZON	ME	620	U2	5	5	Sports
67)	WSNR	NJ	620	U4	3	7.6	Ethnic/religion/Brokered/sports
68)	KPOJ	OR	620	U2	5	5	Talk
69)	WRJZ	TN	620	U2	5	5	Religion/religion: AC
70)	WVMT	VT	620	U4	5	5	Talk/sports
71)	WTMJ	WI	620	U4	50	10	News/talk
72)	KHOW	CO	630	U4	5	5	Talk
73)	WMAL	DC	630	U4	5	5	News/talk
74)	WBMQ	GA	630	U2	5	5	News/talk
75)	KFXD	ID	630	U4	5	5	C&W
76)	KJSL	MO	630	U4	5	5	Religion
77)	WPRO	RI	630	U2	5	5	Talk
78)	KSLR	TX	630	U4	5	5	Religion
79)	KFI	CA	640	U1	50	50	Talk
80)	WGST	GA	640	U4	50	1	News/talk
81)	WNNZ	MA	640	U4	50	1	Talk/sports
82)	KGVW	MT	640	U4	10	1	Religion/gospel
83)	WWJZ	NJ	640	U4	50	0.95	Children's prgrs
84)	WFNC	NC	640	U1	10	1	News/talk
85)	WCRV	TN	640	U2	50	0.48	Religion

#	Call	Sta	kHz	Ant	D	N	Format
86)	WGOC	TN	640	U2	10	0.81	C&W
87)	KSTE	CA	650	U4	21	0.92	News/talk
88)	WMII#	MI	650	U7	30	0.21	
89)	WNMT	MN	650	U2	10	1	News/talk/sports
90)	WSM	TN	650	U1	50	50	C&W
91)	KMTI	UT	650	U4	10	0.9	C&W
92)	WDLT	AL	660	U2	10	0.85	Blues
93)	KTNN	AZ	660	U2	50	50	Navajo/C&W
94)	KGDP	CA	660	U4	10	1	Religion
95)	WBHR	MN	660	U4	10	0.25	Sports
96)	WFAN	NY	660	U1	50	50	Sports
97)	KEYZ	ND	660	U4	5	5	C&W/talk
98)	KZTU	OR	660	U1	10	0.07	News/talk
99)	WLFJ	SC	660	D2	50		Religion
100)	KSKY	TX	660	U2	20	0.7	Talk
101)	KAPS	WA	660	U1	10	1	C&W
102)	KLTT	CO	670	U4	50	1.4	Religion: Talk
103)	WWFE	FL	670	U4	50	1	Spanish: News/talk/sports
104)	KBOI	ID	670	U2	50	50	News/talk
105)	WSCR	IL	670	U1	50	50	Sports
106)	KSXX#	NV	670	U4	10	0.6	
107)	WPMH	VA	670	U5	20	0.003	Religion
108)	KNBR	CA	680	U1	50	50	Sports
109)	WCNN	GA	680	U4	50	10	Sports
110)	WCBM	MD	680	U4	50	20	Talk
111)	WRKO	MA	680	U4	50	50	Talk
112)	WDBC	MI	680	U4	10	1	Religion
113)	KFEQ	MO	680	U4	5	5	Talk/C&W
114)	WPTF	NC	680	U2	50	50	News/talk
115)	WJCE	TN	680	U2	10	5	Nostalgia
116)	KKYX	TX	680	U2	50	10	C&W
117)	WCAW	WV	680	U4	10	0.25	C&W/gospel
118)	WJOX	AL	690	U2	50	0.5	Sports
119)	WOKV	FL	690	U2	50	10	News/talk
120)	KGGF	KS	690	U4	10	5	News/talk/sports
121)	WTIX	LA	690	U4	10	5	News/talk
122)	KTSM	TX	690	U4	10	10	News/talk
123)	WZAP	VA	690	U1	10	0.01	Religion/gospel
124)	WLW	OH	700	U1	50	50	Sports/talk/(n)C&W
125)	KGRV	OR	700	U1	23	0.47	Religion
126)	KSEV	TX	700	U4	15	1	Talk
127)	KALL	UT	700	U3	50	1	Talk
128)	KXLX	WA	700	U2	10	1	C&W
129)	KMIA	AZ	710	U4	22	3.9	Spanish: Mexican
130)	KSPN	CA	710	U2	50	10	Sports
131)	KFIA	CA	710	U4	25	1	Religion
132)	KNUS	CO	710	U3	5	5	News/talk
133)	WAQI	FL	710	U4	50	50	Spanish: News/talk
134)	KEEL	LA	710	U4	50	5	News/talk
135)	KCMO	MO	710	U4	10	5	News/talk
136)	WOR	NY	710	U3	50	50	News/talk
137)	KXMR	ND	710	U7	50	4	Sports
138)	KGNC	TX	710	U4	10	10	News/talk
139)	WFNR	VA	710	D3	10		News/talk/sports
140)	KIRO	WA	710	U2	50	50	News/talk
141)	WDSM	WI	710	U2	10	5	Talk/sports
142)	WRZN	FL	720	U2	10	0.25	Nostalgia
143)	WGN	IL	720	U1	50	50	News/talk/variety
144)	KDWN	NV	720	U2	50	50	News/talk
145)	WQTH#	NH	720	U4	50	0.5	
146)	WGCR	NC	720	D1	10		Gospel/religion
147)	KSAH	TX	720	U4	10	0.89	Spanish: Mexican
148)	KBSU	ID	730	U4	15	0.50	Jazz
149)	WMSP	AL	740	U4	10	0.33	Sports
150)	KBRT	CA	740	U3	10	0.11	Religion: Talk
151)	KCBS	CA	740	U4	50	50	News/talk
152)	WQTM	FL	740	U4	50	50	Sports
153)	WGSM	NY	740	U3	25	0.04	Korean/Brokered
154)	WPAQ	NC	740	U1	10	0.007	Bluegrass
155)	KRMG	OK	740	U4	50	25	News/talk
156)	KTRH	TX	740	U4	50	50	News/talk
157)	WSB	GA	750	U1	50	50	News/talk
158)	KERR	MT	750	U2	50	1	C&W
159)	KMMJ	NE	750	L3	10		C&W/talk
160)	KHWG#	NV	750	U1	10	0.28	
161)	KXL	OR	750	U4	50	20	Talk
162)	KAMA	TX	750	U4	10	1	Spanish: Oldies
163)	KOAL	UT	750	U2	10	6.8	Talk/sports
164)	KMTL	AR	760	D1	10		Gospel/religion
165)	KFMB	CA	760	U2	5	50	News/talk

#	Call	Sta	kHz	Ant	D	N	Format
166)	KKZN	CO	760	U4	50	1	Financial/sports
167)	WLCC	FL	760	U4	10	1	Spanish: Mexican
168)	WVNE	MA	760	U1	25	0.002	Religion
169)	WJR	MI	760	U1	50	50	News/talk
170)	WCHP	NY	760	U4	35	0.01	Religion
171)	KTKR	TX	760	U4	50	1	Sports
172)	KCBC	CA	770	U3	50	1	Religion/gospel
173)	WWCN	FL	770	U4	10	1	Sports
174)	KATL	MT	770	U2	10	1	AC
175)	KKOB	NM	770	U2	50	50	News/talk
176)	WABC	NY	770	U1	50	50	News/talk
177)	KAAM	TX	770	U4	10	1	Nostalgia
178)	KTTH	WA	770	U4	50	5	Talk
179)	WBBM	IL	780	U1	50	50	News
180)	WTME	ME	780	U1	10	0.01	Religion/news
181)	KKOH	NV	780	U2	50	50	News/talk
182)	WWOL	NC	780	D1	10		Religion
183)	KABC	CA	790	U2	5	5	News/talk
184)	WAXY	FL	790	U4	5	5	Nostalgia/talk
185)	WQXI	GA	790	U2	28	1	Sports
186)	KGHL	MT	790	U2	5	5	C&W
187)	KFGO	ND	790	U2	5	5	Talk
188)	WSKO	RI	790	U2	5	5	Sports
189)	WMC	TN	790	U2	5	5	Sports
190)	KBME	TX	790	U4	5	5	Nostalgia
191)	WNIS	VA	790	U3	5	5	News/talk
192)	WAYY	WI	790	U2	5	5	News/talk/sportsan
193)	WCKS	AL	810	U4	50	0.5	C&W
194)	KGO	CA	810	U3	50	50	News/talk
195)	WSJC	MS	810	U2	50	0.5	Religion
196)	WHB	MO	810	U2	50	5	Sports
197)	WGY	NY	810	U1	50	50	News/talk
198)	KBHB	SD	810	U1	25	0.06	C&W
199)	KTBI	WA	810	D1	50		Religion
200)	WMGG	FL	820	U4	50	1	Spanish: Tropical
201)	WNYC	NY	820	U4	10	1	News/talk
202)	WBAP	TX	820	U1	50	50	Sports/talk
203)	KUTR#	UT	820	U8	50	2.5	
204)	WGGM	VA	820	U4	10	1	Religion
205)	KGNW	WA	820	U4	50	5	Religion/talk

	Call	Sta	kHz	Ant	D	N	Format
206)	KFLT	AZ	830	U2	50	1	Religion
207)	KMXE	CA	830	U4	50	20	Spanish: News/talk
208)	KNCO	CA	830	U2	5	5	News/talk
209)	WFGM#	GA	830	U4	50	2.4	
210)	WCRN	MA	830	U4	50	5	Oldies
211)	WCCO	MN	830	U1	50	50	News/talk/sports
212)	KOTC	MO	830	D1	10		C&W
213)	WTRU	NC	830	U4	50	10	Religion
214)	WEEU	PA	830	U4	20	6	AC/news/talk
215)	KMUL#	TX	830	U5	50	0.009	Spanish
216)	KUYO	WY	830	D1	25		Religion
217)	WBHY	AL	840	D1	10		Religion
218)	KPMP#	CA	840	U4	4	5	
219)	WHGH	GA	840	D1	10		UC
220)	WHAS	KY	840	U1	50	50	Talk
221)	KXNT	NV	840	U4	50	25	Talk
222)	WCEO	SC	840	D3	50		Financial/talk
223)	KMAX	WA	840	U1	10	0.28	News/talk/sports
224)	WXJC	AL	850	U4	50	1	Religion/gospel
225)	KOA	CO	850	U1	50	50	News/talk/sports
226)	WRUF	FL	850	U2	5	5	News/talk
227)	WEEI	MA	850	U4	50	50	Sports
228)	WWJC	MN	850	D1	10		Religion/gospel
229)	WQST	MS	850	D3	10		C&W
230)	KFUO	MO	850	L1	5	5	Religion
231)	WRBZ	NC	850	U2	10	5	Sports
232)	WKNR	OH	850	U4	50	4.7	Sports
233)	WNTJ	PA	850	U3	10	10	News/talk
234)	WKVL	TN	850	D3	50		Talk/sports
235)	KEYH	TX	850	U4	10	0.18	Spanish: Mexican
236)	WTAR	VA	850	U4	50	25	Talk/sports
237)	KHHO	WA	850	U4	10	1	Sports
238)	KTRB	CA	860	U4	50	10	News/talk
239)	WDMG	GA	860	U2	5	5	Sports
240)	KKOW	KS	860	U2	10	5	News/talk/sports
241)	KPAM	OR	860	U2	50	5	News/talk
242)	WWDB	PA	860	D3	10		Financial
243)	KKAT	UT	860	U1	10	0.19	C&W
244)	WOAY	WV	860	U1	10	0.01	Gospel/religion
245)	WQRX	AL	870	D1	10		Spanish: Religion
246)	KRLA	CA	870	U4	20	3	News/talk
247)	WWL	LA	870	U3	50	50	News/talk/(n)C&W
248)	WLVP	ME	870	U4	10	1	News/talk
249)	WKAR	MI	870	D3	10		News/talk
250)	KPRM	MN	870	U2	25	1	C&W/talk
251)	WPWT	TN	870	D1	10		Talk
252)	KFLD	WA	870	U1	10	0.25	News/talk/sports
253)	KGHT	AR	880	U2	50	0.22	Gospel
254)	KKMC	CA	880	U4	10	1	Religion
255)	KJJR	MT	880	U1	10	0.5	Talk/sports
256)	KRVN	NE	880	U2	50	50	C&W/talk
257)	KHAC	NM	880	U1	10	0.43	Religion/Navajo
258)	WCBS	NY	880	U1	50	50	News
259)	WRFD	OH	880	D1	23		Religion
260)	KJOJ	TX	880	U4	10	1	Ethnic
261)	KIXI	WA	880	U4	50	10	Nostalgia
262)	WMEQ	WI	880	U2	10	0.21	Talk
263)	KLFF	CA	890	U2	5	5	Religion
264)	KDJQ#	ID	890	U2	50	0.25	
265)	WLS	IL	890	U1	50	50	News/talk
266)	WAMG	MA	890	U4	25	3.4	Spanish: Tropical
267)	WEEZ	MS	890	D1	10		Blues
268)	WBAJ	SC	890	D1	10		Religion
269)	KVOZ	TX	890	U2	10	1	Spanish: Religion
270)	KDXU	UT	890	U2	10	10	News/talk
271)	WKNV	VA	890	D3	10		Gospel/religion
272)	WJWL	DE	900	U4	10	1	Nostalgia
273)	KTIS	MN	900	U4	25	0.3	Religion
274)	KGME	AZ	910	U2	5	5	Sports
275)	KECR	CA	910	U4	5	5	Religion
276)	KNEW	CA	910	U2	5	5	Talk
277)	WLAT	CT	910	U2	5	5	Spanish: Tropical
278)	WTWD	FL	910	U3	5	5	Religion
279)	WFVR	GA	910	U2	5	5	Tourist
280)	WABI	ME	910	U2	5	5	AC/easy listening
281)	WSRP	NC	910	U2	5	5	Spanish: Mexican
282)	KRIO	TX	910	U4	5	5	Spanish: Religion
283)	KOTK	WA	910	U4	5	5	Talk
284)	KARN	AR	920	U2	5	5	News/talk
285)	KDHL	MN	920	U4	5	5	C&W
286)	WHJJ	RI	920	U2	5	5	News/talk
287)	KXLY	WA	920	U1	20	5	News/talk
288)	KHJ	CA	930	U2	5	5	Spanish: Ranchera
289)	WFXJ	FL	930	U2	5	5	Sports
290)	KSEI	ID	930	U2	5	5	Sports
291)	WGIN	NH	930	U2	5	5	News/talk/sports
292)	WPAT	NJ	930	U4	5	5	Ethnic/Spanish
293)	WBEN	NY	930	U2	5	5	News/talk
294)	WKY	OK	930	U2	5	5	News/talk
295)	KYAK	WA	930	U1	10	0.12	Religion
296)	KWRU	CA	940	U4	50	50	Spanish: News/talk
297)	WINZ	FL	940	U2	50	10	Talk
298)	WMAC	GA	940	U2	50	10	News/talk/sports
299)	KPSZ	IA	940	U4	10	5	Religion: AC
300)	WYLD	LA	940	U4	10	0.5	UC/gospel
301)	WCPC	MS	940	U4	50	0.25	Religion/gospel/C&W
302)	KICE	OR	940	U4	10	0.06	Sports
303)	KNNZ	UT	940	U1	10	0.03	News
304)	WKGM	VA	940	U2	10	3.1	Religion
305)	KAHI	CA	950	U4	5	5	Talk/oldies
306)	KKFN	CO	950	U3	5	5	Sports
307)	WTLN	FL	950	U2	12	5	Religion
308)	WNTD	IL	950	U2	1	5	Spanish
309)	WWJ	MI	950	U4	50	50	News
310)	KMTX	MT	950	U2	5	5	Nostalgia
311)	WIBX	NY	950	U3	5	5	News/talk
312)	WPEN	PA	950	U2	5	5	Nostalgia
313)	WORD	SC	950	U2	5	5	Talk
314)	KPRC	TX	950	U2	5	5	News/talk
315)	KJR	WA	950	U4	50	50	Sports
316)	WERC	AL	960	U2	5	5	News/talk
317)	KKNT	AZ	960	U2	5	5	Talk
318)	KABL	CA	960	U3	5	5	Nostalgia
319)	WELI	CT	960	U2	5	5	Talk
320)	WSBT	IN	960	U4	5	5	News/talk
321)	KMA	IA	960	U2	5	5	Talk
322)	WTGM	MD	960	U4	5	5	Sports
323)	WEAV	NY	960	U4	5	5	Talk/sports
324)	KKJX	OR	960	U2	5	5	Spanish: Mexican
325)	WFIR	VA	960	U2	5	5	News/talk
326)	KGET	CA	970	U4	1	5	News/talk
327)	WFLA	FL	970	U4	25	11	News/talk
328)	WGTK	KY	970	U4	5	5	News/talk
329)	WZAN	ME	970	U2	5	5	Talk/sports
330)	KBUL	MT	970	U2	5	5	News/talk
331)	WWDJ	NJ	970	U4	5	5	Religion/religion: AC
332)	WNED	NY	970	U3	5	5	News
333)	WDAY	ND	970	U2	5	5	News/talk
334)	KUPL	OR	970	U2	5	5	C&W
335)	WBGG	PA	970	U4	5	5	Sports
336)	WJMX	SC	970	U2	10	3	Talk
337)	KFWB	CA	980	U1	5	5	News
338)	KDBV	CA	980	U4	10	10	Spanish: Religion
339)	WTEM	DC	980	U4	50	5	Sports
340)	WCAP	MA	980	U4	5	5	Talk
341)	KKMS	MN	980	U3	5	5	Religion
342)	KMBZ	MO	980	U2	5	5	News/talk/sports
343)	WOFX	NY	980	U2	5	5	Sports
344)	WAAV	NC	980	U2	5	5	News/talk/sports
345)	WONE	OH	980	U2	5	5	Sports
346)	WYFN	TN	980	U2	5	5	Religion
347)	WCUB	WI	980	U4	5	5	C&W/talk
348)	KTKT	AZ	990	U4	10	1	News
349)	KATD	CA	990	U4	5	5	Spanish: News/talk
350)	WMYM	FL	990	U4	5	5	Children's prgrs
351)	WDYZ	FL	990	U4	50	14	Children's prgrs
352)	WEEB	NC	990	U1	10	0.02	Talk
353)	WNTW	PA	990	U3	10	0.1	News/talk
354)	WNTP	PA	990	U4	50	10	Talk
355)	WALE	RI	990	U4	50	5	Talk/variety/Spanish
356)	KWAM	TN	990	U4	10	0.45	Talk
357)	WNOX	TN	990	U2	10	10	News/talk/sports
358)	WDJL	AL	1000	D3	10		UC: Gospel
359)	WMVP	IL	1000	U4	50	50	Sports
360)	KKIM	NM	1000	U1	10	0.03	Religion
361)	KTOK	OK	1000	U4	5	5	News/talk
362)	KXRB	SD	1000	U4	10	0.1	C&W
363)	KOMO	WA	1000	U2	50	50	News
364)	KXEM	AZ	1010	U5	15	0.25	News/talk
365)	KIQI	CA	1010	U3	10	0.5	Spanish: News/talk

	Call	Sta	kHz	Ant	D	N	Format
366)	KSIR	CO	1010	U3	25	0.28	News/talk/sports
367)	WIOJ	FL	1010	U4	10	0.14	Religion
368)	WBZZ	FL	1010	U4	50	5	Talk
369)	WGUN	GA	1010	U1	50	0.07	Talk
370)	WMOX	MS	1010	U4	10	1	Talk/sports
371)	KXEN	MO	1010	U4	50	0.5	Religion/religion: AC
372)	WNTK	NH	1010	U1	10	0.03	C&W
373)	WINS	NY	1010	U3	50	50	News
374)	WFGW	NC	1010	U7	50	0.50	Gospel/religion
375)	KBBW	TX	1010	U4	10	2.50	Gospel/religion
376)	KCPW	UT	1010	U1	50	0.01	News
377)	KTNQ	CA	1020	U4	50	50	Spanish: Nostalgia
378)	WJEP	GA	1020	D1	10		Religion: AC
379)	KOIL	NE	1020	U4	50	1.4	C&W
380)	KINF	NM	1020	U4	50	50	AC/religion/talk/sports
381)	KDKA	PA	1020	U1	50	50	News/talk
382)	WRIX	SC	1020	D1	10		Religion/gospel
383)	KEVT	AZ	1030	U4	10	1	Spanish: Mexican
384)	KFAY	AR	1030	U4	10	1	News/talk/sports
385)	WONQ	FL	1030	U4	10	1.7	Spanish: Tropical
386)	WWGB	MD	1030	D3	50		Spanish: Religion
387)	WBZ	MA	1030	U3	50	50	News/talk
388)	WCTS	MN	1030	U4	50	1	Religion
389)	WFTK	NC	1030	D3	50		Spanish: Mexican
390)	KDUN	OR	1030	U1	50	0.63	C&W
391)	WGSF	TN	1030	U12	50	1	Spanish: Mexican
392)	KCTA	TX	1030	U2	50	1	Religion
393)	KMAS	WA	1030	U1	10	1	AC/easy listening
394)	WBGS	WV	1030	D5	10		Gospel/religion
395)	KTWO	WY	1030	U2	50	50	C&W/News/talk
396)	KCBR	CO	1040	D1	15		Religion
397)	WLVJ	FL	1040	U4	25	1.1	Religion
398)	WPBS	GA	1040	D1	12		UC: Gospel
399)	WHO	IA	1040	U1	50	50	News/talk/C&W(n)
400)	WZSK	PA	1040	D1	10		News/talk
401)	WQBB	TN	1040	D1	10		Sports
402)	KTCT	CA	1050	U4	50	10	Sports
403)	KMAP	CA	1050	U5	10	0.007	Religion
404)	WTKA	MI	1050	U3	10	0.5	Sports
405)	KMTA	MT	1050	D1	10		Oldies
406)	WEPN	NY	1050	U3	50	50	Sports
407)	KRCN	CO	1060	U1	10	0.11	Talk
408)	WIXC	FL	1060	U4	10	5	Sports
409)	KBGN	ID	1060	D1	10		Religion
410)	WLNO	LA	1060	U4	50	5	Religion
411)	WBIX	MA	1060	D3	40		Financial
412)	KYW	PA	1060	U3	50	50	News
413)	KGFX	SD	1060	U4	10	1	C&W/talk/sports
414)	KOFY	TX	1060	D1	10		Spanish
415)	KIJN	TX	1060	D3	10		Spanish: Religion
416)	KXPL	TX	1060	D1	10		Spanish: News
417)	KDYL	UT	1060	U1	10	0.14	Nostalgia
418)	WAPI	AL	1070	U2	50	5	News/talk
419)	KNX	CA	1070	U1	50	50	News
420)	WFRF	FL	1070	D1	10		Religion: AC
421)	WIBC	IN	1070	U4	50	10	News/talk
422)	KFTI	KS	1070	U2	10	1	C&W
423)	KVKK#	MN	1070	U2	10	5	
424)	WNCT	NC	1070	U4	10	10	News/talk
425)	WKOK	PA	1070	U2	10	1	News/talk/sports
426)	WCSZ	SC	1070	U4	50	1.5	UC: Gospel
427)	WFLI	TN	1070	U4	50	2.5	Religion/gospel
428)	WDIA	TN	1070	U4	50	5	UC: AC
429)	KKHT	TX	1070	U4	10	5	Religion/talk
430)	WINA	VA	1070	U2	5	5	Talk/sports
431)	WIWS	WV	1070	D1	10		Oldies
432)	WTSO	WI	1070	U4	10	5	Sports
433)	KSCO	CA	1080	U2	10	5	News/talk
434)	WTIC	CT	1080	U2	50	50	News/talk
435)	WVCG	FL	1080	U4	50	10	Spanish: Religion
436)	WHOO	FL	1080	D3	10		Sports
437)	WFTD	GA	1080	D3	10		Spanish: Mexican
438)	KVNI	ID	1080	U2	10	1	Oldies
439)	WKJK	KY	1080	U4	10	1	Talk
440)	KFXX	OR	1080	U4	50	10	Sports
441)	WWNL	PA	1080	D4	50		Religion
442)	KRLD	TX	1080	U2	50	50	News/talk
443)	KSLL	UT	1080	D1	10		C&W
444)	KAAY	AR	1090	U2	50	50	Gospel/religion
445)	KNCR	CA	1090	D1	10		Spanish: Mexican
446)	KMXA	CO	1090	U4	50	0.5	Spanish: Mexican
447)	WNVY	FL	1090	D1	10		UC: Gospel
448)	WBAL	MD	1090	U2	50	50	News/talk/sports
449)	KBOZ	MT	1090	U2	5	5	Talk
450)	WHGG	TN	1090	D1	10		Religion: AC
451)	KYCW	WA	1090	U4	50	50	C&W
452)	KFNX	AZ	1100	U4	50	1	Talk/variety/ethnic
453)	KFAX	CA	1100	U3	50	50	Religion
454)	KNZZ	CO	1100	U12	50	10	News/talk/sports
455)	WCGA	GA	1100	D1	10		Talk
456)	WOMN#	LA	1100	D1	30		C&W
457)	WHLI	NY	1100	D3	10		Nostalgia
458)	WTAM	OH	1100	U1	50	50	News/talk
459)	KDRY	TX	1100	U2	11	1	Religion
460)	WBCA	AL	1110	D1	10		Gospel
461)	KDIS	CA	1110	U4	50	20	Children's prgrs
462)	WTIS	FL	1110	D3	10		Religion/ethnic
463)	WJML	MI	1110	U3	10	0.01	News/talk
464)	KFAB	NE	1110	U2	50	50	News/talk
465)	WBT	NC	1110	U2	50	50	News/talk
466)	KBND	OR	1110	U12	10	5	News/talk
467)	WCKO	VA	1110	D3	50		Religion
468)	WUST	DC	1120	D1	20		Ethnic/UC: Gospel (SS)
469)	WXJO	GA	1120	D1	10		UC: Gospel
470)	KMOX	MO	1120	U1	50	50	Talk/news
471)	KPNW	OR	1120	U3	50	50	News/talk
472)	KANN	UT	1120	U4	10	1	Religion: AC
473)	KSDO	CA	1130	U4	10	10	Spanish: Religion
474)	KRDU	CA	1130	U4	5	6.2	Religion
475)	WLBA	GA	1130	D1	10		Spanish: Mexican
476)	WMGA	GA	1130	U8	10	0.25	Spanish: Mexican
477)	KWKH	LA	1130	U2	50	50	C&W
478)	WDFN	MI	1130	U4	50	10	Sports
479)	KFAN	MN	1130	U4	50	30	Sports
480)	WBBR	NY	1130	U2	50	50	Financial/news
481)	KBMR	ND	1130	D1	10		C&W
482)	KTMR	TX	1130	D3	10		Tejano
483)	WISN	WI	1130	U4	50	10	News/talk
484)	WBXR	AL	1140	D4	15		Religion/gospel
485)	KNWQ	CA	1140	U4	10	2.5	News/talk
486)	KHTK	CA	1140	U4	50	50	Talk/sports
487)	WQBA	FL	1140	U4	50	10	Spanish: News/talk
488)	KGEM	ID	1140	U2	10	10	Nostalgia
489)	KSFN	NV	1140	U2	10	2.5	Talk
490)	KSOO	SD	1140	U2	10	5	News/talk/sports
491)	WRVA	VA	1140	U3	50	50	Talk
492)	KZMQ	WY	1140	D1	10		C&W
493)	KXTA	CA	1150	U4	50	44	Sports
494)	KNRC	CO	1150	U4	10	1	AOR/rock
495)	WDEL	DE	1150	U4	5	5	News/talk/sports
496)	WTMP	FL	1150	U4	10	0.5	UC: AC
497)	KSAL	KS	1150	U2	5	5	News/talk/sports
498)	WJBO	LA	1150	U3	5	5	News/talk
499)	WTTT	MA	1150	U4	5	5	News/talk
500)	KSEN	MT	1150	U4	10	5	Oldies
501)	KKNW	WA	1150	U2	10	6	News
502)	KQQQ	WA	1150	U1	11	0.02	News/talk/sports
503)	WHBY	WI	1150	U4	5	5	News/talk
504)	WMLB	GA	1160	U5	50	0.16	Nostalgia
505)	WYLL	IL	1160	U4	50	5	Religion
506)	WSKW	ME	1160	U1	10	0.73	Sports
507)	WMET	MD	1160	U4	50	1.5	Talk
508)	WVNJ	NJ	1160	U4	20	2.5	Nostalgia
509)	WOBM	NJ	1160	U4	5	8.9	Nostalgia
510)	WJFJ	NC	1160	U2	10	0.5	Gospel
511)	WCCS	PA	1160	U4	10	1	AC/oldies
512)	WAMB	TN	1160	U2	50	1	Nostalgia
513)	KRDY	TX	1160	U4	10	1	Children's prgrs
514)	KBIS#	TX	1160	U4	25	1	Ethnic
515)	KSL	UT	1160	U1	50	50	News/talk
516)	WACV	AL	1170	U4	10	1	News/talk/sports
517)	KLOK	CA	1170	U4	50	5	Spanish: Tropical
518)	KCBQ	CA	1170	U4	50	1.5	Talk
519)	KFAQ	OK	1170	U2	50	50	Talk
520)	WLGO	SC	1170	D1	10		UC: Gospel/talk
521)	KPUG	WA	1170	U2	10	5	Sports
522)	WWVA	WV	1170	U2	50	50	Talk/religion/C&W
523)	KYET	AZ	1180	U1	10	0.25	C&W
524)	KERI	CA	1180	U4	50	10	Religion/talk
525)	VOA	FL	1180	U3	100	100	Spanish

	Call	Sta	kHz	Ant	D	N	Format
526)	WJNT	MS	1180	U12	50	0.5	News/talk
527)	KOFI	MT	1180	U2	50	10	Oldies/talk
528)	KYDZ	NE	1180	U4	25	1	Children's prgrs
529)	WHAM	NY	1180	U1	50	50	News/talk
530)	WMYT	NC	1180	D3	10		Spanish: Religion
531)	WVLZ	TN	1180	D1	10		Sports
532)	KGOL	TX	1180	U4	50	1	Religion/ethnic
533)	KXMX	CA	1190	U4	20	1.3	Ethnic/Spanish
534)	WAFS	GA	1190	D1	25		News/talk
535)	WOWO	IN	1190	U2	50	9.8	News/talk
536)	WBIS	MD	1190	D3	10		Financial/sports
537)	KRFT	MO	1190	D3	10		Sports
538)	KXKS	NM	1190	U1	10	0.02	Spanish: Mexican
539)	WLIB	NY	1190	U4	10	30	Talk
540)	KEX	OR	1190	U2	50	50	Talk
541)	KFXR	TX	1190	U4	50	5	Sports
542)	WBDY	VA	1190	D3	10		Sports
543)	KYAA	CA	1200	U2	25	1	Oldies
544)	WPTK	FL	1200	U4	10	1	News/talk
545)	WRTO	IL	1200	U4	10	2.5	Spanish: Talk
546)	WKOX	MA	1200	U2	10	1	Spanish: Religion
547)	WCHB	MI	1200	U4	50	15	UC: Talk/gospel
548)	WSML	NC	1200	U2	10	1	News/talk/sports
549)	WXIT	NC	1200	D1	10		Talk
550)	KFNW	ND	1200	U2	10	0.7	Religion
551)	WRKK	PA	1200	U4	10	0.25	Talk/sports
552)	WKDA	TN	1200	U2	10	0.5	Spanish: Rock
553)	WOAI	TX	1200	U1	50	50	News/talk
554)	WQLS	AL	1210	U1	10	0.004	Gospel
555)	KQTL	AZ	1210	U2	10	1	Spanish: News/talk
556)	KPRZ	CA	1210	U4	20	10	Religion
557)	WNMA	FL	1210	U4	47	2.5	Spanish: News/talk
558)	WDGR	GA	1210	D1	10		Ethnic
559)	WSKR	LA	1210	U2	10	1	Sports
560)	WLDR	MI	1210	D1	50		C&W
561)	KGYN	OK	1210	U2	10	10	C&W
562)	WPHT	PA	1210	U1	50	50	Talk/sports/nostalgia (SS)
563)	WMPS	TN	1210	U2	10	0.25	AOR
564)	KUBR	TX	1210	U4	10	5	Spanish: Religion
565)	KUNF	UT	1210	U1	10	0.25	Nostalgia/oldies
566)	KNWX	WA	1210	U4	27	10	News/financial
567)	KZTS	WA	1210	U1	10	1	Spanish: Mexican
568)	KHAT	WY	1210	U2	10	1	Oldies
569)	WHK	OH	1220	U3	50	50	Religion/talk
570)	WHNZ	FL	1250	U4	25	5.9	Talk
571)	KKHK	KS	1250	U4	25	3.7	Spanish: Mexican
572)	WKBR	NH	1250	U4	5	5	News/talk
573)	WMTR	NJ	1250	U4	5	5	Oldies
574)	WEAE	PA	1250	U2	5	5	Sports
575)	WDVA	VA	1250	U2	5	5	UC: Gospel/religion
576)	KWSU	WA	1250	ST1	5	5	News/talk
577)	KKDZ	WA	1250	ST2	5	5	Children's prgrs
578)	WEMP	WI	1250	U4	5	5	Religion
579)	KSUR	CA	1260	U4	20	7.5	Oldies
580)	WWRC	DC	1260	U4	5	5	Sports
581)	WSUA	FL	1260	U4	5	5	Spanish: AC
582)	WSDZ	IL	1260	U4	20	5	Children's prgrs
583)	WNDE	IN	1260	U2	5	5	Talk/sports
584)	WMKI	MA	1260	U2	5	5	Children's prgrs
585)	WPNW	MI	1260	U4	10	1	Religion/gospel
586)	KSGF	MO	1260	U2	5	5	News/talk
587)	WNSS	NY	1260	U2	5	5	Sports
588)	WWMK	OH	1260	U4	10	5	Children's prgrs
589)	WRIE	PA	1260	U4	5	5	Nostalgia
590)	WXCE	WI	1260	U4	5	5	News/talk/sports
591)	WRLZ	FL	1270	U2	5	5	Spanish: CHR
592)	WNLS	FL	1270	U2	5	5	News/talk
593)	WKBF	IL	1270	U2	5	5	C&W
594)	WXYT	MI	1270	U4	50	50	Sports/talk
595)	WMKT	MI	1270	U2	5	5	Financial/talk/sports
596)	WWWI	MN	1270	U2	5	5	Talk/sports
597)	KBZZ	NV	1270	U2	13	5	Talk/sports
598)	WTSN	NH	1270	U4	5	5	News/talk/sports
599)	WCGC	NC	1270	U4	10	0.5	Religion
600)	KFLC	TX	1270	U3	5	5	Spanish: Mexican
601)	KXTK	CA	1280	U4	10	2.5	Sports
602)	KBNO	CO	1280	U4	5	5	Spanish: Mexican
603)	WODT	LA	1280	U3	5	5	Sports
604)	WFAU	ME	1280	U2	5	5	Sports
605)	WWTC	MN	1280	U2	5	5	Talk
606)	WADO	NY	1280	U4	50	7.2	Spanish: Talk
607)	WHTK	NY	1280	U2	5	5	Talk/sports
608)	KZNS	UT	1280	U4	10	0.6	Sports
609)	WNAM	WI	1280	U4	5	5	Nostalgia
610)	KPAY	CA	1290	U2	5	5	Talk/sports
611)	KKDD	CA	1290	U4	5	5	Children's prgrs
612)	WJNO	FL	1290	U4	10	4.9	News/talk
613)	WTKS	GA	1290	U2	5	5	News/talk
614)	WWFS	IL	1290	U4	5	5	Sports
615)	KGVO	MT	1290	U2	5	5	News/talk
616)	KKAR	NE	1290	U2	5	5	News/talk
617)	WKBK	NH	1290	U3	5	5	News/talk
618)	WNBF	NY	1290	U2	9.3	5	News/talk
619)	WHKY	NC	1290	U4	50	1	Talk/sports
620)	WHIO	OH	1290	U2	5	5	News/talk
621)	KUMA	OR	1290	U2	5	5	Talk
622)	WRNI	RI	1290	U4	10	10	News/talk/educational
623)	KRGE	TX	1290	U2	5	5	Spanish: Religion
624)	WDZY	VA	1290	U1	25	0.04	Children's prgrs
625)	WMCS	WI	1290	U4	5	5	Talk
626)	KGLO	IA	1300	U4	5	5	News/talk
627)	WJFK	MD	1300	U4	5	5	Sports
628)	WOOD	MI	1300	U3	20	20	News/talk
629)	WTMM	NY	1300	U4	5	5	Sports
630)	WERE	OH	1300	U3	5	5	News/talk
631)	KAPL	OR	1300	U2	20	5	Religion
632)	WNQM	TN	1300	U2	50	5	Religion
633)	KKOL	WA	1300	U2	5	5	News/talk
634)	KMKY	CA	1310	U3	5	5	Children's prgrs
635)	WICH	CT	1310	U4	5	5	AC/easy listening: talk
636)	WLOB	ME	1310	U4	5	5	News/talk
637)	WXDX	MI	1310	U4	5	5	News/talk
638)	KNOX	ND	1310	U2	5	5	News/talk/sports
639)	WDOD	TN	1310	U2	5	5	Nostalgia
640)	KTCK	TX	1310	U4	9	5	Sports
641)	WGH	VA	1310	U4	20	5	Sports
642)	WIBA	WI	1310	U2	5	5	News/talk
643)	KYHN	AR	1320	U2	5	5	News/talk
644)	KCTC	CA	1320	U4	5	5	Nostalgia
645)	WJGR	FL	1320	U2	5	5	News/talk
646)	WLQY	FL	1320	U4	5	5	Ethnic
647)	WARL	MA	1320	U4	5	5	Talk
648)	KOZY	MN	1320	U2	5	5	Oldies
649)	WDER	NH	1320	U4	10	1	Religion
650)	WCOG	NC	1320	U4	5	5	Children's prgrs
651)	WJAS	PA	1320	U2	5	5	Nostalgia
652)	KELO	SD	1320	U2	5	5	News/talk
653)	KXYZ	TX	1320	U2	5	5	Spanish: Religion
654)	KFNZ	UT	1320	U3	5	5	Sports
655)	KJLL	AZ	1330	U2	2	5	Talk
656)	KLBS	CA	1330	U2	0.4	5	Ethnic
657)	KWKW	CA	1330	U2	5	5	Spanish: Talk/sports
658)	KWLO	IA	1330	U4	5	5	Nostalgia
659)	KFH	KS	1330	U2	5	5	Talk
660)	WRCA	MA	1330	U4	5	5	Ethnic
661)	WLOL	MN	1330	U4	9.7	5.1	Religion
662)	WWRV	NY	1330	U4	10	5	Spanish: Religion
663)	KKPZ	OR	1330	U3	5	5	Religion
664)	WFNN	PA	1330	U4	5	5	Sports
665)	WYRD	SC	1330	U2	5	5	News/talk
666)	KSRO	CA	1350	U2	5	5	News/talk/sports
667)	KRNT	IA	1350	U2	5	5	Talk/nostalgia
668)	WSMB	LA	1350	U2	5	5	Talk
669)	WHWH	NJ	1350	U4	5	5	Financial/talk
670)	WTOU	OH	1350	U3	5	5	Sports
671)	KCOR	TX	1350	U2	5	5	Spanish: CHR
672)	WGPL	VA	1350	U4	5	5	UC: Gospel
673)	KPXQ	AZ	1360	U2	50	1	Religion
674)	WDRC	CT	1360	U2	5	5	Talk
675)	KSCJ	IA	1360	U2	5	5	News/talk/sports
676)	WCKY	OH	1360	U2	5	5	Sports
677)	KUIK	OR	1360	U2	5	5	Talk
678)	KAHZ	TX	1360	U4	50	0.89	Spanish: News/talk
679)	KKMO	WA	1360	U1	5	5	Spanish: Mexican
680)	WTAQ	WI	1360	U2	5	5	News/talk
681)	KZSF	CA	1370	U3	5	5	Spanish: Mexican
682)	WCOA	FL	1370	U2	5	5	Talk
683)	KDTH	IA	1370	U2	5	5	Nostalgia
684)	WDEA	ME	1370	U4	5	5	Nostalgia
685)	WWLG	MD	1370	U4	50	7.7	Nostalgia

	Call	Sta	kHz	Ant	D	N	Format
686)	KXTL	MT	1370	U1	5	5	Oldies/talk
687)	WFEA	NH	1370	U4	5	5	Nostalgia
688)	WXXI	NY	1370	U2	5	5	News/talk/variety/jazz
689)	WLTC	NC	1370	U1	12	0.03	UC: Gospel
690)	WSPD	OH	1370	U2	5	5	News/talk/sports
691)	WDEF	TN	1370	U2	5	5	Sports
692)	KTKZ	CA	1380	U4	5	5	Talk
693)	KZFX	CA	1380	U4	5	5	Sports
694)	WWMI	FL	1380	U2	5	5	Children's prgrs
695)	WTJK	IL	1380	U2	5	5	Sports
696)	WKJG	IN	1380	U4	5	5	Sports
697)	WPHM	MI	1380	U4	5	5	AC/News/talk/sports
698)	KLIZ	MN	1380	U2	5	5	Sports
699)	WKDM	NY	1380	U3	5	5	Russian
700)	WKJV	NC	1380	U2	25	1	Gospel/religion
701)	KOTA	SD	1380	U2	5	5	News/talk/sports
702)	WBTK	VA	1380	U4	5	5	Religion
703)	KRKO	WA	1380	U2	5	5	News/talk/sports
704)	KLOC	CA	1390	U4	5	5	Spanish: Mexican
705)	WGRB	IL	1390	U4	5	5	UC: Gospel
706)	WEGP	ME	1390	U2	5	5	Talk
707)	WPLM	MA	1390	U4	5	5	Financial/AC
708)	WROA	MS	1390	U4	5	5	Nostalgia
709)	WFBL	NY	1390	U4	5	5	News/talk
710)	WXTC	SC	1390	U2	5	5	UC: Gospel
711)	WVAA	VT	1390	U2	5	5	C&W
712)	WZHF	VA	1390	U4	5	5	Spanish/ethnic
713)	WRIG	WI	1390	U4	5	5	Talk/nostalgia
714)	WLVV	AL	1410	U2	5	5	UC: Gospel
715)	WPOP	CT	1410	U4	5	5	Sports
716)	WDOV	DE	1410	U4	5	5	News/talk
717)	WMYR	FL	1410	U2	5	5	Children's prgrs
718)	WING	OH	1410	U2	5	5	Sports
719)	KQV	PA	1410	U4	5	5	News
720)	WIZM	WI	1410	U2	5	5	Talk
721)	WRCG	GA	1420	U2	5	5	News/talk
722)	KIGO#	ID	1420	U1	50	0.01	C&W
723)	WIMS	IN	1420	U4	5	5	News/talk/sports
724)	WOC	IA	1420	U4	5	5	News/talk
725)	KTOE	MN	1420	U2	5	5	AC/talk
726)	WRMR	OH	1420	U2	5	5	Talk
727)	WCOJ	PA	1420	U2	5	5	Nostalgia/oldies/talk
728)	WKCW	VA	1420	U1	10	0.01	Spanish: CHR
729)	KITI	WA	1420	U4	5	5	Oldies
730)	KUJ	WA	1420	U2	5	5	Nostalgia/talk
731)	KFIG	CA	1430	U3	5	5	Talk/sports
732)	KMRB	CA	1430	U4	5	5	Chinese
733)	KEZW	CO	1430	U2	10	5	Nostalgia
734)	WTMN	FL	1430	D1	10		UC: Gospel
735)	WLTG	FL	1430	U4	5	5	News/talk
736)	WXNT	IN	1430	U2	5	5	News/talk/sports
737)	WRTH	MO	1430	U4	5	5	Oldies
738)	WNSW	NJ	1430	U2	5	5	Korean/brokered
739)	WENE	NY	1430	U2	5	5	Talka/sports
740)	KTBZ	OK	1430	U4	25	5	Sports/talk
741)	KYKN	OR	1430	U2	5	5	News/talk
742)	WPLN	TN	1430	U2	15	1	Talk/variety
743)	KLO	UT	1430	U4	10	5	Talk
744)	WJAE	ME	1440	U2	5	5	Sports
745)	WVEI	MA	1440	U2	5	5	Sports
746)	WHKW	OH	1440	U4	5	5	Nostalgia
747)	WGVL	SC	1440	U2	5	5	Spanish: CHR/talk
748)	KION	CA	1460	U3	10	10	News/talk
749)	WZNZ	FL	1460	U2	5	5	Sports
750)	WZEP	FL	1460	U1	10	0.18	C&W
751)	KXNO	IA	1460	U2	5	5	Sports
752)	KENO	NV	1460	U4	10	0.62	Sports
753)	WHIC	NY	1460	U2	5	5	Religion
754)	WDDY	NY	1460	U2	5	5	Children's prgrs
755)	WEWO	NC	1460	U4	5	5	UC: Gospel
756)	KLTC	ND	1460	U2	5	5	C&W/talk
757)	WTKT	PA	1460	U2	5	5	Sports
758)	WKDV	VA	1460	U4	5	5	Spanish
759)	KUTY	CA	1470	U4	5	5	Spanish: Mexican
760)	WWNN	FL	1470	U4	50	2.50	Talk
761)	WRGA	GA	1470	U2	5	5	News/talk
762)	WMBD	IL	1470	U4	5	5	News/talk/sports(n)
763)	KWSL	IA	1470	U4	5	5	Sports
764)	WLAM	ME	1470	U3	5	5	Oldies
765)	KLBP	MN	1470	U4	5	5	Nostalgia
766)	WWBG	NC	1470	U4	10	5	Spanish: Mexican
767)	WKAP	PA	1470	U2	5	5	Oldies
768)	KACE#	UT	1470	U4	10	1	
769)	KVNR	CA	1480	U4	5	5	Ethnic
770)	KYOS	CA	1480	U2	5	5	News/talk
771)	WGUS	GA	1480	U2	5	5	C&W
772)	WSAR	MA	1480	U3	5	5	Talk
773)	WGVU	MI	1480	U2	2	5	News/talk
774)	WZRC	NY	1480	U4	5	5	Cantonese
775)	WGFY	NC	1480	U4	4.4	5	Children's prgrs
776)	WHBC	OH	1480	U4	15	5	Oldies/talk
777)	WLMV	WI	1480	U4	5	5	Spanish: CHR
778)	KIEV#	CA	1500	U4	50	4.3	News/talk
779)	KSJX	CA	1500	U4	10	5	Asian/ethnic
780)	WTOP	DC	1500	U4	50	50	News
781)	WLQV	MI	1500	U4	50	10	Religion
782)	KSTP	MN	1500	U2	50	50	News/talk
783)	WICY#	NY	1500	D4	50		Oldies
784)	KFNN	AZ	1510	U3	22	0.1	Financial/talk
785)	KIRV	CA	1510	D3	10		Religion
786)	KSPA	CA	1510	U4	10	1	Nostalgia
787)	KCUV	CO	1510	U4	10	1.3	C&W/bluegrass
788)	WWZN	MA	1510	U7	50	50	Sports
789)	KCTE	MO	1510	D3	10		Talk
790)	WLAC	TN	1510	U2	50	50	News/talk
791)	KLLB	UT	1510	D1	10		Gospel
792)	KGA	WA	1510	U4	50	50	Talk/sports
793)	WAUK	WI	1510	D3	10		Sports
794)	KVTA	CA	1520	U4	10	1	Talk
795)	KDYS	LA	1520	U6	10	0.5	Children's prgrs
796)	WTRI	MD	1520	D3	17		Korean
797)	WIZZ	MA	1520	D3	10		Nostalgia
798)	KOLM	MN	1520	U8	10	0.8	Talk
799)	WWKB	NY	1520	U3	50	50	Oldies/talk
800)	KOMA	OK	1520	U2	50	50	News/talk/religion(n)
801)	KGDD	OR	1520	U3	50	15	Spanish: Mexican
802)	KFBK	CA	1530	U4	50	50	News/talk
803)	KCMN	CO	1530	U1	15	0.01	Nostalgia
804)	WYMM	FL	1530	D3	50		Gospel
805)	WTTI	GA	1530	D4	10		Gospel/religion
806)	WRPM	MS	1530	D1	10		Gospel
807)	WRTP	NC	1530	D3	10		Religion
808)	WSAI	OH	1530	U2	50	50	Oldies
809)	KZNX	TX	1530	D4	10		Sports
810)	KGBT	TX	1530	U8	50	10	Spanish: Mexican/Tejano
811)	KASA	AZ	1540	U3	10	0.01	Spanish/English: Gospel/ religion
812)	KMPC	CA	1540	U4	50	10	Sports
813)	KXEL	IA	1540	U2	50	50	News/talk/religion
814)	WDCD	NY	1540	U3	50	50	Religion
815)	WNWR	PA	1540	D3	50		Ethnic/brokered
816)	WTBI	SC	1540	D1	10		Gospel/religion
817)	KZMP	TX	1540	U4	32	0.75	Spanish: Religion
818)	WREJ	VA	1540	D3	10		UC: Gospel/religion
819)	KXPA	WA	1540	U2	5	5	Spanish: CHR/ethnic
820)	WLOR	AL	1550	U4	50	0.5	UC: AC
821)	KUAZ	AZ	1550	D1	50		Jazz/variety
822)	KYCY	CA	1550	U4	10	10	Talk
823)	WAMA	FL	1550	U1	10	0.13	Spanish: Mexican
824)	WRHC	FL	1550	U4	10	0.5	Spanish/ethnic
825)	WAZX	GA	1550	U4	50	0.5	Spanish: Mexican
826)	WNTN	MA	1550	D1	10		Ethnic
827)	KSFT	MO	1550	U2	5	5	Oldies
828)	WITK	PA	1550	U4	10	0.5	Oldies
829)	WBSC	SC	1550	U2	10	5	Oldies
830)	KMRI	UT	1550	U1	10	0.34	Religion/talk
831)	WKBA	VA	1550	D3	10		Religion/gospel
832)	KRPI	WA	1550	U4	50	10	Punjabi
833)	KKAD	WA	1550	U2	50	12	Talk
834)	KNZR	CA	1560	U2	25	10	News/talk
835)	WRHC#	FL	1560	U4	25	5	Spanish/ethnic
836)	KLNG	IA	1560	D1	10		Religion/gospel
837)	WPAD	KY	1560	U4	10	1	Nostalgia
838)	WQEW	NY	1560	U4	50	50	Children's prgrs
839)	WAGL	SC	1560	D3	50		Spanish: Mexican
840)	KKAA	SD	1560	U4	10	5	News/talk
841)	WVOJ	FL	1570	U1	10	0.03	Spanish: Mexican
842)	KMIK	AZ	1580	U2	50	50	Children's prgrs
843)	KBLA	CA	1580	U4	50	50	Spanish/English: Religion
844)	KWYD	CO	1580	U1	10	0.06	Talk

	Call	Sta	kHz	Ant	D	N	Format
845)	WSRF	FL	1580	U4	10	5	Ethnic/Jamaican
846)	WTCL	FL	1580	D1	10		Gospel
847)	WXRA	KY	1580	U3	10	0.04	Sports
848)	WPGC	MD	1580	U4	50	0.27	UC: Gospel
849)	WLIM	NY	1580	U8	10	0.5	Polish/ethnic
850)	WWGS#	SC	1580	U4	20	5	
851)	KKZZ	CA	1590	U4	5	5	Nostalgia
852)	KLIV	CA	1590	U2	5	5	News/talk
853)	KVGB	KS	1590	U2	5	5	Talk
854)	WSMN	NH	1590	U3	5	5	Financial/talk/sports
855)	WAKR	OH	1590	U2	5	5	AC/OLD: Talk
856)	WARV	RI	1590	U4	5	5	Religion
857)	WKTP	TN	1590	U3	5	5	Nostalgia
858)	KMIC	TX	1590	U2	5	5	Children's prgrs
859)	KLFE	WA	1590	U2	5	5	Religion: Talk/AC
860)	KMNY	CA	1600	U2	5	5	Ethnic
861)	KGST	CA	1600	U2	5	5	Spanish: Mexican
862)	KCKK	CO	1600	U2	5	5	C&W
863)	WOKB	FL	1600	U4	5	5	UC: AC/gospel/ethnic(n)
864)	WAOS	GA	1600	U1	20	0.06	Spanish: Mexican
865)	KCRG	IA	1600	U2	5	5	Sports
866)	WUNR	MA	1600	U3	5	5	SS(d)/ethnic/UC/religion(n)
867)	WMHG	MI	1600	U2	5	5	Nostalgia
868)	WAAM	MI	1600	U4	5	5	News/talk
869)	KZGX	MN	1600	U3	5	5	Oldies
870)	KATZ	MO	1600	U2	5	5	UC: Gospel
871)	KANM	NM	1600	U1	10	0.12	Oldies
872)	WWRL	NY	1600	U4	25	5	UC/ethnic/talk
873)	WMQM	TN	1600	U1	50	0.03	Religion
874)	KVRI	WA	1600	U4	50	10	Punjabi
875)	WRPN	WI	1600	U4	5	5	AC/talk/sports
876)	KALT	TX	1610	U1	10	1	Religion
877)	KSMH	CA	1620	U1	10	1	Religion
878)	WNRP#	FL	1620	U1	10	1	Gospel
879)	KBLI	ID	1620	U1	10	1	Sports
880)	WHLY	IN	1620	U1	10	1	Nostalgia/oldies
881)	KOZN	NE	1620	U1	10	1	Sports
882)	WTAW	TX	1620	U1	10	1	Talk
883)	KYIZ	WA	1620	U1	10	1	UC: AC
884)	WRDW	GA	1630	U1	10	1	Talk/sports
885)	KCJJ	IA	1630	U1	10	1	Talk/sports/AC
886)	KKGM	TX	1630	U1	10	1	Religion
887)	KKWY	WY	1630	U1	10	1	C&W
888)	KDIA	CA	1640	U1	10	1	Religion
889)	WTNI	MS	1640	U1	10	1	News/talk
890)	KFNY	OK	1640	U4	10	1	Comedy/talk
891)	KDZR	OR	1640	U1	10	1	Children's prgrs
892)	KBJA	UT	1640	U1	10	1	Spanish: Talk
893)	WKSH	WI	1640	U1	10	1	Children's prgrs
894)	KWHN	AR	1650	U1	10	1	News/talk
895)	KFOX	CA	1650	U1	10	0.49	Korean
896)	KBJD	CO	1650	U1	10	1	Talk
897)	KCNZ	IA	1650	U1	10	1	News/talk/sports
898)	WHKT	VA	1650	U1	10	1	Children's prgrs
899)	KTIQ	CA	1660	U1	10	1	Spanish: Talk
900)	WCNZ	FL	1660	U1	10	1	Financial/news/talk
901)	KXTR	KS	1660	U1	10	1	Classical
902)	WQSN	MI	1660	U1	10	1	Sports
903)	WWRU	NJ	1660	U2	10	10	Korean
904)	WFNA	NC	1660	U1	10	1	Sports
905)	KQWB	ND	1660	U1	10	1	News/talk
906)	KRZX	TX	1660	U1	10	1	Sports
907)	KXOL	UT	1660	U1	10	1	Oldies
908)	KNRO	CA	1670	U1	10	1	Sports
909)	KHPY	CA	1670	U4	10	9	Spanish: Religion
910)	WMWR	GA	1670	U1	10	1	Talk
911)	WTDY	WI	1670	U1	10	1	Talk
912)	KAVT	CA	1680	U1	10	1	Children's prgrs
913)	WLAA	FL	1680	U1	10	1	Spanish: Mexican
914)	KRJO	LA	1680	U1	10	1	UC: Gospel
915)	WDSS	MI	1680	U1	10	0.68	Children's prgrs
916)	WTTM	NJ	1680	U1	10	1	Ethnic/Asian
917)	KTFH	WA	1680	U1	10	1	Spanish: Mexican
918)	KFSG	CA	1690	U1	10	1	Spanish: Religion
919)	KDDZ	CO	1690	U1	10	1	Children's prgrs
920)	WSWK	GA	1690	U1	10	1	C&W
921)	WRLL	IL	1690	U1	10	1	Oldies
922)	WPTX	MD	1690	U1	10	1	News/talk
923)	WEUV	AL	1700	U1	10	1	UC: Gospel
924)	WJCC	FL	1700	U1	10	1	Spanish: Religion
925)	KBGG	IA	1700	U1	10	1	Spanish: Mexican
926)	KTBK	TX	1700	U1	10	0.7	Sports

Addresses:
1) 495 Elder Avenue, Sand City, CA 93955-3547 – **2)** 2500 Maitland Center Pkwy #401, Maitland, FL 32751-4122 – **3)** 3223 Sillect Ave, Bakersfield, CA 93308-6329 – **4)** 1102 Thompson Bridge Rd, Gainesville, GA 30501-1706 – **5)** 638 West Port Plaza, Saint Louis, MO 63146-3106 – **6)** 500 Corporate Parkway #200, Buffalo, NY 14226-1263 – **7)** 210 N 4th Street, Bismarck, ND 58501-4004 – **8)** 237 Covell Hall - OSU, Corvallis, OR 97331-8524 – **9)** 4050 Eisenhauer Road, San Antonio, TX 78218-3409 – **10)** 557 Scott Street, Wausau, WI 54403-4829 – **11)** 900 Front St, San Francisco, CA 94111-1427 – **12)** 2150 West 29th Ave. #300, Denver, CO 80211-3889 – **13)** 625 N. Michigan Avenue #300, Chicago, IL 60611-3163 – **14)** 420 Western Avenue, South Portland, ME 04106-1704 – **15)** 14 East Central Entrance, Duluth, MN 55811-5508 – **16)** 20 Third Street N #231, Great Falls, MT 59401-3188 – **17)** 117 Ridge Pike, Lafayette Hill, PA 19444-1900 – **18)** 316 Greystone Blvd, Columbia, SC 29210-8007 – **19)** 2885 Interstate 10 E, Beaumont, TX 77702-1001 – **20)** 32 N. Mission Street, Wenatchee, WA 98801-7210 – **21)** 3400 Olive Avenue #400, Burbank, CA 91505-5538 – **22)** 504 N. Reo Street, Tampa, FL 33609-1013 – **23)** 777 Terrace Ave #16, Hasbrouck Heights, NJ 07604-3100 – **24)** 500 Plum Street #100, Syracuse, NY 13204-1427 – **25)** 13 Summerlin Road, Asheville, NC 28806-2800 – **26)** 7461 South Avenue, Youngstown, OH 44512-5789 – **27)** WNAX Bldg - 1609 East Hwy 50, Yankton, SD 57078-6406 – **28)** 3500 Maple Ave. #1600, Dallas, TX 75219-3945 – **29)** 2801 Decker Lake Drive, West Valley City, UT 84119-2330 – **30)** 140 4th Avenue North #340, Seattle, WA 98109-4932 – **31)** 1071 West Shaw Street, Fresno, CA 93771-3702 – **32)** 4192 North John Young Pkwy, Orlando, FL 32804-2696 – **33)** 827 Park Blvd #201, Boise, ID 83712-7782 – **34)** 1200 SW Executive Drive, Topeka, KS 66615-3850 – **35)** 96 Stereo Lane, Paxton, MA 01612-1376 – **36)** 314 E. Front Street, Traverse City, MI 49684-2528 – **37)** 600 Corporate Cir #100, Harrisburg, PA 17110-9787 – **38)** 1111 Virginia Street East, Charleston, WV 25301-2406 – **39)** 308 Victory Road, Quincy, MA 02171-3129 – **40)** 4200 W. Main Street, Kalamazoo, MI 49006-2766 – **41)** 11128 John Galt Blvd #192, Omaha, NE 68137-2371 – **42)** 4002 NC Hwy 42 West, Wilson, NC 27893-7774 – **43)** 1200 Executive Pkwy #440, Eugene, OR 97401-2169 – **44)** 600 Baltimore Drive, Wilkes-Barre, PA 18702-7901 – **45)** 808 East Sprague Avenue, Spokane, WA 99202-2126 – **46)** 9660 Granite Ridge Drive, San Diego, CA 92123-2657 – **47)** 10245 Centurion Pkwy North #109, Jacksonville, FL 32256-0569 – **48)** 600 Old Marion Road NE, Cedar Rapids, IA 52402-2152 – **49)** 711 West 40th Street #350, Baltimore, MD 21211-2190 – **50)** 875 W. 5th Street, Winston-Salem, NC 27101-2505 – **51)** 2400 8th Avenue SW, Jamestown, ND 58401-6623 – **52)** 2650 Thousand Oaks Blvd #4100, Memphis, TN 38118-2451 – **53)** 4180 North Mesa Street, El Paso, TX 79902-1420 – **54)** 500 Washington St. #200, San Francisco, CA 94111-2968 – **55)** 7601 Riviera Blvd, Miramar, FL 33023-6574 – **56)** 715 East Central Entrance, Duluth, MN 55811-5596 – **57)** 4935 Belinder Rd, Westwood, KS 66205-1999 – **58)** 500 4th Street NW, Albuquerque, NM 87102-5324 – **59)** 2323 West 5th Avenue, Columbus, OH 43204-4899 – **60)** 511 Rossanley Drive, Medford, OR 97501-1771 – **61)** 441 North 5th Street, Philadelphia, PA 19123-4089 – **62)** 24 East Greenway Plaza #1900, Houston, TX 77046-2428 – **63)** 2823 W. Lewis Street, Pasco, WA 99301-6700 – **64)** 5300 North Central Ave, Phoenix, AZ 85012-1410 – **65)** 4002 W. Gandy Blvd, Tampa, FL 33611-3410 – **66)** 861 Broadway, Bangor, ME 04401-2916 – **67)** 475 Park Avenue South 27th Flr, New York, NY 10016-6901 – **68)** 4949 SW. Macadam Avenue, Portland, OR 97201-3912 – **69)** 1621 E. Magnolia Avenue, Knoxville, TN 37917-7825 – **70)** 118 Malletts Bay Avenue, Winooski, VT 05404-1916 – **71)** 720 E. Capitol Drive, Milwaukee, WI 53212-1308 – **72)** 4695 S. Monaco Street, Denver, CO 80237-3403 – **73)** 4400 Jenifer St NW #400, Washington, DC 20015-2183 – **74)** 214 Television Circle, Savannah, GA 31406-4519 – **75)** 827 Park Blvd #201, Boise, ID 83712-7782 – **76)** 1215 Fern Ridge Parkway #220, Saint Louis, MO 63141-4406 – **77)** 1502 Wampanoag Trail, Riverside, RI 02915-1075 – **78)** 9601 McAllister Freeway #1200, San Antonio, TX 78216-4686 – **79)** 3400 Olive Avenue #400, Burbank, CA 91505-5538 – **80)** 1819 Peachtree Rd. NE #700, Atlanta, GA 30309-1849 – **81)** 1331 Main Street #5, Springfield, MA 01103-1621 – **82)** 2050 Amsterdam Road, Belgrade, MT 59714-8957 – **83)** 500 Office Center Drive #330, Fort Washington, PA 19034-3214 – **84)** 1009 Drayton Road, Fayetteville, NC 28303-3887 – **85)** 555 S. Perkins Road #201, Memphis, TN 38117-3944 – **86)** 162 Free Hill Road, Gray, TN 37615-3144 – **87)** 1440 Ethan Way #200, Sacramento, CA 95825-2214 – **88)** Manistique, MI – **89)** 807 West 37th Street, Hibbing, MN 55746-2856 – **90)** 2644 McGavock Pike,

Nashville, TN 37214-1223 – **91)** 1600 W 500 Riverlane Rd North, Manti, UT 84642 – **92)** 2800 Dauphin Street #104, Mobile, AL 36606-2400 – **93)** P.O. Box 2569, Window Rock, AZ 86515-2569 – **94)** 2225 Skyway Drive, Santa Maria, CA 93455-1118 – **95)** 1010 2nd St. North, Sauk Rapids, MN 56379-2527 – **96)** 3412 36th Street, Astoria, NY 11106-1214 – **97)** 410 E. 6th Street, Williston, ND 58801-5552 – **98)** 888 SW 5th Avenue #790, Portland, OR 97204-2021 – **99)** 2420 Wade Hampton Blvd, Greenville, SC 29615-1107 – **100)** 6400 North Belt Line Road #110, Irving, TX 75063-6065 – **101)** 2029 Freeway Drive, Mount Vernon, WA 98273-5470 – **102)** 2150 West 29th Ave. #300, Denver, CO 80211-3889 – **103)** 330 SW 27th Avenue #207, Miami, FL 33135-2957 – **104)** 1419 W. Bannock Street, Boise, ID 83702-5234 – **105)** NBC Tower - 455 N. Cityfront Plaza Dr. 6th Flr, Chicago, IL 60611-5579 – **106)** Las Vegas, NV – **107)** 2202 Mt. Jolliff Road, Chesapeake, VA 23321-1416 – **108)** 55 Hawthorne St. #1100, San Francisco, CA 94105-3932 – **109)** 14 Piedmont Ct NE #14, Atlanta, GA 30305-4535 – **110)** 1726 Reisterstown Rd #117, Pikesville, MD 21208-2986 – **111)** 20 Guest Street 3rd Flr, Brighton, MA 02135-2040 – **112)** 604 Ludington Street, Escanaba, MI 49829-3830 – **113)** 4104 Country Lane, Saint Joseph, MO 64506-4921 – **114)** 3012 Highwoods Blvd #200, Raleigh, NC 27604-1031 – **115)** 5904 Ridgeway Center Pkwy, Memphis, TN 38120-4025 – **116)** 8122 Datapoint Drive #500, San Antonio, TX 78229-3296 – **117)** 1111 Virginia Street East, Charleston, WV 25301-2406 – **118)** 244 Goodwin Crest Dr. #300, Birmingham, AL 35209-3700 – **119)** 8000 Belfort Parkway #100, Jacksonville, FL 32256-6971 – **120)** 306 W 8th Street, Coffeyville, KS 67337-5829 – **121)** 4539 N I-10 Service Road West, Metaire, LA 70006-6575 – **122)** 4045 N. Mesa Street, El Paso, TX 79902-1526 – **123)** 11373 Wallace Pike, Bristol, VA 24202-2743 – **124)** 8044 Montgomery Road, Cincinnati, OH 45263-0001 – **125)** 196 Main Street, Winston, OR 97496-9503 – **126)** 11451 Katy Freeway #215, Houston, TX 77079-1322 – **127)** 2801 South Decker Lake Drive, West Valley City, UT 84119-2330 – **128)** 282 Memory Lane, Old Town, ID 83822-9203 – **129)** 1641 E. Osborn Rd #8, Phoenix, AZ 85016-7136 – **130)** 3321 S. La Cienega Blvd, Los Angeles, CA 90016-3114 – **131)** 1425 River Park Dr. #520, Sacramento, CA 95815-4524 – **132)** 3131 S. Vaughn Way #601, Aurora, CO 80014-3516 – **133)** 800 S. Douglas Rd #111, Coral Gables, FL 33134-3187 – **134)** 6341 West Port Avenue, Shreveport, LA 71129-2415 – **135)** 5800 Foxridge Drive, Mission, KS 66205-2333 – **136)** 1440 Broadway - 24th Flr, New York, NY 10018-2374 – **137)** 210 N 4th Street, Bismarck, ND 58501-4004 – **138)** 3505 Olsen Blvd #117, Amarillo, TX 79109-3096 – **139)** 7080 Lee Highway, Radford, VA 24141-8416 – **140)** 1820 Eastlake Avenue East, Seattle, WA 98102-3711 – **141)** 715 East Central Entrance, Duluth, MN 55811-5596 – **142)** 3988 N Roscoe Rd, Hernando, FL 34442-3141 – **143)** 435 N. Michigan Avenue, Chicago, IL 60611-4076 – **144)** 1 South Main Street, Las Vegas, NV 89101-6370 – **145)** 25 Newport Road, New London, NH 03257-4129 – **146)** 3400 New Hendersonville Road, Pisgah Forest, NC 28768-8614 – **147)** 7800 West IH 10 #330, San Antonio, TX 78230-4700 – **148)** 1910 University Drive, Boise, ID 83725-0399 – **149)** 1 Commerce Street #300, Montgomery, AL 36104-3542 – **150)** 3183 Airway Avenue #D, Costa Mesa, CA 92626-4611 – **151)** 865 Battery Street, San Francisco, CA 94111-1503 – **152)** 2500 Maitland Center Pkwy #401, Maitland, FL 32751-4122 – **153)** 13656 39th Street #400, Flushing, NY 11354-5508 – **154)** 2147 Springs Road, Mount Airy, NC 27030-2447 – **155)** 7136 S. Yale Ave. #500, Tulsa, OK 74136-6325 – **156)** 510 Lovett Blvd, Houston, TX 77006-4098 – **157)** 1601 W. Peachtree St. NE, Atlanta, GA 30309-2663 – **158)** 581 N. Reservoir Road, Polson, MT 59860-8677 – **159)** 3205 West North Front Street, Grand Island, NE 68803-4024 – **160)** Fallon, NV – **161)** 0234 S.W. Bancroft Street, Portland, OR 97201-4237 – **162)** 2211 E. Missiouri Ave # S-300, El Paso, TX 79903-3831 – **163)** 1899 Carbonville Road, Helper, UT 84526-2508 – **164)** 2902 East Kiehl Ave, North Little Rock, AR 72120-3280 – **165)** 7677 Engineer Road, San Diego, CA 92111-1582 – **166)** 4695 S. Monaco Street, Denver, CO 80237-3408 – **167)** 1915 North Dale Mabry Hwy #200, Tampa, FL 33607-2555 – **168)** 70 James Street #140, Worcester, MA 01603-1038 – **169)** 3011 W. Grand Blvd #800, Detroit, MI 48202-3086 – **170)** 137 Rapids Road, Champlain, NY 12919-4945 – **171)** 6222 W IH-10 #200, San Antonio, TX 78201-2097 – **172)** 10948 Cleveland Ave. Oakdale, Riverbank, CA 95361-9709 – **173)** 20125 S. Tamiami Trail, Estero, FL 33928-2117 – **174)** 818 Main Street, Miles City, MT 59301-3221 – **175)** 500 4th Street NW, Albuquerque, NM 87102-2102 – **176)** 2 Penn Plaza #1700, New York, NY 10121-1701 – **177)** 3201 Royalty Row, Irving, TX 75062-4961 – **178)** 1820 Eastlake Avenue East, Seattle, WA 98102-3711 – **179)** 630 N. McClurg Court, Chicago, IL 60611-4536 – **180)** 243 Main Street, Norway, ME 04268-5914 – **181)** 595 E. Plumb Lane, Reno, NV 89502-3503 – **182)** 1381 W. Main Street, Forest City, NC 28043-2525 – **183)** 3321 S. LaCienega Blvd, Los Angeles, CA 90016-3197 – **184)** 20450 N.W.Second Ave. Miami, South Miami, FL 33169-2593 – **185)** 3350 Peachtree Rd. NE #1610, Atlanta, GA 30326-1040 – **186)** 222 N. 32nd St - 10th Floor, Billings, MT 59101-1911 – **187)** 1020 S. 25th Street, Fargo, ND 58103-3212 – **188)** 1502 Wampanoag Trail, Riverside, RI 02915-1075 – **189)** 1960 Union Ave, Memphis, TN 38104-4127 – **190)** 510 Lovett Blvd, Houston, TX 77006-4098 – **191)** 500 Dominion Tower - 999 Waterside Drive, Norfolk, VA 23510-3300 – **192)** 944 Harlem Street, Altoona, WI 54720-1127 – **193)** 188 John Turner Broadcast Blvd, Jacksonville, AL 36265-6659 – **194)** 900 Front Street, San Francisco, CA 94111-1450 – **195)** 130 Radio Station Drive, Magee, MS 39111-4399 – **196)** 6721 West 121st Street, Overland Park, KS 66209-2003 – **197)** One Washington Square, Albany, NY 12205-5579 – **198)** P.O. Box 99, Sturgis, SD 57785-0099 – **199)** 55 Alder Street NW #3, Ephrata, WA 98823-1663 – **200)** 1915 North Dale Mabry Hwy #200, Tampa, FL 33607-2555 – **201)** 1 Centre Street #2516, New York, NY 10007-1699 – **202)** 2221 E. Lamar Blvd #300, Arlington, TX 76006-7419 – **203)** Taylorsville, UT – **204)** 4301 W. Hundred Road, Chester, VA 23831-1737 – **205)** 2815 Second Ave. #550, Seattle, WA 98121-1263 – **206)** 7355 N. Orcale Rd. #102, Tucson, AZ 85704-6353 – **207)** 15301 Ventura Blve #200, Sherman Oaks, CA 91403-6625 – **208)** 1255 E. Main St. #A, Grass Valley, CA 95945-5711 – **209)** Sandy Springs, GA – **210)** 1049 Main Street, Worcester, MA 01603-2485 – **211)** 625 2nd Avenue South #200, Minneapolis, MN 55402-1961 – **212)** 932 County Road 448, Poplar Bluff, MO 63901-9018 – **213)** 4405 Providence Lane #D, Winston-Salem, NC 27106-3226 – **214)** 34 North 4th Street, Reading, PA 19601-3996 – **215)** 600 W. 8th Street, Muleshoe, TX 79347-3330 – **216)** 1423 S. Beverly Street, Casper, WY 82609-4131 – **217)** 2621 Ralston Road #B, Mobile, AL 36606-2358 – **218)** Modesto, CA – **219)** 221 Pall Bearer Road, Thomasville, GA 31792-1101 – **220)** 4000 Radio Drive #1, Louisville, KY 40218-4568 – **221)** 6655 W. Sahara Avenue #D208, Las Vegas, NV 89146-0851 – **222)** 108 Columbia Northeast Dr. #F, Columbia, SC 29223-6433 – **223)** 840 West Fairview Street, Colfax, WA 99111-9515 – **224)** 244 Goodwin Crest Drive #G126, Birmingham, AL 35209-3712 – **225)** 4695 S. Monaco St, Denver, CO 80237-3403 – **226)** P.O. Box 14444, Gainesville, FL 32604-2444 – **227)** 20 Guest Street 3rd Flr, Brighton, MA 02135-2040 – **228)** 1120 E. McCuen Street, Duluth, MN 55808-2199 – **229)** 18844 Highway 80, Forest, MS 39074-4410 – **230)** 85 Founders Lane, Saint Louis, MO 63105-3085 – **231)** 5000 Falls of Neuse Road #308, Raleigh, NC 27609-5480 – **232)** 9446 Broadview Road, Broadview Heights, OH 44147-2308 – **233)** 109 Plaza Drive #2, Johnstown, PA 15905-1212 – **234)** 517 Watt Road, Knoxville, TN 37922-1110 – **235)** 3000 Bering Drive, Houston, TX 77057-5708 – **236)** 500 Dominion Tower - 999 Waterside Drive, Norfolk, VA 23510-3300 – **237)** 351 Elliott Avenue West #300, Seattle, WA 98119-4150 – **238)** 5087 E. McKinley Avenue, Fresno, CA 93727-1965 – **239)** 620 Ward Street E, Douglas, GA 31533-0302 – **240)** 1162 East Hwy 126, Pittsburg, KS 66762-8712 – **241)** 888 SW 5th Avenue #790, Portland, OR 97204-2021 – **242)** 555 East City Avenue #330, Bala Cynwyd, PA 19004-1137 – **243)** 434 South Bearcat Drive, Salt Lake City, UT 84115-2543 – **244)** 240 Central Avenue, Oak Hill, WV 25901-3006 – **245)** 2278 Wortham Lane, Grovetown, GA 30813-5103 – **246)** 701 N. Brand Blvd #550, Glendale, CA 91203-1235 – **247)** 1450 Poydras St. #440, New Orleans, LA 70112-6004 – **248)** 447 Congress Street #3B, Portland, ME 04101-3505 – **249)** 283 Comm. Arts Bldg. - M.S.U, East Lansing, MI 48824-1212 – **250)** P.O. Box 49, Park Rapids, MN 56470-0049 – **251)** 340 Edgemont Avenue #100, Bristol, TN 37620-2313 – **252)** 2621 West A Street, Pasco, WA 99301-4702 – **253)** 10000 Warden Rd, North Little Rock, AR 72120-3656 – **254)** 30 East San Joaquin Street #105, Salinas, CA 93901-2946 – **255)** 2432 US Hwy 2 East, Kalispell, MT 59901-2310 – **256)** 1007 Plum Creek Parkway, Lexington, NE 68850 – **257)** P.O. Box 9090, Window Rock, AZ 86515-9090 – **258)** 524 West 57th Street, New York, NY 10019-2924 – **259)** 8101 N. High Street #360, Columbus, OH 43235-1442 – **260)** 3000 Bering Drive, Houston, TX 77057-5708 – **261)** 3650 131st SE #550, Bellevue, WA 98006-1334 – **262)** 619 Cameron Street, Eau Claire, WI 54703-4700 – **263)** 560 Higuera Street #G, San Luis Obispo, CA 93401-3850 – **264)** Meridian, ID – **265)** 190 N. State Street, Chicago, IL 60601-3398 – **266)** 529 Main Street #200, Charlestown, MA 02129-1119 – **267)** 1 Commerce Drive #106, Hattiesburg, MS 39402-1499 – **268)** 241 Riverchase Way #A, Lexington, SC 29072-9470 – **269)** 4501 North McColl Road, McAllen, TX 78504-2431 – **270)** 750 Ridgeview Drive #204, Saint George, UT 84770-2665 – **271)** 1501 Lark Lane, Blacksburg, VA 24060-2658 – **272)** 20200 DuPont Blvd, Georgetown, DE 19947-3105 – **273)** 3003 Snelling Avenue North, Saint Paul, MN 55113-1599 – **274)** 645 E. Missouri Avenue #119, Phoenix, AZ 85012-1370 – **275)** 290 Hegenberger Rd. Oakland, El Cajon, CA 94621-1436 – **276)** 340 Townsend Street #4, San Francisco, CA 94107-1698 – **277)** 330 Main Street, Hartford, CT 06106-1860 – **278)** 504 N. Reo Street, Tampa, FL 33609-1013 – **279)** 3765 N John Young Pkwy, Orlando, GA 32804-3213 – **280)** 184 Target Circle #207, Bangor,

ME 04401-5718 – **281)** 907 Lejeune Blvd, Jacksonville, NC 28540-5916 – **282)** 4300 S. US Highway 281, Edinburg, TX 78539-9650 – **283)** 0700 SW Bancroft Street, Portland, OR 97239-4226 – **284)** 700 Wellington Hills Road, Little Rock, AR 72211-2026 – **285)** 601 Central Avenue North, Faribault, MN 55021-1307 – **286)** 75 Oxford Street, Providence, RI 02905-4722 – **287)** 500 W. Boone Avenue, Spokane, WA 99201-2497 – **288)** 1845 Empire Avenue, Burbank, CA 91504-3402 – **289)** 11700 Central Pkwy, Jacksonville, FL 32224-2600 – **290)** 544 N. Arthur Avenue, Pocatello, ID 83204-3002 – **291)** 815 Lafayette Road, Portsmouth, NH 03801-5406 – **292)** 449 Broadway, New York, NY 10013-2549 – **293)** 500 Corporate Parkway #200, Buffalo, NY 14226-1263 – **294)** 4045 NW 64th Street #600, Oklahoma City, OK 73116-2615 – **295)** 2715 East 31st Street #B, Spokane, WA 99223-4708 – **296)** 4910 E Clinton Way #107, Fresno, CA 93727-1505 – **297)** 7601 Riviera Blvd, Miramar, FL 33023-6574 – **298)** 580 Mulberry St #500, Macon, GA 31201-2768 – **299)** 1416 Locust Street, Des Moines, IA 50309-3014 – **300)** 929 Howard Avenue, New Orleans, LA 70113-1148 – **301)** 1189 North Jackson Street, Houston, MS 38851-8273 – **302)** 969 SW Colorado Avenue, Bend, OR 97702-3120 – **303)** 251 Hilton Drive #200, Saint George, UT 84770-2201 – **304)** 13379 Great Springs Road, Smithfield, VA 23430-6930 – **305)** 986 Lincoln Way #103, Auburn, CA 95603-5244 – **306)** 1095 S. Monaco Pkwy, Denver, CO 80224-1602 – **307)** 1188 Lake View Road, Altamonte Springs, FL 32714-2713 – **308)** 541 North Fairbanks Court #1260, Chicago, IL 60611-3319 – **309)** 26495 American Drive, Southfield, MI 48034-6114 – **310)** 516 Fuller Avenue, Helena, MT 59601-3301 – **311)** 9418 State Route 49, Marcy, NY 13403-2342 – **312)** 1 Bala Plaza #339, Bala Cynwyd, PA 19004-1403 – **313)** 25 Garlington Road, Greenville, SC 29615-4613 – **314)** 510 Lovett Blvd, Houston, TX 77006-4021 – **315)** 351 Elliott Avenue West #300, Seattle, WA 98119-4150 – **316)** 530 Beacon Parkway W #600, Birmingham, AL 35209-3152 – **317)** 2425 E. Camelback Rd #570, Phoenix, AZ 85016-4250 – **318)** 340 Townsend Street #4, San Francisco, CA 94107-1698 – **319)** 495 Benham Street, Hamden, CT 06514-2009 – **320)** 300 W. Jefferson Blvd, South Bend, IN 46601-1580 – **321)** 209 N. Elm Street, Shenandoah, IA 51601-1139 – **322)** 351 Tilghman Road, Salisbury, MD 21804-1920 – **323)** 1500 Hegeman Avenue, Colchester, VT 05446-3116 – **324)** 4509 South 6th St. #201, Klamath Falls, OR 97603-4881 – **325)** 3934 Electric Road, Roanoke, VA 24018-4513 – **326)** 1100 Mohawk St #280, Bakersfield, CA 93309-7417 – **327)** 4002 West Gandy Blvd #A, Tampa, FL 33611-3410 – **328)** 9960 Corporate Campus Drive #3600, Louisville, KY 40223-4070 – **329)** 420 Western Avenue, South Portland, ME 04106-1704 – **330)** 27 N 27th Street, Billings, MT 59101-2357 – **331)** 777 Terrace Ave #6, Hasbrouck Heights, NJ 07604-3112 – **332)** 140 Lower Terrace Street, Buffalo, NY 14202-4303 – **333)** 301 8th Street South, Fargo, ND 58103-1826 – **334)** 222 S.W. Columbia Street #350, Portland, OR 97201-6603 – **335)** 200 Fleet Street 4th Flr, Pittsburgh, PA 15220-2910 – **336)** 181 E. Evans St. #311, Florence, SC 29506-2512 – **337)** 6230 Yucca St, Los Angeles, CA 90028-5295 – **338)** 604 East Chapel Street, Santa Maria, CA 93454-4522 – **339)** 8750 Brookville Rd, Silver Spring, MD 20910-1824 – **340)** 243 Central Street, Lowell, MA 01852-2214 – **341)** 2110 Cliff Road, Eagan, MN 55122-2347 – **342)** 4935 Belinder Rd, Westwood, KS 66205-1937 – **343)** One Washington Square, Albany, NY 12205-5579 – **344)** 3233 Burnt Mill Road #4, Wilmington, NC 28403-2655 – **345)** 101 Pine Street, Dayton, OH 45402-2925 – **346)** 1940 Neelys Bend Road, Madison, TN 37115-5800 – **347)** 1915 Mirro Drive, Manitowoc, WI 54220-6715 – **348)** 3871 North Commerce Drive, Tucson, AZ 85705-2983 – **349)** 730 Harrison Street #300, San Francisco, CA 94107-1260 – **350)** 2150 W 68th Street #202, Hialeah, FL 33016-1802 – **351)** 610 Sycamore Street #220, Celebration, FL 34747-4996 – **352)** 1650 Midland Road , Southern Pines, NC 28387-2111 – **353)** 109 Plaza Drive #2, Johnstown, PA 15905-1212 – **354)** 117 Ridge Pike, Lafayette Hill, PA 19444-1900 – **355)** 1185 North Main Street, Providence, RI 02904-1824 – **356)** 2650 Thousand Oaks Blvd #4100, Memphis, TN 38118-2451 – **357)** 4711 Old Kingston Pike, Knoxville, TN 37919-5207 – **358)** 6420 Stringfield Road NW, Huntsville, AL 35806-1455 – **359)** 190 N. State Street, Chicago, IL 60601-3302 – **360)** 4125 Carlisle Blvd NE, Albuquerque, NM 87107-4848 – **361)** 1900 NW Expressway Street, 50 Penn Place #100, Oklahoma City, OK 73118-1810 – **362)** 3205 S. Meadow Avenue, Sioux Falls, SD 57106-0939 – **363)** 140 4th Avenue North #340, Seattle, WA 98109-4932 – **364)** 4000 North Central Avenue #720, Phoenix, AZ 85012-1978 – **365)** 730 Harrison Street #300, San Francisco, CA 94107-1260 – **366)** 220 State Street, Fort Morgan, CO 80701-2116 – **367)** 10055 Beach Blvd, Jacksonville, FL 32246-4707 – **368)** 5510 W Gray Street #130, Tampa, FL 33609-1035 – **369)** 2901 Mountain Industrial Blvd, Tucker, GA 30084-3011 – **370)** 451 Highway 11 & 80, Meridian, MS 39301-2779 – **371)** 1445 E Chain of Rocks Rd, Granite City, IL 62040 – **372)** 25 Newport Road, New London, NH 03257-4129 – **373)** 888 7th Avenue - 10th floor, New York, NY 10106-1099 – **374)** 1330 US Highway 70 West, Black Mountain, NC 28711-9767 – **375)** 1019 Washington Avenue, Waco, TX 76701-1256 – **376)** Eagle Gate Plaza - 60 East South Temple #120, Salt Lake City, UT 84111-1004 – **377)** 655 N. Central Avenue #2500, Glendale, CA 91203-1447 – **378)** 540 Daisy Lane, Thomasville, GA 31792-9025 – **379)** 5011 Capitol Avenue, Omaha, NE 68132-2921 – **380)** 5206 West 2nd Street, Roswell, NM 88201-8839 – **381)** 1 Gateway Center, Pittsburgh, PA 15222-1465 – **382)** 100 E. Shockley Ferry Road, Anderson, SC 29624-3746 – **383)** 2919 E Broadway Blvd, Tucson, AZ 85716-5301 – **384)** 24 E. Meadow St #1, Fayetteville, AR 72701-5356 – **385)** 1033 Semoran Blvd #253, Casselberry, FL 32707-5758 – **386)** 5210 Auth Road #500, Suitland, MD 20746-4354 – **387)** 1170 Soldiers Field Road, Boston, MA 02134-1004 – **388)** 900 Forestview Lane North, Plymouth, MN 55441-5934 – **389)** 3025 Waughtown Street #G, Winston-Salem, NC 27107-1634 – **390)** 136 North 7th Street, Reedsport, OR 97467-1503 – **391)** 6080 Mount Moriah Road Extension, Memphis, TN 38115-2645 – **392)** 1602 South Brownlee Blvd, Corpus Christi, TX 78404-3134 – **393)** 210 West Cota Street, Shelton, WA 98584-2264 – **394)** 303 8th Street, Point Pleasant, WV 25550-1209 – **395)** 150 North Nichols Avenue, Casper, WY 82601-1816 – **396)** 5050 Edison Ave. #218, Colorado Springs, CO 80915-3450 – **397)** 6600 North Andrews Avenue #160, Fort Lauderdale, FL 33309-2188 – **398)** 1381 Rockbridge Rd. NW, Conyers, GA 30012-3511 – **399)** 1801 Grand Avenue, Des Moines, IA 50309-3309 – **400)** 151 E. 1st Avenue, Everett, PA 15537-1351 – **401)** 1533 Amherst Road, Knoxville, TN 379109 – **402)** 55 Hawthorne St. #1100, San Francisco, CA 94105-3914 – **403)** 3550 Barron Way, Reno, NV 89511-1848 – **404)** 1100 Victors Way #100, Ann Arbor, MI 48108-5220 – **405)** 508 Main Street, Miles City, MT 59301-3047 – **406)** Two Penn Plaza 17th Floor, New York, NY 10121-0101 – **407)** 614 Kimbark Street, Longmont, CO 80501-4911 – **408)** 6305 State Road 46, Mims, FL 32754-5914 – **409)** 3303 E. Chicago Street, Caldwell, ID 83605-6904 – **410)** 401 Whitney Ave #160, Gretna, LA 70056-2573 – **411)** 164 Canal Street, Boston, MA 02114-1809 – **412)** 101 South Independence Mall East, Philadelphia, PA 19106-2597 – **413)** 214 W. Pleasant Drive, Pierre, SD 57501-2472 – **414)** 4296 Park Place, Tyler, TX 75703-1871 – **415)** 205 9th Street, Farwell, TX 79325 – **416)** 2211 E. Missiouri Ave #E239, El Paso, TX 79903-3807 – **417)** 3606 South 500 West, Salt Lake City, UT 84115-4208 – **418)** 244 Goodwin Crest Drive #300, Birmingham, AL 35209-3700 – **419)** 6121 W. Sunset Blvd, Los Angeles, CA 90028-6423 – **420)** 4015 North Monroe Street, Tallahassee, FL 32303-2139 – **421)** 40 Monument Circle #400, Indianapolis, IN 46204-3014 – **422)** 4200 N. Old Lawrence Rd, Wichita, KS 67219-3211 – **423)** , Verndale, MN – **424)** 2929 Radio Station Road, Greenville, NC 27834-0864 – **425)** P.O. Box 1070, Sunbury, PA 17801-0870 – **426)** 200 N. Highway 25 Bypass, Greenville, SC 29617-1108 – **427)** 621 O'Grady Drive, Chattanooga, TN 37419-1305 – **428)** 2650 Thousand Oaks Blvd #4100, Memphis, TN 38118-2451 – **429)** 6161 Savoy Drive #1200, Houston, TX 77036-3363 – **430)** 1140 Rose Hill Drive, Charlottesville, VA 22903-5128 – **431)** 306 S Kanawha Street, Beckley, WV 25801-5619 – **432)** 2651 S. Fish Hatchery Road, Fitchburg, WI 53711-5410 – **433)** 2300 Portola Dr, Santa Cruz, CA 95062-4203 – **434)** 10 Executive Drive, Farmington, CT 06032-2841 – **435)** 2828 W. Flagler Street, Miami, FL 33135-1337 – **436)** 1160 S. Semoran Blvd #B, Orlando, FL 32807-1461 – **437)** 2865 Amwiler Road #650, Doraville, GA 30360-2828 – **438)** 504 E. Sherman Avenue, Coeur d' Alene, ID 83814-2731 – **439)** 4000 Radio Drive #1, Louisville, KY 40218-1568 – **440)** 0700 SW Bancroft St, Portland, OR 97239-4226 – **441)** 5316 William Flynn Hwy #3N, Gibsonia, PA 15044-9646 – **442)** 1080 Ballpark Way, Arlington, TX 76011-5164 – **443)** 163 East 100 North, Price, UT 84501-2501 – **444)** 700 Wellington Hills Road, Little Rock, AR 72211-2026 – **445)** 3560 Hillras Way, Fortuna, CA 95540-9570 – **446)** 5660 Greenwood Plaza Blvd #400, Greenwood Village, CO 80111-2402 – **447)** 2070 N. Palafox Street, Pensacola, FL 32501-2145 – **448)** 3800 Hooper Ave, Baltimore, MD 21211-1313 – **449)** 5445 Johnson Road, Bozeman, MT 59718-8333 – **450)** 340 Edgemont Avenue #100, Bristol, TN 37620-2313 – **451)** 1000 Dexter Avenue North #100, Seattle, WA 98109-3582 – **452)** 2001 N. 3rd Street #102, Phoenix, AZ 85004-1439 – **453)** 39138 Fremont Blvd 3rd Flr, Fremont, CA 94538-1305 – **454)** 1360 E. Sherwood Dr, Grand Junction, CO 81501-7546 – **455)** RR18 Box 280E, Saint Simons Island, GA 31522-9704 – **456)** 3015 East Causeway Approach, Mandeville, LA 70448-3510 – **457)** 234 Airport Plaza Blvd #5, Farmingdale, NY 11735-3938 – **458)** 6200 Oak Tree Blvd 4th Flr, Independence, OH 44131-2510 – **459)** 16414 San Pedro Avenue #575, San Antonio, TX 78232-2277 – **460)** 1318 South Main Street, Atmore, AL 36502-2834 – **461)** 3321 S. La Cienega Blvd, Los Angeles, CA 90016-3114 – **462)** 311 112th Ave. NE, St Petersburg, FL 33716-3394 – **463)** 2175 Click Road, Petoskey, MI 49770-8818 – **464)** 5010 Underwood Avenue, Omaha, NE 68132-2297 – **465)** 1 Julian Price Place, Charlotte, NC 28208-5211 – **466)** 711 NE Butler Market Road, Bend, OR 97701-8083 – **467)** 4801

Columbia Street #202, Virginia Beach, VA 23462-6751 – **468)** 2131 Crimmins Lane, Falls Church, VA 22043-1962 – **469)** 6174 GA Highway 57, Macon, GA 31217-3405 – **470)** 1 South Memorial Drive #600, Saint Louis, MO 63102-2498 – **471)** 1345 Olive Street, Eugene, OR 97401-3924 – **472)** 2201 S. 6th Street, Las Vegas, NV, UT 89104-2999 – **473)** 2310 E. Ponderosa Dr #28, Camarillo, CA 93010-4747 – **474)** 83 East Shaw Avenue #150, Fresno, CA 93710-7622 – **475)** 5815 Westside Road, Austell, GA 30106-3179 – **476)** 5815 Westside Road, Austell, GA 30106-3179 – **477)** 6341 West Port Avenue, Shreveport, LA 71129-2415 – **478)** 27675 Halsted Road, Farmington Hills, MI 48331-3511 – **479)** 1600 Utica Avenue South #400, Minneapolis, MN 55416-1480 – **480)** 499 Park Avenue 15 Flr, New York, NY 10022-1240 – **481)** 3500 E. Rosser Avenue, Bismarck, ND 58501-3398 – **482)** 1302 N Shepherd Drive, Houston, TX 77008-3752 – **483)** 12100 W. Howard Avenue, Milwaukee, WI 53228-1851 – **484)** 2926 Huntsville Hwy #D, Fayetteville, TN 37334-6687 – **485)** 1321 North Gene Autry Trail, Palm Springs, CA 92262-5473 – **486)** 5244 Madison Avenue, Sacramento, CA 95841-3004 – **487)** 800 S. Douglas Rd #111, Coral Gables, FL 33134-3187 – **488)** 5257 Fairview Avenue #260, Boise, ID 83706-1766 – **489)** 6655 W. Sahara #D208, Las Vegas, NV 89146-0851 – **490)** 5100 South Tennis Lane, Sioux Falls, SD 57108-2212 – **491)** 3245 Basie Road, Richmond, VA 23228-3404 – **492)** 1949 Mountain View Drive, Cody, WY 82414-4932 – **493)** 3400 Olive Avenue #400, Burbank, CA 91505-5538 – **494)** 1201 18th Street #220, Denver, CO 80202-1421 – **495)** 2727 Shipley Rd, Wilmington, DE 19810-3299 – **496)** 5207 East Washington Street, Tampa, FL 33619-3437 – **497)** 131 N. Santa Fe Avenue, Salina, KS 67401-2615 – **498)** 5555 Hilton Ave. #500, Baton Rouge, LA 70808-2564 – **499)** 308 Victory Road, Quincy, MA 02171-3129 – **500)** 830 Oilfield Avenue, Shelby, MT 59474-1641 – **501)** 3650 131st Avenue #550, Bellevue, WA 98006-1334 – **502)** 801 Old Wawawai Rd, Pullman, WA 99163-9002 – **503)** 2800 East College Avenue, Appleton, WI 54915-3255 – **504)** 130 Martin Luther King Jr Drive SE, Atlanta, GA 30312-2012 – **505)** 25 NW Point Blvd #400, Elk Grove Village, IL 60007-1030 – **506)** 150 Whitten Road, Augusta, ME 04330-6021 – **507)** 8945 N Westland Drive #302, Gaithersburg, MD 20877-1249 – **508)** 1086 Teaneck Road #4F, Teaneck, NJ 07666-4858 – **509)** 1015 Atlantic City Blvd, Bayville, NJ 08721-3541 – **510)** 60 Courthouse Street, Columbus, NC 28722 – **511)** P.O. Box 1020, Indiana, PA 15701-1020 – **512)** 1617 Lebanon Pike, Nashville, TN 37210-3217 – **513)** 84 NE Loop 410, San Antonio, TX 78216-5802 – **514)** 103 West Main Street, Allen, TX 75013-8070 – **515)** 55 North 300 West, Salt Lake City, UT 84180-1109 – **516)** 4101 Wall Street #A, Montgomery, AL 36106-3656 – **517)** 655 Campbell Technology Pkwy #200, Campbell, CA 95008-5062 – **518)** 9255 Towne Centre Drive #535, San Diego, CA 92121-3038 – **519)** 4590 E. 29th Street, Tulsa, OK 74114-6208 – **520)** 145 Branham View Road, Lexington, SC 29072-2335 – **521)** 2219 Yew Street Road, Bellingham, WA 98229-8855 – **522)** 1015 Main Street #1, Wheeling, WV 26003-2782 – **523)** 812 East Beale Street, Kingman, AZ 86401-5925 – **524)** 110 S. Montclair St #205, Bakersfield, CA 93309-3111 – **525)** VOA - 330 Independence Ave. SW, Washington, DC 20547-0003 – **526)** 1985 Lakeland Drive #212, Jackson, MS 39216-5024 – **527)** 317 First Ave. East, Kalispell, MT 59901-9601 – **528)** 5011 Capitol Avenue, Omaha, NE 68132-2921 – **529)** 207 Midtown Plaza, Rochester, NY 14604-2016 – **530)** 201 North Front Street #805, Wilmington, NC 28401-5089 – **531)** 802 S. Central Avenue, Knoxville, TN 37902-1207 – **532)** 5821 Southwest Freeway #600, Houston, TX 77057-7532 – **533)** 701 N. Brand Blvd #550, Glendale, CA 91203-1235 – **534)** 2970 Peachtree Rd. NW #700, Atlanta, GA 30305-4919 – **535)** 2915 Maples Rd, Fort Wayne, IN 46816-3199 – **536)** 2131 Crimmins Lane, Falls Church, VA 22043-1962 – **537)** 8045 Big Bend Blvd, Saint Louis, MO 63119-2714 – **538)** 5411 Jefferson Street NE #100, Albuquerque, NM 87109-3406 – **539)** 3 Park Avenue, New York, NY 10016-5902 – **540)** 4949 S.W. Macadam Avenue, Portland, OR 97239-3997 – **541)** 14001 North Dallas Pkwy #300, Dallas, TX 75240-7369 – **542)** 900 Bluefield Avenue, Bluefield, WV 24701-2744 – **543)** 495 Elder Avenue, Sand City, CA 93955-3547 – **544)** 2824 Palm Beach Blvd, Fort Myers, FL 33916-1503 – **545)** 625 N. Michigan Avenue #300, Chicago, IL 60611-3163 – **546)** 100 Mount Wayte Avenue, Framingham, MA 01702-5705 – **547)** 3250 Franklin Street, Detroit, MI 48207-4219 – **548)** 875 W. 5th Street, Winston-Salem, NC 27101-2505 – **549)** 738 Blowing Rock Road, Boone, NC 28607-4840 – **550)** 5702 52nd Avenue South, Fargo, ND 58104-5605 – **551)** 1559 W. 4th Street, Williamsport, PA 17701-5650 – **552)** 1617 Lebanon Road, Nashville, TN 37210-3217 – **553)** 6222 West Interstate 10, San Antonio, TX 78201-2097 – **554)** 285 N. Foster St, Dothan, AL 36303-4541 – **555)** 2955 E Broadway Blvd, Tuscon, AZ 85716-5311 – **556)** 9255 Towne Centre Dr. #535, San Diego, CA 92121-3038 – **557)** 8400 NW 52nd Street #101, Miami, FL 33166-5309 – **558)** 6972 Buford Hwy NE, Atlanta, GA 30340-1410 – **559)** 5555 Hilton Avenue #500, Baton Rouge, LA 70808-2564 – **560)** 118 South Union Street #2, Traverse City, MI 49684-5712 – **561)** 2300 North Lelia Street, Guymon, OK 73942-2840 – **562)** 10 Monument Road, Bala Cynwyd, PA 19004-1712 – **563)** 6080 Mount Moriah Road Extension, Memphis, TN 38115-2645 – **564)** 4501 North McColl Road, McAllen, TX 78504-2431 – **565)** 720 Ridgeview Drive #204, Saint George, UT 84770-2678 – **566)** 1820 Eastlake Avenue East, Seattle, WA 98102-3711 – **567)** 706 Butterfield Road, Yakima, WA 98901-2021 – **568)** 302 South 2nd Street #204, Laramie, WY 82070-3650 – **569)** 4 Summit Park Drive #150, Independence, OH 44131-6921 – **570)** 4002 W. Gandy Blvd, Tampa, FL 33611-3410 – **571)** 6220 Kansas Avenue, Kansas City, KS 66111-2125 – **572)** 922 Elm Street #301, Manchester, NH 03101-2012 – **573)** 55 Horsehill Road, Cedar Knolls, NJ 07927-2003 – **574)** 400 Ardmore Blvd, Pittsburgh, PA 15221-3019 – **575)** 1 Radio Lane, Danville, VA 24541-5235 – **576)** Murrow Comm Cntr - WSU, Pullman, WA 99163-3002 – **577)** 200 1st Avenue West #104, Seattle, WA 98119-4291 – **578)** 11800 W. Grange Avenue, Hales Corners, WI 53130-1099 – **579)** 1500 Cotner Avenue, Los Angeles, CA 90025-3303 – **580)** 8750 Brookville Rd, Silver Spring, MD 20910-1824 – **581)** 2100 Coral Way, Coral Gables, FL 33145-2635 – **582)** 638 Westport Plaza, Saint Louis, MO 63146-3106 – **583)** 6161 Fall Creek Rd, Indianapolis, IN 46220-5032 – **584)** 226 Lincoln Street, Allston, MA 02134-1317 – **585)** 425 Centerstone #1, Zeeland, MI 49464 – **586)** 2330 W. Grand Street, Springfield, MO 65802-4900 – **587)** 1064 James Street, Syracuse, NY 13203-2704 – **588)** 1422 Euclid Ave #604, Cleveland, OH 44115-1952 – **589)** 471 Robison Rd West, Erie, PA 16509-5425 – **590)** 328 100th Street, Amery, WI 54001-4024 – **591)** 2500 West Oakridge Road, Orlando, FL 32809-3771 – **592)** 325 John Knox Rd. #G, Tallahassee, FL 32303-4161 – **593)** 3535 E. Kimberly Road, Davenport, IA 52807-2583 – **594)** 26495 American Drive, Southfield, MI 48034-6114 – **595)** 2095 South US Highway 131, Petoskey, MI 49770-9216 – **596)** 305 West Washington Street, Brainerd, MN 56401-2923 – **597)** 300 East 2nd Street #1400, Reno, NV 89501-1566 – **598)** 101 Back Road, Dover, NH 03820-5012 – **599)** 5732 N. Tryon Street, Charlotte, NC 28607-4835 – **600)** 7700 Carpenter Freeway, Dallas, TX 75247-4829 – **601)** 1303 Grand Ave. #233, Arroyo Grande, CA 93420-2462 – **602)** 600 Grant Street #600, Denver, CO 80203-3540 – **603)** 929 Howard Avenue, New Orleans, LA 70113-1148 – **604)** 150 Whitten Road, Augusta, ME 04330-6021 – **605)** 2110 Cliff Road, Saint Paul, MN 55122-2347 – **606)** 485 Madison Ave, New York, NY 10022-5803 – **607)** 207 Midtown Plaza, Rochester, NY 14604-2016 – **608)** 515 South 700 East #1C, Salt Lake City, UT 84102-2802 – **609)** 491 South Washburn Street #400, Oshkosh, WI 54904-6733 – **610)** 2654 Cramer Lane, Chico, CA 95928-8838 – **611)** 2030 Iowa Avenue #A, Riverside, CA 92507-7412 – **612)** 3071 Continental Drive, West Palm Beach, FL 33407-3274 – **613)** 245 Alfred Street, Savannah, GA 31408-3205 – **614)** 331 Fulton Street #1200, Peoria, IL 61602-1475 – **615)** 3250 South Reserve Street #200, Missoula, MT 59801-8236 – **616)** 5011 Capitol Avenue, Omaha, NE 68132-2921 – **617)** 69 Stanhope Avenue, Keene, NH 03431-1577 – **618)** 59-61 Court Street #100, Binghamton, NY 13901-3293 – **619)** 526 Main Avenue SE, Hickory, NC 28602-1103 – **620)** 1414 Wilmington Avenue, Dayton, OH 45420-1568 – **621)** 2003 NW 56th Street, Pendleton, OR 97801-4593 – **622)** 890 Commonwealth Ave, Boston, MA 02215-1205 – **623)** P.O. Box 1290, Weslaco, TX 78599-1290 – **624)** 3220 W. Cary Street #A, Richmond, VA 23221-3402 – **625)** 2979 North Mayfair Road, Milwaukee, WI 53222-4301 – **626)** 341 South Yorktown Pike, Mason City, IA 50401-4533 – **627)** 600 Washington Avenue #301, Baltimore, MD 21204-3916 – **628)** 77 Monroe Center NW, Grand Rapids, MI 49503-2903 – **629)** 800 New Loudon Road #69, Latham, NY 12110-5885 – **630)** 2510 St Clair Avenue NE, Cleveland, OH 44114-4013 – **631)** 7590 Highway 238, Jacksonville, OR 97530-9728 – **632)** 1300 WWCR Avenue, Nashville, TN 37218-3800 – **633)** 2815 2nd Avenue #550, Seattle, WA 98121-1266 – **634)** 900 Front Street, San Francisco, CA 94111-1427 – **635)** Cuprak Rd, Norwich, CT 06360 – **636)** 779 Warren Avenue, Portland, ME 04103-1176 – **637)** 27675 Halsted Road, Farmington Hills, MI 48331-3511 – **638)** P.O. Box 13638, Grand Forks, ND 58208-3638 – **639)** 2615 South Broad Street, Chattanooga, TN 37408-3100 – **640)** 3500 Maple Ave. #1310, Dallas, TX 75219-3931 – **641)** 5589 Greenwich Rd #300, Virginia Beach, VA 23462-6565 – **642)** 2651 S. Fish Hatchery Rd, Madison, WI 53711-5400 – **643)** 311 Lexington Avenue, Fort Smith, AR 72901-3842 – **644)** 5345 Madison Ave, Sacramento, CA 95841-3141 – **645)** 4190 Belfort Road #450, Jacksonville, FL 32216-1405 – **646)** 10800 Biscayne Boulevard #810, Miami, FL 33161-7402 – **647)** 127 Dorrance Street, Providence, RI 02903-2828 – **648)** 507 SE 11th Street, Grand Rapids, MN 55744-3950 – **649)** 8 Lawrence Rd, Derry, NH 03038-4191 – **650)** 4405 Providence Lane #D, Winston-Salem, NC 27106-3226 – **651)** 900 Parish Street, Pittsburgh, PA 15220-3425 – **652)** 500 S. Phillips Avenue, Sioux Falls, SD 57104-6825 – **653)** 7322 Southwest Freeway #1500, Houston, TX 77074-2009 – **654)** 434 Bearcat Drive, Salt Lake City, UT 84115-2543 –

655) 4320 N. Campbell Avenue #234, Tucson, AZ 85718-5473 – **656)** 401 Pacheco Blvd, Los Banos, CA 93635-4227 – **657)** 3301 Barham Blvd #201, Los Angeles, CA 90068-1477 – **658)** 514 Jefferson Street, Waterloo, IA 50701-5422 – **659)** 2120 N. Woodlawn Street #352, Wichita, KS 67208-1881 – **660)** 552 Massachusetts Avenue #201, Cambridge, MA 02139-4088 – **661)** 331 South 11th St, Minneapolis, MN 55404-1006 – **662)** 419 Broadway, Paterson, NJ 07501-2104 – **663)** 4700 SW Macadam Ave #102, Portland, OR 97239-4265 – **664)** 1 Boston Store Place, Erie, PA 16501-2312 – **665)** 25 Garlington Road, Greenville, SC 29615-4613 – **666)** 1410 Neotomas Ave. #200, Santa Rosa, CA 95405-7533 – **667)** 1416 Locust St, Des Moines, IA 50309-3014 – **668)** 1450 Poydras Street #440, New Orleans, LA 70112-1264 – **669)** 619 Alexander Rd 3flr, Princeton, NJ 08540-6003 – **670)** 1867 W. Market Street, Akron, OH 44313-6901 – **671)** 1777 N.E. Loop 410 #400, San Antonio, TX 78217-5217 – **672)** 645 Church St #400, Norfolk, VA 23510-1712 – **673)** 2425 East Camelback Road #570, Phoenix, AZ 85016-4250 – **674)** 869 Blue Hills Ave, Bloomfield, CT 06002-3710 – **675)** 2000 Indian Hills Drive, Sioux City, IA 51104-1602 – **676)** 8044 Montgomery Road, Cincinnati, OH 45263-0001 – **677)** 3355 NE Cornell Road, Hillsboro, OR 97124-5018 – **678)** 2501 Oak Lawn Avenue #690, Dallas, TX 75219-4057 – **679)** 2815 2nd Avenue. #550, Seattle, WA 98121-1266 – **680)** 115 S. Jefferson Street, Green Bay, WI 54301-4534 – **681)** 3031 Tisch Way #3 Plaza West, San Jose, CA 95128-2530 – **682)** 6565 N W Street #270, Pensacola, FL 32505-1797 – **683)** 346 West 8th Street, Dubuque, IA 52001-4649 – **684)** 49 Acme Road, Brewer, ME 04412-1545 – **685)** 1726 Reisterstown Rd #117, Pikesville, MD 21208-2986 – **686)** 750 Dewey Blvd #1, Butte, MT 59701-3200 – **687)** 500 North Commercial Street, Manchester, NH 03101-1151 – **688)** 280 State Street, Rochester, NY 14614-1033 – **689)** 1286 Holland Road, Rock Hill, SC 29732-9748 – **690)** 125 S. Superior Street, Toledo, OH 43602-1790 – **691)** 2615 Broad Street, Chattanooga, TN 37408-3100 – **692)** 1425 River Park Drive #520, Sacramento, CA 95815-4524 – **693)** 903 North Main Street, Salinas, CA 93906-3912 – **694)** 11300 4th Street N, Saint Petersburg, FL 33716-2918 – **695)** 1 Parker Place #485, Janesville, WI 53545-4078 – **696)** 2915 Maples Rd, Fort Wayne, IN 46816-3199 – **697)** 808 Huron Avenue, Port Huron, MI 48060-3705 – **698)** 13225 Dogwood Drive, Baxter, MN 56425-8669 – **699)** 449 Broadway 2nd Floor, New York, NY 10013-2549 – **700)** 70 Adams Hill Road, Asheville, NC 28806-3841 – **701)** 518 St Joseph Street, Rapid City, SD 57701-2717 – **702)** 9401 Courthouse Road #307, Chesterfield, VA 23832-6690 – **703)** 2707 Colby Avenue #1380, Everett, WA 98201-3568 – **704)** 4043 Geer Road, Hughson, CA 95326-9715 – **705)** 233 N Michigan Avenue, Chicago, IL 60601-5519 – **706)** 28 Houlton Road, Presque Isle, ME 04769-5206 – **707)** 17 Columbus Road, Plymouth, MA 02360-4810 – **708)** 10250 Lorraine Road, Gulfport, MS 39503-6005 – **709)** 8456 Smokey Hollow Road, Baldwinsville, NY 13027-8222 – **710)** 4230 Faber Place Drive #100, North Charleston, SC 29405-8512 – **711)** 1 Main Street, Winooski, VT 05404-2228 – **712)** 12216 Parklawn Drive #203, Rockville, MD 20852-1710 – **713)** 557 Scott Street, Wausau, WI 54403-4829 – **714)** 1263 Battleship Pkwy, Spanish Fort, AL 36527-9321 – **715)** 10 Columbus Blvd #24, Hartford, CT 06106-1973 – **716)** 1575 McKee Road #206, Dover, DE 19904-1382 – **717)** 2835 Hanson Street, Fort Myers, FL 33916-7505 – **718)** 717 E. David Road, Dayton, OH 45429-5218 – **719)** Centre City Towers - 650 Smithfield Street, Pittsburgh, PA 15222-3902 – **720)** 201 State Street, La Crosse, WI 54601-3246 – **721)** 1353 13th Avenue, Columbus, GA 31901-2347 – **722)** 2458 Radio Road, Saint Anthony, ID 83445-5403 – **723)** 6405 Olcott Avenue, Hammond, IN 46320-2835 – **724)** 3535 E. Kimberly Rd, Davenport, IA 52807-2583 – **725)** 59346 Madison Avenue, Mankato, MN 56001-8518 – **726)** 26501 Renaissance Parkway, Cleveland, OH 44128-5761 – **727)** 17 West Gay Street, West Chester, PA 19380-3090 – **728)** 320 Maple Avenue East #B, Vienna, VA 22180-4716 – **729)** 1133 Kresky Avenue, Centralia, WA 98531-3789 – **730)** 45 Campbell Road, Walla Walla, WA 99362-9597 – **731)** 351 W Cromwell Avenue #108, Fresno, CA 93711-6115 – **732)** 747 E. Green Street #400, Pasadena, CA 91101-2148 – **733)** 4700 S Syracuse Street #1050, Denver, CO 80237-2713 – **734)** 249 W. University Avenue #B, Gainesville, FL 32601-5211 – **735)** 3100 E. 15th Steert, Panama City, FL 32405-7421 – **736)** 9245 N. Meridian Street #300, Indianapolis, IN 46260-1832 – **737)** 11647 Olive Blvd, Saint Louis, MO 63141-7001 – **738)** 449 Broadway, New York, NY 10013-2549 – **739)** 320 N. Jensen Road, Vestel, NY 13850-2111 – **740)** 2625 South Memorial Drive, Tulsa, OK 74129-2600 – **741)** 4205 Cherry Ave NE, Keizer, OR 97303-4856 – **742)** 630 Mainstream Drive, Nashville, TN 37228-1204 – **743)** 4155 Harrison Blvd #206, Ogden, UT 84403-2497 – **744)** 779 Warren Avene, Portland, ME 04103-1007 – **745)** 20 Guest Street, Brighton, MA 02135-2040 – **746)** 4 Summit Park Drive #150, Independence, OH 44131-6921 – **747)** 7 N. Laurens Street #700, Greenville, SC 29601-2760 – **748)** 903 N. Main Street, Salinas, CA 93906-3912 – **749)** 4190 Belfort Road #450, Jacksonville, FL 32216-1405 – **750)** 449 North 12th Street, Defuniak Springs, FL 32433-0411 – **751)** 1801 Grand Avenue, Des Moines, IA 50309-3362 – **752)** 8755 West Flamingo Road, Las Vegas, NV 89147-8667 – **753)** 6325 Sheridan Drive, Williamsville, NY 14221-4801 – **754)** 52 Corporate Circle #K, Albany, NY 12203-5176 – **755)** 145 Rowan Street #A3, Fayetteville, NC 28301-4901 – **756)** 11291 39th Street SW, Dickinson, ND 58601-9206 – **757)** 600 Corporate Cir #100, Harrisburg, PA 17110-9787 – **758)** 12216 Parklawn Drive #203, Rockville, MD 20852-1710 – **759)** 570 E. Avenue Q9, Palmdale, CA 93550-2354 – **760)** 6699 N. Federal Hwy #200, Boca Raton, FL 33487-1671 – **761)** 20 John Davenport Drive NW, Rome, GA 30165-2536 – **762)** 331 Fulton Street #1200, Peoria, IL 61602-1475 – **763)** 1113 Nebraska Street, Sioux City, IA 51105-1438 – **764)** 447 Congress Street #3B, Portland, ME 04101-3505 – **765)** 331 South 11th Street, Minneapolis, MN 55404-1006 – **766)** 3025 Waughtown Street #G, Winston-Salem, NC 27107-1634 – **767)** 1541 Alta Drive #400, Whitehall, PA 18052-5622 – **768)** Tremonton, UT – **769)** 3101 W. 5th Street, Santa Ana, CA 92703-1897 – **770)** 1020 West Main Street, Merced, CA 95340-4521 – **771)** 432 S. Belair Road, Augusta, GA 30907-9681 – **772)** 1 Home Street, Fall River, MA 02720-5229 – **773)** 301 Fulton Street West, Grand Rapids, MI 49404-6492 – **774)** 449 Broadway 2nd Flr, New York, NY 10013-2549 – **775)** 1100 South Tryon Street #210, Charlotte, NC 28203-4297 – **776)** 550 Market Avenue South, Canton, OH 44702-2103 – **777)** 2740 Ski Lane, Madison, WI 53713-3267 – **778)** 801 K St. 27th Flr, Sacramento, CA 95814-3534 – **779)** 501 Wooster Avenue #C, San Jose, CA 95116-1046 – **780)** 3400 Idaho Avenue NW #200, Washington, DC 20016-3000 – **781)** 29200 Vassar Drive #650, Livonia, MI 48154-2122 – **782)** 3415 University Avenue West, Saint Paul, MN 55114-2099 – **783)** 86 Porter Road, Malone, NY 12953-3701 – **784)** 4800 N. Central Ave. Phoenix, Mesa, AZ 85012-1722 – **785)** 3401 Holland Avenue, Fresno, CA 93722-4197 – **786)** 1045 South East Street, Anaheim, CA 92805-5749 – **787)** 1201 18th Street #220, Denver, CO 80202-1421 – **788)** 1 Van de Graaff Drive #300, Burlington, MA 01803-5171 – **789)** 6721 West 121st Street, Overland Park, KS 66209-2003 – **790)** 55 Music Square West, Nashville, TN 37203-3207 – **791)** 868 East 5900 South, Salt Lake City, UT 84107-7650 – **792)** 1601 E. 57th Avenue, Spokane, WA 99223-6623 – **793)** 1801 Coral Drive, Waukesha, WI 53186-5353 – **794)** 2284 S. Victoria Ave #2-G, Ventura, CA 93003-6626 – **795)** 202 Galbert Road, Lafayette, LA 70506-1806 – **796)** 7601 Little River Turnpike, Annandale, VA 22003-2601 – **797)** 369 Shelburne Road, Greenfield, MA 01301-9653 – **798)** 1220 4th Avenue SW, Rochester, MN 55902-3834 – **799)** 500 Corporate Parkway #200, Buffalo, NY 14226-1265 – **800)** 400 E. Britton Road, Oklahoma City, OK 73114-7507 – **801)** 24 South A Street #C, Washougal, OR 98671-2101 – **802)** 1440 Ethan Way #200, Sacramento, CA 95825-2214 – **803)** 5050 Edison Ave. #218, Colorado Springs, CO 80915-3540 – **804)** 5900 Pickettville Rd, Jacksonville, FL 32254-1172 – **805)** 111 West Crawford Street, Dalton, GA 30720-4202 – **806)** 103 Progress Road, Poplarville, MS 39470-3388 – **807)** 3013 Guess Road, Durham, NC 27705-2634 – **808)** 8044 Montgomery Road, Cincinnati, OH 45263-0001 – **809)** 4314 W Braker Lane #1260, Austin, TX 78759-5362 – **810)** 200 South 10th #600, McAllen, TX 78501-4869 – **811)** 1445 W. Baseline Rd, Phoenix, AZ 85041-7010 – **812)** 2800 28th Street #308, Santa Monica, CA 90405-6205 – **813)** 514 Jefferson Street, Waterloo, IA 50701-5422 – **814)** 4243 Albany Street, Albany, NY 12205-4609 – **815)** 2131 Crimmins Lane, Falls Church, VA 22043-1962 – **816)** 3931 Whitehorse Road, Greenville, SC 29611-5599 – **817)** 5307 E. Mockingbird Lane #500, Dallas, TX 75206-5184 – **818)** 306 West Broad Street, Richmond, VA 23220-4219 – **819)** 114 Lakeside Avenue, Seattle, WA 98122-6542 – **820)** 1900 Memorial Pkwy SW, Huntsville, AL 35801-5002 – **821)** Univ. of Arizona, Tucson, AZ 85721-0067 – **822)** 500 Washington St #450, San Francisco, CA 94111-2938 – **823)** 402 North Reo Street #218, Tampa, FL 33609-1027 – **824)** 330 SW 27th Avenue #207, Miami, FL 33135-2957 – **825)** 2460 Atlanta Road SE, Smyrna, GA 30080-2000 – **826)** 143 Rumford Avenue, Auburndale, MA 02466-1311 – **827)** 4104 Country Lane, Saint Joseph, MO 64506-4921 – **828)** 1049 N Sekol Avenue, Scranton, PA 18504-1040 – **829)** 226 Radio Road, Bennettsville, SC 29512-6183 – **830)** 314 S Redwood Road, Salt Lake City, UT 84104-3536 – **831)** 2043 Tenth Street NE, Roanoke, VA 24012-5309 – **832)** 5538 Imhoff Road, Ferndale, WA 98248-9177 – **833)** 888 SW 5th Avenue #790, Portland, OR 97204-2021 – **834)** 3561 Pegasus Drive #107, Bakersfield, CA 93308-0658 – **835)** 330 SW 27th Avenue #207, Miami, FL 33135-2957 – **836)** 120 South 35th Street #2, Council Bluffs, IA 51501-3203 – **837)** 6000 WKYX WKYO Road, Paducah, KY 42003-9213 – **838)** 2 Penn Plaza 17th Floor, New York, NY 10121-0101 – **839)** 101 S. Woodland Drive, Lancaster, SC 29720-2244 – **840)** 3980 S. Dakota Street, Aberdeen, SD 57401-8585 – **841)** 376 New Berlin Road #8, Jacksonville, FL 32218-3881 – **842)** 2231 E. Camelback Rd #326, Phoenix, AZ 85016-3417 – **843)** 123 S. Figueroa

Street, Los Angeles, CA 90012-2469 – **844)** 614 Kimbark Street, Longmont, CO 80501-4911 – **845)** 4431 Rock Island Road, Tamarac, FL 33319-3101 – **846)** P.O. Box 30, Chattahoochee, FL 32324-0030 – **847)** 2601 Nicholasville Road, Lexington, KY 40503-3307 – **848)** 4200 Parliament Place #300, Lanham, MD 20706-1881 – **849)** 1551 Route 202, Pomona, NY 10970-2936 – **850)** Georgetown, SC – **851)** 2284 Victoria Ave. #2-G, Ventura, CA 93003-6626 – **852)** 750 Story Road, San Jose, CA 95122-2604 – **853)** 1200 Baker Avenue, Great Bend, KS 67530-4523 – **854)** 502 West Hollis Street, Nashua, NH 03062-1356 – **855)** 1795 West Market Street, Akron, OH 44313-7001 – **856)** 19 Luther Avenue, Warwick, RI 02886-4615 – **857)** 222 Commerce Street, Kingsport, TN 37660-4319 – **858)** 3050 Post Oak Blvd #220, Houston, TX 77056-6515 – **859)** 2815 2nd Avenue #550, Seattle, WA 98121-1263 – **860)** 747 E. Green Street #400, Pasadena, CA 91101-2148 – **861)** 1110 E Olive Avenue, Fresno, CA 93728-3535 – **862)** 1095 S. Monaco Pkwy, Denver, CO 80224-1600 – **863)** 1801 Clark Road, Orlando, FL 32868 – **864)** 5815 Westside Rd SW, Austell, GA 30106-3179 – **865)** 501 2nd Avenue SE, Cedar Rapids, IA 52401-1303 – **866)** 160 N. Washington Street #603, Boston, MA 02114-2142 – **867)** 3565 Green Street, Muskegon, MI 49444-3875 – **868)** 4230 Packard Street, Ann Arbor, MI 48108-1597 – **869)** 409 Territorial Street East, Watertown, MN 55388-9285 – **870)** 10155 Corporate Square Drive, Saint Louis, MO 63132-2905 – **871)** 1418 Bonito Suenos Court NW, Albuquerque, NM 87107-7111 – **872)** 333 7th Avenue #1401, New York, NY 10001-5021 – **873)** 3704 Whittier Road, Memphis, TN 38108-2649 – **874)** 4840 Lincoln Road, Blaine, WA 98230-9602 – **875)** 112 Watson Street, Ripon, WI 54971-1327 – **876)** 8919 World Ministry Avenue, Baton Rouge, LA 70810-9000 – **877)** 5945 Franklin Blvd, Sacramento, CA 95824-1114 – **878)** 805 North Main St, Atmore, AL 36502-1209 – **879)** P.O. Box 699, Blackfoot, ID 83221-0699 – **880)** 3371 W. Cleveland Road Ext. #310, South Bend, IN 46628-9780 – **881)** 5011 Capitol Avenue, Omaha, NE 68132-2921 – **882)** 2700 Earl Rudder Freeway South, College Station, TX 77845-5010 – **883)** 2600 S. Jackson Street, Seattle, WA 98144-2499 – **884)** 432 S. Belair Rd, Augusta, GA 30907-9601 – **885)** 4404 SE Napolean St, Iowa City, IA 52240-8143 – **886)** 5787 South Hampton Road #340, Dallas, TX 75232-6335 – **887)** 110 E. 17th Street #205, Cheyenne, WY 82001-4598 – **888)** 3260 Blume Drive #520 Plaza II, Richmond, CA 94806-5715 – **889)** 1909 East Pass Road #D11, Gulfport, MS 39507-3778 – **890)** 316 E. Willow Road, Enid, OK 73701-1514 – **891)** 3030 SW Moody Avenue #210, Portland, OR 97201-4868 – **892)** 2250 S. Redwood Road #4, Salt Lake City, UT 84119-1348 – **893)** W. 223 N. 3251 Shady Lane, Pewaukee, WI 53072-4194 – **894)** 311 Lexington Avenue, Fort Smith, AR 72901-3842 – **895)** 4525 Wilshire Blvd, Los Angeles, CA 90010-3837 – **896)** 3131 S. Vaughn Way #601, Aurora, CO 80014-3516 – **897)** 721 Shirley Street, Cedar Falls, IA 50613-1513 – **898)** 5041 Corporate Woods Drive #165, Virginia Beach, VA 23462-4381 – **899)** 1020 West Main Street, Merced, CA 95340-4521 – **900)** 5043 Tamiami Trail East, Naples, FL 34113-4127 – **901)** 4935 Belinder Road, Westwood, KS 66205-1937 – **902)** 4200 W. Main Street, Kalamazoo, MI 49006-2749 – **903)** 449 Broadway, New York, NY 10013-2549 – **904)** 1520 South Blvd #300, Charlotte, NC 28203-3701 – **905)** 2720 South 7th Avenue SW, Fargo, ND 58103-8710 – **906)** 1018 N. Valley Mills Drive, Waco, TX 76710-4741 – **907)** 515 South 700 East #1C, Salt Lake City, UT 84102-2802 – **908)** 3360 Alta Mesa Drive, Redding, CA 96002-2831 – **909)** 24490 Sunnymead Blvd #215, Moreno Valley, CA 92553-2831 – **910)** 7080 Industrial Highway, Macon, GA 31216-7538 – **911)** 2740 Ski Lane, Madison, WI 53713-3267 – **912)** 139 W. Olive Avenue, Fresno, CA 93728-3035 – **913)** 1801 Clark Road, Orlando, FL 32868 – **914)** 1109 Hudson Lane, Monroe, LA 71201-6003 – **915)** 3777 44th Street SE, Grand Rapids, MI 49512-3945 – **916)** 456 Middlesex Avenue, Metuchen, NJ 08840-1412 – **917)** 2815 2nd Avenue #550, Seattle, WA 98121-1263 – **918)** 3463 Ramona Avenue #15, Sacramento, CA 95826-3827 – **919)** 12136 Bayaud Avenue #125, Lakewood, CO 80228-2115 – **920)** 38 Kenmare Hall NE, Atlanta, GA 30324-2566 – **921)** 223 North Michigan Avenue #2800, Chicago, IL 60601-5916 – **922)** 28095 Three Notch Road #2B, Mechanicsville, MD 20659-3373 – **923)** 2609 Jordan Lane NW, Huntsville, AL 35816-1030 – **924)** 2828 Coral Way #2, Coral Gables, FL 33145-3214 – **925)** 4143 109th Street, Urbandale, IA 50322-7925 – **926)** 3500 Maple Ave. #1310, Dallas, TX 75219-3931

States: AK Alaska, AL Alabama, AR Arkansas, AZ Arizona, CA California, CO Colorado, CT Connecticut, DE Delaware, FL Florida, GA Georgia, HI Hawaii, IA Iowa, ID Idaho, IL Illinois, IN Indiana, KS Kansas, KY Kentucky, LA Louisiana, MA Massachusetts, MD Maryland, ME Maine, MI Michigan, MN Minnesota, MO Missouri, MS Mississippi, MT Montana, NC North Carolina, ND North Dakota, NE Nebraska, NH New Hampshire, NJ New Jersey, NM New Mexico, NV Nevada, NY New York, OH Ohio, OK Oklahoma, OR Oregon, PA Pennsylvania, RI Rhode Island, SC South Carolina, SD South Dakota, TN Tennessee, TX Texas, UT Utah, VA Virginia, VT Vermont, WA Washington, WI Wisconsin, WV West Virginia, WY Wyoming.

FM STATIONS IN MAJOR METROPOLITAN AREAS

NB: Sts of less than 1kW are not shown

Location	State	Callsign	MHz	kW(ERP)
Atlanta Area				
Arcade	GA	WPUP	103.7	25
Athens	GA	WMSL	88.9	20
Athens	GA	WUOG	90.5	26
Athens	GA	WUGA	91.7	6
Athens	GA	WBTS	95.5	74
Athens	GA	WFSH-FM	104.7	100
Atlanta	GA	WRAS	88.5	100
Atlanta	GA	WRFG	89.3	100
Atlanta	GA	WABE	90.1	96
Atlanta	GA	WREK	91.1	40
Atlanta	GA	WCLK	91.9	6
Atlanta	GA	WZGC	92.9	100
Atlanta	GA	WLTM	94.9	100
Atlanta	GA	WKLS	96.1	100
Atlanta	GA	WSB-FM	98.5	100
Atlanta	GA	WNNX	99.7	100
Atlanta	GA	WVEE	103.3	100
Bolingbroke	GA	WWWD	102.1	6
Bostwick	GA	WMOQ	92.3	3
Bowdon	GA	WWVA-FM	105.3	70
Buckhead	GA	WPMA	102.7	8
Buford	GA	WLKQ-FM	102.3	4
Canton	GA	WLCL	105.7	20
Cartersville	GA	WCCV	91.7	7
Clarkesville	GA	WMJE	102.9	16
Cleveland	GA	WAZX-FM	101.9	3
College Park	GA	WWWQ	100.5	27
Coosa	GA	WSRM	95.3	3
Cornelia	GA	WCON-FM	99.3	19
Crawford	GA	WGMG	102.1	10
Cumming	GA	WWEV-FM	91.5	9
Dahlonega	GA	WKHC	104.3	4
Demorest	GA	WPPR	88.3	6
Eatonton	GA	WMGZ	97.7	9
Ellijay	GA	WLJA-FM	93.5	6
Fayetteville	GA	WPZE	97.5	8
Forsyth	GA	WQMJ	100.1	3
Fruithurst	AL	WCKS-FM	102.7	2
Gainesville	GA	WFOX	97.1	100
Gainseville	GA	WYAY	106.7	100
Gray	GA	WYNF	96.5	8
Greensboro	GA	WDDK	103.9	5
Greenville	GA	WKZJ	95.7	3
Griffin	GA	WMVV	90.7	18
Hampton	GA	WHTA	107.9	27
Heflin	AL	WPIL	91.7	1
Hogansville	GA	WMGP	98.1	25
Jackson	GA	WJGA-FM	92.1	2
La Grange	GA	WOAK	90.9	3
La Grange	GA	WALR-FM	104.1	100
Mableton	GA	WAMJ	102.5	3
Manchester	GA	WVFJ-FM	93.3	29
Marietta	GA	WKHX-FM	101.5	100
Peachtree City	GA	WBZY-FM	96.7	2
Roanoke	AL	WELR-FM	102.3	9
Rockmart	GA	WTSH-FM	107.1	50
Rome	GA	WKCX	97.7	4
Rome	GA	WQTU	102.3	1
Roswell	GA	WJZZ-FM	107.5	25
Royston	GA	WPUP	103.7	25
Smyrna	GA	WSTR	94.1	100
Talking Rock	GA	WNSY	100.1	7
The Rock	GA	WKEU-FM	88.9	5
Thomaston	GA	WTGA-FM	101.1	6
Toccoa	GA	WNGC	106.1	100
Trion	GA	WATG	95.7	1
Warm Springs	GA	WJSP-FM	88.1	100
Watkinsville	GA	WXKT	100.1	6
Winder	GA	WYFW	89.5	6
Yates	GA	WWBM	89.7	1
Zebulon	GA	WEKS	92.5	6

Location	State	Callsign	MHz	kW
Boston Area				
Amherst	MA	WFCR	88.5	13
Athol	MA	WNYN-FM	99.9	2
Barnstable	MA	WQRC	99.9	50
Boston	MA	WERS	88.9	5
Boston	MA	WGBH	89.7	100
Boston	MA	WBUR-FM	90.9	12
Boston	MA	WJMN	94.5	9
Boston	MA	WTKK	96.9	23
Boston	MA	WBMX	98.5	9
Boston	MA	WZLX	100.7	22
Boston	MA	WODS	103.3	16
Boston	MA	WBCN	104.1	21
Boston	MA	WMJX	106.7	22
Brockton	MA	WBOT	97.7	3
Brookline	MA	WBOS	92.9	19
Cambridge	MA	WHRB	95.3	3
Chatham	MA	WFCC-FM	107.5	50
Concord	NH	WEVO	89.1	50
Concord	NH	WOTX-FM	102.3	3
Concord	NH	WJYY	105.5	2
Dover	NH	WOKQ	97.5	50
Durham	NH	WUNH	91.3	6
Exeter	NH	WERZ	107.1	6
Fairhaven	MA	WFHN	107.1	5
Falmouth	MA	WFPB-FM	91.9	6
Falmouth	MA	WCIB	101.9	50
Farmington	NH	WMEX	106.5	3
Fitchburg	MA	WXLO	104.5	37
Framingham	MA	WROR-FM	105.7	23
Gloucester	MA	WBOQ	104.9	3
Hampton	NH	WSAK	102.1	3
Harwich Port	MA	WDVT	93.5	3
Haverhill	MA	WXRV	92.5	25
Henniker	NH	WNNH	99.1	3
Hillsboro	NH	WTPL	107.7	1
Hyannis	MA	WPXC	102.9	3
Hyannis	MA	WCOD-FM	106.1	50
Kingston	RI	WRIU	90.3	3
Kittery	ME	WSHK	105.3	2
Lawrence	MA	WQSX	93.7	34
Lowell	MA	WUML	91.5	1
Lowell	MA	WKLB-FM	99.5	37
Lynn	MA	WFNX	101.7	2
Manchester	NH	WZID	95.7	15
Manchester	NH	WGIR-FM	101.1	12
Marshfield	MA	WATD-FM	95.9	2
Mashpee	MA	WTWV	101.1	6
Medford	MA	WXKS-FM	107.9	21
Middletown	RI	WKKB	100.3	2
Narragansett Pier	RI	WAKX	102.7	2
Nashua	NH	WEVS	88.3	4
New Bedford	MA	WJFD-FM	97.3	50
New Bedford	MA	WCTK	98.1	47
Newton	MA	WZBC	90.3	1
North Dartmouth	MA	WSMU-FM	89.3	10
North Dartmouth	MA	WSMU-FM	91.1	1
Orange	MA	WJDF	97.3	6
Orleans	MA	WKPE-FM	104.7	50
Plymouth	MA	WPLM-FM	99.1	50
Portsmouth	NH	WHEB	100.3	50
Providence	RI	WPRO-FM	92.3	39
Providence	RI	WHJY	94.1	50
Providence	RI	WBRU	95.5	19
Providence	RI	WWBB	101.5	28
Providence	RI	WWLI	105.1	50
Provincetown	MA	WOMR	92.1	6
Rochester	NH	WQSO	96.7	3
Sanford	ME	WPHX-FM	92.1	3
Scituate	MA	WSMA	90.5	22
Somersworth	NH	WBYY	98.7	6
South Yarmouth	MA	WOCN-FM	103.9	6
Southbridge	MA	WWFX	100.1	3
Storrs	CT	WHUS	91.7	4
Taunton	MA	WSNE-FM	93.3	30
Tisbury	MA	WMVY	92.7	3
Wakefield-Peacedale	RI	WSKO-FM	99.7	2
Waltham	MA	WCRB	102.5	8
Webster	MA	WORC-FM	98.9	2
Wellfleet	MA	WWTE	90.7	1
West Yarmouth	MA	WXTK	95.1	50
Westborough	MA	WAAF	107.3	20
Westerly	RI	WEEI-FM	103.7	37
Winchendon	MA	WINQ	97.7	6
Woods Hole	MA	WCAI	90.1	1
Woonsocket	RI	WWKX	106.3	1
Worcester	MA	WICN	90.5	8
Worcester	MA	WSRS	96.1	17
Worcester	MA	WAAF	107.3	10
York Center	ME	WUBB	95.3	1
Buffalo Area				
Albion	NY	WJCA	102.1	4
Alfred	NY	WZKZ	101.9	1
Arcade	NY	WCOF	89.5	2
Attica	NY	WLOF	101.7	3
Bradford	PA	WBRR	100.1	2
Brighton	NY	WZNE	94.1	3
Brockport	NY	WBSU	89.1	7
Brockport	NY	WMJQ	104.9	6
Brockport	NY	WMJQ	105.5	6
Buffalo	NY	WBFO	88.7	50
Buffalo	NY	WFBF	89.9	16
Buffalo	NY	WBNY	91.3	1
Buffalo	NY	WBUF	92.9	91
Buffalo	NY	WBLK	93.7	12
Buffalo	NY	WNED-FM	94.5	105
Buffalo	NY	WJYE	96.1	47
Buffalo	NY	WGRF	96.9	24
Buffalo	NY	WDCX	99.5	110
Buffalo	NY	WTSS	102.5	110
Buffalo	NY	WEDG	103.3	49
Buffalo	NY	WHTT-FM	104.1	50
Buffalo	NY	WYRK	106.5	50
Canandaigua	NY	WCIY	88.9	1
Dansville	NY	WDNY-FM	93.9	3
Depew	NY	WBLK	93.7	47
Fairport	NY	WBBF-FM	93.3	4
Fredonia	NY	WBKX	96.5	1
Friendship	NY	WCID	89.1	7
Geneseo	NY	WGSU	89.3	2
Greece	NY	WGMC	90.1	15
Honeoye Falls	NY	WFXF	95.1	50
Hornell	NY	WCKR	92.1	3
Hornell	NY	WKPQ	105.3	43
Houghton	NY	WJSL	90.3	6
Irondequoit	NY	WKGS	106.7	4
Jamestown	NY	WUBJ	88.1	3
Jamestown	NY	WNJA	89.7	6
Jamestown	NY	WCOT	90.9	12
Jamestown	NY	WWSE	93.3	27
Jamestown	NY	WHUG	101.9	6
Niagara Falls	NY	WKSE	98.5	46
North East	PA	WRKT	100.9	4
Olean	NY	WPIG	95.7	43
Olean	NY	WMXO	101.5	1
Palmyra	NY	WZXV	99.7	3
Rochester	NY	WRUR-FM	88.5	3
Rochester	NY	WXXI-FM	91.5	45
Rochester	NY	WBEE-FM	92.5	50
Rochester	NY	WCMF-FM	96.5	50
Rochester	NY	WPXY-FM	97.9	50
Rochester	NY	WBZA	98.9	37
Rochester	NY	WVOR-FM	100.5	50
Rochester	NY	WRMM-FM	101.3	27
Rochester	NY	WDKX	103.9	1
Rochester	NY	WJZR	105.9	3
Russell	PA	WQFX-FM	103.1	3
Salamanca	NY	WQRT	98.3	3
Warsaw	NY	WCOU	88.3	11
Webster	NY	WRCI	102.7	6
Wellsville	NY	WJQZ	103.5	2
Wethersfield Twnshp	NY	WLKK	107.7	20
Chicago Area				
Aurora	IL	WERV-FM	95.9	3
Aurora	IL	WLEY-FM	107.9	21
Benton Harbor	MI	WCNF	94.9	2
Benton Harbor	MI	WHFB-FM	99.9	50
Berrien Springs	MI	WAUS	90.7	50
Bridgman	MI	WYTZ	97.5	4
Buchanan	MI	WSMK	99.1	3

Location	State	Callsign	MHz	kW
Chesterton	IN	WBEW	89.5	50
Chicago	IL	WMBI-FM	90.1	100
Chicago	IL	WBEZ	91.5	8
Chicago	IL	WXRT-FM	93.1	14
Chicago	IL	WLIT-FM	93.9	4
Chicago	IL	WZZN	94.7	4
Chicago	IL	WNUA	95.5	8
Chicago	IL	WBBM-FM	96.3	45
Chicago	IL	WDRV	97.1	8
Chicago	IL	WLUP-FM	97.9	5
Chicago	IL	WFMT	98.7	6
Chicago	IL	WUSN	99.5	50
Chicago	IL	WNND	100.3	7
Chicago	IL	WKQX	101.1	6
Chicago	IL	WKSC-FM	103.5	4
Chicago	IL	WJMK	104.3	48
Chicago	IL	WGCI-FM	107.5	4
Coal City	IL	WRXQ	100.7	2
Crest Hill	IL	WCCQ	98.3	3
Crete	IL	WYCA	102.3	1
Crown Point	IN	WXRD	103.9	3
Dekalb	IL	WNIU	89.5	50
Dekalb	IL	WDEK	92.5	20
Dekalb	IL	WDKB	94.9	3
Dwight	IL	WJEZ	98.9	1
Elmwood Park	IL	WCKG	105.9	50
Flossmoor	IL	WHFH	88.5	2
Gary	IN	WGVE-FM	88.7	2
Genoa	IL	WYRB	106.3	4
Glen Ellyn	IL	WDCB	90.9	5
Hammond	IN	WPWX	92.3	50
Hanna	IN	WHLP	89.9	8
Joliet	IL	WJCH	91.9	50
Joliet	IL	WVIX	93.5	6
Joliet	IL	WSSR	96.7	4
Kankakee	IL	WAWF	88.3	1
Kankakee	IL	WONU	89.7	35
Kankakee	IL	WKCC	91.1	2
Kankakee	IL	WKIF	92.7	3
Kankakee	IL	WVLI	95.1	2
Kentland	IN	WIVR	101.7	3
Knox	IN	WKVI-FM	99.3	3
La Porte	IN	WCOE	96.7	3
Lansing	IL	WSRB	106.3	4
Lowell	IN	WTMK	88.5	2
Lowell	IN	WZVN	107.1	1
Marseilles	IL	WKOT	96.5	3
Michigan City	IN	WEFM	95.9	3
Morris	IL	WBEQ	90.7	1
Morris	IL	WCSJ-FM	103.1	6
Morris	IL	WCFL	104.7	50
Naperville	IL	WONC	89.1	2
New Carlisle	IN	WOZW	102.3	2
Niles	MI	WAOR	95.3	6
Oak Park	IL	WVAZ	102.7	35
Ottawa	IL	WRKX	95.3	4
Park Forest	IL	WRZA	99.9	50
Plano	IL	WSPY-FM	107.1	2
Rensselaer	IN	WLQI	97.7	3
Rochelle	IL	WRHL-FM	102.3	5
Rockford	IL	WNIJ	90.5	50
Seneca	IL	WJDK-FM	95.7	3
Skokie	IL	WTMX	101.9	4
South Bend	IN	WUBS	89.7	2
South Bend	IN	WUBU	106.3	3
St. Joseph	MI	WIRX	107.1	1
Valparaiso	IN	WLJE	105.5	1
Watseka	IL	WGFA-FM	94.1	50
Wilmington	IL	WYKT	105.5	1
Dallas & Fort Worth Area				
Allen	TX	KESN	103.3	100
Arlington	TX	KLTY	94.9	100
Azle	TX	KTCY	101.7	92
Bells	TX	KMKT	93.1	6.8
Benbrook	TX	KDXX	107.1	74
Bonham	TX	KFYZ-FM	98.3	12.5
Bridgeport	TX	KBOC	98.3	40
Campbell	TX	KRVA-FM	107.1	3.6
Commerce	TX	KETR	88.9	100
Cooper	TX	KIKT	93.5	12.4

Location	State	Callsign	MHz	kW
Dallas	TX	KNON	89.3	55
Dallas	TX	KERA	90.1	100
Dallas	TX	KCBI	90.9	100
Dallas	TX	KVTT	91.7	100
Dallas	TX	KZPS	92.5	100
Dallas	TX	KBFB	97.9	100
Dallas	TX	KLUV-FM	98.7	100
Dallas	TX	KJKK	100.3	100
Dallas	TX	WRR	101.1	100
Dallas	TX	KDMX	102.9	100
Dallas	TX	KKDA-FM	104.5	100
Dallas	TX	KLLI	105.3	100
Decatur	TX	KDKR	91.3	57
Decatur	TX	KRNB	105.7	100
Denton	TX	KNTU	88.1	100
Denton	TX	KFZO	99.1	100
Denton	TX	KHKS	106.1	100
Durant	OK	KLAK	97.5	27
Farmersville	TX	KXEZ	92.1	2.7
Flower Mound	TX	KTYS	96.7	93
Fort Worth	TX	KTCU-FM	88.7	10
Fort Worth	TX	KLNO	94.1	100
Fort Worth	TX	KSCS	96.3	100
Fort Worth	TX	KEGL	97.1	100
Fort Worth	TX	KPLX	99.5	100
Fort Worth	TX	KOAI	107.5	53
Fort Worth-Dallas	TX	KDGE	102.1	100
Gainesville	TX	KSOC	94.5	100
Greenville	TX	KIKT	93.5	1.8
Haltom City	TX	KDBN	93.3	50
Highland Park-Dallas	TX	KVIL-FM	103.7	100
Highland Village	TX	KWRD-FM	100.7	100
Hillsboro	TX	KBRQ	102.5	100
Howe	TX	KHYI	95.3	15
Keene	TX	KJCR	88.3	23
Kerens	TX	KRVF	106.9	21.5
Krum	TX	KNOR	93.7	100
Lewisville	TX	KESS-FM	107.9	100
Malakoff	TX	KCKL	95.9	6
Mckinney	TX	KNTU	88.1	100
Mesquite	TX	KEOM	88.5	61
Mineola	TX	KMOO-FM	99.9	6
Muenster	TX	KKDL	106.7	75
Pilot Point	TX	KZMP-FM	104.9	16
Sanger	TX	KVRK	89.7	14
Sanger	TX	KTDK	104.1	11
Springtown	TX	KSQX	89.1	3
Sulphur Springs	TX	KSCH	95.9	6
Whitesboro	TX	KMAD-FM	102.5	18
Denver Area				
Bennett	CO	KSIR-FM	107.1	100
Boulder	CO	KGNU-FM	88.5	1
Boulder	CO	KRKS-FM	94.7	100
Boulder	CO	KBCO-FM	97.3	100
Boulder	CO	KXKL-FM1	105.1	2
Breckenridge	CO	KSMT	102.3	6
Broomfield	CO	KDJM	92.5	57
Brush	CO	KSIR-FM	107.1	100
Canon City	CO	KTLC	89.1	1
Castle Rock	CO	KJMN	92.1	42
Colorado Springs	CO	KEPC	89.7	8
Colorado Springs	CO	KTLF	90.5	20
Colorado Springs	CO	KRCC	91.5	2
Colorado Springs	CO	KSPZ	92.9	79
Colorado Springs	CO	KILO	94.3	83
Colorado Springs	CO	KRDO-FM	95.1	65
Colorado Springs	CO	KKFM	98.1	71
Colorado Springs	CO	KKCS-FM	101.9	72
Commerce City	CO	KBRU-1	101.5	19
Denver	CO	KUVO	89.3	23
Denver	CO	KVOD	90.1	50
Denver	CO	KFMD	95.7	100
Denver	CO	KYGO-FM	98.5	100
Denver	CO	KQMT	99.5	100
Denver	CO	KIMN	100.3	100
Denver	CO	KOSI	101.1	100
Denver	CO	KRFX	103.5	100
Denver	CO	KXKL-FM	105.1	100
Denver	CO	KALC	105.9	100
Denver	CO	KBPI	106.7	100

Location	State	Callsign	MHz	kW
Estes Park	CO	KXDC	102.1	25
Evergreen	CO	KXPK	96.5	100
Fort Collins	CO	KRFC	88.9	3
Fort Collins	CO	KCSU-FM	90.5	10
Fort Collins	CO	KTCL	93.3	100
Fort Collins	CO	KPAW	107.9	100
Fort Morgan	CO	KBRU-FM	101.5	100
Fort Morgan	CO	KBRU-FM	101.7	3
Greeley	CO	KUNC-FM	91.5	81
Greeley	CO	KSME	96.1	100
Hudson	CO	KSIR-FM1	107.1	20
Kremmling	CO	KKHI	106.3	50
Lakewood	CO	KQKS	107.5	100
Limon	CO	KAVD	103.1	100
Longmont	CO	KJCD	104.3	100
Loveland	CO	KXWA	89.7	36
Loveland	CO	KTRR	102.5	50
Manitou Springs	CO	KCME	88.7	12
Manitou Springs	CO	KBIQ	102.7	72
Morrison	CO	KLDV	91.1	100
Parker	CO	KAVD	103.1	100
Pueblo	CO	KCCY	96.9	72
Pueblo	CO	KKMG	98.9	72
Pueblo	CO	KVUU	99.9	79
Pueblo	CO	KGFT	100.7	78
Pueblo	CO	KDZA-FM	107.9	25
Pueblo West	CO	KYZX	103.9	2
Southglenn	CO	KKCS-FM2	101.9	3
Strasburg	CO	KAGM	102.3	25
Timnath	CO	KJAC	105.5	58
Wheat Ridge	CO	KTCL	93.3	28
Widefield	CO	KKLI	106.3	2
Windsor	CO	KUAD-FM	99.1	100
Detroit Area				
Adrian	MI	WLEN	103.9	3
Ann Arbor	MI	WUOM	91.7	110
Ann Arbor	MI	WWWW	102.9	49
Ann Arbor	MI	WQKL	107.1	3
Birmingham	MI	WCSX	94.7	14
Bowling Green	OH	WRQN	93.5	4
Brooklyn	MI	WKHM-FM	105.3	2
Burton	MI	WTAC	89.7	1
Clyde	OH	WHVT	90.5	3
Dearborn	MI	WNIC	100.3	50
Delta	OH	WRWK	106.5	5
Detroit	MI	WRCJ-FM	90.9	42
Detroit	MI	WMXD	92.3	45
Detroit	MI	WDRQ	93.1	27
Detroit	MI	WKQI	95.5	100
Detroit	MI	WDVD	96.3	21
Detroit	MI	WKRK-FM	97.1	50
Detroit	MI	WJLB	97.9	50
Detroit	MI	WVMV	98.7	50
Detroit	MI	WYCD	99.5	18
Detroit	MI	WRIF	101.1	11
Detroit	MI	WDET-FM	101.9	48
Detroit	MI	WMUZ	103.5	50
Detroit	MI	WOMC	104.3	190
Detroit	MI	WMGC-FM	105.1	50
Detroit	MI	WDTJ	105.9	20
Detroit	MI	WDTW	106.7	61
Detroit	MI	WGPR	107.5	50
East Lansing	MI	WKAR-FM	90.5	87
Flint	MI	WFUM-FM	91.1	18
Flint	MI	WDZZ-FM	92.7	3
Flint	MI	WFBE	95.1	50
Flint	MI	WWCK-FM	105.5	25
Flint	MI	WCRZ	107.9	50
Frankenmuth	MI	WRCL	93.7	4
Fremont	OH	WFRO-FM	99.1	20
Gibsonburg	OH	WIMX	95.7	4
Goodland Township	MI	WHYT	88.1	13
Holland	OH	WPOS-FM	102.3	6
Howell	MI	WIIMI-FM	93.5	5
Imlay City	MI	WWKM	89.1	6
Lapeer	MI	WQUS	103.1	3
Leroy Township	MI	WLGH	88.1	10
Lexington	MI	WBTI	96.9	3
Luna Pier	MI	WTWR-FM	98.3	3
Marlette	MI	WBGV	92.5	3
Maumee	OH	WYSZ	89.3	2
Monroe	MI	WDTR	88.1	3
Mount Clemens	MI	WDMK	102.7	50
Oak Harbor	OH	WJZE	97.3	2
Owosso	MI	WRSR	103.9	3
Port Clinton	OH	WXKR	94.5	30
Port Huron	MI	WNFA	88.3	1
Port Huron	MI	WGRT	102.3	3
Port Huron	MI	WSAQ	107.1	6
Sandusky	OH	WVMS	89.5	5
Sandusky	MI	WNFR	90.7	50
Sandusky	MI	WTGV-FM	97.7	3
Sandusky	OH	WCPZ	102.7	50
Swanton	OH	WJUC	107.3	3
Sylvania	OH	WWWM-FM	105.5	4
Toledo	OH	WGTE-FM	91.3	14
Toledo	OH	WVKS	92.5	50
Toledo	OH	WKKO	99.9	50
Toledo	OH	WRVF	101.5	41
Toledo	OH	WIOT	104.7	50
Tuscola	MI	WWBN	101.5	2
Vassar	MI	WOWE	98.9	3
Wauseon	OH	WXQQ	96.9	5
Ypsilanti	MI	WEMU	89.1	16
Houston Area				
Alvin	TX	KACC	89.7	5.6
Baycity	TX	KZBJ	89.5	35
Beaumont	TX	KLBT	88.1	40
Beaumont	TX	KRWP	97.5	100
Beaumont	TX	KTCX	102.5	50
Beaumont	TX	KQQK	107.9	100
Brenham	TX	KULF	94.1	50
Cleveland	TX	KTHT	97.1	100
Columbus	TX	KULM-FM	98.3	6
Conroe	TX	KAXF	88.3	100
Conroe	TX	KHPT	106.9	100
Crystal Beach	TX	KSTB	101.5	6
Crystal Beach	TX	KLTO	105.3	6
Fannett	TX	KZFT	90.5	35
Freeport	TX	KJOJ-FM	103.3	100
Galveston	TX	KYBJ	91.1	15.8
Galveston	TX	KOVE-FM	106.5	100
Hempstead	TX	KEZB	105.3	25
Houston	TX	KUHF	88.7	100
Houston	TX	KPFT	90.1	100
Houston	TX	KTSU	90.9	18.5
Houston	TX	KTRU	91.7	50
Houston	TX	KKRW	93.7	100
Houston	TX	KTBZ-FM	94.5	100
Houston	TX	KHJZ-FM	95.7	100
Houston	TX	KHMX	96.5	100
Houston	TX	KBXX	97.9	100
Houston	TX	KODA	99.1	100
Houston	TX	KILT-FM	100.3	100
Houston	TX	KLOL	101.1	100
Houston	TX	KMJQ	102.1	100
Houston	TX	KLTN	102.9	100
Houston	TX	KRBE	104.1	100
Houston	TX	KHCB-FM	105.7	100
Humble	TX	KSBJ	89.3	100
Huntsville	TX	KSHU	90.5	3
Huntsville	TX	KUST	99.7	7.3
Huntsville	TX	KSAM-FM	101.7	3.7
La Porte	TX	KVST	103.7	100
Lake Jackson	TX	KYBJ	91.1	5
Lake Jackson	TX	KLDE	107.5	98
Liberty	TX	KSHN	99.9	26.5
Livingston	TX	KETX-FM	92.3	32
Missouri City	TX	KPTY	104.9	2.7
Navasota	TX	KHTZ	92.5	6
New Ulm	TX	KNRG	92.3	6
Pasadena	TX	KKBQ-FM	92.9	100
Port Arthur	TX	KQBU-FM	93.3	100
Port Arthur	TX	KTJM	98.5	100
Prairie View	TX	KPVU	91.3	9.8
Santa Fe	TX	KJIC	90.5	7.7
Seabrook	TX	KROI	92.1	100
Willis	TX	KUST	99.7	2.55
Willis	TX	KVST	103.7	15
Winnie	TX	KOBT	100.7	100

Location	State	Callsign	MHz	kW
Kansas Area				
Butler	MO	KMOE	92.1	5
Cameron	MO	KKWK	100.1	50
Carrollton	MO	KMZU	100.7	99
Chillicothe	MO	KRNW	88.9	38
Chillicothe	MO	KCHI-FM	98.5	3
Clinton	MO	KDKD-FM	95.3	17
Concordia	MO	KYRV	88.1	1
Country Club	MO	KJCV	89.7	4
Gallatin	MO	KGOZ	101.7	15
Garden City	MO	KFME-FM	105.1	69
Harrisonville	MO	KCFX	101.1	100
Hiawatha	KS	KNZA	103.9	50
Horton	KS	KAIR-FM	93.7	25
Kansas City	MO	KLJC	88.5	100
Kansas City	MO	KCUR-FM	89.3	100
Kansas City	MO	KKFI	90.1	100
Kansas City	MO	KMXV	93.3	100
Kansas City	KS	KFKF-FM	94.1	100
Kansas City	MO	KCMO-FM	94.9	100
Kansas City	MO	KRBZ	96.5	100
Kansas City	KS	KUDL	98.1	100
Kansas City	MO	KYYS	99.7	100
Kansas City	MO	KSRC	102.1	100
Kansas City	MO	KPRS	103.3	100
Kansas City	MO	KBEQ-FM	104.3	100
Knob Noster	MO	KCVQ	89.7	5
Knob Noster	MO	KXKX	105.7	38
La Monte	MO	KPOW-FM	97.7	100
Lawrence	KS	KJHK	90.7	3
Lawrence	KS	KANU	91.5	100
Lawrence	KS	KLZR	105.9	100
Leavenworth	KS	KQRC-FM	98.9	100
Lee's Summit	MO	KZPL	97.3	55
Lexington	MO	KMJK	107.3	100
Liberty	MO	KWJC	91.9	4
Liberty	MO	WDAF-FM	106.5	100
Malta Bend	MO	KRLI	103.9	12
Marshall	MO	KMMO-FM	102.9	76
Olathe	KS	KCCV-FM	92.3	8
Osage City	KS	KKYD	92.9	8
Ottawa	KS	KCHZ	95.7	98
Richmond	MO	KAYX	92.5	2
Savannah	MO	KSJQ	92.7	50
Shawnee	KS	KMAJ-FM	107.7	90
Silver Lake	KS	KCVT	92.5	7
St. Joseph	MO	KSRD	91.9	10
St. Joseph	MO	KKJO-FM	105.5	100
St. Marys	KS	KQTP	102.9	30
Topeka	KS	KJTY	88.1	100
Topeka	KS	WIBW-FM	94.5	100
Topeka	KS	KWIC	99.3	7
Topeka	KS	KDVV	100.3	100
Topeka	KS	KTPK	106.9	100
Topeka	KS	KMAJ-FM	107.7	100
Warrensburg	MO	KTBG	90.9	97
Windsor	MO	KWKJ	98.5	9
Los Angeles Area				
Anaheim	CA	KFSH-FM	95.9	6
Arcadia	CA	KSSE	107.1	6
Avalon	CA	KLIT	92.7	3
Burbank	CA	KSSE-FM1	107.1	3
Camarillo	CA	KMRO	90.3	7
Camarillo	CA	KOCP	95.9	2
Claremont	CA	KSPC	88.7	3
Compton	CA	KJLH	102.3	6
East Los Angeles	CA	KLAX-FM	97.9	33
Edwards	CA	KEDD	103.9	2
Garden Grove	CA	KEBN	94.3	6
Glendale	CA	KSCA	101.9	5
Inglewood	CA	KRCD	103.9	4
Lancaster	CA	KTLW	88.9	6
Lancaster	CA	KGMX	106.3	3
Long Beach	CA	KKJZ	88.1	30
Long Beach	CA	KBUE	105.5	3
Los Angeles	CA	KXLU	88.9	3
Los Angeles	CA	KPFK	90.7	110
Los Angeles	CA	KUSC	91.5	39
Los Angeles	CA	KHHT	92.3	43
Los Angeles	CA	KCBS-FM	93.1	29
Los Angeles	CA	KZLA-FM	93.9	35
Los Angeles	CA	KTWV	94.7	58
Los Angeles	CA	KLOS	95.5	72
Los Angeles	CA	KXOL-FM	96.3	54
Los Angeles	CA	KLSX	97.1	21
Los Angeles	CA	KYSR	98.7	75
Los Angeles	CA	KKLA-FM	99.5	11
Los Angeles	CA	KKBT	100.3	15
Los Angeles	CA	KRTH-FM	101.1	54
Los Angeles	CA	KIIS-FM	102.7	8
Los Angeles	CA	KOST	103.5	13
Los Angeles	CA	KBIG-FM	104.3	105
Los Angeles	CA	KMZT-FM	105.1	18
Los Angeles	CA	KPWR	105.9	25
Los Angeles	CA	KLVE	107.5	50
Newport Beach	CA	KDLE	103.1	2
Ontario	CA	KZBA	93.5	6
Oxnard	CA	KXLM	102.9	6
Oxnard	CA	KCAQ	104.7	50
Pasadena	CA	KROQ-FM	106.7	7
Redlands	CA	KCAL-FM	96.7	2
Redondo Beach	CA	KZAB	93.5	6
Riverside	CA	KSGN	89.7	3
Riverside	CA	KELT	92.7	6
Rosamond	CA	KLKX	93.5	3
Rosamond	CA	KOSS	105.5	6
San Bernardino	CA	KVCR	91.9	4
San Bernardino	CA	KFRG	95.1	50
San Bernardino	CA	KOLA	99.9	30
San Clemente	CA	KWVE	107.9	105
San Fernando	CA	KBUA	94.3	6
Santa Ana	CA	KWIZ	96.7	6
Santa Ana	CA	KALI-FM	106.3	6
Santa Monica	CA	KCRW	89.9	7
Santa Monica	CA	KDLD	103.1	4
Thousand Oaks	CA	KCLU	88.3	3
Thousand Oaks	CA	KDSC	91.1	5
Thousand Oaks	CA	KMLT	92.7	3
Ventura	CA	KBBY-FM	95.1	13
West Covina	CA	KRCV	98.3	6
West Los Angeles	CA	KCSN-FM1	88.5	1
Miami Area				
Belle Glade	FL	WBGF	93.5	20
Boca Raton	FL	WKIS	99.9	100
Bonita Springs	FL	WRXK-FM	96.1	100
Boynton Beach	FL	WRMB	89.3	100
Clewiston	FL	WAFC-FM	99.5	12
Coral Gables	FL	WVUM	90.5	1
Coral Gables	FL	WHQT	105.1	100
Florida City	FL	WMFL	88.5	8
Fort Lauderdale	FL	WAFG	90.3	3
Fort Lauderdale	FL	WHYI-FM	100.7	100
Fort Lauderdale	FL	WMIB	103.5	100
Fort Lauderdale	FL	WBGG-FM	105.9	100
Fort Lauderdale	FL	WRMA	106.7	100
Goulds	FL	WRTO-FM	98.3	100
Hialeah	FL	WCMQ-FM	92.3	31
Hobe Sound	FL	WOLL	105.5	50
Jupiter	FL	WJBW-FM	106.3	19
Key Largo	FL	WGES	90.9	33
Key Largo	FL	WMKL	91.7	50
Key Largo	FL	WZMQ	106.3	50
Miami	FL	WDNA	88.9	7
Miami	FL	WMCU	89.7	100
Miami	FL	WLRN-FM	91.3	100
Miami	FL	WPYM	93.1	100
Miami	FL	WPOW	96.5	100
Miami	FL	WFLC	97.3	100
Miami	FL	WEDR	99.1	100
Miami	FL	WLYF	101.5	100
Miami	FL	WAMR-FM	107.5	95
Miami Beach	FL	WLVE	93.9	100
Miami Beach	FL	WZTA	94.9	100
North Miami Beach	FL	WXDJ	95.7	40
Palm Beach	FL	WRMF	97.9	100
Pennsuco	FL	WIRP	88.3	6
Plantation Key	FL	WCTH	100.3	100
Plantation Key	FL	WFKZ	103.1	50
Pompano Beach	FL	WMXJ	102.7	100
Riviera Beach	FL	WZZR	94.3	50

Location	State	Callsign	MHz	kW
Rock Harbor	FL	WKLG	102.1	100
Sunrise	FL	WKPX	88.5	3
Tavernier	FL	WKEZ-FM	96.9	25
West Palm Beach	FL	WAYF	88.1	50
West Palm Beach	FL	WXEL	90.7	38
West Palm Beach	FL	WRLX	92.1	7
West Palm Beach	FL	WEAT-FM	104.3	100
West Palm Beach	FL	WIRK-FM	107.9	100
Milwaukee Area				
Arlington Heights	IL	WCLR	88.3	1
Arlington Heights	IL	WKIE	92.7	2
Beaver Dam	WI	WXRO	95.3	6
Belvidere	IL	WXRX	104.9	4
Brookfield	WI	WFMR	106.9	6
Cleveland	WI	WLKN	98.1	6
Columbus	WI	WTLX	100.5	6
De Forest	WI	WHIT-FM	93.1	6
Delafield	WI	WHAD	90.7	72
Des Plaines	IL	WZFS	106.7	50
Dundee	IL	WWYW	103.9	3
Elgin	IL	WJKL	94.3	6
Evanston	IL	WNUR-FM	89.3	7
Evanston	IL	WOJO	105.1	6
Evansville	WI	WKPO	105.9	2
Fond Du Lac	WI	WLWR	91.7	20
Fond Du Lac	WI	WFON	107.1	6
Fort Atkinson	WI	WSJY	107.3	26
Hartford	WI	WTKM-FM	104.9	6
Highland Park	IL	WVIV-FM	103.1	6
Janesville	WI	WJVL	99.9	11
Kenosha	WI	WGTD	91.1	5
Kenosha	WI	WIIL	95.1	50
Kiel	WI	WSTM	91.3	1
Lake Geneva	WI	WLKG	96.1	6
Lomira	WI	WFDL-FM	97.7	18
Marshall	WI	WJWD	90.3	10
Mayville	WI	WMDC	98.7	6
Menomonee Falls	WI	WJMR-FM	98.3	5
Milwaukee	WI	WYMS	88.9	2
Milwaukee	WI	WUWM	89.7	16
Milwaukee	WI	WMSE	91.7	3
Milwaukee	WI	WJZI	93.3	13
Milwaukee	WI	WKTI-FM	94.5	16
Milwaukee	WI	WRIT-FM	95.7	34
Milwaukee	WI	WKLH	96.5	20
Milwaukee	WI	WLTQ	97.3	16
Milwaukee	WI	WMYX-FM	99.1	50
Milwaukee	WI	WLUM-FM	102.1	20
Milwaukee	WI	WLZR	102.9	50
Milwaukee	WI	WVCY-FM	107.7	43
Mukwonago	WI	WFZH	105.3	2
Omro	WI	WPKR	99.5	25
Plymouth	WI	WXER	104.5	6
Port Washington	WI	WPJP	100.1	6
Racine	WI	WEZY	92.1	3
Racine	WI	WKKV-FM	100.7	50
Ripon	WI	WTCX	96.1	4
Sheboygan	WI	WBFM	93.7	6
Sheboygan Falls	WI	WHBZ	106.5	6
Sturtevant	WI	WEXT	104.7	4
Sun Prairie	WI	WXXM	92.1	4
Watertown	WI	WJJO	94.1	50
Waukegan	IL	WXLC	102.3	3
Waukesha	WI	WMIL-FM	106.1	13
Waunakee	WI	WBZU	105.1	6
Wauwatosa	WI	WXSS	103.7	20
West Bend	WI	WBWI-FM	92.5	18
Whitewater	WI	WSUW	91.7	1
Whitewater	WI	WSLD	104.5	6
Whitewater	WI	WKCH	106.5	6
Woodstock	IL	WZSR	105.5	2
Zion	IL	WWDV	96.9	50
Minneapolis Area				
Anoka	MN	KQQL	107.9	100
Atwater	MN	KKLN	94.1	6
Balsam Lake	WI	WLMX-FM	104.9	22
Blooming Prairie	MN	KOWZ-FM	100.9	100
Cambridge	MN	WGVY	105.3	25
Cold Spring	MN	KMXK	94.9	50
Collegeville	MN	KNSR	88.9	100
Collegeville	MN	KSJR-FM	90.1	100
Coon Rapids	MN	WFMP	107.1	22
Dassel	MN	KARP-FM	106.9	7
Durand	WI	WDMO	95.9	4
Eden Prairie	MN	WGVZ	105.7	6
Elk River	MN	KLCI	106.1	9
Faribault	MN	KQCL	95.9	3
Faribault	MN	KBGY	107.5	48
Forest Lake	MN	WLKX-FM	95.9	3
Glencoe	MN	KTTB	96.3	100
Golden Valley	MN	KQRS-FM	92.5	100
Lake City	MN	KLCH	94.9	5
Lake City	MN	KMFX-FM	102.5	9
Lakeville	MN	WGVX	105.1	3
Mankato	MN	KMSU	89.7	20
Mankato	MN	KYSM-FM	103.5	100
Menomonie	WI	WHWC	88.3	71
Minneapolis	MN	KBEM-FM	88.5	2
Minneapolis	MN	KMOJ	89.9	1
Minneapolis	MN	KXXR	93.7	100
Minneapolis	MN	KTCZ-FM	97.1	100
Minneapolis	MN	KTIS-FM	98.5	100
Minneapolis	MN	KSJN	99.5	100
Minneapolis	MN	KJZI	100.3	100
Minneapolis	MN	WLTE	102.9	100
Minneapolis-St. Paul	MN	KNOW-FM	91.1	100
Mora	MN	KBEK	95.5	25
New Prague	MN	KRDS-FM	95.5	6
New Ulm	MN	KXLP	93.1	100
North Mankato	MN	KDOG	96.7	12
Northfield	MN	WCAL	89.3	100
Owatonna	MN	KRFO-FM	104.9	5
Paynesville	MN	KZPK	98.9	47
Pine City	MN	WCMP-FM	100.9	25
Red Wing	MN	KWNG	105.9	12
Rice Lake	WI	WKFX	99.1	44
Richfield	MN	KDWB-FM	101.3	100
River Falls	WI	WRFW	88.7	3
River Falls	WI	WEVR-FM	106.3	6
Rochester	MN	KWWK	96.5	43
Rochester	MN	KRCH	101.7	39
Sartell	MN	KKSR	96.7	50
Sauk Rapids	MN	WHMH-FM	101.7	50
Siren	WI	WXCX	105.7	6
St. Cloud	MN	KVSC	88.1	17
St. Cloud	MN	KCFB	91.5	15
St. Cloud	MN	WWJO	98.1	100
St. Cloud	MN	KCLD-FM	104.7	100
St. Joseph	MN	KKJM	92.9	25
St. Joseph	MN	KCML	99.9	3
St. Louis Park	MN	WXPT	104.1	89
St. Paul	MN	KSTP-FM	94.5	100
St. Paul	MN	KNOF	95.3	6
St. Paul	MN	KEEY-FM	102.1	100
St. Peter	MN	KGAC	90.5	75
St. Peter	MN	KNGA	91.5	9
St. Peter	MN	KRBI-FM	105.5	25
Waite Park	MN	KLZZ	103.7	9
Waseca	MN	KRUE	92.1	10
New York City Area				
Asbury Park	NJ	WJLK-FM	94.3	1
Babylon	NY	WBAB	102.3	6
Bay Shore	NY	WBZO	103.1	3
Belvidere	NJ	WWYY	107.1	1
Briarcliff Manor	NY	WXPK	107.1	2
Bridgeport	CT	WPKN	89.5	10
Bridgeport	CT	WEZN-FM	99.9	28
Brookfield	CT	WRKI	95.1	30
Brookfield	CT	WDBY-FM1	105.5	1
Center Moriches	NY	WLVG	96.1	3
Danbury	CT	WXCI	91.7	3
Danbury	CT	WDAQ	98.3	1
Delaware Township	NJ	WDVR	89.7	5
Dover	NJ	WDHA-FM	105.5	1
Dover Township	NJ	WWNJ	91.1	50
East Orange	NJ	WFMU	91.1	1
Eatontown	NJ	WHTG-FM	106.3	1
Fairfield	CT	WSHU-FM	91.1	20
Freehold Township	NJ	WRDR	89.7	5
Garden City	NY	WZAA	92.7	2

Location	State	Callsign	MHz	kW
Hackettstown	NJ	WNTI	91.9	6
Hamden	CT	WKCI-FM	101.3	15
Hempstead	NY	WKJY	98.3	3
Lake Ronkonkoma	NY	WSHR	91.9	6
Lake Success	NY	WKTU	103.5	17
Long Branch	NJ	WWZY	107.1	5
Medford Lakes	NJ	WVBV	90.5	3
Middletown	NY	WOSR	91.7	2
Middletown	NY	WRRV	92.7	6
Monroe	CT	WMNR	88.1	6
Monticello	NY	WSUL	98.3	2
Mount Hope	NY	WXHD	90.1	1
Mount Kisco	NY	WFAF	106.3	1
New Brunswick	NJ	WRSU-FM	88.7	1
New Brunswick	NJ	WMGQ	98.3	1
New Haven	CT	WYBC-FM	94.3	3
New Haven	CT	WPLR	99.1	16
New Rochelle	NY	WRTN	93.5	3
New York	NY	WNYU-FM	89.1	8
New York	NY	WKCR-FM	89.9	7
New York	NY	WFUV	90.7	50
New York	NY	WNYE	91.5	18
New York	NY	WXRK	92.3	18
New York	NY	WNYC-FM	93.9	6
New York	NY	WPLJ	95.5	19
New York	NY	WQXR-FM	96.3	6
New York	NY	WQHT	97.1	30
New York	NY	WSKQ-FM	97.9	12
New York	NY	WRKS	98.7	6
New York	NY	WBAI	99.5	4
New York	NY	WCBS-FM	101.1	17
New York	NY	WQCD	101.9	30
New York	NY	WNEW	102.7	50
New York	NY	WAXQ	104.3	17
New York	NY	WWPR-FM	105.1	17
New York	NY	WLTW	106.7	17
New York	NY	WBLS	107.5	4
Newark	NJ	WBGO	88.3	5
Newark	NJ	WFME	94.7	37
Newark	NJ	WHTZ	100.3	17
Newark	NJ	WCAA	105.9	2
Newburgh	NY	WGNY-FM	103.1	6
Newton	NJ	WNNJ-FM	103.7	3
Norwalk	CT	WEFX	95.9	3
Ocean Acres	NJ	WBBO	98.5	3
Patchogue	NY	WALK-FM	97.5	39
Patchogue	NY	WBLI	106.1	49
Paterson	NJ	WPAT-FM	93.1	22
Peekskill	NY	WHUD	100.7	50
Pemberton	NJ	WBZC	88.9	19
Point Pleasant	NJ	WRAT	95.9	6
Port Jervis	NY	WTSX	96.7	3
Poughkeepsie	NY	WVKR-FM	91.3	4
Poughkeepsie	NY	WPKF	96.1	4
Poughkeepsie	NY	WPDH	101.5	4
Poughkeepsie	NY	WSPK	104.7	7
Riverhead	NY	WRCN-FM	103.9	2
Smithtown	NY	WFRS	88.9	2
Smithtown	NY	WMJC	94.3	3
South Orange	NJ	WSOU	89.5	2
Stamford	CT	WEDW-FM	88.5	2
Stamford	CT	WKHL	96.7	3
Stony Brook	NY	WUSB	90.1	4
Sussex	NJ	WNJP	88.5	1
Toms River	NJ	WOBM-FM	92.7	1
Trenton	NJ	WWFM	89.1	1
Trenton	NJ	WTSR	91.3	2
Trenton	NJ	WTHK	94.5	50
Trenton	NJ	WPST	97.5	50
Trenton	NJ	WKXW-FM	101.5	16
West Haven	CT	WNHU	88.7	2
West Long Branch	NJ	WMCX	88.9	1
Westhampton	NY	WBON-FM	98.5	3
Westport	CT	WEBE	107.9	50
Zarephath	NJ	WAWZ	99.1	28
Philadelphia Area				
Allentown	PA	WLEV	100.7	11
Allentown	PA	WAEB-FM	104.1	50
Asbury Park	NJ	WJLK-FM	94.3	1
Atlantic City	NJ	WNJN-FM	89.7	6
Atlantic City	NJ	WAYV	95.1	50
Atlantic City	NJ	WFPG-FM	96.9	50
Atlantic City	NJ	WMGM	103.7	50
Atlantic City	NJ	WPUR	107.3	14
Avalon	NJ	WWZK	94.3	3
Bel Air	MD	WHFC	91.1	1
Bethlehem	PA	WZZO	95.1	30
Boyertown	PA	WBYN	107.5	30
Bridgeton	NJ	WNJB-FM	89.3	3
Bridgeton	NJ	WSNJ-FM	107.7	15
Brigantine	NJ	WWFP	90.5	1
Camden	NJ	WKDN	106.9	38
Canton	NJ	WJKS	101.7	3
Cape May	NJ	WWCJ	89.1	15
Cape May	NJ	WAIV	102.3	3
Cape May Court Ho	NJ	WNJZ	90.3	6
Cape May Court Ho	NJ	WGBZ	105.5	3
Cherry Hill	NJ	WSJI	89.5	2
Christiana	DE	WXHL-FM	89.1	1
Dover	DE	WRDX	94.7	50
East Stroudsburg	PA	WESS	90.3	1
Easton	PA	WCTO	96.1	50
Easton	PA	WODE-FM	99.9	50
Egg Harbor City	NJ	WOJZ	104.9	10
Elkton	MD	WOEL-FM	89.9	3
Ephrata	PA	WIOV-FM	105.1	25
Havre De Grace	MD	WXCY	103.7	37
Lancaster	PA	WJTL	90.3	12
Lancaster	PA	WDAC	94.5	19
Lancaster	PA	WLAN-FM	96.9	50
Lebanon	PA	WQIC	100.1	3
Manahawkin	NJ	WYRS	90.7	2
Manahawkin	NJ	WJRZ-FM	100.1	2
Manahawkin	NJ	WCHR-FM	105.7	13
Margate City	NJ	WTTH	96.1	3
Media	PA	WPLY	100.3	35
Milford	DE	WAFL	97.7	3
Millville	NJ	WIXM	97.3	50
Newark	DE	WVUD	91.3	1
North Cape May	NJ	WDOX	106.7	3
Ocean City	NJ	WRTQ	91.3	11
Ocean City	NJ	WTKU	98.3	6
Ocean City	NJ	WKOE	106.3	3
Pennsauken	NJ	WSNJ-FM	107.9	2
Petersburg	NJ	WJSE	102.7	3
Philadelphia	PA	WXPN	88.5	5
Philadelphia	PA	WRTI	90.1	13
Philadelphia	PA	WHYY-FM	90.9	14
Philadelphia	PA	WXTU	92.5	16
Philadelphia	PA	WMMR	93.3	25
Philadelphia	PA	WYSP	94.1	16
Philadelphia	PA	WMWX	95.7	23
Philadelphia	PA	WRDW-FM	96.5	17
Philadelphia	PA	WOGL	98.1	13
Philadelphia	PA	WUSL	98.9	32
Philadelphia	PA	WBEB	101.1	14
Philadelphia	PA	WIOQ	102.1	32
Philadelphia	PA	WMGK	102.9	43
Philadelphia	PA	WSNI-FM	104.5	16
Philadelphia	PA	WDAS-FM	105.3	42
Philadelphia	PA	WJJZ	106.1	23
Pleasantville	NJ	WZBZ	99.3	3
Princeton	NJ	WPRB	103.3	14
Reading	PA	WRFY-FM	102.5	10
Reading	PA	WIOV-FM1	105.1	3
Smyrna	DE	WDSD	92.9	2
Tamaqua	PA	WMGH-FM	105.5	1
Tuckerton	NJ	WBHX	99.7	6
Villas	NJ	WCZT	98.7	6
Vineland	NJ	WVLT	92.1	6
Warminster	PA	WRDV	89.3	1
Wildwood	NJ	WZXL	100.7	38
Wildwood Crest	NJ	WDTH	93.1	4
Wilmington	DE	WSTW	93.7	47
Wilmington	DE	WJBR-FM	99.5	50
Woodbine	NJ	WJPH	89.9	1
Worton	MD	WKHS	90.5	18
St Loius Area				
Alton	IL	KATZ-FM	100.3	50
Ava	IL	WXAN	103.9	3

Location	State	Callsign	MHz	kW
Bethalto	IL	WFUN-FM	95.5	25
Bismarck	MO	KHCR	99.5	4
Bonne Terre	MO	KDBB	104.3	2
Bowling Green	MO	KPVR	94.1	8
Breese	IL	WDLJ	97.5	3
Carlinville	IL	WTSG	90.1	5
Carlinville	IL	WIBI	91.1	50
Carlinville	IL	WOLG	95.9	6
Carlyle	IL	WCXO	96.7	2
Centralia	IL	WRXX	95.3	6
Clayton	MO	KFUO-FM	99.1	100
Columbia	IL	KMJM-FM	104.9	8
Crestwood	MO	KSHE	94.7	100
Cuba	MO	KGNN-FM	90.3	6
De Soto	MO	KDJR	100.1	2
Duquoin	IL	WDQN-FM	95.9	6
East St. Louis	IL	WVRV	101.1	44
Edwardsville	IL	WSIE	88.7	50
Farmington	MO	KSEF	88.9	10
Farmington	MO	KTJJ	98.5	100
Festus	MO	KTBJ	89.3	25
Florissant	MO	KFTK	97.1	100
Godfrey	IL	WLCA	89.9	2
Granite City	IL	WSSM	106.5	90
Greenville	IL	WGEL	101.7	3
Hillsboro	IL	WXAJ	99.7	50
Ironton	MO	KYLS-FM	95.9	3
Jacksonville	IL	WYMG	100.5	50
Jerseyville	IL	WRDA	104.1	39
Litchfield	IL	WSMI-FM	106.1	50
Louisiana	MO	KJFM	102.1	2
Lynnville	IL	WEAI	107.1	6
Mount Vernon	IL	WBMV	89.7	11
Mount Vernon	IL	WAPO	90.5	1
Mount Vernon	IL	WMIX-FM	94.1	50
Mount Vernon	IL	WIBV	102.1	11
Mt. Vernon	IL	WVSI	88.9	4
Nashville	IL	WNSV	104.7	3
Okawville	IL	WIBV	102.1	10
Owensville	MO	KXMO-FM	95.3	37
Park Hills	MO	KBGM	91.1	8
Perryville	MO	KBDZ	93.1	2
Pittsfield	IL	WBBA-FM	97.5	10
Potosi	MO	KNLP	89.7	2
Potosi	MO	KHZR	97.7	6
Ramsey	IL	WJLY	88.3	25
Ramsey	IL	WTRH	93.3	3
Salem	IL	WJBD-FM	100.1	1
St. Charles	MO	KCLC	89.1	35
St. Genevieve	MO	KPNT	105.7	100
St. Louis	MO	KDHX	88.1	42
St. Louis	MO	KWMU	90.7	100
St. Louis	MO	KSIV-FM	91.5	85
St. Louis	MO	WIL-FM	92.3	100
St. Louis	MO	KSD	93.7	100
St. Louis	MO	KIHT	96.3	100
St. Louis	MO	KYKY	98.1	90
St. Louis	MO	KEZK-FM	102.5	100
St. Louis	MO	KLOU	103.3	100
St. Louis	MO	KSLZ	107.7	100
Staunton	IL	WAOX	105.3	10
Steelville	MO	KNSX	93.3	10
Sullivan	MO	KTUI-FM	100.9	3
Troy	MO	KFNS-FM	100.7	6
Union	MO	KLPW-FM	101.7	5
Vandalia	IL	WKRV	107.1	5
Virden	IL	WCVS-FM	96.7	6
Warrenton	MO	KFAV	99.9	11
Washington	MO	KGNV	89.9	1
Washington	MO	KSLQ-FM	104.5	3
White Hall	IL	WRLJ	88.3	2
Woodlawn	IL	WDML	106.9	3

Salt Lake City Area

Location	State	Callsign	MHz	kW
Bountiful	UT	KHTB-3	94.9	1
Bountiful	UT	KURR	99.5	40
Bountiful	UT	KEGA-FM6	101.5	1
Bountiful	UT	KPEB-FM5	103.1	3
Bountiful	UT	KRMF-1	106.1	3
Bountiful	UT	KUDD-FM4	107.9	5
Brigham City	UT	KJQN	100.7	81
Brigham City	UT	KRAR	106.9	81
Centerville	UT	KCPX	105.7	25
Coalville	UT	KCUA	92.5	20
Coalville	UT	KTPM	97.5	89
Coalville	UT	KPEB	103.1	89
Delta	UT	KMGR	95.9	100
Eureka	UT	KUDE-FM3	99.1	11
Eureka	UT	KUDE-FM3	103.9	11
Eureka	UT	KNJQ-3	105.1	11
Evanston	WY	KRMF	106.1	89
Fort Bridger	WY	KNYN	99.1	28
Fort Bridger	WY	KGNT	103.9	89
Franklin	ID	KTPM	97.5	68
Lehi	UT	KNJQ-FM1	105.1	3
Lyman	WY	KBNZ	104.7	89
Manti	UT	KNJQ	105.1	48
Midvale	UT	KQMB	102.7	25
Nephi	UT	KUDE	99.1	83
Nephi	UT	KUDE	103.9	74
North Ogden	UT	KNKL	88.7	7
Oakley	UT	KEGA	101.5	89
Ogden	UT	KWCR-FM	88.1	2
Ogden	UT	KYFO-FM	95.5	100
Ogden	UT	KBZN	97.9	26
Ogden	UT	KBER	101.1	25
Ogden	UT	KEGA-FM1	101.5	5
Ogden	UT	KPQP	101.9	26
Ogden	UT	KDUT-FM3	102.3	6
Ogden	UT	KUDD-FM2	107.9	6
Orem	UT	KOHS	91.7	2
Orem	UT	KENZ	107.5	45
Park City	UT	KXRK-1	96.3	1
Park City	UT	KEGA-FM7	101.5	3
Park City	UT	KPEB-FM3	103.1	3
Pleasant Grove	UT	KPGR	88.1	1
Provo	UT	KBYU-FM	89.1	32
Provo	UT	KHTB	94.9	48
Provo	UT	KXRK	96.3	25
Provo	UT	KUDE-FM1	99.1	5
Provo	UT	KUDE-FM1	103.9	9
Provo	UT	KNJQ-2	105.1	4
Randolph	UT	KDUT	102.3	89
Roy	UT	KUDD	107.9	75
Salt Lake City	UT	KCPW-FM	88.3	2
Salt Lake City	UT	KUER-FM	90.1	38
Salt Lake City	UT	KRCL	90.9	25
Salt Lake City	UT	KUBL-FM	93.3	25
Salt Lake City	UT	KODJ	94.1	40
Salt Lake City	UT	KZHT	97.1	30
Salt Lake City	UT	KBEE	98.7	40
Salt Lake City	UT	KSFI	100.3	25
Salt Lake City	UT	KRSP-FM	103.5	25
Salt Lake City	UT	KSOP-FM	104.3	25
Sandy	UT	KHTB-1	94.9	6
Smithfield	UT	KGNT	103.9	6
Spanish Fork	UT	KOSY-FM	106.5	25
Tooele	UT	KUUU	92.1	10
Tooele	UT	KHTB-2	94.9	5
Tremonton	UT	KBNZ	104.9	100

San Francisco Area

Location	State	Callsign	MHz	kW
Alameda	CA	KNGY	92.7	4
Berkeley	CA	KPFA	94.1	59
Berkeley	CA	KBLX-FM	102.9	7
Concord	CA	KISQ-FM3	98.1	1
Davis	CA	KDVS	90.3	9
Davis	CA	KRRE	104.3	3
Dunnigan	CA	KKFS	105.5	3
Esparto	CA	KTTA	97.9	6
Gilroy	CA	KBAY	94.5	30
Healdsburg	CA	KFGY	92.9	2
Healdsburg	CA	KRSH	95.9	3
Healdsburg	CA	KNOB	96.7	2
Lafayette	CA	KDFC-FM1	102.1	1
Livermore	CA	KKIQ	101.7	5
Lodi	CA	KWIN	97.7	6
Los Altos	CA	KFFG	97.7	3
Manteca	CA	KMRQ	96.7	2
Martinez	CA	KOIT-FM2	96.5	3
Modesto	CA	KATM	103.3	50
Modesto	CA	KHKK	104.1	50

Location	State	Callsign	MHz	kW
Monte Rio	CA	KVRV	97.7	2
Morganhill	CA	KSQQ	96.1	5
Patterson	CA	KOSO	93.1	50
Patterson	CA	KTSE-FM	97.1	1
Pleasanton	CA	KISQ-FM2	98.1	10
Rohnert Park	CA	KJZY-FM1	93.7	3
Rohnert Park	CA	KRPQ	104.9	7
Rohnert Park	CA	KZST-FM2	100.1	1
Sacramento	CA	KEDR	88.1	8
Sacramento	CA	KXJZ	88.9	50
San Francisco	CA	KQED-FM	88.5	110
San Francisco	CA	KUSF	90.3	3
San Francisco	CA	KALW	91.7	2
San Francisco	CA	KBAA	93.3	50
San Francisco	CA	KYLD	94.9	30
San Francisco	CA	KZBR	95.7	7
San Francisco	CA	KOIT-FM	96.5	24
San Francisco	CA	KLLC	97.3	82
San Francisco	CA	KISQ	98.1	75
San Francisco	CA	KSOL	98.9	6
San Francisco	CA	KFRC-FM	99.7	40
San Francisco	CA	KIOI	101.3	125
San Francisco	CA	KDFC-FM	102.1	33
San Francisco	CA	KKSF	103.7	10
San Francisco	CA	KFOG	104.5	14
San Francisco	CA	KITS	105.3	17
San Francisco	CA	KMEL	106.1	69
San Francisco	CA	KEAR	106.9	80
San Francisco	CA	KDFC-FM2	102.1	1
San Jose	CA	KSJS	90.5	2
San Jose	CA	KSJO	92.3	32
San Jose	CA	KUFX	98.5	10
San Jose	CA	KBRG	100.3	15
San Jose	CA	KEZR	106.5	42
San Mateo	CA	KCSM	91.1	12
San Mateo	CA	KSAN	107.7	9
San Rafael	CA	KSFB-FM	100.7	6
Santa Clara	CA	KVVF	105.7	50
Santa Cruz	CA	KZSC	88.1	20
Santa Cruz	CA	KSQL	99.1	1
Santa Rosa	CA	KZST	100.1	6
Santa Rosa	CA	KXFX	101.7	2
Sebastopol	CA	KJZY	93.7	6
Sonoma	CA	KSVY	91.3	3
St.Helena	CA	KVYN	99.3	6
Stockton	CA	KYCC	90.1	50
Stockton	CA	KUOP	91.3	7
Stockton	CA	KJOY	99.3	5
Stockton	CA	KQOD	100.1	6
Stockton	CA	KSTN-FM	107.3	8
Sunnyvale	CA	KCNL	104.9	6
Tracy	CA	KMIX	100.9	6
Tracy	CA	KKIQ-FM2	101.7	1
Walnut Creek	CA	KABL-FM	92.1	3
Walnut Creek	CA	KKIQ-FM3	101.7	1
Walnut Creek	CA	KMEL-FM2	106.1	7
Woodland	CA	KSFM	102.5	50
Seattle Area				
Bellevue	WA	KBCS	91.3	8
Bellevue	WA	KLSY-FM	92.5	80
Bremerton	WA	KRWM	106.9	49
Centralia	WA	KCED	91.3	1
Centralia	WA	KMNT	102.9	87
Chehalis	WA	KACS	90.5	6
Covington	WA	KMCQ	104.5	25
Eatonville	WA	KFNK	104.9	17
Edmonds	WA	KCMS	105.3	54
Elma	WA	KAYO-FM	99.3	41
Elma	WA	KSWW	102.1	25
Everett	WA	KSER	90.7	6
Gig Harbor	WA	KGHP	89.9	2
Mccleary	WA	KGY-FM	96.9	2
Mount Vernon	WA	KMWS	89.7	2
Olympia	WA	KAOS	89.3	1
Olympia	WA	KXXO	96.1	85
Olympia	WA	KFMY-FM1	97.7	4
Olympia	WA	KAYO-FM1	99.3	3
Port Angeles	WA	KNWP	90.1	2
Raymond	WA	KFMY	97.7	44
Roy	WA	KWFJ	89.7	1
Seattle	WA	KNHC	89.5	9
Seattle	WA	KEXP-FM	90.3	3
Seattle	WA	KUBE	93.3	100
Seattle	WA	KMPS-FM	94.1	73
Seattle	WA	KUOW	94.9	100
Seattle	WA	KJR-FM	95.7	100
Seattle	WA	KRQI-FM	96.5	100
Seattle	WA	KING-FM	98.1	58
Seattle	WA	KWJZ	98.9	58
Seattle	WA	KISW	99.9	58
Seattle	WA	KQBZ	100.7	58
Seattle	WA	KPLZ-FM	101.5	100
Seattle	WA	KZOK-FM	102.5	73
Seattle	WA	KNDD	107.7	58
Tacoma	WA	KPLU-FM	88.5	58
Tacoma	WA	KVTI	90.9	51
Tacoma	WA	KXOT	91.7	39
Tacoma	WA	KBSG-FM	97.3	55
Tacoma	WA	KMTT	103.7	58
Tacoma	WA	KBKS-FM	106.1	73
Washington DC Area				
Annapolis	MD	WHFS	99.1	50
Annapolis	MD	WFSI	107.9	50
Arlington	VA	WAVA	105.1	50
Baltimore	MD	WYPR	88.1	16
Baltimore	MD	WEAA	88.9	13
Baltimore	MD	WBJC	91.5	50
Baltimore	MD	WERQ-FM	92.3	37
Baltimore	MD	WPOC	93.1	20
Baltimore	MD	WRBS	95.1	50
Baltimore	MD	WIYY	97.9	14
Baltimore	MD	WLIF	101.9	14
Baltimore	MD	WQSR	102.7	50
Baltimore	MD	WSMJ	104.3	32
Baltimore	MD	WWMX	106.5	8
Bel Air	MD	WHFC	91.1	1
Berryville	VA	WWRE	105.5	3
Bethesda	MD	WARW	94.7	21
Bethesda	MD	WMMJ	102.3	3
Bowling Green	VA	WWUZ	96.9	3
California	MD	WKIK-FM	102.9	4
Cambridge	MD	WINX-FM	94.3	22
Cambridge	MD	WCEM-FM	106.3	6
Catonsville	MD	WXYV	105.7	50
Charles Town	WV	WKSI-FM	98.3	3
Colonial Beach	VA	WGRQ	95.9	2
Columbia	MD	WD2XAB	93.5	2
Culpeper	VA	WPER	89.9	50
Easton	MD	WCEI-FM	96.7	25
Falmouth	VA	WGRX	104.5	3
Federalsburg	MD	WTDK	107.1	4
Frederick	MD	WJTM	88.1	4
Frederick	MD	WFRE	99.9	8
Fredericksburg	VA	WJYJ	90.5	38
Fredericksburg	VA	WFLS-FM	93.3	50
Fredericksburg	VA	WBQB	101.5	50
Front Royal	VA	WZRV	95.3	6
Front Royal	VA	WFQX	99.3	6
Gettysburg	PA	WGTY	107.7	16
Glen Burnie	MD	WWIN-FM	95.9	3
Grasonville	MD	WRNR-FM	103.1	6
Greencastle	PA	WQCM	94.3	4
Hagerstown	MD	WAYZ-FM	104.7	8
Hagerstown	MD	WARX	106.9	16
Halfway	MD	WDLD	96.7	5
Havre De Grace	MD	WXCY	103.7	37
Heathsville	VA	WCNV	89.1	5
Hurlock	MD	WAAI	100.9	1
Lexington Park	MD	WMDM-FM	97.7	6
Manassas	VA	WJFK-FM	106.7	40
Martinsburg	WV	WLTF	97.5	13
Mechanicsville	MD	WSMD-FM	98.3	3
Middletown	MD	WAFY	103.1	1
Morningside	MD	WPGC-FM	95.5	50
Orange	VA	WCUL	98.9	3
Prince Frederick	MD	WBZS-FM	92.7	3
Red Lion	PA	WSOX	96.1	50
Spotsylvania	VA	WYSK-FM	99.3	3
Stephens City	VA	WKSI-FM	98.3	2
Takoma Park	MD	WGTS	91.9	30

Location	State	Callsign	MHz	kW
Tappahannock	VA	WRAR-FM	105.5	6
Towson	MD	WTMD	89.7	10
Waldorf	MD	WWZZ	104.1	50
Warrenton	VA	WBPS-FM	94.3	2
Warrenton	VA	WTOP-FM	107.7	29
Warsaw	VA	WNNT-FM	100.9	3
Washington	DC	WAMU	88.5	50
Washington	DC	WPFW	89.3	50
Washington	DC	WCSP-FM	90.1	36
Washington	DC	WETA	90.9	75
Washington	DC	WKYS	93.9	25
Washington	DC	WHUR-FM	96.3	17
Washington	DC	WASH	97.1	18
Washington	DC	WMZQ-FM	98.7	50
Washington	DC	WIHT	99.5	50
Washington	DC	WBIG-FM	100.3	40
Washington	DC	WWDC-FM	101.1	25
Washington	DC	WGMS-FM	103.5	44
Washington	DC	WRQX	107.3	20
Washington	DC	WRQX	107.3	22
Waynesboro	PA	WWMD	101.5	50
Westminster	MD	WZBA	100.7	27
Williamsport	MD	WCRH	90.5	10
Williamsport	MD	WKMZ	95.9	3
Winchester	VA	WINC-FM	92.5	22
Winchester	VA	WUSQ-FM	102.5	32
Woodbridge	VA	WJZW	105.9	40
Worton	MD	WKHS	90.5	18
York-Hanover	PA	WYCR	98.5	11

ARMED FORCES RADIO & TELEVISION SERVICE

✉ AFRTS Broadcast Center, 1363 Z Street, Bldg. 2730, March Air Reserve Base, CA 92518-2017. ☎ +1 909 413-2236. **Web:** www.afrts.osd.mil or www.afrts.dodmedia.osd.mil.

The AFRTS Broadcast Center, located at March Air Reserve Base near Riverside, California, is the sole programming source for military radio and television outlets overseas. These outlets serve American service men and women, Department of Defense (DoD) civilians, and their families stationed in over 150 countries around the world where English language broadcast service is unavailable or inadequate. Known as AFRTS-BC, the Broadcast Center is responsible for reflecting an accurate cross-section of what is widely available to stateside audiences of the American radio and television industry. The global AFRTS radio and television network service is called AFN, the American Forces Network.

STATIONS: Details of the AFRTS on-air broadcast services are listed under the countries concerned. AFRTS SW services are listed in the International Radio section.

ARMY BROADCASTING SERVICE (ABS)

✉ 601 North Fairfax Street, Suite 340, Alexandria, VA 22314-2040. **Email:** abs@afn.army.mil or myafn@dodmedia.osd.mil
LP: Commander, ABS: Col David R. Apt.

ABS broadcasts for soldiers, civilians and their families serving overseas. The ABS international networks and sts broadcast American radio and television to United States Army soldiers, civilians and their families serving across the globe. ABS manages three Armed Forces Radio & Television Service broadcast networks and two independent broadcast sts. These sts broadcast satellite news, entertainment and information to the majority of United States Army soldiers, civilians and their families stationed overseas.

STATIONS: American Forces Network Europe is the largest ABS broadcast outlet and serves the United States military community in Western Europe, Northern Africa, the Mediterranean and the Balkans – American Forces Korea Network serves the United States military community on the Korean Peninsula – AFN Kwajalein is located in the Marshall Islands – AFN Honduras is located on the Soto Cano Air Base, Honduras. See the various countries for details.

INTERNATIONAL BROADCASTING

Government-operated, private and religious sts on SW are listed in the International Broadcasting section. Some sts of the latter categories also target a domestic audience.

URUGUAY

L.T: UTC -3h (19 Sep-14 Mar: UTC -2h) — **Pop:** 3.4 million — **Pr.L:** Spanish — **E.C:** 50Hz, 220V — **ITU:** URG

MINISTERIO DE DEFENSA NACIONAL

✉ Av. 8 de Octubre 2628, Montevideo.

UNIDAD REGULADORA DE SERVICIOS DE COMUNICACIONES (URSEC)

✉ Calle Uruguay 988 (Casilla de Correo 927), 11100 Montevideo ☎ +598 2 902 8082, 902 7689 🖷 +598 2 901 4074 **Email:** radiodifusion@ursec.gub.uy **Web:** www.ursec.gub.uy
L.P: Presidente: Dr. Fernando Pérez Tabo.

ASOCIACION NACIONAL DE BROADCASTERS URUGUAYOS (ANDEBU)

✉ Carlos Quijano 1264, 11100 Montevideo ☎ + 598 2 902 15215, 908 0037 🖷 +598 2 902 1540 **Web:** www.andebu.com.uy
Email: andebu@adinet.com.uy **Web:** www.andebu.com.uy
Affiliated str´s: 2), 3), 5), 6), 7), 9), 11), 12), 14), 15), 16), 17). 18), 21), 22), 23), 26), 29), 30), 32), 33), 34), 35), 36), 38), 39), 40), 44), 46), 47), 48), 49), 51), 52), 53), 54), 57), 61), 62), 64), 67), 68), 71), 72), 73), 74), 75), 77), 79), 80), 82), 84), 85), 87), 88). All affiliated st's carry "Cadena Andebu" prgr. D 1453-1500.

COOPERATIVA DE RADIO EMISORAS DEL INTERIOR (CORI)

✉ Av. 18 de Julio, Oficina 603, 11000 Montevideo
🖷 +598 2 9086284 **Email:** coriamfm@adinet.com.uy
Affiliated st´s: 5), 12), 18), 20), 21), 23), 28), 30), 31), 35), 39). 40), 46), 47), 48), 50), 51), 56), 57), 58), 59), 60), 63), 67), 69), 70), 72), 73), 74), 76), 77), 78), 80). 84).

RADIOS AM DEL INTERIOR (RAMI)

✉Nueva York 1618, 11800 Montevideo 🖷 +598 2 9047279.
Affiliated st´s: 1), 5), 10), 12), 13), 20), 21), 24), 25), 27), 28), 29), 30), 31), 33), 34), 37), 41), 43), 44), 45), 48), 50), 51), 52), 53), 54), 55), 56), 57), 58), 59), 62), 63), 64), 65), 67), 68), 69), 70), 71), 75), 76), 78), 79), 81), 82), 83), 85), 86), 87), 88), 89).

RED ORO

✉ Rio Negro 1337, Esc. 209, 11100 Montevideo ☎ + 598 2 903-1678/79 🖷 +598 2 900-3916 **Email:** redoro@adinet.com.uy
Affiliated st´s: 1), 10), 13), 22), 24), 25), 27), 33), 37), 43), 44), 52), 54), 55), 65), 68), 80), 81), 82).

MW: ° = also on SW, * = inactive, v = varying freq.

	Call	kHz	kW	Name, location & h. of tr.
1)	CW1	550	58	R. Colonia, Colonia: 24h
2)	CX58	580	5	R. Clarín, Montevideo: 24h
3)	CX4	610	50	R. Rural, Montevideo: 0800-0600 (Sat/Sun 0300)
4)	CX6	°650	50/25	S.O.D.R.E.. Montevideo: 24h (classical)
71)	CW68	680	1/0.7	R. Young, Young: 0900-0300
6)	CX8	690	25/10	R. Sarandí, Montevideo: 24h
7)	CX10	730	5/2.5	R. Continente, Montevideo: 24h
5)	CW27	740	5/1	R.Tabaré, Salto: 0900 (Sun 1100)-0300
8)	CX12	°770	100/25	Radio Oriental, Montevideo: 0850-0600, Sun: 0950-0600
9)	CX14	810	50/25	R. El Espectador, Montevideo: 0830-0600
10)	CW23	820	1/0.5	R. Cultural, Salto: 0800-0300
11)	CX16	850	50	R. Carve, Montevideo: 0730-0400
49)	CX18	890	50/10	R. Sarandi Sport, Montevideo: 24h
12)	CW17	900	3/1	R. Frontera, Artigas: 0900-0300
91)	CX20	°930	50/25	R. Monte Carlo, "la Super R.", Montevideo: 24h
13)	CW96	960	3/1	Radio Yi, Durazno: 1000-0200
14)	CX22	970	20/5	R. Universal, Montevideo: 0900-0400
90)	CX24	1010	20	R. Nuevotiempo, Montevideo: 0900-0400
86)	CW102	1020	0.1	R. Libertadores, Salto: 0900-0300
4)	CX26	°1050	25	S.O.D.R.E.. Montevideo: 1000-0300
15)	CX28	1090	15	R. Imparcial, Montevideo: 24h
78)	CX111	1110	2/1	R. Paso de los Toros, Paso de los Toros: 1100-0200
16)	CW31	1120	10/2	R. Salto, Salto: 1000 (Sun 1100)-0300
17)	CX30	1130	20/5	R. Nacional, Montevideo: 24h, (Sun 0800-0500)
18)	CW116	1160	1	R. Agraria del Uruguay, Cerro Chato: 0830-0130

	Call	kHz	kW	Name, location & h. of tr.
87)	CV116	1160	1/0.25	R. Impacto AM 1160, Mercedes: 0900-0400
19)	CX32	1170	10	Radiomundo, Montevideo: 1100-0300
43)	CX118	°1180	10	LV de Artigas, Artigas: 0900-0300
20)	CW33	1200	2	La Nueva Radio, Florida: 24h
22)	CX121	1210	2	Difusora Soriano, Mercedes: 24h
23)	CV121	1210	2.5/0.25	R. RBC, Piriápolis: 24h
24)	CW121	1210	1	R. El Libertador, Villa Vergara: 0830-0300
21)	CX122	1220	1	R. Reconquista, Rivera: 0945-0300
25)	CW35	1240	5/1	R. Paysandú, "la emisora sin fronteras", Paysandú: 0900-0400
26)	CX36	1250	10	R. Centenario, Montevideo: 24h
27)	CW125	1250	5	R. Bella Unión, Bella Unión: 0900-0300
82)	CW37	1260	3/1	Dif. Rochense, Rocha: 0900-0300
28)	CV127	1270	4/2	R. Cuareim, Artigas: 0900-0300
81)	CX128	1280	3/1	R. "Noticias" Tacuarembó, Tacuarembó: 0900-0300
4)	CX38	°1290	10	S.O.D.R.E.. Montevideo: 1000-0300
30)	CW39	1320	1/0.5	R. LV de Paysandú, Paysandú: 0858-0400
31)	CW132	1320	0.3	R. Fortaleza, Rocha: 0900-0300
32)	CX40	1330	5	R. Fenix, Montevideo: 1000-0600
33)	CW53	1340	10	LV de Melo, Melo: 0800-0300
34)	CW136	1360	1/0.25	R. Rio Branco, Rio Branco: 0930-0230
35)	CW41	1360	2.5/0.5	Broadcasting San José, San José: 0900-0300
36)	CX42	°1370	10/2.5	Emis. Ciudad de Montevideo: 1100-0300
37)	CV137A	1370	0.5/0.25	R. Real, Minas de Corrales:0930-0130
88)	CW137	1370	0.25/0.1	R. San Javier, San Javier: 1000-2400
39)	CW45	v1390	7.5/3	Dif. Treinta y Tres, Treinta y Tres: 0800 (Sun 0900)-0300
40)	CX140	1400	25	R. Zorrilla de San Martin, Tacuarembó: 0900-0300
42)	CX44	1410	10/5	AM Libre, Montevideo: 0800-0400
84)	CW141	1410	1/0.25	R. Turística, Salto
44)	CW43	1420	5	R. Lavalleja, Minas: 0830-0300
45)	CX142	1420	1	R. Felicidad, Paysandú: 1000-0300
46)	CW25	1430	5/1	R. Durazno, Durazno: 0900-0300
47)	CV144	1440	3	AM 1440, Chuy: 24h
48)	CX144	1440	3/0.5	R. Rivera, Rivera: 0830 (Sun 1000)-0300
38)	CX46	1450	10/5	R. América, Montevideo: 0900-0630
83)	CW145	1450	2/0.5	R. Arapey, Salto: 24h
50)	CX146	1460	3/1	R.Carmelo, Carmelo: 0900-0300
29)	CV146	1460	0.25	R. José Batlle y Ordoñez, José Batlle y Ordoñez: 1100-0300
51)	CX147	1470	15	R. Cristal del Uruguay,Las Piedras: 24h
52)	CW147	1470	1/0.5	Abril 1470 AM, Melo: 0830-0330
53)	CW148	°1480	3/0.8	R. Universo, Castillos: 0900-0300
54)	CW43B	1480	5/1.5	R. Internacional, Rivera: 0800-0300
85)	CX148	1480	1/0.7	Difusora Rio Negro, Young
41)	CV149	1490	1/0.25	Em. del Centro, Baltasar Brum
55)	CX149	1490	5/4	R. del Oeste, Nueva Helvecia: 0930-0300
56)	CX151	1510	1/0.25	R. Rincón, Fray Bentos: 1000-0300
57)	CW57	1510	2/0.5	R. San Carlos, San Carlos: 0830-0300
58)	CW151	1510	0.5	R. Ibirapitá, San Gregorio de Polanco: 1000-0200
59)	CX152	1520	2	R. Acuarela, Melo: 0900-0300
60)	CV152	1520	0.1	R. Paz, "la nueva R. ", Guichón: 1000-2300
61)	CX50	1530	5/2.5	R. Independencia, Montevideo: 1000-0400
62)	CW153	1530	0.25	Emisora Cono Sur, Nueva Palmira: 0900-0300
63)	CW154	1540	0.1	R. Charruá, Paysandú: 1000-0300
64)	CX154	1540	0.25	R. Patria, Treinta y Tres: 0800 (Sun 0900)-0300
65)	CV154	1540	1	R. Centro, Cardona: 0900-0200
66)	CV155	1550	1/0.25	R. Agraciada, Mercedes: 0800-0300
67)	CW155	°1550	2	R. Sarandí del Yí, Sarandí del Yí: 1030-0130
68)	CW51	1560	3/0.5	R. Maldonado, Maldonado: 24h
69)	CX156	1560	2/0.5	Dif. Americana, Trinidad: 0930-0130
70)	CV156	1560	1/0.25	R. Vichadero: 1000-0200
72)	CX157	1570	2/0.5	R. Canelones: 1055-0200
89)	CW157A	1570	0.25/0.1	R. Celeste, Tomás Gomensoro: 0900-0300
73)	CW54	1580	0.5	Emisoras del Este, Minas: 0800-0200
74)	CW158	1580	1/0.5	R. San Salvador, Dolores: 24h
75)	CW159	1590	1/0.25	R. Regional- "La Nueva Radio", Lascano: 0900-0300
76)	CV159	1590	0.25	R. Regional, Constitución: 1000-0200
77)	CX159	1590	10	R. Real, Colonia: 0930-0300
79)	CV160	1600	2	Emisora Continental, Pando: 0915-0300
80)	CX160	1600	1	R. Litoral, Fray Bentos: 1000-0300

SW: * = inactive, v = varying freq.

	Call	kHz	kW	Name, location & h. of tr.
36)	CXA42A	6010	10	Em. Ciudad de Montevideo: 1300-2130
49)	CXA61	6045	10	R. Sport, Montevideo: 24h
53)	CWA148	6055	0.02	R. Universo, Castillos (testing)
43)	CXA3	6075	1	LV de Artigas, Artigas: irr.
4)	CXA4	6125	0.35	S.O.D.R.E.:, Montevideo: 1000-0300 (r: CX38 1290)
91)	CXA20	6140	1	R. Monte Carlo. Montevideo: 1030-1630v
67)	CWA155	6154	2	Banda Oriental, Sarandí del Yi: 0130-0300 (n. 6155)
91)	CXA72	9595	1	R. Monte Carlo, Montevideo: 2330-0300v
4)	CXA6	9620	0.35	S.O.D.R.E., Montevideo: 24h (r. CX6 650)
8)	CXA7	11735	1	R. Oriental, Montevideo: 1630-2330v

Addresses and other information

1) Rivadavia 383, 70000 Colonia ☎ +598 522 2461 🖷 +598 522 2961 **Web:** radiocolonia.com **E.mail:** cw1@adinet.com.py - **FM:** 93.5 "FM Mágica" – **2)** Av. 18 de Julio 1516, P.9, Esc. 7, 11200 Montevideo ☎ +598 2 480-6877, 408-2554 🖷 +598 2 401-5841. – **3)** Colonia 2212, piso 2, 11200 Montevideo ☎ +598 2 400-0500 🖷 +598 2 401-4097 **Web:** www.cx4radiorural.com **Email:** ruralcx4@adinet.com.uy – **4)** Sarandí 430, 11000 Montevideo **Web:** www.sodre.gub.uy ☎ +598 2 915 7865 🖷 +598 2 916 1933 - CX6: classical music; CX26 music & spoken word; CX38 "Radio Educativa" 1700-2100. **DX Prgr:** SS1400-1500, 0200-0300 "Radioactividades" on 1050kHz. Re. to Cas, 7011, 11000 Montevideo. – **5)** Av. Uruguay 1416, 50000 Salto ☎🖷 +598 73 33222 – **6)** Enriqueta Compte y Rique 1250, 11800 Montevideo. ☎ +598 2 208-2612 🖷 +598 2 203-6906 **Web:** www.sarandi690.com.uy **Email:** conexion@sarandi690.com.uy - News and talk – **7)** Germán Barbato 1472, 11100 Montevideo ☎ +598 2 902-4038/39/43 🖷 +598 2 902-4038 **Email:** cx10@adinet.com.uy – **8)** Cerrito 475, 11000 Montevideo. **Web:** www.oriental.com.uy **Email:** secretaria@oriental.com.uy +598 2 916 1130. – **9)** Río Branco 1481, 11100 Montevideo. ☎ +598 2 902-3531 🖷 +598 2 908-3044 **Web:** www.espectador.com **Email:** am810@espectador.com,uy – **10)** Lavalleja 48, 50000 Salto ☎🖷 +598 73 24330 - **FM:** 106.5 "Em. del Exodo." – **11)** Mercedes 973, 11100 Montevideo ☎ +598 2 902-6162/63, 902-1350 🖷 +598 2 902-0126 **Email:** carve@ adinet.com.uy **Web:** www.carve.com.uy – **12)** Av. Lecueder 803, 55000 Artigas. ☎ +598 772 2438. 🖷 +598 772 4715 **Email:** am900@adinet.com.uy - **FM:** 88.3 "Frontera FM" – **13)** Zorrilla de San Martín 875, 97000 Durazno ☎ +598 362 2701 🖷 +598 362 3297 **Email:** multimyi@adinet.com.uy – **14)** Av. 18 de Julio, 1220, 3er piso, 11100 Montevideo 🖷 +598 2 902-6050 **Web:** www.22universal.com **Email:** cx22@adinet.com.uy – **15)** Av. del Libertador Brg. Gral. Lavalleja 1708, ap. 101, Edificio Carioca, 11800 Montevideo ☎ +598 2 924-1514. 🖷 +598 2 924-2323 **Email:** radioimparcial@ netgate.com.uy – **16)** Brasil 715, 50000 Salto ☎ +598 733 2515 🖷 +598 733 3414 - **FM:** 88.3 "Emisora del Lago". – **17)** Plaza Independencia 846, EP, 11100 Montevideo ☎ +598 2 902-5640/41/44 🖷 +598 2 902-4800 **Email:** cx30@netgate.com.uy – **18)** Juan Muñoz s/n, 30204 Cerro Chato, Depto. Treinta y Tres ☎ +598 466 2200. 🖷 +598 466 2225. – **19)** Rambla Armenia 1647, Montevideo ☎ +598 2 628-9626 🖷 +598 2 628-9627. – **20)** Antonio Ma. Fernández 800, 94000 Florida ☎ +598 352 2026 **Email:** cw33@adinet.com.uy – **21)** Pantaleón Quesada 725, 40000 Rivera. ☎ +598 622 3807 🖷 +598 622 5893 **Email:** evervier@adinet.com.uy – **22)** Castro y Careaga 568, 75000 Mercedes ☎ +598 562 3430 🖷 +598 562 2977. - **FM:** 89.3 "Em. del Hum". – **23)** Chacabuco y Moreno, 20200 Piriápolis ☎🖷 +598 432 2771 **Web:** www.radiorbc.com.uy **Email:** rbc1210@adinet. com.uy – **24)** Jacinto Ruiz s/n, Villa Vergara, 33000 Treinta y Tres ☎ +598 458 2102 🖷 +598 458 2398 – **25)** 19 de Abril 1009, 60000 Paysandú ☎ 🖷 +598 72 35000. – **26)** Av. 18 de Julio 1357, ap. 202, 11200 Montevideo ☎ +598 2 903-0302 🖷 +598 2 903-0307 **Email:** radio36@internet.com.uy **Web:** www.radio36.com.uy – **27)** Enrique Ferreira 1550, 55100 Bella Unión ☎ +598 779 2058 🖷 +598 779 2078 **Email:** amatista@montevideo.com.uy - **FM:** 105.5 "Stereo Norte FM". – **28)** Av. Lecueder 167, 55000 Artigas. ☎ +598 772 2867 **Email:** racua@adinet.com.uy – **29)** Camino Nacional s/n, 30200 José Batlle y Ordoñez, Depto. de Lavalleja ☎🖷 +598 469 2132 – **30)** 18 de Julio 614, 60000 Paysandú ☎ +598 72 22267 🖷 +598 72 24970 **Email:** cw39@adinet.com.uy – **31)** Zorrilla de S. Martin 200, 27000 Rocha ☎ +598 472 2460 🖷 +598 472 3973. – **32)** Canelones 1969, 11200 Montevideo ☎ 🖷 +598 2 408-3292. – **33)** Remigio Castellanos 721, 37000 Melo ☎ +598 642 2105/2397/3226/7070 🖷 +598 642 5329 **Email:** cw53melo@ adinet.com.uy – **34)** Virrey Arredondo 986, 37100 Rio Branco ☎ +598 675 2009/2831 🖷 +598 675 2009 **Email:** am1360@adinet.com.uy – **35)** Treinta y Tres 890, 80000 San José. ☎ +598 342 6444/6333 🖷 +598 342 6444 **Email:** la41@adinet.com.uy – **36)** Canelones 2061, 11200 Montevideo ☎ +598 2 401-4342/402-0142 🖷 +598 2 402-0700 **Web:** www.emisoraciudaddemontevideo.com.uy – **37)** Dr. Dávison s/n, 40002 Minas de Corrales ☎ +598 658 2073 – **38)** Emilio Frugoni 1312, Montevideo ☎ +598 2 409-0094, 400-2121. 🖷 +598 2 408-

9314. **Email:** americaam@redfacil.com.uy – **39**) Pablo Zufriátegui 1076, 33000 Treinta y Tres ☎🖷 +598 452 2340. – **40**) 18 de Julio 302, 45000 Tacuarembó ☎ +598 632 2950 🖷 +598 622 2538. **Email:** zsm@netgate.com.uy - **FM:** 88.9"Em. de la Música". – **41**) Batlle y Ordóñez y 25 de Agosto, 55001 Baltasar Brum, Artigas ☎🖷 +598 776 2109. **Email:** radiodc@adinet.com.uy – **42**) Garibaldi 2579, Montevideo **Email:** 1410@1410amlibre.com **Web:** www.1410amlibre.com.uy ☎ +598 2 480-2121 🖷 +598 2 486 1633 – **43**) Av. Lecueder 483, 55000 Artigas. ☎ +598 772 3445 🖷 +598 772 4744 **Web:** www.radioartigas.com.uy **Email:** cx118@radioartigas.com.uy **F.Pl.:** 31 metres.- **FM:** 90.7 "Amatista FM". – **44**) José E. Rodó 530, 30000 Minas ☎ 🖷 +598 442 2304. – **45**) 33 Orientales 946,1° piso, 60000 Paysandú. ☎+598 72 24020 🖷 +598 722 4020. – **46**) Br.Gral. Fructoso Rivera 501, 97000 Durazno ☎ +598 362 2015 🖷 +598 362 2058. **Web:** www.radiodurazno.com/ **Email:** am1430@adinet.com.uy - **FM:** 95.1 "City. – **47**) Laguna Negra 174, 27100 Chuy ☎ 🖷 +598 474 2080 – **48**) Dr. Gabriel Anolles 441, 40000 Rivera ☎ 🖷 +598 622 3230 **Email:** cx144@adinet.com.uy – **49**) Enriqueta Compte y Rique 1250, 11800 Montevideo ☎+598 2 204-1630 🖷 +598 2 200-3786 **Web:** www.sport890.com.uy **Email:** sport890@sport890.com.uy – **50**) 19 de Abril 444, 70100 Carmelo ☎ +598 542 3558 🖷 +598 542 2520 **Email:** radiocar@ adinet.com.uy – **51**) Av. Artigas 781, 90200 Las Piedras, Canelones ☎ +598 2 364-4775 🖷 +598 2 364-4814. – **52**) Treinta y Tres 949, 37100 Melo, Depto. de Cerro Largo ☎ +598 642 2387 🖷 +598 642 1700 **Email:** abrilam@abrilam.com.uy **Web:** www.abrilam.com.uy – **53**) Calle Dr. Pedro Emilio Ferrer 1265, 27200 Castillos ☎ 🖷 +598 475 8755 **Email:** radio@universo.com – **54**) Av. Sarandí 792, 40000 Rivera ☎ +598 62 23259 🖷 +598 62 23422 **Web:** www.rivera.com.uy/cw43b **Email:** internac@fastnet.com.uy - **FM:** 94.5 – **55**) Calle Berna 1375, 70201 Nueva Helvecia ☎ +598 554 4409 🖷 +598 554 4217 **Web:** www.corporacionro.com.uy **Email:** deloeste@adinet.com.uy - **FM:** 90.7 "Reflejos" – **56**) 25 de Mayo 3164 al 3168, 65000 Fray Bentos ☎ +598 562 2022 🖷 +598 562 2653. – **57**) Sarandí 775, 20400 San Carlos. ☎+598 42 669575, 664050 🖷 +598 42 669575 **Email:** rsc@adinet.com.uy – **58**) Gral. Artigas 193, 42500 San Gregorio de Polanco, Tacuarembó ☎ +598 639 4017 🖷 +598 639 2495 – **59**) José Pedro Varela 750, Melo ☎ +598 64 22051 🖷 +598 64 23126 **Email:** acuarela@montevideo. com.uy – **60**) Luis Alberto de Herrera 346, 60008 Guichón, Depto. de Paysandú ☎🖷 +598 742 2053 **Email:** radiopaz@adinet.com.uy – **61**) Paysandú 1186, 11100 Montevideo. ☎+598 2 902-3939 🖷 +598 2 902-0628, 902-3671 **Email:** recepcion@conciertofm.com – **62**) José Pedro Varela 1242, 70101 Nueva Palmira, Depto. de Colonia ☎ 🖷 +598 544 6053 **Email:** radio_conosur@hotmail.com – **63**) Ruta Gral Artigas y Francisco Bicudo, 60000 Paysandú ☎ 🖷 +598 722 1817. – **64**) Atanasio Sierra 1040, 33000 Treinta y Tres ☎ +598 452 3532/33 🖷 +598 452 2423. – **65**) Boulevard Cardona s/n y Rivera, 75.200 Cardona 🖷 +598 536 9315. – **66**) José Enrique Rodó 791, 75000 Mercedes - **FM:** 100.3 "Galicia" – **67**) Calle Sarandí del Yi 328, 97100 Sarandí del Yí ☎🖷 +598 367 9155. **Email:** norasan@adinet.com.uy - **FM:** 89.5 "Scala FM" – **68**) Zelmar Michelini 819, 20000 Maldonado ☎ +598 42 23872 🖷 +598 42 22555 **Email:** am1560@adinet.com.uy - **N:** every ½h. **FM:** 103.5 "FM Punta del Este" – **69**) 25 de Agosto 724, 85000 Trinidad ☎ +598 364 2229 🖷 +598 364 3755 – **70**) Bulevar Artigas casi Rivera, 40003 Vichadero ☎ 🖷 +598 654 2018 – **71**) Rincón 1689, 65100 Young 🖷 +598 567 2071 - **72**) J.T. González 434, 90000 Canelones ☎ +598 332 2589/2993 🖷 +598 332 2040 **Email:** cx157101@adinet.com.uy - **FM:** 101.1. – **73**) Treinta y Tres 632, 30000 Minas ☎ +598 442 3092 🖷 +598 442 8714 **Email:** federalfm@adinet.com.uy - **FM:** 107.3 "Federal FM" – **74**) Av. Asencio, 1695, 75100 Dolores, Depto. de Soriano ☎ +598 534 2110 🖷 +598 534 2691 **Email:** radiosan@adinet.com.uy - **FM:** 89.7 "Skorpio" – **75**) Ituzaingó 1149, 27300 Lascano, Depto. de Rocha **Email:** cw159am@adinet.com.uy ☎🖷+598 456 9280 – **76**) Av. Gral. Artigas y Av. Domingo Pérez, 50002 Constitución, Depto. de Salto ☎🖷 +598 764 2051 **Email:** cw159am@adinet.com.uy – **77**) Av. Gral. Flores 468, 70000 Colonia ☎🖷 +598 522 2030. – **78**) 18 de Julio 743, 45100 Paso de los Toros 🖷 +598 664 2333 - **FM:** 91.9 "Toros FM" – **79**) Av. Artigas 932, Galería Solari, local 6, 7 y 8, 91000 Pando, Depto. de Canelones ☎ +598 2 292-2512 🖷 +598 2 292-4440 **Email:** emisoracontinental@hotmail.com – **80**) 18 de Julio y 25 de Agosto, 65000 Fray Bentos ☎ +598 562 3100 🖷 +598 562 3528 – **81**) Ituzaingó 246, 45000 Tacuarembó ☎ +598 632 2898 🖷 +598 632 2495 - **FM:** 92.5 – **82**) Ramirez 127, 27000 Rocha. ☎ +598 472 2250/2650 🖷 +598 472 2650 **Web:** www.difusorarochense.com.uy – **83**) Calle Artigas 1014, 50000 Salto ☎ +598 73 27759 🖷 +598 73 26264. – **84**) Uruguay 533, Galeria Aries, Local 7 y 8, 50000 Salto. ☎ +598 73 39322 🖷 +598 73 24196 – **85**) Rincón 1811, 65100 Young ☎🖷 +598 567 3125 - **FM:** 89.1 "Imagen FM" – **86**) Uruguay 1416, 50000 Salto ☎ +598 73 26272 🖷 +598 73 33222 **Email:** libertadores@mundonet. com.uy – **87**) 18 de Julio 291, 75000 Mercedes ☎ +598 53 25007 🖷 +598 53 23340 – **88**) 27 de Julio casi Basilio Lubkov, San Javier ☎ +598 569 2005 🖷 +598 569 2089 – **89**) 18 de Julio y 19 de Abril, 55002 Tomás Gomensoro, Depto. de Artigas ☎🖷 +598 777 2157 – **90**) Mercedes 973, 11100 Montevideo ☎ +598 2 902-6712 🖷 +598 2 902-9110 **Email:** prensa@portalx.com.uy **Web:** www.nt1010.com.uy – **91**) Av. 18 de Julio 1224, 11100 Montevideo. **Web:** www.radiomontecarlo.com.uy +598 2 901 4433

FM in Montevideo: All st's 10-100 kW.
91.1 R.Futura – 6) 91.9 R.Disney – 92.3 Urbana FM – 19) 93.9 Océano FM – 61) 94.7 Concierto FM – 95.5 Em. del Plata – 96.3 Em. Alfa – 4) 97.1 SODRE – 97.9 M24 – 98.7 Diamante FM – 99.5 Em. del Sol – 100.3 Aire FM – 101.9 Azul FM – 103.7 Millenium Montevideo – 8) 104.3 Radiocero – 105.9 Galaxia FM – 106.7 Energy FM.
In the rest of the country there are 175 FM outlets.

UZBEKISTAN

L.T: UTC +5h — **Pop:** 24 million — **Pr.L:** Uzbek, Russian — **E.C:** 50Hz, 220V — **ITU:** UZB

O'ZBEKISTON RADIOSI (Gov.)

✉ Xorazm ko'chasi 49, 700047 Toshkent. ☎ +998 71 2441210. 🖷 +998 71 2440021. **Email:** uztele@tkt.uz **Web:** www.teleradio.uz
L.P: Chmn: Abdusait Ko'chimov.

LW/MW	kHz	kW	Prgr		kHz	kW	Prgr
Toshkent	162	150	1	Nukus	1062	5	3
Toshkent	576	50	2	Toshkent	1062	10	1
Samarqand	648	10	1	Nukus	1260	20	1
Toshkent	666	30	3	Zarafshon	1269	50	2
Qo'ng'irot	675	5	2	Dang'ara	1323	5	2
Zarafshon	675	5	1	Koson	1323	7	3
Buxoro	711	50	3	Muborak	1332	5	1
Urganch	711	5	3	Samarqand	1539	5	3
Toshkent	756	50	4	Zharqo'rg'on	1593	7	3
Andijon	1062	50	3				

FM (MHz)	UZR1	UZR2	UZR3	UZR4	kW
Toshkent	67.19	69.23	67.97	66.41	17
Toshkent	103.1	104.0	107.8	87.9	4

+ FM tr's in other parts of the country not mentioned.

D.PRGR: UZR1 (O'zbekiston): 0000-2000 in Uzbek. – **UZR2 (Yoshlar):** 0000-2000 in Uzbek. – **UZR3 (Mash'al):** 0000-2100 in Uzbek, exc. Russian 0900-1000. Tx's relay UZR4 in various languages (see below) at 0230-0400 & 1500-1700. – **UZR4 (Do'stlik):** 0000-2000 in Uzbek, Russian (0220-0430 & 0900-1100), Tajik, Kazakh, Kyrgyz. Relays R.Mayak from Russia at 1100-1500 & 1800-2000.
EXTERNAL SERVICE: R. Tashkent International. See International Radio section.

OTHER STATIONS

FM	MHz	kW	Location	Station
8)	88.4	1	Toshkent	Navruz FM
7)	90.0	1	Toshkent	Europa Plus
1A)	100.5	2	Toshkent	Oriat FM
3)	101.0	1	Toshkent	Uzbegim taronasi
3)	101.0	1	Buxoro	Uzbegim taronasi
3)	101.0	1	Navoiy	Uzbegim taronasi
3)	101.0	1	Qo'qon	Uzbegim taronasi
3)	101.0	4	Samarqand	Uzbegim taronasi
3)	101.0	1	Urganch	Uzbegim taronasi
3)	101.0	1	Andijon*	Uzbegim taronasi
3)	101.0	1	Qarshi*	Uzbegim taronasi
3)	101.0	1	Termiz*	Uzbegim taronasi
2)	101.5	0.3	Toshkent	R. Grand
5)	102.0	2	Toshkent	Avtoradio-Xamrox
9)	102.5	-	Jizzakh	Vodiy sadosi
9)	102.7	1	Toshkent	Vodiy sadosi
9)	102.7	5	Andijon	Vodiy sadosi
9)	102.7	1	Buxoro	Vodiy sadosi
9)	102.7	1	Navoiy	Vodiy sadosi
9)	102.7	1	Termiz	Vodiy sadosi
9)	102.7	1	Urganch	Vodiy sadosi
10)	104.5	1	Samarqand	R. Poytaxt
4)	105.2	-	Samarqand	R. Sezam
4)	105.4	0.6	Toshkent	R. Sezam
6)	105.5	-	Jizzakh	R. Sanzar
1B)	106.5	2	Toshkent	Oriat-Dono
9)	106.9	1	Angren	Vodiy sadosi
9)	106.9	1	Qarshi	Vodiy sadosi
9)	106.9	1	Qo'qon	Vodiy sadosi
9)	106.9	1	Kamchik	Vodiy sadosi
10)	107.2	1	Toshkent	R. Poytaxt

*) in preparation

Addresses & other information:
1A,B) Shakhrizabad ko'chasi 1, 700000 Toshkent. Email: os2@oriat.uz.

1A) in Russian and English. Email: fm@oriyat.uz – **2)** A.Temur ko'chasi 108a, 700043 Toshkent. Email: radio@grand.uz – **3)** Murtazaev ko'chasi 10b, 700084 Toshkent. Email: raihon@yahoo.com – **4)** Xalklar do'stligi 42, 700097 Toshkent. Email: sezam@svetaleks.uz – **5)** Abay ko'chasi 6, 700011 Toshkent. Email: hamroh@mail.ru – **6)** Sharaf Rashidov ko'chasi, Jizzakh. – **7)** Bobur ko'chasi 20, 700100 Toshkent. Email: setar1@mail.ru – **8)** Mukumiy ko'chasi 178, 700096 Toshkent. Email: navruz@tps.uz. – **9)** Konaev ko'chasi 39-1A, Mirobod tumani, Toshkent. Email: mtrk@intal.uz – **10)** Movaraunnahr ko'chasi 14, 700000 Tashkent.

VANUATU

L.T: UTC +11h — **Pop:** 193,000 — **Pr.L:** Bislama, English, French — **E.C:** 50Hz, 230V — **ITU:** VUT

VANUATU BROADCASTING AND TELEVISION CORPORATION (VBTC)

P.M.B. 049, Port Vila ☎ +678 22999 ⎙ +678 22026
Web: www.vbtc.com.vu/Radio **L.P:** Head of Prgrs: Abong Thompson.
MW: Emten Lagoon 1125kHz 2kW, Santo 1179kHz 2kW.
SW: Emten Lagoon 7260khz 10/2.5kW (3945/4960kHz inactive)
FM: R Vanuatu, Santo-Luganville 98.1MHz 0.2kW, "Nambawan FM" Port Vila 98.0MHz. 0.25kW; BBC WS 99.0MHz 0.25kW; France Inter 100.0MHz 0.2kW
R. Vanuatu AM: 1900-1115 (Sun 1000). **On 7260kHz:** 1900-1115 (Sun 1000). **N. in English:** 0100W, 0900MF. **N. in French:** 0100W, 1200MF. **Rel. N. from foreign broadcasters:** 2000 (RA English), 2100 (RFI or VOA French), 2200 (exc. Fri/Sat. BBC or RA or RNZI English), 2300 (exc. Fri/Sat. RA or BBC English), 0000MF (RFI French).
Nambawan FM: 1900-1100.
ANN: "Radio Vanuatu", "Yu stap haren naoia Radio Vanuatu"

UCB PACIFIC PARTNERS (VTU)

Radio 90 Laef FM, PO Box 674, Port Vila, Republic of Vanuatu
Email: vanuatu@pacificpartners.org **Web:** www.pacificpartners.org
LP: Stn Mgr: Graham Carter
FM: Radio 90 Laef FM, Port Vila 90.0MHz 0.3kW D.Prgr: French, English & Bislama. **F.PI:** Luganville 91.0MHz (late 2004) and Tanna Is (2005). Run in partnership with Apostolic Life Ministries.

VATICAN CITY STATE

L.T: UTC +1h (27Mar-30 Oct. UTC +2h) — **Pop:** 900 — **E.C:** 50Hz, 220V — **ITU:** CVA

RADIO VATICANA (Rlg.)

Vatican Radio, 00120 Vatican City. ☎ +379 06 6988 3551.
Int. Rel: +39 06 6988 3551. ⎙ +39 06 6988 4565.
Email: promo@vatiradio.va **Web:** www.vaticanradio.org
LP: DG: Rev. Pasquale Borgomeo S.J.;PD: Rev. Federico Lombardi S.J.; TD: Rev. Eugenio Matis S.J.; CE: Rev. Lino Dan S.J.; Head of Int. Rel: Mrs. Solange de Maillardoz; Pub.Relations: F .Papi. Vatican Radio Museum, guided visiting tour C/o Piazza Pio XI 3, contact Mr. Papi.
MW: 585kHz 5kW, 1260kHz 5kW, 1530kHz 300/600kW, 1611kHz 50kW. Operating with reduced power on MW & SW.
FM: 93.3/103.8/105.0MHz 10kW (stereo).
Progr: Europa Programma 1 1530 kHz (1500-2200, 0330-0800)// 93.3MHz 24h; Europa Programma 2 1260kHz/1611kHz 24h (DRM on 1611kHz); ONE o FIVE 105.0MHz 24h (Multil.); Studio A 585kHz 24h(Classic Music)/ Radio Vaticana International Service Roma area 103.8MHz 24h.
ANN: Before all transmissions: Latin: "Laudetur Jesus Christus" (Praised be Jesus Christ), repeated in the language of the broadcast, then station identification – **IS:** "Christus Vincit" – **V.** by QSL-card.

EXTERNAL SERVICE: Vatican Radio
see International Broadcasting section

VENEZUELA

L.T: UTC -4h — **Pop:** 24,120,500 — **Pr.L:** Spanish — **E.C:** 60Hz, 120V — **ITU:** VEN

MINISTERIO DE TRANSPORTES Y COMUNICACIONES

Dir. General Sectorial de Comunicaciónes, Torre Este, piso 35, Parque Central, Caracas ⎙ +58 2 5740753

CAMARA VENEZOLANA DE LA INDUSTRIA DE RADIODIFUSION

Ap. 3955, Caracas 1060 ☎ +58 2 2634855, 2634528 ⎙ +58 2 2614783
MW: Call YV–,
° = also on SW, * = inactive, (r) = repeater, v = varying fq.

	Call	kHz	kW	Name and h. of tr.
AM01)		540	10	LV de Manapiare, San Juan de Manapiare
ZU01)	OY	540	50/25	R.Perijá, La Villa del Rosario: 0900-0400
DC01)	KE	550	50	YVKE Mundial, Caracas: 24h
DC02)	RH	560	50	R.Nacional, Cd. Guayana (r: 630)
TA01)	PJ	560	20/10	R.Exitos "Latina 5-60", Rubio: 1000-0400
AR09)	LX	570	100	R.Rumbos, Villa de Cura: 24h
DC02)		580		R.Nacional, Maturín (r: 630)
ZU02)	MJ	580	50/10	LV de la Fé, Maracaibo: 24h
DC04)	KL	590	20	R.Continente, Caracas: 24h
BA01)	SW	600	15	R.Alto Llano, Sta Bárbara de Barinas: 0900-0500
SU01)	QB	600	10	R.Sucre, Cumaná: 24h
AN01)	XY	610	10	R.Centro 6-10, Cantaura
LA01)	SE	610	10	R.Cristal, Barquisimeto
AP01)	ZC	620	50/25	R.Fé y Alegría Los Llanos,Guasdualito: 0900-0400
ZU03)	NO	620	10	R.Libertad, Cabimas: 0900-0400
DC02)	KA	°630	50/25	R.Nacional "Canal Informativo", Caracas: 24h
AN02)	QO	640	30	Unión Radio Porteñas, Puerto La Cruz: 24h
LA02)	MU	640	10/5	R.Carora, Carora: 1000-0400
AR01)	LH	650	50/20	Aragueña 650, Maracay: 0900-0500
AN03)	QZ	660	10	R.Anaco, Anaco: 0900-0400
DC02)		660		R.Nacional, El Callao (r: 630)
FA01)	NA	660	10	Ondas de los Médanos "Tu R.Popular", Coro: 0900-0400
DC03)	LL	°670	100	R.Rumbos, Caracas: 1000-0500, SS: 24h
BA02)	ZJ	680	10	R.Llanera "R.1400", Barinas: 0900-0500
SU02)	QR	v680	10	R.Continente Cumaná, Cumaná: 1000-0500
LA03)	MR	690	50/20	R.Barquisimeto, Barquisimeto
BO01)	PQ	700	5/2	R.Sur, Puerto Ordaz: 24h
ZU04)	MH	700	10	R.Popular, Maracaibo: 1000-0400
DC05)	KY	710	50/20	R.Capital, Caracas: 1000-0600
AP02)	XE	720	10	R.Elorza, Elorza
NE01)	QE	720	50	R.Venezuela "Oriente", Porlamar: 24h
LA04)	MT	730	10	R.Universo, Barquisimeto
TA02)	OO	730	10	R.Frontera, San Antonio del Táchira
BO02)	NQ	740	50	R.Caroni "Q-FM", Puerto Ordaz
ZU05)	NC	740	10	CNB 740 R.Maracaibo, Maracaibo: 0900-0400
DC06)	KS	750	100	RCR 750 "Radio Caracas", Caracas: 24h
AN04)	QQ	760	10	R.Pto. La Cruz "Doble Q", Pto. La Cruz: 0955-0300
TR01)	SO	760	10	R.Popular 760, Trujillo
DC02)	KK	770	50/20	R.Nacional, Valencia (r: 630)
FA02)	MN	780	10	R.Coro, Coro: 24h
TA03)	OD	°780	50/20	Ecos del Torbes, San Cristóbal: 0900-0400, (SS-0600)
DC02)		790		R.Nacional, Cd.Bolívar (r: 630)
DC07)	KC	790	10	R.Venezuela 7-90, Caracas
LA05)	XM	790	50	R.Minuto "La Barquisimetana", Barquisimeto: 24h
AN05)		810		R.Piritu, Puerto Píritu
CA01)	LP	810	50	Super Radio 810, Valencia: 0900-0500
BO03)	SH	820	50	R.Guayana, Upatá: 0900-0500
FA03)	XG	820	25/10	R.Guadalupana, Coro: 0900-0400
TA04)	KU	820	10	R.Altura 820, La Grita: 1000-0400
DC08)	LT	830	25	R.Sensación, Caracas: 0900-0500
LA04)	MY	840	10	R.Juventud, Barquisimeto
MO01)	UZ	840	10/5	Guarapiche 8-40 "La Primera", Maturín: 24h
CA02)	RV	850	10	RV-850, Valencia
ZU06)	ZC	850	10	R.Fé y Alegría, Maracaibo: 0900-0500
GU01)	YE	860	20/10	Enlace 8-60, Valle de la Pascua
TA05)	OL	860	10	Mundial 8-60, San Cristóbal: 0900-0500
AN06)	RU	870	10	Pueblo CNB 870, Puerto La Cruz
LA11)	MP	870	10	R.Lara, Barquisimeto: 0958-0400
BO04)	YM	880	20/10	R.Venezuela, Puerto Ordaz
DC09)	KV	880	10	R.Deportiva 8-80, Caracas
FA04)		880	10	R.Paraguaná, Punto Fijo: 24h.
AN07)	VO	890	10	R.Oriente, El Tigre
CA03)	LW	890	10	R.América, Valencia: 0900-0400
ZU07)	MD	900	25	R.Venezuela "Mara Ritmo", Maracaibo
DC10)	RQ	910	50/20	R.Q 910, Caracas: 24h
CO01)	QU	920	10/5	R.San Carlos, San Carlos: 0955-0400
NE02)	QX	920	20	R.Nueva Esparta, Porlamar: 1000-0400
AR02)	LJ	930	10	R.Maracay, Maracay: 1000-0600

	Call	kHz	kW	Name and h. of tr.
AN08)	LU	940	10	R.Fé y Alegría El Tigre, El Tigre: 0900-0300
BA03)	ZR	940	15	R.Continental, Barinas
FA05)	NN	940	10	R.Punto Fijo, Punto Fijo: 0900-0500
DC11)	KG	950	50	AM Popular, Caracas: 24h.
MO02)	RB	960	50/20	R.Monagas, Maturín
PO01)		960	25	R.Venezuela "Llanera", Acarigua
TA06)	SS	960	10	R.San Sebastián, San Cristóbal: 1000-0500
AN09)		970	10	Mundial Oriente, Barcelona: 24h
AR03)	LR	970	10	R.Continente 970 Maracay, Maracay: 0900-0400
TR02)	SD	970	15	R.Turismo, Valera: 0855-0355
AN10)	QM	980	10	LV de El Tigre, El Tigre: 1000-0300
DC02)		980		R.Nacional, Maracaibo (r: 630)
DC12)	RT	990	20	R.Tropical "99-0", Caracas: 24h
LA06)	TA	990	10	R.Venezuela "Tricolor", Barquisimeto: 24h
CA04)	NM	1000	10	R.Mil "La Caribeña", Morón: 0900-0400
TA11)	OA°	1000	10	R.Táchira, San Cristóbal: 1000-0400
AR04)	PC	1010	10	R.Aragua, Cagua: 0900-0400
BO05)	QF	1010	10	R Venezuela, Cd.Bolívar: 0900-0400
NE03)	RS	1020	10	R.Mundial Margarita, La Asunción: 0955-0500
YA01)	TW	1020	25	R.Alegría, Chivacoa
ZU08)	MX	1020	50/10	R.Continente Calendario, Maracaibo: 24h
MI01)	TD	1030	25/10	R.Valles del Tuy, Ocumare del Tuy: 0930-0400
PO02)	QY	1030	20	R.Onda 1030, Guanare: 0900-0600
CA05)	LB	1040	20	LV de Carabobo, Valencia: 0900-0400
ME01)	ON	1040	20/10	Mundial Los Andes, Mérida
DC02)	KZ	1050	25	R.Nal. "Canal Musical", Caracas: 1000-0400
DC02)	PO	1050	20	R.Nacional, Cabudare: 1000-0400 (r: 1050)
GU02)	LN	1060	10	R.Guárico, S. Juan de los Morros: 1030-0330
TA07)	OE	1060	10	R.Noticias AM, San Cristóbal
AP03)		1070	10	Superior 1070 Biruaca, San Fernando de Apure: 0930-0400
PO03)		1070	25	Contacto 1070, Ospino: 1000-0400
TA08)	PX	1070	5	R.El Sol, La Fría
ZU09)	MA	1070	10	Mundial Zulia, Maracaibo: 24h
AN11)	QJ	1080	10	R.Barcelona, Barcelona
AR05)	NR	1080	10	R.Venezuela, Maracay: 24h
DC02)		1080	10	R.Nacional, Mérida (F.Pl.)
DC13)	SZ	1090	20	Unión R.1090, Caracas: 24h
YA02)	PB	1090	10	R.Yaracuy "Operadora 1090 AM", S. Felipe: 24h
ZU10)	TG	1090	3	Melódica 1090, Machiques: 0900-0500
BO06)	SV	1100	10	R.Angostura, Cd.Bolívar: 0900-0430
ME02)	OP	1100	10	R.Fe y Alegría, Tovar: 0900-0300
CA06)	RX	1110	10	Unión R.Valencia, Valencia
SU03)	QT	1110	10	R.Carúpano, Carúpano: 0900-0400
AP04)	SK	1120	20/10	R.Dif.del Sur, San Fernando de Apure
MO03)	XZ	1120	5	R.República "La Estación Feliz", Maturín
ZU11)	MF	1120	10	Ondas del Lago "Super Ondas", Maracaibo: 24h
AM02)	PY°	1130	15	R.Amazonas, Puerto Ayacucho: 0830-0400
LA07)	KQ	1130	10	R.Popular, Barquisimeto: 0900-0400
DC16)	RL	1130	20/10	R.Ideal, Maiquetia (Caracas)
NE04)		1140		R.Porlamar "LV del Caribe", Porlamar: 1000-0400
BO07)	QD	1150	10	Ecos del Orinoco, Cd.Bolívar: 24h
FA06)	MV	1150	10	R.Venezuela "Ondas del Caribe", Punto Fijo: 24h
ME03)	OK	1160	1	R.Universidad, Mérida
MI02)	RR	1160	20/10	R.Industrial 1160 Estéreo, Guarenas
PO04)	QV	1170	20/10	R.Acarigua, Acarigua
VA01)	KW	1170	10	Celestial 1170 AM, Maiquetía: 1000-0400
AR06)	LQ	1180	10	LV de la Victoria "Super Suave 11-80", La Victoria
MO04)	OR	1180	10	R.Maturín, Maturín: 0900-0400
ZU12)	NJ	1180	10	R.Petrolera, Cd.Ojeda: 0900-0700
BA04)	RE	1190	20/10	R.Barinas 1190 AM Estéreo, Barinas
BO08)	PF	1190	20/10	Ondas de Libertad, San Félix: 0900-0300
TA09)	ZD	1190	10	R.Dif.Cult. del Táchira "Paz Vital 11-90", San.Cristóbal: 1000-0400
DC14)	OZ	1200	10	R.Tiempo, Caracas: 24h
MO05)	SF	1200	10	R.Dimensión, Caripito: 1000-0300
ZU13)	NH	1200	1	Ondas del Escalante, Sta Bárbara del Zulia: 1000-0300
AN12)	ZT	1210	10	R.Anzoátegui, Barcelona: 24h
AP05)	RD	1220	10	LV de Apure, San Fernando de Apure
CA07)	VM	1220	10/5	R.Valencia, Valencia
ZU14)	ZO	1220	20/10	R.Aeropuerto 1220, Maracaibo: 24h
MI03)	NT	1230	10	R.Barlovento, Caucagua
TR03)	OH°	1230	10	R.Valera, Valera: 0900-0400
DC02)	NV*	1240	50	R.Nal. Punta Tumatey (Prgr: Antena Populares)
BO09)	PZ	1250	20/10	Latina 12-50, Pto Ordaz: 0900-0400
ZU15)	ML	1250	1	R.Cabimas, Cabimas: 1000-0300
DC15)	RM	1260	10	RRB 1260 AM Radiodif. Biblica, "Palabra de Vida", Caracas
YA03)	RY	1260	10	R.Horizonte, Nirgua: 1000-0200
DA01)	TR	1270	5	R.Tucupita, Tucupita: 0900-0500
DC02)		1270	10	R.Nacional, Ureña (r: 630)
ME04)	OU	1270	10	R.Ondas Panamericanas, El Vigía
GU03)	QS	1280	10/5	R.Zaraza, Zaraza: 1000-0300
TR04)	OF	1280	10	R.Trujillo, Trujillo
CA08)	LF	1290	10	R.Puerto Cabello, Puerto Cabello: 24h
DC10)	KH	1300	10/8	R.1300, Caracas: 1000-0400
ZU16)	NS	1300	10	R.Reloj, Maracaibo: 24h.
DC02)	SM	1310	10	R.Nacional, Barcelona (r: 630)
DC02)	SL	1310	1	R.Nacional, Guri (r: 630)
TR05)	TS	1310	5	R.Andina "Sonido 13-10", Isnotú: 0900-0500
AR07)	WP	1320	10/5	R.Apolo, Turmero: 24h
LA08)	SG	1320	10	R.Colonial, El Tocuyo
GU04)	OY	1330	5	R.Los Llanos, Calabozo: 0900-0300
ZU17)	TU	1330	10	R.Regional, Cd.Ojeda: 0900-0500
DC17)	NE	1340	10	R.Uno "AM 1340", Caracas: 24h (R. María)
AN13)	ZZ	1350	5	R.Eclipse "R.Guanipa",El Tigrito: 24h
FA07)	TJ	1350	5	R.Falcón, Puerto Cumarebo
MI04)	TZ	1360	5	R.YVTZ "R.Armonia", Charallave: 1000-0300
YA01)	TW	1360	5	R.Alegría, Chivacoa
ZU18)	TI	1360	10	R.Internacional, Maracaibo: 24h
GU05)	OQ	1370	5	R.La Pascua, Valle de la Pascua: 1000-0400
ME05)	JI	1370	10	R. Continente Cumbre, Mérida: 1000-0400
PO05)	SV	1370	5	R.Portuguesa, Araure: 1000-0400
BO10)	ME	1380	5	R.Fantasía, Cd.Bolivar
CA09)	NG	1380	10	Ondas del Mar, Puerto Cabello: 0900-0359
ZU19)	TL	1380	10	R.Triunfo 13-80, Caja Seca: 0900-0400
DC18)	ZAv	1390	20	R.Fé y Alegría, Caracas: 24h
LA09)	TT	1390	10	R.Terepaima, Cabudare: 24h
ZU20)	ZO	1390	10	R.Lumen 2000, Maracaibo: 1030-0500 (Prgr: R.Católica Mundial)
AN03)	QZ	1400	10	R.Anaco, Anaco: 0900-0400 (cfr 660)
GU06)	NF	1400	1	R.Sabana, El Sombrero: 1000-0200
PO06)	ST	1410	5	R.Turén, Turén: 0900-0400
TR06)	SP	1410	10	R.Simpatía, Valera
DC21)		1420	5	R.Sintonía, Caracas
LA10)	RW	1420	10/5	R.Cardenal, Carora: 1000-0400
ZU21)	NZ	1420	5	R.Marabina 1420, Maracaibo: 24h
AN14)	TP	1430	25	R.Bahía, Puerto La Cruz: 24h
BO11)	TM	1430	10/5	R.Caicara, Caicara del Orinoco
CA10)	NB	1430	10	R.Satélite 14-30, Guacara: 0930-0400
GU07)	RF	1440	5	R.Orituco, Altagracia del Orituco
PO07)	ZI	1440	10	R.Estelar 14-40, Guanare: 0900-0400
TA10)	TY	1440	1	R.Sucesos, Táriba: 0950-0400
BO12)	XC	1450	10/5	R.Mega Visión, San Felix
VA02)	KJ	1450	10/8	Sonera 14-50, Catia La Mar: 0900-0400
ZU22)	ZQ	1450	10	Informativa 14-50, Los Puertos de Altagracia: 0900-0500
TR07)	RJ	1460	5	R.Jardín, Boconó
CA11)	JW	1470	10	R.Latina, Valencia: 24h
SU04)	SY	1470	10	R.Vibración, Carúpano
FA08)		1480		R.Cumarebo, Cumarebo
DC19)	XD	1490	10	La Dinámica, Caracas
ME06)	SQ	1490	1	R.Mérida 14-90, Mérida: 24h
ZU11)	RP	1490	10/5	R.El Sol, Maracaibo: 24h
AR08)		1500		R.Galaxia, San Mateo
SU05)	RZ	1500	10/5	R.2000 AM, Cumaná: -0400
CA12)		1510	20	Informativa "LV del Centro", Güigüe
MI05)	IC	1520	25	R.Bonita La Guapa, Guatire: 0930-0400
YA04)	NP	1530	10	R.San Felipe el Fuerte, San Felipe
MI06)	MV	1550	10	R.Metropolitana, Los Teques: 24h
ZU24)	XO	1550	10/5	R.Impacto, Cd. Ojeda
ME07)	LZ	1560	10/5	R.Dif. Andina, Mérida
GU08)	YV	1580	10/5	R.Venezolana, Calabozo: 1000-0200
SU06)	TK	1580	10/5	Manzanares 15-80, Cumaná: (r: R.Q 910kHz)
ZU25)	YO	1580	10	R Celestial, San Francisco, Maracaibo
DC20)	UD	1590	10	R.Deporte 15-90, Caracas: 24h

SW:
Stations with a (*) are reported to be inactive, but may occasionally be reactivated for variable periods of time.

	Call	kHz	kW	Name and h. of tr.
TA11)	OB	4830	10	R.Táchira, S. Cristóbal: 1100-1400, 2000-0400 irr.
TR03)	OI	*4840	1	R.Valera, Valera
AM02)	PAv	4940	1	R.Amazonas, Pto. Ayacucho:1000-0400 irr
TA03)	OC*	4980	10	Ecos del Torbes, San Cristóbal

Other stations
CNB - CIRCUITO NACIONAL BELFORT
✉ Quinta CNB, Av.Los Naranjos, La Florida, Caracas. **Web:** www.cnb.com.ve.
CIRCUITO AM CENTER
✉ CentroComercialConcresa, Nivel 1, Circuito Center, Prados del Este, Caracas 1080, Edo.Miranda ☎+58 212 976-2013.
Email: feloespinosa@cantv.et.
CIRCUITO RADIAL ALFA OMEGA
✉ Calle 25, Con Calle 67, Sector El Paraíso, frente Al Colegio La Epifanía, Maracaibo, Edo.Zulia ☎+58 261 783-2524.
CIRCUITO POPULAR
✉ Boulevard de Sabana Grande, Torre Provincial, P10, Sabana Grande, Caracas 1050 ☎+58 212 762 5052.
CIRCUITO RADIO CARACAS RADIO
✉ Av.Páez, Quinta RCR, El Paraíso, Caracas 1021 ☎+58 212 481-3590.
CIRCUITO RADIAL CONTINENTE
✉ Calle La Joya, Edif.Cosmos, PH, Chacao, Caracas 1060, Edo.Miranda ☎+58 212 267-3132 🖷+58 212 267-1223 **Web:** http://radiocontinente.tripod.om.ve **Email:** produccion@radiocontinente.zzn.com
CIRCUITO RADIO VENEZUELA
✉ Av.Rómulo Gallegos, Edif.KLM, P12, Ofcs CyD, Los Palos Grandes, Caracas 1062, Edo.Miranda ☎+58 212 286-8492 **Web:** www.radiovenezuela.com.ve **Email**: radiovenezuela@hotmail.com
CIRCUITO SATELITAL RUMBOS
✉ Av.Francisco de Miranda, Multicentro Empresarial del Este, Edif.Libertador, Núcleo A, P7, Chacao, Caracas 1060, Edo.Miranda ☎+58 212 263-3236 🖷+58 212 263-2212 **Email**: radiorumbos@ipnet.work.net
CORPORACIÓN REGIONAL BRADCASTING
✉ Calle 74, Entre Av. 3Dy3E, Edif.Televisa, Sector La Lago, Maracaibo 4002, Edo. Zulia ☎+58 261 792-9217.
GRUPO RADIAL DE ORIENTE
✉ Urb.Tricentenaria, Centro ComercialTricentenaria, P2, Ofcs 03y09, Barcelona 6001, Edo.Anzoátegui ☎+58 281 277-1743.
🖷+58 281 277-1776 **Email:** radioanzoategui@hotmail.com
RADIO CADENA MUNDIAL
✉ Calle Nueva York, Edif.Manzanillo, P2, Las Mercedes, Caracas 1060, Edo.Miranda ☎+58 212 993-9391.
Email: prensayvke@cantv.net.
UNION RADIO
✉ Av.Mohedano, Entre Calle Los Granados y 1ª transversal, Edif.Splendor, La Castellana, Caracas 1060, Edo.Miranda ☎+58 212 263-5133. **Web:** www.unionradio.com.ve.

Addresses and other information:
State abbreviations: AM = Amazonas, AN = Anzoátegui, AP = Apure, AR = Aragua, BA = Barinas, BO = Bolívar, CA = Carabobo, CO = Cojedes, DA = Delta Amacuro, DC = Distrito Capital, FA = Falcón, GU = Guárico, LA = Lara, ME = Mérida, MI = Miranda, MO = Monagas, NE = Nueva Esparta, PO = Portuguesa, SU = Sucre, TA = Táchira, TR = Trujillo, VA = Vargas, YA = Yaracuy, ZU = Zulia.
N.B: These abbreviations are not officially recognized by the Venezuelan Post Office. Letters should therefore carry the full name.
AM00) AMAZONAS
AM01) San Juan de Manapiare ☎+58 248 978-0249. – **AM02)** Av. Bolívar 4 c/c Av. La Guardia, Puerto Ayacucho 7101 ☎ +58 248 521-4892 🖷+58 248 214-769 (Reception reports to: Jorge García Rangel, Calle Roma, Qta Costa Rica N° A-16, Urb.Alto Barinas, Barinas 5201, Barinas, Venezuela).
AN00) ANZOÁTEGUI
AN01) Av. Hospital cruce con Calle Freites, Edif.Radio Centro, Cantura 6007. ☎+58 282 455-1414. – **AN02)** Av. 5 de Julio, Edif. Los Angeles, Sotanos 1y2, Puerto La Cruz 6023. ☎+58 281 265-1953 **Web:** www.unionradio.com.ve/ – **AN03)** Calle Cajigal cruce con Av.Nueva Esparta N° 39, Edif.Radio City, planta baja, Anaco 6003. ☎+58 282 125-2055.– **AN04)** Calle Arismendi N° 20, Edif.Radio Puerto La Cruz, PB, Puerto La Cruz 6023. ☎+58 281 265-3512. – **AN05)** Av. Costanera, frente al malecón, Puerto Píritu 6022. – **AN06)** Av.Municipal,Torre Porteñas, Mezzanina, Ofc. 2-4, Puerto La Cruz 6023. ☎+58 281 267-0870 **Web:** www.cnb.com.ve – **AN07)** Calle Guayana, Centro Comercial Bleu Hill, P1, Local 4, El Tigre 6034. ☎+58 283 235-0902 **Email**: Oriente89cero@terra.com.ve – **AN08)** Av.Simon Rodríguez con 8va Calle Norte, Complejo Cultural Sim+on Rodríguez, El Tigre 6034. ☎+58 283 231-6330 **Web:** www.feyalegria.org/Venezuela **Email**: feyalegria@cantv.net or irfaeltigre@ cantv.net – **AN09)** Av.Intercomunal "Andrés Bello", Centro Comercial Géminis, P3, Local 9, Barcelona 6001. ☎+58 281 276-2986. – **AN10)** Av. Francisco de Miranda N° 196, Al lado del Banco Provincial, El Tigre 6034. ☎+58 283 235-2801. – **AN11)** Av. Miranda cruce con Av.San Carlos, Edif.Radio Barcelona, P2, Barcelona 6001. ☎+58 281 277-2801. – **AN12)** Urb. Tricentenaria, Centro Comercial Tricente-naria, P2, Ofc. 3y9, Barcelona 6001. ☎+58 281 277-1743 **Email**: radioanzoategui@hotmail.com – **AN13)** Av.Intercomunal El Tigre El Tigrito, Detrás de Elite Motors, Casa Amarilla,El Tigrito 6035. ☎+58 283 255-0556 **Email**: eclipse@telcel.net.ve – **AN14)** Av. Municipal, Torre Pelicano, P8, Apto 8-4, Puerto La Cruz 6023. ☎+58 281 269-9522.
AP00) APURE
AP01) Carr. Nacional, Vía Elorza La Arenosa, Edif.Fe y Alegría, Guasdualito 5063. ☎+58 278 332-0233 **Web:** www.feyalegria. org/ve **Email:** rcepeda@cantv.net or feyalegria@cantv.net – **AP02)** Calle 9 con Cra. 4, Municipio Rómulo Gallegos, Elorza 7007. ☎+58 240 929-1051. – **AP03)** Av.Fuerzas Armadas, Edif.Superior, P1, San Fernando de Apure 7001. ☎+58 247 341-0070. – **AP04)** Calle Carlos Rodríguez Rincones, Gobernación del Estado Apure, San Fernando de Apure 7001. ☎+58 247 341-1114. – **AP05)** Av Miranda, Edif.Don António Cestari, San Fernando de Apure 7001. ☎+58 247 341-1768.
AR00) ARAGUA
AR01) Calle Coromoto, Urb.Calicanto, Torre Capitolio, P9, Ofc.B-9, Urb.Calicanto, Maracay 2101. ☎+58 243 246-2809 **Web:** www. unionradio.com.ve **Email:** rb650@telcel.net.ve – **AR02)** Calle Boyacá, Edif. Centro, P9, Ofc. 1, Maracay 2101. ☎+58 243 246-5591. – **AR03)** Av. Miranda Oeste N° 149, Entre Carabobo y Pinhincha, Edif.Canaobre, PH, Maracay 2101. ☎+58 243 246-4560 **Web:** http://radiocontinente.tripod.com.ve/ **Email**: produccion@radiocontinente.zzn.com – **AR04)** Calle Boyacá Nte N° 9, Edif. Radio Aragua, Ofc.1y2, Cagua 2122. ☎+58 244 395-4123. – **AR05)** Urb.Calicanto, Calle Coromoto, Norte 6, Detrás de la Maestranza Cesar Girón, Maracay 2101. ☎+58 243 245-5643 **Web:** www. radiovenezuela.com.ve **Email:** radiovenezuela@hotmail.com – **AR06)** Edif. Veliz, Calle Aldao, frente a la Plaza Rivas, La Victoria 2126 **Web:** www.cnb.com.ve/ – **AR07)** Av.Bermúdez, Torre Apolo, PB, entre Mariño y Bolívar, Turmero 2115. ☎+58 244 6630-2928. – **AR08)** San Mateo. –**AR09)** Calle Páez, N° 138, Detrás del Teatro de La Opera, Maracay 2126. ☎+58 243 232-9835.
BA00) BARINAS
BA01) Cra. 3 N° 7-39, entre Calles 7 y 8, Santa Bárbara de Barinas 5210. ☎+58 278 221-1133. – **BA02)** Av. Sucre Quinta Claret N° 17-46, Barinas 5201. ☎+58 273 552-7976. – **BA03)** Av Marqués del Pumar, Edif.Radio Continental, Barinas 5201. ☎+58 273 552-4021. – **BA04)** Av. Sucre con Av. Agustín Codazzi, Edif. Circuito Sensacional Barinas, Barinas 5201. ☎+58 273 552-24.17 **Web:** www. radiovenezuela.com.ve **Email:** radiovenezuela@hotmail.com
BO00) BOLÍVAR
BO01) Av.Guasipati, Edif. Piarde, PH, Puerto Ordaz 8015. ☎+58 286 922-99.08 **Email:** sur700am@yahoo.com or – **BO02)** Urb.Altavista Calle Caura, Edif. Los Bancos, P4, Puerto Ordaz 8015. ☎+58 286 961-8411 **Email:** cesargonzales1284@hotmail.com – **BO03)** Av.Raúl Leoni, Edif.Antonelli, PB, Upatá 8026. ☎+58 288 221-1457 **Email:** rodriguayana@hotmail.com – **BO04)** Av.Venezuela, Centro Comercial Venezuela, Local 14-15, P1, Urb. Villa Colombia, Puerto Ordaz 8015. ☎+58 286 923-7051 **Web:** www.radiovenezuela. com.ve **Email:** radiovenezuela@hotmail.com – **BO05)** Calle Dalla Costa, Alto N° 5, Cd. Bolívar 8001. ☎+58 285 632-3743 **Web:** www.radiovenezuela.com.ve **Email:** radiovenezuela@hotmail.com – **BO06)** Final Paseo Heres, Edif.Tovar, P2, Cd. Bolívar 8001. ☎+58 285 652-2202. – **BO07)** Paseo Meneses, Centro Comercial Meneses, PA, Locales 11 y 12, Cd. Bolívar 8001. ☎+58 285 632-0413. – **BO08)** Calle México, Parcela El Roble, Detrás de la Estación de Servicio Volfo, Sector La Antena, San Félix 8024. ☎+58 286 932-2366 **Email:** ondasdelibertad@cantv.net – **BO09)** Calle El Tocuyo, Centro Comercial Plaza, P2, Pto Ordaz 8015. ☎+58 286 922-1346. – **BO10)** Av. 17 de Diciembre, Centro Comercial Zamara, Locales 29 y 32, PB, Cd. Bolívar 8001. ☎+58 285 632-6564. (Offices and studios in Cd.Bolívar, transmitter site Cantaura, Anzoátegui). – **BO11)** Calle Constitución N° 78, Caicara del Orinocco 7107. ☎+58 284 666.74.30. – **BO12)** Av.Della Costa, Edif.Flor Motors, PB, San Felix 8024. ☎+58 286 932-2662.
CA00) CARABOBO
CA01) Av.Girardot con Calle Montes de Oca, Edif.Normal, Piso PH, Valencia 2001. ☎+58 241 857-1910 – **CA02)** Av. Bolívar Norte, Edif. Felpo, P7, Ofc. 3-3, Valencia 2001. ☎+58 241 857-5850 – **CA03)** Calle Girardot, Entre Urdaneta y Boyacá N° 98-28, Valencia 2001. ☎+58 241 857-4868 **Email:** tomas@cantv.net – **CA04)** Carr.Panamericana, Edif.Radio Mil, Morón. ☎+58 242 372-0283 – **CA05)** Av. Rosarito, Torre Trebol, P1, Ofc. 13, Urb. Lomas del Este, Valencia 2001. ☎+58 241 857-4111 **Email:** mbranger@mixmail. com – **CA06)** Av.Bolívar Norte, Torre Banavén, P12, Ofc.12-9, Valencia 2001. ☎+58 241 821-1213 **Web:** : www.unionradio.com.ve **Email:** 1110am@unionradio.com.ve – **CA07)** Av.Rotaria, Edif.El Parque, PB Local 2, Urb.Lomas del Este, Valencia 2001. ☎+58 241 857-4864 **Web:** www.radiovenezuela.com.ve **Email:**

radiovenezuela @hotmail.com – **CA08)** Av.Marina, Edif.Diproca, PB, Local 3, Puerto Cabello 2024 ☎+58 242 361-3103 **Web:** www.cnb.com.ve **Web:** http://diproca.com/rpc **Email:** radiorpc@telcel.net.ve – **CA09)** Av. Bolívar, Edif. Sabatino, P1, Urb.Rancho Grande, Puerto Cabello 2024. ☎+58 242 362-3569 **Web:** www.cnb.com.ve/ **Email:** omcm@telcel.net.ve – **CA10)** Final de La Calle Jacinto con Calles Ricaurte y Girardot, Edif.Radio Satélite, Guacara 2015. ☎+58 245 564-0979 **Email:** mbranger@mixmail.com – **CA11)** Av.Montes de Oca, Edif.Don Pelayo, P12, Valencia 2001. ☎+58 241 857-4270 **Web:** www.latina.com.ve/ **Email:** latina@unete.com.ve - **FM:** 99.1. – **CA12)** Av. Miranda,Edif. Padre Cecilio Ávila, PH, Güigüe 2010. ☎+58 245 541-1819.

CO00) COJEDES

CO01) Av.Sucre, Edif.General Manuel Manrique, P3, Local 46, San Carlos 2201. ☎+58 285 433-0051 **Web:** www.unionradio.com.ve **Email:** radiosancarlos@cantv.net

DA00) DELTA AMACURO

DA01) Calle Petión cruse con Calle La Paz, Tucupita 6401. ☎+58 287 721-0022.

DC00) DISTRITO CAPITAL

DC01) Calle Nueva York Cruce con Av.Rio de Janeiro, Edif. YVKE Mundial, P1, Las Mercedes, Caracas 1060, Edo.Miranda. ☎+58 212 993-6242 - 🖷+58 212 993 2267 - **Email:** prensayvke @cantv.net – **DC02)** Final Calle Las Marías, Edif.Radio Nacional de Venezuela, entre Chapellín y Country Club, La Frorida, Caracas 1050, Edo. Miranda. ☎+58 212 730-6022 **Web:** www.rnv.gov.ve **Email:** rnv2000@hotmail.com. – **DC03)** Av.Francisco de Miranda, Multicentro Empresarial del Este, Edif.Libertador, P7, Núcleo A. Chacao, Caracas 1060, Edo Miranda. ☎ +58 212 263-3236 **Web:** www.tycom.com.ve/rumbos **Email:** radiorumbos@ip-net.work.net – **DC04)** Calle La Joya, Edif. Cosmos PH, Chacao, Caracas 1060, Edo Miranda. ☎+58 212 267-3132 **Web:** www.radiocontinente.da.ru/ or http://radiocontinente.tripod.com.ve **Email:** produccion@radiocontinente.zzn.com – **DC05)** Av.Francisco de Miranda, Centro Comercial Los Ruices, P3, Los Ruices, Caracas 1071, Edo Miranda. ☎+58 212 238-1630. – **DC06)** Av. José A. Paez, Quinta RCR, El Paraiso, Caracas 1021, Distrito Capital. ☎+58 212 481-3590 **Web:** www.radionet. com.ve **Email:** jnestares@etheron.net – **DC07)** Av.Rómulo Gallegos, Edif.KLM, P12, Ofc. CyD, Los Palos Grandes, Caracas 1062, Edo Miranda. ☎+58 212 286-84.92 **Web:** www.radiovenezuela.com.ve **Email:** radiovenezuela@hotmail.com. – **DC08)** Av. Santiago de Chile, Quinta Radio Sensación, Los Caobos, Caracas 1050. Disatrito Capital. ☎+58 212 793-6458 **Email:** radiosensacion@cantv.net – **DC09)** Calle Nueva York, Edif.Manzanillo, P2, Las Mercedes, Caracas 1060, Edo Miranda ☎+58 212 993-8321 **Email:** 880am@ trompo.com – **DC10)** Centro Comercial Concresa, Nivel 1, Circuito Center, Prados del Este, Caracas 1080, Edo.Miranda. ☎+58 212 976.20.13 **Email:** feloespinosa@cantv.net . – **DC11)** Boulevard de Sabana Grande, Torre Provincial, P10, Sabana Grande, Caracas 1050, Distrito Capital. ☎+58 212 762-5052 **Email:** radiopopular@cantv. net . – **DC12)** Puente Nuevo a Puerto Escondido, Edif.Torre del Oeste, P1, El Silencio, Caracas 1010, Distrito Capital. (or: Ap.3674, Caracas 1010-A) ☎+58 212 482-1111 **Email:** radiotropical@cantv.net – **DC13)** Av.Mohedano, Entre Calle Los Granados y 1ª transversal, Edif.Splendor, La Castellana, Caracas 1060, Edo.Miranda. ☎+58 212 263-5133 **Web:** www.unionradio.com.ve – **DC14)** Av. Los Mangos N° 49, Qta.Radio Tiempo, La Florida, Caracas 1050-A, Edo.Miranda. ☎+58 212 730-3889 **Email:** radiotiempo@telcel.net.ve – **DC15)** Av. Los Mangos con Av.Valencia Parpacén, Qta.RRB, La Florida, Caracas 1050, Edo.Miranda. ☎+58 212 730-8438 **Web:** http://rrb.org/rrbes/ emissoras/ve **Email:** caracas@etheron.net or rrb-caracas@etheron. net – **DC16)** Centro Comercial Uslar, P15, Ofc. 152, Montalbán, Caracas 1021, Distrito Capital. ☎+58 212 443-6680 **Email:** radioideal@cantvc.net. – **DC17)** Edif. Mundial, Av. Tamanaco, El Rosal, Caracas 1060. – **DC18)** Calle 3B, Edif.C-207, P2, (detrás del McDonald's), La Urbina, Caracas 1070, Edo.Miranda. ☎+58 212 242 2919 **Web:** www.feyalegria.org/Venezuela/ **Email:** radiofya@ cantv.net or radiofyanacional@cantv.net – **DC19)** Av.Boulevard Brasil N° 74, de Santa Ana a Providencia La Pastora, Caracas 1010, Distrito Capital. ☎+58 212 862-6433.**Email:**dinamica@cantv.net – **DC20)** Av. Circunvalación del Sol, Centro Profesional Sta Paula, Torre A, P5 Ofc. 51, Caracas 1061, Edo.Miranda. ☎+58 212 985-2907. **Web:** radiodeporte.8m.com **Email:** radiodeporte@cantv.net – **DC21)** Calle La Joya, Torre Cosmos, P9, Ofc. 9A, Chacao, Caracas 1060, Edo.Miranda. (or: Centro Comercial El Pichacho, P8, San António de los Altos 1204). ☎+58 212 264-0782.

FA00) FALCÓN

FA01) Calle Bolívar, Edif.Don Cosme, P2, Coro 4101. ☎+58 268 253-2095 **Email:** olm660@cantv.net – **FA02)** Calle Bolívar, Edif.Don Cosme, P2, Coro 4101. ☎+58 268 253-1448 **Email:** radiocoro780am @cantv.net – **FA03)** Calle Palmasola cruce Con Calle Federación, Edif.Arquidiocesano, Coro 4101. ☎+58 268 251-5455 **Email:** rguadalu@funflc.org.ve –**FA04)** Urb. Los Caciques, Calle Falcón, Qta.Paraguaná, Punto Fijo 4102. ☎+58 269 246-5194. – **FA05)** Calle Talavera, entre Calles Comercio y Arismendi, Edif.Radio Punto Fijo, Punto Fijo 4102. ☎+58 269 245-1232. – **FA06)** Av.Ecuador, Entre Calles Comercio y Arismendi, Punto Fijo 4102. ☎+58 269 245-6565. – **FA07)** Av.Bolívar, Edif.Colonial Planta Baja, Urb.Alta Vista, Puerto Cumarebo 4167. ☎+58 268 747-1437. – **FA08)** Centro Ciudad Comercial Tamanaco (CCCT), Torre B, P7, Ofc. 704, Chuao, Caracas 1060, Edo Miranda. ☎+58 212 959-0075.

GU00) GUÁRICO

GU01) Av. RómuloGallegos, Edif.Flor de Pascua, Loc 2, Valle de la Pascua 2307. ☎+58 235 341-2860 **Email:** radioenlace860@ cantv.net – **GU02)** Av. Principal. La Moreras, Edif.Ghersy N° 28, San Juan de los Morros 2301. ☎+58 246 431-6494 **Email:** feloespinosa@cantv.net – **GU03)** Calle Concordia, Qta. Puerto Arturo N° 35, Zaraza 2332. ☎+58 238 762-1032 **Web:** www.circuitoz.com/ or htttp://radiocontinente.tripod,com.ve **Email:** circuitoz@hotmail. com – **GU04)** Cra 12, Altos del Teatro Paez, Frente a La Bomba, Calabozo 2312. ☎+58 246 871-3639 **Email:** rlosllanos@telcel.net. ve – **GU05)** Av. 5 de Julio N° 20, Valle de la Pascua 2307. ☎+58 235 341-3255 **Web:** www.unionradio.com.ve – **GU06)** Calle Alegría, Qta.Galia, El Sombrero 2319. ☎+58 246 616-3111. – **GU07)** Calle Andrés Eloy Blanco, Altagracia de Orituco 2320. – **GU08)** Cra 12, Entre Calles 3 y 4 N° 3-57, Calabozo 2312 ☎+58 246 871-1776.

LA00) LARA

LA01) Av. Venezuela con Calles 13 y 14, Edif.Radio Cristal, Barquisimeto 3001. ☎+58 251 252-3610. – **LA02)** Calle Sucre Entre Cras 7 y 8, La Casita, Carora 3040. ☎+58 251 421-6142 **Web:** www.angelfire.com/la/carora/ **Email:** radiocarora@cantv.net or antena@cantv.net - **FM:** 100.5. – **LA03)** Calle 4 con Cra 3, Qta.Técnica, Urb.del Este, Barquisimeto 3002. ☎+58 251 255-1690 **Email:** feloespinosa@cantv.net – **LA04)** Av. Venezuela con Calles 32 y 33, Edif.Don Martín, P4, Apto 4-A, Barquisimeto 3001. ☎+58 251 232-8145 **Web:** http://radiocontinente,tripod.com.ve **Email:** radiouniverso@cantv.net – **LA05)** Av.Pedro León Torres, Centro Comercial Venrol, locales 29 y 30, Barquisimeto 3001. ☎+58 251 446-2494 **Email:** radiominuto@cantv.net – **LA06)** Av. Vargas, Cra 16, Edif. Tricolor, Barquisimeto 3001. ☎+58 251 231-2311 **Web:** www.radiovenezuela.com.ve **Email:** radiovenezuela@hotmail.com – **LA07)** Calle 29, Entre Calles 18 y 19, Casa N° 18-74, Barquisimeto 3001. ☎+58 251 232-5386 **Email:** radiopopular@cantv.net – **LA08)** Calle 10 cruce con Calle 9, Casa S/N, El Tocuyo 3018. ☎ +58 253 663-1040. – **LA09)** Av.Libertador, altos de la Farmacia San Rafael, Cabudare 3023. ☎+58 251 261-1884. – **LA10)** Av. Bolívar, Edif. Guillermo, Locales 2 y 3, Carora 3040. ☎+58 252 421-3292 – **LA11)** Av. Los Leones, Centro Empresarial Caracas, P5, Ofc. 5-2, Barquisimeto 3002. ☎+58 251 255-0981 **Web:** www. unionradio.com.ve/

ME00) MÉRIDA

ME01) Calle 44 N° 3-57, Diagonal al Colegio de Médicos, Mérida 5101. ☎ +58 274 263-0921. – **ME02)** Cra. 4 N° 6-46, Frente a La Plaza Bolívar, Tovar 5143. ☎+58 275 873-3574. – **ME03)** Av. Gonzalo Pico, Bajando por La Facultad de Ingeniería, Qta.Radio Universidad, Mérida 5101. ☎+58 274 252-1931. – **ME04)** Av. Bolívar, Esquina Calle 11, N° 10-87, El Vigía 5145. ☎+58 275 881-4140. – **ME05)** Av.Andrés Bello, Centro Comercial Las Tapias, P3, Ofc.40-41, Mérida 5101. ☎+58 274 266-1355. 🖷+58 274 266-4712 **Web:** http://radiocontinente.tripod.com.ve **Email:** radiocumbre-crc@hotmail.com – **ME06)** Av. 3, Esquina con Calle 22, Mérida 5101. ☎+58 274 263-0466 **Email:** feloespinosa@cantv.net – **ME07)** Av. Urdaneta, Edif. La Huaca, PH, Mérida 5101. ☎+58 274 263-1560 **Web:** www. latinmail.com

MI00) MIRANDA

MI01) Calle Urdaneta N° 29, Edif. Radio Valles del Tuy, P1, Ocumare del Tuy 1209. ☎+58 239 225-0832. **Email:** rvdt1030am@telcel.net. ve – **MI02)** Edif. Electricidad De Caracas, Semi Sotano, Frente a La Plaza Bolívar, Guarenas 1220. ☎+58 212 362-1160 **Email:** rvdt1030am@telcel.net.ve – **MI03)** Calle Real Pantoja, al lado del Estadium De Barlovento, Caucagua 1246. ☎+58 234 662-1045 – **MI04)** Final Av.Tosta Gracía, Resd.Boal, Mezz.2, Charallave 1200. ☎+58 239 248-9984 **Email:** yvtz1360@cantv.net – **MI05)** Av. Concepción con Ricaurta N° 16, Guatire 1221. ☎+58 212 341-4885. **Email:** rbonita@cantv.net – **MI06)** Calle Rivas, Edif. Centro Empresarial, Torre Chocolate, P7, Ofc.7-A y 7-B, Los Teques 1201. ☎+58 212 364-8513 **Email:** metropolitana@hotmail.com

MO00) MONAGAS

MO01) Cra 5 N° 33, Antigua Calle Boyacá, Maturín 6201. ☎+58 291 641-1083. – **MO02)** Av. Bolívar,Edif.Radio Monagas, P1, Maturín 6201. ☎+58 291 641-4495. **FM:** 93.5. – **MO03)** Calle Monagas, Edif. Isnotú, PB, Maturín 6201. ☎+58 291 641-3282 **Email:** rdsn94 @cantv.net – **MO04)** Calle Sucre, Edif.Radio Maturín, PB, Maturín 6201. ☎+58 291 641-1439 **Email:** radiomaturin@cantv.net – **MO05)** Av. Bolívar, Edif.Radio Dimensión, PB, Caripito 6211. ☎+58 291 772-1082 **Email:** mrosque@cantv.net

NE00) NUEVA ESPARTA

NE01) Calle La Marina, Edif.Sta Rita, Nivel 3, Porlamar 6301. ☎+58 295 261-6656 **Web:** www.radiovenezuela.com.ve **Email:** radiovenezuela@hotmail.com – **NE02)** Av. Miranda, Edif.Best, P2,

Porlamar 6301. ☎+58 295 261-2857. – **NE03)** Calle Girardot, Urb.Cocheima, Edif. Doña Teresa, P3, La Asunción 6311. ☎+58 295 242-1383. – **NE04)** Av. 4 de Mayo, Centro Comercial Real, Local 2, Porlamar 6301. ☎ +58 295 263-2626.

PO00) PORTUGUESA

PO01) Av. 36-A, cruce con Av.Las Lagrimas, Qta.Acarigua, frente al Parque Mario Nerio, Acaragua 3301. ☎+58 255 621-3182 **Web:** www.radiovenezuela.com.ve **Email:** radiovenezuela@hotmail.com – **PO02)** Cra 9, Esq. Calle 15, Edif. D'Zonno, P3, Apto 8, Guanare 3310. ☎+58 257 251-0396. – **PO03)** Intercepción de la Autopista José António Páez con Carr.Nacional, Ospino 3319. ☎+58 256 328-2077. – **PO04)** Av. 35 con Calle 29, Edif.Radio Acarigua, Acarigua 3301. ☎+58 255 621-2067 **Web:** publiworldnet.com/radioacarigua/ **Email:** radioacarigua@cantv.net – **PO05)** Av. 24 entre Calles 5 y 6, Araure 3303. – **PO06)** Av. Peñalver con Calle 31, Edif.Los Andes, PB, Turén 3308. – **PO07)** Av. Los Próceres, Urb.Francisco de Miranda, Edif.Radial, Guanare 3310. ☎+58 257 251-5886. 🖷+58 257 253-5476 **Email:** rotelpa@cantv.net

SU00) SUCRE

SU01) Av.Perimetral, Edif.Libertad, P2, Cumaná 6101. ☎+58 293 433-2201. – **SU02)** Av.Gran Mariscal Sucre N° 30, Cumaná 6101. ☎+58 293 451-2090 **Web:** http://radiocontinente.tripod.com.ve/ – **SU03)** Av.Juncal, Edif.Siglo XX, P1, Locales B1 y B-2, Carúpano 6124. ☎+58 294 332-1402 **Web:** www.radiovenezuela.com.ve **Email:** radiovenezuela@hotmail.com – **SU04)** Av. Independencia 141, Edif. Plaza, PB, Carúpano 6124. ☎+58 294 331-0214 **Web:** www.unionradio.com.ve **Email:** solar1015fmvibracion@cantv.net – **SU05)** Av. Santa Rosa 18, Sector La Copita, frente a la Iglesia Santa Rosa de Lima, Cumaná 6101. ☎+58 293 432-2037 **Email:** radio2000@cantv.net – **SU06)** Av. Miranda, Qta.Tere, Cumaná 6101. ☎+58 293 433-4432 **Email:** feloespinosa@cantv.net

TA00) TACHIRA

TA01) Av. 19 N° 13-61, Rubio 5030. ☎+58 276 762-2263. – **TA02)** Av.1 de Mayo (Cra 3), Edif.Centro Civico, P7, San Antonio del Táchira 5007. ☎+58 276 771-2083. – **TA03)** Calle 9 N° 8-16, San Cristóbal 5001. ☎+58 276 341-4189 **Email:** ecos1947@cantv.net – **TA04)** Av. Fco. de Cáceres 9-88, Qta. Delia Mercedes, La Grita 5022. ☎+58 277 881-2583. – **TA05)** Av. Las Lomas, Edif.Primo Centro, Locales 3-12 y 3-13, San Cristóbal 5001. ☎+58 276 341-7524 **Email:** mundial860@cantv.net – **TA06)** Av. 18 de Abril, Qta.Circuito Lider, San Cristóbal 5001. ☎ +58 276 347-4594. – **TA07)** Pasaje Acueducto N° 24-60, Barrio Obrero, San Cristóbal 5001. ☎+58 276 355-0801 **Web:** www.unionradio.com.ve/ – **TA08)** Calle 2, Edif. Illinois, P2, La Fria 5020. ☎+58 277 541-1667. – **TA09)** Av. 19 de Abril con Av. 8, La Concordia, San Cristóbal 5001. ☎+58 276 344-6536. – **TA10)** Cra 4 N° 1-35, Táriba 5017. ☎+58 276 394-0758. – **TA11)** Cra 9 cruce con Calle 9, Edif.El Ciclón, P4, San Cristóbal 5001. ☎+58 276 356-7444.

TR00) TRUJILLO

TR01) Av.Bolívar, Qta.Primera N° 6-96, Antigua Casa Monseñor, Valera 3101. ☎+58 271 221-1651. – **TR02)** Av. Bolívar con Calle 15, Edif.Grasso, P1, Valera 3101. ☎+58 271 234-3755. – **TR03)** Av. 10 entre Calles 9y10, Edif.Radio Valera, Local 9-31, Valera 3101. ☎+58 271 225-3978 **Web:** www.envalera.com/radiovalera **Email:** radiovalera@envalera.com – **TR04)** Calle Independencia N° 10-11, Trujillo 3102. ☎+58 272 236-3080 **Web:** www.cnb.com.ve – **TR05)** Calle Iglesia, José Gregorio Hernández, Isnotu 3109. – **TR06)** Av. 11, entre Calles 12y13 N° 12-56, Valera 3101. ☎+58 271 225-7835 **Email:** simpatia@cantv.net – **TR07)** CalleBolívar, Plaza la Alameda, Edif.Radio Jardín, Boconó 3103. ☎+58 272 652-5574 **Email:** radiojardin@cantv.net

VA00) VARGAS

VA01) Av. Soublette, Edif. Las Américas B, P16, Maiquetía 1161. ☎+58 212 332-5401. – **VA02)** Av. Tacagua, Qta. Sola, Urb.La Atlántida, Catia La Mar 1162. (or: Ap.1812, Caracas 1060; or Edif.Cavendes, P13, Ofc. 1301, Av.Franciso de Miranda, Los Palos Grandes, Caracas 1020), ☎+58 212 351-1683.

YA00) YARACUY

YA01) Av. 10, Entre Calles 7y8, Edif.Alegría, Chivacoa 3202. ☎+58 251 883-1766. – **YA02)** Prolongación 5ta Av.Urb.Andrés Eloy Blanco, Sector la Aduana, San Felipe 3201. ☎+58 254 231-5055. 🖷+58 254 234.3453 **Email:** radioyaracuyam@cantv.net – **YA03)** Urb. Las Tunitas, Av. 4, entre Calles 4 y 5, Nirgua 3205. ☎+58 254 572-2192. – **YA04)** Av.Cartagena, entre Calles 19 y 20, Edif.Radio San Felipe, San Felipe 3201. ☎+58 254 231-5046.

ZU00) ZULIA

ZU01) Calle Central, Edif.Radio Perijá, P2, La Villa del Rosario 4047. ☎+58 263 451-1158. – **ZU02)** Calle 64 Esq.Av. 3e, Edif.La Voz de la Fe, Sector Don Bosco, Maracaibo 4002. (or: P.O.Box 459, Maracaibo 4002-A). ☎+58 261 792-3712 **Web:** www.aciprensa.com/radio/ vene.htm – **ZU03)** Av. El Muelle N° 1, Edif.Radio Libertad, frente a la Plaza Bulívar, Cabimas 4013. ☎+58 264 241-1057 **Web:** www.cnb.com.ve **Email:** orbitafm@telcel.net.ve – **ZU04)** Av. 11 N° 87-46, Edif. 95.5, PB, Sector Veritas, Maracaibo 4002. ☎+58 261 798-5674. – **ZU05)** Av. 25 con Calle Paraíso N° 24-88, Maracaibo 4005. ☎+58 261 759-1182 **Web:** www.cnb.com.ve **Email:** maracaibo@cnb.com.ve – **ZU06)** Av. 3-E N° 63-50, Sector Don Bosco, Maracaibo 4002. ☎+58 261 791-0237 **Web:** www.feyalegria.org/ve **Email:** rfya850@cantv.net or irfamaracaibo@cantv.net or glombardi@cantv.net – **ZU07)** Calle 67 cruce con Av. 27, detrás del Colegio La Epifanía, Sector Santa María, Maracaibo 4005. ☎+58 261 752-8383 **Web:** www.radiovenezuela.com.ve **Email:** radiovenezuela@ hotmail.com – **ZU08)** Av. Edif.Radio Calendario, Sector Grano de Oro, frente al Stadium Alejandro Borges, Maracaibo 4005. ☎+58 261 783-4673 **Web:** www.radiocontinente.da.ru or http://radiocontinente.tripod.com.ve **Email:** produccion@radiocontinente.zzn.com – **ZU09)** Av. 22 con Calle 26, Edif.Radio Zulia, Sector Santa María, Maracaibo 4005. ☎+58 261 752-9614. – **ZU10)** Av. Gral Trias, Machiques 4021, Distrito Perijá. – **ZU11)** Calle 74, Entre Av. 3Dy3E, Edif.Televisa, Sector La Lago, Maracaibo 4002. ☎+58 261 792-9217. – **ZU12)** Calle Manrique, Edif.Raquel, PB, Cd.Ojeda 4019. ☎+58 265 631-3707. – **ZU13)** Av. 5 N° 2-21, Sta Bárbara del Zulia 5148. ☎+58 275 555-2400. – **ZU14)** Av. 3H, Edif.Plaza, Local 2, Sierra Maestra, Maracaibo 4008. ☎+58 261 792-1330. – **ZU15)** Calle 74, Entre Av. 3Dy3E, Edif. Televisa, Sector La Lago, Maracaibo 4002 (or: Av. Andrés Bello, Edif. Ambrosio, Cabimas 4013). (Office in Maracaibo, transmitter site Cabimas) ☎+58 261 792-9217. – **ZU16)** Av. 8 Esq. Calle 73, N° 72-75, Edif. Radiolandia, Sector Santa Rita, Maracaibo 4020. ☎+58 261 797-1539. – **ZU17)** Av.Intercomunal Cabimas-Cd.Ojeda, con Calle La Planta, Cd.Ojeda 4019. ☎+58 265 662-5093. – **ZU18)** Calle 27 con Av.12 N° 12-10, Edif.Camsa, Maracaibo 4002. (or: Calle Bello Lago, Santa Cruz de Mara 4045). (Office in Maracaibo, transmitter site Santa Cruz de Mara). ☎+58 262 867-9400. – **ZU19)** Av. El Terminal, Centro Comercial Nuevo Mundo, Local 2, Caja Seca 3156. ☎+58 271 772-1087. – **ZU20)** Iglesia de María en Pentecostés, Urb.San Jacinto, primera entrada, vía El Moján, Maracaibo 4005. ☎+58 261 757 3779 **Email:** lumen 2000vzla@cantv.net or spev@cantv.net – **ZU21)** Edif.R.Marabina, Av. 25 con Calle 67 N° 24-88, Sector Paraiso, Maracaibo 4002. – **ZU22)** Sector La Salina, Los Puertos de Altagracia 4036. ☎+58 261 791-1712. – **ZU24)** Cra N. Con Av.51, Zona Industrial, Cd.Ojeda 4019. ☎+58 261 751-7540. – **ZU25)** Calle 13, Edif.La Linda, Sector Sierra Maestra, Municipio San Francisco, Maracaibo 4008. ☎+58 261 735-4892.

FM in Caracas: 88.1 Imagen – 88.9 Romántica – 89.7 X FM – 90.3 Unión Noti– 91.1 Nacional (classical) – 91.9 Avila – 92.9 RCR – 94.1 Hot 94 – 95.5 Jazz – 96.3 Estrella – 96.9 X FM – 97.7 Em.Cultural – 99.1 Mágica – 99.9 Éxitos – 101.5 Kys – 102.3 CNB – 102.7 Original –103.3 Stereo 103 – 104.5 Capital – 105.3 Planeta – 105.9 Sonera – 106.5 Fiesta 106 – 106.9 Playa 107 – 107.3 Mega 107 – 107.9 Onda.

VIETNAM

L.T: UTC +7h — **Pop:** 78 million — **Pr.L:** Vietnamese, ethnic — **E.C:** 50Hz, 127/230V — **ITU:** VTN

DÀI TIẾNG NÓI VIỆT NAM (VOV, RADIO THE VOICE OF VIETNAM) (Gov.)

🖃 58 Quan Su Str, Hanoi ☎ +84 (48) 254953 🖷 +84 48255765
Web: www.vov.org.vn Email: qhqt.vov@hn.vnn.vn
L.P: DG: Mr. Vu Van Hien. Dir. of Int. Rel: Ms. Hoang Minh Nguyet. Officer in charge of Technical Section: Mrs. Nguyen Thi Le Quan.

MW:

	kHz	Net	Station (location), schedule
1)	549	2	Hanoi: 2200-1700
1)	558v	2	Ho Chi Minh C. (Quan Tre): 2200-1700
10)	570	P	Ha Giang
11)	572	P	Binh Duong: r. inactive
12)	576	2,P	Khanh Hoa (Nha Trang): 2200-1600
1)	594	1	Danang (Site: An Hai): 2200-1700
2)	610	H	Ho Chi Minh City: 2130-1600*
1)	630	1	Quang Binh (Dong Hoi): 2200-1700
1)	648	1	Binh Dinh (Quy Nhon, Site: An Nhon): 2200-1700
14)	650	P	Bac Giang [Ha Bac]: 1030-1100
1)	657v	1	Ho Chi Minh C. (Quan Tre): 2200-1700
1)	666	1	Khanh Hoa (Nha Trang): 2200-1700
1)	675	1	Hanoi (My Van dt, Hung Yen prov.): 2200-1700
16)	690	1,4	Dac Lac (Buon Me Thuot): 2200-1600*
17)	702	2,Q,D	Danang (Site: An Hai): 2200-1600*
1)	711	1	Can Tho (Thoi Long): 2200-1700
18)	720	P	Dong Nai (Bien Hoa): r. inactive
19)	720	P	Thua Thien Hue (Hue): 2200-1310*
1)	729	2	Quang Binh (Dong Hoi): 2200-1700
60)	740	2,P	Binh Dinh (Quy Nhon, Site: An Nhon): 2200-1700
1)	747	4	Ho Chi Minh City: 2200-1300*
20)	756	P	Long An (Tan An): 2200-1100*

kHz	Net	Station (location), schedule
21) 765	P	Thai Binh: 0300-1250*
22) 782v	P	Nghe An (Vinh): ?2200-?*
1) 783	2	Can Tho (Thoi Long): 2200-1700
23) 818v	P	Dong Thap (Cao Lanh): r. inactive.
47) 819	2,4	Dac Lac (Buon Me Thuot): 2200-1600*
24) 828	P	Son La: 2200-1400*
25) 830	P	Tien Giang (My Tho): 2200-1255*
26) 837	P	Can Tho: 2200-1200*
27) 846	P	Thanh Hoa: 0400-1030*
28) 861	P	Lai Chau
1) 873	4	Can Tho (Thoi Long): 2200-1300*
30) 891	1,P	Lam Dong (Da Lat): 2200-1600*
31) 898v	P	Ha Tinh: 0400-?*
32) 899	P	Vinh Phuc: r. inactive
33) 900	1,P	Kon Tum: 2200-1600*
35) 909	P	Ca Mau [Ming Hai]: 2200-?*
1) 918	1	Cao Bang
38) 930v	P	Ben Tre: 2155-1315*
39) 954	P	Vinh Long: 2200-1145*
37) 970	P	Cao Bang
11) 970	P	Binh Duong: r. inactive
41) 972	1,P	Quang Ngai: 2200-1600*
61) 981	1,P	Gia Lai, Pleiku
36) 999	P	Lang Son
42) 999	2,P	Quang Tri
43) 1000v	P	Quang Binh (Dong Hoi): 0400-0600
44) 1035	P	Quang Ninh (Halong): 2200-?*
45) 1050v	P	Tra Vinh: ?-1130v
46) 1089	P	Kien Giang (Rach Gia):2200-1200*
48) 1098	1,P	Binh Thuan (Phan Thiet): *
49) 1098	P	Lao Cai: 2200-1400*
50) 1116	P	Bac Lieu: 2200-1200*
54) 1116	P	Ha Tay
13) 1125	P	Tay Ninh: 2200-1200*
53) 1170	P	An Giang (Long Xuyen): 2200-1200*
55) 1195	P	Hay Duong: r. Inactive
1) 1242	E	Can Tho (Thoi Long): 2200-0030, 0900-1700
56) 1278	P	Soc Trang: 2200-?*
57) 1280	P	Nam Dinh
58) 1505	P	Ba Ria Vung Tau (Vung Tau): 1000-?

*) Split schedule, see Regional sts below for details.

SW: Freq's of P sts may vary widely. Stations: Hanoi 50kW (Me Tri, G.C: 105.47E 21.01N). Xuan Mai (also known as CK2) 15/50kW (GC: 105.33E 20.43N). Buon Me Thuot 2x20kW (G.C: 108.03E 12.41N).

kHz	Net	Location, schedule
24) 4740v	P	Son La: 2200-0100, 0400-0600, 1200-1400
1) 5035	4	Xuan Mai: H'Mong Sce: 2200-0000, 1130-1330
49) 5597v*	P	Lao Cai
1) 5925	2	Xuan Mai: 2145-1700
1) 5975	1	Hanoi: 2145-1700
1) 6020	4	Buon Me Thuot: 2200-1600
1) 6165	4	Xuan Mai: H'Mong Sce: as 5035kHz
59) 6347v*	P	Yen Bai
28) 6379v	P	Dien Bien: 2200-0030, 0400-0600, 1200-1330
37) 6490v*	P	Cao Bang
49) 6665v*	P	Lao Cai
10) 7156v*	P	Ha Giang
1) 7210	1,4	Buon Me Thuot: 2145-1700
1) 9530	1	Hanoi: 2145-1700)
1) 9650	4	Xuan Mai: Hmong Sce: 0430-0600
1) 9850	4	Xuan Mai: Hmong Sce: 0430-0600
1) 9875	2	Hanoi: 0150v-1000

*) reported inactive.

Networks: 1/2/3: Voice of Vietnam 1st/2nd/3rd national prgr – **4:** Voice of Vietnam minorities network – **D:** Radio & TV Danang – **E:** Voice of Vietnam external services – **H:** Voice of the People of Ho Chi Minh City – **P:** Provincial service – **Q:** Radio & TV Quang Nam (Hoi An, Quang Nam Province). The Thoi Long high-power site (VN2) in the O Mon district, Can Tho Municipality, Mekong delta, is using 1x2000kW and 3x500kW tr's. The My Van site near Hanoi is using 700kW. The Dong Hoi site is using 2x200kW (directional).

FM: All services are also carried by numerous FM sts. Details as available for Hanoi and Ho Chi Minh City are shown here, others in the address section where known.

Location	Local	VOV2	VOV3	VOV5	External
Hanoi (MHz)	90.0+	*102.7	100.0	105.5	101.5
HCMC (MHz)	99.9	-	**104.5	105.7	-

*) High power tr, believed loc: Tam Dao in Vinh Phuc province.**) 10kW. +) ✉ 5 Huynh Thuc Khang, Dong Da District, Hanoi.

Prgrs. from Hanoi

VOV1, news & current affairs: 2200-1600 (Fri 1700). **N:** 2205, 2300, 0100, 0300, 0500, 1100, 1300, 1545.

VOV2, economic, social, cultural & education prgrs: 2200-1600. **N:** 2205, 2300, 0200, 0400, 0600, 1100, 1545.

VOV3, news & music prgrs: 24h on FM (Quang Binh 105.1MHz, Hue 106.1MHz, Danang 106.0MHz (5kW), Qui Nhon, Khanh Hoa 103.1MHz, Mekong Delta 101.0MHz and as above).

VOV4, ethnic language prgrs: Bana, Giarai, K'Hor (Koho): On 690 & 7210kHz: 2200-2300, 2330-2400, 0330-0500, 0930-1100. **Ede (Rade), Xedang (Sedang):** On 819 & 6020kHz: 2200-2300, 0400-0500, 0930-1030. **H'Mong (Ho Mong):** On 5035/6165 or 9650/9850kHz: 2200-2400, 0430-0600, 1130-1330. **N:** 2200, 2300 (rel. Netw.1), 0500, 1100 (rel. Netw. 1), 1200, 1300. **So. Khmer (Kho Me):** On 747/873kHz: 2200-2400, 0200-0600, 0800-1300, incl. VOV1 1100-1200 and further Vietnamese prgr's. Reportedly Ede, Giarai, K'Ho, Bana and M'Nong are now on the air daily at 2200-1600 on 819/6020kHz.

VOV5, prgrs for foreigners: Hanoi 105.5MHz, Ho Chi Minh City 105.7MHz: **Cambodian:** 0800-0830. **Cantonese:** 0000-0030. **Chinese:** 0400-0430, 1100-1130. **English:** 0030-0130, 0500-0600, 0900-1030, 1200-1300, 1400-1500, 1600-1730. **French:** 0130-0230, 0600-0700, 1300-1330. **Indonesian:** 0730-0800. **Japanese:** 0430-0500, 1330-1400. **Lao:** 0700-0730. **Russian:** 0230-0300, 0830-0900. **Spanish:** 1030-1100. **Thai:** 1130-1200. **Vietnamese:** 0300-0400, 1500-1600.

VOV6: Current FM schedule not available.

ANN: Vietnamese: "Dây là Tiéng Nói Viêt Nam, phát thanh tù Hà Nôi, thu dô nuóc Công Hòa Xá Hôi Chu Nghia Viêt Nam". Khmer: "Thini Vitthayu Samlang Vietnam".

Regional stations

General remarks: All schedules are based on monitoring. Further local transmissions are carried by many sts, especially in the 2200-2400, 0330-0630 and 0930-1400 periods, details unknown. A few provincial sts also operate longer hours in daytime on Sunday mornings, especially in the Mekong Delta area. Many provincial sts also relay news from Hanoi, especially at 2300-2330, 0500-0545/0600 and 1100-1130/1145 if they are on air at those times. Relays of Hanoi as a rule are not included in the schedules below. Sts broadcasting only on FM have been omitted.

ANN: Provincial services, usually identify as "Radio & TV (name of province)", in Vietnamese: "Dài Phát Thanh Truyên Hình (name)".

Addresses and other information:

1) National freqs. See above for details – **2)** 3 Nguyen Dinh Chieu, Dist. 1, Ho Chi Minh City. H: 2130-1600. News in Khmer on 610kHz: 0200. - **FM:** 99.9MHz (1100 News in English with ID as "Radio Ho Chi Minh City"). Districts: Binh Chanh (An Lac) 94.3MHz, Cu Chi 106.5MHz, Hoc Mon 93.6MHz, Nha Be 96.5MHz – **10)** Group 8, Tran Phu Ward, Ha Giang Town. P: r. 0300-0330v, 1230 – **11)** National Road 13, Phu Hoa Ward, Thu Dau Mot Town. Binh Duong Province. - **FM:** 92.5MHz – **12)** 70 Tran Phu, Nha Trang. P: ?2230-2200, 0430-0500, 1030-1100 – **13)** 188 Ward 3, 30/4 Rd, Tay Ninh. 2200-2400(Sun 0230), 0400/0430-0515, 1000-1200. - **FM**: 92.7MHz (P) – **14)** Nguyen Van Cu, Bac Giang Town – **16)** 1 Nguyen Chi Thanh, Buon Me Thuot City, Dac Lac. Netw. 4: 2200-2300, 0400-0500, 1130-1230, ? -1400 – **17) Q:** Tran Phu Road, Tan Thanh Ward, Tam Ky Town, Quang Nam: 0415-0445, 1145-1215. - **FM**: 97.6MHz (P). **D:** 19 Le Loi, Da Nang. 0445-0500, 1215-1300 (occ. to 1330). - **FM:** 94.5 (P) – **18)** Dong Khoi Road, Group 3, Tam Hoa Ward, Bien Hoa City, Dong Nai Province. P: 2200-2300, 0430-0530, 1130-1230. - **FM:** 92.5MHz – **19)** 14 Ngo Quyen / 2A Tran Cao Van, Hue City. P: 2200-2330, 0400-0600, 0955-1135 (occ. to 1310). - **FM**: 93.0MHz (P) – **20)** 15/21 1st National Road, Tan An Town. P: 2200-0030, 0430-?, 1000-1100/1210 – **21)** 2 Le Loi St, Thai Binh Town. P: 0300-0500, ? -1250 – **22)** 01 Nguyen Thi Minh Khai, Vinh City, Nghe An Province. P: ?2200-2400, 0400-0600, 1000-? FM: 103.1MHz (P), 98.0MHz (3) – **23)** Tran Phu Road, Ward 1, Cao Lanh Town, Dong Thap Province. P: 2215-2300, 0415-0500v, 1000-1100. - **FM:** 96.5/98.4MHz – **24)** Group 12, Quyet Thang Ward, Son La Town. P: – **25)** 125 Le Thi Hong Gam, Ward 4, My Tho, Tien Giang. P: 2200-?, 0430-0545, 1030-1300. - **FM:** My Tho 96.0MHz. Districts: Cai Be 94.5MHz, Cai Lay 103.5MHz, Chau Thanh (Tan Hiep) 94.0MHz, Cho Gao 88.8MHz, Go Cong Tay (Vinh Binh) 95.3MHz, Tan Phuoc (My Phuoc) 91.5MHz – **26)** 213 30 Thang 4 St, Can Tho City. P: 2200-2400, 0400-0600, 0900-1200 - **FM:** 97.3MHz (P, C) – **27)** 8 Hac Thanh St, Thanh Hoa City. P: 0400-?, 1000-1030 – **28)**

279 Muong Thanh Ward, Dien Bien Phu Town – **30)** 12 Tran Hung Dao, Da Lat City, Lam Dong Province. P: 2230-2300, 2330-2400, 0430-0500, 1030-1100, 1145-1400 – **31)** 28 - Phan Dinh Phung, Ha Tinh Town. P: 0400-0600, 1000-1100, 1145-? - **FM:** 97MHz – **32)** Ngo Quyen Ward, Vinh Yen Town. - **FM:** 89.7MHz– **33)** 258A Phan Dinh Phung St, Kon Tum. P: 2215-2300, 0430-0500, 1030-1100 – **35)** 413 Nguyen Trai, Ward 9, Ca Mau Town. P: 0400-0545, 1000-? – **36)** 9 Hoang Van Thu Rd, Lang Son Town. P: 1030-1100, 1130-1200 - **FM:** 88.2MHz – **37)** Be Van Dan Rd, Cao Bang Town – **38)** Km 98/1 Tran Quoc Tuan, Ward 4, Ben Tre Province. P: 2155-?, 0430-0530, 1200-1315. **FM:** Co Lach 88.5MHz – **39)** 50 Pham Thai Buong, Ward 4, Vinh Long Town, Vinh Long Province. P: 2200-2350(Sat 0215, Sun 0645), 0400-0645, 0900-1145. - **FM:** 90.2MHz. Districts (MHz): Vinh Long Township 93.5, Binh Minh 96.0, Long Ho 98.0, Mang Thit 95.5, Tam Binh 99.7, Tra On 93.2 – **41)** 165 Hung Vuong St, Quang Ngai Town. 1: 2200-2230, 2300-0030, 0500-0600, 0900-1030, 1100-1600. P: 2230-2300, 0430-0500, 1030-1100. - **FM**: 89.6MHz (P) – **42)** Ward 1, Dong Ha Town, Quang Tri Province. - **FM:** 92.5MHz – **43)** 54 Quang Trung St, Dong Hoi – **44)**1 Le Loi Road, Yet Kien Ward, Ha Long City, Quang Ninh Province . P: 2200-2300, 0400(occ. 0430)-0500, 1030-?- **FM:** 97.5MHz – **45)** 18 A Le Loi St, Tra Vinh Town. Prgr's in Vietnamese/Khmer: ?-0015, 0430-0530, 1000-? - **FM:** 96.6MHz– **46)** Dong Da, Vinh Lac, Rach Gia Town. Prgr's in Vietnamese, Khmer: 2200-?(Sun 0230), 0400-0555, 0900-1200 – **47)** 1 Nguyen Chi Thanh, Buon Me Thuot, Dak Lak Province– **48)** Nguyen Tat Thanh Road, Phan Thiet City, Binh Thuan Province. P: 0415-? – **49)** 200 Hoang Lien Road, Coc Leu Ward, Lao Cai. P: 2200-2300, 0330-0430, 0945-1100, 1145-1400. - **FM**: 95.2MHz (P/1) – **50)** Tra Kha, Highway 1A, Ward 8, Bac Lieu. P: 2200-2400, 0955-1200. - **FM:** 93.8MHz – **53)** 45/1 Tran Hung Dao, Long Xuyen City, An Giang Province. P: 2200-0015(Sun0145), 0330-0545, 0900-1200 in Vietnamese/Khmer - **FM:** Districts: Chau Doc 92.1MHz, An Phu 96.0MHz, Tinh Bien 107.1MHz – **54)** 32 To Hieu Road, Ha Dong Town, Ha Tay Province. - **FM**: 96.0MHz (P) – **55)** Bach Dang Rd, Hai Duong City. - **FM:** 104.5MHz – **56)** 357/1, Le Hong Phong, Soc Trang. P: 2200-2400(Sun 0205), 0400-0600, 0900-? – **57)** 255 Han Thuyen Rd, Nam Dinh City – **58)** 7 Thong Nhat Rd, Ward 1, Vung Tau City, Ba Ria-Vung Tao Province. P: 1000-? Possibly inactive. - **FM**: 102.5MHz (P) – **59)** Tran Quoc Toan. **FM:** 92.1MHz (P/1), 98.0 MHz – **60)** 181 Le Hong Phong Rd, Quy Nhon City. - **FM:** 93.2 MHz – **61)** 2 Hung Vuong Rd, Pleiku. **FM:** 93.7MHz.

VIRGIN ISLANDS (American)

L.T: UTC -4h — **Pop:** 123,000 — **Pr.L:** English, Spanish, Creole — **E.C:** 60Hz, 110V — **ITU:** VIR.

MW	Call	kHz	kW	MW	Call	kHz	kW
1)	WSTX	970	5/1	4)	WRRA	1290	0.5/0.29
2)	WVWI	1000	5/1	5)	WSTA	1340	1
3)	WGOD	1090	0.25	4)	WDHP	1620	10/1

FM	Call	MHz	kW	FM	Call	MHz	kW
6)	WIVH	90.1	1	2)	WWKS	101.3	50
7)	WYAC	93.5	9.6	12)	WEVI	101.7	0.9
8)	WJKC	95.1	50	13)	WIUJ	102.9	1.5
8)	WJKC	95.3	27	14)	WAXJ	103.5	6
9)	WIVI	96.1	2.4	15)	WZIN	104.3	44
3)	WGOD	97.9	50	16)	WMNG	104.9	6
10)	WMYP	98.3	1.9	2)	WVJZ	105.3	30
11)	WVIQ	99.5	32	17)	WVGN	107.3	1.4
1)	WSTX	100.3	7/50				

Addresses and other information

1) Family B'casting Inc., Box 3279, Christiansted, St. Croix 00822. ☎ +1 340 773-0390. **Web**: www.wstx.net (Rlg.) – **2)** Knight Quality Stations, Box 8209, St. Thomas 00801. ☎ +1 340 776 1000. **Web**: www.wvwi.net. **Stations:** KISS 101.3 FM (Urban, A/C), 105 JAMZ (CHR/reggae on 105.3) & Radio One (all talk – on 1000kHz) – **3)** Box 305012, St. Thomas 00803-5012. ☎ +1 340 774 4498. (Rlg.). **F.pl.:** 1690kHz – **4)** Box 277, Frederiksted, St. Croix 00841-0277. ☎ +1 340 772 1290. **Web:** www.wrra.vi. (Rlg.). – **5)** Box 1340, Charlotte Amalie, St. Thomas 00804-1340. ☎ +1 340 777 4500. 🖷 +1 340 776 1316. **Web:** www.wsta.com. **ANN:** "Lucky 13" – **6)** Gospel Media Institute, Christiansted, St. Croix. ☎ +1 340 778 2852. **Web**: www.wrgn.com/wivh.htm. **ANN**: "West Indies Voice Of Hope" (Rlg.) – **7)** El Morro Broadcasting, Box 25016, Christiansted, St. Croix 00824. ☎ +1 340 773 3693. **ANN**: Sistema 102 FM. (Spanish) – **8)** Isle 95, 5020 Anchors Way, Christiansted, St. Croix 00824. ☎ +1 340 773 0995. **Web**: www.isle95.com. **ANN:** "Isle 95". (Urban/reggae) – **9)** Box 304383, Charlotte Amalie, St. Thomas 00803 ☎ +1 340 774 1972. **Web**: www.piratevi.com. **ANN**: "Pirate Radio" (Classic rock) – **10)** DBA J&J Broadcasters, PO Box 142755, Arecibo, 00614 PR. (Rlg.) – **11)** JKC Communications, Christiansted, St. Croix. ☎ +1 340 773 9951. **ANN**: "Sunny 99.5" (A/C) – **12)** Frontline Missions Int'l, PO Box 892, Christiansted 00821 – **13)** Virgin Isl. Youth Development Radio, GPO, Govt. of Virgin Isl., St. Thomas 00801. ☎ +1 340 776 1029 – **14)** Reef Broadcasting, Frederiksted. (News, talk) – **15)** Nisky Mail Center, PMB 686, Charlotte Amalie, St. Thomas 00802. ☎ +1 340 776 1043. **Web**: www. buz-zrocks.com **ANN**: "The Buzz" (Current & Classic Rock) – **16)** Choice Communications Corp., Christiansted, St. Croix 00820 ☎ +1 340 713 9666. **Web:** www.viacces.net/radio/mng104. **ANN**: "Moongoose 104.9 FM" (Classic rock/oldies) – **17)** Caribbean Community Broadcasting, Nisky Mail Box, PMP 99-105, St. Thomas 00802. ☎ +1 800 275 6437. **Web**: www.wvgn.org (Public).

VIRGIN ISLANDS (British)

L.T: UTC -4h — **Pop:** 23,000 — **Pr.L:** English — **E.C:** 60Hz, 110V — **ITU:** VRG.

VIRGIN ISLANDS BROADCASTING LTD. (Comm.)

🖃 P.O. Box 78, Road Town, Tortola, BVI ☎ +1 284 494 2250/2430/6994 🖷 +1 284 494 1139 **Email:** zbvi@caribsurf.com **Web:** www.zbviradio.com & www.zbvi.vi. **L.P:** MD: Meritt Herbert. GM: Harvey Herbert. Op's Mgr: Mrs. Sandra Potter-Warrican. Production: Iris Jones. CE: Olin Hester.

MW: ZBVI 780kHz (10kW).

D.Prgr: MF 0930-0200, SS 1100-0200. **N:** W on the h. exc. 1000, 1700, 1900, 0100. Sun 1600, 2000. **Local N:** 1100, 2230.

ANN: "This is ZBVI Radio from Tortola".

ZROD (Comm.)

🖃 Road Town, Tortola, BVI ☎ +1 284 494 5832 🖷 +1 284 494 4564 **L.P:** GM: Rodney Herbert **FM:** 103.7MHz

CARIBBEAN BROADCASTING SYSTEM (Comm.)

🖃 Box 3049, Road Town, Tortola, BVI ☎ +1 284 494 4990 **L.P:** GM: Alvin Korngold **FM:** 91.7/94.3/97.3MHz (10kW). **Stations:** 91.7 ZGOLD – 94.3 ZHIT – 97.3 ZWAVE

ZJVK ISLE 95 (Comm.)

FM: Tortola 90.9MHz 1kW (relay St. Croix, US Virgin Islands).

WALLIS & FUTUNA (French)

L.T: UTC +12h — **Pop:** 15,000 — **Pr.L:** French, Wallisian — **E.C:** 50Hz, 220V — **ITU:** WAL

RADIO WALLIS ET FUTUNA

🖃 B. P. 102, 97911 Mata-Utu, Iles de Wallis et Futuna (par Nouméa, Nouvelle-Calédonie) ☎ +681 722020 🖷 +681 722346 **Web:** www.rfo.fair/wallis/wallis

L.P: SM: Joseph Blasco Head of Inf: Bernard Joyeux

MW: Mata-Utu 1188kHz 2kW **D.Prgr:** 1800-1000

ANN: "Bonjour, vous écoutez Radio Wallis et Futuna" **V.** by letter.

YEMEN

L.T: UTC +3h — **Pop:** 18m — **Pr.L:** Arabic — **E.C:** 50Hz, 220/230V — **ITU:** YEM

MINISTRY OF INFORMATION

🖃 Al-Zubairy St, P.O. Box 19560, San'a ☎ +967 1 215116/7/8 🖷 +967 1 207716 **Web:** www.yemeninfo.gov.ye **Email:** yemen-info@y.net.ye

YEMEN RADIO & TV CORPORATION

🖃 Tech. Dept., PO Box 2371, San'a ☎ +967 1 231181 🖷 +967 1 230761 **Web:** www.yradio.gov.ye **Email:** yradio@y.net.ye **L.P:** Vice Chairman: Abdul Malik Al-Arashi. Tech. Dir: Mohammed H. Bather. **Regional addresses:** P.O. Box 122, **Aden**. P.O. Box 6234, **Taiz**. P.O. Box 8367, **Mukalla**. P.O. Box 3263, **Al-Hudaydah**

MW	kHz	kW	N.	Times
San'a	711	200	G	0300-1900
Alshahr (Mukalla)	760	50	G/L	1500-2300
Al-Hiswah	792	100	2	0300-0800, 1100-2130
San'a	837v	30	2	0300-1700
			G	1700-2300

MW	kHz	kW	N.	Times
Al-Hudaydah	909	-	G/L	1500-2300
San'a	1008v	600	G	1400-2300
Taiz	1071v	30	G/L	0300-2300
Al-Hiswah	1188	-	G	0300-2300

SW: San'a (G.C: 15N22 044E11)

kHz	kW	N.	Times
5950	-	G	0300-1400
6135	-	G	0300-1500
9780v	50	G	0300-0700, 1100-2300

Networks: G= General (San'a) prgr, **2**= Second (Aden) prgr, **L**= Local prgrs (approx. 0600-1800).
FM: San'a 91.1/92.5MHz.
D.Prgr: General prgr. from San'a: 0300-2215. **N**: 0330, 0430, 0600, 0700, 0800, 0900, 1030, 1200, 1400, 1600(local), 1700, 1900, 2000, 2200. **English**: 1800-1900 (repeated next day 0600-0700). **N:** 1800, 1830. **Second prgr. from Aden**: 0300-0800, 1100-2130 (Fri 0255-2130). **N:** 0330, 0430, 0555, 1130, 1230, 1500, 1630(local), 1700, 1800, 1900, 2045. **English:** 1600-1630. **French**: 1705-1730.
IS: Flute. **ANN:** "Idha'atu-l-jumhuriya al-Yamaniya min San'a/Adan". E: "The Republic of Yemen Radio broadcasting from San'a/Aden".

ZAMBIA

L.T: UTC +2h — **Pop:** 10 million — **Pr.L:** English (official), Bemba, Lozi, Lunda, Nyanja, Tonga, Chichewa, others — **E.C:** 50Hz, 230V — **ITU:** ZMB

COMMUNICATIONS AUTHORITY OF ZAMBIA (CAZ)

Plot 3141, Lumumba Rd, P.O. Box 36871, Lusaka ☎ +260 1 241236/246702/246557/240463 Fax +260 1 246701
Web: www.caz.gov.zm **Email:** info@caz.gov.zm

ZAMBIA NATIONAL BROADCASTING CORPORATION (ZNBC)

Mass Media Complex, Alick Nkhata Rd, P.O. Box 50015, Lusaka 10101 ☎ +260 1 253301/252005 Fax +260 1 254013
Web: www.znbc.co.zm **Email:** znbc@microlink.zm **L.P:** DG: Eddy C Mupeso. Dir. Eng: Edward H Mwanza. Dir. of Prgrs: Ben Kangwa. A/Dir. of Finance:Jasat Mwanza. A/Contr. Radio:Emelde Yume. Contr. Regional Contr (North): Margaret Chimanse. Public Rel. Mgr: Mwana Kapeya. Contr. N. & Current Affairs: Nkamu Nkamu.
MW: Livingstone 2x10kW

kHz	Sce.	Times
729	R1	0245-2205
927	R2	0245-2205

SW: Lusaka (G.C:15S30 028E15): 2x100kW.

kHz	Sce.	Times
4910	R1	0245-0515,1555-2205
5915	R1	0515-1555
6165	R2	0245-2205

FM (MHz):	R1	R2	R4
Lusaka	102.6	95.8	88.2
Chipata	93.1	96.3	-
Kitwe	98.7	95.4	92.2
Kabwe	-	-	92.2
Kapiri	97.8	88.2	
Kasama	88.2	92.3	-
Livingstone	-	-	95.5
Mansa	88.6	91.7	-
Ndola	-	-	94.5
Mongu	95.1	91.9	-
Solvezi	95.1	91.6	-
Senkobo	89.3	97.1	88.0

R. One in 7 Zambian languages: 0245-2205. **N. in English** (rel. R2): 0500, (Mon-Sat)0600, 1115, 1800 – **R. Two in English:** 0245-2205. **N:** 0400, 0500, 0600W, 0800W, 1000W, 1115MF, 1400MF, 1600W, 1800, 2000, 2100 – **R. Four (music channel) in English:** 0240-2205. Also rel. VOA.
ANN: R2: "This is Radio Two of ZNBC Radio and Television Network broadcasting from Lusaka". **IS:** "Call of the Fish Eagle".

Other stations:
Breeze FM, P.O. Box 511178, Chipata: 99.6MHz. **Email:** breezefm@zamtel.zm – **Chikuni Community R,** P.O. Box 660239, Monze: 91.8MHz. **Web:** www.chikuniradio.org **Email:** chikuni@sat.signis.net – **R. Choice**, 22nd floor Findeco Houses, P.O. Box 35681, Lusaka: 107.8MHz. **Email:** choice@microlink.zm – **Five FM,** Lusaka: 105.1MHz – **Horn FM,** Lusaka: 94.2MHz – **R. Icengelo** (rlg.), P.O. Box 20694, Kitwe: 89.1MHz in English/Vernac. Also rel. BBC & VOA – **R. Liambayi,** Mongu 101.9MHz – **R. Maria Zambia** (rlg.), P.O. Box 510103, Chipata. **FM:** Kanjala 90MHz 0.3kW 15hrs a day in English/Chichewa **Web:** www.radiomaria.org **Email:** radiomar@zamnet.zm **F.PI**: another tr. in Lusaka – **R. Phoenix**, 12th Floor, ZIMCO House, Cairo Rd, Private Bag E702, Lusaka **Web:** www.radiophoenix.co.zm **Email:** rphoenix@zamnet.zm – **FM**: 0345-2210 (SS 24hrs.) Lusaka 89.5MHz, Kabwe 100MHz, Kitwe 100.5MHz, Chingola 104MHz, Kapiri/Mposhi 104.5MHz, Ndola/Luanshya 107.6MHz. Also rel. VOA – **R. QFM,** 15th floor Indeco House, P.O. Box 30896, Lusaka **Email:** qfm@zamnet.zm **FM:** Lusaka 93.2MHz, Kabwe 96.7MHz, Choma 89.8MHz, Mumbwa 89MHz, Namwala 90.6MHz – **Sky FM,** P.O. Box 31165, Lusaka: freq. not known. **Email:** skyfmbcast@zamtel.zm – **R. Yatsani** (rlg.), P.O. Box 31965, Bauleni, Lusaka: 99.1MHz 2kW 24h in English/Vernac. **Web:** www.yatsani.com **Email:** yatsani@coppernet.zm

BBC African Sce: Lusaka 98MHz.
RFI Afrique: Lusaka 100.4MHz.
Christian Voice (rlg.): **FM**: Lusaka 106.2MHz, Ndola 99.3MHz, Kitwe 105.8MHz. For SW see International Radio section.

ZIMBABWE

L.T: UTC +2h — **Pop:** 12 million — **Pr.L:** English (official), Shona, Ndebele, Chewa — **E.C:** 50Hz, 220V — **ITU:** ZWE

BROADCASTING AUTHORITY OF ZIMBABWE

Block A, Emerald Park 30, The Chase, P.O. Box MP 843, Mt. Pleasant, Harare ☎ +263 4 333032/48 Fax +263 4 333041
Web: www.zim.gov.zw

ZIMBABWE BROADCASTING CORPORATION (ZBC)

Broadcasting Centre, Pockets Hill, P.O. Box HG 444, Highlands, Harare ☎ +263 4 498610, SW station: +263 4 22104 Fax +263 4 498613 **Web:** www.zbc.co.zw/radio.htm **Email:** zbc@zbc.co.zw
Spot FM (Montrose studios): House Enstone Rd, P.O. Box 2279, Bulawayo. **R. Zimbabwe** (Mbare studios): Simon Mazorodze Rd, P.O. Box 9048, Harare. **3FM**: studios in Gweru: 43 5th St, P.O. Box 52, Gweru.
L.P: CEO: Munfaradzi Hwengwere. Hd. Finance: Francis Mamura. Hd. Radio & TV: Abigail Mvududu.

SW: Gweru (G.C: 19S26 029E51) 100kW.

kHz	Prgr	Times
3306	2	1700-0500
4828	4	24h (alt. fq to 5975)
5975	4	24h (alt. fq to 4828)
6045	2	0500-1700

FM (MHz)	R1	R2	R3	R4	kW
Beithbridge	-	98.1	-	105.2	-
Bulawayo	90.0	96.3	99.6	103.1	10
Chiredzi	93.3	95.5	98.8	102.3	-
Chivhu	93.3	96.5	103.3	106.8	-
Gokwe	-	96.8	89.6	103.5	-
Gwanda	105.8	95.4	98.7	102.2	-
Gweru	90.7	93.9	97.2	100.7	5
Harare	92.8	96.0	99.3	102.8	10
Hwange	91.5	98.2	94.7	-	-
Kadoma	88.5	94.8	98.1	101.6	10
Karoi	99.9	96.6	93.4	90.3	-
Kenmur	90.4	93.5	96.7	-	-
Lowveld	101.1	88.0	91.1	94.3	-
Masvingo	106.5	92.9	99.4	102.9	-
Mount Darwin	-	95.2	99.2	102.0	-
Mutare	105.3	89.1	98.7	105.8	3
Mutorashanga	104.7	94.3	91.1	101.1	-
Nyanga	105.5	91.7	94.9	101.7	-
Sabi/Chipinge	94.5	97.8	101.3	-	-
Victoria Falls	92.9	96.1	99.4	-	-

1) S-FM: mainly in English: 24h. **N:** on the h. Also rel. BBC & VOA.
2) R. Zimbabwe: in Shona/Ndebele/English: 24h.
3) Power FM: youth programme in English: 24h. **N:** on the h.
4) National FM: in 14 minority languages: 24h. Joint overnight service with R. Zimbabwe. **N.** in English: 0600, 1130, 1800.
ANN: In addition to programme names: "ZBC" and in connection with news: "Voice of Zimbabwe".
F.PI: "News 247", a daily 24h all-news service on SW.

LONG & MEDIUMWAVE STATION LISTINGS BY REGION

Section Contents

(For country codes please see the Country Code Table in the Reference section)

EUROPE, AFRICA, NEAR & MIDDLE EAST

Abbreviations: AFN=American Forces Network, BBCWS=British Broadcasting Corporation World Service, COPE= Cadena de Ondas Populares Espanolas, DRM=Digital Radio Mondiale, LPAMs=Low Power AM station, OCR=Onda Cero Radio, RFI=Radio France International, RSL=Restricted Service Licences, TWR=Trans World Radio, VOA=Voice of America .

Compiled by Bengt Ericson (Email: bengt.ericson@wrth.com)

kHz	kW	Ctry	Station, location
153	2x1000	ALG	RTA 1, Béchar
153	500/250	D	DLF, Donebach
153	100	NOR	NRK Europakanalen + Reg., Ingöy
153	600	ROU	R.România Actualitati, Brasov
153	300	RUS	R.Yunost, Taldom
162	2000/1000	F	France Inter, Allouis
162	150	RUS	GTRK "Bashkortostan", Ufa
162	1000	TUR	TRT 4, Agri
171	2000	MRC	Medi 1, Nador
171	1200	RUS	R.Chechnya Svob., Tbilisskaya
171	600	RUS	R.Rossii, Bolshakovo
177	500	D	DLRB, Zehlendorf (177)
180	1200	TUR	TRT4, Polatli
183	2000	D	Europe 1, Saarlouis
189	250	GEO	GR1, Dusheti
189	10	I	Raiuno + Regional, Caltanissetta
189	300	ISL	RUV, Gufuskálar
198	2x1000	ALG	RTA 1, Ouargla
198	50	G	BBC R4, Burghead
198	500	G	BBC R4, Droitwich
198	50	G	BBC R4, Westerglen
198	200	POL	PR R. Parlament/PR1, Raszyn
198	150	RUS	R. Mayak, Noginsk
198	150	RUS	R. Mayak, Olgino
198	150	RUS	R. Mayak, Ufa
198	120	TUR	TRT 1,Etimesgut
207	500/250	D	DLF, Aholming
207	100	ISL	RUV, Eidar
207	400	MRC	RTM A, Azilal
207	500	UKR	UR 1, Kyiv
216	2000	F	RMC Info/TWR, Roumoules
225	1000	POL	PR 1, Solec Kujawski
225	600	TUR	TRT 4+Reg, Van
234	500	ARM	AR, Gavar
234	2000	LUX	RTL, Junglinster
243	300	DNK	DR 1, Kalundborg
243	200	TUR	TRT4+Reg, Erzurum
252	1500/750	ALG	RTA 3, Tipaza
252	500/100	IRL	RTÉ 1, Summerhill
252	150	RUS	R. Rossii + Reg., Kazan
261	75	BUL	Horizont + Parliament Channel, Sofia
261	2500	RUS	R. Rossii, Taldom
270	650	CZE	CRo 1, Uherské Hradisté
270	50	RUS	R. Rossii + Reg., Orenburg
279	500	BLR	BR 1, Sasnovy
531	600/300	ALG	RTA 1, Ain-El-Beida
531	50	BOT	RB 1, Maun
531	2.5	D	531 Digital, Burg (silent)
531	10	E	RNE 5 TN, Cordoba
531	20	E	RNE 5 TN, Oviedo
531	10	E	RNE 5 TN, Pamplona
531	10	E	RNE 5 TN, Pontevedra
531	100/200	FRO	Útvarp Foroya, Akraberg
531	600	IRN	R.Sarasarye/VOIRI, Iranshahr
531	500	IRN	Regional, Azarshahr
531	100	ISR	Reshet Alef, Yavne
531	10	MDR	RDP Madeira, Porto Santo
531	50	NIG	Ondo State R. Corp.,Akure
531	14	ROU	R. România Actualitati, Petrosani
531	30	RUS	R. Mayak+Reg.,Cheboksary
531	10	SCG	R. Uzice, Uzice
531	1	SCG	R. Vranje, Vranje
531	160	SUI	Musigwälle, Beromünster
531	10	TZA	R. Tanzania, Dar es Salaam
540	100	AFS	R. Bop, Ga-Rankuwa
540	150	BEL	R.Twee, Waver-Overijse
540	50	E	OCR R. Barcelona, Barcelona
540	2000/1000	HNG	Kossuth R., Solt
540	200	IRN	R. Sarasarye, Mashhad
540	100	KEN	KBC, Voi
540	600	KWT	R. Kuwait 1, Sulaibiyah
540	50	MLI	ORTM, Bamako
540	300	MRC	RTM A/R, Tahadart
540	300	MRC	RTM A/R, Tanger
540	10	MWI	MBC R 1, Mangochi
540	50	NIG	Sokoto State B.C.,Sokoto
540	50	RUS	R. Mayak, Orenburg
540	50	SDN	SRTC, Nyala
549	600/300	ALG	RTA 1, S. Hamadouche
549	1	ARS	BSKSA, Gizan
549	2000	ARS	BSKSA, Qurayyat
549	20	ARS	BSKSA, Rafha
549	50	AZE	AZR 1, Gäncä
549	100	D	DLF, Nordkirchen
549	100	D	DLF, Thurnau
549	20	GAB	RTG 2, Oyem
549	70	IRL	UCB, Dundalk
549	400	IRN	R. Sarasarye, Sirjan
549	150	MDA	R. PMR, Grigoriopol
549	50	NIG	Kano State B.C.,Tukun Tawa
549	50	RUS	R. Mayak, Kaliningrad
549	1200	RUS	R. Mayak, Krasnyy Bor
549	500	RUS	R. Mayak, Kurovskaya
549	50	RUS	R. Mayak, Novocherkassk
549	150	RUS	R. Mayak, Syktyvkar
549	10	SCG	RTK Radio Kosova, Pristina
549	15	SVN	R. Koper, Beli Kriz
558	1	ARS	BSKSA, Jeddah
558	10	CYP	CBC 1, Paphos
558	20	E	RNE5 TN, La Coruna
558	20	E	RNE5 TN, San Sebastian
558	50	E	RNE5 TN, Valencia
558	100	EGY	ERTU, Cairo
558	50	FIN	YLE, Helsinki-Sandhamnen
558	1	G	Spectrum R., London
558	1000	IRN	R. Farhang, Gheslagh
558	20	KEN	KBC, Kapsimotwa
558	10	MWI	MBC R 1, Karonga
558	50	NIG	Cross River State B.C, Calabar
558	10	POR	R. Nacional, Faro (inactive)
558	400	ROU	R.Oltenia Craiova,Tirgu Jiu
558	300	SUI	RSI 1, Monte Ceneri-Cima
558	10	SVN	MMR / R. Slovenija 1, Maribor
558	600	TUR	TRT 1, Denizli
567	25	AFS	Cape Talk, Cape Town
567	5	ARS	BSKSA, Abha + 1 st
567	15	ARS	BSKSA, Afif
567	1.8	D	Radio Multikulti, Berlin
567	5	E	RNE5 TN, Marbella
567	50	E	RNE5 TN, Murcia
567	20	I	Raiuno + Regional, Caltanisetta
567	500	IRL	RTÉ 1, Tullamore
567	50	KEN	KBC, Garissa
567	10	MKD	R. Strumica
567	50	NIG	FRCN Ibadan, Alaho
567	50	NIG	Imo B.C., Owerri
567	-	NIG	Zamfara State R. Mall, Gusau
567	50	ROU	R.România Actualitati, Brasov/S.Mare
567	1000	RUS	R. Rossii + Reg., Dubovka
567	20	SVK	R. Regina Banská Bystrica, R. Sobota
567	6	SVK	R. Regina Banská Bystrica, Zilina
567	300	SYR	ORTAS 1, Damas-Adra
576	50	AFS	R. Metro FM, Meyerton
576	400	ALG	RTA 1, Béchar
576	500	BUL	Christo Botev, Vidin
576	95	D	SWR Cont.Ra., Mühlacker
576	100	E	RNE 5, Barcelona
576	750	IRN	R. Sarasarye/VOIRI, Mahshahr
576	100	LVA	Relays, Kuldiga
576	25	NIG	FRCN Ibadan, Moniya
576	100	OMA	R. Oman, Haima
576	10	POR	R. Renascenca, Braga
576	50	RUS	R. Mayak, Astrakhan
576	100	SDN	SNBC, Khartoum

kHz	kW	Ctry	Station, location
576	100	UGA	R. Uganda, Mawagga
585	1200	ARS	BSKSA, Riyadh
585	5	CVA	R.105, Vatican City
585	600	E	RNE 1, Madrid
585	8	F	FIP, Paris
585	2	G	BBC Scotland, Dumfries
585	600	IRN	R. Quran, Tehran
585	50	NIG	Enugu State B.C., Abakaliki
585	150	RUS	R. Rossii + Reg., Perm
585	350	TUN	RTT, Gafsa
585	10	TZA	R. Tanzania, Chumbum, Zanzibar
594	7	AFG	R. Faryab, Maimana
594	2000	ARS	BSKSA, Duba
594	250	BUL	Horizont, Pleven
594	90	D	hr-Info/MDR Info, Hoher Meissner
594	250	D	hr-Info/MDR Info, Rodgau
594	100	ETH	R. Ethiopia, Bahir Dar
594	20	HRV	HR Glas Hrvatske, Osijek
594	400	IRN	Regional, Shiraz
594	50	MRC	RTM A/R, Oujda
594	25	MWI	MBC R 1, Lilongwe
594	100	NIG	FRCN Kaduna, Jaji
594	100	POR	R. Renascenca, Muge
594	25	RUS	R. Mayak+Reg, Vladikavkaz
594	40	RUS	R. Rossii + Reg., Izhevsk
594	1	SVN	R.Odmev, Cerkno
594	100	SYR	ORTAS 1/2, Sarakeb
594	600	TUR	TRT 4 + Reg., Malatya
603	100	CYP	CBC 3, Nicosia
603	20	D	VoR, Zehlendorf
603	10	E	RNE 5 TN, Palencia
603	50	E	RNE 5 TN, Sevilla
603	100	EGY	ERTU, Barnis
603	300	F	France Info, Lyon
603	0.2	FIN	Radio 603 AM, Mariehamn
603	2	G	BBC R. 4, Newcastle
603	0.1	G	Capital Gold Kent, Littlebourne
603	100	IRN	Regional, Zahedan
603	-	IRQ	Radio Iraq, Baghdad (inactive)
603	10	MDR	RDP Madeira, Pico de Areeiro
603	50	NIG	Borno R. & TV Corp.,Maiduguri
603	50	ROU	Antena Satelor/R.R. Act., Bucuresti
603	14	ROU	R. România Actualitati, Oradea
603	14	ROU	R. România Actualitati, Turnu Severin
603	100/10	TZA	R. Tanzania, Dodoma
612	5	ARS	BSKSA, Hail
612	15	ARS	BSKSA, Khamasin
612	100	BHR	R. Bahrain, Manama
612	600	BIH	BH Radio 1, Sarajevo
612	10	E	RNE 1, Lleida
612	10	E	RNE 1, Vitoria
612	600	IRN	VOIRI, Qasr-e-Shirin
612	0.5	IRQ	R. Kull al-Iraq, Nasiriyah (610)
612	200	JOR	R. Jordan, Amman
612	100	KEN	KBC, Ngong
612	100	LTU	R. Baltic Waves, Vilnius
612	300	MRC	RTM A/R, Sebaa-Aioun
612	50	NIG	Kwara State B.C., Ilorin
612	40	RUS	Narodnoye R./VoR Relay, Moskva
612	150	RUS	R. Mayak, Petrozavodsk
612	5	UKR	BBC, Kyiv
612	5	UKR	BBC, Taranivka
621	7	AFG	R. Paktia, Gardez
621	300	BEL	Première RTBF 1, Wavre
621	100	BOT	RB 1, Selebi-Phikwe
621	100	CNR	RNE 1, Santa Cruz, Tenerife
621	10	E	RNE 1, Avila
621	10	E	RNE 1, Jaén
621	10	E	RNE 1, Palma de Mallorca
621	1000	EGY	ERTU, Batra
621	20	IRN	Regional, Birjand
621	20	NIG	Anambra Broadcasting Sce., Akwa
621	5	RUS	R. Rossii + Reg., Kochubey
621	50	RUS	R. Rossii + Reg., Syktyvkar
621	50	RUS	R. Rossii+Reg, Makhachkala
621	5	SVK	R. Regina Banská Bystrica, Orava
621	50	TZA	R. Tanzania, Mbeya
630	20	ARS	BSKSA, Gizan
630	10	ARS	BSKSA, Najran
630	0.2	G	BBCThree Counties R., Luton
630	2	G	R. Cornwall, Redruth
630	10	KWT	R. Kuwait, Kuwait city
630	2x75	MDG	RNM 1, Antananarivo
630	50	NIG	Rivers State B.C., Pt. Harcourt
630	100	NOR	NRK Europakanalen + Reg., Vigra
630	10	POR	RDP-Antena 1, Montemor + 2 st's
630	400	ROU	Antena Satelor/R.R. Act., Voinesti
630	400	ROU	R. Timisoara/R.R. Act., Ortisoara
630	42	RUS	R. Mayak, Saratov
630	600	TUN	RTT, Tunis-Djedeida
630	300	TUR	TRT 4 + Reg, Cukurova
639	500	CYP	BBC, Zygi
639	30	CZE	CRo 2 + Cro 6, Ostrava-Svinov
639	1500	CZE	CRo 2 + Cro 6, Praha (Liblice)
639	300	E	RNE 1, A Coruña
639	10	E	RNE 1, Albacete
639	20	E	RNE 1, Almeria
639	50	E	RNE 1, Bilbao
639	50	E	RNE 1, Zaragoza
639	400	IRN	VOIRI, Bonab
639	50	KEN	KBC, Garissa
639	1	MKD	R. Stip, Stip
639	25	NIG	Kaduna S.M.C., Katabu(638)
639	200	SDN	SRTC, Juba+ 1 st
639	50	UGA	R. Uganda, Kampala
648	2000	ARS	BSKSA, Jeddah
648	1	AZR	R. Lajes, Lajes
648	50	BOT	RB 1, Mopipi
648	30	BUL	Christo Botev + R. Plovdiv, Plovdiv
648	50	E	RNE 1, Badajoz
648	500	G	BBC W.S., Orfordness
648	50	GMB	Gambia RTV, Bonto
648	10	IRN	Regional, Shahr-e-Kord
648	300	LBY	LJB, Tobruk
648	10	SVN	R. Murski Val, Nemèavci
648	100/10	TZA	R. Tanzania, Nachingwea
648	150	UKR	UR 1, Oktiabrske
657	50	AFS	R. Pulpit / R. Kansel, Meyerton
657	20	ARS	BSKSA, Rafha
657	50	E	RNE 5 TN, Madrid
657	0.5	G	R. Cornwall, Bodmin
657	2	G	R. Wales, Wrexham
657	120	I	Raiuno + RAI International, Napoli
657	25	I	Raiuno + Regional, Bolzano
657	50	I	Raiuno, Torino
657	100	IRN	R. Sarararye, Zahedan
657	200	ISR	Reshet Bet, Yavne
657	100	NIG	FRCN Ibadan, Ibadan
657	150	RUS	R. Rossii, Murmansk
657	100	RUS	R.Rossii+R.ChS., Alpatovo
657	2x50	TZA	R. Tanzania, Dar-es-Salaam
657	100	UAE	Asianet Radio, Sadiyat
657	25	UKR	UR 2/3/FS, Chernivtsi
666	5	ALG	R. Saoura, Tindouf
666	150	D	SWR Cont.Ra, Rohrdorf
666	50	E	SER R. Barcelona, Barcelona
666	0.34	G	Classic Gold 666/954, Exeter
666	0.5	G	R. York, Fulford
666	15	GRC	Filia Radio, Athens
666		IRN	R. Sarararye, Shushtar
666	500	LTU	LR 1, Sitkunai
666	50	NIG	Edo State Broadc.Sce, Benin City
666	10	POR	RDP-Antena 1, Vila Real + 5 st's
666	20	REU	R. Réunion, St. Pierre
666	25	RUS	R. Mayak, Sochi
666	10	SCG	Radio Sombor, Sombor
666	5	SDN	SRTC, Kassala
666	600	SYR	ORTAS 1, Damas-Sabboura
675	5	ARS	BSKSA, Abha
675	20	ARS	BSKSA, Afif
675	100	F	Superloustic, Marseille
675	100	HOL	Arrow Rock Radio, Lopik
675	50	IRN	Regional, Hamadan
675		IRQ	R. Iraq, Baghdad
675	50	KEN	KBC, Marsabit
675	100	LBY	LJB, Benghazi
675	50	MWI	MBC R 1, Ekwendeni
675	25	NIG	R. Oyo, Ojeowode
675	20	NOR	NRK Europakanalen + Reg., Röst
675	50	QAT	QBS, Al Khaisah
675	5	SCG	RTS Beograd 1, Bosilegrad
675	25	UKR	UR1, Uzhhorod
684	50	ARS	BSKSA, Jeddah
684	10	ARS	BSKSA, Riyadh
684	600	E	RNE 1, Sevilla
684	100	ETH	R. Ethiopia, Metu

kHz	kW	Ctry	Station, location
684	100	IRN	Regional , Mashhad
684	-	LBN	V.o.the Opressed,Baalbekk
684	10	MAU	R.Maurice, Malherbes
684	50	NIG	Yobe B. C., Damaturu
684	10	RUS	Relays, St. Petersburg
684	200	SCG	RTS Beograd 1, Aleksinac
684	10	TUN	RTT, Mednine
693	5	ALG	RTA 2, Reggane
693	20	ARS	BSKSA, Tabuk
693	10	AZR	RDP Antena 1 Açores, Santa Barbara
693	25	BOT	RB 1, Sakawe
693	10	CYP	CBC 1, Limassol
693	20	E	RNE 1, Toledo
693	10	E	RNE 1, Tortosa
693	50	G	BBC R. 5 Live, 10 st's
693	150	G	BBC R. 5 Live, Droitwich
693	20	I	Raiuno, Potenza
693	100	IRN	Regional, Bandar-e-Lengeh
693	-	JOR	R. Jordan, unk. location
693	-	LBY	LJBC, unkn. location (690 v.freq.)
693	10	NIG	Kogi State Broadc.Corp., Ochaja
693	20	RUS	Deutsche Welle, Moskva
693	150	RUS	R. Rossii, Ufa
693	5	SCG	RTS Beograd 1, Negotin
693	1	SOM	R. Hargesia, Hargesia
702	100	AFS	702 Talk Radio, Ga-Rankuwa
702	10	AGL	RNA Canal A, Mulenvos
702	40	ARS	BSKSA, Duba
702	10	BUL	Christo Botev, Pirin
702	5	D	NDR Info Spezial, Flensburg
702	5	D	Truck Radio, Jülich
702	10	EGY	ERTU, Asswan
702	10	EGY	ERTU, El Kharga
702	40	F	RMC, Col de la Madone (silent)
702	500	IRN	R. Sarasarye, Bushehr
702	500	IRN	VOIRI, Kiashahr
702	100	KEN	KBC, Meru
702	140	MRC	RTM C, Sebaa-Aioun
702	25	NIG	Taraba State B.S., Wukari
702	800	OMA	BBC W.S., A'Seela
702	40	SVK	R. Regina Kosice + R. Patria, Presov
702	-	SYR	Al-Quds Radio, Southwest Syria
702	1200	TUR	TRT 4, Catalca
711	5	D	SWR Cont.Ra., Ulm+ 1 st
711	5	E	COPE Murcia
711	100	EGY	ERTU, Tanta
711	300	F	France Info, Rennes
711	200	IRN	Regional/VOIRI, Ahwaz
711	50	LBY	LJB, Ghadames
711	50	LBY	LJB, Jefren
711	50	LBY	LJB, Sebha
711	7.5	MRC	RTM A, Sidi-Bennour
711	300	MRC	RTM A/R, Dakhla
711	50	ROU	R. România Actualitati, Sighetul M.
711	7	RUS	R.Rossii + Reg., Naryan-Mar
711	10	SCG	RTS Beograd 1 + R. Nis, Nis
711	100/10	TZA	R. Tanzania, Kigoma
711	50	UKR	UR1, Dokuchalevsk
711	200	YEM	YRTC, San'a
720	20	CNR	RNE 5, Santa Cruz, Tenerife
720	500	CYP	BBC, Zygi
720	85	D	WDR 2/VERA, Langenberg
720	0.75	G	BBC R. 4, Crystal Palace, London
720	10	G	BBC R. 4, Lisnagarvey
720	0.25	G	BBC R. 4, Londonderry
720	750	IRN	Regional /VOIRI, Mahidasht
720	400	IRN	Regional /VOIRI, Tayebad
720	1	MKD	R. Veles, Veles
720	50	NIG	Imo Broadc. Corp., Owerri
720	10	POR	RDP-Antena 1, Porto + 5 st's
720	14	ROU	R.România Actualitati,Sinaia + 2 st's
720	100	TUN	RTT, Sfax-Sidi Mansour (silent)
720	50	TZA	R. Tanzania, Mwanza
729	25	AFS	Klipheuwel (silent)
729	1	D	Bayern 1, Hof/Würzburg
729	10	D	DRM, Putbus
729	10	E	RNE 1, Alicante
729	10	E	RNE 1, Cuenca
729	20	E	RNE 1, Logrono
729	20	E	RNE 1, Malaga
729	100	E	RNE 1, Oviedo
729	10	E	RNE 1, Valladolid
729	0.2	G	BBC Essex, Manningtree
729	150	GRC	ERA 1, Athens
729	10	IRL	RTE 1/R.Cork, Cork
729	25	NIG	Kano State Broadc. Corp., Jogana
729	20	REU	R. Réunion, St. Andre
729	50	RUS	Narodnoye Radio, Samara
729	2x750	UAE	UAE Radio, Sadivat
729	100	UGA	R. Uganda, Butebo
738	600	E	RNE 1, Barcelona
738	5	F	RFI, Paris
738	0.04	G	BBC Hereford&Worcester, W
738	-	IRN	Regional, Dayyer
738	50	MOZ	Antena Nacional, Hillel
738	100	OMA	R. Oman, Salalah
738	5	RUS	WRN Relay, Moskva
747	1	ARS	BSKSA, Najran
747	100	BFA	R. Burkina, Ougadougou
747	500	BUL	Horizont + Foreign Sce, Petrich
747	10	BUL	Horizont + Turkish sce., Salmanrovo
747	20	CNR	RNE 5, Las Palmas
747	10	E	RNE 5 TN, Cádiz
747	10	GMB	Gambia RTV, Basse
747	400	HOL	R. 747 AM, Flevoland
747	150	IRN	Regional, Gonbad
747	100	KEN	KBC, Ngong
747	10	SDN	SRTC, Khartoum
747	5	SDN	SRTC, Port Sudan
747	100	SYR	ORTAS 1, Sarakeb
756	200	D	DLF, Braunschweig
756	100	D	DLF, Ravensburg
756	10	E	R. Euskadi, Bilbao
756	10	EGY	ERTU, Qena
756	2	G	BBC R 4, Redruth
756	1	G	R. Cumbria, Carlisle
756	0.63	G	R. Maldwyn 756, Newton
756	100	IRN	R. Sarasarye / VOIRI, Rasht
756	-	IRQ	R. Ma'alumat, Northern Iraq
756	-	LBN	R. Mashreg, Kfar-Killa
756	25	MWI	MBC R 1, Blantyre
756	25	NIG	Borno Radio & TV Corp., Damagun
756	50	NIG	Niger State Media B.C., Minna
756	100	NIG	R. Oyo, Ibadan
756	2	POR	RDP-Antena 1, Lamego
756	400	ROU	R.R.Cultural+RRI, Lugoj
756	50	YEM	YRTC, Mukalla (760)
765	20	ARS	BSKSA, Khamasin
765	10	ARS	BSKSA, Qurayyat
765	0.5	G	BBC Essex, Chelmsford
765	10	GRC	ERA Regional, Ioannina
765	600	IRN	VOIRI, Chah Bahar
765	50	MOZ	EP de Nampula, Nampula
765	150	RUS	R. Rossii + Reg,Petrozavodsk
765	1	SCG	RTS Beograd 1, Medvedja
765	50	SDN	SRTC, Omdurman
765	300/10	SEN	RTV du Sénégal, Dakar
765	600	SUI	Option Musique, Sottens
765	600	TUR	TRT4+Reg.,Gaziantep
765	75	UKR	R. Maiak, Petrivka
774	50	AGL	EP de Benguela, Benguela
774	2	BIH	R. Tuzla, Tuzla
774	75	BUL	Radio Varna, Varna
774	5	D	WDR 2/VERA, Bonn
774	10	E	RNE 1, 4 st's
774	60	E	RNE 1, Cáceres
774	20	E	RNE 1, Ourense
774	50	E	RNE 1, San Sebastián
774	100	E	RNE 1, Valencia
774	500	EGY	ERTU, Abis
774	1	G	BBC R4, Enniskillen + 1 st
774	0.14	G	Classic Gold 774, Gloucester
774	0.7	G	R. Kent, Littlebourne
774	0.5	G	R. Leeds, Farnley
774	50	HRV	HR Glas Hrvatske, Hvar
774	100	IRN	Regional, Arak
774	600	MRC	RTM A/R, Agadir
774	10	NIG	Taraba State B.S.,Wukari
774	30	RUS	R. Mayak+ Reg., Voronezh
783	20	ALG	RTA 3, Laghouat
783	100	ARS	BSKSA, Dammam
783	100	D	MDR Info, Leipzig
783	50	E	COPE Miramar, Barcelona
783	10	HRV	HR Glas Hrvatske, Buje
783	150	IRN	Regional, Iranshahr
783	50	MTN	R. Mauritanie, Nouakchott

kHz	kW	Ctry	Station, location
783	50	NIG	R. Kogi, Okene
783	10	POR	R. Nacional, Miramar
783	0.2	SCG	R. Stara Pazova 2, Stara Pazova
783	5	SDN	SNBC, Atbara
783	300	SYR	ORTAS 1/E, Tartus
792	50	ARS	BSKSA, Jeddah
792	2	BIH	Radio Banovici, Banovici
792	5	D	NDR Info Spezial, Lingen
792	50	E	SER R. Sevilla, Sevilla
792	300	F	France Info, Limoges
792	1	G	BBC R. Foyle, Londonderry
792	0.275	G	Classic Gold 828/792, Bedford
792	600	GRC	ERA 2/ VOA, Kavala
792	50	IRN	Regional, Zanjan
792	20	LBY	LJB, Sirt
792	25	NIG	R. Oyo, Gambari
792	50	RUS	Regional, Astrakhan
792	5	SVK	R.Slovensko/R.Regina Bratislava, B.
792	100	YEM	YRTC, Al-Hiswah
801	150	AZE	AZR 1, Pirsaat
801	-	AZE	AZR 1, Quba
801	15	AZE	BBC, Baki
801	100	BHR	R. Bahrain, Manama
801	100	D	Bayern 1, München-Ismaning
801	10	D	Bayern 1, Nürnberg-Dillberg
801	25	E	RNE 1, Ciudad Real
801	20	E	RNE 1, Lugo
801	10	E	RNE 1, Zamora + 3 st's
801	2	G	R. Devon, Barnstaple
801	50	IRN	R. Sarasarye, Kashmar
801	2000(?)	JOR	R. Jordan, Ajlun
801	1	NIG	R. Kebbi , Zuru
801	20	NIG	Yobe B..C., Damaturu
801	5	SDN	SRTC, Al-Fashir
810	20	ARS	BSKSA, Hafral Baten
810	20	E	SER R. Madrid, Madrid
810	100	G	BBC Scotland, Burghead
810	5	G	BBC Scotland, Redmoss
810	100	G	BBC Scotland, Westerglen
810	100	IRN	R.Sarasarye, Khorramabad
810	1200	MKD	MR 1 + DW, Ovce Pole
810	50	MOZ	EP da Gaza, Xai-Xai
810	10	MWI	MBC R 1, Bangula
810	500	RUS	R. Mayak, Dubovka
810	20	RUS	VOA relay, Kurkino
810	100	SDN	SRTC, Juba (u.c.)
810	50	UAE	UAE Radio, Maqtaa
810	100	UGA	R. Uganda, Bobi
819	10	E	R. Euskadi, San Sebastián
819	1000	EGY	ERTU, Batra
819	20	F	Sud Radio, Toulouse
819	20	I	Raiuno + Regional, Trieste
819	30	IRN	Regional, Sari
819	10	MAU	R. Mauritius, Malherbes
819	25	MRC	RTM A, Rabat
819	5	SDN	SRTC, Dongola
828	20	ARS	BSKSA, Medinah
828	1	AZR	RDP Antena 1 Açores, Mt.das Cruzes
828	500	BUL	Christo Botev, Shumen
828	50	BUL	Christo Botev, Sofia
828	20/5	D	NDR Info Spezial, Hannover
828	10	D	SWR Cont.ra, Freiburg
828	5	E	SER R. Terrassa, Terrassa
828	100	ETH	R. Ethiopia, Arba Minch
828	0.2	G	BBC Asian Network, Sedgley
828	0.27	G	Classic Gold 828, Bournemouth
828	0.2	G	Classic Gold 828/792, Luton
828	0.12	G	Magic 828, Leeds
828	50	IRN	Regional, Tabas
828	300	LBY	LJB, Sebha
828	50	MRC	RTM A/R, Oujda
828	25	NIG	FRCN Enugu, Enugu
828	1	POR	R. Nacional, 5 st's (inactive)
828	50	RUS	R.Rossii+Reg,Nizhniy Novgorod
828	10	RUS	RFE/RL Relay, St. Petersburg
828	200	SYR	ORTAS 1, Deir-ez-Zor(v.freq.)
828	1	UAE	UAE Radio, al Ain
837	10	AZR	RDP Antena 1 Açores, P. da Barossa
837	10	CNR	R. Popular, Las Palmas
837	10	E	COPE, Burgos
837	5	E	COPE, Eivissa
837	5	E	COPE, El Ferrol
837	10	E	COPE, Sevilla
837	100	ERI	V.o. the Broad Masses, Asmara
837	200	F	France Info, Nancy
837	0.5	G	BBC Asian Network,Freemen's Com.
837	1	G	R. Cumbria, Barrow
837	1	HRV	HR Glas Hrvatske, Gospic
837	300	IRN	Regional, Isfahan
837	10	LBN	R. Lebanon, Amchit
837	1000	LBN	R. Lebanon, Hamat (inactive)
837	10	SCG	RTN, R. Novi Sad, Sombor
837	1	TZA	R. Tanzania, Dar-es-Salaam
837	30	YEM	YRTC, San'a
840	20	TCD	RNT, N`djamena
846	100	AFS	Umhlobo Wenene FM, Komga
846	20	ARS	BSKSA, Buraida
846	100	IRL	R. North, Galway
846	10	IRN	R.Sarasarye, Mianeh
846	5	ISR	Reshet Bet, Zefat
846	100	KEN	KBC, Nyaminia
846	10	NIG	Bauchi R. Corp., Azare
846	150	RUS	R. Radonzeh + Reg., Noginsk
846	42	RUS	R. Rossii + Reg., Elista
846	10	RUS	R. Yunost, Perm
846	20	UAE	UaQ Radio, Umm al Qiwain
850	1	TCD	R. Sarh, Sarh
855	100	ARS	BSKSA, Dammam
855	25	D	DRM test/Special AM tr., Berlin
855	5	D	Truck Radio, Nordkirchen
855	10	E	RNE 1, 5 st's
855	50	E	RNE 1, Camargo
855	5	E	RNE 1, Marbella
855	300	E	RNE 1, Murcia
855	20	E	RNE 1, Pontevedra
855	20	E	RNE 1, Tarragona
855	100	ETH	R. Ethiopia, Harar
855	1	G	R. Devon, Plymouth
855	1	G	R. Lancashire, Preston
855	1.5	G	R. Norfolk, Postwick
855	0.15	G	Sunshine 855, Ludlow
855	10	JOR	R. Jordan, Amman
855	1500	ROU	R. România Actualitati/VOA, Lugoj
855	50	RUS	R. Rossii + Reg. , Kamenka
864	5	AFG	Peace Radio, Kandahar
864	1000	ARM	FS/Relays, Gavar
864	10	BUL	Horizont + Turkish sce., Samuil
864	150	BUL	R. Blagoevgrad, Blagoevgrad
864	7	CZE	CRo 2, Strakonice
864	10	E	RNE 1, Socuellamos
864	500	EGY	ERTU, Santah
864	300	F	La City Radio de Paris, Paris
864	50	IRN	Regional, Qasr-e-Shirin
864	7.5	MRC	RTM A, Errachidia
864	7.5	MRC	RTM A, Laayoune
864	1	SVK	R. Regina Banská Bystrica, Cadca
864	1	SVK	R. Regina Kosice + R. Patria, Snina
873	5	ALG	RTA C, Ghardaia
873	10	ARS	BSKSA, Qassim
873	50	BOT	RB 1, Gansti
873	60	BUL	R. Stara Zagora, Stara Zagora
873	150	D	AFN Power Network, Frankfurt
873	10	E	SER R. Galicia, Stgo de Comp.
873	25	E	SER R. Zaragoza, Zaragoza
873	100	ETH	R. Ethiopia, Addis Ababa
873	0.3	G	R. Norfolk, West Lynn
873	1	G	R. Ulster, Enniskillen
873	22	HNG	Kossuth Radio+Ethnic prgrs, Lakihegy
873	20	HNG	R. Petöfi + R. Pécs, Pécs
873	1	I	Raiuno, Taranto
873	80	LBN	La Voix du Liban, Beirut
873	75	MDA	R. Moldova 1, Chisinau
873	50	MOZ	EP de Sofala, Beira
873	150	RUS	R. Rossii + Reg., Olgino
873	1250	RUS	R. Rossii, Elektrostal
873	50	RUS	R. Rossii, Kaliningrad
873	1200	RUS	R. Rossii, Novosemeykino
873	10	SDN	SRTC, Wad Madani + 1 st.
873	50	SYR	ORTAS 2, Damascus-Adra
873	10	UKR	Reg., Dnipropetrovsk
882	7	AFG	R. Kandahar, Kandahar
882	100	ARS	BSKSA, Dammam
882	20	CNR	R.P. de Tenerife,La Laguna
882	20	D	MDR Info, Wachenbrunn
882	20	E	COM Rádio, Barcelona
882	5	E	COPE Gijón

kHz	kW	Ctry	Station, location
882	10	E	COPE, Alicante
882	5	E	COPE, Málaga
882	5	E	COPE, Valladolid
882	10	EGY	ERTU, Matruh + 1 st
882	100	G	R.Wales,Washford + 3 st's
882	60	IRN	Regional, Mahabad
882	10	ISR	Reshet Bet, Shear-Yashuv
882	50	KEN	KBC, Kitale
882	25	NIG	Capital Sound, Kafanchan
882	30	RUS	R. Mayak+Reg., Stavropol
882	300	SCG	R. Podgorica, Podgorica
882	1	TUN	RTT, Remada (silent)
891	600/300	ALG	RTA 1, Alger
891	30	AZE	AZR 1, Baki
891	20	HOL	R. 538, Hulsberg
891	50	IRN	Regional, Yasuj
891	100	LSO	R. Lesotho, Lancer's Gap
891	-	NIG	Osun State B.C., Osu
891	20	POR	R. Renascenca, Vila Moura
891	50	RUS	R. Yunost, Petrozavodsk
891	600	TUR	TRT4+Reg., Antalya
900	1000	ARS	BSKSA, Qurayyat
900	5	E	COPE, Cáceres
900	5	E	COPE, Granada
900	5	E	COPE, Vigo
900	10	E	R. Popular de Bilbao, Bilbao
900	600	I	Raiuno+RAI International, Milano
900	600	IRN	R. Sarasarye, Tehran
900	100	KEN	KBC, Marania
900	25	NIG	Ogun State B.C., Abeoukuta
900	20	RUS	R. Mayak + Reg., Sovietskiy
900	6	SVK	R. Regina Kosice, Poprad
909	10	AFG	RTV Afghanistan, Kabul
909	10	AZR	R.C.de Angra, Angra do H.(inactive)
909	600	BOT	VOA, Selebi-Phikwe
909	10	E	RNE5 TN, Palma de M.
909	50	G	BBC R.5 Live, 9 st's
909	150	G	BBC R.5 Live, Brookmans Park
909	200	G	BBC R.5 Live,Moorside Edge
909	5	GEO	GR1/R.Ajaria, Batumi
909	50	IRN	R.Sarasarye, Lar
909	20	IRQ	Radio Nahrain, Basra
909	20	LBY	LJB, Giaghboub
909	10	LBY	LJB, Kufra
909	20	MRC	RTM B, Safi
909	50	NIG	FRCN Abuja, Fwagwa Lada
909	400	ROU	R. Cluj, Cluj
909	50	ROU	R. România Actualitati, Timisoara
909	14	ROU	R.Constanta/Ant Satelor, Valu I. Traian
909	5	SDN	SRTC, Malakal
909	20	UGA	R. Uganda, Kampala
909	-	YEM	YRTC, Al-Hudaydah
918	10	CYP	CBC 3, Paphos
918	20	E	R. Intercontinental, Madrid
918	10	EGY	ERTU, Bawti
918	10	EGY	ERTU, Hurghada
918	50	IRN	Regional, Jiroft
918	50	MOZ	R. Cidade, Maputo (inactive)
918	50	NIG	Lagos State B.C., Ikeja
918	50	NIG	R. Benue, Makurdi
918	50	RUS	R. Mayak + Reg., Makhachkala
918	150	RUS	R. Rossii + Reg., Arkhangelsk
918	75	RUS	R.Svobodnaya Rossiya, Moskva
918	300	SVN	R. Slovenija 1, Domzale
918	200	SYR	ORTAS 1, Al-Hassake
927	5	ALG	RTA 1, Timimoun
927	20	ARS	BSKSA, Aflaj
927	300	BEL	R.Een/Sporza, Wolvertem
927	50	GRC	ERA Regional, Zakynthos
927	10	IRN	R.Sarasarye, Dorud
927	50	ISR	Reshet Bet, Akko
927	1	ISR	Reshet Bet, Eilat
927	100	KEN	KBC, Malindi
927	1	POR	R. Renascenca, Evora
927	5	SVK	R. Patria, Kosice
927	25	SVK	R. Patria, Nitra
927	200	TUR	TRT 1, Izmir
936	1	ARS	BSKSA, Riyadh
936	50/10	D	Bremen 1, Bremen
936	20	E	RNE 5 TN, Valladolid
936	20	E	RNE 5 TN, Zaragoza
936	20	E	RNE5 TN, Alicante
936	10	EGY	ERTU, Salum
936	0.18	G	Classic Gold 936/1161, Naish Hill
936	1	G	Fresh Radio, Hawes
936	20	I	Raiuno + Regional, Venezia
936	10	I	Raiuno, Trapani
936	50	IRN	Regional, Urumiyeh
936	10	MKD	R.Gevgelija, Gevgelija
936	100	MRC	RTM C, Agadir
936	5	RUS	R. Rossii + Reg., Matveyevka
936	1	SCG	R. Srem, Ruma
936	100	SYR	ORTAS 1, Homs
936	3	UKR	UR1, Staroblisk
936	1000	UKR	VoR Relay, Lviv
945	25	AGL	R.N'Gola Yetu/Canal A, Mulenvos
945	5	ARS	BSKSA, Hail
945	100	ERI	V.o. the Broad Masses, Asmara
945	300	F	France Blue, Toulouse
945	0.7	G	Capital Gold 1323/945, Bexhill
945	0.2	G	Classic Gold GEM, Derby
945	5	GRC	ERA Regional, Larissa
945	100	IRN	Regional, Dehgolan
945	2.7	LVA	R. Nord, Riga
945	2	MKD	R. Kumanovo, Kumanovo
945	10	NIG	R. Kebbi, Birnin Kebbi
945	14	ROU	R.România Actualitati, Miercurea Ciuc
945	40	RUS	R. Rossii + Reg., Novocherkassk
945	5	SDN	SRTC, Al-Foula
945	20	STP	R. Nacional, Sao Tomé
954	200	CZE	CRo 2 + Cro 6, Brno + 2 st's
954	50	E	OCR Madrid, Madrid
954	0.4	G	Classic Gold 666/954, Torbay
954	0.16	G	Classic Hits, Hereford
954	10	GRC	ERA Regional, Heraklion
954	100	ISR	Reshet Bet, Yavne
954	100	KEN	KBC, Nyaminia
954	1500	QAT	QBS, Al Arish
954	1.7	SWZ	R. Swaziland, Sidvokodvo
954	50	SYR	ORTAS 2, Deir ez-Zor
954	300	TUR	TRT4+Regional, Trabzon
963	1.6	BEN	RTV Bénin, Parakou (inactive)
963	40	BUL	Horizont, Sofia+ 2st's
963	75	BUL	R. Shumen, Shumen
963	100	CYP	CBC 1, Nicosia
963	10	E	R. Euskadi, Vitoria
963	600	FIN	YLE, Pori
963	0.2	G	Asian Sound R., Haslingden
963	0.95	G	Club Asia, E. London
963	50	IRN	R. Sarasarye, Birjand
963	20	KWT	R. Kuwait, Kuwait city
963	50	MOZ	EP de Tete, Tete
963	0.1	POL	Twoje R. Lipsko, Lipsko
963	10	POR	R. Renascenca, Seixal
963	5	RUS	Radiotserkov, Moskva
963	100	SDN	SRTC, Khartoum
963	1	SEN	RTV duSenegal, Orossogui (960)
963	200	TUN	RTT, Tunis-Djedeida
972	50	BOT	RB 1, Sebele
972	100	D	NDR Info Spezial, Hamburg
972	5	E	RNE 1, Cabra
972	2	E	RNE 1, Monf. de Lemos
972	100	ETH	R. Ethiopia, Robe
972	1	G	Club Asia, W. London
972	100	IRN	Regional, Ilam
972	20	LBY	LJB, Sirte
972	5	MRC	RNE 1, Mellilla
972	25	NIG	Katsina State Radio, Katsina
972	10	NIG	R. Kogi, Otite
972	2x50	UAE	UAE Radio, Fujairah
972	500	UKR	VoR Relay, Mykolaiv
981	600/300	ALG	RTA 2, Alger
981	20	ARS	BSKSA, Madinah
981	150	BUL	R. Varna, Varna
981	10	EGY	ERTU, Assiut + 2 st's
981	5	F	Ciel AM, Alfortville (Paris)
981	200	GRC	ERA Sport, Athens-Megara
981	10	I	Regional, Trieste
981	1	IRL	R.Star Country, Emyvale, Co.Monagh
981	100	IRN	R.Sarasarye, Hamadan
981	100	KEN	KBC, Voi
981	10	POR	R. Renascenca, Coimbra + 3 st's
990	50	AGL	EP do Bié, Kuito
990	600	CYP	R.Sawa, Cape Greco
990	100	D	DLR Berlin, Berlin
990	10	E	SER R. Bilbao, Bilbao

kHz	kW	Ctry	Station, location
990	5	E	SER R. Cádiz, Cádiz
990	1	ETH	R. Ethiopia, Addis Ababa
990	1	G	BBC R.5 Live, Tywyn
990	0.1	G	Classic Gold WABC, Wolverhampton
990	0.25	G	Magic AM, Doncaster
990	0.25	G	Magic AM, Doncaster
990	1	G	R. Devon, Exeter
990	1	G	R. Nan Gaidheal,Redmoss
990	400	IRN	R.Sarasarye, Shiraz
990	50	NIG	Bauchi R. Corp, Bauchi
990	10	NIG	NBC, Ikeja
990	1	RUS	R. Mayak, Yuryuzan
990	15	RUS	R. Slavyanka, Moskva
990	1	SCG	R. Pozarevac, Pozarevac
990	100/10	TZA	R. Tanzania, Songea
999	20	ARS	BSKSA, Tabuk
999	50	E	COPE, Madrid
999	5	F	Superloustic, Paris
999	0.25	G	Classic Gold GEM,Nottingham
999	0.8	G	Magic 999, Preston/Blackpool
999	1	G	R. Solent, Fareham
999	0.3	G	Valleys Radio, Aberdare
999	20	I	Raiuno, Rimini + 2 st's
999	50	IRN	R.Sarasarye, Baneh
999	2	IRQ	R. Al-Bilad, Baghdad
999	500	MDA	Relays, Grigoriopol
999	5	MLT	R. Malta 1, Bizbizja
999	300	MRC	RTM A/R, Tanger
999	50	QAT	QBS, Al Khaisah
999	1	SCG	RTS Beograd 2/3, Kladovo
999	100	UGA	R. Uganda, Kabale
1008	1	AGL	R. Luanda, Luanda (1010)
1008	10	BFA	R. Bobo, B.Dioulasso
1008	50	BLR	BR Kanal Kultura, Babrujsk + 3 st's
1008	10	CNR	Punto Radio, Las Palmas
1008	5	E	SER R. Alacant, Alicante
1008	10	E	SER R. Girona, Girona
1008	5	E	SER R.Extremadura, Badajoz
1008	100	EGY	ERTU, El Arish + 2 st's
1008	50	GRC	ERA Regional, Kerkyra
1008	400/200	HOL	R. 10 FM, Zeewolde
1008	50	IRN	Regional, Semnan
1008	-	IRQ	V.o. Fadhilah, Najaf
1008	50	MOZ	EP de Maputo, Maputo
1008	10	NIG	Osun State B.C., Iree
1008	5	RUS	R. Mayak, Tuapse
1008	1	SCG	RTS Beograd 2/3, Beograd
1008	600	YEM	YRTC, San'a
1017	10	AFG	R. Ghazni, Ghazni
1017	5	ALG	RTA 1, Touggourt
1017	20	ARS	BSKSA, Madinah
1017	50	BUL	Horizont + Turkish sce., Kardzhali
1017	100	D	SWR Cont.Ra., Wolfsheim
1017	10	E	RNE5 TN, Burgos
1017	10	E	RNE5 TN. Granada
1017	0.63	G	Classic Gold WABC, Shrewsbury
1017	1	MDR	PEF, Santana
1017	10	NIG	Adamawa B.C., Yola
1017	5	SVK	R. Patria, Bratislava city
1017	25	SVK	R. Patria, Rimavská Sobota.
1017	1200	TUR	TRT 1, Mundanya
1026	5	ALG	RTA 3, Hassi Messaoud
1026	50	BLR	BR Kanal Kultura, Mahilioú + 5 st's
1026	5	E	SER 'R. Salamanca, Salamanca
1026	5	E	SER R. Asturias, Oviedo
1026	5	E	SER R. Jaén, Jaén
1026	5	E	SER R. Jerez, J.de la Frontera
1026	10	E	SER R. Reus, Reus
1026	5	E	SER R. Vigo, Vigo
1026	1.7	G	Downtown Radio, Belfast
1026	1	G	R. Jersey, Trinity
1026	0.5	G	R.Cambrigeshire, Chesterton Fen
1026	100	IRN	Regional, Tabriz
1026	1	IRQ	Radio Iraq, Baghdad (inactive)
1026	50	ISR	Reshet Dalet, Yavne
1026	50	MOZ	EP do Manica, Chimoio
1026	1	MRC	RTM B, Rabat
1026	25	NIG	Jigawa Broadc.Corp., Dutse
1026	7	RUS	R. Mayak, Nyandoma+2 st's
1026	5	SDN	SRTC, Al-Damazin
1035	50	EST	Semeynoye Radio, Tartu
1035	1	G	Easy Radio, London
1035	0.78	G	Northsound Two, Aberdeen
1035	1	G	R.Sheffield, Sheffield
1035	0.32	G	West Sound AM, Ayr
1035	10	I	Raiuno, Pescara
1035	50	IRN	R. Sarasarye, Yazd
1035	-	JOR	R. Jordan, unk.location
1035	100	POR	R. Nacional, Porto Alto
1035	14	SVK	R. Regina Banská Bystrica, B.B.
1035	10	TZA	R. Tanzania,Dar es Salaam
1044	7	AFG	Radio Farah, Farah
1044	10	CYP	CBC 3, Limassol
1044	20	D	MDR Info, Wilsdruff
1044	10	E	SER R. San Sebastian, S.S.
1044	5	E	SER R. Valladolid, Valladolid
1044	150	GRC	R.S.M. 1, Thessaloniki
1044	50	IRN	R. Sarasarye, Dehloran
1044	100	KEN	KBC, Malindi
1044	300	MRC	RTM C, Sebaa-Aioun
1044	40	RUS	R. Svobodna,Moskva
1044	1	SCG	R. Temerin, Temerin
1053	5	E	COPE Castello, Vila Real
1053	25	E	COPE, Zaragoza
1053	500	G	TalkSport,,Droitwich + 12 st's
1053	100	IRN	Regional, Khorramabad
1053	-	IRQ	Radio As-Salam, Baghdad
1053	50	LBY	LJB, Tripoli
1053	10	MRC	RTM A/R, Beni Makada
1053	1000	ROU	R.Iasi, Uricani
1053	10	RUS	R. Mariya, St. Peterburg
1053	50	RUS	Regional, Orenburg
1062	20/1	CZE	Country Radio, Praha
1062	250	DNK	DR P3, Kalundborg
1062	25	I	Raiuno + Regional, Cagliari
1062	2	I	Raiuno + Regional, Catania
1062	10	I	Raiuno, Pisa + 2 st's
1062	50	IRN	Regional, Kerman
1062	10	NIG	Enugu State B.S., Onitsha
1062	0.1	POL	Twoje R. Cmolas, Cmolas
1062	1	POL	Twoje R. Pulawy, Pulawy
1062	10	SCG	R. Jagodina, Jagodina
1062	1	SCG	RTS Beograd 1 + R. Novi Pazar, N.P.
1062	300	TUR	TRT4+Regional, Diyarbakir
1071	25	BOT	RB 1, Jwaneng
1071	50	E	Euskadi Irratia, Bilbao
1071	100	EGY	ERTU, Cairo
1071	1	G	TalkSport, Clipstone + 1st
1071	100	IRN	R. Ma'aref, Qom
1071	-	IRQ	R. Babil, Al-Hilla
1071	1	IRQ	Radio Iraq, Baghdad (inactive)
1071	100	SYR	ORTAS 1/2, Tartus
1071	30	YEM	YRTC, Taiz
1080	20	ARS	BSKSA, Taif
1080	10	E	Onda Cero R., Toledo
1080	5	E	SER R. Coruña, La Coruña
1080	5	E	SER R. Granada, Granada
1080	10	E	SER R. Huesca, Huesca
1080	5	E	SER R. Mallorca, Palma de M.
1080	10	EGY	ERTU, El Minya + 1 st
1080	-	ETH	R. Fana, Addis Ababa
1080	10	GRC	ERA Regional, Orestiada
1080	750	IRN	VOIRI + Regional, Mahshar
1080	5	ISR	Reshet Bet, Jerusalem
1080	100	RUS	R. Rossii + Reg., Kovylkino
1089	25	AGL	RNA Canal A, Mulenvos (1088)
1089	150	ALB	Radio Tirana, Shijak
1089	5	ALG	RTA 1, Adrar
1089	10	ARS	BSKSA, Quaryyat
1089	400	G	Brookmans Park + 7 st's
1089	-	IRN	Regional, Biarjmand
1089	20	NIG	FRCN Lagos, Sogunle
1089	1200	RUS	R. Rossii+Reg+VoR, Tbilisskaya
1089	20	RUS	R. Teos, St. Peterburg
1098	50	AFS	Ikwekwezi FM, Ga-Rankuwa
1098	5	ALG	RTA 1, Ouargla
1098	5	ARS	BSKSA, Dammam
1098	2x50	CYP	BRT Bayrak Radyo 1, Yeni Iskele
1098	25	E	RNE5 TN, Almeria
1098	10	E	RNE5 TN, Avila
1098	5	E	RNE5 TN, Huelva
1098	20	E	RNE5 TN, Lugo
1098	100	IRN	VOIRI, Zabol
1098	7	RUS	R. Rossii + Reg., Chagoda
1098	5	RUS	R. Rossii + Reg., Nikolsk
1098	10	RUS	R. Vatanym, Moscow

kHz	kW	Ctry	Station, location
1098	50	SVK	R. Regina Bratislava, Nitra
1107	400	AFG	RTV Afghanistan, Pol-e-Charkhi
1107	10	D	AFN Power Network, Kaiserslautern
1107	10	D	AFN The Big Gun, Grafenwöhr+2 st's
1107	20	E	RNE5 TN, Caceres
1107	20	E	RNE5 TN, Camargo
1107	10	E	RNE5 TN, Ponferrada
1107	10	E	RNE5 TN, Teruel
1107	25	E	RNE5 TN,Logrono
1107	600	EGY	ERTU, Batra
1107	1.5	G	Moray Firth Radio,Inverness
1107	2	G	TalkSport, Lydd + 5 st's
1107	100	I	Raiuno + RAI International, Roma
1107	10	IRN	Regional, Sabzevar
1107	100	KEN	KBC, Maralal
1107	1	MWI	MBC R 1, Nkhota Kota
1107	25	NIG	FRCN Kaduna, Jaji
1107	150	RUS	Narodnoye Radio, Samara
1107	100	SCG	RTN Beograd 1, Novi Sad
1107	10	UAE	Emirates Radio, Dubai
1116	20	ARS	BSKSA, Shaqra
1116	40	DJI	RTV de Djibouti, Dorale
1116	5	E	SER R. Albacete, Albacete
1116	5	E	SER R. Pontevedra, Pontevedra
1116	1	G	R.Derby, Burnaston Lane
1116	0.5	G	R.Guernsey, Rohais
1116	1	G	Valleys R., Ebbw Vale
1116	5	HNG	Györ R., Mosonmagyaróvár
1116	15	HNG	Kossuth R.+ R. Miskolc, Miskolc
1116	0.5	HOL	R. Bloemendaal, B.
1116	2	I	Raiuno + Regional, Aosta
1116	10	I	Raiuno + Regional, Palermo
1116	60	I	Raiuno, Bologna + 2 st's
1116	200	IRN	Regional, Ardekan
1116	5	MRC	RTM C, Quarzazate
1116	75	RUS	GTRK Yantar. Bolshakovo
1116	5	RUS	KhrTserkObshchKanal, Moskva
1116	30	RUS	R. Rossii + Reg., Sochi
1125	10	BEL	Classic 21 RTBF 4, Houdeng
1125	150	BLR	BR Kanal Kultura, Minsk
1125	5	E	RNE5 TN, Badajoz
1125	10	E	RNE5 TN, Castelló
1125	10	E	RNE5 TN, Toledo
1125	10	E	RNE5 TN, Vitoria
1125	10	E	RNE5 TN,Soria
1125	1	G	R. Wales, Llandrindod Wells
1125	100	HRV	HR Glas Hrvatske, Deanovac
1125	10	IRN	Regional, Nehbandan
1125	500	LBY	LJB, El Beida
1125	1	MDR	RDP Madeira, Ponta do Pargo
1125	20	NGR	La Voix du Sahel, Niamey
1125	-	NIG	Edo State B. Sce., Hievbe
1125	150	RUS	R. Orfey, Olgino
1125	200	SYR	ORTAS 2/E, Al-Hassake
1134	10	AGL	EP de Bengo, Mulenvos
1134	5	E	COPE, Astorga
1134	5	E	COPE, Ciutadella
1134	5	E	COPE, Jerez de la Frontera
1134	5	E	COPE, Pamplona
1134	5	E	COPE, Puertollano
1134	10	E	COPE, Salamanca
1134	0.001	G	BFBS Gurkha Radio (2 st's)
1134	0.001	G	LPAMs
1134	0.001	G	RSLs
1134	600	HRV	HR Glas Hrvatske, Zadar
1134	50	IRN	Regional, Bojnurd
1134	50	KEN	KBC, Kitale
1134	10	KWT	R. Kuwait, Sulaibiyah
1134	10	NIG	Cross River State B.C., Ugaga
1134	75	RUS	R. Mayak, Murmansk + 2 st's
1134	5	RUS	R. Rossii + Reg., Salsk + 2 st's
1134	20	RUS	R. Teos, Kurkino
1143	40	BUL	Horizont, Varna
1143	0.3	D	AFN Big Red Radio, Würzburg + 3 sts
1143	1	D	AFN Power Network, Bitburg + 1 st
1143	1	D	AFN Power Network, Heidelberg
1143	10	D	AFN Power Network, Stuttgart
1143	1	D	AFN SHAPE, Mönchengladbach
1143	5	E	COPE, Jaén
1143	2	E	COPE, Ourense
1143	5	E	COPE, Oviedo
1143	2	E	COPE, Reus
1143	10	EGY	ERTU, Sohag
1143	10	I	Raiuno + Regional, Messina
1143	10	I	Raiuno + Regional, Sassari
1143	50	IRN	R. Sarasarye, Yasuj
1143	10	ISR	Arutz Sheva, Channel 7 (silent)
1143	10	NIG	Crystal Radio, Bida
1143	150	RUS	R. Mayak, Mekhzavod
1143	150	RUS	R. Mayak/VoR, Bolshakovo
1152	10	AGL	EP do Zaire, Mbanza Congo
1152	10	E	RNE5 TN, Albacete
1152	10	E	RNE5 TN, Cartagena
1152	10	E	RNE5 TN, Lleida
1152	20	E	RNE5 TN, Málaga
1152	10	E	RNE5 TN, Zamora
1152	3	G	Capital Gold 1152, Birmingham
1152	0.32	G	Classic Gold 1152, Plymouth
1152	0.8	G	Classic Gold Amber, Norwich
1152	3.6	G	Clyde 2, Glasgow
1152	23.5	G	LBC News, London
1152	1.5	G	Magic 1152, Manchester
1152	1.8	G	Magic 1152, Newcastle
1152	100	IRN	R. Farhang, Tabriz
1152	2/0.2	IRQ	R. Dar As-Salam, Baghdad
1152	50	KEN	KBC, Wajir
1152	950	ROU	R.România Actualitati, Cluj
1152	150	RUS	R. Orfey, Kupavna
1152	-	SDN	SNBC, Khartoum
1152	200	UAE	R. Asia, Ras al Khaimah
1161	5	ALG	RTA, Ain-Salah
1161	500	BUL	Horizont, Stara Zagora + 2 st's
1161	50	E	Euskadi Irratia, San Sebastian
1161	100	EGY	ERTU, Tanta
1161	1	G	BBC Southern Counties R., Bexhill
1161	0.1	G	BBC Three Counties R, Bedford
1161	0.16	G	Classic Gold 936/1161, Swindon
1161	0.35	G	Magic 1161, Hull
1161	1.4	G	Tay AM, Dundee
1161	600	IRN	VOIRI, Qasr-e-Shirin
1161	75	RUS	R. Orfey, Dubovka
1170	10	AGL	EP do Huambo, Huambo
1170	800	BLR	FS/VoR Relays, Sasnovy
1170	0.12	G	Capital Gold 1170/1557, Portsmouth
1170	0.28	G	Classic Gold Amber, Ipswich
1170	0.32	G	Magic 1170, Stockton
1170	0.2	G	Signal Two, Stoke-on-Trent
1170	0.58	G	Swansea Sound, Swansea
1170	750	IRN	R. Sarasarye, Abadan (1169)
1170	50	IRN	R. Sarasarye, Semnan
1170	25	NIG	Ogun State B.C., Abeoukuta
1170	10	POR	R. Nacional, Miramar + 2 st's (inactive)
1170	700	RUS	VoR Relays/BR1/FS, Sasnovy
1170	0.2	SCG	R. BT, Backa Topola
1170	1	SCG	R. Vrnjacka Banja, V.B.
1170	300	SVN	R.Capodistria/R.Slovenija Int., Beli Kriz
1170	50	SWZ	TWR, Mpangela Range
1170	800	UAE	R. Farda, Dhabbayaabiya
1179	20	CNR	R.Clube Tenerife,Santa Cruz
1179	2	E	SER R. Rioja, Logroño
1179	50	E	SER R. Valencia,Valencia
1179	10	EGY	ERTU, Quena
1179	10	EGY	ERTU, Quena
1179	50	GRC	ERA 4/Macedonia 2, Thessaloniki
1179	50	IRN	R. Sarasarye, Gonbad
1179	10	IRQ	R. Voice of Iraq, Baghdad
1179	50	MOZ	EP de Zambézia,Quelimane
1179	200	ROU	R.România Actualitati, Bacau
1179	7	ROU	R.România Actualitati, Resita
1179	300/600	S	SR1/SR4/R.Sweden, Sölvesborg
1188	7	AFG	R. Faryab, Maimana
1188	10	AGL	EP de Malange, Malange
1188	5	BEL	R,Twee, Kuurne
1188	3	D	MDR Info, Reichenbach
1188	10	EGY	ERTU, Ras Gharib
1188	300	IRN	Regional, Tehran
1188	-	IRQ	Voice of Iraq, Baghdad
1188	10	RUS	Deutsche Welle, St. Peterburg
1188	5	RUS	R. 21 vek, Samara
1188	-	YEM	YRTC, Al-Hiswah
1197	40	BLR	BR Kanal Kultura, Viciebsk + 2 st's
1197	150/300	D	VOA/RFE, München
1197	50	E	Euskadi Irratia, Vitoria
1197	25	EGY	ERTU, Alexandria
1197	2	G	Virgin Radio, Hoo + 8 st's
1197	50	IRN	IRIB Golestan, Gonbad

kHz	kW	Ctry	Station, location
1197	100	LSO	Family Radio, Lancer´s Gap
1197	1	MKD	R. Kriva Palanka, K.P.
1197	50	MRC	RTM C, Agadir
1197	14	ROU	R.Târgu Mures/Antena Brasov, Brasov
1197	5	RUS	R. Rossi + Reg., Balakovo + 2 st's
1200	0.5	AFG	R. Khost, Khost
1200		TUR	Cinarli Radyosu, Izmir
1204	2/1	SEN	RTV du Sénégal,Ziguinchor
1205	1	SCG	R. Majdanpek, Majdanpek
1206	300	F	France Info, Bordeaux
1206	50	IRN	R. Sarasarye, Azna
1206	-	IRQ	V.o.People of Kurdistan, Sulaimaniyah
1206	50	ISR	Reshet Dalet, Akko
1206	1	MAU	R.Rodrigues, Citronelle
1206	50	MOZ	EP de Inhambane, Inhambane.
1206	1	RUS	R. Mayak + Reg., Nazran
1206	5	RUS	R. Mayak, Plesetsk
1215	500	ALB	R. Tirana, Fllake
1215	20	ARS	BSKSA, Hafrul Baten
1215	50	BOT	RB1, Mahalapye
1215	2	E	COPE, Córdoba
1215	5	E	COPE, Léon
1215	2	E	COPE, Lorca
1215	5	E	COPE, Santander
1215	200	G	Virgin Radio, Moorside Edge + 13 sts
1215	125	GEO	GR1, Dusheti
1215	50	IRN	Regional, Chalus
1215	0.1	NGR	La Voix du Sahel, Tahoua
1215	1200	RUS	VoR, Bolshakovo
1215	1	SCG	R. Mladenovac, M.
1215	50/10	TZA	R. Tanzania, Arusha
1224	500	BUL	Horizont + Foreign Sce., Vidin
1224	5	E	COPE, Albacete
1224	5	E	COPE, Almería
1224	5	E	COPE, Huelva
1224	5	E	COPE, Lleida
1224	5	E	COPE, Lugo
1224	5	E	COPE, Palma de Mallorca
1224	10	E	R. Popular, San Sebastián
1224	400	IRN	VOIRI, Kerman
1224	20	ISR	Galei Zahal, Beersheba
1224	50	MOZ	EP de Cabo Delg.,Pemba
1224	50	NIG	Plateau RTV Corp., Jos
1224	30	RUS	R. Ura, Elista
1224	1	SCG	R. Backi Petrovac, Backi Petrovac
1233	10	AGL	EP da Huila, Lubango
1233	0.2	BEL	Classic 21 RTBF 4, Liège
1233	600	CYP	RMC/TWR, Cape Greco
1233	0.5	G	Virgin Radio, 5 st's
1233		IRN	R. Sarasarye, Bandar Abbas
1233	50	IRN	Regional, Abadeh
1233	50	KEN	KBC, Marsabit
1233	600	MRC	RTM A/R. Marrakech
1233	100	QAT	QBS, Al Khaisah
1242	150	F	France Info, Marseille
1242	0.32	G	Capital Gold Kent, Maidstone
1242	2	G	Virgin Radio, 4 st's
1242	50	IRN	R. Sarasarye, Zanjan
1242	5	MKD	R. Ohrid, Ohrid
1242	200	OMA	R. Oman, Seeb
1251	0.76	G	Classic Gold Amber, Bury St.Edmunds
1251	0.001	G	LPAMs
1251	25	HNG	Kossuth R+reg.Nyíregyháza, N.
1251	25	HNG	Kossuth R+reg.Szombathely+Györ, Sz.
1251	10	HOL	R. 747 AM , Hulsberg
1251	50	IRN	R. Sarasarye, Kiashahr
1251	500	LBY	LJB+Voice of Africa, Tripoli
1251	10	POR	R. Renascenca, Porto+3 st's
1251	7	RUS	R. Yunost, Izhevsk
1251	7	RUS	R.Mayak+Reg.,Cherkessk + 3 st's
1251	50	UAE	Emirates Radio, Dubai
1260	10	AGL	EP do Kuanza Norte, N'dalatando
1260	5	CVA	Vatican Radio, Vatican City
1260	5	E	SER R. Algeciras, Algeciras
1260	5	E	SER R. Murcia, Murcia
1260	1.6	G	Classic Gold 1260, Bristol
1260	0.64	G	Classic Gold Marcher, Wrexham
1260	0.5	G	R. York, Scarborough
1260	0.29	G	Sabras R., Leicester
1260	1	G	Virgin Radio, Lydd + 1 st
1260	500	GRC	R. Sawa/ERA5, Rhodos
1260	10	IRN	R. Sarasarye, Khur
1260	50	MOZ	EP do Niassa, Lichinga
1260	10	RUS	BBC World Sce, Moskva
1260	10	RUS	BBC World Sce, St. Peterburg.
1269	2	AFS	Chinese Commercial R., Midrand
1269	20	CNR	R. ECCA, Las Palmas
1269	300	D	DLF, Neumunster
1269	5	E	COPE, Badajoz
1269	10	E	COPE, Ciudad Real
1269	10	E	COPE, Figueres
1269	5	E	COPE, Zamora
1269	0.001	G	RSLs
1269	50	IRN	Regional, Khalkhal
1269	20	KEN	KBC, Ngong
1269	100	KWT	R. Kuwait, Sulaibiyah
1269	10	NIG	Taraba State B.S., Jalingo
1269	1	SCG	RTN, Novi Sad (Serbian sce)
1278	50	AFG	RTV Afghanistan, Kabul
1278	25	AGL	EP de Cabinda, Tenda
1278	2.5	BLR	BR 1, Brest
1278	10	EGY	ERTU, Asswan
1278	300	F	France Blue, Strasbourg
1278	0.001	G	BFBS Gurkha Radio
1278	0.001	G	LPAMs
1278	0.43	G	Pulse Classic Gold, Bradford
1278	0.001	G	RSLs
1278	10	GRC	ERA Regional , Florina
1278	100	IRN	Regional, Kermanshah
1278	50	RUS	R.Yunost, Dubovka + 6 st's
1287	2	AFS	Ligwalagwala FM, Welgedacht
1287	5	ALG	RTA C, El Golea
1287	5	ARS	BSKSA, Makkah
1287		BUL	R. Christo Botev, Smolyan
1287	5	E	SER R. Castilla, Burgos
1287	10	E	SER R. Lleida, Lleida
1287	5	E	SER R. Lugo, Lugo
1287	0.001	G	BFBF N. Ireland (10 st's)
1287	0.001	G	BFBS Gurkha Radio (2 st's)
1287	0.001	G	Garrison Radio (3 st's)
1287	0.001	G	LPAMs
1287	100	IRN	Regional, Lar
1287	100	ISR	Galei Zahal, Ramle
1287	2	POR	RDP-Antena 1, Portalegre
1287	50	RUS	R. Yunost, Yazykovo +2 st's
1287	4	SEN	RTV du Sénégal, Kaolack
1296	400	AFG	R. Free Afgh./VOA Rel., Pol-e-Charkhi
1296	10	AGL	EP do Uige, Uige
1296	1	AGL	EP do Zaire, Soyo (1298)
1296	125	AZE	FS/RFE-RL, Pirsaat
1296	150	BUL	Christo Botev, Kardzhali
1296	30	BUL	Christo Botev, Pleven
1296	50	E	COPE, Valencia
1296	500	G	BBC W.S., Orfordness
1296	10	G	R. XL, Birmingham
1296	5	I	Raiuno, La Spezia
1296	50	IRN	R.Sarasarye, Qazvin
1296	-	IRN	Regional, Zahedan
1296	10	SCG	RTS Beograd 1 + R, Vranje, Vranje
1296	600	SDN	SRTC, Reiba
1305	20	ALG	RTA, Constantine
1305	1	ARS	BSKSA, Taif
1305	5	BEL	Classic 21 RTBF 4, Marche
1305	1	BIH	Radio Buzim, Bosanska Krupa
1305	20	E	RNE5 TN, Bilbao
1305	20	E	RNE5 TN, Ciudad Real
1305	10	E	RNE5 TN, León
1305	25	E	RNE5 TN, Ourense
1305	10	EGY	ERTU, Assiut
1305	0.2	G	Capital Gold 1305/1359, Newport
1305	0.15	G	Magic AM, Barnsley
1305	0.5	G	Premier Christian R., Chingford
1305	0.5	G	Premier Christian R., Epsom
1305	50	IRN	Regional, Bushehr
1305	0.5	IRQ	R. Al-Mustaqbal, Baghdad
1305	10	ISR	Galei Zahal, Eilat
1305	50	KEN	KBC, Wajir
1305	100	RUS	R. Druzhba, Moskva-Kupavna
1305	7	RUS	R. Mayak, Serov
1314	1	AGL	EP da Huila, Lubango(1313)
1314	10	AGL	EP do Namibe, Namibe
1314	1000	ARM	Relays, Gavar
1314	20	E	RNE5 TN, Cuenca
1314	10	E	RNE5 TN, Salamanca

kHz	kW	Ctry	Station, location
1314	10	E	RNE5 TN, Tarragona
1314	10	EGY	ERTU, Hurghada + 2 st's
1314	5	F	Loisirs AM(R. du Temps Libre), Paris
1314	10	GRC	ERA Regional , Tripolis
1314	2	I	Raiuno, Matera
1314	10	IRN	Regional, Ardabil
1314	5	MKD	Skopje 2, Skopje
1314	1200	NOR	NRK Europakanalen + Reg., Kvitsöy
1314	7	ROU	Antena Satelor/R.R. Act., Craiova
1314	30	ROU	Antena Satelor/R.R. Act., Timisoara
1314	1	RUS	R. Rossii + Reg., Pleshanovo
1314	50	SYR	ORTAS 2, Sarakeb
1314	1000	UAE	BBC World Sce, Dhabbaya
1323	200	CYP	BBC World Sce, Zygi
1323	150/800	D	VoR, Wachenbrunn
1323	-	ETH	R. Ethiopia, unk. location (1322)
1323	0.5	G	Capital Gold 1323/945, Brighton
1323	50	IRN	Regional, Jolfa
1323	10	MKD	R. Bitola, Bitola
1323	10	MKD	R. Delcevo, Delcevo
1323	1	MKD	R. Gostivar, Gostivar
1323	5	MRC	RTM B, Safi
1323	7	ROU	R. Târgu Mures, T.M.
1323	10	RUS	R.Grad Petrov, St. Peterburg
1323	1	SCG	R. Sid, Sid
1323	100	TZA	Radio One, Moshi
1331	20	NGR	La Voix du Sahel, Meninsoroua
1332	50	CZE	CRo 2 + CRo6, Moravské Budejovice
1332	0.6	G	Classic Gold 1332, Peterborough
1332	1	G	Premier Christian R., London
1332	0.4	G	R. Wiltshire, Lacock
1332	300	IRN	Tehran City Radio, Tehran
1332	1	MDR	RDP Madeira, Senhora do Monte
1332	50	ROU	R.România Actualitati, Galati
1341	1	BFA	R. Burkina, Ouagadougou
1341	5	E	OCR, Almeria
1341	10	E	OCR, Ciudad Real
1341	5	E	SER R. León, León
1341	100	EGY	ERTU, Cairo + 3 st's
1341	100	G	R. Ulster, Lisnagarvey
1341	135	HNG	Magyar Katolikus Radio, Szolnok
1341	10	IRN	R. Sarasarye, Bam
1341	-	IRQ	Voice of Komal, Kirkuk
1341	10	KWT	R. Kuwait, Magwa
1350	1000	ARM	Relays, Gavar
1350	50	BOT	RB 1, Tshabong
1350	10	EGY	ERTU, Quseir
1350	10	F	R. Orient, Nice
1350	0.001	G	Garrison Radio (1 st)
1350	0.001	G	LPAMs
1350	0.001	G	RSLs
1350	30	GEO	Abkhaz State Radio, Soxum
1350	4	GRC	ERA Regional, Pyrgos
1350	5	HNG	R.Györ, Györ
1350	600	IRN	Regional, Shushtar (inactive)
1359	-	AZE	AZR 2, Gäncä
1359	600	E	RNE 1, Madrid
1359	0.2	G	Capital Gold 1305/1359, Cardiff
1359	0.27	G	Classic Gold 1359, Coventry
1359	0.28	G	Classic Gold Breeze, Chelmsford
1359	0.85	G	R. Solent for Dorset, Bournemouth
1359	50	IRN	Regional, Lar
1359	25	NIG	Capital Sound, Zaria
1359	10	NIG	Osun State, B.Corp., Iwo
1359	50	RUS	R. Mayak, Perm
1359	50	UKR	Reg. Donetsk, Dokuchaievsk
1368	10	EGY	ERTU, El Kharga + 1 st
1368	0.5	G	BBC Southern.Counties R., Duxhurst
1368	20	G	Manx Radio, Douglas
1368	0.1	G	R. Wiltshire, Swindon
1368	2	G	R.Lincolnshire, Lincoln
1368	25	I	Raiuno, Firenze
1368	20	IRN	R. Sarasarye, Sari
1368	50	ISR	Galei Zahal,Pilon + 1 st
1368	10	SCG	R. Valjeva, Valjevo
1368	20	SEN	RTV du Sénégal, St Louis
1368	10	SEY	SBC Radio, Victoria
1377	300	F	France Info, Lille
1377	0.08	G	Asian Sound R., Ashton Moss
1377	10	IRN	R. Sarasarye, Chabahar
1377	10	IRN	Regional, Paveh
1377	50	SWZ	R. Cidade, Sandlane
1377	50	TZA	R. Free Africa, Mwanza
1377	7	UKR	Reg., Mykolaiv
1386	10	AGL	EP da Luanda Sul, Saurimo
1386	10	EGY	ERTU, Luxor + 1 st
1386	0.001	G	LPAMs
1386	50	GRC	ERA2/Filia Radio, Athens
1386	50	GUI	R. Rurale, Labé
1386	600	IRN	Regional, Mahshahr (inactive)
1386	100	KEN	KBC, Maralal
1386	500	LTU	Relays, Sitkunai
1386	5	RUS	R. Yunost, Obninsk
1386	1200	RUS	VoR, Bolshakovo
1395	500	ALB	R. Tirana, Fllake
1395	150	ARM	AR, Yerevan
1395	50	IRN	R.Sarasarye, Hajiabad
1395	10	ISR	Galei Zahal, Mitspe Ramon
1395	4	MDG	RNM 1, Antananarivo
1395	10	NIG	Akwa Ibom B.C., Abak
1395	10	NIG	R. Kogi, Egbe
1395	5	RUS	R. Rossii + Reg., Buguruslan
1395	5	RUS	R. Yunost, Volga + 2 st's
1395	20/1	TGO	RTV Togolaise, Lomé
1397	10	NIG	Delta State B.S., Warri
1404	2	AFS	Inwekwezi FM, Welgedacht
1404	10	AGL	EP do Bié, Kuito
1404	20	F	France Bleu,Ajaccio
1404	20/5	F	France Info, Brest+3st's
1404	0.001	G	LPAMs
1404	0.001	G	RSLs
1404	100	GRC	ERA Regional , Komotini
1404	1	I	Radio 106, Salvaterra di Casalgrande
1404	500	IRN	VOIRI, Kiashahr
1404	20	ISR	Galei Zahal, Rama
1404	20	LBY	LBJ, Tripoli
1404	10	MWI	MBC R.1, Chitipa
1404	10	NIG	GBC Yola, Gombe
1404	50	ROU	R.Cluj/Local, Sighetul M.
1413	5	E	RNE5 TN, Girona
1413	10	E	RNE5 TN, Jaén
1413	20	E	RNE5 TN, Vigo
1413	0.04	G	Fresh Radio, Richmond
1413	0.1	G	Fresh Radio, Skipton
1413	0.5	G	Premier Christian R., Dartford Marshes
1413	0.5	G	Premier Christian R., Heathrow
1413	0.5	G	R. Gloucestershire, Berkley Heath
1413	0.5	G	R. Gloucestershire, Bourton-on-the-W.
1413	0.001	G	RSLs
1413	-	IRN	Regional, Estahban
1413	0.5	IRQ	V.o. Workers Communist Party, Baghd.
1413	800	OMA	BBC W.S., A'Seela
1413	30	RUS	R. Yunost, Stavropol
1422	1	AFS	New Panhellenic Voice, Bedfordview
1422	40	ALG	RTA C, O. Fayet
1422	20	ARS	BSKSA, Riyadh
1422	600	D	DLF, Heusweiler
1422	10	EGY	ERTU, Salum + 1 st
1422	100	IRN	R.Sarasarye, Kermanshah
1422	10	MWI	MBC R 1, Matiya
1422	7	ROU	R.România Actualitati, Rm. Valcea
1431	600	DJI	R. Sawa, Arta
1431	0.14	G	Classic Gold 1431/1485, Reading
1431	0.35	G	Classic Gold Breeze, Southend
1431	0.01	G	Fresh Radio, Likley & Settle
1431	0.001	G	LPAMs
1431	2	I	Raiuno, Foggia
1431	200	IRN	R. Sarasarye, Isfahan
1431	0	IRN	R. Sarasarye, Kerman
1431	1	MKD	R. Probistip, Probistip
1431	0.2	SCG	R. Beocin, Beocin
1431	1200	UKR	VoR Relay, Mykolaiv
1440	10	AGL	EP da Luanda Norte, Dundo
1440	1600	ARS	BSKSA, Dammam
1440	20/50	CAF	RTV Centreafricaine, Bangui
1440	300	LUX	RTL Radio / Relays
1440	50	NIG	Gombe State B.C., Yola
1440	5	RUS	RFI, Moskva
1440	10	RUS	RFI, St. Peterburg
1440	10	SCG	RTS Beograd 1, Jagodina
1449	2	G	BBC R.4, Redmoss
1449	0.001	G	LPAMs
1449	0.15	G	R. Cambridgesh/Asian Netw,Gunthorpe
1449	0.001	G	RSLs
1449	50	I	Raiuno, Squinzano + 6 st's
1449	400	IRN	VOIRI, Bandar-e-Torkamen

kHz	kW	Ctry	Station, location
1449	500	LBY	LJB, Misurata
1449	30	MDA	R. Moldova 2, Chisinau
1449	42	RUS	R. Mayak,Monchegorsk. + 6 st's
1449	5	RUS	R. Rossii + Reg., Livny
1449	2	SCG	R. Srbobran, Srbobran
1458	10	AGL	EP do Moxico, Luena
1458	500	ALB	R. Tirana, Fllake
1458	5	G	BBC Asian Network, Langley Mill
1458	5	G	Capital Gold, Manchester.
1458	2	G	R. Devon, Torquay
1458	2	G	R. Newcastle,Wrekenton
1458	0.5	G	R.Cumbria, Whitehaven
1458	125	G	Sunrise Radio, London
1458	2	GIB	GBC R.Gibraltar, Wellington Front
1458	10	IRN	R. Sarasarye, Khoy
1458	10	ISR	Reshet Alef, Eilat
1458	10	ISR	Reshet Alef, Jerusalem
1458	5	MYT	RFO Mayotte, Pamandzi
1458	50	ROU	R. România Actualitati, Constanta
1458	7	RUS	R. Rossii + Reg., Kudymkar
1458	5	RUS	R. Yunost, Valuyki
1458	1	SCG	R. Kladovo, Kladovo
1467	10	AGL	EP do Kuando-Kubango, Menongue
1467	-	ARS	BSKSA, Unkn. Loc.
1467	1000	F	Relays, Romoules
1467	50	F	Superloustic, Col de la Madonne
1467	10	IRN	Regional, Qom
1467	500	MDA	Relays, Grigoriopol
1476	60	AUT	ORF-R.1476, Wien-Bissamberg
1476	150	AZE	AZR 2, Pirsaat
1476	50/20	BEN	R. Bénin, Cotonou (Inactive)
1476	20	COG	R. Congo, Brazzaville (inactive)
1476	10	EGY	ERTU, El Minya + 1 st
1476	0.5	G	County Sound, Guildford
1476	10	IRN	Regional, Marivan
1476	1500	UAE	Emirates Radio, Dubai
1476	20	UKR	R. Bryz, Sevastopol
1485	1	AFS	R. Today, Honeydew
1485	10	AGL	E.P do Kuanza Sul, Sumbe
1485	1	ARS	BSKSA, Jeddah
1485	0.5	ASC	BBC W.S., English Bay
1485	3	BUL	Christo Botev, Haskovo
1485	5	BUL	Horizont, Suvorovo
1485	0.3	D	AFN Bavaria AM, Regensburg
1485	0.3	D	AFN Big Red Radio, Ansbach
1485	0.3	D	AFN The Big Gun, Hohenfels
1485	1	D	DRM-test, Kaiserslautern
1485	1	D	SWR Cont.Ra.,Baden-Baden
1485	5	E	OCR, Antequera
1485	6	E	OCR, Vilanova
1485	5	E	SER R. Alcoi, Alcoi
1485	10	E	SER R. Santander, Santander
1485	10	E	SER R. Zamora, Zamora
1485	10	EGY	ERTU, El Tur
1485	1	ETH	R. Ethiopia, 3 st's
1485	1	G	BBC R 4, Carlisle
1485	1	G	BBC Southern Counties R., Brighton
1485	1	G	Classic Gold 1431/1485, Newbury
1485	2	G	R. Humberside, Hull
1485	2	G	R. Merseyside, Wallasey
1485	1	GRC	ERA 1, Orestiada
1485	1	GRC	ERA Regional, Patras
1485	1	GRC	ERA Regional, Volos
1485	0.25	HNG	Party Radio, Mohács
1485	0.8	HOL	Haagstad R., Rijswijk
1485	2	I	Raiuno, Vicenza
1485	-	IRN	Regional, Izeh
1485	10	IRN	Regional, Jahrom
1485	5	JOR	R. Jordan, Aqaba
1485	1	LBY	LJB, Brak
1485	1	MKD	R. Berovo, Berovo
1485	1	MKD	R. Kicevo, Kicevo
1485	5	MRC	R. Mellilla,Mellilla
1485	1	MRC	RTM C, Casablanca
1485	0.1	NGR	La Voix du Sahel, Difa (1484)
1485	1	NOR	NRK P1, Longyearbyen
1485	1	RUS	R. Rossii, Oktyabrskiy
1485	1	SCG	R. Priboj, Priboj
1485	1	SCG	RTS Beograd 1 + Regional. 5 st's
1485	1	SCG	RTS Beograd 1, Crna Trava
1485	2	SCG	The City Radio, Novi Sad
1485	5	SDN	SRTC, Al-Gadarif
1485	1	SUI	Option Musique, Savièse

kHz	kW	Ctry	Station, location
1485	10	UGA	R. Uganda, Arua
1494	20	F	France Blue, Bastia
1494	20	F	France Info,Clermont Ferrand+2st's
1494	0.001	G	RSLs
1494	100	GRC	ERA Regional, Rhodes
1494	20	IRN	R. Sarasarye, Maku
1494	1000	JOR	R. Jordan, Al Karanah
1494	30	MDA	R. Moldova 1, Cahul + 1 st
1494	600	RUS	VoR, Krasnyy Bor
1494	0.2	SCG	R. Apatin, Apatin
1500	0.4	AFG	R. Bamiyan, Bamiyan
1502	-	MDG	RNM 2, Antananarivo
1503	10	AGL	EP do Benguela , Benguela
1503	0.1	AZR	AFRTS, Lajes
1503	1	BIH	RTV Zavidovici, Zavidovici
1503	5	E	RNE5 TN, La Linea
1503	2	E	RNE5 TN, Monf. de Lemos
1503	25	EGY	ERTU, El Arish
1503	1	G	R.Stoke, Sideway
1503	500	IRN	R. Sarasarye, Bushehr
1503	20	RUS	R. Tsentr/R. Sadko, Moskva
1503	1	SCG	R. Beograd 202, Beograd
1503	20/1	SEN	RTV du Sénégal,Tambacounda.
1503	10	TGO	Radio Kara, Kara
1512	0.1	AFG	R.Herat, Herat
1512	1000	ARS	BSKSA, Jeddah
1512	25/300	BEL	RVI, Wolvertem
1512	100	GRC	ERA Regional, Chania
1512	50	IRN	R. Sarasarye, Ardabil
1512	5	RUS	R. Rossii + Reg., Chaykovskiy
1512	7	RUS	R. Yunost + Reg., Ibresi
1518	2	AFG	R. Mimroz, Zaranj
1521	2000	ARS	BSKSA, Duba
1521	5	E	SER 'R. Castelló, Castelló
1521	0.64	G	Classic Gold 1521, Reigate
1521	100	IRN	R. Farhang, Kiashahr
1521	1	MKD	R.Brod, Makedonski Brod
1521	20	RUS	R. Mayak, Kazan + 1 st
1530	0.4	AFG	R. Nangarhar, Jalalabad
1530	10	AGL	EP de Cabinda, Tenda
1530	7	AZE	RFE-RL/Azad Azärb. R., Baki
1530	300/600	CVA	Vatican R., Vatican City
1530	0.15	G	BBC Essex, Southend-on-Sea
1530	0.52	G	Classic Hits, Worcester
1530	0.74	G	Pulse Classic Gold, Huddersfield
1530	10	IRN	R. Sarasarye, Yazd
1530	0.25	ISL	"Thunder 1530", AFRTS, Keflavik
1530	10	MDR	PEF, Funchal
1530	14	ROU	R.România Actualitati, Mahmudia
1530	14	ROU	R.România Actualitati, Radauti
1530	600	STP	VOA, Pinheira
1539	120/700	D	Evangeliumsrundfunk, Mainflingen
1539	40	DJI	RTV de Djibouti, Dorale
1539	6	E	SER R. Elche-R. Elx, Elx
1539	5	E	SER R. Manresa, Manresa
1539	10	IRN	Regional, Gorgan
1539	40	ISR	Arutz Sheva/Channel 7(silent)
1539	5	RUS	R. Yunost, Sochi
1539	0.2	SCG	R. Odzaci, Odzaci
1548	10	AFS	R. Islam, Lenasia
1548	97.5	G	Capital Gold 1548, London
1548	2.2	G	Forth 2, Edinburgh
1548	1	G	Magic 1548, Liverpool
1548	0.74	G	Magic AM, Sheffield
1548	5	G	R. Bristol & Somerset S., Mangotsfield
1548	10	IRN	R. Sarasarye, Sanandaj
1548	-	IRN	R.Sarasarye, Gach Saran
1548	10	IRN	Regional, Ferdows
1548	10	IRN	Regional, Larijan
1548	600	KWT	R.Sawa, Kuwait City
1548	500	MDA	Relays, Grigoriopol
1548	1	SHN	R. St. Helena, Jamestown
1550	100	ALG	R.Nacional de la RASD,Tindouf
1557	-	AZE	AZR 2, Quba
1557	300	F	France Info, Fontbonne
1557	0.5	G	Capital Gold 1170/1557, Southampton
1557	0.76	G	Classic Gold 1557, Northampton
1557	0.25	G	R. Lancashire, Oxcliffe
1557	20	HRV	R. Osijek, Osijek
1557	50	IRN	R. Sarasarye, Zabol
1557	50	KWT	Unkn. loc. (nonstop music)
1557	150	LTU	Relays, Sitkunai
1566	10	AZR	EECAA, Vila do Porto (inactive)

kHz	kW	Ctry	Station, location
1566	0.8	G	County Sound Radio, Guildford
1566	0.6	G	R.Bristol&Somerset Sound, Taunton
1566	100	IRN	R. Sarasarye, Bandar Abbas
1575	10	E	SER R. Pamplona, Pamplona
1575	5	E	SER R.Córdoba, Córdoba
1575	10	EGY	ERTU, Queseir
1575	5	F	R. Nouveaux Talents, Paris
1575	0.001	G	LPAMs
1575	0.001	G	RSLs
1575	20	GAB	RTG 2, Tchibanga
1575	50	I	Raiuno, Genova + 3 st's
1575	10	IRN	Regional, Ghaen
1575	10	ISR	REQA, Akko
1575	2	MAU	BBC W.S., Bigara
1575	1	NGR	La Voix du Sahel, Niamey
1575	1	SCG	R. Backa Palanka, Backa Palanka
1575	100	UAE	R. Asia, Ras al Khaimah
1580	0.1	AFG	R. Kunar, Asadabad
1584	10	AFG	R. Balkh, Mazar-e-Sharif
1584	1	BIH	R. Bosanska Petrovac, Bos.Petrovac
1584	10	BUL	Horizont, Dobrich
1584	5	E	SER R. Gandía, Gandia
1584	5	E	SER R. Ourense, Ourense
1584	10	EGY	ERTU, Idfu + 1 st
1584	1	F	RMC Info, Metz
1584	0.3	G	BBC Hereford&Worcester, Woofferton
1584	0.2	G	London Turkish R., London
1584	1	G	R.Nottingham,Clipstone
1584	0.21	G	Tay AM, Perth
1584	1	GRC	ERA Regional, Serres
1584	1	GRC	RSA. Amaliadas
1584	7	I	R. Studio X, Momigno (private)
1584	2	I	Raiuno , Terni
1584	10	IRN	Regional, Maku
1584	0.1	IRQ	R. Shrara, Baghdad
1584	1	MKD	R. Radovis, Radovis
1584	5	MRC	R. Olé, Ceuta
1584	1	POR	R. Altitude, Guarda
1584	7	RUS	R. Rossii, Khunzakh
1584	1	SCG	R. Prijepolje, Prijepolje
1584	1	SVN	R.Brezice, Sremic
1584	1	TUR	Voice of Tigris, Eastern Turkey
1584	1	UKR	UR1 + Reg., Verkhovnya
1593	10	EGY	ERTU, Matruh
1593	0.2	IRL	R. Caroline, Cork
1593	150	KWT	VOA/RFE-RL, Kuwait
1593	1	MRC	RTM A/C/R, Marrakech
1593	20	ROU	R. Cluj, Oradea
1593	20	ROU	R. Cluj, Sibiu
1593	14	ROU	R. Târgu Mures, Miercurea Ciuc
1593	14	ROU	R.România Actualitati, Ion Corvin
1593	1	TUR	AFN Incirlik, Incirlik (1590?)
1602	1	ASC	ZD8VR Asc. Radio(USAF)
1602	1	BIH	Nezavisni R. Boston, Sanski Most
1602	25	E	R. Vitoria, Vitoria
1602	5	E	SER 'R. Segovia, Segovia
1602	5	E	SER R. Cartagena
1602	5	E	SER R. Linares, Linares
1602	5	E	SER R. Ontinyent, Ontinyent
1602	10	EGY	ERTU, El Dakhla + 2 st's
1602	1	F	R. Orient, Nîmes
1602	0.25	G	R. Kent, Rusthall
1602	0.001	G	RSLs
1602	1	GRC	ERA 1, Samos
1602	1	GRC	ERA Regional, Kavala
1602	1	GRC	ERA Regional, Kozani
1602	2	I	Raitre, Trieste + 2 st's
1602	-	IRN	R. Sarasarye, Bahabad
1602	-	IRN	R. Sarasarye, Kazerun
1602	-	IRN	Regional, Ahwaz
1602	1	MKD	R. Debar, Debar
1602	1	MKD	R. Resen, Resen
1602	1	QAT	QBS, Doha
1602	1	ROU	R. CNM, Arad
1602	1	ROU	R. Sud-Est, Slobozia
1602	5	RUS	R. Rossii + Reg., Gayny
1602	1	SCG	RTS Beograd 1 + R. Leskovac, L.
1602	1	SCG	RTS Beograd 2/3 + R. Negotin, N.
1602	5	SDN	SRTC, Kadogli
1611	100/50/25	CVA	Vatican R., Santa Maria di Galeria

EAST ASIA & PACIFIC

Abbreviations peculiar to the E.Asia/Pacific section of MW freq. lists: AF = allocated freq. C. = City. PO = Present operation on. Proj. = Projected station. Rptr. = repeater. Trtr = translator. Unk. = Unknown location.
Australia: The numeral preceding the call letters indicates the state: 2 = New South Wales. 3 = Victoria. 4 = Queensland. 5 = South Australia. 6 = Western Australia. 7 = Tasmania. 8 = Northern Territory. ACT = Australian Capital Territory. **China, P.R:** If several locations are listed for one frequency, the power listed applies to the first entry. For full details see country section. A (v) under location indicates variable frequency.
Indonesia: Only RRI stns included. For details of other stns see country section. **Philippines:** Province Abbreviations: Ag Nte = Agusan del Norte; Ag Sur = Agusan del Sur; Ant = Antique; Boh = Bohol; Bat = Batangas; Buk = Bukidnon; Bul = Bulacan; Cag = Cagayan; Cam Nte = Camarines Norte; Cam Sur = Camarines Sur; Dvo Nte = Davao del Norte; Dvo Sur = Davao del Sur; Isa = Isabela; I.Nte = Ilocos Norte; I.Sur = Ilocos Sur; LU = La Union; Lanao Nte = Lanao del Norte; Lanao Sur = Lanao del Sur; Mag = Maguindanao; Mas = Masbate; M Octal = Mindoro Occidental; Mind Or = Mindoro Oriental; Mis Or = Misamis Oriental; Mt Prov = Mountain Province; Neg Occ = Negros Occidental; Neg Or = Negros Oriental; Nva Viz = Nueva Vizcaya; Pam = Pampanga; Pang = Pangasinan; Que = Quezon; Riz = Rizal; S Cot = South Cotabato; S Leyte = Southern Leyte; S Sur = Surigao del Sur; Sor = Sorsogon; Tar = Tarlac; Z Nte = Zamboanga del Norte; Z Sur = Zamboanga del Sur; Zamb = Zambales. **Russia:** Regions in the Asian parts of Russia: Sib. = Siberia. FE = Far East.

kHz	kW	Ctry	Call	Station, location
153	1200	RUS		R.Rossii, Komsomolsk, FE
162	150	RUS		R.Rossii + Reg., Norilsk, Sib.
162	150	RUS		Reg., Yazykovo, Sib.
162	150	UZB		UZR (1), Toshkent
164	500	MNG		MRT (1), Ulaanbaatar
171	500	RUS		R.Rossii + Reg., Oyash, Sib.
171	150	RUS		R.Rossii + Reg., Yakutsk, FE
180	600	RUS		R.Rossii + Reg., Chita, Sib.
180	150	RUS		R.Rossii + Reg., Yelizovo, FE
189	1200	RUS		R.Rossii + Reg., Belogorsk, FE
207	150	RUS		R.Mayak, Tynda, FE
209	75	MNG		MRT (1), Dalanzadgad/Choibalsan
209	30	MNG		MRT (1), Ulgii
216	150	RUS		R.Rossii + Reg., Krasnoyarsk, Sib.
216	30	RUS		R.Rossii + Reg., Birobidzhan, FE
225	1000	RUS		R.Rossii + Rog., Surgut, Sib.
227	75	MNG		MRT (1), Altay
234	250	RUS		R.Rossii + Reg., Angarsk, Sib.
234	1000	RUS		R.Rossii + Reg., Arman, FE
243	500	RUS		R.Rossii + Reg., Razdolnoye, FE
252	150	TJK		TR (1), Yangiyul
261	150	RUS		R.Mayak, Chita (Atamanovka), Sib.
270	150	RUS		R.Rossii + Reg./R.Slovo, Novosibirsk, Sib.
279	500	RUS		R.Rossii + Reg., Yuzhno-Sakhalinsk, FE
279	150	RUS		R.Rossii + Reg., Selenginsk, Sib.
279	150	RUS		R.Rossii + Reg., Yekaterinburg
279	50	RUS		R.Rossii + Reg., Gorno-Altaysk, Sib.
279	150	TKM		Turkmen Radio (1), Asgabat
531	5	AUS	2PM	Port Macquarie
531	5	AUS	3GG	Warragul
531	5	AUS	4KZ	Innisfail
531	0.5	AUS	5RTI	Adelaide (HPONS)
531	10	AUS	6DL	ABC (RR), Dalwallinu
531	10	CHN		ZJ
531	300	IND		AIR (A), Jodhpur
531	10	J	JOQG	NHK (1), Morioka
531	1	J		NHK (1), Nago
531	5	NZL		531 PI, Auckland
531	2	NZL		Solid Gold AM, Alexandra
531	10	PHL	DYDW	Word Bc.Corp., Tacloban C., Leyte
531	5	PHL	DZBR	Kumintang Bc.System, Batangas C., Bat.
531	5	PHL	DXGH	Pacific Bc.System, Gen.Santos C, S Cot

kHz	kW	Ctry	Call	Station, location
531	5	RUS		Avtoradio, Yuzhno-Sakhalinsk, FE
531	25	THA		R.Thailand, Maha Sarakham
540	10	AUS	4QL	ABC (RR), Longreach
540	5	AUS	7SD	Scottsdale
540		CHN		CNR1
540		CHN		NM;QH
540	20	IND		AIR, Aizawl
540	10/2	INS		RRI, Bandung
540	5	J	JOJG	NHK (1), Yamagata
540	5	J	JOMG	NHK (1), Miyazaki
540	1	J	JOSK	NHK (1), Kitakyushu
540	1	J		NHK (1), Matsumoto
540	1	J		NHK (1), Nanao/Ishigaki
540	10	KOR		KBS, Hongseong
540	1	KOR		KBS, Jangsu/Jangheung/Jeomchon
540	5	NZL	1XC	R. Rhema, Tauranga
540	2	NZL	2XV	R. Rhema, New Plymouth
540	300	PAK		PBC, Peshawar
540	10	PHL	DYRB	Radio, Inc., Cebu C.
540	10	PHL	DZWT	Mt.Province BC, Baguio C., Benguet
540	50	RUS		R.Mayak, Orenburg
540	10	SMO	2AP	Samoan Bc.Sce.- 2AP, Apia
540	5	THA		Yaan Kraw, Bangkok
549	50	AUS	2CR	ABC (RR), Orange
549	1200	CHN		FJ (CNR5)
549	10	CHN		NM (2 st's);HEN
549	100	IND		AIR (A), Ranchi
549	10	J	JOAP	NHK (1), Okinawa
549	20	MLA		RTM Sarawak, Kuching
549	5	NZL	2XC	R. Rhema, Gisborne
549	2	NZL		R. Rhema, Kaitaia
549	1	NZL		R. Sport, Nelson
549	5	PHL	DXHM	Catholic Welfare Org., Madong, Mind Or
549	25-500	RUS		R.Mayak, FE , 4 st's (sync.)
549	100	THA		R.Thailand, Lampang
549	10	THA		R.Thailand, Mukdahan
549	40	TJK		TR (3), Dushanbe
549		VTN		Hanoi (2), My Van
550	5	HWA	KMVI	Wailuku, Maui
558	5	AUS	4AM	Atherton (Mareeba)
558	5	AUS	4GY	Gympie
558	50	AUS	6WA	ABC (RR), Wagin
558	2	AUS	7BU	Burnie
558	100	BGD		Bangladesh Betar, Khulna
558	120	CHN		XJ;FJ;NM (2 st's)
558	12	FJI		Fiji Bc.Corp. Ltd. (1), Suva
558	100	IND		AIR (B), Mumbai
558	20	J	JOCR	AMK, Kobe
558	250	KOR	HLQH	KBS, Daegu
558	5	NZL		R. Sport, Invercargill
558	50	PHL	DZXL	Radio Mindanao Netw., Pasig C., NCR
558	50	THA		R.Thailand, Songkhla
558	10	THA		R.Thailand, Kanchanaburi
558	1	TWN	BEH7	Fu Hsing BC (1), Taipei
558		VTN		Ho Chi Min C. (2), Quan Tre (v)
567	0.5	AUS	2BH	Broken Hill
567	10	AUS	4JK	ABC (RR), Julia Creek
567	0.1	AUS	6...	ABC (RR), W.A., 4 st's
567		CHN		CNR1
567	20	CHN		TJ
567	10	GUM	KGUM	"Newstalk 57 AM", Agana
567	20	HKG		RTHK (3), Golden Hill
567	300	IND		AIR, Dibrugarh
567	100	J	JOIK	NHK (1), Sapporo
567	100	KOR	HLKF	KBS, Jeonju
567	200	LAO		R.Nationale Lao, Vientiane
567	10	MLA		RTM Sabah, Tenom (r565)
567	100	NZL	2YA	National R., Wellington
567	300	PAK		PBC, Khuzdar
567	10	PHL	DWRM	Pilippine Bc.Sce., Puerto Princesa, Palawan
567	10	PHL	DWRB	Pilippine Bc.Sce., Naga C., Cam. Sur
567	5	PHL	DXCH	Pacific Bc.System, Cotabato C., Mag.
567	150	RUS		R.Rossii + Reg., Kyzyl, Sib.
567	5	THA		Jor.Sor. 5, Chaiyaphum
570	1	HWA	KQNG	Lihu'e, Kauai
570		VTN		Ha Giang (P)
572		VTN		Binh Duong (P)
576	50	AUS	2RN	ABC (RN), Sydney
576	200	BRM		MRTV, Yangon
576	10	CHN		YN;ZJ(v);HEN;FJ
576	200	IND		AIR, Alappuzha
576	10	J	JOHG	NHK (1), Kagoshima
576	1	J	JODG	NHK (1), Hamamatsu
576	40	KGZ		R.DDD, Osh
576	1	KOR	HLKZ	KBS, Suncheon
576	5	KOR		AFNK, Munsan
576	20	MLA		RTM Sarawak, Miri
576	100	NPL		R.Nepal, Surkhet
576	2	NZL	1XLR	Southern Star, Hamilton
576	10	PHL	DXMF	People's Bc.Sce., Davao C., Dvo Sur
576	10	PHL	DYMR	Pilippine Bc.Sce., Cebu C
576	5	PHL	DZMQ	Pilippine Bc.Sce., Dagupan C., Pang.
576	5	PHL	DZSH	Cebu Bc.Co., Tuguegarao, Cag.
576	150	RUS		R.Mayak, FE, 2 st's, (sync)
576	250-500	RUS		R.Mayak, Sib., 2 st's, (sync)
576	5	THA		Tor.Chor.Dor., Bangkok
576	150	TKM		Turkmen Radio (2/3), Asgabat
576	50	UZB		UZR (2), Toshkent
576		VTN		Khanh Hoa (2/P), Nha Trang
580	0.25	PAQ		R.Manukena
585	5	AUS	2WEB	W.Region Educ.Bc., Bourke
585	5	AUS	6PB	ABC (PNN), Perth
585	10	AUS	7RN	ABC (RN), Hobart
585	20	CBG		Nat.Radio of Cambodia, Steung Treng
585	200	CHN		Southeast BC, FJ
585	50	CHN		JS;JX;SX;HEN;GS
585	300	IND		AIR (A), Nagpur
585	50	INS		RRI, Surabaya
585	10	J	JOPG	NHK (1), Kushiro
585	20	LAO		R.Nationale Lao, Khantabouly
585	2	NZL	2XR	R.Ngati Porou, Ruatoria
585	1000	PAK		PBC, Islamabad
585	5	PHL	DXCP	Catholic Welfare Org., Gen.Santos C., S Cot
585	1	PHL	DYLL	Pilippine Bc.Sce., Iloilo C.
585	10	PNG		PNG Nat.Bc.Corp., Port Moresby
585	1200	RUS		VoR, Belogorsk, FE
585	5	SMA	KJAL	Asia Pac. Media Min.
585	5	THA		Wor.Por. Tho. 15, Chumphon
585	5	THA		Thor.Phor. 3, Phrae
585	1200	TWN		CBS (RTI), Fangliao
590	7.5	HWA	KSSK	Honolulu
594	50	AUS	3WV	ABC (RR), Horsham
594	200	BRU		Tutong
594	300	CHN		XZ;SD
594	1000	IND		AIR (FS), Chinsurah
594	300	J	JOAK	NHK (1), Tokyo
594	10	KOR		KBS, Yeongju
594	5	NZL	3XL	R. Rhema, Timaru
594	2	NZL		R. Rhema, Wanagnui
594	20	PHL	DZBB	GMA Network, Inc., Quezon C., NCR
594	10	PHL	DYWR	Palawan Bc.Corp., Tacloban C., Leyte
594	5	PHL	DXDB	Catholic Welfare Org., Malaybalay, Buk.
594	1000	RUS		R.Mayak, Surgut, Sib.
594	150	RUS		R.Mayak, Krasnoyarsk, Sib.
594	5	THA		Phon.Por.Thor.Or., Bangkok
594	10	TWN	BEH44	Fu Hsing BC (1), Kaohsiung
594	10	TWN	BEH2	Fu Hsing BC (2), Taipei
594	5	TWN	BEH38	Fu Hsing BC (2), Taichung
594		VTN		Danang (1), An Hai
603	10	AUS	2RN	ABC (RN), Nowra
603	10	AUS	4CH	ABC (RR), Charleville
603	2	AUS	6PH	ABC (RR), Port Hedland
603	50	CHN		NM + 25 st's
603	200	IND		AIR, Ajmer
603	5	J	JOKK	NHK (1), Okayama
603	5	J	JOOG	NHK (1), Obihiro
603	500	KOR	HLSA	KBS, Namyang (Seoul)
603	20	MLA		RTM Sabah, Kota Kinabalu
603	5	NZL		R.Waatea, Auckland
603	10	PHL	DZLL	Bicol Bc.System, Naga C., Cam Sur
603	5	PHL	DXPR	R.Mindanao Netw., Pagadian C, Z Sur
603	5	PHL	DZVV	COC Bc.Netw., Vigan, I.Sur
603	30	RUS		R.Mayak, Belogorsk/Skovorodino, FE
603	5	THA		Wor.Por.Tho. 12, Khon Kaen
603	1000	TWN		CBS (RTI), Lukang
610		VTN		Ho Chi Minh C. (H)
612	50	AUS	4QR	ABC (MS), Brisbane
612	10	AUS	6RN	ABC (RN), Dalwallinu
612	100	CHN		FJ;LN;SC
612	10/1	GUM	KUAM	"Isla 61", Agana
612	200	IND		AIR (A), Bangalore
612	100	J	JOLK	NHK (1), Fukuoka

kHz	kW	Ctry	Call	Station, location
612	2	NZL	3XG	R. Rhema, Christchurch
612	10	PAK		PBC (2), Karachi (Landhi)
612	5	PHL	DWSP	Philippine Bc.Corp., Itogon, Benguet
612	10	PHL	DYHP	R.Mindanao Netw., Cebu C.
612	25	RUS		R.Mayak, Norilsk, Sib.
612	10	RUS		R.VBC, Vladivostok
612	5	THA		Wor.Sor.Por., Lop Buri
612	5	THA		Mor.Kor., Chiang Mai
620	5	HWA	KIPA	Hilo (inactive)
620	10	HWA	KIPA-1	Kalaoa-Kona (inactive) (rptr)
620	5	HWA	KIPA-2	Na'alehu (inactive) (rptr)
621	50	AUS	3RN	ABC (RN), Melbourne
621	2	AUS	6EL	Bunbury
621	200	CHN		HL;QH;HB;SC;YN
621	20	HKG		RTHK (P), Golden Hill
621	100	IND		AIR (A), Patna
621	3	J	JOCG	NHK (1), Asahikawa
621	1	J	JOOK	NHK (1), Kyoto
621	1	J		NHK (1), Iidia/Nobeoka
621	10	KOR		KBS, Seogwipo
621	10	KOR		KBS, Taebaek
621	1	KOR		KBS, Yeongdong
621	500	KRE		Pyongyang BS (P/E), Chongjin
621	20	MLA		RTM Sarawak, Sibu
621	2	NZL	4XG	R. Rhema, Dunedin
621	2	NZL		R. Rhema, Whangarei
621	10	PHL	DXDC	R.Mindanao Netw., Davao C., Dvo Sur
621	5	PHL	DZTG	R.Philippines Netw., Tuguegarao, Cag.
621	1	PHL	DZVC	Pilippine Bc.Sce., Virac, Catanduanes
621	50	RUS		R.Rossii + Reg., Khabarovsk, FE
621	100	THA		R.Thailand, Khon Kaen
621	5	TUV	T2U2	R.Tuvalu, Funafuti
621	1	TWN		Taiwan BC, Tahsi
630	10	AUS	2PB	ABC (PNN), Sydney
630	50	AUS	4QN	ABC (RR), Townsville
630	5	AUS	6AL	ABC (RR), Albany
630	0.4	AUS	7RN	ABC (RN), Queenstown
630	100	BGD		Bangladesh Betar (B), Dhaka
630	200	CHN		JX (CNR2)
630	2.5	CKH	ZK1ZC	R.Cook Is., Matavera
630	100	IND		AIR, Thrisoor
630	50	INS		RRI, Makassar
630	10	KOR		KBS, Yeosu
630	5	KOR		KBS, Inje
630	10	NZL	2YZ	National R., Napier
630	100	PAK		PBC (1), Lahore
630	50	PHL	DZMM	ABS-CBN Bc.Corp., Quezon C., NCR
630	5	PHL	DYAG	Cadiz R. And TV Netw., Cadiz C., Cam. Sur
630	500	RUS		VoR, Komsomolsk, FE
630	5	THA		Mor.Thor.Bor. 11, Bangkok
630	10	TWN	BEG51	BCC (I), Ilan
630	10	TWN		Taiwan BC, Sungling
630		VTN		Quang Binh (1), Dong Hoi
639	5	AUS	2HC	Coff's Harbour
639	1	AUS	4MS	ABC (RR), Mossman
639	10	AUS	5CK	ABC (RR), Port Pirie
639	2	AUS	8RN	ABC (RN), Katherine
639	200	CHN		CNR1
639	10	FJI		Fiji Bc.Corp. Ltd. (1), Lautoka
639	100	IND		AIR, Kohima
639	10	J	JOPB	NHK (2), Shizuoka
639	5	J	JOIP	NHK (1), Oita
639	5	J	JOWN	STV, Hakodate
639	50	KOR	HLKC	KBS, Gaebong (Seoul)
639	2	NZL	4YW	National R., Alexandra
639	100	PAK		PBC, Karachi (2) (Landhi)
639	5	PHL	DXKR	R.Mindanao Netw., Koronadal, Cot. Sur
639	1	PHL	DZRL	R.Philippines Netw., Batac, I.Nte
639	75	RUS		R.Rossii + Reg., Omsk, Sib.
639	20	THA		R.Thailand, N. Si Thammarat
639	10	THA		R.Thailand, Lamphun
640	1	LAO		R.Nationale Lao, Vientiane
648	10	AUS	2NU	ABC (RR), Tamworth
648	2	AUS	6GF	ABC (RR), Kalgoorlie
648	150	CHN		GD + 5 st's
648	200	IND		AIR (A), Indore
648	10	J		AFN, Okinawa C.
648	5	J	JOIG	NHK (1), Toyama
648	1	KOR		KBS, Boseong
648	20	MLA		RTM Sarawak, Limbang
648	100	NPL		R.Nepal, Dhankuta
648	10	PHL	DWRH	Pacific Bc.System, Santiago C., Isa.
648	5	PHL	DXMB	R.Mindanao Netw., Malaybalay, Buk.
648	5	PHL	DWPS	We.Philippinnes Bc.Corp., Puerto Princesa, Palawan
648	5	PHL	DYXR	Manila Bc.Co., Cebu C
648	1000	RUS		VoR, Razdolnoye, FE
648	10	SMA	WVUV	Pago Pago (Leone)
648	25	THA		R.Thailand, Khon Kaen
648	1000	TJK		Various relays, Orzu
648		UZB		UZR (1), Samarqand
648		VTN		Binh Dinh (1), An Nhon
650	5	HWA	KHNR	Honolulu
650		VTN		Bac Giang (P), Ha Bac
657	10	AUS	2BY	ABC (RR), Byrock
657	2	AUS	6—	Perth (HPONS)
657	2	AUS	8RN	ABC (RN), Darwin
657	300	CHN		HEN;JL;ZJ
657	200	IND		AIR (A), Kolkata
657	50	KOR	HLKM	KBS, Chuncheon
657	1500	KRE		Pyongyang BS (P), Kangnam
657	20	MLA		RTM, Gerik
657	50	NZL	2YC	Parl. Bc/So.Star, Wellington
657	5	PHL	DXDD	Catholic Welfare Org., Ozamis C., Mis. Occ.
657	5	PHL	DWRN	Naga C., Cam. Sur
657	5	PHL	DYVR	R.Mindanao Netw., Roxas C., Capiz
657	1	PHL	DYES	Philippine Bc.Sce., Borongan, E. Samar
657	1	PHL	DZLU	Satellite Bc.Corp., S.Fernando C., LU
657	5	THA		Jor.Sor. 1, Bangkok
657	20	TWN	BED34	BCC (N), Taipei
657	10	TWN	BEV59	Cheng Sheng BC (2), Taichung
657		VTN		Ho Chi Minh C. (1), Quan Tre (v)
666	5	AUS	2CN	ABC (MS), Canberra
666	2	AUS	4LM	Mt. Isa
666	2	AUS	4CC	Biloela (trtr)
666	1	AUS	6LN	Carnarvon
666	200	CHN		QH+ 9 st's
666	100	IND		AIR (B), New Delhi
666	100	J	JOBK	NHK (1), Osaka
666	20	NCL		R.Nouvelle Caledonie, Noumea
666	50	PHL	DZRH	Manila Bc.Co., Makati C, NCR
666	10	PHL	DXRP	Pilippine Bc.Sce., Davao C., Dvo Sur
666	150	RUS		R.Mayak, Komsomolsk, FE
666	150	RUS		R.Rossii + Reg., Tynda, FE
666	10	RUS		BBC, Yekaterinburg, Sib.
666	5	THA		Thor.Phor. 3, Tak
666	5	THA		Thor.Phor. 2, Surin
666	30	UZB		UZR (3), Toshkent
666		VTN		Khanh Hoa (1), Nha Trang
670	10	HWA	KPUA	Hilo
675	10	AUS	2CO	ABC (RR), Albury
675	5	AUS	6BE	ABC (RR), Broome
675	200	BRU		Serasa
675	200	CHN		NM;ZJ;YN
675	10	HKG		RTHK (6), Peng Chau
675	100	IND		AIR, Itanagar
675	20	IND		AIR, Chhattarpur
675	5	J	JOUG	NHK (1), Yamaguchi
675	5	J	JOVK	NHK (1), Hakodate
675	10	KOR		KBS, Jeonju
675	10	MLA		RTM Sabah, Lahad Datu
675	10	NZL	3YA	National R., Christchurch
675	10	PNG		PNG Bc.Corp., Lae/Wewak
675	5	PHL	DYKC	R.Philippines Netw., Mandaue, Cebu
675	5	PHL	DWLW	Intercontinental Bc.Corp., Laoag C., I.Nte
675	1	PHL	DXGD	Sulu Tawi-Tawi Bc.Found., Bongao, Tawi-Tawi
675	40	RUS		R.Radonezh, Razdolnoye, FE
675	5	THA		Sor.Thor.Ror. 2, Bangkok
675	150	TKM		Turkmen R. (1), Asgabat
675	1	TWN		Cheng Sheng BC, Peikang
675	5	UZB		UZR (1), Zarafshon
675	5	UZB		UZR (2), Qo'ng ' irot
675		VTN		Hanoi (1), My Van
675	10	TKM		Turkmen R. (2/3), Türkmenbasy
684	10	AUS	2KP	ABC (RR), Kempsey
684	4	AUS	6BS	ABC (RR), Busselton
684	1	AUS	8RN	ABC (RN), Tennant Creek
684	1200	CHN		FJ(CNR6) + 9 st's
684	1	TMP		R.Timor-Leste, Dili
684	2.5	FJI		Fiji Bc.Corp Ltd. (1), Labasa
684	100	IND		AIR (A), Kozhikode

kHz	kW	Ctry	Call	Station, location
684	20	IND		AIR, Port Blair
684	10	IND		AIR (C), Srinagar
684	5	J	JOAG	NHK (1), Nagasaki
684	5	J	JODF	IBC, Morioka
684	1	J	JOLO	IBC, Ofunato
684	250	KRE		Pyongyang BS (P), Samgo
684	100	NPL		R.Nepal, Pokhara
684	10	PHL	DYEZ	Manila Bc.Co., Bacolod, Neg. Occ.
684	5	PHL	DWJJ	Kaissar Bc.Netw., Cabanatuan, Nva. Ecija
684	5	PHL	DZCV	Filipinas Bc.Netw.,, Tuguegarao, Cag.
684	1	PHL	DWGW	Intercontinental Bc.Corp., Legaspi C., Albay
684	10	RUS		R.Nakhodka, N., FE
684	5	THA		Thor.Phor. 4, N.Si Thammarat
684	5	THA		Yaan Kraw, Udon Thani
684	10	TWN	BEC22	Han Sheng BS, Taipei
690	10	HWA	KORL	Honolulu
690		VTN		Da Lac (1/4), Buon Me Thuot
693	5	AUS	3EE	Melbourne
693	5	AUS	4KQ	Brisbane (Newstead)
693	0.5	AUS	4KZ	Tully (trtr)
693	0.5	AUS	4LM	Cloncurry (trtr)
693	2	AUS	5SY	ABC (RR), Streaky Bay
693	5	AUS	6WR	R.Stn. 6WR, Kununurra
693	1000	BGD		Bangladesh Betar (A), Dhaka
693	200	CHN		SN
693	1	INS		RRI, Sungai Liat
693	500	J	JOAB	NHK (2), Tokyo
693	20	MLA		RTM Sabah, Kota Kinabalu (r690v)
693	5	NZL		R.Sport, Dunedin
693	10	PHL	DYPH	Manila Bc.Co., Pto.Princesa, Palawan
693	10	PHL	DZTP	Tirad Pass R/TV Bc.Netw., Candon, I.Sur
693	10	PHL	DXBC	R.Mindanao Netw., Butuan, Ag. Nte
693	1	PHL	DXDX	R.Philippines Netw., Gen. Santos C., S.Cot.
693	1	PHL	DYKH	Manila Bc.Co., Kalibo, Aklan
693	150	RUS		R.Rossii, Yazykovo, Sib,
693	25	RUS		R.Rossii + Reg., Anadyr, FE
693	5	THA		Siang Adison, Saraburi
693	10	TWN	BEC25	Han Sheng BS, Taoyuan
693	10	TWN	BEC32	Han Sheng BS, Tainan
700		CHN		LN
702	50	AUS	2BL	ABC (MS), Sydney
702	10	AUS	6KP	ABC (RR), Karratha
702	150	CHN		JS (CRI DS) + 7 st's
702	200	IND		AIR (B/FS), Jalandhar
702		INS		RRI, Manokwari
702	10	J	JOFB	NHK (2), Hiroshima
702	10	J	JOKD	NHK (2), Kitami
702	50	KRE		Korean Central BS (C/R), Chongjin
702	10	NZL	1XP	R.Pacific, Auckland
702		NZL		Newstalk ZB, Rotorua
702	50	PHL	DZAS	FEBC, Valenzuela, NCR
702	7	RUS		R.Mayak, Bratsk, Sib.
702	150	TJK		TR (1), Orzu
702	10	TWN	BEP24	Ching Cha BS, Taichung
702		VTN		Danang (2/Q/D), An Hai
705	2.5	LAO		R.Nationale Lao, Luang Prabang
711	10	AUS	4QW	ABC (RR), St. George
711	10	AUS	7NT	ABC (RR), Launceston
711	20	BRU		S. Hanching (r710v)
711	10	CHN		QH + 7 st's
711	200	IND		AIR, Siliguri
711	500	KOR	HLKA	KBS, Sorae (Seoul)
711	5	NZL	2XP	R.Pacific, Wellington
711	10	PHL	DZLW	Penafrancia Bc.Corp., Naga C., Cam. Sur
711	5	PHL	DXIC	R.Mindanao Netw., Iligan C., Lanao Nte
711	5	PHL	DXRD	Nation Bc.Corp., Davao C., Dvo. Sur
711	5	PHL	DZYI	Nation Bc.Corp., Ilagan, Isa.
711	5	PHL	DYBR	East Visayan Bc., Tacloban, Leyte
711	5	PHL	DZVR	Newsounds Bc.Netw., Laoag, I.Nte
711	7	RUS		R.Vostok Rossii, Khabarovsk, FE
711	5	RUS		R.Rossii, Nikolayevsk, FE
711	5	RUS		R.Rossii + Reg., Okhotsk, FE
711	0.2	RUS		Avtoradio, Abakan, FE
711	20	THA		R.Thailand, U.Ratchathani
711	5	THA		Wor.Por.Thor., Chiang Mai
711	5	THA		Wor.Sor.Por., Lop Buri
711	250	TWN		VO Kuanghua, Hsinfeng
711	10	TWN	BED92	BCC (C), Tainan
711	50	UZB		UZR (3), Buxoro
711	5	UZB		UZR (3), Urganch
711		VTN		Can Tho (1), Thoi Long
720	0.4	AUS	2ML	ABC (RR), Murwillumbah
720	0.05	AUS	2RN	ABC (RN), Armidale
720	2	AUS	3MT	ABC (RR), Omeo
720	4	AUS	4AT	ABC (RR), Atherton
720	50	AUS	6WF	ABC (MS), Perth
720	200	CHN		BJ (CNR2)
720	5	HWA	KUAI	'Ele'ele, Kauai
720	200	IND		AIR (A), Chennai
720	10	INS		RRI, Ambon
720	1	J	JOIL	KBC, Kitakyushu
720	500	KRE		Korean Central BS (C/R), Wiwon (Kanggye)
720	10	NZL	4YZ	National R., Invercargill
720	10	PHL	DYOK	Manila Bc.Co., Iloilo C
720	5	PHL	DZSO	Newsounds Bc.Netw., San Fernando, LU
720	5	PHL	DZJO	Bayanihan Bc.Corp., San Juan, NCR
720	1000	RUS		R.Mayak/VoR, Yuzhno-Sakhalinsk, FE
720	10	THA		R.Thailand, Krabi
720	5	THA		Sor.Thor.Ror. 5, Chon Buri
720	1	TKM		Turkmen Radio (1), Ek-Arça/Etrek
720	10	TWN	BED58	BCC (N), Taichung
720		VTN		Dong Nai (P), Bien Hoa
720		VTN		Thua Thien Hue (P), Hue
729	50	AUS	5RN	ABC (RN), Adelaide
729	150	CHN		JX;HEN
729	100	IND		AIR (A), Guwahati
729	50	J	JOCK	NHK (1), Nagoya
729	50	KRE		Pyongyang BS (P), Sepo
729	20	MLA		RTM Sarawak, Kuching
729	2.5	NZL		R.Sport, Whangarei
729	2	NZL	1YP	National R., Tokoroa
729	0.9	NZL	4XX	Ranfurly R., Ranfurly
729	100	PAK		PBC (2), Peshawar
729	10	PHL	DWPE	Pilippine Bc.Sce., Tuguegarao, Cag.
729	5	PHL	DXOR	Cagayan de Oro C., Mis. Or.
729	5	PHL	DZGB	People's Bc.Netw., Legaspi C., Albay
729	5	PHL	DXMY	R.Mindanao Netw., Cotabato C., Mag.
729	25	THA		R.Thailand, N. Ratchasima
729	0.5	TWN	BEE43	Shih Hsin BS, Taipei
729		VTN		Quang Binh (2), Dong Hoi
738	50	AUS	2NR	ABC (RR), Grafton
738	5	AUS	6MJ	ABC (RR), Manjimup
738	150	CHN		HN; JL; XJ;ZJ
738	200	IND		AIR (A), Hyderabad
738	1	INS		RRI, Jermber
738	10	J	JORR	RBC, Naha, Okinawa
738	5	J	JOLR	KNB, Toyama
738	1	J		KNB, Takaoka
738	100	KOR	HLKG	KBS, Daegu
738	10	MAC		R.Vilaverde
738	5	NZL		R.Pacific, Christchurch
738	60	PHL	DZRB	Pilippine Bc.Sce., Quezon C., NCR
738	20	OCE		R.Tahiti, Mahina
738	50	RUS		R.Novaya volna, Vladivostok, FE
738	40	RUS		R.Rossii + Reg., Chelyabinsk, Sib.
738	25	RUS		R.Rossii + Reg., Palana, FE
738	5	THA		Wor.Por.Tho. 5, Songkhla
738	5	THA		Wor.Por.Tho. 2, Chiang Mai
738	100	TWN	BEL2	Taiwan Chu Yuyeh BS, Penghu
740	150	CBG		Nat.Radio of Cambodia, Phnom Penh
740		VTN		Binh Dinh (2), An Nhon
747	10	AUS	4QS	ABC (RR), Toowoomba
747	5	AUS	6SE	Esperance
747	1	AUS	6FMS	Exmouth
747	2	AUS	7PB	ABC (PNN), Hobart
747	0.2	AUS	8JB	ABC (RR), Jabiru
747		CHN		BJ (CNR9)
747		CHN		AH (CRI DS1)
747	100	CHN		YN + 23 st's
747	300	IND		AIR (A), Lucknow
747	5	INS		RRI, Bengkulu
747	500	J	JOIB	NHK (2), Sapporo
747	100	KOR	HLKH	KBS, Gwangju
747	20	KAZ		R.Liberty, Qaraghandy
747	10	MLA		RTM Sabah, Tawau (r750)
747	5	PHL	DXND	Notre Dame Bc.Corp., Kidapawan, N.Cot.
747	10	PHL	DYHB	R.Mindanao Netw., Bacolod, Neg. Occ.
747	10	PHL	DZJC	Manila Bc.Co., Laoag C, I.Nte
747	10	SMO	2AP	Samoan Bc.Sce.- 2AP, Apia
747	5	THA		Ror.Dor., Bangkok
747	5	THA		Thor.Phor. 2, Udon Thani
747	250	TWN		CBS (RTI), Minhsiung

kHz	kW	Ctry	Call	Station, location
747	10	TWN	BED57	BCC (H), Taipei
747		VTN		Ho Chi Minh City (4)
750	1	CHN		SX;LN
756	5	AUS	2TR	ABC (RR), Taree
756	10	AUS	3RN	ABC (RN), Wangaratta (rptr)
756	2	AUS	6TZ	Margaret River
756		CHN		CNR1
756	100	IND		AIR, Jagdalpur
756	10/2	INS		RRI, Purwokerto
756	10	J	JOGK	NHK (1), Kumamoto
756	100	KOR		KBS, Yeoju
756	10	NZL	1YA	National R., Auckland
756	150	PAK		PBC (1), Quetta (Pishin)
756	1	PHL	DWHL	Beta Bc.Syst., Olongapo C., Zamb.
756	10	PHL	DWRS	Pilippine Bc.Sce., Tayug, Pang.
756	5	PHL	DWNW	Intercontinental Bc.Corp., Naga C., Cam.Sur
756	2	PHL	DXJM	R.Corp.of the Philippines, Butuan C., Ag.Nte
756	5	THA		Nor.Thor.Phor., Narathiwat
756	5	THA		Kor.Wor.Sor. 1, Surin
756	1	TWN		Sheng Li chih Sheng, Makung
756	50	UZB		UZR (4), Toshkent
756		VTN		Long An (P), Tan An
760	10	HWA	KGU	Honolulu
765	4	AUS	2EC	Bega
765	0.5	AUS	4GC	Hughenden (trtr)
765	5	AUS	5CC	Port Lincoln
765	0.1	AUS	6SAT	Tom Price/Paraburdoo. (trtr)
765	0.5	AUS	8HOT	Katherine (trtr)
765	600	CHN		FJ (CNR5)
765	10	CHN		GZ(2 st's); NM; GD;AH
765	200	IND		AIR (A), Dharwad
765	1	INS		RRI, Tual
765	0.2	INS		RRI, Banjarmasin
765	5	J	JOJF	YBS, Kofu
765	5	J	JOPF	KRY, Shunan
765	10	KOR	HLCQ	MBC, Daejeon
765	50	KRE		Korean Central BS (C/R), Hyesan
765	2.5	NZL	2XT	R.Kahungunu, Napier
765	5	PHL	DXGS	Radio, Inc., Gen. Santos C., S.Cot.
765	5	PHL	DYAR	Nation Bc.Corp., Cebu C.
765	5	PHL	DZYT	Nation Bc.Corp., Tuguegarao, Cag.
765	10	PHL	DYPR	Palawan Bc.Corp., Puerto Princesa, Palawan
765	5	RUS		R.Vostok Rossii, Bikin, FE
765	5	THA		Neung.Por.Nor., Lampang
765	5	THA		Thor.Or. 2, Lop Buri
765		VTN		Thai Binh (P)
774	50	AUS	3LO	ABC (MS), Melbourne
774	5	AUS	4TO	Townsville
774	100	CHN		HB;SX;LN
774	100	IND		AIR, Shimla
774	10	INS		RRI, Fak-Fak
774	500	J	JOUB	NHK (2), Akita
774	10	KOR	HLAJ	MBC, Jeju
774	10	KOR	HLAN	MBC, Chuncheon
774	10	MLA		RTM Sabah, Tenom (r777)
774	5	NZL		R.Sport, New Plymouth
774	10	PHL	DXSO	Pilippine Bc.Sce., Marawi C., Lanao Sur
774	25	PHL	DWWW	Interactive Bc.Media, Inc., Quezon C., NCR
774	10	PHL	DYRI	R.Mindanao Netw., Iloilo C
774	1	PHL	DXSM	Pilippine Bc.Sce., Jolo, Sulu
774	5	THA		Sor.Sor.Sor., Udon Thani
774	5	THA		Phon.Mor. 2, Rayong
774	10	TWN	BEV88	Hsien Sheng BC, Taoyuan
774	10	TWN	BEV94	Taiwan BC, Taichung
782		VTN		Nghe An (P), Vinh (v)
783	2	AUS	6VA	Albany
783	2	AUS	8AL	ABC (RR), Alice Springs
783	200	CHN		China Huayi BC, FJ
783	100	CHN		HEB;GD
783	20	HKG		RTHK (5), Golden Hill
783	20	IND		AIR (C), Chennai
783	10	KOR		KBS, Yeongwol
783	10	MLA		RTM Sabah, Sandakan
783	10	NZL	2YB	Access R./Samoan Cap.R., Wellington
783	10	PHL	DXRA	RMC Bc.Co., Inc., Davao C., Dvo Sur
783	5	PHL	DYME	Masbate Comm. Bc.Co., Masbate C.
783	5	PHL	DZNL	Philippine Bc.Corp., San Fernando, LU
783	75	RUS		Russkoye R.Lemma, Vladivostok, FE
783	10	THA		R.Thailand, Ranong
783	5	THA		Thor.Phor. 3, Kamphaeng Phet
783		VTN		Can Tho (2), Thoi Long

kHz	kW	Ctry	Call	Station, location
790	5	HWA	KKON	Kealakekua
792	25	AUS	4RN	ABC (RN), Brisbane
792	200	CHN		GX + 7 st's
792	100	IND		AIR (A), Pune
792	1	J		NHK (1), Takayama/Enbetsu
792	1	J		NHK (1), Takada/Naze
792	50	KOR	HLSQ	Seoul Bc.System, Goyang (Seoul)
792	100	NPL		R.Nepal, Kathmandu
792	5	NZL	1XSR	R.Sport, Hamilton
792	150	PAK		Azad Kashmir Radio, Muzaffarabad
792	10	PHL	DXBN	Pilippine Bc.Sce., Butuan, Ag.Nte
792	5	PHL	DYRR	Ormoc Bc.Co., Ormoc C., Leyte
792	5	PHL	DXPD	People's Bc.Sce., Pagadian, Z.Sur
792	5	PHL	DWGV	GV Bc.System, Angeles C, Pampanga
792	5	PHL	DWES	Rolin Bc.Enterprises, Narra, Palawan
792	50	RUS		R.Rossii + Reg., Aleksandrovsk-Sakh., FE
792	25	RUS		R.Rossii + Reg., Abakan, Sib.
792	20	THA		Wor.Por.Thor., Bangkok
792	10	TWN	BEC33	Han Sheng BS, Hualien
792	1	TWN	BEV79	Keelung BS, Keelung
800	1	LAO		R.Nationale Lao, Muang Hay
801	5	AUS	2RF	Gosford (HPONS)
801	2	AUS	4QY	ABC (RR), Cairns
801	2	AUS	5RM	Berri
801		CHN		AH (CRI DS2)
801		CHN		SD (CRI DS)
801	50	CHN		Zhujiang EBS, GD
801	10	CHN		HEB + 20 st's
801	10	GUM	KTWG	TWR, Agana
801	200	IND		AIR, Jabalpur
801	10	INS		RRI, Semarang
801	1	INS		RRI, Medan
801	500	KRE		Pyongyang BS, Hwadae
801	10	MLA		RTM Sabah, Kudat
801	1	NZL	2XL	R.Rhema, Nelson
801	5	PHL	DWFA	Hypersonic Bc.Center, Sorsogon C.
801	1	PHL	DXBL	Nation Bc.Corp., Bislig, Surigao S.
801	5	PHL	DXES	Consolidated Bc.System, Inc., Gen.Santos C., S.Cot.
801	5	PHL	DYKA	Catholic Welfare Org., San José, Ant.
801	5	PHL	DYWC	Franciscan Bc.Corp., Dumaguete, Neg. Or.
801	10	PHL	DZNC	Newsounds Bc.Netw., Cauayan, Isa.
801	1200	RUS		VoR, Chita (Atamanovka), Sib.
801	5	THA		Thor.Or. 15, Chiang Rai
801	5	THA		Thor.Or. 8, U.Ratchathani
801	5	THA		Mor.Thor.Bor. No. 31, N.Sawan
801	1000	TJK		Various relays, Orzu
801	250	TWN		VO Kuanghua, Kuanyin
801	1	TWN		Chien Kuo BS, Hsinhua
810	10	AUS	2BA	ABC (RR), Bega
810	10	AUS	6RN	ABC (RN), Perth
810	200	CHN		ZJ + 4 st's
810	10	FJI		Fiji Bc.Corp. Ltd. (2), Labasa
810	300	IND		AIR (A), Rajkot
810	7.5	INS		RRI, Merauke
810	50	J		AFN, Tokyo
810	20	KOR	HLCT	MBC, Daegu
810	50	KRE		Korean Central BS (C/R), Kaesong
810	10	NPL		R.Nepal, Dipayal
810	10	NZL	4YA	National R., Dunedin
810	10	PNG		PNG Bc.Corp., Rabaul
810	10	PHL	DZRJ	Rajah Bc.Netw., Manila, NCR
810	150	RUS		R.Rossii + Reg., Razdolnoye, FE
810	50	RUS		R.Mayak, Yekaterinburg, Sib.
810	10	RUS		Avtoradio-Krasnoyarsk, K., Sib.
810	20	THA		R.Thailand, Nong Khai
810	10	THA		R.Thailand, Trang
810	10	TWN	BEV54	Kuo Sheng BC, Changhua
818		VTN		Dong Thap (P), Cao Lanh (v)
819	10	AUS	2GL	ABC (RR), Glen Innes
819	5	AUS	6KW	ABC (RR), Kununurra
819	200	CHN		SX; XJ(2)
819	200	IND		AIR (A), New Delhi
819	5	J	JONK	NHK (1), Nagano
819	20	KOR	HLCN	MBC, Gwangju
819	500	KRE		Korean Central BS (C), Pyongyang
819	20	MLA		RTM Sarawak, Miri
819	10	NZL	1YZ	National R., Rotorua
819	1	PHL	DWMG	Vanguard R.Netw., Solano, Nva Viz
819	10	PHL	DXUM	Mt.Apo Science Found., Davao C, Dvo Sur
819	5	PHL	DWRI	Nation Bc.Corp., Laoag C, I.Nte

kHz	kW	Ctry	Call	Station, location
819	1	PHL	DXSC	Zamboanga C., Z.Sur
819	5	PHL	DYVL	Manila Bc.Co., Tacloban, Leyte
819	10	THA		R.Thailand, Bangkok
819	15	TJK		TR (1), Khujand
819	10	TWN	BED28	BCC (N), Taitung
819	10	TWN	BEP28	Ching Cha BS, Kaohsiung
819	5	TWN	BEV35	Cheng Sheng BC, Taipei
819		VTN		Dac Lac (2/4), Buon me Tuhot
828	10	AUS	3GI	ABC (RR), Sale
828	1	AUS	4GC	Charters Towers
828	10	AUS	6GN	ABC (RR), Geraldton
828	50	CHN		BJ; GD; HEN (2 st's)(v); HB(2 st's)(v)
828	20	IND		AIR, Silchar
828	300	J	JOBB	NHK (2), Osaka
828	10	MLA		RTM Sabah, Lahad Datu
828	2	NZL	2XS	Magic 828, Palmerston No.
828	100	PAK		PBC (1), Karachi
828	5	PHL	DWZR	Hypersonic Bc.Center, Legaspi C., Albay
828	10	PHL	DXCC	R.Mindanao Netw., Cagayan de Oro C., Mis. Or.
828	10	PHL	DYER	Katigbak Entertainment, Pto. Princesa, Palawan
828	1	PHL	DZTC	Radyo Pilipino Corp., Tarlac C.
828	150	RUS		R.Mayak, Kyzyl, Sib.
828	5	THA		Wor.Por.Tho. 4, N.Si Thammarat
828	5	THA		Thor.Phor. 3, Sukhothai
828		VTN		Son La (P)
830	10	HWA	KHVH	Honolulu
830		VTN		Tien Giang (P), My Tho
837	10	AUS	4RK	ABC (RR), Rockhampton
837	1	AUS	6ED	ABC (RR), Esperance
837	0.5	AUS	7XS	Queenstown
837		CHN		CNR1
837	10	CHN		HL;XJ;LN
837	100	IND		AIR (A), Vijayawada
837	10	J	JOQK	NHK (1), Niigata
837	1	J		NHK (1), Nayoro
837	50	KOR	HLKY	CBS, Seoul
837	2	NZL	1YX	National R., Kaitaia
837	2	NZL	1YX	National R., Whangarei
837	5	PHL	DXRE	Nation Bc.Corp., Gen. Santos C., S.Cotab.
837	10	PHL	DYFM	Consolidated Bc.System, Inc., Iloilo C.
837	5	PHL	DZXE	Fairwaves Bc.Netw., Vigan, I.Sur
837	5	THA		Nor.Thor.Phor., Sakon Nakhon
837	10	THA		R.Thailand, Pathum Thani
837	10	TWN	BED43	BCC (C), Taichung
837	1	TWN	BEV56	Sheng Li chih Sheng (1), Tainan
837		VTN		Can Tho (P)
846	10	AUS	2RN	ABC (RN), Canberra
846	5	AUS	4EL	Cairns
846	2	AUS	6CA	ABC (RR), Carnarvon
846	10	BGD		Bangladesh Betar, Bagura
846		CHN		BJ (CRI DS3)
846	20	CHN		SX + 22 st's
846	200	IND		AIR (A), Ahmedabad
846	5	J		NHK (1), Koriyama
846	1	J		NHK (1), Uwajima/Hitoyoshi
846	10	KIR		R.Kiribati, Naranakei, Betio I. (v)
846	10	KOR	HLAU	MBC, Ulsan
846	5	KOR		KBS, Yanggu
846	10	MLA		RTM Sarawak, Kuching
846	2	NZL	2ZD	Newstalk ZB/R.Sport, Masterton
846	50	PHL	DZRV	R.Veritas, Quezon C., NCR
846	10	THA		R.Thailand, Phetchabun
846	250	TWN		VO Kuanghua, Kuanyin
846	10	TWN	BEC38	Han Sheng BS, Penghu
846	10	TWN	BEH56	Fu Hsing BC (2), Kaohsiung
846		VTN		Thanh Hoa (P)
850	5	HWA	KHLO	Hilo
850	1	INS		RRI, Bogor
855	2	AUS	3CR	Community R.Fed.Ltd., Collingwood
855	10	AUS	4QB	ABC (RR), Pialba
855	10	AUS	4QO	ABC (RR), Eidsvold
855	50	CHN		YN (CNR2);XJ
855	20	CLN		SLBC, Periyakulam
855	50	INS		RRI, Medan (P.Cermin)
855	10/2	INS		RRI, Mataram
855	10	KOR	HLCX	MBC, Jeonju
855	500	KRE		Pyongyang BS (P), Sangwon
855	2	NZL	1XH	R.Rhema, Hamilton
855	10	PAK		PBC (2), Quetta

kHz	kW	Ctry	Call	Station, location
855	.1	PHL	DXWG	Intercontinental Bc.Corp., Ilagan C. Lanao Nte
855	10	PHL	DZGE	Filipinas Bc.Netw,., Naga C., Cam.Sur
855	10	PHL	DXGO	Pacific Bc.System, Davao C., Dvo Sur
855	5	PHL	DXZH	Cebu Bc.Co., Zamboanga C., Z.Sur
855	20	RUS		R.3, Petropavlovsk-K., FE
855	5	THA		Mor.Thor.Bor. 12, Prachin Buri
855	10	TWN	BED27	BCC (N), Hualien
855	1	TWN	BEV72	Cheng Sheng BC (1), Chia-i
855	1	TWN	BEV24	Min Pen BC (2), Taipei
861		VTN		Lai Chau (P)
864	2	AUS	4GR	Toowoomba
864	2	AUS	6AM	Northam
864	2	AUS	7RPH	Bc.Sce.for Handicapped Inc., Hobart
864	50	CHN		AH; ZJ (2 stn's);HEN
864	10	HKG		Hong Kong Comm. Bc.Co., Peng Chau
864	100	IND		AIR, Shillong
864	10/2	INS		RRI, Cirebon
864	10	J	JOXR	ROK, Naha, Okinawa
864	5	J	JOPR	FBC, Fukui
864	3	J	JOHE	HBC, Asahikawa
864	3	J	JOQF	HBC, Muroran
864	1	J		HBC, Enbetsu
864	1	J	JOSO	SBC, Matsumoto
864	1	J	JOXN	CRT, Nasu
864	100	KOR	HLKR	KBS, Gangneung
864	250	KRE		Korean Central BS (C/R), Sinuiju
864	10	NZL	4ZA	Newstalk ZB, Invercargill
864	10	PNG		PNG Bc.Corp., Madang
864	10	PHL	DYHH	Siam Bc.Netw.Corp., Bogo, Cebu
864	5	PHL	DZSP	Nation Bc.Corp., San Pablo C., Laguna
864	5	PHL	DWSI	Nation Bc.Corp., Santiago, Isa.
864	5	PHL	DZWM	Catholic Welfare Org., Alaminos, Pang.
864	25	RUS		R.Shanson, Blagoveshchensk, FE
864	10	THA		R.Thailand, Si Sa Ket
864	10	THA		R.Thailand, Tak
864	10	THA		R.Thailand, Phattahalung
864	10	TWN	BED25	BCC (N), Kaohsiung
864	10	TWN	BEV52	Chung Sheng BC, Taichung
870	5	HWA	KAIM	Honolulu
873	5	AUS	2GB	Sydney
873	2	AUS	4—	Innisfail (HPONS)
873	2	AUS	6DB	ABC (RR), Derby
873	100	BGD		Bangladesh Betar, Chittagong
873	200	CHN		HL + 8 st's
873	400	CLN		SLBC, Puttalam
873	300	IND		AIR (B), Jalandhar
873	500	J	JOGB	NHK (2), Kumamoto
873	20	MLA		RTM Sarawak, Limbang
873	1	NZL	3ZE	Newstalk ZB, Ashburton
873	10	PHL	DXJS	Pilippine Bc.Sce., Tandag, S.Sur
873	5	PHL	DXRB	Nation Bc.Corp., Butuan C., Ag.Nte
873	5	PHL	DXRT	Nation Bc.Corp., Jolo, Sulu
873	5	PHL	DZPA	Abra Comm.Bc.Corp., Bangued, Abra
873	5	PHL	DZRC	Filipinas Bc.Netw,., Legaspi C., Albay
873	300	RUS		R.Mayak, Khabarovsk, FE
873	5	THA		Wor.Kor.Thor.Mor., Bangkok
873		VTN		Can Tho (4), Thoi Long
882	2	AUS	3YB	Warrnambool
882	5	AUS	4BH	Brisbane
882	2	AUS	6PR	Perth
882	100	CHN		FJ + 9 st's
882	400	CLN		TWR, Puttalam
882	300	IND		AIR, Imphal
882		INS		RRI, Kendari
882	10	J	JOPK	NHK (1), Shizuoka
882	3	J	JOWS	STV, Kushiro
882	1	J		STV, Esashi
882	20	KOR	HLKI	KBS, Daejon
882	250	KRE		Korean Central BS (C/R), Wonsan
882	75	MNG		MRT (1), Mörön
882	10	NZL	1YC	Parl.Bc./So.Star, Auckland
882	50	PHL	DWIZ	Aliw Bc.Corp., Navotas, NCR
882	10	PHL	DXMS	Notre Dame Bc.Corp., Cotabato C., Mag.
882	10	PHL	DYOG	Pilippine Bc.Sce., Calbayog, W. Samar
882	1	PHL	DXRG	Pilippine Bc.Sce., Gingoog, Mis. Or.
882	10	TWN	BEG77	BCC (N), Hsinchu
882	1	TWN		Feng Ming BC, Penghu
886	0.5	INS		RRI, Serui
891	5	AUS	4TAB	Townsville (HPONS)
891	50	AUS	5AN	ABC (MS), Adelaide

kHz	kW	Ctry	Call	Station, location
891	200	CHN		NX;LN;NM
891	20	IND		AIR, Rampur
891	10	INS		RRI, Malang
891	20	J	JOHK	NHK (1), Sendai
891	250	KOR	HLKB	KBS, Busan
891	5	NZL	2XW	The Breeze, Wellington
891	10	PHL	DYSR	Nat.Council of Churches, Dumaguete C., Neg.Or.
891	5	PHL	DWAR	Caceres Bc.Corp., Naga C., Cam.Sur
891	5	PHL	DZGR	People's Bc.Sce., Tuguegarao, Cag.
891	50	RUS		R.Mayak + Reg., Tyumen, Sib.
891	1000	THA		R.Thailand, Saraburi
891	10	TWN	BED24	BCC (L), Tainan
891	3.5	TWN	BEG78	BCC (I/H), Miaoli
891		VTN		Lam Dong (1/P), Da Lat
898		VTN		Ha Tinh (P) (v)
899		VTN		Vinh Phuc (P)
900	5	AUS	2LM	Lismore
900	5	AUS	2LT	Lithgow
900	2	AUS	6BY	Bridgetown
900	2	AUS	7AD	Devonport
900	2	AUS	8HA	Alice Springs
900	10	CHN		QH (CNR2)
900		CHN		BJ (CRI DS2)
900	100	CHN		YN + 22 st's
900	5	HWA	KNUI	Kahului, Maui
900	100	IND		AIR, Cuddapah
900	5	J	JOHF	BSS, Yonago
900	5	J	JOZR	RKC, Kochi
900	5	J	JOHO	HBC, Hakodate
900	50	KOR	HLKV	MBC, Seoul
900	10	NZL	4YC	Parl.Bc./So.Star, Dunedin
900	10	PNG		PNG Bc.Corp., Goroka
900	5	PHL	DXIP	Southern Bc.Netw., Davao C.
900	5	PHL	DXRZ	R.Mindanao Netw., Zamboanga C., Z .Sur
900	5	PHL	DYOW	Consolidated Bc.System, Inc., Roxas, Capiz
900	5	PHL	DWNE	Nueva Ecija Prov.Gov., Cabanatuan C., Nva Viz
900		VTN		Kon Tum (1/P)
909	120	CHN		SC;TJ + 3 st's
909	100	CHN		FJ (CNR6)
909	100	IND		AIR, Gorakhpur
909	10	INS		RRI, Sorong
909	10	J	JOCB	NHK (2), Nagoya
909	5	J	JOVX	STV, Abashiri
909	10	KOR		KBS, Gumi
909	20	MLA		RTM Sarawak, Sibu
909	5	NZL	2XD	Parl.Bc./So.Star, Napier
909	5	PHL	DYLA	Visayas Mindanao C.of TU, Cebu C
909	5	PHL	DYSP	Republic Bc.System, Pto Princesa, Palawan
909	5	PHL	DZEA	Catholic Welfare Org., Laoag C, I.Nte
909	10	RUS		Studiya Gorod, Yekaterinburg
909	25	THA		R.Thailand, Surin
909	10	THA		R.Thailand, Loei
909	10	TWN	BED79	BCC (C), Kaohsiung
909	10	TWN	BEH3	Fu Hsing BC (1), Taipei
909		VTN		Ca Mau (P), Ming Hai
918	2	AUS	2XL	Cooma
918	2	AUS	4VL	Charleville
918	2	AUS	6NA	Narrogin
918	120	CBG		Nat.Radio of Cambodia, Phnom Penh
918	200	CHN		SD; GX
918	300	IND		AIR, Suratgarh
918	5	J	JOEF	YBC, Yamagata
918	1	J		YBC, Suruoka/Yonezawa
918	1	J		YBC, Shinjo
918	1	J	JOPM	KRY, Shimonoseki
918	1	J	JOPN	KRY, Iwakuni
918	50	KOR		KBS, Yeoncheon
918	2	NZL	3YT	National R., Timaru
918	10	PHL	DZSR	Pilippine Bc.Sce., Quezon C., NCR
918	7/5	RUS		R.Mayak, Sib., 3st's, (synch)
918	10	THA		Sor.Wor.Phor. 1, Chiang Mai
918	10	THA		R.Thailand, Bangkok
918		VTN		Cao Bang (1)
927	5	AUS	3UZ	Melbourne
927	5	AUS	4CC	Gladstone
927	200	CHN		GZ;BJ + 18 st's
927		CHN		FJ (CNR6)
927	2.5	FJI		Fiji Bc.Corp. Ltd. (1), Sigatoka
927	100	IND		AIR, Visakhapatnam
927	25	INS		RRI, Pekanbaru
927	5	J	JOFG	NHK (1), Fukui
927	5	J	JOKG	NHK (1), Kofu
927	1	J		NHK (1), Wakkania/Tsuyama
927	10	KOR		KBS, Buyeo
927	1	KOR		KBS, Hongcheon/Hadong
927	50	KRE		Korean Central BS (C/R), Hwangju (Sariwon)
927	10	MLA		RTM Sabah, Tawau
927	2	NZL	2ZA	Newstalk ZB, Palmerston No.
927	100	PAK		PBC, Khairpur
927	5	PHL	DXMM	Sulu Tawi-Tawi Bc.Found., Jolo,Sulu
927	5	PHL	DXDA	Office of the Governor, San Francisco, Ag.Sur
927	10	PHL	DWBS	Soild North Bc., Vigan, I.Sur
927	5	PHL	DXMD	R.Mindanao Netw., Gen.Santos C., S.Cot
927	5	PHL	DZLG	People's Bc.Sce., Legaspi, Albay
927	20	THA		R.Thailand, Chanthaburi
927	10	THA		R.Thailand, Nong Khai
927	1200	TWN		CBS (RTI), Changchih
930		CHN		ZJ
930		VTN		Ben Tre (P) (v)
936	10	AUS	4PB	ABC (PNN), Brisbane
936	5	AUS	6FX	(PBS), Fitzroy Crossing
936	10	AUS	7ZR	ABC (MS), Hobart
936	200	CHN		AH;NM
936	100	IND		AIR (A), Tiruchirapalli
936	5	J	JONF	MRT, Miyazaki
936	5	J	JOTR	ABS, Akita
936	1	J		MRT, 4 st's
936	10	KOR		KBS, Changwon
936	1	NZL		New Supremo 936, Waiuku
936	100	PAK		Azad Kashmir Radio, Mirpur
936	5	PHL	DXDN	Univ. of Mindanao, Tagum C., Dvo Nte
936	10	PHL	DXIM	Philippine Bc.Sce., Cagayan de Oro C., Mis.Or
936	5	PHL	DWIM	Insular Bc.System, Calapan, Mind.Or.
936	1	PHL	DYKW	R.Philippines Netw., Binalgaban, Neg.Occ
936	1	PHL	DYCC	R.Mindanao Netw., Calbayog C, W. Samar
936	1	PHL	DZXT	R.Corp. of the Philippines, Tarlac C.
936	5	RUS		R.Yunost, Krasnoyarsk, Sib.
936	5	RUS		VBC, Dalnegorsk
936	50	THA		R.Thailand, N. Sawan
936	10	THA		Thor.Phor. 4, Pattani
936	5	TWN	BEC42	Kuo Kuang BS, Taipei
940	10	HWA	KHCM	Honolulu
945	1	AUS	4HI	Dysart (trtr)
945	2	AUS	3UZ	Bendigo (HPONS)
945	400	CHN		CNR (1)
945		CHN		HB;SD
945	100	IND		AIR, Sambalpur
945	5	J	JOXK	NHK (1), Tokushima
945	3	J	JOIQ	NHK (1), Muroran
945	1	J	JOQP	NHK (1), Hikone
945	1	J		NHK (1), Fukue
945	10	KOR		KBS, Boeun
945	2	NZL	2ZG	Newstalk ZB/R.Sport, Gisborne
945	10	PHL	DXDV	Vismin R. and TV Bc.Net, Butuan C., Ag.Nte
945	5	PHL	DXRO	Nation Bc.Corp., Cotabato C., Mag.
945	5	PHL	DYRO	Allied Bc.Center, Inc., Roxas C., Capiz
945	10	SLM	H4B	SIBC, Gizo
945	10	THA		Thor.Or. 1, Bangkok
945	10	THA		Thor.Phor. 2, Kalasin
954	5	AUS	2UE	Sydney
954	0.35	AUS	4EL	Gordonvale (trtr)
954	50	CHN		NM + 7 st's
954	100	IND		AIR, Najibabad
954	10	INS		RRI, Kendari
954	100	J	JOKR	TBS, Tokyo
954	10	MLA		RTM Sarawak, Kuching
954	2	NZL	1XW	R.Pacific, Hamilton
954	0.8	NZL		Puketapu R., Palmerston No.
954	40	PHL	DZEM	Cristian Era Bc.Sce., Quezon City, NCR
954	10	PHL	DWFB	Pilippine Bc.Sce., Laoag C, I.Nte
954	5	PHL	DZAL	Rinconada Bc.Corp., Iriga C., Cam Sur
954	5	PHL	DYMM	Universal Bc.System, Tacloban C., Leyte
954	10	THA		Thor.Or. 10, Phitsanulok
954	10	THA		Thor.Or. 16, Chantaburi
954	20	TWN	BED55	BCC (C), Taipei
954	1	TWN		Yen Sheng BS, Wuho
954	10	TWN	BEV85	Chien Kuo BS, Hsinying
954		VTN		Vinh Long (P)
963	5	AUS	2RG	Griffith
963	5	AUS	4WK	Warwick

kHz	kW	Ctry	Call	Station, location
963	5	AUS	5SE	Mt.Gambier
963	2	AUS	6TZ	Bunbury
963	20	BGD		Bangladesh Betar, Sylhet
963	50	CHN		LN; ZJ; HB;HEB
963	20	IND		AIR, Jalgaon
963	10/2	INS		RRI, Jember
963	5	J	JOTG	NHK (1), Aomori
963	5	J	JOZK	NHK (1), Matsuyama
963	1	J	JOSP	NHK (1), Saga
963	1	J		NHK (1), Yonago/Hagi
963	10	KOR	HLKS	KBS, Jeju
963	10	KOR	HLCR	KBS, Andong
963	10	NZL	3YC	Parl.Bc./So.Star, Christchurch
963	10	PHL	DYMF	People's Bc.Sce., Cebu C.
963	5	PHL	DXYZ	Nation Bc.Corp., Zamboanga C., Z.Sur
963	5	PHL	DZNS	Catholic Welfare Org., Vigan, I.Sur
963	20	RUS		R.Rossii + Reg., Zakamensk, Sib.
963	1	RUS		R.Rossii + Reg., Guzino-Ozersk, Sib.
963	50/10	THA		R.Thailand, Krabi
963	10	THA		Phon Mor. 2, Bangkok
963	10	TWN	BEV84	Taiwan BC, Chunghsing
970		VTN		Cao Bang (P)
970		VTN		Binh Duong (P)
972	0.3	AUS	2DU	Cobar (trtr)
972	5	AUS	2MW	Murwillumbah
972	2	AUS	5PB	ABC (PNN), Adelaide
972	150	CHN		HEN;HL
972	300	IND		AIR (A), Cuttack
972	50	INS		RRI, Surakarta
972	1500	KOR	HLCA	KBS, Dangjin
972	5	NZL	2XG	R.Rhema, Wellington
972	5	PHL	DWTI	Lucena C, Que.
972	5	PHL	DWFR	Pilippine Bc.Sce., Bontoc, Mt.Prov.
972	5	PHL	DXKH	Cebu Bc.Co., Cagayan de Oro C., Mis.Or.
972	1	PHL	DYSM	Cebu Bc.Co., Catarman, N. Samar
972	0.2	RUS		R.Mayak, Yuzhno-Kurilsk, FE
972	10	THA		Nor.Thor.Phor., Phetchabun
972	500	TJK		Various relays, Orzu
972		VTN		Quang Ngai (1/P)
981	5	AUS	2NM	Muswellbrook
981	2	AUS	3HA	Hamilton
981	2	AUS	6KG	Kalgoorlie
981	200	CHN		JL (CNR1)
981	100	IND		AIR, Raipur
981		J		NHK (1), Kisofukushima/Sasebo
981	2	ZL	1YE	National R., Kaikohe
981	10	PHL	DXOW	Radyo Pilipino Corp., Davao C., Dvo Sur
981	10	PHL	DXBR	Consolidated Bc.System, Inc., Butuan C., Ag.Nte
981	10	PHL	DYBQ	Intercontinental Bc.Corp., Iloilo C.
981	5	PHL	DXDR	R.Mindanao Netw., Dipolog, Z.Nte
981	5	PHL	DZRD	Nation Bc.Corp., Dagupan C., Pang.
981	5	PHL	DWMT	Philippine Bc.Corp., Naga C., Cam.Sur
981	25	THA		R.Thailand, Mae Hong Son
981	25	THA		R.Thailand, Yala
981	20	THA		R.Thailand, Nakhon Phanom
981	10	THA		Makaawitthayalei Ratthasapha, Pathum Thani
981	250	TWN		VO Kuanghua, Hsinfeng
981	1	TWN	BEV68	Feng Ming BC (2), Kaohsiung
981		VTN		Gia Lai (1), Pleiku
990	0.25	AUS	3RN	ABC (RN), Albury-Wodonga
990	5	AUS	4RO	Rockhampton
990	2	AUS	6RPH	Foundation for Info.R., Victoria Park
990	0.5	AUS	8GO	ABC (RR), Gove
990	50	CHN		SH;YN;HEB
990	5	HWA	KHBZ	Honolulu
990	300	IND		AIR (A), Jammu
990	10	J	JORK	NHK (1), Kochi
990	10	KOR	HLAP	MBC, Masan
990	500	MNG		MRT (FS), Ulaanbaatar
990	1	NZL		Ace Bc/BBC, Auckland
990	1	NZL		Fifeshire Classics, Nelson
990	15	PHL	DWRT	Trans-Radio Bc.Corp., Makati, NCR
990	5	PHL	DYTH	Pacific Bc.System, Tacloban C., Leyte
990	5	PHI	DZMT	Pacific Bc.System, Laoag, I.Nte
990	5	PHL	DXBM	Republic Bc.System, Cotabato C., Mag.
990	10	THA		Sor.Wor.Phor. 2, N. Ratchasima
990	10	TWN	BEV58	Cheng Sheng BC (1), Taichung
990	10	TWN	BEP34	Ching Cha BS, Hualien
990	1	TWN	BEP38	Ching Cha BS, Ilan
999	2	AUS	2NB	ABC (RR), Broken Hill
999	5	AUS	2ST	Nowra
999	10	BGD		Bangladesh Betar, Thakurgaon
999	20	CBG		Nat.Radio of Cambodia, Battambang
999	200	CHN.		LN + 5 st's
999	20	IND		AIR, Coimbatore
999	1	IND		AIR, Almora
999	150/1	INS		RRI, Jakarta
999	1	J		NHK (1), Fukuyama/Hachinoe
999	1	J		NHK (1), Nakamura
999	10	KOR	HLCL	CBS, Gwangju
999	250	KRE		Korean Central BS (C/R), Hamhung
999	1.5	NZL		Sounz AM, Palmerston No.
999	5	PHL	DYSS	Republic Bc.System, Cebu C.
999	5	PHL	DZEQ	Pilippine Bc.Sce., Baguio C., Benguet
999	5	PHL	DWMI	Katigbak Enterprises, Calapan, Mind.Or.
999	1	PHL	DXHP	R.Mindanao Netw., Bislig, S.Sur
999	1	PHL	DXDC	Pilippine Bc.Sce., Bongao, Tawi-Tawi
999	7	RUS		R.Mayak + Reg., Birobidzhan, FE
999	10	THA		Thor.Phor. 3, Chiang Rai
999	10	THA		Phon.Neung Ror.Or., Bangkok
999	1	TWN	BEV92	Tien Nan BS, Taipei
999		VTN		Lang Son (P)
999		VTN		Quang Tri (2/P)
1000		LAO		R.Nationale Lao, Houa Phan
1000		VTN		Quang Binh (P), Dong Hoi (v)
1008	0.3	AUS	2TAB	Canberra (HPONS)
1008	5	AUS	4TAB	Brisbane (Ipswich)
1008	2	AUS	6TAB	Geraldton (HPONS)
1008	5	AUS	7TAB	Launceston
1008	200	CHN		YN (CNR1)
1008		CHN		BJ (CNR DS3)
1008	10	CHN		SN + 11 st's
1008	100	IND		AIR (B), Kolkata
1008	10	INS		RRI, Madiun
1008	50	J	JONR	ABC, Osaka
1008	50	KOR		KBS, Gangneung
1008	10	NZL	1ZD	Newstalk ZB, Tauranga
1008	120	PAK		PBC (1), Hyderabad
1008	10	PHL	DXXX	R.Philippines Netw., Zamboanga C., Z.Sur
1008	5	PHL	DWBS	Catholic Welfare Org., Sto.Domingo, Albay
1008	5	PHL	DWGO	Subic Bc.Corp., Olongapo C., Zamb.
1008	50	RUS		R.Yunost + Reg., Yelizovo, FE
1008	25	RUS		R.Yunost, Khabarovsk, FE
1008	10	THA		Wor.Por.Tho 3, N.Ratchasima
1008	300	TWN		CBS (RTI), Lukang
1008	10	TWN	BED88	BCC (C), Taitung
1008	1	TWN	BEV60	Cheng Sheng BC, Kaohsiung
1017	5	AUS	2KY	Sydney
1017	0.5	AUS	6WH	ABC (RR), Wyndham
1017	1	AUS	6TAB	Bunbury (HPONS)
1017		CHN		CNR1
1017	200	CHN		JL (CNR8)
1017	10	CHN		HEB; GD
1017	20	IND		AIR (B), Chennai
1017	10	IND		AIR, New Delhi
1017	50	J	JOLB	NHK (2), Fukuoka
1017	10	KOR	HLAW	MBC, Andong
1017	2	NZL		R.Hauraki, Christchurch
1017	10	PHL	DWDW	Intercontinental Bc.Corp., Dagupan C., Pang
1017	10	PHL	DWLC	Pilippine Bc.Sce., Lucena C., Que.
1017	10	PHL	DXRR	Kalayaan Bc.System, Davao C., Dvo Sur
1017	10	PHL	DYRP	Allied Bc.Center, Inc., Iloilo C.
1017	5	PHL	DXSN	Catholic Welfare Org., Surigao C., S. Nte
1017	10	THA		Thor.Or. 5, Prachuap KK
1017	10	TON	A3Z	Tonga Bc.Comm., Nuku'alofa
1017	10	TWN	BED53	BCC (C), Hsinchu
1026	5	AUS	3PB	ABC (PNN), Melbourne
1026	5	AUS	4MK	Mackay
1026	2	AUS	6NW	Port Hedland
1026		CHN		FJ (CNR6)
1026	200	CHN		GZ;BJ + 3 st's
1026	20	IND		AIR (A), Allahabad
1026	5	INS		RRI, Serui
1026	1	KOR		KBS, Geochang/Hwacheon
1026	2	NZL	1ZK	R.Northland, Kaitaia
1026	2	NZL	1ZN	R.Northland, Whangarei
1026	1	NZL	4XSR	R.Sport/So.Star, Invercargill
1026	10	PHL	DZAR	Nation Bc.Corp., Quezon C, NCR
1026	5	PHL	DXMC	People's Bc.Sce., Koronadal, S.Cot.
1026	1	PHL	DXMI	Univ. of Mindanao, Iligan C., Lanao Nte

kHz	kW	Ctry	Call	Station, location
1026	50	THA		R.Thailand, Phitsanulok
1026	10	THA		R.Thailand, Yala
1026	1	TWN		Tien Sheng BS, Yuanli
1026	1	TWN	BEV51	Chung Hua BC (2), Sanchung
1030	10	LAO		R.Nationale Lao (FS), Vientiane
1035	50	CHN		CNR1
1035	10	IND		AIR (B), Guwahati
1035		INS		RRI, Palu
1035	1/5	INS		RRI, Bandar Lampung
1035	1	J	JOIC	NHK (2), Toyama
1035	1	J	JOHD	NHK (2), Takamatsu
1035	1	J		NHK (2), Tsuruoka
1035	10	KOR	HLCP	KBS, Pohang
1035	20	NZL	2ZB	Newstalk ZB, Wellington
1035	120	PAK		PBC, Multan
1035	10	PHL	DYRL	Radyo Pilipino Corp., Bacolod C., Neg.Occ.
1035	5/2.5	PHL	DYUM	Univ. of Mindanao, Ormoc C., Leyte
1035	5	PHL	DZWX	Consolidated Bc.System, Inc., Baguio C., Benguet
1035	10	SLM	H4B1	SIBC, Honiara
1035	10	THA		Phaak Phiset, Bangkok
1035	10	TWN	BED26	BCC (C), Chia-i
1035		VTN		Quang Ninh (P), Halong
1040	10	HWA	KLHT	Honolulu
1044	2	AUS	2UH	ABC (RR), Muswellbrook
1044	0.5	AUS	4WP	ABC (RR), Weipa
1044	2	AUS	5CS	Port Pirie
1044	1	AUS	6BR	ABC (RR), Bridgetown
1044	1000	CHN		JS (FS)
1044	10	CHN		XJ;YN
1044	10	HKG		Metro Bc.Corp., Peng Chau
1044	100	IND		AIR (A), Mumbai
1044	10	INS		RRI, Biak
1044		INS		RRI, Sibolga
1044	10	KOR		KBS, Samcheok/Jecheon
1044	1	KOR		AFNK, Chuncheon
1044	20	MLA		RTM Sarawak, Sri Aman
1044	10	NZL	4ZB	Newstalk ZB, Dunedin
1044	10	PHL	DZNG	Newsounds Bc.Netw., Naga C., Cam. Sur
1044	5	PHL	DXCO	Radyo Pilipino Corp., Cayagan de Oro, Mis. Or
1044	5	PHL	DXLL	R.T.Bc.Specialists Phil., Zamboanga C., Z.Sur
1044	5	PHL	DYMS	Cebu Bc.Co., Catbalogan, W. Samar
1044	1	PHL	DXML	Rural Electrification Corp., Digos, Dvo. Sur
1044	10	THA		Kor.Wor.Sor. 5, Khon Kaen
1044	10	THA		Thor.Phor. 4, N.Si Thammarat
1044	1	TWN	BEV98	Cheng Kung BS, Kaohsiung
1044	5	TWN	BEV64	Yen Sheng BS (1), Hualien
1050		CHN		ZJ
1050		VTN		Tra Vinh (P) (v)
1053	5	AUS	2CA	Canberra, ACT
1053	0.5	AUS	4—	Brisbane (HPONS)
1053	20	BGD		Bangladesh Betar, Rangpur
1053	20	CHN		JL + 10 st's
1053	200	IND		AIR (FS), Tuticorin
1053	20	IND		AIR, Leh
1053	10	INS		RRI, Jayapura
1053	50	J	JOAR	CBC, Nagoya
1053	1500	KRE		Pyongyang BNDF of SK, Haeju
1053	20	MLA		RTM, Mersing (r1055)
1053	2	NZL	2ZP	Newstalk ZB, New Plymouth
1053	10	PHL	DXKD	R.Philippines Netw., Dipolog, Z.Nte
1053	5	PHL	DYSA	Univ. of San Agustin, Iloilo C.
1053	50	RUS		Reg., Orenburg
1053	25	RUS		R.Plyus, Belogorsk, FE
1053	10	RUS		R.Shanson, Krasnoyarsk, Sib.
1053	10	THA		Mor.Thor.Bor. 11, Bangkok
1053	10	THA		Mor.Thor.Bor. 32, Lampang
1055	1	INS		RRI, Surakarta
1060	5	HWA	KHBC	Hilo
1062	2	AUS	4TI	ABC (RR), Thursday Isl.
1062	2	AUS	5MU	ABC (RR), Renmark/Loxton
1062	150	CHN		Zhujiang EBS, GD; HL
1062	10	IND		AIR, Pasighat
1062	50	KOR	HLKQ	KBS, Cheongju
1062	20	MLA		RTM Sarawak, Sibu
1062	1	NZL		R.Sport, Wanganui
1062	40	PHL	DZEC	Eagle Bc.Corp., Quezon C., NRC
1062	5	PHL	DXKI	FEBC, Koronadal C., S. Cot.
1062	5	RUS		Avtoradio, Irkutsk, Sib.
1062	1	RUS		R.Mayak, Ust-Kamchatsk, FE
1062	10	THA		Thor.Or. 9, Udon Thani
1062	10	THA		R.Thailand, Phuket
1062	10	TWN	BED85	BCC (I), Taipei
1062	10	TWN	BED23	BCC (I), Taichung
1062	1	TWN	BEV82	Cheng Sheng BC, Ilan
1062	5	TWN	BEV74	Min Li BS, Pingtung
1062	50	UZB		UZR (3), Andijon
1062	10	UZB		UZR (1), Toshkent
1062	5	UZB		UZR (3), Nukus
1071	5	AUS	3EL	Maryborough
1071	2	AUS	4SB	Kingaroy
1071	2	AUS	6WB	Katanning
1071	50	CHN		TJ + 7 st's
1071	1000	IND		AIR (FS), Rajkot
1071	20	J	JOFK	NHK (1), Hiroshima
1071	5	J	JOWM	STV, Obihiro
1071	100	KAZ		Shygyz Qazaqstan OTRK, Ösqemen
1071	2	NZL	2YE	National R., Masterton
1071		NZL		R.Pacific, Ashburton
1071	5	PHL	DXKT	R.Philippines Netw., Davao C., Dvo Sur
1071	1	PHL	DYXT	Universal Bc.System, Tagbilaran C., Bohol
1071		PHL	DZSL	Talisay, Cam Nte
1071	7	RUS		R.Mayak, Zeya, FE
1071	10	THA		Neung.Por.Nor., Tak
1071	1	TWN	BEV96	Tien Sheng BS, Tainan
1080	2	AUS	2MO	Gunnedah
1080	2	AUS	6IX	Perth
1080	5	AUS	7TAB	Hobart (HPONS)
1080	10	BGD		Bangladesh Betar, Rajshahi
1080	200	CHN		YN (FS)
1080	10	CHN		JS;ZJ(v);GD;HL
1080	5	HWA	KWAI	Honolulu
1080	2/10	INS		RRI, Singaraja
1080	1	INS		RRI, Gorontalo
1080	10	KOR	HLAT	MBC, Yeosu
1080	5	KOR		AFNK, Daegu
1080	1500	KRE		Korean Central BS (C/R), Haeju
1080	10	NZL	1ZB	Newstalk 1ZB, Auckland
1080	10	MRA	KCNM	Inter Island Comm., Chalan Kiya, Saipan
1080	50	PAK		PBC (2), Lahore
1080	5	PHL	DWIN	Eagle Bc.Corp., Dagupan C., Pang.
1080	5	PHL	DWRL	Radio, Inc., Legaspi C., Albay
1080	5	PHL	DXRH	First United Bc.Corp., Zamboanga C., Z.Sur
1080	5	PHL	DYBH	Pacific Bc.System, Bacolod C., Neg Occ
1080	1	PHL	DWAM	Catholic Welfare Org., Batangas C
1080	1	PHL	DXKS	R.Philippines Netw., Surigao, S. Nte
1080	1000	RUS		VoR, Angarsk, Sib.
1080	10	THA		Wor.Por.Tho. 9, N. Sawan
1080	10	THA		Wor.Por.Tho. 16, Yala
1080	10	THA		Wor.Por.Tho. 10, Chiang Rai
1080	5	TKM		Turkmen Radio (1), Serhetabat
1089	5	AUS	2EL	Orange
1089	5	AUS	3WM	Horsham
1089	600	CHN		FJ (CNR6)
1089	200	CHN		LN; HN
1089	20	IND		AIR, Udipi
1089	10	J	JOHB	NHK (2), Sendai
1089	10	KOR	HLCH	KBS, Chungju
1089	20	MLA		RTM, Gerik
1089	2.5	NZL		R.Sport, Palmerston No.
1089	10	PHL	DXCM	Univ. of Mindanao, Cotabato C., Mag.
1089	1	PHL	DYHR	Hypersonic Bc.Center, Calbayog C., W. Samar
1089	5	RUS		R.Rossii + Reg., Tilichiki, FE
1089	10	THA		Neung Por.Nor, Udon Thani
1089	10	THA		Mor.Sor.Thor., Bangkok
1089	10	TWN	BEC31	Han Sheng BS, Yunlin
1089	10	TWN	BEG28	Kaohsiung BS, Kaohsiung
1089	10	TWN	BEH34	Fu Hsing BC (2), Taichung
1089	5	TWN	BEH5	Fu Hsing BC (1), Taipei
1089		VTN		Kien Giang (P), Rach Gia
1098	0.2	AUS	2RN	ABC (RN), Goulburn
1098	2	AUS	4LG	Longreach
1098	2	AUS	6MD	Merredin
1098	5	AUS	7LA	Launceston
1098	10	CHN		ZJ + 17 st's
1098	2/10	INS		RRI, Jambi
1098	0.5/10	INS		RRI, Sumenep
1098	5	J	JOGF	OBS, Oita
1098	5	J	JOSR	SBC, Nagano
1098	1	J	JOSW	SBC, Iida
1098	5	J	JOWO	RFC, Koriyama
1098	1	J	JOMF	NBC, Sasebo

kHz	kW	Ctry	Call	Station, location
1098	150	KAZ		Qazaq Radiosi/BBC, Almaty
1098	20	KOR	HLCJ	KBS, Jinju
1098	25	MHL	V7AD	Marshall Is. BC, Majuro
1098	10	NZL	3ZB	Newstalk ZB, Christchurch
1098	50	PAK		PBC (2), Hyderabad
1098	10	PHL	DWAD	Crusaders Bc.System, Mandaluyong C., NCR
1098	5	PHL	DXCL	Nation Bc.Corp., Cagayan de Oro C., Mis. Or.
1098	75	RUS		R.Vladivostok, V., FE
1098	10	THA		Sor.Wor.Phor. 3, Songkhla
1098	10	THA		R.Thailand, Tak
1098	300	TWN		CBS (RTI), Kouhu
1098		VTN		Binh Thuan (1/P), Phan Thiet
1098		VTN		Lao Cai (P)
1107	5	AUS	2EA	Sydney (SBS)
1107	120	CHN		XJ + 7 st's
1107	20	IND		AIR, Gulbarga
1107	1/10	INS		RRI, Yogyakarta
1107	1/5	INS		RRI, Kupang
1107	20	J	JOCF	MBC, Kagoshima
1107	1	J		MBC, 3 st's
1107	5	J	JOMR	MRO, Kanazawa
1107	1	J		MRO, Nanao
1107	10	KOR	HLAV	MBC, Pohang
1107	2	PNG		R.Milne Bay, Alotau
1107	10	PHL	DWDY	Northeastern Bc.Sce., Cauayan, Isa.
1107	1	PHL	DZOM	Ben Vidyua, Calapan C., Mind.Or.
1107	5	PHL	DXBB	Republic Bc.System, Gen.Santos C., S.Cot.
1107	5	PHL	DYIN	People's Bc.Sce., Kalibo, Aklan
1107	10	THA		Mor.Kor., Samut Sakhon
1107	10	THA		Thor.Phor. 2, Khon Kaen
1110	5	HWA	KAOI	Kihei (Pukalani), Maui
1116	2	AUS	3AK	Melbourne
1116	5	AUS	4BC	Brisbane
1116	2	AUS	6MM	Mandurah
1116	600	CHN		FJ (CNR5)
1116	120	CHN		HL (CNR2)
1116	50	CHN		SC;AH
1116	200	IND		AIR (A), Srinagar
1116	0.3	INS		RRI, Pekanbaru
1116	5	J	JODR	BSN, Niigata
1116	5	J	JOAF	RNB, Matsuyama
1116	1	J	JOAL	RNB, Niihama
1116	1	J	JOAM	RNB, Uwajima
1116	2	NZL	2YX	National R., Nelson
1116	10	PHL	DYTR	Tagbilaran Bc.Corp., Tagbilaran C, Bohol
1116	5	PHL	DXAS	FEBC, Zamboanga C., Z.Sur
1116	5	PHL	DZLB	Univ.of the Philippines, Los Banos, Laguna
1116	10	THA		Thor.Phor. 3, Phitsanulok
1116	10	THA		R.Thailand, Phangnga
1116	3.5	TWN	BED72	BCC (N), Yuli
1116	10	TWN	BEC22	Han Sheng BS, Taipei
1116	10	TWN	BEC30	Han Sheng BS, Ilan
1116	5	TWN	BEP26	Ching Cha BS, Hsinchu
1116	5	TWN	BEP25	Ching Cha BS, Kaohsiung
1116		VTN		Bac Lieu (P)
1116		VTN		Ha Tay (P)
1125	2	AUS	1RPH	Print-Hand.Radio of ACT Inc., Canberra
1125	0.5	AUS	4RO	Gladstone (trtr)
1125	5	AUS	5MU	Murray Bridge
1125	50	CHN		HB(v); HEB
1125	20	IND		AIR, Tezpur
1125	20	IND		AIR, Udaipur
1125		INS		RRI, Pontianak
1125	10	J	JOAD	NHK (2), Naha, Okinawa
1125	1	J	JOIZ	NHK (2), Muroran
1125	1	J	JOLC	NHK (2), Tottori
1125	1	J	JOOC	NHK (2), Obihiro
1125	1	J		NHK (2), Hagi/Nayoro
1125	1	J		NHK (2), Takayama
1125	1	NZL		R.Sport, Napier
1125	0.2	NZL		R.Hauraki, Dunedin
1125	10	PHL	DXGL	PEC Bc.Corp., Butuan C., Ag.Nte
1125	10	PHL	DZWN	Consolidated Bc.System, Inc., Dagupan C., Pang.
1125	5	PHL	DWAS	FEBC, Legaspi C., Albay
1125	5	PHL	DXGM	Republic Bc.System, Davao C., DvoSur
1125	25	THA		R.Thailand, Chanthaburi
1125	5	TWN	BEV36	Cheng Sheng BC, Yunlin
1125	1	TWN	BEP40	Ching Cha BS, Taitung
1125		VTN		Tay Ninh (P)
1125	2	VUT		VBTC, Emten Lagoon

kHz	kW	Ctry	Call	Station, location
1134	2	AUS	2AD	Armidale
1134	5	AUS	3CS	Colac
1134	2	AUS	6TZ	Collie(trtr)
1134	1200	CHN		QH (CNR1)
1134	10	CHN		GD;SN + 4 st's
1134	1000	IND		AIR (N/FS), Chinsurah (Mogra)
1134	1/25	INS		RRI, Banjarmasin
1134	100	J	JOQR	NCB, Tokyo
1134	500	KOR		KBS, Hwaseong
1134	2	NZL	4YQ	National R., Queenstown
1134	10	PHL	DWDD	Dept.of Nat.Defence, Quezon C., NCR
1134		PHL	DXOS	Public Affairs Sce., AFP, Basilan Is., Basilan
1134	5	PHL	DWJS	Rolin Bc.Enterprises, Roxas, Palawan
1134	5	PHL	DXMV	Univ. of Mindanao, Valencia, Buk.
1134	1	PHL	DYRM	Philippine R.Corp., Dumaguete, Neg.Or.
1134	1	PHL	DWBT	Pilippine Bc.Sce., Basco, Batanes
1134	7	RUS		Avtoradio, Khabarovsk, FE
1134	10	THA		Thor.Phor. 2, N.Ratchasima
1134	10	THA		R.Thailand, Lampang
1134	10	TWN	BEG26	Taipei BS, Taipei
1143	2	AUS	2HD	Newcastle
1143	5	AUS	4HI	Emerald
1143	10	CHN		BJ (CNR8)
1143	10	CHN		GS + 26 st's
1143	20	IND		AIR, Ratnagiri
1143	20	IND		AIR, Rohtak
1143	20	J	JOBR	KBS, Kyoto
1143	10	NPL		R.Nepal, Bardibas
1143	2	NZL	1YW	National R., Hamilton
1143	1000	PHL	DWVA	IBB Relay Stn., Poro Pt, Luzon
1143	5	PHL	DYAF	Catholic Welfare Org., Bacolod, Neg.Occ.
1143	7	RUS		R.Mayak, Tayshet, Sib.
1143	10	THA		Or.Sor.Mor.Thor., Bangkok
1143	150	TJK		TR (2)/FS/Various relays, Yangiyul
1143	100	TWN	BEL3	Taiwan Chu Yuyeh BS, Penghu
1147		CHN		HEN
1152	2	AUS	2WG	Wagga Wagga
1152	10	AUS	6RN	ABC (RN), Manjimup
1152	10	CHN		NM (2 st's);LN;HN
1152	2.5	FJI		Fiji Bc.Corp. Ltd. (1), Rakiraki
1152	10	J	JOPC	NHK (2), Kushiro
1152	10	J	JORB	NHK (2), Kochi
1152	10	KOR	HLCW	KBS, Wonju
1152	2	NZL	3ZC	Newstalk ZB, Timaru
1152	100	PAK		PBC, Rawalpindi
1152	5	PHL	DYCM	Masbate Comm. Bc.Co., Bogo, Cebu
1152	50	RUS		R.Rossii + Reg., Komsomolsk, FE
1152	20	RUS		R.Rossii + Reg., Khanty-Mansiysk, Sib.
1152	10	THA		Ror.Dor., Chiang Mai
1152	10	THA		Ror.Dor., Khon Kaen
1152	1	TWN	BED68	BCC (C), Puli
1152	5	TWN	BEV70	Hua Sheng BC (1), Taipei
1161	2	AUS	4FC	Maryborough
1161	10	AUS	5PA	ABC (RR), Naracoorte
1161	1	AUS	7FG	ABC (RR), Fingal
1161	10	BGD		Bangladesh Betar, Rangamati
1161		CHN		CNR1
1161	10	CHN		SD;HB;GX;JS
1161	20	IND		AIR, Thiruvanathapuram
1161	20	KOR	HLKU	MBC, Busan
1161	0.25	KOR		AFNK, Uijeongbu
1161	20	MLA		RTM Sarawak, Sri Aman
1161	5	NZL	2XM	Te Upoko o te Ika, Wellington
1161	10	PHL	DWCM	Philippine Bc.Corp., Dagupan C., Pang.
1161	5	PHL	DYRD	Bohol Chronicle R.Corp., Tagbilaran C, Bohol
1161	5	PHL	DZMD	People's Bc.Netw., Daet, Cam.Nte
1161	5	PHL	DYKR	R.Mindanao Netw., Kalibo, Aklan
1161	1	PHL	DXDS	Univ. of Mindanao, Davao C., Dvo.Sur
1161	20	THA		Wor.Sor.Sor., Bangkok
1161	10	THA		Sor.Thor.Ror. 9, U.Ratchathani
1161	40	TJK		TR (3), Orzu
1161	10	TWN	BED86	BCC (C), Ilan
1161	10	TWN	BED89	BCC (C), Miaoli
1161	1	TWN	BEV67	Feng Ming BC (1), Kaohsiung
1170	5	AUS	2CH	Sydney
1170	10	BGD		Bangladesh Betar (C)/R.Metrowave, Dhaka
1170	10	CHN		SD (3 st's)
1170	5	HWA	KJPN	Honolulu (r. KAIM FM))
1170	1	IND		AIR, Hyderabad
1170	50	INS		RRI, Semarang
1170	500	KOR	HLSR	KBS, Gimje

kHz	kW	Ctry	Call	Station, location
1170	0.4	NZL	1ZW	V. of.Waitomo, Te Kuiti
1170	10	PHL	DXMR	Pilippine Bc.Sce., Zamboanga C., Z.Sur
1170	10	PHL	DZCA	Office of the Civil Defence, Quezon C, NCR
1170	700	PHL		IBB Relay Stn., Poro Pt, Luzon
1170	10	THA		Sor.Thor.Ror. 4, Chantaburi
1170	10	THA		Sor.Thor.Ror. 8, Phitsanulok
1170	1	TWN		Taiwan BC, Kuanhsi
1170		VTN		An Giang (P), Long Xuyen
1175		INS		RRI, Sumenep
1179	5	AUS	3RPH	Ass.for the Blind, Melbourne
1179	1	CHN		HL + 3 st's
1179	20	IND		AIR, Rewa
1179	2/10	INS		RRI, Padang
1179	50	J	JOOR	MBS, Osaka
1179	5	NZL		Ruia Mai, Auckland
1179	5	PHL	DXYK	Republic Bc.System, Butuan C., Ag.Nte
1179		PHL	DXRC	Republic Bc.System, Zamboanga C., Z.Sur
1179	5	PHL	DYCX	GMA Netw., Inc., Bacolod C., Neg.Occ
1179	1	PHL	DZRS	R.Sorsogon Netw., Inc., Sorsogon C.
1179	10	THA		Nor.Thor.Phor, Chiang Rai
1179	10	THA		Sor.Sor.Sor., Bangkok
1179	2.5	TWN		Kuo Sheng BC, Erhlin
1179	2	VUT		VBTC, Santo
1188	2	AUS	2NZ	Inverell
1188	2	AUS	6XM	ABC (RR), Exmouth
1188	300	CHN		YN (FS)
1188	1	CHN		HEB(2 st's)
1188	50	IND		AIR (C), Mumbai
1188	1	INS		RRI, Manado
1188	0.3	INS		RRI, Pekanbaru
1188	10	J	JOKP	NHK (1), Kitami
1188		KAZ		Qazaq Radiosi/BBC, Abay
1188	100	KOR	HLKX	FEBC, Inchon
1188	0.4	NZL	1YR	National R., Rotorua
1188	10	PHL	DXIF	Newsounds Bc.Netw., Cagayan de Oro
				C., Mis.Or.
1188	5	PHL	DZLT	R.Corp. of the Philippines, Lucena C, Que.
1188	5	PHL	DZXO	Vanguard R.Netw., Cabanatuan, Nva. Ecija
1188	5	PHL	DXLX	Consolidated Bc.System, Inc., Iligan,
				Lanao Nte
1188	1	PHL	DYRV	ABS-CBN Bc.Corp., Catbalogan, Samar
1188	5	RUS		R.DVA, Khabarovsk, FE
1188	10	THA		Kor.Wor.Sor. 3, Sakon Nakhon
1188	10	THA		Thor.Phor. 3, Phitsanulok
1188	10	THA		Thor.Phor,Neung, Sa Kaeo
1188	10	TWN	BED32	BCC (C), Hualien
1188	1	TWN	BEV46	Taiwan BC (2), Taipei
1188	1	TWN	BEV57	Sheng Li chih Sheng (2), Tainan
1188	2	WAL		R.Wallis et Futuna, Mata-Utu
1194	0.5	INS		RRI, Mataram
1195		VTN		Hay Duong (P)
1197	1	AUS	4BI	Brisbane
1197	2	AUS	5RPH	Adelaide
1197	600	CHN		XJ (FS)
1197	10	CHN		HL; SH;FJ(v);SD
1197	20	IND		AIR, Tirunelveli
1197	1	IND		AIR, Shillong
1197	1/5	INS		RRI, Palangkaraya
1197	10	J	JOBF	RKK, Kumamoto
1197	1	J		RKK, 3 st's
1197	5	J	JOYF	IBS, Mito
1197	1	J	JOFO	RKB, Kitakyushu
1197	3	J	JOWL	STV, Asahikawa
1197	1	J		STV, 3 st's
1197	1	J		RKC, Nakamura
1197		KAZ		Qazaq Radiosi/BBC, Astana
1197	1	KOR		AFNK, Dongducheon
1197	10	MLA		RTM Sabah, Kudat
1197	2	NZL	2ZW	River City R., Wanganui
1197	5	PHL	DXFE	FEBC, Davao C., Dvo Sur
1197	5	PHL	DYRH	Allied Bc.Center, Inc., Bacolod, Neg. Occ.
1197	5	PHL	DWBA	Satellite Bc.Corp., Bangued, Abra
1197	5	RUS		R.Rossii + Reg., Berezovo, Sib.
1197	0.2	RUS		R.Rossii + Reg., Sib., 4st's
1197	10	THA		Jor.Tor.Lor, Lop Buri
1206	5	AUS	2CC	Canberra, ACT
1206	5	AUS	2GF	Grafton
1206	2	AUS	6TAB	Perth (HPONS)
1206	300	CHN		YN (FS)
1206	150	CHN		JL + 4 st's
1206	2.5	FJI		Fiji Bc.Corp. Ltd. (2), Sigatoka
1206	200	IND		AIR, Bhawanipatna
1206	0.5/10	INS		RRI, Denpasar
1206	1	INS		RRI, Surabaya
1206	1	KOR		KBS, Jeongseon/Cheongsong
1206	20	MLA		RTM Sarawak, Miri
1206	2	NZL	4XO	R.Otago, Dunedin
1206	0.5	NZL	1XHC	Access CR, Hamilton
1206	10	PHL	DWAN	Banahaw Bc.Corp., Quezon C, NCR
1206	5	PHL	DXRS	R.Mindanao Netw., Surigao C, S. Nte
1206	10	THA		R.Thailand, Satun
1206	10	THA		Thor.Phor.Neung, Prachuap KK
1206	100	TWN		CBS (RTI), Minhsiung
1206	10	TWN	BEV62	Taiwan BC, Hsinchu
1210	1	HWA	KZOO	Honolulu
1215	0.35	AUS	2TAB	Bowral (HPONS)
1215	0.25	AUS	4HI	Moranbah (trtr)
1215	0.5	AUS	6NM	ABC (RR), Northam
1215		CHN		CNR2
1215		CHN		GD (CNR7)
1215	10	CHN		XJ
1215	20	IND		AIR (N), New Delhi (Kingsway)
1215	20	IND		AIR, Pudducherri
1215	0.5/10	INS		RRI, Samarinda
1215	2	J	JOBO	KBS, Maizuru
1215	1	J	JOBW	KBS, Hikone
1215	10	KOR	HLAK	MBC, Jinju
1215	1	LAO		R.Nationale Lao, Phonsavan (inactive)
1215	2	NZL	1ZE	Classic Hits, Kaikohe
1215	10	PHL	DYRF	World Bc.Corp., Cebu C.
1215	50	THA		R.Thailand, Surat Thani
1215	10	THA		Kor.Wor.Sor. 2, Phrae
1215	10	THA		Thor.Phor. 2, U. Ratchathani
1215	1	TWN		Tien Sheng BS, Pengshan
1224	5	AUS	2RPH	Sydney
1224	5	AUS	3EA	Melbourne (SBS)
1224	5	AUS	6RN	ABC (RN), Busselton
1224		CHN		FJ (CNR6)
1224	100	CHN		GX; HEB; JS
1224	20	IND		AIR, Kolkata
1224	10	J	JOJK	NHK (1), Kanazawa
1224	20	KOR		KBS, Gwangju
1224	1	MHL		Central Pacific Netw. (AFRTS), Kwajalein
1224	2	NZL	4XF	R.Foveaux, Invercargill
1224	10	PHL	DXED	Eagle Bc.Corp., Davao C., Dvo Sur
1224	10	PHL	DZAG	Pilippine Bc.Sce., Agoo, LU
1224	5	PHL	DWSR	Manila Bc.Co., Lucena, Que.
1224	5	PHL	DWBF	?Pilippine Bc.Sce., Virac, Catanduanes
1224	10	RUS		Ekho Moskvy, Khabarovsk, FE
1224	10	THA		Thor.Or. 4, N.Sawan
1224	10	THA		Thor.Or. 15, Chiang Rai
1224	10	TWN	BED52	BCC (L), Kaohsiung
1224	1	TWN	BEV71	Hua Sheng BC (2), Taipei
1233	10	AUS	2NC	ABC (MS), Newcastle
1233	120	CHN		XJ;HN;JS
1233	20	IND		AIR, Tura
1233	0.2/1/5	INS		RRI, Pontianak
1233		INS		RRI, Bandung
1233	5	J	JOGR	RAB, Aomori
1233	5	J	JOUR	NBC, Nagasaki
1233	1	KOR		KBS, Pyeongchang/Yeongyang
1233	2	NZL		Solid Gold AM, Wellington
1233	5	PHL	DYVS	FEBC, Bacolod, Neg. Occ.
1233	5	PHL	DWRV	R.Veritas, Bayombong, Nva Viz.
1233	20	RUS		R.3, Yelizovo, FE
1233	10	THA		Wor.Por.Tho. 7, Udon Thani
1233	10	THA		Thor.Or. 1, Bangkok
1233	40	TKM		Turkmen Radio (1), Syrtagta
1233	1	TWN		Chung Hua BC, Juifang
1242	5	AUS	3TR	Sale
1242	2	AUS	4AK	Toowoomba
1242	2	AUS	5AU	Port Augusta
1242	2	AUS	8TAB	Darwin (HPONS)
1242	1	CHN		LN; HB(2);YN;AH(v);JX
1242	100	IND		AIR, Varanasi
1242	0.5/5	INS		RRI, Bogor
1242	1	INS		RRI, Bengkulu
1242	100	J	JOLF	NBS, Tokyo
1242	10	KOR	HLSB	MBC, Wonju
1242	2	NZL	1XX	1 Double X, Whakatane
1242	0.1	NZL	1XX	1 Double X, Galatea
1242	20	PHL	DWBL	FBS R.Netw., Pasig C., NCR

kHz	kW	Ctry	Call	Station, location
1242	5	PHL	DXZB	DXZB/TV13 Coop., Inc., Zamboanga C., Z.Sur
1242	5	PHL	DXSY	Tirad Pass R/TV Bc.Netw., Ozamis C, Mis. Occ.
1242	2	RUS		R.Avtos/ORR, Angarsk, Sib.
1242	10	THA		Thor.Phor. 3, Phetchabun
1242	50	THA		R.Thailand, Surat Thani
1242	10	TWN	BED77	BCC (L), Taichung
1242	1	TWN		Yen Sheng BS (2), Hualien
1242	2000	VTN		Can Tho (E), Thoi Long
1250		CHN		ZJ; AH
1250	1	INS		RRI, Bogor
1251	2	AUS	2DU	Dubbo
1251	2	AUS	6NAN	Narrogin
1251		CHN		BJ(CRI DS1)
1251	100	CHN		QH + 19 st's
1251	20	IND		AIR, Sangli
1251	10	INS		RRI, Banda Aceh
1251	1	INS		RRI, Mataram
1251	1	INS		RRI, Singaraja
1251	10	KOR	HLKT	CBS, Daegu
1251	10	PAK		PBC, Loralai
1251	5	NZL	1XG	R.Rhema, Auckland
1251	0.8	NZL		Puketapu R., Palmerston
1251	5	PHL	DXPH	Manila Bc.Co., Prosperidad, Ag.Sur
1251	2.5	PHL	DZMS	People's Bc.Netw., Sorsogon C.
1251	1	PHL	DYRG	Intercontinental Bc.Corp., Kalibo, Aklan
1251	600	RUS		VoR, Ussuriysk, FE
1251	10	THA		Jor.Sor. 3, Roi Et
1251	5	THA		Thor.Or. 6, Bangkok
1251	100	TJK		Various relays, Yangiyul
1251	10	TWN	BEC29	Han Sheng BS, Kaohsiung
1254		CHN		ZJ (v)
1255	20	CBG		Nat.Radio of Cambodia, Sihanoukville
1260	2	AUS	3SR	Shepparton
1260	2	AUS	4MW	Thursday Island
1260	1	AUS	6KA	Karratha
1260	1	CHN		XZ; LN;HN
1260	20	IND		AIR, Ambikapur
1260	20	J	JOIR	TBC, Sendai
1260	10	KOR	HLKL	KBS, Namwon
1260	5	KOR		AFNK, Busan
1260	2	NZL	3XA	"Lite FM", Christchurch
1260	10	PHL	DYDD	Siam Bc.Netw.Corp., Lapu-Lapu C., Cebu
1260	5	PHL	DWMC	Magiliw Comm.Bc.Co., Rosales, Pang.
1260	5	PHL	DXRF	Manila Bc.Co., Davao C., Dvo Sur
1260	5	PHL	DZEL	Eagle Bc.Corp., Lucena C., Que.
1260	10	RUS		R.Radonezh, Yekaterinburg
1260	25	THA		R.Thailand, Chiang Rai
1260	10	TWN	BEP22	Ching Cha BS, Taipei
1260	1	TWN		Cheng Sheng BC, Putzu
1260	20	UZB		UZR (1), Nukus
1269	5	AUS	2SM	Sydney
1269	300	CHN		YN (FS)
1269	200	CHN		FJ; SX; JL; JS
1269	20	IND		AIR, Agartala
1269	20	IND		AIR, Madurai
1269	1	IND		AIR (B), Jaipur
1269	5	J	JOHW	HBC, Obihiro
1269	1	J	JOFM	HBC, Esashi
1269	5	J	JOJR	JRT, Tokushima
1269	1	J		JRT, Ikeda
1269	10	KOR		KBS, Yangju
1269	1	KOR		KBS, Gurye
1269	0.4	NZL	2ZT	Classic Hits, Takaka
1269	10	PHL	DWRC	Republic Bc.System, San Nicolas, I.Nte
1269	10	PHL	DYWB	Consolidated Bc.System, Inc., Bacolod, Neg. Occ
1269	5	PHL	DZVX	Newsounds Bc.Netw., Daet, Cam. Nte
1269	5	RUS		R.Ussuri, Ussuriyisk, FE
1269		RUS		R.Vostok Rossii, Komsomolsk, FE
1269	10	THA		Mor.Kor, Songkhla
1269	10	THA		Kho.Sor.Thor.Bor., Bangkok
1269	10	TWN	BEC44	Han Sheng BS, Penghu
1269	1	TWN	BEV37	Cheng Sheng BC, Taitung
1269	50	UZB		UZR (2), Zarafshon
1270	5	HWA	KNDI	Honolulu
1278	5	AUS	3AW	Melbourne
1278	100	CHN		HEB;HL;FJ;JX
1278	10	IND		AIR (C), Lucknow
1278	50	J	JOFR	RKB, Fukuoka
1278	1	KOR		KBS, Hapcheon
1278	2	NZL	2ZC	Newstalk ZB, Napier
1278	10	PHL	DZRM	Pilippine Bc.Sce., Quezon C, NCR
1278	10	PHL	DXAM	Intercontinental Bc.Corp., Maramag, Buk.
1278	7	RUS		R.Rossii + Reg., Severobaykalsk, Sib.
1278	5	RUS		R.Rossii, Bagdarin, Sib.
1278		VTN		Soc Trang (P)
1280		VTN		Nam Dinh (P)
1287	2	AUS	2TM	Tamworth
1287	10	BGD		Bangladesh Betar, Barishal
1287		CHN		CNR1
1287	10	CHN		YN + 6 st's
1287	100	IND		AIR (A), Panaji
1287	20/25	INS		RRI, Palembang
1287	50	J	JOHR	HBC, Sapporo
1287	150	KGZ		KGR (1), Bishkek
1287	10	KOR	HLAF	MBC, Gangneung
1287	10	KOR	HLAX	MBC, Cheongju
1287	2	NZL	3ZW	Scenicland FM, Westport
1287	5	PHL	DXRC	Republic Bc.System, Zamboanga C., Z.Sur
1287	5	PHL	DZZH	Manila Bc.Co., Sorsogon C.
1287	75	RUS		R.Radonezh, Novosibirsk, Sib.
1287	50	RUS		R.Yunost, Yazykovo, Sib.
1287	7	RUS		R.Rossii + Reg., Shagonar/Chadan, Sib.
1287	5	RUS		R.Rossii + Reg., Kyakhta, Sib.
1287	10	THA		Wor.Por.Tho. 6, U. Ratchathani
1287	10	THA		Sor.Or.Thor., Bangkok
1287	10	TWN	BEC27	Han Sheng BS, Taichung
1287	1	TWN		Min Li BS, Fangliao
1296	5	AUS	4RPH	Brisbane
1296	10	AUS	6RN	ABC (RN), Wagin
1296	300	CHN		YN (FS)
1296	20	CHN		SH + 5 st's
1296	10	IND		AIR, Darbhanga
1296		INS		RRI, Surabaya
1296	10	J	JOTK	NHK (1), Matsue
1296	2.5	NZL	1ZH	Newstalk ZB, Hamilton
1296	10	PHL	DXAB	ABS-CBN Bc.Corp., Davao C., Dvo Sur
1296	5	PHL	DYJJ	Intercontinental Bc.Corp., Roxas C., Capiz
1296	5	PHL	DWPR	Allied Bc.Center, Inc., Dagupan C, Pang.
1296	5	PHL	DWLQ	Allied Bc.Center, Inc., Lucena C., Que.
1296	5	RUS		Ekho Moskvy, Irkutsk, Sib.
1296	10	THA		R.Thailand, Pattani
1296	10	TWN	BED47	BCC (N), Tainan
1296	1	TWN	BEV23	Min Pen BC (1), Taipei
1300	1	CBG		Nat.Radio of Cambodia, Phnom Penh
1305	2	AUS	5RN	ABC (RN), Renmark/Loxton
1305		CHN		CNR2
1305		CHN		SD
1305	20	IND		AIR, Parbhani
1305	10	KOR		KBS, Uljin
1305	2	NZL	4XD	R.Dunedin, D.
1305	10	PHL	DYFX	Eagle Bc.Corp., Cebu C.
1305	7	RUS		R.Mayak, Ust-Kut, Sib.
1305	10	THA		Yaan Kraw, Bangkok
1310	20	MLA		RTM, Mersing (AF 1314)
1314	5	AUS	2TAB	Wollongong (HPONS)
1314	5	AUS	3BT	Ballarat
1314	10	BGD		Bangladesh Betar, Coxbazar
1314	100	CHN		NM (FS)
1314	15	CHN		CQ + 4 st's
1314	10	IND		AIR, Bhuj
1314	1	IND		AIR (B), Cuttack
1314	50	J	JOUF	OBC, Osaka
1314	10	KOR	HLCM	CBS, Jeonbuk
1314	2	NZL	2YW	National R., Gisborne
1314	10	PHL	DWXI	Delta Bc.System, Parañaque, NCR
1314	10	THA		Mor.Kor., Khon Kaen
1314	10	TWN	BEV76	Tien Sheng BS, Chunan
1314	5	TWN	BEP32	Ching Cha BS, Tainan
1323	2	AUS	5DN	Adelaide
1323		CHN		XZ (FS)
1323	100	CHN		JL (FS)
1323	20	CHN		ZJ + 5 st's
1323	20	IND		AIR (C), Kolkata
1323	1	J	JOFP	NHK (1), Fukushima
1323	1	J		NHK (1), Yamada
1323	30	KGZ		R.Liberty, Bishkek
1323	1	KOR		KBS, Yeonggwang/Ulleung
1323	1	NRU		Nauru Bc.Sce., Nauru
1323	10	PHL	DYSI	GMA Netw., Inc., Iloilo C.
1323	5	PHL	DXAD	Muslim Mindanao DMPC, Marawi, Lanao Sur

kHz	kW	Ctry	Call	Station, location
1323	0.25	PHL	DZRK	Pilippine Bc.Sce., Tabuk,Kalinga
1323	10	THA		Thor.Or. 13, Chiang Mai
1323	10	THA		Thor.Or. 7, Surat Thani
1323	7	TJK		TR (1), Dushanbe
1323	1	TWN	BEV45	Taiwan BC (1), Taipei
1323	7	UZB		UZR (3), Koson
1323	5	UZB		UZR (2), Dang'ara
1332	2	AUS	3SH	Swan Hill
1332	5	AUS	4BU	Bundaberg
1332	10	CHN		HEN; JL; FJ; GS
1332	10	IND		AIR, Tezu
1332	10	INS		RRI, Jakarta
1332	50	J	JOSF	Tokai R., Nagoya
1332	10	KOR	HLAO	MBC, Chungju
1332	10	NZL		R.Sport, Auckland
1332	5	PHL	DWAY	Nation Bc.Corp., Cabanatuan, Nva. Ecija
1332	1	PHL	DZKI	R.Philippines Netw., Iriga C., Cam. Sur
1332	10	RUS		Nashe vremya na MV, Irkutsk, Sib.
1332	10	THA		Or.Sor., Bangkok
1332	10	THA		Thor.Or. 14, Maha Sarakham
1332	10	TWN	BEC36	Han Sheng BS, Tsoying
1332	1	TWN		Taiwan BC, Puli
1332	5	UZB		UZR (1), Muborak
1341	5	AUS	2TAB	Newcastle (HPONS)
1341	5	AUS	3—	Geelong (HPONS)
1341	100	CHN		GD (FS)
1341	10	CHN		HL + 6 st's
1341	1	IND		AIR, Kohima
1341	1/5	INS		RRI, Tanjung Pinang
1341	1	J		NHK (1), Iwaki/Minamata
1341	30	KAZ		RL/VOA, Almaty
1341	10	KOR		KBS, Gimpo
1341	2	NZL	2ZN	Newstalk ZB, Nelson
1341	10	PAK		PBC, Bahawalpur
1341	10	PHL	DXRL	Republic Bc.System, Koronadal, S.Cot.
1341	25	THA		R.Thailand, Ubon Ratchathani
1341	20	THA		R.Thailand, Loei
1341	10	THA		R.Thailand, Phangnga
1350	5	AUS	2LF	Young
1350	50	CHN		YN; NM;JX(v);LN
1350	1	FSM	V6A	Moen. Chuuk State
1350	1	IND		AIR (B), Dharwad
1350	20	J	JOER	RCC, Hiroshima
1350	10	KOR	HLAQ	MBC, Samcheok
1350	150	MNG		MRT (1), Ulaanbaatar
1350	1	NZL		R.Sport, Rotorua
1350	10	PHL	DZXQ	Mabuhay Bc.System, Inc., Pasig C., NCR
1350	5	PHL	DXXY	GMA Netw., Inc., Dipolog C., Z.Nte
1350	5	RUS		R.Rossii + Reg., Ust-Kan/Ust-Ulagan, Sib.
1350	10	THA		Wor.Por.Tho. 17, Trang
1350	10	THA		Phon.Neung Ror.Or., Bangkok
1350	10	TWN	BED63	BCC (N), Chia-i
1350	2.5	TWN	BEV50	Chung Hua BC (1), Sanchung
1359	0.2	AUS	3—	Mildura (HPONS)
1359	0.3	AUS	4WK	Toowoomba (trtr)
1359		CHN		CNR1
1359	20	IND		AIR, Bhadravathi
1359	1	INS		RRI, Makassar
1359	1	KOR		AFNK, Songtan
1359	1	NZL	4XC	Resort R., Queenstown
1359	5	PHL	DZYR	Philippine R.Corp., S. Fernando, LU
1359	1	PHL	DYSL	Philippine Bc.Sce., Sogod, S.Leyte
1359	7	RUS		R.Mayak, Ust-Ilimsk, Sib.
1359	5	RUS		R.Mayak, Onguday, Sib.
1359	1	RUS		R.Mayak, Choya/Shebalino, Sib.
1359	10	THA		Thor.Phor. 2, Sakhon Nakhon
1359	5	TWN	BEC40	Han Sheng BS, Hualien
1360	1	CBG		Nat.Radio of Cambodia, Phnom Penh (FS)
1368	2	AUS	2GN	Goulburn
1368	10	CHN		HL;FJ (v);HB
1368	20	IND		AIR (C), New Delhi
1368	5	J	JOHP	NHK (1), Takamatsu
1368	1	J	JOLG	NHK (1), Tottori
1368	1	J		NHK (1), Tsuruoka
1368	1	J	JOTS	HBC, Wakkanai
1368	1	KOR		KBS, Muju
1368	2	KRE		Korean Central BS (E), Pyongyang
1368	1	NZL	1XT	Village R., Tauranga
1368	10	PHL	DXKO	R.Philippines Netw, Cagayan de Oro C, Mis. Or
1368	5	PHL	DWTT	Nation Bc.Corp., Tarlac C.
1368	2.5	PHL	DZBS	R.Philippines Netw., Baguio C., Benguet
1368	1	PHL	DZRA	Catanduanes State College, Virac, Catanduanes
1368	25	THA		R.Thailand, Nan
1368	10	THA		R.Thailand, Buri Ram
1368	10	THA		Thor.Or. 12, N.Pathom
1368	1	TWN		Chin Hsi, Kaohsiung
1370	5	HWA	KITT	Pearl City
1370	10	LAO		R.Nationale Lao, Pakse
1377	5	AUS	3MP	Melbourne
1377	600	CHN		HEN (CNR1)
1377	200	CHN		FJ + 7 st's
1377	20	IND		AIR (B), Hyderabad
1377	5	J	JOUC	NHK (2), Yamaguchi
1377	1	J	JOAC	NHK (2), Nagasaki
1377	1	J		NHK (2), Hachinohe
1377	2	NZL	2XX	R.Sport, Levin
1377	10	PHL	DXKP	R.Philippines Netw., Pagadian C., Z. Sur
1377	75	RUS		R.Yunost, Tavrichanka, FE
1377	50	RUS		R.Yunost, Yekaterinburg, Sib.
1377	5	RUS		R.Mayak, Okha, FE
1377	10	THA		Wor.Phon 4, Phitsanulok
1377	10	THA		R.Thailand, Chumphon
1386	20	CHN		TJ + 4 st's
1386	20	IND		AIR, Gwalior
1386	10	J	JOQC	NHK (2), Morioka
1386	10	J	JOJB	NHK (2), Kanazawa
1386	10	J	JOHC	NHK (2), Kagoshima
1386	5	J	JOKB	NHK (2), Okayama
1386	10	KOR	HLAM	MBC, Mokpo
1386	5	NZL		R.Tarana/R.Korea/Ch.Life CR, Auckland
1386	10	PHL	DXCR	Mt.View College, Valencia, Buk.
1386	5	PHL	DYVW	Catholic Welfare Org., Borongan, E.Samar
1386	50	RUS		R.Liberty/VOA, Khabarovsk, Sib.
1386	5	SLM		SIBC, Lata, Sta. Cruz Is.
1386	10	THA		SW Pheua Kaan Kaset, Bangkok
1386	3.5	TWN	BED87	BCC (I), Hsinchu
1386	3.5	TWN	BED74	BCC (C), Yuli
1395	0.2	AUS	2LG	ABC (RR), Lithgow
1395	5	AUS	5AA	Adelaide
1395	10	CHN		AH (2 st's);NM (2)
1395	20	IND		AIR, Bikaner
1395	1	INS		RRI, Wamena
1395	1	J		AMK, Toyooka
1395	1	J	JOWE	RFC, Wakamatsu
1395	10	KOR		KBS, Cheorwon
1395	2	NZL	4ZW	Newstalk ZB, Oamaru
1395	10	PHL	DYRC	Cebu Bc.Co., Talisay C., Cebu
1395	5	PHL	DZVT	Catholic Welfare Org., San Jose, Min.Occ.
1395	10	RUS		Ekho Moskvy, Krasnoyarsk, Sib.
1395	10	THA		Nor.Thor.Phor., Chiang Rai
1395	10	TWN		Cheng Sheng BC, Tafa
1404	2	AUS	2PK	Parkes
1404	4	AUS	6TAB	Busselton (HPONS)
1404	10	CHN		LN;HB;ZJ
1404	0.1	ICO	VKW	R.VKW, Keeling
1404	20	IND		AIR, Gangtok
1404	10	J	JOVR	SBS, Shizuoka
1404	1	J	JOVO	SBS, Hamamatsu
1404	5	J	JOQL	HBC, Kushiro
1404		KAZ		Qazaq Radiosi/BBC, Qyzylorda
1404	20	KGZ		KGR (1), Jojomel
1404	7	KGZ		KGR (1), Haidarkan/Naryn
1404	1	KGZ		KGR (1), Cholpon-Ata
1404		KGZ		KGR (1), Orgochor
1404	10	KOR	HLKP	CBS, Busan
1404	2.5	NZL	4XL	R.Rhema, Invercargill
1404	10	PAK		PBC, Dera Ismail Khan
1404	1	PHL	DYKB	R.Philippines Netw., Bacolod, Neg. Occ.
1404	25	THA		R.Thailand, Songkhla
1404	10	THA		Jor.Sor. 4, Yasothon
1404	10	THA		Thor.Phor.Neung, Suphan Buri
1404	2.5/5	TMP		R.Timor Kmanek, Dili
1404	10	TWN	BED65	BCC (N), Ilan
1404	10	TWN	BEV78	Yi Shih BS, Keelung
1413	5	AUS	2EA	Newcastle (SBS)
1413	0.5	AUS	3—	Shepparton (HPONS)
1413	10	BGD		Bangladesh Betar, Comilla
1413	100	CHN		XJ + 4 st's
1413		INS		RRI, Sungai Liat
1413	50	J	JOIF	KBC, Fukuoka
1413	2	NZL	1ZO	R.Forestland, Tokoroa
1413	0.1	NZL	3XP	R.Ferrymead/Nga Hou E Wha, Christchurch

kHz	kW	Ctry	Call	Station, location
1413	10	PHL	DXBZ	Baganian Bc.Corp., Dumalinao, Z.Sur
1413	5	PHL	DYXW	Filipinas Bc.Netw., Tacloban C., Leyte
1413	5	PHL	DWRA	Republic Bc.System, Bauio C., Benguet
1413	7	RUS		Russkoye R., Khabarovsk, FE
1413		RUS		R.Rossii, Sangar, FE
1413	10	TWN	BED54	BCC (N), Miaoli
1413	1	TWN	BED67	BCC (N), Puli
1413	3.5	TWN	BED80	BCC (I), Taitung
1420	5	HWA	KKEA	Honolulu
1422	5	AUS	3XY	Melbourne (HPONS)
1422	1	AUS	4AM	Port Douglas (trtr)
1422	2	AUS	6TAB	Wagin (HPONS)
1422	600	CHN		XJ (FS)
1422	20	CHN		SH (2 st's);SX;SC
1422	0.5	CHR	VLU2	Christmas Is. CRS, Phosphate Hill
1422		INS		RRI, Kendari
1422	50	J	JORF	RF, Yokohama
1422	10	PHL	DWBC	United Bc.Netw., Quezon C, NCR
1422	5	PHL	DXMU	Central Mindanao Univ., Musuan, Buk.
1422	5	PHL	DYZD	Bohol Chronicle R.Corp., Ubay, Bohol
1422	1	PHL	DZOR	Zambales Bc.& Dev.Corp., Olongapo C.
1422	5	RUS		R.Rossii, Kuanda, Sib.
1422	10	THA		R.Thailand, Amnat Charoen
1422	10	THA		Phon.Neung Ror.Or., Bangkok
1422	10	THA		Sor.Wor.Phor. 4, Phitsanulok
1422	1	TWN		Chien Kuo BS, Kuanyin
1422	100	TWN		CBS (RTI), Minhsiung
1431	2	AUS	2RN	ABC (RN), Wollongong
1431	2	AUS	6TAB	Calgoorlie (HPONS)
1431	10	CHN		HEB + 6 st's
1431	5	J	JOVF	WBS, Wakayama
1431	5	J	JOZF	GBS, Gifu
1431	1	J	JOWW	RFC, Iwaki
1431	1	J		NBC, Fukue
1431	1	J	JOHL	BSS, Tottori
1431	1	J		BSS, Izumo
1431	2	NZL	2XKC	R.Kidnappers, Hastings
1431	5	PHL	DYRS	Ragde, Vicente & Sons, San Carlos, Neg. Occ.
1431	10	THA		Thor.Or. 3, N.Ratchasima
1431	5	THA		Sor.ThorRor. 6, Songkhla
1431	10	TWN		VO Kuanghua, Chingshui
1440	2	AUS	2PB	ABC (PNN), Canberra
1440	50	CHN		NM (2); GX; LN
1440	1	IND		AIR, Kurseong
1440	50	J	JOWF	STV, Sapporo
1440	3	J		STV, Muroran
1440	1	J		STV, Tomakomai
1440		KAZ		BBC, Qyzylorda
1440	1-0.25	KOR		AFNK, 4 st's
1440	0.2	NZL	1XK	Te Reo o Tauranga Moana, Tauranga
1440	0.1	NZL		Goldrush 14-40, Lawrence
1440	10	PHL	DWDH	Manila Bc.Co., Dagupan C., Pang.
1440	0.01	PHL	DXSI	So.Inst. of Tech., Cagayan de Oro C., Mis.Or.
1440	5	RUS		R.Rossii + Reg., Ust-Koksha/Kosh-Agach, Sib.
1440	10	THA		Wor.Por.Thor. 8, Samut Sakhon
1440	10	THA		Thor.Phor. 2, N. Phanom
1449	5	AUS	2MG	Mudgee
1449	2	AUS	6TAB	Mandurah (HPONS)
1449	20	CHN		JX ; SD(2 st's)
1449	10	FSM	V6AH	Kolonia, Pohnpei
1449	1	IND		AIR, Kanpur
1449	5	J	JOKF	RNC, Takamatsu
1449	5	J	JOQM	HBC, Abashiri
1449	1	J		RNC, Marugame
1449	10	KOR	HLQB	KBS, Ulsan
1449	2	NZL	2YM	National R., Palmerston No.
1449	10	PAK		PBC, Zhob
1449	5	PHL	DXSA	Mindanao Bc.Co., Inc., Marawi C, Lanao Sur
1449	5	PHL	DYAC	Ce.Visayas Coll. of Agr., Baybay, Leyte
1449	10	THA		Wor.Sor.Por., Chumphon
1449	10	THA		Thor.Phor. 3, Phichit
1449	10	TWN	BED48	BCC (I), Kaohsiung
1458	2	AUS	2PB	ABC (PNN), Newcastle
1458	200	CHN		NM;JS
1458	20	IND		AIR, Barmer
1458	20	IND		AIR, Bhagalpur
1458	1	J	JOUO	NBC, Saga
1458	1	J	JOYL	IBS, Tsuchiura
1458	1	J		IBS, Sekijo
1458	1	J	JOWR	RFC, Fukushima
1458	1	J		RCC, Shobara
1458	1	KOR		KBS, Hamyang/Bonghwa
1458	5	MLD		Voice of Maldives, Malé
1458	0.4	NZL	3YW	National R., Westport
1458	10	PHL	DWRF	FEBC, Iba, Zamb.
1458	10	PHL	DYZZ	Siam Bc.Netw.Corp., Gihulngan, Neg.Occ.
1458	10	PHL	DZJV	ZOE Bc.Netw., Calamba, Laguna
1458	10	THA		Sor.Thor.Ror. 3, Phuket
1458	10	THA		Jor.Sor. 6, Si Sa Ket
1460	5	HWA	KRHA	Honolulu
1467	2	AUS	3ML	Mildura
1467	50	CHN		FJ (v);SD;JX
1467	2.5	FJI		Fiji Bc.Corp. Ltd. (2), Rakiraki
1467	100	IND		AIR, Jeypore
1467	1	J	JOVB	NHK (2), Hakodate
1467	1	J	JONB	NHK (2), Nagano
1467	1	J	JOID	NHK (2), Oita
1467	1	J	JOMC	NHK (2), Miyazaki
1467	1	J		NHK (2), Wakkanai
1467	50	KOR	HLKN	KBS, Mokpo
1467	75	KGZ		R.Extol/TWR, Bishkek
1467	5	PHL	DXVP	Catholic Welfare Org., Zamboanga C., Z.Sur
1467	1	PHL	DWVR	R.Veritas, San Jose C., Nva Ecija
1467	100	THA		R.Thailand, Pathum Thani
1467	10	TWN	BED81	BCC (I/H), Huanlien
1467	10	TWN	BED82	BCC (I), Chia-i
1476	0.5	AUS	2—	Penrith (HPONS)
1476	2	AUS	4ZR	Roma
1476	0.2	AUS	5MG	ABC (RR), Mt.Gambier
1476	200	CHN		HL (CNR2)
1476	10	CHN		QH + 7 st's
1476	1	IND		AIR (A), Jaipur
1476	1	J		NHK (2), Iida
1476	700	MLA		RTM Sabah, Kota Kinabalu (r1475)
1476	5	NZL	1XD	BBC WS, Auckland Airport
1476	10	PAK		PBC, Faisalabad
1476	10	PHL	DXRJ	Rajah Bc.Netw., Iligan C., Lanao Nte
1476	1	PHL	DZYA	Radyo Pilipino Corp., Angeles C, Pamp.
1476	1	PHL	DWRB	Ribbon Bc.Netw., Lipa C, Bat
1476	75	RUS		Studiya O'key, Vladivostok, FE
1476	20	RUS		R.Rossii + Reg., Onguday, Sib.
1476	50	THA		R.Thailand, Lamphun
1476	10	TKM		Turkmen R. (1), Türkmenbasy
1485	0.05-0.2	AUS		ABC (RR), 2 st's
1485	0.1	AUS	2RN	ABC (RN), Wilcannia
1485	0.15	AUS	2EA	Wollongong (SBS)
1485	0.25	DGA		AFRTS, Diego Garcia
1485	1	CHN		SD + 13 st's
1485	1	IND		AIR, 7 st's
1485	1	J	JOGO	RAB, Hachinohe
1485	1	J	JOPL	KRY, Hagi
1485	1	KOR		KBS, Gongju/Goheung
1485	5	PHL	DYDH	Pacific Bc.System, Iloilo C.
1485	1	RUS		R.Rossii + Reg., Kamenskoye, FE
1485	1	RUS		R.Rossii, Sib., 3 st's (sync.)
1485	0.2-1	RUS		R.Rossii, FE, 2 st's (sync.)
1485	1/2	RUS		R.Mayak, FE, 2 st's (sync.)
1494	2	AUS	2AY	Albury
1494		CHN		XJ;AH(v); NM
1494	10	FSM	V6AI	Colonia, Yap
1494	10	J	JOYR	RSK, Okayama
1494	1	J		RSK, 5 st's
1494	1	J	JOTL	HBC, Nayoro
1494	0.1	LHW		R.Lord Howe Island
1494	2.5	NZL		R.Sport, Timaru
1494	10	PNG		NBC, Wabag
1494	10	PHL	DWSS	Ultrasonic Bc.System, Pasig C., NCR
1494	5	PHL	DXOC	Radio, Inc., Ozamis C., Mis.Occ.
1494	10	THA		Or.Sor.Mor.Thor., Bangkok
1494	10	TWN	BEE32	Chiao Yu BS, Taipei
1494	5	TWN	BEE34	Chiao Yu BS, Changhua
1500	10	HWA	KUMU	Honolulu
1503	5	AUS	2BS	Bathurst
1503	5	AUS	3KND	(PBS), Port Melbourne
1503	1	CHN		AH(v);HN;ZJ
1503	1	FSM	V6AJ	Tofol, Kosrae
1503	1	IND		AIR (B), Vijayawada
1503	10	J	JOUK	NHK (1), Akita
1503	1	J		NHK (1), Aso
1503	1	KOR		KBS, Gimcheon
1503	5	NZL		R.Sport, Wellington
1503	2.5	NZL		R.Sport, Christchurch
1503	5	PHL	DYBB	GMA Netw., Inc., Roxas C., Capiz
1503	5	RUS		R.Mayak, Salekhard, Sib.

kHz	kW	Ctry	Call	Station, location
1503	5	RUS		Ekho Moskvy, Ussuruyisk, FE
1503	1	RUS		R.Rossii + Reg., Magistralnyy, Sib.
1503	10	THA		Jor.Sor. 2, Surat Thani
1503	7	TJK		R.Mayak/R.Rossii/VoR, Dushanbe
1505		VTN		Ba Ria Vung Tau (P), Vung Tau
1512	10	AUS	2RN	ABC (RN), Newcastle
1512	5	AUS	6BAY	Morawa
1512	10	CHN		GS; NM;SD
1512	20	IND		AIR, Kokrajhar
1512		INS		RRI, Bukittinggi
1512	5	J	JOZB	NHK (2), Matsuyama
1512	1	J		NHK (2), Koriyama/Matsumoto
1512	0.25-0.1	KOR		AFNK, 3 st's
1512	1	NZL	1ZU	King Country R., Taumarunui
1512	0.3	NZL		Coast Access R., Waikanae
1512	10	PAK		PBC, Gilgit
1512	10	PHL	DYAB	ABS-CBN Bc.Corp., Cebu C.
1512	10	THA		Thor.Or. 11, Songkhla
1512	10	THA		Kor.Wor.Sor. 4, Phayao
1512	10	TWN		Ching Cha BS, Hsinchu
1521	2	AUS	2QN	Deniliquin
1521	500	CHN		XJ (FS)
1521	10	CHN		GS + 20 st's
1521	10	IND		AIR, Tawang
1521	1	IND		AIR, Aurangabad
1521	1	J	JOJC	NHK (2), Yamagata
1521	1	J	JOTC	NHK (2), Aomori
1521	1	J	JODC	NHK (2), Hamamatsu
1521	1	J	JOFC	NHK (2), Fukui
1521	1	J		NHK (2), Yonago
1521	1	J		NHK (2), Ishigaki/Nakamura
1521		NZL		Classic GTO, Tauranga
1521	5	RUS		R.Rossii, Boguchany, Sib.
1521	10	THA		Nor.Thor.Phor, Bangkok
1521	1200	TWN		CBS (RTI), Changchih
1530	2	AUS	2VM	Moree
1530	50	CHN		ZJ;JL
1530	20	IND		AIR, Agra
1530	5	J	JOXF	CRT, Utsunomiya
1530	1	J	JODO	BSN, Joetsu
1530	1	J	JOEO	RCC, Fukuyama
1530	1	J		RCC, Mihara
1530	5	KOR		AFNK, Seoul (Yongsan)
1530	2	NZL	2YP	National R., New Plymouth
1530	1/0.3	NZL		"Coast 15-30", Hastings
1530	10	PHL	DZME	Capitol Bc.Center, Quezon C., NCR
1530	5	RUS		R.Mayak, Krasnyy Chikoy, Sib.
1530	10	THA		Wor.Por.Tho. 14, Uttaradit
1530	10	THA		Thor.Phor.Neung, Chanthaburi
1539	1	AUS	2RF	Sydney (HPONS)
1539	10	AUS	5TAB	Adelaide (HPONS)
1539	600	CHN		XJ (FS)
1539	10	CHN		CNR1
1539	20	IND		AIR (B), Panaji
1539	1	KOR		KBS, Gosan
1539	1	NZL	2ZE	R.Sport, Blenheim
1539	5	PHL	DZYM	Philippine R.Corp., San José, Mind. Occ.
1539	10	THA		Phon Ror.Kao, Kanchanaburi
1539	10	TWN	BED78	BCC (I), Tainan
1539	5	UZB		UZR (3), Samarqand
1540	5	HWA	KREA	Honolulu
1548	50	AUS	4QD	ABC (RR), Emerald
1548	200	CHN		SD; HN
1548	600	CLN		DW, Trincomalee
1548	0.99	NZL	1XN	Classic Country, Rotorua
1548	10	PHL	DZSD	GMA Netw., Inc., Dagupan C., Pang.
1548	5	PHL	DZKV	Kaissar Bc.Netw., Lipa C., Bat.
1548	5	PHL	DYDM	Catholic Welfare Org., Maasin C., So.Leyte
1548	10	RUS		R.Mayak + Reg., Aleksandrovsk-Sak., FE
1551	0.1	INS		RRI, Manado
1557	2	AUS	2RE	Taree
1557	0.5	AUS	5TAB	Renmark/Loxton (HPONS)
1557	1	CHN		HEB (2 st's)
1557	10	MHL	V7RR	Micronesia Heatwave, Majuro
1557	2	NZL	2ZH	Newstalk ZB, Hawera
1557	10	PAK		PBC, Skardu
1557	10	RUS		R.Shanson, Vladivostok,. FE
1557	5	RUS		Inta R., Irkutsk, Sib.
1557	10	THA		Siang Adison, Phetchabun
1557	10	THA		R.Thailand, Trat
1557	300	TWN		CBS (RTI), Kouhu
1566	5	AUS	3NE	Wangaratta
1566	0.2	AUS	4GM	ABC (RR), Gympie
1566	10	CHN		HEB;GS;SX
1566	1000	IND		AIR (N), Nagpur (Buttibori)
1566	250/100	KOR	HLAZ	FEBC, Jeju
1566	0.1	NFK	VL2NI	Norfolk Is. Bc.Sce., Kingston
1566	10	PHL	DXID	Ass.of Islamic Dev.Coop., Pagadian C., Z.Sur
1566	10	PHL	DZHH	Philippine Air Force, Pasay C., NCR
1570	0.5	HWA	KUAU	Ha'iku, Maui
1575	5	AUS	2RF	Wollongong (HPONS)
1575	2	CHN		LN;JL
1575	1	J		AFN, Iwakuni
1575	0.6	J		AFN, Misawa
1575	0.25	J		AFN, Sasebo
1575	2.5	NZL	4XS	Hills AM, Dunedin
1575	10	PHL	DXJR	COC Bc.Netw., Cagayan de Oro C., Mis.Or.
1575	30	RUS		R.Yunost + Reg., Yuzhno-Sakhalinsk, FE
1575	0.2	RUS		Ekho Usoloya, Usolye-Sibirskoye, Sib.
1575	1000	THA		IBB Relay Stn., Ayutthaya
1584	0.05-0.2	AUS		ABC (RR), 4 st's
1584	0.2	AUS	2EC	Narooma (trtr)
1584	0.5	AUS	4CC	Rockhampton (trtr)
1584	0.2	AUS	4VL	Cunnamulla (trtr)
1584	10	CHN		SX (2 st's) + 8 st's
1584	0.2	HKG		RTHK (3), Chung Hom Kok
1584	1	IND		AIR, 8 st's
1584	1	KOR		KBS, Danyang/Geumsan
1584	1	KOR		KBS, Sancheong
1584	0.4	NZL	2ZF	R.Marlborough, Picton
1584	0.25	PAK		PBC, Turbat/Chitral/Sibi
1584	5	PAL	T8AA	T8AA Bc.Stn., Koror, Malakal Is.
1584	10	PHL	DYAY	Allied Bc.Center, Inc., Minglanilla, Cebu
1584	1	PHL	DWBR	Dawnbreaker's Found., Talavera, Nva Ecija
1584	1/5	RUS		R.Mayak, Aykhal/Ust-Nera, FE
1584	1	RUS		R.Rossii, Taksimo, Sib.
1584	0.2	RUS		R.Rossii, B.Gora/Khandyra, Sib.
1584	1	RUS		R.Rossii + Reg., Klyuchi/Tigil, FE
1584	5	RUS		R.Svob. Nakhodka, N., Sib.
1584	1	THA		R.Thailand, Loei
1593	0.2	AUS	2—	Murwillumbah (HPONS)
1593	5	AUS	3RG	Melbourne (HPONS)
1593	600	CHN		CNR1
1593	10	CHN		HL (2 st's)
1593	5	FSM	V6AK	Weno, Chuuk
1593	10	IND		AIR (A), Bhopal
1593	10	J	JOQB	NHK (2), Niigata
1593	10	J	JOTB	NHK (2), Matsue
1593	2	NZL		R.Asia Pacific/R.Samoa, Auckland
1593	2	NZL		1593 AM, Christchurch
1593		PHL	DXFM	Radyo Ranaw, Marawi C., Lanao Sur
1593	10	PNG		NBC, Vanimo
1593	50	RUS		R.Yunost, Sib.
1593	10	THA		Neung.Por.Nor., Buri Ram
1593	10	THA		R.Thailand, Ratchaburi
1593	3	TWN		Taiwan Chu Yuyeh BS, Ilan
1593	7	UZB		UZR (3), Zharqo'rg'on
1602	0.05-0.25	AUS		ABC (RR), 3 st's
1602	1	CHN		JS
1602	1	IND		AIR, 10 st's
1602	1	J	JOCC	NHK (2), Asahikawa
1602	1	J	JOKC	NHK (2), Kofu
1602	1	J	JOSB	NHK (2), Kitakyushu
1602	1	J	JOFD	NHK (2), Fukushima
1602	1	J		NHK (2), 6 st's
1602	1	KOR		KBS, Sabuk
1602	2.5	NZL	2XA	R.Reading Service, Levin
1602	0.25	PAK		PBC, Abbottabad
1602	10	PHL	DZUP	Univ. of the Philippines, Quezon C., NCR
1602	1	RUS		R.Rossii, Sib., 3 st's (sync.)
1602	0.2	RUS		R.Rossii, Chumikan, FE
1602	1	RUS		R.Shanson, Zheleznogorsk-Ilimsk, Sib.
1602	1	RUS		R.Mayak, Severo-Kurilsk, FE
1611	0.3-0.4	AUS		8 st's (HPONS)
1620	0.4	AUS		3 st's (HPONS)
1629	0.1-0.4	AUS		7 st's (HPONS)
1638	0.4	AUS	2ME	Sydney (HPONS)
1638	0.4	AUS	3ME	Melbourne (HPONS)
1665	0.4	AUS	2MM	Sydney (HPONS)
1674	1	PHL	DZBF	Mun. of Marikina, Marikina C., NCR
1674	0.01	PHL	DWGI	Guzman Inst. Of Tech, Manila, NCR
1683	0.4	AUS	2—	Sydney (HPONS)
1701	0.4	AUS	2NTC	Sydney (HPONS)
1701	0.1	AUS	4—	Brisbane (HPONS)

NORTH AMERICA

Explanation of listing:
FIRST COLUMN – Call letters. These are required identification for US sts, usually on top of the hour.
SECOND COLUMN – Location. The official Post Office abbreviations are used for US states and Canadian provinces.
THIRD COLUMN – Transmitter powers. A daytime station listed with two powers uses the second one during critical hours (cf. D and U6 below). For stations using a directional antenna the ERP in most cases varies greatly with the direction from the station.
FOURTH COLUMN – Contains authorized operating hours and directional antenna information. The symbols mean as follows: **D** is daytime operation (between local sunrise and local sunset), **D1** without directional antenna, **D2** with directional antenna during critical hours only, **D3** with directional antenna, **D4** with directional antenna, different patterns during critical and non-critical hours, **D5** with directional antenna except during critical hours. **L** is limited time, and means a st. West of the dominant st. can operate from as early as sunrise at the dominant sts location; A st. East of the dominant st. can operate as late as the dominant sts sunset. Number indicates directional pattern as under "U" below. **SH** equals "Specified Hours" as directed by the station license. The number corresponds with the designation for Unlimited stations. SH stations are those which would normally be Unlimited, but due to financial or other considerations have petitioned for a waiver of the minimum schedule of 0600 -2200 local time period. **ST** means "Shares Time". The broadcasting time is shared with a second station on the same frequency. The number corresponds with the designation for Unlimited stations. **U** means Unlimited Time operation, i.e. up to 24 hours a day. **U1** without directional antenna, **U2** with directional antenna at night, **U3** with directional antenna at all hours, same pattern, day and night, **U4** with directional antenna at all hours, different patterns day and night, **U5** with directional antenna daytime, non-directional at night, **U6** with directional antenna at night and during critical hours, **U7** with different directional patterns for day, critical hours and night, **U8** as U7 but non-directional day. **U9** means directional day and night (different patterns), but non-directional during critical hours (usually on reduced power). **U10** means directional during critical hours only**. U11** means separate patterns for daytime and critical hours, nondirectional nigths. **Critical hours** means the periods from sunrise to two hours after sunrise and from two hours before sunset to sunset.
FIFTH COLUMN – Gives an indication of actual operating hours as follows: **NH** normal hours, usually from 18 to 20h a day. **AN** all night operation, i.e. 24h a day most days. **D** daytime, i.e. local sunrise to sunset only. **D*** 0600 local time to local sunset, but with low power (from a few watts to a maximum of 500 watts) before local sunrise if sunrise is later than 0600. A similiar extension of evening hours also exists. **SH** specified hours as fourth column; or special hours, i.e. less than NH, often with breaks during the day.
SCOPE – Because of the vast number of stations in operation in North America it has been found necessary to limit the scope of this list. All US and Canadian st's on the "local" channels (1230, 1240, 1340, 1400, 1450, 1490kHz), except those having more than 1kW power, have been omitted. For the remaining frequencies a lower power limit of 5kW day and/or 1kW night has been set for US st's and 1kW day for Canadian st's. For each frequency the approximate number of omitted low power **(lp)** stations is mentioned. Full details of these stations may be obtained from specialized publications, cf. next paragraph. Frequencies in the AM broadcast band are also used by tourist information stations (TIS). These stations have low or very low powers and are omitted here.
ADDRESSES – In most cases the US Post Office requires a full address to deliver a letter. Complete addresses for all US MW stations may be obtained from the National Radio Club AM Radio Log (see club list for address) and from trade publications (The M Street Radio Directory and others).

Call	Location	kW	Lic	Ops
530kHz				
CIAO	Brampton, ON	1/0.25	U1	AN
540kHz				
KKGO	Costa Mesa, CA	25/0.24	U7	D
KMEO	Carmel Valley, CA	10/0.5	U4	AN
WFLF	Pine Hills, FL	50/46	U4	AN
WDAK	Columbus, GA	5/0.41	U2	AN
KWMT	Fort Dodge, IA	5/0.2	U3	AN
KNOE	Monroe, LA	5/1	U4	AN
KNMX	Las Vegas, NM	5	D3	D
WETC	Wendell, NC	8/0.5	U4	NH
CBT	Grand Falls, NL	10	U1	AN
CBEF	Windsor, ON	2.5/5	U3	AN
CBGA1	New Carlisle, QC	10	U4	AN
CBK	Watrous, SK	50	U1	AN
+lp: USA 12/Can 4				
550kHz				
WASG	Atmore, AL	10/0.143	U1	NH
KTZN	Anchorage, AK	5	U1	AN
KFYI	Phoenix, AZ	5/1	U1	AN
KUZZ	Bakersfield, CA	5	U4	AN
KRAI	Craig, CO	5/0.5	U2	AN
WAYR	Orange Park, FL	5/0.26	U3	AN
WDUN	Gainesville, GA	10/2.5	U2	NH
KFRM	Salina, KS	5/0.11	U3	AN
KTRS	St. Louis, MO	5	U2	AN
KBOW	Butte, MT	5/1	U2	AN
WGR	Buffalo, NY	5	U2	AN
KFYR	Bismarck, ND	5	U2	AN
WKRC	Cincinnati, OH	5/1	U4	AN
KOAC	Corvallis, OR	5	U4	AN
WJMW	Bloomsburg, PA	1	U4	AN
WDDZ	Pawtucket, RI	4.6/3.4	U4	AN
KCRS	Midland, TX	5/1	U4	AN
KTSA	San Antonio, TX	5	U2	AN
WDEV	Waterbury, VT	5/1	U4	NH
WSVA	Harrisonburg, VA	5/1	U2	AN
KARI	Blaine, WA	25/2.5	U4	AN
WSAU	Wausau, WI	15/20	U4	AN
CHLN	Trois-Rivières, QC	10/5	U4	AN
+lp: USA 5				
560kHz				
WOOF	Dothan, AL	5	D1	D*
KVOK	Kodiak, AK	1	U1	NH
KBLU	Yuma, AZ	1	U2	AN
KSFO	San Francisco, CA	5	U2	AN
KLZ	Denver, CO	5	U3	AN
WQAM	Miami, FL	5/1	U1	AN
WIND	Chicago, IL	5	U4	AN
WGAN	Portland, ME	4.8	U3	AN
WFRB	Frostburg, MD	5/0.055	U1	AN
WHYN	Springfield, MA	5/1	U3	AN
WEBC	Duluth, MN	50/5	U4	AN
KWTO	Springfield, MO	5/4	U2	AN
KMON	Great Falls, MT	5	U2	AN
WFIL	Philadelphia, PA	5	U4	AN
WVOC	Columbia, SC	5	U2	AN
WNSR	Brentwood, TN	4.5/0.075	U5	
WHBQ	Memphis, TN	5/1	U4	AN
KLVI	Beaumont, TX	5/5.4	U2	AN
KQC	Wenatchee, WA	5	U2	AN
WJLS	Beckley, WV	4.5/0.5	U2	AN
CHTK	Prince Rupert, BC	1/0.25	U1	AN
CHVO	Carbonear, NL	5	U2	AN
CFOS	Owen Sound, ON	7.5/1	U4	AN
+lp USA 4/Can 2				
570kHz				
WAAX	Gadsden, AL	5/0.5	U2	AN
KCFJ	Alturas, CA	5	D1	D
KLAC	Los Angeles, CA	5	U2	AN
WTBN	Pinellas Park, FL	5	U4	AN
WTNT	Bethesda, MD	5/3	U4	AN
KSNM	Las Cruces, NM	5	D1	D*
WMCA	New York, NY	50/30	U4	AN
WSYR	Syracuse, NY	5	U4	AN
WWNC	Asheville, NC	5	U2	AN
WKBN	Youngstown, OH	5	U2	AN
WNAX	Yankton, SD	5	U2	AN
KLIF	Dallas, TX	5	U4	AN
KNRS	Salt Lake City, UT	5	U3	AN
KVI	Seattle, WA	5	U1	AN
CKWL	Williams Lake, BC	1	U2	AN

Call	Location	kW	Lic	Ops
CFCB	Corner Brook, NL	1	U1	AN
CKGL	Kitchener, ON	10	U3	AN
CKSW	Swift Current, SK	10	U4	AN
CFWH	Whitehorse, YT	5/1	U1	AN
	Nuuk (Godthåb), GRL	25	U1	SH
+lp: USA 4, Can 2				
580kHz				
KRSA	Petersburg, AK	5	U1	AN
KSAZ	Marana, AZ	5/0.39	U2	
KMJ	Fresno, CA	50	U3	AN
KUBC	Montrose, CO	5/1	U2	AN
WDBO	Orlando, FL	5	U2	AN
KIDO	Nampa, ID	5	U2	AN
WILL	Urbana, IL	5/0.1	U4	AN
WIBW	Topeka, KS	5	U2	AN
KJMJ	Alexandria, LA	5/1	U2	NH
WTAG	Worcester, MA	5	U4	AN
WTCM	Traverse City, MI	35/1.1	U4	AN
WKSK	West Jefferson, NC	5/0.34	U1	NH
KTMT	Ashland, OR	1	U4	AN
WHP	Harrisburg, PA	5	U2	AN
WCHS	Charleston, WV	5	U2	AN
WKTY	LaCrosse, WI	5/0.74	U4	AN
CKUA	Edmonton, AB	10	U4	AN
CKXR	Salmon Arm, BC	10/1	U2	AN
CFRA	Ottawa, ON	50/10	U4	AN
CKPR	Thunder Bay, ON	5/1	U1	AN
+lp: USA 8/Can 1				
590kHz				
KHAR	Anchorage, AK	5	U1	AN
KBHS	Hot Springs, AR	5/0.067	U1	
KTIE	San Bernardino, CA	2/1	U4	AN
KTHO	South Lake Tahoe, CA	2.5/0.5	U2	AN
KCSJ	Pueblo, CO	1	U4	AN
WDIZ	Panama City, FL	1.7/2.5	U2	AN
WDWD	Atlanta, GA	5/4.5	U4	AN
KID	Idaho Falls, ID	5/1	U2	NH
KFNS	Wood River, IL	1	U4	AN
WVLK	Lexington, KY	5/1	U4	AN
WEZE	Boston, MA	5	U3	AN
WJMS	Ironwood, MI	5/1	U2	AN
WKZO	Kalamazoo, MI	5	U2	AN
KOMJ	Omaha, NE	5	U1	AN
WROW	Albany, NY	5/1	U4	AN
WGTM	Wilson, NC	5	U4	AN
KUGN	Eugene, OR	5	U2	AN
WARM	Scranton, PA	5	U4	AN
WMBS	Uniontown, PA	1	U2	AN
KLBJ	Austin, TX	5/1	U2	AN
KSUB	Cedar City, UT	5/1	U2	AN
WLVA	Lynchburg, VA	5/1	U4	AN
KQNT	Spokane, WA	5	U1	AN
CFTK	Terrace, BC	1	U3	AN
CFAR	Flin Flon, MB	10/1	U5	AN
CJCW	Sussex, NB	1/0.25	U4	AN
VOCM	St. John's, NL	20/10	U2	AN
CJCL	Toronto, ON	50	U4	AN
CKRS	Jonquière, QC	25/10	U4	AN
+lp: USA 4				
600kHz				
KVNA	Flagstaff, AZ	5/0.5	U2	AN
KAZT	Indio, CA	1	U3	AN
KOGO	San Diego, CA	5	U3	AN
KCOL	Fort Collins, CO	5/0.5	U4	AN
WBWL	Jacksonville, FL	5	U2	AN
WMT	Cedar Rapids, IA	5	U2	AN
WKYH	Paintsville, KY	5/0.043	U1	
WFST	Caribou, ME	5/0.127	U1	
WCAO	Baltimore, MD	5	U3	AN
KGEZ	Kalispell, MT	5/1	U4	NH
WSJS	Winston-Salem, NC	5	U4	AN
KSJB	Jamestown, ND	5	U3	AN
WREC	Memphis, TN	5	U4	AN
KROD	El Paso, TX	5	U2	AN
KTBB	Tyler, TX	5/2.5	U4	AN
CKBD	Vancouver, BC	10	U3	AN
CBNA	St. Anthony, NL	10	U4	AN
CKAT	North Bay, ON	10/5	U4	AN
CJWW	Saskatoon, SK	25/8	U4	AN
+lp: USA 14/Canada 2				
610kHz				
WAGG	Birmingham, AL	5/1	U2	AN
KAVL	Lancaster, CA	4.9/4	U4	NH
KFRC	San Francisco, CA	5	U1	AN
KVLE	Vail, CO	5/0.217	U1	
WIOD	Miami, FL	10	U4	AN
KDAL	Duluth, MN	5	U2	AN
WCSP	Kansas City, MO	5	U1	AN
KOJM	Havre, MT	1	U4	NH
WGIR	Manchester, NH	5/1	U4	AN
KNML	Albuquerque, NM	5	U2	AN
WFNZ	Charlotte, NC	5/1	U4	AN
WTVN	Columbus, OH	5/50	U4	AN
KRTA	Medford, OR	2.5/5	U4	AN
WIP	Philadelphia, PA	5	U3	AN
KILT	Houston, TX	5	U4	AN
KVNU	Logan, UT	5/1	U2	AN
WVBE	Roanoke, VA	5/1	U4	AN
KONA	Tri-Cities, WA	5	U4	AN
CKYL	Peace River, AB	10	U2	AN
CHNL	Kamloops, BC	25/5	U4	AN
CHTM	Thompson, MB	5	U1	AN
CKTB	St. Catherines, ON	10/5	U3	AN
CHNC	New Carlisle, QC	10/5	U3	AN
CKRW	Whitehorse, YT	1	U1	AN
+lp: USA 7/Canada 2				
620kHz				
WJHX	Lexington, AL	5/0.099	U1	
KGTL	Homer, AK	5	U1	NH
KTAR	Phoenix, AZ	5	U2	AN
KIGS	Hanford, CA	1	U2	AN
KJOL	Grand Junction, CO	5/0.85	U1	AN
WDAE	St. Petersburg, FL	5	U2	AN
KWAL	Wallace, ID	1	U2	NH
KMNS	Sioux City, IA		U4	AN
WZON	Bangor, ME	5	U2	AN
WJDX	Jackson, MS	5/1	U2	AN
WSNR	Jersey City, NJ	8.5/5	U4	AN
WHEN	Syracuse, NY	5/1	U2	AN
WDNC	Durham, NC	5.4/1.08	U4	AN
KPOJ	Portland, OR	5	U2	AN
KPOJ	Portland, OR	25/10	U2	F.Pl.
WKHB	Irwin, PA	5.5/0.25	U4	AN
WRJZ	Knoxville, TN	5	U2	AN
KMKI	Plano, TX	5/4.5	U2	AN
WVMT	Burlington, VT	5	U4	AN
WWNR	Beckley, WV	5/0.025	U1	AN
WTMJ	Milwaukee, WI	50/10	U4	AN
CKCM	Grand Falls, NL	10	U3	AN
CKRM	Regina, SK	10	U4	AN
+lp: USA 6				
630kHz				
KJNO	Juneau, AK	5/1	U1	AN
KIAM	Nenana, AK	10/3.1	U1	NH
KIDD	Monterey, CA	1	U4	AN
KHOW	Denver, CO	5	U4	AN
WMAL	Washington, DC	5	U4	AN
WBMQ	Savannah, GA	4.8/0.05	U1	AN
KFXD	Boise, ID	5	U4	AN
WLAP	Lexington, KY	5/1	U4	AN
KJSL	St. Louis, MO	5	U4	AN
KPTT	Reno, NV	5/1	U2	AN
WMFD	Wilmington, NC	0.8/1	U3	AN
KWRO	Coquille, OR	5/0.046	U1	
WPRO	East Providence, RI	5	U2	AN
KSLR	San Antonio, TX	5	U4	AN
KCIS	Seattle, WA	3.9/2.5	U2	AN
WDGY	Hudson, WI	1/2.5	U4	AN
CHED	Edmonton, AB	50	U4	AN
CKOV	Kelowna, BC	5/1	U1	AN
CFCO	Chatham, ON	10/6	U4	AN
CFCY	Charlottetown, PEI	10	U4	AN
CHLT	Sherbrooke, QC	10/5	U4	AN
+lp: Can 1/USA 9				
640kHz				
KYUK	Bethel, AK	10	U1	NH
KFI	Los Angeles, CA	50	U1	AN
WJNA	Royal Palm Beach, FL	7.5/0.4	U2	AN
WJNA	Royal Palm Beach, FL	25	U4	FPl.
WGST	Atlanta, GA	50/1	U4	AN
WOI	Ames, IA	5/1	U2	AN
KTIB	Thibodeaux, LA	5/1	U4	

Call	Location	kW	Lic	Ops
WNNZ	Westfield, MA	50/15	U4	AN
KGVW	Belgrade, MT	10/1	U2	AN
WWJZ	Mt. Holly, NJ	39/0.95	U3	AN
WFNC	Fayetteville, NC	10/1	U1	AN
WHLO	Akron, OH	5/0.5	U4	AN
WWLS	Moore, OK	5/1	U4	AN
WGOC	Blountsville, TN	5/0.81	U4	AN
WCRV	Collierville, TN	50/0.48	U2	AN
CBN	St. John's, NL	10	U1	AN
CFMJ	Toronto, ON	50	U4	AN
+Ip: Can 1/USA 2				
650kHz				
KENI	Anchorage, AK	50	U1	AN
KSTE	Rancho Cordova, CA	21.4/0.92	U4	NH
WSRO	Ashland, MA	5/0.009	U5	AN
WMII	Manistique, MI	30/20/0.2	U7	F.Pl.
WNMT	Nashwauk, MN	10/1	U2	AN
WSM	Nashville, TN	50	U1	AN
KMTI	Manti, UT	10/0.9	U4	AN
KGAB	Orchard Valley, WY	8.6/0.5	U2	AN
CISL	Richmond, BC	10/9	U4	AN
CKGA	Gander, NL	5	U3	AN
CKOM	Saskatoon, SK	10	U4	AN
	Qeqertarsuaq (Godhavn), GRL	5	U1	SH
+Ip: Can 1/USA 2				
660kHz				
WDLT	Fairhope, AL	10/0.85	U2	AN
KFAR	Fairbanks, AK	10	U1	AN
KTNN	Window Rock, AZ	50	U2	AN
KGDP	Orcutt, CA	50/7	U4	AN
WORL	Altamonte Springs, FL	1	U3	
WBHR	Sauk Rapids, MN	10/0.5	U4	
WFAN	New York, NY	50	U1	AN
KEYZ	Williston, ND	5	U4	AN
KZTU	Junction City, OR	10/0.07	U1	
WLFJ	Greenville, SC	50/10	D2	D*
KSKY	Balch Springs, TX	20/2	U2	AN
KAPS	Mt. Vernon, WA	10/1	U1	AN
CFFR	Calgary, AB	50	U4	AN
+Ip: USA 2				
670kHz				
WYLS	York, AL	4.8	D1	D
KDLG	Dillingham, AK	10	U1	NH
KWXI	Glenwood, AR	5	D1	D*
KIRN	Simi Valley, CA	5/3	U4	AN
KIRN	Simi Valley, CA	35	U4	F.Pl.
KLTT	Commerce City, CO	50/1.4	U4	
WWFE	Miami, FL	50/1	U4	AN
KBOI	Boise, ID	50	U2	AN
WSCR	Chicago, IL	50	U1	AN
KSXX	Las Vegas, NV	10/0.6	U4	F.Pl.
WIEZ	Lewiston, PA	5.4	D1	D
WPMH	Claremont, VA	20/0.003	U4	
+Ip: USA 1				
680kHz				
KBRW	Barrow, AK	10	U1	NH
KNBR	San Francisco, CA	50	U1	AN
WCNN	Atlanta, GA	50/10	U4	AN
WCBM	Baltimore, MD	50/20	U4	AN
WRKO	Boston, MA	50	U4	AN
WNZK	Dearborn Heights, MI	2.5	N2	N
WDBC	Escanaba, MI	10/1	U4	AN
KFEQ	St. Joseph, MO	5	U4	AN
KKGR	East Helena, MT	5	D1	D
WINR	Binghamton, NY	5/0.5	U4	AN
WPTF	Raleigh, NC	50	U2	AN
WJCE	Memphis, TN	10/5	U2	AN
KKYX	San Antonio, TX	50/10	U2	AN
KOMW	Omak, WA	5	D1	D
WCAW	Charlestown, WV	10/0.25	U4	AN
CHFA	Edmonton, AB	10	U4	AN
CJOB	Winnipeg, MB	50	U4	AN
CFTR	Toronto, ON	50	U4	AN
+Ip: USA 10				
690kHz				
WJOX	Birmingham, AL	50/0.5	U2	AN
WOKV	Jacksonville, FL	50/10	U2	AN
KGGF	Coffeyville, KS	10/5	U4	NH
WTIX	New Orleans, LA	10/5	U4	AN
KTSM	El Paso, TX	10	U4	AN
WZAP	Bristol, VA	10/0.02	U1	AN
CBU	Vancouver, BC	50	U3	AN
CINF	Montreal, QC	50	U3	AN
CBKF-1	Gravelbourg, SK	5	U2	AN
+Ip: USA 17/Can 6				
700kHz				
KBYR	Anchorage, AK	10	U1	AN
WDMV	Walkersville, MD	5	D3	D
WLW	Cincinnati, OH	50	U1	AN
KGRV	Winston, OR	23/0.47	U1	AN
KSEV	Tomball, TX	15/1	U4	NH
KALL	North Salt Lake, UT	50/1	U4	AN
KJMY	Newport, WA	10/0.6	U2	NH
+Ip: USA 3				
710kHz				
WPMI	Mobile, AL	1	U2	AN
KMIA	Black Canyon City, AZ	22/3.9	U4	
KFIA	Carmichael, CA	25/1	U4	AN
KSPN	Los Angeles, CA	50/10	U2	AN
KNUS	Denver, CO	25/2.7	U4	AN
WAQI	Miami, FL	50	U4	AN
KEEL	Shreveport, LA	50/5	U4	AN
WREM	Monticello, ME	5	D1	D
KCMO	Kansas City, MO	10/5	U4	AN
WOR	New York, NY	50	U3	AN
KXMR	Bismarck, ND	10/13/4	U7	
KGNC	Amarillo, TX	10	U4	AN
WFNR	Christiansburg, VA	10	D3	D
KIRO	Seattle, WA	50	U2	AN
WDSM	Superior, WI	10/5	U2	AN
CKVO	Clarenville, NL	10	U3	AN
CJRN	Niagara Falls, ON	10/5	U4	AN
CKVM	Ville-Marie, QC	10/1	U2	AN
+Ip: USA 14/Can 4				
720kHz				
KOTZ	Kotzebue, AK	10	U1	NH
WRZN	Hernando, FL	10/0.25	U2	NH
WVCC	Hogansville, GA	8	D3	D
WGN	Chicago, IL	50	U1	AN
KDWN	Las Vegas, NV	50	U2	AN
WQTH	Hanover, NH	50/0.5	U4	F.Pl.
WGCR	Pisgah Forest, NC	10	D1	D
KSAH	Universal City, TX	10/0.89	U4	AN
CHTN	Charlottetown, PEI	10/7.5	U2	AN
	Simiutaq, GRL	20	U1	SH
+Ip: USA 1				
730kHz				
WSNI	Thomasville, GA	5	D1	D*
KBSU	Boise, ID	15/0.5	U4	NH
WMTC	Vancleve, KY	13/0.05	U4	
WACE	Chicopee, MA	5/0.008	U1	AN
KURL	Billings, MT	5/0.23	U1	AN
WPIT	Pittsburgh, PA	5/0.02	U1	AN
WSCC	Charleston, SC	5.2/0.1	U5	
WKDL	Alexandria, VA	8/0.025	U1	AN
K...	Hoquiam, WA	1	U3	F.Pl.
CHMJ	Vancouver, BC	50	U4	AN
CKDM	Dauphin, MB	10/5	U2	AN
CKAC	Montreal, ON	50	U3	AN
+Ip: USA 25				
740kHz				
WMSP	Montgomery, AL	10/0.335	U4	
KBRT	Avalon, CA	10/0.113	U3	
KCBS	San Francisco, CA	50	U4	AN
KVOR	Colorado Springs, CO	3.3/1.5	U4	AN
WQTM	Orlando, FL	5/1	U2	AN
WGSM	Huntington, NY	25/0.05	U4	AN
WPAQ	Mt. Airy, NC	10/1/0.007	U1	
K...	Fargo, ND	50/7.5/0.9	U7	F.Pl.
KRMG	Tulsa, OK	50/25	U4	AN
WVCH	Chester, PA	50/0.006	U1	AN
KTRH	Houston, TX	50	U4	AN
KCMC	Texarkana, TX	1	U3	AN
CBX	Edmonton, AB	50	U4	AN
CHWO	Toronto, ON	50	U3	AN
CHCM	Marystown, NL	10	U2	AN
+Ip: USA 16/Can 15				
750kHz				
KFQD	Anchorage, AK	50	U1	AN
WSB	Atlanta, GA	50	U1	AN
WNDZ	Portage, IN	5	D3	D

Call	Location	kW	Lic	Ops
KBNN	Lebanon, MO	5	D1	D
KERR	Polson, MT	50/1	U2	AN
KMMJ	Grand Island, NE	10	L3	D*
KHWG	Fallon, NV	7.5/0.28	U8	F.Pl.
KXL	Portland, OR	50/20	U4	AN
KAMA	El Paso, TX	10/1	U4	AN
KOAL	Price, UT	10/6.8	U2	AN
CBGY	Bonavista Bay, NL	10	U4	AN
CKGB	Timmins, ON	10/5	U2	AN
CKJH	Melfort, SA	25	U2	AN
+Ip: USA 7/Can 2				
760kHz				
KMTL	Sherwood, AR	10	D1	D
KFMB	San Diego, CA	50/5	U2	AN
KKZN	Thornton, CO	50/1	U1	AN
WLCC	Brandon, FL	10/1	U4	
WEFL	Tequesta, FL	3.5/1.5	U4	
KCCV	Overland Park, KS	6/0.2	U4	
WVNE	Leicester, MA	25/8.6	D1	D
WJR	Detroit, MI	50	U1	AN
WCHP	Champlain, NY	35/0.011	U3	
KTKR	San Antonio, TX	50/1	U4	AN
CFLD	Burns Lake, BC	1/0.5	U1	AN
+Ip: USA 3				
770kHz				
WVNN	Athens, AL	7/0.25	U2	AN
KCHU	Valdez, AK	9.7	U1	NH
KCBC	Riverbank, CA	50/1	U4	AN
W...	Nassau Village-Ratliff, FL	50/0.41	U4	F.Pl.
WWCN	North Fort Myers, FL	10/1	U4	AN
KUOM	Minneapolis, MN	25/2.2	U2	D
WEW	St. Louis, MO	10/0.205	U4	
KATL	Miles City, MT	10/1	U2	AN
KKOB	Albuquerque, NM	50	U2	AN
WABC	New York, NY	50	U1	AN
WTOR	Youngstown, NY	9	D3	D
WLWL	Rockingham, NC	5	D1	D
KPBC	Garland, TX	10/1	U4	AN
WYRV	Cedar Bluff, VA	5	D1	D
KTTH	Seattle, WA	50/5	U4	AN
CHQR	Calgary, AB	50	U2	AN
+Ip: USA 5				
780kHz				
WZZX	Lineville, AL	5	D1	D
KNOM	Nome, AK	25/14	U1	NH
KAZM	Sedona, AZ	5/0.25	U2	AN
WBBM	Chicago, IL	50	U1	AN
WTME	Rumford, ME	10/0.018	U1	
WIIN	Ridgeland, MS	5	D1	D
WJAG	Norfolk, NE	1	L1	D*
WCKB	Dunn, NC	7/0.001	U1	
WWOL	Forest City, NC	10	D1	D
KKOH	Reno, NV	50	U2	AN
WABS	Arlington, VA	5	D1	D
CFDR	Dartmouth, NS	50/15	U4	AN
+Ip: USA 4				
790kHz				
WTSK	Tuscaloosa, AL	5	D1	D
KCAM	Glenallen, AK	5	U1	AN
KNST	Tucson, AZ	5/0.5	U3	AN
KURM	Rogers, AR	5/0.5	U2	
KOOR	Clovis, CA	5/2.5	U4	
KWSW	Eureka, CA	5/0.112	U1	
KABC	Los Angeles, CA	5	U2	AN
WLBE	Leesburg, FL	5/1	U2	AN
WAXY	South Miami, FL	5	U4	AN
WQXI	Atlanta, GA	28/1	U2	AN
KBRV	Soda Springs, ID	5	D1	D*
KXXX	Colby, KS	5/0.02	U1	AN
WXXA	Louisville, KY	5/1	U4	AN
WSGW	Saginaw, MI	5/1	U4	AN
KGHL	Billings, MT	5	U2	AN
WTNY	Watertown, NY	1	U2	AN
KFGO	Fargo, ND	5	U2	AN
KWIL	Albany, OR	1	U4	AN
WAEB	Allentown, PA	3.6/1.5	U4	AN
WSKO	Providence, RI	5	U2	AN
WETB	Johnson City, TN	5/0.072	U1	
WMC	Memphis, TN	5	U2	AN
KBME	Houston, TX	5	U4	AN
KFYO	Lubbock, TX	5/1	U4	AN

Call	Location	kW	Lic	Ops
WNIS	Norfolk, VA	5	U3	AN
KGMI	Bellingham, WA	5/1	U2	AN
KJRB	Spokane, WA	5/3.8	U4	AN
WAYY	Eau Claire, WI	5	U2	AN
CFCW	Camrose, AB	50	U4	AN
CFNW	Port au Choix, NL	1	U3	AN
CIGM	Sudbury, ON	50	U4	AN
+Ip: USA 17				
800kHz				
KINY	Juneau, AK	10/7.8	U1	AN
WTMR	Camden, NJ	5/0.5	U4	AN
KQCV	Oklahoma City, OK	2.5/1	U4	AN
KPDQ	Portland, OR	1	U2	AN
WSVS	Crewe, VA	5/0.3	U1	AN
WVHU	Huntington, WV	5/0.185	U1	
WDUX	Waupaca, WI	5/0.5	U4	
CKOR	Penticton, BC	10/0.5	U1	AN
VOWR	St. John's NL	10/2.5	U3	AN
CJBQ	Belleville, ON	10	U4	AN
CKDR	Dryden, ON	1/0.7	U1	AN
CKLW	Windsor, ON	50	U4	AN
CJAD	Montreal, QC	50/10	U4	AN
CHRC	Quebec, QC	50	U3	AN
CHAB	Moose Jaw, SK	10	U2	AN
+Ip: USA 21				
810kHz				
WCKS	Jacksonville, AL	50/0.5	U4	
KGO	San Francisco, CA	50	U3	AN
WEKG	Jackson, KY	5	D1	D*
WHB	Kansas City, MO	50/5	U2	AN
WSJC	Magee, MS	50/0.5	U4	NH
KSWV	Santa Fe, NM	5/0.01	U1	
WGY	Schenectady, NY	50	U1	AN
WQIZ	St. George, SC	5	D1	D*
KBHB	Sturgis, SD	25/0.06	U1	AN
WMGC	Murfreesboro, TN	5/0.006	U1	
KTBI	Ephrata, WA	50/23	D3	D
CKJS	Winnipeg, MB	10	U3	AN
CJVA	Caraquet, NB	10	U2	AN
	Upernavik, GRL	5	U1	SH
+Ip: USA 15				
820kHz				
KCBF	Fairbanks, AK	10	U1	AN
WMGG	Largo, FL	50/1	U2	AN
WCSN	Chicago, IL	5	D1	D
WNYC	New York, NY	10/1	U4	AN
WOSU	Columbus, OH	5/0.8	U2	AN
WBAP	Forth Worth, TX	50	U1	AN
KUTR	Taylorsville, UT	50/10/2.5	U7	F.Pl.
WGGM	Chester, VA	10/1	U4	AN
KGNW	Seattle, WA	50/5	U4	AN
CHAM	Hamilton, ON	50/10	U4	AN
+Ip: USA 4				
830kHz				
KSDP	Sand Point, AK	1	U1	NH
KFLT	Tucson, AZ	50/1	U2	AN
KNCO	Grass Valley, CA	5	U2	NH
KNCO	Grass Valley, CA	25/10	U2	F.Pl.
KMXE	Orange, CA	50/20	U4	AN
WXTO	Hialeah, FL	1	U4	
WFGM	Sandy Springs, GA	50/2.4	U4	F.Pl.
WFNO	Norco, LA	5/0.75	U4	AN
WCRN	Worcester, MA	50	U4	AN
WCCO	Minneapolis, MN	50	U1	AN
KOTC	Kennett, MO	10	D1	D
WTRU	Kernersville, NC	50/10	U2	AN
WEEU	Reading, PA	20/6	U4	AN
KMUL	Farwell, TX	50/0.009	U5	F.Pl.
KUYO	Evansville, WY	25/9.2	D1	D
CKKY	Wainwright, AB	10/3.5	U2	AN
+Ip: USA 3/Can 1				
840kHz				
WBHY	Mobile, AL	10	D1	D
KPMP	Modesto, CA	4/5	U4	F.Pl.
WHGH	Thomasville, GA	10	D1	D
WHAS	Louisville, KY	50	U1	AN
KWDF	Ball, LA	8	D1	D
KTIC	West Point, NE	5	D1	D
KXNT	North Las Vegas, NV	50/25	U3	AN
WCEO	Columbia, SC	50	D3	D
KVJY	Pharr, TX	5/1	U3	AN

Call	Location	kW	Lic	Ops
WKTR	Earlysville, VA	8.2	D3	F.Pl.
KMAX	Colfax, WA	10/0.28	U1	AN
CKBX	100 Mile House, BC	1/0.5	U1	AN
+Ip: USA 9				
850kHz				
WXJC	Birmingham, AL	50/1	U2	AN
KICY	Nome, AK	50	U10	NH
KOA	Denver, CO	50	U1	AN
WRUF	Gainesville, FL	5	U2	AN
WFTL	West Palm Beach, FL	50/24	U4	AN
WPTB	Statesboro, GA	1	U2	AN
WEEI	Boston, MA	50	U4	AN
WGVS	Muskegon, MI	1	U3	AN
WWJC	Duluth, MN	10	D1	D
WQST	Forest, MS	10	D3	D
KFUO	Clayton, MO	5	L1	D
WRBZ	Raleigh, NC	10/5	U2	AN
WKNR	Cleveland, OH	5/0.47	U4	AN
WTNJ	Johnstown, PA	10	U3	AN
WEEU	Reading, PA	20/6	U4	AN
KJON	Carrollton, TX	5	D3	D
WKVL	Knoxville, TN	50	D3	D
KEYH	Houston, TX	10/0.185	U4	AN
WTAR	Norfolk, VA	50/25	U4	AN
KHHO	Tacoma, WA	10/1	U4	AN
CKBA	Athabasca, AB	1	U2	AN
+Ip: USA 10				
860kHz				
KMVP	Phoenix, AZ	1	U2	
KTRB	San Francisco, CA	50/50	U4	AN
WGUL	Dunedin, FL	6.5/1.5	U4	NH
WAEC	Atlanta, GA	5/0.5	U2	
WDMG	Douglas, GA	5	U2	NH
KKOW	Pittsburg, KS	10/5	U2	AN
KPAM	Troutdale, OR	50/5	U2	
WWDB	Philadelphia, PA	10	D3	D
KONO	San Antonio, TX	5/0.9	U2	AN
KKAT	Salt Lake City, UT	10/0.2	U1	AN
WOAY	Oak Hill, WV	10/0.01	U1	AN
CFPR	Prince Rupert, BC	10/2.5	U3	AN
CHAK	Inuvik, NWT	1	U1	AN
CJBC	Toronto, ON	50	U1	AN
CBKF-2	Saskatoon, SK	10	U4	AN
+Ip: USA 26/Can 18				
870kHz				
WQRX	Valley Head, AL	10/4.7	D1	D
KSKO	McGrath, AK	10	U1	AN
KRLA	Glendale, CA	20/3	U4	AN
WWL	New Orleans, LA	50	U3	AN
WMTW	Gorham, ME	10/1	U4	AN
WKAR	East Lansing, MI	10	D3	D
KPRM	Park Rapids, MN	25/1	U2	NH
KLSQ	Whitley, NV	5/0.43	U2	AN
WHCU	Ithaca, NY	5/1	U2	AN
WPWT	Colonial Heights, TN	10	D3	D
KFLD	Pasco, WA	10/0.25	U1	AN
CKIR	Invermere, BC	1/0.25	U3	AN
CFBV	Smithers, BC	1/0.5	U3	AN
+Ip: USA 5/Can 1				
880kHz				
KGHT	Sheridan, AR	50/31/0.22	U2	
KKMC	Gonzales, CA	10	U4	AN
WBKZ	Jefferson, GA	5	D3	D
KJJR	Whitefish, MT	10/0.5	U2	AN
KRVN	Lexington, NE	50	U4	AN
KHAC	Tse Bonito, NM	43/1.2	U1	NH
WCBS	New York, NY	50	U1	AN
WPEK	Fairview, NC	5	D1	D
WRFD	Columbus, OH	23/6.1	D3	D
KWIP	Dallas, OR	5/1	U1	NH
KCMX	Phoenix, OR	1	U1	AN
KJOJ	Conroe, TX	10/1	U4	AN
KIXI	Mercer Island, WA	50/10	U4	AN
WMEQ	Menomonie, WI	10/0.21	U2	AN
CHQT	Edmonton, AB	50	U2	AN
CKKC	Nelson, BC	1/0.7	U3	AN
CKLQ	Brandon, MB	10	U2	AN
+Ip: USA 2				
890kHz				
KBBI	Homer, AK	10	U1	NH
KLFF	Arroyo Grande, CA	5/5	U4	
KDJQ	Meridian, ID	50/0.25	U2	F.Pl.
WLS	Chicago, IL	50	U1	AN
WAMG	Dedham, MA	25/3.4	U4	AN
WEEZ	Laurel, MS	10	D1	D
WBAJ	Blythewood, SC	50/8.5	D1	D
KVOZ	Laredo, TX	10/1	U2	AN
KDXU	St. George, UT	10	U2	AN
WKNV	Fairlawn, VA	10	D3	D
CJDC	Dawson Creek, BC	10	U2	AN
+Ip: USA 5				
900kHz				
KZPA	Fort Yukon, AK	5	U1	AN
KALI	West Covina, CA	1	U4	AN
WJWL	Georgetown, DE	10/1	U4	AN
KTIS	Minneapolis, MN	25/0.3	U4	AN
WCOR	Lebanon, TN	5/0.136	U1	AN
CKMO	Victoria, BC	10	U3	AN
CKDH	Amherst, NS	1	U4	AN
CHML	Hamilton, ON	50	U4	AN
CKTS	Sherbrooke, QC	10	U4	AN
CKBI	Prince Albert, SK	10	U2	AN
	Uummannaq, GRL	5	U1	SH
+Ip: USA 51/Can 3				
910kHz				
KIYU	Galena, AK	12.5	U1	AN
KGME	Phoenix, AZ	5	U2	AN
KLCN	Blytheville, AR	5/0.85	U1	AN
KECR	El Cajon, CA	5	U4	AN
KNEW	Oakland, CA	20/5	U4	AN
KOXR	Oxnard, CA	5/1	U4	AN
KPOF	Denver, CO	5/1	U4	AN
WLAT	New Britain, CT	5	U2	AN
WTWD	Plant City, FL	5	U3	NH
WFVR	Valdosta, GA	5	U2	AN
WSUI	Iowa City, IA	5/4	U2	AN
WNDC	Baton Rouge, LA	1	U3	AN
WABI	Bangor, ME	5	U2	AN
WFDF	Flint, MI	50/1	U4	AN
WALT	Meridian, MS	5/1	U1	AN
KBIM	Roswell, NM	5/0.5	U2	NH
WSRP	Jacksonville, NC	5	U2	AN
KCJB	Minot, ND	5/1	U4	AN
WLTP	Marietta, OH	5/0.04	U5	
KVIS	Miami, OK	1	U3	AN
WAVL	Apollo, PA	5/0.069	U4	AN
WSBA	York, PA	5/1	U4	AN
WJCW	Johnson City, TN	5/1	U4	AN
WEPG	South Pittsburg, TN	5/0.095	U1	AN
KRIO	McAllen, TX	5	U4	AN
KWDZ	Salt Lake City, UT	5/1	U4	AN
WRNL	Richmond, VA	5/1.5	U2	AN
KOTK	Vancouver, WA	10	U4	AN
WHSM	Hayward, WI	5/0.07	U1	AN
CKDQ	Drumheller, AB	50	U4	AN
+Ip: USA 12				
920kHz				
KSRM	Soldotna, AK	5	U1	AN
KARN	Little Rock, AR	5	U2	AN
KVIN	Ceres, CA	0.5/2.5	U4	
KPSI	Palm Springs, CA	5/1	U4	AN
KLMR	Lamar, CO	5/0.5	U2	NH
WMEL	Melbourne, FL	5/1	U4	AN
WGKA	Atlanta, GA	5/0.5	U1	AN
WBAA	West Lafayette, IN	5/1	U2	AN
KYFR	Shenandoah, IA	5/2.5	U2	AN
WBOX	Bogalusa, LA	1	U2	AN
KDHL	Faribault, MN	5	U4	AN
KWAD	Wadena, MN	1	U4	AN
KBAD	Las Vegas, NV	5/0.5	U2	AN
KIHM	Reno, NV	4.6/0.85	U2	AN
WPHY	Trenton, NJ	1	U3	AN
WGHQ	Kingston, NY	5/0.5	U4	AN
WIRD	Lake Placid, NY	5/0.09	U1	AN
WPCM	Burlington, NC	5/0.06	U1	AN
KSHO	Lebanon, OR	1	U3	AN
WHJJ	Providence, RI	5	U2	AN
WYMB	Manning, SC	5/1	U2	
KKLS	Rapid City, SD	5/0.111	U3	
KYST	Texas City, TX	5/1	U4	AN
KVEL	Vernal, UT	5/1	U2	
KXLY	Spokane, WA	20/5	U1	AN

Call	Location	kW	Lic	Ops
WMMN	Fairmont, WV	5/0.2	U1	AN
WOKY	Milwaukee, WI	5/1	U4	AN
CKCQ	Quesnel, BC	10/1	U2	AN
CFRY	Portage la Prairie, MB	25/10	U4	AN
CJCH	Halifax, NS	25	U2	AN
CKNX	Wingham, ON	10/1	U4	AN
+lp: USA 19/Can 3				
930kHz				
WYNI	Monroeville, AL	5/0.048	U1	
WJBY	Rainbow City, AL	5/0.5	U2	
KTKN	Ketchikan, AK	5/1	U1	NH
KNSA	Unalakleet, AK	2.5	U1	
KAFF	Flagstaff, AZ	5/0.031	U1	
KHJ	Los Angeles, CA	5	U2	AN
KIUP	Durango, CO	5/0.1	U1	AN
WFXJ	Jacksonville, FL	5	U2	AN
WLSS	Sarasota, FL	5/3	U4	AN
WMGR	Bainbridge, GA	5/0.5	U2	AN
KSEI	Pocatello, ID	5	U2	AN
WTAD	Quincy, IL	5/1	U2	AN
WAUR	Sandwich, IL	2.5/4.2	U4	AN
WKCT	Bowling Green, KY	5/0.5	U2	NH
WFMD	Frederick, MD	5/2.5	U4	AN
WBCK	Battle Creek, MI	5/1	U4	AN
WSFZ	Jackson, MS	3.8/3.1	U2	NH
KWOC	Poplar Bluff, MO	5/0.5	U2	NH
KLCY	East Missoula, MT	5/1	U2	
KOGA	Ogallala, NE	5/0.5	U4	AN
WGIN	Rochester, NH	5	U2	AN
WPAT	Paterson, NJ	5	U4	AN
WBEN	Buffalo, NY	5	U2	AN
WYFQ	Charlotte, NC	5/1	U2	AN
WDLX	Washington, NC	5/1	U2	AN
WEOL	Elyria, OH	1	U4	AN
WKY	Oklahoma City, OK	5	U2	AN
KAGI	Grants Pass, OR	5/1	U2	AN
KSDN	Aberdeen, SD	5/1	U4	AN
WSEV	Sevierville, TN	5/0.148	U1	
KLUP	San Antonio, TX	5/1	U2	AN
WLLL	Lynchburg, VA	9/0.05	U5	AN
KYAK	Yakima, WA	10/0.127	U1	AN
WRVC	Huntington, WV	5/1	U2	AN
WLBL	Auburndale, WI	5	D1	D
KROE	Sheridan, WY	5/0.117	U1	AN
CJCA	Edmonton, AB	50	U4	AN
CFBC	St. John, NB	50	U4	AN
CJYQ	St. John's, NL	50	U4	AN
+lp: USA 14				
940kHz				
KGMS	Tucson, AZ	5/1	U4	AN
KWRU	Fresno, CA	50	U4	AN
WINZ	Miami, FL	50/10	U2	AN
WMAC	Macon, GA	50/10	U2	AN
WMIX	Mount Vernon, IL	5/1.5	U4	AN
KPSZ	Des Moines, IA	10/5	U4	AN
WYLD	New Orleans, LA	10/0.5	U4	AN
WIDG	St. Ignace, MI	5/0.004	U1	
WCPC	Houston, MS	50/0.25	U4	NH
KVSH	Valentine, NE	5/0.019	U1	
WKYK	Burnsville, NC	4.6/0.25	U2	AN
KICE	Bend, OR	10/0.06	U4	NH
WECO	Wartburg, TN	5	D1	D*
KIXZ	Amarillo, TX	5/1	U4	AN
KNNZ	Cedar City, UT	10/0.039	U1	AN
WNRG	Grundy, VA	5/0.014	U1	
WKGM	Smithfield, VA	10/3.1	U2	AN
CINW	Montreal, QC	50	U3	AN
CJGX	Yorkton, SK	10	U2	AN
+lp: USA 14/Can 2				
950kHz				
KSWD	Seward, AK	1	U1	
KXJK	Forrest City, AR	5/0.087	U1	
KFSA	Fort Smith, AR	1/0.5	U4	AN
KAHI	Auburn, CA	5	U4	AN
KKFN	Denver, CO	5	U3	AN
WTLN	Orlando, FL	12/5	U2	AN
WGTA	Summerville, GA	5	D1	D*
WGOV	Valdosta, GA	5/0.063	U1	
KNJY	Boise, ID	5/0.035	U1	NH
KOZE	Lewiston, ID	5/1	U4	AN
WNTD	Chicago, IL	1/5	U2	AN

Call	Location	kW	Lic	Ops
WXLW	Indianapolis, IN	5/0.11	U3	NH
KOEL	Oelwein, IA	5/0.5	U4	AN
WROL	Boston, MA	5/0.090	U1	AN
WWJ	Detroit, MI	50	U4	AN
KSNB	St. Louis Park, MN	1	U4	AN
WBKH	Hattiesburg, MS	5	D1	D*
KWOS	Jefferson City, MO	5/0.5	U2	NH
KMTX	Helena, MT	5	U2	NH
KNFT	Bayard, NM	5/0.22	U1	AN
WROC	Rochester, NY	1	U2	AN
WIBX	Utica, NY	5	U3	AN
WPEN	Philadelphia, PA	50	U2	AN
WQTK	Moncks Corner, SC	10/6	U4	
WORD	Spartanburg, SC	5	U2	AN
KWAT	Watertown, SD	1	U2	NH
WAKM	Franklin, TN	5/0.08	U1	
KPRC	Houston, TX	5	U2	AN
KJTV	Lubbock, TX	5/0.5	U4	AN
KJR	Seattle, WA	50	U3	AN
WVTS	Charleston, WV	5/1	U2	AN
KMER	Kemmerer, WY	5/0.09	U1	
CFAM	Altona, MB	10	U4	AN
CKNB	Campbellton, NB	10/1	U4	AN
CHER	Sydney, NS	10	U2	AN
+lp: USA 14				
960kHz				
WERC	Birmingham, AL	5	U2	AN
WLPR	Pritchard, AL	5/1	U2	NH
KKNT	Phoenix, AZ	5	U2	AN
KCGS	Marshall, AR	5	D1	D
KIXW	Apple Valley, CA	5/0.02	U1	
KABL	San Francisco, CA	5	U3	AN
WELI	New Haven, CT	5	U2	AN
WGRO	Lake City, FL	0.5/1	U2	NH
WJYZ	Albany, GA	5	D3	D*
WRFC	Athens, GA	5/2.5	U2	AN
WSBT	South Bend, IN	5	U4	AN
KMA	Shenandoah, IA	5	U2	NH
WTGM	Salisbury, MD	5	U4	AN
WFGL	Fitchburg, MA	1	U4	AN
WHAK	Rogers City, MI	5/0.136	U1	
KLTF	Little Falls, MN	5/0.038	U1	
KZIM	Cape Girardeau, MO	5/0.5	U2	NH
KFLN	Baker, MT	5/0.091	U1	
KNEB	Scottsbluff, NE	5/0.35	U4	AN
KNDN	Farmington, NM	5/0.163	U1	NH
WEAV	Plattsburgh, NY	5	U4	NH
WRNS	Kinston, NC	5/1	U2	AN
KGWA	Enid, OK	1	U3	NH
KKJX	Klamath Falls, OR	5	U2	AN
WHYL	Carlisle, PA	5/0.022	U3	AN
WATS	Sayre, PA	5/0.05	U1	AN
KGKL	San Angelo, TX	5/1	U2	AN
KOVO	Provo, UT	5/1	U2	AN
WFIR	Roanoke, VA	5	U2	AN
KALE	Richland, WA	5/1	U2	AN
WTCH	Shawano, WI	1	U2	NSP
CFAC	Calgary, AB	50	U2	AN
CHNS	Halifax, NS	10	U2	AN
CFFX	Kingston, ON	10/5	U4	AN
+lp: USA 15				
970kHz				
WERH	Hamilton, AL	5	D1	D*
WTBF	Troy, AL	5/0.5	U2	NH
KFBX	Fairbanks, AK	10	U1	AN
KVWM	Show Low, AZ	5/0.195	U1	
KNWS	Coachella, CA	5/1	U4	AN
KESP	Modesto, CA	1	U4	AN
WFLA	Tampa, FL	25/11	U4	AN
WNIV	Atlanta, GA	5	D1	D
WFSR	Harlan, KY	5/0.024	U1	NH
WGTK	Louisville, KY	5	U4	AN
KSYL	Alexandria, LA	1	U2	AN
WZAN	Portland, ME	5	U2	AN
WZAM	Ishpeming, MI	5/0.062	U1	AN
WKHM	Jackson, MI	1	U4	AN
KNFX	Austin, MN	5/0.5	U4	AN
KBUL	Billings, MT	5	U2	AN
KJLT	North Platte, NE	5/0.055	U1	
KNUU	Paradise, NV	5/0.5	U4	
WWDJ	Hackensack, NJ	5	U4	AN

Call	Location	kW	Lic	Ops
WNED	Buffalo, NY	5	U3	AN
WOXL	Canton, NC	5/0.03	U1	AN
WDAY	Fargo, ND	5	U2	AN
WFUN	Ashtabula, OH	5/1	U4	AN
KCFO	Tulsa, OK	2.5/1	U4	AN
KUPL	Portland, OR	5	U2	AN
WBGG	Pittsburgh, PA	5	U4	AN
WJMX	Florence, SC	10/3	U2	AN
KIXL	Del Valle, TX	1	U4	
WKCI	Waynesboro, VA	5/1	U4	AN
KTRW	Spokane, WA	5/1	U2	AN
WHA	Madison, WI	5/0.051	U1	
CJYR	Edson, AB	10	U3	AN
+lp: USA 21/Can 1				
980kHz				
KCAB	Dardanelle, AR	5/0.032	U1	
KINS	Eureka, CA	5/0.5	U2	AN
KFWB	Los Angeles, CA	5	U1	AN
KDBV	Salinas, CA	10	U4	AN
WTEM	Washington, DC	50/5	U4	AN
WDVH	Gainesville, FL	5/0.166	U1	AN
WRNE	Gulf Breeze, FL	4/1	U2	AN
WHSR	Pompano Beach, FL	5/2.2	U4	AN
KUPI	Ammon, ID	5/1	U4	AN
WITY	Danville, IL	1	U3	NH
KOKA	Shreveport, LA	5	D1	D*
WCAP	Lowell, MA	5	U4	AN
KKMS	Richfield, MN	5	U3	AN
WAPF	McComb, MS	5/0.152	U1	
KMBZ	Kansas City, MO	5	U2	AN
KVLV	Fallon, NV	5	D1	D*
KMIN	Grants, NM	1	U1	AN
WOFX	Troy, NY	5	U2	AN
WAAV	Wilmington, NC	5	U2	AN
WONE	Dayton, OH	5	U2	AN
WILK	Wilkes-Barre, PA	5/1	U2	AN
KDSJ	Deadwood, SD	5/1	U2	NH
WYFN	Nashville, TN	5	U2	AN
KRTX	Rosenberg, TX	1/4	U2	AN
KSVC	Richfield, UT	11/1	U2	AN
WFHG	Bristol, VA	5/1	U2	AN
KBBO	Selah, WA	5/0.5	U4	AN
WCUB	Two Rivers, WI	5	U4	AN
CKNW	New Westminster, BC	50	U3	AN
CFPL	London, ON	10/5	U4	AN
CKRU	Peterborough, ON	10/5	U4	AN
CJRP	St-Nicolas, QC	10	U4	F.Pl.
CJME	Regina, SA	10/5	U4	AN
+lp: USA 27				
990kHz				
KTKT	Tucson, AZ	10/1	U4	AN
KATD	Pittsburg, CA	5	U4	AN
KTMS	Santa Barbara, CA	5/0.5	U5	NH
KRKS	Denver, CO	6.6/0.39	U2	AN
WMYM	Miami, FL	5	U4	
WDYZ	Orlando, FL	50/14	U4	AN
WDEO	Ypsilanti, MI	9.2/0.25	U4	AN
WLGZ	Rochester, NY	5/2.5	U4	AN
WEEB	Southern Pines, NC	10/0.5	U1	AN
WNTP	Philadelphia, PA	50/10	U4	AN
WNTW	Somerset, PA	10/0.1	U3	AN
WALE	Greenville, RI	50/5	U4	NH
WNOX	Knoxville, TN	10	U2	AN
KWAM	Memphis, TN	10/0.33	U4	AN
KZZB	Beaumont, TX	1	U3	AN
KMSR	Farmersville, TX	7/0.92	U4	AN
WNRV	Narrows, VA	5/0.01	U1	AN
CBW	Winnipeg, MB	50/46	U1	AN
CBY	Corner Brook, NL	10	U3	AN
CKGM	Montreal, QC	50	U4	AN
+lp: USA 25/Can 12				
1000kHz				
WDJL	Huntsville, AL	10	D3	D
WYBT	Blountstown, FL	5	D1	D
WMVP	Chicago, IL	50	U4	AN
WXTN	Lexington, MS	5	D1	D
KKIM	Albuquerque, NM	10/0.04	U1	D*
WLNL	Horseheads, NY	5/2.5	D1	D
KTOK	Oklahoma City, OK	5	U4	AN
KXRB	Sioux Falls, SD	10/0.1	U4	AN
WMUF	Paris, TN	5/2.5	D3	D
KOMO	Seattle, WA	50	U2	AN
+lp: USA 21				
1010kHz				
WCOC	Dora, AL	5/0.041	U1	
KXXT	Tolleson, AZ	15/0.25	U5	AN
KCHJ	Delano, CA	5/1	U4	AN
KIQI	San Francisco, CA	10/1.5	U4	
KSIR	Brush, CO	25/0.28	U3	
WIOJ	Jacksonville Beach, FL	10/0.14	U4	AN
WBZZ	Seffner, FL	50/5	U4	AN
WGUN	Atlanta, GA	50/0.3	U1	AN
WMOX	Meridian, MS	10/1	U4	NH
KXEN	Festus, MO	50/0.5	U4	AN
WNTK	Newport, NH	10/0.037	U1	D
WINS	New York, NY	50	U3	AN
WFGW	Black Mountain, NC	50/0.5	U7	
WHIN	Gallatin, TN	5/0.047	U1	
KTNZ	Amarillo, TX	5/0.5	U4	AN
KLAT	Houston, TX	5/3.6	U4	AN
KBBW	Waco-Marlin, TX	10/2.5	U4	NH
KCPW	Tooele, UT	50/0.013	U1	AN
WRJR	Portsmouth, VA	5/0.449	U3	
CBR	Calgary, AB	50	U4	NH
CFRB	Toronto, ON	50	U4	AN
+lp: USA 20/Can 4				
1020kHz				
KAXX	Eagle River, AK	10	U2	AN
KTNQ	Los Angeles, CA	50	U4	AN
WJEP	Ochlocknee, GA	10	D1	D
KOIL	Plattsmouth, NE	50/1.4	U4	AN
KINF	Roswell, NM	50	U4	NH
KDKA	Pittsburgh, PA	50	U1	AN
WRIX	Homeland Park, SC	10/3	D1	D
CKVH	High Prairie, AB	1/0.4	U1	AN
+lp: USA 2				
1030kHz				
KFAY	Farmington, AR	10/1	U2	AN
KEVT	Cortaro, AZ	10/1	U4	
WONQ	Oviedo, FL	45/0.7	U4	AN
WNVR	Vernon Hills, IL	5//3/1.2	U8	
KBUF	Holcomb, KS	1	U1	AN
WBZ	Boston, MA	50	U3	AN
WWGB	Indian Head, MD	50	D3	D
WUFL	Sterling Heights, MI	5	D3	D
WCTS	Maplewood, MN	50/1	U4	NH
WNOW	Mint Hill, NC	9.4	D3	D
WFTK	Wake Forest, NC	50	D3	D
KDUN	Reedsport, OR	50/0.63	U1	AN
WGSF	Memphis, TN	50/1	U2	AN
KCTA	Corpus Christi, TX	50/1	U2	
KWFA	Tye, TX	5/0.37	U4	F.Pl.
KMAS	Shelton, WA	10/1	U1	AN
WBGS	Point Pleasant, WV	10/2.9	D5	D
KTWO	Casper, WY	50	U2	AN
+lp: USA 8				
1040kHz				
KCBR	Monument, CO	15/2	D1	D
WLVJ	Boynton Beach, FL	25/1.1	U4	AN
WPBS	Conyers, GA	12/5	D1	D
WHO	Des Moines, IA	50	U1	AN
WCHR	Flemington, NJ	4.7/1	U4	AN
WSGH	Lewisville, NC	9.1/0.18	U4	AN
WJTB	North Ridgeville, OH	5/2.5	D1	D
WSKE	Everett, PA	10/4	D1	D
WQBB	Powell, TN	10/3	D3	D
CKST	Vancouver, BC	10	U4	AN
CJMS	St-Constant, QC	5/1.1	U4	
+lp: USA 11				
1050kHz				
KTBA	Tuba City, AZ	5	D1	D
KMAP	Frazier Park, CA	10/0.007	U1	
KTCT	San Mateo, CA	50/10	U4	AN
WROS	Jacksonville, FL	5/0.013	U3	
WFAM	Augusta, GA	5	D1	D*
WTKA	Ann Arbor, MI	10/0.5	U3	AN
KLOH	Pipestone, MN	9/0.4	U4	
KMTA	Miles City, MT	10	D	D
KTBL	Los Ranchos de Albuquerque, NM	1	U3	AN
WEVD	New York, NY	50	U3	AN
KORE	Springfield, OR	5/0.149	U1	D

Call	Location	kW	Lic	Ops
WIQB	Conway, SC	5	D1	D*
WIQB	Conway, SC	25/1	U4	F.Pl.
WCMS	Norfolk, VA	5/0.36	U3	AN
KEYF	Dishman, WA	5/0.26	U1	AN
KBLE	Seattle, WA	5/0.44	U1	NH
WADC	Parkersburg, WV	5/0.144	U1	AN
CKSB	Winnipeg, MB	10	U2	AN
CHUM	Toronto, ON	50	U4	AN
CJNB	North Battleford, SK	10	U2	AN
+lp: USA 44				
1060kHz				
KDUS	Tempe, AZ	5/0.5	U2	AN
KTNS	Oakhurst, CA	5/0.023	U1	
KRCN	Longmont, CO	30/0.111	U1	AN
WIXC	Titusville, FL	50/17/5	U7	AN
WKNG	Tallapoosa, GA	11/5	D1	D*
KBGN	Caldwell, ID	10	D1	D*
WLNO	New Orleans, LA	50/5	U4	AN
WBIX	Natick, MA	40/22/2.5	U4	
WHFB	Benton Harbor, MI	5/2.5	D1	D*
KKVV	Las Vegas, NV	5/0.043	U1	
WILB	Canton, OH	5	D3	D*
KYW	Philadelphia, PA	50	U3	AN
KGFX	Pierre, SD	10/1	U4	AN
KXPL	El Paso, TX	10	D1	D*
KIJN	Farwell, TX	10	D3	D
KOFY	Gilmer, TX	10	D1	D*
KDYL	Salt Lake City, UT	10/0.149	U1	AN
CKMX	Calgary, AB	50	U2	AN
+lp: USA 20				
1070kHz				
WAPI	Birmingham, AL	50/5	U2	AN
KNX	Los Angeles, CA	50	U1	AN
WFRF	Tallahassee, FL	10	D1	D
WIBC	Indianapolis, IN	50/10	U4	AN
KFTI	Wichita, KS	10/1	U2	AN
KVKK	Verndale, MN	10/5	U2	F.Pl.
KHMO	Hannibal, MO	5/1	U4	AN
KATQ	Plentywood, MT	5	D1	D
WTWK	Plattsburgh, NY	5	D1	D
WNCT	Greenville, NC	10	U4	AN
WKOK	Sunbury, PA	10/1	U2	AN
WCSZ	Greenville, SC	50/1.5	U4	AN
WFLI	Lookout Mountain, TN	50/2.5	U4	AN
WDIA	Memphis, TN	50/5	U4	AN
KOPY	Alice, TX	1	U4	AN
KKHT	Houston, TX	10/5	U4	AN
WINA	Charlottesville, VA	5	U2	AN
WIWS	Beckley, WV	10/7.7	D1	D*
WTSO	Madison, WI	10/5	U4	AN
CFAX	Victoria, BC	10	U3	AN
CBA	Moncton, NB	50	U1	AN
CHOK	Sarnia, ON	10	U4	AN
+lp: USA 6/Can 1				
1080kHz				
WKAC	Athens, AL	5/2.5	D1	D
KUDO	Anchorage, AK	10	U1	AN
KSCO	Santa Cruz, CA	10/5	U2	AN
WTIC	Hartford, CT	50	U2	AN
WVCG	Coral Gables, FL	50/10	U4	AN
WHOO	Kissimmee, FL	19/10	D4	D
WFTD	Marietta, GA	50/30	D6	D
KVNI	Coeur d'Alene, ID	10/1	U2	AN
WKJK	Louisville, KY	10/1	U4	AN
WKGX	Lenoir, NC	5/2.5	D1	D*
WKKE	St. Pauls, NC	50/25	D3	D
KFXX	Portland, OR	50/10	U3	AN
WWNL	Pittsburgh, PA	50/25	D3	D*
KRLD	Dallas, TX	50	U2	AN
KSLL	Price, UT	10/5	D1	D
+lp: USA 17/Can 1				
1090kHz				
WWGC	Albertville, AL	5/0.5	D1	D
KAAY	Little Rock, AR	50	U2	AN
KNCR	Fortuna, CA	10	D1	D
KMXA	Aurora, CO	50/0.5	U4	AN
WNVY	Cantonment, FL	10/2.3	D1	D
WSLG	Gonzales, LA	10	D3	D
WBAL	Baltimore, MD	50	U2	AN
WILD	Boston, MA	5/1	D1	D
KBOZ	Bozeman, MT	5	U2	AN

Call	Location	kW	Lic	Ops
WTSB	Selma, NC	9/1.7	D1	D
WHGG	Kingsport, TN	10/1.8	D1	D
KVOP	Plainview, TX	5/0.25	U4	AN
KYCW	Seattle, WA	50	U4	AN
WAQE	Rice Lake, WI	5	D1	D
CKKW	Kitchener, ON	10	U4	AN
+lp: USA 23/Can 4				
1100kHz				
KAGV	Big Lake, AK	10	U1	F.Pl.
KFNX	Cave Creek, AZ	50/1	U4	AN
KFAX	San Francisco, CA	50	U3	AN
KNZZ	Grand Junction, CO	50/10	U2	AN
WWWE	Hapeville, GA	5/3.8	D1	D
WCGA	Woodbine, GA	10	D1	D
WOMN	Franklinton, LA	30/10	D1	F.Pl.
new	Dilworth, MN	50/4.4/1	U2	F.Pl.
KKLL	Webb City, MO	5	D1	D
WHLI	Hempstead, NY	10	D3	D
WTAM	Cleveland, OH	50	U3	AN
KDRY	Alamo Heights, TX	11/1	U2	NH
WTWN	Wells River, VT	5/2	D1	D
+lp: USA 1				
1110kHz				
WBCA	Bay Minette, AL	10/2.5	D1	D
KGFL	Clinton, AR	5/1	D1	D
KDIS	Pasadena, CA	50/20	U4	AN
KLIB	Roseville, CA	5/0.5	U4	AN
WTIS	Tampa, FL	10	D3	D*
WUHN	Pittsfield, MA	5	D3	D
WJML	Petoskey, MI	10/0.01	U4	AN
KFAB	Omaha, NE	50	U2	AN
WCEC	Salem, NH	5	D3	D
KYKK	Humble City, NM	5/2.5	D1	D*
WBT	Charlotte, NC	50	U2	AN
KEOR	Atoka, OK	5	D3	D
KBND	Bend, OR	10/5	U2	AN
WPMZ	East Providence, RI	5	D3	D
WYRM	Norfolk, VA	50	D3	D
+lp: USA 22/Can 2				
1120kHz				
KZSJ	San Martin, CA	5/0.15	U1	
KLIM	Security, CO	10	D3	F.Pl.
WUST	Washington, DC	20/3	D1	D
WXJO	Gordon, GA	10/2.5	D1	D*
WBNW	Concord, MA	5/1	U4	AN
WTWZ	Clinton, MS	7.5/2.5	D1	D
KMOX	St. Louis, MO	50	U1	AN
WSME	Camp Lejeune, NC	6/4.2	D1	D
KPNW	Eugene, OR	50	U3	AN
KANN	Roy, UT	10/1	U2	AN
+lp: USA 13				
1130kHz				
KRDU	Dinuba, CA	5/6	U4	AN
KSDO	San Diego, CA	50/10	U4	AN
WMGA	Moultrie, GA	10/0.25	U2	
WWBF	Bartow, FL	2.5/0.5	U2	NH
WRKY	Murray, KY	1.5/0.5	U8	AN
KWKH	Shreveport, LA	50	U2	AN
WDFN	Detroit, MI	50/10	U4	AN
KFAN	Minneapolis, MN	50/30	U4	AN
WBBR	New York, NY	50	U2	AN
WPYB	Benson, NC	5/1	D1	D
KBMR	Bismarck, ND	10/0.024	U1	
WASP	Brownsville, PA	5/1	D5	D*
KTMR	Edna, TX	10	D3	D
WISN	Milwaukee, WI	50/10	U4	AN
CKWX	Vancouver, BC	50	U4	AN
+lp: USA 21/Can 1				
1140kHz				
WBXR	Hazel Green, AL	15/7.5	D3	D
KSLD	Soldotna, AK	10	U1	AN
KNWQ	Palm Springs, CA	10/2.5	U4	AN
KHTK	Sacramento, CA	50	U4	AN
WQBA	Miami, FL	50/10	U4	AN
WRMQ	Orlando, FL	5	D1	D
KGEM	Boise, ID	10	U2	AN
WVEL	Pekin, IL	5/3.2	D1	D*
WJNZ	Kentwood, MI	5	D3	D
WSAO	Senatobia, MS	5	D1	D
KSFN	Las Vegas, NV	10/2.5	U2	AN
KSOO	Sioux Falls, SD	10/5	U2	AN

Call	Location	kW	Lic	Ops
KYOK	Conroe, TX	5	D1	D
WRVA	Richmond, VA	50	U3	AN
KZMQ	Greybull, WY	10	D1	D
CHRB	High River, AB	50/46	U4	AN
CBI	Sydney, NS	10	U2	AN
+lp: USA 14/Can 4				
1150kHz				
WSPZ	Tuscaloosa, AL	5/1	U2	AN
KCKY	Coolidge, AZ	5/1	U4	AN
KXTA	Los Angeles, CA	50/44	U4	AN
KMXN	Santa Rosa, CA	5	U4	AN
KNRC	Englewood, CO	10/1	U4	AN
WDEL	Wilmington, DE	5	U4	AN
WNDB	Daytona Beach, FL	1	U2	AN
WTMP	Egypt Lake, FL	10/0.5	U4	AN
WJEM	Valdosta, GA	5/0.101	U3	
WGGH	Marion, IL	5	D3	D*
KWKY	Des Moines, IA	1	U4	NH
KSAL	Salina, KS	5	U2	AN
WJBO	Baton Rouge, LA	5	U3	AN
WTTT	Boston, MA	5	U4	AN
KSEN	Shelby, MT	10/5	U4	NH
KDEF	Albuquerque, NM	5/0.5	U2	AN
WRUN	Utica, NY	5/1	U4	AN
WGBR	Goldsboro, NC	5/0.8	U4	NH
WCUE	Cuyahoga Falls, OH	5/0.5	U4	
WIMA	Lima, OH	1	U2	AN
KNED	McAlester, OK	1	U2	AN
KAGO	Klamath Falls, OR	5/1	U2	AN
KRMZ	Portland, OR	5/0.047	U3	
WHUN	Huntingdon, PA	5/0.04	U1	AN
KIMM	Rapid City, SD	5/0.5	U2	AN
WGOW	Chattanooga, TN	5/1	U2	AN
WCRK	Morristown, TN	5/0.5	U2	NH
KSVE	El Paso, TX	5/0.38	U1	AN
KQQQ	Pullman, WA	11/0.027	U2	
KKNW	Seattle, WA	10/6	U2	AN
WELC	Welch, WV	5	D1	D*
WEAQ	Chippewa Falls, WI	5/0.046	U1	
WHBY	Kimberly, WI	5	U3	AN
CKFR	Kelowna, BC	10	U2	AN
CKOC	Hamilton, ON	50	U2	AN
CJRC	Gatineau, QC	50/5	U4	AN
CHGM	Gaspé, QC	5	U2	AN
+lp: USA 31/Can 7				
1160kHz				
W...	Saraland, AL	15/0.25	U2	F.Pl.
WEWC	Callahan, FL	5/0.25	U5	F.Pl.
WMLB	East Point, GA	50/0.16	U5	AN
WYLL	Chicago, IL	50	U4	AN
WBOB	Florence, KY	5/1	U4	AN
WKCM	Hawesville, KY	2.5/1	U2	AN
WSKW	Skowhegan, ME	10/0.73	U1	AN
WMET	Gaithersburg, MD	50/1.5	U4	
WCXI	Fenton, MI	1	U1	NH
WOBM	Lakewood Township, NJ	20/8.9	U4	AN
WVNJ	Oakland, NJ	10/2.5	U4	AN
WABY	Mechanicville, NY	5/0.47	U1	NH
WPIE	Trumansburg, NY	5/0.31	U4	AN
WYRU	Red Springs, NC	5/0.25	U1	NH
WJFJ	Tryon, NC	10/0.5	U2	
WCCS	Homer City, PA	10/1	U4	AN
WYNS	Lehighton, PA	4/1	U4	AN
WAMB	Donelson, TN	50/1	U2	AN
KBIS	Highland Park, TX	25/1	U4	F.Pl.
KENS	San Antonio, TX	10/1	U4	AN
KSL	Salt Lake City, UT	50	U1	AN
WODY	Fieldale, VA	5/0.25	U4	AN
VSB3	Hamilton, Bermuda	1	U1	SH
+lp: USA 3/Can 1				
1170kHz				
WACV	Montgomery, AL	10/1	U4	AN
KJNP	North Pole, AK	50/21	U2	NH
KCBQ	San Diego, CA	50/4.5	U4	AN
KLOK	San Jose, CA	50/5	U4	AN
WAVS	Davie, FL	5/0.25	U2	NH
WLBH	Mattoon, IL	5	D3	D*
KJOC	Davenport, IA	1	U4	AN
WCXN	Claremont, NC	7.7/1	D1	D
WCLN	Clinton, NC	5/1	D1	D
KFAQ	Tulsa, OK	50	U2	AN

Call	Location	kW	Lic	Ops
K...	Bend, OR	50/0.55	U12	F.Pl.
WLGO	Lexington, SC	10/2.5	D1	D
WPLX	Germantown, TN	10/0.009	U4	
KPUG	Bellingham, WA	10/5	U2	AN
WWVA	Wheeling, WV	50	U2	AN
+lp: USA 15/Can 3				
1180kHz				
KYET	Williams, AZ	10/0.25	U1	NH
KERI	Wasco, CA	50/10	U4	AN
–	R Martí, Marathon, FL	100	U3	AN
WZQZ	Trion, GA	5	D1	D
WXLA	Dimondale, MI	10/2	D4	D
WJNT	Pearl, MS	50/0.5	U2	AN
KOFI	Kalispell, MT	50/10	U2	AN
KYDZ	Bellevue, NE	25/1	U4	AN
WHAM	Rochester, NY	50	U1	AN
WMYT	Carolina Beach, NC	10	D3	D
WVLZ	Knoxville, TN	10/2.6	D1	D
KGOL	Humble, TX	50/1	U4	AN
KLAY	Lakewood, WA	5/1	U2	AN
+lp: USA 7				
1190kHz				
KMYL	Tolleson, AZ	5/0.25	U4	AN
KXMX	Anaheim, CA	20/1.3	U4	AN
KXMX	Paramount, CA	25/1	U4	F.Pl.
KVCU	Boulder, CO	6.8/0.11	U1	AN
WAMT	Pine Castle, FL	5	D1	D
WAFS	Atlanta, GA	25/2.3	D1	D
WOWO	Fort Wayne, IN	50/9.8	U2	AN
WBIS	Annapolis, MD	50	D3	D
WBIS	Highland Beach, MD	50	D3	F.Pl.
KKOJ	Jackson, MN	5	D3	D
WBSL	Bay St. Louis, MS	5	D1	D
KRFT	DeSoto, MO	10/0.03	U7	
KPHN	Kansas City, MO	4.2/4.0	U2	AN
KXKS	Albuquerque, NM	10/0.024	U1	
WLIB	New York, NY	10/30	U4	AN
KEX	Portland, OR	50	U2	AN
WSDQ	Dunlap, TN	5/1	D1	D
KFXR	Dallas, TX	50/5	U4	AN
WBDY	Bluefield, VA	10	D3	D
WNWC	Sun Prairie, WI	4.8	D3	D
CFSL	Weyburn, SK	10/5	U2	AN
+lp: USA 18				
1200kHz				
WQLS	Ozark, AL	10/2.5	D1	D
KYAA	Soquel, CA	25/1	U2	
WPTK	Pine Island Center, FL	10/1	U4	AN
WRTO	Chicago, IL	10/2.5	U4	AN
WNSW	Brewer, ME	10	U3	AN
WKOX	Framingham, MA	50	U4	AN
WCHB	Taylor, MI	50/2.1	U4	AN
WTLA	North Syracuse, NY	1	U2	AN
WXIT	Blowing Rock, NC	10/7	D1	D
WSML	Graham, NC	10/1	U2	AN
KFNW	West Fargo, ND	10/0.7	U2	AN
WKST	New Castle, PA	5/1	U2	AN
WRKK	Hughesville, PA	10/0.25	U4	AN
WMIR	Atlantic Beach, SC	6.5/0.01	U1	
WKDA	Nashville, TN	10/0.195	U2	AN
WOAI	San Antonio, TX	50	U1	AN
WAGE	Leesburg, VA	5/1	U2	AN
CFGO	Ottawa, ON	50	U4	AN
+lp: USA 2				
1210kHz				
KQTL	Sahuarita, AZ	10/1	U1	AN
KEBR	Rocklin, CA	5/0.5	U5	AN
KPRZ	San Marcos, CA	20/10	U4	AN
WNMA	Miami Springs, FL	47/2.5	U4	
WKTT	Silver Springs, FL	5/0.25	U2	F.Pl.
WDGR	Dahlonega, GA	10/2.5	D1	D
WILY	Centralia, IL	10/1.1	D6	D
WSKR	Denham Springs, LA	10/1	U2	AN
WLDR	Kingsley, MI	50/2.5	D1	D
KGYN	Guymon, OK	10	U2	AN
WPHT	Philadelphia, PA	50	U1	AN
KOKK	Huron, SD	5/0.9	U4	NH
WMPS	Bartlett, TN	10/0.25	U2	AN
WSBI	Static, TN	10/2.5	D1	D
KUBR	San Juan, TX	10/5	U4	
KUNF	Washington, UT	10/0.25	U1	AN

Call	Location	kW	Lic	Ops
KNWX	Auburn-Federal Way, WA	27.5/10	U1	AN
KZTS	Sunnyside, WA	10/1	U1	NH
KRSV	Afton, WY	5/0.25	U1	AN
KHAT	Laramie, WY	10/1	U2	AN
CKWA	Slave Lake, AB	1	U1	AN
VOAR	St. John's, NL	10	U4	NH
CFYM	Kindersley, SK	1	U1	AN

+Ip: USA 3/Can 1

1220kHz

Call	Location	kW	Lic	Ops
KNTS	Palo Alto, CA	5/0.14	U1	NH
WIBQ	Sarasota, FL	5/0.005	U5	
WSLM	Salem, IN	5	D3	D*
WMGT	Stillwater, MN	5	D1	D
WENC	Whiteville, NC	5	D1	D*
WHK	Cleveland, OH	50	U3	AN
WFAX	Falls Church, VA	5	D1	D*
CJRB	Boissevain, MB	10	U3	AN
CJUL	Cornwall, ON	1	U4	AN
CJRL	Kenora, ON	5/1	U1	AN
CHSC	St. Catharines, ON	10	U4	AN
CFVM	Amqui, QC	10/5	U2	AN
CKSM	Shawinigan, QC	10/2.5	U3	AN

+Ip: USA 42

1230kHz

USA 172 st's mostly 1kW, Canada 19 st's 40W to 1kW

Call	Location	kW	Lic	Ops
CFFB	Iqaluit, NWT	4/1	U1	NH
ZFB	Hamilton, Bermuda	1	U1	NH

1240kHz

USA 156 st's mostly 1kW, Canada 30 st's 40W to 1kW

1250kHz

Call	Location	kW	Lic	Ops
WZOB	Fort Payne, AL	5	D1	D
WAPZ	Wetumpka, AL	5	D1	D*
KHIL	Willcox, AZ	5	D1	D
KPZK	Little Rock, AR	2/1.2	U4	AN
KZER	Santa Barbara, CA	2.5/1	U4	AN
KLLK	Willits, CA	5/2.5	U4	
WHNZ	Tampa, FL	25/5.9	U4	AN
WGL	Fort Wayne, IN	2.3/1.5	U4	NH
KFKU	Lawrence, KS	5	ST2	
KKHK	Kansas City, KS	25/5	U4	AN
WARE	Ware, MA	5/2.5	U4	NH
KBRF	Fergus Falls, MN	5/2.2	U2	AN
WHNY	McComb, MS	5/1	U2	NH
KIKC	Forsyth, MT	5	D1	D*
WKBR	Manchester, NH	5	U4	AN
WMTR	Morristown, NJ	5/7	U4	AN
WGHB	Farmville, NC	5/2.5	U4	NH
WBRM	Marion, NC	5	D1	D
WEAE	Pittsburgh, PA	5	U2	AN
WTMA	Charleston, SC	5/1	U2	AN
KDEI	Port Arthur, TX	5/1	U2	AN
KXDC	San Antonio, TX	1	U2	AN
KNEU	Roosevelt, UT	5	D1	D*
WDVA	Danville, VA	5	U2	AN
WPRZ	Warrenton, VA	5	D3	D
KWSU	Pullman, WA	5/2.5	U1	NH
KKDZ	Seattle, WA	5	U2	D
WYKM	Rupert, WV	5	D1	D*
WEMP	Milwaukee, WI	5	U4	AN
CHSM	Steinbach, MB	10/5	U3	AN
CJYE	Oakville, ON	10	U4	AN
C...	Ottawa, ON	1/0.1	U1	F.Pl.

+Ip: USA 33

1260kHz

Call	Location	kW	Lic	Ops
WYDE	Birmingham, AL	5/1	U2	
KSUR	Beverly Hills, CA	20/7.5	U4	NH
KOIT	San Francisco, CA	5/1	U1	AN
WWRC	Washington, DC	5	U4	AN
WSUA	Miami, FL	50/20	U4	AN
WUFE	Baxley, GA	5	D1	D*
WTJH	East Point, GA	5/0.04	U1	AN
KSSL	Idaho Falls, ID	5	D1	D*
KWEI	Weiser, ID	10/0.06	U1	F.Pl.
WSDZ	Belleville, IL	20/5	U4	AN
WNDE	Indianapolis, IN	5	U2	AN
KFGQ	Boone, IA	5/0.03	U4	
KBRH	Baton Rouge, LA	5/0.127	U1	AN
WMKI	Boston, MA	5	U2	AN
WPNW	Zeeland, MI	10/1	U4	
KTTF	Springfield, MO	5	U2	AN
WBUD	Trenton, NJ	5/1	U4	AN
KTRC	Santa Fe, NM	5/1	U1	F.Pl.
WNSS	Syracuse, NY	5	U2	AN
WKXR	Asheboro, NC	5/0.5	U4	NH
WWMK	Cleveland, OH	10/5	U4	AN
WNXT	Portsmouth, OH	5/1	U4	NH
KWSH	Wewoka, OK	1	U2	NH
WRIE	Erie, PA	5	U4	AN
WPHB	Philipsburg, PA	5	D1	D*
WMUU	Greenville, SC	5	D1	D*
WHYM	Lake City, SC	5	D1	D
KWYR	Winner, SD	5	D1	D*
WNOO	Chattanooga, TN	5	D1	D
WDKN	Dickson, TN	5/0.018	U1	
WCHV	Charlottesville, VA	5/2.5	U4	AN
WXCE	Amery, WI	5	U4	NH
KPOW	Powell, WY	5/1	U2	NH
CFRN	Edmonton, AB	50	U2	AN
CKHJ	Fredericton, NB	10	U2	AN

+Ip: USA 34

1270kHz

Call	Location	kW	Lic	Ops
WIJD	Prichard, AL	5	D1	D*
KDJI	Holbrook, AZ	5	D1	D*
KPBA	Pine Bluff, AR	5	D1	D
KCMJ	Thousand Palms, CA	5/0.75	U4	
KJUG	Tulare, CA	5/1	U2	AN
WRLZ	Eatonville, FL	5	U2	AN
WNOG	Naples, Fl	5/1.9	U4	AN
WNLS	Tallahassee, FL	5	U2	AN
WSHE	Columbus, GA	5	D1	D*
WJJC	Commerce, GA	5	D1	D
KTFI	Twin Falls, ID	5/1	U1	AN
WKBF	Rock Island, IL	5	U2	AN
WFRN	Elkhart, IN	5/1	U4	AN
WWCA	East Chicago, IN	2.5	U3	AN
KSCB	Liberal, KS	5/0.025	U1	AN
WCBC	Cumberland, MD	5/1	U4	AN
WSPR	Springfield, MA	5/1	U4	AN
WMKT	Charlevoix, MI	5	U2	AN
WXYT	Detroit, MI	50	U4	AN
WWWY	Baxter, MN	5	U4	
KWEB	Rochester, MN	5/1	U4	AN
KBZZ	Sparks, NV	13/5	U2	
WTSN	Dover, NH	5	U2	AN5
WHLD	Niagara Falls, NY	5/1	U4	NH
WDLA	Walton, NY	5	D1	D*
WCGC	Belmont, NC	10/0.5	U4	AN
WMPM	Smithfield, NC	5	D1	D*
KRVT	Claremore, OK	1	U2	AN
KAJO	Grants Pass, OR	5	D1	D*
WLBR	Lebanon, PA	5/1	U4	NH
KNWC	Sioux Falls, SD	5/2.2	U4	NH
WLIK	Newport, TN	5/0.5	U2	NH
KFLC	Fort Worth, TX	50/5	U4	AN
WHEO	Stuart, VA	5	D1	D*
KBAM	Longview, WA	5/0.08	U1	
KIML	Gillette, WY	5/1	U2	AN
CHAT	Medicine Hat, AB	10	U2	AN
CJCB	Sydney, NS	10	U2	AN
CFGT	Alma, QC	10/5	U2	AN

+Ip: USA 30/Can 1

1280kHz

Call	Location	kW	Lic	Ops
WWPG	Tuscaloosa, AL	5/0.5	U2	AN
KXTK	Arroyo Grande, CA	10/2.5	U4	AN
KFRN	Long Beach, CA	1	U5	AN
KUYL	Stockton, CA	1	U2	AN
KBNO	Denver, CO	5	U4	AN
WGTX	De Funiak Springs, FL	9/0.046	U4	
WLCG	Macon, GA	5	D1	D*
WBIG	Aurora, IL	2.5/0.5	U4	AN
WGBF	Evansville, IN	5/1	U2	AN
WODT	New Orleans, LA	5	U3	AN
WFAU	Gardiner, ME	5	U2	NH
WEIM	Fitchburg, MA	5/1	U4	NH
WWTC	Minneapolis, MN	5	U2	AN
KVOX	Moorehead, MN	5/1	U4	AN
KDOX	Henderson, NV	5/0.05	U1	
KRZE	Farmington, NM	5/0.108	U1	
WADO	New York, NY	50/7.2	U4	AN
WHTK	Rochester, NY	5	U2	AN
WSAT	Salisbury, NC	1	U2	NH
WYAL	Scotland Neck, NC	5	D1	D*

Call	Location	kW	Lic	Ops
KRVM	Eugene, OR	5/1.5	U2	AN
WHVR	Hanover, PA	5/0.5	U4	AN
WJST	New Castle, PA	4.9/1	U2	NH
WANS	Anderson, SC	5/1	U2	AN
WMCP	Columbia, TN	5/0.5	U4	
KZNS	Salt Lake City, UT	10/0.6	U4	AN
KAQQ	Spokane, WA	5	D3	D*
KIT	Yakima, WA	5/1	U1	AN
WNAM	Neenah, WI	50/5	U4	AN
CHQB	Powell River, BC	1	U3	AN
CFMB	Montreal, QC	50	U4	AN
CJSL	Estevan, SK	10	U4	AN
VSB2	Hamilton, Bermuda	1	U1	AN
+Ip: USA 32/Can 1				
1290kHz				
WOPP	Opp, AL	2.5/0.5	U4	NH
KCUB	Tucson, AZ	1	U1	AN
KUOA	Siloam Springs, AR	5	D1	D*
KPAY	Chico, CA	5	U2	AN
KAZA	San Jose, CA	5	D3	D*
KKDD	San Bernardino, CA	5	U4	AN
WCFI	Ocala, FL	5/1	U2	AN
WBZT	West Palm Beach, FL	10/4.9	U4	AN
WCHK	Canton, GA	5/0.5	U2	AN
WTKS	Savannah, GA	5	U2	AN
KOUU	Pocatello, ID	50/0.024	U5	
WWFS	Peoria, IL	5	U4	AN
KWLS	Pratt, KS	5/0.5	U4	AN
WCBL	Benton, KY	5	D1	D*
WKLB	Manchester, KY	5	D1	D
KGVO	Missoula, MT	5	U2	AN
KKAR	Omaha, NE	7.3/5	U2	AN
WKBK	Keene, NH	5	U3	AN
WNBF	Binghamton, NY	9.3/5	U2	AN
WHKY	Hickory, NC	50/1	U4	AN
WJVC	Jacksonville, FL	5/0.047	U1	AN
WHIO	Dayton, OH	5	U2	AN
KUMA	Pendleton, OR	5	U2	NH
KKSL	Lake Oswego, OR	5	U3	AN
WFBG	Altoona, PA	5/1	U2	AN
WRNI	Providence, RI	5/10	U4	AN
WQMC	Sumter, SC	1	U2	AN
WATO	Oak Ridge, TN	5/0.5	U4	NH
KRGE	Weslaco, TX	5	U2	NH
KWFS	Wichita Falls, TX	5/0.07	U5	AN
WDZY	Colonial Heights, VA	25/0.041	U1	AN
WVOW	Logan, WV	5/1	U2	AN
WMCS	Greenfield, WI	5	U4	AN
WCOW	Sparta, WI	5	D1	D*
KOWB	Laramie, WY	5/1	U4	NH
CFRW	Winnipeg, MB	10	U4	AN
CJBK	London, ON	10	U3	AN
+Ip: USA 29				
1300kHz				
WKXM	Winfield, AL	5	D1	D*
KWCK	Searcy, AR	5	D1	D*
KYNO	Fresno, CA	5/1	U2	AN
KPMO	Mendocino, CA	5/0.077	U1	
KAZN	Pasadena, CA	5/1	U4	AN
KKML	Colorado Springs, CO	5/1	U1	AN
WAVZ	New Haven, CT	1	U2	AN
WTIR	Cocoa Beach, FL	5/1	U4	AN
WFFG	Marathon, FL	2.5	U3	NH
WQBN	Temple Terrace, FL	5/0.16	U5	NH
WMTM	Moultrie, GA	5	D1	D*
KLER	Orofino, ID	5/1	U2	NH
WRDZ	La Grange, IL	5/4.5	U4	AN
KGLO	Mason City, IA	5	U4	AN
WLXG	Lexington, KY	2.5/1	U2	AN
WIBR	Baton Rouge, LA	5/1	U4	AN
KSYB	Shreveport, LA	5	D1	D
WJFK	Baltimore, MD	5	U4	AN
WOOD	Grand Rapids, MI	20	U3	AN
WOAD	Jackson, MS	5/1	U1	AN
KBRL	McCook, NE	5	D3	D*
KPTL	Carson City, NV	5/0.5	U2	AN
WPNH	Plymouth, NH	5	D1	D*
WIMG	Ewing, NJ	3.2/1.3	U4	AN
WXRL	Lancaster, NY	5/2.5	U4	AN
WTMM	Rensselaer, NY	5	U4	AN
WSYD	Mount Airy, NC	5/1	U2	NH

Call	Location	kW	Lic	Ops
WERE	Cleveland, OH	5	U3	AN
KAKC	Tulsa, OK	5/1	U4	AN
KAPL	Phoenix, OR	20/5	U2	NH
WOGY	West Hazelton, PA	5/0.5	U4	AN
KOLY	Mobridge, SD	5	D1	D*
WMTN	Morristown, TN	5	D1	D*
WNQM	Nashville, TN	50/5	U2	AN
KVET	Austin, TX	5/0.99	U4	AN
WKCY	Harrisonburg, VA	5	D1	D*
KKOL	Seattle, WA	50	U4	AN
+Ip: USA 30				
1310kHz				
WJUS	Marion, AL	5	D1	D*
KXAM	Mesa, AZ	5/0.5	U2	AN
KIQQ	Barstow, CA	5/0.5	U4	AN
KMKY	Oakland, CA	5	U3	AN
KFKA	Greeley, CO	5/1	U2	AN
WICH	Norwich, CT	5	U4	AN
WYND	De Land, FL	8.5/0.95	U1	NH
WAUC	Wauchula, FL	5/0.5	U3	
KLIX	Twin Falls, ID	5/2.5	U2	AN
WTLC	Indianapolis, IN	5/1	U2	AN
WDOC	Prestonsburg, KY	5/0.025	U1	
KMBS	West Monroe, LA	5	D1	D*
WLOB	Portland, ME	5	U4	AN
WORC	Worcester, MA	5/1	U4	AN
WXDX	Dearborn, MI	5	U4	AN
WCCW	Traverse City, MI	15/0.13	U1	
KOCR	Joplin, MO	5/1	U4	AN
KEIN	Great Falls, MT	5/1	U1	AN
WADB	Asbury Park, NJ	2.5/1	U4	AN
KKNS	Corrales, NM	5/0.5	U2	AN
WRSB	Canandaigua, NY	1	U4	AN
WVIP	Mount Kisco, NY	5	D3	D*
WTLB	Utica, NY	5/0.5	U4	AN
WISE	Asheville, NC	5/1	U2	AN
WTIK	Durham, NC	5/1	U4	NH
KNOX	Grand Forks, ND	5	U2	AN
KNPT	Newport, OR	5/1	U2	NH
WNAE	Warren, PA	5	D1	D*
WDKD	Kingstree, SC	5	D1	D*
WDOD	Chattanooga, TN	5	U2	AN
WDXI	Jackson, TN	5/1	U2	NH
KTCK	Dallas, TX	9/5	U4	AN
KXTN	San Antonio, TX	5/0.28	U3	
WDCT	Fairfax, VA	5/0.5	U4	NH
WGH	Newport News, VA	20/5	U4	AN
KZXR	Prosser, WA	5	D1	D*
WSLW	White Sulphur Springs, WV	5	D1	D*
WIBA	Madison, WI	5	U2	AN
CHLW	St. Paul, AB	10	U2	AN
CIWW	Ottawa, ON	50	U4	AN
+Ip: USA 26				
1320kHz				
WZZK	Birmingham, AL	5	D1	D*
KYHN	Fort Smith, AR	5	U2	AN
KCTC	Sacramento, CA	5	U4	AN
WATR	Waterbury, CT	5/1	U4	AN
WZMZ	Hollywood, FL	5	U4	AN
WJGR	Jacksonville, FL	5	U2	AN
WAMR	Venice, FL	5/1	U2	AN
WHIE	Griffin, GA	5/0.08	U1	NH
KNCB	Vivian, LA	5	D1	D*
WARL	Attleboro, MA	5	U4	AN
WILS	Lansing, MI	5/1	U4	AN
WDMJ	Marquette, MI	5/0.135	U1	AN
KOZY	Grand Rapids, MN	5	U2	NH
WRJW	Picayune, MS	5	D1	D*
KSIV	St. Louis, MO	5/0.27	U2	AN
KOLT	Scottsbluff, NE	5/1	U2	AN
WDER	Derry, NH	10/5	U4	AN
WHHO	Hornell, NY	5	D1	D*
WCOG	Greensboro, NC	5	U4	AN
WKRK	Murphy, NC	5	D1	D*
WOBL	Oberlin, OH	1	U4	AN
WJAS	Pittsburgh, PA	5	U2	AN
WISW	Columbia, SC	5/2.5	U2	AN
KELO	Sioux Falls, SD	5	U2	AN
WKIN	Kingsport, TN	5/0.5	U2	AN
WMSR	Manchester, TN	5	D1	D*

Call	Location	kW	Lic	Ops
KXYZ	Houston, TX	5.4	U2	AN
KFNZ	Salt Lake City, UT	5	U3	AN
WVNZ	Richmond, VA	5/1.5	U4	AN
KXRO	Aberdeen, WA	5/1	U2	NH
WFHR	Wisconsin Rapids, WI	5/0.5	U2	AN
CHMB	Vancouver, BC	50	U4	AN
CKEC	New Glasgow, NS	25	U2	AN
CJMR	Mississauga, ON	20	U4	AN
+Ip: USA 31/Can 1				
1330kHz				
WPRN	Butler, AL	5	D	D
WZCT	Scottsboro, AL	5/0.5	U2	
KJLL	Tucson, AZ	2/5	U2	AN
KWKW	Los Angeles, CA	5	U2	AN
KLBS	Los Banos, CA	0.5/5	U2	
KSNA	Shasta Lake City	1	U4	F.Pl.
WJNX	Fort Pierce, FL	5/1	U2	AN
WEBY	Milton, FL	25/0.079	U5	NH
WCVC	Tallahassee, FL	5	D1	D*
WMLT	Dublin, GA	5/0.5	U2	AN
WKTA	Evanston, IL	5/0.5	U4	AN
WVHI	Evansville, IN	5/1	U2	AN
KWLO	Waterloo, IA	5	U4	AN
KNSS	Wichita, KS	5	U2	AN
WKDP	Corbin, KY	5	D3	D*
KVOL	Lafayette, LA	5/1	U2	AN
WJSS	Havre de Grace, MD	5/0.5	U2	AN
WRCA	Waltham, MA	5	U4	AN
WRCA	Watertown, MA	25/17	U4	F.Pl.
WTRX	Flint, MI	5/1	U4	AN
WLOL	Minneapolis, MN	9.7/5.1	U4	AN
WFTO	Fulton, MS	5	D1	D*
KGAK	Gallup, NM	5/1	U2	AN
WWRV	New York, NY	10/5	U4	AN
WEBO	Owego, NY	5	D1	D*
WSPQ	Springville, NY	1	U4	AN
KKPZ	Portland, OR	5	U3	AN
WFNN	Erie, PA	5	U4	AN
WYSN	Somerset, PA	5	D3	D*
WPJS	Conway, SC	5/0.027	U1	NH
WYRD	Greenville, SC	5	U2	AN
KLBO	Monahans, TX	5/1	U2	NH
WBTM	Danville, VA	5/1	U2	NH
WOLD	Marion, VA	5	D1	D
WESR	Onley, VA	5	D1	D*
KMBI	Spokane, WA	5	D1	D*
WHBL	Sheboygan, WI	5/1	U4	NH
KOVE	Lander, WY	5/1	U2	NH
CJYM	Rosetown, SK	10	U3	AN
+Ip: USA 30				
1340kHz				
USA 174 st's, mostly with 1kW, Canada 27 st's 20W to 1kW.				
CFYK	Yellowknife, NWT	2.5	U1	AN
ZBM	Hamilton, Bermuda	1	U1	NH
1350kHz				
WGAD	Gadsden, AL	5/1	U2	NH
KTDD	San Bernardino, CA	5/0.6	U4	AN
KSRO	Santa Rosa, CA	5	U2	AN
KGHF	Pueblo, CO	5/0.28	U1	AN
WNLK	Norwalk, CT	2.5/0.5	U4	AN
WINY	Putnam, CT	5	D1	D*
WMMV	Cocoa, FL	1	U2	AN
WFNS	Blackshear, GA	5	D1	D*
WNNG	Warner Robins, GA	15/0.5	U2	
KRLC	Lewiston, ID	5/1	U2	AN
KTIK	Nampa, ID	5	U2	AN
WOAM	Peoria, IL	1	U2	AN
WIOU	Kokomo, IN	5/1	U4	AN
KRNT	Des Moines, IA	5	U2	AN
WSMB	New Orleans, LA	5	U2	AN
WEZS	Laconia, NH	5	D1	D*
WHWH	Princeton, NJ	5	U4	AN
KABQ	Albuquerque, NM	5/0.12	U1	NH
WZNN	Black Mountain, NC	10/0.056	U1	
WTOU	Akron, OH	5	U3	AN
WOYK	York, PA	5/1	U2	AN
WPFM	Darlington, SC	1	U1	
KCOX	Jasper, TX	5/0.04	U1	NH
KCOR	San Antonio, TX	5	U2	AN
KACE	Fillmore, UT	5/1	U2	F.Pl.
WNVA	Norton, VA	5	D1	D*

Call	Location	kW	Lic	Ops
WGPL	Norfolk, VA	5	U4	AN
CKAD	Middleton, NS	1	U3	AN
CKDO	Oshawa, ON	10/5	U4	AN
+Ip: USA 37/Can 5				
1360kHz				
WMOB	Mobile, AL	5	D3	D*
KPXQ	Glendale, AZ	5/1	U2	AN
KFFA	Helena, AR	1	U2	NH
KFIV	Modesto, CA	4/1	U4	AN
KLSD	San Diego, CA	5/1	U1	AN
KHNC	Johnstown, CO	10/0.45	U2	NH
WDRC	Hartford, CT	5	U2	AN
WHNR	Cypress Gardens, FL	5/2.5	U4	AN
WCGL	Jacksonville, FL	5	D1	D
WKAT	Miami, FL	5/1	U1	AN
KSCJ	Sioux City, IA	5	U2	AN
WKYO	Caro, MI	1	U4	AN
WKMI	Kalamazoo, MI	5/1	U2	AN
KKBJ	Bemidji, MN	5/2.5	U2	AN
WNJC	Washington Township, NJ	5/0.8	U4	AN
KBUY	Ruidoso, NM	5/0.2	U1	NH
WYOS	Binghamton, NY	5/0.5	U4	AN
WCHL	Chapel Hill, NC	5/1	U2	AN
WCKY	Cincinnati, OH	5	U2	AN
WWOW	Conneaut, OH	5/0.036	U1	AN
KOHU	Hermiston, OR	4.3/1	U2	AN
KUIK	Hillsboro, OR	5	U2	AN
WPTT	McKeesport, PA	5/1	U2	AN
WPPA	Pottsville, PA	5/0.5	U4	AN
WELP	Easley, SC	5/0.036	U1	
KDJW	Amarillo, TX	5/0.137	U5	
KWWJ	Baytown, TX	5/1	U4	AN
KKTX	Corpus Christi, TX	1	U1	AN
KAHZ	Hurst, TX	50/0.89	U4	AN
WWWJ	Galax, VA	5	D1	D*
WHBG	Harrisonburg, VA	5	D1	D*
KKMO	Tacoma, WA	5	U1	AN
WTAQ	Green Bay, WI	10/5	U4	AN
KRKK	Rock Springs, WY	5/1	U2	AN
+Ip: USA 41				
1370kHz				
KWRM	Corona, CA	5/2.5	U4	AN
KPCO	Quincy, CA	5/0.5	U4	
KZSF	San Jose, CA	5	U4	AN
WOCA	Ocala, FL	5	D1	D*
WCOA	Pensacola, FL	5	U2	AN
WLOP	Jesup, GA	5	D1	D*
WGCL	Bloomington, IN	5/1	U4	NH
KDTH	Dubuque, IA	5	U2	AN
KGNO	Dodge City, KS	5/0.23	U1	AN
WGOH	Grayson, KY	5	D1	D
WDEA	Ellsworth, ME	5	U4	AN
WWLG	Pikesville, MD	50/7.7	U4	AN
WLJW	Cadillac, MI	5/1	U4	NH
KSUM	Fairmont, MN	1	U4	AN
KXTL	Butte, MT	5	U1	AN
WFEA	Manchester, NH	5	U4	AN
WELV	Ellenville, NY	5	D1	D*
WXXI	Rochester, NY	5	U2	AN
WLTC	Gastonia, NC	20/0.03	U1	AN
WLLN	Lillington, NC	5	D3	D*
WTAB	Tabor City, NC	5	D1	D*
WSPD	Toledo, OH	5	U2	AN
KAST	Astoria, OR	1	U2	AN
WKMC	Roaring Spring, PA	5	D3	D*
WDEF	Chattanooga, TN	5	U2	AN
KFRO	Longview, TX	1	U2	AN
KSOP	Salt Lake City, UT	5/0.5	U4	AN
WHEE	Martinsville, VA	5	D1	D*
WVMR	Frost, WV	5	D1	D*
WVLY	Moundsville, WV	5	D1	D*
WCCN	Neillsville, WI	5/0.04	U1	AN
CFOK	Westlock, AB	10	U2	AN
+Ip: USA 37				
1375kHz				
RFO	St. Pierre & Miquelon	20	U1	NH
1380kHz				
WVSA	Vernon, AL	5	D1	D*
KDXE	North Little Rock, AR	5/2.5	U4	
KTKZ	Sacramento, CA	5	U4	AN
KZFX	Salinas, CA	5	U4	AN

Call	Location	kW	Lic	Ops
WFNW	Naugatuck, CT	5/0.5	U4	NH
WTMC	Wilmington, DE	5/1	U4	AN
WELE	Ormond Beach, FL	5/2.5	U4	AN
WWMI	St. Petersburg, FL	5	U2	AN
WAOK	Atlanta, GA	5/4.2	U2	AN
WTJK	South Beloit, IL	5	U2	AN
WKJG	Fort Wayne, IN	5	U4	AN
KCIM	Carroll, IA	1	U4	NH
WYNK	Baton Rouge, LA	5	D3	D*
WPHM	Port Huron, MI	5	U4	NH
KLIZ	Brainerd, MN	5	U2	AN
KSLG	St. Louis, MO	5/1	U4	AN
WMYF	Portsmouth, NH	2.2/5	U4	AN
WABH	Bath, NY	10/0.45	U4	
WKDM	New York, NY	5/13	U4	AN
WKJV	Asheville, NC	25/1	U2	AN
WTOB	Winston-Salem, NC	5/2.5	U4	AN
KXCA	Lawton, OK	1	U4	AN
KMUS	Sperry, OK	7/0.25	U4	F.Pl.
KSRV	Ontario, OR	5/1	U2	NH
KOTA	Rapid City, SD	5	U2	AN
WLRM	Millington, TN	2.5/1	U4	AN
KHEY	El Paso, TX	5/0.5	U1	AN
WSYB	Rutland, VT	5/1	U2	AN
WBTK	Richmond, VA	5	U4	AN
KRKO	Everett, WA	5	U2	AN
WFCL	Clintonville, WI	3.9/1.8	U3	AN
CKPC	Brantford, ON	25	U4	AN
CKLC	Kingston, ON	10	U4	AN

+Ip: USA 36/Can 4

1390kHz

Call	Location	kW	Lic	Ops
WHMA	Anniston, AL	5/1	U2	NH
KLTX	Long Beach, CA	5	U4	AN
KLOC	Turlock, CA	5	U4	AN
WAJD	Gainesville, FL	5	D1	D*
WGRB	Chicago, IL	5	U4	AN
WKIC	Hazard, KY	5	D1	D*
WEGP	Presque Isle, ME	5	U2	
WPLM	Plymouth, MA	5	U4	AN
WLCM	Charlotte, MI	5	D3	D*
KXSS	Waite Park, MN	2.5/1	U4	AN
WROA	Gulfport, MS	5	U4	AN
WMER	Meridian, MS	5	D1	D*
KENN	Farmington, NM	5/1.3	U2	AN
KHOB	Hobbs, NM	5/0.5	U2	AN
WEOK	Poughkeepsie, NY	5	D3	D
WFBL	Syracuse, NY	5	U4	AN
WEED	Rocky Mount, NC	5/0.03	U1	AN
KRRZ	Minot, ND	5/1	U1	AN
WMPO	Middleport, OH	5/0.12	U1	AN
WNIO	Youngstown, OH	9.5/4.8	U2	AN
KCRC	Enid, OK	1	U3	AN
KSLM	Salem, OR	5/0.69	U1	AN
WLAN	Lancaster, PA	5/1	U4	AN
WRSC	State College, PA	2/1	U2	AN
WXTC	Charleston, SC	5	U2	AN
WTJS	Jackson, TN	5/1	U2	NH
KLGN	Logan, UT	5/0.5	U2	AN
WVAA	Burlington, VT	5	U2	AN
WZHF	Arlington, VA	5	U4	AN
KJOX	Yakima, WA	5/0.5	U2	AN
WRIG	Schofield, WI	10/7.2	U4	NH

+Ip: USA 26

1400kHz

USA 176 st's, mostly 1kW; Canada 7 st's, 40W-1kW.

Call	Location	kW	Lic	Ops
CBG	Gander, NL	4	U1	AN

1410kHz

Call	Location	kW	Lic	Ops
WIQR	Prattville, AL	5/1	U4	
WLVV	Mobile, AL	3.9	U3	AN
KERN	Bakersfield, CA	1	U1	AN
KRML	Carmel, CA	2.5/2	U4	NH
KMYC	Marysville, CA	5/1	U4	AN
KCAL	Redlands, CA	5/4	U4	NH
KIIX	Fort Collins, CO	1	U4	AN
WPOP	Hartford, CT	5	U4	AN
WDOV	Dover, DE	5	U4	AN
WMYR	Fort Myers, FL	5	U2	AN
WOBQ	Leesburg, FL	10/0.09	U1	
WHBT	Tallahassee, FL	5/0.18	U1	
WLAQ	Rome, GA	1	U2	AN
KKLO	Leavenworth, KS	5/0.5	U4	AN
KMYR	Wichita, KS	5/1	U4	AN
WHLN	Harlan, KY	5	D1	D*
KRWB	Roseau, MN	1	U2	NH
KOOQ	North Platte, NE	5/0.5	U2	AN
WELM	Elmira, NY	5/1	U4	AN
WSRC	Durham, NC	5/0.29	U4	AN
WING	Dayton, OH	5	U2	AN
KBNP	Portland, OR	5	D1	D
WLSH	Lansford, PA	5/0.06	U3	AN
KQV	Pittsburgh, PA	5	U4	AN
KRIL	Odessa, TX	1	U2	AN
WRIS	Roanoke, VA	5	D1	D*
WSCW	South Charleston, WV	5	D1	D*
WIZM	La Crosse, WI	5	U2	AN
KWYO	Sheridan, WY	5/0.5	U1	AN
CFUN	Vancouver, BC	50	U4	AN
CKSL	London, ON	10	U4	AN

+Ip: USA 38

1420kHz

Call	Location	kW	Lic	Ops
WACT	Tuscaloosa, AL	5	D1	D*
KXOW	Hot Springs, AR	5	D1	D*
KSTN	Stockton, CA	5/1	U4	AN
WLIS	Old Saybrook, CT	5/0.5	U2	AN
WDJA	Delray Beach, FL	5/0.46	U4	NH
WBRD	Palmetto, FL	2.5/1	U4	
WRCG	Columbus, GA	5	U2	AN
KIGO	St. Anthony, ID	50/0.016	U1	F.Pl.
WIMS	Michigan City, IN	5	U4	NH
WOC	Davenport, IA	5	U4	AN
WVJS	Owensboro, KY	5/1	U4	AN
WBSM	New Bedford, MA	5/1	U3	AN
WBEC	Pittsfield, MA	1	U2	AN
KTOE	Mankato, MN	5	U2	AN
WIGG	Wiggins, MS	5	D1	D*
WASR	Wolfeboro, NH	5	D1	D*
WACK	Newark, NY	5/0.5	U4	AN
WLNA	Peekskill, NY	5/1	U4	AN
WRMR	Cleveland, OH	5	U2	AN
WCOJ	Coatesville, PA	5	U2	AN
WCED	DuBois, PA	5/0.5	U2	AN
WEMB	Erwin, TN	5	D1	D*
WKSR	Pulaski, TN	1	U2	AN
WKCW	Warrenton, VA	22/0.06	U1	NH
KITI	Chehalis, WA	5	U4	AN
KUJ	Walla Walla, WA	5/0.93	U1	AN
WTCR	Kenova, WV	5/0.5	U2	AN
CKDY	Digby, NS	1	U3	AN
CKPT	Peterborough, ON	10/5	U4	AN

+Ip: USA 44

1430kHz

Call	Location	kW	Lic	Ops
WFHK	Pell City, AL	5	D1	D
KFIG	Fresno, CA	5	U4	AN
KMRB	San Gabriel, CA	5	U4	AN
KVVN	Santa Clara, CA	1/2.5	U4	AN
KEZW	Aurora, CO	10/5	U2	AN
WTMN	Gainesville, FL	10/0.045	U1	
WOIR	Homestead, FL	5/0.047	U1	AN
WLKF	Lakeland, FL	5/1	U1	AN
WLTG	Panama City, FL	5	U4	AN
WGFS	Covington, GA	5	D1	D*
WEEF	Highland Park, IL	1	U4	
WXNT	Indianapolis, IN	5	U2	AN
WYMC	Mayfield, KY	1	U2	AN
WNAV	Annapolis, MD	5/1	U2	AN
WPNI	Amherst, MA	5	D3	D*
WXKS	Everett, MA	5/1	U2	AN
WION	Ionia, MI	5	D3	D*
WRTH	St. Louis, MO	5	U4	AN
KRGI	Grand Island, NE	5/1	U2	AN
WNSW	Newark, NJ	5	U2	AN
KCRX	Roswell, NM	5/1	U2	NH
WENE	Endicott, NY	5	U2	AN
WDEX	Monroe, NC	2.5	U4	AN
WDJS	Mount Olive, NC	10/0.07	U5	
WFOB	Fostoria, OH	1	U4	NH
KTBZ	Tulsa, OK	25/5	U4	AN
KYKN	Keizer, OR	5	U2	AN
WVAM	Altoona, PA	5/1	U2	AN
WBLR	Batesburg, SC	5	D1	D*
WOWW	Germantown, TN	2.5	U4	
WPLN	Madison, TN	15/1	U2	

Call	Location	kW	Lic	Ops
KEES	Gladewater, TX	5/1	U2	NH
KCOH	Houston, TX	5/1	U4	AN
KLO	Ogden, UT	10/5	U4	AN
WHAN	Ashland, VA	5	D3	D*
WDIC	Clintwood, VA	5	D1	D*
KBRC	Mount Vernon, WA	5/1	U2	AN
KCLK	Asotin, WA	5/1	U4	AN
WEIR	Weirton, WV	1	U4	AN
WBEV	Beaver Dam, WI	1	U2	NH
WQOQ	Durand, WI	15/0.138	U4	
CHKT	Toronto, ON	50	U4	AN
+lp: USA 32				
1440kHz				
WLWI	Montgomery, AL	5/1	U2	AN
KAZG	Scottsdale, AZ	5	D1	D*
KITA	Little Rock, AR	5/0.24	U2	
KVON	Napa, CA	5/1	U4	AN
KDIF	Riverside, CA	1	U1	AN
KUHL	Santa Maria, CA	5/1	U2	AN
KRDZ	Wray, CO	5	D1	D
WWCL	Lehigh Acres, FL	5/1	U4	AN
WPRD	Winter Park, FL	5/1	U2	AN
WGIG	Brunswick, GA	5/1	U2	AN
WGEM	Quincy, IL	5/1	U4	AN
WROK	Rockford, IL	5/0.27	U5	AN
KMAJ	Topeka, KS	5/1	U3	AN
KMLB	Monroe, LA	5/1	U2	AN
WJAE	Portland, ME	5	U2	AN
WVEI	Worcester, MA	5	U4	AN
WMAX	Bay City, MI	5/2.5	U4	AN
WMKM	Inkster, MI	1	U4	AN
KDIZ	Golden Valley, MN	5/0.5	U2	AN
WRBE	Lucedale, MS	5	D1	D
WBLA	Elizabethtown, NC	5	D1	D*
WLXN	Lexington, NC	5/1	U2	AN
WHKW	Warren, OH	5	U4	AN
KMED	Medford, OR	5/1	U1	AN
KODL	The Dalles, OR	5/1	U2	NH
WDCL	Carbondale, PA	5	D1	D*
WGVL	Greenville, SC	5	U2	AN
WZYX	Cowan, TN	5	D1	D*
KPUR	Amarillo, TX	5/1	U2	AN
KEYS	Corpus Christi, TX	1	U2	AN
KTNO	University Park, TX	9/0.35	U4	AN
KETX	Livingston, TX	5	D1	D*
WKLV	Blackstone, VA	5	D1	D*
WHIS	Bluefield, WV	5/0.5	U1	AN
WAJR	Morgantown, WV	5/0.5	U4	AN
WNFL	Green Bay, WI	5/0.5	U4	AN
CKJR	Wetaskiwin, AB	10	U2	AN
1450kHz				
USA 178st's mostly with 1kW, Canada 14 st's 40W-1kW				
CHUC	Cobourg, ON	8/1	U4	AN
VSB1	Hamilton, Bermuda	1	U1	AN
1460kHz				
WMCJ	Cullman, AL	5/0.5	U2	AN
KTYM	Inglewood, CA	5/0.5	U4	AN
KION	Salinas, CA	10	U3	
KCNR	Shasta, CA	1	U1	
KZNT	Colorado Springs, CO	5/0.5	U2	AN
WZEP	DeFuniak Springs, FL	10/0.19	U1	AN
WZNZ	Jacksonville, FL	5	U2	AN
WXEM	Buford, GA	5	D1	D*
KXNO	Des Moines, IA	5	U2	AN
WBPA	Elkhorn City, KY	5	D1	D
WXOK	Baton Rouge, LA	5/1	U2	AN
WBET	Brockton, MA	5/1	U2	AN
WBRN	Big Rapids, MI	5/2.5	U2	NH
KDMA	Montevideo, MN	1	U2	NH
KIRL	St. Charles, MO	5/0.5	U4	AN
KXPN	Kearney, NE	5	D1	D*
KENO	Las Vegas, NV	10/0.65	U4	AN
WIFI	Florence, NJ	5/0.5	U3	AN
WDDY	Albany, NY	5	U2	AN
WHIC	Rochester, NY	5	U2	AN
WEWO	Laurinburg, NC	5	U4	AN
WHBK	Marshall, NC	5/0.14	U1	NH
KLTC	Dickinson, ND	5	U2	AN
WBNS	Columbus, OH	5/1	U2	AN
WTKT	Harrisburg, PA	2.4/4.2	U4	AN
WEMR	Tunkhannok, PA	5/1	U4	AN
WBCU	Union, SC	1	U2	NH
KTFW	Burleson, TX	5/0.7	U4	
WKDV	Manassas, VA	5	U4	AN
WRAD	Radford, VA	5/0.5	U2	AN
KARR	Kirkland, WA	5/2.5	U4	AN
KUTI	Yakima, WA	5/3.7	U2	AN
WBUC	Buckhannon, WV	5/0.025	U1	D*
CJOY	Guelph, ON	50/10	U3	AN
+lp: USA 36/Can 1				
1470kHz				
KUTY	Palmdale, CA	5	U4	AN
KIID	Sacramento, CA	5/1	U4	AN
WMMW	Meriden, CT	2.5	U4	AN
WLVU	Dunedin, FL	5	D1	D*
WWNN	Pompano Beach, FL	50/2.5	U4	AN
WRGA	Rome, GA	5	U2	AN
WCFJ	Chicago Heights, IL	1	U4	AN
WMBD	Peoria, IL	5	U4	AN
KWSL	Sioux City, IA	5	U4	AN
KAIR	Atchison, KS	1	U3	NH
KLCL	Lake Charles, LA	5/0.5	U1	AN
WLAM	Lewiston, ME	5	U3	AN
WJDY	Salisbury, MD	5	D3	D*
WTTR	Westminster, MD	1	U2	AN
WAZN	Marlboro, MA	5	U4	AN
WAZN	Watertown, MA	1.4/3.4	U4	AN
WFNT	Flint, MI	5/1	U4	AN
WKLZ	Kalamazoo, MI	0.8/1	U2	
KLBP	Brooklyn Park, MN	5	U4	AN
WTKO	Ithaca, NY	5/1	U2	AN
WWBG	Greensboro, NC	5	U4	
WJPI	Plymouth, NC	5	D1	D*
WTOE	Spruce Pine, NC	5	D1	D*
WLQR	Toledo, OH	1	U4	AN
WKAP	Allentown, PA	5	U2	AN
WQXL	Columbia, SC	5	D1	D*
WVOL	Berry Hill, TN	5/1	U4	NH
KYYW	Abilene, TX	5/1	U2	AN
KWRD	Henderson, TX	5	D1	D
KNFL	Tremonton, UT	10/1	U4	F.Pl.
WBTX	Broadway, VA	5	D1	D*
WTZE	Tazewell, VA	5/0.75	U1	
KELA	Centralia, WA	5/1	U1	ANH
KBSN	Moses Lake, WA	5/1	U4	AN
WEMM	Huntington, WV	5/0.072	U1	
WBKV	West Bend, WI	2.5	U4	NH
CJVB	Vancouver, BC	50	U4	AN
+lp: USA 39/Can 1				
1480kHz				
WLPH	Irondale, AL	5	D1	D*
WABB	Mobile, AL	5/4.4	U2	AN
KPHX	Phoenix, AZ	5/0.5	U4	AN
KTHS	Berryville, AR	5	D1	D*
KGOE	Eureka, CA	5/0.68	U1	AN
KYOS	Merced, CA	5	U2	AN
KVNR	Santa Ana, CA	5	U4	AN
WVOI	Marco Island, FL	1	U4	AN
WYZE	Atlanta, GA	5/0.04	U1	AN
WGUS	Augusta, GA	5	U2	AN
KRXR	Gooding, ID	5/0.093	U1	AN
WPFR	Terre Haute, IN	5/1	U4	AN
KQAM	Wichita, KS	5/1	U4	AN
WEZC	Neon, KY	5	D1	D*
WSAR	Fall River, MA	5	U3	AN
WGVU	Kentwood, MI	2.5/5	U2	AN
WSDS	Salem Township, MI	0.75/3.8	U4	AN
KAUS	Austin, MN	1	U4	AN
KKCQ	Fosston, MN	5/0.09	U1	NH
KLMS	Lincoln, NE	5/1	U4	AN
KKEL	Hobbs, NM	5/1	U2	AN
WZRC	New York, NY	5	U4	AN
WADR	Remsen, NY	5/0.02	U1	AN
WGFY	Charlotte, NC	4.4/5	U4	AN
WPFJ	Franklin, NC	5/0.01	U1	
WHBC	Canton, OH	15/5	U4	AN
WCNS	Latrobe, PA	0.5/1	U2	AN
WDAS	Philadelphia, PA	5/1	U4	AN
WBBP	Memphis, TN	5	D1	D*
KHCK	Dallas, TX	5/1.9	U4	AN
WNBX	Springfield, VT	5	D1	D*
WPWC	Dumfries-Triangle, VA	5/0.5	U4	AN

Call	Location	kW	Lic	Ops
WTOX	Glen Allen, VA	6.3/1.5	U4	
WTOY	Salem, VA	5	D1	D*
KBMS	Vancouver, WA	1/2.5	U2	AN
WLMV	Madison, WI	5	U4	AN
+lp: USA 39/Can 2				
1490kHz				
USA 177st's, mostly 1kW, Canada 7 st's 40W-1kW				
1500kHz				
KIEV	Culver City, CA	50/4.3	U4	AN
KSJX	San Jose, CA	10/5	U4	AN
WFIF	Milford, CT	5	D3	D
WTOP	Washington, DC	50	U4	AN
WDPC	Dallas, GA	5/0.5	D1	D
WBRI	Indianapolis, IN	5	D3	D
WLQV	Detroit, MI	50/10	U4	AN
KSTP	St. Paul, MN	50	U2	AN
WICY	Malone, NY	50/43	D4	F.Pl.
+lp: USA 30				
1510kHz				
KFNN	Mesa, AZ	22/0.1	U4	D*
KIRV	Fresno, CA	10	D3	D*
KSPA	Ontario, CA	10/1	U4	AN
KZMT	Piedmont, CA	8/0.23	U4	
KCUV	Littleton, CO	10/1.3	U4	AN
WWBC	Cocoa, FL	50/25	D4	D
WWZN	Boston, MA	50	U7	AN
KCTE	Independence, MO	10	D3	D*
KMRF	Marshfield, MO	5/0.16	D3	D
WAHT	Annville-Cleona, PA	5	D3	D
WPGR	Monroeville, PA	5/0.001	U4	
KMSD	Milbank, SD	5/1/0.014	U1	
WLAC	Nashville, TN	50	U2	AN
KQHN	Nederland, TX	5	D3	D
KLLB	West Jordan, UT	10	D1	D
KGA	Spokane, WA	50	U4	AN
WAUK	Waukesha, WI	10	D3	D*
CKOT	Tillsonburg, ON	10	D3	D
+lp: USA 36/Can 1				
1520kHz				
WTLM	Opelika, AL	5	D3	D
KMPG	Hollister, CA	5/3.5	U4	
KVTA	Oxnard, CA	10/1	U4	AN
WHIM	Apopka, FL	5/0.35	U4	D
WHOW	Clinton, IL	5/1	D1	D
WLGC	Greenup, KY	5/0.3	D1	D
KFXZ	Lafayette, LA	10/0.5	U2	AN
WTRI	Brunswick, MD	17	D3	D
WIZZ	Greenfield, MA	10	D3	D
WMLM	St. Louis, MI	1	U4	AN
KOLM	Rochester, MN	10/0.8	U8	AN
KRHW	Sikeston, MO	5/1.6	U7	NH
WWKB	Buffalo, NY	50	U3	AN
WDSL	Mocksville, NC	5/1	D1	D
WARR	Warrenton, NC	5	D1	D
KOKC	Oklahoma City, OK	50	U2	AN
KGDD	Oregon City, OR	50/15	U4	AN
+lp: USA 32				
1530kHz				
KFBK	Sacramento, CA	50	U3	AN
KHPI	Moreno Valley, CA	10/1.3	D3	D
KCMN	Colorado Springs, CO	15/0.016	U1	AN
WDJZ	Bridgeport, CT	5	D3	D
WYMM	Jacksonville, FL	50	D3	D
WTTI	Dalton, GA	10	D3	D
WLMR	Lapeer, MI	5	D3	D
KSMM	Shakopee, MN	8.6/0.01	U3	
WRPM	Poplarville, MS	10/1	D1	D*
WRTP	Durham, NC	10	D3	D
WSAI	Cincinnati, OH	50	U2	AN
KXTD	Wagoner, OK	5	D3	D
KZNX	Creedmore, TX	10/1/0.01	U7	
KGBT	Harlingen, TX	50/10	U2	AN
KCLR	Ralls, TX	5/1	D1	D*
+lp: USA 31/Can 2				
1540kHz				
KASA	Phoenix, AZ	10	D3	D
KMPC	Los Angeles, CA	50/10	U4	AN
KXEL	Waterloo, IA	50	U2	AN
WACA	Wheaton, MD	5	D1	D
WGIP	Exeter, NH	5/2.5	D1	D
WDCD	Albany, NY	50	U3	AN
WNWR	Philadelphia, PA	50	D3	D
WECZ	Punxsutawney, PA	5/1	D1	D
WTBI	Pickens, SC	10/1	D1	D*
KZMP	University Park, TX	32/0.75	U4	AN
KEDA	San Antonio, TX	5/1	U4	AN
WREJ	Richmond, VA	10	D3	D*
KXPA	Bellevue, WA	5	U2	AN
CHIN	Toronto, ON	50/30	U4	AN
+lp: USA 37/Can 2				
1550kHz				
WLOR	Huntsville, AL	50/0.4	U4	AN
KUAZ	Tucson, AZ	50	D1	D
KWRN	Apple Valley, CA	5/0.5	U2	
KXEX	Fresno, CA	5/2.5	U4	AN
KYCY	San Francisco, CA	50/40	U4	AN
WDZK	Bloomfield, CT	5/2.5	U4	NH
WAMA	Tampa, FL	10	D1	D*
WKTF	Augusta, GA	10/0.023	U1	
WAZX	Smyrna, GA	50/0.5	U4	AN
WPFC	Baton Rouge, LA	5	D1	D
WNTN	Newton, MA	10	D1	D
KAPE	Cape Girardeau, MO	5/0.05	U3	AN
KLFJ	Springfield, MO	5/0.03	U1	AN
KSFT	St. Joseph, MO	5	U2	AN
KKJY	Albuquerque, NM	5/0.02	U1	
WITK	Pittston, PA	10/0.5	U4	AN
WBSC	Bennettsville, SC	10/5	U2	NH
WBCV	Bristol, TN	5	D1	D*
KMRI	West Valley City, UT	10/0.5	U2	
WKBA	Vinton, VA	10	D3	D
WVAB	Virginia Beach, VA	5/0.01	U1	AN
KRPI	Ferndale, WA	50/10	U2	AN
KKAD	Vancouver, WA	50/12	U2	AN
WXVA	Charles Town, WV	5	D1	D*
WTUX	Madison, WI	5	D3	D*
CBE	Windsor, ON	10	U3	NH
+lp: USA 43/Can 1				
1560kHz				
WTKN	Daleville, AL	50/2.5	D1	D
KNZR	Bakersfield, CA	25/10	U2	AN
WRHC	Coral Gables, FL	45/4.4	U4	AN
WINV	Beverly Hills, FL	5/4.1	D1	D
WINT	Melbourne, FL	5	D1	D*
KLNG	Council Bluffs, IA	10/2.1	D1	D
WPAD	Paducah, KY	10/5	U4	AN
KMBH	Joplin, MO	10	D3	D*
WQEW	New York, NY	50	U4	AN
WCNW	Fairfield, OH	5/1	L3	D*
WTOD	Toledo, OH	5	D3	D*
WAGL	Lancaster, SC	50	D4	D*
KKAA	Aberdeen, SD	10/5	U4	AN
WWRO	Nashville, TN	10	D3	D*
KILE	Bellaire, TX	5	D3	D
KTXZ	West Lake Hills, TX	2.5	U4	AN
K...	Burbank, WA	50/15/1.4	U7	F.Pl.
KZIZ	Sumner, WA	5//3.3/2.4	U12	D*
+lp: USA 36/Can 1				
1570kHz				
KCVR	Lodi, CA	5/0.5	U4	AN
KPRO	Riverside, CA	5/0.2	U1	AN
KTGE	Salinas, CA	5/0.5	U4	AN
KSXT	Loveland, CO	7/0.018	U1	AN
WTWB	Auburndale, FL	5	D1	D*
WVOJ	Fernandina Beach, FL	10/0.03	U1	
WSSA	Morrow, GA	5/0.05	U1	
WFRL	Freeport, IL	5/0.5	U3	AN
WKDB	Baltimore, MD	5	D1	D*
KBCV	Hollister, MO	5/3	U4	F.Pl.
WFLR	Dundee, NY	5/0.44	U1	AN
K...	Warrenton, OR	50/1	U4	F.Pl.
WISP	Doylestown, PA	5/0.95	U3	AN
WNKX	Centerville, TN	5	D1	D*
WCLE	Cleveland, TN	5/0.08	U1	AN
WTRB	Ripley, TN	28/0.5	U4	D
WLKD	Minocqua, WI	5	D1	D
CKMW	Winkler, MB	10	U4	AN
CFAV	Laval, QC	10	U4	
+lp: USA 63				
1580kHz				
KMIK	Tempe, AZ	50	U2	AN
KBLA	Santa Monica, CA	50	U4	AN

Call	Location	kW	Lic	Ops
KWYD	Colorado Springs, CO	10	D1	D
WNFT	Bithlo, FL	10	D3	D
WTCL	Chattahoochee, FL	10	D1	D
WSRF	Fort Lauderdale, FL	10/5	U4	AN
WEAM	Columbus, GA	2.3/1	U2	
WXRA	Georgetown, KY	10	D3	D
KXZZ	Lake Charles, LA	1	U2	AN
WPGC	Morningside, MD	50/0.27	U4	AN
WZZJ	Pascagoula, MS	5	D3	D
WLIM	Patchogue, NY	10/0.5	U7	AN
WVKO	Columbus, OH	5/0.29	U4	AN
KGAL	Lebanon, OR	1	U3	AN
WDAB	Travelers Rest, SC	5/0.01	U1	AN
WNPZ	Knoxville, TN	5/1	D1	D
WLIJ	Shelbyville, TN	5	D1	D
WPUV	Pulaski, VA	5/1	D1	D
CHUC	Cobourg, ON	10	U4	F.Pl.
+lp: USA 50				
1590kHz				
WVNA	Tuscumbia, AL	5/1	U2	AN
KLIV	San Jose, CA	5	U2	AN
KKZZ	Ventura, CA	5	U4	AN
WPSL	Port St. Lucie, FL	5	D1	D
WRXB	St. Petersburg Beach, FL	5/1	U4	AN
WALG	Albany, GA	5/1	U4	AN
WQCH	LaFayette, GA	5	D1	D*
WONX	Evanston, IL	3.5/1	U2	NH
WAIK	Galesburg, IL	5/0.005	U3	AN
WNTS	Beach Grove, IN	5/0.5	U4	AN
KVGB	Great Bend, KS	5	U2	AN
WJRO	Glen Burnie, MD	1	U4	AN
WTVB	Coldwater, MI	5/1	U2	AN
KCNN	East Grand Forks, MN	5/1	U2	NH
WZRX	Jackson, MS	5/1	U2	AN
KQLO	Sun Valley, NV	5	D1	D*
WSMN	Nashua, NH	5	U3	AN
WAUB	Auburn, NY	0.5/1	U4	AN
WA3D	Drockport, NY	1	U4	AN
WGGO	Salamanca, NY	5	D1	D*
WHPY	Clayton, NC	5	D3	D*
WAKR	Akron, OH	5	U2	AN
KMBD	Tillamook, OR	5/1	U2	NH
WCBG	Chambersburg, PA	5/1	U2	AN
WPWA	Chester, PA	2.5/1	U2	AN
WARV	Warwick, RI	5	U4	AN
WKTP	Jonesborough, TN	5	U3	AN
KELP	El Paso, TX	50/0.8	U4	NH
KYOK	Houston, TX	5	U2	AN
KDAV	Lubbock, TX	1	U4	AN
WFTH	Richmond, VA	5	D1	D*
KLFE	Seattle, WA	5	U2	AN
WIXK	New Richmond, WI	5	D1	D*
+lp: USA 50				
1600kHz				
WEUP	Huntsville, AL	5/0.5	U2	AN
WXVI	Montgomery, AL	5/1	U4	AN
KXEW	S. Tucson, AZ	2.5/1	U4	AN
KNWA	Bellefonte, AR	5	D1	D
KGST	Fresno, CA	5	U2	AN
KMNY	Pomona, CA	5	U2	AN
KUBA	Yuba City, CA	5/2.5	U2	AN
KCKK	Lakewood, CO	5	U2	AN
WIBF	Dover, DE	5/1	U2	AN
WQOP	Atlantic Beach, FL	5/0.09	U1	
WMNE	West Palm Beach, FL	5/4.7	U3	AN
WAOS	Austell, GA	20/0.067	U1	
KCRG	Cedar Rapids, IA	5	U2	AN
WUNR	Boston, MA	5	U3	AN
WHNP	East Longmeadow, MA	2.5	U4	AN
WAAM	Ann Arbor, MI	5	U4	AN
WMHG	Muskegon, MI	5	U2	AN
KZGX	Watertown, MN	5	U3	AN
KATZ	St. Louis, MO	6/3.5	U4	AN
KANM	Albuquerque, NM	5/0.13	U1	AN
WEHH	Elmira Heights-Horseheads, NY	5	D1	D
WWRL	New York, NY	25/5	U4	AN
WTZQ	Hendersonville, NC	5/0.21	U1	AN
KEED	Eugene, OR	5/1	U2	AN
WHJB	Bedford, PA	5	D1	D*
WMQM	Lakeland, TN	50/0.035	U1	
KQXX	Brownsville, TX	1	U4	NH
KRVA	Cockrell Hill, TX	5/1	U4	AN
KOGT	Orange, TX	1	U4	AN
KOKE	Pflugerville, TX	5/0.7	U4	
KRRD	Centerville, UT	5/1	U2	AN
WXMY	Saltville, VA	10/0.1	U4	
KVRI	Blaine, WA	50/10	U4	AN
WZZW	Milton, WV	5	D1	D*
WKKX	Wheeling, WV	5	D1	D*
WRPN	Ripon, WI	5	U4	NH
+lp: USA 37				
1610kHz				
KALT	Atlanta, TX	10/1	U1	
CJWI	Montreal	1	U1	AN
1620kHz				
KSMH	Auburn, CA	10/1	U1	AN
WNRP	Gulf Breeze, FL	10/1	U1	
KBLI	Blackfoot, ID	10/1	U1	
WHLY	South Bend, IN	10/1	U1	AN
KOZN	Bellevue, NE	10/1	U1	AN
WTAW	College Station, TX	10/1	U1	AN
KYIZ	Renton, WA	10/1	U1	AN
1630kHz				
WRDW	Augusta, GA	10/1	U1	AN
KCJJ	Iowa City, IA	10/1	U1	AN
KKGM	Fort Worth, TX	10/1	U1	
KKWY	Fox Farm, WY	10/1	U1	AN
1640kHz				
KDIA	Vallejo, CA	10/1	U1	AN
WTNI	Biloxi, MS	10/1	U1	AN
KFNY	Enid, OK	10/1	U1	
KDZR	Lake Oswego, OR	10/1	U1	AN
KBJA	Sandy, UT	10/1	U1	AN
WKSH	Sussex, WI	10/1	U1	AN
1650kHz				
KWHN	Fort Cmith, AR	10/1	U1	AN
KFOX	Torrance, CA	10/0.49	U1	AN
KBJD	Denver, CO	10/1	U1	AN
KCNZ	Cedar Falls, IA	10/1	U1	AN
KBIV	El Paso, TX	8.5/0.85	U1	
WHKT	Portsmouth, VA	10/1	U1	AN
1660kHz				
KTIQ	Merced, CA	10/1	U1	
WCNZ	Marco Island, FL	10/1	U1	AN
KXTR	Kansas City, KS	10/1	U1	AN
WQSN	Kalamazoo, MI	10/1	U1	AN
WWRU	Jersey City, NJ	10	U2	AN
WFNA	Charlotte, NC	10/1	U1	AN
KQWB	West Fargo, ND	10/1	U1	AN
KRZX	Waco, TX	10/1	U1	AN
KXOL	Brigham City, UT	10/1	U1	AN
1670kHz				
KHPY	Moreno Valley, CA	10/9	U4	
KNRO	Redding, CA	10/1	U1	AN
WMWR	Dry Branch, GA	10/1	U1	AN
WTDY	Madison, WI	10/1	U1	AN
1680kHz				
KAVT	Fresno, CA	10/1	U1	AN
WLAA	Winter Garden, FL	10/1	U1	AN
KRJO	Monroe, LA	10/1	U1	
WDSS	Ada, MI	10/0.68	U1	AN
WTTM	Lindenwold, NJ	10/1	U1	AN
KTFH	Seattle, WA	10/1	U1	AN
1690kHz				
KFSG	Roseville, CA	10/1	U1	
KDDZ	Arvada, CO	10/1	U1	AN
WSWK	Avondale Estates, GA	10/1	U1	
WRLL	Berwyn, IL	10/1	U1	
WPTX	Lexington Park, MD	10/1	U1	AN
1700kHz				
WEUV	Huntsville, AL	10/1	U1	AN
WJCC	Miami Springs, FL	10/1	U1	AN
KBGG	Des Moines, IA	10/1	U1	AN
KVNS	Brownsville, TX	8.8/0.88	U1	AN
KTBK	Sherman, TX	10/0.7	U1	AN

CENTRAL AMERICA, CARIBBEAN AND MEXICO

Abbreviations: Broadc.=Broadcasting, Corp.=Corporation, Em=Emisora, LV=La Voz, Nal=Nacional, Nat=National, Sce=Service.
Call signs: Costa Rica TI_, Cuba CM_, Dominican Republic HI_, El Salvador YS_, Guatemala TG_, Honduras HR_, Mexico XE_, Nicaragua YN_, Panama HO_

Email: tore.larsson@beta.telenordia.se

kHz	kW	Ctry	Call	Station, location
530	18	CTR	CAL	R. Sinfonola, Cartago
530		CUB		R. Rebelde
530	100	TCA		R. Vision Cristiana Internacional
535	10	GRD		Grenada Broadcasting Network
540	1	CUB	HV	R. Rebelde, Sancti Spíritus
540	5	DOM	CM	R. ABC, Sto Domingo
540	0.025	GTM		R. Amistad, San Pedro de Laguna
540		GTM		R. Cobán, Cobán
540	1	HND	OW	R. Atlántida, La Ceiba
540		HND		R. Nuevo Mundo, Tegucigalpa
540	5/0.2	MEX	HS	La Norteñita, Los Mochis
540	1/0.25	MEX	TX	La Ranchera de Paquime, Nuevo Casas Grandes
540	5/1	MEX	MIT	LV de BalunCanán, Comitán
540	25	MEX	SURF	Oldies 540, Tijuana
540	0.5	MEX	WA	W Radio, Monterrey
540	150	MEX	WA	W Radio, San Luis Potosí
540	25	NCG	OW	R. Corporación, Managua
540	10	PNR	PU	R. 540 AM, Panamá
540	10	PNR	U23	R. Mía, David
540	5	SLV	HV	R.Restauración, San Salvador
550	20/2	CTR	SCL	R. Santa Clara, Cd. Quesada
550	10	CUB	DN	R. Rebelde, Guantánamo
550	1	CUB		R. Rebelde, Manzanillo
550	30	CUB		R. Rebelde, Pinar del Río
550	0.5	HND	XD	R. Manantial, Sta Rosa de Copán
550	1	HND	XT	R. X, Tegucigalpa
550	1.5	JMC		RJR Llandilo (Westmoreland)
550	5/0.15	MEX	PL	La Super Estación, Cd. Cuauhtémoc
550	1/0.25	MEX	ZK	Poder 55, Tepatitlán
550	5/0.35	MEX	QW	QW La Poderosa, Mérida
550	1.5/0.25	MEX	HLL	R. Mar, Salina Cruz
550	5/0.15	MEX	TNC	R. Nayarit, Tepic
550	1/0.25	MEX	ACD	R. Sensación, Acapulco
550	5/0.25	MEX	KL	Romántica 550, Jalapa
550	10	NCG	CH	R. 19 de Julio "la 19", Chinandega
550	5	PTR	WPAB	Cadena R. Puerto Rico, Ponce
550	2	SLV	FG	R.Variedades, Sonsonate
555	10	SCN		Ziz R.
560	5	CUB		R. Rebelde, Moa,
560	5	DOM	AA	R. Ritmos, Santiago
560	10	GTM	RV	R. 5-60, Guatemala
560	1	GTM		R. Quetzal, Malacatán
560	1	HND	OS	R. Castilla, Tocoa
560	1	HND	OY	R. Jupiter, Comayagua
560	5	HND	RZ	R. Juticalpa, Juticalpa
560	1	HND	OT	R. Montserrat, Danlí
560	1	HND	PX	R. Tropical "Cadena Radial Reloj", San Pedro Sula
560	5/0.5	MEX	GIK	Acerera, Monclova
560	10/1	MEX	MZA	La Buena Onda del Pacífico, Cihuatlán
560	1/0.5	MEX	QAA	La Poderosa, Chetumal
560	5/0.25	MEX	SRD	La Que Suave, Santiago Papasquiaro
560	10/0.25	MEX	XZ	La Z, Zacatecas
560	2/0.25	MEX	IN	LV del Valle, Cintalapa
560	5/0.5	MEX	OC	R. Chapultepec, México
560	1/0.5	MEX	YO	R. Lobo/R. 5-60, Huatabampo
560	30	NCG		R. 5-60 "La Poderosa", Managua
560	1	PNR	H2	RPC Radio, Colón
570	6.5	CTR	CDL	R. Libertad, Desamparados
570	30	CUB	DC	R. Reloj, Santa Clara
570	10/5	DOM	MS	R. Cristal, Sto Domingo
570	1	GTM	PA	R. Palmeras, Escuintla
570	1	HND	OX	R. El Triunfo, Choluteca
570	10	HTI		Vision 2000,Port-au-Prince
570	5/0.5	MEX	BJB	La Estación del Barrilito/R. Alegría, Monterrey
570	1/0.25	MEX	TJ	La Invasora/R. Alegría, Torreón
570	2/1.7	MEX	LQ	R. Fórmula, Primera Cadena Nacional, Morelia
570	10/1	MEX	VX	R. Fórmula/La Grande de Tabasco, Villahermosa
570	5/0.25	MEX	OA	R. Mexicana, Oaxaca
570	5/1	MEX	VJP	R. Xicotepec, Xicotepec de Juárez
570	2.5	MEX	ME	Radio Valladolid "La Poderosa de Oriente", Valladolid
570	5/0.5	MEX	KZX	Tejano KZK, Cd.Guzmán
570	2.5/0.25	MEX	UK	U-K, Caborca
570	5	NCG		R. 5-70, Chinandega
570	5	PNR	S	R. Soberana, Panamá
570	10	SLV	KT	R.Cadena Central, La Libertad
580	5	CUB	DF	R. Rebelde, Baracoa
580	10	CUB	AM	R. Rebelde, Mantua
580	3	DOM	AS	R. Montecristi, Montecristi
580	5	GTM	Y	R. Progreso, Guatemala
580	3	HND	ZQ	R. Tegucigalpa, Tegucigalpa
580	1	HND	OU	R. Unión, Gracias
580		HND	EO	Super Estrella de Occidente, Sta Rosa de Copán
580	1.5	JMC		RJR Baileys Vale (St. Mary)
580	1/0.5	MEX	DZ	Canal 58, Córdoba
580	10/1	MEX	AV	Canal 58/R. Guadalajara, Guadalajara
580	1/0.25	MEX	UE	Imperio, Tuxtla Gutiérrez
580	1/0.2	MEX	BJ	La Ranchera, Cd.Victoria
580	5/2.5	MEX	MU	La Rancherita del Aire, Piedras Negras
580	1/0.25	MEX	YI	Mix AM, Cancún
580	1/0.25	MEX	HO	R. 13/La Fuerza de la Palabra, Cd.Obregón
580	5/0.7	MEX	FI	R. Mexicana, Chihuahua
580	0.25	MEX	UAQ	R. Universidad, Querétaro
580	1	NCG	EA	R. 5-80, Managua
580	10	PNR	H4	RPC Radio, David
580	10	PTR	WKAQ	R. Reloj, San Juan
590	5	CTR	RN	R. Nacional, San José
590	30	CUB	HI	R. Rebelde, Santa Clara
590	10	DMA		Hillsborough
590	10/5	DOM	DV	R. Santa María, La Vega
590	5	GTM	RQ	R. Quiché, Sta Cruz del Quiché
590	1	HND	OV	LV de Lepaguare, Juticalpa
590		HND		R. Agricola, El Zamorano
590	1	HTI		R. Ti Moun,Port-au-Prince
590	1	MEX	XA	Exa, Hermosillo
590	5/0.5	MEX	FD	La Consentida, Reynosa
590	10/1	MEX	CJU	La Explosiva, Puerto Vallarta
590	1/0.25	MEX	GTO	La Nueva R. Cañon, León
590	1	MEX	E	R. Fiesta Mexicana, Durango
590	1	MEX	OM	R. Fórmula, Coatzacoalcos
590	5/1	MEX	ZZZ	R. Z, Tapachula
590	2 1/2	MEX	PH	Tuya 590, México
590	10	PNR	H3	RPC Radio, Chitré
600	150	CUB	KV	R. Rebelde, Urbano Noris,
600		DOM		R. Studio 600 AM, Sto Domingo
600		DOM	SD	R. Televisión Dominicana, El Seybo
600	1	GTM	RC	Emisoras Unidas Campesina, Escuintla
600	5/1	MEX	BB	La Comadre, Acapulco
600	5/1	MEX	HW	La Estación del Poder, Rosario
600	5/1	MEX	CV	La Gran Compañía, Cd.Valles
600	5/0.5	MEX	OB	La Máquina Musical, Pichucalco
600	1	MEX	DN	La Mexicana, Torreón
600	1/0.5	MEX	MN	La Regiomontaña, Monterrey
600	10	MEX	LAZ	La Z, Cd.Guzmán
600	10/1	MEX	OCH	Quién Radio, Ocosingo
600	1	MEX	TA	R. Fórmula, Zitácuaro
600	20/1	MEX	Z	R. Fórmula,Tercera Cadena Nacional, Mérida
600	10	NCG	LD	La Nueva Ya, Managua
600	5	PTR	WAEL	R. 600, Mayagüez
600	3	SLV	NK	Vox FM, San Salvador
610	4	CTR	RSU	R. María, San José
610	1	CUB	AN	R. Rebelde, Bahía Honda
610	1	CUB	HI	R. Reloj, Trinidad

kHz	kW	Ctry	Call	Station, location
610	5/1	DOM	JR	R. Amanecer, Santiago
610	1	DOM	SD	R. Televisión Dominicana, Pedernales
610	0.5	GTM	GA	R. Alianza, Guatemala
610	10	HND	LD	R. América "LV Informativo del Pueblo", Tegucigalpa
610	10	HND	LD	R. América, Sta Rosa de Copán
610	0.2	HTI		R. L'Eternal est Grand, Port-au-Prince
610	5/0.5	MEX	BX	La B-X, Sabinas
610	1/0.5	MEX	GS	La Ley, Guasave
610	1/0.5	MEX	KZ	LV del Istmo, Tehuantepec
610	1/0.5	MEX	JA	Mundo 610, Jalapa
610	1	MEX	SAC	R. Lobo, Saltillo
610	10/1	MEX	UF	Stereo Mía, Uruapan
610	5/0.1	MEX	EL	Super Canal 610/La L, Fresnillo
610	10	PNR	HM	RPC Radio, Panamá
610	0.2 5/1	PTR	WEXS	X-61, Patillas
610	10	SLV	SS	R.El Salvador, Morazán
610	50	TRD		National Broadcasting Network
620	10	ATG		Antigua & Barbuda Broadcasting Service
620	30	CUB	GN	R. Rebelde, Colón
620	1	CUB	KF	R. Rebelde, Moa
620	10	DOM	SD	R. Televisión Dominicana, Sto Domingo
620	5	GTM	PQ	R. 6-20, San Cristóbal
620	1	HND	LD	R. América, Comayagua
620	1	HND	LD	R. América, Juticalpa
620	1	HND	LP17	R. Continental, San Pedro Sula
620	1/0.25	MEX	GH	Bonita, Reynosa
620	1/0.5	MEX	CK	Digital 620, Durango
620	5/1	MEX	BU	La Norteñita, Chihuahua
620	5	MEX	SS	La Tropical, Ensenada
620	50/10	MEX	NK	R. 6-20, México
620	2.5/0.5	MEX	WZ	R. 6-20, San Luis Potosí
620	1/0.25	MEX	KX	R. Cultural de la Zona Maya, Felipe Carillo Puerto
620	2.5/0.11	MEX	HGR	R. Fórmula 620, Villahermosa
620	5/1	MEX	OO	R. Triunfadora, Tepic
620	50	NCG	N	R. Nicaragua, Managua
630	5	CUB		R. Progreso, Pinar del Río
630	1	DOM	SD	R. Televisión Dominicana, San Juan
630		GTM	EL	R. El Porvenir, Sta Elena
630	1	HND	LD	R. América, Choluteca
630	1	HND	LD	R. América, La Ceiba
630	1	HTI		Rdf Jeremienne, Jeremie
630	1	HTI		V. des ODS, Port-au-Prince
630	5	MEX	JR	Coral 630, Zihuatanejo
630	5/0.25	MEX	OPE	Exa, Mazatlán
630	1/0.5	MEX	CCQ	La Nueva Coqueta, Cancún
630	50	MEX	FB	La Nueva F-B Romántica, Monterrey
630	10/0.75	MEX	FU	LV Amiga de AM, Cosamaloapan
630	2/0.25	MEX	FX	R. 6-30, Guaymas
630	1/0.15	MEX	ERO	R. Tamaulipas, Altamira
630	10/0.5	MEX	JB	Radiarte 630, Guadalajara
630	1	PNR		R. Capital, Panamá
630	1	PNR	J35	R. Provincias, Chitré
630	5	PTR	WUNO	NotiUno, San Juan
630	10	SLV	LN	R. Promesa, San Salvador
640	20	CTR	AD	R. Rica, San José
640	50	CUB	BC	R. Progreso, Guanabacoa
640	10	CUB	DQ	R. Progreso, Las Tunas
640	5	CUB	DD	R. Rebelde, Las Mercedes
640	10	DOM	SD	R. Televisión Dominicana, Santiago
640	40	GDL	-	R. Guadeloupe, Point-à-Pitre
640	10	GTM	W	R. Nacional "LV de Guatemala", Guatemala
640		HND		LV de Centroamérica, Sta Rosa de Copán
640		HND		R. Estéreo Canaan, Sta Bárbara
640	1	HND	NN4	R. Televisión, Tegucigalpa
640	1	MEX	JUA	La Caliente, Cd.Juárez
640	50	MEX	NQ	La N-Q/R. 6-40, Tulancingo
640	1/0.25	MEX	TAM	La Poderosa, Cd.Victoria
640	5/1	MEX	WM	R. 6-40, San Cristóbal de las Casas
640	10/1	MEX	HHI	R. Uno, Hidalgo del Parral
640	1	MEX	HDL	XEHDL, Huajuapán de León
640	10	NCG	LN	R. Ranchera "La Mera, Mera", Managua
640	2.5	PNR		Caracol, La Palma
640	2.5	PNR	K22	R.CPR, Colón
650	1	CUB	DC	R. Rebelde, Media Luna
650	1	CUB	KU	R. Rebelde, Stgo de Cuba
650	15/5	DOM	AT	R. Universal, Sto Domingo
650		HND		LV de Centroamérica, La Ceiba
650	25	HND	VW	LV de Centroamérica, San Pedro Sula
650		HND		LV de Centroamérica, Siguatepeque
650	15	HND	LD	R. América, Danlí
650	1	HND		R. Católica Olancho, Olanchito
650		HND		R. Turquesa, Siguatepeque
650	2/0.1	MEX	TNT	65 La Ley, Los Mochis
650	1	MEX	VG	Éxtasis, Mérida
650	5/0.25	MEX	CHH	La Explosiva, Chilpancingo
650	5/0.2	MEX	PX	La Voz del Ángel, Puerto Ángel
650	5/1	MEX	ZM	La Zamorana, Zamora
650	2.5/0.1	MEX	VSS	R. 13/La Fuerza de la Palabra, Hermosillo
650	1/0.5	MEX	VILL	R. Felicidad, Villahermosa
650	10/0.5	MEX	EJ	R. Paraíso, Puerto Vallarta
650	0.5	MEX	RCG	XERCG, Cd. Acuña
650	10/8	NCG	RD	R. Diriangén "La Super D", Granada
650	12	NCG	RI	R. Septentrión, Matagalpa
650	5	PNR	S22	R. Mía "Cadena Nacional", Panamá
655	10	SLV	SS	R.El Salvador, San Salvador
660	30	CUB	HG	R. Progreso, Santa Clara
660	3	DOM	AM	R. Visión Cristiana, Santiago
660	3	GTM	Q	R. Nacional "LV de Quetzaltenago",
660	3	HND	NN18	LV de Honduras, La Ceiba
660	5	HTI		R. Lumiere, Port-au-Prince
660	3	LCA		R. St Lucia, Castries
660	50	MEX	EY	La Consentida, Aguascalientes
660	5/1	MEX	AR	La Mexicana, Tampico
660	2.5/0.25	MEX	SJC	La Tremenda, San José del Cabo
660	10/0.25	MEX	FZ	Noti-Radio 6-60, Monterrey
660	1	MEX	CPR	R. Chan Santa Cruz-LV de los Mayas, Félipe Carillo Puerto
660	1/0.5	MEX	YG	R. Fiesta Mexicana, Matías Romero
660	1/0.5	MEX	WX	R. Fórmula, Durango
660	5/1	MEX	ACB	Radio 6-60, Cd.Delicias
660	50	MEX	DTL	XEDTL -60, México
660	5	PNR		La Nueva Exitosa, Sabana Grande
660	1	PNR	F33	RPC Radio, Bocas del Toro
670	10	CTR	RM	R. Monumental, San José
670	50	CUB	BA	R. Rebelde, Arroyo Arenas
670	5	DOM	BS	R. Dial, San Pedro de Macorís
670	1	DOM	SD	R. Televisión Dominicana, Barahona
670	10	GTM	RT	Emisoras Unidas Central, Guatemala
670	1	HND	NN20	LV de Honduras, Sta Rosa de Copán
670	10	HND	N	LV de Honduras, Tegucigalpa
670	5/0.25	MEX	IS	La Rancherita Consentida, Cd.Guzmán
670	5	MEX	SIC	R. ACIR, Córdoba
670	1/0.1	MEX	QG	R. Lobo, Querétaro
670	5/0.25	MEX	TOR	R. Ranchita, Torreón
670		NCG	RC	R. Caribe, Puerto Cabezas
670	5	PNR	LY	R. Hogar, Panamá
680	1	CUB	HN	R. Progreso, Cienfuegos
680	1	CUB	DB	R. Progreso, Stgo de Cuba
680	10	CUB	JV	R. Rebelde, Ciego de Ávila
680	3	DOM	JX	R. Zamba, San Ignacio de Sabaneta
680	10	GTM	VP	R. Norte, Cobán
680	1	HND	NN7	LV de Honduras, Danlí
680	1	HND	NN10	LV de Honduras, Juticalpa
680	10	HND	NN8	LV de Honduras, San Pedro Sula
680	10	HND	NN2	LV de Honduras, Siguatepeque
680	10	HND	NN11	LV de Honduras, Tocoa
680	5	MEX	OAX	Aro AM, Oaxaca
680	1/0.25	MEX	FO	Energía 6-80, Chihuahua
680	1	MEX	CHG	Fiesta Mexicana, Chilpancingo
680	2. 5/1	MEX	PY	Foro 6-80, Mérida
680	1/0.1	MEX	FJ	La Consentida, Teziutlán
680	1/0.5	MEX	ORO	La Tremenda, Guasave
680	10/5	MEX	LG	LG, La Grande, León
680	1	MEX	SON	R. ACIR, Hermosillo
680	5/0.5	MEX	KQ	R. Mexicana, Tapachula
680	10/2	NCG	AM	R. La Primerísima, Managua
680	5	PNR	F32	Súper Z Stereo, David
680	5	PNR		Voz Sin Fronteras, Metetí
680	0.4/0.4	PTR	WAPA	Arecibo (synchr. WAPA)
680	10	PTR	WAPA	Cadena WAPA "Guapa", San Juan
690	50	AIA		The Caribbean Beacon
690	20	CUB		R. Progreso, Jovellanos
690	10	DOM	AW	R. Guarachita, Sto Domingo
690	1	GTM	VB	R. Tamazulapa, Jutiapa
690	1	HND	NN3	LV de Honduras, Choluteca
690	1	HND	NN9	LV de Honduras, Tela
690	10	HTI		V. des Travailleurs, Port-au-Prince
690	77.5	MEX	TRA	Extra Sports, Tijuana
690	50/5	MEX	N	La 69, México
690	10/1	MEX	RG	La Deportiva 6-90/La R-G, Monterrey
690	10/0.25	MEX	ST	La Invasora, Mazatlán
690	1.5/0.5	MEX	XL	La Ley, Pátzcuaro

kHz	kW	Ctry	Call	Station, location
690	2/0.25	MEX	AFA	La Más Picuda, Coatzacoalcos
690	5/1	MEX	CS	La Z/La Grande de Manzanillo, Manzanillo
690	50/1	MEX	MA	M-A/La Madre de Todas, Fresnillo
690	10/5	NCG	RH	R. Hermanos, Matagalpa
690	5	PNR		R. Evangelio Vivo, Panamá
690	10	PNR	R43	R. Veraguas, Santiago
700	10	CTR	JC	R. Sonora, San José
700	1	CUB	DU	R. Enciclopedia, Guantánamo
700		CUB		R. Progreso, Baracoa
700	1	CUB	GA	R. Rebelde, Sancti Spíritus
700	1.5	DOM	DC	R. Mao, Mao, Valverde
700	15	GTM	HR	R. Mundial, Guatemala
700	5	HND	GP	R. Reloj, Tegucigalpa
700	1.5	JMC		RJR Hague (Trelawny)
700	2.5/0.1	MEX	VC	Canal 70, Córdoba
700	1/0.25	MEX	GD	La Poderosa, Hidalgo del Parral
700	5	MEX	PUJ	LV del Corazón de la Selva, X'pujil
700	5	MEX	LX	R. Mexicana, Zitácuaro
700	1	MEX	DKR	R. Red, Guadalajara
700	10	NCG	MM	R. Managua, Managua
700	5	SLV	UU	Más Hits FM, San Salvador
700	10	VCT		R. St. Vincent and The Grenadines
710	30	CUB	JN	R. Rebelde, Camagüey
710	10	CUB	KJ	R. Rebelde, Holguín
710	150	CUB	W	R. Rebelde, La Julia
710	50	CUB	HQ	R. Rebelde, Santa Clara
710		DOM	WP	Onda del Caribe, San Cristóbal
710	1	GTM	XL	R. Tecún Umán, Quetzaltenango
710	1	HND	UP	Estéreo Rey, San Pedro Sula
710	1	HND	NN13	LV de Honduras, Olanchito
710	3	HND	RH	LV de Occidente, Sta Rosa de Copán
710	2.5	HND	KN	LV de Olancho, Catacamas
710	2	HND	LK	R. Comayagua/LV Católica, Comayagua
710	5/1	MEX	BL	La Poderosa, Culiacán
710	10/1	MEX	DP	La Ranchera de Cuauhtémoc, Cd.Cuauhtémoc
710	1/0.25	MEX	RL	La R-L de Colima, Colima
710	1/0.25	MEX	PS	La Super Grupera, Empalme
710	5/0.25	MEX	LZ	La Z, Torreón
710	10/1	MEX	MP	R. 7-10, Mexico
710	5/0.25	MEX	YK	R. Familiar, Mérida
710	1/0.25	MEX	SMR	R. Fórmula, San Luis Potosí
710	1	MEX	MAR	R. Inolvidable, Acapulco
710	1	MEX	RK	R. Korita, Tepic
710	4. 5/1	MEX	ON	R. Mexicana, Tuxtla Gutiérrez
710	1/0.25	MEX	OLA	R. Ola, Tampico
710	5/0.5	MEX	RPO	R. Variedades, Oaxaca
710	10	PNR	Q51	KW Continente, Panamá
710	5	PNR	B52	Ondas del Caribe, Bocas del Toro
710	10/0.75	PTR	WKJB	KJB, Mayagüez
720	1	CUB	HC	R. Rebelde, Cienfuegos
720	5	DOM	AQ	R. Norte, Santiago
720	1	GTM	RO	R. Corona, Morales
720	1	HND	NN3	R. Caribe, La Ceiba
720	1	HND	NG	Super Stereo Costa Sur, Choluteca
720	1	HTI		R. Lumiere, Petite Riv.
720	10	JMC		RJR Innswood (St. Catherine)
720	1/0.25	MEX	QZ	La Máquina Musical, San Juan de los Lagos
720	1/0.5	MEX	VU	La Poderosa, Mazatlán
720	5/0.25	MEX	DE	R. Fórmula, Primera Cadena Nac., Saltillo
720	25/0.25	MEX	AVR	R. Fórmula, Primera Cadena Nac., Veracruz
720	2	MEX	CPQ	Ritmo 720, Félipe Carillo Puerto
720	10	NCG	RC	R. Católica, Managua
720	10	PNR	B50	R. República, Chitré
720	1	SLV	RA	R. Paz, San Salvador
730	20	CTR	HB	R. 730, San José
730	10	CUB	BB	R. Progreso, Nueva Gerona
730	10	DOM	Z	R. HIZ, Broadcasting Nac., Sto Domingo
730	10	GTM	N	R. Cultural, Guatemala
730	0.25	HND	XG	R. Cadena Dial, Sta Bárbara
730	1	HND	TG	R. Exitos, Tegucigalpa
730	100	MEX	X	Estado W, México
730	1	MEX	PQ	La 73/La Sabrosita, Cd.Muzquiz
730	3.5/0.5	MEX	GDL	La Explosiva, Zapotlanejo
730	10	MEX	PET	LV de los Mayas, Peto
730	5	MEX	EBC	R. Felicidad, Ensenada
730	10/5	MEX	VF	R. Villaflores, Villaflores
730	10	MEX	LBC	XELBC, Loreto
730	10	NCG	NS	R. Segovia, Ocotal
730	20	TRD		Trinidad Broadcasting Company
740	20	CUB	JL	R. Progreso, Camagüey
740	1	DOM	EF	R. Cayacoa, Higüey
740	1	GTM	HF	Emisoras UnidasTacaná, San Marcos
740	1	HND	IH	7-40 La Super, Juticalpa
740	1	HND	QQ	R. Intibucañá, La Esperanza
740	1	HND	NN23	R. Satélite, San Pedro Sula
740	1	HTI		R. Lumiere, Pignon
740	1	MEX	VAY	Bonita, Puerto Vallarta
740	1/0.5	MEX	LZ	El Planeta, Aguascalientes
740	5/1	MEX	CW	La Z, Los Mochis
740	2/1	MEX	GF	R. Fiesta 740 AM, Gutiérrez Zamora
740	10/1	MEX	QN	R. Fórmula 7-40, Torreón
740	1	MEX	CAQ	R. Fórmula, Cancún
740	5/1	MEX	OF	Romántica 7-40, Cortázar
740	5/1	MEX	KV	Stereo Vida, Villahermosa
740	50	NCG	RS	R. Sandino "La S Grande", Managua
740	2.6	PNR	R44	La Exitosa de Chorrera, La Chorrera
740	5	PNR	N26	R. Cristal, David
740	0.5/0.1	PTR	WIAC	Cadena R. Puerto Rico, Ponce (synchr)
740	10	PTR	WIAC	Cadena R. Puerto Rico, San Juan
750	1	CUB	HV	R. Progreso, Trinidad
750	5	DOM	DB	R. Cristo es el Señor, Santiago
750	1	GTM	AJ	R. Tropicana "Circuito Dos", Escuintla
750	1	HND	XK	LV de la Mosquitia, Puerto Lempira
750	1	HND	TU	R. Trujillo, Trujillo
750	1/0.1	MEX	CORO	Arco Iris 750, Loma Bonita
750	10/1	MEX	URM	Fiesta Mexicana, Uruapán
750	1/0.75	MEX	OH	La Chiquita, Camargo
750	5	MEX	JMN	LV de los Cuatro Pueblos, Jesús María
750	5/0.5	MEX	DGO	R. Capital, Durango
750	10/0.25	MEX	TI	R. Fiesta, La Más Picuda, Tempoal
750	5/0.25	MEX	KOK	R. Fórmula, Acapulco
750	1/0.25	MEX	CSI	R. Mexicana, Culiacán
750	1/0.1	MEX	RASA	XERASA, San Luis Potosí
750	5	PNR		R. Inolvidable, Chitré
750	10	SLV	SS	R.El Salvador, Santa Ana
760	20	CTR	LX	R. Columbia, San José
760	1	CUB		R. Reloj, La Habana (occasional)
760	10	CUB	CD	R. Reloj, Las Mercedes
760	5	DOM	CO	R. Cordillera, Sto Domingo
760	5	GTM	HB	Nueva R. Super, Guatemala
760	2.5	HND	XW	R. Comayagüela/Stereo Azul, Comayagüela
760	1	HND	CG	R. Copán Galel, La Entrada
760	2	HTI		R. Lumiere, Cayes
760	70/5	MEX	ABC	ABC Radio, México
760	5/0.25	MEX	EB	La Comadre, Cd.Obregón
760	10/0.25	MEX	ZZ	La Ke Buena/Gallito, Guadalajara
760	0.25	MEX	EQ	La Pantera, San Luis Potosí
760	5/0.5	MEX	YW	Mexicanísima, Mérida
760	8/1	MEX	RA	R. Chiapas, San Cristóbal las Casas
760	5/0.1	MEX	NY	R. Geny, Nogales
760	10	NCG		Ultravisión de Nicaragua, Managua
760	5	PNR	XO	LV del Istmo, Panamá
760	5	PTR	WORA	NotiUno, Mayagüez
770	10	DOM	MD	R. Popular, Santiago
770	1	GTM	BX	R. Fraternidad, Quetzaltenango
770	0.5	HND	MV	R. Aguán, Olanchito
770	1	HND	RO	R. Majestad "LV del Guayape", Juticalpa
770	10	HND	NN21	R. Norte, San Pedro Sula
770		HND		R. Sui Generis, Comayagua
770	1.5	JMC		RJR Grove Place (Manchester)
770	1/0.1	MEX	JJR	La Ke Guapa, Los Mochis
770	5/1	MEX	SUR	La Más Bonita, Chilapa
770	1/0.1	MEX	ML	La Ranchera, Apatzingán
770	1/0.25	MEX	HB	La Rancherita, Hidalgo del Parral
770	10/1	MEX	IH	La Unica, Fresnillo
770	5/0.5	MEX	QRV	R. Costenita, Veracruz
770	5/0.2	MEX	ACH	R. Fórmula, Monterrey
770	1	MEX	HUA	XEHUA, Sta Cruz Huatulco
770	1	MEX	MRO	XEMRO, Matias Romero
770	10	PNR	L83	R. Nacional Herrera, Chitré
770	10	SLV	KL	R.Cadena YSKL,San Salvador
780	10	CTR	RA	R. América, San José
780		CUB		R. Rebelde
780	0.5	DOM	BO	R. Constanza, Constanza
780	1	GTM	CK	R. Sultana del Oriente, Zacapa
780	1	HND	SE	Estéreo Sol 2000, Choluteca
780		HND		R. Amapala, Amapala
780		HND		R. Sonora, La Ceiba
780	10	HTI		Eben-Ezer, Mirebalais
780	0.5	HTI		R. Lumiere, Jeremie
780	5/1	MEX	SFT	La Triple T/La Caliente, San Fernando
780	5	MEX	GLO	LV de la Sierra Juárez, Guelato de Juárez
780	2. 5/1	MEX	XY	LV del Balsas, Cd.Altamirano
780	10/0.5	MEX	LD	R. Costa, Autlán

kHz	kW	Ctry	Call	Station, location
780	1/0.25	MEX	MTS	R. Fórmula, Tampico
780	5/0.5	MEX	MF	R. Nostalgia, Monclova
780	5/0.5	MEX	TS	R. Tapachula, Tapachula
780	5/1	MEX	ZN	Stereo Digital, Celaya
780	1	NCG	AD	R. Deportes, Managua
780	10	PNR	B55	R. Chiriquí, David
780	5	SLV	KL	R.Cadena YSKL, San Miguel
780	1	SLV	KL	R.Cadena YSKL, Sonsonate
780	1	SLV	KL	R.Cadena YSKL, Sta Ana
780	1	SLV	KL	R.Cadena YSKL, Usulután
780	10	VRG	ZBVI	Virgin Islands Broadcasting
790	10	BRB		Stacom Network
790	30	CUB	AQ	R. Reloj, Pinar del Río
790	5	DOM	L	LV del Trópico, Sto Domingo
790	3	GTM	O	R. Festival, Guatemala
790	1	HND	IR	R. Feliz, Sta Bárbara
790	3	HND	TG2	R. Satélite, Tegucigalpa
790	2. 5/1	MEX	UP	Candela, Tizimín
790	50/1	MEX	RC	Formato 21, México
790	25/5	MEX	VA	La Emisora del Hogar, Villahermosa
790	1/0.25	MEX	GZ	La Pantera, Torreón
790	1/0.5	MEX	FE	La Pura Ley, Nuevo Laredo
790	1/0.25	MEX	SU	R. 790, Mexicali
790	20/1	MEX	BI	R. B-I, Aguascalientes
790	1	MEX	GAJ	R. Fórmula, Primera Cadena Nac., Guadalajara
790	5/0.75	MEX	NT	R. La Paz, La Paz
790	1/0.5	MEX	COV	R. Lobo, Poza Rica
790	5/0.4	MEX	RPC	R. Ranchito, Chihuahua
790	6	PNR		Caracol, Santiago
800	100	ATN	PJB	TWR, Bonaire
800	5	CTR	W	R. Unica, San José
800	1	CUB	DT	R. Progreso, Manzanillo
800		DOM	VM	R. Bonao, Bonao
800	1	GTM	YZ	R. Rosa, Chiquimulilla
800	1	HND	DL	R. Corporación, Comayagua
800	1	HND	LP26	R. Sonora, Danlí
800	0.5	MEX	SPM	ESPN Radio 800, Tijuana
800	5/1	MEX	GX	Fiesta Mexicana, San Luis de la Paz
800	10	MEX	DD	La Doble D/La Pezada, Montemorelos
800	2/0.25	MEX	ZR	La Formula, Zaragoza
800	5	MEX	QT	La Poderosa, Veracruz
800	3	MEX	ZV	LV de la Montaña, Tlapa de Comonfort
800	1/0.25	MEX	AN	R. Alegría, Ocotlán
800	50	MEX	ROK	R. Cañon Láser, Cd.Juárez
800	5/1	MEX	UI	R. Comitán, Comitán
800	1	NCG		R. 800, Managua
800	3	PNR		Tropical 800, Las Tablas
800	10	SLV	AX	R.María El Salvador, San Salvador
810	1	BAH	ZNS3	Broadcasting Corporation of the Bahamas
810	10	CUB	DW	R. Progreso, Guantánamo (rep on 814kHz)
810	1	DOM	AV	R. Baní, Baní
810		DOM	RN	R. Novel, Santiago
810		GTM		R. Moapán, Sta Elena
810	1	HND	VC	LV Evangélica, La Ceiba
810	3	HND	MA	R. Mundial, San Pedro Sula
810	3	HND	LP24	R. Valle, Choluteca
810	0.05	HTI		R. Atlantique, Gonaives
810	1/0.5	MEX	IM	Bonita, Saltillo
810	1/0.15	MEX	AGR	Éxtasis Digital, Acapulco
810	10/0.25	MEX	UX	La Tremenda, Tepic
810	5/0.25	MEX	RSV	R. Alegría, Cd.Obregón
810	50/1	MEX	FW	R. Estrella, Tampico
810	1/0.15	MEX	OE	R. Éxitos, Tapachula
810	1/0.25	MEX	ZC	R. Felicidad, Río Grande
810	2/0.25	MEX	MQ	R. Fórmula, Segunda Cadena Nac., Mérida
810	2.5/1	MEX	HT	R. Huamantla, Huamantla
810	1	MEX	SB	R. Mexicana, Santa Bárbara
810	1/0.1	MEX	RI	R. Rey, Reynosa
810	1/0.5	MEX	EMM	R. Salmantina, Salamanca
810	3/0.25	MEX	MAX	Radiomax, Tecomán
810	5/0.15	MEX	RB	Sol Estéreo, Cozumel
810	0.1	MEX	IC	XEIC, Campeche
810	1	PNR	G	R. 10, Panamá
810	50	PTR	WKVM	AM-81, San Juan
810	1	SLV	DA	R.Imperial, Sonsonate
810	2	SLV	FA	R.Lorenzana, San Vicente
820	2.5	CTR	GC	R. Centro AM, San José
820	10	CUB	CA	R. Ciudad de la Habana, Santa Catalina
820	10	CUB	JT	R. Progreso, Ciego de Avila
820	5/1	DOM	AZ	Bachatera 8-20, Santiago
820	10	GTM	TO	R. Internacional, Guatemala
820	5	HND	LD	R. Moderna, Tegucigalpa
820	7/3	HND	KW	R. Sultana, Sta Rosa de Copán
820	10	HTI		R. Tropicale, Port-au-Prince
820	1/0.5	MEX	DRD	Energy, Durango
820	2.5/0.1	MEX	KG	Golden Hits, Córdoba
820	10/0.1	MEX	BA	La Consentida, Guadalajara
820	1	MEX	BM	La Ranchera, La Mera, San Luis Potosí
820	0.75	MEX	ESC	R. Escárcega, Escárcega
820	5/0.25	MEX	ZQ	R. Futurama, Villahermosa
820	1	MEX	GRC	R. Guerrero, Coyuca de Catalán
820	1/0.25	MEX	UDO	R. Universidad de Occidente, Los Mochis
820	1/0.5	MEX	YN	Sonido 820, Oaxaca
820	3/0.5	MEX	MVS	Zona 820, Mexicali
820	20	NCG	OL	R. Ondas de Luz, Managua
820	3	PNR	F28	R. Ritmo Chiriquí, David
820	50	SCN		R. Paradise
830	5	CUB		R. Reloj, Holguín
830	10	DOM	JB	R. HIJB, Sto Domingo
830	5	GTM	AV	R. Satélite, Mazatenango
830	1	HND	JB	Cadena Radial Impacto, Comayagua
830	1	HND	VQ	R. Excelsior, Juticalpa
830	1	HND	RU	R. Uno, San Pedro Sula
830	10/0.5	MEX	LK	La L-K, Zacatecas
830	5	MEX	IK	La Norteñita, Piedras Negras
830	3/0.25	MEX	LN	La Super Llegadora, Linares
830	5/1	MEX	VQ	La Superestación/La Grande, Culiacán
830	5	MEX	PUR	LV de los Purépechas, Cheran
830	10	MEX	ITE	R. Capital, México
830	1/0.25	MEX	TLX	R. Tlaxiaco, Tlaxiaco
830	10	NCG	RZ	R. Zinica "Alegre Corazón Costeño", Bluefields
830	5	PNR	R56	R. Península, Macaracas
830	5	SLV	PX	R.Pax, San Miguel
840	10	CUB	HW	Doblevé, Santa Clara
840	1	CUB	BQ	R. Enciclopedia, La Fé
840	1	CUB	DQ	R. Progreso, Las Tunas
840	1	CUB	KC	R. Revolución, Stgo de Cuba
840	1	DOM	AB	R. Isabel de Torres, Puerto Plata
840	0.35	GTM	SM	LV de San Marcos, San Marcos
840	1	HND	CR	Dif. Cristiana de Radio "DCR", Choluteca
840	10	HTI		R. 4VEH, Cap Haitien
840	0.5	MEX	CUC	Casa de la Cultura de Campeche, Campeche
840	5/1	MEX	XXX	Fiesta Mexicana/Fiesta Digital, Tamazula
840	1	MEX	MY	La Cañerita, Cd.Mante
840	2.5/0.1	MEX	PV	La Fiera Tropical, Papantla
840	5/0.5	MEX	FG	La Pachanga, Celaya
840	10/1	MEX	IO	La Ranchera, Tuxtla Gutiérrez
840	1/0.25	MEX	TEY	R. Sensación, Tepic
840	5	NCG	NR	R. Noticias, Managua
840	10	PNR	L80	R. Nacional, Panamá
840	5	PTR	WXEW	NotiUno/R. Victoria, Yabucoa
840	10	SLV	FB	R.Santa Bíblia, San Salvador
850	20	CTR	W	R. Tigre, San José
850	1	CUB	HL	R. Progreso, Trinidad
850	1	CUB		R. Reloj, Nueva Gerona
850	5	DOM	UA	R. Clarín, Santiago
850	5	DOM	GA	R. Guarocuya, Barahona
850	10	GTM	X	R. Ciro, Guatemala
850	10	HND	UP	R. Centro, Tegucigalpa
850	0.5	HND	IF	R. Inspiración, La Entrada
850		HND		R. Misionera, Sta Bárbara
850	0.25	HTI		R. Petion-Ville, Port-au-Prince
850	5/1	MEX	MIA	Bonita, Guadalajara
850	0.5	MEX	ZF	Éxtasis, Mexicali
850	10	MEX	TQ	La Q Internacional, Orizaba
850	5/1	MEX	M	R. Exitos, Chihuahua
850	4/1	MEX	JAQ	R. Felicidad, Jalpan
850	1/0.2	MEX	US	R. Universidad de Sonora, Hermosillo
850	5	PNR	T61	La Exitosa de Chiriquí, David
850	1	PNR		La Exitosa de Colón, Colón
850	5/1	PTR	WABA	Waba "La Grande", Aguadilla
860	10	ATN	PJZ-86	R. Curom, Willemstad
860	10	CUB	BL	R. Progreso, Arroyo Arenas
860	1	CUB	DB	R. Reloj, Baracoa
860	10	DOM	UA	R. Clarín, Sto Domingo
860	1	GTM	FP	R. Nal. Tikal, Flores
860	0.5	HND	LS	R. Dinorama, La Paz
060	10	HND	BS	R. San Pedro, San Pedro Sula
860	3	HTI		R. Men Kontre, Cayes
860	5/0.25	MEX	DB	Canal 86, Tonalá
860	5/0.5	MEX	DU	D-U la que le gusta, Durango
860	1/0.15	MEX	ZX	La Comadre, Tenosique
860	1/0.25	MEX	NW	La Radio de la Ciudad, Culiacán
860	5	MEX	MO	R. 86/La Poderosa AM Estéreo, Tijuana

kHz	kW	Ctry	Call	Station, location
860	5	MEX	CCM	R. Caribe, Cancún
860	5	MEX	CTL	R. Chetumal, Chetumal
860	5/0.5	MEX	RRF	R. Felicidad, Mérida
860	1/0.25	MEX	TW	R. Fiesta/La Sabrosona, Tampico
860	5/1	MEX	PLA	R. Mexicana, Aguascalientes
860	5/0.1	MEX	AL	R. Mundo, Manzanillo
860	1/0.5	MEX	ZOL	R. Noticias 860, Cd.Juárez
860	5/2	MEX	NL	R. Recuerdo, Monterrey
860	50/10	MEX	UN	R. UNAM, México
860	5	NCG		Ultravisión de Nicaragua, Managua
860	10	PNR	L55	R. Reforma, Chitré
860	1	SLV	RC	R.Tecana, Sta Ana
870	5	CTR	UCR	R. Universidad de Costa Rica, San José
870	1	CUB	DT	R. Reloj, Sancti Spíritus
870	10	DOM	VG	R. La Vega, La Vega
870	0.5	GTM	L	R. Victoria, Mazatenango
870	5	HND	H9	R. Honduras, La Ceiba
870	3	HND	H4	R. Honduras, Nacaome
870	5	HND	H10	R. Honduras, Puerto Lempira
870	1	HTI		R. Express, Jacmel
870	1/0.5	MEX	AMO	AMO 870, Irapuato
870	10	MEX	TAR	LV de la Sierra Tarahumara, Guachochi
870	5/0.25	MEX	ACC	LV del Puerto, Puerto Escondido
870	1/0.25	MEX	FIL	R. Fórmula, Mazatlán
870	1	MEX	GRO	R. Guerrero, Acapulco
870	1/0.1	MEX	LY	R. Moderna, Morelia
870	1/0.1	MEX	NG	R. Nueva Generación, Huauchinango
870	10	NCG	CD	R. Centro, Juigalpa
870	5.5	PNR	HO	R. Libre, Panamá
870	5	PTR	WQBS	La Gran Cadena QBS, San Juan
870	10	SLV	AR	R.Renacer, San Salvador
880	30	CUB	AF	R. Progreso, Pinar del Río
880	1	DOM	OR	AM-88, Mao, Valverde
880	10	GTM	J	R. Nuevo Mundo, Guatemala
880	10	HND	H5	R. Honduras, Sta Rosa de Copán
880	10	HND	H	R. Honduras, Tegucigalpa
880	5	HND	MD	R. Yoro, Yoro
880	0.3	HTI		R. Independance, Gonaives
880	10/2	MEX	PNK	Canal 88/Superestación, Los Mochis
880	10/0.1	MEX	TC	Estéreo Mayrán, Torreón
880	1	MEX	EM	La EM Mexicana, Río Verde
880	1	MEX	YV	La Invasora, Córdoba
880	20/1	MEX	AAA	R. 8-80/La Triple A, Guadalajara
880	5/0.25	MEX	V	R. Fórmula, Primera Cadena Nac., Chihuahua
880	1/0.1	MEX	IG	RCN La Grande de Iguala, Iguala
880	10/0.5	MEX	QQQ	Super Q, Villahermosa
880	10	NCG	AT	R. El Pensamiento, Managua
880	2.5	PNR		Caracol, Bocas del Toro
880	2.5	PNR		Caracol, Chiriquí
880	1	PNR	B51	R. Visión Panamá, Colón
880	1/0.5	PTR	WYKO	La Poderosa 880, Sabana Grande
880	1	SLV	CD	R.Ritmo, Stgo de María
890	10	CTR	HOT	R. Fabulosa, San José
890	80	CUB	DZ	R. Progreso, Chambas
890	1	CUB	HD	R. Progreso, Santa Clara
890	4/5	DOM	PJ	R. Continental, Sto Domingo
890	1	GTM	HU	R. Escuintla, Escuintla
890	1	HND	H2	R. Honduras, Comayagua
890	1	HND	H6	R. Honduras, El Paraíso
890	10	HND	H7	R. Honduras, Juticalpa
890	1	HND	H8	R. Honduras, Olanchito
890	10	HND	H3	R. Honduras, San Pedro Sula
890	10	HND	H9	R. Honduras, Siguatepeque
890	1	HND	UP5	R. Satélite, Danlí
890	0.5	HTI		R. Trans Artibonite, Gonaives
890	1	HTI		V. du Nord'est, Forte Liberte
890	1/0.25	MEX	BY	La Consentida, Tuxpam
890	1/0.5	MEX	POR	La Explosiva, Putla de Guerrero
890	10/1	MEX	NZ	La Sinaloense, Culiacán
890	5/0.5	MEX	AK	R. Consentida, Acámbaro
890	5/1	MEX	YQ	R. Fresnillo, Fresnillo
890	20/1	MEX	FRT	R. Frontera, Comitán
890	1/0.25	MEX	PNA	R. Joya, Tepic
890	5/1	MEX	PC	Sonido Estrella, Zacatecas
890	5	PNR	Q62	R. Ritmo Stereo, Chitré.
890	0.25	PTR	WFAB	WFAB, Ceiba
890	3	SLV	LA	R.Musical, Sta Ana
895	10	SCN		Voice of Nevis
900	10	BRB		Caribbean Broadcasting Corporation
900	50	CUB	KP	R. Progreso, Cacocum
900	5	DOM	AJ	R. Amanecer, San Pedro de Macorís
900	5/1	DOM	EN	R. Puerto Plata, Puerto Plata
900		DOM	FK	R. Super Mega, Neiba
900	1	GTM	MA	R. Amatique, Puerto Barrios
900	1	HND	UP7	R. Satélite, Choluteca
900	1	HND	UP6	R. Satélite, La Ceiba
900	1/0.75	MEX	TAK	La K-900, Tapachula
900		MEX	DT	La Reina, Cd.Cuahtémoc
900	10/2.5	MEX	OK	R. ACIR, Monterrey
900	250	MEX	W	W Radio, México
900	50	MEX	WB	W Radio, Veracruz
900	5	NCG	RT	R. Tiempo, Managua
900	10	PNR	HA	Caracol, Panamá
900	2	SLV	QJ	R.El Tiempo, San Salvador
910	1	CTR	JQM	R. Metrópolis, San José
910	10	CUB	FA	R. Cadena Agramonte, Camagüey
910		CUB	CA	R. Ciudad de la Habana
910	10	CUB	BL	R. Metropolitana, La Lisa
910	5	CUB	GL	R. Reloj, Bolondrón
910	5	DOM	LB	R. 91 "La Grande", Bonao
910	10	GTM	KL	R. Emperador, Guatemala
910	10	HND	VS	R. Católica "LV de Suyapa", Tegucigalpa
910	2.5	HND	NM	R. Comunidad, Ocotepeque
910	0.5	HND	VH	R. Corona, La Entrada
910	0.5	HTI		R. Kyskeya, Port-au-Prince
910	0.5	HTI		R. Neg Combit, Port-au-Prince
910	10/1	MEX	NAY	La Buena Onda del Pacífico, Nuevo Vallarta
910	5/0.1	MEX	ACM	R. Exitos, Cárdenas
910	10/0.5	MEX	OL	R. Impacto, Teziutlán
910	1/0.25	MEX	AO	R. Mexicana, Mexicali
910	5/0.1	MEX	ACN	R. Uno, León
910	5	NCG		R. Jinotega, Jinotega
910	3	PNR	L85	R. Nacional, Colón
910	10	PNR		R. Nacional, Darién
910	10	PNR	L81	R. Nacional, David
910	4.2	PTR	WPRP	NotiUno, Ponce
920	1	CUB		R. Progreso, Pilón
920	1	CUB	GL	R. Reloj, Moa
920	10	DOM	BA	R. 9-20 AM-Stereo "Power", Sto Domingo
920	0.2	GTM	RS	R. Sur, Escuintla
920	5	HND	SK	R. Catacamas, Catacamas
920	1	HND	H11	R. Honduras, Danlí
920	1	HND	RM	R. Sistema, Comayagua
920	1	HND	ZV	R. Variedades, San Pedro Sula
920	5/0.5	MEX	CQ	C-Q/La Ranchera de Culiacán, Culiacán
920	1	MEX	ZAR	Inolvidable 920, Puebla
920	5/1	MEX	RE	La Comadre/Salvatierra, Celaya
920	1/0.25	MEX	MJ	La Coqueta, Piedras Negras
920	5/0.2	MEX	RCA	La Joya, Torreón
920	5/1	MEX	HQ	La Mejor, Hermosillo
920	10/0.25	MEX	LT	Oasis 920, Guadalajara
920	1/0.15	MEX	PNX	R. Costa, Pinotepa Nacional
920	10/0.5	MEX	VV	R. Diversión, Tuxtla Gutiérrez
920	1.5/0.5	MEX	TEB	R. Mar, Campeche
920	1	MEX	LCM	R. Mexicana, Cd.Lázaro Cárdenas
920	1/0.25	MEX	QD	R. Noticias 920, Chihuahua
920	10	NCG	W	R. Mundial, Managua
920	5	PNR	S56	R. Mía de Los Santos, Los Santos
930	5	CTR	RCR	R. Costa Rica, San José
930	10	CUB	JS	R. Reloj, Ciego de Ávila
930	1	CUB	GB	R. Reloj, La Jaiba
930	1	CUB	KN	R. Reloj, Stgo de Cuba
930	10	DOM	CK	Ondas del Yaque, Santiago
930	5	GTM	JL	Em. Unidas Imperial, San Pedro Carchá
930	5	HTI		R. Cap Haitien, Cap Haitien
930	0.1	HTI		R. Echo 2000, Val. de Jacmel
930	2/1	MEX	CY	Banda 930, Huejutla
930	1/0.25	MEX	SHT	Digital 930, Saltillo
930	1	MEX	TTT	La Rocola, Colima
930	10/1	MEX	U	La U de Veracruz, Veracruz
930	5	MEX	TLA	LV de la Mixteca, Tlaxiaco
930	2.5/0.2	MEX	UL	R. Fórmula, Primera Cadena Nac., Progreso
930	5/0.5	MEX	MK	R. Mexicana, Huixtla
930	10/1	MEX	QS	Romance en Radio, Fresnillo
930	1	MEX	ZU	Sonido ZU Poder Musical, Zacapu
930	1	MEX	RLA	XERLA, Santa Rosalía
930	10	PNR	R46	La Nueva Exitosa de Panamá, Panamá
930	2	PNR	K85	Mi Preferida Estéreo, Pto Armuelles
930	2.5	PTR	WYAC	Cadena R. Puerto Rico, Cabo Rojo
930	1	SLV	TG	R.Cadena Sonora, Ahuachapán
930	1	SLV	TG	R.Cadena Sonora, San Miguel
930	5	SLV	TG	R.Cadena Sonora, San Salvador
930	1	SLV	TG	R.Cadena Sonora, Sonsonate
930	1	SLV	TG	R.Cadena Sonora, Sta Ana

kHz	kW	Ctry	Call	Station, location
930	1	SLV	TG	R.Cadena Sonora, Usulután
940	1	CUB		R. Progreso, Sancti Spíritus
940	10	CUB	GU	R. Reloj, Central España
940	10	CUB		R. Reloj, Holguín
940	5	GTM	TL	LV del Hogar "R.Paz", Guatemala
940	1	GTM	TL	LV del Hogar "R.Paz", Sacatepeque
940	1	HND	BO	R. Cadena Occidental, La Entrada
940	1	HND	CR	R. Dif. Cristiana de Radio "DCR", Tegucigalpa
940	0.25	HTI		R. St Marc, St Marc
940	0.2	HTI		Rdf Jacmelienne, Jacmel
940	50	MEX	Q	Besame 9-40, México
940	1/0.1	MEX	WV	Fiesta Mexicana, Mexicali
940	1	MEX	RKS	La Poderosa, Reynosa
940	15	MEX	YJ	La Y-J Mexicana, Sabinas
940	1	MEX	HE	LV 9-40, Atotonilco
940	1	MEX	REC	R. Fiesta, Reforma
940	10	PTR	WIPR	WIPR R. Dif de Puerto Rico, San Juan
950	10	CUB		R. Reloj, La Habana
950	1	CUB		R. Reloj, Mayarí Arriba
950	10	DOM	G	R. Popular, Sto Domingo
950	1	GTM	AF	R. Indiana, Mazatenango
950	1	HND	QL	Centro Radial Hondureño, Siguatepeque
950	1.5	HND	ZE	R. Cortés AM, Puerto Cortés
950	0.5	HND	PS	R. Sistema Popular, Danlí
950	1/0.5	MEX	CAA	Azul 95, Aguascalientes
950	1/0.25	MEX	MAB	Canal Internacional, Cd.del Carmen
950	1/0.25	MEX	TUG	Dimensión 9-50, Tuxtla Gutiérrez
950	10/0.1	MEX	PB	La Grande, Hermosillo
950	2. 5/1	MEX	ZE	La Invasora, Santiago Ixcuintla
950	5/0.5	MEX	MEX	La Mexicana, Cd.Guzmán
950	5	MEX	OJN	LV de la Chinantla, San Lúcas Ojitlán
950	5	MEX	ACA	R. ACIR, Acapulco
950	5/0.5	MEX	ORF	R. Amor, Los Mochis
950	17/5	MEX	KAM	R. Fórmula Californias, Tijuana
950	5/1	MEX	CEL	R. Lobo, Cortazar
950	5/1	MEX	RN	R. Naranjera, Monterey
950	1/0.25	MEX	FA	R. Rama/R Amor, Chihuahua
950	1	MEX	TO	Romántica, Tampico
950	2.5	NCG	CC	R. Rumbos de Rivas, Rivas
950	2.5	PNR		Caracol, Las Mercedes, Colón
950	3	PNR	L84	R. Nacional, Penonomé
950	1	SLV	HG	R.Cristo Te Llama, San Miguel
960	5	CTR	CS	Premium Radio, San José
960	1	CUB	GF	R. Enciclopedia, Matanzas
960	0.25	CUB	JD	R. Musical, Ciego de Avila
960	10	CUB	DJ	R. Reloj, Guantánamo
960	5/1	DOM	FF	LV del Atlántico, Puerto Plata
960	1	GTM	RU	Em. Unidas Utatlán, Sta Cruz del Quiché
960	1	HND	YF	R. Fergusón, Choluteca
960	1	HND	RD3	R. Sangrelaya, Sangrelaya
960	0.3	HTI		R. Carillon, Port-au-Prince
960	5/0.15	MEX	TAP	Imperio, Tapachula
960	5/1	MEX	K	La Estación Grande de Nuevo, Laredo
960	1	MEX	MM	La Grupera, Morelia
960	5/0.5	MEX	ROO	La Voz de Quintana Roo, Chetumal
960	10/5	MEX	HK	LV de Guadalajara, Guadalajara
960	1/0.25	MEX	CZ	Perfil 9-60, San Luis Potosí
960	1/0.1	MEX	FAMA	R. 960 La Fama, Cd.Camargo
960	1/0.5	MEX	IQ	R. ACIR, Cd.Obregón
960	1/0.5	MEX	UQ	R. Variedades, Zihuatanejo
960	1/0.5	MEX	GB	Romántica, Coatzacoalcos
960	1/0.25	MEX	OZ	Satélite, Jalapa
960	1	MEX	XC	Super Mil, Taxco
960	1/0.1	MEX	KS	Super Mix, Saltillo
960	2.5	NCG		LV del Trópico Húmedo, San Carlos
960	1	PNR	M33	CHT Stereo Digital, David
960	1/1.7	PTR	WCHQ	Quebradillas
960	0.5	SLV	TW	R.Centro, Sonsonate
970	10	DOM	VP	R. Olímpica, La Vega
970	5	GTM	AX	R. Continental, Guatemala
970	0.25	HND	AS	LV de la Frontera, Ocotepeque
970		HND		R. Copán, Copán
970	2	HND	TL	R. Milenium, Tegucigalpa
970	5/0.5	MEX	MH	Candela Tropicaliente, Mérida
970	10/0.5	MEX	ZAZ	De Mil Amores 9-70, Zacatecas
970	50/5	MEX	J	La J Mexicana, Cd.Juárez
970	10/1	MEX	VT	La Primera Estación de Tabasco, Villahermosa
970	5/0.25	MEX	EZ	La Super Z, Caborca
970	1/0.25	MEX	CJ	R. Apatzingán, Apatzingán
970	100	MEX	RFR	R. Fórmula, Primera Cadena Nac., México
970	1	MEX	O	R. Gallito, Matamoros
970	10/1	MEX	VOX	R. Mujer, Mazatlán
970	1	MEX	UG	R. Universidad de Guanajuato, Guanajuato
970	3	PNR	S97	Ondas Centrales, Santiago
970	5	SLV	MS	R.UTEC, San Salvador
970	5/1	VIR	WSTX	Family Broadcasting Inc, Christiansted
980	20	CTR	RI	R. Favorita, San José
980	5	CUB	CO	El Periodico del Aire, Sapo
980	1	CUB	KR	La Voz del Níquel, Moa
980	1	CUB	DE	R. Reloj, Bayamo
980	5	DOM	FA	LV Cultural de las Fuerzas Armadas, Sto Domingo
980	1	GTM	MQ	R. Retama, San Marcos
980		HND	VC	LV Evangélica, Siguatepeque
980	1	HND	RD2	R. Emperador, Campamento
980	2	HND	ZC	R. Monumental, San Pedro Sula
980	1	HND	YG	R. Tocoa, Tocoa
980	10/0.2	MEX	LC	Dual Stereo, La Piedad
980	1/0.25	MEX	KE	KE-98 Acción Digital, Navojoa
980	1	MEX	JK	La Comadre, Cd.Delicias
980	1/0.25	MEX	FF	La Norteña, Matehuala
980	1/0.5	MEX	FQ	LV de la Ciudad del Cobre, Cananea
980	5/0.5	MEX	NR	R. 980, Nueva Rosita
980	1	MEX	XT	R. Fiesta, Tepic
980	5	MEX	QO	R. Romance, Cosamaloapan
980	10/1	MEX	TU	R. Tampico, Tampico
980	1	NCG	VA	R. Redención Internacional, Managua
980	1	PNR		R. Mía, Bocas del Toro
990	1	CUB	AP	R. Guamá, San Luís
990	5	DOM	SA	R. Cibao, Santiago
990	1	GTM	AL	R. Perla de Oriente, Chiquimula
990	3.5	HND	VO	R. Paz, Choluteca
990	0.2	HTI		R. Cacique, Port-au-Prince
990	1	MEX	ATM	A Toda Máquina, Morelia
990	1/0.25	MEX	UM	Candela Valladolid, Valladolid
990	1	MEX	IU	Estéreo Cristal, Oaxaca
990	1/0.1	MEX	BC	La Buena Onda, Cd.Guzmán
990	10	MEX	TG	La Grande del Sureste, Tuxtla Gutiérrez
990	50	MEX	T	La T Grande, Monterrey
990	5/0.25	MEX	HZ	R. 9-90, La Paz
990	10/1	MEX	ID	R. Alamo, Alamo
990	10/1	MEX	FP	R. Alegría, Jalpa
990	5/0.25	MEX	ER	R. Lobo, Cd.Cuauhtémoc
990	5/3	MEX	CL	Rocola 990, Mexicali
990	5	PNR		R. Impacto, Panamá
990	1	PTR	WPRA	R. Mil, Mayagüez
990	1	SLV	AT	R.UPA "La radio de los niños", San Salvador
1000	10/1	CTR	MIL	Mil FM, San José
1000	10	CUB	AC	R. Guamá, Los Palacios
1000	1	CUB	JB	R. Musical, Camagüey
1000	1	CUB	HB	R. Musical, Sancti Spíritus
1000	5/1	DOM	HG	R. Beller, Dajabón
1000	0.5	HND	MH	LV del Junco, Sta Bárbara
1000	1	HND	XZ	Unión R., Tegucigalpa
1000	5/1	MEX	TAC	Audio Mil de Chiapas, Tapachula
1000	1/0.5	MEX	RZ	Bonita, León
1000	1	MEX	MMS	Inolvidable, Mazatlán
1000	5/0.25	MEX	MYL	Juvemil, Mérida
1000	1/0.25	MEX	MIL	La Comadre, Los Mochis
1000	5/1	MEX	FV	La Rancherita, Cd.Juárez
1000	1	MEX	CSV	La Tremenda, Coatzacoales
1000	1/0.1	MEX	NLT	Laredo Radio, Nuevo Laredo
1000	50/20	MEX	OY	R. Mil "Tradición y Excelencia en Radio", México
1000	1/0.5	MEX	HPC	R. Mil, Hidalgo del Parral
1000	10	NCG	FF	R. Mil, Managua
1000	10	PNR	K36	R. Poderosa "La Fuerte", Aguadulce
1000	1	SLV	HH	Estación H, Sta Ana
1000	5/1	VIR	WVWI	Knight Quality Sts, St Thomas
1010	10	CUB	AP	R. Guamá, Guane
1010	1	CUB	KM	R. Musical, Holguín
1010	5	CUB		R. Reloj, Jobabo
1010	10	DOM	JA	R. Comercial, Sto Domingo
1010	1	GTM		R. Caribe, Izabal
1010	1	GTM	XI	R. Emmanuel, Nebaj
1010	1	HND	CD	R. Constelación. Juticalpa
1010	1	HND	LP23	R. Moderna, El Progreso
1010		HND		R. Sonora, San Pedro Sula
1010	5/0.5	MEX	WS	Inolvidable, Culiacán
1010	1/0.25	MEX	KD	K de Oro, Cd.Acuña
1010	5/1	MEX	VK	La Ke Buena, Torreón
1010	1/0.5	MEX	FM	La Máquina Tropical, Veracruz
1010	10/1	MEX	PA	La Prendida, Puebla

kHz	kW	Ctry	Call	Station, location
1010	5	MEX	TUMI	LV de la Sierra Oriente, Tuxpán
1010	1	MEX	HGO	R. Hidalgo, Huejutla
1010	5/0.5	MEX	LO	R. Lobo Latino, Chihuahua
1010	2.5/0.5	MEX	XN	R. Ures, Ures
1010	1/0.5	MEX	DX	R. Variedades, Ensenada
1010	50/5	MEX	HL	W Radio 1010, Guadalajara
1010	5	NCG	HG	R. LV del Pinar, Ocotal
1010	3	PNR	L86	R. Nacional, Bocas del Toro
1020	2	CTR	TIC	R. Mil Veinte, San José
1020	1	CUB	AP	R. Guamá, Bahía Honda
1020		CUB		R. Reloj
1020	10	DOM	TS	R. Enriquillo, Tamayo
1020	5	GTM	CM	R. Frontera, Pajapita
1020	1	HND	UW	R. Michel, La Ceiba
1020	1	HND	MP	R. Moropocai, Nacaome
1020	5/0.5	MEX	PR	Estéreo Vida, Poza Rica
1020	1	MEX	VE	La Comadre, Colima
1020	2.5/0.5	MEX	KH	R. Centro, Querétaro
1020	1	MEX	PIC	R. Hits, Tepic
1020	2. 5/1	MEX	OU	Sensación Estéreo, Huajuapan de León
1020	1/0.1	MEX	WO	Sol Estéreo Frontera, Chetumal
1020	5	PNR		R. Ancón, Panamá
1020	1	PTR	WOQI	R. Coquí/Gigante, Adjuntas
1020	5	SLV	CA	R.Internacional, San Salvador
1020	20	TCA		Caribbean Christian Radio
1030	1	CUB	AX	R. Guamá, La Palma
1030		CUB		R. Musical
1030	10	DOM	DL	R. Novedades, Santiago
1030	10	GTM	UX	R. Panamericana, Guatemala
1030	1	HND	UP3	Estéreo Mil, Tegucigalpa
1030	1	HND	YF	R. Ticante, Ocotepeque
1030		HTI		R. Guinen, Port-au-Prince
1030	1/0.5	MEX	VP	La Estación del Puerto, Acapulco
1030	1/0.25	MEX	BCC	La Gaviota Musical, Cd.del Carmen
1030	5/1	MEX	LJ	La Ke Buena, Lagos de Moreno
1030	5	MEX	SDD	La Tremenda, Ensenada
1030	10/0.25	MEX	VFS	LV de la Frontera Sur, Las Margaritas
1030	2.5	MEX	NKA	LV del Gran Pueblo, Félipe Carillo Puerto
1030	50/5	MEX	QR	R. Centro, México
1030	10/1	MEX	MPM	R. Fama/El Fuerte, Los Mochis
1030	5/0.5	MEX	YC	R. Fórmula, Cd.Juárez
1030	1/0.5	MEX	TEKA	R. Teca, Ixtepec
1030	1	MEX	GQ	R. Variedades, Los Reyes
1030	5/0.15	MEX	IE	Stereo 1030 AM, Matehuala
1030	1/0.5	MEX	PAV	W Radio, Tampico
1030	2	NCG	LL	R. Masaya, Masaya
1030	10	PTR	WOSO	El Oso, San Juan
1030	1	SLV	RM	R.Frontera, Ahuachapán
1040	10	CTR	AC	R. Fides, San José
1040	2	CTR	HG	R. Nosara, Hojancha
1040	1	CUB	KT	R. Victoria, Puerto Padre
1040	10	DOM	ON	La Mezcla, Sto Domingo
1040	1	GTM	JP	R. Oriental, Jalapa
1040	3	HND	NN22	Exitos, San Pedro Sula
1040	10/5	HND	ZX	La Primerísima, Olanchito
1040		HND	VC	LV Evangélica, Juticalpa
1040	1	HND	FX	R. Musical, Catacamas
1040	1	HND	MJ	R. Renovación, Comayagua
1040	10	MEX	CH	R. Capital, Toluca
1040	2. 5/1	MEX	GR	R. Favorita, Jalapa
1040	5/0.25	MEX	HES	R. Luz, Chihuahua
1040	10/1	MEX	BBB	R. Mujer, Guadalajara
1040	5	MEX	PLE	R. Palanque, Palenque
1040	1/0.25	MEX	GYS	Super Banda, Guaymas
1040	1/0.25	MEX	SAG	Tu Radio 1040, Irapuato
1040	2	NCG	VJ	LV de Jinotega, Jinotega
1040	3	PNR		LV del Mamoni, Panamá
1040	2.5	PNR	J2	Ondas del Canajagua, Las Tablas
1040	5/0.2	PTR	WZNA	Zona 1040/Super Kadena Noticias, Moca
1050	10	CUB	KT	R. Victoria, Las Tunas
1050	10	DOM	CB	R. Hispaniola, Santiago
1050	5/1	GTM	SL	LV de los Cuchumatanes, Huehuetenango
1050	1	HND		Estéreo Ceiba, La Ceiba
1050	1/0.5	MEX	IP	Fiesta Mexicana, Uruapán
1050	2.5/0.5	MEX	ZUM	La Invasora, Chilpancingo
1050	1	MEX	VUC	La Norteñita, Allende
1050	100	MEX	G	La Ranchera de Monterrey, Monterrey
1050	10/1	MEX	BCS	R. Cultural Surcalifornia, La Paz
1050	35/2.5	MEX	QOO	R. Pirata, Cancún
1050	5	MEX	JF	R. Sensación, Tierra Blanca
1050	10/5	MEX	TAB	R. Tabasco, Villahermosa
1050	7	MEX	DC	Satélite, Aguascalientes

kHz	kW	Ctry	Call	Station, location
1050	10/1	MEX	D	W Radio, Mexicali
1050	3	PNR		Caribe Stereo, Colón
1060	1	CTR	LX	R. Columbia, Liberia
1060	1	CTR	LX	R. Columbia, San Isidro del General
1060	5	CUB	DX	Cadena CMKS, Baracoa
1060		CUB		R. 26, Matanzas
1060	1	CUB	KT	R. Victoria, Amancio Rodríguez
1060		DOM	AJ	R. Amanecer, San Francisco de Macorís
1060	1	DOM	XF	R. Azua, Azua
1060	1	DOM	RV	R. Mar, San Pedro de Macorís
1060	10	GTM	T	R. Favorita, Guatemala
1060	2	HND	VW	LV de Centroamérica, Tegucigalpa
1060		HND		R. Mineria, Sta Cruz de Yojoa
1060	0.5	HND	FA	R. Peña Blanca, Sta Barbara
1060	100/20	MEX	EP	R. Educación, México
1060	1	NCG		LV del Atlántico, Bluefields
1060	1	NCG	JJ	R. Juvenil, Managua
1060	3.5	PNR	J60	R. LV de Panamá "La Auténtica", Panamá
1060	5/0.5	PTR	WCGB	Iniciativa Mil 60, Juana Díaz
1070	10	CUB	KS	Cadena CMKS, Guantánamo
1070	1	CUB	AS	R. Guamá, Pinar del Río
1070	5/1	DOM	BI	HIBI R. 1070, San Francisco de Macorís
1070	3/2	GTM	D	LV de Occidente, Quetzaltenango
1070	3	HND	GR	Cadena Guaymuras, El Paraíso
1070	1	HND	XM	R. Meridiano, Choluteca
1070	2.5	HND	LP26	R. Siguatepeque, Siguatepeque
1070	1	HND	LE	R. Unica AM, San Pedro Sula
1070		HND		R. Unión Evangélica, Catacamas
1070		HND		R. ZAZ Stereo, Danlí
1070	1/0.2	MEX	AGS	Bonita, Acapulco
1070	1/0.25	MEX	OBS	La Norteña 1070, Cd.Obregón
1070	1/0.1	MEX	MI	La Poderosa, Minatitlán
1070	5	MEX	ANT	LV de las Huastecas, Tancanhuitz de Santos
1070	1/0.25	MEX	EI	Momentos 10-70, San Luis Potosí
1070	1/0.25	MEX	IT	R. Interactiva, Cd.del Carmen
1070	5/1	MEX	SP	R. Juventud Unica, Guadalajara
1070	1/0.25	MEX	GY	R. Lobo, Tehuacán
1070	1/0.5	MEX	RPR	Retro, Tuxtla Gutiérrez
1070	10	PNR		R. Nacional, Los Santos
1070	3	PNR		Radio Estéreo Mi Favorita, Penonomé
1070	2.5	PTR	WMIA	WMIA/R. Arecibo, Arecibo
1070	1	SLV	AN	LV de los Ausoles, Ahuachapán
1080	19	CTR	FC	Faro del Caribe, San José
1080	10	CUB	CH	R. Cadena Habana, Güines
1080	1	DOM	MC	R. Ambar, Sto Domingo
1080	1	GTM	LU	R. Viva, Zacapa
1080	1	HND	ID	R. Miramar, Tela
1080	20	HTI		R. Nationale, Port-au-Prince
1080	10/0.25	MEX	XK	1080 R. Mundo, Poza Rica
1080	1/0.5	MEX	CN	Fuerza 1080, Irapuato
1080	1/0.25	MEX	PAB	R. Celebridad, La Paz
1080	1/0.25	MEX	DY	R. Gallo, San LuisRíoColorado
1080	1/0.5	MEX	UU	R. Variedades, Colima
1080	5	MEX	JLV	Sistema Jalisciense, Puerto Vallarta
1080	5/0.25	MEX	TUL	Sistema XEGEM "R. Mexiquense", Tultitlán
1080		NCG	LC	R. 15 de Septiembre, Managua
1080	5	PNR		CNB, Chiriquí
1080	5	PNR	J24	CNB, Panamá
1080	0.25	PTR	WLEY	Motivos 1080, Cayey
1080	5	SLV	ME	R.CRET, San Salvador
1080	1	SLV		R.CRET, Sta Ana
1090	1	CUB	KO	R. Angulo, Moa
1090	1.5	CUB	CH	R. Cadena Habana, La Salud
1090	1	CUB	AP	R. Guamá, Santa Lucia
1090	3/1	DOM	JM	R. Amistad, Santiago
1090	1	DOM	RB	R. Jimaní, Jimaní
1090	10	GTM	Z	Emisoras Unidas Central, Guatemala
1090	1	HND	WC	Cadena Radial Samaritano, Tegucigalpa
1090	1	HND	NN27	Exitos, Sta Rosa de Copán
1090	10/0.25	MEX	FC	Frequencia Cordial, Mérida
1090	1/0.5	MEX	IL	La Grupera 1090, Veracruz
1090	5/1	MEX	HR	La HR/R. ACIR, Puebla
1090	1	MEX	WL	La Romantica, Nuevo Laredo
1090	10/0.5	MEX	MCA	MCA 1090, Pánuco
1090	5/0.25	MEX	AU	Que Buena, Monterrey
1090	2. 5/1	MEX	XE	R. Fórmula, Primera Cadena Nac., Querétaro
1090	50	MEX	PRS	The Mighty 1090, Rosarito
1090	5/1	MEX	LB	Tremenda 10-90, La Barca
1090	5	NCG	AI	R. Alma Latina, Estelí
1090	10	PNR	L82	R. Urracá Civilista, Santiago
1090	0.5/0.7	PTR	WSOL	R. Sol, San Germán
1090	3	SLV	MG	R.1090, Atiquizaya

kHz	kW	Ctry	Call	Station, location
1090	0.25	VIR	WGOD	WGOD, St Thomas
1100	10	ATG		Grenville R., St John's (inactive)
1100	0.25	ATN	PJL-3	R. Caribe, Willemstad
1100	5	CTR	SCR	R. Chorotega, Santa Cruz
1100	1	CUB	KO	R. Angulo, Banes
1100	1	CUB	CH	R. Cadena Habana, La Habana
1100	1	DOM	PS	R. Nagua, Nagua
1100	1	DOM	MP	R. Ocoa, San José de Ocoa
1100	1	DOM	HD	R. Oriente, San Pedro de Macorís
1100	1	GTM	SR	R. Superior, Coatepeque
1100	1	HND	VS	LV de Suyapa "R. Católica", Juticalpa
1100	1	HND	ND	R. Esperanza, La Esperanza
1100	1	HND	VL	R. Lux, Olanchito
1100	1	HND	VA	R. Tiempo/R. Fama, San Pedro Sula
1100	1/0.25	MEX	PO	R. ACIR, San Luis Potosí
1100	5/0.5	MEX	TGO	R. Alegría Digital, Tlaltenango
1100	5/1	MEX	BV	R. Alegría, Moroleón
1100	1	MEX	GRM	R. Guerrero, Ometepec
1100	4	MEX	CAN	R. Mundo Maya Turquesa, Cancún
1100	1/0.5	MEX	NAS	Radiante 1100, Navojoa
1100	1	MEX	BAC	XEBAC, Bahía Asunción
1100	5	PNR	M92	R. Sabrosa, Panamá
1100	3	SLV	RF	R.Ranchera, San Salvador
1110	10	CUB	KO	R. Angulo, Holguín
1110		CUB		R. Cadena Habana
1110	2.5	DOM	TC	R. Jarabacoa, Jarabacoa
1110	1/0.5	DOM	OS	R. Marién, Dajabón
1110	1	GTM	MK	R. Verapaz, Cobán
1110	0.5	HND	ME	R. El Patio, La Ceiba
1110		HND		R. Sonora, Choluteca
1110	1/0.5	MEX	WR	Classics 11-10, Cd.Juárez
1110	1	MEX	OQ	Dimensión Gape 1110, Reynosa
1110	1/0.2	MEX	PVJ	Energía Vallarta La Líder, Puerto Vallarta
1110	1/0.5	MEX	ES	La Radio Viva, Chihuahua
1110	5/1	MEX	LEO	La Rancherita, León
1110	1/0.25	MEX	VS	Maxima, Hermosillo
1110	0.25	MEX	PU	Patronato Cultural Monclova, Monclova
1110	50	MEX	RED	R. Red, México
1110	0.5	MEX	TED	XETED, Teotitlán de Flores Magon
1110	0.5	MEX	TUX	XETUX, Tuxtepec
1110	1	NCG	MT	R. Momotombo, La Paz Centro
1110		PNR		LV Podrosa, Los Santos
1110	2.5/0.5	PTR	WVJP	R. Caguas/Criolla, Caguas
1110	2.5	SLV	CL	R.Horizonte, San Miguel
1120	1	ATN	PJE-3	R. Statia, St. Eustasius
1120		CTR		Unción Radio, San José
1120	1	CUB	KO	R. Angulo, Mayarí
1120	5	CUB	CH	R. Cadena Habana, Artemisa
1120		CUB		R. Rebelde
1120		DOM		R. Antillas, Barahona
1120	10	DOM	CN	R. Metro 1120 AM Stereo, Sto Domingo
1120		DOM	CN	R. Metro, Samaná
1120	0.5	GTM	C	R. Uno 120 AM, Guatemala
1120	2	HND	YL	R. Fiesta, Tegucigalpa
1120		HND		R. Marchala, Ocotepeque
1120	1	HND	DG	R. Oriental "RCO", Danlí
1120	10	HTI		R. Magic, Port-au-Prince
1120	1/0.1	MEX	POP	La Preciosa, Puebla
1120	1	MEX	MX	MVS Noticias, Mexicali
1120	1/0.5	MEX	GV	R. ACIR, Querétaro
1120	2/0.25	MEX	ZB	R. Oro, Oaxaca
1120	1/0.5	MEX	TR	R. Panorámica, Cd.Valles
1120	1/0.25	MEX	RUY	R. Universidad, Mérida
1120	1/0.5	MEX	UNO	R. Uno, Guadalajara
1120	5/0.5	MEX	TQE	XETQE, Tenosique
1120	5	NCG	CP	R. CEPAD "El Arco Iris Del Amor", Managua
1120		PNR		LV Poderosa, Colón
1120	5	PNR	M21	R. Sonora, Panamá
1120	2.6/5	PTR	WMSW	R. Once/La Gran W, Hatillo
1120	3	SLV	LR	R.Voz que Clama en Desierto, San Salvador
1130	5	CUB	KO	R. Angulo/Ecos del Sagua, Sagua de Tánamo
1130	1	CUB	HA	R. Enciclopedia, Santa Clara
1130	10/1	DOM	RL	La Mezcla, Santiago Cadena de Noticias
1130	1	GTM	VR	Em. Unidas LV de la Costa Sur, Retalhuleu
1130	1	HND	HP	R. Pinares, Siguatepeque
1130	5	HND	PL	R. Progreso, El Progreso
1130	1	HND	BI	R. San Francisco, San Francisco de la Paz
1130	1/0.25	MEX	MOS	Banda Sonora, Los Mochis
1130	10/1	MEX	ZL	La Grupera, Jalapa
1130	5	MEX	ETCH	LV de los Tres Ríos, Etchojoa
1130	10/5	MEX	TOL	R. Lobo, Toluca
1130	1	MEX	LUP	R. Lupita, Las Varas
1130	1/0.1	MEX	FN	R. Moderna, Uruapan
1130	1	MEX	HN	Rockola, Nogales
1130		PNR		LV Poderosa, Chiriquí
1130	2.5	PNR	U80	R. Sensación, Aguadulce
1130	0.2/0.7	PTR	WOIZ	R. Antillas, Guayanilla
1130	1	SLV	LG	R.Chaparrastique, San Miguel
1130	1	SLV	AJ	R.Moderna, Sta Ana
1140	1.5	CTR	VAL	R. Nueva, Guápiles
1140	1	CUB	KX	R. Bayamo, Media Luna
1140	5	CUB	CH	R. Cadena Habana, La Habana
1140		CUB		R. Ciudad Banderas
1140	5	CUB	CG	R. Enciclopedia, Loma de la Cruz
1140	5	DOM	RA	R. Anacaona, San Juan de la Maguana
1140		HND	VC	LV Evangélica, Choluteca
1140	1	HND	AP	R. Mercurio, Choluteca
1140	1	HND	UN	R. Palmeras, La Ceiba
1140	5/0.1	MEX	TE	1140 Punto Digital, Tehuacán
1140	5/1	MEX	XF	La Grupera, León
1140	1	MEX	LIA	La Tremenda, Morelia
1140	50	MEX	MR	M-R 140 AM, Música Romántica, Monterrey
1140	10	MEX	SOS	R. Uno, Agua Prieta
1140	1	MEX	PEC	XEPEC, San Bartolo Tutotepec
1140	2.5	MEX	TEC	XETEC, Tecpatan
1140	5	PNR	B49	R. Panamericana, Panamá
1140	10	PTR	WQII	Once Q, San Juan
1140	10	SLV	TS	R.El Mundo, San Salvador
1150	10	CUB	KX	R. Bayamo, Entronque Bueycito
1150	5	DOM	AS	Onda Musical, Sto Domingo
1150	1	GTM	RR	R. Fiesta, Guatemala
1150	5	HND	AV	Ondas del Ulúa, Sta Bárbara
1150		HND		R. Universal, Tegucigalpa
1150	0.25	HTI		R. Caraibes, Port-au-Prince
1150	20/10	MEX	CMQ	El Fonógrafo/Canal 115, México
1150	1/0.5	MEX	JS	JS Digital, Hidalgo del Parral
1150	5/0.3	MEX	SO	La Coqueta, Cd.Obregón
1150	1.5/0.5	MEX	TVR	La Nueva Azul, Tuxpam
1150	10/1	MEX	XP	La Super Buena, Tuxtepec
1150	1/0.25	MEX	BF	La Tremenda, San Pedro
1150	1	MEX	RM	R. Fórmula, Mexicali
1150	20/0.5	MEX	AD	R. Metrópoli, Guadalajara
1150	1	MEX	QUE	R. Querétaro, Querétaro
1150	10/0.15	MEX	UAS	R. Universidad, Culiacán
1150	5/1	MEX	RTM	Zonido Zeta, Macuspana
1150	5	NCG	UW	R. Darío, León
1150	5	PNR		Ecos de Pedasí, Pedasí
1150	1	SLV	CF	Estéreo Mi Consentida, San Miguel
1160	10	ATG		Caribbean R. Lighthouse
1160	3	CTR	LX	R. Columbia, Puntarenas
1160		CUB	KX	R. Bayamo, Pilón
1160	5/1	DOM	BE	Radiolandia, Santiago
1160	1	GTM	RI	R. Izabal, Morales
1160	1	HND	HZ	R. Bethel, Taujica
1160	0.5	HND	GF	R. El Paraíso, El Paraíso
1160	5	HND	QN	R. LV del Atlántico, Puerto Cortés
1160	1	HND	QL2	R. Sentimentos, Siguatepeque
1160	1/0.1	MEX	IW	Canal Juvenil, Uruapan
1160	5/0.25	MEX	BE	Imversa Radio, Perote
1160	2.5/0.5	MEX	VW	R. Sensación, Acámbaro
1160	1/0.1	MEX	GI	Reyna de las Huastecas, Tamazunchale
1160	1	NCG	HM	R. Satélite, Estelí
1160	5	PNR		Ecos de Pedasí, Pedasí
1160	5	PNR	C20	Ondas Chiricanas, David
1160	10	PNR	WK	R. Metrópolis, Panamá
1160	5/2.5	PTR	WBQN	Super Borinquén, Barceloneta-Manatí
1160	1	SLV	RG	R.Corporación, Sta Ana
1160	3	SLV	CL	R.Horizonte, San Salvador
1170	10	CUB	KS	Cadena CMKS, Maisí
1170		DOM	JS	Cadena Espacial, Azua
1170	5	GTM	RL	R. Cadena Landívar, Quetzaltenango
1170	2	HND	AF	R. Atenea "La Internacional", Choluteca
1170	1	HND	AZ3	R. Hits, La Ceiba
1170	10	HTI		R. Soleil, Port-au-Prince
1170	1/0.5	MEX	MDA	La Ley 11-70, Monclova
1170	10/1	MEX	UVA	La Rancherita, Aguascalientes
1170	1/0.1	MEX	JTF	Prisma Musical, Zacoalco de Torres
1170	5/1	MEX	FEM	R. Felicidad, Hermosillo
1170	2. 5/1	MEX	ZS	R. Hit, Coatzacoalcos
1170	1	MFX	IB	Super Banda/Punto de Vista, Caborca
1170	1/0.25	MEX	RLK	Super Stereo Miled, Atlacomulco
1170	5	MEX	RT	Voz 1170, Reynosa
1170	10/0.5	MEX	CD	XECD 1170 R. De Verdad, Puebla
1170	5	NCG		R. Máxima, Masaya

kHz	kW	Ctry	Call	Station, location
1170	0.2	PTR	WLEO	Zona Metro del Sur, Ponce
1170		SLV	CR	R.Cristo Viene, San Miguel
1175	0.5	SLV	CB	LV del Pacifico, Sonsonate
1180	20	CTR	PJ	R. Victoria, Heredia
1180	50	CUB	BA	R. Rebelde, Villa María
1180	1	CUB	DB	R. Reloj, Mayarí Arriba
1180	10	DOM	BE	R. Mil, Sto Domingo
1180	10	GTM	T	R. Sonora, Guatemala
1180	1/0.8	HND	CY	R. Congolon, Gracias
1180	1	HND	AZ	R. Taxi, Tegucigalpa
1180		HND		Sta Bárbara Estéreo, Sta Bárbara
1180	10/1	MEX	GN	La Gigante, Piedras Negras
1180	1	MEX	YA	La Picosa, Irapuato
1180	10	MEX	FR	R. Felicidad, México
1180	0.5	MEX	AH	R. Hit, Juchitán
1180	10	MEX	UBS	R. Universidad Autonoma de Baja California Sur, La Paz
1180	1/0.25	MEX	DCH	Romántica 11-80, Cd.Delicias
1180	10	PNR		China Visión Panamá, Panamá
1180	10	PNR		R. Belén, Santiago
1180	5	SLV	VG	R.VEA-Voz Evangélica de América, San Salvador
1190	1	CUB		R. 26, La Caridad
1190	1	CUB	GL	R. Sancti Spíritus, Trinidad
1190	10	DOM	AG	Azul 11-90 Bachatisima, Santiago
1190	1	HND	GK	R. Brassabola, Minas de Oro
1190	0.5	HND	FS	R. Familiar, Morazan
1190	1	HND	PO	R. Sta María de la Luz, Gualaco
1190	1	HND	ZQ	R. Tegucigalpa, San Pedro Sula
1190	0.3	HTI		R. Grand Anse, Jeremie
1190	5/0.5	MEX	TOT	Éxtasis Digital, Tampico
1190	5/0.25	MEX	PP	La Comadre, Orizaba
1190	5/0.5	MEX	JPA	La Grande/Red W, Cuernavaca
1190	50/10	MEX	WK	La W de Guadalajara, Guadalajara
1190	10/0.1	MEX	CT	Morena, Monterrey
1190	0.5/0.1	MEX	MBC	R. Hablada, Mexicali
1190	5/0.1	MEX	PZ	R. Norteña, Cd.Juárez
1190	2.5/0.5	MEX	SOL	R. Sol, Cd.Hidalgo
1190	10/0.5	MEX	RV	R. Villa, Villahermosa
1190	10/5	PTR	WBMJ	WBMJ Rock Radio Network, San Juan
1200	5	CTR	AM	R. Cucú, San José
1200	1	CUB	BS	R. Ariguanabo, San Antonio de los Baños
1200	10	CUB	KC	R. Revolución, Palma Soriano
1200	1	CUB	GL	R. Sancti Spíritus/LV de Yaguajay, Yaguajay
1200	1	DOM	MR	R. Caracol, Azua
1200	1	GTM	RJ	R. Jutiapa, Jutiapa
1200	1	HND	DS	R. Nacaome, Nacaome
1200	1	MEX	ZI	Canal Festivo 120, Zacapu
1200	1/0.5	MEX	QY	Inolvidable 1200 AM, Toluca
1200	1	MEX	AGA	La Bonita, Aguascalientes
1200	1/0.25	MEX	WT	La Buenísima, Culiacán
1200	1/0.25	MEX	YF	R. Fórmula, Primera Cadena Nac., Hermosillo
1200	0.25	MEX	ITC	R. Tecnológico, Celaya
1200	1/0.3	MEX	PW	Tu Música, Poza Rica
1200	1	MEX	PAS	XEPAS, Punta Abrejos
1200	1	PTR	WGDL	R. Grito/La Radioemisora Lareña, Lares
1200	10	SLV	MM	R.Familiar, San Salvador
1200	1	SLV	KJ	R.Sirama, San Miguel
1210	1	CUB	KC	R. Revolución, Chivirico
1210	1	CUB	KC	R. Revolución, Mayarí Arriba
1210	10	CUB	GL	R. Sancti Spíritus, Sancti Spíritus
1210	5	DOM	CJ	R. Merengue, San Francisco de Macorís
1210		DOM	AH	R. VEN - Voz Evangelica Nac., Sto Domingo
1210	10/5	GTM	MX	Coco Radio, Guatemala
1210	1	HND	HO	Estéreo Maya, La Entrada
1210	1	HND	RO	R. Capital, Comayagüela
1210	1	HND	SI	R. Impacto, Tela
1210	1	HTI		R. Plus, Port-au-Prince
1210	50/5	MEX	BCO	La Poderosa Voz de Colima, Colima
1210	5	MEX	COPA	LV de los Vientos, Copainalá
1210	5/1	MEX	PUE	Méxicana 1210, Puebla
1210	10/0.25	MEX	BD	R. Centro, Jalapa
1210	5/1	MEX	VZ	R. La Veraz, Acayacan
1210	1	PNR	E91	R. El Mundo, Panamá
1210	5	PTR	WHOY	R. Hoy, Salinas
1210	1	SLV	CG	R.La Paz, Zacatecoluca
1220	1	CTR	Q	R. Casino, Limón
1220	10	CUB	GY	R. 26, Central España
1220		DOM		R. Bemba, Sto Domingo
1220	1	GTM	MT	R. Amiga, Antigua
1220	1	HND	QO	R. Costeña Ebenezer, San Pedro Sula
1220	0.5	HND	JM	R. Destellos de Luz, Sabá
1220	10/1	HND	GW	R. Patria, Catacamas
1220	1	HND	YS	R. Suari, Marcala
1220	1	HTI		V. du Plateau Central, Hinche
1220	100	MEX	B	La B Grande, México
1220	1/0.25	MEX	DKN	R. Fórmula, Guadalajara
1220	2.5	MEX	SAL	R. Universidad, Saltillo
1220	1	NCG	VA	R. América, Managua
1230	3	CUB	GJ	R. 26, Unión de Reyes
1230	1	DOM	PM	R. Moca, Moca
1230		GTM		R. América, Cuyotenango
1230	1	GTM	AT	R. Atlántida, Puerto Barrios
1230	0.25	HND	SM	R. Samaritano, San Marcos de Colón
1230	10	HND	QW	R. Tela, Tela
1230	1	HTI		V. de L'ave Maria, Cap Haitien
1230	20/1	MEX	TVH	La Morena, Villahermosa
1230	1	MEX	TCP	La Romántica, Tehuacan
1230	1/0.25	MEX	EX	R. Fórmula, Culiacán
1230	1	MEX	LP	R. Pía, La Piedad
1230	5	NCG	MNG	R. Manantial, Nueva Guinea
1230	1	PTR	WNIK	R. Unica, Arecibo
1240	1	BAH	ZNS2	Broadcasting Corporation of the Bahamas
1240	1	CTR	LX	R. Columbia, Nicoya
1240	10	CUB	GW	R. 26, Bolondrón
1240	5/1	DOM	CV	R. Barahona, Barahona
1240	1	DOM	AU	R. Revelación, Puerto Plata
1240	5	GTM	K	R. Luz, Guatemala
1240	1	HND	ZC	R. Monumental, Tegucigalpa
1240	1	HND	VN	R. Venus, Sta Bárbara
1240	1	HTI		Haiti Internationales, Port-au-Prince
1240	1	MEX	BQ	Estelar 12-40/R. Mexicana, Guaymas
1240	1	MEX	VM	La Estación del Amor, Piedras Negras
1240	2.5/0.5	MEX	OV	La Picosa, Orizaba
1240	1/0.25	MEX	S	La Tamaulipeca, Tampico
1240	1	MEX	WG	R. Amor, Cd.Juárez
1240	1	MEX	LM	R. Capital, Tuxtla Gutiérrez
1240	2. 5/1	MEX	SI	R. Felicidad, Santiago Ixcuintla
1240	1	MEX	IZ	R. Fórmula,Tercera Cadena Nac., Monterrey
1240	2. 5/1	MEX	CE	R. Hit 12-40, Oaxaca
1240	1	MEX	RD	R. Lobo, Pachuca
1240	1	MEX	CG	R. Mexicana, Nogales
1240	5/0.5	MEX	RPA	R. Ranchito, Morelia
1240	1/0.25	MEX	BN	Radiola, Cd.Delicias
1240	1	NCG		R. Restauración, Managua
1240	1	PNR	M56	Faro de David, David
1240	1/5	PTR	WALO	R. Oriental/Cadena R. Puerto Rico, Humacao
1240	0.5	SLV	MT	R.Metapán, Metapán
1240	1	SLV	QN	R.Norteña, San Miguel
1250	0.25	CUB	KS	R. Bayamo, Imías
1250	1	CUB	HS	R. Caibarién, Caibarién
1250	5	DOM	RJ	El Sonido del Este "Digital", La Romana
1250	5	DOM	BC	LV del Progreso, San Francisco de Macorís
1250	1	GTM		LV Cristiana, Totonicapán
1250	1	GTM	PY	R. Payakí, Esquipulas
1250	1	HND	CC	R. Cadena Continental, Comayagua
1250	1	HND	YN	R. Latina, Danlí
1250		HND		R. Sonaguera, Sonaguera
1250	0.5	HND	QV	R. Subirana, Yoro
1250	1	HND	AT	Super R., San Pedro Sula
1250	10/1	MEX	DK	DK 12-50, Guadalajara
1250	2.5/0.5	MEX	PI	La Consentida, Chilpancingo
1250	1	MEX	TF	La Jarocha, Veracruz
1250	5/0.25	MEX	MG	Máxima 1250/La R.Impresionante, Arriaga
1250	1/0.5	MEX	SC	R. 1250, Sabinas
1250	5/0.5	MEX	DL	R. 13/Fuerza de la Palabra, Hermosillo
1250	5/0.1	MEX	JX	R. Fórmula, Segunda Cadena Nac., Querétaro
1250	5/0.25	MEX	AT	R. Imagen, Hidalgo del Parral
1250	5/0.5	MEX	SJ	R. Saltillo, Saltillo
1250	5/0.5	MEX	ZT	R. Tribuna 12-50, Puebla
1250	1/0.25	MEX	TEJ	Sistema XEGEM "R. Mexiquense", Tejupilco
1250	2.5	NCG	CR	Cadena Radial Samaritano, Condega
1250	5	PNR	LY	R. Hogar, Penonomé
1250	0.2 5/1	PTR	WJIT	R. Hit, Sabana
1260	5	CTR	HM	R. Emaús, San Vito de Coto Brus
1260	5	CUB	BF	R. Enciclopedia, Arroyo Arenas
1260	1	CUB	GH	R. Victoria de Girón, Torriente
1260	1	DOM	T	R. Recuerdos, Sto Domingo
1260	1	HND	ZR	R. 1260, La Ceiba
1260	1	HND	YF2	R. San Marcos, San Marcos de Colón
1260	5/0.25	MEX	WGR	Estéreo Vida, Monclova
1260	1/0.25	MEX	ZH	La Estación que es Escucha, Salamanca
1260	1	MEX	TBV	La Poderosa, Tierra Blanca
1260	5/0.5	MEX	SA	La Sabrosita/La Mejor, Culiacán

kHz	kW	Ctry	Call	Station, location
1260	5	MEX	JAM	LV de la Costa Chica, Santiago Jamiltepec
1260	50/10	MEX	L	R. ACIR, México
1260	10/1	MEX	JY	R. Ambiente, Autlán
1260	1/0.25	MEX	R	R. Linares, Linares
1260	1	MEX	MTV	R. Lobo de Mina, Minatitlán
1260	5/1	MEX	XR	R. Mensajera, Cd.Valles
1260	5/0.15	MEX	OG	R. Ranchito, Ojinaga
1260	5/2.5	MEX	RO	R. Recuerdo, Aguascalientes
1260	1/0.25	MEX	MW	R. San Luis, San Luis Río Colorado
1260	1	MEX	QL	Sonido Brillante, Zamora
1260	2.5/0.8	PTR	WISO	R. Wiso/Cadena WAPA, Aguadilla
1260	2.5	PTR	WISO	R. Wiso/Cadena WAPA, Ponce
1260	3	SLV	AA	R.Abba, San Salvador
1270		ABW		R. 1270
1270	10	CUB	BN	R. Caribe, Nueva Gerona
1270	1	CUB	GF	R. Enciclopedia, Varadero
1270	10	CUB		R. Reloj, Camagüey
1270	1	DOM	TA	R. Ambiente, Baní
1270	5	DOM	DA	R. Hit 12-70, Santiago
1270	2.5	GTM	CQ	R. Exclusiva, Guatemala
1270	1	HND	OF	Ecos del Celaque, Gracias
1270	1	HND	NQ	R. Sonora, Tegucigalpa
1270	1/0.5	MEX	GL	Digital 12-70, Navojoa
1270	0.5/0.15	MEX	WN	El Fonógrafo del Recuerdo, Torreón
1270	1/0.25	MEX	RRR	La Invasora 12-70, Poza Rica
1270	10/0.15	MEX	RPL	La Poderosa, León
1270	1/0.1	MEX	QH	R. Sinfonía, Ixmiquilpán
1270	0.5	MEX	AZ	R. Zeta 13, Tijuana
1270	1	MEX	VHT	Romántica 12-70, Villahermosa
1270	5/0.5	MEX	RRT	Solar 1270, Cd.Madero
1270	5/0.5	MEX	AX	Tu Frecuencia 1080, Oaxaca
1270	1.5/0.5	MEX	HD	Universidad Juárez del Estado de Durango, Durango
1270	3	NCG	RA	R. Amistad, Matagalpa
1270	3	PNR	J22	R. Tipy Q, Panamá
1270	1	SLV	QZ	R.W "LV de la Verdad en Oriente", San Miguel
1280	2	CTR	HT	R. Alajuela, Alajuela
1280	1	CUB	KW	R. Mambí, Stgo de Cuba
1280	1	CUB	JC	R. Rectángulo/R.Guaimaro, Guaimaro
1280		DOM	JH	Cadena Espacial, Sto Domingo
1280	1	DOM	HZ	R. Clave, Monte Plata
1280	2.5	GTM	VY	R. Zamaneb, Salamá
1280	1	HND	BU	R. Digital, San Pedro Sula
1280		HND		R. Monserrat, El Paraíso
1280	1	HND	AM	R. Olanchito, Olanchito
1280	1	HND	BN	R. San Miguel, Marcala
1280	3	HTI		R. Metropole, Port-au-Prince
1280	1/0.5	MEX	BW	La Pantera, Chihuahua
1280	1/0.1	MEX	KY	LV de la Costa de Chiapas, Huixtla
1280	2.5/1	MEX	CAM	Mix, Campeche
1280	2/1	MEX	AG	R. Cafetal, Córdoba
1280	1/0.5	MEX	EG	R. Fórmula Puebla, Puebla
1280	10/0.5	MEX	BON	R. Fórmula,Tercera Cadena Nac., Guadalajara
1280	2.5/0.15	MEX	SQ	R. San Miguel. San Miguel de Allende
1280	1	MEX	TUT	R. Tamaulipas, Tula
1280	10/1	MEX	AW	Teleradio, Monterrey
1280	5/1	PTR	WCMN	NotiUno/R. Centro, Arecibo
1280		SLV		R.Emaús, San Vicente
1280	1	SLV	QV	R.Galaxia, Sta Ana
1290	1	CUB	HW	Doblevé, Rancho Veloz
1290	5	CUB	BQ	R. Enciclopedia, La Habana
1290	5	CUB	CS	R. Progreso, La Pastora
1290		CUB		R. Taino, La Habana
1290		DOM	BD	R. Jánico, Jánico
1290		GTM		R. Miramundo "LV del Ejercito", Zacapa
1290	0.5	GTM	TU	R. Nal. de Totonicapán, Totonicapán
1290	1	HND	NN26	R. Choluteca, Choluteca
1290	1	HND	GS	R. HRGS/Bay Island Christian Network, Utila
1290	1/0.5	MEX	IX	Enlace Digital 12-90, Sahuayo
1290	1	MEX	IY	Espectacular 12-90, Río Verde
1290	10/1	MEX	NX	Fiesta Mexicana, Mazatlán
1290	5/0.25	MEX	FAC	La Mera Mera, Salvatierra
1290	2.5	MEX	QIN	LV de las Montañas/LV del Valle, San Quintín
1290	7	MEX	DA	R. 13/La Fuerza de la Palabra, México
1290	0.25	MEX	TH	R. Palizada, Palizada
1290	1/0.25	MEX	AP	Romántica 1290, Cd.Obregón
1290	10	PNR		RCM Noticias, David
1290	10	PNR		RCM Noticias, Guararé
1290	10	PNR	S23	RCM Noticias, Panamá (R. Cadena Milenium)
1290	1	SLV	MA	R.Chalatenango, Chalatenango

kHz	kW	Ctry	Call	Station, location
1290	0.5/0.29	VIR	WRRA	WRRA, Frederiksted
1300	1	ATN	PJD-2	The Voice of St. Maarten, Philipsburg
1300	7.5	CTR	LC	La Fuente Musical, Cartago
1300	1	CUB	DA	R. Enciclopedia, Las Tunas
1300		CUB		R. Portada de la Libertad, Niquero
1300	1	DOM	KQ	R. Dos, Sto Domingo
1300	1	HND	LH	LV de la Amistad, Tegucigalpa
1300	5	HND	LR	R. Sta Rosa, Sta Rosa de Copán
1300		HTI		R. Vision Nouvelle, Port-au-Prince
1300	1	MEX	KW	Bonita, Morelia
1300	1/0.1	MEX	XW	Estéreo Vida, Nogales
1300	1/0.25	MEX	JL	La 130, La Ley, Guamuchil
1300	1/0.15	MEX	LE	R. 13, Tampico
1300	50	MEX	P	R. 13/R. Centro, Cd.Juárez
1300	10/0.75	MEX	XV	R. Capital, León
1300	1/0.25	MEX	AWL	R. Jacala,Jacala
1300	1/0.5	MEX	SW	R. Madera, Cd.Madera
1300	1/0.1	MEX	HU	R. Tropical, Martinez de la Torre
1300	1	NCG	R	Canal 130 AM, Managua
1300	5	PNR	I417	R. Baha'í, Boca del Monte
1300	1	PTR	WTIL	R. Util/Cadena R. Puerto Rico, Mayagüez
1300		SLV	KG	R.Llanera "La Campechana", San Miguel
1300	5	SLV	LV	W-LV de la Verdad, San Salvador
1310	1	CUB	HW	Doblevé, Sagua La Grande
1310	1	CUB	JW	R. Santa Cruz, Santa Cruz del Sur
1310	1	DOM	MH	R. Real, La Vega
1310	1	GTM	AN	R. LV de los Altos, Quetzaltenango
1310	2.5	HND	VC	LV Evangélica, San Pedro Sula
1310	0.5	HND	JH	R. Colón, Tocoa
1310	1	HND	YN	R. Latina, Danlí
1310	1	HND	RL	R. Libertad, Marcala, La Paz
1310	1/0.25	MEX	HY	13-10 La Jefa, Querétaro
1310	10/0.25	MEX	TIA	Alma de México, Guadalajara
1310	2. 5/1	MEX	HV	HV 1310 AM, Veracruz
1310	1	MEX	GRT	Jaguar 1310, Taxco
1310	5/0.25	MEX	AM	La M Grande, Matamoros
1310	5/0.1	MEX	VB	R. 13, Monterrey
1310	1	MEX	C	R. Enciso, Tijuana
1310	5/1	MEX	HIT	R. Felicidad, Puebla
1310	1	MEX	TRC	R. Gazeta de la Tierra Norte, Tepetzintla
1310	0.25	MEX	HJ	R. Petatlán, Petatlán
1310	1/0.1	MEX	FH	R. Plan de Agua Prieta, Agua Prieta
1310	1/0.25	MEX	RU	R. Universidad, Chihuahua
1310	10	MEX	LPZ	R. Variedades, La Paz
1310	1	MEX	BTS	XEBTS, Bahía de Tortugas
1310	10/1	NCG	SC	R. San Cristóbal, Chinandega
1310	12	PNR		R. María, Panamá
1310	5	SLV	RV	R.Veritas, Stgo de María
1320	1	ABW		R. Holland Aruba
1320	0.5	CUB	AD	R. Artemisa, Artemisa (cfr 1330)
1320	1	CUB	HA	R. Enciclopedia, Sancti Spíritus
1320	1	CUB	DA	R. Enciclopedia, Stgo de Cuba
1320	1/0.5	DOM	BZ	R. Centro, San Juan de la Maguana
1320	1	GTM	ME	R. Quesada, Jutiapa
1320	1	HND	MG	R. Bahía "La Super Grande", La Ceiba
1320	1	HND	GM	R. Ilusión, Choluteca
1320		HND		R. Super K, Nacaome
1320	0.25	MEX	NM	Expresión Total, Aguascalientes
1320	2. 5/1	MEX	FRO	Fiesta Mexicana, Villahermosa
1320	5/0.25	MEX	JZ	La Campera, Cd.Jimenez
1320	5/1	MEX	UH	La Consentida, Tuxtepec
1320	10/0.1	MEX	CPN	La Mexicana 1320, Piedras Negras
1320	5/0.5	MEX	RJ	La Ranchera, Mazatlán
1320	20/0.5	MEX	NI	Mix, Uruapán
1320	20	MEX	D	R. Bienestar/Monitor, México
1320	1/0.25	MEX	SR	R. Cachanía, Santa Rosalia
1320	5/2.3	PTR	WSKN	Super Kadena Noticias, San Juan
1320	1	SLV	AH	R.Emanuel, La Unión
1330	0.5	CUB	AD	R. Jaruco, Artemisa (cfr 1320)
1330	1	CUB		R. Portada de la Libertad, Holguín
1330	3	DOM	VC	R. Visión Cristiana, Sto Domingo
1330	5.5	GTM	MU	Unión Radio "LV de la Esperanza"
1330	1	HND	SW	R. Evangélica, Tegucigalpa
1330	1	HND	FL	R. Florida, La Entrada
1330	10	HTI		R. Haiti Inter, Port-au-Prince
1330	1/0.1	MEX	RP	Èxtasis Digital, Cd.Madero
1330	2. 5/1	MEX	HTY	Inolvidable, Martínoz de la Torre
1330	2/0.25	MEX	AJ	La Imagen de la R en Satillo, Saltillo
1330	0.5	MEX	MAC	La Poderosa, Manzanillo
1330	4/0.25	MEX	WQ	La Superestación, Monclova

kHz	kW	Ctry	Call	Station, location
1330	1	MEX	EV	R. Festival, Izúcar de Matamoros
1330	5/0.2	MEX	BO	R. Variedades, Irapuato
1330	5	NCG	GA	R. Matagalpa, Matagalpa
1330	5	PNR		LV Poderosa, Panamá
1330	2/1.5	PTR	WENA	La Buena del Sur, Yauco
1330	5	SLV	HQ	R.Cristo Te Llama, San Salvador
1340	6	CTR	HR	R. Sideral, San Ramón
1340	1	CUB	DO	R. Banes, Banes
1340	10	CUB	FL	R. Ciudad del Mar, Palmira
1340	3	DOM	FA	LV Cultural de las Fuerzas Armadas, Moca
1340	10	GTM	CO	Em. Unidas LV del Trópico, Coatepeque
1340	1	HND	JC	R. Colonial, Comayagua
1340	10	HND	HH	R. El Mundo, San Pedro Sula
1340	1	HND	ED	R. Red, Olanchito
1340	2	MEX	SL	Cancionero 13-40, San Luis Potosí
1340	1	MEX	APM	Candela, Apatzingán
1340	1	MEX	AA	La Caliente, Mexicali
1340	1	MEX	QB	La Divertida, Tulancingo
1340	0.25/0.1	MEX	RCH	La Pantera, Ojinaga
1340	1	MEX	QE	La Perla Camaronera, Escuinapa
1340	1	MEX	NV	La Sabrosita, Monterrey
1340	1	MEX	OS	La Super Tremenda, Cd.Obregón
1340	1	MEX	DH	La Tremenda Tropical, Cd.Acuña
1340	1	MEX	MT	Magia 13-40, Matamoros
1340	1	MEX	YR	R. 13, Teapa
1340	5/0.25	MEX	LU	R. Esmeralda, Cd.Serdán
1340	1	MEX	RPV	R. Festival, Cd.Victoria
1340	5/1	MEX	DKT	R. Ranchito, Guadalajara
1340	1	MEX	CI	Romántica 1340, Acapulco
1340	5/1	MEX	ASM	Romántica 13-40, Cuernavaca
1340	1	MEX	CR	Stereo Mía, Morelia
1340	5/1	MEX	BK	Super Grupera, Nuevo Laredo
1340	1	NCG	OS	R. Ondas Sonoras, Managua
1340	2.5	PNR		R. Tipical, Las Tablas
1340	0.95	PTR	WWNA	R. Tiempo/R. Una, Aguadilla
1340	1	SLV	XW	R.Novedades, Usulután
1340	1	VIR	WSTA	WSTA, St Thomas
1350	1	CUB	FL	R. Ciudad del Mar, Aguada de Pasajeros
1350	10	CUB	KY	R. Libertad, Puerto Padre
1350	1	DOM	JD	Ondas del Yuna, Bonao
1350	1	DOM	PM	R. Rutas Musical, La Romana
1350	1	GTM	MC	R. Monja Blanca, Cobán
1350	1	HND	JV	LV de San Lorenzo, San Lorenzo
1350		HND		R. Estelar, La Ceiba
1350	0.25	HTI		R. Dame Marie, Dame Marie
1350	1	MEX	TM	El Heraldo de la Frontera, Naco
1350	1/0.25	MEX	ZD	La Doña de la Frontera, Camargo
1350	5/1	MEX	CAH	La Popular 13-50, Cacahoatán
1350	5/1	MEX	QK	La R. de los Ciudadanos, México
1350	5	MEX	CTZ	LV de la Sierra Norte, Cuetzalán
1350	6/1	MEX	LBL	R. Centro, San Luis Río Colorado
1350	5/0.5	MEX	TB	R. Laguna, Torreón
1350	1	NCG	GF	R. Ondas del Sur, Jinotepe
1350	5	PNR	Z38	R. Integridad, Panamá
1350	2.5	PTR	WEGA	R. Las Vegas, Vega Baja
1360		CTR	CA	R. Celestial, San José
1360	1	CUB	FA	R. Cadena Agramonte, Rodolfo Ramírez Esquível
1360		DOM	XZ	R. Listín, Sto Domingo
1360	10	GTM	LK	R. Tic Tac "LV del Tiempo", Guatemala
1360		HND		R. Continente, Trinidad
1360	1	HND	BS	R. San Pedro, Tegucigalpa
1360	5	HND	GH	R. Sta Bárbara, Sta Bárbara
1360	5	HTI		R. Liberte, Port-au-Prince
1360	1/0.4	MEX	DI	Éxtasis Digital, Chihuahua
1360	1/0.15	MEX	DQ	La Comadre, San Andrés Tuxtla
1360	1/0.25	MEX	Y	La Grupera, Celaya
1360	5/0.5	MEX	UD	La U de Tuxtla, Tuxtla Gutiérrez
1360	5	MEX	ZON	LV de la Sierra de Zongolica, Zongolica
1360	1	MEX	XM	R. Jerez, Jerez de García Salinas
1360	1/0.5	MEX	KF	Stereomil 1360, La K-F, Iguala
1360	5/1	PTR	WCHQ	C-H-Q, Camuy
1360	5	SLV	FM	Super Radio, San Salvador
1370	1	CUB	FA	R. Cadena Agramonte, Nuevitas
1370	1	CUB	DF	R. Granma, Manzanillo
1370	1	CUB	DV	R. Siboney, Stgo de Cuba
1370	5	DOM	FA	LV Cultural de las Fuerzas Armadas, Elías Piña
1370	5	DOM	RP	R. Seybo, El Seybo
1370	1	GTM	AC	LV de Colomba, Colomba
1370	1.5	HND	TR	R. Danlí, Danlí
1370	1	HND	ST	R. Fraternidad, San Pedro Sula
1370	1	HND	SZ	R. Sta Bárbara, Siguatepeque
1370	0.5	HTI		R. Citadelle, Cap Haitien
1370	1	HTI		Rdf Cayenne, Cayes
1370	5/1	MEX	A	El Eco de las Murallas, Campeche
1370	10	MEX	MON	R. Fórmula, Monterrey
1370	5	MEX	HF	R. Fórmula, Nogales
1370	5	MEX	GNK	R. Mexicana, Nuevo Laredo
1370	1/0.5	MEX	HG	R. Norteña, Mexicali
1370	5/1.5	MEX	JE	R. Reyna, Dolores Hidalgo
1370	5/1	MEX	UAA	R. Universidad, Aguascalientes
1370	1/0.5	MEX	SV	R. Universidad, Morelia
1370	1/0.25	MEX	RPU	Sonido Z, Durango
1370	10/1	MEX	PJ	Super Deportiva, Guadalajara
1370	1	NCG	RE	R. Somoto, Somoto
1370	1	PNR	B64	R. Sitrachilco, Pto Armuelles
1370	5/2.5	PTR	WIVV	WIVV Rock Radio Network, Viequez Isl
1370	1	SLV	KO	R Lluvia de Bendición, San Miguel
1380	1	CTR	MS	R. Guanacaste, Liberia
1380	1	CTR	MS	R. Guanacaste, San José
1380	10	CUB	FA	R. Cadena Agramonte, Central Brasil
1380	5/1	DOM	SC	R. Nacional, Santiago
1380	1	GTM	EB	R. Momostenango Educativa, Momostenango
1380	0.5	HND	AH	R. Redención, Jutiapa
1380	1	HND	EJ	R. Voz Evangélica, Choluteca
1380	0.7	HTI		R. Port au Prince, Port-au-Prince
1380	5/0.15	MEX	GW	Expansión W, Cd.Victoria
1380	1/0.1	MEX	VD	La V-D, Allende
1380	10/1	MEX	TP	R. Sensación. Jalapa
1380	50/5	MEX	CO	Romántica 13-80, México
1380	1/0.25	MEX	RS	Romántica 1380, Torreón
1380	10	PNR		R. América, Panamá
1380	1	PTR	WOLA	R. Prócer, Barranquitas
1390	1	CUB	BT	R. Jaruco, Jaruco
1390	1	DOM	AR	R. San Cristóbal
1390	5	GTM	YC	R. Istmania, Guatemala
1390	1	HND	VC	LV Evangélica, Sta Rosa de Copán
1390	10/5	HND	VC	LV Evangélica, Tegucigalpa
1390	5/0.2	MEX	TY	La Mexicana, Tecomán
1390	5/0.1	MEX	XO	La Super Buena, Cd.Mante
1390	5/0.1	MEX	KT	La Súper Estación, Tecate
1390	5/1	MEX	TL	LV de la Huasteca, Tuxpan
1390	5/0.15	MEX	QC	LV de Pto Penasco "Rocky Point", Pto Peñasco
1390	1	MEX	OR	Mix 13-90, Reynosa
1390	1/0.25	MEX	CTA	R. Cuautla, Cuautla
1390	10/0.25	MEX	RW	R. Formula, Primera Cadena Nac., León
1390	0.5	MEX	ZG	R. Mezquital y Huasteca Hidalguense, Ixmiquilpán
1390	6	PNR		R. Mundo Internacional, Colón
1390	1	PTR	WISA	Cadena Radio Puerto Rico, Isabela
1390		SLV		R.Sinaí, San Salvador
1400	12	CTR	CJ	R. Sinaí, San Isidro del General
1400	1	CUB	FA	R. Cadena Agramonte/R. Guaimaro, Guaimaro
1400	1	CUB	GX	R. Musical, Matanzas
1400	1	DOM	AC	Ondas del Valle, La Vega
1400	5	GRD		The Harbour Light Of The Windwards
1400	1	GTM	RB	R. Porteña, Puerto Barrios
1400	1	HND	AU	R. Alegre, Sava Colón
1400	1	HND	JJ	R. Estéreo Punto, Comayagua
1400	1	HND	YT	R. Estrella de Oro, San Pedro Sula
1400		HND	JU	R. Punto, Comayagua
1400	1	MEX	VI	Fantasía 99-1, San Juan del Río
1400	1/0.25	MEX	LH	La Gardenia Musical, Acaponeta
1400	2. 5/1	MEX	XI	La I de Ixtapan, Ixtapan de la Sal
1400	5/1	MEX	AC	La Ke Buena, Aguascalientes
1400	0.5	MEX	WU	La Poderosa, Matehuala
1400	1	MEX	KJ	La Rancherita, Acapulco
1400	1	MEX	PF	La Rancherita, Ensenada
1400	5/1	MEX	OJ	R. Horizonte, Cd.Lázaro Cárdenas
1400	1/0.25	MEX	FS	R. Matamoros, Izúcar de Matamoros
1400	1	MEX	I	R. Morelia, Morelia
1400	1	MEX	SH	R. Sabinas, Cd.Sabinas
1400	1/0.5	MEX	AB	R. Santa Ana, Santa Ana
1400	1	MEX	UBJ	R. Universidad Benito Juárez, Oaxaca
1400	10	NCG		R. María, Managua
1400	10	PNR	T40	Digital Radio Luz, La Chorrera
1400	1	PTR	WIDA	R. Vida, Carolina
1400	1	SLV	JI	LV del Litoral, Usulután
1410	1	CUB	JW	R. Cadena Agramonte, Sta Cruz

kHz	kW	Ctry	Call	Station, location
1410	1	CUB	AL	R. Enciclopedia, Pinar del Río
1410	3/0.5	DOM	CH	R. 14-10, Barahona
1410	1/0.5	DOM	JJ	R. Grí-Grí, Río San Juan
1410	1	DOM	AE	R. Revelación en América, Sto Domingo
1410	3	DOM	RM	R. Sol, Higüey
1410	5	GTM	GH	R. Xelajú, Quetzaltenango
1410	1	HND	DD	LV de Atlántida, La Ceiba
1410	1	HND	SY	R. Voz Evangélica del Pacifico, San Lorenzo
1410	1	HTI		V. de Nord-ouest, Port de Paix
1410	2 1/2	MEX	KB	Canal 14-10, Guadalajara
1410	5/0.5	MEX	IR	Estelar 14-10, Cd.Valles
1410	10/0.5	MEX	CF	La Mexicana, Los Mochis
1410	5/0.25	MEX	AS	La Tamaulipeca, Nuevo Laredo
1410	2/1	MEX	ZHO	R. Fama, Zihuatanejo
1410	2 1/2	MEX	BS	R. Sinfonola, México
1410	1/0.25	MEX	CUA	R. Universidad, Campeche
1410	1/0.1	MEX	YD	Super Banda, Torreón
1410	3/1	NCG	RA	La Estación de la Amistad, León
1410	5	PNR	H779	R. Mensabé, Las Tablas
1410	1	PTR	WRSS	R. Progreso, San Sebastián
1420	5	CTR	RP	R. Pampa, Nicoya
1420		CUB	JH	R. Grito de Baire, Contramaestre
1420	0.25	CUB		R. Llanuras, Colón
1420	15	DOM	FD	R. Oro, Cotuí
1420	1	GTM	RP	R. Verdad, Guatemala
1420	1	HND		LV de las Fuerzas Armadas, Comayagüela
1420	1	HND	SL	R. Stereo Actualidad, Trinidad
1420	0.5	HTI		R. Messie Continental, Dessalines
1420	1	MEX	PK	Inolvidable, Pachuca
1420	10/1	MEX	WE	La Estación Familiar, Irapuato
1420	1	MEX	KMX	La Super X, Sayula
1420	5/0.5	MEX	F	Línea 1420, Cd.Juárez
1420	1	MEX	AFQ	Mariachi Stereo, Minatitlan
1420	1	MEX	EW	R. Fórmula, Matamoros
1420	2	MEX	XX	R. Mexicana 14-20/Doble X, Tijuana
1420	1	MEX	WF	R. Mexicana, Cuernavaca
1420	2.5/0.25	MEX	WJ	R. Popular, Tehuacán
1420	5/1	MEX	H	R. Tremenda, Monterrey
1420	1	PTR	WUKQ	R. Universidad Católica, Ponce
1420	1	SLV	UCA	R.Universitaria, San Salvador
1430	12	CTR	RSC	R. San Carlos, Cd. Quesada
1430	10	CUB	JY	R. Surco/R. Amanecer, Primero de Enero
1430	3	DOM	JC	R. Emanuel, Santiago
1430	1.2	GTM	AG	LV de Huehuetenango
1430	1	HND	IC	La R. del 70, Puerto Cortés
1430	1	HND	SJ	R. Futura, Tocoa
1430	1	HND	VM	R. Maranatha, La Paz
1430	1	HND	TP	R. Recuerdos, Juticalpa
1430	0.8	HTI		R. MBC, Port-au-Prince
1430	5/1	MEX	OX	Doble Impacto/O-Equis, Cd.Obregón
1430	1	MEX	COC	La ACIR, Colima
1430	1/0.25	MEX	RAC	La Número Uno de Campeche, Campeche
1430	2/0.15	MEX	WD	Poder de la Radio, Cd.Miguel Alemán
1430	1/0.2	MEX	CA	R. Éxitos, Ixtepec
1430	5/1	MEX	LL	R. Onda, Veracruz
1430	5/0.1	MEX	TT	R. Tlaxcala, Tlaxcala
1430	5	NCG	LE	R. Liberación "La Tayacana", Estelí
1430	7.5	PNR		R. Kids, Panamá
1430	5	PTR	WNEL	NotiUno/ R. Tiempo, Caguas
1440	10	CUB	JP	R. Surco, Ciego de Avila
1440	1	DOM	FS	R. Bahía, Nagua
1440	5	DOM	AK	R. Cristocéntrico, Sto Domingo
1440	5	DOM	AD	R. San Juan, San Juan de la Maguana
1440	0.5	GTM	MS	R. Nal., Mazatenango
1440	5	HND	RD	Dimensión R, La Ceiba
1440	0.5	HND	RY	R. Mía, San Marcos de Colón
1440	10/1	MEX	CCC	Estadio 1440, Guadalajara
1440	7	MEX	EST	La 14-40, La Reina del Hogar, México
1440	5/0.5	MEX	VSD	La Señal del Progreso, Cd. Constitución
1440	1	MEX	NAC	LV de los Chontales, Nacajuca
1440	25	NCG	RM	R. Maranatha, Managua
1450	1	CUB	BU	R. Güines, Güines
1450	1	CUB	JF	R. Maboa, Amancio Rodríguez
1450		DOM		R. Alfa y Omega, Sto Domingo
1450	10	DOM	AC	R. Util, Salcedo
1450	1	GTM	LG	R. Epoca, Guatemala
1450	1	HND	BR	R. Cultural, La Entrada
1450	1	HND	XZ2	R. Titania, Tegucigalpa
1450	1	MEX	JM	1450 Bombazo Vallenato, Monterrey
1450	1	MEX	VH	Activa 14-50, Matamoros
1450	1	MEX	BP	Bonita, Torreón
1450	1/0.25	MEX	ED	ED Contigo, Ameca
1450	10/1	MEX	CU	La Rancherita, Los Mochis
1450	2/1	MEX	RY	LV del Sur, Arcelia
1450	10	MEX	NA	R. Alegría, Querétaro
1450	0.5	MEX	DJ	R. Clave, Magdalena
1450	1/0.25	MEX	CM	R. Festival, Cd.Mante
1450	1	MEX	GC	R. Impacto, Sahuayo
1450	1	MEX	KM	R. Mina/Onda 14-50, Minatitlán
1450	1	MEX	JD	R. Mundo 14-50, Poza Rica
1450	1/0.25	MEX	ARE	R. Pegüis, Ojinaga
1450	1/0.25	MEX	TD	Su Favorita, Tecuala
1450	0.5	MEX	PNO	XEPNO, Santiago Pinotepa Nacional
1450	5	PNR		R. Melodía, Panamá
1450	1	PTR	WCPR	R. Coamo, Coamo
1450	1	SLV	KR	R.Restauración, San Miguel
1460	2	CTR	LX	R. Columbia, Limón
1460	1	CUB	HZ	R. Cadena Agramonte/R. Cubitas, Sola
1460	0.5	DOM	AN	R. Renacimiento, Hato Mayor del Rey
1460	2.5	GTM	RN	R. Petén, Flores
1460	0.5	HND	CX	LV de Patuca, Catacamas
1460	2.5	HND	GC	R. Conga, San Pedro Sula
1460	0.5	HND	OC	R. Ranchera, Yoro
1460	1	HND	QX	Radiolandia, Comayagua
1460	0.2	HTI		V. du Nord, Cap Haitien
1460	5/0.5	MEX	KC	Estéreo Exitos, Oaxaca
1460	1/0.1	MEX	JH	Inolvidable, Jalapa
1460	1/0.25	MEX	HX	R. Fama 14-60, Cd.Obregón
1460	10/0.5	MEX	GRA	R. Guerrero, Acapulco
1460	6. 5/1	MEX	CB	R. Ranchito, San Luis Río Colorado
1460	0.25	MEX	XQ	R. Universidad, San Luis Potosí
1460	0.5	PNR	D42	LV de Almirante, Bocas del Toro
1460	0.5	PTR	WRRE	R. La Fabulosa, Juncos
1460	0.5	PTR	WLRP	R. Raíces, San Sebastián
1470	1	CUB	GE	R. Ciudad Banderas, Cárdenas
1470	1	DOM	DE	LV de la Alabanza, San Francisco de Macorís
1470		DOM	CV	R. Emisoras Unidas, Duvergé
1470		DOM	CH	R. Sur, Barahona
1470	0.5	HND	SA	R. Luz y Verdad, La Ceiba
1470	0.5	HTI		R. Lakansyel, Port-au-Prince
1470	5/0.25	MEX	CAV	Estéreo Imagen, Durango
1470	10/0.25	MEX	HI	Heraldo Internacional, Cd.Miguel Alemán
1470	1/0.5	MEX	IND	LV Sierra Hidalguense, Tlanchinol
1470	1/0.1	MEX	ACE	Magia Digital, Mazatlán
1470	50/15	MEX	AI	R. Fórmula, Tercera Cadena Nac., México
1470	10/5	MEX	RCN	R. Hispaña, Tijuana
1470	2.5/0.5	MEX	BAL	R. Voz Maya de México, Bécal
1470	1	NCG	RY	R. Yarrince, Boaco
1470	5	PNR		R. La Primerísima, Panamá
1470	1/2.5	PTR	WKCK	R. Cumbre, Orocovis
1480	1	CTR	AW	R. Caracol, Puntarenas
1480	0.25	CUB	JI	R. Florida, Florida
1480	5	DOM	AH	R. Villa, Sto Domingo
1480	5	GTM	HB	R. Buenas Nuevas, Guatemala
1480	1	HND	MI	LV de Misiones "R. MI", Comayagüela
1480	1	HND	WP	R. Soberanía, San Marcos, Ocotepeque
1480	1/0.1	MEX	XU	La Poderosa, Monclova
1480	2.5	MEX	CARH	LV del Pueblo Hña-hñu, Cardonal
1480	5/1	MEX	NS	R. 14-80, Navojoa
1480	1/0.5	MEX	HM	R. Alegría/H-M, Cd.Delicias
1480	2.5/0.1	MEX	VIC	R. Tamaulipas, Cd.Victoria
1480	10/0.5	MEX	TDK	Tancherita y Regional, Monterrey
1480	20/5	MEX	ZJ	XEZJ El 1480 AM, Guadalajara
1480	5	PTR	WMDD	R. Tropical 14-80, Fajardo
1490	1	CUB	LW	R. Camoa, San José de las Lajas
1490	1	CUB	DH	R. Mayarí, Mayarí,
1490	1	DOM	AP	LV del Cibao, Santiago
1490	1	GTM	DS	R. LV de Atitlán, Santiago Atitlán
1490	1	GTM	RE	R. Modelo, Retalhuleu
1490	1/0.5	HND	RA	R. Juventud, Sonaguera
1490	1	HND	OM	R. Omega "Sonido Internacional", La Esperanza
1490	1.2	HND	GO	R. Porteña, Puerto Cortés
1490	1/0.25	MEX	DR	Digital 99, Empalme
1490	1	MEX	AQ	La AQ, Agua Prieta
1490	5/2.5	MEX	YZ	La Podorosa, Aguascalientes
1490	2.5/0.2	MEX	SK	La Super K, Cd.Ruiz
1490	5/1	MEX	GT	R. Alegría, Zamora
1490	1	MEX	MS	R. Mexicana, Matamoros
1490	1	MEX	CJC	R. Net, Cd.Juárez

kHz	kW	Ctry	Call	Station, location
1490	1	MEX	YT	R. Teocelo, Teocelo
1490	2. 5/1	MEX	KN	R. Variedades, Huetamo
1490	3.6/0.8	PTR	WDEP	Super Kadena Noticias "La Isla", Ponce
1500	15	CTR	RC	R. Cima, Cd. Quesada
1500	1	CUB	DA	R. Enciclopedia, Holguín
1500	0.25	CUB	KQ	R. Majaguabo, San Luis
1500	0.5	DOM	PA	R. Color, Higüey
1500		DOM	RD	R. Juan Pablo Duarte, Elías Piña
1500		HND		R. Sion, La Ceiba
1500	1	HND	TX	R. Victoria, Choluteca
1500	10	HTI		Haiti Flambeau Caraibes, Port-au-Prince
1500	0.4	MEX	JQ	La Explosiva, Parras
1500	1/0.5	MEX	FL	La FL, Guanajuato
1500	50/5	MEX	DF	R. Fórmula, Segunda Cadena Nac., México
1500	1	NCG	PT	R. Minuto, Managua
1500	1/0.25	PTR	WMNT	R. Atenas, Manatí
1500	1	SLV	CS	R.Fides, Usulután
1510	1	CUB	DA	R. Enciclopedia, Moa,
1510	10/3	DOM	BL	R. Pueblo, Sto Domingo
1510	5	GTM	DX	R. Centroamericana "Nueva RCA"
1510	1	HND	EM	R. Emanuel, Ocotepeque
1510	1	HND	YK	R. Gualcho, Tegucigalpa
1510	50	MEX	QI	La Sultana, Monterrey
1510	0.25	MEX	HUI	R. Huichapan, Huichapan
1510	0.5	MEX	JPM	R. Veracruz, La Antigua Veracruz
1510	5	PNR	A95	Hosanna R, Panamá
1510	1	PTR	WSQD	R. Voz, Lajas
1520	2	CTR	ECC	R. Cartago, Cartago
1520	1	CUB	KZ	R. Pitan, Mella
1520	1	DOM	WJ	R. Samaná "R. 15-20", Samaná
1520	1	GTM	RS	R. Superior, Coatepeque
1520		GTM		R. Taysal, Sta Elena de la Cruz
1520	1	HND	CR	Dif. Cristiana de Radio "DCR", San Pedro Sula
1520		HND		R. Manantial de Vida Eterna, Juticalpa
1520	5	HND	RG	R. Providencia, Danlí
1520		HND		R. Rios de Agua Viva, Siguatepeque
1520	1	HND	HJ	R. Santiago, Yoro
1520	5	MEX	JCC	Bonita, Cd.Juárez
1520	1	MEX	VO	La Furia, San Rafael
1520	1	MEX	YP	La Juvenil, El Limón
1520	2	MEX	ART	La Señal de las Estrellas, Jojutla
1520	1	MEX	EH	R. Exitos, San Luis Río Colorado
1520	1/0.25	MEX	ATL	Sistema XEGEM "R. Mexiquense" Atlacomulco
1520	1	NCG	RF	R. Flash, Managua
1520	2.5	PTR	WVOZ	R. Voz, San Juan
1530	1	CUB	IX	R. Morón, Morón
1530		DOM	JN	R. 1530, Santiago
1530	10/0.1	MEX	SD	La Ley, Silao
1530	50/1	MEX	UR	La Positiva, México
1530	0.5	NCG	RST	LV de Sta Teresa, Sta Teresa
1530	3	PNR		R. Avivamiento, Panamá
1530	1/0.25	PTR	WUPR	Exitos 15-30, Utuado
1540	50	BAH	ZNS1	Broadcasting Corporation of the Bahamas
1540		CTR		Enlace Radio, Pavas
1540	1	CUB		R. Juvenil, Holguín
1540	1	CUB	ES	R. Sagua, Sagua La Grande
1540	1	DOM	BU	LV de La Romana, La Romana
1540	1	DOM	FP	R. Criolla Comercial, Sto Domingo
1540	1	GTM		R. Cultura y Deportes, Guatemala
1540		HND	YK	R. Nuevo Mundo "Cadena Radial Reloj", Tegucigalpa
1540	1/0.25	MEX	NC	Inolvidable 15-40, Celaya
1540	5	MEX	HOS	La Poderosa, Hermosillo
1540	2. 5/1	MEX	RTP	R. Impacto Estéreo Digital, San Martín Texmelucán
1540	0.5/0.1	MEX	STN	R. Red, Monterrey
1540	1	PTR	WIBS	R. Caribe/Cadena R. Puerto Rico, Guayama
1550	1	CUB	JQ	R. Nuevitas, Nuevitas
1550	1	HND	JO	R. Campeona, Comayagua
1550	1	HND	KR	R. Kristel, Juticalpa
1550	1	HND	JX	R. Nueva Vida, San Pedro Sula
1550	1	MEX	XOO	La O de Oro, El Oro
1550	5/0.25	MEX	NU	La Rancherita, Nuevo Laredo
1550	10/1	MEX	BG	R. 15-50/La B-G, Tijuana
1550	1	MEX	REL	R. Michoacán, Morelia
1550	10	MEX	RUV	R. Universidad Veracruzana, Jalapa
1550	0.25	PTR	WKFE	R. Café, Yauco
1550	5	SLV		R.Sanidad Divina, San Salvador
1560	6	CTR	RN	R. Nicoya, Nicoya
1560	1	CUB	BQ	R. Enciclopedia, Ciego de Avila
1560	1/0.5	DOM	PZ	R. Pedernales, Pedernales
1560	1	DOM	GL	R. Unica, Santiago
1560	10	HTI		V. de L'esperance, Port-au-Prince
1560	1	MEX	JPV	La Nueva Radio Viva, Cd. Juárez
1560	5	MEX	RIO	La Poderosa, Ixtlán del Río
1560	5	MEX	SE	LV de Campeche, Champotón
1560	1/0.25	MEX	MAS	Más 1560, Salamanca
1560	5/1	MEX	LAC	R. Azul, Cd.Lázaro Cárdenas
1560	1	MEX	ZW	R. Diversión, Cerritos
1560	20/0.15	MEX	CHZ	R. Lagarto, Chiapa de Corzo
1560	50/10	MEX	INFO	R. Monitor, México
1560	5	MEX	HUO	XEHUO, Huantla de Jiménez
1560	5	NCG	CN	R. América, Managua
1560	10	PNR		R. Adventista de Panamá, Panamá
1560	5	PTR	WRSJ	WRSJ, Bayamón
1570		CUB	BQ	R. Enciclopedia, Las Tunas
1570	10	DOM	AJ	R. Amanecer, Sto Domingo
1570	10	GTM	VE	VEA - Voz Evengélica de América,
1570	2.5	HND	RF	R. Cadena Nac. de Noticias "RCN", Tegucigalpa
1570	100	MEX	RF	La Poderosa, Cd.Acuña
1570	6/1	MEX	LBL	R. Centro, San Luis Río Colorado
1570	1/0.1	PTR	WPPC	R. Felicidad, Peñuelas
1580	0.25	CTR	RCC	R. Cultural de Corredores, Cd. Neily
1580	0.25	CTR	RCLS	R. Cultural Los Santos, San Marcos
1580	0.25	CTR	RCM	R. Cultural Maleku, Tonjibe
1580	0.25	CTR	RCLC	R. Cultural, La Cruz
1580	0.25	CTR	RCL	R. Cultural, Los Chiles
1580	10	CTR		R. Mi País, Siquirres
1580	1	CUB	FA	R. Cadena Agramonte,Santa Cruz del Sur
1580	1	DOM	PK	R. Neiba, Neiba 0900-0400
1580	1	HND	CR	Dif. Cristiana de Radio "DCR", La Esperanza
1580	50	MEX	DM	La Grande de Sonora, Hermosillo
1580	1/0.25	MEX	LI	LV del Sur, Chilpancingo
1580	1/0.5	MEX	AF	R. Felicidad, Apaseo el Grande
1580	1	MEX	VAB	Super Stereo Miled, Valle del Bravo
1580	1	PNR		Resplandor Estéreo, Panamá
1580	5/2.5	PTR	WEKO	R. Voz, Morovis
1580	5	SLV	CZ	R.Cadena Cuscatlán, San Salvador
1590	2	CTR	LGJ	R. 16, Grecia
1590		CUB	BQ	R. Progreso, Manzanillo
1590	5	DOM	AC	R. Libertad, Santiago
1590	1	GTM	XC	R. Triunfadora, Chimaltenango
1590		HND		R. Perla, El Progreso
1590	1	HND	IK	R. San Antonio, San Pedro Sula
1590	50/10	MEX	VOZ	Bonita AM, México
1590	1/0.25	MEX	BZ	Inolvidable, Cd.Delicias
1590	1	MEX	IRG	La Campirana, Irapuato
1590	1	MEX	HC	R. Bahía, Ensenada
1590	1/0.1	MEX	PT	R. Misantla, Misantla
1590	10	MEX		Valladolid (CP)
1590	1	PTR	WXRF	R. Voz/R. 15-90, Guayama
1600	0.25	CTR		LV de Talamanca
1600	3/2	CTR	JV	R. 88 Stereo, San Isidro del General
1600	0.25	CTR	RCN	R. Cultural Nicoyano, Nicoya
1600	0.25	CTR	RCBA	R. Cultural, Buenos Aires
1600	0.25	CTR	RCP	R. Cultural, Pital
1600	0.25	CTR	RCT	R. Cultural, Turrialba
1600	0.25	CTR	RCU	R. Cultural, Upala
1600	2/1	CTR	MMCH	R. Golfito, Pto Golfito
1600	1.5	CTR	MQ	R. Pococí, Guápiles
1600	0.25	CTR		R. Quepos, Pto Quepos
1600	5	DOM	FG	R. Revelación en América, Sto Domingo
1600	5	GTM	ML	R. María "LV de la Familia", Guatemala
1600	1	HND	PC	R. Luz y Vida, San Luís
1600	1	MEX	TPA	R. Guerrero, Tlapa de Comonfort
1600	2.5/0.25	MEX	GEM	Sistema XEGEM "R. Mexiquense", Metepec
1600	1	MEX	AE	Texano Hits, Cd.Acuña
1600	5	PTR	WLUZ	R. Luz/Romántica 1600, Bayamón
1610	50	AIA		The Caribbean Beacon
1610	0.25	MEX	UACH	R. Universidad Autónoma de Chapingo, Chapingo
1620		DOM	SR	R. Taina/Planeta, San Pedro de Macorís
1620	10/1	VIR	WDHP	WDHP, Frederiksted
1630	10/1	MEX	UT	R. Universidad, Mexicali
1640	1/0.5	DOM		R. Juventus Don Bosco, Sto Domingo
1660	10/1	PTR	WGIT	Gigante 16-60, Canóvanas
1700	10	MEX	KTT	La Romantica, Tecate

SOUTH AMERICA

(excluding Brazil)

Note: Brazil has been excluded to save space – see country entry for frequencies

Abbreviations: Dif=Difusora, Em=Emisora, LV=La Voz, Nal=Nacional, n=notional, SF=Santafé.

kHz	kW	Ctry	Call	Station, location
530	3/1	ARG		R. República, San Justo
530	1	EQA	DC1	R. Iris "LV de la Comunidad", Quito
530	15	FLK		Falkland Islands Broadcasting Station
540	10/5	ARG	LU17	R. Golfo Nuevo, Pto. Madryn
540	25/1	ARG	LRA14	R. Nal., Santa Fé
540	5	ARG	LRA25	R. Nal.,Tartagal
540	1	CHL	CD54	R. Calle Calle Saval, Valdivia
540	1	CHL	CB54	R. Ignacio Serrano, Melipilla
540	20	CLM	HJKA	R. Auténtica, SF de Bogotá
540	25	EQA	FA2	R. Tropicana "Canal 540", Guayaquil
540	12	PRU	OBX4E	R. Inca del Perú, Lima
540	1	PRU	OCX2D	R. San Antonio, Trujillo
540	1	PRU	OBX4E	R. Inca del Perú, Lima
540	1	PRU	OCX2D	R. San Antonio, Trujillo
540	10	VEN		LV de Manapiare, San Juan de Manapiare
540	50/25	VEN	OY	R. Perijá, La Villa del Rosario
550	1	CHL	CD55	R. LV. de la Tierra, Angol
550	1	CHL	CC55	Radiodifusión Americana, Penco
550	50	CLM	HJHF	R. Dif. Nal., Marinilla (rel
550	50	CLM	HJZQ	R. Dif. Nal., Neiva (rel
550	50	EQA	GM1	R. Reloj "5-50", Quito
550	10	FLK		BFBS, Bush Rincon
550	20/12	PRG	ZP16	R. Parque, Ciudad del Este
550	58	URG	CW1	R. Colonia, Colonia
550	50	VEN	KE	YVKE Mundial, Caracas
560	25/5	ARG	LV1	R. Colón, San Juan
560	10/5	ARG	LT15	R. del Litoral, Concordia
560	25/5	ARG	LRA13	R. Nal., Bahia Blanca
560	25/15	ARG	LRA9	R. Nal., Esquel
560	25/1	ARG	LRA16	R. Nal., La Quiaca
560	15	BOL	CP-	R. El Mundo, La Paz
560	25/10	CLM	HJPF	LV de la Pampa, Maicao
560	10	CLM	HJGS	R. Dif. Nal., Tunja (rel
560	25	EQA	RN2	C. R. E. Satelital, Guayaquil
560	10	GUY		Guyana Broadcasting Corp., Georgetown
560	1	PRU		R. Mover de Dios, Huancayo
560	1	PRU	OBU1F	R. OBU1F, Coscomba
560	2	PRU	OBZ4L	R. Oriente, Lima
560	20/10	VEN	PJ	R. Exitos "Latina 5-60", Rubio
560	50	VEN	RH	R. Nacional, Cd. Guayana
570	1	ARG		R. del Centro, Lomas de Mirador
570	50	CHL	CB57	R. Agricultura, Santiago
570	100	CLM	HJND	R. Dif. Nacional de Colombia, SF de Bogotá
570	10	EQA	CE1	R. El Sol, Quito
570	1	PRG	ZP15	R. LV del Amambay, Pedro Juan Caballero
570	1	PRG	ZP15	R. S. Roque González de Sta. Cruz, Ayolas
570	1	PRU	OAU1M	R. Univ. Nal. Pedro Ruiz Gallo, Lambayeque
570	100	VEN	LX	R. Rumbos, Villa de Cura
580	10	ARG	LU20	R. Chubut "La 20," Trelew
580	25/5	ARG	LW1	R. Univ. Nal. de Córdoba, Córdoba
580	25	BOL	CP91	R. Panamericana, La Paz
580	50/10	CLM	HJHP	R. Dif. Nal., Cali (rel
580	10	EQA	PC2	R. Uno, Guayaquil
580	1	PRU	OCY2L	R. El Sol, La Esperanza
580	10	PRU	OAX2E	R. Marañón, Jaén
580		PRU	OAX4M	R. Maria, Lima
580	5	URG	CX58	R. Clarín, Montevideo
580	50/10	VEN	MJ	LV de la Fé, Maracaibo
580		VEN		R. Nacional, Maturín
590	50/5	ARG	LS9	R. Continental, Buenos Aires
590	4	ARG	LV12	R. Independencia, San Miguel de Tucumán
590	25	ARG	LRA30	R. Nal., San Carlos de Bariloche
590	10	CHL	CD59	R. Chilena "Solonoticias", Punta Arenas
590	1	CHL	CC59	R. Hebrón, Concepción
590	1	CHL	CA59	R. Santa Maria de Guadalupe, Antofagasta
590	50	CLM	HJCR	W Radio, Medellín
590	10	EQA	SP1	R. Carrousel, Quito
590	5	PRG	ZP32	R. Ycuámandyyú, Villa de S. Pedro
590	1	PRU	OCX6V	R. Catedral, Miraflores, Arequipa
590		PRU		R. del Sur, Arequipa
590	20	VEN	KL	R. Continente, Caracas
600	20/5	ARG	LU5	R. Neuquén
600	10	BOL	CP190	R. ACLO, Sucre
600	1	BOL	CP-	Radioemisoras del Recobro, La Paz
600	10	CHL	CB60	R. Monumental, Santiago
600	10	CHL	CD60	R. Tricolor, Osorno
600	50	CLM	HJHJ	R. Libertad, Barranquilla
600	2	CLM	HJZ95	R. UWA Unipa, Ricaurte el Diviso
600	50	EQA	XY2	R. Nal. del Ecuador, Guayaquil
600	10	PRU	OBZ4W	R. Cora, Lima
600	1	PRU	OBX2B	R. Star, Trujillo
600	1	PRU	OAU7A	R. Tropicana, Cusco
600	15	VEN	SW	R. Alto Llano, Sta Bárbara de Barinas
600	10	VEN	QB	R. Sucre, Cumaná
610	5/1	ARG		R. General San Martín, Villa Lynch
610	1	ARG	LRK201	R. Solidaridad, Añatuya
610	5	CHL	CD61	R. Puerto Aysen, Puerto Aysén
610	30	CLM	HJKL	La Cariñosa 6-10, SF de Bogotá
610	50	CLM	HJD90	R. Dif.Nal., Uríbia
610	10	EQA	MJ1	R. Caravana, Quito
610	10/1	PRG	ZP30	R. ZP30, LV del Chaco Paraguayo, Filadelfia
610	1	PRU	OBU1E	R. Santa Rosa, Sullana
610	50	URG	CX4	R. Rural, Montevideo
610	10	VEN	XY	R. Centro 6-10, Cantaura
610	10	VEN	SE	R. Cristal, Barquisimeto
620	25/5	ARG	LRA28	R. Nal., La Rioja
620	25/5	ARG	LRA26	R. Nal., Resistencia
620	25/7	ARG	LRA18	R. Nal., Río Turbio
620	25/5	ARG	LT17	R. Provincia de Misiones, Posadas
620	10/5	ARG	LV4	R. San Rafael, do
620	20	BOL	CP63	R. San Gabriel, La Paz
620	1	CHL	CC62	R. Bío-Bío, Concepción
620	1	CHL	CA62	R. Norte Verde, Ovalle
620	50/20	CLM	HJEL	Colmundo, Cali
620	10	CLM	HJVP	Colmundo, Cartagena
620	50	EQA	XY3	R. Nal. del Ecuador, Loja
620	10	PRG	ZP40	R. Ñasaindý, San Estanislao (R. 619-616.6v)
620	0.4	PRU	OAX2N	R. Chepen, Chepen
620	10	PRU	OBU4B	R. del Sur, San Isidro
620	50/25	VEN	ZC	R. Fé y Alegría Los Llanos,Guasdualito
620	10	VEN	NO	R. Libertad, Cabimas
630	25/5	ARG	LU4	R. Dif. Patagonia Argentina, Comodoro Rivadavia
630	25/5	ARG	LS5	R. Rivadavia, Buenos Aires
630	25/5	ARG	LW8	R. San Salvador de Jujuy
630		BOL	CP204	R. Tarija
630	10	CHL	CB63	R. Stela Maris, Valparaíso
630	10	CLM	HJWC	LV del Guainía, Puerto Inírida
630	10	CLM	HJFD	R. Manizales, Manizales
630	10	EQA	HA2	Ondas Quevedeñas, Quevedo
630	1	PRU	OBU1A	R. OBU1A, Piura
630	1	PRU	OAU7N	R. Univ.Nal.San Antonio Abad, Cusco
630	50/25	VEN	KA	R. Nacional "Canal Informativo", Caracas
640	10/5	ARG	LU18	R. El Valle, "640 AM", General Roca
640	25/5	ARG	LRA24	R. Nal., Río Grande
640	10/5	ARG	LV15	R. Villa Mercedes
640		BOL	CP204	R. Tarija
640	10	CHL	CD64	R. Temuco Cooperativa AM, Temuco
640	10	CLM	HJBJ	RCN, Santa Marta
640		EQA		R. Morena, Guayaquil
640	50	EQA	XY1	R. Nal. del Ecuador, Quito
640	8	PRG	ZP19	R. Caaguazú, Coronel Oviedo:
640	1	PRU	OAU1Y	R. La Luz, José Leonardo Ortiz
640	10	PRU	OBX7B	R. Onda Azul, Puno
640	10	PRU	OAZ4K	R. Pacifico, Lima
640	10/5	VEN	MU	R. Carora, Carora
640	30	VEN	QO	Unión Radio Porteñas, Puerto La Cruz
650	3	ARG		La Nueva Radio, Florida
650	15	BOL	CP263	R. Dif. Integración, El Alto
650	100	CLM	HJKH	RCN Antena 2, SF de Bogotá
650	5	EQA	FD4	R. Visión Manta, Manta
650	15	PRG	ZP4	R. Uno, Asunción
650	1.5	PRU	OBU2P	R. Estación Universal, Huambos
650	1	PRU	OAX2N	R. Reginal del Norte, Trujillo
650	50/25	URG	CX6	S.O.D.R. E.. Montevideo
650	50/20	VEN	LH	Aragueña 650, Maracay

kHz	kW	Ctry	Call	Station, location
660	1/0.25	ARG	LT41	R. LV del Sur Entrerriano, Gualeguaychú
660		ARG		R. Popular, Claypole
660	1	BOL	CP-	R. ABC, Santa Cruz
660	50	CHL	CB66	R. Chilena "Solonoticias", Santiago
660	25	CLM	HJQS	Colmundo, Cúcuta
660	20	CLM	HJJM	R. Auténtica, Cali
660	30	EQA	LG2	R. Carrousel, Guayaquil
660	6/10	PRG	ZP26	R. Itapirú, Cd. del Este
660	10	PRU	OCX4R	La Inolviable 660 AM, Lima
660	5	PRU	OCX1U	R. J.H.C., Chiclayo
660	1	PRU	OCX4L	R. Chinchaycocha, Junin
660	10	VEN	NA	Ondas de los Médanos "Tu R. Popular", Coro
660		VEN		R. Nacional, El Callao
660	10	VEN	QZ	R. Anaco, Anaco
670	25/5	ARG	LT4	R. Dif. Misiones, Posadas
670	25/5	ARG	LRI209	R. Mar del Plata, do
670	3	ARG	LRA52	R. Nal., Chos Malal
670	25/5	ARG	LRA11	R. Nal., Comodoro Rivadavia
670	10	CLM	HJR33	R. U.I.S - Universidad Industrial de Santander, Bucaramanga
670	50	CLM	HJPL	RCN Antena 2, Medellín
670	12/5	EQA	FF1	R. Jesús del Gran Poder, Quito
670	10	PRU	OAX7H	R. Nacional del Perú, Puno
670	100	VEN	LL	R. Rumbos, Caracas
680	25	ARG	LT3	R. Cerealista "AM 680", Rosario
680		ARG		R. Melody, Remedios de Escalada
680	25/5	ARG	LV6	R. Nihuil, Mendoza
680	25/5	ARG	LU12	R. Río Gallegos, do
680	5	BOL	CP274	R. Andina, La Paz
680	10	CHL	CA68	R. Chilena "Solonoticias", Calama
680	10	CHL	CC68	R. Cooperativa, Concepción
680	25/12	EQA	VP2	Sistema de Emis. Atalaya, Guayaquil
680	10/1	PRG	ZP11	R. Caritas, Asunción
680		PRU		CP, Cusco
680	5	PRU	OAX5E	Emisora del Pacifico, Ica
680	0.5	PRU	OBX2L	R. Amauta, Chócope
680	5	PRU	OCY2Y	R. San Luis, Jaén
680	20	PRU	OBX4A	R. Tigre, San Isidro
680	1/0.7	URG	CW68	R. Young, Young
680	10	VEN	QR	R. Continente Cumaná, Cumaná
680	10	VEN	ZJ	R. Llanera "R. 1400", Barinas
690	10/3	ARG	LU19	LV de Comahue, Cipoletti
690		ARG		R. Maranatha en las Nubes, Lomas del Mirador
690	25/5	ARG	LRA4	R. Nal. Salta
690	10	CHL	CD69	R. Estrella del Mar, Ancud
690	10	CHL	CB69	R. Santiago, Santiago
690	50/12	CLM	HJCZ	R. Recuerdos, SF de Bogotá
690	50	EQA	JB1	LV de los Andes, Quito
690	5	EQA	FA4	Sucre Portoviejo, Portoviejo
690	1	PRU	OCX1W	CPN Radio, Chiclayo
690	0.5	PRU	OBX6Q	R. Comercial, La Joya
690	25/10	URG	CX8	R. Sarandí, Montevideo
690	50/20	VEN	MR	R. Barquisimeto, Barquisimeto
693	1.5	PRU	OCX1T	R. Horizonte, Chiclayo
700	25/5	ARG	LV3	R. Córdoba
700	5	CHL	CD70	R. Magallanes, Punta Arenas
700	1	CHL	CA70	R. Nibsan, Copiapó
700	1	CHL	CD70	R. Valdivia, Valdivia
700	120	CLM	HJCX	W Radio, Cali
700	50	EQA	RS2	Sucre Guayaquil, Guayaquil
700	1	GUY		Guyana Broadcasting Corp., Linden
700	10	PRG	ZP12	R. Carlos Antonio López, "LV del Neembucú", Pilar
700	1	PRU	OBU4J	R. La Luz, Huancayo
700	1	PRU	OBZ4H	R. Aeropuerto, San Miguel
700	10	PRU	OBX1U	R. Cutivalú "LV del Desierti", Castilla
700	1	PRU	OCY2H	R. Sausal Superior, Sausal
700	1	PRU	OBU7K	R. Teleducional, Maras
700	10	VEN	MH	R. Popular, Maracaibo
700	5/2	VEN	PQ	R. Sur, Puerto Ordaz
710	50	ARG	LRL202	R. Diez, Buenos Aires
710	25/5	ARG	LRA19	R. Nal., Pto. Iguazú
710	25/5	ARG	LRA17	R. Nal., Zapala
710	10	BOL	CP50	R. Pío XII, Siglo Veinte
710	5	CLM	HJYD	R. La Paz, Paipa
710	10	CLM	HJNX	R. Super, Medellín
710	8	EQA	ER5	Escuelas Radiofónicas Populares, Riobamba
710	1	PRU	OAU6L	R. Amor, Arequipa
710	10	PRU	OCX7I	R. Ncional del Peru, Puerto Maldonado
710	5	PRU	OBX5Q	R. Programas del Perú
710	50/20	VEN	KY	R. Capital, Caracas
720	25/5	ARG	LV10	R. de Cuyo, Mendoza
720	1	ARG	LRA59	R. Nal., Gobernador Gregores
720	10	BOL	CP27	R. La Cruz del Sur, La Paz
720	2.5	BOL	CP148	R. Yungas, Chulumani
720	30	CLM	HJAN	Emisoras Unidas, Barranquilla
720	50	CLM	HJZX	R. Dif. Nal., Rionegro (rel
720	25	CLM	HJVO	Transmisora Quindío, Armenia
720	10	EQA	GB4	LV de Portoviejo, Portoviejo
720	5	EQA	MO3	R. Matovelle "HCM-3", Loja
720	5	EQA	IC1	R. Municipal, Quito
720	10	EQA	UE3	R. Unica, Machala
720	25	PRG	ZP17	R. Pa'i Puku, Teniente Irala Férnandez
720	1	PRU	OBU7D	R. Alegria, Wanchaq
720	1	PRU	OAU1Q	R. Frecuencia Oceánica, Lambayque
720	25	PRU	OAX2J	R. Nacional del Perú, Trujillo
720	10	PRU	OAU4E	R. Sideral, La Oroya
720	10	VEN	XE	R. Elorza, Elorza
720	50	VEN	QE	R. Venezuela "Oriente", Porlamar
725	5	SUR		SRS, Paramaribo (inactive)
730	10/1	ARG	LU23	Em. Lago Argentino, El Calafate
730		ARG		R. Excelsior, Monte Grande
730	25/5	ARG	LRA27	R. Nal., Catamarca
730	20/5	ARG	LRA3	R. Nal., Santa Rosa
730	3	BOL	CP165	R. Mensaje, Montero
730	1	CHL	CD73B	R. Aysén, Pto. Aysén
730	1	CHL	CD73	R. Camila, Los Angeles
730	10	CHL	CB73	R. Cooperativa AM, Valparaíso
730	100	CLM	HJCU	La 730, SF de Bogotá
730	15	CLM	HJTJ	R. Uno, Montería
730	10	EQA	MG2	R. Guayaquil, Guayaquil
730	50/5	PRG	ZP7	R. Cardinal, Asunción
730	10	PRU	OAZ7S	LV de la Esperanza, Juliaca
730	10	PRU	OAX1D	R. del Pacifico, Piura
730	5	PRU		R. Maria, Cajamarca
730	50	PRU	OAX4G	R. Programas del Peru
730	5/2.5	URG	CX10	R. Continente, Montevideo
730	10	VEN	OO	R. Frontera, San Antonio del Táchira
730	10	VEN	MT	R. Universo, Barquisimeto
740	25/5	ARG	LRH251	R. Chaco, Resistencia
740	5	ARG		R. Cooperativa, Buenos Aires
740	1	ARG	LRA55	R. Nal., Alto Río Senguer
740	1	ARG	LRI200	R. Puerto Deseado
740	10	CLM	HJHB	Ecos de Pasto, Pasto
740	50	CLM	HJNS	R. Guatapurí, Valledupar
740	10	EQA	SE4	R. Libertad, Chone
740	10	EQA	GC1	R. Melodía "Canal 7-40", Quito
740	10	PRU	OAX6C	R. Continental, Arequipa
740	1	PRU	OCX2X	R. El Puerto, Pascamayo
740	1	PRU	OBU7C	Rede Latino, Cusco
740	5/1	URG	CW27	R. Tabaré, Salto
740	10	VEN	NC	CNB 740 R. Maracaibo, Maracaibo
740	50	VEN	NQ	R. Caroni "Q-FM", Puerto Ordaz
750	5/3	ARG		R. del Pueblo, Buenos Aires
750	50	CLM	HJDK	Caracol Colombia, Medellín
750	5	CLM	HJLH	LV de Yopal, Yopal
750	30	EQA	RC2	Caravana, Guayaquil
750	1	PRG	ZP42	LV de la Policía Nacional, Asunción
750	5	PRU	OCX4X	R. Altura, Cerro de Pasco
750	3	PRU	OBX2R	R. Oriental, Jaén
750	100	VEN	KS	RCR 750 "Radio Caracas", Caracas
760	25/5	ARG	LU6	R. Atlántica, Mar del Plata
760	18	BOL	CP29	R. Fides, La Paz
760	50	CHL	CB76	R. Cooperativa, Santiago
760	30/10	CLM	HJAJ	RCN, Barranquilla
760	25	EQA	QR1	R. Quito "LV de la Capital", Quito
760	10	GUY		Guyana Broadcasting Corp., Georgetown
760	0.5	PRU	OBX2K	R. Andino, Otuzco
760	10	PRU	OBZ4X	Radiomar, Chorillos
760	10	VEN	SO	R. Popular 760, Trujillo
760	10	VEN	QQ	R. Pto. La Cruz "Doble Q", Pto. La Cruz
770		ARG		R. Urbana, Lomas del Mirador
770	5	BOL	CP116	R. Cosmos, Cochabamba
770		BOL	CP-	R. Popular, Santa Cruz (CP)
770	10	CHL	CD77	R. Agricultura, Temuco
770	1	CHL	CD77	R. Cooperativa, Castro
770	100	CLM	HJJX	RCN, SF de Bogotá
770	25/12	EQA	MF2	R. El Telégrafo, Guayaquil
770	5	PRU	OAX8M	LV de la Selva, Iquitos
770	1.5	PRU	OCX1T	R. Horizonte, Chiclayo
770	2.5	PRU	OAU7D	R. OAU7D, Macusani
770	5	PRU	OBX6H	Radiomar, Uchumayo
770	100/25	URG	CX12	Radio Oriental, Montevideo
770	50/20	VEN	KK	R. Nacional, Valencia
780	25/5	ARG	LV8	R. Libertador, Mendoza

kHz	kW	Ctry	Call	Station, location
780	5	ARG	LRA12	R. Nal. Santo Tomé
780	5/1	ARG	LRA10	R. Nal., Ushuaía
780	5	ARG	LRF210	R. Tres, Trelew
780	10	CHL	CD78	R. Sago AM, Osorno
780	10	CLM	HJZG	LV del Valle, Cali
780	10/5	CLM	HJZW	R. Almirante, Riohacha
780	10/2	EQA	CM1	Nueva R. Colón, Quito
780	1.5	EQA	RG4	R. Mía, Manta
780	30	PRG	ZP70	R. Primero de Marzo, Asunción
780	10	PRU	OAZ7S	LV de la Esperanza, Juliaca
780	1	PRU		R. Coremarca, Bambamarca
780	10	PRU	OAX1K	R. Nacional del Perú, Tumbes
780	3	PRU	OAX4X	R. Victoria,Lima
780	50/20	VEN	OD	Ecos del Torbes, San Cristóbal
780	10	VEN	MN	R. Coro, Coro
790	5	ARG	LV19	R. Malargüe
790	25/5	ARG	LR6	R. Mitre "AM 80," Buenos Aires
790	25/5	ARG	LRA22	R. Nal., San Salvador de Jujuy
790	5	ARG	LT46	R. Provincia, Bernardo de Irigoyen
790	50	CLM	HJDC	R. Caracol, Medellín
790	50	CLM	HJZR	R. Dif. Nal., Villavicencio (rel
790	50	CLM	HJBU	R. Dif. Nal., Zambrano (rel
790		EQA		R. Paraíso, Maldonado
790		EQA		Su Radio 790 AM, Otavalo
790	5	PRU	OAZ7H	R. Armonia, Wanchaq
790	10	PRU	OAX2I	R. Programas del Perú, Trujillo
790	50	VEN	XM	R. Minuto "La Barquisimetana", Barquisimeto
790		VEN		R. Nacional, Cd.Bolívar
790	10	VEN	KC	R. Venezuela 7-90, Caracas
800	5/1	ARG	LT43	R. Mocoví, Charata
800	1/0.25	ARG	LV23	R. Rio Atuel, General Alvear
800	24/5	ARG	LU15	R. Viedma
800	1	BOL	CP-	R. Churuquella, Sucre
800	5	BOL	CP265	R. Libertad, La Paz
800	0.25	BOL	CP157	R. Santa Clara, Sorata
800	5/1	CHL	CB80	R. Santa Maria de Guadalupe, Viña del Mar
800	100	CLM	HJBW	RCN, Bucaramanga
800	25	EQA	ML2	K 800, Guayaquil
800	5	EQA	FB1	R. Sensación 800, Quito
800	5/3	PRG	ZP27	R. Mbaracayú, Saltos del Guairá
800	1	PRU	OBU4D	Emp. de Communicaciones Vida, Huancayo
800	0.5	PRU	OAU4H	R. La Luz, Huaral
800	1	PRU	OBX5B	R. Maria, Ica (F.P.I.)
800	0.3	PRU	OBX6A	R. Porteña, Arequipa
800	1	PRU	OCX1P	Telecom de Norte, Piura
810	200	CLM	HJCY	Caracol Colombia, SF de Bogotá
810	5	EQA	VT2	R. Atalaya, El Milagro
810		EQA		Sucre Ambato, Ambato
810	1	PRU	OAU2G	R. Apocali, Trujillo
810	10	PRU	OAX7V	R. Programas del Perú, Juliaca
810	50/25	URG	CX14	R. El Espectador, Montevideo
810		VEN		R. Piritu, Puerto Píritu
810	50	VEN	LP	Super Radio 810, Valencia
820	5	ARG	LRI208	Estacion 820, Lomas de Zamora
820	1/0.25	ARG	LRK221	R. Ciudad Perico, Perico
820	25/5	ARG	LRA8	R. Nal., Formosa
820	5/1	ARG	LU24	R. Tres Arroyos
820	10	BOL	CP35	Radiodifusoras Altiplano, La Paz
820	1	CHL	CD82	R. Concordia, La Unión
820	10/1	CHL	CA82	R. Gabriela Mistral, La Serena
820	1	CHL	CC82	R. Maria Inmaculada, Concepción
820	0.25	CHL	CA82	R. Pampa, Pedro de Valdivia
820	10/5	CHL	CB82	Radioemisora Carabineros de Chile, Santiago
820	50	CLM	HJED	Caracol Colombia, Cali
820	10	CLM	HJAD	R. Vigía, Cartagena
820	1	EQA	RF4	Canal Manabita, Portoviejo
820	5	EQA	VI5	R. LV de Ingapirca, Cañar
820	25	EQA	UP1	R. Unión, Quito
820	20	PRU	OAX4O	R. Libertad, Lima
820	0.5	PRU	OBX2J	R. Nuevo Continene, Cajamarca
820	1	PRU	OCX6J	R. Paraiso, Camaná
820	1/0.5	URG	CW23	R. Cultural, Salto
820	10	VEN	KU	R. Altura 820, La Grita
820	25/10	VEN	XG	R. Guadalupana, Coro
820	50	VEN	SH	R. Guayana, Upatá
830		ARG		R. Filadelfia, Isidro Casanovas
830	1/0.5	ARG	LT21	R. Municipal, Alvear
830	5/1	ARG	LV18	R. Municipal, San Rafael
830	25	ARG	LU14	R. Provincia de Santa Cruz, Rio Gallegos
830	10/5	ARG	LT8	R. Rosario, do
830	25	CLM	HJDM	R. Reloj, Medellín
830	25	EQA	RM2	R. Huancavilca, Guayaquil
830	4.5	EQA	RP5	R. Promoción, Riobamba
830	1	PRU	OAU4C	CPN Radio, El Tambo
830	1	PRU	OCX2Y	CPN Radio, Trujillo
830	1	PRU	OAZ7U	R. Inti Raymi, Santiago
830	1	PRU	OAX3Y	R. La Selva, Rupa-Rupa
830	10	PRU	OAX6D	R. Nacional del Perú, Tacna
830	25	VEN	LT	R. Sensación, Caracas
840	25/5	ARG	LU2	R. Bahía Blanca, do
840	1	ARG		R. General Belgrano, Buenos Aires
840	10/5	ARG	LT12	R. General Madariaga, Paso de los Libres
840	25/5	ARG	LV9	R. Salta, do
840	10	CHL	CB84	R. Portales, Valparaíso
840	10	CHL	CD84	R. Santa María, Coyhaique
840	30	CLM	HJKK	H J Doble K, Neiva
840	30	CLM	HJBI	Ondas del Caribe, Santa Marta
840	1	EQA	EM4	R. Costa Azul, Portoviejo
840	50	EQA	PN1	R. Vigía "LV de la Policia Nacional", Quito
840	5	PRG	ZP6	R. Guairá, Villarrica
840	1	PRU	OCX1N	CPN Radio, Piura
840	1	PRU	OBX6Y	R. Azul, Arequipa
840	1	PRU	OAX3S	R. Casma, Casma
840	1	PRU	OAU2E	R. Frequencia, San Ignacio
840	10/5	VEN	UZ	Guarapiche 8-40 "La Primera", Maturín
840	10	VEN	MY	R. Juventud, Barquisimeto
850	10	ARG		LV de Amérca, San Miguel
850	1	BOL	CP160	R. 21 de Diciembre, Mina Catavi
850	5	BOL	CP210	R. María Auxiliadora, Montero
850	50	CLM	HJKC	W Radio, SF de Bogotá
850	0.5	EQA	GB7	R. Nal. Espejo, El Puyo
850	20/12	EQA	VS2	R. San Francisco, Guayaquil
850		PRU	OBU7Z	Instituto de Desarrollo, Puno
850	40	PRU	OAX4A	R. Nacional del Perú, Lima
850	1	PRU	OAU7J	R. Quispicanchi, Urcos
850	1	PRU	OCX2F	R. Selecta, Virú
850	50	URG	CX16	R. Carve, Montevideo
850	10	VEN	ZC	R. Fé y Alegría, Maracaibo
850	10	VEN	RV	RV-850, Valencia
860	5/1	ARG		R. Municipal, Chilecito
860	1	ARG	LRA56	R. Nal., Perito Moreno
860	10	BOL	CP8	R. Nueva América, La Paz
860		BOL	CP185	R. Paitití, Guayaramerín
860	10	CHL	CC86	R. Nueva Inés de Suárez, Concepción
860	50	CLM	HJNJ	LV del Cañaguate, Valledupar
860	10	CLM	HJFP	Voces de Occidente, Buga
860	10	EQA	PC1	R. Positiva, Quito
860	25	PRG	ZP28	LV de la Cordillera, Caacupé
860		PRU	OAU2J	CPN Radio, Cajamarca
860	5	PRU	OAU5Q	R. Educativo Macedonia, Ayacucho
860	3	PRU	OCX1M	R. Nuevo Norte, Sullana
860	20/10	VEN	YE	Enlace 8-60, Valle de la Pascua
860	10	VEN	OL	Mundial 8-60, San Cristóbal
870	100	ARG	LRA1	R. Nal., Buenos Aires
870	5	CLM	HJGD	Em. Reina de Colombia, Chiquinquirá
870	10	CLM	HJLA	LV del Tolima, Ibagué
870	25	CLM	HJSB	R. Mar Caribe Internacional, Barranquilla
870	5	CLM	HJZH	Vida AM, Medellín
870	20	EQA	NY2	R. Cristal "RCQ", Guayaquil
870	1	EQA	GS6	R. Píllaro, Píllaro
870	2.5	PRU	OCX4D	R. Huancayo, Huancayo
870	5	PRU	OAU7O	R. Libertad, Puno
870	1	PRU	OCX7R	R. Mundo, Wanchaq
870	10	PRU	OBX1F	R. Programas del Perú, Chiclayo
870	1	PRU	OCX6F	R. TV Impacto, Arequipa
870	10	VEN	RU	Pueblo CNB 870, Puerto La Cruz
870	10	VEN	MP	R. Lara, Barquisimeto
874	0.6	BOL	CP-	LV del Campesino, Sipe Sipe
875		BOL	CP-	R. Eucaliptos, Eucaliptos
879	1	PRU	OAU1G	R. San Pedro Chanel, Sullana
880	10	ARG	LU14	R. Provincia de Santa Cruz, Las Heras
880		ARG		R. Cualidad, Monte Grande
880		BOL	CP-	R. Inca, El Alto
880	10	CHL	CB88	R. Colo Colo, Santiago
880	20	CLM	HJGE	Caracol Colombia, Bucaramanga
880	10	CLM	HJFH	R. Regional Independiente, Anserma
880	50/40	EQA	RP1	R. Católica Nacional, Quito
880	1	PRU	OAX2P	R. Sintonia, Trujillo
880	10	PRU	OBZ4N	R. Union, Lima
880	10	VEN	KV	R. Deportiva 8-80, Caracas
880	10	VEN		R. Paraguaná, Punto Fijo
880	20/10	VEN	YM	R. Venezuela, Puerto Ordaz
890	25/5	ARG	LV11	Emisora Santiago del Estero, do
890	25/5	ARG	LU33	R. Pampeana, Santa Rosa
890		ARG		R. Soberania, Buenos Aires
890	1	CHL	CC89	R. Interamericana, Concepción

kHz	kW	Ctry	Call	Station, location
890	10	CHL	CA89	R. León XIII, Pozo Almonte
890	20	CHL	CD89	R. Nal., Punta Arenas
890	10	CLM	HJCE	R. Continental, SF de Bogotá
890	0.25	CLM	HK093	R. Ecos de Soledad, Soledad
890	20	CLM	HJPM	R. Galeón, Santa Marta
890	1	EQA	TL5	Ondas del Chimborazo, Riobamba
890	25/20	EQA	RS3	R. Superior, Machala
890	5	PRG	ZP33	R. Tres de Febrero, Itá
890	1	PRU	OBX7S	R. Bahá'í del Lago Titicaca, Chiucuito
890	1	PRU	OAU2N	R. Libertad, Cajamarca
890	50/10	URG	CX18	R. Sarandi Sport, Montevideo
890	10	VEN	LW	R. América, Valencia
890	10	VEN	VO	R. Oriente, El Tigre
900		ARG		R. Municipal, 25 de Mayo
900	25/5	ARG	LT7	R. Provincia, Corrientes
900	0.25	BOL	CP79	R. Em. LV Nacional, Tarija
900		BOL	CP20	R. Popular, La Paz
900	1	CHL	CB90	Cablenoticias, Valparaíso
900	1	CHL	CD90	R. LV de la Costa, Osorno
900	5	CHL	CA90	R. Manantial, Copiapó
900	1	CHL	CC90	R. Ñuble, Chillán
900	10	CLM	HJEY	LV de Cali, Cali
900	15/5	CLM	HJDD	R. Super, Cúcuta
900	1	EQA	RR5	R. Carrousel, Cuenca
900	5	EQA	OF4	R. Chone, Chone
900	10	EQA	VA1	Sucre Quito, Quito
900	10	PRU	OBX4X	R. Canal N, Lima
900	1	PRU	OAU7I	R. Frecuencia Telerad, Cusco
900	1	PRU	OBX6K	R. Nevada, Uchumayo
900	1	PRU	OAU2Q	R. Nor Oriental, Jaén
900		PRU	OAX3E	R. Ribereña, Aucaycu
900	1	PRU	OCX1D	R. Sensacional, Ferreñafe
900	3/1	URG	CW17	R. Frontera, Artigas
900	25	VEN	MD	R. Venezuela "Mara Ritmo", Maracaibo
902	1	BOL	CP-	R. Central Misionera, Cochabamba
905	1.5	BOL	CP83	R. Norte, Montero
910	25/5	ARG	LR5	R. La Red, Buenos Aires
910	50/5	ARG	LRA23	R. Nal.,San Juan
910	15	CLM	HJS52	Colombia Mía, Florencia, CA
910	10	CLM	HJDO	LV del Rio Grande, Medellín
910	1	CLM	HJTT	Ondas del Porvenir, Samacá
910	30	CLM	HJMY	RCN, San Andrés
910	2	EQA	BO2	R. Espectáculo, Guayaquil
910	5	EQA	GE5	R. Mundial, Riobamba
910	1	PRU	OAU5M	R. Lider, Ayacucho
910	1	PRU	OAU7G	R. Vision de Altiplano, Juliaca
910	50/20	VEN	RQ	R. Q 910, Caracas
920	1	BOL	CP-	R. Encuentro, Sucre
920	0.3	BOL	CP-	R. San Andres de Topohoco, Topohoco (CP)
920	1	CHL	CD92	R. 920, Temuco
920	10	CLM	HJSJ	Colmundo, Ibagué
920	30	CLM	HJAA	Emisoras Fuentes, Cartagena
920	10	CLM	HJJN	Ondas del Mayo, Pasto
920	10	EQA	RU3	Compañía Radiofonica Orense, Machala
920	1	EQA	AB1	R. Democrácia "La Cariñosa", Quito
920		EQA		R. Peripa, El Empalme
920	10/100	PRG	ZP1	R. Nal. del Paraguay, Asunción: 24h
920	1	PRU	OAU6G	R. La Heróica, Tacna
920	1	PRU	OAX9V	R. Marginal, Tocache
920	1	PRU	OBX2S	R. Ollantay, Virú
920	1	PRU	OCX7M	R. Programas del Perú, Cusco
920	10	PRU	OBX1J	R. Programas del Peru, Piura (rel.
920	0.1	PRU	OCX5C	R. Stelar, Chinca Alta
920	1	PRU	OAU4D	R. Super AM, Sta. Rosa de Sacco
920	20	VEN	QX	R. Nueva Esparta, Porlamar
920	10/5	VEN	QU	R. San Carlos, San Carlos
930		ARG		R. Alfa, Villa Ballester
930	25/5	ARG	LV7	R. Tucumán, San Miguel de Tucumán
930	5/1	ARG	LV28	R. Villa María, do
930	10	CHL	CA93	R. El Cobre, Antofagasta
930	10	CHL	CB93	R. Nuevo Mundo, Santiago
930	10	CHL	CD93	R. Reloncaví, Puerto Montt
930	10	CLM	HJCS	LV de Bogotá, SF de Bogotá
930	5	EQA	VI2	Canal Tropical, Guayaquil
930	5	EQA	BA6	R. Ambato, Ambato
930		PRU		R. Colca, Juliaca
930	1	PRU	OCX2V	R. Inti, Chepén
930	1	PRU	OAU1X	R. La Favorita, Olmos
930	5	PRU	OAX4E	R. Modern - "R. Papa", Lima
930	2.5	PRU	OBX6T	R. Yaravi, Arequipa
930	50/25	URG	CX20	R. Monte Carlo, "la Super R. ", Montevideo
930	10	VEN	LJ	R. Maracay, Maracay
940	3/5	ARG	LRH200	R. Chajarí, do
940	20/5	ARG	LRJ241	R. Dimensión, San Luís
940	1	BOL	CP-	Chuquisaca XXI Comunicación, Sucre (CP)
940		BOL	CP145	R. Metropolitana, La Paz
940	1	CHL	CA94	R. 9-40, Copiapó
940	1	CHL	CB94	R. Valentín Letelier, Valparaíso
940	10	CLM	HJGB	R. Calima, Cali
940	25	CLM	HJTL	RCN, Cúcuta
940		EQA		R. Austral del Ecuador, Cuenca
940	5	EQA	BZ1	R. Dif. de la Casa de la Cultura Ecuatoriana, Quito
940	1	PRU	OBU4E	R. Comericial, Jauja
940	1	PRU	OBX7L	R. Willkamayu, Wanchaq
940	1	PRU	OAY2F	R. Wipimsa, "Waicocha Radio", Huamachuco
940	15	VEN	ZR	R. Continental, Barinas
940	10	VEN	LU	R. Fé y Alegría El Tigre, El Tigre
940	10	VEN	NN	R. Punto Fijo, Punto Fijo
941	0.8	BOL	CP-	R. San Lorenzo, Colcapirhua
950	25/5	ARG	LR3	R. Belgrano, Buenos Aires
950	25/5	ARG	LT16	R. Esmeralda, Roque Saénz Peña
950	3	BOL	CP-	R. Yurac Molino, Chimboata
950	1	CLM	HJUJ	Armonias Boyacenses, Motavita
950	15	CLM	HJFN	Caracol Colombia, Pereira
950		EQA		Chasquis del Norte, Ibarra
950	10	EQA	DE2	GRD - Grupo Radial Delgado, Guayaquil
950	3	EQA	UE5	R. Colta "LV de la Asociación", Colta
950	1	PRU	OBX2G	R. Cutervo, Cutervo
950	1	PRU	OBX9L	R. Estacón Láser, Rioja
950	10	PRU	OAZ7T	R. Instituto Comunicacion Pututo, Puno
950	1	PRU	OAU5K	R. La Luz, Ayacucho
950	1	PRU	OBX3S	R. Programas del Perú, Chimbote
950	50	VEN	KG	AM Popular, Caracas
960	25/1	ARG	LRA6	R. Nal., Mendoza
960	10/3	ARG	LU13	R. Necochea, do
960		BOL	CP-	R. Huayna Potosí, Tiawanaku (CP)
960	1	BOL	CP93	R. Kollasuyo, Potosí
960	10	CHL	CB96	R. Carrera, Santiago
960	10	CHL	CD96	R. Polar, Punta Arenas
960	1	CLM	HJHX	Candela AM, Bucaramanga
960	50	CLM	HJHN	Caracol Colombia, Magangué
960	1	EQA	JX6	LV del Santuario, Baños
960	1	EQA	NC1	R. Cosmopolita, Quito
960	1	EQA	SA5	Sononda Internacional, Cuenca
960		PRU		R. Concierto Santa Monica, Espinar
960	1	PRU	OCY4V	R. Constelación, Huancayo
960	1	PRU	OBX8H	R. Diez, Iquitos
960	12	PRU	OBX6S	R. Hispania, Mariano Melgar
960	10	PRU	OAX4D	R. Panamericana, Lima
960	3	PRU	OBX1Y	R. WST, Chiclayo
960	3/1	URG	CW96	Radio Yi, Durazno
960	50/20	VEN	RB	R. Monagas, Maturín
960	10	VEN	SS	R. San Sebastián, San Cristóbal
960	25	VEN		R. Venezuela "Llanera", Acarigua
965	10	EQA	OT1	R. Católica Nacional., Sto Domingo de los Colorados
970		ARG		NCN/Cadena de la Nueva Conciencia, Villa Insuperable
970	25/15	ARG	LV2	R. General Paz, Córdoba
970	1/0.25	ARG	LT25	R. Guaraní, Curuzú Cuatiá
970	10	BOL	CP30	R. Santa Cruz, Santa Cruz
970	1	CHL	CD97A	R. Austral, Valdivia
970	1	CHL	CA97	R. Calama, Calama
970	1	CHL	CC97	R. Lautaro, Talca
970	1	CHL	CD97B	R. Patagonia Chilena, Coyhaique
970	30	CLM	HJVK	Armonias del Caquetá, Florencia
970	0.25	CLM	HKX59	R. Quimbaya, Calarca
970	10	CLM	HJCI	R. Super, SF de Bogotá
970	10	CLM	HJME	RCN Guajira, Maicao
970	20	EQA	AW2	R. Católica Nal. del Ecuador, Guayaquil
970	1	EQA	MB1	R. Imperio, Ibarra
970	10	PRG	ZP9	R. 9-70 AM, Asunción
970	1	PRU	OBX5A	R. Comericial Sonora, Ica
970	1	PRU	OAU3B	R. Huaraz, Huaraz
970	1	PRU	OBX1V	R. La Capullana, Sullana
970	1	PRU	OAU2K	R. Lider del Norte, Cajamarca
970	1	PRU	OAU7A	R. Tropicana, Wanchaq
970	1	PRU	OBU7B	R. Virgin de Copacabana, Juliaca
970	20/5	URG	CX22	R. Universal, Montevideo
970	10	VEN		Mundial Oriente, Barcelona
970	10	VEN	LR	R. Continente 970 Maracay, Maracay
970	15	VEN	SD	R. Turismo, Valera
980	10/3	ARG	LU37	R. General Pico "R. 37",
980	25/10	ARG		R. Luján AM, Valcheta
980	5	ARG	LT39	R. Victoria

kHz	kW	Ctry	Call	Station, location
980		ARG		Sintonia de Vida, El Talar
980		BOL	CP-	R. Concordia, Oruro (CP)
980	5	BOL	CP192	R. Esperanza, Aiquile
980	2.5	BOL	CP118	R. Mar AM, La Paz
980	5	CHL	CB98	R. Agricultura, Valparaíso
980	1	CHL	CA98	R. Univ. Católica del Norte, Arica
980	15	CLM	HJJV	La Vallenata, Cúcuta
980	100	CLM	HJES	RCN, Cali
980	1	EQA	JI5	R. El Prado, Riobamba
980	5	PRG	ZP31	R. Mburucuyú, Pedro Juan Caballero
980	1	PRU	OAU5O	R. OAU5O, Querobamba
980	1	PRU	OBU4H	R. OBU4H, Huancayo
980	1	PRU	OAU6F	R. Universidad, Arequipa
980	1	PRU	OAU1N	Radio y Sonido, Lambayque
980	10	VEN	QM	LV de El Tigre, El Tigre
980		VEN		R. Nacional, Maracaibo
990	25/5	ARG	LRH203	AM 990, Formosa
990	1	ARG	LRJ201	R. Calingasta, Barreal
990	25/5	ARG	LR4	R. Splendid AM 990, Buenos Aires
990	1	CHL	CC99	R. El Roble, Parral
990	5	CLM	HJHI	LV de Garagoa, Garagoa
990	100	CLM	HJDB	RCN, Medellín
990	15	EQA	EW2	Frecuencia Mil, Guayaquil
990	4	EQA	OL5	R. América, Cuenca
990	25	EQA	GH1	R. Tarquí, Quito
990		PRU		CP - Perunao de Com., Chimbote
990	10	PRU	OAX6K	R. Continental, Tacna
990	0.5	PRU	OBX2M	R. Contumaza, Contumaza
990	10	PRU	OBX4J	R. Disco, Miraflores
990	1	PRU	OBU1C	R. OBU1C, Sechuar
990	1	PRU	OBX8E	R. Programas del Perú, Iquitos
990	20	VEN	RT	R. Tropical "99-0", Caracas
990	10	VEN	TA	R. Venezuela "Tricolor", Barquisimeto
1000	1/0.25	ARG	LT42	R. del Iberá, Mercedes
1000	1/0.25	ARG	LU16	R. Río Negro, Villa Regina
1000	10	BOL	CP220	R. Bahá'í de Bolivia, Caracollo
1000	3	BOL	CP119	R. Dif. Trópico, Trinidad
1000	1	BOL	CP-	R. Mística de Comunicaciones, La Paz (CP)
1000	1	BOL	CP	R. Piraí, Santa Cruz
1000	10	CHL	CB100	R. RRB, Santiago
1000	10	CLM	HJJG	R. Dif. Nal., Manizales (rel
1000	50	CLM	HJZP	R. Dif. Nal., Yopal (rel
1000	0.8	CLM		R. Panamericana, Cajibío
1000	15	CLM	HJAQ	RCN, Cartagena
1000	1	EQA	NT3	Dinamita Mil, Catamayo
1000	1	EQA	CR1	R. Alegría, Sto Domingo de los Colorados
1000	5/1	PRG	ZP36	R. Mil, San Antonio
1000		PRU		CP - Huancayo
1000	2	PRU	OAU2P	R. Bambamarca, Bambamarca
1000	1	PRU	OAU1P	R. California, Lambayque
1000	1	PRU	OBX6R	R. Endesa, Paucarpata
1000	0.5	PRU		R. Huarmaca, Huarmaca
1000	1	PRU	OBX5W	R. Lircay, Lircay
1000		PRU		R. LV de Campesino, Paucartambo
1000	2	PRU	OAZ7P	R. Prensa el Dia, Cusco
1000	10	VEN	NM	R. Mil "La Caribeña", Morón
1000	10	VEN	OA	R. Táchira, San Cristóbal
1010	1/0.25	ARG	LW2	R. Emis. Tartagal
1010		ARG		R. Oasis, Victoria
1010	20/10	ARG	LV16	R. Rio Cuarto, do
1010	1	ARG	LRA28	R. Nal., La Rioja
1010		ARG		R. Onda Latina, Buenos Aires
1010		ARG		Sintonia Ghost, Lanús
1010		BOL	CP-	R. LV de Sipe Sipe, Sipe Sipe
1010	10	CHL	CD101	R. Chilena "Solonoticias", Temuco
1010	10	CLM	HJOP	Caracol Barranquilla, Barranquilla
1010	15	CLM	HJJR	Caracol Colombia, Neiva
1010	10/5	CLM	HJBN	LV del Galeras, Pasto
1010	20	CLM	HJZD	R. Panzenú, Montería
1010	10	CLM	HJCN	R. Reloj, SF de Bogotá
1010	10	CLM	HJIX	R. Yarima, Barrancabermeja
1010	3	EQA	RZ2	R. Amiga, Guayaquil
1010	1	EQA	RC4	R. Cenit, Portoviejo
1010	2.5	EQA	RV5	R. Visión, Cuenca
1010	15	EQA	NR6	TSB R. Lider, Ambato
1010	1	PRU	OAU5G	R. Amistad,Abancay
1010	1	PRU	OAX7F	R. Ayaviri "LV Melgar", Ayavirl
1010		PRU		R. LV de las Huaringas, Huancabamba
1010	1.5	PRU	OBX2P	R. San Francisco, Cajamarca
1010	1	PRU	OBZ1C	R. Sonora, Tumbes
1010	20	URG	CX24	R. Nuevotiempo, Montevideo
1010	10	VEN	QF	R Venezuela, Cd.Bolívar
1010	10	VEN	PC	R. Aragua, Cagua
1020	1	ARG	LRA58	R. Nal., Río Mayo
1020	10/5	ARG	LT10	R. Univ. Nal. del Litoral, Santa Fé
1020	10	BOL	CP4	R. Illimani, La Paz
1020	5	CHL	CC102	R. Amiga, Talca
1020	10	CLM	HJDQ	Emisora Claridad, Medellín
1020	10	CLM	HJKS	LV del Llano, Villavicencio
1020	15	CLM	HJDZ	R. Primavera, Bucaramanga
1020	10	CLM	HJFT	R. Super, Ibagué
1020	10	CLM	HJFQ	RCN, Pereira
1020	3	EQA	GO3	Canal Estelar, Santa Rosa
1020	5	EQA	HR1	R. Quitumbe "LV del Orgullo", Quito
1020	5/3	EQA	CR6	R. Surcos, Guaranda
1020	25/10	PRG	ZP14	R. Ñandutí, Asunción
1020	1	PRU	OBU4F	R. Cristo Vivea, Huancayo
1020	1	PRU	OBU7O	R. Informes, Sivuani
1020	1	PRU	OAU6J	R. Internacional, Tacna
1020	1	PRU	OBU1D	R. La Luz, Piura
1020	1	PRU	OBX3U	R. Nacional, Chimbote
1020	0.1	URG	CW102	R. Libertadores, Salto
1020	25	VEN	TW	R. Alegría, Chivacoa
1020	50/10	VEN	MX	R. Continente Calendario, Maracaibo
1020	10	VEN	RS	R. Mundial Margarita, La Asunción
1030	25/5	ARG	LS10	R. del Plata, Buenos Aires
1030	10	CHL	CC103	R. Chilena "Solonoticias", Concepción
1030	1	CHL	CD103A	R. Chiloé, Castro
1030	1	CHL	CB103	R. Progreso, Talagante
1030	10	CLM	HJDJ	LV de los Libertadores, Duitama
1030	15	CLM	HJRF	Ondas del Cesar, Aguachica
1030	5	CLM		Ondas del Vaupés, Mitú
1030	1	CLM	HJGX	R. Progreso de Córdoba, Lorica
1030	30	CLM	HJER	RCN Antena 2, Cali
1030	5	EQA	RF2	R. Punto 1030, Guayaquil
1030	1	PRU	OCX7O	R. HG-AM, Cusco
1030	3	PRU		R. Imperio, Huamachuco
1030	1	PRU	OAX7N	R. LV del Altiplano, Puno
1030	1	PRU	OCX6L	R. San Luis, Arequipa
1030	20	VEN	QY	R. Onda 1030, Guanare
1030	25/10	VEN	TD	R. Valles del Tuy, Ocumare del Tuy
1040		BOL	CP-	R. Bolivianísima, La Paz (CP)
1040	1	BOL	CP208	R. Sipe Sipe, Quillacollo
1040	1	BOL	CP113	R. Villazón, Villazón
1040	1	CHL	CD104	R. Payne AM, Puerto Natales
1040	1	CHL	CD104	R. Raíces, Curacautín
1040	15	CLM	HJUB	Colmundo, Pasto
1040	15	CLM	HJCJ	Colmundo, SF de Bogotá
1040	10	CLM	HJSY	La Caucana 10-40, Popayán
1040	15	CLM	HJFM	LV de Armenia, Armenia
1040	15	CLM	HJBF	LV del Norte, Cúcuta
1040	15	CLM	HJAI	R. Tropical, Barranquilla
1040	3	EQA	CW1	LV del Valle, Machachi
1040	3	EQA	GB6	R. Colosal, Ambato
1040	10/5	EQA	EV5	R. Splendit, Cuenca
1040	5	PRG	ZP43	R. Arapisandú, San Ignacio
1040	1	PRU	OAU7H	Multimedio Sistena de R. , Espinar
1040	1	PRU	OAZ1D	R. Alas Peruanas, Piura
1040	1	PRU	OBX5U	R. Andina del Pacifico, Ica
1040	10	PRU	OBX4O	R. Em. Nor-Oriente, Miraflores (ex. R. Exito)
1040	1	PRU	OBX2O	R. Nor Oriente, Jaén
1040	20	VEN	LB	LV de Carabobo, Valencia
1040	20/10	VEN	ON	Mundial Los Andes, Mérida
1050		ARG		R. Conurbana, Gregorio de Laferrere
1050		ARG		R. Federal, Lanús
1050	5	BOL	CP233	R. El Mundo, Santa Cruz
1050	1	CHL	CD105	R. Armonía, Osorno
1050	15	CLM	HJBB	Caracol Colombia, Valledupár
1050	10	CLM	HJFZ	La Cariñosa del Centro, Espinal
1050	5	CLM	HJIO	LV de la Conquista, Granada
1050	10	CLM	HJLZ	LV del Cinaruco/Caracol, Arauca
1050	10	CLM	HJGU	R. Bucarica, Bucaramanga
1050	10	CLM	HJNG	R. Palmira, Palmira
1050	10	CLM	HJDR	R. Unica, Medellín
1050	15	CLM	HJTJ	R. Uno, Montería
1050	5	EQA	RQ2	R. Motivación, Guayaquil
1050	5/3	EQA	IM1	R. Municipal, Ibarra
1050	1	PRU	OBX8F	CPN Radio, Iquitos
1050	1	PRU	OBX6D	R. Bethel, Arequipa
1050	1	PRU	OBZ4J	R. Bolognesi, Huancayo
1050	1	PRU		R. Campesina, Cajamarca
1050	1	PRU	OCX2B	R. Maria, Chepén
1050	1	PRU	OAZ7Q	R. San Augistín, Juliaca
1050	25	URG	CX26	S.O.D.R. E.. Montevideo
1050	20	VEN	PO	R. Nacional, Cabudare
1050	25	VEN	KZ	R. Nal. "Canal Musical", Caracas

kHz	kW	Ctry	Call	Station, location
1060		ARG		R. Restauración, Llavallol
1060	10	BOL	CP57	R. Eco 2000, La Paz
1060	0.5	BOL	CP181	R. LV de la Frontera, Pto. Suárez
1060	1.5	BOL	CP-	R. Noticias, Oruro
1060	50	CHL	CB106	R. Santa Maria de Guadalupe, Santiago
1060	1	CLM	HJMG	Caracol Colombia, Turbo
1060	1	CLM	HJYX	Caracoli, Sincelejo
1060	5	CLM	HJLY	R. Delfín, Riohacha
1060	10	CLM	HJMV	R. Furatena, Chiquinquirá
1060	15	CLM	HJOV	R. Surcolombiana, Neiva
1060	15	CLM	HJFJ	RCN Caldas, Manizales
1060	5	EQA	MG6	R. Ecos del Pueblo, Saquisilí
1060		EQA		R. Fiesta, Machala
1060		EQA		R. Richi, El Empalme
1060	0.05	GUF		R. F.O. Guyane, St. Laurent du Maroní
1060	3	PRG	ZP13	R. Boquerón, Alberdi
1060	5	PRU	OAU1C	CPN Radio, Tumbes
1060		PRU		R. La Luz, Ilo
1060	1	PRU	OCY4D	R. Mil Sesenta, Lima
1060		PRU	OAU7U	R. OAU7U, Cusco
1060	5	PRU	OCY2O	R. Sudamerica, Cutervo
1060	10	VEN	LN	R. Guárico, S. Juan de los Morros
1060	10	VEN	OE	R. Noticias AM, San Cristóbal
1070	25/5	ARG	LR1	R. El Mundo, Buenos Aires
1070	20	CLM	HJAH	Em. Atlántico, Barranquilla
1070	30	CLM	HJCG	R. Santa Fé, SF de Bogotá
1070	15	CLM	HJVR	R. Super, Popayán
1070	1	EQA	VP1	R. Libertad, Quito
1070	1	EQA	RS1	R. Lubakán, Santo Domingo de los Colorados
1070	5	EQA	CJ5	R. LV de Tomebamba, Cuenca
1070	10	GUF		R. F.O. Guyane, Matoury
1070	3	PRU	OBX9J	R. Andes, Tarapoto
1070	0.2	PRU	OAX5A	R. San Juan, San Juan de Marcona
1070	1	PRU	OAU6K	R. Trinidad, Arequipa
1070	1	PRU	OAU1J	R. Vida, Chiclayo
1070	1	PRU	OBX4G	R. Visión, San Ramón
1070	25	VEN		Contacto 1070, Ospino
1070	10	VEN	MA	Mundial Zulia, Maracaibo
1070	5	VEN	PX	R. El Sol, La Fría
1070	10	VEN		Superior 1070 Biruaca, San Fernando de Apure
1075	0.5	BOL	CP173	R. Agricultura, Portachuelo
1080	25/5	ARG	LU3	R. del Sur, Bahía Blanca
1080	10/1	ARG		R. Departamento Minas, Andacollo
1080	25/5	ARG	LW4	R. Orán/R. Maria
1080	1	BOL	CP291	R. Dif. Colosal, Sucre
1080		BOL	CP-	R. Em.Comunitaria Pachacuti, Letanía (CP)
1080	1	CHL	CD108	R. Los Confines, Angol
1080	1	CHL	CA108	R. Río Elqui, Vicuña
1080	10	CLM	HJAW	LV de Montería, Montería
1080	10	CLM	HJMH	Melodía AM, Floridablanca
1080	10	CLM	HJKT	R. Autentica/R. Macarena, Villavicencio
1080	15	CLM	HJJS	R. Pontoná, La Dorada
1080	10	CLM	HJJF	R. Popular, Cali
1080	10	CLM	HJAX	R. Recuerdos, Medellín
1080	1	EQA	AB4	R. Contacto, Manta
1080	10	EQA	BH6	R. Latacunga, Latacunga
1080	10	EQA	KD2	R. Tigre, Guayaquil
1080	10	PRG	ZP25	Radiodif. Nanawa, Luque
1080		PRU		CP, Puno
1080	1	PRU	OAU2L	R. Andes, Cajamarca
1080	1	PRU	OCX6X	R. Futura, Ilo
1080	10	PRU	OAU4I	R. La Luz, Lima // 1340
1080	2.2	PRU	OAX7S	R. Salkantay, CuscO
1080	1.5	PRU	OBX1D	v R. San Miguel, Piura
1080	10	VEN	QJ	R. Barcelona, Barcelona
1080		VEN		R. Nacional, Mérida (F.Pl.)
1080	10	VEN	NR	R. Venezuela, Maracay
1090		ARG		R. Nuestras Raíces, Valentin Alsina
1090		ARG		R. Sintonia, José C.Paz
1090	3	BOL	CP45	R. Cultura, Cochabamba
1090	5/1	CHL	CC109	R. Chilena "Solonoticias", Talca
1090	15	CLM	HJBC	Caracol Colombia, Cúcuta
1090	10	CLM	HJIG	Caracol Colombia, Florencia
1090	10	CLM	HJIH	Caracol Colombia, Sogamoso
1090	1	CLM	HJJB	LV de los Pijaos, Guamo
1090	10	CLM	HJIA	Ondas del Nevado, Manizales
1090	5	CLM	HJOM	R. Bucanero, Cartagena
1090	5	EQA	VI1	R. Irfeyal "Fe y Alegría", Quito
1090	1	PRU	OBX6X	R. Amistad, Arequipa
1090	1	PRU	OAU5F	R. Apoyo El Agrario, Aucara
1090	1	PRU	OBX2A	R. Cajabamba, Cajabamba
1090	15	URG	CX28	R. Imparcial, Montevideo
1090	3	VEN	TG	Melódica 1090, Machiques
1090	10	VEN	PB	R. Yaracuy "Operadora 1090 AM", S. Felipe
1090	20	VEN	SZ	Unión R. 1090, Caracas
1100		ARG		R. Estilo, Glew
1100		BOL	CP-	R. Chaka, Pucarani
1100	4	BOL	CP137	R. Mundial, La Paz
1100	1/0.75	BOL	CP55	R. Universidad de Oruro
1100	10	CHL	CB110	R. Integridad, Viña del Mar
1100	1	CHL	CA110	R. La Portada, Antofagasta
1100	15	CLM	HJAT	Caracol Colombia, Barranquilla
1100	10	CLM	HJCN	Caracol, SF de Bogotá Radiodifusión Biblica
1100	5/1	CLM	HJGI	Em. José António Galán/LV de Colombia, Socorro
1100	5	CLM	HJMK	Emisora Ideal, Planeta Rica
1100	2	CLM	HJEF	LV del Vichada, Puerto Carreño
1100	15	CLM	HJYZ	R. Super, Neiva
1100	10	EQA	FW2	R. Alegría, Guayaquil
1100	5/2	EQA	GR6	R. Novedades, Latacunga
1100	1.5	EQA	LE7	R. Oriental, Tena
1100	5	PRG	ZP71	R. Ñu Vera, Capitán Bado
1100	1	PRU	OAZ4W	R. Programas del Perú, Lima
1100	1	PRU		R. Altura, Huarmaca
1100		PRU	OCX4S	R. Imperial "LV de la Provincia", Cañete
1100	0.5	PRU	OAX9J	R. Lamas, Lamas
1100	1	PRU	OBX7Z	R. LTC, Juliaca
1100	1	PRU	OBX1L	R. Star, Chiclayo
1100	1	PRU	OCY4G	Sonorama Radio, Huancayo
1100	10	VEN	SV	R. Angostura, Cd.Bolívar
1100	10	VEN	OP	R. Fe y Alegría, Tovar
1110	25/5	ARG	LS1	R. de la Ciudad/La Once Diez, Buenos Aires
1110	10	CHL	CD111	R. La Frontera, Temuco
1110	1	CLM	HJNC	Ecos del Combeima, Ibagué
1110	1	CLM	HJPA	LV de las Islas, San Andrés
1110	5	CLM	HJGP	LV del Río Arauca, Arauca
1110	10	CLM	HJDI	R. Bolivariana, Medellín
1110	15	CLM	HJZE	R. Piragua, Sincelejo
1110	10	CLM	HJEW	R. Reloj, Cali
1110	10	CLM	HJJP	RCN, Villavicencio
1110	5	CLM	HJGQ	Transmisora Surandes, Andes
1110	10	EQA	JR1	Hoy La Radio, Quito
1110	5	EQA	JC5	R. Ondas Azuayas, Cuenca
1110	5	EQA	RP6	R. Pelileo, Pelileo
1110	1	PRU	OCX6P	R. Austral, Ilo
1110	0.5	PRU	OCX1R	R. Centro Popular, La Union
1110	5	PRU	OCX7T	R. Comer, Cusco
1110	1	PRU	OBX3B	R. Heroica, Huaraz
1110	1	PRU	OCX2U	R. Jaén, Jaén
1110	1	PRU	OAU4J	R. Sonora, Los Olivios
1110	2/1	URG	CX111	R. Paso de los Toros, Paso de los Toros
1110	10	VEN	QT	R. Carúpano, Carúpano
1110	10	VEN	RX	Unión R. Valencia, Valencia
1115	1	BOL	CP-	R. Difusoras Independencia, Atocha
1120	25/5	ARG	LV5	R. Sarmiento, San Juan
1120		BOL	CP-	R. Celestial El Milagro, El Alto
1120	0.5	BOL	CP-	R. Em. Winay Khantati, Tiawanaku (CP)
1120	1	BOL	CP184	R. Estación El Dorado, Trinidad
1120	10	CLM	HJKQ	Caracol Colombia, Tunja
1120	10	CLM	HJTI	Colmundo R. 24, Cúcuta
1120	5	CLM	HJQ92	Colombia Mía, Yopal, CS
1120	5	CLM	HJJC	R. Matecaña, Pereira
1120	15	CLM	HJGH	R. Reloj, Bucaramanga
1120	2	EQA	EB1	Canal 1120, San Gabriel
1120	5	EQA	FV2	Estación Intercontinental, Guayaquil
1120	10	EQA	LE1	R. Dif. Marañon, Sto Domingo de los Colorados
1120	3	EQA	AS7	R. Variedades del Puyo, El Puyo
1120	10	PRG	ZP24	R. Nuevo Mundo, San Lorenzo
1120	1.5	PRU	OBX2I	R. Dinamica, Trujillo
1120	1	PRU	OCX6U	R. Municipal, Cerro Colorado
1120	5	PRU	OAX8A	R. Nacional del Perú, Iquitos
1120	1	PRU	OAU5H	R. Quispillaccta, Ayacucho
1120	10/2	URG	CW31	R. Salto, Salto
1120	10	VEN	MF	Ondas del Lago "Super Ondas", Maracaibo
1120	20/10	VEN	SK	R. Dif.del Sur, San Fernando de Apure
1120	5	VEN	XZ	R. República "La Estación Feliz", Maturín
1125	0.5	BOL	CP-	R. Cruceña, Cotoca
1125	0.3	BOL	CP-	R. Em. Cooperativa Poopó, Poopó
1130		ARG		R. Argentina, Buenos Aires
1130	25/5	ARG	LRA21	R. Nal., Santiago del Estero
1130	10	ARG		R. Tropicana, Buenos Aires (nom
1130	10	CLM	HJAC	Em. Riomar, Barranquilla
1130	1	CLM	HJNN	Ondas del Río, Magangué
1130	15	CLM	HJQQ	R. Reloj, Pasto
1130	15	CLM	HJVA	Vida AM, SF de Bogotá
1130	5	EQA	PV6	R. Centro, Ambato

kHz	kW	Ctry	Call	Station, location
1130	5/3	EQA	RD1	R. Punto, Ibarra
1130		EQA		R. Sibimbe, Ventanas
1130	1	PRU	OAU5A	R. Armonia, Abancay
1130	2.6	PRU	OAX4N	R. Bacán, Lince
1130	1	PRU	OAZ4S	R. Chanchamayo, Chanchamayo
1130	1.2	PRU	OAX2V	R. Los Andes, Cjamarca
1130	1	PRU	OAU7B	R. San Gabriel, Juliaca
1130	3	PRU	OAX9Q	R. San Martin, Tarapoto
1130	20/5	URG	CX30	R. Nacional, Montevideo
1130	15	VEN	PY	R. Amazonas, Puerto Ayacucho
1130	20/10	VEN	RL	R. Ideal, Maiquetia (Caracas)
1130	10	VEN	KQ	R. Popular, Barquisimeto
1140	5/1.5	ARG	LU22	R. Tandil, Tandil
1140	2	BOL	CP-	R. Pico Verde, Chulumani
1140	75	CHL	CB114	R. Nal., Santiago
1140	10	CLM	HJRW	Caracol Villavicencio, Villavicencio
1140	10	CLM	HJKO	LV de la Victoria, Cartagena
1140	10	CLM	HJCL	R. Girardot, Girardot
1140	10	CLM	HJDL	R. Paisa "La Cariñosa de Antioquia", Medellín
1140		CLM		R. Piendamo, Piendamo
1140	10	CLM	HJRN	RCN, Barbosa
1140	10	EQA	AZ5	R. Alfa Musical, Cuenca
1140	1.5	EQA	FB2	R. Cóndor, Guayaquil
1140	4	EQA	MF4	R. Rumbos, Portoviejo
1140	5	EQA	IR1	Raíz 11-40, Quito
1140	5/3	PRG	ZP22	R. Panambí Verá, Villarrica
1140	1	PRU	OAX3R	R. Bahia, Chimbote
1140	0.5	PRU	OAX5W	R. Chinchaysuyo, Chinca Alta
1140	1	PRU	OAX6L	R. Concordia, Arequipa
1140		PRU	OAU1T	R. Fraternal, Ferreñafe
1140	1.5	PRU	OBX1W	R. Piura, Piura
1140	1	PRU	OCY4C	R. Programas del Perú, Pilcomayo
1140		VEN		R. Porlamar "LV del Caribe", Porlamar
1143	1	BOL	CP-	R. Colonia, Yapacani
1145	1	BOL	CP19	R. Chuquiago Musical, La Paz
1150		ARG		Concepto AM 11-50, Buenos Aires
1150	10/5	ARG	LT9	R. Brigadier López, Santa Fé
1150	1	ARG	LRA51	R. Nal., Jáchal
1150	10	ARG	LRA2	R. Nal., Viedma
1150	1	ARG	LRH202	R. Tupá Mbaé, Posadas
1150		BOL		R. 24 de Noviembre, Eucaliptos
1150	0.2	BOL	CP194	R. Chaco, Yacuíba
1150	0.5	BOL	CP71	R. El Cóndor, Oruro
1150	0.3	BOL	CP-	R. Guaqui, Guaqui
1150	15	CLM	HJFI	Caracol Colombia, Armenia
1150	1	CLM	HJGJ	La Vallenata, Duitama
1150	1	CLM	HJTE	LV del Chocó, Quibdó
1150	10	CLM	HJBT	R. Catatumbo, Ocaña
1150	5	CLM	HJSQ	R. Robledo/RCN Antena 2, Cartago
1150	5	CLM	HJFP	RCN, Neiva
1150	10	EQA	GB5	LV de Riobamba "Antena 1", Riobamba
1150	1	EQA	BC7	R. El Cisne, Nueva Loja
1150	10	EQA	AV3	R. Luz y Vida, Loja
1150	0.5	PRU	OCY2E	R. Chasqui Llacta, San Marcos
1150	2.5	PRU	OAU7K	R. Lider, Juliaca
1150	10	PRU	OAX8D	R. Loreto, Iquitos
1150	5	PRU	OBU4K	R. Mineria, Cerro de Pasco
1150	2.5	PRU	OCX7Q	R. Universal, Wanchaq
1150	10	VEN	QD	Ecos del Orinoco, Cd.Bolívar
1150	10	VEN	MV	R. Venezuela "Ondas del Caribe", Punto Fijo
1160	5/10	ARG	LRH253	R. Cataratas, Pto. Iguazú
1160	10/2.5	ARG	LU32	R. Coronel Olavarría, Olavarría
1160	1	ARG	LRA57	R. Nal., El Bolsón
1160	5	BOL	CP317	R. Centenario, "La Nueva", Sta. Cruz
1160	10	BOL	CP132	R. Continental, La Paz
1160	1	BOL	CP98	R. Nuevo Mundo, Sucre
1160	3/1	BOL	CP78	R. RTC, Cochabamba
1160	1	CHL	CC116	R. Ancoa, Linares
1160	1	CHL	CD116	R. Baha'i, Temuco
1160	10	CLM	HJS31	Colombia Mía, Barrancabermeja
1160	15	CLM	HJOC	Ecos de Colombia, SF de Bogotá
1160	5	CLM	HJAZ	Meridiano Radio, Montería
1160	15	CLM	HJAU	Ondas del Orteguaza, Florencia
1160		CLM		Ondas del Puerto, La Virginia
1160	10	CLM	HJBL	R. Aeropuerto, Barranquilla
1160	5	CLM	HJZV	R. Las Lajas, Ipiales
1160	10	CLM	HJEC	R. San José de Cúcuta, Cúcuta
1160	10	CLM	HJEV	R. Unica, Cali
1160		EQA		LV del Pueblo, Azoguez
1160	1	EQA	WD4	R. Cenit, Portoviejo
1160	2	EQA	CP1	R. Presidente, Quito
1160	1	EQA	UR6	R. Runatacuyaj, Latacunga
1160	2	EQA	VR3	R. Vía, Machala

kHz	kW	Ctry	Call	Station, location
1160	10	PRG	ZP72	R. Antena 2, Asunción
1160	5	PRU	OAX4C	R. 1160 Noticias, Lima
1160	1	PRU	OCX7Z	R. del Sur, Puerto Maldonado
1160	1	PRU	OBX5O	R. Huanta 2000, Huanta
1160	1	PRU	OBX5O	R. Huanta 2000, Huanta
1160	1	PRU	OAX9A	R. Imagen, Tarapoto
1160	0.3	PRU	OAX2C	R. Libertad, Trujillo
1160	1	PRU	OBX5M	R. Luren, Ica
1160	1	PRU	OBX6G	R. Nacional del Perú, Moquegua
1160	1	PRU	OAU2T	R. OAU2T, Chota
1160	1	PRU	OCX1S	Radiales Nor Oriental del Marañon, Chiclayo
1160	1	URG	CW116	R. Agraria del Uruguay, Cerro Chato
1160	1/0.25	URG	C116	R. Impacto AM 1160, Mercedes
1160	20/10	VEN	RR	R. Industrial 1160 Estéreo, Guarenas
1160	1	VEN	OK	R. Universidad, Mérida
1170	5	ARG		R. Mi País, Hurlingham
1170	25/3	ARG	LRA29	R. Nal., San Luis
1170	3	CHL	CD117	R. Natales, Puerto Natales
1170	10	CLM	HJNW	Caracol Colombia, Cartagena
1170	5	CLM	HJWA	LV del Guaviare, San José del Guaviare
1170	10	CLM	HJE74	Meridiano 70, Arauca
1170	10	CLM	HJPB	Ondas de Macondo, Valledupar
1170	10	CLM	HJBX	Ondas del Meta, Villavicencio
1170	10	CLM	HJKW	R. Nutibara, Medellín
1170	10	CLM	HJGA	R. Recuerdos, Tunja
1170	1	CLM	HJJE	RCN, Tuluá
1170	10	EQA	JM4	R. Antena Libre, Esmeraldas
1170	5	EQA	JV5	R. Central, Riobamba
1170	5	EQA	RV2	R. Filadelfia, Guayaquil
1170		PRU		R. Bethel, Cusco
1170	0.5	PRU	OCX7Y	R. Constelación, Puno
1170	1	PRU	OCX4Y	R. COSAT, Satipo
1170	1	PRU	OBX8M	R. La Luz, Iquitos
1170	1	PRU	OAU2M	R. Layzon, Cajamarca
1170	1	PRU	OAZ3K	R. Nor Peruano Chimbote
1170	10	PRU	OBX6L	R. Programas del Perú, Arequipa
1170	1	PRU	OCX1B	R. San Juan, Talara
1170	10	URG	CX32	Radiomundo, Montevideo
1170	10	VEN	KW	Celestial 1170 AM, Maiquetía
1170	20/10	VEN	QV	R. Acarigua, Acarigua
1180		BOL	CP-	R. Amanecer, Potosí
1180	5	BOL	CP-	R. Central, Oruro
1180	1	BOL	CP235	R. Emisora Ingavi, Viacha
1180	1	BOL	CP-	Radioemisora 20 de Septiembre, Arbieto
1180	50	CHL	CB118	R. Portales, "la primera de Chile", Santiago
1180	15	CLM	HJFX	Caracol Colombia, Manizales
1180		CLM		Em. Coorpurabá, Apartadó
1180	20	CLM	HJGK	R. Santander 2, Bucaramanga
1180	10/5	CLM	HJJT	RCN, Ibagué
1180	12.5	EQA	LR1	Nueva Em. Central, Quito
1180	4	EQA	DP5	R. Cuenca, Cuenca
1180	1.2	EQA	R1	R. Familiar, Julio Andrade
1180	5	EQA		R. Trébol AM, Zaruma
1180	5/1	PRG	ZP52	R. Coronel Oviedo - RCO-AM, Coronel Oviedo
1180	1	PRU	OCX2A	R. America, Quiruvilca
1180	1	PRU	OAZ1C	R. Chulucanas, Chulucanas
1180	1	PRU		R. La Luz, Jaen
1180	1	PRU	OCY4Z	R. Libertad "R. RLJ", Junin
1180	10	URG	CX118	LV de Artigas, Artigas
1180	10	VEN	LQ	LV de la Victoria, La Victoria
1180	10	VEN		R. Maturín, Maturín
1180	10	VEN	NJ	R. Petrolera, Cd.Ojeda
1190	25/5	ARG	LR9	R. América, Buenos Aires
1190	50	ARG	LRA15	R. Nal., San Miguel de Tucumán
1190	10	CLM	HJCT	LV de la Costa, Barranquilla
1190	15	CLM	HJEO	Ondas del Valle, Cartago
1190	1	CLM	HJKI	R. Barají, Sahagún
1190	10	CLM	HJCV	R. Cordillera, SF de Bogotá
1190	10	CLM	HJKG	R. Mira, Tumaco
1190	2	EQA	DE2	Estudio 11-90, Guayaquil
1190	1	EQA	RF6	R. El Sol, Pujilí
1190		PRG	ZP45	LV de la Libertad, Henendarias
1190	5	PRU	OBX3D	R. Ancash, Huaraz
1190	10	PRU	OAX1E	R. Chiclayo, Chiclayo
1190	1.5	PRU	OCX6G	R. Encuentro, Yanahuara
1190	2	PRU	OAX7B	R. Twantinsuyo, Cusco
1190	20/10	VEN	PF	Ondas de Libertad, San Félix
1190	20/10	VEN	RE	R. Barinas 1190 AM Estéreo, Barinas
1190	10	VEN	ZD	R. Dif.Cult. del Táchira, San.Cristóbal
1195	1	BOL	CP108	R. Independencia, Quillacollo
1195		CLM		Ondas del Ranchería, Barrancas
1200	5/1.5	ARG	LT6	R. Goya
1200	1	ARG		R. Nal. Mendoza, Valle de Uspallata

kHz	kW	Ctry	Call	Station, location
1200	0.25	BOL	CP171	R. 24 de Noviembre, Arani
1200		BOL	CP-	R. Cuarzo de Comunicaciones, La Paz (CP)
1200	5	BOL	CP32	R. Oriental, Santa Cruz
1200	10	CHL	CD120	R. Agricultura, Los Angeles
1200	1	CHL	CA120	R. Almirante Blanco Encalada, Tocopilla
1200	10	CLM	HJBV	Caracol Colombia, Cartagena
1200	10	CLM	HJCD	Em. Nueva Epoca, Fusagasugá
1200	10	CLM	HJLR	La Cariñosa, Sogamoso
1200	10	CLM	HJBZ	Ondas del Riohacha, Riohacha
1200	15	CLM	HJIJ	R. 1200 "LV de la Raza", Medellín
1200	10	CLM	HJNF	R. Super, Cali
1200	5	EQA	RE2	LV del Trópico, Quevedo
1200	5	EQA	RM5	R. El Mercurio, Cuenca
1200		EQA		R. Filadelfia, Quito
1200	1	EQA	MP4	R. La Grande, Bahía de Caráquez
1200	5	EQA	CS1	R. Super K, Sangolquí
1200		EQA		R. U Cadena Sur, Sta Rosa
1200	10	PRG	ZP44	R. Libre, Fernando de la Mora
1200	1	PRU	OAU2A	Frecuencia Pedagogica, Cajamarca
1200	3	PRU	OAU4G	R. Andes, Huancayo
1200	3	PRU	OAX4B	R. Cadena, Lima
1200	1	PRU	OBX5X	R. Comercial, Abancay
1200	1	PRU	OCX7S	R. Cultura, Juliaca
1200		PRU		R. La Luz, Pucallapa
1200		PRU		R. La Luz, Tacna
1200	2	URG	CW33	La Nueva Radio, Florida
1200	1	VEN	NH	Ondas del Escalante, Sta Bárbara del Zulia
1200	10	VEN		R. Dimensión, Caripito
1200	10	VEN	OZ	R. Tiempo, Caracas
1210	5/1	ARG	LRI229	R. Las Flores
1210		ARG		R. Mailín, Gregorio de Laferrere
1210	10	CHL	CD121	R. Armonía, Puerto Montt
1210	1	CHL	CC121	R. Universidad de Talca, Talca
1210	5	CHL	CB121	R. Valparaíso, Valparaíso
1210	10	CLM	HJBE	La Cariñosa, Cúcuta
1210	10	CLM	HJFR	R. Recuerdos, Neiva
1210	10	CLM	HJBQ	RCN Antena 2, Pereira
1210	10	EQA	VC3	R. Centinela del Sur "CDS", Loja
1210	20	EQA	BJ2	R. El Mundo, Guayaquil
1210	3	EQA	JM6	R. Sira, Ambato
1210	1	PRU	OCY4T	R. Galaxia, Satipo
1210	1	PRU		R. Municipalidad, Aybaca
1210	1	PRU	OAX7M	R. Quillabamba, Santa Ana
1210	1	PRU	OAX2Q	R. Universo, Trujillo(rel.
1210	2	URG	CX121	Difusora Soriano, Mercedes
1210	1	URG	CW121	R. El Libertador, Villa Vergara
1210	25/0.25	URG	C121	R. RBC, Piriápolis
1210	10	VEN	ZT	R. Anzoátegui, Barcelona
1220	5/1	ARG	LRL328	LV del Aire - "Cadena Eco", Buenos Aires
1220		ARG		R. del Norte, Pres. Roque Sanez Peña
1220	1	BOL	CP162	R. Batallón Topáter, Oruro
1220		BOL	CP-	R. El Cóndor, Arque
1220	1	BOL	CP67	R. Splendid, La Paz
1220	10	CHL	CD122	R. Santa Maria de Guadalupe, Temuco
1220	1	CHL	CA122	Soc. Morales y Morales y Cia., La Serena
1220	10	CLM	HJKR	R. María, SF de Bogotá
1220	15	CLM	HJFF	R. Reloj, Barranquilla
1220	10	CLM	HJNM	R. Viva Cultural Bolívar, Ipiales
1220	10	CLM	HJAV	RCN, Montería
1220	10	CLM	HJMT	RCN, San Gil
1220	3/5	EQA	EB6	Ecos de Bolívar, Guaranda
1220	10	EQA	AP1	Sistema de Radiodif. Marañon, Quito
1220	3	PRU	OCX1X	R. Gran Plaza, Chiclayo
1220	1	PRU	OAU5N	R. La Luz, Ica
1220	4	PRU	OAX6X	R. Melodia, Arequipa
1220	1	URG	CX122	R. Reconquista, Rivera
1220	10	VEN	RD	LV de Apure, San Fernando de Apure
1220	20/10	VEN	ZO	R. Aeropuerto 1220, Maracaibo
1220	10/5	VEN	VM	R. Valencia, Valencia
1230	25/5	ARG	LT2	R. Gral. San Martín, "R. 2", Rosario
1230		ARG		R. La Bendición, General Pico
1230	5/1	ARG	LW5	R. Libertador, General San Martín
1230		ARG		R. Litoral, Isidro Casanova
1230	10	CLM	HJBR	Caracol Tunja, Tunja
1230	15	CLM	HJGV	Colmundo, Bucaramanga
1230	10	CLM		Minuto de Dios, Cartagena
1230	10	CLM	HJIL	Minuto de Dios, Medellín
1230	10	CLM	HJKL	R. Calidad "La Cariñosa", Cali
1230	1	CLM	HJTP	R. Colina, Girardot
1230	1	CLM	HJMJ	RCN Antena 2, Maicao
1230	3	EQA	RI1	Centro Radiofónico de Imbabura, Ibarra
1230	1	EQA	RL6	LV de Saquisilí y Libertador, Saquisilí
1230	15	EQA	FV2	R. Galáctica, Guayaquil
1230	3	EQA	MV5	R. Popular, Cuenca
1230	5	EQA	FG4	Sucre Esmeraldas, Esmeraldas
1230	3	PRG	ZP21	R. Oriental, 'La radio del Pueblo', Caaguazú
1230	1	PRU	OAX2T	R. Albújar, Guadalupa
1230	1	PRU	OBX4Z	R. LV de Oxapampa, Oxapampa
1230	0.5	PRU	OBX7J	R. Madre de Dios, Puerto Maldonado
1230		PRU	OAU7V	R. OAU7V, Juliaca
1230	1	PRU	OBX2C	R. Otuzco, Otuzco
1230	1	PRU	OBZ4Y	R. Selleciones, Tarma
1230	10	VEN	NT	R. Barlovento, Caucagua
1230	10	VEN	OH	R. Valera, Valera
1240	1	ARG		Onda Marina, Mar del Plata
1240		ARG		R. Vida, Monte Grande
1240	2	BOL	CP16	R. Los Andes, Tarija
1240	1	BOL	CP180	R. San Miguel, Arani
1240		BOL	CP-	R. Achocalla, Achocalla
1240	0.25	CHL	CA124	R. Principal Chuquicamata, Calama
1240	10	CHL	CB124	R. Universidad de Santiago, Santiago
1240	5	CLM	HJGN	R. Barrancabermeja
1240	5	CLM	HJJA	R. Buenaventura, Buenaventura
1240	1	CLM	HJGO	R. Caribabare, Saravena
1240	10	CLM	HJFG	RCN, Calarca
1240	5	EQA	RF3	R. Fenix, Zaruma
1240	1	EQA	PA1	R. Metropolitana, Quito
1240		EQA	LA5	R. Sonorama, Riobamba
1240		PRU		CP, Bagua Grande
1240		PRU		CP, Ica
1240	1	PRU	OAU2Y	R. Bolivar, Bolivar
1240	10	PRU	OAU4V	R. Cumbre, Chilca
1240	1	PRU	OAU3C	R. La Luz, Chimbote
1240	5	PRU	OAU6D	R. Lider, Arequipa
1240	1	PRU	OCX1C	R. Sechura, Sechura
1240		PRU	OBX7M	R. Túpac Amaru, Sicuani
1240	5/1	URG	CW35	R. Paysandú, Paysandú
1240	50	VEN	NV	R. Nal. Punta Tumatey (Prgr
1250	1	ARG		R. Estirpe Nal., "La Radio", San Justo
1250	1	BOL	CP26	R. Amboró, Santa Cruz
1250	0.1	BOL	CP47	R. Frontera, Cobija
1250	2.5	BOL	CP54	R. La Plata, "LV de la Capital", Sucre
1250	0.5	BOL	CP69	R. Nacional, Cochabamba
1250	0.4	BOL	CP65	R. Oruro, Oruro
1250	0.5	BOL	CP17	R. Sararenda, Camiri
1250		BOL		R. Uncia, Uncia
1250	10	CHL	CD125	R. Armonía, Valdivia
1250	1	CHL	CA125	R. Santa Maria de Guadalupe, La Serena
1250	10	CLM	HJOK	Em. ABC, Barranquilla
1250	1	CLM	HJEM	LV de Corozal, Corozal
1250	10	CLM	HJCA	R. Capital, SF de Bogotá
1250	15	CLM	HJHS	R. Reloj, Cúcuta
1250	1.5	CLM	HJFV	R. Viva Canal 12-50, Pasto
1250	3	EQA	MY1	LV del Triunfo, Sto Domingo de los Colorados
1250	10	EQA	EM1	Ondas Carchenses, Tulcán
1250	10	EQA	HB2	R. Tricolor, Guayaquil
1250	1	PRG	ZP3	R Libertad,.
1250	1	PRU	OAU2V	HGV, Santa Cruz
1250	1	PRU	OBZ1B	R. B.N.S., Talara Alta
1250	5	PRU	OAX4L	R. Miraflores, Miraflores
1250	1	PRU	OAX8P	R. Pucallapa, Pucallapa
1250	3	PRU	OBX7A	R. Solar, Cusco
1250	5	URG	CW125	R. Bella Unión, Bella Unión
1250	10	URG	CX36	R. Centenario, Montevideo
1250	20/10	VEN	PZ	Latina 12-50, Pto Ordaz
1250	1	VEN	ML	R. Cabimas, Cabimas
1260		ARG		R. Fortaleza Cristiana, Rafael Castillo
1260	25/5	ARG	LT14	R. General Urquiza, Paraná
1260	2	BOL	CP14	Radioemisoras Unidas, La Paz
1260	1	CHL	CC126	R. Condell, Curicó
1260	10	CHL	CA126	R. Nal., Arica
1260	10	CHL	CD126	R. Santa Maria de Guadalupe, Punta Arenas
1260	5	CLM	HJNO	Bésame AM, Duitama
1260	5	CLM	HJDV	Caracol Colombia, Ibagué
1260	1	CLM	HJHU	Caracol Colombia, San Andrés
1260	5	CLM	HJLX	Minuto de Dios Eco Llanero, Villavicencio
1260	2	CLM	HJOU	Ondas del Amazonas, Leticia
1260	5	CLM	HJDA	R. Autentica, Medellín
1260	5	CLM	HJET	R. María, Cali
1260	5	CLM	HJTM	R. Sonar, Ocaña
1260	5	CLM	HJOH	RCN Cesar, Valledupar
1260	10	EQA	MO1	LV del Santuario del Quinche, Quito
1260	1	EQA	RB3	R. Benemérita, Sta Rosa
1260	3	EQA	RO6	R. Calidad, Ambato
1260	2	EQA	PB5	R. Contacto XG, Cuenca
1260	1	PRG	ZP34	R. Cultura, Villarrica

kHz	kW	Ctry	Call	Station, location
1260	1	PRU		R. Ebenezer, Bambamarca
1260	1	PRU	OAZ1A	R. Ferrañafe, Ferrañafe
1260	1	PRU		R. La Luz, Huanuco
1260	1	PRU	OBX6D	R. Mundial, Arequipa
1260	0.3	PRU	OBX5S	R. Nacional del Perú, Ayacucho
1260	1	PRU	OCX10	R. Nor Puruana, Chiclayo
1260		PRU		R. Periodico, Chimbote
1260		PRU	OAU7K	R. Stereo Nevada, Espinar
1260	3/1	URG	CW37	Dif. Rochense, Rocha
1260	10	VEN	RY	R. Horizonte, Nirgua
1260	10	VEN	RM	RRB 1260 AM Radiodif. Biblica, Caracas
1265	0.4	BOL	CP-	R. Uncía, Uncía
1270	5	ARG	LRA20	R. Nal., Las Lomitas
1270	50/10	ARG	LS11	R. Provincia de Buenos Aires, La Plata
1270	1	BOL	CP134	R. Vanguardia, Colquiri
1270	10	CHL	CB127	R. Festival, Viña del Mar
1270	5	CLM	HJTX	Bésame AM, Bucaramanga
1270	1	CLM	HJIM	Colmundo, Pereira
1270	5	CLM	HJQ99	Colombia Mía, San José del Guaviare, GV
1270	5	CLM	HJKD	La Cariñosa, Neiva
1270	1.5	CLM	HJKJ	LV de Curumaní, Curumaní
1270	1	CLM	HJSV	LV de Orito, Orito
1270	5	CLM	HJBM	R. Internacional, Honda
1270	1	CLM	HJXQ	R. Melodía, Ubaté
1270	2	CLM	HJAR	RCN Antena 2, Cartagena
1270	3	EQA	LD4	R. Junín, Junín
1270	15	EQA	UM2	R. Universal, Guayaquil
1270	1	PRU	OAX8T	R. Eco, Iquitos
1270	1	PRU	OCX2Z	R. Estacion Latina, Cepén
1270	2	PRU	OAU7S	R. Horizonte, Cusco
1270	0.4	PRU	OAZ4H	R. Huacho, Huacho
1270	0.4	PRU	OBZ4T	R. La Merced, Chanchamayo
1270	1	PRU	OAU1S	R. Nor Paita, Paita
1270	4/2	URG	C127	R. Cuareim, Artigas
1270		VEN		R. Nacional, Ureña
1270	10	VEN	OU	R. Ondas Panamericanas, El Vigía
1270	5	VEN	TR	R. Tucupita, Tucupita
1275	0.5	BOL	CP187	R. Chané, Mineros
1276	1	PRU	OAU1R	R. Gotas del Oro, Urrunaga
1280		ARG		R. Eco Porteña, Buenos Aires
1280		ARG		R. Nuestra Señora de Itatí, Morón
1280	10/5	ARG	LU11	R. Trenque Lauquén, Trenque Lauquén
1280	1	CHL	CC128	R. Arturo Prat Chacón AM, San Carlos
1280	10	CHL	CD128	R. del Sur "En Voz Alta", Osorno
1280	5	CLM	HJLR	Caracol Colombia, Pasto
1280	5	CLM	HJRP	Ecos de Tibú, Tibú
1280	5	CLM	HJHO	Impacto Popular, San Juan del Cesar
1280	1	CLM	HJNQ	LV del Río Suárez, Barbosa
1280	5	CLM	HJSO	R. Playa Mendoza, Barranquilla
1280	5	CLM	HJTK	R. Super, Caicedonia
1280	5	CLM	HJCM	R. Sur, Pitalito
1280	5	CLM	HJMB	R. Suroeste, Concordia
1280	5	CLM	HJKN	R. Unica, SF de Bogotá
1280	1	EQA	IN4	LV del Sur de Manabí, Jipijapa
1280	1	EQA	NW5	R. Canal Tropical, Riobamba
1280	2	EQA	RP3	R. Continental, Arenillas
1280	20	PRG	ZP53	R. LV del Este, Cd. del Este
1280		PRU	OBX3C	R. Alopesa, Chimbote
1280	0.5	PRU	OBX6P	R. Fénix, Camaná
1280	1	PRU	OAU1R	R. Gotas del Oro, Urrunaga
1280	1	PRU	OAX3Y	R. La Selva, Rupa-Rupa (r
1280	1	PRU	OBX2F	R. Moderna, Cajamarca
1280	3/1	URG	CX128	R. "Noticias" Tacuarembó, Tacuarembó
1280	10	VEN	OF	R. Trujillo, Trujillo
1280	10/5	VEN	QS	R. Zaraza, Zaraza
1290	1	ARG	LRI371	R. Amanacer, Reconquista
1290		ARG		R. Cristal, Lanús
1290	5/1	ARG	LRJ212	R. Murialdo, Villa Nueva de Guaymallén
1290		ARG		R. Provincia, Mariano Acosta
1290	1	BOL	CP212	Radiodifusoras Minería, Oruro
1290	0.25	CHL	CA129	R. Coya, María Elena
1290	1	CHL	CD129	R. Mulchen, Mulchen
1290	5	CLM	HJSZ	Colombia Mía, Saravena, AR
1290	5	CLM	HJTH	LV de las Estrellas "R. Ritmos", Medellín
1290	5	CLM	HJNE	LV del Ariari, Granada
1290	5	CLM	HJEB	LV del Turismo, Santa Marta
1290	5	CLM	HJOI	R. Chacurí, Sampués
1290	5	CLM	HJMC	R. Viva 12-90, Cali
1290	5	CLM	HJKY	RCN, Girardot
1290	1	EQA	OF2	Canal Milagreño, El Milagro
1290	3	EQA	JA5	LV del Río Tarqui, Cuenca
1290	0.5	EQA	VM6	R. Once de Noviembre, Latacunga
1290	1	EQA	NS1	R. Popular, Atuntaqui
1290		PRU		CP, La Oroya
1290	10	PRU	OAX9N	R. Nor Oriental, Bagua Grande
1290	1	PRU	OCX1Q	R. Programas del Perú, Tumbes
1290	1	PRU	OCX6B	R. Trebol, Mariano Melgar
1290		PRU		R. TV Sonorama, Trujillo
1290	1	PRU	OBU4Q	S & RD, Hualmay
1290	10	URG	CX38	S.O.D.R. E., Montevideo
1290	10	VEN	LF	R. Puerto Cabello, Puerto Cabello
1300		ARG		R. Identidad, Buenos Aires
1300		ARG		R. Metropolitana, Luís Guillón
1300	10/5	ARG	LRA5	R. Nal., Rosario
1300	5	BOL	CP-	R. Bandera Beniana, Trinidad
1300	0.3	BOL	CP168	R. Chichas, Siete Suyos
1300	1	BOL	CP-	R. Coronel Eduardo Avaroa, Sta. Cruz
1300	1	BOL	CP82	R. Fides, Potosí
1300	0.15	BOL	CP127	R. Juan XXIII, Uyuni
1300	2.5	BOL	CP51	R. Loyola, Sucre
1300	15/6	BOL	CP-	R. Sol, "Poder de Diós", La Paz
1300	1	CHL	CD130	R. Cabo de Hornos, Pto. Williams
1300	10	CHL	CD130	R. Chilena "Solonoticias", Valdivia
1300	5	CHL	CB130	R. Tierra, Santiago
1300	5	CLM	HJOG	LV de las Antillas, Cartagena
1300	5	CLM	HJNB	Onda 5, Bucaramanga
1300	5	CLM	HJIN	R. Eucha, Belalcázar
1300	5	CLM	HJEA	R. Lumbí, Mariquita
1300	5	CLM	HJLD	R. Reloj, Pereira
1300	5	CLM	HJUA	R. Sindamanoy, Mocoa
1300	5	CLM	HJRB	R. Super, Tunja
1300	5	EQA	DC2	R. Cenit, Guayaquil
1300	5	EQA	R1	R. Festival, Sto Domingo de los Colorados
1300		EQA		R. La Paz, Guaranda
1300	2/1	EQA	RS7	R. Sucumbios, Nueva Loja
1300	1	PRU	OAZ4B	R. Andina, Huancayo
1300	5	PRU	OAX4S	R. Comas, Comas
1300	0.4	PRU	OAX6P	R. Comercial Latina, Tacna
1300	1	PRU	OAU1U	R. Frecuencia Lider, Morrop
1300	0.5	PRU	OAX30	R. Huascarán, Independencia
1300	0.3	PRU	OAX7X	R. Juliaca, Juliaca
1300		PRU		R. La Luz, Tarapoto
1300	5	PRU	OAX7P	R. Misercordia, Cusco
1300		PRU	OAZ8B	R. Nuevo Mundo, Pucallapa
1300	1	PRU	OAU2I	R. Paraiso, Cajabamba
1300	10/8	VEN	KH	R. 1300, Caracas
1300	10	VEN	NS	R. Reloj, Maracaibo
1310	1	ARG		R. Dr. Gregorio Alvarez, Piedra del Aguila
1310		ARG		R. Integracion, Buenos Aires
1310	1	ARG	LRA42	R. Nal., Gualeguaychú
1310		ARG		R. Panamericana, Gregorio de Laferrere
1310	10	BOL	CP68	R. San Rafael, Cochabamba
1310	5	CLM	HJDG	Caracol Colombia, Monteria
1310	5	CLM	HJJZ	Colorín ColorRadio, SF de Bogotá
1310	5	CLM	HJAK	LV de la Patria, Barranquilla
1310	5	CLM	HJWD	Micrófono Civico, Palermo
1310	5	CLM	HJLM	R. Santa Bárbara
1310	5	CLM	HJTQ	R. Tasajero, Cúcuta
1310	5	CLM	HJIR	RCN Urabá, Apartadó
1310	0.5	EQA	AI5	Eco de los Andes, Cumanda
1310	1	EQA	CP3	LV de El Oro, Pasaje
1310	20	EQA	GB1	R. Nal. Espejo, Quito
1310	3	EQA	CI5	T. V. O. "El Poder Mágico de la Fé", Biblián
1310	1	PRU	OBX2D	R. Chota, Chota
1310	1	PRU	OBX4L	R. Irvisa, Huacho
1310	1	PRU	OAU6N	R. MCV, Paucarpata
1310	1	PRU	OBX8L	R. Vision Amazonia, Iquitos
1310	5	VEN	TS	R. Andina "Sonido 13-10", Isnotú
1310	10	VEN	SM	R. Nacional, Barcelona
1310	1	VEN	SL	R. Nacional, Guri
1320	5/3	ARG	LU10	R. Azul
1320	0.25	ARG	LV24	R. Manantiales, Tunuyán
1320		ARG		R. Mística, Libertad
1320		ARG		R. Sentir, Remedios de Escalada
1320		BOL	CP-	R. Panorama, Achocalla
1320		BOL	CP-	R. Tawantinsuyo, Taraco (CP)
1320	0.25	CHL	CA132	R. Estrella del Norte, Vallenar
1320	1	CHL	CD132	R. Lincoyan, Mulchén
1320	5	CLM	HJNO	La Cariñosa, Girardot
1320	5	CLM	HJMS	R. El Sol, Barrancabarmeja
1320	5	CLM	HJHT	R. Guateque, Guateque
1320	5	CLM	HJQI	R. Leda Internacional, San Andrés
1320	1	CLM	HJNK	R. Luna, Palmira
1320	1	CLM	HJTA	R. María, Medellín
1320	5	CLM	HJLV	R. Onda Fantastica, Fundación
1320	10	EQA	JD6	R. Continental, Ambato

kHz	kW	Ctry	Call	Station, location
1320	3	EQA	FR2	R. Guayaquil, Babahoyo
1320	0.5	EQA	OB7	R. Nacional Limón, Limón Indanza
1320	1	EQA	VO4	R. Stéreo Carrizal, Calceta
1320		PRU		CP. Olmos
1320	1	PRU	OBX2Q	R. Frecuencia Popular, Chepén
1320	1	PRU	OBU4I	R. Majestad, Huancayo
1320	1	PRU	OAX3U	R. Miramar, Chimbote
1320	10	PRU	OAX4A	R. Nacional del Perú (R. La Cronica), Lima
1320	1	PRU	OAU5C	R. Perú, Abancay
1320	3	PRU	OAU7W	R. Peru, Juliaca
1320	0.3	URG	CW132	R. Fortaleza, Rocha
1320	1/0.5	URG	CW39	R. LV de Paysandú, Paysandú
1320	10/5	VEN	WP	R. Apolo, Turmero
1320	10	VEN	SG	R. Colonial, El Tocuyo
1330	3	ARG		R. Cadena Central, Bernal
1330	3/3.5	BOL	CP176	R. América, Oruro
1330	1	BOL	CP112	R. Frontera, Yacuíba
1330	3	CHL	CB133	R. Metropolitana, Santiago
1330	3/1.5	CHL	CD133	R. Vicente Pérez Rosales, Puerto Montt
1330	0.25	CLM	HKR33	Alcadía de Salamina, Salamina
1330	5	CLM	HJLS	Caracol Colombia, Popayán
1330	5	CLM	HJNR	La Caliente 13-30, San Gil
1330	5	CLM	HJFE	La Cariñosa Amiga, Pereira
1330	1	CLM	HJMP	LV de Aguachica, Aguachica (cfR. 1500)
1330	5	CLM	HJAP	R. Autentica, Cartagena
1330	1	CLM	HJRD	R. Coopeñol, El Peñol
1330	3	EQA	O1	GRC AM-Grupo Radial Carisma, El Angel
1330		EQA		Lomas Stereo 2000, Guayaquil
1330	5	EQA	RV3	R. El Oro, Machala
1330	2	EQA	LW5	R. Misión Cristiana Internacional, Cuenca
1330	3	EQA		R. Misión Cristiana Internacional, Quito
1330	5	PRG		R. Chaco Boreal, Asunción
1330	1	PRU	OAU1A	R. Dos Mil, Chiclayo
1330	1	PRU	OVX6E	R. Ondas del Misti, Mariano Melgar
1330	0.5	PRU	OAU5L	R. San Juan. San Juan Bautista
1330	1	PRU	OCX7K	R. San Miguel, Wanchaq
1330	5	URG	CX40	R. Fenix, Montevideo
1330	5	VEN	OY	R. Los Llanos, Calabozo
1330	10	VEN	TU	R. Regional, Cd.Ojeda
1340		ARG		R. Tradicional, Ituzaingó
1340		BOL	CP-	R. Dif. La Misión, La Paz (CP)
1340	1	BOL	CP24	R. Grigotá, Santa Cruz
1340	0.5	BOL	CP-	R. Jach'a Suyu, Corocoro
1340	0.35	BOL	CP146	R. San Francisco, Apolo
1340	0.5	BOL	CP-	Radiodifusora Copacabana, Copacabana
1340	10	CHL	CB134	R. Caracola, Valparaíso
1340	1	CHL	CC134	R. La Discusión, Chillán
1340	1	CHL	CD134	R. Panguipulli, Panguipulli
1340	0.5	CLM	HJVL	Brisas del Catatumbo, Tibú
1340	5	CLM	HJIS	La Cariñosa, Buenaventura
1340	1	CLM	HJNP	R. Comunal, Nariño
1340	5	CLM	HJPY	R. Lemas, Cúcuta
1340	5	CLM	HJFA	R. Olimpica AM, Barranquilla
1340	1	CLM	HJNY	R. Unica, Bucaramanga
1340	5	CLM	HJFB	R. Uno, SF de Bogotá
1340	5	CLM	HJHA	RCN Nariño, Pasto
1340	5	CLM	HJHY	RCN Sucre, Sincelejo
1340		EQA		LV de su amiga, Esmeraldas
1340	2.5	EQA	VP5	LV del Volcan, Penipe
1340	1	EQA	SF2	R. Fluminense, Babahoyo
1340	5	EQA	RT6	R. Paz y Bien, Ambato
1340	1	EQA		R. Regional, Loja
1340		PRU		CP, Iglesia de Dios, Nuevo Chimbote
1340	0.2	PRU	OAZ4M	R,Huaral, Huaral
1340	0.5	PRU	OAX5D	R. Chinca, Chinca Alta
1340	5.5	PRU	OAU4Q	R. Colonial, Pucasana
1340		PRU		R. Comercial Sudamericana, Juliaca
1340		PRU		R. Comercial, Molendo
1340	1	PRU	OAU4N	R. Jauja, Jauja
1340	1	PRU	OAU2S	R. Shalom, Cajamarca
1340	10	URG	CW53	LV de Melo, Melo
1340	10	VEN	NE	R. Uno "AM 1340", Caracas
1350	25/5	ARG	LS6	R. Buenos Aires, "RBA"
1350	5/1	ARG		R. Sucesos, Córdoba
1350	1	BOL	CP-	América Radiodifusión, Sucre
1350	2.5/0.1	BOL	CP28	R. Cochabamba, "CBA"
1350	2.5	BOL	CP214	R. Ichilo, Yapacaní
1350	1	CHL	CA135	R. Riquelme, Coquimbo
1350	1	CHL	CD135	R. San Carlos, Ancud
1350	0.25	CLM	HKZ98	Alcaldía de Caicedonia, Caicedonia
1350	5/1	CLM	HJHW	Em. Ecos del Río, Puerto Boyacá
1350	1	CLM		R. Cultural 2001, Pailitas
1350	10	CLM	HJEN	R. Fabulosa, Cali
1350	5	CLM	HJDS	R. Ondas de la Montaña, Medellín
1350	1	CLM	HJMN	R. Perijá, Codazzi
1350	5	CLM	HJHL	R. Reloj, Ibagué
1350	5	CLM	HJOC	RCN Antena 2, Santa Marta
1350	5	CLM	HJLO	RCN Antena 2/R. Uno, Caucasia
1350	1	EQA	PU1	LV de Sto Domingo, Sto Domingo. de los Colorados
1350	5	EQA	PZ1	R. Rumichaca, Tulcán
1350	2/1	EQA	SF5	R. San Fernando, San Fernando
1350	3	EQA	VP2	Teleradio AM, Guayaquil
1350	1	PRU	OAU1H	R. Capimag, Chiclayo
1350	1	PRU	OBX6F	R. Ilo, Ilo
1350	1	PRU	OBU7E	R. Lider, Cusco
1350		PRU	OBX8D	R. Super, Pucallpa
1350	5	VEN	ZZ	R. Eclipse "R. Guanipa",El Tigrito
1350	5	VEN	TJ	R. Falcón, Puerto Cumarebo
1352	1	PRU	OAX3N	R. Ondas del Huallaga, Huanuco
1355	0.25	BOL	CP154	R. Armonía, Cliza
1360	1	BOL	CP143	R. Libertad, Villazón
1360	5	BOL	CP270	Radiodifusoras Jiménez, El Alto
1360	5	CHL	CC136	R. Universidad del Bío Bío, Concepción
1360	5	CLM	HJTU	Caracol Cartagena, Cartagena
1360	1	CLM	HJRA	Eco 13-60 "La Superestación", Pereira
1360	10/5	CLM	HJPK	LV de Abejorral, Abejorral
1360		CLM	HJRX	LV de la Comarca, Miraflores
1360	5	CLM	HJMI	R. Autentica, Melgar
1360	1	CLM	HJKV	R. Láser, Zapatoca
1360	1	CLM	HJSD	R. Morichal, San Martín
1360	0.5	CLM		R. Segovia, Segovia
1360	3	EQA	EG4	LV del Carmen, El Carmen
1360	3	EQA	MT	Oyambaro AM, Tumbaco
1360	1	EQA	RJ5	R. América, Riobamba
1360	5	EQA	HG3	R. Jerusalem AM, Machala
1360	1	PRG	ZP37	R. Yby Ya'u, Ybu Ya'u
1360	2.5	PRU	OUA7L	R. Continente, Juliaca
1360	1	PRU	OBZ5Z	R. Cruz del Sur, Palpa
1360	1	PRU	OBZ1A	R. del Norte, Sullana
1360	1	PRU	OAU4O	R. Hecaburt, Tarma
1360	0.2	PRU	OAU3A	R. Intercontinental, Yungay
1360	1	PRU	OCX6T	R. Luza, Paucarpata
1360	5	PRU	OCY2I	R. Santa Monica, Chota
1360	2.5	PRU	OAX7R	R. Sicuani, Sicuani
1360	1	PRU	OBX2N	R. Super Uno, Santiago de Cao
1360	2.5/0.5	URG	CW41	Broadcasting San José, San José
1360	1/0.25	URG	CW136	R. Rio Branco, Rio Branco
1360	5	VEN	TW	R. Alegría, Chivacoa
1360	10	VEN	TI	R. Internacional, Maracaibo
1360	5	VEN	TZ	R. YVTZ "R. Armonia", Charallave
1370		ARG		AM-1370, Isidro Casanova
1370	1	ARG	LRA54	R. Nal., Ingeniero Jacobacci
1370	1	BOL	CP133	R. Agricultura, Achacachi
1370	0.15	BOL	CP186	R. Libertad, Cliza
1370	0.5	BOL	CP158	R. LV de Minero, Siglo XX
1370	5/3	BOL	CP288	Radiodifusoras Coral, Oruro
1370	1	CHL	CD137	R. Conun Huenu "La Popular", Temuco
1370	1	CLM	HJBD	La Nueva R. Guaimaral, Cúcuta
1370	10	CLM	HJBO	Minuto de Dios, Barranquilla
1370	5	CLM	HJKX	R. Mundial, SF de Bogotá
1370	1	CLM	HJJQ	RCN Antena 2, Zarzal
1370	10	CLM	HJEQ	RCN Cauca, Popayán
1370	2.5	CLM	HJNU	RCN, Rionegro
1370	2	EQA	JS1	Ecos Andinos, Pimampiro
1370	5	EQA	VO2	LV del Milagro, El Milagro
1370		EQA		R. El Rocio, Biblián
1370	2	EQA	RP7	R. Pastaza, El Puyo
1370	5	EQA	ER3	R. Progreso, Loja
1370		PRU	OAX6T	R. Moquegua, Moquegua
1370		PRU	OBX9A	R. Palmera
1370		PRU		R. S. Miguel Arcangel, S.Migeul de Pallaques
1370	1	PRU	OAZ7J	R. Santa Monica, Wanchaq
1370	1	PRU	OCX5A	R. Sudamericana, Abanacy
1370	0.5	PRU	OAZ4O	R. Tres de Octubre (R. Cosmos), Huacho
1370	10/2.5	URG	CX42	Emis. Ciudad de Montevideo
1370	0.5/0.25	URG	C137A	R. Real, Minas de Corrales
1370	0.25/0.1	URG	CW137	R. San Javier, San Javier
1370	10	VEN	JI	R. Continente Cumbre, Mérida
1370	5	VEN	OQ	R. La Pascua, Valle de la Pascua
1370	5	VEN	SV	R. Portuguesa, Araure
1371	1	PRU	OAU1W	R. OAU1W, Chiclayo
1380		ARG		R. La Voz, Monte Chingolo
1380		ARG		R. Los Toldos, Los Toldos
1380	0.25	BOL	CP221	R. 16 de Noviembre, Sacaba
1380	1.5	BOL	CP342	R. Bandera Tricolor, Cochabamba

kHz	kW	Ctry	Call	Station, location
1380		BOL	CP-	R. Em.Trunupa, Tiawanaku (CP)
1380	0.5	BOL	CP227	R. Luis de Fuentes, Tarija
1380		BOL	CP-	R. Misericordia, El Alto
1380	1	BOL	CP-	R. Global AM, Sucre (CP)
1380	50	CHL	CB138	R. Corporación, Santiago
1380	1	CLM	HJEJ	Armonías del Palmar, Palmira
1380	2.5	CLM	HJJD	Armony Records, Medellín
1380	3	CLM	HJLG	LV de La Dorada, La Dorada
1380	5	CLM	HJID	R. Potencia Latina, La Plata
1380	5	CLM	HJMM	R. Recuerdos, Valledupar
1380	5	CLM	HJEE	RCN, Tunja
1380	1	EQA	OA3	Impacto AM, Piñas
1380	5	EQA	C1	R. Cristal "RCQ", Quito
1380	5	EQA		R. Mera, Ambato
1380	3	EQA	WV7	R. Morona, Macas
1380	7	EQA	VL7	R. Multicolor, Tulcán
1380	1	PRG	ZP8	R. Concepción, "LV del Norte"
1380		PRU		CP, Huancayo
1380	1	PRU	OCY4U	R. ABC, Lima
1380	1	PRU	OAX2W	R. Atahualpa, Cajamarca
1380	1	PRU	OBZ1D	R. Bellavista, Bellavista
1380	2.5	PRU	OAX6O	R. San Martin, Arequipa
1380	10	VEN	NG	Ondas del Mar, Puerto Cabello
1380	5	VEN	ME	R. Fantasía, Cd.Bolivar
1380	10	VEN	TL	R. Triunfo 13-80, Caja Seca
1382	1	PRU	OBX3I	R. Pilco Mozo, Huanucio
1390	1	ARG	LRA6	R. Nal., Mendoza, Valle de Uspallata
1390		ARG		R. Ribera Sud, Ingeniero Budge
1390		ARG		R. Tradición, Isidro Casanova
1390	10	ARG	LR11	R. Univ., La Plata
1390	0.25	BOL	CP169	R. LV Minera del Sud, Mina Telamayu
1390	1	CLM	HJZY	LV de la Misericordia, Bucaramanga
1390	5	CLM	HJFO	LV de los Andes, Manizales
1390	5	CLM	HJYW	R. Autentica, Pacho
1390	5	CLM	HJFY	R. Avenida, Espinal
1390	0.1	CLM		R. Ciudad de Antioquia, Santa Fé de Antioquia
1390	1	EQA	HE4	LV de Esmeraldas, Esmeraldas
1390	3	EQA	DN5	R. Atenas, Riobamba
1390	5	EQA	EA5	R. Tropicana "Canal 13-90", Cuenca
1390	1.5	EQA	IE1	R. Uno, Urcuquí
1390	1	PRU	OCX7U	R. Cultura, Yunguy
1390	1	PRU	OAU7T	R. Enlace, Kunturkanki
1390	1	PRU	OAU2Z	R. La Luz, Trujillo
1390		PRU		R. Neptuno, Mollendo
1390	1	PRU	OAU1V	R. Tropical, Morrop
1390	7.5/3	URG	CW45	Dif. Treinta y Tres, Treinta y Tres
1390	20	VEN	ZA	R. Fé y Alegría, Caracas
1390	10	VEN	ZO	R. Lumen 2000, Maracaibo
1390	10	VEN	TT	R. Terepaima, Cabudare
1395	0.1	BOL	CP-	R. Horizontes, Huanuni
1400	10/1	ARG	LRG202	R. Cumbre, Neuquén
1400		ARG		R. Gamma, Valentin Alsina
1400		ARG		R. Fantastica, Lujan
1400		BOL	CP-	R. Comunidad, Patacamaya
1400	1	BOL	CP174	R. Libertador, Santa Cruz
1400	5	BOL	CP3	R. Nacional de Bolivia, La Paz
1400	5	CHL	CD140	R. Belén, Puerto Montt
1400	5	CHL	CD140	R. La Amistad, Los Angeles
1400	1	CHL	CA140	R. Tarapacá, Iquique
1400	0.25	CLM	HKZ22	Alcaldía de Majagual, Majagual
1400	0.25	CLM	HKZ25	Alcaldía de Ovejas, Ovejas
1400	0.25	CLM		Brisas del Sinú, Tierralta
1400	1	CLM	HJTY	Caracol Colombia, Vélez
1400	1	CLM	HJIT	Ecos del Atrato, Quibdó
1400	5	CLM	HJKM	Em. Mariana de Bogotá, SF de Bogotá
1400	2.5	CLM	HJD31	LV de Cimitarra, Cimitarra
1400	1	CLM	HJWY	LV de los Samanes
1400	5	CLM	HJDF	LV de Niquel, Montelíbano
1400	1.5	CLM		LV de Samaniego, Samaniego
1400	0.45	CLM		R. Cañaveral, Morales
1400	5	CLM	HJJJ	R. Ipiales, Ipiales
1400	5	CLM	HJAS	RCN Antena 2, Barranquilla
1400	5	CLM	HJHM	RCN Antena 2, Calarca
1400	1	CLM	HJLL	RCN Antena 2, Santa Bárbara
1400	1	CLM	HJBK	Voz Grancolombia, Cúcuta
1400		EQA		Impacto 1400 AM, Latacunga
1400	5	EQA	VZ7	R. LV de Zamora, Zamora
1400	10	EQA	FL2	R. Z Uno, Guayaquil
1400	2.5	PRU	OBX4W	R. Callao, Lima
1400	1	PRU	OCX5B	R. Interandina, Pisco
1400	1	PRU	OAX7I	R. La Hora, Cuzco
1400	0.5	PRU	OAX6J	R. Landa, Arequipa
1400	1	PRU	OCX1A	R. MDY, Talara Alta
1400	1	PRU	OAU2H	R. OAU2H, Cajamarca
1400	1	PRU	OBX4H	R. Selecciones, Tarma
1400	25	URG	CX140	R. Zorrilla de San Martin, Tacuarembó
1400	10	VEN	QZ	R. Anaco, Anaco
1400	1	VEN	NF	R. Sabana, El Sombrero
1410	5/0.25	ARG		R. Folklorismo, José Léon Suárez
1410	0.25	BOL	CP124	R. Atlántida, Oruro
1410	0.25	BOL	CP-	R. Roboré, Roboré
1410	1	CHL	CD141	R. Loncoche, Loncoche
1410	3	CHL	CB141	R. Quinta Región, Valparaíso
1410	0.25	CLM	HKP86	Alcaldía de Chiquinquira, Chiquinquira
1410	5	CLM	HJDU	Em. Cultural Universidad de Antioquia, "R. Universidad", Medellín
1410	2	CLM	HJP79	R. Evangélica, Uribia
1410	5	CLM	HJEI	R. Guadalajara, Buga
1410	1	CLM	HKP79	R. Universidad, Tunja
1410	5	CLM	HJFS	RCN Antena 2, Honda
1410	1	EQA	FR4	LV de Quinindé, Quinindé
1410	1	EQA		Ondas Cisnerias, Riobamba
1410	1	EQA	GC5	R. Centro Gualaceo, Gualaceo
1410	1	EQA	EC1	R. El Tiempo "Em.del Amor", Quito
1410	1	EQA	CQ2	R. Presidente "LV del Pueblo", El Milagro
1410	2	PRG	ZP35	La Voz de Misiones, S. Juan Bautista
1410		PRU	OBX8I	Dif.Comercial, Pucallapa
1410	1	PRU	OAX2Y	R. Heróica, Trujillo
1410	1	PRU	OBU1H	R. La Luz, Tumbes
1410		PRU		R. Olmos, Olomos
1410	1	PRU	OBZ4V	R. Universal, Santa Maria
1410	10/5	URG	CX44	AM Libre, Montevideo
1410	1/0.25	URG	CW141	R. Turística, Salto
1410	10	VEN	SP	R. Simpatía, Valera
1410	5	VEN	ST	R. Turén, Turén
1415		PRU	OAU2R	R. Cajamarca, Cajamarca
1417	5	PRG	ZP42	R. Güyrá Campana, Horqueta (n. 1420)
1420		ARG		R. Génesis 2000, General Conesa
1420		ARG	LRJ359	R. Granaderos Puntanos, San Luis
1420		ARG		R. Mágica, Lanús
1420	1	BOL	CP49	R. Centro, Cochabamba
1420		BOL	CP-	R. Em. Omasuyo Andina, Achacachi (CP)
1420	1.5	BOL	CP254	R. Guadalquivir, Tarija
1420	1	BOL	CP-	R. Real Audiencia, Sucre
1420	1	CHL	CC142	R. Maule, Cauquenes
1420	1	CHL	CB142	R. Panamericana, Santiago
1420	5	CLM	HJBH	Caracol Colombia/R. Magdalena, Santa Marta
1420	1	CLM	HJD23	Ecos de Frontino, Frontino
1420	1	CLM	HJLE	La Cariñosa, Ibagué
1420	5	CLM	HJAP	R. Autentica, Cartagena
1420	1	CLM	HJSN	R. Lenguerque, Zapatoca
1420	5	CLM	HJHK	R. Reloj, Manizales
1420	1	EQA	NR3	LV de Huaquillas, Huaquillas
1420		EQA	VN7	LV del Napo, Tena
1420	3	EQA	RN1	R. Bahá'í, Otavalo
1420	1	EQA	MA6	R. Nuevos Exitos, Salcedo
1420	5	PRU	OBX2U	R. Ilucan, Cutervo
1420		PRU	OBU7L	R. OBU7L, Yanaoca
1420	1	PRU	OAZ8Z	R. Oriente, Yurimaguas
1420	1	PRU	OBZ4G	R. San Isidro, Lima
1420	1	URG	CX142	R. Felicidad, Paysandú
1420	5	URG	CW43	R. Lavalleja, Minas
1420	10/5	VEN	RW	R. Cardenal, Carora
1420	5	VEN	NZ	R. Marabina 1420, Maracaibo
1420	5	VEN		R. Sintonía, Caracas
1426	0.2	PRU	OCX1H	R. San Jose, La Union
1430	0.25	ARG	LRI235	R. Balcarce, do
1430		ARG		R. Imagén, Castelar
1430		ARG		R. José de S. Martín, "la Pionera", El Jagüel
1430	1/0.25	ARG	LV26	R. Río Tercero
1430	1/0.25	ARG	LT24	R. San Nicolás
1430	0.25	BOL	CP193	R. 23 de Marzo, Tupiza
1430	0.15	BOL	CP-	R. Centinela, Tupiza
1430	0.25	BOL	CP141	R. Nuestra Señora de Burgos, Mizque
1430	1	CHL	CC143	R. Chilena "Solo Noticias", Rancagua
1430	1	CLM	HJIU	Armonías del Ingrumá, Riosucio
1430	5	CLM	HJPW	Colmundo, Barranquilla
1430	5	CLM	HJKU	Em. Kennedy, SF de Bogotá
1430	1	CLM	HJEG	LV de Belalcázar, Popayón
1430	0.5	CLM	HJG42	R. Alejandría, Alejandría
1430	2	CLM	HJBP	R. Cariongo, Pamplona
1430	0.25	CLM	HKX73	R. Ciudad de Pereira, Pereira
1430	0.25	CLM	HJX61	R. Dif. Cultural del Quindío, Armenia
1430	5	CLM	HJQX	R. Majagual, Corozal
1430	0.5	CLM	HKK38	R. Manantial, Sibundoy

kHz	kW	Ctry	Call	Station, location
1430	1	CLM	HJCK	R. Sensación, Yarumal
1430	2	CLM	HJMF	R. Venus, Puerto Berrío
1430	5	EQA	CV3	Ondas del Zamora, Loja
1430	10	EQA	MB2	R. Federal, Virgen de Fátima
1430	3.5	EQA	GF1	R. Futura 14-30, Quito
1430	5	EQA	JC6	R. Guaranda, Guaranda
1430	1	PRU	OAZ7M	CPN Radio, Cusco
1430	1	PRU	OAZ3H	R. Chavin, Chimbote
1430		PRU		R. Forestal, San Vincente de Cañete
1430	1	PRU	OBX3E	R. Huarmey, Huarmey
1430	1	PRU	OAU6M	R. Lider, Tacna
1430		PRU		R. Red, Andina
1430	1	PRU	OBX2T	R. Santa Bárbara, Ascope
1430	0.5	PRU	OAZ4V	R. Universal, El Tambo
1430	1	PRU	OBX9H	R. Utcubamba, Bagua Grande
1430	5/1	URG	CW25	R. Durazno, Durazno
1430	25	VEN	TP	R. Bahía, Puerto La Cruz
1430	10/5	VEN	TM	R. Caicara, Caicara del Orinoco
1430	10	VEN	NB	R. Satélite 14-30, Guacara
1440	0.25	ARG	LU36	R. Coronel Suárez
1440	1/0.5	ARG		R. General Obligado, Reconquista
1440		ARG		R. Impacto, Tapiales
1440	1/0.25	ARG	LV20	R. Laboulaye
1440	1	ARG	LRA53	R. Nal., S. Martín de los Andes
1440	1/0.25	ARG	LV27	R. Rural, San Francisco
1440	1	BOL	CP61	R. Batallón Colorados, La Paz
1440	0.25	BOL	CP-	R. Bolivia, Cochabamba
1440		BOL	CP-	R. LV de Juno, Tiraque (CP)
1440	0.5	BOL	CP-	R. Oriente, Camiri
1440	2/1	BOL	CP107	R. Yaguarí, Vallegrande
1440		BOL	CP-	Sistema de Comunicaciones Horizontes, Sucre
1440	1	CHL	CA144	R. Agricultura, La Serena
1440	1	CHL	CC144	R. El Sembrador, Chillán
1440	1	CHL	CA144	R. Santa Maria de Guadalupe, Arica
1440	0.25	CLM	HKT58	Alcaldía de Ubala, Ubala
1440	5	CLM	HJNZ	Colmundo, Medellín
1440	5	CLM	HJBM	R. Internacional, Honda
1440	5	CLM	HJEK	R. Reloj, Tuluá
1440	1	CLM	HJIB	RCN Caquetá, Florencia
1440	5	CLM	HJGM	RCN, Sogamoso
1440	2.8	EQA	OV5	Ondas del Volante, Azogues
1440	2	EQA	RC6	R. Antología, Caluma
1440	3/5	EQA	AQ6	R. Fenix, Latacunga
1440	2.5	EQA	DY4	R. Iris, Esmeraldas
1440	5	EQA	DF1	R. Panorama, Ibarra
1440	5	EQA	MD7	R. Puyo, El Puyo
1440	2	PRU	OBX1T	R. Cooperativa Tumán, Chiclayo
1440	1	PRU	OAX6R	R. El Tiempo, Cayma
1440	1	PRU	OAU2O	R. Frecuencia VH, Celendin
1440	1	PRU	OAZ3O	R. LV de Pomebamba, Pomebamba
1440	1	PRU	OAU7M	R. Satelite, Sicuani
1440	3	URG	C144	AM 1440, Chuy
1440	3/0.5	URG	CX144	R. Rivera, Rivera
1440	10	VEN	ZI	R. Estelar 14-40, Guanare
1440	5	VEN	RF	R. Orituco, Altagracia del Orituco
1440	1	VEN	TY	R. Sucesos, Táriba
1441	1	PRU	OAX4K	R. Imperial, Lima (n.f.
1445	0.5	BOL	CP-	Super Broadcasting Alborada, Santa Cruz
1445	0.5	CLM		Em. R. Unión, La Palma
1450	0.5	ARG		R. Ciudad, Remedios de Escalada
1450	5/1	ARG		R. Las Cuarenta, San Juan
1450		ARG		R. Presencia, Martinez
1450		BOL	CP-	R. Amanacer, Huari
1450		BOL	CP-	R. Amazonia, Cobija
1450	1	BOL	CP62	R. Em. Bolivia, Oruro
1450	1	BOL	CP262	R. Verde y Blanco, Santa Cruz
1450	5	CHL	CC145	R. Libertad, Curicó
1450	1	CHL	CD145	R. Santa Maria de Guadalupe, Puerto Varas
1450	1	CHL	CB145	R. Universidad Técnica "Federico Santa María", Valparaíso
1450	5	CLM	HJNL	La Cariñosa, Manizales
1450	0.5	CLM		LV del Cauca, El Bordo
1450	5	CLM	HJHH	R. Católica Metropolitana, Bucaramanga
1450	5	CLM	HJBY	R. Ciudad de Flandes, Flandes
1450	0.2	CLM		R. LV del Nordeste, Remedios
1450	1	CLM	HJMX	R. Mancomoján, Carmen de Bolívar
1450	1	CLM	HJE20	R. María, Urrao
1450	1	EQA	SC1	AS La Radio, Tabacundo
1450	10	EQA	SC5	R. Calidad, Riobamba
1450	1	EQA	DR	R. Minutera, Guayaquil
1450	1	EQA	SE2	R. Santa Elena, Santa Elena
1450	1	PRU	OBX4K	R. Fortaleza, Barranca
1450	1.5	PRU	OCX2J	R. San Juan, Trujillo

kHz	kW	Ctry	Call	Station, location
1450	1	PRU	OCX7W	R. Santa Rosa, Santa Ana
1450	10/5	URG	CX46	R. América, Montevideo
1450	2/0.5	URG	CW145	R. Arapey, Salto
1450	10	VEN	ZQ	Informativa 14-50, Los Puertos de Altagracia
1450	10/5	VEN	XC	R. Mega Visión, San Felix
1450	10/8	VEN	KJ	Sonera 14-50, Catia La Mar
1453	1	PRU	OAU2W	R. San Miguel, San Miguel
1455	0.5	BOL	CP-	R. Magnal, Capinota
1457	1	PRU	OAX1V	R. Sullana "LV de Chira", Sullana
1460	1	ARG	LRK146	R. 21, Yerba Buena
1460		ARG		R. Almirante Brown, San José
1460		ARG		R. Contacto, Ituzaingó
1460		ARG		R. Iuminemos el Mundo, Ezeiza
1460	0.25	ARG	LU30	R. Maipú
1460		ARG		R. Nativa, Claypole
1460	0.1	ARG	LU34	R. Pigüé
1460	1/0.25	ARG	LT29	R. Venado Tuerto
1460	1	CHL	CC146	R Armonía, Concepción
1460	10	CHL	CA146	R. Antofagasta, Antofagasta
1460	1	CHL	CB146	R. Yungay, Santiago
1460	2.5	CLM	HJFL	Agustiniana Minuto de Dios, San Agustín
1460	0.25	CLM	HKY73	Alcaldía de San Andrés, San Andrés
1460	5	CLM	HJJW	Em. Nuevo Continente, SF de Bogotá
1460	1	CLM	HJMN	LV de Amalfi, Amalfi
1460	5	CLM	HJTF	Ondas del Darién, Turbo
1460	1	CLM	HJE26	R. Capiro, La Ceja
1460	5	CLM	HJJH	R. Ciudad Milagro, Armenia
1460	1	CLM	HJIW	R. Monumental, Cúcuta
1460	1	CLM	HJAL	R. Sincelejo, Sincelejo
1460	5	CLM	HJVH	R. Uno, Barranquilla
1460	5	CLM	HJZU	RCN Antena 2, Pasto
1460	5	EQA	AA7	LV de Gualaquiza, Gualaquiza
1460	5	EQA	CL3	R. Cariamanga, Cariamanga
1460	5	EQA	IC6	R. Nuevos Horizontes, Latacunga
1460	1	PRU	OBX6C	R. Bahia, Mollendo
1460	1	PRU	OBX3A	R. Chimu, Chimbote
1460	1	PRU	OBU2E	R. Comercial, Jaén
1460	10	PRU	OAX7W	R. El Sol de los Andes, Juliaca
1460	1	PRU	OBX2Y	R. Estelar, Guadalupe
1460	1	PRU	OBX9B	R. Frecuencia popular, Rioja
1460	0.5	PRU	OCY4I	R. Imperial, Junin
1460	2.5	PRU	OAX5K	R. Internacional, Pisco
1460	1	PRU	OAZ4F	R. La Oroya, La Oroya
1460		PRU	OBU7M	R. OBU7M, Marcapata
1460	1	PRU	OAX1V	R. Sullana "LV de Chira", Sullana
1460	0.25	URG	C146	R. José Batlle y Ordoñez, J. Batlle y Ordoñez
1460	3/1	URG	CX146	R. Carmelo, Carmelo
1460	5	VEN	RJ	R. Jardín, Boconó
1461		BOL	CP-	R. LV del Pueblo de Dios, Cochabamba
1470		ARG		Cadena 14-70, Lanús
1470	0.25	ARG	LU26	R. Coronel Dorrego
1470	1/0.25	ARG	LT20	R. Junín
1470		ARG		R. Mburucuya, José León Suarez
1470	1	ARG		R. Municipal, Luis Beltrán
1470	1/0.25	ARG	LT26	R. Nuevo Mundo, Colón
1470	1/0.25	ARG	LT28	R. Rafaela
1470	0.25	BOL	CP215	R. Cordech, Alcalá
1470	1	CHL	CB147	R. Sargento Aldea, San Antonio
1470	0.25	CLM	HKO96	Alcaldía de Baranoa, Baranoa
1470	5	CLM	HJPX	Colmundo, Cartagena
1470	0.25	CLM	HJS20	Ecos de Palo Cabildo, Palo Cabildo
1470	5	CLM	HJTB	Ondas de Ibagué, Ibagué
1470	5	CLM	HJHQ	R. Futurama, Pacho
1470	5	CLM	HJIM	R. Popular, Medellín
1470	5	CLM	HJNT	R. Restauración, Cali
1470	1	CLM	HJIF	R. Tres Fronteras, Puerto Asís
1470	1	CLM	HJB63	R. Uno, Iza
1470	5	EQA	JC1	Ecos de Cayambe, Cayambe
1470	1.5	EQA	LD2	R. Ecos de Naranjito, Naranjito
1470	5	EQA		R. San Juan, Ambato
1470	20	PRU	OAU4B	CPN Radio, Lima
1470	1	PRU	OAX7G	R. Cusco, Cusco
1470	1	PRU	OAU6E	R. del Sur, Arequipa
1470	1	PRU	OCX2G	R. Occidenta, Quiruvilca
1470	0.8	PRU	OAX6M	R. Tacna, Tacna
1470	1/0.5	URG	CW147	Abril 1470 AM, Melo
1470	15	URG	CX147	R. Cristal del Uruguay,Las Piedras
1470	10	VEN	JW	R. Latina, Valencia
1470	10	VEN	SY	R. Vibración, Carúpano
1475		BOL	CP-	R. Tiraque, Tiraque
1475	1	PRU	AOZ7G	R. Espinar, Yauri
1476	5	PRU	OBX2U	R. Ilucan, Cutervo
1480		ARG		La R. del Corazón, Tablada

kHz	kW	Ctry	Call	Station, location
1480	0.25	ARG	LU27	R. Dolores
1480	0.1	BOL	CP-	Patrimonio Radiodifusión, Potosí
1480		BOL	CP-	R. Amor de Diós, La Paz
1480	1	BOL	CP-	R. Charcas AM, Sucre (CP)
1480	1/0.8	BOL	CP-	R. Chiwalaki, Vacas
1480		BOL	CP-	R. Domingo Savio, Villa Independencia
1480		BOL	CP-	R. Em. Ayni, Corapata (CP)
1480	1/0.25	CHL	CA148	R. Amanecer, Ovalle
1480	1	CHL	CD148	R. General Baquedano, Valdivia
1480	1	CHL	CC148	R. La Amistad AM, Tomé
1480	0.25	CLM	HKR44	Alcaldía de Victoria, Victoria
1480	0.25	CLM		LV del Samán, Bochalema
1480	1	CLM	HJVB	R. Guayabal, Armero, Guayabal
1480	2.5	CLM	HJOD	R. Rodadero, Santa Marta
1480	1	CLM	HJTC	R. Sonsón, Sonsón (n.f.1490)
1480	5	CLM	HJFC	R. Unica, Pereira
1480	5	CLM	HJTZ	RCN Antena 2, Bucaramanga
1480	3	EQA	WP5	R. Atlántida, Alausí
1480	3	EQA	JV4	R. LV de Jipijapa, Jipijapa
1480	1	EQA	MC1	R. Municipal, Cotacachi
1480	5	EQA	CY6	R. Popular de La Maná, La Maná
1480	3	EQA	BS3	Sucre Machala, Machala
1480	5	PRG	ZP20	R. América, Ñemby
1480	1	PRG	ZP23	R. Mariscal Francisco Solano López, Bella Vista Norte
1480	0.6	PRU	OCX2C	R. Comercial, Virú
1480	0.6	PRU	OCX2C	R. Comercial, Virú
1480	1	PRU	OCX4V	R. K´ler, Paramonga
1480	1	PRU	OAU4A	R. Laser, Santa Rosa de Sacco
1480	1	PRU	OAU4A	R. Laser, Santa Rosa de Sacco
1480	0.5	PRU	OBU2H	R. San Lorenzo, Socota
1480	1	PRU	OCX1L	R. Supercontinental, Chulucanas
1480	1/0.7	URG	CX148	Difusora Rio Negro, Young
1480	5/1.5	URG	CW43B	R. Internacional, Rivera
1480	3/0.8	URG	CW148	R. Universo, Castillos
1480		VEN		R. Cumarebo, Cumarebo
1485	1	BOL	CP135	R. LV del Valle, Punata
1490		ARG		R. Canaán Celestial, Isidro Casanova
1490	0.1	ARG	LU25	R. Carhué, Carhué
1490	1	ARG	LV22	R. Huinca Renancó
1490		ARG		R. Vida AM, Mar del Plata
1490	0.25	BOL	CP-	R. Mairana, Mairana
1490	0.25	BOL	CP196	R. Moxos, San Ignacio de Moxos
1490	0.35	BOL	CP198	R. Pedro Domingo Murillo, Quime
1490	1	BOL	CP172	R. San José, San José, Oruro
1490	5	CHL	CA149	R. Alicanto, Salvador
1490	1	CHL	CB149	R. El Canelo de Nos AM, San Bernardo
1490	5	CHL	CD149	R. Malleco, Victoria
1490	0.2	CLM	HJJ76	Alcaldía de El Peñon, El Peñon
1490	0.2	CLM	HKW24	Alcaldía de Guaitarilla, Guaitarilla
1490	5	CLM	HJBS	Em. Punto Cinco, SF de Bogotá
1490	5	CLM	HJZB	LV de los Robles, Tuluá
1490	1	CLM	HJJO	LV de San Marcos, San Marcos
1490	5	CLM	HJAY	Onda Nueva, Barranquilla
1490	8	CLM	HJAG	R. Garzón, Garzón
1490	1	EQA	VY2	La R. Dinámica, Guayaquil
1490	3	EQA	AI6	R. Moderna, Píllaro
1490	5	EQA	SM5	R. Santa María, Azogues
1490	2.5	EQA	AE4	R. Unión, Esmeraldas
1490	1	PRU	OAX8F	R. Atlantida, Iquitos
1490	1	PRU	OBU7I	R. Chaski, Maras
1490	1	PRU	OCX7P	R. Emisora Frontera, Puno
1490	1	PRU	OAX1L	R. Imperio, Chiclayo
1490	1	PRU	OBU4N	R. La Luz, Cerro de Pasco
1490	1.3	PRU	OAX6Q	R. Minuto, Cerro Colorado
1490	0.3	PRU	OAX5N	R. Nazca, Nazca
1490	1/0.25	URG	C149	Em. del Centro, Baltasar Brum
1490	5/4	URG	CX149	R. del Oeste, Nueva Helvecia
1490	10	VEN	XD	La Dinámica, Caracas
1490	10/5	VEN	RP	R. El Sol, Maracaibo
1490	1	VEN	SQ	R. Mérida 14-90, Mérida
1495	2.5	BOL	CP152	El Mundo Radiodifusión, Sacaba
1495		BOL	CP-	R. Domingo Savio, Villa Independencia (n
1500	5/1	ARG	LRI214	R. Bonaerense, Llavallol
1500		ARG		R. En Realidad, Capilla del Señor
1500	0.04	ARG	LU1	R. Libertador General S. Martín, Lisandro Olmos
1500	1/0.25	ARG		R. Municipal, Gral. Conesa
1500	0.25	ARG	LT34	R. Nuclear, Zárate
1500	0.25	ARG	LT22	R. Nueva Era, Pehuajó
1500	1/0.25	ARG	LT45	R. San Javier
1500	1/0.25	ARG	LV25	R. Unión, Bell Ville
1500	5/1	BOL	CP1	R. Chuquisaca, El Alto
1500	1	BOL	CP238	R. Sagrado Corazón, Mineros
1500	1	CHL	CC150	R. Centenario, San Javier
1500	1	CHL	CA150	R. Santa Maria de Guadalupe, Iquique:
1500	1	CHL	CD150	R. Tierra del Fuego, Puerto Porvenir
1500	1	CHL	CB150	R. Trasandina, Los Andes
1500	5	CLM	HJSH	Ecos del Ricaurte, Moniquirá
1500	5	CLM	HJLJ	La Básica 1500, Cali
1500	1	CLM	HJMP	LV de Aguachica, Aguachica (cfR. 1330)
1500	1	CLM	HKT71	Macheta
1500	5	CLM	HJUW	R. María, Manizales
1500	5	CLM	HJTW	R. Sumapaz, Fusagasugá
1500	5	EQA	HG2	LV del Río Vinces, Vinces
1500	1	EQA	RO1	R. Otavalo, Otavalo
1500	5	EQA	AD4	R. Satélite, El Carmen
1500	1	PRU	OAU6B	R. Bulevar, Tacna
1500	1	PRU	OCX7G	R. Chancis, Sicuani
1500	1	PRU	OBX2X	R. Comercial, Trujillo
1500	1/3	PRU	OBX3J	R. Luz y Sonido, Huanuco
1500		PRU		R. San Pedro, San Pablo
1500	10	PRU	OBX4I	R. Santa Rosa, Lima
1500	1	PRU	OAU4W	R. Wanka, Huancayo
1500	10/5	VEN	RZ	R. 2000 AM, Cumaná
1500		VEN		R. Galaxia, San Mateo
1505	1.5	EQA	OY7	Ondas del Río Yacuambí, Yacuambí
1510		ARG		LV del Oeste,Libertad
1510		ARG		R. Alabanza, Guernica
1510	1/0.25	ARG	LV21	R. Champaqui, Villa Dolores
1510		ARG		R. Sentimento Litoral, Banfield
1510	0.25	BOL	CP102	R. 27 de Diciembre, Villamontes
1510	1/0.5	CHL	CA151	R. Luís Alvarez Sierra. Illapel
1510	1	CHL	CC151	R. Rancagua, Rancagua
1510	1	CHL	CD151	R. Teniente Merino, Lebu
1510	0.25	CLM	HKZ94	Alcaldía de Buenaventura, Buenaventura
1510	0.25	CLM	HKZ98	Alcaldía de Caicedonia, Caicedonia
1510	0.25	CLM	HKZ93	Alcaldía de Versalles, Versalles
1510	1	CLM	HJHX	Candela AM, Bucaramanga
1510	1	CLM	HKY41	Colombia Mía, Barrancabermeja, SS
1510	5	CLM	HJD24	LV de La Unión, La Unión
1510	0.5	CLM		LV de los Cedros, Libanó
1510	1	CLM	HJA22	LV de San Luis, San Luis de Gaceno
1510	1	CLM	HJZA	R. Estrella, Armenia
1510	0.5	EQA	HD2	Inst. Oceanográfico de la Armada, Guayaquil
1510	0.5	EQA	RC5	LV de la Juventud, Cañar
1510	3	EQA	JV7	R. Ecos del Oriente, Lago Agrio
1510	5	EQA		R. Monumental, Quito
1510		EQA		R. Net, Ambato
1510	1	EQA	RY6	R. Runacunapac Yachana, Simiátug
1510	10	EQA	UC3	R. Unión Calvense, Cariamanga
1510	1	PRU	OCX6Q	R. Alegria, Arequipa
1510	1	PRU	OBX8K	R. Centro de los Medios, Sepahua
1510	1	PRU	OBX7P	R. El Sur, Wanchaq
1510	1	PRU	OAU4M	R. Flores de Campo, Barranca
1510		PRU	OCX2O	R. Inca, Los Baños del Inca
1510	1	PRU	OAX5F	R. LV Huamanga, Nazca
1510	1	PRU	OBU1B	R. OBU1B, Olmos
1510	1	PRU	OCX4J	R. Tarma, Tarma
1510	1	PRU	OCX1V	R. Tumbes, Tumbes
1510	2.5	PRU	OAU2U	R. Virgin, Huamachuco (ex.R. Los Andes)
1510	0.5	URG	CW151	R. Ibirapitá, San Gregorio de Polanco
1510	1/0.25	URG	CX151	R. Rincón, Fray Bentos
1510	2/0.5	URG	CW57	R. San Carlos, San Carlos
1510	20	VEN		Informativa "LV del Centro", Güigüe
1517	1	PRU	OCX2O	R. Inca, Los Baños del Inca
1520		ARG		AM Reverendo Aquiles Acosta, S. Justo
1520	5/1	ARG		R. Chascomús
1520	0.25	ARG	LT38	R. Gualeguay
1520		ARG		R. Metropolitana, Ciudadela
1520		ARG		R. Modelo, Monte Grande
1520	0.25	BOL	CP207	R. LV del Cobre, Corocoro
1520		BOL	CP-	R. Melodía, Oruro
1520		BOL	CP-	R. Nueva Esperanza, El Alto
1520	1	BOL	CP179	R. Petrolera, Sta. Cruz
1520	0.1	CHL	CD152	R. Aníbal Pinto, Lautaro
1520	1	CHL	CB152	R. Integración, San Antonio
1520	1	CHL	CC152	R. Nueva Soboranía, Linares
1520	0.25	CLM	HKT20	Alcaldía de Montería, Montería
1520	0.1	CLM	HKW43	Alcaldía de Tangua, Tangua
1520	15	CLM	HJRL	Antena de los Andes, Santa Rosa de Cabal
1520	0.3	CLM		Brisas del Palmar, Caucasia

kHz	kW	Ctry	Call	Station, location
1520	0.25	CLM	HJT21	Colombia Mía, Tierralta, CO
1520	1	CLM	HJMZ	Ecos de la Sierra Flor, Sincelejo
1520	1	CLM	HJJ98	Em. Una Voz de la Frontera, Puerto Santander
1520	5	CLM	HJLI	Estación Latina, SF de Bogotá
1520	1	CLM	HJMA	LV de Suroeste, Jericó
1520	1	CLM	HJAM	R. Altamizal, Dolores
1520	0.5	CLM	HKS24	R. Cristalares Timbío, Timbío
1520	5	CLM	HJLQ	R. Minuto, Barranquilla
1520	1	CLM	HKW37	R. Universidad, Pasto
1520	1	CLM	HJV37	R. Pueblo Viejo, Zipacon
1520		CLM		Sonoradio 1520 AM, Viterbo
1520	2.5	EQA	RI5	LV de Guamote, Guamote
1520	1	EQA	RN2	LV de Naranjal, El Naranjal
1520	1	EQA	TI1	R. Ibarra, Ibarra
1520	5	EQA	EB4	R. Manta, Manta
1520	1	PRU	OAX1C	R. Delcar, Chiclayo
1520		PRU		R. Fuentes Mollo, Espinar
1520	5	PRU	OAU7Y	R. OAU7Y, Juliaca
1520	1	PRU	OAU5J	R. Virgin de Carmen, Huancavelica
1520	1	PRU	OAX9X	R. Vision, Janjui
1520	2	URG	CX152	R. Acuarela, Melo
1520	0.1	URG	C152	R. Paz, "la nueva R. ", Guichón
1520	25	VEN	IC	R. Bonita La Guapa, Guatire
1530		ARG		LV del Futuro, Merlo
1530	1	ARG	LRJ200	R. Centro Morteros, Morteros
1530		ARG		R. Contemporánea, Lomas de Zamora
1530	0.5	BOL	CP111	R. Em. Ballivián, San Borja
1530	0.5	BOL	CP111	R. Em. Ballivián, San Borja
1530	0.25	BOL	CP200	R. Litoral, Llica
1530	1	CHL	CD153	R. Calbuco, Calbuco
1530	1	CHL	CC153	R. Corporación, Lota
1530	1	CHL	CA153	R. Juan Godoy, Copiapó
1530	1	CHL	CB153	R. Nexo, Quillota
1530	0.25	CLM	HKN85	Alcaldía de Anza, Anza
1530	0.1	CLM	HKS58	Alcaldía de El Copey, El Copey
1530	0.25	CLM	HKN57	Alcaldía de San Juan de Uraba, S. J. de Uraba
1530	0.25	CLM	HJV82	Alcaraván Radio, Puerto Lleras
1530	1	CLM	HJJB	Caracol Sevilla, Sevilla
1530	0.25	CLM	HKN65	Colombia Mía, Caucasia, AN
1530	1	CLM	HKR73	Ecos del Pacífico, Guapí
1530		CLM	HKS56	Fascinación AM, Becerril
1530	5	CLM	HJDN	LV de la Misericordia, Medellín
1530	5	CLM	HJOZ	LV de la Prov. de Padilla, San Juan del Cesar
1530		CLM		R. Integración, Morales
1530	5	EQA	MP2	LV de la Península, La Libertad
1530	5	EQA	CC5	Ondas Cañaris AM, Azogues
1530	1	EQA	MZ6	R. Dorado, Pelileo
1530	3	EQA	VP5	R. LV de Pallatanga, Pallatanga
1530	5	EQA	JY4	R. Uno, La Concordia
1530	1	PRU	OBX3H	CPN Radio, Chimbote
1530	1	PRU	OBZ4S	R. 15-15, Huancayo
1530	2	PRU	OAU2P	R. Bambamarca, Bambamarca
1530	0.5	PRU	OAZ7F	R. dif. Espinar, Yauri (R. Confraternidad)
1530	1	PRU	OCX1Y	R. Leomar, Bellavista
1530	10	PRU	OBU4C	R. Milena, Lima
1530		PRU		R. Ondas del Sur Oriente, Quillabamba
1530		PRU		R. Universidad, San Juan Bautista
1530	0.25	URG	CW153	Emisora Cono Sur, Nueva Palmira
1530	5/2.5	URG	CX50	R. Independencia, Montevideo
1530	10	VEN	NP	R. San Felipe el Fuerte, San Felipe
1540		ARG		AM 15 - 40, Buenos Aires
1540		ARG		R. Fuego, Longchamps
1540	0,25	ARG	LT35	R. Mon, Pergamino
1540	0.25	ARG	LU28	R. Tuyú, General Madariaga
1540	0.8	BOL	CP-	R. Sariri, Escoma
1540	0.25	BOL	CP-	R. Tutuka, Vilaque (CP)
1540	1	CHL	CC154	R. Central, Chillán
1540	1	CHL	CD154	R. San José de Alcudia, Río Bueno
1540	1	CHL	CB154	R. Sudamérica, Santiago
1540	0.25	CLM	HKP50	Alcaldía de Arjona, Arjona
1540	0.15	CLM	HKR80	Alcaldía de Sacama, Sacama
1540	1	CLM	HKZ52	Colombia Mía, Chaparral, TO
1540	1	CLM	HJB89	Em. Brisas del Río Chico, Belmira
1540		CLM	HJD89	LV del Nevado Cumbal, Melgar
1540	1	CLM	HJHD	LV del Petróleo, Barrancabermeja
1540	0.25	CLM		LV Dorada, Segovia
1540	2	CLM	HJRQ	R. Austral, Túquerres
1540	5	CLM	HJZF	R. Cóndor "Em. Universitaria", Manizales
1540	0.25	CLM		R. El Sur, San Vicente de Chucurí
1540	0.5	EQA	MH	Cotopaxi Digital, Latacunga
1540	0.25	EQA	VB7	LV del Upano, Macas
1540	1	EQA	DP1	R. Caracol, Quito
1540	3	EQA	FM2	R. Cristal, Babahoyo
1540		EQA		R. Flecha AM, Machala
1540	1	EQA	P1	R. Mira. Mira
1540	1	PRU	OBZ4U	R. Barranca, Barranca
1540	0.3	PRU	OBX4N	R. Corporacion, Cerro de Pasco
1540	1	PRU	OAU2X	R. Espacial, Otuzco
1540	1	PRU	OCX7V	R. Los Andes, Cusco
1540	1	PRU	OBX1B	R. LV de la Frontera, Tumbes
1540	1	PRU	OAU6A	R. M-U, Arequipa
1540	2	PRU	OBU2A	R. Mundial AM, Trujillo
1540	1	URG	C154	R. Centro, Cardona
1540	0.1	URG	CW154	R. Charruá, Paysandú
1540	0.25	URG	CX154	R. Patria, Treinta y Tres
1545		BOL	CP-	R. Emisoras Villamontes, Villamontes
1545	0.35	BOL	CP191	R. Mejillones, Tarata
1545	1	PRU	OAX9X	R. Vision, Janjui
1550	0.25	ARG	LT32	R. Chivilcoy
1550	0.25	ARG	LT40	R. LV de la Paz, La Paz
1550	0.25	ARG	LT33	R. Nueve de Julio
1550	5/0.25	ARG	LT23	R. Regional, San Jenaro Norte
1550		ARG		R. Tiempo, Mar del Plata
1550		ARG		R. Trompeta de Diós, Isidro Casanova
1550		ARG		R. Urkupiña, Buenos Aires
1550	10	BOL	CP115	R. Caranavi, Caranavi
1550	1	BOL	CP205	R. Tamengo, Pto. Quijarro
1550	1	CHL	CC155	R. Manuel Rodríguez, San Fernando
1550	1	CHL	CB155	R. Provincia AM, Putaendo
1550	0.25	CHL	CD155	R. Regional, Traiguén
1550	0.1	CLM	HKW53	Alcaldía de El Tablón, El Tablón
1550	0.1	CLM	HKW55	Alcaldía de Guachucal, Guachucal
1550	0.25	CLM	HKW50	Alcaldía de Mallama, Mallama
1550	5	CLM	HJQD	Caracol Armenia, Armenia
1550	1	CLM	HKV38	Colombia Mía, Pitalito, HU
1550	0.25	CLM	HKX29	Colombia Mía, Tibú, NS
1550	5	CLM	HJUN	LV del Río Arma, Aguadas
1550	5	CLM	HJZI	MCI Radio 15-50, SF de Bogotá
1550	0.5	CLM		Ondas del Nechí, Campamento
1550	5	CLM	HJCB	R. El Sol, Barranquilla
1550	1	CLM	HJLT	R. Renacer en Cristo, Cali
1550	5	EQA	AD5	LV de Chaguarurco, Santa Isabel
1550	2	EQA	AD2	LV del Triunfo, El Triunfo
1550	1	EQA	RA7	R. Amazonas, Archidona
1550	2	EQA	EI6	R. Montalvo, Ambato
1550	1	PRU	OAU3D	R. Cruz, Chimbote
1550	1	PRU	OCX7A	R. Cultura, Puno
1550	1	PRU	OBX4P	R. Independencia, Lima
1550	1	PRU	OCX2R	R. OCX2R, Chota
1550	1	PRU	OBX5J	R. San Cristobal, Carmen Alto (R. Maria)
1550	1	PRU	OAX1D	R. Superior, Monsefú
1550	1/0.25	URG	C155	R. Agraciada, Mercedes
1550	2	URG	CW155	R. Sarandí del Yí, Sarandí del Yí
1550	10/5	VEN	XO	R. Impacto, Cd. Ojeda
1550	10	VEN	MW	R. Metropolitana, Los Teques
1555	0.5	CLM		R. Parroquial, El Santuario
1560		ARG		R. Almirante Brown, Rafael Calzada
1560		ARG		R. Castañares, Ituzaingó
1560		ARG		R. Ebenezer, Ezeiza
1560	2.5/1.5	ARG	LT11	R. Gral. Francisco Ramírez, Villaguay
1560		ARG		R. Renecar, Quilmes Oeste
1560	0.5	BOL	CP-	1° de Octubre, Capinota
1560	1	BOL	CP255	R. Occidental, Oruro
1560	0.5	BOL	CP-	R. Urkupiña, Quillacollo
1560	1	CHL	CB156	R. Manantial, Talagante
1560	5/3	CHL	CA156	R. Parinacota, Putre
1560	1	CHL	CD156	R. Parque Nacional, Villarrica
1560	0.25	CLM	HKO35	Alcaldía de Cañasgordas, Cañasgordas
1560	0.25	CLM	HK90	Alcaldía de Villavicencio, Villavicencio
1560	5	CLM	HJLP	La Cariñosa, Tuluá
1560	1	CLM	HJPZ	R. Codazzi, Codazzi
1560	0.5	CLM	HKS65	R. Tamalameque, Tamalameque
1560	5	CLM	HJCP	RCN Antena 2, Arbelaez
1560	1	CLM	HJXZ	Sta María de la Paz, Medellín
1560	0.2	CLM	HK90	Villavicencio
1560	5	CLM	HJHE	Voces Rovirenses, Málaga
1560	1.5	EQA	ZD1	Ecos Culturales de Urcuquí, Urcuquí
1560	2	EQA	TR3	LV del Guabo, El Guabo
1560	2	EQA	CS2	R. Sideral, Daule
1560	1	PRU	OCX6N	R. La Union, Arequipa
1560	1	PRU	OAZ7N	R. Maria, Wanchaq
1560	0.5	PRU	OBX2J	R. Nuvo Continente, Cajamarca

kHz	kW	Ctry	Call	Station, location
1560	1	PRU	OBU4G	R. San Sebastian, Yauyos
1560	2/0.5	URG	CX156	Dif. Americana, Trinidad
1560	3/0.5	URG	CW51	R. Maldonado, Maldonado
1560	1/0.25	URG	C156	R. Vichadero
1560	10/5	VEN	LZ	R. Dif. Andina, Mérida
1564	0.5	PRU	OBU2H	R. San Lorenzo, Socota
1570		ARG		R. Interactiva, Ciudad Madero
1570		ARG		R. Nuevo Mundo, General Pinto
1570	1	ARG		R. Rocha, La Plata
1570	0.5	BOL	CP-	R. 1° de Mayo, 1° de Mayo
1570	0.25	CHL	CD157	R. Acuarela, Nueva Imperial
1570	7	CHL	CC157	R. Familia del Maule, Talca
1570	1	CHL	CC157	R. Niebla, Rancagua
1570	0.25	CLM	HKX78	Alcaldía de Balboa, Balboa
1570	0.15	CLM	HKU42	Alcaldía de Cajica, Cajica
1570	0.25	CLM	HKQ83	Alcaldía de Maripi, Maripi
1570	0.25	CLM	HKQ82	Alcaldía de Sta María, Sta María
1570	0.25	CLM	HKP58	Alcaldía de Sta Rosa Sur, Sta Rosa Sur
1570	2	CLM	HKX52	Arc. Armada de Colombia, Pto Leguizamo
1570	1	CLM	HJE96	Colombia Mía, Palmira, VA
1570		CLM		LV de Fomeque, Fomeque
1570	1	CLM	HJC22	R. Ciudad Dabeiba, Dabeiba
1570	1	CLM	HJTG	R. María, Machetá
1570	0.1	CLM	HKX80	R. Marsella, Marsella
1570	1	CLM	HJZT	R. Sensación, Manizales
1570	0.2	CLM	HKR66	R. Universidad de la Amazonia, Florencia
1570	0.5	CLM	HJR66	Timbiqui Estéreo, Timbiqui
1570	0.5	EQA		Ondas Quereñas, Quero
1570	1	EQA		R. LV Espirítu Santo de Dios, Manta
1570	10	EQA	PG1	R. Nucanchic, Maldonado
1570		PRG		R. Oriental AM 1570, Caaguazú
1570	1	PRU	OAU7Z	Em.Comercial Oriunda Eco, Juliaca
1570	1	PRU	OBX3N	R. Chasquie, Yungay
1570	1	PRU	OCX1Z	R. La Nueva Esperanza, Tambo Grande
1570	1	PRU	OBX3M	R. San Martin, Huanuco
1570	1	PRU	OCX6I	R. Willy, Uraca
1570	2/0.5	URG	CX157	R. Canelones
1570	0.25/0.1	URG	CW157A	R. Celeste, Tomás Gomensoro
1577	1	PRU	OAU2E	R-.Frecuencia, San Ignacio
1578	1	BOL	CP237	R. Don Bosco, Kami
1580	1	ARG		R. Activa, Longchamps
1580	0.25	ARG	LT36	R. Chacabuco
1580	0.25	ARG	LT27	R. LV del Montiel, Villaguay
1580		ARG		R. Música, Educación y Cultura, Caseros
1580		ARG		R. Planeta, Rosario, SF
1580		ARG		R. Tradición, San Martín
1580	1	BOL	CP-	R. Andrés Ibáñez, Santa Cruz
1580		BOL	CP-	R. El Fuego del Espíritu Santo, El Alto
1580	1	CHL	CC158	R. Colchagua, Santa Cruz
1580	0.5	CHL	CD158B	R. Continental, Collipulli
1580	0.25	CHL	CD158A	R. Millaray, Cañete
1580	0.25	CLM	HKU42	Alcaldía de Cajica, Cajica
1580	0.1	CLM	HKW74	Alcaldía de Pupiales, Pupiales
1580	0.25	CLM	HKT34	Alcaldía de San Antero, San Antero
1580		CLM		Alcaldía de Yaguará, Yaguará
1580	5	CLM	HJRM	Caracol Colombia, Sincelejo
1580	1	CLM	HJLC	LV del Banco, El Banco
1580	0.15	CLM	HKS46	R. Alcaldía de Padilla, Padilla
1580	5	CLM	HJQT	R. Mar, SF de Bogotá
1580	5	CLM	HJQZ	R. María, Barranquilla
1580	1	CLM	HJDE	R. Miraflores, Rovira
1580	5	CLM	HJSQ	R. Robledo/RCN Antena 2, Cartago
1580	1	CLM	HJKB	R. Zulima, Villa del Rosario
1580	0.5	EQA	CP2	Canal del Pueblo, Samborondón
1580	1	EQA	LF1	Ecos de Orellana, Machachi
1580	3	EQA	TP5	Ecos del Portete, Girón
1580	5	EQA	VA4	Estación de la Alegría, Esmeraldas
1580	0.25	EQA	AB3	Ondas de Paltas, Catacocha
1580	1	PRU		R. Central, Bellavista
1580	3/1	PRU	OBX1M	R. Naylamp, Lambayeque
1580	1	PRU	OAU4P	R. San Juan, Tarma
1580	0.5	URG	CW54	Emisoras del Este, Minas
1580	1/0.5	URG	CW158	R. San Salvador, Dolores
1580	10/5	VEN	TK	Manzanares 15-80, Cumaná
1580	10	VEN	YO	R Celestial, San Francisco, Maracaibo
1580	10/5	VEN	YV	R. Venezolano, Calabozo
1584	0.5	PRU	OBX7Q	R. El Triunfo, Cusco
1584	0.5	PRU	OBX7Q	R. El Triunfo, Cusco
1587	1	PRU	OAU5A	R. Armonia, Abancay
1590		ARG		R. Guaviyú, Gregorio de Laferrere
1590		ARG		R. Jesucristo es el Rey, Lomas de Zamora
1590	3	BOL	CP155	R. Bermejo, Bermejo
1590		BOL	CP-	R. Globo, La Guardia
1590		BOL	CP-	R. Kollasuyo Marka, Tiawanaku
1590	0.5	BOL	CP-	R. Producciones Pusisuyu, Oruro
1590	5	CHL	CD159	Em. Tepual, Llanquihue
1590	1	CHL	CB159	R. Aconcagua, San Felipe
1590	0.25	CHL	CC159	R. Rengo, Rengo
1590		CLM	HKS72	Alcaldía de La Gloria, La Gloria
1590	1	CLM	HJQM	Ecos de la Miel, Samaná
1590	5	CLM	HJIP	Em. Nuevo Continente, Envigado
1590	5	CLM	HJWB	Minuto de Dios Sra del Socorro, Socorro
1590		CLM		Ondas del Rioseco, Rioseco
1590		CLM		R. Espacial, Andalucía
1590	1	EQA	RZ1	R. Mensaje, Cayambe
1590	1	EQA	QT6	R. Panamericana, Quero
1590	0.25	EQA	AS2	R. Record, La Libertad
1590	0.2	PRG		R. Villeta, Villeta
1590	1	PRU	OBU2C	Agro Radio, Trujillo
1590	2	PRU	OAZ4Z	R. Agricultura "La Peruanísima" Lima
1590	1	PRU	OCX6S	R. Mundo, Arequipa
1590	1	PRU	OCX6S	R. Mundo, Arequipa
1590	1	PRU	OAU7C	R. Publicidad Lider, Juliaca
1590	10	URG	CX159	R. Real, Colonia
1590	1/0.25	URG	CW159	R. Regional- "La Nueva Radio", Lascano
1590	0.25	URG	C159	R. Regional, Constitución
1590	10	VEN	UD	R. Deporte 15-90, Caracas
1600	1.2	ARG		R. Armonia, José Ingenieros
1600		ARG		R. Belgrano, Junín
1600		ARG		R. Copacabana, Gregorio de Laferrere
1600		ARG		R. Fénix, General Viamonte
1600	0.5	BOL	CP153	R. Continental, Punata
1600	1	BOL	CP-	R. La Voz de Dios, El Alto
1600	0.25	CHL	CD160	Millalebu-La Regalona AM, Temuco
1600	0.25	CHL	CC160A	R. Llacolén, Concepción
1600	0.25	CHL	CB160A	R. Nuevo Tiempo, Santiago
1600	0.25	CHL	CB160B	Radiocable, Viña del Mar
1600	0.15	CLM	HKZ79	Alcaldía de Cajamarca, Cajamarca
1600	0.25	CLM	HKO63	Alcaldía de Jardín, Jardín
1600	0.25	CLM	HKX83	Alcaldía de La Celia, Celia
1600	0.25	CLM	HKT39	Alcaldía de Valencia, Valencia
1600	0.15	CLM	HKZ77	Alcaldía de Venadillo, Venadillo
1600	5	CLM	HJHV	Armonías Zipaquireñas, Zipaquirá
1600	5	CLM	HKO72	Colombia Mía, Carepa, AN
1600		CLM	HKX84	Em. Mundial, Dosquebradas
1600	0.25	CLM		LV de Aranzazu
1600	0.25	CLM	HKR52	LV de Colina, Risaralda
1600	1	CLM		LV del Rosario, Junín
1600		CLM		R. Bello Horizonte, Pesca
1600		CLM		R. Fortaleza, Sogamoso
1600	0.25	CLM		R. Impacto Cristiano, Popayán
1600	0.25	CLM	HJF33	R. Restauración, Cali
1600		EQA		Ilusión AM, Quito
1600		EQA		Ondas de Caluma "R. del Pueblo", Caluma
1600	1	EQA	JP2	R. Consular, Playas
1600	3	EQA	PB5	R. Intiñán, Girón
1600		PRU		CP, Huancayo
1600	1	PRU	OCY2D	R. Internacional, San Pablo
1600	2	URG	C160	Emisora Continental, Pando
1600	1	URG	CX160	R. Litoral, Fray Bentos
1610	0.5	ARG		R. Buenas Nuevas, Laboulaye
1610		ARG		R. Exitos, Ituzaingó
1610	0.05	ARG		R. Luz del Mundo, Rafael Calzada
1610		ARG		R. Maranata AM, Puerto Iguazú
1610		CLM		Armonías de Occidente, Medellín
1610	3	EQA	TP5	Ecos del Portete, Girón
1610	0.1	PRG		R. Colegio Tecnico Municipal
1610		PRU		R. Carabamba, Julcánn
1610	0.5	PRU		R. Flor de los Andes, José Luis Bustamente y Rivero
1610		PRU		R. Haquira, Haquira
1613	1	CLM		R. Ideal, Umbita
1620		ARG		R. Italia,Villa Martelli
1620	10	ARG		R. Tropicana, Buenos Aires
1630		ARG		AM Restauración, Hurlingham
1630	1/5	ARG		R. Buen Ayre (Red 92), La Plata
1640		ARG		R. Boanerges, Posadas
1640		ARG		R. Libre, Buenos Aires
1650		ARG		R. Fortaleza, Ezeiza
1680		ARG		R. Getro, Lanús Oeste
1690	1/0.25	ARG		R. Apocalipsis II, San Justo

INTERNATIONAL RADIO

Section Contents

Initial entries for each letter, see Main Index for full details.

Features & Reviews

National Radio

LW and MW Listings by Region

International Radio

Television

Reference

Note: The three-letter codes after each frequency are transmitter site codes. These, and the area/country codes under **Area,** can all be decoded by referring to the tables in the Reference Section. Where a frequency has an asterisk, etc. after it, see the 'Notes' section of the main entry for explanation.

ALASKA (U.S. State)

KNLS INTERNATIONAL (Rlg)

P.O. Box 473, Anchor Point, AK 99556, USA.
☎ +1 904 2358262.
Email: knls@aol.com **Web:** www.knls.org (English); www.knls.net (Russian); www.smzg.org (Mandarin)
WCBC Studios: 605 Bradley Court, Franklin, TN 37067, USA.
☎ +1 615 3718707. 🖷 +1 615 3718791.
Email: info@worldchristian.org **Web:** www.worldchristian.org
L.P: WCBC: Pres.: Charles Caudill; Exec. Producer: Dale Ward; Dir of Engineering: Kevin K. Chambers.
SW: [NLS] Anchor Point, AK (G.C. 59N45 151W44) 2 x 100kW
kHz: *7355, 7365, 9615, 9690, 11765*

Winter Schedule 2004

English	Days	Area	kHz
0800-0900	daily	Pac	7365nls*, 11765nls**
1300-1400	daily	EAs	9690nls
Mandarin	**Days**	**Area**	**kHz**
1000-1100	daily	CHN	7355nls*, 9690nls**
1200-1300	daily	CHN	7355nls*, 9690nls**
1400-1500	daily	CHN	9615nls
1500-1600	daily	CHN	7355nls
1600-1700	daily	CHN	7355nls***, 9615nls****
Russian	**Days**	**Area**	**kHz**
0900-1000	daily	RUS	7365nls***, 9690nls****
1100-1200	daily	RUS	7365nls***, 9690nls****
1700-1800	daily	RUS	7355nls*, 9615nls**

ANN: English: "You are listening to station KLNS broadcasting from the top of the world, Anchor Point, Alaska"
V: QSL-card. Rec. acc. For email rpt, the subject should be "Reception Report" (no quotes).
NOTES: Owned by World Christian Broadcasting, Inc. (WCBC). KNLS amends its schedule 4 times a year. WCBC is going to begin constructing a SW relay station in Southern Africa (see Madagascar). Key: * To 30 Jan; ** from 30 Jan; *** to 27 Feb; **** from 27 Feb to 27 Mar 2005.

ALBANIA

RADIO TIRANA (Pub)

Rruga Ismail Qemali 11, Tirana, Albania.
☎ +355 4 222481. 🖷 +355 4 222481.
Email: rtsh_international@hotmail.com **Web:** rtsh.sil.at/foreign.htm
L.P: Dir: Martin Leka; Tech Dir: Irfan Mandija; Head of RTV Monitoring: Mrs. Drita Çiço.
MW: [FLA] Fllaka (G.C. 41N22 019E30) 1215/1395/1458kHz 500kW
SW: [CER] Cërrik (G.C. 41N20 019E36) 2 x 50, 4 x 100kW; [SHI] Shijak (G.C. 41N20 019E33) 3 x 100kW
SAT: Eutelsat W2
kHz: *1395, 1458, 5955, 5995, 6115, 6205, 7105, 7120, 7160, 7210, 7240*

Winter Schedule 2004

Albanian	Days	Area	kHz
0000-0130	daily	NAm	6115shi
0730-0900	daily	Eu	1458fla
0730-1000	daily	Eu	7105shi
0900-1000	daily	Eu	1395fla
1500-1630	daily	Eu	1458fla
2130-2300	daily	Eu	6205shi
English	**Days**	**Area**	**kHz**
0245-0300	.twtfss	NAm	6115shi, 7160shi
0330-0400	.twtfss	NAm	6115shi, 7160shi
1945-2000	mtwtfs.	Eu	6115shi, 7210shi
2230-2300	mtwtfs.	Eu	7120shi
French	**Days**	**Area**	**kHz**
2000-2030	mtwtfs.	Eu	6115shi
German	**Days**	**Area**	**kHz**
1900-1930	mtwtfs.	Eu	1458fla, 7240shi
Greek	**Days**	**Area**	**kHz**
1645-1700	mtwtfs.	Eu	1458fla
Italian	**Days**	**Area**	**kHz**
0530-0600	mtwtfs.	Eu	5955shi
Serbian	**Days**	**Area**	**kHz**
2115-2130	mtwtfs.	Eu	1458fla
2215-2230	mtwtfs.	Eu	5995shi
Turkish	**Days**	**Area**	**kHz**
1630-1645	mtwtfs.	ME	1458fla

ANN: Albanian: "Radio Tirana per bashkatdhetaret"; English: "This is Radio Tirana"; French: "Ici Tirana"; Italian: "Parla Tirana"; German: "Hier ist Tirana"; Greek: "Sas milun ta Tirana"; Serbian: "Govori Tirana"; Turkish: "Burasi Tiran Radyosu"
V: QSL-card.
NOTES: Radio Tirana is the External Sce of the public broadcaster Albanian Radio&TV (Radiotelevizioni Shqiptar).
Broadcasters using sites in this country:
BBG-VOA uses: (FLA). See stn entry in: **USA**, INT Section
China R. Int'l uses: (FLA). See stn entry in: **CHN**, INT Section
Deutsche Welle uses: (FLA). See stn entry in: **D**, INT Section
TWR Europe uses: (SHI). See stn entry in: **AUT**, INT Section
TWR Europe uses: (FLA). See stn entry in: **AUT**, INT Section

ANGOLA

RÁDIO NACIONAL DE ANGOLA (Gov)

C.P. 1329, Luanda, Angola.
☎ +244 2 321638. 🖷 +244 2 391234.
Email: rna@rna.ao **Web:** www.rna.ao
L.P: GD: Manuel Rabelais; Tech Dir: Cândido R. Pinto.
MW: [CAZ] Cazenga (G.C. 08S53 015E56) 945kHz 25kW
SW: [MUL] Luanda, Mulenvos (G.C. 08S53 013E20) 1 x 5, 1 x 50, 2 x 100kW
kHz: *945, 7217*

Winter Schedule 2004

English	Days	Area	kHz
2100-2200	daily	Af	945caz, 7217mul*
French	**Days**	**Area**	**kHz**
2000-2100	daily	Af	945caz, 7217mul*

ANN: English: "This is Luanda, the International Service of the Angolan National Radio"
V: QSL-card.
NOTES: Key: * Variable frequency.

ANGUILLA (British)

THE CARIBBEAN BEACON (UNIVERSITY NETWORK RELAY) (Rlg)

See The University Network (USA).
P.O. Box 690, Anguilla, British West Indies.
☎ +1 809 4974340. 🖷 +1 809 4974311.
L.P: Chief Engineer: Kevon Mooney.
MW: [AIA] The Valley (G.C. 18N13 063W01) 690kHz 100kW, 1610kHz 200kW
SW: [AIA] The Valley (G.C. 18N13 063W01) 1 x 100kW
FM: The Valley 100.1MHz 35kW
V: QSL-card.
NOTES: Carries programming from Gene Scott's "University Network" (see main entry under "USA" for schedules).
Broadcasters using sites in this country:
Dr Gene Scott uses: (AIA). See stn entry in: **USA**, INT Section

ANTIGUA & BARBUDA

CARIBBEAN RELAY COMPANY LTD.

P.O. Box 1203, St John's, Antigua.
☎ +1 268 4620436. 🖷 +1 268 4620487.
Email: acm_crc@candw.ag
L.P: Mgr: Dave Rayney; Assistant Mgr: Peter Ippendorf; Secretary: David George.

SW: [ATG] St John's (G.C. 17N06 061W48) 4 x 250kW
FM: St John's 98.1MHz (rel. BBCWS)
V: QSL-card.
NOTES: Established 1975 as a jointly owned BBC/Deutsche Welle relay facility.

Broadcasters using sites in this country:
BBC World Sce uses: (ATG). See stn entry in: **G**, INT Section
Deutsche Welle uses: (ATG). See stn entry in: **D**, INT Section

ARGENTINA

RADIODIFUSIÓN ARGENTINA AL EXTERIOR (RAE) (Pub)

✉ Casilla de Correo 555, Correo Central, C1000WAF Buenos Aires, Argentina.
☎ +54 11 43256368. 🖷 +54 11 43259433.
Email: rae@radionacional.gov.ar **Web:** www.radionacional.gov.ar
L.P: Dir: Marcela Campos.
SW: [BUE] Buenos Aires, General Pacheco (G.C. 36S43 058W22) 2 x 50, 1 x 100kW
kHz: *6060, 9690, 11710, 15345*

Winter Schedule 2004

English	**Days**	**Area**	**kHz**
0200-0300	mtwtf..	Am	11710bue
1800-1900	mtwtf..	Eu	9690bue, 15345bue
French	**Days**	**Area**	**kHz**
0300-0400	mtwtf..	Am	11710bue
2000-2100	mtwtf..	Eu,NAf	9690bue, 15345bue
German	**Days**	**Area**	**kHz**
2100-2200	mtwtf..	Eu,NAf	9690bue, 15345bue
Italian	**Days**	**Area**	**kHz**
1900-2000	mtwtf..	Eu	9690bue, 15345bue
Japanese	**Days**	**Area**	**kHz**
1000-1200	mtwtf..	FE	11710bue
Portuguese	**Days**	**Area**	**kHz**
0000-0200	mtwtf..	Am	11710bue
Spanish	**Days**	**Area**	**kHz**
1200-1400	mtwtf..	Am	15345bue
2000-2200	.....s.	Eu,NAf	11710bue, 15345bue
2000-2200	.....s.	Am,Eu	6060bue
2200-2300	mtwtf..	Eu,NAf	6060bue, 11710bue, 15345bue
2300-2400	mtwtf..	Am,Eu	6060bue, 11710bue, 15345bue

ANN: English: "This is R.A.E., the International Service of the Argentine Radio"
V: QSL-card.
NOTES: RAE is the External Sce of Servicio Oficial de Radiodifusión (SOR).

ARMENIA

VOICE OF ARMENIA (Pub)

✉ A. Manukyan Street 5, 375025 Yerevan, Armenia.
☎ +374 1 558010. 🖷 +374 1 551513.
Email: pr@armradio.am **Web:** www.armradio.am
L.P: Dir: Levon V. Ananikyan.
LW/MW/SW: Leased from Republican Broadcasting Centre.
kHz: *234, 864, 4810, 9965*

Winter Schedule 2004

Arabic	**Days**	**Area**	**kHz**
1745-1815	daily	WAs,ME	4810yer
1745-1815	daily	ME	864gav
Armenian	**Days**	**Area**	**kHz**
0300-0330	daily	SAm	9965gav
1845-1905	mtwtfs.	Eu	9965gav
1845-1905	mtwtfs.	WAs,ME	4810yer
Azeri	**Days**	**Area**	**kHz**
1345-1400	.....ss	ME	864gav
1345-1400	.....ss	WAs,ME	4810yer
1345-1415	mtwtf..	ME	864gav
1345-1415	mtwtf..	WAs,ME	4810yer
English	**Days**	**Area**	**kHz**
1925-1945	mtwtfs.	Eu	9965gav
1925-1945	mtwtfs.	WAs,ME,Eu	4810yer
Farsi	**Days**	**Area**	**kHz**
0330-0400	daily	WAs,ME	4810yer
0330-0400	daily	ME	864gav
French	**Days**	**Area**	**kHz**
1945-2000	daily	WAs,ME,Eu	4810yer
1945-2000	daily	Eu	9965gav
Georgian	**Days**	**Area**	**kHz**
1305-1315	daily	WAs	234gav
German	**Days**	**Area**	**kHz**
1900-1925	daily	Eu	9965gav
1900-1925	daily	WAs,ME,Eu	4810yer
Kurdish	**Days**	**Area**	**kHz**
1430-1500	daily	ME	864gav
1430-1500	daily	WAs,ME	4810yer
Spanish	**Days**	**Area**	**kHz**
0330-0345	daily	SAm	9965gav
Turkish	**Days**	**Area**	**kHz**
1400-1430	.....ss	ME	864gav
1400-1430	.....ss	WAs,ME	4810yer
1415-1430	mtwtf..	ME	864gav
1415-1430	mtwtf..	WAs,ME	4810yer
Yiddish	**Days**	**Area**	**kHz**
1315-1345	daily	WAs	234gav

ANN: Armenian: "Yerevan e khosum, yeterum Hayastani Dzayn"; English: "You are listening to the Voice of Armenia"; French: "Ici Erevan. Vous écoutez la Voix d'Armenie"
IS: "Spring" by Gomitas Vartabad, and "Dance of the Rose Maidens" from the Kayane ballet suite by Aram Khachaturyan.
V: QSL-card. Rp (1 IRC).
NOTES: The Voice of Armenia is the External Sce of the public service Armenian National Radio (Hayastani Azgain Radio).

REPUBLICAN BROADCASTING CENTRE (Tx Operator)

✉ Yerevan, Armenia.
LW: [GAV] Gavar (G.C. 40N25 45E11) 234kHz 500kW
MW: [GAV] Gavar (G.C. 40N25N 45N11E) 864/1314/1350kHz 1000kW
SW: [YER] Yerevan, Arinj (G.C. 40N10 44E34) 1 x 50, 2 x 100kW; [GAV] Gavar (G.C. 40N25 45E11) 3 x 100, 3 x 1000kW
NOTES: The Republican Broadcasting Centre is the national transmitter network owner. The facilities are leased to domestic and foreign customers. In the seasonal SW schedules coordinated by the HFCC, the transmissions from Yerevan and Gavar can be found under the code "ERV".

AR RADIO INTERCONTINENTAL (Broker)

✉ 153, Nork Marash 13th St., 375047 Yerevan, Armenia.
☎ +374 1 551143. 🖷 +374 1 554600.
Email: president@mediaconcern.am **Web:** www.mediaconcern.am
L.P: DG: Hrachya Kostanyan; Tech Dir: Tigran Khanamiryan.

Broadcasters using sites in this country:
BBG-R.Free Asia uses: (GAV). See stn entry in: **USA**, INT Section
BBG-RFE/RL uses: (GAV). See stn entry in: **USA**, INT Section
BBG-VOA uses: (GAV). See stn entry in: **USA**, INT Section
Deutsche Welle uses: (GAV). See stn entry in: **D**, INT Section
FEBA Radio uses: (GAV). See stn entry in: **G**, INT Section
R.Santec uses: (GAV). See stn entry in: **D**, INT Section
TWR Europe uses: (GAV). See stn entry in: **AUT**, INT Section
VO Russia (VOR) uses: (GAV). See stn entry in: **RUS**, INT Section
VOR-RKS uses: (GAV). See stn entry in: **RUS**, INT Section
VOR-RMR uses: (GAV). See stn entry in: **RUS**, INT Section

ASCENSION ISLAND (British)

BBC ATLANTIC RELAY STATION

✉ English Bay, Ascension Island.
☎ +247 4458. 🖷 +247 6135.
Email: niki.roy@atlantis.co.ac
L.P: Transmitter Eng: Nicola Nicholls.
SW: [ASC] English Bay (G.C. 07S54 014W23) 6 x 250kW
V: QSL-letter for direct rpt.
NOTES: Owned by the BBC and operated by VT Merlin Communications (see UK). Carries relays of BBC and other international broadcasters.

Broadcasters using sites in this country:
BBC World Sce uses: (ASC). See stn entry in: **G**, INT Section
FEBA Radio uses: (ASC). See stn entry in: **G**, INT Section
R.Japan uses: (ASC). See stn entry in: **J**, INT Section
R.Prague uses: (ASC). See stn entry in: **CZE**, INT Section
RAI Int'l uses: (ASC). See stn entry in: **I**, INT Section
RCI uses: (ASC). See stn entry in: **CAN**, INT Section
RFI uses: (ASC). See stn entry in: **F**, INT Section
UN Radio uses: (ASC). See stn entry in: **UNO**, INT Section

AUSTRALIA

RADIO AUSTRALIA (Pub)

P.O. Box 428G, Melbourne, VIC 3001, Australia.
☎ +61 3 96261898. Fax +61 3 96261899.
Email: english@ra.abc.net.au **Web:** radioaustralia.net.au
L.P: GM: Jean-Gabriel Manguy; PD: Tony Hastings; Chief Eng: Nigel Holmes.
SW: Leased from Broadcast Australia. Also leases air time at the Darwin facilities of Voice International.
SAT: Pas 2.
kHz: *5995, 6020, 6080, 7240, 9475, 9500, 9560, 9580, 9590, 9630, 9660, 9710, 9730, 9875, 11550, 11650, 11660, 11690, 11695, 11750, 11820, 11880, 12010, 12080, 13620, 13630, 15110, 15160, 15230, 15240, 15415, 15515, 17715, 17750, 17775, 17795, 17855, 21725, 21740, 21780*

Winter Schedule 2004

BBC WS	**Days**	**Area**	**kHz**
2200-2300	daily	Pac	9660brn, 12080brn
English	**Days**	**Area**	**kHz**
0000-0100	daily	Pac	15240shp
0000-0130	daily	As	17775dar
0000-0200	daily	Pac	17715shp
0030-0400	daily	As	15415shp
0100-0700	daily	Pac	15240shp
0200-0500	daily	Pac	21725shp
0200-0900	daily	Pac	15515shp
0430-0500	daily	As	15415shp
0500-0800	daily	As	15160shp
0530-0800	daily	As	15415shp
0700-0800	daily	Pac	15240shp
0800-0900	daily	Pac	5995brn, 9710shp
0800-1130	daily	As	15240shp
0800-1400	daily	Pac	9580shp
0800-1600	daily	Pac	9590shp
0830-0900	daily	As	15415shp
0900-1300	daily	Pac	11880shp
0930-1100	daily	As	15415shp
1100-1300	daily	As	9475shp
1100-1400	daily	Pac	5995brn, 6020shp, 9560shp
1400-1600	daily	As	11750shp
1400-1800	daily	Pac	5995shp, 6080shp
1430-1900	daily	As	9475shp
1500-1530	......s	Eu	9875rmp+
1600-2000	daily	Pac	9710shp
1700-2100	daily	Pac	9580shp, 11880shp
1800-2000	daily	Pac	6080shp, 7240shp
1900-2130	daily	As	9500shp
2000-2100	.....ss	Pac	6080shp, 7240shp
2000-2200	daily	Pac	11650shp, 12080brn
2100-0700	daily	Pac	13630shp
2100-2130	daily	As	11695shp
2100-2200	daily	Pac	9660brn
2100-2300	daily	Pac	15515shp
2200-2330	daily	As	15240dar
2200-2400	daily	As	13620dar, 15230shp
2200-2400	daily	Pac	21740shp
2300-0200	daily	Pac	17795shp
2300-0800	daily	Pac	9660brn
2300-1200	daily	Pac	12080brn
2330-0900	daily	As	17750shp
2330-2400	daily	As	15415shp
Indonesian	**Days**	**Area**	**kHz**
0000-0030	daily	As	11690sng, 15415shp, 17855dar
0400-0430	daily	As	15415shp, 17855dar, 21780tin
0500-0530	daily	As	15415shp, 17855dar
0800-0830	daily	As	15415shp
0800-0930	daily	As	11550tai
0900-0930	daily	As	15415shp
2130-2330	daily	As	9630dar, 11550tai, 11695shp, 15415shp
Khmer	**Days**	**Area**	**kHz**
2300-2330	daily	As	9730sng
Mandarin	**Days**	**Area**	**kHz**
1300-1430	daily	As	9475shp, 11660shp, 12010sng
Tok Pisin	**Days**	**Area**	**kHz**
0900-1100	daily	Pac	5995brn, 6020shp, 9710shp
2000-2100	mtwtf..	Pac	6080shp, 7240shp
Vietnamese	**Days**	**Area**	**kHz**
0530-0600	daily	As	17855dar
2330-2400	daily	As	11820dar, 15110tai

ANN: English: "This is Radio Australia broadcasting from studios in Melbourne, Victoria"
IS: "Waltzing Matilda" prior to opening on all freqs. Foreign language broadcasts start with the laugh of the Kookaburra.
V: QSL-card.
NOTES: Radio Australia is the External Sce of the public service Australian Broadcasting Corporation (ABC). Key: + DRM. Frequency usage of offshore relays is subject to variation.

HCJB WORLD RADIO AUSTRALIA (Rlg)

P.O. Box 691, Melbourne, VIC 3001, Australia.
☎ +61 3 97614844. Fax +61 3 97614061.
Email: office@hcjb.org.au
P.O. Box 291, Kilsyth, VIC 3137, Australia.
L.P: Dir: David Maindonald; Freq Mgr: Ian Williams.
SW: [KNX] Kununurra (G.C. 15S45 128E44) 1 x 100kW
kHz: *11750, 15390, 15405, 15425, 15525, 15560*

Winter Schedule 2004

Chhattisgarhi	**Days**	**Area**	**kHz**
1415-1430	..t....	As	15405knx
English	**Days**	**Area**	**kHz**
0000-0100	daily	EAs	15525knx
0100-0230	daily	As	15560knx
0230-0300	......s	As	15560knx
0800-1100	daily	Pac	11750knx
1100-1230	daily	SEA	15425knx
1230-1300	daily	SEA	15405knx
1330-1400	......s	As	15405knx
1430-1800	daily	As	15390knx
2230-2400	.....s.	EAs	15525knx
Hindi	**Days**	**Area**	**kHz**
1400-1415	daily	As	15405knx
1415-1430	......s	As	15405knx
Hmar	**Days**	**Area**	**kHz**
1415-1430	....f..	As	15405knx
Indonesian	**Days**	**Area**	**kHz**
1300-1330	daily	SEA	15405knx
Malayalam	**Days**	**Area**	**kHz**
1415-1430	..w....	As	15405knx
Mandarin	**Days**	**Area**	**kHz**
2230-2400	mtwtf..	EAs	15525knx
Meitei	**Days**	**Area**	**kHz**
1415-1430	.....s.	As	15405knx
Nepali	**Days**	**Area**	**kHz**
1415-1430	.t.....	As	15405knx
Punjabi	**Days**	**Area**	**kHz**
1415-1430	m......	As	15405knx
Urdu	**Days**	**Area**	**kHz**
0230-0300	mtwtfs.	As	15560knx
1330-1400	mtwtfs.	As	15560knx

ANN: English: "The Voice of the Great Southland"
V: QSL-card.
NOTES: Part of HCJB's World Radio Network, see USA for corporate headquarters.

VOICE INTERNATIONAL (Rlg)

P.O. Box 1104, Buderim, QLD 4556, Australia.
☎ +61 7 54771555. Fax +61 7 54771727.

Email: voice@voice.com.au **Web:** www.voice.com.au
L.P: Corporate Relations Mgr: Richard Daniel.
SW: [DAR] Darwin (G.C. 12S25 136E37) 5 x 250, 1 x 300kW
kHz: *7245, 11685, 11840, 11955, 13685, 13790, 15165, 15250, 15365, 17635, 17820*

Winter Schedule 2004

English	Days	Area	kHz
0900-1030	daily	IND	11955dar
0900-1430	daily	CHN	13685dar
1100-1730	daily	IND	13685dar
1500-1730	daily	IND	11840dar
1800-2030	daily	IND	11685dar
Indonesian	**Days**	**Area**	**kHz**
0400-1000	daily	INS	17820dar
1000-1300	daily	INS	15365dar
1300-1700	daily	INS	7245dar
2300-0200	daily	INS	15250dar
Mandarin	**Days**	**Area**	**kHz**
0700-1300	daily	CHN	17635dar
1300-1800	daily	CHN	13790dar
2200-0100	daily	CHN	15165dar

V: QSL-card. Rp.
NOTES: Voice International Ltd is a branch of Christian Vision (see United Kingdom for corporate details). The station was launched in 2000, when Christian Vision purchased the Darwin transmitter site from Radio Australia.
PUBS: Monthly "Newsletter" available by E-mail (see website for details).

BROADCAST AUSTRALIA (Tx Operator)

655 Pacific Highway, St Leonards, NSW 2065, Australia.
☎ +61 2 84254666. Fax +61 2 94370825.
Email: info@broadcastaustralia.com.au
Web: www.broadcastaustralia.com.au
L.P: Chmn: Gerry Moriarty; CEO: Scott Davies.
SW: [SHP] Shepparton (G.C. 36S20 145E25) 7 x 100kW; [BRN] Brandon (G.C. 19S31 147E20) 3 x 10kW.
NOTES: Broadcast Australia is the national transmitter network operator.
Broadcasters using sites in this country:
BBC World Sce uses: (BRN). See stn entry in: **G**, INT Section

AUSTRIA

RADIO ÖSTERREICH 1 (ORF) (Pub)

Argentinierstrasse 30a, A-1040 Wien, Austria.
☎ +43 1 5010116060. Fax +43 1 5010116066.
Email: servicecenter@orf.at **Web:** oe1.orf.at
L.P: DG: Dr. Monika Lindner; Tech. Dir: Andreas Gall.
SW: [MOS] Moosbrunn (G.C. 48N00 016E28) 5 x 100, 2 x 300, 1 x 500kW
SAT: Astra 1H
kHz: *5945, 6155, 7325, 9870, 13675, 13730, 17855, 17870*

Winter Schedule 2004

German/Various	Days	Area	kHz
0000-0030	daily	CAm	7325mos
0030-0100	daily	NAm	7325mos
0400-0500	daily	ME	17870mos
0500-1830	daily	Eu	13730mos
0500-2310	daily	Eu	6155mos
1300-1400	daily	As,AUS	17855mos
1600-1700	daily	NAm	13675sac
1830-2310	daily	Eu	5945mos
2330-2400	daily	SAm	9870mos

V: QSL-card. Rec. acc.
NOTES: he German language transmissions are relays of the ORF Home Sce prgr "Österreich 1" and news magazines in English ("Report from Austria") and Spanish ("Noticiero de Austria") , details see e1.orf.at/service/international. ORF is also offering air time at its SW transmitter site in Moosbrunn for leasing to international broadcasters.

TRANS WORLD RADIO EUROPE (Rlg)

Postfach 141, A-1235 Wien, Austria.
☎ +43 1 863120. Fax +43 1 8631220.
Email: eurofreq@twr-europe.at **Web:** www.twr.org
kHz: *216, 864, 999, 1233, 1350, 1395, 1467, 1494, 1548, 5855, 5885, 6105, 6130, 6230, 6235, 6240, 7160, 7180, 7210, 7225, 7330, 7355, 7375, 7380, 9495, 9870, 9945, 9960, 11865*

Winter Schedule 2004

Arabic	Days	Area	kHz
0255-0300	daily	ME	1233cgr
0300-0315	.....ss	ME	1233cgr
0300-0330	mtwtf..	ME	1233cgr
0315-0330	.....s.	ME	1233cgr
2015-2030	....f..	Eu	1395fla
2025-2044	.t.....	ME	1233cgr
2025-2059	m.wtfss	ME	1233cgr
2044-2059	.t.....	ME	1233cgr
2059-2100	daily	ME	1233cgr
2100-2115	.t.....	ME	1233cgr
2100-2215	m.wtfss	ME	1233cgr
2100-2300	......s	NAf	1467rou
2115-2215	.t.....	ME	1233cgr
2130-2300	.....s.	NAf	1467rou
2200-2215	mtw....	NAf	1467rou
2200-2300	...tf..	NAf	1467rou
2215-2230	m......	NAf	1467rou
2215-2230	.tw....	NAf	1467rou
2230-2300	mtw....	NAf	1467rou
2300-2315	......s	NAf	1467rou
2300-2315	mtwtfs.	NAf	1467rou
2315-2330	m......	NAf	1467rou
Armenian	**Days**	**Area**	**kHz**
0400-0430	daily	WAs	864gav
1633-1648	.....ss	WAs	7375shi, 9945shi
1633-1703	mtwtf..	WAs	7375shi, 9945shi
Assyrian	**Days**	**Area**	**kHz**
0315-0330	......s	ME	1233cgr
Balkan	**Days**	**Area**	**kHz**
1830-1845	daily	Eu	1548gri
Bayash	**Days**	**Area**	**kHz**
2015-2030	...t...	Eu	1467rou
Belarusian	**Days**	**Area**	**kHz**
1457-1527	m......	Eu	7330shi, 9495mos
2030-2100	m......	Eu	999gri
Bosnian	**Days**	**Area**	**kHz**
1925-1940	.....ss	Eu	1395fla
2045-2115	.....ss	Eu	1395fla
Bulgarian	**Days**	**Area**	**kHz**
1800-1830	daily	Eu	1548gri
Croatian	**Days**	**Area**	**kHz**
2030-2045	daily	Eu	1395fla
2045-2115	mtwtf..	Eu	1395fla
Czech	**Days**	**Area**	**kHz**
1700-1715	mt.tf..	Eu	6240ekb, 7180ekb
2130-2200	daily	Eu	1395fla
English	**Days**	**Area**	**kHz**
0745-0920	......s	Eu	9870mco, 11865shi
0800-0920	mtwtf..	Eu	9870mco, 11865shi
0815-0850	.....s.	Eu	9870mco, 11865shi
1710-1725	daily	CAs	864gav, 5885gav
2315-2330	.....s.	Eu	1467rou
2315-2345	......s	Eu	1467rou
Estonian	**Days**	**Area**	**kHz**
2030-2100	.....ss	Eu	1494spb
Farsi	**Days**	**Area**	**kHz**
1725-1840	daily	ME	7355shi, 9960shi
1810-1840	mtwtfs.	ME	864gav
1840-1910	daily	ME	864gav
1910-1940	daily	ME	5855gav, 7375shi
2015-2030	.w.....	Eu	1395fla
French	**Days**	**Area**	**kHz**
0328-0358	......s	Eu	216rou
0341-0356	mtwtfs.	Eu	216rou
German	**Days**	**Area**	**kHz**
0445-0515	daily	Eu	1467rou
0930-0945	mtwtfs.	Eu	6230mco, 7160mco
0930-1015	......s	Eu	6230mco, 7160mco
1400-1430	......s	Eu	6230mco, 7160mco
1430-1500	daily	Eu	6230mco, 7160mco
2030-2100	.....ss	Eu	1467rou
2030-2130	mtwtf..	Eu	1467rou
Hebrew	**Days**	**Area**	**kHz**
2000-2100	daily	ME	1350gav

Hungarian	Days	Area	kHz
0930-0945	.twtfs.	Eu	6105jul, 7210jul
1630-1700	daily	Eu	6240ekb
1940-2015	daily	Eu	1395fla
Italian	**Days**	**Area**	**kHz**
1945-2015	mtwtf..	Eu	1467rou
Kabyle	**Days**	**Area**	**kHz**
2100-2130	.....s.	NAf	1467rou
2130-2200	mtwtf..	NAf	1467rou
Kalderash	**Days**	**Area**	**kHz**
1915-1945	mtwtf..	Eu	1548gri
Karakalpak	**Days**	**Area**	**kHz**
1740-1755	m......	CAs	864gav, 5885gav
Kazakh	**Days**	**Area**	**kHz**
1630-1645	mtwtf..	CAs	1467bis
1725-1740	mtwt...	CAs	864gav, 5885gav
Kyrgyz	**Days**	**Area**	**kHz**
1715-1730	mtwt...	CAs	1467bis
Lithuanian	**Days**	**Area**	**kHz**
2000-2030	.....ss	Eu	1494spb
Macedonian	**Days**	**Area**	**kHz**
1915-1945	......s	Eu	1548gri
Mandarin	**Days**	**Area**	**kHz**
2015-2030	..w....	Eu	1467rou
Norwegian	**Days**	**Area**	**kHz**
2030-2100	mtwtf..	Eu	1494spb
Polish	**Days**	**Area**	**kHz**
0615-0630	daily	Eu	6235shi, 7380shi
1545-1600	......s	Eu	6240ekb, 7380shi
1600-1630	daily	Eu	6240ekb, 7380shi
2015-2030	m......	Eu	1395fla
Qashqai	**Days**	**Area**	**kHz**
1840-1855	......s	ME	7355shi, 9960shi
Romanian	**Days**	**Area**	**kHz**
1700-1730	.....s.	Eu	6240ekb, 7180ekb
1845-1915	daily	Eu	1548gri
1915-1945	.....s.	Eu	1548gri
2015-2030	...t...	Eu	1467rou
Russian	**Days**	**Area**	**kHz**
1442-1457	m......	RUS	7330shi, 9495mos
1442-1527	.....ss	RUS	7330shi, 9495mos
1442-1557	.twtf.s	RUS	7330shi, 9495mos
1527-1557	m......	RUS	7330shi, 9495mos
1630-1715	.....ss	CAs	1467bis
1645-1715	mtwtf..	CAs	1467bis
1740-1810	mtwtf..	CAs	864gav, 5885gav
1810-1840	......s	WAs	864gav
1845-1900	.....ss	Eu	999gri
2000-2030	....f..	WAs	1350gav
2000-2030	mt....s	Eu	999gri
2015-2030	......s	Eu	1395fla
2015-2030	.....s.	Eu	999gri
2030-2100	.mtwtfs	Eu	999gri
Serbian	**Days**	**Area**	**kHz**
1910-1940	mtwtf..	Eu	1395fla
1945-2000	daily	Eu	1548gri
Slovak	**Days**	**Area**	**kHz**
0630-0645	mtwtf..	Eu	6130jul, 7380shi
1130-1200	.....s.	Eu	6130jul, 7225jul
2115-2130	daily	Eu	1395fla
Slovenian	**Days**	**Area**	**kHz**
2015-2030	......s	Eu	1467rou
Sorani	**Days**	**Area**	**kHz**
1910-1925	daily	ME	864gav
2015-2030	...t...	ME	1395fla
Sous	**Days**	**Area**	**kHz**
2015-2030	......s	NAf	1467rou
Spanish	**Days**	**Area**	**kHz**
2015-2030	....f..	Eu	1467rou
Swedish	**Days**	**Area**	**kHz**
2000-2030	mtwtf..	Eu	1494spb
Tamazight	**Days**	**Area**	**kHz**
2015-2030	m......	NAf	1467rou
Tarifit	**Days**	**Area**	**kHz**
2015-2030	.t.....	NAf	1467rou
Turkish	**Days**	**Area**	**kHz**
1930-2000	daily	TUR	1350gav
2015-2030	.t...s.	TUR	1395fla
Turkmen	**Days**	**Area**	**kHz**
1725-1740	....fss	CAs	864gav, 5885gav
1740-1755	.....s.	CAs	864gav, 5885gav
Ukrainian	**Days**	**Area**	**kHz**
1830-1845	.....ss	Eu	999gri
1830-1900	mtwtf..	Eu	999gri
2000-2015	.....s.	Eu	999gri
2000-2030	..wtf..	Eu	999gri
Uzbek	**Days**	**Area**	**kHz**
1730-1745	daily	CAs	1467bis
1755-1810	.....ss	CAs	864gav
Vlax	**Days**	**Area**	**kHz**
1915-1945	mtwtf..	Eu	1548gri

ANN: English: "This is Trans World Radio. The following programme is in the ... Language"
V: QSL-card.
NOTES: TWR branch; see USA for corporate headquarters. TWR Europe closed its office in Monaco at the end of 2004.
Broadcasters using sites in this country:
AWR uses: (MOS). See stn entry in: **USA**, INT Section
BBC World Sce uses: (MOS). See stn entry in: **G**, INT Section
FEBA Radio uses: (MOS). See stn entry in: **G**, INT Section
RCI uses: (MOS). See stn entry in: **CAN**, INT Section
VO Vietnam uses: (MOS). See stn entry in: **VTN**, INT Section
Wales R. Int'l uses: (MOS). See stn entry in: **G**, INT Section

AZERBAIJAN

VOICE OF AZERBAIJAN (Gov)

M. Hüseyn Street 1, AZ 1011 Baki, Azerbaijan.
☎ +994 12 4927851. Fax +994 12 4398505.
Email: root@aztv.baku.az **Web:** www.aztv.az
MW/SW: Leased from Teleradio IB
kHz: *1296, 6110*

Winter Schedule 2004

Arabic	Days	Area	kHz
1700-1800	daily	ME	1296pir, 6110gan
Azeri	**Days**	**Area**	**kHz**
0315-0400	daily	ME	1296pir, 6110gan
1400-1600	daily	ME	1296pir, 6110gan
English	**Days**	**Area**	**kHz**
1800-1830	daily	ME	1296pir, 6110gan
Farsi	**Days**	**Area**	**kHz**
1100-1200	daily	ME	1296pir, 6110gan
French	**Days**	**Area**	**kHz**
1330-1400	daily	ME	1296pir, 6110gan
German	**Days**	**Area**	**kHz**
1300-1330	daily	ME	1296pir, 6110gan
Russian	**Days**	**Area**	**kHz**
1830-1900	daily	ME	1296pir, 6110gan
Turkish	**Days**	**Area**	**kHz**
1200-1300	daily	ME	1296pir, 6110gan

ANN: Azeri: "Danisir Baki"; Arabic: "Huna Baku, idha'at jumhuryat Azerbaijan"; English: "This is the Voice of Azerbaijan"
V: QSL-card.
NOTES: The Voice of Azerbaijan is the External Sce of the State Radio-TV Company of Azerbaijan. The frequencies are currently drifting around 6111 and 1295kHz.

TELERADIO IB (Tx Operator)

A. Abaszadä küç. 2, AZ 1073 Baki, Azerbaijan.
☎ +994 12 4988066. Fax +994 12 4983325.
Email: teleradio@bakinter.net **Web:** teleradio.rabita.az
L.P: Dir: Räcäb Abdurahmanov.
MW: [BAK] Baki (G.C. 40N22 049E53) 801kHz 15kW; [PIR] Pirsaat (G.C. 39N55 049E25) 1296kHz 125kW
SW: [GAN] Gäncä (G.C. 40N37 046E20) 2 x 100, 1 x 170kW
NOTES: Teleradio IB, a subsidiary of the Azerbaijani Ministry for Telecommunications and Information Technology, is the owner of the transmitter facilities in Azerbaijan.
Broadcasters using sites in this country:
BBC World Sce uses: (BAK). See stn entry in: **G**, INT Section

BANGLADESH

BANGLADESH BETAR (Pub)

External Services, P.O. Box 2204, Dhaka 1000, Bangladesh.
☎ +880 2 505113. Fax +880 2 8612021.
Email: ts-betar@bdonline.com **Web:** www.moi-gob.org/bater.htm
L.P: Deputy DG & Dir External Sce: A. S. M. S. Apel Mahmood.
SW: [DKA] Dhaka, Khabirpur (G.C. 23N43 090E26) 2 x 250kW
kHz: *7185, 9550*

Winter Schedule 2004

	Days	Area	kHz
Arabic	**Days**	**Area**	**kHz**
1600-1630	daily	ME	7185dka
Bangla	**Days**	**Area**	**kHz**
1630-1730	daily	ME	7185dka
1915-2000	daily	Eu	7185dka
English	**Days**	**Area**	**kHz**
1230-1300	daily	SAs,SEA	7185dka, 9550dka*
1815-1900	daily	Eu	7185dka, 9550dka*
English (VO Islam)	**Days**	**Area**	**kHz**
1745-1815	daily	Eu	7185dka, 9550dka*
Hindi	**Days**	**Area**	**kHz**
1515-1545	daily	IND	7185dka, 9550dka*
Nepali	**Days**	**Area**	**kHz**
1315-1345	daily	NPL	7185dka, 9550dka*
Urdu	**Days**	**Area**	**kHz**
1400-1430	daily	PAK	7185dka, 9550dka*

ANN: English: "This is the External Service of Bangladesh Betar"
IS: Local composition of violin and tanpura
V: QSL-card. Rpt to Senior Engineer (Research Wing). Email rpt to rrc@aitlbd.net
NOTES: Key: * May be inactive.

BELARUS

BELARUSKAJE RADYJO (Gov)

See National Radio Section.
kHz: *1170, 7170, 7255, 11960*

Winter Schedule 2004

	Days	Area	kHz
Belarusian	**Days**	**Area**	**kHz**
0500-0700	daily	RUS	1170sas, 7170mns
1000-1100	daily	RUS	1170sas, 11960mns
1600-1800	daily	RUS	1170sas*, 7255mns*

V: QSL-card.
NOTES: SW frequencies for domestic coverage: see National Radio section. Key: * incl. prgr's from regional studios.

RADIO BELARUS (Gov)

Cyrvonaja Street 4, 220807 Minsk, Belarus.
☎ +375 17 2395830. Fax +375 17 2848574.
Email: radio-minsk@tvr.by **Web:** www.tvr.by
L.P: Dir: Navum Halpiarovic; Head English Dept: Vjacaslaú Lakcjušyn; Head German Dept: Alena Charaševic.
MW/SW: Leased from Belaruskaje Radyjotelevizijny Peredajucy Centr
kHz: *5970, 7105, 7210, 7340*

Winter Schedule 2004

	Days	Area	kHz
Belarusian	**Days**	**Area**	**kHz**
0100-0130	daily	Eu	5970mns, 7210mns
0130-0200	mtwtfs.	Eu	5970mns, 7210mns
0230-0300	mtwtfs.	Eu	5970mns, 7210mns
1900-1930	daily	Eu	7105mns, 7340mns
2030-2100	daily	Eu	7105mns, 7340mns
2100-2130	mtwtfs.	Eu	7105mns, 7340mns
2130-2200	daily	Eu	7105mns, 7340mns
English	**Days**	**Area**	**kHz**
0200-0230	mtw.s.	Eu	5970mns, 7210mns
0230-0300	......s	Eu	5970mns, 7210mns
1930-2000	mt.tf..	Eu	7105mns, 7340mns
2100-2130	......s	Eu	7105mns, 7340mns
German	**Days**	**Area**	**kHz**
0200-0230	...t..s	Eu	5970mns, 7210mns
1930-2000	..w..ss	Eu	7105mns, 7340mns
Russian	**Days**	**Area**	**kHz**
0130-0200	......s	Eu	5970mns, 7210mns
2000-2030	daily	Eu	7105mns, 7340mns

ANN: Belarusian: "Havoryc Radyjostancyja Belarus"; English: "This is Radio Belarus"; German: "Hier ist die Radiostation Belarus"
V: QSL-card.
NOTES: Radio Belarus is the External Sce of the National State Radio-TV Company of Belarus.

BELARUSKAJE RADYJOTELEVIZIJNY PEREDAJUCY CENTR (Tx Operator)

vul. Engelsa 22, 220030 Minsk, Belarus.
☎ +375 17 2270845. Fax +375 17 2271084.
L.P: Dir: H.S.Rossa
MW: [SAS] Sasnovy (G.C. 53N24 028E32) 1170kHz 700kW
SW: [MNS] Minsk, Kalodziscy (G.C. 53N58 027E47) 1 x 75, 1 x 150, 1 x 250kW
NOTES: Belaruskaje Radyjotelevizijny Peredajucy Centr, a subsidiary of the Ministry of Post & Telecommunications, is the national transmitter network operator. It leases tx's to domestic and foreign customers.
Broadcasters using sites in this country:
VO Russia (VOR) uses: (SAS). See stn entry in: **RUS**, INT Section
VOR-RKS uses: (SAS). See stn entry in: **RUS**, INT Section
VOR-RMR uses: (SAS). See stn entry in: **RUS**, INT Section

BELGIUM

RADIO VLAANDEREN INTERNATIONAAL (RVI) (Pub)

P.O. Box 26, B-1043 Brussels, Belgium.
☎ +32 2 7413807. Fax +32 2 7416295.
Email: info@rvi.be **Web:** www.rvi.be
L.P: SM: Wim Jansen; Freq Mgr: Hector De Cuyper.
MW: [WOL] Wolvertem (G.C. 50N57 004E18) 1512kHz 300kW
SAT: Astra 1H, Hotbird 3
kHz: *1512, 5910, 5960, 5965, 5985, 7490, 9590, 9925, 9945, 11730, 13690, 13790, 13800, 15195, 15230, 15530, 17690, 17745*

Winter Schedule 2004

	Days	Area	kHz
Dutch	**Days**	**Area**	**kHz**
0530-0600	daily	Am	9590bon
0600-0630	daily	CAf	15530mey
0600-0630	daily	Eu	9925msk
0600-0630	daily	SEu	5965jul
0630-0700	daily	Eu	9925msk
0630-0700	daily	SEu	5965jul
0700-0800	daily	Eu	1512wol, 15195arm
0700-0800	daily	SEu	5965jul
0800-0900	daily	Eu	15195arm
0800-0900	daily	SEu	9590skn
1130-1200	......s	Eu	1512wol
1130-1200	......s	CAf	17745mey
1200-1230	daily	As,AUS	9945irk, 17690tac
1200-1230	daily	CAf	17745mey
1200-1230	daily	Eu	1512wol, 15195msk
1200-1230	daily	SEu	13690rmp
1400-1700	......s	SEu	13690skn
1400-1700	......s	Eu	13800msk
1800-1900	daily	SEu	15230sac
1900-2000	daily	CAf,SAf	13790dha
1900-2000	daily	Eu	1512wol, 7490arm
1900-2000	daily	Eu,ME	5910jul
1900-2000	daily	SEu	15230sac
1900-2100	......s	Eu	5985jul
2100-2200	daily	Eu	1512wol, 7490arm
2100-2200	daily	SEu	5960skn
2230-2300	daily	Am	11730bon
English	**Days**	**Area**	**kHz**
0500-0530	daily	Am	9590bon
0800-0830	daily	Eu	1512wol, 5965jul
1130-1200	daily	As,AUS	9945irk
1830-1900	daily	Eu,ME	5910jul
2030-2100	daily	Eu	1512wol, 7490arm
2200-2230	daily	Am	11730bon
French	**Days**	**Area**	**kHz**
1800-1815	daily	Eu	1512wol, 7490arm
2015-2030	daily	Eu	1512wol, 7490arm
German	**Days**	**Area**	**kHz**
1815-1830	daily	Eu	1512wol, 1512wol, 7490arm, 7490arm
2000-2015	daily	Eu	1512wol, 7490arm

ANN: Dutch: "Dit is Radio Vlaanderen Internationaal"; English: "Brussels Calling"; French: "Ici Bruxelles"; German: "Hier ist Brüssel"

IS: Starting: "Tussen Maas en Schelde"
V: QSL-card.
NOTES: RVI is the External Sce of the public broadcaster Vlaamse Radio en Televisie (VRT). Prgr's in English, French and German are no longer carried on SW after the end of the winter season from March 2005.

RTBF INTERNATIONAL (Pub)

Bureau 3C23, 52 Bd Reyers, B-1044 Bruxelles, Belgium.
☎ +32 2 7374014. Fax +32 2 7373032.
Email: rtbfi@rtbf.be **Web:** www.rtbf.be
L.P: Dir: Gerard Delacroix.
SW: [WAV] Wavre (G.C. 50N44 004E34) 1 x 100, 2 x 250kW
kHz: *9970, 15570, 17570, 17580, 21565*

Winter Schedule 2004

French	Days	Area	kHz
0555-0815	mtwtf..	CAf	17580jul
0555-1100	.....ss	CAf	17580jul
0600-2200	daily	SEu	9970wav
1055-1230	daily	CAf	21565jul
1455-1805	.....ss	CAf	17570jul
1525-1805	mtwtf..	CAf	15570jul
1805-2200	daily	CAf	9970wav

V: QSL-card.
NOTES: Transmissions are relays of RTBF Home Sce prgr's.

MAEVA FM INTERNATIONAL (Comm)

P.O. Box 550, B-1000 Brussels, Belgium.
☎ +32 9 2270487.
Email: maevaradio@hotmail.com **Web:** www.maevafm.com
L.P: Head: Eric Hofman.
kHz: *6015*

Winter Schedule 2004

Dutch	Days	Area	kHz
1300-1500	.....s.	Eu	6015jul

NOTES: Maeva FM is a domestic commercial broadcaster.

TDP (Broker)

c/o Ludo Maes, P.O. Box 1, B-2310 Rijkevorsel, Belgium.
☎ +32 33 147800. Fax +32 33 141212.
Email: info@transmitter.org **Web:** www.airtime.be
L.P: Owner: Ludo Maes.
V: QSL-card (for brokered transmissions). Rp.
NOTES: TDP Radio is brokering air time for prgr's with political or religious background. Details and schedule can be found at: www.airtime.be/schedule.html.

RADIO TRAUMLAND

Based in Belgium
kHz: *5925*

Winter Schedule 2004

German	Days	Area	kHz
1400-1515	....f..	Eu	5925jul**
1400-1515	......s	Eu	5925jul
1515-1600	......s	Eu	5925jul*

NOTES: Key: * 5 Dec 2004 only; ** 24 Dec 2004 only.

TDPRADIO

P.O. Box 1, B-2310 Rijkevorsel, Belgium.
☎ +32 33 147800. Fax +32 33 141212.
Email: daniel@tdpradio.com **Web:** www.tdpradio.com
L.P: Prgr Mgr: Daniël Versmissen; Technical Mgr: Ludo Maes.
kHz: *6015, 7240, 7375, 7590, 11900*

Winter Schedule 2004

English	Days	Area	kHz
1100-1200	.....s.	Eu	7240fle+
1200-1300	.....s.	Eu	6015jul
1500-1600	.....s.	Eu	6015jul+
1600-1700	.....s.	NAm	11900sac+
2000-2100	.....s.	Eu	7375tld+, 7590arm
Music	**Days**	**Area**	**kHz**
1100-1200	.....s.	Eu	7240fle+

V: QSL-card.
NOTES: TDPradio broadcasts dance music mixes of Belgian Club DJs. Key: + DRM.

Broadcasters using sites in this country:
Deutsche Welle uses: (WOL). See stn entry in: **D**, INT Section
RNWO uses: (WOL). See stn entry in: **HOL**, INT Section

BOSNIA & HERZEGOVINA

INTERNATIONAL RADIO OF SERBIA & MONTENEGRO RELAY STATION

KTCB, 76300 Bijeljina, Bosnia & Herzegovina.
SW: [BIJ] Bijeljina (G.C. 44N42 10E10) 2 x 500kW
NOTES: The transmitting station is owned and operated by the Int'l Radio of Serbia & Montenegro, see Serbia & Montenegro.
Broadcasters using sites in this country:
Int'l R.SerbMon uses: (BIJ). See stn entry in: **SCG**, INT Section

BOTSWANA

IBB RELAY STATION BOTSWANA

IBB Transmitting Station, Private Bag 38, Selebi-Phikwe, Botswana.
Email: rnelson@bot.ibb.gov
L.P: SM: Rodney Nelson.
MW: [SEL] Selebi-Phikwe (G.C. 22S01 027E50) 909kHz 600kW
SW: [BOT] Moepeng Hill (G.C. 21S57 027E39) 4 x 100kW
Broadcasters using sites in this country:
BBG-Studio 7 uses: (BOT). See stn entry in: **USA**, INT Section
BBG-VOA uses: (BOT). See stn entry in: **USA**, INT Section

BRAZIL

RADIOBRÁS (Gov)

C.P. 259, Brasília, DF, CEP 70359-970, Brasil.
☎ +55 61 3274124 Fax + 55 61 3271377
Email: radionacionaldobrasil@radiobras.gov.br **Web:** www.radiobras.gov.br
L.P: Pres: Eugênio Bucci, Head of Radio Dept: Marcia Detoni.
SW: [BRA] Brasília (G.C. 15S51 047W56) 7 x 250kW
kHz: *9665*

Winter Schedule 2004

Portuguese	Days	Area	kHz
0500-0700	daily	SAm,Af	9665bra
1900-2100	daily	SAm,Af	9665bra

V: QSL-card.
Broadcasters using sites in this country:
China R. Int'l uses: (BRA). See stn entry in: **CHN**, INT Section

BULGARIA

RADIO BULGARIA (Pub)

P.O. Box 900, 1000 Sofia, Bulgaria.
☎ +359 2 9336733. Fax +359 2 650560.
Email: radiobulgaria@bnr.bg **Web:** www.bnr.bg
Studios: 4, Dragan Tsankov Blvd., 1040 Sofia, Bulgaria.
L.P: PD: Angel Nedialkov; Freq Mgr: Ivo Ivanov.
MW/SW: Leased from Bulgarian Telecommunications Comp.
kHz: *747, 1224, 5800, 5900, 6000, 7200, 7400, 7500, 9400, 9500, 9600, 9700, 11500, 11600, 11700, 11900, 13600, 13800, 15700, 17500*

Winter Schedule 2004

Albanian	Days	Area	kHz
0630-0700	mtwtf..	EEu	1224vdn, 5900pld
0700-0800	.....ss	EEu	1224vdn, 5900pld
1200-1230	daily	EEu	7200pld
1700-1730	daily	EEu	1224vdn, 5900pld
2000-2100	daily	EEu	747pet, 1224vdn, 5900pld
Bulgarian	**Days**	**Area**	**kHz**
0100-0200	daily	NAm	7400pld, 9700pld
0100-0200	daily	SAm	7500pld, 11500pld
0500-0600	.....ss	EEu	1224vdn, 5800sof, 5900pld, 7500sof
0500-0600	.....ss	WEu	9500pld, 11500pld
0530-0600	mtwtf..	WEu	9500pld, 11500pld
0530-0600	mtwtf..	EEu	1224vdn, 5800sof, 5900pld, 7500sof
1100-1130	daily	EEu	7200pld, 11600sof, 13600sof
1100-1130	daily	WEu	11700pld, 15700pld
1300-1500	daily	EEu	1224vdn
1300-1500	daily	WEu	11700pld, 15700pld
1600-1700	daily	EEu	1224vdn, 5800sof, 5900pld, 7500sof

Bulgarian	Days	Area	kHz
1600-1700	daily	SAf	17500pld
1600-1700	daily	ME	9400pld
1900-2000	daily	EEu	747pet, 1224vdn, 5900pld
1900-2100	daily	ME	7400pld
1900-2100	daily	WEu	7200pld
English	**Days**	**Area**	**kHz**
0000-0100	daily	NAm	7400pld, 9700pld
0300-0400	daily	NAm	7400pld, 9700pld
0730-0800	daily	WEu	11600pld, 13600pld
1230-1300	daily	WEu	11700pld, 15700pld
1830-1900	daily	WEu	5800pld, 7500pld
2200-2300	daily	WEu	5800pld, 7500pld
French	**Days**	**Area**	**kHz**
0200-0300	daily	NAm	7400pld, 9700pld
0700-0730	daily	WEu	11600pld, 13600pld
1200-1230	daily	WEu	11700pld, 15700pld
1800-1830	daily	WEu	5800pld, 7500pld
2100-2200	daily	WEu	5800pld, 7500pld
German	**Days**	**Area**	**kHz**
0600-0630	daily	WEu	9500pld, 11500pld
1130-1200	daily	WEu	11700pld, 15700pld
1730-1800	daily	WEu	5800pld, 7500pld
2000-2100	daily	WEu	5800pld, 7500pld
Greek	**Days**	**Area**	**kHz**
0600-0630	mtwtf..	EEu	1224vdn, 5900pld
0600-0700	…..ss	EEu	1224vdn, 5900pld
1130-1200	daily	EEu	7200pld
1730-1800	daily	EEu	747pet, 1224vdn, 5900pld
2100-2200	daily	EEu	747pet, 1224vdn, 5900pld
Russian	**Days**	**Area**	**kHz**
0000-0100	daily	CAs	9400pld
0400-0500	daily	EEu	1224vdn, 5800sof, 7500sof
0600-0630	daily	EEu	5800sof, 7500sof
1130-1200	daily	EEu	11600sof, 13600sof
1500-1600	daily	CAs	9400pld
1500-1600	daily	EEu	1224vdn, 5800sof, 7500sof
1700-1730	daily	EEu	5800sof, 7500sof
1900-2000	daily	EEu	5800sof, 7500sof
Serbian	**Days**	**Area**	**kHz**
0700-0730	mtwtf..	EEu	1224vdn, 5900pld
0800-0900	…..ss	EEu	1224vdn, 5900pld
1230-1300	daily	EEu	7200pld
1800-1830	daily	EEu	747pet, 1224vdn, 5900pld
2200-2300	daily	EEu	747pet, 1224vdn, 5900pld
Spanish	**Days**	**Area**	**kHz**
0000-0100	daily	SAm	7500pld, 11500pld
0200-0300	daily	CAm	9400pld
0200-0300	daily	SAm	7500pld, 11500pld
0700-0730	daily	SEu	11900pld, 13800pld
1200-1230	daily	SEu	11600pld, 13600pld
1730-1800	daily	SEu	9600pld, 11600pld
2200-2300	daily	SEu	7400pld, 9400pld
Turkish	**Days**	**Area**	**kHz**
0600-0630	daily	ME	6000pld, 7400pld
1100-1130	daily	ME	6000pld, 7400pld
1830-1900	daily	ME	747pet, 1224vdn, 7400pld

ANN: Bulgarian: "Tuk e Radio Bâlgarija"; English: "This is Radio Bulgaria"; French: "Ici Radio Bulgarie"; German: "Hier spricht Radio Bulgarien"; Albanian: "Ju flet Radio Bulgaria"; Greek: "Akute to Radio Vulgaria"; Russian: "V efire Radio Bolgariya"; Serbian: "Govorit Radio Bugarska"; Spanish: "Ésta es Radio Bulgaria"; Turkish: "Burasi Bulgaristan Radyosu"

IS: Starting: The first music phrase from "Bulgarian Suite" for orchestra by Pancho Vladigerov

V: QSL-card. Rp (1 IRC). Rec acc.

NOTES: Radio Bulgaria is the External Sce of the public-service Bulgarian National Radio (Bâlgarsko Nacionalno Radio).

BULGARIAN TELECOMMUNICATIONS COMPANY (Tx Operator)

✉ Totleben blvd. 8, 1606 Sofia, Bulgaria.
☎ +359 2 9320844. 🖷 +359 2 9515550.
Email: central.office@btc.bg **Web:** www.btc.bg

MW: [PET] Petrich (G.C. 41N42 023E18) 747kHz 500kW; [VDN] Vidin (G.C. 43N39 022E40) 1224kHz 500kW

SW: [PLD] Plovdiv, Padarsko (G.C. 42N04 024E41) 3 x 250, 2 x 500kW; [SOF] Sofia, Kostinbrod (G.C. 42N40 023E20) 1 x 15, 4 x 50, 3 x 100, 1 x 250kW

NOTES: The Bulgarian Telecommunications Company is the national transmitter network operator in Bulgaria. It leases out its tx's to national and international customers.

Broadcasters using sites in this country:
VO Iran. Nation uses: (SOF). See stn entry in: **IRN**, CTB Section
Voice Africa uses: (SOF). See stn entry in: **G**, INT Section

CANADA

RADIO CANADA INTERNATIONAL (Pub)

✉ P.O. Box 6000, Montreal, Quebec, H3C 3A8, Canada.
☎ +1 514 5977500. 🖷 +1 514 5977760.
Email: info@rcinet.ca **Web:** www.rcinet.ca

L.P: Mgr: Jean Larin; French and English Prgr's: Elzbieta Olechowska; Foreign language Prgr's: Roger Tetrault; Engineering: Jaques Bouliane; Audience Relations: Bill Westenhaver; Schedules: Steve Lemay.

SW: [SAC] Sackville, NB (G.C. 45N53 064W19) 3 x 100, 6 x 250kW (also leased to foreign customers).

SAT: Asiasat 2, Hotbird 6, IntelSat 707, Telstar 12

kHz: *1233, 5840, 5850, 5985, 5995, 6025, 6160, 6190, 7195, 7235, 7265, 7370, 9515, 9525, 9535, 9555, 9565, 9615, 9635, 9665, 9670, 9710, 9730, 9755, 9760, 9770, 9790, 9800, 9810, 9815, 9880, 11725, 11730, 11835, 11845, 11865, 11875, 11905, 11935, 11975, 12015, 12045, 13650, 13655, 13730, 15140, 15180, 15245, 15305, 17735, 17765, 17820, 17835*

Winter Schedule 2004

Arabic	Days	Area	kHz
0330-0400	daily	ME	5840hor, 6025wer, 9615wer
0430-0500	daily	ME	7265skn, 9760wer
2015-2045	daily	ME,NAf	5995skn, 9615skn, 12015sac
2215-2245	daily	ME	1233rou
English	**Days**	**Area**	**kHz**
0000-0100	daily	As,CHN	9880xia
0100-0300	daily	NAm,Car,SAm	6190sac, 9755sac, 9810sac
1200-1300	daily	As,CHN	9670yam, 11730yam
1300-1330	daily	As,CHN	9670yam, 11730yam
1300-1600	daily	NAm,Car	9515sac, 13655sac, 17820sac
1400-1430	daily	WEu	9815fle+
1400-1700	daily	NAm,Car	9515sac, 13655sac, 17820sac
1500-1600	daily	IND	5985kim, 9635xia, 11975xia
1800-1900	daily	NAf	5850hor, 7370kas, 9770kas, 11875wer, 15140sac
2000-2300	daily	NAm,Car	15180sac
2100-2200	daily	Eu	5850hor, 9770sac
2200-2300	daily	NAm	9800sac+
2230-2300	daily	CHN	6160kim, 7195kim, 9730yam
French	**Days**	**Area**	**kHz**
1100-1300	daily	NAm,Car	9515sac
1100-1400	daily	NAm,Car	9515sac
1430-1500	daily	As,CHN	5985yam, 9535yam
1600-2000	daily	NAm,Car	17835sac
1700-2000	daily	NAm,Car	17835sac
1900-2000	daily	NAf	11845wer, 13650sac, 15140dha, 17735sac
2000-2100	daily	Eu	5850hor, 7235skn, 9710sac, 11725sac
2100-2200	daily	NAf	7235skn, 9565skn, 11845sac
2200-2300	daily	NAf	9665mos, 11835asc
2300-2400	daily	NAm,Car	15180sac

Mandarin	Days	Area	kHz
0000-0030	daily	As,CHN	9565kim
2200-2230	daily	CHN	6160kim, 7195kim, 9730yam
2300-2330	daily	CHN	6160kim, 7195yam, 9525kim, 12045yam
Portuguese	**Days**	**Area**	**kHz**
2000-2030	daily	B	15305sac, 17765sac
2100-2130	daily	B	15305sac, 17765sac
2230-2300	daily	B	11905sac, 15245sac
2330-2400	daily	B	11905sac, 13730sac
Russian	**Days**	**Area**	**kHz**
1600-1630	daily	RUS	5840hor, 9555wer, 11935wer, 13650rmp
1700-1730	daily	RUS	9555skn**, 11935skn**
Spanish	**Days**	**Area**	**kHz**
0000-0030	daily	Car,SAm	9755sac, 11865sac
0030-0100	daily	Car,SAm	9755sac, 11865sac
0100-0130	daily	MEX,CUB	9790sac
0300-0330	daily	Car,SAm	6190sac, 9755sac, 9810sac
2300-2330	daily	SAm	11905sac, 13730sac
Ukrainian	**Days**	**Area**	**kHz**
1630-1700	daily	UKR	9555skn*, 11935skn*

ANN: English: "This is Radio Canada International"; French: "Ici Radio Canada Internationale"
IS: First bar of Canadian National Anthem
V: QSL-card.
NOTES: Radio Canada International is the External Sce of the public service Canadian Broadcasting Corporation (CBC). Relayed via Voice of Lebanon, 2015-2045 daily in Arabic on 93.3, 93.4 and 93.6MHz FM to Beirut and Bekaa areas of Lebanon. Key: * until 30 Nov 2004. ** from 1 Dec 2004 + DRM
Broadcasters using sites in this country:
BBC World Sce uses: (SAC). See stn entry in: **G**, INT Section
China R. Int'l uses: (SAC). See stn entry in: **CHN**, INT Section
Deutsche Welle uses: (SAC). See stn entry in: **D**, INT Section
HCJB uses: (SAC). See stn entry in: **EQA**, INT Section
Hmong Lao Radio uses: (SAC). See stn entry in: **LAO**, CTB Section
R.Japan uses: (SAC). See stn entry in: **J**, INT Section
R.Korea Int'l uses: (SAC). See stn entry in: **KOR**, INT Section
R.Österreich 1 uses: (SAC). See stn entry in: **AUT**, INT Section
R.Sweden uses: (SAC). See stn entry in: **S**, INT Section
RNWO uses: (SAC). See stn entry in: **HOL**, INT Section
RVI uses: (SAC). See stn entry in: **BEL**, INT Section
TDPradio uses: (SAC). See stn entry in: **BEL**, INT Section
VO the NASB uses: (SAC). See stn entry in: **USA**, INT Section
VO Vietnam uses: (SAC). See stn entry in: **VTN**, INT Section

CHILE

VOZ CRISTIANA – VOZ CRISTA (Rlg)

✉ Castilla 490-3, Santiago 3, Chile.
☎ +56 2 8557046. Fax +56 2 8557053.
Email: comentarios@vozcristiana.com
Web: www.vozcristiana.com (Spanish); www.vozcrista.com (Portuguese)
✉ Studios: P.O. Box 2889, Miami, FL 33144, USA.
L.P: Reg Dir Americas: Juan Mark Gallardo; General Op's Dir (Chile): Samuel Svensson.
SW: [SGO] Santiago de Chile (G.C. 33S27 070W41) 8 x 100kW
kHz: *6070, 9635, 9780, 11745, 11890, 15375, 15475, 15585, 17660, 17680*

Winter Schedule 2004

Portuguese	Days	Area	kHz
0400-1100	daily	B	11890sgo
1100-2300	daily	B	17660sgo
2100-0100	daily	B	15475sgo
2300-0400	daily	B	11745sgo
Spanish	**Days**	**Area**	**kHz**
0000-0600	daily	SAm	15375sgo
0000-1200	daily	SAm	6070sgo
0100-0400	daily	CAm	15585sgo
0600-1200	daily	SAm	9780sgo
1200-2400	daily	SAm	9635sgo
1200-2400	daily	CAm	17680sgo

ANN: Spanish: "Radio Voz Cristiana"; Portuguese: "Radio Voz Cristã"
V: QSL-card.
NOTES: A branch of Christian Vision, established 1998; see United Kingdom for corporate details.
Broadcasters using sites in this country:
China R. Int'l uses: (SGO). See stn entry in: **CHN**, INT Section

CHINA (People's Rep. of)

CHINA RADIO INTERNATIONAL (Gov)

✉ P.O. Box 4216, Beijing 100040, China.
☎ +86 10 68891676. Fax +86 10 68891582.
Email: crieng@cri.com.cn **Web:** www.cri.com.cn
L.P: GD: Zhang Zhenhua; CE: Yu Jikai; Dir English Sce: Xia Jixuan.
MW: [BEI] Beijing (G.C. 39N57 116E27) 1251kHz; [CAH] Changchun (G.C. 43N48 125E23) 1017/1323kHz 100kW; [DOF] Dongfang (G.C. 18N54 108E39) 603/684kHz; [GDG] Guangdong Province (*) 1341kHz; [HEI] Heilongjiang Province (*) 1116kHz; [JIA] Jiangsu Province (*) 1044kHz; [KAS] Kashi (G.C. 39N20 075E46) 1197/1422/1539kHz 600kW; [KUN] Kunming (G.C. 25N10 102E50) 1080kHz 200kW, 1296kHz 300kW; [LHA] Lhasa (G.C. 29N30 090E59) 1323kHz; [NEI] Nei Menggu Autonomous Region (*) 1314kHz; [URU] Ürümqi (Wurumchi) (G.C. 43N35 087E30) 1521kHz 500kW; [YUN] Yunnan Province (*) 1188/1206/1269kHz; Unknown site (*) 963kHz. (*) Exact location not known.
SW: [BEI] Beijing (G.C. 39N57 116E27) 14 x 100, 2 x 350kW; [DOF] Dongfang (G.C. 18N54 108E39) 1 x 100, 6 x 150kW; [GEM] Golmud [Ge'ermu] (G.C. 36N24 094E59) 4 x 100kW; [HUH] Hohhot (G.C. 41N12 111E30) 6 x 50, 4 x 100kW; [JIN] Jinhua (G.C. 28N07 119E39] 2 x 100, 3 x 500kW; [KAS] Kashi (G.C. 39N20 075E46) 2 x 100, 8 x 500kW; [KUN] Kunming (G.C. 25N10 102E50) 2 x 100, 2 x 500kW; [LHA] Lhasa (G.C. 29N30 090E59) 13 x 100kW; [LIN] Lingshi (G.C. 36N52 111E40) 6 x 100kW; [NNN] Nanning (G.C. 22N47 108E11) 2 x 100kW; [SZG] Shijiazhuang (G.C. 38N04 114E28) 6 x 100, 2 x 500kW; [URU] Ürümqi [Wurumchi] (G.C. 43N35 087E30) 9 x 100, 8 x 500kW; [XIA] Xi'an, two sites: Xi'an (G.C. 34N12 108E54) 6 x 100, 2 x 120, 2 x 150kW, Baoji (G.C. 34N30 107E10) 6 x 100kW
kHz: *558, 603, 684, 963, 1017, 1044, 1080, 1116, 1170, 1188, 1215, 1269, 1296, 1323, 1341, 1386, 1422, 1440, 1458, 1467, 1521, 1548, 1557, 5905, 5915, 5955, 5960, 5965, 5975, 5990, 6005, 6010, 6020, 6040, 6075, 6100, 6105, 6115, 6140, 6145, 6150, 6165, 6175, 6180, 6190, 7105, 7110, 7120, 7130, 7140, 7150, 7160, 7170, 7180, 7190, 7200, 7215, 7220, 7225, 7235, 7240, 7245, 7255, 7260, 7265, 7290, 7295, 7305, 7315, 7325, 7335, 7340, 7345, 7350, 7360, 7405, 9365, 9435, 9440, 9460, 9490, 9510, 9525, 9535, 9550, 9560, 9570, 9580, 9585, 9590, 9600, 9610, 9615, 9620, 9635, 9640, 9645, 9655, 9665, 9670, 9675, 9685, 9690, 9695, 9700, 9720, 9725, 9730, 9745, 9755, 9765, 9770, 9785, 9790, 9795, 9855, 9860, 9865, 9870, 9880, 9885, 11600, 11640, 11650, 11660, 11675, 11680, 11685, 11700, 11730, 11760, 11770, 11775, 11780, 11800, 11825, 11850, 11860, 11870, 11875, 11880, 11885, 11900, 11940, 11945, 11955, 11970, 11975, 11980, 11990, 12000, 12110, 13600, 13610, 13620, 13630, 13640, 13650, 13670, 13675, 13685, 13700, 13715, 13720, 13790, 15100, 15110, 15120, 15125, 15135, 15140, 15145, 15160, 15165, 15180, 15210, 15230, 15245, 15250, 15260, 15320, 15340, 15350, 15400, 15415, 15435, 15440, 15465, 15505, 15600, 15670, 17490, 17540, 17625, 17630, 17650, 17670, 17680, 17690, 17710, 17720, 17730, 17735, 17740, 17755, 17785, 17880, 17890*

Winter Schedule 2004

Albanian	Days	Area	kHz
1600-1700	daily	Eu	1215fla
1800-1900	daily	Eu	1215fla
1900-1930	daily	Eu	7265uru
1900-2000	daily	Eu	7130kas
1930-2000	daily	Eu	6020szg
2100-2130	daily	Eu	6145iss
Amoy	**Days**	**Area**	**kHz**
0100-0200	daily	FE	6140kun, 7180xia, 15100xia, 17680bei
0100-0200	daily	SEA	9460kun, 9550kun, 9695kas, 11945kun
1400-1500	daily	SEA	11650xia, 15340xia
Arabic	**Days**	**Area**	**kHz**
1600-1700	daily	NAf,ME	9610kas
1600-1700	daily	NAf	7245kun, 17880bko
1600-1700	daily	CAf,EAf	15125bko
1600-1700	daily	ME	7130spb, 7160kas
1830-1930	daily	CAf	11640bko

Arabic	Days	Area	kHz
1830-1930	daily	ME	6175kas
1830-1930	daily	ME,EAf	7200krv
1830-1930	daily	NAf	13685bko
1830-1930	daily	NAf,ME	7315kun
2100-2200	daily	NAf	9725uru
2100-2200	daily	NAf,ME	7260kun, 9695kas

Bangla	Days	Area	kHz
0200-0300	daily	SAs	9655kun, 11640kun
1300-1400	daily	SAs	9600xia, 9610kun, 11640kun

Bulgarian	Days	Area	kHz
1700-1800	daily	Eu	1458fla
1830-1900	daily	Eu	6020szg, 7265kas, 9860jin
2030-2100	daily	Eu	6145iss, 7160xia

Burmese	Days	Area	kHz
1130-1200	daily	SEA	1269yun, 9880kun, 11780xia
1300-1400	daily	SEA	1188yun, 9880kun, 11780xia

Cambodian	Days	Area	kHz
0000-0100	daily	SEA	684dof, 9765kas
1030-1130	daily	SEA	684dof, 15160xia, 17680kun
1200-1300	daily	SEA	9440kun, 17680xia
1400-1500	daily	SEA	15180xia, 17710xia
2300-2400	daily	SEA	684dof, 9765kas

Cantonese	Days	Area	kHz
0400-0500	daily	NAm	9790hab
1000-1100	daily	AUS,NZL	15440kun, 17755xia
1000-1100	daily	Eu	17670kas
1100-1200	daily	SEA	9590kun, 15340xia, 17785xia
1700-1800	daily	FE	7220jin, 9770uru
1900-2000	daily	Eu,RUS	7255kas
1900-2000	daily	Eu	9770kas
2300-2400	daily	SEA	9460kun, 9610kas, 11945kun, 15400bei
2300-2400	daily	FE	6140kun, 7315kun, 15100xia, 15260xia

Chaozhou	Days	Area	kHz
1100-1200	daily	SEA	9440kun, 11875kun
1800-1900	daily	FE	6040uru, 7220jin

Czech	Days	Area	kHz
1900-1930	daily	Eu	6020szg
1900-2000	daily	Eu	1386sit, 7150uru
1930-2000	daily	Eu	7305iss
2230-2330	daily	Eu	1458fla

English	Days	Area	kHz
0000-0100	daily	As	7180kas
0000-0200	daily	As	6075kas
0000-0200	daily	Eu	7345kas
0100-0200	daily	NAm	6005sac, 9580hab
0100-0200	daily	As	7180kas
0100-0400	daily	SAs	11770kas
0200-0300	daily	SAs	13640kas
0300-0400	daily	NAm	9690nob, 9790hab
0300-0400	daily	SAs	15110uru
0400-0500	daily	NAm	6190sac, 9755guf
0400-0600	daily	NAm	9560sac
0500-0600	daily	NAm	6190sac
0500-0700	daily	FE	11770kas
0500-0900	daily	FE	11880kun
0500-0900	daily	SAs	15350kas, 15465kas, 17540kas
0600-0700	daily	ME	15140uru
0600-0700	daily	NAm	6115kas
0700-0900	daily	Eu	1215fla
0800-1200	daily	Eu	17490uru
0900-1100	daily	Pac	15210kun, 17690jin
0900-1500	daily	Pac	17490kas
1000-1100	daily	NAm	6040sac
1100-1200	daily	NAm	5960sac
1200-1300	daily	AUS,NZL	15415kun
1200-1300	daily	SEA	684dof, 1188yun, 1269yun

English	Days	Area	kHz
1200-1300	daily	As	9730kun
1200-1400	daily	Eu	13790kas
1200-1400	daily	OC	9795uru, 11760kun
1200-1400	daily	SEA	11980kun
1200-1400	daily	SEA,PHL	1341gdg
1300-1400	daily	Eu	13790kas
1300-1400	daily	NAm	9570hab, 11885sac, 17625sgo
1300-1400	daily	As	15180xia
1300-1400	daily	AUS,NZL	11900kun
1300-1500	daily	Eu	13610kas
1300-1500	daily	NAm	15230sac
1400-1500	daily	As	11675kun, 11760uru
1400-1500	daily	Eu	9700kas, 9795uru
1400-1500	daily	SAs	1422kas, 9560kas
1400-1600	daily	NAm	7405jin, 13675sac, 17730hab
1400-1600	daily	WAf	17630bko
1400-1600	daily	EAf	13685bko
1500-1600	daily	G	558lnd
1500-1600	daily	As	7160uru, 9785jin
1500-1700	daily	Eu	9435kas, 9525kas
1600-1700	daily	Eu	7255uru
1600-1800	daily	SEA	1080kun
1600-1800	daily	Af	9570xia
1600-1800	daily	SAf	11900xia
1600-1800	daily	SAs	1323lha
1700-1800	daily	Eu	7255kas
1700-2100	daily	Eu	6100qiq
1900-2000	daily	Af	9585kun
1900-2100	daily	Af	7295kas
1900-2100	daily	NAf	9440bei
2000-2100	daily	EAf	13630bko
2000-2100	daily	Eu	1386sit, 1440mrn, 7190kas
2000-2130	daily	Af	11640bko
2000-2200	daily	Eu	9600kas, 9855uru
2100-2130	daily	EAf	13630bko
2100-2200	daily	Eu	7190kas
2200-2300	daily	Eu,NAm	7170tld
2300-2400	daily	As	5975kas, 7180kas
2300-2400	daily	NAm	5990hab, 6040sac, 11970sac

Esperanto	Days	Area	kHz
1100-1200	daily	FE	9510xia
1100-1200	daily	J	7150jin
1300-1400	daily	SEA	9440nnn, 11650xia
1700-1800	daily	Eu	1215fla
1930-2030	daily	Eu	9745uru
1930-2030	daily	Eu,NAf	7265uru
2200-2300	daily	SAm	9860bei, 11700bei

Farsi	Days	Area	kHz
1500-1530	daily	ME	6165uru, 11700kun
1800-1830	daily	ME	7130spb
1800-1900	daily	ME	7140kun, 9670uru

French	Days	Area	kHz
0400-0600	daily	Eu	15110kas
0800-1000	daily	Eu	17650uru
1600-1700	daily	Eu	9700kas
1830-2030	daily	Eu,NAf	7350uru
1830-2030	daily	WAf,CAf	9645kun
2030-2130	daily	Eu	7215sam
2030-2230	daily	EAf	13630bko
2030-2230	daily	Eu	7200uru, 11660xia
2100-2200	daily	Eu	1440mrn
2130-2230	daily	NAf	11975bko

German	Days	Area	kHz
0600-0800	daily	Eu	15245uru, 17720uru
1800-2000	daily	Eu	1440mrn, 7170kas, 9615uru, 11760kas
2100-2200	daily	Eu	1386sit

Hakka	Days	Area	kHz
0000-0100	daily	FE	6140kun, 9610kas, 15100xia, 15260xia
0000-0100	daily	SEA	9460kun, 9550kun, 11945kun, 15400bei

Hakka	Days	Area	kHz
1600-1700	daily	EAf	11825xia
1600-1700	daily	FE	9770uru

Hausa	Days	Area	kHz
1730-1830	daily	WAf	11640bko, 13670bko
1830-1900	daily	WAf	9570kas, 11730kun

Hindi	Days	Area	kHz
0300-0400	daily	SAs	11640kas, 13720kas, 15350kas, 15465kas
1300-1400	daily	SAs	1422kas, 9635kas, 11675uru
1500-1600	daily	SAs	1323lha
1500-1600	daily	ME	7120kas
1500-1700	daily	SAs	1269yun, 7235kas, 9690uru
1600-1700	daily	SAs	5915kas, 7120kas

Hungarian	Days	Area	kHz
1900-1930	daily	Eu	7110jin, 9860uru
2000-2100	daily	Eu	1458fla
2030-2100	daily	Eu	6020szg, 9585kas
2130-2200	daily	Eu	6145iss, 7120uru

Indonesian	Days	Area	kHz
0830-0930	daily	SEA	15135kun, 17735kun
1030-1130	daily	SEA	11700kun, 15135kun
1330-1430	daily	SEA	11955kun, 15135kun

Italian	Days	Area	kHz
1800-1900	daily	Eu	1458fla, 7150jin, 7340kas
2030-2130	daily	Eu	7180kas, 7265uru

Japanese	Days	Area	kHz
0930-1530	daily	FE	1044jia
0930-1530	daily	J	7190bei

Korean	Days	Area	kHz
1100-1300	daily	FE	1323cah
1100-1500	daily	FE	1017cah, 5965bei

Lao	Days	Area	kHz
1230-1330	daily	SEA	7360kun, 9785kun
1430-1530	daily	SEA	1080kun, 7360kun, 9675kun

Malay	Days	Area	kHz
0930-1030	daily	SEA	15135kun, 17680kun
1230-1330	daily	SEA	11955kun, 15600kun

Mandarin	Days	Area	kHz
0000-0100	daily	NAm	9790sac
0000-0100	daily	NAm,Car	6040sac
0100-0200	daily	FE	13640kas
0200-0300	daily	NAm	9580hab
0200-0300	daily	NAm,Car	9690nob
0300-0400	daily	FE	13600kas
0300-0400	daily	NAm	9720guf
0400-0500	daily	FE	11770kas, 11880kun
0400-0500	daily	SAs	15350kas, 17540kas
0600-0700	daily	Eu	17650kas
0700-0800	daily	Eu	17650uru
0900-1000	daily	FE	9665bei
0900-1000	daily	SEA	15110xia
0900-1000	daily	AUS,NZL	15125bei, 15440kun, 17670kun
0900-1100	daily	FE	15250kun
0900-1100	daily	SEA	11980kun, 15340xia, 17785xia
1000-1200	daily	Eu	17650uru
1500-1600	daily	SAs	9560kas
1500-1600	daily	Eu	9700kas
1730-1830	daily	WAf,CAf	9645kun
1730-1830	daily	Eu,NAf	6150szg, 7120uru
1730-1830	daily	NAf,ME	7160uru, 7315kun, 9745kun
1800-2000	daily	FE	11940kas
2000-2100	daily	Eu	7120szg, 7335jin
2000-2100	daily	ME	9685kun, 9865kun
2000-2100	daily	NAf,ME	7245kas
2100-2200	daily	Eu	1557sit
2200-2300	daily	G	558lnd
2200-2300	daily	SEA	7220kun, 9460kun, 11945kun, 15400bei
2200-2300	daily	SAf	7190uru
2200-2300	daily	FE	5955bei, 6140kun, 7180xia, 7315kun, 15260xia
2200-2300	daily	ME	7265kun
2230-2300	daily	CAf	15505bko
2230-2400	daily	NAf	11975bko
2300-2400	daily	Af	7170bko

Mongolian	Days	Area	kHz
1100-1200	daily	MNG	5955bei, 7110huh
1200-1300	daily	MNG	5990huh, 7255bei
1200-1300	daily	CAs,RUS	5915huh
1400-1500	daily	CAs,RUS	5915huh
1400-1500	daily	MNG	5990huh, 7255bei

Nepali	Days	Area	kHz
0230-0330	daily	NPL	13790kun, 15320xia
1400-1500	daily	NPL	7160kun, 9600xia
1400-1500	daily	SEA	1269yun
1500-1600	daily	NPL	7215kun
1500-1600	daily	SAs	9535xia

Pashto	Days	Area	kHz
0200-0230	daily	ME	9765kas, 11860kas
0200-0230	daily	SAs	17890bei
1500-1600	daily	ME	9665kas
1500-1600	daily	ME,SAs	11880kun
1530-1600	daily	ME	6165uru

Polish	Days	Area	kHz
2000-2030	daily	Eu	6020szg, 6145iss
2000-2100	daily	Eu	1557sit, 7150uru
2030-2100	daily	Eu	7110jin
2130-2230	daily	Eu	1458fla

Portuguese	Days	Area	kHz
0000-0100	daily	SAf	11850guf
0000-0100	daily	SAm	7245xia, 11680bei
1900-2000	daily	Eu	7225xia, 7335jin
1900-2000	daily	NAf	9620xia
1900-2000	daily	Af	7180xia
1900-2000	daily	SAf	9535xia, 13630bko
1930-2000	daily	Af	11640bko
2200-2300	daily	B	7245xia
2200-2300	daily	SAm	5990bei
2300-2400	daily	SAm	13650hab

Romanian	Days	Area	kHz
1700-1730	daily	Eu	1548gri
1800-1900	daily	Eu	1215fla
1900-1930	daily	Eu	7305iss
1900-2000	daily	Eu	6145uru
1930-2000	daily	Eu	7110jin
2000-2030	daily	Eu	1548gri

Russian	Days	Area	kHz
0000-0100	daily	FE	5990huh
0000-0100	daily	RUS	7110huh, 9870bei
0000-0200	daily	CAs,RUS	1521uru, 5905kas
0300-0400	daily	CAs,RUS	5905kas
0300-0400	daily	RUS	15435bei, 17710bei, 17740xia
1000-1100	daily	RUS	7110huh
1000-1100	daily	FE	9695bei
1000-1200	daily	RUS	7255bei, 7290jin
1000-1200	daily	CAs,RUS	5915huh
1000-1200	daily	FE	1116hei
1000-1500	daily	FE	1323lha
1000-1600	daily	RUS	963—
1100-2000	daily	CAs,RUS	1521uru
1200-1300	daily	Eu	9590szg
1200-2000	daily	CAs,RUS	5905kas
1300-1400	daily	RUS	5990huh, 7255bei, 9675bei
1300-1400	daily	CAs,RUS	5915huh
1430-1630	daily	Eu,RUS	1467gri
1500-1600	daily	CAs,RUS	5915huh
1500-1600	daily	RUS	5990huh, 6105qiq, 6180uru, 7245xia, 7255bei
1600-1700	daily	RUS	5965bei
1600-1800	daily	Eu	9885bei
1600-1800	daily	RUS	6040uru, 7265uru, 9765kas

Russian	Days	Area	kHz
1700-1800	daily	RUS	5965bei, 7105xia, 9795uru
1700-2000	daily	RUS	7245xia, 9365bei
1800-1900	daily	RUS	7190szg, 7255uru, 9535xia
1800-2000	daily	Eu	1557sit
2000-2100	daily	RUS	7255xia, 9730xia
2300-2400	daily	CAs,RUS	5905kas, 5955bei
2300-2400	daily	RUS	5990huh, 7110huh
Serbian	**Days**	**Area**	**kHz**
1730-1800	daily	Eu	1548gri
2000-2030	daily	Eu	7130kas, 7180uru, 9585kas
2030-2100	daily	Eu	1548gri
2100-2130	daily	Eu	7110jin, 7160xia
2200-2300	daily	Eu	1215fla
Sinhala	**Days**	**Area**	**kHz**
1400-1500	daily	SAs	7265kas, 11900jin, 15145kun
1400-1500	daily	SEA	1188yun
2330-0030	daily	SAs	9490kun, 11700kas
Spanish	**Days**	**Area**	**kHz**
0000-0100	daily	MEX	9745bon
0000-0100	daily	NAm,Car	5990hab
0000-0100	daily	SAm	7160xia, 15120hab
0000-0300	daily	SAm	11650xia
0200-0300	daily	NAm,Car,SAm	13685guf
0300-0400	daily	SAm	9560sac, 9665bra
2100-2300	daily	Eu	6020szg
2100-2300	daily	Eu,NAf	9640kas
2200-2300	daily	Eu,NAf	7120uru
2200-2300	daily	Car,SAm	13700sac
2300-2400	daily	SAm	7160xia, 7245xia
Swahili	**Days**	**Area**	**kHz**
1600-1700	daily	EAf	11600xia, 12000kas
1630-1700	daily	EAf	12000kas
1700-1730	daily	EAf	11640bko, 15125bko
Tagalog	**Days**	**Area**	**kHz**
1130-1200	daily	SEA,PHL	1341gdg
1130-1230	daily	PHL	11700xia, 12110kun
1430-1500	daily	PHL	12110kun
1430-1500	daily	SEA,PHL	1341gdg
Tamil	**Days**	**Area**	**kHz**
0200-0300	daily	FE	15260kun
0200-0300	daily	SAs	11870kas, 13715kas
1400-1500	daily	SAs	9665kun, 11685kas
1500-1600	daily	SAs	11800kas, 13620kas
Thai	**Days**	**Area**	**kHz**
1130-1230	daily	SEA	7360kun, 9785kun
1330-1430	daily	SEA	1080kun, 7360kun, 9785kun
Turkish	**Days**	**Area**	**kHz**
1400-1430	daily	TUR	15165uru, 15670kun
1600-1630	daily	TUR	6165uru, 7325xia
1900-1930	daily	TUR	7215jin, 9655kun
1930-2000	daily	Eu	1170arm
Urdu	**Days**	**Area**	**kHz**
0100-0200	daily	SAs	7240kas, 9695kas
1400-1600	daily	SAs	1422kas, 9610kun, 11775kas
Vietnamese	**Days**	**Area**	**kHz**
1100-1200	daily	SEA	1296kun, 9550kun, 11990xia
1300-1500	daily	SEA	1296kun
1300-1600	daily	SEA	9550kun
1300-1700	daily	SEA	603dof, 11990xia
1400-1700	daily	SEA	684dof
1600-1700	daily	SEA	6010kun, 7360kun
2300-2400	daily	SEA	7220xia

ANN: Arabic: "Idha'at as-Sin ad-Duwaliyah"; Mandarin: "Zhongguo guoji guangbo diantai"; English: "This is China Radio International, broadcasting from Beijing"; German: "Hier ist Radio China International", Indonesian: "Inilah CRI, China Radio International"; Japanese: "Kochirawa Pekin Hoso, Chugoku Kokusai Hosokyoku desu"; Korean: "Jungguk gukje bangsonggugimnida"; Malay: "Inilah Radio Antarabangsa China, dalam bahasa Melayu"; Mongolian: "Hyatadyn Olon Ulsyn Radio"; Spanish: "Esta es Radio Internacional de China"; Swahili: "Hii ni Radio China kimataifa"; Vietnamese: "Day la dai phatthanh quoc te Trung quoc"
IS: First 4 bars of "The East is Red"
V: QSL-card.
NOTES: China Radio International (CRI) is the External Sce produced under the roof of the State Administration of Radio, Film and Television of the P.R. of China (SARFT). CRI also rents out air time on some of its tx's to foreign broadcasters.

Broadcasters using sites in this country:
BBC World Sce uses: (HKG). See stn entry in: **G**, INT Section
RCI uses: (XIA). See stn entry in: **CAN**, INT Section
RCI uses: (KAS). See stn entry in: **CAN**, INT Section
REE uses: (XIA). See stn entry in: **E**, INT Section
REE uses: (BEI). See stn entry in: **E**, INT Section
RFI uses: (XIA). See stn entry in: **F**, INT Section
RFI uses: (KUN). See stn entry in: **F**, INT Section
RFI uses: (DOF). See stn entry in: **F**, INT Section
RFI uses: (BEI). See stn entry in: **F**, INT Section
VO Russia (VOR) uses: (YUN). See stn entry in: **RUS**, INT Section
VO Russia (VOR) uses: (DOF). See stn entry in: **RUS**, INT Section

COSTA RICA

THE CARIBBEAN BEACON (UNIVERSITY NETWORK RELAY) (Rlg)

✉ Contact info: see The University Network (USA).
SW: [CHA] Cahuita (G.C. 09N45 082W54) 2 x 20, 1 x 40, 2 x 50kW
V: QSL-card (contact address see USA).
NOTES: Carries programming from Gene Scott's "University Network" (see USA).

RADIO EXTERIOR DE ESPAÑA RELAY STATION

✉ Radio Nacional de España, c/o Delegación en Costa Rica, Apartado 677-2010, Zapote, San José, Costa Rica.
☎ +506 2329471. 🖷 +506 2329340.
SW: [CRI] Cariari de Pococí (G.C. 10N00 083W30) 3 x 100kW

RADIO FOR PEACE INTERNATIONAL

✉ P.O. Box 75, Ciudad Colón, Costa Rica.
Email: info@rfpi.org **Web:** www.rfpi.org
✉ P.O. Box 3165, Newberg, OR 97132-5165, USA.
L.P: GM: James Latham.
NOTES: RFPI is currently available via webcasting only, the SW broadcasts ceased in November 2003. RFPI is hoping to return to SW at a later stage.

Broadcasters using sites in this country:
Dr Gene Scott uses: (CHA). See stn entry in: **USA**, INT Section
REE uses: (CRI). See stn entry in: **E**, INT Section

CROATIA

GLAS HRVATSKE (VOICE OF CROATIA) (Pub)

✉ Prisavlje 3, 10000 Zagreb, Croatia.
☎ +385 1 6342602. 🖷 +385 1 6343305.
Email: voiceofcroatia@hrt.hr **Web:** www.hrt.hr/hr/glashrvatske
L.P: Chief editor: Ivana Jadresic
MW/SW: Uses tx's provided by Odašiljaci i veze d.o.o.
SAT: Hotbird 6, NSS 806, Optus B3, Telstar 5
kHz: *594, 774, 783, 1125, 1134, 6165, 7285, 7365, 9470, 9830, 13820*

Winter Schedule 2004

Croatian	Days	Area	kHz
0500-1000	daily	Eu	7365dea*
0500-1800	daily	Eu	9830dea*
0500-2400	daily	Eu	6165dea*
Various	**Days**	**Area**	**kHz**
0000-0600	daily	NAm	7285jul
0000-2400	daily	Eu	594osi, 774hva, 783buj, 1125dea
0500-0800	daily	NZL,AUS	9470jul
0600-1000	daily	NZL,AUS	13820jul
1300-0530	daily	Eu	1134zad
2300-0400	daily	SAm	7285jul

ANN: Croatian: "Hrvatski Radio, kratki val"; English: "This is Croatian Radio, you are listening to the Voice of Croatia"
IS: Tune to Dubrovnik's poem "Lovely, Dear, Sweet Liberty" played on celeste.
V: QSL-card.

NOTES: A service of the public broadcaster Hrvatska Radiotelevizija (HRT) for listeners abroad. "Glas Hrvatske" consists of Home Sce prgr's in Croatian, plus newscasts in English 0200-0215, 0600-0603, 1000-1003, 1500-1503, 1600-1630, 1800-1803, 2200-2215; Spanish 0230-0245, 2230-2245; and prgr's in Italian (produced by HR R.Rijeka) MF 1400-1430 and Hungarian (produced by HR R.Osijek) MF 1630-1700. Key: * Relay Domestic Sce HRT1 in Croatian.

ODAŠILJACI I VEZE D.O.O. (Tx Operator)
Vlaška 106, 10000 Zagreb, Croatia.
☎ +385 1 4646160. Fax +385 1 4646161.
Web: www.oiv.hr
MW: [BUJ] Buje (G.C. 45N24 013E40) 783kHz 10kW; [DEA] Deanovac (G.C. 45N41 016E27) 1125kHz 100kW; [HVA] Hvar (G.C. 43N11 016E25) 774kHz 50kW; [OSI] Osijek (G.C. 45N38 018E41) 594kHz 10kW; [ZAD] Zadar (G.C. 44N06 015E15) 1134kHz 600kW
SW: [DEA] Deanovac (G.C. 45N41 016E27) 10 x 10, 1 x 100kW
NOTES: Odašiljaci i veze is the national transmitter network operator.

CUBA

RADIO HABANA CUBA (Gov)
Apartado 6240, La Habana, Cuba.
☎ +53 7 791053. Fax +53 7 795007.
Email: radiohc@enet.cu **Web:** www.radiohc.cu
L.P: DG: Milagro Hernandez Cuba; Chief Editor: Pedro Otero Cabañas; Technical Dir: Justo Moreno García; Head of Correspondence Dpt: Lourdes Lopéz.
SW: Leased from Radiocuba
kHz: *5965, 6000, 6060, 9505, 9550, 9600, 9655, 9820, 11670, 11760, 11800, 11875, 12000, 13360, 13680, 13750, 15230, 17705, 17750*

Winter Schedule 2004

	Days	Area	kHz
Arabic	**Days**	**Area**	**kHz**
2030-2100	daily	Eu	13360hab
Creole	**Days**	**Area**	**kHz**
0100-0130	daily	Car	9550hab
2130-2200	daily	Car	9505hab
2230-2300	daily	Car	9505hab
English	**Days**	**Area**	**kHz**
0100-0500	daily	NAm	6000hab, 9820hab
0500-0700	daily	Car	6060hab, 9550hab, 9655hab
0500-0700	daily	NAm	9820hab, 11760hab
2030-2130	daily	Car	9505hab
2030-2130	daily	NAm	11760hab
2300-2400	daily	Car	9550hab
Esperanto	**Days**	**Area**	**kHz**
0700-0730	......s	NAm	9820hab
1500-1530	......s	NAm	11760hab
1930-2000	......s	NAm	11760hab
2330-2400	......s	VEN	9600hab
2330-2400	......s	CAm	9505hab
French	**Days**	**Area**	**kHz**
0000-0100	daily	Car	9550hab
0130-0200	daily	Car	9550hab
2000-2030	daily	NAm	11760hab
2130-2200	daily	NAm	11760hab
2200-2230	daily	Car	9505hab
Guarani	**Days**	**Area**	**kHz**
2230-2300	daily	SAm	17705hab
2330-2400	daily	SAm	17705hab
Portuguese	**Days**	**Area**	**kHz**
2000-2030	daily	Eu	13360hab
2200-2230	daily	B	17705hab
2300-2330	daily	B	17705hab
2300-2400	daily	B	15230hab
Quechua	**Days**	**Area**	**kHz**
0000-0030	daily	SAm	17705hab
Spanish	**Days**	**Area**	**kHz**
0000-0100	daily	NAm	6000hab, 9820hab
0000-0500	daily	ARG	15230hab
0000-0500	daily	Car	9505hab, 9655hab
0000-0500	daily	MEX	5965hab
0000-0500	daily	VEN	9600hab
0100-0500	daily	NAm	11760hab
0200-0500	daily	Car	9550hab
0300-0500	daily	CHL	11875hab
Spanish	**Days**	**Area**	**kHz**
1100-1500	daily	Am	6000hab
1100-1500	daily	VEN	11800hab
1100-1500	daily	NAm	11760hab, 12000hab
1100-1500	daily	ARG	15230hab
1100-1500	daily	Car	9550hab
1400	......s	B	17750hab*
1400	......s	CAm	13680hab*
1400	......s	Car	11670hab*
1400	......s	CHL	11875hab*
1400	......s	NAm	13750hab*
2100-2300	daily	Car	6060hab, 9550hab
2100-2300	daily	Eu	13360hab
2100-2300	daily	SAm	15230hab
2300-0100	mtwtf..	NAm	6000hab, 11875hab

ANN: English: "This is Radio Havana, Cuba"
V: QSL-card. Online form: www.radiohc.cu/ingles/diexismo.htm
NOTES: Radio Habana Cuba is the External Sce of the state-owned Instituto Cubano de Radio y Television (ICRT). Key: * A Lo Presidente. Frequencies and schedule are subject to variation.

RADIOCUBA (Tx Operator)
Habana, Cuba.
☎ +53 7 8607181. Fax +53 7 8603107.
Email: dirgeneral@radiocuba.cu **Web:** www.radiocuba.cu
L.P: DG: Julio Antonio González García.
SW: [HAB] La Habana; two sites: Bauta (G.C. 23N00 082W30) 1 x 7.5, 2 x 10, 4 x 20, 3 x 30, 7 x 100kW; Bejucal (G.C. 22N55 082W23) 4 x 250kW
NOTES: Radiocuba, a subsidiary of the Ministry of Information and Communications, is the national transmitter network operator.
Broadcasters using sites in this country:
China R. Int'l uses: (HAB). See stn entry in: **CHN**, INT Section
R.Nac.Venezuela uses: (HAB). See stn entry in: **VEN**, INT Section

CYPRUS

CYPRUS BROADCASTING CORPORATION (Pub)
P.O. Box 24824, 1397 Nicosia, Cyprus.
☎ +357 22862000. Fax +357 22314050.
Email: rik@cybc.com.cy **Web:** www.cybc.com.cy
L.P: GD: Marios Mavrikios.
SW: Leased fromVT Merlin Communications.
SAT: Sirius 2
kHz: *6180, 7210, 9760*

Winter Schedule 2004

Greek	Days	Area	kHz
2215-2245	....fss	SEu	6180cyp, 7210cyp, 9760cyp

ANN: Greek: "Radiofonikon Idryma Kyprou"
IS: "Avkoritssa" (guitar)
V: QSL-card. Rec. acc.
NOTES: The transmissions are relays of CBC's Home Sce prgr's for Cypriots living in the UK.

RADIO IBRAHIM (Rlg)
P.O. Box 56500, 3312 Limassol, Cyprus.
☎ +357 99447768. Fax +357 25338394.
Email: mail@radioibrahim.com **Web:** www.radioibrahim.com
L.P: Dir: Oskar Lindén.
MW: Leased from RTRN (see Russia)
SAT: Amos
kHz: *1170, 7340, 9835*

Winter Schedule 2004

Arabic	Days	Area	kHz
1900-2030	daily	ME	9835sam
2000-2100	daily	NAf	7340jul
2000-2130	daily	ME	1170arm

V: QSL-card. Email rpt to dx@radioibrahim.com.
NOTES: A station owned by the Swedish IBRA mission. Broadcasts in Standard Arabic and a number of Arabic dialects.

MONTE CARLO RADIODIFFUSION RELAY STATION (Tx Operator)
Cape Gkroko, Cyprus.
MW: [CGR] Cape Gkreko (G.C. 34N59 034E06) 990kHz 600kW (operated by IBB), 1233kHz 1200kW
NOTES: Transmitting station owned by Monte Carlo Radiodiffusion, see Monaco for corporate details.

BBC MIDDLE EAST RELAY STATION
P.O. Box 4912, Limassol, Cyprus.
+357 24332511. +357 24332595.
L.P: Sen. Eng: S. Welch.
MW: [CYP] Zygi (G.C. 34N43 033E19) 639/720kHz 500kW, 1323kHz 200kW
SW: [CYP] Zygi (G.C. 34N43 033E19) 2 x 250, 8 x 300kW
V: QSL-card for direct rpt.
NOTES: Owned by the BBC and operated by VT Merlin Communications (see UK). Carries relays of BBC and other international broadcasters.
Broadcasters using sites in this country:
BBC World Sce uses: (CYP). See stn entry in: **G**, INT Section
BBC World Sce uses: (CGR). See stn entry in: **G**, INT Section
BBG-R. Sawa uses: (CGR). See stn entry in: **USA**, INT Section
TWR Europe uses: (CGR). See stn entry in: **AUT**, INT Section

CYPRUS (Northern)

RADIO BAYRAK INTERNATIONAL (Gov)
Bayrak Radio Television Corporation, P.O. Box 417, Lefkosa, via Mersin 10, Turkey.
+90 392 2255555. +90 392 2254991.
Email: brt@brtk.net **Web:** www.brtk.net
L.P: DG: Hüseyin Gür?an.
SW: [ISK] Yeni Iskele (G.C. 35N13 033E55) 1 x 25kW
FM: Sinandagi 87.8MHz 10kW, Selvilitepe 105.0MHz 5kW
SAT: Türksat 1C
kHz: *6150*

Winter Schedule 2004

Various	Days	Area	kHz
0000-2400	daily	ME,NAf	6150isk

V: QSL-folder.
NOTES: Foreign language channel of the state broadcaster Bayrak Radyo Televizyon Kurumu (BRTK). News: 1200-1215 (Greek), 1215-1225 (English), Tue-Sat 1600-1610 (Arabic, Russian, German), 1730-1740 (English), 1800-1810 (Greek). Headlines in English and Greek: Tue-Sat 1000-1003 & 1400-1403.

CZECH REPUBLIC

RADIO PRAGUE (Pub)
Vinohradská 12, 12099 Praha 2, Czech Republic.
+420 2 24218349. +420 2 21552903.
Email: cr@radio.cz **Web:** www.radio.cz
L.P: Dir: Miroslav Krupicka.
SW: Leased from Ceské Radiokomunikace A.S.
FM: 92.6MHz
kHz: *5830, 5840, 5930, 6055, 6200, 7345, 9415, 9430, 9435, 9450, 9865, 9880, 11600, 11640, 11665, 13580, 15255, 15710, 21745*

Winter Schedule 2004

Czech	Days	Area	kHz
0030-0100	daily	SAm	5930lit
0030-0100	daily	NAm	7345lit
0230-0300	daily	NAm	6200lit
0230-0300	daily	SAm	7345lit
0330-0400	daily	NAm	6200lit, 7345lit
0930-1000	daily	EAf,ME	21745lit
0930-1000	daily	SEu	11600lit
1030-1100	daily	SAs,WAf	21745lit
1200-1230	daily	Eu	11640lit
1200-1230	daily	SAs,AUS	21745lit
1330-1400	daily	WEu	7345lit
1330-1400	daily	Eu	6055lit
1430-1500	daily	EAf,NAm	21745lit
1630-1700	daily	CAf,WAf	15710lit
1630-1700	daily	WEu	5930lit
1830-1900	daily	As,AUS	9415lit
1830-1900	daily	WEu	5930lit
2030-2100	daily	SEA,AUS	9430lit
2030-2100	daily	WEu	5930lit
2200-2230	daily	SAm,Eu	9435lit
2200-2230	daily	SEu,SAm	5930lit
English	**Days**	**Area**	**kHz**
0100-0130	daily	NAm	6200lit, 7345lit
0200-0230	daily	NAm	6200lit, 7345lit
0400-0430	daily	NAm	6200lit, 7345lit
0430-0500	daily	ME,SAs	9865lit, 11600lit
0800-0830	daily	Eu	7345lit, 9880lit
1000-1030	daily	SAs,WAf	21745lit
1130-1200	daily	EAf,ME	21745lit
1130-1200	daily	Eu	11640lit
1400-1430	daily	EAf,NAm	21745lit
1700-1730	daily	CAf,WAf	15710lit
1700-1730	daily	Eu	5930lit
1800-1830	daily	As,AUS	9415lit
1800-1830	daily	Eu	5930lit
2100-2130	daily	Eu,NAm	5930lit
2100-2130	daily	SEA,AUS	9430lit
2230-2300	daily	WAf	7345lit
2230-2300	daily	NAm	5930lit
2330-2400	daily	NAm	5930lit, 7345lit
French	**Days**	**Area**	**kHz**
0700-0730	daily	SEu	7345lit
0700-0730	daily	WEu	5930lit
0830-0900	daily	SEu	11600lit
0830-0900	daily	WEu	9880lit
1730-1800	daily	WEu	5930lit
1730-1800	daily	CAf	15710lit
1930-2000	daily	SEu,NAf	9430lit
1930-2000	daily	WEu	5930lit
2300-2330	daily	NAm	5930lit, 7345lit
German	**Days**	**Area**	**kHz**
0730-0800	daily	Eu	7345lit
0730-0800	daily	WEu	5930lit
1100-1130	daily	Eu	7345lit
1100-1130	daily	WEu	9880lit
1300-1330	daily	WEu	7345lit
1300-1330	daily	Eu	6055lit
1600-1630	daily	WEu	5930lit
1730-1800	daily	WEu	5840arm
Russian	**Days**	**Area**	**kHz**
0500-0530	daily	EEu	6055lit
0500-0530	daily	EEu,SAs	11600lit
1230-1300	daily	EEu	6055lit
1230-1300	daily	EEu,SAs	21745lit
1530-1600	daily	EEu	5930lit
1530-1600	daily	EEu,SAs	9450lit
1900-1930	daily	EEu	5830nsb
Spanish	**Days**	**Area**	**kHz**
0000-0030	daily	SAm	5930lit, 7345lit, 11665asc
0130-0200	daily	CAm	6200lit, 7345lit
0300-0330	daily	CAm	6200lit
0300-0330	daily	SAm	7345lit
0900-0930	daily	SEu	11600lit, 15255lit
1500-1530	daily	SEu	11600lit, 13580lit
1900-1930	daily	SEu	5930lit, 9430lit
2000-2030	daily	SEu	5930lit, 9430lit
2130-2200	daily	SEu,SAm	5930lit, 9435lit

ANN: English: "Welcome to Radio Prague, the External Service of Czech Radio".
IS: Fanfare from Dvorák's 9th Symphony ("From the New World") played on French horn.
V: QSL-card. Rec. acc.
NOTES: Radio Prague is the External Sce of the public service Czech Radio (Ceský Rozhlas). Also in English, Mon-Thurs 1805-1820 for Prague area on 92.6MHz FM.

CESKÉ RADIOKOMUNIKACE A.S. (Tx Operator)
U Nákladového nádrazí 3144, 130 00 Praha 3, Czech Republic.
+420 2 42411111. +420 2 42417595.
Email: cra@cra.cz **Web:** www.cra.cz
Broadcasting Division: Mahlerovy sady 1, 130 00 Praha 3, Czech Republic.
+420 2 42418901. +420 2 42418858.
SW: [LIT] Litomysl (G.C. 49N48 016E10) 3 x 100kW
NOTES: Ceské Radiokomunikice A.S.is the national transmitter network owner.

DENMARK

WORLD MUSIC RADIO (WMR) (Comm)

P.O. Box 112, DK-8900 Randers, Denmark.
☎ +45 70222222. Fax +45 70222888.
Email: wmr@wmr.dk **Web:** www.wmr.dk
L.P: Owner & MD: Stig Hartvig Nielsen.
SW: [KRP] Karup, Ilskov (G.C. 56N15 009E04) 1 x 10kW; second site under preparation.
FM: Galten 104.2MHz (0.16kW)
kHz: *5815, 15810*

Winter Schedule 2004

English	Days	Area	kHz
0000-2400	daily	Eu	5815krp, 15810krp*

ANN: English: "International music radio - this is World Music Radio WMR"
V: QSL-card. Rp preferred.
NOTES: Key: * Transmissions are planned to resume from a new site in East Jutland in the first half of 2005, projected power between 0.5 - 10kW.

DJIBOUTI

IBB RELAY STATION DJIBOUTI

IBB Transmitting Station, Arta, Djibouti.
MW: [ART] Arta (G.C. 11N52 042E84) 1431kHz 600kW
Broadcasters using sites in this country:
BBG-R. Sawa uses: (ART). See stn entry in: **USA**, INT Section

ECUADOR

HCJB (LA VOZ DE LOS ANDES) (Rlg)

Casilla 17-17-691, Quito, Ecuador.
☎ +593 2 2266808. Fax +593 2 2267263.
Email: vozandes@hcjb.org.ec **Web:** www.hcjb.org.ec
L.P: Freq Mgr: Doug Weber.
MW: [QUI] Quito, Pifo (G.C. 00S14 078W20) 690kHz 50kW
SW: [QUI] Quito, Pifo (G.C. 00S14 078W20) 2 x 25, 2 x 50, 4 x 100, 1 x 500kW; SSB tx's: 2 x 1, 2 x 25kW
kHz: *690, 1251, 3220, 3995, 6050, 6080, 6125, 9745, 9765, 9785, 11700, 11760, 11920, 11960, 12005, 12020, 12025, 12040, 15140, 15295, 21455*

Winter Schedule 2004

Arabic	**Days**	**Area**	**kHz**
2100-2230	daily	NAf	12025sac
Bashkir	**Days**	**Area**	**kHz**
1700-1715	......s	CAs	11760rmp
English	**Days**	**Area**	**kHz**
1100-1330	daily	Eu,Oc	21455qui*
1100-1330	daily	NAm,SAm	12005qui
Georgian	**Days**	**Area**	**kHz**
1715-1730	......s	WAs	11760rmp
German (High)	**Days**	**Area**	**kHz**
0230-0300	daily	MEX	9785qui
0700-0730	daily	Eu	9765qui
0700-0730	daily	Eu,Oc	21455qui*
1630-1700	daily	Eu	3995jul
2300-2400	daily	SAm	12040qui
German (Low)	**Days**	**Area**	**kHz**
0200-0230	daily	MEX	9785qui
0730-0800	daily	Eu	9765qui
0730-0800	daily	Eu,Oc	21455qui*
1600-1630	daily	Eu	3995jul
2230-2300	daily	SAm	12040qui
Huarani	**Days**	**Area**	**kHz**
1030-1100	daily	SAm	6050qui
Portuguese	**Days**	**Area**	**kHz**
0800-0930	daily	B	9745qui
0800-0930	daily	Eu,Oc	21455qui*
1530-1800	daily	B	15295qui
2300 0230	daily	B	11920qui, 12020qui
Quichua	**Days**	**Area**	**kHz**
0000-0300	daily	SAm	3220qui
0830-1000	daily	SAm	6125qui
0830-1030	daily	EQA	690qui
0830-1200	daily	SAm	3220qui
0830-1400	daily	SAm	6080qui
Quichua	**Days**	**Area**	**kHz**
0930-1100	daily	Eu,Oc	21455qui*
2100-0300	daily	SAm	6080qui
2130-2400	daily	SAm	9745qui
Russian	**Days**	**Area**	**kHz**
1715-1730	mtwtfs.	RUS	11760rmp
Spanish	**Days**	**Area**	**kHz**
0100-0500	daily	MEX	9745qui
1030-0500	daily	EQA	690qui
1100-1300	daily	CUB	11960qui
1100-1500	daily	SAm	6050qui, 15140qui
1300-1500	daily	MEX	11960qui
1330-1500	daily	Eu,Oc	21455qui*
1900-0500	daily	EQA	6050qui
2000-0500	daily	Eu,Oc	21455qui*
2100-2300	daily	SAm	15140qui
2300-0100	daily	NAm,SAm	11700qui
Tajik	**Days**	**Area**	**kHz**
1700-1715	.t.t...	CAs	11760rmp
Tatar	**Days**	**Area**	**kHz**
1700-1715	....fs.	RUS	11760rmp
Turkmen	**Days**	**Area**	**kHz**
1700-1715	daily	CAs	1251—**
Uzbek	**Days**	**Area**	**kHz**
1645-1700	daily	CAs	1251—**
1700-1715	m.w....	CAs	11760rmp

ANN: English: "This is the Voice of the Andes, HCJB, in Quito, Ecuador, South America"
V: QSL-card. Rp (1 IRC). Rec. acc. but cannot be returned.
NOTES: Part of HCJB's World Radio Network; see USA for corporate headquarters. Key: * AM-compatible USB with reduced carrier; ** Tx site not listed on request of HCJB.

EGYPT

EGYPTIAN RADIO (Gov)

See National Radio section.
kHz: *11665, 12050, 15115*

Winter Schedule 2004

Arabic	**Days**	**Area**	**kHz**
0700-1100	daily	WAf	15115abz*
1100-0300	daily	NAm,Eu	12050abz*
1900-0030	daily	EAf,CAf	11665abz**

ANN: Arabic (General Prgr): "Idha'at Jumhuriyat Masr al'arabiya min al-qahira"
V: QSL-card.
NOTES: Relays of Home Sce prgr's in Arabic for listeners abroad. Key: * General Programme ** Voice of the Arabs.

RADIO CAIRO (Gov)

P.O. Box 1186, 11511 Cairo, Egypt.
☎ +20 2 5789461. Fax +20 2 5789491.
Email: englishprog@ertu.org **Web:** www.ertu.org
Email: freqmag@menanet.net **Web:** www.ertu.gov.eg
L.P: Pres ERTU: Hassan Hamed; Chmn. Broadc. Sector: Omar Batisha; Chmn. Eng. Sector: Hamdy Emara.
SW: [ABS] Abis (G.C. 31N10 030E05) 8 x 250, 1 x 500kW; [ABZ] Abu Zaabal (G.C. 30N16 031E22) 13 x 100, 1 x 250, 4 x 500kW
kHz: *6230, 7115, 7120, 7270, 9415, 9735, 9780, 9855, 9950, 9988, 9990, 11655, 11695, 11725, 11755, 11790, 11855, 15115, 15135, 15155, 15335, 15365, 15375, 15425, 15480, 15620, 15670, 15715, 17670, 17775, 17810*

Winter Schedule 2004

Afar	**Days**	**Area**	**kHz**
1530-1630	daily	EAf,CAf	15155abz
Albanian	**Days**	**Area**	**kHz**
1600-1800	daily	ALB	9950abs
Amharic	**Days**	**Area**	**kHz**
1730-1900	daily	EAf,SAf	15155abz
Arabic	**Days**	**Area**	**kHz**
0030-0430	daily	NAm	7115abz
1015-1215	daily	ME,AFG	17775abz
1300-1600	daily	WAf	15365abs
2000-2200	daily	AUS	7270abs
2330-0045	daily	CAm,SAm	11755abz
2330-0045	daily	SAm	9735abs

Azeri	**Days**	**Area**	**kHz**
1400-1530	daily	AZE	11655abs
Bambara	**Days**	**Area**	**kHz**
1930-2030	daily	WAf	15375abz
Bangla	**Days**	**Area**	**kHz**
1330-1430	daily	SAs	17670abz
English	**Days**	**Area**	**kHz**
0200-0330	daily	NAm	11855abz
1215-1330	daily	SAs	17670abz
1630-1830	daily	CAf,SAf	9855abs
2030-2200	daily	WAf	15375abz
2115-2245	daily	Eu	9990abs
2300-0030	daily	NAm	11725abz
Farsi	**Days**	**Area**	**kHz**
1330-1530	daily	IRN	15480abz
French	**Days**	**Area**	**kHz**
2000-2115	daily	Eu	9990abs
2030-2230	daily	WAf	15335abs
Fulani	**Days**	**Area**	**kHz**
1915-2030	daily	WAf	15425abz
German	**Days**	**Area**	**kHz**
1900-2000	daily	Eu	9990abs
Hausa	**Days**	**Area**	**kHz**
1800-2100	daily	WAf	9780abs
Hindi	**Days**	**Area**	**kHz**
1500-1600	daily	SAs	15135abz
Indonesian	**Days**	**Area**	**kHz**
1315-1450	daily	SEA	15715abs
Italian	**Days**	**Area**	**kHz**
1800-1900	daily	Eu	9988abs
Lingala	**Days**	**Area**	**kHz**
1830-1915	daily	CAf,SAf	9855abs
Malay	**Days**	**Area**	**kHz**
1215-1315	daily	SEA	15715abs
Ndebele	**Days**	**Area**	**kHz**
1730-1815	daily	CAf,SAf	15620abs
Oulof/Wolof	**Days**	**Area**	**kHz**
1830-1930	daily	WAf	15375abz
Pashto	**Days**	**Area**	**kHz**
1430-1600	daily	AFG	15670abs
Portuguese	**Days**	**Area**	**kHz**
2215-2330	daily	SAm	11790abz
Russian	**Days**	**Area**	**kHz**
1800-1900	daily	RUS	7120abz
Shona	**Days**	**Area**	**kHz**
1645-1730	daily	CAf,SAf	15620abs
Somali	**Days**	**Area**	**kHz**
1630-1730	daily	EAf,CAf	15155abz
Spanish	**Days**	**Area**	**kHz**
0045-0200	daily	NAm	11855abz
0045-0200	daily	SAm	9415abs
0045-0200	daily	CAm	11755abz
Swahili	**Days**	**Area**	**kHz**
1530-1730	daily	EAf,CAf	17810abz
Tajik	**Days**	**Area**	**kHz**
1230-1330	daily	TJK	15480abz
Thai	**Days**	**Area**	**kHz**
1115-1215	daily	SEA	15715abs
Turkish	**Days**	**Area**	**kHz**
1600-1800	daily	TUR	6230abs
Urdu	**Days**	**Area**	**kHz**
1600-1800	daily	SAs	15115abz
Uzbek	**Days**	**Area**	**kHz**
1530-1630	daily	UZB	11695abz
Yoruba	**Days**	**Area**	**kHz**
2100-2200	daily	WAf	9780abs
Zulu	**Days**	**Area**	**kHz**
1600-1645	daily	CAf,SAf	15620abs

ANN: English: "You are tuned to Radio Cairo"
V: QSL-card.
NOTES: Radio Cairo is the External Sce of the Egyptian Radio & TV Union.

ESTONIA

RADIO TALLINN (Pub)

Gonsiori 21, EE-15020 Tallinn, Estonia.
☎ +372 6114446. Fax +372 6114369.
Email: english@er.ee **Web:** www.er.ee/tallinn
FM: Tallinn 103.5MHz 0.75kW
V: QSL-card.
NOTES: Radio Tallinn is a foreign language channel of the public broadcaster Eesti Raadio. Available on FM and via Internet, no shortwave transmissions. Programmes in English and Esperanto.

ETHIOPIA

RADIO ETHIOPIA (Gov)

P.O. Box 1020, Addis Ababa, Ethiopia.
☎ +251 1 551011. Fax +251 1 552263.
Email: sisayhaile@yahoo.com
Web: www.angelfire.com/biz/radioethiopia
L.P: Head: Moges Taffese; Head English Prgr: Edea Melessee.
SW: [GJW] Gedja Jewe (G.C. 08N47 038E38) 3 x 100kW
kHz: *7165, 9561*

Winter Schedule 2004

Afar	**Days**	**Area**	**kHz**
1300-1400	daily	EAf,ME	9561gjw*
1300-1400	daily	EAf	7165gjw*
Arabic	**Days**	**Area**	**kHz**
1400-1500	daily	EAf,ME	9561gjw*
1400-1500	daily	EAf	7165gjw*
English	**Days**	**Area**	**kHz**
1600-1700	daily	EAf,ME	9561gjw*
1600-1700	daily	EAf	7165gjw*
French	**Days**	**Area**	**kHz**
1700-1800	daily	EAf,ME	9561gjw*
1700-1800	daily	EAf	7165gjw*
Somali	**Days**	**Area**	**kHz**
1200-1300	daily	EAf,ME	9561gjw*
1200-1300	daily	EAf	7165gjw*

ANN: English: "This is the External Service of Radio Ethiopia"
V: QSL-card.
NOTES: External Sce of the national state broadcaster Radio Ethiopia. Key: * Frequency variable

FINLAND

YLE RADIO FINLAND (Pub)

FI-00024 Yleisradio, Finland.
☎ +358 9 14801. Fax +358 9 14801169.
Email: rfinland@yle.fi **Web:** www.yle.fi/rfinland
L.P: Head: Juhani Niinisto.
MW/SW: Uses tx's provided by Digita Oy
SAT: Asiasat 2, Hotbird 6, Intelsat 707, Thor 3
kHz: *558, 963, 5970, 6120, 7160, 7195, 7270, 9560, 9595, 9600, 9610, 9630, 9730, 9805, 9815, 11755, 11865, 13665, 15330, 15400, 17730, 17810, 17820, 17840, 21800*

Winter Schedule 2004

Finnish	**Days**	**Area**	**kHz**
0000-0115	daily	Eu	558hel
0000-2225	daily	Eu	963por
0120-0255	......s	Eu	558hel
0120-0300	mtwtfs.	Eu	558hel
0345-0915	twtfss	Eu	558hel
0350-0915	m......	Eu	558hel
0400-0505	......s	EAf	11865por
0400-0505	......s	Eu,EAf	9815por
0400-0600	mtwtfs.	Eu,EAf	9815por
0400-0600	mtwtfs.	Eu,EAf,RUS	11865por
0500-0505	......s	Eu,EAf,RUS	6120por
0500-0700	mtwtfs.	EAf	6120por
0500-2010	mtwtfs.	Eu,RUS	6120por
0550-0600	......s	EAf	11865por
0550-0600	......s	Eu,EAf	9815por
0550-0700	......s	EAf	6120por
0550-1955	......s	Eu,RUS	6120por
0600-0800	daily	As,AUS	11755por
0600-0900	daily	SAm	11755por
0600-1900	daily	Eu,WAf	11755por

Finnish	Days	Area	kHz
0700-0800	daily	WAf	6120por
0700-0900	daily	As,AUS	9560por
0700-0900	daily	SAm	9560por
0700-0900	daily	Eu,WAf	9560por
0730-0900	......ss	As,AUS	21800por
0930-1045	daily	As,AUS	17730por
0955-2000	daily	Eu	558hel
1100-1200	daily	As,AUS	17820por
1100-1200	daily	EAf	21800por
1100-1200	daily	Eu	21800por
1200-1300	daily	WAf,SAm	21800por
1300-1400	daily	NAm	15400por
1300-1450	daily	NAm	17840por
1400-1450	daily	As,AUS	7195por
1400-1450	daily	Eu,EAf,RUS	7195por
1500-1600	daily	EAf	11755por
1500-1600	daily	Eu,RUS	7195por
1600-1640	daily	SAm	17730por
1600-1640	daily	SAm,NAm	13665por
1655-1700	mtwtfs.	SAm	17730por
1655-1700	mtwtfs.	SAm,NAm	13665por
1700-1740	daily	Eu,EAf,RUS	9610por
1700-2100	daily	WAf	6120por
1800-1840	daily	Eu,EAf,RUS	7270por
1800-1840	daily	As,AUS	7270por
1900-2000	daily	Eu,EAf	9805por
2000-2010	......s	Eu,RUS	6120por
2045-2230	mtwtfs.	Eu	558hel
2050-2230	......s	Eu	558hel
2130-2150	daily	As,AUS	7160por
2200-2225	daily	WAf,SAm	5970por
2230-2400	daily	Eu	558hel, 963por
2330-2355	daily	As,AUS	9730por

Latin	Days	Area	kHz
0255-0300	......s	Eu	558hel
0345-0350	m......	Eu	558hel
0955-1000	m......	As,AUS	17810por
1355-1400	m......	As,AUS	9595por
1655-1700	......s	SAm	17730por
1655-1700	......s	SAm,NAm	13665por
1955-2000	......s	Eu,RUS	6120por
2045-2050	......s	Eu	558hel

Russian	Days	Area	kHz
0300-0345	daily	Eu	558hel
0915-0955	daily	Eu	558hel
0915-0955	m......	As,AUS	17810por
0915-1000	.twtfss	As,AUS	17810por
1000-1200	.....s.	As,AUS	9600por
1315-1355	m......	As,AUS	9595por
1315-1400	.twtfss	As,AUS	9595por
2000-2045	daily	Eu	558hel

Swedish	Days	Area	kHz
0115-0120	daily	Eu	558hel
0505-0550	......s	EAf	11865por
0505-0550	......s	Eu,EAf	9815por
0505-0550	......s	Eu,EAf,RUS	6120por
1045-1055	daily	As,AUS	17730por
1200-1300	......s	As,AUS	15330por
1400-1800	daily	Eu,WAf	9630por
1450-1500	daily	As,AUS	7195por
1450-1500	daily	Eu,EAf,RUS	7195per
1450-1500	daily	NAm	17840por
1500-1600	daily	As,AUS	7195por
1640-1655	daily	SAm	17730por
1640-1655	daily	SAm,NAm	13665por
1740-1800	daily	Eu,EAf,RUS	9610por
1840-1900	daily	As,AUS	7270por
1840-1900	daily	Eu,EAf,RUS	7270por
2150-2155	daily	As,AUS	7160por
2225-2230	daily	Eu	558hel, 963por
2225-2230	daily	WAf,SAm	5970por
2355-2400	daily	As,AUS	9730por

V: YLE does not verify reception reports, rpt should be sent to Digita Oy.
NOTES: External Sce of the public broadcaster Suomen Yleisradio (YLE). The Finnish and Swedish language segments are YLE Home Sce prgr's (mainly live relays, some are timeshifted recordings).

DIGITA OY (Tx Operator)

P.O. Box 135, FI-00521 Helsinki, Finland.
☎ +358 20 411711.
Email: info@digita.fi **Web:** www.digita.fi
L.P: Dir: Dr. Pauli Heikkilä.
MW: [HEL] Helsinki (G.C. 60N11 024E49) 558kHz 50kW, [POR] Pori (G.C. 61N28 021E35) 963kHz 600kW
SW: [POR] Pori (G.C. 61N28 021E35) 1 x 100, 1 x 250, 3 x 500kW
V: QSL-card. Rpt to Digita Oy, Shortwave Centre, Makholmantie 79, FI-28660 Pori, Finland (E-mail: la-asema.pori@digita.fi).
NOTES: Digita Oy is the national Finnish transmitter network operator, a joint stock company owned by the public broadcaster YLE (51%) and TDF-Télédiffusion de France (49%).

SCANDINAVIAN WEEKEND RADIO

P.O. Box 99, FI-34801 Virrat.
☎ +358 400 995559. 🖷 +358 3 4755776.
Email: info@swradio.net **Web:** www.swradio.net
L.P: Chief Editor: Esa Saunamäki; QSL Manager: Teemu Lehtimäki; Contact: Alpo Heinonen.
MW: [VIR] Virrat (G.C. 62N23 023E37) 1602kHz 0.1kW
SW: [VIR] Virrat (G.C. 62N23 023E37) 1 x 0.05, 1 x 0.1kW
kHz: *1602, 5980, 5990, 6170, 11690, 11720*

Winter Schedule 2004

English/Finnish	Days	Area	kHz
0700-1200	…..s.	Eu	6170vir*, 11690vir*
1200-1800	…..s.	Eu	5980vir*
1200-1900	…..s.	Eu	11720vir*
1800-1900	…..s.	Eu	5990vir*
1900-2200	…..s.	Eu	5980vir*, 11690vir*
2200-0700	….f..	Eu	5980vir*, 11720vir*
2200-2200	….f..	NEu	1602vir*

V: QSL-card. Rp (2 IRC's/2 US-$). Rpt form available on website.
NOTES: SWR is on the air on the first Saturday of each month for 24h, starting midnight local time (corresponding to Fri 2200 UTC winter, Fri 2100 UTC summer) and also Christmas Day. 1602kHz to become operational during 2005.

FRANCE

RADIO FRANCE INTERNATIONALE (RFI) (Pub)

BP 9516, F-75016 Paris, France.
☎ +33 1 42301212. 🖷 +33 1 42303071.
Email: english.service@rfi.fr **Web:** www.rfi.fr
Studios: 116 Av. du Président Kennedy, F-75016 Paris.
L.P: Pres: Jean-Paul Cluzel; DG: Benoît Paumier; Dir of Communication: Christine Berbudeau.
MW/SW: Leased from TDF
kHz: *684, 747, 1098, 1296, 3965, 4890, 5905, 5915, 5925, 5945, 5990, 6010, 6015, 6045, 6085, 6090, 6120, 6175, 6185, 7135, 7140, 7160, 7180, 7270, 7280, 7315, 7430, 9555, 9565, 9580, 9595, 9655, 9730, 9790, 9800, 9805, 9830, 11600, 11615, 11665, 11670, 11685, 11700, 11705, 11725, 11845, 11850, 11955, 11965, 11995, 12015, 12025, 12075, 13640, 15155, 15160, 15170, 15210, 15275, 15300, 15315, 15515, 15530, 15605, 17610, 17620, 17630, 17710, 17770, 17800, 17850, 17860, 21580, 21620, 21645, 21685, 21760*

Winter Schedule 2004

Albanian	Days	Area	kHz
0700-0730	daily	EEu	9805iss, 11670iss

Arabic
See Radio Monte Carlo-Moyen Orient

Creole	Days	Area	kHz
1330-1400	daily	CAm,Car	17860guf

English	Days	Area	kHz
0400-0430	daily	EAf,IOc	9555iss*, 9805gab, 11995iss**
0500-0530	daily	EAf,IOc	11850gab, 11995iss*, 15155iss**
0600-0630	daily	EAf,IOc	15155iss, 17800iss
0600-0630	daily	WAf	9595asc
0700-0800	daily	WAf	11700gab*, 11725gab*, 15605gab*, 15605gab**
1200-1230	daily	EAf,IOc	21620iss
1200-1230	daily	WAf	15275asc
1400-1500	daily	IND	7180xia*, 9580xia**

English	Days	Area	kHz
1400-1500	daily	ME,IND	17620iss
1600-1700	daily	CAf	9730mey, 17850iss
1600-1700	daily	NAf	11615iss
1600-1700	daily	WAf	15160mey
1600-1730	daily	EAf,IOc	15605iss
1600-1730	daily	EAf,ME	11615iss

French	Days	Area	kHz
0100-0200	daily	IND	15605bei*, 17710xia**
0130-0200	daily	CAm,Car	9800guf
0300-0400	daily	CAf,EAf,IOc	7135mey
0300-0400	daily	ME	5945iss*, 7315iss**
0300-0600	daily	CAf	9790iss
0400-0500	daily	CAf	4890gab, 7135iss, 7270asc
0400-0500	daily	ME	7315iss*, 9555iss**
0400-0500	daily	NAf	3965iss
0400-0600	daily	EAf,ME	15210dha
0430-0500	daily	EAf,IOc	9555iss*, 11995iss**
0500-0600	daily	NAf,CAf	7135iss**
0500-0600	daily	CAf	6175gab, 11700iss, 15300iss**
0500-0600	daily	ME	9555iss*, 11685iss**
0500-0600	daily	NAf	3965iss*, 5925iss
0530-0545	daily	EEu	5990iss
0530-0600	daily	EAf,IOc	11995iss*, 15155iss**
0600-0700	daily	CAf	15300iss, 17770kig, 17850iss**
0600-0700	daily	NAf	5925iss*, 7135iss
0600-0700	daily	NAf,WAf	9790iss**
0600-0700	daily	WAf	7135iss*, 9790iss*, 11700iss
0630-0700	daily	EAf,IOc	17800iss
0630-0700	daily	WAf	9595asc
0700-0800	daily	CAf	15170mey, 17850iss
0700-0800	daily	NAf	7135iss*
0700-0800	daily	NAf,WAf	9790iss, 11700iss
0700-0800	daily	WAf	9790iss*, 15300iss**, 17620iss**
0700-0900	daily	WAf	15315iss
0700-1600	daily	CAf	21580iss
0800-1000	daily	NAf	15300iss
0800-1000	daily	WAf	17620iss
0800-1130	daily	NAf,WAf	15300iss
0800-1600	daily	NAf	11845iss
0900-1600	daily	WAf	21685iss
1000-1100	daily	CAf	17850iss
1030-1200	daily	FE	7140yam
1030-1200	daily	SEA	9830yam
1100-1130	daily	Atl	6175iss
1100-1130	daily	NAf	15300iss
1100-1130	daily	NAm	15515iss
1100-1200	daily	CAm,Car	11670guf
1100-1200	daily	SEA	11600bei
1100-1400	daily	CAf	17850mey
1100-1400	daily	WAf	17620iss
1200-1400	daily	NAf	15300iss
1200-1700	daily	WAf	15300iss
1200-1800	daily	NAf	15300iss
1230-1300	daily	CAm,Car	15515guf
1230-1300	daily	EAf,IOc	21620iss
1230-1300	daily	WAf	21760mey
1300-1330	daily	CAm,Car	17860guf
1300-1400	daily	SEA	684dof
1500-1600	daily	CAf	17850iss
1600-1700	daily	CAf	15300iss*, 21580iss**
1600-1700	daily	SEA	1296kun, 6090kun
1600-1700	daily	WAf	17620iss
1700-1800	daily	NAf,CAf	15300iss
1700-1800	daily	WAf	11965iss*, 15300iss*, 15300iss**, 17620iss**
1800-1900	daily	NAf,CAf	15300iss**
1800-1900	daily	CAf	9790iss*
1800-2000	daily	NAf	7315iss
1800-2000	daily	WAf	11965iss
1800-2100	daily	NAf,WAf	9790iss
1800-2100	daily	WAf	11955gab
1800-2200	daily	CAf	11705iss
1800-2200	daily	NAf	7315iss
1900-2200	daily	CAf	7160mey, 9790iss
1900-2200	daily	NAf	6175iss
2000-2200	daily	NAf	7315iss
2100-2200	daily	NAf	3965iss
2100-2200	daily	WAf	7315iss, 9790gab
2300-0030	daily	SEA	17710yam
2300-0100	daily	FE,SEA	12025nsb
2300-2400	daily	SEA	12075vld

Khmer	Days	Area	kHz
1200-1300	daily	SEA	11600xia, 12015irk

Lao	Days	Area	kHz
1100-1200	daily	SEA	12015irk

Mandarin	Days	Area	kHz
0930-1030	daily	FE	5945irk, 9655yam
1200-1300	daily	FE	7140yam, 7430nsb
2200-2300	daily	FE	747min, 1098kou, 7315vld, 7430nsb

Marine Weather	Days	Area	kHz
1130-1200	daily	Atl	6175iss
1130-1200	daily	CAm,Car	17610iss, 21645iss
1130-1200	daily	NAf,WAf	15300iss
1130-1200	daily	NAm	13640iss, 15515iss

Pashto	Days	Area	kHz
1600-1630	daily	ME	6010tac, 9565dha
1800-1900	daily	ME	5990tac, 6015dha

Polish	Days	Area	kHz
0545-0600	daily	EEu	5990iss
1700-1800	daily	EEu	6085iss
2200-2300	daily	EEu	5915iss

Portuguese	Days	Area	kHz
1700-1800	daily	WAf	11995iss*, 15530iss**
1700-1800	daily	EAf,IOc	12015gab
2000-2100	daily	CAf	11965iss

Romanian	Days	Area	kHz
1600-1700	daily	EEu	9805iss
2100-2200	daily	EEu	6185iss, 7135iss

Russian	Days	Area	kHz
0400-0430	daily	EEu	5990iss, 6045iss, 7280iss
1400-1430	daily	EEu	11665iss*, 15515iss, 15605iss, 17850iss**
1900-2000	daily	EEu	5905iss, 7135iss

Serbian	Days	Area	kHz
0600-0630	daily	EEu	6175iss, 7315iss
1500-1600	daily	EEu	9805iss, 11670iss
2000-2100	daily	EEu	3965iss, 6090iss

Spanish	Days	Area	kHz
0100-0130	daily	CAm,Car	9800guf
1200-1230	daily	CAm,Car	15515guf
1600-1630	daily	CAm,Car	17860guf
1800-1830	daily	CAm,Car	17630guf
2100-2130	daily	CAm,Car	17630guf

Vietnamese	Days	Area	kHz
1400-1500	daily	SEA	6120yam
1500-1600	daily	SEA	1296kun

ANN: French: "Ici Paris, Radio France Internationale"
IS: "La Marseillaise"
V: QSL-card.
NOTES: RFI is the External Sce of the public broadcaster Radio France. RFI's Arabic prgr's see under Radio Monte Carlo Moyen-Orient. Key: * from 31 October 04 - 27 February 2005; ** from 27 February 2005 - 27 March 2005.

RADIO MONTE CARLO MOYEN–ORIENT (RMC–MO)

116, Avenue du President Kennedy, F-75220 Paris 16, France.
☎ +33 1 56401717. Fax +33 1 56401700.
Email: contact@rmc-mo.com **Web:** www.rmc-mo.com
P.O. Box 2026, Nicosia, Cyprus.
L.P: GM: Christophe Carbonnier.
MW/SW: Leased from Monte Carlo Radiodiffusion (MW) and TDF (SW)
kHz: *3965, 5925, 7135, 7325, 9790, 12025*

Winter Schedule 2004

Arabic	Days	Area	kHz
0500-0600	daily	NAf	3965iss*, 5925iss, 7135iss**
1600-1700	daily	NAf	7325iss*, 12025iss
1600-1800	daily	NAf	9790iss
1700-1800	daily	NAf	7325iss

V: QSL-card.
NOTES: Radio Monte Carlo Moyen-Orient is the Arabic service of Radio France Internationale (RFI), it is a member of the RFI group since the end of 1996. Key: * from 31 October 04 - 27 February 2005; ** from 27 February 2005 - 27 March 2005. Schedule shown is RFI's Arabic Service.

GOLOS PRAVOSLAVIYA (LA VOIX DE L'ORTHODOXIE) (Rlg)

BP 416-08, F-75366 Paris CEDEX 08, France.
☎ +33 1 49770366. Fax +33 1 43534066.
Email: voix.orthodoxie@wanadoo.fr **Web:** www.russie.net/orthodoxie/vo
Studio in Russia: nab. Leyt.Shmidta 39, 199034 St.Petersburg, Russia.
☎ +7 812 3232867. Fax +7 812 3232867.
kHz: *9355*

Winter Schedule 2004

Russian	Days	Area	kHz
1630-1700	.t.f..	RUS	9355alm

V: QSL-card.
NOTES: Russian-orthodox station, launched in 2000. Uses same freq throughout the year, but tr's are 1 hour earlier in summer (DST in Russia).

TÉLÉDIFFUSION DE FRANCE S.A. (TDF) (Tx Operator)

21-27 rue Barbès, F-92120 Montrouge, France.
☎ +33 1 49651000. Fax +33 1 46574850.
Email: jacques.gruson@tdf.fr **Web:** www.tdf.fr
Radio Division: 10 rue d'Oradour-sur-Glane, F-75732 Paris Cedex 15, France.
☎ +33 1 55951553. Fax +33 1 55952137.
L.P: GD: Philippe Levrier; Freq Mgr: Jacques Gruson.
MW: [PRS] Paris (G.C. 48N51 002E20) 738kHz 5kW
SW: [ISS] Issoudun (G.C. 46N56 001E59) 21 x 500kW
NOTES: TDF is the national French transmitter network operator with shortwave transmitting facilities in France and French Guiana. Leases out its tr's to national and foreign broadcasters.

Broadcasters using sites in this country:
China R. Int'l uses: (ISS). See stn entry in: **CHN**, INT Section
R.Taiwan Int'l uses: (ISS). See stn entry in: **TWN**, INT Section
RCI uses: (ROU). See stn entry in: **CAN**, INT Section
TWR Europe uses: (ROU). See stn entry in: **AUT**, INT Section
TWR Europe uses: (MCO). See stn entry in: **AUT**, INT Section
Vatican Radio uses: (ROU). See stn entry in: **CVA**, INT Section
VO Africa uses: (ISS). See stn entry in: **LBY**, INT Section

FRENCH GUIANA

TÉLÉDIFFUSION DE FRANCE RELAY STATION

Direction TDF Outre-Mer, BP 7024, 97307 Cayenne Cedex, French Guiana.
☎ +33 5 94350550.
Email: fabrice.esnay@tdf.fr
SW: [GUF] Montsinéry (G.C. 04N54 052W36) 6 x 500kW
V: QSL-card.
Broadcasters using sites in this country:
China R. Int'l uses: (GUF). See stn entry in: **CHN**, INT Section
R.Japan uses: (GUF). See stn entry in: **J**, INT Section
RFI uses: (GUF). See stn entry in: **F**, INT Section

GABON

AFRICA NO.1 (Comm)

193 Rue du Faubourg Poissonniere, F-75009 Paris, France.
☎ +241 760001. Fax +241 742133.
Web: www.africa1.com
☎ +33 1 55075801. Fax +33 1 55079748.
L.P: Pres: Louis Barthélémy Mapangou; Dir Techn: Gaston Ombolo Ki-Obo; Dir Prgrs. & Adv: Augustin Letamba.
SW: [MOY] Moanda, Moyabi (G.C. 01S40 013E31) 5 x 500kW
FM: FM Relays in some African countries.
SAT: Atlantic Bird 3, Astra 1H, NSS 7
kHz: *9580, 15475, 17630*

Winter Schedule 2004

French	Days	Area	kHz
0500-2300	daily	Af	9580gab
0700-1600	daily	Af	17630gab
1600-2100	daily	Af	15475gab

V: QSL-card.
NOTES: Africa 1 is owned by Africa Média S.A. Some capacities of the transmitter facilities are leased to international broadcasters.
Broadcasters using sites in this country:
R.Japan uses: (GAB). See stn entry in: **J**, INT Section
RFI uses: (GAB). See stn entry in: **F**, INT Section

GEORGIA

RADIO GEORGIA (Gov)

M. Kostava Street 68, T'bilisi 0171, Georgia.
☎ +995 32 360063. Fax +995 32 955137.
Email: foraf@geotvr.ge **Web:** www.geotvr.ge
L.P: Dir European Dept: Irina Gegechkori; Dir Int'l Rel: Nana Chibalashvili.
SW: Leased from Georgian Radio&TV Centre
kHz: *4540, 6080, 6180, 11805, 11910*

Winter Schedule 2004

Armenian	Days	Area	kHz
1515-1545	daily	ARM	6080dsh
Azeri	**Days**	**Area**	**kHz**
1600-1630	daily	AZE	4540dsh
English	**Days**	**Area**	**kHz**
0630-0700	daily	Eu	11805dsh
0830-0900	daily	Eu	11910dsh
0930-1000	daily	ME	11910dsh
1630-1700	daily	ME	6180dsh
French	**Days**	**Area**	**kHz**
0800-0830	daily	Eu	11910dsh
Georgian	**Days**	**Area**	**kHz**
0500-0600	.t.t...	ME	6080dsh
0630-0800	.t.t...	ME	6080dsh
1000-1030	daily	ME	11910dsh
1600-1700	.....ss	ME	6080dsh
1700-1730	daily	ME	6180dsh
1730-1900	.....ss	ME	6080dsh
German	**Days**	**Area**	**kHz**
0700-0730	daily	Eu	11805dsh
Russian	**Days**	**Area**	**kHz**
0600-0630	daily	Eu	11805dsh

ANN: Georgian: "Laparakobs T'bilisi"; German: "Hier ist Georgien"; English: "This is Georgia"; Russian: "Govorit Gruziya"
V: QSL-card.
NOTES: Radio Georgia is the External Sce of the state owned Georgian National Broadc. Corp. (Saqartvelos Teleradio Korporacia). Due to budget limitations, the transmissions may not always be daily.

GEORGIAN RADIO & TV CENTRE (Tx Operator)

P.O. Box 160, T'bilisi 0008, Georgia
☎ +995 32 935421. Fax +995 32 995492.
Email: telecenter@iberiapac.ge
SW: [DSH] Dusheti (G.C. 42N03 044E41) 1 x 50, 2 x 100kW
NOTES: Georgian Radio&TV Centre is the national transmitter network operator in Georgia. It provides SW facilities for Radio Georgia.

GERMANY

DEUTSCHE WELLE (Pub)

D-53111 Bonn, Germany.
☎ +49 228 4290. Fax +49 228 4293000.
Email: online@dw-world.de **Web:** www.dw-world.de
Studios: Kurt-Schumacher-Str. 3, D-53113 Bonn, Germany.
L.P: GD: Erik Bettermann; MD Radio: Joachim Lenz; MD Marketing, Distribution, Technology: Peter Senger.
SW: Leased from Deutsche Telekom
SAT: AMC 1, Asiasat 2, Astra 1F, Hotbird 6, Intelsat 707, Nilsat 101, Nimiq 1/2, Pas 7/9/10

kHz: *693, 810, 999, 1188, 1215, 1350, 1458, 1512, 1548, 3995, 5905, 5910, 5925, 5945, 5975, 5980, 6030, 6045, 6075, 6090, 6100, 6130, 6140, 6145, 6170, 6180, 6205, 6225, 6245, 7130, 7145, 7175, 7195, 7200, 7210, 7225, 7240, 7245, 7250, 7285, 7290, 7305, 7400, 9395, 9430, 9495, 9535, 9545, 9560, 9565, 9585, 9610, 9615, 9640, 9655, 9690, 9710, 9715, 9720, 9735, 9745, 9755, 9770, 9775, 9780, 9790, 9800, 9815, 9870, 9875, 11690, 11695, 11720, 11785, 11795, 11810, 11865, 11890, 11895, 11905, 11945, 11955, 11970, 11975, 11985, 11990, 12015, 12025, 12035, 12045, 12945, 13645, 13735, 13780, 15110, 15145, 15190, 15205, 15275, 15330, 15335, 15410, 15440, 15470, 15490, 15595, 15605, 15680, 17485, 17545, 17610, 17630, 17700, 17710, 17800, 17820, 17845, 17860, 21560, 21640, 21665, 21675, 21780, 21820, 21840*

Winter Schedule 2004

Albanian	**Days**	**Area**	**kHz**
0630-0645	daily	ALB	1215fla
0630-0700	daily	ALB	6045wer, 7195nau
1200-1230	daily	ALB	810sko, 7175wer, 9770wer
1600-1630	daily	ALB	810sko, 7210wer, 15470sin
Amharic	**Days**	**Area**	**kHz**
1400-1450	daily	ETH	11810kig, 21840wer
Arabic	**Days**	**Area**	**kHz**
1300-1330	daily	ME,NAf	15470sin, 17485wer, 21780sin, 21820wer
1400-1430	daily	ME,NAf	15145sin, 17485nau, 21560trm
1430-1500	daily	ME,NAf	15145sin, 17485nau, 21560trm, 21780wer, 21820sin
1600-1630	daily	ME,NAf	9745wer, 9755kig, 11975nau, 17800kig
2000-2130	daily	ME,NAf	6130nau*, 9495wer, 11865sin, 11890trm
2100-2130	daily	ME,NAf	1350gav
Bangla	**Days**	**Area**	**kHz**
0100-0200	daily	SAs	7285wer, 9615trm
Bosnian	**Days**	**Area**	**kHz**
0700-0715	daily	BIH	6045wer, 7195nau
1300-1330	daily	BIH	7175wer, 9770wer
1700-1715	daily	BIH	6130wer, 15470sin
Bulgarian	**Days**	**Area**	**kHz**
0500-0530	daily	BUL	7200sin
0600-0630	daily	BUL	7195nau
1030-1100	daily	BUL	11970nau
1230-1300	daily	BUL	9770wer
Croatian	**Days**	**Area**	**kHz**
0900-0915	daily	SEu	9770wer
1330-1400	daily	SEu	7175wer
1500-1515	daily	SEu	7175wer
Dari	**Days**	**Area**	**kHz**
0830-0850	daily	AFG	11895dha, 15145arm
1330-1400	daily	AFG	17545wer, 21820wer
English	**Days**	**Area**	**kHz**
0000-0100	daily	SAs	1548trm, 6030trm, 7290wer
0400-0500	daily	CAf,EAf	6180kig, 9545kig, 9710wer
0500-0600	daily	CAf,SAf	7285wer, 9565kig, 12035kig, 15410dha
0600-0700	daily	WAf	7225sin, 7225wer, 11785wer, 15410kig
0600-1000	daily	Eu	6140jul
0600-1000	daily	ME,NAf	21675trm+
1300-1600	daily	Eu	6140jul
1600-1700	daily	SAs	1548trm, 6170trm, 7225trm, 11695wer
1900-2000	daily	EAf	6180kig, 11865sin, 13780wer, 17800sin
2000-2100	daily	CAf,SAf	12025trm, 13780wer, 15205wer, 15410trm
2100-2200	daily	WAf	9615wer, 13780trm, 15410kig
2200-2300	daily	EAs	6180trm, 6225alm
2300-2330	daily	NAm	9800sac+
2300-2400	daily	SEA	7250trm, 9815trm, 12035kig
English/German	**Days**	**Area**	**kHz**
0700-1000	daily	Eu	5975wer+
0800-1400	daily	Eu	15440sin+
0900-1100	daily	Eu	17700sin+
1000-1300	daily	Eu	6140jul+
1100-1155	daily	Eu	17710sin+
1200-1400	daily	Eu	9655wer+
1400-1555	daily	Eu	17800sin+
1400-1559	daily	Eu	6130wer+
1600-0700	daily	Eu	3995wer+
1600-1900	daily	Eu	6140jul+
Farsi	**Days**	**Area**	**kHz**
1730-1800	daily	IRN	9495wer
1730-1930	daily	IRN	6245nsb, 11695trm
1800-1900	daily	IRN	7175nau, 12945kig
French	**Days**	**Area**	**kHz**
1200-1300	daily	Af	15410kig, 15470sin, 17610wer, 17800kig, 21665wer
1600-1700	daily	Af	12035sin, 15145kig, 15680wer, 17630wer, 21560sin
1700-1800	daily	Af	9535kig, 9735sin, 12035wer, 13645wer, 15410kig
German	**Days**	**Area**	**kHz**
0000-0200	daily	NAm,MEX	9655kig
0000-0200	daily	SAm	11690kig
0000-0200	daily	NAm,Car	6100atg
0000-0200	daily	Eu,NAf	6075wer
0000-0200	daily	Eu	6075sin
0000-0200	daily	SAm,NAm	9545sin
0200-0400	daily	Eu	6075sin
0200-0400	daily	Eu,NAf	6075wer
0200-0400	daily	Eu,NAf,ME	6075nau
0200-0400	daily	NAm	6145wer
0200-0400	daily	NAm,Car	9640atg, 9870kig
0200-0400	daily	NAm,MEX	6100sac
0300-0400	daily	RUS	693msk, 1188spe
0400-0500	daily	NAm,MEX	6100bon
0400-0600	daily	Eu	6075sin
0400-0600	daily	NAm,MEX	6145wer
0400-0600	daily	Eu,NAf	6075wer
0400-0600	daily	NAm,Car	9640atg
0500-0600	daily	NAm,MEX	6100atg
0500-0600	daily	RUS	693msk, 1188spe
0600-0800	daily	Eu	6075sin
0600-0800	daily	Eu,NAf	6075wer, 9545nau
0600-0800	daily	Eu,NAf,ME	13780wer
0600-0800	daily	NZL,AUS	9690atg, 9735wer, 11985atg
0600-0800	daily	RUS	693msk, 1188spe
0600-0800	daily	SEA,AUS	21640trm
0700-0800	daily	Eu	3995wer
0800-1000	daily	SEA,AUS,NZL	21640trm
0800-1000	daily	RUS	693msk, 1188spe
0800-1000	daily	NZL,AUS	9690atg, 9735wer
0800-1000	daily	Eu,NAf,ME	13780wer
0800-1000	daily	Eu	6075wer
0800-1000	daily	Eu,NAf	9545nau
1000-1200	daily	SEA,AUS,NZL	21840nau
1000-1200	daily	Eu	6075wer
1000-1200	daily	Eu,ME	13780wer
1000-1200	daily	Eu,NAf	9545nau
1000-1200	daily	FE,SEA	5910ppk, 7400irk, 15605alm, 17845trm
1000-1200	daily	RUS	693msk, 1188spe
1200-1400	daily	Eu	6075wer
1200-1400	daily	Eu,ME	13780wer
1200-1400	daily	Eu,NAf	9545nau
1200-1400	daily	FE,SEA	5910ppk, 7400irk, 9395alm, 17845trm
1200-1400	daily	RUS	693msk, 1188spe
1200-1400	daily	Eu,As,ME	17630nau
1400-1430	daily	SAs	1548trm
1400-1500	daily	RUS	693msk, 1188spe
1400-1600	daily	Eu,CAs,ME	15275kig

German	Days	Area	kHz
1400-1600	daily	SAs	9655trm
1400-1600	daily	Eu,ME	13780wer
1400-1600	daily	Eu,As,ME	15680nau
1400-1600	daily	Eu	6075wer
1400-1600	daily	Eu,NAf	9545nau
1500-1600	daily	Eu	1512wol
1600-1700	daily	Eu	1512wol
1600-1800	daily	Eu	6075wer
1600-1800	daily	Eu,NAf	9545nau
1600-1800	daily	ME,CAs	11795kig
1600-1800	daily	NAf,ME	13780wer
1600-1800	daily	SAs	9655trm
1600-1800	daily	SAs,SEA	9545wer
1700-1800	daily	Eu	6075sin
1700-1800	daily	SAs	1548trm
1800-2000	daily	Am	17860kig
1800-2000	daily	Eu	6075sin, 6075wer
1800-2000	daily	Eu,NAf	9545nau
1800-2000	daily	NAf,CAf	11795nau
1800-2000	daily	NAf,WAf	9735wer
1800-2000	daily	SAf	11945kig
1800-2000	daily	Af,ME	15275trm
2000-2200	daily	NAf,CAf	11795nau
2000-2200	daily	SAm,NAf	9545nau
2000-2200	daily	NAf,WAf	9735wer
2000-2200	daily	Eu,NAf	6075wer
2000-2200	daily	Eu	6075sin
2000-2200	daily	Am	17860kig
2000-2200	daily	SAf	11945kig
2100-2200	daily	RUS	693msk, 1188spe
2200-2300	daily	RUS	693msk, 1188spe
2200-2400	daily	Am	11955sin
2200-2400	daily	Eu	6075sin
2200-2400	daily	Eu,NAf	6075wer
2200-2400	daily	NAm,Car	9780atg, 11990sac
2200-2400	daily	SAm	9545sin, 11690kig

Hausa	Days	Area	kHz
0630-0700	daily	WAf	7240sin, 9565wer, 15440kig
1300-1350	daily	WAf	15410kig, 17800kig, 21665wer
1800-1900	daily	WAf	9430wer, 12015sin, 17800kig

Hindi	Days	Area	kHz
1515-1600	daily	SAs	1548trm, 7225trm, 9585trm, 15605wer

Indonesian	Days	Area	kHz
1200-1250	daily	INS	9655trm, 17820trm, 21820dha
2200-2250	daily	INS	9610trm, 9720kig, 12035kig

Kiswahili	Days	Area	kHz
0300-0400	daily	SAf,EAf	6180kig, 7195kig, 9565sin, 9710wer
1000-1050	daily	SAf,EAf	9875kig, 12045kig, 15410kig, 21780wer
1500-1600	daily	SAf,EAf	9735kig, 12025kig, 21820wer

Macedonian	Days	Area	kHz
0730-0800	daily	MKD	810sko, 9775wer
1000-1030	daily	MKD	810sko, 9770wer
1400-1430	daily	MKD	7175wer

Mandarin	Days	Area	kHz
1030-1055	daily	CHN	6205kna, 15145trm, 15190sng, 17820trm
1300-1350	daily	CHN	6225nsb, 13735sng, 15330trm, 15490trm
2300-2350	daily	CHN	6090dha, 6225alm, 9560trm

Pashto	Days	Area	kHz
0800-0830	daily	AFG	11895dha, 15145arm
1400-1430	daily	AFG	17545wer, 21820wer

Polish	Days	Area	kHz
1300-1330	daily	POL	7130wer, 9735wer
1730-1800	daily	POL	7240sin

Portuguese	Days	Area	kHz
0500-0545	daily	Af	9545wer, 9755kig

Romanian	Days	Area	kHz
1100-1300	daily	ROM	11970nau*

Romany	Days	Area	kHz
1130-1200	......s	SEu	11905wer, 15275wer

Russian	Days	Area	kHz
0100-0200	daily	FE	15145ppk, 15595trm
0100-0200	daily	RUS	5925wer, 15110vld
0200-0300	daily	CAs	7305nau, 15335trm
0200-0300	daily	RUS	5905wer
0300-0400	daily	CAs	15335trm
0300-0400	daily	RUS	5905nau
0400-0500	daily	Eu,CAs	1188spe, 7145wer, 15110kig
0400-0500	daily	RUS	693msk
0500-0630	daily	Eu	5910nau, 7305wer, 17700kig
0600-0630	daily	RUS	999gri
1500-1600	daily	RUS	693msk, 1188spe, 7145wer, 9715wer, 11720wer
1600-1700	daily	RUS	693msk, 999gri, 1188spe, 7145wer, 9715wer
1700-1900	daily	RUS	693msk, 1188spe, 5980wer, 7145wer, 9715trm
1900-2000	daily	RUS	693msk, 999gri, 1188spe, 5980wer, 7145wer, 9715trm
2000-2100	daily	RUS	693msk, 1188spe, 5980wer, 6180wer, 7145sin

Sanskrit	Days	Area	kHz
1545-1600	daily	SAs	1548trm, 9585trm, 15605wer
1545-1600	m......	SAs	7225trm**

Serbian	Days	Area	kHz
0715-0730	daily	SEu	6045wer, 7195nau
1030-1100	daily	SEu	810sko, 7175wer, 9770wer
1430-1500	daily	SEu	7175wer, 9770wer
2100-2115	daily	SEu	1458fla, 7245sin, 11905kig

Turkish	Days	Area	kHz
0630-0700	daily	TUR	9615wer, 11905wer
1130-1200	mtwtfs.	TUR	11905wer, 15275wer
1530-1600	daily	TUR	9790nau, 15470sin

Ukrainain	Days	Area	kHz
0530-0600	daily	UKR	999gri, 5945wer, 7200sin

Urdu	Days	Area	kHz
1430-1515	daily	SAs	1548trm, 7225trm, 15605wer
1700-1730	daily	SAs	9495wer, 11695trm

ANN: German: "Hier ist die Deutsche Welle"; English: "This is DW Radio"; Russian: "Nemetskaya Volna"

V: QSL-card. Rpt to DW - Technische Beratung.

NOTES: Deutsche Welle is a public service broadcaster established to serve German nationals abroad as well as foreign listeners around the world. DW owns relay stations in Portugal, Rwanda and Sri Lanka. Transmissions in some Asian languages are jammed in the target area. Relayed at certain times in Bucharest (ROM) on 88.5MHz, in Prstina (SCG) on 88.6MHz, in Sofia (BUL) on 95.7MHz, in Kigali (RRW) on 96.0MHz, in Tirana (ALB) on 106.0 and DAB in Berlin (D) area on 199.360MHz. Additional broadcasts may be heard at other times on FM/DAB frequencies. Key: + DRM; * until 15 Feb 2005; ** every 2nd Monday.

EVANGELISCHE MISSIONS–GEMEINDEN (Rlg)

✉ Evangelische Missions-Gemeinden, Jahnstrasse 9, D-89182 Bernstadt, Germany.
☎ +49 7348 948026. 🖷 +49 7348 948027.
kHz: *6015, 9815, 11840*

Winter Schedule 2004

German	Days	Area	kHz
1130-1200	.....ss	Eu	6015jul

Russian	Days	Area	kHz
1200-1205	.....s.	RUS	11840jul

Russian	**Days**	**Area**	**kHz**
1205-1230	.....s.	RUS	11840nau
1600-1630	.....s.	RUS	9815wer

V: QSL-card.
NOTES: Rebroadcasts prgr's of various protestant missions.

EVANGELIUMSRADIO HAMBURG (Rlg)

Postfach 920741, D-21137 Hamburg, Germany.
☎ +49 40 7027025. Fax +49 40 85408861.
Email: evangeliums-radio-hamburg@t-online.de
Web: www.evr-hamburg.de
kHz: *6045*

Winter Schedule 2004

German	**Days**	**Area**	**kHz**
1000-1100	......s	Eu	6045jul

V: QSL-card.

EVANGELIUMS–RUNDFUNK (Rlg)

Berliner Ring 62, D-35576 Wetzlar, Germany.
☎ +49 6441 9570. Fax +49 6441 957120.
Email: info@erf.de **Web:** www.erf.de
MW: Leased from Deutsche Telekom
kHz: *1539*

Winter Schedule 2004

Arabic	**Days**	**Area**	**kHz**
0400-0430	m......	Eu	1539mnf
0445-0500	.t....	Eu	1539mnf
Croatian	**Days**	**Area**	**kHz**
0400-0415	....f.s	Eu	1539mnf
0445-0500	....f..	Eu	1539mnf
Farsi	**Days**	**Area**	**kHz**
0400-0430	.t....	Eu	1539mnf
French	**Days**	**Area**	**kHz**
0430-0445	daily	Eu	1539mnf
German	**Days**	**Area**	**kHz**
0500-0400	daily	Eu	1539mnf
Greek	**Days**	**Area**	**kHz**
0445-0500	m......	Eu	1539mnf
Russian	**Days**	**Area**	**kHz**
0400-0430	..w....	Eu	1539mnf
0445-0500	..w....	Eu	1539mnf
Sorani	**Days**	**Area**	**kHz**
0445-0500	.....s.	Eu	1539mnf
Spanish	**Days**	**Area**	**kHz**
0415-0430	....f..	Eu	1539mnf
0445-0500	......s	Eu	1539mnf
Turkish	**Days**	**Area**	**kHz**
0400-0430	...t....	Eu	1539mnf
0445-0500	...t....	Eu	1539mnf

V: QSL-card.
NOTES: TWR partner station. Produces German prgr's for TWR Europe (see Austria) and relays certain TWR prgr's.

LUTHERISCHE STUNDE (Rlg)

Postfach 1162, 27363 Sottrum, Germany.
☎ +49 4264 2436. Fax +49 4264 2437.
Email: info@lutherischestunde.de
Web: www.lutherischestunde.de
kHz: *603, 1215, 1323, 1386, 1440, 6235, 7300*

Winter Schedule 2004

German	**Days**	**Area**	**kHz**
1830-1840	...t....	Eu	1440mrn
1845-1900	..w....	Eu	603bln, 1215klg, 1323wbr, 1386klg, 6235spb, 7300arm

V: QSL-letter.

MISSIONSWERK ARCHE (Rlg)

Doerriesweg 7, D-22525 Hamburg, Germany
☎ +49 40 547050. Fax +49 40 54705299.
Email: info@arche-gemeinde.de **Web:** www.arche-gemeinde.de
kHz: *6015*

Winter Schedule 2004

German	**Days**	**Area**	**kHz**
1200-1215	......s	Eu	6015jul

NOTES: Transmissions were due to start on 2 January 2005.

MISSIONSWERK HEUKELBACH (Rlg)

D-51700 Bergneustadt, Germany.
☎ +49 2261 94537. Fax +49 2261 94537.
Email: info@missionswerk-heukelbach.de **Web:** www.missionswerk-heukelbach.de
kHz: *603, 1215, 1323, 1386, 1440, 6095, 6235, 7300*

Winter Schedule 2004

German	**Days**	**Area**	**kHz**
0315-0330	mt..f..	Eu	1440mrn
0345-0400	.....s.	Eu	1440mrn
0515-0530	......s	Eu	1440mrn, 6095jun+
1745-1800	daily	Eu	1440mrn
1845-1900	mt.tfss	Eu	603bln, 1215klg, 1323wbr, 1386klg, 6235spb, 7300arm

V: QSL-card.
NOTES: Key: + DRM

RADIO SANTEC (Rlg)

Postfach 5643, D-97006 Würzburg, Germany.
☎ +49 931 3903264. Fax +49 931 3903195.
Email: info@radio-santec.com **Web:** www.radio-santec.com
Studio: Marienstrasse 1, D-97070 Würzburg, Germany.
kHz: *603, 1143, 1215, 1323, 1386, 5775, 5945, 6045, 6145, 6195, 6235, 7105, 7125, 7145, 7180, 7230, 7300, 7330, 7370, 7390, 7570, 9480, 9495, 9965, 11840*

Winter Schedule 2004

English	**Days**	**Area**	**kHz**
0100-0130	......s	IND	7145jul
1800-1830	......s	Af	11840jul
1900-1930	ISR		
2100-2130	....f..	Eu,As	5775mil
2200-2230	.t.....	Eu	1323wbr
French	**Days**	**Area**	**kHz**
1600-1630	......s	CAf	9495jul
2030-2100	....f..	Eu,Af	1323wbr, 7230spb, 7300arm, 7370sam, 7390msk, 9480msk
German	**Days**	**Area**	**kHz**
0545-0600	daily	Eu	1323wbr
1200-1300	.....s.	Eu	6045jul
1230-1330	......s	Eu	6045jul
1655-1700	daily	Eu	603bln, 1215klg, 1323wbr, 1386klg, 6145msk, 7300arm
1800-1900	......s	Eu	603bln, 1215klg, 1323wbr, 1386klg, 6235spb, 7300arm
1830-1900	.t...s.	Eu	603bln, 1215klg, 1323wbr, 1386klg, 6235spb, 7300arm
1930-2000	..w....	Eu	603bln, 1215klg, 1323wbr, 6145msk, 7300arm
Italian	**Days**	**Area**	**kHz**
2200-2230	..w....	Eu	1323wbr
Polish	**Days**	**Area**	**kHz**
1830-1900	..w....	Eu	1143klg, 7125jul
Portuguese	**Days**	**Area**	**kHz**
0045-0100	m.....s	SAm	7330msk, 7390sam, 7570orz, 9965gav
Spanish	**Days**	**Area**	**kHz**
0150-0200	mtwtf..	SAm	5945arm, 6195spb, 7125jul, 7180gri, 7330msk, 7390sam, 7570orz, 9965gav

ANN: German: "Hier hören Radio Santec"; English: "You are listening to Radio Santec"
V: QSL-card.
NOTES: Radio ministry of the the Universal Life Church (Universelles Leben).

HAMBURGER LOKALRADIO

Hamburger Lokalradio, Kulturzentrum Lola, Lohbrügger Landstrasse 8, D-21031 Hamburg, Germany.
☎ +49 40 72692422. Fax +49 40 72692423.
Email: m.kittner@freenet.de **Web:** www.hhlr.de
kHz: *5925, 6045*

Winter Schedule 2004

German	Days	Area	kHz
1000-1100	.....s.	Eu	6045jul*
1000-1600	.....s.	Eu	5925jul**

NOTES: Hamburger Lokalradio is a non-commercial community radio station. Planned transmission period: * until 29 Jan 2005; ** 25 Dec 2004 - 1 Jan 2005.

DEUTSCHE TELEKOM T–SYSTEMS MEDIABROADCAST (Tx Operator)

Am Propsthof 51, D-53121 Bonn, Germany.
+49 228 7090.
Email: mediabroadcast.marketing@t-systems.com
Web: www.t-systems.de
MW: [BLN] Berlin (G.C. 52N30 013E20) 603kHz 5kW; [MNF] Mainflingen (G.C. 58N00 008E59) 1539kHz 700kW; [WBR] Wachenbrunn (G.C. 50N29 010E33) 1323kHz 1000kW
SW: [JUL] Jülich (G.C. 50N57 006E22) 12 x 100kW; [NAU] Nauen (G.C. 52N38 012E54) 4 x 500kW; [WER] Wertachtal (G.C. 48N05 010E41) 16 x 500kW
V: QSL-card (for relayed stn's). Rpt for Jülich transmissions: T-Systems Regional MediaBroadcast Cologne, Merscher Höhe, D-52428 Jülich, Germany.
NOTES: DTK T-Systems is a major transmitter network operator in Germany. DTK owns the SW transmitting centres in Jülich, Nauen and Wertachtal which it leases out to Deutsche Welle and various international broadcasters. The DTK MW tr's in Wachenbrunn and Berlin are rented by the Voice of Russia (see Russia).

IBB RELAY STATIONS GERMANY

Headquarters: IBB Transmitting Station, Ismaning, Germany.
Email: jlambert@ger.ibb.gov
L.P: SM: Jim Lambert.
MW: [ISM] Ismaning (G.C. 48N15 011E45) 1197kHz 300kW
SW: [BIB] Biblis (G.C. 49N41 008E29) 11 x 100kW; [LAM] Lampertheim (G.C. 49N36 008E33) 8 x 100kW
Broadcasters using sites in this country:
AWR uses: (JUL). See stn entry in: **USA**, INT Section
BBG-R.Farda uses: (LAM). See stn entry in: **USA**, INT Section
BBG-R.Free Asia uses: (LAM). See stn entry in: **USA**, INT Section
BBG-R.Free Asia uses: (WER). See stn entry in: **USA**, INT Section
BBG-RFE/RL uses: (BIB). See stn entry in: **USA**, INT Section
BBG-RFE/RL uses: (ISM). See stn entry in: **USA**, INT Section
BBG-RFE/RL uses: (LAM). See stn entry in: **USA**, INT Section
BBG-VOA uses: (BIB). See stn entry in: **USA**, INT Section
BBG-VOA uses: (ISM). See stn entry in: **USA**, INT Section
BBG-VOA uses: (JUL). See stn entry in: **USA**, INT Section
BBG-VOA uses: (LAM). See stn entry in: **USA**, INT Section
Bozy Glos uses: (JUL). See stn entry in: **POL**, INT Section
BVB uses: (NAU). See stn entry in: **G**, INT Section
BVB uses: (WER). See stn entry in: **G**, INT Section
BVB uses: (JUL). See stn entry in: **G**, INT Section
Chr.Sc.Herold uses: (NAU). See stn entry in: **USA**, INT Section
Chr.Sc.Herold uses: (WER). See stn entry in: **USA**, INT Section
Chr.Sc.Herold uses: (JUL). See stn entry in: **USA**, INT Section
Dem.VO Burma uses: (JUL). See stn entry in: **BRM**, CTB Section
Gospel for Asia uses: (WER). See stn entry in: **USA**, INT Section
HCJB uses: (JUL). See stn entry in: **EQA**, INT Section
IBRA Radio uses: (JUL). See stn entry in: **S**, INT Section
Maeva FM Int'l uses: (JUL). See stn entry in: **BEL**, INT Section
Minivan Radio uses: (JUL). See stn entry in: **MLD**, CTB Section
Overcomer Min. uses: (JUL). See stn entry in: **USA**, INT Section
R. Cimarrona uses: (JUL). See stn entry in: **URG**, CTB Section
R.Free Syria uses: (JUL). See stn entry in: **SYR**, CTB Section
R.Freundes-D. uses: (WBR). See stn entry in: **SUI**, INT Section
R.Freundes-D. uses: (BLN). See stn entry in: **SUI**, INT Section
R.Ibrahim uses: (JUL). See stn entry in: **CYP**, INT Section
R.Réveil uses: (JUL). See stn entry in: **SUI**, INT Section
R.Rhino Int'l uses: (JUL). See stn entry in: **UGA**, CTB Section
R.Taiwan Int'l uses: (JUL). See stn entry in: **TWN**, INT Section
R.Traumland uses: (JUL). See stn entry in: **BEL**, INT Section
R.VO Women uses: (JUL). See stn entry in: **IRN**, CTB Section
R.Xoriyo uses: (JUL). See stn entry in: **SOM**, CTB Section
RCI uses: (WER). See stn entry in: **CAN**, INT Section
RTBF Int'l uses: (JUL). See stn entry in: **BEL**, INT Section
RVI uses: (JUL). See stn entry in: **BEL**, INT Section
TDPradio uses: (JUL). See stn entry in: **BEL**, INT Section
TWR Europe uses: (JUL). See stn entry in: **AUT**, INT Section
VO Croatia uses: (JUL). See stn entry in: **HRV**, INT Section
VO Dem. Eritrea uses: (JUL). See stn entry in: **ERI**, CTB Section
VO Eth. Medhin uses: (JUL). See stn entry in: **ETH**, CTB Section
VO Eth.Unity uses: (JUL). See stn entry in: **ETH**, CTB Section
VO Oromo Liber. uses: (JUL). See stn entry in: **ETH**, CTB Section
VO Russia (VOR) uses: (BLN). See stn entry in: **RUS**, INT Section
VO Russia (VOR) uses: (JUL). See stn entry in: **RUS**, INT Section
VO Russia (VOR) uses: (WBR). See stn entry in: **RUS**, INT Section
VOR-RKS uses: (BLN). See stn entry in: **RUS**, INT Section
VOR-RKS uses: (JUL). See stn entry in: **RUS**, INT Section
VOR-RKS uses: (WBR). See stn entry in: **RUS**, INT Section
VOR-RMR uses: (BLN). See stn entry in: **RUS**, INT Section
VOR-RMR uses: (JUL). See stn entry in: **RUS**, INT Section
VOR-RMR uses: (WBR). See stn entry in: **RUS**, INT Section
Waymarks Int'l uses: (JUL). See stn entry in: **USA**, INT Section

GREECE

RADIOFONIKOS STATHMOS MAKEDONIAS (ERT3) (Pub)

P.O. Box 11312, 54110 Thessaloniki, Greece.
+30 2310299400. +30 2310299550.
Email: eupro@ert3.gr **Web:** www.ert3.gr
SW: [AVL] Avlida (G.C. 38N23 023E36) 1 x 100kW
SAT: Hotbird 3
kHz: *7450, 9935*

Winter Schedule 2004

Greek	Days	Area	kHz
1100-1550	daily	Eu	9935avl
1600-2350	daily	Eu	7450avl

ANN: Greek: "Edo Thessaloniki, Radiofonikos Stathmos Makedonias, Trito Programma, Vrahea"
V: QSL-card.
NOTES: ERT3 is a regional station of the public broadcaster ERT, transmitting on MW & FM in Northern Greece (see National Radio section) and on SW for Greek listeners in Europe.

VOICE OF GREECE (ERA5) (Pub)

Messogion 432, 15342 Aghia Paraskevi Attikis, Athens, Greece.
+30 2106066308. +30 2106066309.
Email: era5@ert.gr **Web:** www.ert.gr
L.P: MD: Gina Vogiatzoglou; Head of Prgrs: Angeliki Barka; Planning Eng: D. Angelogiannis.
MW: Uses facilities provided by IBB
SW: [AVL] Avlida (G.C. 38N23 023E36) 1 x 100kW, 5 x 250kW. Also leases tx's from IBB.
FM: Athens 107.0MHz
SAT: Thaicom 3
kHz: *792, 1260, 5865, 7430, 7475, 9375, 9420, 9770, 11645, 11750, 12105, 15485, 15630, 15650, 21530*

Winter Schedule 2004

Albanian	Days	Area	kHz
1800-1830	daily	Eu	7430avl
Arabic	**Days**	**Area**	**kHz**
1400-1430	daily	Eu	7430avl
Bulgarian	**Days**	**Area**	**kHz**
1730-1800	daily	Eu	7430avl
English	**Days**	**Area**	**kHz**
1930-2000	daily	Eu	7430avl
French	**Days**	**Area**	**kHz**
1830-1900	daily	Eu	7430avl
German	**Days**	**Area**	**kHz**
1430-1500	daily	Eu	7430avl
Greek	**Days**	**Area**	**kHz**
0000-0200	daily	Eu	5865avl, 7475avl, 9420avl
0000-0200	daily	Af,SAm,AUS	12105avl
0000-0300	daily	Eu,Atl	7475avl
0000-0300	daily	Atl	9420avl
0000-0300	daily	Eu	5865avl
0000-0400	daily	ME	15650kav
0000-0600	daily	NAm	5865avl, 7475avl, 9420avl
0200-0500	daily	Eu	7475avl, 9420avl
0200-0500	daily	Eu,Atl	5865avl
0300-0550	daily	Atl	7475avl

Greek	Days	Area	kHz
0300-0600	daily	Atl	9420avl
0300-0600	daily	Eu,Atl	5865avl
0400-0600	daily	ME,AUS	12105avl
0400-0900	daily	AUS	15650kav
0600-0700	daily	Eu,Atl	9420avl
0600-0900	daily	ME	15650kav
0600-0900	daily	ME,AUS	21530kav
0700-0900	daily	J,AUS,Pac	9770dln
0700-1000	daily	Af	11645avl
0800-1000	daily	Atl	9420avl, 15630avl
1100-1200	daily	Eu	9375kav, 15630avl
1100-1400	daily	J,Pac	15650kav
1100-1950	daily	Atl	15630avl
1100-2000	daily	Atl	9420avl
1200-1300	daily	Eu	9375kav, 15630avl
1200-1300	daily	UZB	15650avl
1200-1500	daily	NAm	11750dln
1300-1400	daily	Eu	9375kav, 9420avl, 15630avl
1400-1500	daily	Eu	9375kav, 9420avl, 15630avl
1500-1600	daily	Eu	7475kav, 9420avl, 15630avl
1500-2200	.....ss	NAm	15485dln
1600-1800	daily	Eu	7475kav, 9420avl, 15630avl
1600-2200	mtwtf..	NAm	15485dln
1730-1800	daily	Eu	792kav
1800-1900	daily	Eu	7475kav, 9420avl
1800-1950	daily	Eu,Af	15630avl
1900-1950	daily	Eu	7475kav, 15630avl
1900-2000	daily	Eu	9420avl
1900-2050	daily	SAm,Af	15630avl
2000-2100	daily	Eu	7475kav, 9375kav, 9420avl
2000-2130	daily	Eu	792kav
2000-2300	daily	Atl	7475kav, 9420kav
2100-2200	daily	Eu	7475kav, 9420kav
2100-2300	daily	ME,AUS	9375kav, 12105kav
2200-2300	daily	Eu	792kav, 7475kav, 9420kav
2300-2400	daily	SAm,Af	9375avl
2300-2400	daily	Eu,Atl	5865avl, 7475kav, 9420kav
2300-2400	daily	AUS	12105kav
Greek/Arabic	**Days**	**Area**	**kHz**
1200-1400	daily	AUS	15650kav
Greek/Arabic /German	**Days**	**Area**	**kHz**
0900-1400	daily	Eu	1260rho
1100-1400	daily	Eu,ME	15650avl
Greek/English	**Days**	**Area**	**kHz**
0500-0550	daily	Eu	7475kav
0500-0600	daily	Eu	5865avl, 9420avl
0600-0650	daily	Eu	5865avl
0600-0700	daily	Eu,Atl	15630avl
0700-1000	daily	Eu	9420avl, 15630avl
Greek/Various	**Days**	**Area**	**kHz**
0900-1700	daily	Eu	792kav
Polish	**Days**	**Area**	**kHz**
1900-1930	daily	Eu	7430avl
Romanian	**Days**	**Area**	**kHz**
1600-1630	daily	Eu	7430avl
Russian	**Days**	**Area**	**kHz**
1500-1530	daily	Eu	7430avl
Serbian	**Days**	**Area**	**kHz**
1700-1730	daily	Eu	7430avl
Spanish	**Days**	**Area**	**kHz**
1530-1600	daily	Eu	7430avl
Turkish	**Days**	**Area**	**kHz**
1630-1700	daily	Eu	7430avl

ANN: Greek: "ERA pente, Foni tis Elladas"
V: QSL-card.
NOTES: The Voice of Greece (ERA 5) is the External Sce of the public broadcaster Elliniki Radiofonia Teleorassi (ERT). Some prgr's are relays of ERT's domestic multilingual channel R.Filia.

IBB RELAY STATION GREECE

IBB Transmitting Station, Dasochori Xanthi, Kavala, Greece.
Email: gwise@gre.ibb.gov
L.P: SM: Gary Wise.
MW: [KAV] Kavala (G.C. 40N52 024E50) 792kHz 600kW; [RHO] Rhodos (G.C. 36N18 028E00) 1260kHz 500kW
SW: [KAV] Kavala (G.C. 40N52 024E50) 2 x 50, 12 x 250kW
Broadcasters using sites in this country:
BBG-AapkiDunyaa uses: (KAV). See stn entry in: **USA**, INT Section
BBG-R. Sawa uses: (RHO). See stn entry in: **USA**, INT Section
BBG-R.Farda uses: (KAV). See stn entry in: **USA**, INT Section
BBG-RFE/RL uses: (KAV). See stn entry in: **USA**, INT Section
BBG-VOA uses: (KAV). See stn entry in: **USA**, INT Section

GUAM

KSDA (ADVENTIST WORLD RADIO) (Rlg)

P.O. Box 8990, Agat, Guam 96928.
☎ +1 671 5652000. Fax +1 671 5652983.
Email: aproffice@awr.org
SW: [SDA] Agat, Facpi Point (G.C. 13N20 144E39) 4 x 100kW
kHz: *5985, 6045, 6195, 7150, 9780, 11560, 11610, 11675, 11685, 11690, 11695, 11700, 11755, 11800, 11825, 11850, 11870, 11895, 11900, 11935, 11940, 11980, 11985, 12010, 12120, 15185, 15245, 15260, 15320, 15430, 15480, 15495, 15660, 17635, 17880*

Winter Schedule 2004

Assami	Days	Area	kHz
1330-1400	..w...s	As	15660sda
Bangla	**Days**	**Area**	**kHz**
1300-1330	daily	As	15660sda
Burmese	**Days**	**Area**	**kHz**
0000-0030	daily	As	17635sda
1400-1430	daily	As	11940sda
Chin	**Days**	**Area**	**kHz**
1430-1500	daily	As	11940sda
English	**Days**	**Area**	**kHz**
1600-1630	daily	As	15495sda
1630-1700	daily	As	11980sda
1730-1800	daily	ME	11560sda
2130-2200	daily	EAs	11980sda, 12010sda, 12010sda
2230-2300	daily	SEA	11850sda, 15320sda
English	**Days**	**Area**	**kHz**
1000-1030	daily	EAs	11900sda
1000-1030	daily	SEA	11870sda
1130-1200	daily	SEA	15260sda
1330-1400	daily	EAs	11980sda
1330-1400	mt.tfs.	As	15660sda
1600-1630	daily	As	15480sda
Hindi	**Days**	**Area**	**kHz**
1530-1600	daily	As	15245sda
1700-1730	daily	ME	11675sda
Indonesian	**Days**	**Area**	**kHz**
1100-1130	daily	SEA	15260sda
2200-2230	daily	SEA	11850sda, 15320sda
Japanese	**Days**	**Area**	**kHz**
1300-1330	daily	EAs	11755sda, 11980sda
2100-2130	daily	EAs	11980sda, 12010sda
Kannada	**Days**	**Area**	**kHz**
1530-1600	daily	As	15185sda
Karen	**Days**	**Area**	**kHz**
0030-0100	daily	EAs,SEA	17635sda
1430-1500	daily	EAs,SEA	15660sda
Khmer	**Days**	**Area**	**kHz**
1330-1400	daily	SEA	11695sda
Korean	**Days**	**Area**	**kHz**
1200-1300	daily	EAs	9780sda
2000-2100	daily	EAs	6195sda
2000-2100	daily	SEA	6045sda
Malayalam	**Days**	**Area**	**kHz**
1530-1600	daily	As	11985sda
Mandarin	**Days**	**Area**	**kHz**
0000-0200	daily	EAs	17880sda
0100-0200	daily	EAs	17635sda
1000-1100	daily	EAs	15260sda, 15430sda
1100-1200	daily	EAs	11895sda, 12120sda

Mandarin	Days	Area	kHz
1100-1500	daily	EAs	11825sda
1200-1300	daily	EAs	11690sda, 12120sda
1400-1500	daily	EAs	11800sda
2100-2200	daily	EAs	7150sda
2100-2200	daily	As	5985sda
2200-2300	daily	EAs	11685sda, 17880sda
2300-2400	daily	EAs	11700sda, 11850sda, 17880sda
Marathi	**Days**	**Area**	**kHz**
1530-1600	daily	As	11935sda
Mizo	**Days**	**Area**	**kHz**
1500-1530	daily	As	11610sda
Mongolian	**Days**	**Area**	**kHz**
1030-1100	daily	EAs	11900sda
Panjabi	**Days**	**Area**	**kHz**
1500-1530	daily	WAs	11935sda
Sinhala	**Days**	**Area**	**kHz**
1400-1430	daily	As	15660sda
Tagalog	**Days**	**Area**	**kHz**
1030-1100	daily	SEA	11870sda
1700-1730	daily	ME	11560sda
Tamil	**Days**	**Area**	**kHz**
1500-1530	daily	As	11985sda
1730-1800	daily	ME	11675sda
Telugu	**Days**	**Area**	**kHz**
1500-1530	daily	As	15185sda
Urdu	**Days**	**Area**	**kHz**
1600-1630	daily	As	11980sda
Vietnamese	**Days**	**Area**	**kHz**
2300-2400	daily	SAE	15320sda

ANN: English: "From the Beautiful island of Guam in the West Pacific, this is Adventist World Radio, the Voice of Hope"
V: QSL-card. Rp.
NOTES: AWR branch and transmitting stn; see USA for corporate headquarters.

KTWR (TRANS WORLD RADIO GUAM) (Rlg)

P.O. Box 8780, Agat, Guam 96928.
☎ +1 671 4779701. Fax +1 671 4772838.
Email: ktwrfreq@guam.twr.org **Web:** gumwww.twr.org
SW: [TWR] Merizo (G.C. 13N17 144E40) 5 x 100kW
kHz: *7455, 9415, 9465, 9585, 9635, 9865, 9910, 9920, 9975, 11690, 11695, 11840, 11895, 12080, 12105, 12130, 13630, 13690, 13715, 13765, 15200, 15225, 15275, 15330*

Winter Schedule 2004

Balinese	Days	Area	kHz
0900-0915	mt..fss	EAs	15200twr
Burmese	**Days**	**Area**	**kHz**
1200-1300	daily	As	9975twr
Cantonese	**Days**	**Area**	**kHz**
1400-1500	daily	As	9975twr
2300-2400	daily	As	13765twr
Chinese (Mix)	**Days**	**Area**	**kHz**
1300-1330	daily	As	9975twr
English	**Days**	**Area**	**kHz**
0730-0900	.....ss	SEA	15225twr
0740-0900	mtwtf..	SEA	15225twr
0815-0930	.....ss	Pac,Oc	11840twr
0815-0930	mtwtf..	Pac,Oc	11840twr
1500-1630	daily	As,EAf	12105twr
Hakka	**Days**	**Area**	**kHz**
0900-0930	daily	As	12130twr
Hindi	**Days**	**Area**	**kHz**
1330-1400	daily	As	12080twr
Indonesian	**Days**	**Area**	**kHz**
0930-1100	daily	SEA	15330twr
1100-1200	daily	SEA	15200twr
Japanese	**Days**	**Area**	**kHz**
1215-1300	daily	EAs	9465twr
2115-2200	daily	As	11690twr
Javanese	**Days**	**Area**	**kHz**
1100-1200	daily	SEA	15275twr
Khmer	**Days**	**Area**	**kHz**
1300-1330	daily	SEA	11695twr
Korean	**Days**	**Area**	**kHz**
1445-1615	daily	EAs	9920twr
Madurese	**Days**	**Area**	**kHz**
0915-1000	daily	EAS	15200twr
Mandarin	**Days**	**Area**	**kHz**
0930-1100	daily	As	9865twr, 9910twr
0930-1600	daily	As	12130twr
1100-1615	daily	As	7455twr
1330-1400	daily	As	9975twr
1400-1600	daily	EAs	9415twr
2200-2245	daily	As	12130twr
2245-2330	daily	As	13630twr
2300-2330	daily	As	13690twr
Sgaw Karen	**Days**	**Area**	**kHz**
1330-1400	daily	SEA	9585twr
Sundanese	**Days**	**Area**	**kHz**
1000-1030	daily	SEA	15200twr
Swatow	**Days**	**Area**	**kHz**
1200-1230	daily	As	11895twr
Torajanese	**Days**	**Area**	**kHz**
0900-0915	..wt...	EAs	15200twr
Vietnamese	**Days**	**Area**	**kHz**
1100-1200	daily	SEA	9635twr
1400-1445	daily	SEA	9920twr
2230-2300	daily	SEA	13715twr

ANN: English: "This is your Station for Inspiration, KTWR, Agana"; "This is the voice of Trans World Radio Pacific, Agana"
IS: "We've a story to tell the Nations", played on an organ.
V: QSL-card. Rp. (3 IRC's for airmail reply, one for surface mail). Rec. acc. Online rpt form: gumwww.twr.org/ktwrmonrep.htm.
NOTES: TWR branch and transmitting stn; see USA for corporate headquarters.
Broadcasters using sites in this country:
AFN Feeder uses: (BAR). See stn entry in: **USA**, INT Section
TWR India uses: (TWR). See stn entry in: **IND**, INT Section

HAWAII (U.S. State)

KWHR – WORLD HARVEST RADIO (Rlg)

Contact details: see World Harvest Radio (USA).
SW: [WHR] Naalehu (G.C. 19N02 155W40) 2 x 100kW
kHz: *9930, 11565, 15220, 17510*

Winter Schedule 2004

English	Days	Area	kHz
0600-1000	daily	Oc	11565whr
1000-1200	.....ss	Oc	11565whr
English/Various	**Days**	**Area**	**kHz**
0200-0400	daily	SEA	17510whr
0400-0600	daily	SEA	15220whr
0600-1900	daily	SEA	9930whr

ANN: English: "This is World Harvest Radio, the International service of LeSea Broadcasting Corporation. KWHR transmits from Naalehu, Hawaii in the United States of America"
V: QSL-card.
Broadcasters using sites in this country:
AFN Feeder uses: (PEH). See stn entry in: **USA**, INT Section
BBG-R.Free Asia uses: (WHR). See stn entry in: **USA**, INT Section
Fang Guang M.R. uses: (WHR). See stn entry in: **USA**, INT Section
R.Free Vietnam uses: (WHR). See stn entry in: **VTN**, CTB Section

HUNGARY

RADIO BUDAPEST (Pub)

Bródy Sándor u. 5-7, H-1800 Budapest, Hungary.
☎ +36 1 328 8108. Fax +36 1 3287004.
Email: nki@radio.hu **Web:** www.radiobudapest.radio.hu
L.P: Dir: László Krassó; Freq. Mgr: Ferenc Horváth.
SW: Leased from Antena Hungária
SAT: Hotbird 6
kHz: *3975, 6025, 7160, 9580, 9710, 9735, 9775, 9825, 9870, 11675, 11785, 12010, 21560*

Winter Schedule 2004

English	Days	Area	kHz
0200-0230	daily	NAm	9775jbr
0330-0400	daily	NAm	9775jbr
1600-1630	......s	Eu	6025jbr, 9580jbr
2000-2030	daily	Eu	3975jbr, 6025rso
2200-2230	daily	Eu	6025rso
2200-2230	daily	SAf	12010jbr

French	Days	Area	kHz
1700-1730	daily	Eu	3975jbr, 6025rso
2100-2130	daily	Eu	6025jbr, 9710jbr
German	**Days**	**Area**	**kHz**
1300-1400	......s	Eu	6025jbr, 12010jbr
1500-1600	......s	Eu	6025jbr, 9735jbr
1800-1900	......s	Eu	3975jbr, 6025rso
1830-1900	mtwtfs.	Eu	3975jbr, 6025rso
2030-2100	mtwtfs.	Eu	3975jbr, 6025rso
Hungarian	**Days**	**Area**	**kHz**
0000-0100	m......	SAm	12010jbr
0100-0200	daily	NAm	9870jbr
0230-0330	daily	NAm	9775jbr
0500-1300	......s	Eu	6025jbr
0500-1700	mtwtfs.	Eu	6025jbr
1200-1300	daily	SAf	21560jbr
1400-1500	......s	Eu	6025jbr
1900-2000	daily	Eu	3975jbr, 6025jbr
1900-2000	daily	SAf	11675rso
2000-2100	daily	SAf	11785jbr
2200-2300	daily	NAm	9825jbr
2300-2400	daily	Eu	6025jbr
2300-2400	daily	SAm	12010jbr
Italian	**Days**	**Area**	**kHz**
1730-1800	daily	Eu	3975jbr, 6025rso
2130-2200	daily	Eu	3975jbr, 6025jbr
Russian	**Days**	**Area**	**kHz**
0400-0430	daily	Eu	3975jbr, 6025rso
1630-1700	......s	Eu	3975jbr, 6025jbr
1800-1830	mtwtfs.	Eu	3975jbr, 6025rso
2030-2100	......s	Eu	3975jbr, 6025rso
Spanish	**Days**	**Area**	**kHz**
0430-0500	daily	Eu,NAf	3975jbr, 6025rso
2230-2300	daily	Eu,NAf	6025jbr, 7160rso

ANN: English: "This is Radio Budapest, Hungary"; German: "Hier ist Radio Budapest"
V: QSL-card. Rec. acc.
NOTES: Radio Budapest is the External Sce of the public broadcaster Magyar Rádió.

ANTENNA HUNGÁRIA RT. (Tx Operator)
P.O. Box 447, H-1519 Budapest, Hungary.
☎ +36 1 2036060. Fax +36 1 464-525.
Email: antennah@ahrt.hu **Web:** www.ahrt.hu
SW: [JBR] Jászberény (G.C. 47N35 019E52) 2 x 100*, 2 x 250kW. Key: * Transfered from the Székesfehérvár site which was closed in October 2004. The move was due to be completed in May 2005.
NOTES: Antena Hungária is the national Hungarian transmitter network operator. Leases out its transmitters to national and international customers.
Broadcasters using sites in this country:
BBG-RFE/RL uses: (JBR). See stn entry in: **USA**, INT Section
BBG-VOA uses: (JBR). See stn entry in: **USA**, INT Section

ICELAND

RÍKISÚTVARPIÐ (Pub)
Efstaleiti 1, 150 Reykjavík, Iceland.
☎ +354 515300. Fax +354 5153010.
Email: frettir@ruv.is **Web:** www.ruv.is
L.P: Dir: Dóra Ingvadóttir.
SW: Leased from Iceland Telecom
kHz: *12115, 13865*

Winter Schedule 2004

Icelandic	Days	Area	kHz
1215-1300	daily	Eu	13865rey
1410-1440	daily	NAm	13865rey
1755-1825	daily	Eu	12115rey
1835-1905	daily	NAm	13865rey
2300-2335	daily	NAm	12115rey

ANN: Icelandic: "Útvarp Reykjavík"
V: QSL-card.
NOTES: Relays of Home Sce newscasts. RÚV is the public service broadcaster in Iceland. Transmissions are in AM-compatible R3E modulaton (USB with -6dB carrier reduction).

ICELAND TELECOM (Tx Operator)
Síminn v/Austurvöll, IS-150 Reykjavík, Iceland.
Email: reyrad@simi.is **Web:** www.siminn.is
SW: [REY] Reykjavík (G.C. 64N05 021W50) 1 x 20kW
NOTES: Iceland Telecom is the owner of Gufunes Telecom Centre, a utility transmitting facility in Reykjavík. It is leasing out one SW tx to the pubcaster Ríkisutvarpið (RÚV) for relaying of newscasts.
Broadcasters using sites in this country:
AFN Feeder uses: (GVK). See stn entry in: **USA**, INT Section

INDIA

ALL INDIA RADIO (Pub)
External Services Division, P.O. Box 500, New Delhi-110001, India.
☎ +91 11 23715411. Fax +91 11 23710057.
Email: esd@air.org.in **Web:** www.allindiaradio.org
Studios: Akashvani Bhavan, 1 Sansad Marg, New Delhi-110001, India.
L.P: CEO Prasar Bharati Corp: K S Sarma; Dir External Sces: P.M. Iyer.
MW: [JAL] Jalandhar (G.C. 31N19 075E18) 702kHz 300kW; [KKT] Chinsurah (G.C. 22N55 088E25) 594/1134kHz 1000kW; [RAJ] Rajkot (G.C. 22N22 070E41) 1071kHz 1000kW*; [TUT] Tuticorin (G.C. 08N48 078E12) 1053kHz 200kW. Key: * Not in use during winter 2004-2005, new 1000kW tx is being installed.
SW: [ALG] Aligarh (G.C. 28N00 078E06) 4 x 250kW; [BGL] Bangalore, Doddaballapur (G.C. 13N14 077E13) 6 x 500kW; [GKP] Gorakhpur (G.C. 23N52 083E28) 1 x 50kW; [DEL] Delhi , two sites: Khampur (G.C. 28N50 077E09) 7 x 250kW; Kingsway (G.C. 28N43 077E12) 3 x 50, 2 x 100kW; [MUM] Mumbai (G.C. 19N11 072E49) 1 x 100kW; [PAN] Panaji (G.C. 15N28 073E51) 2 x 250kW
SAT: AsiaStar, Insat 2E, AfriStar
kHz: *594, 702, 1053, 1134, 3945, 4860, 5990, 6045, 6155, 6165, 7115, 7125, 7250, 7255, 7410, 9445, 9575, 9595, 9620, 9635, 9690, 9705, 9810, 9820, 9835, 9875, 9905, 9910, 9950, 11585, 11620, 11645, 11710, 11715, 11730, 11735, 11740, 11775, 11840, 11850, 11935, 11985, 12025, 13605, 13620, 13645, 13695, 13710, 13770, 13795, 15020, 15050, 15075, 15140, 15155, 15175, 15185, 15235, 15260, 15770, 15795, 17510, 17670, 17705, 17715, 17740, 17800, 17810, 17845, 17860, 17875, 17895*

Winter Schedule 2004

Arabic	Days	Area	kHz
0430-0530	daily	ME	11730del, 13620bgl, 15770alg, 17845del*
1730-1945	daily	ME	9905alg, 11585del, 13620bgl
Baluchi	**Days**	**Area**	**kHz**
1500-1600	daily	PAK	6165del, 9620alg, 11585del
Bangla	**Days**	**Area**	**kHz**
0300-0430	daily	BGD	594kkt
0800-1100	daily	BGD	594kkt
1445-1515	daily	BGD	1134kkt
1600-1730	daily	BGD	1134kkt
Burmese	**Days**	**Area**	**kHz**
1215-1315	daily	BRM	11620alg, 11710del
Dari	**Days**	**Area**	**kHz**
0300-0345	daily	AFG	9835del, 9910alg, 11735alg
1315-1415	daily	AFG	7255alg, 7410del, 9910del
English	**Days**	**Area**	**kHz**
1000-1100	daily	AUS,NZL	13710bgl, 17510del, 17895alg
1000-1100	daily	CLN	1053tut, 15260del
1000-1100	daily	EAs	15020alg, 15235bgl, 17800bgl
1330-1500	daily	EAs,SEA	9690bgl, 11620del, 13710bgl
1530-1545	daily	SAs	7255alg, 9820pan, 9910del, 11740pan
1745-1945	daily	WEu	7410del, 9950del, 11620alg
1745-1945	daily	NAf	9445bgl, 13605bgl, 15155alg
1745-1945	daily	EAf	11935mum, 15075del, 17670del
2045-2230	daily	WEu	7410del, 9445bgl, 9950del

English	**Days**	**Area**	**kHz**
2045-2230	daily	AUS,NZL	9910alg, 11620bgl, 11715pan
2245-0045	daily	EAs	9950alg, 11645del, 13605bgl
2245-0045	daily	EAs,SEA	9705pan, 11620del, 13605bgl
Farsi	**Days**	**Area**	**kHz**
0400-0430	daily	IRN	11730del, 15770alg, 17845del
1615-1730	daily	IRN	7115pan, 9905alg, 11585del
French	**Days**	**Area**	**kHz**
1945-2030	daily	NAf	9905alg, 13605bgl, 13620bgl
Gujarati	**Days**	**Area**	**kHz**
0415-0430	daily	EAf,MAU	15075bgl, 15185alg, 17715del
1515-1600	daily	EAf,MAU	11620bgl, 15175bgl
Hindi	**Days**	**Area**	**kHz**
0315-0415	daily	EAf,MAU	15075bgl, 15185alg, 17715del
0315-0415	daily	ME	11840pan, 13695bgl, 15075bgl
0430-0530	daily	EAf,MAU	15075bgl, 15185alg, 17715del
1615-1730	daily	EAf,MAU	9950del, 15075del, 17670del
1615-1730	daily	ME	7410alg, 12025pan, 13770bgl
1945-2045	daily	WEu	7410del, 9950del
2300-2400	daily	EAs,SEA	9910alg, 11740pan, 13795alg
Indonesian	**Days**	**Area**	**kHz**
0845-0945	daily	SEA	15770alg, 17510del, 17875alg
Kannada	**Days**	**Area**	**kHz**
0215-0300	daily	ME	11985bgl, 15075bgl
Malayalam	**Days**	**Area**	**kHz**
1730-1830	daily	ME	7115pan, 12025pan
Mandarin	**Days**	**Area**	**kHz**
1145-1315	daily	EAs	11840del, 15795bgl, 17705bgl
Nepali	**Days**	**Area**	**kHz**
0130-0230	daily	NPL	594kkt, 3945gkp, 7250pan, 9810pan, 11715del
0700-0800	daily	NPL	7250gkp, 9595del, 11850del
1330-1430	daily	NPL	1134kkt, 3945gkp, 4860del, 11775pan
Pashto	**Days**	**Area**	**kHz**
0215-0300	daily	AFG,PAK	9835del, 9910alg, 11735alg
1415-1530	daily	AFG,PAK	7255alg, 7410del, 9910del
Punjabi	**Days**	**Area**	**kHz**
0800-0830	daily	PAK	702jal
1230-1430	daily	PAK	702jal
Russian	**Days**	**Area**	**kHz**
1615-1715	daily	EEu	9875del, 11620bgl, 15140del
Saraiki	**Days**	**Area**	**kHz**
1130-1200	daily	PAK	702jal
Sindhi	**Days**	**Area**	**kHz**
0100-0200	daily	PAK	5990alg, 7125del, 9635alg
1230-1500	daily	PAK	6165del, 9620alg, 11585del
Sinhala	**Days**	**Area**	**kHz**
0045-0115	daily	CLN	1053tut, 11740pan, 11985del
1300-1500	daily	CLN	1053tut, 9820pan, 15050del
Swahili	**Days**	**Area**	**kHz**
1515-1615	daily	EAf	9950del, 13605alg, 17670del
Tamil	**Days**	**Area**	**kHz**
0000-0045	daily	CLN	1053tut, 9835del, 11740pan, 11985del
0000-0045	daily	SEA	9910alg, 11740pan, 13795alg
0115-0330	daily	CLN	1053tut
1100-1300	daily	CLN	1053tut
1115-1215	daily	CLN	15050del, 17860del
1115-1215	daily	SEA	13710bgl, 15770alg, 17810pan
1500-1530	daily	CLN	1053tut
Telugu	**Days**	**Area**	**kHz**
1215-1245	daily	SEA	13710bgl, 15770alg, 17810pan
Thai	**Days**	**Area**	**kHz**
1115-1200	daily	SEA	13645alg, 15235pan, 17740del
Tibetan	**Days**	**Area**	**kHz**
1215-1330	daily	CHN	1134kkt, 9575del, 11775pan
Urdu	**Days**	**Area**	**kHz**
0015-0430	daily	PAK	702jal, 6155del, 9595del
0100-0430	daily	PAK	11620del
0530-0600	daily	ARS	11730del, 17845del
0830-1130	daily	PAK	702jal, 7250gkp, 9595alg, 11620del
1430-1735	daily	PAK	3945gkp
1430-1930	daily	PAK	702jal, 4860del, 6045del

ANN: English: "This is the General Overseas Service of All India Radio"; Hindi: "Yeh Akashvani ki videsh prasaran sewa hai"; Tamil: "Idi Akashvani videsh sewai"; Sinhala: "Me All India Radio videshiya sevayai"; Nepali: "Yo All India Radio ho"; Dari: "Inja Delhi"
V: QSL-card. Rpt to the Director (Spectrum Management & Synergy): Y.K.Sharma, All India Radio, Room No.204, Akashvani Bhavan, New Delhi-110001. Tel/fax: 91-11-23421062, 23421145. E-mail: spectrum-manager@air.org.in
NOTES: External Sce of the national public broadcaster Prasar Bharati Corporation. Key: * Haj season only.

TRANS WORLD RADIO INDIA (Rlg)

L-15, Green Park, New Delhi 110016, India.
☎ +91 11 6852568. Fax +91 11 6868049.
kHz: *882, 7365, 7430, 7535, 7560, 9445, 12080*

Winter Schedule 2004

Assami	**Days**	**Area**	**kHz**
0015-0045	mtwtf..	As	7430alm
Awadhi	**Days**	**Area**	**kHz**
0100-0115	.....s.	As	9445tac, 9445tac
Baduga	**Days**	**Area**	**kHz**
1445-1500	……s	SAs	882put
Bangla	**Days**	**Area**	**kHz**
0045-0100	mtwtf..	As	7430alm
1245-1300	.....s.	As	7560tch
1445-1515	mtwtf..	As	7535irk
2230-2300	daily	SAs	882put
Banjara	**Days**	**Area**	**kHz**
1230-1245	mtwtf..	SAs	882put
1245-1315	daily	SAs	882put
Bhili	**Days**	**Area**	**kHz**
1630-1645	…..ss	SAs	882put
1815-1845	mtwtf..	SAs	882put
Bhojpuri	**Days**	**Area**	**kHz**
1415-1500	mtwtf..	As	7560tch
Boro	**Days**	**Area**	**kHz**
1330-1345	......s	As	12080twr
Brajbhas	**Days**	**Area**	**kHz**
1300-1315	.....ss	As	7535irk
Bundelkhandi	**Days**	**Area**	**kHz**
1315-1330	.....ss	As	7560tch
1330-1345	.....s.	As	7560tch
Chakma	**Days**	**Area**	**kHz**
0000-0015	......s	As	7430alm
Chhattisgarhi	**Days**	**Area**	**kHz**
1430-1445	…..ss	SAs	882put
1600-1615	mt…..	SAs	882put
1715-1745	mtwtf..	SAs	882put

Chowdhary	**Days**	**Area**	**kHz**
2300-2315	m......	SAs	882put
Dari	**Days**	**Area**	**kHz**
1600-1630	.....ss	As	7365sam
Deccani	**Days**	**Area**	**kHz**
1345-1400	......s	SAs	882put
1645-1700	.....s.	SAs	882put
1745-1815	mtwtf..	SAs	882put
Dhodiya	**Days**	**Area**	**kHz**
1345-1400	.....ss	As	7535irk
Dogri	**Days**	**Area**	**kHz**
1245-1300	mtwtf..	As	7535irk
Dzongkha	**Days**	**Area**	**kHz**
1400-1415	mtwtf..	As	7560tch
English	**Days**	**Area**	**kHz**
1130-1215	daily	SAs	882put
1215-1230	.....ss	SAs	882put
1315-1330	.....s.	As	7535irk
1645-1700	......s	SAs	882put
1700-1730	.....ss	SAs	882put
Gamit	**Days**	**Area**	**kHz**
1330-1345	.....ss	As	7535irk
Garhwali	**Days**	**Area**	**kHz**
1230-1245	mtwtf..	As	7535irk
Gondi	**Days**	**Area**	**kHz**
1545-1615	..wtfss	SAs	882put
Gujarati	**Days**	**Area**	**kHz**
1400-1415	.....ss	SAs	882put
1700-1715	mtwtf..	SAs	882put
2300-2330	..wtfss	SAs	882put
Hindi	**Days**	**Area**	**kHz**
0100-0115	.....s	As	9445tac, 9445tac
0115-0130	.....ss	As	9445tac, 9445tac
1230-1400	mtwtf..	As	7560tch
1300-1315	.....s.	As	7560tch
1315-1330	......s	As	7535irk
1430-1500	.....ss	As	7560tch
1845-1915	mtwtf..	SAs	882put
Ho	**Days**	**Area**	**kHz**
1300-1315	......s	As	7560tch
1545-1600	mt.....	SAs	882put
Kannada	**Days**	**Area**	**kHz**
0045-0200	mtwtf..	SAs	882put
1215-1230	mtwtf..	SAs	882put
1330-1345	......s	SAs	882put
Kashmiri	**Days**	**Area**	**kHz**
1245-1300	.....s.	As	7535irk
Kokborok	**Days**	**Area**	**kHz**
0000-0015	.....s.	As	7430alm
2345-0015	mtwtf..	As	7430alm
Konkani	**Days**	**Area**	**kHz**
0030-0045	daily	SAs	882put
0045-0100	.....ss	SAs	882put
Kotuwalia	**Days**	**Area**	**kHz**
1315-1330	.....ss	SAs	882put
Koya	**Days**	**Area**	**kHz**
0100-0115	.....ss	SAs	882put
Kui	**Days**	**Area**	**kHz**
1245-1300	......s	As	7560tch
Kukna	**Days**	**Area**	**kHz**
1615-1630	.....s.	SAs	882put
Kumauni	**Days**	**Area**	**kHz**
1230-1245	.....ss	As	7535irk
Kuruk	**Days**	**Area**	**kHz**
0030-0045	.....ss	As	9445tac
Kutchi	**Days**	**Area**	**kHz**
1315-1345	mtwtf..	SAs	882put
Magahi	**Days**	**Area**	**kHz**
0030-0045	......s	As	7430alm
Maithili	**Days**	**Area**	**kHz**
0045-0100	.....ss	As	9445tac
1330-1400	mtwtf..	As	7535irk
Malayalam	**Days**	**Area**	**kHz**
2330-2400	daily	SAs	882put
Manipuri	**Days**	**Area**	**kHz**
2345-2400	.....ss	As	7430alm
Marathi	**Days**	**Area**	**kHz**
1430-1445	mtwtf..	SAs	882put
1445-1500	mtwtfs.	SAs	882put
1615-1630	mtwtf..	SAs	882put
Marwari	**Days**	**Area**	**kHz**
1330-1345	......s	As	7560tch
Mavchi	**Days**	**Area**	**kHz**
2315-2330	mt.....	SAs	882put
Mewadi	**Days**	**Area**	**kHz**
1230-1245	.....ss	As	7560tch
Mundari	**Days**	**Area**	**kHz**
0030-0045	.....s.	As	7430alm
Muslimi Bengali	**Days**	**Area**	**kHz**
1330-1345	......s	As	12080twr
Nepali	**Days**	**Area**	**kHz**
0030-0145	mtwtf..	As	9445tac
Newari	**Days**	**Area**	**kHz**
1245-1300	......s	As	7535irk
Oriya	**Days**	**Area**	**kHz**
1500-1515	daily	SAs	882put
1515-1545	..wtfss	SAs	882put
Pashto	**Days**	**Area**	**kHz**
1600-1630	mtwtf..	As	7365sam
Punjabi	**Days**	**Area**	**kHz**
1400-1445	mtwtf..	As	7535irk
Sadari	**Days**	**Area**	**kHz**
0045-0100	.....ss	As	7430alm
Santali	**Days**	**Area**	**kHz**
1345-1400	......s	As	12080twr
1415-1430	.....ss	As	7560tch
Sindhi	**Days**	**Area**	**kHz**
1630-1700	mtwtf..	SAs	882put
Soura	**Days**	**Area**	**kHz**
1230-1245	.....ss	SAs	882put
Tamil	**Days**	**Area**	**kHz**
0000-0030	daily	SAs	882put
Telegu	**Days**	**Area**	**kHz**
1330-1345	.....s.	SAs	882put
1345-1400	mtwtfs.	SAs	882put
1400-1415	mtwtf..	SAs	882put
1415-1430	daily	SAs	882put
1515-1545	mt.....	SAs	882put
Tibetan	**Days**	**Area**	**kHz**
0015-0030	.....ss	As	7430alm
Tulu	**Days**	**Area**	**kHz**
0115-0200	.....ss	SAs	882put
Urdu	**Days**	**Area**	**kHz**
1300-1330	mtwtf..	As	7535irk
Varli	**Days**	**Area**	**kHz**
1615-1630	......s	SAs	882put
Vasavi	**Days**	**Area**	**kHz**
2300-2315	t......	SAs	882put

V: QSL-card.

NOTES: TWR branch, see USA for corporate headquarters.

Broadcasters using sites in this country:
R.Sed.Kashmir uses: (DEL). See stn entry in: **PAK**, CTB Section

INDONESIA

VOICE OF INDONESIA (Pub)

P.O. Box 1157, Jakarta, Indonesia.
☎ +62 21 3846817. 🖷 +62 21 3457134.
Email: voi@rri-online.com **Web:** www.rri-online.com
SW: [JAK] Jakarta, Cimanggis (G.C. 06S12 106E51) 2 x 50, 3 x 100kW, 8 x 250kW
kHz: *15150*

Winter Schedule 2004

Arabic	**Days**	**Area**	**kHz**
1600-1700	daily	FE,SEA	15150jak*
Bahasa Indonesia	**Days**	**Area**	**kHz**
0300-0400	daily	FE,SEA	15150jak*
1300-1400	daily	ME,SAs,SEA	15150jak*
English	**Days**	**Area**	**kHz**
0200-0300	daily	FE,SEA,AUS	15150jak*
0800-0900	daily	FE,SEA,AUS	15150jak*
2000-2100	daily	FE,SEA,AUS	15150jak*

French	Days	Area	kHz
1900-2000	daily	Eu,NAf,ME	15150jak*
German	**Days**	**Area**	**kHz**
1800-1900	daily	Eu,NAf,ME	15150jak*
Japanese	**Days**	**Area**	**kHz**
1130-1200	daily	FE,SEA,AUS	15150jak*
Korean	**Days**	**Area**	**kHz**
1200-1300	daily	FE,SEA,AUS	15150jak*
Malay	**Days**	**Area**	**kHz**
0900-1000	daily	FE,SEA,AUS	15150jak*
Mandarin	**Days**	**Area**	**kHz**
1030-1130	daily	FE,SEA,AUS	15150jak*
Spanish	**Days**	**Area**	**kHz**
1700-1800	daily	Eu,NAf,ME	15150jak*
Thai	**Days**	**Area**	**kHz**
1000-1030	daily	FE,SEA,AUS	15150jak*

ANN: English: "From Jakarta, you are listening to the Voice of Indonesia". Key: * Variable Frequency. Alternative frequencies: 9525kHz and 11785kHz.
V: QSL-card.
NOTES: The Voice of Indonesia is the External Sce of the state broadcaster Radio Republik Indonesia.

IRAN

VOICE OF THE ISLAMIC REPUBLIC OF IRAN (VOIRI) (Gov)

P.O. Box 19395-6767, Tehran, Iran.
☎ +98 21 2042808. 🖷 +98 21 2051635.
Email: englishradio@irib.ir **Web:** www.irib.ir/worldservice
L.P: Pres: Dr Ali Larijani; Dir Int'l Rel: M.Safdari.
MW: [BNB] Bonab (G.C. 37N20 046E05) 639kHz 400kW; [BNT] Bandar-e Torkeman (G.C. 36N54 054E04) 1449kHz 400kW; [CHB] Chah Bahar (G.C. 25N17 060E37) 765kHz 600kW, 1377kHz 10kW; [IRS] Iranshar (G.C. 27N12 060E42) 531kHz 600kW; [KER] Kerman (G.C. 29N59 056E46) 1224kHz 600kW; [KIA] Kiashar (G.C. 36N14 053E33) 702/1404kHz 500kW; [MHD] Mahidasht (G.C. 34N16 046E48) 720kHz 750kW; [MHS] Mahshahr (G.C. 30N55 049E15) 576/1080kHz 750kW; [MKU] Maku (G.C. 39N17 044E30) 1584kHz 10kW; [QSH] Qasr-e Shirin (G.C. 34N31 045E35) 612/1161kHz 600kW; [REZ] Rezayeh (G.C. 37N32 045E05) 936kHz 50kW; [RSH] Rasht (G.C. 37N10 049E40) 756kHz 100kW; [TYB] Tayebad (G.C. 34N43 060E48) 720kHz 400kW; [ZAB] Zabol (G.C. 31N02 061E29) 1098kHz 100kW
SW: [AHW] Ahwaz (G.C. 31N20 048E40) 2 x 250kW; [KAM] Tehran, Kamalabad (G.C. 35N46 051E27) 10 x 100, 3 x 250, 1 x 350, 12 x 500kW; [MAS] Mashhad (G.C. 36N15 059E33) 4 x 500kW; [SIR] Sirjan (G.C. 29N27 055E41) 10 x 500kW; [ZAH] Zahedan (G.C. 29N28 060E53) 2 x 500kW
SAT: Arabsat 2D, Hotbird 3, Telstar 5
kHz: *576, 612, 639, 702, 720, 765, 1080, 1098, 1161, 1224, 1449, 3985, 5905, 5945, 5955, 5970, 5990, 6005, 6010, 6015, 6035, 6040, 6065, 6095, 6100, 6110, 6120, 6125, 6130, 6140, 6145, 6175, 6180, 6185, 6190, 6200, 7125, 7130, 7135, 7165, 7170, 7180, 7205, 7210, 7225, 7230, 7235, 7250, 7265, 7270, 7275, 7295, 7305, 7320, 7325, 7335, 9500, 9505, 9510, 9545, 9555, 9565, 9575, 9580, 9590, 9595, 9610, 9615, 9635, 9660, 9685, 9695, 9705, 9710, 9735, 9740, 9750, 9755, 9770, 9775, 9785, 9790, 9825, 9835, 9855, 9860, 9865, 9895, 9905, 9920, 9940, 11610, 11670, 11695, 11705, 11745, 11750, 11870, 11910, 11950, 12025, 13640, 13645, 13720, 13740, 13745, 13760, 13790, 15085, 15150, 15165, 15200, 15205, 15235, 15260, 15275, 15320, 15340, 15365, 15440, 15460, 15480, 15530, 15545, 17560, 17590, 17660, 17680, 17690, 17745, 17810, 21645, 21770, 21810*

Winter Schedule 2004

Albanian	Days	Area	kHz
0630-0730	daily	Eu	15235kam, 15340sir
1830-1930	daily	Eu	6100sir, 7165kam
2030-2130	daily	Eu	6100sir, 9740kam
Arabic	**Days**	**Area**	**kHz**
0000-2400	daily	ME	1224qsh
0130-0330	daily	ME	612qsh
0230-1430	daily	ME	13760zah, 13790kam
0330-1030	daily	ME	765chb
0330-1630	daily	ME	576mhs
0430-1630	daily	ME	612qsh
0530-1630	daily	NAf,ME	15545sir
1630-0230	daily	ME	1080mhs
Arabic	**Days**	**Area**	**kHz**
1630-0530	daily	NAf,ME	6065mas
1630-2130	daily	ME	1161qsh
1830-2130	daily	ME	765chb
Arabic (Vo Palestine)	**Days**	**Area**	**kHz**
0330-0430	daily	ME	7250kam, 9505sir
Armenian	**Days**	**Area**	**kHz**
0300-0330	daily	ME	7295sir
0930-1000	daily	ME	9695kam, 15260sir
1630-1730	daily	ME	6185sir, 7230sir
Azeri	**Days**	**Area**	**kHz**
0330-0530	daily	ME	9860sir
1430-1700	daily	ME	702kia, 6200sir
Bengali	**Days**	**Area**	**kHz**
0030-0130	daily	SAs	765chb, 5905kam, 6185kam
0830-0930	daily	ME	11705sir
1430-1530	daily	SAs	9545kam, 9565kam, 9940kam
Bosnian	**Days**	**Area**	**kHz**
0530-0630	daily	EEu	15235kam, 15340sir
1730-1830	daily	EEu	7295sir, 9705kam
2130-2230	daily	EaEu	7235sir
2130-2230	daily	EEu	9710kam
Dari	**Days**	**Area**	**kHz**
0300-0630	daily	ME	720mhd, 1098zab, 11910kam, 13740ahw
0830-1430	daily	ME	720mhd, 1098zab, 13720ahw
1030-1500	daily	ME	9920kam
English	**Days**	**Area**	**kHz**
1030-1130	daily	ME	702kia
1030-1130	daily	SAs	15460kam, 15480kam
1030-1130	daily	WAs	765chb
1530-1630	daily	SAs	9610sir, 9940kam
1930-2030	daily	Eu	6110kam, 7320sir
1930-2030	daily	SAf	9855sir, 11695kam
English (Vo Justice)	**Days**	**Area**	**kHz**
0130-0230	daily	NAm	6120kam, 9580sir
French	**Days**	**Area**	**kHz**
0630-0730	daily	Eu,NAf	21645sir
0630-0730	daily	Eu	17590kam
1830-1930	daily	Af	9565kam
1830-1930	daily	Eu	6180kam, 9755sir
Georgian	**Days**	**Area**	**kHz**
1700-1800	daily	ME	702kia
German	**Days**	**Area**	**kHz**
0730-0830	daily	Eu	15085kam, 21770sir
1730-1830	daily	Eu	6110kam, 9500sir
Hausa	**Days**	**Area**	**kHz**
0600-0700	daily	WAf	17810sir, 21810sir
1830-1930	daily	WAf	7335kam, 9775sir
Hebrew	**Days**	**Area**	**kHz**
0430-0500	daily	ME	7250kam, 9590sir
1900-1930	daily	Eu	3985ahw
1900-1930	daily	ME	5970kam
Hindi	**Days**	**Area**	**kHz**
0230-0300	daily	SAs	15165sir, 15205sir
1430-1530	daily	SAs	9865kam, 13745sir
Indonesian	**Days**	**Area**	**kHz**
1230-1330	daily	SEA	15200sir, 15275kam
2230-2330	daily	SEA	7275kam, 9685sir
Italian	**Days**	**Area**	**kHz**
0630-0730	daily	Eu	15085kam, 17560kam
1930-2000	daily	Eu	7295sir, 9615kam
Japanese	**Days**	**Area**	**kHz**
1300-1330	daily	FE	9510kam, 9770sir
2100-2130	daily	FE	6125sir, 7180sir
Kazakh	**Days**	**Area**	**kHz**
0130-0230	daily	CAs	7135sir, 7265sir
1300-1400	daily	ME	9660sir, 11745kam
Kurdish	**Days**	**Area**	**kHz**
0330-0430	daily	ME	612qsh, 639bnb, 6145kam, 9825sir
1330-1630	daily	ME	639bnb, 5990kam

Mandarin	Days	Area	kHz
1200-1300	daily	FE	9895kam, 11670kam, 13645sir, 15150sir
2330-0030	daily	FE	7130sir, 7325sir, 9635kam

Pashto	Days	Area	kHz
0230-0330	daily	ME	765chb, 6095kam, 6140sir
0730-0830	daily	ME	1098zab, 15440ahw
1230-1330	daily	ME	765chb, 6175sir, 9790sir, 11870kam
1430-1530	daily	ME	765chb, 1098zab, 7270sir
1630-1730	daily	ME	6005ahw, 6015sir

Russian	Days	Area	kHz
0300-0330	daily	CAs	702kia
0300-0330	daily	RUS,CAs	6040kam, 7125sir
0500-0530	daily	CAs,FE	17680sir, 17745sir
0500-0530	daily	RUS	12025kam, 15530sir
1430-1530	daily	CAs	1449ban
1430-1530	daily	RUS	9575sir
1430-1530	daily	RUS,CAs	7165kam, 9735ahw
1700-1800	daily	RUS	7170ahw
1700-1800	daily	RUS,CAs	3985kam
1800-1900	daily	RUS	6035sir, 7305kam
1930-2030	daily	UKR,CAs	702kia
1930-2030	daily	RUS	3985kam, 7205sir

Spanish	Days	Area	kHz
0030-0230	daily	CAm,SAm	9555kam
0030-0330	daily	SAm	9905kam
0530-0630	daily	Eu	15320sir, 17590kam
2030-2130	daily	CAm,SAm	11610sir
2030-2130	daily	Eu	7130kam, 9750sir

Swahili	Days	Area	kHz
0330-0430	daily	EAf	13640sir, 15260kam
0830-0930	daily	EAf	17660kam, 17690kam
1730-1830	daily	EAf	11750sir
1730-1830	daily	EAf,ME	9595kam
1800-1830	daily	ME	702kia

Tajik	Days	Area	kHz
0100-0230	daily	CAs	720mhd, 5955sir, 6175kam
1600-1730	daily	CAs	720mhd, 5945kam, 5955sir

Turkish	Days	Area	kHz
0430-0600	daily	ME	15260kam, 15365kam
1600-1730	daily	ME	7125kam, 9705kam
1830-1930	daily	ME	639bnb, 702kia

Turkmen	Days	Area	kHz
0000-0500	daily	ME	1449bnt
1530-1830	daily	ME	1449bnt

Urdu	Days	Area	kHz
0130-0230	daily	SAs	765chb, 6010kam, 6190sir, 7210ahw
1330-1430	daily	ME	9835kam
1330-1430	daily	SAs	765chb, 6175sir, 11950kam
1530-1730	daily	SAs	765chb, 7270kam
1730-1800	daily	SAs	6130sir, 7225kam

Uzbek	Days	Area	kHz
0230-0300	daily	SAs	6175kam, 9785sir
1500-1600	daily	SAs	5945kam, 5955sir

ANN: English: "This is the Voice of the Islamic Republic of Iran"; Farsi: "Inja Tehran ast, seda-ye jomhuri-ye eslami-ye Iran"; French: "Ici Tehran, la Voix de la République Islamique de l'Iran"; Russian: "Govorit Tegeran, Golos Islamskoy Respubliki Iran"; Arabic: "Huna Tahran - Sawt al Jumhuriya al Islamiya fi Iran"
V: QSL-card. Rec. acc.
NOTES: The Voice of the Islamic Republic of Iran is the External Sce of the state broadcaster IRIB.

ISRAEL

KOL ISRAEL (THE VOICE OF ISRAEL) (Pub)

P.O. Box 1082, Jerusalem 91010, Israel.
☎ +972 2 248715. Fax +972 2 302327.
Email: raphaelk@iba.org.il **Web:** www.iba.org.il
SW: Leased from Bezeq.
SAT: Hotbird 3
kHz: *5915, 6280, 7520, 7545, 9345, 9390, 9985, 11585, 11605, 13850, 15615, 15640, 15760, 17535, 17600*

Winter Schedule 2004

Amharic/Tigrinya	Days	Area	kHz
1900-1945	daily	NAm,Eu	11585isr, 11605isr
1900-1945	daily	NAf	9390isr

Arabic	Days	Area	kHz
0345-2215	daily	ME	5915isr

English	Days	Area	kHz
0430-0445	daily	CAm,AUS	17600isr
0430-0445	daily	NAm,Eu	6280isr, 7545isr
1030-1045	daily	NAm,Eu	15640isr, 17535isr
1830-1845	daily	NAm,Eu	9390isr, 11585isr, 11605isr
2000-2025	daily	NAm,Eu	6280isr, 9390isr
2000-2025	daily	SAf	15615isr

Farsi	Days	Area	kHz
1500-1600	....fs.	IRN	9985isr, 11605isr
1500-1600	....fs.	NAm,Eu	17535isr
1500-1625	mtwt..s	NAm,Eu	17535isr
1500-1625	mtwt..s	IRN	9985isr, 11605isr, 13850isr*, 15640isr*

French	Days	Area	kHz
0445-0500	daily	NAm,Eu	6280isr, 7545isr
1100-1115	daily	NAm,Eu	15640isr, 17535isr
1800-1815	daily	NAm,Eu	9390isr, 11585isr, 11605isr
2030-2045	daily	Eu,CAm	6280isr
2030-2045	daily	NAm,Eu	7520isr, 9390isr

Hebrew	Days	Area	kHz
0000-0430	daily	NAm,Eu	7545isr
0500-0600	daily	NAm,Eu	7545isr
0500-1700	daily	NAm,Eu	15760isr
0600-1030	daily	NAm,Eu	17535isr
1115-1455	daily	NAm,Eu	17535isr
1700-0500	daily	NAm,Eu	9345isr
2100-2215	daily	SAm	7520isr
2200-2400	daily	NAm,Eu	6280isr

Hungarian	Days	Area	kHz
1945-2000	daily	Eu	9390isr, 11585isr, 11605isr

Ladino	Days	Area	kHz
1045-1100	daily	NAm,Eu	15640isr, 17535isr

Romanian	Days	Area	kHz
1845-1900	daily	ROU	9390isr, 11585isr, 11605isr

Russian	Days	Area	kHz
2100-2200	daily	NAm,Eu	6280isr
2100-2200	daily	RUS	9390isr

Spanish	Days	Area	kHz
1815-1830	daily	NAm,Eu	9390isr, 11585isr, 11605isr
2045-2100	daily	Eu,CAm	6280isr
2045-2100	daily	NAm,Eu	9390isr
2045-2100	daily	SAm,SAf	7520isr

Spanish/Ladino	Days	Area	kHz
1600-1625	.....s.	Eu	15640isr
1600-1625	.....s.	NAm,Eu	17535isr

Yiddish	Days	Area	kHz
1700-1725	daily	NAm,Eu	11605isr
1700-1725	daily	Eu	9390isr
1700-1725	daily	Eu,CAm	17535isr

ANN: Yiddish: "Hert zu der yisrael odizie im yiddish fyn yerushaalayion"; English: "This is Kol Israel broadcasting from Jerusalem"; French: "Ici Kol Israel, Radiodiffusion Israelienne"
V: QSL-email
NOTES: Relays of Kol Israel's Home Sce networks. All SW transmissions due to cease on 31 December 2004. More information on the private website www.israelradio.org. Key: * Alternate/additional frequency, when conditions require.

BEZEQ (THE ISRAEL TELECOMMUNICATIONS CORP. LTD.) (Tx Operator)

P.O. Box 1088, Jerusalem 91010, Israel.
☎ +972 36 264562. Fax +972 36 264559.
Email: mosheor@bezeq.com **Web:** www.bezeq.com
SW: [ISR] Yavne (G.C. 31N52 034E45) 1 x 100, 4 x 300, 1 x 500kW
NOTES: Bezeq is the national transmitter network operator in Israel. Kol Israel is Bezeq's main customer.

ITALY

RAI INTERNATIONAL (Pub)
P.O. Box 320, I-00100 Roma, Italy.
☎ +39 6 33542526. Fax +39 6 33170767.
Email: raiinternational@rai.it **Web:** www.raiinternational.rai.it
L.P: Dir: Roberto Morrione.
SW: Uses tx's provided by RAI WAY
SAT: Asiasat 2, Eutelsat W4, Hotbird 1, Nahuel 1, Pas 2/7/9/10
kHz: *567, 900, 1332, 5965, 5985, 5990, 6000, 6010, 6035, 6040, 6060, 6110, 6125, 6130, 6140, 7230, 7290, 9570, 9655, 9670, 9755, 9760, 9840, 9850, 11670, 11680, 11765, 11800, 11815, 11855, 11875, 11880, 11895, 11900, 11920, 11985, 15250, 15320, 17780, 21520, 21550, 21710*

Winter Schedule 2004

	Days	Area	kHz
Amharic	**Days**	**Area**	**kHz**
0435-0455	daily	EAf,ME	11985rom
Arabic	**Days**	**Area**	**kHz**
0600-0620	daily	EAf,ME	11985rom
1330-1345	daily	Eu,Med	567rom
1330-1355	daily	E,NAf	9670rom, 11800rom
1430-1455	daily	NAf	11900rom
1630-1655	daily	EAf,ME	6040rom, 11670rom
2025-2045	daily	E,NAf	6010rom, 7290rom
2135-2155	daily	NAf	6010rom, 7290rom
Bulgarian	**Days**	**Area**	**kHz**
1540-1600	daily	EEu	11985rom
Croatian	**Days**	**Area**	**kHz**
1435-1455	daily	EEu	9850rom
Czech	**Days**	**Area**	**kHz**
1810-1825	daily	EEu	5990rom
2135-2155	daily	EEu	6125rom
Danish	**Days**	**Area**	**kHz**
2000-2020	.t.t..s	WEu	6035rom, 9760rom
English	**Days**	**Area**	**kHz**
0055-0115	daily	NAm	11800rom
0445-0500	daily	E,NAf	5965rom, 7230rom
0445-0500	daily	NAf	6000rom
1935-1955	daily	WEu	6035rom, 9760rom
2025-2045	daily	EAf,ME	6040rom, 11880rom
2025-2045	daily	NAf	6040rom, 11880rom
2205-2230	daily	As,FE,J	11895rom
Esperanto	**Days**	**Area**	**kHz**
2000-2020	…..s.	WEu	6035rom, 9760rom
French	**Days**	**Area**	**kHz**
0115-0130	daily	NAm	11800rom
1530-1555	daily	WEu	5985rom, 9570rom, 11680rom
1630-1655	daily	E,NAf	9570rom, 11895rom
German	**Days**	**Area**	**kHz**
1415-1435	daily	EEu	9850rom
1805-1825	daily	WEu	6110rom, 9760rom
Greek	**Days**	**Area**	**kHz**
1520-1540	daily	EEu	11985rom
Hungarian	**Days**	**Area**	**kHz**
1935-1955	daily	EEu	6130rom
Italian	**Days**	**Area**	**kHz**
0130-0230	daily	SAm	6110asc
0130-0230	daily	CAm	11765asc
0130-0315	daily	NAm	11800rom
0130-0315	daily	SAm	9840rom
0435-0445	daily	E,NAf	5965rom, 7230rom
0435-0445	daily	NAf	6000rom
0455-0530	daily	EAf,ME	11985rom
0630-1300	daily	EEu	11800rom
1000-1100	daily	AUS,Oc	11920sng
1350-1730	daily	SAm	21550rom**
1350-1730	daily	CAf	21710rom**
1350-1730	daily	Eu	9670rom**
1350-1730	daily	NAm	21520rom**
1400-1425	daily	NAm	17780rom, 21520rom
1500-1525	daily	E,NAf	9670rom, 11800rom
1500-1525	daily	Med	9670rom, 11800rom
1500-1525	daily	NAf	11900rom
1555-1625	daily	WEu	5985rom, 9570rom, 11680rom
Italian	**Days**	**Area**	**kHz**
1700-1800	daily	CAf	11875rom, 15250rom, 15320asc
1700-1800	daily	E,NAf	9755rom, 11895rom
1700-1800	daily	EAf,ME	6140rom, 11875rom
1830-1905	daily	NAm	11800rom, 15250rom, 17780rom
2200-0400	daily	Eu,Med	900rom, 1332rom
2240-0055	daily	SAm	9840rom
2240-0055	daily	NAm	11800rom
2300-0500	daily	Med	6060rom*
Lithuanian	**Days**	**Area**	**kHz**
0505-0525	daily	EEu	5965rom
Polish	**Days**	**Area**	**kHz**
1840-1900	daily	EEu	5990rom
2210-2225	daily	EEu	6125rom
Portuguese	**Days**	**Area**	**kHz**
0115-0130	daily	SAm	9840rom
2050-2110	daily	E,NAf	6010rom, 7290rom
2050-2110	daily	EAf,ME	11880rom
2050-2110	daily	CAf	11880rom, 15250rom
Romanian	**Days**	**Area**	**kHz**
0530-0550	daily	EEu	5965rom
2115-2135	daily	EEu	6125rom
Russian	**Days**	**Area**	**kHz**
0345-0405	daily	RUS	5965rom, 9655rom
0600-0620	daily	RUS	9670rom, 11800rom
1335-1355	daily	EEu	9670rom, 11670rom
1605-1625	daily	RUS	9655rom, 11815rom
2000-2020	daily	RUS	6125rom, 9670rom
Serbian	**Days**	**Area**	**kHz**
1910-1930	daily	EEu	6130rom
Slovak	**Days**	**Area**	**kHz**
1825-1840	daily	EEu	5990rom
2155-2210	daily	EEu	6125rom
Slovenian	**Days**	**Area**	**kHz**
1400-1415	daily	EEu	9850rom
Somali	**Days**	**Area**	**kHz**
0530-0550	daily	EAf,ME	11985rom
1910-1930	daily	EAf,ME	11855rom
Spanish	**Days**	**Area**	**kHz**
0055-0115	daily	SAm	9840rom
0315-0335	daily	NAm	11800rom
0315-0335	daily	SAm	9840rom
2110-2130	daily	E,NAf	6010rom, 7290rom
Swedish	**Days**	**Area**	**kHz**
2000-2020	m.w.f..	WEu	6035rom, 9760rom
Turkish	**Days**	**Area**	**kHz**
1500-1520	daily	EEu	11985rom
Ukrainian	**Days**	**Area**	**kHz**
0405-0425	daily	EEu	5965rom, 9655rom

ANN: Italian: "RAI International programmi in lingua Italiana"; English: "This is the Italian Radio and Television Service broadcasting from Rome"; French: "Ici la Radio Italienne"; German: "Hier ist der Italienische Auslandssendedienst".
V: QSL-card.
NOTES: RAI International is the External Sce of the public broadcaster Radiotelevisione Italiana (RAI). Key: * Notturno dall'Italia; ** Sundays 1350-1730, broadcasts may be reduced or stopped for news or sports coverage.

RAIWAY (Tx Operator)
Via Teulada 66, I-00195 Roma, Italy.
☎ +39 6 33177022. Fax +39 6 33177022.
Email: raiway@rai.it **Web:** www.raiway.rai.it
SW: [ROM] Roma, Prato Smeraldo (G.C. 41N48 012E31) 6 x 100kW

IRRS–SHORTWAVE (NEXUS–IBA)
P.O. Box 11028, I-20110 Milano, Italy.
☎ +39 2 2666971. Fax +39 2 70638151.
Email: info@nexus.org **Web:** www.nexus.org
L.P: CEO: Alfredo E. Cotroneo.
SW: [MIL] Milano (G.C. 45N27 009E11) 1 x 20kW. Also leases air time on behalf of customers on facilities with 100kW or more at unconfirmed locations.
kHz: *5775, 13840, 15665*

Winter Schedule 2004

Arabic/Spanish	Days	Area	kHz
1100-1200	....f..	Eu,WAf	15665mil
English/German/ Italian	**Days**	**Area**	**kHz**
0800-1300	.....ss	Eu,NAf	13840mil
2000-2130	mtwt.ss	Eu,NAf	5775mil
2000-2200	....f..	Eu,NAf	5775mil

IS: S/on: Triumphal Scene from Aida (Giuseppe Verdi); S/off: Prisoners' Chorus (Giuseppe Verdi).

V: QSL-card. Rp. Rpt by email to reports@nexus.org. Due to budget constraints, not all reports may be acknowledged. Listeners are encouraged to send reports direct to the programme producers using addresses given during broadcasts.

NOTES: NEXUS-IBA is a 24h Internet radio station and provider of shortwave air time for prgr producers. Details of relayed stations and current schedule can be found at: www.nexus.org/NEXUS-IBA/Schedules.

Broadcasters using sites in this country:
R.Santec uses: (MIL). See stn entry in: **D**, INT Section
Radio Six Int'l uses: (MIL). See stn entry in: **G**, INT Section

JAPAN

RADIO JAPAN (NHK WORLD) (Pub)

NHK World Radio Japan, NHK 150-8001, Japan.
☎ +81 3 34651111. 🖷 +81 3 34811350.
Email: info@intl.nhk.or.jp **Web:** www.nhk.or.jp/nhkworld
L.P: DG: T.Sato.
SW: Leased from KDDI
SAT: Pas 8/9/10, Galaxy 3C
kHz: *5955, 5960, 5975, 6030, 6035, 6090, 6110, 6115, 6120, 6135, 6145, 6165, 6175, 6180, 6190, 7105, 7115, 7140, 7200, 7225, 7230, 9505, 9530, 9535, 9540, 9560, 9575, 9660, 9685, 9695, 9710, 9750, 9825, 9835, 9875, 11665, 11690, 11705, 11710, 11715, 11730, 11740, 11760, 11770, 11785, 11815, 11840, 11855, 11860, 11865, 11890, 11895, 11910, 11920, 11970, 12045, 13630, 13650, 13660, 15195, 15220, 15325, 15355, 15400, 15590, 17560, 17585, 17605, 17650, 17675, 17685, 17720, 17780, 17810, 17820, 17825, 17835, 17845, 17860, 17870, 21600, 21610, 21630, 21670, 21755, 21820*

Winter Schedule 2004

Arabic	Days	Area	kHz
0400-0430	daily	ME,Af	17780eka
0700-0730	daily	ME,Af	15220asc
Bengali	**Days**	**Area**	**kHz**
0630-0700	daily	SAs	11890eka, 15590yam
1230-1300	daily	SAs	11890eka
Burmese	**Days**	**Area**	**kHz**
1030-1100	daily	SEA	11740sng
1230-1300	daily	SEA	9695yam
2320-2340	daily	SEA	13650yam
English	**Days**	**Area**	**kHz**
0000-0015	daily	SEA	13650yam, 17810yam
0000-0100	daily	NAm	6145sac
0100-0200	daily	As	17845yam
0100-0200	daily	SEA	11860sng, 17810yam
0100-0200	daily	SAs	15325yam
0100-0200	daily	SAm	17835yam
0100-0200	daily	Oc	17685yam
0100-0200	daily	ME,NAf	6030rmp, 17560yam
0100-0200	daily	NAm,CAm	17825yam
0300-0400	daily	Oc	21610yam
0500-0600	daily	Eu	5975rmp
0500-0600	daily	NAm	6110sac
0500-0600	daily	SEA	17810yam
0500-0700	daily	Oc	21755yam
0500-0700	daily	As	15195yam
0500-0700	daily	Eu	7230wof
0600-0700	daily	FE,RUS	11715yam, 11760yam
0600-0700	daily	HWA	17870yam
0600-0700	daily	NAm,CAm	11690yam
0600-0700	daily	SEA	11740sng
1000-1100	daily	Oc	21755yam
1000-1100	daily	Eu	17585dha
1000-1100	daily	ME,NAf	17720dha
1000-1200	daily	SEA	9695yam
1000-1200	daily	As	11730yam
1000-1200	daily	NAm	6120sac
English	**Days**	**Area**	**kHz**
1400-1500	daily	Oc	11840eka
1400-1600	daily	SAs	9875yam
1400-1600	daily	SEA	7200yam
1500-1600	daily	As	6190yam
1500-1600	daily	NAm,CAm	9505yam
1700-1800	daily	SAf	15355gab
1700-1800	daily	NAm,CAm	9535yam
1700-1800	daily	Eu	11970yam
1700-1800	....f..	Eu	9875rmp+
2100-2200	daily	Eu	6090skn, 6180skn
2100-2200	daily	HWA	21670yam
2100-2200	daily	NAm	17825yam
2100-2200	daily	Oc	6035sng
2100-2200	daily	CAf	11855asc
Farsi	**Days**	**Area**	**kHz**
0230-0300	daily	ME,NAf	17780eka
0830-0900	daily	ME,NAf	17675eka
French	**Days**	**Area**	**kHz**
0500-0530	daily	ME,NAf	17820eka
0630-0700	daily	Eu	11970gab
1230-1300	daily	WAf	15400asc
1230-1300	daily	CAf	17870asc
1630-1650	daily	ME,NAf	7105yam
1800-1820	daily	Af	9685yam, 11785yam
1800-1820	daily	Eu	11970yam
German	**Days**	**Area**	**kHz**
0600-0630	daily	Eu	11970gab
1100-1130	daily	Eu	9660skn, 11710skn
Hindi	**Days**	**Area**	**kHz**
0700-0730	daily	SAs	11890eka, 15590yam
1300-1330	daily	SAs	11890eka
Indonesian	**Days**	**Area**	**kHz**
0930-1000	daily	SEA	9695yam
1130-1200	daily	SEA	13660yam
1230-1300	daily	SEA	13660yam
2300-2320	daily	SEA	17810yam
2340-2400	daily	SEA	13650yam
Italian	**Days**	**Area**	**kHz**
0530-0545	daily	Eu	11970gab
1030-1045	daily	Eu	21820gab
Japanese	**Days**	**Area**	**kHz**
0200-0300	daily	As	17845yam
0200-0300	daily	SAm	17835yam
0200-0300	daily	SEA	11860sng
0200-0400	daily	Oc	17685yam
0200-0500	daily	As	15195yam
0200-0500	daily	SEA	17810yam
0200-0500	daily	NAm	5960sac
0200-0500	daily	SAs	15325yam
0300-0400	daily	SAm	9660guf
0300-0500	daily	ME,NAf	17560yam
0300-0500	daily	NAm,CAm	17825yam
0700-0800	daily	As	15195yam
0700-0800	daily	FE	6145yam, 6165yam
0700-0800	daily	HWA	17870yam
0700-0900	daily	SEA	17860yam
0700-1000	daily	SEA	11740sng
0700-1000	daily	Oc	11920sng, 21755yam
0800-1000	daily	Af	17650asc
0800-1000	daily	Eu	11710skn
0800-1000	daily	ME,NAf	17720dha
0800-1000	daily	NAm,CAm	9540yam
0800-1000	daily	SAm	9530guf
0800-1000	daily	SAm,HWA	9825yam
0800-1000	daily	SAs	15590yam
0800-1700	daily	As	9750yam
0900-1600	daily	SEA	11815yam
1300-1500	daily	NAm	11705sac
1500-1700	daily	NAm,CAm	9535yam
1500-1700	daily	SAs	12045sng
1500-1700	daily	Af	21630asc
1600-1900	daily	As	6035yam
1600-1900	daily	SEA	7200yam
1700-1800	daily	Eu	9750rmp
1700-1800	daily	SAm	21600guf
1700-1800	daily	SAs	11865sng

Japanese	Days	Area	kHz
1700-1900	daily	Oc	7140yam
1700-1900	daily	ME,NAf	9575dha
1700-1900	daily	Eu	6175skn
1700-1900	daily	SAm,HWA	9835yam
1800-1900	daily	Af	15355gab
1900-2100	daily	Oc	6035sng
2000-2100	daily	As	6165yam
2000-2100	daily	Eu	11970yam
2000-2200	daily	SEA	7225yam
2000-2400	daily	As	11910yam
2000-2400	daily	SEA	11665yam
2100-2200	daily	SAs	9560yam
2200-2300	daily	SAm	15220asc
2200-2300	daily	Oc	11770eka
2200-2300	daily	NAm	17825yam
2200-2300	daily	ME,NAf	7115dha
2200-2300	daily	CAm	11895guf, 17825yam
2200-2300	daily	Eu	6115skn
2300-2400	daily	SAm	17605bon
Korean	**Days**	**Area**	**kHz**
0430-0500	daily	As	17845yam
0530-0600	daily	As	17845yam
1115-1145	daily	As	6090yam
1230-1300	daily	As	6190yam
1400-1430	daily	As	6190yam
2210-2230	daily	As	9560yam
Malay	**Days**	**Area**	**kHz**
1200-1230	daily	SEA	9695yam, 13660yam
1300-1330	daily	SEA	9695yam
2240-2300	daily	SEA	17810yam
Mandarin	**Days**	**Area**	**kHz**
0400-0430	daily	As	17845yam
0500-0530	daily	As	17845yam
0600-0630	daily	SEA	17860yam
1200-1230	daily	SEA	11740sng
1200-1230	daily	As	6190yam
1300-1330	daily	As	6190yam
1430-1500	daily	As	6190yam
2230-2250	daily	As	9560yam
2240-2300	daily	SEA	13650yam
2340-2400	daily	SEA	13630yam, 17810yam
Portuguese	**Days**	**Area**	**kHz**
0230-0300	daily	SAm	9660guf
1030-1100	daily	SAm	9530guf
Russian	**Days**	**Area**	**kHz**
0330-0400	daily	As	17845yam
0430-0500	daily	Eu	11970gab
0530-0600	daily	RUS	11715yam, 11760yam
0800-0830	daily	RUS	6145yam, 6165yam
1130-1200	daily	Eu	11710skn
1330-1400	daily	As	6190yam
1840-1900	daily	Eu	11970yam
1900-1920	daily	RUS	5955yam
Spanish	**Days**	**Area**	**kHz**
0400-0430	daily	SAm	9660guf
0500-0530	daily	CAm	11895guf
0500-0530	daily	Eu	11970gab
1000-1030	daily	CAm	9540yam
1000-1030	daily	SAm	9530guf, 9710yam
1820-1840	daily	Eu	11970yam
Swahili	**Days**	**Area**	**kHz**
0330-0400	daily	CAf	6135asc
1300-1330	daily	CAf	17870asc
Swedish	**Days**	**Area**	**kHz**
0545-0600	daily	Eu	11970gab
1045-1100	daily	Eu	21820gab
Thai	**Days**	**Area**	**kHz**
1130-1200	daily	SEA	11740sng
1330-1400	daily	SEA	7200yam
2300-2320	daily	SEA	13650yam
Urdu	**Days**	**Area**	**kHz**
0730-0800	daily	SAs	11890eka, 15590yam
Vietnamese	**Days**	**Area**	**kHz**
1100-1130	daily	SEA	13660yam
1230-1300	daily	SEA	11740sng
2320-2340	daily	SEA	17810yam

ANN: English: "This is Radio Japan, NHK World network, Tokyo"; German: "Hier ist Radio Japan, NHK WORLD"; Indonesian: "Inilah Radio Jepang, NHK World, siaran bahasa Indonesia"; Japanese: "Kochirawa NHK Warudo, Rajio Nippon, NHK no kokusaihoso desu"; Korean: "Yeogineun Radio Ilbon, NHK Worldeumnida"; Mandarin: "Zheli shi riben guoji guangbo diantai, NHK huanqiu guangbowang"
IS: Interval signal music "Kazoe Uta"
V: QSL-card.
NOTES: Radio Japan is the External Sce of the public broadcaster NHK. The Japanese programmes include relays of NHK domestic Radio 1. Key: + DRM

KDDI CORPORATION (Tx Operator)
3-2 Nishi-Shinjyuku 2-Chome Shinjyuku-Ku 163-8003, Tokyo 102-8401, Japan.
☎ +81 3 33475711. Fax +81 3 33475845.
Web: www.kddi.com
SW: [YAM] Sanwa, Yamata (G.C. 36N10 139E50) 4 x 100, 7 x 300kW
Broadcasters using sites in this country:
BBC World Sce uses: (YAM). See stn entry in: **G**, INT Section
RCI uses: (YAM). See stn entry in: **CAN**, INT Section
RFI uses: (YAM). See stn entry in: **F**, INT Section

JORDAN

RADIO JORDAN (JRTV) (Gov)
P.O. Box 909, Amman, Jordan.
☎ +962 6 4757410. Fax +962 6 4207862.
Email: eng@jrtv.gov.jo **Web:** www.jrtv.com
L.P: Dir Foreign Sces: Haytham Al-Etoom.
SW: [AKA] Al Karanah (G.C. 31N44 036E26) 3 x 500kW
SAT: Arabsat 2D/3A
kHz: *6105, 9830, 11690, 11810, 11960, 15290, 15435*

Winter Schedule 2004

Arabic	Days	Area	kHz
0300-0600	daily	NAm,Eu	15435aka*
0400-0815	daily	ME,As	11810aka*
0600-0815	daily	Eu	11960aka*
1130-1300	daily	ME,As	11810aka*
1130-1300	daily	Eu,NAf	15290aka*
1600-2300	daily	ME,SEA	6105aka*
1830-2100	daily	Eu	9830aka*
2000-2200	daily	SAm	15435aka*
Arabic (Armed forces)	**Days**	**Area**	**kHz**
1300-1600	daily	ME,As	11810aka*
English	**Days**	**Area**	**kHz**
1400-1730	daily	NAm,Eu	11690aka*

ANN: Arabic: "Huna 'amman, Idha'atu-l-mamlaka al-urduniyya al-hashimiyya"; English: "This is Radio Jordan, broadcasting from Amman". Key: * Sign on and off times vary.
V: QSL-card. Rec. acc.
NOTES: Relays of Home Sce prgr's in Arabic and English.

KAZAKHSTAN

KAZTELERADIO (Tx Operator)
pr. Al-Farabi 118, 480090 Almaty, Kazakhstan.
SW: [ALM] Almaty, Dmitriyevka (G.C. 43N31 077E00) 9 x 100kW ; [QAR] Qaraturyq (G.C. 43N39 077E56) 4 x 1000kW. Code used in seasonal HFCC schedules: "A-A".
NOTES: Kazteleradio is the national transmitter network owner in Kazakhstan. It leases out its facilities to domestic and international broadcasters.
Broadcasters using sites in this country:
BBG-R.Free Asia uses: (ALM). See stn entry in: **USA**, INT Section
Dem.VO Burma uses: (ALM). See stn entry in: **BRM**, CTB Section
Deutsche Welle uses: (ALM). See stn entry in: **D**, INT Section
Golos Pravosl. uses: (ALM). See stn entry in: **F**, INT Section
TWR India uses: (ALM). See stn entry in: **IND**, INT Section

KOREA, NORTH (D.P.R.)

VOICE OF KOREA (Gov)
Voice of Korea, Pyongyang, Democratic People's Republic of Korea.
☎ +850 2 3816035. Fax +850 2 3814416.
MW/SW: Uses tx's provided by the Ministry of Telecommunications.

SAT: Thaicom 3
kHz: *621, 3250, 3560, 4405, 6070, 6195, 6520, 6575, 7140, 7505, 7580, 9325, 9335, 9345, 9660, 9850, 9975, 11335, 11710, 11735*

Winter Schedule 2004

Arabic	Days	Area	kHz
1500-1600	daily	ME,Af	3560pyo, 9975kuj, 11735kuj
1900-2000	daily	ME,Af	9975kuj, 11735kuj
1900-2000	daily	SAf	3560pyo, 9660kuj, 11710kuj

English	Days	Area	kHz
0100-0200	daily	CAm,SAm	6520kuj, 7580kuj, 11735kuj
0100-0200	daily	CHN	3560pyo, 6195kuj, 7140kuj, 9345kuj
0200-0300	daily	SEA	4405pyo, 9325kuj, 11335kuj
0300-0400	daily	CHN	3560pyo, 6195kuj, 7140kuj, 9345kuj
1000-1100	daily	CAm,SAm	3560pyo, 9335kuj, 11710kuj
1000-1100	daily	SEA	9850kuj, 11735kuj
1300-1400	daily	NAm	9335kuj, 11710kuj
1300-1400	daily	Eu	4405pyo, 9325kuj, 11335kuj
1500-1600	daily	Eu	4405pyo, 9325kuj, 11335kuj
1500-1600	daily	NAm	9335kuj, 11710kuj
1600-1700	daily	ME,NAf	3560pyo, 9975kuj, 11735kuj
1900-2000	daily	Eu	4405pyo, 9325kuj, 11335kuj
2100-2200	daily	Eu	4405pyo, 9325kuj, 11335kuj

French	Days	Area	kHz
0100-0200	daily	SEA	4405pyo, 9325kuj, 11335kuj
0300-0400	daily	CAm,SAm	6520kuj, 7580kuj, 11735kuj
1100-1200	daily	CAm,SAm	9335kuj, 11710kuj
1100-1200	daily	SEA	3560pyo, 9850kuj, 11735kuj
1400-1500	daily	Eu	4405pyo, 9325kuj, 11335kuj
1400-1500	daily	NAm	9335kuj, 11710kuj
1600-1700	daily	Eu	4405pyo, 9325kuj, 11335kuj
1600-1700	daily	NAm	9335kuj, 11710kuj
1800-1900	daily	SAf	3560pyo, 9660kuj, 11710kuj
1800-1900	daily	ME,Af	9975kuj, 11735kuj
2000-2100	daily	Eu	4405pyo, 9325kuj, 11335kuj

German	Days	Area	kHz
1600-1700	daily	Eu	6575kuj, 7505kuj
1800-2000	daily	Eu	6575kuj, 7505kuj

Japanese	Days	Area	kHz
0700-0850	daily	J	621cho, 3250pyo, 6520kuj, 7580kuj
0900-1050	daily	J	621cho, 3250pyo, 6070kng, 6520kuj, 7580kuj
1100-1250	daily	J	621cho, 3250pyo, 6070kng, 6520kuj, 7580kuj
2100-2150	daily	J	621cho, 3250pyo, 6520kuj
2200-2350	daily	J	621cho, 3250pyo, 6520kuj, 7580kuj, 7580kuj

Korean (CBS)	Days	Area	kHz
0900-0950	daily	CHN	4405pyo, 7140kuj, 9345kuj
1200-1250	daily	SEA	3560pyo, 9850kuj, 11735kuj
1200-1250	daily	CAm,SAm	9335kuj, 11710kuj
1400-1450	daily	SEA	3560pyo, 9850kuj, 11735kuj
1700-1750	daily	Eu	4405pyo, 9325kuj, 11335kuj
1700-1750	daily	NAm	9335kuj, 11710kuj
2000-2050	daily	SAf	3560pyo, 9660kuj, 11710kuj
2000-2050	daily	Eu	6575kuj, 7505kuj
2000-2050	daily	ME,NAf	9975kuj, 11735kuj
2300-2350	daily	CHN	3560pyo, 7140kuj, 9345kuj, 9975kuj, 11735kuj
2300-2350	daily	Eu	4405pyo, 9325kuj, 11335kuj

Korean (R.Pyongyang)	Days	Area	kHz
0000-0050	daily	CHN	3560pyo, 6195kuj, 7140kuj, 9345kuj
0700-0750	daily	CHN	4405pyo, 7140kuj, 9345kuj
0900-0950	daily	Eu	9325kuj, 11335kuj
0900-0950	daily	FE	3560pyo, 9975kuj, 11735kuj
1000-1050	daily	CHN	4405pyo, 7140kuj, 9345kuj
1200-1250	daily	CHN	4405pyo, 7140kuj, 9345kuj
1300-1350	daily	Eu	6575kuj, 7505kuj

Mandarin	Days	Area	kHz
0000-0100	daily	SEA	4405pyo, 9325kuj, 11335kuj
0200-0300	daily	CHN	3560pyo, 6195kuj, 7140kuj, 9345kuj
0300-0400	daily	SEA	4405pyo, 9325kuj, 11335kuj
0800-0900	daily	CHN	4405pyo, 7140kuj, 9345kuj
1100-1200	daily	CHN	4405pyo, 7140kuj, 9345kuj
1300-1400	daily	SEA	3560pyo, 9850kuj, 11735kuj
2100-2300	daily	CHN	3560pyo, 7140kuj, 9345kuj, 9975kuj, 11735kuj

Russian	Days	Area	kHz
0700-0800	daily	FE	3560pyo, 9975kuj, 11735kuj
0700-0800	daily	Eu	9325kuj, 11335kuj
0800-0900	daily	Eu	9325kuj, 11335kuj
0800-0900	daily	FE	3560pyo, 9975kuj, 11735kuj
1400-1600	daily	Eu	6575kuj, 7505kuj
1700-1800	daily	Eu	6575kuj, 7505kuj

Spanish	Days	Area	kHz
0000-0100	daily	CAm,SAm	6520kuj, 7580kuj, 11735kuj
0200-0300	daily	CAm,SAm	6520kuj, 7580kuj, 11735kuj
1700-1800	daily	ME,NAf	3560pyo, 9975kuj, 11735kuj
1800-1900	daily	Eu	4405pyo, 9325kuj, 11335kuj
2200-2300	daily	Eu	4405pyo, 9325kuj, 11335kuj

ANN: Korean: "Joson Jung-ang Pangsong-imnida", "Pyongyang Pangsong-imnida"; Arabic: "Sawt Kuriya"; English: "This is Voice of Korea"; French: "La Voix de la Corée"; German: "Stimme Koreas"; Japanese: "Choson no koe hoso desu"; Chinese: "Chaoxian zhi sheng guangbo diantai"; Russian: "Govorit Golos Korei"; Spanish: "Aqui la Voz de Corea"

IS: Song of General Kim Il Sung. Opening music for Korean sce: Nat. Anthem.

V: QSL-card.

NOTES: The Voice of Korea is the External Sce of the Radio & TV Broadcasting Committee of the Dem. People's Rep. of Korea.

MINISTRY OF POSTS & TELECOMMUNICATIONS (Tx Operator)
Oesong-dong, Central District, Pyongyang, Democratic People's Republic of Korea.
☎ +850 2 3813180. +850 2 3814418.
Email: mptird@co.chesin.com
L.P: Dir: Sung Su Ri.
MW: [CHO] Chongjin (G.C. 41N47 129E50) 621kHz 500kW
SW: [KNG] Kanggye (G.C. 40N58 126E36) 5 x 200kW; [KUJ] Kujang (G.C. 40N05 125E05) 5 x 200kW; [PYO] Pyongyang (G.C. 39N05 125E23) 10 x 200kW; Unknown location: 4 x 250kW
NOTES: The Mininstry of Posts and Telecommunications is owning and operating the transmitter network in the Dem. People's Rep. of Korea.

KOREA, SOUTH (Rep. of)

RADIO KOREA INTERNATIONAL (Gov)
18 Yeouido-dong, Yeongdeungpo-gu, Seoul 150-790, Rep. of South Korea.
☎ +82 2 7813650. +82 2 7813694.
Email: rki@kbs.co.kr **Web:** rki.kbs.co.kr
L.P: Pres: Jung, Yun Joo; D.G.: Nam, Sun Hyun Exec. Dir: Park, Young Suck.
MW: [KIM] Kimjae (G.C. 35N50 126E50) 1170kHz 500kW
SW: [HWA] Hwasung (G.C. 37N13 126E47) 2 x 10, 5 x 100kW; [KIM] Kimjae (G.C. 35N50 126E50) 8 x 100, 3 x 250kW
kHz: *1170, 3955, 5955, 5975, 6065, 6135, 6170, 7150, 7180, 7235, 7275, 9515, 9535, 9560, 9570, 9580, 9640, 9650, 9770, 9805, 9870, 9875, 11795, 11810, 15210, 15575*

Winter Schedule 2004

Arabic	**Days**	**Area**	**kHz**
1900-2000	daily	ME,Af	7180rmp
1900-2000	daily	ME	15575kim
2000-2100	daily	ME	7150kim
English	**Days**	**Area**	**kHz**
0200-0300	daily	NAm	9560sac, 15575kim
0200-0300	daily	SAm	11810kim
0800-0900	daily	Eu	9640kim
0800-0900	daily	SEA	9570kim
1200-1300	daily	NAm	9650sac
1300-1400	daily	SEA	9570kim, 9770kim
1430-1500	daily	Eu	9770kim
1530-1600	.....f..	Eu	9875rmp+
1600-1700	daily	Af	9870kim
1600-1700	daily	FE	5975hwa
1900-2000	daily	Eu	7275kim
1900-2000	daily	FE	5975hwa
2100-2130	daily	Eu	3955skn
French	**Days**	**Area**	**kHz**
0800-0900	daily	Eu	15210kim
1600-1700	daily	ME	7150kim
1700-1800	daily	Af	9870kim
1800-1900	daily	ME	15575kim
2000-2100	daily	Eu	5955skn
German	**Days**	**Area**	**kHz**
0700-0800	daily	Eu	15210kim
2000-2100	daily	Eu	3955skn
Indonesian	**Days**	**Area**	**kHz**
0000-0100	daily	SEA	9805kim
1200-1300	daily	SEA	9570kim
1400-1500	daily	SEA	9570kim
2200-2300	daily	SEA	9805kim
Japanese	**Days**	**Area**	**kHz**
0000-0100	daily	NAm	15575kim
0000-0100	daily	SAm	11810kim
0800-0900	daily	FE	5975hwa, 7275kim
1100-1200	daily	FE	7275kim
1200-1300	daily	FE	1170kim, 5975hwa, 6135hwa
1400-1500	daily	FE	5975hwa, 7275kim
Korean	**Days**	**Area**	**kHz**
0100-0200	daily	NAm	15575kim
0300-0400	daily	SAm	9650sac, 11810kim
0700-0800	daily	Eu	9535skn
0900-1000	daily	Eu	15210kim
0900-1100	daily	Eu	9640kim
0900-1100	daily	FE	5975hwa, 7275kim
0900-1100	daily	SEA	9570kim
1000-1100	daily	FE	1170kim
1200-1300	daily	FE	7275kim
1600-1800	daily	Eu	7275kim
1600-1800	daily	ME	15575kim
1700-1900	daily	Eu	9515kim
1700-1900	daily	FE	5975hwa
1700-1900	daily	ME	7150kim
1800-2000	daily	Af	9870kim
2100-2300	daily	FE	5975hwa
Mandarin	**Days**	**Area**	**kHz**
1130-1230	daily	CHN	6065kim
1200-1300	daily	SEA	9770kim
1300-1400	daily	FE	1170kim, 5975hwa, 6135hwa, 7275kim
2000-2100	daily	FE	5975hwa
2100-2200	daily	CHN	6170kim
2300-2400	daily	Eu	7275kim
2300-2400	daily	FE	5975hwa
2300-2400	daily	SEA	9805kim
Russian	**Days**	**Area**	**kHz**
1100-1200	daily	FE	1170kim, 5975hwa, 6135hwa
1600-1700	daily	Eu	9515kim
1800-1900	daily	Eu	7235rmp, 7275kim
1900-2000	daily	Eu	9515kim
1900-2000	daily	ME	7150kim
2000-2100	daily	Eu	7275kim
Spanish	**Days**	**Area**	**kHz**
0100-0200	daily	SAm	11810kim
0700-0800	daily	Eu	9640kim
1000-1100	daily	Eu	15210kim
1000-1100	daily	SAm	9580kim
1100-1200	daily	Sam	11795sac
2000-2100	daily	Eu	9515kim

ANN: Yeogineun Daehanminguk Seoul-eseo bonaedeurineun Hanguk Bangsong Gongsa, KBS-e gukje bangsong, Radio Hangugimnida"; English: "This is Radio Korea International of the KBS"; Japanese: "Kochirawa Rajio Kankoku, KBS-no kokusai hoso desu"; Mandarin: "Zheli shi Hanguo guoji guangbo diantai"; Indonesian: " Inilah siaran Radio Korea Internasional, KBS yang dipancarkan langsung dari ibu kota Republik Korea Seoul"
IS: Korean children's song "Dar-a Dar-a Balgeun Dar-a (Oh, bright moon)" played by a glockenspiel. Original music "Dawn" composed by Kim Hee Jyo with KBS symphony orchestra.
V: QSL-card.
NOTES: Radio Korea International is the External Sce of the state broadcaster Korean Broadcasting System (KBS). Key: + DRM

FAR EAST BROADCASTING CO. – KOREA (Rlg)
P.O. Box 88, Seoul 121-707, Rep. of South Korea.
☎ +82 2 3200114. +82 2 3200229.
Email: febcadm@febc.net **Web:** www.febc.net
MW: [JEJ] HLAZ Jeju (G.C. 33N28 126E23) 1566kHz 250kW; [SEO] HLKX Seoul (G.C. 37N34 126E58) 1188kHz 100kW
kHz: *1188, 1566*

Winter Schedule 2004

English	**Days**	**Area**	**kHz**
1100-1230	daily	SEA	1188seo
1500-1515	.twt...	SEA	1566jej
Japanese	**Days**	**Area**	**kHz**
1230-1345	daily	J	1566jej
Mandarin	**Days**	**Area**	**kHz**
1100-1130	daily	CHN	1566jej
1230-1700	daily	CHN	1188seo
1345-1500	.twt...	CHN	1566jej
1345-1730	m...fss	CHN	1566jej
1515-1730	.twt...	CHN	1566jej
Russian	**Days**	**Area**	**kHz**
1730-1800	daily	RUS	1566jej

V: QSL-card.
NOTES: A division of Far East Broadcasting Company Inc.; see USA for corporate details.

Broadcasters using sites in this country:
BBC World Sce uses: (KIM). See stn entry in: **G**, INT Section
RCI uses: (KIM). See stn entry in: **CAN**, INT Section

KUWAIT

RADIO KUWAIT (Gov)

P.O. Box 193, Safat, 13002 Kuwait.
☎ +965 2423774. Fax +965 2456660.
Email: radiokuwait@radiokuwait.org **Web:** www.radiokuwait.org
Email: info@moinfo.gov.kw
Web: www.moinfo.gov.kw/KBS/index.html
L.P: Under Secretary Broadc. Affairs: Dr. Abdulazeez Al-Mansour.
SW: [KBD] Kabd, Sulaibiyah (G.C. 29N16 047E53) 5 x 500kW
kHz: *6055, 9750, 9855, 9880, 11675, 11990, 13620, 15110, 15495, 15505, 17885*

Winter Schedule 2004

Arabic	**Days**	**Area**	**kHz**
0200-0500	daily	ME	6055kbd
0200-0530	daily	NAm	11675kbd
0200-1315	daily	NAf	15495kbd
0400-0800	daily	ME	15505kbd
0500-0900	daily	ME	6055kbd+
0500-0930	daily	ME	15110kbd
0900-1300	daily	ME	6055kbd
0930-1300	daily	Eu,NAm	13620kbd+
1200-1600	daily	FE,Pac	17885kbd
1300-1600	daily	SAs	15110kbd
1300-1605	daily	Eu,NAm	13620kbd
1300-1730	daily	NAf	9880kbd+
1315-1800	daily	Eu,NAm	11990kbd
1730-2130	daily	NAf	9880kbd
1800-2200	daily	Eu,NAm	15505kbd
1800-2400	daily	CAf	15495kbd
1800-2400	daily	Eu,NAm	9855kbd
2200-0200	daily	NAm	11675kbd+
Farsi	**Days**	**Area**	**kHz**
0800-1000	daily	ME	9750kbd
Filipino	**Days**	**Area**	**kHz**
1000-1200	daily	PHL	17885kbd
Holy Quran	**Days**	**Area**	**kHz**
1015-1740	daily	CAf	15505kbd
Urdu	**Days**	**Area**	**kHz**
1600-1800	daily	SAs	15110kbd

ANN: Arabic: "Huna al-Kuwait"
V: QSL-folder. Rec. acc.
NOTES: The Arabic prgr's are relays of Home Sce networks. Key: + DRM

IBB RELAY STATION KUWAIT

IBB Transmitting Station, Kuwait.
Email: wpatterson@kuw.ibb.gov
L.P: SM: Walter Patterson.
MW: [KWT] Kabd (G.C. 29N31 047E41) 1548kHz 600kW, 1593kHz 150kW
SW: [KWT] Kabd (G.C. 29N31 047E41) 3 x 250kW
Broadcasters using sites in this country:
BBG-R. Sawa uses: (KBD). See stn entry in: **USA**, INT Section
BBG-R.Ashna uses: (KBD). See stn entry in: **USA**, INT Section
BBG-R.Free Afg. uses: (KBD). See stn entry in: **USA**, INT Section
BBG-R.Free Iraq uses: (KBD). See stn entry in: **USA**, INT Section
BBG-VOA uses: (KBD). See stn entry in: **USA**, INT Section

LAOS

RADIO NATIONALE LAO (Gov)

P.O. Box 310, Vientiane, Laos.
☎ +856 21 212432. Fax +856 21 212430.
Email: laonatradio@lnr.org.la **Web:** www.lnr.org.la
L.P: GD: Bounthan Inthaxay; Dep. GD: Keungkham Vilayasith; MD (Tech.): D. Sisombath.
SW: [VIE] Vientiane (G.C. 17N58 102E33) 1 x 3kW
kHz: *7145*

Winter Schedule 2004

Khmer	**Days**	**Area**	**kHz**
0000-0030	daily	SEA	7145vie*
1230-1300	daily	SEA	7145vie*
Thai	**Days**	**Area**	**kHz**
0500-0530	daily	SEA	7145vie*
1130-1200	daily	SEA	7145vie*
Vietnamese	**Days**	**Area**	**kHz**
1200-1230	daily	SEA	7145vie*
2330-2400	daily	SEA	7145vie*

IS: National Anthem
V: QSL-card. No IRC's required.
NOTES: Broadcasts often irratic. 7145kHz inactive at all other times. Also broadcasts foreign service on 97.25MHz FMKey: * Frequency variable.

LATVIA

BROADCAST RELAY SERVICES

c/o KREBS TV, P.O. Box 371, LV-1010 Riga, Latvia.
☎ +371 9224105.
Email: tesug@parks.lv
L.P: Owner KREBS TV: Raimonds Kreicbergs.
MW/SW: Leased from LVRTC
kHz: *9290*

Winter Schedule 2004

Various	**Days**	**Area**	**kHz**
1200-2000	.....ss	Eu	9290ulb

NOTES: Relay service for prgr producers and radio stations, provided by KREBS TV. The facilities are available 24/7, actual transmission times vary acc. to bookings.

LATVIJAS VALSTS RADIO IR TELEVIZIJAS CENTRS (LVRTC) (Tx Operator)

Erglu iela 7, LV-1012 Riga, Latvia.
☎ +371 7108704. Fax +371 7315577.
Email: info@lvrtc.lv **Web:** www.lvrtc.lv
MW: [KUL] Kuldiga (G.C. 56N58 021E58) 576kHz 100kW
SW: [ULB] Riga, Ulbroka (G.C. 56N56 024E17) 1 x 100kW
NOTES: LVRTC is the national transmitter network operator.

LEBANON

VOICE OF CHARITY (SAWT AL–MAHABBA) (Rlg)

P.O. Box 850, Jounieh, Lebanon.
☎ +961 9 918090. Fax +961 9 930272.
Email: email@radiocharity.org.lb **Web:** www.radiocharity.org
L.P: Dir: Father Fadi Tabet.
FM: Beirut 106.0MHz (24h)
kHz: *11715*

Winter Schedule 2004

Arabic	**Days**	**Area**	**kHz**
0530-0600	daily	LBN	11715smg

ANN: Arabic: "Sawt Al-Mahabba"
V: QSL-letter.
NOTES: Founded in 1984 and broadcasting on SW since May 1996. On FM in Lebanon in Arabic, English, French, Armenian: see National Radio section.

LIBERIA

VOICE OF LIBERTY (LBNC RADIO) (Rlg)

P.O. Box 4759, Monrovia, Liberia.
Email: morgan@wjie.com (USA)
USA: P.O. Box 197309, Louisville, KY 40259, USA.
SW: [MON] Monrovia (G.C. 06N18 010W40) 1 x 10kW
FM: Monrovia 102.1MHz
kHz: *11515*

Winter Schedule 2004

English	**Days**	**Area**	**kHz**
1200-1800	daily	WAf	11515mon

V: QSL-letter.
NOTES: A station run by WJIE in Louisville KY, USA. The tx was relocated from an earlier SW project in Southern Lebanon.

LIBYA

VOICE OF AFRICA (LIBYAN JAMAHIRIYA BROADC. CORP.) (Gov)

P.O. Box 4677, Soug al Jama, Tripoli, Libya.
☎ +218 21 4449106. Fax +218 21 4446875.
Email: africavoice@hotmail.com **Web:** www.ljbc.net
P.O. Box 17, Hamrun, Malta.

SW: [TRI] Tripoli (G.C. 32N54 013E11), several sites: Sabrata (G.C. 32N47 012E29) 9 x 500kW and unknown location: 5 x 10, 19 x 100kW. Mainly leases tx's from TDF (see France).
kHz: *711, 1251, 9485, 11635, 11715, 11860, 15220, 15615, 15660, 17695, 17840, 21485, 21675, 21695*

Winter Schedule 2004

Arabic	Days	Area	kHz
1000-0400	daily	NAf, Eu	1251tri
1000-0400	daily	NAf	711—
1000-1400	daily	Af	21695iss
1100-1230	daily	NAf,WAf	17695iss, 21485iss
1100-1500	daily	Af	21675iss
1600-1800	daily	NAf,WAf	15220iss
1700-1800	daily	NAf,WAf	15615iss
1700-1800	daily	Af	15660iss, 17840iss
1700-1900	daily	NAf,WAf	11860iss
1800-1900	daily	WAf	9485iss
1800-2030	daily	Af	11715iss
1800-2130	daily	Af	11635iss

ANN: Arabic: "Huna saut Afrikiya min al-Jamahiriya al-Ozma"; English: "The Voice of Africa from the Great Jamahiriya"
V: QSL-card.
NOTES: The Voice of Africa is the External Sce of the Libyan Jamahirya Broadcasting Corporation. News in English and French have been reported irregulary around the following times: 1140, 1735, 1820, 1920, 2030, 2120.

LJBC SERVICE FOR IRAQ (Gov)
kHz: *11180, 11660, 11890*

Winter Schedule 2004

Arabic	Days	Area	kHz
1200-1300	daily	IRQ	11180—*, 11660—*, 11890—*
1800-1900	daily	IRQ	11180—*, 11660—*, 11890—*
2100-2200	daily	IRQ	11180—*, 11660—*, 11890—*

ANN: Arabic: "Al-Markaz al'Aam l'il-Idha'at al-Mowagaha min al-Jamahirya al-Ozma, Resalah el as-Sha'ab al-Rafidayn"
NOTES: Key: * AM compatible single sideband.

LITHUANIA

RADIO VILNIUS (Pub)
Konarskio g. 49, LT-03123 Vilnius, Lithuania.
☎ +370 5 2363021. Fax +370 5 2363208.
Email: radiovilnius@lrt.lt **Web:** www.lrt.lt
L.P: Dir News Dept: Audrius Braukyla.
MW/SW: Leased from LRTC
kHz: *666, 7325, 9710, 9875*

Winter Schedule 2004

English	Days	Area	kHz
0030-0100	daily	NAm	9875sit
0930-1000	daily	Eu	9710sit
1900-1930	daily	Eu	666sit
2330-2400	daily	NAm	7325sit
Lithuanian	**Days**	**Area**	**kHz**
0000-0030	daily	NAm	9875sit
0900-0930	daily	Eu	9710sit
2300-2330	daily	NAm	7325sit

ANN: English: "This is Radio Vilnius"; Lithuanian: "Vilniaus radijas uzsieniui"
V: QSL-card.
NOTES: Radio Vilnius is produced by the news department of the public-service Lithuanian National Radio (Lietuvos radijas).

LIETUVOS RADIJO IR TELEVIZIJOS CENTRAS (LRTC) (Tx Operator)
Sausio 13-osios g. 10, LT-04347 Vilnius, Lithuania.
☎ +370 5 2525300. Fax +370 5 2525325.
Email: info@lrtc.net **Web:** www.lrtc.net
MW: [SIT] Kaunas, Sitkunai (G.C. 55N02 023E49) 666/1386kHz 500kW, 1557kHz 150kW; [VLN] Vilnius (G.C. 54N42 025E13) 612kHz 100kW
SW: [SIT] Kaunas, Sitkunai (G.C. 55N02 023E49) 1 x 100kW
NOTES: LRTC is the national transmitter network operator.

RADIO BALTIC WAVES INTERNATIONAL (RBWI)
P.O. Box 3245, LT-02002 Vilnius, Lithuania.
☎ +370 5 2652532. Fax +370 5 2652532.
Email: radio@balticwaves.cjb.net
L.P: Dir: Rolandas Stirblys; Project coordinator: Rimantas Pleikys.
MW/SW: Leased from LRTC
V: QSL-card (for relayed stn's).
NOTES: RBWI is providing relay facilities for international broadcasters.
Broadcasters using sites in this country:
BBG-RFE/RL uses: (VLN). See stn entry in: **USA**, INT Section
China R. Int'l uses: (SIT). See stn entry in: **CHN**, INT Section
VOR-RKS uses: (VLN). See stn entry in: **RUS**, INT Section
VOR-RMR uses: (VLN). See stn entry in: **RUS**, INT Section

LUXEMBOURG

RTL GROUP (Comm)
45, boulevard Pierre Frieden, L-1543 Luxembourg.
☎ +352 42 1422175. Fax +352 42 1422756.
Web: www.rtlgroup.com
MW/SW: Uses tx's provided by Broadcasting Center Europe.
kHz: *5990, 6095*

Winter Schedule 2004

French	Days	Area	kHz
0000-2400	daily	Eu	5990jun+
German	**Days**	**Area**	**kHz**
0000-2400	daily	Eu	6095jun+

NOTES: The RTL Group is Europe's largest TV, radio and production company, majority-owned by Bertelsmann AG (Germany). 5990 carries RTL French, 6095 RTL Das Oldieradio in German from 1 Jan 2005. Key: + DRM

BROADCASTING CENTER EUROPE (BCE) (Tx Operator)
45, boulevard Pierre Frieden, L-1543 Luxembourg.
☎ +352 42 1427703. Fax +352 42 1424809.
Email: eugene_muller@bce.lu **Web:** www.bce.lu
L.P: Head of TV & Radio Transmissions: Eugène Muller.
MW: [MRN] Marnach (G.C. 50N02 006E04) 1440kHz 1200kW
SW: [JUN] Junglinster (G.C. 49N40 006E19) 2 x 250kW (used exclusively in DRM mode)
V: QSL-card. Online report form available at www.bce.lu/transmission/lwsw/report.
NOTES: BCE was founded in January 2000 as a result of the merge of different technical entities of the RTL Group. BCE is part of RTL Group Technical Division and owns several high power transmitters in Luxembourg. Apart from carrying RTL programmes, the facilities are being leased out to international customers.
Broadcasters using sites in this country:
China R. Int'l uses: (MRN). See stn entry in: **CHN**, INT Section
Lutherische Std uses: (MRN). See stn entry in: **D**, INT Section
Miss.Heukelbach uses: (MRN). See stn entry in: **D**, INT Section
Miss.Heukelbach uses: (JUN). See stn entry in: **D**, INT Section
R.Freundes-D. uses: (MRN). See stn entry in: **SUI**, INT Section

MACEDONIA

RADIO MAKEDONIJA (Pub)
blvd. "Goce Delcev" bb, 1000 Skopje, FYR Macedonia.
☎ +389 2 321193. Fax +389 2 311821.
Email: radiomakedonija@mr.com.mk **Web:** www.mr.com.mk/biljana.htm
MW: Leased from Makedonska Radiodifuzija
kHz: *810*

Winter Schedule 2004

Albanian	Days	Area	kHz
2000-2030	daily	Eu	810sko
Bulgarian	**Days**	**Area**	**kHz**
1900-1930	daily	Eu	810sko
Greek	**Days**	**Area**	**kHz**
1930-2000	daily	Eu	810sko
Serbian	**Days**	**Area**	**kHz**
2030-2100	daily	Eu	810sko

V: QSL-letter.
NOTES: External Sce of the public-service broadcaster Makedonsko Radio.

MAKEDONSKA RADIODIFUZIJA (Tx Operator)
blvd. "Goce Delcev" bb, 1000 Skopje, FYR Macedonia.
☎ +389 2 297100. +389 2 225520.
Email: radiodifuzija@jpmrd.gov.mk **Web:** www.jpmrd.gov.mk
MW: [SKO] Skopje, Ovce Pole (G.C. 42N00 021E25) 810kHz 1200kW
V: QSL-letter (for transmissions on 810kHz).
NOTES: Makedonska Radiodifuzija is the national transmitter network provider.
Broadcasters using sites in this country:
Deutsche Welle uses: (SKO). See stn entry in: **D**, INT Section

MADAGASCAR

RADIO NEDERLAND WERELDOMROEP RELAY STATION
P.O. Box 404, Antananarivo, Madagascar.
SW: [MDC] Talata Volonondry (G.C.18S43 047E37) 2 x 50, 2 x 300kW
V: QSL-card for direct rpt.

WORLD CHRISTIAN BROADCASTING INC. RELAY STATION (Rlg)
Headquarters: 605 Bradley Court, Franklin, TN 37067, USA.
SW: [MHJ] Mahajanga (G.C. 15S40 046E21) 1 x 100kW (under construction)
NOTES: Owned by World Christian Broadcasting, Inc. (USA). WCBC runs the station KNLS International, see under Alaska.
Broadcasters using sites in this country:
AWR uses: (MDC). See stn entry in: **USA**, INT Section
Dem.VO Burma uses: (MDC). See stn entry in: **BRM**, CTB Section
R.Sweden uses: (MDC). See stn entry in: **S**, INT Section
Radio Nile uses: (MDC). See stn entry in: **SDN**, CTB Section
RNWO uses: (MDC). See stn entry in: **HOL**, INT Section
VO People uses: (MDC). See stn entry in: **ZWE**, CTB Section

MALAYSIA

VOICE OF MALAYSIA (Pub)
P.O. Box 11272, 50740 Kuala Lumpur, Malaysia.
☎ +60 3 22887824. +60 3 22847594.
Email: vom@rtm.net.my **Web:** www.rtm.net.my
MW: [TUA] Tuaran (G.C. 06N11 116E12) 1475kHz 700kW
SW: [KAJ] Kajang (G.C. 03N01 101E46) 9 x 100, 2 x 500kW
kHz: *1475, 6025, 6100, 6175, 9750, 11885, 15295*

Winter Schedule 2004

Arabic	**Days**	**Area**	**kHz**
1530-1700	daily	ME,NAf	15295kaj
Bahasa Indonesia	**Days**	**Area**	**kHz**
1000-1400	daily	INS	6175kaj, 9750kaj
Bahasa Malaysia	**Days**	**Area**	**kHz**
0830-1030	daily	ME,NAf,Oc	15295kaj
1700-1900	daily	INS	6175kaj, 9750kaj
Bahasa Malaysia (Voice of Islam)	**Days**	**Area**	**kHz**
1400-1700	daily	MLA	6025kaj
1400-1700	daily	INS	6175kaj, 9750kaj
Burmese	**Days**	**Area**	**kHz**
1430-1530	daily	BRM	6100kaj
English	**Days**	**Area**	**kHz**
0600-0825	daily	INS	6175kaj, 9750kaj
0600-0825	daily	AUS,NZL	15295kaj
English (Voice of Islam)	**Days**	**Area**	**kHz**
0300-0600	daily	INS	6175kaj, 9750kaj
0300-0600	daily	AUS,NZL	15295kaj
Mandarin	**Days**	**Area**	**kHz**
1030-1230	daily	Oc,INS	15295kaj*
1030-1230	daily	FE	11885kaj*
Tagalog	**Days**	**Area**	**kHz**
1030-1300	daily	PHL	1475tua
Thai	**Days**	**Area**	**kHz**
1300-1430	daily	THA	6100kaj

ANN: Malay: "Inilah suara Malaysia"; English: "This is the Voice of Malaysia"
IS: First bar of Nat. Anthem "Negara Ku" (Chimes)
V: QSL-card. Rec. acc.
NOTES: The Voice of Malaysia is the External Sce of the public service Radio Televisyen Malaysia (RTM). Key: * News at 1100 in Cantonese.

MALI

CHINA RADIO INTERNATIONAL RELAY
SW: [BKO] Bamako, Kati (G.C. 12N39 008W01) 2 x 100kW
V: QSL-card (rpt to CRI in China).
NOTES: The shortwave facilities are leased by CRI from Radiodiffusion-Télévision Mali (ORTM).
Broadcasters using sites in this country:
China R. Int'l uses: (BKO). See stn entry in: **CHN**, INT Section

MARSHALL ISLANDS

GOSPEL RADIO RELAY STATION (Rlg)
Contact info: see WJIE, USA.
SW: [MAJ] Majuro (G.C. 007N09 171E12) 1 x 100kW (projected)
NOTES: In 2003, the US religious broadcaster WJIE announced plans to build a SW relay station for religious programming, in cooperation with the local station V7AD.

MOLDOVA

RADIO MOLDOVA INTERNATIONAL (RMI) (Pub)
str. Miorita 1, MD-2028 Chisinau, Moldova.
☎ +373 22 723379.
Email: info@trm.md **Web:** www.trm.md/radio/default_en.asp
L.P: Dept. Head: Iurie Moraru
V: QSL-card.
NOTES: RMI is the External Sce of the public broadcaster Radio Moldova. Available only via Internet, no shortwave transmissions.

PRIDNESTROVYE

RADIO DMR (Gov)
ul. Rozy Lyuksemburg 10, MD-3300 Tiraspol, Moldova.
☎ +373 533 35570. +373 533 32245.
Email: radiopmr@inbox.ru **Web:** www.president-pmr.org/radio
MW/SW: Uses tx's provided by Pridnestrovskiy radiotsentr
kHz: *999, 5960*

Winter Schedule 2004

English	**Days**	**Area**	**kHz**
1700-1710	mtwt...	Eu	5960gri
1700-1730	....f..	Eu	5960gri
French	**Days**	**Area**	**kHz**
1710-1720	.t.t...	Eu	5960gri
German	**Days**	**Area**	**kHz**
1710-1720	m.w....	Eu	5960gri
Russian	**Days**	**Area**	**kHz**
1800-1830	daily	Eu	999gri

ANN: English: "Here is the Radio of the Dniester Moldavian Republic"; Russian: "Vy slyshayete programma 'Pridnestrovye'"
V: QSL-letter.
NOTES: Produced by the state broadcaster of the self-proclaimed Dniester Moldavian Republic (Pridnestrovye) in Eastern Moldova, in cooperation with the state news agency Olvia-Press.

PRIDNESTROVSKIY RADIOTSENTR (Tx Operator)
Maiac, Pridnestrovye, Moldova.
MW: [GRI] Grigoriopol, Maiac (G.C. 47N14 029E24) 999/1467/1548kHz 1000kW (mostly run with 500kW)
SW: [GRI] Grigoriopol, Maiac (G.C. 47N14 029E24) 5 x 1000kW
NOTES: Pridnestrovskiy Radiotsentr (situated in the self-proclaimed Dniester Moldavian Republic in Eastern Moldova) provides high power MW & SW transmitting facilities.
Broadcasters using sites in this country:
China R. Int'l uses: (GRI). See stn entry in: **CHN**, INT Section
Dengê Mezop. uses: (GRI). See stn entry in: **IRQ**, CTB Section
Deutsche Welle uses: (GRI). See stn entry in: **D**, INT Section
Family Radio uses: (GRI). See stn entry in: **USA**, INT Section
R.International uses: (GRI). See stn entry in: **IRN**, CTB Section
R.Payam-e Doost uses: (GRI). See stn entry in: **USA**, INT Section
R.Santec uses: (GRI). See stn entry in: **D**, INT Section
The Arabic R. uses: (GRI). See stn entry in: **SYR**, CTB Section
TWR Europe uses: (GRI). See stn entry in: **AUT**, INT Section
VO Russia (VOR) uses: (GRI). See stn entry in: **RUS**, INT Section
VOR-RKS uses: (GRI). See stn entry in: **RUS**, INT Section
VOR-RMR uses: (GRI). See stn entry in: **RUS**, INT Section

MONACO

MONTE CARLO RADIODIFFUSION (MCR) (Tx Operator)
10-12 quai Antoine 1er, MC-98000 Monte Carlo, Monaco.
+377 97974700. +377 97974707.
Email: mcradiodiffusion@mcr.mc **Web:** www.mcr.mc
L.P: DG: Jean Pierre Margossian.
LW: [ROU] Roumoules, France (G.C. 43N51 006E09) 216kHz 2000kW
MW: [ROU] Roumoules, France (G.C. 43N51 006E09) 1467kHz 1000kW
SW: [MCO] Fontbonne, Mont Agel, France (G.C. 43N44 007E26) 2 x 100, 1 x 500kW
NOTES: MCR (a subsidiary of Télédiffusion de France) is the national transmitter network owner in Monaco and also maintains high power transmitting centres in France and Cyprus.

MONGOLIA

VOICE OF MONGOLIA (Pub)
P.O. Box 365, Ulaanbaatar 13, Mongolia.
+976 1 327900. +976 1 323096.
Email: mr@mongol.net
L.P: Dir. Foreign Sce: Mrs B. Narantuya, Mail Editor: Z. Densmaa.
MW: [UBA] Ulaanbaatar (G.C. 47N55 107E00) 990kHz 500kW
SW: [UBA] Ulaanbaatar, Khonkhor (G.C. 47N55 107E00) 3 x 50, 1 x 100, 1 x 250, 1 x 500kW
kHz: *990, 12015, 12085*

Winter Schedule 2004

English	Days	Area	kHz
1000-1030	daily	As	12085uba
1500-1530	daily	Eu	12015uba
2000-2030	daily	Eu	12015uba
Japanese	**Days**	**Area**	**kHz**
0830-0900	daily	As	12085uba
1200-1230	daily	As	12085uba
Mandarin	**Days**	**Area**	**kHz**
0930-1000	daily	As	990uba, 12085uba
1130-1200	daily	As	990uba, 12085uba
Mongolian	**Days**	**Area**	**kHz**
0900-0930	daily	As	990uba, 12085uba
1030-1100	daily	As	990uba, 12085uba
Russian	**Days**	**Area**	**kHz**
1100-1130	daily	As	990uba
1330-1400	daily	Eu	12015uba

ANN: Mongolian: "Ulaanbaataraas yarij baina"; English: "This is the Voice of Mongolia"
V: QSL-card. Rec. acc. (non returnable), Rp (2 IRC's or 1 US-$) appreciated.
NOTES: The Voice of Mongolia is the External Sce of the Mongolian National Radio & TV.
Broadcasters using sites in this country:
BBG-R.Free Asia uses: (UBA). See stn entry in: **USA**, INT Section

MOROCCO

RADIODIFFUSION–TÉLÉVISION MAROCAINE (RTM) (Gov)
BP 1042, 10000 Rabat, Morocco.
+212 37 766880. +212 37 766888.
Email: belghiti@rtm.gov.ma **Web:** www.rtm.ma
L.P: Dir Radio: Mohamed El Boukili; Dir Foreign Broadcasting: Abdelouahad Belghiti Alaoui; Dir Foreign Rel: Abdelkader Bouazza.
SW: [NAD] Nador (G.C. 35N03 002W55) 1 x 250kW; also leases tx's from IBB.
SAT: Arabsat 2B/2D/3A, Astra 1E, Eutelsat W2, Hotbird 6
kHz: *5980, 7135, 15335, 15340, 15345*

Winter Schedule 2004

Arabic	Days	Area	kHz
0000-0500	daily	SEu,NAf,ME	5980mor
0900-1500	daily	SEu,NAf,ME	15340nad
1100-1500	daily	Eu	15335mor
1500-2200	daily	NAf,EAf,ME	15345nad
2200-2400	daily	Eu	7135mor

ANN: Arabic: "Huna Ribat, idha'atu-l-mamlaka al Maghribiyya"
V: QSL-card. Rec. acc. Rp.
NOTES: Relays of Home Sce prgr's for listeners abroad.

RADIO MÉDITERRANÉE INTERNATIONALE (MEDI 1) (Comm)
BP 2055, 90000 Tanger, Morocco.
+212 39 936363. +212 39 935755.
Email: medi1@medi1.com **Web:** www.medi1.com
LW: [NAD] Nador (G.C. 35N03 002W55) 171kHz 2000kW
SW: [NAD] Nador (G.C. 35N03 002W55) 1 x 250kW
SAT: Astra 1H
kHz: *171, 9575*

Winter Schedule 2004

French/Arabic	Days	Area	kHz
0000-2400	daily	NAf,ME,Eu	171nad, 9575nad

ANN: French: "Ici Medi 1, Radio Méditerranée Internationale"
V: QSL-card.
NOTES: Also relayed on FM in Morocco and France.

IBB RELAY STATION MOROCCO
IBB Transmitting Station, Briech, Morocco.
+212 39 932481. +212 39 935571.
Email: dduckworth@mor.ibb.gov
L.P: SM: Darrel Duckworth.
SW: [MOR] Briech (G.C. 35N34 005W58) 10 x 500kW
Broadcasters using sites in this country:
BBG-AapkiDunyaa uses: (MOR). See stn entry in: **USA**, INT Section
BBG-R.Farda uses: (MOR). See stn entry in: **USA**, INT Section
BBG-RFE/RL uses: (MOR). See stn entry in: **USA**, INT Section
BBG-Studio 7 uses: (MOR). See stn entry in: **USA**, INT Section
BBG-VOA uses: (MOR). See stn entry in: **USA**, INT Section

NETHERLANDS

RADIO NEDERLAND WERELDOMROEP (INDEPENDENT FOUNDATION)
P.O. Box 222, 1200 JG Hilversum, Netherlands.
+31 35 6724211. +31 35 6724207.
Email: letters@rnw.nl **Web:** www.rnw.nl
L.P: GD: Lodewijk Bouwens; Freq Mgr: Jan Willem Drexhage.
SW: Leased from NOZEMA
SAT: Asiasat 2, Astra 1G, Intelsat 707, Optus 1C, Pas 7, Thaicom 3, Telstar 12
kHz: *1512, 5955, 6015, 6020, 6120, 6165, 7120, 7125, 7240, 7285, 7315, 7380, 9345, 9525, 9590, 9625, 9715, 9790, 9795, 9800, 9845, 9890, 9895, 9940, 11655, 11675, 11895, 11935, 12065, 12070, 12080, 13700, 13820, 13840, 15315, 15530, 15595, 17580, 17725, 17810, 17815, 17875, 21480*

Winter Schedule 2004

Dutch	Days	Area	kHz
0300-0400	daily	NAm	6165bon
0300-0400	daily	CAm,MEX	9590bon
0600-0700	daily	Eu	1512wol, 5955hor, 7125fle
0600-0700	daily	NAm	6165bon
0600-0800	daily	SEu	6015fle
0700-0800	daily	AUS,NZL	9625bon, 11655bon
0700-0900	daily	SEu	9895fle
0700-1700	.....ss	WEu	5955fle
0700-1715	mtwtf..	WEu	5955fle
0800-0900	daily	SEu	11935fle
0900-1600	.....ss	SEu	9895fle, 13700fle
0930-1015	mtwtfs.	SUR	6020bon
1200-1300	daily	Eu	7240fle+
1200-1300	daily	NAm	9890bon
1300-1400	daily	SEA	17815mdc
1300-1400	daily	SAs	21480mdc
1300-1400	daily	FE,EAs,SEA	7380ppk
1300-1400	daily	EAs,SEA	9940khb
1300-1400	daily	SEA,AUS	12070tac
1600-1700	daily	ME	13840mdc
1600-1700	daily	SEu	11655fle
1600-1800	daily	SEu	9895fle, 13700mdc
1700-1715	.....ss	Eu	5955hor
1700-1800	daily	SAf	6020mdc
1700-1800	daily	EAf	11655fle
1715-1800	daily	Eu	5955hor
2100-2200	daily	SUR,B	15315bon
2100-2200	daily	WAf	17810bon
2100-2200	daily	CAf	7120mdc, 9895mdc

Dutch	Days	Area	kHz
2200-2300	daily	SAm	15315bon
2300-2400	daily	SAm	15315bon
2300-2400	daily	SAm,Car	9525sac
English	**Days**	**Area**	**kHz**
0000-0100	daily	NAm	9845bon
0100-0200	daily	NAm	6165bon
0400-0500	daily	NAm	6165bon, 9590bon
1000-1100	daily	AUS,NZL	9790bon
1000-1100	daily	EAs	13820khb
1000-1100	daily	EAs,SEA	12065irk
1000-1100	daily	FE	7315ppk
1000-1100	.....s.	Eu	7240fle+
1000-1200	mtwtf.s	Eu	7240fle+
1200-1300	daily	NAm	11675bon
1200-1300	daily	Eu	7240fle+
1400-1600	daily	SAs	9345tac, 12080mdc, 15595mdc
1430-1500	daily	Eu	7240fle+
1800-1900	daily	SAf	6020mdc
1800-2000	daily	EAf	9895fle
1800-2100	daily	CAf,WAf	11655mdc
1900-2100	.....ss	NAm	15315bon, 17725bon, 17875sac
1900-2100	daily	CAf,SAf	7120mdc
1900-2100	daily	WAf	17810bon
2000-2100	daily	WAf	9895fle
2100-2200	daily	NAm	15530bon+
2130-2200	daily	NAm	9800sac+
2200-2300	daily	Eu	1512wol
Indonesian	**Days**	**Area**	**kHz**
1100-1200	daily	INS	9795sng
1100-1300	daily	INS	17580mdc, 21480mdc
1200-1300	daily	INS	9795sng
2200-2300	daily	INS	7285mdc
2200-2400	daily	INS	6120sng, 9590mdc
2300-2400	daily	INS	11895mdc
Spanish	**Days**	**Area**	**kHz**
0000-0200	daily	SAm	9895mdc, 15315bon
0200-0300	daily	MEX,Car	9590bon
0200-0300	daily	CAm	6165bon
0200-0400	daily	CAm,Car	9895mdc
1100-1130	daily	Car,NAm	6165bon
1100-1200	daily	SAm	9715bon
1200-1230	daily	CAm	9715bon
2200-2300	daily	NAm	15530bon+
2300-2400	daily	SAm	9895fle

ANN: English: "This is Radio Netherlands, the Dutch International Service"; Spanish: "Transmite R. Nederland desde la ciudad de Hilversum en Holanda"; Indonesian: "Inilah Radio Nederland di Hilversum dengan siaran dalam bahasa Indonesia"
V: QSL-card.
NOTES: RNW is an independently funded public broadcaster serving Dutch citizens abroad, listeners in the former Dutch colonies and an international audience around the world. RNW owns shortwave transmitting stn's in Netherlands Antilles and Madagascar, it leases out airtime at these facilities to other broadcasters as well. Key: + DRM transmissions, * To 3rd April 2005, ** June to August 2005.

INFORADIO
P.O. Box 140, 5590 AC Heeze, Netherlands.
Email: info@inforadio.nl **Web:** www.inforadio.nl
SW: Considers leasing air time from Deutsche Telekom Jülich (see Germany) and via WRMI Miami (see USA)
V: QSL-card. Email rpts to receptionreport@inforadio.nl.
NOTES: Established as news service for Dutch holidaymakers during summer months. No transmissions in recent years, activity in 2005 is uncertain.

NOZEMA (Tx Operator)
P.O. Box 6, 3400 AA IJsselstein, Netherlands.
☎ +31 30 6862400. Fax +31 30 6881448.
Email: nozema@nozema.nl **Web:** www.nozema.nl
SW: [FLE] Flevo, Zeewolde (G.C. 52N21 005E27) 1 x 100, 4 x 500kW
NOTES: NOZEMA is the national transmitter network operator and the owner of the Flevo shortwave transmitting station. It leases out the Flevo facilities to Radio Nederland Wereldomroep.

Broadcasters using sites in this country:
R.Sweden uses: (FLE). See stn entry in: **S**, INT Section
RCI uses: (FLE). See stn entry in: **CAN**, INT Section
TDPradio uses: (FLE). See stn entry in: **BEL**, INT Section

NETHERLANDS ANTILLES

TRANS WORLD RADIO BONAIRE (Rlg)
P.O. Box 388, Bonaire, Netherlands Antilles.
☎ +599 7178800. Fax +599 7178808.
Email: 800am@twr.org **Web:** www.gospelcom.net/twr/bonaire
MW: [BON] Bonaire (G.C. 12N06 068W17) 800kHz 100kW
FM: Bonaire 89.5MHz
kHz: *882*

Winter Schedule 2004

Baniua	Days	Area	kHz
0045-0100	.....s.	CAm,SAm	882bon
English	**Days**	**Area**	**kHz**
1800-1900	daily	CAm,SAm	882bon
Kreyol	**Days**	**Area**	**kHz**
1600-1630	.....ss	CAm,SAm	882bon
1600-1645	mtwtf..	CAm,SAm	882bon
Macuxi	**Days**	**Area**	**kHz**
0045-0100	......s	CAm,SAm	882bon
Portuguese	**Days**	**Area**	**kHz**
0000-0045	.....ss	CAm,SAm	882bon
0000-0100	mtwtf..	CAm,SAm	882bon
1500-1600	daily	CAm,SAm	882bon
2300-2400	daily	CAm,SAm	882bon
Spanish	**Days**	**Area**	**kHz**
0100-0415	daily	CAm,SAm	882bon
0800-1000	daily	CAm,SAm	882bon
1300-1500	daily	CAm,SAm	882bon
1630-1700	.....ss	CAm,SAm	882bon
1700-1800	daily	CAm,SAm	882bon

ANN: English: "This is the international sound of the Caribbean, Trans World Radio, Bonaire"
V: QSL-card.
NOTES: TWR branch and transmitting stn; see USA for corporate headquarters.

RADIO NEDERLAND WERELDOMROEP RELAY STATION
P.O. Box 45, Kralendijk, Netherlands Antilles.
SW: [BON] Bonaire (G.C. 12N12 068W18) 1 x 250, 2 x 300kW
V: QSL-card for direct rpt
NOTES: Owned by Radio Nederland Wereldomroep; RNW leases out air time also to other broadcasters.

Broadcasters using sites in this country:
AWR uses: (BON). See stn entry in: **USA**, INT Section
China R. Int'l uses: (BON). See stn entry in: **CHN**, INT Section
Deutsche Welle uses: (BON). See stn entry in: **D**, INT Section
R.Japan uses: (BON). See stn entry in: **J**, INT Section
R.Sweden uses: (BON). See stn entry in: **S**, INT Section
RNWO uses: (BON). See stn entry in: **HOL**, INT Section
RVI uses: (BON). See stn entry in: **BEL**, INT Section

NEW ZEALAND

RADIO NEW ZEALAND INTERNATIONAL (RNZI) (Pub)
P.O. Box 123, Wellington, New Zealand.
☎ +64 4 4741437. Fax +64 4 4741433.
Email: info@rnzi.com **Web:** www.rnzi.com
L.P: CEO & Chief Editor: Peter Cavanagh; Tech. Mgr: Adrian Sainsbury.
SW: [RAN] Rangitaiki (G.C. 38S50 176E25) 2 x 100kW
kHz: *9870, 9875, 9885, 11980, 15265, 15530, 15720, 17675*

Winter Schedule 2004

English	Days	Area	kHz
0400-0800	daily	Pac,Eu,NAm	15720ran
0800-1100	daily	Pac,NAm	9885ran
1100-1300	daily	Pac,As	15530ran
1300-1650	daily	Pac	9870ran
1500-1530	.....s.	Eu	9875rmp+
1650-1750	daily	Pac	9870ran
1750-1850	daily	Pac	11980ran

English	Days	Area	kHz
1850-2240	daily	Pac,Eu	15265ran
2240-0400	daily	Pac,NAm	17675ran

ANN: Maori: "Te reo irirangi O te Moana-nui-a-kiwa"; English: "This is Radio New Zealand International, the voice of the Pacific"
V: QSL-card. Rp (2 IRC's). Rec. not accepted.
NOTES: RNZI is the External Sce of the public broadcaster Radio New Zealand. The SW transmissions are in English with news in various Pacific languages. Pacific Press Review in French: Sun/Mon 2040-2050. Key: + DRM

NIGERIA

VOICE OF NIGERIA (Gov)

Broadcasting House, Ikoyi, P.M.B. 40003, Falomo, Lagos, Nigeria.
☎ +234 1 2693078. Fax +234 1 2691944.
Email: info@voiceofnigeria.org **Web:** www.voiceofnigeria.org
L.P: DG: Alhaji Abubakar Jijiwai; PD: Alhaji Ayodele Sulaiman; News Dir: Ben Egbuna.
SW: [IKO] Ikorodu (G.C. 07N23 003E56) 3 x 250kW
kHz: *7255, 9690, 11770, 15120*

Winter Schedule 2004

Arabic	Days	Area	kHz
1500-1530	daily	NAf,ME	11770iko
English	**Days**	**Area**	**kHz**
0455-0700	daily	Eu,Af	15120iko*
1000-1500	daily	Eu,Af	15120iko*
1700-2100	daily	WAf	7255iko
French	**Days**	**Area**	**kHz**
0700-0800	daily	Eu,Af	15120iko*
2100-2200	daily	Eu,Af	15120iko*
Fulfulde	**Days**	**Area**	**kHz**
2100-2200	daily	WAf	7255iko
Hausa	**Days**	**Area**	**kHz**
0800-1000	daily	WAf	7255iko
2200-2300	daily	WAf	7255iko
Swahili	**Days**	**Area**	**kHz**
1600-1630	daily	EAf	9690iko

ANN: English: "This is the Voice of Nigeria"
IS: As Home Sce. Also bells playing the first bars of the National Anthem 15 mins. before the commencement of each block period.
V: QSL-card.
NOTES: The Voice of Nigeria is the External Sce of the Federal Radio Corporation of Nigera (FRCN). Key: * Alternative frequency 17800kHz. Schedule subject to change.

NORTHERN MARIANA IS. (U.S.)

FAR EAST BROADCASTING CO. – SAIPAN (KFBS) (Rlg)

P.O. Box 500209, Saipan, MP 96950-0209, CNMI, USA.
☎ +1 670 3229088. Fax +1 670 3223060.
Email: saipan@febc.org **Web:** www.febc.org
L.P: Dir: Robert Springer.
SW: [FBS] Saipan, Marpi (G.C. 15N16 145E48) 4 x 100kW
kHz: *9465, 11580, 11650, 12090, 12120, 15580*

Winter Schedule 2004

Chuvash	Days	Area	kHz
1530-1545	.....s.	RUS	9465fbs
German	**Days**	**Area**	**kHz**
1545-1600	..w....	CAs	9465fbs
Hmong	**Days**	**Area**	**kHz**
1400-1430	..w....	SEA	12120fbs
Indonesian	**Days**	**Area**	**kHz**
0830-1130	daily	SEA	15580fbs
Kazakh	**Days**	**Area**	**kHz**
1545-1600	....fs.	CAs	9465fbs
Koho	**Days**	**Area**	**kHz**
1400-1430	......s	SEA	12120fbs
Kyrgyz	**Days**	**Area**	**kHz**
1530-1545	....f..	CAs	9465fbs
Mandarin	**Days**	**Area**	**kHz**
0800-1400	daily	SEA	11580fbs
Mari	**Days**	**Area**	**kHz**
1530-1545	..w....	RUS	9465fbs
Mongolian (Chi)	**Days**	**Area**	**kHz**
1100-1115	daily	SEA	11650fbs
Mongolian (Halh)	**Days**	**Area**	**kHz**
1115-1130	daily	SEA	11650fbs
Ossetic	**Days**	**Area**	**kHz**
1545-1600	...t...	RUS	9465fbs
Russian	**Days**	**Area**	**kHz**
0900-1100	daily	RUS	11650fbs
1130-1400	daily	RUS	11650fbs
1400-1530	daily	RUS	9465fbs
Sasak	**Days**	**Area**	**kHz**
1130-1200	daily	SEA	15580fbs
Tatar	**Days**	**Area**	**kHz**
1530-1545	m......	RUS	9465fbs
1545-1600	mt.....	RUS	9465fbs
Udmurt	**Days**	**Area**	**kHz**
1530-1545	.t....s	RUS	9465fbs
1545-1600	......s	RUS	9465fbs
Uzbek	**Days**	**Area**	**kHz**
1530-1545	...t...	CAs	9465fbs
Vietnamese	**Days**	**Area**	**kHz**
1300-1330	daily	SEA	12120fbs
1400-1430	mt.tfs.	SEA	12120fbs
2230-2330	daily	SEA	12090fbs

V: QSL-card. Rp. (2 IRC's). Rec. acc.
NOTES: A division of Far East Broadcasting Company Inc.; see USA for corporate details.

IBB "ROBERT E. KAMOSA" TRANSMITTING STATION

IBB "Robert E. Kamosa" Transmitting Station, P.O. Box 504969, Saipan, MP 96950, USA.
☎ +670 2331624. Fax +670 2331614.
Email: gshirk@mar.ibb.gov
L.P: SM: Gary Shirk.
SW: [SAI] Saipan, Agingan Point (G.C. 15N07 145E42) 3 x 100kW; [TIN] Tinian (G.C. 15N03 145E36) 2 x 250, 6 x 500kW
NOTES: IBB owned transmitting station; maintenance & operation to be transferred to a private contractor for the period 1 July 2005 - 30 June 2006 (with 4 x 1-year extension options).
Broadcasters using sites in this country:
BBG-R.Free Asia uses: (TIN). See stn entry in: **USA**, INT Section
BBG-R.Free Asia uses: (SAI). See stn entry in: **USA**, INT Section
BBG-RFE/RL uses: (TIN). See stn entry in: **USA**, INT Section
BBG-VOA uses: (TIN). See stn entry in: **USA**, INT Section
BBG-VOA uses: (SAI). See stn entry in: **USA**, INT Section
R.Australia uses: (TIN). See stn entry in: **AUS**, INT Section

NORWAY

NORKRING (Tx Operator)

Telenor Broadcast, N-1331 Fornebu, Norway
☎ +47 67892000. Fax +47 67893614.
Email: norkring@telenor.com **Web:** www.norkring.no
SW: [KVI] Kvitsøy (G.C. 59N04 005E27) 3 x 500kW. The transmitter site in Sveio is being dismantled.

OMAN

RADIO SULTANATE OF OMAN (Gov)

P.O. Box 600, 113 Muscat, Oman.
☎ +968 603888. Fax +968 604629.
Email: tvradio@omantel.net.om **Web:** www.oman-tv.gov.om
L.P: Dir Foreign Sce: Shakar Al-Araimi; Dir Engineering: Mohd Salim AL Morhouby; Freq Mgr: Salim Al-Nomani.
SW: [SEB] Seeb (G.C. 23N40 058E10) 1 x 100kW; [THU] Thumrayt (G.C. 17N38 053E56) 1 x 100kW
SAT: Arabsat 2B/2C/3A, Hotbird 4, Nilesat 101
kHz: *6085, 6190, 9515, 13640, 15140, 15355, 15375, 17590, 17630*

Winter Schedule 2004

Arabic	Days	Area	kHz
0200-0400	daily	ME	6085seb
0200-0400	daily	EAf	15355thu
0400-0600	daily	ME	9515seb
0400-0600	daily	EAf	17590thu
0600-1000	daily	Eu,ME	17630thu
0600-1400	daily	ME	13640seb
1400-1800	daily	ME,EAf	15375seb
1500-1800	daily	Eu,ME	15140thu
1800-2000	daily	ME,EAf	6190seb

Arabic	Days	Area	kHz
1800-2000	daily	EAf	15355thu
2000-2200	daily	ME,EAf	6085seb
2000-2200	daily	Eu,ME	13640thu
English	**Days**	**Area**	**kHz**
1400-1500	daily	Eu,ME	15140thu

ANN: Arabic: "Idha'atu Saltanat Oman min Muscat"
V: QSL-folder.
NOTES: Relays of Home Sce programmes in Arabic and English.

BBC EASTERN RELAY STATION

✉ A'Seela, Oman.
MW: [SLA] A'Seela (G.C. 21N57 059E27) 702/1413kHz 800kW
SW: [SLA] A'Seela (G.C. 21N57 059E27) 3 x 250kW
V: QSL-card for direct rpt.
NOTES: Owned by the BBC and operated by VT Merlin Communications (see UK). Carries relays of BBC and other international broadcasters.
Broadcasters using sites in this country:
BBC World Sce uses: (SLA). See stn entry in: **G**, INT Section

PAKISTAN

RADIO PAKISTAN (Gov)

✉ Broadcasting House, Constitution Avenue, Islamabad 4400, Pakistan.
☎ +92 51 9210689. 🖷 +92 51 9201861.
Email: cnoradio@isb.comsats.net.pk **Web:** www.radio.gov.pk
L.P: GD: S Auwar Mehmood; Dir.Tech: Muhammad Iqbel; Dir. Overseas Liaison: Muhammad Sharif Shad.
SW: [ISL] Islamabad, Rawat (G.C. 33N27 073E12) 5 x 100kW
kHz: *4850, 4955, 5860, 6060, 7375, 7465, 7530, 7570, 9340, 9390, 9400, 9585, 11550, 11565, 11570, 11580, 11850, 15100, 15485, 15625, 15725, 17485, 17495, 17835*

Winter Schedule 2004

Arabic	Days	Area	kHz
1815-1900	daily	WAf,NAf,ME	9340isl
1815-1900	daily	NAf,ME	7465isl
Assami	**Days**	**Area**	**kHz**
0045-0115	daily	SAs	9340isl, 11565isl
Bangla	**Days**	**Area**	**kHz**
0115-0200	daily	SAs	9340isl, 11565isl
1200-1245	daily	SAs	11550isl, 15625isl
Dari	**Days**	**Area**	**kHz**
1515-1545	daily	ME	4955isl, 5860isl
English	**Days**	**Area**	**kHz**
1600-1615	daily	EAf,SAf	11850isl, 15725isl
1600-1615	daily	NAf,ME	9390isl
1600-1615	daily	WAf,NAf,ME	11570isl
Farsi	**Days**	**Area**	**kHz**
1715-1800	daily	ME	5860isl, 7570isl
Gujarati	**Days**	**Area**	**kHz**
0400-0430	daily	EAf,SAf	9340isl, 11565isl
Hindi	**Days**	**Area**	**kHz**
0215-0300	daily	SAs	9340isl, 11565isl
1100-1145	daily	SAs	9340isl, 11570isl
Mandarin	**Days**	**Area**	**kHz**
1200-1230	daily	SAs,FE	9585isl, 11570isl
Nepali	**Days**	**Area**	**kHz**
1245-1315	daily	SAs	11550isl, 15625isl
Pashto	**Days**	**Area**	**kHz**
1445-1515	daily	ME	4955isl
Russian	**Days**	**Area**	**kHz**
1415-1500	daily	RUS	7375isl, 9340isl
Sinhala	**Days**	**Area**	**kHz**
1015-1045	daily	SAs	15625isl, 17495isl
Tamil	**Days**	**Area**	**kHz**
0315-0345	daily	SAs	15625isl, 17485isl
0945-1015	daily	SAs	15625isl, 17495isl
Turkish	**Days**	**Area**	**kHz**
1630-1700	daily	NAf,ME	9340isl, 11565isl
Uighur	**Days**	**Area**	**kHz**
1330-1400	daily	ME	4850isl, 6060isl
Urdu	**Days**	**Area**	**kHz**
0045-0215	daily	SAs,SEA,AUS	11580isl, 15485isl
0500-0700	daily	NAf,ME	11570isl, 15100isl
0500-0700	daily	WAf,NAf,ME	17835isl
0800-1104	daily	Eu	15100isl, 17835isl
1330-1530	daily	NAf,ME	9390isl, 11570isl
1700-1900	daily	Eu	7530isl, 9400isl
1800-1900	daily	ME	7570isl
1915-0045	daily	WAf,NAf,ME	7570isl

ANN: English: "This is Radio Pakistan"; Urdu: "Ye Radio Pakistan hai"
V: QSL-card.
NOTES: External Sce of the Pakistan Broadcasting Corp.

PALAU

T8BZ – THE VOICE OF HOPE (Rlg)

✉ P.O. Box 66, Koror, Republic of Palau 96940.
☎ +680 4882162. 🖷 +680 4882163.
Email: hamadmin@palaunet.com **Web:** vohasia.in2000.com
L.P: Chief engineer: Bentley Chan.
SW: [HBN] Medorn (G.C. 07N27 134E28) 4 x 100kW
kHz: *9955, 9965, 9985, 12160, 13840, 15725, 15745*

Winter Schedule 2004

Various	Days	Area	kHz
0600-1700	daily	SEA	9965hbn
0700-1600	daily	SEA,Oc	15725hbn, 15745hbn
0700-1600	daily	SEA	9985hbn
0800-1700	daily	SEA	9955hbn
1000-1600	daily	SEA,Oc	12160hbn, 13840hbn
2100-2400	daily	SEA	9985hbn
2200-2400	daily	SEA	9955hbn, 9965hbn

V: QSL-card.
NOTES: Transmitting station owned by High Adventure Ministries; see USA for corporate details. Former callsign: KHBN (unofficially still used). Registered freq's shown, actual usage varies; some capacities are leased to other broadcasters.
Broadcasters using sites in this country:
BBG-R.Free Asia uses: (HBN). See stn entry in: **USA**, INT Section

PHILIPPINES

RADYO PILIPINAS OVERSEAS (Gov)

✉ 4/F Bldg.,Visayas Ave., Q.C., Manila 1103, Philippines.
☎ +63 2 9242267. 🖷 +63 2 9242745.
Email: bbs@ops.gov.ph **Web:** www.pbs.gov.ph
L.P: SM: Magtanggol Rodriguez.
SW: Uses facilities provided by IBB
kHz: *11730, 11890, 12015, 15120, 15190, 15270*

Winter Schedule 2004

Tagalog/English	Days	Area	kHz
0200-0330	daily	ME	12015pht, 15120pht, 15270pht
1730-1930	daily	ME	11730pht, 11890pht, 15190pht

ANN: English: "This is Radyo Pilipinas, the Overseas Radio of the Phillipines Broadcasting Service"
V: QSL-card. Rp (2 IRC's). Rec. acc.
NOTES: Radyo Pilipinas Overseas is the External Sce of the state-owned Philippine Broadcasting Service - Bureau of Broadcast Services (PBS-BBS).

FAR EAST BROADCASTING CO. – PHILIPPINES (Rlg)

✉ P.O. Box 1, Valenzuela City 0560, Philippines.
☎ +63 2 2925603. 🖷 +63 2 2924982.
Email: info@febc.org.ph **Web:** www.febc.ph
L.P: Dir: Efren M. Pallorina; Head of Prgrs: Peter McIntyre; Head of PR: Priscilla R. Calica.
SW: [BOC] Bocaue, Bulacan (G.C. 14N48 120E55) 3 x 50, 1 x 100kW; [IBA] Iba, Zambales (G.C. 15N20 119E58) 2 x 100kW
kHz: *7375, 7400, 9405, 9420, 9435, 9795, 9920, 12065, 12090, 12095, 15335, 15405, 15435, 15450, 15465*

Winter Schedule 2004

Akha	Days	Area	kHz
0000-0015	.....ss	SEA	12090boc
Atsi	**Days**	**Area**	**kHz**
0115-0130	...tfs.	BRM	15465boc
Bahnar	**Days**	**Area**	**kHz**
1115-1145	....f..	VTN	9920boc
Batak-Toba	**Days**	**Area**	**kHz**
1030-1100	daily	INS	15450boc

Black Tai	**Days**	**Area**	**kHz**
1130-1145	mtwtfs.	VTN	9920boc
Bru	**Days**	**Area**	**kHz**
1130-1145	.t.....	VTN	9920boc
Burmese	**Days**	**Area**	**kHz**
1230-1300	daily	BRM	9420boc
1430-1530	daily	BRM	9420boc
2330-0100	daily	BRM	15465boc
Cantonese	**Days**	**Area**	**kHz**
1430-1530	daily	CHN	7400boc
Chin-Asho	**Days**	**Area**	**kHz**
1330-1345	mtw...s	BRM	9420boc
Chin-Daai	**Days**	**Area**	**kHz**
1315-1330	daily	BRM	9420boc
Chin-Khumi	**Days**	**Area**	**kHz**
1330-1345	...tfs.	BRM	9420boc
Chin-Tedim	**Days**	**Area**	**kHz**
1345-1400	...tfs.	BRM	9420boc
Chin-Thado	**Days**	**Area**	**kHz**
0100-0115	daily	BRM	15435boc
Chrau	**Days**	**Area**	**kHz**
1130-1200	......s	VTN	9920boc
Chru	**Days**	**Area**	**kHz**
1130-1145	..w....	VTN	9920boc
Eastern Cham	**Days**	**Area**	**kHz**
1115-1130	..w....	VTN	9920boc
Hmong Blue	**Days**	**Area**	**kHz**
1100-1130	...t.s.	SEA	12095boc
2300-2330	...t.s.	SEA	15335boc
Hmong White	**Days**	**Area**	**kHz**
1100-1130	mtw.f.s	SEA	12095boc
1300-1330	daily	SEA	12095boc
2300-2330	mtw.f.s	SEA	15335boc
Hre	**Days**	**Area**	**kHz**
1300-1330	.t.....	VTN	9920boc
Indonesian	**Days**	**Area**	**kHz**
0900-1000	daily	INS	12095boc
1000-1030	daily	INS	15450boc
2230-2330	daily	INS	9435boc
Jarai	**Days**	**Area**	**kHz**
1300-1330	m...f..	VTN	9920boc
Jeh	**Days**	**Area**	**kHz**
1130-1145	...t...	VTN	9920boc
Jingpho	**Days**	**Area**	**kHz**
1145-1200	daily	BRM	9420boc
Karen-Pao	**Days**	**Area**	**kHz**
1100-1115	daily	BRM	9420boc
Karen-Pwo	**Days**	**Area**	**kHz**
0100-0115	...tfs.	BRM	15465boc
Karen-Sgaw	**Days**	**Area**	**kHz**
1345-1400	mtw...s	BRM	9420boc
Katu	**Days**	**Area**	**kHz**
1115-1130	.t.....	VTN	9920boc
Khmer	**Days**	**Area**	**kHz**
1200-1300	daily	CBG	7375iba
1300-1315	..wtfss	CBG	7375iba
Khmu	**Days**	**Area**	**kHz**
1045-1100	daily	SEA	12095boc
1330-1400	daily	LAO	12095boc
Koho	**Days**	**Area**	**kHz**
1145-1200	m......	VTN	9920boc
1300-1330	...t..s	VTN	9920boc
Komering	**Days**	**Area**	**kHz**
0900-0930	m.w.f..	INS	15450boc
Lahu	**Days**	**Area**	**kHz**
0015-0030	daily	SEA	12090boc
Lao	**Days**	**Area**	**kHz**
1130-1200	daily	SEA	12095boc
2230-2300	daily	LAO	9795boc
Lisu	**Days**	**Area**	**kHz**
1215-1230	daily	BRM	9420boc
1400-1430	daily	BRM	9420boc
Mandarin	**Days**	**Area**	**kHz**
0530-0900	daily	CHN	15450iba
0800-0900	daily	CHN	15405boc
0900-1600	daily	CHN	9405iba
Mandarin	**Days**	**Area**	**kHz**
1230-1500	daily	CHN	9420boc
2300-0100	daily	CHN	12065iba
Maru	**Days**	**Area**	**kHz**
0115-0130	mtw...s	BRM	15465boc
Meitei	**Days**	**Area**	**kHz**
0115-0130	daily	BRM	15435boc
Mien	**Days**	**Area**	**kHz**
1200-1230	daily	VTN	12095boc
1230-1300	...t...	SEA	12095boc
2330-2400	daily	VTN	9795boc
Minangkabau	**Days**	**Area**	**kHz**
0930-1000	daily	INS	15450boc
Mnong	**Days**	**Area**	**kHz**
1145-1200	.t.....	VTN	9920boc
Mon	**Days**	**Area**	**kHz**
1115-1145	daily	BRM	9420boc
Muong	**Days**	**Area**	**kHz**
1115-1130	...t...	VTN	9920boc
Naga-Makware	**Days**	**Area**	**kHz**
1300-1315	daily	BRM	9420boc
Nung	**Days**	**Area**	**kHz**
1115-1130	m......	VTN	9920boc
Ogan	**Days**	**Area**	**kHz**
0900-0930	.t.t.ss	INS	15450boc
Palaung-Pale	**Days**	**Area**	**kHz**
0100-0115	mtw...s	BRM	15465boc
Rade	**Days**	**Area**	**kHz**
1300-1330	..w..s.	VTN	9920boc
Rawang	**Days**	**Area**	**kHz**
1200-1215	daily	BRM	9420boc
Rengao	**Days**	**Area**	**kHz**
1145-1200	...t...	VTN	9920boc
Roglai	**Days**	**Area**	**kHz**
1145-1200	..w....	VTN	9920boc
Sasak	**Days**	**Area**	**kHz**
1000-1030	daily	INS	12095boc
Sedang	**Days**	**Area**	**kHz**
1145-1200	....f..	VTN	9920boc
Shan	**Days**	**Area**	**kHz**
0000-0045	daily	BRM	15435boc
Shan-Chinese	**Days**	**Area**	**kHz**
0045-0100	mtw....	SEA	15435boc
Shan-Khamti	**Days**	**Area**	**kHz**
0045-0100	......s	BRM	15435boc
Stieng	**Days**	**Area**	**kHz**
1115-1130	.....ss	VTN	9920boc
Tai-lu	**Days**	**Area**	**kHz**
1030-1045	daily	SEA	12095boc
2345-2400	daily	SEA	12090boc
Wa	**Days**	**Area**	**kHz**
0030-0045	daily	SEA	12090boc
White Tai	**Days**	**Area**	**kHz**
1145-1200	.....s.	VTN	9920boc

ANN: English: "You are tuned to FEBC Radio International"
V: QSL-card. Rp. preferred (3 IRC's).
NOTES: A division of Far East Broadcasting Company Inc.; see USA for corporate details.

RADIO VERITAS ASIA (Rlg)

P.O. Box 2642, Quezon City, Manila 1166, Philippines.
☎ +63 2 9390012. 🖷 +63 2 9381940.
Email: rvaprogram@rveritas-asia.org **Web:** www.rveritas-asia.org
L.P: SM: Rev. Fr. Carlos S. Lariosa; Tech Dir: Engr. Honorio L. Llavore.
SW: [PUG] Palauig (G.C. 15N28 119E50) 1 x 50, 3 x 250kW
kHz: *6190, 7265, 9505, 9520, 9570, 9670, 9805, 11725, 11765, 11780, 11790, 11795, 11820, 11850, 11895, 15225, 15350, 15450, 15520, 15530, 17830*

Winter Schedule 2004

Bangla	**Days**	**Area**	**kHz**
0100-0130	daily	As	11790pug
1400-1430	daily	As	11725pug
Burmese	**Days**	**Area**	**kHz**
1130-1200	daily	As	15450pug
2330-2400	daily	As	9805pug

Cantonese	Days	Area	kHz
2200-2230	daily	EAs	9805pug
Hindi	**Days**	**Area**	**kHz**
0130-0200	daily	As	11790pug
1330-1400	daily	As	11725pug
Hmong	**Days**	**Area**	**kHz**
1000-1030	daily	SEA	11780pug
Indonesian	**Days**	**Area**	**kHz**
1200-1230	daily	SEA	11795pug
2300-2330	daily	SEA	9505pug, 11820pug
Kachin	**Days**	**Area**	**kHz**
0030-0100	daily	SEA	9505pug
1230-1300	daily	SEA	15225pug
Karen	**Days**	**Area**	**kHz**
0000-0030	daily	SEA	11795pug
1200-1230	daily	SEA	15225pug
Mandarin	**Days**	**Area**	**kHz**
1000-1200	daily	EAs	9520pug
2100-2300	daily	EAs	6190pug
Russian	**Days**	**Area**	**kHz**
0230-0330	daily	RUS	17830pug
Sinhala	**Days**	**Area**	**kHz**
0000-0030	daily	As	11820pug
1330-1400	daily	As	9520pug
Tagalog	**Days**	**Area**	**kHz**
1500-1530	daily	SEA	11765pug
1530-1600	..w.f.s	SEA	11765pug
2230-2300	daily	SEA	7265pug
Tamil	**Days**	**Area**	**kHz**
0030-0100	daily	As	15520pug
1400-1430	daily	As	9520pug
Telugu	**Days**	**Area**	**kHz**
0100-0130	daily	As	15530pug
1430-1500	daily	As	9520pug
Urdu	**Days**	**Area**	**kHz**
0200-0230	daily	As	15350pug
1430-1500	daily	As	11725pug
Vietnamese	**Days**	**Area**	**kHz**
0130-0230	daily	SEA	15530pug
1030-1130	daily	SEA	11850pug
1300-1330	daily	SEA	11850pug
2330-2400	daily	SEA	9670pug
Zomi-Chin	**Days**	**Area**	**kHz**
0230-0300	daily	SEA	11895pug
1500-1600	daily	SEA	9570pug

ANN: English: "This is Radio Veritas Asia, broadcasting from Quezon City, Philippines"
V: QSL-card.
NOTES: Catholic station, on the air since 1969. Owned by the "Philippine Radio Educational and Information Center" (PREIC), composed of Filipino bishops and professionals.

IBB RELAY STATION PHILIPPINES (PORO PT.)

IBB Transmitting Station, Poro Point, San Fernando, La Unión, Philippines.
☎ +63 72 8882747. Fax +63 72 8885133.
Email: sdaitch@phi.ibb.gov
L.P: Transmitter Plant Supervisor: Sheldon Daitch.
MW: [PHP] Poro Point (G.C. 16N37 120E17) 1143kHz 1000kW, 1170kHz 800kW

IBB RELAY STATION PHILIPPINES (TINANG)

IBB Transmitting Station, Barangay Tinang, Concepción, Tarlac, Philippines.
☎ +63 45 9820254. Fax +63 45 9821402.
Email: dbrewer@phi.ibb.gov
L.P: SM: Dennis G. Brewer.
SW: [PHT] Tinang (G.C. 15N21 120E37) 3 x 50, 12 x 250kW
Broadcasters using sites in this country:
BBG-AapkiDunyaa uses: (PHT). See stn entry in: **USA**, INT Section
BBG-RFE/RL uses: (PHT). See stn entry in: **USA**, INT Section
BBG-VOA uses: (PHT). See stn entry in: **USA**, INT Section
BBG-VOA uses: (PHP). See stn entry in: **USA**, INT Section
Vatican Radio uses: (PUG). See stn entry in: **CVA**, INT Section

POLAND

RADIO POLONIA (Pub)

P.O. Box 46, 00-977 Warszawa, Poland.
☎ +48 22 6459262. Fax +48 22 6455917.
Email: radio.polonia@radio.com.pl **Web:** www.radio.com.pl/polonia
L.P: Dir: Juliusz M. Maliszewski.
SW: Leased from TP EmiTel
SAT: Hotbird 1
kHz: *5965, 6000, 6035, 6050, 6095, 6110, 6150, 6180, 6200, 7180, 7185, 7210, 7220, 7265, 7270, 7275, 7285, 9525, 11820*

Winter Schedule 2004

Belarusian	Days	Area	kHz
1430-1530	daily	Eu	6035wwa, 7180wwa
1730-1800	daily	Eu	6050wwa
English	**Days**	**Area**	**kHz**
1300-1400	daily	Eu	9525wwa, 11820wwa
1800-1900	daily	Eu	7220wwa, 7265wwa
Esperanto	**Days**	**Area**	**kHz**
1600-1625	daily	Eu	7270wwa, 7285wwa
1900-1925	daily	Eu	7285wwa
German	**Days**	**Area**	**kHz**
1230-1300	daily	Eu	5965wwa, 9525wwa
1630-1655	daily	Eu	7270wwa
2030-2055	daily	Eu	6110wwa, 6150wwa
Polish	**Days**	**Area**	**kHz**
1130-1200	daily	Eu	5965wwa, 7285wwa
1630-1730	daily	Eu	6050wwa
2200-2300	daily	Eu	6050wwa, 7265wwa
Russian	**Days**	**Area**	**kHz**
1200-1230	daily	Eu	6180wwa, 7285wwa
1400-1430	daily	Eu	6035wwa, 7275wwa
1530-1555	daily	Eu	7180wwa
1900-1930	daily	Eu	6095wwa
2000-2055	daily	Eu	6200wwa, 7185wwa
Ukrainian	**Days**	**Area**	**kHz**
1530-1600	daily	Eu	6000wwa
1930-2000	daily	Eu	6095wwa, 7210wwa

ANN: Polish: "Tu Polskie Radio, Warszawa"; English: "This is Polish Radio, Warsaw", "This is Radio Polonia"
V: QSL-card.
NOTES: Radio Polonia is the External Sce of the public broadcaster Polskie Radio.

BOZY GLOS W CZASACH OSTATECZNYCH (Rlg)

Wydawnictwo Cezary Mikolajczyk, ul. Przegrodka 44, 43-400 Cieszyn, Poland.
☎ +48 33 3796795.
Email: kontakt@radio.zapraszamy.pl **Web:** radio.zapraszamy.pl
kHz: *6015*

Winter Schedule 2004

Polish	Days	Area	kHz
1630-1700	......s	Eu	6015jul

NOTES: The broadcasts are in English with Polish voice-over.

TP EMITEL (Tx Operator)

ul. Wadowicka 8W, 30-415 Kraków, Poland.
☎ +48 12 2637355. Fax +48 12 2637611.
Email: sekretariat@emitel.pl **Web:** www.emitel.pl
SW: [WWA] Warszawa, Leszczynka (G.C. 52N02 020E53) 5 x 100kW
NOTES: TP EmiTel, a subsidiary of Telekomunikacje Polska S.A. (TP), is a major transmitter network owner in Poland.

PORTUGAL

RDP INTERNACIONAL (Pub)

Apartado 1011, 1001 Lisboa Codex, Portugal.
☎ +351 21 3820000. Fax +351 21 3820165.
Email: rdpinternacional@rdp.pt **Web:** www.rdp.pt
L.P: Dir. Jaime Marques de Almeida.
SW: [LIS] São Gabriel (G.C. 38N45 008W40) 6 x 100, 2 x 300kW. Also leases tx from Deutsche Welle Relay Station.
SAT: Asiasat 2, Hotbird 2
kHz: *7310, 9410, 9460, 9670, 9715, 9755, 9815, 11630, 11635, 11660, 11825, 11875, 11960, 11980, 13700, 13770, 15140, 15460, 15535, 15540, 15555, 15575, 15690, 17680, 17710, 17745, 17825, 21655, 21830*

Winter Schedule 2004

Portuguese	Days	Area	kHz
0000–0300	.twtfs.	NAm	9410lis, 9715lis
0000–0300	.twtfs.	VEN	13700lis
0000–0300	.twtfs.	B	11980lis, 13770lis
0600–0855	mtwtf..	Eu	9755lis
0600–1300	mtwtf..	Eu	9815lis
0745–0900	mtwtf..	Eu	11660sin
0800–1055	.....ss	B,WAf	17710lis
0800–1455	.....ss	Eu	11875lis, 15575lis
0800–1655	.....ss	Af	21830lis
0900–1055	mtwtf..	Eu	11875lis
0930–1100	.....ss	Eu	9815sin
1100–1300	mtwtf..	B,WAf	21655lis
1100–1300	mtwtf..	Eu	15140lis
1100–1300	mtwtf..	Af	21830lis
1100–2100	.....ss	B,WAf	21655lis
1300–1700	.....ss	NAm	15575lis
1300–1700	mtwtf..	NAm	15575lis*
1300–1800	.....ss	VEN	17745lis
1400–1600	mtwtf..	ME,IND	15690lis
1500–1755	.....ss	Eu	11635lis
1500–1800	.....ss	Eu	11960lis
1700–1900	.....ss	NAm	17825lis
1700–1900	mtwtf..	NAm	17825lis*
1700–2000	.....ss	Af	17680lis
1700–2000	mtwtf..	Af	17680lis
1700–2000	mtwtf..	B,WAf	21655lis
1700–2000	mtwtf..	Eu	9460lis
1800–2100	mtwtf..	VEN	15535lis*
1800–2100	.....ss	Eu	9460lis, 11630lis
1800–2100	.....ss	VEN	15535lis
1900–2100	.....ss	NAm	15540lis**
1900–2400	mtwtf..	NAm	15540lis*
2000–2400	.....ss	Af	9670lis*
2000–2400	.....ss	B,WAf	15555lis*
2000–2400	.....ss	Eu	7310lis*, 9460lis*
2000–2400	mtwtf..	Af	11825lis*
2000–2400	mtwtf..	B,WAf	15555lis*
2000–2400	mtwtf..	Eu	7310lis*, 9460lis*
2100-2400	.....ss	VEN	15460lis*
2100–2400	mtwtf..	VEN	15460lis*

ANN: Portuguese: "RDP Internacional - Rádio Portugal a emitir dos seus estúdios em Lisboa".
IS: Opens with brief tune on a Portuguese guitar, followed by national anthem and announcement. Closes with National Anthem, preceded by time gong
V: QSL-card. Rec. acc.
NOTES: RDP Internacional is the External Sce of the public broadcaster Radiodifusão Portuguesa (RDP). Key: * Special Transmissions; ** Sometimes extended until 2400.
PUBS: Schedule twice yearly (available per fax +351 21 3871381 or Email: redes@rtp.pt).

DEUTSCHE WELLE RELAY STATION
Profunk GmbH, Sines, Portugal.
SW: [SIN] Sines (G.C. 37N57 008W45) 3 x 250kW
Broadcasters using sites in this country:
Deutsche Welle uses: (SIN). See stn entry in: **D**, INT Section

ROMANIA

RADIO ROMANIA INTERNATIONAL (Pub)
P.O. Box 111, 70756 Bucuresti, Romania.
☎ +40 1 2222556. +40 1 2232613.
Email: rri@rri.ro **Web:** www.rri.ro
L.P: Deputy DG & Head RRI: Doru Vasile Ionescu.
MW/SW: Leased from Radiocomunicatii S.A.
SAT: Eutelsat W2, Hotbird 6
kHz: *5965, 6015, 6040, 6055, 6105, 6110, 6125, 6130, 6135, 6140, 6145, 6175, 6180, 7105, 7120, 7125, 7130, 7135, 7140, 7145, 7160, 7180, 7220, 7275, 9510, 9515, 9520, 9525, 9540, 9545, 9565, 9570, 9575, 9610, 9635, 9650, 9655, 9690, 9745, 11710, 11730, 11740, 11870, 11885, 11895, 11935, 11940, 11960, 15105, 15145, 15150, 15160, 15170, 15250, 15260, 15280, 15315, 15370, 15380, 15430, 17720, 17735, 17745, 17755, 17775, 17790, 17810, 17820, 17825, 17845*

Winter Schedule 2004

Arabic	Days	Area	kHz
0730-0800	daily	NAf	15280gal, 17720tig
0730-0800	daily	ME	15145tig, 17755gal
1500-1600	daily	ME	9655tig
1500-1600	daily	NAf	17820tig
Aromanian	**Days**	**Area**	**kHz**
1600-1630	daily	MKD	6175tig
1800-1830	daily	MKD	7130tig
2000-2030	daily	MKD	6130tig
English	**Days**	**Area**	**kHz**
0100-0200	daily	AUS	9510gal, 11740tig
0100-0200	daily	NAm	6140tig, 9690gal
0400-0500	daily	IND	11870gal, 15250gal
0400-0500	daily	NAm	6125tig, 9515tig
0630-0700	daily	WEu	9565tig, 11710tig
1300-1400	daily	WEu	15105tig, 17745tig
1800-1900	daily	WEu	5965tig, 7130tig
2130-2200	daily	WEu	6055gal, 7145gal
2130-2200	daily	NAm	6015tig, 9540tig
2300-2400	daily	NAm	6180tig, 9610tig
2300-2400	daily	WEu	6135gal, 7105gal
French	**Days**	**Area**	**kHz**
0200-0300	daily	CAN	6130gal, 9690gal
0600-0630	daily	WEu	7160gal, 7180tig, 9565tig, 9650gal
1100-1200	daily	NAf	15315gal, 17790tig
1100-1200	daily	WEu	15260tig, 17845gal
1700-1800	daily	WEu	6110gal, 7135gal
2000-2030	daily	WEu	6055gal, 7120gal
German	**Days**	**Area**	**kHz**
0700-0730	daily	WEu	7160gal, 7275tig, 9635tig, 9655gal
1200-1300	daily	WEu	9610tig, 9690gal, 11730tig, 11940gal
1900-2000	daily	WEu	6140tig, 7140tig
Italian	**Days**	**Area**	**kHz**
1630-1700	daily	I	7105tig
1830-1900	daily	I	6110tig
2030-2100	daily	I	6130tig
Mandarin	**Days**	**Area**	**kHz**
0500-0530	daily	CHN	15160tig, 17735tig
1400-1430	daily	CHN	9635tig, 11885tig
Romanian	**Days**	**Area**	**kHz**
0800-0900	......s	ME,IRN,AFG	15370tig, 15430gal, 17735gal, 17810tig
0900-1000	......s	ME,NAf	15380gal, 15430tig, 17745gal, 17775tig
1000-1100	......s	NAf,Eu	15260gal, 15380tig, 17735tig, 17825gal
1300-1400	daily	EEu	15170gal, 17825gal
1500-1600	daily	WEu	11740gal, 15150gal
1730-1800	daily	ISR	6055tig, 7220tig
1800-1900	daily	EEu	6040gal, 7140gal
1900-2000	daily	WEu	6040gal, 7125gal
Russian	**Days**	**Area**	**kHz**
0530-0600	daily	RUS	6055tig, 7135tig
1430-1500	daily	RUS	7120tig, 9520tig
1600-1700	daily	RUS	6125tig, 7135tig
Serbian	**Days**	**Area**	**kHz**
1530-1600	daily	SCG	7105tig
1730-1800	daily	SCG	6135tig
1930-2000	daily	SCG	6105tig
Spanish	**Days**	**Area**	**kHz**
0000-0100	daily	ARG	9745tig, 11960tig
0000-0100	daily	MEX	9525gal, 11935gal
0300-0400	daily	ARG	9545tig, 11895tig
0300-0400	daily	MEX	9690gal, 11870gal
2000-2100	daily	E	7140gal, 9570gal
2200-2300	daily	ARG	9575tig, 11940tig
Ukrainian	**Days**	**Area**	**kHz**
1500-1530	daily	UKR	6145tig
1700-1730	daily	UKR	6135tig
1900-1930	daily	UKR	6175tig

ANN: English: "This is Bucharest, Radio Romania International"
V: QSL-card.

NOTES: Radio Romania International is the External Sce of the public broadcaster Radio Romania. A part of the Romanian language prgr's are relays of Home Sce networks.

SN RADIOCOMUNICATII S.A. (Tx Operator)
Bd. Libertatii 14, sector 5, 050706 Bucuresti, Romania.
+40 1 3073045. +40 1 3149798.
Email: info@snr.ro **Web:** www.snr.ro
MW: [LUG] Lugoj (G.C. 45N41 021E55) 756kHz 400kW
SW: [GAL] Bacau, Galbeni (G.C. 46N44 026E50) 2 x 120, 2 x 250kW; [TIG] Bucuresti, Tiganesti (G.C. 44N42 026E06) 4 x 250kW
NOTES: SN Radiocomunicatii is the national transmitter network owner, providing SW facilities for Radio Romania International.

RUSSIA

VOICE OF RUSSIA (VOR) – WORLD SERVICE (Gov)
Pyatnitskaya 25, 115326 Moscow, Russia.
+7 095 9506278. +7 095 2302828.
Email: letters@vor.ru **Web:** www.vor.ru
L.P: MD: Armen Oganesyan.
MW/SW: Leased from RTRN
SAT: Asiasat 3S, Express 3A
kHz: *234, 585, 603, 612, 630, 648, 720, 801, 936, 972, 999, 1080, 1143, 1170, 1215, 1251, 1269, 1314, 1323, 1386, 1431, 1467, 1494, 1503, 1548, 3955, 4940, 4965, 4975, 5910, 5920, 5925, 5930, 5940, 5945, 5950, 5995, 6000, 6005, 6030, 6125, 6130, 6145, 6170, 6175, 6195, 6205, 6235, 7130, 7150, 7155, 7170, 7180, 7215, 7220, 7230, 7240, 7260, 7290, 7300, 7305, 7310, 7315, 7320, 7330, 7335, 7340, 7350, 7355, 7360, 7365, 7370, 7380, 7390, 7400, 7415, 7420, 7445, 7510, 7570, 9465, 9470, 9480, 9495, 9710, 9720, 9770, 9800, 9830, 9865, 9885, 9900, 9945, 11500, 11510, 11655, 12005, 12010, 12025, 12030, 12060, 12110, 13665, 15425, 15460, 15475, 15540, 15570, 15595, 15780, 17495, 17525, 17570, 17665, 17695, 21790*

Winter Schedule 2004

Albanian	**Days**	**Area**	**kHz**
1600-1630	daily	Eu	1548gri, 7320msk, 7340spb
Arabic	**Days**	**Area**	**kHz**
1500-1600	daily	ME	12005arm, 12030spb
1600-1700	daily	ME	1170arm, 1314gav, 1431smf, 7215sam, 7510dsb, 12005arm, 12030spb, 12060msk
1600-1700	daily	NAf	9480spb
1600-1700	daily	NAf,ME	5925arm, 9710msk
1700-1800	daily	NAf,ME	5925arm, 9710msk
1700-1800	daily	ME	1170arm, 1314gav, 1431smf, 7130spb, 7215msk, 7510dsb, 12005arm, 12030spb, 12060msk
1700-1800	daily	NAf	9480spb
1800-1830	daily	ME	7130spb
1800-1900	daily	NAf,ME	5925arm
1800-1900	daily	ME	1170arm, 1314gav, 7130spb, 12005arm, 12030spb, 12060msk
2300-2400	daily	ME	6175jul
Bangla	**Days**	**Area**	**kHz**
1530-1600	daily	As	7305nvs, 9800arm, 9885sam**, 9900sam*
Bulgarian	**Days**	**Area**	**kHz**
1800-1900	daily	Eu	1467gri, 5920spb, 7370sam
2000-2100	daily	Eu	1467gri, 6000sam
Croatian/Serbian	**Days**	**Area**	**kHz**
1630-1800	daily	Eu	1548gri, 5920spb, 6000msk, 7340spb, 7370sam
2100-2230	daily	Eu	1548gri, 6000sam
Czech	**Days**	**Area**	**kHz**
1845-1930	daily	Eu	1170sas, 6030spb, 7310msk, 7380ekb
Darl/Pashto	**Days**	**Area**	**kHz**
1300-1500	daily	WAs	648orz, 801orz, 972orz, 4940dsb, 4965dsb, 4975dsb, 9885sam**, 9900sam*, 11655arm

English	**Days**	**Area**	**kHz**
0200-0300	daily	NAm	7180gri, 7350smg, 15425ppk, 15475kna, 15595ppk
0200-0500	daily	As	17695tch
0300-0400	daily	NAm	7150arm, 7180gri, 7350smg, 12010kna, 15425ppk, 15475kna, 15595ppk
0400-0500	daily	Eu	603bln, 1548gri
0400-0500	daily	NAm	7150arm, 7180gri, 12010kna, 15425ppk, 15595ppk
0500-0600	daily	Eu	603bln
0600-0700	daily	Eu	603bln, 1323wbr
0600-0800	daily	AUS,NZL	17665irk, 21790irk
0700-0900	daily	Eu	12010spb, 12060spb
0700-1000	daily	Eu	603bln, 1323wbr, 15780tld+
0800-0900	daily	AUS,NZL	17495orz, 17525orz, 17570tch, 17665irk, 21790irk
0800-1000	daily	As	1251dsb, 17570tch
0900-1000	daily	AUS,NZL	17495orz, 17525orz, 17570tch, 17665irk
1500-1600	daily	Eu	12060tld+
1500-1600	daily	As	1251dsb, 5945nvs, 6205tch, 7260vld, 7315sam*, 7350tch, 7415ppk, 9900sam**, 11500orz, 12025msk
1530-1600	daily	ME	972orz
1600-1700	daily	As	972orz, 4940dsb, 4965dsb, 4975dsb, 7260vld, 7415ppk
1600-1700	daily	Eu	6130msk, 7290msk
1600-1700	daily	ME	972orz, 4940dsb, 4965dsb, 4975dsb, 6005arm, 9470msk
1700-1800	daily	As	648orz, 1251dsb, 1269yun, 5910irk, 5945nvs, 7415ppk
1700-1800	daily	ME	648orz, 1251dsb, 9470msk, 9830msk
1800-1900	daily	Af	11510gav
1800-1900	daily	ME	1251dsb, 9830msk
1800-1900	daily	As	1251dsb, 5910irk, 5945nvs, 7415ppk
1800-1900	.....ss	Eu	1494spb, 5950arm, 6175arm
1800-1900	daily	Eu	7290msk
1900-2000	daily	Af	7335tch, 11510gav
1900-2000	daily	Eu	6175arm, 6235spb, 7290msk, 7400msk
2000-2100	daily	Eu	6145msk, 6235spb, 7290msk, 7330msk
2100-2200	daily	Eu	6235spb, 7300arm, 7330msk
Farsi	**Days**	**Area**	**kHz**
1500-1600	daily	ME	7215sam, 7510dsb
1500-1700	daily	ME	648orz
Finnish	**Days**	**Area**	**kHz**
1800-1830	mtwtf..	Eu	1494spb, 5950arm, 6175arm
French	**Days**	**Area**	**kHz**
1700-1800	daily	Eu	7330msk
1700-1800	daily	Eu,Af	6130msk, 7390msk
1700-1800	daily	Af	7335tch, 11510gav
1800-1900	daily	Af	7230spb**, 7335tch, 7420msk*
1800-1900	daily	Eu	6145msk, 7330msk, 7420msk
1800-1900	daily	Eu,Af	6130msk
1900-2000	daily	Af	7230spb**, 7420msk*
1900-2000	daily	Eu,Af	5950spb, 7390msk
1900-2000	daily	Eu	7215sam, 7230spb**, 7330msk, 7420msk*
1900-2000	daily	Eu, Af	6130msk

French	Days	Area	kHz
2000-2100	daily	Af	5940msk, 7230spb**, 7420msk*
2000-2100	daily	Eu	1323wbr, 5950spb, 7230spb**, 7300arm, 7420msk*
2000-2100	daily	Eu,Af	6130msk, 7390msk, 9480msk
2100-2130	daily	Af	7170smg
2100-2200	daily	Eu	1323wbr

German	Days	Area	kHz
1000-1100	daily	Eu	603bln, 1323wbr, 9720klg, 15540arm, 15780tld+
1100-1200	daily	Eu	603bln, 1323wbr
1200-1300	daily	Eu	603bln, 1323wbr, 1386klg*, 12060tld+
1600-1700	daily	Eu	603bln, 1215klg, 1323wbr, 1386klg, 6145msk, 7300arm
1700-1800	daily	Eu	603bln, 1215klg, 1323wbr, 1386klg, 6145msk, 7290msk, 7300arm
1800-1900	daily	Eu	603bln, 1215klg, 1323wbr, 1386klg, 6235spb, 7300arm
1900-2000	daily	Eu	603bln, 1215klg, 1323wbr, 6145msk, 7300arm

Greek	Days	Area	kHz
1800-1900	daily	Eu	1431smf, 1467gri, 5920spb, 6000sam, 7355ekb, 9830msk

Hindi	Days	Area	kHz
1300-1400	daily	As	1269yun, 7350tch, 9800arm, 11500orz, 12025msk
1500-1530	daily	As	972orz, 7305nvs, 9800arm, 9885sam**, 9900sam*

Hungarian	Days	Area	kHz
1800-1845	daily	Eu	1170sas, 6030spb, 7380ekb

Italian	Days	Area	kHz
1700-1800	daily	Eu	6000msk, 7380ekb

Japanese	Days	Area	kHz
1200-1400	daily	EAs	630kna, 720iuj, 5920kna, 7155kna

Korean	Days	Area	kHz
1000-1100	daily	EAs	648vld, 3955vld, 5920kna, 6125irk, 9465nvs
1200-1300	daily	EAs	648vld, 3955vld, 5995nvs, 6125irk
1400-1500	daily	EAs	1323wbr, 3955vld

Mandarin	Days	Area	kHz
1100-1200	daily	EAs	585blg, 1251vld, 5920kna, 5930vld, 6145khb, 7220khb
1200-1300	daily	EAs	585blg, 1251vld, 5930vld, 6145khb, 7220khb, 7305nvs
1300-1400	daily	EAs	585blg, 1251vld, 7220khb
1400-1500	daily	EAs	585blg, 801tch, 1080irk, 1251vld, 5930vld, 7220khb

Mongolian	Days	Area	kHz
1300-1400	daily	MNG	801tch, 1080irk, 5930vld, 7305nvs

Norwegian	Days	Area	kHz
1830-1900	.t.t...	Eu	1494spb, 5950arm, 6175arm

Polish	Days	Area	kHz
1800-1900	daily	Eu	1143klg, 7215sam

Portuguese	Days	Area	kHz
0000-0100	daily	B	7330msk, 7390sam, 7570orz

Portuguese	Days	Area	kHz
0000-0100	daily	Eu	603bln
2100-2130	daily	Eu	6145msk, 7400msk

Romanian	Days	Area	kHz
1600-1700	daily	Eu	999gri, 7320msk**, 7380ekb, 7420msk*

Russian	Days	Area	kHz
0200-0300	daily	ME	648orz, 972smf, 5995jul
0200-0300	daily	TJK	1503dsb, 1503dsb
0200-0300	daily	NAm	7150arm, 7240smf, 7260msk, 7350smg, 12110kna, 13665ppk
0200-0300	daily	SAm	6195spb
0200-0400	daily	Eu	936smf
0300-0400	daily	NAm	7240smf, 7260msk, 12110kna, 13665ppk
0300-0400	daily	SAm	7330msk
1300-1400	daily	As	5995irk, 6145khb
1300-1400	daily	SEA	7260vld, 9495kna, 9770irk, 15460msk, 17570msk
1300-1400	daily	ME	9830msk
1300-1400	daily	CAs	7365sam, 15460msk, 15570msk
1300-1400	daily	CAs,ME	1143dsb
1300-1400	daily	Eu	936smf, 972smf, 999gri, 1431smf, 1548gri, 12060tld+
1300-1500	daily	AUS,NZL	9770irk
1400-1500	daily	Eu	12060tld+
1400-1500	daily	ME	7315sam, 9830msk, 9900sam
1400-1500	daily	CAs,ME	1251dsb
1400-1500	daily	CAs	15570msk
1400-1500	daily	As	5995irk, 6205tch
1400-1500	daily	SEA	7260vld, 9495kna, 9770irk, 15460msk, 17570msk
1600-1700	daily	As	5945nvs
1600-1700	daily	CAs,ME	1251dsb
1600-1700	daily	ME	1314gav, 7315sam, 9900sam
1800-1900	daily	Eu	603bln, 7400msk
1800-1900	daily	ME	7360msk
2000-2100	daily	Eu	612msk, 1215klg, 7310msk, 7400msk
2000-2100	daily	ME	7445msk
2000-2100	daily	Eu,ME	6170gri
2000-2200	daily	ME	7445msk
2000-2200	daily	WAs	234gav
2100-2200	daily	Eu	999gri, 1215klg
2100-2200	daily	ME	7445msk

Slovak	Days	Area	kHz
1930-2000	daily	Eu	1170sas, 6030spb, 7310msk, 7380ekb

Spanish	Days	Area	kHz
0100-0200	daily	SAm	5945arm, 6195spb, 7180gri, 7330msk, 7390sam, 7570orz
0100-0300	daily	Eu	603bln
0200-0300	daily	SAm	5945arm, 7330msk, 7390sam, 7570orz, 9945orz
2130-2200	daily	Eu	6145msk, 7400msk

Swedish	Days	Area	kHz
1830-1900	daily	Eu	1494spb, 5950arm, 6175arm

Turkish	Days	Area	kHz
1500-1600	daily	ME	1170arm, 6005arm, 9470msk, 9830msk

Urdu	Days	Area	kHz
1200-1300	daily	As	7305nvs, 7350tch, 9800arm, 9865nvs, 11500orz, 12025msk
1400-1500	daily	As	7305nvs, 7350tch, 9800arm, 11500orz, 12025msk

Vietnamese	Days	Area	kHz
1200-1300	daily	As	603dof, 6205tch, 15460msk*, 17570tch**

ANN: English: "This is Moscow, you are tuned to the World Service of the Voice of Russia'"
V: QSL-card.
NOTES: The Voice of Russia (VOR) is the External Sce produced under the roof of the Allrussian State Broadcasting Company (VGTRK).Transmissions in Russian consist of Voice of Russia World Service (see schedule above), Radiokanal "Sodruzhestvo" and "Russkoye Mezhdunaronoye Radio" (see entries below). Key: * To 5 Mar 2005; ** From 6 Mar 2005.

VOR – RADIOKANAL SODRUZHESTVO (RKS) (Gov)

kHz: *234, 603, 612, 648, 936, 972, 999, 1143, 1170, 1314, 1323, 1431, 1503, 1548, 7445, 9555, 9820, 9865, 9875, 9900*

Winter Schedule 2004

Russian	Days	Area	kHz
0300-0400	daily	Eu	972orz, 1170sas
0300-0400	daily	CAs	648orz, 1503dsb
0900-1000	daily	Eu	936lvi, 972smf, 1170sas
1000-1100	daily	Eu	612vln, 936lvi, 972smf
1100-1300	daily	Eu	612vln, 936lvi, 972smf, 1170sas
1300-1400	daily	CAs	1503dsb
1300-1400	daily	Eu	612vln, 1170sas
1400-1500	daily	CAs	9875tch
1400-1500	daily	Eu	7445msk
1400-1600	daily	CAs	1503dsb
1400-1600	daily	Eu	612vln, 936lvi, 972smf, 999gri, 1143klg, 1170sas, 1431smf, 1548gri
1500-1600	daily	Eu	7445msk
1500-1600	daily	As	9555jul
1500-1600	daily	CAs	9875tch
1600-1700	daily	Eu	936lvi, 972smf, 1431smf
1600-1700	daily	CAs	1503dsb
1600-1800	daily	Eu	7445msk, 9865spb
1700-1800	daily	CAs	1503dsb
1700-1800	daily	Eu	936lvi, 972smf
1800-1900	daily	CAs	648orz, 1503dsb
1800-1900	daily	Eu	972orz, 7445msk, 9820msk
1900-2000	daily	CAs	648orz, 1503dsb
1900-2000	daily	Eu	7445msk
1900-2000	daily	WAs	9900sam
2200-2300	daily	WAs,ME	1314gav
2200-2300	daily	Eu	603bln, 1323wbr
2200-2300	daily	WAs	234gav

ANN: Russian: "Radiokompaniya Golos Rossii predlagayet 'Radiokanal Sodruzhestvo'"

VOR – RUSSKOYE MEZHDUNARODNOYE RADIO (RMR) (Gov)

kHz: *234, 603, 612, 801, 936, 972, 999, 1089, 1143, 1170, 1215, 1314, 1323, 1386, 1494, 1548, 5965, 5975, 5990, 5995, 7125*

Winter Schedule 2004

Russian	Days	Area	kHz
0200-0400	daily	ME	5995jul
0300-0400	daily	CAs	801orz
0400-0500	daily	CAs	801orz
0400-0500	daily	Eu	1170arm, 1170sas
0500-0600	daily	Eu	1170sas, 1548gri
0600-0700	daily	Eu	1548gri
0700-0800	daily	Eu	1170sas, 1548gri
0800-0900	daily	Eu	612vln, 1170sas, 1548gri
0900-1000	daily	Eu	603bln, 612vln, 1170sas
1000-1100	daily	Eu	1215klg
1100-1300	daily	WAs	234gav
1300-1600	daily	WAs	234gav
1300-1600	daily	Eu	603bln, 1143klg, 1323wbr, 1386klg
1500-1700	daily	Eu	1143klg
1700-1800	daily	Eu	1089arm, 1143klg
1800-2000	daily	Eu	936lvi, 972smf, 1089arm, 1143klg
2000-2100	daily	CAs	1143dsb
2000-2100	daily	Eu	603bln, 936lvi, 1089arm, 1143klg
2000-2100	daily	WAs	1314gav
2000-2200	daily	ME	5965jul, 5975jul
2100-2200	daily	CAs	1143dsb
2100-2200	daily	Eu	603bln, 1143klg, 1494spb
2100-2200	daily	ME	5990jul
2200-2300	daily	Eu	999gri, 1170sas
2300-0600	daily	NAm	7125gri
2300-2400	daily	Eu	999gri

ANN: Russian: "Radiokompaniya Golos Rossii predlagayet programmu 'Russkoye Mezhdunarodnoye Radio"

RADIO RADONEZH (Rlg)

ul. Pyatnitskaya 25, 115326 Moskva, Russia.
☎ +7 095 9506356. 🖷 +7 095 9506356.
Email: radonezh@radonezh.ru **Web:** www.radrad.ru/radio
SW: Leased from RTRN
kHz: *7465*

Winter Schedule 2004

Russian	Days	Area	kHz
1700-2000	daily	Eu	7465nvs, 7465nvs

V: QSL-card.
NOTES: A station of the Moscow Patriarchate of the Russian Orthodox Church. Relays for domestic audience: see National Radio section.

RUSSIAN TELEVISION AND RADIO BROADCASTING NETWORK (RTRN) (Tx Operator)

ul. Ak.Korolyova 13, 129515 Moscow, Russia.
☎ +7 095 2175141. 🖷 +7 095 2175228.
Email: rtrs1@relcom.ru **Web:** www.rtrs.ru
L.P: GD: Gennadiy Sklyar.
MW: [ARM] Krasnodar, Tbilisskaya (G.C. 45N29 040E07) 1089/1170kHz 1200kW; [BLG] Belogorsk (G.C. 50N30 128E18) 585kHz 1200kW; [MSK] Moskva, Kurkino (G.C. 55N45 037E18) 612kHz 40kW; [IRK] Angarsk (G.C. 52N25 103E40) 1080kHz 1000kW; [IUJ] Yuzhno-Sakhalinsk, Vestochka (G.C. 46N50 142E54) 720kHz 1000kW; [KLG] Sovetsk, Bolshakovo (G.C. 54N54 021E43) 1143kHz 150kW, 1215/1386kHz 1200kW (1386kHz will be closed in 2007); [KNA] Komsomolsk-na-Amure (G.C. 50N39 136E55) 630kHz 500kW; [SPB] St.Peterburg, Krasnyy Bor (G.C. 59N39 030E42) 1494kHz 600kW; [TCH] Chita, Atamanovka (G.C. 51N50 113E43) 801kHz 1200kW; [VLD] Vladivostok, Ussuriysk (G.C. 43N32 131E57) 648/1251kHz 1000kW
SW: [MSK] Moskva (G.C. 55N45 037E18), Moscow sites in detail: [TLD] Taldom (G.C. 56N44 037E38) 12 x 100, 4 x 250, 3 x 1000kW; [KRV] Kurovskaya (G.C. 55N34 039E09) 2 x 80, 8 x 100, 1 x 150, 6 x 250kW; [LES] Lesnoy (G.C. 56N04 037E58) 1 x 150, 15 x 250kW. Other sites in Russia: [ARM] Krasnodar, Tbilisskaya (G.C. 45N29 040E07) 8 x 100, 1 x 250, 4 x 1000kW; [EKB] Yekaterinburg (G.C. 56N55 060E36) 20 x 100kW; [IRK] Irkutsk, Angarsk (G.C. 52N25 103E40) 2 x 100, 4 x 250, 2 x 2000kW; [KHB] Khabarovsk (G.C. 48N33 135E15) 7 x 100, 4 x 120kW; [KLG] Sovetsk, Bolshakovo (G.C. 54N54 021E43) 9 x 80kW; [KNA] Komsomolsk-na-Amure (G.C. 50N39 136E55) 4 x 100; 1 x 200, 2 x 250kW; [NVS] Novosibirsk, two sites: Novosibirsk (G.C. 55N04 082E58) 23 x 100kW, Oyash (G.C. 55N31 083E45) 3 x 1000kW; [PPK] Petropavlovsk, Yelizovo (G.C. 52N59 158E39) 4 x 100, 2 x 250kW; [SAM] Samara (G.C. 53N17 050E15) 10 x 100, 3 x 200, 6 x 250kW; [SPB] St.Peterburg, Krasnyy Bor (G.C. 59N39 030E42) 18 x 200kW; [TCH] Chita, Atamanovka (G.C. 51N50 113E43) 1 x 100, 2 x 250, 2 x 1000kW; [VLD] Vladivostok, Razdolnoye (G.C. 43N32 131E57) 2 x 100, 2 x 120, 2 x 200, 3 x 250, 2 x 1000kW
NOTES: RTRN is the national transmitter network operator in Russia. Leases out its facilities to domestic and international customers.

RADIOAGENCY–M (Broker)

ul. Demyana Bednogo 24, 123308 Moscow, Russia.
☎ +7 095 1919161. 🖷 +7 095 1918591.
Email: abat@radioagency.ru **Web:** www.radioagency.ru
L.P: Dir: Anatoliy Batyushkin.
NOTES: Radioagency-M is brokering air time for high power medium and shortwave tx's owned by RTRN in Russia.

Broadcasters using sites in this country:
BBC World Sce uses: (MSK). See stn entry in: **G**, INT Section
BBC World Sce uses: (VLD). See stn entry in: **G**, INT Section
BBC World Sce uses: (SPE). See stn entry in: **G**, INT Section
BBC World Sce uses: (ARM). See stn entry in: **G**, INT Section
BBC World Sce uses: (EKB). See stn entry in: **G**, INT Section
BBC World Sce uses: (IRK). See stn entry in: **G**, INT Section
BBG-R.Free Asia uses: (VLD). See stn entry in: **USA**, INT Section
BBG-R.Free Asia uses: (IRK). See stn entry in: **USA**, INT Section
BBG-VOA uses: (PPK). See stn entry in: **USA**, INT Section
BBG-VOA uses: (VLD). See stn entry in: **USA**, INT Section
BBG-VOA uses: (IRK). See stn entry in: **USA**, INT Section
BBG-VOA uses: (NVS). See stn entry in: **USA**, INT Section
BVB uses: (KHB). See stn entry in: **G**, INT Section
BVB uses: (VLD). See stn entry in: **G**, INT Section
BVB uses: (ARM). See stn entry in: **G**, INT Section
China R. Int'l uses: (ARM). See stn entry in: **CHN**, INT Section
China R. Int'l uses: (TLD). See stn entry in: **CHN**, INT Section
China R. Int'l uses: (SPB). See stn entry in: **CHN**, INT Section
China R. Int'l uses: (KRV). See stn entry in: **CHN**, INT Section
China R. Int'l uses: (SAM). See stn entry in: **CHN**, INT Section
Degar Voice uses: (NVS). See stn entry in: **VTN**, CTB Section
Deutsche Welle uses: (ARM). See stn entry in: **D**, INT Section
Deutsche Welle uses: (PPK). See stn entry in: **D**, INT Section
Deutsche Welle uses: (SPE). See stn entry in: **D**, INT Section
Deutsche Welle uses: (VLD). See stn entry in: **D**, INT Section
Deutsche Welle uses: (NSB). See stn entry in: **D**, INT Section
Deutsche Welle uses: (MSK). See stn entry in: **D**, INT Section
Deutsche Welle uses: (KNA). See stn entry in: **D**, INT Section
Deutsche Welle uses: (IRK). See stn entry in: **D**, INT Section
FEBA Radio uses: (MSK). See stn entry in: **G**, INT Section
FEBA Radio uses: (NVS). See stn entry in: **G**, INT Section
FEBA Radio uses: (SAM). See stn entry in: **G**, INT Section
FEBA Radio uses: (ARM). See stn entry in: **G**, INT Section
FEBA Radio uses: (IRK). See stn entry in: **G**, INT Section
Lutherische Std uses: (KLG). See stn entry in: **D**, INT Section
Lutherische Std uses: (SPB). See stn entry in: **D**, INT Section
Lutherische Std uses: (ARM). See stn entry in: **D**, INT Section
Miss.Heukelbach uses: (SPB). See stn entry in: **D**, INT Section
Miss.Heukelbach uses: (ARM). See stn entry in: **D**, INT Section
Miss.Heukelbach uses: (KLG). See stn entry in: **D**, INT Section
Qala Aturaya uses: (MSK). See stn entry in: **IRQ**, CTB Section
Qala Aturaya uses: (ARM). See stn entry in: **IRQ**, CTB Section
Quê Huong R. uses: (VLD). See stn entry in: **VTN**, CTB Section
R.Freundes-D. uses: (KLG). See stn entry in: **SUI**, INT Section
R.Freundes-D. uses: (MSK). See stn entry in: **SUI**, INT Section
R.Freundes-D. uses: (ARM). See stn entry in: **SUI**, INT Section
R.Ibrahim uses: (ARM). See stn entry in: **CYP**, INT Section
R.Ibrahim uses: (SAM). See stn entry in: **CYP**, INT Section
R.Kumru uses: (ARM). See stn entry in: **S**, INT Section
R.Prague uses: (ARM). See stn entry in: **CZE**, INT Section
R.Prague uses: (NSB). See stn entry in: **CZE**, INT Section
R.Santec uses: (KLG). See stn entry in: **D**, INT Section
R.Santec uses: (SPB). See stn entry in: **D**, INT Section
R.Santec uses: (MSK). See stn entry in: **D**, INT Section
R.Santec uses: (SAM). See stn entry in: **D**, INT Section
R.Santec uses: (ARM). See stn entry in: **D**, INT Section
R.VO Oro.Lib.Fr uses: (SAM). See stn entry in: **ETH**, CTB Section
RFI uses: (IRK). See stn entry in: **F**, INT Section
RFI uses: (VLD). See stn entry in: **F**, INT Section
RFI uses: (NSB). See stn entry in: **F**, INT Section
RNWO uses: (IRK). See stn entry in: **HOL**, INT Section
RNWO uses: (KHB). See stn entry in: **HOL**, INT Section
RNWO uses: (PPK). See stn entry in: **HOL**, INT Section
RVI uses: (IRK). See stn entry in: **BEL**, INT Section
RVI uses: (MSK). See stn entry in: **BEL**, INT Section
RVI uses: (ARM). See stn entry in: **BEL**, INT Section
TDPradio uses: (ARM). See stn entry in: **BEL**, INT Section
TDPradio uses: (TLD). See stn entry in: **BEL**, INT Section
TWR Europe uses: (SPB). See stn entry in: **AUT**, INT Section
TWR Europe uses: (EKB). See stn entry in: **AUT**, INT Section
TWR India uses: (IRK). See stn entry in: **IND**, INT Section
TWR India uses: (TCH). See stn entry in: **IND**, INT Section
TWR India uses: (SAM). See stn entry in: **IND**, INT Section
Vatican Radio uses: (TCH). See stn entry in: **CVA**, INT Section
Vatican Radio uses: (KHB). See stn entry in: **CVA**, INT Section
Vatican Radio uses: (NVS). See stn entry in: **CVA**, INT Section
VO Liberty-Erit uses: (SAM). See stn entry in: **ERI**, CTB Section
VO Oromia uses: (SAM). See stn entry in: **ETH**, CTB Section

RWANDA

DEUTSCHE WELLE RELAY STATION

Kigali, Rwanda.
SW: [KIG] Kigali (G.C. 01S53 030E04) 4 x 250kW
Broadcasters using sites in this country:
Deutsche Welle uses: (KIG). See stn entry in: **D**, INT Section
FEBA Radio uses: (KIG). See stn entry in: **G**, INT Section
RFI uses: (KIG). See stn entry in: **F**, INT Section

SÃO TOMÉ E PRINCÍPE

IBB RELAY STATION SÃO TOMÉ

IBB Transmitting Station, P.O. Box 522, São Tomé, São Tomé e Príncipe.
Email: clewis@sto.ibb.gov
L.P: SM: Charles Lewis.
MW: [SAO] Pinheira (G.C. 00N18 006E46) 1530kHz 600kW
SW: [SAO] Pinheira (G.C. 00N18 006E46) 4 x 100kW
Broadcasters using sites in this country:
BBG-Studio 7 uses: (SAO). See stn entry in: **USA**, INT Section
BBG-VOA uses: (SAO). See stn entry in: **USA**, INT Section

SAUDI ARABIA

SAUDI RADIO (Gov)

P.O. Box 61718, Riyadh-11575, Saudi Arabia.
☎ +966 1 4425170. Fax +966 1 4041692.
Email: inform.eng@awalnet.net.sa **Web:** www.saudiradio.net
L.P: GM: Suleiman Al-Kalifa; Dir of Engineering and Freq Management: Suleiman Al-Samnan.
SW: [JED] Jeddah (G.C. 21N32 039E10) 6 x 50, 2 x 100kW; [RIY] Riyadh (G.C. 24N30 046E23) 4 x 350, 8 x 500kW
SAT: Asiasat 2, Arabsat 2C/2D/3A, Hotbird 2/4, NSS 7, Telstar 5/12
kHz: *9525, 9555, 9580, 9675, 9730, 9870, 11740, 11745, 11785, 11820, 11855, 11915, 11935, 13710, 15170, 15205, 15275, 15315, 15345, 15380, 15435, 17560, 17615, 17730, 17740, 17760, 17775, 17785, 17805, 17895, 21460, 21495, 21505, 21600, 21640, 21670, 21705*

Winter Schedule 2004

Arabic	**Days**	**Area**	**kHz**
0600-0900	daily	ME	17730riy
0600-0900	daily	Eu	17740riy
0900-1200	daily	Eu	21705riy
0900-1200	daily	NAf	17805riy
1200-1500	daily	Eu	21640riy
1200-1500	daily	NAf	21505riy
1700-1800	daily	Eu	15435riy
1700-1800	daily	NAf	15315riy
1800-2300	daily	Eu	9870riy
1800-2300	daily	NAf	9555riy
Arabic (Call of Islam)	**Days**	**Area**	**kHz**
1500-1700	daily	Eu	15435riy
1500-1700	daily	NAf	15315riy
Arabic 2nd prgr	**Days**	**Area**	**kHz**
0300-0600	daily	ME	9580jed
0300-0900	daily	ME	9675riy
0600-1700	daily	ME	11855jed
1700-2200	daily	EAf,ME	9580jed
Bambara	**Days**	**Area**	**kHz**
1700-1800	daily	CAf	17775riy
Bengali	**Days**	**Area**	**kHz**
1600-1700	daily	SAs	15345riy
Farsi	**Days**	**Area**	**kHz**
1400-1600	daily	WAs	11745riy
French	**Days**	**Area**	**kHz**
0800-1000	daily	WAf	17785riy
1400-1600	daily	WAf	21600riy
Holy Quran	**Days**	**Area**	**kHz**
0300-0600	daily	RUS	15170riy
0300-0800	daily	RUS	17895riy
0600-0900	daily	ME	15380riy
0600-1700	daily	ME	11785riy
0900-1200	daily	ME	11935riy

Holy Quran	**Days**	**Area**	**kHz**
0900-1200	daily	SAs,EAs	21495riy
0900-1200	daily	SEA	17615riy
1200-1400	daily	ME	15380riy
1200-1400	daily	SEA	21600riy
1200-1500	daily	NAf	17895riy
1300-1600	daily	EAf	21460riy
1500-1800	daily	NAf	13710riy
1600-1800	daily	CAf	17560riy
1600-1800	daily	Eu	15205riy
1800-2300	daily	CAf	11740riy
1800-2300	daily	Eu	11820riy
1800-2300	daily	NAf	11915riy
Indonesian	**Days**	**Area**	**kHz**
1000-1200	daily	SEA	21670riy
Pashto	**Days**	**Area**	**kHz**
1600-1700	daily	WAs	9525riy
Somali	**Days**	**Area**	**kHz**
0400-0500	daily	EAf	17760riy
Swahili	**Days**	**Area**	**kHz**
0500-0600	daily	EAf	17760riy
Turkish	**Days**	**Area**	**kHz**
0400-0600	daily	ME	15275riy
Urdu	**Days**	**Area**	**kHz**
1200-1400	daily	SAs	15345riy
Uzbek	**Days**	**Area**	**kHz**
1400-1600	daily	CAs	9730riy

ANN: Arabic (General Prgr): "Idha'at al mamlaka alarabiya al saudiyah min al Riyadh"
IS: 'Ud' (Oriental Lute). Opens and closes with National Anthem.
V: QSL-card. Rpt to Frequency Mgr.
NOTES: The SW transmissions in Arabic are relays of Home Sce prgr's.

SERBIA & MONTENEGRO

INTERNATIONAL RADIO OF SERBIA & MONTENEGRO (Gov)

Hilandarska 2/IV, 11000 Beograd, Serbia & Montenegro.
☎ +381 11 3244455. 🖷 +381 11 3232014.
Email: radioyu@bitsyu.net **Web:** www.radioyu.org
L.P: Dir: Milena Jokic; Head of Prgrs: Dr. Zivorad Djordjevic.
kHz: *6100, 7115, 7130, 7220, 9580, 9680, 11800, 11835*

Winter Schedule 2004

Albanian	**Days**	**Area**	**kHz**
1800-1815	daily	ALB	6100bij
Arabic	**Days**	**Area**	**kHz**
1530-1600	daily	ARS	11800bij
Bulgarian	**Days**	**Area**	**kHz**
1815-1830	daily	BUL	6100bij
English	**Days**	**Area**	**kHz**
0100-0130	mtwtfs.	NAm,WEu	7115bij
0200-0230	daily	NAm,WEu	7130bij
1330-1400	daily	AUS	11835bij
1930-2000	daily	WEu	6100bij
2200-2230	daily	Eu	6100bij
French	**Days**	**Area**	**kHz**
1700-1730	daily	WEu	6100bij
2130-2200	daily	Eu	6100bij
German	**Days**	**Area**	**kHz**
1730-1800	daily	WEu	6100bij
2100-2130	mtwtf.s	WEu	6100bij
Greek	**Days**	**Area**	**kHz**
1645-1700	daily	GRC	6100bij
Hungarian	**Days**	**Area**	**kHz**
1630-1645	daily	HNG	6100bij
Italian	**Days**	**Area**	**kHz**
1830-1900	daily	WEu	6100bij
Mandarin	**Days**	**Area**	**kHz**
2330-2400	daily	CHN	9580bij
Russian	**Days**	**Area**	**kHz**
1600-1630	daily	RUS	6100bij
1900-1930	daily	RUS	6100bij
Serbian	**Days**	**Area**	**kHz**
0030-0100	mtwtfs.	NAm,WEu	7115bij
0030-0130	……s	NAm,WEu	7115bij
0130-0200	daily	NAm,WEu	7115bij
1400-1530	daily	AUS	11835bij
2030-2100	mtwtf.s	Eu	6100bij
2030-2130	…..s.	Eu	6100bij
Spanish	**Days**	**Area**	**kHz**
0000-0030	daily	SAm	9680bij
2000-2030	daily	E	7220bij

ANN: English: "This is the International Radio of Serbia and Montenegro"; Serbian: "Medjunarodni Radio Srbija i Crna Gora"
V: QSL-card. Rec. acc.

SEYCHELLES

BBC INDIAN OCEAN RELAY STATION

P.O. Box 448, Victoria, Mahé, Seychelles.
☎ +248 78496. 🖷 +248 78500.
Email: resey@seychelles.net
L.P: Resident Eng: Barrie Elding.
SW: [SEY] Mahé (G.C. 04S36 055E28) 2 x 250kW
V: QSL-card for direct rpt.
NOTES: Owned by the BBC and operated by VT Merlin Communications (see UK). Carries relays of BBC and other international broadcasters.
Broadcasters using sites in this country:
BBC World Sce uses: (SEY). See stn entry in: **G**, INT Section

SINGAPORE

RADIO SINGAPORE INTERNATIONAL (Gov)

P.O. Box 5300, Singapore 912899.
☎ +65 63597662. 🖷 +65 62591357.
Email: info@rsi.com.sg **Web:** www.rsi.com.sg
L.P: PD Chinese Sce: Mrs Chin Kwee Chin; PD English Sce: Ms Sakuntala Gupta; Senior PD Malay/Indonesian Sce: Ms Zainab Rahim; Freq Mgr: Mr Andoor Ravindra.
SW: [SGP] Singapore (G.C. 01N24 103E51) 6 x 250kW
SAT: Asiasat 3S, Palapa C2
kHz: *6000, 6080, 6120, 6150, 6185, 7235*

Winter Schedule 2004

English	**Days**	**Area**	**kHz**
1100-1400	daily	SEA	6080sgp, 6150sgp
Indonesian	**Days**	**Area**	**kHz**
1200-1400	daily	SEA	6120sgp, 7235sgp
Malay	**Days**	**Area**	**kHz**
0900-1200	daily	SEA	6120sgp, 7235sgp
Mandarin	**Days**	**Area**	**kHz**
1100-1400	daily	SEA	6000sgp, 6185sgp

ANN: Malay: "Radio Singapura Internasional"; Mandarin: "Xinjiapo guoji guangbo diantai"
V: QSL-card.
NOTES: Radio Singapore International is the External Sce of the national broadcaster MediaCorp Singapore, MediaCorp Radio.

BBC FAR EAST RELAY STATION

51 Turut Track, Singapore 718930.
☎ +65 67937511. 🖷 +65 67937834.
SW: [SNG] Kranji (G.C. 01N25 103E44) 4 x 100, 5 x 250kW
V: QSL-card for direct rpt.
NOTES: Owned by the BBC and operated by VT Merlin Communications (see UK). Carries relays of BBC and other international broadcasters.
Broadcasters using sites in this country:
BBC World Sce uses: (SGP). See stn entry in: **G**, INT Section
Deutsche Welle uses: (SNG). See stn entry in: **D**, INT Section
R.Australia uses: (SNG). See stn entry in: **AUS**, INT Section
R.Japan uses: (SNG). See stn entry in: **J**, INT Section
RAI Int'l uses: (SNG). See stn entry in: **I**, INT Section
RNWO uses: (SNG). See stn entry in: **HOL**, INT Section

SLOVAKIA

RADIO SLOVAKIA INTERNATIONAL (Pub)

P.O. Box 55, 81755 Bratislava, Slovak Republic.
☎ +421 7 57273737. 🖷 +421 7 52496282.
Email: englishsection@slovakradio.sk **Web:** www.rsi.sk
L.P: Chief Editor: Ladislav Kubiš.
SW: Leased from Slovenské Telekomunikácie

kHz: *5915, 6055, 7230, 7345, 9440, 9445, 9460, 9485, 11600, 11610, 11990, 13715, 15460*

Winter Schedule 2004

English	**Days**	**Area**	**kHz**
0100-0130	daily	SAm	9440rso
0100-0130	daily	NAm	7230rso
0700-0730	daily	AUS	13715rso, 15460rso
1730-1800	daily	Eu	5915rso, 6055rso
1930-2000	daily	Eu	5915rso, 7345rso
French	**Days**	**Area**	**kHz**
0200-0230	daily	NAm	7230rso
0200-0230	daily	SAm	9440rso
1800-1830	daily	Eu	5915rso, 6055rso
2030-2100	daily	Eu	5915rso, 7345rso
German	**Days**	**Area**	**kHz**
0730-0800	daily	Eu	5915rso, 6055rso
1430-1500	daily	Eu	6055rso, 7345rso
1700-1730	daily	Eu	5915rso, 6055rso
1900-1930	daily	Eu	5915rso, 7345rso
Russian	**Days**	**Area**	**kHz**
1400-1430	daily	EEu,CAs	9440rso, 11990rso
1600-1630	daily	EEu,CAs	5915rso, 11990rso
1830-1900	daily	EEu,CAs	5915rso, 9485rso
Slovak	**Days**	**Area**	**kHz**
0130-0200	daily	NAm	7230rso
0130-0200	daily	SAm	9440rso
0730-0800	daily	AUS	13715rso, 15460rso
1630-1700	daily	Eu	5915rso, 6055rso
2000-2030	daily	Eu	5915rso, 7345rso
Spanish	**Days**	**Area**	**kHz**
0230-0300	daily	SAm	7230rso, 9440rso
1530-1600	daily	Eu	9445rso, 11600rso
2100-2130	daily	SAm	9460rso, 11610rso

ANN: English: "You are listening to Radio Slovakia International"
V: QSL-card.
NOTES: Radio Slovakia International is the External Sce of the public-service Slovak Radio (Slovenský Rozhlas).

SLOVENSKÉ TELEKOMUNIKÁCIE A.S. (Tx Operator)

Radiokomunikácie o.z., Cesta na Kamzik 14, 810 05 Bratislava, Slovak Republic.
☎ +421 7 5020489. Fax +421 7 5020537.
Email: marketing@telekom.sk **Web:** www.telecom.sk
SW: [RSO] Rimavská Sobota (G.C. 48N23 020E00) 4 x 250kW; [VKO] Vel'ké Kostolany (G.C. 48N31 017E44) 2 x 100kW
NOTES: Radiokomunikácie o.z., a division of Slovenské Telekomunikácie, is the owner of the transmitter networks in the Slovak Republic and provides the SW facilities for Radio Slovakia International.
Broadcasters using sites in this country:
R.Budapest uses: (RSO). See stn entry in: **HNG**, INT Section

SOUTH AFRICA

CHANNEL AFRICA (Pub)

P.O. Box 91313, Auckland Park 2006, South Africa.
☎ +27 11 7142255. Fax +27 11 7142072.
Email: meyerhelen@channelafrica.org
Web: www.channelafrica.org
L.P: Exec. Editor: Thami Ntenteni; Technical Dept: Helen Meyer.
SW: Leased from Sentech
kHz: *3345, 7240, 7390, 9565, 9685, 11825, 11875, 15220, 15285, 17770, 17780*

Winter Schedule 2004

English	**Days**	**Area**	**kHz**
0300-0355	daily	EAf,CAf	7390mey
0300-0500	daily	SAf	3345mey
0500-0555	daily	WAf	11875mey
0500-0700	daily	SAf	7240mey
0600-0655	daily	WAf	15220mey
0700-0800	daily	SAf	11825mey
1000-1200	daily	SAf	11825mey
1400-1600	daily	SAf	11825mey
1500-1555	daily	EAf,CAf	17770mey
1700-1755	daily	WAf	15285mey
1900-2200	daily	SAf	3345mey
French	**Days**	**Area**	**kHz**
0400-0455	daily	CAf	9565mey
1600-1655	daily	WAf	15285mey
Lozi	**Days**	**Area**	**kHz**
0900-1000	daily	SAf	11825mey
1300-1400	daily	SAf	11825mey
Nyanja	**Days**	**Area**	**kHz**
0800-0900	daily	SAf	11825mey
1200-1300	daily	SAf	11825mey
Swahili	**Days**	**Area**	**kHz**
0300-0355	daily	EAf,CAf	9685mey
1500-1555	daily	EAf,CAf	17780mey

ANN: English: "You're listening to Channel Africa coming to you from Johannesburg"
IS: Birds chirping and native melody.
V: QSL-card.
NOTES: Channel Africa is the External Sce of the public-service South African Broadcasting Corporation (SABC).

SENTECH PTY. (Tx Operator)

Private Bag X06, Honeydew 2040, South Africa.
☎ +27 11 4714400. Fax +27 11 6917107.
Email: ottok@sentech.co.za **Web:** www.sentech.co.za
L.P: Chmn: Dr Stephen Mncube; CEO: Dr Sebiletso Mokone-Matabane.
SW: [MEY] Meyerton, Tygerberg (G.C. 26S35 028E08) 10 x 100, 4 x 250, 4 x 250, 3 x 500kW
V: QSL-card (for relayed stations).
NOTES: Sentech Pty. is the owner of the transmitter networks in South Africa. Sentech is renting out air time on its SW facilities in Meyerton to various customers.

AMATEUR RADIO MIRROR INTERNATIONAL

P.O. Box 90438, Garsfontein 0042, South Africa.
☎ +27 11 6752393. Fax +27 11 6752793.
Email: armi@sarl.org.za
Web: www.sarl.org.za/public/ARMI/ARMI.asp
SW: Leased from Sentech.
kHz: *3215, 9750, 17700*

Winter Schedule 2004

English	**Days**	**Area**	**kHz**
0800-0900	……s	SAf	9750mey
0800-0900	……s	EAf,CAf	17700mey
1900-2000	m……	SAf	3215mey

V: QSL-card.
NOTES: AMRI is a weekly prgr about amateur radio, shortwave listening and electronics produced by the South African Radio League.
Broadcasters using sites in this country:
AWR uses: (MEY). See stn entry in: **USA**, INT Section
BBC World Sce uses: (MEY). See stn entry in: **G**, INT Section
FEBA Radio uses: (MEY). See stn entry in: **G**, INT Section
RFI uses: (MEY). See stn entry in: **F**, INT Section
RVI uses: (MEY). See stn entry in: **BEL**, INT Section
SW Radio Africa uses: (MEY). See stn entry in: **ZWE**, CTB Section
TWR Africa uses: (MEY). See stn entry in: **SWZ**, INT Section
UN Radio uses: (MEY). See stn entry in: **UNO**, INT Section
VO Biafra Int'l uses: (MEY). See stn entry in: **NIG**, CTB Section

SPAIN

RADIO EXTERIOR DE ESPAÑA (REE) (Pub)

Apartado 156202, E-28080 Madrid, Spain.
☎ +34 1 3461149. Fax +34 1 3461815.
Email: ree.rne@rtve.es **Web:** www.rtve.es/rne/ree
L.P: Dir: Javier Garrigos Fernandez; Foreign Language Prgr's: Jose J. Amorena Zabalza.
SW: [NOB] Noblejas, Toledo (G.C. 39N57 003W26) 2 x 250, 6 x 350kW
kHz: *5970, 5985, 6040, 6050, 6055, 6095, 6125, 6920, 7150, 7270, 7275, 9535, 9595, 9620, 9630, 9655, 9660, 9665, 9680, 9690, 9710, 9765, 11625, 11795, 11815, 11880, 11890, 11910, 11945, 12035, 13720, 15125, 15170, 15195, 15385, 15585, 17595, 17715, 17755, 17770, 17850, 21540, 21570, 21610, 21700*

Winter Schedule 2004

Arabic	**Days**	**Area**	**kHz**
1700-1900	mtwtf..	Eu	21610nob
1900-2100	mtwtf..	Af	7270nob
1900-2100	mtwtf..	Eu	12035nob

2000-2100	.....ss	Eu	12035nob
2000-2200	.....ss	Af	7270nob
English	**Days**	**Area**	**kHz**
2000-2100	mtwtf..	Af	9595nob
2000-2100	mtwtf..	Eu	9680nob
2200-2300	.....ss	Eu	9680nob
2200-2300	.....ss	Af	9595nob
French	**Days**	**Area**	**kHz**
1800-1900	mtwtf..	Eu	9655nob
1900-2000	mtwtf..	Eu	7150nob
1900-2000	mtwtfs.	Af	9595nob
1900-2000	.....ss	Eu	12035nob
2100-2200	......s	Af	9595nob
2300-0200	daily	Am	6055nob
2300-2400	.....ss	Eu	6095nob
German	**Days**	**Area**	**kHz**
1700-1730	m..t...	Eu	9665nob
Russian	**Days**	**Area**	**kHz**
1700-1730	mtwtf..	Eu	15195nob
Sefardi	**Days**	**Area**	**kHz**
0115-0145	.t.....	Am	11795nob
0415-0445	.t.....	Am	9690nob
1825-1855	m......	Eu	17770nob
Spanish	**Days**	**Area**	**kHz**
0000-0300	daily	SAm	11815cri
0200-0400	daily	NAm	6050nob
0200-0600	daily	CAm	6040cri
0200-0600	daily	NAm	11880cri
0400-0500	daily	SAm	6920nob
0400-0600	daily	NAm	6055nob
0400-0600	daily	SAm	5970nob
0500-0700	daily	ME	11890nob
0600-0800	.....ss	Eu	5985nob
0600-0800	daily	Eu	9710nob
0600-0900	daily	Eu	12035nob
0700-0900	.....ss	AUS	21610nob
0700-0900	daily	AUS	17770nob
0800-1000	mtwtf..	SAm	21570nob
0800-1300	daily	Eu	13720nob
0900-1000	daily	Eu	15585nob
0900-1500	daily	Af	21540nob
0900-1700	daily	ME	21610nob
1000-1100	mtwtf..	SAm	11815cri
1000-1200	daily	J	9660bei
1000-1700	daily	SAm	21570nob
1000-1800	mtwtf..	NAm	17595nob
1100-1200	mtwtf..	CAm	5970cri
1100-1200	mtwtf..	NAm	15170cri
1200-1300	mtwtf..	SAm	11815cri
1200-1400	mtwtf.s	NAm	15170cri
1200-1400	daily	PHL	11910xia
1200-1400	mtwtf.s	CAm	5970cri
1200-1600	......s	SAm	15125cri
1200-1800	.....ss	SAm	21700nob
1300-1400	.....ss	Eu	13720nob
1300-1700	daily	Eu	15585nob
1400-1500	......s	CAm	5970cri
1500-1600	......s	CAm	9765cri
1500-1600	......s	NAm	17850cri
1500-1700	daily	Af	15385nob
1500-1900	daily	Af	17755nob
1600-1800	.....ss	CAm	9765cri
1600-2300	.....ss	NAm	17850cri
1700-1800	.....ss	SAm	15125cri
1700-1900	daily	SAm	17715nob
1700-2200	.....ss	Eu	9665nob
1700-2300	daily	Eu	7275nob
1800-2000	daily	CAm	9765cri
1800-2000	daily	SAm	15125cri
1800-2100	.....ss	SAm	17595nob
1900-2100	......s	Af	17755nob
1900-2300	daily	NAm	9630nob
2000-2300	.....ss	CAm	9765cri
2000-2300	.....ss	SAm	15125cri
2100-2200	.....s.	SAm	17595nob
2100-2200	mtwtf..	Af	11625nob
2200-2300	.....s.	Af	11625nob

Spanish	Days	Area	kHz
2200-2300	daily	NAf	7270nob
2300-0200	daily	SAm	11945nob
2300-0400	daily	SAm	9620nob
2300-0500	daily	SAm	6125nob
2300-0500	daily	NAm	9535nob

ANN: Spanish: "Radio Exterior de España"; Arabic: "Idha'atu Isbania al-Jariyia"; English: "This is Radio Exterior de Espana, broadcasting from Madrid"; French: "Radio Extérieure d'Espagne"; German: "Hier ist der spanische Auslandssender Radio Exterior de España"

V: QSL-card.

NOTES: REE is the External Sce of the public broadcaster Radio Nacional de España.

AKHBAR MUFRIHA (Rlg)

Apartado 353, E-29080 Malaga, Spain.

Email: akhbar@akhbarmufriha.com **Web:** www.akhbarmufriha.com

L.P: SM: Andy Braio.

kHz: *12025*

Winter Schedule 2004

Arabic	Days	Area	kHz
2100-2230	daily	NAf	12025skn

V: QSL-card.

NOTES: Prgr for listeners in the Arab World, produced by IBRA Radio (Sweden) and HCJB (USA).

Broadcasters using sites in this country:

China R. Int'l uses: (NOB). See stn entry in: **CHN**, INT Section

SRI LANKA

RADIO SRI LANKA (SLBC) (Pub)

P.O. Box 574, Colombo 7, Sri Lanka.

☎ +94 11 2697491. 🖷 +94 11 2691568.

Email: chmnslbc@sltnet.lk **Web:** www.slbc.lk

Studios: Independence Square, Colombo 7, Sri Lanka.

L.P: Chmn/DG: Hudson Samarasinghe; Dir Engineering: Sanath Panawennage.

SW: [EKA] Colombo, Ekala (G.C. 07N06 079E54) 10 x 10, 3 x 35, 2 x 100, 2 x 300kW

kHz: *6005, 6010, 7300, 9770, 11775, 11905, 15745*

Winter Schedule 2004

English	Days	Area	kHz
0025-0430	daily	As	6005eka, 9770eka, 15745eka
1225-1545	daily	As	6005eka, 9770eka, 15745eka
1900-2000	.....s	Eu	6010wof
Hindi	**Days**	**Area**	**kHz**
0050-0430	daily	As	7300eka, 11905eka
1330-1530	daily	As	7300eka, 11905eka
Kannada	**Days**	**Area**	**kHz**
0800-0830	daily	As	7300eka, 11905eka
Malayalam	**Days**	**Area**	**kHz**
1000-1130	daily	As	7300eka, 11905eka
Sinhala	**Days**	**Area**	**kHz**
1600-1900	daily	ME	11775eka
Tamil	**Days**	**Area**	**kHz**
1130-1330	daily	As	7300eka, 11905eka
Telugu	**Days**	**Area**	**kHz**
0830-1000	daily	As	7300eka, 11905eka

ANN: English: "This is the Sri Lanka Broadcasting Corporation", "This is the All Asia Service of Radio Sri Lanka"

IS: Melody on drums

V: QSL-card. Rp.

NOTES: Radio Sri Lanka is the External Sce of the public-service Sri Lanka Broadcasting Corporation (SLBC).

TRANS WORLD RADIO SRI LANKA (Rlg)

P.O. Box 364, 91 Wijerama Mawatha, Colombo 7, Sri Lanka.

☎ +94 1 685235. 🖷 +94 1 685245.

L.P: Reg Dir: N. Emil Jebasingh.

MW: [PUT] Puttalam (G.C. 07N58 079E47) 882kHz 400kW

V: QSL-card.

NOTES: TWR branch and transmitting stn; for corporate headquarters see USA. Schedule see under TWR India.

DEUTSCHE WELLE RELAY STATION

Correspondence: 92/2, D.S. Senanayake Mawatha, Colombo 7, Sri Lanka

☎ +94 1 699449 Fax +94 1 699450

L.P: Resident Engineer: R. Groschkus.

MW: [TRM] Trincomalee (G.C. 08N44 081E10) 1548kHz 600kW

SW: [TRM] Trincomalee, Perkara (G.C. 08N44 081E10) 1 x 250kW, 2 x 300kW

V: QSL-card. Rpt to DW Bonn, not to relay stn.

NOTES: Schedule see under DW (Germany).

IBB RELAY STATION SRI LANKA

IBB Transmitting Station, c/o US Embassy, 210 Galle Rd., Colombo 10, Sri Lanka.

☎ +94 32 55931.

Email: gbritt@sri.ibb.gov

L.P: SM: Glenn Britt.

SW: [IRA] Iranawila (G.C. 07N32 079E30) 3 x 250, 4 x 500kW

Broadcasters using sites in this country:

BBG-AapkiDunyaa uses: (IRA). See stn entry in: **USA**, INT Section

BBG-R.Ashna uses: (IRA). See stn entry in: **USA**, INT Section

BBG-R.Farda uses: (IRA). See stn entry in: **USA**, INT Section

BBG-R.Free Afg. uses: (IRA). See stn entry in: **USA**, INT Section

BBG-R.Free Asia uses: (IRA). See stn entry in: **USA**, INT Section

BBG-RFE/RL uses: (IRA). See stn entry in: **USA**, INT Section

BBG-VOA uses: (IRA). See stn entry in: **USA**, INT Section

Deutsche Welle uses: (TRM). See stn entry in: **D**, INT Section

R.Japan uses: (EKA). See stn entry in: **J**, INT Section

TWR India uses: (PUT). See stn entry in: **IND**, INT Section

SWAZILAND

TRANS WORLD RADIO SWAZILAND (Rlg)

P.O. Box 64, Manzini, Swaziland.

☎ +268 5052781. Fax +268 5055333.

Email: jburnett@twraro.org.za **Web:** www.twrafrica.org

Correspondence: P.O. Box 4232, Kempton Park 1620, South Africa.

☎ +27 11 9742885. Fax +27 11 9749960.

Email: info@twr.org.za **Web:** www.twr.org.za

L.P: Pres: Thomas J. Lowell, Regional Dir (Africa): Rev. Stephen Boakye-Yiadom, St. Dir.: Lee Lowell; Dir. of Prgs: Rev Andrew MacDonald; Chief Eng.: Steve Stavropolous; Freq. Mgr: James Burnett.

MW: [MAN] Manzini (G.C. 26S34 031E59) 1170kHz 50kW

SW: [MAN] Manzini, Mpangela (G.C. 26S34 031E59) 4 x 25, 1 x 50, 3 x 100kW. Also leases tx's from Sentech (South Africa)

kHz: *1170, 3200, 3240, 4760, 4775, 6070, 6100, 6120, 6130, 7215, 7225, 7265, 7315, 9475, 9500, 9510, 9525, 9585, 9620, 9660, 9675, 9695, 9720, 9930, 11640, 15330*

Winter Schedule 2004

Amharic	**Days**	**Area**	**kHz**
0330-0345	....fss	EAf	7215mey
1700-1730	daily	EAf	9930mey
1730-1800	.....s.	EAf	9930mey
Bambara	**Days**	**Area**	**kHz**
1810-1840	daily	CAf	9720mey
Bemba	**Days**	**Area**	**kHz**
1700-1715	.....s.	WAf	6130man
Chewa	**Days**	**Area**	**kHz**
0400-0430	daily	CAf	6100man
0430-0500	mtwtf..	CAf	6100man
1600-1630	daily	CAf	6130man
1630-1700	daily	CAf	6130man
1700-1715	mtwtf..	CAf	6130man
Chokwe	**Days**	**Area**	**kHz**
1820-1835	daily	SAf	6130man
English	**Days**	**Area**	**kHz**
0300-0330	......s	SAf	3200man
0430-0600	mtwtf..	SAf	4775man
0430-0900	mtwtf..	SAf	6120man
0500-0800	.....ss	SAf	4775man
0500-0900	daily	CAf	9500man
0600-0605	.....ss	CAf	11640mey
0600-0635	mtwf..	CAf	11640mey
0600-0900	.....ss	SAf	6120man
1600-1630	.....ss	SAf	6070man
English	**Days**	**Area**	**kHz**
1700-2030	daily	SAf	3200man
1700-2035	daily	SAf	1170man
1730-1900	daily	EAf	9500man
Ewe	**Days**	**Area**	**kHz**
1930-1945	.....ss	CAf	9510mey
Fiote	**Days**	**Area**	**kHz**
1905-1920	....f...	SAf	6130man
French	**Days**	**Area**	**kHz**
1510-1525	.....s.	SAf	9585man
1755-1825	.....ss	CAf	9620mey
1840-1925	mtwt.ss	CAf	9720mey
1935-1950	daily	CAf	9525man
1950-2020	.....ss	CAf	9525man
1950-2020	m......	CAf	9525man
Fulfulde	**Days**	**Area**	**kHz**
1830-1900	daily	NAf,CAf	9510mey
German	**Days**	**Area**	**kHz**
0400-0430	mtwtf..	SAf	4775man, 6120man
0400-0500	.....ss	SAf	4775man, 6120man
Hadiya	**Days**	**Area**	**kHz**
1645-1700	.....ss	EAf	9930mey
Hausa	**Days**	**Area**	**kHz**
1830-1900	daily	CAf	9695mey
Igbo	**Days**	**Area**	**kHz**
1945-2000	.....s.	CAf	9510mey
1945-2015	......s	CAf	9510mey
Juba	**Days**	**Area**	**kHz**
1657-1712	.mtwtfs	EAf	9660mey
1657-1727	m.....s	EAf	9660mey
Kambaata	**Days**	**Area**	**kHz**
1645-1700	...tf..	EAf	9930mey
Kanuri	**Days**	**Area**	**kHz**
1900-1915	daily	CAf	9695mey
Kikongo	**Days**	**Area**	**kHz**
1850-1905	.twtfss	SAf	6130man
Kimbundu	**Days**	**Area**	**kHz**
1950-2005	daily	SAf	6130man
Kimwani	**Days**	**Area**	**kHz**
1747-1802	......s	EAf	9475man
1802-1817	.....s.	EAf	9475man
Kirundi	**Days**	**Area**	**kHz**
1600-1630	daily	CAf	9675mey
Lingala	**Days**	**Area**	**kHz**
1905-1935	daily	CAf	9525man
Lomwe	**Days**	**Area**	**kHz**
0340-0355	daily	SAf	4775man
1525-1555	daily	WAf	7315man
Luchazi	**Days**	**Area**	**kHz**
1905-1920	..w....	SAf	6130man
Lunyaneka	**Days**	**Area**	**kHz**
1905-1920	.....ss	SAf	6130man
Luvale	**Days**	**Area**	**kHz**
1850-1905	m......	SAf	6130man
Makua	**Days**	**Area**	**kHz**
1455-1510	.....s.	WAf	7315man
1510-1525	daily	WAf	7315man
Malagasy	**Days**	**Area**	**kHz**
1440-1510	mtwtf..	SAf	9585man
1510-1525	mtwtf.s	SAf	9585man
Moore	**Days**	**Area**	**kHz**
1910-1925	....f..	WAf	9720mey
1925-1940	mtwtf..	WAf	9720mey
Ndau	**Days**	**Area**	**kHz**
0330-0345	daily	SAf	3240man
1645-1700	daily	WAf	4760man
Ndebele	**Days**	**Area**	**kHz**
0300-0330	mtwtfs.	SAf	3200man
1600-1630	mtwtf..	SAf	6070man
Oromo	**Days**	**Area**	**kHz**
1645-1700	mtw....	EAf	9930mey
1730-1800	mtwtf.s	EAf	9930mey
Portuguese	**Days**	**Area**	**kHz**
1440-1455	.....s.	WAf	7315man
1440-1510	mtwtf.s	WAf	7315man
1630-1645	m..t.s.	WAf	4760man

Portuguese	**Days**	**Area**	**kHz**
1905-1920	mt.t...	SAf	6130man
1920-1950	daily	SAf	6130man
2005-2035	......s	SAf	6130man
Pulaar	**Days**	**Area**	**kHz**
1755-1825	mtwtf..	CAf	9620mey
Sena	**Days**	**Area**	**kHz**
1703-1718	daily	WAf	7265mey
Shangaan	**Days**	**Area**	**kHz**
1600-1630	.....ss	WAf	4760man
1630-1645	.tw.f..	WAf	4760man
Shona	**Days**	**Area**	**kHz**
0300-0330	daily	SAf	3240man
1545-1600	...fss	SAf	6070man
1630-1659	daily	SAf	6070man
Sidamo	**Days**	**Area**	**kHz**
0330-0345	..wt...	EAf	7215mey
Siswati	**Days**	**Area**	**kHz**
1600-1630	daily	SAf	1170man
Somali	**Days**	**Area**	**kHz**
1625-1655	daily	EAf	9660mey
Songhai	**Days**	**Area**	**kHz**
1840-1910	....f..	CAf	9720mey
1925-1940	.....s.	CAf	9720mey
Swahili	**Days**	**Area**	**kHz**
0300-0345	daily	EAf	7225man
1702-1717	mt.tfss	EAf	9475man
1717-1747	daily	EAf	9475man
1747-1802	.....s.	EAf	9475man
1747-1817	mtwtf..	EAf	9475man
Tshwa	**Days**	**Area**	**kHz**
1600-1630	mtwtf..	WAf	4760man
1630-1645	......s	WAf	4760man
Umbunbu	**Days**	**Area**	**kHz**
1750-1820	mtwtf..	EAf	6130man
Umbundu	**Days**	**Area**	**kHz**
1835-1850	daily	SAf	6130man
Urdu	**Days**	**Area**	**kHz**
1400-1415	daily	WAs	15330man
Yao	**Days**	**Area**	**kHz**
1718-1733	daily	WAf	7265mey
1733-1748	.t..f.s	WAf	7265mey
Yoruba	**Days**	**Area**	**kHz**
1900-1930	daily	CAf	9510mey
Zulu	**Days**	**Area**	**kHz**
1630-1700	daily	SWZ	1170man

ANN: English: "This is Trans World Radio Swaziland"
IS: Last Bar bar of "We've a story to tell the Nations" on Hand Bells
V: QSL-folder. IRC's appreciated (3 IRC's for airmail reply).
NOTES: TWR branch and transmitting stn; for corporate headquarters see USA.

SWEDEN

RADIO SWEDEN (SR INTERNATIONAL) (Pub)

SE-10510 Stockholm, Sweden.
☎ +46 8 7847288. Fax +46 8 6676283.
Email: radiosweden@sr.se **Web:** www.radiosweden.org
☎ Listeners Response: +46-8-7847238.
L.P: MD: Anne Sseruwagi; Listeners sces: Victoria Padin; Freq Mgr: Anders Backlin.
MW/SW: Uses tx's provided by Teracom
SAT: Hotbird 6, Sirius 2
kHz: *1179, 5830, 5840, 5850, 6010, 6065, 7240, 7420, 9375, 9490, 9510, 9800, 9865, 11550, 13580, 15240, 21810*

Winter Schedule 2004

Assyrian	**Days**	**Area**	**kHz**
1700-1715	.....s.	ME	7420hor
Belarusian	**Days**	**Area**	**kHz**
1800-1830	......s	Eu	5830hort
1930-2000	......s	Eu	5830hort
English	**Days**	**Area**	**kHz**
0130-0200	daily	As	11550mdc
0230-0300	daily	NAm	6010sac
0330-0400	daily	NAm	6010sac
0730-0800	......s	Eu	1179sol
1330-1400	daily	As	7420hor
1330-1400	daily	Eu	7240fle+
1330-1400	daily	ME,As	11550hor
1330-1400	daily	NAm	15240hor
1430-1500	daily	ME,As	11550hor
1430-1500	daily	NAm	15240sac
1830-1900	mtwtfs.	Eu	1179sol, 6065hor
2000-2030	mtwtfs.	Eu	1179sol
2030-2100	daily	Eu	6065hor
2030-2100	daily	Eu,ME,AUS	7420hor
2230-2300	daily	Eu	1179sol, 6065hor
2330-2400	daily	NAm	9800sac+
Estonian	**Days**	**Area**	**kHz**
1800-1830	.....s.	EEu	6065hor
German	**Days**	**Area**	**kHz**
0700-0730	......s	Eu	1179sol
1300-1330	daily	Eu	7240fle+
1730-1800	daily	Eu	1179sol
1800-1830	mtwtfs.	Eu	6065hor
1930-2000	mtwtfs.	Eu	1179sol, 6065hor
1930-2030	......s	Eu	1179sol, 6065hor
Kurdish	**Days**	**Area**	**kHz**
1730-1745	......s	ME	7420hor
1730-1800	m......	ME	7420hor
Latvian	**Days**	**Area**	**kHz**
1630-1645	mtwtf..	EEu	5850hor
1715-1730	mtwtf..	EEu	1179sol, 6065hor
Romany	**Days**	**Area**	**kHz**
1700-1730	......s	Eu,ME	1179sol, 7420hor
1930-2000	.....s.	Eu	5840hor
Russian	**Days**	**Area**	**kHz**
1400-1430	daily	EEu	9865hor
1500-1530	daily	EEu	5850hor
1500-1530	mtwtfs.	EEu	1179sol
1800-1830	daily	EEu	5830hor
1930-2000	daily	EEu	5830hor
2000-2030	mtwtfs.	EEu	6065hor
2030-2100	daily	EEu	1179sol
Swedish	**Days**	**Area**	**kHz**
0000-0030	daily	SAm	9490sac
0100-0130	daily	As	11550mdc
0100-0130	daily	SAm	9490sac
0200-0230	daily	NAm	6010sac
0300-0330	daily	NAm	6010sac
0430-0600	mtwtf..	Af,ME	9490sac*
0455-0700	......s	Eu	1179sol*
0455-0700	mtwtf..	Eu	1179sol*
0455-0900	.....s.	Eu	1179sol*
0500-0700	mtwtf..	Eu	6065hor*
0555-0800	mtwtf..	Eu,Af,ME	9490hor*
0700-0900	.....s.	Eu	1179sol**
0700-0900	.....s.	Eu,Af,ME	6065hor**, 9490hor**
0800-1000	......s	Eu,Af,ME	6065hor*, 9490hor*
1100-1110	mtwtf..	As,NZL	7420hor**
1100-1110	mtwtf..	Eu,Af,ME	9490hor**
1100-1130	.....ss	As,NZL	7420hor
1100-1130	.....ss	Eu,Af,ME	9490hor
1130-1140	mtwtf..	Af,ME	21810hor**
1130-1140	mtwtf..	As	11550hor**
1130-1140	mtwtf..	SAm,NZL,AUS	9490bon**
1130-1200	.....ss	Af,ME	21810hor
1130-1200	.....ss	As	11550hor
1130-1200	.....ss	SAm,NZL,AUS	9490bon
1200-1210	mtwtf..	NAm	15240hor**
1200-1230	.....ss	NAm	15240hor
1300-1315	mtwtf..	As,NZL	7420hor
1300-1315	mtwtf..	NAm	15240hor
1300-1330	.....ss	As,NZL	7420hor
1300-1330	.....ss	NAm	15240hor
1315-1330	mtwtf..	As,AUS	11550hor
1315-1330	mtwtf..	NAm	15240hor
1400-1415	mtwtf..	As,AUS	11550hor
1400-1415	mtwtf..	NAm	15240sac
1400-1430	.....ss	As,AUS	11550hor
1400-1430	.....ss	NAm	15240sac
1415-1430	mtwtf..	NAm	15240sac

Swedish	Days	Area	kHz
1415-1430	mtwtf..	As,NZL	7420hor
1500-1530	daily	ME,As	11550hor
1500-1530	daily	NAm	15240hor
1545-1600	daily	NAm	15240hor*
1545-1715	mtwtfs.	Eu	1179sol*, 6065hor*
1545-1730	......s	Eu	1179sol*, 6065hor*
1600-1630	daily	Eu,ME	5850hor
1645-1700	.....ss	Eu,Af,SAm	13580hor*
1645-1700	.....ss	Eu	1179sol*
1645-1700	.....ss	Eu,Af,ME	7420hor*
1645-1715	mtwtf..	Eu,Af,SAm	13580hor*
1645-1715	mtwtf..	Eu	1179sol*
1645-1715	mtwtf..	Eu,Af,ME	7420hor*
1730-1800	daily	Eu	6065hor
1800-1900	......s	Eu	1179sol****, 6065hor****
1900-1930	daily	Eu	1179sol, 6065hor
1900-1930	daily	Eu,Af	9375hor
1900-1930	daily	ME	7420hor
2000-2030	daily	Eu,ME,AUS	7420hor
2100-2200	daily	Eu	1179sol***, 6065hor***
2100-2200	daily	Eu,Af,SAm	9510hor***
2200-2230	daily	Eu	1179sol, 6065hor
2300-2330	daily	Eu	1179sol

ANN: English: "This is Radio Sweden"; German: "Hier ist Radio Schweden, Stockholm"; Swedish: "Här är Radio Sweden, Stockholm"; Russian: "Govorit Stokgolm"
IS: "To the Wide, Wide World" (electronic music composed by Ralph Lundsten)
V: QSL-card. Cassettes not accepted.
NOTES: External Sce of the public broadcaster Sveriges Radio (SR). External Sce of the public broadcaster Sveriges Radio (SR). Most of the Swedish language transmissions are relays of SR Home Sce prgr's. Key: * P1; ** P4; *** P1/P3; **** P4 Sport; + DRM; † Every second Sunday (replaces Russian language broadcast).

IBRA RADIO (Rlg)

SE-14199 Stockholm, Sweden.
☎ +46 8 6089600. Fax +46 8 6089650.
Email: ibra@ibra.se **Web:** www.ibra.org
kHz: *7340, 9520, 9610, 9660*

Winter Schedule 2004

Arabic	Days	Area	kHz
2000-2100	daily	NAf	7340jul
Bambara	**Days**	**Area**	**kHz**
2000-2015	mt.....	WAf	9610jul
English	**Days**	**Area**	**kHz**
1830-1845	daily	EAf	9520jul
Hausa	**Days**	**Area**	**kHz**
1915-1930	mtwt..s	WAf	9610jul
Joula	**Days**	**Area**	**kHz**
1945-2000	....fss	WAf	9610jul
Malinke	**Days**	**Area**	**kHz**
1930-1945	....fs.	WAf	9610jul
Moore	**Days**	**Area**	**kHz**
1930-1945	mt....s	WAf	9610jul
Somali	**Days**	**Area**	**kHz**
1730-1800	daily	EAf	9660jul
Songhai	**Days**	**Area**	**kHz**
1930-2000	..wt...	WAf	9610jul
Swahili	**Days**	**Area**	**kHz**
1730-1845	daily	EAf	9520jul
Tamajeq	**Days**	**Area**	**kHz**
1915-1930	....fs.	WAf	9610jul
Wolof	**Days**	**Area**	**kHz**
2000-2015	.....ss	WAf	9610jul
Zarma	**Days**	**Area**	**kHz**
2000-2015	..wtf..	WAf	9610jul

V: QSL-card.
NOTES: IBRA Radio is the radio ministry of the Swedish Pentecostal Movement (Pingstkyrkan), established 1955. See also Radio Ibrahim (Cyprus) and Radyo Kumru (Sweden).

RADYO KUMRU (Rlg)

Herrhagsvägen 291, SE-79176 Falun, Sweden.
☎ +46 23 17620.
Email: lidya@radiokumru.com **Web:** www.radyokumru.com
kHz: *1170*

Winter Schedule 2004

Turkish	Days	Area	kHz
1900-1930	daily	TUR	1170arm

NOTES: Radyo Kumru is a prgr for Turkish listeners produced by IBRA Radio.

TERACOM (Tx Operator)

P.O. Box 1366, SE-17227 Sundbyberg, Sweden.
☎ +46 8 55542000. Fax +46 8 55542001.
Email: info@teracom.se **Web:** www.teracom.se
MW: [SOL] Sölvesborg (G.C. 55N59 014E40) 1179kHz 600kW
SW: [HOR] Hörby (G.C. 55N49N 013E44) 3 x 500kW
NOTES: Teracom is the national Swedish transmitter network operator, providing the SW facilities for Radio Sweden.
Broadcasters using sites in this country:
RCI uses: (HOR). See stn entry in: **CAN**, INT Section
RNWO uses: (HOR). See stn entry in: **HOL**, INT Section

SWITZERLAND

RADIO FREUNDES–DIENST (Rlg)

Missionswerk Freundes-Dienst, CH-5023 Biberstein, Switzerland.
☎ +41 62 8272727. Fax +41 62 8273440.
Email: info@freundesdienst.org **Web:** www.freundesdienst.org
kHz: *603, 1215, 1323, 1440, 6145, 7300*

Winter Schedule 2004

German	Days	Area	kHz
0445-0500	mtwtf..	Eu	1440mrn
1830-1845	mtw.fss	Eu	1440mrn
1925-1930	.t....s	Eu	603bln, 1215klg, 1323wbr, 6145msk, 7300arm

V: QSL-card.

RADIO RÉVEIL (Rlg)

Les Chapons 4, CH-2022 Bevaix, Switzerland.
☎ +41 32 8461655. Fax +41 32 8462547.
Email: contact@paroles.ch **Web:** www.paroles.ch
kHz: *11840*

Winter Schedule 2004

French	Days	Area	kHz
1830-1900	...t...	CAf	11840jul

ANN: French: "Radio Réveil Paroles de Vie"
V: QSL-letter.

DIGITAL RADIO MONDIALE CONSORTIUM (DRM)

DRM Project Office, P.O. Box 360, CH-1218 Grand-Saconnex, Genève, Switzerland.
☎ +41 2 27172718. Fax +41 2 27172718.
Email: projectoffice@drm.org **Web:** www.drm.org
L.P: Project administrator: Anne Fechner.
NOTES: The DRM consortium, formed in 1998 and consisting of broadcasters and manufacturers, is aiming at developing and promoting digital radio in the broadcasting bands below 30 MHz.

ICRC RADIO

Red Cross Broadcasting Service, 19 Ave de la Paix, CH-1202 Genève, Switzerland.
☎ + 41 22 7346001. Fax +41 22 7332057.
Web: www.icrc.org
ANN: English: "This is Geneva, the Red Cross Broadcasting Service"
V: QSL-card.
NOTES: ICRC Radio transmissions are organized by the International Red Cross during emergency situations in the world, aired via leased tx's.

SYRIA

RADIO DAMASCUS (Gov)

P.O. Box 4702, Damascus, Syria.
☎ +963 11 720700. Fax +963 11 2234336.
Email: radio@rtv.gov.sy **Web:** www.rtv.gov.sy
L.P: GD: Khudr Omran; Dir Eng: M.Bara; Dir Public Rel: Mrs. Awafet Haffar; Dir Admin & Finance: Zuheir Breidi.

MW: [AHA] Al Hassake (G.C. 36N28 040E45) 1125kHz 200kW; [TAR] Tartus (G.C. 34N50 035E50) 783kHz 600kW
SW: [ADR] Adra (G.C. 33N27 036E30) 4 x 500kW
SAT: Hotbird 3
kHz: *783, 1125, 12085, 13610*

Winter Schedule 2004

Arabic	**Days**	**Area**	**kHz**
1100-1400	daily	NAf,ME	12085adr*, 13610adr
2205-2320	daily	NAf,SAm	12085adr*13610adr
English	**Days**	**Area**	**kHz**
2005-2205	daily	Eu, NAm,Oc	12085adr*, 13610adr
French	**Days**	**Area**	**kHz**
1905-2005	daily	Eu, NAm	12085adr*, 13610adr
German	**Days**	**Area**	**kHz**
1805-1905	daily	Eu	12085adr*, 13610adr
Hebrew	**Days**	**Area**	**kHz**
1600-1830	daily	ME	783tar, 1125aha
Russian	**Days**	**Area**	**kHz**
1700-1805	daily	Eu	13610adr
1830-1900	daily	Eu	783tar, 1125aha
Spanish	**Days**	**Area**	**kHz**
2320-0030	daily	SAm	12085adr*, 13610adr
Turkish	**Days**	**Area**	**kHz**
1600-1700	daily	ME	12085adr*, 13610adr

ANN: Arabic: "Idha'atu-l-jumhuriyati-l'arabiyya as-suriyya min dimashq"; English: "You are listening to Radio Damascus, the External Service of the Syrian Broadcasting System"; French: "Ici Damas"; Hebrew: "Kol Damasek"
IS: Guitar
V: QSL-card.
NOTES: Radio Damascus is the External Sce of the state broadcaster Organisme de la Radio-TV Arabe Syrienne (ORTAS). Key: * Irregular.

TAIWAN (Rep. of China)

BROADCASTING CORPORATION OF CHINA (BCC)

✉ 375 Sungchian Rd., Chungshan Ward, Taipei 104, Taiwan.
☎ +886 2 25019688. 🖷 +886 2 25018834.
Email: pr@bcc.com.tw **Web:** www.bcc.com.tw
MW: [CHG] Changchih (G.C. 22N39 120E30) 927/1521kHz 1200kW; [FAN] Fangliao (G.C. 22N22 120E36) 585kHz 1200kW, 1503kHz 600kW; [KOU] Kouhu (G.C. 23N35 120E10) 1098/1557kHz 300kW; [LUK] Lukang (G.C. 24N03 120E24) 603kHz 1000kW, 1008kHz 300kW; [MIN] Minhsiung (G.C. 23N29 120E27) 747kHz 250kW, 1206/1422kHz 100kW
SW: [HUW] Huwei (G.C. 23N43 120E25) 4 x 100, 1 x 300kW; [KOU] Kouhu (G.C. 23N35 120E10) 3 x 100kW; [MIN] Minhsiung (G.C. 23N29 120E27) 1 x 50kW; [PAO] Paochung (G.C 23N43 120E18) 5 x 100kW; [TAI] Taipei, Pali (G.C. 25N05 121E27) 5 x 100kW; [TNN] Tainan (G.C 23N11 120E38) 4 x 250kW; [TSH] Tamsui (G.C. 25N13 121E29) 3 x 300kW
V: QSL-card. Rec. acc.
NOTES: Joint Stock Company: 96.95% of the shares belong to the Hua-Hsia Investment Holding Co., owned by Taiwan's Nationalist Party (KMT). In accordance with changes in the broadcasting law, KMT is obliged to sell all stakes to BCC until Dec 2006. Transmissions to Asia are jammed in parts of the target area; some frequencies may change temporarily due to interference.

RADIO TAIWAN INTERNATIONAL (RTI)

✉ 55 Pei'an Road, Tachih, Taipei 104, Taiwan.
☎ +886 2 28856168. 🖷 +886 2 28867088.
Email: rti@rti.org.tw **Web:** www.rti.org.tw
L.P: Chairman: Feng-jenq Lin.
MW/SW: See Broadcasting Corp. of China.
kHz: *603, 747, 927, 1008, 1098, 1206, 1422, 1503, 1521, 1557, 3955, 3965, 5810, 5820, 5950, 6085, 6105, 6120, 6145, 6150, 6170, 7105, 7130, 7135, 7185, 7270, 7315, 9355, 9415, 9465, 9495, 9565, 9610, 9635, 9660, 9680, 9690, 9780, 9790, 11605, 11635, 11640, 11650, 11665, 11680, 11710, 11715, 11720, 11725, 11740, 11755, 11760, 11780, 11795, 11815, 11825, 11875, 11885, 11890, 11915, 11935, 11940, 11985, 15130, 15175, 15215, 15245, 15265, 15270, 15290, 15320, 15395, 15430, 15440, 15465, 15525, 15580, 15610, 17845*

Winter Schedule 2004

Arabic	**Days**	**Area**	**kHz**
1600-1700	daily	ME	11890tnn
1800-1900	daily	ME	11890tnn
Burmese	**Days**	**Area**	**kHz**
1130-1300	daily	SEA	11680pao
1500-1600	daily	SEA	9465huw
Cantonese	**Days**	**Area**	**kHz**
0100-0200	daily	NAm	5950yfr, 15440yfr
0100-0200	daily	SEA	15290tnn
0200-0300	daily	SEA	15610pao
0500-0600	daily	NAm	5950yfr, 9680yfr
0500-0600	daily	SEA	15320pao
1000-1100	daily	SEA	11635pao, 15525pao
1000-1100	daily	Oc	11715tnn
1000-1200	daily	SEA	15270pao
1100-1300	daily	CHN	1206min
1200-1400	daily	CHN	6105kou
1200-1400	daily	SEA	11915tnn
2200-2300	daily	Eu	5820yfr
English	**Days**	**Area**	**kHz**
0200-0300	daily	EAs	15465pao
0200-0300	daily	SEA	11875tnn
0200-0300	daily	NAm	5950yfr, 9680yfr
0300-0400	daily	NAm	5950yfr
0300-0400	daily	SAm	15215yfr
0300-0400	daily	SEA	15320pao
0700-0800	daily	NAm	5950yfr
0800-0900	daily	SEA	9610tnn
1100-1200	daily	SEA	7105pao
1200-1300	daily	EAs	7130min
1400-1500	daily	SEA	15265tnn
1600-1700	daily	CHN, SAs	11815pao
1800-1900	daily	Eu	3965iss
2200-2300	daily	Eu	9355yfr
French	**Days**	**Area**	**kHz**
0700-0800	daily	Eu	5810yfr
1900-2000	daily	Eu	3955skn
2000-2100	daily	Eu	9635tnn, 11665yfr
2000-2100	daily	NAm	15440yfr
2200-2300	daily	Af	7315iss
German	**Days**	**Area**	**kHz**
0600-0700	daily	Eu	5810yfr
1800-1900	daily	Eu	9565tai
1900-2000	daily	Eu	6170skn
2100-2200	daily	Eu	11665yfr
Hakka	**Days**	**Area**	**kHz**
0000-0100	daily	NAm	5950yfr
0200-0300	daily	NAm	15440yfr
0300-0400	daily	SEA	15610pao
0900-1000	daily	SEA	15465pao
1000-1200	daily	CHN	6105kou
1100-1200	daily	SEA	11635pao, 15465pao
1300-1400	daily	SEA	15175huw
1400-1500	daily	SEA	11915tnn
1700-1800	daily	SEA	11875tnn
Hokkien (Amoy)	**Days**	**Area**	**kHz**
0000-0100	daily	NAm	15440yfr
0000-0200	daily	SEA	11875tnn
0500-0700	daily	SEA	15580pao
0500-0700	daily	CHN	1008luk
0500-0900	daily	CHN	1422min
0700-1100	daily	SEA	1206min
1000-1100	daily	EAs	11605tnn
1000-1100	daily	SEA	15465pao
1200-1300	daily	SEA	11715tnn
1300-1400	daily	SEA	11635pao, 15465pao
2100-2200	daily	NAm	15130yfr
Indonesian	**Days**	**Area**	**kHz**
1000-1200	daily	SEA	11725pao, 11940tsh
1200-1300	daily	SEA	7105pao, 11635pao
1400-1500	daily	SEA	11875tnn
Japanese	**Days**	**Area**	**kHz**
0800-0900	daily	EAs	11605tnn
1100-1200	daily	EAs	7130min, 11605tnn
1300-1400	daily	EAs	7130min, 11605tnn
Korean	**Days**	**Area**	**kHz**
0300-0330	daily	EAs	15465pao
1200-1230	daily	EAs	9415huw
1400-1430	daily	EAs	9415huw

Mandarin	Days	Area	kHz
0000-0200	daily	CHN	11640kou
0100-0200	daily	SAm	11825yfr, 15215yfr
0100-0500	daily	CHN	11940huw
0200-0500	daily	SEA	15290tnn
0300-0500	daily	CHN	1008luk, 15215huw
0300-0800	daily	CHN	1557kou
0400-0500	daily	NAm	5950yfr, 9680yfr
0400-0500	daily	SEA	15320huw
0400-0600	daily	SEA	15270pao
0400-0600	daily	CHN	11640kou, 11985huw, 15430huw
0400-1000	.....ss	CHN	603luk
0500-0600	daily	CAm	9495yfr
0500-0800	.....ss	CHN	15215huw
0600-0900	.....ss	CHN	11985huw, 15430huw
0600-1000	.....ss	CHN	11640kou
0600-1000	daily	CHN	11795huw
0700-0900	.....ss	CHN	1008luk
0900-1000	daily	SEA	11605tnn, 11635pao, 11940pao, 15525pao
0900-1000	daily	Oc	11715tnn
0900-1000	.....ss	CHN	6085tnn, 7185kou, 11665kou
0900-1100	daily	CHN	9415pao
0900-1300	daily	CHN	15395huw
0900-1400	daily	CHN	7270tsh
0900-1500	daily	CHN	1422min
0900-1700	daily	CHN	1008luk, 9780huw
1000-1100	daily	CHN	747min, 927chg
1000-1400	daily	CHN	11640kou
1000-1500	daily	CHN	6085tnn
1000-1600	daily	CHN	603luk
1000-1700	daily	CHN	7185kou, 11665tnn
1100-1200	daily	Oc	11715tnn
1100-1200	mtw.fss	CHN	747min, 927chg
1100-1400	daily	CHN	11875tnn
1100-1700	daily	CHN	11780huw
1200-1300	daily	EAs	11605tnn
1200-1300	daily	SEA	15465pao
1200-1700	daily	CHN	1521chg
1300-1400	daily	SEA	15265tnn
1300-1500	daily	CHN	927chg
1300-1500	daily	SEA	7105pao
1300-1700	daily	CHN	1098kou
1400-1700	daily	CHN	9680huw
1400-1800	daily	CHN	6145kou, 7130min
1900-2000	daily	Eu	9565tai, 11760yfr
2200-0300	daily	CHN	11710huw
2200-2300	daily	Eu	3965iss
2200-2400	daily	NAm	5950yfr, 15440yfr
2200-2400	daily	SEA	11635pao
2200-2400	daily	CHN	603luk, 1008luk
2300-0200	daily	CHN	11885huw, 15245huw
2300-0300	daily	CHN	9660huw
2300-0500	daily	CHN	1422min
2300-2400	daily	SEA	9790kou
2300-2400	daily	CHN	747min, 1206min, 6150kou

Mongolian	Days	Area	kHz
1000-1100	daily	CHN, MNG	11985huw

Russian	Days	Area	kHz
1100-1200	daily	RUS	11985huw
1300-1400	daily	RUS	11935tnn
1700-1800	daily	RUS	7135iss

Spanish	Days	Area	kHz
0200-0300	daily	SAm	15215yfr, 17845yfr
0400-0500	daily	NAm	11740yfr
0600-0700	daily	NAm	5950yfr
2000-2100	daily	Eu	6120jul
2300-2400	daily	SAm	9690yfr, 11720yfr

Thai	Days	Area	kHz
0600-0700	daily	SEA	15270pao
1400-1500	daily	SEA	11635pao, 15465pao
1500-1600	daily	SEA	1503fan, 11650kou
2200-2300	daily	SEA	1503fan
2200-2400	daily	SEA	11755pao

Tibetan	Days	Area	kHz
1300-1400	daily	CHN	9415huw

Vietnamese	Days	Area	kHz
0900-1000	daily	SEA	15270pao
1500-1600	daily	SEA	11915tnn
2200-2300	daily	SEA	9790tnn

ANN: English: "This is Radio Taiwan International"; Indonesian: "Inilah Radio Taiwan Internasional"; Japanese: "Kochirawa Taiwan Kokusai Hoso, CBS, Chukaminkoku Chuohosokyoku no nihongobangumi desu"; Korean: "Yeogineun Junghwa Minguk Taipei, RTI hangugeo bangsong, Taiwanui sorimnida"; Mandarin: "Cheli shih CBS, Taipei Kuochi chih sheng"
NOTES: Formed in 1996 when the Broadcasting System of the Ministry of Defense was joined with the international section of the Broadcasting Corporation of China.

VOICE OF KUANGHUA (KUANGHUA SHENG)

Contact info see National Radio section, Han Sheng radio station.
SW: [KUA] Kuanyin (G.C. 25N02 121E09) 1 x 100kW
ANN: Mandarin: "Zhin zha Han sheng guan bo tien tai, Kuang hua zhi sheng"
NOTES: The Voice of Kuanghua is the mainland channel of Han Sheng (Voice of Han), a national radio network operated by Tang-Yun Broadcasting Inc. (linked with the Department of Defense).

Broadcasters using sites in this country:
AWR uses: (TAI). See stn entry in: **USA**, INT Section
BBC World Sce uses: (TAI). See stn entry in: **G**, INT Section
Family Radio uses: (TAI). See stn entry in: **USA**, INT Section
Family Radio uses: (KOU). See stn entry in: **USA**, INT Section
Hmong Lao Radio uses: (TAI). See stn entry in: **LAO**, CTB Section
R.Australia uses: (TAI). See stn entry in: **AUS**, INT Section
RFI uses: (MIN). See stn entry in: **F**, INT Section
RFI uses: (KOU). See stn entry in: **F**, INT Section
Sound of Hope uses: (TAI). See stn entry in: **USA**, INT Section
VO China uses: (TAI). See stn entry in: **CHN**, CTB Section

TAJIKISTAN

RADIO TAJIKISTAN (Gov)

Chapayev Street 31, 734025 Dushanbe, Tajikistan.
☎ +992 372 277417. 🖷 +992 372 211198.
Web: radio.tojikiston.com
MW/SW: Leased from Teleradiokom
kHz: *1143, 7245*

Winter Schedule 2004

Arabic	Days	Area	kHz
0400-0415	daily	ME	1143dsb, 7245dsb
1700-1715	daily	ME	1143dsb, 7245dsb

Dari	Days	Area	kHz
0100-0200	daily	WAs	1143dsb, 7245dsb
0300-0345	daily	WAs	1143dsb, 7245dsb
1400-1500	daily	WAs	1143dsb, 7245dsb
1600-1645	daily	WAs	1143dsb, 7245dsb

English	Days	Area	kHz
0345-0400	daily	WAs, ME	1143dsb, 7245dsb
1645-1700	daily	WAs, ME	1143dsb, 7245dsb

Farsi	Days	Area	kHz
0200-0300	daily	ME	1143dsb, 7245dsb
0415-0500	daily	ME	1143dsb, 7245dsb
1500-1600	daily	ME	1143dsb, 7245dsb
1715-1800	daily	ME	1143dsb, 7245dsb

ANN: English: "This Radio Tajikistan World Service, the Republic of Tajikistan"; Dari: "In ja Radyoi Tojikiston, Jumhuriye Tojikiston"; Tajik: "Injo Radioi Tojikiston, Jumhurii Tojikiston"
V: QSL-letter.
NOTES: Radio Tajikistan is the External Sce of the State Committee for TV and Radio Broadcasting.

TELERADIOKOM (Tx Operator)

Internatsionalnaya Street 85, 734001 Dushanbe, Tajikistan.
☎ +992 372 212517. 🖷 +992 372 210912.
L.P: GD: R.M. Masharifov.
MW: [DSB] Dushanbe, Yangiyul (G.C. 38N29 068E48) 1143kHz 150kW, 1251kHz 100kW; [ORZ] Orzu (G.C. 37N32 068E42) 648/801kHz 1000kW, 972/1161kHz 500kW
SW: [DSB] Dushanbe, Yangiyul (G.C. 38N29 068E48) 1 x 50, 5 x 100kW; [ORZ] Orzu (G.C 37N32 068E42) 2 x 1000kW

NOTES: Teleradiokom, a subsidiary of the Telecommunications Ministry, is the national transmitter network owner. Leases out its facilities to national and international broadcasters. In the seasonal coordinated schedules distributed by the HFCC, the transmissions from Dushanbe and Orzu are listed under the code "DB".
Broadcasters using sites in this country:
BBC World Sce uses: (DSB). See stn entry in: **G**, INT Section
BBG-AapkiDunyaa uses: (ORZ). See stn entry in: **USA**, INT Section
BBG-R.Farda uses: (DSB). See stn entry in: **USA**, INT Section
BBG-R.Free Asia uses: (DSB). See stn entry in: **USA**, INT Section
BBG-RFE/RL uses: (DSB). See stn entry in: **USA**, INT Section
BBG-VOA uses: (ORZ). See stn entry in: **USA**, INT Section
R.Santec uses: (ORZ). See stn entry in: **D**, INT Section
VO Russia (VOR) uses: (DSB). See stn entry in: **RUS**, INT Section
VO Russia (VOR) uses: (ORZ). See stn entry in: **RUS**, INT Section
VOR-RKS uses: (DSB). See stn entry in: **RUS**, INT Section
VOR-RKS uses: (ORZ). See stn entry in: **RUS**, INT Section
VOR-RMR uses: (DSB). See stn entry in: **RUS**, INT Section
VOR-RMR uses: (ORZ). See stn entry in: **RUS**, INT Section

THAILAND

RADIO SARANROM (Gov)

✉ Sri Ayudhya Road, Bangkok 10400, Thailand.
☎ +66 28435095. 🖷 +66 26435093.
Web: back.to/rs
L.P: Dir Broadcasting Div: Narumit Hinshiranan.
MW: Uses facilities provided by IBB
kHz: *1575*

Winter Schedule 2004

Thai	Days	Area	kHz
1030-1100	daily	SEA	1575bph
1100-1130	mtwtf..	SEA	1575bph
1200-1230	mtwtf..	SEA	1575bph
1500-1530	mtwtf..	SEA	1575bph
2230-2400	mtwt..s	SEA	1575bph

V: QSL-card.
NOTES: Service for Thai's living in South East Asia, funded by the Ministry of Foreign Affairs.

RADIO THAILAND (Gov)

✉ 236, Vibhavadi Rangsit Road, Ding Daeng, Bangkok 10400, Thailand.
☎ +66 2 2770943. 🖷 +66 2 2774022.
Email: amporns@mozart.inet.co.th **Web:** www.prd.go.th
L.P: Head of External Sce: Mrs. Amporn Samosorn.
SW: [BAN] Bangkok, Pathum Thani (G.C. 14N01 100E31) 3 x 10, 1 x 50, 1 x 100kW. Most freq's via tx's provided by IBB.
kHz: *5890, 6040, 6070, 7115, 7160, 7285, 7305, 9535, 9680, 9725, 9810, 9840, 11805, 11855, 13780*

Winter Schedule 2004

Burmese	Days	Area	kHz
1145-1200	daily	SEA	6040udo, 6070ban, 7115ban
English	**Days**	**Area**	**kHz**
0000-0030	daily	EAf	9680udo
0030-0100	daily	NAm,Car	5890grv
0300-0330	daily	NAm	5890dln
0530-0600	daily	Eu	13780udo
1230-1300	daily	SEA,Pac	9810udo
1400-1430	daily	SEA,Pac	9725udo
1900-2000	daily	Eu	9840udo
2030-2045	daily	Eu	9535udo
French	**Days**	**Area**	**kHz**
2015-2030	daily	Eu	9535udo
German	**Days**	**Area**	**kHz**
2000-2015	daily	Eu	9535udo
Indonesian	**Days**	**Area**	**kHz**
1215-1230	daily	SEA	6070ban, 7115ban, 11805udo
Japanese	**Days**	**Area**	**kHz**
1300-1315	daily	FE	7160udo
Khmer	**Days**	**Area**	**kHz**
1115-1130	daily	SEA	6070ban, 7115ban, 7305udo
Lao	**Days**	**Area**	**kHz**
1130-1145	daily	SEA	6040udo, 6070ban, 7115ban
Malay	**Days**	**Area**	**kHz**
1200-1215	daily	SEA	6070ban, 7115ban, 11805udo
Mandarin	**Days**	**Area**	**kHz**
1315-1330	daily	FE	7160udo
Thai	**Days**	**Area**	**kHz**
0100-0200	daily	NAm	5890grv
0330-0430	daily	NAm	5890dln
1000-1100	daily	SEA	7285udo
1330-1400	daily	SEA	7160udo
1800-1900	daily	ME	11855udo
2045-2115	daily	Eu	9535udo
Vietnamese	**Days**	**Area**	**kHz**
1100-1115	daily	SEA	6070ban, 7115ban, 7305udo

ANN: English: "This is HSK9, Radio Thailand World Service broadcasting from Bangkok"
IS: Gong
V: QSL-card.
NOTES: Radio Thailand (World Service) is the External Sce of the Thai Government's Public Relations Department.

BBC ASIA RELAY STATION

✉ P.O. Box 20, Muang, Nakhon Sawan, 60000, Thailand.
☎ +66 56227275. 🖷 +66 56227277.
SW: [NAK] Nakhon Sawan (G.C. 15N49 100E04) 4 x 250kW
V: QSL-card for direct rpt.
NOTES: Owned by the BBC and operated by VT Merlin Communications (see UK). Carries relays of BBC and other international broadcasters.

IBB RELAY STATION THAILAND (BANGKOK)

✉ IBB Transmitting Station, Rangsit-Bangpoon Road, Bangkok, Thailand.
☎ +66 25815191.
MW: [BHP] Ban Phachi, Rasom (G.C. 14N24 100E47) 1575kHz 1000kW

IBB RELAY STATION THAILAND (UDON THANI)

✉ IBB Transmitting Station Udon Thani, c/o US Embassy Thailand - IBB Box UD APOAP 96546, USA.
SW: [UDO] Udon Thani, Ban Dung (G.C. 17N25 102E48) 7 x 500kW
Broadcasters using sites in this country:
BBC World Sce uses: (NAK). See stn entry in: **G**, INT Section
BBG-AapkiDunyaa uses: (UDO). See stn entry in: **USA**, INT Section
BBG-R.Ashna uses: (UDO). See stn entry in: **USA**, INT Section
BBG-R.Farda uses: (UDO). See stn entry in: **USA**, INT Section
BBG-R.Free Afg. uses: (UDO). See stn entry in: **USA**, INT Section
BBG-RFE/RL uses: (UDO). See stn entry in: **USA**, INT Section
BBG-VOA uses: (UDO). See stn entry in: **USA**, INT Section
BBG-VOA uses: (BPH). See stn entry in: **USA**, INT Section
VOIRI uses: (BAN). See stn entry in: **IRN**, INT Section

TUNISIA

RADIO–TÉLÉVISION TUNISIENNE (ERTT) (Gov)

✉ 71, ave. de la Liberté, Tunis 1002, Tunisia.
☎ +216 1 287300. 🖷 +216 1 785146.
Email: info@radiotunis.com **Web:** www.radiotunis.com
L.P: DG Radio: Kamel Omranc; Tech Dir: Said Aljane.
MW: [TUN] Tunis (G.C. 36N48 010E10) 963kHz 200kW
SW: [SFA] Sfax, Sidi Mansour (G.C. 34N48 010E53) 3 x 100, 2 x 500kW
SAT: Arabsat 2D/3A, Eutelsat W2, Hotbird 3, Intelsat Americas 5
kHz: *963, 7190, 7225, 7275, 9720, 11730, 11950, 12005, 15450, 17735*

Winter Schedule 2004

Arabic	Days	Area	kHz
0200-0500	daily	NAf,ME	9720sfa, 12005sfa
0400-0700	daily	NAf	7190sfa
0400-0700	daily	Eu	7275sfa
1200-1600	daily	NAf,ME	15450sfa, 17735sfa
1400-1700	daily	NAf	11950sfa
1400-1700	daily	Eu	11730sfa
1600-2100	daily	NAf,ME	9720sfa, 12005sfa
1600-2400	daily	Eu	7225sfa
1700-2400	daily	NAf	7190sfa

English	Days	Area	kHz
1915-1930	daily	NAf,Eu	963tun

French	Days	Area	kHz
0500-1900	daily	NAf,Eu	963tun
2000-0100	daily	NAf,Eu	963tun

German	Days	Area	kHz
1900-1915	daily	NAf,Eu	963tun

Italian	Days	Area	kHz
1945-2000	daily	NAf,Eu	963tun

Spanish	Days	Area	kHz
1930-1945	daily	NAf,Eu	963tun

ANN: Arabic: "Idha'atu-l-gumhuriya at-tunisiyya"
V: QSL-card. Rpt in Arabic or French to L'Office National de la Télédiffusion (ONT), Cité Ennassim I - Bourjel, BP 399, Tunis 1080, Tunisia. Email: ont@ati.tn.
NOTES: The SW programmes are relays of Home Sce channels.

TURKEY

VOICE OF TURKEY (Pub)

P.O. Box 333, Yenisehir, Ankara 06443, Turkey.
☎ +90 312 4909842. Fax +90 312 4909846.
Email: genel.sekreterlik@trt.net.tr **Web:** www.trt.net.tr
Studios: TRT/Oran Sitesi A Blok No: 427, Ankara 06109, Turkey.
L.P: Head of Foreign Sces: Oktay Samiloglu; International Tech Rel: Elif Soyata Arslan.
SW: [CAK] Çakirlar (G.C. 39N58 032E40) 3 x 250, 2 x 500kW; [EMR] Emirler (G.C. 39N29 032E51) 5 x 500kW
SAT: Eutelsat Sesat, Hotbird 6, Intelsat 907, Optus A3/C1, Pas 8, Telstar 5, Thaicom 3, Türksat 1C
kHz: *5955, 5965, 5980, 6020, 6050, 6055, 6095, 6110, 6120, 6135, 6185, 7115, 7140, 7155, 7205, 7240, 7275, 7295, 7300, 9510, 9525, 9560, 9595, 9625, 9780, 9840, 11690, 11705, 11795, 11835, 11895, 11910, 11925, 11955, 11980, 15105, 15155, 15160, 15195, 15225, 15245, 15320, 17690, 17700, 17720, 17860*

Winter Schedule 2004

Albanian	Days	Area	kHz
1230-1330	daily	Eu	11910cak

Arabic	Days	Area	kHz
1000-1200	daily	As	15245emr
1000-1200	daily	As,Af	15105emr
1500-1700	daily	Af	15195emr
1500-1700	daily	As,Af	6120cak

Azeri	Days	Area	kHz
0800-0930	daily	As	11835cak, 15160emr
1500-1600	daily	As	5965emr

Bosnian	Days	Area	kHz
1900-2000	daily	Eu	6110cak

Bulgarian	Days	Area	kHz
1430-1530	daily	Eu	7140emr

Croatian	Days	Area	kHz
1700-1730	daily	Eu	9595emr

English	Days	Area	kHz
0400-0500	daily	As,Af	7240emr
0400-0500	daily	Eu,NAm	6020emr
1330-1430	daily	As,AUS	15195emr
1330-1430	daily	Eu	15155emr
1930-2030	daily	Eu	6055emr
2130-2230	daily	As,AUS	9525emr
2300-2400	daily	Eu,NAm	7275emr

Farsi	Days	Area	kHz
0930-1030	daily	As	11795cak, 17690emr
1330-1500	daily	As	11705cak

French	Days	Area	kHz
2030-2130	daily	Af	6050cak
2030-2130	daily	Eu	7155emr

Georgian	Days	Area	kHz
0800-0900	daily	As	11690emr

German	Days	Area	kHz
1230-1330	daily	Eu	17700emr
1830-1930	daily	Eu	7205emr

Greek	Days	Area	kHz
1130-1230	daily	Eu	9840emr
1130-1230	daily	As	7295cak
1530-1630	daily	Eu	6185emr

Hungarian	Days	Area	kHz
1030-1130	daily	Eu	15160emr

Kazakh	Days	Area	kHz
1600-1700	daily	As	7295emr

Kyrgyz	Days	Area	kHz
1700-1800	daily	As	6095cak

Macedonian	Days	Area	kHz
0900-1000	daily	Eu	11895emr

Mandarin	Days	Area	kHz
1200-1300	daily	As	15320emr

Romanian	Days	Area	kHz
1030-1130	daily	Eu	9560cak

Russian	Days	Area	kHz
1400-1500	daily	As	11980emr
1800-1900	daily	As	6135emr

Serbian	Days	Area	kHz
1430-1500	daily	Eu	9510emr

Spanish	Days	Area	kHz
1730-1800	daily	Eu	9780emr

Tatar	Days	Area	kHz
1600-1700	daily	As	5980emr

Turkish	Days	Area	kHz
0500-0800	daily	As	17690emr
0500-1000	daily	As	11925emr
0800-1700	daily	As,Af,Eu	11955cak
1000-1300	daily	As,AUS	17720emr
1100-1600	....f..	Af	17860emr
1300-1700	daily	As,AUS	9625emr
1700-2200	daily	Eu	5980emr
1700-2300	daily	As,Af	6120emr
1700-2300	daily	As,AUS	9560emr
1800-2300	daily	Af	9840cak
2200-0800	daily	Eu,NAm	7300emr

Turkmen	Days	Area	kHz
1630-1730	daily	As	5965emr

Urdu	Days	Area	kHz
1300-1400	daily	As	15225emr

Uzbek	Days	Area	kHz
0200-0300	daily	As	7115emr
1800-1900	daily	As	5955cak

ANN: English: "This is the Voice of Turkey"; German: "Hier ist die Stimme der Türkei"; Turkish: "Burasi Türkiye'nin Sesi Radyosu"; Spanish: "Esta es La Voz de Turquia".
V: QSL-card.
NOTES: The Voice of Turkey is the External Sce of the public service Turkish Radio-TV Corporation, TRT (Türkiye Radyo-Televizyon Kurumu).

UKRAINE

RADIO UKRAINE INTERNATIONAL (Gov)

Kreschatyk 26, 01001 Kyiv, Ukraine.
☎ +380 44 2282534. Fax +380 44 2287356.
Email: vsru@nrcu.gov.ua **Web:** www.nrcu.gov.ua
L.P: Dir RUI: Oleksandr Dyky; Chief Editor, English Section: Zhanna Mescherska.
MW/SW: Leased from Concern RRT
kHz: *657, 5840, 7400, 7420, 7440, 7490, 7555, 15620*

Winter Schedule 2004

English	Days	Area	kHz
0100-0200	daily	NAm	7440smf
0400-0500	daily	NAm	7440smf
1200-1300	daily	Eu	15620khr
2200-2300	daily	Eu	5840khr

German	Days	Area	kHz
0000-0100	daily	Eu	5840khr
1800-1900	daily	Eu	7555khr
2100-2200	daily	Eu	7555khr

Romanian	Days	Area	kHz
1800-1830	daily	Eu	657crn
2030-2100	daily	Eu	657crn
2200-2230	daily	Eu	657crn

Ukrainian	Days	Area	kHz
0000-0100	daily	NAm	7440smf
0100-0600	daily	RUS	7420khr
0200-0400	daily	NAm	7440smf
0600-0900	daily	RUS	7490khr
0900-1200	daily	Eu	15620khr
1300-1400	daily	Eu	15620khr

Ukrainian	Days	Area	kHz
1400-1800	daily	RUS	7400khr
1900-2100	daily	Eu	7555khr
2300-2400	daily	Eu	5840khr

ANN: Ukrainian: "Hovorit Kyiv, Vsesvitnia sluzhba Radio Ukrayiny"; English: "This is Radio Ukraine International"
V: QSL-card.
NOTES: Radio Ukraine International is the External Sce of the state broadcaster Natsionalna Radiokompaniia Ukraini (NRKU).

CONCERN RRT (Tx Operator)
vul. Dorohozhytska 10, 04112 Kyiv, Ukraine.
☎ +380 44 4408766. Fax +380 44 4408450.
Email: vvu@concernbrt.kiev.ua **Web:** www.rrt.com.ua
L.P: Pres: Volodymyr O. Ischuk.
MW: [CRN] Chernivtsi (G.C. 28N20 025E55) 657kHz 30kW; [KHR] Kharkiv, Taranivka (G.C. 49N38 036E07) 612kHz 5kW; [KYV] Kyiv, Brovary (G.C. 50N31 030E46) 612kHz 5kW; [LVI] Lviv, Krasne (G.C. 49N51 024E40) 936kHz 1000kW; [SMF] Mykolaiv, Luch (G.C. 46N49 032E14) 972/1431kHz 1200kW
SW: [KHR] Kharkiv, Taranivka (G.C. 49N38 036E07) 4 x 100kW; [KYV] Kyiv, Brovary (G.C. 50N31 030E46) 4 x 100kW; [LVI] Lviv, Krasne (G.C. 49N51 024E40) 2 x 1000kW; [SMF] Mykolaiv, Luch (G.C. 46N49 032E14) 1 x 100, 2 x 250, 2 x 1000, 2 x 1200kW
NOTES: Concern RRT is the national transmitter network owner. Leases out its facilities to domestic and international customers.
Broadcasters using sites in this country:
BBC World Sce uses: (SMF). See stn entry in: **G**, INT Section
BBC World Sce uses: (KYV). See stn entry in: **G**, INT Section
VO Russia (VOR) uses: (SMF). See stn entry in: **RUS**, INT Section
VOR-RKS uses: (SMF). See stn entry in: **RUS**, INT Section
VOR-RKS uses: (LVI). See stn entry in: **RUS**, INT Section
VOR-RMR uses: (SMF). See stn entry in: **RUS**, INT Section
VOR-RMR uses: (LVI). See stn entry in: **RUS**, INT Section

UNITED ARAB EMIRATES

EMIRATES RADIO (Gov)
P.O. Box 1695, Dubai, United Arab Emirates.
☎ +971 4 370255. Fax +971 4 374111.
Email: radio@dubaitv.gov.ae **Web:** www.dubaitv.gov.ae
L.P: GD: Ahmed Saeed al Gaoud.
MW: [DBA] Dubai (G.C. 25N14 055E16) 1476kHz 1500kW
SW: [DBA] Dubai (G.C. 25N14 055E16) 3 x 300, 1 x 500kW
SAT: Asiasat 2, Telstar 12
kHz: *11795, 11950, 12005, 13630, 13675, 15370, 15395, 15400, 15435, 17830, 17865, 17890, 21605, 21700*

Winter Schedule 2004

Music	Days	Area	kHz
0200-0400	daily	NA	12005dba, 15400dba, 17890dba
0200-0600	daily	NA,Pac	13675dba
0400-0600	daily	Pac	17830dba, 21700dba
0400-0600	daily	FE	15435dba
0600-1700	daily	Eu	17865dba, 21605dba
0600-2100	daily	Eu	15395dba
1000-1200	daily	NAf	15370dba
1200-2100	daily	NAf	13630dba
1700-2100	daily	Eu	11795dba, 11950dba, 13675dba

ANN: Arabic: "Idha'at al imarat al Arabiyyah al Mutahhida min Dubai"; English: "This is Emirates Radio from Dubai"
V: QSL-card.
NOTES: The SW transmissions are relays of Emirates Radio Dubai Home Sce programmes in Arabic and English.

EMIRATES MEDIA (Tx Operator)
Dhabbaya, United Arab Emirates.
Web: www.emi.co.ae
MW: [DHA] Dhabbaya (G.C. 24N11 054E14) 1170kHz 800kW, 1314kHz 1000kW, 1539kHz 60kW. One additional 800kW tx to be commissioned in 2005.
SW: [DHA] Dhabbaya (G.C. 24N11 054E14) 4 x 500kW
NOTES: The Dhabbiya transmitting station is owned by Emirates Media. VT Merlin Communications (UK) was appointed to operate and maintain the Emirate's short- and mediumwave transmitters until 2011.

Broadcasters using sites in this country:
AWR uses: (DHA). See stn entry in: **USA**, INT Section
BBC World Sce uses: (DHA). See stn entry in: **G**, INT Section
BBG-R.Farda uses: (DHA). See stn entry in: **USA**, INT Section
BBG-R.Free Asia uses: (DHA). See stn entry in: **USA**, INT Section
BVB uses: (DHA). See stn entry in: **G**, INT Section
Deutsche Welle uses: (DHA). See stn entry in: **D**, INT Section
FEBA Radio uses: (DHA). See stn entry in: **G**, INT Section
Gospel for Asia uses: (DHA). See stn entry in: **USA**, INT Section
R.Japan uses: (DHA). See stn entry in: **J**, INT Section
R.Mustaqbal uses: (DHA). See stn entry in: **ETH**, CTB Section
R.UNMEE uses: (DHA). See stn entry in: **ETH**, CTB Section
RCI uses: (DHA). See stn entry in: **CAN**, INT Section
RFI uses: (DHA). See stn entry in: **F**, INT Section
RVI uses: (DHA). See stn entry in: **BEL**, INT Section
Salaam Watandar uses: (DHA). See stn entry in: **AFG**, CTB Section

UNITED KINGDOM

BBC WORLD SERVICE (Pub)
P.O. Box 76, Strand, London WC2B 4PH, United Kingdom.
☎ +44 20 72403456. Fax +44 20 75571258.
Email: worldservice.letters@bbc.co.uk
Web: www.bbc.co.uk/worldservice
L.P: Dir:Richard Sambrook; Deputy Dir World Sce: Nigel Chapman; Chief Editor: Mark Byford; Dir News & Programme Commissioning: Bob Jobbins; Dir, Regions: Andrew Taussig; Head of English Programmes Commissioning: Penny Tuerk.
LW: [DRO] Droitwich (G.C. 52N18 002W06) 198kHz 500kW (leased from Crown Castle International)
MW/SW: Uses tx's provided by VT Merlin Communications Ltd
kHz: *612, 639, 648, 666, 675, 702, 720, 801, 1251, 1260, 1296, 1314, 1323, 1413, 1503, 3255, 3390, 3915, 5875, 5965, 5970, 5975, 5990, 5995, 6005, 6010, 6015, 6020, 6030, 6035, 6050, 6060, 6065, 6080, 6090, 6105, 6110, 6130, 6135, 6140, 6150, 6155, 6170, 6190, 6195, 7105, 7110, 7115, 7120, 7130, 7135, 7140, 7150, 7160, 7165, 7180, 7185, 7190, 7195, 7205, 7210, 7225, 7230, 7235, 7255, 7260, 7265, 7295, 7320, 7325, 7330, 7430, 7435, 9410, 9510, 9515, 9525, 9530, 9540, 9565, 9580, 9600, 9605, 9610, 9630, 9635, 9660, 9670, 9680, 9685, 9695, 9740, 9750, 9790, 9795, 9815, 9825, 9855, 9870, 9875, 9895, 9915, 11670, 11675, 11680, 11685, 11695, 11725, 11730, 11740, 11750, 11760, 11765, 11785, 11820, 11835, 11845, 11850, 11855, 11860, 11865, 11920, 11925, 11935, 11940, 11945, 11955, 11965, 12010, 12035, 12095, 13615, 13640, 13650, 13660, 13700, 13755, 15105, 15115, 15155, 15180, 15190, 15245, 15265, 15280, 15285, 15310, 15325, 15360, 15390, 15400, 15405, 15420, 15425, 15470, 15485, 15510, 15555, 15565, 15575, 17585, 17610, 17615, 17640, 17690, 17695, 17760, 17780, 17790, 17810, 17820, 17830, 17850, 17870, 17885, 21455, 21470, 21490, 21515, 21590, 21630, 21640, 21660*

Winter Schedule 2004

Albanian	Days	Area	kHz
0630-0700	daily	SEu	7210rmp, 9635cyp, 11845cyp
1330-1445	......s	SEu	9750cyp, 15115skn
1415-1445	mtwtfs.	SEu	9750cyp, 15115skn
1800-1830	daily	SEu	6050cyp, 6130skn, 7105rmp
2100-2115	mtwtf..	SEu	6050cyp, 7150rmp, 7205sla

Arabic	Days	Area	kHz
0000-0200	daily	ME	702sla
0000-0300	daily	ME	639cgr, 6105rmp, 7140skn, 9915skn
0000-2400	daily	ME	720cgr
0300-0445	daily	ME	9915skn
0300-0600	daily	ME	11740cyp
0300-0600	mtwtfs.	ME	7140cyp, 13660cyp
0300-1200	......s	ME	13660cyp
0300-2400	......s	ME	7140cyp
0330-0600	daily	ME	15180sla
0330-2400	daily	ME	639cgr
0400-0600	daily	NAf	6110skn
0400-0730	daily	NAf	7325rmp
0430-0930	daily	ME	1314dha
0445-0600	daily	NAf	9915rmp, 9915skn
0600-0730	daily	NAf	9915skn
0600-0800	daily	ME	11740cyp

Arabic	Days	Area	kHz
0600-0900	daily	ME	15180cyp
0600-1200	mtwtfs.	ME	13660arm
0730-1100	daily	NAf	17610skn
0800-1800	daily	ME	11820cyp
0900-1130	daily	ME	21455mos
0900-1630	daily	ME	15555cyp
0900-1800	daily	NAf	15180rmp
1030-1300	mtwt.ss	ME	1314dha
1100-1630	daily	NAf	17585skn
1130-1300	....f..	ME	1314dha
1200-1800	daily	NAf	13660skn
1200-2400	mtwtfs.	ME	7140cyp
1500-2400	daily	ME	702sla
1630-1800	daily	NAf	11680cyp
1630-2000	daily	ME	6030sla
1700-2100	daily	ME	9915cyp
1800-2100	daily	NAf	6110rmp, 11680skn
1800-2400	daily	NAf	9915cyp
2000-2200	daily	ME	1314dha, 6030sla
2100-2400	daily	ME	5875rmp
2100-2400	daily	NAf	6110skn

Azeri	Days	Area	kHz
0400-0415	mtwtf..	CAs	801bak
1000-1030	mtwtf..	CAs	801bak
1530-1600	mtwtfs.	CAs	801bak
1800-1830	daily	CAs	801bak, 5875cyp, 7195rmp, 9750cyp
1900-2000	daily	CAs	801bak

Bangla	Days	Area	kHz
0030-0100	daily	SAs	6065sla, 9790nak, 11850sgp
1330-1400	daily	SAs	7225nak, 7430tac, 11835sgp
1630-1700	daily	SAs	5990nak, 7205sgp, 9605sgp

Brazilian	Days	Area	kHz
2230-2300	daily	SAm	9870asc, 11965atg, 15390asc

Burmese	Days	Area	kHz
0000-0030	daily	SEA	6065nak, 9580sgp, 11850sgp
1345-1430	daily	SEA	7135sgp, 9540sgp, 11685sgp, 13615cyp

Dari	Days	Area	kHz
0030-0100	daily	ME	1314dha, 1413sla, 6020cyp, 7165cyp
0130-0200	daily	ME	1314dha, 6020cyp, 7165cyp, 17615nak
0200-0230	daily	CAs	1251dsb
0230-0300	daily	ME	5875rmp, 6020cyp, 7320rmp
0830-0900	daily	ME	15420cyp, 17870sla
0930-1000	mtwt.ss	ME	1314dha
0930-1000	daily	ME	15420cyp, 17870sla
0930-1000	daily	CAs	1251dsb
1030-1100	daily	ME	15420cyp, 17870sla
1400-1500	daily	CAs	1251dsb
1400-1500	daily	ME	1314dha, 9635cyp, 13755nak
1400-1500	daily	WEu	6195skn
1600-1615	daily	ME	9795cyp, 11785nak

English	Days	Area	kHz
0000-0030	daily	FE	11945yam, 17615nak
0000-0030	daily	ME	1314dha
0000-0030	daily	SEA	3915sgp
0000-0100	daily	NAm	6010sac
0000-0100	daily	SAs	5970sla, 11955nak
0000-0100	daily	SEA	9740sgp, 9740sgp
0000-0200	daily	ME	9410cyp
0000-0200	daily	SEA	6195sgp
0000-0300	daily	SAm	9825skn, 12095asc
0000-0300	daily	SAs	15310nak, 17790sgp
0000-0300	daily	SEA	15360sgp
0000-0330	daily	RUS	1260msk
0000-0400	daily	Car	5975atg
0000-0530	daily	FE	15280nak

English	Days	Area	kHz
0000-2400	daily	HKG	675hkg
0000-2400	daily	ME	1323cgr
0000-2400	daily	WEu	648orf
0030-0100	daily	FE	17615nak
0030-0100	daily	SAs	9580sgp
0055-0330	daily	RUS	666ekb
0100-0300	daily	SAs	11955sla
0100-0400	daily	CAm	9525yfr
0200-0230	daily	SAs	1413sla
0200-0300	daily	EAf	9750sey
0200-0300	daily	WAs	6195cyp
0200-0300	daily	ME	9410cyp
0245-0300	daily	EAf	11865sey
0300-0330	daily	NAf	639cgr
0300-0400	daily	EAf	9750cyp, 12035sey
0300-0400	daily	Eu	9410skn
0300-0400	daily	ME	1413sla
0300-0400	daily	RUS	6195rmp, 9410cyp
0300-0400	daily	SAf	6005asc
0300-0400	daily	WAf	11765mey
0300-0500	daily	WAs	11760cyp
0300-0500	daily	CAs	15575sla
0300-0500	daily	FE	17760nak
0300-0500	daily	SAf	3255mey, 6190mey
0300-0500	daily	SEA	15360nak
0300-0600	daily	WAf	7160asc
0300-0600	daily	SAs	15310sla
0300-0700	daily	SAs	17790nak
0300-1030	daily	FE	21660nak
0330-0600	daily	EAf	15420sey
0330-0700	......s	RUS	666ekb, 1260msk, 1260spe
0400-0500	daily	EAf	12035cyp
0400-0500	daily	WAf	11765mey
0400-0500	daily	NAm	6010sac
0400-0500	daily	Car,SAm	5975atg
0400-0500	daily	RUS	6195rmp
0400-0600	daily	CAm	6135dln
0400-0600	daily	Eu	6195skn, 9410cyp
0400-0600	daily	RUS	9410rmp
0400-0705	daily	WAf	6005asc
0430-0800	.....ss	UKR	612kyv
0500-0530	.....ss	EAf	17885sey
0500-0600	daily	ME	11760sla
0500-0600	mtwtf..	EAf	17885sey
0500-0600	mtwtfs.	WAs	15575cyp
0500-0700	.....s.	RUS	666ekb, 1260msk, 1260spe
0500-0700	daily	EAf	17640cyp
0500-0700	daily	Eu	15565cyp
0500-0700	daily	WAf	11765mey
0500-0700	daily	WEu	9410skn
0500-0800	daily	WEu	6195rmp
0500-0900	daily	SEA	11955nak, 15360sgp, 15360sgp
0500-1000	daily	SEA	17760sgp
0500-1500	......s	WAs	15575cyp
0500-1700	daily	SAf	6190mey, 11940mey
0530-0545	daily	Eu	6010skn, 9815rmp
0600-0700	daily	WEu	7160skn
0600-0700	mtwtf..	RUS	666ekb, 1260msk, 1260spe
0600-0700	mtwtf..	UKR	612kyv
0600-0700	daily	RUS	12095wof
0600-0730	mtwtf..	ME	15575smf
0600-0900	daily	Eu	9410skn
0600-1200	.....s.	ME	15575smf
0600-1400	.....ss	EAf	17885sey
0600-1800	daily	SAs	15310nak
0630-0645	.....ss	Eu	9875cyp
0630-0700	daily	WAf	15400asc
0700-0720	daily	WAf	6005asc
0700-0800	mtwtf..	UKR	612kyv
0700-0800	daily	WEu	17830rmp
0700-0800	daily	WAf	11765asc
0700-0800	daily	RUS	12095wof

English	Days	Area	kHz
0700-1000	mtwtf..	WAf	15400asc
0700-1130	.....ss	WAf	15400asc
0700-1400	daily	ME	11760sla
0700-1500	daily	Eu	17640skn
0700-1600	daily	SAs	17790sla
0700-1700	daily	Eu	12095wof
0700-1700	daily	WEu	15485skn
0700-1800	daily	RUS	15565rmp
0715-0730	daily	RUS	666ekb, 1260msk, 1260spe
0730-0900	daily	RUS	666ekb, 1260msk, 1260spe
0800-1000	mtwtf..	WAf	17830asc
0800-1300	daily	SAf	21470sey
0800-1400	mtwtf..	EAf	17885sey
0800-1500	daily	RUS	17640wof
0800-2100	.....ss	WAf	17830asc
0900-1000	.....s.	SEA	6195nak, 6195sgp, 9740sgp
0900-1000	mtwtf..	SAm	15190asc
0900-1030	......s	SEA	6195nak
0900-1030	daily	FE	9605yam, 15360nak
0900-1100	mtwtf..	SEA	6195nak
0900-1100	mtwtf.s	SEA	6195sgp
0900-1100	.....ss	SAm	15190asc
0900-1200	mtwtf..	ME	15575smf
0900-1600	mtwtf.s	SEA	9740sgp
0915-0930	daily	RUS	666ekb, 1260msk, 1260spe
0930-1000	daily	RUS	666ekb, 1260msk, 1260spe
1000-1100	mtwtf..	Car	6195atg
1000-1100	.....s.	SEA	6195nak, 6195sgp
1000-1100	daily	RUS	666ekb, 1260msk, 1260spe
1000-1400	daily	FE	17760nak
1000-1400	.....ss	Car	6195atg
1000-1500	daily	Eu	7320rmp+
1000-1600	.....s.	SEA	9740sgp
1030-1100	daily	FE	9605yam, 11945nak, 21660nak
1030-1100	daily	SEA	15285sgp
1100-1130	daily	Car,SAm	15190atg
1100-1130	mtwtf..	WAf	15400asc
1100-1130	daily	SAm	17790asc
1100-1130	.....ss	SAm	15190asc
1100-1130	mtwtf..	Car	6195atg
1100-1700	daily	SEA	6195sgp
1100-2100	mtwtf..	WAf	17830asc
1115-1130	daily	RUS	666ekb, 1260msk, 1260spe
1130-1145	daily	SEA	7135sgp, 11920nak
1130-1200	mtwtf..	Car,SAm	15190atg
1130-1200	daily	RUS	666ekb, 1260msk, 1260spe
1130-1200	mtwtf..	Car	6195atg
1130-1700	.....ss	Car,SAm	15190atg
1200-1230	mtwtf..	Car	6195atg
1200-1230	mtwtf..	Car,SAm	15190atg
1200-1300	daily	RUS	666ekb, 1260msk, 1260spe
1200-1500	mtwtfs.	WAs	15575cyp
1230-1245	daily	CAf	21640asc
1230-1245	daily	WAf	17780asc
1230-1245	daily	WEu	15425wof
1230-1400	mtwtf..	Car	6195atg
1230-1700	mtwtf..	Car,SAm	15190atg
1300-1400	daily	ME	1314dha
1300-1400	daily	SAs	1413sla
1300-1400	daily	EAf	15420sey
1300-1900	daily	SAf	21470asc
1305-1400	mtwtf..	RUS	666ekb, 1260msk, 1260spe
1315-1330	.....ss	RUS	666ekb, 1260msk, 1260spe
1330-1345	daily	WAf	15105asc, 17810asc

English	Days	Area	kHz
1330-1600	.....ss	RUS	666ekb, 1260msk, 1260spe
1400-1415	mtw....	EAf	11860sey, 15420sey
1400-1415	mtw....	Eu	21490rmp
1400-1500	daily	UKR	612kyv
1400-1600	daily	FE	7160nak
1400-1700	daily	EAf	21660cyp
1445-1500	mtwtfs.	SAs	1413sla, 6140sla, 7205sla, 15245nak
1500-1530	daily	EAf	11860sey, 15420sey, 21490mey
1500-1600	daily	SAs	5975sgp
1500-1600	daily	RUS	12095wof
1500-2300	daily	WAf	15400asc
1530-1545	daily	SAs	9600sgp, 11685sgp
1530-1600	daily	UKR	612kyv
1600-1700	daily	Eu	9410wof
1600-1700	daily	RUS	12095wof
1600-1700	daily	WAs	17790cyp
1600-1700	daily	WEu	17820rmp
1600-1800	daily	SAs	3915sgp, 11750sgp
1600-1800	daily	SEA	7160sgp
1600-1830	daily	SAs	5975nak
1600-1915	daily	WEu	1296orf+
1615-1700	.....ss	EAf	11860sey, 15420sey, 21490mey
1630-1700	mtwtf..	EAf	15420sey
1700-1745	daily	EAf	6005sey, 9630sey
1700-1800	daily	Eu	12095wof
1700-1800	daily	WEu	17820skn
1700-1900	daily	RUS	12095wof
1700-1900	daily	EAf	15420mey
1700-2000	daily	Eu	6195cyp, 6195skn
1700-2200	daily	Eu	9410cyp
1700-2200	daily	SAf	3255mey, 6190mey
1700-2300	daily	WEu	6195rmp
1730-1745	daily	WAf	9685mey
1730-1745	daily	EAf	7230mey
1730-1745	daily	SAf	3390mey
1730-1800	daily	UKR	612kyv
1730-1800	daily	Eu	6015skn, 7190rmp
1730-1800	daily	RUS	5875cyp
1800-1830	daily	ME	1413sla
1800-1830	daily	SAs	11750nak
1800-2000	daily	WEu	13700skn
1830-1845	m.w....	Eu	6050cyp, 6130skn, 7105rmp
1830-2000	daily	SAs	5975nak
1830-2100	daily	EAf	6005sey, 9630sey
1900-2100	daily	ME	1413sla
1900-2100	daily	SAf	12095asc
1915-1930	daily	WAf	15105asc, 17885asc
1930-2000	daily	Eu	1296orf
2000-2100	daily	Eu	1296orf
2000-2100	mtwtf..	UKR	612kyv
2000-2130	......s	RUS	1260msk
2000-2200	......s	RUS	666ekb, 1260spe
2000-2230	.....ss	UKR	612kyv
2000-2300	daily	Eu	6195cyp
2100-2130	mtwtf..	Car	5975atg
2100-2130	.....s.	RUS	1260msk
2100-2130	.....ss	Car	5975atg
2100-2200	daily	SEA	6195nak
2100-2200	daily	SAs	3915sgp
2100-2200	.....s.	RUS	666ekb, 1260spe
2100-2200	daily	FE	6110yam
2100-2200	daily	SAf	6005sey
2100-2300	daily	EAf	9605sey
2100-2400	daily	FE	5965nak
2100-2400	daily	SAm	12095asc
2105-2400	daily	WEu	1296orf+
2110-2130	mtwtf..	Car,SAm	11675atg
2115-2130	mtwtf..	SAm	15390grv
2130-2145	.t.f..	SAm	11680rmp
2130-2200	mtwtf..	RUS	666ekb, 1260spe
2130-2230	mtwtf..	UKR	612kyv
2130-2400	daily	Car	5975atg
2130-2400	daily	RUS	1260msk

English	Days	Area	kHz
2200-2300	daily	Pac	9660brn
2200-2300	daily	SAs	7105sla
2200-2300	daily	SEA	11955sgp
2200-2400	daily	ME	1314dha
2200-2400	daily	SEA	6195sgp, 9740sgp, 9740sgp
2300-2400	daily	FE	11945yam, 15280nak
2300-2400	daily	SEA	3915sgp, 11955nak
2300-2400	daily	WEu	6195rmp
2330-2400	daily	FE	6170kim

Farsi	Days	Area	kHz
0230-0300	daily	ME	1413sla, 7165cyp, 9875cyp, 11750sla
0230-0330	daily	CAs	1251dsb
0230-0430	daily	ME	1314dha
0300-0400	daily	ME	9875rmp
0300-0430	daily	ME	7165cyp, 11750cyp
0400-0430	daily	ME	9875rmp
0930-1030	mtwt.ss	ME	12035dha
0930-1030	daily	ME	21515skn
0930-1130	....f..	ME	1314dha, 12035dha
1000-1030	daily	CAs	1251dsb
1030-1130	....f..	ME	21515skn
1600-1700	daily	ME	1413sla, 9915cyp
1600-1700	daily	WEu	6195skn
1600-1800	daily	ME	13755nak
1600-2000	daily	ME	1314dha, 6090sla, 9510sgp
1615-1700	daily	CAs	1251dsb
1730-2000	daily	CAs	1251dsb
1800-2000	daily	ME	11935nak
1830-1900	daily	ME	1413sla

French	Days	Area	kHz
0430-0500	daily	WAf	6155asc, 7105asc
0430-0500	daily	EAf	17885sey
0600-0630	daily	NAf	7180rmp, 11680cyp
0600-0630	daily	WAf	7105asc, 9610asc
0700-0730	daily	CAf	17695mey
0700-0730	daily	WAf	15105asc
1200-1230	daily	NAf	15425wof
1200-1230	daily	WAf	17780asc, 21640asc
1800-1830	daily	NAf	9815wof
1800-1830	daily	SAf	7230mey
1800-1830	daily	WAf	15105asc, 17885asc, 21630asc

Hausa	Days	Area	kHz
0530-0600	daily	WAf	6135asc, 7105asc, 9610asc
1345-1415	daily	WAf	15105asc, 17810asc, 21640asc
1930-2000	daily	WAf	11855asc, 15105asc, 17885asc

Hindi	Days	Area	kHz
0100-0130	daily	SAs	1413sla, 6065sla, 7110tac, 7320cyp, 11750sgp, 15510nak
0230-0300	daily	SAs	11725sla, 15405nak, 15510irk, 17615nak
1400-1445	daily	SAs	7430tac, 11920sgp
1400-1445	mtwtfs.	SAs	1413sla, 6140sla, 7205sla, 15245nak
1400-1500	......s	SAs	1413sla, 6140sla, 7205sla, 15245nak
1700-1730	daily	SAs	1413sla, 6065nak, 7205sgp, 7235sla, 9605nak

Indonesian	Days	Area	kHz
1100-1130	daily	SEA	7135sgp, 9510sgp, 11920nak
1300-1330	daily	ME	6030sla
1300-1330	daily	SEA	6035nak, 7135sgp, 9540sgp, 11945sgp
2200-2300	daily	SEA	3915sgp, 6080sgp, 7235sgp, 9510nak

Kazakh	Days	Area	kHz
1300-1330	mtwtf..	CAs	15155rmp, 17690rmp

Kinyarwanda/ Kirundi	Days	Area	kHz
0530-0600	.....ss	EAf	15400mey, 17885sey
1630-1700	mtwtf..	EAf	11860sey, 21490mey

Mandarin	Days	Area	kHz
1100-1300	daily	CHN	11945nak, 21660nak
1100-1530	daily	CHN	9605yam
1100-1530	daily	FE	7330vld, 15285sgp
1300-1530	daily	CHN	6090kim, 7105nak
2200-2300	daily	CHN	6110nak, 7160nak, 11945yam
2200-2330	daily	CHN	6170kim, 7150sla, 9580nak

Nepali	Days	Area	kHz
1500-1530	daily	SAs	7430tac, 9600sgp, 11685sgp

Pashto	Days	Area	kHz
0100-0130	daily	ME	1314dha
0100-0130	daily	SAs	17615nak
0100-0130	daily	WAs	6020cyp, 7165cyp
0200-0230	daily	WAs	6020cyp, 7165cyp
0200-0230	daily	ME	1314dha
0200-0230	daily	SAs	17615nak
0300-0330	daily	ME	6150dha
0300-0330	daily	WAs	6020rmp, 9510cyp
0900-0930	daily	SAs	17870sla
0900-0930	daily	WAs	15420cyp
1000-1030	daily	SAs	17870sla
1000-1030	daily	WAs	15420cyp
1000-1030	mtwt.ss	ME	1314dha
1100-1130	daily	SAs	17870sla
1100-1130	daily	WAs	15420cyp
1500-1600	daily	ME	1314dha
1500-1600	daily	SAs	13755nak
1500-1600	daily	WAs	7190cyp
1500-1600	daily	WEu	6195skn
1615-1630	daily	SAs	11785nak
1615-1700	daily	WAs	9795cyp
1630-1700	daily	SAs	11785nak

Portuguese	Days	Area	kHz
0430-0500	daily	SAf	3390mey, 6135mey, 7205mey
2030-2100	daily	SAf	3390mey, 6135mey, 7205mey
2030-2100	daily	WAf	9565skn, 11695rmp, 11855asc

Romanian	Days	Area	kHz
0600-0615	daily	SEu	9875cyp
0615-0630	.....ss	SEu	9875cyp
1200-1230	daily	SEu	11680cyp
1600-1630	daily	SEu	6050cyp
1900-1930	daily	SEu	6050cyp

Russian	Days	Area	kHz
0200-0230	daily	CAs	801bak
0300-0305	daily	CAs	801bak
0300-0330	daily	RUS	5875rmp, 7265cyp, 9670sla
0305-0330	daily	CAs	801bak
0330-0400	daily	CAs	1251dsb
0330-0430	.....s.	UKR	612kyv
0330-0430	mtwtfs.	RUS	6065skn, 7265cyp
0330-0500	mtwtf..	UKR	612kyv
0330-0500	mtwtfs.	RUS	5875rmp, 5875wof, 7230rmp, 9670cyp
0330-0505	.....s.	CAs	1260msk
0330-0505	.....s.	RUS	666ekb, 1260spe
0330-0535	mtwtf..	CAs	1260msk
0330-0535	mtwtf..	RUS	666ekb, 1260spe
0430-0500	mtwtfs.	RUS	11845cyp
0500-0530	mtwtf..	RUS	6020wof, 7295rmp, 9670wof, 11845cyp
0530-0600	mtwtf..	CAs	1260msk
0530-0600	mtwtf..	RUS	666ekb, 1260spe
0700-0715	daily	CAs	1260msk
0700-0715	daily	RUS	666ekb, 1260spe
0900-0915	daily	CAs	1260msk
0900-0915	daily	RUS	666ekb, 1260spe
1000-1006	daily	CAs	1260msk

Russian	Days	Area	kHz
1000-1006	daily	RUS	666ekb, 1260spe
1100-1115	daily	CAs	1260msk
1100-1115	daily	RUS	666ekb, 1260spe
1300-1305	mtwtf..	CAs	1260msk
1300-1305	mtwtf..	RUS	666ekb, 1260spe
1300-1315	.....ss	RUS	666ekb, 1260spe
1300-1315	.....ss	CAs	1260msk
1400-2130	mtwtf..	CAs	1260msk
1400-2130	mtwtf..	RUS	666ekb, 1260spe
1600-1700	daily	UKR	612kyv
1600-2000	......s	CAs	1260msk
1600-2000	......s	RUS	666ekb, 1260spe
1600-2100	.....s.	CAs	1260msk
1600-2100	.....s.	RUS	666ekb, 1260spe
1630-1633	......s	CAs	7435msk
1630-1700	......s	CAs	7435msk
1630-1700	.....s.	CAs	7435msk
1730-1900	daily	RUS	11670wof, 13640rmp
1730-2000	daily	RUS	7325cyp, 9635cyp, 9825wof
1830-1900	daily	CAs	801bak
1900-2000	daily	RUS	5875cyp, 5990rmp, 11925rmp+
2000-2030	mtwtf..	RUS	5875cyp, 5990rmp, 7325cyp, 9635cyp, 9825wof
2000-2100	.....s.	RUS	5875cyp, 5990rmp, 7325cyp, 9635cyp, 9825wof
2000-2100	.....s.	CAs	801bak
2000-2130	mtwtf..	CAs	801bak
2100-2130	mtwtf..	UKR	612kyv

Serbian	Days	Area	kHz
0500-0515	daily	SEu	6130wof, 7210rmp, 9510cyp
0545-0600	daily	SEu	6010rmp, 7210cyp, 9510cyp
1130-1145	daily	SEu	11680cyp, 13650rmp, 15325wof
1700-1730	daily	SEu	6050cyp, 7255wof, 9635rmp

Sinhala	Days	Area	kHz
1515-1545	daily	SAs	6140sla, 9680sgp

Somali	Days	Area	kHz
1100-1130	daily	EAf	17850cyp, 21590dha
1400-1500	...tf..	EAf	11860sey, 15420sey, 21490rmp
1415-1500	mtw..ss	EAf	11860sey, 15420sey, 21490rmp
1800-1830	daily	EAf	6005sey, 9630sey, 9695wof

Spanish	Days	Area	kHz
0000-0115	daily	CAm,SAm	6110atg
0000-0115	daily	SAm	5875skn, 6110asc, 9855asc, 11765asc
0000-0115	daily	CAm	5875rmp
0115-0130	.twtfs.	CAm,SAm	6110atg
0115-0130	.twtfs.	SAm	5875skn, 6110asc, 9855asc, 11765asc
0115-0130	.twtfs.	CAm	5875rmp
0300-0345	daily	CAm	7325rmp, 7325skn
0300-0345	daily	CAm,SAm	6110atg
0300-0345	daily	SAm	5995dln, 9515dln
0345-0400	.twtfs.	CAm	7325rmp, 7325skn
0345-0400	.twtfs.	CAm,SAm	6110atg
0345-0400	.twtfs.	SAm	5995dln, 9515dln
1100-1130	mtwtf..	CAm	9670atg
1100-1130	mtwtf..	Car	6110grv
1100-1130	mtwtf..	SAm	6130dln, 17820asc
1300-1330	mtwtf..	SAm	6130dln, 9670dln, 15325grv

Swahili	Days	Area	kHz
0300 0330	daily	EAf	7235rmp, 9610mey, 11865sey
0400-0430	daily	EAf	7185asc, 11730sey, 15400mey
1530-1615	.....ss	EAf	11860sey, 15420sey, 21490mey
1530-1630	mtwtf..	EAf	11860sey, 15420sey, 21490mey
1745-1800	daily	EAf	6005sey, 7230mey, 9630sey

Tajik	Days	Area	kHz
1500-1530	daily	CAs	1251dsb, 7180cyp, 11670skn

Tamil	Days	Area	kHz
1545-1615	daily	SAs	6140sla, 7205nak, 9680sgp

Thai	Days	Area	kHz
1230-1300	daily	ME	15265cyp
1230-1300	daily	SEA	7135sgp, 9540sgp
2330-2400	daily	ME	7185cyp
2330-2400	daily	SEA	6060sla, 9580sgp

Turkish	Days	Area	kHz
0500-0530	mtwtf..	SEu	6010skn, 7130rmp
0900-1000	......s	SEu	7120cyp, 9410cyp
1600-1700	daily	SEu	5875rmp, 9530rmp, 12010skn
2030-2100	mtwtf..	SEu	7115rmp, 9670skn

Ukrainian	Days	Area	kHz
0500-0600	mtwtf..	UKR	612kyv, 5875rmp, 7260skn, 9895cyp
0600-0606	mtwtf..	UKR	612kyv
0700-0706	mtwtf..	UKR	612kyv
0800-0806	mtwtf..	UKR	612kyv
0900-0905	mtwtf..	UKR	612kyv
1000-1006	mtwtf..	UKR	612kyv
1500-1530	daily	UKR	612kyv, 11865rmp, 13640skn, 15470rmp
1700-1730	daily	UKR	612kyv, 5875cyp, 6015skn, 7190rmp

Urdu	Days	Area	kHz
0130-0200	daily	SAs	1413sla, 6065sla, 7320cyp, 11750sla, 15510nak
1500-1545	daily	SAs	7205nak
1500-1600	daily	SAs	1413sla, 6035sla, 9510cyp, 11920sgp
1730-1800	daily	SAs	1413sla, 6065nak, 7205sgp, 7235sla, 9605nak

Uzbek	Days	Area	kHz
1600-1630	.....ss	CAs	7325cyp, 7435msk, 9635sla
1600-1700	mtwtf..	CAs	7325cyp, 7435msk, 9635sla
1700-1730	daily	CAs	1251dsb

Vietnamese	Days	Area	kHz
1430-1500	daily	SEA	1503tai, 6135sgp, 7135sgp, 11685sgp
2300-2400	daily	SEA	6080nak, 7105sgp, 11685sgp

ANN: English: "This is London, you are listening to the World Service of the BBC"
V: Does not verify reception reports.
NOTES: BBC World Sce prgr's in English and other languages are relayed by local st's in many countries. Full details can be found on the BBCWS website. Transmissions in some Asian languages are being jammed in the target area.

BIBLE VOICE BROADCASTING (Rlg)

P.O. Box 200, Leeds, LS26 0WW, United Kingdom.
☎ +44 1900 826522.
Email: mail@biblevoice.org **Web:** www.biblevoice.org
kHz: *5945, 6015, 6175, 7105, 7155, 7185, 7205, 7210, 7220, 7295, 9460, 9470, 9730, 12005, 12065, 13810, 17565*

Winter Schedule 2004

Amharic	Days	Area	kHz
1630-1730	...t.s.	EAf	13810jul
1630-1800	..w....	EAf	13810jul

Arabic	Days	Area	kHz
0500-0530	m.w....	ME	12065arm
0500-0545	....f..	ME	12065arm

Arabic	**Days**	**Area**	**kHz**
0845-1015	....f..	ME	17565jul
1700-1715	.twtf..	ME	7155wof
1700-1730	m......	ME	7155wof
1715-1830	m.w.f..	ME	9730jul
1800-1830	.t.t...	ME	9730jul
1900-1945	...t...	ME	9470nau
1930-1945	....f..	CAf	7295jul
Bangla	**Days**	**Area**	**kHz**
0030-0100	.....ss	As	7205dha
1500-1530	......s	As	7185tac
1500-1530	....f..	As	7185tac
Cantonese	**Days**	**Area**	**kHz**
1215-1230	...tfss	EAs	5945khb
Chinese (Mix)	**Days**	**Area**	**kHz**
1215-1245	.t.....	EAs	5945khb
English	**Days**	**Area**	**kHz**
0030-0100	.....ss	As	7105dha
0730-0945	....	Eu	5945jul
0800-0915	.....s.	Eu	5945jul
0815-0845	..w.f..	Eu	5945jul
1130-1200	.....ss	EAs	5945khb
1215-1245	..w....	EAs	5945khb
1230-1235	....f..	EAs	5945khb
1230-1245	...t...	EAs	5945khb
1230-1315	......s	EAs	5945vld
1400-1415	...t...	As	7185tac
1400-1500	.....ss	As	7185tac
1500-1600	.....s.	As	12005jul
1630-1900	......s	ME	9460jul
1645-1715	..w.f..	ME	9460jul
1645-1715	m......	ME	9460jul
1645-1745	...t...	ME	9460jul
1645-1800	.t.....	ME	9460jul
1645-1830	.....s.	ME	9460jul
1800-1815	.....s.	ME	7210jul
1800-1830	......s	Eu	6015jul
1800-1900	.....ss	ME	9730jul
1800-1900	..w.f..	ME	9460jul
1900-1930	.....s.	CAf	7295jul
1900-1930	......s	Eu	6015jul
1900-1930	......s	ME	9460jul
1900-2000	.....s.	Eu	6015jul
1900-2000	.....s.	ME	9470nau
1900-2015	....f.s	ME	9470nau
1915-1930	....f..	CAf	7295jul
1930-2000	......s	CAf	7295jul
1945-2015	....f..	WAf	7220wer
Farsi	**Days**	**Area**	**kHz**
1800-1900	......s	ME	7210jul
1815-1900	.....s.	ME	7210jul
French	**Days**	**Area**	**kHz**
1930-2000	.....s.	CAF	7295jul
Hebrew	**Days**	**Area**	**kHz**
1815-1900	.t.....	ME	9460jul
Hindi	**Days**	**Area**	**kHz**
0000-0030	.....ss	As	6175dha
1400-1500	....f..	As	7185tac
1415-1445	...t...	As	7185tac
1530-1600	......s	As	12005jul
Japanese	**Days**	**Area**	**kHz**
1215-1230	m......	EAs	5945khb
1235-1250	....f..	EAs	5945khb
Nepali	**Days**	**Area**	**kHz**
1445-1500	...t...	As	7185tac
Punjabi	**Days**	**Area**	**kHz**
1530-1600	....f..	As	12005jul
Russian	**Days**	**Area**	**kHz**
1800-1815	.t.....	ME	9460jul
1830-1900	......s	Eu	6015jul
1915-1930	mtwtf..	Eu	6015jul
Tagalog	**Days**	**Area**	**kHz**
1830-1900	......s	ME	9460jul
Tigrinya	**Days**	**Area**	**kHz**
1630-1730	mt..f..	EAf	13810jul
Urdu	**Days**	**Area**	**kHz**
1500-1600	.t.....	As	12005jul
Vietnamese	**Days**	**Area**	**kHz**
1200-1215	daily	EAs	5945khb

V: QSL-card.

NOTES: Joint radio mission of Bible Voice (UK) and High Adventure Gospel Communication Ministries (Canada) since July 2002.

CHRISTIAN VISION (THE VOICE) (Rlg)

✉ P.O. Box 3040, West Bromwich, West Midlands, B70 0EJ, United Kingdom.
☎ +44 121 5226087. 🖷 +44 121 5226083.
Email: deborahcollier@christianvision.com **Web:** www.christianvision.com

kHz: *9680, 9760, 9855, 11850, 13630, 13765*

Winter Schedule 2004

English	**Days**	**Area**	**kHz**
1000-1100	m......	Eu	9760rmp+
1800-2000	daily	CAf,WAf	9680sof
Hindi	**Days**	**Area**	**kHz**
0100-0400	daily	IND	11850tac
0400-1100	daily	IND	13630tac
1100-1400	daily	IND	13765tac
1400-1700	daily	IND	9855tac

V: QSL-card.

NOTES: Christian Vision Ltd was founded in 1998 with corporate headquarters in the UK. The prgr's for Africa and Asia are produced in the UK, the prgr's for Latin America in the USA. For schedules, see the Christian Vision foreign transmitting sites in Australia (Voice International), Chile (Voz Cristiana/Voz Crista) and Zambia (Christian Voice). Key: + DRM

FEBA RADIO (Rlg)

✉ Ivy Arch Road, Worthing BN14 8BX, United Kingdom.
☎ +44 1903 237281. 🖷 +44 1903 205294.
Email: info@feba.org.uk **Web:** www.feba.org.uk

L.P: Chief Executive: Mr John Bartlett.

kHz: *5985, 6125, 6180, 7265, 7330, 7340, 7365, 7370, 9445, 9450, 9485, 9530, 9550, 9660, 9820, 9840, 9860, 9885, 11675, 11985, 12125, 15125, 15205, 15525*

Winter Schedule 2004

Amharic	**Days**	**Area**	**kHz**
1600-1630	...tfss	Af	12125mey
1630-1700	daily	Af	12125mey
1633-1700	daily	Af	9885kig
Arabic	**Days**	**Area**	**kHz**
0400-0500	mtwt..s	ME	15525sam
0400-0530	....fs.	ME	15525sam
1903-2030	daily	Af	9550kig
Badaga	**Days**	**Area**	**kHz**
0100-0115	....fs.	As	7365gav
Balti	**Days**	**Area**	**kHz**
1500-1515	m..tf.s	WAs	9445nvs
Baluchi	**Days**	**Area**	**kHz**
0215-0230	....fss	WAs	5985dha
1730-1745	.....ss	WAs	9840msk
Bangla	**Days**	**Area**	**kHz**
0030-0045	mtwt...	As	7265tac
1230-1315	....f..	As	9485tac
1300-1315	mtwt.ss	As	9485tac
Bhili	**Days**	**Area**	**kHz**
1330-1345	m......	As	11675dha
Bhojpuri	**Days**	**Area**	**kHz**
0030-0045	....fs.	As	7265tac
Brahui	**Days**	**Area**	**kHz**
0215-0230	mtwt...	WAs	5985dha
Brij	**Days**	**Area**	**kHz**
1330-1345	.t.....	As	11675dha
Chhattisgarhi	**Days**	**Area**	**kHz**
1230-1245	...t...	As	9485tac
1230-1300	.....s.	As	9485tac
Dari	**Days**	**Area**	**kHz**
0215-0245	daily	WAs	7370sam, 9860sam
1600-1630	daily	WAs	7330arm
Dhivehi	**Days**	**Area**	**kHz**
1600-1615	..w.fs.	As	7340irk

Dinka	**Days**	**Area**	**kHz**
1530-1545	daily	Af	12125mey
English	**Days**	**Area**	**kHz**
1400-1415	daily	WAs	9445nvs
1500-1515	daily	As	7340irk
1515-1600	daily	As	7340irk
1730-1745	....f..	WAs	9840msk
Farsi	**Days**	**Area**	**kHz**
0630-0800	....f..	ME	9660dha
1630-1730	mtw.fss	ME	9840msk
1630-1745	...t...	ME	9840msk
French	**Days**	**Area**	**kHz**
1830-1900	daily	CAf,WAf	15125asc
Gujarati	**Days**	**Area**	**kHz**
1330-1400	....f.s	As	11675dha
1345-1400	mtwt.s.	As	11675dha
Guragena	**Days**	**Area**	**kHz**
1600-1630	mtw....	Af	12125mey
Hassinya/Pulaar	**Days**	**Area**	**kHz**
2145-2215	...tf..	WAf	11985asc
Hazaragi	**Days**	**Area**	**kHz**
0245-0300	daily	WAs	7370sam, 9860sam
1630-1645	daily	WAs	7330arm
Hindi	**Days**	**Area**	**kHz**
0030-0100	.....s.	As	7265tac
0045-0100	m.w.fs.	As	7265tac
0100-0130	daily	As	9820mos
1400-1500	....fs.	As	9530dha
1415-1500	mtw...s	As	9530dha
1445-1500	...t...	As	9530dha
Hindko	**Days**	**Area**	**kHz**
0230-0245	mtwtfs.	WAs	9450nvs
Kangri	**Days**	**Area**	**kHz**
1315-1330	.....s.	As	11675dha
Kannada	**Days**	**Area**	**kHz**
0100-0130	...t..s	As	7365gav
0115-0130	m.w.fs.	As	7365gav
1445-1500	....fs.	As	7340irk
Kumauni	**Days**	**Area**	**kHz**
1315-1345	.....s.	As	11675dha
Lambadi	**Days**	**Area**	**kHz**
1445-1500	m.....s	As	7340irk
Magahi	**Days**	**Area**	**kHz**
0045-0100	...t...	As	7265tac
Makonde	**Days**	**Area**	**kHz**
1545-1600	daily	Af	12125mey
Malay	**Days**	**Area**	**kHz**
1600-1615	...t...	As	7340irk
Malayalam	**Days**	**Area**	**kHz**
0530-0630	....f..	ME	6125dha
1400-1430	mtw...s	As	7340irk
1400-1445	...tfs.	As	7340irk
Marathi	**Days**	**Area**	**kHz**
0130-0145	daily	As	9820mos
Marwari	**Days**	**Area**	**kHz**
1330-1345	...t...	As	11675dha
Mundari	**Days**	**Area**	**kHz**
1230-1245	m.w....	As	9485tac
Nepali	**Days**	**Area**	**kHz**
1230-1300	t....s	As	9485tac
Nuer	**Days**	**Area**	**kHz**
1500-1530	daily	Af	12125mey
Oriya	**Days**	**Area**	**kHz**
0045-0100	.t.....	As	7265tac
1245-1300	m.wt...	As	9485tac
Oromo	**Days**	**Area**	**kHz**
1700-1730	daily	Af	6180dha
Pashto	**Days**	**Area**	**kHz**
0200-0215	daily	WAs	7370sam, 9860sam
0230-0245	daily	WAs	5985dha
1530-1600	daily	WAs	7330arm
Pothwari	**Days**	**Area**	**kHz**
0215-0230	.tw....	WAs	9450nvs
Punjabi	**Days**	**Area**	**kHz**
0115-0130	.....s.	As	9820mos
0200-0215	..w....	WAs	9450nvs
Punjabi	**Days**	**Area**	**kHz**
0215-0230	m...fs.	WAs	9450nvs
1315-1330	mt.tf..	As	11675dha
1315-1345	..w....	As	11675dha
1500-1515	.t.....	WAs	9445nvs
Sindhi	**Days**	**Area**	**kHz**
0200-0215	....fss	WAs	5985dha
Sinhala	**Days**	**Area**	**kHz**
0500-0530	....f..	ME	6125dha
1600-1615	mt....s	As	7340irk
Siraiki	**Days**	**Area**	**kHz**
0200-0215	mtwt...	WAs	5985dha
Somali	**Days**	**Area**	**kHz**
1700-1730	daily	Af	9885kig
Tamil	**Days**	**Area**	**kHz**
0030-0100	...tfss	As	7365gav
0030-0115	mtw....	As	7365gav
1445-1500	.t.t...	As	7340irk
Telugu	**Days**	**Area**	**kHz**
0130-0200	daily	As	7365gav
1430-1445	mt....s	As	7340irk
1430-1500	..w....	As	7340irk
Tibetan	**Days**	**Area**	**kHz**
1200-1230	daily	As	15205dha
Tigrinya	**Days**	**Area**	**kHz**
1730-1757	daily	Af	9885kig
Tulu	**Days**	**Area**	**kHz**
0115-0130	.t.....	As	7365gav
Turkmen	**Days**	**Area**	**kHz**
1730-1745	mtw....	WAs	9840msk
Urdu	**Days**	**Area**	**kHz**
0115-0130	....f..	As	9820mos
0200-0215	mt..fs.	WAs	9450nvs
0200-0230	...t...	WAs	9450nvs
0200-0245	.....s.	WAs	9450nvs
1400-1415	mtw...s	As	9530dha
1400-1445	...t...	As	9530dha
1415-1500	mt.tf.s	WAs	9445nvs
1415-1515	..w..s.	WAs	9445nvs
Uzbek	**Days**	**Area**	**kHz**
1645-1700	daily	WAs	7330arm

V: Does not verify reception reports.
NOTES: A division of Far East Broadcasting Company Inc.; see USA for corporate details.

RADIO EZRA (Rlg)

P.O. Box 674, Stockton on Tees, TS18 3WR, United Kingdom. ☎ +44 1642 887546. Fax +44 1642 887546.
Email: info@radioezra.com **Web:** www.radioezra.com
L.P: Producer: John D. Hill
ANN: English: "Blessed be Yahweh, the God of our fathers. You're tuned to Radio Ezra and you're listening to the Light of Israel radio broadcast"
V: QSL-letter.
NOTES: Radio Outreach Project of the World Karaite Movement. Not on the air at editorial deadline, leases air time on European tx several times per year, as funds allow.

VT MERLIN COMMUNICATIONS LTD. (Tx Operator)

20 Lincoln's Inn Fields, London WC2A 3ED, United Kingdom. ☎ +44 20 79690000. Fax +44 20 79366223.
Email: marketing@merlincommunications.com
Web: www.vtplc.com/merlin
L.P: Chief Executive: Fiona Lowry; Marketing Mgr: Laura Jelf.
MW: [ORF] Orfordness (G.C. 52N10 001E57) 648/1296kHz 500kW
SW: [RMP] Rampisham (G.C. 50N48 002W38) 10 x 500kW; [SKN] Skelton (G.C. 54N44 002W54) 11 x 250, 6 x 300kW; [WOF] Woofferton (G.C. 52N19 002W43) 6 x 250, 4 x 300kW
NOTES: VT Merlin Communications Ltd., part of VT Group plc, owns and operates the medium and shortwave sites in the UK that are used by the BBC World Service. It also operates the British overseas relay stations under a management contract. While the BBCWS is Merlin's primary customer, Merlin also leases out its facilities to a variety of other broadcasters.

RADIO SIX INTERNATIONAL

PO Box 600, Glasgow G41 5SH Scotland.
☎ +44 141 427 0531.

Email: letters@radiosix.com **Web:** www.radiosix.com
L.P: Prgr Dir.: Tony Currie; Chief Engineer: Leo Currie.
SW: Relayed via IRRS in Italy and WBCQ in USA.
kHz: *5105, 5775, 13840*

Winter Schedule 2004

English	Days	Area	kHz
0000-0200	daily	NAm,Eu	5105bcq**
0800-0900	......s	Eu,ME	13840mil*
0930-1030	.....s.	Eu,ME	13840mil*
2000-2100	...t...	Eu,ME	5775mil*

ANN: English: "Around the clock, around the world, Radio Six International"
V: QSL-card. Rp.
NOTES: Radio Six International is a not-for-profit station set up and run by a handful of professional broadcasters. The station plays music mainly by unsigned performers, and solicits new music from musicians around the world. The station has been in existence in one form or another since 1963. Key: * Second week in month only; ** alternate frequency 7415kHz.
PUBS: "Radio news", monthly

WALES RADIO INTERNATIONAL

✉ Pros Kairon, Crymych, Pembrokeshire, SA41 3QE, Wales, United Kingdom.
☎ +44 1437 563361. 🖷 +44 1239 831390.
Email: jennyob@wri.cymru.net **Web:** wri.cymru.net
SW: Leased from VT Merlin Communications Ltd
kHz: *3955, 6005, 7110, 17625*

Winter Schedule 2004

English	Days	Area	kHz
0300-0330	.....s.	NAm	6005rmp
1130-1200	.....s.	Oc	17625rmp
2130-2200	....f..	WEu	7110mos
2130-2200	....f..	Eu	3955skn

ANN: English: "Wales Radio International"; Welsh: "Radio Rhyngwladol Cymru"
V: QSL-card.
NOTES: Wales Radio International is a project initiated by the studio company Preseli Radio Productions in association with public and private sector partners in order to raise awareness of the heritage, culture, music and economic base of Wales.

WORLD RADIO NETWORK

✉ P.O. Box 1212, London SW8 2ZF, United Kingdom.
☎ +44 20 78969000. 🖷 +44 20 78969007.
Email: email@wrn.org **Web:** www.wrn.org
L.P: MD: Karl Miosga.
SAT: Astra 2B, Hotbird 5, Telstar 5, Thaicom 3
NOTES: WRN is a multichannel 24h news and information network via satellite and Internet, carrying prgr's from major world broadcasters. The WRN feeds can be heard on numerous AM/FM radio stations and cable around the globe. WRN is also brokering shortwave transmitter air time.

Broadcasters using sites in this country:
Akhbar Mufriha uses: (SKN). See stn entry in: **E**, INT Section
BBG-R.Farda uses: (WOF). See stn entry in: **USA**, INT Section
BBG-RFE/RL uses: (WOF). See stn entry in: **USA**, INT Section
BBG-VOA uses: (WOF). See stn entry in: **USA**, INT Section
Brigham YU R. uses: (RMP). See stn entry in: **USA**, INT Section
China R. Int'l uses: (LND). See stn entry in: **CHN**, INT Section
HCJB uses: (RMP). See stn entry in: **EQA**, INT Section
Leading The Way uses: (RMP). See stn entry in: **USA**, INT Section
Peace Radio uses: (RMP). See stn entry in: **AFG**, CTB Section
R.Australia uses: (RMP). See stn entry in: **AUS**, INT Section
R.Japan uses: (RMP). See stn entry in: **J**, INT Section
R.Japan uses: (SKN). See stn entry in: **J**, INT Section
R.Japan uses: (WOF). See stn entry in: **J**, INT Section
R.Korea Int'l uses: (SKN). See stn entry in: **KOR**, INT Section
R.Korea Int'l uses: (RMP). See stn entry in: **KOR**, INT Section
R.Ndeke Luka uses: (WOF). See stn entry in: **CAF**, CTB Section
R.Sri Lanka uses: (WOF). See stn entry in: **CLN**, INT Section
R.Taiwan Int'l uses: (SKN). See stn entry in: **TWN**, INT Section
RCI uses: (RMP). See stn entry in: **CAN**, INT Section
RCI uses: (SKN). See stn entry in: **CAN**, INT Section
RNZI uses: (RMP). See stn entry in: **NZL**, INT Section
RVI uses: (RMP). See stn entry in: **BEL**, INT Section
RVI uses: (SKN). See stn entry in: **BEL**, INT Section
Salaam Watandar uses: (RMP). See stn entry in: **AFG**, CTB Section
Sudan R. Sce uses: (WOF). See stn entry in: **SDN**, CTB Section
UN Radio uses: (RMP). See stn entry in: **UNO**, INT Section
UN Radio uses: (SKN). See stn entry in: **UNO**, INT Section
VO Eritr.People uses: (RMP). See stn entry in: **ERI**, CTB Section
VO Vietnam uses: (SKN). See stn entry in: **VTN**, INT Section

UNITED NATIONS

UNITED NATIONS RADIO

✉ UN Secretariat Building, Room S-850A, New York, NY 10017, USA.
☎ +1 212 9635201. 🖷 +1 212 9631307.
Email: unradio@un.org
Web: www.un.org/av/radio/news/latenews.htm
kHz: *7170, 7265, 9565, 9810, 17810, 21535*

Winter Schedule 2004

Arabic	Days	Area	kHz
1830-1845	mtwtf..	ME	7265rmp, 9810skn
English	**Days**	**Area**	**kHz**
1730-1745	mtwtf..	WAf,CAf	17810asc
1730-1745	mtwtf..	ME	9565skn
1730-1745	mtwtf..	EAf	7170mey
French	**Days**	**Area**	**kHz**
1700-1715	mtwtf..	SAf	7170mey
1700-1715	mtwtf..	NAf	9565skn
1700-1715	mtwtf..	CAf,SAf	21535mey

ANN: English: "United Nations Radio in New York"
V: QSL-card.

See also Radio UNMEE in: ETH, CTB Section

UNITED STATES OF AMERICA

AMERICAN FORCES RADIO AND TELEVISION SERVICE (AFRTS) (Gov)

✉ AFRTS Broadcast Center, 1363 Z Street, Bldg. 2730, March ARB, CA 92518-2017, USA.
☎ +1 909 4132236. 🖷 +1 909 4132457.
Web: www.myafn.net/radio/shortwave
SW: [BAR] Barrigada, Guam (G.C. 13N34 144E50); [DGA] Diego Garcia (G.C. 07S03 072E04); [GVK] Grindavík, Iceland (G.C. 63N50 022W26); [KEW] Key West, FL (G.C. 24N34 081W45); [PEW] Pearl Harbour, Hawaii (G.C. 21N25 158W09); [ROR] Roosevelt Roads, Puerto Rico (G.C. 18N23 067W11).
kHz: *4319, 5446, 5765, 6350, 7507, 7590, 9980, 10320, 12133, 12579, 13362*

Winter Schedule 2004

English	Days	Area	kHz
0000-2400	daily	Atl	5446kew, 7507ror, 7590gvk, 9980gvk, 12133kew
0200-1400	daily	Pac	12579dga
0600-1800	daily	Pac	6350peh
0800-2200	daily	Pac	5765bar
1400-0200	daily	Pac	4319dga
1800-0600	daily	Pac	10320peh
2200-0800	daily	Pac	13362bar

ANN: English: "You're listening to AFN"; "This is National Public Radio"
V: QSL-card.
NOTES: The shortwave transmissions are aired from U.S. bases on maritime frequencies and are USB feeds for U.S. Navy vessels. AFRTS left SW in 1986, but resumed SW feeds in 1998 after changing from analogue to digital satellite distribution. The AFRTS shortwave frequencies are carrying the AFN Interruptible Voice Channel (IVC), consisting mainly of a relay of National Public Radio (NPR). The IVC is often interrupted with live sport events.

BBG – RADIO AAP KI DUNYAA (Gov)

✉ 330 Independence Avenue SW, Washington, DC 20237, USA.
☎ +1 202 6191933.
Email: urdu@voanews.com **Web:** www.voanews.com/urdu
L.P: Head of Urdu Service: Dr. Brian Q. Silver.
kHz: *972, 6170, 7260, 9510, 9705, 9785, 11730, 11975, 12150, 15540*

Winter Schedule 2004

Urdu	Days	Area	kHz
0100-0200	daily	SAs	6170mor, 9705udo, 11730udo
1400-0200	daily	SAs	972orz

Urdu	Days	Area	kHz
1400-1500	daily	SAs	9510kav, 12150ira, 15540kav
1700-1800	daily	SAs	7260udo, 9785pht, 11975ira

ANN: Urdu: "Radio Aap Ki Dunyaa"
V: QSL-card.
NOTES: BBG funded station for listeners in Pakistan, launched May 2004.

BBG – RADIO ASHNA (Gov)

330 Independence Avenue SW, Washington, DC 20237, USA.
kHz: *1296, 9335, 11685, 11730, 11750, 11770, 11835, 11995, 12140, 15615*

Winter Schedule 2004

Dari	Days	Area	kHz
0130-0230	daily	AFG	1296kab, 9335ira, 11995kbd
1500-1530	daily	AFG	1296kab, 12140kbd, 15615kbd
1630-1730	daily	AFG	1296kab, 11685kbd, 11770udo
1800-1830	daily	AFG	1296kab, 11730kbd, 11770udo
1930-2030	daily	AFG	1296kab, 11835kbd
Pashto	**Days**	**Area**	**kHz**
0030-0130	daily	AFG	1296kab, 9335ira, 11995kbd
1430-1500	daily	AFG	1296kab, 12140kbd, 15615kbd
1530-1630	daily	AFG	1296kab, 12140kbd, 15615kbd
1730-1800	daily	AFG	1296kab, 11730kbd, 11770udo
1830-1930	daily	AFG	1296kab, 11750kbd

ANN: Dari: "In Radyoi Ashna"; Pashto: "Da VOA Ashna Radyo"
V: QSL-card.
NOTES: BBG funded service for listeners in South West Asia, produced by VOA.

BBG – RADIO FARDA (Gov)

1201 Connecticut Avenue NW, Washington, DC 20036, USA.
☎ +1 202 8287220. +1 202 8287239.
Email: comment@radiofarda.com **Web:** www.radiofarda.com
Studios: Vinohradská 1, 110 00 Prague 1, Czech Republic.
☎ +420 2 21121111. +420 2 21123013.
L.P: Dir: Andres Ilves.
kHz: *1170, 6140, 7105, 7550, 7580, 9335, 9435, 9585, 9785, 9795, 11845, 12015, 13680, 15290, 15410, 15690, 17595, 17675*

Winter Schedule 2004

Farsi	Days	Area	kHz
0000-2400	daily	ME	1170dha
0030-0230	daily	ME	15690ira
0030-0400	daily	ME	9585mor
0030-0600	daily	ME	9795lam
0230-0400	daily	ME	7105kav
0400-0600	daily	ME	12015kav
0400-0830	daily	ME	9585lam
0600-0800	daily	ME	17675kav
0600-0830	daily	ME	15290kav
0800-1030	daily	ME	11845ira
0830-1400	daily	ME	13680kav, 15690ira
1030-1230	daily	ME	17595udo
1230-1700	daily	ME	9435kav
1400-1700	daily	ME	15410wof
1400-1900	daily	ME	13680lam
1700-1900	daily	ME	7580ira, 11845lam
1900-2000	daily	ME	6140dsb
1900-2130	daily	ME	7550ira, 9335ira
2000-2130	daily	ME	9785udo

ANN: Farsi: "Radio Farda"
V: QSL-card.
NOTES: BBG funded station for listeners in Iran, launched in December 2002. Produced in the RFE/RL studios in Prague, Czech Republic. The transmissions are jammed in the target area.

BBG – RADIO FREE AFGHANISTAN (Gov)

1201 Connecticut Avenue NW, Washington, DC 20036, USA.
☎ +1 202 4576900. +1 202 4576992.
Email: afghan@rferl.org **Web:** www.azadiradio.org
Studios: Vinohradská 1, 110 00 Prague 1, Czech Republic.
☎ +420 2 21122370. +420 2 21123245.
L.P: Dir: Andres Ilves (temp.).
kHz: *1296, 9335, 11940, 12140, 15690, 17595, 17775, 19010, 21690*

Winter Schedule 2004

Dari	Days	Area	kHz
0330-0430	daily	AFG	1296kab, 9335ira, 11940kbd, 15690ira
0530-0630	daily	AFG	1296kab, 11940kbd, 19010kbd, 21690udo
0730-0830	daily	AFG	1296kab, 11940kbd, 17595udo, 19010kbd
0930-1030	daily	AFG	1296kab, 11940kbd, 17595udo, 19010kbd
1130-1230	daily	AFG	1296kab, 11940kbd, 19010kbd
1330-1430	daily	AFG	1296kab, 12140kbd, 17775kbd
Pashto	**Days**	**Area**	**kHz**
0230-0330	daily	AFG	1296kab, 9335ira, 11940kbd, 15690ira
0430-0530	daily	AFG	1296kab, 11940kbd, 19010kbd, 21690udo
0630-0730	daily	AFG	1296kab, 11940kbd, 17595udo, 19010kbd
0830-0930	daily	AFG	1296kab, 11940kbd, 17595udo, 19010kbd
1030-1130	daily	AFG	1296kab, 11940kbd, 19010kbd
1230-1330	daily	AFG	1296kab, 11940kbd, 12140kbd, 17595udo

ANN: Dari: "Radyoi Afghonistani Azad"; Pashto: "Da Azad Afghanistan Radyo"
V: QSL-card.
NOTES: BBG funded station for listeners in Afghanistan, launched in January 2001. Produced in the RFE/RL studios in Prague, Czech Republic.

BBG – RADIO FREE ASIA (RFA) (Gov)

2025 M Street NW, Washington, DC 20036, USA.
☎ +1 202 5304900. +1 202 5307794.
Email: info@rfa.org **Web:** www.rfa.org
L.P: Pres: Richard Richter.
kHz: *6010, 7185, 7210, 7415, 7455, 7460, 7470, 7480, 7495, 7515, 7530, 7540, 7550, 7560, 9355, 9365, 9385, 9455, 9490, 9570, 9625, 9645, 9670, 9690, 9775, 9825, 9845, 9875, 9885, 9905, 9930, 11510, 11520, 11535, 11540, 11580, 11605, 11695, 11720, 11740, 11775, 11785, 11790, 11795, 11830, 11870, 11900, 11945, 11950, 11965, 11970, 11995, 12105, 13625, 13670, 13710, 13720, 13725, 13745, 13760, 13800, 13815, 13830, 13865, 15150, 15185, 15210, 15215, 15220, 15255, 15270, 15385, 15395, 15430, 15435, 15470, 15485, 15510, 15545, 15550, 15555, 15565, 15660, 15665, 15680, 17495, 17515, 17525, 17540, 17565, 17570, 17615, 17720, 17730, 17880, 21540, 21570, 21625, 21715*

Winter Schedule 2004

Burmese	Days	Area	kHz
0030-0130	daily	SEA	11535dsb, 13710sai, 13815ira, 15210tin
1300-1400	daily	SEA	9355dsb, 11795tin, 12105ira, 15215tin
Cantonese	**Days**	**Area**	**kHz**
1400-1500	daily	CHN	9825tin, 11950sai, 15255tin
2200-2300	daily	CHN	9570sai, 9845hbn, 11740tin, 11775tin
Khmer	**Days**	**Area**	**kHz**
1230-1330	daily	SEA	11510alm, 13725ira, 15395tin
2230-2330	daily	SEA	7185ira, 9930hbn, 15485tin
Korean	**Days**	**Area**	**kHz**
1500-1700	daily	FE	7210irk, 11870sai, 13625tin
2100-2300	daily	FE	7460uba, 9385tin, 11785sai, 13625tin
2200-2300	daily	FE	9455tin

Lao	Days	Area	kHz
0000-0100	daily	SEA	11830ira, 13830alm, 15545tin
1100-1200	daily	SEA	9355sai, 9775tin, 15555ira, 15680alm
Mandarin	**Days**	**Area**	**kHz**
0300-0600	daily	CHN	21540tin
0300-0700	daily	CHN	13625tin, 13760tin, 15150tin, 15665tin, 17495dsb, 17525dsb, 17615sai, 17880sai
1500-1800	daily	CHN	9905hbn, 17565tin
1500-2000	daily	CHN	11945tin, 13670tin
1500-2200	daily	CHN	7540dsb, 13745tin, 15510tin
1600-2200	daily	CHN	9455sai
1700-2200	daily	CHN	9355sai
1800-2000	daily	CHN	7455dsb, 11790tin
1900-2200	daily	CHN	9875hbn, 11970tin
2000-2100	daily	CHN	11900sai
2000-2200	daily	CHN	9885tin, 11950tin
2300-2400	daily	CHN	7540dsb, 9905hbn, 11775tin, 11995sai, 13800tin, 15430tin, 15550tin
Tibetan	**Days**	**Area**	**kHz**
0100-0300	daily	SAs	7560gav, 9670wer, 11695dha, 15220tin, 15660dsb, 17730uba
0600-0700	daily	SAs	17515dsb, 17540gav, 17720uba, 21570tin, 21715dha
1100-1400	daily	SAs	7470uba, 9365gav, 11540dsb, 13625tin, 15435dha
1200-1400	daily	SAs	15185sai
1500-1600	daily	SAs	7470uba, 7495dsb, 11520gav, 15385dha
2300-2400	daily	SAs	6010dha, 7415dsb, 7470uba, 7550gav, 9875lam
Uighur	**Days**	**Area**	**kHz**
0100-0200	daily	CHN	7480dsb, 9365dsb, 9645dha, 9690dha, 15270tin, 17570tin
1600-1700	daily	CHN	7515dsb, 7530dsb, 9625dha, 11720tin, 13725ira
Vietnamese	**Days**	**Area**	**kHz**
1400-1500	daily	SEA	9365dsb, 9455sai, 9930whr, 11535alm, 11605tin, 13725hbn, 13865ira, 15470tin, 21625ira
2330-0030	daily	SEA	7515dsb, 9490alm, 9930hbn, 11580uba, 11605tin, 11965tin, 13720sai, 13865ira, 15565vld

ANN: At the start of the transmission period on each frequency in English: "This is Radio Free Asia. The following program is in ..."
V: QSL-card. Rpt to AJ Janitschek, Radio Free Asia, 2025 M. Street NW, Washington, DC 20036, USA. Email: qsl@rfa.org
NOTES: BBG funded station, launched in September 1996 and aimed at listeners in East & South East Asia. Due to political sensitivities, RFA does not wish to disclose the location of its transmitter sites. Transmissions are being jammed in parts of the target area.

BBG – RADIO FREE EUROPE/RADIO LIBERTY (RFE/RL) (Gov)

1201 Connecticut Avenue NW, Washington, DC 20036, USA.
☎ +1 202 4576900. 🖷 +1 202 4576992.
Email: webmaster@rferl.org **Web:** www.rferl.org
Studios: Vinohradská 1, 110 00 Prague 1, Czech Republic.
☎ +420 2 21121111. 🖷 +420 2 21123013.
L.P: Pres: Thomas A. Dine; Dir of Broadcasting: Michele DuBach; Dir of Communications: Donald Jensen.

kHz: *612, 864, 1143, 1197, 3965, 4760, 4995, 5955, 5980, 5985, 6055, 6095, 6105, 6115, 6135, 6140, 6150, 6160, 6170, 6180, 7115, 7145, 7155, 7165, 7175, 7190, 7195, 7220, 7235, 7245, 7255, 7260, 7265, 7275, 7280, 7295, 7490, 7565, 9315, 9325, 9355, 9505, 9520, 9555, 9565, 9570, 9595, 9605, 9620, 9625, 9635, 9650, 9675, 9680, 9695, 9705, 9715, 9725, 9770, 9805, 9825, 9830, 9835, 9840, 9850, 9865, 11665, 11685, 11705, 11730, 11740, 11765, 11785, 11790, 11795, 11805, 11815, 11835, 11875, 11885, 11895, 11905, 11910, 11930, 12015, 12020, 12040, 13640, 13810, 15110, 15120, 15130, 15160, 15170, 15205, 15215, 15250, 15345, 15370, 15410, 15460, 15590, 17610, 17680, 17695, 17730, 17805, 17845, 17865, 21690*

Winter Schedule 2004

Albanian (Kosovo)	Days	Area	kHz
2000-2030	daily	SEu	9565mor
2000-2030	daily	Eu	7175bib, 11765mor
Armenian	**Days**	**Area**	**kHz**
1500-1600	daily	CAs	11895bib
Avar/Chechen/ Circassian	**Days**	**Area**	**kHz**
0500-0600	daily	CAs	9595kav, 9770bib, 11785lam
1800-1900	daily	CAs	7565ira, 9595bib, 9840lam
Azeri	**Days**	**Area**	**kHz**
0400-0500	daily	CAs	9605kav
1600-1700	daily	CAs	9605lam
1900-2000	daily	CAs	9605bib
Belarusian	**Days**	**Area**	**kHz**
0400-0600	daily	Eu	612vln, 6140lam, 7190mor
1600-1800	daily	Eu	9865bib, 15460mor
1600-2200	daily	Eu	612vln
1800-1900	daily	Eu	9865mor
1800-2000	daily	Eu	6150bib
1900-2000	daily	Eu	9865lam
2000-2200	daily	Eu	7165kav, 9865mor
Georgian	**Days**	**Area**	**kHz**
0600-0700	daily	CAs	9850kav
1500-1600	daily	CAs	9325ira
Kazakh	**Days**	**Area**	**kHz**
0000-0100	daily	CAs	6135kav, 7145kav, 7490ira
0200-0400	daily	CAs	7145kav, 11795udo, 21690pht
1200-1300	daily	CAs	9520udo, 15110lam, 17680kav
1400-1500	daily	CAs	6055udo, 17695lam
1400-1600	daily	CAs	15205kav
1500-1600	daily	CAs	4995dsb, 6055pht
Kyrgyz	**Days**	**Area**	**kHz**
1300-1330	daily	CAs	9315ira, 11685udo, 15120ira
1400-1430	daily	CAs	9315ira, 12015lam, 15120lam
1500-1600	daily	CAs	9825kav, 11790wof
1500-1700	daily	CAs	7260udo
1600-1700	daily	CAs	9675pht, 9825lam
Romanian	**Days**	**Area**	**kHz**
1600-1630	mtwtf..	Eu	7165bib, 9725bib
1900-2000	mtwtf..	Eu	3965bib, 9725mor
Russian	**Days**	**Area**	**kHz**
0000-0100	daily	RUS	6095lam
0000-0200	daily	RUS	9520kav
0100-0200	daily	RUS	6095bib
0300-0400	daily	RUS	6105lam, 7115kav, 9680kav
0300-0500	daily	RUS	9520jbr
0300-0600	daily	RUS	5955bib
0300-0700	daily	RUS	7220lam
0400-0500	daily	RUS	6105kav
0400-0600	daily	RUS	9680mor, 9715lam
0500-0700	daily	RUS	9520kav, 13810ira
0600-0700	daily	RUS	11885bib
0600-0900	daily	RUS	9680bib, 17845udo
0700-0900	daily	RUS	9520lam, 11885lam, 15205lam, 15250pht
0900-1100	daily	RUS	9355tin, 9725pht, 11930pht, 15410udo

Russian	Days	Area	kHz
1100-1300	daily	RUS	15120lam, 15215kav, 17805lam
1100-1400	daily	RUS	9805lam, 11885lam, 17730kav
1300-1400	daily	RUS	11895bib, 15130lam, 15370lam
1500-1600	daily	RUS	9520lam, 11805bib, 11885lam, 15370mor
1500-1700	daily	RUS	7220lam, 15130mor
1600-1700	daily	RUS	9520mor, 12040bib
1600-1800	daily	RUS	6105lam, 11805mor
1700-1800	daily	RUS	7220jbr, 9505kav, 9520kav, 11885bib
2000-2100	daily	RUS	9650bib
2000-2200	daily	RUS	7265pht, 9520udo, 9620udo
2000-2300	daily	RUS	7220kav
2000-2400	daily	RUS	6105lam
2100-2300	daily	RUS	5955kav
2200-0200	daily	RUS	7175lam
2200-2300	daily	RUS	9865lam
2200-2400	daily	RUS	9520bib
2300-0200	daily	RUS	5985kav, 7155kav, 7220kav
Serbian	**Days**	**Area**	**kHz**
0000-0100	daily	Eu	1197ism, 6115bib, 9725mor
0330-0430	daily	Eu	1197ism
0830-0900	daily	Eu	9565bib, 11730mor, 15170mor
1400-1430	daily	Eu	9555bib, 11885mor, 15170mor
1700-1800	daily	Eu	1197ism, 7115mor, 7245bib, 9695bib
1830-1900	daily	Eu	7155bib
1830-2000	daily	Eu	9705wof, 11815mor
1900-2000	daily	Eu	7155lam
2100-2200	daily	Eu	7175bib, 7265bib, 9680mor
2300-0100	daily	Eu	7115mor
2300-2400	daily	Eu	1197ism, 6115lam, 9725mor
Tajik	**Days**	**Area**	**kHz**
0100-0200	daily	CAs	4760dsb, 7275kav
0100-0300	daily	CAs	9830udo
0200-0400	daily	CAs	7275lam, 11665udo
0300-0400	daily	CAs	9830ira
1400-1500	daily	CAs	11795lam, 11835kav
1400-1700	daily	CAs	9695udo
1500-1630	daily	CAs	11910udo
1500-1700	daily	CAs	11705mor
1630-1700	daily	CAs	4760dsb
Tatar/Bashkir	**Days**	**Area**	**kHz**
0400-0500	daily	RUS	7255bib, 9635kav
0600-0700	daily	CAs,RUS	9570kav, 11730bib
1600-1700	daily	RUS	6180kav, 9505lam
2000-2100	daily	CAs,RUS	7195lam, 7295kav
Turkmen	**Days**	**Area**	**kHz**
0200-0300	daily	CAs	864gav, 6160dsb, 7295kav, 9770ira
0300-0400	daily	CAs	9770kav, 15160ira, 17865udo
1400-1500	daily	CAs	9565bib, 13640lam, 15345kav
1500-1600	daily	CAs	15160kav
1500-1700	daily	CAs	11875mor
1500-1800	daily	CAs	9770bib
1530-1600	daily	CAs	864gav
1600-1800	daily	CAs	11740kav
1700-1800	daily	CAs	9625lam
Ukrainian	**Days**	**Area**	**kHz**
0400-0500	mtwtfs.	RUS	7115mor
0400-0500	mtwtfs.	Eu	6170bib, 9725mor
0600-0700	mtwtf..	Eu	5980bib, 7245lam, 9725mor
1700-1800	mtwtf..	Eu	7280kav

Ukrainian	Days	Area	kHz
1700-1800	mtwtf..	RUS	9725mor
1700-1800	mtwtf..	EEu	11905mor
1800-1900	daily	RUS	9725mor
1800-2000	daily	EEu	11905mor
1800-2000	daily	Eu	7280kav
1900-2000	daily	Eu	7235mor
Uzbek	**Days**	**Area**	**kHz**
0100-0200	daily	CAs	864gav
0200-0300	daily	CAs	7190lam
0200-0400	daily	CAs	9725udo, 15590udo
0300-0400	daily	CAs	7190kav
1300-1400	daily	CAs	1143dsb
1600-1800	daily	CAs	9835kav, 12020bib, 17610ira

ANN: RFE: Albanian: "Ju flet Radio Europa e Lire"; Bosnian/Makedonian/Serbian: "Radio Svobodna Evropa"; Moldovan (Romanian): "Aici e Radio Europa Libera". R. Liberty: Armenian: "Yeterum e Azatutyun Radiokayane"; Azeri: "Danisir Azadlyq Radiosu"; Belarusian: "Havoryc Radyjo Svaboda"; Georgian: "Laparakobs Radio Tavisupleba"; Kazakh: "Azattyq Radiosinan sövlep turmiz"; Kyrgyz: "Azattiq Radioyosinan söylöbüz"; Russian: "Govorit Radio Svoboda"; Tajik: "Injo Radioi Ozodi"; Tatar: "Azatliq Radiosi söyli"; Turkmen: "Gepleýär Azatlyk Radiosy"; Ukrainian: "Hovorit Radio Svoboda"; Uzbek: "Ozodlik Radiosidan gapiramiz"
V: QSL-card.
NOTES: BBG funded station for listeners in East & South East Europe and the successor states to the former USSR. RFE (launched 1950) and RL (launched 1951) were merged into one station in 1975. The studios were originally located in Munich, Germany and were moved to Prague, Czech Republic in 1995. The volume of the language services is reviewed every year, some services are provided only via satellite or webcasting.

BBG – RADIO FREE IRAQ (Gov)

✉ 1201 Connecticut Avenue NW, Washington, DC 20036, USA.
☎ +1 202 4576900. 🖷 +1 202 4576992.
Email: iraq@rferl.org **Web:** www.iraqhurr.org
✉ Studios: Vinohradská 1, 110 00 Prague 1, Czech Republic.
☎ +420 2 21121111. 🖷 +420 2 21123013.
L.P: Dir: David Newton
SAT: Hotbird 3, AsiaSat 2D
kHz: *1593*

Winter Schedule 2004

Arabic	Days	Area	kHz
0200-0300	daily	ME	1593kbd
0400-0700	daily	ME	1593kbd
1500-1700	daily	ME	1593kbd
2100-2300	daily	ME	1593kbd

ANN: Arabic: "Idha'at al-Iraq al-khar min Prag"
V: QSL-card.
NOTES: BBG funded station for listeners in Iraq, launched in October 1998. Produced in the RFE/RL studios in Prague, Czech Republic.

BBG – RADIO MARTÍ (Gov)

✉ 4201 NW 77th Ave, Miami, FL 33166, USA.
☎ +1 305 4377000. 🖷 +1 305 4377016.
Email: martinoticias@ocb.ibb.gov **Web:** www.martinoticias.com
L.P: Dir: Pedro V. Roig; Dir Tech. Operations: Michael F. Pallone (mpallone@ocb.ibb.gov).
kHz: *1180, 5745, 5980, 6030, 7365, 7405, 9565, 9805, 11775, 11930, 13820, 15330, 17670*

Winter Schedule 2004

Spanish	Days	Area	kHz
0000-0400	daily	CUB	7365grv, 11775grv
0000-2400	daily	CUB	1180mth
0300-0400	daily	CUB	7405grv
0400-0700	.twtfss	CUB	9805grv, 11775grv
0400-1000	.twtfss	CUB	6030grv, 7405grv
0700-1000	.twtfss	CUB	5980dln, 7365dln
1000-1200	daily	CUB	6030dln
1000-1300	daily	CUB	5980dln, 7365dln
1000-1400	daily	CUB	5745grv
1200-1500	daily	CUB	7405grv
1300-1930	daily	CUB	13820grv
1300-2400	daily	CUB	11930grv
1400-2000	daily	CUB	15330grv

Spanish	Days	Area	kHz
1500-2200	daily	CUB	17670dln
1930-0300	daily	CUB	13820dln
2000-2200	daily	CUB	9565grv
2200-0400	daily	CUB	6030grv
2200-2400	daily	CUB	15330dln

ANN: Spanish: "Radio Marti"
V: QSL-card.
NOTES: BBG funded station for listeners in Cuba, launched in May 1985. Also at various times on 531 (airborne Commando Solo transmissions) and 1610kHz (relayed via WDHP, Virgin Islands). Transmissions are jammed in the target area. Additional transmitter on the Turks & Caicos Islands (1570kHz, 50kW) is under construction.

BBG – RADIO SAWA (Gov)

330 Independence Avenue SW, Washington, DC 20237, USA.
☎ +1 202 6191941. Fax +1 202 6190428.
Email: comments@radiosawa.com **Web:** www.radiosawa.com
L.P: Dir: Gary Thatcher.
kHz: *990, 1260, 1431, 1548*

Winter Schedule 2004

Arabic	Days	Area	kHz
0000-0400	daily	Af	1431art
0000-2400	daily	NAf	990cgr
0000-2400	daily	ME	1548kbd
1500-0800	daily	ME	1260rho
1600-2400	daily	Af	1431art

ANN: Arabic: "Radio Sawa"
V: QSL-card.
NOTES: BBG funded station for young Arab listeners in the Middle East, launched in March 2002. Produced in the VOA studios in Washington, D.C. (on satellite & FM: 24h).

BBG – STUDIO 7 (Gov)

330 Independence Avenue SW, Washington, DC 20237, USA.
☎ +1 202 2034230. Fax +1 202 2034230.
Email: studio7@voanews.com **Web:** www.voanews.com/zimbabwe
kHz: *909, 11975, 17895*

Winter Schedule 2004

English	Days	Area	kHz
1740-1800	daily	ZMB	909bot, 11975sao, 17895mor
Ndebele	**Days**	**Area**	**kHz**
1720-1740	daily	ZMB	909bot, 11975sao, 17895mor
Shona	**Days**	**Area**	**kHz**
1700-1720	daily	ZMB	909bot, 11975sao, 17895mor

V: QSL-card.
NOTES: BBG funded station for listeners in Zimbabwe, launched in April 2003. Produced in the VOA studios.

BBG – VOICE OF AMERICA (VOA) (Gov)

330 Independence Avenue SW, Washington, DC 20237, USA.
☎ +1 202 4017000. Fax +1 202 6191241.
Email: letters@voa.gov **Web:** www.voanews.com
L.P: Dir: David Jackson.
kHz: *648, 756, 792, 909, 1143, 1197, 1215, 1296, 1395, 1458, 1530, 1575, 1593, 3980, 3985, 4940, 4960, 5890, 5905, 5955, 5985, 5990, 5995, 6015, 6025, 6030, 6035, 6040, 6045, 6050, 6060, 6080, 6105, 6110, 6135, 6140, 6160, 6170, 6180, 7105, 7110, 7115, 7125, 7130, 7135, 7140, 7145, 7150, 7155, 7165, 7175, 7190, 7200, 7205, 7215, 7220, 7235, 7255, 7260, 7265, 7270, 7280, 7290, 7295, 7340, 7390, 7405, 7570, 9325, 9435, 9480, 9485, 9495, 9505, 9520, 9525, 9530, 9535, 9540, 9545, 9555, 9560, 9565, 9575, 9590, 9595, 9620, 9635, 9645, 9650, 9655, 9670, 9675, 9680, 9685, 9705, 9710, 9720, 9725, 9750, 9760, 9775, 9780, 9785, 9790, 9795, 9800, 9805, 9810, 9815, 9830, 9835, 9845, 9850, 9875, 9885, 9890, 9980, 11520, 11655, 11665, 11680, 11690, 11700, 11705, 11715, 11730, 11760, 11770, 11775, 11780, 11785, 11790, 11805, 11820, 11825, 11835, 11855, 11870, 11875, 11885, 11890, 11895, 11915, 11925, 11930, 11935, 11965, 11975, 11985, 11990, 11995, 12010, 12015, 12040, 12065, 12080, 12110, 12140, 13600, 13640, 13645, 13650, 13710, 13715, 13735, 13740, 13755, 13765, 13800, 13865, 15105, 15130, 15150, 15160, 15185, 15205, 15210, 15220, 15225, 15240, 15250, 15255, 15265, 15290, 15305, 15320, 15370, 15385, 15395, 15425, 15445, 15460, 15515, 15530, 15545, 15580, 15585, 15615, 15665, 15750, 17555, 17565, 17580, 17640, 17705, 17715, 17730, 17740, 17750, 17765, 17770, 17785, 17855, 17895, 21480, 21485, 21540, 21570, 21580*

Winter Schedule 2004

Albanian	Days	Area	kHz
0600-0630	daily	Eu	1215fla, 6030bib, 7115wof, 9635mor
1700-1730	daily	Eu	5990bib, 11665mor, 11855bib
1930-2000	daily	Eu	1458fla, 7115wof, 9565mor
Amharic	**Days**	**Area**	**kHz**
1800-1830	daily	EAf	11690kav, 13755bot, 13800ira
1830-1900	.....ss	EAf	11690kav, 13755bot, 13800ira
Azeri	**Days**	**Area**	**kHz**
1830-1900	daily	CAs	9750lam, 9800ira, 11770mor
Bangla	**Days**	**Area**	**kHz**
0130-0200	daily	SAs	11520ira, 15160pht, 15210ira
1600-1700	daily	SAs	1575bph, 7280udo, 11520ira, 15185pht
Bosnian	**Days**	**Area**	**kHz**
1600-1615	mtwtf..	Eu	1197ism
2230-2300	mtwtf..	Eu	792kav, 1197ism
Burmese	**Days**	**Area**	**kHz**
1130-1200	daily	SEA	1575bph, 6140udo, 9890ira, 15225pht
1430-1500	daily	SEA	1575bph, 5955pht, 9325ira, 11965pht
2330-2400	daily	SEA	6135udo, 7260ira, 9710pht
Cantonese	**Days**	**Area**	**kHz**
1300-1400	daily	CHN	9705sai, 11930tin
1300-1500	daily	CHN	1143php, 15160pht
1400-1500	daily	CHN	9705sai, 11930tin
Creole	**Days**	**Area**	**kHz**
1230-1300	mtwtf..	Car	9535grv, 11890grv, 15265grv
1730-1800	daily	Car	15385grv, 17565grv, 21540dln
2200-2230	daily	Car	9525grv, 9670grv, 21540dln
Croatian	**Days**	**Area**	**kHz**
0530-0600	daily	Eu	756lam, 1197ism, 1395fla, 7165bib, 9635bib, 9655mor
1930-2000	daily	Eu	1197ism, 6050bib, 7105bib, 7270wof
English	**Days**	**Area**	**kHz**
0000-0030	daily	EAs	15290pht
0000-0030	daily	SEA,Pac	11760udo
0000-0030	daily	SEA	1575bph, 7215pht, 9890pht, 15185pht
0000-0030	daily	Pac	17740pht
0000-0030	daily	AFG	11995kbd
0000-0030	daily	ME	1593kbd
0030-0100	daily	EAs	15290pht
0030-0100	daily	EAs,Pac	17740pht
0030-0100	daily	ME	1593kbd
0030-0100	daily	SEA	1575bph, 9890pht
0030-0100	daily	SEA,Oc	15185pht
0030-0100	daily	SEA,Pac	7215pht
0100-0130	daily	ME	1593kbd
0100-0200	daily	SAs	7200kav, 11705udo, 11820ira, 17740pht
0130-0200	.twtfs.	ME	1593kbd
0130-0200	.twtfs.	SAm	7405grv, 9775grv, 13740dln
0200-0300	mtwtf..	SAs	7200kav, 11705udo, 11820ira, 17740pht
0300-0330	daily	EAf,SAf	7340bot
0300-0400	daily	Af	6035bot
0300-0430	daily	Af	1530sao, 9885bot
0300-0500	daily	Af	6080sao, 7290sao
0300-0630	daily	Af	909bot
0400-0500	daily	Af	4960sao, 9575grv, 9775bot

English	Days	Area	kHz
0500-0600	daily	Af	6035grv, 6080sao, 6105sao, 7295mor
0500-0600	daily	EAf,SAf	13710bot
0600-0630	daily	Af	6035grv, 6105sao, 11995kav
0600-0630	daily	EAf,SAf	13710bot
0600-0700	daily	Af	1530sao, 6080sao, 7295mor, 11835bot
0700-0900	daily	Af	5995mor, 6080sao, 11655bot
0900-1200	daily	ME	13865ira, 15615kav, 17555kav
1100-1130	…..ss	SEA	1575bph
1200-1230	daily	EAs	1143php
1200-1300	daily	Pac	11715pht
1200-1300	daily	SEA	6110pht, 15665ira
1200-1400	daily	EAs	9760pht
1200-1400	daily	SEA,Pac	9645udo
1200-1500	daily	SAs,SEA	9760pht
1200-1500	daily	CHN	11705pht
1300-1500	daily	SAs,SEA	6110pht
1400-1500	daily	SEA	15425pht
1400-1500	daily	SEA,Pac	15425pht
1400-1500	daily	SAs,SEA	9645pht
1400-1600	daily	SAs	7125udo
1500-1530	…..ss	SEA	1575bph
1500-1530	daily	EAs	9760pht, 9795pht
1500-1530	daily	SAs,SEA	6110pht, 9760pht
1500-1530	daily	SEA	15460udo
1500-1600	daily	ME	9685kav
1500-1600	mtwtf..	EAf	13865ira
1500-1600	daily	SAs	9645ira
1500-1600	daily	EAs	7175udo
1500-1600	mtwtf..	Af	13600sao, 17715bot, 17895bot
1500-1600	daily	EAs,SEA	11780ira, 13735ira
1500-1700	daily	ME	11835lam, 15255kav
1530-1600	daily	EAs	9760pht, 9795pht
1530-1600	daily	SAs,SEA	6110pht, 9760pht
1530-1600	daily	SEA	1575bph, 15460udo
1600-1700	mtwtf..	SAs,SEA	6160pht, 9760pht
1600-1700	daily	Af	909bot, 1530sao, 13600sao, 15445bot, 17640mor, 17715sao, 17895bot
1600-1700	daily	ME	9685kav
1600-1700	mtwtf..	CHN	1143php
1600-1700	mtwtf..	SAs	7125udo, 9645ira
1600-2200	daily	Af	15240mor
1700-1800	daily	EAf,SAf	15445bot
1700-2000	daily	Af	13710udo
1800-2000	daily	Af	17895bot
1800-2200	daily	Af	909bot, 6035sao, 11975sao
1900-2000	daily	ME	9785kav, 12015udo, 13640mor
1900-2030	daily	Af	4940sao
1900-2200	daily	Af	15580grv
2000-2100	daily	ME	1593kbd
2000-2200	daily	Af	1530sao, 13710bot
2030-0030	daily	AFG	1296kab
2030-2100	…..ss	Af	4940sao
2030-2230	daily	AFG	11835kbd
2200-2400	daily	EAs	15290pht
2200-2400	daily	EAs,Pac	17740pht
2200-2400	daily	SEA	7215pht, 9890pht, 15185pht, 15305ira
2230-2300	daily	CHN	9545pht, 9785udo, 13755tin
2230-2330	daily	AFG	11935kbd
2230-2400	….fs.	SEA	1575bph
2300-2400	daily	EAs	6180udo, 7205udo, 9780pht, 11655udo, 15150pht
2300-2400	daily	ME	1593kbd
2330-2400	daily	SEA	7130udo, 9620udo, 11805pht, 13640tin, 15205pht
2330-2400	daily	AFG	11995kbd

Farsi	Days	Area	kHz
0300-0400	daily	ME	1593kbd, 7200kav, 9435kav, 17855ira
1700-1800	daily	ME	12110jul
1700-1900	daily	ME	6160kav, 9680lam
1700-2000	daily	ME	1593kbd
1800-1900	daily	ME	648orz, 9495jul
1900-2000	daily	ME	6160bib, 9680jul, 9980ira

French	Days	Area	kHz
0530-0600	mtwtf..	Af	1530sao
0530-0630	mtwtf..	Af	5890grv, 7265mor, 9480grv, 9505wof
1830-1900	daily	Af	1530sao, 9815bot, 12080bot, 13735sao, 15220mor, 17580grv, 21485grv
1830-2030	daily	Af	11985sao
1900-2000	daily	Af	1530sao, 9815bot, 12080bot, 13735sao, 15220mor, 17580grv, 21485grv
2000-2030	daily	Af	9815bot, 12080bot, 13735sao, 15220mor, 21485grv
2030-2100	…..ss	Af	9780sao, 9815bot, 11775sao, 12080bot, 15220mor, 21485grv
2100-2130	mtwtf..	Af	5985wof, 9780sao, 9815bot, 21485grv

Georgian	Days	Area	kHz
1630-1700	daily	CAs	11925kav, 12140ira, 13645mor

Hausa	Days	Area	kHz
0500-0530	daily	Af	1530sao, 4960sao, 7105sao, 9885mor
1500-1530	daily	Af	7135sao, 9810sao, 11680sao
1800-1830	…..s.	Af	1530sao, 4940sao, 9830sao, 11825sao, 17785mor
2030-2100	mtwtf..	Af	4940sao, 9780sao, 9815bot, 11775sao, 12080bot, 15220mor, 21485grv

Hindi	Days	Area	kHz
0030-0100	daily	SAs	5955kav, 7135ira, 11730udo
1600-1700	daily	SAs	6060udo, 9595kav, 11730ira

Indonesian	Days	Area	kHz
1130-1230	daily	SEA	7215pht, 7255udo, 9720udo, 15160sai
1400-1500	…tfs.	SEA	11760tin, 11985pht, 15105udo
2200-2330	daily	SEA	7130udo, 9620udo, 11805pht, 15205pht

Khmer	Days	Area	kHz
1330-1430	daily	SEA	1575bph, 5955pht, 9325ira, 11965pht
2200-2230	daily	SEA	1575bph, 6060pht, 7260ira, 9535pht, 13640tin

Kinyarwanda/ Kirundi	Days	Area	kHz
0330-0430	daily	Af	7340bot, 9785sao, 11915sao
1600-1630	…..s.	Af	17785mor
1600-1630	…..s.	EAf	11665kav, 11965sao

Korean	Days	Area	kHz
1300-1400	daily	FE	648vld, 5985udo, 7235tin, 9555udo, 15250tin

Korean	Days	Area	kHz
1400-1500	daily	EAs	9555pht
1400-1500	daily	FE	7235tin, 15250tin
2000-2100	daily	FE	5995pht, 7110udo, 11825udo
2030-2100	daily	FE	12065ppk

Kurdish	Days	Area	kHz
0500-0600	daily	ME	5995bib, 7115mor, 11855kav
1400-1500	daily	ME	1593kbd, 13740kav, 15530mor, 17750mor
1700-1800	daily	ME	7145kav, 7570ira, 9325ira
1900-2000	daily	ME	6040kav, 7255kav, 9325ira

Lao	Days	Area	kHz
1230-1300	daily	SEA	1575bph, 6030udo, 7215pht, 11930pht

Mandarin	Days	Area	kHz
0000-0200	daily	CHN	7190udo, 9545pht
0000-0300	daily	CHN	11925pht, 15395pht, 17765pht, 21580tin
0700-1000	daily	CHN	15515udo
0700-1100	daily	CHN	11855udo, 11965udo, 12010pht, 13650tin, 13765udo
0900-1100	daily	CHN	9845pht, 15665sai
1000-1100	daily	CHN	15515udo
1100-1200	daily	CHN	1143php
1100-1300	daily	CHN	9530pht, 11965pht
1100-1400	daily	CHN	12040pht
1100-1500	daily	CHN	6160pht, 9680pht, 11785udo
1200-1300	daily	CHN	11995tin
1300-1500	daily	CHN	7390nvs, 9790pht
2200-2300	daily	CHN	5905irk, 6025pht, 6045udo, 7140udo

Oromo	Days	Area	kHz
1600-1630	mtwtf..	EAf	11715kav, 11965sao, 15750ira

Portuguese	Days	Area	kHz
0430-0500	daily	Af	1530sao, 5890grv, 6015bot, 9480grv, 9675sao
1700-1730	daily	Af	15545bot
1700-1800	daily	Af	1530sao, 11775sao
1730-1800	daily	Af	9805bot, 21485grv
1800-1830	mtwtf..	Af	1530sao, 7290udo, 9805bot, 21485grv

Russian	Days	Area	kHz
1400-1500	daily	RUS	11805bib, 11895bib, 15130mor, 15320lam, 15370mor, 17730lam
1800-1900	daily	RUS	6105kav, 7220jbr, 11885mor
1800-2000	daily	RUS	3980bib, 9520kav, 9650mor
1900-2000	daily	RUS	6105lam, 7220lam, 9505lam, 9750wof

Serbian	Days	Area	kHz
0630-0700	daily	Eu	1458fla, 6035bib, 7105mor, 7115wof
2030-2100	daily	Eu	792kav, 7175bib, 9505mor, 9805mor
2200-2230	mtwtf..	Eu	756lam, 7155wof, 9540mor, 9655mor

Spanish	Days	Area	kHz
0100-0200	daily	SAm	9480dln, 9560dln, 9885grv, 11700dln, 11990dln
1100-1200	daily	SAm	9535grv
1100-1230	daily	SAm	11890grv, 15265grv
1200-1230	daily	SAm	9480dln, 9535grv, 13715grv

Swahili	Days	Area	kHz
1630-1700	daily	EAf	17580bot, 17705bot, 21480sao
1700-1730	mtwtf..	EAf	17580bot, 17705bot, 21480sao

Tibetan	Days	Area	kHz
0000-0100	daily	SAs	7200udo, 7255kav, 9555udo
0400-0600	daily	SAs	15585udo, 17770udo, 21570ira
1400-1500	daily	SAs	6015ira, 7115udo, 11790gav, 12040pht

Tigrinya	Days	Area	kHz
1630-1700	mtwtf..	EAf	11715kav, 11965mor, 15750ira

Turkish	Days	Area	kHz
0430-0500	mtwtf..	TUR	792kav, 7200kav, 9835bib, 9850mor
1130-1200	mtwtf..	TUR	9555kav, 11870kav, 15150lam
1900-2000	daily	TUR	792kav, 9485jul, 9590lam, 11875mor

Ukrainian	Days	Area	kHz
0500-0600	daily	Eu	3985bib, 6170bib, 9875mor
2100-2130	daily	Eu	7295mor, 9650bib, 11875mor

Vietnamese	Days	Area	kHz
1300-1330	daily	SEA	1575bph, 9325ira, 9890pht, 15150pht
1500-1600	daily	CHN	1143php
1500-1600	daily	SEA	5955pht, 7150pht, 9725sai, 9780ira
2230-2330	daily	SEA	6060pht, 7260ira, 9535pht, 13640tin

ANN: At the start and end of the transmission period on each frequency, English: "This is the Voice of America, Washington DC, sign-ing on/off". Before all foreign language programs: "This is the Voice of America. The following program is in... (language)."
V: QSL-card. Email rpts to qsl@voa.gov.
NOTES: Launched 1942 under the roof of the U.S. Foreign Information Service (FIS), 1953-1994 financed by the U.S. Information Agency (USIA). BBG funded since April 1994. Some transmissions in Asian languages are being jammed in the target area.

BROADCASTING BOARD OF GOVERNORS (BBG) (Gov)

✉ 330 Independence Avenue SW, Washington, DC 20237, USA.
☎ +1 202 4013736. 🖷 +1 202 4016605.
Email: jmower@ibb.gov **Web:** www.bbg.gov
L.P: Chmn: Kenneth Y. Tomlinson; Exec. Dir: Brian T. Conniff; Communications Coordinator: Joan Mower.
NOTES: On 1 October 1999, the Broadcasting Board of Governors (BBG) became the independent, autonomous entity responsible for all U.S. government and government sponsored, non-military, international broadcasting. While the "Broadcasting Board of Governors" is the legal name given to the Federal entity encompassing all U.S international broadcasting services, the day-to-day broadcasting activities are carried out by the individual BBG international broadcasters: the Voice of America (VOA), Radio Sawa, Radio Farda, Radio Free Afghanistan, Radio Free Iraq, Radio Free Europe/Radio Liberty (RFE/RL), Radio Free Asia (RFA), Radio and TV Martí, with the assistance of the International Broadcasting Bureau (IBB).

INTERNATIONAL BROADCASTING BUREAU (IBB) (Gov)

✉ 330 Independence Avenue SW, Washington, DC 20237, USA.
☎ +1 202 4017000. 🖷 +1 202 6191241.
Email: pubaff@ibb.gov **Web:** www.ibb.gov
✉ Transmitting Sites: Greenville Site A: 10000 Cherry Run Road, Greenville, NC 27834, USA. Greenville Site B: 3919 VOA Site B Road, Grimesland, NC 27837, USA. Delano: 110015 Melcher Road, Delano, CA 93215, USA.
L.P: Dir: Seth Cropsey; Freq Mgr: Dan Ferguson; SM Tx Site Delano: Michael Hardegen (mhardegen@del.ibb.gov); SM Tx Site Greenville: David Strawman (dstrawman@grn.ibb.gov).
MW: [MTH] Marathon Key, FL (G.C. 24N43 081W03) 1180kHz 100kW
SW: [DLN] Delano, CA (G.C. 35N45 119W10) 4 x 250kW; [GRV] Greenville, NC (G.C. 35N35 077W22) 6 x 50, 6 x 250, 11 x 500kW
V: QSL-card. Email rpts to jvodenik@del.ibb.gov (John Vodenick), Delano transmitting stn.

NOTES: Under the supervision of the Broadcasting Board of Governors (BBG), the International Broadcasting Bureau (IBB) provides the administrative and engineering support for U.S. government-funded non-military international broadcast services. The IBB Office of Engineering and Technical Services manages, operates and maintains a network of domestic and overseas transmitting stations in Botswana, Djibouti, Germany, Greece, Kuwait, Morocco, Philippines, Northern Mariana Islands, São Tomé, Sri Lanka, Thailand and USA. In addition, the IBB is leasing high power transmitter facilities from network operators in various countries, incl. Afghanistan, Armenia, Germany, Hungary, Kazakhstan, Mongolia, Tajikistan, Taiwan, United Arab Emirates and United Kingdom.

ADVENTIST WORLD RADIO (AWR) (Rlg)

12501 Old Columbia Pike, Silver Spring, ML 20904, USA.
☎ +1 301 6806304. 🖷 +1 301 6806303.
Email: info@awr.org **Web:** www.awr.org
L.P: Regional dir: Africa: Samuel Misiani; Asia/Pacific: Akinori Kaibe; Europe: Bert Smit.
kHz: *3215, 3345, 6040, 6095, 6165, 6175, 7210, 7235, 9530, 9550, 9655, 9695, 9760, 9770, 9800, 9830, 9875, 11680, 11720, 11730, 11785, 11845, 11910, 11915, 11925, 12025, 12130, 15135, 15215, 15225, 15255, 15295, 15365, 15385, 15440, 15445, 17595*

Winter Schedule 2004

Afar	**Days**	**Area**	**kHz**
1430-1500	daily	EAf	15440mos
Amharic	**Days**	**Area**	**kHz**
0300-0330	daily	EAf	9760dha
Arabic	**Days**	**Area**	**kHz**
1930-2000	m.w....	NAf	9800jul
Arabic	**Days**	**Area**	**kHz**
1900-1930	daily	NAf	9800jul
Arabic	**Days**	**Area**	**kHz**
0400-0430	daily	ME	7210mos
0430-0500	daily	NAf	9875mos
1700-1730	daily	ME	11915mos
1730-1800	daily	NAf	11785mos
1830-1900	daily	NAf	12025mos
Bangla	**Days**	**Area**	**kHz**
1230-1300	daily	As	15135dha
Bari	**Days**	**Area**	**kHz**
1800-1830	m......	EAf	9530mos
Bulgarian	**Days**	**Area**	**kHz**
0500-0600	daily	Eu	6095jul
Dyula	**Days**	**Area**	**kHz**
2000-2030	daily	CAf	9770mos
English	**Days**	**Area**	**kHz**
1800-1830	..w.f..	EAf	9530mos
English	**Days**	**Area**	**kHz**
0200-0230	daily	WAs	6175mos
1200-1230	daily	As	15135dha
1530-1600	daily	As	15225dha
1800-1830	daily	SAf	3215mey, 3345mey
1800-1900	daily	EAf	11925mey
2000-2030	daily	CAf	15295mey
2030-2100	daily	CAf	15295mey
2100-2130	daily	WAf	9830mos
2130-2200	daily	WAf	9830mos
Farsi	**Days**	**Area**	**kHz**
0330-0400	daily	ME	6040mos
1630-1700	daily	ME	11910mos
French	**Days**	**Area**	**kHz**
2000-2030	daily	CAf	11845mey, 15365mey
2000-2030	daily	NAf	9695jul
2030-2100	daily	WAf	9800mos
German	**Days**	**Area**	**kHz**
1600-1630	daily	Eu	7235mos
Hausa	**Days**	**Area**	**kHz**
1930-2000	daily	CAf	15255mey
Hindi	**Days**	**Area**	**kHz**
1530-1600	daily	As	15215dha
Igbo	**Days**	**Area**	**kHz**
1930-2000	daily	CAf	15365mey
Italian	**Days**	**Area**	**kHz**
1000-1100	......s	Eu	11730jul
Juba Arabic	**Days**	**Area**	**kHz**
1800-1830	.t...s.	EAf	9530mos
Kabyle	**Days**	**Area**	**kHz**
1930-2000	...t..s	NAf	9800jul
Malagasy	**Days**	**Area**	**kHz**
0230-0330	daily	MDG	3215mdc
1528-1628	daily	MDG	3215mdc
Mandarin	**Days**	**Area**	**kHz**
1300-1330	mtwtf..	EAs	15385dha
1330-1500	daily	EAs	15385dha
Masai	**Days**	**Area**	**kHz**
1730-1800	daily	CAf	12130mey
Moru	**Days**	**Area**	**kHz**
1800-1830	...t..s	EAf	9530mos
Nepali	**Days**	**Area**	**kHz**
1500-1530	daily	As	15225dha
Oromo	**Days**	**Area**	**kHz**
0300-0330	daily	EAf	9550dha
Panjabi	**Days**	**Area**	**kHz**
1500-1530	daily	As	15215dha
Russian	**Days**	**Area**	**kHz**
0300-0330	daily	CAs	9655dha
1330-1400	daily	CAs	9530dha
Somali	**Days**	**Area**	**kHz**
1630-1700	daily	EAf	17595dha
Spanish	**Days**	**Area**	**kHz**
2300-0057	daily	CAm	6165bon
Swahili	**Days**	**Area**	**kHz**
1700-1730	daily	CAf	12130mey
Tachelhit	**Days**	**Area**	**kHz**
1930-2000	.t..fs.	NAf	9800jul
Tigrinya	**Days**	**Area**	**kHz**
0330-0400	daily	EAf	9760dha
Uighur	**Days**	**Area**	**kHz**
1300-1330	.....ss	EAs	15385dha
Urdu	**Days**	**Area**	**kHz**
0230-0300	daily	WAs	6175mos
1400-1430	daily	WAs	15440mos
1600-1630	daily	WAs	11680mos
Vietnamese	**Days**	**Area**	**kHz**
0100-0200	.....s.	SEA	15445tai
1400-1500	daily	SEA	11720tai
Yoruba	**Days**	**Area**	**kHz**
2030-2100	daily	CAf	11845mey

ANN: English: "This is Adventist World Radio, the Voice of Hope"; French: "Ici la Radio Mondiale Adventiste, la Voix d l'Esperance"; German: "Sie hören Adventist World Radio, die Stimme der Hoffnung"
IS: Different arrangements of the melody "Lift Up the Trumpet".
V: QSL-card.
NOTES: Owned by Adventist Broadcasting Service, Inc. The AWR prgr's are recorded in Program Partner studios; they are usually located in countries where the respective prgr languages are spoken. AWR owns the transmitting station KSDA in Guam, for other transmissions it rents air time on shortwave tx's in many parts of the world.

BYU RADIO (Rlg)

2000 Ironton Blvd., Provo, UT 84606, USA.
☎ +1 866 7472346. 🖷 +1 801 3788478.
Email: byuradio@byu.edu **Web:** www.byuradio.org
SAT: Echostar 7, Intelsat Americas 5
kHz: *9875*

Winter Schedule 2004

English	**Days**	**Area**	**kHz**
1400-1500	......s	Eu	9875rmp+

ANN: English: "BYU Radio"
NOTES: BYU Radio is run by the Church of Jesus Christ of Latter-day Saints (LDS). Key: + DRM

CHRISTIAN SCIENCE HEROLD (Rlg)

One Norway Street C04-10, Boston, MA 02115-3195, USA.
☎ +1 617 4502893. 🖷 +1 617 4502893.
Email: herold@csps.com **Web:** www.tfccs.com
kHz: *6015, 7220, 9890*

Winter Schedule 2004

English	**Days**	**Area**	**kHz**
1800-1830	.t.....	WAf,NAf	7220jul
1830-1900	...t...	EAf,CAf	7220nau

German	Days	Area	kHz
1000-1100	......s	Eu	6015jul

Russian	Days	Area	kHz
1900-1935	.....s.	Eu	9890wer*
1935-2000	.....s.	Eu	9890jul*

NOTES: Produced by the Christian Science Publishing Society (The First Church of Christ, Scientist). Key: * Fortnightly (uneven weeks).

FANG GUANG MING RADIO (Rlg)

P.O. Box 93436, City of Industry, CA 91715, USA.
☎ +1 309 2185334.
Email: editor@falundafaradio.org **Web:** www.falundafaradio.org
kHz: *9930, 17510*

Winter Schedule 2004

Mandarin	Days	Area	kHz
0200-0300	.twtfs.	As	17510whr
1500-1600	daily	As	9930whr

ANN: Mandarin: "Shijie Falun Dafa diantai, "Zheli shi Fang Guang Ming diantai"
V: QSL-card.
NOTES: On the air since July 2000. Produced by members of the Falun Gong movement in the USA. Transmissions are jammed in parts of East Asia.

FAR EAST BROADCASTING COMPANY, INC. (Rlg)

P.O. Box 1, La Mirada, CA 90637-0001, USA.
☎ +1 562 9474651. +1 562 9430160.
Email: contactinfo@febi.org **Web:** www.febi.org
Email: febc@febc.org **Web:** www.febc.org
L.P: Pres: Gregg Harris.
NOTES: Far East Broadcasting Company, Inc. maintains more than 35 recording studios in various countries producing religious programming for listeners in the Far East. For schedules see FEBA Radio (United Kingdom), Far East Broadcasting Company (Korea), Far East Broadcasting Company (Philippines), KFBS Saipan (Northern Mariana Islands).

GOSPEL FOR ASIA (Rlg)

1800 Golden Trail Court, Carrollton, TX 75010, USA.
☎ +1 972 3007777. +1 972 3007778.
Email: info@gfa.org **Web:** www.gfaradio.org
L.P: Pres: Dr K.P. Yohannan.
kHz: *6145, 9495, 9765, 9785, 13590, 13650, 13790, 15170*

Winter Schedule 2004

Language / Time	Days	Area	kHz
Adi			
2345-2400	.....ss	IND	6145dha
Assamese			
2345-2400	mtw....	IND	6145dha
Awadhi			
1515-1530	.....ss	IND,SEA	13650wer
Bagri			
0030-0045	mt.....	IND,ME	9495wer
Banjara			
1615-1630	mt.....	IND	9785dha
Bengali			
2330-2345	mtw....	IND	6145dha
Bengali (Mulslimi)			
1445-1500	....f..	IND,SEA	13650wer
2330-2345	...tf..	IND	6145dha
2345-2400	....f..	IND,SEA	9765wer
Bhojpuri			
0015-0030	....f..	IND,SEA	9765wer
0115-0130	mt.....	IND,ME	9495wer
1515-1530	....f..	IND,SEA	13650wer
Bodo			
0000-0015	mt.....	IND,SEA	9765wer
2300-2315	..wt...	IND	6145dha
Bundelkhandi			
1545-1600	mt.....	IND,ME	13790wer
Burmese			
1445-1500	..wt...	IND,SEA	13650wer
2315-2330	....f..	IND	6145dha
2345-2400	..wt...	IND,SEA	9765wer
Chakma			
0015-0030	mt.....	IND,SEA	9765wer
2300-2315	mt.....	IND	6145dha
Chhattisgarhi			
1530-1545	mt.....	IND,ME	13590wer
Chin			
1445-1500	mt.....	IND,SEA	13650wer
2300-2315	....f..	IND	6145dha
2345-2400	mt.....	IND,SEA	9765wer
Dari			
1530-1545	.....s.	IND,ME	13590wer
1615-1630	..w....	IND	9785dha
Divehi			
0000-0015	.....ss	IND	6145dha
Dogri			
1600-1615	...tf..	IND,ME	13590wer
Dzongkha			
1430-1445	mtw....	IND,SEA	13650wer
Garwali			
0030-0045	.....ss	IND,ME	9495wer
Gujarati			
1245-1300	..wtf..	IND	15170dha
1600-1615	mt.....	IND,ME	13590wer
Hindi			
0100-0115	....f..	IND,ME	9495wer
0115-0130	..wtfss	IND,ME	9495wer
0115-0130	mtwtf..	IND	6145dha
1430-1445	...tfss	IND,SEA	13650wer
1615-1630	daily	IND,ME	13590wer
2330-2345	daily	IND,SEA	9765wer
Kangri			
0045-0100	.....ss	IND,ME	9495wer
Kannada			
0000-0015	mtwtf..	IND	6145dha
Karbi			
1445-1500	.....ss	IND,SEA	13650wer
2300-2315	.....s.	IND	6145dha
2345-2400	.....ss	IND,SEA	9765wer
Kashmiri			
1230-1245	..wt...	IND	15170dha
Kokborok			
2315-2330	mt.....	IND	6145dha
2330-2345	.....ss	IND	6145dha
Konkani			
1615-1630	.....ss	IND	9785dha
Koya			
1245-1300	.....ss	IND	15170dha
Kuruk			
0000-0015	..wt...	IND,SEA	9765wer
Lepcha			
1500-1515	.tw....	IND,SEA	13650wer
2315-2330	.....s.	IND	6145dha
Magahi			
0000-0015	....f..	IND,SEA	9765wer
1500-1515	...tf..	IND,SEA	13650wer
Maithili			
1530-1545	..wt...	IND,ME	13590wer
Malayalam			
0015-0045	daily	IND	6145dha
1600-1615	daily	IND	9785dha
Marathi			
0100-0115	.....ss	IND,ME	9495wer
1600-1615	.....ss	IND,ME	13590wer
Marwari			
0100-0115	mt.....	IND,ME	9495wer
1615-1630	....f..	IND	9785dha
Meitei			
1500-1515	.....ss	IND,SEA	13650wer
2315-2330	..wt...	IND	6145dha
Mundari			
0045-0100	..w....	IND,ME	9495wer
1515-1530	..wt...	IND,SEA	13650wer
Nepali			
1300-1330	daily	IND	15170dha
Oriya			
1230-1245	....fss	IND	15170dha
Pashto			
1530-1545	......s	IND,ME	13590wer
1615-1630	...t...	IND	9785dha

Punjabi	Days	Area	kHz
0100-0115	..wt...	IND,ME	9495wer
1245-1300	mt....	IND	15170dha
1600-1615	..w....	IND,ME	13590wer
Rajasthani	**Days**	**Area**	**kHz**
0045-0100	mt.....	IND,ME	9495wer
Sadri	**Days**	**Area**	**kHz**
0030-0045	..w....	IND,ME	9495wer
Santali	**Days**	**Area**	**kHz**
0015-0030	..wt...	IND,SEA	9765wer
1545-1600	..wt...	IND,ME	13590wer
Sharchhokpa	**Days**	**Area**	**kHz**
1515-1530	mt.....	IND,SEA	13650wer
Sherpa	**Days**	**Area**	**kHz**
1500-1515	m......	IND,SEA	13650wer
Sindhi	**Days**	**Area**	**kHz**
1545-1600	......s	IND,ME	13590wer
Sinhala	**Days**	**Area**	**kHz**
0115-0130	.....ss	IND	6145dha
Tamil	**Days**	**Area**	**kHz**
0100-0115	daily	IND	6145dha
Telugu	**Days**	**Area**	**kHz**
0045-0100	daily	IND	6145dha
Tibetan (Amdo)	**Days**	**Area**	**kHz**
0000-0015	.....ss	IND,SEA	9765wer
2300-2315	......s	IND	6145dha
Tibetan (Lasa)	**Days**	**Area**	**kHz**
0015-0030	.....ss	IND,SEA	9765wer
2315-2330	......s	IND	6145dha
Tulu	**Days**	**Area**	**kHz**
2345-2400	...tf..	IND	6145dha
Urdu	**Days**	**Area**	**kHz**
0045-0100	...tf..	IND,ME	9495wer
1230-1245	mt.....	IND	15170dha
1545-1600	....fs.	IND,ME	13590wer
Various	**Days**	**Area**	**kHz**
1330-1430	daily	IND,ME	13590wer
Vasavi	**Days**	**Area**	**kHz**
0030-0045	...tf..	IND,ME	9495wer
1530-1545	....f..	IND,ME	13590wer

V: QSL-card.
NOTES: Owned by Gospel for Asia, Inc.

HCJB WORLD RADIO (Rlg)

☐ P.O. Box 39800, Colorado Springs, CO 80949-9800, USA.
☎ +1 719 5909800. 🖷 +1 719 5909801.
Email: info@hcjb.org **Web:** www.hcjb.org
L.P: SM: John E. Beck; Program Director: Alex Saks; Freq. Mgr: Douglas Weber.
V: QSL-card.
NOTES: Owned by World Radio Missionary Fellowship, Inc. HCJB, founded 1931, was the world's first missionary broadcaster; it has ministries in more than 100 countries and broadcasts in nearly 120 languages and dialects. For schedules, see HCJB La Voz de Los Andes (Ecuador) and HCJB World Radio Australia (Australia).

HIGH ADVENTURE MINISTRIES (Rlg)

☐ P.O. Box 197569, Louisville, KY 40259, USA.
☎ +1 502 9687550. 🖷 +1 502 9687580.
Email: mail@highadventure.net **Web:** www.highadventure.net
NOTES: High Adventure Ministries Inc. is operating the shortwave station T8BZ (Palau), owns shares in the SW station WJIE and is brokering air time for international radio ministries.

KAIJ INTERNATIONAL (Rlg)

☐ 22720 SE 410th Street, Enumclaw, WA 98022, USA.
☎ +1 360 8251099. 🖷 +1 360 8254517.
L.P: Dir: Michael L. Parker.
SW: [AIJ] Frisco, TX (G.C. 33N13 096W52) 1 x 50, 1 x 100kW
ANN: English: "KAIJ, Dallas, Texas USA"
V: QSL-card. Rp.
NOTES: Owned by Two If By Sea Broadcasting Corporation. Carries programming of Gene Scott's "University Network" (schedules see under "University Network").

KIMF (Rlg)

☐ Owner: 9746 6th Street, Rancho Cucamonga, CA 91730, USA.
☎ +1 909 4664793. 🖷 +1 909 3704862.
Email: jkpimf@msn.com
L.P: Owner: James Planck.
SW: [IMF] Pinon, NM (G.C. 32N37 105W24) 1 x 50kW (F.PI)
NOTES: Projected stn, funded by the International Fellowship of Churches.

KJES (Rlg)

☐ Our Lord's Ranch, 230 High Valley Rd., Vado, NM 88072, USA.
☎ +1 505 2332090. 🖷 +1 505 2333019.
Email: kjes@aol.com
L.P: Pres: Fr Rick Thomas; GM: Michael Reuter.
SW: [JES] Vado, NM (G.C. 32N08 106W35) 1 x 5, x 50kW
kHz: *7555, 11715, 15385*

Winter Schedule 2004

English/Spanish	Days	Area	kHz
0200-0330	daily	NAm	7555jes
1400-1700	daily	NAm	11715jes
1900-2100	daily	SEA,AUS	15385jes

ANN: English: "This is KJES Radio, broadcasting from the Lord's Ranch"
V: QSL-card. Rp.
NOTES: Catholic station; transmissions are part of a rehabilitation programme for young people. Licensed since November 1992, original tests began in 1989. Registered freq's shown, actual usage varies. At editorial deadline the stn was on the air irregulary with backup tx, while the main tx was under repair.

KTBN SHORTWAVE RADIO (Rlg)

☐ P.O. Box A, Santa Ana, CA 92711, USA.
☎ +1 714 7311000. 🖷 +1 714 7300661.
Email: comments@tbn.org **Web:** www.tbn.org
L.P: SM: Cheryl Gilroy.
SW: [TBN] Salt Lake City, UT (G.C. 40N39 112W03) 1 x 100kW
kHz: *7505, 15590*

Winter Schedule 2004

English	Days	Area	kHz
0000-1600	daily	NAm	7505tbn
1600-2400	daily	NAm	15590tbn

ANN: English: "This is the Trinity Broadcasting Network. This has been the superpower KTBN, Salt Lake City, Utah, USA"
V: QSL card. Rp. preferred (1 IRC). Rpt to KTBN Radio QSL Manager, Cheryl Gilroy, 2442 Michelle Drive Tustin, CA 92780, USA.
NOTES: Owned by Trinity Broadcasting Network, Inc. Began operating in December 1990, simulcasts the audio of TBN TV programmes. A closure of the stn is under consideration.

KVOH – LA VOZ DE RESTAURACIÓN (Rlg)

☐ P.O. Box 56320, Los Angeles, CA 90056, USA.
☎ +1 323 7662454. 🖷 +1 323 7662458.
Email: comentarios@restauracion.com
Web: www.restauracion.com
☐ Studio: 4409 W. Adams blvd., Los Angeles, CA 90007, USA.
SW: [VOH] Rancho Simi, CA (G.C. 34N15 118W38) 2 x 50kW
kHz: *9975, 17775*

Winter Schedule 2004

Spanish	Days	Area	kHz
0100-0800	daily	CAm	9975voh
1300-1500	daily	CAm	9975voh
1500-0100	daily	CAm	17775voh

ANN: English: "This is KVOH, La Voz de Restauración Broadcasting"; Spanish: "Ésta es KVOH, La Voz de Restauración"
V: QSL-card.
NOTES: Owned by Iclesias de Restauración Inc. Registered freq's shown, 9975kHz not recently in use.

LEADING THE WAY (Rlg)

☐ P.O. Box 20100, Atlanta, GA 30325, USA.
☎ +1 404 8410100. 🖷 +1 404 8410117.
Email: webmail@leadingtheway.org
Web: www.leadingtheway.org
L.P: CEO: Dr. Michael Youssef.
kHz: *9800*

Winter Schedule 2004

Farsi	Days	Area	kHz
1700-1730	mt..f..	ME	9800rmp

RADIO PAYAM–E DOOST (Rlg)

P.O. Box 765, Great Falls, VA 22066, USA.
☎ +1 703 6718888. +1 301 2926947.
Email: payam@bahairadio.org **Web:** www.bahairadio.org
SAT: Telstar 5/12
kHz: *7460, 7480*

Winter Schedule 2004

Farsi	Days	Area	kHz
0230-0315	.twtf.s	ME	7460gri
1800-1845	.twtf.s	ME	7480gri

ANN: Farsi: "Radio Payam-e Doost"
NOTES: Payam-e Doost ("Message from a friend) is a satellite radio station run by members of the Baha'i Faith in the USA. Relays on shortwave started November 1999.

THE OVERCOMER MINISTRY (Rlg)

P.O. Box 69, Walterboro, SC 29488, USA.
☎ +1 843 5384202. +1 843 5384202.
Email: rgstair@overcomerministry.org **Web:** www.overcomerministry.org
L.P: Owner: Ralph G. Stair.
SAT: Hotbird 6
kHz: *5070, 5765, 6110, 6870, 7465, 9985, 12160, 13810, 15825*

Winter Schedule 2004

English	Days	Area	kHz
0400-0900	daily	NAm,CAm	6870rmi
0400-1300	daily	CAm,Af	5765wcr
0600-0800	daily	NAm,Eu	5070wcr
0900-1100	daily	NAm,Eu	5070wcr
1300-1600	daily	NAm,CAm	7465wcr
1300-1600	daily	Eu,ME	13810jul
1300-1600	daily	Eu	6110jul
1600-1700	mtwtfs.	NAm	9985wcr
2100-2130	......s	NAm	15825wcr
2100-2200	daily	NAm	9985wcr
2100-2200	.....s	NAm	12160wcr
2200-0400	daily	NAm,CAm	7465wcr

ANN: English: "You have been listening to the International Broadcast - The Overcomer"
V: QSL-card. Rpt to overcomer@overcomerministry.com.
NOTES: Owned by Faith Cathedral Fellowship, Inc

THE UNIVERSITY NETWORK (DR GENE SCOTT) (Rlg)

P.O. Box 1, Los Angeles, CA 90053, USA.
☎ +1 818 2408151.
Web: www.drgenescott.com
L.P: Owner: Dr. Eugene Scott.
SAT: AMC 3, Intelsat Americas 6
kHz: *5030, 5755, 5935, 6090, 6150, 7375, 9725, 11755, 11870, 13750, 13815, 13845*

Winter Schedule 2004

English	Days	Area	kHz
0000-1200	daily	NAm,SAm	6150cha
0000-1200	daily	CTR	7375cha
0000-1200	daily	CAm,Eu,Af	5030cha
0000-1400	daily	SEA	5935wcr
0000-1400	daily	NAm,SEA	5755aij
0000-2400	daily	SAm	9725cha
1000-2200	daily	CAm	11755aia
1200-2400	daily	NAm	13750cha
1200-2400	daily	CTR	11870cha
1400-2400	daily	SEA	13845wcr
1400-2400	daily	NAm,SEA	13815aij
2200-1000	daily	CAm	6090aia

V: Does not verify reception reports.
NOTES: Owns shortwave relay stn's in Anguilla and Costa Rica ("The Carribean Beacon"), see country entries for details. The [CHA] freq's 7375 and 13750kHz have been observed drifting around 7373 and 13746kHz lately.

TRANS WORLD RADIO (TWR) (Rlg)

P.O. Box 8700, Cary, NC 27512, USA.
☎ +1 919 4603700. +1 919 4603702.
Email: info2@twr.org **Web:** www.twr.org
L.P: Pres & CEO: Dr. David G. Tucker.
V: QSL-card.
NOTES: TWR owns transmitting facilities in Guam (KTWR), Netherlands Antilles, Sri Lanka and Swaziland, see TWR branches in these countries for schedules. For TWR Europe schedules, see Austria.

WAYMARKS INTERNATIONAL MINISTRIES (Rlg)

P.O. Box 2324, Macon, GA 31203, USA.
☎ +1 912 7501422.
Email: lorenwilson@waymarks.org **Web:** www.waymarks.org
L.P: Radio pastor: Loren H. Wilson.
kHz: *5945, 13820*

Winter Schedule 2004

English	Days	Area	kHz
0030-0045	......s	As	5945jul
English/Arabic	**Days**	**Area**	**kHz**
1400-1430	.....s.	ME	13820jul
1445-1500	.....s.	ME	13820jul
1500-1515	......s	ME	13820jul
1545-1600	......s	ME	13820jul
1600-1630	......s	ME	13820jul

WBOH/WTJC – FUNDAMENTAL BROADCASTING NETWORK (FBN) (Rlg)

520 Roberts Road, Newport, NC 28570, USA.
☎ +1 252 2236088. +1 252 2232201.
Email: fbn@fbnradio.com **Web:** www.fbnradio.com
L.P: Missionary and Chief Engineer: David Robinson.
SW: [BOH] Newport, NC (G.C. 34N47 076W56) WBOH 1 x 50kW; [TJC] Newport, NC (G.C. 34N47 076W53) WTJC 1 x 50kW
kHz: *5920, 9370*

Winter Schedule 2004

English	Days	Area	kHz
0000-2400	daily	NAm	5920boh, 9370tjc

V: QSL-card.
NOTES: Owned by Paxson Communications Corporation. FBN includes the shortwave stn's WTJC ("Working Till Jesus Comes") and WBOH ("Worldwide Beacon of Hope").

WEWN – GLOBAL CATHOLIC NETWORK (ETWN) (Rlg)

5817 Old Leeds Rd., Irondale, AL 35210-2164, USA.
☎ +1 205 2712900. +1 205 2712926.
Email: radio@ewtn.com **Web:** www.ewtn.com
L.P: SM: Richard Jones; Freq. Mgr: Joseph A. Dentici; Affiliate Eng Mgr: Glen Tapley.
SW: [EWN] Vandiver, AL (G.C. 33N30 086W28) 4 x 500kW
kHz: *5825, 7425, 7570, 9955, 9975, 11530, 11615, 11875, 13615, 15695, 15745, 17595*

Winter Schedule 2004

English	Days	Area	kHz
0000-1300	daily	NAm	5825ewn
0500-0800	daily	Eu	7570ewn
1300-1600	daily	NAm	9955ewn
1600-2000	daily	Eu	15695ewn
1600-2200	daily	NAm	13615ewn
2000-2200	daily	WAf	17595ewn
2200-2400	daily	Eu	15695ewn
2200-2400	daily	NAm	9975ewn
Spanish	**Days**	**Area**	**kHz**
0000-1300	daily	CAm	5825ewn
0500-0800	daily	SAm	11615ewn
0800-1300	daily	SAm	11875ewn
1300-1400	daily	CAm	7425ewn
1300-1600	daily	CAm	9955ewn
1300-2300	daily	SAm	15745ewn
1400-2300	daily	CAm	11530ewn
1600-2200	daily	CAm	13615ewn
2200-2400	daily	CAm	9975ewn
2300-0500	daily	SAm	11530ewn
2300-1300	daily	CAm	7425ewn

ANN: English: "This is WEWN, Global Catholic Radio, Birmingham Alabama, USA"
V: QSL-card. Rp (3 IRC's).

NOTES: Owned by the Eternal Word TV Network, Inc. Began broadcasting in December 1992.

WHRA – WORLD HARVEST RADIO (Rlg)

See World Harvest Radio.

SW: [HRA] Greenbush, ME (G.C. 45N08 068W34) 1 x 500kW

kHz: *5835, 5850, 7580, 9455, 17560, 17650*

Winter Schedule 2004

English	Days	Area	kHz
0000-0400	daily	Af	7580hra
0400-0500	daily	Af	5850hra
0500-0600	daily	Af	5835hra
0600-0800	daily	Af	7580hra
1300-1600	daily	Af	17560hra
1600-2100	daily	Af	17650hra
2100-2400	daily	Af	9455hra

ANN: English: "This is World Harvest Radio, the International Service of LeSea Broadcasting Corporation. WHRA transmits from Greenbush, Maine in the United States of America"

V: QSL-card.

WHRI – WORLD HARVEST RADIO (Rlg)

See World Harvest Radio.

SW: [HRI] Noblesville, IN (G.C 40N01 085W57) 2 x 100kW

NOTES: The SW station WHRI has been closed down, the transmissions have been transfered to the newly purchased station WSHB.

WINB (Rlg)

P.O. Box 88, Red Lion, PA 17356, USA.

+1 717 2445360. Fax +1 717 2460363.

Email: winb40th@yahoo.com **Web:** www.winb.com

L.P: Sales & Freq Mgr: Hans Johnson.

SW: [INB] Red Lion, PA (G.C. 39N54 076W35) 1 x 50kW

kHz: *9320, 13570*

Winter Schedule 2004

English	Days	Area	kHz
1100-1300	daily	CAm	9320inb
1300-2300	daily	CAm	13570inb
2300-0500	daily	CAm	9320inb

ANN: English: "This is WINB, Red Lion, Pennsylvania in the United States of America"

V: QSL-card.

NOTES: Owned by World International Broadcasters, Inc. Nominal schedule shown, actual usage may vary.

WJIE INTERNATIONAL SHORTWAVE (Rlg)

P.O. Box 197309, Louisville, KY 40259, USA.

+1 502 9681220. Fax +1 502 9644228.

Email: morgan@wjie.org **Web:** www.wjiesw.com

L.P: GM: Doc Burkhart.

SW: [JCR] Millerstown, KY (G.C. 37N26 086W02) 4 x 50kW (2 tx's out of service), 1 x 100kW

kHz: *7490, 13595*

Winter Schedule 2004

English	Days	Area	kHz
0000-2400	daily	NAm	7490jcr, 13595jcr

V: QSL-card.

NOTES: Owned by Word Broadcasting Network, Inc. Callsign WJCR until 2002 under different ownership. WJIE is involved in several missionary SW transmitter projects in Africa: LCBN Radio/R. Liberty in Liberia and a planned stations in Uganda and the Marshall Islands.

WMLK (Rlg)

P.O. Box C, Bethel, PA 19507, USA.

+1 717 9334518.

Email: aoy@wmlkradio.net **Web:** www.wmlkradio.net

L.P: Directing Elder: Jacob O. Meyer; Operating Engineer Gary A. McAvin.

SW: [MLK] Bethel, PA (G.C. 40N29 076W17) 1 x 50kW. Installed 250kW tx not yet operational.

kHz: *9265*

Winter Schedule 2004

English	Days	Area	kHz
1600-2100	mtwtfs.	Eu,ME	9265mlk

ANN: English: "This is Radio Station WMLK"

V: QSL-card. Rp.

NOTES: Owned by the Assemblies of Yahweh.

WORLD HARVEST RADIO (WHRA/WHRI/KWHR/WSHB) (Rlg)

P.O. Box 12, South Bend, IN 46624, USA.

+1 574 2918200. Fax +1 574 2919043.

Email: whr@lesea.com **Web:** www.whr.org

LeSEA Broadcasting, 61300 S Ironwood Rd, South Bend, IN 46614, USA

Web: www.lesea.com

L.P: GM: Peter Sumrall; CE: Douglas Garlinger; Freq Consultant: Douglas Garlinger; Sales/Program Coordinator: Joseph Brashier.

V: QSL-card.

NOTES: World Harvest Radio is a shortwave radio network owned by LeSEA Broadcasting, Inc. It includes the stations WHRI & WHRA (see above), KWHR (see Hawaii), and since 2004 WSHB (see above).

WRNO WORLDWIDE (Rlg)

P.O. Box 895, Fort Worth, TX 76101, USA.

+1 817 8509990. Fax +1 817 8509994.

Email: hope@goodnewsworld.org **Web:** www.wrnoworldwide.org

L.P: Chmn: Robert E. Mawire.

SW: [RNO] New Orleans, LA (G.C. 29N50 090W07) 1 x 0.15kW (estimated power)

kHz: *7355, 7395, 15420*

Winter Schedule 2004

English	Days	Area	kHz
0300-1600	daily	NAm,CAm	7395rno
1600-2300	daily	NAm,CAm	15420rno
2200-0300	daily	NAm,CAm	7355rno

ANN: English: "From New Orleans, Louisiana, your listening to WRNO Worldwide broadcasting from the United States of America"

IS: When the Saints go marching in

V: QSL-card. Rp. (2 IRC's).

NOTES: Owned by Good News World Outreach. Licensed for 50kW, but using low power radio amateur equipment in recent years. The original 50kW tx belonging to the stn when it was bought from the previous owner in 2001, had caught fire and burnt out. Registered freq's shown; on the air irregulary.

WSHB – WORLD HARVEST RADIO (Rlg)

See World Harvest Radio.

Transmitter: WSHB Cypress Creek: 1030 Shortwave Lane, Pineland, SC 29934, USA.

+1 803 6255551. Fax +1 803 6255559.

SW: [SHB] WSHB Cypress Creek, SC (G.C. 32N41 081W08) 2 x 500kW

kHz: *5835, 5860, 5970, 7315, 7535, 9495, 9840, 15105, 15665*

Winter Schedule 2004

English	Days	Area	kHz
0800-1100	daily	NAm,Eu,Af	5860shb
1100-1300	daily	NAm,Eu,Af	7535shb
1300-2200	daily	NAm,Eu,Af	9840shb
2200-0800	daily	NAm,Eu,Af	7535shb
English/Spanish	**Days**	**Area**	**kHz**
0100-0500	mtwtf..	NAm,SAm	5835shb
0100-0600	.....ss	NAm,SAm	7315shb
0500-0600	mtwtf..	NAm,SAm	5970shb
0600-1000	daily	NAm,SAm	7315shb
1000-1300	daily	NAm,SAm	9495shb
1300-1900	daily	NAm,SAm	15105shb
1900-2200	daily	NAm,SAm	15665shb
2300-0100	daily	NAm,SAm	7315shb

ANN: English: "This is World Harvest Radio International broadcasting over WSHB in Cypress Creek, South Carolina"

V: QSL-card.

NOTES: WSHB was purchased by LeSEA Broadcasting in 2004.

WWBS (Rlg)

P.O. Box 18174, Macon, GA 31209, USA.

+1 912 7451485.

Email: wwbsradio@aol.com

Studio: 965 Hickory Ridge Drive, Macon, GA 31204-1018, USA.

L.P: Owner: Charles C. Josey †

SW: [WBS] Macon, GA (G.C. 32N50 083W38) 1 x 50kW

ANN: English: "WWBS Macon, Georgia, United States of America"

V: QSL-letter.

NOTES: Launched in December 1998; went silent when the owner Charles C. Josey died in 2003.

WWCR – WORLDWIDE CHRISTIAN RADIO (Rlg)

1300 WWCR Avenue, Nashville, TN 37218, USA.
☎ +1 615 2551300. +1 615 2551311.
Email: wwcr@wwcr.com **Web:** www.wwcr.com
L.P: Pres: Fred P. Westenberger; GM: George McClintock; Op's Mgr: Adam W.Lock, Sr.
SW: [WWR] Nashville, TN (G.C. 36N13 086W54) 4 x 100kW
kHz: *3210, 5070, 5765, 7465, 9985, 12160, 15825*

Winter Schedule 2004

English	Days	Area	kHz
0000-1000	daily	NAm,Eu,NAf	3210wcr**
0300-1300	daily	CAm,Af	5765wcr*
0400-1300	daily	CAm,Af	5765wcr**
1000-1100	daily	NAm,Eu,NAf	9985wcr*, 9985wcr**
1100-2100	daily	NAm,Eu,NAf	15825wcr*
1100-2200	daily	NAm,Eu,NAf	15825wcr**
1300-1600	daily	NAm,Eu	9985wcr*, 9985wcr**
1300-1600	daily	CAm,Af	7465wcr*, 7465wcr**
1600-2200	daily	NAm,Eu	12160wcr*
1600-2200	daily	CAm,Af	9985wcr*, 9985wcr**
1600-2300	daily	NAm,Eu	12160wcr**
2100-2300	daily	NAm,Eu,NAf	9985wcr*
2200-0300	daily	CAm,Af	7465wcr*
2200-0400	daily	CAm,Af	7465wcr**
2200-1300	daily	NAm,Eu	5070wcr*
2200-2400	daily	NAm,Eu,NAf	9985wcr**
2300-1000	daily	NAm,Eu,NAf	3210wcr*
2300-1300	daily	NAm,Eu	5070wcr**

ANN: English: "This is World Wide Christian Radio-WWCR, Nashville, Tennessee USA"
V: QSL-card. Rp. preferred (1 IRC). Rec. acc.
NOTES: Owned by WNQM, Inc. Two tx's are used exclusively for programming of the Overcomer Ministry and the University Network. Key: * To 28 Feb 2005; ** From 1 - 27 Mar 2005.

WWRB (Rlg)

P.O. Box 7, Manchester, TN 37349-0007, USA.
☎ +1 931 8410492. +1 931 8410492.
Email: dfrantz@tennessee.com **Web:** www.wwrb.org
Studio: 6755 Shady Grove Road, Morrison, TN 37357, USA.
L.P: Owner & CE: Dave Frantz.
SW: [GTG] McCaysville, GA (G.C. 34N58 084W22) 1 x 50kW (standby); [WRB] Manchester, TN (G.C. 35N29 086W02) 4 x 50, 1 x 100kW
kHz: *3185, 5050, 5085, 5745, 9320, 12172*

Winter Schedule 2004

English	Days	Area	kHz
1300-2300	daily	NAm,Eu	9320wrb
1300-2300	......s	Atl,Eu,NAf	12172wrb*
2300-0600	daily	NAm,SEA	5050wrb
2300-0600	daily	NAm,Eu	5085wrb
2300-0600	daily	NAm	3185wrb, 5745wrb

V: QSL-card. Email rpts not accepted.
NOTES: Owned by Blue Ridge Communications, Inc. Registered freq's shown, actual usage varies. Key: * AM-compatible USB with reduced carrier (nominal frequency: 12170kHz), this freq is intended mainly for sailors in the Atlantic Ocean.

WYFR – FAMILY RADIO (Rlg)

290 Hegenberger Rd., Oakland, CA 94621, USA.
☎ +1 510 5686200. +1 510 6337983.
Email: intl@familyradio.com **Web:** www.familyradio.com
Studio: 10400 NW 240th Street, Okeechobee, FL 34972, USA.
☎ +1 863 7630281. +1 863 7631034.
L.P: Pres: Harold Camping; Dir Tech: Wesley D. Becker; PM: Thomas A. Schaff; Dir Int'l Rel: Richard H. Homeres.
SW: [YFR] Okeechobee, FL (G.C. 27N28 080W56) 2 x 50, 10 x 100kW
kHz: *1557, 5820, 5985, 6085, 7250, 7360, 7580, 9280, 9355, 9690, 11565, 11665, 11740, 11855, 11885, 15170, 15215, 15400, 15565, 17575, 17845, 21525*

Winter Schedule 2004

Arabic	Days	Area	kHz
2000 2100	daily	WAf	21525yfr
2200-2245	daily	Eu,NAf	11665yfr
2200-2245	daily	WAf	15565yfr
English	**Days**	**Area**	**kHz**
2000-2200	daily	Eu	7580yfr
2000-2200	daily	Eu,NAf	7360gri
2000-2200	daily	SAm	17575yfr
2005-2200	daily	Eu	5820yfr
2104-2200	daily	WAf	15565yfr
2200-2245	daily	WAf	21525yfr
2200-2300	daily	SAm	9690yfr
2200-2345	daily	NAm	11740yfr
2300-2400	daily	SAm	15170yfr, 15400yfr
2300-2400	daily	CAm	5985yfr, 11855yfr
French	**Days**	**Area**	**kHz**
2300-2400	daily	NAm	6085yfr
German	**Days**	**Area**	**kHz**
2000-2100	daily	Eu	9355yfr
2100-2145	daily	Eu	11565yfr
Mandarin	**Days**	**Area**	**kHz**
2100-2400	daily	CHN	7250tai, 9280tai
2200-0300	daily	CHN	1557kou
Portuguese	**Days**	**Area**	**kHz**
2100-2200	daily	WAf	21525yfr
2200-2245	daily	Eu	7580yfr
2200-2245	daily	SAm	17575yfr
2300-0145	daily	SAm	11885yfr
Spanish	**Days**	**Area**	**kHz**
2000-2300	daily	CAm	5985yfr, 11855yfr
2100-2200	daily	Eu	9355yfr
2305-0045	daily	SAm	17845yfr
2305-0100	daily	SAm	15215yfr

ANN: English: "This is your Family Radio, International Broadcast Station WYFR, Okeechobee, Florida, the United States of America"; German: "Dies ist Ihr Familienradio, die internationale Radiostation WYFR, in Okeechobee, Florida, Vereinigte Staaten von Amerika"
V: QSL-card. No tapes accepted.
NOTES: Owned by Family Stations, Inc.

PAN AMERICAN BROADCASTING (Broker)

20410 Town Center Lane, Suite 200, Cupertino, CA 95014, USA.
☎ +1 408 9962033. +1 408 2526855.
Email: info@panambc.com **Web:** www.panambc.com
L.P: Pres: Gene Bernald.
NOTES: Pan American Broadcasting is brokering air time for production studios of religious broadcasts.

COMMANDO SOLO (U.S. MILITARY)

Pennsylvania Air National Guard, 193rd Special Operations Wing, 81 Constellation Court, Middletown, PA 17057-5086, USA.
☎ +1 717 9482490. +1 717 9482490.
Email: pa.193sow@paharr.ang.af.mil **Web:** www.paharr.ang.af.mil
MW/SW: Multiple tx's onboard Lockheed EC130J airplanes: 1kW FM, 10kW MW/SW
V: QSL-letter.
NOTES: The 193rd Special Operations Wing under the U.S. Air Force Special Operations Command is conducting air borne radio/tv transmisions ("PsyOps") from Lockheed EC130J planes (recently replacing earlier EC130E's planes). Current target: Cuba (see Radio Martí). Earlier missions: Southwest Asia in 1970, Grenada in 1983, Panama in 1989, Southwest Asia ("Desert Shield" and "Desert Storm") in 1990/91, Haiti 1994, Balkans 1997/98, Southwest Asia in 2001-2003 ("Operation Freedom").

SOUND OF HOPE RADIO NETWORK

2520 Wyandotte Street, Suite A, Mountain View, CA 94043, USA.
☎ +1 866 4327764. +1 415 2765861.
Email: englishfeedback@soundofhope.org
Web: www.soundofhope.org
L.P: Dir: Allen Zeng.
kHz: *11765*

Winter Schedule 2004

Mandarin	Days	Area	kHz
1600-1700	daily	CHN	11765tai

ANN: Mandarin: "Xi Wang Zhi Sheng"
NOTES: Sound of Hope Radio Network Inc. is a global provider of Chinese language news and cultural programming for the Chinese community in over 20 major cities in US, Canada, Australia, Germany, Sweden, Denmark, Taiwan, and mainland China.

VOICE OF THE NASB

P.O. Box 526852, Miami, FL 33152, USA.
Email: radiomiami9@cs.com
kHz: *6870, 11900*

Winter Schedule 2004

English	Days	Area	kHz
0300-0330	......s	NAm	6870rmi
1700-1730	.....s.	NAm	11900sac+

V: QSL-card.
NOTES: The Voice of the NASB is a weekly broadcast, produced by WRMI in cooperation with members of the National Association of Shortwave Broadcasters (NASB). Key: + DRM

WBCQ – THE PLANET
97 High Street, Kennebunk, MA 04043, USA.
☎ +1 207 9857547.
Email: wbcq@gwi.net **Web:** www.wbcq.us; www.wbcq.com
Transmitter site: 274 East Road, Monticello, Maine 04760 USA.
L.P: Owner: Allan Weiner.
SW: [BCQ] Monticello, ME (G.C. 46N20 067W50) 4 x 50kW
kHz: *5105, 7415, 9330, 17495*

Winter Schedule 2004

English	Days	Area	kHz
0000-2400	daily	CAm	5105bcq*
1200-1600	daily	CAm	9330bcq*
1200-2300	daily	CAm	17495bcq*
1300-1000	daily	CAm	7415bcq

ANN: English: "This is WBCQ, in Monticello, Maine broadcasting from the USA"
V: QSL-card. Rp (1 IRC).
NOTES: Leases out air time, mainly to religious prgr producers. Actual schedule varies acc. too bookings. Key: * AM-compatible SSB with reduced carrier

WRMI – RADIO MIAMI INTERNATIONAL
P.O. Box 526852, Miami, FL 33152, USA.
☎ +1 305 5599764. 🖷 +1 305 5598186.
Email: info@wrmi.net **Web:** www.wrmi.net
L.P: GM: Jeff White; CE: Indalecio Espinosa.
kHz: *6870, 9955, 15725*

Winter Schedule 2004

English/Spanish	Days	Area	kHz
0000-1000	.twtfs.	NAm	6870rmi
0300-1000	m.....s	NAm	6870rmi
1000-1300	daily	CAm	9955rmi
1300-2400	daily	NAm	15725rmi

ANN: English: "This is WRMI, Radio Miami International"
V: QSL-card.
NOTES: Licensed since 1994, WRMI is providing air time for prgr's by various production companies (mainly in English and Spanish). The latest schedule can be found at www.wrmi.net/pages/714011/index.htm. Transmissions of certain prgr's aimed at a Cuban audience are jammed in the target area.

Broadcasters using sites in this country:
BBC World Sce uses: (YFR). See stn entry in: **G**, INT Section
BBC World Sce uses: (GRV). See stn entry in: **G**, INT Section
BBC World Sce uses: (DLN). See stn entry in: **G**, INT Section
Conv.entre Cub. uses: (RMI). See stn entry in: **CUB**, CTB Section
Foro Mil.Cubano uses: (RMI). See stn entry in: **CUB**, CTB Section
Junta Patr.Cub. uses: (RMI). See stn entry in: **CUB**, CTB Section
R.Oriente Libre uses: (RMI). See stn entry in: **CUB**, CTB Section
R.Taiwan Int'l uses: (YFR). See stn entry in: **TWN**, INT Section
R.Thailand uses: (GRV). See stn entry in: **THA**, INT Section
R.Thailand uses: (DLN). See stn entry in: **THA**, INT Section
Radio Six Int'l uses: (BCQ). See stn entry in: **G**, INT Section
Trova Libre uses: (RMI). See stn entry in: **CUB**, CTB Section
VO Greece uses: (DLN). See stn entry in: **GRC**, INT Section

UZBEKISTAN

RADIO TASHKENT INTERNATIONAL (Gov)
Xorezm Street 49, 700047 Toshkent, Uzbekistan.
☎ +998 71 1338920. 🖷 +998 71 1440021.
Email: ino@uzpak.uz **Web:** ino.uzpak.uz
L.P: Head: Sherzat Gulyamov.
SW: Leased from RRDTK
kHz: *5025, 5040, 5060, 5975, 6025, 6165, 7160, 7185, 7215, 7285, 9375, 9540, 9715, 11905, 15330*

Winter Schedule 2004

Arabic	Days	Area	kHz
1700-1730	daily	ME	5975tac, 7285tac
1900-1930	daily	ME	5975tac, 7285tac
Dari	**Days**	**Area**	**kHz**
0130-0200	daily	WAs	5975tac, 6165tac, 7160tac
1520-1550	daily	WAs	5975tac, 6025tac, 7285tac
English	**Days**	**Area**	**kHz**
0100-0130	daily	Eu	5975tac
0100-0130	daily	WAs	6165tac, 7160tac
1200-1230	daily	WAs	6025tac
1200-1230	daily	As	5060tac, 9715tac
1200-1230	daily	Eu	5975tac
1330-1400	daily	WAs	6025tac
1330-1400	daily	As	5060tac, 9715tac
1330-1400	daily	Eu	5975tac
2030-2100	daily	Eu	5025tac, 11905tac
2030-2100	daily	Eu,NAf	7185tac
2130-2200	daily	Eu	5025tac, 11905tac
2130-2200	daily	Eu,NAf	7185tac
Farsi	**Days**	**Area**	**kHz**
1630-1700	daily	WAs	5975tac, 7285tac
1830-1900	daily	WAs	5975tac, 7285tac
German	**Days**	**Area**	**kHz**
1935-2030	daily	Eu	5025tac, 11905tac
Hindi	**Days**	**Area**	**kHz**
1300-1330	daily	As	5060tac, 5975tac, 6025tac, 9715tac
1430-1500	daily	As	5060tac, 5975tac, 6025tac, 9715tac
Mandarin	**Days**	**Area**	**kHz**
1330-1400	daily	As	5040tac
1430-1500	daily	As	5040tac
Pashto	**Days**	**Area**	**kHz**
0200-0230	daily	WAs	5975tac, 6165tac, 7160tac
Turkish	**Days**	**Area**	**kHz**
0600-0630	daily	ME	15330tac
1700-1730	daily	ME	9540tac
Uighur	**Days**	**Area**	**kHz**
1400-1430	daily	As	5040tac
Urdu	**Days**	**Area**	**kHz**
1230-1300	daily	As	5060tac, 5975tac, 6025tac, 9715tac
1400-1430	daily	As	5060tac, 5975tac, 6025tac, 9715tac
Uzbek	**Days**	**Area**	**kHz**
0230-0330	daily	As	9375tac, 9540tac
0230-0330	daily	ME	5975tac, 7215tac
1550-1630	daily	As	9540tac
1550-1630	daily	Eu	5975tac
1550-1630	daily	WAs	6025tac, 7285tac
1730-1830	daily	WAs	6025tac, 7285tac
1730-1830	daily	As	9540tac
1730-1830	daily	Eu	5975tac

ANN: English: "This is Radio Tashkent International calling"; Uzbek: "Toskentdan gapiramiz"
V: QSL-card.
NOTES: Radio Tashkent International is the External Sce of the State Radio & TV Company of Uzbekistan (O'zbekiston teleradiokompaniyasi).

RADIOALOQA, RADIOESHITTIRISH VA TELEVIDENIYA DAVLAT KORXONASI (RRDTK) (Tx Operator)
Xisor Street 88, 700188 Toshkent, Uzbekistan.
☎ +998 71 1443445. 🖷 +998 71 2210555.
Email: soatov@prrt.ccc.uz **Web:** www.crrt.cc.uz
L.P: GD: Xoliq Sodiqovich Soatov.
SW: [TAC] Toshkent (G.C. 41N13 069E09) 19 x 100kW
NOTES: RRTDK, a division of the State Communications and Information Agency of Uzbekistan, is the national transmitter network operator in Uzbekistan. It leases out its facilities to national and international clients.

Broadcasters using sites in this country:
BBC World Sce uses: (TAC). See stn entry in: **G**, INT Section
BVB uses: (TAC). See stn entry in: **G**, INT Section
FEBA Radio uses: (TAC). See stn entry in: **G**, INT Section
IBC Tamil Radio uses: (TAC). See stn entry in: **CLN**, CTB Section

RFI uses: (TAC). See stn entry in: **F**, INT Section
RNWO uses: (TAC). See stn entry in: **HOL**, INT Section
RVI uses: (TAC). See stn entry in: **BEL**, INT Section
TWR India uses: (TAC). See stn entry in: **IND**, INT Section
Vatican Radio uses: (TAC). See stn entry in: **CVA**, INT Section
VO Tibet uses: (TAC). See stn entry in: **CHN**, CTB Section
Voice Africa uses: (TAC). See stn entry in: **G**, INT Section

VATICAN CITY STATE

VATICAN RADIO (Rlg)

Piazza Pia 3, I-00120 Vatican City.
☎ +3906 69883945. Fax +3906 69883463.
Email: sedoc@vatiradio.va **Web:** www.vaticanradio.org
L.P: GD: Rev. Pasquale Borgomeo S.I; PD: Rev. Federico Lombardi S.I; Tech Dir: Rev. Lino Dan S.I; CE: Pier Vincenzo Giudici; Head of Int'l Rel: Mrs. Solange de Maillardoz.
MW: [SMG] Santa Maria di Galeria 1530kHz 600kW, 1611kHz 50kW; [VAT] Vatican City 585/1260kHz 5kW
SW: [SMG] Santa Maria di Galeria (G.C. 42N03 012E19) 4 x 100, 5 x 500kW; [VAT] Vatican City (G.C. 41N54 012E27) 1 x 10, 1 x 80kW
kHz: *585, 1260, 1467, 1530, 1611, 4005, 5885, 5895, 5910, 6020, 6145, 6185, 6205, 7250, 7305, 7335, 7360, 7365, 7370, 9585, 9600, 9605, 9645, 9660, 9695, 9755, 9850, 9865, 11625, 11715, 11740, 11805, 11850, 11910, 12070, 13765, 13770, 15235, 15570, 15595, 17515, 21850*

Winter Schedule 2004

Albanian	Days	Area	kHz
0620-0700	daily	Eu	1260vat, 1611smg
2000-2020	daily	Eu	1260vat, 1611smg, 6185smg, 7250smg

Amharic	Days	Area	kHz
0400-0415	daily	EAf	7360smg, 9660smg
1630-1645	daily	EAf	13765smg, 15570smg

Angelus	Days	Area	kHz
1100-1115	......s	Eu	585vat, 1611smg+, 5885vat, 9645smg, 11740smg, 15595smg, 17515smg, 21850smg
1100-1130	......s	Af	15595smg, 21850smg
1100-1130	......s	As	15595smg, 17515smg
1100-1130	......s	Eu	1530smg, 1611smg+

Arabic	Days	Area	kHz
0500-0530	daily	Eu	1260vat
0500-0530	daily	ME	9645smg
0500-0530	daily	As	11715smg
0500-0530	daily	NAf	9645smg, 11715smg
0745-0800	mtwtfs.	Eu	1530smg, 5885vat, 7250smg, 9645smg, 15595smg
0745-0800	mtwtfs.	ME	15595smg
0745-0800	mtwtfs.	NAf	7250smg, 9645smg, 15595smg
1630-1700	daily	Eu	1260vat
1630-1700	daily	ME	11625smg, 15595smg
1630-1700	daily	NAf	11625smg, 15595smg
2145-2200	daily	Eu	1530smg, 4005vat, 5885vat, 7250smg
2145-2200	daily	NAf	7250smg

Armenian	Days	Area	kHz
0310-0330	daily	Eu	1260vat, 6185smg, 9645smg
1330-1400	daily	Eu	1611smg, 7365smg, 9585smg, 11715smg

Belarusian	Days	Area	kHz
0420-0440	daily	Eu	1260vat, 6185smg, 7335smg
1800-1820	daily	Eu	1260vat, 1611smg, 6185smg, 7365smg

Bulgarian	Days	Area	kHz
0540-0600	daily	Eu	1611smg, 6185smg, 7335smg
1920-1940	daily	Eu	1260vat, 1611smg, 6185smg, 7365smg

Chinese (Mass)	Days	Area	kHz
1230-1300	.....s.	EAs	13770smg, 15235smg

Croatian	Days	Area	kHz
0350-0410	daily	Eu	1530smg, 4005vat

Croatian	Days	Area	kHz
1750-1810	daily	Eu	1467rou, 1530smg, 4005vat, 5885vat, 7250smg

Czech	Days	Area	kHz
0410-0425	daily	Eu	1530smg, 4005vat, 5885vat
1830-1845	daily	Eu	1467rou, 1530smg, 4005vat, 5885vat, 7250smg

English	Days	Area	kHz
0140-0200	daily	As	7335smg, 9865smg
0250-0315	daily	NAm	7305smg, 9605smg
0300-0330	daily	As	12070nvs
0300-0330	daily	Af	7360smg
0500-0530	daily	Af	7360smg, 9660smg, 11625smg
0600-0620	daily	Eu	1530smg, 4005vat, 5885vat, 7250smg
0630-0700	daily	Af	9660smg, 11625smg, 13765smg
0730-0745	mtwtfs.	Af	9645smg, 15595smg
0730-0745	mtwtfs.	As	15595smg
0730-0745	mtwtfs.	Eu	585vat, 1530smg, 4005vat, 5885vat, 6185smg, 7250smg, 9645smg, 11740smg, 15595smg
1030-1100	mtwtfs.	Eu	585vat, 1611smg+, 5885vat
1530-1600	daily	As	9865tac, 11850smg, 13765smg
1715-1730	daily	Eu	585vat, 1530smg, 4005vat, 5885vat, 7250smg, 9645smg, 15595smg
1730-1800	daily	Af	11625smg, 13765smg, 15570smg
1730-1800	daily	As	15595smg
2000-2030	daily	Af	7365smg, 9755smg, 11625smg
2040-2100	m......	Eu	1260vat, 1611smg, 6185smg
2050-2110	daily	Eu	585vat, 1530smg, 4005vat, 5885vat, 7250smg

English (Mass)	Days	Area	kHz
1130-1230	....f..	As	15595smg, 17515smg
1130-1300	....f..	Af	15595smg, 17515smg
1530-1630	.....s.	As	9865tac, 11850smg, 13765smg
1630-1600	.....s.	Af	9865tac, 11850smg, 13765smg

Esperanto	Days	Area	kHz
2020-2030	......s	Eu	585vat, 1530smg, 4005vat, 5885vat
2020-2030	..wt...	Eu	1260vat, 1611smg, 6185smg, 7250smg
2250-2300	......s	Eu	585vat, 1530smg, 1611smg+, 4005vat, 5885vat

French	Days	Area	kHz
0230-0250	daily	NAm	7305smg, 9605smg
0230-0300	daily	Af	7360smg
0430-0500	daily	Af	7360smg, 9660smg
0540-0600	daily	Eu	1530smg, 4005vat, 5885vat, 7250smg
0600-0530	daily	Af	9660smg, 11625smg, 13765smg
0715-0730	mtwtfs.	Eu	585vat, 1530smg, 4005vat, 5885vat, 6185smg, 7250smg, 9645smg, 11740smg, 15595smg
0715-0730	mtwtfs.	Af	9645smg, 15595smg
0715-0730	mtwtfs.	As	15595smg
1200-1300	mtwtfs.	Eu	585vat, 1611smg+, 5885vat

French	Days	Area	kHz
1700-1715	daily	Eu	585vat, 1530smg, 4005vat, 5885vat, 7250smg, 9645smg, 15595smg
1700-1730	daily	Af	13765smg, 15570smg
1700-1730	daily	As	15595smg
2030-2050	daily	Eu	585vat, 1530smg, 4005vat, 5885vat, 7250smg
2030-2145	daily	Af	7365smg, 9755smg, 11625smg

Ge'ez Liturgy	Days	Area	kHz
0930-1000	......s	Af	15595smg, 17515smg

German	Days	Area	kHz
0520-0540	daily	Eu	1530smg, 4005vat, 5885vat, 7250smg
1500-1515	daily	Eu	5885vat, 7250smg, 9645smg
1920-1940	daily	Eu	1467rou, 1530smg, 4005vat, 5885vat, 7250smg

Hindi	Days	Area	kHz
0040-0100	daily	As	7335smg, 9865smg
0200-0220	daily	As	12070nvs
1430-1450	daily	As	9865tac, 11850smg, 13765smg

Hungarian	Days	Area	kHz
0440-0500	daily	Eu	1530smg, 4005vat, 5885vat
1810-1830	daily	Eu	1467rou, 1530smg, 4005vat, 5885vat, 7250smg

Italian	Days	Area	kHz
0620-0630	daily	Eu	585vat, 1530smg, 4005vat, 5885vat, 6185smg, 7250smg
0700-0715	mtwtfs.	Af	9645smg, 15595smg
0700-0715	mtwtfs.	As	15595smg
0700-0715	mtwtfs.	Eu	585vat, 1530smg, 4005vat, 5885vat, 6185smg, 7250smg, 9645smg, 11740smg, 15595smg
1100-1115	mtwtfs.	Eu	585vat, 1611smg+, 5885vat
1115-1200	......s	Eu	585vat, 1611smg+, 5885vat
1300-1315	daily	As	1611smg+, 15595smg
1300-1330	daily	Eu	1611smg+
1300-1400	daily	Eu	585vat, 5885vat, 9645smg, 11740smg, 15595smg, 21850smg
1300-1530	daily	Af	15595smg, 21850smg
1530-1600	....f..	Eu	5885vat, 7250smg, 9645smg
1630-1700	daily	Eu	585vat, 1530smg, 5885vat, 7250smg, 9645smg
2000-2020	daily	Eu	585vat, 1530smg, 4005vat, 5885vat
2020-2040	m......	Eu	1260vat, 1611smg, 6185smg
2200-2230	daily	Eu	4005vat, 5885vat
2230-2250	daily	Eu	585vat, 1530smg, 1611smg+, 4005vat, 5885vat

Italian (Mass)	Days	Area	kHz
0830-0900	c	Eu	585vat, 7250smg

Latin (Mass)	Days	Area	kHz
0630-0700	daily	Af	9645smg, 15595smg
0630-0700	daily	As	15595smg
0630-0700	daily	Eu	585vat, 1530smg, 4005vat, 5885vat, 6185smg, 7250smg, 9645smg, 11740smg, 15595smg

Latvian	Days	Area	kHz
0500-0520	daily	Eu	6185smg, 7335smg
1840-1900	daily	Eu	1260vat, 1611smg, 6185smg, 7365smg, 9585smg

Lithuanian	Days	Area	kHz
0440-0500	daily	Eu	1260vat, 6185smg, 7335smg
1820-1840	daily	Eu	1260vat, 1611smg, 6185smg, 7365smg, 9585smg

Malayalam	Days	Area	kHz
0120-0140	daily	As	7335smg, 9865smg
0240-0300	daily	As	12070nvs
1510-1530	daily	As	9865tac, 11850smg, 13765smg

Mandarin	Days	Area	kHz
1230-1300	mtwtf.s	EAs	6020pug, 13770smg, 15235smg
2200-2315	daily	EAs	6145smg, 7305smg, 9600khb

Music	Days	Area	kHz
1530-1600	mtwt.ss	Eu	5885vat, 7250smg, 9645smg

Oriental Liturgy	Days	Area	kHz
0930-1000	......s	Eu	11740smg, 15595smg, 17515smg

Papal Audience	Days	Area	kHz
0915-0930	..w....	Eu	585vat, 1611smg+, 5885vat

Polish	Days	Area	kHz
0500-0520	daily	Eu	1530smg, 4005vat, 5885vat, 7250smg
1515-1530	daily	Eu	5885vat, 7250smg, 9645smg
1900-1920	daily	Eu	1467rou, 1530smg, 4005vat, 5885vat, 7250smg

Portuguese	Days	Area	kHz
0030-0100	daily	Eu	1260vat
0030-0100	daily	SAm	7305smg, 9605smg
0530-0600	daily	Af	9660smg, 11625smg, 13765smg
0900-1000	mtwtfs.	Eu	1260vat
1000-1130	mtwtfs.	Eu	1260vat
1000-1130	mtwtfs.	SAm	21850smg
1415-1500	daily	Eu	1260vat, 9645smg, 11740smg
1500-1600	...t...	Eu	1260vat
1600-1630	daily	Eu	1260vat
1800-1900	daily	Af	11625smg, 13765smg, 15570smg
2130-2145	daily	Eu	1530smg, 4005vat, 5885vat, 7250smg

Romanian	Days	Area	kHz
0520-0540	daily	Eu	1611smg, 6185smg, 7335smg
1900-1920	daily	Eu	1260vat, 1611smg, 6185smg, 7365smg

Romanian Liturgy	Days	Area	kHz
0710-0745	c	Eu	7250smg, 9645smg

Rosary	Days	Area	kHz
1940-2000	......s	Eu	585vat, 7365smg
1940-2000	daily	Eu	585vat, 1530smg, 4005vat, 5885smg, 9755smg
1940-2000	daily	As	9755smg
1940-2000	daily	Af	7365smg, 9755smg, 11625smg

Russian	Days	Area	kHz
0330-0400	daily	Eu	1260vat, 7335smg, 9645smg
1330-1400	daily	Eu	1260vat, 5895vat, 9695smg, 11805smg
1710-1740	daily	Eu	1611smg, 6185smg, 7365smg, 9585smg, 11715smg

Russian	Days	Area	kHz
2100-2130	daily	Eu	1260vat, 5910smg, 7370smg, 9585smg

Scandinavian languages	Days	Area	kHz
0600-0620	daily	Eu	1260vat, 1611smg, 6185smg, 7335smg
1940-2000	daily	Eu	1260vat, 1611smg, 6185smg, 7250smg

Slovak	Days	Area	kHz
0425-0440	daily	Eu	1530smg, 4005vat, 5885vat
1845-1900	daily	Eu	1467rou, 1530smg, 4005vat, 5885vat, 7250smg

Slovenian	Days	Area	kHz
0330-0350	daily	Eu	1530smg, 4005vat
1730-1750	daily	Eu	1467rou, 1530smg, 4005vat, 5885vat, 7250smg

Somali	Days	Area	kHz
0345-0400	.....s	EAf	7360smg, 9660smg
1615-1630	.....s.	EAf	13765smg, 15570smg

Spanish	Days	Area	kHz
0100-0145	daily	Eu	1260vat
0100-0145	daily	SAm	7305smg, 9605smg, 11910smg
0145-0230	daily	SAm	7305smg, 9605smg, 11910smg
0315-0400	daily	SAm	7305smg, 9605smg
0900-0915	mtwtfs.	Eu	585vat, 1611smg+, 5885vat
1130-1200	mtwtfs.	SAm	21850smg
1130-1200	mtwtfs.	Eu	1260vat
1400-1415	daily	Eu	585vat, 1260vat, 1611smg, 9645smg, 11740smg
1500-1600	m...f..	Eu	1260vat
1730-1800	daily	Eu	1260vat
1900-1940	.....s.	Af	9755smg, 11625smg
2110-2130	daily	Eu	585vat, 1530smg, 4005vat, 5885vat, 7250smg

Swahili	Days	Area	kHz
0330-0345	daily	Af	7360smg, 9660smg
1600-1615	daily	Af	13765smg, 15570smg

Tagalog	Days	Area	kHz
2020-2030	....f..	Eu	1260vat, 1611smg

Tamil	Days	Area	kHz
0100-0120	daily	As	7335smg, 9865smg
0220-0240	daily	As	12070nvs
1450-1510	daily	As	9865tac, 11850smg, 13765smg

Tigrinya	Days	Area	kHz
0415-0430	daily	EAf	7360smg, 9660smg
1645-1700	daily	EAf	13765smg, 15570smg

Ukrainian	Days	Area	kHz
0400-0420	daily	Eu	1260vat, 6185smg, 7335smg
1740-1800	daily	Eu	1611smg, 6185smg, 7365smg, 9585smg

Ukrainian Liturgy	Days	Area	kHz
0715-0730	c	Eu	1611smg, 9850smg, 11740smg

Urdu	Days	Area	kHz
0025-0040	m..t...	As	7335smg, 9865smg
1415-1430	..w...s	As	11850smg, 13765smg

Vespers	Days	Area	kHz
1600-1630	daily	Eu	5885vat, 7250smg, 9645smg

Vietnamese	Days	Area	kHz
1315-1415	daily	SEA	6205tch, 17515smg
2315-2400	daily	SEA	7305smg, 9600smg

ANN: Before all transmissions: Latin: "Laudetur Jesus Christus" (Praised be Jesus Christ), repeated in the language of the broadcast, then station identification. English: "This is the English program of Vatican Radio"

V: QSL-card.

NOTES: Key: + DRM. Some broadcasts are on Sundays and Holy Days only.

Broadcasters using sites in this country:

VO Charity uses: (SMG). See stn entry in: **LBN**, INT Section

VO Russia (VOR) uses: (SMG). See stn entry in: **RUS**, INT Section

VENEZUELA

RADIO NACIONAL VENEZUELA – ANTENA INTERNACIONAL (Gov)

✉ Final calle Las Marías, El Pedregal de Chapellin, Caracas D.F., Zona Postal 1050, Venzuela.
☎ +58 2 7306666. 🖷 +58 2 7311457.
Email: ondacortavenezuela@hotmail.com **Web:** www.rnv.gov.ve
L.P: Dir: Helena Salcedo.
SW: Leased from Radiocuba (see Cuba)
kHz: *6000, 9550, 9820, 11760, 11875, 13680, 13740, 15230, 17705*

Winter Schedule 2004

Spanish	Days	Area	kHz
1900-2000	daily	NAm	13740hab*
2000-2100	daily	SAm	15230hab*, 17705hab*
2000-2100	daily	NAm	13680hab*
2000-2100	daily	Car	9550hab*
2100-2200	daily	SAm	6000hab*, 11875hab*
2300-2400	daily	NAm	9820hab*, 11760hab*
2300-2400	daily	CAm,SAm	13680hab*

ANN: Spanish: "Vd. escucha Radio Nacional de Venezuela, Antena Internacional"
V: QSL-card.
NOTES: Key: * Schedule and frequencies subject to change.

VIETNAM

VOICE OF VIETNAM (VOV) (Gov)

✉ 58 Quán Sú Street, Hanoi, Vietnam.
☎ +84 4 9344231. 🖷 +84 4 9344230.
Email: qhqt.vov@hn.vnn.vn **Web:** www.vov.org.vn
L.P: Chmn: Prof. Dr. Vu Van Hien; Chief Editor: Dinh The Loc.
MW: [OMO] Ô Môn (G.C. 10N04 125E39) 1242kHz 2000kW
SW: [HAN] Hanoi, Me Tri (G.C. 20N59 105E52) 2 x 50kW; [VNI] Son Tay (G.C. 21N12 105E22) 11 x 100kW
FM: Hanoi 105.5MHz, Ho Chi Minh City 105.7MHz
kHz: *1242, 5955, 5970, 6175, 7220, 7280, 7285, 9550, 9730, 9840, 12020*

Winter Schedule 2004

Cantonese	Days	Area	kHz
1130-1200	daily	As	9840vni, 12020vni
1330-1400	daily	As	9840vni, 12020vni
1530-1600	daily	As	9840vni, 12020vni
2230-2300	daily	As	9840vni, 12020vni

English	Days	Area	kHz
0100-0200	daily	CAm	6175sac
0230-0300	daily	CAm	6175sac
0330-0400	daily	CAm	6175sac
1100-1130	daily	SEA	1242omo
1100-1130	daily	As	7285han
1230-1300	daily	As	9840vni, 12020vni
1500-1530	daily	SAs	1242omo
1500-1530	daily	As	7285han, 9840vni, 12020vni
1600-1630	daily	Eu,ME	7220vni, 7280vni, 9550vni, 9730vni
1600-1630	daily	SEA	1242omo
1800-1830	daily	Eu	5955mos
1800-1830	daily	Eu,ME	7280vni, 9730vni
1900-1930	daily	Eu,ME	7280vni, 9730vni
2030-2100	daily	Eu,ME	7220vni, 7280vni, 9550vni, 9730vni
2330-2400	daily	As	9840vni, 12020vni

French	Days	Area	kHz
1200-1230	daily	As	7285han
1200-1230	daily	SEA	1242omo
1300-1330	daily	As	7285han
1300-1330	daily	SEA	1242omo
1630-1700	daily	Eu,ME	7220vni, 9550vni

French	Days	Area	kHz
1630-1700	daily	SEA	1242omo
1830-1900	daily	Eu,ME	7280vni, 9730vni
1930-2000	daily	Eu	5955mos
1930-2000	daily	Eu,ME	7280vni, 9730vni
2100-2130	daily	Eu,ME	7220vni, 7280vni, 9550vni, 9730vni
Indonesian	**Days**	**Area**	**kHz**
1030-1100	daily	As	9840vni, 12020vni
1300-1330	daily	As	9840vni, 12020vni
1430-1500	daily	As	9840vni, 12020vni
1430-1500	daily	SEA	1242omo
2300-2330	daily	As	9840vni, 12020vni
Japanese	**Days**	**Area**	**kHz**
1100-1130	daily	As	9840vni, 12020vni
1200-1230	daily	As	9840vni, 12020vni
1400-1430	daily	As	9840vni, 12020vni
2130-2200	daily	As	9840vni, 12020vni
2130-2200	daily	Eu,ME	7220vni, 9550vni
Khmer	**Days**	**Area**	**kHz**
1030-1100	daily	As	7285han
1230-1300	daily	As	7285han
1230-1300	daily	SEA	1242omo
2230-2300	daily	As	7285han
2230-2300	daily	SEA	1242omo
Lao	**Days**	**Area**	**kHz**
1330-1430	daily	As	7285han
1330-1430	daily	SEA	1242omo
2300-2400	daily	SEA	1242omo
2300-2400	daily	As	7285han
Mandarin	**Days**	**Area**	**kHz**
1100-1130	daily	As	7220vni, 9550vni
1200-1230	daily	As	7220vni, 9550vni
1300-1330	daily	As	7220vni, 9550vni
2200-2230	daily	As	7220vni, 9550vni, 9840vni, 12020vni
Russian	**Days**	**Area**	**kHz**
1130-1200	daily	As	7220vni, 9550vni
1230-1300	daily	As	7220vni, 9550vni
1630-1700	daily	Eu,ME	7280vni, 9730vni
2000-2030	daily	Eu	5970skn
2000-2030	daily	Eu,ME	7280vni, 9730vni
Spanish	**Days**	**Area**	**kHz**
0300-0330	daily	CAm	6175sac
0400-0430	daily	NAm	6175sac
Thai	**Days**	**Area**	**kHz**
1130-1200	daily	As	7285han
1130-1200	daily	SEA	1242omo
1430-1500	daily	As	7285han
1530-1600	daily	As	7285han
1530-1600	daily	SEA	1242omo
2200-2230	daily	SEA	1242omo
2200-2230	daily	As	7285han
Vietnamese	**Days**	**Area**	**kHz**
0000-0100	daily	As	7285han
0130-0230	daily	NAm	6175sac
0430-0530	daily	NAm	6175sac
1500-1600	daily	Eu,ME	7220vni, 9550vni
1700-1800	daily	Eu,ME	7280vni, 9730vni
1830-1930	daily	Eu	5955mos
2030-2130	daily	Eu	5970skn

ANN: English: "You are listening to the Voice of Vietnam"
V: QSL-card.
NOTES: The External Sce of the national broadcaster Voice of Vietnam.

ZAMBIA

CHRISTIAN VOICE (Rlg)
Private Bag E606, Lusaka, Zambia.
☎ +260 1 274251. 🖷 +260 1 274526.
Email: feedback@voiceafrica.net **Web:** www.voiceafrica.net
☎ +44 121 5226087. 🖷 +44 121 5226083.
L.P: SM: Charles Maboshe; Transmitter Eng: John Kawele.
SW: [LUS] Lusaka (G.C. 15S30 028E15) 1 x 100kW
kHz: *4965, 6065, 9865*

Winter Schedule 2004

English	Days	Area	kHz
0400-0700	daily	SAf,CAf	6065lus
0700-1700	daily	SAf,CAf	9865lus
1700-0400	daily	SAf,CAf	4965lus

ANN: English: "This is Radio Christian Voice"
V: QSL-letter.
NOTES: Christian Voice (Zambia) Ltd is a branch of Christian Vision (see United Kingdom for corporate details), launched in December 1994.

VERIFICATIONS

You have spent a lot of time and effort on your QSL collection, but what will happen to it if you leave the listening hobby or pass away? It will probably be lost or discarded.

The Committee to Preserve Radio Verifications – a committee of the Association of North American Radio Clubs – will preserve this valuable material for future hobbyists to enjoy and appreciate. The CPRV collection is housed at the Library of American Broadcasting, University of Maryland, U.S.A. For information, send an SASE or two IRCs to:

Committee to Preserve Radio Verifications
Jerry Berg, Chair
38 Eastern Avenue
Lexington, MA 02421, U.S.A.
jsberg@rcn.com
Visit our website at
http://www.ontheshortwaves.com

CLANDESTINE AND OTHER TARGET BROADCASTS

Clandestine Broadcasts (Clan) are politically-motivated broadcasts produced by groups opposed to the government of the target country. Other Target Broadcasts are produced by non-governmental or governmental organisations and targetted at zones of regional or local conflict. Most COTBs are transmitted via the facilities of international transmitter operators.

Target: AFGHANISTAN

PEACE RADIO (RADIO SOLH)

kHz: *11810, 15265, 17710, 21620*

Winter Schedule 2004

Various	Days	Area	kHz
0200-0500	daily	WAs	11810rmp
0700-1200	daily	WAs	21620rmp
1200-1300	daily	WAs	17710rmp
1300-1500	daily	WAs	15265rmp
1500-1630	daily	WAs	17710rmp

ANN: Dari: "Radio Solh"; Pashto: "Sola Radyo"
NOTES: On shortwave since October 2004. Operated by U.S. Forces.

SALAAM WATANDAR

c/o Internews Afghanistan, Baharistan, Karti-Parwan, Kabul, Afghanistan.
☎ +93 70 257455.
Email: johnfxwest@yahoo.co.uk
Web: www.internews.org/regions/centralasia/afghanistan.htm
L.P: Radio Network Coordinator: Sanjar Qiam.
FM: Relayed by local FM stn's in Afghanistan.
SAT: Hotbird 6
kHz: *7230, 17720*

Winter Schedule 2004

Dari/Pashto	Days	Area	kHz
0130-0300	daily	AFG	7230dha
1330-1500	daily	AFG	17720rmp

V: QSL-email.
NOTES: Radio show produced by the "Internews" organisation, primarily fed by satellite to local radio stations in Afghanistan for rebroadcasting.

Target: CENTRAL AFRICAN REPUBLIC

RADIO NDEKE LUKA

c/o PNUD, BP 872, Bangui, Central African Republic.
☎ +236 610652.
Email: ndekeluka@hotmail.com
Fondation Hirondelle, 3 Rue Traversiere, CH-1018 Lausanne, Switzerland.
Web: www.hirondelle.org
L.P: Head of project: Reinhard Moser.
FM: Bangui 100.8MHz 1kW (24h)
kHz: *11785*

Winter Schedule 2004

Various	Days	Area	kHz
1830-1930	daily	CAF	11785wof

ANN: French: "Vous écoute Radio Ndeke Luka"
V: QSL-card.
NOTES: On shortwave since September 2003. Broadcasts in Sango and French. Radio Ndeke Luka is a local FM station in the capital Bangui, established by the Swiss-based "Fondation Hirondelle" in March 2000.

Target: CHINA (People's Rep. of)

VOICE OF CHINA (Clan)

P.O. Box 273538, Concord, CA 94527, USA.
☎ +1 510 6872354. Fax +1 510 6877396.
Email: info@china21century.org **Web:** www.china21century.org
L.P: Exec. Producer: Lily Hu.
kHz: *7270, 11940*

Winter Schedule 2004

Mandarin	Days	Area	kHz
0800-0900	daily	CHN	11940tai
2300-2400	daily	CHN	7270tai

ANN: Mandarin: "Zhongguo zhi yin"
V: QSL-card.
NOTES: On the air since April 1991. A prgr produced by the "Foundation for China in the 21st Century", a U.S.-based non-profit organisation. The "Voice of China" prgr is aired via a tx in Taiwan. Transmissions are jammed in the target area.

VOICE OF TIBET (Clan)

Admin. & Studio: St. Olavs gate 24, N-0166 Oslo, Norway.
☎ + 47 22112700. Fax +47 22115474.
Email: voti@online.no **Web:** www.vot.org
Main Editorial Office: Narthang Building, Gangchen Kyishong, Dharamsala-176215, H.P., India.
☎ +91 1892 228179. Fax +91 1892 224913.
L.P: Project manager: Øystein Alme; Project coordinator: Chophel Norbu; Chief Editor (India): Karma Yeshi.
kHz: *9395, 15690, 17525, 17540*

Winter Schedule 2004

Mandarin	Days	Area	kHz
1230-1245	daily	CHN	17525tac
1500-1515	daily	CHN	15690tac*, 17540tac
1550-1605	daily	CHN	9395tac*, 17540tac
Tibetan	**Days**	**Area**	**kHz**
1215-1230	daily	CHN	17525tac
1430-1500	daily	CHN	15690tac*, 17540tac
1520-1550	daily	CHN	9395tac*, 17540tac

ANN: Mandarin: "Zheli shi Nuowei Ziyou Xizang zhi Sheng Guangbo Diantai huayi jiemu"; Tibetan: "'Di nor we bod kyi rlung 'phrin khang yin"
V: QSL-card.
NOTES: On the air since July 1996. Licensed radio station in Norway, run by the "Voice of Tibet Foundation". Established by the organisations "Worldview Rights", the "Norwegian Human Rights House" and the "Norwegian Tibet Committee". Transmissions are jammed in the target area, frequencies are often changed. Key: * alternative frequencies which have been reported to include 7520kHz.

Target: COLOMBIA

LA VOZ DE LA RESISTENCIA (Clan)

Correspondence: FARC-EP Comision Internacional, Apartado Postal 27-552, México D.F. 06761, Mexico.
Email: elbarcino@laneta.apc.org **Web:** www.farcep.org (FARC-EP)
FM: Network of mobile and stationary FM transmitters in the FARC-EP controlled areas.
kHz: *6120, 6240*

Winter Schedule 2004

Spanish	Days	Area	kHz
0000-0040	daily	CLM	6120—, 6240—

NOTES: Operated by "Fuerzas Armadas Revolucionaris de Columbia - Ejercito del Pueblo" (FARC-EP). Extensive transmissions on FM, limited on SW. Jammed.

Target: CUBA

CONVERSANDO ENTRE CUBANOS (Clan)

P.O. Box 520562, Miami, FL 33152, USA.
Email: exclub@aol.com
L.P: Press Dir: Justo Gabriel Quintana
kHz: *9955*

Winter Schedule 2004

Spanish	Days	Area	kHz
0100-0130	......s	CUB	9955rmi
0230-0300	m......	CUB	9955rmi

ANN: Spanish: "Conversando entre Cubanos"
V: QSL-card.
NOTES: On the air since the 1990s. A prgr produced by the "Association of Ex-Political Prisoners of Cuba" (ExClub). Jammed in the target area.

FORO MILITAR CUBANO (Clan)

P.O. Box 140305, Coral Gables, FL 33114-0305, USA.
☎ +1 305 4472713. Fax +1 305 2050311.
Email: webmaster@veteranscava.org
Web: www.veteranscava.org
kHz: *9955*

Winter Schedule 2004

Spanish	Days	Area	kHz
0000-0100	......s	CUB	9955rmi
1200-1300	....f..	CUB	9955rmi

ANN: Spanish: "Foro Militar Cubano"
NOTES: On the air since September 1997. A prgr produced by the "Cuban American Veterans Association". Jammed in the target area.

JUNTA PATRIÓTICA CUBANA (Clan)

P.O. Box 7799, Washington, D.C. 20044, USA.
☎ +1 703 5780160. Fax +1 703 5781587.
Email: cabenedi@juntapatriotica.org
Web: www.juntapatriotica.org
L.P: Contact: Dr. Roberto Rodriguez de Aragon.
kHz: *9955*

Winter Schedule 2004

Spanish	Days	Area	kHz
1200-1230	m......	CUB	9955rmi

ANN: Spanish: "Junta Patriótica Cubana"
NOTES: On the air since September 1997. A prgr produced by the "Junta Patriótica Cubana" (JPC). Jammed in the target area.

RADIO ORIENTE LIBRE

c/o WRMI, P.O. Box 526852, Miami, FL 33152, USA.
kHz: *9955*

Winter Schedule 2004

Spanish	Days	Area	kHz
0130-0230	m......	CUB	9955rmi
0200-0300	......s	CUB	9955rmi
1200-1300	.t.....	CUB	9955rmi

ANN: Spanish: "Radio Oriente Libre"
NOTES: On the air since 2001. Jammed in the target area.

TROVA LIBRE

c/o WRMI, P.O. Box 526852, Miami, FL 33152, USA
L.P: Producer: Michael Mendéz.
kHz: *9955*

Winter Schedule 2004

Spanish	Days	Area	kHz
0000-0015	m......	CUB	9955rmi
1115-1130	......s	CUB	9955rmi
1200-1215	...t...	CUB	9955rmi

ANN: Spanish: "Trova Libre"
NOTES: On the air since August 2004.

Target: ERITREA

VOICE OF DEMOCRATIC ERITREA (Clan)

Postfach 1946, D-65409 Rüsselsheim, Germany.
Email: mghebresel@aol.com
Web: www.nharnet.com/radio/radiopage.htm
kHz: *9820, 12015*

Winter Schedule 2004

Arabic	Days	Area	kHz
1530-1600	.....s.	ERI	9820jul
1730-1800	...t...	ERI	12015jul
Tigrinya	**Days**	**Area**	**kHz**
1500-1530	.....s.	ERI	9820jul
1700-1730	...t...	ERI	12015jul

ANN: Arabic: "Sawt Eritrea al-dimuqratiya"; Tigrinya: "Dmtsi Democrasiyawet Writrea"
V: QSL-letter.
NOTES: On the air since March 2000. Produced by the "Eritrean Liberation Front - Revolutionary Council" (ELF-RC).

VOICE OF LIBERTY – ERITREA (Clan)

P.O. Box 115500, Atlanta, GA 30210, USA.
Email: vol@eritrea1.org **Web:** www.eritrea1.org
kHz: *15675*

Winter Schedule 2004

Various	Days	Area	kHz
0600-0700	..w...s	ERI	15675sam

ANN: Arabic: "Huna sawt al-shariyah"; Tigrinya: "Dmtsi Harnet Writrea"
NOTES: On the air since February 2004. Produced by the "Eritrean People's Liberation Front - Democratic Party" (EPLF-DP). Prgr's are in Tigrinya and Arabic.

VOICE OF PEACE AND DEMOCRACY (Clan)

c/o Voice of the Tigray Revolution, P.O. Box 450, Mek'ele, Ethiopia.
kHz: *5500, 6350*

Winter Schedule 2004

Arabic/Tigrinya	Days	Area	kHz
0315-0400	mtwtf..	ERI	5500—, 6350—
1420-1450	mtwtf..	ERI	5500—, 6350—

ANN: Arabic: "Sawt al-salam wal dimuqratiya"; Tigrinya: "Huna Writrea kumana Demokrasiyana radiyonya"
NOTES: On the air since February 1999. A prgr produced in the studios of the Ethiopian broadcaster Voice of the Revolution of Tigray (see National Radio section) and transmitted via its tx's. Broadcasts in Arabic, Kunama and Tigrinya. Tx location is Mek'ele, Ethiopia (10kW).

VOICE OF THE ERITREAN PEOPLE (Clan)

Based in Sweden.
Email: webmaster@eritreana.com
Web: www.eritreana.com/voep.htm
kHz: *13690*

Winter Schedule 2004

Tigrinya	Days	Area	kHz
1730-1830	......s	ERI	13690rmp

ANN: Tigrinya: "Ezi dmtsi hzbi Writrea eyu"
V: QSL-email.
NOTES: On the air since December 2001. Linked with the "Eritrean National Alliance" (ENA) and the "Eritrean Liberation Front - National Congress" (ELF-NC).

Target: ETHIOPIA

RADIO VOICE OF OROMO LIBERATION FRONT (Clan)

Based in Canada.
Email: rsqbo@yahoo.com **Web:** www.oromia.org/rsqbo/rsqbo.htm
kHz: *7590*

Winter Schedule 2004

Oromo	Days	Area	kHz
1700-1730	m..t...	ETH	7590sam

ANN: Oromo: "Radiyoo Sagalee Qabsoo Bilisummaa Oromoo"
NOTES: On the air since November 2003. Produced by the "Oromo Liberation Front" (OLF). The OLF also produces the prgr "Voice of Oromo Liberation" (see separate entry).

VOICE OF ETHIOPIAN MEDHIN (Clan)

Postfach 111423, D-60049 Frankfurt, Germany.
☎ +49 69 66366672. Fax +49 69 66366674.
Email: voiceofmedhin@medhin.org **Web:** www.medhin.com
kHz: *9820*

Winter Schedule 2004

Amharic	Days	Area	kHz
1600-1700	......s	ETH	9820jul

ANN: Amharic: "Yih ye Ethiopia Medhin dimts new"
V: QSL-card.
NOTES: On the air since June 2000. A prgr produced by the "Ethiopian Medhin Democratic Party" (MEDHIN).

VOICE OF ETHIOPIAN UNITY (Clan)

Finote Democracy, P.O. Box 10573, 1001 EN Amsterdam, Netherlands.
Email: efdpu@finote.org **Web:** www.finote.org
USA: Finote Democracy, P.O. Box 88675, Los Angeles, CA 90009, USA.
kHz: *7220*

Winter Schedule 2004

Amharic	Days	Area	kHz
1830-1930	..w...s	ETH	7220jul

ANN: Amharic: "Yih Finote Demokrasi ye Ethiopia andinet dimts"
V: QSL-letter.
NOTES: On the air since January 2000. A prgr produced by "Finote Democracy", a group of Ethiopians in Europe and the USA. Linked with the "Ethiopian People's Revolutionary Party".

VOICE OF OROMIA (Clan)

P.O. Box 17662, Atlanta, GA 30316, USA.
Email: sagaloromo@aol.com **Web:** www.voiceoforomiyaa.com
L.P: Producer: Mahdi H.Muudee.
kHz: *7590*

Winter Schedule 2004			
Oromo	**Days**	**Area**	**kHz**
1730-1800	m......	ETH	7590sam

ANN: Oromo: "Raadiyoo Sagalee Oromiyaa"
V: QSL-email.
NOTES: On the air since December 2001. A prgr produced by Voice of Oromia Radio, Inc., promoting the cultural heritage of the Oromia region.

VOICE OF OROMO LIBERATION (Clan)

Postfach 510620, D-13366 Berlin, Germany.
☎ +49 30 4941036. Fax +49 30 4943372.
Email: sbo13366@aol.com
Web: www.oromoliberationfront.org/sbo.html
L.P: Secr. SBO Committee: Taye Teferra.
kHz: *9820*

Winter Schedule 2004			
Oromo	**Days**	**Area**	**kHz**
1700-1800	.tw.f.s	ETH	9820jul

ANN: Oromo: "Kun Sagalee Bilisummaa Oromoo"
V: QSL-letter.
NOTES: On the air since July 1988 (transmitting from outside of Ethiopian territory since 1996). Produced by the "Oromo Liberation Front" (OLF). Another OLF produced prgr is "Radio Voice of Oromo Liberation Front" (see separate entry).

RADIO MUSTAQBAL

1000 Potomac Street, NW, Suite 350, Washington, DC 20007, USA.
☎ +1 202 5723700. Fax +1 202 2986038.
Email: ahoussein@edc.org **Web:** www.edc.org
kHz: *15370, 15385*

Winter Schedule 2004			
Somali	**Days**	**Area**	**kHz**
0630-0700	mt.t...	ETH	15370dha
1130-1200	mt.t...	ETH	15385dha

NOTES: On the air since January 2004. Educational prgr's for Somali speakers in Southern Ethiopia. A project by Education Development Center, Inc., financed by USAID.

RADIO UNMEE

P.O. Box 3001, Addis Ababa, Ethiopia.
☎ +251 1 443396.
Email: bakari@un.org
Web: www.un.org/Depts/dpko/unmee/radio.htm
Eritrea: P.O. Box 5805, Asmara, Eritrea.
☎ +291 1 150411.
L.P: Producer: Diane Bailey.
kHz: *21460, 21550*

Winter Schedule 2004			
Various	**Days**	**Area**	**kHz**
0900-1000	......s	EAf	21460dha
1030-1130	.t.....	EAf	21550dha

V: QSL-card.
NOTES: On the air since January 2001. A project of the UN Peacekeeping Mission in Ethiopia and Eritrea. Broadcasts in Amharic, Arabic, Oromo, Tigre, Tigrinya and English.

Target: INDIA (Kashmir)

VOICE OF JAMMU KASHMIR FREEDOM MOVEMENT (Clan)

P.O. Box 102, Muzaffarabad, Azad Kashmir, Pakistan.
Email: harakat@muslimsonline.com
Web: www.harkatulmujahideen.org
L.P: Contact: Islam ud Din But.
kHz: *5102, 5990, 7235*

Winter Schedule 2004			
Kashmiri/English	**Days**	**Area**	**kHz**
0230-0400	daily	IND	5990—
0745-0845	daily	IND	7235—
1300-1430	daily	IND	5102—*

ANN: Kashmiri: "Sada-i Hurriyat-i Jammu Kashmir"
V: QSL-letter. No rp.
NOTES: On the air since 1991 (1991-1999 broadcasting as "Voice of Independent Kashmir"). Produced by the political organisation "Harkat ul-Mujahideen" (until 1998 named "Harkat ul-Ansar"). Broadcasts in Kashmiri, English and Urdu. Presumed to use tx's of the Pakistan BC Corp. in Rawat (Islamabad). Key: * Variable frequency.

Target: INTERNATIONAL WATERS

INFORMATION RADIO/RADIO ONE

c/o US Navy, Maritime Liaison Office (MARLO), P.O. Box 116 (NSA-MARLO), Juffair, Bahrain.
☎ +973 17 853925. Fax +973 17 853930.
Email: marlo.bahrain@me.navy.mil **Web:** www.me.navy.mil/marlo
kHz: *6125, 15500*

Winter Schedule 2004			
Various	**Days**	**Area**	**kHz**
0300-1400	daily	ITW	6125—
1400-0300	daily	ITW	15500—*

ANN: Dari: "Radyoi Malumati"; Farsi: "Radyo Malumat-e"; Pashto: "Ma'lumat Radyo"; English: "Radio One", "CFM Radio"
V: QSL-letter.
NOTES: On the air since April 2004. The mission of MARLO is to facilitate the exchange of information between the U.S. Navy and the commercial shipping community in the U.S. Central Command's area of responsibility. The broadcasts are in Arabic, Dari, Farsi, Hindi, Pashto, Urdu, and English and are aimed at the crews of ships sailing in the waters along the Arabic peninsula. The tx's are currently located on Coalition Forces vessels. – Key: * USB.

Target: IRAN

RADIO INTERNATIONAL (Clan)

P.O. Box 1499, London WC1N 3XX, United Kingdom.
☎ +44 771 4611099.
Email: radio7520@yahoo.com **Web:** www.radio-international.org
kHz: *7490*

Winter Schedule 2004			
Farsi	**Days**	**Area**	**kHz**
1730-1815	daily	IRN	7490gri

ANN: Farsi: "In Radyo Anternacional ast"
V: QSL-email.
NOTES: On the air since December 1999. A prgr produced by the 'Worker-Communist Party of Iran' (WCP). Transmissions are jammed in the target area.

RADIO VOICE OF WOMEN (Clan)

P.O. Box 15205, Boston, MA 02215, USA.
☎ +1 617 5901665.
Email: radio@wfafi.org **Web:** www.wfafi.org
kHz: *9495*

Winter Schedule 2004			
Farsi	**Days**	**Area**	**kHz**
1900-1930	.....s.	IRN	9495jul

ANN: Farsi: "Radyo Seda-ye Zan"
NOTES: On the air since November 2004. Produced by the "Women's Forum Against Fundamentalism in Iran" (WFAFI).

VOICE OF IRANIAN KURDISTAN (Clan)

Reportedly based in Salah Al-Din, Iraqi Kurdistan. Correspondence France: c/o AFK, BP 102, F-75623 Paris, Cedex 13, France.
☎ +33 145856431. Fax +33 145852093.
Email: pdkiran@club-internet.fr **Web:** www.pdk-iran.org
Canada: PDKI Canada Bureau, P.O. Box 29010, London, ON, N6G 2V3, Canada.
Email: pdkicanada@pdki.org **Web:** www.pdki.org
kHz: *3970, 4860*

Winter Schedule 2004			
Farsi	**Days**	**Area**	**kHz**
0500-0530	daily	IRN	3970—*, 4860—*
1530-1700	daily	IRN	3970—*, 4860—*
Kurdish	**Days**	**Area**	**kHz**
0250-0500	daily	IRN	3970—*, 4860—*
1430-1530	daily	IRN	3970—*, 4860—*

ANN: Farsi: "In Seda-ye Kordestan-e Iran"; Kurdish: "Erê Dengê Kurdistanî Îran"
V: QSL-email.
NOTES: On the air 1973-1975 and again since 1980. Produced by the "Democratic Party of Iranian Kurdistan" (PDKI). Tx's presumed to be located in northeastern Iraq; transmissions are jammed in the target area. Key: * Variable frequency.

VOICE OF IRANIAN REVOLUTION (Clan)

c/o C.D.C.R.I., P.O. Box 70445, SE-10725 Stockholm, Sweden.
Email: cpi@cpiran.org **Web:** www.cpiran.org (CPI)
kHz: *3880, 4380, 6420*

Winter Schedule 2004

Kurdish	Days	Area	kHz
0325-0430	daily	IRN	3880—*, 4380—*, 6420—*
1425-1530	daily	IRN	3880—*, 4380—*, 6420—*

ANN: Kurdish: "Erê Dengê Sorsî Îran"
V: QSL-letter.
NOTES: On the air since 1983. Produced by the "Communist Party of Iran" (CPI). The CPI also produces the prgr "Voice of the Communist Party of Iran" (see separate entry below). Tx's presumed to be located in northeastern Iraq. Transmissions are jammed in the target area. Key: * In order to escape from jamming, each frequency is constantly changed in 5kHz steps (ranging 3870–3880, 4360-4390, 6415-6420kHz).

VOICE OF KOMALA (Clan)

Postfach 800272, D-51002 Köln, Germany.
☎ +1 561 7605814 (USA). Fax +1 561 7605814 (USA).
Email: radiokomala@komala.org
Web: www.komala.org/radio/rindex.htm
kHz: *1612, 3930, 4610*

Winter Schedule 2004

Farsi	Days	Area	kHz
0355-0425	daily	IRN	1612, 3930*, 4610*
1755-1835	daily	IRN	1612, 3930*, 4610*
Kurdish	**Days**	**Area**	**kHz**
0325-0355	daily	IRN	1612, 3930*, 4610*
1655-1755	daily	IRN	1612, 3930*, 4610*

ANN: Farsi: "In Seda-ye Komala"; Kurdish: "Erê Dengê Komala"
V: QSL-letter.
NOTES: On the air since October 2001. Produced by the "Komala Party - Iranian Kurdistan". Tx's presumed to be located in northeastern Iraq; transmissions are jammed in the target area. Key: * Variable Frequency

VOICE OF THE COMMUNIST PARTY OF IRAN (Clan)

c/o C.D.C.R.I., P.O. Box 70445, SE-10725 Stockholm, Sweden.
Email: cpi@cpiran.org **Web:** www.cpiran.org (CPI)
kHz: *3880, 4380, 6420*

Winter Schedule 2004

Farsi	Days	Area	kHz
0325-0430	daily	IRN	3880—*, 4380—*, 6420—*
1555-1830	daily	IRN	3880—*, 4380—*, 6420—*

ANN: Farsi: "In Seda-ye Hezb-e Komonist-e Iran"
V: QSL-letter.
NOTES: On the air since 1983. Produced by the "Communist Party of Iran" (CPI). The CPI also produces the prgr "Voice of the Iranian Revolution" (see separate entry above). Tx's presumed to be located in North Eastern Iraq; transmissions are jammed in the target area. Key: * In order to escape from jamming, each frequency is constantly changed in 5kHz steps (ranging 3870–3880, 4360-4390, 6415-6420kHz).

VOICE OF THE IRANIAN NATION (Clan)

Email: radiomelate@yahoo.com
kHz: *15660*

Winter Schedule 2004

Farsi	Days	Area	kHz
1430-1500	daily	IRN	15660sof

ANN: Farsi: "Inja Seda-ye Mellat-e Iran-e"
NOTES: On the air since August 2004. Transmissions are jammed in the target area.

VOICE OF THE STRUGGLE OF IRANIAN KURDISTAN (Clan)

Based in Salah al-Din, Iraqi Kurdistan.
Email: postmaster@khabat.org **Web:** www.khabat.org
kHz: *4250*

Winter Schedule 2004

Kurdish	Days	Area	kHz
0300-0400	daily	IRN	4250—*
1600-1700	daily	IRN	4250—*

ANN: Kurdish: "Erê Dengê Xebatî Kurdistanî Îran"
NOTES: On the air since 1985. Produced by the "Revolutionary Khabat Organization of Iranian Kurdistan". Tx presumed to be located in northeastern Iraq; transmissions are jammed in the target area. Key: * variable frequency.

Target: IRAQ

VOICE OF MUJAHEDIN (Clan)

c/o Islamic Republic of Iran Broadcasting, P.O. Box 15875-4344, Tehran, Iran.
Web: www.radiomojahedin.com
FM: 90.1MHz
SAT: Hotbird 3
kHz: *720*

Winter Schedule 2004

Arabic	Days	Area	kHz
0500-2000	daily	IRQ	720—

ANN: Arabic: "Idha'at Sawt al-Mujahedin"
NOTES: On the air since April 2003. Produced in the studios of Iran's state broadcaster Islamic Republic of Iran Broadcasting (IRIB), supporting the Shi'a "Supreme Council for the Islamic Revolution in Iraq" (SCIRI). The Tx is located in western Iran.

VOICE OF REBELLIOUS IRAQ (Clan)

c/o SCIRI, 27a Old Gloucester St., London WC1N 3XX, United Kingdom.
☎ +44 207 3716815. Fax +44 207 3712886.
Email: sciri@btinternet.com **Web:** www.sciri.btinternet.co.uk (SCIRI)
kHz: *864*

Winter Schedule 2004

Arabic	Days	Area	kHz
0800-2330	daily	IRQ	864—*

ANN: Arabic: "Sawt al-Iraq al-Tha'ir"
NOTES: On the air since March 1991 via tx's of the Iranian state broadcaster IRIB, produced by the Shi'a "Supreme Council for the Islamic Revolution in Iraq" (SCIRI). Status uncertain at editorial deadline, last observation September 2004. Key: * Last observed schedule

DENGÊ MEZOPOTAMYA (VOICE OF MESOPOTAMIA)

c/o Roj NV, Fabriekstraat 6, B-9470 Denderleeuw, Belgium.
☎ +32 53 648827. Fax +32 53 680779.
Email: info@denge-mezopotamya.com
Web: www.denge-mezopotamya.com
L.P: SM: Zerdest Peri.
SAT: Hotbird 3 (24h)
kHz: *11530*

Winter Schedule 2004

Kurdish	Days	Area	kHz
0500-1700	daily	ME	11530gri

ANN: Kurdish: "Radyoya Dengê Mezopotamya"
NOTES: On the air since May 2001. Produced by the Kurdish-Belgian media production company Roj NV. Linked with the "Kurdistan Freedom and Democracy Congress" (KADEK), which until April 2002 was named "Kurdistan Workers' Party" (PKK). Broadcasts to Kurdish settled areas in Iraq, Turkey and Iran in 5 Kurdish dialects: Hawrami, Kurmanji, Luri, Sorani and Zazaki.

QALA ATURAYA

c/o LAROS, Arbat ul. 28/1, 121002 Moscow, Russia.
☎ +7 095 2411425. Fax +7 095 2411756.
kHz: *612, 1170*

Winter Schedule 2004

Assyrian	Days	Area	kHz
1600-1700	.....s.	RUS	612msk
1600-1700	.....s.	ME	1170arm

V: QSL-card.
NOTES: On the air since January 1993. A weekly prgr produced by the "International Russian League of Assyrians" (LAROS).

Target: KOREA, NORTH (D.P.R.)

RADIO ECHO OF HOPE (Clan)

Based in South Korea.
kHz: *3985, 6348*

Winter Schedule 2004

Korean	Days	Area	kHz
0300-0600	daily	KRE	3985—, 6348—
1200-1500	daily	KRE	3985—, 6348—
1500-1800	daily	KRE	3985—, 6348—

ANN: Korean: "Huimang-e meari pangsong-imnida"
NOTES: Until June 1973 broadcasting under the name "The Voice of Reunification". Believed to be operated by the South Korean National Intelligence Service. Tx's are located in Gimpo, Kyonggi-do, South Korea. Jammed in the target area.

VOICE OF THE PEOPLE (Clan)

Based in South Korea.
kHz: *3912, 6600*

Winter Schedule 2004

Korean	Days	Area	kHz
1100-1500	daily	KRE	3912—, 6600—
1500-1900	daily	KRE	3912—, 6600—

ANN: Korean: "Yoginun Choson Nodongja Ch'ongdongmaeng-eso ponaedurinun inmine sori pangsong-imnida"
NOTES: On the air since June 1985. Claims to be run by the Korean Worker's Union, but is believed to be operated by the South Korean Armed Forces. Tx's are located in Goyang (3912) and Gimpo (6600), South Korea. Jammed in the target area.

Target: LAOS

HMONG LAO RADIO (Clan)

P.O. Box 6426, St. Paul, MN 55106, USA.
+1 651 2920774. +1 651 2920795.
Email: info@hmonglaoradio.org **Web:** www.hmonglaoradio.org
L.P: Prgr Coordinator: Wachai Xiong.
kHz: *9515, 15260*

Winter Schedule 2004

Hmong	Days	Area	kHz
0100-0200	..w.f..	SEA	15260tai
0100-0200	..w.f..	NAm	9515sac

ANN: Hmong: "Xovtooj Cua Hmoob Lostsuas"
V: QSL-letter.
NOTES: On shortwave since May 2002. A prgr for Hmong speakers in Laos, South East Asia and North America, produced by United Lao Movement for Democracy, Inc. (ULMD).

Target: LEBANON

RADIO MASHREQ (Clan)

Correspondence: P.O. Box 52341, 4062 Limassol, Cyprus.
Email: radio@carmelnews.org **Web:** www.carmelnews.org
5505 Connecticut Avenue N.W., Washington, D.C. 20015, USA.
+1 202 4680261. +1 202 4680261.
FM: 99.1MHz
SAT: Hotbird 4
kHz: *756*

Winter Schedule 2004

Arabic	Days	Area	kHz
0430-1300	daily	ME	756—

ANN: Arabic: "Al-idha'at al-Mashriqiyah"
NOTES: On the air since January 2001 (tests since December 2000). Run by the news agency "Carmelnews", prgr's are in Arabic and Hebrew. Radio Mashreq took over the MW frequency from 'Voice of the South' (the South Lebanon Army's mouthpiece) which was operating until May 2000 on 756kHz from Kfar-Killa (Southern Lebanon). Current location is presumed to be Northern Israel.

Target: MALDIVES

MINIVAN RADIO (Clan)

64 Milford Street, Salisbury SP1 2BP, United Kingdom.
+44 1722 504330.
Email: admin@friendsofmaldives.co.uk
Web: www.friendsofmaldives.co.uk
L.P: Producer: Ahmed Naseer.
kHz: *11810*

Winter Schedule 2004

Dhivehi	Days	Area	kHz
1600-1700	daily	MLD	11810jul

ANN: Dhivehi: "Mee Dhivehi Minivan Radio"
V: QSL-letter.
NOTES: On the air since August 2004. Produced by the UK-based opposition group "Friends of Maldives", linked with the "Maldivian Democratic Party". Transmissions are jammed in the target area.

Target: MYANMAR

DEMOCRATIC VOICE OF BURMA (Clan)

P.O. Box 6720, N-0130 Oslo, Norway.
+47 22868486. +47 22868471.
Email: comments@dvb.no **Web:** www.dvb.no
L.P: Dir: Aye Chan Naing.
kHz: *5905, 5945, 17495*

Winter Schedule 2004

Burmese	Days	Area	kHz
1430-1530	daily	BRM	5905alm, 17495mdc
2330-0030	daily	BRM	5945jul

ANN: Burmese: "Democratic Myanmar a-Than"
V: QSL-card.
NOTES: On the air since July 1992. Founded by the exile organisation "National Coalition Government of the Union of Burma". DVB holds a Norwegian broadcasting license. Broadcasts are in Burmese, with 15 mins per transmission allocated to the Arakan, Chin, Karen, Karenni, Kayan, Kachin, Mon and Shan languages.

Target: NEPAL

MAOIST REBEL FM STATIONS (Clan)

n/a
Email: info@cpnm.org (CPNM) **Web:** www.cpnm.org (CPNM)
FM: multiple mobile FM transmitters (typically 500 Watts) with changing locations to avoid detection. Reported frequencies: 95.1 (Karhmamndu valley), 100 MHz.
NOTES: Local FM services (several hours daily), operated by the "Communist Party of Nepal (Maoists)" (CPNM): Radio Janabadi Ganatantra, Rolpa; Bheri-Karnali Broadcasting Service; Seti-Mahakali Broadcasting Service.

Target: NIGERIA

VOICE OF BIAFRA INTERNATIONAL (Clan)

733 15th Street NW, Suite 700, Washington, D.C. 20005, USA.
+1 202 3472983.
Email: biafrafoundation@yahoo.com
Web: www.biafraland.com/vobi.htm
L.P: MD: Oguchi Nkwocha.
kHz: *7380*

Winter Schedule 2004

Various	Days	Area	kHz
2100-2200	.....s.	NIG	7380mey

ANN: English: "This is Voice of Biafra International, coming to you from Washington, D.C."
V: QSL-card.
NOTES: On the air since September 2001. Produced by the U.S.-based 'Biafra Foundation'. Prgr's are in Igbo and English.

Target: PAKISTAN (Kashmir)

RADIO SEDAYEE KASHMIR (Clan)

c/o All India Radio (AIR), Akashvani Bhavan, Sansad Marg, New Delhi-110001, India.
kHz: *6100, 9890*

Winter Schedule 2004

Dogri	Days	Area	kHz
0310-0330	daily	PAK	6100del
0810-0830	daily	PAK	9890del
1510-1530	daily	PAK	6100del
Kashmiri	**Days**	**Area**	**kHz**
0230-0310	daily	PAK	6100del
0730-0810	daily	PAK	9890del
1430-1510	daily	PAK	6100del

ANN: Urdu: "Sedayee Kashmir Radio"
NOTES: On the air since early 2003. Radio Sedayee Kashmir is a prgr representing the views of the Indian government in the dispute with Pakistan over Kashmir. It is transmitted via SW facilities of AIR in Delhi.

Target: SOMALIA

RADIO XORIYO (Clan)

P.O. Box 27618, Toronto, ON M3A 3B8, Canada
Email: radioxoriyo@ogaden.com
Web: www.ogaden.com/radio_Freedom.htm
kHz: *9820*

Somali	Days	Area	kHz
Winter Schedule 2004			
1630-1700	.t..f..	EAf	9820jul

ANN: Somali: "Ku soo dhawaada Radio Xoriyo codkii ummadda Ogadeniya"
V: QSL-email.
NOTES: On the air since May 2000. A prgr produced by the "Ogaden National Liberation Front" (ONLF), addressing listeners in the Ogaden territory spreading across parts of Somalia and Ethiopia.

Target: SRI LANKA

IBC TAMIL RADIO
3 College Fields, Prince George's Road, Colliers Wood, London SW19 2PT, United Kingdom.
☎ +44 208 1000011. Fax +44 208 1000003.
Email: radio@ibctamil.co.uk **Web:** www.ibctamil.co.uk
L.P: Dir of Prgr: S.Shivaranjith.
SAT: Astra 1C, Hotbird 3
kHz: *7450*

Winter Schedule 2004

Tamil	Days	Area	kHz
0000-0100	daily	CLN	7450tac

V: QSL-letter.
NOTES: On shortwave since August 1997. IBC Tamil is a 24h satellite radio station, licensed in the UK.

Target: SUDAN

VOICE OF FREEDOM AND RENEWAL (Clan)
SNA/SAF, Culture and Information Office, P.O. Box 9257, Asmara, Eritrea.
☎ +291 1 184803. Fax +291 1 182865.
Email: infosaf@eol.com.er **Web:** www.safsudan.com (SAF)
L.P: SAF Secretary for Culture & Information: Fathi Abdelaziz.
kHz: *6985*

Winter Schedule 2004

Arabic	Days	Area	kHz
0400-0500	daily	SDN	6985—*
1430-1600	daily	SDN	6985—*

ANN: Arabic: "Sawt al-hurriyah wa al-tajdid, sawt Sudan al-jadid"
V: QSL-letter.
NOTES: On the air since April 1998 (with interruptions). Operated by the "Sudan Alliance Forces" (SAF)/ "Sudan National Alliance" (SNA). Broadcasts in Arabic and other languages of Sudan. The station purchased a 10kW SW tx and claimed to broadcast from Kassala in southern Sudan. Independent sources indicate that this tx is located in the Eritrean capital Asmara. Key: * Status uncertain at editorial deadline.

VOICE OF SUDAN (Clan)
P.O. Box 4961, Asmara, Eritrea. In UK: 16 Cameret Court, Lorne Gardens, London W11 4XX, United Kingdom.
Web: www.ndasudan.org (NDA)
L.P: NDA SG Office Dir: Abdullahi F. El Mahdi.
kHz: *7999*

Winter Schedule 2004

Arabic	Days	Area	kHz
1230-1300	daily	SDN	7999—*
1530-1600	daily	SDN	7999—*

ANN: Arabic: "Sawt al-Sudan, sawt al-dimuqratiyah wa al-salam, itha'at al-tajamu al-watani al-dimuqrati"
V: QSL-letter.
NOTES: Appeared first in 1990/1991, then again in 1995-2000. Most recent resumption in April 2003. Operated by the Sudanese opposition grouping "National Democratic Alliance" (NDA). Tx's are presumed to be located in Asmara, Eritrea. Key: * Variable frequency.

RADIO NILE
Plot No 15, Komi Crescent, Lusira, 338829 Kampala, Uganda.
☎ +256 41 220334.
Email: hope@africaonline.co.ug **Web:** www.radiovoiceofhope.net
P.O. Box 19318, 3501 DH Utrecht, Netherlands.
L.P: Editor: Jane Namadi
kHz: *12060, 15320*

Winter Schedule 2004

Various	Days	Area	kHz
0430-0500	mt...ss	SDN	12060mdc, 15320mdc,

V: QSL-card.
NOTES: On the air since December 2001. Radio Nile (formerly known as Voice of Hope) is a project initiated by the New Sudan Council of Churches, sponsored by the Dutch public broadcaster NCRV, Radio Nederland Wereldomroep, and several religious and humanitarian organisations. It is a registered non-government organisation (NGO) in Uganda. The objective is to promote peace and reconciliation among the conflicting groups in South Sudan. The broadcasts are in Arabic and English.

SUDAN RADIO SERVICE
c/o EDC, P.O. Box 4392, 00100 Nairobi, Kenya.
☎ +254 20 570906. Fax +254 20 576520.
Email: srs@edc.org **Web:** www.sudanradio.org
1000 Potomac Street, NW, Suite 350, Washington, D.C. 20007, USA.
L.P: Radio Prgr Advisor: Jeremy Groce.
kHz: *9625, 11715, 11795, 15530*

Winter Schedule 2004

Various	Days	Area	kHz
0300-0500	mtwtf..	SDN	9625wof
0500-0600	mtwtf..	SDN	11795wof
1500-1700	mtwtf..	SDN	15530wof
1700-1800	mtwtf..	SDN	11715wof

ANN: English: "You are listening to the Sudan Radio Service on ... kHz"
V: QSL-letter.
NOTES: On the air since July 2003. SRS is a project of Education Development Center, Inc. (USA). It is funded by the U.S. Agency for International Development (USAID) for the period 2003-2006. The broadcasts are in English, Arabic, Juba-Arabic, Bari, Dinka, Nuer, Shiluck, Zande.

Target: SYRIA

RADIO FREE SYRIA (Clan)
P.O. Box 59730, Potomac, MD 20859, USA.
☎ +359 89 9812923 (Bulgaria). Fax +49 30 69088573 (Germany).
Email: admin@radiofreesyria.net **Web:** www.radiofreesyria.net (Arabic); www.radiofreesyria.org (English)
L.P: Project Manager: Ali Hajj-Husayn.
kHz: *9495*

Winter Schedule 2004

Arabic	Days	Area	kHz
1900-2000	....f.s	SYR	9495jul

ANN: Arabic "Sawt Syria al-hurrah"
NOTES: On shortwave since June 2004. Produced by the U.S.-based "Reform Party of Syria"(RPS). Plans to expand the broadcasting time.

THE ARABIC RADIO (Clan)
BCM Box 2789, London WC1N 3XX, United Kingdom.
Email: ced@arabicsyradio.org **Web:** www.arabicsyradio.org
kHz: *7470, 7510, 12085*

Winter Schedule 2004

Arabic	Days	Area	kHz
0430-0500	daily	SYR	7510—
1600-1630	daily	SYR	12085—, 7470gri

ANN: Arabic: "Al-idha'at al-arabiyyah"
NOTES: On the air since July 2002. Produced by the "Syrian Human Rights Committee" (SHRC). Presumed to lease air time on tx's in Eastern Europe.

Target: UGANDA

RADIO RHINO INTERNATIONAL – AFRICA (RRIA)
c/o Allerweltshaus, Körnerstr. 77-79, D-50823 Köln, Germany.
☎ +49 162 8854486. Fax +49 221 9912927.
Email: mail@radiorhino.org **Web:** www.radiorhino.org
L.P: Dir: Godfrey Elum Ayoo.
kHz: *17870*

Winter Schedule 2004

English	Days	Area	kHz
1500-1530	mtwtf..	UGA	17870jul

ANN: English: "You are listening to Radio Rhino International Africa"
V: QSL-letter.
NOTES: On the air since September 2003. Prgr produced by the organisation "Voice of the Voiceless International-Uganda eV" (VOVI-Uganda eV), formed by Ugandan exiles.

Target: URUGUAY

RADIO CIMARRONA

c/o Allerweltshaus, Körnerstr. 77-79, D-50823 Köln, Germany
☎ +49 221 5103002. Fax +49 221 5891480.
Email: radiocimarrona@hotmail.com **Web:** www.testimonios.org
kHz: *9480*

Winter Schedule 2004

Spanish	Days	Area	kHz
2200-2300	m.....s	URG	9480jul

ANN: Spanish: "Están escuchando Radio Cimarrona"
NOTES: On the air since October 2004. Produced by the staff of Radio Testimonios, Montevideo, Uruguay with support from Allerweltshaus, Germany.

Target: VIETNAM

DEGAR VOICE (Clan)

P.O. Box 171114, Spartanburg, SC 29301, USA.
☎ +1 864 5760698. Fax +1 864 5951940.
Email: degar@montagnard-foundation.org
Web: www.montagnard-foundation.org
L.P: Project coordinator: Kok Ksor.
kHz: *7125*

Winter Schedule 2004

Various	Days	Area	kHz
1300-1330	mt.t.s.	VTN	7125nvs

V: QSL-letter.
NOTES: On the air since July 2003. Degar Voice is a prgr for the Degar people (Montagnards) in the Vietnamese Highlands, produced by Radio Radicale, Italy for the Montagnard Foundation (which is linked with the 'Transnational Radical Party' - TRP). The prgr's are in Vietnamese and local languages. Transmissions are jammed in the target area. Alternative frequencies: 7180 and 7480kHz.

QUÊ HUONG RADIO

2670 South White Road, Suite 165, San Jose, CA 95148, USA.
☎ +1 408 2233130. Fax +1 408 2233131.
Email: qhradio@aol.com **Web:** www.quehuongradio.org
L.P: SM: Nguyên Khôi.
kHz: *15680*

Winter Schedule 2004

Vietnamese	Days	Area	kHz
1200-1300	mtwtfs.	VTN	15680vld

ANN: Vietnamese: "Quê Huong Radio"
V: QSL-card.
NOTES: On shortwave since November 1999. Quê Huong Radio ("Fatherland Radio") is produced by Dai Phat Thanh Quê Huong Inc., the owner of the radio station KZSJ 1120kHz in San Jose, California.

RADIO FREE VIETNAM

Correspondence: P.O. Box 29245, New Orleans, LA 70189, USA.
☎ +1 504 2542303. Fax +1 504 2542305.
Email: rfvla@aol.com **Web:** www.radiofreevietnam.com
L.P: Dir: Ky-Son Vuong.
kHz: *9930*

Winter Schedule 2004

Vietnamese	Days	Area	kHz
1230-1300	mtwtf..	VTN	9930whr

ANN: Vietnamese: "Dài Viêt Nam tu do"
V: QSL-letter.
NOTES: On shortwave since August 2001. Radio Free Vietnam is broadcast from studios in Washington, D.C.

Target: WEST BANK & GAZA (Palest. Authority)

AL-QUDS RADIO (Clan)

P.O. Box 5092, Damascus, Syria.
L.P: Dir: Abu Shadi
FM: 107.4MHz (24h)
kHz: *702*

Winter Schedule 2004

Arabic	Days	Area	kHz
0500-1400	daily	PSE	702—

ANN: Arabic: "Al-quds, al-idha'ah al-arabiyah al-Filastiniyah ala tariq tahrir al-ard wa al-insan"
NOTES: On the air since January 1988. Operated by the "Popular Front for the Liberation of Palestine - General Command" (PFLP-GC). The tx's are located in southwestern Syria.

Target: WESTERN SAHARA

RADIO NACIONAL DE LA R.A.S.D. (Clan)

37000 Tindouf-Rabouni, Algeria.
☎ +213 49 923525.
Email: rasdradio@yahoo.es **Web:** web.jet.es/rasd/amateur4.htm
Correspondence: c/o Mission de la RASD, BP 10, El Mouradia, 16000 Alger, Algeria.
kHz: *1550, 7460*

Winter Schedule 2004

Arabic	Days	Area	kHz
0600-0830v	daily	NAf	1550—, 7460—
1800-2400	daily	NAf	1550—, 7460—
Spanish	**Days**	**Area**	**kHz**
1700-1800	daily	NAf	1550—
1800-2400	daily	NAf	7460—

ANN: Arabic: "Al-idha'ah al-wataniyah li-jumhuriyah al-arabiyah al-Sahrawiyah al-dimokratiyah"; Spanish: "Ésta es la Radio Nacional de la República Arabe Saharaui Democrática"
V: QSL-letter.
NOTES: On the air since 1975. Operated by the "Polisario Front". The SW tx is located in Rabouni (20kW), the MW tx in Tindouf (100kW). Transmissions are jammed in the target area.

RADIO4PEACE

c/o Radio K Centrale, via della Beverara 125/L, I-40131 Bologna, Italy.
☎ +39 51 19984183. Fax +39 51 19984184.
Email: radioforpeace@libero.it
Web: www.radiokcentrale.org/radio4peace.htm
L.P: Prgr coordinator: Gabriella Podobnich.
kHz: *15665*

Winter Schedule 2004

Arabic/Spanish	Days	Area	kHz
1100-1200	....f..	NAf	15665—

NOTES: On the air since April 2004. A prgr produced by Radio K Centrale and the organisation COSPE (Cooperazione per lo sviluppo dei paesi emergenti).

Target: ZIMBABWE

SW RADIO AFRICA (Clan)

P.O. Box 243, Borehamwood, Herts WD6 4WA, United Kingdom.
☎ +44 20 83871441.
Email: mail@swradioafrica.com **Web:** www.swradioafrica.com
L.P: Tech Mgr: Keith Farquharson.
kHz: *4880, 6145*

Winter Schedule 2004

Various	Days	Area	kHz
1600-1900	daily	ZMB	4880mey*, 6145mey**

ANN: English: "SW Radio Africa, Zimbabwe's Independent Voice"
V: QSL-card.
NOTES: On the air since December 2001. Operated by a London based group of Zimbabwean exiles. Broadcasts in English, Ndebele and Shona. Key: * May-Aug, ** Aug-May (For exact dates see website).

VOICE OF PEOPLE (Clan)

P.O. Box CY 3093, Causeway, Harare, Zimbabwe.
☎ +263 91 308052.
Email: voxpop@ecoweb.co.zw
L.P: MD: John Masuku.
kHz: *7120*

Winter Schedule 2004

Various	Days	Area	kHz
1700-1800	daily	ZMB	7120mdc

ANN: English: "Radio VOP"
V: QSL letter.
NOTES: On the air since June 2000. Funded by the "Soros Foundation", run by former staff of the Zimbabwe Broadcasting Corporation (ZBC). The prgr "Voice of People" strives to broadcast ideas and information for the general development of the country, socially, politically and culturally. Transmissions are in English, Ndebele, Shona.

SHORTWAVE STATIONS OF THE WORLD

November 2004 - World Copyright WRTH Publicaions Ltd.

Stations in **bold** are Standard Time/Frequency transmissions. For country and site codes, see relevant tables in reference section. Stations marked as 'dom' in the site column are domestic/national broadcasts. DRM transmissions are marked with a '+' after the frequency.

kHz	kW	Ctry	Site	Station, location
2310	50	AUS	dom	N. Terr. SW Sce, VL8A, Alice Springs
2325	50	AUS	dom	N. Terr. SW Sce, VL8T, Tennant Creek
2340		CHN	dom	Fujian N, Fuzhou
2350		KRE	dom	Korean Cent. B'casting Stn, Sariwon
2380	0.25	B	dom	R. Educadora, Limeira
2390	0.5	MEX	dom	R. Huayacocotla, Huayacocotla
2410	10	PNG	dom	R. Enga
2420	0.5	B	dom	R. São Carlos, São Carlos
2460	1	B	dom	Super R. Alvorada, Rio Branco
2470	0.25	B	dom	R. Cacique, Sorocaba
2485	50	AUS	dom	N. Terr. SW Sce, VL8K, Katherine
2491	0.25	B	dom	R. Oito de Setembro, Descalvado
2500	**10**	**CHN**	**—**	**BPM**
2500	**10**	**USA**	**—**	**WWV**
2500	**10**	**HWA**	**—**	**WWVH**
2850		KRE	dom	Korean Cent. B'casting Stn., Pyongyang
2960	0.3	INS	dom	RPDT2 Manggarai, Ruteng
3040		CTR	dom	R. Puntarenas
3173		PRU	dom	R. Municipal, Distrito de Panao
3185	65	USA	WRB	WWRB
3200	35	SWZ	MAN	TWR Africa
3200	50	SWZ	MAN	TWR Africa
3205	1	B	dom	R. Ribeirão Preto
3205	5	B	dom	R. Vale do Rio Madeira, Humaitá
3205	10	PNG	dom	R. West Sepik
3210	100	USA	WCR	WWCR
3215	100	AFS	MEY	Adventist World R. (AWR)
3215	50	MDG	MDC	Adventist World R. (AWR)
3215	100	AFS	MEY	Amateur R. Mirror Int'l
3215		MDG	dom	R. Feon'ny Filazantsara, Tanarive
3220	8	EQA	QUI	HCJB
3220		KRE	dom	Korean Central B'casting Stn, Hamhung
3220	8	EQA	dom	LV de los Andes/TWR, Quito
3220	10	PNG	dom	R. Morobe
3223	50	IND	dom	All India Radio, Shimla
3230	50	AUS	dom	N. Terr. SW Sce, VL8A, Alice Springs
3230	1	PRU	dom	R. El Sol de Los Andes, Juliaca
3230	100	NPL	dom	R. Nepal, Khumaltar
3232	10	INS	dom	RRI Bukittinggi
3235	1	B	dom	R. Guarujá Paulista, Guarujá
3235	1	PRU	dom	R. Luz y Sonido, Huánuco
3235	10	PNG	dom	R. West New Britain
3240	25	SWZ	MAN	TWR Africa
3245	1	B	dom	R. Clube, Varginha
3245	10	PNG	dom	R. Gulf
3250		KRE	dom	Pyongyang B'casting Stn, Pyongyang
3250	1	HND	dom	R. Luz y Vida, San Luís
3250	50	KRE	PYO	VO Korea
3255	100	AFS	MEY	BBC World Service
3255	1	B	dom	R. Educ. 6 de Agosto, Xapuri
3255	5	B	dom	R. Transamazônica, Senador Guiomard
3259	0.6	J	dom	Nippon Hoso Kyokai, Fukuoka 1
3260	10	PNG	dom	R. Madang
3260	1	EQA	dom	R. Stéreo Carrizal, Calceta
3267	10	INS	dom	RRI Gorontalo
3275	10	PNG	dom	R. Southern Highlands
3280	2.5	EQA	dom	LV del Napo, Tena,R. María
3280	1	PRU	dom	R. Ilucan, Cutervo
3280		CHN	dom	V.O.Pujiang, Shanghai
3288	10	MDG	dom	R. Nasionaly Malagasy, Antananarivo
3290	10	PNG	dom	R. Central
3290	0.5	EQA	dom	R. Centro, Ambato
3290	1	PRU	dom	R. Horizonte, Chiclayo
3300	10	GTM	dom	R. Cultural, Guatemala
3305	10	PNG	dom	R. Western
3306	100	ZWE	dom	Zimbabwe B'casting Corp., Gweru
3310	10	BOL	dom	R. Mosoj Chaski, Cochabamba
3315	50	IND	dom	All India Radio, Bhopal
3315	50	AUS	dom	N. Terr. SW Sce, VL8T, Tennant Creek
3315	10	PNG	dom	R. Manus
3316	10	SRL	dom	Sierra Leone B'casting Sce, Goderich
3320		KRE	dom	Pyongyang B'casting Stn, Pyongyang
3320	100	AFS	dom	R. Sonder Grense, Meyerton
3320	1	PRU	dom	R. Sudamérica, Cutervo
3325	0.2	GTM	dom	R. Maya, Barillas
3325	2.5	B	dom	R. Mundia, São Paulo
kHz	**kW**	**Ctry**	**Site**	**Station, location**
3325	10	PNG	dom	R. North Solomons
3325	10	INS	dom	RRI Palangkaraya
3326	50	NIG	dom	National B'casting Commission, Lagos
3330	**5**	**CAN**	**—**	**CHU**
3330	5	PRU	dom	R. Ondas del Huallaga, Huánuco
3335	10	PNG	dom	R. East Sepik
3340		HND	dom	R. Misiones Int. "R. MI", Comayagüela
3344	0.5	BOL	dom	R. Ayopaya, Independencia
3345	100	AFS	MEY	Adventist World R. (AWR)
3345	100	AFS	MEY	Channel Africa
3345	10	PNG	dom	R. Oro
3345	10	INS	dom	RRI Ternate
3350		KRE	dom	Korean Cent. B'casting Stn., Pyongsong
3350	0.1	BOL	dom	R. 27 de Diciembre, Villamontes
3350	1	PRU	dom	R. Bambamarca, Bambamarca
3350	5	PRU	dom	R. Oriente, Yurimaguas
3355	10	PNG	dom	R. Simbu
3360	2.5	EQA	dom	LV del Upano, Macas
3360	1	GTM	dom	R. LV de Nahualá, Nahualá
3365	50	IND	dom	All India Radio, Delhi
3365	1	B	dom	R. Cultura, Araraquara
3365	10	PNG	dom	R. Milne Bay
3370	50	AUS	dom	N. Terr. SW Sce, VL8K, Katherine
3370	1	PRU	dom	R. Huancabamba, Huancabamba
3373	0.3	J	dom	Nippon Hoso Kyokai, Osaka 2
3375	5	B	dom	R. Clube, Dourados
3375	5	B	dom	R. Educadora, Guajará Mirim
3375	5	B	dom	R. Equatorial, Macapá
3375	5	B	dom	R. Municipal, São Gabriel da Cachoeira
3375	1	PRU	dom	R. San Antonio, Callalli (irR.)
3375	10	PNG	dom	R. Western Highlands
3380	1	EQA	dom	CRI-Centro Radiofónico de Imbabura, Ibarra
3380	50	MWI	dom	Malawi B'casting Corporation, Limbe
3380	1	GTM	dom	R. Chortís, Jocotán
3380	1	BOL	dom	R. Cumbre, Tazna
3385	10	PNG	dom	R. East New Britain
3385		INS	dom	RRI Kupang
3390	10	IND	dom	All India Radio, Gangtok
3390	100	AFS	MEY	BBC World Service
3390	1	PRU	dom	R. Cutervo, Cutervo
3390	1	BOL	dom	R. Emisoras Camargo
3395	10	PNG	dom	R. Eastern Highlands
3395	1	PRU	dom	R. Internacional, Comas
3420		BOL	dom	R. Melodía, Bermejo
3480		KRE	dom	PBNDFSK, Wonsan
3493	0.5	BOL	dom	R. Padilla, Padilla
3560	1.5	B	dom	R. Difusora, Brasiléia
3560	50	KRE	PYO	VO Korea
3579		INS	dom	RSPK Ngada
3607	0.9	J	dom	Nippon Hoso Kyokai, Tokyo 1
3810	**1**	**EQA**	**—**	**HD2IOA**
3815	0.2	GRL	dom	Kalaalit Nunaata Radioa, Tasiilaq
3850	80	PNG	dom	R. Independent Mekamui
3880		—	—	VO Iranian Revolution
3880		—	—	VO the Communist Party of Iran
3900	7.5	CHN	dom	Hulun Buir-Ch, Hailar
3905	10	PNG	dom	R. New Ireland
3905	10	INS	dom	RRI Merauke
3912		—	—	VO the People
3915	100	SNG	SGP	BBC World Service
3920		KRE	dom	Korean Cent. B'casting Stn., Hyesan
3930	10	KOR	dom	KBS, Hwaseong
4930		—	—	VO Komala
3935	1	NZL	dom	R. Reading Service, Levin
3940		KRE	dom	Korean Cent. B'casting Stn., Chongjin
3945	50	IND	GKP	All India Radio (AIR)
3945	50	IND	dom	All India Radio, Gorakhpur
3950	50	CHN	dom	Xinjiang-Ch, Urumqi
3955	250	G	SKN	R. Korea Int'l
3955	250	G	SKN	R. Taiwan Int'l
3955	100	RUS	VLD	VO Russia (VOR)
3955	250	G	SKN	Wales Radio Int'l
3960		KRE	dom	Korean Cent. B'casting Stn., Kanggye

kHz	kW	Ctry	Site	Station, location
3960	10	INS	dom	RRI Palu
3965	100	D	BIB	BBG - RFE/RL
3965	250	F	ISS	R. France Int'l (RFI)
3965	500	F	ISS	R. France Int'l (RFI)
3965	500	F	ISS	R. Monte Carlo-MO
3965	250	F	ISS	R. Taiwan Int'l
3970		KRE	dom	Korean Cent. B'casting Stn., Wonsan
3970	0.3	J	dom	Nippon Hoso Kyokai, Nagoya 1
3970	0.6	J	dom	Nippon Hoso Kyokai, Sapporo 1
3970		—	—	VO Iranian Kudistan
3975	250	HNG	JBR	R. Budapest
3976		INS	dom	RRI Pontianak
3980	100	D	BIB	BBG - VO America (VOA)
3985	100	D	BIB	BBG - VO America (VOA)
3985	100	CHN	dom	CNR 2, Golmud
3985		B	—	R. Echo of Hope
3985	250	IRN	AHW	VO the Islamic Rep. of Iran
3985	500	IRN	KAM	VO the Islamic Rep. of Iran
3990	15	CHN	dom	Gannan, Hezuo
3990	50	CHN	dom	Xinjiang-Ug, Urumqi
3995	500	D	WER	Deutsche Welle
3995	100	D	JUL	HCJB
3995+	200	D	WER	Deutsche Welle
4000	50	CHN	dom	Nei Menggu-Ch, Hohhot
4000	5	INS	dom	RRI Kendari
4005	10	CVA	VAT	Vatican Radio
4010	100	KGZ	dom	Kyrgyz Radio, Bishkek, KGR1
4025		IRQ	dom	VO the People of Kurdistan, Sulaimaniyah
4052	0.8	GTM	dom	R. Verdad, Chiquimula
4085		IRQ	dom	VO Iraqi Kurdistan, Salah al Deen
4116	0.25	B	dom	R. Difusora, Sena Madureira
4160		IRQ	dom	VO Independence, Kurdistan
4190	50	CHN	dom	CNR 8, Beijing
4195	10	KEN	dom	Kenya B'casting Corporation, Langata
4220	15	CHN	dom	Qinghai-Tb, Xining
4244		**B**	—	**PPR**
4250		—	—	VO the Struggle of Iran. Kurd.
4319	3	DGA	DGA	AFRTS (AFN Feeder)
4330	15	CHN	dom	Xinjiang-Kz, Urumqi
4380		—	—	VO Iranian Revolution
4380		—	—	VO the Communist Party of Iran
4386	0.5	PRU	dom	R. Imperio, Chiclayo
4405	50	KRE	PYO	VO Korea
4409	0.5	BOL	dom	R. Eco, Reyes
4422		BOL	dom	Radioemisora Reyes, Reyes
4427	1	PRU	dom	R. Bambamarca, Bambamarca
4435	0.5	PRU	dom	R. Nyalamp, Lambayeque
4450		KRE	dom	PBNDFSK, Pyongyang
4450	0.25	BOL	dom	R. Estación Frontera, Cobija
4460	100	CHN	dom	CNR 1, Beijing
4461	1	PRU	dom	R. Nor Andina, Celendin
4472	1	BOL	dom	R. Movima, Santa Ana del Yacuma
4485	1	PRU	dom	R. Frecuencia VH, Celendin
4500	50	CHN	dom	Xinjiang-Mo, Urumqi
4525	50	CHN	dom	Nei Menggu-Mo, Hohhot
4530	0.12	BOL	dom	R. Hitachi, Guayaramerín
4534	0.5	PRU	dom	R. Horizonte, Chiclayo
4540	100	GEO	DSH	R. Georgia
4557		KRE	dom	PBNDFSK, Haeju
4599	1	BOL	dom	Radio Emisoras Villamontes
4600	0.2	BOL	dom	R. Perla del Acre, Cobija:
4605	1	INS	dom	RRI Serui
4610		—	—	VO Komala
4620	50	CHN	dom	Nei Menggu-Ch, Hohhot
4635	50	TJK	dom	R. Tojikiston
4649	1	LAO	dom	R. Nationale Lao, Sam Neua, HP
4649	1	BOL	dom	R. Santa Ana, Santa Ana del Yacuma
4682	1	BOL	dom	R. Paitití, Guayaramerín
4699	0.5	GTM	dom	R. Amistad, San Pedro La Laguna
4702		BOL	dom	R. Eco, San Borja
4717	1	BOL	dom	R. Yatun Ayllu Yura, Yura
4720	0.5	BOL	dom	R. Abaroa, Riberalta
4722		BOL	dom	R. Uncia, Uncia
4732	0.7	BOL	dom	R. La Palabra, Santa Ana del Yacuma
4740		VTN	dom	VO Vietnam, Son La
4750	15	CHN	dom	Qinghai-Ch, Xining
4750	1	SDN	dom	R. Peace, Southern Sudan
4750		PRU	dom	R. San Francisco Solano, Sondor
4750	20	INS	dom	RRI Makassar
4751	0.5	PRU	dom	R. Huanta 2000, Huanta
4754	5	B	dom	R. Dif. do Maranhão, São Luís

kHz	kW	Ctry	Site	Station, location
4755	10	B	dom	R. Educação Rural, Campo Grande
4755	0.5	PRU	dom	R. Huanta 2000, Huanta
4760	10	IND	dom	All India Radio, Leh
4760	10	IND	dom	All India Radio, Port Blair
4760	100	TJK	DSB	BBG - RFE/RL
4760	1	LBR	dom	Liberia B'casting System, Monrovia
4760	25	SWZ	MAN	TWR Africa
4762		BOL	dom	R. Guanay, Guanay
4763		BOL	dom	R Chicha, Tocla
4765	10	B	dom	R. Integração, Cruzeiro do Sul
4765	5	B	dom	R. Rural, Santarém
4765	50	COG	dom	Telediffusion du Congo, Brazzaville
4770	50	NIG	dom	Nat. B'casting Commission, Kaduna
4770	5	EQA	dom	R. Centinela del Sur, Loja
4770	5	PRU	dom	R. Inca del Peru, Lince
4775	50	IND	dom	All India Radio, Imphal
4775	5	B	dom	R. Amarela, Rolim de Moura
4775	1	B	dom	R. Congonhas, Congonhas
4775	5	B	dom	R. Liberal, Belém
4775	1	B	dom	R. Portal da Amazônia, Cuiabá
4775	0.4	PRU	dom	R. Tarma, Tarma
4775	25	SWZ	MAN	TWR Africa
4775	50	SWZ	MAN	TWR Africa
4780	1	GTM	dom	R. Cultural Coatán, San Sebastián Coatán
4780	50	DJI	dom	RTD, Djibouti (Doraleh)
4781	3	EQA	dom	R. Oriental, Tena
4781	1	PRU	dom	R. Satelite, Santa Cruz
4781		BOL	dom	R. Tacana, Tumupasa
4784	100	MLI	dom	Office de Radiodif. TV. du Mali, Kati
4785	50	CHN	dom	Nei Menggu-Mo, Hohhot
4785	1	B	dom	R. Brasil, Campinas
4785	10	B	dom	R. Caiari, Porto Velho
4785	10	EQA	dom	R. Federación Shuar, Sucúa
4785	5	B	dom	R. Ribamar, São Luís
4785	5	CLM	dom	R. Super, Ibagué
4788	1	BOL	dom	R. Em. Ballivián, S. Borja
4790	1	PRU	dom	R. Atlantida, Iquitos
4790		INS	dom	RRI Fak-Fak
4795	15	KGZ	dom	Kyrgyz Radio, Bishkek, KGR1
4795	3	EQA	dom	LV de los Caras, Bahía de Caráquez
4795	1	B	dom	R. Difusora, Aquidauana
4795	50	RUS	dom	R. Rossii, Selenga
4796		BOL	dom	R. Mallku, Uyuni
4800	50	IND	dom	All India Radio, Hyderabad
4800	100	CHN	dom	CNR 1, Golmud
4800	100	LSO	dom	Lesotho Nat. B'casting Sce, Lancer's Gap
4800	1	GTM	dom	R. Buenas Nuevas, San Sebastián
4802	0.5	BOL	dom	R. Mamoré, Guayaramerín
4805	10	B	dom	R. Dif. do Amazonas, Manaus
4805	0.5	B	dom	R. Itatiaia, Belo Horizonte
4810	100	ARM	YER	VO Armenia
4810	0.5	MEX	dom	XERTA R. Transcontinental, México
4815	1	EQA	dom	R. Buen Pastor, Saraguro
4815	10	B	dom	R. Difusora, Londrina
4815	100	BFA	dom	Radiodif. Nat. du Burkina, Ouagadougou
4819	5	HND	dom	LV Evangélica, Tegucigalpa
4820	50	IND	dom	All India Radio, Kolkata
4820	50	BOT	dom	R. Botswana, Sebele
4820	50	CHN	dom	Xizang-Ch, Lhasa
4824	10	PRU	dom	LV de la Selva, Iquitos
4825	10	B	dom	R. Canção Nova, Cachoeira Paulista
4825	5	B	dom	R. Educadora, Bragança
4825	0.5	GTM	dom	R. Mam, Cabricán
4826	0.3	PRU	dom	R. Sicuani "LV de Canchis", Sicuani
4828	100	ZWE	dom	Zimbabwe B'casting Corp. Gweru
4830	50	IND	dom	All India Radio, Jammu
4830	15	CHN	dom	China Huayi BC, Fuzhou
4830	10	MNG	dom	Mongoliin Radio, Altay
4830	1	BOL	dom	R. Grigotá, Santa Cruz
4830	10	VEN	dom	R. Táchira, S. Cristóbal
4832	0.5	HND	dom	R. Litoral, La Ceiba
4835	50	AUS	dom	N. Terr. SW Sce, VL8A, Alice Springs
4835	100	MLI	dom	Office de Radiodif. Tv. du Mali, Kati
4835	5	B	dom	R. Atalaia, Corumbá
4835	1	CLM	dom	R. Buenaventura, Buenaventura
4835	1	PRU	dom	R. Marañon, Jaen
4835	0.3	PRU	dom	R. Sicuani "LV de Canchis", Sicuani
4840	50	IND	dom	All India Radio, Mumbai
4840	15	CHN	dom	Heilongjiang N, Shangzhi
4840	1	VEN	dom	R. Valera, Valera
4845	10	B	dom	R. Cultura, Manaus

kHz	kW	Ctry	Site	Station, location
4845	1.25	GTM	dom	R. K'ekchi, Fray Bartolomé de las Casas
4845	100	MTN	dom	R. Mauritanie, Nouakchott
4845	1	B	dom	R. Meteorologia Paulista, Ibitinga
4845	0.3	COD	dom	R. Tangazeni Kristo, Aru
4845	100	MLA	dom	Radio Television Malaysia, Kajang
4850	50	IND	dom	All India Radio, Kohima
4850	3	EQA	dom	R. Luz y Vida, Loja
4850	100	PAK	ISL	R. Pakistan
4855	1	B	dom	R. Por Um Mundo Melhor, G.V.
4855	2.5	B	dom	R. Tropical da Barra, Barra do Garças
4856	1	PRU	dom	R. La Hora, Cusco
4860	50	IND	DEL	All India Radio (AIR)
4860	50	IND	dom	All India Radio, Delhi
4860	10	EQA	dom	R. Federación Shuar, Sucúa
4860		—	—	VO Iranian Kudistan
4864	1	BOL	dom	R. Em. 16 de Marzo, Mina Bolívar
4865	5	B	dom	R. Alvorada, Londrina
4865	5	BOL	dom	R. Centenario "La Nueva", Santa Cruz
4865	5	B	dom	R. Missões da Amazônia, Óbidos
4865	5	B	dom	R. Verdes Florestas, Cruzeiro do Sul
4870		EQA	dom	LV del Upano, Macas, R. María
4870		INS	dom	RRI Wamena
4870	1	MWI	dom	Trans World R. Malawi, Lilongwe
4871	10	INS	dom	RRI Sorong
4875	10	BOL	dom	R. La Cruz del Sur, La Paz
4875	10	B	dom	R. Roraima, Boa Vista
4880	50	IND	dom	All India Radio, Lucknow
4880	100	BGD	dom	Bangladesh Betar, Shavar
4880	1	PRU	dom	R. Comas, Lima
4880	100	AFS	MEY	SW Radio Africa
4885	5	CLM	dom	Ondas del Meta, Villavicencio
4885	1	B	dom	R. A Voz do Coração Imaculado, Anápolis
4885	10	B	dom	R. Clube do Pará, Belém
4885	5	B	dom	R. Dif. Acreana, Rio Branco
4886	1	BOL	dom	R. Sararenda, Camiri
4886	0.8	PRU	dom	R. Virgin del Carmen, Huancavelica
4890	100	PNG	dom	Port Moresby
4890	1	PRU	dom	R. Chota, Chota
4890	250	GAB	GAB	R. France Int'l (RFI)
4890		PRU	dom	R. Macedonia, Arequipa
4895	50	IND	dom	All India Radio, Kurseong
4895		CLM	dom	Colombia Estéreo/Em de Creer, Melgar
4895	10	MNG	dom	Mongoliin Radio, Mörön
4895	5	B	dom	R. Bare, Manaus
4895	5	B	dom	R. Novo Tempo, Campo Grande
4895	10	MLA	dom	R. Television Malaysia Sarawak, Stapok
4899	1	PRU	dom	R. Huanta, Huanta
4900	1	EQA	dom	LV de Saquisilí y Libertades, Saquisilí
4900	50	CHN	dom	V.O.Strait Amoy, Fuzhou
4901	0.75	BOL	dom	R. Em. San Ignacio, San Ignacio de Moxos
4904		BOL	dom	R. San Miguel, Riberalta
4905	1	B	dom	R. Araguaia, Araguaína
4905	1	PRU	dom	R. La Oroya, La Oroya
4905	5	B	dom	R. Nova Relógio, Rio de Janeiro
4905	50	CHN	dom	Xizang-Tb, Lhasa
4910	50	IND	dom	All India Radio, Jaipur
4910	0.5	HND	dom	LV de la Mosquitia, Puerto Lempira
4910	50	AUS	dom	N. Terr. SW Sce, VL8T, Tennant Creek
4910	100	ZMB	dom	Zambia Nat. B'casting Corp., Lusaka
4915	3	CLM	dom	Armonías del Caquetá, Florencia
4915	50	GHA	dom	Ghana B'casting Corporation, Accra
4915	10	B	dom	R. CBN Anhanguera, Goiânia
4915	10	PRU	dom	R. Cora, Lima
4915	25	B	dom	R. Dif., Macapá
4919	12	EQA	dom	R. Quito "LV de la Capital", Quito
4920	50	IND	dom	All India Radio, Chennai
4920		INS	dom	RRI Biak
4920	50	CHN	dom	Xizang-Tb, Lhasa
4925	0.5	B	dom	R. Difusora, Taubaté
4925	5	B	dom	R. Educação Rural, Tefé
4925	10	INS	dom	RRI Jambi
4930	15	CHN	dom	Honghe, Gejiu
4930		DOM	dom	R. Barahona, Barahona
4930	1	HND	dom	R. Costeña Ebenezer, San Pedro Sula
4930	1	PRU	dom	R. LV dc Huarinjas, Huancabamba
4930		PRU	dom	R. San Miguel, Cusco
4930	50	TKM	dom	Türkmen Radiosi, Asgabat
4935	1	B	dom	R. Capixaba, Vitória
4935	2.5	B	dom	R. Difusora, Jataí
4939	1.5	BOL	dom	R. Norte, Montero
4940	50	IND	dom	All India Radio, Guwahati

kHz	kW	Ctry	Site	Station, location
4940	100	STP	SAO	BBG - VO America (VOA)
4940	1	VEN	dom	R. Amazonas, Pto. Ayacucho
4940	1	PRU	dom	R. San Antonio, Villa Atalaya
4940	15	CHN	dom	V.O.Strait N, Fuzhou
4940	100	TJK	DSB	VO Russia (VOR)
4945	1	B	dom	Emiss. Rural A Voz do São
4945	1	B	dom	R. Difusora, Poços de Caldas
4945	10	BOL	dom	R. Illimani, La Paz
4945	7.5	B	dom	R. Progresso, Porto Velho
4950	50	IND	dom	All India Radio, Srinagar
4950	1	EQA	dom	R. Bahá'í, Otavalo
4950	5	PRU	dom	R. Madre de Dios, Puerto Maldonado
4950	15	AGL	dom	R. Nacional de Angola, Mulenvos
4950		CHN	dom	V.O.Pujiang, Shanghai
4955	2.5	B	dom	R. Clube, Rondonópolis
4955	5	PRU	dom	R. Cultural Amauta, Huanta
4955	10	B	dom	R. Marajoara, Belém
4955	100	PAK	ISL	R. Pakistan
4955	100	PAK	dom	R. Pakistan, Islamabad
4956	1	B	dom	R. Cultura, Campos dos Goitacazes
4960	50	IND	dom	All India Radio, Ranchi
4960	100	STP	SAO	BBG - VO America (VOA)
4960	1	PNG	dom	Catholic Radio Network, Vanimo
4960	1	HND	dom	R. Buenas Nuevas, Puerto Lempira
4960	5	EQA	dom	R. Federación Shuar, Sucúa
4960	5	DOM	dom	R. Villa/Cima100/Super QFM, Sto Domingo
4965	100	ZMB	LUS	Christian Voice
4965	5	B	dom	R. Alvorada, Parintins
4965	1	B	dom	R. Poty, Natal
4965	1	PRU	dom	R. Santa Monica, Wanchaq
4965	100	TJK	DSB	VO Russia (VOR)
4970	50	IND	dom	All India Radio, Shillong
4975	10	CHN	dom	Fujian N, Fuzhou
4975	1	CLM	dom	Ondas del Orteguaza, Florencia
4975	1	B	dom	R. Iguatemi, Osasco
4975	1	B	dom	R. Mundial, São Paulo
4975	5	PRU	dom	R. Pacifico, Lima
4975	5	B	dom	R. Timbira do Maranhão, São Luís
4975	100	TJK	DSB	VO Russia (VOR)
4976	10	UGA	dom	R. Uganda
4980	10	VEN	dom	Ecos del Torbes, San Cristóbal
4980		PRU	dom	LV de las Huarinjas, Huancabamba
4980	1	BOL	dom	R. Batallón Topater, Oruro
4980	50	CHN	dom	Xinjiang-Ug, Urumqi
4985	10	B	dom	R. Brasil Central, Goiânia
4990	50	IND	dom	All India Radio, Itanagar
4990	10	CHN	dom	Hunan N, Xiangtan
4990	1	SUR	dom	R. Apintie, Paramaribo
4991	1	BOL	dom	R. Animas, Animas
4992	5	PRU	dom	R. Ancash, Huaraz
4995	100	TJK	DSB	BBG - RFE/RL
4996	2	PRU	dom	R. Andina, Huancayo
4996	**50**	**RUS**	**—**	**RWM**
4998	**10**	**E**	**—**	**EBC**
5000	**10**	**CHN**	**—**	**BPM**
5000	**10**	**TWN**	**—**	**BSF**
5000	**1**	**EQA**	**—**	**HD2IOA**
5000	**10**	**KOR**	**—**	**HLA**
5000	**10**	**ARG**	**—**	**LOL 1**
5000	**10**	**USA**	**—**	**WWV**
5000	**10**	**HWA**	**—**	**WWVH**
5000	**2**	**VEN**	**—**	**YVTO**
5005	1	PRU	dom	R. LTC, Juliaca
5005	100	NPL	dom	R. Nepal, Khumaltar
5005	50	GNE	dom	R. Nacional de Guinea Ecuatorial, Bata
5010	50	IND	dom	All India Radio, Thiruvananthap.
5010	1	DOM	dom	R. Cristal Int., Sto Domingo
5010	1	HND	dom	R. Misiones Int., Comayagüela
5010	100	MDG	dom	R. Nasionaly Malagasy, Antananarivo
5014	1	PRU	dom	R. Altura, Cerro de Pasco
5015	1	B	dom	R. Brasil Tropical, Cuiabá
5015	1	B	dom	R. Copacabana, Rio de Janeiro
5015	1	B	dom	R. Pioneira, Teresina
5015	20	TKM	dom	Türkmen Radiosi, Asgabat
5020	1	CLM	dom	Ecos del Atrato, Quibdó
5020	5	PRU	dom	R. Horizonte, Chachapoyas
5020	10	SLM	dom	Solomon Is Broadc. Corp.
5025	50	AUS	dom	N. Terr. SW Sce, VL8K, Katherine
5025	10	BEN	dom	Office de Radiodif. et Tv du Benin, Parakou
5025	5	B	dom	R. Morimoto, Ji-Paraná
5025	5	PRU	dom	R. Quillabamba, Quillabamba

kHz	kW	Ctry	Site	Station, location
5025	10	CUB	dom	R. Rebelde
5025	100	UZB	TAC	R. Tashkent Int'l
5025	5	B	dom	R. Vale do Xingu, Altamira,
5025	1	B	dom	Super R. Borborema, Campina Grande
5026	10	UGA	dom	R. Uganda
5027	10	PAK	dom	R. Pakistan, Quetta
5030	100	CHN	dom	CNR 1, Beijing
5030	30	CTR	CHA	Dr Gene Scott (Univ.Netw.)
5030	5	PRU	dom	R. Virgin, Huamachuco
5030	10	MLA	dom	R. Television Malaysia Sarawak, Stapok
5030	100	BFA	dom	Radiodif. Nat. du Burkina, Ouagadougou
5030	1	TON	dom	Tonga B'casting Commission
5035	10	B	dom	R. Aparecida, Aparecida
5035	5	B	dom	R. Educação Rural, Coari
5035	50	VTN	dom	VO Vietnam, Xuan Mai
5039	1	PRU	dom	R. Libertad, Junín
5040	50	IND	dom	All India Radio, Jeypore
5040	10	CHN	dom	Fujian N, Fuzhou
5040	10	EQA	dom	LV del Upano, Macas
5040	50	BRM	dom	R. Myanmar, Yangon
5040	50	UZB	TAC	R. Tashkent Int'l
5045	10	B	dom	R. Cultura do Pará, Belém
5045	1	B	dom	R. Guarujá Paulista, Guarujá
5047	100	TGO	dom	R. Nat. Tchadienne, N'Djaména-Gredia
5050	50	IND	dom	All India Radio, Aizawl
5050	15	CHN	dom	Guangxi FBS, Nanning
5050	100	PAK	dom	R. Pakistan, Islamabad
5050	10	TZA	dom	R. Tanzania, Dar es Salaam
5050	50	CHN	dom	V.O.Strait L, Fuzhou
5050	65	USA	WRB	WWRB
5055	5	CTR	dom	Faro del Caribe, San José
5055	1	B	dom	R. Difusora, Cáceres
5055	10	GUF	dom	R. F.O. Guyane, Matoury
5055	5	B	dom	R. Jornal A Crítica, Manaus
5060	100	UZB	TAC	R. Tashkent Int'l
5060	50	CHN	dom	Xinjiang-Ch, Urumqi
5066	1	COD	dom	R. Candip, Bunia
5070	100	USA	WCR	The Overcomer Ministry
5070	100	USA	WCR	WWCR
5075		CHN	dom	V.O.Pujiang, Shanghai
5080	100	PAK	dom	R. Pakistan, Islamabad
5085	65	USA	WRB	WWRB
5102	10	—	—	VO Jammu Kashmir Freed. Movem.
5105	50	USA	BCQ	Radio Six International
5105		USA	BCQ	WBCQ
5119	1	PRU	dom	R. Ondas del Sur Oriente, Quillabamba
5153	0.2	BOL	dom	R. Galaxia, Guayaramerín
5240	50	CHN	dom	Xizang-Tb, Lhasa
5385	0.3	PRU	dom	R. Huarmaca, Huarmaca
5420	50	CHN	dom	CNR 8, Beijing
5428	0.3	J	dom	Nippon Hoso Kyokai, Osaka 2
5446	3	USA	KEW	AFRTS (AFN Feeder)
5460		PRU	dom	R. LV Bolivar, Bolivar
5470	0.5	PRU	dom	R. San Nicolas, Rodriguez de Mendoza
5487		PRU	dom	Reina de la Selva, Chachapoyas
5500		PRU	dom	R. San Miguel, San Miguel
5500		BOL	dom	R. Virgen de Remedios, Tupiza
5500	10	—	—	VO Peace and Democracy
5500	10	ETH	dom	Voice of the Tigray Revolution, Mekelle
5580	0.25	BOL	dom	R. San José, San José de Chiquitos
5585	0.3	CLM	dom	R. Juventud, Pasto
5597		VTN	dom	VO Vietnam, Lao Cai
5678		PRU	dom	R. Ilucan, Cutervo
5700	0.1	PRU	dom	R. Frecuencia, San Ignacio
5745	250	USA	GRV	BBG - R. Martí
5745	100	USA	WRB	WWRB
5755	100	USA	AIJ	Dr Gene Scott (Univ.Netw.)
5765	3	GUM	BAR	AFRTS (AFN Feeder)
5765	100	USA	WCR	The Overcomer Ministry
5765	100	USA	WCR	WWCR
5770	10	BRM	dom	Defence Forces B'casting Unit
5770	1	NCG	dom	R. Miskut, Puerto Cabezas
5775	100	I	MIL	IRRS Shortwave
5775	20	I	MIL	IRRS Shortwave
5775	20	I	MIL	R. Santec
5775	20	I	MIL	Radio Six International
5800	100	BUL	SOF	R. Bulgaria
5800	500	BUL	PLD	R. Bulgaria
5810	100	USA	YFR	R. Taiwan Int'l
5815	10	DNK	dom	World Music R. , Karup
5815	10	DNK	KRP	World Music Radio (WMR)
5820	100	USA	YFR	R. Taiwan Int'l
5820	100	USA	YFR	WYFR - Family Radio
5825	0.1	CHL	dom	R. Triunfal Evangélica, Santiago
5825	500	USA	EWN	WEWN
5830	250	RUS	NSB	R. Prague
5830	500	S	HOR	R. Sweden
5835	100	USA	HRA	WHRA - World Harvest R.
5835	500	USA	SHB	WSHB - World Harvest R.
5840	350	S	HOR	R. Canada Int'l (RCI)
5840	250	RUS	ARM	R. Prague
5840	500	S	HOR	R. Sweden
5840	100	UKR	KHR	R. Ukraine Int'l (RUI)
5850	350	S	HOR	R. Canada Int'l (RCI)
5850	500	S	HOR	R. Sweden
5850	100	USA	HRA	WHRA - World Harvest R.
5855	100	ARM	GAV	TWR Europe
5860	100	PAK	ISL	R. Pakistan
5860	50	CHN	dom	V.O.Jinling, Nanjing
5860	500	USA	SHB	WSHB - World Harvest R.
5865	250	GRC	AVL	VO Greece (ERA5)
5875	250	CYP	CYP	BBC World Service
5875	300	CYP	CYP	BBC World Service
5875	300	G	SKN	BBC World Service
5875	300	G	WOF	BBC World Service
5875	500	G	RMP	BBC World Service
5885	100	ARM	GAV	TWR Europe
5885	100	CVA	SMG	Vatican Radio
5885	80	CVA	VAT	Vatican Radio
5890	250	USA	GRV	BBG - VO America (VOA)
5890	250	USA	DLN	R. Thailand
5890	500	USA	GRV	R. Thailand
5895	5	SDN	dom	R. Peace, Nuba Mountains
5895	250	RUS	dom	R. Rossii, Moskva
5895	80	CVA	VAT	Vatican Radio
5900	250	BUL	PLD	R. Bulgaria
5905	250	RUS	IRK	BBG - VO America (VOA)
5905	100	CHN	KAS	China Radio Int'l
5905	200	KAZ	ALM	Democratic VO Burma
5905	500	D	NAU	Deutsche Welle
5905	500	D	WER	Deutsche Welle
5905	500	F	ISS	R. France Int'l (RFI)
5905	500	IRN	KAM	VO the Islamic Rep. of Iran
5910	500	D	NAU	Deutsche Welle
5910	250	RUS	PPK	Deutsche Welle
5910		CLM	dom	LV de tu Conciencia, Lomalinda (Meta)
5910	100	D	JUL	R. Vlaanderen Int'l (RVI)
5910	500	CVA	SMG	Vatican Radio
5910	250	RUS	IRK	VO Russia (VOR)
5915	100	CHN	HUH	China Radio Int'l
5915	100	CHN	KAS	China Radio Int'l
5915	50	ISR	ISR	Kol Israel
5915	250	F	ISS	R. France Int'l (RFI)
5915	150	SVK	RSO	R. Slovakia Int'l
5915	250	SVK	RSO	R. Slovakia Int'l
5915	100	ZMB	dom	Zambia National B'casting Corp., Lusaka
5920	50	USA	BOH	Fundamental BC Network
5920	240	RUS	KNA	VO Russia (VOR)
5920	240	RUS	SPB	VO Russia (VOR)
5925	50	CHN	dom	CNR 5, Beijing
5925	500	D	WER	Deutsche Welle
5925	100	D	JUL	Hamburger Lokalradio
5925	500	F	ISS	R. France Int'l (RFI)
5925	500	F	ISS	R. Monte Carlo-MO
5925	250	RUS	dom	R. Rossii, Moskva
5925	100	D	JUL	Radio Traumland
5925	250	RUS	ARM	VO Russia (VOR)
5925	50	VTN	dom	VO Vietnam, Xuan Mai
5927	1	BOL	dom	Radiodifusoras Minería, Oruro
5930	1	B	dom	R. Guarujá Paulista, Guarujá
5930	100	CZE	LIT	R. Prague
5930	50	RUS	dom	R. Rossii, Monchegorsk
5930	100	RUS	VLD	VO Russia (VOR)
5935	100	USA	WCR	Dr Gene Scott (Univ.Netw.)
5935	100	RUS	dom	R. Rossii, Arman
5935	50	CHN	dom	Xizang-Ch, Lhasa
5939	1	PRU	dom	R. Melodia, Arequipa
5940	100	RUS	dom	R. Rossii, Arman
5940	250	RUS	MSK	VO Russia (VOR)
5945	100	D	JUL	Bible Voice B'casting
5945	100	RUS	KHB	Bible Voice B'casting
5945	250	RUS	VLD	Bible Voice B'casting

kHz	kW	Ctry	Site	Station, location
5945	100	CHN	dom	CNR 1, Beijing
5945	100	D	JUL	Democratic VO Burma
5945	500	D	WER	Deutsche Welle
5945	500	F	ISS	R. France Int'l (RFI)
5945	500	RUS	IRK	R. France Int'l (RFI)
5945	100	AUT	MOS	R. Österreich 1
5945	500	RUS	ARM	R. Santec
5945		BOL	dom	R. Virgen de Remedios, Tupiza
5945	100	RUS	NVS	VO Russia (VOR)
5945	500	RUS	ARM	VO Russia (VOR)
5945	500	IRN	KAM	VO the Islamic Rep. of Iran
5945	100	D	JUL	Waymarks Int'l Ministries
5949	1	PRU	dom	R. Bethel, Arequipa
5950	15	CHN	dom	Heilongjiang Ko
5950	10	GUY	dom	Nat. Comms Network, Sparendaam
5950	100	USA	YFR	R. Taiwan Int'l
5950	500	RUS	ARM	VO Russia (VOR)
5950	500	RUS	SPB	VO Russia (VOR)
5950		YEM	dom	Yemen R., San'a
5952	5	BOL	dom	R. Pío XII, Siglo Veinte
5954	1	CTR	dom	R. Casino, Limón
5955	100	D	BIB	BBG - RFE/RL
5955	250	GRC	KAV	BBG - RFE/RL
5955	250	GRC	KAV	BBG - VO America (VOA)
5955	250	PHL	PHT	BBG - VO America (VOA)
5955	150	CHN	BEI	China Radio Int'l
5955	5	CLM	dom	LV de los Centauros, Villavicencio
5955	0.5	GTM	dom	R. Cultural, Guatemala
5955	10	B	dom	R. Gazeta, São Paulo
5955	300	J	YAM	R. Japan (NHK World)
5955	250	G	SKN	R. Korea Int'l
5955	500	HOL	FLE	R. Nederland Wereldomroep
5955	500	S	HOR	R. Nederland Wereldomroep
5955	100	ALB	SHI	R. Tirana
5955	500	IRN	SIR	VO the Islamic Rep. of Iran
5955	500	TUR	CAK	VO Turkey
5955	100	AUT	MOS	VO Vietnam (VOV)
5960	250	CAN	SAC	China Radio Int'l
5960	500	MDA	GRI	R. DMR
5960	250	CAN	SAC	R. Japan (NHK World)
5960	1	NZL	dom	R. Reading Service, Levin
5960	250	G	SKN	R. Vlaanderen Int'l (RVI)
5960	50	CHN	dom	Xinjiang-Ch, Urumqi
5960	50	CHN	dom	Yunnan ED, Kunming
5965	50	IND	dom	All India Radio, Jammu
5965	250	THA	NAK	BBC World Service
5965	150	CHN	BEI	China Radio Int'l
5965	300	CHN	BEI	China Radio Int'l
5965		EQA	dom	LV del Upano/Deal Tena, Tena
5965	10	PNG	dom	NBC Mt. Hagen
5965	250	CUB	HAB	R. Habana Cuba
5965	1	BOL	dom	R. Nacional de Huanuni, Huanuni
5965	7.5	B	dom	R. Nova Visão, Santa Maria
5965	100	POL	WWA	R. Polonia
5965	250	ROU	TIG	R. Romania Int'l (RRI)
5965	100	D	JUL	R. Vlaanderen Int'l (RVI)
5965	100	MLA	dom	Radio Television Malaysia, Kajang
5965	100	I	ROM	RAI International
5965	500	TUR	EMR	VO Turkey
5965	100	D	JUL	VOR - Russkoye Mezhd. Radio
5970	250	OMA	SLA	BBC World Service
5970	15	CHN	dom	Gannan, Hezuo
5970	250	BLR	MNS	R. Belarus
5970	100	CTR	CRI	R. Exterior de España (REE)
5970	350	E	NOB	R. Exterior de España (REE)
5970	10	B	dom	R. Itatiaia, Belo Horizonte
5970	500	IRN	KAM	VO the Islamic Rep. of Iran
5970	250	G	SKN	VO Vietnam (VOV)
5970	500	USA	SHB	WSHB - World Harvest R.
5970	500	FIN	POR	YLE R. Finland
5975	250	ATG	ATG	BBC World Service
5975	250	SNG	SGP	BBC World Service
5975	250	THA	NAK	BBC World Service
5975	100	CHN	KAS	China Radio Int'l
5975	5	CLM	dom	R. Autentica, Villavicencio
5975	1	PRG	dom	R. Guairá, Villarrica
5975	500	G	RMP	R. Japan (NHK World)
5975	100	KOR	HWA	R. Korea Int'l
5975	100	UZB	TAC	R. Tashkent Int'l
5975	50	VTN	dom	VO Vietnam, Hanoi
5975	100	D	JUL	VOR - Russkoye Mezhd. Radio
5975	100	ZWE	dom	Zimbabwe B'casting Corp., Gweru
5975+	200	D	WER	Deutsche Welle
5980	250	USA	DLN	BBG - R. Martí
5980	100	D	BIB	BBG - RFE/RL
5980	500	D	WER	Deutsche Welle
5980	5	PRU	dom	R. Chasqui, Cusco
5980	10	EQA	dom	R. Federación Shuar, Sucúa
5980	10	B	dom	R. Guarujá, Florianópolis
5980	10	MLA	dom	Radio Tv. Malaysia Labuan, Kota Kinabalu
5980	250	MRC	MOR	RTMarocaine
5980	0.1	FIN	VIR	Scandinavian Weekend R.
5980	500	TUR	EMR	VO Turkey
5985	50	IND	dom	All India Radio, Ranchi
5985	250	GRC	KAV	BBG - RFE/RL
5985	300	G	WOF	BBG - VO America (VOA)
5985	250	THA	UDO	BBG - VO America (VOA)
5985	250	UAE	DHA	FEBA Radio
5985	100	GUM	SDA	KSDA (AWR Guam)
5985	300	J	YAM	R. Canada Int'l (RCI)
5985	100	KOR	KIM	R. Canada Int'l (RCI)
5985	250	E	NOB	R. Exterior de España (REE)
5985	100	D	JUL	R. Vlaanderen Int'l (RVI)
5985	100	I	ROM	RAI International
5985	50	COG	dom	Telediffusion du Congo, Brazzaville
5985	50	USA	YFR	WYFR - Family Radio
5986	50	BRM	dom	R. Myanmar, Yangon
5990	250	IND	ALG	All India Radio (AIR)
5990	500	G	RMP	BBC World Service
5990	250	THA	NAK	BBC World Service
5990	100	D	BIB	BBG - VO America (VOA)
5990	100	CHN	BEI	China Radio Int'l
5990	100	CHN	HUH	China Radio Int'l
5990	250	CUB	HAB	China Radio Int'l
5990	15	CHN	dom	Qinghai-Tb, Xining
5990	100	ETH	dom	R. Ethiopia, Gedja
5990	250	F	ISS	R. France Int'l (RFI)
5990	500	F	ISS	R. France Int'l (RFI)
5990	100	UZB	TAC	R. France Int'l (RFI)
5990	250	B	dom	R. Senado, Brasília
5990	100	I	ROM	RAI International
5990	0.1	FIN	VIR	Scandinavian Weekend R.
5990	10	—	—	VO Jammu Kashmir Freed. Movem.
5990	500	IRN	KAM	VO the Islamic Rep. of Iran
5990	100	D	JUL	VOR - Russkoye Mezhd. Radio
5990+	50	LUX	JUN	RTL
5995	250	USA	DLN	BBC World Service
5995	100	D	BIB	BBG - VO America (VOA)
5995	250	MRC	MOR	BBG - VO America (VOA)
5995	250	PHL	PHT	BBG - VO America (VOA)
5995	100	MLI	dom	Office de Radiodif. Tv du Mali, Kati
5995	10	AUS	BRN	R. Australia
5995	100	AUS	SHP	R. Australia
5995	300	G	SKN	R. Canada Int'l (RCI)
5995	100	ALB	SHI	R. Tirana
5995	100	D	JUL	VO Russia (VOR)
5995	100	RUS	IRK	VO Russia (VOR)
5995	100	RUS	NVS	VO Russia (VOR)
5995	100	D	JUL	VOR - Russkoye Mezhd. Radio
5996	1	BOL	dom	R. Loyola, Sucre
6000	10	IND	dom	All India Radio, Leh
6000		EQA	dom	LV del Upano, Macas
6000	250	SNG	dom	Mediacorp R. , Kranji
6000	250	BUL	PLD	R. Bulgaria
6000	10	B	dom	R. Guaíba, Porto Alegre
6000	250	CUB	HAB	R. Habana Cuba
6000	250	CUB	HAB	R. Nac.Venezuela - Canal Int'l
6000	100	POL	WWA	R. Polonia
6000	250	SNG	SGP	R. Singapore Int'l
6000	100	I	ROM	RAI International
6000	240	RUS	SAM	VO Russia (VOR)
6000	250	RUS	MSK	VO Russia (VOR)
6005	250	ASC	ASC	BBC World Service
6005	250	SEY	SEY	BBC World Service
6005	250	CAN	SAC	China Radio Int'l
6005	100	D	dom	Deutschlandradio, Berlin-Britz
6005	0.3	J	dom	Nippon Hoso Kyokai, Nagoya 1
6005	0.6	J	dom	Nippon Hoso Kyokai, Sapporo 1
6005	100	RUS	dom	R. Nalch./R. Cherk, Tbiliskaya
6005	10	CLN	EKA	R. Sri Lanka (SLBC)
6005	100	RUS	ARM	VO Russia (VOR)
6005	250	IRN	AHW	VO the Islamic Rep. of Iran

kHz	kW	Ctry	Site	Station, location
6005	500	G	RMP	Wales Radio Int'l
6010	250	CAN	SAC	BBC World Service
6010	300	G	SKN	BBC World Service
6010	500	G	RMP	BBC World Service
6010	500	UAE	DHA	BBG - R. Free Asia (RFA)
6010	100	CHN	KUN	China Radio Int'l
6010	100	CHN	dom	CNR 2/8, Tianshui
6010	10	URG	dom	Em. Ciudad de Montevideo
6010	0.4	CLM	dom	LV de tu Conciencia, Lomalinda (Meta)
6010	100	UZB	TAC	R. France Int'l (RFI)
6010	5	B	dom	R. Inconfidência, Belo Horizonte
6010	1	MEX	dom	R. Mil Onda Corta, México
6010	1	CHL	dom	R. Parinacota, Putre
6010	300	G	WOF	R. Sri Lanka (SLBC)
6010	350	CAN	SAC	R. Sweden
6010	100	I	ROM	RAI International
6010	5	BLR	dom	State TV & Radio Co, Brest
6010	500	IRN	KAM	VO the Islamic Rep. of Iran
6015	300	G	SKN	BBC World Service
6015	100	BOT	BOT	BBG - VO America (VOA)
6015	250	CLN	IRA	BBG - VO America (VOA)
6015	100	D	JUL	Bible Voice B'casting
6015	100	D	JUL	Bozy Glos
6015	100	D	JUL	Christian Science Herold
6015	100	D	JUL	Ev. Missions-Gemeinden
6015	100	KOR	dom	KBS, Hwaseong
6015	100	D	JUL	Maeva FM Int'l
6015	100	D	JUL	Missionwerk Arche
6015	10	BOL	dom	R. El Mundo, Santa Cruz
6015	250	UAE	DHA	R. France Int'l (RFI)
6015	500	HOL	FLE	R. Nederland Wereldomroep
6015	250	ROU	TIG	R. Romania Int'l (RRI)
6015	100	D	JUL	TDPradio
6015	50	TZA	dom	VO Tanzania, Dole
6015	500	IRN	SIR	VO the Islamic Rep. of Iran
6015	15	CHN	dom	Xinjiang-Kz, Urumqi
6015+	40	D	JUL	TDPradio
6020	50	IND	dom	All India Radio, Shimla
6020	250	CYP	CYP	BBC World Service
6020	300	G	WOF	BBC World Service
6020	500	G	RMP	BBC World Service
6020	500	CHN	SZG	China Radio Int'l
6020	100	AUS	SHP	R. Australia
6020	10	B	dom	R. Gaúcha, Porto Alegre
6020	250	ATN	BON	R. Nederland Wereldomroep
6020	250	MDG	MDC	R. Nederland Wereldomroep
6020	3	PRU	dom	R. Victoria, Lima
6020	250	PHL	PUG	Vatican Radio
6020	500	TUR	EMR	VO Turkey
6020	20	VTN	dom	VO Vietnam, Buon Me Thuot
6025	15	CHN	dom	Alxa-Ch, Bayanhot
6025	250	PHL	PHT	BBG - VO America (VOA)
6025	1	DOM	dom	R. Amanecer Internacional, Sto Domingo
6025	100	HNG	JBR	R. Budapest
6025	250	HNG	JBR	R. Budapest
6025	150	SVK	RSO	R. Budapest
6025	250	SVK	RSO	R. Budapest
6025	250	D	WER	R. Canada Int'l (RCI)
6025	10	BOL	dom	R. Illimani, La Paz
6025	0.7	PRG	dom	R. Nal. del Paraguay, Asunción
6025	100	UZB	TAC	R. Tashkent Int'l
6025	100	MLA	dom	Radio Television Malaysia, Kajang
6025	100	MLA	KAJ	VO Malaysia
6030	50	IND	dom	All India Radio, Delhi
6030	250	OMA	SLA	BBC World Service
6030	250	USA	DLN	BBG - R. Martí
6030	250	USA	GRV	BBG - R. Martí
6030	100	D	BIB	BBG - VO America (VOA)
6030	250	THA	UDO	BBG - VO America (VOA)
6030	0.1	CAN	dom	CFVP, Calgary
6030	100	CHN	dom	CNR 1, Beijing
6030	250	CLN	TRM	Deutsche Welle
6030	1	BOL	dom	R. ABC, Santa Cruz
6030	10	B	dom	R. Globo, Rio de Janeiro
6030	500	G	RMP	R. Japan (NHK World)
6030	10	COD	dom	R. Okapi, Kinshasa
6030	5	RUS	dom	R. Rossii, Perm
6030	10	CHL	dom	R. Santa María, Coyhaique
6030	250	RUS	SPB	VO Russia (VOR)
6035	250	OMA	SLA	BBC World Service
6035	250	THA	NAK	BBC World Service
6035	100	BOT	BOT	BBG - VO America (VOA)
6035	100	D	BIB	BBG - VO America (VOA)
6035	100	STP	SAO	BBG - VO America (VOA)
6035	250	USA	GRV	BBG - VO America (VOA)
6035	50	BTN	dom	Bhutan B'casting Service
6035	5	CLM	dom	LV del Guaviare, San José del Guaviare
6035	250	J	YAM	R. Japan (NHK World)
6035	250	SNG	SNG	R. Japan (NHK World)
6035	100	POL	WWA	R. Polonia
6035	100	I	ROM	RAI International
6035	500	IRN	SIR	VO the Islamic Rep. of Iran
6035	50	CHN	dom	Yunnan BS, Kunming
6037	1.5	BOL	dom	R. Tropico, Trinidad
6040	300	AUT	MOS	Adventist World R. (AWR)
6040	50	IND	dom	All India Radio, Jeypore
6040	250	GRC	KAV	BBG - VO America (VOA)
6040	250	CAN	SAC	China Radio Int'l
6040	500	CHN	URU	China Radio Int'l
6040	10	PNG	dom	NBC Alotau
6040	7.5	B	dom	R. Clube Paranaense, Curitiba
6040	100	CTR	CRI	R. Exterior de España (REE)
6040	250	ROU	GAL	R. Romania Int'l (RRI)
6040	250	THA	UDO	R. Thailand
6040	100	I	ROM	RAI International
6040	5	BLR	dom	State TV & Radio Co, Hrodna
6040	500	IRN	KAM	VO the Islamic Rep. of Iran
6045	250	IND	DEL	All India Radio (AIR)
6045	500	THA	UDO	BBG - VO America (VOA)
6045	500	D	WER	Deutsche Welle
6045	100	D	JUL	Evangeliumsradio Hamburg
6045	100	D	JUL	Hamburger Lokalradio
6045	100	GUM	SDA	KSDA (AWR Guam)
6045	50	CHN	dom	Nei Menggu-Ch, Hohhot
6045	500	F	ISS	R. France Int'l (RFI)
6045	1	BOL	dom	R. Libertad, La Paz
6045	100	D	JUL	R. Santec
6045	10	URG	dom	R. Sport, Montevideo
6045	0.25	MEX	dom	R. Universidad, San Luis Potosí
6045	100	ZWE	dom	Zimbabwe B'casting Corp., Gweru
6047	10	PRU	dom	R. Santa Rosa, Lima
6050	250	CYP	CYP	BBC World Service
6050	300	CYP	CYP	BBC World Service
6050	100	D	BIB	BBG - VO America (VOA)
6050	50	EQA	QUI	HCJB
6050	50	NIG	dom	National B'casting Commission, Ibadan
6050	350	E	NOB	R. Exterior de España (REE)
6050	10	B	dom	R. Guarani, Belo Horizonte
6050	100	POL	WWA	R. Polonia
6050	10	MLA	dom	R. Television Malaysia Sarawak, Sibu
6050	500	TUR	CAK	VO Turkey
6050	50	CHN	dom	Xizang-Ch, Xi'an
6054	3	BOL	dom	R. Juan XXIII, San Ignacio de Velasco
6055	250	PHL	PHT	BBG - RFE/RL
6055	250	THA	UDO	BBG - RFE/RL
6055	350	E	NOB	R. Exterior de España (REE)
6055	500	KWT	KBD	R. Kuwait
6055	100	CZE	LIT	R. Prague
6055	250	ROU	GAL	R. Romania Int'l (RRI)
6055	250	ROU	TIG	R. Romania Int'l (RRI)
6055	150	SVK	RSO	R. Slovakia Int'l
6055	0.02	URG	dom	R. Universo, Castillos
6055	50	RRW	dom	R.dif. de la Republique Rwandaise, Kigali
6055	500	TUR	EMR	VO Turkey
6055+	500	KWT	KBD	R. Kuwait
6060	250	OMA	SLA	BBC World Service
6060	250	PHL	PHT	BBG - VO America (VOA)
6060	250	THA	UDO	BBG - VO America (VOA)
6060	100	NMB	dom	Namibian B'casting Corp., Windhoek
6060	250	CUB	HAB	R. Habana Cuba
6060	30	ARG	dom	R. Nacional Buenos Aires
6060	100	PAK	ISL	R. Pakistan
6060	5	RUS	dom	R. Rossii, Yakutsk
6060	10	B	dom	R. Tupi, Curitiba
6060	100	I	ROM	RAI International
6060	50	ARG	BUE	Rdif. Argentina al Exterior
6060	15	CHN	dom	Sichuan LF, Xichang
6065	50	IND	dom	All India Radio, Kohima
6065	300	G	SKN	BBC World Service
6065	250	OMA	SLA	BBC World Service
6065	250	THA	NAK	BBC World Service
6065	100	ZMB	LUS	Christian Voice

kHz	kW	Ctry	Site	Station, location
6065	150	CHN	dom	CNR 2, Beijing
6065	250	KOR	KIM	R. Korea Int'l
6065	1	BOL	dom	R. Mauro Nuñez, Villa Serrano
6065	500	S	HOR	R. Sweden
6065	500	IRN	MAS	VO the Islamic Rep. of Iran
6070	1	CAN	dom	CFRX, Toronto
6070	7.5	B	dom	R. Capital, Rio de Janeiro
6070	10	THA	BAN	R. Thailand
6070	5	BLR	dom	State TV & Radio Co, Brest
6070	25	SWZ	MAN	TWR Africa
6070	125	KRE	KNG	VO Korea
6070	100	CHL	SGO	Voz Cristiana/Voz Crista
6075	100	CHN	KAS	China Radio Int'l
6075	500	D	NAU	Deutsche Welle
6075	500	D	WER	Deutsche Welle
6075	250	POR	SIN	Deutsche Welle
6075	1	URG	dom	LV de Artigas, Artigas
6075	100	RUS	dom	R. Rossii, Arman
6075	50	CHN	dom	Yushu
6080	250	SNG	SGP	BBC World Service
6080	250	THA	NAK	BBC World Service
6080	100	STP	SAO	BBG - VO America (VOA)
6080	100	CHN	dom	CNR 1, Golmud
6080	8	EQA	QUI	HCJB
6080	7.5	CHN	dom	Hulun Buir-Mo, Hailar
6080	10	PNG	dom	NBC Daru
6080	100	AUS	SHP	R. Australia
6080	5	B	dom	R. CBN Anhanguera, Goiânia
6080	100	GEO	DSH	R. Georgia
6080	10	B	dom	R. Novas de Paz, Curitiba
6080	1	CHL	dom	R. Patagonia Chilena,Coyhaique
6080	250	SNG	SGP	R. Singapore Int'l
6080	150	BLR	dom	State TV & Radio Co, Minsk
6085	50	IND	dom	All India Radio, Delhi
6085	10	IND	dom	All India Radio, Gangtok
6085	100	D	dom	Ismaning, München
6085	250	F	ISS	R. France Int'l (RFI)
6085	50	RUS	dom	R. Rossii, Krasnoyarsk
6085	5	BOL	dom	R. San Gabriel, La Paz
6085	100	OMA	SEB	R. Sultanate of Oman
6085	300	TWN	TNN	R. Taiwan Int'l
6085	100	USA	YFR	WYFR - Family Radio
6090	250	KOR	KIM	BBC World Service
6090	250	OMA	SLA	BBC World Service
6090	100	CHN	dom	CNR 2, Golmud
6090	250	UAE	DHA	Deutsche Welle
6090	100	AIA	AIA	Dr Gene Scott (Univ.Netw.)
6090	50	NIG	dom	Nat. B'casting Commission, Kaduna
6090	10	B	dom	R. Bandeirantes, São Paulo
6090	10	CHL	dom	R. Esperanza, Temuco
6090	150	CHN	KUN	R. France Int'l (RFI)
6090	250	F	ISS	R. France Int'l (RFI)
6090	300	G	SKN	R. Japan (NHK World)
6090	100	J	YAM	R. Japan (NHK World)
6090	10	LBR	dom	R. Veritas, Monrovia
6090	100	AIA	dom	The Caribbean Beacon, The Valley
6095	100	D	JUL	Adventist World R. (AWR)
6095	100	D	BIB	BBG - RFE/RL
6095	100	D	LAM	BBG - RFE/RL
6095	350	E	NOB	R. Exterior de España (REE)
6095	100	POL	WWA	R. Polonia
6095	500	IRN	KAM	VO the Islamic Rep. of Iran
6095	500	TUR	CAK	VO Turkey
6095+	50	LUX	JUN	Missionwerk Heukelbach
6095+	50	LUX	JUN	RTL
6100	500	CHN	QIQ	China Radio Int'l
6100	250	ATG	ATG	Deutsche Welle
6100	250	ATN	BON	Deutsche Welle
6100	250	CAN	SAC	Deutsche Welle
6100	250	BIH	BIJ	Int'l R. of Serbia&Monten.
6100		KRE	dom	Korean Cent. B'casting Stn., Kanggye
6100	5	RUS	dom	R. Rossii, Kyzyl
6100	100	IND	DEL	R. Sedayee Kashmir
6100	100	SWZ	MAN	TWR Africa
6100	100	MLA	KAJ	VO Malaysia
6100	500	IRN	SIR	VO the Islamic Rep. of Iran
6105	500	G	RMP	BBC World Service
6105	100	D	LAM	BBG - RFE/RL
6105	250	GRC	KAV	BBG - RFE/RL
6105	100	D	LAM	BBG - VO America (VOA)
6105	250	GRC	KAV	BBG - VO America (VOA)
6105	100	STP	SAO	BBG - VO America (VOA)
6105	0.25	MEX	dom	Candela FM, Mérida
6105	500	CHN	QIQ	China Radio Int'l
6105	5	B	dom	R. Canção Nova, Cachoeira Paulista
6105	5	B	dom	R. Cult. Filadelfia, Foz do Iguaçu
6105	500	JOR	AKA	R. Jordan (JRTV)
6105	10	BOL	dom	R. Panamericana, La Paz
6105	50	ROU	TIG	R. Romania Int'l (RRI)
6105	100	TWN	KOU	R. Taiwan Int'l
6105	10	CTR	dom	R. Universidad de Costa Rica , San José
6105	100	D	JUL	TWR Europe
6110	50	IND	dom	All India Radio, Srinagar
6110	250	ASC	ASC	BBC World Service
6110	250	ATG	ATG	BBC World Service
6110	300	G	SKN	BBC World Service
6110	500	G	RMP	BBC World Service
6110	300	J	YAM	BBC World Service
6110	250	THA	NAK	BBC World Service
6110	250	USA	GRV	BBC World Service
6110	250	PHL	PHT	BBG - VO America (VOA)
6110	250	CAN	SAC	R. Japan (NHK World)
6110	100	POL	WWA	R. Polonia
6110	250	ROU	GAL	R. Romania Int'l (RRI)
6110	50	ROU	TIG	R. Romania Int'l (RRI)
6110	250	ASC	ASC	RAI International
6110	100	I	ROM	RAI International
6110	100	D	JUL	The Overcomer Ministry
6110	100	AZE	GAN	VO Azerbaijan
6110	500	IRN	KAM	VO the Islamic Rep. of Iran
6110	500	TUR	CAK	VO Turkey
6110	50	CHN	dom	Xizang-Tb, Lhasa
6115	100	D	BIB	BBG - RFE/RL
6115	100	D	LAM	BBG - RFE/RL
6115		CHN	KAS	China Radio Int'l
6115	10	CLM	dom	LV del Llano, Villavicencio
6115	300	G	SKN	R. Japan (NHK World)
6115	100	ALB	SHI	R. Tirana
6115	10	PRU	dom	R. Union, Lima
6115	75	BLR	dom	State TV & Radio Co, Minsk
6115	50	COG	dom	Telediffusion du Congo, Brazzaville
6115	50	CHN	dom	V.O.Strait Amoy, Fuzhou
6120		—	—	LV de la Resistencia
6120	300	J	YAM	R. France Int'l (RFI)
6120	10	B	dom	R. Globo, São Paulo
6120	250	CAN	SAC	R. Japan (NHK World)
6120	250	SNG	SNG	R. Nederland Wereldomroep
6120	10	CUB	dom	R. Rebelde/Reloj
6120	250	SNG	SGP	R. Singapore Int'l
6120	100	D	JUL	R. Taiwan Int'l
6120	1	MEX	dom	R. Tapachula, Tapachula
6120	25	SWZ	MAN	TWR Africa
6120	50	SWZ	MAN	TWR Africa
6120	500	IRN	KAM	VO the Islamic Rep. of Iran
6120	500	TUR	CAK	VO Turkey
6120	500	TUR	EMR	VO Turkey
6120	50	CHN	dom	Xinjiang-Ug, Urumqi
6120	100	FIN	POR	YLE R. Finland
6120	250	FIN	POR	YLE R. Finland
6120	500	FIN	POR	YLE R. Finland
6125	100	CHN	dom	CNR 1, Shijiazhuang
6125	250	UAE	DHA	FEBA Radio
6125	100	EQA	QUI	HCJB
6125	350	E	NOB	R. Exterior de España (REE)
6125	0.25	—	—	R. One/Information R.
6125	250	ROU	TIG	R. Romania Int'l (RRI)
6125	100	I	ROM	RAI International
6125	0.35	URG	dom	S.O.D.R. E.:, Montevideo
6125	100	RUS	IRK	VO Russia (VOR)
6125	500	IRN	SIR	VO the Islamic Rep. of Iran
6130	300	G	SKN	BBC World Service
6130	300	G	WOF	BBC World Service
6130	250	USA	DLN	BBC World Service
6130	500	D	NAU	Deutsche Welle
6130	500	D	WER	Deutsche Welle
6130	0.6	J	dom	Nippon Hoso Kyokai, Fukuoka 1
6130	50	LAO	dom	R. Nationale Lao, Vientiane
6130	250	ROU	GAL	R. Romania Int'l (RRI)
6130	50	ROU	TIG	R. Romania Int'l (RRI)
6130	100	I	ROM	RAI International
6130	100	SWZ	MAN	TWR Africa
6130	50	SWZ	MAN	TWR Africa

kHz	kW	Ctry	Site	Station, location
6130	100	D	JUL	TWR Europe
6130	250	RUS	MSK	VO Russia (VOR)
6130	500	IRN	SIR	VO the Islamic Rep. of Iran
6130	50	CHN	dom	Xizang-Tb, Lhasa
6130+	200	D	WER	Deutsche Welle
6135	250	AFS	MEY	BBC World Service
6135	250	ASC	ASC	BBC World Service
6135	250	SNG	SGP	BBC World Service
6135	250	USA	DLN	BBC World Service
6135	250	GRC	KAV	BBG - RFE/RL
6135	250	THA	UDO	BBG - VO America (VOA)
6135	10	KOR	dom	KBS, Hwaseong
6135	25	B	dom	R. Aparecida, Aparecida
6135	250	ASC	ASC	R. Japan (NHK World)
6135	10	KOR	HWA	R. Korea Int'l
6135	250	ROU	GAL	R. Romania Int'l (RRI)
6135	50	ROU	TIG	R. Romania Int'l (RRI)
6135	10	BOL	dom	R. Santa Cruz, Santa Cruz
6135	30	MDG	dom	R. Nasionaly Malagasy, Antananarivo
6135	500	TUR	EMR	VO Turkey
6135		YEM	dom	Yemen R., San'a
6140	250	OMA	SLA	BBC World Service
6140	100	TJK	DSB	BBG - R. Farda
6140	100	D	LAM	BBG - RFE/RL
6140	250	THA	UDO	BBG - VO America (VOA)
6140	100	CHN	KUN	China Radio Int'l
6140	50	CHN	dom	CNR 6, Beijing
6140	100	D	JUL	Deutsche Welle
6140	5	CLM	dom	Melodía Bogotá, SF de Bogotá
6140	10	PNG	dom	NBC Wewak
6140	1	URG	dom	R. Monte Carlo, Montevideo
6140	10	CUB	dom	R. Rebelde/Reloj
6140	250	ROU	TIG	R. Romania Int'l (RRI)
6140	1	SRL	dom	R. UNAMSIL, Freetown
6140	60	BDI	dom	Radiodif. Nat. du Burundi, Gitega
6140	100	I	ROM	RAI International
6140	500	IRN	SIR	VO the Islamic Rep. of Iran
6140+	100	D	JUL	Deutsche Welle
6141		PRU	dom	R. Concordia, Arequipa
6145	500	CHN	URU	China Radio Int'l
6145	250	F	ISS	China Radio Int'l
6145	500	F	ISS	China Radio Int'l
6145	500	D	WER	Deutsche Welle
6145	250	UAE	DHA	Gospel for Asia
6145	15	CHN	dom	Qinghai-Ch, Xining
6145	250	RUS	MSK	R. Freundes-Dienst
6145	250	CAN	SAC	R. Japan (NHK World)
6145	300	J	YAM	R. Japan (NHK World)
6145	50	ROU	TIG	R. Romania Int'l (RRI)
6145	250	RUS	MSK	R. Santec
6145	100	TWN	KOU	R. Taiwan Int'l
6145	100	AFS	MEY	SW Radio Africa
6145	500	CVA	SMG	Vatican Radio
6145	100	RUS	KHB	VO Russia (VOR)
6145	199	RUS	KHB	VO Russia (VOR)
6145	250	RUS	MSK	VO Russia (VOR)
6145	500	IRN	KAM	VO the Islamic Rep. of Iran
6150	50	IND	dom	All India Radio, Itanagar
6150	25	CYP	dom	Bayrak R. , Yeni Yskele
6150	250	UAE	DHA	BBC World Service
6150	100	D	BIB	BBG - RFE/RL
6150	500	CHN	SZG	China Radio Int'l
6150	50	CTR	CHA	Dr Gene Scott (Univ.Netw.)
6150	250	SNG	dom	Mediacorp R. , Kranji
6150	25	CYP	ISK	R. Bayrak Int'l
6150	100	POL	WWA	R. Polonia
6150	7.5	B	dom	R. Record, São Paulo
6150	5	RUS	dom	R. Rossii, Perm,
6150	50	RUS	dom	R. Rossii, Yakutsk
6150	250	SNG	SGP	R. Singapore Int'l
6150	100	TWN	KOU	R. Taiwan Int'l
6150		THA	dom	R. Thailand
6154	2	URG	dom	Banda Oriental, Sarandí del Yi
6155	100	IND	DEL	All India Radio (AIR)
6155	250	ASC	ASC	BBC World Service
6155	150	CHN	dom	CNR 2, Beijing
6155	10	BOL	dom	R. Fides, La Paz
6155	300	AUT	MOS	R. Österreich 1
6155	50	GUI	dom	Radiodif. Tv Guineenne, Conakry
6160	100	TJK	DSB	BBG - RFE/RL
6160	100	D	BIB	BBG - VO America (VOA)
6160	250	GRC	KAV	BBG - VO America (VOA)
6160	250	PHL	PHT	BBG - VO America (VOA)
6160	1	CAN	dom	CBC, St. John's
6160	0.5	CAN	dom	CBC, Vancouver
6160	100	KOR	KIM	R. Canada Int'l (RCI)
6160	1	ARG	dom	R. Malargüe, Malargüe
6160	10	PRU	dom	R. Milenia, Lima
6160	1	B	dom	R. RGS, Porto Alegre
6160	10	B	dom	R. Rio Mar, Manaus
6160	40	RUS	dom	R. Rossii, Arkhangelsk
6165	150	ATN	BON	Adventist World R. (AWR)
6165	250	IND	DEL	All India Radio (AIR)
6165	500	CHN	URU	China Radio Int'l
6165	100	CHN	dom	CNR 1, Golmud
6165	50	CHN	dom	CNR 6, Beijing
6165	10	HRV	DEA	Glas Hrvatske
6165	300	J	YAM	R. Japan (NHK World)
6165	250	ATN	BON	R. Nederland Wereldomroep
6165	100	UZB	TAC	R. Tashkent Int'l
6165	100	TCD	dom	R. dif. Nat Tchadienne, N'Djaména-Gredia
6165	50	VTN	dom	VO Vietnam, Xuan Mai
6165	100	ZMB	dom	Zambia Nat. B'casting Corp., Lusaka
6170	250	KOR	KIM	BBC World Service
6170	250	MRC	MOR	BBG - R. Aap Ki Dunyaa
6170	100	D	BIB	BBG - RFE/RL
6170	100	D	BIB	BBG - VO America (VOA)
6170	250	CLN	TRM	Deutsche Welle
6170	7.5	B	dom	R. Cultura, São Paulo
6170	250	KOR	KIM	R. Korea Int'l
6170	300	G	SKN	R. Taiwan Int'l
6170	0.1	FIN	VIR	Scandinavian Weekend R.
6170	500	MDA	GRI	VO Russia (VOR)
6173	1	PRU	dom	R. Tawantinsuyo, Cusco
6175	300	AUT	MOS	Adventist World R. (AWR)
6175	250	UAE	DHA	Bible Voice B'casting
6175		CHN	KAS	China Radio Int'l
6175	100	CHN	dom	CNR 1, Beijing
6175	2.5	CTR	dom	Faro del Caribe, San José
6175	100	NMB	dom	Namibian B'casting Corp., Windhoek
6175	0.9	J	dom	Nippon Hoso Kyokai, Tokyo 1
6175	250	F	ISS	R. France Int'l (RFI)
6175	500	F	ISS	R. France Int'l (RFI)
6175	250	GAB	GAB	R. France Int'l (RFI)
6175	250	G	SKN	R. Japan (NHK World)
6175	50	ROU	TIG	R. Romania Int'l (RRI)
6175	100	MLA	dom	Radio Television Malaysia, Kajang
6175	100	MLA	KAJ	VO Malaysia
6175	100	D	JUL	VO Russia (VOR)
6175	100	RUS	ARM	VO Russia (VOR)
6175	500	IRN	KAM	VO the Islamic Rep. of Iran
6175	500	IRN	SIR	VO the Islamic Rep. of Iran
6175	250	CAN	SAC	VO Vietnam (VOV)
6176	15	CHN	dom	Shaanxi N, Xi'an
6180	250	GRC	KAV	BBG - RFE/RL
6180	250	THA	UDO	BBG - VO America (VOA)
6180	500	CHN	URU	China Radio Int'l
6180	250	CYP	CYP	Cyprus Broadc. Corporation
6180	250	CLN	TRM	Deutsche Welle
6180	500	D	WER	Deutsche Welle
6180	250	RRW	KIG	Deutsche Welle
6180	250	UAE	DHA	FEBA Radio
6180	100	GEO	DSH	R. Georgia
6180	300	G	SKN	R. Japan (NHK World)
6180	250	B	dom	R. Nacional da Amazônia, Brasília
6180	7.5	ARG	dom	R. Nacional Mendoza
6180	100	POL	WWA	R. Polonia
6180	250	ROU	TIG	R. Romania Int'l (RRI)
6180	500	IRN	KAM	VO the Islamic Rep. of Iran
6185	15	CHN	dom	China Huayi BC, Fuzhou
6185	10	MEX	dom	R. Educación, México
6185	250	F	ISS	R. France Int'l (RFI)
6185	250	SNG	SGP	R. Singapore Int'l
6185	500	CVA	SMG	Vatican Radio
6185	500	IRN	KAM	VO the Islamic Rep. of Iran
6185	500	IRN	SIR	VO the Islamic Rep. of Iran
6185	500	TUR	EMR	VO Turkey
6188	1	PRU	dom	R. Oriente, Yurimaguas
6190	50	IND	dom	All India Radio, Delhi
6190	100	AFS	MEY	BBC World Service
6190	250	CAN	SAC	China Radio Int'l
6190	100	CHN	dom	CNR 2, Golmud

kHz	kW	Ctry	Site	Station, location
6190	15	D	dom	Deutschlandfunk, Berlin-Britz
6190	100	CAN	SAC	R. Canada Int'l (RCI)
6190	100	J	YAM	R. Japan (NHK World)
6190	300	J	YAM	R. Japan (NHK World)
6190		B	dom	R. Senado Federal, Brasília
6190	100	OMA	SEB	R. Sultanate of Oman
6190	250	PHL	PUG	R. Veritas Asia
6190	5	BLR	dom	State TV & Radio Co, Mahilioú
6190	500	IRN	SIR	VO the Islamic Rep. of Iran
6190	15	CHN	dom	Xinjiang-Mo, Urumqi
6193	1	PRU	dom	R. Cusco, Cusco
6195	250	ATG	ATG	BBC World Service
6195	250	CYP	CYP	BBC World Service
6195	300	G	SKN	BBC World Service
6195	500	G	RMP	BBC World Service
6195	250	SNG	SGP	BBC World Service
6195	250	THA	NAK	BBC World Service
6195	100	GUM	SDA	KSDA (AWR Guam)
6195	50	CHN	dom	Nei Menggu-Mo, Hohhot
6195	500	RUS	SPB	R. Santec
6195	200	KRE	KUJ	VO Korea
6195	500	RUS	SPB	VO Russia (VOR)
6200	100	POL	WWA	R. Polonia
6200	100	CZE	LIT	R. Prague
6200	500	IRN	SIR	VO the Islamic Rep. of Iran
6200	50	CHN	dom	Xizang-Tb, Xi'an
6205	250	RUS	KNA	Deutsche Welle
6205	100	ALB	SHI	R. Tirana
6205	500	RUS	TCH	Vatican Radio
6205	500	RUS	TCH	VO Russia (VOR)
6210	0.8	COD	dom	R. Kahuzi, Bukavu
6210	10	ETH	dom	Radio Fana, Addis Ababa
6215		ARG	dom	R. Baluarte, Puerto Iguazú
6225	500	KAZ	ALM	Deutsche Welle
6225	250	RUS	NSB	Deutsche Welle
6225	100	PAK	dom	R. Pakistan, Islamabad
6230	250	EGY	ABS	R. Cairo
6230	100	F	MCO	TWR Europe
6235	200	RUS	SPB	Lutherische Stunde
6235	200	RUS	SPB	Missionwerk Heukelbach
6235	200	RUS	SPB	R. Santec
6235	100	ALB	SHI	TWR Europe
6235	200	RUS	SPB	VO Russia (VOR)
6240		—	—	LV de la Resistencia
6240	100	RUS	EKB	TWR Europe
6245	250	RUS	NSB	Deutsche Welle
6250		KRE	dom	Pyongyang B'casting Stn, Pyongyang
6250	10	GNE	dom	R. Nacional de Guinea Ecuatorial, Malabo
6260	15	CHN	dom	Qinghai-Ch, Xining
6277	0.4	PRU	dom	R. Apurimac, Abancay
6280	300	ISR	ISR	Kol Israel
6329		PRU	dom	R. LV de Faique
6340		IRQ	dom	VO Iraqi Kurdistan, Salah al Deen
6347		VTN	dom	VO Vietnam, Yen Bai
6348		—		R. Echo of Hope
6350	3	HWA	PEH	AFRTS (AFN Feeder)
6350	10	—	—	VO Peace and Democracy
6350	10	ETH	dom	Voice of the Tigray Revolution, Mekelle
6379		VTN	dom	VO Vietnam, Dien Bien
6400		KRE	dom	Pyongyang B'casting Station, Kanggye
6420		—	—	VO Iranian Revolution
6420		—		VO the Communist Party of Iran
6490		VTN	dom	VO Vietnam, Cao Bang
6500	7.5	CHN	dom	Qinghai-Tb, Xining
6520		PRU	dom	R. Paucartambu, Paucartambo
6520	200	KRE	KUJ	VO Korea
6536	1	PRU	dom	R. Huancabamba, do (R. La Ponderosa)
6537		BOL	dom	R. LV del Campesino, Sipe Sipe
6560		PRU	dom	Estacion Dos, Huancabamba
6575	200	KRE	KUJ	VO Korea
6586		BOL	dom	R. Nueva Esperanza, El Alto
6600		—	—	VO the People
6665		VTN	dom	VO Vietnam, Lao Cai
6674		PRU	dom	R. Super Sencacion, Huancabamba
6724		PRU	dom	R. Cielo, Chiclayo
6798	1	PRU	dom	R. Ondas del Rio Mayo, Nueva Cajamarca
6820		PRU	dom	LV de las Huarinjas, Huancabamba
6822		SOM	dom	R. Mogadishu
6870	50	USA	RMI	The Overcomer Ministry
6870	50	USA	RMI	VO the NASB
6870	50	USA	RMI	WRMI - R. Miama Int'l

kHz	kW	Ctry	Site	Station, location
6884		PRG	dom	LV del Chaco Paraguayo, Chaco
6890	0.8	SOM	dom	R. Galkayo, Puntland
6895		PRU	dom	R. San Miguel, San Miguel de El Faique
6920	350	E	NOB	R. Exterior de España (REE)
6937	20	CHN	dom	Yunnan Minor, Kunming
6940	10	ETH	dom	Radio Fana, Addis Ababa
6950	100	CHN	dom	CNR 1, Shijiazhuang
6957		PRU	dom	R. LV de Campesino, Huarmaca
6960		SOM	dom	R. Shabele, Mogadishu
6973	10	ISR	dom	Galei Tzahal (Defence Forces R.)
6985	10	—	—	VO Freedom and Renewal
7002		SOM	dom	R. Banadir
7100	100	ERI	dom	VO Broad Masses of Eritrea, Sela'i Da'iro
7105	50	IND	dom	All India Radio, Lucknow
7105	250	ASC	ASC	BBC World Service
7105	500	G	RMP	BBC World Service
7105	250	OMA	SLA	BBC World Service
7105	250	SNG	SGP	BBC World Service
7105	250	THA	NAK	BBC World Service
7105	250	GRC	KAV	BBG - R. Farda
7105	100	D	BIB	BBG - VO America (VOA)
7105	250	MRC	MOR	BBG - VO America (VOA)
7105	100	STP	SAO	BBG - VO America (VOA)
7105	250	UAE	DHA	Bible Voice B'casting
7105	150	CHN	XIA	China Radio Int'l
7105	50	CHN	dom	Nei Menggu-Ch, Hohhot
7105	250	BLR	MNS	R. Belarus
7105	300	J	YAM	R. Japan (NHK World)
7105	100	PAK	dom	R. Pakistan, Islamabad
7105	250	ROU	GAL	R. Romania Int'l (RRI)
7105	50	ROU	TIG	R. Romania Int'l (RRI)
7105	100	D	JUL	R. Santec
7105	100	TWN	PAO	R. Taiwan Int'l
7105	100	ALB	SHI	R. Tirana
7105	20	MDG	dom	R. Nasionaly Malagasy, Antananarivo
7110	200	UZB	TAC	BBC World Service
7110	250	THA	UDO	BBG - VO America (VOA)
7110	100	CHN	HUH	China Radio Int'l
7110	600	CHN	JIN	China Radio Int'l
7110	100	CHN	dom	CNR 1, Shijiazhuang
7110	100	ETH	dom	R. Ethiopia, Gedja
7110	10	UGA	dom	R. Uganda
7110	5	BLR	dom	State TV & Radio Co, Hrodna
7110	100	AUT	MOS	Wales Radio Int'l
7115	250	IND	PAN	All India Radio (AIR)
7115	10	IND	dom	All India Radio, Port Blair
7115	500	G	RMP	BBC World Service
7115	250	GRC	KAV	BBG - RFE/RL
7115	250	MRC	MOR	BBG - RFE/RL
7115	250	G	WOF	BBG - VO America (VOA)
7115	300	G	WOF	BBG - VO America (VOA)
7115	250	MRC	MOR	BBG - VO America (VOA)
7115	500	THA	UDO	BBG - VO America (VOA)
7115	250	BIH	BIJ	Int'l R. of Serbia&Monten.
7115	500	EGY	ABZ	R. Cairo
7115	500	UAE	DHA	R. Japan (NHK World)
7115	10	THA	BAN	R. Thailand
7115		INS	dom	RRI Fak-Fak
7115	500	TUR	EMR	VO Turkey
7120	50	IND	dom	All India Radio, Jaipur
7120	300	CYP	CYP	BBC World Service
7120	500	CHN	KAS	China Radio Int'l
7120	500	CHN	SZG	China Radio Int'l
7120	500	CHN	URU	China Radio Int'l
7120	50	CHN	dom	CNR 8, Lingshi
7120	250	EGY	ABZ	R. Cairo
7120	250	MDG	MDC	R. Nederland Wereldomroep
7120	250	ROU	GAL	R. Romania Int'l (RRI)
7120	250	ROU	TIG	R. Romania Int'l (RRI)
7120	100	ALB	SHI	R. Tirana
7120	50	MDG	MDC	VO People
7120	15	CHN	dom	Xinjiang-Kg, Urumqi
7125	100	IND	DEL	All India Radio (AIR)
7125	250	THA	UDO	BBG - VO America (VOA)
7125	500	RUS	NVS	Degar Voice
7125	500	HOL	FLE	R. Nederland Wereldomroep
7125	250	ROU	GAL	R. Romania Int'l (RRI)
7125	100	D	JUL	R. Santec
7125	50	GUI	dom	Radiodif. Tv. Guineenne, Conakry
7125	500	IRN	KAM	VO the Islamic Rep. of Iran
7125	500	IRN	SIR	VO the Islamic Rep. of Iran

kHz	kW	Ctry	Site	Station, location
7125	500	MDA	GRI	VOR - Russkoye Mezhd. Radio
7125	50	CHN	dom	Xizang-Tb, Xi'an
7130	50	IND	dom	All India Radio, Shillong
7130	500	G	RMP	BBC World Service
7130	250	THA	UDO	BBG - VO America (VOA)
7130	500	CHN	KAS	China Radio Int'l
7130	400	RUS	SPB	China Radio Int'l
7130	150	CHN	dom	CNR 2, Xi'an
7130	500	D	WER	Deutsche Welle
7130	250	BIH	BIJ	Int'l R. of Serbia&Monten.
7130	50	MWI	dom	Malawi B'casting Corporation, Limbe
7130	250	ROU	TIG	R. Romania Int'l (RRI)
7130	50	ROU	TIG	R. Romania Int'l (RRI)
7130	100	TWN	MIN	R. Taiwan Int'l
7130	50	TWN	MIN	R. Taiwan Int'l
7130	10	MLA	dom	R. Television Malaysia Sarawak, Stapok
7130	500	RUS	SPB	VO Russia (VOR)
7130	500	IRN	KAM	VO the Islamic Rep. of Iran
7130	500	IRN	SIR	VO the Islamic Rep. of Iran
7135	100	SNG	SGP	BBC World Service
7135	250	CLN	IRA	BBG - VO America (VOA)
7135	100	STP	SAO	BBG - VO America (VOA)
7135	250	AFS	MEY	R. France Int'l (RFI)
7135	250	F	ISS	R. France Int'l (RFI)
7135	500	F	ISS	R. France Int'l (RFI)
7135	500	F	ISS	R. Monte Carlo-MO
7135	250	ROU	GAL	R. Romania Int'l (RRI)
7135	250	ROU	TIG	R. Romania Int'l (RRI)
7135	500	F	ISS	R. Taiwan Int'l
7135	250	MRC	MOR	RTMarocaine
7135	500	IRN	SIR	VO the Islamic Rep. of Iran
7140	100	IND	dom	All India Radio, Delhi
7140	50	IND	dom	All India Radio, Hyderabad
7140	300	CYP	CYP	BBC World Service
7140	300	G	SKN	BBC World Service
7140	500	THA	UDO	BBG - VO America (VOA)
7140	500	CHN	KUN	China Radio Int'l
7140	150	CHN	dom	CNR 2, Beijing
7140	100	CHN	dom	CNR 2, Golmud
7140	300	J	YAM	R. France Int'l (RFI)
7140	100	J	YAM	R. Japan (NHK World)
7140	250	ROU	GAL	R. Romania Int'l (RRI)
7140	250	ROU	TIG	R. Romania Int'l (RRI)
7140	50	RUS	dom	R. Rossii, Yakutsk
7140	200	KRE	KUJ	VO Korea
7140	250	TUR	EMR	VO Turkey
7145	250	GRC	KAV	BBG - RFE/RL
7145	250	GRC	KAV	BBG - VO America (VOA)
7145	500	D	WER	Deutsche Welle
7145	250	POR	SIN	Deutsche Welle
7145	3	LAO	VIE	R. Nationale Lao
7145	250	ROU	GAL	R. Romania Int'l (RRI)
7145	100	D	JUL	R. Santec
7145	5	BLR	dom	State TV & Radio Co, Mahilioŭ
7150	50	IND	dom	All India Radio, Delhi
7150	50	IND	dom	All India Radio, Imphal
7150	500	G	RMP	BBC World Service
7150	250	OMA	SLA	BBC World Service
7150	250	PHL	PHT	BBG - VO America (VOA)
7150	500	CHN	URU	China Radio Int'l
7150	600	CHN	JIN	China Radio Int'l
7150	100	CHN	dom	CNR 2, Tianshui
7150	100	GUM	SDA	KSDA (AWR Guam)
7150	350	E	NOB	R. Exterior de España (REE)
7150	250	KOR	KIM	R. Korea Int'l
7150	500	RUS	ARM	VO Russia (VOR)
7155	100	D	BIB	BBG - RFE/RL
7155	100	D	LAM	BBG - RFE/RL
7155	250	GRC	KAV	BBG - RFE/RL
7155	300	G	WOF	BBG - VO America (VOA)
7155	250	G	WOF	Bible Voice B'casting
7155	10	PAK	dom	R. Pakistan, Quetta
7155	250	RUS	KNA	VO Russia (VOR)
7155	500	TUR	EMR	VO Turkey
7155	50	CHN	dom	Xinjiang-Ch, Urumqi
7156		VTN	dom	VO Vietnam, Ha Giang
7160	50	IND	dom	All India Radio, Chennai
7160	250	ASC	ASC	BBC World Service
7160	300	G	SKN	BBC World Service
7160	250	SNG	SGP	BBC World Service
7160	250	THA	NAK	BBC World Service
7160	100	CHN	KAS	China Radio Int'l
7160	100	CHN	XIA	China Radio Int'l
7160	150	CHN	XIA	China Radio Int'l
7160	500	CHN	KUN	China Radio Int'l
7160	500	CHN	URU	China Radio Int'l
7160	150	SVK	RSO	R. Budapest
7160	250	AFS	MEY	R. France Int'l (RFI)
7160	250	ROU	GAL	R. Romania Int'l (RRI)
7160	200	UZB	TAC	R. Tashkent Int'l
7160	250	THA	UDO	R. Thailand
7160	100	ALB	SHI	R. Tirana
7160	100	F	MCO	TWR Europe
7160	250	FIN	POR	YLE R. Finland
7165	300	CYP	CYP	BBC World Service
7165	100	D	BIB	BBG - RFE/RL
7165	250	GRC	KAV	BBG - RFE/RL
7165	100	D	BIB	BBG - VO America (VOA)
7165	50	CHN	dom	Nei Menggu-Ch, Hohhot
7165	100	ETH	GJW	R. Ethiopia
7165	100	NPL	dom	R. Nepal, Khumaltar
7165	500	IRN	KAM	VO the Islamic Rep. of Iran
7170	150	BLR	MNS	Belaruskaje Radyjo 1
7170	500	CHN	KAS	China Radio Int'l
7170	100	MLI	BKO	China Radio Int'l
7170	250	RUS	TLD	China Radio Int'l
7170	100	SNG	dom	Mediacorp R. , Kranji
7170	100	AFS	MEY	United Nations Radio
7170	250	CVA	SMG	VO Russia (VOR)
7170	250	IRN	AHW	VO the Islamic Rep. of Iran
7170	50	CHN	dom	Xizang-Ch, Lhasa
7175	100	D	BIB	BBG - RFE/RL
7175	100	D	LAM	BBG - RFE/RL
7175	100	D	BIB	BBG - VO America (VOA)
7175	250	THA	UDO	BBG - VO America (VOA)
7175	500	D	NAU	Deutsche Welle
7175	500	D	WER	Deutsche Welle
7180	50	IND	dom	All India Radio, Bhopal
7180	300	CYP	CYP	BBC World Service
7180	500	G	RMP	BBC World Service
7180	100	CHN	KAS	China Radio Int'l
7180	100	CHN	XIA	China Radio Int'l
7180	500	CHN	KAS	China Radio Int'l
7180	500	CHN	URU	China Radio Int'l
7180	120	CHN	XIA	R. France Int'l (RFI)
7180	500	G	RMP	R. Korea Int'l
7180	100	POL	WWA	R. Polonia
7180	250	ROU	TIG	R. Romania Int'l (RRI)
7180	500	MDA	GRI	R. Santec
7180	100	RUS	EKB	TWR Europe
7180	500	MDA	GRI	VO Russia (VOR)
7180	100	ERI	dom	VO Broad Masses of Eritrea, Sela'i Da'iro
7180	500	IRN	SIR	VO the Islamic Rep. of Iran
7185	250	BGD	DKA	Bangladesh Betar
7185	250	ASC	ASC	BBC World Service
7185	250	CYP	CYP	BBC World Service
7185	250	CLN	IRA	BBG - R. Free Asia (RFA)
7185	250	UZB	TAC	Bible Voice B'casting
7185	50	BRM	dom	R. Myanmar, Yangon
7185	100	POL	WWA	R. Polonia
7185	100	AFS	dom	R. Sonder Grense, Meyerton
7185	100	TWN	KOU	R. Taiwan Int'l
7185	50	UZB	TAC	R. Tashkent Int'l
7190	50	IND	dom	All India Radio, Guwahati
7190	250	CYP	CYP	BBC World Service
7190	500	G	RMP	BBC World Service
7190	100	D	LAM	BBG - RFE/RL
7190	250	GRC	KAV	BBG - RFE/RL
7190	250	MRC	MOR	BBG - RFE/RL
7190	500	THA	UDO	BBG - VO America (VOA)
7190	150	CHN	BEI	China Radio Int'l
7190	500	CHN	KAS	China Radio Int'l
7190	500	CHN	SZG	China Radio Int'l
7190	500	CHN	URU	China Radio Int'l
7190	500	TUN	SFA	RT Tunisienne (ERTT)
7195	100	IND	dom	All India Radio, Mumbai
7195	500	G	RMP	BBC World Service
7195	100	D	LAM	BBG - RFE/RL
7195	500	D	NAU	Deutsche Welle
7195	250	RRW	KIG	Deutsche Welle
7195	100	J	YAM	R. Canada Int'l (RCI)
7195	100	KOR	KIM	R. Canada Int'l (RCI)

kHz	kW	Ctry	Site	Station, location
7195	10	UGA	dom	R. Uganda
7195	50	CHN	dom	Xinjiang-Ug, Urumqi
7195	250	FIN	POR	YLE R. Finland
7200	250	GRC	KAV	BBG - VO America (VOA)
7200	500	THA	UDO	BBG - VO America (VOA)
7200	500	CHN	URU	China Radio Int'l
7200	200	RUS	KRV	China Radio Int'l
7200	250	POR	SIN	Deutsche Welle
7200	250	BUL	PLD	R. Bulgaria
7200	100	J	YAM	R. Japan (NHK World)
7200	100	RUS	dom	R. Rossii, Yakutsk
7200	100	SDN	dom	Sudan Radio and TV Corp., Omdurman
7205	500	AFS	MEY	BBC World Service
7205	250	OMA	SLA	BBC World Service
7205	250	SNG	SGP	BBC World Service
7205	250	THA	NAK	BBC World Service
7205	250	THA	UDO	BBG - VO America (VOA)
7205	250	UAE	DHA	Bible Voice B'casting
7205	500	IRN	SIR	VO the Islamic Rep. of Iran
7205	500	TUR	EMR	VO Turkey
7210	300	AUT	MOS	Adventist World R. (AWR)
7210	50	IND	dom	All India Radio, Kolkata
7210	250	CYP	CYP	BBC World Service
7210	500	G	RMP	BBC World Service
7210	250	RUS	IRK	BBG - R. Free Asia (RFA)
7210	100	D	JUL	Bible Voice B'casting
7210	250	CYP	CYP	Cyprus Broadc. Corporation
7210	500	D	WER	Deutsche Welle
7210	50	CHN	dom	Nei Menggu-Mo, Hohhot
7210	30	BEN	dom	Office de Radiodif. et Tv. du Benin, Cotonou
7210	150	BLR	MNS	R. Belarus
7210	100	POL	WWA	R. Polonia
7210	100	ALB	SHI	R. Tirana
7210	100	D	JUL	TWR Europe
7210	250	IRN	AHW	VO the Islamic Rep. of Iran
7210	20	VTN	dom	VO Vietnam, Buon Me Thuot
7215	250	PHL	PHT	BBG - VO America (VOA)
7215	50	PHL	PHT	BBG - VO America (VOA)
7215	150	CHN	JIN	China Radio Int'l
7215	500	CHN	KUN	China Radio Int'l
7215	250	RUS	SAM	China Radio Int'l
7215	15	AGL	dom	R. Nacional de Angola, Mulenvos
7215	100	UZB	TAC	R. Tashkent Int'l
7215	250	AFS	MEY	TWR Africa
7215	240	RUS	MSK	VO Russia (VOR)
7215	240	RUS	SAM	VO Russia (VOR)
7215		CHN	dom	Xizang-Ch, Lhasa
7217	15	AGL	MUL	R. Nacional de Angola
7220	100	D	LAM	BBG - RFE/RL
7220	250	GRC	KAV	BBG - RFE/RL
7220	250	HNG	JBR	BBG - RFE/RL
7220	100	D	LAM	BBG - VO America (VOA)
7220	250	HNG	JBR	BBG - VO America (VOA)
7220	125	D	WER	Bible Voice B'casting
7220	100	CHN	KUN	China Radio Int'l
7220	100	CHN	XIA	China Radio Int'l
7220	150	CHN	JIN	China Radio Int'l
7220	100	D	JUL	Christian Science Herold
7220	125	D	NAU	Christian Science Herold
7220	250	BIH	BIJ	Int'l R. of Serbia&Monten.
7220	100	POL	WWA	R. Polonia
7220	250	ROU	TIG	R. Romania Int'l (RRI)
7220	100	CAF	dom	Radiodif.-Tv. Centrafricaine, Bangui-Bimbo
7220	100	D	JUL	VO Ethiopian Unity
7220	100	RUS	KHB	VO Russia (VOR)
7220	100	VTN	VNI	VO Vietnam (VOV)
7225	250	THA	NAK	BBC World Service
7225	150	CHN	XIA	China Radio Int'l
7225	250	CLN	TRM	Deutsche Welle
7225	500	D	WER	Deutsche Welle
7225	250	POR	SIN	Deutsche Welle
7225	300	J	YAM	R. Japan (NHK World)
7225	100	PAK	dom	R. Pakistan, Islamabad
7225	500	TUN	SFA	RT Tunisienne (ERTT)
7225	100	SWZ	MAN	TWR Africa
7225	100	D	JUL	TWR Europe
7225	500	IRN	KAM	VO the Islamic Rep. of Iran
7230	50	IND	dom	All India Radio, Kurseong
7230	250	AFS	MEY	BBC World Service
7230	500	AFS	MEY	BBC World Service
7230	500	G	RMP	BBC World Service
7230	120	CHN	dom	CNR 1, Beijing
7230	300	G	WOF	R. Japan (NHK World)
7230	500	RUS	SPB	R. Santec
7230	150	SVK	RSO	R. Slovakia Int'l
7230	100	BFA	dom	Radiodif. Nat du Burkina, Ouagadougou
7230	100	I	ROM	RAI International
7230	250	UAE	DHA	Salaam Watandar
7230	400	RUS	SPB	VO Russia (VOR)
7230	500	IRN	SIR	VO the Islamic Rep. of Iran
7230	15	CHN	dom	Xinjiang-Mo, Urumqi
7235	300	AUT	MOS	Adventist World R. (AWR)
7235	50	IND	dom	All India Radio, Delhi
7235	500	G	RMP	BBC World Service
7235	250	OMA	SLA	BBC World Service
7235	100	SNG	SGP	BBC World Service
7235	250	MRC	MOR	BBG - RFE/RL
7235	250	MRA	TIN	BBG - VO America (VOA)
7235	500	MRA	TIN	BBG - VO America (VOA)
7235	100	CHN	KAS	China Radio Int'l
7235	250	SNG	dom	Mediacorp R. , Kranji
7235	300	G	SKN	R. Canada Int'l (RCI)
7235	500	G	RMP	R. Korea Int'l
7235	250	SNG	SGP	R. Singapore Int'l
7235		INS	dom	RRI Palu
7235	5	BLR	dom	State TV & Radio Co, Mahilioú
7235	10	—	—	VO Jammu Kashmir Freed. Movem.
7235	500	IRN	SIR	VO the Islamic Rep. of Iran
7240	50	IND	dom	All India Radio, Mumbai
7240	100	AFS	MEY	Channel Africa
7240	100	CHN	KAS	China Radio Int'l
7240	250	POR	SIN	Deutsche Welle
7240	100	AUS	SHP	R. Australia
7240	100	ALB	SHI	R. Tirana
7240	500	UKR	SMF	VO Russia (VOR)
7240	500	TUR	EMR	VO Turkey
7240	50	CHN	dom	Xizang-Ch, Lhasa
7240+	40	HOL	FLE	R. Nederland Wereldomroep
7240+	40	HOL	FLE	R. Sweden
7240+	40	HOL	FLE	TDPradio
7245	100	D	BIB	BBG - RFE/RL
7245	100	D	LAM	BBG - RFE/RL
7245	100	CHN	XIA	China Radio Int'l
7245	200	CHN	XIA	China Radio Int'l
7245	500	CHN	KAS	China Radio Int'l
7245	500	CHN	KUN	China Radio Int'l
7245	250	POR	SIN	Deutsche Welle
7245	100	MTN	dom	R. Mauritanie, Nouakchott
7245	50	AGL	dom	R. Nacional de Angola, Mulenvos
7245	100	TJK	DSB	R. Tajikistan World Sce
7245	100	TJK	dom	R. Tojikiston
7245	250	AUS	DAR	Voice International
7250	250	IND	PAN	All India Radio (AIR)
7250	50	IND	GKP	All India Radio (AIR)
7250	50	IND	dom	All India Radio, Gorakhpur
7250	250	CLN	TRM	Deutsche Welle
7250	250	CVA	SMG	Vatican Radio
7250	500	IRN	KAM	VO the Islamic Rep. of Iran
7250	100	TWN	TAI	WYFR - Family Radio
7255	250	IND	ALG	All India Radio (AIR)
7255	250	IND	dom	All India Radio, Aligarh
7255	300	G	WOF	BBC World Service
7255	100	D	BIB	BBG - RFE/RL
7255	250	GRC	KAV	BBG - VO America (VOA)
7255	250	THA	UDO	BBG - VO America (VOA)
7255	250	BLR	MNS	Belaruskaje Radyjo 1
7255	100	CHN	XIA	China Radio Int'l
7255	150	CHN	BEI	China Radio Int'l
7255	500	CHN	KAS	China Radio Int'l
7255	500	CHN	URU	China Radio Int'l
7255	25	BOT	dom	R. Botswana, Sebele
7255	250	NIG	IKO	VO Nigeria
7260	300	G	SKN	BBC World Service
7260	250	THA	UDO	BBG - R. Aap Ki Dunyaa
7260	250	THA	UDO	BBG - RFE/RL
7260	250	CLN	IRA	BBG - VO America (VOA)
7260	500	CHN	KUN	China Radio Int'l
7260	50	MNG	dom	Mongoliin Radio, Ulaanbaatar
7260	10	VUT	dom	Vanuatu Bc. & Tv Corp., Emten Lagoon
7260	500	RUS	MSK	VO Russia (VOR)
7260	500	RUS	VLD	VO Russia (VOR)
7265	250	CYP	CYP	BBC World Service

kHz	kW	Ctry	Site	Station, location
7265	100	D	BIB	BBG - RFE/RL
7265	250	PHL	PHT	BBG - RFE/RL
7265	250	MRC	MOR	BBG - VO America (VOA)
7265	100	CHN	KAS	China Radio Int'l
7265	500	CHN	KUN	China Radio Int'l
7265	500	CHN	URU	China Radio Int'l
7265	100	UZB	TAC	FEBA Radio
7265	300	G	SKN	R. Canada Int'l (RCI)
7265	100	POL	WWA	R. Polonia
7265	250	PHL	PUG	R. Veritas Asia
7265	2.5	BLR	dom	State TV & Radio Co, Hrodna
7265	250	AFS	MEY	TWR Africa
7265	500	G	RMP	United Nations Radio
7265	500	IRN	SIR	VO the Islamic Rep. of Iran
7270	100	IND	dom	All India Radio, Chenai
7270	250	G	WOF	BBG - VO America (VOA)
7270	50	CHN	dom	Nei Menggu-Mo, Hohhot
7270	500	EGY	ABS	R. Cairo
7270	350	E	NOB	R. Exterior de España (REE)
7270	250	ASC	ASC	R. France Int'l (RFI)
7270	100	POL	WWA	R. Polonia
7270	300	TWN	TSH	R. Taiwan Int'l
7270	100	MLA	dom	R. Television Malaysia Sarawak, Stapok
7270	100	TWN	TAI	VO China
7270	500	IRN	KAM	VO the Islamic Rep. of Iran
7270	500	IRN	SIR	VO the Islamic Rep. of Iran
7270	250	FIN	POR	YLE R. Finland
7275	100	D	LAM	BBG - RFE/RL
7275	250	GRC	KAV	BBG - RFE/RL
7275	100	CHN	dom	CNR 1, Beijing
7275	7.5	CHN	dom	Guizhou Sat., Guiyang
7275	100	NIG	dom	National B'casting Commission, Abuja
7275	250	E	NOB	R. Exterior de España (REE)
7275	250	KOR	KIM	R. Korea Int'l
7275	100	POL	WWA	R. Polonia
7275	250	ROU	TIG	R. Romania Int'l (RRI)
7275	500	TUN	SFA	RT Tunisienne (ERTT)
7275	500	IRN	KAM	VO the Islamic Rep. of Iran
7275	500	TUR	EMR	VO Turkey
7275	50	CHN	dom	Xinjiang-Ug, Urumqi
7280	50	IND	dom	All India Radio, Guwahati
7280	250	GRC	KAV	BBG - RFE/RL
7280	250	THA	UDO	BBG - VO America (VOA)
7280	500	F	ISS	R. France Int'l (RFI)
7280	50	CHN	dom	V.O.Strait L, Fuzhou
7280	100	VTN	VNI	VO Vietnam (VOV)
7285	500	D	WER	Deutsche Welle
7285	100	D	JUL	Glas Hrvatske
7285	100	MLI	dom	Office de Radiodif. Tv. du Mali, Kati
7285	250	MDG	MDC	R. Nederland Wereldomroep
7285	100	POL	WWA	R. Polonia
7285	100	UZB	TAC	R. Tashkent Int'l
7285	250	THA	UDO	R. Thailand
7285	50	VTN	HAN	VO Vietnam (VOV)
7290	50	IND	dom	All India Radio, Thiruvananthap.
7290	100	STP	SAO	BBG - VO America (VOA)
7290	250	THA	UDO	BBG - VO America (VOA)
7290	600	CHN	JIN	China Radio Int'l
7290	100	CHN	dom	CNR 1, Beijing
7290	500	D	WER	Deutsche Welle
7290	1	NZL	dom	R. Reading Service
7290	100	I	ROM	RAI International
7290		INS	dom	RRI Nabire
7290	250	RUS	MSK	VO Russia (VOR)
7295	50	IND	dom	All India Radio, Aizawl
7295	500	G	RMP	BBC World Service
7295	125	GRC	KAV	BBG - RFE/RL
7295	250	GRC	KAV	BBG - RFE/RL
7295	250	MRC	MOR	BBG - VO America (VOA)
7295	100	D	JUL	Bible Voice B'casting
7295	500	CHN	KAS	China Radio Int'l
7295	100	MLA	dom	Radio Television Malaysia, Kajang
7295	500	IRN	SIR	VO the Islamic Rep. of Iran
7295	250	TUR	CAK	VO Turkey
7295	500	TUR	EMR	VO Turkey
7300	500	RUS	ARM	Lutherische Stundo
7300	500	RUS	ARM	Missionwerk Heukelbach
7300	500	RUS	ARM	R. Freundes-Dienst
7300	500	RUS	ARM	R. Santec
7300	10	CLN	EKA	R. Sri Lanka (SLBC)
7300	500	RUS	ARM	VO Russia (VOR)
7300	500	TUR	EMR	VO Turkey
7305	250	F	ISS	China Radio Int'l
7305	100	CHN	dom	CNR 1, Shijiazhuang
7305	500	D	NAU	Deutsche Welle
7305	500	D	WER	Deutsche Welle
7305	250	THA	UDO	R. Thailand
7305	500	CVA	SMG	Vatican Radio
7305	250	RUS	NVS	VO Russia (VOR)
7305	500	RUS	NVS	VO Russia (VOR)
7305	500	IRN	KAM	VO the Islamic Rep. of Iran
7306	1	I	dom	R. Europe, Pioltello
7310	250	RUS	dom	R. Rossii, Moskva
7310	300	POR	LIS	RDP Internacional
7310	240	RUS	MSK	VO Russia (VOR)
7310	50	CHN	dom	Xinjiang-Ch, Urumqi
7315	150	CHN	KUN	China Radio Int'l
7315	500	CHN	KUN	China Radio Int'l
7315	120	CHN	dom	CNR 2, Xi'an
7315	250	F	ISS	R. France Int'l (RFI)
7315	500	F	ISS	R. France Int'l (RFI)
7315	500	RUS	VLD	R. France Int'l (RFI)
7315	250	RUS	PPK	R. Nederland Wereldomroep
7315	500	F	ISS	R. Taiwan Int'l
7315	50	SWZ	MAN	TWR Africa
7315	250	RUS	SAM	VO Russia (VOR)
7315	500	USA	SHB	WSHB - World Harvest R.
7320	300	CYP	CYP	BBC World Service
7320	500	G	RMP	BBC World Service
7320	10	PAK	dom	R. Pakistan, Peshawar
7320	100	RUS	dom	R. Rossii, Arman
7320	250	RUS	MSK	VO Russia (VOR)
7320	500	IRN	SIR	VO the Islamic Rep. of Iran
7320+	500	G	RMP	BBC World Service
7325	250	CYP	CYP	BBC World Service
7325	300	G	SKN	BBC World Service
7325	500	G	RMP	BBC World Service
7325	100	CHN	XIA	China Radio Int'l
7325	500	F	ISS	R. Monte Carlo-MO
7325	300	AUT	MOS	R. Österreich 1
7325	100	LTU	SIT	R. Vilnius
7325	500	IRN	SIR	VO the Islamic Rep. of Iran
7330	300	RUS	VLD	BBC World Service
7330	200	RUS	ARM	FEBA Radio
7330	500	RUS	MSK	R. Santec
7330	100	ALB	SHI	TWR Europe
7330	250	RUS	MSK	VO Russia (VOR)
7330	500	RUS	MSK	VO Russia (VOR)
7335	600	CHN	JIN	China Radio Int'l
7335	**5**	**CAN**	**—**	**CHU**
7335	100	CHN	dom	CNR 2, Tianshui
7335	250	CVA	SMG	Vatican Radio
7335	500	RUS	TCH	VO Russia (VOR)
7335	500	IRN	KAM	VO the Islamic Rep. of Iran
7340	100	BOT	BOT	BBG - VO America (VOA)
7340	500	CHN	KAS	China Radio Int'l
7340	250	RUS	IRK	FEBA Radio
7340	100	D	JUL	IBRA Radio
7340	150	BLR	MNS	R. Belarus
7340	100	D	JUL	R. Ibrahim
7340	200	RUS	SPB	VO Russia (VOR)
7340	15	CHN	dom	Xinjiang-Kz, Urumqi
7345	500	CHN	KAS	China Radio Int'l
7345	100	CHN	dom	CNR 1, Beijing
7345	100	CZE	LIT	R. Prague
7345	200	CZE	LIT	R. Prague
7345	50	RUS	dom	R. Rossii, Yakutsk
7345	150	SVK	RSO	R. Slovakia Int'l
7350	500	CHN	URU	China Radio Int'l
7350	100	CHN	dom	CNR 2, Tianshui
7350	15	CHN	dom	Heilongjiang N, Wuchang
7350	100	CVA	SMG	VO Russia (VOR)
7350	500	RUS	TCH	VO Russia (VOR)
7350+	500	RUS	TCH	VO Russia (VOR)
7355	100	ALS	NLS	KNLS International
7355	100	ALB	SHI	TWR Europe
7355	150	RUS	EKB	VO Russia (VOR)
7355	0.15	USA	RNO	WRNO Worldwide
7360	100	IND	dom	All India Radio, Delhi
7360	100	CHN	KUN	China Radio Int'l
7360	100	CHN	dom	CNR 2/8, Tianshui
7360	500	CVA	SMG	Vatican Radio

kHz	kW	Ctry	Site	Station, location
7360	250	RUS	MSK	VO Russia (VOR)
7360	300	MDA	GRI	WYFR - Family Radio
7365	250	USA	DLN	BBG - R. Martí
7365	250	USA	GRV	BBG - R. Martí
7365	100	ARM	GAV	FEBA Radio
7365	10	HRV	DEA	Glas Hrvatske
7365	100	ALS	NLS	KNLS International
7365	250	RUS	SAM	TWR India
7365	500	CVA	SMG	Vatican Radio
7365	240	RUS	SAM	VO Russia (VOR)
7370	250	RUS	SAM	FEBA Radio
7370	1	PRG	dom	R. América, Ñemby
7370	100	CHN	KAS	R. Canada Int'l (RCI)
7370	250	RUS	SAM	R. Santec
7370	500	CVA	SMG	Vatican Radio
7370	200	RUS	SAM	VO Russia (VOR)
7371	0.05	PRG	dom	R. Colegio Tecnico Municipal
7375	150	CHN	dom	CNR 2, Beijing
7375	40	CTR	CHA	Dr Gene Scott (Univ.Netw.)
7375	50	PHL	IBA	FEBC Philippines
7375	100	PAK	ISL	R. Pakistan
7375	100	ALB	SHI	TWR Europe
7375+	35	RUS	TLD	TDPradio
7380	250	RUS	PPK	R. Nederland Wereldomroep
7380	100	ALB	SHI	TWR Europe
7380	240	RUS	EKB	VO Russia (VOR)
7380	100	AFS	MEY	VO Biafra Int'l
7385	50	CHN	dom	Xizang-Tb, Lingshi
7390	200	RUS	NVS	BBG - VO America (VOA)
7390	500	AFS	MEY	Channel Africa
7390	250	RUS	MSK	R. Santec
7390	500	RUS	SAM	R. Santec
7390	250	RUS	MSK	VO Russia (VOR)
7390	500	RUS	SAM	VO Russia (VOR)
7395	0.15	USA	RNO	WRNO Worldwide
7400	100	BUL	dom	R. Bulgaria, Varna
7400	250	RUS	IRK	Deutsche Welle
7400	100	PHL	BOC	FEBC Philippines
7400	250	BUL	PLD	R. Bulgaria
7400	500	BUL	PLD	R. Bulgaria
7400	100	UKR	KHR	R. Ukraine Int'l (RUI)
7400	200	RUS	MSK	VO Russia (VOR)
7405	250	USA	GRV	BBG - R. Martí
7405	250	USA	GRV	BBG - VO America (VOA)
7405	600	CHN	JIN	China Radio Int'l
7410	250	IND	ALG	All India Radio (AIR)
7410	250	IND	DEL	All India Radio (AIR)
7415	100	TJK	DSB	BBG - R. Free Asia (RFA)
7415	250	RUS	PPK	VO Russia (VOR)
7415		USA	BCQ	WBCQ
7420	50	IND	dom	All India Radio, Guwhati
7420	500	S	HOR	R. Sweden
7420	100	UKR	KHR	R. Ukraine Int'l (RUI)
7420	240	RUS	MSK	VO Russia (VOR)
7425	500	USA	EWN	WEWN
7430	200	UZB	TAC	BBC World Service
7430	500	RUS	NSB	R. France Int'l (RFI)
7430	200	KAZ	ALM	TWR India
7430	250	GRC	AVL	VO Greece (ERA5)
7435	250	RUS	MSK	BBC World Service
7435		COD	dom	R. Télévision Nationale Congolaise,
7440	1000	UKR	SMF	R. Ukraine Int'l (RUI)
7445	250	RUS	MSK	VO Russia (VOR)
7445	250	RUS	MSK	VOR - Radiokanal Sodruzhestvo
7450	100	UZB	TAC	IBC Tamil Radio
7450	100	GRC	AVL	RS Makedonias (ERT3)
7455	500	TJK	DSB	BBG - R. Free Asia (RFA)
7455	100	GUM	TWR	KTWR (TWR Guam)
7460	250	MNG	UBA	BBG - R. Free Asia (RFA)
7460	20	ALG	dom	R. Nacional de la R. A.S.D
7460	500	MDA	GRI	R. Payam-e Doost
7460	20	—		Radio Nacional de la RASD
7465	100	PAK	ISL	R. Pakistan
7465	100	RUS	NVS	Radio Radonezh
7465	100	USA	WCR	The Overcomer Ministry
7465	100	USA	WCR	WWCR
7470	250	MNG	UBA	BBG - R. Free Asia (RFA)
7470	500	MDA	GRI	The Arabic Radio
7475	100	GRC	AVL	VO Greece (ERA5)
7475	250	GRC	AVL	VO Greece (ERA5)
7475	250	GRC	KAV	VO Greece (ERA5)
7480	250	TJK	DSB	BBG - R. Free Asia (RFA)
7480	500	MDA	GRI	R. Payam-e Doost
7490	250	CLN	IRA	BBG - RFE/RL
7490	500	MDA	GRI	R. International
7490	100	UKR	KHR	R. Ukraine Int'l (RUI)
7490	200	RUS	ARM	R. Vlaanderen Int'l (RVI)
7490	50	USA	JCR	WJIE International Shortwave
7495	250	TJK	DSB	BBG - R. Free Asia (RFA)
7500	100	BUL	SOF	R. Bulgaria
7500	250	BUL	PLD	R. Bulgaria
7500	500	BUL	PLD	R. Bulgaria
7505	100	USA	TBN	KTBN Shortwave R.
7505	200	KRE	KUJ	VO Korea
7507	3	PTR	ROR	AFRTS (AFN Feeder)
7507		PTR	dom	AFRTS, Roosevelt Roads (USB)
7510		—		The Arabic Radio
7510	100	TJK	DSB	VO Russia (VOR)
7515	200	TJK	DSB	BBG - R. Free Asia (RFA)
7520	300	ISR	ISR	Kol Israel
7530	200	TJK	DSB	BBG - R. Free Asia (RFA)
7530	1	SOM	dom	R. Hargeisa, Somaliland
7530	100	PAK	ISL	R. Pakistan
7535	250	RUS	IRK	TWR India
7535	500	USA	SHB	WSHB - World Harvest R.
7540	500	TJK	DSB	BBG - R. Free Asia (RFA)
7545	250	ISR	ISR	Kol Israel
7550	500	CLN	IRA	BBG - R. Farda
7550	500	ARM	GAV	BBG - R. Free Asia (RFA)
7555	50	USA	JES	KJES
7555	100	UKR	KHR	R. Ukraine Int'l (RUI)
7560	500	ARM	GAV	BBG - R. Free Asia (RFA)
7560	200	RUS	TCH	TWR India
7565	250	CLN	IRA	BBG - RFE/RL
7570	500	CLN	IRA	BBG - VO America (VOA)
7570	100	PAK	ISL	R. Pakistan
7570	500	TJK	ORZ	R. Santec
7570	500	TJK	ORZ	VO Russia (VOR)
7570	500	USA	EWN	WEWN
7580	500	CLN	IRA	BBG - R. Farda
7580	200	KRE	KUJ	VO Korea
7580	100	USA	HRA	WHRA - World Harvest R.
7580	100	USA	YFR	WYFR - Family Radio
7590	10	ISL	GVK	AFRTS (AFN Feeder)
7590	250	RUS	SAM	R. VO Oromo Liberation Front
7590	100	RUS	ARM	TDPradio
7590	250	RUS	SAM	VO Oromia
7600	**1**	**EQA**	**—**	**HD2IOA**
7620	50	CHN	dom	CNR 6, Beijing
7935	100	CHN	dom	CNR 1, Lingshi
7999		—		VO Sudan
8634		**B**	**—**	**PPR**
9170	50	CHN	dom	CNR 6, Beijing
9181	0.3	J	dom	Nippon Hoso Kyokai, Osaka 2
9265	50	USA	MLK	WMLK
9280	100	TWN	TAI	WYFR - Family Radio
9290	100	LVA	ULB	Relay Services
9315	250	CLN	IRA	BBG - RFE/RL
9320	50	USA	INB	WINB
9320	65	USA	WRB	WWRB
9325	125	CLN	IRA	BBG - RFE/RL
9325	250	CLN	IRA	BBG - VO America (VOA)
9325	200	KRE	KUJ	VO Korea
9330		USA	BCQ	WBCQ
9335	250	CLN	IRA	BBG - R. Farda
9335	250	CLN	IRA	BBG - R. Free Afghanistan
9335	250	CLN	IRA	BBG R. Ashna
9335	200	KRE	KUJ	VO Korea
9340	100	PAK	ISL	R. Pakistan
9340	100	PAK	dom	R. Pakistan, Islamabad
9345	250	ISR	ISR	Kol Israel
9345	100	UZB	TAC	R. Nederland Wereldomroep
9345	200	KRE	KUJ	VO Korea
9355	100	MRA	SAI	BBG - R. Free Asia (RFA)
9355	250	TJK	DSB	BBG - R. Free Asia (RFA)
9355	250	MRA	TIN	BBG - RFE/RL
9355	200	KAZ	ALM	Golos Pravoslaviya
9355	100	USA	YFR	R. Taiwan Int'l
9355	100	USA	YFR	WYFR - Family Radio
9365	500	ARM	GAV	BBG - R. Free Asia (RFA)
9365	200	TJK	DSB	BBG - R. Free Asia (RFA)
9365	150	CHN	BEI	China Radio Int'l

kHz	kW	Ctry	Site	Station, location
9365	1	AFG	dom	Peace R. , Bagram
9370	50	USA	TJC	Fundamental BC Network
9375	500	S	HOR	R. Sweden
9375	100	UZB	TAC	R. Tashkent Int'l
375	100	GRC	AVL	VO Greece (ERA5)
9375	250	GRC	KAV	VO Greece (ERA5)
9380	50	CHN	dom	CNR 5, Beijing
9385	250	MRA	TIN	BBG - R. Free Asia (RFA)
9390	250	ISR	ISR	Kol Israel
9390	100	PAK	ISL	R. Pakistan
9395	500	KAZ	ALM	Deutsche Welle
9395	100	UZB	TAC	VO Tibet
9400	250	BUL	PLD	R. Bulgaria
9400	500	BUL	PLD	R. Bulgaria
9400	100	PAK	ISL	R. Pakistan
9405	100	PHL	IBA	FEBC Philippines
9410	250	CYP	CYP	BBC World Service
9410	300	G	SKN	BBC World Service
9410	300	G	WOF	BBC World Service
9410	500	G	RMP	BBC World Service
9410	100	POR	LIS	RDP Internacional
9415	100	GUM	TWR	KTWR (TWR Guam)
9415	250	EGY	ABS	R. Cairo
9415	100	CZE	LIT	R. Prague
9415	100	TWN	HUW	R. Taiwan Int'l
9415	100	TWN	PAO	R. Taiwan Int'l
9420	100	PHL	BOC	FEBC Philippines
9420	100	GRC	AVL	VO Greece (ERA5)
9420	250	GRC	AVL	VO Greece (ERA5)
9420	250	GRC	KAV	VO Greece (ERA5)
9425	500	IND	dom	All India Radio, Bangalore
9430	500	D	WER	Deutsche Welle
9430	100	CZE	LIT	R. Prague
9435	250	GRC	KAV	BBG - R. Farda
9435	250	GRC	KAV	BBG - VO America (VOA)
9435	500	CHN	KAS	China Radio Int'l
9435	100	PHL	BOC	FEBC Philippines
9435	100	CZE	LIT	R. Prague
9440	100	CHN	NNN	China Radio Int'l
9440	150	CHN	BEI	China Radio Int'l
9440	150	CHN	KUN	China Radio Int'l
9440		CHN	dom	CNR 8, Lingshi
9440	150	SVK	RSO	R. Slovakia Int'l
9445	500	IND	BGL	All India Radio (AIR)
9445	500	RUS	NVS	FEBA Radio
9445	150	SVK	RSO	R. Slovakia Int'l
9445	200	UZB	TAC	TWR India
9450	500	RUS	NVS	FEBA Radio
9450	100	CZE	LIT	R. Prague
9455	100	MRA	SAI	BBG - R. Free Asia (RFA)
9455	250	MRA	TIN	BBG - R. Free Asia (RFA)
9455	100	CHN	dom	CNR 1, Lingshi
9455	100	USA	HRA	WHRA - World Harvest R.
9460	100	D	JUL	Bible Voice B'casting
9460	150	CHN	KUN	China Radio Int'l
9460	100	CHN	dom	CNR 1/8, Lingshi
9460	150	SVK	RSO	R. Slovakia Int'l
9460	100	POR	LIS	RDP Internacional
9460	300	POR	LIS	RDP Internacional
9465	100	MRA	FBS	Far East Broadcasting Company
9465	100	GUM	TWR	KTWR (TWR Guam)
9465	100	TWN	HUW	R. Taiwan Int'l
9465	200	RUS	NVS	VO Russia (VOR)
9470	250	IND	dom	All India Radio, Aligarh
9470	250	D	NAU	Bible Voice B'casting
9470	100	D	JUL	Glas Hrvatske
9470	250	RUS	MSK	VO Russia (VOR)
9470	15	CHN	dom	Xinjiang-Kz, Urumqi
9475	100	AUS	SHP	R. Australia
9475	100	SWZ	MAN	TWR Africa
9480	250	USA	DLN	BBG - VO America (VOA)
9480	250	USA	GRV	BBG - VO America (VOA)
9480	100	CHN	dom	CNR 2/8, Tianshui
9480	100	D	JUL	R. Cimarrona
9480	500	RUS	MSK	R. Santec
9480	100	RUS	dom	R/S Tihkiy Okean, Razdolnoye
9480	250	RUS	SPB	VO Russia (VOR)
9480	500	RUS	MSK	VO Russia (VOR)
9485	100	D	JUL	BBG - VO America (VOA)
9485	100	UZB	TAC	FEBA Radio
9485	150	SVK	RSO	R. Slovakia Int'l
9485	500	F	ISS	VO Africa (LJBC)
9490	200	KAZ	ALM	BBG - R. Free Asia (RFA)
9490		CHN	KUN	China Radio Int'l
9490	100	ATN	BON	R. Sweden
9490	350	CAN	SAC	R. Sweden
9490	500	S	HOR	R. Sweden
9490	50	CHN	dom	Xizang-Tb, Xi'an
9495	100	D	JUL	BBG - VO America (VOA)
9495	500	D	WER	Deutsche Welle
9495	250	D	WER	Gospel for Asia
9495	100	D	JUL	R. Free Syria
9495	100	D	JUL	R. Santec
9495	100	USA	YFR	R. Taiwan Int'l
9495	100	D	JUL	R. Voice of Women
9495	100	AUT	MOS	TWR Europe
9495	250	RUS	KNA	VO Russia (VOR)
9495	500	USA	SHB	WSHB - World Harvest R.
9500	100	CHN	dom	CNR 1, Shijiazhuang
9500	100	AUS	SHP	R. Australia
9500	500	BUL	PLD	R. Bulgaria
9500	100	SWZ	MAN	TWR Africa
9500	500	IRN	SIR	VO the Islamic Rep. of Iran
9505	100	D	LAM	BBG - RFE/RL
9505	250	GRC	KAV	BBG - RFE/RL
9505	100	D	LAM	BBG - VO America (VOA)
9505	300	G	WOF	BBG - VO America (VOA)
9505	250	MRC	MOR	BBG - VO America (VOA)
9505	250	CUB	HAB	R. Habana Cuba
9505	300	J	YAM	R. Japan (NHK World)
9505	7.5	B	dom	R. Record, São Paulo
9505	0.2	PRU	dom	R. Tacna, Tacna
9505	250	PHL	PUG	R. Veritas Asia
9505	500	IRN	SIR	VO the Islamic Rep. of Iran
9510	250	CYP	CYP	BBC World Service
9510	300	CYP	CYP	BBC World Service
9510	250	SNG	SGP	BBC World Service
9510	250	THA	NAK	BBC World Service
9510	125	GRC	KAV	BBG - R. Aap Ki Dunyaa
9510	100	CHN	XIA	China Radio Int'l
9510	250	ROU	GAL	R. Romania Int'l (RRI)
9510	500	S	HOR	R. Sweden
9510	500	AFS	MEY	TWR Africa
9510	500	IRN	KAM	VO the Islamic Rep. of Iran
9510	250	TUR	EMR	VO Turkey
9510	15	CHN	dom	Xinjiang-Mo, Urumqi
9515	250	USA	DLN	BBC World Service
9515	50	CHN	dom	CNR 2, Beijing
9515	100	CAN	SAC	Hmong Lao Radio
9515	100	CAN	SAC	R. Canada Int'l (RCI)
9515	250	CAN	SAC	R. Canada Int'l (RCI)
9515	100	KOR	KIM	R. Korea Int'l
9515	250	KOR	KIM	R. Korea Int'l
9515	10	B	dom	R. Novas de Paz, Curitiba
9515	250	ROU	TIG	R. Romania Int'l (RRI)
9515	100	OMA	SEB	R. Sultanate of Oman
9520	100	D	BIB	BBG - RFE/RL
9520	100	D	LAM	BBG - RFE/RL
9520	250	GRC	KAV	BBG - RFE/RL
9520	250	HNG	JBR	BBG - RFE/RL
9520	250	MRC	MOR	BBG - RFE/RL
9520	250	THA	UDO	BBG - RFE/RL
9520	250	GRC	KAV	BBG - VO America (VOA)
9520	100	D	JUL	IBRA Radio
9520	50	CHN	dom	Nei Menggu-Ch, Hohhot
9520	100	PNG	dom	Port Moresby
9520	250	ROU	TIG	R. Romania Int'l (RRI)
9520	250	PHL	PUG	R. Veritas Asia
9525	50	USA	YFR	BBC World Service
9525	250	USA	GRV	BBG - VO America (VOA)
9525	500	CHN	KAS	China Radio Int'l
9525	100	KOR	KIM	R. Canada Int'l (RCI)
9525	250	CAN	SAC	R. Nederland Wereldomroep
9525	100	POL	WWA	R. Polonia
9525	250	ROU	GAL	R. Romania Int'l (RRI)
9525	500	ARS	RIY	Saudi Radio
9525	100	SWZ	MAN	TWR Africa
9525	500	TUR	EMR	VO Turkey
9525	250	INS	dom	Voice of Indonesia, Cimanggis
9530	300	AUT	MOS	Adventist World R. (AWR)
9530	250	UAE	DHA	Adventist World R. (AWR)
9530	500	G	RMP	BBC World Service

kHz	kW	Ctry	Site	Station, location
9530	250	PHL	PHT	BBG - VO America (VOA)
9530	100	CHN	dom	CNR 2/8, Tianshui
9530	250	UAE	DHA	FEBA Radio
9530	300	GUF	GUF	R. Japan (NHK World)
9530	10	B	dom	R. Nova Visão, Santa Maria
9530	50	VTN	dom	VO Vietnam, Hanoi
9535	250	PHL	PHT	BBG - VO America (VOA)
9535	250	USA	GRV	BBG - VO America (VOA)
9535	100	CHN	XIA	China Radio Int'l
9535	150	CHN	XIA	China Radio Int'l
9535	250	RRW	KIG	Deutsche Welle
9535	0.6	J	dom	Nippon Hoso Kyokai, Fukuoka 1
9535	0.6	J	dom	Nippon Hoso Kyokai, Sapporo 1
9535	300	J	YAM	R. Canada Int'l (RCI)
9535	350	E	NOB	R. Exterior de España (REE)
9535	300	J	YAM	R. Japan (NHK World)
9535	300	G	SKN	R. Korea Int'l
9535	250	THA	UDO	R. Thailand
9540	250	SNG	SGP	BBC World Service
9540	250	MRC	MOR	BBG - VO America (VOA)
9540	300	J	YAM	R. Japan (NHK World)
9540	250	ROU	TIG	R. Romania Int'l (RRI)
9540	100	UZB	TAC	R. Tashkent Int'l
9545	250	PHL	PHT	BBG - VO America (VOA)
9545	500	D	NAU	Deutsche Welle
9545	500	D	WER	Deutsche Welle
9545	250	POR	SIN	Deutsche Welle
9545	250	RRW	KIG	Deutsche Welle
9545	250	ROU	TIG	R. Romania Int'l (RRI)
9545	10	SLM	dom	Solomon Is Broadc. Corp.
9545	500	IRN	KAM	VO the Islamic Rep. of Iran
9550	250	UAE	DHA	Adventist World R. (AWR)
9550	250	BGD	DKA	Bangladesh Betar
9550	150	CHN	KUN	China Radio Int'l
9550	250	RRW	KIG	FEBA Radio
9550	0.9	J	dom	Nippon Hoso Kyokai, Tokyo 1
9550	250	CUB	HAB	R. Habana Cuba
9550	250	CUB	HAB	R. Nac.Venezuela - Canal Int'l
9550	10	COD	dom	R. Okapi, Kinshasa
9550	10	B	dom	R. RGS, Porto Alegre
9550	100	VTN	VNI	VO Vietnam (VOV)
9552	7.5	INS	dom	RRI Makassar
9555	100	D	BIB	BBG - RFE/RL
9555	250	GRC	KAV	BBG - VO America (VOA)
9555	250	PHL	PHT	BBG - VO America (VOA)
9555	250	THA	UDO	BBG - VO America (VOA)
9555	500	THA	UDO	BBG - VO America (VOA)
9555	250	D	WER	R. Canada Int'l (RCI)
9555	100	G	SKN	R. Canada Int'l (RCI)
9555	300	G	SKN	R. Canada Int'l (RCI)
9555	500	F	ISS	R. France Int'l (RFI)
9555	500	ARS	RIY	Saudi Radio
9555	500	IRN	KAM	VO the Islamic Rep. of Iran
9555	100	D	JUL	VOR - Radiokanal Sodruzhestvo
9560	250	USA	DLN	BBG - VO America (VOA)
9560	250	CAN	SAC	China Radio Int'l
9560	100	CHN	KAS	China Radio Int'l
9560	250	CLN	TRM	Deutsche Welle
9560	100	AUS	SHP	R. Australia
9560	300	J	YAM	R. Japan (NHK World)
9560	250	CAN	SAC	R. Korea Int'l
9560	250	TUR	CAK	VO Turkey
9560	500	TUR	EMR	VO Turkey
9560	50	CHN	dom	Xinjiang-Ug, Urumqi
9560	500	FIN	POR	YLE R. Finland
9561	100	ETH	GJW	R. Ethiopia
9565	300	G	SKN	BBC World Service
9565	250	USA	GRV	BBG - R. Martí
9565	100	D	BIB	BBG - RFE/RL
9565	250	MRC	MOR	BBG - RFE/RL
9565	250	MRC	MOR	BBG - VO America (VOA)
9565	250	AFS	MEY	Channel Africa
9565	500	D	WER	Deutsche Welle
9565	250	POR	SIN	Deutsche Welle
9565	250	RRW	KIG	Deutsche Welle
9565	300	G	SKN	R. Canada Int'l (RCI)
9565	100	KOR	KIM	R. Canada Int'l (RCI)
9565	250	UAE	DHA	R. France Int'l (RFI)
9565	250	ROU	TIG	R. Romania Int'l (RRI)
9565	250	TWN	TAI	R. Taiwan Int'l
9565	20	B	dom	R. Tupi, Curitiba
9565	300	G	SKN	United Nations Radio
9565	500	IRN	KAM	VO the Islamic Rep. of Iran
9570	100	MRA	SAI	BBG - R. Free Asia (RFA)
9570	250	GRC	KAV	BBG - RFE/RL
9570	100	CHN	KAS	China Radio Int'l
9570	100	CHN	XIA	China Radio Int'l
9570	250	CUB	HAB	China Radio Int'l
9570	100	CHN	dom	CNR 2, Golmud
9570	100	KOR	KIM	R. Korea Int'l
9570	250	ROU	GAL	R. Romania Int'l (RRI)
9570	250	PHL	PUG	R. Veritas Asia
9570	100	I	ROM	RAI International
9575	50	IND	DEL	All India Radio (AIR)
9575	50	IND	dom	All India Radio, Delhi
9575	500	USA	GRV	BBG - VO America (VOA)
9575	500	UAE	DHA	R. Japan (NHK World)
9575	250	MRC	NAD	R. Méditerranée Int'l
9575	250	ROU	TIG	R. Romania Int'l (RRI)
9575	500	IRN	SIR	VO the Islamic Rep. of Iran
9580	250	GAB	GAB	Africa No.1
9580	100	SNG	SGP	BBC World Service
9580	250	THA	NAK	BBC World Service
9580	250	CUB	HAB	China Radio Int'l
9580	250	BIH	BIJ	Int'l R. of Serbia&Monten.
9580	0.25	PHL	dom	Philippine Fed. Catholic Broadc., Marulas
9580	250	AUS	SHP	R. Australia
9580	250	HNG	JBR	R. Budapest
9580	120	CHN	XIA	R. France Int'l (RFI)
9580	250	KOR	KIM	R. Korea Int'l
9580	50	ARS	JED	Saudi Radio
9580	500	IRN	SIR	VO the Islamic Rep. of Iran
9585	100	D	LAM	BBG - R. Farda
9585	250	MRC	MOR	BBG - R. Farda
9585	500	CHN	KAS	China Radio Int'l
9585	500	CHN	KUN	China Radio Int'l
9585	250	CLN	TRM	Deutsche Welle
9585	100	GUM	TWR	KTWR (TWR Guam)
9585	10	B	dom	R. CBN (Globo), São Paulo
9585	100	PAK	ISL	R. Pakistan
9585	100	SWZ	MAN	TWR Africa
9585	250	CVA	SMG	Vatican Radio
9590	100	D	LAM	BBG - VO America (VOA)
9590	150	CHN	KUN	China Radio Int'l
9590	500	CHN	SZG	China Radio Int'l
9590	100	CHN	dom	CNR 1, Golmud
9590	100	AUS	SHP	R. Australia
9590	250	ATN	BON	R. Nederland Wereldomroep
9590	250	MDG	MDC	R. Nederland Wereldomroep
9590	250	ATN	BON	R. Vlaanderen Int'l (RVI)
9590	250	G	SKN	R. Vlaanderen Int'l (RVI)
9590	500	IRN	SIR	VO the Islamic Rep. of Iran
9595	100	IND	DEL	All India Radio (AIR)
9595	250	IND	ALG	All India Radio (AIR)
9595	250	IND	DEL	All India Radio (AIR)
9595	250	IND	dom	All India Radio, Aligarth
9595	100	D	BIB	BBG - RFE/RL
9595	250	GRC	KAV	BBG - RFE/RL
9595	250	GRC	KAV	BBG - VO America (VOA)
9595	350	E	NOB	R. Exterior de España (REE)
9595	250	ASC	ASC	R. France Int'l (RFI)
9595	1	URG	dom	R. Monte Carlo, Montevideo
9595	500	IRN	KAM	VO the Islamic Rep. of Iran
9595	250	TUR	EMR	VO Turkey
9595	250	FIN	POR	YLE R. Finland
9598	1	MEX	dom	R. UNAM-Universidad Nacional Autónoma
9600	100	SNG	SGP	BBC World Service
9600	150	CHN	XIA	China Radio Int'l
9600	500	CHN	KAS	China Radio Int'l
9600	250	BUL	PLD	R. Bulgaria
9600	250	CUB	HAB	R. Habana Cuba
9600	7.5	B	dom	R. MEC, Rio de Janeiro
9600	500	CVA	SMG	Vatican Radio
9600	100	RUS	KHB	Vatican Radio
9600	50	CHN	dom	Xinjiang-Ch, Urumqi
9600	250	FIN	POR	YLE R. Finland
9605	300	J	YAM	BBC World Service
9605	250	SEY	SEY	BBC World Service
9605	100	SNG	SGP	BBC World Service
9605	250	THA	NAK	BBC World Service
9605	100	D	BIB	BBG - RFE/RL
9605	100	D	LAM	BBG - RFE/RL

kHz	kW	Ctry	Site	Station, location
9605	250	GRC	KAV	BBG - RFE/RL
9605	250	CVA	SMG	Vatican Radio
9610	500	AFS	MEY	BBC World Service
9610	250	ASC	ASC	BBC World Service
9610	100	CHN	KAS	China Radio Int'l
9610	150	CHN	KUN	China Radio Int'l
9610	500	CHN	KAS	China Radio Int'l
9610	50	CHN	dom	CNR 8, Beijing
9610	250	CLN	TRM	Deutsche Welle
9610	100	D	JUL	IBRA Radio
9610	250	ROU	TIG	R. Romania Int'l (RRI)
9610	250	TWN	TNN	R. Taiwan Int'l
9610	50	COG	dom	Telediffusion du Congo, Brazzaville
9610	500	IRN	SIR	VO the Islamic Rep. of Iran
9610	500	FIN	POR	YLE R. Finland
9615	500	CHN	URU	China Radio Int'l
9615	250	CLN	TRM	Deutsche Welle
9615	500	D	WER	Deutsche Welle
9615	100	ALS	NLS	KNLS International
9615	250	D	WER	R. Canada Int'l (RCI)
9615	100	G	SKN	R. Canada Int'l (RCI)
9615	7.5	B	dom	R. Cultura, São Paulo
9615	500	IRN	KAM	VO the Islamic Rep. of Iran
9620	250	IND	ALG	All India Radio (AIR)
9620	250	THA	UDO	BBG - RFE/RL
9620	250	THA	UDO	BBG - VO America (VOA)
9620	100	CHN	XIA	China Radio Int'l
9620	150	CHN	dom	CNR 2, Beijing
9620	350	E	NOB	R. Exterior de España (REE)
9620	0.35	URG	dom	S.O.D.R. E., Montevideo
9620	500	AFS	MEY	TWR Africa
9625	500	UAE	DHA	BBG - R. Free Asia (RFA)
9625	100	D	LAM	BBG - RFE/RL
9625		CAN	dom	CBC, North Quebec via Sackville
9625	15	BOL	dom	R. Fides, La Paz
9625	250	ATN	BON	R. Nederland Wereldomroep
9625	300	G	WOF	Sudan Radio Service
9625	500	TUR	EMR	VO Turkey
9630	250	SEY	SEY	BBC World Service
9630	100	CHN	dom	CNR 1, Golmud
9630	10	CHL	dom	R. Agricultura, Santiago
9630	10	B	dom	R. Aparecida, Aparecida
9630	250	AUS	DAR	R. Australia
9630	350	E	NOB	R. Exterior de España (REE)
9630	250	FIN	POR	YLE R. Finland
9635	250	IND	ALG	All India Radio (AIR)
9635	250	CYP	CYP	BBC World Service
9635	300	CYP	CYP	BBC World Service
9635	500	G	RMP	BBC World Service
9635	250	OMA	SLA	BBC World Service
9635	250	GRC	KAV	BBG - RFE/RL
9635	100	D	BIB	BBG - VO America (VOA)
9635	250	MRC	MOR	BBG - VO America (VOA)
9635	100	CHN	KAS	China Radio Int'l
9635	100	GUM	TWR	KTWR (TWR Guam)
9635	100	MLI	dom	Office de Radiodif. Tv. du Mali, Kati
9635	100	CHN	XIA	R. Canada Int'l (RCI)
9635	250	ROU	TIG	R. Romania Int'l (RRI)
9635	250	TWN	TNN	R. Taiwan Int'l
9635	500	IRN	KAM	VO the Islamic Rep. of Iran
9635	100	CHL	SGO	Voz Cristiana/Voz Crista
9640	500	CHN	KAS	China Radio Int'l
9640	250	ATG	ATG	Deutsche Welle
9640	250	KOR	KIM	R. Korea Int'l
9645	500	UAE	DHA	BBG - R. Free Asia (RFA)
9645	250	CLN	IRA	BBG - VO America (VOA)
9645	250	PHL	PHT	BBG - VO America (VOA)
9645	250	THA	UDO	BBG - VO America (VOA)
9645	500	CHN	KUN	China Radio Int'l
9645	100	CHN	dom	CNR 1, Beijing
9645	5	CTR	dom	Faro del Caribe, San José
9645	7.5	B	dom	R. Bandeirantes, São Paulo
9645	100	CVA	SMG	Vatican Radio
9645	500	CVA	SMG	Vatican Radio
9650	100	D	BIB	BBG - RFE/RL
9650	100	D	BIB	BBG - VO America (VOA)
9650	250	MRC	MOR	BBG - VO America (VOA)
9650	250	CAN	SAC	R. Korea Int'l
9650	250	ROU	GAL	R. Romania Int'l (RRI)
9650	100	AFS	dom	R. Sonder Grense, Meyerton
9650	50	VTN	dom	VO Vietnam, Xuan Mai
9655	250	UAE	DHA	Adventist World R. (AWR)
9655	250	MRC	MOR	BBG - VO America (VOA)
9655	150	CHN	KUN	China Radio Int'l
9655	500	CHN	KUN	China Radio Int'l
9655	100	CHN	dom	CNR 1, Lingshi
9655	250	CLN	TRM	Deutsche Welle
9655	250	RRW	KIG	Deutsche Welle
9655	350	E	NOB	R. Exterior de España (REE)
9655	300	J	YAM	R. France Int'l (RFI)
9655	250	CUB	HAB	R. Habana Cuba
9655	10	CUB	dom	R. Rebelde/Reloj
9655	250	ROU	GAL	R. Romania Int'l (RRI)
9655	250	ROU	TIG	R. Romania Int'l (RRI)
9655	100	I	ROM	RAI International
9655+	200	D	WER	Deutsche Welle
9660	10	AUS	BRN	BBC World Service
9660	250	UAE	DHA	FEBA Radio
9660	100	D	JUL	IBRA Radio
9660	1	BOL	dom	R. ABC, Santa Cruz
9660	10	AUS	BRN	R. Australia
9660	120	CHN	BEI	R. Exterior de España (REE)
9660	300	G	SKN	R. Japan (NHK World)
9660	300	GUF	GUF	R. Japan (NHK World)
9660	100	TWN	HUW	R. Taiwan Int'l
9660	500	AFS	MEY	TWR Africa
9660	500	CVA	SMG	Vatican Radio
9660	200	KRE	KUJ	VO Korea
9660	500	IRN	SIR	VO the Islamic Rep. of Iran
9665	250	B	BRA	China Radio Int'l
9665	100	CHN	KAS	China Radio Int'l
9665	150	CHN	BEI	China Radio Int'l
9665	150	CHN	KUN	China Radio Int'l
9665		KRE	dom	Korean Cent. B'casting Stn., Pyongyang
9665	300	AUT	MOS	R. Canada Int'l (RCI)
9665	350	E	NOB	R. Exterior de España (REE)
9665	10	B	dom	R. Marumby, Florianópolis
9665	250	B	BRA	Radiobrás
9670	250	ATG	ATG	BBC World Service
9670	250	CYP	CYP	BBC World Service
9670	250	G	WOF	BBC World Service
9670	300	G	SKN	BBC World Service
9670	250	OMA	SLA	BBC World Service
9670	250	USA	DLN	BBC World Service
9670	500	D	WER	BBG - R. Free Asia (RFA)
9670	250	USA	GRV	BBG - VO America (VOA)
9670	500	CHN	URU	China Radio Int'l
9670	100	J	YAM	R. Canada Int'l (RCI)
9670	250	PHL	PUG	R. Veritas Asia
9670	100	I	ROM	RAI International
9670	300	POR	LIS	RDP Internacional
9675	250	PHL	PHT	BBG - RFE/RL
9675	100	STP	SAO	BBG - VO America (VOA)
9675	150	CHN	KUN	China Radio Int'l
9675	300	CHN	BEI	China Radio Int'l
9675	100	CHN	dom	CNR 1, Beijing
9675	100	PNG	dom	Port Moresby
9675	10	B	dom	R. Canção Nova, Cachoeira Paulista
9675	7.5	PRU	dom	R. Pacifico, Lima
9675	500	ARS	RIY	Saudi Radio
9675	250	AFS	MEY	TWR Africa
9677	5	AZE	dom	Ädälän Säsi Radiosu, Stepanakert
9680	100	SNG	SGP	BBC World Service
9680	100	D	BIB	BBG - RFE/RL
9680	250	GRC	KAV	BBG - RFE/RL
9680	250	MRC	MOR	BBG - RFE/RL
9680	100	D	JUL	BBG - VO America (VOA)
9680	100	D	LAM	BBG - VO America (VOA)
9680	250	PHL	PHT	BBG - VO America (VOA)
9680	250	BIH	BIJ	Int'l R. of Serbia&Monten.
9680	350	E	NOB	R. Exterior de España (REE)
9680	100	TWN	HUW	R. Taiwan Int'l
9680	100	USA	YFR	R. Taiwan Int'l
9680	250	THA	UDO	R. Thailand
9680	250	INS	dom	RRI Jakarta, Cimanggis
9680	100	BUL	SOF	The Voice - Africa
9685	500	AFS	MEY	BBC World Service
9685	250	GRC	KAV	BBG - VO America (VOA)
9685	250	AFS	MEY	Channel Africa
9685	500	CHN	KUN	China Radio Int'l
9685	7.5	B	dom	R. Gazeta, São Paulo
9685	300	J	YAM	R. Japan (NHK World)

kHz	kW	Ctry	Site	Station, location
9685	500	IRN	SIR	VO the Islamic Rep. of Iran
9690	500	IND	BGL	All India Radio (AIR)
9690	500	UAE	DHA	BBG - R. Free Asia (RFA)
9690	500	CHN	URU	China Radio Int'l
9690	350	E	NOB	China Radio Int'l
9690	100	CHN	dom	CNR 8, Lingshi
9690	250	ATG	ATG	Deutsche Welle
9690	100	ALS	NLS	KNLS International
9690	350	E	NOB	R. Exterior de España (REE)
9690	250	ROU	GAL	R. Romania Int'l (RRI)
9690	100	USA	YFR	R. Taiwan Int'l
9690	10	MDG	dom	R. Nasionaly Malagasy, Antananarivo
9690	50	ARG	BUE	Rdif. Argentina al Exterior
9690	250	NIG	IKO	VO Nigeria
9690	100	USA	YFR	WYFR - Family Radio
9695	100	D	JUL	Adventist World R. (AWR)
9695	300	G	WOF	BBC World Service
9695	100	D	BIB	BBG - RFE/RL
9695	250	THA	UDO	BBG - RFE/RL
9695	100	CHN	KAS	China Radio Int'l
9695	300	CHN	BEI	China Radio Int'l
9695	500	CHN	KAS	China Radio Int'l
9695	300	J	YAM	R. Japan (NHK World)
9695	7.5	B	dom	R. Rio Mar, Manaus
9695	500	AFS	MEY	TWR Africa
9695	500	CVA	SMG	Vatican Radio
9695	500	IRN	KAM	VO the Islamic Rep. of Iran
9700	500	CHN	KAS	China Radio Int'l
9700	500	BUL	PLD	R. Bulgaria
9704	100	ETH	dom	R. Ethiopia, Gedja
9705	250	IND	PAN	All India Radio (AIR)
9705	250	THA	UDO	BBG - R. Aap Ki Dunyaa
9705	300	G	WOF	BBG - RFE/RL
9705	100	MRA	SAI	BBG - VO America (VOA)
9705	100	NGR	dom	La Voix Du Sahel, Niamey
9705	7.5	B	dom	R. Nacional, Rio de Janeiro
9705		CHN	dom	V.O.Pujiang, Shanghai
9705	500	IRN	KAM	VO the Islamic Rep. of Iran
9705	15	CHN	dom	Xinjiang-Kg, Urumqi
9710	250	PHL	PHT	BBG - VO America (VOA)
9710	100	CHN	dom	CNR 1, Shijiazhuang
9710	500	D	WER	Deutsche Welle
9710	100	AUS	SHP	R. Australia
9710	250	HNG	JBR	R. Budapest
9710	250	CAN	SAC	R. Canada Int'l (RCI)
9710	350	E	NOB	R. Exterior de España (REE)
9710	100	J	YAM	R. Japan (NHK World)
9710	100	LTU	SIT	R. Vilnius
9710	250	RUS	MSK	VO Russia (VOR)
9710	500	IRN	KAM	VO the Islamic Rep. of Iran
9715	100	D	LAM	BBG - RFE/RL
9715	250	CLN	TRM	Deutsche Welle
9715	500	D	WER	Deutsche Welle
9715	250	ATN	BON	R. Nederland Wereldomroep
9715	100	UZB	TAC	R. Tashkent Int'l
9715	100	POR	LIS	RDP Internacional
9717	1	BOL	dom	R. La Platal, Sucre
9720	250	THA	UDO	BBG - VO America (VOA)
9720	500	GUF	GUF	China Radio Int'l
9720	150	CHN	dom	CNR 2, Baoji
9720	250	RRW	KIG	Deutsche Welle
9720	500	TUN	SFA	RT Tunisienne (ERTT)
9720	250	AFS	MEY	TWR Africa
9720	500	AFS	MEY	TWR Africa
9720	120	RUS	KLG	VO Russia (VOR)
9722	1	PRU	dom	R. Victoria, Lima
9725	100	D	BIB	BBG - RFE/RL
9725	250	MRC	MOR	BBG - RFE/RL
9725	250	PHL	PHT	BBG - RFE/RL
9725	250	THA	UDO	BBG - RFE/RL
9725	100	MRA	SAI	BBG - VO America (VOA)
9725	500	CHN	URU	China Radio Int'l
9725	50	CTR	CHA	Dr Gene Scott (Univ.Netw.)
9725	7.5	B	dom	R. Clube Paranaense, Curitiba
9725	250	THA	UDO	R. Thailand
9730	100	D	JUL	Bible Voice B'casting
9730	100	CHN	XIA	China Radio Int'l
9730	150	CHN	KUN	China Radio Int'l
9730	100	CHN	dom	CNR 2, Tianshui
9730	100	SNG	SNG	R. Australia
9730	300	J	YAM	R. Canada Int'l (RCI)
9730	100	AFS	MEY	R. France Int'l (RFI)
9730	500	ARS	RIY	Saudi Radio
9730	100	VTN	VNI	VO Vietnam (VOV)
9730	500	FIN	POR	YLE R. Finland
9731	50	BRM	dom	R. Myanmar, Yangon
9735	500	D	WER	Deutsche Welle
9735	250	POR	SIN	Deutsche Welle
9735	250	RRW	KIG	Deutsche Welle
9735	250	HNG	JBR	R. Budapest
9735	250	EGY	ABS	R. Cairo
9735	100	PRG	dom	R. Nal. del Paraguay, Asunción
9735	250	IRN	AHW	VO the Islamic Rep. of Iran
9740	250	SNG	SGP	BBC World Service
9740	500	IRN	KAM	VO the Islamic Rep. of Iran
9743	10	INS	dom	RRI Sorong
9745	5	BHR	dom	Bahrain Radio & Television Corp.
9745	250	ATN	BON	China Radio Int'l
9745	500	CHN	KUN	China Radio Int'l
9745	500	CHN	URU	China Radio Int'l
9745	500	D	WER	Deutsche Welle
9745	100	EQA	QUI	HCJB
9745	250	ROU	TIG	R. Romania Int'l (RRI)
9750	100	AFS	MEY	Amateur R. Mirror Int'l
9750	250	CYP	CYP	BBC World Service
9750	300	CYP	CYP	BBC World Service
9750	250	SEY	SEY	BBC World Service
9750	100	D	LAM	BBG - VO America (VOA)
9750	250	G	WOF	BBG - VO America (VOA)
9750	50	CHN	dom	Nei Menggu-Mo, Hohhot
9750	500	G	RMP	R. Japan (NHK World)
9750	300	J	YAM	R. Japan (NHK World)
9750	500	KWT	KBD	R. Kuwait
9750	100	MLA	dom	Radio Television Malaysia, Kajang
9750	100	MLA	KAJ	VO Malaysia
9750	500	IRN	SIR	VO the Islamic Rep. of Iran
9755	500	GUF	GUF	China Radio Int'l
9755	100	CHN	dom	CNR 2, Tianshui
9755	250	RRW	KIG	Deutsche Welle
9755	250	CAN	SAC	R. Canada Int'l (RCI)
9755	100	I	ROM	RAI International
9755	300	POR	LIS	RDP Internacional
9755	500	CVA	SMG	Vatican Radio
9755	500	IRN	SIR	VO the Islamic Rep. of Iran
9760	250	UAE	DHA	Adventist World R. (AWR)
9760	250	PHL	PHT	BBG - VO America (VOA)
9760	300	CYP	CYP	Cyprus Broadc. Corporation
9760	250	D	WER	R. Canada Int'l (RCI)
9760	100	I	ROM	RAI International
9760+	33	G	RMP	The Voice - Africa
9765	100	CHN	KAS	China Radio Int'l
9765	500	CHN	KAS	China Radio Int'l
9765	250	D	WER	Gospel for Asia
9765	100	EQA	QUI	HCJB
9765	100	CTR	CRI	R. Exterior de España (REE)
9770	300	AUT	MOS	Adventist World R. (AWR)
9770	250	CLN	IRA	BBG - RFE/RL
9770	100	D	BIB	BBG - RFE/RL
9770	250	GRC	KAV	BBG - RFE/RL
9770	500	CHN	KAS	China Radio Int'l
9770	500	CHN	URU	China Radio Int'l
9770	500	D	WER	Deutsche Welle
9770	250	CAN	SAC	R. Canada Int'l (RCI)
9770	100	CHN	KAS	R. Canada Int'l (RCI)
9770	250	KOR	KIM	R. Korea Int'l
9770	100	CLN	EKA	R. Sri Lanka (SLBC)
9770	250	USA	DLN	VO Greece (ERA5)
9770	500	RUS	IRK	VO Russia (VOR)
9770	500	IRN	SIR	VO the Islamic Rep. of Iran
9775	500	MRA	TIN	BBG - R. Free Asia (RFA)
9775	100	BOT	BOT	BBG - VO America (VOA)
9775	250	USA	GRV	BBG - VO America (VOA)
9775	150	CHN	dom	CNR 2, Beijing
9775	500	D	WER	Deutsche Welle
9775	250	HNG	JBR	R. Budapest
9775	500	IRN	SIR	VO the Islamic Rep. of Iran
9780	250	CLN	IRA	BBG - VO America (VOA)
9780	250	PHL	PHT	BBG - VO America (VOA)
9780	100	STP	SAO	BBG - VO America (VOA)
9780	250	ATG	ATG	Deutsche Welle
9780	100	GUM	SDA	KSDA (AWR Guam)
9780		CHN	dom	Qinghai-Ch, Xining

kHz	kW	Ctry	Site	Station, location
9780	250	EGY	ABS	R. Cairo
9780	100	TWN	HUW	R. Taiwan Int'l
9780	500	TUR	EMR	VO Turkey
9780	100	CHL	SGO	Voz Cristiana/Voz Crista
9780	50	YEM	dom	Yemen R., San'a
9785	125	PHL	PHT	BBG - R. Aap Ki Dunyaa
9785	250	THA	UDO	BBG - R. Farda
9785	250	GRC	KAV	BBG - VO America (VOA)
9785	100	STP	SAO	BBG - VO America (VOA)
9785	500	THA	UDO	BBG - VO America (VOA)
9785	150	CHN	KUN	China Radio Int'l
9785	600	CHN	JIN	China Radio Int'l
9785	250	UAE	DHA	Gospel for Asia
9785	100	EQA	QUI	HCJB
9785	500	IRN	SIR	VO the Islamic Rep. of Iran
9790	250	THA	NAK	BBC World Service
9790	250	PHL	PHT	BBG - VO America (VOA)
9790	250	CAN	SAC	China Radio Int'l
9790	250	CUB	HAB	China Radio Int'l
9790	500	D	NAU	Deutsche Welle
9790	250	CAN	SAC	R. Canada Int'l (RCI)
9790	500	F	ISS	R. France Int'l (RFI)
9790	250	GAB	GAB	R. France Int'l (RFI)
9790	500	F	ISS	R. Monte Carlo-MO
9790	250	ATN	BON	R. Nederland Wereldomroep
9790	250	TWN	KOU	R. Taiwan Int'l
9790	250	TWN	TNN	R. Taiwan Int'l
9790	500	IRN	SIR	VO the Islamic Rep. of Iran
9795	250	CYP	CYP	BBC World Service
9795	100	D	LAM	BBG - R. Farda
9795	250	PHL	PHT	BBG - VO America (VOA)
9795	500	CHN	URU	China Radio Int'l
9795	100	PHL	BOC	FEBC Philippines
9795	100	SNG	SNG	R. Nederland Wereldomroep
9795	250	SNG	SNG	R. Nederland Wereldomroep
9800	300	AUT	MOS	Adventist World R. (AWR)
9800	100	D	JUL	Adventist World R. (AWR)
9800	250	CLN	IRA	BBG - VO America (VOA)
9800	500	G	RMP	Leading The Way
9800	500	GUF	GUF	R. France Int'l (RFI)
9800	500	RUS	ARM	VO Russia (VOR)
9800+	40	CAN	SAC	Deutsche Welle
9800+	70	CAN	SAC	R. Canada Int'l (RCI)
9800+	70	CAN	SAC	R. Nederland Wereldomroep
9800+	70	CAN	SAC	R. Sweden
9800+	500	RUS	ARM	VO Russia (VOR)
9805	250	USA	GRV	BBG - R. Martí
9805	100	D	LAM	BBG - RFE/RL
9805	100	BOT	BOT	BBG - VO America (VOA)
9805	250	MRC	MOR	BBG - VO America (VOA)
9805	250	F	ISS	R. France Int'l (RFI)
9805	250	GAB	GAB	R. France Int'l (RFI)
9805	100	KOR	KIM	R. Korea Int'l
9805	250	PHL	PUG	R. Veritas Asia
9805	500	FIN	POR	YLE R. Finland
9810	250	IND	PAN	All India Radio (AIR)
9810	100	STP	SAO	BBG - VO America (VOA)
9810	100	CHN	dom	CNR 1, Nanning
9810	100	CHN	dom	CNR 2, Xi'an
9810	250	CAN	SAC	R. Canada Int'l (RCI)
9810	250	THA	UDO	R. Thailand
9810	300	G	SKN	United Nations Radio
9815	300	G	WOF	BBC World Service
9815	500	G	RMP	BBC World Service
9815	100	BOT	BOT	BBG - VO America (VOA)
9815	250	CLN	TRM	Deutsche Welle
9815	250	D	WER	Ev. Missions-Gemeinden
9815	100	POR	LIS	RDP Internacional
9815	250	POR	SIN	RDP Internacional
9815	500	FIN	POR	YLE R. Finland
9815+	40	HOL	FLE	R. Canada Int'l (RCI)
9820	250	IND	PAN	All India Radio (AIR)
9820	250	IND	dom	All India Radio, Panaji
9820	150	CHN	dom	CNR 2, Xi'an
9820	300	AUT	MOS	FEBA Radio
9820		CHN	dom	Guangxi FBS, Nanning
9820	250	CUB	HAB	R. Habana Cuba
9820	250	CUB	HAB	R. Nac.Venezuela - Canal Int'l
9820	10	B	dom	R. Nove de Julho, São Paulo
9820	100	D	JUL	R. Xoriyo
9820	100	D	JUL	VO Democratic Eritrea
9820	100	D	JUL	VO Ethiopian Medhin
9820	100	D	JUL	VO Oromo Liberation
9820	200	RUS	MSK	VOR - Radiokanal Sodruzhestvo
9825	250	G	WOF	BBC World Service
9825	300	G	SKN	BBC World Service
9825	250	MRA	TIN	BBG - R. Free Asia (RFA)
9825	100	D	LAM	BBG - RFE/RL
9825	250	GRC	KAV	BBG - RFE/RL
9825	250	HNG	JBR	R. Budapest
9825	100	J	YAM	R. Japan (NHK World)
9825	1	KIR	dom	Radio Kiribati, Tarawa
9825	500	IRN	SIR	VO the Islamic Rep. of Iran
9830	300	AUT	MOS	Adventist World R. (AWR)
9830	250	CLN	IRA	BBG - RFE/RL
9830	250	THA	UDO	BBG - RFE/RL
9830	100	STP	SAO	BBG - VO America (VOA)
9830	100	CHN	dom	CNR 1, Beijing
9830	100	HRV	DEA	Glas Hrvatske
9830	300	J	YAM	R. France Int'l (RFI)
9830	500	JOR	AKA	R. Jordan (JRTV)
9830	200	RUS	MSK	VO Russia (VOR)
9835	100	IND	DEL	All India Radio (AIR)
9835	250	IND	DEL	All India Radio (AIR)
9835	50	IND	dom	All India Radio, Delhi
9835	250	GRC	KAV	BBG - RFE/RL
9835	100	D	BIB	BBG - VO America (VOA)
9835	200	RUS	SAM	R. Ibrahim
9835	300	J	YAM	R. Japan (NHK World)
9835	500	IRN	KAM	VO the Islamic Rep. of Iran
9835	50	CHN	dom	Xinjiang-Ch, Urumqi
9840	100	D	LAM	BBG - RFE/RL
9840	250	RUS	MSK	FEBA Radio
9840	250	THA	UDO	R. Thailand
9840	100	ROM	ROM	RAI International
9840	500	TUR	CAK	VO Turkey
9840	500	TUR	EMR	VO Turkey
9840	100	VTN	VNI	VO Vietnam (VOV)
9840	500	USA	SHB	WSHB - World Harvest R.
9845	80	PLW	HBN	BBG - R. Free Asia (RFA)
9845	250	PHL	PHT	BBG - VO America (VOA)
9845	100	CHN	dom	CNR 1, Beijing
9845	250	ATN	BON	R. Nederland Wereldomroep
9850	250	GRC	KAV	BBG - RFE/RL
9850	250	MRC	MOR	BBG - VO America (VOA)
9850	100	I	ROM	RAI International
9850	250	CVA	SMG	Vatican Radio
9850	200	KRE	KUJ	VO Korea
9850	50	VTN	dom	VO Vietnam, Xuan Mai
9855	250	ASC	ASC	BBC World Service
9855	500	CHN	URU	China Radio Int'l
9855	250	EGY	ABS	R. Cairo
9855	500	KWT	KBD	R. Kuwait
9855	100	UZB	TAC	The Voice - Africa
9855	500	IRN	SIR	VO the Islamic Rep. of Iran
9860	100	CHN	BEI	China Radio Int'l
9860	500	CHN	JIN	China Radio Int'l
9860	500	CHN	URU	China Radio Int'l
9860	100	CHN	dom	CNR 1, Beijing
9860	250	RUS	SAM	FEBA Radio
9860	500	IRN	SIR	VO the Islamic Rep. of Iran
9865	100	D	BIB	BBG - RFE/RL
9865	100	D	LAM	BBG - RFE/RL
9865	250	MRC	MOR	BBG - RFE/RL
9865	500	CHN	KUN	China Radio Int'l
9865	100	ZMB	LUS	Christian Voice
9865	100	GUM	TWR	KTWR (TWR Guam)
9865	100	CZE	LIT	R. Prague
9865	500	S	HOR	R. Sweden
9865	250	CVA	SMG	Vatican Radio
9865	100	UZB	TAC	Vatican Radio
9865	500	RUS	NVS	VO Russia (VOR)
9865	500	IRN	KAM	VO the Islamic Rep. of Iran
9865	250	RUS	SPB	VOR - Radiokanal Sodruzhestvo
9870	250	ASC	ASC	BBC World Service
9870	150	CHN	BEI	China Radio Int'l
9870	250	RRW	KIG	Deutsche Welle
9870	250	HNG	JBR	R. Budapest
9870	100	KOR	KIM	R. Korea Int'l
9870	100	NZL	RAN	R. New Zealand Int'l (RNZI)
9870	300	AUT	MOS	R. Österreich 1
9870	500	ARS	RIY	Saudi Radio

kHz	kW	Ctry	Site	Station, location
9870	100	F	MCO	TWR Europe
9875	300	AUT	MOS	Adventist World R. (AWR)
9875	250	IND	DEL	All India Radio (AIR)
9875	250	CYP	CYP	BBC World Service
9875	300	CYP	CYP	BBC World Service
9875	500	G	RMP	BBC World Service
9875	100	D	LAM	BBG - R. Free Asia (RFA)
9875	80	PLW	HBN	BBG - R. Free Asia (RFA)
9875	250	MRC	MOR	BBG - VO America (VOA)
9875	250	RRW	KIG	Deutsche Welle
9875	300	J	YAM	R. Japan (NHK World)
9875	100	LTU	SIT	R. Vilnius
9875	50	VTN	dom	VO Vietnam, Hanoi
9875	500	RUS	TCH	VOR - Radiokanal Sodruzhestvo
9875+	35	G	RMP	Brigham Young Univ. Radio
9875+	125	G	RMP	R. Australia
9875+	75	G	RMP	R. Japan (NHK World)
9875+	125	G	RMP	R. Korea Int'l
9875+		G	RMP	R. New Zealand Int'l (RNZI)
9880	100	CHN	KUN	China Radio Int'l
9880	100	CHN	XIA	R. Canada Int'l (RCI)
9880	500	KWT	KBD	R. Kuwait
9880	100	CZE	LIT	R. Prague
9880+	500	KWT	KBD	R. Kuwait
9885	500	MRA	TIN	BBG - R. Free Asia (RFA)
9885	100	BOT	BOT	BBG - VO America (VOA)
9885	250	MRC	MOR	BBG - VO America (VOA)
9885	250	USA	GRV	BBG - VO America (VOA)
9885	150	CHN	BEI	China Radio Int'l
9885	250	RRW	KIG	FEBA Radio
9885	100	NZL	RAN	R. New Zealand Int'l (RNZI)
9885	250	RUS	SAM	VO Russia (VOR)
9890	250	CLN	IRA	BBG - VO America (VOA)
9890	250	PHL	PHT	BBG - VO America (VOA)
9890	100	D	JUL	Christian Science Herold
9890	125	D	WER	Christian Science Herold
9890	100	CHN	dom	CNR 1, Lingshi
9890	250	ATN	BON	R. Nederland Wereldomroep
9890	100	IND	DEL	R. Sedayee Kashmir
9895	250	CYP	CYP	BBC World Service
9895	500	HOL	FLE	R. Nederland Wereldomroep
9895	250	MDG	MDC	R. Nederland Wereldomroep
9895	500	MDG	MDC	R. Nederland Wereldomroep
9895	500	IRN	KAM	VO the Islamic Rep. of Iran
9900	100	CHN	dom	CNR 1,Beijing
9900	250	RUS	SAM	VO Russia (VOR)
9900	250	RUS	SAM	VOR - Radiokanal Sodruzhestvo
9905	250	IND	ALG	All India Radio (AIR)
9905	80	PLW	HBN	BBG - R. Free Asia (RFA)
9905	0.2	PRG	dom	R. América, Villeta
9905	500	IRN	KAM	VO the Islamic Rep. of Iran
9910	250	IND	ALG	All India Radio (AIR)
9910	250	IND	DEL	All India Radio (AIR)
9910	250	IND	dom	All India Radio, Aligarh
9910	100	GUM	TWR	KTWR (TWR Guam)
9915	300	CYP	CYP	BBC World Service
9915	300	G	SKN	BBC World Service
9915	500	G	RMP	BBC World Service
9920	100	PHL	BOC	FEBC Philippines
9920	100	GUM	TWR	KTWR (TWR Guam)
9920	100	IRN	KAM	VO the Islamic Rep. of Iran
9925	250	RUS	MSK	R. Vlaanderen Int'l (RVI)
9930	100	HWA	WHR	BBG - R. Free Asia (RFA)
9930	50	PLW	HBN	BBG - R. Free Asia (RFA)
9930	100	HWA	WHR	Fang Guang Ming Radio
9930	100	HWA	WHR	KWHR - World Harvest R.
9930	100	HWA	WHR	R. Free Vietnam
9930	250	AFS	MEY	TWR Africa
9935	100	GRC	AVL	RS Makedonias (ERT3)
9940	100	RUS	KHB	R. Nederland Wereldomroep
9940	500	IRN	KAM	VO the Islamic Rep. of Iran
9945	250	RUS	IRK	R. Vlaanderen Int'l (RVI)
9945	100	ALB	SHI	TWR Europe
9945	500	TJK	ORZ	VO Russia (VOR)
9950	250	IND	ALG	All India Radio (AIR)
9950	250	IND	DEL	All India Radio (AIR)
9950	250	EGY	ABS	R. Cairo
9955	50	USA	RMI	Conversando entre Cubanos
9955	50	USA	RMI	Foro Militar Cubano
9955	50	USA	RMI	Junta Patriótica Cubana
9955	50	USA	RMI	R. Oriente Libre
9955	50	PLW	HBN	T8BZ - VO Hope
9955	50	USA	RMI	Trova Libre
9955	500	USA	EWN	WEWN
9955	50	USA	RMI	WRMI - R. Miama Int'l
9960	100	ALB	SHI	TWR Europe
9965	500	ARM	GAV	R. Santec
9965	50	PLW	HBN	T8BZ - VO Hope
9965	500	ARM	GAV	VO Armenia
9970	100	BEL	WAV	RTBF International
9975	100	GUM	TWR	KTWR (TWR Guam)
9975	50	USA	VOH	KVOH - La Voz de Restauración
9975	200	KRE	KUJ	VO Korea
9975	500	USA	EWN	WEWN
9980	10	ISL	GVK	AFRTS (AFN Feeder)
9980	250	CLN	IRA	BBG - VO America (VOA)
9983	0.2	PRG	dom	R. América, Villeta
9985	250	ISR	ISR	Kol Israel
9985	50	PLW	HBN	T8BZ - VO Hope
9985	100	USA	WCR	The Overcomer Ministry
9985	100	USA	WCR	WWCR
9988	250	EGY	ABS	R. Cairo
9990	250	EGY	ABS	R. Cairo
9996	**50**	**RUS**	**—**	**RWM**
10000	**10**	**CHN**	**—**	**BPM**
10000	**10**	**ARG**	**—**	**LOL 2**
10000	**10**	**USA**	**—**	**WWV**
10000	**10**	**HWA**	**—**	**WWVH**
10320	3	HWA	PEH	AFRTS (AFN Feeder)
10330	500	IND	dom	All India Radio, Bangalore
11180		—		LJBC Sce for Iraq
11335	200	KRE	KUJ	VO Korea
11500	250	BUL	PLD	R. Bulgaria
11500	500	BUL	PLD	R. Bulgaria
11500	500	TJK	ORZ	VO Russia (VOR)
11510	200	KAZ	ALM	BBG - R. Free Asia (RFA)
11510	500	ARM	GAV	VO Russia (VOR)
11515	5	LBR	MON	VO Liberty
11520	500	ARM	GAV	BBG - R. Free Asia (RFA)
11520	250	CLN	IRA	BBG - VO America (VOA)
11530	300	MDA	GRI	Dengê Mezopotamya
11530	500	USA	EWN	WEWN
11535	200	KAZ	ALM	BBG - R. Free Asia (RFA)
11535	200	TJK	DSB	BBG - R. Free Asia (RFA)
11540	200	TJK	DSB	BBG - R. Free Asia (RFA)
11550	250	TWN	TAI	R. Australia
11550	100	PAK	ISL	R. Pakistan
11550	250	MDG	MDC	R. Sweden
11550	500	S	HOR	R. Sweden
11560	100	GUM	SDA	KSDA (AWR Guam)
11565	100	HWA	WHR	KWHR - World Harvest R.
11565	100	PAK	ISL	R. Pakistan
11565	100	USA	YFR	WYFR - Family Radio
11570	100	PAK	ISL	R. Pakistan
11580	250	MNG	UBA	BBG - R. Free Asia (RFA)
11580	100	MRA	FBS	Far East Broadcasting Company
11580	100	PAK	ISL	R. Pakistan
11585	250	IND	DEL	All India Radio (AIR)
11585	100	ISR	ISR	Kol Israel
11590	15	CHN	dom	V.O.Strait N, Fuzhou
11600	150	CHN	XIA	China Radio Int'l
11600	100	BUL	SOF	R. Bulgaria
11600	250	BUL	PLD	R. Bulgaria
11600	500	BUL	PLD	R. Bulgaria
11600	120	CHN	BEI	R. France Int'l (RFI)
11600	120	CHN	XIA	R. France Int'l (RFI)
11600	100	CZE	LIT	R. Prague
11600	150	SVK	RSO	R. Slovakia Int'l
11605	250	MRA	TIN	BBG - R. Free Asia (RFA)
11605	250	ISR	ISR	Kol Israel
11605	300	ISR	ISR	Kol Israel
11605	250	TWN	TNN	R. Taiwan Int'l
11610	150	CHN	dom	CNR 2, Beijing
11610	100	GUM	SDA	KSDA (AWR Guam)
11610	150	SVK	RSO	R. Slovakia Int'l
11610	500	IRN	SIR	VO the Islamic Rep. of Iran
11615	500	F	ISS	R. France Int'l (RFI)
11615	500	USA	EWN	WEWN
11620	250	IND	ALG	All India Radio (AIR)
11620	250	IND	DEL	All India Radio (AIR)
11620	500	IND	BGL	All India Radio (AIR)
11620	250	IND	dom	All India Radio, Delhi

kHz	kW	Ctry	Site	Station, location
11620	50	CHN	dom	CNR 5, Beijing
11625	350	E	NOB	R. Exterior de España (REE)
11625	100	CVA	SMG	Vatican Radio
11630	100	CHN	dom	CNR 1/8, Lingshi
11630	100	POR	LIS	RDP Internacional
11635	100	TWN	PAO	R. Taiwan Int'l
11635	100	POR	LIS	RDP Internacional
11635	500	F	ISS	VO Africa (LJBC)
11640	100	CHN	KAS	China Radio Int'l
11640	150	CHN	KUN	China Radio Int'l
11640	100	MLI	BKO	China Radio Int'l
11640	100	CZE	LIT	R. Prague
11640	100	TWN	KOU	R. Taiwan Int'l
11640	500	AFS	MEY	TWR Africa
11645	250	IND	DEL	All India Radio (AIR)
11645	100	GRC	AVL	VO Greece (ERA5)
11650	100	CHN	XIA	China Radio Int'l
11650	100	MRA	FBS	Far East Broadcasting Company
11650	100	AUS	SHP	R. Australia
11650	5	RUS	dom	R. Rossii, Perm,
11650	100	TWN	KOU	R. Taiwan Int'l
11655	100	BOT	BOT	BBG - VO America (VOA)
11655	250	THA	UDO	BBG - VO America (VOA)
11655	250	EGY	ABS	R. Cairo
11655	250	ATN	BON	R. Nederland Wereldomroep
11655	500	HOL	FLE	R. Nederland Wereldomroep
11655	250	MDG	MDC	R. Nederland Wereldomroep
11655	10	CUB	dom	R. Rebelde/Reloj
11655	250	RUS	ARM	VO Russia (VOR)
11660	120	CHN	XIA	China Radio Int'l
11660	120	CHN	dom	CNR 2, Xi'an
11660		—	—	LJBC Sce for Iraq
11660	100	AUS	SHP	R. Australia
11660	250	POR	SIN	RDP Internacional
11665	250	THA	UDO	BBG - RFE/RL
11665	250	GRC	KAV	BBG - VO America (VOA)
11665	250	MRC	MOR	BBG - VO America (VOA)
11665	100	EGY	ABZ	Egyptian Radio
11665	250	F	ISS	R. France Int'l (RFI)
11665	300	J	YAM	R. Japan (NHK World)
11665	250	ASC	ASC	R. Prague
11665	300	TWN	KOU	R. Taiwan Int'l
11665	300	TWN	TNN	R. Taiwan Int'l
11665	100	USA	YFR	R. Taiwan Int'l
11665	100	USA	YFR	WYFR - Family Radio
11670	300	G	SKN	BBC World Service
11670	300	G	WOF	BBC World Service
11670	150	CHN	dom	CNR 2, Beijing
11670	250	F	ISS	R. France Int'l (RFI)
11670	250	GUF	GUF	R. France Int'l (RFI)
11670	250	CUB	HAB	R. Habana Cuba
11670	100	I	ROM	RAI International
11670	500	IRN	KAM	VO the Islamic Rep. of Iran
11675	250	ATG	ATG	BBC World Service
11675	500	CHN	KUN	China Radio Int'l
11675	500	CHN	URU	China Radio Int'l
11675	250	UAE	DHA	FEBA Radio
11675	100	GUM	SDA	KSDA (AWR Guam)
11675	250	SVK	RSO	R. Budapest
11675	500	KWT	KBD	R. Kuwait
11675	250	ATN	BON	R. Nederland Wereldomroep
11675+	500	KWT	KBD	R. Kuwait
11680	300	AUT	MOS	Adventist World R. (AWR)
11680	250	CYP	CYP	BBC World Service
11680	300	G	SKN	BBC World Service
11680	500	G	RMP	BBC World Service
11680	100	STP	SAO	BBG - VO America (VOA)
11680	150	CHN	BEI	China Radio Int'l
11680		KRE	dom	Korean Cent. B'casting Stn., Kanggye
11680	100	TWN	PAO	R. Taiwan Int'l
11680	100	I	ROM	RAI International
11685	250	SNG	SGP	BBC World Service
11685	250	THA	UDO	BBG - RFE/RL
11685	250	KWT	KBD	BBG R. Ashna
11685	100	CHN	KAS	China Radio Int'l
11685	100	CHN	dom	CNR 2/8, Tianshui
11685	100	GUM	SDA	KSDA (AWR Guam)
11685	500	F	ISS	R. France Int'l (RFI)
11685	250	AUS	DAR	Voice International
11690	250	GRC	KAV	BBG - VO America (VOA)
11690	250	RRW	KIG	Deutsche Welle
11690	100	GUM	SDA	KSDA (AWR Guam)
11690	100	GUM	TWR	KTWR (TWR Guam)
11690	250	SNG	SNG	R. Australia
11690	300	J	YAM	R. Japan (NHK World)
11690	500	JOR	AKA	R. Jordan (JRTV)
11690	10	COD	dom	R. Okapi, Kinshasa
11690	0.1	FIN	VIR	Scandinavian Weekend R.
11690	500	TUR	EMR	VO Turkey
11695	500	G	RMP	BBC World Service
11695	500	UAE	DHA	BBG - R. Free Asia (RFA)
11695	250	CLN	TRM	Deutsche Welle
11695	500	D	WER	Deutsche Welle
11695	100	GUM	SDA	KSDA (AWR Guam)
11695	100	GUM	TWR	KTWR (TWR Guam)
11695	100	AUS	SHP	R. Australia
11695	100	EGY	ABZ	R. Cairo
11695	500	IRN	KAM	VO the Islamic Rep. of Iran
11700	250	USA	DLN	BBG - VO America (VOA)
11700	100	CHN	KAS	China Radio Int'l
11700	100	CHN	XIA	China Radio Int'l
11700	150	CHN	BEI	China Radio Int'l
11700	500	CHN	KUN	China Radio Int'l
11700	100	EQA	QUI	HCJB
11700	100	GUM	SDA	KSDA (AWR Guam)
11700	500	BUL	PLD	R. Bulgaria
11700	500	F	ISS	R. France Int'l (RFI)
11700	250	GAB	GAB	R. France Int'l (RFI)
11705	250	MRC	MOR	BBG - RFE/RL
11705	250	PHL	PHT	BBG - VO America (VOA)
11705	500	THA	UDO	BBG - VO America (VOA)
11705	500	F	ISS	R. France Int'l (RFI)
11705	250	CAN	SAC	R. Japan (NHK World)
11705	500	IRN	SIR	VO the Islamic Rep. of Iran
11705	500	TUR	CAK	VO Turkey
11710	50	IND	DEL	All India Radio (AIR)
11710	50	IND	dom	All India Radio, Delhi
11710	100	CHN	dom	CNR 1, Beijing
11710	300	G	SKN	R. Japan (NHK World)
11710	250	ROU	TIG	R. Romania Int'l (RRI)
11710	300	TWN	HUW	R. Taiwan Int'l
11710	100	ARG	BUE	Rdif. Argentina al Exterior
11710	200	KRE	KUJ	VO Korea
11715	250	IND	DEL	All India Radio (AIR)
11715	250	IND	PAN	All India Radio (AIR)
11715	250	GRC	KAV	BBG - VO America (VOA)
11715	250	PHL	PHT	BBG - VO America (VOA)
11715	50	USA	JES	KJES
11715	300	J	YAM	R. Japan (NHK World)
11715	250	TWN	TNN	R. Taiwan Int'l
11715	300	G	WOF	Sudan Radio Service
11715	100	CVA	SMG	Vatican Radio
11715	250	CVA	SMG	Vatican Radio
11715	500	F	ISS	VO Africa (LJBC)
11715	100	CVA	SMG	VO Charity
11720	100	TWN	TAI	Adventist World R. (AWR)
11720	500	MRA	TIN	BBG - R. Free Asia (RFA)
11720	100	CHN	dom	CNR 1, Shijiazhuang
11720	500	D	WER	Deutsche Welle
11720	100	USA	YFR	R. Taiwan Int'l
11720	0.1	FIN	VIR	Scandinavian Weekend R.
11725	250	OMA	SLA	BBC World Service
11725	500	EGY	ABZ	R. Cairo
11725	250	CAN	SAC	R. Canada Int'l (RCI)
11725	250	GAB	GAB	R. France Int'l (RFI)
11725	10	B	dom	R. Novas de Paz, Curitiba
11725	250	TWN	PAO	R. Taiwan Int'l
11725	250	PHL	PUG	R. Veritas Asia
11730	100	D	JUL	Adventist World R. (AWR)
11730	250	IND	DEL	All India Radio (AIR)
11730	250	SEY	SEY	BBC World Service
11730	250	THA	UDO	BBG - R. Aap Ki Dunyaa
11730	100	D	BIB	BBG - RFE/RL
11730	250	MRC	MOR	BBG - RFE/RL
11730	250	CLN	IRA	BBG - VO America (VOA)
11730	250	THA	UDO	BBG - VO America (VOA)
11730	250	KWT	KBD	BBG R. Ashna
11730	500	CHN	KUN	China Radio Int'l
11730	300	J	YAM	R. Canada Int'l (RCI)
11730	300	J	YAM	R. Japan (NHK World)
11730	250	PHL	PHT	R. Pilipinas Overseas
11730	250	ROU	TIG	R. Romania Int'l (RRI)

kHz	kW	Ctry	Site	Station, location
11730	250	ATN	BON	R. Vlaanderen Int'l (RVI)
11730	500	TUN	SFA	RT Tunisienne (ERTT)
11734	50	TZA	dom	VO Tanzania, Dole
11735	250	IND	ALG	All India Radio (AIR)
11735	50	B	dom	R. Nova Visão, Santa Maria
11735	1	URG	dom	R. Oriental, Montevideo
11735	200	KRE	KUJ	VO Korea
11740	250	IND	PAN	All India Radio (AIR)
11740	250	IND	dom	All India Radio, Panaji
11740	300	CYP	CYP	BBC World Service
11740	500	MRA	TIN	BBG - R. Free Asia (RFA)
11740	250	GRC	KAV	BBG - RFE/RL
11740	50	CHN	dom	CNR 2, Beijing
11740	250	SNG	SNG	R. Japan (NHK World)
11740	250	ROU	GAL	R. Romania Int'l (RRI)
11740	250	ROU	TIG	R. Romania Int'l (RRI)
11740	100	USA	YFR	R. Taiwan Int'l
11740	500	ARS	RIY	Saudi Radio
11740	100	CVA	SMG	Vatican Radio
11740	100	USA	YFR	WYFR - Family Radio
11745	500	ARS	RIY	Saudi Radio
11745	500	IRN	KAM	VO the Islamic Rep. of Iran
11745	100	CHL	SGO	Voz Cristiana/Voz Crista
11750	300	CYP	CYP	BBC World Service
11750	250	OMA	SLA	BBC World Service
11750	100	SNG	SGP	BBC World Service
11750	250	SNG	SGP	BBC World Service
11750	250	THA	NAK	BBC World Service
11750	250	KWT	KBD	BBG R. Ashna
11750	100	CHN	dom	CNR 1, Shijiazhuang
11750	100	AUS	KNX	HCJB World R. Australia
11750	100	AUS	SHP	R. Australia
11750	250	USA	DLN	VO Greece (ERA5)
11750	500	IRN	SIR	VO the Islamic Rep. of Iran
11755	100	AIA	AIA	Dr Gene Scott (Univ.Netw.)
11755	100	GUM	SDA	KSDA (AWR Guam)
11755	500	EGY	ABZ	R. Cairo
11755	100	TWN	PAO	R. Taiwan Int'l
11755	250	FIN	POR	YLE R. Finland
11755	500	FIN	POR	YLE R. Finland
11760	250	CYP	CYP	BBC World Service
11760	250	OMA	SLA	BBC World Service
11760	500	MRA	TIN	BBG - VO America (VOA)
11760	500	THA	UDO	BBG - VO America (VOA)
11760	500	CHN	KAS	China Radio Int'l
11760	500	CHN	KUN	China Radio Int'l
11760	500	CHN	URU	China Radio Int'l
11760	100	CHN	dom	CNR 1, Shijiazhuang
11760	500	G	RMP	HCJB
11760	250	CUB	HAB	R. Habana Cuba
11760	300	J	YAM	R. Japan (NHK World)
11760	250	CUB	HAB	R. Nac.Venezuela - Canal Int'l
11760	100	USA	YFR	R. Taiwan Int'l
11765	250	AFS	MEY	BBC World Service
11765	250	ASC	ASC	BBC World Service
11765	250	MRC	MOR	BBG - RFE/RL
11765	100	ALS	NLS	KNLS International
11765	20	B	dom	R. Tupi, Curitiba
11765	250	PHL	PUG	R. Veritas Asia
11765	250	ASC	ASC	RAI International
11765	100	TWN	TAI	Sound of Hope
11770	250	MRC	MOR	BBG - VO America (VOA)
11770	250	THA	UDO	BBG R. Ashna
11770	100	CHN	KAS	China Radio Int'l
11770	300	CLN	EKA	R. Japan (NHK World)
11770	250	NIG	IKO	VO Nigeria
11770	50	CHN	dom	Xinjiang-Ch, Urumqi
11775	250	IND	PAN	All India Radio (AIR)
11775	500	MRA	TIN	BBG - R. Free Asia (RFA)
11775	250	USA	GRV	BBG - R. Martí
11775	100	STP	SAO	BBG - VO America (VOA)
11775	100	CHN	KAS	China Radio Int'l
11775	300	CLN	EKA	R. Sri Lanka (SLBC)
11775	100	AIA	dom	The Caribbean Beacon, The Valley
11780	250	CLN	IRA	BBG - VO America (VOA)
11780	100	CHN	XIA	China Radio Int'l
11780	50	CHN	dom	CNR 8, Lingshi
11780	250	B	dom	R. Nal. da Amazônia, Brasília
11780	300	TWN	HUW	R. Taiwan Int'l
11780	250	PHL	PUG	R. Veritas Asia
11785	300	AUT	MOS	Adventist World R. (AWR)
11785	250	THA	NAK	BBC World Service
11785	100	MRA	SAI	BBG - R. Free Asia (RFA)
11785	100	D	LAM	BBG - RFE/RL
11785	500	THA	UDO	BBG - VO America (VOA)
11785	500	D	WER	Deutsche Welle
11785	250	HNG	JBR	R. Budapest
11785	7.5	B	dom	R. Guaíba, Porto Alegre
11785	300	J	YAM	R. Japan (NHK World)
11785	250	G	WOF	R. Ndeke Luka
11785	500	ARS	RIY	Saudi Radio
11785	250	INS	dom	Voice of Indonesia, Cimanggis
11790	500	MRA	TIN	BBG - R. Free Asia (RFA)
11790	250	G	WOF	BBG - RFE/RL
11790	100	ARM	GAV	BBG - VO America (VOA)
11790	500	EGY	ABZ	R. Cairo
11790	250	PHL	PUG	R. Veritas Asia
11795	500	MRA	TIN	BBG - R. Free Asia (RFA)
11795	100	D	LAM	BBG - RFE/RL
11795	250	THA	UDO	BBG - RFE/RL
11795	500	D	NAU	Deutsche Welle
11795	250	RRW	KIG	Deutsche Welle
11795	300	UAE	DBA	Emirates Radio
11795	350	E	NOB	R. Exterior de España (REE)
11795	250	CAN	SAC	R. Korea Int'l
11795	100	TWN	HUW	R. Taiwan Int'l
11795	250	PHL	PUG	R. Veritas Asia
11795	300	G	WOF	Sudan Radio Service
11795	250	TUR	CAK	VO Turkey
11800	100	CHN	KAS	China Radio Int'l
11800	150	CHN	dom	CNR 2, Beijing
11800	250	BIH	BIJ	Int'l R. of Serbia&Monten.
11800	100	GUM	SDA	KSDA (AWR Guam)
11800	250	CUB	HAB	R. Habana Cuba
11800	100	I	ROM	RAI International
11805	100	D	BIB	BBG - RFE/RL
11805	250	MRC	MOR	BBG - RFE/RL
11805	100	D	BIB	BBG - VO America (VOA)
11805	250	PHL	PHT	BBG - VO America (VOA)
11805	100	GEO	DSH	R. Georgia
11805	10	B	dom	R. Globo, Rio de Janeiro
11805	250	THA	UDO	R. Thailand
11805	500	CVA	SMG	Vatican Radio
11810		CHN	dom	CNR 8, Lingshi
11810	250	RRW	KIG	Deutsche Welle
11810	100	D	JUL	Minivan Radio
11810	500	G	RMP	Peace Radio
11810	500	JOR	AKA	R. Jordan (JRTV)
11810	250	KOR	KIM	R. Korea Int'l
11815	250	MRC	MOR	BBG - RFE/RL
11815	50	CHN	dom	CNR 8, Beijing
11815	7.5	B	dom	R. Brasil Central, Goiânia
11815	100	CTR	CRI	R. Exterior de España (REE)
11815	300	J	YAM	R. Japan (NHK World)
11815	100	TWN	PAO	R. Taiwan Int'l
11815	100	I	ROM	RAI International
11820	300	CYP	CYP	BBC World Service
11820	250	CLN	IRA	BBG - VO America (VOA)
11820	250	AUS	DAR	R. Australia
11820	100	POL	WWA	R. Polonia
11820	250	PHL	PUG	R. Veritas Asia
11820	500	ARS	RIY	Saudi Radio
11825	100	STP	SAO	BBG - VO America (VOA)
11825	250	THA	UDO	BBG - VO America (VOA)
11825	100	AFS	MEY	Channel Africa
11825	100	CHN	XIA	China Radio Int'l
11825	100	GUM	SDA	KSDA (AWR Guam)
11825	100	USA	YFR	R. Taiwan Int'l
11825	300	POR	LIS	RDP Internacional
11830	50	IND	dom	All India Radio, Delhi
11830	250	CLN	IRA	BBG - R. Free Asia (RFA)
11830	10	B	dom	R. CBN Anhanguera, Goiânia
11835	250	SNG	SGP	BBC World Service
11835	250	GRC	KAV	BBG - RFE/RL
11835	100	BOT	BOT	BBG - VO America (VOA)
11835	100	D	LAM	BBG - VO America (VOA)
11835	250	KWT	KBD	BBG - VO America (VOA)
11835	250	KWT	KBD	BBG R. Ashna
11835	150	CHN	dom	CNR 2, Xi'an
11835	250	BIH	BIJ	Int'l R. of Serbia&Monten.
11835	250	ASC	ASC	R. Canada Int'l (RCI)
11835	250	TUR	CAK	VO Turkey

kHz	kW	Ctry	Site	Station, location
11840	250	IND	DEL	All India Radio (AIR)
11840	250	IND	PAN	All India Radio (AIR)
11840	100	D	JUL	Ev. Missions-Gemeinden
11840	250	D	NAU	Ev. Missions-Gemeinden
11840	100	GUM	TWR	KTWR (TWR Guam)
11840	300	CLN	EKA	R. Japan (NHK World)
11840	100	D	JUL	R. Réveil
11840	15	RUS	dom	R. Rossii, Yu-Sakhal.
11840	100	D	JUL	R. Santec
11840	250	AUS	DAR	Voice International
11845	100	AFS	MEY	Adventist World R. (AWR)
11845	250	CYP	CYP	BBC World Service
11845	500	CLN	IRA	BBG - R. Farda
11845	100	D	LAM	BBG - R. Farda
11845	150	CHN	dom	CNR 2, Xi'an
11845	250	CAN	SAC	R. Canada Int'l (RCI)
11845	250	D	WER	R. Canada Int'l (RCI)
11845	500	F	ISS	R. France Int'l (RFI)
11850	100	IND	DEL	All India Radio (AIR)
11850	250	SNG	SGP	BBC World Service
11850	500	GUF	GUF	China Radio Int'l
11850	100	GUM	SDA	KSDA (AWR Guam)
11850	250	GAB	GAB	R. France Int'l (RFI)
11850	100	PAK	ISL	R. Pakistan
11850	250	PHL	PUG	R. Veritas Asia
11850	100	UZB	TAC	The Voice - Africa
11850	500	CVA	SMG	Vatican Radio
11855	250	ASC	ASC	BBC World Service
11855	100	D	BIB	BBG - VO America (VOA)
11855	250	GRC	KAV	BBG - VO America (VOA)
11855	500	THA	UDO	BBG - VO America (VOA)
11855	1	B	dom	R. Aparecida, Aparecida
11855	500	EGY	ABZ	R. Cairo
11855	250	ASC	ASC	R. Japan (NHK World)
11855	250	THA	UDO	R. Thailand
11855	100	I	ROM	RAI International
11855	50	ARS	JED	Saudi Radio
11855	100	USA	YFR	WYFR - Family Radio
11860	250	SEY	SEY	BBC World Service
11860		CHN	KAS	China Radio Int'l
11860	100	CHN	dom	CNR 1, Beijing
11860	250	SNG	SNG	R. Japan (NHK World)
11860	250	INS	dom	RRI Jakarta, Cimanggis
11860	500	F	ISS	VO Africa (LJBC)
11860	50	CHN	dom	Xizang-Ch, Lhasa
11865	500	G	RMP	BBC World Service
11865	250	SEY	SEY	BBC World Service
11865	250	POR	SIN	Deutsche Welle
11865	250	CAN	SAC	R. Canada Int'l (RCI)
11865	250	SNG	SNG	R. Japan (NHK World)
11865	100	ALB	SHI	TWR Europe
11865	500	FIN	POR	YLE R. Finland
11870	100	MRA	SAI	BBG - R. Free Asia (RFA)
11870	250	GRC	KAV	BBG - VO America (VOA)
11870	100	CHN	KAS	China Radio Int'l
11870	40	CTR	CHA	Dr Gene Scott (Univ.Netw.)
11870	100	GUM	SDA	KSDA (AWR Guam)
11870	250	ROU	GAL	R. Romania Int'l (RRI)
11870	500	IRN	KAM	VO the Islamic Rep. of Iran
11875	250	MRC	MOR	BBG - RFE/RL
11875	250	MRC	MOR	BBG - VO America (VOA)
11875	500	AFS	MEY	Channel Africa
11875	500	CHN	KUN	China Radio Int'l
11875	250	D	WER	R. Canada Int'l (RCI)
11875	250	CUB	HAB	R. Habana Cuba
11875	250	CUB	HAB	R. Nac.Venezuela - Canal Int'l
11875	100	TWN	TNN	R. Taiwan Int'l
11875	250	TWN	TNN	R. Taiwan Int'l
11875	100	I	ROM	RAI International
11875	300	POR	LIS	RDP Internacional
11875	500	USA	EWN	WEWN
11880	500	CHN	KUN	China Radio Int'l
11880	10	PNG	dom	Port Moresby
11880	100	AUS	SHP	R. Australia
11880	100	CTR	CRI	R. Exterior de España (REE)
11880	100	I	ROM	RAI International
11885	100	D	BIB	BBG - RFE/RL
11885	100	D	LAM	BBG - RFE/RL
11885	250	MRC	MOR	BBG - RFE/RL
11885	250	MRC	MOR	BBG - VO America (VOA)
11885	250	CAN	SAC	China Radio Int'l
11885	250	ROU	TIG	R. Romania Int'l (RRI)
11885	100	TWN	HUW	R. Taiwan Int'l
11885	100	MLA	KAJ	VO Malaysia
11885	100	USA	YFR	WYFR - Family Radio
11885	50	CHN	dom	Xinjiang-Ug, Urumqi
11890	250	USA	GRV	BBG - VO America (VOA)
11890	250	CLN	TRM	Deutsche Welle
11890				LJBC Sce for Iraq
11890	100	E	NOB	R. Exterior de España (REE)
11890	300	CLN	EKA	R. Japan (NHK World)
11890	250	PHL	PHT	R. Pilipinas Overseas
11890	250	TWN	TNN	R. Taiwan Int'l
11890	100	CHL	SGO	Voz Cristiana/Voz Crista
11895	100	D	BIB	BBG - RFE/RL
11895	100	D	BIB	BBG - VO America (VOA)
11895	250	UAE	DHA	Deutsche Welle
11895	100	GUM	SDA	KSDA (AWR Guam)
11895	100	GUM	TWR	KTWR (TWR Guam)
11895	300	GUF	GUF	R. Japan (NHK World)
11895	250	MDG	MDC	R. Nederland Wereldomroep
11895	10	B	dom	R. RGS, Porto Alegre
11895	250	ROU	TIG	R. Romania Int'l (RRI)
11895	250	PHL	PUG	R. Veritas Asia
11895	100	I	ROM	RAI International
11895	250	TUR	EMR	VO Turkey
11900	100	MRA	SAI	BBG - R. Free Asia (RFA)
11900	500	CHN	KUN	China Radio Int'l
11900	500	CHN	XIA	China Radio Int'l
11900	600	CHN	JIN	China Radio Int'l
11900	100	GUM	SDA	KSDA (AWR Guam)
11900	250	BUL	PLD	R. Bulgaria
11900	100	I	ROM	RAI International
11900+	70	CAN	SAC	TDPradio
11900+	70	CAN	SAC	VO the NASB
11905	250	MRC	MOR	BBG - RFE/RL
11905	50	CHN	dom	CNR 6, Beijing
11905	500	D	WER	Deutsche Welle
11905	250	RRW	KIG	Deutsche Welle
11905	250	CAN	SAC	R. Canada Int'l (RCI)
11905	300	CLN	EKA	R. Sri Lanka (SLBC)
11905	240	UZB	TAC	R. Tashkent Int'l
11910	300	AUT	MOS	Adventist World R. (AWR)
11910	250	THA	UDO	BBG - RFE/RL
11910	120	CHN	XIA	R. Exterior de España (REE)
11910	100	GEO	DSH	R. Georgia
11910	300	J	YAM	R. Japan (NHK World)
11910	100	CVA	SMG	Vatican Radio
11910	100	IRN	KAM	VO the Islamic Rep. of Iran
11910	250	TUR	CAK	VO Turkey
11915	300	AUT	MOS	Adventist World R. (AWR)
11915	100	STP	SAO	BBG - VO America (VOA)
11915	100	CHN	dom	CNR 2, Tianshui
11915	10	B	dom	R. Gaucha, Porto Alegre
11915	250	TWN	TNN	R. Taiwan Int'l
11915	500	ARS	RIY	Saudi Radio
11915	200	RUS	dom	Tatarstan dulk, Samara
11920	100	SNG	SGP	BBC World Service
11920	250	THA	NAK	BBC World Service
11920	250	EQA	QUI	HCJB
11920	250	SNG	SNG	R. Japan (NHK World)
11920	250	SNG	SNG	RAI International
11925	100	AFS	MEY	Adventist World R. (AWR)
11925	250	GRC	KAV	BBG - VO America (VOA)
11925	250	PHL	PHT	BBG - VO America (VOA)
11925	100	CHN	dom	CNR 1, Lingshi
11925	10	B	dom	R. Bandeirantes, São Paulo
11925	500	TUR	EMR	VO Turkey
11925+	500	G	RMP	BBC World Service
11930	250	USA	GRV	BBG - R. Martí
11930	250	PHL	PHT	BBG - RFE/RL
11930	250	MRA	TIN	BBG - VO America (VOA)
11930	250	PHL	PHT	BBG - VO America (VOA)
11935	100	IND	MUM	All India Radio (AIR)
11935	250	THA	NAK	BBC World Service
11935	250	KWT	KBD	BBG - VO America (VOA)
11935	50	CHN	dom	CNR 5, Beijing
11935	100	GUM	SDA	KSDA (AWR Guam)
11935	250	D	WER	R. Canada Int'l (RCI)
11935	300	G	SKN	R. Canada Int'l (RCI)
11935	7.5	B	dom	R. Clube Paranaense, Curitiba
11935	500	HOL	FLE	R. Nederland Wereldomroep

kHz	kW	Ctry	Site	Station, location
11935	250	ROU	GAL	R. Romania Int'l (RRI)
11935	250	TWN	TNN	R. Taiwan Int'l
11935	500	ARS	RIY	Saudi Radio
11940	100	AFS	MEY	BBC World Service
11940	250	KWT	KBD	BBG - R. Free Afghanistan
11940	300	CHN	KAS	China Radio Int'l
11940	100	GUM	SDA	KSDA (AWR Guam)
11940	50	CBG	dom	R. Cambodia, Steung Meanchey
11940	250	ROU	GAL	R. Romania Int'l (RRI)
11940	250	ROU	TIG	R. Romania Int'l (RRI)
11940	100	TWN	HUW	R. Taiwan Int'l
11940	100	TWN	PAO	R. Taiwan Int'l
11940	100	TWN	TSH	R. Taiwan Int'l
11940	100	TWN	TAI	VO China
11945	300	J	YAM	BBC World Service
11945	250	SNG	SGP	BBC World Service
11945	250	THA	NAK	BBC World Service
11945	250	MRA	TIN	BBG - R. Free Asia (RFA)
11945	150	CHN	KUN	China Radio Int'l
11945	250	RRW	KIG	Deutsche Welle
11945	250	E	NOB	R. Exterior de España (REE)
11950	100	MRA	SAI	BBG - R. Free Asia (RFA)
11950	250	MRA	TIN	BBG - R. Free Asia (RFA)
11950	300	UAE	DBA	Emirates Radio
11950	250	B	dom	Radiobrás, Brasília
11950	500	TUN	SFA	RT Tunisienne (ERTT)
11950	500	IRN	KAM	VO the Islamic Rep. of Iran
11950	50	CHN	dom	Xizang-Ch, Lhasa
11955	250	OMA	SLA	BBC World Service
11955	250	SNG	SGP	BBC World Service
11955	250	THA	NAK	BBC World Service
11955	500	CHN	KUN	China Radio Int'l
11955	250	POR	SIN	Deutsche Welle
11955	250	GAB	GAB	R. France Int'l (RFI)
11955	250	TUR	CAK	VO Turkey
11955	250	AUS	DAR	Voice International
11960	250	BLR	MNS	Belaruskaje Radyjo 1
11960	100	CHN	dom	CNR 1, Beijing
11960	100	EQA	QUI	HCJB
11960	100	MLI	dom	Office de Radiodif. Tv. du Mali, Kati
11960	500	JOR	AKA	R. Jordan (JRTV)
11960	250	ROU	TIG	R. Romania Int'l (RRI)
11960	300	POR	LIS	RDP Internacional
11965	250	ATG	ATG	BBC World Service
11965	500	MRA	TIN	BBG - R. Free Asia (RFA)
11965	250	MRC	MOR	BBG - VO America (VOA)
11965	250	PHL	PHT	BBG - VO America (VOA)
11965	100	STP	SAO	BBG - VO America (VOA)
11965	500	THA	UDO	BBG - VO America (VOA)
11965	500	F	ISS	R. France Int'l (RFI)
11965	7.5	B	dom	R. Record, São Paulo
11970	500	MRA	TIN	BBG - R. Free Asia (RFA)
11970	250	CAN	SAC	China Radio Int'l
11970	500	D	NAU	Deutsche Welle
11970	500	GAB	GAB	R. Japan (NHK World)
11970	300	J	YAM	R. Japan (NHK World)
11975	250	CLN	IRA	BBG - R. Aap Ki Dunyaa
11975	100	STP	SAO	BBG - Studio 7
11975	100	STP	SAO	BBG - VO America (VOA)
11975	100	MLI	BKO	China Radio Int'l
11975	500	D	NAU	Deutsche Welle
11975	200	RUS	dom	Kamchatka ryb, Yelizovo
11975	100	CHN	XIA	R. Canada Int'l (RCI)
11975	15	CHN	dom	Xinjiang-Kg, Urumqi
11980	100	CHN	KUN	China Radio Int'l
11980	150	CHN	KUN	China Radio Int'l
11980	0.5	UKR	dom	Dniprovska khvylia, Zaporizhia
11980	100	GUM	SDA	KSDA (AWR Guam)
11980	100	NZL	RAN	R. New Zealand Int'l (RNZI)
11980	100	POR	LIS	RDP Internacional
11980	500	TUR	EMR	VO Turkey
11985	250	IND	DEL	All India Radio (AIR)
11985	500	IND	BGL	All India Radio (AIR)
11985	50	PHL	PHT	BBG - VO America (VOA)
11985	100	STP	SAO	BBG - VO America (VOA)
11985	250	ATG	ATG	Deutsche Welle
11985	250	ASC	ASC	FEBA Radio
11985	100	GUM	SDA	KSDA (AWR Guam)
11985	100	TWN	HUW	R. Taiwan Int'l
11985	100	I	ROM	RAI International
11990	250	USA	DLN	BBG - VO America (VOA)
11990	150	CHN	XIA	China Radio Int'l
11990	250	CAN	SAC	Deutsche Welle
11990	500	KWT	KBD	R. Kuwait
11990	150	SVK	RSO	R. Slovakia Int'l
11995	100	MRA	SAI	BBG - R. Free Asia (RFA)
11995	250	GRC	KAV	BBG - VO America (VOA)
11995	250	KWT	KBD	BBG - VO America (VOA)
11995	500	MRA	TIN	BBG - VO America (VOA)
11995	250	KWT	KBD	BBG R. Ashna
11995	500	F	ISS	R. France Int'l (RFI)
12000	100	CHN	KAS	China Radio Int'l
12000	250	CUB	HAB	R. Habana Cuba
12005	100	D	JUL	Bible Voice B'casting
12005	300	UAE	DBA	Emirates Radio
12005	250	EQA	QUI	HCJB
12005	500	TUN	SFA	RT Tunisienne (ERTT)
12005	100	RUS	ARM	VO Russia (VOR)
12010	300	G	SKN	BBC World Service
12010	250	PHL	PHT	BBG - VO America (VOA)
12010	100	GUM	SDA	KSDA (AWR Guam)
12010	100	SNG	SNG	R. Australia
12010	250	HNG	JBR	R. Budapest
12010	100	RUS	KNA	VO Russia (VOR)
12010+	200	RUS	SPB	VO Russia (VOR)
12015	250	GRC	KAV	BBG - R. Farda
12015	100	D	LAM	BBG - RFE/RL
12015	250	THA	UDO	BBG - VO America (VOA)
12015	250	POR	SIN	Deutsche Welle
12015	250	CAN	SAC	R. Canada Int'l (RCI)
12015	250	GAB	GAB	R. France Int'l (RFI)
12015	500	RUS	IRK	R. France Int'l (RFI)
12015	250	PHL	PHT	R. Pilipinas Overseas
12015	100	D	JUL	VO Democratic Eritrea
12015	50	MNG	UBA	VO Mongolia
12020	100	D	BIB	BBG - RFE/RL
12020	100	EQA	QUI	HCJB
12020	100	VTN	VNI	VO Vietnam (VOV)
12025	300	AUT	MOS	Adventist World R. (AWR)
12025	250	G	SKN	Akhbar Mufriha
12025	250	IND	PAN	All India Radio (AIR)
12025	250	CLN	TRM	Deutsche Welle
12025	250	RRW	KIG	Deutsche Welle
12025	250	CAN	SAC	HCJB
12025	500	RUS	NSB	R. France Int'l (RFI)
12025	500	F	ISS	R. Monte Carlo-MO
12025	500	RUS	MSK	VO Russia (VOR)
12025	500	IRN	KAM	VO the Islamic Rep. of Iran
12025+	500	RUS	MSK	VO Russia (VOR)
12030	240	RUS	SPB	VO Russia (VOR)
12035	250	CYP	CYP	BBC World Service
12035	250	SEY	SEY	BBC World Service
12035	250	UAE	DHA	BBC World Service
12035	500	D	WER	Deutsche Welle
12035	250	POR	SIN	Deutsche Welle
12035	250	RRW	KIG	Deutsche Welle
12035	350	E	NOB	R. Exterior de España (REE)
12040	100	D	BIB	BBG - RFE/RL
12040	250	PHL	PHT	BBG - VO America (VOA)
12040	100	EQA	QUI	HCJB
12045	250	RRW	KIG	Deutsche Welle
12045	300	J	YAM	R. Canada Int'l (RCI)
12045	250	SNG	SNG	R. Japan (NHK World)
12050	500	EGY	ABZ	Egyptian Radio
12055	100	CHN	dom	CNR 1/8, Lingshi
12060	250	MDG	MDC	The Radio Nile
12060	200	RUS	SPB	VO Russia (VOR)
12060	240	RUS	MSK	VO Russia (VOR)
12060	35	RUS	TLD	VO Russia (VOR)
12065	250	RUS	PPK	BBG - VO America (VOA)
12065	250	RUS	ARM	Bible Voice B'casting
12065	100	PHL	IBA	FEBC Philippines
12065	250	RUS	IRK	R. Nederland Wereldomroep
12070	100	UZB	TAC	R. Nederland Wereldomroep
12070	250	RUS	NVS	Vatican Radio
12075	500	RUS	VLD	R. France Int'l (RFI)
12075	250	RUS	dom	R. Rossii, Moskva
12080	100	BOT	BOT	BBG - VO America (VOA)
12080	100	CHN	dom	CNR 2, Tianshui
12080	100	GUM	TWR	KTWR (TWR Guam)
12080	10	AUS	BRN	R. Australia
12080	250	MDG	MDC	R. Nederland Wereldomroep

kHz	kW	Ctry	Site	Station, location
12080	100	GUM	TWR	TWR India
12085	500	SYR	ADR	R. Damascus
12085		—	—	The Arabic Radio
12085	100	MNG	UBA	VO Mongolia
12085	250	MNG	UBA	VO Mongolia
12090	100	MRA	FBS	Far East Broadcasting Company
12090	100	PHL	BOC	FEBC Philippines
12095	250	ASC	ASC	BBC World Service
12095	250	G	WOF	BBC World Service
12095	100	PHL	BOC	FEBC Philippines
12105	250	CLN	IRA	BBG - R. Free Asia (RFA)
12105	100	GUM	TWR	KTWR (TWR Guam)
12105	100	GRC	AVL	VO Greece (ERA5)
12105	250	GRC	AVL	VO Greece (ERA5)
12105	250	GRC	KAV	VO Greece (ERA5)
12110	100	D	JUL	BBG - VO America (VOA)
12110	100	CHN	KUN	China Radio Int'l
12110	250	RUS	KNA	VO Russia (VOR)
12115	20	ISL	REY	Ríkisútvarpið
12120	100	MRA	FBS	Far East Broadcasting Company
12120	100	GUM	SDA	KSDA (AWR Guam)
12125	250	AFS	MEY	FEBA Radio
12130	100	AFS	MEY	Adventist World R. (AWR)
12130	100	GUM	TWR	KTWR (TWR Guam)
12133	3	USA	KEW	AFRTS (AFN Feeder)
12140	250	KWT	KBD	BBG - R. Free Afghanistan
12140	250	CLN	IRA	BBG - VO America (VOA)
12140	250	KWT	KBD	BBG R. Ashna
12150	250	CLN	IRA	BBG - R. Aap Ki Dunyaa
12160	50	PLW	HBN	T8BZ - VO Hope
12160	100	USA	WCR	The Overcomer Ministry
12160	100	USA	WCR	WWCR
12172	65	USA	WRB	WWRB
12579	3	DGA	DGA	AFRTS (AFN Feeder)
12945	250	RRW	KIG	Deutsche Welle
13105		B	—	PPR
13360	250	CUB	HAB	R. Habana Cuba
13362	3	GUM	BAR	AFRTS (AFN Feeder)
13570	50	USA	INB	WINB
13580	100	CZE	LIT	R. Prague
13580	500	S	HOR	R. Sweden
13590	250	D	WER	Gospel for Asia
13595	50	USA	JCR	WJIE International Shortwave
13600	100	STP	SAO	BBG - VO America (VOA)
13600	100	CHN	KAS	China Radio Int'l
13600	100	BUL	SOF	R. Bulgaria
13600	250	BUL	PLD	R. Bulgaria
13600	500	BUL	PLD	R. Bulgaria
13605	250	IND	ALG	All India Radio (AIR)
13605	500	IND	ALG	All India Radio (AIR)
13610	100	CHN	KAS	China Radio Int'l
13610	100	CHN	dom	CNR 1, Nanning
13610	500	SYR	ADR	R. Damascus
13615	300	CYP	CYP	BBC World Service
13615	500	USA	EWN	WEWN
13620	500	IND	BGL	All India Radio (AIR)
13620	100	CHN	KAS	China Radio Int'l
13620	250	AUS	DAR	R. Australia
13620	500	KWT	KBD	R. Kuwait
13620+	500	KWT	KBD	R. Kuwait
13625	500	MRA	TIN	BBG - R. Free Asia (RFA)
13630	100	MLI	BKO	China Radio Int'l
13630	300	UAE	DBA	Emirates Radio
13630	100	GUM	TWR	KTWR (TWR Guam)
13630	100	AUS	SHP	R. Australia
13630	300	J	YAM	R. Japan (NHK World)
13630	100	UZB	TAC	The Voice - Africa
13640	300	G	SKN	BBC World Service
13640	500	G	RMP	BBC World Service
13640	100	D	LAM	BBG - RFE/RL
13640	500	MRA	TIN	BBG - VO America (VOA)
13640	250	MRC	MOR	BBG - VO America (VOA)
13640	100	CHN	KAS	China Radio Int'l
13640	500	F	ISS	R. France Int'l (RFI)
13640	100	OMA	SEB	R. Sultanate of Oman
13640	100	OMA	THU	R. Sultanate of Oman
13640	500	IRN	SIR	VO the Islamic Rep. of Iran
13645	250	IND	ALG	All India Radio (AIR)
13645	250	MRC	MOR	BBG - VO America (VOA)
13645	500	D	WER	Deutsche Welle
13645	500	IRN	SIR	VO the Islamic Rep. of Iran
13650	500	G	RMP	BBC World Service
13650	500	MRA	TIN	BBG - VO America (VOA)
13650	250	CUB	HAB	China Radio Int'l
13650	250	D	WER	Gospel for Asia
13650	250	CAN	SAC	R. Canada Int'l (RCI)
13650	500	G	RMP	R. Canada Int'l (RCI)
13650	300	J	YAM	R. Japan (NHK World)
13655	250	CAN	SAC	R. Canada Int'l (RCI)
13660	250	CYP	CYP	BBC World Service
13660	300	G	SKN	BBC World Service
13660	200	RUS	ARM	BBC World Service
13660	100	J	YAM	R. Japan (NHK World)
13665	240	RUS	PPK	VO Russia (VOR)
13665	500	FIN	POR	YLE R. Finland
13670	500	MRA	TIN	BBG - R. Free Asia (RFA)
13670	100	MLI	BKO	China Radio Int'l
13670	50	CHN	dom	Xinjiang-Ug, Urumqi
13675	250	CAN	SAC	China Radio Int'l
13675	300	UAE	DBA	Emirates Radio
13675	250	CAN	SAC	R. Österreich 1
13680	100	D	LAM	BBG - R. Farda
13680	250	GRC	KAV	BBG - R. Farda
13680	250	CUB	HAB	R. Habana Cuba
13680	250	CUB	HAB	R. Nac.Venezuela - Canal Int'l
13680		CUB	dom	R. Reloj
13685	500	GUF	GUF	China Radio Int'l
13685	100	MLI	BKO	China Radio Int'l
13685	250	AUS	DAR	Voice International
13690	100	GUM	TWR	KTWR (TWR Guam)
13690	250	G	RMP	R. Vlaanderen Int'l (RVI)
13690	250	G	SKN	R. Vlaanderen Int'l (RVI)
13690	500	G	RMP	VO the Eritrean People
13695	500	IND	BGL	All India Radio (AIR)
13700	300	G	SKN	BBC World Service
13700	250	CAN	SAC	China Radio Int'l
13700	100	CHN	dom	CNR 1, Lingshi
13700	500	HOL	FLE	R. Nederland Wereldomroep
13700	250	MDG	MDC	R. Nederland Wereldomroep
13700	100	POR	LIS	RDP Internacional
13710	500	IND	BGL	All India Radio (AIR)
13710	100	MRA	SAI	BBG - R. Free Asia (RFA)
13710	100	BOT	BOT	BBG - VO America (VOA)
13710	250	THA	UDO	BBG - VO America (VOA)
13710	500	ARS	RIY	Saudi Radio
13715	250	USA	GRV	BBG - VO America (VOA)
13715	100	CHN	KAS	China Radio Int'l
13715	100	GUM	TWR	KTWR (TWR Guam)
13715	150	SVK	RSO	R. Slovakia Int'l
13720	100	MRA	SAI	BBG - R. Free Asia (RFA)
13720	100	CHN	KAS	China Radio Int'l
13720	350	E	NOB	R. Exterior de España (REE)
13720	250	IRN	AHW	VO the Islamic Rep. of Iran
13725	250	CLN	IRA	BBG - R. Free Asia (RFA)
13725	50	PLW	HBN	BBG - R. Free Asia (RFA)
13730	250	CAN	SAC	R. Canada Int'l (RCI)
13730	100	AUT	MOS	R. Österreich 1
13735	250	CLN	IRA	BBG - VO America (VOA)
13735	100	STP	SAO	BBG - VO America (VOA)
13735	100	SNG	SNG	Deutsche Welle
13740	250	GRC	KAV	BBG - VO America (VOA)
13740	250	USA	DLN	BBG - VO America (VOA)
13740	250	CUB	HAB	R. Nac.Venezuela - Canal Int'l
13740	250	IRN	AHW	VO the Islamic Rep. of Iran
13745	500	MRA	TIN	BBG - R. Free Asia (RFA)
13745	500	IRN	SIR	VO the Islamic Rep. of Iran
13750	30	CTR	CHA	Dr Gene Scott (Univ.Netw.)
13750	250	CUB	HAB	R. Habana Cuba
13755	250	THA	NAK	BBC World Service
13755	100	BOT	BOT	BBG - VO America (VOA)
13755	500	MRA	TIN	BBG - VO America (VOA)
13760	500	MRA	TIN	BBG - R. Free Asia (RFA)
13760	500	IRN	ZAH	VO the Islamic Rep. of Iran
13765	500	THA	UDO	BBG - VO America (VOA)
13765	100	GUM	TWR	KTWR (TWR Guam)
13765	100	UZB	TAC	The Voice - Africa
13765	500	CVA	SMG	Vatican Radio
13770	500	IND	BGL	All India Radio (AIR)
13770	300	POR	LIS	RDP Internacional
13770	500	CVA	SMG	Vatican Radio
13780	250	CLN	TRM	Deutsche Welle
13780	500	D	WER	Deutsche Welle

kHz	kW	Ctry	Site	Station, location
13780	250	THA	UDO	R. Thailand
13790	500	CHN	KAS	China Radio Int'l
13790	500	CHN	KUN	China Radio Int'l
13790	250	D	WER	Gospel for Asia
13790	250	UAE	DHA	R. Vlaanderen Int'l (RVI)
13790	500	IRN	KAM	VO the Islamic Rep. of Iran
13790	250	AUS	DAR	Voice International
13795	250	IND	ALG	All India Radio (AIR)
13800	250	MRA	TIN	BBG - R. Free Asia (RFA)
13800	250	CLN	IRA	BBG - VO America (VOA)
13800	250	BUL	PLD	R. Bulgaria
13800	250	RUS	MSK	R. Vlaanderen Int'l (RVI)
13810	250	CLN	IRA	BBG - RFE/RL
13810	100	D	JUL	Bible Voice B'casting
13810	100	D	JUL	The Overcomer Ministry
13815	250	CLN	IRA	BBG - R. Free Asia (RFA)
13815	100	USA	AIJ	Dr Gene Scott (Univ.Netw.)
13820	250	USA	DLN	BBG - R. Martí
13820	250	USA	GRV	BBG - R. Martí
13820	100	D	JUL	Glas Hrvatske
13820	100	RUS	KHB	R. Nederland Wereldomroep
13820	100	D	JUL	Waymarks Int'l Ministries
13830	200	KAZ	ALM	BBG - R. Free Asia (RFA)
13840	20	I	MIL	IRRS Shortwave
13840	250	MDG	MDC	R. Nederland Wereldomroep
13840	20	I	MIL	Radio Six International
13840	50	PLW	HBN	T8BZ - VO Hope
13845	100	USA	WCR	Dr Gene Scott (Univ.Netw.)
13850	250	ISR	ISR	Kol Israel
13865	250	CLN	IRA	BBG - R. Free Asia (RFA)
13865	250	CLN	IRA	BBG - VO America (VOA)
13865	20	ISL	REY	Ríkisútvarpið
14670	**5**	**CAN**	**—**	**CHU**
14996	**50**	**RUS**	**—**	**RWM**
15000	**10**	**CHN**	**—**	**BPM**
15000	**10**	**TWN**	**—**	**BSF**
15000	**10**	**USA**	**—**	**WWV**
15000	**10**	**HWA**	**—**	**WWVH**
15006	**10**	**E**	**—**	**EBC**
15020	250	IND	ALG	All India Radio (AIR)
15050	250	IND	DEL	All India Radio (AIR)
15075	100	IND	DEL	All India Radio (AIR)
15075	500	IND	BGL	All India Radio (AIR)
15085	500	IRN	KAM	VO the Islamic Rep. of Iran
15100	200	CHN	XIA	China Radio Int'l
15100	100	PAK	ISL	R. Pakistan
15105	250	ASC	ASC	BBC World Service
15105	250	THA	UDO	BBG - VO America (VOA)
15105	250	ROU	TIG	R. Romania Int'l (RRI)
15105	200	RUS	dom	Tatarstan dulk., Samara
15105	500	TUR	EMR	VO Turkey
15105	500	USA	SHB	WSHB - World Harvest R.
15110	100	D	LAM	BBG - RFE/RL
15110	100	CHN	KAS	China Radio Int'l
15110	100	CHN	URU	China Radio Int'l
15110	100	CHN	XIA	China Radio Int'l
15110	250	RRW	KIG	Deutsche Welle
15110	200	RUS	VLD	Deutsche Welle
15110	250	TWN	TAI	R. Australia
15110	500	KWT	KBD	R. Kuwait
15115	300	G	SKN	BBC World Service
15115	100	EGY	ABZ	Egyptian Radio
15115	100	EGY	ABZ	R. Cairo
15120	250	CLN	IRA	BBG - RFE/RL
15120	100	D	LAM	BBG - RFE/RL
15120	250	CUB	HAB	China Radio Int'l
15120	250	PHL	PHT	R. Pilipinas Overseas
15120	250	NIG	IKO	VO Nigeria
15125	300	CHN	BEI	China Radio Int'l
15125	100	MLI	BKO	China Radio Int'l
15125	250	ASC	ASC	FEBA Radio
15125	100	CTR	CRI	R. Exterior de España (REE)
15125	250	INS	dom	RRI Jakarta, Cimanggis
15130	100	D	LAM	BBG - RFE/RL
15130	250	MRC	MOR	BBG - RFE/RL
15130	250	MRC	MOR	BBG - VO America (VOA)
15130	100	USA	YFR	R. Taiwan Int'l
15135	250	UAE	DHA	Adventist World R. (AWR)
15135	500	IND	dom	All India Radio, Delhi
15135	100	CHN	KUN	China Radio Int'l
15135	500	CHN	KUN	China Radio Int'l
15135	500	EGY	ABZ	R. Cairo
15135	7.5	B	dom	R. Record, São Paulo
15140	250	IND	DEL	All India Radio (AIR)
15140	100	CHN	URU	China Radio Int'l
15140	100	EQA	QUI	HCJB
15140	250	CAN	SAC	R. Canada Int'l (RCI)
15140	250	UAE	DHA	R. Canada Int'l (RCI)
15140	100	OMA	THU	R. Sultanate of Oman
15140	300	POR	LIS	RDP Internacional
15145	150	CHN	KUN	China Radio Int'l
15145	250	CLN	TRM	Deutsche Welle
15145	250	POR	SIN	Deutsche Welle
15145	250	RRW	KIG	Deutsche Welle
15145	250	RUS	PPK	Deutsche Welle
15145	500	RUS	ARM	Deutsche Welle
15145	250	ROU	TIG	R. Romania Int'l (RRI)
15150	500	MRA	TIN	BBG - R. Free Asia (RFA)
15150	100	D	LAM	BBG - VO America (VOA)
15150	250	PHL	PHT	BBG - VO America (VOA)
15150	50	PHL	PHT	BBG - VO America (VOA)
15150	250	ROU	GAL	R. Romania Int'l (RRI)
15150	250	INS	JAK	VO Indonesia
15150	500	IRN	SIR	VO the Islamic Rep. of Iran
15150	250	INS	dom	Voice of Indonesia, Cimanggis
15155	250	IND	ALG	All India Radio (AIR)
15155	500	G	RMP	BBC World Service
15155	100	EGY	ABZ	R. Cairo
15155	500	F	ISS	R. France Int'l (RFI)
15155	500	TUR	EMR	VO Turkey
15160	250	CLN	IRA	BBG - RFE/RL
15160	250	GRC	KAV	BBG - RFE/RL
15160	100	MRA	SAI	BBG - VO America (VOA)
15160	250	PHL	PHT	BBG - VO America (VOA)
15160	100	CHN	XIA	China Radio Int'l
15160	100	AUS	SHP	R. Australia
15160	250	AFS	MEY	R. France Int'l (RFI)
15160	250	ROU	TIG	R. Romania Int'l (RRI)
15160	500	TUR	EMR	VO Turkey
15165		CHN	URU	China Radio Int'l
15165	500	IRN	SIR	VO the Islamic Rep. of Iran
15165	250	AUS	DAR	Voice International
15170	250	MRC	MOR	BBG - RFE/RL
15170	250	UAE	DHA	Gospel for Asia
15170	100	CTR	CRI	R. Exterior de España (REE)
15170	250	AFS	MEY	R. France Int'l (RFI)
15170	250	ROU	GAL	R. Romania Int'l (RRI)
15170	500	ARS	RIY	Saudi Radio
15170	100	SDN	dom	Sudan Radio and TV Corp., Omdurman
15170	100	USA	YFR	WYFR - Family Radio
15175	500	IND	BGL	All India Radio (AIR)
15175	100	TWN	HUW	R. Taiwan Int'l
15180	250	CYP	CYP	BBC World Service
15180	500	G	RMP	BBC World Service
15180	250	OMA	SLA	BBC World Service
15180	100	CHN	XIA	China Radio Int'l
15180	100	CHN	dom	CNR 1, Lingshi
15180	250	CAN	SAC	R. Canada Int'l (RCI)
15185	250	IND	ALG	All India Radio (AIR)
15185	50	IND	dom	All India Radio, Delhi
15185	100	MRA	SAI	BBG - R. Free Asia (RFA)
15185	250	PHL	PHT	BBG - VO America (VOA)
15185	50	PHL	PHT	BBG - VO America (VOA)
15185	100	GUM	SDA	KSDA (AWR Guam)
15190	250	ASC	ASC	BBC World Service
15190	250	ATG	ATG	BBC World Service
15190	100	SNG	SNG	Deutsche Welle
15190	5	B	dom	R. Inconfidência, Belo Horizonte
15190	250	PHL	PHT	R. Pilipinas Overseas
15195	350	E	NOB	R. Exterior de España (REE)
15195	300	J	YAM	R. Japan (NHK World)
15195	200	RUS	ARM	R. Vlaanderen Int'l (RVI)
15195	250	RUS	MSK	R. Vlaanderen Int'l (RVI)
15195	500	TUR	EMR	VO Turkey
15200	100	GUM	TWR	KTWR (TWR Guam)
15200	250	B	dom	R. Nacional da Amaz0nia, Brasília
15200	500	IRN	SIR	VO the Islamic Rep. of Iran
15205	100	D	LAM	BBG - RFE/RL
15205	250	GRC	KAV	BBG - RFE/RL
15205	50	PHL	PHT	BBG - VO America (VOA)
15205	500	D	WER	Deutsche Welle
15205	250	UAE	DHA	FEBA Radio

kHz	kW	Ctry	Site	Station, location
15205	500	ARS	RIY	Saudi Radio
15205	500	IRN	SIR	VO the Islamic Rep. of Iran
15210	500	MRA	TIN	BBG - R. Free Asia (RFA)
15210	250	CLN	IRA	BBG - VO America (VOA)
15210	100	CHN	KUN	China Radio Int'l
15210	250	UAE	DHA	R. France Int'l (RFI)
15210	250	KOR	KIM	R. Korea Int'l
15215	250	UAE	DHA	Adventist World R. (AWR)
15215	500	MRA	TIN	BBG - R. Free Asia (RFA)
15215	250	GRC	KAV	BBG - RFE/RL
15215	100	TWN	HUW	R. Taiwan Int'l
15215	100	USA	YFR	R. Taiwan Int'l
15215	2.5	B	dom	R. Timbira, São Luís
15215	100	USA	YFR	WYFR - Family Radio
15220	500	MRA	TIN	BBG - R. Free Asia (RFA)
15220	250	MRC	MOR	BBG - VO America (VOA)
15220	500	AFS	MEY	Channel Africa
15220	100	HWA	WHR	KWHR - World Harvest R.
15220	250	ASC	ASC	R. Japan (NHK World)
15220	500	F	ISS	VO Africa (LJBC)
15225	250	UAE	DHA	Adventist World R. (AWR)
15225	50	PHL	PHT	BBG - VO America (VOA)
15225	100	GUM	TWR	KTWR (TWR Guam)
15225	250	PHL	PUG	R. Veritas Asia
15225	500	TUR	EMR	VO Turkey
15230	250	CAN	SAC	China Radio Int'l
15230	100	AUS	SHP	R. Australia
15230	250	CUB	HAB	R. Habana Cuba
15230	250	CUB	HAB	R. Nac.Venezuela - Canal Int'l
15230	250	CAN	SAC	R. Vlaanderen Int'l (RVI)
15235	250	IND	PAN	All India Radio (AIR)
15235	500	IND	BGL	All India Radio (AIR)
15235	500	CVA	SMG	Vatican Radio
15235	500	IRN	KAM	VO the Islamic Rep. of Iran
15240	250	MRC	MOR	BBG - VO America (VOA)
15240	100	AUS	SHP	R. Australia
15240	250	AUS	DAR	R. Australia
15240	250	CAN	SAC	R. Sweden
15240	500	S	HOR	R. Sweden
15245	250	THA	NAK	BBC World Service
15245	500	CHN	URU	China Radio Int'l
15245	100	GUM	SDA	KSDA (AWR Guam)
15245	250	CAN	SAC	R. Canada Int'l (RCI)
15245	100	TWN	HUW	R. Taiwan Int'l
15245	500	TUR	EMR	VO Turkey
15250	250	PHL	PHT	BBG - RFE/RL
15250	500	MRA	TIN	BBG - VO America (VOA)
15250	100	CHN	KUN	China Radio Int'l
15250	250	ROU	GAL	R. Romania Int'l (RRI)
15250	100	I	ROM	RAI International
15250	250	AUS	DAR	Voice International
15255	100	AFS	MEY	Adventist World R. (AWR)
15255	500	MRA	TIN	BBG - R. Free Asia (RFA)
15255	250	GRC	KAV	BBG - VO America (VOA)
15255	100	CZE	LIT	R. Prague
15260	50	IND	DEL	All India Radio (AIR)
15260	50	IND	dom	All India Radio, Delhi
15260	100	CHN	XIA	China Radio Int'l
15260	150	CHN	KUN	China Radio Int'l
15260	100	TWN	TAI	Hmong Lao Radio
15260	100	GUM	SDA	KSDA (AWR Guam)
15260	250	ROU	GAL	R. Romania Int'l (RRI)
15260	250	ROU	TIG	R. Romania Int'l (RRI)
15260	500	IRN	KAM	VO the Islamic Rep. of Iran
15260	500	IRN	SIR	VO the Islamic Rep. of Iran
15265	300	CYP	CYP	BBC World Service
15265	250	USA	GRV	BBG - VO America (VOA)
15265	500	G	RMP	Peace Radio
15265	1	B	dom	R. Globo, São Paulo
15265	100	NZL	RAN	R. New Zealand Int'l (RNZI)
15265	250	TWN	TNN	R. Taiwan Int'l
15265	250	B	dom	Radiobras, Brasília
15270	500	MRA	TIN	BBG - R. Free Asia (RFA)
15270	150	CHN	dom	CNR 2, Beijing
15270	250	PHL	PHT	R. Pilipinas Overseas
15270	100	TWN	PAO	R. Taiwan Int'l

kHz	kW	Ctry	Site	Station, location
15275	250	CLN	TRM	Deutsche Welle
15275	500	D	WER	Deutsche Welle
15275	250	RRW	KIG	Deutsche Welle
15275	100	GUM	TWR	KTWR (TWR Guam)
15275	250	ASC	ASC	R. France Int'l (RFI)
15275	500	ARS	RIY	Saudi Radio
15275	500	IRN	KAM	VO the Islamic Rep. of Iran
15280	250	THA	NAK	BBC World Service
15280	250	ROU	GAL	R. Romania Int'l (RRI)
15285	100	SNG	SGP	BBC World Service
15285	500	AFS	MEY	Channel Africa
15290	250	GRC	KAV	BBG - R. Farda
15290	250	PHL	PHT	BBG - VO America (VOA)
15290	500	JOR	AKA	R. Jordan (JRTV)
15290	250	TWN	TNN	R. Taiwan Int'l
15295	100	AFS	MEY	Adventist World R. (AWR)
15295	100	EQA	QUI	HCJB
15295	100	MLA	KAJ	VO Malaysia
15295	250	MLA	KAJ	VO Malaysia
15300	100	CHN	dom	CNR 1, Beijing
15300	500	F	ISS	R. France Int'l (RFI)
15305	250	CLN	IRA	BBG - VO America (VOA)
15305	250	CAN	SAC	R. Canada Int'l (RCI)
15310	250	OMA	SLA	BBC World Service
15310	250	THA	NAK	BBC World Service
15315	500	F	ISS	R. France Int'l (RFI)
15315	250	ATN	BON	R. Nederland Wereldomroep
15315	250	ROU	GAL	R. Romania Int'l (RRI)
15315	500	ARS	RIY	Saudi Radio
15320	100	D	LAM	BBG - VO America (VOA)
15320	100	CHN	XIA	China Radio Int'l
15320	100	GUM	SDA	KSDA (AWR Guam)
15320	100	TWN	HUW	R. Taiwan Int'l
15320	100	TWN	PAO	R. Taiwan Int'l
15320	250	ASC	ASC	RAI International
15320	250	MDG	MDC	The Radio Nile
15320	500	IRN	SIR	VO the Islamic Rep. of Iran
15320	500	TUR	EMR	VO Turkey
15325	300	G	WOF	BBC World Service
15325	250	USA	GRV	BBC World Service
15325	1	B	dom	R. Gazeta, São Paulo
15325	300	J	YAM	R. Japan (NHK World)
15330	250	USA	DLN	BBG - R. Martí
15330	250	USA	GRV	BBG - R. Martí
15330	250	CLN	TRM	Deutsche Welle
15330	100	GUM	TWR	KTWR (TWR Guam)
15330	100	UZB	TAC	R. Tashkent Int'l
15330	100	SWZ	MAN	TWR Africa
15330	500	FIN	POR	YLE R. Finland
15335	250	CLN	TRM	Deutsche Welle
15335	100	PHL	BOC	FEBC Philippines
15335	250	EGY	ABS	R. Cairo
15335	250	MRC	MOR	RTMarocaine
15340	100	CHN	XIA	China Radio Int'l
15340	250	MRC	NAD	RTMarocaine
15340	500	IRN	SIR	VO the Islamic Rep. of Iran
15345	250	GRC	KAV	BBG - RFE/RL
15345	100	ARG	BUE	Rdif. Argentina al Exterior
15345	250	MRC	NAD	RTMarocaine
15345	500	ARS	RIY	Saudi Radio
15350	100	CHN	KAS	China Radio Int'l
15350	250	PHL	PUG	R. Veritas Asia
15355	500	GAB	GAB	R. Japan (NHK World)
15355	100	OMA	THU	R. Sultanate of Oman
15360	100	SNG	SGP	BBC World Service
15360	250	SNG	SGP	BBC World Service
15360	250	THA	NAK	BBC World Service
15365	100	AFS	MEY	Adventist World R. (AWR)
15365	250	EGY	ABS	R. Cairo
15365	500	IRN	KAM	VO the Islamic Rep. of Iran
15365	250	AUS	DAR	Voice International
15370	100	D	LAM	BBG - RFE/RL
15370	250	MRC	MOR	BBG - RFE/RL
15370	250	MRC	MOR	BBG - VO America (VOA)
15370	100	CHN	dom	CNR 1, Shijiazhuang
15370	300	UAE	DBA	Emirates Radio

kHz	kW	Ctry	Site	Station, location
15370	250	ROU	TIG	R. Romania Int'l (RRI)
15370	250	UAE	DHA	Radio Mustaqbal
15375	100	EGY	ABZ	R. Cairo
15375	100	OMA	SEB	R. Sultanate of Oman
15375	100	CHL	SGO	Voz Cristiana/Voz Crista
15380	100	CHN	dom	CNR 1, Beijing
15380	250	ROU	GAL	R. Romania Int'l (RRI)
15380	250	ROU	TIG	R. Romania Int'l (RRI)
15380	500	ARS	RIY	Saudi Radio
15385	250	UAE	DHA	Adventist World R. (AWR)
15385	500	UAE	DHA	BBG - R. Free Asia (RFA)
15385	250	USA	GRV	BBG - VO America (VOA)
15385	50	USA	JES	KJES
15385	350	E	NOB	R. Exterior de España (REE)
15385	250	UAE	DHA	Radio Mustaqbal
15390	250	ASC	ASC	BBC World Service
15390	250	USA	GRV	BBC World Service
15390	100	CHN	dom	CNR 1/8, Lingshi
15390	100	AUS	KNX	HCJB World R. Australia
15395	500	MRA	TIN	BBG - R. Free Asia (RFA)
15395	250	PHL	PHT	BBG - VO America (VOA)
15395	500	UAE	DBA	Emirates Radio
15395	100	TWN	HUW	R. Taiwan Int'l
15400	250	AFS	MEY	BBC World Service
15400	250	ASC	ASC	BBC World Service
15400	150	CHN	BEI	China Radio Int'l
15400	500	UAE	DBA	Emirates Radio
15400	250	ASC	ASC	R. Japan (NHK World)
15400	100	USA	YFR	WYFR - Family Radio
15400	500	FIN	POR	YLE R. Finland
15405	250	THA	NAK	BBC World Service
15405	100	PHL	BOC	FEBC Philippines
15405	100	AUS	KNX	HCJB World R. Australia
15410	300	G	WOF	BBG - R. Farda
15410	250	THA	UDO	BBG - RFE/RL
15410	250	CLN	TRM	Deutsche Welle
15410	250	RRW	KIG	Deutsche Welle
15410	250	UAE	DHA	Deutsche Welle
15415	500	CHN	KUN	China Radio Int'l
15415		CHN	dom	CNR 8, Lingshi
15415	100	AUS	SHP	R. Australia
15415	1	B	dom	R. Clube, Ribeirão Preto
15420	250	AFS	MEY	BBC World Service
15420	300	CYP	CYP	BBC World Service
15420	250	SEY	SEY	BBC World Service
15420	0.15	USA	RNO	WRNO Worldwide
15425	300	G	WOF	BBC World Service
15425	50	PHL	PHT	BBG - VO America (VOA)
15425	100	AUS	KNX	HCJB World R. Australia
15425	250	EGY	ABZ	R. Cairo
15425	100	RUS	PPK	VO Russia (VOR)
15430	500	MRA	TIN	BBG - R. Free Asia (RFA)
15430	100	GUM	SDA	KSDA (AWR Guam)
15430	250	ROU	GAL	R. Romania Int'l (RRI)
15430	250	ROU	TIG	R. Romania Int'l (RRI)
15430	100	TWN	HUW	R. Taiwan Int'l
15435	500	UAE	DHA	BBG - R. Free Asia (RFA)
15435	150	CHN	BEI	China Radio Int'l
15435	300	UAE	DBA	Emirates Radio
15435	100	PHL	BOC	FEBC Philippines
15435	500	JOR	AKA	R. Jordan (JRTV)
15435	500	ARS	RIY	Saudi Radio
15440	300	AUT	MOS	Adventist World R. (AWR)
15440	500	CHN	KUN	China Radio Int'l
15440	250	RRW	KIG	Deutsche Welle
15440	100	USA	YFR	R. Taiwan Int'l
15440	250	IRN	AHW	VO the Islamic Rep. of Iran
15440+	90	POR	SIN	Deutsche Welle
15445	100	TWN	TAI	Adventist World R. (AWR)
15445	100	BOT	BOT	BBG - VO America (VOA)
15450	100	PHL	BOC	FEBC Philippines
15450	100	PHL	IBA	FEBC Philippines
15450	250	PHL	PUG	R. Veritas Asia
15450	500	TUN	SFA	RT Tunisienne (ERTT)
15460	250	MRC	MOR	BBG - RFE/RL
15460	250	THA	UDO	BBG - VO America (VOA)
15460	150	SVK	RSO	R. Slovakia Int'l
15460	100	POR	LIS	RDP Internacional
15460	250	RUS	MSK	VO Russia (VOR)
15460	500	IRN	KAM	VO the Islamic Rep. of Iran
15460+	250	RUS	MSK	VO Russia (VOR)
15465	100	CHN	KAS	China Radio Int'l
15465	100	PHL	BOC	FEBC Philippines
15465	100	TWN	PAO	R. Taiwan Int'l
15470	500	G	RMP	BBC World Service
15470	500	MRA	TIN	BBG - R. Free Asia (RFA)
15470	250	POR	SIN	Deutsche Welle
15475	250	GAB	GAB	Africa No.1
15475	250	RUS	KNA	VO Russia (VOR)
15475	100	CHL	SGO	Voz Cristiana/Voz Crista
15476	10	ATA	dom	R. Nacional Arcangel San Gabriel
15480	100	CHN	dom	CNR 1, Beijing
15480	100	GUM	SDA	KSDA (AWR Guam)
15480	100	EGY	ABZ	R. Cairo
15480	500	IRN	KAM	VO the Islamic Rep. of Iran
15483	0.2	PRG	dom	R. América, Villeta
15485	300	G	SKN	BBC World Service
15485	500	MRA	TIN	BBG - R. Free Asia (RFA)
15485	100	PAK	ISL	R. Pakistan
15485	250	USA	DLN	VO Greece (ERA5)
15490	250	CLN	TRM	Deutsche Welle
15495	100	GUM	SDA	KSDA (AWR Guam)
15495	500	KWT	KBD	R. Kuwait
15500	150	CHN	dom	CNR 2, Beijing
15500	0.25		—	R. One/Information R.
15505	100	MLI	BKO	China Radio Int'l
15505	500	KWT	KBD	R. Kuwait
15510	250	RUS	IRK	BBC World Service
15510	250	THA	NAK	BBC World Service
15510	500	MRA	TIN	BBG - R. Free Asia (RFA)
15515	500	THA	UDO	BBG - VO America (VOA)
15515	100	AUS	SHP	R. Australia
15515	250	F	ISS	R. France Int'l (RFI)
15515	500	F	ISS	R. France Int'l (RFI)
15515	250	GUF	GUF	R. France Int'l (RFI)
15520	100	BGD	dom	Bangladesh Betar, Shavar
15520	250	PHL	PUG	R. Veritas Asia
15525	250	RUS	SAM	FEBA Radio
15525	100	AUS	KNX	HCJB World R. Australia
15525	100	TWN	PAO	R. Taiwan Int'l
15530	250	MRC	MOR	BBG - VO America (VOA)
15530	500	F	ISS	R. France Int'l (RFI)
15530	100	NZL	RAN	R. New Zealand Int'l (RNZI)
15530	250	PHL	PUG	R. Veritas Asia
15530	250	AFS	MEY	R. Vlaanderen Int'l (RVI)
15530	300	G	WOF	Sudan Radio Service
15530	500	IRN	SIR	VO the Islamic Rep. of Iran
15530+	10	ATN	BON	R. Nederland Wereldomroep
15535	100	POR	LIS	RDP Internacional
15540	250	GRC	KAV	BBG - R. Aap Ki Dunyaa
15540	50	CHN	dom	CNR 2, Beijing
15540	100	POR	LIS	RDP Internacional
15540	250	RUS	ARM	VO Russia (VOR)
15545	500	MRA	TIN	BBG - R. Free Asia (RFA)
15545	100	BOT	BOT	BBG - VO America (VOA)
15545	500	IRN	SIR	VO the Islamic Rep. of Iran
15550	500	MRA	TIN	BBG - R. Free Asia (RFA)
15550	100	CHN	dom	CNR 1, Beijing
15555	250	CYP	CYP	BBC World Service
15555	250	CLN	IRA	BBG - R. Free Asia (RFA)
15555	100	POR	LIS	RDP Internacional
15560	100	AUS	KNX	HCJB World R. Australia
15565	300	CYP	CYP	BBC World Service
15565	500	G	RMP	BBC World Service
15565	250	RUS	VLD	BBG - R. Free Asia (RFA)
15565	100	USA	YFR	WYFR - Family Radio
15570	100	CHN	dom	CNR 2/8, Tianshui
15570		CUB	dom	R. Rebelde
15570	100	D	JUL	RTBF International
15570	250	CVA	SMG	Vatican Radio
15570	250	RUS	MSK	VO Russia (VOR)
15575	250	UKR	SMF	BBC World Service

kHz	kW	Ctry	Site	Station, location
15575	250	OMA	SLA	BBC World Service
15575	100	KOR	KIM	R. Korea Int'l
15575	250	KOR	KIM	R. Korea Int'l
15575	100	POR	LIS	RDP Internacional
15580	250	USA	GRV	BBG - VO America (VOA)
15580	100	MRA	FBS	Far East Broadcasting Company
15580	100	TWN	PAO	R. Taiwan Int'l
15585	500	THA	UDO	BBG - VO America (VOA)
15585	250	E	NOB	R. Exterior de España (REE)
15585	100	CHL	SGO	Voz Cristiana/Voz Crista
15590	250	THA	UDO	BBG - RFE/RL
15590	100	USA	TBN	KTBN Shortwave R.
15590	300	J	YAM	R. Japan (NHK World)
15595	250	CLN	TRM	Deutsche Welle
15595	250	MDG	MDC	R. Nederland Wereldomroep
15595	250	CVA	SMG	Vatican Radio
15595	100	RUS	PPK	VO Russia (VOR)
15600	100	CHN	KUN	China Radio Int'l
15605	500	D	WER	Deutsche Welle
15605	500	KAZ	ALM	Deutsche Welle
15605	120	CHN	BEI	R. France Int'l (RFI)
15605	500	F	ISS	R. France Int'l (RFI)
15605	250	GAB	GAB	R. France Int'l (RFI)
15610	100	TWN	PAO	R. Taiwan Int'l
15615	250	GRC	KAV	BBG - VO America (VOA)
15615	250	KWT	KBD	BBG R. Ashna
15615	300	ISR	ISR	Kol Israel
15615	500	F	ISS	VO Africa (LJBC)
15620	250	EGY	ABS	R. Cairo
15620	100	UKR	KHR	R. Ukraine Int'l (RUI)
15625	100	PAK	ISL	R. Pakistan
15630	100	GRC	AVL	VO Greece (ERA5)
15640	250	ISR	ISR	Kol Israel
15640	300	ISR	ISR	Kol Israel
15650	100	GRC	AVL	VO Greece (ERA5)
15650	250	GRC	KAV	VO Greece (ERA5)
15660	200	TJK	DSB	BBG - R. Free Asia (RFA)
15660	100	GUM	SDA	KSDA (AWR Guam)
15660	500	F	ISS	VO Africa (LJBC)
15660	100	BUL	SOF	VO Iranian Nation
15665	500	MRA	TIN	BBG - R. Free Asia (RFA)
15665	250	CLN	IRA	BBG - VO America (VOA)
15665	100	MRA	SAI	BBG - VO America (VOA)
15665	100	I	MIL	IRRS Shortwave
15665	100	—	—	Radio4Peace
15665	500	USA	SHB	WSHB - World Harvest R.
15670	150	CHN	KUN	China Radio Int'l
15670	50	CHN	dom	CNR 8, Lingshi
15670	250	EGY	ABS	R. Cairo
15675	250	RUS	SAM	VO Liberty - Eritrea
15680	200	KAZ	ALM	BBG - R. Free Asia (RFA)
15680	500	D	NAU	Deutsche Welle
15680	500	D	WER	Deutsche Welle
15680	250	RUS	VLD	Quê Huong Radio
15690	250	CLN	IRA	BBG - R. Farda
15690	250	CLN	IRA	BBG - R. Free Afghanistan
15690	100	POR	LIS	RDP Internacional
15690	100	UZB	TAC	VO Tibet
15695	500	USA	EWN	WEWN
15700	500	BUL	PLD	R. Bulgaria
15710	50	CHN	dom	CNR 5, Beijing
15710	100	CZE	LIT	R. Prague
15715	250	EGY	ABS	R. Cairo
15720	100	NZL	RAN	R. New Zealand Int'l (RNZI)
15725	100	PAK	ISL	R. Pakistan
15725	50	PLW	HBN	T8BZ - VO Hope
15725	50	USA	RMI	WRMI - R. Miama Int'l
15745	35	CLN	EKA	R. Sri Lanka (SLBC)
15745	50	PLW	HBN	T8BZ - VO Hope
15745	500	USA	EWN	WEWN
15750	500	CLN	IRA	BBG - VO America (VOA)
15760	250	ISR	ISR	Kol Israel
15770	250	IND	ALG	All India Radio (AIR)
15780	35	RUS	TLD	VO Russia (VOR)
15780+	35	RUS	TLD	VO Russia (VOR)
15785	10	ISR	dom	Galei Tzahal (Defence Forces R.)
15795	500	IND	BGL	All India Radio (AIR)
15810	10	DNK	dom	World Music R. , Karup
15810	10	DNK	KRP	World Music Radio (WMR)
15825	100	USA	WCR	The Overcomer Ministry
15825	100	USA	WCR	WWCR
15880	50	CHN	dom	CNR 6, Beijing
17194		B	—	PPR
17485	500	D	NAU	Deutsche Welle
17485	500	D	WER	Deutsche Welle
17485	100	PAK	ISL	R. Pakistan
17490	500	CHN	KAS	China Radio Int'l
17490	500	CHN	URU	China Radio Int'l
17495	500	TJK	DSB	BBG - R. Free Asia (RFA)
17495	50	MDG	MDC	Democratic VO Burma
17495	100	PAK	ISL	R. Pakistan
17495	500	TJK	ORZ	VO Russia (VOR)
17495		USA	BCQ	WBCQ
17500	500	BUL	PLD	R. Bulgaria
17510	250	IND	DEL	All India Radio (AIR)
17510	100	HWA	WHR	Fang Guang Ming Radio
17510	100	HWA	WHR	KWHR - World Harvest R.
17515	200	TJK	DSB	BBG - R. Free Asia (RFA)
17515	250	CVA	SMG	Vatican Radio
17515	500	CVA	SMG	Vatican Radio
17525	200	TJK	DSB	BBG - R. Free Asia (RFA)
17525	500	TJK	ORZ	VO Russia (VOR)
17525	100	UZB	TAC	VO Tibet
17535	250	ISR	ISR	Kol Israel
17540	500	ARM	GAV	BBG - R. Free Asia (RFA)
17540	100	CHN	KAS	China Radio Int'l
17540	100	UZB	TAC	VO Tibet
17545	500	D	WER	Deutsche Welle
17550	100	CHN	dom	CNR 1, Beijing
17555	250	GRC	KAV	BBG - VO America (VOA)
17560	300	J	YAM	R. Japan (NHK World)
17560	500	ARS	RIY	Saudi Radio
17560	500	IRN	KAM	VO the Islamic Rep. of Iran
17560	100	USA	HRA	WHRA - World Harvest R.
17565	500	MRA	TIN	BBG - R. Free Asia (RFA)
17565	250	USA	GRV	BBG - VO America (VOA)
17565	100	D	JUL	Bible Voice B'casting
17565	100	CHN	dom	CNR 1, Beijing
17570	500	MRA	TIN	BBG - R. Free Asia (RFA)
17570	100	D	JUL	RTBF International
17570	250	RUS	TCH	VO Russia (VOR)
17570	500	RUS	MSK	VO Russia (VOR)
17575	100	USA	YFR	WYFR - Family Radio
17580	100	BOT	BOT	BBG - VO America (VOA)
17580	250	USA	GRV	BBG - VO America (VOA)
17580	100	CHN	dom	CNR 1, Lingshi
17580	250	MDG	MDC	R. Nederland Wereldomroep
17580	100	D	JUL	RTBF International
17585	300	G	SKN	BBC World Service
17585	500	UAE	DHA	R. Japan (NHK World)
17590	100	OMA	THU	R. Sultanate of Oman
17590	500	IRN	KAM	VO the Islamic Rep. of Iran
17595	250	UAE	DHA	Adventist World R. (AWR)
17595	250	THA	UDO	BBG - R. Farda
17595	250	THA	UDO	BBG - R. Free Afghanistan
17595	350	E	NOB	R. Exterior de España (REE)
17595	250	MRC	MOR	RTMarocaine
17595	500	USA	EWN	WEWN
17600	300	ISR	ISR	Kol Israel
17600	250	RUS	dom	R. Rossii, Moskva
17605	100	CHN	dom	CNR 1, Beijing
17605	250	ATN	BON	R. Japan (NHK World)
17610	300	G	SKN	BBC World Service
17610	250	CLN	IRA	BBG - RFE/RL
17610	500	D	WER	Deutsche Welle
17610	500	F	ISS	R. France Int'l (RFI)
17615	250	THA	NAK	BBC World Service
17615	100	MRA	SAI	BBG - R. Free Asia (RFA)
17615	100	CHN	dom	CNR 1, Shijiazhuang
17615	500	ARS	RIY	Saudi Radio
17620	500	F	ISS	R. France Int'l (RFI)
17625	100	CHL	SGO	China Radio Int'l

kHz	kW	Ctry	Site	Station, location
17625	50	CHN	dom	CNR 2,Beijing
17625	500	G	RMP	Wales Radio Int'l
17630	250	GAB	GAB	Africa No.1
17630	100	MLI	BKO	China Radio Int'l
17630	500	D	NAU	Deutsche Welle
17630	500	D	WER	Deutsche Welle
17630	500	GUF	GUF	R. France Int'l (RFI)
17630	100	OMA	THU	R. Sultanate of Oman
17635	100	GUM	SDA	KSDA (AWR Guam)
17635	250	AUS	DAR	Voice International
17640	250	CYP	CYP	BBC World Service
17640	250	G	WOF	BBC World Service
17640	300	G	SKN	BBC World Service
17640	250	MRC	MOR	BBG - VO America (VOA)
17650	500	CHN	KAS	China Radio Int'l
17650	500	CHN	URU	China Radio Int'l
17650	250	ASC	ASC	R. Japan (NHK World)
17650	100	USA	HRA	WHRA - World Harvest R.
17660	500	IRN	KAM	VO the Islamic Rep. of Iran
17660	100	CHL	SGO	Voz Cristiana/Voz Crista
17665	250	RUS	IRK	VO Russia (VOR)
17670	250	IND	DEL	All India Radio (AIR)
17670	250	USA	DLN	BBG - R. Martí
17670	500	CHN	KAS	China Radio Int'l
17670	500	CHN	KUN	China Radio Int'l
17670	500	EGY	ABZ	R. Cairo
17675	250	GRC	KAV	BBG - R. Farda
17675	300	CLN	EKA	R. Japan (NHK World)
17675	100	NZL	RAN	R. New Zealand Int'l (RNZI)
17680	250	GRC	KAV	BBG - RFE/RL
17680	100	CHN	KUN	China Radio Int'l
17680	100	CHN	XIA	China Radio Int'l
17680	150	CHN	KUN	China Radio Int'l
17680	300	CHN	BEI	China Radio Int'l
17680	300	POR	LIS	RDP Internacional
17680	500	IRN	SIR	VO the Islamic Rep. of Iran
17680	100	CHL	SGO	Voz Cristiana/Voz Crista
17685	300	J	YAM	R. Japan (NHK World)
17690	500	G	RMP	BBC World Service
17690	600	CHN	JIN	China Radio Int'l
17690	200	UZB	TAC	R. Vlaanderen Int'l (RVI)
17690	500	IRN	KAM	VO the Islamic Rep. of Iran
17690	500	TUR	EMR	VO Turkey
17695	500	AFS	MEY	BBC World Service
17695	100	D	LAM	BBG - RFE/RL
17695	500	F	ISS	VO Africa (LJBC)
17695	250	RUS	TCH	VO Russia (VOR)
17700	250	AFS	MEY	Amateur R. Mirror Int'l
17700	250	RRW	KIG	Deutsche Welle
17700	500	TUR	EMR	VO Turkey
17700+	90	POR	SIN	Deutsche Welle
17705	500	IND	BGL	All India Radio (AIR)
17705	100	BOT	BOT	BBG - VO America (VOA)
17705	250	CUB	HAB	R. Habana Cuba
17705	250	CUB	HAB	R. Nac.Venezuela - Canal Int'l
17710	100	CHN	XIA	China Radio Int'l
17710	300	CHN	BEI	China Radio Int'l
17710	500	G	RMP	Peace Radio
17710	120	CHN	XIA	R. France Int'l (RFI)
17710	300	J	YAM	R. France Int'l (RFI)
17710	300	POR	LIS	RDP Internacional
17710+	90	POR	SIN	Deutsche Welle
17715	250	IND	DEL	All India Radio (AIR)
17715	100	BOT	BOT	BBG - VO America (VOA)
17715	100	STP	SAO	BBG - VO America (VOA)
17715	100	AUS	SHP	R. Australia
17715	350	E	NOB	R. Exterior de España (REE)
17720	250	MNG	UBA	BBG - R. Free Asia (RFA)
17720	500	CHN	URU	China Radio Int'l
17720	500	UAE	DHA	R. Japan (NHK World)
17720	250	ROU	TIG	R. Romania Int'l (RRI)
17720	500	G	RMP	Salaam Watandar
17720	500	TUR	EMR	VO Turkey
17725	250	ATN	BON	R. Nederland Wereldomroep
17730	250	MNG	UBA	BBG - R. Free Asia (RFA)
17730	250	GRC	KAV	BBG - RFE/RL

kHz	kW	Ctry	Site	Station, location
17730	100	D	LAM	BBG - VO America (VOA)
17730	250	CUB	HAB	China Radio Int'l
17730	500	ARS	RIY	Saudi Radio
17730	500	FIN	POR	YLE R. Finland
17735	100	CHN	KUN	China Radio Int'l
17735	250	CAN	SAC	R. Canada Int'l (RCI)
17735	250	ROU	GAL	R. Romania Int'l (RRI)
17735	250	ROU	TIG	R. Romania Int'l (RRI)
17735	500	TUN	SFA	RT Tunisienne (ERTT)
17740	250	IND	DEL	All India Radio (AIR)
17740	250	PHL	PHT	BBG - VO America (VOA)
17740	100	CHN	XIA	China Radio Int'l
17740	250	ARS	RIY	Saudi Radio
17745	250	ROU	GAL	R. Romania Int'l (RRI)
17745	250	ROU	TIG	R. Romania Int'l (RRI)
17745	250	AFS	MEY	R. Vlaanderen Int'l (RVI)
17745	100	POR	LIS	RDP Internacional
17745	500	IRN	SIR	VO the Islamic Rep. of Iran
17750	250	MRC	MOR	BBG - VO America (VOA)
17750	100	AUS	SHP	R. Australia
17750	250	CUB	HAB	R. Habana Cuba
17755	100	CHN	XIA	China Radio Int'l
17755	350	E	NOB	R. Exterior de España (REE)
17755	250	ROU	GAL	R. Romania Int'l (RRI)
17760	100	SNG	SGP	BBC World Service
17760	250	THA	NAK	BBC World Service
17760	500	ARS	RIY	Saudi Radio
17765	250	PHL	PHT	BBG - VO America (VOA)
17765	250	CAN	SAC	R. Canada Int'l (RCI)
17770	500	THA	UDO	BBG - VO America (VOA)
17770	500	AFS	MEY	Channel Africa
17770	350	E	NOB	R. Exterior de España (REE)
17770	250	RRW	KIG	R. France Int'l (RFI)
17775	250	KWT	KBD	BBG - R. Free Afghanistan
17775	50	USA	VOH	KVOH - La Voz de Restauración
17775	250	AUS	DAR	R. Australia
17775	500	EGY	ABZ	R. Cairo
17775	250	ROU	TIG	R. Romania Int'l (RRI)
17775	500	ARS	RIY	Saudi Radio
17780	250	ASC	ASC	BBC World Service
17780	250	AFS	MEY	Channel Africa
17780	300	CLN	EKA	R. Japan (NHK World)
17780	100	I	ROM	RAI International
17785	250	MRC	MOR	BBG - VO America (VOA)
17785	100	CHN	XIA	China Radio Int'l
17785	500	ARS	RIY	Saudi Radio
17790	250	ASC	ASC	BBC World Service
17790	250	CYP	CYP	BBC World Service
17790	250	OMA	SLA	BBC World Service
17790	100	SNG	SGP	BBC World Service
17790	250	THA	NAK	BBC World Service
17790	250	ROU	TIG	R. Romania Int'l (RRI)
17795	100	AUS	SHP	R. Australia
17800	500	IND	BGL	All India Radio (AIR)
17800	250	POR	SIN	Deutsche Welle
17800	250	RRW	KIG	Deutsche Welle
17800	500	F	ISS	R. France Int'l (RFI)
17800+	90	POR	SIN	Deutsche Welle
17805	100	D	LAM	BBG - RFE/RL
17805	500	ARS	RIY	Saudi Radio
17810	250	IND	PAN	All India Radio (AIR)
17810	250	ASC	ASC	BBC World Service
17810	100	EGY	ABZ	R. Cairo
17810	100	J	YAM	R. Japan (NHK World)
17810	300	J	YAM	R. Japan (NHK World)
17810	250	ATN	BON	R. Nederland Wereldomroep
17810	250	ROU	TIG	R. Romania Int'l (RRI)
17810	250	ASC	ASC	United Nations Radio
17810	500	IRN	SIR	VO the Islamic Rep. of Iran
17810	500	FIN	POR	YLE R. Finland
17815	10	B	dom	R. Cultura, São Paulo
17815	250	MDG	MDC	R. Nederland Wereldomroep
17820	250	ASC	ASC	BBC World Service
17820	300	G	SKN	BBC World Service
17820	500	G	RMP	BBC World Service
17820	250	CLN	TRM	Deutsche Welle

kHz	kW	Ctry	Site	Station, location
17820	100	CAN	SAC	R. Canada Int'l (RCI)
17820	300	CLN	EKA	R. Japan (NHK World)
17820	250	ROU	TIG	R. Romania Int'l (RRI)
17820	250	AUS	DAR	Voice International
17820	500	FIN	POR	YLE R. Finland
17825	300	J	YAM	R. Japan (NHK World)
17825	250	ROU	GAL	R. Romania Int'l (RRI)
17825	100	POR	LIS	RDP Internacional
17830	250	ASC	ASC	BBC World Service
17830	500	G	RMP	BBC World Service
17830	500	UAE	DBA	Emirates Radio
17830	250	PHL	PUG	R. Veritas Asia
17835	250	CAN	SAC	R. Canada Int'l (RCI)
17835	1.5	SLV	dom	R. Imperial, Sonsonate
17835	100	J	YAM	R. Japan (NHK World)
17835	100	PAK	ISL	R. Pakistan
17840	500	F	ISS	VO Africa (LJBC)
17840	500	FIN	POR	YLE R. Finland
17845	250	IND	DEL	All India Radio (AIR)
17845	250	THA	UDO	BBG - RFE/RL
17845	250	CLN	TRM	Deutsche Welle
17845	300	J	YAM	R. Japan (NHK World)
17845	250	ROU	GAL	R. Romania Int'l (RRI)
17845	100	USA	YFR	R. Taiwan Int'l
17845	100	USA	YFR	WYFR - Family Radio
17850	250	CYP	CYP	BBC World Service
17850	100	CTR	CRI	R. Exterior de España (REE)
17850	250	AFS	MEY	R. France Int'l (RFI)
17850	250	F	ISS	R. France Int'l (RFI)
17850	500	F	ISS	R. France Int'l (RFI)
17855	250	CLN	IRA	BBG - VO America (VOA)
17855	250	AUS	DAR	R. Australia
17855	300	AUT	MOS	R. Österreich 1
17860	100	IND	DEL	All India Radio (AIR)
17860	100	IND	dom	All India Radio, Delhi
17860	250	RRW	KIG	Deutsche Welle
17860	500	GUF	GUF	R. France Int'l (RFI)
17860	300	J	YAM	R. Japan (NHK World)
17860	500	TUR	EMR	VO Turkey
17865	250	THA	UDO	BBG - RFE/RL
17865	300	UAE	DBA	Emirates Radio
17870	250	OMA	SLA	BBC World Service
17870	250	ASC	ASC	R. Japan (NHK World)
17870	100	J	YAM	R. Japan (NHK World)
17870	100	AUT	MOS	R. Österreich 1
17870	100	D	JUL	R. Rhino Int'l Africa
17875	250	IND	ALG	All India Radio (AIR)
17875	250	CAN	SAC	R. Nederland Wereldomroep
17880	100	MRA	SAI	BBG - R. Free Asia (RFA)
17880	100	MLI	BKO	China Radio Int'l
17880	100	GUM	SDA	KSDA (AWR Guam)
17885	250	ASC	ASC	BBC World Service
17885	250	SEY	SEY	BBC World Service
17885	500	KWT	KBD	R. Kuwait
17890	100	CHN	BEI	China Radio Int'l
17890	100	CHN	dom	CNR 1, Beijing
17890	300	UAE	DBA	Emirates Radio
17895	250	IND	ALG	All India Radio (AIR)
17895	250	MRC	MOR	BBG - Studio 7
17895	100	BOT	BOT	BBG - VO America (VOA)
17895	500	ARS	RIY	Saudi Radio
19010	250	KWT	KBD	BBG - R. Free Afghanistan
20000	**10**	**USA**	**—**	**WWV**
21455	100	AUT	MOS	BBC World Service
21455	1	EQA	QUI	HCJB
21460	250	UAE	DHA	R. UNMEE
21460	500	ARS	RIY	Saudi Radio
21470	250	ASC	ASC	BBC World Service
21470	250	SEY	SEY	BBC World Service
21480	100	STP	SAO	BBG - VO America (VOA)
21480	250	MDG	MDC	R. Nederland Wereldomroep
21485	250	USA	GRV	BBG - VO America (VOA)
21485	500	F	ISS	VO Africa (LJBC)
21490	500	AFS	MEY	BBC World Service
21490	500	G	RMP	BBC World Service
21495	500	ARS	RIY	Saudi Radio
21505	500	ARS	RIY	Saudi Radio
21515	300	G	SKN	BBC World Service
21520	100	I	ROM	RAI International
21525	100	USA	YFR	WYFR - Family Radio
21530	250	GRC	KAV	VO Greece (ERA5)
21535	500	AFS	MEY	United Nations Radio
21540	500	MRA	TIN	BBG - R. Free Asia (RFA)
21540	250	USA	DLN	BBG - VO America (VOA)
21540	350	E	NOB	R. Exterior de España (REE)
21550	250	UAE	DHA	R. UNMEE
21550	100	I	ROM	RAI International
21560	250	CLN	TRM	Deutsche Welle
21560	250	POR	SIN	Deutsche Welle
21560	250	HNG	JBR	R. Budapest
21565	100	D	JUL	RTBF International
21570	500	MRA	TIN	BBG - R. Free Asia (RFA)
21570	250	CLN	IRA	BBG - VO America (VOA)
21570	350	E	NOB	R. Exterior de España (REE)
21580	250	MRA	TIN	BBG - VO America (VOA)
21580	500	F	ISS	R. France Int'l (RFI)
21590	250	UAE	DHA	BBC World Service
21600	300	GUF	GUF	R. Japan (NHK World)
21600	500	ARS	RIY	Saudi Radio
21605	300	UAE	DBA	Emirates Radio
21610	350	E	NOB	R. Exterior de España (REE)
21610	100	J	YAM	R. Japan (NHK World)
21620	500	G	RMP	Peace Radio
21620	500	F	ISS	R. France Int'l (RFI)
21625	250	CLN	IRA	BBG - R. Free Asia (RFA)
21630	250	ASC	ASC	BBC World Service
21630	250	ASC	ASC	R. Japan (NHK World)
21640	250	ASC	ASC	BBC World Service
21640	250	CLN	TRM	Deutsche Welle
21640	500	ARS	RIY	Saudi Radio
21645	500	F	ISS	R. France Int'l (RFI)
21645	500	IRN	SIR	VO the Islamic Rep. of Iran
21655	100	POR	LIS	RDP Internacional
21655	300	POR	LIS	RDP Internacional
21660	250	CYP	CYP	BBC World Service
21660	250	THA	NAK	BBC World Service
21665	500	D	WER	Deutsche Welle
21670	100	J	YAM	R. Japan (NHK World)
21670	500	ARS	RIY	Saudi Radio
21675	500	F	ISS	VO Africa (LJBC)
21675+	90	CLN	TRM	Deutsche Welle
21685	500	F	ISS	R. France Int'l (RFI)
21690	250	THA	UDO	BBG - R. Free Afghanistan
21690	250	PHL	PHT	BBG - RFE/RL
21695	500	F	ISS	VO Africa (LJBC)
21700	300	UAE	DBA	Emirates Radio
21700	350	E	NOB	R. Exterior de España (REE)
21705	500	ARS	RIY	Saudi Radio
21710	100	I	ROM	RAI International
21715	500	UAE	DHA	BBG - R. Free Asia (RFA)
21725	100	AUS	SHP	R. Australia
21740	100	AUS	SHP	R. Australia
21745	100	CZE	LIT	R. Prague
21755	100	J	YAM	R. Japan (NHK World)
21760	250	AFS	MEY	R. France Int'l (RFI)
21770	500	IRN	SIR	VO the Islamic Rep. of Iran
21780	500	D	WER	Deutsche Welle
21780	250	POR	SIN	Deutsche Welle
21780	250	MRA	TIN	R. Australia
21790	250	RUS	IRK	VO Russia (VOR)
21800	500	FIN	POR	YLE R. Finland
21810	500	S	HOR	R. Sweden
21810	500	IRN	SIR	VO the Islamic Rep. of Iran
21820	500	D	WER	Deutsche Welle
21820	250	POR	SIN	Deutsche Welle
21820	250	UAE	DHA	Deutsche Welle
21820	500	GAB	GAB	R. Japan (NHK World)
21830	100	POR	LIS	RDP Internacional
21840	500	D	NAU	Deutsche Welle
21840	500	D	WER	Deutsche Welle
21850	250	CVA	SMG	Vatican Radio

International Broadcasts in English, French, German, Portuguese and Spanish

ENGLISH

0000	English	Area	kHz
0000-0015	R.Japan	SEA	13650yam, 17810yam
0000-0030	BBC World Sce	FE	11945yam, 17615nak
0000-0030	BBC World Sce	ME	1314dha
0000-0030	BBC World Sce	SEA	3915sgp
0000-0030	BBG-VOA	SEA,Pac	11760udo
0000-0030	BBG-VOA	AFG	11995kbd
0000-0030	BBG-VOA	EAs	15290pht
0000-0030	BBG-VOA	SEA	1575bph, 7215pht, 9890pht, 15185pht
0000-0030	BBG-VOA	ME	1593kbd
0000-0030	BBG-VOA	Pac	17740pht
0000-0030	R.Thailand	EAf	9680udo
0000-0100	BBC World Sce	SAs	5970sla, 11955nak
0000-0100	BBC World Sce	NAm	6010sac
0000-0100	BBC World Sce	SEA	9740sgp, 9740sgp
0000-0100	China R. Int'l	As	7180kas
0000-0100	Deutsche Welle	SAs	1548trm, 6030trm, 7290wer
0000-0100	HCJB Australia	EAs	15525knx
0000-0100	R.Australia	Pac	15240shp
0000-0100	R.Bulgaria	NAm	7400pld, 9700pld
0000-0100	RCI	As,CHN	9880xia
0000-0100	R.Japan	NAm	6145sac
0000-0100	RNWO	NAm	9845bon
0000-0130	R.Australia	As	17775dar
0000-0200	BBC World Sce	SEA	6195sgp
0000-0200	BBC World Sce	ME	9410cyp
0000-0200	China R. Int'l	As	6075kas
0000-0200	China R. Int'l	Eu	7345kas
0000-0200	R.Australia	Pac	17715shp
0000-0200	Radio Six Int'l	NAm,Eu	5105bcq
0000-0300	BBC World Sce	SAs	15310nak, 17790sgp
0000-0300	BBC World Sce	SEA	15360sgp
0000-0300	BBC World Sce	SAm	9825skn, 12095asc
0000-0330	BBC World Sce	RUS	1260msk
0000-0400	BBC World Sce	Car	5975atg
0000-0400	WHRA (WHR)	Af	7580hra
0000-0530	BBC World Sce	FE	15280nak
0000-1000	WWCR	NAm,Eu,NAf	3210wcr
0000-1200	Dr Gene Scott	CAm,Eu,Af	5030cha
0000-1200	Dr Gene Scott	NAm,SAm	6150cha
0000-1200	Dr Gene Scott	CTR	7375cha
0000-1300	WEWN	NAm	5825ewn
0000-1400	Dr Gene Scott	NAm,SEA	5755aij
0000-1400	Dr Gene Scott	SEA	5935wcr
0000-1600	KTBN	NAm	7505tbn
0000-2400	AFN Feeder	Atl	5446kew, 7507ror, 7590gvk, 9980gvk, 12133kew
0000-2400	BBC World Sce	ME	1323cgr
0000-2400	BBC World Sce	WEu	648orf
0000-2400	BBC World Sce	HKG	675hkg
0000-2400	Dr Gene Scott	SAm	9725cha
0000-2400	WBCQ	CAm	5105bcq
0000-2400	FBN	NAm	5920boh, 9370tjc
0000-2400	WJIE	NAm	7490jcr, 13595jcr
0000-2400	World Music R.	Eu	5815krp, 15810krp
0025-0430	R.Sri Lanka	As	6005eka, 9770eka, 15745eka
0030-0045	Waymarks Int'l	As	5945jul
0030-0100	BBC World Sce	FE	17615nak
0030-0100	BBC World Sce	SAs	9580sgp
0030-0100	BBG-VOA	SEA,Oc	15185pht
0030-0100	BBG-VOA	EAs	15290pht
0030-0100	BBG-VOA	SEA	1575bph, 9890pht
0030-0100	BBG-VOA	ME	1593kbd
0030-0100	BBG-VOA	EAs,Pac	17740pht
0030-0100	BBG-VOA	SEA,Pac	7215pht
0030-0100	BVB	As	7105dha
0030-0100	R.Thailand	NAm,Car	5890grv
0030-0100	R.Vilnius	NAm	9875sit
0030-0400	R.Australia	As	15415shp
0055-0115	RAI Int'l	NAm	11800rom
0055-0330	BBC World Sce	RUS	666ekb
0100	**English**	**Area**	**kHz**
0100-0130	BBG-VOA	ME	1593kbd
0100-0130	Int'l R.SerbMon	NAm,WEu	7115bij
0100-0130	R.Prague	NAm	6200lit, 7345lit
0100-0130	R.Santec	IND	7145jul
0100-0130	R.Slovakia Int.	NAm	7230rso
0100-0130	R.Slovakia Int.	SAm	9440rso
0100-0130	R.Taskent Int'l	Eu	5975tac
0100-0130	R.Taskent Int'l	WAs	6165tac, 7160tac
0100-0200	BBG-VOA	SAs	7200kav, 11705udo, 11820ira, 17740pht
0100-0200	China R. Int'l	NAm	6005sac, 9580hab
0100-0200	China R. Int'l	As	7180kas
0100-0200	R.Japan	SEA	11860sng, 17810yam
0100-0200	R.Japan	SAs	15325yam
0100-0200	R.Japan	Oc	17685yam
0100-0200	R.Japan	NAm,CAm	17825yam
0100-0200	R.Japan	SAm	17835yam
0100-0200	R.Japan	As	17845yam
0100-0200	R.Japan	ME,NAf	6030rmp, 17560yam
0100-0200	RNWO	NAm	6165bon
0100-0200	R.Romania Int'l	NAm	6140tig, 9690gal
0100-0200	R.Romania Int'l	AUS	9510gal, 11740tig
0100-0200	R.Ukraine Int'l	NAm	7440smf
0100-0200	VO Korea	CHN	3560pyo, 6195kuj, 7140kuj, 9345kuj
0100-0200	VO Korea	CAm,SAm	6520kuj, 7580kuj, 11735kuj
0100-0200	VO Vietnam	CAm	6175sac
0100-0230	HCJB Australia	As	15560knx
0100-0300	BBC World Sce	SAs	11955sla
0100-0300	RCI	NAm,Car,SAm	6190sac, 9755sac, 9810sac
0100-0400	BBC World Sce	CAm	9525yfr
0100-0400	China R. Int'l	SAs	11770kas
0100-0500	R.Habana Cuba	NAm	6000hab, 9820hab
0100-0700	R.Australia	Pac	15240shp
0130-0200	BBG-VOA	ME	1593kbd
0130-0200	BBG-VOA	SAm	7405grv, 9775grv, 13740dln
0130-0200	R.Sweden	As	11550mdc
0140-0200	Vatican Radio	As	7335smg, 9865smg
0200	**English**	**Area**	**kHz**
0200-0230	BBC World Sce	SAs	1413sla
0200-0230	Int'l R.SerbMon	NAm,WEu	7130bij
0200-0230	R.Belarus	Eu	5970mns, 7210mns
0200-0230	R.Budapest	NAm	9775jbr
0200-0230	R.Prague	NAm	6200lit, 7345lit
0200-0300	BBC World Sce	WAs	6195cyp
0200-0300	BBC World Sce	ME	9410cyp
0200-0300	BBC World Sce	EAf	9750sey
0200-0300	BBG-VOA	SAs	7200kav, 11705udo, 11820ira, 17740pht
0200-0300	China R. Int'l	SAs	13640kas
0200-0300	R.Korea Int'l	SAm	11810kim
0200-0300	R.Korea Int'l	NAm	9560sac, 15575kim
0200-0300	R.Taiwan Int'l	SEA	11875tnn
0200-0300	R.Taiwan Int'l	EAs	15465pao
0200-0300	R.Taiwan Int'l	NAm	5950yfr, 9680yfr
0200-0300	RAE	Am	11710bue
0200-0300	VO Indonesia	FE,SEA,AUS	15150jak
0200-0300	VO Korea	SEA	4405pyo, 9325kuj, 11335kuj

0200	English	Area	kHz
0200-0300	VO Russia (VOR)	NAm	7180gri, 7350smg, 15425ppk, 15475kna, 15595ppk
0200-0330	R.Cairo	NAm	11855abz
0200-0500	R.Australia	Pac	21725shp
0200-0500	VO Russia (VOR)	As	17695tch
0200-0900	R.Australia	Pac	15515shp
0200-1400	AFN Feeder	Pac	12579dga
0230-0300	HCJB Australia	As	15560knx
0230-0300	R.Belarus	Eu	5970mns, 7210mns
0230-0300	R.Sweden	NAm	6010sac
0230-0300	VO Vietnam	CAm	6175sac
0245-0300	BBC World Sce	EAf	11865sey
0245-0300	R.Tirana	NAm	6115shi, 7160shi
0250-0315	Vatican Radio	NAm	7305smg, 9605smg
0300	**English**	**Area**	**kHz**
0300-0330	BBC World Sce	NAf	639cgr
0300-0330	BBG-VOA	EAf,SAf	7340bot
0300-0330	R.Thailand	NAm	5890dln
0300-0330	TWR Africa	SAf	3200man
0300-0330	Vatican Radio	As	12070nvs
0300-0330	Vatican Radio	Af	7360smg
0300-0330	VO the NASB	NAm	6870rmi
0300-0330	Wales R. Int'l	NAm	6005rmp
0300-0355	Channel Africa	EAf,CAf	7390mey
0300-0400	BBC World Sce	WAf	11765mey
0300-0400	BBC World Sce	ME	1413sla
0300-0400	BBC World Sce	SAf	6005asc
0300-0400	BBC World Sce	RUS	6195rmp, 9410cyp
0300-0400	BBC World Sce	Eu	9410skn
0300-0400	BBC World Sce	EAf	9750cyp, 12035sey
0300-0400	BBG-VOA	Af	6035bot
0300-0400	China R. Int'l	SAs	15110uru
0300-0400	China R. Int'l	NAm	9690nob, 9790hab
0300-0400	R.Bulgaria	NAm	7400pld, 9700pld
0300-0400	R.Japan	Oc	21610yam
0300-0400	R.Taiwan Int'l	SAm	15215yfr
0300-0400	R.Taiwan Int'l	SEA	15320pao
0300-0400	R.Taiwan Int'l	NAm	5950yfr
0300-0400	VO Korea	CHN	3560pyo, 6195kuj, 7140kuj, 9345kuj
0300-0400	VO Russia (VOR)	NAm	7150arm, 7180gri, 7350smg, 12010kna, 15425ppk, 15475kna, 15595ppk
0300-0430	BBG-VOA	Af	1530sao, 9885bot
0300-0500	BBC World Sce	WAs	11760cyp
0300-0500	BBC World Sce	SEA	15360nak
0300-0500	BBC World Sce	CAs	15575sla
0300-0500	BBC World Sce	FE	17760nak
0300-0500	BBC World Sce	SAf	3255mey, 6190mey
0300-0500	BBG-VOA	Af	6080sao, 7290sao
0300-0500	Channel Africa	SAf	3345mey
0300-0600	BBC World Sce	SAs	15310sla
0300-0600	BBC World Sce	WAf	7160asc
0300-0630	BBG-VOA	Af	909bot
0300-0700	BBC World Sce	SAs	17790nak
0300-1030	BBC World Sce	FE	21660nak
0300-1300	WWCR	CAm,Af	5765wcr
0300-1600	WRNO Worldwide	NAm,CAm	7395rno
0330-0400	R.Budapest	NAm	9775jbr
0330-0400	R.Sweden	NAm	6010sac
0330-0400	R.Tirana	NAm	6115shi, 7160shi
0330-0400	VO Vietnam	CAm	6175sac
0330-0600	BBC World Sce	EAf	15420sey
0330-0700	BBC World Sce	RUS	666ekb, 1260msk, 1260spe
0345-0400	R.Tajikistan	WAs, ME	1143dsb, 7245dsb
0400	**English**	**Area**	**kHz**
0400-0430	RFI	EAf,IOc	9555iss, 9805gab, 11995iss
0400-0430	R.Prague	NAm	6200lit, 7345lit
0400-0500	BBC World Sce	WAf	11765mey
0400-0500	BBC World Sce	EAf	12035cyp
0400-0500	BBC World Sce	Car,SAm	5975atg
0400-0500	BBC World Sce	NAm	6010sac
0400-0500	BBC World Sce	RUS	6195rmp
0400-0500	BBG-VOA	Af	4960sao, 9575grv, 9775bot
0400-0500	China R. Int'l	NAm	6190sac, 9755guf
0400-0500	Deutsche Welle	CAf,EAf	6180kig, 9545kig, 9710wer
0400-0500	RNWO	NAm	6165bon, 9590bon
0400-0500	R.Romania Int'l	IND	11870gal, 15250gal
0400-0500	R.Romania Int'l	NAm	6125tig, 9515tig
0400-0500	R.Ukraine Int'l	NAm	7440smf
0400-0500	VO Russia (VOR)	Eu	603bln, 1548gri
0400-0500	VO Russia (VOR)	NAm	7150arm, 7180gri, 12010kna, 15425ppk, 15595ppk
0400-0500	VO Turkey	Eu,NAm	6020emr
0400-0500	VO Turkey	As,Af	7240emr
0400-0500	WHRA (WHR)	Af	5850hra
0400-0600	BBC World Sce	CAm	6135dln
0400-0600	BBC World Sce	Eu	6195skn, 9410cyp
0400-0600	BBC World Sce	RUS	9410rmp
0400-0600	China R. Int'l	NAm	9560sac
0400-0700	Christian Voice	SAf,CAf	6065lus
0400-0705	BBC World Sce	WAf	6005asc
0400-0800	RNZI	Pac,Eu,NAm	15720ran
0400-0900	Overcomer Min.	NAm,CAm	6870rmi
0400-1300	Overcomer Min.	CAm,Af	5765wcr
0400-1300	WWCR	CAm,Af	5765wcr
0430-0445	Kol Israel	CAm,AUS	17600isr
0430-0445	Kol Israel	NAm,Eu	6280isr, 7545isr
0430-0500	R.Australia	As	15415shp
0430-0500	R.Prague	ME,SAs	9865lit, 11600lit
0430-0600	TWR Africa	SAf	4775man
0430-0800	BBC World Sce	UKR	612kyv
0430-0900	TWR Africa	SAf	6120man
0445-0500	RAI Int'l	E,NAf	5965rom, 7230rom
0445-0500	RAI Int'l	NAf	6000rom
0455-0700	VO Nigeria	Eu,Af	15120iko
0500	**English**	**Area**	**kHz**
0500-0530	BBC World Sce	EAf	17885sey
0500-0530	RFI	EAf,IOc	11850gab, 11995iss, 15155iss
0500-0530	RVI	Am	9590bon
0500-0530	Vatican Radio	Af	7360smg, 9660smg, 11625smg
0500-0555	Channel Africa	WAf	11875mey
0500-0600	BBC World Sce	ME	11760sla
0500-0600	BBC World Sce	WAs	15575cyp
0500-0600	BBC World Sce	EAf	17885sey
0500-0600	BBG-VOA	EAf,SAf	13710bot
0500-0600	BBG-VOA	Af	6035grv, 6080sao, 6105sao, 7295mor
0500-0600	China R. Int'l	NAm	6190sac
0500-0600	Deutsche Welle	CAf,SAf	7285wer, 9565kig, 12035kig, 15410dha
0500-0600	R.Japan	SEA	17810yam
0500-0600	R.Japan	Eu	5975rmp
0500-0600	R.Japan	NAm	6110sac
0500-0600	TWR Africa	SAf	4775man
0500-0600	VO Russia (VOR)	Eu	603bln
0500-0600	WHRA (WHR)	Af	5835hra
0500-0700	BBC World Sce	WAf	11765mey
0500-0700	BBC World Sce	Eu	15565cyp
0500-0700	BBC World Sce	EAf	17640cyp
0500-0700	BBC World Sce	RUS	666ekb, 1260msk, 1260spe
0500-0700	BBC World Sce	WEu	9410skn
0500-0700	Channel Africa	SAf	7240mey
0500-0700	China R. Int'l	FE	11770kas
0500-0700	R.Habana Cuba	Car	6060hab, 9550hab, 9655hab
0500-0700	R.Habana Cuba	NAm	9820hab, 11760hab
0500-0700	R.Japan	As	15195yam

0500	**English**	**Area**	**kHz**
0500-0700	R.Japan	Oc	21755yam
0500-0700	R.Japan	Eu	7230wof
0500-0800	BBC World Sce	WEu	6195rmp
0500-0800	R.Australia	As	15160shp
0500-0800	WEWN	Eu	7570ewn
0500-0900	BBC World Sce	SEA	11955nak, 15360sgp, 15360sgp
0500-0900	China R. Int'l	FE	11880kun
0500-0900	China R. Int'l	SAs	15350kas, 15465kas, 17540kas
0500-0900	TWR Africa	CAf	9500man
0500-1000	BBC World Sce	SEA	17760sgp
0500-1500	BBC World Sce	WAs	15575cyp
0500-1700	BBC World Sce	SAf	6190mey, 11940mey
0530-0545	BBC World Sce	Eu	6010skn, 9815rmp
0530-0600	R.Thailand	Eu	13780udo
0530-0800	R.Australia	As	15415shp
0600	**English**	**Area**	**kHz**
0600-0605	TWR Africa	CAf	11640mey
0600-0620	Vatican Radio	Eu	1530smg, 4005vat, 5885vat, 7250smg
0600-0630	BBG-VOA	EAf,SAf	13710bot
0600-0630	BBG-VOA	Af	6035grv, 6105sao, 11995kav
0600-0630	RFI	EAf,IOc	15155iss, 17800iss
0600-0630	RFI	WAf	9595asc
0600-0630	R.Nationale Lao	SEA	7145vie
0600-0635	TWR Africa	CAf	11640mey
0600-0655	Channel Africa	WAf	15220mey
0600-0700	BBC World Sce	RUS	12095wof
0600-0700	BBC World Sce	UKR	612kyv
0600-0700	BBC World Sce	RUS	666ekb, 1260msk, 1260spe
0600-0700	BBC World Sce	WEu	7160skn
0600-0700	BBG-VOA	Af	1530sao, 6080sao, 7295mor, 11835bot
0600-0700	China R. Int'l	ME	15140uru
0600-0700	China R. Int'l	NAm	6115kas
0600-0700	Deutsche Welle	WAf	7225sin, 7225wer, 11785wer, 15410kig
0600-0700	R.Japan	NAm,CAm	11690yam
0600-0700	R.Japan	FE,RUS	11715yam, 11760yam
0600-0700	R.Japan	SEA	11740sng
0600-0700	R.Japan	HWA	17870yam
0600-0700	VO Russia (VOR)	Eu	603bln, 1323wbr
0600-0730	BBC World Sce	ME	15575smf
0600-0800	Overcomer Min.	NAm,Eu	5070wcr
0600-0800	VO Russia (VOR)	AUS,NZL	17665irk, 21790irk
0600-0800	WHRA (WHR)	Af	7580hra
0600-0825	VO Malaysia	AUS,NZL	15295kaj
0600-0825	VO Malaysia	INS	6175kaj, 9750kaj
0600-0900	BBC World Sce	Eu	9410skn
0600-0900	TWR Africa	SAf	6120man
0600-1000	Deutsche Welle	ME,NAf	21675trm+
0600-1000	Deutsche Welle	Eu	6140jul
0600-1000	KWHR (WHR)	Oc	11565whr
0600-1200	BBC World Sce	ME	15575smf
0600-1400	BBC World Sce	EAf	17885sey
0600-1800	AFN Feeder	Pac	6350peh
0600-1800	BBC World Sce	SAs	15310nak
0630-0645	BBC World Sce	Eu	9875cyp
0630-0700	BBC World Sce	WAf	15400asc
0630-0700	R.Georgia	Eu	11805dsh
0630-0700	R.Romania Int'l	WEu	9565tig, 11710tig
0630-0700	Vatican Radio	Af	9660smg, 11625smg, 13765smg
0700	**English**	**Area**	**kHz**
0700-0720	BBC World Sce	WAf	6005asc
0700-0730	R.Slovakia Int.	AUS	13715rso, 15460rso
0700-0800	BBC World Sce	WAf	11765asc
0700-0800	BBC World Sce	RUS	12095wof
0700-0800	BBC World Sce	WEu	17830rmp
0700-0800	BBC World Sce	UKR	612kyv
0700-0800	Channel Africa	SAf	11825mey

0700	**English**	**Area**	**kHz**
0700-0800	R.Australia	Pac	15240shp
0700-0800	RFI	WAf	11700gab, 11725gab, 15605gab, 15605gab
0700-0800	R.Taiwan Int'l	NAm	5950yfr
0700-0900	BBG-VOA	Af	5995mor, 6080sao, 11655bot
0700-0900	China R. Int'l	Eu	1215fla
0700-0900	VO Russia (VOR)	Eu	12010spb, 12060spb
0700-1000	BBC World Sce	WAf	15400asc
0700-1000	VO Russia (VOR)	Eu	603bln, 1323wbr, 15780tld+
0700-1130	BBC World Sce	WAf	15400asc
0700-1400	BBC World Sce	ME	11760sla
0700-1500	BBC World Sce	Eu	17640skn
0700-1600	BBC World Sce	SAs	17790sla
0700-1700	BBC World Sce	Eu	12095wof
0700-1700	BBC World Sce	WEu	15485skn
0700-1700	Christian Voice	SAf,CAf	9865lus
0700-1800	BBC World Sce	RUS	15565rmp
0715-0730	BBC World Sce	RUS	666ekb, 1260msk, 1260spe
0730-0745	Vatican Radio	As	15595smg
0730-0745	Vatican Radio	Eu	585vat, 1530smg, 4005vat, 5885vat, 6185smg, 7250smg, 9645smg, 11740smg, 15595smg
0730-0745	Vatican Radio	Af	9645smg, 15595smg
0730-0800	R.Bulgaria	WEu	11600pld, 13600pld
0730-0800	R.Sweden	Eu	1179sol
0730-0900	BBC World Sce	RUS	666ekb, 1260msk, 1260spe
0730-0900		KTWR	SEA 15225twr
0730-0945	BVB	Eu	5945jul
0740-0900		KTWR	SEA 15225twr
0745-0920	TWR Europe	Eu	9870mco, 11865shi
0800	**English**	**Area**	**kHz**
0800-0830	R.Prague	Eu	7345lit, 9880lit
0800-0830	RVI	Eu	1512wol, 5965jul
0800-0900	Am.R.Mirr Int'l	EAf,CAf	17700mey
0800-0900	Am.R.Mirr Int'l	SAf	9750mey
0800-0900	KNLS Int'l	Pac	7365nls, 11765nls
0800-0900	R.Australia	Pac	5995brn, 9710shp
0800-0900	R.Korea Int'l	SEA	9570kim
0800-0900	R.Korea Int'l	Eu	9640kim
0800-0900	Radio Six Int'l	Eu,ME	13840mil
0800-0900	R.Taiwan Int'l	SEA	9610tnn
0800-0900	VO Indonesia	FE,SEA,AUS	15150jak
0800-0900	VO Russia (VOR)	AUS,NZL	17495orz, 17525orz, 17570tch, 17665irk, 21790irk
0800-0915	BVB	Eu	5945jul
0800-0920	TWR Europe	Eu	9870mco, 11865shi
0800-1000	BBC World Sce	WAf	17830asc
0800-1000	VO Russia (VOR)	As	1251dsb, 17570tch
0800-1100	HCJB Australia	Pac	11750knx
0800-1100	RNZI	Pac,NAm	9885ran
0800-1100	WSHB (WHR)	NAm,Eu,Af	5860shb
0800-1130	R.Australia	As	15240shp
0800-1200	China R. Int'l	Eu	17490uru
0800-1300	BBC World Sce	SAf	21470sey
0800-1400	BBC World Sce	EAf	17885sey
0800-1400	R.Australia	Pac	9580shp
0800-1500	BBC World Sce	RUS	17640wof
0800-1600	R.Australia	Pac	9590shp
0800-2100	BBC World Sce	WAf	17830asc
0800-2200	AFN Feeder	Pac	5765bar
0815-0845	BVB	Eu	5945jul
0815-0850	TWR Europe	Eu	9870mco, 11865shi
0815-0930	KTWR	Pac,Oc	11840twr
0830-0900	R.Australia	As	15415shp
0830-0900	R.Georgia	Eu	11910dsh
0900	**English**	**Area**	**kHz**
0900-1000	BBC World Sce	SAm	15190asc

0900	English	Area	kHz
0900-1000	BBC World Sce	SEA	6195nak, 6195sgp, 9740sgp
0900-1000	VO Russia (VOR)	AUS,NZL	17495orz, 17525orz, 17570tch, 17665irk
0900-1030	BBC World Sce	SEA	6195nak
0900-1030	BBC World Sce	FE	9605yam, 15360nak
0900-1030	Voice Int'l	IND	11955dar
0900-1100	BBC World Sce	SAm	15190asc
0900-1100	BBC World Sce	SEA	6195nak
0900-1100	BBC World Sce	SEA	6195sgp
0900-1100	China R. Int'l	Pac	15210kun, 17690jin
0900-1100	Overcomer Min.	NAm,Eu	5070wcr
0900-1200	BBC World Sce	ME	15575smf
0900-1200	BBG-VOA	ME	13865ira, 15615kav, 17555kav
0900-1300	R.Australia	Pac	11880shp
0900-1430	Voice Int'l	CHN	13685dar
0900-1500	China R. Int'l	Pac	17490kas
0900-1600	BBC World Sce	SEA	9740sgp
0915-0930	BBC World Sce	RUS	666ekb, 1260msk, 1260spe
0930-1000	BBC World Sce	RUS	666ekb, 1260msk, 1260spe
0930-1000	R.Georgia	ME	11910dsh
0930-1000	R.Vilnius	Eu	9710sit
0930-1030	Radio Six Int'l	Eu,ME	13840mil
0930-1100	R.Australia	As	15415shp
1000	**English**	**Area**	**kHz**
1000-1030	R.Prague	SAs,WAf	21745lit
1000-1030	VO Mongolia	As	12085uba
1000-1100	All India R.	CLN	1053tut, 15260del
1000-1100	All India R.	AUS,NZL	13710bgl, 17510del, 17895alg
1000-1100	All India R.	EAs	15020alg, 15235bgl, 17800bgl
1000-1100	BBC World Sce	Car	6195atg
1000-1100	BBC World Sce	SEA	6195nak, 6195sgp
1000-1100	BBC World Sce	RUS	666ekb, 1260msk, 1260spe
1000-1100	China R. Int'l	NAm	6040sac
1000-1100	Voice Africa	Eu	9760rmp+
1000-1100	R.Japan	Eu	17585dha
1000-1100	R.Japan	ME,NAf	17720dha
1000-1100	R.Japan	Oc	21755yam
1000-1100	RNWO	EAs,SEA	12065irk
1000-1100	RNWO	EAs	13820khb
1000-1100	RNWO	Eu	7240fle+
1000-1100	RNWO	FE	7315ppk
1000-1100	RNWO	AUS,NZL	9790bon
1000-1100	VO Korea	CAm,SAm	3560pyo, 9335kuj, 11710kuj
1000-1100	VO Korea	SEA	9850kuj, 11735kuj
1000-1100	WWCR	NAm,Eu,NAf	9985wcr, 9985wcr
1000-1200	Channel Africa	SAf	11825mey
1000-1200	KWHR (WHR)	Oc	11565whr
1000-1200	R.Japan	As	11730yam
1000-1200	R.Japan	NAm	6120sac
1000-1200	R.Japan	SEA	9695yam
1000-1200	RNWO	Eu	7240fle+
1000-1400	BBC World Sce	FE	17760nak
1000-1400	BBC World Sce	Car	6195atg
1000-1500	BBC World Sce	Eu	7320rmp+
1000-1500	VO Nigeria	Eu,Af	15120iko
1000-1600	BBC World Sce	SEA	9740sgp
1000-2200	Dr Gene Scott	CAm	11755aia
1030-1045	Kol Israel	NAm,Eu	15640isr, 17535isr
1030-1100	BBC World Sce	SEA	15285sgp
1030-1100	BBC World Sce	FE	9605yam, 11945nak, 21660nak
1030-1100	Vatican Radio	Eu	585vat, 1611smg+, 5885vat
1030-1130	VOIRI	SAs	15460kam, 15480kam
1030-1130	VOIRI	ME	702kia
1030-1130	VOIRI	WAs	765chb

1100	English	Area	kHz
1100-1130	BBC World Sce	SAm	15190asc
1100-1130	BBC World Sce	Car,SAm	15190atg
1100-1130	BBC World Sce	WAf	15400asc
1100-1130	BBC World Sce	SAm	17790asc
1100-1130	BBC World Sce	Car	6195atg
1100-1130	BBG-VOA	SEA	1575bph
1100-1130	VO Vietnam	SEA	1242omo
1100-1130	VO Vietnam	As	7285han
1100-1200	China R. Int'l	NAm	5960sac
1100-1200	R.Taiwan Int'l	SEA	7105pao
1100-1200	TDPradio	Eu	7240fle+
1100-1230	FEBC Korea	SEA	1188seo
1100-1230	HCJB Australia	SEA	15425knx
1100-1300	R.Australia	As	9475shp
1100-1300	RNZI	Pac,As	15530ran
1100-1300	WINB	CAm	9320inb
1100-1300	WSHB (WHR)	NAm,Eu,Af	7535shb
1100-1330	HCJB	NAm,SAm	12005qui
1100-1330	HCJB	Eu,Oc	21455qui
1100-1400	R.Australia	Pac	5995brn, 6020shp, 9560shp
1100-1400	R.Singapore Int	SEA	6080sgp, 6150sgp
1100-1700	BBC World Sce	SEA	6195sgp
1100-1730	Voice Int'l	IND	13685dar
1100-2100	BBC World Sce	WAf	17830asc
1100-2100	WWCR	NAm,Eu,NAf	15825wcr
1100-2200	WWCR	NAm,Eu,NAf	15825wcr
1115-1130	BBC World Sce	RUS	666ekb, 1260msk, 1260spe
1130-1145	BBC World Sce	SEA	7135sgp, 11920nak
1130-1200	BBC World Sce	Car,SAm	15190atg
1130-1200	BBC World Sce	Car	6195atg
1130-1200	BBC World Sce	RUS	666ekb, 1260msk, 1260spe
1130-1200	BVB	EAs	5945khb
1130-1200	R.Prague	Eu	11640lit
1130-1200	R.Prague	EAf,ME	21745lit
1130-1200	RVI	As,AUS	9945irk
1130-1200	Wales R. Int'l	Oc	17625rmp
1130-1215	TWR India	SAs	882put
1130-1700	BBC World Sce	Car,SAm	15190atg
1200	**English**	**Area**	**kHz**
1200-1230	BBC World Sce	Car,SAm	15190atg
1200-1230	BBC World Sce	Car	6195atg
1200-1230	BBG-VOA	EAs	1143php
1200-1230	RFI	WAf	15275asc
1200-1230	RFI	EAf,IOc	21620iss
1200-1230	R.Taskent Int'l	As	5060tac, 9715tac
1200-1230	R.Taskent Int'l	Eu	5975tac
1200-1230	R.Taskent Int'l	WAs	6025tac
1200-1300	BBC World Sce	RUS	666ekb, 1260msk, 1260spe
1200-1300	BBG-VOA	Pac	11715pht
1200-1300	BBG-VOA	SEA	6110pht, 15665ira
1200-1300	China R. Int'l	AUS,NZL	15415kun
1200-1300	China R. Int'l	SEA	684dof, 1188yun, 1269yun
1200-1300	China R. Int'l	As	9730kun
1200-1300	RCI	As,CHN	9670yam, 11730yam
1200-1300	R.Korea Int'l	NAm	9650sac
1200-1300	RNWO	NAm	11675bon
1200-1300	RNWO	Eu	7240fle+
1200-1300	R.Taiwan Int'l	EAs	7130min
1200-1300	R.Ukraine Int'l	Eu	15620khr
1200-1300	TDPradio	Eu	6015jul
1200-1400	BBG-VOA	SEA,Pac	9645udo
1200-1400	BBG-VOA	EAs	9760pht
1200-1400	China R. Int'l	SEA	11980kun
1200-1400	China R. Int'l	SEA,PHL	1341gdg
1200-1400	China R. Int'l	Eu	13790kas
1200-1400	China R. Int'l	OC	9795uru, 11760kun
1200-1500	BBC World Sce	WAs	15575cyp
1200-1500	BBG-VOA	CHN	11705pht
1200-1500	BBG-VOA	SAs,SEA	9760pht

1200	English	Area	kHz
1200-1600	WBCQ	CAm	9330bcq
1200-1800	VO Liberty	WAf	11515mon
1200-2300	WBCQ	CAm	17495bcq
1200-2400	Dr Gene Scott	CTR	11870cha
1200-2400	Dr Gene Scott	NAm	13750cha
1215-1230	TWR India	SAs	882put
1215-1245	BVB	EAs	5945khb
1215-1330	R.Cairo	SAs	17670abz
1225-1545	R.Sri Lanka	As	6005eka, 9770eka, 15745eka
1230-1235	BVB	EAs	5945khb
1230-1245	BBC World Sce	WEu	15425wof
1230-1245	BBC World Sce	WAf	17780asc
1230-1245	BBC World Sce	CAf	21640asc
1230-1245	BVB	EAs	5945khb
1230-1300	Bangladesh Bet.	SAs,SEA	7185dka, 9550dka
1230-1300	HCJB Australia	SEA	15405knx
1230-1300	R.Bulgaria	WEu	11700pld, 15700pld
1230-1300	R.Thailand	SEA,Pac	9810udo
1230-1300	VO Vietnam	As	9840vni, 12020vni
1230-1315	BVB	EAs	5945vld
1230-1400	BBC World Sce	Car	6195atg
1230-1700	BBC World Sce	Car,SAm	15190atg

1300	English	Area	kHz
1300-1000	WBCQ	CAm	7415bcq
1300-1330	RCI	As,CHN	9670yam, 11730yam
1300-1400	BBC World Sce	ME	1314dha
1300-1400	BBC World Sce	SAs	1413sla
1300-1400	BBC World Sce	EAf	15420sey
1300-1400	China R. Int'l	AUS,NZL	11900kun
1300-1400	China R. Int'l	Eu	13790kas
1300-1400	China R. Int'l	As	15180xia
1300-1400	China R. Int'l	NAm	9570hab, 11885sac, 17625sgo
1300-1400	KNLS Int'l	EAs	9690nls
1300-1400	R.Korea Int'l	SEA	9570kim, 9770kim
1300-1400	R.Polonia	Eu	9525wwa, 11820wwa
1300-1400	R.Romania Int'l	WEu	15105tig, 17745tig
1300-1400	VO Korea	Eu	4405pyo, 9325kuj, 11335kuj
1300-1400	VO Korea	NAm	9335kuj, 11710kuj
1300-1500	BBG-VOA	SAs,SEA	6110pht
1300-1500	China R. Int'l	Eu	13610kas
1300-1500	China R. Int'l	NAm	15230sac
1300-1600	Deutsche Welle	Eu	6140jul
1300-1600	RCI	NAm,Car	9515sac, 13655sac, 17820sac
1300-1600	Overcomer Min.	Eu,ME	13810jul
1300-1600	Overcomer Min.	Eu	6110jul
1300-1600	Overcomer Min.	NAm,CAm	7465wcr
1300-1600	WEWN	NAm	9955ewn
1300-1600	WHRA (WHR)	Af	17560hra
1300-1600	WWCR	CAm,Af	7465wcr, 7465wcr
1300-1600	WWCR	NAm,Eu	9985wcr, 9985wcr
1300-1650	RNZI	Pac	9870ran
1300-1900	BBC World Sce	SAf	21470asc
1300-2200	WSHB (WHR)	NAm,Eu,Af	9840shb
1300-2300	WINB	CAm	13570inb
1300-2300	WWRB	Atl,Eu,NAf	12172wrb
1300-2300	WWRB	NAm,Eu	9320wrb
1305-1400	BBC World Sce	RUS	666ekb, 1260msk, 1260spe
1315-1330	BBC World Sce	RUS	666ekb, 1260msk, 1260spe
1315-1330	TWR India	As	7535irk
1330-1345	BBC World Sce	WAf	15105asc, 17810asc
1330-1400	HCJB Australia	As	15405knx
1330-1400	Int'l R.SerbMon	AUS	11835bij
1330-1400	R.Nationale Lao	SEA	7145vie
1330-1400	R.Sweden	ME,As	11550hor
1330-1400	R.Sweden	NAm	15240hor
1330-1400	R.Sweden	Eu	7240fle+
1330-1400	R.Sweden	As	7420hor
1330-1400	R.Taskent Int'l	As	5060tac, 9715tac
1330-1400	R.Taskent Int'l	Eu	5975tac
1330-1400	R.Taskent Int'l	WAs	6025tac
1330-1430	VO Turkey	Eu	15155emr
1330-1430	VO Turkey	As,AUS	15195emr
1330-1500	All India R.	EAs,SEA	9690bgl, 11620del, 13710bgl
1330-1600	BBC World Sce	RUS	666ekb, 1260msk, 1260spe

1400	English	Area	kHz
1400-0200	AFN Feeder	Pac	4319dga
1400-1415	BBC World Sce	EAf	11860sey, 15420sey
1400-1415	BBC World Sce	Eu	21490rmp
1400-1415	BVB	As	7185tac
1400-1415	FEBA Radio	WAs	9445nvs
1400-1430	RCI	WEu	9815fle+
1400-1430	R.Prague	EAf,NAm	21745lit
1400-1430	R.Thailand	SEA,Pac	9725udo
1400-1500	BBC World Sce	UKR	612kyv
1400-1500	BBG-VOA	SEA	15425pht
1400-1500	BBG-VOA	SEA,Pac	15425pht
1400-1500	BBG-VOA	SAs,SEA	9645pht
1400-1500	BVB	As	7185tac
1400-1500	Brigham YU R.	Eu	9875rmp+
1400-1500	China R. Int'l	As	11675kun, 11760uru
1400-1500	China R. Int'l	SAs	1422kas, 9560kas
1400-1500	China R. Int'l	Eu	9700kas, 9795uru
1400-1500	RFI	ME,IND	17620iss
1400-1500	RFI	IND	7180xia, 9580xia
1400-1500	R.Japan	Oc	11840eka
1400-1500	R.Sult.of Oman	Eu,ME	15140thu
1400-1500	R.Taiwan Int'l	SEA	15265tnn
1400-1600	BBC World Sce	FE	7160nak
1400-1600	BBG-VOA	SAs	7125udo
1400-1600	Channel Africa	SAf	11825mey
1400-1600	China R. Int'l	EAf	13685bko
1400-1600	China R. Int'l	WAf	17630bko
1400-1600	China R. Int'l	NAm	7405jin, 13675sac, 17730hab
1400-1600	R.Australia	As	11750shp
1400-1600	R.Japan	SEA	7200yam
1400-1600	R.Japan	SAs	9875yam
1400-1600	RNWO	SAs	9345tac, 12080mdc, 15595mdc
1400-1700	BBC World Sce	EAf	21660cyp
1400-1700	RCI	NAm,Car	9515sac, 13655sac, 17820sac
1400-1730	R.Jordan	NAm,Eu	11690aka
1400-1800	R.Australia	Pac	5995shp, 6080shp
1400-2400	Dr Gene Scott	NAm,SEA	13815aij
1400-2400	Dr Gene Scott	SEA	13845wcr
1430-1500	R.Korea Int'l	Eu	9770kim
1430-1500	RNWO	Eu	7240fle+
1430-1500	R.Sweden	ME,As	11550hor
1430-1500	R.Sweden	NAm	15240sac
1430-1800	HCJB Australia	As	15390knx
1430-1900	R.Australia	As	9475shp
1445-1500	BBC World Sce	SAs	1413sla, 6140sla, 7205sla, 15245nak

1500	English	Area	kHz
1500-1515	FEBC Korea	SEA	1566jej
1500-1515	FEBA Radio	As	7340irk
1500-1530	BBC World Sce	EAf	11860sey, 15420sey, 21490mey
1500-1530	BBG-VOA	SEA	15460udo
1500-1530	BBG-VOA	SEA	1575bph
1500-1530	BBG-VOA	SAs,SEA	6110pht, 9760pht
1500-1530	BBG-VOA	EAs	9760pht, 9795pht
1500-1530	R.Australia	Eu	9875rmp+
1500-1530	RNZI	Eu	9875rmp+
1500-1530	R.Rhino Int'l	UGA	17870jul
1500-1530	VO Mongolia	Eu	12015uba
1500-1530	VO Vietnam	SAs	1242omo
1500-1530	VO Vietnam	As	7285han, 9840vni, 12020vni

1500	English	Area	kHz
1500-1555	Channel Africa	EAf,CAf	17770mey
1500-1600	BBC World Sce	RUS	12095wof
1500-1600	BBC World Sce	SAs	5975sgp
1500-1600	BBG-VOA	EAs,SEA	11780ira, 13735ira
1500-1600	BBG-VOA	Af	13600sao, 17715bot, 17895bot
1500-1600	BBG-VOA	EAf	13865ira
1500-1600	BBG-VOA	EAs	7175udo
1500-1600	BBG-VOA	SAs	9645ira
1500-1600	BBG-VOA	ME	9685kav
1500-1600	BVB	As	12005jul
1500-1600	China R. Int'l	G	558lnd
1500-1600	China R. Int'l	As	7160uru, 9785jin
1500-1600	RCI	IND	5985kim, 9635xia, 11975xia
1500-1600	R.Japan	As	6190yam
1500-1600	R.Japan	NAm,CAm	9505yam
1500-1600	TDPradio	Eu	6015jul+
1500-1600	VO Korea	Eu	4405pyo, 9325kuj, 11335kuj
1500-1600	VO Korea	NAm	9335kuj, 11710kuj
1500-1600	VO Russia (VOR)	Eu	12060tld+
1500-1600	VO Russia (VOR)	As	1251dsb, 5945nvs, 6205tch, 7260vld, 7315sam, 7350tch, 7415ppk, 9900sam, 11500orz, 12025msk
1500-1630		KTWR	As,EAf 12105twr
1500-1700	BBG-VOA	ME	11835lam, 15255kav
1500-1700	China R. Int'l	Eu	9435kas, 9525kas
1500-1730	Voice Int'l	IND	11840dar
1500-2300	BBC World Sce	WAf	15400asc
1515-1600	FEBA Radio	As	7340irk
1530-1545	All India R.	SAs	7255alg, 9820pan, 9910del, 11740pan
1530-1545	BBC World Sce	SAs	9600sgp, 11685sgp
1530-1600	BBC World Sce	UKR	612kyv
1530-1600	BBG-VOA	SEA	1575bph, 15460udo
1530-1600	BBG-VOA	SAs,SEA	6110pht, 9760pht
1530-1600	BBG-VOA	EAs	9760pht, 9795pht
1530-1600	R.Korea Int'l	Eu	9875rmp+
1530-1600	Vatican Radio	As	9865tac, 11850smg, 13765smg
1530-1600	VO Russia (VOR)	ME	972orz
1530-1630	VOIRI	SAs	9610sir, 9940kam

1600	English	Area	kHz
1600-1615	R.Pakistan	WAf,NAf,ME	11570isl
1600-1615	R.Pakistan	EAf,SAf	11850isl, 15725isl
1600-1615	R.Pakistan	NAf,ME	9390isl
1600-1630	KSDA	As	15495sda
1600-1630	R.Budapest	Eu	6025jbr, 9580jbr
1600-1630	TWR Africa	SAf	6070man
1600-1630	VO Vietnam	SEA	1242omo
1600-1630	VO Vietnam	Eu,ME	7220vni, 7280vni, 9550vni, 9730vni
1600-1700	BBC World Sce	RUS	12095wof
1600-1700	BBC World Sce	WAs	17790cyp
1600-1700	BBC World Sce	WEu	17820rmp
1600-1700	BBC World Sce	Eu	9410wof
1600-1700	BBG-VOA	CHN	1143php
1600-1700	BBG-VOA	SAs,SEA	6160pht, 9760pht
1600-1700	BBG-VOA	SAs	7125udo, 9645ira
1600-1700	BBG-VOA	Af	909bot, 1530sao, 13600sao, 15445bot, 17640mor, 17715sao, 17895bot
1600-1700	BBG-VOA	ME	9685kav
1600-1700	China R. Int'l	Eu	7255uru
1600-1700	Deutsche Welle	SAs	1548trm, 6170trm, 7225trm, 11695wer
1600-1700	R.Ethiopia	EAf	7165gjw
1600-1700	R.Ethiopia	EAf,ME	9561gjw
1600-1700	RFI	NAf	11615iss
1600-1700	RFI	WAf	15160mey
1600-1700	RFI	CAf	9730mey, 17850iss
1600-1700	R.Korea Int'l	FE	5975hwa
1600-1700	R.Korea Int'l	Af	9870kim
1600-1700	R.Taiwan Int'l	CHN, SAs	11815pao
1600-1700	TDPradio	NAm	11900sac+
1600-1700	Overcomer Min.	NAm	9985wcr
1600-1700	VO Korea	ME,NAf	3560pyo, 9975kuj, 11735kuj
1600-1700	VO Russia (VOR)	Eu	6130msk, 7290msk
1600-1700	VO Russia (VOR)	ME	972orz, 4940dsb, 4965dsb, 4975dsb, 6005arm, 9470msk
1600-1700	VO Russia (VOR)	As	972orz, 4940dsb, 4965dsb, 4975dsb, 7260vld, 7415ppk
1600-1730	RFI	EAf,ME	11615iss
1600-1730	RFI	EAf,IOc	15605iss
1600-1800	BBC World Sce	SAs	3915sgp, 11750sgp
1600-1800	BBC World Sce	SEA	7160sgp
1600-1800	China R. Int'l	SEA	1080kun
1600-1800	China R. Int'l	SAf	11900xia
1600-1800	China R. Int'l	SAs	1323lha
1600-1800	China R. Int'l	Af	9570xia
1600-1830	BBC World Sce	SAs	5975nak
1600-2000	R.Australia	Pac	9710shp
1600-2000	WEWN	Eu	15695ewn
1600-2100	WHRA (WHR)	Af	17650hra
1600-2100	WMLK	Eu,ME	9265mlk
1600-2200	BBG-VOA	Af	15240mor
1600-2200	WEWN	NAm	13615ewn
1600-2200	WWCR	NAm,Eu	12160wcr
1600-2200	WWCR	CAm,Af	9985wcr, 9985wcr
1600-2300	WRNO Worldwide		NAm,CAm 15420rno
1600-2300	WWCR	NAm,Eu	12160wcr
1600-2400	KTBN	NAm	15590tbn
1615-1700	BBC World Sce	EAf	11860sey, 15420sey, 21490mey
1630-1700	BBC World Sce	EAf	15420sey
1630-1700	KSDA	As	11980sda
1630-1700	R.Georgia	ME	6180dsh
1630-1830	R.Cairo	CAf,SAf	9855abs
1630-1900	BVB	ME	9460jul
1645-1700	R.Tajikistan	WAs, ME	1143dsb, 7245dsb
1645-1700	TWR India	SAs	882put
1645-1715	BVB	ME	9460jul
1645-1745	BVB	ME	9460jul
1645-1800	BVB	ME	9460jul
1645-1830	BVB	ME	9460jul
1650-1750	RNZI	Pac	9870ran

1700	English	Area	kHz
1700-0400	Christian Voice	SAf,CAf	4965lus
1700-1710	R.DMR	Eu	5960gri
1700-1730	R.DMR	Eu	5960gri
1700-1730	R.Prague	CAf,WAf	15710lit
1700-1730	R.Prague	Eu	5930lit
1700-1730	TWR India	SAs	882put
1700-1730	VO the NASB	NAm	11900sac+
1700-1745	BBC World Sce	EAf	6005sey, 9630sey
1700-1755	Channel Africa	WAf	15285mey
1700-1800	BBC World Sce	Eu	12095wof
1700-1800	BBC World Sce	WEu	17820skn
1700-1800	BBG-VOA	EAf,SAf	15445bot
1700-1800	China R. Int'l	Eu	7255kas
1700-1800	R.Japan	Eu	11970yam
1700-1800	R.Japan	SAf	15355gab
1700-1800	R.Japan	NAm,CAm	9535yam
1700-1800	R.Japan	Eu	9875rmp+
1700-1800	VO Russia (VOR)	As	648orz, 1251dsb, 1269yun, 5910irk, 5945nvs, 7415ppk
1700-1800	VO Russia (VOR)	ME	648orz, 1251dsb, 9470msk, 9830msk
1700-1900	BBC World Sce	RUS	12095wof
1700-1900	BBC World Sce	EAf	15420mey

1700	English	Area	kHz
1700-2000	BBC World Sce	Eu	6195cyp, 6195skn
1700-2000	BBG-VOA	Af	13710udo
1700-2030	TWR Africa	SAf	3200man
1700-2035	TWR Africa	SAf	1170man
1700-2100	China R. Int'l	Eu	6100qiq
1700-2100	R.Australia	Pac	9580shp, 11880shp
1700-2100	VO Nigeria	WAf	7255iko
1700-2200	BBC World Sce	SAf	3255mey, 6190mey
1700-2200	BBC World Sce	Eu	9410cyp
1700-2300	BBC World Sce	WEu	6195rmp
1710-1725	TWR Europe	CAs	864gav, 5885gav
1715-1730	Vatican Radio	Eu	585vat, 1530smg, 4005vat, 5885vat, 7250smg, 9645smg, 15595smg
1730-1745	BBC World Sce	SAf	3390mey
1730-1745	BBC World Sce	EAf	7230mey
1730-1745	BBC World Sce	WAf	9685mey
1730-1745	FEBA Radio	WAs	9840msk
1730-1745	UN Radio	WAf,CAf	17810asc
1730-1745	UN Radio	EAf	7170mey
1730-1745	UN Radio	ME	9565skn
1730-1800	BBC World Sce	RUS	5875cyp
1730-1800	BBC World Sce	Eu	6015skn, 7190rmp
1730-1800	BBC World Sce	UKR	612kyv
1730-1800	KSDA	ME	11560sda
1730-1800	R.Slovakia Int.	Eu	5915rso, 6055rso
1730-1800	Vatican Radio	Af	11625smg, 13765smg, 15570smg
1730-1800	Vatican Radio	As	15595smg
1730-1900	TWR Africa	EAf	9500man
1740-1800	BBG-Studio 7	ZMB	909bot, 11975sao, 17895mor
1745-1945	All India R.	EAf	11935mum, 15075del, 17670del
1745-1945	All India R.	WEu	7410del, 9950del, 11620alg
1745-1945	All India R.	NAf	9445bgl, 13605bgl, 15155alg
1750-1850	RNZI	Pac	11980ran
1800	**English**	**Area**	**kHz**
1800-0600	AFN Feeder	Pac	10320peh
1800-1815	BVB	ME	7210jul
1800-1830	BBC World Sce	SAs	11750nak
1800-1830	BBC World Sce	ME	1413sla
1800-1830	BVB	Eu	6015jul
1800-1830	Chr.Sc.Herold	WAf,NAf	7220jul
1800-1830	R.Prague	Eu	5930lit
1800-1830	R.Prague	As,AUS	9415lit
1800-1830	R.Santec	Af	11840jul
1800-1830	VO Azerbaijan	ME	1296pir, 6110gan
1800-1830	VO Vietnam	Eu	5955mos
1800-1830	VO Vietnam	Eu,ME	7280vni, 9730vni
1800-1830		AWR	EAf 9530mos
1800-1900	BVB	ME	9460jul
1800-1900	BVB	ME	9730jul
1800-1900	RCI	NAf	5850hor, 7370kas, 9770kas, 11875wer, 15140sac
1800-1900	RNWO	SAf	6020mdc
1800-1900	R.Polonia	Eu	7220wwa, 7265wwa
1800-1900	R.Romania Int'l	WEu	5965tig, 7130tig
1800-1900	R.Taiwan Int'l	Eu	3965iss
1800-1900	RAE	Eu	9690bue, 15345bue
1800-1900	TWR Bonaire	CAm,SAm	882bon
1800-1900	VO Russia (VOR)	Af	11510gav
1800-1900	VO Russia (VOR)	As	1251dsb, 5910irk, 5945nvs, 7415ppk
1800-1900	VO Russia (VOR)	ME	1251dsb, 9830msk
1800-1900	VO Russia (VOR)	Eu	1494spb, 5950arm, 6175arm
1800-1900	VO Russia (VOR)	Eu	7290msk
1800-2000	BBC World Sce	WEu	13700skn
1800-2000	BBG-VOA	Af	17895bot

1800	English	Area	kHz
1800-2000	Voice Africa	CAf,WAf	9680sof
1800-2000	R.Australia	Pac	6080shp, 7240shp
1800-2000	RNWO	EAf	9895fle
1800-2030	Voice Int'l	IND	11685dar
1800-2100	RNWO	CAf,WAf	11655mdc
1800-2200	BBG-VOA	Af	909bot, 6035sao, 11975sao
1815-1900	Bangladesh Bet.	Eu	7185dka, 9550dka
1830-1845	BBC World Sce	Eu	6050cyp, 6130skn, 7105rmp
1830-1845	IBRA Radio	EAf	9520jul
1830-1845	Kol Israel	NAm,Eu	9390isr, 11585isr, 11605isr
1830-1900	Chr.Sc.Herold	EAf,CAf	7220nau
1830-1900	R.Bulgaria	WEu	5800pld, 7500pld
1830-1900	R.Sweden	Eu	1179sol, 6065hor
1830-1900	RVI	Eu,ME	5910jul
1830-2000	BBC World Sce	SAs	5975nak
1830-2100	BBC World Sce	EAf	6005sey, 9630sey
1850-2240	RNZI	Pac,Eu	15265ran
1900	**English**	**Area**	**kHz**
1900-1930	BVB	Eu	6015jul
1900-1930	BVB	CAf	7295jul
1900-1930	BVB	ME	9460jul
1900-1930	R.Santec	ISR	
1900-1930	R.Vilnius	Eu	666sit
1900-1930	VO Vietnam	Eu,ME	7280vni, 9730vni
1900-2000	Am.R.Mirr Int'l	SAf	3215mey
1900-2000	BBG-VOA	ME	9785kav, 12015udo, 13640mor
1900-2000	BVB	Eu	6015jul
1900-2000	BVB	ME	9470nau
1900-2000	China R. Int'l	Af	9585kun
1900-2000	Deutsche Welle	EAf	6180kig, 11865sin, 13780wer, 17800sin
1900-2000	R.Korea Int'l	FE	5975hwa
1900-2000	R.Korea Int'l	Eu	7275kim
1900-2000	R.Sri Lanka	Eu	6010wof
1900-2000	R.Thailand	Eu	9840udo
1900-2000	VO Korea	Eu	4405pyo, 9325kuj, 11335kuj
1900-2000	VO Russia (VOR)	Eu	6175arm, 6235spb, 7290msk, 7400msk
1900-2000	VO Russia (VOR)	Af	7335tch, 11510gav
1900-2015	BVB	ME	9470nau
1900-2030	BBG-VOA	Af	4940sao
1900-2100	BBC World Sce	SAf	12095asc
1900-2100	BBC World Sce	ME	1413sla
1900-2100	China R. Int'l	Af	7295kas
1900-2100	China R. Int'l	NAf	9440bei
1900-2100	RNWO	NAm	15315bon, 17725bon, 17875sac
1900-2100	RNWO	WAf	17810bon
1900-2100	RNWO	CAf,SAf	7120mdc
1900-2130	R.Australia	As	9500shp
1900-2200	BBG-VOA	Af	15580grv
1900-2200	Channel Africa	SAf	3345mey
1915-1930	BBC World Sce	WAf	15105asc, 17885asc
1915-1930	BVB	CAf	7295jul
1915-1930	RT Tunisienne	NAf,Eu	963tun
1925-1945	VO Armenia	WAs,ME,Eu	4810yer
1925-1945	VO Armenia	Eu	9965gav
1930-2000	BBC World Sce	Eu	1296orf
1930-2000	BVB	CAf	7295jul
1930-2000	Int'l R.SerbMon	WEu	6100bij
1930-2000	R.Belarus	Eu	7105mns, 7340mns
1930-2000	R.Slovakia Int.	Eu	5915rso, 7345rso
1930-2000	VO Greece	Eu	7430avl
1930-2030	VOIRI	Eu	6110kam, 7320sir
1930-2030	VOIRI	SAf	9855sir, 11695kam
1930-2030	VO Turkey	Eu	6055emr
1935-1955	RAI Int'l	WEu	6035rom, 9760rom
1945-2000	R.Tirana	Eu	6115shi, 7210shi
1945-2015	BVB	WAf	7220wer

2000	English	Area	kHz
2000-2025	Kol Israel	SAf	15615isr
2000-2025	Kol Israel	NAm,Eu	6280isr, 9390isr
2000-2030	R.Budapest	Eu	3975jbr, 6025rso
2000-2030	R.Sweden	Eu	1179sol
2000-2030	Vatican Radio	Af	7365smg, 9755smg, 11625smg
2000-2030	VO Mongolia	Eu	12015uba
2000-2100	BBC World Sce	Eu	1296orf
2000-2100	BBC World Sce	UKR	612kyv
2000-2100	BBG-VOA	ME	1593kbd
2000-2100	China R. Int'l	EAf	13630bko
2000-2100	China R. Int'l	Eu	1386sit, 1440mrn, 7190kas
2000-2100	Deutsche Welle	CAf,SAf	12025trm, 13780wer, 15205wer, 15410trm
2000-2100	R.Australia	Pac	6080shp, 7240shp
2000-2100	REE	Af	9595nob
2000-2100	REE	Eu	9680nob
2000-2100	RNWO	WAf	9895fle
2000-2100	Radio Six Int'l	Eu,ME	5775mil
2000-2100	TDPradio	Eu	7375tld+, 7590arm
2000-2100	VO Indonesia	FE,SEA,AUS	15150jak
2000-2100	VO Russia (VOR)	Eu	6145msk, 6235spb, 7290msk, 7330msk
2000-2130	BBC World Sce	RUS	1260msk
2000-2130	China R. Int'l	Af	11640bko
2000-2200	BBC World Sce	RUS	666ekb, 1260spe
2000-2200	BBG-VOA	Af	1530sao, 13710bot
2000-2200	China R. Int'l	Eu	9600kas, 9855uru
2000-2200	R.Australia	Pac	11650shp, 12080brn
2000-2200	WEWN	WAf	17595ewn
2000-2200	Family Radio	SAm	17575yfr
2000-2200	Family Radio	Eu,NAf	7360gri
2000-2200	Family Radio	Eu	7580yfr
2000-2230	BBC World Sce	UKR	612kyv
2000-2300	BBC World Sce	Eu	6195cyp
2000-2300	RCI	NAm,Car	15180sac
2005-2200	Family Radio	Eu	5820yfr
2005-2205	R.Damascus	Eu, NAm,Oc	12085adr, 13610adr
2025-2045	RAI Int'l	EAf,ME	6040rom, 11880rom
2025-2045	RAI Int'l	NAf	6040rom, 11880rom
2030-0030	BBG-VOA	AFG	1296kab
2030-2045	R.Thailand	Eu	9535udo
2030-2100	BBG-VOA	Af	4940sao
2030-2100	R.Sweden	Eu	6065hor
2030-2100	R.Sweden	Eu,ME,AUS	7420hor
2030-2100	R.Taskent Int'l	Eu	5025tac, 11905tac
2030-2100	R.Taskent Int'l	Eu,NAf	7185tac
2030-2100	RVI	Eu	1512wol, 7490arm
2030-2100	VO Vietnam	Eu,ME	7220vni, 7280vni, 9550vni, 9730vni
2030-2130	R.Habana Cuba	NAm	11760hab
2030-2130	R.Habana Cuba	Car	9505hab
2030-2200	R.Cairo	WAf	15375abz
2030-2230	BBG-VOA	AFG	11835kbd
2040-2100	Vatican Radio	Eu	1260vat, 1611smg, 6185smg
2045-2230	All India R.	WEu	7410del, 9445bgl, 9950del
2045-2230	All India R.	AUS,NZL	9910alg, 11620bgl, 11715pan
2050-2110	Vatican Radio	Eu	585vat, 1530smg, 4005vat, 5885vat, 7250smg

2100	English	Area	kHz
2100-0700	R.Australia	Pac	13630shp
2100-2130	BBC World Sce	RUS	1260msk
2100-2130	BBC World Sce	Car	5975atg
2100-2130	China R. Int'l	EAf	13630bko
2100-2130	R.Australia	As	11695shp
2100-2130	R.Belarus	Eu	7105mns, 7340mns
2100-2130	R.Korea Int'l	Eu	3955skn
2100-2130	R.Prague	Eu,NAm	5930lit
2100-2130	R.Prague	SEA,AUS	9430lit
2100-2130	R.Santec	Eu,As	5775mil
2100-2130	Overcomer Min.	NAm	15825wcr
2100-2200	BBC World Sce	SAs	3915sgp
2100-2200	BBC World Sce	SAf	6005sey
2100-2200	BBC World Sce	FE	6110yam
2100-2200	BBC World Sce	SEA	6195nak
2100-2200	BBC World Sce	RUS	666ekb, 1260spe
2100-2200	China R. Int'l	Eu	7190kas
2100-2200	Deutsche Welle	WAf	9615wer, 13780trm, 15410kig
2100-2200	R.Australia	Pac	9660brn
2100-2200	RCI	Eu	5850hor, 9770sac
2100-2200	R.Japan	CAf	11855asc
2100-2200	R.Japan	NAm	17825yam
2100-2200	R.Japan	HWA	21670yam
2100-2200	R.Japan	Oc	6035sng
2100-2200	R.Japan	Eu	6090skn, 6180skn
2100-2200	R.Nac.de Angola	Af	945caz, 7217mul
2100-2200	RNWO	NAm	15530bon+
2100-2200	Overcomer Min.	NAm	12160wcr
2100-2200	Overcomer Min.	NAm	9985wcr
2100-2200	VO Korea	Eu	4405pyo, 9325kuj, 11335kuj
2100-2200	VO Russia (VOR)	Eu	6235spb, 7300arm, 7330msk
2100-2300	BBC World Sce	EAf	9605sey
2100-2300	R.Australia	Pac	15515shp
2100-2300	WWCR	NAm,Eu,NAf	9985wcr
2100-2400	BBC World Sce	SAm	12095asc
2100-2400	BBC World Sce	FE	5965nak
2100-2400	WHRA (WHR)	Af	9455hra
2104-2200	Family Radio	WAf	15565yfr
2110-2130	BBC World Sce	Car,SAm	11675atg
2115-2130	BBC World Sce	SAm	15390grv
2115-2245	R.Cairo	Eu	9990abs
2130-2145	BBC World Sce	SAm	11680rmp
2130-2200	BBC World Sce	RUS	666ekb, 1260spe
2130-2200	KSDA	EAs	11980sda, 12010sda, 12010sda
2130-2200	RNWO	NAm	9800sac+
2130-2200	R.Romania Int'l	NAm	6015tig, 9540tig
2130-2200	R.Romania Int'l	WEu	6055gal, 7145gal
2130-2200	R.Taskent Int'l	Eu	5025tac, 11905tac
2130-2200	R.Taskent Int'l	Eu,NAf	7185tac
2130-2200	Wales R. Int'l	Eu	3955skn
2130-2200	Wales R. Int'l	WEu	7110mos
2130-2230	BBC World Sce	UKR	612kyv
2130-2230	VO Turkey	As,AUS	9525emr
2130-2400	BBC World Sce	RUS	1260msk
2130-2400	BBC World Sce	Car	5975atg

2200	English	Area	kHz
2200-0300	WRNO Worldwide	NAm,CAm	7355rno
2200-0300	WWCR	CAm,Af	7465wcr
2200-0400	Overcomer Min.	NAm,CAm	7465wcr
2200-0400	WWCR	CAm,Af	7465wcr
2200-0800	AFN Feeder	Pac	13362bar
2200-0800	WSHB (WHR)	NAm,Eu,Af	7535shb
2200-1000	Dr Gene Scott	CAm	6090aia
2200-1300	WWCR	NAm,Eu	5070wcr
2200-2230	Int'l R.SerbMon	Eu	6100bij
2200-2230	R.Budapest	SAf	12010jbr
2200-2230	R.Budapest	Eu	6025rso
2200-2230	R.Santec	Eu	1323wbr
2200-2230	RVI	Am	11730bon
2200-2245	Family Radio	WAf	21525yfr
2200-2300	BBC World Sce	SEA	11955sgp
2200-2300	BBC World Sce	SAs	7105sla
2200-2300	BBC World Sce	Pac	9660brn
2200-2300	China R. Int'l	Eu,NAm	7170tld
2200-2300	Deutsche Welle	EAs	6180trm, 6225alm
2200-2300	R.Bulgaria	WEu	5800pld, 7500pld
2200-2300	RCI	NAm	9800sac+
2200-2300	REE	Af	9595nob
2200-2300	REE	Eu	9680nob

2200	English	Area	kHz
2200-2300	RNWO	Eu	1512wol
2200-2300	R.Taiwan Int'l	Eu	9355yfr
2200-2300	R.Ukraine Int'l	Eu	5840khr
2200-2300	Family Radio	SAm	9690yfr
2200-2330	R.Australia	As	15240dar
2200-2345	Family Radio	NAm	11740yfr
2200-2400	BBC World Sce	ME	1314dha
2200-2400	BBC World Sce	SEA	6195sgp, 9740sgp, 9740sgp
2200-2400	BBG-VOA	EAs	15290pht
2200-2400	BBG-VOA	EAs,Pac	17740pht
2200-2400	BBG-VOA	SEA	7215pht, 9890pht, 15185pht, 15305ira
2200-2400	R.Australia	As	13620dar, 15230shp
2200-2400	R.Australia	Pac	21740shp
2200-2400	WEWN	Eu	15695ewn
2200-2400	WEWN	NAm	9975ewn
2200-2400	WWCR	NAm,Eu,NAf	9985wcr
2205-2230	RAI Int'l	As,FE,J	11895rom
2230-2300	BBG-VOA	CHN	9545pht, 9785udo, 13755tin
2230-2300	KSDA	SEA	11850sda, 15320sda
2230-2300	RCI	CHN	6160kim, 7195kim, 9730yam
2230-2300	R.Prague	NAm	5930lit
2230-2300	R.Prague	WAf	7345lit
2230-2300	R.Sweden	Eu	1179sol, 6065hor
2230-2300	R.Tirana	Eu	7120shi
2230-2330	BBG-VOA	AFG	11935kbd
2230-2400	BBG-VOA	SEA	1575bph
2230-2400	HCJB Australia	EAs	15525knx
2240-0400	RNZI	Pac,NAm	17675ran
2245-0045	All India R.	EAs,SEA	9705pan, 11620del, 13605bgl
2245-0045	All India R.	EAs	9950alg, 11645del, 13605bgl

2300	English	Area	kHz
2300-0030	R.Cairo	NAm	11725abz
2300-0200	R.Australia	Pac	17795shp
2300-0500	WINB	CAm	9320inb
2300-0600	WWRB	NAm	3185wrb, 5745wrb
2300-0600	WWRB	NAm,SEA	5050wrb
2300-0600	WWRB	NAm,Eu	5085wrb
2300-0800	R.Australia	Pac	9660brn
2300-1000	WWCR	NAm,Eu,NAf	3210wcr
2300-1200	R.Australia	Pac	12080brn
2300-1300	WWCR	NAm,Eu	5070wcr
2300-2330	Deutsche Welle	NAm	9800sac+
2300-2400	BBC World Sce	FE	11945yam, 15280nak
2300-2400	BBC World Sce	SEA	3915sgp, 11955nak
2300-2400	BBC World Sce	WEu	6195rmp
2300-2400	BBG-VOA	ME	1593kbd
2300-2400	BBG-VOA	EAs	6180udo, 7205udo, 9780pht, 11655udo, 15150pht
2300-2400	China R. Int'l	As	5975kas, 7180kas
2300-2400	China R. Int'l	NAm	5990hab, 6040sac, 11970sac
2300-2400	Deutsche Welle	SEA	7250trm, 9815trm, 12035kig
2300-2400	R.Habana Cuba	Car	9550hab
2300-2400	R.Romania Int'l	WEu	6135gal, 7105gal
2300-2400	R.Romania Int'l	NAm	6180tig, 9610tig
2300-2400	VO Turkey	Eu,NAm	7275emr
2300-2400	Family Radio	SAm	15170yfr, 15400yfr
2300-2400	Family Radio	CAm	5985yfr, 11855yfr
2315-2330	TWR Europe	Eu	1467rou
2315-2345	TWR Europe	Eu	1467rou
2330-0900	R.Australia	As	17750shp
2330-2400	BBC World Sce	FE	6170kim
2330-2400	BBG-VOA	AFG	11995kbd
2330-2400	BBG-VOA	SEA	7130udo, 9620udo, 11805pht, 13640tin, 15205pht
2330-2400	R.Australia	As	15415shp
2330-2400	R.Prague	NAm	5930lit, 7345lit
2330-2400	R.Sweden	NAm	9800sac+
2330-2400	R.Vilnius	NAm	7325sit
2330-2400	VO Vietnam	As	9840vni, 12020vni

1100	English (mass)	Area	kHz
1130-1230	Vatican Radio	As	15595smg, 17515smg
1130-1300	Vatican Radio	Af	15595smg, 17515smg

1500	English (mass)	Area	kHz
1530-1630	Vatican Radio	As	9865tac, 11850smg, 13765smg

1600	English (mass)	Area	kHz
1630-1600	Vatican Radio	Af	9865tac, 11850smg, 13765smg

1700	English (vo Islam)	Area	kHz
1745-1815	Bangladesh Bet.	Eu	7185dka, 9550dka

FRENCH

0000	French	Area	kHz
0000-0100	R.Habana Cuba	Car	9550hab
0000-2400	RTL	Eu	5990jun+

0100	French	Area	kHz
0100-0200	RFI	IND	15605bei, 17710xia
0100-0200	VO Korea	SEA	4405pyo, 9325kuj, 11335kuj
0115-0130	RAI Int'l	NAm	11800rom
0130-0200	RFI	CAm,Car	9800guf
0130-0200	R.Habana Cuba	Car	9550hab

0200	French	Area	kHz
0200-0230	R.Slovakia Int.	NAm	7230rso
0200-0230	R.Slovakia Int.	SAm	9440rso
0200-0300	R.Bulgaria	NAm	7400pld, 9700pld
0200-0300	R.Romania Int'l	CAN	6130gal, 9690gal
0230-0250	Vatican Radio	NAm	7305smg, 9605smg
0230-0300	Vatican Radio	Af	7360smg

0300	French	Area	kHz
0300-0400	RFI	ME	5945iss, 7315iss
0300-0400	RFI	CAf,EAf,IOc	7135mey
0300-0400	RAE	Am	11710bue
0300-0400	VO Korea	CAm,SAm	6520kuj, 7580kuj, 11735kuj
0300-0600	RFI	CAf	9790iss
0328-0358	TWR Europe	Eu	216rou
0341-0356	TWR Europe	Eu	216rou

0400	French	Area	kHz
0400-0455	Channel Africa	CAf	9565mey
0400-0500	RFI	NAf	3965iss
0400-0500	RFI	CAf	4890gab, 7135iss, 7270asc
0400-0500	RFI	ME	7315iss, 9555iss
0400-0600	China R. Int'l	Eu	15110kas
0400-0600	RFI	EAf,ME	15210dha
0430-0445	EvangeliumsRdfk	Eu	1539mnf
0430-0500	BBC World Sce	EAf	17885sey
0430-0500	BBC World Sce	WAf	6155asc, 7105asc
0430-0500	RFI	EAf,IOc	9555iss, 11995iss
0430-0500	Vatican Radio	Af	7360smg, 9660smg
0445-0500	Kol Israel	NAm,Eu	6280isr, 7545isr

0500	French	Area	kHz
0500-0530	R.Japan	ME,NAf	17820eka
0500-0600	RFI	NAf	3965iss, 5925iss
0500-0600	RFI	CAf	6175gab, 11700iss, 15300iss
0500-0600	RFI	NAf,CAf	7135iss
0500-0600	RFI	ME	9555iss, 11685iss
0500-1900	RT Tunisienne	NAf,Eu	963tun
0500-2300	Africa No.1	Af	9580gab
0530-0545	RFI	EEu	5990iss
0530-0600	BBG-VOA	Af	1530sao
0530-0600	RFI	EAf,IOc	11995iss, 15155iss
0530-0600	R.Nationale Lao	SEA	7145vie

0500	**French**	**Area**	**kHz**
0530-0630	BBG-VOA	Af	5890grv, 7265mor, 9480grv, 9505wof
0540-0600	Vatican Radio	Eu	1530smg, 4005vat, 5885vat, 7250smg
0555-0815	RTBF Int'l	CAf	17580jul
0555-1100	RTBF Int'l	CAf	17580jul

0600	**French**	**Area**	**kHz**
0600-0530	Vatican Radio	Af	9660smg, 11625smg, 13765smg
0600-0630	BBC World Sce	WAf	7105asc, 9610asc
0600-0630	BBC World Sce	NAf	7180rmp, 11680cyp
0600-0630	R.Romania Int'l	WEu	7160gal, 7180tig, 9565tig, 9650gal
0600-0700	RFI	CAf	15300iss, 17770kig, 17850iss
0600-0700	RFI	NAf	5925iss, 7135iss
0600-0700	RFI	WAf	7135iss, 9790iss, 11700iss
0600-0700	RFI	NAf,WAf	9790iss
0600-2200	RTBF Int'l	SEu	9970wav
0630-0700	RFI	EAf,IOc	17800iss
0630-0700	RFI	WAf	9595asc
0630-0700	R.Japan	Eu	11970gab
0630-0730	VOIRI	Eu	17590kam
0630-0730	VOIRI	Eu,NAf	21645sir

0700	**French**	**Area**	**kHz**
0700-0730	BBC World Sce	WAf	15105asc
0700-0730	BBC World Sce	CAf	17695mey
0700-0730	R.Bulgaria	WEu	11600pld, 13600pld
0700-0730	R.Prague	WEu	5930lit
0700-0730	R.Prague	SEu	7345lit
0700-0800	RFI	CAf	15170mey, 17850iss
0700-0800	RFI	NAf	7135iss
0700-0800	RFI	WAf	9790iss, 15300iss, 17620iss
0700-0800	RFI	NAf,WAf	9790iss, 11700iss
0700-0800	R.Taiwan Int'l	Eu	5810yfr
0700-0800	VO Nigeria	Eu,Af	15120iko
0700-0900	RFI	WAf	15315iss
0700-1600	Africa No.1	Af	17630gab
0700-1600	RFI	CAf	21580iss
0715-0730	Vatican Radio	As	15595smg
0715-0730	Vatican Radio	Eu	585vat, 1530smg, 4005vat, 5885vat, 6185smg, 7250smg, 9645smg, 11740smg, 15595smg
0715-0730	Vatican Radio	Af	9645smg, 15595smg

0800	**French**	**Area**	**kHz**
0800-0830	R.Georgia	Eu	11910dsh
0800-0900	R.Korea Int'l	Eu	15210kim
0800-1000	China R. Int'l	Eu	17650uru
0800-1000	RFI	NAf	15300iss
0800-1000	RFI	WAf	17620iss
0800-1000	Saudi Radio	WAf	17785riy
0800-1130	RFI	NAf,WAf	15300iss
0800-1600	RFI	NAf	11845iss
0830-0900	R.Prague	SEu	11600lit
0830-0900	R.Prague	WEu	9880lit

0900	**French**	**Area**	**kHz**
0900-1600	RFI	WAf	21685iss

1000	**French**	**Area**	**kHz**
1000-1100	RFI	CAf	17850iss
1030-1200	RFI	FE	7140yam
1030-1200	RFI	SEA	9830yam
1055-1230	RTBF Int'l	CAf	21565jul

1100	**French**	**Area**	**kHz**
1100-1115	Kol Israel	NAm,Eu	15640isr, 17535isr
1100-1130	RFI	NAf	15300iss
1100-1130	RFI	NAm	15515iss
1100-1130	RFI	Atl	6175iss
1100-1200	RFI	SEA	11600bei
1100-1200	RFI	CAm,Car	11670guf
1100-1200	R.Romania Int'l	WEu	15260tig, 17845gal
1100-1200	R.Romania Int'l	NAf	15315gal, 17790tig
1100-1200	VO Korea	SEA	3560pyo, 9850kuj, 11735kuj
1100-1200	VO Korea	CAm,SAm	9335kuj, 11710kuj
1100-1300	RCI	NAm,Car	9515sac
1100-1400	RCI	NAm,Car	9515sac
1100-1400	RFI	WAf	17620iss
1100-1400	RFI	CAf	17850mey

1200	**French**	**Area**	**kHz**
1200-1230	BBC World Sce	NAf	15425wof
1200-1230	BBC World Sce	WAf	17780asc, 21640asc
1200-1230	R.Bulgaria	WEu	11700pld, 15700pld
1200-1230	VO Vietnam	SEA	1242omo
1200-1230	VO Vietnam	As	7285han
1200-1300	Deutsche Welle	Af	15410kig, 15470sin, 17610wer, 17800kig, 21665wer
1200-1300	Vatican Radio	Eu	585vat, 1611smg+, 5885vat
1200-1400	RFI	NAf	15300iss
1200-1700	RFI	WAf	15300iss
1200-1800	RFI	NAf	15300iss
1230-1300	RFI	CAm,Car	15515guf
1230-1300	RFI	EAf,IOc	21620iss
1230-1300	RFI	WAf	21760mey
1230-1300	R.Japan	WAf	15400asc
1230-1300	R.Japan	CAf	17870asc

1300	**French**	**Area**	**kHz**
1300-1330	RFI	CAm,Car	17860guf
1300-1330	R.Nationale Lao	SEA	7145vie
1300-1330	VO Vietnam	SEA	1242omo
1300-1330	VO Vietnam	As	7285han
1300-1400	RFI	SEA	684dof
1330-1400	VO Azerbaijan	ME	1296pir, 6110gan

1400	**French**	**Area**	**kHz**
1400-1500	VO Korea	Eu	4405pyo, 9325kuj, 11335kuj
1400-1500	VO Korea	NAm	9335kuj, 11710kuj
1400-1600	Saudi Radio	WAf	21600riy
1430-1500	RCI	As,CHN	5985yam, 9535yam
1455-1805	RTBF Int'l	CAf	17570jul

1500	**French**	**Area**	**kHz**
1500-1600	RFI	CAf	17850iss
1510-1525	TWR Africa	SAf	9585man
1525-1805	RTBF Int'l	CAf	15570jul
1530-1555	RAI Int'l	WEu	5985rom, 9570rom, 11680rom

1600	**French**	**Area**	**kHz**
1600-1630	R.Santec	CAf	9495jul
1600-1655	Channel Africa	WAf	15285mey
1600-1700	China R. Int'l	Eu	9700kas
1600-1700	Deutsche Welle	Af	12035sin, 15145kig, 15680wer, 17630wer, 21560sin
1600-1700	RFI	SEA	1296kun, 6090kun
1600-1700	RFI	CAf	15300iss, 21580iss
1600-1700	RFI	WAf	17620iss
1600-1700	R.Korea Int'l	ME	7150kim
1600-1700	VO Korea	Eu	4405pyo, 9325kuj, 11335kuj
1600-1700	VO Korea	NAm	9335kuj, 11710kuj
1600-2000	RCI	NAm,Car	17835sac
1600-2100	Africa No.1	Af	15475gab
1630-1650	R.Japan	ME,NAf	7105yam
1630-1655	RAI Int'l	E,NAf	9570rom, 11895rom
1630-1700	VO Vietnam	SEA	1242omo
1630-1700	VO Vietnam	Eu,ME	7220vni, 9550vni

1700	**French**	**Area**	**kHz**
1700-1715	UN Radio	CAf,SAf	21535mey
1700-1715	UN Radio	SAf	7170mey
1700-1715	UN Radio	NAf	9565skn
1700-1715	Vatican Radio	Eu	585vat, 1530smg, 4005vat, 5885vat, 7250smg, 9645smg,

1700 **French**	**Area**	**kHz**
		15595smg
1700-1730 Int'l R.SerbMon	WEu	6100bij
1700-1730 R.Budapest	Eu	3975jbr, 6025rso
1700-1730 Vatican Radio	Af	13765smg, 15570smg
1700-1730 Vatican Radio	As	15595smg
1700-1800 Deutsche Welle	Af	9535kig, 9735sin, 12035wer, 13645wer, 15410kig
1700-1800 R.Ethiopia	EAf	7165gjw
1700-1800 R.Ethiopia	EAf,ME	9561gjw
1700-1800 RFI	WAf	11965iss, 15300iss, 15300iss, 17620iss
1700-1800 RFI	NAf,CAf	15300iss
1700-1800 R.Korea Int'l	Af	9870kim
1700-1800 R.Romania Int'l	WEu	6110gal, 7135gal
1700-1800 VO Russia (VOR)	Eu,Af	6130msk, 7390msk
1700-1800 VO Russia (VOR)	Eu	7330msk
1700-1800 VO Russia (VOR)	Af	7335tch, 11510gav
1700-2000 RCI	NAm,Car	17835sac
1710-1720 R.DMR	Eu	5960gri
1730-1800 R.Prague	CAf	15710lit
1730-1800 R.Prague	WEu	5930lit
1755-1825 TWR Africa	CAf	9620mey

1800 **French**	**Area**	**kHz**
1800-1815 Kol Israel	NAm,Eu	9390isr, 11585isr, 11605isr
1800-1815 RVI	Eu	1512wol, 7490arm
1800-1820 R.Japan	Eu	11970yam
1800-1820 R.Japan	Af	9685yam, 11785yam
1800-1830 BBC World Sce	WAf	15105asc, 17885asc, 21630asc
1800-1830 BBC World Sce	SAf	7230mey
1800-1830 BBC World Sce	NAf	9815wof
1800-1830 R.Bulgaria	WEu	5800pld, 7500pld
1800-1830 R.Slovakia Int.	Eu	5915rso, 6055rso
1800-1900 REE	Eu	9655nob
1800-1900 RFI	NAf,CAf	15300iss
1800-1900 RFI	CAf	9790iss
1800-1900 R.Korea Int'l	ME	15575kim
1800-1900 VO Korea	SAf	3560pyo, 9660kuj, 11710kuj
1800-1900 VO Korea	ME,Af	9975kuj, 11735kuj
1800-1900 VO Russia (VOR)	Eu,Af	6130msk
1800-1900 VO Russia (VOR)	Eu	6145msk, 7330msk, 7420msk
1800-1900 VO Russia (VOR)	Af	7230spb, 7335tch, 7420msk
1800-2000 RFI	WAf	11965iss
1800-2000 RFI	NAf	7315iss
1800-2100 RFI	WAf	11955gab
1800-2100 RFI	NAf,WAf	9790iss
1800-2200 RFI	CAf	11705iss
1800-2200 RFI	NAf	7315iss
1805-2200 RTBF Int'l	CAf	9970wav
1830-1900 BBG-VOA	Af	1530sao, 9815bot, 12080bot, 13735sao, 15220mor, 17580grv, 21485grv
1830-1900 FEBA Radio	CAf,WAf	15125asc
1830-1900 R.Réveil	CAf	11840jul
1830-1900 VO Greece	Eu	7430avl
1830-1900 VO Vietnam	Eu,ME	7280vni, 9730vni
1830-1930 VOIRI	Eu	6180kam, 9755sir
1830-1930 VOIRI	Af	9565kam
1830-2030 BBG-VOA	Af	11985sao
1830-2030 China R. Int'l	Eu,NAf	7350uru
1830-2030 China R. Int'l	WAf,CAf	9645kun
1840-1925 TWR Africa	CAf	9720mey

1900 **French**	**Area**	**kHz**
1900-2000 BBG-VOA	Af	1530sao, 9815hnt, 12080bot, 13735sao, 15220mor, 17580grv, 21485grv
1900-2000 RCI	NAf	11845wer, 13650sac, 15140dha, 17735sac
1900-2000 REE	Eu	12035nob
1900-2000 REE	Eu	7150nob
1900-2000 REE	Af	9595nob
1900-2000 R.Taiwan Int'l	Eu	3955skn
1900-2000 VO Indonesia	Eu,NAf,ME	15150jak
1900-2000 VO Russia (VOR)	Eu,Af	5950spb, 7390msk
1900-2000 VO Russia (VOR)	Eu, Af	6130msk
1900-2000 VO Russia (VOR)	Eu	7215sam, 7230spb, 7330msk, 7420msk
1900-2000 VO Russia (VOR)	Af	7230spb, 7420msk
1900-2200 RFI	NAf	6175iss
1900-2200 RFI	CAf	7160mey, 9790iss
1905-2005 R.Damascus	Eu, NAm	12085adr, 13610adr
1930-2000 BVB	CAF	7295jul
1930-2000 R.Prague	WEu	5930lit
1930-2000 R.Prague	SEu,NAf	9430lit
1930-2000 VO Vietnam	Eu	5955mos
1930-2000 VO Vietnam	Eu,ME	7280vni, 9730vni
1935-1950 TWR Africa	CAf	9525man
1945-2000 VO Armenia	WAs,ME,Eu	4810yer
1945-2000 VO Armenia	Eu	9965gav
1945-2030 All India R.	NAf	9905alg, 13605bgl, 13620bgl
1950-2020 TWR Africa	CAf	9525man

2000 **French**	**Area**	**kHz**
2000-0100 RT Tunisienne	NAf,Eu	963tun
2000-2030 AWR	CAf	11845mey, 15365mey
2000-2030 AWR	NAf	9695jul
2000-2030 BBG-VOA	Af	9815bot, 12080bot, 13735sao, 15220mor, 21485grv
2000-2030 R.Habana Cuba	NAm	11760hab
2000-2030 R.Romania Int'l	WEu	6055gal, 7120gal
2000-2030 R.Tirana	Eu	6115shi
2000-2100 RCI	Eu	5850hor, 7235skn, 9710sac, 11725sac
2000-2100 R.Korea Int'l	Eu	5955skn
2000-2100 R.Nac.de Angola	Af	945caz, 7217mul
2000-2100 R.Taiwan Int'l	NAm	15440yfr
2000-2100 R.Taiwan Int'l	Eu	9635tnn, 11665yfr
2000-2100 RAE	Eu,NAf	9690bue, 15345bue
2000-2100 VO Korea	Eu	4405pyo, 9325kuj, 11335kuj
2000-2100 VO Russia (VOR)	Eu	1323wbr, 5950spb, 7230spb, 7300arm, 7420msk
2000-2100 VO Russia (VOR)	Af	5940msk, 7230spb, 7420msk
2000-2100 VO Russia (VOR)	Eu,Af	6130msk, 7390msk, 9480msk
2000-2115 R.Cairo	Eu	9990abs
2000-2200 RFI	NAf	7315iss
2015-2030 R.Thailand	Eu	9535udo
2015-2030 RVI	Eu	1512wol, 7490arm
2030-2045 Kol Israel	Eu,CAm	6280isr
2030-2045 Kol Israel	NAm,Eu	7520isr, 9390isr
2030-2050 Vatican Radio	Eu	585vat, 1530smg, 4005vat, 5885vat, 7250smg
2030-2100 AWR	WAf	9800mos
2030-2100 BBG-VOA	Af	9780sao, 9815bot, 11775sao, 12080bot, 15220mor, 21485grv
2030-2100 R.Santec	Eu,Af	1323wbr, 7230spb, 7300arm, 7370sam, 7390msk, 9480msk
2030-2100 R.Slovakia Int.	Eu	5915rso, 7345rso
2030-2130 China R. Int'l	Eu	7215sam
2030-2130 VO Turkey	Af	6050cak
2030-2130 VO Turkey	Eu	7155emr
2030-2145 Vatican Radio	Af	7365smg, 9755smg, 11625smg
2030-2230 China R. Int'l	EAf	13630bko

2000	French	Area	kHz
2030-2230	China R. Int'l	Eu	7200uru, 11660xia
2030-2230	R.Cairo	WAf	15335abs

2100	French	Area	kHz
2100-2130	BBG-VOA	Af	5985wof, 9780sao, 9815bot, 21485grv
2100-2130	R.Budapest	Eu	6025jbr, 9710jbr
2100-2130	VO Russia (VOR)	Af	7170smg
2100-2130	VO Vietnam	Eu,ME	7220vni, 7280vni, 9550vni, 9730vni
2100-2200	China R. Int'l	Eu	1440mrn
2100-2200	R.Bulgaria	WEu	5800pld, 7500pld
2100-2200	RCI	NAf	7235skn, 9565skn, 11845sac
2100-2200	REE	Af	9595nob
2100-2200	RFI	NAf	3965iss
2100-2200	RFI	WAf	7315iss, 9790gab
2100-2200	VO Nigeria	Eu,Af	15120iko
2100-2200	VO Russia (VOR)	Eu	1323wbr
2130-2200	Int'l R.SerbMon	Eu	6100bij
2130-2200	R.Habana Cuba	NAm	11760hab
2130-2230	China R. Int'l	NAf	11975bko

2200	French	Area	kHz
2200-2230	R.Habana Cuba	Car	9505hab
2200-2300	RCI	NAf	9665mos, 11835asc
2200-2300	R.Taiwan Int'l	Af	7315iss

2300	French	Area	kHz
2300-0030	RFI	SEA	17710yam
2300-0100	RFI	FE,SEA	12025nsb
2300-0200	REE	Am	6055nob
2300-2330	R.Prague	NAm	5930lit, 7345lit
2300-2400	RCI	NAm,Car	15180sac
2300-2400	REE	Eu	6095nob
2300-2400	RFI	SEA	12075vld
2300-2400	Family Radio	NAm	6085yfr

GERMAN

0000	German	Area	kHz
0000-0100	R.Ukraine Int'l	Eu	5840khr
0000-0200	Deutsche Welle	SAm	11690kig
0000-0200	Deutsche Welle	Eu	6075sin
0000-0200	Deutsche Welle	Eu,NAf	6075wer
0000-0200	Deutsche Welle	NAm,Car	6100atg
0000-0200	Deutsche Welle	SAm,NAm	9545sin
0000-0200	Deutsche Welle	NAm,MEX	9655kig
0000-2400	RTL	Eu	6095jun+

0200	German	Area	kHz
0200-0230	R.Belarus	Eu	5970mns, 7210mns
0200-0400	Deutsche Welle	Eu,NAf,ME	6075nau
0200-0400	Deutsche Welle	Eu	6075sin
0200-0400	Deutsche Welle	Eu,NAf	6075wer
0200-0400	Deutsche Welle	NAm,MEX	6100sac
0200-0400	Deutsche Welle	NAm	6145wer
0200-0400	Deutsche Welle	NAm,Car	9640atg, 9870kig

0300	German	Area	kHz
0300-0400	Deutsche Welle	RUS	693msk, 1188spe
0315-0330	Miss.Heukelbach	Eu	1440mrn
0345-0400	Miss.Heukelbach	Eu	1440mrn

0400	German	Area	kHz
0400-0430	TWR Africa	SAf	4775man, 6120man
0400-0500	Deutsche Welle	NAm,MEX	6100bon
0400-0500	TWR Africa	SAf	4775man, 6120man
0400-0600	Deutsche Welle	Eu	6075sin
0400-0600	Deutsche Welle	Eu,NAf	6075wer
0400-0600	Deutsche Welle	NAm,MEX	6145wer
0400-0600	Deutsche Welle	NAm,Car	9640atg
0445-0500	R.Freundes-D.	Eu	1440mrn
0445-0515	TWR Europe	Eu	1467rou

0500	German	Area	kHz
0500-0400	EvangeliumsRdfk	Eu	1539mnf

0500	German	Area	kHz
0500-0600	Deutsche Welle	NAm,MEX	6100atg
0500-0600	Deutsche Welle	RUS	693msk, 1188spe
0515-0530	Miss.Heukelbach	Eu	1440mrn, 6095jun+
0520-0540	Vatican Radio	Eu	1530smg, 4005vat, 5885vat, 7250smg
0545-0600	R.Santec	Eu	1323wbr

0600	German	Area	kHz
0600-0630	R.Bulgaria	WEu	9500pld, 11500pld
0600-0630	R.Japan	Eu	11970gab
0600-0700	R.Taiwan Int'l	Eu	5810yfr
0600-0800	China R. Int'l	Eu	15245uru, 17720uru
0600-0800	Deutsche Welle	Eu,NAf,ME	13780wer
0600-0800	Deutsche Welle	SEA,AUS	21640trm
0600-0800	Deutsche Welle	Eu	6075sin
0600-0800	Deutsche Welle	Eu,NAf	6075wer, 9545nau
0600-0800	Deutsche Welle	RUS	693msk, 1188spe
0600-0800	Deutsche Welle	NZL,AUS	9690atg, 9735wer, 11985atg

0700	German	Area	kHz
0700-0730	R.Georgia	Eu	11805dsh
0700-0730	R.Romania Int'l	WEu	7160gal, 7275tig, 9635tig, 9655gal
0700-0730	R.Sweden	Eu	1179sol
0700-0800	Deutsche Welle	Eu	3995wer
0700-0800	R.Korea Int'l	Eu	15210kim
0730-0800	R.Prague	WEu	5930lit
0730-0800	R.Prague	Eu	7345lit
0730-0800	R.Slovakia Int.	Eu	5915rso, 6055rso
0730-0830	VOIRI	Eu	15085kam, 21770sir

0800	German	Area	kHz
0800-1000	Deutsche Welle	Eu,NAf,ME	13780wer
0800-1000	Deutsche Welle	SEA,AUS,NZL	21640trm
0800-1000	Deutsche Welle	Eu	6075wer
0800-1000	Deutsche Welle	RUS	693msk, 1188spe
0800-1000	Deutsche Welle	Eu,NAf	9545nau
0800-1000	Deutsche Welle	NZL,AUS	9690atg, 9735wer

0900	German	Area	kHz
0930-0945	TWR Europe	Eu	6230mco, 7160mco
0930-1015	TWR Europe	Eu	6230mco, 7160mco

1000	German	Area	kHz
1000-1100	Chr.Sc.Herold	Eu	6015jul
1000-1100	Evangeliumsrad.	Eu	6045jul
1000-1100	Hamburger Lokal	Eu	6045jul
1000-1100	VO Russia (VOR)	Eu	603bln, 1323wbr, 9720klg, 15540arm, 15780tld+
1000-1200	Deutsche Welle	Eu,ME	13780wer
1000-1200	Deutsche Welle	SEA,AUS,NZL	21840nau
1000-1200	Deutsche Welle	FE,SEA	5910ppk, 7400irk, 15605alm, 17845trm
1000-1200	Deutsche Welle	Eu	6075wer
1000-1200	Deutsche Welle	RUS	693msk, 1188spe
1000-1200	Deutsche Welle	Eu,NAf	9545nau
1000-1600	Hamburger Lokal	Eu	5925jul

1100	German	Area	kHz
1100-1130	R.Japan	Eu	9660skn, 11710skn
1100-1130	R.Prague	Eu	7345lit
1100-1130	R.Prague	WEu	9880lit
1100-1200	VO Russia (VOR)	Eu	603bln, 1323wbr
1130-1200	Ev.Miss.Gemeind	Eu	6015jul
1130-1200	R.Bulgaria	WEu	11700pld, 15700pld

1200	German	Area	kHz
1200-1215	M-werk Arche	Eu	6015jul
1200-1300	R.Romania Int'l	WEu	9610tig, 9690gal, 11730tig, 11940gal
1200-1300	R.Santec	Eu	6045jul
1200-1300	VO Russia (VOR)	Eu	603bln, 1323wbr, 1386klg, 12060tld+
1200-1400	Deutsche Welle	Eu,ME	13780wer
1200-1400	Deutsche Welle	Eu,As,ME	17630nau
1200-1400	Deutsche Welle	FE,SEA	5910ppk, 7400irk,

1200	German	Area	kHz
			9395alm, 17845trm
1200-1400	Deutsche Welle	Eu	6075wer
1200-1400	Deutsche Welle	RUS	693msk, 1188spe
1200-1400	Deutsche Welle	Eu,NAf	9545nau
1230-1300	R.Polonia	Eu	5965wwa, 9525wwa
1230-1330	R.Santec	Eu	6045jul
1230-1330	VO Turkey	Eu	17700emr
1300	**German**	**Area**	**kHz**
1300-1330	R.Prague	Eu	6055lit
1300-1330	R.Prague	WEu	7345lit
1300-1330	R.Sweden	Eu	7240fle+
1300-1330	VO Azerbaijan	ME	1296pir, 6110gan
1300-1400	R.Budapest	Eu	6025jbr, 12010jbr
1400	**German**	**Area**	**kHz**
1400-1430	Deutsche Welle	SAs	1548trm
1400-1430	TWR Europe	Eu	6230mco, 7160mco
1400-1500	Deutsche Welle	RUS	693msk, 1188spe
1400-1515	R.Traumland	Eu	5925jul
1400-1515	R.Traumland	Eu	5925jul
1400-1600	Deutsche Welle	Eu,ME	13780wer
1400-1600	Deutsche Welle	Eu,CAs,ME	15275kig
1400-1600	Deutsche Welle	Eu,As,ME	15680nau
1400-1600	Deutsche Welle	Eu	6075wer
1400-1600	Deutsche Welle	Eu,NAf	9545nau
1400-1600	Deutsche Welle	SAs	9655trm
1415-1435	RAI Int'l	EEu	9850rom
1430-1500	R.Slovakia Int.	Eu	6055rso, 7345rso
1430-1500	TWR Europe	Eu	6230mco, 7160mco
1430-1500	VO Greece	Eu	7430avl
1500	**German**	**Area**	**kHz**
1500-1515	Vatican Radio	Eu	5885vat, 7250smg, 9645smg
1500-1600	Deutsche Welle	Eu	1512wol
1500-1600	R.Budapest	Eu	6025jbr, 9735jbr
1515-1600	R.Traumland	Eu	5925jul
1545-1600	KFBS	CAs	9465fbs
1600	**German**	**Area**	**kHz**
1600-1630	AWR	Eu	7235mos
1600-1630	R.Prague	WEu	5930lit
1600-1700	Deutsche Welle	Eu	1512wol
1600-1700	VO Korea	Eu	6575kuj, 7505kuj
1600-1700	VO Russia (VOR)	Eu	603bln, 1215klg, 1323wbr, 1386klg, 6145msk, 7300arm
1600-1800	Deutsche Welle	ME,CAs	11795kig
1600-1800	Deutsche Welle	NAf,ME	13780wer
1600-1800	Deutsche Welle	Eu	6075wer
1600-1800	Deutsche Welle	Eu,NAf	9545nau
1600-1800	Deutsche Welle	SAs,SEA	9545wer
1600-1800	Deutsche Welle	SAs	9655trm
1630-1655	R.Polonia	Eu	7270wwa
1655-1700	R.Santec	Eu	603bln, 1215klg, 1323wbr, 1386klg, 6145msk, 7300arm
1700	**German**	**Area**	**kHz**
1700-1730	REE	Eu	9665nob
1700-1730	R.Slovakia Int.	Eu	5915rso, 6055rso
1700-1800	Deutsche Welle	SAs	1548trm
1700-1800	Deutsche Welle	Eu	6075sin
1700-1800	VO Russia (VOR)	Eu	603bln, 1215klg, 1323wbr, 1386klg, 6145msk, 7290msk, 7300arm
1710-1720	R.DMR	Eu	5960gri
1730-1800	Int'l R.SerbMon	WEu	6100bij
1730-1800	R.Bulgaria	WEu	5800pld, 7500pld
1730-1800	R.Prague	WEu	5840arm
1730-1800	R.Sweden	Eu	1179sol
1730-1830	VOIRI	Eu	6110kam, 9500sir
1745-1800	Miss.Heukelbach	Eu	1440mrn

1800	German	Area	kHz
1800-1830	R.Sweden	Eu	6065hor
1800-1900	R.Budapest	Eu	3975jbr, 6025rso
1800-1900	R.Santec	Eu	603bln, 1215klg, 1323wbr, 1386klg, 6235spb, 7300arm
1800-1900	R.Taiwan Int'l	Eu	9565tai
1800-1900	R.Ukraine Int'l	Eu	7555khr
1800-1900	VO Indonesia	Eu,NAf,ME	15150jak
1800-1900	VO Russia (VOR)	Eu	603bln, 1215klg, 1323wbr, 1386klg, 6235spb, 7300arm
1800-2000	China R. Int'l	Eu	1440mrn, 7170kas, 9615uru, 11760kas
1800-2000	Deutsche Welle	NAf,CAf	11795nau
1800-2000	Deutsche Welle	SAf	11945kig
1800-2000	Deutsche Welle	Af,ME	15275trm
1800-2000	Deutsche Welle	Am	17860kig
1800-2000	Deutsche Welle	Eu	6075sin, 6075wer
1800-2000	Deutsche Welle	Eu,NAf	9545nau
1800-2000	Deutsche Welle	NAf,WAf	9735wer
1800-2000	VO Korea	Eu	6575kuj, 7505kuj
1805-1825	RAI Int'l	WEu	6110rom, 9760rom
1805-1905	R.Damascus	Eu	12085adr, 13610adr
1815-1830	RVI	Eu	1512wol, 1512wol, 7490arm, 7490arm
1830-1840	Lutherische Std	Eu	1440mrn
1830-1845	R.Freundes-D.	Eu	1440mrn
1830-1900	R.Budapest	Eu	3975jbr, 6025rso
1830-1900	R.Santec	Eu	603bln, 1215klg, 1323wbr, 1386klg, 6235spb, 7300arm
1830-1930	VO Turkey	Eu	7205emr
1845-1900	Lutherische Std	Eu	603bln, 1215klg, 1323wbr, 1386klg, 6235spb, 7300arm
1845-1900	Miss.Heukelbach	Eu	603bln, 1215klg, 1323wbr, 1386klg, 6235spb, 7300arm
1900	**German**	**Area**	**kHz**
1900-1915	RT Tunisienne	NAf,Eu	963tun
1900-1930	R.Slovakia Int.	Eu	5915rso, 7345rso
1900-1930	R.Tirana	Eu	1458fla, 7240shi
1900-2000	R.Cairo	Eu	9990abs
1900-2000	R.Romania Int'l	WEu	6140tig, 7140tig
1900-2000	R.Taiwan Int'l	Eu	6170skn
1900-2000	VO Russia (VOR)	Eu	603bln, 1215klg, 1323wbr, 6145msk, 7300arm
1905-1925	VO Armenia	WAs,ME,Eu	4810yer
1905-1925	VO Armenia	Eu	9965gav
1920-1940	Vatican Radio	Eu	1467rou, 1530smg, 4005vat, 5885vat, 7250smg
1925-1930	R.Freundes-D.	Eu	603bln, 1215klg, 1323wbr, 6145msk, 7300arm
1930-2000	R.Belarus	Eu	7105mns, 7340mns
1930-2000	R.Santec	Eu	603bln, 1215klg, 1323wbr, 6145msk, 7300arm
1930-2000	R.Sweden	Eu	1179sol, 6065hor
1930-2030	R.Sweden	Eu	1179sol, 6065hor
1935-2030	R.Taskent Int'l	Eu	5025tac, 11905tac
2000	**German**	**Area**	**kHz**
2000-2015	R.Thailand	Eu	9535udo
2000-2015	RVI	Eu	1512wol, 7490arm
2000-2100	R.Bulgaria	WEu	5800pld, 7500pld
2000-2100	R.Korea Int'l	Eu	3955skn
2000-2100	Family Radio	Eu	9355yfr
2000-2200	Deutsche Welle	NAf,CAf	11795nau
2000-2200	Deutsche Welle	SAf	11945kig

2000	**German**	**Area**	**kHz**
2000-2200	Deutsche Welle	Am	17860kig
2000-2200	Deutsche Welle	Eu	6075sin
2000-2200	Deutsche Welle	Eu,NAf	6075wer
2000-2200	Deutsche Welle	SAm,NAf	9545nau
2000-2200	Deutsche Welle	NAf,WAf	9735wer
2030-2055	R.Polonia	Eu	6110wwa, 6150wwa
2030-2100	R.Budapest	Eu	3975jbr, 6025rso
2030-2100	TWR Europe	Eu	1467rou
2030-2130	TWR Europe	Eu	1467rou
2100	**German**	**Area**	**kHz**
2100-2130	Int'l R.SerbMon	WEu	6100bij
2100-2145	Family Radio	Eu	11565yfr
2100-2200	China R. Int'l	Eu	1386sit
2100-2200	Deutsche Welle	RUS	693msk, 1188spe
2100-2200	R.Taiwan Int'l	Eu	11665yfr
2100-2200	R.Ukraine Int'l	Eu	7555khr
2100-2200	RAE	Eu,NAf	9690bue, 15345bue
2200	**German**	**Area**	**kHz**
2200-2300	Deutsche Welle	RUS	693msk, 1188spe
2200-2400	Deutsche Welle	Am	11955sin
2200-2400	Deutsche Welle	Eu	6075sin
2200-2400	Deutsche Welle	Eu,NAf	6075wer
2200-2400	Deutsche Welle	SAm	9545sin, 11690kig
2200-2400	Deutsche Welle	NAm,Car	9780atg, 11990sac

0200	**German (low)**	**Area**	**kHz**
0200-0230	HCJB	MEX	9785qui
0700	**German (low)**	**Area**	**kHz**
0730-0800	HCJB	Eu,Oc	21455qui
0730-0800	HCJB	Eu	9765qui
1600	**German (low)**	**Area**	**kHz**
1600-1630	HCJB	Eu	3995jul
2200	**German (low)**	**Area**	**kHz**
2230-2300	HCJB	SAm	12040qui

PORTUGUESE

0000	**Portuguese**	**Area**	**kHz**
0000-0045	TWR Bonaire	CAm,SAm	882bon
0000-0100	China R. Int'l	SAf	11850guf
0000-0100	China R. Int'l	SAm	7245xia, 11680bei
0000-0100	TWR Bonaire	CAm,SAm	882bon
0000-0100	VO Russia (VOR)	Eu	603bln
0000-0100	VO Russia (VOR)	B	7330msk, 7390sam, 7570orz
0000-0200	RAE	Am	11710bue
0000-0300	RDP Int'l	B	11980lis, 13770lis
0000-0300	RDP Int'l	VEN	13700lis
0000-0300	RDP Int'l	NAm	9410lis, 9715lis
0030-0100	Vatican Radio	Eu	1260vat
0030-0100	Vatican Radio	SAm	7305smg, 9605smg
0045-0100	R.Santec	SAm	7330msk, 7390sam, 7570orz, 9965gav
0100	**Portuguese**	**Area**	**kHz**
0115-0130	RAI Int'l	SAm	9840rom
0200	**Portuguese**	**Area**	**kHz**
0230-0300	R.Japan	SAm	9660guf
0400	**Portuguese**	**Area**	**kHz**
0400-1100	Voz Cristã	B	11890sgo
0430-0500	BBC World Sce	SAf	3390mey, 6135mey, 7205mey
0430-0500	BBG-VOA	Af	1530sao, 5890grv, 6015bot, 9480grv, 9075sao
0500	**Portuguese**	**Area**	**kHz**
0500-0545	Deutsche Welle	Af	9545wer, 9755kig
0500-0700	Radiobrás	SAm,Af	9665bra
0530-0600	Vatican Radio	Af	9660smg, 11625smg, 13765smg
0600	**Portuguese**	**Area**	**kHz**
0600-0855	RDP Int'l	Eu	9755lis
0600-1300	RDP Int'l	Eu	9815lis
0700	**Portuguese**	**Area**	**kHz**
0745-0900	RDP Int'l	Eu	11660sin
0800	**Portuguese**	**Area**	**kHz**
0800-0930	HCJB	Eu,Oc	21455qui
0800-0930	HCJB	B	9745qui
0800-1055	RDP Int'l	B,WAf	17710lis
0800-1455	RDP Int'l	Eu	11875lis, 15575lis
0800-1655	RDP Int'l	Af	21830lis
0900	**Portuguese**	**Area**	**kHz**
0900-1000	Vatican Radio	Eu	1260vat
0900-1055	RDP Int'l	Eu	11875lis
0930-1100	RDP Int'l	Eu	9815sin
1000	**Portuguese**	**Area**	**kHz**
1000-1130	Vatican Radio	Eu	1260vat
1000-1130	Vatican Radio	SAm	21850smg
1030-1100	R.Japan	SAm	9530guf
1100	**Portuguese**	**Area**	**kHz**
1100-1300	RDP Int'l	Eu	15140lis
1100-1300	RDP Int'l	B,WAf	21655lis
1100-1300	RDP Int'l	Af	21830lis
1100-2100	RDP Int'l	B,WAf	21655lis
1100-2300	Voz Christiana	B	17660sgo
1300	**Portuguese**	**Area**	**kHz**
1300-1700	RDP Int'l	NAm	15575lis
1300-1700	RDP Int'l	NAm	15575lis
1300-1800	RDP Int'l	VEN	17745lis
1400	**Portuguese**	**Area**	**kHz**
1400-1600	RDP Int'l	ME,IND	15690lis
1415-1500	Vatican Radio	Eu	1260vat, 9645smg, 11740smg
1440-1455	TWR Africa	WAf	7315man
1440-1510	TWR Africa	WAf	7315man
1500	**Portuguese**	**Area**	**kHz**
1500-1600	TWR Bonaire	CAm,SAm	882bon
1500-1600	Vatican Radio	Eu	1260vat
1500-1755	RDP Int'l	Eu	11635lis
1500-1800	RDP Int'l	Eu	11960lis
1530-1800	HCJB	B	15295qui
1600	**Portuguese**	**Area**	**kHz**
1600-1630	Vatican Radio	Eu	1260vat
1630-1645	TWR Africa	WAf	4760man
1700	**Portuguese**	**Area**	**kHz**
1700-1730	BBG-VOA	Af	15545bot
1700-1800	BBG-VOA	Af	1530sao, 11775sao
1700-1800	RFI	WAf	11995iss, 15530iss
1700-1800	RFI	EAf,IOc	12015gab
1700-1900	RDP Int'l	NAm	17825lis
1700-1900	RDP Int'l	NAm	17825lis
1700-2000	RDP Int'l	Af	17680lis
1700-2000	RDP Int'l	B,WAf	21655lis
1700-2000	RDP Int'l	Eu	9460lis
1730-1800	BBG-VOA	Af	9805bot, 21485grv
1800	**Portuguese**	**Area**	**kHz**
1800-1830	BBG-VOA	Af	1530sao, 7290udo, 9805bot, 21485grv
1800-1900	Vatican Radio	Af	11625smg, 13765smg, 15570smg
1800-2100	RDP Int'l	VEN	15535lis
1800-2100	RDP Int'l	VEN	15535lis
1800-2100	RDP Int'l	Eu	9460lis, 11630lis
1900	**Portuguese**	**Area**	**kHz**
1900-2000	China R. Int'l	Af	7180xia
1900-2000	China R. Int'l	Eu	7225xia, 7335jin
1900-2000	China R. Int'l	SAf	9535xia, 13630bko
1900-2000	China R. Int'l	NAf	9620xia
1900-2100	Radiobrás	SAm,Af	9665bra
1900-2100	RDP Int'l	NAm	15540lis
1900-2400	RDP Int'l	NAm	15540lis

1900	Portuguese	Area	kHz
1905-1920	TWR Africa	SAf	6130man
1920-1950	TWR Africa	SAf	6130man
1930-2000	China R. Int'l	Af	11640bko

2000	Portuguese	Area	kHz
2000-2030	RCI	B	15305sac, 17765sac
2000-2030	R.Habana Cuba	Eu	13360hab
2000-2100	RFI	CAf	11965iss
2000-2400	RDP Int'l	Af	11825lis
2000-2400	RDP Int'l	B,WAf	15555lis
2000-2400	RDP Int'l	Eu	7310lis, 9460lis
2000-2400	RDP Int'l	Af	9670lis
2005-2035	TWR Africa	SAf	6130man
2030-2100	BBC World Sce	SAf	3390mey, 6135mey, 7205mey
2030-2100	BBC World Sce	WAf	9565skn, 11695rmp, 11855asc
2050-2110	RAI Int'l	EAf,ME	11880rom
2050-2110	RAI Int'l	CAf	11880rom, 15250rom
2050-2110	RAI Int'l	E,NAf	6010rom, 7290rom

2100	Portuguese	Area	kHz
2100-0100	Voz Cristã	B	15475sgo
2100-2130	RCI	B	15305sac, 17765sac
2100-2130	VO Russia (VOR)	Eu	6145msk, 7400msk
2100-2200	Family Radio	WAf	21525yfr
2100-2400	RDP Int'l	VEN	15460lis
2100-2400	RDP Int'l	VEN	15460lis
2130-2145	Vatican Radio	Eu	1530smg, 4005vat, 5885vat, 7250smg

2200	Portuguese	Area	kHz
2200-2230	R.Habana Cuba	B	17705hab
2200-2245	Family Radio	SAm	17575yfr
2200-2245	Family Radio	Eu	7580yfr
2200-2300	China R. Int'l	SAm	5990bei
2200-2300	China R. Int'l	B	7245xia
2215-2330	R.Cairo	SAm	11790abz
2230-2300	RCI	B	11905sac, 15245sac

2300	Portuguese	Area	kHz
2300-0145	Family Radio	SAm	11885yfr
2300-0230	HCJB	B	11920qui, 12020qui
2300-0400	Voz Christiana	B	11745sgo
2300-2330	R.Habana Cuba	B	17705hab
2300-2400	China R. Int'l	SAm	13650hab
2300-2400	R.Habana Cuba	B	15230hab
2300-2400	TWR Bonaire	CAm,SAm	882bon
2330-2400	RCI	B	11905sac, 13730sac

SPANISH

0000	Spanish	Area	kHz
0000-0015	Trova Libre	CUB	9955rmi
0000-0030	Int'l R.SerbMon	SAm	9680bij
0000-0030	RCI	Car,SAm	9755sac, 11865sac
0000-0030	R.Prague	SAm	5930lit, 7345lit, 11665asc
0000-0040	LV Resistencia	CLM	6120—, 6240—
0000-0100	China R. Int'l	NAm,Car	5990hab
0000-0100	China R. Int'l	SAm	7160xia, 15120hab
0000-0100	China R. Int'l	MEX	9745bon
0000-0100	Foro Mil.Cubano	CUB	9955rmi
0000-0100	R.Bulgaria	SAm	7500pld, 11500pld
0000-0100	R.Habana Cuba	NAm	6000hab, 9820hab
0000-0100	R.Romania Int'l	MEX	9525gal, 11935gal
0000-0100	R.Romania Int'l	ARG	9745tig, 11960tig
0000-0100	VO Korea	CAm,SAm	6520kuj, 7580kuj, 11735kuj
0000-0115	BBC World Sce	CAm	5875rmp
0000-0115	BBC World Sce	SAm	5875skn, 6110asc, 9855asc, 11765asc
0000-0115	BBC World Sce	CAm,SAm	6110atg
0000-0200	RNWO	SAm	9895mdc, 15315bon
0000-0300	China R. Int'l	SAm	11650xia
0000-0300	REE	SAm	11815cri
0000-0400	BBG-R.Martí	CUB	7365grv, 11775grv
0000-0500	R.Habana Cuba	ARG	15230hab
0000-0500	R.Habana Cuba	MEX	5965hab
0000-0500	R.Habana Cuba	Car	9505hab, 9655hab
0000-0500	R.Habana Cuba	VEN	9600hab
0000-0600	Voz Christiana	SAm	15375sgo
0000-1200	Voz Christiana	SAm	6070sgo
0000-1300	WEWN	CAm	5825ewn
0000-2400	BBG-R.Martí	CUB	1180mth
0030-0100	RCI	Car,SAm	9755sac, 11865sac
0030-0230	VOIRI	CAm,SAm	9555kam
0030-0330	VOIRI	SAm	9905kam
0045-0200	R.Cairo	CAm	11755abz
0045-0200	R.Cairo	NAm	11855abz
0045-0200	R.Cairo	SAm	9415abs
0055-0115	RAI Int'l	SAm	9840rom

0100	Spanish	Area	kHz
0100-0130	Conv.entre Cub.	CUB	9955rmi
0100-0130	RCI	MEX,CUB	9790sac
0100-0130	RFI	CAm,Car	9800guf
0100-0145	Vatican Radio	Eu	1260vat
0100-0145	Vatican Radio	SAm	7305smg, 9605smg, 11910smg
0100-0200	BBG-VOA	SAm	9480dln, 9560dln, 9885grv, 11700dln, 11990dln
0100-0200	R.Korea Int'l	SAm	11810kim
0100-0200	VO Russia (VOR)	SAm	5945arm, 6195spb, 7180gri, 7330msk, 7390sam, 7570orz
0100-0300	VO Russia (VOR)	Eu	603bln
0100-0400	Voz Christiana	CAm	15585sgo
0100-0415	TWR Bonaire	CAm,SAm	882bon
0100-0500	HCJB	MEX	9745qui
0100-0500	R.Habana Cuba	NAm	11760hab
0100-0800	KVOH	CAm	9975voh
0115-0130	BBC World Sce	CAm	5875rmp
0115-0130	BBC World Sce	SAm	5875skn, 6110asc, 9855asc, 11765asc
0115-0130	BBC World Sce	CAm,SAm	6110atg
0130-0200	R.Prague	CAm	6200lit, 7345lit
0130-0230	R.Oriente Libre	CUB	9955rmi
0145-0230	Vatican Radio	SAm	7305smg, 9605smg, 11910smg
0150-0200	R.Santec	SAm	5945arm, 6195spb, 7125jul, 7180gri, 7330msk, 7390sam, 7570orz, 9965gav

0200	Spanish	Area	kHz
0200-0300	China R. Int'l	NAm,Car,SAm	13685guf
0200-0300	R.Bulgaria	SAm	7500pld, 11500pld
0200-0300	R.Bulgaria	CAm	9400pld
0200-0300	RNWO	CAm	6165bon
0200-0300	RNWO	MEX,Car	9590bon
0200-0300	R.Oriente Libre	CUB	9955rmi
0200-0300	R.Taiwan Int'l	SAm	15215yfr, 17845yfr
0200-0300	VO Korea	CAm,SAm	6520kuj, 7580kuj, 11735kuj
0200-0300	VO Russia (VOR)	SAm	5945arm, 7330msk, 7390sam, 7570orz, 9945orz
0200-0400	REE	NAm	6050nob
0200-0400	RNWO	CAm,Car	9895mdc
0200-0500	R.Habana Cuba	Car	9550hab
0200-0600	REE	NAm	11880cri
0200-0600	REE	CAm	6040cri
0230-0300	Conv.entre Cub.	CUB	9955rmi
0230-0300	R.Slovakia Int.	SAm	7230rso, 9440rso

0300	**Spanish**	**Area**	**kHz**
0300-0330	RCI	Car,SAm	6190sac, 9755sac, 9810sac
0300-0330	R.Prague	CAm	6200lit
0300-0330	R.Prague	SAm	7345lit
0300-0330	VO Vietnam	CAm	6175sac
0300-0345	BBC World Sce	SAm	5995dln, 9515dln
0300-0345	BBC World Sce	CAm,SAm	6110atg
0300-0345	BBC World Sce	CAm	7325rmp, 7325skn
0300-0400	BBG-R.Martí	CUB	7405grv
0300-0400	China R. Int'l	SAm	9560sac, 9665bra
0300-0400	R.Romania Int'l	ARG	9545tig, 11895tig
0300-0400	R.Romania Int'l	MEX	9690gal, 11870gal
0300-0500	R.Habana Cuba	CHL	11875hab
0315-0335	RAI Int'l	NAm	11800rom
0315-0335	RAI Int'l	SAm	9840rom
0315-0400	Vatican Radio	SAm	7305smg, 9605smg
0330-0345	VO Armenia	SAm	9965gav
0345-0400	BBC World Sce	SAm	5995dln, 9515dln
0345-0400	BBC World Sce	CAm,SAm	6110atg
0345-0400	BBC World Sce	CAm	7325rmp, 7325skn
0400	**Spanish**	**Area**	**kHz**
0400-0430	R.Japan	SAm	9660guf
0400-0430	VO Vietnam	NAm	6175sac
0400-0500	REE	SAm	6920nob
0400-0500	R.Taiwan Int'l	NAm	11740yfr
0400-0600	REE	SAm	5970nob
0400-0600	REE	NAm	6055nob
0400-0700	BBG-R.Martí	CUB	9805grv, 11775grv
0400-1000	BBG-R.Martí	CUB	6030grv, 7405grv
0415-0430	EvangeliumsRdfk	Eu	1539mnf
0430-0500	R.Budapest	Eu,NAf	3975jbr, 6025rso
0445-0500	EvangeliumsRdfk	Eu	1539mnf
0500	**Spanish**	**Area**	**kHz**
0500-0530	R.Japan	CAm	11895guf
0500-0530	R.Japan	Eu	11970gab
0500-0700	REE	ME	11890nob
0500-0800	WEWN	SAm	11615ewn
0530-0630	VOIRI	Eu	15320sir, 17590kam
0600	**Spanish**	**Area**	**kHz**
0600-0700	R.Taiwan Int'l	NAm	5950yfr
0600-0800	REE	Eu	5985nob
0600-0800	REE	Eu	9710nob
0600-0900	REE	Eu	12035nob
0600-1200	Voz Christiana	SAm	9780sgo
0700	**Spanish**	**Area**	**kHz**
0700-0730	R.Bulgaria	SEu	11900pld, 13800pld
0700-0800	R.Korea Int'l	Eu	9640kim
0700-0900	REE	AUS	17770nob
0700-0900	REE	AUS	21610nob
0700-1000	BBG-R.Martí	CUB	5980dln, 7365dln
0800	**Spanish**	**Area**	**kHz**
0800-1000	REE	SAm	21570nob
0800-1000	TWR Bonaire	CAm,SAm	882bon
0800-1300	REE	Eu	13720nob
0800-1300	WEWN	SAm	11875ewn
0900	**Spanish**	**Area**	**kHz**
0900-0915	Vatican Radio	Eu	585vat, 1611smg+, 5885vat
0900-0930	R.Prague	SEu	11600lit, 15255lit
0900-1000	REE	Eu	15585nob
0900-1500	REE	Af	21540nob
0900-1700	REE	ME	21610nob
1000	**Spanish**	**Area**	**kHz**
1000-1030	R.Japan	SAm	9530guf, 9710yam
1000-1030	R.Japan	CAm	9540yam
1000-1100	REE	SAm	11815cri
1000-1100	R.Korea Int'l	Eu	15210kim
1000-1100	R.Korea Int'l	SAm	9580kim
1000-1200	BBG-R.Martí	CUB	6030dln
1000-1200	REE	J	9660bei

1000	**Spanish**	**Area**	**kHz**
1000-1300	BBG-R.Martí	CUB	5980dln, 7365dln
1000-1400	BBG-R.Martí	CUB	5745grv
1000-1700	REE	SAm	21570nob
1000-1800	REE	NAm	17595nob
1030-0500	HCJB	EQA	690qui
1100	**Spanish**	**Area**	**kHz**
1100-1130	BBC World Sce	Car	6110grv
1100-1130	BBC World Sce	SAm	6130dln, 17820asc
1100-1130	BBC World Sce	CAm	9670atg
1100-1130	RNWO	Car,NAm	6165bon
1100-1200	BBG-VOA	SAm	9535grv
1100-1200	REE	NAm	15170cri
1100-1200	REE	CAm	5970cri
1100-1200	R.Korea Int'l	Sam	11795sac
1100-1200	RNWO	SAm	9715bon
1100-1230	BBG-VOA	SAm	11890grv, 15265grv
1100-1300	HCJB	CUB	11960qui
1100-1500	HCJB	SAm	6050qui, 15140qui
1100-1500	R.Habana Cuba	NAm	11760hab, 12000hab
1100-1500	R.Habana Cuba	VEN	11800hab
1100-1500	R.Habana Cuba	ARG	15230hab
1100-1500	R.Habana Cuba	Am	6000hab
1100-1500	R.Habana Cuba	Car	9550hab
1115-1130	Trova Libre	CUB	9955rmi
1130-1200	Vatican Radio	Eu	1260vat
1130-1200	Vatican Radio	SAm	21850smg
1200	**Spanish**	**Area**	**kHz**
1200-1215	Trova Libre	CUB	9955rmi
1200-1230	BBG-VOA	SAm	9480dln, 9535grv, 13715grv
1200-1230	Junta Patr.Cub.	CUB	9955rmi
1200-1230	R.Bulgaria	SEu	11600pld, 13600pld
1200-1230	RFI	CAm,Car	15515guf
1200-1230	RNWO	CAm	9715bon
1200-1300	Foro Mil.Cubano	CUB	9955rmi
1200-1300	REE	SAm	11815cri
1200-1300	R.Oriente Libre	CUB	9955rmi
1200-1400	REE	PHL	11910xia
1200-1400	REE	NAm	15170cri
1200-1400	REE	CAm	5970cri
1200-1400	RAE	Am	15345bue
1200-1500	BBG-R.Martí	CUB	7405grv
1200-1600	REE	SAm	15125cri
1200-1800	REE	SAm	21700nob
1200-2400	Voz Christiana	CAm	17680sgo
1200-2400	Voz Christiana	SAm	9635sgo
1300	**Spanish**	**Area**	**kHz**
1300-1330	BBC World Sce	SAm	6130dln, 9670dln, 15325grv
1300-1400	REE	Eu	13720nob
1300-1400	WEWN	CAm	7425ewn
1300-1500	HCJB	MEX	11960qui
1300-1500	KVOH	CAm	9975voh
1300-1500	TWR Bonaire	CAm,SAm	882bon
1300-1600	WEWN	CAm	9955ewn
1300-1700	REE	Eu	15585nob
1300-1930	BBG-R.Martí	CUB	13820grv
1300-2300	WEWN	SAm	15745ewn
1300-2400	BBG-R.Martí	CUB	11930grv
1330-1500	HCJB	Eu,Oc	21455qui
1400	**Spanish**	**Area**	**kHz**
1400	R.Habana Cuba	Car	11670hab
1400	R.Habana Cuba	CHL	11875hab
1400	R.Habana Cuba	CAm	13680hab
1400	R.Habana Cuba	NAm	13750hab
1400	R.Habana Cuba	B	17750hab
1400-1415	Vatican Radio	Eu	585vat, 1260vat, 1611smg, 9645smg, 11740smg
1400-1500	REE	CAm	5970cri

1400	**Spanish**	**Area**	**kHz**
1400-2000	BBG-R.Martí	CUB	15330grv
1400-2300	WEWN	CAm	11530ewn
1500	**Spanish**	**Area**	**kHz**
1500-0100	KVOH	CAm	17775voh
1500-1530	R.Prague	SEu	11600lit, 13580lit
1500-1600	REE	NAm	17850cri
1500-1600	REE	CAm	9765cri
1500-1600	Vatican Radio	Eu	1260vat
1500-1700	REE	Af	15385nob
1500-1900	REE	Af	17755nob
1500-2200	BBG-R.Martí	CUB	17670dln
1530-1600	R.Slovakia Int.	Eu	9445rso, 11600rso
1530-1600	VO Greece	Eu	7430avl
1600	**Spanish**	**Area**	**kHz**
1600-1630	RFI	CAm,Car	17860guf
1600-1800	REE	CAm	9765cri
1600-2200	WEWN	CAm	13615ewn
1600-2300	REE	NAm	17850cri
1630-1700	TWR Bonaire	CAm,SAm	882bon
1700	**Spanish**	**Area**	**kHz**
1700-1800	REE	SAm	15125cri
1700-1800	R.Nac.RASD	NAf	1550—
1700-1800	TWR Bonaire	CAm,SAm	882bon
1700-1800	VO Indonesia	Eu,NAf,ME	15150jak
1700-1800	VO Korea	ME,NAf	3560pyo, 9975kuj, 11735kuj
1700-1900	REE	SAm	17715nob
1700-2200	REE	Eu	9665nob
1700-2300	REE	Eu	7275nob
1730-1800	R.Bulgaria	SEu	9600pld, 11600pld
1730-1800	Vatican Radio	Eu	1260vat
1730-1800	VO Turkey	Eu	9780emr
1800	**Spanish**	**Area**	**kHz**
1800-1830	RFI	CAm,Car	17630guf
1800-1900	VO Korea	Eu	4405pyo, 9325kuj, 11335kuj
1800-2000	REE	SAm	15125cri
1800-2000	REE	CAm	9765cri
1800-2100	REE	SAm	17595nob
1800-2400	R.Nac.RASD	NAf	7460—
1815-1830	Kol Israel	NAm,Eu	9390isr, 11585isr, 11605isr
1820-1840	R.Japan	Eu	11970yam
1900	**Spanish**	**Area**	**kHz**
1900-0500	HCJB	EQA	6050qui
1900-1930	R.Prague	SEu	5930lit, 9430lit
1900-1940	Vatican Radio	Af	9755smg, 11625smg
1900-2000	R.Nac.Venezuela	NAm	13740hab
1900-2100	REE	Af	17755nob
1900-2300	REE	NAm	9630nob
1930-0300	BBG-R.Martí	CUB	13820dln
1930-1945	RT Tunisienne	NAf,Eu	963tun
2000	**Spanish**	**Area**	**kHz**
2000-0500	HCJB	Eu,Oc	21455qui
2000-2030	Int'l R.SerbMon	E	7220bij
2000-2030	R.Prague	SEu	5930lit, 9430lit
2000-2100	R.Korea Int'l	Eu	9515kim
2000-2100	R.Nac.Venezuela	NAm	13680hab
2000-2100	R.Nac.Venezuela	SAm	15230hab, 17705hab
2000-2100	R.Nac.Venezuela	Car	9550hab
2000-2100	R.Romania Int'l	E	7140gal, 9570gal
2000-2100	R.Taiwan Int'l	Eu	6120jul
2000-2200	BBG-R.Martí	CUB	9565grv
2000-2200	RAE	Eu,NAf	11710bue, 15345bue
2000-2200	RAE	Am,Eu	6060bue
2000-2300	REE	SAm	15125cri
2000-2300	REE	CAm	9765cri
2000-2300	Family Radio	CAm	5985yfr, 11855yfr
2015-2030	TWR Europe	Eu	1467rou
2030-2130	VOIRI	CAm,SAm	11610sir

2000	**Spanish**	**Area**	**kHz**
2030-2130	VOIRI	Eu	7130kam, 9750sir
2045-2100	Kol Israel	Eu,CAm	6280isr
2045-2100	Kol Israel	SAm,SAf	7520isr
2045-2100	Kol Israel	NAm,Eu	9390isr
2100	**Spanish**	**Area**	**kHz**
2100-2130	RFI	CAm,Car	17630guf
2100-2130	R.Slovakia Int.	SAm	9460rso, 11610rso
2100-2200	REE	Af	11625nob
2100-2200	REE	SAm	17595nob
2100-2200	R.Nac.Venezuela	SAm	6000hab, 11875hab
2100-2200	Family Radio	Eu	9355yfr
2100-2300	China R. Int'l	Eu	6020szg
2100-2300	China R. Int'l	Eu,NAf	9640kas
2100-2300	HCJB	SAm	15140qui
2100-2300	R.Habana Cuba	Eu	13360hab
2100-2300	R.Habana Cuba	SAm	15230hab
2100-2300	R.Habana Cuba	Car	6060hab, 9550hab
2110-2130	RAI Int'l	E,NAf	6010rom, 7290rom
2110-2130	Vatican Radio	Eu	585vat, 1530smg, 4005vat, 5885vat, 7250smg
2130-2200	R.Prague	SEu,SAm	5930lit, 9435lit
2130-2200	VO Russia (VOR)	Eu	6145msk, 7400msk
2200	**Spanish**	**Area**	**kHz**
2200-0400	BBG-R.Martí	CUB	6030grv
2200-2300	China R. Int'l	Car,SAm	13700sac
2200-2300	China R. Int'l	Eu,NAf	7120uru
2200-2300	R.Bulgaria	SEu	7400pld, 9400pld
2200-2300	R. Cimarrona	URG	9480jul
2200-2300	REE	Af	11625nob
2200-2300	REE	NAf	7270nob
2200-2300	RNWO	NAm	15530bon+
2200-2300	R.Romania Int'l	ARG	9575tig, 11940tig
2200-2300	RAE	Eu,NAf	6060bue, 11710bue, 15345bue
2200-2300	VO Korea	Eu	4405pyo, 9325kuj, 11335kuj
2200-2400	BBG-R.Martí	CUB	15330dln
2200-2400	WEWN	CAm	9975ewn
2230-2300	R.Budapest	Eu,NAf	6025jbr, 7160rso
2300	**Spanish**	**Area**	**kHz**
2300-0057	AWR	CAm	6165bon
2300-0100	HCJB	NAm,SAm	11700qui
2300-0100	R.Habana Cuba	NAm	6000hab, 11875hab
2300-0200	REE	SAm	11945nob
2300-0400	REE	SAm	9620nob
2300-0500	REE	SAm	6125nob
2300-0500	REE	NAm	9535nob
2300-0500	WEWN	SAm	11530ewn
2300-1300	WEWN	CAm	7425ewn
2300-2330	RCI	SAm	11905sac, 13730sac
2300-2400	China R. Int'l	SAm	7160xia, 7245xia
2300-2400	R.Nac.Venezuela	CAm,SAm	13680hab
2300-2400	R.Nac.Venezuela	NAm	9820hab, 11760hab
2300-2400	RNWO	SAm	9895fle
2300-2400	R.Taiwan Int'l	SAm	9690yfr, 11720yfr
2300-2400	RAE	Am,Eu	6060bue, 11710bue, 15345bue
2305-0045	Family Radio	SAm	17845yfr
2305-0100	Family Radio	SAm	15215yfr
2320-0030	R.Damascus	SAm	12085adr, 13610adr

N.B. not all transmissions are daily, please check main schedules under the appropriate country for full details.
Frequencies marked with '+' indicate a DRM broadcast.

International DRM Broadcasts

0000	Language	Area	Station	kHz
0000-0100	English	NAm	BBC World Sce	6010sac
0000-0200	Arabic	NAm	R.Kuwait	11675kbd
0000-0400	Various	Eu	(TDF)*	3965iss
0000-1000	Various	Eu	Deutsche Welle	3995wer
0000-2400	French	Eu	RTL Radio	5990jun
0000-2400	German	Eu	RTL Oldieradio	6095jun

0100	Language	Area	Station	kHz
0100-0200	English	NAm	CRI	6080sac

0400	Language	Area	Station	kHz
0400-0500	English	NAm	BBC World Sce	6010sac

0500	Language	Area	Station	kHz
0500-0900	Arabic	ME	R.Kuwait	6055kbd
0515-0530	German	Eu	Miss.Heukelbach	6095jun
0500-1600	Various	Eu	(TDF)	6175iss

0600	Language	Area	Station	kHz
0600-1000	English	ME,NAf	Deutsche Welle	21675trm
0630-1200	Various	Eu	Deutsche Welle	7265wer
0600-1700	Various	NAf	(TDF)	15790iss
0600-1800	Various	Eu	(TDF)*	3965iss

0700	Language	Area	Station	kHz
0700-1000	English	Eu	VO Russia	15780tld
0700-1000	Various	Eu	Deutsche Welle	5975wer

0800	Language	Area	Station	kHz
0800-1400	Various	Eu	Deutsche Welle	15440sin

0900	Language	Area	Station	kHz
0900-1100	Various	Eu	Deutsche Welle	17700sin
0900-1430	Various	Eu	Vatican Radio	1611smg
0930-1300	Arabic	Eu	R.Kuwait	13620kbd

1000	Language	Area	Station	kHz
1000-1100	English (Sat)	Eu	RNWO	7240fle
1000-1100	English (Mon)	Eu	Christian Voice	9760rmp
1000-1100	German	Eu	VO Russia	15780tld
1000-1200	English (Sun-Fri)	Eu	RNWO	7240fle
1000-1300	Various	Eu	Deutsche Welle	6140jul
1000-1500	English	Eu	BBC World Sce	7320rmp

1100	Language	Area	Station	kHz
1100-1155	Various	Eu	Deutsche Welle	17710sin
1100-1200	Music (Sat)	Eu	TDPradio	7240fle

1200	Language	Area	Station	kHz
1200-1300	Dutch/English	Eu	RNWO	7240fle
1200-1300	German	Eu	VO Russia	12060tld
1200-1400	Various	Eu	Deutsche Welle	9655wer

1300	Language	Area	Station	kHz
1300-1330	German	Eu	R.Sweden	7240fle
1300-1330	Music (Sun)	Eu	HCJB Just Jazz	9565rmp
1300-1500	Russian	Eu	VO Russia	12060tld
1300-1900	Various	NAm	(TDF)	17875iss
1315-1730	Arabic	NAf	R.Kuwait	9880kbd
1330-1400	English	Eu	R.Sweden	7240fle

1400	Language	Area	Station	kHz
1400-1430	English	Eu	RCI	7240fle
1400-1500	English (Sun)	Eu	Brigham YU. R.	9875rmp
1400-1555	Various	Eu	Deutsche Welle	17800sin
1400-1600	Various	Eu	Deutsche Welle	6130wer
1430-1500	English	Eu	RNWO	7240fle

1500	Language	Area	Station	kHz
1500-1515	German	Eu	Vatican Radio	7240fle
1500-1530	English (Fri)	Eu	RFI	9875rmp
1500-1530	English (Sat)	Eu	RNZI	9875rmp
1500-1600	Music (Sat)	Eu	TDPradio	6015jul
1500-1600	English	Eu	VO Russia	12060tld
1530-1600	English (Fri)	Eu	R.Korea Int'l	9875rmp
1500-1530	English (Sat)	Eu	R.Australia	9875rmp

1600	Language	Area	Station	kHz
1600-1700	Music (Sat)	NAm	TDPradio	11900sac
1600-1700	English (Fri)	Eu	R.Taiwan Int'l	9875rmp
1600-1900	Various	Eu	Deutsche Welle	6140jul
1600-1915	English	Eu	BBC World Sce	1296orf
1600-2400	Various	Eu	Deutsche Welle	3995wer

1700	Language	Area	Station	kHz
1700-1730	English (Sat)	NAm	VO the NASB	11900sac
1700-1800	English (Fri)	Eu	R.Japan	9875rmp

1900	Language	Area	Station	kHz
1900-2000	Russian	RUS	BBC World Sce	11925rmp
1900-2000	Various	Eu	(TDF)*	3965iss

2000	Language	Area	Station	kHz
2000-2100	Music (Sat)	Eu	TDPradio	7375tld
2055-2130	English	NAm	Vatican Radio	9800sac

2100	Language	Area	Station	kHz
2100-2200	English	NAm	RNWO	15530bon
2100-2200	English	NAm	RNWO	15530bon
2105-2400	English	Eu	BBC World Sce	1296orf
2130-2200	English	NAm	RNWO	9800sac

2200	Language	Area	Station	kHz
2200-2300	English	NAm	RCI	9800sac
2200-2300	Spanish	NAm	RNWO	15530bon
2200-2300	Various	Eu	Vatican Radio	1611smg
2200-2400	Arabic	NAm	R.Kuwait	11675kbd

2300	Language	Area	Station	kHz
2300-2330	English	NAm	Deutsche Welle	9800sac
2330-2400	English	NAm	R.Sweden	9800sac
2300-2400	Various	Eu	(TDF)*	3965iss

All transmissions are daily exc. where stated. *) From 1 Jan 2005
Compiled: 15 November 2004

TELEVISION

Section Contents

Initial entries for each letter, see Main Index for full details

AFGHANISTAN

Colour: PAL — **System:** B.

RADIO-TELEVISION AFGHANISTAN (RTA) (Gov)
P.O. Box 544, Kabul. ☎ +93 25460/25373.
L.P: DG: Dr Saeed Makhdom Raheen
Station: Kabul chE11 (217.25 MHz vision/222.75 MHz sound).
D.Prgr: daily 1315-1900 +Fri:0430-0730.News in Dari: 1430-1435 and 1500-1530 daily. News in Pashto: Fri.0530-0535 and 1600-1630 daily.

Provincial stations
Herat TV, Herat, chE7
Kandahar TV, Kandahar.
Nangahar TV, Jalalabad.
Balkh TV, Mazar-e Sharif.
Badakhshan TV, Faizabad.

ALASKA (US State)

Colour: NTSC — **System:** M.

STATIONS:
KTUU-TV Ch 2. Box 102880, Anchorage, AK 99510
L.P. Gen. Mgr: Al Bramstedt Jr. **D.Prgr.** 2230 (Sat/Sun 0000)-0900.
KATN-TV Ch 2. P.O. Box 74730, Fairbanks, AK 99701.
KTOO-TV* Ch 3. Capital Community Broadc. Inc, 224 Fourth Str, Juneau 99801
L.P. Pres. & Gen. Mgr: D. Rinker. Dir. Tec: J.W. Foster. **D.Prgr.** 1930 (Sat/Sun 1530)-0800.
KJNP-TV Ch 4. Evangelistic Alaska Missionary Fellowship, Box "O", North Pole 99705
L.P. Pres. & Dir: D.L. Nelson. Dir. Tec: E. Nichols.
KYUK-TV* Ch 4. Bethel Broadc. Inc, Box 468, Bethel 99559
L.P. Dir. Gen:J. Brigham.
KTBY-TV* Ch 4. KTBY Inc, 1840 S. Bragnaw Str, Anchorage 99508
L.P: Gen. Mgr: R.V. Bradley. Dir. Tec: E. Gjernes.
KAKM-TV Ch 7. Alaska Public Television Inc, 2677 Providence Dr, Anchorage 99508
L.P Gen. Mgr: E. Sackett. Dir. Tec: F. Mengel.
KJUD-TV Ch 8. 1107 West Eighth St., Suite 2, Juneau, AK 99801.
KUAC-TV* Ch 9. University of Alaska, Fairbanks 99701
L.P St. Mgr: Kathryn Jensen. Dir. Tec: David L. Walstad. **D.Prgr.**1800-0900.
KTVA-TV Ch 11. Northern TV Inc, Box 102200, Anchorage 99510
L.P Dir. Tec: D. Milsap. **D.Prgr.** 1700-1100.
KTVF-TV Ch 11. Northern TV Inc, Box 950, Fairbanks 99707
D.Prgr. 1700-1100.
KIMO-TV Ch 13. Alaska 13 Corp, 2700 Tudor Rd., Anchorage 99507
L.P Pres: D.L. Triplett.
KTNL-TV Ch 13. Sitka Broadc. Co. Inc, Box 2668, Sitka 99835
L.P Gen. Mgr: D. Etulain.
D.Prgr. Mon-Fri 1900-0900, Sat 1700-0900, Sun 1400-0800.
All comm. exc. * = Educational.

ALBANIA

Colour: PAL. — **Systems:** B & G

RADIOTELEVISIONi SHQIPTAR (Gov)
Rr. "Ismail Qemali" 11, Tirana. ☎ +355 42 26332 🖷 +355 42 56058 **L.P:** DG: Albert Minga. Dir. TVSH: Eduard Mazi.
Stations: Tirana City ch11, Dajt ch57, Korfuz ch47, Qafe Prush ch5/27/39, Homesh ch5/32, Mide ch12, Tarabosh ch6, Petresh ch6, Cervenake ch11, Korce ch8, Kerculle ch5, Mile ch12, Sopot ch7, Llogara ch11, Gilave ch9, Berat ch10, Lushnje-Blerimi ch11, Zvernec ch12. **D.Prgr:** 0600-2300. **F.Pl:** 2nd Channel.

ALGERIA

Colour: PAL — **System:** B

ENTREPRISE NATIONALE DE TÉLÉVISION (E.N.T.V.) (Gov)
Poste Restante 16004, Algiers. ☎ +213 (2) 1476935 🖷 +213 (2) 1741755
L.P: DG: Zemzoum Zoubir. Dir. of Inf: M. Ibrahim. Dir. Tec: M. El Ksouri. Dir. Ext. Rel: M. Bey.
D.Prgr: 1500-2300 (Thurs/Sat/Sun 1300-2400). News, cultural prgrs, films, drama and comedy prgrs in Arabic and French.

ANDORRA

Colour: PAL/SECAM — **System:** B/G, L

ANDORRA TELEVISIÓ (Telivisió Pública)
Baixada del Moli, n°24, Andorra la Vella. ☎ +376 873777. 🖷 +376 863242 **Email:** orta@andorra.ad **Web:** www.andorra.at.
L.P: DG: Enric Castellet. Ed. in Chief: Montserrat Talarn. Prod: Raimon Cartró. Chief Tech: Josep Mª Samper. Chief of Prog: Lluis Quintana. Chief of Info: Jordi Pifarré.

ANGOLA

Colour: PAL — **System:** I.

TELEVISÃO PUBLICA DE ANGOLA (Gov)
Avenida Ho-Chi-Min, P.O. Box 2604, Luanda. ☎ +244 (2) 320326. 🖷 +244 (2) 323622. **Web:** www.tpa.ao
L.P: MD: Carlos Chunha. Head of Prgrs: António Pedreira.
Station: ch9 13kW (ERP) + st's at Benguela, Huambo, Lubango, Namibe, Cabinda, Bié
D.Prgrs: 1730-2300 (Mon-Fri), 1400-2300 (Sat), 0900-2300 (Sun).

ANGUILLA

Colour: NTSC — **System:** M

CHANNELS 3&9
Broadcast Center Anguilla, Crocus Hill. ☎ +1 264 4973919 🖷 +1 264 4973909.
D.Prgr: 24h

ANTARCTICA

Colour: NTSC — **System**: M

AMERICAN FORCES ANTARCTIC NETWORK (AFAN McMurdo)
"Operation Deep Freeze", Fleet Post Office, San Francisco, California 96692, USA.
D.Prgr: The US Navy Antarctic support group operates six cable TV channels. incl. occ. local prgrs on ch13.

ANTIGUA & BARBUDA

Colour: NTSC — **System:** M.

ANTIGUA & BARBUDA BROADC. SERVICE (Gov)
Public Information Division, Galstron's Palace, Old Parnham Road, St. John's. ☎ +1 (268) 462 0010. 🖷 +1 (268) 462 4442. **Email:** absradio@cmatt.zzn.com. **Web:** www.cmattcomm.com.
L.P: Gen.Mgr. (TV):Trevor Parker.
Stations: ABS-TV chA10 50/20kW H.
D.Prgr: 0530-0100 (mon-Fri); 0530-0200 (Sat-Sun)
Relay: Montserrat ch13 10kW.

CTV ENTERTAINMENT SYSTEMS (Comm)
25 Long Str, Box 1536, St. Johns. ☎ + 1 (809) 4620346. 🖷 + 1 (809) 4624211 **L.P:** Prgr. Dir: J. Cox.
Cable Television only.

ARGENTINA

Colour: PAL — **System:** N.

ASOCIACIÓN DE TELERADIODIFUSORAS ARGENTINAS (ATA)
Av. Córdoba 323, 6to., 1054 Buenos Aires. ☎ +54 (1) 312-4208/4219/4533. 🖷 +54 (1) 312-4208.
L.P: Pres: Alejandro Enrique Massot. CE: Enrique Parodi.

CANAL 7
Avenida Figueroa Alcorta 2977 1425 Buenos Aires ☎802-6001/6
CANAL 9
Av. Dorrego 1708, 1414 Buenos Aires
CANAL 11
Pavon 2444 - Buenos Aires C.P.(1248) ☎943-2555
ARTEAR Arte Radiotelevisivo Argentino
Lima 1261 (C.P. 1138) Capital Federal. ☎4305-0013 **Email:** infotrece@artear.com.ar **Web:** artear.com.ar
L.P: Marketing Dir: Jorge Vaillant
CANAL 13
Lima 1261, Constitucion, Capital Federal ☎ 4305 0013 4370 1281

ARMENIA

Colour: SECAM — **Systems:** D & K.

ARMENIAN NATIONAL TELEVISION (Pub)
Hovsepyan Str. 26, Nork, 375047 Yerevan. ☎ +374 1 558505. +374 1 562460. **Email:** director@armtv.com **Web:** www.armtv.com
L.P: Dir: Armen Arzumanyan.

ARMENIA TV (Comm)
Yeghvard Highway 1, 375054 Yerevan. ☎ +374 1 365161. +374 1 365161. **Email:** message@armeniatv.am **Web:** www.armeniatv.am **L.P:** Dir: Bagrat Sarkissyan.

ARUBA

Colour: NTSC — **System:** M.

ARUBA BROADCASTING CO. - ATV
Royal Plaza Suite 223, Oranjestad ☎+297 (8) 38 150 +297 (8) 38 750

TELE ARUBA (Comm)
Pos Chiquito 1-A, PO Box 392, Oranjestad. ☎ + 297 (8) 57302. + 297 (8) 51683. **Web:** telearuba.aw
L.P. Gen. Mgr: Mrs. Jane Lampkin. CE: Miguel Roga.
Station: chA13 3/0.6kW H.
D.Prgr: 2030-0400.

AUSTRALIA

Colour: PAL. **System:** B.

AUSTRALIAN BROADCASTING CORPORATION (ABC)
ABC Ultimo Centre, 700 Harris St, Ultimo, NSW 2007 ☎ +61 (2) 8333 1500. +61 (2) 8333 5305. **Web:** www.abc.net.au **Email:** comments@your.abc.net.au
L.P: Chairman: Donald McDonald, MD: Russell Balding, Dir Television: Sandra Levy.The 'National Television Service' is controlled by the Australian Broadcasting Corporation which is responsible to Parliament through the Minister for Transport and Communications.
D.Prgrs: Mon-Fri 2100-1400; Sat/Sun 24h.
Also 'Homestead and Community Broadcasting Satellite Service' (HACBSS) in 12 250 to 12 750 MHz band, B-MAC encoded.

SPECIAL BROADCASTING SERVICE (SBS)
Locked bag 028, Crows Nest NSW 1585 ☎ +61 (2) 9430 2828. +61 (2) 9430 3700 **Web:** www.sbs.com.au
L.P: MD: Nigel Milan, Head. TV: Rod Webb.

IMPARJA TELEVISION PTY LTD.
PO Box 2924, Alice Springs, NT 0871. ☎ +61 89 523744, +61 89 531014.
This st. is owned by the Central Australian Aboriginal Media Association (CAAMA).

COMMERCIAL TV STATIONS:
FEDERATION OF AUSTRALIAN COMMERCIAL TELEVISION STATIONS
44A Avenue Rd, Mossman, NSW 2088. ☎ +61 (2) 960 2622. + 61 (2) 969 3520.

Main Networks:
THE SEVEN NETWORK
Television Centre, Mobbs Lane, Epping, NSW 2121. ☎ +61 (2) 858 7777. +61 (2) 858 7888.
Web: www.seven.com.au
(5 owned and 9 affiliated st's).

THE NINE NETWORK
P.O. Box 27, Willoughby, NSW 2068. ☎ +61 (2) 9906 9999. +61 (2) 9958 2279. **Web:** ninenet.com.au

NETWORK 10 AUSTRALIA
P.O. Box 10, Lane Cove, NSW 2066. ☎ +61 (2) 887 0222.

AUSTRIA

Colour: PAL — **Systems:** B & G.

ÖSTERREICHISCHER RUNDFUNK
ORF-Zentrum Wien, 1136 Wien, Würzburgasse 30.
☎ 43 1 878780 +43 1 5010 118701 **Web:** www.orf.at
L.P: DG: Dr Monika Lindner. Dirs. of TV: Dr. Reinhard Scolik, Gerhard Draxler. Tech.Dir: Andreas Gall. Head of Intl Rel: Christiane Veigl
Stations: System B ch1-12, System G ch21-68.
D.Prgr: Prgr. 1: 24h. **Prgr. 2:** 24h.

AZERBAIJAN

Colour: PAL — **Systems:** D & K

AZÄRBAYCAN DÖVLÄT TELEVIZIYASI (Gov)
Mehdi Hüseyn Str. 1, 370011 Baki. ☎ +994 12 984720. +994 12 972020. **Email:** root@aztv.baku.az **Web:** www.aztv.az
L.P: Dir: Nizami Xudiyev

AZORES (Portuguese)

Colour: PAL—**System:** B&G

RTP-RADIO E TELEVISÃO DE PORTUGAL (public, partly comm.)
R. Ernesto do Canto, 40, 9500-312 Ponta Delgada, S. Miguel. ☎ +351 (296) 202 700. **Email:** rtp@rtp.pt
Stations: RTP-1 (from mainland) and RTP Açores are broadcast over 10 tr's + 70 relays
D. Prgrs: RTP Açores: Sun-Thurs 0900-0100, Fri&Sat 0900-0230; RTP-1 (see Portugal)

SIC-SOCIEDADE INDEPENDENTE DE COMUNICAÇÃO (comm.)
(cf. PORTUGAL)
Available in the Açores via cable only.

TVI-TELEVISÃO INDEPENDENTE, S.A. (comm.)
(cf. PORTUGAL)
Available in the Açores via cable only.

AFRTS (US Air Force)
Detachment 3, Air Force European Broadc. Squadron, APO New York, NY. 09406-5000, USA
Station: (System M): Base Aérea das Lajes, isl. of Terceira, chA8 1kW H, 9760 Praia da Vitória, Terceira.
D. Prgr: 0900-0200 (Fri/Sat 0400).

BAHAMAS

Colour: NTSC — **System:** M.

BAHAMAS TELEVISION (owned and operated by the Broadc. Corp. of the Bahamas)
P.O. Box N-1347, Third Terrace, Centerville, Nassau. ☎ +1 (242) 322 4623. +1 (242) 322 3924.
Email: bcbcorp@mail.bahamas.net.bs.
Web: www.cba.org.uk/bahamas.htm.
L.P: Exec. Chm: Calsey Johnson, MP. General Manager: Mr Edwin S. Lightbourn.
Station: ZNS ch13 50kW (ERP).
D.Prgr: 2200 (Sat 2100, Sun 2000)-0400.

BAHRAIN

Colour: PAL — **Systems:** B & G.

BAHRAIN TELEVISION (Gov, Comm)
P.O. Box 1075, Bahrain. ☎ +973 781888/686000. Fax +973 681544. **Email:** brtcnews@batelco.com.bh
L.P: Dir: Dr. H. Al-Umran. Head of Prgrs: Fowzia Zainal. Head of Mktg: Maria Khoury. Dir. Pub. Rel: Ahmed Al Sherooqi.
Station: chE4, chE44, chE55, ch57.
D.Prgr: ch4: Main Arabic ch. loc. & int. news, cultural and variety prgrs, Arabic & English feature films.
ch44: Satellite broadcasts, loc. & int. sports. Also rel. Egypt satellite ch.
ch55: Main English ch. Also rel. CNN.
ch57: Transmits BBC World Sce. TV, 24h.

BANGLADESH

Colour: PAL — **System:** B/G.

NATIONAL BROADCASTING AUTHORITY BANGLADESH TELEVISION (Gov, Comm)
121 Kazi Nazrul Islam Ave., Shahbag, Dhaka-1000 ☎ +880 (2) 9330 131-9 Fax +880 (2) 831 2927.**Email:** btv-news@bttb.net.bd
L.P: DG: A.K.M. Mustafizur Rahman. Dep. DG (Prgrs): Md Mahbubul Alam. Dep. DG (News): Faruque Alamgir. Chief Eng: Md Moyeedul Hoq Chowdhury.
One main tr., 15 relays throughout country.
D.Prgr: av.12hrs, more Fri and Sat. Also carries prgrs of BBC, CNN and the Open University **F.Pl:** 2nd channel.

Private TV: The government. has decided to allow private TV stns to operate .

BARBADOS

Colour: NTSC — **System:** M.

CARIBBEAN BROADCASTING CORP. (Gov, Comm)
P.O. Box 900, Pine Hill, Bridgetown. ☎ +1 (246) 429 2041. Fax +1 (246) 429 4795.**Email:** cbc@caribsurf.com
L.P: Sen. Chrmn: John Williams, Head Tech. Servcs: Keith Alleyne
Station: CBC-TV ch8 60/30kW, ch 9, ch14, ch18, ch22, ch26.
D.Prgr: Channel 8: Mon-Fri 0940-1400 and 2000-0330, Sat 1200-0430, Sun 1200-0330.
Cable TV: A Gov. Sce, STV, provides two additional subscription ch's.

BELARUS

Colour: SECAM — **Systems:** D & K.

PERŠY NACYJANALNY TELEKANAL (Gov)
Makaionka Str. 9, 220807 Minsk. ☎ +375 17 2634301. Fax +375 17 2648182. **Email:** reklama@tv1.belpak.minsk.by **Web:** www.tvr.by

BELGIUM

Colour: PAL — **Systems:** B & H.

VLAAMSE RADIO EN TELEVISIEOMROEP (VRT)
1043 Brussels. ☎ +32 (2) 741 3111. Fax +32 (2) 734 9351. **Web**: www.vrt.be; www.tv1.be; www.ketnet.be; www.canvas.be. **Email**: info@vrt.be
L.P: MD: Mr Bert De Graeve, Dir.TV: Ms Christina von Wackerbarth, Dir. Prod: Mr Jan Cuypers.
Stations: ch2-11 System B, ch21-68 system H. NICAM stereo audio.
D.Prgr: BRT1: 1400-2200. **BRT2:** 1800 (Sun 1300)-2230.

RADIO TELEVISION BELGE DE LA COMMUNAUTE CULTURELLE FRANCAISE (RTBF)
1044 Brussels. ☎ +32 (2) 737 2111. Fax +32 (2) 737 4357.
L.P: PD: G. Lovites.
Stations: ch2-11 System B, ch21-68 system H. NICAM stereo audio.
D.Prgr: RTBF1: 24h. **RTBF2:** 24 h. **Télé 21:** 1800 (Sat 1600, Sun 1300)-2200.

BELGISCHES RUNDFUNK UND FERNSEHZENTRUM DER DEUTSCHSPACHIGEN GEMEINSCHAFT BELGIENS (BRF)
Kehrweg 11, B-4700 Eupen. ☎ +32 87 591111. Fax +32 87 591199. **Web:** www.brf.be **Email:** tv@brf.be
LP: Dr. of BRF: H. Engels, Chief Editor TV: A. Homann, CE: J. Schifflers.

VTM (Vlaamse Televisie Maatschappij)
1800 Vilvoorde. ☎ +32 (2) 255 32 11.
L.P: PR: Mark Van Lombeek. Commercial TV Service in Dutch on cable only.

CANAL PLUS (Comm)
Chaussee de Lauvain 656, 1050 Brussels. ☎ +32 (2) 7300 211. Fax +32 (2) 732 1848

RTL-TVi (Comm)
rue Cockx 6, 1160 Brussels. ☎ +32 (2) 640 51 50. Fax +32 (2) 640 9307. **Web:** www. rtl.be
Station: ch27 (tr located in Dudelange, Luxembourg).
D.Prgr in French: 12h daily.

TV-5 - Europe
Station: Bruxelles ch56 1kW H.
Rebroadcasts the TV-5 satellite sce.

BELIZE

Colour: NTSC — **System:** M.

TROPICAL VISION (Comm)
48 Albert Cattouse Bldg, Regent Str, P.O. Box 89, Belize City. ☎ +501 77246/7/8 Fax +501 (2) 75040
Station: ch 7.

BAYMEN BROADCASTING NETWORK (Comm)
27 Baymen Ave., Belize City. ☎ + 501 (2) 44400. Fax +501 (2) 31242
Station: ch 9.

BENIN

Colour: SECAM. — **System:** K.

OFFICE DE RADIODIF. ET TV DE BENIN (ORTB) (Gov)
P.O. Box 366, Cotonou. ☎ +229 3010628.
L.P: Dir. Gen: Nicolas Benon. Dir. TV: Michèle Badarou. Chief of Sce. (TV): Marcellin Illougbade. Head of Prgrs: Didier Falde.
Station: ch4 20kW.
D.Prgr: Mon-Fri 1800-2100, Sat/Sun 1700-2200.

BERMUDA

Colour: NTSC — **System:** M.

BERMUDA BROADCASTING COMPANY Ltd.
P.O. Box HM 1450, Hamilton. ☎ +441 (295) 1450. Fax +441 (295) 1658. **Email:** inbda@ibi.bm
L.P.: CEO: Kenneth DeFontes, Stn Mngr TV: Mike Bishop, Chief Engineers: Ed Tucker, Fred Blanchette **Stations:** VSB-TV, ch11, ch4 (cable) **D.Prgr:** 24 h

LOCAL STATIONS
There are three local commercial television stations in Bermuda. Reception is island-wide and no special cabling or antennas are required.
Stations: ZFB-TV, ch7, operated by the Bermuda Broadcasting Company Ltd. (US ABC affiliate);
ZBM-TV, ch9, operated by the Bermuda Broadcasting Company Ltd (US CBS affilate);
VSB-TV, ch11, operated by DeFontes Broadcasting Television Ltd. (US NBC Affiliate).

BHUTAN

Colour: unk — **System:** unk

BHUTAN BROADCASTING SERVICE (Pub.)
P.O. Box 101, Thimpu. ☎ +975 2 2286/22533/23071 Fax +975 2

23073 Web: www.bbs.com.bt Email: request@bbs.com.bt **L.P**: Exec. Dir: Sonam Tsho. **H of tr.:** 1500-1700 daily on Ch 5, 1kW

BOLIVIA

Colour: NTSC — **System:** M&N.

ASOCIACION TELEVISION BOLIVIANO (ATB)
Av. Argentina N #2057, La Paz. ☎ +591 (2) 229922. 🖷 +591 (2) 227935. **Web**: www.atb.com.bo

RED UNO DE BOLIVIA
Romecin Campos #592, La Paz. ☎ +591 (2) 421111. 🖷 +591 (2) 415101. **Web**: www.bolivianet.com/reduno **Email:** reduno@net-mail.tfnet.org
Stations: 9 member stns on chs 2, 9, 11, 13

TELEVISION BOLIVIANO
Cas. 4837, La Paz.
Stations: Ch 2 and 6 relays

BOLIVISION
Av Santa Cruz esq, Tres pasos al frente, Santa Cruz. ☎ +591 (3) 3524544. 🖷 +591 (3) 3530707. **Web**: www.bolivision.net **Email:** bolivision@cotas.com.bo
L.P: Pres: Ing. Ernesto Asbún Gazaui; DG: Fernando Perez F. de Córdova
Stations: Ch 4

BOSNIA & HERZEGOVINA

Colour: PAL — **Systems:** B & G.

JAVNI RTV SERVIS BOSNE I HERCEGOVINE (Public Broadcasting Service of Bosnia & Herzegovina, PBS-BiH)
Bulevar Meše Selimovica 12, 71000 Sarajevo. ☎ +387 33 461101. 🖷 +387 33 464061. **Email:** kontakt@pbsbih.ba
Web: www.pbsbih.ba
L.P: Dir BHT1: Lazar Petrovic.
NOTES: produces national channel "BHT1"
Federacija Bosna i Hercegovina
FTV (Pub.)
Bulevar Meše Selimovica 12, 71000 Sarajevo. ☎ +387 33 455102. 🖷 +387 33 455103. **Email:** press@rtvfbih.ba **Web:** www.rtvbih.ba
Republika Srpska
RADIO TELEVIZIJA REPUBLIKE SRPSKE (RTRS) (Pub)
ul. Kralja Petra I Karadordevica 129, 78000 Banja Luka. ☎ +387 51 317661. 🖷 +387 51 301922. **Email:** marketing@rtrs.tv
Web: www.rtrs-bl.com

BOTSWANA

Colour: PAL — **System:** I

BOTSWANA TV (Gov.)
Private Bag 0060, Gaborone. ☎ +267 3658000. 🖷 +267 3164416.
Web: www.btv.gov.bw
L.P: Gen. Mngr: Simon Moilwa.
Station: ch. not known.
D.Prgr. in English: not determined.

BRAZIL

Colour: PAL — **System:** M.
All st's comm. exc. where indicated.

ASSOCIACÃO BRASILEIRA DE EMISSORAS DE RADIO E TELEVISÃO (ABERT).
Hotel Nacional, s/5 a 8, C.P. 040-280, 70322-900 Brasilia, DF. ☎ +55 61 224 4600. 🖷 +55 61 321 7583.

SEARA — Serviços Associados de Rádio Ltda, Rua do Livramento 189, 20021 Rio de Janeiro, RJ. ☎ +55 (61) 243 2225

CENTRO NACIONAL DE TELEVISAO - CNT
Rua General Padhilla 134 Sao Cristovao ☎ +55 21 2589 0909 🖷 +55 21 2580 5897

REDE CULTURA
Rua Cenno Sbrighi 378, Agua Branca, Sao Paulo ☎ +55 (011) 3874 3122 **Web:** www.tvcultura.com.br
L.P: Pres: Antonio Carlos Caruso-Ronca;Sec: Jose Eduardo Bandeira de Mello

REDE GLOBO
Cerqueira Cesar 01419 903, Sao Paulo ☎ +55 11 3177 9692 **Web:** www.redeglobo5.globo.com.br
Stations: 91 broadcasting & affiliated sts

BRITISH INDIAN OCEAN TERRITORY

Colour: NTSC — **System:** M.

ARMED FORCES RADIO AND TELEVISION SERVICE (AFRTS)
Naval Media Center Detachment - Diego Garcia, PSC 466 Box 14, FPO, AP 96595-0014. ☎ +246 370 3680/3685. 🖷 +246 370 3681.
Email: Dgar@mediacen.navy.mil.
L.P: Not specific - as personnel rotate on a yearly basis.
Station: ch8 Island 8/AFN - 250 W, ch10 NewSports 10 - 250 W, ch12 Tropical 12 - 250 W.
D.Prgr: 24 hr.

BRUNEI DARUSSALAM

Colour: PAL — **System:** B

RADIO TELEVISION BRUNEI (RTB) (Gov)
Jabatan Perdana Menteri, Bandar Seri Begawan 2042, Negara Brunei Darussalam. ☎ +673 (2) 243 111. 🖷 +673 (2) 241882. **Web:** www.rtb.gov.bn. **Email:** rtbdir@brunet.bn
L.P: Dir: Pengiran Dato Ismail Mohamed; Ass. Dir. TV: Mrs Pengiran Datin Hajah Normah Daud
Stations: Bt. Subok ch5 10kW H; Bt. Andulau ch8 20kW H.
D.Prgr: 0800 (Fri/Sun 0030) -1600.

BULGARIA

Colour: SECAM, PAL — **Systems:** D/K

BÅLGARSKA NACIONALNA TELEVIZIJA (Pub)
ul. San Stefano 29, 1504 Sofija. ☎ +359 2 661149. 🖷 +359 2 9634045. **Email:** press@bnt.bg **Web:** www.bnt.bg
L..P: GD: Emil Vladkov.

BTV (Comm)
Nacionalen Dvorec na Kulturata, 1463 Sofija. ☎ +359 2 9176800. 🖷 +359 2 9521483. **Email:** pr@btv.bg **Web:** www.btv.bg
L..P: CEO: Albert Parsons.

NOVA TELEVIZIJA (Comm)
bul. N. Vabcarov 55, Expo 2000 P.K., 1507 Sofija. ☎ +359 2 9331840. 🖷 +359 2 9331820. **Email:** office@ntv.bg **Web:** www.ntv.bg
L..P: Chwmn: Silva Nikolova Zurleva.

BURKINA FASO

Colour: SECAM — **System:** K

TÉLÉVISION NATIONALE DU BURKINA (Gov)
1 T.N.B. 995 Boulevard de la Révolution: 01 B.P. 2530, Ouagadougou 01. ☎ + 226 324271. 🖷 + 226 324809. **Email:** tnb@mcc.gov.bf **Web:** www.tnb.bf.
L.P: DG: Mme Aline Koala.
Station: Ouagadougou & Bobodioulasso ch6 50/10W V.
D.Prgr: Tues-Thurs 1200-1430, 1800-2300; Fri 1200-2300; Sat-Sun 0800-2300 **Projected:** Ouagadougou 10kW H.

BURUNDI (Rep.)

Colour: SECAM — **System:** K.

TÉLÉVISION NATIONALE DU BURUNDI (Gov)
B.P. 1900, Bujumbura. ☎ +257 2247 60

L.P: DG: Louis-Marie Nindorera; Hd. of Prgr: Leonidas; Director TV: Clément Kirahagazwi.
Station: ch 25 0.5kW
D.Prgr: 1600 (Sat/Sun 1400)-2200.

CAMBODIA

Colour: PAL — **System:** B/G.

TVK (National Television of Cambodia)

26 Monivong Boulevard, Phnom Penh 12202.
☎ +855 23 724 149. +855 23 426 407. **Email:** tvk@camnet.gov.kh
Web: www. tvk.gov.kh
L.P: St. Mgr: Tan Yan. TD: Uy Thuon.
Stations: Phnom Penh chE7 10kW **D.Prgr:** 0715 PM-0745 PM.

INTERNATIONAL BROADCASTING CORP. Ltd. (IBC)

Borei Keila Street No. 169, Sangkat Vealvong, Phnom Penh City.
☎ +855 (23) 66061, 66064. +855 (23) 66063

Cambodian TV Network

33 Sihanouk Street (Street 274), Phnom Penh ☎ +855 12 800800 +855 12 801801 **Station:** Phnom Penh ch21

TV3 (Phonm Penh Municipality TV)

2 Bvd Confederation de la Russie (Street 112), Sangat Monorom, Khan 7 Makra, Phnom Penh. +855 (23) 360 80. **Web:** www.camnet.com.kh/tv3 **Station:** Phnom Penh ch E3 10 kW TRP.

TV CHANNEL 5 (TV FARC, Royal Cambodian Armed Forces)

Street 169, Borei Keila, Phnom Penh 12253. ☎ +855 (23) 366 061-2. +855 (23) 366 063 **Station:** Phnom Penh ch E5 10kW TRP

CAMBODIAN TV STATION CHANNEL 9 (CTV9)

18 Street 562, Toul Kok, Phnom Penh 12151. ☎ +855 (23) 880 874.
Email: tv9@camnet.com.kh **Web:** www.tv9.com.kh
Station: Phnom Penh ch E9 10kW TRP

APSARA TV

69,Street 57 (Corner Street 370), Sangat Beung Keng Kang 1, Khan Chamcarmon, Phnom Penh. ☎ +855 (23) 303 002. +855 (23) 214 302.
Web: www.apsaratv.com.kh **Station:** Phnom Penh ch E11 10kW TRP

BAYON TV

Khom Prek Samrong, Takhmau, Kandal Province. ☎ +855 (23) 363 695. +855 (23) 363 795. **Web:** www. bayontv.com.kh
Stations: Takhmau)(Phnom Penh area) chE27 250 kW ERP; Siem Reap ch E8; Takhao (Kampong Cham) ch E12.

CAMEROON

Colour: PAL — **System:** B

CAMEROON RADIO AND TELEVISION (CRTV) (Gov)

P.O. Box 1634, Yaoundé. ☎ +2372140 77/21 40 88 +237 204340. Douala ☎ +237 42 6060/7211/9440. **Web:** www.crtv.com
L.P: Dir. Gen: Pr. Gervais Mendoze.
Stations: ch 5 10kW

Stations:
TV Max (Comm.)
Canal 2 Broadcasts cultural prgrs to the capital and west of the country.

CANADA

Colour: NTSC — **System:** M

Public TV Networks

CANADIAN BROADCASTING CORPORATION/ SOCIÉTÉ RADIO-CANADA (Publicly owned)

181 Queen St., P.O. Box 3220, Station C, Ottawa ON K1Y 1E4. ☎ +1 613 288 6000. +1 613 288 6335. **Web:** www.cbc.radio-canada.ca
LP: President and CEO, Robert Rabinovitch. Chair, Board of Directors: Carole Taylor. Vice-President, and Chief Technology Officer: Raymond Carnovale. Vice-President, Comm.: Bill Chambers. Sen. Dir. Corporate Comm.: Martine Ménard.
English Networks: Box 500, Station A, Toronto ON M5W 1E6. ☎ +1 416 205 3311. **Web:** www.cbc.ca
L.P: Exec. VP, English Television: Richard Stursberg. Editor in Chief CBC News (radio & TV) Current Affairs, Newsworld & cbc.ca: Tony Burman. Deputy Dir., English Comm.: Bridget Hoffer.
Stations: CBRT Calgary AB ch9 325kW, CBXT Edmonton AB ch5 318kW, CBUT Vancouver BC ch2 100kW, CBWT Winnipeg MB ch6 100kW, CBAT Saint John NB ch4 100kW, CBYT Corner Brook NF ch5 15.7kW, CBNT St. John's NF ch8 356kW, CBHT Halifax NS ch3 100kW, CBIT Sydney NS ch5 100kW, CBOT Ottawa ON ch4 100kW, CBLT Toronto ON ch5 100kW, CBET Windsor ON ch9 201kW, CBCT Charlottetown PEI ch13 325kW, CBMT Montreal PQ ch6 100kW, CBVE Quebec PQ ch5 13.9kW, CBKT Regina SK ch9 250kW + relay tr's. **NB:** Stations identify as 'CBC Television'.
French Networks: Box 6000, Montreal PQ H3C 3A8. ☎ +1 514 597 6000. **Web:** www.radio-canada.ca
L.P: Exec. VP, French Television: Daniel Gourd. GM Communications TV: André Beaudet. GM Information TV: Louis Lalande.
Stations: CBRFT Calgary AB ch16 4.4kW, CBXFT Edmonton AB ch11 90kW, CBUFT Vancouver BC ch26 68kW, CBWFT Winnipeg MB ch3 59kW, CBAFT Moncton NB ch11 325kW, CBHFT Halifax NS ch13 3.9kW, CBOFT Ottawa ON ch9 252kW, CBLFT Toronto ON ch25 1928kW, CBEFT Windsor ON ch54 144kW, CBFT Montreal PQ ch2 100kW, CBVT Quebec PQ ch11 317kW, CBST Sept îles PQ ch13 20kW, CBKFT Regina SK ch13 235kW + relay tr's.

SOCIÉTÉ DE TÉLÉDIFFUSION DU QUEBEC (Télé-Québec)

800 rue Fullum, Montreal PQ H2K 3L7. ☎ +1 514 521 2424 +1 514 525 5511. **Web:** www.telequebec.qc.ca
L.P: Dir. Gen: Robert Normand. Head of Prgrs: Mario Clément.

TVO (English) & TFO (French)

Box 200, Station Q, Toronto ON M4T 2T1. ☎ +1 416 484 2600. +1 416 484 7771. **Web:** www.tvo.org. **Web (French):** www.tfo.org
Station: TVO (CICA) ch19 1080kW + relay tr's throughout Ontario.
NB: English stations identify as 'TVO'.

Private TV Networks

CANWEST GLOBAL TV

3100 TD Centre, 201 Portage Ave., Winnipeg MB R3B 3L7. ☎ +1 204 956 2025. +1 204 947 9841. **Web:** www.canada.com/globaltv
L.P: President and CEO: Leonard Asper. Chief Operating Officer: Richard C. Camilleri.
Stations: CICT Calgary AB ch2 100kW, CITV Edmonton AB ch13 325kW, CISA Lethbridge AB ch7 325kW, RDTV (CKRD) Red Deer AB ch6 100kW, CHBC Kelowna BC ch2 3.7kW, CKVU Vancouver BC ch10 325kW, CH (CHEK)Victoria BC ch6 100kW, CKND Winnipeg MB ch9 325kW, CIHF-2 Saint John NB ch12 35.5kW, CIHF Halifax/Dartmouth NS ch8 20kW, CH (CHCH)Hamilton ON ch11 325kW, CIII Toronto ON ch41 732kW, CH (CJNT) Montreal PQ ch62 11kW, CKMI-1 Montreal PQ ch46 33kW, CKMI Quebec PQ ch20 86.2kW, CFRE Regina SK ch11 325kW, CFSK Saskatoon SK ch4 100kW + relay tr's. **NB:** Stations identify as 'Global' or 'CH'.

CHUM TELEVISION

299 Queen St. W., Toronto ON M5V 2Z5. ☎ +1 416 591 5757. +1 416 591 7791. **Web:** www.chumlimited.com/television
L.P: Exec. VP: Stephen Tapp. VP Public Affairs: Sarah Crawford. VP Production: Marcia Martin. VP Planning & Regulatory Affairs: Peter Miller.
Stations: CITY-TV (CKVU)Vancouver ch10 325kW, New VI (CIVI)Victoria BC ch53 23kW, New VR (CKVR)Barrie ON ch3 100kW, New PL (CFPL)London ON ch10 325kW, New RO (CHRO)Ottawa/Pembroke ON ch5 100kW, CITY-TV Toronto ON ch57 310kW, New WI (CHWI)Windsor/Wheatley ON ch16 492kW, New NX (CKNX)Wingham ON ch8 260kW + relay tr's.

CTV Inc. (Division of Bell Globemedia)

9 Channel Nine Court, Scarborough ON M1S 4B5. ☎ +1 416 332 5000. +1 416 332 5283. **Web:** www.ctv.ca
L.P: CEO: Ivan Fecan. Pres. CTV Inc.: Rick Brace. Senior VP Corporate and Public Affairs. Paul Sparkes. Senior VP CTV Stations Group: Elaine Ali. Pres. CTV Prgr and Chair of CTV Media Group: Susanne Boyce. Senior VP Engineering and Operations: Allan Morris.
Stations: CFCN Calgary AB ch4 100kW, CFCN Lethbridge AB ch13 139kW, CFRN Edmonton AB ch3 609kW, CTV British Columbia (CIVT)Vancouver BC ch32 2000kW, CKY Winnipeg MB ch7 325kW, ATV (CKCW)Moncton NB ch2 100kW, ATV (CKLT)Saint John NB ch9

325kW, ATV (CJCH)Halifax NS ch5 100kW, ATV (CJCB)Sydney NS ch4 180kW, CKCO Kitchener ON ch13 325kW, MCTV (CKNY)North Bay ON ch10 132.6kW, CJOH Ottawa ON ch13 325kW, MCTV (CITO)Timmins ON ch3 100kW, CFTO Toronto ON ch9 325kW, MCTV (CHBX)Sault Ste. Marie ON ch2 100kW, MCTV (CICI)Sudbury ON ch5 100kW, CFCF Montreal PQ ch12 325kW, CIPA Prince Albert SK ch9 325kW, CKCK Regina SK ch2 100kW, CFQC Saskatoon SK ch8 325kW, CICC Yorkton SK ch10 56kW + relay tr's.

LE RESEAU DE TELEVISION (TVA)
2600 boul. de Maisonneuve, Montreal PQ H2L 4P2. ☎ +1 514 526 9251. **Web:** tva.canoe.com
Stations: CHAU Carleton PQ ch5 81.7kW, CJPM Chicoutimi PQ ch6 100kW, CHOT Hull/Ottawa PQ ch40 684kW, CFTM Montreal PQ ch10 325kW, CFCM Quebec PQ ch4 100kW, CFER Rimouski PQ ch11 325kW, CIMT Rivière du Loup PQ ch9 275.4kW, CFEM Rouyn-Noranda PQ ch13 346kW, CHLT Sherbrooke PQ ch7 300kW, CHEM Trois-Rivières PQ ch8 325kW + relay tr's.

TÉLÉVISION QUATRE SAISONS (TQS) Inc.
612, rue St-Jacques, Montreal PQ H3C 5R1. ☎ +1 514 271 3535. **Web:** www.tqs.ca.

CANARY ISLANDS

Colour: PAL — **Systems:** B & G.

TELEVISION ESPAÑOLA EN CANARIAS
TVE1: Plazoleta de Milton 1, 35005 Las Palmas de Gran Canaria. ☎ +34 922 455300. **TVE2:** 69 Calle Buenos Aires, 38005 Santa Cruz de Tenerife. ☎ +34 922 609000. **D.Prgr. TVE1** & **TVE2:** 24h

AUTONOMIC TV
Avenida de Madrid, 38005 Santa Cruz de Tenerife. ☎ +34 922 844100 & Calle Cochabamba 7, El Cebadal, 35008 Las Palmas de Gran Canaria. ☎ +34 922 218100. **D.Prgr.** 24h

Local Stations
CANAL BUENAS NUEVAS Calle Sao Paulo 45, Santa Cruz de Tenerife. ☎ +34 22 279442 **Station:** Cebadal ch21.– **CANARYVISION** Calle Arequipa 10, Santa Cruz de Tenerife. ☎ +34 22 470366 **Station:** Cebadal ch25.– **TELE GRAN CANARIA** Calle Sao Paulo 46, Santa Cruz de Tenerife. ☎ +34 22 464722 **Station:** ch40. – **ONDA TELEVISION MASPALOMAS (OTM 6)** Calle Galdar 48, San Agustin, Playa del Ingles. ☎ +34 22 772445, 773737 **Stations:** Guia ch42, Cumbre ch46. – **LIBERTAD TELEVISION** Avda. Escaleritas 112, Escaleritas. ☎ +34 22 251440. **Station:** Escaleritas ch50. – **ANTENA 3 TELEVISION** Eduardo Benot 3, Santa Cruz de Tenerife. ☎ +34 22 275242 **Stations:** Cumbre ch36, Isleta ch38. – **CANAL 7 DEL ATLANTICO** Calle Numancia, 38006 Santa Cruz de Tenerife

CAYMAN ISLANDS

Colour: NTSC — **System:** M

CAYMAN INTERNATIONAL TV NETWORK (Comm.)
P.O. Box 30563 SMB, Grand Cayman. ☎ +1 345 9452739
L.P: GM: Mike Martin.
D.Prgr. 24h.

CENTRAL AFRICAN REPUBLIC

Colour: SECAM — **System:** K.

RADIODIFFUSION-TÉLÉVISION CENTRAFRIQUE
P.O. Box 940, Bangui. ☎ +236 613242.
L.P: MD: Paul Service; Hd. of Prgrs: Henri-Gustav Hytayu.
Stations: n/a.

CHAD

Colour: SECAM — **System:** D.

TÉLÉTCHAD (Gov)
B.P. 74, N'Djamena. ☎ +235 52 3554.
L.P: Dir: Hourmadji Houssa Doumgor. Adj. Dir: Houssa Dago.
Station: N'Djamena ch7 (offset) 100W.
D.Prgr. in French/Arabic: 1800-2100 4 days per week.

CHILE

Colour: NTSC — **System:** M.

TVN CHILE (Gov)
Bellavista 0990, Providencia, Santiago. ☎ +56 (2) 7077777. 🖷 +56 (2) 7380040 **Web:** www.tvchile.cl
L.P: Pres: Marco Colodro Hadjes; Dir Prgr: Eugenio Garcia Ferrada.
D.Prgr: 1200 (Sat/Sun 1400)-0500.

RED TELEVISIVA MEGAVISIÓN S.A.
Av. Vicuña Mackenna, 1348, Santiago. ☎ +56 (2) 81008200. 🖷 56 (2) 8108204. **LP:** GM Ernesto Corona Bozzo.

CHILEVISION S.A. (Comm)
Ines Matte Urrejola, 0825, Santiago. ☎ +56 (2) 7372227. 🖷 56 (2) 7377923.**Email:** chilevis.ionsa001@chilnet.cl **Web:** www.cisneros.com/companies/broadcast/chilevision.htm
Stations: chA11 60/30kW (+ relay st. at Valparaíso ch10).
D.Prgr: 2145-0430.

TELETRECE
Inés Matte Urrejola 0848, Santiago. ☎ +56 (2) 514000. 🖷 +56 (2) 377044.**Web:** www.reuna.cl/teletrece

RED DE RADIOTELEVISION DE LA UNIVERSIDAD DEL NORTE (TELENORTE)
Carrera 1625, Antofagasta. ☎ +56 222496
L.P: GM: Juan Carlos Salas Floras.
Stations: ch3 Antofagasta, ch11 Arica, ch12 Iquique +7 low power sts.
D. Prgr: 1735-0435.

CORPORACION DE TELEVISION DE LA UNIVERSIDAD CATOLICA DE VALPARAÍSO
Agua Santo Alto 2455 (Casilla 4059), Viña del Mar. ☎ +56 (32) 610140. 🖷 +56 (32) 610505.**Email:** ucvtelev.ision@chilnet.cl
Stations: chA4 (Valparaíso), chA5 (Santiago), ch7 (Puerto Montt), chA8 (La Serena).

RADIO COOPERATIVA TELEVISION S.A.
Antonio Bellet 223, Santiago. ☎ +56 (2) 2360066. 🖷 +56 (2) 2352320. **Email:** canalroc.kpop002@chilnet.cl
Station: chE2.

MEGAVISION S.A.
Av. Vicuña Mackenna 1348, Santiago. ☎ +56 (2) 5555400. 🖷 +56 (2) 5518916. **Email:** megavisi.onsa001@chilnet.cl
Station: chE9.

CHINA (People's Rep. of)

Colour: PAL — **System:** D

CHINA CENTRAL TELEVISION (CCTV) (Gov.)
11 Fuxing Lu, Haidian, Beijing 100859, China. ☎ +86 10 6850 0114. 🖷 +86 10 6850 8743.**Web:** www.cctv.com
L.P: Dir: Zhao Huayong.
1st Prgr (Comprehensive Channel): 2200-1800 on ch2 (Beijing).
2nd Prgr (Economy, life and service Channel): 2200-1800 on ch8 (Beijing).
3rd Prgr (Entertainment Channel): 2200-1700 on satellite.
4th Prgr (International Channel): 24hrs on satellite.
5th Prgr (Sports Channel):.2200-1815 on satellite.
6th Prgr (Movies Channel):. 2200-1800 on satellite.
7th Prgr (Children, military and agriculture Channel):.2200-1700 on satellite.
8th Prgr (Television drama Channel):. 2200-1700 on satellite.
9th Prgr (English Channel): 24hrs on satellite.
10th Prgr (Science and education Channel): 2200-1740 on satellite.
11st Prgr (Opera Channel): 2200-1600 on satellite.
12nd Prgr (Channel West): 2355-1925 on satellite.
News Channel: 24hrs on satellite
Children's Channel: 2155-1500 on ch15 (Beijing).
Music Channel: 2200-1600 on ch33 (Beijing).

Anhui TV 355 Tongcheng Nanlu, Hefei, Anhui 230066. ☎+86 551 3414074. **Web:** www.ahtv.com.cn

Beijing TV 3 Xi-sanhuan Beilu, Haidian Qu, Beijing 100081. ☎+86 10 68419806. **Web:** www.btv.com.cn
Chongqing TV 68 Yuzhou Lu, Chongqing 400041. ☎+86 23 68602789. **Web:** www.ccqtv.com
Fujian TV 2 Gutian Lu, Fuzhou, Fujian 350001. ☎+86 591 3310945. **Web:** www.fjtv.net
Fujian South East TV 2 Gutian Lu, Fuzhou, Fujian 350001. ☎+86 591 3315838. **Web:**www.setvad.com.cn
Gansu TV 226 Donggang Xilu, Lanzhou, Gansu 730000. ☎+86 931 8266396. **Web:** www.gstv.com.cn
Guangdong TV 331 Huangshi Donglu, Guangzhou, Guangdong 510066. ☎+86 20 83355188. **Web:** www.gdtv.com.cn
Guangdong Southern TV 331 Huangshi Donglu, Guangzhou, Guangdong 510066. ☎+86 20 83320978. **Web:** www.tvscn.com
Guangxi TV 73 Minzu Dadao, Nanning, Guangxi 530022. ☎+86 771 5851315. **Web:** www.gxtv.com.cn
Guizhou TV 261 Qingyun Lu, Guiyang, Guizhou 550002. ☎+86 851 5812692.
Hainan TV 36 Nanhang Xilu, Haikou, Hainan 570206. ☎+86 898 66814396. **Web:** www.hainantv.com.cn
Hebei TV 100 Jianhua Nandajie, Shijiazhuang, Hebei 050031. ☎+86 311 5077842. **Web:** www.hebtv.com.cn
Henan TV 18 Zhenghua Lu, Zhengzhou, Henan 450008. ☎+86 371 8268888. **Web:** www.hntv.ha.cn
Heilongjiang TV 181 Zhongshan Lu, Harbin, Heilongjiang 150001. ☎+86 451 2636501.**Web:** www.hljtv.com
Hubei TV Zijin Cun, Liangdao Jie,Wuchang Qu, Wuhan , Hubei 430071. ☎+86(27)7839221. **Web:** www.hbtv.com.cn
Hunan TV 314 Deya Lu, Changsha, Hunan 410003. ☎+86 731 4801111. **Web:** www.hunantv.com
Inner Mongolia TV 55 Xinhua Dajie, Hohhot, Nei Menggu 010058. ☎+86 471 6962041.**Web:** www.nmgtv.com.cn
Jilin TV 11 Xinmin Dajie, Changchun, Jilin 130021. ☎+86 431 5653924. **Web:** www.chinajilin.com.cn/jltv
Jiangsu TV 4 Beijing Donglu, Nanjing, Jiangsu 210008. ☎+86 25 7711539.**Web:** www.jsgd.com.cn
Jiangxi TV 207 Hongdu Zhong Dadao, Nanchang, Jiangxi 330046. ☎+86 791 8319746. **Web:** www.jxtv.com
Liaoning TV 79 Wenhua Lu, Heping Qu, Shenyang, Liaoning 110003. ☎+86 24 23186352. **Web:** www.lntv.com.cn
Ningxia TV 39 Gulou Beijie,Yinchuan 750001. ☎+86 951 6013862. **Web.** www.nxtv.com.cn
Qinghai TV 6 Kunlun Lu, Xining, Qinghai 810001. ☎+86 971 6144148.
Shandong TV 81 Jingshi Lu, Jinan, Shandong 250001. ☎+86 531 5036841. **Web:** www.sdtv.com.cn
Shanxi TV 318 Yingze Dajie, Taiyuan, Shanxi 030001. ☎+86 351 4036680. **Web:** www.shanxitv.com
Shaanxi TV 336 Chang'an Nanlu, Xi'an, Shaanxi 710061. ☎+86 29 5252900. **Web:** www.sxtvs.com
Shanghai TV 651 Nanjing Xilu, Shanghai 200041. ☎+86 21 62565899. **Web:** www.stv.sh.cn
Shanghai Oriental TV 2000 Dongfang Lu, Pudong Xinqu, Shanghai 200125.☎+86 21 58812000. **Web:** www.shotv.com
Sichuan TV 40 Dongsheng Jie, Chengdu, Sichuan 610015. ☎+86 28 86636065.**Web:** www.sctv.com
Tianjin TV 143 Weijin Lu, Heping Qu, Tianjin 300071. ☎+86 22 23345613. **Web:** www.ctjtv.com.cn
Tibet TV 149 Beijing Zhonglu, Lhasa, Xizang 850000,☎+86 891 6834768. **Web:** www.xztv.com.cn
Xinjiang TV 84 Tuanjie Lu, Urumqi, Xinjiang 830044. ☎+86 991 2561420. **Web:**www.xj-tv.com.cn
Yunnan TV 182 Renmin Xilu, Kunming, Yunnan 650031. ☎+86 871 5325313. **Web:** www.yntv.com.cn
Zhejiang TV 111 Moganshan Lu, Hangzhou, Zhejiang 310005. ☎+86 571 8077050. **Web:** www.cztv.com.cn

CHINA EDUCATION TELEVISION (CETV Gov.)
160 Fuxingmennei Dajie, Xicheng Qu, Beijing 100031. ☎ +86 10 6641 9055. 🖷 +86 10 6608 4298. **Web:** www.cetv.edu.cn

COLOMBIA

Colour: NTSC — **System:** M.

INSTITUTO NACIONAL DE RADIO Y TELEVISION (INRAVISION)
Centro Administrativo Nacional, Via Eldorado, Bogotá. ☎ +57 (1) 2220700. 🖷 +57 (1) 222 0800
L.P: Exec. Dir: Jose Jorgo Dangorich Castro.
Inravision leases airtime to 26 comm. companies. The three largest are:

CADENA UNO (Inravision) (Gov)
Av El Dorado, Cra 46 CAN, Bogotá ☎ +57 222 0700 🖷 +57 222 2765 **Email:** cadena1@latino.net.co
L.P.: VP TV: Alvaro Osorio Mejia

Caracol
AA 9291, Santafé de Bogot. ☎ +57 (1) 337 8866. 🖷 +57 (1) 337 7126. **Web:** latina.latina.net.co/empresa/caracol. **Key st:** Manjui ch7.

Punch
Carrera 28, 49-98 Bogotá. ☎ +57 (1) 2174750.
Key st: Manjui ch9.

RTI
Calle 19 N 4-56 Piso 2, Bogotá. ☎ +57 (1) 282 7700. 🖷 +57 (1) 284 9012. ✆ 43294.
L.P: Pres: Patricio Wills. Head of Prgrs: Patricio Wills.
Key st: Manjui ch11.
Network III: Manjui (1) ch A 11 668kW.
D. Prgrs: 1630-1830 (Comm), 1830-2130 (Educ.), 2100-0500 (Comm)

CONGO (Dem. Rep.)

Colour: SECAM — **System:** K.

OZRT (Gov)
B.P. 3171, Kinshasa, Gombe 3164. ☎ +243 23171.
L.P: Dir. Gen: B. Dongo. Dir. Tec: S. Lepamabla
D.Prgr: Mon/Tues/Thurs/Fri 1130-1330 & 1630-2300, Wed 1130-2300, Sat/Sun 0900-2300. Relayed on Intelsat 66°E, C-band. Tr's from inland towns are dependent on power supplies (i.e. fuel availability).

PRIVATE/COMMERCIAL STATIONS

ANTENNE A (Private/Comm)
Av. du Port 4, Building Forescom 2e floor, Kinshasa/Gombe. P.O. Box 2681 Kinshasa 1. ☎ +243 21736/24818/25308
L.P: P.D.G: A Pinhas; Dir Gen: Igal Avivi Neirson; Tech Dir: Ranny Ranny Shoket.
D.Prgr: Mon-Fri: 1430-0030, Sat1430-0130, Sun 1000-2330.

CANAL Z (Comm)
6, av. du Port, Kinshasa/Gombe, P.O. Box 614 Kinshasa I. ☎ +243 20239.
L.P: Dir Gen: Frederic Flasse
Station: Kinshasa UHF ch23
D.Prgr: 1500-2400

CONGO (Rep.)

Colour: SECAM — **System:** K.

RADIODIFFUSION TÉLÉVISION CONGOLAISE
2241, Brazzaville. ☎ +242814574/814273/814030.
L.P: D.G: J.F. Sylvestre SOUKA.
Station: ch7 10/20kW H.
D.Prgr: 1730-2300

COOK ISLANDS

Colour: PAL — **System:** B.

COOK ISLANDS BROADCASTING CORPORATION (Gov)
P.O. Box 126, Avarua, Rarotonga. ☎ +682 29460. 🖷 +682 21907 Cook Islands Television (CITV).
Stations: VHF ch1 & 6
D.Prgr: 6h a day, 5 days a week.

COSTA RICA

Colour: NTSC — **System:** M.

Corporación Costaricense de Televisión (Comm.)
P.O. Box 2860, 1000 San José. ☎ +506 312222

L.P: Dir. Gen: M. Sotela B. **D.Prgr.** 1530-0700.

Multivision
Apt 4666, 1000 San José. ☎ +506 334444. 🖷 +506 211734
L.P: Dir: Arnaldo Vargas V.
D.Prgr. 1600-0600.

Televisora de Costa Rica
Apt 3876, San José. ☎ +506 322222.
D.Prgr. 1730-0600 (+ 9 repeaters).

Rede Nacional de Televísion
Apt 7-1980, San José. ☎ +506 200071
L.P: Dir. Gen: Dr. Ch. Zelaya Goodman
D.Prgr. 2200-0400 (+ 2 repeaters).

Universidad de Costa Rica
San Pedro, Montes de Doa, San José ☎ +506 340463. 🖷 +506 256950.
L.P: Dir. Gen: Dr. Sergio Guevara Fallas
D.Prgr: 1600-2200.

CROATIA

Colour: PAL — **System:** B & H

HRVATSKA TELEVIZIJA (HTV)
Prisavlje 3, Zagreb, Croatia. ☎ + 385 (1) 616 3366. 🖷 + 385 (1) 616 3392. ✆ 21477 HTV RH. **Web:** www.hrt.hr
L.P: GM: Ivan Parac. Head of Prgrs: Hloverka Srzic-Novak. Head of Int. Rel. Dept: Marija Nemcic.
D.Prgr: HTV1: 0700-2300; HTV2: 1000-2300; HTV3: 0800-2400.

OTV (Open TV)
Teslina 7, Zagreb, 10000. ☎ +385 (1) 424 124. 🖷 +385 (1) 455 1386.

REGIONAL STATIONS

SLAVONSKA TELEVIZIJA OSIJEK
Hrvatske Republike 20, Osijek 31000. ☎ +385 (31) 124 666. 🖷 +385 31 124 111.

TV MARJAN
Savska bb, Split 21000. ☎ +385 (21) 364 525. 🖷 +385 (21) 523 455.

VINKOVACKA TELEVIZIJA
Genschera 2, Vinkovci, 32000 Croatia. ☎ +385 (32) 331 990. 🖷 +385 (32) 331 985.

ZADARSKA TELEVIZIJA
Molotska bb, Zadar, 23000 Croatia. ☎ +385 (23) 311 791. 🖷 +385 (23) 314 749.

CUBA

Colour: NTSC — **System:** M.

I
NSTITUTO CUBANO DE RADIODIFUSION (Gov)
Television Nacional, Calle M No. 313, Vedado, La Habana. Estudios en Pinar del Rio, Ciudad de la Habana, Santa Clara, Nueva Gerona, Camagüey, Holgüí, Santiago de Cuba & Guantánamo.

TELE REBELDE
Mazón No. 52, Vedado, La Habana. ☎ +537 (32) 3369. ✆ 511661.
L.P: VP: Gary Gonzalez.
Studios in Santiago de Cuba, Holguín & La Habana.
D. Prgr: 2257-0500.

CUBAVISION (Gov)
Calle M No. 313, Vedado, La Habana.
D.Prgr: 2227-0500.

AFRTS (US Navy)
US Naval Base, P.O. Box 22, FPO New York, NY 09406.
Station: Guantanamo Bay chA8 0.35kW.

CYPRUS

Colour: PAL — **System:** B & G

CYPRUS BROADCASTING CORPORATION (CyBC)
P.O.Box 24824, 1397 Nicosia, ☎ 22422231, 22862000. 🖷 22314050. **Email**: rik@cybc.com.cy **Web:** www.cybc.com.cy
LP: Pres: Antonis Drakos, Gen. Mngr: Michalis Stylianou, Head T.V.: Michalakis Tofarides, Head News & Current Affairs: Vangelis Louca.
Stations: CyBC1 6, 38, CyBC2 31, CYBC2, 22.

MEGA
P.O.Box: 27400, 1644 Nicosia, 20, Agios Avgoustinos Str., Archangelos, 2054 Strovolos, ☎ 22477777, 🖷 22355138, **Email**: director@logos.cy.net **Web:** www.logos.cy.net,
L.P: Gen. Mngr: Petros Protopapas, Head News & Current Affairs: Andreas Hadjikyriakos.
Stations: ch24, 25, 34, 42, 57, 46, 64,

ANTENNA T.V.
Sophocleous 15, Aglantzia, P.O.Box: 20923, 1655 Nicosia, ☎22311111, 🖷 22314959
L.P: Pres: Loukis Papaphilippou, Gen Mngr: Stelios Malekos, Head News: George Tsalakos, Chief Eds: Andros Michaelides, Petros Pashas.
Stations: ch48, 35, 60, 41, 63, 65, 23, 26, 67, 24, 56, 37, 42,

LUMIERE T.V. Ltd.(Comm Pay-TV service)
1 Diogenous Str., Block A, 1st and 2nd floor, 2122 Nicosia, ☎ 22357272, 🖷 22354649, 22354638
L.P: Gen. Mngr: Akis Avraamides
Stations: ch26, 63, Encoded signal.

SIGMA
P.O. Box: 21836, 1513 Nicosia, ☎ 22357070, 🖷 22352237 **Web:** www.sigma.com.cy
L.P: Pres/GenMngr: Costis Hadjicostis, Prgr Mngr: Constantinos Odysseos, Head News: Dinos Menelaou.
Stations: ch37, 46, 58, 69, 26.

ALPHA T.V.
Corner Makarios and Karpenisiou, Xenios Commercial Centre, 7th floor, 1648 Nicosia, P.O.Box 26811, ☎ 22763000, 🖷 22760001
L.P: Dir Gen/Pres: Andreas Hassikos.
Stations: ch52, 56, 34.

CAPITAL TV
Limasol. ☎ +357 (25) 577577.
D.Prgr: Mon-Fri. p.m; Sat + Sun: longer hrs. More info not available.

BFBS Akrotiri (SSVC)
BFPO 57, Dhekelia Mil 381. ☎ +357 (474) 8518
Stations: ch 69 and 66 in ESBA, ch 60 and 68 in the WSBA.
D.Prgrs: relays of English prgrs. + live prgrs. from satellite.

NORTHERN CYPRUS

Colour: PAL — **System:** B & G

BAYRAK RADIO & TELEVISION CORP. (Turkish Cypriot State Broadcaster)
Dr. Fazil Kucuk Bulvari, BRT Sitesi, Lefkosa-KTC, via Mersin 10, Turkey. ☎ +90 (392) 225 5555/225 6159. 🖷 +90 (392) 3332. **Email:** brttv@cc.emu.edu.tr **Web:** www.cc.emu.edu.tr/~BRT.
L.P: DG: Ismet Kotak. Head of Tr's: A.Ziya Dİncer. Head of Admin: Süleyman Türem. Head of Prgrs: Hüseyin Cobanoglu. Head of Sales: Mehmet Kircailiar. Head of Int. N: Huriye Dimililer.
Stations: Sinan dagi ch8 100kW (Prgr. 2) – Selvilitepe ch40 450kW (Prgr. 3), ch44 450kW (Prgr. 1) + 4 relay st's.
D.Prgrs: 0355-2330 (UHF) ch21, ch44. Broadcasts are Turkish language only.

CZECH REPUBLIC

Colour: PAL — **System**: D/K

CESKÁ TELEVIZE (Czech Television) (Public Service)
Praha, Kavcí Hory, 140 70 Praha 4 ☎ +420 261 131 111 **Web:** www.czech-tv.cz
L.P: DG: Jirí Janecek. PD: Eva Vrtisková. **D.Prgr: CT1:** 24h. **CT2:** 24h

PRIVATE STATIONS:
NOVA TV
✉ Krízeneckého nám. 5, 152 52 Praha 5 ☎ +420 233 100 111
Web: www.nova.cz
L.P: DG: Petr Dvorák. PD: Líba Smuclerová
D.Prgr: 24h

PRIMA TV
✉ Na Zertvách 24, 180 00 Praha 8 Liben ☎ +420 266 700 111 **Web:** www.prima-tv.cz
L.P: DG: Martin Dvorák. PD: Milos Zahradník.
D.Prgr: 24h

DENMARK

Colour: PAL — **System:** B

DR (Gov.)
✉ TV-Byen, DK-2860 Søborg. ☎ +45 35203040. 🖷 +45 35202644. **Web:** www.dr.dk . **E-mail**: dr@dr.dk
L.P: DG: vacant. Dir. TV: Jørgen Ramskov. Dir. News (radio & TV): Lisbeth Knudsen. Head of DR1: Lars Grarup. Head of DR2: Mette Davidsen Nielsen & Gitte Rabøl. Head of TV-International: Finn Rowold. Head of sales dept.: Helene Auroe. Head of Production: Bent Fjord.
D.Prgr: DR1: MF 0530-0030, Sat 0700-0100, Sun 0800-0100. **N:** 0600, 0700, 1100, 1730, 2000. **DR2:** MF 1430-2330, Sat 1130-0030, Sun 1350-2330. **N:** 16,00, 2130.

TV 2 (Gov., Comm.)
✉ Rugaardsvej 25, DK-5100 Odense C. ☎ +45 65911244. 🖷 +45 65913322. **Web:** www.tv2.dk. **E-mail**: tv2@tv2.dk
L.P: DG: Peter Parbo. Dir. Sales & Marketing: Flemming Rasmussen. Dir. Finances: Anders Kronborg. Head of News: Michael Dyrby. Head of Prgr's: Bo Damgaard. Head of Tech. Dept: Lars Esben Hansen. Head of TV 2 Zulu: Palle Strøm & Keld Reinicke. Head of TV 2 Charlie: Frode Munksgaard.
D.Prgr: TV 2/Danmark: MF 0455-0130 MF, SS 0700-0130 **N:** 0600, 0700, 0800, 1100, 1500, 1700, 1800, 2100. **TV 2/Zulu:** 0600-0100. **TV2/Charlie**: 1100-2300.
Regional Prgrs: 1000-1100, 1110-1140, 1505-1510, 1710-1714, 1830-1900, 2120-2125 (excl. SS).
TV2/Bornholm, Brovangen 1, 3720 Aakirkeby. ☎ +45 56975400. 🖷 +45 53975095. **TV2/Fyn,** Olfert Fischers Vej 31, 5220 Odense SØ. ☎ +45 63156000. 🖷 +45 63156060. **TV2/Lorry,** Allégade 7-9, 2000 Frederiksberg. ☎ +45 38385535. 🖷 +45 38883111. **TV2/Midt-Vest,** Søvej 2, 7500 Holstebro. ☎ +45 97403300. 🖷 +45 97401444. **TV2/Nord,** Søparken 4, 9440 Åbybro. ☎ +45 96969696. 🖷 +45 96969679 **TV/Syd,** El-vej 2 B, Seest, 6000 Kolding. ☎ +45 76303132. 🖷 +45 76303199. **TV2/Øst,** Kildemarksvej 7, 4760 Vordingborg. ☎ +45 55365656. 🖷 +45 55364595. **TV2/Østjylland,** Skejbyparken 1, 8200 Århus N. ☎ +45 87424242. 🖷 +45 87424287.

PRIVATE STATIONS:
TV3 (Comm,)
✉ Wildersgade 8, DK-1408 København K. ☎ +45 77305500. 🖷 +45 77305510. **Web:** www.tv3.dk. **E-mail**: tv3@viasat.dk
L.P: Dir.: Jesper Grønholt. Head of prgr's: Susanne Teilmann. Head of sales: Christian Bechmann.
D.Prgr: TV3: MF 0530-0400. SS: 0500-0400. **TV3+:** Mon-Fri: 0510-0400. Sat: 0630-0400. Sun: 1000-0400

TVDANMARK (Comm.)
✉ Mileparken 20 A, DK-2740 Skovlunde. ☎ +45 70101010. 🖷 +45 32699699. **Web:** www.kanal5.dk and www.tvdanmark.dk .
L.P: GM: Henrik Ravn. PD: Jacob Mejlhede. Head of Sales: Jan Hjøllund.
D.Prgr: Kanal 5: 0700-0200. **TvDanmark 2:** 0500-0200

DK4
✉ Rådmandsgade 55, DK-2200 København N. ☎ +45 70253535. 🖷 +45 70243593. **Web:** www.dk4.dk. **E-mail**: post@dk4.dk
L.P: Dir: Stig Holbøll Hasner.
D.Prgr: 24h

Local TV Stations: Several organizations are on the air, especially in Copenhagen. Almost all stations carry TvDanmark2 for most of the day.

DJIBOUTI

Colour: SECAM — **System:** B.

RADIO TÉLÉVISION DE DJIBOUTI (Gov)
✉ P.O. Box 97, Djibouti. ☎ +253 352294. 🖷 +253 356502.
L.P: DG: Abdi Atteyeh Abdi.
Station: Djibouti ch7.
D.Prgr: 35h p/week.

DOMINICA

Colour: NTSC — **System:** M

MARPIN-TV (Comm)
✉ P.O. Box 382, Roseau. ☎ +1 (767) 4484107. 🖷 +1 (767) 4482965
L.P: Prgr. Mgr: Ron Abraham.

DOMINICAN REPUBLIC

Colour: NTSC — **System:** M

RadioTelevisión Dominicana/CerTV (Gov.)
✉ Av. Dr. Tejeda Florentino 8, Sto. Domingo. ☎ +1 809 689-1220/2120
L.P: Dir: George Rodriguez. **Chs:** 4, 17

Private Stations:
Antena Latina: Av. Independencia, Sto. Domingo. ☎ +1 809 532-2531 **Ch:** 7 – **Cadena de Noticias:** C/ Dr Defillo 4, Sto. Domingo ☎ +1 809 683-8100 **Ch:** 37 – **Canal 25:** Av. General Lopez, Santiago. ☎ +1 809 583-2525 **Ch:** 25 – **Canal 27:** Av. Luperon, Sto. Domingo ☎ +1 809 566-9596 **Ch:** 27 – **Color Vision**, Corporación Dominicana de Radio & TV, Av. Emilio Morel, Sto. Domingo ☎ +1 809 556-5876 **Ch:** 9 – **Digital 15:** Av. San Martin, Sto. Domingo. ☎ +1 809 689-8151 **Ch:** 15 – **Digital Vision:** Av. Constitución 101, San Cristobal ☎ +1 809 528-5690 **Ch:** 63 – **Mango TV:** Av. 27 de Febrero 308, Sto. Domingo ☎ +1 809 472-5466 **Ch:** 59 – **Medios Educativa/Canal del Sol:** C/ Cub Scout 19, Sto. Domingo. ☎ +1 809 687-2953/2952 **Chs:** 6, 65 – **Radioemisoras Unidas:** Av. Tirandentes 35, Sto. Domingo ☎ +1 809563-3202 **Ch:** 57 – **Supercanal 33:** C/ Rafael A Sanchez, Sto. Domingo ☎ +1 809 537-3833 **Ch:** 33 – **Teleamerica:** Av. Abraham Lincoln 1015, Sto. Domingo ☎ +1 809 562-4747 **Ch:** 47 – **Teleantillas**: Autopista Duarte Km.7½, Sto. Domingo. ☎ +1 809 567-7751 **Ch:** 2 – **Telecentro/TXns Y Proyecciones:** Av. Pasteur 204, Sto. Domingo. ☎ +1 809 687-9161 **Chs:** 13, 31 – **Telecoral:** Av. Independencia 59, Sto. Domingo ☎ +1 809 592-4838 **Ch:** 39 – **Telefuturo:** Av. 27 de Febrero 371, Sto. Domingo ☎ +1 809 472-3364 **Ch:** 23 – **Telemicro:** Av. San Martin, Sto. Domingo. ☎ +1 809 689-5555 **Ch:** 5 – **Telesistema:** Av. 27 de Febrero 52, Sto. Domingo ☎ +1 809 563-6661 **Ch:** 11 – **Teleuniverso:** Av. Las Carreras 1, Santiago ☎ +1 809 241-0066 **Ch:** 29 – **Televida:** Expreso V Centenario, Sto. Domingo ☎ +1 809 685-4100 **Ch:** 41

Note: From 1 Jan 2005 put 829 before 809 for all telephone numbers.

EASTER ISLAND

Colour: PAL — **System:** B.

TV RAPANUI
✉ Hanga Roa, Isla de Pascua. ☎ +5639 223291
L.P: Dir. Gen: J. Edmund Paoa. Head Tec. Sce's: J. Pont Chavez.
Station: ch (unknown). **D.Prgr:** 0000-0600

EAST TIMOR

Colour: PAL — **System:** G

TV TIMOR-LESTE
✉ Edifício da Rádio e Televisão, Rua de Caicoli, Díli. ☎+670 3321825. **Email**: tv@rttl.org
L.P: Mgr: Antonio Diaz.
Stations: Dili ch7 1.5 kW, Baucau ch12.
D.Prgr: 2230-1200 in Tetum, Portuguese and English. Own prgrs in Tetum plus relays of RTP, ABC Australia.& BBC

ECUADOR

Colour: NTSC — **System:** M.

Corporación Ecuatoriana de Televisión, Casilla 1239, Guayaquil. ☎ +593 (4) 300150. 🖷 +593 (4) 303677.**D.Prgr.** 1200-0600.
Canal 2 Quito, Murgeon 732, Quito. ☎ +593 (2) 540877 **D.Prgr** 1930-0730 (Sun 1330-0700).
Telecuenca, Canal Universitaria Catolica, Casilla 400, Cuenca. ☎ +593 827862. **D.Prgr** 1600-0400.
Teleamazonas, Av. Diguja 529 y Brazil, Quito. ☎ +593 (2) 430313. Canal 4 Guayaquil S.A, 9 de Octubre 1200, Guayaquil. ☎ +593 (4) 308194.
Canal 6 Esmeraldas, Cas. 108, Esmeraldas. ☎ +593 (2) 710090. **D.Prgr** 2300-0400.
Canal 8 Quito, Cas. 3888, Quito. ☎ +593 (2) 244888 **D.Prgr** 1730-0530.
Manavision S.A, Apt. 50, Portoviejo **D.Prgr** 1930-0530.
Canal 10, Guayaquil, Casilla 673, Guayaquil. ☎ +593 (4) 391555 **D.Prgr** 1130-1430, 1630-0500 (+14 relays).
Canal 13 Quito, Rumipampa 1039, Quito. ☎ +593 (2) 242758.
Televisora Nacional, Bosmediano 447 y José Carbo, P.O. Box 6615, Quito.

EGYPT

Colour: PAL — **System:** B & G.

EGYPTIAN RADIO AND TV UNION (ERTU) (Gov)

✉ TV Bldg, Cornish El-Nil, Cairo 11511. ☎ +20 (2) 5757155 **Web:** www.ertu.gov.eg.
L.P: Chmn of TV: Zainab Swidan.
Stations: Cairo: **Prgr 1** Ch5, **Prgr 2** Ch9, **Prgr 3** Ch7, **Prgr 4** Ch40, **Prgr 5** Ch46, **Prgr 6** Ch43, **Prgr 7** Ch34, **Prgr 8** Ch26, **Nile TV** Ch22, **Nile News** Ch38. All the 71 other stations carry the 1st Prgr and most cary the 2nd Prgr. There are 8 national & 3 local terrestrial channels.

EL SALVADOR

Colour: NTSC — **System:** M.

Canal Dos SA(Comm), Ap. Postal 720, San Salvador. ☎ +503 236744 **D.Prgr** 1730-0530.
Canal Cuatro(Comm), Ap. Postal 720, San Salvador. ☎ +503 244633 **D.Prgr** 2100(Sat/Sun 1500)-0600.
Canal Seis (Comm), Km. 6, Carretera Panamericana a Santa Tecla, San Salvador. ☎ +503 235122 **D.Prgr** 2300 (Sat/Sun 1700)-0600.
Television Cultural Educativa, Ap. Postal 4, Santa Tecla. ☎ +503 280499 **L.P:** Dir. Gen: Maura Echaverria **D.Prgr** 1300-0500
Television Cultural Educativa Canal 10, ✉ Ap. Postal No. 104, Neuva San Salvador. ☎ +503 228 0499 or 228 4599. 🖷 +503 228 0973. **Email:** tydiez@es.com.sv. **LP:** D.G. Tomás W. Panameño

EQUATORIAL GUINEA

Colour: SECAM — **System:** B.

TELEVISION NACIONAL (Gov)

✉ Malabo Bioko Norte.
L.P: Dir: Antonio Nkulu Oye.
Station: chE2.

ESTONIA

Colour: PAL — **Systems:** B/D & K.

EESTI TELEVISIOON - ETV (Pub)

✉ Faehlmanni 12, 15029 Tallinn. ☎ +372 6284100. 🖷 +372 6284114. **Email:** etv@etv.ee **Web:** www.etv.ee
L..P: MD: Ilmar Raag.

KANAL 2 (Comm)

✉ Maakri 23a, 10145 Tallinn. ☎ +372 6662450. 🖷 +372 6662451. **Email:** info@kanal2.ee **Web:** www.kanal2.ee
L..P: Dir: Urmas Oru.

TV3 VIASAT (Comm)

✉ Peterburi tee 81, 11415 Tallinn. ☎ +372 6220200. 🖷 +372 6220201 **Email:** tv3@ tv3.ee **Web:** www.tv3.ee
L..P: MD: Toomas Vara.

ETHIOPIA

Colour: PAL — **System:** B (Pol=H).

ETHIOPIAN TELEVISION (Gov)

✉ P.O. Box 5544, Addis Ababa. ☎ +251 (1) 516977. 🖷 +251 (1) 512686.
L.P: St. Mgr: Teshome Asrat. TD: Taye Zewde. Film Buyer: Mrs. Meaza Zewde.
D.Prgr: Mon-Fri 1900-2230, Sat/Sun 1800-2400 (Sun 2300)

FALKLAND ISLANDS (British)

Colour: PAL — **System:** I.

FALKLAND ISLANDS BROADCASTING SERVICE (BFBS)

✉ BFBS Falkland Islands, Mount Pleasant, BFPO 655.☎ 32179. 🖷32193.
L.P: St.Mgr: Steve Johnston.
Station: Mount Pleasant ch 24 UHF/100 W. Port Stanley ch 30 UHF/15 W. Rebros ch40UHF.
D.Prgr: 4 h. of taped broadcasts from BBC and ITV London.

FAROE ISLANDS (Danish)

Colour: PAL — **System:** B & G

SJÓNVARP FØROYA (SvF)

✉ M. A. Winthersgøta 2, Postboks 21, 110 Tórshavn. ☎ +298 340400. 🖷 +298 318815. **Web:** www.svf.fo. **E-mail:** svf@svf.fo
L.P: GM: Mikkjal Helmsdal. Dir. of Adm: Sámal J. Samuelsen. Head of Technical Dept: Carsten Arnskov. Head of News: Katrin Petersen.
D. Prgr.: Mon-Thu 1830-2400, Fri 1830-0200, Sat 1600-0200 and Sun 1400-0100.

Sat. relays on UHF: MTV Europe, BBC Prime, BBC World, TV3 and Eurosport.

FIJI

Colour: NTSC — **System:** M.

FIJI TELEVISION LTD

✉ PO Box 2442, Govnt. Bldngs, Suva. ☎ +679 305100. 🖷 +679 305077Web: www.fijitv.com.fj**Email:** fijitv@is.com.fj
L.P: Chief Exec: Ken Clark; Hd Prgr: Richard Broadbridge.
Stations: Fiji 1, Sky Fiji

FIJI BROADCASTING SERVICE LTD

✉ PO BOX 334, Suva ☎ +679 3304518 🖷 +679 301643 **Web**: www.radiofiji.org **Email:** fbcl@is.com.fj
L.P.: Acting CEO: Francis Herman

FINLAND

Colour: PAL — **Systems:** B & G.

YLEISRADIO OY (Non-comm, Public Broadc. Service)

✉ TV-1, Box 96, FIN-00024, Finland. ☎ +358 (0) 14801. 🖷 +358 (0) 1480 5148 **FST (Swedish Language TV)**, Box 83, FIN-00024 ☎ +358 (0) 14801. 🖷 +358 (0) 1481256. **TV-2,** Box 196, FIN-33101 Tampere. ☎ +358 (31) 345 6111. ⓣ 22749. 🖷 +358 (31) 345 6892.
L.P: Dir. TV: H. Lehmusto; Dir. Prgr TV-1: A. Gartz; Dir Prgr TV-2: A. Hoffren; Dir. Swedish lge Radio & TV: A. Sandelrin; Dir Prgrs: J. Harms.

MTV Oy (Comm)

✉ 00033 MTV3, Finland ☎ +358 (0) 15001. 🖷 +358 (0) 1500707.
L.P: Pres: E. Pilkama. Exec. Vice Pres: J. Paavela. Prgr. Dir: T. Äijälä. News Dir. (Editor-in-chief): P. Hyvârinen. Tec. Dir: H. Marsalo. Marketing Dir: Eero Aalto. Sales Dir: Heikki Rotko. Vice Pres (communications): J. Mietinen. Comm. Mgr: M. Paaso. Proj. Mgr: M. Rainbird (FinnImage)

Prgrs: Own production & acquisition programmes on 3rd network (MTV3).

MTV 3 FINLAND/OY KOLMOSTELEVISIO AB (Comm., subsiduary of MTV Oy)
00033 MTV3, Finland. ☎ +358 (0) 15001. 🖷 +358 (0) 150 0677.
L.P: Man. Dir: J-P. Louhelainen. Prgr Dir: J. Sairanen.
Prgrs: (produced by Swedish television, SVT) approx. 60h weekly.

FRANCE

Colour: SECAM — **System:** L.

TÉLÉVISION FRANÇAISE 1 (TF1) (Priv Comm)
1 quai du Point du Jour, 92656 Boulogne-Billancourt.Cedex ☎ +33 1 41 41 12 34. 🖷 +33 1 41 41 28 40. **Web:** www.tf1.fr
L.P: Pres. & DG: Patrick Le Lay
D.Prgrs: 24 h. **UHF:** 3408 transmitters NICAM stereo.

FRANCE TÉLÉVISIONS (Public Television)
7 esplanade Henri de France, F-75907 Paris cedex 15. ☎ +33 1 56 22 60 00. 🖷 +33 1 56 22 90 90. **Web:** www.francetelevisions.fr
L.P: Pres.: Marc Tessier
France Télévision controls public television networks: France 2, France 3, France 5 and RFO (in french overseas territories).

FRANCE 2 (Public Television)
7 esplanade Henri de France, F-75907 Paris cedex 15. ☎ +33 1 56 22 42 42. 🖷 +33 1 56 22 55 82. **Web:** www.france2.fr
L.P: DG: Christopher Baldelli. **D.Prgrs:** 24 h.
UHF: 3557 transmitters NICAM stereo.

FRANCE 3 (Public Television)
7 esplanade Henri de France, F-75907 Paris cedex 15. ☎ +33 1 56 22 30 30. 🖷 +33 1 56 22 73 42. **Web:** www.france3.fr
L.P: DG: Rémy Pflimlin
D.Prgrs: 24 h. **UHF:** 3599 transmitters NICAM stereo.

FRANCE 5 (Educational, Public Television)
10 rue Horace Vernet, 92785 Issy les Moulineaux Cedex 9. ☎ +33 1 56 22 91 91. 🖷 +33 1 56 22 95 95. **Web:** www.france5.fr
L.P: DG: Daniel Goudineau
D.Prgrs: 0200-1800. **UHF:** 1078 transmitters NICAM stereo

ARTE (Cultural, Public Television)
4 quai du Chanoine Winterer, 67080 Strasbourg Cedex. ☎ +33 3 88 14 22 22. 🖷 +33 3 88 14 22 00. **Web:** www.arte-tv.com
L.P: Pres.: Jobst Plog
D.Prgrs: 1800-0200. (using FRANCE 5 txs).

CANAL PLUS (Private)
85/89 Quai André Citroën, 75711 Paris Cedex 15. ☎ +33 1 44 25 10 00. **Web:** www.canalplus.fr
L.P: Pres.: Bertrand Meheut
D.Prgrs: 24 h. **VHF:** 204 and **UHF:** 33 transmitters
Canal Plus is a subscription network. The signals are mostly coded and subscribers need a decoder. Times for uncoded signals: W 0600-0730, 1130-1300, 1730-2000.

M6 Metropole TV (Priv. Comm.)
89/91 avenue Charles de Gaulle, F-92575 Neuilly sur Seine Cedex. ☎ +33 1 41 92 66 66. 🖷 +33 1 41 92 66 10. **Web:** www.m6.fr
L.P: Pres. Nicolas de Tavernost.
D.Prgrs: 24h. **UHF:** 1285 transmitters – NICAM stereo

PRIVATE LOCAL STATIONS

AB7 TELEVISION
2 bis bld Joseph Cugnot 42160 Andrézieux Bouthéon. ☎ +33 4 77 36 54 54. 🖷 +33 4 77 55 16 95.
Stations: Saint Heand ch52 1.2 kW, Saint Galmier ch41 0,7 kW

CANAL 32
7 r Raymond Aron, 10120 Saint André les Vergers. ☎ +33 3 25 72 32 32. 🖷 +33 3 25 72 31 99
Station: Troyes ch32 0.93 kW

CLERMONT 1ERE
40 rue Morel Ladeuil, 63000 Clermont-Ferrand. ☎ +33 4 73 17 66 66. 🖷 +33 4 73 17 66 67. **Web:** www.clermont1ere.com
Station: Clermont-Ferrand ch64 1 kW.

TELE 102
22 rue de l'Hôtel de Ville, 85103 Les Sables d'Olonne. ☎ & 🖷 +33 2 51 95 95 95. **Web:** www.tele102.com
Stations: Les Sables d'Olonne ch48 2.5 kW + Lp. ch59 9 W.

TELE LYON METROPOLE (TLM)
15 bd Yves Farge, 69363 Lyon Cedex 07. ☎ +33 4 72 71 10 90. 🖷 +33 4 72 71 10 95. **Web:** www.tlm.fr
Stations: Lyon ch49 9.1 kW, Lyon (town) ch25 5 kW, Caluire et Cuire ch38 25 W.

TELE TOULOUSE (TLT)
1 allée Jacques Chaban-Delmas, BP 15828, 31004 Toulouse Cedex 5. ☎ +33 5 62 30 30 30. 🖷 +33 5 62 30 30 31. **Web:** www.teletoulouse.com
Stations: Toulouse ch37 2kW, Muret ch63 40W.

TELE SUD VENDEE (TSV)
100 av. du Maréchal de Lattre de Tassigny, 85400 Luçon. ☎ +33 2 51 29 00 94. 🖷 +33 2 51 27 66 85.
Stations: Luçon ch52 4 kW, La Tranche sur Mer ch55 155 W, Mareuil sur Lay Dissay ch31 96 W, Fontenay le Comte ch45 5 W.

TLP LUBERON
Mairie, Cours Aristide Briand, 04280 Céreste. ☎ +33 4 92 79 00 15. 🖷 +33 4 92 79 00 03. **Web:** www.tvlocales-depays.com.
Stations: Céreste ch52 70W, Manosque ch47 55 W, Villemus ch56 40W, Forcalquier ch 44 15 W, Dauphin ch27 2W.

TMC
6 bis quai Antoine 1er, Monte Carlo 98090, Monaco. ☎ +377 92 16 54 80. 🖷 +377 92 16 54 81. **Web:** www.tmc.tv
241, boulevard Péreire, 75017 Paris. ☎ +33 1 58 05 58 05. 🖷 +33 1 58 05 59 95.
Stations: Marseille ch35 160kW, Toulon ch33 25kW, Marseille (town) ch51 22kW, Avignon ch57 4,4kW, Nîmes ch58 0,1kW. Other tx's see under Monaco.

TV7 BORDEAUX
73 av. Thiers, 33100 Bordeaux. ☎ +33 5 57 54 77 77. 🖷 +33 5 57 54 77 80. **Web:** www.tv7bordeaux.fr
Station: Bordeaux ch40 21 kW, Bordeaux (town) ch55 55 W.

TV8 MONT BLANC
route Pontets, 74320 Sevrier. ☎ +33 4 50 52 69 69. 🖷 +33 4 50 19 06 12. **Web:** www.tv8montblanc.com
Stations: Chambéry ch36 4 kW, Annemasse ch57 3.8Kw, Cluses ch47 1.8kW, +32 Lp. stations under 1kW.

FRENCH GUIANA

Colour: SECAM — **System:** K.

RFO-GUYANE
BP 7013, Cayenne Cedex. ☎ +594 299900. 🖷 +590 302649
L.P: Dir: Henri Neron. T.D: Daniel Beugin.
Stations: Cayenne chK4 0.1kW, +8 low power repeaters.
D.Prgr: 2100-0130.

ANTENNE CREOLE (Priv, Comm)
31 avenue Louis Pasteur, 97300 Cayenne. ☎ +594 31 2020
Stations: Kourou ch44 1kW, Cayenne ch39 3kW

FRENCH POLYNESIA

Colour: SECAM — **System:** K.

TELE TAHITI
Radio Télévision Française d'OutreMer (RFO), B.P. 125, Papeete, F-98 713 Polynésie Française. ☎ +689 430551. 🖷 +689 413155. **Email:** rfopolyfr@mail.pf **Web:** www.tahiti-explorer.com/rfo.html
L.P: Dir. Claude Ruben. Chief Editor: Patrick Durand Gaillard. Dir. of Prgrs: Jean-Raymond Bodin.
Stations: Papeete chK4 0.1kW H, Mont Marau chK8 0.5kW H, Vaitape chK7 0.2kW V, Taravao chK4 0.1kW H (+ 8 low power repeaters).
D.Prgr: 0400 (Sat/Sun 0200)-0830.

COMMERCIAL STATIONS

CANAL POLYNESIE (Priv, Comm)
Colline de Putiaoro, Papeete
Stations: Taravao ch26 2kW, Mont Marau ch43 55 kW, Punaauia ch55 1.2kW + 9 low power repeaters.
N.B: Canal Polynesie is a subscription sce and the signal is encrypted except: 1630-1720, 2225-2325, 0415-0610.
D.Prgr: W 1630-1100 Sun 24h

GABON

Colour: SECAM — **System:** K.

RADIODIFFUSION-TÉLÉVISION GABONAISE (Gov)
B.P. 10150, Libreville. ☎ +241 732152. 🖷 +241 732153.
L.P: DG (TV): Jules César Lekogho.
Stations: Libreville chK4 & K8 2kW H, Port Gentil chK10 0.1kW H, Moanda 1kW (relay) + 5 low power relay sts.
D.Prgr: 1800-2200; ch10: 1800-2100 (relay Libreville).

GALAPAGOS ISLANDS

Colour: NTSC — **System:** M.

TELEGALAPAGOS (Cult)
Misión Franciscana, Puerto Baquerizo Moreno, Isla San Cristobal, Galapagos, Ecuador. ☎ +593 (5) 520-144. 🖷 +593 (5) 520-372.
LP: Dir. Gen: Mons. Manuel Valarezo. GM: Freddy López Valarezo. Dir. Tec: Germán Chiriboga. Film Buyer: Remigio Andrade.
Station: chA13
D.Prgr: 2000-0400.

GAMBIA

Colour: PAL — **System:** B.

GAMBIA RADIO TELEVISION SERVICES
Mile 7, Banjul. ☎ +220 373918. 🖷 +220 495102/495923. **Web:** www.grts.com
L.P: DG: Bora Mboge.

GEORGIA

Colour: SECAM — **Systems:** D & K.

GEORGIAN TELEVISION (Gov)
M. Kostava Street 68, 380071 Tbilisi. ☎ +995 32 362294. 🖷 +995 32 368665. **Email:** irc@geotvr.ge **Web:** www.geotvr.ge

GERMANY

Colour: PAL — **System:** B.

DEUTSCHE WELLE (DW-TV) (Pub)
DW-Berlin, Voltastr. 6, D-13355, Berlin. ☎ +49 (30) 4646 -0. 🖷 +49 (30) 4646-8405. **Email:** info@dw-world.de. **Web:** dw-world.de

L.P: DG: Erik Bettermann. Dir: Christoph Lanz.

ARD (PROGRAMMDIREKTION DEUTSCHES FERNSEHEN)
Arnulfstrasse 42, 80335 München. ☎ +49 (89) 59 00 01 🖷 +49 (89) 5900 3249
L.P: PD: Dr. Günter Struve. TD. Chrmn: Ingo Dahrendorf. Film Buyer: Klaus Lackschewitz
NB: The ARD is an umbrella organisation representing regionalized German public radio- and tv broadcasters. The ARD is responsible for the first public tv network (ARD Eins) and third public tv programs.
ARD members:
-Bayerischer Rundfunk Fernsehen, Rundfunkplatz 1, 80335 München. ☎ +49 (89) 59 00 2433 🖷 +49 (89) 5900 3199.
-Hessischer Rundfunk Fernsehen, Bertramstrasse 8, 60320 Frankfurt. ☎ + 49 (69) 1551 🖷 +49 (69) 1552 900
-MDR Fernsehen, Kantstrasse 71-73, 04275 Leipzig. ☎ +49 (341) 22760 🖷 +49 (341) 5663 544
-NDR Fernsehen, Rothenbaumchaussee 132, 20149 Hamburg. ☎ +49 (40) 4131 🖷 +49 (40) 4476 02
-ORB Fernsehen, August-Bebel-Strasse 25-53, 14482 Potsdam-Babelsberg. ☎ +49 (331) 72 36 00 🖷 +49 (331) 77395
-Radio Bremen Fernsehen, Hans-Bredow-Strasse 10, 28307 Bremen. ☎ +49 (421) 2460 🖷 +49 (421) 246 2010/1010
-Saarländischer Rundfunk Fernsehen, Funkhaus Halberg, 66100 Saarbrücken. ☎ +49 (681) 6020 🖷 +49 (681) 6023 874
-SDR Fernsehen, Neckarstrasse 230, 70190 Stuttgart. ☎ +49 (711) 929 1 🖷 +49 (711) 929 2600
-SFB Fernsehen/B 1, Masurenallee 8-14, W-14057 Berlin. ☎ +49 (30) 3031 0 🖷 +49 (30) 301 50 62
-SWF Fernsehen, Hans-Bredow-Strasse, 76530 Baden-Baden. P.O. Box 820, 76485 Baden-Baden. ☎ +49 (7221) 92 0 🖷 +49 (7221) 92 20 13
-WDR Fernsehen, Appellhoffplatz 1, D-50667 Köln. ☎ +49 (221) 22 00 🖷 +49 (221) 2204 800
D.Prgr: ARD Eins, Germany's first public tv network, broadcasts nationwide 24h (except for 2 ½ hrs. in the evening when regional tv from 13 tv centers is relayed). In 1992 ARD together with Germany's second public tv network ZDF, started broadcasting a common breakfast tv program called "Morgenmagazin" (Mon-Fri 0600-0800). Germany's third program comprises a combination of seven separate channels: **NDR/RB** in **"N 3"**; **MDR** in **"MDR 3"**; **ORB** in **"ORB 3"**; **WDR** in **"WDR Fernsehen"**; **HR** in **"HR 3"**; **SWF/SDR/Saarländischer Rundfunk** in **"Südwest 3"**; **Bayerischer Rundfunk** in **"BR 3"**.

ZWEITES DEUTSCHES FERNSEHEN (ZDF)
P.O. Box 4040, 55030 Mainz. ☎ +49 (6131) 70 1 🖷 +49 (6131) 7021 57
L.P: Gen.Dir: Prof.Dr. Dieter Stolte; TD: Dr. Albert Ziemer; Film Buyer: Dr. Hans-Jürgen Steimer
D.Prgr: The ZDF is Germany's second public tv network, broadcasting nationwide 24h.

COMMERCIAL TV STATIONS

N24 TELEVISION
Gutenbergstrasse 1, D-85774 Unterfoehring. ☎ +49 (89) 9507-10. 🖷 +49 (89) 9507/7194. **Email:** info@24.de. **Web:** www.n24.de.
D.Prgr: N24 is a commercial all-news TV channel, broadcastinggeneral and economic news 18h, with updated news bulletins every 30 min.

SAT EINS
Martin Luther Strasse 1, 10777 Berlin, Germany. ☎ +49 (30) 21241 0 🖷 +49 (30) 21241 140
L.P: Man Dir: Hans Grimm; Hd. of News: Heinz Klaus Mertes; Film Buyer: Akim Andorfer
D.Prgr: This commercial satellite tv station, set up by a number of German publishing houses, broadcasts 24h. Reg. prgr. from Hannover, Dortmund, Mainz, Stuttgart, München at 1630-1700 UTC.

RTL FERNSEHEN
Aachenerstrasse 1036, 50858 Cologne, Germany. ☎ +49 (221) 456 0 🖷 +49 (221) 456 4290
D.Prgr: Originally Luxembourg's German language tv channel, but due to German legal rules currently operating from Cologne. RTL Fernsehen broadcasts 24 hrs. with loc. prgrs. (Hamburg, Essen, Frankfurt, Mannheim, München, Berlin) from 1700-1730.
N.B: Also relayed via ECS II f1 (13° East)

RTL-2
Bavariafilmplatz 7, 82031 Grünwald. ☎ +49 (89) 641850. 🖷 +49 (89) 64185999.
Stations: Aschaffenburg ch21; Augsburg ch58; Bayreuth ch46; Deggendorf ch52; München ch27; Nürnberg ch53; Regensburg ch48; Rosenheim ch50; Weilheim ch47; Würzburg ch34/56 (ASTRA 19.2° East)

SUPER RTL - RTL DISNEY FERNSEHEN GmbH & Co. KG
Richard-Byrd-Strasse 6, D-50829, Cologne. ☎ +49 (221) 9155-1080. 🖷 +49 (221) 9155-279. **Email:** kommikation@superrtl.de.
Stations: Hamburg ch34. Joint MD and CEO: Peter T. Heimes, Claude Schmitt.

DEUTSCHES SPORTFERNSEHEN (DSF)
Bahnhofstrasse 27, 85774 Unterföhring. ☎ +49 (89) 95002 0 🖷 +49 (89) 9500 2392
L.P: Man.Dir: Dr. Dieter Hahn; Prgr. Dir: Rudolf Brückner; Marketing Dir: Kai Blasberg **D.Prgr:** 24h. Sports & Leisure.

VOX
Richard-Byrd-Strasse 6, D-50829, Cologne. ☎ +49 (221) 9534 0 🖷 +49 (221) 9534 440

PRO SIEBEN
Bahnhofstrasse 27, 85774 Unterföhring. ☎ +49 (89) 9507 1000.

N-TV
Taubenstr. 1, 10117 Berlin. ☎ +49 (30) 201900.

GHANA

Colour: PAL — **System:** B.

GHANA BROADCASTING CORPORATION
P.O. Box 1633, Accra. ☎ +233 (21) 221161. 🖷 +233 (21) 773240 **Web:** www.gbg.ncs.com.gh **Email:** gtv@ncs.com.gh
L.P: DG: Eva Lokka. Dir. of TV: Wallace Bampoe-Addo.
D.Prgr: 0500-0100 Incl. relays of CNN International, Deutsche Welle and CFI.

TV3 details n/a.

METRO TV details n/a.

GIBRALTAR

Colour: PAL — **System:** B & G.

GBC TELEVISION (partly comm)
Broadcasting House, 18 So. Barrack Rd, Gibraltar.
☎ +350 79760. 🖷 +350 78673. **Email:** gbc@gibnet.gi
L.P: GM: George Valarino. Senior Eng: John Tewkesbury.
Station: chE6 0.2/0.4kW H (+ low power repeaters ch12, 53, 56).
D.Prgr: rel BBC World + local prgrs.

GREECE

Colour: PAL — **Systems:** B & G.

ELLINIKI TILEORASSI-1 (ET1)
Leophoros Mesogeion 136, 153 42 Agia Paraskevi. ☎ +30 210 7701911. 🖷 +30 210 6352263 Web: www.ert.gr
L.P: DG: Panos Panayotu. **D.Prgr:** 0800-2400 (approx).

NEA ELLINIKI TILEORASSI-2 (ET2)
Leophoros Mesogeion 136, 153 42 Agia Paraskevi. ☎ +30 210 6066000 🖷 +30 210 7797776 Web: www.ert.gr
L.P: DG: George Stamatelppoulos **D.Prgr:** 0800-2400 (approx).

ET3 (regional channel for Macedonia)
Angelaki 16, 546 21 Thessaloniki. ☎ +30 2310 299400. 🖷 +30 2310 236466 **Web:** www.ert3.gr **L.P:** DG: Hichalis Alexandridis.
Station: Thessaloniki ch23/27 H (local prgrs), Pillo (Volos) ch 44H, Kavala ch 35H, Parnitha ch 52H, Ymi Hos ch 31H, Thassos Isl. ch 26H, Florina ch 39H, Polygyros ch 21H. **D.Prgr:** 0800-2400 (approx).

KANALI VOULIS
Parliament House, Athens. **L.P:** Dir: Konstantin Alavanos
Station: Athens and 17 local relays. Hotbird satellite. **D.Prgr:** 1600(0830 when parliament is in session)-2330

PRIVATE STATIONS:
902 TV, Leoforos Irakliou 145, 142 31 Nea Ionia ☎ +30 210 2592802 **Web:** www.902.gr National coverage inc. Hotbird and Hellas satellites – **Alpha TV,** Pavlou Mela 25, 182 33 Rentis. ☎ +30 210 4897777 **Email:** alpha@alphatv.gr **Web:** www.alphaworld.gr. Ch 33/24/3/63 – **Alter TV,** Ag Paraskevi 36-38, 121 32 Peristeri. ☎ +30 210 5707000 🖷 +30 210 5707070 **Web:** www.alter.gr Ch 27/62/68 – **Antenna TV,** 10-12 Kifissias Ave 10-12, 151 25 Maroussi ☎ +30 210 6886100 🖷 +30 210 6886632 **Web:** www.ant1.gr – **FilmNet/NetMed,** Kiffiseos 8, 115 26 Athens ☎ +30 210 6602000.**Web:** netmed.gr. Ch 8/53/60 – **Mega Channel,** Alamanas 1/Dolfon, 151 25, Athens. ☎ +30 210 6994224. 🖷 +30 210 6899046. **Web:** www.megatv.com – **Star Channel,** Dimitros 37, 177 78 Tavros ☎ +30 210 3421201 🖷 +30 210 3452190 – **Teleasty,** Praxitelouys 58, 176 74 Kalithea ☎ +30 210 9407000 Ch 32 Athens and National coverage inc. Hotbird and Intelsat satellites

AFN TV (U.S. Mil)
Station: chA2 Iraklion, A6.

GREENLAND

Colour: PAL — **System:** B

KNR TV (Gov)
Kalaallit Nunaata Radioa TV, P.O. Box 1007, DK-3900 Nuuk. ☎ +299 361500. 🖷 +299 325042. **Web:** www.knr.gl. **E-mail:** knr@knr.gl
L.P: MD: Lars Lennert-Sandgreen.
D.Prgr: MF 1750-0300, Sat 1700-0500, Sun 1300-0330
N: Greenlandic: 2230-2255. **Danish:** 2100-2130 & 0000-0100 (rebroadcasts from DR TV).
Some 85 % of prgrs originate from DR TV and TV 2/Danmark.

PRIVATE STATIONS (local TV):
Tusaat TV Aasiaat, Box 20, 3950 Aasiaat – **Arctic TV,** Box 420, 3952 Ilulissat – **Arfivik-TV,** Box 138, Qeqertarsuaq – **Nanortalik TV,** Box 11, 3922 Nanortalik – **Nuuk TV,** Box 1016, 3900 Nuuk – **Paamiut TV,** Box 229, 3940 Paamiut – **Qaqortoq TV,** Box 55, 3920 Qaqortoq – **Qeqertaq TV:** B-84, Qeqertaq, 3952 Ilulissat – **Sisimiut TV,** Box 1004, 3911 Sisimiut.

GRENADA

Colour: NTSC — **System:** M.

GRENADA BROADCASTING NETWORK LTD (GBN).
Morne Jaloux, P.O. Box 535, St. George's, Grenada. ☎ +1 (473) 440 1252 🖷 +1 (473) 440 4180 **Email:** gbn@caribsurf.com
L.P: Gen Mngr: Richard Purcell Sen. Eng: Kennedy Bowen
Station: ch7 (4kW), ch11 (5kW).

GUADELOUPE

Colour: SECAM — **System:** K.

RFO-GUADELOUPE
B.P. 402, F-97163 Point-à-Pitre Cedex. ☎ +590 939696. 🖷 +590 939682.
L.P: Dir: R.Surjus. Editor-in-Chief: Philippe Goudé. PD: L.Francil. Head Communications Dept: Sonia Gémieux.
Stations: Basse Terre chK5 2kW + low power repeaters.
D.Prgr: 1900-0230.

SAINT MARTIN
An RFO st. is operating on chK7 0.1kW relaying RFO Guadeloupe.

COMMERCIAL STATIONS

ARCHIPEL 4 (Priv, Comm)
Résidence Les Palmiers, Gabarre 2, 97110 Pointe a Pitre. ☎ +590 8363 50
Stations: Morne a Louis ch53 1.3kW

CANAL ANTILLES (Priv, Comm)
2 lot. Les Jardins de Houelbourg, 97122 Baie Mahault. ☎ +590 26 8179
Stations: Morne a Louis ch 58 1.3kW, Basse-Terre ch42 60kW + 5 low power repeaters under 1kW.
N.B: Canal Antilles is a subscription sce and the signal is encrypted except: 1120-1130, 1630-1730, 1820-0010.
D. Prgr: W 1100-0500 Sun 24h

TCI GUADELOUPE (Priv, Comm)
Montauban, 97190 Gosier.
Station: Basse-Terre ch32 60kW

GUAM

Colour: NTSC — **System:** M.

KUAM TELEVISION (Comm)
Pacific Telestations, P.O. Box 368, Agana 96910. ☎ +671 637/5826, 6376397. 🖷 +671 6379865, 6379870.
L.P: Pres: L.S. Berger. Gen. Mgr: Greg Perez. Dir. Tec: K. Tydingco.
Station: chA8 21.9/3.8kW

D.Prgr: Mon-Fri 2000-1400 (also rel. CBS/NBC prgrs).

KGTF TELEVISION (Educ)

Guam Educational Telecommunications Corporation, P.O. Box 21449, Guam, Marianas Is. 96921. ☎ +671 7342207. +671 7345483. **L.P:** GM: Joseph E. Tighe. TD: Edmond Cheung. Film Buyer: Doris Gallo.
Station: chA12 27.6/5.5kW. **F.PI.** ch 14 (Saipan & Tinian); ch 16 (Rota).
D.Prgr: 2000-1300.

KTGM-TV

692 Marine Dr, Tamuning 96911. ☎ +671 6498814. +671 6490371 **Station:** chA14.

GUATEMALA

Colour: NTSC — **System:** M.

Stations: (all Comm except TGCE-TV):
TGV-TV. Radio-Television Guatemala, Apt. 1367, Guatemala. ☎ +502 (2) 922491. **L.P.** Pres: Lic. M. Kestler F. Dir. Tec: E. Sandoval **D.Prgr.** 1200-0600 (+ 2 repeaters).
TGCE-TV. Television Cultural Educativa, 4a Calle 18-38, Zona 1, Guatemala. ☎ +502 (2) 531913 **D.Prgr.** 2200-0500.
TGVG-TV. Televisiete, Apt. Postal 1242, Guatemala. ☎ +502 (2) 62216. **D.Prgr.** 1800-0600 (+ 3 repeaters).
TGMO-TV. Teleonce, Ca. 20, 5-02, Zona 10, Guatemala. ☎ +502 (2) 682165 **D.Prgr.** 1800-0600 (+ 2 repeaters).
TGSS-TV. Trecevision, 3a Calle 10-70, Zona 10, Guatemala. ☎ +502 (2) 63266.**D.Prgr.** 1800-0600 (+ 12 repeaters)

GUINEA

Colour: PAL — **System:** K.

RADIODIFFUSION TÉLÉVISION GUINÉENNE (Gov)

B.P. 391, Conakry. ☎ +224 442205.
L.P: Dir. Gen: B. Camara. Dir. of Prgrs: B. Kaba.
Stations: Conakry ch 5 1kW + Kindia ch4 0.2 kW, Faranah ch5 0.5kW, Labé ch7 8kW, Mamou/Mali ch9 0.2kW, Kankan ch9 1kW.
D.Prgr: 1700-2000 (approx)

GUINEA-BISSAU

Colour: PAL — **System:** K.

RADIOTELEVISAO DE GUINEA-BISSAU (Gov)

C.P. 178, Bissau. ☎ +245 221924.
L.P: Dir. Gen: Samuel Fernandes

GUYANA

Colour: NTSC — **System:** M.

GUYANA TELEVISION BROADCASTING CO LTD (Gov)

Homestretch Av, D'Urban Park,Georgetown. ☎ +592 (227) 1566
Email: guyanatelevision@hotmail.com
L.P: Chairman: Oscar Phillips; Ch Engnr: Dennis Bernard.
Station: Georgetown ch10 0.04kW.
D.Prgr: Sun 1500-1600, repeated 2100-2200.
Two private TV stations relay U.S. satellite sce

HAITI

Colour: NTSC — **System:** M.

TÉLÉVISION NATIONALE D'HAITI (Gov., Cult)

P.O. Box 13400 Delmas 33, Port-au-Prince. ☎ +509 (1) 63324/64049/62202.
L.P: Dir: Mme. Jacqueline André.
Stations: Port-au-Prince chA8 0.3kW, chA10 5kW.
D.Prgr: Mon-Fri 2100-0400 in French & Creole.
F.PI: chA12 Cap. Haïtien.

TÉLÉ HAITI S.A. (Comm)

B.P. 1126, Boulevard Harry Truman, Port-au-Prince. ☎ +509 (1) 23000. **L.P:** Dir: Walter Bussenius. Operates cable TV 24h in Port-au-Prince area

LA 2 S.A. 14 Ave Marie Jeanne, Port-au-Prince.
TÉLÉ ECLAIR 526 Rte de Delmas, Port-au-Prince.
RADIO TV GRANDE ANSE 54 bis, Rue Eugene Margron, Jeremie.
TÉLÉ MAX B.P. 654, Delmas 19, Port-au-Prince.
SUPER CANAL Rue Vertieres, en Face Odn, Cap-Haitien.
TV NORD'OUEST Rue B. Sylvain, Port-de-Paix.
TRANS AMERICA TELEVISION 27 Rue Roger, Gonaives.
TÉLÉ KAY TIMOUN Boutilliers, Port-au-Prince.
PVS ANTENNE 16 95 Bourdon, Port-au-Prince.
TÉLÉ HORIZON B.P. 11174/Carrefour, Port-au-Prince.
TÉLÉVISION CHRETIENNE B.P. 1600, Port-au-Prince.
TÉLÉ REPUBLIQUE D'HAITI 135 Ave Martin Luther King, Port-au-Prince.
TVA Rue Liberte, Gonaives.
SOGETEL B.P. 2511, Port-au-Prince.

HAWAII

Colour: NTSC — **System:** M.

Stations (all Comm)
KAAH-TV Ch 26. All American Network, 1152 Smith Str, Honolulu. ☎ 96817-5101. **Web:** www.aatv.org/kaah/index.html; kaah@xc.org. **L.P:** GM: Bob Papisan. CE: Don Porter.
KAIE-TV Ch 38. Pacifica Broadcasting Corp. (Proposed station).
KAII-TV Ch 7. (Relay of KHON-TV Ch 2).
KAMN-TV Ch 61. Kahului, Maui. **Web:** trinity@maui.net. **L.P:**Pres.: Juliet R. Harvey.
KBFD Ch 32. The Allen Broadc. Corp, 1188 Bishop Str, Honolulu.☎ 96813-3300.**Web:** www.kbfd.com.**L.P:** Pres./GM: Kea-Sung Chung. 96813-3314.
KFVE-TV Ch 5. KFVE Joint Venture (Guam Cable TV and King Broadcasting Corp.), managed by KHNL-TV, 150-B Pu'uhale Road, Honolulu.☎96819-2282. **Web:** www.khnl.com. **L.P:**D.Eng: Keith Aotaki. GM: John L. Fink.
KGMB-TV Ch 9. Lee Enterprises, 1534 Kapiolani Blvd, Honolulu. ☎ 96814-3799. **Web:** www.kgmb.com. **L.P:**GM: Richard T "Dick" Grimm.
KGMD-TV Ch 9. Hilo, Big Island. (Relay of KGMB-TV Ch 9).
KGMV-TV Ch 3. Wailuku, Maui. (Relay of KGMB-TV).
KHAI-TV Ch 20. Honolulu Family TV Ltd, 735 Sheridan Str, Honolulu 96814-3095.
KHAW-TV Ch 11. Hilo, Big Island. (Relay of KHON-TV Ch 2).
KHBC-TV Ch 2. Hilo Broadc. Corp, Box 4250 Hilo, Big Island. ☎ 96720-0520. Relay of KHNL-TV Ch13.
KHET-TV Ch 11. Hawaii Public Broadc. Authority, 2350 Dole Str, Honolulu. ☎ 96822-2495. **Email:** khettv@khet.pbs.org. **Web:** www.khet.org. **L.P:** ED/GM Don Robbs.
KHNL-TV Ch 13. (educational) King Broadc. Co, 315 Sand Island Access Rd, Honolulu, HI. ☎ 96819-2295. **Web:** www.khnl.com. **L.P:** GM: John L. Fink. D.Eng: Keith Aotaki.
KHON-TV Ch 2. Emmis TV License Corp., 388 Pi'ikoi Str, Honolulu. ☎ 96814-4243. **Web:** www.khon.com.
KHVO-TV Ch 13. Hilo, Big Island. (Relay of KITV-TV Ch 4).
KHVO-DT Ch 18. Hilo, Big Island. (HDTV relay of KITV-DT).
KIKU-TV Ch 20. KHLS Inc., 2021 Marina Business Plaza, 197 Sand Island Access Rd, Honolulu. ☎ 96819-4901. **Web:** www.kikutv.com; kikutv@lava.net. **L.P:** GM: Joanne Ninomiya.
KITV-TV Ch 4. KITV Argyle Television, Inc, One Archer Bldg, Suite 4, 801 South King Street, Honolulu. ☎ 96813-3008. **Web:** www.kitv.com.
KITV-DT Ch 40. Honolulu. (HDTV simulcast of KITV-TV).
KLEI-TV Ch 6. 'Aina'e Company Ltd.
KMAU-TV Ch 12. Wailuku, Maui. (Relay of KITV-TV Ch 4).
KMAU-DT Ch 29. Wailuku, Maui. (HDTV proposed relay station of KITV-TV).
KMEB-TV Ch 10. (Relay of KHET-TV Ch 11).
KMGT-TV Ch 26. Mauna Kea Broadc. Co, 970 N. Kalaheo Ave, Honolulu 96734-1892.
KPXO-TV Ch 66. Paxon Hawaii License, Inc., 601 Waimanu Warehouse, 875 Waimanu Str., Honolulu. ☎ 96813-5267. **Web:** www.paxtv.com/kpxo.
KWHE-TV Ch 14. LeSEA Broadcasting Corp., 502 Century Sq., 1188 Bishop Street, Honolulu. ☎ 98613-3302. **Web:** www.lesea.com/kwhe.htm **L.P:**GM: Pete Sumrall. CE: Mauro Pena.
KWHH-TV Ch 14. Hilo, Big Island. (Relay of KWHE-TV Ch 14).
KWHM-TV Ch 21. Wailuku, Maui. (Relay of KWHE-TV Ch 14).

K56EX-TV Ch 56. The Mabuhay Channel, 1172 North King Str, Honolulu. ☎ 96817-3346. **L.P:** Pres. Victor Agmata, Jr.

HONDURAS (Rep.)

Colour: NTSC — **System:** M.

Stations (all Comm)
HRJS-TV Ch 2 & 9. Corp. Centroamericana de Comunicaciones, S.A. de C.V, Apt. Postal 120, San Pedro Sula **L.P:** Pres: J.J. Sikaffy. Exec. Vice Pres: F.J. Sikaffy. Dir. Tec: R. Beurket & A. Pinto **D. Prgr:** 1530-0400 (+ 2 relays).
JRCV-TV Ch 3 & HRTS-TV Ch 7. Telesistema Hondureño, Apt. Postal 642, Tegucigalpa **D. Prgr:** 1530-0400 (+ 6 relays).
HRTG-TV Ch 5 & 8. Compañia Televisora Hondureña, Apt. Postal 734, Tegucigalpa **D. Prgr:** 1230-0400 (+ 9 relays). ☎ +504 (32) 7835. 🖷 +504 (32) 0097.
HRLP-TV Ch 4 & 7. Compañia Centroamericana de TV, Apt. Postal 68, Tegucigalpa **D. Prgr:** 1430-0400.
HRNQ-TV Ch 13. Cruceña de Televísion, Casilla 3424, Tegucigalpa **L.P:** Pres: Lic. Ivo Kuljis F. Dir. Gen: Lic. Walter Gasser Diaz C. **D. Prgr:** 1700-0800.
HRGJ-TV Ch 6. Compañia Broadcasting, Apt. Postal 882, Barrio Rio Piedras **D. Prgr:** 1130-0500

HONG KONG

Colour: PAL — **System:** I.

TELEVISION BROADCASTS LIMITED
🖃 TV City, Clear Water Bay Road, Kowloon, HK. ☎ +852 2335 9123. 🖷+ 852 2358 1300. **Email:** tvbpr@tvb.com.hk. **Web:** www.tvb.com.hk. **L.P:** MD: Mr. Louis Page. GM: Mr. T. K. Ho. Film Buyer: Ms. Sophia Chan (Jade Channel), Ms. Cecilia Tan (Pearl Channel).
Stations: chE21 & chE25, 10kW.
D.Prgr: Jade network on ch21: 2245-2030 (approx). Pearl network on ch25: 0000 (Sat 0100, Sun 0030)-1730 (approx).

ASIA TELEVISION LIMITED
🖃 81 Broadcast Drive, Kowloon. ☎ +852 2992 8888. 🖷 +852 2338 0438. ✆ HX44680. **Cable:** ASIATV. **Email:** atv@hkatv.com **Web:** www.hkatv.com
L.P: CEO: Mr. Mark Lee; Dep CEO: Mr. Clarence Chang; Controller: Mr. Jermyn Lynn
Stations: chE23 & chE27, 10kW.
D.Prgr: Home Channel in Chinese on ch23: 2230-1930. World Channel in English on ch27: 24h.

RADIO TELEVISION HONG KONG
🖃 PO Box 70200, Kowloon Central PO, ☎ +852 2339 6300 🖷 +852 2338 0279 **Email:** admin@rthk.org.hk **Web:** rthk.org.hk
L.P.: Dir Broadcasting: Chu Pui-hing
Prgrs aired through TVB, ATV and Wharf Cable.

HUNGARY

Colour: PAL — **Systems:** D & K

MAGYAR TELEVÍZIÓ (MTV, public service)
🖃 Szabadság tér 17, 1810 Budapest, 5. ☎ +36 1 353-3200. **Email:** web@mtv.hu **Web:** www.mtv.hu
L.P: Pres: Károly Mendrezczky
Stations: m1 (19 relays + 107 repeaters Ch 41+ Ch01 Budapest), + carries regional programs in Szeged , Pécs. **m2** (only sat.: Hot Bird 3: 12,130 GHz)
D.Prgr: m1: 0440-approx.0100 **m2:** 24h

DUNA TV (public service)
🖃 1016 Budapest, Mészáros u. 48-54. ☎ +36 1 489-1200. **Web:** www.dunatv.hu
L.P: Pres: István Pekár
Stations: only sat. Hot Bird 4: 10,815 GHz
D.Prgr: 24h **NB:** 0510-0530 Relays Radio Vatican in Hungarian Public Service prgrs provided to Hungarians in the Carpathian Basin

PRIVATE COMMERCIAL STATIONS

TV2
🖃 1145 Budapest, Róna utca 174. ☎ +36 (1) 467-6400. 🖷 +36 (1) 467-6500. **Web:** www.tv2.hu (MTM-SBS Group)
Stations: 13 relays+ 57 repeaters. Ch 58 Budapest
D.Prgr: 0450- approx.0100

RTL KLUB
🖃 1117 Budapest, Fehérvári út 84. ☎ +36 (1) 382-8282 🖷 +36 (1) 382-8283 **Email**: rtlklub@rtlklub.hu **Web:** www.rtlklub.hu (CLT-UFA Group)
Stations: 12 relays + 35 repeaters. Ch 24 Budapest
D.Prgr: 0530- approx.0100

Major National TV Transmitters (Public+Comm.)

	m1	tv2	RTL-Klub	kW
Budapest	01+41	58	24	
Kabhegy	012	22	57	
Kékes	08	36	53	
Komádi	07	32	49	
Nagykanizsa	01	60	31	
Pécs	49	32	02	
Szentes	010	23	57	
Tokaj	43	60	26	

LOCAL STATIONS:

FIX.TV
🖃 Budapest Ady Endre utca 19. ☎ +36 (1). 438-5380
Ch. 26 Budapest 1 kW

VIASAT 3
🖃 1037 Budapest, Kiscelli u. 104. ☎ +36 (1) 453-4575. 🖷 +36 (1) 453-4576 **Email:** info@viasat3.hu
Ch. 47 Budapest 100W

+ 45 other municipal stts in larger cities on the UHF band, all 100W.

ICELAND

Colour: PAL — **Systems:** B & G.

RÚV - SJÓNVARPIÐ (Pub)
🖃 Efstaleiti 1, 150 Reykjavík. ☎ +354 515 3900. 🖷 +354 515 3008. **Email:** istv@ruv.is **Web:** www.ruv.is
L.P: Dir: Bjarni Guðmundsson

STÖÐ 2 (Comm)
🖃 Krókhalsi 6, 112 Reykjavík. ☎ +354 515 6000. 🖷 +354 515 6810. **Email:** postur@iu.is **Web:** www.stod2.is

SKJÁREINN (Comm)
🖃 Skipholti 31, 105 Reykjavík. ☎ +354 595 6000. 🖷 +354 595 6001. **Email:** info@s1.is **Web:** www.s1.is
L.P: Dir: Árni þór Vigfússon

INDIA

Colour: PAL — **System:** B

PRASAR BHARATI (Broadcasting Corporation of India) (Pub)
🖃 2nd Floor, PTI Building, Parliament Street, New Delhi 110001 ☎ +91 11 23382094 🖷 +91 11 23386507
L.P: Chmn: MV Kamath, CEO: K.S. Sharma

DOORDARSHAN INDIA (Gov., semi-comm.)
🖃 Directorate General of Doordarshan, Mandi House, Copernicus Marg, New Delhi-110001 ☎ +91 11 23382094-99 🖷 +91 11 23386507 **Web:** www.ddindia.com
L.P: DG: S.Y. Quaraishi Eng.-in-Chief: R.K. Gupta
News: Doordarshan Kendra, Akashvani Bhavan, 1 Sansad Marg, New Delhi-110 001. ☎ +91 11 23382021/23715411. Add. DG (News): Swagat Ghose
Programming: Central Production Centre, Doordarshan, Asiad Village Complex, Siri Fort, New Delhi-110 016. ☎ +91 11 26462539 Add. DG (Prog): Ms Omita Paul

Channels: 22 channels: DD-1 National, DD-2 Metro, DD-Sports, DD-News, DD-Bharati, Malayalam, Tamil, Oriya, Bengali, Telugu, Kannada, Marathi, Gujarati, Kashmiri, Assamese, Punjabi, Rajasthan, Uttar Pradesh, Madhya Pradesh, Bihar, DD India DD-Gyandarshan.
Programme Production Centres: 56 **Transmitters:** 1432.
The DD programmes are networked via the following satellites: INSAT,

2B, 2C, 2DT, 2E, PAS-4, Thaicom.
Output (hours per week): 1485

INDONESIA

Colour: PAL — **System:** B

TELEVISI REPUBLIK INDONESIA TVRI (Gov)
Jalan Gerbang Pemuda, Senayan, Jakarta 10270 ☎ +62 (21) 3846 740 🖷 +62 (21) 5737 152. **Web:** www.tvri.co.id
L.P: MD: Azis Husein. TD: Djoko Widayat. Film Buyer: Adi Kasno.
D.Prgr: W 0930-1630 (Sat 1700), Sun & Holidays 0100-0630, 0930-1630. **English:** 1130-1200. **N:** 1130.

COMMERCIAL STATIONS:
RCTI (PT Rajawali Citra Televisi Indonesia)
Jl. Raya Perjuangan No. 3, kb. Jeruk, Jakarta 11000.
☎ +62 (21) 530 3550 🖷 +62 (21) 549 3852 **Web:** www.rcti.co.id
L.P: Pres Dir: Mr. Muchamad Ralie Siregar; TM: Mr Doopy Irwan
Stations: Ambon ch12, Balikpapan ch36, Batam ch43, Denpasar ch35, Jakarta ch43, Makassar ch33, Malang ch40, Manado ch30, Semarang ch33 **D.Prgr:** 90 hrs per week.

SCTV (PT Surya Citra Televisi)
Graha SCTV 2nd floor, Jl. Gatot Subroto Kav 21, Jakarta 12930. ☎ +62 (21) 522 5555. 🖷 +62 (21) 522 4777.**Web:** www.sctv.co.id
L.P.: Dir. Op.: Lanny Ratulangi
Stations: Balikpapan ch34, Bandung ch52, Banjarmasin ch34, Batam ch47, Dili ch11, Makassar ch35, Malang ch46, Manado ch34, Mataram ch45, Medan ch35, Solo ch44, Surabaya ch43, Yogjakarta ch34

TPI (PT Cipta Televisi Pendidikan Indonesia)
Jalan Pintu II - Taman Mini Indonesia Indah, Pondok Gede, Jakarta Timur 13810. ☎ +62 (21) 841 2473 to 83 (HQ). 🖷 +62 (21) 841 2470/1 **Web:** www.tpi.co.id
L.P: Sa'Dullah Sulchan; GM: Syamsudin C. Haesy
Stations: Jakarta chE37 80 kW TRP
D.Prgr: Mon-Fri: 2230-1800, Sat: 2230-1800

ANTEVE (PT Cakrawala Andalas Televisi)
Mulia Center Building, 19th Floor, Jl. HR Rasuna Said Kav. X-6 No.8, Jakarta 12940. ☎ +62 (21) 522 2084 to 86, 522 9175. 🖷 +62 (21) 522 2087. **Web:** www.anteve.uninet.net.id/an2/index0.html
L.P: GM: Mr. Dennis M. Cabalfin
Stations: Jakarta ch E47 40 kW TRP + approx 9 relays.

IVM (PT. Indosiar Visual Mandiri)
Jl. Damai No 11, Daan Mogot, Jakarta 11510. ☎ +62 (21) 567 2222, 568 8888. 🖷 +62 (21) 565 2221
Web: www.indosiar.com
Stations: Jakarta ch E41 + approx 16 relays

BALI TV
Jl Kebo Iwa 63A, Denpasar, Bali. or PO Box 3788 Denpasar. ☎ +62 (361) 427372. 🖷 +62 (361) 426949. **Web:** www.balitv.tv
Station: South Bali ch39 10 kW TRP

GLOBAL TV (PT Global Informasi Bermutu)
Jl Jend. Ahmad Yani 31, Jakarta 13230.☎ +62 (21) 489 1223. 🖷 +62 (21) 475 3559. **Web:** www.globaltv.co.id
Station: Jakarta ch E51 + approx 5 relays

JTV (PT Jawa Pos)
Graha Pena Building, Jl. Ahmad Yani 88, Surabaya, East Java.
L.P: Gen Mngr: Agus Mustofa.
Station: Surabaya ch E36 2kW TRP +3 relays

LATIVI (PT Lativi Media Karya)
Kawasan Industri Pulo Gadung,
Jl Rawa Teratai II No 2, Jakarta Timur 13260. ☎ +62 (21) 461 3545. 🖷 +62 (21) 461 6255. **Web:** www.lativi.com
Station: Jakarta ch E53 + approx 5 relays

METRO TV (PT Media Televisi Indonesia)
Jl. Pilar Mas Raya Kav. A-D., Kedoya, Kebon Jeruk, Jakarta 11520. ☎ +62 (21) 5830 0077. 🖷 +62 (21) 581 6365. **Web:** www.metrotvnews.com
Station: Jakarta ch E57 + at least 2 relays.

TRANS TV (PT Televisi Transformasi Indonesia)
Jl. Kapten Tendean Kav. 12-14A, Jakarta 12790. ☎ +62 (21) 794 4240. 🖷 +62 (21) 799 2600. **Web:** www. transtv.co.id
Station: Jakarta chE29 + approx 5 relays.

TV7 (PT Duta Visual Nusantara)
Wisma Dharmala Sakti Lt. 3, Jl. Jend. Sudirman Kav. 32, Jakarta 10220. ☎ +62 (21) 570 9777. 🖷 +62 (21) 570 8008-9.
Station: Jakarta ch E49 + at least 3 relays.

IRAN

Colour: SECAM — **System:** B.

ISLAMIC REPUBLIC OF IRAN BROADCASTING (Gov)
P.O. Box 19395 3333, Tehran; P.O. Box 15875-4344, Tehran ☎ +98 (21) 298053, 290079, 96715150. 🖷 +98 (21) 295056 **Web:** irib.com
L.P: Pres: H.E. Dr. Ali Larijani. Gen Dir. Int. Affairs: Dr. A. Ghasemzadeh.
D.Prgr: Network I: 0545-1200 & 1600-2400 (on holidays 1400-2400). **Network II:** 0800-1300 & 1400-2400. **Network III:** 0830-1100 & 1730-2300

Local st's (28) Abadan, Ahwaz, Alamdeh, Ardebil, Baharlo, Bakhtaran, Bandar-Abbas, Booshehr, Esfahan, Hamedan, Kerman, Khoramabad, Kohe Genon, Kohe Noor, Kosangar, Mashhad, Oromieh, Rasht, Sanandaj, Sari, Shahrkord, Shiraz, Tabriz, Tehran, Yazd, Zahedan, Zanjan, Zibakenar + 450 low power repeaters.

IRAQ

Colour: SECAM — **System:** B.

IRAQI TV (Gov)
Salhiya Baghdad. ☎ +964 (1) 884 4412, 884 4413. 🖷 +964 (1) 541 0480. **L.P:** Unknown. **Stations:** Baghdad & Mosul

IRELAND

Colour: PAL — **System:** I.

RADIO TELEFIS EIREANN (Statutory Corporation)
Donnybrook, Dublin 4. ☎ +353 (1) 208 3111. 🖷 +353 (1) 208 3080. **Web:** www.rte.ie/tv/
L.P: MD: Joe Mulholland
D.Prgr: RTE1: Mon-Sun 24hr. **RTE2:** Mon-Fri 0730-0200, Sat 0600-0200, Sun 0600-0300

TG4 (Irish-language service): Mon-Fri 1030-0200, Sat 0900-0200, Sun 0800-0200. From 0200 Euronews is broadcast. Web: www.tg4.ie

TV THREE
Westgate Business Park, Ballymount, Dublin 24. ☎ +353 (1) 419 3333. 🖷 +353 (1) 419 3317.

ISRAEL

Colour: PAL — **Systems:** B & G

ISRAEL TELEVISION (operated by the IBA)
P.O. Box 7139, Jerusalem 91071. ☎ +972 (2) 530 1333. 🖷 +972 (2) 629 1862 **Web:** www.iba.org.il
L.P: DG: Motty Eden.
Ch. 1 in Hebrew/Arabic: 24h Broadcasts Israel Educational TV (see below) 0600-1530 (Fri 1430). (Sat: no trs)
Ch. 3 (33): broadcasts via satellite, and VHF-10 Haifa area

CHANNEL 2
5 Kanfey Nesharim, PO Box 34122, Jerusalem 95464. ☎ +972 (2) 655 6222. 🖷 +972 (2) 655 6286 **L.P:** Man. Dir: N. Shay.
Stations: Eitanim chE22 50kW (ERP), Acco ch E27 2kW, Beersheba chE35 6kW **D.Prgr:** 0400-0300v in Hebrew and Arabic

ISRAEL EDUCATIONAL TELEVISION
14 Klausner Str, Ramat Aviv, Tel Aviv. ☎ +972 (3) 646 6666. 🖷 +972 (3) 642 7091 **L.P:** DG: Ms. Yaffa Zigovsky, Dir. Prog. Ms. Dvorah Morag, Dir. of Eng: Mr. Shlomo Kassif **Prgrs** broadcast on Ch1 & Ch2 and cable.

WEST BANK & GAZA

PALESTINIAN BROADCASTING CORP. TV
Palestine National Authority PBC, Gaza, PO Box 4025 Al Remal. ☎ +972 (7) 282 4681/2. 📠 +972 (7) 282 5804.
L.P: Dir Gen: Mr. Hisham Makki. Dir Eng: Mr Mohammed Saker.
Station: (UHF) Naplose ch5, Khan Younis ch21, Jericho ch21 (very low power), Kasser-Elhakim (Gaza) ch23, Ramallah ch25, Halhul, ch30, Jenine ch31, Betjala ch34, VHF ch4.
D.Prgr: 12 hrs (up to 18hrs during holiday periods).

WATAN TV (Priv.)
Al-kulliyah al Ahliyah Street, Ramallah. ☎ +297 (2) 2980053 📠 +297 (2) 2959253. **Email:** wattan@p-ol.com. **Web:** www.wattan.com **Station:** (UHF) ch42 with 0.5kW. **D.Pgr:** 0800-2000.

ITALY

Colour: PAL — **Systems:** B (VHF), G (UHF)

RADIOTELEVISIONE ITALIANA
Direzione Centrale TV, Viale Mazzini 14, 00195 Roma.
☎ +39 (6) 38781. 📠 +39 (6) 3226070. **Web:** www.rai.it **Email:** portale@rai.it
L.P: Chmn: Antonio Baldassarre. GM: Flavio Cattaneo. Dir TG1: Clemente Mimum. Dir TG2: Mauro Mazza. Dir TG3: Antonio Di Bella.Dir.TGRegionali: Angela Buttiglione. Dir. Raisport : Fabrizio Maffei. Dir. Televideo: Antonio Bagnardi. Dir.TV RAI-International: Roberto Morrione. PR: Marcello del Bosco.
Stations: Rome: RAI 1 chG, RAI 2 ch28, RAI 3 ch43.

RUNDFUNKANSTALT SÜDTIROL (RAS) (Public Statutory Body of the Autonomous Province of Southern Tyrol)
Europaalee 164A, I-39100 Bozen. ☎ +39 (0471) 546666. 📠 +39 (0471) 200378. **Web:** www.ras.bz.it **Email:** info@ras.bz.it
L.P: Pres. Helmuth Hendrich, Dir. Georg Plattern.
Stations: RAS1 (relay ORF-FS1); RAS2 (relay ZDF); RAS3 (relay ORF-FS2+SRG).

PRIVATE TV STATION NETWORKS
There are about 500 privately operated TV sts in Italy, mostly on local service. Due to space limitations, only those sts with nationwide networks are mentioned.
All stations 24h unless stated otherwise

Canale 5, Mediaset, Viale Europa 48, Palazzo dei Cigni, IT-20093 Cologno Monzese (MI). ☎ +39 02 25141. 📠 +39 02 25147715. **Web:** www.canale5.com **Email:** canale5@mediaset.it
Canale Italia, Serenissima Tv, Via Pacinotti 1/8,IT-350030 Rubano(PD). ☎ +39 049 8733111. 📠 +39 049 8733190. **Web:** www.serenissima.tv. **Email:** redazione@serenissimatv.com
Italia 7 Gold Tele City,Telestar,Amica 8,Amica9,Telecity,Via A. Gramsci 27/29, IT-15060 Castelletto d'Orba (AL). ☎ +39 0143 827012. 📠 +39 0143 830236. **Web:** www.telecity.it **Email:** info@telecity.it
Italia 1, Mediaset, Viale Europa 48, Palazzo dei Cigni, It-20093 Cologno Monzese (MI). ☎ +39 02 25141. 📠 +39 02 25147715. **Web:** www.italia1.com **Email:** italia1@mediasetit
Junior TV, Via Mambretti 9/13, IT-20157 Milano (MI). ☎ +39 02 332131. 📠 +39 02 33200514.
La 7, Via della Pineta Sacchetti 229, IT-00166 Roma (RM) ☎ +39 06 355841 . 📠 +39 06 355 84257. **Web:** www.la7.tv **Email:** la7@la7.tv
MTv, Corso Europa 7, IT-20122 Milano (MI). ☎ +39 02 7621171. 📠 +39 02 7621227. **Web:** www.mtv.it **Email:** segreteria@mtvne.com
Odeon TV,Tvitalia, Via Tavecchia 43/45, IT-20017 Rho (MI). ☎ +39 02 935151. 📠 +39 02 9304378. **Web:** www.telereporter.net **Email:** info@telereporter.net
Rete 4, Mediaset, Viale Europa 48, Palazzo dei Cigni, IT-20093 Cologno Monzese (MI). ☎ +39 02 25141. 📠 +39 02 25147715. **Web:** www.rcto4.com **Email:** rete4@mediaset.it
Sat 2000, Via Aurelia 786, IT-00165 Roma (RM). ☎ +39 06 665081. 📠 +39 06 66508581. **Web**: www.sat2000.it **Email:** sat2000@sat2000.it
Tele Market, Via Villanuova 38, IT-25030 Roncadelle (BS). ☎ +39 030 3510215. 📠 +39 030 2583341. **Web**: www.telemarket.it **Email**: info@telemarket.it.

IVORY COAST

Colour: SECAM — **System:** K.

TÉLÉVISION IVOIRIENNE (Gov)
08 B.P. 883, Abidjan 08. ☎ +225 439039. 📠 +225 222297.
L.P: Dir. Gen: Mamadou Berté.

D.Prgrs: 1st Prgr: Mon-Wed 1200-1330 & 1900-2300, Thurs 1200-1300 & 1600-2300, Sat 1200-0130, Sun 1030-2330. **2nd Prgr:** Mon-Fri 2030-2300, Sat 1600-2030 (Sun no transmissions). **Bouaké Regional Prgrs:** Thurs 1200-1300, Fri 1700-1830.

JAMAICA

Colour: NTSC — **System:** M.

TELEVISION JAMAICA LTD - TVJ(Comm)
Box 100, Kingston 10. ☎ +1 (876) 926 5620/9. 📠 +1 (876) 929 1029 .**Email:** tvjadmin@cwjamaica.com
L.P: Chairman: Milton Samuda; Hd. Prgrs: Marcia Forbes
Station: HWT ch 7, 8, 9, 10, 11, 12, 13.
D.Prgr: 2200(Sat 1930, Sun 1900)-0500

CVM TELEVISION LTD
69 Constant Spring Rd, Kingston 10 ☎ +1 (876) 931 9400-3 📠 +1 (876) 931 1573 **Web:** www.cvmtv.com
L.P.: Chairman: Neville Blythe, Pres: Dr. David McBean, Prgrs/Ops Mngr: Tomlin Ellis.

Stations

St. Andrew:	Coopers Hill	Ch. 9
St. Thomas:	Rowlandsfield	Ch. 12
St. Thomas:	Cabbage Hill	Ch. 4
St. Catherine:	Marley Hill	Ch. 4
St. Mary:	Berry Hill	Ch. 4
St. James	Kemp Shot	Ch. 4
St. James	Flower Hill	Ch. 11
St. Ann:	Lillyfield	Ch. 10
St. Ann:	Ocho Rios	Ch. 8
Manchester:	Huntley	Ch. 8
Westmoreland:	Chafton	Ch. 7
Portland:	Shotover	Ch. 13

JAPAN

Colour: NTSC — **System:** M

NIPPON HOSO KYOKAI (NHK) (Japan Broadc. Corp.) (non Gov., non Comm.)
2-1, Jinnan 2-chome, Shibuya-ku, Tokyo 150-8001. ☎ +81 3 3465 1111. **Web:** www.nhk.or.jp

JAPAN NEWS NETWORK (JNN)
Key st: TBS Radio & Communications, Inc. (Comm.)
3-6, Akasaka 5-chome, Minato-ku, Tokyo 107-8006. ☎ +81 3 3746 1111. **Web:** www.tbs.co.jp

NIPPON NEWS NETWORK (NNN)
Key st: Nippon Television Network Corp. (Comm.)
6-1, Higashishinbashi 1-chome, Minato-ku, Tokyo 105-7444. ☎ +81 3 6215 1111. **Web:** www.ntv.co.jp

FUJI NEWORK SYSTEM (FNS)
Key st: Fuji Television Network, Inc. (Comm.)
4-8, Daiba 2-chome, Minato-ku, Tokyo 137-8088. ☎ +81 3 5500 8888. **Web:** www.fujitv.co.jp

ALL NIPPON NEWS NETWORK (ANN)
Key st: TV Asahi Corp. (Comm.)
9-1, Roppongi 6-chome, Minato-ku, Tokyo 106-8001. ☎ +81 3 6406 1111. **Web:** www.tv-asahi.co.jp

TXN NETWORK
Key st: TV Tokyo Corp. (Comm.)
3-12, Toranomon 4-chome, Minato-ku, Tokyo 105-8012. ☎ +81 3 3432 1212. **Web:** www.tv-tokyo.co.jp

ARMED FORCES RADIO & TV SERVICE (U.S. Mil.)
(Misawa) OLAA, AFPBS, APO San Francisco 96519 (Okinawa) Det 2, AFPBS, APO San Francisco 96239
Stations: Misawa ch66 1kW, Iwakuni ch66 0.4kW, Okinawa ch8 40kW + additional st's at Yokota(Tokyo) & Sasebo on cable only.

JORDAN

Colour: PAL — **Systems:** B.

JORDAN RADIO & TELEVISION CORPORATION
Umm al-Hiran, P.O. Box 1041, Amman. ☎ +962 (6) 5773 +962 (6) 4757512. **Email:** jtv@jrtv.gov.jo **Web:** www.jrtv.com./index.html.
L.P: DG: Ayman al-Safadi; Dir Tel: Abdul-Halim Arabiat
Stations: JRTV1: in Arabic; **JRTV2** in English, French, Hebrew, Arabic. **1st Prgr (in stereo):** Suweilih chE3 104kW H, Aqaba ch9 5kW, Ras Munif-Ajlun ch9 500kW H, Deir Alla ch26 6kW H + low power repeaters. **2nd Prgr:** Aqaba ch5 5kW H, Suweilih ch6 108kW H, Ras Munif-Ajlun ch11 500kW H, Deir Alla ch29 6kW H + low power repeaters. **D.Prgr:** 0000-2359

KAZAKHSTAN

Colour: SECAM — **Systems:** D & K.

QAZAQ TELEVIZIYASY (Gov)
Zheltoqsan köshesi 177, 480013 Almaty. ☎ +7 3272 635579. +7 3272 631207.

KHABAR (Gov) Respublik alana 13, 480013 Almaty. ☎ +7 3272 625091. +7 3272 696505. E-mail: Web: www.khabar.kz
NOTES: produces 2 TV channels: Khabar and Yel Arna.

KTK (Comm)
Respublik alana 13, 480013 Almaty. ☎ +7 3272 583657. +7 3272 583693. **Email:** ktk@ktk.caravan.kz **Web:** www.ktk.kz
L.P: Dir: Andrey Osadtsyuk.

NTK (Comm)
Respublik alana 13, 480013 Almaty. ☎ +7 3272 634255 +7 3272 582467. **Email:** ntk@ntk.kz **Web:** www.ntk.kz
L.P: GD: Anuar Salkimbayev.

KENYA

Colour: PAL — **System:** B.

KENYA BROADCASTING CORPORATION (Gov, Comm)
Box 30456, Harry Thuku Road, Nairobi 00100. ☎ +254 20 334567. +254 20 220675 **Email:** kbctv@swiftkenya,com. **Web:** www.kbc.co.ke.
L.P: Chmn: James Kangwana, MD: Wachira Waruru. TV Prog. Mngr: Joseph Murema
Stations: Channel One: ch4 (Limuru) 10/1kW, ch2 (Timboroa) 10/1 kW, ch6 (Nakuru)10/1kW, ch6 (Mazeras) 5/10kW, ch8 (Kisii) 2kW, ch9 (Webuye), ch10 (Nyeri) 10/1kW, ch11 (Nyambene)10/1kW. **D.Prgr:** 0330-2100, multilingual in English and Swahili, incl. relays of CNN, CCTV (China) and DWTV.
Metro TV: ch31 (Nairobi). **D.Prgr:** 1400-2100MF (1100-2100SS), incl. relays of M-Net (South Africa)

COMMERCIAL STATIONS
KENYA TELEVISION NETWORK (KTN-TV)
P.O. Box 56985, Nairobi. ☎ +254 20 227122. +254 20 214467.
Web: www.kenyaweb.com/ktn/ktn.html
L.P: Chmn: Mwakio Sio. MD: Sam Shollei. CEO: Steve Crozier. Mktg. Mgr: Patrick Ndeda. Tech. Mgr: Francis Kimore.
Stations: UHF ch 57 (Eldoret), ch59 (Nairobi), ch61 (Kisumu), ch12 (Mombasa), ch58 (Nakuru), ch54 (Nyeri)
D.Prgr: 24hrs with own programming, also incl. relays of CNN.

STELLA TV
P.O. Box 56985, Nairobi. ☎ +254 20 2712982. +254 20 2713146. **Stations:** UHF ch 37 (Eldoret), ch56 (Nairobi), ch30 (Kisumu), ch55 (Mombasa), ch54 (Nakuru), ch43 (Nyeri), ch55 (Machakos)
D.Prgr: 24hrs incl. relays of Sky News

CITIZEN TV
P.O. Box 7468, Nairobi. ☎ +254 20 2721415. +254 20 2724220 Email: citizen@clubinternetk.com **Stations:** ch 39 (Nairobi), ch50 (Nyeri) **L.P:** Owner: Samuel Macharia, Ed.: Herman Igambi

NATION TV
P.O. Box 49010, Nairobi. ☎ +254 20 3208000 +254 20 213946. **Stations:** ch42 (Nairobi), ch33 (Kisumu), ch40 (Mazeras), ch47 (Eldoret), ch51 (Nyeri)

KIRIBATI

Colour: PAL — **System:** B.

RADIO KIRIBATI
Broadcasting House, P.O. Box 78, Bairiki, Taiwara, Rep. of Kiribati, Central Pacific. ☎ (686) 21187. (686) 21096 **Email:** bpa@tskl.net.ki
L.P.: Gen. Mngr: Timeon Ioane
Station & D.Prgr: details unknown

KOREA (North, DPR)

Colour: PAL/NTSC — **System:** D & K/M

THE RADIO AND TELEVISION BROADCASTING COMMITTEE OF THE DEMOCRATIC PEOPLE'S REPUBLIC OF KOREA (KRT) (Gov.)
Chonsung-dong, Moranbong District, Pyongyang. ☎ +850 2 816 035.
L.P: Chairm: Cha, Sung Su; Dir: Chun, Li-Ji; Head of Tech: Chol, Li-Yong.
D.Prgr: W 0900-1400; Sun: 0000-0300, 0600-1400.

MANSUDAE TELEVISION
Mansudae, Pyongyang.
Station: ch5 350kW(ERP).
D.Prgr: Sun: 0100-0400, 0700-1300.

KOREAN EDUCATIONAL & CULTURAL TELEVISION
Pyongyang.
Stations: Pyongyang ch9 140kW(ERP),.Kaesong ch8 30kW(ERP)
D.Prgr: W 1000-1300; Sun: 0300-1300.

KOREA (South, Rep.)

Colour: NTSC — **System:** M

KOREAN BROADCASTING SYSTEM (KBS) (Public Corporation)
18 Yeouido-dong Yeoungdeungpo-gu, Seoul 150-790. ☎ +82 2 781 2001/2, 781 1460/1, 781 5108. +82 2 781 2099, 781 1496-7, 781 5199. **Web:** www.kbs.co.kr
L.P: Pres & CEO: Jung, Yun Joo. Man. Dir.(TV): Chang, Youn Taik. Man. Dir.(Broadc.Engineering): Hong, Soo Wan. Dir. Int. Rel. Div: Choi, Choon Ae.
Stations: 1st prgr: ch4: Yeosu – ch5: Seoul, Ulsan – ch6: Changwon, Daejeon – ch7: Jeonju – ch8: Daegu, Chuncheon – ch9: Seoul, Busan, Gangneung – ch10: Jinju, Cheongju, Wonju – ch11: Gwangju – ch12: Andong, Chungju, Jeju – ch13: Pohang – ch27: Mokpo – 2nd prgr: ch6: Gangneung – ch7: Seoul, Busan – ch10: Jeju – ch13: Jeonju – ch20: Pohang – ch22: Chuncheon – ch23: Andong – ch24: Yeosu, Cheongju – ch25: Gwangju – ch27: Ulsan, Jinju – ch29: Mokpo – ch30: Chungju – ch31: Wonju – ch38: Daegu – ch42: Daejeon – ch45: Changwon.
D.Prgr.: 1st prgr: W 2100-0405, 0700-1650; Sat: 2100-1730; Sun: 2100-1710; 2nd prgr: W 2100-0415, 0700-1645; Sat/Sun: 2100-1800.

KOREA EDUCATIONAL BROADCASTING SYSTEM (EBS) (Public Corporation)
92-6, Umyeon-dong, Seocho-gu. Seoul 137-791. ☎ +82 2 521 1586/1988/1989/1357. +82 2 521 0241/522 8043. **Web:** www.ebs.co.kr
Stations: ch13: Seoul – ch19: Gangneung, Gwangju – ch20: Jeju – ch21: Ulsan, Chungju – ch23: Busan – ch26: Pohang – ch28: Chuncheon – ch29: Andong – ch30: Yeosu – ch32: Jinju – ch39: Mokpo – ch39: Daejeon, Changwon – ch40: Wonju – ch43: Seoul – ch44: Daegu – ch45: Jeonju.
D.Prgr: W 2100-0300, 0630-1630; Sat/Sun: 2100-1620.

MUNHWA BROADCASTING CORP. (MBC) (Comm.)
31 Yeouido-dong Yeoungdeungpo-gu, Seoul 150-728. ☎ +82 2 789 2851/3521. +82 2 782 3094/0294. **Web:** www.imbc.com
Stations: ch5: Andong – ch6: Pohang – ch7: Mokpo, Jeju – ch8: Daejeon, Jinju – ch9: Gwangju – ch10: Daegu, Jeonju, Chuncheon – ch11: Seoul, Busan – ch13: Masan – ch22: Samcheok – ch28: Yeosu – ch31: Gangneung – ch33: Ulsan, Cheongju – ch34: Wonju – ch36: Chungju.
D.Prgr: W 2100-0400, 0700-1620; Sat/Sun: 2100-1700.

SEOUL BROADCASTING SYSTEM (SBS) (Comm.)
920 Mok-dong, Yangcheon-gu, Seoul 158-725. ☎ +82 2 2061 0006. +82 2 2113 3169. **Web:** www.sbs.co.kr
Station: HLSQ-TV ch6.
D.Prgr: W 2100-0400, 0700-1655; Sat/Sun: 2100-1700.
Local Network: KBC (Gwangju), TBC (Daegu), TJB (Daejeon), PSB (Busan), UBC (Ulsan), JTV (Jeonju), CJB (Cheongju), GTB (Chuncheon), JIBS(Jeju).

KYUNG-IN BROADCASTING LTD.(iTV) (Comm.)
: 587-46, Hagik-dong, Nam-gu, Incheon 402-040. ☎+82 32 830 1000. +82 32 865 6300. **Web:** www.itv.co.kr
Station: HLDO-TV ch15. **Relay st:** ch4.
D.Prgr: W 2100-0300, 0700-1610; Sat/Sun: 2100-1600.

AMERICAN FORCES NETWORK KOREA (US Mil.)
Unit #15324, APO AP 96205-0097, USA. ☎ +82 2 7914 6495.
Stations: ch2: Palgonsan, Dongdeucheon, Busan, Jinhae, Hoideok, Wonju, Gunsan – ch6: Munsan – ch12: Chuncheon, Daegu, Daejon – ch13: Gwangju – ch34: Seoul – ch49: Osan, Suseong, Daegu – ch70: Pyeongtaek, Dongdeucheon – ch75: Dongdeucheon.
D.Prgr: 24H.

KUWAIT

Colour: PAL — **System:** B & G

KUWAIT TELEVISION (Gov)
Television of the State of Kuwait, P.O. Box 621 Safat, 13007 Safat, Kuwait. ☎ +965 (24) 23774. +965 (24) 56660/39667. **Web:** www.moinfo.kw.gov.
L.P: Minister: H.E. Dr. Sa'ad Mohammed bin Teflah Al-Ajmi; Asst. Under Secr. for Broadcasting Affairs: Dr. Abdulazeez Al-Mansour ; Dir. of Eng. (TV): Abdulazeez Albagli.
Stations: KTV1 in Arabic: ch8, ch24, ch26, ch38, ch59. 0500-2200.
KTV2. in English: ch10, ch28, ch39, ch65:Sat-Wed: 1200-2100, Thurs-Fri: 1100-2100.
KTV3. (sports) in English and Arabic: ch5, ch47 Sat-Fri (occasional)
4th Prgr. (Arabic and English entertainment): ch12, ch39, ch45. Sat-Fri: 1000-0500.

OTHER STATIONS
MBC (Middle East Broadcasting Centre), Arabic relay ch12, Sat-Thu. 1100-0030, Fri 0900-0030, Sun-Wed. 1200-2400
ESC (Egyptian Satellite Channel), Arabic relay ch5, Sat-Fri. 24h.
Kuwait Space Channel: ARABSAT 1C 31° East.

KYRGYZSTAN

Colour: SECAM — **Systems:** D & K.

KYRGYZ TELEVISION (Gov)
Jash Gvardiya blvd. 59, 720300 Bishkek. ☎ +996 312 253404. +996 312 651064. **Email:** rkaktr@elcat.kg.

LAOS

Colour: PAL — **System:** B

LAO NATIONAL TELEVISION (TVNL) (Gov)
P.O. Box 5635, Sivilay Village, Vientiane ☎ +856 21 412183 +856 21 710182 **L.P:** DG: Kheckheo Soisaya
Stations: Vientiane stations: ch9 (5kW), ch23 (0.1kW), ch12 (1kW); Savannakhet station: ch12 (1kW)
D.Prgr: ch9, 2330-0030 (Sat-Sun 2330-0230), evening prgr.:1130-1600; ch23, 2330-0400; ch12, 2330-0030, 1000-1600; Savannakhet station: 1130-1600

LAO TELEVISION CHANNEL 3
PO Box 860, Thatluang Road, Ban Nongbone, Vientiane ☎ +856 21 315449 +856 21 215628
Station: Vientiane ch3 10kW

LATVIA

Colour: PAL — **Systems:** D & K.

LATVIJAS TELEVIZIJA - LTV (Pub)
Zakusalas krastmala 3, 1509 Riga. ☎ +371 7200314 +371 7200025. **Email:** ltv@ltv.lv. **Web:** www.ltv.lv.
L.P: Dir: Uldis Grava.
NOTES: produces 2 programmes: LTV-1 and LTV-7

LNT (Comm)
Elijas iela 17, 1050 Riga. ☎ +371 7070200. + 371 7821128.
Email: lnt@lnt.lv. **Web:** www.lnt.lv
L.P: DG: Andrejs Ekis.

TV3 VIASAT (Comm)
Mukusalas iela 72b, 1004 Riga. ☎ +371 7629366. + 371 7600599. **Email:** tv3@tv3.lv. **Web:** www.tv3.lv

LEBANON

Colour: SECAM — **Systems:** B & G.

TÉLÉ-LIBAN (Gov)
B.P. 115054, Hazmieh, Beirut. ☎ +961 (1) 405100. +961 (1) 457253 **L.P:** DG: Jean-Claude Boulos.
D.Prgrs: 1st and 2nd Prgr (Arabic/French/English): 1000-2200; **N. in English:** 1600 (Prgr. 1). **N. in French:** 1615 (Prgr. 2). **3rd Prgr.** (French/English) 1630-2200.

MIDDLE EAST TELEVISION (Comm)
P.O. Box 5689, Nicosia, Cyprus (Studios in Marjayoun).
Addr. in USA: 977 Centreville Turnpike, Virginia Beach, VA 23463-0001, USA. ☎ +1 (804) 579 3419. +1 (804) 579 3417.
L.P: GM: Wes Hylton. Prgr. Mgr: Tom Foley.
Station: chE12 100kW (Pol:V) – chE5 10W.
D.Prgrs: 1130-2200 (approx) in English & Arabic.
N. in English: 1700.

LEBANESE BROADC. CORP. INT. (Comm)
P.O. Box 16-5853 Beirut. ☎ +961 (9) 938938. +961 (9) 937916.
Email: lbcsat@lbcsat.com.lb **Web:** www.lbcsat.com.lb
L.P: SM: Pierre Al Daher. TD: Nasim Boustany. Film Buyer: Selim El-Azar.
Stations: ch12H 60kW; ch33H 325kW; ch10H 35kW, ch9H 35kW; ch5H 35kW.
D.Prgr: 0445-2200.

FUTURE TELEVISION (Comm)
White House, Rue Spears, Sanayeh, Beirut, Lebanon. ☎ +961 (1) 355355 +961 (1) 753232 **Email:** future@future.com.lb **Web:** www.future.com.lb
Stations: ch28, ch37, ch46, ch52.
D.Prgr: 1100-2200.

MURR TELEVISION (MTV) (Comm)
Fouad Chehab Ave (P.O. Box 166000) - Fassouh -MTV Bldg. ☎ +961 (1) 217000. +961 (1) 215215. **Email:** mtv@mtv.com.lb
Web: www.mtv.cm.lb
L.P: Pres: Michel El Murr.
Stations: ch28, ch38, ch43, ch45, ch48, ch58, ch68.
D.Prgr: 0700-0200.

LESOTHO

Colour: PAL — **System:** I

LESOTHO NATIONAL BROADCASTING SERVICES
P.O. Box 552, Maseru 100. ☎ +266 323561. +266 310003.
L.P: Contr. TV: Molikuoa Tau
D.Prgr: 7h daily.

LIBERIA

Colour: PAL — **System:** B

LIBERIAN BROADCASTING CORPORATION (Gov. Comm)

P.O. Box 10-594, Monrovia. ☎ +231 271250.
L.P: DG: Jesse B. Karnley.
Station: ELTV chE6 1/0.1kW + 4 low power repeaters.
D.Prgr: W 1815 (Sat 1615)-2300; Sun 1415-2230.

LIBYA

Colour: PAL — **System:** B

LIBYAN JAMAHIRIYA BROADCASTING (Gov)

P.O. Box 333, Tripoli ☎ +218 21 3332451.
L.P: Dir: Youssif Debri.
Station: One terrestrial & satellite channel. **D.Prgr:** 1700-2230.

LITHUANIA

Colour: PAL — **Systems:** D/K

LIETUVOS TELEVIZIJA - LTV (Pub)

Konarskio g. 49, 03123 Vilnius. ☎ +370 5 2363100. 🖷 +370 5 236 3208. **Email:** lrt@lrt.lt. **Web:** www.lrt.lt.
L.P: Dir: Šarunas Kalinauskas.
NOTES: LTV produces two programmes - LTV1 and LTV2.

LNK (Comm)

Šeškines g. 20, 07156 Vilnius. ☎ +370 5 2431058. 🖷 +370 5 2123924. **Email:** lnk@lnk.lt **Web:** www.lnk.lt
L.P: Dir: Zita Sarakiene

TV3 VIASAT (Comm)

Nemencines pl. 4, 10102 Vilnius. ☎ +370 5 2316131. 🖷 +370 5 2784530. **Email:** biuras@tv3.lt **Web:** www.tv3.lt

BALTIJOS TELEVIZIJA (Comm)

Laisves pr. 60, 05120 Vilnius. ☎ +370 5 2780805. 🖷 +370 5 2428907. **Email:** info@btv.lt **Web:** www.btv.lt
L.P: Dir. Gen: Gintaras Songaila.

LUXEMBOURG

Colour: PAL & SECAM — **Systems:** B, L & G.

CLT Multi Media

45, blvd Pierre Frieden, L-1543 Luxembourg-Kirchberg. ☎ +352 421421. 🖷 +352 42142-2760 **Web:** www.cltmulti.com
L.P: MD: Rémy Sautter.
CLT Multi Media operates various terrestrial and satellite-delivered TV services serving Belgium, France, German, Italy, Luxembourg, The Netherlands and Poland. It is also a major shareholder in Channel 5 (UK). **Terrestrial tr's:** Dudelange ch7 (System B) 100/25kW H, Dudelange ch21 (System L) 1000/100kW, Dudelange ch27 (System G) 1000/100kW (2 studios), ch24 100kW.

RTL 9 in French: W 1045-1210, 1600-2230 (Sat 1400-2240); Sun 1100-2200 on ch21 (SECAM) for French viewers and ch27 (PAL) for Belgium & Luxembourg.
RTL-4 in Dutch & Multilingual: Luxembourg ch. 41 (30kW).
Club RTL (French for Belgium): ch27.

RTL Télé Lëtzebuerg (local sce. of CLT)

45, blvd Pierre Frieden, L-1543 Luxembourg-Kirchberg. ☎ +352 421 427400. 🖷 +352 421 427438. **Web:** www.rtl.lu
D. Prgr: in Luxembourgish: MF 1700-1900, Sat 1730-1900, Sun 1800-1930.

MACAU

Colour: PAL — **System:** I.

TELEDIFUSÃO DE MACAU (TDM SARL)

P.O. Box 446, Macau. ☎ +853 520204/6. 🖷 +853 520 208. **Web**: tdm.com.mo **Email:** prog@tdm.com.mo
L.P: Chairman: Stanley Ho; Exec. Vice Chairman: Maria do Carmo Figueiredo.
Stations: Portuguese Ch30 0.2kW+1 repeater of 10W; English Ch32 0.2kW+1 repeater of 10W. **D.Prgr:** Portuguese Channel: appr. 1058-1600; Chinese Channel 2330-0100, 1015-1600.

MACEDONIA

Colour: PAL — **Systems:** B & H

MAKEDONSKA RADIODIFUZIJA (Gov)

bul Goce Delcev bb, 1000 Skopje. ☎ +389 2 3117 301. 🖷 +389 2 3225 520. **Web**: www.jpmrd.gov.mk

TELEVIZIJA MAKEDONIJE (Gov)

Dolno Nerezi bb, 1000 Skopje. ☎ +389 2 258-230.
Stations (Prgrs 1, 2, 3):
Boskija: Ch 8(**1**)/57(**2**). Bukovik: Ch 6(**1**)/55(**2**). Vodno: Ch 9/26/36. Golak: Ch 5(**1**)/38(**2**). Mali Vlaj: Ch 9/44/50. Pelister: Ch 4/29/33. Popova Sapka: Ch 10(**1**)/38(**2**). Stogovo: Ch 6(**1**)/31(**2**). Turtel: Ch 11(**1**)/22(**2**). Crni Vrv: Ch 6(**1**)/30(**2**)
1st Prgr: D.Prgr: Mon-Thurs 0740-0200, Fri 0740-0330, Sat-Sun 0740-0200. **2nd Prgr: D.Prgr:** Mon-Sat, 0900-0030, Sun 0740-0030
3rd Prgr: BBC and minority languages.

TELEVIZIJA SITEL (Com)

1000 Skopje, "G.Station" bb, Skopje. ☎ +389 2 311 6566 🖷 +389 2 3114898 **Email:**sitel@unet.com.mk **Web:** www.sitel.com.mk
L.P: GM: Mr. Goran Ivanovski. Tech.D: Mr. Tase Seizov.
D.Prgr: ch24/ch57/ch64: 24 h

A1 NEZAVISNA TELEVIZIJA (Comm)

1000 Skopje, "Pero Nakov" bb. ☎ +389 2 255 1111. 🖷 +389 2 255 1133 **Email:**altv@unet.com.mk
Web: www.soros.org.mk/a1/index.htm
L.P: Prop: Mr. Ramkovski Velija. GM: Mrs. Gordana Stoshich.
D.Prgr: ch33/ch47/ch60/ch65: 24 hrs.

MADAGASCAR

Colour: SECAM — **System:** K.

RADIO TELEVISION MALAGASY (Gov)

P.O. Box 442, Antananarivo. ☎ +261 (2) 21784.
L.P: Dir: M. Rabesahala.
Stations: Antananarivo ch5 1kW H + 36 low power st's.
D.Prgr: 1600-1930. News bulletins in Malagasy and French.
Television broadcasts in Madagascar increasingly reflect the division of the country into two political camps, following the elections of 2001.

MALAGASY BROADCASTING SYSTEM TV (MBS TV) (Comm.)

L.P: Owned by self-declared president, Marc Ravalomanana.
D.Prgr: range of prgs including evening news bulletins in Malagasy and English

MADAGASCAR TELEVISION (MA-TV) (Comm.)

Web: www.matvonline.tv
L.P: Owned by Andriambelo family.
D.Prgr: Broadcasts only in Antananarivo.

TV-5 Europe (a Belgian st. broadcasting in French) and **TF1** (a French independent st) can be received by satellite through two local satellite channel providers.

MADEIRA

Colour: PAL — **System:** B&G

RTP-RÁDIO E TELEVISÃO DE PORTUGAL, SGPS (Partly Comm.)

Caminho de Santo António,140, 9000 321 Funchal
☎ +351-291 709 100. 🖷 +351-291 741 859. **Email:** rtp@rtp.pt
Web: www.rtp.pt
Stations: RTP-1 (from mainland) and RTP Madeira are brodcast from 2 tr's plus 40 relays. **D.Prgr:** RTP Madeira 24h; RTP-1 see Portugal.

SIC-SOCIEDADE INDEPENDENTE DE COMUNICAÇÃO
(cf. PORTUGAL) Available in Madeira via cable only.
TVI-TELEVISÃO INDEPENDENTE, S.A.
(cf. PORTUGAL) Available in Madeira via cable only.

MALAWI

Colour: PAL — **System:** B.

Malawi Television
Private bag 268, Blantyre. ☎ +265 675033 Fax 265 672627. **Email:** tvmalawi@malawi.net
L.P: DG Benson M Tembo, Tech. Super Harry Chuma

MALAYSIA

Colour: PAL — **System:** B.

Peninsular Malaysia

RADIO TELEVISYEN MALAYSIA (RTM) (Gov)
Dept. of Broadc, Angkasapuri, Kuala Lumpur 50614.
☎ +60 (3) 2282 5333 Fax +60 (3) 2282 5103 **Web:** www.rtm.net.my
L.P: DG: Barbara E. Edmonds; MD TV: Hasiah Ariffin; Dir of Prgrs: Yoong Rafidah Yacob
D.Prgr: TV1 in Malay: 2145-1900. **TV2** in Malay, English, Mandarin and Tamil: 0050-1705.

SYSTEM TV MALAYSIA BERHAD (TV3)
Sri Pentas (Ground Floor, South Wing) No. 3, Persiaran Banjar Utama, 47800 Petaling Jaya Selangor Darul Ehsan.
☎ +60 (3) 716 6333. Fax +60 (3) 716 133.
L.P: MD: Hisham Abdul Rahman. Senior Gen. Mgr. Progr. Haji Khalil Mohd Zain. Eng. Mgr: Rahmad A Kadir.
Stations: Kuala Lumpur ch12 124/25kW H.
Repeater st's of high power in Kuantan (ch 11), Ipoh (ch 11), Gunung Ledang (ch 12), Johore Bahru (ch 26), Kedah (ch 29), Kota Bharu (ch 27), Kuala Terengganu (ch 11), Dungun (ch 27), Tampin (ch 23), Taiping (ch 41), Kuching (ch 12), Sibu (ch 11), Kota Kinabalu (ch 29), Ulu Kali (ch 29) & Machang (ch 11).
D. Prgrs: 2300-1630

8TV
Metropolitan TV sdn bhd, Sri Pentas, 3 Persiaran Bandar Utama, 47800 Petaling Jaya, Selangor Darul Ehsan ☎ +60 3 7728 8282 Fax +60 3 7726 8282 Web: www.8tv.com.my
Stations: Gunung Ulu Kali chE27, Bukit Besi chE58 + 2 relays on UHF. 8TV is affiliated to TV3 **D. Prgrs:** 0400-1900

CHANNEL 9
Lot 31, Jalan Pelukis U1/46, Temasya Industrial Park, 40150 Shah Alam, Selangor Darul Ehsan ☎ +60 3 5568 5999 Web: www.ch-9.tv
Stations: Gunung Ulu Kali chE42 + 3 relays on UHF **D. Prgrs:** 0200-1630/1700

NTV7 (Nat Seven Sdn Bhd) (Comm)
7, Jalan Jurubina U1/18, Hicom-Glenmarie Industrial Park, 40000 Shah Alam, Selangor Darul Ehsan. ☎ +60 (3) 5569 1777. Fax +60 (3) 5569 2515. **Web:** www.ntv7.com.my
Stations: Kuala Lumpur ch E35; Kuching ch E27, Bukit Besi chE7 + 14 relays on UHF. **D. Prgrs:** 0400-1700 (SS 0100-1700/1800). Limited separate programming for Sabah and Sarawak is carried by Kuching and relays.

East Malaysia

TV MALAYSIA SABAH AND SARAWAK (Gov)
P.O. Box 1016, 88614 Kota Kinabalu. ☎ +60 (88)52711.
L.P: Prgr. Contr: M.A. Mahmood.
D.Prgrs: as for Peninsular Malaysia.

MALDIVES

Colour: PAL — **System:** B.

TELEVISION MALDIVES (Gov)
Buruzu Magu, 20-04 Male ☎ +960 323 105, 324 10 Fax +960 325 083.
L.P: DG: Mr Samarubuloo Ibrahim Manik
Station: ch7 1kW H.
D.Prgr: 0300-0500 (Fri), 1200-1620.

MALI

Colour: SECAM — **System:** B.

RADIODIFFUSION TÉLÉVISION DU MALI
B.P. 171, Bamako. ☎ +223 (21) 4621/2019/4727. Fax +223 (21) 4205. **Email:** ortm@spider.toolnet.org.
L.P: DG: Sidki Konate.
Stations: Bamako ch5 10kW + 2 repeaters.
D.Prgr: 1700-0000. (Sat/Sun and public holidays. 1000-0000).

MALTA

Colour: PAL — **System:** B/H

PUBLIC BROADCASTING SERVICES LTD .
75 St. Luke's Road, Gwardamangia MSD 01. ☎ +356 21225051. Fax +356 21244601.
Email: info@pbs.com.mt **Web:** www.pbs.com.mt
L.P: Chmn: Chief Justice Prof. J.J. Cremona. Chief Exec: Albert Marshall. Head of TV: Joe Galea. TV Prgr. Mgr: Sylvana Cristina.
Station: Ch. H-E10 10/2.5kW / Ch 55-68 1 kW
D.Prgr: 24 h.(relay of BBC WS in the night)
Station: Ch12 (cable) - The Community Channel
☎ +356 22913360. Fax +22913312. **Email**: cea@pbs.com.mt
D. Prgr: 24 h (also relay of DW and Euronews)

SUPER 1 TV
Rainbow Productions Ltd, Marsa Ind. Estate, Marsa HMR 15. ☎ +356 21235313. Fax +356 21240717. **E-mail:** news@super1.com **Web:** www.super1.com/tv.asp.
L.P.: Chairman: Mr. Renald Dalli (renald.dalli@super1.com). Chief Executive Officer: Albert Marshall (marshall@super1.com) Group Head - TV Broadcasting: Mrs. Ruth Vella (rvella@super1.com) (Operated by Maltese Labour Party)
Station: Ch 29 10kW / Ch 39-45-49 kW
D.Prgr: 24 hours.

SMASH TV
4 Thisle Lane, Paola PLA19. ☎ +356 21697829. Fax +356 21697830. **E-mail**: smash@vol.net.mt **Web**: www.smashmalta.com
L.P: Head: Jesmond Saliba.
Station: Ch 44 10kW / Ch 52 1 kW
D.Prgr: 24 hours

NET TV
Triq Herbert Ganado, Pieta HMR 08. ☎ +356 21243641. Fax +356 21242886 **E-mail**:antona@vol.net.mt
Web: www.nettv.com.mt
L.P: Chairman: Joe Saliba. Broadcast Manager: Anton Attard.
Station: Ch 50 10kW / Ch 45-62-66 1 kW
D.Prgr: 24 hours

EDUCATIONAL CHANNEL
Maria Regina School, Triq Mile End - Hamrun ☎ +356 21239274. Fax +356 21240701 **Email**: education22@euroweb.net.mt **Web:** www.geocities.com/m175363
L.P.: Acting Head: Stephen Florian (stephen.florian@gov.mt)
Station: Ch 22 (cable)
D.Prgr: 0730-2200.

MOVIE CHANNEL
Melita Cable plc., Gasan Centre, Mriehel By-Pass, Mriehel BKR14 ☎ +356 21490030. Fax +356 22745050 **Email**: info@melitacable.com
Web: www.melitacable.com
Station: Ch 45 (cable)

SPORTS CHANNEL
Melita Cable plc., Gasan Centre, Mriehel By-Pass, Mriehel BKR14 ☎ +356 21490030. Fax +356 22745050 **Email**: info@melitacable.com
Web: www.melitacable.com
Station: Ch 47-48 (cable).

MARSHALL ISLANDS

Colour: NTSC — **System:** M.

MBC-TV
☐ Marshall Islands Broadcasting Company, Majuro 96960. ☎ +692 6253413.

AFRTS TELEVISION (Department of Defense)
☐ Box 23, APO San Francisco, CA 96555, USA.
L.P: Netw. Mgr: Larry Malinowski. **Stations:** ch9, ch13 0.25kW (24 h to Kwajalein Island & Roi-Namur Island).

MARTINIQUE

Colour: SECAM — **System:** K.

SOCIÉTÉ NATIONAL DE RADIO-TÉLÉVISION D'OUTRE MER (RFO)
☐ B.P. 662, F-97263 Fort de France Cedex. ☎ +596 595200.Web: rfo.fr
L.P: Dir: Fred Jouhoud. CE: Jean Claude Arrivé.
Stations: Fort de France ch4 1kW (+ 9 relay st's). Pol: V.
D. Prgr: 18hrs + daily from 0600

COMMERCIAL STATIONS

ATV ANTILLES TELEVISION (Priv, Comm)
☐ 28 rue Arawaks, 97200 Fort de France. ☎ +596 75 4444. 🖷 +596 75 5565
Stations: La Trinite ch39 7kW, Fort de France ch44 8 kW, La Morne Rouge ch52 1.4 kW, Riviere Pilote ch34 0.19kW

CANAL ANTILLES (Priv, Comm)
☐ Centre Commercial La Galléria, 97232 Le Lamentin. ☎ +596 50 5787
Stations: La Trinite ch25 7 kW, Le Morne Rouge ch46 1.4kW, Port de France ch29 8kW, Saint Pierre ch34 0.6kW, Riviere Pilote ch50 0.19 kW.

TCI MARTINIQUE-TELE CARAIBES INTERNATIONAL (Priv, Comm)
☐ Immeuble RCI/TCI-Zone industrielle-97232 Le Lamentin.
☎ +596 510606. 🖷 +596 518562.
D. Prgr: 11:00 a.m. - noon-(rel. T.F.I. & Euronews)

MAURITANIA

Colour: SECAM — **System:** B.

TÉLÉVISION NATIONALE (Gov)
TVM (Television du Mauritanie) ☐ B.P. 5522, Nouakchott. ☎ +222 53303.
Station: Nouakchott chE5 (2x1kW).
D.Prgr: 2000-2245.

MAURITIUS

Colour: SECAM — **System:** B.

MAURITIUS BROADCASTING CORP. (Comm)
☐ 1 Louis Pasteur Str, Forest Side. ☎ +230 675 5001/2. 🖷 +230 675 7332. **Web:** www.mbc@intnet.mu
L.P: DG: Hootesh Ramburn; Dir. Eng: Mr. Amoordalingum Pather.
D.Prgr: ch MBC1, MBC2, MBC3, MBC4 (Pay TV), MBC5 (Pay TV), Rodrigues TV. 0000-2359 hrs.

MAYOTTE

Colour: SECAM — **System:** K.

R.F.O.—MAYOTTE
☐ B.P. 103, F-97610 Pamandzi, Ile de Mayotte. ☎ +269 601017. 🖷 +269 601852.**Web:** www.rfo.fr
L.P: St. Dir: Robert Xavier. Dir. Tec: Serge Sulpice-Timothee.
Stations: Lavigie ch 9H 100W, Mamadzou ch 7H 50W, Lima Combanich 4H 200W.
D.Prgr: Mon-Fri 1100-2100, Sat/Sun 0800-2100.

MEXICO

Colour: NTSC. — **System:** M.

TELEVISIÓN AZTECA SA de CV (Priv, Comm)
☐ Periférico Sur 4121, Col, Fuentes del Pedregal, 14140 ☎ +52 (5) 645-4080/5959 **Email:**webtv@tvazteca.com
Web: www.tvazteca.com.mx
L.P: Pres. Ricardo B. Salinas Pliego.
D.Prgr: ch Red Nacional 7 (XHIMT), Red Nacional 13 (XHDF).

XEIPN (Instituto Politécnico Nacional)
☐ Carpio 475, Col. Casco de Santo Tomás,11340. ☎ +52 (5) 356-1111. **Email:** medioc11@mail.oncetv.ipn.mx **Web:** www.oncetv.ipn.mx.
L.P: D.G: Lic. Alejandra Lajous, Vargas.
D.Prgr: XEIPN-TV ch 11.

TELEVISIÓN METROPOLITANA SA de CV
☐ Calzada de Tlaplan 583 Col. Alamos, 03400.☎ +52 (5) 538-3256/4162/3413. **Web:** www.canal22.com.mx
L.P: Dir. José Maria Pérez Gay.
D.Prgr: (UHF) XEIMT-TV ch 22.

CNI (Corporación de Noticias e Información)
☐ Monte Escandinavos 105, Lomas de Chapultepec, 11000. ☎ +52 (5) 202-0186. **Web:** www.cni40.com.mx.
L.P: Pres. Javier Moreno Valle.

TELEVISA SA de CV
☐ Ave. Chapultepec 18, 0672. ☎ +52 (5) 709-3333. **Web:** www.televisa.com.mx.
L.P: Pres. Emilio Azcárraga Jean.
Stations: Cadena Canal 2, Cadena Canal 4, Cadena Canal 5 & Cadena Canal 9.

MICRONESIA

Colour: NTSC — **System:** M

TV STATION POHNPEI (Comm)
☐ KPON-TV, Central Micronesia Communications, P.O. Box 460, Kolonia, Pohnpei, FSM 96941.
L.P: Pres: Bernard Hegenberger. Dir. Tec: David Cliffe.
Station: Pohnpei chA7 1kW + cable TV on ch's 4,5,9.

TV-STATION TRUK (Comm)
☐ Truk State, FSM 96942.
Station: TTTK chA7 0.1kW. **D.Prgr:** 0400-1200 (approx).

TV-STATION YAP (Gov)
☐ WAAB-TV, Yap State, FSM 96943.
Station: chA7 1kW. **D.Prgr:** 0400-1200 (approx)

MOLDOVA

Colour: SECAM — **Systems:** D & K

MOLDOVA 1 (Pub)
☐ str. Hâncesti 64, 2018 Chisinau. ☎ +373 22 739534. 🖷 +373 22 739157. **Email:** tvnewstv@cni.md **Web:** www.trm.tm
L.P: Dir: Victor Tabirta.

MONACO

Colour: SECAM & PAL — **Systems:** L & G.

TÉLÉ MONTE CARLO (Comm)
☐ Monte Carlo TMC, 6 Quai Antoine 1er, MC-98000 Monaco. ☎ +3393 505940. 🖷 +3393 250109. **Web:** www.cecchigori.com/tv
L.P: Pres: Jean-Louis Medecin. Dir. Prgrs: George Giaveret.
Stations: chF8 (L/SECAM) 50kW(ERP), ch30(L/SECAM) 500kW, ch33(G/PAL) 0.05kW, ch35(G/PAL) 40kW, ch39(L/SECAM) 0.02kW.
D.Prgr: French 1800-2400 on ch 8, 30, 39. (See also listing of relay st's in France). **Italian: TMC1 & TMC 2:** 1000-2400 on ch 33, 35

MONGOLIA

Colour: SECAM — **Systems:** D & K.

MONGOLIIN TELEVIZ (Pub)
Huvisgalyn zalm 3, Ulaanbaatar 11. ☎ +976 1 23 801. Fax +976 1 327 234. **Email:** mrtv@magicnet.mn
L.P: Dir: Ts. Enkhbat.

MONTSERRAT

Colour: NTSC — **System:** M.

ANTILLES TV LIMITED (Comm)
P.O. Box 342, Plymouth, Montserrat. ☎ +1 (664) 491 2226. Fax +1 (664) 491 4511.
L.P: Gen. Mgr: K. Osborne. Dir. Tec: Z.A. Joseph.
Station: Chance Pic chA7 (48kW towards Dominica, 3kW towards Antigua & St. Kitts).
D.Prgrs: 1000-1110, 2000-0400 (Fri/Sat 0700).

MOROCCO

Colour: SECAM — **System:** B.

RADIODIFFUSION TÉLÉVISION MAROCAINE (Gov)
1, rue Al Brihi, Rabat. ☎ +212 (7) 704963. Fax +212 (7) 722047.
L.P: DG: Mohamed Tricha. Dir. of TV: Mohamed Issari. Head of Ext. Rel: A. Bekkali Abdellatif.
D.Prgr. in Arabic/French: Mon-Thurs 1215-1415 & 1700-0100v, Fri/Sat/Sun 1215-0100v.

2M INTERNATIONAL (Comm)
KM7, 300 route de Rabat, Casablanca. ☎ +212 (2) 354444. Fax +212 (2) 354071.
L.P: MD: Tawfik Bennani-Smires. Tech. Dir: Driss Anouar. Comm. Dir: Mouhaddab Khadija.
D.Prgr: 15h daily, partly subscription.
F.Pl: Pan-African satellite sce.

MOZAMBIQUE

Colour: PAL — **System:** B.

TELEVISÃO DE MOÇAMBIQUE - TVM (Gov)
C.P. 2675, Maputo. ☎ +258 744788 or 741395. **Web:** tvm.co.mz
L.P: Dir Prgr: Armando Chavana Dt.Tec: Jaime Ferreira. Film Buyer: Arlando Tembe.
Station: Maputo ch33 1kW.
D.Prgr: 24h weekly.

MYANMAR

Colour: NTSC — **System:** M

MYANMAR TV (Gov)
426 Pyay Rd, Yangon ☎ +95 (1) 535 553 Fax +95 (1) 534 211
Email: mrtv@mptmail.net.mm
D.Prgr: 0700-0900; 1100-1500 (Sat+ Sun); 1600-2230

There is limited information available concerning this former Burmese broadcaster. It is known that there are over 100 relays throughout the country. The Military Government also operates a second network, **Myawaddy TV,** in major cities . ☎ +95 (1) 620 270.

NAMIBIA

Colour: PAL — **System:** I.

NAMIBIAN BROADCASTING CORPORATION
P.O. Box 321, Windhoek 9000. ☎ +264 (61) 291 3111. Fax +264 (61) 216 209. **Email:** pr@nbc.com.na.
L.P: DG: Penny Uukunde; Gen Mngr TV: Claudia likela
D.Prgrs: Mon-Fri: 1200-2400, Sat-Sun: 0800-2400. All main bdcsts in English.

NAURU

Colour: PAL — **System:** K

NAURU TELEVISION
Govnt Offices, Yaren District,Rep. of Nauru, Central Pacific. ☎ +674 4443113 Fax +674 444 3153
L.P: Mgr: Briar-Rose Nagaya; Tech Eng: Jason Harris

NEPAL

Colour: PAL — **System:** B & G.

NEPAL TELEVISION (NTV) (Gov)
Nepal Television Corporation, P O Box 3826, Singha Durba, Kathmandu. ☎ +977 1 259334 Fax +977 1 228312
Email: neptv@ccsl.com.np
L.P: Chmn Suresh Kumar Pudasaini, Gen Mgr Durganath Sharma

NETHERLANDS

Colour: PAL — **System:** B & G.

NEDERLANDSE OMROEPPROGRAMMA STICHTING (NOS)
Sumatralaan 45, 1217 GP Hilversum, P.O. Box 26600, 1202 JT Hilversum. ☎ +31 (35) 6779222. Fax +31 (35) 6772649
L.P: Dir. Radio and TV: Ruurd Bierman; Hd. Comm: F. de Vries
Board Members: drs. A. Grewel; mr A. Herstel (NCRV); ds. A. van der Veer (EO); S.H. Piersma (VPRO); K. van Doodewaard (TROS); mr H.J.E. Bruins Slot (NPS); G.H. Veringa (SEO); dr. D.Th. Kuiper; prof mr A.J.C.M. Geers; mr B. Staal.

NEDERLANDSE PROGRAMMA STICHTING (NPS)
P.O. Box 29000, 1202 MA Hilversum. ☎ +31 (35) 6779333. Fax +31 (35) 6774517
L.P: Dir: W.J.M. van Beusekom

NB: The Dutch prgrs. are provided by the NOS, NPS and seven broadcasting organizations:

Algemene Omroepvereniging AVRO, 's Gravelandseweg 52, 1217 ET Hilversum, Postbus 2 1200 JA Hilversum. ☎ +31 (35) 6717911 Fax +31 (35) 6717439
-Vereniging Evangelische Omroep EO, Oude Amersfoortseweg 79a, 1213 AC Hilversum, Postbus 21000, 1202 BB Hilversum. ☎ +31 (35) 6474747. Fax +31 (35) 6474727
-Katholieke Radio Omroep KRO, Emmastraat 52, 1213 AL Hilversum, Postbus 23000, 1202 EA Hilversum. ☎ +31 (35) 6713911 Fax +31 (35) 6237345
-Nederlandse Christelijke Radio Vereniging NCRV, Bergweg 30, 1217 SC Hilversum, Postbus 25000, 1202 HB Hilversum. ☎ +31 (35) 6719911 Fax +31 (35) 6719285
-TROS, Lage Naarderweg 45-47, 1217 GN Hilversum, Postbus 28450, 1202 LL Hilversum. ☎ +31 (35) 6715715 Fax +31 (35) 6715236
-Omroepvereniging VARA, Heuvellaan 50, 1217 JN Hilversum, Postbus 175, 1200 AD Hilversum. ☎ +31 (35) 6711911 Fax +31 (35) 6711333
-Omroepvereniging VPRO, 's Gravelandseweg 63-73, 1217 EH Hilversum, Postbus 11, 1200 JC Hilversum. ☎ +31 (35) 6712911 Fax +31 (35) 6712254
D.Prgr: Ned 1: AVRO/KRO/NCRV; Ned 2: EO/NOS/TROS; Ned 3: NPS/VARA/VPRO.

NETHERLANDS ANTILLES

Colour: NTSC — **System:** M.

TELE CURAÇAO (Gov, Comm)
P.O. Box 415, Curaçao. ☎ +599 (9) 61288. Fax +599 (9) 614138.
L.P: Gen. Mgr: Norbert Hendrikse. Prgr. Mgr: H. van der Beist. Dir. Tec: J. Rufina.
Station: chA8 20/5kW H/A6
D.Prgr: 2000-0345.
Cable TV: Telecuraçao also provides a cable service relaying various U.S. satellite networks and two Venezuelan channels.

LEEWARD BROADCASTING CORPORATION — TELEVISION
P.O. Box 375, Philipsburg, St. Maarten.
Station: chA7 5kW.
D.Prgr: 2030 (Sun 1800)-0300 (approx); Sat also 1200-1300.

A Gov. st. on chA6 is reported operating from Saba.

NEW CALEDONIA

Colour: SECAM — **System:** K.

RFO-TV (Gov)
Radio Télévision Française d'Outre Mer (RFO), BP G3 Mont Coffin, F-98848 Nouméa cedex. ☎ +687 274327. 🖷 +687 281252
L.P: Dir: Alain Le Garrec.
Stations: Mont Do chK4 2 x 1kW H, Noumea chK8 0.4kW H, Lifou chK7 0.4kW H (+ 25 low power repeaters).
D.Prgr: 2 channels, 8h a day, in French.

PRIVATE STATIONS:
CANAL CALEDONIE (Priv, Comm)
8 rue de Verneilh, Noumea
Stations: Noumea Mt Coffyn ch43 11kW, Noumea (Town) ch33 0.06kW, Noumea Mt Koghi ch25 9kW
N.B: Canal Caledonie is a subscription sce and the signal is encrypted except: 1945-2020, 0125-0225, 0715-0910.
D. Prgr: W1945-1400 Sun 24h.

NEW ZEALAND

Colour: PAL — **System:** B.

TELEVISION NEW ZEALAND Ltd.
P.O. Box 3819, Auckland. ☎ +64 (9) 916 7000. 🖷 +64 (9) 916 7934
L.P: CEO: Ian Fraser; H. Operations & Tech.: Neil Andrew
Stations: Channel One: Wellington ch1 100/20 kW H, Auckland ch2 100/20 kW H, Christchurch ch3 100/20 kW H, Dunedin ch2 50/10 kW H + relay st's at Hamilton ch1 100/20 kW V, Palmerston North ch2 100/20 kW V, Invercargill ch1 1/0.1 kW H + 18 medium and 412 low powered relay st's.
D.Prgr: 2100 (Sat 1900, Sun 2000)-1200 (Fri 1300, Sat 1400).

Channel Two: Auckland ch4 300/30 kW H, Wellington ch5 300/30 kW H, Christchurch ch3 300/30 kW H, Dunedin ch4 300/25 kW H + repeaters at Hamilton ch3 100/20 kW H, Palmerston North ch4 300/30 kW V, Invercargill ch3 1/0.1 kW H + 17 medium and 240 low powered repeaters.
D.Prgr: 1830-1200. Weekends 24hrs.

PRIME TELEVISION
1 John Glenn Ave., PBox 302 193, North Harbour, Auckland ☎ +64 (9) 414 0700 🖷+64 (9) 414 0701 **Web:** primetv.co.nz **Email:** info@primetv.co.nz **D.Prgr:** Free to air to most viewers in major cities, also available to Sky subscribers.

TAB TRACKSIDE
P.O. Box 388-99 Wellington Mail Centre, NX. ☎ +64 (4) 576 6999. 🖷 +64 (4) 576 6996. **Email:** corporate@tab.co.nz
L.P: Ops. Mgr.: Richard Ellerington.
Stations: Auckland ch55 150/15kW, ch53 100/20kW, ch58 50/5kW; Waikato ch56 100/20kW, ch50 50/5kW, ch47 50/5kW; Palmerston North ch ; Wellington ch56 150/15kW, ch58 100/20kW; Christchurch ch48 65/7kW.
D.Prgr: Fri 2200-0930, Mon 2330-0600, Tues 2345-0610, Thur 2250-1000.

TV3 (Comm)
P.O. Box 5185, Auckland. ☎ +64 (9) 779 730. 🖷 +64 (9) 366 7029.
L.P: Head of Netw. Programming: Kel Geddes.
Stations: Auckland ch7 100/20kW; Wellington ch11 100/20kW; Christchurch ch6 100/20kW; Dunedin ch10 100/20kW; Hamilton ch9 100/20kW; Palmerston North ch7 100/20kW; Invercargill ch7 1/0.1kW. (+ 11 medium powered relay sts)
D.Prgr: Auckland ch7 H, Christchurch ch6 H, Hamilton ch9 V, Invercargill ch7 H, Wellington ch11 H, Dunedin ch10 H, Palmerston North ch7 V.

CANTERBURY TELEVISION (CTV)
196 Gloucester Street, Christchurch.
D.Prgr: 0500-1200 UTC, Fri 2300-Sat 1200
Station: ch48 65kW.

SKY NETWORK TELEVISION (pay-tv)
P.O. Box 9059, Auckland. ☎ +64 (9) 525 5555. 🖷 +64 (9) 525 5725
Stations: Auckland ch27/29/30V (movies), ch31/33/52V (sports), ch43/45/54 (news); Waikato ch28/30V/31V (movies), ch32/34V/27V (sports), ch44/46V/51V (news); Palmerston North ch30 (movies), ch34 (sports), ch46 (news; Wellington ch28/30V/30/49 (movies), ch32/34V/34/53 (sports), ch44/54V/54/47 (news); Christchurchch30 (movies), ch34 (sports), ch46 (news).

NICARAGUA

Colour: NTSC — **System:** M.

TELEVICENTRO SA (Comm)
Apdo Postal 688, Managua ☎ +505 (268) 2222. **Email:** canal2@ibw.com.ni
Station: ch2, 25kW

NUEVA IMAGEN SA
Del Montoya, 1c al Sur, 1c al Este, Managua. ☎ +505 (266) 3420 🖷 +505 (266) 3467
Station: ch4.

CANAL 6
3 1/2 Carretera Sur Contig o Shell, Managua ☎ +505 (266) 0118. 🖷 +505 (266) 6522
Station: ch6 25kW. Sistema Sandinista de TV

TELENICA
Apdo Postal 3611, Mansión Teodolinda 1c al Sur, y ½ Abajo. ☎ +505 (266) 5021. 🖷 +505 (266) 5024.
Station: ch8

CANAL 10
Mansión Teodolinda, 2c, al Ote. ☎ +505 (266) 5021
Station: ch10.

NICAVISIÓN
Apdo 2766, Managua ☎ +505 (266) 0691. 🖷 +505 (266) 1424
Station: ch12.

TELEVISIÓN CRISTIANA de NICARAGUA
De la Casa de Obrero, 5c. al Sur y 2c. Arriba. ☎ +505 (266) 8688. 🖷 +505 (268) 3132.
Station: ch21.

TELESAT
Carretera a Masaya Km. 4½, Motorama ½c al Su, Managua. ☎ +505 (267) 0170
Station: ch23.

NIGER

Colour: SECAM — **System:** K.

TÉLÉ-SAHEL (Gov)
B.P. 309, Niamey. ☎ +227 723155.
L.P: Dir. Gen: DG: Abdou Souley. TD: Zoudi Issouf.
D.Prgr: 0630-1130, 1430-1730.

TÉNÉRE TV (Comm.)
B.P. 13600, Niamey. ☎ +227 736574.
D.Prgr: 1500-1800

NIGERIA

Colour: PAL — **Systems:** B.

NIGERIAN TELEVISION AUTHORITY (Gov)
Ahmadu Bello Way, Victoria Island, Lagos ☎ +234 1 267297, and **Abuja office**:NTA Headquarters, Garki, Abuja ☎ +234 9 2346907 🖷 +234 9 2345914
L.P: DG Ben Murray Bruce; Exec Dir Prgrs: Peter Igho, Exec. Dir. Eng.: Sunday Ibok

NTA ch10 100kW 210.25MHz (VHF). **D.Prgr:** 0830-2215 hrs. Multilingual bcsts for domestic market, with news bulletins in English. **NTA 2** ch5 100kW 175.25MHz (VHF) **D.Prgr:** 24h. English language. **Note:** NTA has Federal offices in each state capital which transmit NTA programming on a variety of VHF & UHF frequencies. Each state also has a Public broadcast station.

MINAJ BROADCAST INTERNATIONAL (Comm)
130/132 Ladipo St, Matori, PO Box 3975, Mushin Lagos ☎ +234 (1) 452 9203-4 🖷 +234 (1) 452 8500. **Email:** minaj@minaj-hq.com. **Web:** www.minaj.com
L.P.: Exec. Chairman: Mike Ajegbo; Head MBI: Cecilia Shobola; Head Minaj Systems TV: Chris Maduka
D.Prgr: ch43, ch41, 0500-2259 hrs. English language broadcasts for the African and Caribbean TV market, terrestrial and satellite transmission

DBN TELEVISION (Comm)
65 Awolowo Rd, PO Box 51162, Ikoyi, Lagos ☎ +234 (1) 269 0051 🖷 +234 (1) 269 3888 **Email:** info@dbninternational.net
L.P: CEO: Osa Sonny Adun; Head Prod: Ugo Afam-Mordi
Station: Ch32, 559.25MHz
D.Prgr: over 90 hours of weekly prgrs. At present DBN covers SW Nigeria; there are plans to extend this nationwide.

NIUE

Colour: PAL — **System:** B.

NIUE TV
Broadcasting Corp. of Niue, P.O. Box 68, Alofi. ☎ +683 4026. 🖷 +683 4217
L.P: GM: Hima Douglas
D.Prgr: ch6 and repeat on ch8. Daily broadcast times not specified.

NORFOLK ISLAND

Colour: PAL — **System:** B.

NORFOLK ISLAND TELEVISION SCE. (Gov)
New Cascade Rd, Norfolk Island 2899, Australia. ☎ +672 (3) 22137. 🖷 +672 (3) 23298.
Station: Mt. Pitt ch7 0.02kW V.
D.Prgr: rel. ABC, SBS & Central 7 TV from Australia .

N. MARIANA ISLANDS (US Commonw.)

Colour: NTSC — **System:** M.

MICRONESIA BROADC. CORPO. (Comm)
c/o KUAM, Box 368, Agana, Guam 96920.
L.P: Pres: H. Scott Killgore. Gen. Mgr: T. Dickey. Asst. Gen. Mgr: A. Ocambo. Technician: M. Madaing.
Stations: WSZE-TV ch10 0.5kW (Saipan)
D.Prgr: 0600-1400..

NORWAY

Colour: PAL — **Systems:** B & G.

NORSK RIKSKRINGKASTING - (non-comm. enterprise operated by an independent public foundation)
0340 Oslo. ☎ +47 23047000. ☎ **Inf.Dpt:** +47 81565900. 🖷 **Inf. Dpt:**+47 75122777. **Email:** info@nrk.no **Web:** www.nrk.no
L.P: DG: John G Bernander.
D.Prgr: NRK-1 0800-0100v **NRK-2** 24h. During daytime and night interactive TV. Some NRK-2 transmitters are leased to private organisations during daytime.
Regional Prgrs: NRK-1 split in 9 regional news broadcasts MF 1740-1758 and (not Friday)1955-2000. **Transmitters:** Satellite and terrestrial VHF/UHF.

TV-Norge (Priv Comm)
Postboks 11 Sentrum, 0101 Oslo. ☎ +47 21022000. 🖷 +47 22051000. **Web:** www.tvnorge.no **L.P:** MD: Morten Aass.
D.Prgr: 24h. Night and morning interactive TV. **Transmitters:** Satellite and terrestrial UHF network through cooperation with 17 local/regional TV-stations.

TV-2 (Priv Comm)
Postboks 7222, 5002 Bergen. ☎ +47 55908070. 🖷 +47 55908090. **Web:** www.tv2.no **L.P:** MD: Kåre Valebrokk.
D.Prgr: 24h. Night and morning interactive TV. **Transmitters:** Satellite and terrestrial UHF network (438 transmitters).

OMAN

Colour: PAL — **Systems:** B & G.

SULTANATE OF OMAN TELEVISION (Gov)
P.O. Box 600, 113 Muscat, Oman. ☎ +968 603888. 🖷 +968 604629. **Email:** tvradio@omantel.net.om
L.P: DG:Salum Habsi. DG (Engineering): Moh'd Salim Al Marhouby.
D.Prgr: 24hrs.

PAKISTAN

Colour: PAL — **System:** B.

PAKISTAN TELEVISION CORPORATION LTD
PO Box 1221, Islamabad. ☎ +92 (51) 921 5528 🖷 +92 (51) 920 3406 (Prgr. Centres at Lahore, Karachi, Peshawar, Quetta and Islamabad). **Web:** ptv.com.pk
L.P: MD: Yousaf Baig Mirza; Dir Engineering: Akhtar Mehmood Dada.
D.Prgr: 1130-1930. **N:** 1400, 1600.
Stations: PTV1, PTV2, PTV3 and cable PTV World.

SHALIMAR TELEVISION NETWORK (STN)
P.O. Box 1246, Islamabad. ☎ +92 (51) 856 171. 🖷 +92 (51) 261 225.
L.P: MD: M Arshad Choudhry. CE: Agha Nasir.
Stations: STN operates from 22 cities.
D.Prgr: 24 h

PALAU

Colour: NTSC — **System:** M.

STV-TV KOROR (Comm)
Koror, Palau 96940.
L.P: Mgr: David Nolan. Technician: Ray Omelen.
Station: Ngermit, Koror ch7 0.1kW.
D.Prgr: 0400-1400.

PANAMA

Colour: NTSC — **System:** M.

TELEVISORA NACIONAL - CANAL 2
Apdo. postal. 6-3092, El Dorado, Panamá ☎ +507 236 2222. 🖷 +507 236 2987. **Web:** www.tvn.com
L.P: Pres: Stanley Motta. Dir. Gen: Pedro Diaz Dir. Production: Miguel Carrera **D.Prgr:** Sun-Thurs: 0600-1230; Fri + Sat: 24 hrs. 650 kW

TELEMETRO - CANAL 13
Calle 50, 6 Urbanización Obarrio, Ciudad de Panamá . Apdo. postal 8-116, Zona 8, Panamá . ☎ +507 269 2122 🖷 +507 269 2720.**Web:** www.telemetro.com.pa **L.P:** Pres: Fernando Eleta Almarán. Dir. Prgr: Analida LópeZ **D.Prgr:** National, Mon-Sun: 0600-1230. 10kW

RPC TELEVISION - CANAL 4
Av 11y Cl28, Panamá ☎ +507 225 0160 🖷 +507 225 0705. **Web:** www.rpctv.com **D.Prgr:** National, daily 0600-1230 32kW.

FETV - CANAL 5
Apdo..6-7295, El Dorado, Panamá. ☎ +507 230 8000. 🖷 +507 230 1955 **Web:** www.fetv.org **L.P:** Dir. Gen. Manuel Santiago Blanquer i Planells **D.Prgr:** National, Mon-Sat: 0800-1200; Sun: 0750-1200.20kW

RADIO Y TELEVISIÓN EDUCATIVA - CANAL ONCE
Curundú. Diagonal al Ministerio de Obras Publicas, Estafeta Universitaria, Universidad de Panamá. ☎ +507 232 8188. 🖷 +507 232 8100. **Email:** rtvel@ancon.up.ac.pa **L.P** Dir. Gen: Ariel Rosas
D.Prgr: Prov. Panamá , Colón, Prov.Centrales, Sant. de Veraguas y Darien: Daily 0730-2300

CADENA MILENIUM RCM - CANAL 21
Via Ricardo J. Alfaro, Edificio Bel Air, Planta Baja, Local 1, Apdo. postal 87-1989, Zona 7, Panamá. ☎ +507 360 0808. 🖷 +507 360 0831. **Web:** www.rcmtv.pa **L.P:** Pres: Alfredo Prieto. Dir. Gen: Julio Miller.

D.Prgr:Prov. Panamá: 24 hrs.

HOSANNA VISION CANAL 37
Ave. Martin Sosa, Ed. Hosanna Vision (A.P. Hosanna, El Dorado 6-7981), Panamá ☎ +507 223 3075. +507 269 9421
Email: hosannaradioytv@hotmail.com **L.P:** Rev. Edwin Alvarez

CANAL +23
Plaza Hispanidad, Ave. 12 de Octubre, (Ap. 6A-9292 El Dorado), Panamá ☎ +507 261 8823. +507 261 7613 Email: sofia@+23.tv
L.P: Antonio Frangías

CANAL 29
Avenida Ricardo J. Alfaro, Sun Tower Mall, Piso 2, Apdo. postal 1465, Balboa, Ancón Panamá ☎ +507 236 7824 +507 236 7825
Email: canal29@pty.com **L.P:** Dir: Enrique Sánchez **D.Prgr:** Rel. 24 hrs

PAPUA NEW GUINEA

Colour: PAL — **Systems:** B & G.

NATIONAL BROADCASTING CORPORATION OF PAPUA NEW GUINEA
PO Box 1359, Boroko NCD ☎+675 (3) 257 175 +675 (3) 256 296
L.P: MD: Kristoffa Ninkama

EMTV (Comm)
Media Niugini Pty. Ltd, P.O. Box 443, Boroko NCD. ☎ +675 3257322. +675 3254450. **Email:** emtv@datec.com.pg. **Web:** www.emtv.com.pg.
L.P: Chief Exec: Steve Moorhouse. CE: Kevin Saban. News Director: John Eggins
Stations: Burns Peak ch9 1.1kW, Air Niugini Hill ch31 0.17kW, Garden City ch68 0.02kW (all Port Moresby area)
F.Pl: st's at Mt. Hagen, Goroka, Lae, Rabaul.
D.Prgr: 12 h daily in English and Tok Pisin, 7 days a week.

PARAGUAY

Colour: PAL — **System:** N.

SISTEMA NACIONAL DE TELEVISIÓN (SNT),
Av. Carlos Antonio Lopez 572, Asunción. ☎ +595 21 424222. **Web:** www.sntparaguay.com.
Main station: Cerro Corá ch9 + 8 repeaters

RED PRIVADA DE COMUNICACIONES (RPC)
Comendador Nicolás Bo y Guaranies, Lambaré, Asunción. ☎ +595 21 332823. **Web:** www.rpc.com.py.
Main station: Asunción ch13 + 12 repeaters

CHANNEL 2 RED GUARANÍ
Yegros, 437 - Piso 21, Asunción. ☎ +595 21 446358. **Web:** www.tvdos.com.py
Main station: Asunción ch2 + 2 repeaters

TELEFUTURO
Andrade c/ O'Higgins, Villa Morra, Asunción. ☎ +595 21 608756. **Web:** www.telefuturo.com.py.
Main station: Asunción ch4 + 26 repeaters

TELEVISIÓN DIRIGIDA (TVD)
Simón Bolívar 294 esq, Iturbe, Asunción. ☎ +595 21 4173500. **Web:** www.tvd.com.py
25 digital subscription channels in Asunción

AGENCIA PARAGUAYA DE NOTÍCIAS "CIMA TV"
Av. Mariscal Estigarríbia c/ Brasil, Asunción. ☎ +595 21 214202. **Web:** www.supernet.com.py/usuarios/apn
3 digital subscription channels in Asunción

PERU

Colour: NTSC — **System:** M.

COMPAÑIA LATINOAMERICANA DE RADIODIFUSION S.A
Av. San Felipe 968, Jesús Mariá, Lima 11. ☎ +51 (14) 707272. +51 (14) 712688.

COMPAÑIA PERUANA DE RADIODIFUSION
Cas. 1192, Lima. **L.P:**Dir. Gen: M. M. Arbulu B. Man. Dir: N. Gonzalez U. Dir. Tec: D. Capella. Operates st's in Piura(ch2 2 kW), Chiclayo(ch 4 5 kW), Trujillo(ch 6 2 kW), Tacna(ch 9 2 kW), Huancayo(ch 4 2 kW) + 59 repeaters **D.Prgr:** 1000-0600.

PANAMERICANA DE TELEVISION
Av. Arequipa 1110, Lima. **D.Prgr:** 1500-0600 (+ 14 relay st's).

EMPRESA DE CINE, RADIO Y TELEVISION PERUANA
José Galvez 1040, Lima.**L.P:** Pres: Carlos Guillen B. **D.Prgr:** 1900-0400 (+ 39 repeaters).

ANDINA DE TELEVISION
Arequipa 3570, San Isidro, Apartado 270077, Lima. **Web:** atv.com.pe **D.Prgr:** 1900-0400.

RBC TELEVISION
Juan de la Fuente 453, Miraflores, Lima.

DIFUSORA UNIVERSAL DE TELEVISION
Paseo de la República 6099, San Antonio, Miraflores, Lima **L.P:** Exec. Pres: J.L. Banchero H. **D.Prgr:** 2200-0400.

EMPRESA RADIODIFUSORA 1160 TV
Apt. Postal 2355, Lima.**D.Prgr:** 800-0500.

PHILIPPINES

Colour: NTSC — **System:** M.

NATIONAL TELECOMMUNICATIONS COMMISSION (Department of Transportation and Communications)
855 Vibal Bldg, Esda Corner Times Str, Quezon City.
L.P: Commissioner: Josefina Lichauco. Dep. Commissioners: Aloysius R. Santos, Florentino L. Ampil. Chief, Broadcast Sce. Dept: Carlos D. Saliuan Jr.

PEOPLE'S TELEVISION NETWORK, INC (Gov)
Broadcast Complex, Visayas Ave, Quezson City 1100. ☎ +63 (2) 920 6521. +63 (2) 920 4342 **Email:** ptv4@l-next.net
L.P: Chairm: Ms Mia A. Concio; GM: Mr Ramon S. Diez; CE: Mr Antonio M Leduna
Stations: PTV 4, D.Prgr: 0425 (Sat/Sun 0300)-1730.

RPN Channel 9,
Broadcast City, Capitol Hills, Quezon City ☎+ 63 (2) 977 661**Web:** rpn9.com
D.Prgr: 0230-1600
.

ABS-CBN BROADCASTING CORPORATION
Eugenio Lopez Jnr St, Quezon C. ☎ +63 (2) 411 1166
Web: abs-cbn.com
L.P: Chairman: Eugenio Lopez III; VP TV Engineering: Eduardo D. Flores
D.Prgr: Mon-Fri 2300-1530 (Sat/Sun 0000-1730).

REPUBLIC BROADCASTING SYSTEM
EDSA, Diliman, Quezon City, Metro Manila.
D.Prgr: Mon-Fri 0800-0130, Sat 0730-0130, Sun 0730-0200.

ARMED FORCES RADIO & TV SERVICE (U.S. Mil)
Det 1, AFPBS, APO San Francisco 96274, USA.
Stations: Olongapo ch14 0.25kW, Angeles City ch17 1kW, San Miguel ch40 0.03kW, Baguio ch14 0.3kW, San Fernando ch17 0.25kW, Capas ch17 25W.

POLAND

Colour: PAL — **Systems:** D & K.

TELEWIZJA POLSKA S.A. (Pub)
ul. Woronicza 17, 00-999 Warszawa. ☎ +48 22 5478000. +48 22 5478000. **Email:** tvp@tvp.pl **Web:** www.tvp.com.pl
L.P: DG: Wojciech Kabarowski
NOTES: produces 2 programmes, TVP1 and TVP2.

TV Polsat (Comm)
ul. Ostrobramska 77, 04-175 Warszawa. ☎ +48 22 5145533. +48 22 5145550. **Email:** poczta@polsat.com.pl **Web:** www.polsat.com.pl

TVN (Comm)
ul. Augustówka 3, 02-981 Warszawa. ☎ +48 22 8566060. +48 22 8566666 **Email:** tzn@tvn.pl **Web:** www.tvn.pl

TV4 (Comm)
ul. Gen. Okulickiego 6, 05-500 Piaseczno. ☎ +48 22 756 9711. Fax +48 22 7503090. **Email:** sekretariat@tv4.pl **Web:** www.tv4.pl

PORTUGAL

Colour: PAL — **System:** B & G

RTP-RÁDIO E TELEVISÃO DE PORTUGAL, SGPS (Pub, part comm.)
Av. Marchal Gomes da Costa, 37, 1800-255 Lisboa. ☎ +351 21 794 7000. Fax +35 21 794 7570 **Email:** rtp@rtp.pt **Web:** www.rtp.pt / www.dois.pt **LP:** Chmn: Almerindo Marques.
Stations: RTP-1 (carries comm. advs.) & "A 2:" via 38 trs + 287 relays; RTPi and RTP-Africa avail. on satellite; Norte TV via cable only; RTP-Açores and RTP-Madeira (cf. respective entries).
D.Prgr: RTP-1: 24h; "A 2:": 24h; RTPi 24h; RTP-Africa 24h; Norte TV: 24h

SIC-SOCIEDADE INDEPENDENTE DE COMUNICAÇÃO, S.A. (comm.)
Estrada da Outurela 119, 2795 Carnaxide ☎ +351 21 417 9550 Fax +351 21 417 3118.
Email: contacto@siconline.pt **Web:** www.sic.pt
LP: Chmn: Francisco Pinto Balsemão. **D.Prgr:** 0645-0330 via 19 trs+115 relays. SIC also has other chs available via cable only.

TVI, TELEVISÃO INDEPENDENTE, S.A. (comm.)
R. Mário Castelhano, 40, Queluz de Baixo, 2749-502 Barcarena ☎ +351 21 434 7500. Fax +351 21 435 5076
Email: relacoes.exteriores@iol.pt **Web:** www.tvi.iol.pt
LP: Chmn: Miguel Pais do Amaral. **D.Prgr:** 24 h via 21 tr's + 36 relays.

PUERTO RICO

Colour: NTSC — **System:** M.

TELEVICENTRO DE PUERTO RICO
Aptdo 362050, San Juan 00936-2059 ☎ +787 792 4444 **Web:** televicentropr.com
L.P.: DG: Jose Ramos
D.Prgr: 1210-0500 (+ 8 relay sts).

SFN Communications Inc
GPO Box 2060, San Juan 00938.

Telecinco Inc
Box 43, Mayagüez 00708 **L.P:** St. Mgr. & Film Buyer: E. Bado. Dir. Tec: G.A. Bonet. **D.Prgr:**1200-0400.

Ponce TV Corpo
Isabel Esq Montaner, Ponce 00731 **L.P:** Pres: L.T. Muniz.

American Colonial Broadc. Corp
Box S-4189, San Juan 00905. **D.Prgr:** 1230-0430 — 8b) rel. 8.

Western Broadc. Corp. of Puerto Rico
Box 1200, Mayagüez 00709 **D.Prgr:** 1245-0500 (partly rel. st. 3).

QATAR

Colour: PAL — **System:** B

QATAR TELEVISION SERVICE (Gov)
Min. of Information and Culture, QTV. P.O. Box 1944, Doha. ☎ +974 89 4444. Fax +974 86 4511.
L.P. Asst. Under Secretary for Radio & TV: Mr. Abdul Rahman Saif Al-Madhadi. Dir. of TV: Mr. Saad Al-Rumehi. Dir of Eng: Mr. Hussain A. Jaffar. Dir of News: Mr. Abdullah Al Haj
Stations: Channnel 1 bdcst in Doha ch9 in Arabic 200kW, Jamiliyah ch11 in Arabic (repeater) 600kW, Doha ch37 in English 695kW, ch49 (repeater), Jamiliyah ch 52 (repeater)
D.Prgr: 0000-0000 24 hrs. Arabic language.

AL JAZEERA SATELLITE CHANNEL
PO Box 22300, Doha. ☎ +974 4382777 Fax +974 4426864 **Web:** www.aljazeera.net **Email:** chief@al-jazirah.com
D.Prgr: News, business, sport, documentaries.

REUNION

Colour: SECAM — **System:** K.

SOCIÉTÉ NATIONALE DE RADIO-TÉLÉVISION FRANÇAISE D'OUTRE-MER (RFO)
1, rue Jean-Chatel, F-97716 Saint-Denis. ☎ +262 406767. Fax +262 406771.
L.P: Head Prgrs and Prod: Gérard Hoarau. Editor in Chief, TV:Claude Regent
Stations: P. Textor chK'9 0.5kW + 18 low power repeaters.
D.Prgr: Prgr.I: 1300 (Sat/Sun 1100)-1930; Prgr.II: no times available.

PRIVATE STATIONS:

ANTENNE REUNION (Priv, Comm)
33 Chemin Vavangues, 97400 Saint Denis. ☎ +262 48 2828. Fax +26248 2829
Stations: Saint Leu ch36 1kW, Sainte Suzanne ch42 2kW, Le Port ch57 9kW, Saint Pierre ch61 2kW, Saint Joseph ch55 1,7kW, Saint Benoit ch26 2,4kW, Saint Denis ch33 2kW, Piton Textor ch56 2kW.
D.Prgr: 0830-1830

CANAL REUNION (Priv, Comm)
35 Chemin Vavangues, 97400 Saint Denis. ☎ +262 29 0202. Fax +262 29 1709
Stations: Saint Joseph ch52 1.7kW, Sainte Suzanne ch39 2kW, Le Port ch54 9kW, Saint Denis ch25 2kW, Piton Textor ch53 2kW, Saint Pierre ch26 2kW.
D. Prgr: 0245-2200, Sun 24h

TV SUD (Priv, Comm)
10 rue Aristide Briand, 97430 Le Tampon. ☎ +262 57 4242
Stations: Saint Pierre ch58 2kW, Les Avirons ch60 0.72kW
D.Prgr: 1400-1800

TV-4 (Priv, Comm)
8 chemin Fontbrune, 97400 Saint Denis. ☎ +262 52 7373
Stations: Saint Leu ch49 1kW, Saint Denis ch52 2kW, Sainte Suzanne ch31 2kW, Le Port ch65 9kW, Piton Textor ch63 2kW
D.Prgr: 0230-2130

ROMANIA

Colour: PAL — **System:** D & G

RADIOTELEVIZIUNEA ROMÂNÂ (Gov)
TVR 1 and TVR 2
191 Calea Dorobanti, sector 1, Bucharest. ☎ +40 (1) 230 6290. Fax +40 (1) 212 1427. **Email:** romania@tvr.ro. **Web:** www.tvr.ro.
L.P: DG: Dumitru Popa. PD: Mamase Radnev.
D.Prgr: 0400-2200 (VHF) chR4. Terrestrial, Satellite, and Internet bdc-sts for Global and Domestic market, giving regional and national news features.

PRIVATE STATIONS:
More than 80 local st's are operating incl. 8 st's in Bucharest are as follows:
Antena 1, Bd. Ficusului 44A, sector 1, Bucharest. ☎ +40 (1) 2303202/2301184. Fax +40 (1) 2327707. **Email:** office@antenal.ro. **Web:** www.antenal.ro
L.P: DG: F. Bratescu.
D.Pgr: 0000-2359, ch57. Terrestrial, Satellite, and Internet Bdcsts in Romanian.

Canal 31, 155 Piata Victorei Di, 7th Floor, 70411 Bucharest. ☎ +40 (1) 210 6628 **L.P:** DG: Adrian Sirlon.

Canalul de Stiri, Calea Victorei 133-5, s 1, Bucharest. ☎ +40 (1) 312 4348. Fax +40 (1) 312 0349.

Pro TV, Bd. Pache Protopopescu 109, Bucharest. ☎ +40 (1) 250 1430/250 1401. Fax +40 (1) 312 4218 **Email:** doinita@protv.ro. **Web:** www.protv.ro **D.Prgr:** 2300-2259, ch31. Terrestrial bdcsts of mainly news and issues of the day/week in Romanian language. A second service of Pro TV International exists as a distict satellite service

Tele 7 ABC, Calea Victoriei 155, Sector 1,Bucharest. ☎ +40 (1) 650 1339 Fax +40 (1) 611 6576 **L.P:** DG: Mihai Tatulia.

Tele America, Blvd. Armata Poporului 1-3, s6, Bucharest. ☎ +40 (1) 311 0419. 🖷 +40 (1) 311 0417.

Tele Europa Nova, Dr. Lister 6, s5, Bucharest. ☎ +40 (1) 623 6661. 🖷 40 (1) 312 1324.

TV Sigma, Armata Poporului Blvd. 1, complex LeuFacultatea de Electronic Crp A, Et 8, Bucharest. ☎ +40 (1) 631 4734 **L.P:** MD: Constantin Crbu.

RUSSIA

Colour: SECAM — **Systems:** D & K.

PERVYY KANAL (Gov)
✉ ul. Ak. Korolyova 12, 127000 Moskva. ☎ +7 095 2179838. 🖷 +7 095 2151976. **Email:** dip@1tv.ru **Web:** www.1tv.ru
L.P: Dir: Konstantin Ernst.

KANAL ROSSIYA (Gov)
✉ ul. Shabolovka 37, 115162 Moskva. ☎ +7 095 2348600. 🖷 +7 095 2142347. **Email:** ivanovavi@rtr-tv.ru **Web:** www.rutv.ru **L.P:** Chmn: Oleg Dobrodeyev.

KANAL KULTURA (Gov)
✉ ul. Malaya Nikitskaya 24 , 123995 Moskva. ☎ +7 095 2900421. 🖷 +7 095 2900421. **Email:** kultura@tvkultura.ru **Web:** www.tvkultura.ru **L.P:** DG: Tatyana Paykhova.

NTV (Comm)
✉ ul. Ak. Korolyova 12, 127000 Moskva. ☎ +7 095 2177895. 🖷 +7 095 2175103. **Email:** info@ntv-tv.ru **Web:** www.ntv-tv.ru
L.P: Dir: Nikolay Senkevich

TV TSENTR (Comm)
✉ ul. Bolshaya Tatarskaya 33-1, 115184 Moskva. ☎ +7 095 9593900. **Email:** press@tvc.ru **Web:** www.tvc.ru
L.P: DG: Oleg M. Poptsov.

REN-TV (Comm)
✉ Zubovskiy bul. 17-1, 119847 Moskva. ☎ +7 095 2465933. 🖷 +7 095 2460655. **Email:** press@rentv.dol.ru **Web:** www.ren-tv.ru
L.P: GD: Boris I. Mints

TNT (Comm)
✉ ul. Trifonovskaya 57-3, 129272 Moskva. ☎ +7 095 2178188. 🖷 +7 095 7481490. **Email:** tht@tht.ru **Web:** www.tht.ru
L.P: GM: Andrey V. Skutin.

STS (Comm)
✉ ul. 3-ya Khoroshevskaya 12, 123298 Moskva. ☎ +7 095 7974126. 🖷 +7 095 7974101. **Email:** ctc@ctc-tv.ru **Web:** www.ctc-tv.ru
L.P: DG: Roman E. Petrenko.

DARYAL TV (Comm)
✉ ul. Ak. Korolyova 4/4, 129515 Moskva. ☎ +7 095 7893818. 🖷 +7 095 7893824. **Email:** sales@dtv.ru **Web:** www.dtv.ru
L.P: DG: Mart Luik.

MTV-RUSSIA (Comm)
✉ Perviy Shipkovskiy pereulok 1-1, 115093 Moskva. ☎ +7 095 7893818. 🖷 +7 095 7893824. **Email:** sales@dtv.ru **Web:** www.dtv.ru
L.P: DG: Mart Luik.

RWANDA

Colour: SECAM — **System:** K1

RWANDAISE RADIO & TV (Gov.)
✉ B.P. 83, Kigali. ☎ +250 77519. 🖷 +250 77520.
L.P: Dir: Aiyoko Augustin

TELE 10 (Comm.)
✉ B.P. 4307, Kigali. ☎ +250 86531
L.P: CEO: Eugene Nyagahene

SAMOA

Colour: PAL — **System:** B.

TELEVISE SAMOA CORPORATION
✉ P.O. Box 3691, Apia. ☎ + 685 26641. 🖷 +685 24789.**Email:** ceotvsamoa@samoa.ws
L.P: CEO: Ms Faiesea Lei Sam-Matafeo
Stations: Apia ch11 10W; Mount Vaea ch8 50W; Faleasiu ch10 10W; Mount Aflau ch4 50W, Mount Fiamoe ch6 10W; Api Park ch5 5W
D.Prgr: 0600-0000 Local prgrs plus BBC World, TVNZ..

SAMOA (American)

Colour: NTSC — **System:** M.

KVZK-TV (Gov)
✉ Office of Public Information, PO Box 3511, Pago Pago 96799
☎ + 684 6334191. 🖷 +684 6331044
L.P: Dir: Vaoita Sava. Dir. Tec: Robert Blauvelt.
Stations: chA2/A4/A5 (72kW).
D.Prgr: ch2 & 5: 1830-1000; ch4: 1830-1100.

SAN MARINO

Colour: PAL — **Systems**: B&G

SAN MARINO RTV (Gov.)
✉ Viale J.F.Kennedy 13, RSM-47890, Rep. San Marino.
☎ +378 549 882000. 🖷 +378 549 882840
L.P: DG: Raviele Gianni
Station: ch51 10kW.

SÃO TOMÉ E PRINCÍPE

Colour: PAL — **System:** B & G.

TELEVISÃO DE SÃO TOMÉ E PRINCÍPE
✉ P.O. Box 393, S. Tomé, Republica de S. Tomé e Princípe, Africa.
☎ +239 (12) 21041/22970 🖷 +239 (12) 21942.
L.P: Dir: Carlos Teixeira d'Alva
Stations: One 2kW transmitter in S. Tomé and one 10W transmitter in Principe covering 80% of the area. Channels: 11, 7, 5.
D.Prgr: RTP Internaçional is also relayed.

SAUDI ARABIA

Colour: SECAM — **System:** G

SAUDI ARABIAN TELEVISION (Gov)
✉ P.O. Box 570, Riyadh 11421 ☎ +966 1 4014440. 🖷 +966 1 4044192/4054176
L.P: Sulaiman Al-Samnan, Director of Frequency Management, Ministry of Information.
Ch1: (Arabic): Sat-Wed 0700-0930, 1400-2130; Thurs/Fri: 0700-2130.
Ch2: (English): 1400-2130 (Thurs/Fri also 0600-0900)

SENEGAL

Colour: SECAM — **System:** K

Radiodiffusion Télévision Sénégalaise (RTS) (Gov)
✉ B.P. 1765, Dakar. ☎ +221 949 1212. 🖷 +221 223490.
L.P: DG: Guila Thiam. Dir. of TV Sces: Babacar Diagne. Dir. of Tech. Sces: Seydou Diallo. Head of Ext. Affairs: Ka Aissatou. Dir. Comm. and External Affairs: Mouhamed Faye
Station: Dakar ch7 10kW
D.Prgr: 1200-2400 (Sat-Sun 1000-0100)

CANAL HORIZONS Sénégal (Pay TV Sce)
✉ 31 ave. Albert Sarraut (B.P. 1390), Dakar. ☎ +221 232525. 🖷 221 233030.
L.P: Pres: Fara N'Diaye. DG: Jacques Barbier de Crozes. Dep. DG: Anne Marie Senghor. Tech. Coordinator: Issa Laye Diop.

SERBIA & MONTENEGRO

Colour: PAL—**System:** B&G.

UDRUZENJE RADIOTELEVIZIJE SRBIJE I CRNE GORE d.O.O.

✉ Permanent Services. Television Department: Beogradska 70, 11000 Beograd. ☎ +381 11 433718 Fax +381 11 434023. **Email:** yrtcoord@eunet.yu – **Televizija Srbije-Televizija Beograd:** Takovska 10, 11000 Beograd. ☎ +381 11 3212000. **Email:** irena@rts.co.yu – **Televizija Vojvodine-Televizija Novi Sad:** Kamenicki put 45, 21000 Novi Sad. ☎ +381 21 56855 – **Televizija Crne Gore:** Cetinski put bb, 81000 Podgorica. ☎ +381 81 41529. **Stations** (System B) (ch2-12), System G (ch21-69)

SERBIA

TV Srbije-TV Beograd Prgrs 1, 2, 3
Kopaonik: ch3(**1**)/4(**2**), 50/1000kW. Jastrebac: ch5/27/33, 100/1000/1000kW. Avala: ch6/22/28, 100/1000/30kW. Deli Jovan: ch6/23/43, 10/50/100kW. Tornik: ch7/53/59, 1/50/50kW. Besna Kobila: ch8/49/59, 10/300/300kW. Ovcar: ch8/42/56, 10/400/10kW. Maljen: ch9/26/32, 5/2.5/250kW. Crveni Cot: ch10/24/30, 100/1000/1000kW. Tupiznica: ch10/25/31, 35/500/500kW. Crni Vrh: ch11/35/38, 35/500/500kW. Cer: ch7/37/34, 3/300/300kW
TV Srbije-TV Novi Sad Prgrs 1, 2, 3
Subotica: ch5(**1**)/43(**2**), 35/1000kW. Venac: ch41(**1**)/48(**3**), 1000/1000kW. Vrsac: ch39(**1**)/56(**2**), 1000/1000kW
BK Television (Priv/Comm)
✉ Bulevar Nikole Tesle 42a, Beograd. ☎ +381 11 319 3752. 🖷 +381 11 319 3706/319 3135. **Email:** info@bktv.com. **Web:** www.bktv.com. **D.Prgr:** 24hr (VHF) ch12, (UHF) ch61.

Kosovo (UN Mandate)
Radio Televizione Kosovës-RTK: ✉ Mother Teresa bb, 38000 Pristina. ☎ +381 38 231211, fax +381 38 249074 Web: www.rtk-live.com **L.P:** Dir: Lridon Cahani. ch23/9/12/7
RTV21 (comm): Media House, 38000 Pristina. ch37/24/55/48

MONTENEGRO

TV Crne Gore Prgrs 1, 2, 3, 4: Bjelasica: ch6/12/37/(62/43), 100/100/1/500/1kW. Sudjina Glava: ch12/6/24/39, 5/5/15/15kW. Sjenica: ch6/33/23/(25/29), 1.5/15/15/15kW. Lustica: ch4/26/33/(39/42), 1/10/10/10kW. Lov´cen: ch8/31/10/(35/67), 100/1000/20/1000/500kW. Volujica: ch6/12/24/38, 1/1/10/10kW. Muzura: ch12/23/33/(43/53), 1/10/10/10/10kW.

SEYCHELLES

Colour: PAL — **System:** B.

SEYCHELLES BROADCASTING CORPORATION

✉ P.O. Box 321, Hermitage, Mahe. ☎ +248 224161. 🖷 +248 225641 **Email:** sbcradtv@seychelles.sc
L.P: MD: Ibrahim Afif. Chief Editor (TV): Ms. Marie-Claire Elizabeth.
Stations: La Misère chE2 1kW, St. Louis chE7 6kW + 9 low power repeaters.
D.Prgr: Mon-Fri 1345-1830, Sat 1200-1830, Sun 1000-1830

SIERRA LEONE

Colour: PAL — **System:** B.

SIERRA LEONE BROADCASTING SERVICE (Gov. Comm)

✉ Private Mailbag, Freetown. ☎ + 232 (22) 40403/40906. **Email:** slbs@sierratel.sl
L.P: DG: Mrs Gina Banda-Thomas; Sen Eng. (TV): Steve Konteh
Station: chE2 1kW H, chE7 126kW H.
D.Prgr: 1745-2330.

SINGAPORE

Colour: PAL— **System:** B.

MEDIACORP TV SINGAPORE LTD

✉ Caldecott Broadcast Centre, Andrew Rd. Singapore, 299939. ☎ +65 633 33888. 🖷 +65 625 38119. **Web:** mediacorptv.com
L.P: CEO: Mdm Chua Foo Yong.
Stations:
Singapore's largest broadcaster, operating 5 free-to-air channels:
ch5 (in English) entertainment 24h
ch8 (in Chinese) entertainment 24h
Suria (in Malay) information and entertainment
Central (ch12) children's, arts, Indian prgrs
TV Mobile digital

SPH MEDIAWORKS (Singapore Press Holdings)

✉ 82 Genting Lane News, Centre Singapore 349567. ☎ +65 6319 7988. 🖷 +656744 3318. **Web:** www.sphmediaworks.com.
Stations: operates 2 networks:
Channel U: ch E28 in Chinese; Channel i: ch E30 in English.

SLOVAKIA

Colour: PAL, SECAM — **Systems** B/G, D/K

SLOVENSKÁ TELEVÍZIA

✉ Mlýnská Dolina 28, Bratislava 845 45. ☎ +42 (7) 723001. 🖷 +42 (7) 729 440.
L.P: DG: Jozef Darmo. PD: Milan Polak. Int. Rel: Mikulas Gavala.
D.Prgr: ST1 (PAL) Mon-Fri 0900-1200, 1600-2330, Sat 0830-0045, Sun 0825-2400;
ST2 (SECAM privatized).

MARKÍZA TV (Comm)

✉ Drobneho 27, 841 01 Bratislava. ☎ +42 (2) 68274103. 🖷 +42 (2) 5249 5744 **Web**: markiza.sk
L.P: CEO: Pavol Rusko.

SLOVENIA

Colour: PAL — **Systems:** B & H

TELEVIZIJA SLOVENIJA

✉ Kolodvorska 2-4, 60111 Ljubljana. ☎ +38 (61) 131 1333. 🖷 +38 (61) 131 9171. **Web:** www.rtvs.si
L.P: DG: Zarko Petan. PD (TV): Janez Lombergar. Int. Rel: Boris Bergant.
Prgr. 1: Mon-Fri 0750-2215 (Thu 2300, Fri 2330), Sat 0700-1115, 1330-2345, Sun 0725-2230.
Prgr. 2: Mon-Fri 1430-2300, Sat 1530-0030, Sun 0900-2300.

TV KOPER-CAPODISTRIA

✉ Ulica OF 12, Koper 6000, ☎ +386 (66) 48505 **Web:** www.rtvslo.si/html/ccenter-koper
D.Prgr: ch27 and ch58. Mon-Fri 1245-2400, Sat 0900-2400, Sun 0930-2400.

PRIVATE STATIONS

KANAL A

✉ Tivolska 50 pp 44, 61101 Ljubljana. ☎ +386 (61) 133 4133. 🖷 +386 (61) 133 4222 **Email:** television@kanal-a.si
L.P: Pres: Douglas Fulton

MMTV

✉ Zorgova 70, 61231 Ljubljana. ☎ +386 (61) 161 2525. 🖷 +386 (61) 374 554.
L.P: Pres: Marjan Meglic. PD: Andrej Meglic. CE: Tomislav Kalan.

POP TV

✉ Kranjceva 26, SI-1521 Ljubljana. ☎ +386 (1) 589 3313 🖷 +386 (1) 534 1118 **Email:** info@pop-tv.si
L.P: Gen. Dir: Marjan Jurenec.

SOMALIA

Colour: PAL — **System:** B.

MINISTRY OF INFORMATION

✉ P.O. Box 1748.
L.P: Dir. of TV project: A. Ali Askar. Dir. Tec: A. Hassan.
Station: ch6 1kW.
D.Prgrs: 1700-2000 (Fri 2100).

SOUTH AFRICA

Colour: PAL — **System:** I.

SENTECH (PTY) LTD.

Private Bag X06, Honeydew 2040. ☎ +27 (11) 471 4400. Fax +27 (11) 471 4653. **Web:** www.sentech.co.za
L.P: Chief Exec.Officer: Dr Sebilesto Mokone-Matabane. Chief Operations Officer: Gladwyn Marumo. Chief Financial Officer: Giel Naude.
Sentech is responsible for the signal distribution of all radio and TV services in South Africa.

SOUTH AFRICAN BROADCASTING CORPORATION (SABC)

(Head Office): Broadcasting Centre, Auckland Park, Johannesburg 2092/Private Bag XI, Auckland Park 2006. ☎ +27 (11) 714 9111. Fax +27 (11) 714 3106. **Web:** www.sabc.co.za
L.P: Chmn (Board): Dr Vincent Maphai. Group Chief Exec: Peter Matlare Chief Exec. (Operations): Solly Mokoetle. Head TV News: Jimi Matthews.
CCIR System 1 (PAL colour) used on bands III/IV/V using ch4-13 (174-254MHz) and 21-68 (470-845MHz), chs 12/38 not used. Sound/Vision spacing is + 6MHz.
Stations:
SABC-1 D.Prgr: 0400-0615 (Mon-Fri), 1300 (Sat 0400, Sun 1130)-2200 (Sat 2230). **SABC-2**, **SABC-3 D.Prgrs:** broadcasts in various languages. SABC-1, SABC-2, SABC-3 and **Bop TV** operate on terrestrial and satellite platforms.
Africa2Africa and **SABC Africa News** operate on satellite.

M-NET TELEVISION (Pay channel, Comm, Priv)

P.O. Box 4950, Randburg 2125. ☎ +27 (11)329 5156. Fax +27 (11) 329 5166
L.P: PD: Sheryl Raine. Mktg. Dir: Etienne Heyns. Head of PR: John Badenhorst.
Stations: Bloemfontein ch6 (H), Alverstone & Pt. Elizabeth ch10 (H), Constantiaberg ch11 (V), Pretoria ch21 (H), Johannesburg ch39 (H) + 16 repeaters, Durban ch10, Cape Town ch11, George ch7, Newcastle ch62.
D.Prgr: Mon-Fri 0830-1030 & 1300-2300; Sat/Sun 0500-2300. **Indian Prgr:** Sun 0530-0830. **Portuguese Prgr:** Sun 0830-1130.
M-Net and **CSN (Community Services Network)** are terrestrial pay channels distributed on networks operated by Sentech (Pty) Ltd.

E-TV (Comm.)

☎ +27 (21) 481 4500.
L.P: Chief Exec. Marcel Golding.
Distributed on an extensive transmitter network operated by Sentech (Pty) Ltd.

SPAIN

Colour: PAL — **Systems:** B & G.

RADIOTELEVISION ESPAÑOLA (RTVE) (Gov)

Prado del Rey, 280023 Madrid. Torrespaña C/ O'Donnell 77, 28007 Madrid ☎ +34 (1) 346 875. Fax +34 (1) 581 7125 **Web:** www.rtve.es/rtve/
L.P: Dir. Gen: Jordi Garcia Candau. Ex.Dir.TVE, S.A: Ramón Colom Esmatges. Dir. of Int. Coop: Alfonso Callego. TD: Francisco Baquedano. Film Buyer: Fernando Moreno.
Stations: (System B & G): Powers = ERP. Audio powers 10% of vision powers indicated.

N.B: TVE's 1st. and 2nd. prgr. are also relayed via satellite. The 1st. prgr is relayed under the name TVE Internacional.
TVE 1st Prgr. 0800-0230 (24 H. at weekends).
TVE 2nd Prgr. 0800-0200.

TV Networks in autonomous areas:

TELEVISIO DE CATALUNYA (Aut)

Televisió de Catalunya, S.A. (TV3 and Canal 33) Jacint Verdaguer, s/n 08970- Sant Joan Despí, Catalunya. ☎ +34 (9) 3 499 9333. Fax +34 (9) 3 473 1964
L.P: Dir: Jaume Ferrús i Estopa. T.D: Pere Vila. Film Buyer: Jaume Santacana.
D.Prgr: TV3 1115-0030, Canal 33 1900-2400.

TV DE GALICIA (TVG)

Apt. 707, San Marcos (Santiago de Compostela). ☎ +34 (981) 560640. Fax +34 (981) 560629. **Email:** crtvg@crtvg.es.
L.P: Dir: Anxo Quintanilla Louzao.
Station: ch 42. In Galician: 1200 (Sun 1030)-2300 (approx).

TELEVISIO VALENCIANA (Gov) CANAL 9

46100 Burjassot, Valencia. ☎ +34 (6) 364 1100. Fax +34 (6) 363 9516.
L.P: GM: Amaden Fabregat-Manes. MD: Rafael Cano-Baron.

TV VASCA-EUSKAL TELEBISTA (Gov)

Barria Lurreta, 48200 Durango (Vizcaya). ☎ +34 (94) 6816600. Fax +34 (94) 6816526. Telex 34441.
L.P: Dir: Koldo Anasagasti.
Stations: ch 42 (ETB-1) & ch 49 (ETB-2) +160 low power st's.
D.Prgr: ETB-1 1400-2000 – ETB-2 1430-2100.

COMMERCIAL STATIONS:

ANTENA TELEVISION (Antena 3)

Carretera San Sebastian de los Reyes, 28700 Madrid ☎ +34 (1) 6320500. Fax +34 (1) 6327144
L.P: Pres: Javier de Godó; G.M: Manuel Martín Ferrand; Film Buyer: Condorcet da Silva Costa.

Projected Autonomous Networks:
Radiotelevision Madrid, Radiotelevision Navarra, TV Andalucia, TV Cantabria & TV Valenciana.

TELEVISION MURCIANA

Plateraa 44, 230001 Murcia
☎ +34 (68) 212 224. Fax +34 (68) 214 673

SRI LANKA

Colour: PAL — **System:** B.

INDEPENDENT TELEVISION NETWORK (ITN)

Wickramasinghepura, Battaramulla. ☎ +94 (1) 864591. Fax +94 (1) 864595. **Email:** itnch@slt.lk **Web:** itnsl.lk
L.P: Chairm: Mr Newton Gunaratne; DE: Mr W.S.E. Fernando
Station: Wickramasinghepura: Yatiyantota ch12 100kW (ERP), Deniyaya ch9 20kW (ERP), Nayabedde ch12 3kW (ERP).
D.Prgr: 1800-2300 (approx), 0900-2300 (w/ends).

SRI LANKA RUPAVAHINI CORPORATION (SLRC)

P.O. Box 2204, Colombo 7. ☎ +94 (1) 580136. Fax +94 (1) 580929.
Cable: Rupavahini.
L.P: DG: Mr. Laxman Perera. Dep. DG (Prgrs):Mr. Sugath Watagedera. Dep. DG (Comm): Ms. Kamala Senaweera. Dep. DG (Eng): Mr. Amal Punchihewa.
Stations: Pidurutalagala ch5 20kW, Kokavil ch8 20 kW, Sooriyakanda ch11 200W +6 other low power repeaters.
D.Prgrs: 0600-0100.

TELSHAN NETWORK (PVT) Ltd. (TNL TV)

Innagale Estate Dampe-Piliyandala. ☎ +94 (1) 575436 430 859 Fax +94 (1) 575436,574 962
L.P: Chairm MD: Mr. Shantilal Nilkant Wickremesinghe
Stations: Colombo ch 21 22kW; Piliyandala ch 26 22kW, ch 3 20kW; Nuweraeliya ch 4 40kW; Polgahawela ch 3 1kW; Ratnapura ch 26 1kW; Hantana (Kandy) ch21 22kW.

EAP NETWORK (PVT) LTD.

676 Galle Rd, Colombo 3. ☎ +94 (1) 503819 (9 lines). Fax +94 (1) 503788. **Email:** eapnet@slt.lk
L.P: Chairperson: Mrs. Soma Edirisinghe. MD: Jeevaka Edirisinghe. Dir/GM: Rosmand Senaratne.
D.Prgr: 24h. ETV1 rel. Sky News. ETV2 rel. Star TV.

MTV CHANNEL (PVT) LTD.

7, Braybrook Pl., Colombo 2. ☎ +94 (1) 75 340111 Fax +94 (1) 340116 **Web:** www.yesfmonline.com
L.P: Tech Dir: Nimal P. Gooneratne
Stations: Depanama ch23 1kW, Nuwaraeliya ch25 1kW.
D.Prgr: 24h. Rel. BBC World + local prgrs 1130-1700

ST KITTS & NEVIS

Colour: NTSC — **System:** M.

ZIZ TELEVISION (Gov, Comm)
P.O. Box 331, Basseterre, St. Kitts. ☎ +1 (869) 465 2621. 🖷 +1 (869) 465-5624. **Email:** zbc@thecable.net
L.P: GM: Mr. Linkon Maynard; TV Prod Mngr: Barry Thomas
Stations: Basseterre chA5 20/5kW H. + 3 repeaters.
D.Prgr: 2000-0430.

ST LUCIA

Colour: NTSC — **System:** M.

HELEN TV (Comm)
P.O. Box 621, Le Morne Castries.
☎ +1 (758) 4522 693. 🖷 +1 (758) 454 1737.
L.P: MD: Linford Fevrier. CE: Stephenson Anius.
Station: ch's 4 & 11.

CABLEVISION
George Gordon Bld., Bridge Str. Castries, St. Lucia. P.O. Box 111, Castries. ☎ (758) 452 3301. 🖷 +1 (758) 453 2544.
Station: ch's 16 on CATV.

ST PIERRE ET MIQUELON

Colour: SECAM — **System:** K.

SOCIETE NATIONALE DE RADIO TÉLÉVISION FRANÇAISE D'OUTRE MER (RFO)
BP 4227, F-97500 St. Pierre et Miquelon. ☎ +508 411111. 🖷 +508 412219
L.P: Dir: Joseph Eden.
Stations (Pol H)
1st Prgr: St. Pierre chK4 0.1kW, chK8 0.5kW, chK39 5W – Miquelon chK6 0.1kW.
2nd Prgr: St. Pierre chK31 0.5kW, chK55 0.05kW – Miquelon chK56 0.2kW.
D.Prgr: 1st Prgr: 1800 (SS 1500)-0400. **2nd Prgr:** 2115-0330

ST VINCENT

Colour: NTSC — **System:** M.

ST. VINCENT & THE GRENADINES BROADCASTING CORPORATION Ltd.
P.O. Box 617, Kingstown. ☎ +1 (809)-4561078. 🖷 +1 (809) 4561015.
Web: www.nbcsvg.com **Email:** svgbc@caribsurf.com
L.P: Gen. Mngr: Corlita Ollivierre.
Station: ch9. Relay sts. ch's 7, 11, 13 varying between 5-30 W. 1500-0900.
Coverage area: St. Vincent, Grenadines, St. Lucia & Grenada.

SUDAN

Colour: PAL — **System:** B.

SUDAN TELEVISION (Gov, Comm)
P.O. Box 1094, Omdurman. ☎ +249 (11) 55022.
L.P: Head of Directorate: Hadid al-Sira.
Stations: Omdurman chE5 5kW H, Gezira chE7 10kW, Atbara chE9 0.5kW.
D.Prgr: 1500-2200.

SURINAME

Colour: NTSC — **System:** M.

SURINAAMSE TELEVISIE STICHTING (STVS) (Gov./Comm)
P.O. Box 535, Paramaribo. Letita Vriesdelaan 5. ☎ +597 473032/473021. 🖷 +597 477216. **Email:** stvs@sr.net.
L.P: K. Moerli.
Stations: Wageningen ch7 0.10kW, Paramaribo ch8 1kW, Moango ch9 0.01kW, Caranis ch10 0.10kW, Nickerie ch11 1kW.
D.Prgr: 2130-0300 (+ Sat 1500-2130, Sun 1400-1700).

ALGEMONE TELEVISIE VERZORGING (ATV) (Comm)
P.O. Box 1839, v't hogerhuysstraat, Paramaribo. ☎ +597 404661, +597 474242. 🖷 +597 402660. **Email:** cooman@sr.net.
L.P: G. Cooman.
Stations: Para ch2 1kW, Wageningen ch6 0.25kW, Caranis ch12 0.4kW, Nickerie ch13 0.5kW.
D.Prgr: 1115-0320

AMPiES BROADCASTING CORPORATION (Comm)
P.O. Box 885, Maystraat 57, Paramaribo. ☎ +597 465092/499166. 🖷 +597 464680. **Email:** info@abcsuriname.com
L.P: H. Kamperveen.
Stations: Paramaribo ch4 1kW.

RADIO APINTI (Comm)
P.O. Box 595, Veriengde Gemenetandsweg 37, Paramaribo. ☎ +597 400455/400450. 🖷 +597 400684. **Email:** apinti@sr.net
L.P: Ch Vervuurt.
Stations: Paramaribo ch10 1kW.

RAPAR BROADCASTING NETWORK n.v. (Comm)
P.O. Box 975, Veriengde Coppenarnestraat 34, Paramaribo. ☎ +597 499895/497772/498881. 🖷 +597 493121.
L.P: M.R. Pierkhan.
Stations: Paramaribo ch5 2kW.

RASONIC
Bataviastraat 2, Nickerie. ☎ +597 (023) 1447. 🖷 +597 (023) 2534.
L.P: P. Sookha.
Stations: Nickerie ch7 1kW.

RADIKA n.v.
P.O. Box 1083, Indira Gandhiweg 165, Paramaribo. ☎ +597 482800/482910. 🖷 +597 481868.
L.P: n/a.
Stations: Paramaribo ch14 1kW.

SWAZILAND

Colour: PAL — **Systems:** B & G.

SWAZILAND TELEVISION AUTHORITY
Swazi TV, P.O. Box A146, Swazi Plaza, Mbabane. ☎ +268 43036/7. 🖷 +268 42093.
L.P: MD: Dan S. Lamini.
Stations: Bulembu ch5 1.5kW H, Ntondozi ch15 15kW H + 7 relay st's.
D.Prgr. in English: 1600-2100, (VHF) ch4, ch9, (UHF) ch21. Multilingual bdcsts (Siswati and English). After closedown (2305 variable) station rlys two South Africal popular music channels: Channel O, and MCM Africa.

SWEDEN

Colour: PAL — **Systems:** B & G.

TERACOM
This company has the responsibility for the distribution of the prgrs produced by Sveriges Television AB and TV4 AB.
HQ: Medborgarplatsen 3, Stockholm (Box 17666, S-118 92 Stockholm). ☎ +46 (8) 671200. 🖷 +46 (8) 671 2000.
L.P: Pres. & CEO: Valdemar Persson.

SVERIGES TELEVISION AB (Non-Comm)
Oxenstiernsgatan 26-34, SE-105 10 Stockholm. **Postal** S-105 10 Stockholm. ☎ +46 (8) 784 0000 🖷 +46 (8) 784 1500. **Web:** www.svt.se
L.P: Chmn. Allan Larsson. Head SVT Tech Resources: Sven Bohlin.
Stations: SVT1, SVT2

TV4 AB (Comm)
Tegeluddsvägen 3, S-115 79 Stockholm. ☎ +46 (8) 459 4000 🖷 +46 (8) 459 4444 **Web:** www.tv4.se
L.P: MD: Torbjörn Larsson; Hd. of Inf.: Helena Dryssen; Hd. of Prgrs: Jan Scherman; Hd. of News: Sven Irving; Hd. of Eng: Anders Ahl. Hd. of Sales: Gunnar Sjögren.

FINNISH TELEVISION RELAY
Stockholm (Nacka) ch39 1000kW(ERP). Pol H.
Relay of Finnish Prgr II: Mon-Fri 1530-2115, Sat 1200-2200, Sun 1200-2115.
+ 2 lp st.

SWITZERLAND

Colour: PAL — **Systems:** B & G.

SBC—SWISS BROADCASTING CORPORATION
The SBC's Television programme services are an integral part of the Swiss Broadcasting Corporation.
SBC, Giacomettistrasse 3, CH-3000 Berne 15. ☎ +41 (31) 3509111. +41 (31) 3509256.
L.P: Pres. SRG: Eric Lehmann. DG: Armin Walpen. Secr. Gen & Dir. Legal Dept: Beat Durrer. Dir. Finance: François Landgraf. Dir. Eng: Hans Strassmann. Dir. Human Resources: Edi Koch. Television Affairs: Tiziana Mona. Radio Affairs: Félix Bollmann. Dir. Communication & Marketing and Press Officer: RJosefa Haas.
Prgr. Sce. in German: TV Dir: Peter Schellenberg, Schweizer Fernsehen DRS, Fernsehstrasse 1-4, 8052 Zürich. ☎ +41 (1) 305 6611. +41 (1) 305 5660.**Web:** www.srg-ssr.ch/srg/
Prgr. Sce. in French: TV Dir: Guillaume Chenevière, Télévision suisse romande, TSR, 20 Quai Ernest Ansermet. B.P. 234, 1211 Geneva 8. ☎ +41 (22) 708 9911. +41 (22) 7811908. TV Prgr. Dir:Raimond Vouillamoz. **Web:** www.tsr.ch
Prgr. Sce. in Italian: RTSI, Radiotelevisione Svizzera di lingua italiana, Via Canevascini, P.O. Box 6903, Lugano.Reg. Dir: M. Blaser, TV Prgr Dir: D. Balestra. ☎ +41 (91) 58 5111. +41 (91) 589150. Studio Televisione, Casella postale, CH-6949 Comano. ☎ +41 (91) 585111. +41 (91) 585355.
Web: www.rtsi.ch/

SCHWEIZ 4/SUISSE 4/SVIZZERA 4 (Pub)
Giacomettistrasse 1. CH-3000 Bern 15, Switzerland. ☎ +41 (31) 350 9444. +41 (31) 350 9725.
L.P: Dir: Dario Rabbiani
D.Prgr: National multi-lingual TV channel in cooperation with private program producers.
Prgrs as follows:

Schweizer Fernsehen DRS:	DRS1, TSR2, TSI2
Télévision Suisse romande:	TSR1, DRS2, TSI1
Televisione Svizzera italiana:	TSI1, DRS3, TSR3
Schweiz 4:	DRS4, TSR4, TSI4

SYRIA

Colour: PAL — **System:** B.

SYRIAN ARAB TELEVISION (Gov)
Ommayyad Square, Damascus. ☎ +963 (11) 720700. +963 (11) 720700.
L.P: DG: Khudr Omran. Dir. Eng: M. Bara. Dir. PR: Mrs. Awafet Haffar.
Prgr 1: 1100 (Fri 0700)-2130.
Prgr 2 in Arabic/English/French: 1700-2130

TAIWAN (Rep. of China)

Colour: NTSC — **System:** M.

CHINA TELEVISION COMPANY- CTV (Comm)
No. 120 Chung-Yang Road, Nankang District, Taipei. ☎ +886 (2) 783 8308. +886 (2) 782 6007.
L.P: Pres: Hu Ping Chung. CE: Mr. Chen.
Stations: BEF21 chA9 180/40kW (No. Taiwan), BEF22 chA10 150/17kW (Ce. Taiwan), BEF23 chA9 180/80/20kW (So. Taiwan).
D.Prgr: W 0400-0500, 0930-1515; Sat 0450-1615; Sun 0250-1515.

CHINESE TELEVISION SERVICE- CTS (Comm)
100 Kuang Fu South Road, Taipei. ☎ +886 (2) 751 0321. +886 (2) 751 6019.
L.P: Chmn: Chicn Chiu Yee. Pres: Shih-shung Wu. CE: Shiao Ho Whu.
D.Prgr: W 2320-0120, 0340-1600; Sun 2320-1600.

EDUCATIONAL TV
D.Prgr: W 1030-1435, Sun 1130-1505.

TAIWAN TELEVISION ENTERPRISE - TTV (Comm)
No. 10, Pa Te Rd, Section 3, Taipei 10560. ☎ +886 (2) 7711515. +886 (2) 7413626.
L.P: Chmn: Ching-Teh Hsu. Pres: Walter C.H. Wang. Executive vice president: Wei-Yung Lee. Vice president: Hsiang-chuan Hsiung. Vice president: Shen-Wen Lee. Manager, Engineering Department: To-Hui Yang. Manager, Business Department: Wen-Lung Liu. Film buyer: Nancy Hu. Manager, News Department: Victor S.T. Chang. Manager, Sports Department: Jason Liao. Manager, Program Department: Sheng Chu-yu. Dir. Inf. Center: Ko-Jan Hwang.
D.Prgr: Mon-Fri 2159-0030, 0311-0810, 0839-1610; Sat 0244-1740; Sun 2339-1610.

TAJIKISTAN

Colour: SECAM — **Systems:** D & K

TAJIK TELEVISION (Gov)
Bekhzod Str. 7, 734013 Dushanbe. ☎ +992 372 224357 +992 372 213459. **Email:** subkh@tajikistan.com

TANZANIA

Colour: PAL — **System:** B.

TELEVISION ZANZIBAR TVZ (Gov)
P.O. Box 314, Zanzibar. ☎ +255 (54) 32816/7.
L.P: MD: Jama A. Simba. TD: George H. Majaliwa. Film Buyer: Jaffar S. Kassingo; Prod. Mgr: Abdulhamid H. Dau.
Stations: Unguja chE21 40kW, Pemba chE9 40kW (ERP).
D.Prgr: 1645-1900 (Sat/Sun/National Holidays 1645-2000).

INDEPENDENT TELEVISION (ITV)
PO Box 4374, Dar es Salaam ☎ +255 (22) 277 5914 **Email:** itv@ipp.co.tz **Web:** www.ippmedia.com
L.P.: MD: Ms Joyce Mhaville
Stations: Dar es Salaam UHF ch24
D. Prgr:1400-1505/1700-1800 (weekdays), local prgr. Sundays and Tuesdays from 1600-1630

THAILAND

Colour: PAL — **Systems:** B&M.

TELEVISION OF THAILAND - TVT (Gov)
90-91 New Phetchaburi Road, Huay Khwang, Bangkok 10320. ☎ +66 (0) 2318 2110. +66 (0) 2318 2991.
Web: www.prd.go.th/tvthai.asp
Stations: Bangkok ch11 200kW (ERP) + 21 relay st's.
D.Prgrs: 0930-1400.

BANGKOK ENTERTAINMENT CO. Ltd.
(Licensed through Mass Communications Organisation of Thailand).
Floors 7, 15, 16, The Emporium Tower, Sukhumvit Road, Khlong Tan, Khlong Toey, Bangkok 10110.☎ +66 (0) 2262 3333. +66 (0) 2204 1384-5. **Web:** www.tv3.co.th
L.P: Prgr. Dir: Pravit Maleenont. TD: Manoontham Thachai.
Stations: Bangkok ch3 650 kW + 32 relay st's not mentioned.
D.Prgr: Mon-Fri 1400-2400, SS 0800-2400.

MASS COMMUNICATIONS ORGANISATION. OF THAILAND - MCOT
63/1 Rama IX Road, Huay Khwang, Bangkok 10320. ☎ +66 (0) 2201 6346/6000/6310. +66 (0) 2245 1960. **Web:** www.mcot.or.th or www.thaitv9.tv
Stations: Bangkok ch9 20/4kW + 32 relay st's not mentioned.
D.Prgrs: 0850 (Sat/Sun 0025)-1700.

THE ARMY TELEVISION HSA-TV (Gov, Comm)
210 Phaholyothin Rd, Sanam Pao. Bangkok 10400.
☎ +66 (0) 2271 0060-9. +66 (0) 2271 2515. **Web:** www.tv5.co.th
L.P: DG: Maj. Gen. Vijit Junapart.
Stations: Bangkok ch5 20/4kW + 18 relay st's not mentioned.
D.Prgr: 0900 (Sat/Sun 0100)-1700.

BANGKOK BROADCASTING TELEVISION - BBTV (Comm)
P.O. Box 4-56, Bangkok 10900. ☎ +66 (0) 2272 0010. +66 (0) 2701976. **Web:** www.ch7.com.

L.P: St. Man: Chatchur Karnasuta. TD: Supoch Sangsayan.
Stations: Bangkok ch7 20kW + 22 relay st's not mentioned.
D.Prgr: 0900 (Sat/Sun 0100)-1700.

ITV (ITV Public Co Ltd)
Floors 12, 17, 21, 22, SCB Park Plaza East Tower 3, 19 Ratchadaphisek Road, Lat Yao, Chatchuchak, Bangok 10900. ☎ +66 (0) 2937 8080. **Web:** www.itv.co.th
Stations: Bangkok ch E29 1000 kW ERP + approx 45 relays on UHF

TOGO

Colour: SECAM — **System:** K

TÉLÉVISION TOGOLAISE (Gov)
B.P. 3286, Lomé. ☎ +228 215357. 🖷 +228 215786.
L.P: Dir. of TV: Yao Martin Ahiavee. Tech. Dir: Vokou Raphaël Soumsa. Film Buyer: Ayi Léopold Mamavi.
Stations: Mt. Agou ch6 10KW V, Lomé ch8 1kW H, Aldjo-Kadara ch8 10kW H + 2 relay st's.
D.Prgr: Mon-Fri 1830-2230, Sat/Sun 1230-2400.

TONGA

Colour: NTSC — **System:** M

TONGA BROADCASTING COMMISSION
PO Box 36, Nuku'alofa ☎ +676 (23) 295 555
Email: a3z-mgt@kalianet.to **L.P.:** Contrlr Prgrs: Mateaki Heimuli; Contrlr TV: Taulupe Aleamotu'a **Station:** 'Television Tonga'

ASTL-TV3 (Comm)
P.O. Box 66, Nuku'alofa. ☎ +676 22325. 🖷 +676 22811
L.P: Pres: Latu Tupouniua
Station: Nuku'alofa ch3 50W
D.Prgr: Mo-Sat 1800-2000 & 0300-1000; Sun 0400-0900.

OCEANIA BROADCASTING NETWORK LTD
P.O. Box 91, Nuku'alofa. ☎ +676 23314. 🖷 +676 23658

TRINIDAD & TOBAGO

Colour: NTSC — **System:** M.

NATIONAL BROADCASTING NETWORK LTD.
Television House. 11A Maraval Rd., P.O. Box 665, Port of Spain. ☎ +1 (809) 622-4141-4. 🖷 +1 (809) 622-0344. **Email:** nbnl@nbn.co.tt
L.P: CEO: John Barsotti; Chief Eng: Augustus Shannon
Stations: ch2 12/6kW, ch13 2/0.2kW , ch4, ch16.
D.Prgr: 0940-0400.

CARIBBEAN COMMUNICATIONS NETWORK -CCN
Express House, 35-37 Independence Sq, Port-of-Spain, Trinidad ☎ +1 (868) 627 8806 **Web:** www.trinidadexpress.com
L.P.: Chairm: Kenneth Gordon; Operations Mngr: Lennor Alcindor
Stations: CCN-TV6 on 3 channels: ch6, ch18, ch19

TUNISIA

Colour: SECAM — **System:** B & G.

ENTREPRISE DE LA RADIODIFFUSION-TÉLÉVISION TUNISIENNE E.R.T.T. (GOV)
71, Ave de la Liberté, 1002 Tunis Belvedere. ☎ +216 (1) 287300, 782700 . 🖷 +216 (1) 781058.
L.P: Dir: Abdeh Afidh Hardudm.

Network I (Arabic). **Network II:** (French) **D.Prgrs:** Netw.1600-2300.

TURKEY

Colour: PAL — **System:** B.

TURKISH RADIO TELEVISION CORPORATION
TRT-TV Department, TRT Sitesi A Blok 427 Oran, Ankara 06109. ☎ +90 312 4900379. 🖷 +90 312 4901109.
Email: genel.sekreterlik@trt.net.tr**Web:** www.trt.net.tr
L.P: Head of TV Dept: Nilgun Artun; Dir Ankara TV: Gürkan Elçy; Prod. Dir: Bengü Sertalp; Tech Dir: Sükrü Sipka.
TRT1 24 hrs. **TRT2:** M-F 1700-0100, SS 0930-0300(Sun 0100). **TRT3** Wed/Thu/Sat/Sun1340-2400, Mon/Tue/Fri 1700-0100. **TRT4** 1330-2400.

UNIVERSITE TECHNIQUE
Stations: Istanbul chE4, 0.5kW.

TURKMENISTAN

Colour: PAL — **Systems:** D & K

TURKMEN TELEVISION (Gov)
Mollanepes Str. 3, 744000 Asgabat. ☎ +993 12 351515. 🖷 +993 12 356850.
NOTES: provides 3 programmes - Altyn Asyr Türkmenistan, Miras and Yaslyk.

TURKS & CAICOS ISLANDS

Colour: NTSC— **System:** M

TURKS & CAICOS TELEVISION
P.O. Box 80, Pond Street, Grand Turk ☎ +649 946 4866 🖷 +649 946 4790 **Email:** wivcabletv@tciway.tc **L.P:** MD Peter Stubbs

TUVALU

Colour: PAL — **System:** B

THE TUVALU MEDIA CORPORATION
Private Mail Bag, Funafuti, Tuvalu
☎ +688 20139 🖷 +688 20732 **Email:** media@tuvalu.tv
L.P: CEO/General Manager Mrs Tia Taui

UGANDA

Colour: PAL — **System:** B (Pol=H).

UGANDA TELEVISION (Gov)
P.O. Box 4260, Kampala. ☎ +256 41 345 376. **Email:** combroad@infocom.co.ug
L.P: Head TV: Mrs Proscovia Njuki; Head Engineer: Godfrey Lugya
Stations: Kampala chE5, Lira chE7, Masaka chE8, Mbale chE8, Mbarara chE10, Soroti chE10. Gulu chE9, Jinja chE11
D.Prgr: Mon-Fri 1500-2100; Sat/Sun 1200-2100.

UKRAINE

Colour: SECAM — **Systems:** D & K

NATSIONALNA TELEKOMPANIA UKRAINY (Gov)
vul. Melnykova 42, 04119 Kyiv. ☎ +380 44 2413909. 🖷 +380 44 2468848. **Email:** office@firstnational.kiev.ua **Web:** www.fn.com.ua
L.P: Dir: Ihor Storozhuk.

1+1 (Comm)
vul. Kreschatyk 7/11, 01001 Kyiv. ☎ +380 44 4900101. 🖷 +380 44 4907097. **Email:** info@base.1plus1.net **Web:** www.1plus1.tv
L.P: DG: Oleksandr Rodnianskyi.

INTER (Comm)
vul. Dmytrivska 30, 01601 Kyiv. ☎ +380 44 4906765. 🖷 +380 44 4906765. **Email:** program@inter.ua **Web:** www.inter.kiev.ua

UNITED ARAB EMIRATES

Colour: PAL — **Systems:** B & G.

UNITED ARAB EMIRATES TELEVISION SERVICE (Gov)
P.O. Box 637, Abu Dhabi. ☎ +971 (2) 452000. 🖷 +971 (2) 461823.
Web: www.ecssr.ac.ae/05uae.6television.html
L.P: Hd. of Eng: Mustafa Hamouda Ishag. Dir. Gen: Ali Obaid.
Stations: chE5 (Abu Dhabi), E7 (Al Ain), E2 (Dubai). Broadcasts Ajman TV Channel 4 on ch26.

U.A.E. RADIO AND TELEVISION-DUBAI (Gov)
P.O. Box 1695, Dubai. ☎ +971 (4) 470255.
Web: www.dubaitv.gov.ae **Email:** commercial@dubaitv.gov.ael
L.P: Dir. Gen: Abdul G. Al Sayeed Ibrahim. Contr. of Prgrs: Nasib Bitar. Contr. of Eng: Ahmed Najeeb.
Stations (Systems B & G): Audio powers are 1/10 of the vision powers indicated.
D.Prgrs: Arabic (prgr. 1) on chs 2, 10 & 41: 1200 (Fri 1000)-2130 (or 2030). **English** (prgr. 2) on ch33: **D.Prgr:** 12 hrs daily via Nilesat satellite.

SHARJAH TV (Gov)
P.O. Box 111, Sharjah. ☎ +971 (6) 547755.
Stations: ch22 (foreign prgrs), 54 (Arabic).
D.Prgr: 1300-2000 (in Arabic).

SHOWTIME
PO Box 502211, Dubai Media City, Dubai. ☎ +971 4 367 7000.
Web: www.showtimeuae.com. **Email:** feedback@showtimeuae.com
Digital satellite pay-TV network for Middle East and North Africa.

UNITED KINGDOM

Colour: PAL — **System:** I

BRITISH BROADCASTING CORPORATION
BBC Television Centre, Wood Lane, London W12 7RJ. ☎ +44 208 743 8000. 🖷 +44 208 749 7520.
L.P: Dir.TV: Jana Bennett. Contr. BBC1: Lorraine Heggessey. Contr. BBC2: Roly Keating. Contr. BBC3: Stuart Murphy. Contr. BBC4: Janice Hadlow. Dir. World Srvc: Nigel Chapman.
Stations: BBC1, BBC2, BBC3 (FTA digital) BBC4 (FTA digital), CBeebies & CBBC (children's FTA digital), BBC News 24 (FTA digital)
D.Prgr: 24h

S4C, WELSH FOURTH CHANNEL AUTHORITY
Clos Sophia, Cardiff, CF1 9XY. ☎ +44 (2920) 747444. 🖷 +44 (2920) 754444. **Web:** www.s4c.co.uk **Email:** S4C@s4c.co.uk.

INDEPENDENT TELEVISION NETWORK
Anglia Television Ltd, Anglia House, Norwich NR1 3JG ☎ 01603 615151 🖷 01603 631032 Web: www.anglia.tv.co.uk
Border Television Plc, The Television Centre, Carlisle CA1 3NT ☎ 01228 525101 🖷 01228 541384 Web: www.border-tv.com
Carlton Television, 101 St Martin's Lane, London WC2N 4AZ ☎ 020 7240 4000 🖷 020 7615 1775 Web: www.carltontv.co.uk
Carlton Broadcasting - Central region, Central Court, Gas Street, Birmingham B1 2JT ☎ 0121 6439898 🖷 0121 6344898 Web: www.carlton.com
Channel Television Ltd, The Television Centre, St Helier, Jersey, Channel Islands JE1 3ZD ☎ 01534 816816 🖷 01534 816817 Web: www.channeltv.co.uk
Grampian Television Ltd, Television Centre, Craigshaw Business Park, West Tullos, Aberdeen AB12 3QH ☎ +01224 848848 Web: www.grampian.co.uk
Granada Television Ltd, Quay Street, Manchester M60 9EA ☎ 0161 832 7211 🖷 0161 827 2141 Web: www.granadamedia.com
HTV (Cymru) Wales, The Television Centre, Culverhouse Cross, Cardiff CF5 6XJ ☎ 02920 590590 🖷 02920 597183 Web: www.htv-wales.co.uk
London Weekend Television Limited, The London Television Centre, Upper Ground, London SE1 9LT ☎ 020 7620 1620 🖷 020 7261 1290 Web: www.lwt.co.uk
Meridian Broadcasting Ltd, Television Centre, Southampton SO14 0PZ ☎ 023 8022 2555 🖷 023 8033 5050 Web: www.meridian.tv.co.uk
Scottish Television plc, 200 Renfield Street, Glasgow G2 3PR ☎ 0141 300 3000 🖷 0141 300 3030 Web: www.scottishtv.co.uk
Tyne Tees Television Ltd, The Television Centre, City Road, Newcastle upon Tyne NE1 2AL ☎ 0191 261 0181 🖷 0191 261 2302
Ulster Television plc, Havelock House, Ormeau Road, Belfast BT7 1EB ☎ 028 9032 8122 🖷 028 9024 6695 Web: www.u.tv
Carlton Broadcasting - Westcountry region, Langage Science Park, Plymouth PL7 5BQ ☎ 01752 333333 🖷 01752 333444 Web: www.carlton.com/westcountry
Yorkshire Television Ltd, The Television Centre, Leeds LS3 1JS ☎ 0113 2438283 🖷 0113 2445107 Web: www.granadamedia.com
GMTV Ltd, The London Television Centre, Upper Ground, London SE1 9TT ☎ 202 7827 7000 🖷 020 7827 7001 Web: www.gmtv.co.uk

CHANNEL FOUR TELEVISION CORPORATION
124 Horseferry Road, London SW1P 2TX ☎ 020 7396 4444 🖷 020 7306 8366 Web: www.channel4.com

CHANNEL 5 BROADCASTING LTD
22 Long Acre, London WC2E 9LY ☎ 020 7550 5555 🖷 020 7550 5554 Web: www.channel5.co.uk **L.P:** CEO: David Elstein. Chief Operating Officer: Ian Ritchie. Dir. Prgrs: Dawn Airey. Dir. Sales: Nick Milligan. Dir. Marketing & Communications: David Brook.

INDEPENDENT TELEVISION NEWS
200 Gray's Inn Road, London WC1X 8XZ ☎ +44 (0)207 833 3000 🖷 +44 (0) 207 430 4868 Web: www.itn.co.uk

UNITED STATES OF AMERICA

Colour: NTSC — **System:** M

ABC TELEVISION DIVISION (Comm)
ABC, Inc., 500 S. Buena Vista Street, Burbank, CA 91521-4551 ☎ +1 (818) 460-7477 **Web:** www.abctelevision.com
Owned stations: WABC-TV/New York, WLS-TV/Chicago, KGO-TV/San Francisco, KABC-TV/Los Angeles, KTRK-TV/Houston, KFSN-TV/Fresno, CA, WPVI-TV/Philadelphia, WTVD-TV/Durham, North Carolina. **Affiliates:** approx. 220.

AMC, Bravo, IFC, WE (Comm)
200 Jericho Quad, Jericho, NY 11753 ☎ 516 803-3000 🖷 516 803-3003 **Web:** www.rainbow-media.com

America One Television (Comm)
6125 Airport Freeway, Suite 100, Ft. Worth, TX 76117 ☎ +1 817 546-1400 **Web:** www.americaone.com

Black Entertainment Television (Comm)
1900 West Place NE, Washington, DC 20018 ☎ +1 202 608-2000

Cartoon Network (Comm)
11050 Techwood Drive, Atlanta, GA 30318
Web: www.cartoonnetwork.com

CNN (Comm)
One CNN Center, P.O. Box 105366, Atlanta, GA 30348.
Web: www.cnn.com

CBS, Inc. (Comm)
51 West 52nd Str, New York, NY 10019. ☎ +1 (212) 975-4321. 🖷 +1 (212) 975 7452. **Email:** marketing@cbs.com **Web:** www.cbs.com
Owned Stations: WCBS-TV, New York; WBBM-TV, Chicago; KCBS-TV, Los Angeles; WCIX-TV Miami; WCCO TV, Minneapolis; WBAY TV, Green Bay. **Affiliated Stations:** 200.

Discovery Channel (Comm)
One Discovery Place, Silver Spring, MCD 20910-3354 **Web:** www.discovery.com

FOX TELEVISION NETWORK (Comm)
P.O. Box 900, Beverly Hills CA 90213-0900. ☎ +1 (310) 277 2211. **Email:** foxnet@delphi.com **Web:** www.foxnetwork.com

NATIONAL BROADCASTING COMPANY (Comm)
30 Rockefeller Plaza, New York, NY 10112. ☎ +1 (212) 664-2074. 🖷 +1 (212) 664 7541. **Web:** www.nbc.com
NBC Television Stations: WNBC-TV, New York; WRC-TV, Washington; WMAQ-TV, Chicago; WKYC-TV, Cleveland; KNBC-TV, Los Angeles; WCAU-TV, Philadelphia; KCNC-TV, Denver; WTVJ-TV, Miami. **Affiliated stations:** 208.

PUBLIC BROADCASTING SERVICE (Non-comm)
1320 Braddock Place, Alexandria, VA 22314-1698. ☎ +1 (703) 739-5000. 🖷 +1 703 739-0775 **Web:** www.pbs.org
L.P: Pres. and Chief Exec: Ervin S. Duggan. Senior V-Pres. and General Counsel: Gregory Ferenbach **Member Stations:** 349.

United Paramount Network (UPN) (Comm)
P.O. Box 251735, Los Angeles, CA 90025. **Web:** www.upn.com

Univision (Spanish Language Network) (Comm)
605 Third Ave, New York, NY 10158-0180. ☎ +1 (212) 455 5200. **Web:** www.univision.net

The History Channel
☐ A&E Television Networks, 235 East 45th Street, New York, NY 10017 **Web:** www.historychannel.com

Warner Brothers Television Network (WB)
☐ 4000 Warner Blvd, Bldg. #34R, Burbank, CA 91522. ☎ +1 (818) 954 6479. **Email:** wbnetwork@aol.com **Web:** www.tv.warnerbros.com

Local stations: There over 1,500 TV stations across the U.S. The major cities have st's affiliated to each of the above-mentioned networks, and there are additional local st's which generally broadcast movies, and re-runs of older programs.

Armed Forces Radio & TV Service Broadcast Center (AFRTS-BC) (Mil)
☐ 1363 Z Street, Bldg 2730, March ARB, CA 92518. 🖷 +1 (909) 413-2234. **Web:** www.dodmedia.osd.mil/afrts_bc/ahome.htm
L.P: Dir. Programming: Robert W. Matheson. Dir. Eng. & Op's: Bruce V. Ziemienski.

American Forces Network on TV (AFN-ON TV)
American military television broadcasts can be accessed in the following overseas locations: Antarctica, Cuba, Germany, Italy, Japan, South Korea, Puerto Rico, Iceland, Spain, Honduras, Turkey, and Diego Garcia. For further details: **Web:** www.afrts.osd.mil/afnontv

TV Marti (Gov)
TV Marti is the television broadcasting service of the United States Information Agency, Office of Cuban Broadcasting.
☐ Washington, D.C. 20547, USA. ☎ +1 (202) 501-7210. 🖷 +1 (202) 208-7808 **L.P:** Ag. Dir. Office of Cuba Broadcasting: Dr. Rolando Bonachea. Dir. of Tech. Op's (OCB): Michael Pallone.
Stations: VHF ch13 (0830-1100).

URUGUAY

Colour: PAL — **System:** N.

Stations: (all commercial)

Tele-Artigas*, Lecueder 291, 55000 Artigas **L.P:** Dir. Gen: Carlos F. Falco.
D.Prgr: 1800-0300.
Televisora Colonia, W. Barbot 172, 70000 Colonia **L.P:** Dir. Gen. G. de Gonzáles.
Río de los Pájaros TV*, Av. España 1629, 60000 Paysandú **L.P:** Dir Gen: A. Davison. Dir. Tec: H. Caporale.
Monte Carlo TV Color, Paraguay 2253, 11800 Montevideo
L.P: Dir. Gen: H. Romay. Film Buyer: M. Fonticiella. Dir. Tec: J. Spinella
D.Prgr: 1830/0400 (Sat/Sun 1300-0400)
Canal 5 S.O.D.R.E, Bulevar Artigas 2552, Montevideo.**L.P:** Gen. Man: Julio Frade. Dir. Tec: Pedro Narancio.
Tele-Rocha*, Av. O. de los Santos 105, 27000 Rocha **L.P:** Dir. Gen: M. Scherchener. Dir. Tec: J. Regalo. Film Buyer: L. Castillo.
Radiotelevisión "Zorilla de San Martín"*, 18 de Julio 302, 45000 Tucuarembó **L.P:** Dir. Gen: D. Dini. S. St. Mgr: G. Valdés G.; Dir. Tec: G. Acosta. Film Buyer: Jose Abbondanza.
D.Prgr: 2030 -0330.
Canal 8 TV Melo, 18 de Julio 572, 37000 Melo, Cerro Largo
L.P: Dir: Raul Figueredo. Dir. Tec: Eduardo Baptista.
Canal 8 Rosario TV Color, Ruta 2 Km. 136.500, 70200 Rosario, Colonia **L.P:** Dir: H. Fripp.
Televisora Salto Grande*, Av. Viera 1280, 50000 Salto
L.P: Dir. Gen: Dr. Carlos A. Gelpi. Dir. Tec: K. Muguerza.
Canal 9 del Este TV Color*, Av. Artigas 879, 20000 Maldonado
L.P: Dir. Gen: M. Scherschener. Dir. Tec: Fernando Bareño. Film Buyer: J. López
D.Prgr: 2000-0400.
Telediez*, General Rivera s/n, 55100 Bella Unión, Artigas
L.P: Dir. Gen: C. Gelpi.
SAETA TV Canal 10*, Dr. Lorenzo Carnelli 1234, 11200 Montevideo
L.P: Dir. Gen: J. de Feo. Dir. Tec: Oscar Inchausti. Film Buyer: H. Villar
D.Prgr: Mon-Fri 1930.
Tevediez*, Sarandí 705, 40000 Rivera **L.P:** Dir. Gen: A. Pereira.
D.Prgr: 2000-0300.
Canal 11, Punta del Este, Cantegril Country Club, 20100 Punta del Este, Maldonado **L.P:** Dir. Gen: D. Romay
D.Prgr: 1830-0400.
Televisora Treinta y Tres*, Pablo Zufriategui 226, Treinta y Tres **L.P:** Dir. Gen: A. Pinho. St. Mgr: A. Lagos. Dir. Tec: D. Ponce.
Canal 12, Río Uruguay, Cno. San Salvador s/n, 65000 Fray Bentos, Río Negro **L.P:** Dir. Gen: D. Romay.
Melo TV*, Castellanos 723, 37000 Melo, Cerro Largo
L.P: Dir. Gen: R. Lucas. Dir. Tec: C. Britos. Film Buyer: J. Lucas.
Teledoce Televisora Color*, Enriqueta Compte y Riqué 1276, 11800 Montevideo
L.P: Dir. Gen: H. Scheck. Dir. Tec: M. Donnangelo. Film Buyer: C. Restano
D.Prgr: 1810 (Sat 1600, Sun 1330)-0400.
TV Cerro del Verdún*, Treinta y Tres 632, 30000 Minas, Lavalleja
L.P: Dir. Gen: C. Falco. Dir. Tec: J. Rodriguez.
* = affiliated to ANDEBU (Associación Nac de Broadcasters Uruguayos)

UZBEKISTAN

Colour: SECAM — **Systems:** D & K

UZBEK TELEVISION (Gov)
☐ Navoi Str. 69, 700011 Toshkent. ☎ +998 71 410062. 🖷 +998 71 440030. **Email:** odil@usis.uz **Web:** www.teleradio.uz
NOTES: produces 4 TV channels - O'zbekiston, Yoshlar, Toshkent and Xalqaro.

VANUATU

Colour: SECAM. — **System:** D/K

TV BLONG VANUATU
☐ Vanuatu Broadcasting and Television Corp, PMB 049, Port Vila. ☎ +678 22999. 🖷 +678 22026
L.P: Gen.Mgr: Maki Simelum; Tech. Mngr: Willie Daniel

VENEZUELA

Colour: NTSC — **System:** M.

CAMARA VENEZOLANA DE LA TELEVISION
(Organization for private TV stations).
☐ Ap. 60423, Chacao, Caracas 1050. ☎ +58 (2) 7814608.
L.P: Pres. H. Ponsdomenech.

TELEVISORA NACIONAL TVN (Gov)
☐ Ap. 3979, Caracas 1010-A. ☎ +58 (2) 239 9811
D.Prgr: 1800-0400 (actually relaying VTV).
Stations: Anzoategui ch13 64kW; Carobobo ch6 67kW; Bolivar ch5 57kW; D. Federal ch5 279kW; Falcon ch5 50kW; Lara ch13 64kW; Merida ch13 2kW; Tachira ch13 72kW; Tachira ch2 5kW; Zulia ch6 61kW.

VENEZOLANA DE TELEVISION "5" (Gov)
☐ Ap. 2979, Caracas 1050. ☎ +58 (2) 239 9811. 🖷 +58 (2) 35734.
Stations: Caracas (Central St): chA5 210/105kW.
D.Prgr: 2200-0400 (approx)

VENEZOLANA DE TELEVISION "8" (Gov)
☐ Ap. 2979, Caracas 1050. ☎ +58 (2) 349571.
Stations: Caracas (Central st): chA8 190/95kW.
D.Prgr: 1600-0600 (approx)

OTHER STATIONS

AMAVISION (Cult & Rlgs)
☐ Calle Selesiano, Colegio Pio XI, Puerto Ayacucho, Amazonas. ☎ +58 (2) 987 6190. **D.Prgr:** 2200-0200 **Stations:** Puerto Ayacucho ch7 6kW

CANAL 10
☐ Av. Francisco de Miranda, con Principal de los Ruices, Centro Empresarial Miranda PHD, Caracas. ☎ +58 (2) 239 8679. 🖷 +58 (2) 239 7757. **Station:** Caracas ch10.

CANAL METROPOLITANO DE TELEVISION (Comm)
☐ Av. Circumvalacion El Sol, Centro Professional Santa Paula, Torre B, Piso 4, Santa Paula, Caracas. ☎ +58 (2) 987 6190. 🖷 +58 (2) 985 4856. **D. Prgr:** 2100-0400 **Stations:** Caracas ch51

NCTV (Comm)
☐ Urv. La Paz, Avenida 57 y Maracaibo, Maracaibo. ☎ +58 (61) 512662. 🖷 +58 (61) 512729. **L.P:** Dir: Gustavo Ocando Yamarte. **Station:** Maracaibo chA11 108/54kW (est). **D.Prgr:** 1600-0400.

OMNIVISION (Comm)
Calle Milan, Edif. Omnivision, Los Ruices Sur, Caracas. ☎ +58 (2) 256 3586/256 5011. 🖷 +58 (2) 256 4482. **D. Prgr:** 24 hrs.
RADIO CARACAS TELEVISION RCTV(Comm)
Ap. 2057, Caracas. ☎ +58 (2) 256 3696. 🖷 +58 (2) 256 1812.
L.P.: DG:Alberto Ravell. **D.Prgrs:** 24 hrs.
TELEVISORA ANDINA DE MERIDA (Cult & Rlgs)
Av. Bolivar, Calle 23 entre Av. 4-5, Merida 5101. ☎ +58 (74) 525 785. 🖷 +58 (74) 520 098. **D.Prgr:**1400-0200
Stations: Merida ch6 20kW; Tachira ch3 33kW.
TELE BOCONO (Cult)
Calle 3, Qta. Caleuche, El Saman. Bocono. ☎ +58 (72) 521 27. 🖷 +58 (72) 524 85. **D. Prgr:** 2100-0300.
Stations: Trujillo ch13 4kW.
TELECARIBE (Comm)
Centro Banaven (Cubo Negro), Torre C, Piso 1, of C-12, Chuao, Caracas. ☎ +58 (2) 911 964/913 089. **D. Prgr:** 1000-0400
Stations: Anzoategui ch9 50kW; Nueva Esparta ch12 30kW.
TELECENTRO (Comm)
Avenide Pedro León Torres, esquina de la calle 47, Edificio Telecentro, Barquisimeto, (3001) Lara. ☎/🖷 +58 51 460 917/4525 27.
L.P.: Dir: Jorge Felix. **D.Prgr:** 1030-0400.
Station: Lara ch11 100kW.
TV GUAYANA (Comm)
Puerto Ordaz, Bolivar. ☎ +58 (86) 2299 08
D.Prgr: 2100-0300. **Stations:** Bolivar ch12 125kW, ch13 80kW
TELESOL (Comm)
Calle Sucre no 15, Cumana, Sucre. ☎ +58 (93) 6620 59. 🖷 +58 (93) 6627 75. **D.Prgr:** 1800-0200. **Station:** Sucre ch7 12kW
TELEVEN (Comm)
C.C. Los Chaguaramos, Caracas. ☎ +58 (2) 6617 511. 🖷 +58 (2) 6625 300. **L.P.:** Pres: Omar Camero Z; VP Engineering: Gustavo Rosario Krasner. **D.Prgr:** 24 hrs.
TELEVISORA REGIONAL DEL TACHIRA (Comm)
Av. Libertador, edif. Servicios Unidos, Piso 3, San Cristobal, Tachira. ☎ +58 (76) 4473 66. 🖷 +58 (76) 4652 77
D. Prgr: 2000-0200 **Stations:** Tachira ch6 144kW.
TELEVISORA DE ORIENTE, TVO (Comm)
Puerto la Cruz, Anzoategui. ☎ +58 (82) 6621 63
D.Prgr: 1800-0300. **Station:** Anzoategui ch5 50kW.
VENEVISION (Comm)
Av. La Salle, Edif, Venevision,Colinas de Los Caobos, Caracas. ☎ +58 (2) 782 0111**Web:** www.venevision.com
L.P: Pres: Carlos Bardasano. GM: Manuel Fraiz Grijalba. Eng. Mgr: German Landaeta. PR: Mariela Castio.
Stations: Caracas (Central st): chA4 132/66kW.
D.Prgr: 24 hrs.

VIETNAM

Colour: PAL — **System:** D&K

VIETNAM TELEVISION (Gov)
43 Nguyen Chi Thanh Street, Ba Dinh, Hanoi. ☎ +84 (4) 835 4992. 🖷 +84 (4) 835 0882. **Web:** www.vtv.org.vn
L.P: DG: Vu Van Hien; Dir of loc. TV: Nguyen Van Nhuong.
Stations: Hanoi VTV1: ch9, VTV2: ch11, VTV3: ch22 10/20kW; Ho Chi Minh City VTV1: ch21, VTV3: ch28 50kW; Hue ch7, ch9, ch22, Cantho VTV1: ch46, VTV3: ch49; DaNang ch9, ch12 5kW; Tam Dao ch3. Many VTV relay stations and provincial and city TV stations are also operating.
D.Prgr: VTV1: 1900-2300; VTV2: 0600-1000, 1900-2130: VTV3: 1400-1900 (Sun 1400-1900 + after 2300)

VIRGIN ISLANDS (American)

Colour: NTSC — **System:** M.

WBNB-TV
Box 1947, Charlotte Amalie, St. Thomas 00801.
☎ +1 (809) 774-0300. 🖷 +1 (809) 776-3511.
L.P: Sen. Vice Pres: J. Potter. St. Mgr: P. Stull.
Station: WBNB-TV chA10 113/76kW.

CARIBBEAN COMM. CORP.
1 Beltjen Place, St. Thomas, V1 00802. ☎ +809 77621 50. 🖷 +809 774 5029.
L.P: Hd. of Sales: Randolph H. Knight; MD: Andrea L. Martin.

VIRGIN ISLANDS PUBLIC TV-SYSTEM
Box 7879, Charlotte Amalie, St. Thomas 00801. ☎ +1 (809) 774-6255. 🖷 +1 (809) 774 7092.
L.P: Gen. Mngr: Lori J.E. Rawlins
Station: WTJX-TV chA12 31.6/6.32kW.

VIRGIN ISLANDS (British)

Colour: NTSC — **System:** M.

VIRGIN ISLANDS BROADCASTING LTD (Comm)
P.O. Box 78, Road Town,Tortola☎ +1 (284) 494 2250. **Email:** zbvi@surfbvi.com **Web:** www.zbvi.com
L.P. Gen Mngr: Harvey Herbert
Station: chA5 30/3kW.

BVI CABLE TV
P.O. Box 644, Road Town, Tortola. ☎ (284) 494 3205. **Email:** adrian_labennett@emcom.vi
L.P: Gen. Mngr: Adrian LaBennett

WALLIS & FUTUNA

Colour: SECAM — **System:** K.

RADIODIFFUSION FRANCAISE D'OUTRE-MER (RFO)
B.P. 102, Mata Utu, 98600 Uvea, Iles de Wallis-et-Futuna, Pacifique sud (par Nouméa, Nouvelle-Calédonie). ☎ +681 722020. 🖷 +681 722346 **Email:** rfo.wallis@wallis.co.nc
L.P: Tech. Dir: Taniela Heafala
Stations: ch6 & ch9
D.Prgr: 0600-0000

YEMEN

Colour: PAL — **System:** B.

YEMEN RADIO & TV CORP. (Gov)
P.O. Box 2182, Sana'a. ☎ +967 (1) 230654. 🖷 +967 (1) 230761.
L.P: Dir's: Ali Caleh Algamrah, Mohammed Abdul Gawi.
Stations: chE5 (0.2kW), chE6 (2 st's, 4 & 1kW), chE7 (2kW), chE8 (4kW), chE10 (4kW), chE11 (1kW), chE12 (2kW) + low power repeaters.
D.Prgr: 1300-2100.

ZAMBIA

Colour: PAL — **System:** B.

ZAMBIA NATIONAL BROADCASTING CORPORATION (Gov)
Broadcasting House, P.O.Box 50015, Lusaka 10101☎ +260 (1) 254 989 **Email:** znbctv@zamtel.zm
L.P: DG: Eddy Mupeso; Tech Dir: Edward Mwanza
Stations: Solwezi ch3, Kitwe ch9, Kapiri Mposhi ch6, Lusaka ch10, Pemba ch8, Senkobo ch10, Kasama ch8, Chipata ch11, Mubwa ch8,
D.Prgrs: Mon-Thur. 1700-2230; Fri-Sat 1500-2400; Sun 1500-2230.

ZIMBABWE

Colour: PAL — **System:** B.

ZIMBABWE BROADCASTING CORPORATION (Statutory Body, Comm)
P.O. Box HG 444, Highlands, Harare. ☎ +263 (4) 498 930 🖷 +263 (4) 482 000 **Email:** zbc@zbc.co.zw. **Web:** www.zbc.co.zw
L.P: Head Broadcast Tech: Oswell Chakwanda; Head TV: Abigail Mvududu
D.Prgr: ZBCTV One: 0600-2400

JOY TV (formerly ZBC 2)
Flame Lily Broadcasting (Pvt) Ltd, PO Box MP1310, Mount Pleasant, Harare ☎ +263 (4) 870567. **Email:** joytv@africaonline.co.zw. **Web:** www.africaonline.co.zw/joytv
D.Prgr: 0400-1500 (VHF) ch7, English language relay of ZBC. 1500-2300, English language broadcasts incl BBC World News.

CHARACTERISTICS OF TELEVISION SYSTEMS (as indicated in CCIR Report 624-3, XVIth Plenary Assembly, Dubrovnik, 1986)

System	Number of lines	Channel width MHz.	Vision band-width MHz.	Vision/Sound separation MHz.	Vestigial side-band MHz.	Vision mod.	Sound mod.
B	625	7	5	+5.5	0.75	Neg.	FM
D	625	8	6	+6.5	0.75	Neg.	FM
G	625	8	5	+5.5	0.75	Neg.	FM
H	625	8	5	+5.5	1.25	Neg.	FM
I	625	8	5.5	+5.996	1.25	Neg.	FM
K	625	8	6	+6.5	0.75	Neg.	FM
L	625	8	6	+6.5	1.25	Pos.	AM
M	525	6	4.2	+4.5	0.75	Neg.	FM
N	625	6	4.2	+4.5	0.75	Neg.	FM

N.B: Channels L2, L3, L4, Vision/Sound separation is -6.5 MHz. (France)

CHANNEL INFORMATION

(Vision carrier frequencies in MHz.)

VHF Channels:

West European "E" Channels

2 = 48.25	5 = 175.25	9 = 203.25
2A = 49.75	6 = 182.25	10 = 210.25
3 = 55.25	7 = 189.25	11 = 217.25
4 = 62.25	8 = 196.25	12 = 224.25

Italy

A = 53.75	D = 175.25	G = 201.25
B = 59.75	E = 183.75	H = 210.25
C = 82.75	F = 192.25	H1 = 217.25

Ireland

A = 45.75	E = 183.75	H = 207.25
B = 53.75	F = 191.25	I = 215.25
C = 61.75	G = 199.25	J = 223.25
D = 175.25		

France

2 = 55.75	5 = 176	8 = 200
3 = 60.50	6 = 184	9 = 208
4 = 63.75	7 = 192	10 = 216

East European "R" Channels

1 = 49.75	5 = 93.25	9 = 199.25
2 = 59.25	6 = 175.25	10 = 207.25
3 = 77.25	7 = 183.25	11 = 215.25
4 = 85.25	8 = 191.25	12 = 223.25

North/South America

2 = 55.25	6 = 83.25	10 = 193.25
3 = 61.75	7 = 175.25	11 = 199.25
4 = 67.25	8 = 181.25	12 = 204.25
5 = 77.25	9 = 187.25	13 = 211.25

Japan

1 = 91.25	5 = 177.25	9 = 199.25
2 = 97.25	6 = 183.25	10 = 205.25
3 = 103.25	7 = 189.25	11 = 211.25
4 = 171.25	8 = 193.25	12 = 217.25

Australia

0 = 46.25	5 = 102.25	8 = 189.25
1 = 57.25	5A = 138.25	9 = 196.25
2 = 64.25	6 = 175.25	10 = 209.25
3 = 86.25	7 = 182.25	11 = 216.25
4 = 95.25		

New Zealand

1 = 45.25	4 = 175.25	7 = 196.25
2 = 55.25	5 = 182.25	8 = 203.25
3 = 62.25	6 = 189.25	9 = 210.25

China (P.R.)

1 = 49.75	5 = 85.25	9 = 192.25
2 = 57.75	6 = 168.25	10 = 200.25
3 = 65.75	7 = 176.25	11 = 208.25
4 = 77.25	8 = 184.25	12 = 216.25

South Africa

4 = 175.25	7 = 199.25	10 = 223.25
5 = 183.25	8 = 207.25	11 = 231.25
6 = 191.25	9 = 215.25	13 = 247.43

Morocco

4 = 163.25	7 = 187.25	9 = 203.25
5 = 171.25	8 = 195.25	10 = 211.25
6 = 179.25		

French Overseas Territories

4 = 175.25	6 = 191.25	8 = 207.25
5 = 183.25	7 = 199.25	9 = 215.25

UHF Channels:

North/South America

14 = 471.25	33 = 585.25	52 = 699.25
15 = 477.25	34 = 591.25	53 = 705.25
16 = 483.25	35 = 597.25	54 = 711.25
17 = 489.25	36 = 603.25	55 = 717.25
18 = 495.25	37 = 609.25	56 = 723.25
19 = 501.25	38 = 615.25	57 = 729.25
20 = 507.25	39 = 621.25	58 = 735.25
21 = 513.25	40 = 627.25	59 = 741.25
22 = 519.25	41 = 633.25	60 = 747.25
23 = 525.25	42 = 639.25	61 = 753.25
24 = 531.25	43 = 645.25	62 = 759.25
25 = 537.25	44 = 651.25	63 = 765.25
26 = 543.25	45 = 657.25	64 = 771.25
27 = 549.25	46 = 663.25	65 = 777.25
28 = 555.25	47 = 669.25	66 = 783.25
29 = 561.25	48 = 675.25	67 = 789.25
30 = 567.25	49 = 681.25	68 = 795.25
31 = 573.25	50 = 687.25	69 = 801.25
32 = 579.25	51 = 693.25	

UHF TV channels 70-83 were discontinued. (to be used by radio)

Europe/Africa

21 = 471.25	38 = 607.25	55 = 743.25
22 = 479.25	39 = 615.25	56 = 751.25
23 = 487.25	40 = 623.25	57 = 759.25
24 = 495.25	41 = 631.25	58 = 767.25
25 = 503.25	42 = 639.25	59 = 775.25
26 = 511.25	43 = 647.25	60 = 783.25
27 = 519.25	44 = 655.25	61 = 791.25
28 = 527.25	45 = 663.25	62 = 799.25
29 = 535.25	46 = 671.25	63 = 807.25
30 = 543.25	47 = 679.25	64 = 815.25
31 = 551.25	48 = 687.25	65 = 823.25
32 = 559.25	49 = 695.25	66 = 831.25
33 = 567.25	50 = 703.25	67 = 839.25
34 = 575.25	51 = 711.25	68 = 847.25
35 = 583.25	52 = 719.25	69 = 855.25
36 = 591.25	53 = 727.25	
37 = 599.25	54 = 735.25	

Australia

28 = 527.25	42 = 625.25	56 = 723.25
29 = 534.25	43 = 632.25	57 = 730.25
30 = 541.25	44 = 639.25	58 = 737.25
31 = 548.25	45 = 646.25	59 = 744.25
32 = 555.25	46 = 653.25	60 = 751.25
33 = 562.25	47 = 660.25	61 = 758.25
34 = 569.25	48 = 667.25	62 = 765.25
35 = 576.25	49 = 674.25	63 = 772.25
36 = 583.25	50 = 681.25	64 = 779.25
37 = 590.25	51 = 688.25	65 = 786.25
38 = 597.25	52 = 695.25	66 = 793.25
39 = 604.25	53 = 702.25	67 = 800.25
40 = 611.25	54 = 709.25	68 = 807.25
41 = 618.25	55 = 716.25	69 = 814.25

China (P.R.)

13 = 471.25	21 = 534.25	29 = 637.25
14 = 479.25	22 = 543.25	30 = 645.25
15 = 487.25	23 = 551.25	31 = 653.25
16 = 495.25	24 = 559.25	32 = 661.25
17 = 503.25	25 = 605.25	33 = 669.25
18 = 511.25	26 = 613.25	34 = 677.25
19 = 519.25	27 = 621.25	36 = 693.25
20 = 527.25	28 = 629.25	

N.B: Japan Channel 13-62 = No./So. America Channel 14-63

REFERENCE

Section Contents

TRANSMITTER SITES

Location & Decode Tables

INTERNATIONAL TRANSMITTER SITES

Code	Site	Ctry	Lat	Long	SW	MW
ABS	Abis	EGY	31N10	030E05	✓	×
ABZ	Abu Zaabal	EGY	30N16	031E22	✓	×
ADR	Adra	SYR	33N27	036E30	✓	×
AHA	Al Hassake	SYR	36N28	040E45	×	✓
AHW	Ahwaz	IRN	31N20	048E40	✓	×
AIA	The Valley	AIA	18N13	063W01	✓	✓
AIJ	Dallas, TX	USA	33N13	096W52	✓	×
AKA	Al Karanah	JOR	31N44	036E26	✓	×
ALG	Aligarh	IND	28N00	078E06	✓	×
ALK	Al Khaisah	QAT	25N25	051E25	✓	×
ALM	Almaty	KAZ	43N31	077E00	✓	×
ARM	Tbilisskaya	RUS	45N29	040E07	✓	✓
ART	Arta	DJI	11N52	042E84	×	✓
ASC	Ascension	ASC	07S54	014W23	✓	×
ATG	Antigua	ATG	17N06	061W48	✓	×
AVL	Avlida	GRC	38N23	023E36	✓	×
BAK	Baki	AZE	40N22	049E53	×	✓
BAN	Pathum Thani	THA	14N01	100E31	✓	×
BAR	Barrigada, GU	GUM	13N34	144E50	✓	×
BCQ	Monticello, ME	USA	46N20	067W50	✓	×
BEI	Beijing	CHN	39N57	116E27	✓	✓
BGL	Bangalore	IND	13N14	077E13	✓	×
BIB	Biblis	D	49N41	008E29	✓	×
BIJ	Bijeljina	BIH	44N42	019E10	✓	×
BIS	Bishkek	KGZ	42N54	074E37	✓	×
BKO	Bamako	MLI	12N39	008W01	✓	×
BLG	Belogorsk	RUS	50N30	128E18	×	✓
BLN	Berlin	D	52N30	013E20	×	✓
BNB	Bonab	IRN	37N20	046E05	×	✓
BNT	Bandar-e Torkeman	IRN	36N54	054E04	×	✓
BOC	Bocaue	PHL	14N48	120E55	✓	×
BOH	Newport, NC (WBOH)	USA	34N47	076W56	✓	×
BON	Bonaire	ATN	12N12	068W18	✓	✓
BOT	Moepeng Hill	BOT	21S57	027E39	✓	×
BPH	Ban Rasom	THA	14N24	100E47	×	✓
BRA	Brasília	B	15S51	047W56	✓	×
BRN	Brandon	AUS	19S31	147E20	✓	×
BUE	Buenos Aires	ARG	36S43	058W22	✓	×
BUJ	Buje	HRV	45N24	013E40	×	✓
CAH	Changchun	CHN	43N48	125E23	×	✓
CAK	Çakirlar	TUR	39N58	032E40	✓	×
CAZ	Cazenga	AGL	08S53	015E56	×	✓
CER	Cërrik	ALB	41N20	019E36	✓	×
CGR	Kavo Gkreko	CYP	34N59	034E06	×	✓
CHA	Cahuita	CTR	09N45	082W54	✓	×
CHB	Chah Bahar	IRN	25N17	060E37	×	✓
CHG	Changchih	TWN	22N39	120E30	×	✓
CHO	Chongjin	KRE	41N47	129E50	×	✓
CNI	Chennai	IND	13N08	080E07	✓	×
CRI	Cariari de Porocí	CTR	10N00	083W30	✓	×
CRN	Chernivtsi	UKR	28N20	025E55	×	✓
CYP	Zygi	CYP	34N43	033E19	✓	✓
DAR	Darwin	AUS	12S25	136E37	✓	×
DBA	Dubai	UAE	25N14	055E16	✓	✓
DEA	Deanovac	HRV	45N41	016E27	✓	✓
DEL	New Delhi	IND	28N43	077E12	✓	×
DGA	Diego Garcia	DGA	07S03	072E04	✓	×
DHA	Dhabbaya	UAE	24N11	054E14	✓	✓
DKA	Dhaka	BGD	23N43	090E26	✓	×
DLN	Delano, CA	USA	35N45	119W10	✓	×
DOF	Dongfang	CHN	18N54	108E39	✓	✓
DRO	Droitwich	G	52N18	002W06	×	✓
DSB	Yangiyul	TJK	38N29	068E48	✓	✓
DSH	Dusheti	GEO	42N03	044E41	✓	×
EKA	Ekala	CLN	07N06	079E54	✓	×
EKB	Yekaterinburg	RUS	56N55	060E36	✓	✓
EMR	Emirler	TUR	39N29	032E51	✓	×
EWN	Vandiver, AL	USA	33N30	086W28	✓	×
FAN	Fangliao	TWN	22N22	120E36	×	✓
FBS	Marpi, MP	MRA	15N16	145E48	✓	×
FLA	Fllaka	ALB	41N22	019E30	×	✓
FLE	Flevo	HOL	52N21	005E27	✓	×
GAB	Moyabi	GAB	01S40	013E31	✓	×
GAL	Galbeni	ROU	46N44	026E50	✓	×
GAN	Gäncä	AZE	40N37	046E20	✓	×
GAV	Gavar	ARM	40N25	045E11	✓	✓
GDG	Guangdong (Prov.)	CHN	-	-	×	✓
GEM	Golmud	CHN	36N24	094E59	✓	×
GJW	Gedja	ETH	08N47	038E38	✓	×
GKP	Gorakhpur	IND	23N52	083E28	✓	×
GRI	Grigoriopol	MDA	47N14	029E24	✓	✓
GRV	Greenville, NC	USA	35N35	077W22	✓	×
GTG	McCayesville, GA	USA	34N58	084W22	✓	×
GUF	Montsinery	GUF	04N54	052W36	✓	×
GVK	Grindavík	ISL	63N50	022W26	✓	×
HAB	La Habana	CUB	23N00	082W30	✓	×
HAN	Hanoi	VTN	20N59	105E52	✓	×
HBN	Medorn, PL	PLW	07N27	134E28	✓	×
HEI	Heilongjiang (Prov.)	CHN	-	-	×	✓
HEL	Helsinki	FIN	60N11	024E49	×	✓
HKG	Hongkong	CHN	22N03	114E02	×	✓
HOR	Hörby	S	55N49	013E44	✓	×
HRA	Greenbush, ME	USA	45N08	068W34	✓	×
HUH	Hohhot	CHN	41N12	111E30	✓	×

Code	Site	Ctry	Lat	Long	SW	MW
HUW	Huwei	TWN	23N43	120E25	✓	×
HVA	Hvar	HRV	43N11	016E25	×	✓
HWA	Hwasung	KOR	37N13	126E47	✓	×
IBA	Iba	PHL	15N20	119E58	✓	×
IKO	Ikorodu	NIG	07N23	003E56	✓	×
IMF	Pinon, NM	USA	32N37	105W24	✓	×
INB	Red Lion, PA	USA	39N54	076W35	✓	×
IRA	Iranawila	CLN	07N32	079E30	✓	×
IRK	Angarsk	RUS	52N25	103E40	✓	✓
IRS	Iranshar	IRN	27N12	060E42	×	✓
ISK	Yeni Iskele	CYP	35N13	033E55	✓	×
ISL	Islamabad	PAK	33N27	073E12	✓	✓
ISM	Ismaning	D	48N15	011E45	✓	✓
ISR	Yavne	ISR	31N52	034E45	✓	×
ISS	Issoudun	F	46N56	001E59	✓	×
IUJ	Vestochka	RUS	46N50	142E54	✓	✓
JAK	Jakarta	INS	06S12	106E51	✓	×
JAL	Jalandhar	IND	31N19	075E18	×	✓
JBR	Jászberény	HNG	47N35	019E52	✓	×
JCR	Millerstown, KY	USA	37N26	086W02	✓	×
JED	Jeddah	ARS	21N32	039E10	✓	×
JEJ	Jeju	KOR	33N28	126E23	×	✓
JES	Vado, NM	USA	32N08	106W35	✓	×
JIA	Jiangsu (Prov.)	CHN	-	-	×	✓
JIN	Jinhua	CHN	28N07	119E39	✓	×
JUL	Jülich	D	50N57	006E22	✓	×
JUN	Junglinster	LUX	49N40	006E19	✓	×
KAB	Kabul	AFG	34N35	069E12	×	✓
KAJ	Kajang	MLA	03N01	101E46	✓	×
KAM	Kamalabad	IRN	35N46	051E27	✓	×
KAS	Kashi	CHN	39N20	075E46	✓	✓
KAV	Kavala	GRC	40N52	024E50	✓	✓
KBD	Kabd	KWT	29N16	047E53	✓	✓
KER	Kerman	IRN	29N59	056E46	×	✓
KEW	Key West, FL	USA	24N34	081W45	✓	×
KHB	Khabarovsk	RUS	46N33	135E15	✓	×
KHR	Kharkiv	UKR	49N38	036E07	✓	×
KIA	Kiashar	IRN	36N14	053E33	×	✓
KIG	Kigali	RRW	01S53	030E04	✓	×
KIM	Kimjae	KOR	35N50	126E50	✓	✓
KKT	Chinsurah	IND	22N55	088E25	×	✓
KLG	Bolshakovo	RUS	54N54	021E43	✓	✓
KNA	Komsomolsk-na-Amure	RUS	50N39	136E55	✓	✓
KNG	Kanggye	KRE	40N58	126E36	✓	×
KNX	Kununurra	AUS	15S45	128E44	✓	×
KOU	Kouhu	TWN	23N35	120E10	✓	✓
KRP	Karup	DNK	56N15	009E04	✓	×
KRV	Kurovskaya	RUS	55N34	039E09	✓	×
KUA	Kuanyin	TWN	25N02	121E09	✓	×
KUJ	Kujang	KRE	40N05	125E05	✓	×
KUL	Kuldiga	LVA	56N58	021E58	×	✓
KUN	Kunming	CHN	25N10	102E50	✓	✓
KVI	Kvitsøy	NOR	59N04	005E27	✓	×
KWT	Kuwait	KWT	29N31	047E41	✓	✓
KYV	Kyiv	UKR	50N31	030E46	✓	✓
LAM	Lampertheim	D	49N36	008E33	✓	×
LES	Lesnoy	RUS	56N04	037E58	✓	×
LHA	Lhasa	CHN	29N30	090E59	✓	✓
LIN	Lingshi	CHN	36N52	111E40	✓	×
LIS	São Gabriel	POR	38N45	008W40	✓	×
LIT	Litomysl	CZE	49N48	016E10	✓	×
LND	London (Spectrum R.)	G	51N24	000W04	×	✓
LUG	Lugoj	ROU	45N41	021E55	×	✓
LUK	Lukang	TWN	24N03	120E24	×	✓
LUS	Lusaka	ZMB	15S30	028E15	✓	×
LVI	Lviv	UKR	49N51	024E40	✓	✓
MAN	Manzini	SWZ	26S34	031E59	✓	✓
MAS	Mashhad	IRN	36N15	059E33	✓	×
MCO	Fontbonne	F	43N44	007E26	✓	×
MDC	Talata Volonondry	MDG	18S43	047E37	✓	×
MEX	Mexico City	MEX	19N16	099W03	✓	×
MEY	Meyerton	AFS	26S35	028E08	✓	×
MHD	Mahidasht	IRN	34N16	046E48	×	✓
MHJ	Mahajanga	MDG	15S40	046E21	✓	×
MHS	Mahshar	IRN	30N55	049E15	×	✓
MIL	Milano	I	45N27	009E11	✓	×
MIN	Minhsiung	TWN	23N29	120E27	✓	✓
MKU	Maku	IRN	39N17	044E30	×	✓
MLK	Bethel, PA	USA	40N29	076W17	✓	×
MNF	Mainflingen	D	58N00	008E59	×	✓
MNS	Minsk	BLR	53N58	027E47	✓	×
MON	Monrovia	LBR	06N18	010W40	✓	×
MOR	Briech	MRC	35N34	005W58	✓	×
MOS	Moosbrunn	AUT	48N00	016E28	✓	×
MRN	Marnach	LUX	50N02	006E04	×	✓
MSK	Moskva	RUS	55N45	037E18	✓	✓
MTH	Marathon Key, FL	USA	24N43	081W03	×	✓
MUL	Mulenvos	AGL	08S53	013E20	✓	×
MUM	Mumbai	IND	19N11	072E49	✓	×
NAD	Nador	MRC	35N03	002W55	✓	✓
NAK	Nakhon Sawan	THA	15N49	100E04	✓	×
NAU	Nauen	D	52N38	012E54	✓	×
NEI	Nei Menggu A.R. (Prov.)	CHN	-	-	×	✓
NLS	Anchor Pt, AK	ALS	59N45	151W44	✓	×
NNN	Nanning	CHN	22N47	108E11	✓	×
NOB	Noblejas	E	39N57	003W26	✓	×
NSB	Novosibirsk	RUS	55N04	082E58	✓	×
NVS	Oyash	RUS	55N31	083E45	✓	×
OMO	Ô Môn	VTN	10N04	125E39	×	✓
ORF	Orfordness	G	52N10	001E57	×	✓
ORZ	Orzu	TJK	37N32	068E42	✓	✓
OSI	Osijek	HRV	45N38	018E41	×	✓
PAN	Panaji	IND	15N28	073E51	✓	×
PAO	Paochung	TWN	23N43	120E18	✓	×
PEH	Pearl Harbour, HI	HWA	21N25	158W09	✓	×
PET	Petrich	BUL	41N42	023E18	×	✓
PHP	Poro Point	PHL	16N37	120E17	×	✓
PHT	Tinang	PHL	15N21	120E37	✓	×
PIR	Pirsaat	AZE	39N55	049E25	×	✓
PLD	Plovdiv	BUL	42N04	024E41	✓	×
POR	Pori	FIN	61N28	021E35	✓	✓
PPK	Yelizovo	RUS	52N59	158E39	✓	×
PRS	Paris	F	48N51	002E20	×	✓
PUG	Palauig	PHL	15N28	119E50	✓	×
PUT	Puttalam	CLN	07N58	079E47	×	✓
PYO	P'yongyang	KRE	39N05	125E23	✓	×
QAR	Qaraturyq	KAZ	43N39	077E56	✓	×
QIQ	Qiqihar	CHN	47N02	124E03	✓	×
QSH	Qasr-e Shirin	IRN	34N31	045E35	×	✓
QUI	Quito	EQA	00S14	078W20	✓	✓

Code	Site	Ctry	Lat	Long	SW	MW
RAJ	Rajkot	IND	22N22	070E41	×	✓
RAN	Rangitaiki	NZL	38S50	176E25	✓	×
REY	Reykjavík	ISL	64N05	021W50	✓	×
REZ	Rezayeh	IRN	37N32	045E05	×	✓
RHO	Rhodos	GRC	36N18	028E00	×	✓
RIY	Riyadh	ARS	24N30	046E23	✓	×
RMI	Miami, FL	USA	25N54	080W22	✓	×
RMP	Rampisham	G	50N48	002W38	✓	×
RNO	New Orleans, LA	USA	29N50	090W07	✓	×
ROM	Prato Smeraldo	I	41N48	012E31	✓	×
ROR	Roosevelt Roads	PTR	18N23	067W11	✓	×
ROU	Roumoules	F	43N51	006E09	×	✓
RSO	Rimavská Sobota	SVK	48N23	020E00	✓	×
SAC	Sackville	CAN	45N53	064W19	✓	×
SAI	Saipan, MP	MRA	15N07	145E42	✓	×
SAM	Samara	RUS	53N17	050E15	✓	×
SAO	Pinheira	STP	00N18	006E46	✓	✓
SAS	Sasnovy	BLR	53N24	028E32	×	✓
SDA	Agat, GU	GUM	13N20	144E39	✓	×
SEB	Seeb	OMA	23N40	058E10	✓	×
SEL	Selebi-Phikwe	BOT	22S01	027E50	×	✓
SEO	Seoul	KOR	37N34	126E58	×	✓
SEY	Mahé	SEY	04S36	055E28	✓	×
SFA	Sfax	TUN	34N48	010E53	✓	×
SGO	Santiago	CHL	33S27	070W41	✓	×
SGP	Singapore	SNG	01N24	103E51	✓	×
SHB	Cypress Greek, SC	USA	32N41	081W08	✓	×
SHI	Shijak	ALB	41N20	019E33	✓	×
SHP	Shepparton	AUS	36S20	145E25	✓	×
SIN	Sines	POR	37N57	008W45	✓	×
SIR	Sirjan	IRN	29N27	055E41	✓	×
SIT	Sitkunai	LTU	55N02	023E49	✓	✓
SKN	Skelton	G	54N44	002W54	✓	×
SKO	Skopje	MKD	42N00	021E25	×	✓
SLA	A'Seela	OMA	21N57	059E27	✓	✓
SMF	Mykolaiv	UKR	46N49	032E14	✓	✓
SMG	S. Maria di Galeria	CVA	42N03	012E19	✓	✓
SNG	Kranji	SNG	01N25	103E44	✓	×
SOF	Sofia	BUL	42N40	023E20	✓	×
SOL	Sölvesborg	S	56N02	014E34	×	✓
SPB	Krasnyy Bor	RUS	59N39	030E42	✓	✓
SPE	St. Peterburg	RUS	59N52	030E28	×	✓
SZG	Shijiazhuang	CHN	38N04	114E28	✓	×
TAC	Toshkent	UZB	41N13	069E09	✓	×
TAI	Taipei	TWN	25N05	121E27	✓	×
TAR	Tartus	SYR	34N50	035E50	×	✓
TBN	Salt Lake City, UT	USA	40N39	112W03	✓	×
TCH	Atamanovka	RUS	51N50	113E43	✓	✓
THE	Thessaloniki	GRC	40N31	022E57	✓	×
THU	Thumrayt	OMA	17N38	053E56	✓	×
TIG	Tiganesti	ROU	44N42	026E06	✓	×
TIN	Tinian, MP	MRA	15N03	145E36	✓	×
TJC	Newport, NC (WJIE)	USA	34N47	076W53	✓	×
TLD	Taldom	RUS	56N44	037E38	✓	×
TNN	Tainan	TWN	23N11	120E38	✓	×
TRI	Tripoli	LBY	32N54	013E11	✓	×
TRM	Trincomalee	CLN	08N44	081E10	✓	✓
TSH	Tamshui	TWN	25N13	121E29	✓	×
TUA	Kota Kinabalu	MLA	06N11	116E12	✓	✓
TUN	Tunis	TUN	36N48	010E10	×	✓
TUT	Tuticorin	IND	08N48	078E12	×	✓
TWR	Merizo, GU	GUM	13N17	144E40	✓	×
TYB	Tayebad	IRN	34N43	060E48	×	✓
UBA	Ulaanbaatar	MNG	47N55	107E00	✓	✓
UDO	Udon Thani	THA	17N42	103E16	✓	×
ULB	Ulbroka	LVA	56N56	024E17	✓	×
URU	Ürümqi	CHN	43N35	087E30	✓	✓
VAT	Vatican City	CVA	41N54	012E27	✓	✓
VDN	Vidin	BUL	43N39	022E40	×	✓
VIE	Vientiane	LAO	17N58	102E33	✓	×
VIR	Virrat	FIN	62N23	023E37	✓	✓
VLD	Razdolnoye	RUS	43N32	131E57	✓	✓
VLN	Vilnius	LTU	54N42	025E13	×	✓
VNI	Son Tay	VTN	21N12	105E22	✓	×
VOH	Rancho Simi, CA	USA	34N15	118W38	✓	×
WAV	Wavre	BEL	50N44	004E34	✓	×
WBR	Wachenbrunn	D	50N29	010E33	×	✓
WBS	Macon, GA	USA	32N50	083W38	✓	×
WCR	Nashville, TN	USA	36N13	086W54	✓	×
WER	Wertachtal	D	48N05	010E41	✓	×
WHR	Naalehu, HI	HWA	19N02	155W40	✓	×
WOF	Woofferton	G	52N19	002W43	✓	×
WOL	Wolvertem	BEL	50N57	004E18	×	✓
WRB	Manchester, TN	USA	35N29	086W02	✓	×
WUS	Falls Church, VA (WUST)	USA	38N52	077W10	×	✓
WWA	Warszawa	POL	52N04	020E52	✓	×
XIA	Xi'an	CHN	34N12	108E54	✓	×
YAM	Tokyo	J	36N10	139E50	✓	×
YER	Yerevan	ARM	40N14	044E34	✓	×
YFR	Okeechobee, FL	USA	27N28	080W56	✓	×
YUN	Yunnan (Prov.)	CHN	-	-	×	✓
ZAB	Zabol	IRN	31N02	061E29	×	✓
ZAD	Zadar	HRV	44N06	015E15	×	✓
ZAH	Zahedan	IRN	29N28	060E53	✓	×
—	Not Specified	-	-	-	×	×

TARGET AREA CODES

Code	Target Area
Af	Africa
Am	Americas
As	Asia
Atl	Atlantic
CAf	Central Africa
CAm	Central America
Car	Caribbean
CAs	Central Asia
EAf	Eastern Africa
EAs	Eastern Asia
EEu	Eastern Europe
Eu	Europe
FE	Far East
IOc	Indian Ocean
ME	Middle East
Med	Mediterranean
NAf	Northern Africa
NAm	North America
Oc	Oceania
Pac	Pacific
SAf	Southern Africa
SAm	South America
SAs	Southern Asia
SEA	South East Asia
SEu	Southern Europe
WAf	Western Africa
WAs	Western Asia
WEu	Western Europe

DOMESTIC SW TRANSMITTER SITES

Ctry	Site	Lat	Long
ARG	Malargüe	35S30	069W35
ARG	Mendoza	32S50	068W47
ARG	Puerto Iguazú	25S36	054W34
ATA	Base Esperanza	63S24	056W59
AUS	Alice Springs	23S42	133E53
AUS	Humpty Doo	12S37	131E17
AUS	Katherine	14S28	132E16
AUS	Tennant Creek	19S40	134E10
AZE	Stepanakert	39N48	046E45
B	Altamira	03S13	052W15
B	Anápolis	16S20	048W58
B	Aparecida	23S00	045W00
B	Aquidauana	20S27	055W45
B	Araguaína	07S16	048W18
B	Araraquara	21S47	048W10
B	Barra do Garças	15S54	052W15
B	Belém	01S27	048W29
B	Belo Horizonte	19S54	043W54
B	Boa Vista	02N51	060W43
B	Bragança	01S02	046W46
B	Brasiléia	11S00	068W44
B	Cáceres	16S05	057W40
B	Cachoeira	22S39	045W01
B	Campinas	22S54	047W06
B	Campo Grande	20S24	054W35
B	Campos dos Got.	21S46	041W21
B	Coari	04S08	063W07
B	Congonhas	20S30	043W53
B	Corumbá	19S01	057W39
B	Cruzeiro do Sul	07S40	072W39
B	Cuiabá	15S32	056W05
B	Curitiba	25S23	049W10
B	Descalvado	21S53	047W40
B	Dourados	22S09	054W52
B	Florianópolis	27S35	048W31
B	Foz do Iguaçu	25S34	054W33
B	Goiânia	16S43	049W18
B	Gov. Valadares	18S51	041W57
B	Guajará Mirim	10S50	065W21
B	Guarujá	23S55	046W17
B	Humaitá	07S31	063W01
B	Ibitinga	21S43	048W47
B	Jataí	17S58	051W45
B	Ji-Paraná	10S50	061W58
B	Limeira	22S34	047W25
B	Londrina	23S18	051W13
B	Macapá	00N04	051W04
B	Manaus	03S04	060W00
B	Natal	05S47	035W13
B	Óbidos	01S52	055W30
B	Osasco	23S30	046W30
B	Parintins	02S38	056W45
B	Petrolina	09S22	040W30
B	Pocos de Caldas	21S48	046W33
B	Porto Alegre	30S03	051W10
B	Porto Velho	08S45	063W54

Ctry	Site	Lat	Long
B	Ribeirão Preto	21S10	047W44
B	Rio Branco	09S59	067W49
B	Rio de Janeiro	22S57	043W13
B	Rolim de Moura	13S04	062W16
B	Rondonópolis	16S29	054W37
B	Santa Maria	29S42	053W42
B	Santarém	02S26	054W41
B	São Carlos	22S02	047W53
B	S.Gabriel da Ca.	00S09	067W03
B	São Luís	02S34	044W16
B	São Paulo	23S33	046W39
B	Sena Madureira	09S04	068W40
B	Sdr. Guiomard	10S10	067W50
B	Sorocaba	23S29	047W27
B	Taubaté	23S00	045W36
B	Tefé	03S24	064W45
B	Teresina	05S09	042W46
B	Varginha	21S33	045W25
B	Vitória	20S19	040W21
B	Xapuri	10S40	068W30
BDI	Gitega	03S29	029E56
BEN	Cotonou	06N21	002E25
BEN	Parakou	09N20	002E38
BFA	Ouagadougou	12N22	001W31
BGD	Shavar	23N27	090E12
BLR	Brest	52N18	023E54
BLR	Hrodna	53N54	024E00
BLR	Mahilioú	53N55	030E17
BOL	Animas	20S58	066W18
BOL	Bermejo	22S10	064W42
BOL	Camargo	20S38	065W15
BOL	Camiri	20S03	063W32
BOL	Caranavi	15S49	067W33
BOL	Cobija	11S01	068W45
BOL	Cochabamba	17S23	066W11
BOL	El Alto	16S30	068W12
BOL	Guanay	12S31	066W50
BOL	Guayaramerín	10S51	065W23
BOL	Huaca	20S26	064W57
BOL	Huanuni	18S47	066W48
BOL	Independencia	17S04	066W49
BOL	La Paz	16S30	068W08
BOL	Las Romas	16S55	065W22
BOL	Mina Bolívar	18S29	066W53
BOL	Montero	17S15	063W15
BOL	Oruro	17S58	067W07
BOL	Padilla	19S18	064W20
BOL	Reyes	14S18	067W23
BOL	Riberalta	10S59	066W06
BOL	Rurrenabaque	14S28	067W34
BOL	San Borja	14S52	066W53
BOL	S.Ignacio de Mo.	14S56	065W38
BOL	S.Ignacio de Vel.	16S22	060W57
BOL	S.José de Chiq.	17S53	060W45
BOL	Sta. Ana del Yac.	13S45	065W32
BOL	Santa Cruz	17S46	063W11

Ctry	Site	Lat	Long
BOL	Siglo Veinte	18S23	066W38
BOL	Sipe Sipe	17S27	066W22
BOL	Sucre	19S02	065W18
BOL	Tazna	20S41	066W22
BOL	Trinidad	14S48	064W48
BOL	Uyuni	20S27	066W50
BOL	Villa Abecia	20S57	065W13
BOL	Villa Montes	14S18	062W21
BOL	Villa Serrano	19S07	064W20
BOL	Villa Yapacani	17S24	063W50
BOL	Yura	20S02	066W10
BOT	Sebele	24S34	025E58
BRM	Taunggyi	20N47	097E02
BRM	Yegu	16N52	096E10
BTN	Thimphu	27N28	089E39
BUL	Varna	43N03	027E40
CAF	Bangui	04N21	018E35
CAN	Calgary	50N54	113W52
CAN	St. John's	47N34	052W49
CAN	Toronto	43N30	079W38
CAN	Vancouver	49N08	123W12
CHL	Coyhaique	45S30	072W06
CHL	Putre	18S12	069W35
CHL	Temuco	38S41	072W35
CHN	Baoji	34N30	107E10
CHN	Bayanhot	38N58	105E35
CHN	Fuzhou	26N06	119E24
CHN	Gejiu	23N21	103E08
CHN	Guiyang	26N25	106E36
CHN	Hailar	49N02	119E45
CHN	Hezuo	35N06	102E54
CHN	Nanjing	32N02	118E44
CHN	Nanning	22N47	108E11
CHN	Shanghai	31N15	121E29
CHN	Shangzhi	45N02	128E00
CHN	Tianshui	34N33	105E42
CHN	Wuchang	44N54	127E11
CHN	Xiangtan	27N30	112E30
CHN	Xichang	27N49	102E14
CHN	Xining	36N38	101E36
CLM	Bogotá	04N38	074W05
CLM	Buenaventura	03N54	077W02
CLM	Florencía	01N37	075W37
CLM	Ibagué	04N26	075W13
CLM	Lomalinda	07N09	074W35
CLM	Melgar	04N12	074W39
CLM	Pasto	01N13	077N17
CLM	Puerto Lleras	03N16	073W22
CLM	Quibdó	05N40	076W38
CLM	S. José del Guav.	02N34	072W38
CLM	Villavicencio	04N09	073W28
COD	Aru	02N52	030E51
COD	Bukavu	02S30	028E50
COD	Bunia	01N32	030E11
COD	Goma	01S41	029E13
COD	Kinshasa	04S23	015E23

Ctry	Site	Lat	Long
COD	Lubumbashi	11S41	027E32
COD	Mbandaka	00N04	018E17
COG	Brazzaville	04S15	015E18
CTR	Limón	10N00	083W02
CTR	San José	09N56	084W05
D	Mühlacker	48N57	008E51
D	Rohrdorf	48N01	009E07
DOM	Barahona	18N13	071W07
DOM	Santo Domingo	18N30	069W57
EQA	Ambato	01S13	078W37
EQA	Bahía de Caráq.	00S60	080W42
EQA	Calceta	00S51	080W07
EQA	Cuena	02S53	078W59
EQA	Ibarra	00N21	078W08
EQA	Loja	03S59	079W12
EQA	Macas	02S22	078W08
EQA	Otavalo	0018N	078W11
EQA	Riobamba	01S40	078W40
EQA	Saquisilí	00S58	078W24
EQA	Saraguro	03S42	079W18
EQA	Sta Rosa de Quij.	00S17	077W46
EQA	Sto Dom. d.l.C.	00S13	079W09
EQA	Sucúa	02S28	078W10
EQA	Tena	01S00	077W48
ERI	Asmara	15N32	038E55
ETH	Addis Ababa	08N58	038E43
ETH	Mek'ele	13N32	039E33
GAB	Libreville	00N25	009E26
GEO	Soxum	43N00	041E00
GHA	Accra	05N31	000W10
GNE	Bata	01N48	009E46
GNE	Malabo	03N45	008E47
GTM	Barillas	15N19	091W26
GTM	Cabricán	14N50	091W30
GTM	Chiquimula	14N48	089W32
GTM	Cobán	15N28	090W20
GTM	Fray Bartolomé	15N20	090W20
GTM	Guatemala	14N55	090W28
GTM	Jocotán	14N49	089W23
GTM	Nahualá	14N50	090W20
GTM	S.Pedro La Lag.	14N46	091W11
GTM	S.Sebastián Huh.	1510N	091W20
GTM	S.Sebastián Coa.	1530N	091W30
GTM	Santiago Atitlán	14N39	091W12
GUF	Matoury	04N54	052W20
GUI	Conacry	09N32	013W40
GUY	Sparendaam	06N49	058W10
HND	Comayagüela	14N15	087W20
HND	La Ceiba	15N45	086W45
HND	Puerto Lempira	15N12	083W51
HND	San Luís	15N08	088W25
HND	San Pedro Sula	15N29	088W01
HND	Tegucigalpa	14N05	087W14
I	Caltanissetta	37N30	014E04
IND	Aizawl	23N43	092E43
IND	Bhopal	23N10	077E30

Ctry	Site	Lat	Long
IND	Gangtok	27N20	088E40
IND	Guwahati	26N06	091E35
IND	Hyderabad	17N20	078E33
IND	Imphal	24N44	093E58
IND	Itanagar	27N12	093E42
IND	Jaipur	26N54	075E50
IND	Jammu	32N45	075E00
IND	Jeypore	18N51	082E40
IND	Kohima	25N39	094E06
IND	Kolkata	22N27	088E18
IND	Kurseong	26N55	088E19
IND	Leh	34N09	077E35
IND	Lucknow	26N53	081E03
IND	Port Blair	11N40	092E44
IND	Ranchi	23N24	085E22
IND	Shillong	25N34	091E56
IND	Shimla	31N00	077E05
IND	Srinagar	34N00	074E50
IND	Thiruvananthap.	08N29	076E59
INS	Bajawa	08S46	120E59
INS	Biak	01S10	136E06
INS	Bukittinggi	00S18	100E22
INS	Fakfak	03S51	132E20
INS	Gorontalo	00N33	123E05
INS	Jambi	01S38	103E34
INS	Kendari	03S38	122E26
INS	Makassar	05S10	119E25
INS	Merauke	08S33	140E27
INS	Palangkaraya	02S02	117E10
INS	Palu	00S54	119E52
INS	Pontianak	00S05	109E16
INS	Ruteng	08S35	120E28
INS	Serui	01S48	136E26
INS	Sorong	00S52	131E25
INS	Ternate	00N48	127E23
INS	Wamena	03S50	138E38
ISR	Lod	32N00	034E90
J	Fukuoka	33N33	130E27
J	Nagara	35N28	140E13
J	Nagoya	35N03	136E58
J	Nemuro	43N18	145E34
J	Osaka	34N33	135E31
J	Sapporo	43N05	141E37
J	Shobu	36N04	139E38
KEN	Langata	01S23	036E46
KGZ	Bishkek	42N54	074E37
KIR	Tarawa	01N21	172E56
KRE	Haeju	38N00	125E07
KRE	Hamhung	39N56	127E39
KRE	Hyesan	41N04	128E02
KRE	P'yongsong	40N05	124E24
KRE	Sariwon	38N05	125E08
KRE	Wonsan	39N05	127E25
LAO	Xam Nua	20N25	104E04
LSO	Maseru	29S19	027E33
MDG	Feonarive	18S50	047E35
MDG	Sabotsy	18S55	047E32
MEX	Huayacocotla	20N34	098W27
MEX	Mérida	20N58	089W37
MEX	San Luis Potosí	22N01	100W59
MEX	Tapachula	14N08	092W04
MLA	Kuching	01N33	110E20
MLA	Sibu	02N18	111E49
MLD	Malé	06N20	073E 00
MNG	Altay	46N30	096E10
MNG	Mörön	49N28	100E10
MTN	Nouakchott	18N07	015W57
NCG	Puerto Cabezas	14N02	083W25
NGR	Niamey	12N30	002E06
NIG	Abuja	09N00	007E16
NIG	Enugu	06N27	007E27
NIG	Ibadan	07N23	003E54
NIG	Kaduna	10N45	007E33
NIG	Lagos	06N34	003E21
NMB	Windhoek	22S33	017E13
NPL	Khumaltar	27N42	085E12
NZL	Levin	40S37	175E18
PAK	Peshawar	34N00	071E30
PAK	Quetta	30N15	067E00
PHL	Marulas	14N41	120E59
PNG	Alotau	10S18	150E28
PNG	Daru	09S05	143E10
PNG	Goroka	06S02	145E22
PNG	Kavieng	02S34	150E48
PNG	Kerema	07S59	145E46
PNG	Kieta	06S15	155E37
PNG	Kimbe	05S36	150E10
PNG	Kundiawa	06S00	144E57
PNG	Lae	06S45	147E00
PNG	Lorengau	02S01	147E15
PNG	Madang	05S14	145E45
PNG	Mendi	06S13	143E39
PNG	Mt. Hagen	05S54	144E13
PNG	Panguna	05S28	143E40
PNG	Popondetta	08S45	148E15
PNG	Port Moresby	09S27	147E11
PNG	Rabaul	04S13	152E12
PNG	Vanimo	02S40	141E17
PNG	Wabag	05S28	143E40
PNG	Wewak	03S35	143E40
PRG	Asunción	25S16	057W38
PRG	Ñemby	25S22	057W36
PRG	Villeta	25S31	057W33
PRU	Abancay	13S37	072W52
PRU	Andahuaylas	13S39	073W24
PRU	Anta	13S08	074W24
PRU	Aramango	05S24	078W27
PRU	Arequipa	16S25	071W32
PRU	Ayabaca	05S30	080W30
PRU	Ayacucho	13S10	074W15
PRU	Ayaviri	14S53	070W35
PRU	Bagua Grande	05S47	078W26
PRU	Bambamarca	06S43	078W34
PRU	Bolívar	07S16	077W47
PRU	Cajabamba	07S37	078W03
PRU	Cajamarca	07S09	078W32
PRU	Callalli	15S51	072W51
PRU	Celendín	06S53	078W09
PRU	Cerro Colorado	08S56	078W27
PRU	Chachapoyas	06S10	077W50
PRU	Chaupimarca	10S24	076W28
PRU	Chiclayo	06S47	079W47
PRU	Chincheros	13S31	073W43
PRU	Chiriaco	05S09	078W21
PRU	Chota	06S21	078W39
PRU	Comas	11S57	077W04
PRU	Cusco	13S32	071W57
PRU	Cutervo	06S23	078W51
PRU	Huamachuco	07S50	078W01
PRU	Huancabamba	05S17	079W28
PRU	Huancavelica	12S45	075W03
PRU	Huancayo	12S05	075W12
PRU	Huanta	12S54	074W13
PRU	Huánuco	09S55	076W11
PRU	Huaraz	09N33	077W31
PRU	Huarmaca	05S34	079W32
PRU	Huayllay	11S01	076W21
PRU	Iquitos	03S51	073W13
PRU	Jaén	05S45	078W51
PRU	Jerillo	06S03	076W56
PRU	Juliaca	15S29	070W09
PRU	Junín	11S11	076W00
PRU	La Merced	11S03	075W16
PRU	La Oroya	11S36	075W54
PRU	Lambayeque	06S36	079W45
PRU	Layas	06S34	078W44
PRU	Líma	12S06	077W03
PRU	Lonya Grande	05S46	078W31
PRU	Moquegua	17S12	070W56
PRU	Moyobamba	06S04	076W58
PRU	Nuev. Cajamarca	06S30	077W30
PRU	Otuzco	07S54	078W35
PRU	Oxapampa	10S34	075W24
PRU	Panao	09S54	075W58
PRU	Parcoy	07S58	077W26
PRU	Pardo Miguel N.	06S30	077W30
PRU	Paucartambo	10S54	075W51
PRU	Pomabamba	08S50	077W28
PRU	Pucallpa	08S23	074W32
PRU	Puerto Maldon.	12S37	069W11
PRU	Puno	15S56	070W01
PRU	Quillabamba	12S49	072W41
PRU	Recobamba	06S54	078W15
PRU	Retamas	07S58	077W25
PRU	Rioja	06S02	077W10
PRU	Rodrigues de M.	06S19	077W28
PRU	San Ignacio	05S09	079W00
PRU	S.Juan de Lurig.	12S02	077W01
PRU	San Miguel	07S03	078W54
PRU	S.Miguel de El F.	05S17	079W28
PRU	San Pablo	07S45	074W59
PRU	Santa Cruz	06S40	079W00
PRU	S.Maria de Nie.	04S35	077W54
PRU	Satipo	11S16	074W41
PRU	Sicuani	14S15	071W12
PRU	Sondor	05S30	079W30
PRU	Tabaconas	05S19	079W17
PRU	Tacna	18S00	070W13
PRU	Tarapoto	06S31	076W29
PRU	Tarma	11S28	075W41
PRU	Tayabamba	08S17	077W18
PRU	Tingo María	09S08	075W54
PRU	Tocache	08S11	076W31
PRU	Trujillo	08S06	079W00
PRU	Villa Atalaya	10S44	073W46
PRU	Yurimaguas	05S54	076W07
RUS	Arkhangelsk	64N24	041E32
RUS	Arman	59N46	150E10
RUS	Krasnoyarsk	56N01	092E54
RUS	Kyzyl	51N42	094E23
RUS	Monchegorsk	67N55	033E01
RUS	Perm	57N59	056E18
RUS	Selenga	51N50	107E38
RUS	Yakutsk	62N01	129E48
RUS	Yazykovo	54N19	047E22
SDN	Narus	04N46	033E35
SDN	Omdurman	15N30	032E28
SLM	Honiara	09S25	160E03
SLV	Sonsonate	13N43	089W44
SOM	Baydhabo	03N07	043E39
SOM	Boosaaso	11N17	049E11
SOM	Gaalkacyo	06N46	047E26
SOM	Hargeysa	09N33	044E03
SOM	Mogadishu	02N01	045E18
SRL	Freetown	08N30	011W30
SRL	Goderich	08N30	013W14
SUR	Paramaribo	05N49	055W12
TCD	N'Djaména	12N08	015E03
TGO	Togblekope	06N16	001E12
THA	Pathum Thani	14N03	100E43
TKM	Asgabat	37N57	058E53
TZA	Dar es Salaam	06S50	039E14
UGA	Kampala	00N20	032E36
UGA	Entebbe	00N04	032E27
UKR	Zaporizhia	47N08	035E02
URG	Artigas	30S25	056W29
URG	Castillos	34S16	053W56
URG	Sarandí del Yi	33S22	055W38
URG	Montevideo	34S50	056W18
VEN	Puerto Ayacucho	05N35	067W40
VEN	San Cristóbal	07N46	072W15
VEN	S. Juan de los C.	11N10	068W25
VEN	Valera	09N19	070W36
VTN	Buôn Mê Thuôt	12N40	108E12
VTN	Cao Bang	22N40	106E16
VTN	Hà Giang	22N50	104E59
VTN	Lai Châu	22N04	103E10
VTN	Lào Cai	22N30	103E57
VTN	Son La	21N20	103E55
VTN	Xuân Mai	20N43	105E33
VTN	Yên Bai	21N43	104E54
VUT	Port-Vila	17S44	168E33
YEM	Sana'a	15N22	044E11
ZWE	Gweru	19S26	029E51

N.B. For coordinates of sites that are jointly used for national and international services: please see the International Transmitter Sites table.

COUNTRY CODES USED IN WRTH

Code	Country
—	Not Specified
ABW	Aruba
AFG	Afghanistan
AFS	South Africa
AGL	Angola
AIA	Anguilla
ALB	Albania
ALG	Algeria
ALS	Alaska
AND	Andorra
AOE	Western Sahara
ARG	Argentina
ARM	Armenia
ARS	Saudi Arabia
ASC	Ascension Island
ATA	Antarctica
ATG	Antigua and Barbuda
ATN	Netherlands Antilles
AUS	Australia
AUT	Austria
AZE	Azerbaijan
AZR	Azores
B	Brazil
BAH	Bahamas
BDI	Burundi
BEL	Belgium
BEN	Benin
BER	Bermuda
BFA	Burkina Faso
BGD	Bangladesh
BHR	Bahrain
BIH	Bosnia & Herzegovina
BIO	British Indian Ocean Territory
BLR	Belarus
BLZ	Belize
BOL	Bolivia
BOT	Botswana
BRB	Barbados
BRM	Myanmar
BRU	Brunei Darussalam
BTN	Bhutan
BUL	Bulgaria
CAF	Central African Republic
CAN	Canada
CBG	Cambodia
CHL	Chile
CHN	China (People's Rep. of)
CHR	Christmas Island
CKH	Cook Islands
CLM	Colombia
CLN	Sri Lanka
CME	Cameroon
CNR	Canary Islands
COD	Congo (Dem. Rep.)
COG	Congo (Rep.of)
COM	Comoros
CPV	Cape Verde
CTI	Ivory Coast
CTR	Costa Rica
CUB	Cuba
CVA	Vatican City State
CYM	Cayman Islands
CYP	Cyprus
CZE	Czech Republic
D	Germany
DGA	Diego Garcia
DJI	Djibouti
DMA	Dominica
DNK	Denmark
DOM	Dominican Republic
E	Spain
EGY	Egypt
EQA	Ecuador
ERI	Eritrea
EST	Estonia
ETH	Ethiopia
F	France
FIN	Finland
FJI	Fiji
FLK	Falkland Islands
FRO	Faroe Islands
FSM	Micronesia
G	United Kingdom
GAB	Gabon
GAL	Galapagos Islands
GDL	Guadeloupe
GEO	Georgia
GHA	Ghana
GIB	Gibraltar
GMB	Gambia
GNB	Guinea-bissau
GNE	Equatorial Guinea
GRC	Greece
GRD	Grenada
GRL	Greenland
GTM	Guatemala
GUF	French Guiana
GUI	Guinea
GUM	Guam
GUY	Guyana
HKG	Hong Kong
HND	Honduras
HNG	Hungary
HOL	Netherlands
HRV	Croatia
HTI	Haiti
HWA	Hawaii
I	Italy
ICO	Cocos (Keeling) Is
IND	India
INS	Indonesia
IRL	Ireland
IRN	Iran
IRQ	Iraq
ISL	Iceland
ISR	Israel
ITW	International Waters
J	Japan
JMC	Jamaica
JOR	Jordan
KAZ	Kazakhstan
KEN	Kenya
KGZ	Kyrgyzstan
KIR	Kiribati
KOR	Korea, South (Rep. of)
KRE	Korea, North (D.P.R.)
KWT	Kuwait
LAO	Laos
LBN	Lebanon
LBR	Liberia
LBY	Libya
LCA	St Lucia
LHW	Lord Howe Island
LIE	Liechtenstein
LSO	Lesotho
LTU	Lithuania
LUX	Luxembourg
LVA	Latvia
MAC	Macao
MAU	Mauritius
MCO	Monaco
MDA	Moldova
MDG	Madagascar
MDR	Madeira
MEX	Mexico
MHL	Marshall Islands
MKD	Macedonia
MLA	Malaysia
MLD	Maldives
MLI	Mali
MLT	Malta
MNG	Mongolia
MOZ	Mozambique
MRA	Northern Mariana Is
MRC	Morocco
MRT	Martinique
MSR	Monserrat
MTN	Mauritania
MWI	Malawi
MYT	Mayotte
NCG	Nicaragua
NCL	New Caledonia
NFK	Norfolk Island
NGR	Niger
NIG	Nigeria
NIU	Niue
NMB	Namibia
NOR	Norway
NPL	Nepal
NRU	Nauru
NZL	New Zealand
OCE	French Polynesia
OMA	Oman
PAK	Pakistan
PAQ	Easter Island
PHL	Philippines
PLW	Palau
PNG	Papua New Guinea
PNR	Panama
POL	Poland
POR	Portugal
PRG	Paraguay
PRU	Peru
PSE	West Bank & Gaza (Palestine Authority)
PTR	Puerto Rico
QAT	Qatar
REU	Reunion
ROU	Romania
RRW	Rwanda
RUS	Russia
S	Sweden
SCG	Serbia & Montenegro
SCN	St Kitts and Nevis
SDN	Sudan
SEN	Senegal
SEY	Seychelles
SHN	St Helena
SLM	Solomon Islands
SLV	El Salvador
SMA	American Samoa
SMO	Samoa
SMR	San Marino
SNG	Singapore
SOM	Somalia
SPM	St. Pierre and Miquelon
SRL	Sierra Leone
STP	São Tomé e Princípe
SUI	Switzerland
SUR	Suriname
SVK	Slovakia
SVN	Slovenia
SWZ	Swaziland
SYR	Syria
TCA	Turks & Caicos Is
TCD	Chad
TGO	Togo
THA	Thailand
TJK	Tajikistan
TKM	Turkmenistan
TMP	East Timor
TOK	Tokelau
TON	Tonga
TRC	Tristan Da Cunha
TRD	Trinidad & Tobago
TUN	Tunisia
TUR	Turkey
TUV	Tuvalu
TWN	Taiwan (Rep. of China)
TZA	Tanzania
UAE	United Arab Emirates
UGA	Uganda
UKR	Ukraine
UNO	United Nations
URG	Uruguay
USA	United States of America
UZB	Uzbekistan
VCT	St Vincent & Grenadines
VEN	Venezuela
VIR	Virgin Islands (American)
VRG	Virgin Islands (British)
VTN	Vietnam
VUT	Vanuatu
WAL	Wallis & Futuna
YEM	Yemen
ZMB	Zambia (Rep. of)
ZWE	Zimbabwe

STANDARD TIME & FREQUENCY TRANSMISSIONS

A guide to what STFTs are and how to use them

What are STFTs?

Standard Time and Frequency Transmissions (STFTs) are continuous transmissions of 'beeps' or 'pips' every second, with the time in UTC announced on the minute. They are often referred to as 'Time Signals'. Some stations broadcast for 24 hours a day while other stations run for a few hours each day or, in some cases, only on certain days of the week.

Using STFTs

STFTs are invaluable aids for the radio user. Not only do they allow listeners to synchronise station clocks to UTC but they are also a handy tool for checking propagation and reception paths. Their most useful role for serious shortwave listeners, however, is for checking that equipment is performing as it should and to test for receiver error.

Checking Performance

It is possible to carry out tests on a variety of frequencies ranging from 2500 to 20000kHz. First select an appropriate set of STFT's, perhaps by saving them into a set of memory channels if your radio has the facility. A quick check can be made for the characteristic ticks and pulses to ensure that there is a good reception path and that the STFT is currently active, before moving on to the tests themselves. Don't forget that it is essential to allow the radio to warm up for an hour or so before starting these tests.

The object of the exercise is to mix the incoming STFT signal with an internally generated signal from the radio's Beat Frequency Oscillator (BFO) and then tune the radio until the resulting whistle drops down to zero. This process of tuning for 'zero beat' then ensures that the radio is on exactly the same frequency as the transmission – any error shown on the dial will be the receiver error and any drift in tone will be receiver drift.

For most radios it will suffice to select either upper or lower sideband mode with a wide filter setting and use a loudspeaker or pair of headphones having a good low frequency audio performance. Many SW receivers have internal speakers which are not very good when it comes to reproducing low notes so are useless for this procedure.

As you carefully tune down and hear the note drop, you should find that the S-meter needle starts to fluctuate. This means that you are very close to 'zero beat'. The lower the rate of S-meter needle movement, the nearer you are to the end point. At this stage you will probably not be able to hear much in the headphones apart from a near silent carrier, and the meter will be your best guide as it will be indicating the 'phase error' between the STFT and your BFO. When your needle moves at its slowest rate, you have reached zero beat. Make a note of the dial reading as this will show the receiver error.

For those radios with particularly good filters, which may prevent a 'zero beat' approach, a similar technique can be used by switching to CW mode. This method requires the use of an audio digital frequency meter – ask around at your radio club and you will probably find one. First of all, refer to the manual and find the 'CW offset' frequency. This is the audio frequency which the receiver will produce when it is exactly tuned to the carrier of the STFT. Common values are 600Hz to 800Hz. Some radios allow the user to programme the CW offset, so make sure that it has not been changed before you start the tests.

The procedure is essentially the same as has just been described, except that you will be tuning the radio until the DFM reads 600Hz exactly, then the receiver dial will show you any error. By repeating this test on a number of frequencies, you can be confident that your radio is accurate, or at least be aware of any errors or developing problems, and of course these are handy techniques for testing a radio you are considering buying.

STFT Transmissions, Stations & Addresses

ARGENTINA

✉ Servicio de Hidrografía Naval, Observatorio Naval, Av. España 2099, 1107 Buenos Aires, Argentina. **Email:** onba@rina.hidro.gov.ar **Web:** www.hidro.gov.ar

Location	Callsign	kHz	kW	Mode	Schedule
Buenos Aires	LOL	5000	2	CW	1100-1200, 1400-1500 1700-1800, 2000-2100 2300-2400
Buenos Aires	LOL	10000	2	CW	1100-1200, 1400-1500 1700-1800, 2000-2100 2300-2400

BELARUS

✉ n/a.

Location	Callsign	kHz	kW	Mode	Schedule°
Maladziecna	RJH69	*25	300	CW	0706-0747

NOTES: *) :27-:30 on 25.1, :32-:35 on 25.5, :38-:41 on 23, :44-:47 on 20.5kHz; °) 1h earlier in summer (DST in Belarus)

CANADA

✉ Radio Station CHU, National Research Council of Canada, 1200 Montreal Road, Bldg M-36, Ottawa, Ontario, K1A 0R6, Canada

☎ +1 613 9935698. 📠 +1 613 9521394. **Email:** radio.chu@nrc.ca **Web:** www.nrc-cnrc.gc.ca

Location	Callsign	kHz	kW	Mode	Schedule
Ottawa	CHU	3330	10	USB	24h
	CHU	7335	3	USB	24h
	CHU	14670	3	USB	24h

CHINA (P.R.)

✉ National Time Service Center (NTSC), National Academy of Science, P.O. Box 18, Linshan (Lintong), Shaanxi, P.R.China ☎ +86 29 83890344. 📠 +86 29 83890196. **Email:** kyc@ntsc.ac.cn **Web:** www.ntsc.ac.cn

Location	Callsign	kHz	kW	Mode	Schedule
Linshan	BPM	2500	10	AM	0900-0100
	BPM	5000	20	AM	24h
	BPM	10000	20	AM	24h
	BPM	15000	20	AM	0100-0900

ECUADOR

✉ Instituto Oceanográfico de la Armada, Casilla 5940, Guayaquil, Ecuador ☎ + 593 4 2481300. 📠 +593 4 2485166. **Email:** inocar@inocar.mil.ec **Web:** www.inocar.mil.ec

Location	Callsign	kHz	kW	Mode	Schedule
Guayaquil	HD2IOA	1510		AM	24h
	HD2IOA	3810	1	LSB	0000-1200
	HD2IOA	5000	1	LSB	1200-1300
	HD2IOA	7600	1	LSB	1300-2400

FRANCE

✉ Bureau National de Métrologie - Systèmes de Référence Temps Espace (BNM-SYRTE), 61 avenue de l'Observatoire, F-75014 Paris, France. ☎ +33 140512213. 📠 +33 143255542 **Email:** info.bnm-syrte@obspm.fr **Web:** opdaf1.obspm.fr

Location	Callsign	kHz	kW	Mode	Schedule
Allouis	-	162	2000*	PSK	24h

NOTES: The tx is provided by Télédiffusion de France (TDF) and carries the France-Inter radio prgr. *) 1000kW at nighttime

GERMANY

✉ Physikalisch-Technische Bundesanstalt (PTB), Bundesallee 100, D-38116 Braunschweig, Germany. ☎ +49 531 5920. 📠 +49 531 5923008. **Email:** time@ptb.de **Web:** www.ptb.de

Location	Callsign	kHz	kW	Mode	Schedule
Mainflingen	DCF77	77.5	50	CW+PSK	24h

NOTES: Tx is leased from Deutsche Telekom T-Systems.

JAPAN

✉ National Institute of Information and CommunicationsTechnology (NICT), Applied Research and Standards Frequency Division, Japan Standard Time Group, 4-2-1, Nukui-Kitamachi, Koganei, Tokyo 184-8795. ☎ +81 42 3277567. 📠 +81 42 3276689. **Web:** jjy.crl.go.jp

Location	Callsign	kHz	kW	Mode	Schedule
Ohtakadoyayama	JJY	40	10	CW	24h
Haganeyama	JJY	60	10	CW	24h

KOREA, SOUTH

✉ Time & Frequency Laboratory, Korea Research Institute of Standard & Science, P.O. Box 102, Yuseong Daejeon 305-600, Rep. of Korea. ☎ +82 42 8685114. 📠 +82 42 8611494. **Web:** krissol.kriss.re.kr

Location	Callsign	kHz	kW	Mode	Schedule
Daejeon	HLA	5000	2	AM	24h

KYRGYZSTAN

✉ n/a

Location	Callsign	kHz	kW	Mode	Schedule°
Bishkek	RJH66	*25	300	CW	0406-0447, 1006-1047

NOTES: *) :27-:30 on 25.1, :32-:35 on 25.5, :38-:41 on 23, :44-:47 on 20.5kHz °) 1h earlier in summer (DST in Kyrgyzstan)

RUSSIA

✉ Russian State Time Frequency Service, Institute of Metrology for Time and Space (IMVP), GP "VNIIFTRI", Moscow Region, Mendeleevo 141570, Russia. **Email:** mark@imvp.aspnet.ru **Web:** www.vniiftri.ru

Location	Callsign	kHz	kW	Mode	Schedule°
Arkhangelsk	RJH77	*25	300	CW	0906-0947
N.Novgorod	RJH99	*25	300	CW	0506-0547
Khabarovsk**	RAB99	*25	300	CW	0206-0247, 0606-0647
Angarsk	RTZ	50	10	CW	
Moskva	RBU	66.66	20	AM	24h
Moskva	RWM	4996	5	CW	24h
Moskva	RWM	9996	5	CW	24h
Moskva	RWM	14996	8	CW	24h

NOTES: *) :27-:30 on 25.1, :32-:35 on 25.5, :38-:41 on 23, :44-:47 on 20.5kHz; **) status uncertain; °) 1h earlier in summer (DST in Russia).

SWITZERLAND

✉ Bundesamt für Metrologie und Akkreditierung (METAS), Lindenweg 50, CH-3003 Bern-Wabern, Switzerland. ☎ +41 31 3234645. 📠 +41 31 3233210. **Email:** laurent-guy.bernier@metas.ch **Web:** www.metas.ch

Location	Callsign	kHz	kW	Mode	Schedule
Prangins	HBG	75	20	CW	24h

TAIWAN

✉ Standard Frequency & Time Transmission in Taiwan (BSF), Telecommunication of Laboratories, P.O. Box 71, Chung-li, 320, Taiwan ☎ +886 3 4244447. 📠 +886 3 4245474 **Email:** csliao@cht.com.tw **Web:** www.stdtime.gov.tw

Location	Callsign	kHz	kW	Mode	Schedule
Chung-li	BSF	5000	2	AM	24h
	BSF	15000	2	AM	24h

UNITED KINGDOM

✉ National Physical Laboratory, Queens Road, Teddington, Middlesex, TW11 0LW, United Kingdom. 📠 +44 20 89436458. **Email:** time@npl.co.uk **Web:** www.npl.co.uk

Location	Callsign	kHz	kW	Mode	Schedule
Rugby	MSF	60	15	CW	24h

NOTES: Tx is leased from British Telecom

UNITED STATES OF AMERICA

✉ National Institute of Standards and Technology (NIST), Physics Laboratory, Time & Frequency Division, 325 Broadway, Mailcode 847.00, Boulder, CO 80305-3328, USA. ☎ +1 303 4973295. 📠 +1 303 4976461 **Web:** www.boulder.nist.gov; www.bldrdoc.gov/timefreq

✉ NIST radio station WWV, 2000 East County Rd.58, Ft. Collins, CO 80524. **Email:** nist.radio@boulder.nist.gov

Location	Callsign	kHz	kW	Mode	Schedule
Boulder, CO	WWVB	60	50	AM	24h
	WWV	2500	2.5	AM	24h
	WWV	5000	10	AM	24h
	WWV	10000	10	AM	24h
	WWV	15000	10	AM	24h
	WWV	20000	2.5	AM	24h

✉ NIST radio station WWVH, P.O. Box 417, Kekaha, Kauai, HI 96752. **Email:** wwvh@boulder.nist.gov

Location	Callsign	kHz	kW	Mode	Schedule
Kekaha, HI	WWVH	2500	5	AM	24h
	WWVH	5000	10	AM	24h
	WWVH	10000	10	AM	24h
	WWVH	15000	10	AM	24h

VENEZUELA

✉ Dirección de Hidrografía y Navegación, Estación Transmisora YVTO, Apartado Postal 6745, Caracas, Venezuela. **Email:** dhn@truevision.net **Web:** www.dhn.armada.mil.ve

Location	Callsign	kHz	kW	Mode	Schedule
Caracas	YVTO	5000	2	AM	24h

CLUBS FOR DXERS & INTERNATIONAL LISTENERS

This section lists non-commercial hobby clubs serving international radio enthusiasts. Some are oriented to programme listening, and others to DXing, the reception of low power or distant stations. In most cases, bulletins are produced on a regular basis. Sample copies are generally available for return postage (3 or 4 IRCs). Unless otherwise stated, all clubs are international, publish bulletins in English (E), (F = French, G = German, I = Italian, S = Spanish) and cover all aspects of the hobby. This list does not include clubs run by commercial publications or by individual broadcasters.

EUROPE

European DX Council, P.O. Box 18120, 50129, Firenze, Italy. Umbrella organization of DX Clubs in Europe. Secretary General Luigi Cobisi, Assistant Secretary General: Paolo Morandotti Email: sg@edxc.org Web: www.edxc.org

AUSTRIA: **Assoziation Junger DXer in Österreich,** ADXB-OE, Postfach 1000, 1082 Wien. Tel. +43 2287 5162. (G) Email: adxbsuess@aon.at Web: www.adxb-oe.org Publication: *ADXB-OE Rundschreiben* quartely. Annual DX camp.

BELGIUM: **DX-Antwerp**, P.O. Box 16, B-2660 Hoboken (Flemish). Email: dxa@dxa.be Web: www.dxa.be – **Radio Contact**, Avenue des Croix de Guerre, 94, 1120 Brussels Email: fred.quentin@infonie.be

BULGARIA: **Association of Balkan Cross-band DXers**, ABCDX, c/o Rumen Pankov, P.O.Box 199, 1000 Sofia-C – **Bulgarian DX Club plus Satellite**, c/o Ivan Penev, P.O. Box 47, Sofia 11, Bulgaria 1111. Email: penev@internet-bg.net

CZECH REPUBLIC/SLOVAK REPUBLIC: **Czechoslovak DX Club**, c/o Václav Dosoudil, Horní 9, 768 21 Kvasice. (Czech/Slovak/E). Email: mail@dx.cz Web: www.dx.cz Publication: *Radio Revue* (Czech)

DENMARK: **Danish Shortwave Club International**, Tavleager 31, 2670 Greve. Email: kaj.bredahl@post.tele.dk Web: www.dswci.org – **Dansk DX Lytter Klub**, P.O.Box 392, 8100 Aarhus C (Danish). Email: ddxlk@ddxlk.net Web: www.ddxlk.net Publication: *DX-Focus (alt om radio)* (Danish)

FINLAND: **Suomen DX-liitto**, P.O.Box 454, 00101 Helsinki (Umbrella organization of Finnish language DX Clubs) Email: toimisto@sdxl.org (Finnish/E) Web: www.sdxl.org Publication: *Radiomaailma* (Finish/E) – **Finlands Svenska DX-Förbund r.f**, P.O. Box 9, 68601 Jakobstad (Umbrella organization of various Swedish-language DX clubs in Finland). Email: cristere@alcom.aland.fi Web: www.saunalahti.fi/~bkl/fsdxf.htm (Swedish).

FRANCE: **Amitié Radio**, B.P.56, 94002 Creteil Cédéx (F). Email: roland.paget@wanadoo.fr Web: http://amitie.multimania.com Publication: *A l'Ecoute du Monde* (F) – **Association Union des Ecouteurs Français**, B.P. 31, 92242 Malakoff Cédéx (F, also publishes magazine on disk in F/E) Email: tsfinfo@magic.fr Web: www.radiocom.org – **Monde & Radiodiffusion**, 65, Montée des Princes, 84100 Orange (F/E) – **Radio Club de la Poste**, Marcel Lecerf, 13 avenue St Michel, 54220 Malzéville – **Radio Club du Perche**, 12 rue du Grand Thuret, 72320 Greez sur Roc. – **Radio Club International Ondes Courtes**, 19 lot Saturne, 26120 Malissard – **Radio DX Club d'Auvergne**, Centre Municipal P. et M. Curie, 2 bis, Rue du Clos Perret, 63100 Clermont-Ferrand. Tel/Fax: +04 73 37 08 46.

GERMANY: **ADDX** (der Assoziation deutschsprachiger Kurzwellenhörer) (G). Jointly issues *Radio-Kurier* magazine with AGDX. Email: dfp@addx.de. Web: www.addx.de – **AGDX** (Arbeitsgemeinschaft DX e.V.) is the umbrella organisation of German-speaking shortwave listeners clubs. The member clubs from Germany and Austria are: **ADXB-DL,** Assoziation Junger DXer e.V. (Germany) – **ADXB-OE,** Assoziation Junger DXer in Oesterreich (Austria) – **KWFS,** Kurzwellenfreunde Sachsen (Germany) – **WWDXC,** Worldwide DX Club (Germany; has non-German-speaking members world-wide) Members of the AGDX clubs receive the German-language magazine *Radio-Kurier – weltweit horen*, an international magazine for long-distance broadcast reception. WWDXC produces an English-language DX magazine. The postal address of AGDX e.V. is: P.O. Box 1214, 61282 Bad Homburg, Germany. Tel: +49 6102 2861 Fax: +49 6102 800999.

National Clubs:

ADDX e.V., Postfach 130124,D 40551 Düsseldorf .Tel. +49 211 790636. Fax: +49 211 793272. (G) Email: kurier@addx.de Web: www.addx.de – **Assoziation Junger DXer, adxb-DL e.V.**, c/o Thomas Schubaur, Am Hansenhohl 9, 86470 Thannhausen. Tel. +49 8281 798230 (18-20 MEZ). Fax: +49 8281 798231. (G) Email: DL1TS@t-online.de Web: home.t-online.de/home/dl1ts/adxb-dl. – **Arbeitsgemeinschaft DX, AGDX e.V.**, Postfach 1214, 61282 Bad Homburg. Tel. +49 89 3122 1852 (abends). (G) Email: agdx@swl.net Web: www.swl.net/agdx – **Power from Heaven, Christlicher DX Club PfH**, c/o Marcel Goerke, Friedrich-Ebert-Str.11, 52249 Eschweiler (G). Email: pfh_club@web.de Web: www.evr-hamburg.de – **UKW/TV AK, UKW/TV Arbeitskreis der AGDX**, c/o H.-J. Kuhlo, Wilhelm Leuschner Str. 293B. 64347 Griesheim. Tel. +49 6155 66300. Büro (Mo-Fr 8-15h): Tel. +49 6151 836486 Fax: +49 6151 835090. (G) Email: sekretariat@ ukwtv.de Web: www.ukwtv.de **WWDXC**, Postfach 1214, 61282 Bad Homburg, Tel. +49 6172 390918 (abends). Fax: +49 6102 800999. Email: mail@wwdxc.de Web: www.wwdxc.de

Regional Clubs (all G):

Berliner Empfangsamateure e.V., Verein für Rundfunk-Fernempfang, Postfach 200113, 13511 Berlin. Tel. +49 30 3323953. Fax: +49 30 3323953. Email: W.G.Lehmann@t-online.de – **Deutscher Welt Radio Club, DWRC e.V.**, c/o Bernd Schilling, Hüling 11, D 53332 Bornheim. Tel. +49 2222 62517 – **East and West Radio Club,** c/o Adolf Schwegeler, Bahnhofstr. 56, 50374 Erftstadt , Tel. +49 2235 45046. Fax: +49 2235 45046. Email: info@eawrc.de Web: www.eawrc.de – **Eastside Radiogeschichte**, c/o Jens Adolph, 04159 Leipzig-Wahren. Publication: *Eastside Radiogeschichte* Email: ctu33jens@yahoo.com – **Hamburger Freunde des Rundfunkfernempfangs**, c/o Dieter Schäfer, Am Sportplatz 18, 24629 Kisdorf. Tel. +49 4193 93407 (to 1900 hr). Email: DL1LAD@darc.de – **Kurzwellenfreunde Brand**, c/o Hans-Jürgen Schmelzer, Mitterteicher Str. 15, 95643 Tirschenreuth. Email: hugotir@t-online.de – **Kurzwellenclub Schwalmtal,** c/o Helmut Reitzer Jr., Willy Rösler Str. 41, 41366 Schwalmtal. Tel. +49 2163 30052. Fax: +49 2163 30052. Email: dk0kws@qsl.net Web: www.qsl.net/dk0kws – **Kurzwellen-freunde Rhein-Ruhr,** Postfach 101555, 45815, Elsenkirchen Email: kwfr.ge@t-online.de Web: www.kwfr.de – **Kurzwellenfreunde Sachsen,** c/o AGDX e.V., Postfach 1214, 61242 Bad Homburg. Email: DK5TL@qsl.net Web: www.swl.net/agdx/KWFS.html – **Kurzwellen-freunde Wuppertal, KWFW**, Postfach 220342, 42373 Wuppertal. Tel.: +49 202 602472 (abends). Fax: +49 202 606742 – **Kurzwellenhörerklub Saar, SWLCS,** Postfach 1230, D 66585 Merchweiler. Tel. +49 6825 8380. Fax: +49 6825 8380 Email: p_hell@freenet.de Web: www.swlcs.com – **Neandertal DX-Club**, c/o Veit Pelinski, Morper Allee 34, 40699 Erkrath – **Oldenburger Kurzwellenfreunde**, c/o Olaf C. Hänßler, Sandweg 98, 26135 Oldenburg, Tel. +49 441 12632. Email: olaf.haenssler@ informatik.uni-oldenburg.de – **Radio Hörer Club International,** c/o Hans-Joachim Brustmann, Straße am Park 16, 04209 Leipzig. Tel. +49 341 4211160. Email: info@ww-rundfunk.de Web: www.rhci.de – **Radio Japan Club Brilon,** c/o Reinhard Reese, Niederbeckstr. 23, 40472 Düsseldorf. Tel: +49 160 6940759. Email: rreese@gmx.net – **Rhein-Main-Radio-Club,** Postfach 700849, 60558 Frankfurt. Email: eamrmrc@t-online.de Web: www.rmrc.de

HUNGARY: **FM DX Club**, Email. fmdx@ha5kfu.hu – **Hungarian DX Club**, Beke ut 85, 2519 Piliscsev (Hungarian) Email: tibor.szilagyi@skf.com

IRELAND: **Irish DX Radio Club**, c/o Edward Dunne, 17 Anville Drive, Kilmacud, Stillorgan, Co. Dublin (E) Email: irishdxclub@ hotmail.com Publication: *MediaWatch* (E) by email.

ITALY: **Associazione Italiana Radioascolto (A.I.R.)**, C.P. 1338, 10100 Torino A.D.(TO) (I) Publication: *Radiorama*. Web: www.arpnet.it/air Email: air@ arpet.it – **BCL Sicilia Club**, c/o Roberto Scaglione, Casella Postale 119/Succ 34, 90144 Palermo (PA) (I) Web: www.bclnews.it Email: info@bclnews.it – **Coordinamento del Radioascolto, (CO.RAD)**, c/o Dario Monferini (Umbrella organisation of various Italian DX Clubs operating only on the WEB) (I) Web: www.corad.net Email: info@corad.net – **FM-DX Italy**, c/o Fabrizio Carnevalini (operating only on Web) (FM-TV DX) Email: fabrizio58it@yahoo.it – **Gruppo Ascolto MondoRadio DX club**, c/o Salvo Micciché, Via Alighieri 27, 97018 Scicli (RG) (I) Web: listen.to/mondoradio Email: mondoradio.dx@tiscali.it – **Gruppo d'Ascolto della Marca Trevigiana**, C.P. 3, Succ. 10, 31100 Treviso (TV) (I) Web: www.geocities.com/CapeCanaveral/Hall/2875/GAMT Email: gamt@ntt.it – **Gruppo d'Ascolto due Mari**, C.P. 1099, 74100 Taranto Centro (TA) (I/E) Web: fly.to/gadm Email: tarantodx@hotmail.com – **Gruppo d'Ascolto Radio dello Stretto**, c/o Giovanni Sergi, Via Sibari 40, 98149 Camaro Inferiore (MS) (I) Publication: *Radio Notizie* (quarterly) Web: www.garst.da.ru Email: gsergi5050@hotmail.com – **Gruppo D'Ascolto RadioTelevisivo della Sicilia**, c/o: Gioacchino Stallone, Via Sappusi 11, Lotto 27, interno 3, 91025 Marsala (TP).(I) (only local) – **Gruppo Radioascolto Liguria**, c/o Riccardo Storti, Via Sapri 34/51, 16134 Genova (GE) (I). Web: utenti.lycos.it/gral Email: ristort@tin.it – **Gruppo Radioascolto Utility World**, (Web only) (Utility) Email: qrirell@tin.it – **Play-DX**, c/o Dario Monferini, Via Davanzati 8, 20158 Milano (MI) (I/E/S) (specialises in difficult DX) Web: www.playdx.com Email: info@playdx.com – **Quelli del Faialllo**, (Independent Group operating only on the Web) c/o:Enrico Oliva, Web: www.faiallo.org/faiallo.html Email: info@faiallo.org

NETHERLANDS: **Benelux DX Club**, Postbus 583, 3700 AN ZEIST, The Netherlands. Email: h.louwsma@chello.nl Web: www.bdxc.nl Publication: *BDXC-Bulletin* (Dutch/E)

NORWAY: **DX Listeners' Club**, c/o Jan Alvestad, Vigdelsveien 637B, 4054 Tjelta (Norwegian). Email: dxnews@dxlc.com Web: www.dxlc.com

RUSSIA: **Club of DX-ers**, c/o Vadim Alexeew, P.O.Box 65, 125581 Moscow (Russian/E/G) Email: gusev@itep.ru. Web: www.radio.hobby.ru. -- **Irkutsk DX Club**: c/o Feodor Brazhnikov, P.O. Box 3036, 664059 Irkutsk. Email: feodor@ pp.irkutsk.ru Web: www.irkutsk.com/radio -- **Russian DX League**, c/o Anatoly Klepov, ul. Tvardovskogo 23-365, 123458 Moscow (Russian/E) Email: dx-league@mtu-net.ru Web: rusdx.narod.ru -- **Sankt-Peterburg DX Club**, c/o Alexey Osipov, P.O.Box 46, 195213 Sankt-Peterburg. Email: dxspb@softhome.net – **Tomsk DX Club**, c/o Vladimir Kovalenko, Tomsk (Russian/ English). Email: tomskdx@mail.ru – **Novosibirsk DX Club**, c/o Igor Yaremenko, Novosibirsk (Russian/English). Email: dxer@yandex.ru Web: www.dxing.hotbox.ru

SPAIN: **Asociación DX Barcelona**, P.O. Box 335, 08080 Barcelona (S). Email: adxb@redestb.es Web: www.redestb.es/adxb Publication: *Mundo DX* (S) – **Asociación Española de Radioescucha (AER)**, P.O. Box 4031, 28080 Madrid (S). Email: sedano@lander.es Web: www.aer-dx.org – **Mediterranean DX Group**, P.O. Box 4212. 41080 Sevilla Email: medidx@svq.servicom.es Web: www.geocities.com/SiliconValley/4847

SWEDEN: **Arctic Radio Club**, c/o Tore Larsson, Frejagatan 14A, 521 43 Falköping (MW, Swe/E) Email: tore.larsson@beta.telenordia.se – **Sveriges DX Förbund**, Box 3108, SE-103 62 Stockholm. (Swedish, umbrella organization of over 30 clubs). Email: ordf@sdxf. org Web: www.sdxf.org

SWITZERLAND: **Radio-und Fernseh-Club Basel und Umgebung, RFCB**, Postfach 67, CH 4027 Basel, Switzerland, Email: info@rfcb.ch Web: www.rfcb.ch

UNITED KINGDOM: **British DX Club**, 126 Bargery Rd, Catford, London SE6 2LR Email: secretary@bdxc.org.uk Web: www.bdxc.org.uk Publication: *Communication* (E) – **International Shortwave League**, c/o John Raynes, 267 Pelham Rd., Immingham N.E. Lincs DN40 1JU (Also amateur radio). Email: www.geocitiesiswl @g0bwg.freeserve.co.uk Web: www. freespace.virgin.net/nigel.dyche – **Medium Wave Circle**, 59 Moat Lane , Luton LU3 1UU (LW/MW only) Email: contact@mwcircle.org Web: www.mwcircle.org – **World DX Club**, 17 Motspur Drive, Northampton NN2 6LY. Email: mikewb@dircon.co.uk and mark@dxradio.demon.co.uk. For North American details see USA. Publication: *Contact* (E).

AFRICA

IVORY COAST: **DX-Ivoire**, c/o Jibirila Liasu, 20 B.P. 197 Abidjan 20 (F).

NIGERIA: **Africa DX Association**, c/o Mr. Friday I. Okoloise, NITEL, P.M.B. 23, Lafia, Plateau State. – **International DX Club**, Emmanuel Ezeani, P.O. Box 1633, Sokoto, Sokoto State. Email: idxerclub@yahoo.com and emmanuel_ezeani@yahoo.com

TUNISIA: **Club des Auditeurs et de l'Amitié**, c/o De Riadh Sakka, Route de Gremda Merkez Sahnoun, 3012 Sfax (F).

SÃO TOMÉ E PRÍNCIPE: **Clube DX-STP**, c/o Leal Bouças, Av. 12 de Julho, Vila Maria (C.P. 490), São Tomé. Email: petterboudx@hotmail.com Web: www.estome.net/vitrina/dx.htm

SOUTH AFRICA: **South African DX Club**, P.O. Box 18008, Hillbrow 2038.

TOGO: **Club Inter Amitié Radio**, CCF B.P. 2090, Lomé (F) – **Groupe Endoc**, B.P. 2667, Lomé (F)

UGANDA: **International DX Club of East Africa**, c/o Ouma Samuel, PB 565, Iganga. ☎ +256 77444201 Email: samuel.ouma@talk21.com, or 077444201@ mtnconnect.co.ug

ASIA

BANGLADESH: **Aurora Listeners' Club**, c/o Miss Kakali Rani, Harida Khalsi-6403, Madhnagar-Natore-6400, Bangladesh – **Basupara DX Listeners Club**, c/o Asfaqul Alam, Basupara, Nandangachi, Rajshahi 6260, E-mail: bdxls@uymail.com – **International Radio Listeners Club**, Konabari, P.O.Nilnagor, Gazipur, Dhaka (E/Bengali) – **Online DX Forum**, c/o MD Azizul Alam Al-Amin, Gourhanga, Ghoramara, Rajshahi-6100. Email: mtech@ rajbd.com. – **'Rose' DW Listeners Club**, c/o Ashik Eqbal "Tokon", Luximpur Greater Rd, GPO Box 56, Rajshahi 6000.Publication: *Dxnet* (Bengali) Email: rosedwlc@yahoo.com Web: www.rosedwlc.tk

INDIA: **Apollo DX International**, c/o Deepak Kumar Das, Dholi Sakra-843105, Distt-Muzaffarpur (Bihar). Email: deepakdx@rediffmail.com – **Ardic DX Club**, Room 6, Sherif Mansion, 10 Nallathambi Street, Triplicane, Chennai-600 005, Tamil Nadu. Publications: *Dxers Guide* (E), *Sarvadesa Vanoli* (Tamil). Email: ardicdxclub@yahoo.co.in Web: www.geocities.com/ardicdxclub/vanoli – **Chaudhary Srota Sangh**, c/o Santosh Kumar (President), Kharauna Jairam, Kharauna Dih, 843113, Distt-Muzaffarpur (Bihar), India – **El Nino Electronics DX Club**, c/o Partha Sarathi Goswami, Kishalay, College Road, Siliguri 734 401, Darjeeling, West Bengal. Email: info@elnino.gq.nu Web: www.elnino.gq.nu – **Foreign Radio Listeners' Club,** c/o Prasenjit Bhakat, Ghoradhara, P.O Jhargram 721507, W. Bengal. 🖹 +91 3221 256084 – **Globe Radio DX Club, GRDXC**, c/o Harjot Singh Brar, P.O Box 158, Chandigarh 160 017. Email: grdxc@yahoo.co.in Web: www.geocities.com/grdxc/index/html – **Paribar Bandhu SWL Club**, c/o Mr. Anand Mohan Bain, Indira Colony, Baloda Bazar 493332, Raipur-Chattisgarh. Email: anandmohan10@yahoo.com – **Universal DX League**, c/o Kanwarjit Sandhu, P.O. Box: 1128, Chandigarh-160 015. Email: udxl@hotmail.com – **World DX Club & Library**, c/o Baidyanath Upadhyaya, At Khairabarigaon, P.O. Khawrang, Udalguri 784509, Darrang, Assam – **World DXing Club**, c/o Mr Madhab Ch. Sagour, 60 Jan Md Ghat Road, P.O. Box Naihati 743 165, 24 Parganas (North), West Bengal. Email: m_sagour@ yahoo.co.in – **Youth International Radio Listeners' Club**, c/o Mr. Pranab Kumar Roy, Vill + PO, Shyamnagar, 741 155, Via Palashipara , Nadia, West Bengal. Publications: *Etherbarta* (Bengali) *Radio Monitors' Guide* (E). Email: etherbarta@hotmail.com Web: www.geocities.com/rmg_yirlc

INDONESIA: **Indonesian DX Club**, P.O. Box 2001 DPPS, Depok 16432, Indonesia (E/Indonesian). Email: idxc@hotmail.com Web: www.idxc.org

JAPAN: **Asian Broadcasting Institute**, C.P.O. Box 1334, Tokyo 100-8693 (J). Email: info@abiweb.jp Web: www.abiweb.jp – **Indonesian DX Circlc Japan**, c/o Atusnori Ishida, 1-16-201 Teranishi, Saichi-cho, Iwakura-shi, Aichi 42-0036 (J) – **Japan BCL Federation**, 1-9-23 Tadao, Machida City, Tokyo 194-0035. Email: mywave@m2.ocv.ne.jp (J) – **Japanese Association of DXers**, P.O. Box 1766, Tokyo 100-91 (J/E) – **Japan Short Wave Club**, P.O. Box 29, Sendai Central 980-8691 (J/E) Fax: +81 22 227 4194 Email: jswchq@ hotmail.com – **Nagoya DXers Circle**, c/o Shigenori Aoki, 2-51 Kasumori-cho, Nakamura-ku, Nagoya 453-0855 Web:

http://newswire.ndxc.org – **Radio Nuevo Mundo**, c/o Tetsuyu Hirahara, 5-6-6 Nukuikita, Koganei-shi, Tokyo 184-0015.

NEPAL: **Friendship Radio Club**, Tanki Sinwari 5, District Morang, Biratnagar – **Listeners' Club of Nepal**, (Reg. No.144), P.O Box 126, Biratnagar-4. – **Small Giant Radio Listener Club**, (Reg. No.17), Kathmandu. Web: www.smallgiantradiolistenerclub.cjb.net

PAKISTAN: **National Society of Pakistani DXers**, E-161/1, Iqbal Park, opposite Adil Hospital, Defence Housing Society Rd, Lahore Cantt. – **Pakistan Aafaqie Lehrain Society (PALS)**, c/o Asrar Chaudhary, Dusehra Ground, Sheikhupura, 39350, Punjab, Pakistan. Newsletter *Aafaqie Lehrain*, (Urdu with E section). – **Pakistani Shortwave Listeners Association**, 38/2-Habib Colony, Bahawalpur 63108. Tel. +92 621 887590. Fax +92 621 874060. Publication: *Radio World* (by email). Email: urlc@mul.paknet.com.pk – **Pakistan: Wonderful World of Shortwave (WWSW)**, c/o Baber Shehzad, 43 Habib Colony, Bahawalpur-63108 Email: baber73@yahoo.com, Publication: *News Letter of Pakistani DX-ers* (by email).

SRI LANKA: **Union of Asian DXers**, c/o Victor Goonetilleke, "Shangri-La" 298 Kolamunne, Piliyandala.

TAJIKISTAN: **DX Listeners' Club**, c/o Ibrahim Rustamov, Navobod Str. 36-36, Isfara 735920, Sogd Region. (E/G/Russian/Tajik/Farsi). Email: i_rustam@swissinfo.org

PACIFIC

South Pacific Association of Radio Clubs Email: clarkb@sparc.org.nz. (Umbrella organization of most Australian and NZ DX Clubs).

AUSTRALIA: **Australian Radio DX Club Incorporated**, c/o John Wright, 15 Olive Crescent, Peakhurst, 2210 NSW. Email: dxer@ fl.net.au Web: www.ardxc.fl.net.au – **The Electronic DX Press** (EDXP), Web-based club offering many member services. Web: http://edxp.org – **The Australian DXing Association**, c/o Bob Padula, 404 Mont Albert Road, Mont Albert, Victoria 3127. Email: ausdx@edxp.org Web: http://ausdx.edxp.org

NEW ZEALAND: **New Zealand Radio DX League**, P.O. Box 3011, Auckland. Web: http://radiodx.com/spdxr/subscription – **New Zealand DX Radio Association**, c/o R.Dickson, 88 Cockerell Str, Brockville, Dunedin.

NORTH AMERICA

Association of North American Radio Clubs (ANARC), 529 Sandy Lane, Franklin, OH 45005-2065. Umbrella organization for most North American DX Clubs. Send 2 IRC's for more information about the association and its member clubs. Web: www.anarc.org

CANADA: **Canadian International DX Club**, P. O. Box 67063-Lemoyne, St. Lambert, PQ J4R 2T8. Email: CIDXclub@yahoo.com Web: www.anarc.org/cidx/ – **Club Ondes Cortes du Quebec**, 5120 35ème rue, Grand-Mère, PQ G9T 3N6 (F). Email: dduplessis@ infoteck.qc.ca – **Ontario DX Association**, 155 Main St N, Apt. 313, Newmarket, ON L3Y 8C2. Email: odxa@rogers.com Web: www.odxa.on.ca

MEXICO: Audio Pico DX Club, c/o César Granillo, Apartado 309, 94301 Orizaba, Ver – **Club DX Miguel Auza**, c/o Luis Antero Aguilar, Apartado Postal 38, 98330 Miguel Auza, Zacatecas – **Consultorio DX**, c/o Miguel Angel Rocha Gámez, Ap. Postal 31, 31820 Ascensión, Chih – **Nayarit DX Club**, P.O. Box 62, 63001 Tepic. Email: naydx@tepic.megared.net.mx – **Sociedad de Ingenieros Radioescuchas**, c/o Cesar Fernandez de Lara Garcia, Ap. Postal 203, Admon. No.1, C.P. 91701 Veracruz, Ver. Email: fedela@ hotmail.com or fedela@veracruz.podernet.com.mx

USA: **All Ohio Scanner Club**, 20 Philip Drive, New Carlisle, OH 45344-9108 (non-broadcast Public Service Bands only). Email: n8oay@sprintmail.com Web: www.aosc.rpmdp.com – **American Shortwave Listeners Club**, 16182 Ballad Lane, Huntington Beach, CA 92649-2204. Email: wdx6aa@earthlink.net Web: http://communitylink.ocnow.com/groups/aswlc – **Association of Clandestine Enthusiasts**, P.O. Box 1, Belfast, NY 14711-0001. Email: acehdq@localnet.com Web: www.frn.net/ace – **Chicago Area DX Club**, Email: dxchicago@earthlink.net – **DecaloMania**, 9705 Mary NW, Seattle. WA 98117 (for collectors of station promo. items and airchecks). Email: bytheway@atk.com. Web: www.anarc.org/decal – **DX Audio Service**, P.O. Box 164, Mannsville, NY 13661-0164 (for sight-impaired listeners). Email: gnbc@wcoil.com Web: www.wcoil.com/~gnbc/ – **International Radio Club of America**, P.O Box 1831, Perris, CA 92572-1831 (mediumwave only) Email: phil_tekno@yahoo.com Web: www.geocities.com/Heartland/5792/info.htm – **Lone Star DX Association**, c/o Jim Bass, 2709 Monarch Drive, Arlington, TX 76006 Email: jwbass@autoeloan.com Web: www.dxer.org/lsdxa – **Longwave Club of America**, 45 Wildflower Road, Levittown, PA 19057 Web: www.users.aol.com/lwcanews – **Memphis Area Shortwave Hobbyists**, P.O. Box 3888, Memphis, TN 38173 – **Miami Valley DX Club (MVDXC)**, Box 292132, Columbus, OH 43229 Email: dhammer@freenet.columbus.oh.us. Web: www.anarc.org/mvdxc – **Michigan Area Radio Enthusiasts**, P.O. Box 530933, Livonia, MI 48153-0933 Email: xx024@detroit.freenet.org Web: www.detroit.freenet.org/sigs/l-radio/ – **Minnesota DX Club (MDXC)**, 16330 Germane Ct W Rosemount, MN 55068. Web: www.anarc.org/mdxc/ – **National Radio Club**, P.O. Box 164, Mannsville, NY 13661-0164 (MW only.) Email: plsbcbdxer@aol.com Web: www.nrcdxas.org – **North American Shortwave Association**, 45 Wildflower Road, Levittown, PA 19057 (SW only) Publication: *The Journal* and *Flashsheet*. (by email) Email: weoliver@comcast.net Web: www.anarc.org/ naswa – **Pacific Northwest, British Columbia DX Club**, c/o Bruce Portzer, 6546 19th Ave NE, Seattle WA 98115. Email: bytheway@atk.com Web: www.anarc.org/ pnbcdxc – **Southern California Area DXers**, c/o Bill Fisher Sr., 6398 Pheasant Drive, Buena Park, CA 90620-1356. Email: billfishernow @netzero.net Web: http://communitylink.ocnow.com/ groups/scads – **World DX Club (N. America)**, Mr. R. A. D'Angelo, 2216 Burkey Drive, Wyomissing, PA 19610. Email: rdangelo3@aol.com – **Worldwide TV-FM DX Association**, PO Box 501, Somersville, CT 06072. Publication: *VHF-UHF Digest*. (FM and TV dxing) Web: www.anarc.org/wtfda.

SOUTH AMERICA

ARGENTINA: **Asociación DX del Littoral**, Casilla 406, Rosario (Santa Fé) – **Grupo DX Suquia**, c/o Carolina J.G. Vandenberghe, Estafeta Rivera Indarte, C.C. No.26, 5149 Córdoba – **Grupo Radioescucha Argentino**, Marcelo A. Cornachioni, Alvarez Thomas 248, 1832 Lomas de Zamora, Buenos Aires (S) Email: dxline@arnet.com.ar

BRAZIL: **Clube DX-ista da Amazônia**, a/c Djaci Franklin Soares da Silva, Tv. Angustura 1961, apto. 1205 – Pedreira, 66087-710 Belem, PA. Email: cdxa@ig.com.br Web: http://www.geocities.com/cdxpara – **DX Clube do Brasil**, C.P. 384, 09701-970 São Bernardo do Campo (P) Email: dxcp@yahoogroups.com Web: www.ondascurtas.com – **Santa Rita DX Clube**, Caixa Postal 4, 58300-970 Santa Rita, Paraiba. Email: srdxc@bol.com.br Web: www.srdxclube.hpg .com.br.

CHILE: **Amigos Radioescuchas de Santiago**, Casilla 183, La Cisterna, Santiago 14 (S). Email: dxars@yahoo.com or hlopez@ inter-access.cl – **Club Diexista de Chile**, Calle 3 Poniente 55, Talca. Email: chiledxclub@mixmail.com Web: www.lanzadera.com/ chiledxclub – **Comision de Radioescuchas de Federachi**, c/o Héctor Frías Jofre, Dr. Eduardo Cruz Coke 389, 3° piso, (Cas. 260-2) Santiago. (S). Email: ce3fzl@yahoo.com Web: www.federachi.cl

URUGUAY: **Asociación Diexman Uruguay**, P.O. Box 6008, C.P. 11000 Montevideo (S). Email: cx4ban@adinet.com.uy or rialv@ network.bbs.com.uy – **DX Club Montevideo**, Calle Batovi 2068, 11800 Montevideo. Email: dxclubmontevideo@yahoo.com

VENEZUELA: **Asociación Diexista de Venezuela**, P.O. Box 65657, Caracas 1066-A (S) Email: marl1@hotmail.com – **Club Diexistas de la Amistad**, c/o Ing. Santiago San Gil Gonzáles, P.O. Box 202, Barinas 5201-A, Estado Barinas. (S). Email: americaenantena @hotmail.com Web: www.lanzadera.com/ radioficionado – **Venezuelan QSL Help**, c/o Winter Monges, P.O. Box 1.116, Barquisimeto 3001-A, Lara. Email: wintermonges@ yahoo.com Web: www.members.tripod.com/~wintermonges/ index.html

SELECTED INTERNET RESOURCES FOR DXers & LISTENERS

GENERAL PAGES:

DXing.com: www.dxing.com
DXing.info: www.dxing.info
A Global Radio Portal: www.radiointel.com
Hard-Core-DX: www.hard-core-dx.com
History of SW: www.ontheshortwaves.com
Radio-directory: www.radiodirectory.com
Radio-portal: www.radio-portal.org
Radio Homepage of Martin Schöch: www.schoechi.de
Russian SWL/DX Site (Russian): www.radio.hobby.ru
World of Radio: www.worldofradio.com
1000 Lakes DX Page: www.geocities.com/Colosseum/Park/3232/dx.htm

DATABASES & SCHEDULES:

ADDX Non-English Frequency List:: dxworld.com/cgi-bin/hfp.sh
African Medium Wave Guide: www.angelfire.com/tx5/dxamtexas/AMWG.htm
Broadcasting in South & South East Asia: www.asiawaves.net
Central American & Caribbean Broadcasting: www.stevenwiseblood.com
DX & Other Interesting Programs Guide: dxworld.com/cgi-bin/speedx.sh
Eike Bierwirth's DX page: www.eibi.de.vu
Eldorado for LA Dxers: members01.chello.se/mwm/eldorado/index.html
European Medium Wave Guide: users.pandora.be/hermanb/Emwg
International Listening Guide: www.ilgradio.com/ilgradio.htm
NA on the air (partly Finnish): www.diccons.com/radio/koje.htm
Online DX Logbook: www.odxl.org.uk
Pacific Asian Log: www.qsl.net/n7ecj
Shortwave Radio Resource Center: shortwave.hfradio.org
WWW Shortwave Listening Guide: www.anarc.org/naswa/swlguide

NEWS SOURCES AND BULLETINS:

BC-DX Top News: www.wwdxc.de/topnews.htm
Clandestine Radio Watch: groups.yahoo.com/group/crwatch
DX-listening Digest: www.worldofradio.com/dxldmid.html
Electronic DX Press: members.tripod.com/~bpadula/edxp.html
Moskovskiy Informatsionniy DX-Bulletin (Russian): www.internews.ru/rts
Shortwave Bulletin: www.hard-core-dx.com/swb
Signal: dxsignal.info/indexen.htm
Ydun's MW Page: www.ydunritz.com

ONLINE RADIO:

www.live365.com – www.shoutcast.com – www.tvradionetwork.com – www.comfm.com/live/radio

RECEIVER SOFTWARE:

Computer Supported SW Listening: home.planet.nl/~jarkest/swl/swl.html
Software Geared to the Shortwave Hobbyist: www.fineware-swl.com

IDENTIFICATION:

Interval Signals Online: www.intervalsignalsonline.com
National Anthems: www.national-anthems.net

PROPAGATION:

Solar Terrestrial Activity Report: www.dxlc.com/solar
Space Weather Alerts, Warnings and Forecasts: sec.noaa.gov

MAILING LISTS:

A-DX Mailingliste (G): www.ratzer.at/A_DX_Info.php
AMFMTVDX list: mailman.qth.net/mailman/listinfo/amfmtvdx
Conexion Digital (S): www.topica.com/lists/conexion.digital
Cumbre DX: cs2.ralabs.com/mailman/listinfo/cumbredx
FM & TV DX Lists: www.fmdx.com
Lists at Yahoogroups.com: AM-SW-DXing – AMPirateRadio – atividadedx (Portuguese) – bclnews (I) – condiglist (S) – dexismo (Portuguese) – DRM-L – dxradio – dx_india – globe-radio-dx – LatinMWDX – mwdx – NoticiasDX (S) – ondescourtes (F) – open_dx (Russian) – playdx2001 (I) – radioescutas (Portuguese) – RealDX – recradioshortwave – shortwave – shortwavedxing – shortwavelistening – ShortWaveRadio – ShortwaveRadios – shortwave-radio – shortwaves – swedx (Swedish) – thebasicsofshortwave
Hard-Core-DX Email List: www2.hard-core-dx.com/mailman/listinfo/hard-core-dx
SW-ITA (I): mailman.qth.net/mailman/listinfo/sw-ita
SW Programs: www.topica.com/lists/swprograms

ABBREVIATIONS & SYMBOLS USED IN THIS HANDBOOK

✉ = Address
☎ = Telephone
🖷 = Fax

A/C = Alternate Current
acc. = accepted
Admin. = Administration
alt. = alternate, alternative
Ann. = Announcement
Ap. = Apartado
Assoc. = Association
Asst. = Assistant
Av. = Avenida (Port.)
Avda. = Avenida (Sp.)
Ave. = Avenue
B.P. = Boite Postale
B'caster = Broadcaster
Bldg = Building
Broadc. = Broadcast(ing)
C.P. = Case/Caixa Postal, Construction Permit
Cad. = Cadena
Cas. = Casilla
Cd. = Ciudad
Ce. = Central
CEO = Chief Executive Officer
cf. = refer to
Ch. = Channel
Chmn. = Chairman
Cl. = Club(e)
Clan. = Clandestine
Co. = Company
comm. = commercial
Contr. = Controller
Corp. = Corporation
Cra. = Carrera
Cult. = Cultura, Cultural
D = Daily
d = Directional antenna
D.Prgr = Daily Programmes
D/C = Direct Current
DAB = Digital Audio Broadcasting
Dem. = Democratic
Dep. = Deputy
Dept. = Department
Depto. = Departamento
Desp. = Despacho
DG = Director General
Dif. = Difusora, Difusão
Diff. = Diffusion
Dir. = Director
Div. = Division
DRM = Digital Radio Mondiale
DSB = Double Side Band
DST = Daylight Saving Time

DVB = Digital Video Broadcasting
DX = Long Distance
E.C. = Electric Current
Ea. = East(ern)
Edif. = Edificio
Educ. = Education(al), Educación (Sp.)
Em. = Emis(s)ora
Eng. = Engineer(ing)
ERP = Effective Radiated Power
Esq. = Esquina
est. = estimated
Est. = Estado
exc. = except
excl. = excluding
exec. = executive
ext. = external
F.Pl. = Future Plan(s)
fed. = federal
For. Rel. = Foreign Relations
Fr. = Father
Freq. = Frequency
Fri = Friday
FS = Foreign Service
Ft. = Fort
G.C. = Geographical Coordinates
GD = General Director
gen. = general
GM = General Manager
Gov. = Government(al)
Gte. = Gerente (Sp. & Port.)
H = Horizontal Pol.
h = Hour
HQ = Headquarters
HS = Home Service
i.e. = that is
ID = (Station) Identification
Inc. = Incoporated
incl. = including, includes
Inf. = Information
int'l = international
IRC = International Reply Coupon
irr. = irregular
IS = Interval Signal
Isl. = Island(s)
kHz = kilohertz
L = Local
L.P = Leading Personnel
L.T = Local Time
Langs. = Languages
Lp. = low power (transmitter)
LSB = Lower Side Band
Ltd. = Limited
LV = La Voz

LW = Longwave
max. = maximum
MD = Managing Director
MF = Mondays-Fridays
Mgr. = Manager
MHz = megahertz
mil. = military
Min. = Ministry, Ministerio, Ministério
mins = Minutes
Mon = Monday
Mpal. = Municipal (Sp.)
Mpo. = Município (Port.)
Mt = Mount
MW = mediumwave
N. = News
n.f. = nominal frequency
n/a = not available
nal. = nacional
nat. = national
nd = omnidirectional Antenna
NE = North East(ern)
Netw. = Network
No. = Number, North
nom. = nominal
Nte. = Norte
NW = North West(ern)
occ. = occasional(ly)
Ops = Operations
Org. = Organisation
Ote. = Oeste
P.O. = Post Office
P.R. = Public Relations
PD = Programme Director
pl. = planned
Pol. = Polarisation
Pop. = Population
Pr. = Praça
Pr.L. = Principal Language(s)
Pres. = President
Prgr(s). = Programme(s)
Prod. = Production
Prov. = Province
Pt. = Point
Pte. = Presidente
Pto. = Puerto
Pub. = Public service
Pubs. = Publication(s)
QSL = Confirmation of Reception
R. = Radio, Rádio
r. = reported, repeater
Radiodif. = Radiodifusion, Radiodifus(s)ora
Rec. = Recording(s)
reg. = regional
Rel. = Relay(s), Relations

Rep. = Republic
Rev. = Reverend
rlg. = religious
Rp. = Return Postage
Rpt. = (Reception) Report
S. = San(ta), Sán, Santo
s/off = sign off
s/on = sign on
SAE = Self Addressed Envelope
Sat = Saturday
Sce. = Service
Sched. = Schedule
SE = South East(ern)
Secr. = Secretary
Sen. = Senior
SM = Station Manager
So. = South
Soc. = Sociedad (Span.), Sociedade (Port.)
Sp. = Spanish
SS = Sat/Sun
SSB = Single Side Band
St. = Saint, Station, Street
Stn. = Station
Str. = Street, Strasse
Su. = Summer
Sun = Sunday
Superv. = Supervisor
SW = shortwave South West(ern)
Syst. = System
TD = Technical Director
techn. = technical
Thu = Thursday
Tr. = Transmitter, transmission
TRP = Transmitter Power
Tue = Tuesday
tx = transmitter
u.c. = under construction
Univ. = University
USB = Upper Side Band
UTC = Coordinated Universal Time
V. = Verification, Vertical Pol.
v. = varying
viz. = namley
VO = Voice of
VP = Vice President
W = Weekdays (Mon-Sat)
We. = West(ern)
Wed = Wednesday
Wi. = Winter
Wrp. = Weather Report

ABBREVIATIONS OF BROADCASTERS' NAMES

AFN	=	American Forces Network
AFRTS	=	American Forces Radio and Television Service
Am.R.Mirr Int'l	=	Amateur Radio Mirror International
AWR	=	Adventist World Radio
Bangladesh Bet.	=	Bangladesh Betar
BBC	=	British Broadcasting Corporation
BBG	=	Broadcasting Board of Governors
BBG-AapkiDunyaa	=	BBG - Radio Aap Ki Dunyaa
BBG-R.Free Afg.	=	BBG - Radio Free Afghanistan
BBG-RFE/RL	=	BBG - Radio Free Europe/Radio Liberty
BCC	=	Broadcasting Corporation of China
Bozy Glos	=	Bozy Glos w Czasach Ostatecznych
Brigham YU R.	=	Brigham Young University Radio
BVB	=	Bible Voice Broadcasting
Chr.Sc.Herald	=	Christian Science Herald
Conv.entre Cub.	=	Conversando Entre Cubanos
Cyprus BC Corp.	=	Cyprus Broadcasting Corporation
Dem.VO Burma	=	Democratic Voice of Burma
Dengê Mezop.	=	Dengê Mezopotamya (Voice of Mesopotamia)
Dr Gene Scott	=	The Caribbean Beacon (University Network Relay)
DRM	=	Digital Radio Mondiale
Ev. Miss. Gemeind	=	Evangelische Missions-Gemeinden
Evangeliumsrad.	=	Evangeliumsradio Hamburg
EvangeliumsRdfk	=	Evangeliums-Rundfunk
Family Radio	=	WYFR - Family Radio
Fang Guang M.R.	=	Fang Guang Ming Radio
FBN	=	Fundamental Broadcasting Network (WBOH/WTJC)
FEBC	=	Far East Broadcasting Company, Inc.
Foro Mil.Cubano	=	Foro Militar Cubano
Golos Pravosl.	=	Golos Pravoslaviya (La Voix de L'orthodoxie)
HAM	=	High Adventure Ministries
Hamburger Lokal	=	Hamburger Lokalradio
IBB	=	International Broadcasting Bureau
Int'l R.SerbMon	=	International Radio of Serbia & Montenegro
Junta Patr.Cub.	=	Junta Patriótica Cubana
KAIJ	=	KAIJ International
KFBS	=	FEBC - Saipan
KSDA	=	KSDA (Adventist World Radio)
KTWR	=	KTWR (Trans World Radio Guam)
LRTC	=	Lietuvos Radijo ir Televizijos Centras
Lutherische Std	=	Lutherische Stunde
LV Resistencia	=	La Voz de la Resistencia
LVRTC	=	Latvijas Valsts Radio ir Televizijas Centrs
Maeva FM Int'l	=	Maeva FM International
MCR	=	Monte Carlo Radiodiffusion
Medi 1	=	Radio Méditerranée Internationale
Miss.Heukelbach	=	Missionswerk Heukelbach
M-werk Arche	=	Missionswerk Arche
Overcomer Min.	=	The Overcomer Ministry
R. Freundes-D.	=	Radio Freundes-Dienst
R. Nac.RASD	=	Radio Nacional de la R.A.S.D.
R. Nac.Venezuela	=	Radio Nacional Venezuela - Antena Internacional
R. One/Inform.R.	=	Information Radio/Radio One
R. Pilipinas	=	Radyo Pilipinas Overseas
R. Sed.Kashmir	=	Radio Sedayee Kashmir
R. Sult.of Oman	=	Radio Sultanate of Oman
R. Tajikistan	=	Radio Tajikistan
R. VO Oro.Lib.Fr	=	Radio Voice of Oromo Liberation Front

Radio Cuba	=	Radio Habana Cuba
Radio Mashreq	=	Radio Mashreq
RAE	=	Radiodifusión Argentina Al Exterior
RAI	=	Radiotelevisione Italiana
RBWI	=	Radio Baltic Waves International
RCI	=	Radio Canada International
RDP	=	Radiodifusão Portuguesa
REE	=	Radio Exterior de España
RFI	=	Radio France Internationale
RFPI	=	Radio for Peace International
RMC-MO	=	Radio Monte Carlo Moyen-Orient
RMI	=	Radio Moldova International
RNWO	=	Radio Nederland Wereldomroep
RNZI	=	Radio New Zealand International
RRDTK	=	Radioaloqa, Radioeshittirish va Televideniya Davlat Korxonasi
RS Makedonias	=	Radiofonikos Stathmos Makedonias (ERT3)
RT Tunisienne	=	Radio-Télévision Tunisienne (ERTT)
RTMarocaine	=	Radiodiffusion-Télévision Marocaine (RTM)
RTRN	=	Russian Television and Radio Broadcasting Network
RVI	=	Radio Vlaanderen Internationaal
Scan.Weekend R.	=	Scandinavian Weekend Radio
TDF	=	Télédiffusion de France
TWR	=	Trans World Radio
TWR Africa	=	Trans World Radio Swaziland
UN Radio	=	United Nations Radio
VO Africa	=	Voice of Africa - Libyan Jamahiriya Broadcasting Corporation
VO C.P.I.	=	Voice of the Communist Party of Iran
VO Croatia	=	Glas Hrvatske (Voice of Croatia)
VO Dem. Eritrea	=	Voice of Democratic Eritrea
VO Eritr.People	=	Voice of the Eritrean People
VO Eth. Medhin	=	Voice of Ethiopian Medhin
VO Eth.Unity	=	Voice of Ethiopian Unity
VO Freedom&Ren.	=	Voice of Freedom and Renewal
VO Iran. Nation	=	Voice of the Iranian Nation
VO Iran.Kurdist	=	Voice of Iranian Kurdistan
VO Iranian Rev.	=	Voice of Iranian Revolution
VO JKashFrMovem	=	Voice of Jammu Kashmir Freedom Movement
VO Liberty-Erit	=	Voice of Liberty - Eritrea
VO Oromo Liber.	=	Voice of Oromo Liberation
VO Peace&Dem.	=	Voice of Peace and Democracy
VO Reb. Iraq	=	Voice of Rebellious Iraq
VO Str.Iran.Kur	=	Voice of the Struggle of Iranian Kurdistan
VOA	=	Voice of America
Voice Africa	=	Christian Vision (The Voice)
VOIRI	=	Voice of the Islamic Republic of Iran
VOR	=	Voice of Russia
VOR-RKS	=	VOR - Radiokanal Sodruzhestvo
VOR-RMR	=	VOR - Russkoye Mezhdunarodnoye Radio
VOV	=	Voice of Vietnam
Voz Christiana	=	Voz Cristiana - Voz Crista
Waymarks Int'l	=	Waymarks International Ministries
WBCQ	=	WBCQ - The Planet
WEWN	=	WEWN - Global Catholic Network (ETWN)
WHR	=	World Harvest Radio
WRMI	=	WRMI - Radio Miami International
WRN	=	World Radio Network
WWCR	=	Worldwide Christian Radio

MAIN COUNTRY INDEX

ADVERTISERS' INDEX

ADVERTISING SALES

Advertising sales manager:

Beth Leinbach
2698 Green Cove Road
Brasstown, NC 28902
USA
Tel/fax: +1 828 389 4007
e-mail: bleinbach@brmemc.net

Advertising sales rep (Europe):

Enrico Callerio
Media Age srl
via Stefano Jacini 4
20121 Milano
ITALY
Tel: +39 02 876038
Fax: +39 02 86450149
e-mail: callerio@monitor-radiotv.com